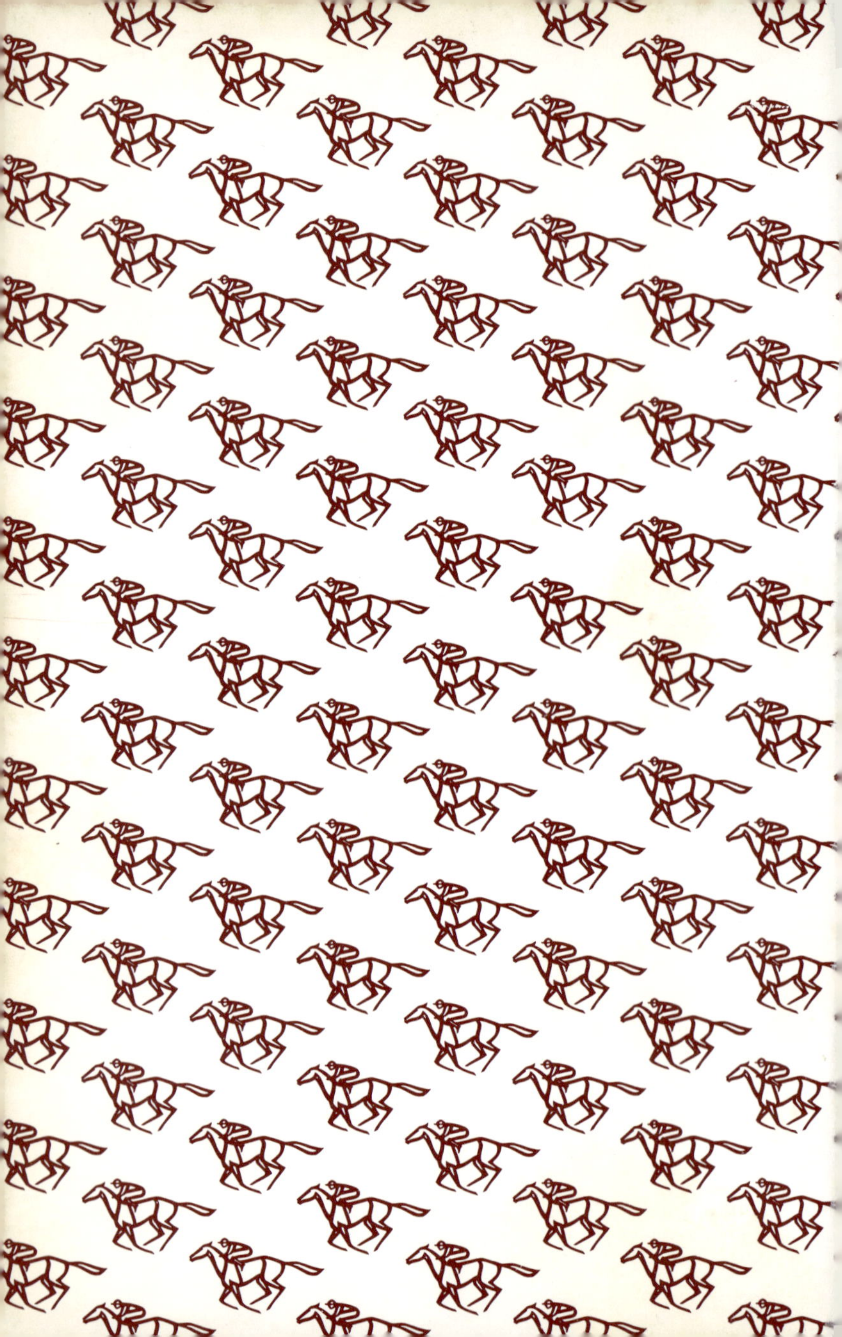

AGE, WEIGHT & DISTANCE TABLE

A. STEEPLECHASES

Dist	Age	Jan	Feb	Mar	Apr	May	Aug	Sept	Oct	Nov	Dec
2m	5	12—2	12—3	12—4	12—5	12—6	12—7	12—7	12—7	12—7	12—7
	4	11—5	11—6	11—7	11—8	11—9	11—11	11—12	11—13	12—0	12—1
2¼m	5	12—2	12—3	12—4	12—5	12—6	12—7	12—7	12—7	12—7	12—7
	4	11—5	11—6	11—7	11—8	11—9	11—11	11—12	11—13	12—0	12—1
2½m	5	12—1	12—2	12—3	12—4	12—5	12—7	12—7	12—7	12—7	12—7
	4	11—4	11—5	11—6	11—7	11—8	11—10	11—11	11—12	11—13	12—0
2¾m	5	12—0	12—1	12—2	12—3	12—4	12—6	12—7	12—7	12—7	12—7
	4	11—3	11—4	11—5	11—6	11—7	11—9	11—10	11—11	11—12	11—13
3m	5	12—0	12—1	12—2	12—3	12—4	12—6	12—7	12—7	12—7	12—7
	4	11—2	11—4	11—5	11—6	11—7	11—9	11—10	11—11	11—12	11—13
3¼m	5	11—13	12—0	12—1	12—2	12—3	12—5	12—6	12—7	12—7	12—7
	4	11—1	11—3	11—4	11—5	11—6	11—8	11—9	11—10	11—11	11—12
3½m	5	11—13	12—0	12—1	12—2	12—3	12—5	12—6	12—7	12—7	12—7
	4	11—0	11—2	11—3	11—5	11—6	11—8	11—9	11—10	11—11	11—12

B. HURDLE RACES

Dist	Age	Jan	Feb	Mar	Apr	May	Aug	Sept	Oct	Nov	Dec
2m	5	12—7	12—7	12—7	12—7	12—7	12—7	12—7	12—7	12—7	12—7
	4	11—13	12—0	12—1	12—2	12—3	12—5	12—5	12—6	12—6	12—7
	3						11—6	11—8	11—9	11—11	11—12
2¼m	5	12—7	12—7	12—7	12—7	12—7	12—7	12—7	12—7	12—7	12—7
	4	11—12	11—13	12—0	12—1	12—2	12—4	12—5	12—5	12—6	12—6
	3						11—5	11—7	11—8	11—9	11—10
2½m	5	12—7	12—7	12—7	12—7	12—7	12—7	12—7	12—7	12—7	12—7
	4	11—11	11—12	11—13	12—0	12—1	12—3	12—4	12—5	12—6	12—6
	3						11—4	11—6	11—7	11—8	11—9
2¾m	5	12—6	12—7	12—7	12—7	12—7	12—7	12—7	12—7	12—7	12—7
	4	11—10	11—11	11—12	11—13	12—0	12—3	12—4	12—5	12—5	12—6
	3									11—7	11—8
3m	5	12—6	12—6	12—7	12—7	12—7	12—7	12—7	12—7	12—7	12—7
	4	11—8	11—10	11—11	11—12	11—13	12—2	12—3	12—4	12—5	12—5
	3									11—6	11—7

For 6-y-o's and older, use 12-7 in all cases

Note—Race distances in the above tables are shown only at ¼-mile intervals. For races of 2m 1f use the 2¼-mile table weights; for races of 2m 3f use 2½ miles; and so forth. For races over odd distances, the nearest distance shown in the table should be used: thus, for 2m 100 yards, use the table weights for 2m; for 3m 300 yards use 3¼ miles, and so on. Races over distances longer than 3½ miles should be treated as 3½-mile races.

CHASERS & HURDLERS 1989/90

A Timeform Publication Price £59.00

A Timeform Publication

Managing Director: Reg Griffin

Compiled and produced by

G. Greetham, B.A., G. F. Walton, Dip.A.D. (Directors), J. D. Newton, B.A. (Editor-in-Chief), E. K. Wilkinson (Editor), S. D. Rowlands, B.A. (Handicapper), J. H. Brazier, D. E. Carr, M.A., G. Crowther, M. T. Greenwood, W. Hughes and D. Sheard.

ISBN 0 900599 51 0

CONTENTS

FOREWORD

'Chasers & Hurdlers 1989/90' deals individually, in alphabetical sequence, with every horse that ran over the sticks in the 1989/90 season (including on the all-weather tracks), plus a number of Irish horses that did not race here. For each of these horses is given (1) its age, colour and sex, (2) its breeding, (3) a form summary giving details of all its performances during the past season, (4) a rating of its merit, (5) a commentary upon its racing or general characteristics as a racehorse, with some suggestions, perhaps, regarding its potentialities in 1990/91 and (6) the name of the trainer in whose charge it was on the last occasion it ran.

The book is published with a twofold purpose. Firstly, it is intended to have permanent value as a review of the exploits and achievements of the more notable of our chasers and hurdlers in the 1989/90 season. Thus, while the commentaries upon the vast majority of the horses are, of necessity, in note form, the best horses are more critically examined, and the short essays upon them are illustrated by half-tone portraits and photographs of some of the races in which they ran. Secondly, the book is designed to help the punter to analyse races, and the Explanatory Notes which follow this Foreword contain instructions for using the data.

October, 1990

INDEX TO PHOTOGRAPHS

PORTRAITS & SNAPSHOTS

Elementary	7 b.g.	Busted–Santa Vittoria (Ragusa)	*Jacqueline O'Brien*	254
Elfast	7 b.g.	Neltino– Niagara Rhythm (Military)	*W. W. Rouch & Co*	256
Fidway	5 b.g.	Fidel–Galway Maid (Jimmy Reppin)	*W. W. Rouch & Co*	274
Forest Sun	5 ch.g.	Whistling Deer– Sun Spray (Nice Guy)	*W. W. Rouch & Co*	287
Formula One	8 b.g.	Ardoon–Little Dipper (Queen's Hussar)	*Bernard Parkin*	289
For The Grain	6 b.g.	Nishapour–Some Dame (Will Somers)	*Dinah Nicholson*	290
Fort Noel	7 br.g.	Bonne Noel–Fortellina (Fortino II)	*Rex Coleman*	291
Four Trix	9 gr. or ro.g.	Peacock–Merry Chariot (Blue Chariot)	*Timeform*	295
Freeline Finishing	6 b.g.	Furry Glen–Superday (Straight Deal)	*Fiona Vigors*	297
Ghofar	7 ch.g.	Nicholas Bill– Royale Final (Henry The Seventh)	*W. W. Rouch & Co*	314
Golden Celtic	6 b.g.	Rare One–Cooleen (Tarqogan)	*Rex Coleman*	321
Grabel	7 b.m.	Bold Owl–Gay Dawn (Gay Fandango)	*Jacqueline O'Brien*	330
Highfrith	7 ch.m.	Deep Run– Lulu's Daughter (Levanter)	*Timeform*	355
Jinxy Jack	6 b.g.	Random Shot– True Or False (Varano)	*Timeform*	387
Joyful Noise	7 b.g.	Lighter– Roadway Mistress (Mandamus)	*Jacqueline O'Brien*	394
Judges Fancy	6 b.g.	Monksfield– Knollwood Court (Le Jean)	*Bernard Parkin*	396
Kribensis	6 gr.g.	Henbit–Aquaria (Double-U-Jay)	*John Crofts*	421
Long Engagement	9 b.g.	Mandalus–Selk Fly (Selko)	*Dinah Nicholson*	442
Lucky Verdict	4 b.g.	Touching Wood– Noor (Mill Reef)	*Bernard Parkin*	447
Lumberjack	6 b.g.	Big Spruce– Snip (Shautung)	*Timeform*	449
Mander's Way	5 b.g.	Furry Glen–Art Mistress (Master Owen)	*Rex Coleman*	457
Man O'Magic	9 br.g.	Manado—Garrucha (Prince Taj)	*W. W. Rouch & Co*	461
Master Bob	10 b.g.	Pitpan–Good Calx (Khalkis)	*Fiona Vigors*	467
Midfielder	4 ch.g.	Formidable– Pampas Flower (Pampered King)	*Bernard Parkin*	478
Midnight Train	9 b.g.	Oats–Gail Borden (Blue Chariot)	*W. W. Rouch & Co*	481
Miinnehoma	7 b.g.	Kambalda–Mrs Cairns (Choral Society)	*Bernard Parkin*	484
Mixed Blends	8 b.m.	The Parson–Biowen (Master Owen)	*Jacqueline O'Brien*	496
Morley Street	6 ch.g.	Deep Run–High Board (High Line)	*W. W. Rouch & Co*	503
Mr Frisk	11 ch.g.	Bivouac–Jenny Frisk (Sunacelli)	*Fiona Vigors*	517
Mweenish	8 b.g.	Callernish–No Trix (No Argument)	*W. W. Rouch & Co*	523
Nick The Brief	8 b.g.	Duky–Roman Twilight (Romulus)	*Bernard Parkin*	536

RACE PHOTOGRAPHS

EXPLANATORY NOTES

The aim of this annual and of Timeform (Chasing Edition) is to supply accurate information as to the merit and the racing character of every horse racing over the sticks, and to present it in a form in which it may be of the greatest practical use in assessing the prospects of the runners in a race.

TIMEFORM RATINGS

The merit of each horse is given as a rating, in pounds, the rating being the number of pounds which the horse's performances would entitle it to receive in a universal handicap embracing all horses worth a rating in training, in which the ratings range from around 175 (12st 7lb) for the very best horses down to below 60 for the worst horses. A horse rated at 155 is thus approximately 20 lb below the top of the handicap; and a horse rated at 168 is to be regarded as 4 lb better than another rated at 164. Ratings preceded by a c relate to steeplechasing, the others, in a lighter type-face, to hurdle racing.

This explains what the ratings are; but of course individual ratings are not actually allocated in this way, merely by 'inspection'. The rating of any horse is a result of careful examination of its running against other horses. We maintain a 'running' handicap of all horses in training throughout the season, or, to be strictly accurate, two handicaps, one for hurdlers and one for chasers.

THE LEVEL OF THE RATINGS

At the close of each season all the horses that have raced are re-handicapped from scratch, and each horse's rating is revised. It is also necessary to adjust the general level of the handicap, so that the mean of all the ratings is kept at the same standard level from year to year. This explains why, in this book, the ratings are, in general, different from those in the final issue of the 1989/90 Timeform Chasing series.

USING THE RATINGS

In using Timeform to assess the prospects of the various runners in any race, the first proceeding is to find out which of them are most favoured by the weights by using the ratings to evaluate the chances of all the runners purely on a handicap basis. This involves adjusting each horse's rating to take into account its age and actual weight it has to carry. The second proceeding is to examine the comments on the horses with a view to considering what factors, other than weight, might also affect the outcome of the race.

Steeplechase ratings, preceded by c, should not be confused with hurdle ratings. A steeplechase rating should never be used to assess the chance of a horse in a hurdle race, and hurdle ratings should never be used when the race being dealt with is a steeplechase. Where a horse has raced over fences and also over hurdles its ratings as a chaser and hurdler are printed one above the other, the steeplechase rating (c) being placed above the hurdle rating. Thus with

REGALITY **c157**
143

the top figure, 157, is the rating to be used in steeplechases, and the one below, 143, is for use only in hurdle races. The procedure for making age and weight adjustments to the ratings (i.e. for the calculation of Race Ratings) is as follows:-

A. Horses of the Same Age

If the horses all carry the same weight there are no adjustments to be made, and the horses with the highest ratings have the best chances. If the horses carry different weights, jot down their ratings, and to the rating of each horse add one point for every pound the horse is set to carry less than 12st 7lb, or subtract one point for every pound he has to carry more than 12st 7lb. When the ratings have been adjusted in this way the highest resultant figure indicates the horse with the best chance at the weights.

Example (any distance: any month of the season)

Teucer	5 yrs (11-0) . .	Rating 140 . .	add 21	161
Kiowa	5 yrs (10-7) . .	Rating 125 . .	add 28	153
Golden Age	5 yrs (10-4) . .	Rating 120 . .	add 31	151

Teucer has the best chance, and Golden Age the worst

B. Horses of Different Ages

In this case reference must be made to the Age, Weight and Distance Table printed on the page facing the front cover. Treat each horse separately, and compare the weight it has to carry with the weight prescribed for it in the appropriate table, according to the age of the horse, the distance of the race and the month of the year. Then, add one point to the rating for each pound the horse has to carry less than the weight given in the table: or, subtract one point from the rating for every pound he has to carry more than the weight prescribed by the table. The highest resultant figure indicates the horse most favoured by the weights.

Example (2¾m Steeplechase in January)
(Table Weights: 8-y-o 12-7; 7-y-o 12-7; 5-y-o 12-0)

Black Book	8 yrs (12-8) . .	Rating 140 . .	subtract 1 . .	139
Pressman	7 yrs (12-3) . .	Rating 132 . .	add 4	136
Copyright	5 yrs (12-2) . .	Rating 150 . .	subtract 2 . .	148

Copyright has the best chance, and Pressman the worst

Example (3m Hurdle race in March)
(Table Weights: 9-y-o 12-7; 5-y-o 12-7; 4-y-o 11-11)

Oxer	9 yrs (10-12) . .	Rating 110 . .	add 23	133
Clairval	5 yrs (10-7) . .	Rating 119 . .	add 28	147
Gallette	4 yrs (10-7) . .	Rating 128 . .	add 18	146

Clairval has the best chance, and Oxer the worst

JOCKEYSHIP AND RIDERS' ALLOWANCES

There is just one further point that arises in evaluating the chances of the horse on the basis of their ratings: the question of jockeyship in general, and riders' allowances in particular. The allowance which may be claimed by a rider is given to enable such riders to obtain race-riding experience against experienced jockeys. For the purposes of rating calculations it should, in general, be assumed that the allowance the rider is able to claim (3lb, 5lb or 7lb) is nullified by his or her inexperience. Therefore, *the weight adjustment to the ratings should be calculated on the weight allotted by the handicapper, or determined by the conditions of the race,* and no extra addition should be made to a rating because the horse's rider claims an allowance.

The above is the general routine procedure. But of course there is no reason why the quality of jockeyship should not be taken into account in assessing the chances of horses in a race. Quite the contrary. Nobody would question that the jockeyship of a first-class rider is worth a pound or two, and occasionally a claiming rider comes along who is riding quite as well as the average jockey long before losing the right to claim. There is no reason whatever why, after the age and weight adjustments have been made to the ratings, small additional allowances should not be made for these matters of jockeyship. This, however, is a matter which must be left to the discretion of the reader.

WEIGHING UP A RACE

The ratings tell you which horses in a particular race are most favoured by the weights; but complete analysis demands that the racing character of each horse, as set out in the commentary upon it, is also studied carefully to see if there is any reason why the horse might be expected not to run up to its rating. It counts for little that a horse is thrown in at the weights if it has no pretensions whatever to staying the distance, or is unable to act on the prevailing going.

These two matters, suitability of distance and going, are, no doubt, the most important points to be considered. But there are others. For example, the ability of a horse to accommodate himself to the conformation of the track. Then there is the matter of pace versus stamina: as between two stayers of equal merit, racing over a distance suitable to both, firm going, or a small field with the prospect of a slowly-run race, would favour the one with the better pace and acceleration, whereas dead or soft going, or a big field with the prospect of a strong gallop throughout the race, would favour the sounder stayer. There is also the matter of the horse's ability and dependability as a jumper and of its temperament: nobody would be in a hurry to take a short price about a horse with whom it is always an even chance whether he will get round or not, or whether he will consent to race.

A few minutes spent checking up on these matters in the commentaries upon the horses concerned will sometimes put a very different complexion on a race from that which is put upon it by the ratings alone. We repeat, therefore, that the correct way to use Timeform, or this annual volume, in the analysis of individual races is, first to use the ratings to find out which horses are most favoured by the weights, and second, to check through the comments on the horse to see what factors other than weight might also affect the outcome of the race.

Incidentally, in setting out the various characteristics, requirements and peculiarities of each horse in the commentary upon him, we have always expressed ourselves in as critical a manner as possible, endeavouring to say just as much, and no whit more than the facts seem to warrant. Where there are clear indications, and definite conclusions can be drawn with fair certainty, we have drawn them: if it is a matter of probability or possibility we have put it that way, being careful not to say the one when we mean the other; and where real conclusions are not to be drawn, we have been content to state the facts. Furthermore, when we say that a horse *may not* be suited by hard going, we do not expect the reader to treat it as though we had said that the horse *is not* suited by hard going. In short, both in our thinking and in the setting out of our views we have aimed at precision.

THE FORM SUMMARIES

The form summaries enclosed in the brackets list each horse's performances in sequence, and show three items of information for each outing. The race distance is given in furlongs, steeplechase form figures are prefixed by the letter 'c' and N.H. Flat race form figures by the letter 'F', the others relating to form over hurdles, that on an all-weather surface being prefixed by the letter 'a'. Runs in N.H. Flat races are not recorded in the ratings.

The going is symbolised as follows: h = hard or very firm; f = firm (turf) or fast (all-weather); m = fairly good, or on the firm side of good; g = good (turf) or standard (all-weather); d = dead, or on the soft side of good; s = soft, sticky or holding (turf) or slow (all-weather); v = heavy, very heavy or very holding.

Placings are indicated, up to sixth place, by the use of superior figures, an asterisk being used to denote a win; and superior letters are used to convey what happened to the horse during the race: F = fell (F^3 denotes remounted and finished third); pu = pulled up; ur = unseated rider; bd = brought down; r = refused; su = slipped up; ro = ran out; co = carried out.

Thus, [1989/90 F16g 16s* c18g^{pu} 16f^2 c20v^F] states that in the 1989/90 jumping season the horse ran five times; unplaced in a 2m N.H. Flat race on good going, winning a 2m hurdle race on soft going, being pulled up in a 2¼m steeplechase on good going, running second in a 2m hurdle race on firm going and falling in a 2½m steeplechase on heavy going; all races on turf.

Where sale prices are given they are in guineas unless otherwise stated. The prefix IR denotes Irish guineas.

THE RATING SYMBOLS

The following symbols, attached to the ratings, are to be interpreted as stated:-

p the horse is likely to make more than normal progress and to improve on his rating.

P there is convincing evidence, or, to say the least, a very strong presumption that the horse is capable of form much better than he has so far displayed.

\+ the horse may be rather better than we have rated him.

d the horse appears to have deteriorated, and might no longer be capable of running to the rating given.

§ a horse of somewhat unsatisfactory temperament; one who may give his running on occasions, but cannot be relied upon to do so.

§§ an arrant rogue or thorough jade; so temperamentally unsatisfactory as to be not worth a rating.

x moderate or sketchy jumper.

xx a very bad jumper, so bad as to be not worth a rating.

? The use of a query without a rating implies that although the horse has form, his merit is impossible to assess with confidence. If used in conjunction with a rating this symbol implies that the rating is based on inadequate or unsatisfactory data, or that the rating is suspect.

CHASERS & HURDLERS 1989/90

Horse	*Commentary*	*Rating*
AARON'S ROD	4 br.c. Mansingh (USA)–Belinda Mede (Runnymede) [1989/90 $16g^{pu}$ $a16s^{6}$] poor maiden on Flat (has been blinkered): no sign of ability in juvenile hurdles: sold 680 gns Doncaster March Sales. *M. J. Charles.*	—
ABADARE (USA)	6 b.g. Robellino (USA)–Latonia Thrush (Tudor Minstrel) [1989/90 16m $16f^{6}$ $22m^{3}$ 22d $a20g^{6}$] smallish, workmanlike gelding: poor novice hurdler: stays 2¾m: acts on firm and yielding going. *J. A. Pickering.*	68
ABADJERO	7 ch.g. Owen Dudley–Sultry One (Tropique) [1989/90 20m* $c20f^{F}$] won conditional jockeys handicap hurdle at Perth in August: stayed 2½m: acted on hard going: dead. *A. Fowler.*	98
ABANDON HOPE	8 b.g. Hell's Gate–Summer Solstice (Naucetra) [1989/90 16d $25d^{pu}$ 24d 28f $24m^{ur}$ $24h^{pu}$ 20m $24f^{4}$] leggy, lengthy, workmanlike gelding: poor novice hurdler: best effort in 3m amateur riders event at Hexham final start. *J. G. Thorpe.*	60
ABAN WAY	8 br.g. Aban–Good Way (Good Apple) [1989/90 20g* 16m* 16g* $16v^{3}$ $20d^{2}$] big gelding: said to have been hobdayed and had soft palate operation: much improved hurdler who won novice events at Wetherby and Newcastle and novice handicap at Ayr in November: beaten a head by Midland Glenn in novice event at Newcastle in February (quickened to lead between last 2, hung badly left run-in and caught on line): stays 2½m: yet to race on very firm going, acts on any other. *G. Richards.*	118 +
ABBERLEY	5 br.m. Idiot's Delight–Polarita (Arctic Kanda) [1989/90 18d 16g 20g 27s] rather leggy mare: first foal: dam winning staying hurdler: well beaten in novice hurdles, including seller. *P. D. Evans.*	—
ABBEYBRANEY	11 b.g. Giolla Mear–Bank Rate (Deep Run) [1989/90 $c17f^{F}$] tall, rather leggy, plain gelding: modest chaser: destroyed after falling at Newton Abbot in July: was headstrong and best with forcing tactics at around 2m: acted on firm and dead ground. *P. D. Cundell.*	c— —
ABBEY BRAVE	7 ch.g. Avocat–Garnerstown Queen (Push On) [1989/90 $19g^{bd}$ 18d $c24f^{3}$ $c24d^{pu}$ $c26g^{5}$ c25g $c25g^{F}$ $c24d^{pu}$ $c26g^{5}$ $c25f^{4}$ $c24f^{2}$ c25m] leggy gelding: poor novice hurdler/chaser: stays well: acts on firm going: ridden by 7-lb claimer last 4 starts. *J. A. Pickering.*	c83 —
ABBEYDORE	8 b.g. Rouser–Cagaleena (Cagirama) [1989/90 24g $21d^{5}$ $22m^{pu}$] lengthy, workmanlike gelding: handicap hurdler: remote fifth of 19 at Ludlow in March: unlikely to stay beyond 2½m: possibly unsuited by extremes of going. *G. J. Powell.*	—
ABBEY DREAM	6 b.g. Martinmas–Lady Begorra (Roi Soleil) [1989/90 $16m^{pu}$ $16f^{F}$ $16s^{pu}$] compact gelding: of little account. *A. P. James.*	—
ABBOT OF FURNESS	6 b.g. The Parson–Chestnut Fire (Deep Run) [1989/90 $16m^{2}$] won NH Flat race in 1988/9: favourite, 2 lengths second to Hot Company in 13-runner novice event at Perth in September on hurdling debut: looked likely to improve but wasn't seen out again. *G. Richards.*	87
ABBOTSHAM	5 b.g. Ardross–Lucy Platter (FR) (Record Token) [1989/90 $c25m^{2}$ $24f^{pu}$ $21m^{3}$ $16m^{5}$] angular gelding: winning hurdler: jumped boldly when 8 lengths second to Wellington Brown in hunter chase at Wincanton in March: stays 25f: acts on any going: should improve sufficiently to win a small race over fences. *O. J. Carter.*	c**88** p 94

ABBOTTS VIEW 6 b.g. Monksfield–In View Lass (Tepukei) [1989/90 16g^{4} 16g^{6} 16s* 16d* 16d^{3} 16m* 16f^{2} 16f^{F}] sturdy, workmanlike gelding: won novice handicap hurdles at Bangor and Warwick and novice hurdle at Sandown: fell fatally at Cheltenham in April: acted on good to firm and soft going. *C. P. E. Brooks.*
116

ABBREVIATION 7 b.g. Torus–Worldling (Linacre) [1989/90 c16f* c16g^{bd} c16f^{pu} c20g^{2} 20g^{4}] leggy, short-backed gelding: smart hurdler at his best: ran moderately final start (January): jumped soundly in main when winning novice chase at Cheltenham in October in canter from only other finisher: showed no zest when beaten a distance by Celtic Shot at Kempton 2 months later (2 finished): seems suited by 2½m: yet to race on heavy going, acts on any other: tends to flash tail under pressure and looks a difficult ride (appears to do just enough). *J. T. Gifford.*
c96 +
—

ABDERA 5 ch.m. Ahonoora–Gentian (Roan Rocket) [1989/90 19h*] medium-sized, sparely-made mare: third foal: dam won over 10.5f in France: well beaten in maiden race on Flat in August: won novice hurdle at Hereford later in month by 8 lengths from Sakr, making running and jumping well in main: seemed sure to win more races but wasn't seen out again. *M. C. Pipe.*
101 p

ABDICATOR 10 ch.g. Levanter–Saffron Princess (Thriller) [1989/90 c21g^{5} c28m* c27s^{pu} c24g^{2} c24d^{6}] big, deep-girthed gelding: finished alone in 2-runner handicap chase at Kelso in November: led until last and kept on gamely when going down narrowly to Tartan Trademark on same course in December: suited by a test of stamina: acts on soft going: sketchy jumper. *J. K. M. Oliver.*
c**102**

ABERCROMBY CHIEF 5 br.g. Buckskin (FR)–Free For Ever (Little Buskins) [1989/90 F16d^{5} 16g] second foal: dam, winner of NH Flat race in Ireland, half-sister to smart hurdler Potato Merchant and useful hurdler Stag Hill: fifth in NH Flat race at Kelso in February: behind in novice hurdle on same course following month. *J. K. M. Oliver.*
—

ABEROY 11 ch.g. Abercorn–Maroyal (Rage Royal) [1989/90 18m^{3} 16f^{3} c21f* c20f* c24m* a22g* c24f^{3} c20g* c21g^{4} c20m^{2} c20f^{2}] sturdy, workmanlike gelding: wide-margin winner of handicap chases at Wincanton and Uttoxeter (both conditional jockeys) and Huntingdon early in season: also in good form in second half of season, and won novice hurdle at Southwell and a handicap chase at Huntingdon: effective with forcing tactics over 2m and stays 3¼m, but is ideally suited by 2½m: yet to show his form on very soft ground, acts on any other: has worn a severe bridle and a dropped noseband: seems suited by a sharp track: sometimes makes mistakes: genuine. *M. J. Ryan.*
c**104**
94

ABHA GUYA 7 b.g. Over The River (FR)–Pegs Guya Guya (Rotharraingt) [1989/90 F16h* F16f^{4} 16f a20g^{3} 22v^{pu} 24s 16g a16g^{6}] strong, compact non-thoroughbred gelding: first foal: dam unraced: won point-to-point and NH Flat race in Ireland: sold out of D. Kiely's stable 22,000 gns Doncaster August Sales: made all in NH Flat race at Hexham in October (hung left closing stages): poor form over hurdles: blinkered last start: has raced with tongue tied down. *Ronald Thompson.*
64

ABLE DAN 9 ch.g. Full of Hope–Set Piece (Firestreak) [1989/90 16f^{6} c20m^{5} c16m^{4} c22m c20f^{5}] good-topped gelding: poor novice hurdler and winning point-to-pointer/steeplechaser: headstrong but probably stays 2½m: acts on hard going and possibly unsuited by heavy. *R. W. Fidler.*
c**68**
—

ABLE LEADER 4 b.g. Beldale Flutter (USA)–Buckham Barn (Lorenzaccio) [1989/90 16f^{6} 18m^{4} 16s* 16d^{pu} 16f] robust gelding: has scope: lightly-raced maiden on Flat: showed promise over hurdles prior to winning juvenile event at Plumpton in December by 3 lengths from Good Spark: ran poorly in good juvenile company afterwards (never going well final start, in March): should stay beyond 2m: acts on soft going. *J. T. Gifford.*
107

ABLE SAILOR 10 gr.g. Abwah–Shipwrecked (Javelot) [1989/90 c24g^{pu} c25f^{4} c24g^{pu}] workmanlike gelding: one-time useful hunter chaser, but is a poor performer nowadays: needs further than 2m and stays 3m: acts on any ground, but best run on soft: has worn blinkers. *C. Smith.*
c—
—

ABLE VALE 4 b.f. Formidable (USA)–Valeur (Val de Loir) [1989/90 16s^{pu} 16s a16g^{2} 16d^{2} 16f* 16m* 16f^{2} 16m^{5}] compact filly: half-sister to winning hurdler Vision of Wonder (by Tyrnavos): winning 1½m plater on Flat: sold out of H. Candy's stable 4,600 gns Newmarket Autumn Sales: won 4-y-o fillies selling hurdle at Wolverhampton (bought in 3,500 gns) in March and novice handicap hurdle at Warwick in May: will prove best at around 2m at present: acts well on
94

firm ground: seemed not to be putting it all in on fourth outing: claimer ridden. *R. J. Holder.*

ABNEGATION 5 b.g. Abednego–Autumn Magic (Arctic Slave) [1989/90 F16g^{5}] brother to novice hurdler Burnt Prophet and half-brother to smart Irish hurdler/useful chaser Barney Burnett (by Le Bavard): dam won 2¼m hurdle: 21 lengths fifth behind Jodami in NH Flat race at Kelso in March: yet to race over hurdles or fences. *J. H. Johnson.*

ABOVE BOARD 5 ch.g. Cut Above–Lady Ector (USA) (King Pellinore (USA)) [1989/90 20g] angular, workmanlike gelding: no worthwhile form over hurdles. *R. McDonald.* —

ABOVE THE WIND 5 b.h. High Top–Golden Windlass (Princely Gift) [1989/90 a18g^{6} a20g^{4}] workmanlike horse: winning hurdler: well beaten in 2 races at Southwell, second a seller: best form at 2m: acts on soft going and probably unsuited by firm: blinkered second outing 1988/9. *W. Clay.* —

A BOY NAMED SIOUX 10 b.g. Idiot's Delight–Susanella (Eborneezer) [1989/90 c26g^{3} c26v^{3} c25g^{2} c26m^{3} c26m^{2}] smallish, dipped-backed gelding: handicap chaser: ran creditably apart from on final start: stays well: acts on any going: has won for an amateur. *S. T. R. Stevens.* c**102** —

ABSENT MINDS 4 br.f. Lir–Forgotten (Forlorn River) [1989/90 16g 17m^{pu}] lightly-made filly: first foal: dam winning point-to-pointer: no form over hurdles: bolted before start and reluctant to race on debut. *B. R. J. Young.* — §

ABSOLUTE BEGINNER 8 ch.g. Crash Course–Move Along Gypsy (Menelek) [1989/90 c22d^{ur} c20g^{5}] sturdy gelding: winning point-to-pointer: novice hurdler/chaser: has shown ability in steeplechases but often let down by his jumping: stays 3m. *Capt. T. A. Forster.* c— x —

ABSOLUTELY HUMMING 4 ch.g. Absalom–Hum (Crooner) [1989/90 16s a16g^{6}] lengthy, good-quartered gelding: modest handicapper on Flat, probably stays 1m: well beaten in novice event and a seller over hurdles: looks headstrong. *J. Sutcliffe.* —

ABSONANT 8 ch.m. Absalom–Chance Belle (Foggy Bell) [1989/90 c20f*] well-made mare: poor handicap hurdler: jumped well, made most and ran on strongly to win novice chase at Sedgefield in September by 12 lengths from Greenheart: not seen out again: worth a try over further than 2½m: acts on any going: has worn a crossed noseband. *Mrs G. R. Reveley.* c93 —

ABU MUSLAB 6 b. or br.h. Ile de Bourbon (USA)–Eastern Shore (Sun Prince) [1989/90 18s 16g^{bd} 21d^{6}] sturdy horse: seemed suited by longer trip when sixth in 21f maiden hurdle at Warwick in March: tailed off in seller on reappearance. *G. F. Edwards.* 84

ACCESSOFHORNCHURCH 4 ch.g. Coquelin (USA)–The Saltings (FR) (Morston (FR)) [1989/90 16g^{pu} 16g 16d 16g^{5}] sparely-made gelding: modest 7f winner on Flat: sold out of R. Boss's stable 4,400 gns Doncaster October Sales: little sign of ability over hurdles: blinkered third start. *E. H. Owen jun.* —

ACCLAIM 10 b.g. Record Token–Acolyte (Roan Rocket) [1989/90 c16g^{4} c16d^{pu} c16g^{4} c20f^{F} c16m^{2} c16g^{4}] sturdy, angular gelding: winning hurdler/chaser: form in 1989/90 only when blinkered on fifth outing: takes good hold and unlikely to stay much beyond 2m: possibly unsuited by very soft ground, acts on any other: needs to improve his jumping over fences: sold to C. Popham 3,500 gns Ascot June Sales. *N. J. Henderson.* c99 ? —

ACEFACE 5 ch.g. Anfield–Silvera (Ribero) [1989/90 16f* 19f^{5} 20s^{6} a20g^{5} 24m] smallish, sturdy gelding: won conditional jockeys handicap hurdle at Worcester in August: well below form afterwards (off course 5 months after second start): stays 2½m: probably acts on any going: blinkered nowadays. *W. Clay.* 87

ACE OF DIAMONDS 4 ch.f. Spur On–Seven Diamonds (Turnpike) [1989/90 F16f F16f^{6}] first foal: dam never ran: behind in NH Flat races at Hexham in April and May: yet to race over hurdles. *F. S. Storey.*

ACE OF SPIES 9 b.g. He Loves Me–Belle Bergere (Faberge II) [1989/90 c24g* c24g^{4}] tall, leggy gelding: fairly useful chaser: usually a sketchy jumper and sometimes takes little interest, but was always travelling well when winning handicap at Cheltenham in November by 15 lengths from Bigsun: badly hampered 5 out and not recover when remote fourth to Bonanza Boy in limited handicap at Chepstow in December: stays 3m: acts on any going: sometimes blinkered or visored. *Mrs G. E. Jones.* c**132** § — §

ACHILLEAN 7 b.g. Wolver Hollow–Prime Thought (Primera) [1989/90 c—
c20g^{ur} c20m^{pu}] workmanlike gelding: behind in 2 races on Flat at 3 yrs: won a
point-to-point in 1989: blundered second, jumped to the right from sixth and was
behind when pulled up twelfth in novice chase at Warwick in November
(reportedly broke blood vessel). *O. Sherwood.*

ACHILTIBUIE 6 b.g. Roscoe Blake–Gorgeous Gertie (Harwell) [1989/90 16g
16f^{6} 16g^{3} 16f^{2} 16f^{2} 20g^{pu} 18h* 16g^{pu} 16f^{2}] leggy, good-topped gelding: made all in 83
3-runner novice handicap hurdle at Kelso in May: stays 2¼m: acts on hard
ground. *W. H. Crawford.*

ACONITUM 9 b.g. Fair Season–The Yellow Girl (Yellow God) [1989/90 a16g^{6}] c— §
strong, medium-sized, angular gelding: winning hurdler and novice chaser: — §
ungenuine and isn't one to trust nowadays: acts on soft going: blinkered final start
1988/9. *J. R. Jenkins.*

ACRE HILL 6 gr.g. Alias Smith (USA)–Acolyte (Roan Rocket) [1989/90 16g*
20g^{4} 16m^{2} 20f^{5}] workmanlike gelding with scope: will make a chaser: won novice 111
hurdle at Cheltenham in January by 20 lengths: best subsequent effort when 3
lengths second to Tildarg in similar event at Sandown in March: likely to prove
best at around 2m on a galloping track for time being: seems suited by a sound
surface. *N. J. Henderson.*

ACROSS THE LAKE 6 b.g. Over The River (FR)–Golden Highway (Royal
Highway) [1989/90 22g^{3} 20g^{F} 24m^{5} 20d^{5} 20g^{2} 20g^{2} 27g* 20d^{2} 24f^{3} 27f^{3}] angular, 103
workmanlike gelding: won handicap hurdle at Sedgefield in February: best other
effort on next start: stays well: best form with give in the ground: amateur or
claimer ridden. *Mrs S. A. Bramall.*

ACROW LINE 5 b.g. Capricorn Line–Miss Acrow (Comedy Star (USA))
[1989/90 16g^{r}] leggy, close-coupled gelding: successful over 1¾m on Flat in 1989: — §
in need of race, jumped slowly before refusing fourth in novice hurdle at
Towcester in December. *J. C. Fox.*

ACTINIUM (FR) 7 br.h. Labus (FR)–Activity (FR) (Montevideo) [1989/90
18d^{2} 16m^{pu}] rangy horse: 2 lengths second to Just The Ticket in Sir Ken Novices' 98
Hurdle at Worcester in November, swishing tail under pressure and finding no
extra flat: pulled up lame at Ascot later in month and not seen out again: will stay
beyond 2¼m: acts on dead going. *J. R. Jenkins.*

ACTRESS 4 b.f. Known Fact (USA)–Tin Tessa (Martinmas) [1989/90 16d]
modest 7f winner on Flat: tailed-off last of 11 finishers in juvenile hurdle at —
Newcastle in February. *J. Wharton.*

ADAMS IMPRINT 7 ch.g. Buckskin (FR)–Kobylka (David Jack) [1989/90 c**82**
c21f^{4}] lengthy gelding: winning hurdler: made mistakes in latter stages when 24 —
lengths fourth to Knight Oil in novice chase at Windsor in November: will stay
3m: yet to race on soft ground, acts on any other. *J. A. C. Edwards.*

ADELAURE (FR) 5 b.g. Rose Laurel–Sonade (FR) (Jefferson) [1989/90 20g
22g 22g] rangy gelding: well beaten over hurdles. *J. S. King.* —

ADEN APOLLO 9 ch.g. Apollo Eight–Fuchsia Cottage (Ossian II) [1989/90 c**120**
24m c20g^{2}] tall gelding: fair chaser: creditable second to Villierstown in handicap —
at Ayr in November: well behind in handicap hurdle on reappearance: stays 2½m:
acts well in the mud and is probably unsuited by firm ground: blinkered once in
1985/6. *T. Craig.*

ADJARAYN 5 b.g. Top Ville–Adayra (FR) (Le Haar) [1989/90 20f^{5} 20m^{6} 16h^{F}
a16g/ smallish, lengthy gelding: poor novice hurdler: well beaten in 1999/90: best —
form at 2m with give in the ground: has run blinkered and visored. *J. R. Jenkins.*

ADMIRAL DEXTER 7 ch.g. Apollo Eight–Fuchsia Cottage (Ossian II)
[1989/90 20m^{pu}] plain, good-bodied gelding: brother to fair chaser Aden Apollo: —
dam moderate stayer on Flat: broke a leg in novice hurdle at Wetherby in May. *R.
M. Whitaker.*

ADMIRAL'S LEAP 6 ch.g. Quayside–Sailor's Will (Laurence O) [1989/90
16m^{3} 21d^{6} 22v* 22g^{2}] rather leggy, workmanlike gelding: won novice hurdle at 110
Folkestone in February by 2 lengths from Rivertino: blinkered, 12 lengths second
to The Illywhacker at Windsor following month, jumping none too fluently and
coming under pressure some way out: will stay 3m: acts well on heavy going. *F.
Walwyn.*

ADMIRE-A-MORE 6 b.m. Le Coq d'Or–Wynsomemore (Game Rights)
[1989/90 16d^{4} 16g 22g* 20d] small, workmanlike mare: seemed suited by longer 93
trip when winning 2¾m mares novice hurdle at Kelso in December by 2½ lengths

from Radical Lady, coming from behind to lead last: ran poorly next time: will stay 3m. *Mrs W. R. Tullie.*

ADMITTED 8 b.g. New Member–Desila (FR) (Silex) [1989/90 c25f^{pu} c24m^{F} c21m^{pu}] very lightly raced and no sign of ability. *Mrs S. D. Williams.* c—

ADROMITOS 7 b.g. Camden Town–Lady Gerardina (Levmoss) [1989/90 16g^{F} 16g 16g^{6} 16m^{5}] medium-sized, well-made gelding: third foal: dam quite modest 1½m winner: poor novice hurdler. *B. J. Curley.* 79

ADVENTURES 10 ch.g. Gingerbread Man–Meigle Talent (Bay of Biscay) [1989/90 c24d^{4} c22m^{3}] strong, lengthy gelding: fair point-to-pointer, winner in February and April: rallied run-in when just over 5 lengths fourth to Mademist Susie in maiden hunter chase at Leicester in March: ran moderately last start: stays 3m. *R. S. Elwell.* c88

AERIALIST 12 b.g. High Line–Bellardita (Derring-Do) [1989/90 c20m^{pu} c20m^{pu}] wiry gelding: novice hurdler/chaser: pulled up lame last outing: has started slowly, and did so on reappearance: not one to trust. *Mrs T. D. Pilkington.* c— § — §

AESCULAPIUS 9 ch.g. Mansingh (USA)–Silver Love (USA) (The Axe II) [1989/90 18f^{4}] compact gelding: selling hurdler: no form for a long time: no sign of ability in steeplechases: acts on any going: has been tried in blinkers. *T. M. Jones.* c— —

AFALTOUN 5 b.g. High Line–Afeefa (Lyphard (USA)) [1989/90 c16m^{5} c16d^{F} c16s^{ur}] workmanlike gelding: novice hurdler: made running and was 5 lengths clear of eventual 20-length winner Master Rajh when falling at the last in novice chase at Nottingham in January: held when unseating rider 2 out in similar race following month: jumped soundly in main each time: pulls hard and will prove best over an easy 2m. *D. R. Gandolfo.* c**104** ? —

AFARISTOUN (FR) 6 b.g. Top Ville–Afrique (FR) (Exbury) [1989/90 16m^{3} 16g^{4} 16d 16g^{4} 16d 16m 24f^{2}] lengthy, sparely-made, angular gelding: useful hurdler: best efforts of season on first, fourth and final starts, on last occasion weakening run-in when 6 lengths second to Picador over 3m at Ascot (had seemed best at around 2m previously): probably acts on any going: suited by a strongly-run race. *J. A. C. Edwards.* 135

AFFAIRE DE COEUR 6 b.m. Imperial Fling (USA)–Creake (Derring-Do) [1989/90 18g^{4} 16g^{3} 18g^{5} 18s a16g* a16g^{2}] lengthy mare: handicap hurdler: won at Lingfield in January: creditable second on same course following month: stays 2¼m: probably acts on any going. *J. Ffitch-Heyes.* 102

AFRICAN AFFAIR 5 br.g. Be My Native (USA)–Moment of Weakness (Pieces of Eight) [1989/90 16f] small, sparely-made gelding: jumped moderately and never dangerous both completed outings over hurdles. *R. M. Whitaker.* —

AFRICAN MINSTREL 5 b.g. Longleat (USA)–Bewitched (African Sky) [1989/90 16g^{3} 16g^{pu}] lightly-made gelding: only form when third in selling hurdle at Hereford in November: blinkered 3 times in 1988/9. *R. T. Juckes.* 64

AFRICAN SAFARI 6 b.g. Daring March–African Berry (African Sky) [1989/90 16m a16g^{6} c16f^{2} c16m^{F} a16g^{3} a16g^{4} a16s^{3} a16g^{5} a16g^{2} a16g^{4}] leggy, rather dipped-backed gelding: plating-class 7f handicapper on Flat: poor novice selling hurdler: beaten comfortably in 2-runner novice chase at Leicester in December: unlikely to stay much beyond 2m: blinkered ninth outing (ran well): sold 4,300 gns Ascot May Sales. *P. D. Cundell.* c? 78

AFRICAN SPIRIT 6 b.g. African Sky–Relic Spirit (Relic) [1989/90 16m^{4} 17f* 16s^{3} 16g* 16g 17g^{bd}] compact gelding: held up when winning novice handicap hurdles at Doncaster and Wetherby in December: will always be best at around 2m: acts on firm going. *R. M. Whitaker.* 91

A FRIEND OF MINE 4 b.g. Noalto–Merency (Meldrum) [1989/90 16v 16g 16s^{6} a16s* a18g^{3} a20g^{2}] rather sparely-made gelding: showed little in maiden on Flat in 1989: won 4-runner juvenile handicap hurdle at Lingfield in January: creditable second to easy winner Go Nobley in novice event on same course in March: stays 2½m: acts on slow going. *M. H. Tompkins.* 84

AFTER FOUR 6 gr.g. Roselier (FR)–Caherelly Cross (Royal Buck) [1989/90 c24s^{2} c24v c20s^{4} c26f^{3}] workmanlike ex-Irish gelding: second foal: dam unraced: won point-to-point in 1989: in frame in novice chases, showing only poor form: stays 3¼m: probably acts on any going. *R. B. Francis.* c82

AFTER THE GLOOM 5 ch.g. Bay Express–Heaven And Earth (Midsummer Night II) [1989/90 16f^{4} 16m^{5} 16m* 16d 16d 16d^{2} 16s^{3} 16s 16d 16f^{5} 20f^{6}] plain gelding: selling hurdler: bought in 2,600 gns after winning conditional jockeys event at Leicester in December: ran creditably most subsequent starts, pulled up 79 feelingly final one: seems to stay 2½m: acts on any going: ridden by 7-lb claimer. *J. A. Pickering.*

AFTER THE NUMBER 5 b.g. Le Moss–Fly Fuss (Little Buskins) [1989/90 F16f] first foal: dam unraced half-sister to several winning jumpers: behind in NH Flat race at Warwick in May: yet to race over hurdles or fences. *O. Sherwood.*

AFTERTHOUGHT (NZ) 5 b.g. Prince Simbir (NZ)–Two Lettres (NZ) (Aureate) [1989/90 F16m6] New Zealand-bred gelding: 19 lengths sixth of 17 behind Captain Dibble in NH Flat race at Sandown in March: yet to race over hurdles or fences. *N. J. Henderson.*

AFTER YOU 7 b.g. Choral Society–Scoupland (Bowsprit) [1989/90 22spu 22gpu] workmanlike gelding: half-brother to winning staying jumper Venturer (by Random Shot): dam placed over hurdles in Ireland: behind when pulled up sixth in novice hurdles. *T. Reid.* —

AGAINST THE GRAIN 9 b.g. Oats–Bench Game (King's Bench) [1989/90 c24g c29s5 c28g* c36fpu] leggy, close-coupled gelding: useful chaser on his day: returned to form when staying on strongly to win handicap at Wolverhampton in February by 8 lengths from Comedy Lane: behind when hampered fourteenth and was eventually pulled up in Seagram Grand National at Liverpool in April: stays extremely well: probably acts on any going: ran moderately when visored once: tends to run in snatches: suited by a strongly-run race. *D. Nicholson.* **c123** —

AGE OF DISCRETION 8 b.g. Rymer–Miss Lara (Master Owen) [1989/90 c20m c25m5 c24g c24mur c26gpu c21m5] strong, medium-sized gelding: pulled up only outing over hurdles: led until unseating rider last in novice event at Market Rasen in April, only sign of ability over fences. *J. C. McConnochie.* c— —

AGREE TO DIFFER 5 ch.g. Werrion–Lustrous Lady VII (pedigree unknown) [1989/90 aF16g5 16f6] non-thoroughbred gelding: first foal: dam never ran: no sign of ability in NH Flat race at Lingfield in February and novice selling hurdle at Towcester in May. *K. C. Bailey.* —

AHALIN 8 ch.g. Laurence O–Reaper's Own (Master Owen) [1989/90 c25f3 c20f3] winning point-to-pointer: beaten about 25 lengths when third in hunter chases at Towcester (behind Eastern Chant) and Uttoxeter (behind John Corbet) in May: blinkered in latter. *Mrs H. J. Clarke.* c75

AHERLOW GLEN 6 b.g. Le Bavard (FR)–Bit of Fashion (Master Owen) [1989/90 16g2 F16v4 24g* 21s5 21s c22d* c24s4 c20f c24g2 c19m3] rangy, rather unfurnished Irish gelding: first foal: half-brother to winning hurdler On The Hooch (by Over The River): dam behind in maiden hurdle in Ireland: won maiden hurdle at Wexford in October and novice chase at Leopardstown in December: creditable second in handicap chase at Fairyhouse in April: ran as though something was amiss at Liverpool on eighth start: stays 3m: best form with give in the ground. *T. Carberry, Ireland.* **c113** 110

AH HELLO 9 b.g. Brave Invader (USA)–Rose Militia (Martial) [1989/90 c21f* c21f2 c21dpu c20s5 c20d c21m3 c20mpu] big, deep-girthed gelding: modest novice hurdler: left clear 3 out when winning novice chase at Market Rasen in July: third in novice hunter chase at Fakenham in March: stays 25f: seems to act on any going. *J. R. Bostock.* c82 —

AH JIM LAD 6 b.g. Jimsun–Gigante Rossa (Mount Hagen (FR)) [1989/90 17g 20d] leggy gelding with some scope: lightly-raced novice hurdler: runner-up over 2¾m in 1988/9: travelled well to 2 out on reappearance: never dangerous in useful company next start (February). *A. P. Stringer.* —

AHLAVAI 5 ch.g. Quayside–Play The Part (Deep Run) [1989/90 F16g] second foal: dam unraced half-sister to smart hurdler/useful chaser Snowtown Boy: behind in NH Flat race at Kempton in February: yet to race over hurdles or fences. *G. B. Balding.*

AH WHISHT 11 b.g. Giolla Mear–Green Fern (Menelek) [1989/90 c24v* c25m2 c25g*] big, strong gelding: good Irish hunter chaser: made all at Thurles in February and Punchestown in April, scoring by 20 lengths in quite valuable event on latter course: stays well: goes particularly well in the mud: jumps well. *Pat P. Hogan, Ireland.* **c126 +**

AICNAL 4 b.f. Ile de Bourbon (USA)–Skelbrooke (Mummy's Pet) [1989/90 16g 20g 21d4 20m3] leggy, light-framed filly: half-sister to winning hurdler Lesclacha (by Homing): in frame in 2m minor event on Flat: easily best effort over hurdles when third to Qannaas in handicap at Uttoxeter in April: shapes like a thorough 98 stayer: sold out of M. Camacho's stable 7,400 gns Doncaster November Sales after first start. *R. Hollinshead.*

AIMEE JANE (USA) 5 gr.m. Our Native (USA)–Look Out Liz (USA) (The Axe II) [1989/9 17f4] made all in juvenile hurdle in 1988/9: favourite, always behind in handicap in July: raced too freely to stay 2¾m final outing 1988/9: acts on hard ground: wears blinkers: sold 3,000 gns Ascot August Sales. *M. C. Pipe.* —

AINSTY FOX 6 b.g. Majestic Current (USA)–Roba's Folly (Blue And Grey) [1989/90 c16g4 c20gpu c20g3 c16gur c16g2 c16dF c16m3 c16m c20gur c20d* c20d] leggy, rather angular gelding: poor novice hurdler: ridden by 7-lb claimer, stayed on well to lead close home when winning handicap chase at Sedgefield in January by short head from Captain Mor: better suited by 2½m than 2m: acts on good to soft going: jumps rather sketchily. *B. Ellison.* **c92** —

AIR BROKER (NZ) 9 b.g. Oakville–Sweet Canyon (NZ) (Headland II) [1989/90 c16m2 c20g3 c24s* c24d* c25f3 c25m*] small gelding: had good season, and won handicap chases at Windsor, Huntingdon and Wincanton, beating Highway Express 2 lengths on last-named course in April: suited by 3m: acts on any going: consistent. *R. Akehurst.* **c109** —

AIR COMMANDER 5 br.g. Strong Gale–Southern Slave (Arctic Slave) [1989/90 16m3 16mpu 16g* 16f] angular, light-bodied gelding: brother to novice hurdler Southerly Buster and half-brother to quite useful Irish jumper Running Slave (by Deep Run): dam sister to very useful staying chaser Arctic Actress: held up when winning novice hurdle at Worcester in March: around 13 lengths seventh to Vazon Bay in quite valuable novice handicap at Cheltenham following month: will be suited by further: tends to hang left and may prove best on left-handed track. *O. Sherwood.* 102

AIRLET 9 b.m. Kinglet–Romany Domador (Romany Air) [1989/90 c19f] sturdy mare: winning point-to-pointer: little form otherwise: refused final outing 1988/9. *A. C. D. Joynson.* c—

AIRLY BEACON 6 b.m. Scallywag–Wayside Dancer (Road House II) [1989/90 F17h5 20mpu] tall, deep-girthed mare: chasing type: sister to novice hurdler Skeletor and half-sister to winning hurdler Shaw Brow (by Mandrake Major): dam won 1m seller: last of 5 in NH Flat race at Carlisle in October: tailed off when pulled up 3 out in novice hurdle on same course following month. *C. Parker.* —

AIR STREAK 6 br.m. Air Trooper–Regent Street (Autre Prince) [1989/90 21v5 21v 21fpu] sturdy, compact mare: modest novice hurdler: no worthwhile form in 1989/90: stays 21f: acts on soft going. *A. J. Wilson.* —

AIR VIEW 5 b.m. Heroic Air–Ladyville (Lord Nelson (FR)) [1989/90 16g 16f 16f6 16m] small mare: placed in 5f sellers on Flat: poor novice selling hurdler. *J. R. Bosley.* 59

AISHOLT 5 ch.m. Avocat–Bryophila (FR) (Breakspear II) [1989/90 16g6 16d 22gur] rather sparely-made mare: showed ability in novice hurdles at Wincanton in January and February: tailed off when unseating rider 3 out over 2¾m: claimer ridden. *K. Bishop.* 72

AISKEW FLUTTER 7 b. or br.g. Move Off–Flicka (Balidar) [1989/90 17gF] big, lengthy, plain gelding: tubed: half-brother to 2 winners, including sprinter Mary Maguire (by Warpath), and to modest novice hurdler Pongee's Girl (by Pongee): pulled hard, had lost place when falling fourth in novice hurdle at Carlisle in February. *S. G. Payne.* —

AIX LA CHAPELLE 5 b.m. Bustino–Charming Thought (USA) (Stage Door Johnny) [1989/90 F16d 16fpu] half-sister to fairly useful Flat performer/winning 2½m hurdler Mitilini (by Julio Mariner): dam disappointing maiden: behind in NH Flat race and when pulled up in novice hurdle. *Miss M. J. Benson.* —

AJALITA 4 ch.f. Move Off–Citrine (Meldrum) [1989/90 16g*] plating-class maiden on Flat, stays 1½m and acts on soft going: claimer ridden, bought in 5,600 gns after winning juvenile selling hurdle at Market Rasen in June by 4 lengths from Casbatina: will stay further. *M. J. Ryan.* 76 p

AKDAM (USA) 5 b.h. Arctic Tern (USA)–Dancers Countess (USA) (Northern Dancer) [1989/90 17v* 16d5 16s5 16d 16f*] leggy, angular horse: useful performer at up to 1¼m on Flat, in good form in 1990: sold out of H. Thomson Jones's stable 21,000 gns Newmarket Autumn Sales: won juvenile hurdle at Newton Abbot in January and novice event at Worcester in April: well beaten in between: will stay 104 beyond 17f: acts on any going: amateur ridden first 3 starts. *R. F. Johnson Houghton.*

AKRASH VALLEY 5 gr. or ro.g. Ardross–Haloom (Artaius (USA)) [1989/90
16v^{3}] well-made gelding: mid-division in NH Flat race in 1988/9: 14 lengths third 81 p
behind Dudley in novice hurdle at Folkestone in February (one pace in latter
stages): likely to do better over further: sold 4,600 gns Ascot June Sales. *Mrs J. Pitman.*

AKROTIRI BAY 6 b.g. Ya Zaman (USA)–Felin Geri (Silly Season) [1989/90
20g^{4} 16d 16s^{3} 16v 16s^{6} 25f^{4}] lengthy gelding: poor novice hurdler: stays 2½m: 75
acts on soft going (well beaten on heavy): blinkered final start 1988/9: has run
creditably for an amateur and a claimer: sold 4,000 gns Ascot May Sales. *R. C. Price.*

ALA AMRIK 5 gr. or ro.g. Prince Tenderfoot (USA)–Negligence (Roan
Rocket) [1989/90 17f^{pu} 17g^{pu}] sturdy, lengthy gelding: no sign of ability over —
hurdles. *R. Callow.*

A LAD INSANE 9 br.g. Al Sirat (USA)–Endora (Royal Palm) [1989/90 c16m c**94** §
c16s^{4} c16g^{pu} c20g^{pu} c16g^{3} c16m^{4} c20f^{2} c24f^{3} c20g^{F}] compact gelding: modest —
hurdler/novice chaser: close second when falling last in novice handicap won by
Mr Entertainer at Worcester on final start: stays 3m: yet to race on heavy going,
acts on any other: often amateur or claimer ridden: visored sixth start 1988/9:
carries head high and isn't one to trust. *K. C. Bailey.*

ALAICBRUN 5 b.g. Golden Love–Carrigal (Deep Run) [1989/90 20d^{6} 20g^{5}
20s^{6} 20g^{4} 20m^{pu}] leggy, lengthy gelding: poor novice hurdler: will be suited by 83
further than 2½m. *R. Earnshaw.*

AL-AMARADY 8 ch.g. Tumble Wind (USA)–Allanooka (Be Friendly) [1989/90 c—
c17f^{4} c20f^{pu} c19f^{3} 16f^{6} 20f] compact gelding: poor winning hurdler: poor novice —
chaser: stays 2½m: acts on any going: sometimes blinkered (not when
successful) and ran visored last start: seems suited by forcing tactics. *R. E. Peacock.*

ALAN BALL 4 b.g. Broadsword (USA)–Keshoon (Sheshoon) [1989/90 F16f^{3}]
first foal: dam moderate staying hurdler: 11 lengths third of 16 behind Raido in NH
Flat race at Uttoxeter in April: yet to race over hurdles. *Miss S. J. Wilton.*

ALANERRY 10 br.g. Alanrod–Kerry B (Paddy's Birthday) [1989/90 16d 22g] c—
compact gelding: poor novice selling hurdler: pulled up all outings over fences: —
acts on soft going: blinkered nowadays. *W. G. Morris.*

ALAOUI 8 ch.g. Al Sirat (USA)–Sunny Sunset (Sunny Way) [1989/90 25g^{2} c**106**
a20g* c25m^{3} a24g* 21d^{pu} a20g a18g^{2} 24m* 20f* 20f^{3} 21m* 22m^{2}] workmanlike 118
gelding: had a good season: won novice hurdles at Southwell (2), Chepstow and
Hexham and an amateur riders hurdle at Fakenham: good second in minor hurdle
at Stratford final start: modest chaser: effective at 2m and stays 3m: probably acts
on any going: tends to sweat. *Mrs S. Oliver.*

ALARM CALL (USA) 7 b.h. Alleged (USA)–Sunelianne (USA) (Cyane)
[1989/90 26v^{F} 21d^{pu} 22g^{pu}] strong horse: fair winning juvenile hurdler: lightly —
raced and no form over hurdles since. *N. R. Mitchell.*

ALASKA RUN 8 ch.g. Deep Run–Snow Slave VI (Arctic Slave) [1989/90 c—
c20g^{pu} c20d^{F}] rangy gelding: has been hobdayed: modest winning hurdler: very —
lightly-raced novice over fences: bred to stay at least 2½m: acts on soft going. *D. Nicholson.*

AL ASOOF (USA) 5 gr.g. Shareef Dancer (USA)–Jet Quick (USA)
(Determine) [1989/90 20m^{pu} 16d] sturdy gelding: useful juvenile hurdler in —
1988/9: stiff task, weakened before 2 out when tenth of 11 finishers in Scottish
Champion Hurdle at Ayr in April: stays 2¼m: best form on a yielding surface. *P. R. Hedger.*

ALBERT PLACE 4 ch.c. Ahonoora–Holiday Regrets (Silly Season) [1989/90
16g] well beaten on Flat: sold out of Mrs L. Piggott's stable 4,000 gns Doncaster —
November Sales: behind in novice hurdle at Kelso in March, weakening 3 out. *K. A. Morgan.*

ALBERT THE GREAT 7 ch.g. Meldrum–Bath Miss (Appiani II) [1989/90
16g* 16f^{2} 16d 16g* 16m^{pu}] compact gelding: handicap hurdler: won at Kelso in 96
October and Ayr following month: pulled up, apparently lame, final start: best at
2m: acts on any going: blinkered last 3 starts in 1986/7. *P. Liddle.*

ALCATRAZ (FR) 6 b.g. Nadjar (FR)–Ancholia (High Line) [1989/90 a20g^{4}
21m^{5} 21m 24m 24m] leggy gelding: handicap hurdler: best effort of season on 102 ?

third start: stays 3m: acts on soft going and good to firm: blinkered nowadays. *J. Ringer.*

ALCAZABA 8 b.g. Comedy Star (USA)–Miss Pimm (Gentle Art) [1989/90 c20m c21fpu] sturdy gelding: winning selling hurdler: no form since 1985/6, including in novice chases (jumped badly last start): form only at around 2m: acts on soft going: ridden by 7-lb claimer: has worn blinkers, including when successful. *Mrs R. Williams.* c— —

ALCHEMIC (NZ) 6 br.g. Bold Venture (NZ)–Poldhullie (Polyfoto) [1989/90 F12g3 16g 16g] rangy, sparely-made gelding: third in NH Flat race at Market Rasen in November: in rear in novice hurdles at Ludlow and Wolverhampton (jumped sketchily). *M. H. B. Robinson.* —

ALDAHE 5 ch.g. Dalsaan–Alanood (Northfields (USA)) [1989/90 16g 16d] workmanlike gelding: winning sprinter on Flat: well beaten in novice hurdle and a maiden event at Edinburgh: pulls hard and barely stays 2m. *T. Craig.* —

ALDAJA 4 b.c. Mill Reef (USA)–Lady Constance (Connaught) [1989/90 a16g 16mpu] fifth foal: half-brother to fair 1m winner Zaytoon (by Formidable) and fair 6f 2-y-o winner Bahrain Star (by Star Appeal), latter also successful over hurdles: dam winner over 5f and 7f at 2 yrs: no sign of ability in juvenile hurdles: sold 1,800 gns Ascot December Sales. *R. J. O'Sullivan.* —

AL DIFFA (USA) 4 b.c. Star de Naskra (USA)–General Partner (USA) (Understanding) [1989/90 16m5 16fur 16gpu] sturdy, workmanlike colt: won over 1½m on Flat at 3 yrs: sold out of H. Thomson Jones's stable 17,000 gns Newmarket July Sales: showed a little ability when fifth in juvenile hurdle at Windsor in November: let down by his jumping afterwards: blinkered final start. *R. V. Smyth.* 78

ALDINGTON BELL 7 b.g. Legal Eagle–Dear Catalpa (Dear Gazelle) [1989/90 16m6 16f* 16h5] leggy gelding: selling hurdler: lightly raced since 1987/8: comfortably justified favouritism at Ludlow in April (bought in 5,400 gns): not certain to stay much beyond 2m: acts well on hard ground: blinkered once in 1987/8 and on last 2 starts: usually ridden by cliimer. *C. C. Trietline.* 95

ALDINGTON PRINCE 4 b.g. Creetown–Dear Catalpa (Dear Gazelle) [1989/90 16m 16d 17vpu 16s 16g4 16d3] good-bodied gelding: half-brother to winning hurdler Aldington Bell (by Legal Eagle): well beaten on Flat: dropped in class and ridden by 5-lb claimer, 11 lengths third behind Sally's Dove in 19-runner selling hurdle at Bangor in March. *C. C. Trietline.* 67

ALDINO 7 ch.g. Artaius (USA)–Allotria (Red God) [1989/90 16g* 16m* 16m3 16g5 16g* 16s5 16f 16d3] small, angular, sparely-made gelding: very useful hurdler: won Ring & Brymer Hurdle at Kempton and 3-runner minor event at Huntingdon in October, and New Year's Day Hurdle at Windsor (looked none too keen when beating Beldale Star 2½ lengths): easily best subsequent effort when 145

New Year's Day Hurdle, Windsor—a third win of the season for Aldino

Mr J. Hobbs's "Al Hashimi"

8 lengths third behind impressive Sayparee in Scottish Champion Hurdle (limited handicap) at Ayr in April: doesn't stay 2½m: ideally suited by give in the ground and acts on heavy: usually visored or blinkered: has edged left under pressure: has a turn of foot and is suited by waiting tactics. *O. Sherwood.*

ALDRA BOND 5 ch.g. Gold Song–Petite Case (Upper Case (USA)) [1989/90 20f* 20m* 16g3] sparely-made gelding: successful in novice hurdles at Hexham in September and November: good third behind Ramilie in handicap on same course later in November: stays 2½m: acts on firm ground: visored, found nothing from 2 out final start 1988/9: retained by trainer 5,000 gns Doncaster November Sales. *G. M. Moore.* 115

ALEDAN 9 b.g. Raise You Ten–Melodic Beat (Melodic Air) [1989/90 c20d c21m6 c24spu c26v6 c26f c25h3 c25mpu] big, angular gelding: poor novice hurdler/chaser: stays 25f: acts on any going: blinkered final outing 1987/8. *G. Ripley.* c79 —

ALEXANDRA KATRINE 4 b.f. Precocious–Sipapu (Targowice (USA)) [1989/90 16g 16f] good-quartered filly: moderate sprint maiden on Flat (possibly ungenuine): no sign of ability in juvenile maiden hurdle at Wincanton and fillies seller at Wolverhampton in second half of season. *R. F. Johnson Houghton.* —

ALEXANDRA PALACE 9 b.g. Warpath–Alexandra (Song) [1989/90 c19m3 c24dF] rangy gelding: poor hurdler/chaser: third in hunter chase at Hereford in April: probably stays 3m: acts on firm ground and is possibly unsuited by heavy: visored last outing: sold 3,400 gns Ascot July Sales. *Miss Susan Rodway.* c85 —

ALEXA'S BOY 6 b.g. African Sky–Regal Step (Ribero) [1989/90 17f^4 16m 16d^5 17g^3 17g 17v] leggy gelding: poor novice selling hurdler: best effort of season on fourth start: acts on heavy going. *T. B. Hallett.* 62

AL FAYES 6 b.g. Ya Zaman (USA)–None-So-Pretty (Never Say Die) [1989/90 16m] lightly-raced novice hurdler: no sign of ability. *T. Casey.* —

AL HASHIMI 6 b.g. Ile de Bourbon (USA)–Parmesh (Home Guard (USA)) [1989/90 c16d^{ur} c16s^5 c16d* c16m*] big, lengthy, angular gelding: modest novice hurdler: always travelling well when successful twice over fences at Chepstow, in novice handicap in March and quite well-contested novice event (by 7 lengths from Pendennis) in April: best at 2m: acts on any going with possible exception of heavy: jumps well in the main and is sure to win more races over fences. *D. Nicholson.* c**127** p —

ALI' CARRENA 5 br.g. Town And Country–Classic Hand (Some Hand) [1989/90 F16m aF13g^4] first foal: dam unraced: well beaten in NH Flat races: dead. *J. R. Jenkins.*

ALICE'S BOY 9 b.g. Tycoon II–Small Dragon (Pendragon) [1989/90 24s^6 c20v^3 c20d^4 c24g^F c26g^4] sturdy gelding: carries plenty of condition: poor chaser: barely stays 3m: probably acts on any going, but goes well in the mud: sometimes jumps deliberately. *R. B. Francis.* c82 + —

ALICIAN BRIDGE 9 br.g. Over The River (FR)–Pontnos (Kythnos) [1989/90 24g^{pu} 20g] lengthy, sparely-made gelding: very lightly-raced novice hurdler: dead. *D. Lee.* —

ALIDAN 6 b.g. Golden Love–Priest's Sister (Bluerullah) [1989/90 F16m 16f] tall, deep-girthed gelding: first foal: dam unraced half-sister to fair staying chaser Priest's Rock: tailed off in NH Flat race and a Leicester novice hurdle in first half of season: sold 3,000 gns Doncaster March Sales. *M. J. Wilkinson.* —

ALI MOURAD 5 ch.g. Final Straw–Paper Sun (Match III) [1989/90 16f 16d^{pu} 20g^2 16m* 16g^3 16m 16m* 20s 17f^5 16f^6 16m^4 20g^6] compact gelding: won selling handicap hurdles at Towcester in December (bought in 3,400 gns) and January (conditional jockeys event, sold out of E. Wheeler's stable 2,400 gns): also ran well ninth to eleventh starts: stays 2½m: acts on any going: blinkered nowadays: has run in snatches. *C. Smith.* 88

ALISON GREY 7 gr.m. Jellaby–Alice (Parthia) [1989/90 17m^5] small, lengthy mare: half-sister to several winners, including quite useful staying hurdler Wonder Wood (by High Line): dam never ran: needed race, late headway when remote fifth of 10 finishers behind Iama Zulu in novice hurdle at Devon & Exeter in April. *P. J. Hobbs.* —

ALISTAIRS GIRL 7 b.m. Connaught–Miss Hubbard (New Brig) [1989/90 16f^4 16m^4 16d* 20m 16s c20g^4 c16v^{pu} c16g* c16d^5 c16d^4 c16m^4 c16d c20f^2 c16d^2 c16f^3] strong, workmanlike mare: has a round action: shows traces of stringhalt: 15-length winner of novice hurdle at Ayr in November and novice handicap chase at Catterick in February: hard-pulling front runner, best at around 2m: has run respectably on firm going, but is probably suited by give in the ground: usually taken to post early or late: inconsistent. *W. G. Reed.* c**88** + 88

ALKINOR REX 5 ch.g. Welsh Pageant–Glebehill (Northfields (USA)) [1989/90 16d* 16g^3 16d^F 16d] rather sparely-made gelding: fair performer on Flat, successful at up to 1¼m: won novice hurdle at Windsor in January in good style by 15 lengths from Le Chat Noir: 6 lengths third behind Stratford Ponds at Kempton following month: stiff task and not disgraced in Scottish Champion Hurdle at Ayr on final start: may be suited by stiffer test of stamina: acts on dead going. *M. E. D. Francis.* 119

ALKIONIS 4 b.c. Dominion–Norfolk Gal (Blakeney) [1989/90 17v^{pu} 16d 16d 17m 17m^3 16f] smallish, sparely-made colt: lightly raced and no worthwhile form on Flat: poor novice over hurdles: has looked a difficult ride: blinkered last 3 outings. *Mrs A. Knight.* 67

ALL ACTION 4 b.g. Rapid River–Palace Tor (Dominion) [1989/90 16f^4 16m 17h* 16f^3 a16g 16h] lightly-raced maiden on Flat: won 4-runner selling hurdle at Carlisle in September (bought out of W. A. Stephenson's stable 4,000 gns): well beaten last 2 starts (off course almost 6 months in between). *M. T. Bowker.* 77

ALL AFLOAT 6 b.g. Oats–Flotilla (Alcide) [1989/90 16g 20v^5 16s^{pu}] lengthy, workmanlike gelding: will make a chaser: sixth living foal: dam modest staying half-sister to good 1964 2-y-o Leonardo: bit backward, blundered last when remote fifth behind Lucky Verdict in novice hurdle at Chepstow in January, only sign of ability: will stay well. *Capt. T. A. Forster.* 77

ALL AGREED 9 b.g. Jaazeiro (USA)–Tynwald Hill (Rarity) [1989/90 16m a16gpu] smallish, sturdy gelding: handicap hurdler: in clear second place when — pulled up lame approaching last in race won by Hill Beagle at Southwell in January: acts on firm ground. *R. Brotherton.*

ALLENELLA 10 br.g. Derek H–Nella The Nipper (Inside Straight) [1989/90 **c83** c27g c27g4 c27d2 c27dF] workmanlike gelding: poor maiden point-to-pointer and novice chaser: stayed well: dead. *M. S. Vernon.*

ALLEN'S ROCK 6 b.g. Abednego–Larne (Giolla Mear) [1989/90 22s3 22s3] angular gelding: brother to winning hurdler Hunter Buoy: third in novice hurdles 98 at Folkestone in December, on second occasion beaten around 12 lengths by Senegalais: stays 2¾m: has worn crossed noseband. *N. A. Gaselee.*

ALLERYBAR 10 br.g. New Brig–Lucky Burn (Lucky Brief) [1989/90 c24dbd] c— winning point-to-pointer: prominent when brought down eleventh in hunter chase at Ayr in April. *R. J. Kyle.*

ALLGALLO 6 br.g. Ballynockan–Some Hope (Gallo Gallante) [1989/90 16g 17m* 20g6 16f] first foal: won novice hurdle at Carlisle in April: below form 92 subsequently: seems best at around 2m: acts on good to firm ground. *C. Parker.*

ALLIED LAD 5 ch.g. Monksfield–Miss Evelin (Twilight Alley) [1989/90 F16f] second foal: half-brother to winning hurdler Henlin (by Lord Henham): dam unraced half-sister to Brown Chamberlin: around 16 lengths seventh of 10 to Norman Conqueror in NH Flat race at Newbury in March: yet to race over hurdles or fences. *K. C. Bailey.*

ALL INTENT (USA) 8 b.g. Alleged (USA)–Dear Intent (USA) (Intentionally) c— [1989/90 16m c21fF 16spu a20g6 a16g5 16f4 20m4 c20m4 c20g 20m4] smallish, 80 well-made gelding: winning selling hurdler and novice chaser: form only on sixth, seventh and last starts: stays 2½m: best form on firm ground: claimer ridden when successful. *G. Thorner.*

ALL JEFF (FR) 6 b.g. Jefferson–Fromentel (FR) (Timour) [1989/90 c**141** + 20d4 c19g* c21gbd c22g2 c24g2 c24fF c20f* c22g*] 109 +

Cagnes-sur-Mer, an early-season venue on the Cote d'Azur popular with certain British Flat trainers and owners over the years, played host in the latest season to a British-trained chaser in the shape of the very useful novice All Jeff. All Jeff, formerly trained in France, paid three visits at around the turn-of-the-year to give his owner, who was on holiday in the vicinity, the opportunity to see him in action. All Jeff, ridden by Landau who'll be remembered for his association with Lean Ar Aghaidh in Britain, made his chasing debut in the Prix Alain du Breil and adapted to the French fences well; he was always prominent in the nineteen-furlong contest and came home a two-length winner. All Jeff fared less well in his next race, being brought down at the second, but turned in a game effort in the valuable Prix de la Ville de Nice on his last appearance in France, making the running until unable to hold off Le Clos Marville in the closing stages. Altogether he earned around £18,000 in win and place prize-money in his short stay. He continued to run well on his return to Britain, and following a second to Arctic Call in a novice chase at Newbury he tackled the best staying novices in the Sun Alliance Chase at Cheltenham in March. Although the outsider of nine, All Jeff was in the process of running an extremely good race when falling at the third last when a close fifth and just in front of eventual winner Garrison Savannah. All Jeff's jumping up to that point had been none too fluent and he appeared to run in snatches, but he had been travelling well when coming to grief. He gained compensation later in the month in the British Aerospace Rapier Novices' Chase at Sandown, overcoming some sticky jumping in the early stages to land the odds by six lengths from Brandeston, and, more importantly, in April in the Tattersalls Novice Chase at Fairyhouse. He put up easily his best performance in Ireland, when leading after the last and pulling away on the run-in to beat Renagown and subsequent Tattersalls Gold Cup Handicap Chase winner Mixed Blends by five lengths and eight.

All Jeff is the fourth foal of the unraced Fromentel; her first three, Chardone, Claodia (both by Olmeto) and All Choisy (by Kouban) have all been successful over jumps in France. Fromentel is a half-sister to two middle-distance Flat winners, and a daughter of Quick Dip, a winner at up to a mile and a quarter. Quick Dip is a full sister to Fast Dip, who was a good-class performer at up to a mile and a quarter, and Major Dip a winner at up to nine and a half furlongs. Their dam, Miss Dip, unplaced on the Flat, is a half-sister to the 1951 Eclipse winner Mystery IX. All Jeff is by the French stallion Jefferson, a top-class racehorse who stayed a mile and a quarter. His most notable progeny are the French-trained 1979 St Leger winner Son of Love and the good French stayer Marson.

All Jeff (FR) (b.g. 1984)	Jefferson (ch 1967)	Charlottesville (b 1957)	Prince Chevalier
			Noorani
		Monticella (ch 1955)	Cranach
			Montenica
	Fromentel (FR) (b 1976)	Timour (b 1964)	Dan Cupid
			Cerisoles II
		Quick Dip (b 1962)	Fast Fox
			Miss Dip

All Jeff, a neat gelding, showed nothing as a two-year-old, but was a successful hurdler in 1987/8 when trained by A. Chelet. Transferred to Lambourn the following season, he showed a good deal of promise on his British debut when seventh in the Long Walk Hurdle at Ascot. He failed to fulfil that in his two subsequent races in 1988/9, his trainer reporting the horse to have been suffering from a virus. All Jeff is effective at around two and a half miles and stays three miles. He seems to act on any going. *C. P. E. Brooks.*

ALL OVER THE WORLD 6 b.g. Kind of Hush–Bosworth Moll (Henry The Seventh) [1989/90 17m* 20f^{3} 16m 22f^{3} 25f^{6} 24g 24m^{4} 24m^{3} 27g 20d^{6} 25m^{6} 20g] workmanlike gelding: half-brother to a winning jumper in Spain by Neltino: poor performer on Flat nowadays: won novice hurdle at Cartmel in August: ran creditably on occasions afterwards, including in slowly-run race over 3m eighth start: acts on firm going: trained until after eleventh outing by D. Smith. *J. R. Fort.* 89

ALL SHOOK UP 4 b.c. All Systems Go–Mary of Scots (Relic) [1989/90 18g^{pu}] quite modest at 2 yrs: tailed off when pulled up 2 out in juvenile hurdle at Fontwell in December: sold 1,550 gns Ascot February Sales. *P. Howling.* —

ALLTEN GLAZED 13 b.g. Ragapan–Elands Kop (Tiepolo II) [1989/90 c16d^{6} c20g c20g^{2} c16v*] strong gelding: modest chaser nowadays: won conditional jockeys handicap at Ayr in January by 10 lengths (left clear when Tactico, who was upsides, fell 2 out): best form at up to 2½m: suited by give in the ground and acts on heavy. *M. P. Naughton.* c**112** —

ALLYFAIR 5 gr.m. Scallywag–Spartan Blonde (Spartan General) [1989/90 F16f^{4}] first foal: dam unraced: around 19 lengths fourth of 9 to Wessex Warrior in NH Flat race at Wincanton in March: yet to race over hurdles or fences. *Mrs J. G. Retter.*

ALMA GOLD 5 b.g. Sonnen Gold–Au Pair (Runnymede) [1989/90 F17m^{ur} F16d] small gelding: fourth foal: half-brother to winning sprinter and prolific winning chaser Yangtse-Kiang (by Rapid River): dam placed at up to 1¼m: mid-division in NH Flat race at Catterick in February: yet to race over hurdles or fences. *J. J. O'Neill.*

ALMANZORA 6 ch.g. Proverb–Serrulata (Raise You Ten) [1989/90 16d^{3}] leggy, lengthy gelding: has scope: third in NH Flat race at Towcester in 1988/9 and in novice hurdle on same course (unable to quicken run-in and beaten 6½ lengths by Greysby) in February: will stay further: should improve, particularly over further. *Mrs J. Pitman.* 93 p

ALMERIMAR 6 b.g. Home Guard (USA)–Melaleuca (Levmoss) [1989/90 16d^{5} 16g^{pu} a16g^{6} c16d^{4} c16f^{3} c16g^{3} c17f^{ur} c16g^{4} c17f^{2}] leggy, good-topped gelding: poor novice hurdler/chaser: unlikely to stay much beyond 2m: acts on firm ground: often finds little: sold 7,600 gns Ascot June Sales. *N. J. Henderson.* c**87** 80

ALMONDBURY 9 b.g. Moulton–Phoenix Rose (Frankincense) [1989/90 c20d^{3} c27g^{3}] big gelding: novice hurdler/winning chaser: travelled strongly until lack of peak fitness told from last in handicap chase at Sedgefield in February on second start: suited by 3m or more: best runs on good ground. *M. W. Easterby.* c**101** —

ALMOOJID 4 b.c. Sadler's Wells (USA)–Irish Bird (USA) (Sea Bird II) [1989/90 17d^{pu}] ex-Irish colt: closely related to top-class middle-distance performer Assert (by Be My Guest) and half-brother to Irish St Leger winner —

Eurobird (by Ela-Mana-Mou), Prix du Jockey-Club winner Bikala (by Kalamoun) and winning hurdler Irish Gantlet (by Run The Gantlet): placed over 1½m on Flat in September: sold out of D. K. Weld's stable 6,600 gns Newmarket Autumn Sales: tailed off when pulled up 2 out in juvenile hurdle at Devon & Exeter in January. *J. H. Baker.*

ALMOST CAUGHT 9 ch.m. Nearly A Hand–Kitty Fisher (Track Spare) c—
[1989/90 c17g^F 21v a16g^5 a20g^6 21d^6] lightly-built mare: novice hurdler/chaser 79
and poor point-to-pointer: showed ability over hurdles third and last starts: ran poorly in selling company in between: stays well: acts on soft going. *R. G. Frost.*

ALNASRIC PETE (USA) 4 b.c. Al Nasr (FR)–Stylish Pleasure (USA) (What
A Pleasure (USA)) [1989/90 16s] fair 1m winner on Flat: well-beaten eighth of 11 to —
Dark Desire in juvenile hurdle at Sandown in February, weakening in latter stages. *G. Harwood.*

ALO' BABY 4 gr.g. Julio Mariner–Bellarina (Rugantino) [1989/90 18f^4] second
foal: dam poor hurdler and novice chaser: poor maiden plater on Flat, has run 63
blinkered: fourth of 6 in juvenile selling hurdle at Fontwell in October. *J. R. Jenkins.*

ALPHA LADY 4 b.f. Daring March–Fair Persuasion (Fair Season) [1989/90
16m^{pu} 16d^{pu} 16d^{pu}] lengthy filly: poor plater on Flat: tailed off when pulled up in —
juvenile hurdles: blinkered last start. *Mrs S. Armytage.*

ALPHA ONE 5 ch.g. Belfalas–Clonaslee Foam (Quayside) [1989/90 F17d F17m^4] second foal: dam won NH Flat race in Ireland: 13 lengths fourth to Merry Master in NH Flat race at Carlisle in April: yet to race over hurdles or fences. *W. A. Stephenson.*

ALPHASONIC (USA) 6 b.g. Super Concorde (USA)–My Kinda Lady (USA) c—
(Canadian Gil (CAN)) [1989/90 20f^2 22f* 21m^2 20f* 24d* 25g^4 22m 22v^3 25f 115
24m^4 24f*] big, lengthy gelding: successful in novice hurdles at Fontwell and Cheltenham and handicap at Kempton in first half of season, and in handicap at Ascot (beat Master Barn ¾ length after being under pressure from some way out) in May: poor form in novice chases: thorough stayer: best form on ground no softer than dead: wears blinkers: sold to K. Bailey 7,200 gns Ascot June Sales. *G. Harwood.*

ALPHIN PIKE 5 b.g. Lochnager–Bombay Duck (Ballyciptic) [1989/90 20d^{pu}
16g 16m 22s 20g^{pu}] sturdy gelding: half-brother to 3 winners on Flat, including —
Bombil (by The Brianstan), also successful over hurdles: no sign of ability. *J. A. C. Edwards.*

AL SAHIL (USA) 5 b.g. Riverman (USA)–Tobira Celeste (USA) (Ribot)
[1989/90 16s^5 16g^5] smallish, workmanlike gelding: lightly raced on Flat, but 76
successful over 1m at 3 yrs: sold out of H. Thomson Jones's stable 11,000 gns Newmarket Autumn Sales: beaten fair way but showed some ability when fifth in novice hurdles at Folkestone and Plumpton in mid-season. *J. White.*

ALSAYEGH 10 b.g. Auction Ring (USA)–Sky Green (Skymaster) [1989/90 c—
c25m^{pu}] leggy, sparely-made gelding: poor novice hurdler/chaser/point-to- —
pointer: refused final outing 1986/7. *Capt V. Lloyd-Davies.*

AL'S SON 9 br.g. Al Sirat (USA)–Fanny's Daughter (London Gazette) [1989/90 **c78** x
c18h* 21f^3 c21m^5 c17m^3 c26f^3] leggy, sparely-made gelding: poor novice hurdler: 64
landed the odds in slowly-run amateur riders novice chase at Fontwell in August: third in similar company afterwards: probably stays 3¼m: acts on any going: has been blinkered: moderate jumper. *J. White.*

ALTAGHADERRY ROSE 10 ch.m. Ete Indien (USA)–Altaghaderry Queen c—
(Giolla Mear) [1989/90 c24g^{ur} c27m^{pu}] leggy, sparely-made mare: winning point-to-pointer/steeplechaser: stays very well: acts on good to firm ground and ran poorly on soft: wears blinkers: sold out of C. Saunders' stable 1,900 gns Doncaster November Sales. *P. Pittendrigh.*

ALTE-XPRESS 11 ch.g. Mon Capitaine–Aerial Orchid (Perspex) [1989/90 c—
c24m^{pu}] winning point-to-pointer/steeplechaser: no worthwhile form for a long —
time: blinkered once: sold out of P. Cowley's stable 2,700 gns Ascot December Sales. *Mrs R. Murdoch.*

ALTOBELLI 6 b.g. Northern Treat (USA)–Imagination (FR) (Dancer's Image
(USA)) [1989/90 16g^F a16g^4 16g^2 16f 16g] good-topped gelding: poor handicapper 86
on Flat, successful over 1½m in August: best effort in novice hurdles when second at Hereford in November: reportedly swallowed tongue fourth start: sold 2,500 gns Ascot July Sales. *P. Mitchell.*

ALTO CUMULUS 8 gr.g. Random Shot–Aughalion (Pals Passage) [1989/90 16d 16d6 16s3] strong, deep-bodied gelding: modest novice hurdler/chaser: only form of season when staying-on 8 lengths third behind Free Justice in novice handicap hurdle at Hereford in March: acts on dead going and good to firm: blinkered final start 1987/8. *N. A. Gaselee.* c— 83

ALTOUNTASH 6 b.h. Labus (FR)–Alannya (FR) (Relko) [1989/90 24f2 24d 20fpu 22m2 24d] rangy horse: handicap hurdler: first outing for 5 months, ½-length second to Fane Banks at Fairyhouse in April: trained prior to then by I. Wardle and was runner-up at Uttoxeter in October: stays 3m: acts well on firm ground: has run well when sweating. *F. Lennon, Ireland.* 114

ALTRAFAN 7 b.g. Gay Fandango (USA)–Tomanaha (USA) (Tom Fool) [1989/90 20f5] leggy, workmanlike gelding: won selling hurdle in 1988/9: ran moderately only start 1989/90 (September): should stay beyond 2½m: no form on very soft ground, acts on any other: often amateur ridden: sold 1,050 gns Ascot November Sales. *G. Harwood.* —

ALUMNUS 12 br.g. Falaise (USA)–Beige Etoile (French Beige) [1989/90 17h6 26f6 21m6] selling hurdler: well beaten in 1989/90: of little account in steeplechases: has worn blinkers. *N. R. Mitchell.* c— x —

ALVECOTE MAGIC 6 gr.g. Anfield–Sawk (Sea Hawk II) [1989/90 16g 16m2] workmanlike gelding: 1m winner at 2 yrs, but lightly raced and little worthwhile form on Flat since: bandaged and carrying plenty of condition, 2½ lengths second to Flying in conditional jockeys selling hurdle at Lingfield in January: likely to prove best over sharp 2m. *D. J. Wintle.* 83

ALWAYS AWAY 6 ch.g. Quayside–Safe Return (Canisbay) [1989/90 F16g 16s 16g] workmanlike gelding: ninth foal: half-brother to winning hurdler/chaser More One Way (by Arapaho): dam poor plater: well beaten in NH Flat race and novice hurdles. *C. C. Trietline.* —

ALWAYS DANGEROUS 8 br.g. Celtic Cone–Sally Ann III (Port Corsair) [1989/90 c20d3 c16gF] smallish, workmanlike gelding: handicap hurdler: novice chaser: under pressure and had just been headed by eventual winner Beau Guest when falling last at Edinburgh in January: stays 2½m: probably acts on any going: has been tried in blinkers: ridden by 7-lb claimer in 1989/90. *G. M. Moore.* c96 —

ALWAYS FLAT BROKE 6 b. or br.g. Flatbush–Poor Girl (Richboy) [1989/90 F12g] second living foal: dam never ran: tailed off in NH Flat race at Hexham in March: yet to race over hurdles or fences. *P. Liddle.*

ALWAYS GREAT 4 b.g. Vaigly Great–Jinja (St Paddy) [1989/90 17f3 16f6 16f a16g2 a16g a16g5] small gelding: sprint maiden on Flat: sold out of T. M. Jones's stable 2,700 gns Ascot 2nd June Sales: poor juvenile selling hurdler: races freely and barely stays 2m: has worn severe bridle: reportedly suffered oxygen starvation after first start. *W. Clay.* 65

ALWAYS NATIVE (USA) 9 b. or br.g. Our Native (USA)–Mountain Memory (USA) (Groton) [1989/90 c16gpu] leggy gelding: has been tubed: winning selling hurdler: no form over fences: pulls hard and barely stays 2m: acts on good to soft going. *G. P. Kelly.* c— —

ALWAYS TAKE PROFIT 4 ch.g. Noalto–Pour Moi (Bay Express) [1989/90 16v a18g5 16g] in frame over 7f at 2 yrs, but no form on Flat in 1989: no worthwhile form in selling hurdles: sold 740 gns Doncaster March Sales. *C. N. Allen.* —

ALWAYS TALKING 9 b.g. Bishop of Orange–Brogeen Lass (Bright As Gold) [1989/90 c20m5 c22d3 c26gpu 21f5] lengthy, angular gelding: successful in point-to-point and NH Flat race in Ireland: third to Toureen Prince at Nottingham in February, best effort in novice chases: tailed off in novice hurdle final outing: will stay 3m: trained by O. Sherwood first 3 starts. *B. Richmond.* c89 —

ALZAMINA 4 b.f. Alzao (USA)–Timinala (Mansingh (USA)) [1989/90 17g4 16g 16f4 a16gpu] leggy filly: quite modest sprint maiden on Flat: bad form over hurdles, including in sellers. *J. White.* 54

AMANDA JANE (USA) 6 b.m. State Dinner (USA)–Roman Edge (USA) (Vertex) [1989/90 20gur 25m6 20f4] sparely-made mare: lightly-raced novice hurdler: poor form: probably stays 3m: sold out of P. Cundell's stable 3,000 gns Ascot August Sales. *C. Smith.* 71

AMANDA'S PRINCE 6 b.g. Chukaroo–Moon Ray (Halation) [1989/90 F16m] half-brother to temperamental winning hurdler/chaser Prince Moon (by Ampney Prince): dam won over hurdles: eleventh of 19 behind Will I Fly in NH Flat race at Sandown in March: yet to race over hurdles or fences. *G. B. Balding.*

Trillium Handicap Hurdle, Ascot—the blinkered Ambassador gets the better of Smart Performer despite hitting the last

AMAREDO 4 b.c. Akarad (FR)–Amila (Great Nephew) [1989/90 16m* 16s^{6} 20s^{pu} 16s^{pu} 16f] smallish, workmanlike colt: claimed out of L. Cumani's stable 87 ?
£12,001 after finishing second in 1½m claimer on Flat in 1989: won juvenile hurdle at Warwick in September: off course 3 months afterwards and ran poorly on return: should stay 2½m: possibly unsuited by soft ground. *M. C. Pipe.*

AMARI KING 6 b.g. Sit In The Corner (USA)–Maywell (Harwell) [1989/90 c115
c16g* c16d* c16m^{F}] workmanlike gelding: no worthwhile form over hurdles: won —
novice handicap chase at Folkestone in December and handicap chase at Warwick (quickened to lead approaching 2 out when scoring easily by 6 lengths from Bee Garden) in January: in process of running an excellent race when falling 2 out in amateur riders handicap at Sandown in March: likely to prove best at around 2m: acts on dead ground: still has something to learn about jumping, but should win more races over fences. *Capt. T. A. Forster.*

AMATORY 7 ch.g. Junius (USA)–Amatrice (Appiani II) [1989/90 16g a20g^{2} 20h^{5}] compact gelding: handicap hurdler: 2 lengths second to Parentus at 100
Lingfield in February: would have finished upsides runner-up but for going lame in amateur riders handicap at Plumpton following month: stays 2½m: acts on firm going: blinkered sixth start 1988/9 and last 2 outings: sold out of K. Bailey's stable 4,300 gns Ascot November Sales. *C. L. Popham.*

AMBASSADOR 7 ch.g. General Assembly (USA)–Klairlone (Klairon) [1989/90 16f* 17v^{5} 16d* 16d 16m 16f^{5} 16f^{2} 16f*] robust gelding: useful hurdler: 137
won at Taunton in December and Ascot in January and April (beat Smart Performer 1½ lengths in Trillium Handicap Hurdle, despite bad mistake last): best at 2m: acts on any going with possible exception of heavy: usually wears blinkers, visored sixth start: showed no enthusiasm when racing with tongue tied down once in 1987/8: suited by a strongly-run race. *M. C. Pipe.*

AMBERGATE 9 b.g. Forlorn River–Jackie's Joy (Skymaster) [1989/90 22f* c94
25f* 24m^{2} 26d^{2} 24f^{2} 24g^{4} c24d^{2} c24g^{4} c24d^{2} c20f^{3} c24h* c24g^{2}] tall, angular 123
gelding: fair hurdler: won 2 handicaps at Kelso in October: beat Solicitor's Choice a length in novice chase at Hexham in April: hampered run-in when third in similar event at Newcastle following month (later placed second): stays 25f: probably acts on any going: sometimes amateur ridden: blinkered tenth start: game. *W. A. Stephenson.*

AMBIANCE 11 gr.g. Three Legs–Ambient (Amber Rama (USA)) [1989/90 16g c—
25d^{pu} c16m^{5} c20f^{pu}] good-bodied gelding: lightly-raced winning hurdler, —

evidently difficult to train: looked none too keen in selling handicap second start: jumped none too fluently and never dangerous in novice event on chasing debut: stays 21f: acts on good to firm and dead going: suited by forcing tactics: sometimes blinkered or visored. *B. Stevens.*

AMBUSCADE (USA) 4 ch.c. Roberto (USA)–Gurkhas Band (USA) (Lurullah) [1989/90 16g* 16d* 16d* 16m4 16m4] workmanlike colt: fair form at 2 yrs, since placed over 2m on Flat: sold out of G. Harwood's stable 9,200 gns Newmarket Autumn Sales: won novice hurdle at Catterick in January and 2 juvenile hurdles at Kelso following month: showed much better form when fourth at Newcastle and Liverpool, on latter course finishing in good style when beaten 11 lengths by Sybillin in Glenlivet Anniversary Hurdle: will be suited by further: not a fluent jumper. *G. M. Moore.* 127

AMENHOTEP (NZ) 5 br.h. Star Wolf–Pendeen (Knight's Romance) [1989/90 F16m 16h4] eighth of 17 in NH Flat race at Sandown in March: tended to jump slowly when fourth of 6 finishers to The Pursewarden in novice hurdle at Taunton following month. *D. H. Barons.* 71

AMETHEA 8 ch.m. True Song–Spartan's Legacy (Spartan General) [1989/90 c24gr c20s6 c25g c24m6 c26sur c26g4 c24f6 c24f5 c24m c24gpu c20d] lengthy mare: no form over hurdles since 1986/7: poor novice chaser: stays 3m: best form with give in the ground: has been tried in blinkers and a crossed noseband: reluctant to race on occasions. *T. N. Bailey.* **c79** § —

AMRULLAH 10 br.g. High Top–Ravenshead (Charlottown) [1989/90 c16f3 c20f4 c20d4 c20g4 c24gpu c20v5 c20s6] big, good-topped gelding: has shown plenty of ability over hurdles and fences, but is thoroughly irresolute: has been blinkered and visored. *J. J. Bridger.* c§§ §§

AMWAJ 6 gr.g. Tumble Wind (USA)–Centennial Rose (Runnymede) [1989/90 16g 21d 20dur 21dpu] compact gelding: modest novice hurdler: well beaten in handicaps in 1989/90: stays 2½m: acts on firm going. *A. W. Denson.* —

AMY'S MYSTERY 9 b. or br.g. Bivouac–Mystery Trip (Kadir Cup) [1989/90 c25f4] won point-to-points in March and April: made mistakes in closing stages when tailed-off fourth in maiden hunter chase at Cartmel in May. *Clifford Thompson.* c—

ANBAK (USA) 5 ch.g. Riverman (USA)–Virgin (FR) (Zeddaan) [1989/90 16g5 16g 16g 17g6 a20g 16dpu 16f] small, lightly-made gelding: poor novice selling hurdler: little form in 1989/90: sometimes visored or blinkered: looks a difficult ride: sold out of K. Morgan's stable 2,400 gns Ascot November Sales after second start: sold privately 1,250 gns Ascot May Sales. *M. B. James.* —

ANBANREE 7 b. or br.m. Al Sirat (USA)–April Shade (Harwell) [1989/90 16m3] smallish mare: won 3 novice hurdles in 1988/9: good third behind Atig in handicap at Worcester in April: suited by sharp 2m: acts on firm ground: has hung under pressure: has won for an amateur. *D. J. G. Murray-Smith.* 107

ANCIENT CROSS 6 ch.m. Celtic Cone–Crossacres (Spiritus) [1989/90 F17m 22gpu 20s 17g 20d] lengthy, angular mare: fourth foal: half-sister to poor novice chaser Kemcross (by Kemal): dam won two 25f chases: behind in NH Flat race and novice hurdles: claimer ridden. *R. Layland.* —

ANDHRA 4 b.f. Indian King (USA)–Altara (GER) (Tarim) [1989/90 a16gpu] sparely-made filly: maiden plater on Flat, placed over 7f: behind when pulled up lame after 3 out in juvenile hurdle at Southwell in November. *J. Wharton.* —

ANDORRA 8 gr.g. Godswalk (USA)–Lady Sioux (USA) (Apalachee (USA)) [1989/90 c20d4] leggy gelding: very lightly raced but has shown fairly useful form over hurdles: needed race when well-beaten last of 4 finishers in novice event at Huntingdon in February on chasing debut, but wasn't knocked about after being hampered at the twelfth: not certain to stay beyond 2¾m: form only on good ground over hurdles: jumped well at Huntingdon and is sure to do better over fences. *J. G. FitzGerald.* c— p —

ANDREW 7 b.g. Le Coq d'Or–Turkish Suspicion (Above Suspicion) [1989/90 c21g4 c24g2 c27gpu c24g4 c27spu c28d3 c33dpu] strong gelding: winning hurdler/chaser: in frame in handicaps at Ayr in November and Kelso in December and February: stays well: acts on soft going: suited by forcing tactics. *S. J. Leadbetter.* **c94** —

ANDROMAHOS 8 b. or br.g. Derrylin–Foxhorn (SWE) (Hornbeam) [1989/90 16m3 16m5 c16m] sparely-made gelding: poor novice selling hurdler: made c— 60 mistakes on chasing debut but showed signs of a little ability: has run visored. *D. Burchell.*

ANDROS PRINCE 5 b.g. Blakeney–Ribamba (Ribocco) [1989/90 27g^{2} 22s*
20g^{2} 24d^{2}] leggy gelding: handicap hurdler: made all at Ayr in January: made 121
running when runner-up afterwards at Newcastle and Wetherby (no extra
approaching last, beaten 5 lengths by Yorkshire Holly): stays well: acts on soft
going: to be trained by Miss H. Knight. *M. W. Easterby.*

ANDY BOY 6 b.g. Mr Fordette–Killonan Lass (The Parson) [1989/90 16m^{2}
16d^{6} 16s^{co} 16s^{3} 16m 20f^{2} 16f^{3} 16m^{3} 16m^{pu}] good-topped, workmanlike gelding: 96
placed 5 times over hurdles, showing modest form: ran poorly when blinkered
final outing: tended to carry head high sixth start: stays 2½m when conditions
aren't testing: probably acts on any going. *T. Casey.*

ANFIELD SALLY 4 b.f. Anfield–Bargain Line (Porto Bello) [1989/90 16g
16f^{pu}] sparely-made filly: poor 1m plater on Flat: last in juvenile hurdle at —
Wetherby in November: ran as though something was amiss in a seller later in
month: has joined J. FitzGerald. *R. M. Whitaker.*

ANGEL'S DREAM 6 b.m. King's Ride–Angel's Halo (Aureole) [1989/90 16g^{5}
20s^{5} 16d 21m*] compact mare: amateur ridden, showed improved form to win 89
novice handicap hurdle at Newton Abbot in April by 3 lengths from Treble
Trouble: stays 21f: evidently suited by top-of-the-ground: ran in snatches on
hurdling debut: trained until after second outing by K. Bailey. *P. J. Hobbs.*

ANGELS KISS 4 b.f. Taufan (USA)–Mexican Girl (Gala Performance (USA))
[1989/90 16d^{3} a16g^{3} 18m^{2} 16m^{3} 16f^{6}] leggy filly: placed over 7f on Flat when 81
trained by Miss S. Hall: placed in juvenile and novice hurdles: likely to prove best
at around 2m: acts on good to firm and good to soft going. *Mrs J. L. Robson.*

ANGELS KISS (SWE) 5 b.g. Atlantic Boy–Cielo-Azzurro (He Loves Me)
[1989/90 16d^{F}] tall gelding: middle-distance performer on Flat in Sweden, winner —
7 times from 35 starts (successful 3 times in 1989): 20/1 and wearing crossed
noseband, took good hold and soon clear but jumped erratically and fell when
trying to refuse fifth (held narrow advantage) in novice hurdle at Towcester in
February. *M. C. Pipe.*

ANGLIA VALE 5 ch.g. Chukaroo–Silmira (Grey Mirage) [1989/90 aF16g^{5}
aF13g] behind in NH Flat races: yet to race over hurdles or fences. *G. Roe.*

ANGLO BRASIL 5 ch.g. Hardboy–Unsinkable Sarah (Mon Capitaine)
[1989/90 F16d F17m] brother to quite useful staying chaser Charter Hardware and
half-brother to 2 winning jumpers, notably smart chaser Direct Line (by Straight
Lad): dam unraced half-sister to very smart hurdler Boxer: mid-division in NH
Flat races in February and April: yet to race over hurdles or fences. *Mrs R. Wharton.*

ANGUS HABIT 4 ch.g. Henbit (USA)–Molly Malone (Bold Lad (IRE))
[1989/90 16m^{pu}] placed over 1m on Flat when trained by G. Huffer: tailed off when —
pulled up 3 out in conditional jockeys selling hurdle at Huntingdon in December.
J. D. Czerpak.

ANHAAR 5 b.m. Ela-Mana-Mou–Chilblains (Hotfoot) [1989/90 21g 20s^{5} 22d]
small, lightly-made mare: poor novice hurdler: has run in a seller: probably stays —
21f: acts on heavy going. *G. H. Yardley.*

ANMICHELLE 4 b.f. Martinmas–Touchy Miss (Tachypous) [1989/90 F16g
16f^{pu}] 420 2-y-o: first foal: dam ran twice: tailed off in NH Flat race and when —
pulled up in juvenile hurdle at Wetherby (not jump well). *D. Lee.*

ANNABEN 7 ch.m. Hotfoot–Northern Empress (Northfields (USA)) [1989/90 c—
17h^{2}] sparely-made mare: poor novice selling hurdler/chaser: seems to stay 60
2½m: evidently suited by give in the ground: suitable mount for a claimer: often
blinkered: sold 3,000 gns Ascot September Sales. *R. T. Juckes.*

ANN DU FEU 5 b.m. Tyrnavos–Rebecca (Quorum) [1989/90 16m^{6}] poor
middle-distance maiden on Flat: tailed off in mares novice hurdle at Huntingdon in —
September. *J. R. Jenkins.*

ANNETTE'S DELIGHT 11 b.g. Idiot's Delight–On Safari (King Hal) c94
[1989/90 c16f^{4} c17m^{3} c16m^{F} c16m^{4} c16s^{3} c16s^{ur} c17v* c18s^{3} c16f^{3} c16g^{ur} c16m* —
c16m^{4} c17m^{4}] medium-sized, lengthy gelding: won selling handicap chase at
Newton Abbot in January (no bid) and amateur riders handicap at Plumpton in
April: best form at around 2m: acts on any going: has worn crossed noseband:
occasionally makes mistakes. *G. G. Gracey.*

ANNETTE'S VENTURE 8 ch.g. Kemal (FR)–Boon Adventure (London c**106**
Gazette) [1989/90 c16m c20g* c20f^{wo} c26g^{4} c26g* c20m^{2} c24s* c25s^{2} c24g^{3} —
c25m^{6}] sparely-made, plain gelding: novice hurdler: gaining fourth win over
fences when beating Page of Gold 5 lengths in handicap at Fakenham in
December: successful earlier in novice events at Uttoxeter and Ludlow (walked
over) and a conditional jockeys handicap at Fontwell: stays 3¼m: acts on heavy
going and good to firm: has looked difficult ride: sometimes jumps moderately:
trained until after fourth start by R. Lee. *B. Stevens.*

ANNICOMBE RUN 6 b.m. Deep Run–Purcella (Straight Lad) [1989/90 16g^{6}
16g^{5} 16d^{5} 20d^{2}] smallish, workmanlike mare: half-sister to winning hurdler Tarqa 91
(by Tarqogan) and fair hurdler/winning chaser Macusla (by Lighter): dam
successful in a bumpers race and over hurdles: 5 lengths second to Junior Parker
in novice hurdle at Sedgefield in March, best effort: stays 2½m. *R. Lee.*

ANNIE DE POMME 6 ch.m. Leander–Pomme (Polic) [1989/90 16g 16g]
lengthy, sparely-made mare: well beaten in novice hurdles. *Mrs J. H. Chadwick.* —

ANNIE'LL DO 5 ch.m. Horage–Anaglogs Daughter (Above Suspicion)
[1989/90 F16g^{4} F16m^{3} 16g^{F} 16m 18s 16g^{4} 16m^{pu}] small mare: third foal: dam —
top-class chaser: in frame in NH Flat races in October when trained by J. Pearce:
well beaten in novice hurdles. *H. B. Hodge.*

ANNIE RA 8 br.m. Ra (USA)–Annie (Damremont) [1989/90 c16g^{3}] leggy, c**85**
sparely-made mare: winning hurdler/chaser: last of 3 finishers in handicap at —
Southwell in November: takes a good hold, and best form at 2m: acts on soft going:
has worn a tongue strap: ridden by 7-lb claimer. *W. Clay.*

ANNIES ROSE 5 br.g. Soldier Rose–Easy Action (Negotiation) [1989/90
21m^{pu} 16s^{pu}] sparely-made gelding: third foal: dam poor novice hurdler, placed at —
up to 17f: tailed off when pulled up in novice hurdles at Warwick. *P. A. Pritchard.*

ANNSOFAIR 6 ch.m. Dubassoff (USA)–Fair Georgina (Silver Cloud) [1989/90
16m 16m^{3} 16m^{6}] leggy, sparely-made mare: poor novice hurdler: jumps none too 63
fluently: sold 1,300 gns Ascot November Sales. *A. J. Chamberlain.*

ANOTHER BARNEY 6 ch.g. Stetchworth (USA)–Another Reef (Take A
Reef) [1989/90 F16g^{5} 16g 22m 16m 16g^{6} 16f 16m^{3} 16f^{4}] second foal: dam unraced: 84
novice hurdler: in frame in conditional jockeys selling hurdle at Huntingdon
(found little) and claimer at Chepstow (best effort) in the spring: form only at 2m:
acts on firm going: reportedly broke blood vessel fifth start: sold 2,700 gns
Doncaster Spring Sales. *J. R. Jenkins.*

ANOTHER BOLUS 8 gr.g. Yankee Gold–Pretty Candy (Candy Cane) c**136**
[1989/90 c16f^{F} c16m* c16g^{F}] medium-sized gelding: won handicap chase at —
Wincanton in December easily by 10 lengths from The A Train: fell third following
month: should stay 2½m: acts on good to firm and soft going: has tongue tied
down. *Mrs I. McKie.*

ANOTHER BOY 4 br.g. Manor Farm Boy–Haverhill Lass (Music Boy)
[1989/90 16g^{ur} 16g^{pu}] sparely-made gelding: lightly-raced maiden on Flat: tried to
refuse and unseated rider first in juvenile hurdle in October: pulled up soon after —
being hampered and mistake first in novice claimer later in month. *A. Bailey.*

ANOTHER BROWNIE 11 br.g. Giolla Mear–Another Rose (Trouville) c—
[1989/90 20f^{pu} 17f c17g^{4} c19d^{pu} c17v^{5} a18g^{4}] lengthy, sturdy ex-Irish gelding: 75
winning hurdler and one-time useful chaser: on the downgrade and has been
beaten in selling company: stays 3m well: acts on heavy going: trained until after
second outing by R. Whitford: sold 1,200 gns Ascot February Sales. *Mrs J.
Wonnacott.*

ANOTHER BUCK 5 b.g. Celtic Cone–Clay Duck (Dicta Drake) [1989/90
16d^{6}] lengthy, unfurnished gelding: has scope: brother to fair hurdler Bitter Buck 82 p
and half-brother to 3 winning jumpers, including very useful chaser Clayside (by
Quayside) and quite useful chaser Clutterbuck (by Mandamus): dam, out-and-out
stayer on Flat and winner over hurdles, half-sister to smart chaser Clear Cut and
grandam of Celtic Shot: 14/1 and green, not knocked about once outpaced from
third last when around 18 lengths sixth to Egypt Mill in slowly-run 9-runner
novice hurdle at Ascot in January: sure to do better. *C. P. E. Brooks.*

ANOTHER COLUMBUS 7 b.m. St Columbus–Milk River (Another River)
[1989/90 16m 21f^{F} 20m^{pu}] medium-sized, leggy mare: no sign of ability in novice
hurdles. *W. J. Smith.* —

ANOTHER CORAL 7 br.g. Green Shoon–Myralette (Deep Run) [1989/90 c**129** +
c16g* c16g* c16g^{2} c16s^{3} c16m^{F}] tall, leggy, lengthy gelding: winning hurdler: —

Coventry Novices' Chase, Cheltenham—
eventual winner Another Coral and Campsea-Ash (right) dispute the lead

jumped well in the main when winning novice chases at Cheltenham in November and January (quickened to lead after 2 out when scoring by 4 lengths from Elfast): ran lack-lustre race when 17 lengths third to Wink Gulliver in Daniel Homes Novices' Chase at Ascot in February: always likely to be best at around 2m: acts on soft going and good to firm: tends to be on toes and is usually taken early to post: fell heavily in final race (Arkle Challenge Trophy at Cheltenham). *D. Nicholson.*

ANOTHER CRUISE 5 gr.g. Cruise Missile–Another Dove (Grey Love) [1989/90 16m^{3} 21d 20d^{6} 19f^{5}] leggy, angular gelding: second foal: dam, fair 2m hurdler, from a successful jumping family: has shown ability in novice hurdles: ran moderately last outing: trained previously by M. Brown. *R. J. Price.* 87

ANOTHER DYER 6 ch.g. Deep Run–Saint Society (Saint Denys) [1989/90 F17m^{3} 16d 20g 20g^{6}] big, lengthy gelding: has plenty of scope: first foal: dam won NH Flat race and 3m hurdle in Ireland: third in NH Flat race: has shown ability all starts in novice hurdles, on last 2 running on steadily without being knocked about at all (not seen out after January): will stay 3m: capable of better. *G. Richards.* 89 p

ANOTHER FOUNTAIN 4 b.g. Royal Fountain–Another Joyful (Rubor) [1989/90 17g^{pu}] workmanlike gelding with some scope: first foal: dam winning 2m hurdler: bit backward and very green, not fluent and was well behind when pulled up before last in juvenile hurdle at Carlisle in January. *J. E. Dixon.* —

ANOTHER HALF 10 ch.g. Hot Grove–Alentejo (Privy Councillor) [1989/90 c19m^{pu}] big, dipped-backed gelding: poor chaser: has been beaten in a seller: pulled up in a point-to-point in March and hunter chase following month: stays 21f: acts on heavy going: moderate jumper: sold privately out of H. Fleming's stable 2,200 gns Doncaster October Sales. *Mrs E. J. Richards.* c— x —

ANOTHER MEMBER 6 b.g. New Member–Silver Peace (Gallup Poll) [1989/90 F16f F16g 16g^{pu} 17v^{pu}] rangy, unfurnished gelding: has scope: fourth foal: brother to winning hurdler Peaceful Member and winning point-to-pointer Allgold Member: dam won 2 novice hurdles: well beaten in NH Flat races and pulled up both outings over hurdles. *R. J. Hodges.* —

ANOTHER NICK 4 ch.g. Nicholas Bill–Another Move (Farm Walk) [1989/90 16g^{3}] leggy gelding: brother to quite useful hurdler Tancred Sand: lightly-raced 92

staying maiden on Flat (has shown ability): in need of race, outpaced before last when 5½ lengths third behind Sagaman in juvenile hurdle at Newcastle in December: will be suited by further. *J. M. Jefferson.*

ANOTHER NONSENSE 6 ch.g. Mr Fluorocarbon–Gosforth Lady (Linacre)
[1989/90 16f 16f^{F}] lightly-made, angular gelding: modest novice hurdler: dead. *J.* —
L. Spearing.

ANOTHER NORFOLK 9 ch.g. Pamroy–Norfolk House (Cantab) [1989/90 c?
c20m^{6} c24m^{pu} c25m^{3}] lengthy gelding: winning hurdler: 15 lengths third of 5 to —
High Ham Blues in novice chase at Wolverhampton in January: stays 3m:
probably acts on any going. *B. A. McMahon.*

ANOTHER RUMOUR 6 b. or br.m. The Parson–Another Lady VI (Anthony)
[1989/90 16m^{pu} 19d^{pu} a20g^{4} 25g] workmanlike non-thoroughbred mare: half- 60
sister to Park Moss (by Beau Tudor), hurdle/chase winner in Ireland over
extended 2m: dam never ran: completed course only once in point-to-points in
1989: no form over hurdles. *C. J. Hitchings.*

ANOTHER SCALLY 7 b.m. Scallywag–Gouly Duff (Party Mink) [1989/90
20m^{pu} a18g^{4} a24g^{5} 17m^{4} a16g^{4} 20m^{pu}] poor plater over hurdles: best form at 69
around 2m. *C. J. Dingwall.*

ANOTHER SCHEDULE 9 ch.g. Beau Tudor–Mo Sgeal Fein (Kabale) **c112**
[1989/90 c21g^{3} c24m^{4} c20s^{2} c25m^{2} c25g^{ur} c20s^{6} 24f^{6} 25f^{3}] strong, deep-girthed 103
gelding: fair chaser and modest hurdler: best effort over fences when short-head
second to Crock-Na-Nee at Bangor on third start: stays 25f: probably acts on any
going: pulls hard, wears a dropped noseband and is suited by racing up with the
leaders: tends to sweat and be on toes in preliminaries. *C. P. E. Brooks.*

ANOTHER SEASON 6 b.g. Ya Zaman (USA)–Another Tune (Red God)
[1989/90 16h^{5} 16f^{6} 16g^{6} a18g^{4} 18s^{6} a16g^{6}] leggy gelding: won 1¼m seller on Flat 65
in 1989: poor novice selling hurdler: has run blinkered: trained until after
reappearance by A. Moore. *D. W. Browning.*

ANOTHER SEEKER 8 ch.g. Status Seeker–Foolish Lady (Signa Infesta) **c83** x
[1989/90 c20m^{6} 24f 21g^{5} c24s^{3} c24m] good sort: winning hurdler: poor novice —
chaser (makes mistakes, and looked none too keen last start): best at around 2m:
has won on heavy going but best run on good to firm: blinkered final start in 1988/9
and last 3 outings: has won for a 7-lb claimer. *C. L. Popham.*

ANOTHER SMOKEY 7 ch.g. Rouser–Smokey Princess (My Smokey) c—
[1989/90 c22m] medium-sized gelding: looked none too keen when tailed off on — §
hurdling debut: well beaten in novice hunter chase in May: runner-up in a
point-to-point earlier: best left alone. *Stan Saunders.*

ANOTHER STRIPLIGHT 7 ch.g. Pauper–Hill Invader (Brave Invader c78
(USA)) [1989/90 c27g^{2} c24g^{5} c21d^{3} c24d^{5}] big, lengthy gelding: shows traces of —
stringhalt: poor novice hurdler/chaser: stays 3m: best form on an easy surface:
blinkered last outing: usually ridden by 7-lb claimer nowadays. *P. A. Blockley.*

ANOTHER STUBBS 11 ch.g. Stubbs Gazette–Burlington Miss (Burlington c—
II) [1989/90 c27f^{F} c26m^{pu} c25h^{pu}] ex-Irish gelding: winning point-to-pointer/
hunter chaser: no form in hunter chases in Britain (has jumped moderately): has
been tried in blinkers. *H. W. Braddick.*

ANOTHER TROUP 8 b.g. Beau Charmeur (FR)–Ballinabranna (Vivi c81 +
Tarquin) [1989/90 c20g^{4} c26s^{5} c24d c20v^{3} c24g c32f c24f^{6}] workmanlike gelding: —
modest novice hurdler/chaser: made several mistakes last 2 starts: suited by a
test of stamina: acts on heavy going: amateur ridden, often at overweight:
blinkered last 3 starts. *R. D. Townsend.*

ANOTHER VULGAN 9 b.g. Vulgan Slave–Milk River (Another River) c—
[1989/90 c22g] maiden hunter chaser: no sign of ability. *W. John Smith.*

ANQUETIL 4 b. or br.g. Valiyar–Racemosa (Town Crier) [1989/90 18h^{5} 16d
16g 16g] little worthwhile form in varied company on Flat, when trained by J. —
Sutcliffe: soundly beaten in juvenile hurdles and a claimer. *C. Holmes.*

ANRIKA 7 gr.m. Riki Lash–Barbary Ann (Barbary Pirate) [1989/90 16f 25f] c—
leggy, workmanlike mare: poor novice hurdler: pulled up on chasing debut: —
changed hands 1,700 gns Doncaster August Sales: sold 2,500 gns Ascot February
Sales: subsequently placed in 2 point-to-points. *D. Lee.*

ANSTEY BOY 5 gr.g. Decoy Boy–Miss Twiggy (Tycoon II) [1989/90 16m]
neat gelding: poor maiden miler on Flat, has run visored: ridden by 7-lb claimer, —
tailed off both starts over hurdles. *C. N. Allen.*

ANSWERS PLEASE 6 b.m. Don–Whichcombe (Huntercombe) [1989/90 c20m^{F} c21f* c21d^{F} c20m^{3} c20g^{F} c24d^{pu} c24f* c26m^{2} c21m*] leggy mare: poor novice hurdler: won novice chases at Towcester in November, Ludlow in April and Towcester again in May: let down by her jumping most other outings over fences: stays 3m: acts on firm ground: trained until after sixth start by R. Smyly. *N. A. Gaselee.* **c103** p —

ANSWER TO PRAYER 11 b.g. Random Shot–Mam'zelle Dolly (Saint Crespin III) [1989/90 c19m] strong gelding: fortunate winner of novice chase in 1986/7: deteriorated temperamentally subsequently and refused to race 3 times: modest point-to-pointer nowadays, successful in May: tailed off in hunter chase (started slowly) previous month: stays 2¼m: acts on any going: has been tried in blinkers and a visor. *A. Jeffries.* c— § —

ANTHONY HILL 9 ch.g. Politico (USA)–Second Glance (Prince Hansel) [1989/90 c20g^{pu}] behind in NH Flat race in 1986: tailed off when pulled up in novice event in February on chasing debut. *N. Bycroft.* c—

ANTIBIOTIC 6 ch.g. Sunyboy–Alex M (Kadir Cup) [1989/90 c22d^{pu}] strong gelding: tailed off when pulled up in novice hurdles and a novice chase (bit backward). *J. B. Sayers.* c— —

ANTIGUAN SMILE 5 ch.g. Croghan Hill–Evan's Love (Master Owen) [1989/90 F13m^{2} F16f^{4} 16g^{ur} 16g^{2}] leggy gelding: fifth foal: dam unraced: in frame in NH Flat races at Perth and Wetherby in October: led until the last when going down by 1½ lengths to Uncle Ernie in novice hurdle on latter course in December. *B. E. Wilkinson.* 93

ANTINOUS 6 ch.g. Hello Gorgeous (USA)–Marthe Meynet (Welsh Pageant) [1989/90 c16g^{F} c16g* c16g* c17f* c16g^{3} c20d* c20v^{3} c16s^{F} c16m^{4} c16m^{4}] **c139** —

Antinous and 25/1-shot Mister Point were the latest representatives from Peter Easterby's stable to contest the Arkle Challenge Trophy at Cheltenham. Easterby has a fine record in the race and won it in 1978 with subsequent Gold Cup winner Alverton, in 1981 with Clayside and in 1983

Freebooter Novices' Chase, Doncaster—Antinous is clear at the last

with Ryeman. Starfen, Karenomore and Nohalmdun are other well-known chasers of his to have run in the race. Antinous, with eight races over fences behind him, lined up one of the most experienced runners in the field; he'd shown useful form and started seventh favourite at 14/1. In his customary position at the rear, he had been produced with what looked to be a well-timed run to challenge the leading trio of Young Snugfit, Comandante and Kiichi, when he made a crucial mistake at the second last. The mistake effectively ended Antinous' chance of winning, though he stayed on most strongly under pressure from the last to finish just over two lengths fourth behind Comandante. Fortune also deserted Antinous in his races either side of Cheltenham. In the Nottinghamshire Novices' Chase at Nottingham won by Cashew King, Antinous was a close third and seemingly travelling best when falling two out, and in the Perrier Jouet Novices' Chase at Liverpool won by Boutzdaroff, he held every chance when badly hampered by the subsequently-disqualified Blazing Walker at the second last and all but unseated his rider. Not all misfortune went the way of Antinous though. When winning the four-runner Freebooter Novices' Chase at Doncaster in December on his fourth start, he looked destined for the runner-up spot when the leader Greenheart fell two out. Prior to Doncaster Antinous had won novice events at Ayr and Market Rasen, and picked up a similar event over two and a half miles at Warwick on his sixth start.

Antinous (ch.g. 1984)	Hello Gorgeous (USA) (ch 1977)	Mr Prospector (b 1970)	Raise A Native
			Gold Digger
		Bonny Jet (b 1959)	Jet Jewel
			Bonny Bush
	Marthe Meynet (b 1973)	Welsh Pageant (b 1966)	Tudor Melody
			Picture Light
		Lovely Lark (ch 1965)	Larkspur
			Lovely Gale

Antinous, a leggy, sparely-made gelding, probably lacks the scope to make the top class, but if learning to jump consistently well he is likely to give a good account of himself in good-class handicaps, in much the same way Nohalmdun has done. Though a winner over two and a half miles, Antinous is, like Nohalmdun, best at around two miles. He seems to act on any going. Antinous, now a winner of twelve races, is the fourth and most successful owner-bred produce of the unraced Marthe Meynet. Her first three foals were also winners—the fair sprinter Batoni (by Realm), two-year-old seller winner Luisa Millar (by Wollow) and winning hurdler Qurrat Al Ain (by Wolver Hollow). Marthe Meynet is a half-sister to four Flat winners, notably Tudor Rhapsody, fairly useful at up to a mile, and Matsufugi Ehsu, Japan's top-rated two-year-old of 1974, out of the seven-furlong winner Lovely Lark, in turn a daughter of Lovely Gale, runner-up in the 1962 Irish One Thousand Guineas. *M. H. Easterby.*

ANVADABO 5 br.g. Kafu–Tassie (Lochnager) [1989/90 aF14g F12f] third foal: brother to quite modest Flat maiden Ryan's Way and half-brother to Irish 1m and 8.5f winner Noora Beag (by Ahonoora): dam ran once in Ireland: tailed off in NH Flat races in November and March: yet to race over hurdles or fences. *R. T. Juckes.*

ANY MORE 7 b.m. Space King–Indy-Ann (Indian Ruler) [1989/90 22g^{pu} 25g^{pu}] lightly raced and seems of little account. *J. A. Hellens.* —

A 1 PAPER CHASER 6 ch.g. The Parson–Summerville Lass (Deep Run) [1989/90 22v^{pu} 20g^{pu} 24m^{pu}] well beaten in NH Flat races: behind when pulled up in novice hurdles. *Miss S. J. Wilton.* —

APACHE RYTHEM 7 b.g. Elvaston–Semi Quaver (Seminole II) [1989/90 20m^{pu}] medium-sized, sparely-made gelding: seems of little account. *R. G. Frost.* —

APOLLO KING 4 b.g. Indian King (USA)–Mehudenna (Ribero) [1989/90 18m^{2} 16f* 16s^{6} 18s^{4} a16s^{2} a20g^{3}] compact gelding: half-brother to novice selling hurdler Brokers Choice (by Malinowski): placed at up to 1½m on Flat: won juvenile hurdle at Warwick in December: good second in juvenile handicap at Lingfield in January: best form at 2m: probably acts on any going. *P. Mitchell.* 99

APPELLANT 5 b.h. Star Appeal–St Louis Sue (FR) (Nonoalco (USA)) [1989/90 16d 16d^{4} 16s^{pu} 16g^{4}] smallish, workmanlike horse: won 1m seller on Flat 71 in 1989: best effort over hurdles when 14 lengths fourth behind Fiery Sun in selling handicap at Catterick in January, final start: pulls hard and is a difficult ride. *D. H. Topley.*

APPLE LANE (USA) 10 ch.g. Star Envoy (USA)–Queen of Diamonds (USA) (Alcibiades) [1989/90 a16g^{2}] ex-Irish gelding: won NH Flat race in August, 1984: 78
12 lengths second to Horatian in novice claimer at Lingfield in February on hurdling debut. *B. J. Curley.*

APPLE MAGIC 4 ch.g. Current Magic–Lucky Apple (Levmoss) [1989/90 F12g 16g^{pu}] second foal: dam showed little worthwhile form on Flat and over —
hurdles: tailed off in NH Flat race at Hexham and when pulled up 2 out in juvenile hurdle at Perth in the spring. *D. McCaskill.*

APPLE PIP 4 ch.f. Takachiho–Apple At Night (Carnival Night) [1989/90 aF14g] first foal: dam won over hurdles and placed in chases: tailed off in NH Flat race at Southwell in February: yet to race over hurdles. *Mrs S. Lamyman.*

APPLETON 4 ch.g. Quayside–Beagle Bay (Deep Run) [1989/90 F16m] half-brother to winning hurdler Hill Beagle (by Goldhill): dam half-sister to winning jumpers Henry The Fifth and Some Surprise: mid-division in NH Flat race at Sandown in March: yet to race over hurdles. *Mrs J. Pitman.*

APPLIED SIGNS 5 b.m. Tycoon II–Arctic Lion (Arctic Slave) [1989/90 F17f^{4}] fifth foal: sister to poor animal Lion Lodge: dam lightly-raced novice hurdler/chaser: 21 lengths fourth behind Saskia's Pride in NH Flat race at Doncaster in March: yet to race over hurdles or fences. *B. C. Morgan.*

APRIL FLOWER 5 ch.m. Parva Stella–Paddys Flyer (Paddy's Stream) [1989/90 F17m F16v 16g 20d^{pu}] leggy mare: third foal: half-sister to winning Irish —
point-to-pointer Pancratic (by Pitpan): dam unraced half-sister to fairly useful hurdler and winning chaser Rufus T Firefly: well beaten in NH Flat races and novice hurdles: sold 1,050 gns Doncaster March Sales. *J. Parkes.*

APRIL'S BABY 6 b.m. Paico–Manhattan Brandy (Frankincense) [1989/90 F16f^{6} F17m 16d^{6} 17g 20d] unfurnished, leggy mare: second foal: sister to winning 72 x
Irish hurdler Jimmy's Brandy: dam, maiden on Flat and over hurdles, refused to race 5 times: failed to complete course in 2 point-to-points in 1989 (refused on first occasion): poor form over hurdles, including in seller: jumped badly on hurdling debut. *Miss C. J. E. Caroe.*

AQUA VERDE 11 b.g. Auction Ring (USA)–Regal Guard (Realm) [1989/90 c**84** ?
a20g^{4} 21f^{4} 22m^{2} a22g^{6} 27g^{5} c18s^{pu} 24d^{5} a24g^{5} c20m^{4} c20m^{5} c21m^{pu} c20f c24m^{4} 79 d
16g^{6} 23f^{6}] neat gelding: fairly useful point-to-pointer: poor novice hurdler/chaser: stays 27f: acts on firm and dead going: sometimes blinkered or visored: sold 2,700 gns Ascot July Sales. *A. S. Reid.*

ARABIAN BLUES 7 gr.g. Jellaby–Abercourt (Abernant) [1989/90 21h^{2} 17h^{5}] c—
leggy, sparely-made gelding: novice hurdler: seems to have lost his form: showed —
no aptitude for chasing in novice event in 1988/9: best form at 2m in the mud. *S. Dow.*

ARABLE LAND 6 ch.g. Crofter (USA)–Piccadilly Lil (Pall Mall) [1989/90 16g 16d 16m^{5} 16d^{2} 16d* 16s^{5} 17d^{3} 16m* 20f^{3}] big, workmanlike gelding: no bid when 80
winning selling handicap hurdles at Leicester (conditional jockeys) and Plumpton (landed a gamble by 4 lengths from Donosti) in second half of season: form only at around 2m: acts on good to firm and dead going (well beaten on very soft). *D. J. Wintle.*

ARAGON GIRL 4 ch.f. Aragon–Hi Love (High Top) [1989/90 16g^{pu} a16g 16d 16m^{pu}] angular filly: poor maiden on Flat: sold out of E. Eldin's stable 2,000 gns —
Newmarket Autumn Sales: no sign of ability over hurdles, including in sellers: blinkered last start. *K. A. Ryan.*

ARAMA 4 b.g. Sallust–Facade (Double Jump) [1989/90 18f^{3} a16g^{pu} 16m^{pu}] half-brother to winning hurdler Greg (by My Swanee): soundly beaten on Flat: 65
sold out of M. Haynes's stable 850 gns Ascot May (1989) Sales: only form over hurdles third of 6 in seller at Fontwell in October. *R. P. C. Hoad.*

ARAPAHO CHIEF 5 b.g. Arapaho–Nevada-Credo (Credo) [1989/90 F16f] brother to quite moderate jumpers Nevada Prince and Mister Boot: dam never ran: tailed off in NH Flat race at Cheltenham in April: yet to race over hurdles or fences. *R. Brotherton.*

ARASTOU 7 br.g. Pitskelly–High Lake (Quisling) [1989/90 20h*] smallish gelding: lightly-raced hurdler: easily landed the odds in 3-runner handicap at 108

Plumpton in August: stays 2½m: acts on hard and dead ground: not one to trust implicitly. *Miss B. Sanders.*

ARBITRAGE 9 b.g. Monsanto (FR)–Sideshow (Welsh Pageant) [1989/90 16s 24g a20gpu 16m3 19f 16m4 19hpu] small, good-bodied gelding: handicap hurdler: only form of season when in frame at Wolverhampton in March and Worcester following month: third in novice event in 1988/9 on chasing debut: jumped moderately next outing: stays 3m: acts on any going: blinkered fourth outing 1986/7, visored last 2 starts 1988/9 and second in 1989/90. *B. Forsey.* c— 79

ARCHIE'S NEPHEW 9 b.g. Royben–Lady London (London Gazette) [1989/90 c21dur] leggy, close-coupled gelding: winning hurdler/point-to-pointer/ hunter chaser: needed race only start in hunter chases in 1990: subsequently placed in 2 point-to-points: suited by long distances and the mud. *R. Barber.* c— —

ARCTIC ADVENTURE 7 b.g. Slim Jim–Lady Marcia (Arctic Slave) [1989/90 c20spu c24mpu] leggy, workmanlike gelding: yet to complete course over hurdles or fences. *Miss J. Eaton.* c— —

ARCTIC BARON 5 b.g. Baron Blakeney–Learctic (Lepanto (GER)) [1989/90 20f2 22m2 25g5 20dpu 22g5 20g] lengthy gelding: moderate novice hurdler: should be suited by further than 2¾m: yet to race on heavy going, acts on any other: blinkered fourth and fifth outings: looks a difficult ride. *Miss J. Thorne.* 105

ARCTIC CALL 7 b.g. Callernish–Polar Lady (Arctic Slave) [1989/90 c24g* c24f* c24sur c25m2 c24gF c24g* c25m2] c**144** p —

Two of the North's more interesting chasing prospects, Young Snugfit and Arctic Call, were transferred to Oliver Sherwood's yard in Upper Lambourn prior to the start of the latest season. Young Snugfit, a useful hurdler with Mick Easterby, took well to fences, winning his first three completed starts and going on to finish a close third in the Arkle Challenge Trophy Chase at Cheltenham. Arctic Call, a winning hurdler with the now-retired Mrs Dickinson, restricted to one outing in 1988/9 following a soft palate operation, was let down by his jumping for a while after making a promising start over fences for his new stable. But fitted with blinkers on his last two appearances he showed himself one of the season's leading novices. On the first of them, conceding weight to virtually all of his

Oxfordshire Novices' Chase, Newbury—
Arctic Call (right) makes it two wins from two runs over fences

Wickham Novices' Chase, Newbury—
a good tussle between Arctic Call (right) and All Jeff who've drawn well clear

seventeen rivals in the Wickham Novices' Chase at Newbury in March, Arctic Call gave a fine front-running performance: he set a good pace, battled with All Jeff over the last four fences and held on to win by three lengths, the pair drawing a distance clear of third-placed Ballinhassig and subsequent National Hunt Chase Challenge Cup winner Topsham Bay. In the Mumm Club Novices' Chase at Liverpool the following month, Arctic Call put up his best performance to date. He again set a strong pace, and looked like taking a lot of beating when still in front and kicked for home three fences out. Eventually Royal Athlete, conceding 6 lb, wore him down and beat him half a length but Arctic Call finished well clear of the remainder headed by leading Irish novices Cahervillahow and Mixed Blends.

Arctic Call had looked a fair novice in the making when winning his first two races in November, a BMW Series qualifier at Kempton by two lengths from Cliffalda and the Oxfordshire Novices' Chase at Newbury nine days later by one and a half lengths from Folk Dance. On each occasion he settled the issue with a turn of foot in the latter stages. Arctic Call's jumping, not put under pressure in those two relatively slowly-run races, initially failed him in stronger company. He failed to get past the ninth in well-contested novice chases at Haydock and Kempton, and though not wholly disgraced when seven lengths second to High Ham Blues at Wolverhampton in between, he jumped deliberately throughout and could make no impression after a mistake two out. Arctic Call's jumping at Liverpool was still less than fluent—he tended to miss out the odd fence. But improvement in that department will come with more experience. Still relatively lightly raced, Arctic Call will be an interesting contender for the top long-distance handicaps in 1990/1. Kempton's Racing Post Chase, on a course where front runners have a good record, could be a long-term target.

<table>
<tr><td rowspan="4">Arctic Call
(b.g. 1983)</td><td rowspan="2">Callernish
(br 1977)</td><td>Lord Gayle
(b 1965)</td><td>Sir Gaylord
Sticky Case</td></tr>
<tr><td>Azurine
(b 1957)</td><td>Chamossaire
Blue Dun</td></tr>
<tr><td rowspan="2">Polar Lady
(b 1962)</td><td>Arctic Slave
(b 1950)</td><td>Arctic Star
Roman Galley</td></tr>
<tr><td>Solar Lady
(ch 1950)</td><td>Foroughi
Solar Lass</td></tr>
</table>

Callernish died at the start of the latest season, in which his reputation as a sire of jumpers was further enhanced by the performances of such as

Call Me Later, Cushinstown and Mweenish. From his second crop, Arctic Call is the eleventh foal of Polar Lady, a winner over hurdles and fences in Ireland. Her dam, winning jumper Solar Lady, also bred the fair Irish chaser Fort Sun. Polar Lady produced six winners prior to Arctic Call, most notably Polar Nomad (by Mandalus), successful in the four-mile-one-furlong Tote Eider Handicap Chase at Newcastle in 1989. Though Arctic Call will probably stay extreme distances, he has a turn of foot and doesn't need a thorough test of stamina. Arctic Call won two ordinary novice hurdles on heavy going in 1987/8; easily his best form over fences has been on a sound surface. *O. Sherwood.*

ARCTIC CAVALIER 8 br.g. Paddy's Stream–Charming Hostess (Khalkis) **c109**
[1989/90 c20f^{2} c19d^{3} c20g^{2} c20d^{F} c20d^{2} c20d^{F}] close-coupled, rather sparely-made gelding: winning hurdler: moderate chaser: destroyed after breaking his back when falling at Warwick in March: stayed 2½m: acted on soft going: blinkered when successful in 1987/8 and also last 2 starts that season. *Mrs J. Pitman.* —

ARCTIC ELLE 4 gr.f. Baron Blakeney–Learctic (Lepanto (GER)) [1989/90 16f^{pu}] sturdy filly: second foal: sister to moderate novice hurdler Arctic Baron: dam ran 3 times over hurdles: 66/1 and carrying condition, jumped moderately and tailed off when pulled up 3 out in 9-runner juvenile hurdle at Cheltenham in October. *Miss J. Thorne.* —

ARCTICFLOW (USA) 5 ch.g. Arctic Tern (USA)–Bold Flora (USA) (Bold Favorite (USA)) [1989/90 16s 20g 16h^{3} 17m^{3}] good-bodied gelding: poor novice hurdler: should be suited by further than 2m: trained by Mrs J. Ramsden until after second start. *N. B. Thomson.* 68

ARCTIC KEN 7 ch.g. Stanford–Peggy Dell (Sovereign Gleam) [1989/90 16f^{4} 16m^{2} 16g^{4} 16m^{3}] small, sparely-made gelding: quite modest mile handicapper on Flat: in frame in novice hurdles: needs to improve his jumping. *William Price.* 88

ARCTIC MARINER 12 b.g. Spitsbergen–Mariners Delight (Fortina) c—
[1989/90 c24s^{pu} c17v^{6} c25d^{pu}] workmanlike gelding: behind in novice hurdles: —
winning point-to-pointer: no sign of ability in steeplechases. *J. B. Shears.*

ARCTIC OATS 5 ch.m. Oats–Arctic Festival (Arctic Slave) [1989/90 aF14g* F17f* a16g^{2} a16g^{3}] half-sister to winning hurdlers Bassnimoor (by Jimmy Reppin), Milly Kelly (by Murrayfield) and fairly useful staying hurdler Singlecote (by Tycoon II): dam unraced: won NH Flat race at Southwell in November, and dead-heated for similar event at Doncaster following month: placed in novice hurdles on former course in February and March: will be suited by further. *W. W. Haigh.* 77

ARCTIC PADDY 7 ch.g. Paddy's Stream–Chorabelle (Choral Society) **c86**
[1989/90 c25f^{3}] strong gelding: fair point-to-pointer, successful in February: in frame in hunter chases: will be suited by very long distances: needs to brush up his jumping. *R. G. Russell.*

ARCTIC SKYLIGHT 6 ch.g. Lighter–Arctic Dawn (Arctic Slave) [1989/90 20d^{2} 16g* 20m] angular, workmanlike gelding: showed promise on hurdling debut, and 4 days later won 7-runner novice event at Catterick in March by 3 lengths from Spartona: headstrong, and will prove best at around 2m at present. *G. Richards.* 97

ARCTIC SONG 11 ch.g. True Song–Arctic Halo (Arctic Slave) [1989/90 c—
c21d^{pu}] useful-looking gelding: showed some ability in latter of 2 races in novice —
hurdles in 1983/4 when trained by J. Webber: won 3 point-to-points in 1987: pulled up in hunter chase at Wincanton in February. *J. M. B. Pugh.*

ARCTIC SPARKLER 10 gr.g. Arctic Kanda–Tandridge Lane (Exploitation) c—
[1989/90 c24g^{4}] won a point-to-point in May: no promise in 2 hunter chases. *Mrs A. B. Garton.*

ARCTIC TEAL 6 b.g. Town And Country–Arctic Warbler (Deep Run) [1989/90 20d^{6} 22m* 24g^{F} 25f 25m^{4} 24f^{3}] good-bodied, workmanlike gelding: will make a chaser: won handicap hurdle at Wincanton in December: creditable fourth behind Sip of Orange in quite valuable handicap at Liverpool in April: eased considerably run-in when remote last of 3 at Cheltenham later in month: stays 3m: acts on heavy and good to firm going: has won for a claimer. *O. Sherwood.* 138

ARCTIC WOLF 5 gr.g. Belfort (FR)–Shahnavaz (Ribero) [1989/90 aF16g^{pu}] 3,000 4-y-o: second foal: dam won at up to 9.5f in France: tailed off when pulled up

5f out in NH Flat race at Southwell in January: sold 1,200 gns Ascot April Sales: yet to race over hurdles or fences. *Mrs S. Oliver.*

ARDBRIN 7 ch.g. Bulldozer–Hazels Fancy (Prefairy) [1989/90 16d 20g^5 20f^2
19f*] well-made, close-coupled gelding: fair hurdler: made much of running when 127
winning handicap at Taunton in March comfortably by ¾ length from Squire Jim: running subject of stewards inquiry second start, jockey reported horse to be ungenuine: blinkered next outing, running creditably: stays 2½m: acts on any going. *B. J. Curley.*

ARDCRONEY CHIEF 4 ch.g. Connaught–Duresme (Starry Halo) [1989/90 F16m^4 F16m] half-brother to several winners, including hurdler Cimarron (by Carnival Dancer): dam placed over 7f at 2 yrs: showed ability in NH Flat races at Sandown in March and Liverpool following month: yet to race over hurdles. *D. R. Gandolfo.*

ARDEN 6 b.g. Ardross–Kereolle (Riverman (USA)) [1989/90 16g* 16m* 21g^6
16m^{ur}] close-coupled gelding: very useful but inconsistent on Flat, winner over 119
2m in 1989: won Wanderer Hurdle at Ayr (by 3 lengths from Aston Express) in October and novice event at Ascot (made most) following month: ran as though something was amiss third start: subsequently off course 3½ months (unseated rider first on his return): looked headstrong and jumped less than fluently at Ascot (tends to jump left): should stay beyond 2m: acts on good to firm ground: injured final start. *C. P. E. Brooks.*

ARDENT SPY 13 br.g. Saucy Kit–Ida Spider (Ben Novus) [1989/90 c24d^3 c**101**
c26m^{ur} c24g^5 c26g* c26m^4] leggy, lightly-made gelding: modest chaser —
nowadays: won handicap at Uttoxeter in May by ½ length from Proverity: needs a thorough test of stamina: acts on any going but is ideally suited by give in the ground. *W. Clay.*

ARDESEE 10 ch.g. Le Coq d'Or–Katie Little (Nulli Secundus) [1989/90 c26s^{pu} c**107**
c30v^{pu} c33v^2 c33d^4 c28d^2 c32g^{pu} c33d^{pu}] plain gelding: modest staying chaser —
nowadays: runner-up at Ayr in January and Sedgefield in March: acts on heavy going: usually jumps soundly. *D. J. Wintle.*

ARDMORE CLASSIC 7 b.g. He Loves Me–Classical Music (Santa Claus)
[1989/90 18f^5 16m^{pu} 22m^5 a16g^4] leggy gelding: poor novice hurdler: visored —
second start: sold 1,250 gns Ascot February Sales. *R. Lee.*

ARDORAN 4 ch.g. Little Wolf–Smoke Creek (Habitat) [1989/90 16m 20m^6 16m
16d 16f^{pu}] medium-sized gelding: irresolute staying handicapper on Flat: sold out 73
of M. Bell's stable 9,400 gns Newmarket Autumn Sales: poor form in juvenile hurdles: pulled up lame last outing (March). *Miss S. J. Wilton.*

Kennel Gate Novices' Hurdle, Ascot—Arden is Peter Scudamore's 1,139th winner, breaking Francome's career record for a jump jockey in Britain

ARDOUR 4 b.g. Ardross–Evita (Reform) [1989/90 16f a16g^{3} a16g* a16g* a20g^{2} a20g^{3} 16m^{ur} 17f^{2}] lightly-made gelding: middle-distance maiden on Flat, claimed out of W. Jarvis' stable £12,051 after finishing second in June: made most to win juvenile hurdles at Southwell in November and January: below his best in seller last outing: tried to run out previous start (in process of running a good race): probably stays 2½m: races freely and suited by forcing tactics. *M. C. Pipe.* — 95 +

ARDRA DUKE 6 ch.g. Deep Run–Astrella Celeste (Menelek) [1989/90 20f^{2} 20f^{2} 19f^{3} 19f^{F} c19g^{3} c16m^{3} c16f^{4} c20g^{3} c20g^{6} a18g^{pu}] lengthy, rather spasely-made gelding: modest novice hurdler/chaser: best form at around 2½m: acts on firm and dead ground: blinkered fifth start, visored final outing 1988/9: ran out once: usually ridden by claimer nowadays. *F. Jordan.* — c89 + / 91 §

ARD T'MATCH 5 b.g. Ardross–Love Match (USA) (Affiliate (USA)) [1989/90 16g^{6} 20f^{6} 21g^{2} 20g^{2} 21d^{5} 20f 17m] sturdy gelding: second in Challow Hurdle at Newbury in December and in handicap at Kempton following month: ran a good race when eleventh to Regal Ambition in Sun Alliance Novices' Hurdle at Cheltenham on penultimate start but poorly next time: stays 2½m: gives impression may prove suited by an easy surface: blinkered last 5 outings. *R. Simpson.* — 111

ARENA AUCTION 8 b.g. Relko–My Sweetie (Bleep-Bleep) [1989/90 c20f^{pu}] robust gelding: little form since winning selling hurdle in 1986/7: pulled up lame after bad mistake fifth in novice chase in March: acts on dead ground. *R. J. Hodges.* — c— / —

AREN'T WE ALL 11 b. or br.g. Impecunious–Solette (Solonaway) [1989/90 c26f^{2} c25m^{2} c26s^{pu}] lengthy, lightly-made gelding: winning point-to-pointer: runner-up in novice chase at Newton Abbot and handicap chase at Devon & Exeter in September: ran as though something was amiss in January, only subsequent outing: stays well: acts on firm ground: amateur ridden: has worn blinkers: trained until after second start by N. Ayliffe. *G. F. Edwards.* — c78 / —

ARGELITH 4 b.g. Runnett–Miss Redmarshall (Most Secret) [1989/90 16m^{ur} 16g^{6} a18g^{4}] half-brother to novice hurdler Sequestrator (by African Sky): plating-class maiden on Flat: sold out of R. Whitaker's stable 850 gns Doncaster October Sales after hurdling debut: blinkered, well beaten in sellers subsequently. *B. Ellison.* — —

ARGES 9 ch.g. Morston (FR)–Buss (Busted) [1989/90 18d^{pu}] small, lightly-made gelding: winning hurdler at around 2m: acted on any going: dead. *C. L. Popham.* — —

ARIBIE 4 b. or br.f. Konigsstuhl (GER)–Arita (FR) (Kronzeuge) [1989/90 16s^{2} 17d^{pu}] sparely-made, angular filly: quite modest middle-distance performer on Flat: sold out of N. Callaghan's stable 2,300 gns Newmarket Autumn Sales: 10 lengths second to Fox Path in selling hurdle at Bangor in December: pulled up in similar company at Devon & Exeter following month: subsequently successful on Flat. *P. Leach.* — 72

ARISTOS 6 b.g. Derring Rose–Forest Fun (Pardao) [1989/90 17d^{5} c24g^{pu} c24d^{pu} 21s* 21d^{ur} 22m^{3} 24d^{2}] workmanlike, good-quartered gelding: winning point-to-pointer: won novice handicap hurdle at Sandown in February: good second to Babil in novice hurdle at Chepstow following month: no form in novice chases: stays well: acts on soft going and seems unsuited by top-of-the-ground: tends to sweat and be edgy in preliminaries (wasn't at Sandown or Chepstow). *J. A. B. Old.* — c— / 102

ARIZONA 9 b.g. Warpath–Shenandoah (Mossborough) [1989/90 c26m^{pu}] workmanlike gelding: NH Flat race winner: no worthwhile form in novice hurdles: poor point-to-pointer: tailed off when pulled up in a hunter chase at Newton Abbot in May. *M. P. Murdoch.* — c— / —

ARIZONA EXPRESS 6 ch.g. Viking (USA)–Nothing On (St Chad) [1989/90 c20f^{pu}] leggy gelding: no worthwhile form over hurdles, including in a seller, and in point-to-points: blinkered, pulled up, reportedly lame, in novice hunter chase in May: looks ungenuine and isn't to be relied upon. *S. C. Haimes.* — c— / — §

ARJUNA 5 b.g. Shirley Heights–Karsavina (Silly Season) [1989/90 16g^{5}] leggy gelding: seventh foal: half-brother to 3 winners on Flat: dam half-sister to Triumph Hurdle winner and winning chaser Peterhof: 100/1, 23 lengths fifth to Forest Sun in 21-runner novice hurdle at Kempton in February on debut, staying on without being subjected to a hard ride: should improve. *P. J. Hobbs.* — 83 p

ARK INVADER 11 b.g. Brave Invader (USA)–Welcome Home (Kythnos) [1989/90 16f^{5}] big, plain gelding: seems of little account. *W. Storey.* — c— / —

ARLECCHINO 8 br.g. Al Sirat (USA)–Pearl Creek (Gulf Pearl) [1989/90 c22s^pu] sturdy gelding: maiden point-to-pointer: tailed off in a novice hurdle and in novice hunter chases. *S. C. Haimes.* c— —

ARMAGRET 5 b.g. Mandrake Major–Friendly Glen (Furry Glen) [1989/90 16d4 16g5 20g* 20g4 25g2 16d5 20m* 20f2 24f6] lengthy, workmanlike gelding: won handicap hurdles at Newcastle in December and March (claimer ridden): best form at 2½m: acts on any going. *B. E. Wilkinson.* 111

ARMALA 5 ch.g. Deep Run–Bardicate (Bargello) [1989/90 16g^pu] strong, lengthy gelding: half-brother to several winners, notably very useful chaser Green Bramble (by Green Shoon) and quite useful chasers Deviner (by Pry) and Polyfemus (by Pollerton): dam unraced half-sister to 3 jumping winners, including Topham Trophy winner Artic Ale: carrying a lot of condition, tailed off when pulled up 2 out in novice hurdle at Worcester in March on debut. *S. T. Harris.* —

AROUND AND ABOUT 6 br.g. Roselier (FR)–Like Now (Cracksman) [1989/90 16g 16s 16m] leggy, angular gelding: eighth foal: dam unplaced in Irish NH Flat races: behind in novice hurdles. *Andrew Turnell.* —

AROUND THE CLOCK 9 br.g. Majestic Streak–Silk Grace (Shantung) [1989/90 c16d c16f5] light-framed gelding: lightly-raced novice hurdler: winning point-to-pointer: tailed off in hunter chases in 1990: sold 800 gns Ascot June Sales. *D. A. Shone.* c— —

ARPAL BREEZE 5 ch.g. Deep Run–Arpal Magic (Master Owen) [1989/90 F16f3 F17m F13d2] workmanlike gelding: third foal: half-brother to novice hurdler Arpal Blitz (by Politico): dam, half-sister to several winning jumpers, behind all outings over hurdles: placed in NH Flat races at Catterick in October and Kelso in January: yet to race over hurdles or fences. *R. Allan.*

ARPAL FOREVER 6 b.g. Deep Run–Arpal Magic (Master Owen) [1989/90 22g5 16f6 16d5] leggy, angular gelding: poor novice hurdler: has worn crossed noseband (raced freely second start). *R. Allan.* 90 ?

ARRANDALE 4 b.f. Tickled Pink–Dawn Affair (Entanglement) [1989/90 16f4 16m4 16m^pu] poor sprint plater on Flat: poor form in selling company over hurdles: sold 1,000 gns Doncaster October Sales. *J. Parkes.* 67

ARRAN VIEW 4 br.g. Aragon–Shadow Play (Busted) [1989/90 16g6 16g 16s6 16d2 16g2 16f2] leggy gelding: half-brother to winning hurdler My Buddy (by Mummy's Game): modest maiden miler on Flat: sold out of P. Calver's stable 4,400 gns Doncaster September Sales: runner-up in claiming hurdles at Stratford (amateur ridden) and Worcester and in juvenile event at Uttoxeter (edged right run-in when going down by a neck to Snugfit's Image): likely to prove best at 2m. *B. Llewellyn.* 95

ARROW DANCER 4 b.g. Gorytus (USA)–Rose And Honey (Amber Rama (USA)) [1989/90 16v 16h3 16m4 18f3] leggy gelding: in frame at up to 1m on Flat: sold out of P. Cole's stable 10,000 gns Ascot December Sales: poor form over hurdles: takes good hold and best form at 2m on top-of-the-ground. *R. J. O'Sullivan.* 78

ARROWOOD JUNCTION (USA) 10 b.g. Junction (USA)–Promised Princess (USA) (Promised Land) [1989/90 c25m^pu] close-coupled, narrow gelding: winning point-to-pointer: lightly raced and no sign of ability over hurdles or in steeplechases. *N. T. Eley.* c— —

ARRY OPEFUL 8 b.g. Full of Hope–Carolsky (Dynastic) [1989/90 c24m^F c21m c16f2 c16m4] poor maiden point-to-pointer/steeplechaser: 50/1 when beaten ½ length by stable-companion Night Guest in 4-runner event at Hexham in September: changed hands 7,200 gns Doncaster September Sales. *P. Monteith.* c79 —

ARSONIST 5 ch.g. Ardross–Dragonist (Dragonara Palace (USA)) [1989/90 16f5 16m2 16m5 16m* 16f* 22m^pu] lengthy gelding: fair handicapper at up to 1¾m on Flat at 3 yrs, when trained by W. Jarvis: comfortable winner of 2 novice hurdles at Towcester in May, making all for an easy 15-length success on latter occasion: should stay beyond 2m: acts on firm ground: claimer ridden first 3 outings: collapsed after race on third start and ran as though something was amiss final one. *A. G. Blackmore.* 103

ARTAIUS STAR 6 b.g. Artaius (USA)–Godwyn (Yellow God) [1989/90 16f*] workmanlike gelding: has looked less than genuine and was well ridden to win conditional jockeys selling handicap hurdle (no bid) at Market Rasen in August by 83

½ length from Co-Tack: suited by a sharp 2m and firm ground: sold 2,700 gns Doncaster August Sales. *J. J. O'Neill.*

ARTESIUM 8 b.g. Artaius (USA)–Idle Waters (Mill Reef (USA)) [1989/90 20dpu 21s 28f4 24m 21m4 20m6] small gelding: winning hurdler: beaten in seller last start: probably stays 3½m: acts on hard ground: has run well for a claimer: sold 1,300 gns Ascot June Sales. *M. J. Wilkinson.* 68

ARTFUL ABBOT 6 ch.g. The Parson–She's Clever (Clever Fella) [1989/90 c17d c16v4 c16mpu c16fr 16f* 20m3 16f 16f] lengthy, well-made gelding: made all in handicap hurdle at Worcester in March: seemed to run extremely well when 3½ lengths third behind Sayparee in Martell Hurdle (Handicap) at Liverpool following month, leading until 2 out: ran moderately next outing, stiff task when well beaten last start: poor form in novice chases (refused to race on fourth outing): stays 2½m: probably acts on any going. *J. Webber.* c84 § 115

ARTFUL ARTHUR 4 b.g. Rolfe (USA)–Light of Zion (Pieces of Eight) [1989/90 F16f] first live foal: dam poor plater on Flat and over hurdles: tailed off in NH Flat race at Warwick in May: yet to race over hurdles. *R. Dickin.*

ARTIC CHIEF 9 b.g. Owen Anthony–Freezing Point (March Past) [1989/90 c18f2] sparely-made gelding: novice hurdler: winning chaser: beaten a distance when second at Fontwell in August: stays 2¼m: acts on firm going. *T. M. Jones.* c— x —

ART TRAIL 6 gr.g. Aristocracy–Bally Sovereign (Supreme Sovereign) [1989/90 F16g* 18d2 22vpu 16s* 16mpu] won both completed starts in point-to-points in 1989 and a NH Flat race at Fairyhouse in January: made most to win novice hurdle at Tipperary following month: destroyed after breaking leg in Waterford Crystal Supreme Novices' Hurdle at Cheltenham in March: stayed 2¼m: acted on soft going. *Patrick G. Kelly, Ireland.* 114

ARTY SCHWEPPES (USA) 4 ch.g. Super Concorde (USA)–Mon Solange (USA) (Bold Reason) [1989/90 16gpu] workmanlike gelding: won 2m handicap on Flat in 1989: sold out of R. J. R. Williams' stable 10,000 gns Newmarket Autumn Sales: blinkered, tailed off when pulled up 2 out in juvenile hurdle at Uttoxeter in April. *Miss S. J. Wilton.* —

ARUM LILY 6 b.m. Bustino–Lys River (FR) (Lyphard (USA)) [1989/90 16f3 16m6 16g 16f2 17m6] smallish, good-quartered mare: won 6 times in modest company over hurdles in 1988/9: not so good in 1989/90: stays 2¾m: acts on any going except very soft: trained first 2 outings by G. Richards. *T. A. K. Cuthbert.* 96

ASAAF (USA) 7 b.g. Cutlass (USA)–Honky Chateau (USA) (Quadrangle) [1989/90 16g] small gelding: won Irish NH Flat race in 1987: poor novice over hurdles: tailed off all 5 outings in Britain. *A. W. Denson.* —

ASARGAR 4 b.c. Gorytus (USA)–Astara (Nishapour (FR)) [1989/90 F17f F16f3 F16m6 16m] 1,300 2-y-o: first foal: dam, 7f and 11.5f winner, half-sister to Prix de Diane winner Crepellana and daughter of useful stayer Astana, a half-sister to French Derby winner Philius: third behind Norman Conqueror in NH Flat race at Newbury in March: mid-division in novice hurdle at Worcester following month. *Mrs Gill E. Jones.* —

ASCENMOOR 11 b.g. Ascendant–Honeymoor (Pardao) [1989/90 24f2] leggy gelding: winning hurdler/chaser: first form for some time ½-length second to easy winner Plaza Toro in handicap hurdle at Uttoxeter in September: stays 3m: acts on any going: sometimes sweats: blinkered fourth and fifth starts 1988/9: moderate jumper of fences. *S. R. Bowring.* c— x 85

ASCERTALMOOR 9 b.g. Ascertain (USA)–Sally Rowanne (Haris II) [1989/90 c25fF] successful in 3 point-to-points in 1990: jumped boldly and was holding slight lead and going well when falling 4 out in hunter chase won by Park Shade at Cheltenham in May: looked probable winner there and should win a novice hunter chase. *A. D. Wardall.* c96 p

ASCOT LAD 5 ch.g. Broadsword (USA)–Aunt Livia (Royalty) [1989/90 F16f2 F16m*] second foal: half-brother to promising novice hurdler Sunninghill Celtic (by Celtic Cone): dam, well behind in 2 outings over hurdles, daughter of a useful staying hurdler: won quite valuable 5-runner NH Flat race at Sandown in April by ½ length from King Credo: yet to race over hurdles or fences. *D. Nicholson.*

AS GOOD AS GOLD 4 ch.g. Oats–Goldyke (Bustino) [1989/90 16g* 16m5 20g 16f 20m2] useful-looking gelding: has scope: first known foal: dam winning hurdler/chaser: poor maiden on Flat: won juvenile hurdle at Newbury in November (went left at the last): good second to Repeat The Dose in novice handicap at Huntingdon in April: stays 2½m. *G. B. Balding.* 108

ASHFIELD BOY 6 gr.g. Scallywag–Confident Girl (Quorum) [1989/90 aF13g^5 F12g] behind in NH Flat races: sold 4,200 gns Ascot May Sales: yet to race over hurdles or fences. *C. Smith.*

ASHMAE 8 b.g. Anax–Solentown (Town Crier) [1989/90 a20g^5 18f^2] leggy, sparely-made gelding: poor novice hurdler: stays 2¼m: acts on any going. *A. S. Neaves.* 78

ASHTON DANCER 6 b.m. Humdoleila–Savette (Frigid Aire) [1989/90 27f^6] leggy mare: lightly raced and no sign of ability. *T. H. Caldwell.* —

ASIGH 8 ch.g. Miami Springs–Misty Hill (Hill Clown (USA)) [1989/90 c20s* c24d^{pu}] big, plain gelding: lightly-raced winning point-to-pointer: bit backward, jumped soundly in the main to win hunter chase at Uttoxeter in February by 12 lengths from Fibreguide Tech: tailed off when pulled up in similar race following month: stays 2½m: acts on soft going. *M. Meade.* **c87**

ASK FOR MORE 5 b.g. Proverb–Primrose Walk (Charlottown) [1989/90 F14v F16g] fifth foal: half-brother to winning Irish hurdler/chaser Yellow Road (by Fine Blade): dam placed at up to 7f at 2 yrs: well beaten in NH Flat races in the spring: yet to race over hurdles or fences. *J. A. C. Edwards.*

ASK JEAN 11 gr.m. Ascertain (USA)–Fort Jean (Fortina) [1989/90 c24d^2 c24f^4 c24g^4] tall, lengthy, plain mare: very useful point-to-pointer: couldn't quicken from the last when 4 lengths second to Mademist Susie in maiden hunter chase at Leicester in March, best effort: acts on dead ground. *A. C. D. Sellers.* **c84**

ASK MOSS 5 ch.g. Le Moss–Triple Fire (Deep Run) [1989/90 22g^2 20g^6 21d^3 20d^{pu}] workmanlike ex-Irish gelding: second foal: dam unraced sister to 2 winners in Ireland and half-sister to fairly useful chaser Darc Hansel: won point-to-point in 1989: placed in novice hurdles at Wincanton in January and Newbury (4 lengths third behind Devil's Valley) following month: hung left and soon beaten at Doncaster in between: pulled up lame last outing: will stay 3m. *G. B. Balding.* 102

ASQUITH (USA) 4 ch.g. Golden Act (USA)–Sweet Patina (USA) (Moonsplash (USA)) [1989/90 16m 16f 16f] rather sparely-made gelding: successful in 1m claimer on Flat in July (has been tried in blinkers): sold out of W. Haggas' stable 9,500 gns Doncaster August Sales: poor form over hurdles, including in a conditional jockeys seller last start (blinkered, pulled hard): sold 3,200 gns Newmarket Autumn Sales. *N. Tinkler.* 62

ASSAGLAWI 8 b.g. Troy–Queen's Counsellor (Kalamoun) [1989/90 c20m^2 c24m* c24m* c24g^2 c20f*] angular, good-bodied gelding: fairly useful hurdler: won novice chases at Worcester and Nottingham (handicap, made most) in October and Huntingdon (jumped soundly, led last to score by 8 lengths from Mshahara) in November: stays 3m: acts on firm and dead ground. *Miss H. C. Knight.* **c110** —

ASSULTAN 6 ch.g. Troy–Plum Run (USA) (Run The Gantlet (USA)) [1989/90 a16g^{pu}] compact, useful-looking gelding: capable of fair form over hurdles but is thoroughly temperamental: refused to race 3 times and was reluctant to race last 2 outings (blinkered only start of 1989/90): sometimes ridden in spurs. *B. J. Curley.* §§

ASTICOT 8 ch.g. Posse (USA)–Noirima (Right Tack) [1989/90 25d^{pu} 17v^{pu} 20d^2 20s* 20d^3 16f] lightly-made gelding: selling hurdler: attracted no bid after winning handicap at Sedgefield (made most) in February: creditable third in non-seller on same course following month: ran poorly last outing: stays 2½m (well beaten over further): probably acts on any going: has worn blinkers. *D. J. Wintle.* c— 83

ASTON EXPRESS 7 b.g. Decent Fellow–Kilbride Lady VI (Menelek) [1989/90 16g^2 20d^4 c24d^2 c20s* c20v^2 c16s^F c16d] medium-sized, good-bodied gelding: fairly useful hurdler: won novice chase at Ayr in January: put up much better performance when 8 lengths second of 3 finishers to Carrick Hill Lad in West of Scotland Pattern Novices' Chase on same course later in month: reportedly suffered heart problems after only outing 1988/9: needs testing conditions when racing at 2m and stays 3m: acts on heavy going. *G. M. Moore.* **c129** 125

ASTRABEE 5 b.g. Show-A-Leg–Manatay (Brilliant Blue) [1989/90 20m^4 16m^5] tall gelding: well beaten on Flat: 33/1 and carrying condition, hampered run-in when 5 lengths fourth to Major Effort in 16-runner novice hurdle at Huntingdon (pulled hard) in April, better effort. *R. F. Marvin.* 88

ASTRASEAL 5 ch.g. Blue Refrain–Lady Farrier (Sheshoon) [1989/90 22g] tall gelding: well beaten over hurdles. *W. Carter.* —

ASTRE RADIEUX (FR) 5 b.g. Gay Mecene (USA)–Divine Etoile (USA) (Nijinsky (CAN)) [1989/90 16g4 16g4 16m5 22d c16s2 c16m2 c20d* c16s2 c20d2 c16g* c21d* c20g*] c**124** p 84

The Festive Spirit Novices' Chase, run at Chepstow on Coral Welsh National day in December, has been the starting point for several good young chasers. The only novice chase of the season confined to four-year-olds, it's been won in recent years by Pukka Major and Sure Metal and has seen the chasing debut of such useful performers as Tom's Little Al and Rig Steel. The latest running was well up to standard. Its winner Brandeston went on to success in the quite valuable Chivas Regal Amateur Riders' Novice Handicap Chase at Liverpool in April. The next three home are now also winners over fences and runner-up Astre Radieux has the makings of a useful handicapper. Just a poor novice over hurdles, placed twice from eight starts, Astre Radieux was a revelation once sent chasing. He did well to finish within two and a half lengths of Brandeston at Chepstow, staying on well having been virtually tailed off on the home turn. Ridden more forcefully to take advantage of his good jumping, Astre Radieux won four of his last six races over fences, novice events at Warwick, Hexham, Ayr and Perth, the last two handicaps. Making the running in what beforehand had looked a competitive Eglinton Cup at Ayr in April, Astre Radieux had the field on the stretch a long way out. Well on top turning into the straight, he kept on strongly to win by eight lengths from Romany King. At Perth six days later neither a 6-lb penalty nor a mistake at the final fence could stop his following up by twenty lengths from hat-trick-seeking Quassimi. On his only venture outside novice company, Astre Radieux's jumping stood the test of being taken on in front by The Leggett in a handicap at Haydock, his defeat attributable in no small measure to a typically strong ride by Scudamore on the winner. Taking on largely run-of-the-mill company in a busy first season over fences gave Astre Radieux plenty of time to learn his job. It also means that he's still

Eglinton Cup (Novices' Handicap Chase), Ayr—
Astre Radieux turns a competitive-looking race into a procession

Mr Trevor Hemmings' "Astre Radieux"

rated low enough to qualify for 0-125 handicaps, at least at the start of the next season, and is sure to win more races. With further improvement probable, Astre Radieux is likely to be troubling all but the best on handicap terms.

Astre Radieux (FR) (b.g. 1985)	Gay Mecene (USA) (b or br 1975)	Vaguely Noble (b 1965)	Vienna
			Noble Lassie
		Gay Missile (b 1967)	Sir Gaylord
			Missy Baba
	Divine Etoile (USA) (ch 1973)	Nijinsky (b 1967)	Northern Dancer
			Flaming Page
		Directoire (ch 1967)	Gun Bow
			Bold Consort

Astre Radieux is Flat-bred, by Gay Mecene, a very good middle-distance performer at his best, out of a seven-furlong two-year-old winner. The next two dams were also successful as two-year-olds, Bold Consort being a sister to top two-year-olds Bold Lad (USA) and Successor. Divine Etoile, half-sister to the very useful 1976 two-year-old Borodine and to smart middle-distance filly La Dorga, has bred four other winners, including successful French jumper Val des Etoiles (by Val de l'Orne). A winner over an extended mile in the French provinces as a three-year-old when trained by Mme C. Head, Astre Radieux runs as though he'll stay three miles over jumps. A workmanlike gelding, he's shown his form on ground ranging from good to firm through to soft. Blinkered on his last two outings in 1988/9, Astre Radieux raced most genuinely over fences in the latest season: he appeared to tie up slightly on the run-in when successful at Warwick, but was subsequently reported to have broken a blood vessel. *S. Mellor.*

ASTURIAS 7 b.g. Artaius (USA)–Tanaka (Tapalque) [1989/90 16g^{4} 16g^{3} 16d^{6} 16g^{6} 16g^{2}] smallish, workmanlike gelding: quite a modest hurdler: placed in 93 handicaps at Catterick in February and Perth in April: seems suited by a sharp 2m: best form with give in the ground. *J. M. Jefferson.*

AS YOU WERE 8 b.g. Beau Charmeur (FR)–Leaney Escort (Escart III) c**104** [1989/90 c16g^{3} c25f*] useful point-to-pointer, winner twice in March and once in May: won hunter chase at Warwick later in May by 2 lengths from Sweet Diana: stays 3m: acts on firm ground. *J. M. Turner.*

ATHENS GATE (USA) 6 ch.h. Lydian (FR)–Pago Miss (USA) (Pago Pago) [1989/90 16m^{2} 16m^{2} 16g^{3} 16g^{3} 16g^{4}] small horse: fair handicapper on Flat, winner 114 ? over 9f in 1989: sold out of J. W. Watts's stable 16,500 gns Newmarket Autumn Sales: neck second to Arden in novice hurdle at Ascot in November: below that form in similar events afterwards and is possibly unreliable: jumps none too fluently: sold 3,400 gns Doncaster June Sales. *N. Tinkler.*

ATHLETES' WEEK 7 b.g. Cure The Blues (USA)–Milveagh (Milesian) c— [1989/90 20d^{pu} 16m 25g^{pu}] small, close-coupled gelding: poor novice selling — hurdler: successful in a point-to-point in 1989: no worthwhile form in steeplechases. *R. Brotherton.*

ATIG (FR) 7 gr.g. Kenmare (FR)–Pardala (Pardal) [1989/90 16m^{pu} 16g 16s 16m^{3} 16m* 16g*] rangy gelding: handicap hurdler: beat Swift Ascent both times 102 when successful at Worcester in April (by 5 lengths) and May (by 1½ lengths): races only at around 2m: acts on good to firm and soft going: has hung left under pressure. *G. B. Balding.*

ATKINSONS 9 gr.g. Oats–For Sure (Fortino II) [1989/90 c16d^{4} c16g*] leggy, c**115** x close-coupled gelding: fair chaser: jumped better than usual when winning — handicap at Market Rasen in November gamely by 1½ lengths from Ringmore: best form at 2m: suited by give in the ground: blinkered tenth start 1987/8: has worn a crossed noseband: usually a moderate jumper. *Mrs G. R. Reveley.*

ATLAAL 5 b.g. Shareef Dancer (USA)–Anna Paola (GER) (Prince Ippi (GER)) [1989/90 16g^{2} 16f* 16d* 16d^{2} 16g* 16s^{3} 16m^{5} 16d] 133

In the spring of 1988 Atlaal was introduced into the Derby betting after winning a maiden event at Nottingham on his racecourse debut. His being trained by Henry Cecil, rather than his achievements, was responsible for Atlaal's position in the market. Further victories at York and Newbury, while confirming that Atlaal was a useful performer, showed him to be some way short of classic standard. Atlaal was to run only once more before being sent to the Newmarket Autumn Sales, where his present connections were able to pick him up for only 7,400 guineas. That he was subsequently operated on for a soft palate would go some way to explaining why he was bought so cheaply. Horses of similar ability would normally be expected to fetch at least five times as much. Atlaal's first outing over hurdles suggested that he was going to prove a bargain, for he ran a race full of

Bic Razor Lanzarote Handicap Hurdle, Kempton—eventual winner Atlaal (centre) is only third behind Osric and Deep Sensation (No. 4) at the last

promise in finishing five lengths third to Urizen in the Stroud Green Hurdle. However, he ran as though something was amiss at Windsor shortly afterwards, and his weak finishing effort when next seen out over hurdles at Newbury in November suggested that his problems were by no means behind him. Atlaal was soon to dispel any doubts concerning his fitness. By the end of the year he'd won run-of-the-mill novice events at Newbury and Stratford. And in January, following a good second to Forest Sun in the Tolworth Hurdle at Sandown, Atlaal took the Bic Razor Lanzarote Handicap at Kempton, a race won by his stable-companion Grey Salute a year earlier. The only novice in the thirteen-runner field, Atlaal turned in a very game effort at Kempton. In fifth place and looking held approaching two out, Atlaal battled his way into contention approaching the last, and a good jump there took him to the quarters of the leader Osric. Continuing to respond to pressure from Dunwoody, Atlaal collared Osric close home to win by a head. Atlaal ran up to his form on his next two starts, when two lengths third behind Whatever You Like in the A. F. Budge Novices' Hurdle at Ascot and when ten lengths fifth behind Fidway in the Seagram 100 Pipers Top Novices' Hurdle at Liverpool. But he was some way below his best in the Scottish Champion Hurdle at Ayr in April, and wasn't seen out again.

Atlaal (b.g. 1985)	Shareef Dancer (USA) (b 1980)	Northern Dancer (b 1961)	Nearctic
			Natalma
		Sweet Alliance (b 1974)	Sir Ivor
			Mrs Peterkin
	Anna Paola (GER) (ch 1978)	Prince Ippi (b 1969)	Imperial
			Prinzess Addi
		Antwerpen (ch 1972)	Waldcanter
			Adelsweihe

Mr Oliver Donnelly's "Atlaal"

Atlaal is the product of two classic winners, his sire Shareef Dancer having won the Irish Derby and his dam Anna Paola the Preis der Diana, which is the German equivalent of the Oaks. Anna Paola, the top filly at two years and three years in Germany, is a half-sister to Aspros, the champion two-year-old in Germany in 1979 and one of the best three-year-olds to race there in 1980. Atlaal was the first winner produced by Anna Paola; her three-year-old filly by Wassl, named Anna Petrovna, won over a mile and a quarter in May: Atlaal, who probably acts on any going, gives the impression that he'll always be best at around two miles over hurdles, and he's likely to be contesting several of the prestigious handicaps run over that distance in the next season. The Tote Gold Trophy at Newbury, which was also won by Grey Salute in 1989, will surely be on the agenda. Atlaal, a tall, close-coupled gelding, has sweated up slightly on occasions but it hasn't affected his performance. *J. R. Jenkins.*

ATLANTIC CEDAR 4 b.g. Touching Wood (USA)–Enchanted (Song) [1989/90 16g 16g 21f^2 20f 20d] leggy gelding: lightly-raced maiden on Flat when trained by R. Hannon, best effort over 7f at 2 yrs: 8 lengths second to Loaningdale in 7-runner novice hurdle at Newbury in March: swished tail and looked reluctant next start: stays 2½m: acts on firm ground: one to treat with caution. *P. Hayward.* 92 §

ATLANTIC PIRATE 7 ch.g. Some Hand–Atlantic Princess (Four Burrow) [1989/90 c26m^{pu}] tall gelding: no sign of ability in NH Flat race and over hurdles and fences. *T. B. Hallett.* c— —

ATRABATES 10 b.m. Precipice Wood–Stanegate (Coliseum) [1989/90 22m 24v 25f 25m^5 24m^6 26f^4] lengthy, rather sparely-made mare: useful hurdler in 1986/7: modest nowadays: best effort of 1988/9 when 19½ lengths fifth behind Sip of Orange in quite valuable handicap at Liverpool in April: fell second in novice chase in 1987/8: stays well: has won on firm going but well suited by plenty of give: has won for a claimer: wears blinkers. *O. Sherwood.* c— 115

ATTAVANTE 8 ch.m. Derrylin–Angor (Lorenzaccio) [1989/90 20d^{pu}] sparely-made mare: lightly-raced novice hurdler: stays 2½m: has run creditably for a 7-lb claimer. *D. Lee.* —

ATTIC WIT (FR) 4 b.g. Shirley Heights–Laughing Matter (Lochnager) [1989/90 F16f^2] first foal: dam, modest sprinter, half-sister to dams of Jester and Reesh: refused to enter stalls only intended outing on Flat: neck second to Cards And Kisses in 13-runner NH Flat race at Hereford in May: yet to race over hurdles. *R. J. Holder.*

ATTRACTIVE (NZ) 6 ch.g. Imposing (AUS)–Mi Gold (NZ) (Gold Sovereign) [1989/90 22v c16g^5 c20g^{bd} c20m^F c26g^{pu}] lengthy gelding: little promise in novice events over hurdles and fences. *M. H. B. Robinson.* c— —

AUCTIONEERS MOLL 7 b.m. Pardigras–Jostling (Clear Run) [1989/90 17g 17d^{pu}] lengthy, shallow-girthed mare: no worthwhile form in novice hurdles: pulled up lame in November. *P. Leach.* —

AUCTION LAW (NZ) 6 ch.g. Pevero–High Plateau (NZ) (Oncidium) [1989/90 20g* 22g* 20d^2 24g* 24s^{pu}] rather leggy gelding: improved hurdler in 1989/90, who was successful in handicaps at Cheltenham (conditional jockeys event), Haydock and Kempton: travelled strongly until 4 out, but soon behind and pulled up 2 out in better company final start: stays 3m: acts on soft going (won NH Flat race on top-of-the-ground). *D. H. Barons.* 132

AUCTION TIME 7 br.g. Auction Ring (USA)–Autumn Flush (Rustam) [1989/90 18g] sturdy gelding: won novice hurdle at Fontwell in 1987/8: always behind in handicap on same course in December: stays 2¼m: acts on heavy going: sold 1,500 gns Ascot June Sales. *R. Akehurst.* —

AUERSBERG 7 ch.g. Hard Fought–Holernzaye (Sallust) [1989/90 16f^5] sturdy gelding: selling hurdler: needed race only outing in 1989/90: raced too freely over 2½m: acts on good to firm and heavy going: blinkered last 3 starts of 1988/9: sold 950 gns Ascot November Sales: inconsistent. *A. D. Brown.* —

AUGHANVILLA 7 b.g. Pry–Coolcanute (Hardicanute) [1989/90 c18g^2 c18s^F c16d^3 c21d* c19s^3 c20v^2 c22d* c25m^5 c25g^4] Irish gelding: winning hurdler: won novice chases at Thurles in January and Fairyhouse (Dawn Run Novices' Chase by 12 lengths from Larchmont) in March: over 25 lengths fifth to Royal Athlete in Mumm Club Chase at Liverpool in April: stays 25f: acts on any going. *P. McCreery, Ireland.* **c125** —

Mrs R. Wilson's "Auntie Dot"

AUGHAVOGUE 8 b. or br.g. Golden Love–Deirdre's Joy (Cadmus II) [1989/90 c20d^{3} c20d^{3} c20s^{5} c20f^{pu}] rather sparely-made gelding: useful chaser: ran creditably first 3 outings, but was pulled up lame on last (March): best at around 2½m: acts on firm and dead going. *C. D. Broad.* **c135** —

AUGHWILLIAM 10 ch.g. Le Bavard (FR)–Snipe Walk (Cracksman) [1989/90 16g^{pu} c20d^{2} c24s^{pu}] sparely-made gelding: winning hurdler: still needed race, made a few mistakes when going down by 10 lengths to Lauderdale Lad in novice chase at Worcester in November: pulled up and dismounted following month and wasn't seen out again: stays 3m: acts on heavy going. *D. R. Gandolfo.* c89 —

AUGUST FOLLY 10 b.m. Idiot's Delight–Highway Holiday (Jimmy Reppin) [1989/90 c20d^{pu}] workmanlike mare: modest form in point-to-points: no worthwhile form in steeplechases (unlikely to stay 3m). *P. Davis.* c— —

AUGUST (USA) 9 b.g. Sensitive Prince (USA)–Polynesian Charm (USA) (What A Pleasure (USA)) [1989/90 17m^{4} 20f^{3} 16m^{2}] medium-sized gelding: handicap hurdler: in frame early in season: stays 2½m: acts on any going: has looked none too keen. *Denys Smith.* 84

AUK EYE (NZ) 6 b.g. Auk (USA)–Horafama (NZ) (Patron Saint) [1989/90 20d^{6} 20s* 22g* 22d*] plain gelding: successful in novice hurdle at Worcester (carried head high on run-in) in January, novice handicap at Stratford in March and 23-runner handicap at Ayr in April: easily best performance on last-named course when scoring by 6 lengths from Gunner Mac, despite whipping round at start: will stay 3m: acts on soft going: ridden by 3-lb claimer: should improve further, and will win more races. *K. White.* 129 p

AULD JAKE 10 b.g. Giolla Mear–Jamestown Girl (Harwell) [1989/90 c24m2] winning hurdler/chaser in Ireland: successful in a point-to-point in May: went down by ½ length to Turn Blue in hunter chase at Fakenham later in month: stays 3m: acts on firm going. *W. J. Tolhurst.* c93 —

AULD YUD 9 ch.g. Scallywag–Lucy Lady (Space King) [1989/90 c20m2 c24gur 22f* 25fpu] sturdy gelding: won slowly-run novice hurdle at Kelso in October: second to Carrolls Grove in novice event at Perth in September, best effort in steeplechases: probably stays 2¾m: acts on firm ground: blinkered second start: makes mistakes. *P. Monteith.* c86 86

AUNTIE DOT 9 b.m. Hallodri (ATA)–Dream Isle (Indian Ruler) [1989/90 c20f2 c20g3 c20g3 c25v3 c20d5 c20f4 c22m c20f2 c22m* c22m3] tall, sparely-made mare: useful chaser: won handicap at Stratford in May by 5 lengths from Gala's Image: ran creditably most other starts: stays 2¾m: acts on any going except perhaps very firm: usually jumps well: races keenly: has run well when sweating and on toes in preliminaries. *J. Webber.* c135 —

AUNTIE GLADYS 4 ch.f. Great Nephew–Vitalise (Vitiges (FR)) [1989/90 20gpu] leggy filly: quite modest maiden on Flat, in frame at up to 1¼m (has been blinkered): jumped poorly and tailed off when pulled up 2 out in juvenile hurdle at Kempton in December. *C. E. Brittain.* —

AUNT ISMAY 7 b.m. Riboboy (USA)–Ramuk's Queen (Queen's Hussar) [1989/90 20fpu 20d] sparely-made mare: poor novice hurdler: placed in a point-to-point in March: stays 19f: acts on firm going: sold 950 gns Ascot June Sales. *D. J. Wintle.* —

AUSTHORPE SUNSET 6 b.g. Majestic Maharaj–Kings Fillet (King's Bench) [1989/90 20f* 16g 20s 17f5 20m5 20f* 16f] medium-sized, rather sparely-made gelding: fair front-running hurdler: won handicaps at Doncaster in December and Wetherby (beat Armagret 10 lengths) in April: below form in between, and well beaten last start (stiff task and looked lean): stays 2½m when conditions aren't testing: acts on any going: usually claimer ridden: takes a good hold. *Mrs R. Wharton.* 122

AUTHORSHIP (USA) 4 b. or br.g. Balzac (USA)–Piap (USA) (L'Aiglon (USA)) [1989/90 16g* a16g3 a16g*] winning stayer on Flat: won juvenile hurdle at Fakenham in October and handicap at Southwell (landed the odds comfortably by 4 lengths from Cherry Chap) in January: will stay beyond 2m. *W. J. Musson.* 86

AUTO ALICK 6 b.g. Amboise–Auto Sam (Even Say) [1989/90 20g] very lightly-raced novice hurdler: no worthwhile form. *M. H. Easterby.* —

AUTUMN GALE 4 b.g. Strong Gale–Whistling Gold (Whistling Wind) [1989/90 F16v4 aF14g a20g 20gsu] IR 4,200Y, resold 4,000Y, 14,000 2-y-o: half-brother to 1¼m winner and successful staying hurdler Whistling Tiger (by Tower Walk) and winners in Hong Kong and Malaysia: dam ran twice: well beaten in NH Flat races: last of 7 in selling hurdle at Southwell in February. *R. O'Leary.* —

AUTUMN GOLD (NZ) 5 ch.g. The Expatriate–Golden Flame (NZ) (Drumfire) [1989/90 F16g 17vur 16g 21d] workmanlike gelding: tailed off in novice hurdles. *D. H. Barons.* —

AUTUMN SPORT 9 b.g. Mossberry–Bounteous Sport (Bounteous) [1989/90 20d 24m c20dbd c20d2 c26gpu c20gF] leggy, sparely-made gelding: fair hurdler in 1987/8: runner-up in novice chase at Bangor in March: spoilt his chance with mistakes last 2 starts: should be suited by 3m: best form with give in the ground (tailed off on top-of-the-ground second start). *J. A. C. Edwards.* c98 —

AUTUMN ZULU 11 gr.g. Wishing Star–Autumn Lulu (London Gazette) [1989/90 c26spu c20gpu c20d] workmanlike, shallow-girthed gelding: moderate chaser at his best: no worthwhile form in 1989/90: probably needs further than 2m nowadays, and should stay beyond 21f: acts well in the mud (yet to race on top-of-the-ground over jumps): front runner. *Miss L. Bower.* c— —

AVARICE 4 ch.c. Persian Bold–Parsimony (Parthia) [1989/90 F12g] half-brother to several winners, including smart sprinter Scarcely Blessed (by So Blessed) and very useful 5f to 7f winner Petty Purse (by Petingo): dam won July Cup and is half-sister to good sprinters Mummy's Pet and Arch Sculptor: well beaten in NH Flat race at Market Rasen in March: yet to race over hurdles. *T. Kersey.*

AVENIO (FR) 6 ch.g. Connaught–Poppea Sabina (FR) (Zeddaan) [1989/90 16d 16mpu 16f] lengthy gelding: poor novice hurdler: tailed off in a seller last start: — §

refused to race first outing: blinkered last 2 starts: sold 1,450 gns Doncaster Spring Sales. *G. M. Moore.*

AVERON 10 b.g. Averof–Reluctant Maid (Relko) [1989/90 16f 16m a16g^{4}] c—
useful-looking gelding: handicap hurdler: best effort in 1989/90 when moderate 92
fourth of 5 at Lingfield in December: third in a novice chase in 1986/7: stays 2¼m: acts on heavy going and possibly unsuited by firm: sometimes claimer ridden: has won when sweating. *C. P. Wildman.*

AVIONNE 5 b.m. Derrylin–Concorde Lady (Hotfoot) [1989/90 17h* 17f^{pu}]
leggy mare: prolific winning selling hurdler: won at Devon & Exeter in August, 101 ?
making all to beat sole opponent Carpet Capers (retained 6,250 gns): pulled up lame after last in non-selling handicap at Newton Abbot over week later and wasn't seen out again: has raced only at around 2m: acts on any going. *M. C. Pipe.*

AVONMOUTHSECRETARY 4 b.f. Town And Country–Star Display
(Sparkler) [1989/90 16f^{3} 16g 20g 16g^{4} 16v^{5} 16s^{2} 18s^{3} 20g^{4}] workmanlike filly: 92
carries condition: poor maiden on Flat: modest form in juvenile and novice hurdles: made numerous mistakes last start: should stay beyond 2½m: acts on soft going: has worn near-side and off-side pricker. *R. J. Holder.*

AYRES ROCK 9 b.h. Shirley Heights–Brazen Faced (Bold And Free) [1989/90
16d 16m^{pu}] compact horse: novice selling hurdler: best form at 2m: acts on heavy —
going. *B. K. Wells.*

AZUSA 7 b.g. Radetzky–Beguiling (Tower Walk) [1989/90 16g* 16f^{F} 17m* 16g^{6}
16d^{5} 16f^{3}] workmanlike gelding: former selling hurdler: won handicap hurdles at 96
Hexham (conditional jockeys) in March and Carlisle in April: races only at around 2m: acts on any going: blinkered once in 1986/7: usually wears a crossed noseband: has looked a difficult ride. *Miss M. K. Milligan.*

B

BABIL 5 b.g. Welsh Pageant–Princess Eboli (Brigadier Gerard) [1989/90 16m^{4}
16g^{2} 21g* 22g* 20d 20f* 24d* 20f* 24f^{2}] rather sparely-made gelding: fourth 134
foal: dam, useful 1½m winner, half-sister to fairly useful hurdler/chaser Canio (by Welsh Pageant): fair 1¼m winner on Flat (has looked ungenuine): sold out of P. Walwyn's stable 15,000 gns Newmarket July Sales: won 5 of his 9 starts over hurdles in 1989/90, namely minor contest at Newbury and novice events at

Hen Harrier Novices' Hurdle, Ascot—Babil (left) outstays Stratford Ponds

Wolverhampton, Doncaster, Chepstow (made all) and Ascot: good 2 lengths second of 3 to Picador in handicap at Cheltenham last start: stays 3m: acts on firm and dead ground. *N. A. Twiston-Davies.*

BABY ALEX 6 br.g. Derrylin–Nello (USA) (Charles Elliott (USA)) [1989/90 16h² 16f^F 16f 16h² 16f⁵ 16g⁶] neat gelding: novice selling hurdler: ran creditably in non-sellers first and fourth outings: found little under pressure last start: suited by sharp 2m: best run on hard ground. *C. J. Vernon Miller.* 71

BABY ASHLEY 4 b.f. Full of Hope–Nello (USA) (Charles Elliott (USA)) [1989/90 16f² 16f⁶ 16g 16g⁵ 16g^pu a16g³ a16g² a16g³] lengthy, dipped-backed filly: half-sister to novice selling hurdler Baby Alex (by Derrylin): lightly-raced maiden on Flat: novice selling hurdler: hung right and found nothing under pressure on first start: trained until after third outing by P. Feilden. *D. Morris.* 74

BABY BOY 9 b.h. Mummy's Pet–Lucent (Irish Ball (FR)) [1989/90 a16g⁵ 16g⁵ a16g⁶ 16m⁴ 19f 22m⁴] close-coupled horse: poor hurdler: has been beaten in a seller: made mistakes and was behind when falling on chasing debut: best form at 2m on an easy surface: sometimes blinkered: trained until after third start by T. Hallett. *B. Forsey.* c— 82

BABY SIGH 8 bl. or br.g. African Sky–Frances Jordan (Prince Regent (FR)) [1989/90 c17f² c17f⁴ c16m³ c16f³ c16d³ 19f⁴ 22m⁵] leggy, close-coupled gelding: poor handicap hurdler/novice chaser: sweated and ran in snatches fourth start, jumped moderately next time: stays 19f: acts on any going: blinkered final outing 1986/7: takes a good hold: often amateur ridden over hurdles. *G. Stickland.* c71 —

BACCAROLE 5 b.g. Ballad Rock–Eastern Saint (Welsh Saint) [1989/90 16s^pu 16s^pu 16s^pu] leggy gelding: seems of little account over hurdles. *Mrs A. Knight.* —

BACHELOR OF LAW 9 br.g. Cantab–Tangle Down (Tangle) [1989/90 c26g^pu c24g^pu] strong gelding: poor form in point-to-points: poor novice hurdler/chaser: stays well. *Mrs W. Fullerton.* c— —

BACHELOR'S PET 4 b.g. Petorius–Smile For Me Diane (Sweet Revenge) [1989/90 16m 16g⁵] sturdy, quite attractive gelding: plating-class maiden on Flat, probably stays 1¼m (has run blinkered and visored): fifth of 6 in novice claimer at Edinburgh in January: made mistakes and looked a difficult ride previous outing. *D. Burchell.* 69

BACK BEFORE DARK 6 b.g. Silly Prices–Willow Path (Farm Walk) [1989/90 16g 22d c20g^pu c16g^pu c17g c24g^pu] compact gelding: first foal: dam, poor staying novice hurdler, sister to winning jumper Willow Walk and half-sister to very useful hunter chaser Jaunty Jane: novice hurdler/chaser: no sign of ability. *J. K. M. Oliver.* c— —

BACKPACKER 10 b.g. New Brig–Preston Deal (Straight Deal) [1989/90 c24m^pu c29g^pu c25f c33d^pu c24d^ur c26m^ro] leggy, angular gelding: poor novice hurdler: winning chaser: let down by his jumping in 1989/90: stays 3m: form only on an easy surface: often amateur ridden over hurdles: usually taken early to post and sometimes mounted on track. *G. P. Enright.* c— x —

BACKSTREET GIRL 6 b.m. Joshua–Lady C (Princely Gift) [1989/90 F16m] half-sister to several winners, including very useful hunter chaser Mr Mellors (by Precipice Wood): dam ran once: in rear in NH Flat race at Sandown in March: yet to race over hurdles or fences. *R. G. Frost.*

BACK TO FORM 5 ch.g. Homing–Alezan Dore (Mountain Call) [1989/90 17d 17g^r] sturdy gelding: novice selling hurdler: reluctant to race, eventually refused after fourth on last start: trainer ridden. *Miss S. Waterman.* — §

BACKTONICA 5 b.m. Rolfe (USA)–Minica (Prince des Loges) [1989/90 18f^pu] first foal: dam poor Flat maiden: 66/1, tailed off when pulled up sixth in 6-runner novice hurdle at Fontwell in October on debut. *C. White.* —

BADGERS GIFT 4 br.g. Warpath–Bravade (Blast) [1989/90 16v 16g 16v 19s⁴ 20f⁵] lengthy gelding: half-brother to fair hurdler So Brave (by So Blessed): dam, sister to very useful Rhodomantade, won 1m seller: of little account: visored last start. *T. H. Caldwell.* —

BADGERS MEAD 8 b.g. Bishop of Orange–Ballynock (Belgrave) [1989/90 c24f^pu c24m^pu c20d⁴] leggy non-thoroughbred gelding: first reported foal: dam unraced sister to winning Irish chaser/point-to-pointer King Cacador: poor winning point-to-pointer: no sign of ability in novice chases. *C. Sporborg.* c—

BAD HABITS 10 b.g. Habat–Ribofleur (Ribero) [1989/90 20m⁴ c20d* c24g³ c20s³ c21s⁵ c20g⁴] compact gelding: novice hurdler: fortunate 12-length winner of conditional jockeys handicap chase at Kempton in November, being left in lead c87 78 when clear leader Mister Feathers unseated his rider at the last: probably stays 3m: acts on hard and dead ground. *G. P. Enright.*

BADIHAR (USA) 6 ch.g. Nijinsky (CAN)–Mofida (Right Tack) [1989/90 22m4 16d 25d6 25fF 20m5] big, good-topped gelding: fair hurdler: best effort of season when 5 lengths fifth behind Sayparee in valuable handicap at Liverpool in April, giving impression he'll be suited by a return to further: probably stays 3m: acts on heavy and good to firm going: has won for a claimer. *D. J. G. Murray-Smith.* 121

BADRAKHANI (FR) 4 b.g. Akarad (FR)–Burnished Gold (Breton) [1989/90 16s3 16dF 16g* 16v* 16g4 16d3 16f 16g4] smallish, close-coupled ex-French gelding: sixth foal: half-brother to 3 French winners: dam, 9.5f winner in France, daughter of sister to Vaguely Noble: placed at around 1¼m in 1989 when trained by A. de Royer-Dupre: won juvenile hurdles at Windsor and Plumpton in January: creditable third behind Question of Degree in juvenile handicap at Newbury in March: acts on heavy going: seems suited by waiting tactics. *N. J. Henderson.* 113

BAD TRADE 8 ch.g. Over The River (FR)–Churchtown Lass (Master Owen) [1989/90 c20d2 c17d3 c20d4 c24f4 c22m] rather angular ex-Irish gelding: fair chaser: placed at Leicester and Kelso (ran very well but found little run-in when 3½ lengths third behind Raise An Argument in minor event) within 3 days in March: stays 2½m: best form with plenty of give in the ground: gives impression he needs holding up for as long as possible. *W. A. Stephenson.* **c118** —

BAFFINLAND 9 ch.g. Pauper–Clody Miss (Gilles de Retz) [1989/90 c21g6] stocky gelding: won a point-to-point in 1989: has made mistakes and shown no sign of ability in 2 starts in steeplechases. *Mrs M. M. Saul.* c—

BAGGRAVE LAD 5 ch.g. Over The River (FR)–Bawnaro (Tarqogan) [1989/90 F16g2] IR 15,000 gns 3-y-o: second foal: dam unraced half-sister to Bregawn: 10 lengths second of 15 to Dalby Dash in NH Flat race at Uttoxeter in December: yet to race over hurdles or fences. *Mrs J. Pitman.*

BAGS 6 br.m. Heres–Dream Buck (Pinturischio) [1989/90 20dpu 20s] small, lightly-made, leggy mare: winning hurdler: very reluctant to race first outing: showed ability on chasing debut: well beaten over 2½m: acts on dead going: tends to sweat. *J. C. Fox.* c— — §

BAHRAIN BRIDGE 5 b.g. Formidable (USA)–Hide Out (Habitat) [1989/90 22m 19g3 22g3 16gpu a20g* a20g* a20g2 a20g6] smallish, good-bodied gelding: won handicap hurdle and novice hurdle at Lingfield within 4 days in February: 106

Tommy Whittle Chase, Haydock—Baies (No. 5) joins issue with Rinus at the last

good second to Olympus Reef in handicap on same course later in month: stiff task last start: stays 2¾m: acts on dead going and good to firm. *A. W. Denson.*

BAIES 8 br.g. Raise You Ten–Peppardstown (Javelot) [1989/90 c24s* c29g^{4} c25m^{3}] compact, sturdy gelding: useful chaser: beat The Thinker a short head in Tommy Whittle Chase at Haydock in December: ran creditably in useful handicap company at Sandown afterwards, finding little first occasion, blinkered second: probably stays 29f: yet to race on very firm ground, acts on any other: deliberate jumper: has won when sweating: has given impression he has his own ideas about the game. *C. P. E. Brooks.* **c144** —

BAITIN TIME 4 b.g. Sweet Monday–Mashin Time (Palm Track) [1989/90 16s^{6}] lightly-raced maiden plater at 2 yrs: weakened 3 out when 23 lengths sixth of 8 behind Leigh Boy in novice hurdle at Ayr in March. *R. H. Goldie.* — p

BAJAN BREEZE 4 b.f. Tumble Wind (USA)–Cristalga (High Top) [1989/90 16m 17f^{F} 17m^{pu}] half-sister to fair hurdler Au Bon (by Song): lightly-raced maiden on Flat: sold out of C. Wall's stable 1,550 gns Newmarket July Sales: no form in juvenile hurdles: pulls very hard: sold 675 gns Ascot November Sales. *D. J. Wintle.* —

BAJAN SUNSHINE 11 b.g. Reliance II–Nyanga (Never Say Die) [1989/90 c20g^{6} c25m* c24m* c28g^{2} c32v^{F} c24m^{pu} c21m^{4}] good-bodied gelding: useful chaser: usually looks unenthusiastic but did nothing wrong when winning from small fields at Wincanton in October and Newbury in November: good second to Royal Cedar at Cheltenham later in month: took little interest last 2 starts: stays well: acts on any going with possible exception of heavy: usually visored or blinkered nowadays: usually jumps well. *C. P. E. Brooks.* **c140** § —

BAKER CONTRACT 5 ch.g. Roman Warrior–Toe Tapper (Record Run) [1989/90 16d] robust gelding: poor sprint maiden on Flat: bit backward and sweating, tailed-off last in novice hurdle at Stratford in November. *J. M. Bradley.* —

BAKHUR 5 b.m. Bustino–Tumble Judy (Tumble Wind (USA)) [1989/90 F 16m^{F}] sixth foal: half-sister to useful 6f and 7f winner Cutting Wind (by Sharpen Up), later successful in USA: dam unraced: broke a leg in NH Flat race at Huntingdon in October. *G. G. Gracey.*

BALA BOY 7 b.g. Black Minstrel–Slave-Lady (Menelek) [1989/90 c20m^{6} c20g^{5} c24d] leggy gelding: has a round action: poor novice hurdler/chaser: weakened very quickly run-in, giving impression something was amiss, final outing (January). *T. T. Bill.* **c78** —

BALANCED REALM (USA) 7 b.g. Lines of Power (USA)–Brown Hare (USA) (Coursing) [1989/90 16f] workmanlike, good-quartered gelding: poor novice hurdler: ran in a seller last time. *T. Casey.* —

BALAO 4 ch.f. Mr Fluorocarbon–Bombay Duck (Ballyciptic) [1989/90 20m^{5} 16g] close-coupled filly: half-sister to 3 winners on Flat, including Bombil (by The Brianstan) who was also successful over hurdles: maiden plater on Flat: fifth in juvenile hurdle at Uttoxeter in December, better effort: claimer ridden. *R. Hollinshead.* 71

BALASANI (FR) 4 b.c. Labus (FR)–Baykara (Direct Flight) [1989/90 16f^{F} 16g^{3} 16g 16g] smallish, lengthy colt: successful in 1½m maiden race on Flat in France when trained by A. de Royer-Dupre: poor form in juvenile hurdles: needs to improve his jumping. *J. R. Jenkins.* 83

BALCRAIG BOY 5 ch.g. Le Soleil–Marnie's Girl (Crooner) [1989/90 16d] rangy, angular gelding: second in NH Flat race at Hexham in 1988/9: sold out of Mrs G. Reveley's stable 14,000 gns Doncaster August Sales: blinkered and ridden by 3-lb claimer, jumped none too fluently when tailed-off last of 8 in novice hurdle at Hereford in November. *K. C. Bailey.* —

BALIBRAY 4 b.g. Balidar–Our Mother (Bold Lad (IRE)) [1989/90 16m^{5}] modest maiden on Flat, stays 1m: over 30 lengths fifth of 9 finishers behind Native Friend in juvenile hurdle at Perth in August: sold 850 gns Doncaster November Sales. *G. M. Moore.* —

BALIDARIUS 5 b.h. Balidar–Siconda (Record Token) [1989/90 16m^{F} 16m^{F} 16g a16g] sparely-made horse: of little account on Flat and over hurdles: has worn crossed noseband. *R. C. Armytage.* —

BALI DOWN LAD 6 b.g. Balinger–Duckdown (Blast) [1989/90 16g] angular gelding: fourth foal: half-brother to Celtic Shot (by Celtic Cone): dam winning hurdler: jumped moderately when tailed off in novice hurdle at Wincanton in January on debut: sold 925 gns Ascot February Sales. *C. P. E. Brooks.* —

BALIGAY 5 b.m. Balidar–Gaygo Lady (Gay Fandango (USA)) [1989/90 17f] quite a modest 6f and 7f winner on Flat: claimer ridden, tailed off in novice event at Newton Abbot in August on hurdling debut. *R. J. Hodges.* —

BALINGER BILL 7 ch.g. Balinger–Berkeley Belle (Runnymede) [1989/90 F16g 20v^{pu}] strong gelding: yet to complete course in 3 point-to-points: bit backward, well beaten in NH Flat race at Ludlow in December: tailed off when pulled up in novice hurdle at Chepstow following month. *A. P. Jones.* —

BALINGLANCE 8 b.g. Balinger–Greek Glance (Athenien II) [1989/90 25g] small, workmanlike gelding: poor novice hurdler: stays 3m: acts on soft going: ridden by claimer: often wears blinkers. *R. Layland.* —

BALITO (NZ) 9 ch.g. Bally Royal–Lenita (NZ) (His Grace (NZ)) [1989/90 c25h* c25m^{3}] lengthy, sparely-made gelding: none too fluent a jumper of fences but won 4-runner novice event at Hereford in August: good third in hunter chase at Wincanton in March: stays 25f: probably acts on any going: blinkered nowadays: refused to race once in 1988/9 and was reluctant to start at Hereford: sold 5,200 gns Ascot May Sales. *D. H. Barons.* **c94** § —

BALLAD RULER 4 ch.g. Ballad Rock–Jessamy Hall (Crowned Prince (USA)) [1989/90 16f 16m 16s a20g^{3} a18g^{2} 16f^{6} 19m] angular gelding: temperamental maiden on Flat, best effort at 1¼m: sold out of B. Hanbury's stable 4,600 gns Newmarket Autumn Sales: placed in novice hurdles at Lingfield: no other form: visored last start. *P. A. Pritchard.* 66

BALLATICO 7 b. or br.g. Ballad Rock–Sweetham (Tudenham) [1989/90 16v a16g^{3}] won 2m novice handicap hurdle at Tramore in 1987/8: winner 3 times on Flat in 1988 (plating-class form in Britain in 1989): remote third in handicap hurdle at Lingfield in January: acts on heavy going. *J. R. Jenkins.* —

BALLIMINSTER 5 b.g. Balinger–Merry Minuet (Trumpeter) [1989/90 16g 20d 22m^{3}] sturdy gelding: first form over hurdles 22 lengths third behind Miinnehoma in 2¾m novice event at Fontwell (still bit backward) in December. *C. T. Nash.* 95 ?

BALLINAGORE GAA 9 br.g. Random Shot–Duessa (Linacre) [1989/90 c16d] good-bodied gelding: lightly-raced novice hurdler/chaser: wears a severe bridle. *M. Scudamore.* c— —

BALLINAVEEN 10 b.g. Peacock (FR)–Fugacity (Sugared) [1989/90 c24m* c24m c22d^{ur} c20s^{2} c20d^{4} c25f^{4} c24f^{3} c24m^{pu}] leggy, workmanlike gelding: has been hobdayed: won 5 point-to-points in 1989: jumped better than previously (though rather low) and showed first form in steeplechases when winning novice event at Leicester in December: also ran well fourth and fifth starts, but poorly on last: stays 3m: acts on soft and good to firm ground. *C. R. Saunders.* **c97**

BALLINCAR BOY 7 b.g. Deep Run–Rugged More (Rugged Man) [1989/90 18d 16g^{2} 16g c16m^{pu}] tall, angular ex-Irish gelding: first foal: dam winning Irish hurdler: won NH Flat race in 1988/9: modest novice hurdler: broke blood vessel when pulled up in novice chase in January: dead. *Miss H. C. Knight.* c— 97

BALLINHASSIG 6 b.g. Slippered–Rathcreevagh (Harwell) [1989/90 F16s^{5} c21s^{3} c16m^{3} c20d^{2} c24g^{3} c32f^{3}] well-made ex-Irish gelding: second foal: dam poor Flat maiden/point-to-pointer in Ireland: won 4 point-to-points in 1989: fifth in NH Flat race at Galway in October (trained until after then by T. Costello): has shown ability all starts in steeplechases: stays 3m (weakened after 3 out when tried over 4m): jumps soundly and should win a steeplechase. *John R. Upson.* **c106**

BALLYANTO 5 b.g. Lepanto (GER)–Ballyarctic (Arcticeelagh) [1989/90 16f^{4} 17d^{6} 17d 17m^{5} 16f^{5}] sparely-made gelding: modest novice hurdler: returned to his best when 10 lengths fifth to Vazon Bay in quite valuable novice handicap at Cheltenham in April, last start: should stay beyond 2m: acts on firm and soft ground. *Miss J. Thorne.* 99

BALLYBELL 5 ch.g. Prince Mab (FR)–Lydien (Sandford Lad) [1989/90 16g 16g 20g^{pu} 16d 16g 16g^{6} 16f^{5}] well-made gelding: only worthwhile form over hurdles when 16½ lengths sixth to Nineofus in novice event at Kelso in March. *J. L. Gledson.* 67

BALLY CODE 11 ch.g. Ballyglitter–Water Sprite II (Silver Kumar) [1989/90 c25m^{pu} c20m^{pu}] sturdy, good-bodied gelding: novice hurdler/chaser: won a point-to-point in 1987. *A. Barrow.* c— —

BALLYDALY EXPRESS 7 b.g. Distinctly (USA)–Indien Wine (Ete Indien (USA)) [1989/90 22d* 20g^{2} 22d^{3}] rangy gelding: will make a chaser: won a point-to-point and NH Flat race in Ireland early in 1988: won moderately-run 93 novice hurdle at Ayr in November: staying-on length second to Schiehallion on same course in December, but ran moderately there following month: will stay 3m: acts on dead going. *G. Richards.*

BALLYDURROW 13 ch.g. Doon–Even Tint (Even Money) [1989/90 a16g* a16g^{F}] 119

'There is no greater sorrow than to
recall a time of happiness when in misery.'

If the renovations at Southwell during the winter weren't quite sufficient to recreate Dante's vision of hell, his lines seemed appropriate to the time there in early-March when that grand old campaigner Ballydurrow was fatally injured in a fall on the all-weather surface, running in a 0-125 handicap in front of a handful of spectators. It is always sad to lose a hardy perennial like Ballydurrow, but the surroundings did make the loss somehow more poignant. All-weather hurdle races are no great spectacle or draw. The races tend to be uncompetitive, there seem to be problems with the hurdles themselves, and although there are few fallers the impression is that there is a greater incidence of serious injury.

Ballydurrow won nine of his forty-five races and a total of £37,753 over hurdles and a further twelve from sixty-five starts and £53,020 on the Flat. Despite those statistics, he was better over hurdles. A smart performer in his prime, his most notable victory came in 1984 when he won the Ekbalco Hurdle by two lengths from Browne's Gazette. On his next outing he went down by six lengths to the same horse in the Food Brokers & Primula 'Fighting Fifth' Hurdle, also at Newcastle, which began a sequence of four consecutive seconds in that event. Ballydurrow's last victory came at Southwell in February when he ran out an easy winner of a handicap hurdle. The next time, he was beginning to make his challenge two out when he fell, breaking a shoulder.

Ballydurrow (ch.g. 1977)	Doon (ch 1965)	Polly's Jet (ch 1953)	Polynesian
			Mary's Dell
		Bright Idea (ch 1958)	Never Say Die
			Bright Unus
	Even Tint (ch 1967)	Even Money (br 1955)	Krakatao
			Vendome
		Royal Tint (br 1958)	Snow King
			La Tinta

Ballydurrow was the third and final live foal out of the unraced Even Tint. His sire Doon came second to Vaguely Noble in the Observer Gold Cup and won over a mile as a three-year-old before being sent to race in America. Doon was returned to stand here, then was exported to Holland after the season in which he covered Even Tint. Ballydurrow was a big, strong gelding, the type to make a chaser although he was never raced over the larger obstacles; he usually jumped hurdles well. Raced only at around two miles, he was always held up and had a very useful turn of foot which he could produce on any type of going. *R. F. Fisher.*

BALLYEDEN 6 br.m. Beau Charmeur (FR)–Mac's Wish (Three Wishes) [1989/90 21v^{pu} 20d 20d^{3} 24m] sturdy ex-Irish mare: third foal: sister to winning chaser Kelsale: dam unraced half-sister to very useful Irish staying chaser Owen's Image: won point-to-point in 1989: 14 lengths third behind stable-companion False Economy at Carlisle in March, best effort in novice hurdles: should be suited by 3m (well beaten when tried at trip): sold 8,000 gns Ascot June Sales. *J. A. C. Edwards.* 85

BALLY FRENCHMAN 6 b.g. Le Dauphin–Border Bally (Bally Russe) [1989/90 20m 20v^{2} 21d^{3} 21d] workmanlike gelding: novice selling hurdler: will stay beyond 21f: acts on heavy going: usually blinkered, but has run well without them: sweating first 2 starts. *A. R. Davison.* 71

BALLYGRENNAN 8 ch.g. Golden Love–Feale-Side Nook (Laurence O) [1989/90 c24d^{r}] medium-sized gelding: maiden point-to-pointer: still carrying condition, reluctant to race and tailed off when refusing at the sixth in hunter chase at Nottingham in February. *Miss Mary Hamilton Ellis.* c– §

BALLYHANE 9 ch.g. Crash Course–Golden Approach (Golden Vision) [1989/90 c24g^{2} c26f^{5} c24g^{3} c24g^{2} c24s^{5} c24g^{4}] rangy, good sort: very smart c**156** ?
—

chaser: best efforts in 1989/90 when placed in valuable handicaps at Wetherby (edged left run-in when very close third behind Durham Edition and Nick The Brief) and Ascot (7 lengths second to Zuko) on third and fourth starts: ran poorly on last 2 outings, and possibly had something amiss: stays 25f: acts on any going: suited by a strongly-run race and waiting tactics: sometimes bandaged. *J. T. Gifford.*

BALLYHEELAN 9 b. or br.g. Ballymore–In My Time (Levmoss) [1989/90 c24v^F 16f 16f^5 16f^3 24g^pu] strong, workmanlike gelding: winning hurdler: only form in 1989/90 in seller and claimer third and fourth starts: novice chaser: stays 2¾m: seems to act on any going: usually blinkered or visored over hurdles: trained by G. McGuinness first outing. *S. J. Leadbetter.* c— 87 ?

BALLYLANE 6 ch.g. Touch Paper–Angelic Princess (Native Prince) [1989/90 17m^pu] strong gelding: sixth foal: dam Irish 9f winner: needing race, tailed off when pulled up 3 out in novice hurdle at Carlisle in November on debut. *J. E. Dixon.* —

BALLYMILAN 13 b.g. Milan–Ballyfin (Soldado) [1989/90 c24g^4 c25m^3] compact gelding: poor performer nowadays. *F. Sheridan.* c— —

BALLYMORE PARK 5 b.g. Ballymore–Tiltress (Tiepolo II) [1989/90 16d^ur 16g^3] neat gelding: 1½m seller winner on Flat: would have won selling hurdle at Hexham in December but for unseating rider last: carrying condition, jumped none too fluently when 8½ lengths third behind Just Pulham in similar event at Wetherby following month (wandered under pressure): will be suited by 2½m: gives impression he'll do best in blinkers. *G. M. Moore.* 81

BALLYNEETY 10 br.g. Bargello–Aunt Irene (Paddy's Birthday) [1989/90 c26m^2] a twin: fair winning point-to-pointer, successful in March and April (twice): 10 lengths second to Meister in hunter chase at Newton Abbot in May. *Mrs M. D. Hartley.* c**91**

BALLYNICK 6 ch.g. Balinger–Ellen Mavourneen (Tiepolo II) [1989/90 F16m* F16m] angular, sturdy gelding: first foal: dam fair hurdler and showed plenty of ability only start over fences: won 17-runner NH Flat race at Towcester in January: always behind in well-contested event at Liverpool in April: yet to race over hurdles or fences. *N. J. Henderson.*

BALLY REBEL 6 b.m. First Footman–Crisp And Easy (Crisp And Even) [1989/90 c25s^F] angular mare: tailed-off last in novice hurdle: bit backward, fell at the second in maiden hunter chase in March. *Dennis Bell (Cwmbran).* c— —

BALLY RUE (USA) 4 b.g. Ballydoyle (CAN)–Honeymoon Miss (FR) (Arctic Tern (USA)) [1989/90 16g^2 16v* 16g^co 16d* 16d^2 16f 16m^3 16g* 16d^4 16g* 16g*] rather angular Irish gelding: first foal: dam unraced half-sister to several winners, including Le Bavard: 9.5f maiden winner and placed at up to 2m on Flat: won juvenile hurdles at Gowran Park in November, Leopardstown following month and Fairyhouse in April, and handicap hurdles at Killarney and Gowran Park (put up a smart performace to beat Frantesa 6 lengths) in May: 8 lengths third behind Sybillin in Glenlivet Anniversary Hurdle at Liverpool seventh start: acts on good to firm and heavy going: ridden by claimer or amateur (unable to claim sixth to ninth outings). *J. S. Bolger, Ireland.* 135

BALLY SHINE 9 ch.g. Shiny Tenth–Sunny Maid (Ballymoss) [1989/90 20g^pu] first foal: dam lightly-raced maiden on Flat and over hurdles: tailed off when pulled up 3 out in novice hurdle at Uttoxeter in December. *O. Brennan.* —

BALLYVAUGHAN LADY 4 ch.f. Burslem–Liangold (Rheingold) [1989/90 16d] half-sister to winning hurdler Reel Guilt (by Imperial Fling): well beaten on Flat: pulled hard and weakened 2 out when eighth in 16-runner juvenile hurdle won by Swift Waters at Ludlow in March. *D. Haydn Jones.* —

BALLY WAY 13 b.g. Bally Russe–Way Up (Three Wishes) [1989/90 c25m^ur] lightly-raced point-to-pointer, but has shown fairly useful form (winner in May): unseated rider at the tenth in hunter chase at Towcester later in month. *M. J. Hill.* c—

BALLYWEST 12 ch.g. Lord Ha Ha–Bally Decent (Wrekin Rambler) [1989/90 20g^5 16m^3 24g a16g^3 a20g^5 a16g^4 16f^6 20m^6] small, sparely-made, plain gelding: inconsistent handicap hurdler: poor form in 1989/90 (amateur ridden): poor form in point-to-points in 1989: stays 2¾m: acts on any going: occasionally blinkered. *B. R. Cambidge.* 65

BALLYWILLWILL 4 b.g. Wolver Hollow–Nuageuse (Prince Regent (FR)) [1989/90 16m* 16g* 16g] workmanlike, angular ex-Irish gelding: half-brother to 4 winners, including 5f to 7f winner Cumulus (by Relko) and 1m winner Cloudless 105 ?

Mr Edward J. Kearns's "Bally Rue"

Sky (by He Loves Me): dam won 4 times over 5f in Ireland: in frame over 1m on Flat: successful by 5 lengths in juvenile hurdles at Roscommon (beat Good Spark) in August and Navan in September when trained by P. Prendergast: well beaten in similar contest won by Major Inquiry at Cheltenham in November. *P. J. Anderson.*

BALMUR 5 b.g. Balinger–Merebimur (Charlottown) [1989/90 16m] dipped-backed gelding: well beaten in juvenile hurdle and a novice hurdle. *Mrs J. E. Croft.* —

BALNERINO 7 b.m. Rolfe (USA)–Cotillion (Gala Performance (USA)) [1989/90 c16d c16g6 c16v6 c16mF a16g6] strong, compact mare: poor hurdler: well beaten in novice chases, making mistakes second start: acts on firm ground (well beaten on heavy). *J. C. McConnochie.* c— 76

BALTIMORE TO PARIS (USA) 5 b.m. Lord Avie (USA)–Solimile (Solinus) [1989/90 16mur 17f 24gpu] seems of little account. *P. Liddle.* —

BALUCHI 9 b.g. Gunner B–Atlantica (Tulyar) [1989/90 22m3 c20g5 c24g* c20m4 c24m* c20d5 c24s3 c25d5 c20m2 c20f2 c24f* c24g2 c24m* c24d c25f*] medium-sized, rather narrow gelding: winning hurdler: quite useful chaser: won handicaps at Market Rasen in November, Ludlow in January, Southwell (2) in April and Hereford (by 2½ lengths from Quilantaro) in May: suited by a strongly-run race at 2m and stays 3m, at least when conditions aren't testing: acts on any going: successful with and without blinkers: suitable mount for a claimer: genuine: has won 6 times at Ludlow. *B. Preece.* c**126** 124

BALVENIE 6 ch.g. Le Bavard (FR)–Arctic Free (Master Buck) [1989/90 22s6 21g] rangy gelding: well-beaten sixth behind Golden Celtic in novice hurdle at Folkestone in December: behind in Challow Hurdle at Newbury later in month. *P. R. Hedger.* —

BANBRIDGE 7 ch.g. Paddy's Stream–Glenroid (Polaroid) [1989/90 c16d* c16f2 c16g3 c16g2 c17f3] tall gelding: won handicap chase at Worcester in November: best subsequent effort when ½-length second to With Gods Help at c**122** § —

Stratford in April on fourth start: stays 19f: acts on any going: jumps soundly: usually led in at start nowadays: didn't go through with his effort second and third outings. *D. Nicholson.*

BANGKOK BOSS 4 b.f. Balinger–Fare (Le Dieu d'Or) [1989/90 F16m] third foal: dam showed no form on Flat or over hurdles: last of 11 in NH Flat race at Huntingdon in April: yet to race over hurdles. *J. L. Spearing.*

BANKER MASON (USA) 4 b.c. Sadler's Wells (USA)–Alwah (USA)
(Damascus (USA)) [1989/90 16g] first foal: dam unraced half-sister to 2 winning —
jumpers: changed hands 7,400 gns Newmarket Autumn Sales: won over 1¼m on Flat in December: ninth behind La Castana in claiming hurdle at Market Rasen later in month: sold 7,000 gns Doncaster January Sales. *N. A. Callaghan.*

BANKERS CREDIT 7 b.g. Pollerton–Blue Bleep VII (pedigree unknown)
[1989/90 F16m a20g^{pu}] non-thoroughbred gelding: third foal: half-brother to —
winning Irish chaser No Grandad (by Strong Gale): dam unraced: tailed off in NH Flat race and when pulled up in novice hurdle: dead. *Mrs E. H. Heath.*

BANKER'S GOSSIP 6 b.g. Le Bavard (FR)–Gracious View (Sir Herbert)
[1989/90 20s^{6} 22d^{4} 24d^{6} a24g^{2} 24f^{2} 24m^{3}] medium-sized, good-quartered 105
gelding: type to carry condition: second in novice hurdles at Southwell in February and Bangor following month: claimer ridden, good third behind Lotschen Lady in handicap at Towcester in April: stays 3m: acts on firm and dead going: lacks turn of foot. *D. Nicholson.*

BANK-JOB 5 ch.g. Don–Royal Performance (Klairon) [1989/90 F16v^{6} 16v]
workmanlike, plain gelding: third foal: half-brother to a winner abroad: dam won —
over 1m in Ireland: well beaten in NH Flat race at Ayr in January: still bit backward, tailed off in novice hurdle at Chepstow following month. *B. Ellison.*

BANK VIEW 5 ch.g. Crofter (USA)–Stony Ground (Relko) [1989/90 16d^{5}
16g 16s* 16v* 16m^{F}] 149

Bank View's second season over hurdles ended with a fall at the second flight in the Waterford Crystal Champion Hurdle at Cheltenham. That Bank View was in the line-up there suggests he'd made satisfactory progress since his juvenile days, when he'd won five of his ten starts and developed into a useful hurdler. That certainly was the case, though his starting price of 50/1 represented a fair reflection of his prospects of winning the Champion Hurdle. Bank View will need to improve a good deal further if he's to trouble the best. Bank View didn't enter the Champion

Daily Mail Racecall Champion Hurdle Trial, Haydock—33/1-shot Bank View leads over the last from Milford Quay and Vicario di Bray

*Noel McCabe Distributors Hurdle, Leopardstown—
Bank View (left) wins for his new owners*

Hurdle picture until January, when he won the Daily Mail Racecall Champion Hurdle Trial at Haydock. It was an unexpected success, for having shown little when on the backward side on his first two outings Bank View was allowed to start at 33/1, the outsider of the seven runners. The market was headed by Vicario di Bray, winner of the race the previous year and thought likely to show a return to that form under similarly testing conditions. Both Vicario di Bray and Bank View were ridden with restraint as Milford Quay set a good gallop, Bank View racing in last place until making steady headway towards the end of the back straight. Bank View and Vicario di Bray came through to challenge the leader at the second last, the trio drawing clear of the remainder, and it was Bank View who found the better pace to take a narrow advantage at the last. Keeping on gamely under strong pressure on the run-in, Bank View was always holding Vicario di Bray. He had a length and a half to spare over that horse at the line, with Milford Quay a further four lengths away in third. Bank View, having changed ownership in the meantime, faced an easier task and duly justified favouritism in a listed race in Ireland the following month, but not before giving his supporters some anxious moments. The Noel McCabe Distributors Hurdle, a listed race for four- and five-year-olds run at Leopardstown, was one of the season's most eventful contests. There was a bizarre start to proceedings, with all but one of the eight jockeys seeming intent on dropping their mounts in behind, and this allowed the 50/1-shot All That Crack to build up a massive lead. At the fourth last All That Crack was roughly a furlong clear, but it wasn't until after jumping the third last that the remaining runners took up the chase in earnest. Bank View was the nearest pursuer and quickly began to peg back the tiring leader, but then early in the straight he veered markedly right towards the chase track and it took a few cracks of the whip to get him back on course. It wasn't until the last flight that Bank View took over in the lead, but he continued to wander on the run-in and had to be driven right out to hold the late challenge of Vestris Abu by two lengths. Bank View looked a difficult ride that day, and his success was due in no small part to the strength of his jockey McCourt.

Bank View (ch.g. 1985)	Crofter (USA) (ch 1977)	Habitat (b 1966)	Sir Gaylord
			Little Hut
		Marie Curie (ch 1970)	Exbury
			Ela Marita
	Stony Ground (ch 1976)	Relko (b 1960)	Tanerko
			Relance III
		Peach Stone (b 1968)	Mourne
			La Melba

Bank View is the fourth foal of Stony Ground, a half-sister to the fairly useful ten-furlong performer Florida Son and daughter of a half-sister to Breton, the top French two-year-old of 1969. The first three foals of Stony Ground, who won over one and a half miles in Ireland, were also winners and included Bank View's full brother Green Croft, a winner on the Flat in Italy and later over hurdles in Ireland. Bank View himself has won four races on the Flat, all over a mile. Tried in blinkers and a visor on the Flat, Bank View hadn't looked in need of either over hurdles until giving his wayward performance at Leopardstown. Apparently Bank View is none the worse for his fall at Cheltenham, and he'll be back in action in the next season, when he should win more races in all but the top company. Bank View, a compact gelding, is always likely to be best at around two miles. He's suited by give in the ground and acts on heavy going. *N. Tinkler.*

BANNEROL (USA) 7 b.g. Smarten (USA)–Queen's Standard (USA) (Hoist The Flag (USA)) [1989/90 20f*] leggy, useful-looking gelding: won novice hurdle at Market Rasen in August by 8 lengths from Ardra Duke despite running in snatches and wandering under pressure: should stay beyond 2½m: suited by top-of-the-ground. *Mrs S. A. Bramall.* 98

BANNISTER 5 b.g. Known Fact (USA)–Swiftfoot (Run The Gantlet (USA)) [1989/90 16m 17g^{pu} 16m^{5}] sparely-made gelding: very little form on Flat since fairly useful winner at 2 yrs (headstrong): dropped in class, 21 lengths fifth to La Castana in conditional jockeys selling hurdle at Huntingdon in December: has worn net muzzle: trained first start by C. C. Elsey. *N. Kernick.* 75

BANQUE D'OR 6 b.m. Le Coq d'Or–Gilzie Bank (New Brig) [1989/90 22d^{pu}] leggy mare: no promise in novice hurdles. *R. McDonald.* —

BANTEL BALOCCO 5 ch.g. River Beauty–Sleigh Lady (Lord Gayle (USA)) [1989/90 16m 17m^{5} 16m^{4} 17h^{F}] lengthy gelding: poor novice hurdler: dead. *P. Monteith.* —

BANTEL BUCCANEER 8 b.g. Jellaby–Highview Jill (Proud Chieftain) [1989/90 16g 22d 20g^{5} c20d^{3} c21d^{3}] tall, rather sparely-made gelding: quite a modest hurdler: third in novice chases at Newcastle in February (3 lengths behind Mister Point) and Ayr in April (13 lengths behind Astre Radieux): stays 21f: suited by plenty of give in the ground: wore protective bandages on knees last start. *J. K. M. Oliver.* c**91** 94

BARACUS 7 b.g. Lepanto (GER)–Pendon Fare (Stupendous) [1989/90 c21m^{su} c20m^{4} c20v^{pu}] tall, rather leggy gelding: novice hurdler/chaser: no sign of ability: tends to sweat. *C. L. Popham.* c— —

BARAOORA 8 gr.g. Bruni–Tory Island (Majority Blue) [1989/90 c18f^{pu} a16g^{4}] tall, well-made gelding: winning hurdler: placed in novice chases and a conditional jockeys selling chase: stays 2¼m: seems suited by a sharp track and a sound surface: blinkered first start: sold 1,700 gns Ascot February Sales. *R. J. O'Sullivan.* c— —

BARA PEG 9 b.m. Random Shot–Borderina (Border Chief) [1989/90 c16d c16g^{5} c20s^{pu} c26g^{3} c24m^{pu} c24s^{3} c25s^{2} c25m^{2} c26g^{4}] tall, workmanlike mare: winning hurdler: placed in varied company over fences, showing poor form: suited by a test of stamina: acts on any going: often sweats: tends to make the odd mistake. *T. M. Jones.* c**86** —

BARATIJO 5 b.g. Krayyan–Another Match (Sovereign Path) [1989/90 16d] sparely-made gelding: of little account: wears blinkers. *G. P. Kelly.* —

BAR FLY (FR) 4 ch.g. Salmon Leap (USA)–Breathalyser (Alcide) [1989/90
16m^{F} a16g^{4}] modest maiden on Flat when trained by M. W. Easterby, only form in 73
1989 at 5f: 11 lengths fourth to Mehtab in juvenile hurdle at Southwell (made a
couple of mistakes) in March: barely stays 2m and is likely to prove suited by a
sharp track: sold 1,200 gns Ascot April Sales. *M. C. Pipe.*

BARGE BOY 6 b.g. Jimsun–Barge Mistress (Bargello) [1989/90 16s^{5}] novice
hurdler: first race for over a year, around 15 lengths fifth behind Bourbon Spirit at 85
Sandown in February, staying on well closing stages. *J. A. B. Old.*

BARJIM 7 ch.g. Slim Jim–Baru (Rubor) [1989/90 16g] compact, workmanlike
gelding: no sign of ability: dead. *M. A. Barnes.* —

BARLEY LOAF 7 b.g. Barley Hill–Motherly Love (Little Buskins) [1989/90 c—
F16h^{3} F12m^{4} aF14g^{5} 22s a16g^{4} c24s^{pu} c16g] tall, rather sparely-made —
non-thoroughbred gelding: half-brother to a poor animal by Garnered: dam never
ran: showed ability in NH Flat races: no form over hurdles or fences. *J. White.*

BARLEY MOW 4 b.g. Wolverlife–Ellette (Le Levanstell) [1989/90 16g 16m^{6}
16g^{6} 16g^{2} a16g* a16g^{3} a16g^{5} 17m* 16f^{pu} 20g^{5}] leggy, close-coupled gelding: 96
maiden on Flat: won juvenile hurdles at Southwell in February and Carlisle in
April: unlikely to stay much beyond 2m: acts on good to firm ground. *N. Bradley.*

BARMOSS 5 b.g. Le Moss–Bartlemy Hostess (Bargello) [1989/90 F16f] first
foal: dam winning Irish hurdler: around 28 lengths seventh of 12 to Bollinger in
NH Flat race at Ascot in April: yet to race over hurdles or fences. *G. B. Balding.*

BARNABY BENZ 6 b.g. Lochnager–Miss Barnaby (Sun Prince) [1989/90
16m^{2} 16g^{3} 17f^{2} 16s^{3} 16g^{3}] dipped-backed, good-quartered gelding: placed in 83
novice handicap hurdles in first half of season: has raced only at around 2m:
probably acts on any going: visored final start. *M. H. Easterby.*

BARNACK 4 b. or br.g. Montekin–Damastown's Lady (Rarity) [1989/90 16g^{3} c—
17d 17g c17g] no sign of ability on Flat: tailed-off last of 3 finishers in juvenile —
hurdle at Fakenham in October: sold out of A. Bailey's stable 3,000 gns
Newmarket Autumn Sales: no form in France subsequently. *T. Civel, France.*

BARNACLE BILL 7 ch.g. Nicholas Bill–Matsui (Falcon) [1989/90 16g c17g^{6} c—
c16g^{F}] leggy gelding: raced much too freely to stay 2m over jumps: sold privately —
out of I. Campbell's stable 2,200 gns Doncaster August Sales: dead. *M. Smith.*

BARN BRAE 8 b.g. Derek H–La Raine (Majority Blue) [1989/90 c24d^{6} c20g^{2} **c91**
c21m^{6} c20f^{3} c16f^{2} c16m^{2}] angular, workmanlike gelding: winning chaser: placed
in hunter chase and handicaps in 1990: stays 21f, at least when conditions aren't
testing: below form on heavy going, acts on any other: often amateur ridden. *J. P. Leigh.*

BARNBROOK AGAIN 9 b.g. Nebbiolo–Single Line (USA) (Rash **c174**
Prince) [1989/90 c20g^{F} c17f* c20f^{3} c24g^{2} c24d* c16f* c20f*] —

'About the best thing in racing is when two good horses single themselves out from the rest of the field and have a long-drawn-out struggle.' George Lambton's *Men and Horses I Have Known*, first published in 1924, remains arguably the finest racing autobiography of them all and Lambton's memorable account of the famous finish between Ard Patrick and Sceptre in the Eclipse has been quoted many times. Lambton's book describes an era long ago but it is a fund of racing wisdom and always rewards re-reading. His perception of the ideal horse-race is one that many would share and it was duplicated in the latest edition of the Queen Mother Champion Chase which produced as thrilling a finish as any all season. The reigning two-mile champion Barnbrook Again crossed the final fence almost in unison with his young challenger Waterloo Boy (winner of the previous year's Arkle Challenge Trophy) and the pair became locked in an epic duel that those lucky enough to have seen will remember for a long time. The issue lay between them on the flat—Sabin du Loir, only a couple of lengths down at the last, could do no more—and they battled it out magnificently up the hill. Showing tremendous resolution, Barnbrook Again proved just the stronger, holding on to a narrow lead gained setting off up the run-in; but Waterloo Boy, fighting back magnificently, pressed him all the way to the line, both horses tending to drift right as they came under extreme pressure. There was never more than half a length—the winning distance—between the pair and Waterloo Boy earned almost as much credit for his

Byrne Brothers Compton Chase, Newbury—
Barnbrook Again leads Golden Friend over the first

performance as did the winner for his. Feroda stayed on after the last to pass Sabin du Loir close home for third, seven lengths behind Waterloo Boy; the only hard-luck story concerned Pearlyman, the champion in 1987 and 1988, who returned lame after being pulled up almost immediately after making a mistake at the third last where he was still moving comfortably.

The sequel to the finish of the Queen Mother Champion Chase—the riders of Barnbrook Again and Waterloo Boy were suspended for misuse of the whip—is also discussed in the essay on Waterloo Boy. Suffice to say here that there was little or no sign that the average racegoer at Cheltenham was offended by the forceful riding of Davies and Dunwoody; there seemed general amazement among the Press when the news of the stewards inquiry and subsequent bans reached them at around the time of the sixth race (the Champion Chase had been the second of the day). It was widely agreed that Davies and Dunwoody were harshly treated by the stewards and, though neither rider appealed, their suspensions brought into focus the injustice of the present guidelines on the use of the whip when commonsense is not applied. The guidelines recommend that the stewards 'should consider enquiring into any case where a rider has used his whip more than ten times . . . after the penultimate obstacle in a steeplechase or hurdle race'. Davies and Dunwoody received their suspensions for 'using their whips excessively'. The Cheltenham stewards could, and should, have made allowances for the fact that riding a finish up the steep climb from the last at Cheltenham takes longer than riding a finish on the average track, and that in a tight finish riders are always likely to make more use of the whip. Both Davies and Dunwoody used the whip correctly, keeping in rhythm with their mounts, both of which responded right up to the finishing post.

The Queen Mother Champion Chase was only the second race that Barnbrook Again had contested over the minimum distance since his victory at Cheltenham twelve months earlier. He had carried top weight to victory at Newbury at the end of November in the North Street Handicap which he won in course-record time by a length, driven out, from Springholm (received 27 lb), the only one of his rivals to complete the course. Barnbrook Again's two most recent outings had been at three miles—in the King George VI Rank Chase at Kempton on Boxing Day and in the Byrne Brothers Compton Chase at Newbury in February—and a final choice about his Cheltenham Festival objective wasn't made until the eleventh hour. Barnbrook Again's trainer made his views plain in a *Timeform Interview*:

'Barnbrook Again is a very high-class horse whatever the distance, a true professional . . . but I don't think he's really as strong at three miles as he is at up to two and a half. There aren't many three-mile chasers who could beat him, and if Desert Orchid was to be retired tomorrow "Barney" would be a very strong contender to take his crown. But if you're going to talk about the very highest level . . . you'd have to think he'd be better having his energies channelled in the most profitable direction which would be to aim him at the Queen Mother Champion Two Mile Chase which he won last year'. Barnbrook Again was left in the Gold Cup at the overnight stage, reportedly as a precaution against any mishap befalling him in the early stages of the Champion Chase which was run the day before. He'd have been a worthy contender for steeplechasing's most prestigious championship and should be seriously considered if he's in the Gold Cup field another year. Barnbrook Again has shown his best form so far at up to two and a half miles but his record at three miles comprises only two races, a creditable second to Desert Orchid in the King George VI Rank Chase on his first attempt at the trip and an easy victory in the Byrne Brothers Compton Chase. Barnbrook Again never seriously challenged Desert Orchid at Kempton and in finishing eight lengths behind his stable companion gave the impression that three miles stretched his stamina (though he had seven lengths to spare over third-placed Yahoo). Judged on his performance at Kempton, Barnbrook Again's prospects of getting the Gold Cup distance of three and a quarter miles in testing conditions wouldn't be good—but we doubt he'd be allowed to tackle the race on soft or heavy going (he acts on any but would be much better suited by the distance of the Queen Mother Champion Chase if ground conditions placed a big premium on stamina).

We'd have had a better idea about Barnbrook Again's capabilities at three miles if his main rival, the subsequent Gold Cup runner-up Toby Tobias, had completed the course in the Compton Chase. Toby Tobias, who

Queen Mother Champion Chase, Cheltenham—Barnbrook Again and Waterloo Boy draw away from Sabin du Loir and Feroda

started 11/8 on, was disputing the lead with Barnbrook Again when unseating his rider at the tenth, too far out to say how the race would have unfolded. Barnbrook Again, who had set a good gallop in the early part of the race, wasn't challenged afterwards and went on to beat the out-of-form 1989 Gold Cup runner-up Yahoo by a distance with Golden Friend last of three finishers. Three of Barnbrook Again's seven races in the latest season were over two and a half miles, a distance which arguably suits him better than two, judged on his very impressive victory at Cheltenham's mid-April fixture in the South Wales Showers Caradon Mira Silver Trophy Chase, a valuable conditions event sponsored by one of his owners and won, incidentally, by the latest Gold Cup winner Norton's Coin in 1989. Barnbrook Again had run a little below his best over the course and distance in the A. F. Budge Gold Cup in December (when third under 12-0 to the lightweights Clever Folly and Welsh Oak) but he produced an exceptional performance in the Silver Trophy. The outsider Sure Metal set a tremendous gallop over the early fences and Barnbrook Again maintained the pace, jumping with zest and fluency, after taking over from Sabin du Loir at the twelfth; he was clear four from home and ran out a clear-cut winner, ten lengths in front of Pegwell Bay, who received 10 lb, with Sabin du Loir, fading from three out, more than twelve lengths further back in fourth. By our reckoning Barnbrook Again's display was the best of the season from any steeplechaser with the exception of the best of Desert Orchid's performances.

Barnbrook Again's pedigree has been discussed at length in previous Annuals. His sire the Two Thousand Guineas winner Nebbiolo didn't stay in the Derby but at stud he has been more of an influence for stamina than speed, the average distance of races won by his progeny on the Flat at three years and upwards being eleven furlongs. Barnbrook Again's dam Single Line, who comes from a very successful family, won five races over sprint distances in North America, but she is a three-parts sister to the Coaching Club American Oaks winner Magazine (grandam, incidentally, of the Daily

South Wales Showers Caradon Mira Silver Trophy Chase, Cheltenham—Barnbrook Again puts up a tremendous performance

Mr Mel Davies' "Barnbrook Again"

Barnbrook Again (b.g. 1981)	Nebbiolo (ch 1974)	Yellow God (ch 1967)	Red God
			Sally Deans
		Novara (br 1965)	Birkhahn
			Norbelle
	Single Line (USA) (b or br 1969)	Rash Prince (b 1960)	Prince John
			Prompt Impulse
		Day Line (b or br 1963)	Day Court
			Fast Line

Express Triumph Hurdle winner Rare Holiday) and has bred the middle-distance Flat winners Ski Lift (by Mount Hagen) and Single Viking (by Viking). Barnbrook Again began his career on the Flat—he was trained until after his four-year-old days by Mellor—and won a handicap over 11.7 furlongs at Windsor as a three-year-old when he was placed over a mile and three quarters. The versatile Barnbrook Again has won seventeen of his twenty-eight races over jumps, finished second on six occasions and third four times. He is very game and genuine, though he wore blinkers (for the only time in his career) when third in the 1987 Champion Hurdle. Barnbrook Again is a sound jumper of fences and every inch a weight-carrying chaser in appearance, being a robust, good sort. The only time he has failed to reach a place over the sticks was on his reappearance at Kempton in the latest season; his jumping that day was nowhere near his usual standard and he was well behind his rivals Pegwell Bay and Panto Prince when falling six from home. Barnbrook Again was distressed afterwards and veterinary examination diagnosed a heart murmur. He showed no sign of any problem in his subsequent races; hopefully, there'll be no recurrence of whatever ailed him. His first major target in the next season was due to have been the King George VI Rank Chase in which he should have played a prominent role, Desert Orchid or no Desert Orchid. Unfortunately, at the time of writing, Barnbrook Again's participation looks very doubtful. He suffered a pre-season injury that could keep him out of action for the best part of the season, if not the whole of it. *D. R. C. Elsworth.*

BARNEY BURNETT 10 ch.g. Le Bavard (FR)–Autumn Magic (Arctic Slave) c**139**
[1989/90 c24g^{2} c24d c25v c24s^{2} c20v c20v* c28m^{2}] useful Irish chaser: made all in handicap at Punchestown in February: 12 lengths second to Desert Orchid in Jameson Irish Grand National at Fairyhouse in April: stays well: acts on good to firm and heavy going: blinkered fifth outing 1988/9 and last 4 in 1989/90. *R. Walsh, Ireland.*

BARNEY O'NEILL 4 gr.c. Ballad Rock–Lapis Lazuli (Zeddaan) [1989/90 F16d] half-brother to 3 winners, notably smart 1m to 1¼m winner Farioffa (by Hotfoot): dam 2-y-o 5f winner: behind in NH Flat race at Kelso in February: yet to race over hurdles. *J. J. O'Neill.*

BARNSDALE 5 ch.h. Ahonoora–Marfisa (Green God) [1989/90 aF13g^{3} aF13g* aF13g*] fourth foal: half-brother to 1986 2-y-o 7f seller winner Gillot Bar (by Rarity) and a winner in Italy by Fordham: dam won 6 races in Italy: won NH Flat races at Lingfield in February and March (made all, by 10 lengths): yet to race over hurdles or fences. *D. M. Grissell.*

BARON SAFEGUARD 4 gr.g. Baron Blakeney–Be Spartan (Spartan General) [1989/90 F16g] fourth foal: half-brother to Langshott Manor (by Celtic Cone), placed in a NH Flat race: dam unraced half-sister to a winning staying chaser: tailed off in NH Flat race at Market Rasen in April: yet to race over hurdles. *W. T. Kemp.*

BARON TWO SHOES 4 gr.g. Baron Blakeney–Win Shoon Please
(Sheshoon) [1989/90 F16m 16g 16s^{2} 22f^{4} 16m^{2} 16m] compact, workmanlike 90
gelding: second foal: dam novice selling hurdler: behind in NH Flat race in January: modest form over hurdles: ran moderately last 2 starts: stays 2¾m: acts on firm and soft going. *N. A. Gaselee.*

BARONY 9 ch.m. Ribston–Sherry (King's Coup) [1989/90 c20g^{pu} c27s^{pu}] c— x
compact mare: seems of no account over hurdles: maiden point-to-pointer: made —
mistakes and was tailed off when pulled up in novice chases in February. *J. E. Swiers.*

BARONY ISLE 9 b.g. Cagirama–Specific Day (Specific) [1989/90 c17f^{F} c20d^{4} c88 ?
c20g^{3} c20s^{6}] strong, rangy gelding: novice hurdler: handicap chaser: ran —
moderately final start (February): stays 2½m: acts on soft ground: has sweated up and got very much on toes. *C. W. Thornton.*

BARRERA LAD (USA) 10 ch.g. Barrera (USA)–Misty Joy (USA) (Misty
Day) [1989/90 16m^{4} 16m^{2} 16m^{F}] compact gelding: handicap hurdler: good second 91 +
at Windsor in November: disputing lead when falling last at Huntingdon following month: best at 2m: acts on any going: ridden by an amateur or claimer. *R. D. Townsend.*

BARRISH 4 b.c. Wassl–Rowa (Great Nephew) [1989/90 16g^{3}] sturdy colt:
fairly useful middle-distance stayer on Flat, winner in 1990: sold out of A. 87 p
Stewart's stable 17,000 gns Newmarket Autumn Sales: not knocked about when 14 lengths third behind Iveagh House in juvenile maiden hurdle at Wincanton in February (took good hold and jumped none too fluently): sure to improve. *R. Akehurst.*

BARRYSVILLE 14 b. or br.g. Woodville II–Barryscourt (Straight Lad) c—
[1989/90 c25m^{pu}] strong gelding: handicap chaser: no form for some time: often —
blinkered nowadays. *P. Burgoyne.*

BARSBRIDGE LAD 10 b.g. Little Buskins–Hills of Fashion (Tarqogan) c83
[1989/90 16f 16d c21g^{pu} c20d^{5} c26s^{F} c20d^{pu}] leggy gelding: poor novice —
hurdler/chaser: pulled up after badly hampered third on final outing (February): suited by 2½m. *R. C. Spicer.*

BARSHARE 5 ch.g. Longleat (USA)–Grill Room (Connaught) [1989/90 F16m
16d] workmanlike gelding: seventh foal: dam ran twice: well beaten in NH Flat —
race and novice hurdle at Market Rasen. *R. C. Spicer.*

BARSTOX BOY 5 b.g. Touch Boy–Siciliana (Sicilian Prince) [1989/90 16d^{pu}] no promise in 2 outings over hurdles, latest a seller. *I. Anderson.* —

BARTINAS STAR 10 b.g. Le Bavard (FR)–Bartina (Bargello) [1989/90 c20m^{F} c20f^{3} c20m^{ur} c16g^{5} c20f^{ur}] leggy, rather angular gelding: winning hurdler: moderate chaser nowadays: suited by 2½m: yet to show his form on heavy ground, acts on any other: goes best fresh. *P. J. Bevan.* **c105** —

BARTONDALE 5 br.m. Oats–Miss Boon (Road House II) [1989/90 F16s F16m] unfurnished mare: fifth foal: half-sister to maiden point-to-pointer Vareck (by Sagaro): dam useful hurdler and fair chaser: well beaten in NH Flat races: yet to race over hurdles or fences. *G. Thorner.*

BARTON RISE 10 b. or br.m. Raise You Ten–Love All (Arctic Chevalier) [1989/90 c20f^{5} c16d^{pu} c25f^{2}] rangy mare: carries plenty of condition: poor chaser: probably stays 3m: acts on firm going: blinkered sixth outing 1988/9. *J. A. C. Edwards.* **c87** ? —

BARTRES 11 ch.g. Le Bavard (FR)–Gail Borden (Blue Chariot) [1989/90 c24d^{pu} c20g c21d^{2} c20s^{3} c20g^{F} c20f c36f] lengthy, plain, raw-boned gelding: fairly useful chaser: best efforts of season on third and fourth starts: eighth of 20 finishers behind Mr Frisk in Seagram Grand National at Liverpool in April: stays well: acts on any going: usually held up: has hung under pressure and has worn blinkers (not in last 2 seasons). *D. J. G. Murray-Smith.* **c135** —

BARTRYN 5 b.m. Barley Hill–Tarylin (Military) [1989/90 16m^{6} a18g^{4} a16g 16s^{ur} a16g^{5}] workmanlike mare: poor novice hurdler: has run in a seller. *Mrs J. E. Croft.* 58

BARUT (USA) 5 b.g. Lines of Power (USA)–Brookbourn (USA) (Kennedy Road (CAN)) [1989/90 16m 16m] leggy, quite good-topped gelding: no sign of ability over hurdles, giving impression something might be amiss: blinkered final start 1988/9: races freely. *R. Champion.* —

BASIC FUN 4 b.f. Teenoso (USA)–Sirenivo (USA) (Sir Ivor) [1989/90 16g* 16d* a16g* a16g^{2} a16g^{2} 16g^{3} 16g^{2} 16g^{3} 16f*] small, sparely-made filly: dam half-sister to 2 successful jumpers: maiden on Flat, probably stays 1¾m: sold out of P. Walwyn's stable 3,800 gns Doncaster November Sales: won conditional jockeys selling hurdle at Ludlow (bought in 5,600 gns), juvenile claimer at Nottingham (claimed out of J. Spearing's stable £9,026), novice hurdle at Southwell and juvenile claimer at Sedgefield (claimed by J. Spearing £9,001): best efforts on good going: good mount for a claimer. *C. R. Beever.* 93

BASILEA 7 b.g. Strong Gale–Katie Kumar (Silver Kumar) [1989/90 c19s^{2} c20g^{3} 18s] well-made gelding: one-time useful hurdler: winning chaser: creditable second over fences at Hereford in December: refused and unseated rider at the last (remounted) next time: stays 2½m: acts on heavy going: refused at the first third outing in 1988/9. *Capt. T. A. Forster.* **c114** § —

BASIL THYME 10 ro.g. Scallywag–Savette (Frigid Aire) [1989/90 c16g^{pu} c16m^{2} c16v^{3} c20m^{4}] tall gelding: novice hurdler: winning chaser: in frame in handicaps in 1989/90: suited by 2½m: acts on any going: moderate jumper. *T. N. Bailey.* c85 x —

BASKET WEAVE (FR) 9 b.g. Weavers' Hall–Manyra (FR) (Abdos) [1989/90 22m^{pu} 24g 22m^{F} 25g 21d^{4} 20s 21s* 25g 25d] lengthy gelding: handicap hurdler: returned to his best when winning at Towcester in February: well beaten afterwards: stays 25f: acts on any going: has won for a claimer. *G. B. Balding.* 107

BASRULLAH 9 b.g. Bluerullah–Bassom's Peach (Bassompierre) [1989/90 c24g^{F} c24g^{ur} c24m^{r} 28f^{6}] close-coupled, sparely-made gelding: winning point-to-pointer: novice hurdler/chaser: yet to complete course in steeplechases, but would probably have finished second in handicap at Fakenham in February but for falling 3 out: beaten when refusing at the last next start. *K. C. Bailey.* c— x —

BASTINADO 7 ch.g. Bustino–Strathspey (Jimmy Reppin) [1989/90 20m^{pu}] third foal: dam half-sister to 2 winning jumpers: quite modest handicapper on Flat, seems best around 1¼m: sold out of I. Balding's stable 5,000 gns Newmarket Autumn Sales: tailed off when pulled up 2 out in novice hurdle at Sedgefield in March: sold 1,100 gns Doncaster Spring Sales. *P. A. Blockley.* —

BATCHWORTH HILL 8 b.g. Balinger–Royal Rally (Royal Record II) [1989/90 c21f^{F}] workmanlike gelding: half-brother to good staying chaser Lesley Ann (by Menelek): won 2 point-to-points in 1989: fell second on steeplechasing debut. *C. Holmes.* c—

BATH STREET BOY 5 b.g. Baptism–Lancashire Lass (King's Troop) [1989/90 17m^{pu} 16d^{pu}] of little account. *Miss G. M. Rees.* —

BATTALION (USA) 6 b.h. Vaguely Noble–Blazon (USA) (Ack Ack (USA)) [1989/90 16g^{6} 16g^{5} 16d 16g^{2} 20d* 21m* 24f*] 153 p

Battalion's performances in his first season over hurdles, when he showed himself a very useful novice, led us to draw the wrong conclusions as to his distance requirements. A free-going type with a turn of foot, he seemed likely to prove best at around two miles. However, Battalion didn't get off the mark in his second season until tried over two and a half miles; and he showed easily his best form when winning the Keith Prowse Long Distance Hurdle over three miles at Ascot in April. At least he fulfilled one of our predictions by developing into a smart performer. Because of the prevailing firm ground the Keith Prowse Long Distance Hurdle, worth over £15,000 to the winner, attracted only eight runners, four of whom looked to have little chance of winning. And with the going much too lively for Rendlesham Hurdle winner Old Dundalk, the race looked to rest between Battalion and Milford Quay, both racing over three miles for the first time, and Maelkar, a useful handicapper who'd finished second in the Coral Golden Hurdle Final at Cheltenham. Milford Quay didn't help his cause by racing freely and he soon dropped away once Battalion had taken his measure with four to jump. Maelkar, who'd been ridden with restraint, now posed the only threat to Battalion, but the latter was still two lengths up and travelling strongly turning for home, and he put the issue beyond doubt when quickening going to the second last. Maelkar could do no more and Battalion, who continued to run on strongly until eased close home, had six lengths to spare at the line. It was a most convincing display. Battalion's earlier wins were gained in handicaps at Wolverhampton and Sandown. Though apparently unsuited by very soft going Battalion confirmed at Wolverhampton that he's not inconvenienced by ground which is just on the soft side of good. Judging by his subsequent efforts, though, it would seem that a firm surface suits him ideally.

Battalion (USA) (b.h. 1984)	Vaguely Noble (b 1965)	Vienna (ch 1957)	Aureole
			Turkish Blood
		Noble Lassie (b 1956)	Nearco
			Belle Sauvage
	Blazon (USA) (b 1976)	Ack Ack (b 1966)	Battle Joined
			Fast Turn
		Too Bald (b or br 1964)	Bald Eagle
			Hidden Talent

Battalion is no stranger to the sales ring, having passed through it on three occasions. As a yearling he fetched 200,000 dollars, and his owner Sheikh Mohammed was to lose heavily on his investment. The winner of

Balvenie Malt Whisky Handicap Hurdle, Sandown—Battalion defies top weight

Keith Prowse Long Distance Hurdle, Ascot—Battalion has quickened clear of Maelkar

only one race, a maiden event at Bath, in two seasons' racing on the Flat, Battalion was sold on for just 8,000 guineas at the Newmarket Autumn Sales in 1987. Battalion remained in training with John Dunlop for one more year, winning a ten-furlong handicap at Goodwood, then was returned to the same sales, where he proved in much greater demand. His present connections had to go to 34,000 guineas to secure him, but they've had no cause to regret their investment. It is understandable that Battalion should fetch such a considerable sum as a yearling. By the Prix de l'Arc de Triomphe winner Vaguely Noble, Battalion is the second foal of Blazon, an extremely well-bred mare who won four races in the USA. Blazon is a half-sister to numerous winners, notably the 1986 Breeders' Cup Juvenile winner Capote and Exceller, the latter a high-class French middle-distance stayer who went on to show himself a tip-top performer in the States. The second dam Too Bald, a high-class stakes winner, is a daughter of the Kentucky Oaks winner Hidden Talent. Battalion is still an entire and should have a future at stud, but there are more races to be won with him over hurdles first. A compact, rather lightly-made individual who jumps well, the game and genuine Battalion will be a force to reckon with in all the top long-distance events given suitable ground conditions. *C. P. E. Brooks.*

BATTIS BAY 11 b.g. Deep Run–Gay Hat (High Hat) [1989/90 c24m^{6}] sturdy gelding: moderate point-to-pointer: well beaten only completed outing in hunter chases. *Tim Brown.* c—

BATTLEAXE 6 b.g. Kampala–Fine Flame (Le Prince) [1989/90 16f] small gelding: selling hurdler: needed race only outing of season (July): has raced only at around 2m: acts on heavy going: blinkered third start 1988/9. *Miss G. M. Rees.* —

BATTLE DRUM 9 b. or br.g. Bustino–Ring Rose (Relko) [1989/90 16s^{4} 16d] lightly-raced novice hurdler: not at all knocked about either outing 1989/90: best run at 2m. *D. H. L. Nugent.* —

BATTLE FLEET 7 ch.m. Alias Smith (USA)–Impregnable (Never Say Die) [1989/90 c24d^{pu}] workmanlike mare: winning point-to-pointer, successful twice in March: tailed off when pulled up in maiden hunter chase at Leicester earlier in month. *Mrs Richard Plummer.* c—

BATTLE OF WITS 9 b.g. Tug of War–Glenvale Princess (Prince Hansel) [1989/90 a20g^{pu} c17g^{pu} c16g^{6}] sturdy gelding: poor hurdler/novice chaser: stays 2½m. *T. W. Cunningham.* c— —

BATTLEPLAN 5 b.g. Hard Fought–Zoly (USA) (Val de L'Orne (FR)) [1989/90 16g^{6} a24g^{2} a24g^{3} a20g^{5} 24g^{2} 16m^{3} 21f^{3}] compact gelding: selling hurdler: 81

effective at 2m and stays 3m: acts on good to firm and dead going (below his best on heavy and very firm): often claimer ridden: visored third to fifth starts 1988/9: sold 4,200 gns Doncaster June Sales. *K. A. Morgan.*

BATTLE STANDARD 4 ch.g. Battle Hymn–Rose Bridges (Calpurnius) [1989/90 16m^{4} 16f^{6}] 5,600Y, 1,000 2-y-o: smallish, sturdy gelding: sixth foal: half-brother to a winner in Italy: dam, plater, stayed 1¼m: poor form in early-season juvenile hurdles: has pulled hard and worn crossed noseband. *Mrs I. McKie.* 66

BATTLE STING 6 b.g. Hard Fought–Mrs Bee (Sallust) [1989/90 17m* 16f^{3} 20h^{2}] close-coupled gelding: won conditional jockeys handicap hurdle at Cartmel in August: barely stays 2½m: acts on any going, except possibly heavy: not raced after October. *Mrs S. A. Ward.* 83

BATTLE'S TOWN BOY 8 b.g. Crash Course–Fair Trouble (Prefairy) [1989/90 c21m^{4} c24g^{3}] leggy, lengthy gelding: no sign of ability over hurdles: poor novice over fences (jumps poorly): stays 3m: has run creditably for a 7-lb claimer. *Mrs V. C. Ward.* c— x —

BATU 9 ch.g. Sparkler–Amber Star (Amber Rama (USA)) [1989/90 16m^{5} c20m^{F}] leggy, lightly-made gelding: poor hurdler: winning chaser: stays 3m: appears suited by firm ground: usually wears blinkers: suitable mount for a claimer: jumps moderately. *N. J. Wheeler.* c— x —

BATU PAHAT 4 b.f. Impecunious–Dicopin (Deauville II) [1989/90 16g^{2} 16g^{2} a16g^{pu}] seventh foal: dam quite a useful staying hurdler: staying maiden on Flat: runner-up in 2 juvenile hurdles: dead. *W. G. M. Turner.* 87

BAVARD ASH 7 ch.g. Le Bavard (FR)–Merrybash (Pinzari) [1989/90 c24f* c24g^{F}] tall, sparely-made gelding: winning hurdler: landed the odds in 4-runner novice event at Leicester in November on chasing debut, despite jumping none too fluently and to his left: led until falling sixth next outing, following month: stays very well: acts on any going: tail swisher. *R. Lee.* c**89** —

BAVARD BAY 6 b. or br.g. Le Bavard (FR)–Winterwood (Bargello) [1989/90 20g^{4}] ex-Irish gelding: fourth foal: brother to Irish NH Flat race winner Roborough: dam never ran: well beaten in NH Flat races in 1988/9: won a point-to-point in March: over 35 lengths fourth behind Goodshot Rich in novice hurdle at Perth following month: should improve. *G. Richards.* 87 p

BAWNRUADH 5 ch.g. Wrens Hill–Oldtown Princess VI (Chou Chin Chow) [1989/90 24m* 20m^{pu} 24g 20g] non-thoroughbred gelding: won novice hurdle at Perth in August: well beaten afterwards (not raced after November): bolted before start second outing: stays 3m. *J. Parkes.* 83

BAY BRIDGE 9 b.g. New Brig–Tarik (Even Money) [1989/90 c20d^{ro} c22s^{4} c24d^{5} c26m^{2} c24f^{2} c24g* c24f* c26m^{2}] close-coupled gelding: well beaten in novice hurdles: won hunter chases at Market Rasen and Wetherby (by a neck from Freddie Teal) in May: stays 3¼m: acts on firm going. *W. A. Stephenson.* c**98** —

BAY CHASER 7 b.g. Hasty Word–Darlinski (Swing Easy (USA)) [1989/90 16m 20d c16s^{F} c16g c24f^{pu}] robust, workmanlike gelding: seems of little account: sold 1,400 gns Doncaster Spring Sales. *W. Storey.* c— —

BAYFORD ENERGY 4 ch.g. Milford–Smiling (Silly Season) [1989/90 16g^{pu} 20s^{4}] lengthy gelding: half-brother to several winners: dam successful hurdler: poor winning stayer on Flat: last of 4 in poor juvenile claiming hurdle at Sedgefield in February. *R. M. Whitaker.* 79 ?

BAY FOX 5 b.g. Bay Express–Gay Vixen (Healaugh Fox) [1989/90 16m 16g^{5} 16s] workmanlike gelding: no worthwhile form. *P. Beaumont.* 64

BAY POND 8 b.g. Grundy–Summer Bloom (Silly Season) [1989/90 25d^{pu}] smallish, sparely-made gelding: winning selling hurdler: suited by testing conditions when racing at 2m and stays 2¼m (unlikely to stay 25f): acts on any going: blinkered once: has run creditably for a claimer: bit backward only outing 1989/90 (November). *J. White.* —

BAYRAM (FR) 8 br.g. Blakeney–Zarin (GER) (Arjon) [1989/90 c20g^{pu} c26s^{5} c24s^{pu} c24g^{pu}] compact ex-Irish gelding: winning hurdler/chaser: showed nothing in 1989/90: stays 3m: acts on heavy going. *T. J. Etherington.* c— —

BAYSHAM (USA) 4 b.c. Raise A Native–Sunny Bay (USA) (Northern Bay (USA)) [1989/90 17d^{5} 16d] close-coupled colt: sold out of G. Harwood's stable 5,000 gns Newmarket Autumn Sales: better effort over hurdles when fifth in juvenile event at Devon & Exeter in January: ran well over 6f in 1990. *B. R. Millman.* 83

BAY TERN (USA) 4 b.c. Arctic Tern (USA)–Unbiased (USA) (Foolish Pleasure (USA)) [1989/90 16g* 20g*] lightly-raced maiden on Flat, placed over 1¼m: sold out of L. Cumani's stable 10,000 gns Newmarket Autumn Sales: unbeaten in 2 outings over hurdles at Perth, namely juvenile event in April (made most) and handicap (led 2 out to beat Paco's Boy 4 lengths, pair clear) in May: stays 2½m: should improve again. *C. Weedon.* 109 p

BAY WINDOW 6 b.g. Bay Express–Broken Record (Busted) [1989/90 16d6] no worthwhile form over hurdles: sold 2,000 gns Doncaster Spring Sales. *I. Campbell.* —

B B S BIDFORD 5 b.m. Legal Eagle–Dear Catalpa (Dear Gazelle) [1989/90 18h6] small mare: poor novice selling hurdler. *C. C. Trietline.* —

BEACHAMWELL 8 b.g. Record Run–Mishabo (Royalty) [1989/90 c17m4 c16gF] strong, lengthy, chasing type: winning hurdler: carrying condition, 29 lengths fourth to Courtbrook in novice handicap at Doncaster in January on chasing debut: sweated and needed race when tailed off over 2¾m: acts on dead going: sold 1,500 gns Ascot April Sales. *M. Skinner.* c— —

BEACH TIGER 6 gr.g. Java Tiger–Lido Light (Good Light) [1989/90 c20gpu c26vur c25gpu 21d5 21s 21d] lengthy, angular gelding: sixth living foal: dam, daughter of a half-sister to Champion Hurdle winner Anzio, won over hurdles: won a point-to-point in Ireland in 1989: bought 15,500 gns Doncaster Spring (1989) Sales: no worthwhile form in novice chases but has shown signs of ability: poor form over hurdles: should stay beyond 21f. *J. S. King.* c— 88

BEACONSIDE 13 b.g. Pardigras–Erica June (Langton Heath) [1989/90 c21gpu c24dpu c25f* c25m3 c36gpu c25m2 c25fpu] tall gelding: handicap chaser: won at Hereford in April: suited by a test of stamina: acts on any going: claimer ridden: blinkered nowadays. *Mrs E. M. Brooks.* c**102** —

BEAN DREAMS 5 b.g. Prince Bee–Travelling Fair (Vienna) [1989/90 16g2 20g*] leggy, good-topped gelding: half-brother to winning hurdler Dibbinsdale Lad (by Sandford Lad): 1¾m seller winner on Flat: won selling hurdle at Sedgefield in November despite hanging left in latter stages (bought in 4,500 gns): stays 2½m: claimer ridden. *W. H. Bissell.* 87

BEARNA NA GAOITHE 8 b.g. Floriferous–Kedrah Lassie (No Argument) [1989/90 F16f* F16m2 16f6 16f 24mpu] big, workmanlike ex-Irish gelding: won a point-to-point in 1988: successful in NH Flat race at Wexford in August: well beaten in novice hurdles: trained by P. Flynn until after second start. *A. P. James.* —

BEAR'S PICNIC 4 b.g. Furry Glen–Three Dieu (Three Dons) [1989/90 F14v] sixth foal: half-brother to fair chaser Hand Over (by Quayside) and winning selling hurdler Top Pryal (by Prominer): dam, quite useful over hurdles and fences, stayed 3m: tailed off in NH Flat race at Ayr in April: yet to race over hurdles. *M. H. Easterby.*

BEAU CHARM 6 b.g. Beau Charmeur (FR)–Anona-Anona (Alcide) [1989/90 16gF] ex-Irish gelding: placed all 4 starts in point-to-points: better for race, behind when falling fourth in novice hurdle at Kempton in February. *J. T. Gifford.* —

BEAU CROFT LASS 5 ch.m. Beau Charmeur (FR)–Niagara Lass (Prince Hansel) [1989/90 F16g 16s 16f] small mare: fifth foal: half-sister to winning hurdler McGillicuddy (by Abednego): dam half-sister to staying chaser The Songwriter: well beaten in novice hurdle and a selling handicap. *C. C. Trietline.* —

BEAU ECHARPE 5 b.m. Relkino–Rapidus (Sharpen Up) [1989/90 16gF 20g6] 1¼m seller winner on Flat: sold out of D. Morley's stable 10,000 gns Newmarket Autumn Sales: well beaten in mares novice hurdle at Market Rasen in June. *N. J. Henderson.* —

BEAU GUEST (FR) 8 ch.g. Be My Guest (USA)–Belle Zed (FR) (Zeddaan) [1989/90 17m2 16d3 16m3 16m3 16g2 c16g* c16g2 c16sur c16d3 16m3] leggy, close-coupled gelding: handicap hurdler: ran creditably in 1989/90: wide-margin winner of novice chase at Edinburgh in January: travelling strongly just behind eventual winner Wink Gulliver when unseating rider 2 out in Daniel Homes Novices' Chase at Ascot in February: jumped none too fluently penultimate outing: best at 2m: probably acts on any going: usually claimer ridden: usually held up: sometimes sweats. *J. Parkes.* c**105** + 105

BEAULIEU BAY 6 b.g. Longleat (USA)–Peta's Bay (I Say) [1989/90 16f5] sparely-made gelding: winning hurdler: second in conditional jockeys selling handicap at Huntingdon in August (hung left and demoted to fifth): unlikely to stay much beyond 2m: acts on firm and dead ground: ridden by claimer: wears 87 visor or blinkers: probably needs holding up for as long as possible. *K. G. Wingrove.*

BEAU NASH 6 b.g. Prince Tenderfoot (USA)–Dominica (GER) (Zank)
[1989/90 16g 16s^3 16g^2] compact gelding: novice hurdler: races only at 2m: acts on 81
soft going: hung badly left final start. *A. P. Stringer.*

BEAU N'IDOL 11 b.g. New Brig–Minibelle (Straight Cut) [1989/90 c25m^5] c**76**
smallish, slightly dipped-backed gelding: moderate chaser: fairly useful winning —
point-to-pointer: about 25 lengths fifth to Wellington Brown in hunter chase at
Wincanton in March: stays 27f: has run moderately on extremes of ground. *Mrs G. P. P. Stewart.*

BEAU PARI 6 b.g. Beau Charmeur (FR)–Raised-in-Paris (Raise You Ten)
[1989/90 16f^2 20d* 20s^4 20d* 25g^3 20f^3] compact gelding: won novice hurdles at 117 +
Worcester in November and Ascot (in good style) in January: good third in novice
handicap at Cheltenham final start in April, running on strongly having been given
a lot to do (jockey reported horse hadn't come down hill well): gives impression
may prove best at up to 2½m: acts on firm and dead going. *J. T. Gifford.*

BEAU RANGER 12 ch.g. Beau Chapeau–Sand Martin (Menelek) [1989/90 c**161** ?
c20g] strong, compact gelding: top-class chaser at his best: made a couple of —
mistakes when around 10 lengths seventh to Joint Sovereignty in Mackeson Gold
Cup at Cheltenham in November: best form at 2½m to 3m: acts on any going:
usually a bold jumper but makes the odd mistake: front runner. *M. C. Pipe.*

BEAU ROLANDO 4 b.g. Teenoso (USA)–Fabulous Luba (Luthier) [1989/90
16g 16d^4 16d* 16g* 16g^3 16g* 16g* 16g^4 16g 17f^{pu}] leggy gelding: well beaten in 90
maiden on Flat: successful over hurdles in claimers at Sedgefield (2) and
Edinburgh and a seller at Catterick (bought in 3,200 gns): ran moderately
afterwards: races freely and unlikely to stay beyond 2m at present: acts on dead
going and probably unsuited by firm: trained until after ninth start by N. Tinkler.
R. T. Juckes.

BEAU ROSE 7 b.g. Beau Charmeur (FR)–Rosantus (Anthony) [1989/90 c27g* c**96**
c27g^3 c25g^3 c24m^2 c26f^2] well-made gelding: winning hurdler: jumped well and —
made all in minor chase at Sedgefield (third course win) in November: ran well
next 3 starts: stays well: acts on firm ground: sold 14,500 gns Ascot June Sales to
be trained by C. Trietline. *T. P. Tate.*

BECTIVE BOY 8 ch.g. Wolverlife–Al Radegonde (St Alphage) [1989/90 16d c—
20m^{pu} 16m 16g^{pu} c16g^6] leggy, rather sparely-made gelding: novice hurdler: no —
form in 1989/90, including in novice chase: stays 2½m: acts on heavy going. *Miss L. Bower.*

BEDE LADY 4 b.f. Montekin–Devine Lady (The Parson) [1989/90 17f^5] small
filly: half-sister to winning Irish hurdler Fortune Favours (by Tanfirion): poor —
maiden plater on Flat: sold out of C. Tinkler's stable 1,250 gns Doncaster
September Sales: blinkered, pulled hard and jumped moderately in juvenile
selling hurdle at Newton Abbot: sold 800 gns Doncaster January Sales. *R. T. Juckes.*

BEDROCK 7 b.g. Town And Country–Restful (Ribero) [1989/90 16g^5 16d^6 16m
16f^6 21f* a22g^5 16g] smallish gelding: selling hurdler: won poor 4-runner 80
non-selling handicap at Warwick in December: effective at 2m and probably
stayed 25f: seemed to act on any going: successful with and without blinkers:
often claimer ridden: dead. *P. Davis.*

BEECH GROVE 9 b.g. Random Shot–Fauteuil (Faubourg II) [1989/90 c25f^F] c**90** x
strong, workmanlike gelding: quite modest hurdler: has fallen 4 times from 6 —
starts in steeplechases (every chance when coming down 4 out in hunter chase
won by Park Shade at Cheltenham in May): should stay beyond 21f: won
point-to-points in April and May. *Miss C. Gordon.*

BEECH PARK 6 b.g. Salluceva–Whitford (Master Owen) [1989/90 16g^4 20s^4 c**98**
21m^F a20g^4 c24h* c21m^2 c26f^3] angular gelding: modest novice hurdler: won 85
novice handicap at Ludlow in May on chasing debut: easily better subsequent
effort on next start: stays 3m: acts on hard ground. *D. Nicholson.*

BEECH ROAD 8 ch.g. Nearly A Hand–North Bovey (Flush Royal) c—
[1989/90 16f^3 20g* 20d* 18s^2 16m^4 16m*] 168

Beech Road's term of office as Champion Hurdler lasted just the twelve months, but there's no sign yet that age is taking its toll. He'd been in good form in the run-up to the Festival and was by no means disgraced behind Kribensis in conditions very different from those in 1989 when he'd won the title by beating Celtic Chief and Celtic Shot. The ground then had been on the soft side; now it was getting on towards firm. On both occasions waiting tactics were employed on Beech Road, and on this second occasion he was left with a lot to do to come from last place at the fourth flight of hurdles. He began to make progress at the next and, taken to the outside as before, quickened really well to get just behind the leader going to the second last. Ridden along, he stayed on strongly to dispute the lead momentarily approaching the last but he could do no more, and was eventually beaten just over four lengths into fourth place. Beech Road returned home slightly unsound but soon came right again. However, he did not meet his chief remaining objectives, the Sandeman Aintree Hurdle and the International Hurdle in Kentucky, either of which must have been far more informative than the race finally chosen for him, the Welsh Champion Hurdle at Chepstow, where he gave an exhibition round of jumping against three inferior opponents, starting at 3/1 on.

Probably the most negative aspect of Beech Road's season was that he ran only four times before the Champion Hurdle. He might have run even fewer. After he'd made a highly promising reappearance, with an eye-catching third behind Cruising Altitude in the Bula Hurdle at Cheltenham in December, connections' first moves were to scrap plans to go to Leopardstown over Christmas for the Bookmakers Hurdle and announce that he'd be trained single-mindedly for the big race, there being just the possibility of a warm-up in the National Spirit Challenge Trophy at Fontwell in February. Fortunately for the public, a change of heart saw his also taking in two more events, the Spa Hurdle and the Bishops Cleeve Hurdle, both run at Cheltenham in January. Neither taxed him unduly. He had only one opponent in the Spa Hurdle—Chatam. Given a rare chance to make the running Beech Road was as quick and fluent as ever at the hurdles, though he went no pace between them until descending the hill; Chatam stayed in touch throughout but could never draw level and was beaten a length and a half. There were only five runners in the Bishops Cleeve Hurdle, and again no strong pace. In the course of winning it by fifteen lengths from Slalom, Beech Road looked well on the way towards his peak. And by the time the National Spirit had been run he stood out as the one they all had to beat in the Champion Hurdle as long as the ground remained soft. Beech Road was unable to repeat his previous season's Fontwell win over Vagador but ran him to a head giving 14 lb. As the ground began to dry up, so confidence in Beech Road's chances began to fade while that in Kribensis' grew, and it was somewhat surprising that Beech Road

Spa Hurdle, Cheltenham—Beech Road beats sole-opponent Chatam

Welsh Champion Hurdle, Chepstow—Beech Road makes all

proved the stronger in the market on the course after the pair had opened up co-favourites. He started at 2/1; he'd been 50/1 in 1989.

Beech Road (ch.g. 1982)	Nearly A Hand (ch 1974)	Busted (b 1963)	Crepello
			Sans Le Sou
		Petite Chou (ch 1966)	Hook Money
			Bettine
	North Bovey (ch 1963)	Flush Royal (b 1945)	Majano
			Altamira
		Desla's Own (gr 1946)	Owenstown
			Desla's Star

There is little to add to Beech Road's pedigree details set out in *Chasers & Hurdlers 1988/89*. He was the last of a long line of foals out of the winning handicap hurdler North Bovey, her tenth and easily best winner from as many runners over jumps. North Bovey's dam Desla's Own, a sister to the Cheltenham Gold Cup winner Roddy Owen, won on the Flat and over hurdles and turned out to be a first-rate broodmare, with the Naas November Handicap winner Miss Patsy and North Bovey's brother, the useful chaser Hound Tor, among her offspring. Beech Road's sire Nearly A Hand, effective from a mile and a half upwards, injured a leg when finishing third in the Cesarewitch as a three-year-old. After a year off, during which he covered a full book of mares, he was returned to the track and, in a short spell, came close to reproducing his very useful best.

Beech Road, a leggy, sparely-made gelding, is effective at two miles to two and a half miles. He is capable of high-class form on a firm surface, but plenty of give in the ground suits him better and is particularly desirable for him when he's in top company at the minimum trip. His prospects for the next Champion Hurdle, provided he keeps fit and well, rest heavily on the going. If it comes up soft we shouldn't be in the least surprised to see him emulate Comedy of Errors' feat of regaining the championship the year after he lost it. Whatever his fate in the Champion Hurdle, Beech Road is still too

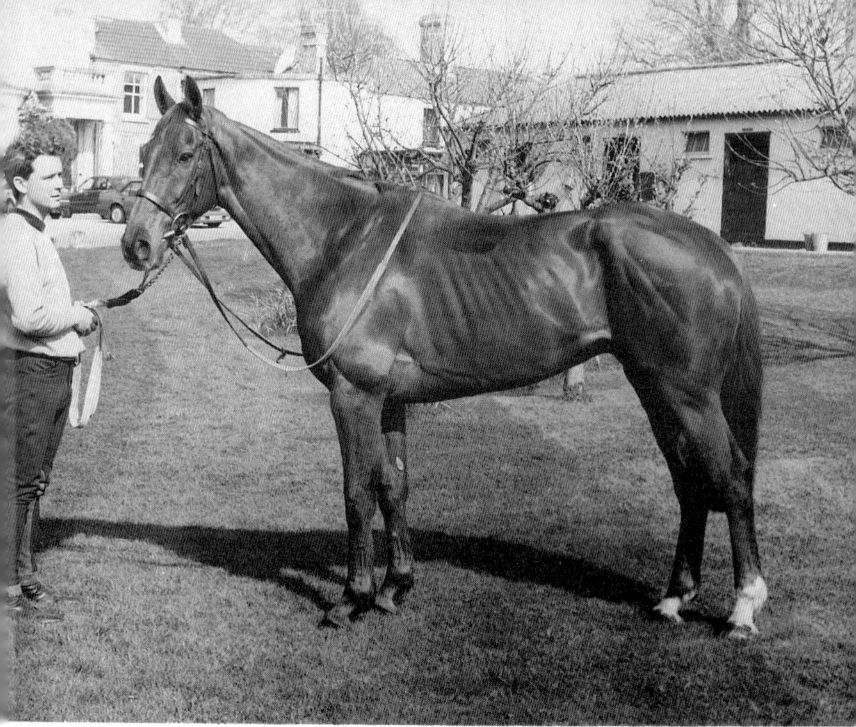

Mr Tony Geake's "Beech Road"

good a horse not to win more than his share of the conditions races on offer. His jumping is as quick and fluent as any of his contemporaries', and his turn of foot superior to most. *G. B. Balding.*

BEECHWOOD COTTAGE 7 ch.g. Malinowski (USA)–Drora (Busted) [1989/90 16m a16g5] modest performer on Flat, successful over 1m in January: novice hurdler: well beaten in lady and amateur riders handicaps in 1989/90: unlikely to stay beyond 2m: possibly unsuited by heavy going. *A. Bailey.* —

BEECHWOOD SAILOR 9 b.g. Owen Dudley–Ma Mitte (FR) (Faristan) [1989/90 c24g4 c24f4 c24f4] small, close-coupled gelding: novice hurdler: winning point-to-pointer: poor novice hunter chaser: probably stays 3m: acts on firm and dead ground. *P. Spottiswood.* c**82** —

BEE GARDEN 9 b.g. Giolla Mear–Regency View (Royal Highway) [1989/90 c16d2 c16d6 c16d2 c16v4 c16d2 c21s6 c16g4] strong, compact gelding: handicap chaser: headstrong and best form at around 2m: acts on soft going: usually blinkered: not one to trust. *P. G. Bailey.* c**97** § —

BEEKMAN STREET 4 b.c. Jalmood (USA)–Plato's Retreat (Brigadier Gerard) [1989/90 16f* 22g6] modest staying handicapper on Flat: sold out of C. Thornton's stable 28,000 gns Doncaster November Sales: won novice hurdle at Worcester in April by 15 lengths: weakened after 3 out when well beaten over 2¾m at Stratford later in month: acts on firm going. *I. P. Wardle.* 104

BEERA QUEST 11 br.g. Caballero–Kellsboro' Rocket (Master Rocky) [1989/90 c26f* c25h*] smallish, compact gelding: fair winning point-to-pointer: c**106** —

won hunter chases at Newton Abbot (novice event) and Devon & Exeter (beat Pardi's Gift 25 lengths despite jumping left in latter stages) in May: stays well: acts on hard going. *S. C. Horn.*

BEETEE YOU 7 b.g. Royalty–Jinkin (King's Troop) [1989/90 c16f4 c20f2] tall gelding: handicap chaser: better effort early in season on second start: stays 2½m: acts on hard ground: claimer ridden. *T. T. Bill.* **c85** —

BEGET 10 ro.g. Be Friendly–Easy To Love (Infatuation) [1989/90 c16d] workmanlike gelding: winning point-to-pointer: poor novice hunter chaser, best effort over 2m. *B. R. Hughes.* c—

BEJAYJAY 6 b.m. Ya Zaman (USA)–Happy Ridan (Ridan (USA)) [1989/90 22dpu 21spu 24g 22d] close-coupled mare: winning Irish hurdler: little form in Britain (looked a difficult ride second start): stays 2½m: acts on heavy going: has worn blinkers. *C. C. Trietline.* —

BE KAFUL 4 b.f. Kafu–Lobela (Lorenzaccio) [1989/90 16m] little worthwhile form at 2 yrs: sold out of J. Wainwright's stable 900 gns Doncaster June Sales: ridden by 7-lb claimer, last of 13 finishers in juvenile hurdle at Perth in September. *T. W. Cunningham.* —

BEL COURSE 8 b.g. Crash Course–Belen (Milesian) [1989/90 21f 16d6 17g4 c17g3 c25f2 25m 16g3 20d* 22m5] tall, rather leggy gelding: looks a chaser: handicap hurdler: ridden by 7-lb claimer, made most when winning by 20 lengths at Worcester in May: well beaten next time: made mistakes when second in novice chase at Doncaster in March: stays 3m: seems to act on any going: blinkered last 2 starts 1987/8: ran a moody race third outing: trained until after sixth start by J. McConnochie. *J. Webber.* **c89** 107 ?

BEL CREATION 6 br.m. Creative Plan (USA)–Linbel (Linacre) [1989/90 20fpu] winning hurdler: bit backward only outing of season (October): form only at 2m: acts on heavy going. *G. H. Yardley.* —

BELDALE STAR 7 b.g. Beldale Flutter (USA)–Little White Star (Mill Reef (USA)) [1989/90 16m* 16mF 18m3 16g6 16g2 16s] smallish, sparely-made gelding: useful front-running hurdler: won minor event at Warwick in November: 2½ lengths second to Aldino in New Year's Day Hurdle at Windsor: well beaten in quite valuable limited handicap at Nottingham 6 weeks later: successful over 2¼m, but seems ideally suited by 2m on a sharp track: probably acts on any going. *R. Akehurst.* 143

BELFIL (USA) 4 ch.f. Believe It (USA)–Filter (USA) (Sir Ivor) [1989/90 16g5 a16g 16g4 16g 16m] sparely-made filly: plating-class maiden on Flat: sold out of R. Armstrong's stable 3,200 gns Doncaster November Sales: poor juvenile selling hurdler: barely stays 2m: ran poorly on good to firm ground. *K. A. Morgan.* 63

BELFORT GIPSY 4 b.g. Belfort (FR)–Tringa (GER) (Kaiseradler) [1989/90 16gpu] small, good-quartered gelding: half-brother to a winning jumper abroad by Grand Conde: modest sprint maiden: sold out of S. Norton's stable 2,300 gns Newmarket Autumn Sales: tailed off when pulled up in selling hurdle at Wetherby in January (jumped poorly). *J. Norton.* —

BELGOOLY 5 b.g. Bulldozer–Canoe (Milesian) [1989/90 F16g4 F16g4 F16g] half-brother to Irish NH Flat race winners Samson's Hollow (by Le Prince) and Wrensborough (by Flair Path): dam never ran: fourth in NH Flat races at Catterick and Kelso in March: blinkered final start: yet to race over hurdles or fences. *M. H. Easterby.*

BELHAVEN BILL 4 ch.g. Windjammer (USA)–Correct Approach (Right Tack) [1989/90 16gpu 16mpu] leggy gelding: half-brother to novice hurdler Rostherne (by Crimson Beau): sprint maiden on Flat: sold out of R. Holder's stable 4,500 gns Ascot July Sales: tailed off when pulled up in juvenile hurdles. *G. G. Gracey.* —

BELHAVEN SPECIAL 4 b.f. Ile de Bourbon (USA)–Saran (Le Levanstell) [1989/90 16g 18f3] half-sister to winning hurdler Thrucham Lad (by Double-U-Jay): maiden on Flat: sold out of R. Holder's stable 2,000 gns Ascot July Sales: 16 lengths third behind Mo Ichi Do in juvenile selling handicap at Fontwell in March, better effort over hurdles. *A. Moore.* 76

BELINDA VARD 8 ch.m. Le Bavard (FR)–Enslavement (Arctic Slave) [1989/90 c16g3 c20g] leggy, sparely-made mare: poor novice hurdler/chaser: stays 2½m: acts on soft going: well beaten when sweating and on toes final start (November). *R. C. Armytage.* **c77** —

BELLA DELITE 4 b.f. Uncle Pokey–Lady Letitia (Le Bavard (FR)) [1989/90 F16d 16d^{pu} 17m^{pu}] first foal: dam, winning Irish hurdler, half-sister to Wayward Lad: little promise in NH Flat race and 2 juvenile hurdles: sold 5,000 gns Doncaster Spring Sales. *D. McCain.* —

BELLA NOAL 4 b.f. Noalto–Nimble Fingers (Burglar) [1989/90 16g^{pu} 16s^{F} a18g^{3}] workmanlike filly: no worthwhile form on Flat and in juvenile hurdles: dead. *W. T. Kemp.* —

BELLA SOFIE 6 ch.m. Sallust–Kath (Thatch (USA)) [1989/90 16g^{pu} 16g^{6} 16g] sturdy mare: no sign of ability over hurdles, including in a seller. *I. Semple.* —

BELLAVENTURE 4 b.f. Gleason (USA)–Adventure Run (Deep Run) [1989/90 F16g] first foal: dam poor maiden point-to-pointer: well beaten in NH Flat race at Catterick in March: yet to race over hurdles. *D. Moffatt.*

BELLE DE MONT 4 b.f. Montekin–Magic Lady (Gala Performance (USA)) [1989/90 16m 16m 16m 16s 16m^{pu}] sparely-made filly: poor maiden on Flat: no promise over hurdles, including in sellers. *T. Kersey.* —

BELLEPHERON 7 b.h. Bellypha–Une Pavane (FR) (Caro) [1989/90 20g* 16m^{5}] sparely-made horse: attracted no bid after winning novice selling handicap hurdle at Sedgefield in November: good fifth in non-seller at Hexham later in month: stays 2½m: acts on good to firm ground: didn't go through with effort first start 1988/9, and isn't one to trust implicitly. *W. Storey.* 85 §

BELL GLASS (FR) 4 gr.g. Bellypha–Greener Pastures (FR) (Rheingold) [1989/90 16f^{2} 16g^{2}] leggy, useful-looking ex-French gelding: fourth foal: half-brother to 2 French Flat winners: dam, 2-y-o 8.5f winner who later showed very useful form over middle distances, half-sister to French St Leger winner Henri Le Balafre: fairly useful on Flat, winner 3 times at up to 11f in 1989 when trained by J. Hammond: second in maiden hurdle at Newbury (pulled hard) in March and juvenile event at Fairyhouse (easily better effort, beaten 1½ lengths by Bally Rue having jumped left throughout) following month: sold J. Jenkins 32,000 gns Doncaster Spring Sales: should win races over hurdles. *C. P. E. Brooks.* 128

BELLIVER PRINCE 10 ch.g. Rugantino–Sharon (Sunny Way) [1989/90 20s c21v^{4} c20v^{6}] sturdy, good-bodied gelding: winning hurdler/chaser: no form in 1989/90: stayed 21f: best form with give in the ground: successful for a claimer: dead. *G. L. Roe.* c— —

BELMOREDEAN 5 ch.g. Be My Guest (USA)–Hanna Alta (FR) (Busted) [1989/90 16d^{pu}] lengthy gelding: half-brother to novice hurdler Khattaf (by Kris): fairly useful 1½m handicapper on Flat when trained by A. Stewart: bit backward, pulled hard and was tailed off when pulled up fifth in listed novice event at Chepstow in March on hurdling debut. *R. J. O'Sullivan.* —

BELON BRIG 9 b.m. New Brig–Oyster Eye (Wrekin Rambler) [1989/90 c24f^{3} c24g*] lengthy, shallow-girthed mare: made a lot of the running and jumped well when winning 5-runner handicap chase at Wetherby in November easily by 8 lengths from Polar Nomad: stays 3m: acts on any going. *J. K. M. Oliver.* c**100** —

BELOW ZERO 7 ch.g. Northfields (USA)–Indigine (USA) (Raise A Native) [1989/90 22m^{2} 22g^{3} 22m^{pu} 22d^{F} 20g^{pu} a20g^{5} 16m^{4} 16m 21f^{2} 21m^{3} 20d^{4} 26m^{pu}] close-coupled gelding: handicap hurdler: stays 2¾m (ran poorly over 3¼m final start): seems to act on any going: usually held up: has looked less than keen under pressure on occasions, but has won for a claimer. *L. J. Codd.* 85

BELPENEL 4 ch.g. Pharly (FR)–Seldovia (Charlottown) [1989/90 16g 16d 16g 16d 16g 16m 16g*] sparely-made gelding: modest maiden on Flat (stays 1¼m): claimed out of B. Hills's stable £10,150 in 1989: won selling handicap hurdle at Uttoxeter in April (bought in 3,500 gns): blinkered fourth, fifth and final outings. *B. L. Key.* 75 +

BELSIR 8 ch.g. Al Sirat (USA)–Lovely Sister (Menelek) [1989/90 20f^{4} c24f^{2} 21m* c20f^{2} c21m c20d* 16v^{4} 17g^{2} c24d^{6} c20g c24d c20v^{3} c18m^{2} 19d c28m^{pu} c16g^{4} 16g 16f^{2}] smallish, lengthy Irish gelding: half-brother to fair chaser Tristram Shandy (by Super Slip): fairly useful hurdler/chaser: won handicaps over hurdles at Limerick and over fences at Tralee early in season: jumped deliberately when behind in Mackeson Gold Cup at Cheltenham on tenth start: effective at 2m and stays 3m: acts on any going. *R. Nevin, Ireland.* c**144** 126

BELSTONE FOX 5 br.g. Buckskin (FR)–Winter Fox (Martinmas) [1989/90 F16g 16g] rangy, unfurnished gelding: has scope: first foal: dam unraced: eighth in NH Flat race at Warwick in December: mid-division in novice hurdle won by — p

Forest Sun at Kempton in February: wasn't at all knocked about and should do better. *D. Nicholson.*

BELVOIR BOY 8 gr.g. Workboy–Silver Phase (First Phase) [1989/90 c16dpu c25m4 c26fpu] leggy, angular, plain gelding: tubed: of no account. *Mrs Sandra C. Oliver.* c— —

BEMAS 9 ch.m. Levanter–Mistyacre (Linacre) [1989/90 c22gpu] of little account. *Pete Nicholas.* c— —

BEN 4 ch.g. Seymour Hicks (FR)–Kirin (Tyrant (USA)) [1989/90 aF14g2 aF16g4] fifth living foal: half-brother to winning hurdler Fiddlers Three (by Orchestra) and sprint winner Amenable (by Kampala): dam, useful Irish 7f and 1m winner, half-sister to fairly useful hurdler Lir: in frame in NH Flat races at Southwell in February: sold 2,700 gns Doncaster Spring Sales: yet to race over hurdles. *C. W. Thornton.*

BENCREIGH 6 ch.g. New Member–Bistro Blue (Blue Streak) [1989/90 20mF 22g5] tall, leggy gelding: poor novice hurdler: best run at 2½m: dead. *D. J. Wintle.* 68

BENDICKS 8 b.g. Young Generation–Mint (Meadow Mint (USA)) [1989/90 c16g4 c17gF3 c16m4 c16v* c16m2 c16d4 c17d3] rangy, workmanlike gelding: first form for a long time when winning handicap chase at Chepstow in January: ran well next and final starts: best at around 2m: acts on good to firm and heavy going: has won in blinkers over hurdles. *A. Moore.* c97 + —

BENGAL WAY 5 b. or br.h. Boreen (FR)–Santal Air (Ballyciptic) [1989/90 F16g] fifth foal: half-brother to winning point-to-pointer Thames Air (by Crash Course): dam unraced half-sister to quite useful Irish chaser Brave Air: tailed off in NH Flat race at Catterick in March: yet to race over hurdles or fences. *C. C. Trietline.*

BENGHAZI 6 b. or br.g. Politico (USA)–Numerous (New Brig) [1989/90 F16d6] first foal: dam never ran: 25 lengths sixth behind Cab On Target in NH Flat race at Kelso in February: yet to race over hurdles or fences. *A. M. Thomson.*

BEN HEAD 8 b.g. Crash Course–Arctic Deer (Arctic Slave) [1989/90 20s 16g5 c20vF c16dF] close-coupled, deep-girthed gelding with scope: Irish NH Flat race winner: modest form in novice hurdles: hasn't got beyond the second over fences: will be suited by return to further than 2m. *Capt. T. A. Forster.* c— 88

BENISA RYDER 7 ch.g. Stanford–Bamstar (Relko) [1989/90 17m2] short-backed gelding: handicap hurdler: ran respectably at Newton Abbot in May (first outing for 18 months): form only at around 2m: acts on firm ground (unimpressive in appearance, ran poorly on soft going final start 1988/9). *M. C. Pipe.* 113

BENJAMIN LANCASTER 6 b.g. Dubassoff (USA)–Lancaster Rose (Canadel II) [1989/90 17mpu 17d 21m6] little sign of ability over hurdles. *T. B. Hallett.* —

BEN LAIR 12 b.g. Pitpan–Denny's Folly (Saint Denys) [1989/90 c19m] big, rangy gelding: winning chaser: modest point-to-pointer nowadays: tailed off in hunter chase in April: stays 3m: acts on heavy going. *D. H. Godfrey.* c—

BEN LEDI 6 b.g. Strong Gale–Balacco (Balidar) [1989/90 c21fF c17m* c20fF c16m2 c16hsu 16g 16v 16f 17m 19f4 21mF] leggy, workmanlike gelding: novice hurdler: won novice chase at Cartmel in August: best form at 2m (clear when falling 3 out over 21f on first outing): acts on firm and dead ground (well beaten on heavy): pulls hard: sometimes blinkered (looked none too keen once): sold out of J. J. O'Neill's stable 8,000 gns Ascot October Sales after fifth outing. *Mrs J. Wonnacott.* c84 84

BEN MACK 5 b.g. Pas de Seul–Fallig Lied (King's Company) [1989/90 F16g 16spu a18gpu] leggy gelding: fourth foal: half-brother to a winner in Belgium by Broxted: dam won in Belgium: tailed off in NH Flat race and when pulled up in 2 outings over hurdles: sold 2,500 gns Doncaster Spring Sales. *C. J. Bell.* —

BENOIT 5 ch.g. Coquelin (USA)–Crepello's Last (Crepello) [1989/90 16g] compact gelding: no promise over hurdles. *N. B. Thomson.* —

BEN OLIVER 5 ch.g. Celtic Cone–Lor Darnie (Dumbarnie) [1989/90 20v3 20fur] workmanlike gelding: won 3 NH Flat races in 1988/9: third in novice hurdle at Haydock in March: losing place when hampered and unseated rider fifth in Sun Alliance Novices' Hurdle at Cheltenham later in month: dead. *M. H. Easterby.* 99

BEN THE BOMBER 5 b.g. Beau Charmeur (FR)–Barnwellsgrove (George Spelvin (USA)) [1989/90 F16s F16f] tall gelding: first foal: dam poor Irish maiden:

well behind in NH Flat races at Warwick and Uttoxeter in the spring: yet to race over hurdles or fences. *J. A. C. Edwards.*

BEN TIRRAN 6 b. or br.g. Takachiho–Portate (Articulate) [1989/90 17m² 16f* 17m⁶] leggy gelding: first outing for 7 months, won maiden hurdle at Hexham in March: moderate sixth at Carlisle following month: will stay beyond 2m: acts on firm ground. *Mrs S. Lamyman.* 91

BENTLEY 7 ch.g. Legal Tender–Dream Isle (Indian Ruler) [1989/90 c16m⁶ c20dpu] big, lengthy, angular gelding: novice hurdler/chaser: well beaten in 1989/90: stays 2½m: acts on dead going: wears a crossed noseband: sweated on reappearance. *Mrs J. E. Croft.* c— —

BE PATIENT MY SON 9 b.g. Stanford–Try My Patience (Balliol) [1989/90 16f 20f⁶ 20f⁴] workmanlike gelding: winning point-to-pointer: poor novice hurdler, only form when fourth over 2½m in April. *Miss C. J. E. Caroe.* 73 ?

BERESFORDS GIRL 5 b.m. Furry Glen–Hansel's Queen (Prince Hansel) [1989/90 F16g 16s 16s⁶] leggy, workmanlike mare: fourth foal: dam placed in Irish NH Flat races: no form in novice hurdles: sweating and edgy final start (February). *R. J. Holder.* 79

BERGEN BABY 9 ch.g. Spitsbergen–Cleo Baby (Dicta Drake) [1989/90 c25f³] workmanlike gelding: novice hurdler: won 3 point-to-points in April: no form in steeplechases. *W. H. Barons.* c— —

BERKANA RUN 5 ch.g. Deep Run–Geraldine's Pet (Laurence O) [1989/90 F16m F17f] third foal: dam poor Irish maiden: behind in NH Flat races at Hexham and Doncaster in first half of season: yet to race over hurdles or fences. *B. R. Cambidge.*

BERKLEY EXPRESS 4 b.f. The Brianstan–Deise Girl (Stranger) [1989/90 a16g] temperamental sprint maiden on Flat: tailed off in selling hurdle at Southwell: sold 1,100 gns Ascot November Sales. *J. G. M. O'Shea.* —

BERLIN OR BUST 6 b.g. Sonnen Gold–Milly Monroe (Lochnager) [1989/90 c24dpu c16dpu] leggy gelding: novice hurdler: pulled up in mid-season novice chases: form only at 2m. *M. H. Easterby.* c— —

BERRYS CRUISE 5 ch.m. Cruise Missile–Quick Walk (Farm Walk) [1989/90 F16f] third foal: dam unraced: tailed off in NH Flat race at Ludlow in April: yet to race over hurdles or fences. *L. J. Codd.*

BERTHELIER 6 ch.g. Mandrake Major–Marton Lady (March Past) [1989/90 16fpu 16fpu] leggy, sparely-made gelding: no form at 2 yrs: pulled up in selling hurdles. *N. Waggott.* —

BERYL'S JOKE 6 b.g. Double Form–Rockeater (Roan Rocket) [1989/90 16g 20g⁶ 20f 24m² 24m 22m⁵ 17h³] good-topped gelding: novice hurdler: made most to 2 out when second at Chepstow in April (ridden by 3-lb claimer), easily best effort: stays 3m: acts on firm going: sometimes blinkered (including last 6 starts): has looked a difficult ride: inconsistent. *J. H. Baker.* 108 ?

BESCABY BOY 4 b.g. Red Sunset–Charo (Mariacci (FR)) [1989/90 16s³ 16d² 16d* 16m³] smallish, angular gelding: fair miler on Flat: changed hands 8,600 gns Ascot November Sales: won juvenile hurdle at Market Rasen in March: claimer ridden, very good third behind Rouyan in quite valuable juvenile handicap at Newcastle later in month: unlikely to stay beyond 2m: successful on dead going, but best run on good to firm: sure to win more races. *J. Wharton.* 127

BESSACARR BOY 9 b.g. Ahonoora–Falcade (Falcon) [1989/90 c17d c20g³ c24gpu c24g⁵ c20gF c20m⁵ c24gpu] workmanlike, good-quartered gelding: has been hobdayed: winning chaser: ran badly in 1989/90: stays 2¾m: possibly unsuited by very soft ground, acts on any other. *G. Richards.* c— —

BEST EFFORT 4 ch.g. Try My Best (USA)–Lunaria (USA) (Twist The Axe (USA)) [1989/90 16g 17v⁵ 16d⁵ 16f⁵] placed over 1¼m on Flat: sold out of M. Francis' stable 15,500 gns Newmarket Autumn Sales: modest form over hurdles, best effort on third start: worth a try over further: gives impression unsuited by heavy ground. *R. J. Holder.* 95

BEST EMPEROR (USA) 4 gr.c. Secreto (USA)–Port Aransas (USA) (Quack (USA)) [1989/90 F16s F16g] sturdy colt: fourth foal: half-brother to a winner in North America by Sharpen Up: dam winning stayer: unplaced in 2 NH Flat races (tailed off, having moved poorly to post, on first occasion): yet to race over hurdles. *J. Mackie.*

BEST INTENT 13 ch.g. Bivouac–Frigid Frolic (Arctic Slave) [1989/90 25h^{pu} 26f^{4} c20m^{ur} c20g^{4} c24f^{2}] compact gelding: poor novice hurdler/chaser and winning point-to-pointer: stays 3m: acts on firm ground: has worn blinkers. *T. N. Bailey.* **c74** —

BEST SMILE (USA) 7 ch.g. Blushing Groom (FR)–Hartebeest (USA) (Vaguely Noble) [1989/90 20g^{3} 22s^{pu}] compact gelding: lightly-raced novice hurdler: 100/1, staying-on 35 lengths third behind File Concord in 16-runner race at Kempton in January: tailed off when pulled up fifth at Fontwell following month: should stay beyond 2½m. *G. P. Enright.* 81

BE SURPRISED 4 ch.g. Dubassoff (USA)–Buckenham Belle (Royben) [1989/90 16d 16g] angular gelding: has scope: third foal: half-brother to a winner in Italy by Baragoi: dam plater: behind in juvenile hurdles at Newbury, still needing race final start. *A. Moore.* —

BE TENDER 4 b.f. Prince Tenderfoot (USA)–The Habit of Being (Busted) [1989/90 16d 17f 16d 16d^{5} 20d a18g] small filly: poor plater on Flat, stays 1½m: fifth in selling handicap at Market Rasen, only worthwhile form over hurdles: visored all bar hurdling debut. *J. S. Wainwright.* 69

BET OLIVER 7 b.m. Kala Shikari–Lor Darnie (Dumbarnie) [1989/90 16s^{pu}] compact mare: lightly raced and of little account. *D. C. Jermy.* —

BETRIM 6 b.g. Dubassoff (USA)–Horoscope (Romany Air) [1989/90 17d 20s^{2} 20s^{4} 21d] tall gelding: novice hurdler: best effort of season on second start: stays 2½m: acts on soft going. *R. J. Holder.* 92

BETSY BOOP 5 b.m. Pauper–Day Fiddle (Harwell) [1989/90 F16m^{6} F16f F16m^{3} 22g a20g^{5} 16g^{pu} 16g 16g] leggy mare: half-sister to National Hunt Chase winner Hazy Dawn (by Official): dam never ran: no sign of ability over hurdles, including in sellers: blinkered sixth and eighth starts. *R. O'Leary.* —

BETTER TIMES AHEAD 4 ro.g. Scallywag–City's Sister (Maystreak) [1989/90 16m^{2} 16s^{ur} 16g^{ur} 17d^{2}] compact gelding: second foal: half-brother to winning hurdler Sweet City (by Sweet Monday): dam, from a good jumping family, won at up to 13f on Flat and was in frame at 2m over hurdles: still in need of race, staying-on ½-length second to Cornet in juvenile hurdle at Carlisle in March: will be suited by further: acts on dead going: should win a race. *G. Richards.* 102

BETTY'S LAST 8 ch.m. Sousa–Betty's Kiss (Khalkis) [1989/90 16m^{pu}] sparely-made mare: well beaten over hurdles: has been tried in blinkers. *H. Willis.* —

BETTY'S PEARL 9 ch.g. Gulf Pearl–Paiukiri (Ballyciptic) [1989/90 c20s* c20g^{ur}] strong, workmanlike gelding: winning point-to-pointer: well beaten over hurdles: jumped soundly when winning amateur riders handicap chase at Folkestone in January: stays 2½m: probably acts on any going. *G. Harwood.* c**100** —

BETWEEN THE SHEETS 5 b.g. Crooner–Miss Chianti (Royben) [1989/90 17h* 20f* 17h* 16g^{4} 16f^{3} 16g^{2} 20d 16d^{3} 17d^{6}] leggy gelding: made all in novice hurdles at Devon & Exeter (2, both handicaps) and Worcester in August: ran creditably when placed afterwards: best form at 2m: probably acts on any going. *W. Carter.* 92

BEWITCHING WIND 5 ch.g. Windjammer (USA)–Tantra (Song) [1989/90 16m] leggy gelding: no sign of ability in selling hurdles. *D. Burchell.* —

BHARKAT 4 b.g. Beldale Flutter (USA)–Cienaga (Tarboosh (USA)) [1989/90 16s 16s 16d a20g^{5} 16f^{4} 17m^{5} 16g^{4} 16g 20g^{3} 21f^{3} 21f* 20f^{2} 22m*] small gelding: quite modest maiden on Flat: sold out of R. Boss's stable 4,000 gns Doncaster October Sales: won selling handicap hurdle at Towcester (bought in 2,600 gns) and novice handicap at Stratford (beat Shy Hiker ½ length) late in season: stays 2¾m: suited by a firm surface: visored fifth to eighth starts: ridden by 7-lb claimer nowadays: game. *J. Norton.* 95

BIBSKELLY 8 br.g. Pitskelly–Piedita (High Hat) [1989/90 19s 16m^{6} 16f] leggy gelding: behind in NH Flat race in 1986/7: no sign of ability over hurdles, including in a seller. *B. K. Wells.* —

BIBULOUS 6 b.g. Bybicello–Ginger Up (Dieu Soleil) [1989/90 c22d^{pu}] well-made gelding: no worthwhile form over hurdles or in a novice chase: sold 1,500 gns Doncaster March Sales. *C. C. Trietline.* c— —

BICKERMAN 7 b.h. Mummy's Pet–Merry Weather (Will Somers) [1989/90 16f^{4} 16g* 16g^{3} 16g^{2} 16m^{6} 16f^{F} 16f^{3} 16g^{5} a16g^{3} a20g^{5} 16f*] lightly-made horse: handicap hurdler: won at Uttoxeter in October and April: pulls hard and is best 94 forcing pace at 2m: acts on hard going and probably unsuited by soft: often claimer ridden: sometimes blinkered, including when successful. *J. L. Spearing.*

BICKERSTAFFE 9 br.g. Workboy–Siciliana (Sicilian Prince) [1989/90 21fpu] workmanlike gelding: winning hurdler: has shown no aptitude for chasing: stays 2¾m, at least when conditions aren't testing: acts on any going: usually blinkered in 1986/7: has found little. *R. Callow.* c— x —

BICKFIELD 7 b. or br.g. Leander–Blandford Dancer (Blandford Lad) [1989/90 16d 20dpu c25dpu] big, workmanlike gelding: poor novice hurdler/chaser. *A. G. Harris.* c— —

BIDDERS LAD 5 ch.g. Ring Bidder–Anniversary Token (Record Token) [1989/90 16mF] sparely-made, shallow-girthed gelding: poor maiden on Flat, stays 9f: tailed off when falling 4 out in minor hurdle at Warwick in September (pulled hard). *R. M. Whitaker.* —

BIDDING FAIR 7 b. or br.g. Auction Ring (USA)–Starlit Way (Pall Mall) [1989/90 20spu 16g] sparely-made ex-Irish gelding: fourth foal: half-brother to Irish 7f winner Afef John (by Monseigneur): dam, 5f winner, half-sister to 3 useful Flat winners: little promise on Flat, in point-to-points and over hurdles. *T. Laxton.* —

BIDSTON MILL 5 ch.g. Main Reef–Allotria (Red God) [1989/90 18f2 16mpu 20m 25m] small, dipped-backed gelding: plater over hurdles: off course 6 months after first start, no subsequent form: stays 2½m: acts on any going: visored second outing 1988/9, usually blinkered since. *R. A. Bennett.* 83

BIETSCHHORN HUT 8 gr.g. Bruni–Hopeful Step (Hopeful Venture) [1989/90 c19s5 c20gF c17d 21spu] narrow, leggy gelding: winning hurdler: no form over fences (makes mistakes): well beaten over 2¾m: acts on heavy going: blinkered twice over hurdles: tends to carry head rather high: has won for a 7-lb claimer. *D. R. Gandolfo.* c— —

BIG ALICK 4 br.c. Another Realm–Abercorn Flyer (Silly Season) [1989/90 17fpu 18h6] half-brother to poor novice hurdler Solo Player (by Blue Refrain): no form on Flat and over hurdles. *W. T. Kemp.* —

BIG BEAR 4 ch.c. Tolomeo–Alma Ata (Bustino) [1989/90 16mF] placed over 1¼m on second of 2 starts on Flat, when trained by L. Cumani: would have won novice hurdle at Newcastle in very good style but for falling fatally at the last. *K. A. Morgan.* 113 ?

BIG BELL BOY 5 ch.h. Scallywag–Miss Quay (Quayside) [1989/90 16g3 17m4 16m3 16gF 17g] lengthy, workmanlike horse: modest novice hurdler: should stay 2½m: acts on dead going and good to firm. *Denys Smith.* 92

BIG CHIEF 5 b.g. Gorytus (USA)–Maybe So (So Blessed) [1989/90 16g 16g 16d2 16d6 a16g3] workmanlike gelding: maiden on Flat: sold out of W. Hastings-Bass's stable 2,500 gns Ascot May Sales: placed in claimer and a seller over hurdles: barely stayed 2m: dead. *Miss L. C. Siddall.* 72

BIG DECISION 7 ch.g. Whistlefield–Last Card (Remainder) [1989/90 c20v3 c16d3 c20f2] plain, sparely-made gelding: well beaten over hurdles: won a point-to-point in February: placed in hunter chases: may prove best at up to 2½m: acts on good to firm and heavy going. *Mrs Ann Taylor.* **c84** —

BIG DIAMOND (FR) 6 b.g. Bikala–Diathese (FR) (Diatome) [1989/90 16s2 16s4 16g 20g 16m*] leggy, sparely-made gelding: handicap hurdler: won at Fakenham in March: best at 2m: acts on soft going and good to firm. *I. Campbell.* 109

BIG FINISH 5 b.g. Persian Bold–Azurn (Klairon) [1989/90 a20g* a20g* a20s3] sparely-made gelding: wide-margin winner of maiden hurdle and novice handicap at Lingfield in January: stayed 2½m: dead. *Miss B. Sanders.* 102

BIG MINSTREL 5 b.g. Black Minstrel–Magic Money (Even Money) [1989/90 F16g6] half-brother to winning point-to-pointers Noble Love and Golden Magic (both by Golden Love): dam never ran: around 30 lengths sixth of 15 behind Snitton Lane in NH Flat race at Market Rasen in April: yet to race over hurdles or fences. *R. Simpson.*

BIGNOR HILL 5 b.g. Hardboy–Marvellous Risk (Mon Capitaine) [1989/90 F16f3] sixth foal: dam won Irish NH Flat race: 13 lengths third of 12 behind stable-companion Bollinger in NH Flat race at Ascot in April: yet to race over hurdles or fences. *J. T. Gifford.*

BIG ORDER 6 b. or br.g. Buckskin (FR)–Newcastle Lady (Tarqogan) [1989/90 F16g] first foal: dam never ran: mid-division in NH Flat race at Uttoxeter in December: yet to race over hurdles or fences. *Mrs H. Parrott.*

BIG OSCAR 6 b.g. Gala Performance (USA)–Lupious (Cantab) [1989/90 21m3 21m 24m] tall, angular gelding: poor novice hurdler. *K. C. Bailey.* 67

BIG RED 6 ch.g. Final Straw–Cut Loose (High Top) [1989/90 16m* 16f* 16d 16g 16g5 20f3 20f3 20f3] strong gelding: won 2 novice hurdles at Wincanton in November: ran creditably last 3 starts: stays 2½m: acts on firm ground. *Andrew Turnell.* 112

BIGSUN 9 b.g. Sunyboy–Stella Roma (Le Levanstell) [1989/90 c24g2 c24d4 c32g* c25d3 c25f* c36f6] c**144** —

The favourite and second favourite for the Seagram Grand National, Brown Windsor and Bigsun, were both conceived at the Conduit Farm Stud, Churchill, Oxford, which houses their respective sires Kinglet and Sunyboy. Brown Windsor and Bigsun had each advertised his National claims on the final day of the Cheltenham Festival meeting, the former winning the Cathcart Challenge Cup, the latter the Ritz Club National Hunt Handicap Chase. In winning the National Hunt Handicap Bigsun broke the twenty-five-furlong course record established by his stable-companion Charter Party when winning the 1986 running of the race. A clutch of course records—there were ten in all—were a feature of the 1990 Festival. A good gallop throughout, particularly over twenty-five furlongs in fast conditions, is essential for Bigsun who is a dour stayer lacking a turn of speed. The strong early pace made by Pharoah's Laen set the race up for a horse of Bigsun's type. Prominent from the start, no doubt ridden with a view to making sure that he could bring his stamina into play, Bigsun was under pressure to hold his position around halfway, and dropped back to sixth or seventh before being brought to the outside going to the top of the hill for the final time and moving forward again. Pharoah's Laen was still travelling strongly when pulled up lame immediately after jumping the third last, leaving Seagram in front ahead of the hard-ridden Bigsun. Bigsun still hadn't made much impression on Seagram's lead approaching the last, but after a good jump there he responded well. Despite being carried to his right and then edging further right out of the way of the tiring Seagram he led close home and won by a head with Boraceva eight lengths away third, twenty lengths clear of fourth-placed Golden Friend.

On the first two days of the Grand National meeting, Seagram, Boraceva and Golden Friend all acquitted themselves well in their respective races and the form of the Ritz Club Chase seemed sound. Bigsun looked in fine fettle in the paddock before the National and wasn't sweating as on occasions in the past. In the race though, he was a disappointment. Despite a strong gallop, he never got into the contest and ran well below his best in finishing sixth to Mr Frisk, beaten over fifty-five lengths by the winner and over twenty-five lengths by fourth-placed Brown Windsor. Quite possibly the Ritz Club drained more than was realized out of Bigsun; he wasn't seen out after the National.

Bigsun had also run lack-lustre races on his first two outings of the campaign, but he did look in need of the race on the first and probably still hadn't come to himself on the second. Bigsun returned to something like his best in the quite valuable four-mile A.S.W. Handicap Chase at Cheltenham on New Year's Day, for which he started at odds on in a field of four. There was only a sedate gallop until seven from home, where Midnight Madness quickened past long-time leader Memberson. Bigsun, who'd been held up, had half a dozen lengths to make up at the final open ditch, six out, but he improved gradually to challenge Midnight Madness at the last and ran on strongly up the hill to win by a length, with Memberson, the only other finisher, beaten a distance. Bigsun was then returned to Cheltenham for the Charterhouse Mercantile Chase later in January, his only other start prior to the Festival meeting. Again there were only four runners but this time Bigsun faced a stiff task and ran as well as could reasonably be expected to finish third behind the rapidly-improving Toby Tobias and the smart Irish mare Maid of Money, beaten ten lengths and fifteen. Bigsun isn't up to

Ritz Club National Hunt Handicap Chase, Cheltenham—Bigsun (left) wears down Seagram

beating the best at level weights, but he should win another good-class staying handicap when conditions are in his favour—he is ideally suited by top-of-the-ground, though he has run respectably on soft.

Bigsun (b.g. 1981)	Sunyboy (b 1970)	Mourne (ch 1954)	Vieux Manoir
			Ballynash
		Fair Bid (b 1952)	My Babu
			Market Fair
	Stella Roma (b 1970)	Le Levanstell (b 1957)	Le Lavandou
			Stella's Sister
		Roman Nose (b 1955)	Nosca
			Roman Figurehead

Bigsun, a sturdy gelding, fetched 36,000 guineas as an unraced four-year-old at the Doncaster Spring Sales. That figure was a big step up on anything he'd attracted on the three occasions he'd been through the sale-ring in Ireland, when IR 6,600 guineas was the most paid for him. One reason for the increase in interest in Bigsun was probably because Sunyboy, second in the Irish St Leger and later the Queen Mother's three-hundredth winner as an owner when successful in the 1976 Fernbank Hurdle at Ascot, had sired several horses who'd run with distinction in the 1984/5 season. These included the promising Tawridge, Sun Rising, Hunter River and Elmboy, who'd won the Christies Foxhunter Challenge Cup at Cheltenham. In addition, one of Bigsun's half-brothers, Androma (by Andrea Mantegna), had just won the William Hill Scottish National at Ayr for the second year in succession. At that time the dam Stella Roma had produced another winning jumper in the selling hurdler Le Touquet (by Town Crier) and two fillies who won on the Flat, Argenta (by Town Crier) and Woodhall (by Shiny Tenth). Stella Roma is also the dam of Mulloch Brae, a sister to Bigsun, who won a nineteen-furlong novice hurdle for the Nicholson stable in 1988/9. Stella Roma herself ran as a two-year-old without showing any form. She is

Mr John F. Horn's "Bigsun"

a sister to the useful Irish sprinter Breide's Wood and half-sister to several other winners, including the hurdler Credulous. Their dam Roman Nose, out of a half-sister to the good jumping stallion Arctic Slave, raced only as a two-year-old and was successful over six furlongs. *D. Nicholson.*

BIG WHITE CHIEF 9 gr.g. Warpath–Compulsion (Aggressor) [1989/90 22d3 22g* 20vur 20g3 20g4 20s2 20d3 20s*] tall, leggy gelding: blind off-side: handicap hurdler: progressive form in 1989/90: won at Wolverhampton in December and Haydock (rallied gamely to beat Brompton Road ¾ length) in March: stays well: has won on hard going but is ideally suited by a soft surface: sometimes hangs but is thoroughly genuine. *B. A. McMahon.* 129

BIJOU GEORGIE 9 b.m. Rhodomantade–Crown Caper (Royal Buck) [1989/90 c25g6 c16d4 c22f3 c22g3] workmanlike mare: winning point-to-pointer/hunter chaser: best effort of season on final start: best form at around 2½m with give in the ground: blinkered nowadays. *Mrs Carrie Janaway.* c84

BILBROOK 8 b.g. Pardigras–Gay Heath (Langton Heath) [1989/90 c17v* c16g6] leggy, sparely-made gelding: blind off-side: novice hurdler: won conditional jockeys handicap chase at Newton Abbot in January: ran well in novice event at Wolverhampton following month (made a few mistakes): stays 21f: acts on heavy going: has worn a crossed noseband. *G. A. Ham.* c92 —

BILL AND COUP 5 br.m. Nicholas Bill–Counter Coup (Busted) [1989/90 16m 16m6 16s 22g 16f3] small, workmanlike mare: poor novice hurdler: form only at 2m: best efforts on top-of-the-ground. *K. A. Morgan.* 68

BILLAN TARA 4 b.f. Nicholas Bill–Celtic Tara (Welsh Saint) [1989/90 F16g5] second foal: half-sister to an Irish maiden by Lochnager: dam winning hurdler:

just over 9 lengths fifth to Flowing River in 15-runner NH Flat race at Edinburgh in January: yet to race over hurdles. *C. B. B. Booth.*

BILLBOARD 5 b.m. Martin John–Bella Berenice (King's Leap) [1989/90 17m^{5}
16m* 17f^{3} 17g^{4}] smallish ex-Irish mare: eighth live foal: half-sister to useful 79
stayer on Flat Monkey Corners (by Ballymore), also a 2m hurdle winner: dam never ran: poor middle-distance maiden on Flat: won mares novice hurdle at Stratford in September, best effort in Britain: will stay beyond 2m: acts on good to firm ground: ridden by 7-lb claimer: not raced after October. *G. A. Ham.*

BILL CORNWALL 11 b.g. Sunnyboy–Vulgans Deal (Straight Deal) [1989/90 c— x
c20v^{F}] smallish, close-coupled gelding: no sign of ability over hurdles: moderate —
jumper in steeplechases, but has won point-to-points: blinkered once. *David Pritchard.*

BILLHEAD 4 b.g. Nicholas Bill–Time-Table (Mansingh (USA)) [1989/90 16f^{2}
16g^{pu} 16g a16g 16g^{pu}] tall, leggy gelding: placed at up to 1¼m on Flat: sold out of J. 81
W. Watts's stable 6,200 gns Doncaster September Sales: second in juvenile hurdle at Cheltenham in October: seemed to lose his way afterwards. *B. Preece.*

BILLILLA 7 ch.g. Nicholas Bill–Thorganby Bella (Porto Bello) [1989/90 16m^{pu}
16s* 16s^{3} 16s] rather leggy gelding: won handicap hurdle at Huntingdon in 106
December: only other form of season on next start: stays 2¼m: acts on heavy going: amateur ridden last 3 starts. *P. G. Bailey.*

BILLION MELODY 8 b.g. Billion (USA)–Thistle (Highland Melody)
[1989/90 16g 16s^{6} 17f 16f^{2} 24g* 16g^{5} 16m^{3}] leggy, sparely-made gelding: handicap 97
hurdler: held up when winnning at Bangor in April: outpaced over 2m both subsequent outings (ran well nonetheless final start) and will be suited by return to further: stays 3m: best on a sound surface: usually amateur ridden nowadays. *A. W. Jones.*

BILL NORMAL 5 ch.h. Ballyglitter–Petite Piece (Major Portion) [1989/90
16d^{F} a16g^{pu}] small horse: poor novice selling hurdler: visored last start 1988/9. —
Mrs Jill Evans.

BILLSHA 4 b.f. Ahonoora–Sanjana (GER) (Priamos (GER)) [1989/90 16d^{4} 16f^{3}
16m*] quite modest maiden miler on Flat when trained by B. Hanbury: won 90
juvenile hurdle at Stratford in May pushed out by 5 lengths from Snappy Date: unlikely to stay much beyond 2m: acts on good to firm ground: amateur ridden. *B. R. Cambidge.*

BILLY'S DANCER 7 ch.g. Piaffer (USA)–Hay-Hay (Hook Money) [1989/90
a16g^{4} a16g^{3} a16g^{6}] close-coupled gelding: novice hurdler: poor form in handicaps 72
in 1989/90. *W. Wilson.*

BILLY STRAYHORN 6 b.g. Northfields (USA)–Tanaka (Tapalque) [1989/90
16s^{6}] angular, rather dipped-backed gelding: won Irish NH Flat race in 1988: 68 p
bought 45,000 gns Tattersalls November (1988) Sales: tired 2 out when around 27 lengths sixth behind Fifth Amendment in novice event at Leicester in January on hurdling debut: will improve. *S. Mellor.*

BILLY TOBIN 10 br.g. Bivouac–Romayne (Rubor) [1989/90 20f^{F} 25m* 25f^{6} c—
20m 27g^{5} 22d 20d 17d 22g 25m^{F}] tall, lengthy gelding: handicap hurdler: won at 84
Cartmel in August: no form over fences: stayed 25f: seemed suited by firm going: dead. *S. G. Payne.*

BILOXI BLUES 8 gr.g. Blue Refrain–Haunting (Lord Gayle (USA)) [1989/90 c**126**
c21m^{4} c20m^{3} c20f^{F} 16f^{6} 22m c20f^{2} c20f^{3} c25m* c24g^{3} c24f^{2} c26m*] strong, —
close-coupled gelding: fairly useful hurdler/chaser: won over fences at Hereford in April and Newton Abbot in May: stays 25f: seems best on top-of-the-ground: takes a good hold. *K. C. Bailey.*

BIN DAAHIR (USA) 4 ch.c. Blushing Groom (FR)–Bolt From The Blue
(USA) (Blue Times (USA)) [1989/90 a16g 16g^{pu} a20s^{pu}] compact colt: little —
worthwhile form on Flat: sold out of P. Walwyn's stable 3,200 gns Newmarket Autumn Sales: no sign of ability over hurdles: visored first start: dead. *M. J. Haynes.*

BINFIELD EXPRESS (USA) 9 b.g. An Act (USA)–Like A Train (USA) c—
(Great Sun (USA)) [1989/90 16d] big gelding: novice hurdler: bit backward only —
outing 1989/90: has fallen in 2 point-to-points and only start in steeplechases. *G. Richards.*

BINKLEY (FR) 4 ch.c. Bikala–Jinkitis (Irish Love) [1989/90 a16g^{3} a20g^{4}
20m] leggy colt: poor 1½m maiden on Flat: sold out of Sir Mark Prescott's stable 74

5,600 gns Newmarket Autumn Sales: poor juvenile hurdler: stays 2½m. *I. Campbell.*

BINLEY 6 b.g. Dublin Taxi–Peachy (Reliance II) [1989/90 F12m F16m] third foal: half-brother to Cheeky Rupert (by Runnymede), a winning stayer on Flat and over hurdles: mid-division in 2 NH Flat races in October: dead. *B. Ellison.*

BIRCHGREY LADY 5 br.m. Strong Gale–Willow Wand (Wolver Hollow) [1989/90 16g^{ur} a16g^{5} 17m] sparely-made, leggy mare: poor novice selling hurdler: races only at around 2m: acts on dead going: trained first outing by P. Mitchell. *J. G. M. O'Shea.* 67

BIRD BATH 4 ch.f. Longleat (USA)–Red Lory (Bay Express) [1989/90 a16g^{pu} 16f 16f 16f^{pu}] small, lightly-made filly: plating class on Flat in Britain, won over 6f in Holland in 1989: bought for 1,900 gns Doncaster September Sales: no sign of ability over hurdles: sold out of S. Avery's stable 1,600 gns Doncaster January Sales after first start. *R. W. Swiers.* —

BIRD OF SPIRIT 10 b.g. Hot Brandy–Bird of Honour (Dark Heron) [1989/90 c26d^{pu} c24s^{pu} c20d^{F}] tall, good-quartered gelding: one-time fair hurdler: winning chaser: running a fair race when falling last at Chepstow in March, only sign of ability in 1989/90: stays 3¼m when conditions aren't testing: acts on heavy going: moderate jumper. *M. Scudamore.* c98 x —

BIRKBECK LAD 5 b.g. Rarity–Supreme Pet (Supreme Sovereign) [1989/90 F16f^{4}] unplaced in 2 NH Flat races: yet to race over hurdles or fences. *T. Casey.*

BIRLING JACK 9 b.g. Bronze Hill–Fortilage (Fortina) [1989/90 c24g^{ur} c25d^{3} c25s^{5} c33d^{3}] big, strong gelding: fairly useful chaser: good third to Four Trix in William Hill Scottish National (Handicap Chase) at Ayr in April, final start: let down by his jumping earlier in season: stays well: acts on heavy going. *J. A. C. Edwards.* c130

BIRMINGHAM'S PRIDE 4 br.f. Indian King (USA)–Cooliney Dancer (Dancer's Image (USA)) [1989/90 a18g* a16g^{3} 16v^{2} a18g^{3}] compact filly: plater on Flat: won juvenile hurdle at Southwell in January: stayed 2¼m: acted on heavy going: claimer ridden: dead. *R. Hollinshead.* 84

BIRSTWITH (USA) 5 gr.h. Valdez (USA)–La Chaumiere (Thatch (USA)) [1989/90 16d^{4} 16s 16g^{2} 16d^{2}] angular horse: fair performer on Flat, won over 1¼m 98

New Year Handicap Chase, Haydock—Bishops Yarn revels in the mud

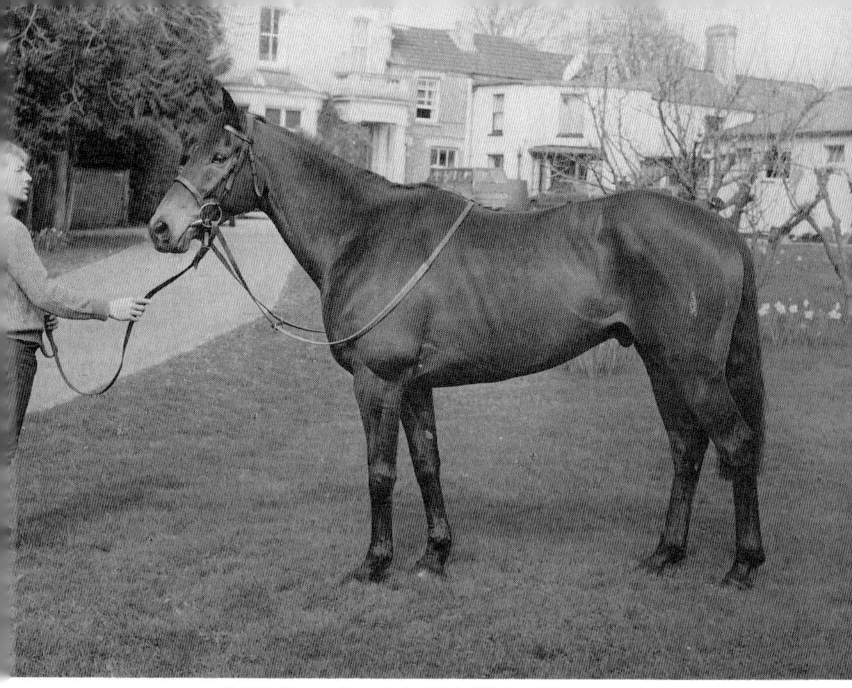

British Thoroughbred R & B Plc's "Bishops Yarn"

in 1990: placed in novice and maiden hurdles at Edinburgh: barely stays 2m. *C. W. C. Elsey.*

BISHOPDALE 9 ch.g. Proverb–Garryduff Lady (Deep Run) [1989/90 c24m* c21g* c24f^{2} c24g* c24d^{F2} c26f* c26m^{F}] leggy gelding: poor mover: fairly useful chaser: had a very successful first half of season, winning at Perth, Market Rasen (twice) and Doncaster: in process of running a good race when falling 2 out only outing in second half of season (March): stays well: acts on any going: usually held up: jumps none too fluently: has plenty of ability, but doesn't always go through with his effort. *W. A. Stephenson.* c **134** — §

BISHOPSFORD 4 b.g. Henbit (USA)–Arena (Sallust) [1989/90 16f^{6} 16g 16m^{5} 16f 16g^{5} 16d^{6}] sparely-made, rather angular gelding: maiden middle-distance plater on Flat: sold out of Sir Mark Prescott's stable 5,200 gns Ascot July Sales: poor plater over hurdles. *N. Waggott.* 83

BISHOPS YARN 11 br.g. Tycoon II–Lilac Veil (Dumbarnie) [1989/90 c20g^{pu} c20v* c24s^{2} c21d^{F} c24v^{4}] short-coupled, workmanlike gelding: carries plenty of condition: smart chaser: won quite valuable handicap at Haydock in January by 3 lengths from Midnight Count: good second to Nick The Brief in Peter Marsh Chase (limited handicap) on same course later in month: much better suited by 3m than shorter distances: suited by plenty of give in the ground: jumps soundly: takes a strong hold and is suited by waiting tactics: has a good turn of foot. *G. B. Balding.* c **153** —

BISPHAM BAY 6 ch.g. Caruso–Miss Sunacelli (Sunacelli) [1989/90 c20f a20g c20g^{pu} c16g c20m^{5} c24m^{pu}] sparely-made gelding: little sign of ability: blinkered second start: tends to sweat: unruly in preliminaries third outing. *J. P. Smith.* c— —

BIT OF A CASE 8 b.m. Reformed Character–Midland Rose (Mugatpura) [1989/90 17f^{F}] fourth foal: half-sister to winning staying hurdler Beni (by No —

Royal Fern Novices' Chase, Ascot—a valuable race for horses that haven't won over fences; Bizage Motors is preceded only by a loose horse over the last

Argument): dam half-sister to Mackeson Gold Cup and Hennessy Cognac Gold Cup winner Red Candle: behind when breaking leg in novice hurdle at Newton Abbot in August. *K. Bishop.*

BIT OF A CHANCE 6 br.m. Lord Ha Ha–Romany Miss (Master Owen)
[1989/90 22m^{pu} 25f^{4} 22m 20m^{3} 20d^{3} 21d^{2} a18g^{pu}] sparely-made, smallish mare: 112
handicap hurdler: pulled up lame run-in final start: worth another chance over further than 21f on easy ground: acts on soft going: has run well for a claimer: often sweats up: has been taken down early. *R. Lee.*

BIT OF A CLOWN 7 b.g. Callernish–Gusserane Lark (Napoleon Bonaparte) **c96**
[1989/90 c21d^{2} c25g^{2} c25s^{3} c24g^{4}] rangy gelding with scope: won 2 point-to-points in 1989: modest form in novice chases, jumping none too fluently: stays 25f: acts on soft going: blinkered last 2 outings: needs to improve his jumping. *Mrs I. McKie.*

BIT OF A DANDY 9 ch.g. Le Bavard (FR)–Fair People (Varano) [1989/90 c—
c25f^{4}] lengthy gelding: winning hurdler/point-to-pointer: sketchy jumper in —
novice chases, little promise: appeared suited by 2½m and a firm surface over hurdles. *L. C. Corbett.*

BIT ON EDGE 4 b.f. Henbit (USA)–Border's Edge (Habitat) [1989/90 16g^{pu}]
leggy filly: well beaten both outings on Flat: bit backward, tailed off when pulled —
up 2 out in juvenile hurdle at Ayr in November. *J. S. Wilson.*

BITTER BUCK 7 ch.m. Celtic Cone–Clay Duck (Dicta Drake) [1989/90 16s^{2}
16s* 16m] close-coupled mare: went down by a head to Riverhead in novice 123
hurdle at Sandown in February and following month won similar event at Haydock easily by 15 lengths: dropped out quickly 3 out in Waterford Crystal Supreme Novices' Hurdle at Cheltenham (second favourite): will stay 2½m: acts on soft going, and probably unsuited by top-of-the-ground. *C. P. E. Brooks.*

BIVADELL 10 ch.m. Bivouac–Delilah Dell (The Dell) [1989/90 c24f^{pu}] maiden c—
point-to-pointer, placed in 1990: tailed off when pulled up in novice hunter chase in May. *S. A. Blyth.*

BIXIO 6 gr.g. Absalom–Brescianina (Hugh Lupus) [1989/90 c16g5 c16dF c20gpu 20d 17g6 24d3 25g 16f6 17m5 24gpu 24h2 24f3] small, plain gelding: placed in amateur riders maiden hurdles at Hexham last 2 outings: no form over fences: suited by 3m: acts on hard and dead ground: blinkered fifth to seventh and last 2 starts. *J. I. A. Charlton.* c— 78

BIZAGE MOTORS 6 b.g. Oats–Cherry Lodge (Charlottesvilles Flyer) [1989/90 22m4 22g5 16s c21g2 c24f* c25fpu c26g3 c24f*] well-made gelding: no form in novice hurdles: won Royal Fern Novices' Chase at Ascot in April (idled run-in and just held on from Golden Fox) and 3-runner novice chase at Chepstow (made heavy weather of beating Montgomery) following month: moderate third at Uttoxeter in between: stays 3m: acts on firm going: blinkered last 4 outings. *Mrs J. Pitman.* c**102** —

BIZARRE CASE 6 b.g. Gleason (USA)–Little Cygnet (My Swanee) [1989/90 F17h3 F16m aF14g] useful-looking gelding: first foal: dam, placed over hurdles in Ireland, is half-sister to several winning jumpers, including very useful Irish performer Royal Dipper and smart hurdler Henry Mann: third of 5 in NH Flat race at Carlisle in October: well behind in similar events afterwards: yet to race over hurdles or fences. *R. F. Fisher.*

BLACK COMEDY 7 b.h. Blakeney–Laughing Goddess (Green God) [1989/90 16g3 16d] sturdy, compact horse: novice hurdler: has been beaten in a seller: ran creditably both starts in 1989/90: worth a try over further than 2m: acts on good to firm and dead ground: has had tongue tied down and worn a crossed noseband: unseated rider when trying to duck out once in 1988/9. *J. Mackie.* 87

BLACKGUARD (USA) 4 ch.g. Irish River (FR)–Principle (USA) (Viceregal (CAN)) [1989/90 16d 16d4 a16g2 16m* 16f] well-made gelding: modest maiden miler on Flat, evidently needs soft ground: won juvenile hurdle at Stratford in May: will do best over a sharp 2m: acts on good to firm ground (showed promise on dead): blinkered last 3 outings: sold 5,200 gns Ascot June Sales. *Mrs J. Pitman.* 89

BLACK HUMOUR 6 b.g. Buckskin (FR)–Artiste Gaye (Artist's Son) [1989/90 16d* 16g*] workmanlike, rather angular gelding: half-brother to numerous winners, notably Gaye Brief and Gaye Chance (both by Lucky Brief): dam unraced: successful in novice hurdles at Hereford in November and Uttoxeter (impressive 12-length winner from Britannia Bell) following month: will stay 2½m: jumps well: sure to win more races. *C. P. E. Brooks.* 113 p

BLACK MOCCASIN 7 b.g. Buckskin (FR)–Lovely Bio (Double-U-Jay) [1989/90 20s3 20g* 25g5] strong, deep-girthed gelding: will make a chaser: won 2 NH Flat races in 1987/8: looked useful novice hurdler in the making when third behind Regal Ambition at Chepstow in December and when winning by a length from Remittance Man at Doncaster following month: ran as though something was amiss in valuable event at Newbury in March (made mistakes and tailed off from 4 out): should be suited by a stiff test of stamina: acts on soft going. *Mrs J. Pitman.* 116 +

BLACK MONKEY 8 b.g. Monksfield–Black Grouse (Black Rock) [1989/90 22m 21dpu c21g] strong, good-bodied gelding: winning hurdler: looked unenthusiastic second start: hasn't taken to jumping fences: should be suited by further than 2½m: acts on soft going: blinkered final outing 1988/9 and 1989/90 (looked sour in paddock). *P. R. Hedger.* c— —

BLACK ROCK 5 br.m. Rymer–Gadabout (Galivanter) [1989/90 F16v F16f] third foal: sister to a poor animal: dam poor novice hurdler: tailed off in NH Flat races at Haydock and Uttoxeter: yet to race over hurdles or fences. *E. H. Owen jun.*

BLACKSBURG 5 b.g. Black Minstrel–Meneplete (Menelek) [1989/90 aF16g2 F16g F16g2] seventh foal: dam unraced sister to Benvalla and Full Measure and half-sister to Malya Mal: 3 lengths second to stable-companions Happyoats and Snitton Lane in NH Flat races at Southwell and Market Rasen respectively: yet to race over hurdles or fences. *J. G. FitzGerald.*

BLACK SPOUT 9 b.g. Nonoalco (USA)–One In A Million (Rarity) [1989/90 16m 16fpu] sparely-made gelding: novice selling hurdler: has worn a crossed noseband: sold 750 gns Ascot October Sales. *C. J. Bell.* —

BLACK SPUR 8 br.g. Spur On–Ravenside (Marcus Superbus) [1989/90 c20m* c24m2 c24g3 c25mF c24d3 c25sur c24d* c25g3 c24f2 c20dpu] workmanlike, angular gelding: modest chaser: successful in handicaps at Hexham (bolted before start) in November and Edinburgh in February: stiffish task final c**108** —

Dennys Gold Medal Novices' Chase, Leopardstown—
Blitzkreig leads The Committee over the last

outing: stays 3m: acts on any going: usually jumps well and makes the running. *J. I. A. Charlton.*

BLACK THORNPRINCE 7 ch.g. Random Shot–Record Bee (Roll of Honour) [1989/90 c27s^{pu} c25g^{F}] rangy, workmanlike gelding: chasing type: no form in a novice hurdle and 2 novice chases. *P. A. Blockley.* c— —

BLACKWELL BOY (USA) 9 gr.g. Vigors (USA)–Aces Full (USA) (Round Table) [1989/90 c24d^{3} c27g^{F} c24d c25g c25s^{ur} c24d c24f^{pu}] big gelding: handicap chaser: no form after first outing: stays well: seems to act on any going except very soft: best in blinkers. *A. P. James.* c— —

BLAKEHOLME 5 ch.g. Over The River (FR)–Fun Princess (Prince Hansel) [1989/90 F16d F16g^{pu} 17m^{5}] fourth foal: brother to winning hurdler/chaser Thames Trader: dam never ran: no sign of ability in NH Flat races: staying-on 21 lengths fifth behind Allgallo in novice hurdle at Carlisle in April. *G. Richards.* 73 p

BLAKE RUN 6 b.m. Sexton Blake–Evening In May (Sole Mio (USA)) [1989/90 24f^{pu}] small mare: no form in selling hurdles. *Miss S. J. Wilton.* —

BLAKE'S PROGRESS 4 b.c. Blakeney–Patosky (Skymaster) [1989/90 16f* 16f^{2} 16g^{2} 17g^{3}] smallish, sparely-made colt: claimed £12,001 after winning 1¾m claimer on Flat in 1989: led around halfway when successful in juvenile hurdle at Plumpton in October: ran well subsequently, though jumped slowly final start (December): will stay beyond 17f: acts on firm ground: blinkered. *M. C. Pipe.* 102

BLAKES SON 5 b.g. Blakeney–Susanna (USA) (Nijinsky (CAN)) [1989/90 20m*] compact gelding: impressive length winner from Platonic Affair of handicap hurdle at Market Rasen in September: not seen out again: stays 2½m when conditions aren't testing: acts on firm and dead ground: blinkered last 2 starts 1988/9: found little fifth outing 1988/9. *M. W. Easterby.* 126

BLAKESWARE GOLD 4 ch.g. Vaigly Great–Presentable (Sharpen Up) [1989/90 16fF 16f* 16g4 16g* 16f2] leggy, close-coupled gelding: useful plater at up to 1¼m on Flat: won juvenile hurdle at Hexham (jumped poorly) in October and novice hurdle at Newcastle (claimer ridden) in May: good second of 3 to Full Monty at Hexham final start: may not stay much beyond 2m: acts on firm ground. *G. M. Moore.* 94

BLANDELL BEAUTY 6 b.m. Mummy's Pet–Maria Luiza (Stradavinsky) [1989/90 16hpu] tall, leggy mare: seems of little account: headstrong: broke blood vessel only outing 1989/90. *R. P. C. Hoad.* — x

BLAZE HILL 8 b. or br.m. Spur On–Miss Gail (I Say) [1989/90 22gpu] seventh foal: half-sister to a poor animal by Maystreak: dam ran once: behind when pulled up 4 out in mares novice hurdle at Kelso in December on debut. *V. Thompson.* —

BLAZING AWAY 4 gr.g. Blazing Saddles (AUS)–Norton Princess (Wolver Hollow) [1989/90 16fF 16fpu 16m] plating-class maiden on Flat: no worthwhile form over hurdles: dead. *L. J. Barratt.* —

BLAZING WALKER 6 ch.g. Imperial Fling (USA)–Princess Kofiyah (High Line) [1989/90 c21m2 c21g* c20g* c20m* c20m* c20s2 c16g* c20vur c20v4 c16m3dis c20f2 c19f2] tall, lengthy gelding: useful hurdler: successful in novice chases at Ayr, Wetherby and Newcastle (3): best performance under 12-7 in novice handicap on last-named course on seventh start: below his best subsequently, particularly next 2 starts: jumped badly right 2 out and disqualified after finishing around 12 lengths third behind Boutzdaroff in valuable novice event at Liverpool in April: effective from 2m to 3m: acts on good to firm and soft going (possibly not at his best on heavy): sweating second start 1988/9 and on reappearance: jumps to his right and may prove best on a right-handed track. *W. A. Stephenson.* c**140** ? —

BLENDERS CHOICE 8 b.g. Cavo Doro–Harriny (Floribunda) [1989/90 c17f* c19f*] workmanlike gelding: modest hurdler: won novice chases at Newton Abbot in August and Hereford (3-runner event, by 20 lengths) in September: stays 2½m: acts on hard going. *J. S. King.* c**98** —

BLICO 6 b.h. Miner's Lamp–Ethiopia (Will Somers) [1989/90 17m 16m6] maiden on Flat, has looked headstrong: easily better effort in novice hurdles when 19 lengths sixth behind Straight Gold at Worcester in April. *S. Pike.* 86

BLITZKREIG 7 gr.g. General Ironside–Tyrone Typhoon (Typhoon) [1989/90 c18d* c18g3 c16s* c18v2 c16m5 c18m* c25g2] c**143** —

Peter Hopkins, a prominent National Hunt owner for the past decade or so thanks to such as Lumen, Here's Why, Homeson, Captain Dawn, Abbreviation and Persian Style, announced he was giving up in May. His horses, to be passed on to his son and reportedly to stay with their current stables, didn't make it so successful a final season as could have been expected. The smart but enigmatic hurdler Vicario di Bray failed to win a race; promising novice chaser Green Willow suffered a set-back and wasn't seen out after November; and leading Irish novice Blitzkreig was sold privately immediately prior to putting up his best performance in winning the EBF Power Gold Cup Chase at Fairyhouse in April. Blitzkreig made simple work of collecting the IR £12,700 prize for his new owner at Fairyhouse. Leading from the fifth fence, he was clear in the straight and was eased before the finish, reached three lengths ahead of Arkle Trophy runner-up Kiichi to whom he was conceding 7 lb. Blitzkreig confirmed himself one of the best

EBF Power Gold Cup Chase, Fairyhouse— Blitzkreig has the race sewn up

Mr J. P. McManus' "Blitzkreig"

novices in Ireland eight days later when runner-up to Mixed Blends, conceding a stone, in the EBF Tattersalls Gold Cup (Handicap) over twenty-five furlongs at Punchestown. He looked the probable winner when stretching the field with some fine jumps down the back straight on the final circuit and when still going well in the lead at the third last. However, he had to be niggled at from two out, found only one pace as Mixed Blends challenged before the last and eventually went down by eight lengths. Blitzkreig had raced previously only at up to two and a quarter miles, over which distance he'd made a successful chasing debut at Fairyhouse in November. He showed his effectiveness over the minimum trip in the Dennys Gold Medal Novice Chase at Leopardstown the following month, winning by one and a half lengths from The Committee, the pair eight lengths clear of Toureen Prince in third. A good second to Derrymore Boy in the Diners Club Chase at Punchestown in February, Blitzkreig started shortest priced of the three Irish challengers for the Arkle Trophy at Cheltenham the following month at 8/1. He ran a little below his best in finishing fifth to Comandante, being outpaced by the principals in the latter stages having briefly threatened at the top of the hill. In hindsight he might have been better served by the forcing tactics adopted subsequently: Blitzkreig lacks the turn of foot to quicken past the best two-milers in fast conditions.

Blitzkreig's dam Tyrone Typhoon gained her only success over hurdles over thirteen furlongs in a maiden at Clonmel as a four-year-old. Her first three winning produce stayed at least three miles, including Blitzkreig's full brother Kingswood Kitchens. Her latest, the winning

Blitzkreig (gr.g. 1983)	General Ironside (gr 1973)	Sea Hawk II (gr 1963)	Herbager
			Sea Nymph
		Come Dancing (b 1967)	Northern Dancer
			Come In Please
	Tyrone Typhoon (br 1969)	Typhoon (br 1958)	Honeyway
			Kingsworthy
		Rahat-Lakoum (br 1963)	Sayajirao
			Turkish Melody

hurdler Typhoon Lucy (by Laurence O), has shown her form only at two miles to date. The next two dams won on the Flat in Ireland, Rahat-Lakoum being a sister to One Thousand Guineas third and Irish Oaks runner-up Indian Melody. A lengthy gelding, Blitzkreig was bought for only 1,900 guineas at Doncaster as a yearling. He won twice in a season and a half hurdling, showing fairly useful form. Blitzkreig has already shown himself significantly better over fences and should improve further. His fine jumping will stand him in good stead in open company and he's sure to win more races. We formed the impression from his running at Punchestown that Blitzkreig may prove best at around two and a half miles, over which distance the Durkan Brothers International EBF Punchestown Chase and the Black And White Whisky Champion Chase at Leopardstown seem likely targets for him. He has yet to race on very firm ground but acts on any other. *E. J. O'Grady, Ireland.*

BLOODHOUND 11 b.g. Armagnac Monarch–Miss Angle (Autre Prince) [1989/90 c26f^{pu} c26f^{F} c18f^{ur}] big, rangy, plain gelding: type to carry condition: winning point-to-pointer/hunter chaser: no form in 1990: stays 3¼m: acts on hard ground. *Mrs J. R. French.* c—

BLOODLESS COUP 8 b.g. Free State–Freely Given (Petingo) [1989/90 16g 16g 20g^{5}] sturdy gelding: modest staying handicapper on Flat in 1986: first sign of ability in novice hurdles when remote fifth to File Concord over 2½m at Kempton in January, making good late headway without being knocked about: will be suited by stiffer test of stamina. *C. C. Elsey.* 77

BLOXHAM 5 b.g. The Brianstan–Sur Les Roches (Sea Break) [1989/90 16g c16g^{F} c16g^{2}] lengthy, sparely-made gelding: little worthwhile form over hurdles: 12 lengths second to Over The Firs in maiden chase at Perth in April. *F. Jordan.* c88 —

BLUEBERRY KING 7 b.g. Sunyboy–Messalina (Pirate King) [1989/90 16d^{5} c16d* c17g* c16g^{6} c20f^{6}] big, workmanlike gelding: has a round action: very useful chaser: won Frogmore Handicap Chase at Ascot in December by 15 lengths from Springholm: beat only other finisher Mzima Spring 12 lengths in handicap at Newbury later in month: ran as though needing race when 9 lengths sixth in 2½m c**144** —

Frogmore Handicap Chase, Ascot—Blueberry King gives a good display of jumping

Pell-mell Partners' "Blueberry King"

Cathcart Challenge Cup won by Brown Windsor at Cheltenham in March: best form at 2m: acts on good to firm and dead ground: jumps well. *Andrew Turnell.*

BLUEBIRDINO 11 ch.g. Bustino–Blue Bird (Majority Blue) [1989/90 25f^{pu}] lengthy gelding: winning hurdler: tailed off when pulled up in hunter chase in 1988: stayed 2¾m: probably acted on any going: dead. *A. M. Thomson.* c— —

BLUE CHATEAU 4 ch.g. Longleat (USA)–La Sinope (FR) (Thatch (USA)) [1989/90 16g] won 2 sellers at up to 1¼m on Flat in 1989: jumped moderately when tailed off in juvenile hurdle at Haydock in November. *C. Tinkler.* —

BLUECHER 9 br.g. Radetzky–Fulcrum Miss (USA) (Fulcrum) [1989/90 c21s] sparely-made gelding: fair chaser at best: no form since 1986/7, though runner-up in 2 point-to-points in April: stays 2½m: acts on any going. *G. J. D. Wragg.* c— —

BLUE DANUBE (USA) 6 ch.g. Riverman (USA)–Wintergrace (USA) (Northern Dancer) [1989/90 c16s^{6} c16s^{5} c16d c20v^{pu} c16d c18s^{5}] medium-sized, rather sparely-made ex-Irish gelding: winning hurdler/chaser: behind in handicap chases in Britain, latest a seller: stays 2¾m: acts on heavy going and good to firm: usually visored or blinkered nowadays. *D. R. Gandolfo.* c— —

BLUE DART 10 ch.g. Cantab–Maisie Owen (Master Owen) [1989/90 c20v c21d^{4} c26v^{pu} c20d^{5}] strong gelding: modest chaser nowadays: stays 3¼m: acts on heavy going. *Capt. T. A. Forster.* c**112** —

BLUE DISC 5 br.g. Disc Jockey–Kaotesse (Djakao (FR)) [1989/90 16f 16g 16g^{2} 16f* 16g^{3} a16g^{4} 18s^{6} a16g^{3} a16g 16m^{6}] sturdy gelding: selling hurdler: ridden by 5-lb claimer, won at Taunton in December (bought in 4,000 gns): placed in similar company afterwards: best form at 2m: acts on firm ground: blinkered last 8 starts: has looked reluctant. *J. R. Jenkins.* 77 §

BLUE FINCH 6 b.g. Bustino–Blue Linnet (Habitat) [1989/90 16s 20m^{4} a20g^{5} 16s 21f^{pu} a20g] leggy, angular gelding: poor novice hurdler: has run in a seller: best effort at 2½m on good to firm ground: blinkered final start. *J. R. Jenkins.* 75

BLUEGRASS LADY 4 b.f. Last Fandango–Gifted Lady (Divine Gift) [1989/90 F17m] fifth foal: dam winner over 2m on Flat in Ireland: behind in NH Flat race at Carlisle in April: yet to race over hurdles. *R. J. Eckley.*

BLUE GRIT 4 b.g. Thatching–Northern Wisdom (Northfields (USA)) [1989/90
16d 16m^6 17m^6 16g^5] angular gelding: little form on Flat: sold out of R. J. R. 83
Williams' stable 5,200 gns Newmarket Autumn Sales: easily best effort over hurdles when fifth to Logamimo in juvenile claimer at Market Rasen in April. *R. W. Dods.*

BLUE MARBLE 8 ch.g. Flair Path–Blue Nimbus (Majority Blue) [1989/90 c— x
c16f^{ro}] rangy gelding: has shown signs of ability over hurdles: has made mistakes —
in 2 novice chases, running out when tailed off in October: tends to sweat up. *F. Murphy.*

BLUE MEMBER 6 ch.m. New Member–Blue Dancer (Blue Streak) [1989/90 c—
c24g^{ur} 24d^{pu} 16f^{pu}] leggy, rather angular mare: sister to Dancing Member, fourth —
in a NH Flat race: dam of little account over hurdles: pulled up in 2 point-to-points in 1989: unseated rider first in novice event on steeplechasing debut: looks of little account over hurdles. *A. P. Jones.*

BLUE RAINBOW 7 ch.m. Balinger–Metaxa (Khalkis) [1989/90 c16v* c16s^4 c94
c20v^4 c17h^2 c21m^F c19f^{ur} c16f*] lengthy, narrow mare: winning hurdler: won —
novice chases at Chepstow (mares event) in January and Hereford (left clear last when beating London Windows 8 lengths) in May: effective at 17f and probably stays 2¾m: acts on any going: game: sold privately 5,000 gns Ascot June Sales. *M. C. Pipe.*

BLUE RAVINE 11 gr.g. Peacock (FR)–Darton View (Deep Run) [1989/90 c32f c101
c24f^{ur} c26m^3 c33d^6 c24f* c25m* c26m*] leggy, close-coupled gelding: novice —
hurdler and winning point-to-pointer: won hunter chases at Hexham (maiden) in April, Towcester in May and Stratford (by 2½ lengths from Bay Bridge) in June: stays very well: acts on any going but goes particularly well on firm: game. *R. R. Lamb.*

BLUFF COVE 8 ch.g. Town Crier–Dolly Dickins (Double-U-Jay) [1989/90
26d^{pu} 20d^2 25m^3] compact gelding: lightly raced over hurdles of late but ran very 147
well when always-prominent 2½ lengths third behind Trapper John in Waterford Crystal Stayers' Hurdle at Cheltenham in March: suited by a good test of stamina: probably acts on any going: in good form on Flat in 1990. *R. Hollinshead.*

BLUFF KNOLL 7 b.g. New Brig–Tacitina (Tacitus) [1989/90 c27s*] tall, c128
strong, close-coupled gelding: fair hurdler: put up a fairly useful performance —
when winning handicap chase at Ayr in December, beating Samfen easily by 12 lengths, but wasn't seen out again: stays well: acts on heavy going and possibly unsuited by firm: still has something to learn about jumping. *R. Brewis.*

BLUSHING RIBERO 4 ch.c. Coquelin (USA)–Roses (Ribero) [1989/90 16g^4
a18g] no worthwhile form on Flat: well beaten in claimer and a novice event over —
hurdles: sold 900 gns Doncaster March Sales. *J. Parkes.*

BLUSHING TIMES 5 b.h. Good Times (ITY)–Cavalier's Blush (King's
Troop) [1989/90 F16g^3 F16f 20d^4 16d^5 16g^5 20g 17g^6 16d 16g] rather 84
dipped-backed horse: novice hurdler: ran poorly last 2 starts: visored or blinkered last 6 outings. *G. R. Oldroyd.*

BLUSTERY FELLOW 5 b.g. Strong Gale–Paulas Fancy (Lucky Guy)
[1989/90 16f^F 20s^6] medium-sized, well-made gelding: fourth foal: half-brother to 88
2 poor Irish animals: dam unraced: looked likely to finish close second when falling last in novice hurdle at Wincanton in November: lost touch from 3 out when well beaten over 2½m following month: reportedly sustained hairline fracture of pastern afterwards. *O. Sherwood.*

BOARDMANS STYLE 12 b.g. Giolla Mear–Caroline's Money (Even Money) c114
[1989/90 c17f^2 c18f* c16f* c19f* c16h^3 c25g^{ur} c16h* c19f*] lengthy, workmanlike —
gelding: front-running handicap chaser: won from small fields at Fontwell and Hereford (twice) early in season and at Taunton and Hereford in May: best up to 2½m: acts on any going: bolted and withdrawn on intended first start: usually taken early to start subsequently (led to post sixth outing): tends to jump to his right. *M. C. Pipe.*

BOBATWO 7 ch.m. Son of Shaka–Coffee Bob (Espresso) [1989/90 16f^5 16f^6]
sparely-made mare: of little account. *A. Moore.* —

BOBBY BURNS 9 b.g. Riboboy (USA)–Spring Exploit (Exploitation) [1989/90 c—
c24g^{pu}] lengthy gelding: winning hurdler/chaser: won a point-to-point in March: —

well beaten when pulled up in hunter chase following month: stays at least 2¾m: acts on good to firm and soft going. *Mrs O. Vaughan-Jones.*

BOBBY KELLY 8 ch.g. Le Bavard (FR)–Very Very (Vulgan) [1989/90 c24dpu] rangy, rather leggy gelding: maiden hurdler and winning chaser: stayed well: acted on heavy going: dead. *D. Nicholson.* c— —

BOBBY ON THE BANK 4 ch.g. Monsanto (FR)–Dewberry (Bay Express) [1989/90 16d2 16g3] small gelding: plating-class 9f winner on Flat: travelled well for a long way but weakened in closing stages in juvenile hurdles at Ayr (claimer) in December and Catterick (seller) following month: barely stays 2m and will prove suited by a sharp track. *M. J. O'Neill.* 74

BOB-CAM 6 ch.g. Scallywag–Stolen Girl (Mountain Call) [1989/90 F12m] third foal: dam unraced half-sister to 2 winners, one a point-to-pointer: failed to complete course in 2 point-to-points in 1989: tailed off in NH Flat race at Bangor in October: yet to race over hurdles or in steeplechases. *J. Parfitt.*

BOB'S DREAM 5 b.g. Ranksborough–Frimley's Alana (Lear Jet) [1989/90 16f 16f] tall, shallow-girthed gelding: half-brother to winning sprinter Tachyon Park (by Frimley Park): dam sprinter: well beaten at 2 yrs and in novice hurdles. *E. A. Wheeler.* —

BOB TISDALL 11 ch.g. Deep Run–Amphibian (Zarathustra) [1989/90 c24g4 c24g4 c25mco c25f6 c36f] strong, lengthy, plain gelding: useful chaser: burly, seemed to run very well when 18 lengths fourth to Desert Orchid in King George VI Rank Chase at Kempton in December on reappearance: returned lame after being carried out third outing and was tailed off last 2 (in Seagram Grand National at Liverpool on final one): suited by a distance of ground and an easy surface nowadays: blinkered fifth start 1988/9: usually races up with pace: trained until after second start by J. Edwards. *N. A. Gaselee.* **c141** ? —

BOCA CHIMES 5 b.g. Welsh Saint–Howzat (Habat) [1989/90 16g6 16m4 16d 22g* 21d3 22gpu 22g] small gelding: won handicap hurdle at Windsor in January: first race for 6 weeks, stiffish task in novice handicap final start: stays 2¾m: acts on good to firm and dead ground. *D. R. Gandolfo.* 96

BOHEA DESTROYER 5 b.g. Crofter (USA)–Bold Kate (Bold Lad (IRE)) [1989/90 16f5 16g 18s] leggy gelding: modest performer at his best on Flat, stays 1½m: poor form in novice and claiming hurdles. *P. Burgoyne.* 74

BOLD ACCLAIM 9 b.g. Persian Bold–Pride of Kilcarn (Klairon) [1989/90 24dpu c24fpu] tall, leggy gelding: handicap chaser: tailed off when pulled up in handicaps in November: stays well: seems to act on any going: blinkered twice in 1984/5. *J. Joseph.* c— —

BOLD AD 6 b.m. Bold Owl–Norma's Way (Great White Way (USA)) [1989/90 16f3 16m] strong, plain mare: poor novice selling hurdler: reportedly finished lame final start (December). *J. I. A. Charlton.* 62

BOLD ANSWER 7 b.g. Bold Owl–Subtle Answer (Stephen George) [1989/90 16gpu c16gpu 16m 16f4 23f6 23f] smallish, workmanlike gelding: winning selling hurdler: little worthwhile form in 1989/90: made mistakes when pulled up on chasing debut: stays 21f: acts on firm and dead ground: blinkered once and visored 4 times in 1988/9. *Miss G. M. Rees.* c— —

BOLD CADET 5 b.g. Sandhurst Prince–Bold Lady (Persian Bold) [1989/90 17m4 16m6 16d 16g3 16d 16gur 20m6 16s6 16g3 16s 16s4] smallish, rather leggy ex-Irish gelding: first foal: dam won over 9f at 2 yrs: placed at up to 1¼m on Flat: poor novice over hurdles: best form at 2m with give in the ground: often blinkered: has worn a tongue strap: reared and unseated rider start sixth outing: trained first start by A. Bunyan. *C. F. C. Jackson.* 79

BOLD CARL 7 b.g. Carlburg–Aerial Orchid (Perspex) [1989/90 20g] leggy gelding: winning staying hurdler: well beaten only start since 1987/8: acts on firm going. *D. R. Greig.* —

BOLD CHOICE 4 b.g. Auction Ring (USA)–Inner Pearl (Gulf Pearl) [1989/90 16g6 16g3 16s3 16g 16m2 18f3 16m* 16f2] leggy gelding: placed at up to 1½m on Flat: sold out of M. Stoute's stable 9,400 gns Newmarket Autumn Sales: 20-length winner of 3-runner juvenile hurdle at Towcester in April: ridden halfway when good second to Ivors Guest in juvenile handicap at Ascot following month: will stay further than 2¼m: acts on firm ground: well beaten in blinkers fourth start. *J. Joseph.* 100

BOLD FRED 8 br.g. Bold Owl–Kit-O-Kate (Raccolto) [1989/90 20dpu 24f2 22m6] big, strong, chasing type: sixth foal: half-brother to 2 poor performers: dam 71 novice hurdler and poor point-to-pointer: second in maiden hurdle at Hexham in May: out of his depth next time: stays 3m: acts on firm ground: likely to prove best on a galloping track. *R. J. Eckley.*

BOLD FURY 7 ch.g. Bold Lad (IRE)–Falassa (Relko) [1989/90 17f* 16m^{pu} 16m
16f^{5} 16d^{3} 22m^{3} 17d^{pu}] compact, workmanlike gelding: won novice hurdle at 93
Newton Abbot very early in season: ran well when third in 2¾m handicap at Wincanton in November, but poorly when next seen out 7 weeks later: ran in seller fourth outing: acts on firm ground: has worn a crossed noseband. *J. D. Roberts.*

BOLD GAMBLE 4 ch.g. Bold Owl–Subtle Queen (Stephen George) [1989/90
16g^{5} a16g^{5} a16g^{2} 16g^{3} a18g^{pu}] small gelding: 7.5f seller winner on Flat (best form 84
on a soft surface): placed in selling hurdle at Southwell and claimer at Market Rasen: pulled up, reportedly lame, final start (January). *Ronald Thompson.*

BOLD GRENADIER 9 b.g. Soldier Rose–Classical Air (Melodic Air) c—
[1989/90 c22f^{5} c24m^{4} c26f^{pu}] small, close-coupled gelding: poor novice —
hurdler/chaser: stays well: seems suited by firm ground: ran out second start in 1987/8: sometimes blinkered. *B. Smart.*

BOLD GUARD 5 ch.g. Bold Lad (IRE)–Mrs Foodbroker (Home Guard (USA))
[1989/90 16g^{2} 17m 16s 16g 16g^{6} 16v 16s 16d^{2} 16s 16m 21f^{pu}] compact ex-Irish 104 d
gelding: fourth foal: dam placed over 1m: 7f winner at 2 yrs: maiden hurdler: well beaten in 3 outings in Britain: unlikely to stay much beyond 2m: acts on heavy going and possibly unsuited by a firm surface: sometimes blinkered: trained until after eighth outing by D. Hughes. *P. D. Cundell.*

BOLD ILLUSION 12 ch.g. Grey Mirage–Savette (Frigid Aire) [1989/90 20d^{5}
16g* 16s^{F}] sparely-made gelding: game and genuine handicap hurdler: made most 113
and stayed on strongly when winning at Warwick in December: fell first 2 months later: probably stays 2¾m: acts on any going: usually jumps well: good mount for a claimer. *M. W. Eckley.*

BOLD IMP 5 bl.h. Dubassoff (USA)–Woodlands Girl (Weepers Boy) [1989/90
16g^{6} 16m^{pu}] compact horse: poor novice hurdler: off course 4 months between 82
starts: acts on dead going. *R. Akehurst.*

BOLD IMPRESSION 9 b.g. Random Shot–Jeanette Marie (Fighting Don) c—
[1989/90 25h 16m^{4} a20g* 19s^{6} 20m a20g^{4} 16m 17m] neat gelding: handicap 78
hurdler: gambled on when winning at Southwell in November: easily best effort afterwards when fourth on same course: ran best race over fences when second in novice event in 1988/9: stays 2½m, at least when conditions aren't testing: blinkered once in 1988/9 and last 3 starts. *J. Parfitt.*

BOLD IN COMBAT 7 b.g. Junius (USA)–Malmsey (Jukebox) [1989/90 c24f^{2} **c93** §
24f] small gelding: one-time fair hurdler: ran moderately in October: won 2 novice — §
chases in 1988/9: second of 3 in handicap at Southwell in August: stays well: suited by a sound surface and acts on hard going: blinkered once in 1987/8 and on last 4 outings: runs in snatches, and probably not genuine. *T. Casey.*

BOLD KING'S HUSSAR 7 ch.g. Sunyboy–Oca (O'Grady) [1989/90 c17g^{F} c**100**
c16s^{6} c16g* c20d^{4} c20d^{4} c16g c20d^{5} c20f] big, lengthy gelding: one-time fairly —
useful hurdler: won novice chase at Warwick in December: ran creditably on occasions afterwards: stays 2½m: acts on any going: sometimes sweating and edgy in preliminaries. *Mrs S. Armytage.*

BOLD LAMENT 9 b.g. Rhett Butler–Ameliorate (Reform) [1989/90 c17d^{5} c**109**
c20g* c24v^{2} c25s^{pu} c24d^{ur}] sparely-made gelding: winning hurdler: won novice —
chase at Folkestone in January: clear of remainder when going down by a length in similar race at Chepstow later in month: had stiff task fourth start: stays 3m: acts on heavy going: blinkered twice in 1987/8. *N. J. Henderson.*

BOLD LILLY 4 b.f. Montekin–Topless Dancer (Northfields (USA)) [1989/90
17f^{r} 16f^{pu} 17d^{pu} 18v^{pu}] leggy filly: modest maiden on Flat (probably stays 1¼m), —
when trained by W. Elsey: of little account over hurdles: refused at the fifth on hurdling debut. *N. G. Ayliffe.*

BOLD MAC 4 b.g. Comedy Star (USA)–Northern Empress (Northfields
(USA)) [1989/90 16f 16g] modest 1m winner on Flat: behind in juvenile hurdles in —
first half of season: sold out of N. Gaselee's stable 5,700 gns Ascot October Sales after first outing. *D. R. Gandolfo.*

BOLD PROTEST 6 b.m. Indian King (USA)–Lady Tycoon (No Mercy) [1989/90 aF13g] first foal: sister to useful Flat stayer Tonkawa: dam won at 1¼m:

well beaten in NH Flat race at Lingfield in March: yet to race over hurdles or fences. *Pat Mitchell.*

BOLD REPUBLIC 4 gr.g. Nishapour (FR)–Gallant Believer (USA) (Gallant Romeo (USA)) [1989/90 16s[5] 16d] modest winner at up to 1½m on Flat: kept on under tender handling when fifth in novice hurdle at Nottingham in February: weakened 3 out in juvenile event at Newcastle 5 days later. *T. D. Barron.* — p

BOLD REVENGE 8 b.g. Sweet Revenge–Bold Raillery (Tyrant (USA)) [1989/90 c16f[pu] 16g 16h c17m[3] c17f[5]] leggy gelding: winning point-to-pointer: poor maiden hurdler/chaser: has run in a seller. *B. T. Crawford.* c— —

BOLD SINGER 4 b.g. Ballad Rock–Grande Maison (Crepello) [1989/90 16m 16d 16d[pu]] tall gelding: poor maiden on Flat: of little account over hurdles. *T. J. Etherington.* —

BOLD SPARTAN 7 b.g. Bold Owl–Spartan's Girl (Spartan General) [1989/90 c24f[2] c26m[bd] c24g[pu]] rangy gelding: novice hurdler: winning chaser: second in BMW Series Chase qualifier at Newcastle in October: pulled up lame final start (February): stays 3m: acts on firm and dead going. *J. K. M. Oliver.* **c91** —

BOLD SPIRIT 7 b.g. Derrylin–Bold Pioneer (Wolver Hollow) [1989/90 17g[pu] 21s[pu]] modest form in novice hurdles in 1987/8: tailed off when pulled up both starts subsequently: form only at 2m: possibly unsuited by a soft surface: often blinkered. *B. Stevens.* —

BOLD TRY 5 ch.g. Try My Best (USA)–Persian Polly (Persian Bold) [1989/90 16m* 16m[4] 20f[pu]] successful twice at around 1m on Flat in 1989, second time in a seller (sold out of P. Cole's stable 4,500 gns): won claiming hurdle at Perth in September: well beaten in seller in November: tailed off when pulled up in novice handicap 4½ months later: sold out of N. Tinkler's stable 2,600 gns Doncaster January Sales. *K. A. Ryan.* 89

BOLLINGER 4 ch.g. Balinger–Jolly Regal (Jolly Good) [1989/90 F16f*] first foal: dam showed little worthwhile form over hurdles: 5/1, won 12-runner NH Flat race at Ascot in April by 12 lengths from Quaker Bob: yet to race over hurdles. *J. T. Gifford.*

BOLLIN GORGEOUS 4 b.f. Hello Gorgeous (USA)–Treberth (Gay Fandango (USA)) [1989/90 17f[4] a16g[3] 16m[2] 16s* 16s* a18g[2] a20g[3]] small, sparely-made filly: poor mover: claimed out of M. H. Easterby's stable £6,776 after winning 7f claimer on Flat in September: won selling handicap hurdle at Leicester in January (bought in 6,200 gns) and juvenile claimer at Uttoxeter following month: below form at 2½m: acts on soft going: blinkered third start: usually claimer or amateur ridden: trained fourth and fifth starts by Miss S. Wilton. *C. R. Beever.* 92

BOLLIN TINO 4 ch.c. Bustino–Strong Light (Fortino II) [1989/90 16m] neat colt: poor maiden on Flat (has worn blinkers): shaped with plenty of promise when seventh in juvenile hurdle at Market Rasen in September, but not seen out again. *M. H. Easterby.* — p

BOLSHOI BOY 6 ch.g. Proverb–Cherrywood (Vulgan) [1989/90 16m[3] 16m* 22v] strong, lengthy gelding: sweating and edgy, made all in novice hurdle at Uttoxeter in December: faded from 4 out when tailed off over 2¾m later in month: should stay beyond 2m: acts on good to firm ground. *Mrs S. Oliver.* 95

BONANZA BOY 9 b.g. Sir Lark–Vulmid (Vulgan) [1989/90 c24g* c30s* c26f c36f c33d[pu]] **c165** —

Bonanza Boy became the first horse to win the Coral Welsh National in successive years when he beat Cool Ground fifteen lengths at Chepstow in December carrying 11-11, 24 lb more than in 1988 and the biggest weight of any Welsh National winner since Limonali (11-12) in 1961. Bonanza Boy is on the small side and sparely made for a chaser—as was Limonali incidentally—but that was by no means the first time he'd proved himself under a big weight, and on his only previous start of the season he defied 11-10 to win the Rehearsal Chase, a limited handicap on the same course, easily by ten lengths from Run And Skip. That success earned Bonanza Boy a 4-lb penalty for the Welsh National. He still looked well treated though, with only Stearsby and Little Polveir of his eleven opponents set to carry their original allotted weight. In addition, the latter's rider put up 5 lb overweight and both Little Polveir and Stearsby looked in need of the race, in contrast to Bonanza Boy who looked in the peak of condition and who also

Coral Welsh National, Chepstow—Bonanza Boy wins it for the second year in succession

had the testing underfoot conditions in which he revels. None of that should take much away from Bonanza Boy, however, and he confirmed that under the right conditions he is a tip-top staying chaser. His performance was made more meritorious by the fact that he lost at least half a dozen lengths when swerving to avoid the fallen Remedy The Malady six fences from home. Prior to the incident Bonanza Boy, who invariably takes some time to warm up in his races, hadn't been travelling or jumping particularly well as Remedy The Malady set a searching gallop. Bonanza Boy had just begun to improve and was full of running when hampered by the fall of the leader. He recovered quickly, was soon back with the leaders and had the race sewn up bar a fall shortly after being sent on approaching four out.

Bonanza Boy's tendency to jump deliberately on occasions is not the handicap against lesser dyed-in-the-wool staying handicappers that it is against top-class performers. With conditions in his favour he'd finished tailed-off fourth, a distance behind the first three having lost touch soon after halfway, in the 1989 Tote Cheltenham Gold Cup. The generally held view of that performance was that Bonanza Boy had run below his best because of the gruelling race he'd had when winning the Racing Post Handicap Chase at Kempton less than three weeks earlier. In order to give him every chance to give of his best in the latest Gold Cup, Bonanza Boy didn't run between Chepstow and Cheltenham. He looked in fine shape in the paddock at Cheltenham and was sent off second favourite at 15/2 in a field of twelve. In the race—on good to firm—it soon became obvious that Bonanza Boy wasn't jumping quickly enough to maintain a prominent position. He stuck to his task, but was tailed-off last of the eight finishers behind Norton's Coin at the end. On firm ground at Liverpool in the Seagram Grand National three weeks later, Bonanza Boy was never able to land a blow but completed the course for the second year in succession, finishing sixteenth—he was eighth in 1989—tailed off on both occasions. Ground conditions were more in his favour in the William Hill Scottish National at Ayr on his only subsequent outing and he started a well-backed favourite at 6/1 against twenty-seven opponents. Unfortunately for his supporters, Bonanza Boy ran badly and was well tailed off when pulled up

Mr S. Dunster's "Bonanza Boy"

after the first fence on the final circuit. He'd given a similar performance in the 1989 Whitbread Gold Cup following his exertions in the Grand National. Hopefully, he'll return refreshed after a summer's break, in which case he should continue to give a good account of himself in long-distance handicap chases when there's plenty of give in the ground. Another Welsh National seems an obvious target for him in the first half of the season.

Bonanza Boy (b.g. 1981)	Sir Lark (b 1968)	Larkspur (ch 1959)	Never Say Die
			Skylarking
		Miss Cossie (b 1957)	Le Lavandou
			Monkey-Puzzler
	Vulmid (b 1967)	Vulgan (b 1943)	Sirlan
			Vulgate
		Midair (ch 1952)	Airborne
			Geoffrey's Lady

Bonanza Boy is the only one of his dam's six foals to have won. Vulmid herself was lightly raced and showed no sign of ability. She is a half-sister to several winning jumpers, including the smart hurdler Midsprite, winner of the 1971 Aldsworth Hurdle (now the Sun Alliance Novices') at Cheltenham. Their dam Midair, out of a Cesarewitch third, was a fair stayer on the Flat and successful at up to three miles over hurdles. Bonanza Boy's sire Sir Lark was a thoroughly game and genuine stayer who is probably best remembered for his head defeat by Bonne Noel in the 1973 Johnnie Walker

Ebor, after leading until the last strides. Both Sir Lark and Bonanza Boy ran moderately the only time they were tried in blinkers. *M. C. Pipe.*

BONANZA REBEL 8 ch.g. Belfalas–Speckled Leinster (Prefairy) [1989/90 22m6 20d] big, leggy gelding: second in NH Flat race in 1986/7, when trained by P. Hobbs: no worthwhile form in 2 novice hurdles but showed signs of ability in fair company on second start: likely to be suited by extreme distances. *M. C. Pipe.* — p

BONNE ARME 9 ch.g. Bonne Noel–Laud (Dual) [1989/90 22gpu 24s 21d 20s 22dpu] rather sparely-made gelding: handicap hurdler: well beaten in 1989/90: stays 3m but likely to prove best at up to 2½m when conditions are very testing: acts on heavy going: good mount for a 7-lb claimer. *O. O'Neill.* —

BONNIE ARTIST 6 ch.g. Caruso–Bonnie Ribema (Three Dons) [1989/90 c21f4 c24f3 c20f3 c24m3 c24g* c24f* c27g* c24m* c25f2 c24g3 c24mF] leggy, rather lightly-made gelding: won novice chase at Ayr and BMW Series Chase qualifier at Newcastle in October, and weakly-contested novice chases at Sedgefield and Newcastle (made mistakes) following month: went down by ¾ length to Wont Be Gone Long in BMW Series Final (Handicap) at Cheltenham in December: first race for nearly 4 months on final outing: stays 3m: acts on firm going: genuine. *W. A. Stephenson.* c**105**

BONNIE BELLE 10 b.m. Pitpan–Brave Bella (Sicilian Prince) [1989/90 c20vF c24dpu] ex-Irish mare: useful point-to-pointer: placed over hurdles in 1985/6 and in hunter chases in 1987/8 when trained by M. Donohoe: no sign of ability in Britain. *Mrs T. Arthur.* c— —

BONNIE BOY 10 b.g. Bonne Noel–Loughamaire (Brave Invader (USA)) [1989/90 16f3 16h5] lightly-raced novice hurdler: poor form. *R. G. Frost.* 72

BONNIE DUNDEE 6 b.g. Leading Man–Dragon Lass (Cheval) [1989/90 22g 24d 24g6 20g5 20f3 20m3 20m* 24g2 24g2] smallish, workmanlike gelding: claimer ridden, won novice handicap hurdle at Carlisle in April: runner-up in handicaps at Perth (amateur riders) and Uttoxeter (beaten a neck by Deep And Even): stays 3m: best form on good ground. *J. A. C. Edwards.* 102

BONN JOVY GREY 5 gr.h. Grey Ghost–Gemma Jean (Derek H) [1989/90 16f 16f 16d] plain horse: well behind in 2 races at 2 yrs and in 3 novice hurdles. *F. Watson.* —

BONNY PRINCE IVOR 8 b.g. Ivotino (USA)–Lady Impeccable (Dalesa) [1989/90 21mpu 25h] lightly-made gelding: winning selling hurdler: tailed off in non-seller in September: suited by 2¾m: acts on firm going. *C. G. Roach.* —

BON RETOUR 5 ch.m. Sallust–Marphousha (FR) (Shirley Heights) [1989/90 a16g2 16d a18gpu a16g] small, sparely-made mare: first form over hurdles when second in mares novice handicap at Lingfield in January: ran moderately in selling company afterwards. *J. Parkes.* 72

BONUS BOY 5 ch.g. Vital Season–Martini Girl (Vilmoray) [1989/90 F12m 16gpu 16f 16g] sparely-made gelding: no sign of ability. *A. J. Chamberlain.* —

BOOKIE BASHER 7 b. or br.g. Derring Rose–Wine Spy (Quisling) [1989/90 22dpu] poor novice over hurdles: has run in a seller: reportedly broke blood vessel in 1988/9. *R. O'Leary.* —

BOOK OF GOLD 5 b.g. The Parson–Bright Record (Royal Record II) [1989/90 16g6 16spu] good-bodied gelding: half-brother to quite useful hurdler/very useful hunter chaser Gratification (by Gala Performance) and winning jumper Deep Ridge (by Deep Run): dam, half-sister to top-class 1971/2 juvenile hurdler Official, was unplaced on Flat and over hurdles: backward, looked inexperienced in novice hurdles at Ascot in January and February (quite valuable event). *J. T. Gifford.* — p

BOOK OF RUNES 5 b.g. Deep Run–Wychelm (Allangrange) [1989/90 F16g2] second living foal: half-brother to moderate hurdler Dutchelm (by Quayside): dam won 2m hurdle in Ireland: 1½ lengths second to stable-companion Storm Island in NH Flat race at Perth in May: yet to race over hurdles or fences. *J. A. C. Edwards.*

BORACEVA 7 b.g. Salluceva–Boreen Queen (Boreen (FR)) [1989/90 c24mF c24mF c21m4 c24d5 c33d5 c29d* c25f3 c25m4 c33dpu] workmanlike, good-quartered gelding: useful chaser: jumped better than previously in season and put up an improved performance when impressive winner of handicap at Warwick in March: not disgraced when in frame in Ritz Club National Hunt Handicap Chase at Cheltenham later in month and quite valuable handicap at Liverpool in April: ran a c**140**

lack-lustre race final start: stays very well, but has a turn of foot: has won on top-of-the-ground but is suited by plenty of give. *G. B. Balding.*

BORADAWRA 4 ch.f. Boreen (FR)–Goldaw (Gala Performance (USA)) [1989/90 F16m] first foal: dam, in frame in Irish maiden hurdles, half-sister to 2 winning jumpers, including fairly useful chaser Boreen Daw: in rear in NH Flat race at Sandown: yet to race over hurdles. *M. C. Pipe.*

BORCALINE 8 b.g. Skyliner–Call God (Red God) [1989/90 c20f^{pu}] ex-Irish c—
gelding: half-brother to winning Irish hurdler Borcaglen (by Furry Glen): dam —
never ran: maiden hurdler/winning chaser: in frame in a point-to-point in Britain in May: tailed off when pulled up in hunter chase later in month: acts on firm ground: usually blinkered in 1988/9, including when successful. *V. A. G. Verrall.*

BORDEAUX BEAU 6 b.g. French Vine–Fiddlers Bee (Idiot's Delight)
[1989/90 16f^{F} 16g^{2} 16d^{2} 20d^{4}] big, lengthy, rather unfurnished gelding: has scope: 100
third foal: dam well beaten in 2 races on Flat: runner-up in novice hurdles at Leicester and Towcester: fair fourth in 2½m event at Wolverhampton in February: owner ridden last 2 starts (likely to do better with stronger handling). *O. Sherwood.*

BORDER ARCHER 6 br.g. Lighter–Inishdooey (Bargello) [1989/90 16g^{6} c—
22m^{3} c20g^{5}] lengthy gelding: won NH Flat race in 1988/9: poor novice hurdler: 76
tailed off in novice event on chasing debut: races freely and will probably prove best at 2m at present. *P. J. Hobbs.*

BORDER BURG 13 b.g. Perhapsburg–Border Knife (Border Legend) c**103**
[1989/90 c26f c25m* c25m^{5}] big, strong gelding: carries plenty of condition: very good hunter chaser at his best: odds on, scrambled home by ½ length from Castle Andrea in 4-runner contest at Towcester in April: successful in a point-to-point later in month: seems not to stay extreme distances: acts on any going: usually jumps well. *J. S. Delahooke.*

BORDER CHERRY 6 b.m. Deep Run–Brown Cherry (Master Buck)
[1989/90 20s^{pu} 21v 22s^{pu} 21d^{pu}] smallish, sparely-made mare: half-sister to —
winning Irish point-to-pointer Anyone Else (by Quisling) and poor novice chaser Pigeon Island (by Geneal Ironside): dam placed in a point-to-point in Ireland: no sign of ability in novice hurdles: pulled up lame final start. *T. N. Bailey.*

BORDER FOLLY 5 b.g. Dalsaan–My Folly (Salvo) [1989/90 16d^{4} 18d^{4}] rangy
gelding with plenty of scope: fourth in novice hurdles at Kelso in January and 92 p
February: gives impression will stay beyond 2¼m: type to progress. *J. S. Haldane.*

BORDER GAMBLER 6 br.m. Strong Gale–Golden Hansel (Prince Hansel)
[1989/90 22g^{4}] fourth in mares novice event at Kelso in December, easily better 79
effort over hurdles. *W. A. Stephenson.*

BORDER KING 8 ch.g. Sagaro–Piper's Gold (Jimmy Reppin) [1989/90 16f^{3} c—
17g^{4}] big, angular gelding: modest novice hurdler: claimer ridden when good third 97
at Wincanton in November: remote fourth in similar event at Devon & Exeter following month (conditional jockeys event): always behind on chasing debut: will be suited by return to further than 2m (stays 19f): acts on firm ground. *D. R. C. Elsworth.*

BORDER LOCH 6 b.g. Lochnager–Sea Chant (Julio Mariner) [1989/90 16m^{4}
20m^{3} 24g^{pu}] sturdy gelding: poor novice hurdler: pulled up lame in selling 78
handicap in October. *P. Davis.*

BORDER OAK 8 b.g. Majestic Streak–Purple Gem (Rubor) [1989/90 c16v^{2} c**93**
c20d^{F} c16d^{F} c16g^{ur} c16m c24f* c22f^{2} c24d^{pu} c24h^{3} c24h^{wo} c24g^{4}] strong, rangy —
gelding: modest novice hurdler: made virtually all to win novice chase at Hexham in March and walked over on same course in May: made mistakes when well beaten ninth and final starts: stays 3m: acts on any going. *J. I. A. Charlton.*

BORDER PERIL 8 br.g. Politico (USA)–Ayr Peril (Bay of Biscay) [1989/90 c—
c27m^{pu}] workmanlike gelding: winning hurdler: successful in 5 point-to-points in —
1989: struggling halfway and well behind when pulled up (reportedly lame) in hunter chase at Sedgefield: acts on firm going. *Mrs V. Scott Watson.*

BORDER'S LEGACY 5 br.m. Cut Above–Border Honour (Above Suspicion)
[1989/90 20g^{3} 20d^{3}] lengthy mare: third in novice hurdles at Ayr in December and 83
Newcastle in February: will stay 3m. *J. S. Wilson.*

BORDER SPARK 7 br.g. Lighter–Border Gloria (Border Chief) [1989/90 c—
16g^{ro} 20m^{4} 20g^{2} 24m* c20s^{ro} c24g^{F}] strong gelding: chasing type: won 89
slowly-run 3m novice handicap hurdle at Newcastle in November: fell fatally in

novice chase at Wetherby in January: best form with give in the ground: suited by strong handling (ran out when claimer ridden first and fifth starts). *G. Richards.*

BORDER SUN 12 b.g. Sunnyboy–Sweet Orchid (Border Chief) [1989/90 c22m^F c25f^4] tall, leggy gelding: won a point-to-point in March: maiden hunter chaser: looked temperamental when tailed off final start: stays 3m: acts on firm ground: blinkered last 3 outings 1985/6. *P. A. Deal.* c— —

BOREEN JEAN 6 ch.m. Boreen (FR)–Kitty Quin (Saucy Kit) [1989/90 19g^F 20d^F 22d^5 16d 16s^4] sturdy mare: no worthwhile form in novice hurdles, though has shown signs of ability. *J. M. Bukovets.* —

BOREEN KING 9 b. or br.g. Boreen (FR)–Proverb's Bride (Proverb) [1989/90 c24g^4 c24d^{pu} c24s^{pu} c20d^{pu} c28g^5] strong, round-barrelled gelding: winning chaser: no worthwhile form in 1989/90: well suited by a test of stamina: acts on soft ground. *S. Mellor.* c— —

BOREHAM DOWN 11 b.g. High Top–Woodwind (FR) (Whistling Wind) [1989/90 24m^{pu} 16f^6 20f^3] strong, compact gelding: selling hurdler: not raced after September: poor novice chaser: stays 3m: acts on any going: moderate jumper of fences: headstrong: sometimes blinkered: temperamental. *N. Bycroft.* c— § — §

BORE HILL PRINCESS 5 b.m. Imperial Fling (USA)–Domicile (Dominion) [1989/90 F16m^3 F16h^2 F17h^5 a16g^4] angular mare: first foal: half-sister to modest 7f handicapper Premier Prince (by King of Spain): dam, lightly raced, from family of Risk Me: beaten fair way in NH Flat races: fourth in novice hurdle at Southwell in November. *W. G. M. Turner.* 62

BORENCO 9 br.m. Boreen (FR)–Enco's Lek (Menelek) [1989/90 c24g^{ur} c26g^{pu} c18m^3 c26s^{pu} 16s c16d^{ur} c20s^3 c16v^6] strong, lengthy mare: placed several times in point-to-points: won hunter chase in Ireland in 1986/7: tailed off completed outings in 1989/90: stays 3m: acts on firm ground. *W. T. Kemp.* c— —

BORLEAFRAS 10 b.g. Sassafras (FR)–Levers Leap (King's Leap) [1989/90 c20m^3 c17m c20m^4 c20f^3 c16d^6 16d 22g^6 16s] sturdy gelding: poor performer nowadays: usually let down by his jumping in steeplechases: stays 2½m: acts on any going: rather headstrong: has worn a brush pricker: sold 1,500 gns Doncaster Spring Sales. *D. Moffatt.* c**84** x —

BORROWDALE 8 b.g. Golden Love–Fragrant Blossom (Straight Deal) [1989/90 c25g^{pu} c24d c24m^{pu} c24f^2 c24m^F c25m^{ur}] strong, workmanlike gelding: winning chaser: little form in 1989/90: stays 3m: best effort on good to firm ground: has won when visored: blinkered last 2 starts: claimer ridden when successful. *T. T. Bill.* c— —

BORUFUS 4 b.g. Sunley Builds–Song of Pride (Goldhills Pride) [1989/90 16f 16f^{pu} 16g 16g 16d^{pu} 16d^4 16g 16m 16m^{pu}] small, sparely-made gelding: only sign of ability when fourth in conditional jockeys claiming hurdle at Catterick in February: visored in sellers afterwards. *R. Thompson.* 64

BORVACALL 6 b.m. Ovac (ITY)–Call God (Red God) [1989/90 21h^3 17f^2 17h^2 17f] workmanlike mare: in frame in selling company over hurdles: ran poorly final start (August): tailed off over 21f: form only on top-of-the-ground: blinkered last 2 starts: unreliable. *W. G. Turner.* 70 §

BOSCEAN CHIEFTAIN 6 b.g. Shaab–Indian Stick (Indian Ruler) [1989/90 21f^3 26f^F 25h* 25f^F 25g^6 24f* 24f^4] leggy gelding: handicap hurdler: won at Ludlow in September and Taunton in December: first run for 5 months, fair fourth to Lapiaffe at Chepstow in May: stays 3m: probably acts on any going. *J. A. Bennett.* 112

BOSCHENDAL 8 b.g. Orange Bay–Bronze Princess (Hul A Hul) [1989/90 c22f^4 c20f^6 c24m^F c26f^5 25m^2 25f*] tall, leggy gelding: handicap hurdler: beat sole opponent Eskimo Mite by 2½ lengths at Huntingdon in May: makes mistakes in novice chases, but was challenging when falling at the last at Huntingdon in April: seems suited by 3m: acts well on top-of-the-ground: claimer or amateur ridden when successful: blinkered final 2 starts 1987/8 (ran out on first occasion). *R. Curtis.* c83 x 92

BOTANY BLADE 8 ch.g. Fine Blade (USA)–Vagrant Lass (Peter Jones) [1989/90 c24d^2 24g^{pu}] modest novice hurdler: runner-up in a point-to-point in February and hunter chase at Market Rasen (carried head high and looked none too keen under pressure) in March: runs like a thorough stayer: acts on soft ground: blinkered once in 1986/7 and final start. *M. Avison.* c89 —

BOTHAM 10 ch.g. Deep Run–Ballyowen (Arctic Slave) [1989/90 c20f^5 c24m^4 c33d^{pu} c24g^{ur}] big, strong, good sort: winning chaser: best effort of 1989/90 c— —

season on reappearance: stays 27f: acts on any going: sometimes makes mistakes. *J. K. M. Oliver.*

BOTTLE BASHER 5 b.m. Le Soleil–Mrs Walker (Border Chief) [1989/90 21d] leggy mare: well beaten in maiden hurdle at Warwick in March. *J. Ringer.* —

BOUNDEN DUTY (USA) 4 b.g. His Majesty (USA)–Inward Bound (USA) (Grey Dawn II) [1989/90 16d5 16gur] well-made, good sort: successful over 1m on Flat in France in 1989 when trained by A. Fabre: showed signs of fair amount of ability in Tote Placepot Hurdle at Kempton in February, starting to weaken when unseating rider 2 out: likely to prove best at around 2m. *G. Harwood.* 100

BOURBON ROSE 4 b.f. Ile de Bourbon (USA)–Tantot (Charlottown) [1989/90 16f] sparely-made, angular filly: half-sister to a fair 6f 2-y-o winner by Darby Creek Road: dam modest middle-distance performer: showed some promise in 1m maiden in September when trained by G. Cottrell: tailed-off last in juvenile hurdle at Cheltenham in December. *P. Leach.* —

BOURBON SPIRIT 5 b.g. Ile de Bourbon (USA)–Indoor Games (Habitat) [1989/90 16s* 16m2] won NH Flat race in 1989: won novice hurdle at Sandown in February: second on same course following month: dead. *M. E. D. Francis.* 105

BOURNE LANE 5 ch.g. Pollerton–Cherry Princess (Prince Hansel) [1989/90 F16m] half-brother to several winners, notably very useful staying chaser Omerta (by Quayside): well beaten in NH Flat race at Huntingdon in April: yet to race over hurdles or fences. *G. B. Balding.*

BOUTZDAROFF 8 ch.g. Dubassoff (USA)–Love Seat (King's Bench) [1989/90 c17m2 c16g* c17g* c16m* c16m* c16g2] c**137** —

Jimmy FitzGerald paid Boutzdaroff an interesting compliment when discussing the horse in the *Timeform Interview* in January. 'We've schooled him over fences and he jumps so well that, if I had the courage, I wouldn't mind riding him myself'. At that time Boutzdaroff had still to make his seasonal reappearance, and anybody taking the trainer's hint would have been well rewarded, for Boutzdaroff had his best season yet. His best and easily most important performance in it came when he won the Perrier Jouet Novices' Chase at Liverpool in April. Boutzdaroff was fourth

Perrier Jouet Novices' Chase, Liverpool—
Boutzdaroff (No. 9) and Young Snugfit in unison at the last

Robinson Publications Ltd's "Boutzdaroff"

favourite, with preference in the betting for Young Snugfit and Antinous, second and fourth in the Arkle Challenge Trophy at Cheltenham, and Elfast. The betting proved to be a fair guide with the first four in the market four of the first five to cross the line. Boutzdaroff, a late ride for Byrne, who'd been on board stable-companion Sybillin when winning the juvenile hurdle earlier in the afternoon, made steady progress from around halfway and was one of five virtually line abreast at the penultimate fence. With Blazing Walker continuing to jump badly to his right, severely hampering Antinous in the process, and Campsea Ash weakening, Young Snugfit and Boutzdaroff began to pull clear approaching the last. Boutzdaroff pecked on landing and it looked momentarily as if Young Snugfit was going to gain compensation for his narrow defeat at Cheltenham, but, recovering quickly, Boutzdaroff under hands-and-heels riding maintained a narrow advantage to the finish. The pair, separated by a head, finished twelve lengths clear of Blazing Walker, subsequently disqualified for hampering Antinous, with Elfast, who stayed on in the closing stages having made a bad mistake, fourth and Antinous fifth. Boutzdaroff had picked up three chases prior to Liverpool, novice events at Edinburgh and Doncaster and the five-runner Burnt Oak and Special Cargo Novices' Chase at Sandown. In the last-named event, he accounted for Pendennis by a head, but the latter would have undoubtedly won but for a bad mistake at the second last. Boutzdaroff possibly hadn't fully recovered from his exertions at Liverpool when narrowly beaten at 2/1-on in a novice event at Bangor two weeks later. Even so, he would probably have won had his jockey not been a trifle over-confident after quickening into what looked to be a winning lead at the second last.

Boutzdaroff, as his trainer indicated, is a very sound jumper in the main—though he does tend to jump to his right in the latter stages—and

Boutzdaroff (ch.g. 1982)	Dubassoff (USA) (b 1969)	Sea Bird II (ch 1962)	Dan Cupid
			Sicalade
		Love Lyric (b 1955)	Prince Chevalier
			Riding Rays
	Love Seat (b 1968)	King's Bench (b 1949)	Court Martial
			King's Cross
		Criterion Maid (b 1959)	Borealis
			Pirate's Daughter

this should enable him to win more two-mile races when conditions are in his favour. However, a sound surface and a sharp track are essential for him, and this will almost certainly limit his chances. The Mansion House Handicap at Doncaster and the Captain Morgan Aintree Handicap on Grand National Day would seem ideal targets. Boutzdaroff, a workmanlike gelding, is a half-brother to five Flat winners here and abroad, including sprinter Resin (by Frankincense) and two-year-olds Bernadine (by Farm Walk) and Flitterdale (by Abwah). The dam Love Seat is an unraced sister to The Diddler, a useful winner of numerous races from five furlongs to a mile in the 'sixties, and a half-sister to Pin Cry who won over two miles on the Flat and was placed over hurdles in Ireland. Their dam Criterion Maid, a quite modest middle-distance Flat maiden, was a half-sister to two Flat winners, notably Kentra who was a fairly useful winner from five furlongs to two miles. *J. G. FitzGerald.*

BOWS PRINCESS 4 b.f. Warpath–Bow Baby (Bowsprit) [1989/90 F12g F16g^ur F16g 16m^pu] half-sister to 4 poor performers: dam never ran: has looked thoroughly temperamental in NH Flat races and a juvenile hurdle (blinkered). *B. T. Crawford.* — §

BOXER REBELLION 4 ch.f. Royal Boxer–Rosefox (Owen Anthony) [1989/90 a16g] third foal: dam poor plater on Flat and over hurdles: claimer ridden, tailed off in seller at Southwell in November on hurdling debut. *J. M. Bradley.* —

Sleaford Handicap Hurdle, Market Rasen—
Brabazon and the blinkered Kings Rank fight out the finish

P. H. Betts (Holdings) Ltd's "Brabazon"

BOXING BELLE 7 b.m. Royal Boxer–Saucy Upham (Saucy Kit) [1989/90 F16g 16g^{pu} 20d^{pu}] smallish, workmanlike mare: first foal: dam, half-sister to several winning jumpers, modest hurdler who stayed 3m: tailed off when pulled up in novice hurdles: jumped poorly final start. *Mrs H. B. Dowson.* —

BOY JAMIE 6 ch.g. Nicholas Bill–Petard (Mummy's Pet) [1989/90 16g 16d 16h^{4}] close-coupled gelding: plating-class handicapper on Flat (suited by 1¼m) when trained by J. Payne: well beaten in novice hurdles: seemed ill at ease on hard ground final start. *J. White.* —

BOYNTON 7 b.g. Riboboy (USA)–Lingdale Lady (Sandford Lad) [1989/90 16d^{3}] sturdy, quite attractive gelding: fell in a point-to-point in 1988: very lightly-raced novice hurdler: ran as though in need of race when third at Sedgefield in January. *J. H. Johnson.* 86

BOY PAINTER 7 ch.g. Gunner B–Sister Anne (Mourne) [1989/90 16g 16g 16g^{pu} 16d^{pu} 16g] tall, rather sparely-made, workmanlike gelding: winning hurdler: well beaten in 1989/90 (whipped round start fourth outing): seems to need a soft surface: pulls hard: usually claimer ridden: blinkered once in 1988/9. *J. R. Fort.* —

BOYSTEROUS BOY 6 br.g. Balinger–Oyster Eye (Wrekin Rambler) [1989/90 20g 20g 22v^{6}] lengthy, rather sparely-made gelding: well beaten in NH Flat races and novice hurdles: sometimes makes mistakes: blinkered final start. *J. K. M. Oliver.* —

BRABAZON (USA) 5 b.g. Cresta Rider (USA)–Brilliant Touch (USA) (Gleaming (USA)) [1989/90 20f^{3} 21g^{3} 24s* 24d* 24s^{3} 25m^{5}] leggy, quite good-topped gelding: improved with his races over hurdles, on final start under 5 lengths fifth to Trapper John in Waterford Crystal Stayers' Hurdle at Cheltenham: 145

successful earlier in handicap at Market Rasen and novice event at Leicester: thorough stayer: acts on any going: suited by racing up with the pace: useful. *M. H. Tompkins.*

BRABINER KING 5 ch.g. Posse (USA)–High Finale (High Line) [1989/90 F16g] fourth foal: half-brother to very useful 7f and 9f winner My Generation, useful 6f to 1m winner Que Sympatica (both by Young Generation) and fair 17f Flat winner Ecran (by Kings Lake): dam, winner over 1¼m, is sister to Park Hill winner Quay Line: tailed off in NH Flat race at Ayr in November: yet to race over hurdles or fences. *C. Parker.*

BRACELET 5 ch.m. Balidar–Asnoura (MOR) (Asandre (FR)) [1989/90 20d^{pu}
16m^{3}] plain mare: third in novice hurdle at Wincanton in December, first form. *P.* 76
J. Hobbs.

BRADBURY STAR 5 b.g. Torus–Ware Princess (Crash Course) [1989/90
20f* 21g* 20g* 20f* 20g^{2} 16m^{F} 16f^{6}] rangy gelding: much improved hurdler who 141
won handicaps at Plumpton (amateur riders), Sandown (conditional jockeys), Kempton and Cheltenham in first half of last season: would probably have finished good second to Moody Man but for falling 2 out in William Hill Imperial Cup at Sandown in March: outpaced in latter stages of quite valuable event at Liverpool following month (will be suited by return to further): stays 21f: yet to show his form on heavy going, probably acts on any other: useful. *J. T. Gifford.*

BRADMORE'S VISION 4 b.c. Vision (USA)–Plum Run (USA) (Run The
Gantlet (USA)) [1989/90 16d 16f^{5} 20m* 17h* 17h^{F}] sparely-made colt: 91
half-brother to fair but ungenuine hurdler Assultan (by Troy): poor form at 2 yrs: won selling hurdles at Chepstow in April and Devon & Exeter following month: in lead but under pressure when falling last in novice claimer on latter course: stays 2½m: acts on hard ground: sold only 1,000 gns Newmarket July Sales. *M. C. Pipe.*

BRADSHAW 5 b. or br.g. Bay Express–Time-Table (Mansingh (USA))
[1989/90 16g 16f^{6} 20g] leggy, good-topped gelding: poor novice hurdler: jumped —
moderately final start (December). *Denys Smith.*

Mr James Campbell's "Bradbury Star"

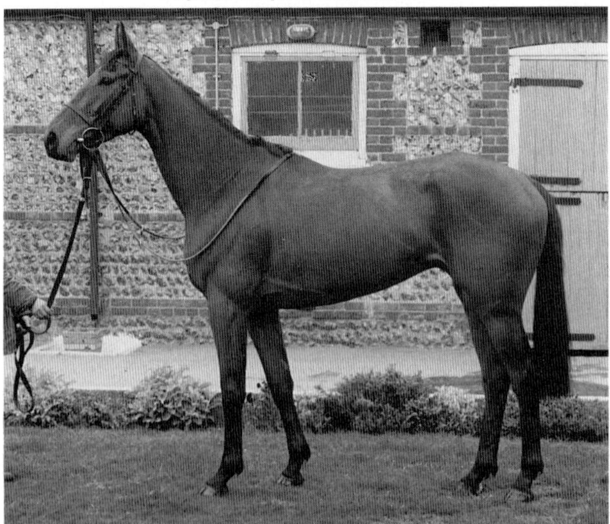

Chivas Regal (Amateur Riders) Novices' Handicap Chase, Liverpool—Brandeston leads Pendennis and Imadyna (left)

BRADWALL 6 br.g. Strong Gale–Sweet Season (Silly Season) [1989/90 16d 16g c16g4 c16s3 c20gF c20d6] lengthy gelding: has scope: novice hurdler: in frame in novice chases at Wolverhampton (none too fluent) and Haydock (jumped left in latter stages) in January: seemed not to stay 2½m final start. *G. B. Barlow.* c**89** —

BRAMBER 4 b.f. Castle Keep–Hartnell Dream (Grundy) [1989/90 16fpu] leggy, sparely-made filly: quite modest form at up to 7f on Flat: sold out of J. Dunlop's stable 4,400 gns Newmarket July Sales: tailed off when pulled up 3 out in juvenile hurdle at Cheltenham in October, giving impression something was amiss (wore crossed noseband). *M. C. Pipe.* —

BRANDESTON 5 b.g. Northern Treat (USA)–Fussy Budget (Wolver Hollow) [1989/90 16m 16m6 16s5 c16s* c16g* c16g3 c20spu c20f2 c20f* c16mF] compact, good-bodied gelding: won novice chases at Chepstow in December, Wolverhampton in January and Liverpool in April: made most on final circuit and ran on gamely to win Chivas Regal Amateur Riders Novices' Chase (Handicap) on last-named course by 4 lengths from Imadyna: led until falling 5 out in race won by Al Hashimi at Chepstow in April: stays 2½m: acts on any ground: sometimes sweating: jumps boldly but makes the odd mistake. *G. A. Hubbard.* c**122** p 81

BRANDY HAMBRO 9 b.g. Hot Brandy–Ice Bird (Fighting Charlie) [1989/90 c20g3 c28g5 c27s4 c24gpu c20g6] big, lengthy, rather plain gelding: moderate chaser: below form in 1989/90: stays well: acts well in the mud: usually jumps boldly. *C. Parker.* c**109** —

BRANSTOWN SUNSET 6 b.g. Red Sunset–Lydja (Hethersett) [1989/90 a16g*] neat gelding: former selling hurdler: won handicap at Lingfield in November: not seen out again: stays 2¼m: possibly unsuited by very firm ground, acts on any other: blinkered once in 1988/9: has won for a claimer. *P. Butler.* 79

BRASSEYS COPSE 11 ch.g. New Member–Glensharragh (Blue Lightning) [1989/90 c24m3 c25mpu c25f5] angular gelding: novice chaser: stayed on in latter stages when third in handicap at Ludlow in January: had stiff task final outing: stays 3m. *Miss J. Horwood.* c— —

BRAVE BANNER 9 b.g. Brave Invader (USA)–Fainne Nua (Paddy's Birthday) [1989/90 24f^{pu}] tailed off in 2 NH Flat races and pulled up in 3 point-to-points in Ireland: second favourite, disputed lead until weakening and pulled up lame run-in in 3m amateur riders maiden hurdle at Hexham in May. *J. Parkes.* —

BRAVE DEFENDER 6 ch.g. Niniski (USA)–Hirsova (Gulf Pearl) [1989/90 c16g^2 c18g^4 24f^2] leggy gelding: one-time quite useful hurdler: blinkered, second to Red Ruddel at Ascot in November (edged right run-in): promising second to Young Snugfit in novice chase at Kempton (not particularly fluent): ruined his chance with mistakes when well beaten in similar race next outing: stays 3m: acts on any going: has looked a difficult ride and tends to run in snatches: sold 8,000 gns Ascot February Sales. *N. J. Henderson.* c**95** 119

BRAVE SETANTA 5 b.g. Hillandale–Kasarose (Owen Dudley) [1989/90 22g^2 22g^6 22v^6 16v 20m^2 20m^6 24m^4] sparely-made gelding: novice hurdler: stays 3m: best form on a sound surface: blinkered third and fourth starts. *F. J. O'Mahony.* 91

BRAVE SONG 11 b.g. Busted–Net Call (Song) [1989/90 20m c24s^4 c24g^{pu} c26s^{pu}] lengthy gelding: has had a soft palate operation: one-time useful point-to-pointer: poor hunter chaser nowadays: tailed off in handicap hurdle on reappearance. *A. W. Jones.* c— —

BRAVO STAR (USA) 5 b.g. The Minstrel (CAN)–Stellarette (CAN) (Tentam (USA)) [1989/90 16g^4 21g^{ur} 20g 22g^2 18s^4 20d a20g^3 a20g^4 a24g* 21g^2 22f^3 26m^6] small, strong gelding: handicap hurdler: won at Lingfield in March: tailed off final outing: stays 3m: acts on firm ground: less than a fluent jumper: has won for a claimer: has found little: usually wears blinkers (ran well when visored ninth to eleventh starts): sold out of P. Mitchell's stable 7,000 gns Ascot May Sales after penultimate start. *P. R. Rodford.* 96

BREAK EVEN 6 b.g. Decent Fellow–Zepps (Reliance II) [1989/90 F16f^4 F16g* F16m^5 20g 16s] big, leggy ex-Irish gelding: fourth foal: dam unraced: won NH Flat race at Leopardstown in June (trained until after next start by J. Maxwell): well beaten in novice hurdles at Haydock: dead. *Mrs S. A. Bramall.* —

BREAKFAST BELLE 5 b.m. Oats–Beau Wonder (Veiled Wonder (USA)) [1989/90 18s^{pu}] second foal: dam, behind in 3 races over hurdles, half-sister to out-and-out stayer Reine Beau: tailed off when pulled up 2 out in mares novice hurdle at Fontwell in January on debut. *D. M. Grissell.* —

BREAKFAST CAR 8 b.g. Oats–Drawing Room Car (Chingacgook) [1989/90 c16m* c16g^3 c16v^2 c16s^2 c18f*] leggy, narrow gelding: fair chaser: won handicaps at Plumpton in November and Fontwell (held up, led run-in to beat Silver Cannon 2 lengths) in March: stays 2½m: acts on any going. *D. M. Grissell.* c**119** —

BREAKOUT 6 ch.g. High Line–Wolverhants (Wolver Hollow) [1989/90 20s^4 18s^4] leggy gelding: fair winning stayer on Flat (goes well with forcing tactics): sold out of D. Elsworth's stable 1,650 gns Newmarket Autumn Sales: modest novice hurdler. *J. L. Harris.* ?

BREAK OUT (FR) 5 ch.h. Bikala–Lyphaora (Lyphard (USA)) [1989/90 16g^4 c20g*] workmanlike, rather sparely-made horse: first live foal: dam, minor winner at 1½m in France, is half-sister to Dankaro: well beaten in 2 races on Flat in France at 3 yrs: placed over hurdles and fences at Auteuil in 1988/9: travelled well much of race when fourth in novice hurdle at Huntingdon in November: left in lead at the third and made rest to win novice chase at Plumpton in December: not seen out again: stays 2½m. *C. P. E. Brooks.* c**86** p 88 p

BREAK THE CHAIN 5 br.g. Callernish–Lovely Daisy (Menelek) [1989/90 F16m 16m^5 16d 16d 20f^3 20m^3] lightly-made gelding: third foal: dam, a maiden, half-sister to successful Irish jumper Ballon Bush: third in novice handicap hurdles at Hexham and Wetherby (seemed unsuited by being held up in slowly-run race): stays 2½m: acts on firm ground. *W. A. Stephenson.* 90

BREAK THE DUCK 4 b.f. Absalom–Bally Tudor (Henry The Seventh) [1989/90 16f] plain filly: little worthwhile form on Flat: behind in juvenile hurdle at Market Rasen: dead. *Miss G. M. Rees.* —

BREEZY SAILOR 4 ch.g. Tumble Wind (USA)–Bouganville (Gulf Pearl) [1989/90 16f^4 16m^F 16m 16m 16g^5 a16g^4 17f^{ur} 16m] small, sparely-made gelding: in frame over sprint distances at 2 yrs, but well beaten on Flat in 1989: poor form in juvenile hurdles: tailed off in selling handicaps last 2 outings: barely stays 2m: blinkered fourth to sixth and final starts. *R. Thompson.* 64

BREGA 6 ch.g. Free State–Dauphiness (Supreme Sovereign) [1989/90 17m^{pu} 16m^{pu}] tailed off when pulled up all 3 starts over hurdles, last 2 sellers. *F. S. Storey.* —

BREGUET 7 b.m. Rouser–Span (Pan II) [1989/90 25f^{6}] compact mare: poor maiden on Flat: tailed-off last in novice event at Doncaster in December on hurdling debut. *N. Tinkler.* —

BREMHILL ROSIE 7 b.m. Celtic Cone–Bay Rambler (Wrekin Rambler) [1989/90 16g* 22d^{pu} 21f^{pu}] smallish, sturdy mare: fourth foal: half-sister to Irish NH Flat race winner Simaroy (by Sagaro): dam successful over 2m on Flat and over hurdles in Ireland: won novice hurdle at Leicester in January: ran as though something amiss next time and was pulled up lame when in touch in valuable mares novice handicap at Newbury final start. *O. Sherwood.* 87 +

BRENDAN OLIVIA 10 b.g. Belfalas–Three Rings (Straight Lad) [1989/90 c17g^{pu} c20d^{5} c20v^{F} c21v^{3} c20v^{4} c16g^{6}] sturdy ex-Irish gelding: winning hurdler/chaser: probably needs further than 2m and stays 2¾m (finished lame when tried at 3m): best form with give in the ground and acts on heavy going: formerly trained by C. J. Power. *T. B. Hallett.* **c99** —

BRENT RIVERSIDE 7 b.g. Track Spare–Queen's Bronze (King's Troop) [1989/90 20g^{pu} 16f^{4} 17d^{F} 16m^{5} 16f] good-topped gelding: handicap hurdler: looked probable winner when falling 2 out at Devon & Exeter in November: ran moderately afterwards (gave impression something amiss final start (November) and subsequently had a tie-back operation): probably stays 19f: acts on any going: good mount for a claimer. *G. B. Balding.* 114

BRIANSTON BELL 11 br.g. The Brianstan–Saucy Belle (Pendragon) [1989/90 16f^{pu}] leggy gelding: winning hurdler/chaser early in 1987/8: pulled up lame before third in April on reappearance: best at around 2m: acts very well on top-of-the-ground: good mount for a claimer. *W. Clay.* c— —

BRIARQUEEN 6 b. or br.m. The Brianstan–Queen of The Kop (Queen's Hussar) [1989/90 16m^{pu} a16g^{pu}] lengthy mare: poor plater at 2 yrs on Flat: pulled up all 3 outings over hurdles, including a seller. *W. G. Morris.* —

BRICKET WOOD 5 b.g. Black Minstrel–Royal Bonnet (Beau Chapeau) [1989/90 16g^{6}] eighth foal: dam unraced half-sister to Cheltenham Gold Cup winner Davy Lad: under strong pressure halfway, but stayed on steadily when sixth in novice hurdle at Towcester in December: will be suited by further: should improve. *N. A. Gaselee.* 80 p

BRIDE FOR A DAY (USA) 4 gr.f. Runaway Groom (CAN)–Angel One (USA) (Son Ange (USA)) [1989/90 a16g^{6} a16g 16d^{6} 16f^{6} 16g 24m^{pu}] light-framed filly: half-sister to a winner in North America: dam unplaced from 4 starts: poor juvenile hurdler: ridden by 7-lb claimer. *W. Clay.* 61

BRIDESBAY BOY 10 b.g. Vitiges (FR)–Leto (High Top) [1989/90 c25m^{pu}] workmanlike gelding: winning point-to-pointer: tailed off when pulled up in hunter chase in March. *T. J. Paget.* c—

BRIDGETOWN LAD 9 b.g. Super Slip–Princess Caroline (Red Pins) [1989/90 c24s^{pu} c22d^{6} c25s^{pu} c21d^{3}] strong, good-bodied gelding: carries plenty of condition: poor novice chaser: effective at 2m and stays 3¼m: yet to race on top-of-the-ground. *J. C. McConnochie.* c83

BRIEF GLANCE 5 b.m. Official–Second Glance (Prince Hansel) [1989/90 16g] sparely-made mare: mid-division in NH Flat race: claimer ridden, tailed off in novice event at Worcester in December on hurdling debut. *G. Price.* —

BRIEFING 5 gr.m. Rusticaro (FR)–Brief Agenda (Levmoss) [1989/90 16m^{3} 16m^{5} 20g^{ur} 21d 17m^{pu}] small ex-Irish mare: sixth foal: half-sister to Flat winners Bold And Brief and Ladenda (both by Bold Lad (IRE)): dam, placed over 9.5f in France, daughter of 1000 Guineas winner Pourparler: has shown a little ability on Flat: poor novice over hurdles: pulled up, reportedly lame, final start: probably stays 2½m: trained on hurdling debut by J. Bolger, and next 2 starts by D. Wintle. *P. J. Hobbs.* 81 ?

BRIERY FILLE 5 b.m. Sayyaf–Zeddera (FR) (Zeddaan) [1989/90 16g^{ur} 16g] lengthy mare: won 2 sellers at up to 1m on Flat in 1989: sold out of R. J. R. Williams' stable 5,400 gns Newmarket Autumn Sales: keeping on when unseating rider last in novice hurdle at Ayr in December: seventh in maiden event at Edinburgh later in month. *R. W. Dods.* —

BRIGADIER BILL 5 ch.g. Nicholas Bill–Sailing Brig (Brigadier Gerard) [1989/90 16f^{2}] plating-class middle-distance maiden on Flat: jumped slowly in 76

latter stages when second in novice hurdle at Southwell in August. *Mrs G. R. Reveley.*

BRIGADIERS GLORY 4 ch.f. Castle Keep–Join The Club (Dance In Time (CAN)) [1989/90 17f^{pu} 16d^{ur} 16s^{5}] smallish filly: little promise in selling hurdles: won 11f claimer on Flat in 1990: sold 2,600 gns Doncaster June Sales. *B. A. McMahon.* —

BRIGAND GIRL 8 b.m. New Brig–Tillside (Lucky Brief) [1989/90 20s 24s^{2} 24s^{5}] sparely-made mare: novice hurdler: runner-up in conditional jockeys handicap at Haydock in January: struggling halfway final start (February): well suited by a good test of stamina: acts on soft going. *Mrs Jill Evans.* 88

BRIGG MELODY 9 ch.m. Oedipus Complex–In For A Penny (Soletra) [1989/90 20g^{5} 20f^{pu} 20g^{pu}] lightly raced and no worthwhile form over hurdles. *J. G. Thorpe.* —

BRIGGS BUILDERS 6 b.g. Absalom–Quenlyn (Welsh Pageant) [1989/90 16g* c16f^{4}] rangy gelding: placed over 7f in Britain at 2 yrs, subsequently won 3 times on Flat in Belgium and has also won twice over hurdles there, at Ostend in 1988 and in July: jumped none too fluently but showed some promise when fourth in novice chase at Windsor in November. *J. R. Jenkins.* c**76** + ?

BRIGHT BARLEY 6 ch.g. Native Bazaar–Laughing Corn (Meadow Court) [1989/90 16g^{2} 22v^{6} 20v] angular, plain gelding: brother to a winner in Malaysia: dam unraced: made mistakes when 25 lengths second in novice hurdle at Stratford in October: weakened from 3 out over longer trips afterwards: not raced after January. *P. J. Hobbs.* 80

BRIGHT CORNER 5 br.m. Sit In The Corner (USA)–Bright Performance (Gala Performance (USA)) [1989/90 F16g 16g 17v^{5} a16g] small mare: fourth foal: dam in frame over hurdles and fences: poor form in novice hurdles. *R. G. Frost.* 66

BRIGHT DANCER 5 ch.m. Move Off–Toadpool (Pongee) [1989/90 16f*] unfurnished mare: successful in novice hurdle at Newcastle (wore crossed noseband) in October, quickening to lead after 2 out and beating Kharif 6 lengths (tended to edge left run-in): had shown ability previous season. *Mrs G. R. Reveley.* 87 +

BRIGHT HONEY 10 ch.m. Duc d'Orleans–Honey Bright (Right Boy) [1989/90 a16g] little worthwhile form over hurdles. *B. Richmond.* —

BRIGHT HOUR 5 ro.g. Kabour–Amber Vale (Warpath) [1989/90 16m] lengthy gelding: showed a little ability in NH Flat races: no worthwhile form over hurdles, including in a seller. *D. W. Chapman.* —

BRIGHT INTERVALS 8 br.g. Condorcet (FR)–Sun Spray (Nice Guy) [1989/90 c20g^{pu} c22m^{F} c20f^{pu}] medium-sized gelding: fairly useful chaser at best: ran poorly in 1989/90: stays 2½m: acts on good to firm and soft going: headstrong: suited by sharp track: usually jumps well: has worn a tongue strap. *C. P. E. Brooks.* c— —

BRIGHTLING BOY 5 ch.g. Deep Run–Susan La Salle (Master Owen) [1989/90 F16f F16f^{3}] non-thoroughbred gelding: first foal: dam poor maiden hurdler in Ireland: 15 lengths third behind Croghan Rose in NH Flat race at Huntingdon in May: yet to race over hurdles or fences. *D. M. Grissell.*

BRIGHT-ONE 5 b.m. Electric–Lady Doubloon (Pieces of Eight) [1989/90 16f* 16m^{4} 16f*] quite modest maiden on Flat, stays 1¼m: won novice hurdles at Southwell in August and Sedgefield following month: reportedly broke blood vessel in between: acts on firm going. *J. G. FitzGerald.* 84

BRIGHT SAPPHIRE 4 b.g. Mummy's Pet–Bright Era (Artaius (USA)) [1989/90 16f^{2} 16m^{3} 16m^{4} 16m^{2} a16g^{6} 17d^{5}] small, sparely-made gelding: selling hurdler: good second to Norquay in handicap at Uttoxeter fourth start: better effort afterwards on final start: wore a hood third start: acts on good to firm ground: changed hands 3,300 gns Ascot December Sales. *D. Burchell.* 81

BRIG'S GAZELLE 8 b.m. Lord Nelson (FR)–Cliburn New Cut (New Brig) [1989/90 c27g c16s^{6} c20g^{pu} 20f^{3} 16h^{5} 16f^{4} 16f^{5}] leggy, sparely-made mare: poor novice hurdler/chaser: stays 2½m: acts on hard and dead ground: usually amateur or claimer ridden. *I. Park.* c— 75 ?

BRILLIANT BAY 5 b.g. Hello Gorgeous (USA)–Cala-Vadella (Mummy's Pet) [1989/90 16m^{pu} 16g^{5} 16m^{5} 16f^{4}] compact gelding: poor novice hurdler: visored first start. *M. D. I. Usher.* 79

BRILLIANT WISH 7 b.g. Green Shoon–Shinaro (Straight Deal) [1989/90 20m^{3} 27g^{2} 20s^{3} 20d 24g^{4} a18g* a16g^{4} a16g^{4} 20f^{3}] leggy gelding: won novice 86 hurdle at Southwell in February: stays well: probably acts on any going. *R. F. Fisher.*

BRIMSTONE HILL 7 b.g. Dynastic–Trysting Day (Black Tarquin) [1989/90 20s4 16d] smallish, sturdy gelding: third in novice hurdle in 1988/9: bit backward when well beaten in similar events in 1989/90: should be suited by further than 2m. *Capt. T. A. Forster.* —

BRIMTO PANEDRY 5 b.g. Maculata–Miss Buck (Master Buck) [1989/90 16f 16gpu 20g a18g c20dpu c20gpu] smallish gelding: was of little account and probably temperamental to boot: dead. *P. J. Bevan.* c— —

BRINKSWAY 4 ch.c. Electric–Nom de Plume (Aureole) [1989/90 16m3] half-brother to fair 2m hurdler Topleigh (by High Top): plating-class maiden on Flat: third in juvenile hurdle at Perth in August: dead. *J. J. O'Neill.* 95

BRINKWATER 14 b.g. Super Slip–Yes Gail (Brilliant Gail) [1989/90 c16h* c16m* c16f* c20m*] workmanlike gelding: won 2 handicap chases at Plumpton and a selling handicap chase at Bangor (no bid) in August, and an amateur riders handicap chase at Huntingdon (finished alone) in September: stays 3m: acts on hard ground. *J. White.* c**101** —

BRITANNIA BELL 5 br.g. Pitskelly–Saintly Angel (So Blessed) [1989/90 16d6 16g2 16g4 17gF] sparely-made gelding: half-brother to winning selling hurdler Hallowed (by Wolver Hollow): modest miler on Flat, well beaten in 1989 (needs give in ground): in frame in novice hurdles at Uttoxeter and Warwick in December: beaten when falling heavily last in handicap at Doncaster following month: will prove best at a sharp 2m. *M. Brittain.* 95

BROAD BEAM 10 b.g. Averof–Angel Beam (SWE) (Hornbeam) [1989/90 c16m* c17f2 c16d3 c16g3 c16m3 c16s2 c16g2 c16g2 c17v4 c20d2 c16m6 c22m c18h2 c24g5 c16m2 c16m*] rangy, strongly-made gelding: inconsistent handicap chaser: won at Worcester in September and Stratford (easily by 20 lengths from Mr Quick) in June: stays 2½m: probably acts on any going: takes strong hold: finds little under pressure. *P. J. Hobbs.* c**124** § —

BROAD BRIDGE 4 b.f. Broadsword (USA)–Tye Bridge (Idiot's Delight) [1989/90 16fbd 16g] workmanlike filly: first reported foal: dam lightly-raced daughter of sister to useful staying chaser Bentley Boy: fair performer on Flat, winning over 5f at 2 yrs and in frame over 9f in 1989 (acts on hard ground): going well when brought down approaching 2 out in juvenile hurdle at Cheltenham in October: well beaten at Kempton later in month (jockey reported that the filly had lost her confidence after slipping going to the first): not seen out again. *J. R. Jenkins.* —

BROAD STREET 7 br.g. Balliol–Ballyarctic (Arcticeelagh) [1989/90 c21d2] rangy gelding: poor novice hurdler: in frame in novice chases, showing modest form: not raced after November: gives impression he'll prove best at up to 2½m: acts on good to firm and dead going. *A. D. Brown.* c87 —

BROADWELL 6 ch.g. Floriferous–Dromos (Cracksman) [1989/90 20spu] rangy gelding: little sign of ability in 2 novice hurdles. *Capt. T. A. Forster.* —

BROCHE (FR) 9 b.g. Nonoalco (USA)–Tyrant's Vale (FR) (Tyrant (USA)) [1989/90 c16m2 c16m3 c17m5 c20gF c24m2 c20spu c16gF] lengthy gelding: selling hurdler: modest chaser: fell fatally at Wincanton in January: best form at around 2m: acted on hard going (unsuited by soft). *Mrs H. Parrott.* c97 —

BROCKHILL BOY 8 b.g. Paddy Boy–Well Endowed (Meldrum) [1989/90 c20s2 c22s* c20d* c24dur c25fur] strong gelding: fourth foal: dam, poor novice hurdler, is daughter of a moderate staying chaser: second in 2 point-to-points in 1989: won novice hunter chases at Nottingham and Ludlow: in lead when unseating rider at Ayr (3 out) and Cheltenham (6 out): stays 2¾m: acts on soft going. *Edward Wood.* c96

BROCTUNE GREY 6 gr.m. Warpath–Hitesca (Tesco Boy) [1989/90 26d* 24g6 21d 25f] small, plain, sparely-made mare: in good form on Flat in 1989 and made a winning reappearance over hurdles in Lang Whang Hurdle at Ayr in November: below her best in handicaps afterwards: stays very well: acts on firm ground and dead going. *Mrs G. R. Reveley.* 118

BRODERIE ANGLAISE 4 b.f. Night Shift (USA)–Emblazon (Wolver Hollow) [1989/90 16f2] leggy filly: placed over 1m on Flat: sold out of Lord John FitzGerald's stable 5,600 gns Newmarket December Sales: always-prominent second in juvenile fillies selling hurdle at Wolverhampton (pulled hard) in March: should improve. *J. Ringer.* 74

BROKEN BRAE 6 b.g. Silly Prices–Penny Pink (Spartan General) [1989/90 16d 16g] has stringhalt: second in NH Flat race in 1987/8: behind both outings in novice hurdles. *C. Parker.* —

BROKEN FLIGHT 13 b.g. Busted–Shortwood (Skymaster) [1989/90 c20s^bd] smallish, lengthy gelding: selling hurdler: fair winning point-to-pointer/selling chaser: would probably have finished second but for being brought down 2 out in amateur riders handicap at Folkestone in January: probably needs further than 2m and stays 2¾m: acts on any going: sometimes blinkered (including when successful): good mount for an inexperienced rider. *J. D. J. Davies.* c— —

BROKEN LINE 4 br.g. Dara Monarch–Bustina (FR) (Busted) [1989/90 17m^F 16g 16g^6 16s^5 20f* 16g] sparely-made gelding: modest maiden on Flat: sold out of P. Cole's stable 5,600 gns Newmarket July Sales: improved form when winning selling handicap hurdle (no bid) at Uttoxeter in April: suited by 2½m and firm ground. *W. Clay.* 80

BROKERS CHOICE 8 ch.g. Malinowski (USA)–Mehudenna (Ribero) [1989/90 16s 17d] workmanlike gelding: novice selling hurdler: tailed off in non-sellers in 1989/90: no form in 2 novice chases in 1987/8: best run at 2m on dead ground. *T. W. Donnelly.* c— —

BROMPTON ROAD 7 b.g. Derring Rose–London Gem (London Gazette) [1989/90 17f^4 25g^2 22d^5 24s* 22v* 24g^2 20s^2 25m^pu] workmanlike gelding: handicap hurdler: won at Bangor in December (made all) and Ayr in January: pulled up lame final start: whipped round and unseated rider at start once in 1988/9: stays 3m: acts on heavy going: game. *D. Moffatt.* 112

BRONZE EFFIGY 8 ch.g. Vaigly Great–Sea Fern (Klondyke Bill) [1989/90 c22d^3 c21d^6 c24v^pu c25s^2 c24d^pu c25f^pu] small, leggy gelding: winning hurdler/novice chaser: never travelling well last 2 outings: suited by a good test of stamina: best form with give in the ground: good mount for an amateur. *M. Henriques.* c99 —

BRONZE FINAL 7 br.g. Track Spare–Bronze Foliage (Bois Le Roi) [1989/90 c20m^F c21m* c21f^ur c21d^3 c20d^F c20d^F c20m^F] leggy, close-coupled gelding: winning hurdler: won novice chase at Wincanton in October: had just taken lead when falling last in handicap at Huntingdon in April on final start: stays 21f: acts on good to firm and dead ground: makes mistakes. *J. T. Gifford.* c**109** x —

BRONZE HEAD 12 b.g. Bronze Hill–Linnhead (Lauso) [1989/90 c20d^3 c27m^4 c24g* c24d^3] smallish, sparely-made gelding: hunter chaser: led from halfway when winning at Kelso in March: good third behind very easy winner Mystic Music at Perth in May: suited by a good test of stamina: has won on heavy ground but better form under less testing conditions. *A. G. Bonas.* c**106** —

BRONZEKNOWE 11 b.g. Bronze Hill–Naughty Tara (Black Tarquin) [1989/90 c24f* c24d^6] winning point-to-pointer: won hunter chase at Kelso in April by a short head from Northern Meadow: always behind in similar race next time: stays 3m: acts on any going. *W. Hamilton.* c**99**

BROOKENFIELD 5 ch.g. Town And Country–Classic Lady (Gratitude) [1989/90 aF16g aF16g 16m 16d 22g 16f] lengthy gelding: ninth reported foal: half-brother to winning selling hurdler Classic Owen (by Owen Anthony): dam won twice over 5f at 2 yrs as Cool In The Pool: well beaten in NH Flat races and novice hurdles. *J. R. Jenkins.* —

BROOKMOUNT 8 ch.g. Bonne Noel–Neater (Double Jump) [1989/90 c21m^3 c20f^F] tall, good sort: useful chaser: third of 5 to Toby Tobias in minor chase at Wincanton in December: suffered a fatal fall at Cheltenham in March: took keen hold and appeared not to stay 2½m: best form with give in the ground. *J. T. Gifford.* c**135** —

BROOKSIDE KING 10 ch.g. True Song–Spartan Clover (Spartan General) [1989/90 c24m^ur c26m^3] lengthy, plain gelding: winning point-to-pointer/hunter chaser: in lead when unseating rider 2 out at Fakenham in May: far from disgraced when remote third to Mystic Music in Horse And Hound Cup at Stratford in June, best effort: suited by a test of stamina: probably acts on any going. *H. Hutsby.* c**114**

BROOKTINO 5 b.g. Neltino–Binney Brook (Roman Warrior) [1989/90 16g 16g^6 16d 16d] lengthy, sparely-made gelding: staying maiden on Flat (has worn a visor): novice hurdler: ran well when remote sixth behind Sudden Victory at Kempton in January: well beaten next start, and below his best final outing (February). *Mrs P. Sly.* 92 ?

BROTHER ANDREW 4 ch.g. Sandalay–Dusky Smile (Dusky Boy) [1989/90 F16g] sixth foal: dam won 2½m hurdle in Ireland: behind throughout in NH Flat race at Market Rasen in April: yet to race over hurdles. *W. A. Stephenson.*

BROUGHTON MANOR 5 b.m. Dubassoff (USA)–Welcome Honey (Be Friendly) [1989/90 17m5 17fpu 17m3] second reported foal: half-sister to a poor Flat performer by Drumrunie: dam won 1m claiming race: yet to complete course in point-to-points (refused once): 2¾ lengths third behind Father John in poor maiden hurdle at Newton Abbot. *Mrs J. G. Retter.* 68

BROWN BEAR BOY (USA) 8 b.g. San Feliou (FR)–Gabriele (USA) (Protanto (USA)) [1989/90 16f4 17f2 16m2 16f4 16f4 20f2 20m3] compact, workmanlike gelding: poor handicap hurdler: not raced after October: acts on firm going: sold 675 gns Ascot April Sales. *Miss S. J. Wilton.* 91

BROWN BLAZER 12 b.g. Rugantino–Miss Ormond (Vulgan) [1989/90 c26f c26f5] lengthy gelding: no worthwhile form in novice hurdles or steeplechases, but has been placed in point-to-points: blinkered final outing 1984/5. *D. A. Cundle.* c— —

BROWNHILL LASS 9 ch.m. Sunyboy–Miss Craigie (New Brig) [1989/90 c24g3 c24s5 c17d5 c24v* c24vpu c24dpu] lengthy, workmanlike mare: moderate chaser: beat only other finisher in quite valuable handicap at Ayr in February: had very stiff task next outing, but ran poorly on final start: ideally suited by further than 2m nowadays and stays 3m well: acts on heavy going. *R. H. Goldie.* **c102** —

BROWN PEPPER 4 b.g. Sharpo–Petrary (Petingo) [1989/90 16s2 16s2 16v2] neat gelding: placed at up to 1m on Flat: made much of running when second in 3 races over hurdles at Folkestone, on final start beaten 5 lengths by easy winner Sharpgun in juvenile event in January: should win a race over hurdles. *R. Akehurst.* 95

BROWN RIFLE 10 bl.g. Scottish Rifle–Mother Brown (Candy Cane) [1989/90 a16g3 16g6 16v3 16s3 a18g2] small, narrow gelding: modest hurdler: placed in claimers last 3 starts: not raced after February: barely stays 2½m: possibly unsuited by very firm ground, acts on any other. *D. Burchell.* 92

BROWNSIDE BRIG 5 b.g. Goldhill–Tumlin Brig (New Brig) [1989/90 F13d F16g 16g4] first foal: dam in frame in NH Flat race in Ireland: behind in 2 NH Flat races: well-beaten fourth of 5 in novice hurdle at Catterick. *J. S. Haldane.* —

BROWN SMASHER 7 br.g. Proverb–Brown Rum (Le Tricolore) [1989/90 F16g 24dpu 24dsu 24fpu] big, angular gelding: fifth reported foal: half-brother to winning chasers Bargello Son (by Bargello) and The Royal Comrie (by Master Buck): dam sister to winning chaser: tailed off when pulled up in novice hurdles (pulls hard). *A. P. James.* —

BROWN WINDSOR 8 b.g. Kinglet–Cauldron (Kabale) [1989/90 c20g* c26f2 c24d3 c26g2 c20f* c36f4] **c150** —

Brown Windsor's hard race in the Whitbread Gold Cup as a seven-year-old novice did him no harm. He went close to more big-handicap wins over fences in the latest season, besides winning a feature event at the Cheltenham Festival—the Cathcart Challenge Cup—and finishing fourth in the Seagram Grand National. Although he wasn't seen out after Liverpool he again emerged unscathed, and he should pick up more races. Brown Windsor's main targets in 1990/1 are likely to be the same as they were in 1989/90, the Hennessy Cognac Gold Cup at Newbury and the National; as then, his other appearances may be rather limited in number. Apparently he tends to get shin-sore with racing. Whenever that happens, usually around Christmas, he is given a break from training and brought back a fresh horse in the spring. Brown Windsor made four starts and reached December 30th before his holiday this time, starting in an Arlington Premier Series Qualifier at Sandown which he won very easily from two opponents, and ending with the Save & Prosper Mandarin Handicap at Newbury which he lost narrowly to Polyfemus after a less fluent round of jumping than usual. In between had come the Hennessy and the SGB Handicap at Ascot, the one worth over £30,000 to the winner, the other worth over £26,000. As in the Mandarin, Brown Windsor went down by a neck in the Hennessy. He could be seen to be thriving physically and started 7/4 favourite in a substandard field, proven on firmish going and reasonably handicapped in the light of his Whitbread performance. He looked the winner as he moved up to challenge at the last but just couldn't contain Ghofar despite responding to pressure up to the line. This performance, his best up to that point (and arguably still the best of his career) was followed by one nearly as good in the SGB, on some of the season's first softish ground in the South. He finished third to 33/1-shot Solidasarock and Panto Prince, beaten five lengths and three quarters of a length, coming back at the first two from the last after they'd quickened the better when what had been a steadily-run affair had begun in earnest six out.

By the turn of the year Brown Windsor was beginning to look like a horse for whom a stiff test of stamina had become essential. However, when he was returned to the track in the spring the Cathcart was chosen (in preference to the Gold Cup) for his Grand National warm-up. 'This horse is no mug at two and a half miles', said the trainer beforehand. So it proved in a strongly-run race on top-of-the-ground. He jumped superbly tracking the leader Blueberry King. Turning for home, where Blueberry King had weakened, it seemed as though Multum In Parvo possessed the best finishing speed but Brown Windsor held on by a short head under strong driving. Obviously, a run of this nature by a proven stayer was a very encouraging trial, and he started 7/1 favourite at Liverpool handicapped right up to his best. For a young horse making his first acquaintance with the National course Brown Windsor ran creditably, given a copybook ride by John White who finished runner-up on the stable's The Tsarevich in 1987. The horse raced close up towards the inside; he jumped the fences extremely well apart from showing some hesitancy at the big third, and travelled smoothly until beginning to tire from second Valentine's; though beaten crossing the Melling Road, he stuck on gamely to keep Lastofthe-brownies out of the frame, more than thirty lengths behind Mr Frisk.

Brown Windsor (b.g. 1982)	Kinglet (b 1970)	Pampered King (b 1954)	Prince Chevalier
			Netherton Maid
		War Ribbon (br 1955)	Anwar
			Last Rank
	Cauldron (b 1969)	Kabale (b 1955)	Chamossaire
			Curia
		Cheerful Biddy (b 1961)	Buckhound
			Winsome Biddy

Brown Windsor is related to a horse who completed the course in three successive Nationals—his dam Cauldron is a half-sister to Biddy Hansel,

Cathcart Challenge Cup, Cheltenham—
Brown Windsor and Multum In Parvo (No. 9) take the last

Mr W. Shand Kydd's "Brown Windsor"

the maternal grandam of Attitude Adjuster, a highest-placed fifth in 1988. Cauldron was a good-looking staying hunter chaser. She won at Wolverhampton as a five-year-old ridden by Lord Oaksey, and at Folkestone as a six-year-old ridden by Brown Windsor's owner-breeder. The first of her three previous foals, Premier Charlie (by Prince de Galles), showed quite useful form over fences and was suited by two and a half miles or more. The grandam Cheerful Biddy never ran but produced several other winners, including the fairly useful hurdler Supathene, and was a half-sister to the top-class hunter chaser Some Man.

Brown Windsor is still on the leggy side but is quite an attractive individual. As a racehorse he is a very handy type to have in the stable—one good enough to get in the weights in most of the best handicaps in the country, able to win at two and a half miles given a strong enough pace and to stay extreme distances, a fine jumper able to act on firm going and good to soft. The doubts about his ability to act on very soft mentioned in the previous *Chasers & Hurdlers* arise from his below-par performance behind Pragada in the 1988 Coral Golden Handicap Hurdle Final at Cheltenham. *N. J. Henderson.*

BRUFF ACADEMY 9 b. or br.g. Crash Course–My Dayan (Palestine) c— [1989/90 c17m c20m5 c16d] tall gelding: has stringhalt: handicap chaser: well below his best in 1989/90: best form at around 2m: acts on firm going: sometimes amateur or claimer ridden. *R. Paisley.*

BRULEE 6 b.m. Balinger–Rough Crossing (Deep Run) [1989/90 16g a16g]
small, workmanlike mare: no form over hurdles. *Mrs E. H. Heath.* —

BRUNI BABY (FR) 9 bl.g. Bruni–Amicable (USA) (Bold Ruler) [1989/90 **c74**
c20f^{F} c16m^{4} c20m^{3} c25m^{ur} 18f^{2} 20f^{2} 20f^{3}] leggy, good-topped gelding: usually 88
looks well: novice hurdler: finished lame at Cheltenham in October final start:
handicap chaser: ran moderately in 1989/90: probably stays 3m: acts on firm
going: blinkered last 3 starts over fences in 1988/9. *J. B. Sayers.*

BRUNONI 6 b.m. Ovac (ITY)–Bramble Leaf (Even Money) [1989/90 16d^{pu}
a18g^{2} a16g^{2}] close-coupled mare: second in 2 novice handicap hurdles at Lingfield 72
in March, beaten 3 lengths by Distant Relation on final outing: stays 2¼m. *P. G. Bailey.*

BRUNTON PARK 12 b.g. Raise You Ten–Sister Drake (Dicta Drake) **c112**
[1989/90 c24f^{2} c24m^{3}] rangy gelding: fair chaser: good second in handicap chase —
at Southwell in September: ran moderately later in month: stays well: probably
acts on any going: good jumper. *J. R. Jenkins.*

BRUSSELS SPROUTS 8 ch.g. Kambalda–Sandcast (Sandford Lad) [1989/90 c—
c20d^{pu}] ex-Irish gelding: winning hurdler/chaser at up to 2¼m: no form for a long —
time: acts on heavy going. *K. C. Bailey.*

BRYANSBI 6 b.m. Golden Passenger–Psidium's Gal (Psidium) [1989/90
17d^{pu}] fifth living foal: dam winning hurdler, stayed 19f: no sign of ability in novice —
hurdles. *J. A. B. Old.*

BRYMA 10 b. or br.g. Rymer–Saucy Walk (Saucy Kit) [1989/90 c20v c21g c—
c20d^{pu} c24m^{F}] lengthy gelding: winning chaser: led until headed and falling last —
at Chepstow in April: barely stayed 3m when conditions were testing: probably
acted on any going: successful with and without blinkers: usually raced up with
pace: didn't always go through with his effort: dead. *B. Palling.*

BRYN FLIER 5 b.g. Shaab–Chingley Lass (Entanglement) [1989/90 17f^{4}]
half-brother to novice hurdler Broad Wood (by I'm Alright Jack): dam, winner —
over hurdles and fences, stayed well: 25/1 and claimer ridden, always behind when
distant last of 4 in novice hurdle at Newton Abbot in July (running subject of
stewards inquiry, trainer fined £125 for schooling in public): not seen out again:
sold 2,700 gns Doncaster September Sales. *D. C. Jermy.*

BRYN TANGLE 11 b.m. Peter Wrekin–Phigaro's Tangle (Tangle) [1989/90 c—
c17g^{5}] leggy, plain mare: placed in point-to-points: well beaten both starts in
steeplechases. *R. G. Frost.*

BUBBLING BROOK 8 b.g. Paddy's Stream–Airport Miss (Levanter)
[1989/90 20m 25f^{ur}] close-coupled, good-bodied gelding: winning point-to- —
pointer: poor maiden over hurdles: probably stayed 3m: seemed to act on any
going: dead. *P. F. Craggs.*

BUCHANAN (USA) 15 gr.g. Dancer's Image (USA)–Fiery Diplomat (USA) c—
(Diplomat Way) [1989/90 c16f^{pu} 17m*] compact gelding: selling hurdler: beat ?
Bushy Bay a head in match at Cartmel in August: poor form over fences: stays
2¼m: seems to act on any going: blinkered once: often races with tongue tied
down. *M. C. Chapman.*

BUCK AND SKIP 6 ch.g. Buckskin (FR)–Cool Amanda (Prince Hansel) c—
[1989/90 c16g^{F} c21d^{pu} 21d 21d^{pu}] rather sparely-made, angular gelding: fifth —
living foal: half-brother to winning jumpers Captain Lowe (by Mon Capitaine),
Auspiciousoccasion (by Deep Run) and Earl Hansel (by Hardboy): dam unraced:
no sign of ability. *J. S. King.*

BUCKANNARA 5 ch.g. Baptism–Penny Maes (Welsh Saint) [1989/90 17m^{pu}]
behind in NH Flat races: pulled up lame after 2 out in novice hurdle at Cartmel in —
August. *I. Semple.*

BUCKBY FOLLY 8 br.m. Netherkelly–Pavement Artist (Tiepolo II) [1989/90 **c91**
c20g^{3} c21d^{bd}] big, workmanlike mare: winning hurdler: novice chaser: staying-on —
third behind Radical Lady in mares event at Newcastle in January, giving
impression would have won ridden closer to the pace (left with a lot to do after a
mistake at the tenth): stays 2½m: acts on soft going: capable of winning over
fences but needs to improve her jumping. *M. J. Camacho.*

BUCKFAST ABBEY 10 ch.g. Deep Run–High School (Even Money) **c124**
[1989/90 c17m* c16f* c16g*] big, lengthy gelding: much improved and won —
early-season handicap chases at Huntingdon, Cheltenham and Kempton, beating
Thar-An-Bharr ¾ length on last-named course: races only at around 2m: seems

to act on any going: ridden by claimer: has reportedly broken blood vessels. *P. W. Harris.*

BUCKHORN 11 ch.g. Bladon–Cottage Myth (Rhythmic) [1989/90 c20f* c16fF] robust gelding: won a point-to-point in March and hunter chase at Ascot (by a length from Purnago) in April: fell seventh next time: stays 25f: acts on firm and dead going. *R. H. Buckler.* c**111**

BUCKO 13 b. or br.g. Royal Buck–Tame Cindy (No Argument) [1989/90 c20d6 c24vpu c22mpu] big, strong, slightly-dipped backed gelding: one-time very useful chaser: ran a moody race second outing: pulled up after being hampered at the third final start: stays 25f (well beaten over further): acts on soft going: usually blinkered nowadays: free-running sort, suited by forcing tactics. *J. G. FitzGerald.* c— —

BUCKOAK 8 br.g. Buckskin (FR)–Tycoonello (Tycoon II) [1989/90 21m6 20vsu] lengthy gelding: little sign of ability in novice hurdles. *D. Williams.* —

BUCKS GREEN 12 b.g. Owen Anthony–Belle Arc (Archive) [1989/90 c26f2] strong, compact gelding: modest handicap chaser when trained by J. Gifford: well beaten in 2 point-to-points and finished 25 lengths second of 4 in hunter chase in 1989/90: stays 3m: acts on any going. *D. V. Cornelius.* c**67** —

BUCKSHEE BOY 8 ch.g. Buckskin (FR)–Old Hand (Master Owen) [1989/90 22g 24g5 c20g* c24s5] lengthy, rather sparely-made gelding: handicap hurdler: 33/1, made successful debut over fences in 10-runner handicap at Newbury in December, jumping soundly in the main, staying on strongly to lead in closing stages and win going away by 2 lengths from Clara Mountain: well beaten in valuable novice event won by Royal Athlete at Ascot in February: reportedly suffered leg trouble afterwards: stays 3m: acts on soft going and is possibly unsuited by firm: blinkered final start over hurdles: jumps hurdles very well. *J. Pilkington.* c**121** —

BUCKSSIV 4 b.f. Buckskin (FR)–Shenton Park (Indigenous) [1989/90 F16f] seventh foal: dam placed over hurdles in Ireland: behind in NH Flat race at Cheltenham: yet to race over hurdles. *A. P. James.*

BUCKSWILL 6 b.g. Liboi (USA)–Berganza (Grey Sovereign) [1989/90 16g5 18g2 16m 18g 16d 16gF 16f6 a20g6] small, angular gelding: novice selling hurdler: stays 2¼m: best form with give in the ground: visored eighth start 1988/9. *Mrs Barbara Waring.* 77

BUCK TO 5 b.m. Buckskin (FR)–Laurebon (Laurence O) [1989/90 F14v] first reported foal: dam winning Irish hurdler: tailed off in NH Flat race at Ayr: yet to race over hurdles or fences. *R. H. Goldie.*

BUDDINGTON 5 b.g. Celtic Cone–Goolagong (Bargello) [1989/90 16d3 16g5 16s6] rangy gelding with plenty of scope: sixth foal: half-brother to a poor animal by Mandrake Major: dam, quite a useful staying hurdler/chaser, is sister to useful chaser Lord Browndodd: modest form in novice hurdles: shapes like a stayer and will be very well suited by longer distances. *Capt. T. A. Forster.* 91

BUDDY HOLLY (NZ) 5 b.g. Leader of The Band (USA)–Annie Day (NZ) (Battle-Waggon) [1989/90 F16g 16g 22g3 22s] compact, workmanlike gelding: remote third in conditional jockeys novice hurdle at Wolverhampton in January: well beaten on much softer ground following month: will stay further than 2¾m. *N. J. Henderson.* 83

BUILDERS GOLD 4 b.c. On Your Mark–Linanbless (So Blessed) [1989/90 17m4 16f6 17h*] rather sparely-made colt: plating-class maiden on Flat: easily beat sole opponent in juvenile hurdle at Carlisle in October: ran poorly when blinkered second start. *J. J. O'Neill.* 83 ?

BUILDMARK 4 ch.f. Longleat (USA)–Crescentia (Crepello) [1989/90 16g] leggy, sparely-made filly: placed over 1¼m on Flat in October: weakened quite badly in straight when well beaten in juvenile maiden hurdle at Wincanton in February. *W. G. M. Turner.* —

BULLET TRAIN 7 ch.g. Paddy's Stream–Irish Beauty (Even Money) [1989/90 c20g5 c16d2 c20gpu] rangy gelding: winning hurdler: 10 lengths second to Mercurius in novice handicap chase at Ayr in January: tailed off when pulled up in similar event at Bangor in April: stays 2½m (pulled hard and weakened 4 out when tried over 2¾m): acts on dead going: claimer ridden: sold privately out of J. Parkes's stable 4,000 gns Doncaster March Sales. *Mrs S. J. Smith.* c85 —

BULLY BOY 7 ch.g. Margouillat (FR)–Chere Madame (Karabas) [1989/90 c17m* c16f* c17d4 c16g2 c17m2] angular, sparely-made gelding: poor novice hurdler: made all in handicap chase at Huntingdon and novice handicap at c**91** —

Edinburgh in December: in frame in novice handicaps at Huntingdon (2) and Edinburgh afterwards: keen front runner, unlikely to stay beyond 17f: acts on firm going: trained until after fourth start by W. Brooks. *D. W. Browne.*

BUMBLES FOLLY (NZ) 9 ch.g. Sea Anchor–Casurina (NZ) (Oakville) [1989/90 c24d2 c27g5 c27s* c25g4 c26v*] compact, workmanlike gelding: fair chaser: won handicaps at Taunton in December and Fontwell (ridden by 7-lb claimer, beat Mountaico 4 lengths) in February: stays 27f: suited by plenty of give in the ground. *D. H. Barons.* c**119** —

BUMPTIOUS BOY 6 b.g. Neltino–Bellardita (Derring-Do) [1989/90 16g4 16d4 17g4 16m* 16mF 16m2 16m5] compact gelding: won handicap hurdle at Wincanton in April: good second at Stratford following month: ran moderately final outing: should stay beyond 2m: acts on good to firm ground. *A. J. Wilson.* 96

BURANNPOUR 10 br.g. Wolver Hollow–Bubunia (Wild Risk) [1989/90 c24gpu c25s6 c29dpu c24dpu] tall, narrow gelding: useful chaser in 1987/8: no form in 1989/90: needs a good test of stamina: used to go well in the mud: sometimes makes mistakes: visored final outing. *G. B. Balding.* c— —

BURGLARS WALK 10 b.g. Godswalk (USA)–Pay Roll (Burglar) [1989/90 c24g3 c26g2 c20spu] lengthy, angular gelding: modest hurdler/chaser at his best: remote second of 3 over fences in October: badly hampered at the seventh 2 months later: stays 3m: acts well on top-of-the-ground: usually bandaged behind: often fails to impress in paddock. *R. Curtis.* c? —

BURGOYNE 4 b.g. Ardross–Love Match (USA) (Affiliate (USA)) [1989/90 20g2 16s2 21s5] medium-sized gelding: brother to novice hurdler Ard T'Match: dam, ran twice, from family of top German horses Neckar and Naxos: won 2 claimers at around 1½m on Flat in October (claimed out of H. Cecil's stable £21,001 after second occasion): 3 lengths second to Sayyure in juvenile hurdle at Kempton in December: well below that form on soft ground afterwards: stays 2½m. *M. H. Easterby.* 108

BURGUNDY 11 b.g. Bustino–Land of Fire (Buisson Ardent) [1989/90 24mpu] light-bodied gelding: winning hurdler: pulled up lame last 2 outings: stays well: yet to race on very firm ground, acts on any other. *C. J. T. Alexander.* —

BURKES PROGRESS 4 b. or br.f. Tyrnavos–Pushkar (Northfields (USA)) [1989/90 a16g4 a20g2 a16g2 16f6] plating-class 7f winner on Flat when trained by R. O'Leary: runner-up in juvenile hurdles at Southwell in February (seller) and March: soon outpaced in conditional jockeys selling handicap at Newcastle later in month: stays 2½m: sold 1,500 gns Doncaster March Sales. *T. D. Barron.* 77

BURNDITCH BOY 11 b.g. More Music–Tummel (Lord Fox) [1989/90 c27m2] leggy, sparely-made gelding: winning hurdler and novice chaser: poor form in point-to-points: ridden along most of way when 12 lengths second to Edenspring in hunter chase at Sedgefield in March: needs a good test of stamina: acts well in the mud: jumps deliberately: tends to race in snatches and needs plenty of driving: refused penultimate start 1987/8. *Peter Sawney.* c**89** § —

BURNING BRIGHT 7 b.g. Star Appeal–Lead Me On (King's Troop) [1989/90 22g4] rather leggy, sparely-made gelding: winning stayer on Flat in 1990: showed ability in novice event at Folkestone in December on second start over hurdles. *R. Curtis.* 78

BURNSWARK 9 b.g. Cagirama–Madam Law (Manicou) [1989/90 c20s5 c24dpu c27f3] smallish, sparely-made gelding: novice hurdler: fair winning point-to-pointer: poor novice hunter chaser. *Miss L. I. McBride.* c**80** —

BURNT FINGERS 6 ch.g. Busted–Madame's Share (Major Portion) [1989/90 20s2 16s] lengthy gelding: quite modest staying handicapper on Flat, successful twice in 1989: second in novice event at Bangor in December, better effort over hurdles: will stay 3m. *J. White.* 94

BURTONWOODS BEST 4 b.g. Longleat (USA)–Abbey Rose (Lorenzaccio) [1989/90 a16g3 a16g2 a16g3 a20g*] rather leggy, angular gelding: plating-class maiden on Flat, stays 8.5f: claimer ridden, successful in novice hurdle at Southwell in January by neck from Valiant Boy, pair well clear: bought out of W. Haigh's stable 5,500 gns after finishing second in seller on same course previous month: stays 2½m. *T. Kersey.* 90 +

BUSH GUIDE 14 b.g. Flatbush–Guide Post (Guide) [1989/90 c24m5] strong, compact gelding: one-time fairly useful chaser: placed in point-to-points in 1990: over 20 lengths fifth to Ready Steady in hunter chase at Newcastle in March: well c**87**

suited by a good test of stamina: probably acts on any going: game front runner: jumps soundly: wears bandages behind. *Mrs V. S. Jackson.*

BUSH MAID 7 ch.m. Flatbush–Sewing Maid (So Blessed) [1989/90 16g 16d^4 27s 20g^6 20d] small, sturdy mare: poor novice selling hurdler: sold 1,300 gns Ascot April Sales. *P. Liddle.* 58

BUSHY BAY 16 b.g. Polyfoto–Latest Bird (Pardal) [1989/90 17m^2] lengthy gelding: poor selling hurdler: head second to Buchanan in match at Cartmel in August: no form over fences (jumps poorly): stays 23f: sometimes wears blinkers or a visor. *M. C. Chapman.* c— x ?

BU-SOFYAN 6 b.g. Runnett–London Spin (Derring-Do) [1989/90 16g^{pu}] smallish, angular gelding: fair winner at up to 1m on Flat: no form over hurdles. *M. Madgwick.* —

BUSORM 10 ch.g. Bustino–Wrekinianne (Reform) [1989/90 16g^{pu} 16m^{pu}] small gelding: seems of little account nowadays. *M. C. Chapman.* —

BUSTAMENTE 7 b.g. Busted–Blessed Damsel (So Blessed) [1989/90 22v 22d^3 21s^5 21d^4] workmanlike gelding: modest novice hurdler: will stay 3m. *J. White.* 92

BUSTED SPRING 9 b.g. Crash Course–Rose of Spring (Golden Vision) [1989/90 c20f* c20m^4 c24m^2 c20f^2 c20h^2 c24g^{ur} c25m^3 c20f^{ur} c24f^{pu} c20g^{pu} c22m^{pu} c20d^3] big gelding: poor novice hurdler: won poorly-contested novice chase at Bangor in August: soundly beaten afterwards, jumping moderately: stays 2½m: acts on firm ground. *K. White.* **c80** x —

BUSTEELE 6 b.g. Bustino–Narration (USA) (Sham (USA)) [1989/90 16f^{pu}] fourth in NH Flat race at Warwick in 1989: second favourite, made mistakes and behind when pulled up in novice hurdle at Taunton in March. *N. J. Henderson.* —

BUSY MITTENS 9 ch.m. Nearly A Hand–Busy Buskins (Little Buskins) [1989/90 c20s^5 c16v c20g^4 c17d^F c16f^{pu}] leggy, rather sparely-made mare: modest novice hurdler: poor novice chaser: stays 2½m: acts on heavy going: blinkered twice in 1988/9 (ran in snatches on one occasion) and final 3 outings. *M. McCourt.* c**73** —

BUTLERS PET 11 b.g. Mummy's Pet–Reluctant Maid (Relko) [1989/90 c16d^4 c20g^{pu} c16m^{bd} c19d^{pu} c17v^3 c16d* c16d^2 c16g^6] rangy gelding: moderate chaser: edged left close home when winning handicap at Nottingham in February: again hung left under pressure when second in similar race at Stratford later in month: ran moderately final start: stays 17f: acts on any going. *T. B. Hallett.* c**103** —

BUTLERS WHARF 5 b.g. Burslem–Regal Promise (Pitskelly) [1989/90 16m 16f^F] lengthy, workmanlike gelding: untrustworthy middle-distance handicapper on Flat, when trained by D. Morley: behind in novice hurdles in October and March (looked reluctant to jump and fell 2 out). *R. Hollinshead.* —

BUTT AND BEN 6 b.g. Crofter (USA)–Aileen's Belle (The Parson) [1989/90 c16g^4 c20d^{pu} c20m^6] rangy gelding: handicap hurdler: poor form in novice chases: will prove best at around 2m. *F. Walwyn.* c**74** —

BUZZARDS CREST 5 ch.g. Buzzards Bay–Diamond Talk (Counsel) [1989/90 16d 16s^{pu}] close-coupled gelding: half-brother to several winners, including winning hurdler Corn Street (by Decoy Boy): 7f winner at 2 yrs but lightly raced and little form on Flat subsequently: no sign of ability in novice hurdle and a claimer: barely stays 2m. *H. J. Collingridge.* —

BWANA KALI 8 b.g. Kala Shikari–Modom (Compensation) [1989/90 16h^3 17h^2 20m 16d^6 16f^6 16f* 16s a16g^3 a16s^{pu}] close-coupled gelding: won novice handicap hurdle at Warwick in December: pulled up and dismounted after last final start (January): poor novice over fences: best form at around 2m on a sound surface. *J. A. Bennett.* c— 72

BY CHOICE 4 ch.g. Sallust–Jamie's Girl (Captain James) [1989/90 16f^F 16f^4 16f] small, sparely-made gelding: won 1¼m claimers on Flat in June (claimed out of R. J. R. Williams' stable £12,010) and July: poor form over hurdles, including in a seller: not raced after October: sold 4,100 gns Newmarket Autumn Sales. *N. Tinkler.* 62

BY LINE 6 b.m. High Line–Mount Hala (Mount Hagen (FR)) [1989/90 16m* 17h* 19h*] tall mare: shows traces of stringhalt: modest hurdler: successful in early-season handicaps at Worcester, Devon & Exeter (idled in front) and Taunton: stays 19f: acts on hard ground: headstrong: has sweated badly on occasions: blinkered third start 1988/9. *F. Walwyn.* 98

C

CABALLINE 6 ch.g. Last Fandango–Rosalia (Tower Walk) [1989/90 18f4 22g4 20g 22g4 18g c18spu] leggy gelding: tubed: winning hurdler: ran creditably first 2 starts, but well below form afterwards, including in sellers: tailed off when pulled up in novice event on chasing debut: stays 2¾m: best run on good ground. *M. J. Haynes.* c— 87 d

CABANAX 8 ch.g. Anax–Cabaletta (Double Jump) [1989/90 20mpu] strong, good-bodied gelding: lightly-raced winning hurdler: behind when pulled up lame before last in amateur riders handicap at Carlisle in November: should stay beyond 17f: acts on heavy going: amateur ridden. *Miss J. Salkeld.* —

CABBIE'S BOY 4 ch.g. Dublin Taxi–Petriva (Mummy's Pet) [1989/90 F16g 16f 16fpu] 2,100Y: first foal: dam unraced: no sign of ability in novice hurdle and a juvenile claimer (blinkered). *J. J. O'Neill.* —

CAB ON TARGET 4 br.g. Strong Gale–Smart Fashion (Carlburg) [1989/90 F16d*] second foal: dam, winner of NH Flat race in Ireland, sister to very smart staying chaser Everett and half-sister to several winning jumpers: won 21-runner NH Flat race at Kelso in February by 10 lengths from Over The Styx: yet to race over hurdles. *Mrs G. R. Reveley.*

CACHE FLEUR (FR) 4 ch.g. Kashneb (FR)–Blanche Fleur (FR) (Mont Blanc II) [1989/90 F16s* F16g5 F16f2] unfurnished gelding: dam lightly raced on Flat in France: made much of running when winning NH Flat race at Warwick in February: 15 lengths second to Piper's Son in similar event at Ascot in April: yet to race over hurdles. *M. C. Pipe.*

CADFORD GIRL 6 ch.m. Nearly A Hand–Claverton (Gold Form) [1989/90 22m4 25g 21f* 21v* 21v a24g2 22d 22d3 22g] small mare: won mares novice hurdle at Warwick and a novice handicap hurdle at Newton Abbot in December: best effort afterwards on penultimate start: probably stays 3m: acts on any going: well ridden by 7-lb claimer J. Neaves. *W. G. M. Turner.* 90

CAERNARVON ROYAL 5 ch.g. Main Reef–Berserk (Romulus) [1989/90 16f 16f2] small, light-framed gelding: winning sprinter on Flat: second in novice selling hurdle at Taunton in December: unlikely to stay much beyond 2m. *R. J. Hodges.* 75

CAFFIERI (USA) 7 b.g. Youth (USA)–Effeffvee (USA) (Tom Rolfe) [1989/90 c20v5 c17d6 c16vF] smallish, workmanlike gelding: modest hurdler: well beaten in novice chases: form only at 2m: acts on heavy going: wore blinkers last 4 starts 1987/8 (seems suited by them): good mount for a claimer. *J. R. Upson.* c— —

CAHERVILLAHOW 6 b. or br.g. Deep Run–Bargara (Bargello) [1989/90 c24g* c21g* c19d* c20vF c20v* c25m3] c**143** p —

The dearth of established good-class chasers trained in Ireland continues. Maid of Money has been retired to the paddocks; Hungary Hur, Weather The Storm and Wolf of Badenoch all died during the season; Super Furrow is approaching the veteran stage and Carvill's Hill is beset by training difficulties. All of which leaves the top Irish prizes wide open to challenges from enterprising British stables. However, the home defences will be bolstered next season by several very useful novices with the potential to take high rank over fences. Cahervillahow, Kiichi, Mixed Blends and The Committee all made the frame in top novice events in Britain in the latest season, and Blitzkreig and Welcome Pin showed very smart form in their native country, with such as Roc de Prince, Derrymore Boy and On The Other Hand close behind.

The lightly-raced Cahervillahow in particular looks a very good chaser in the making. Unbeaten in his first four completed outings over fences, he did very well to finish third behind Royal Athlete in the Mumm Club Novices' Chase at Liverpool in April. Jumping none too fluently, he came off the bridle after a very bad mistake at the twelfth then got back in touch before another mistake at the third last put paid to his chance; he stayed on to be beaten ten and a half lengths at the finish. Cahervillahow's earlier form on much softer ground entitles him to be regarded as one of the two best novices trained in Ireland along with Blitzkreig. He beat a good horse each time when winning run-of-the-mill novice chases at Clonmel (from Cloney Grange) and Thurles (by twelve lengths from Roc de Prince) in November.

*Irish National Hunt Novice Chase Series Final, Leopardstown—
Cahervillahow starts to go clear from The Committee*

But it was in the newly-instituted Irish National Hunt Novice Chase Series that Cahervillahow really showed his mettle. He got the better of one-time useful hurdler Welcome Pin by a length in a qualifier at Naas in January, the pair finishing fifteen lengths clear of On The Other Hand and chasing debutant Cloughtaney.

Cahervillahow again met On The Other Hand, winner of his next two starts, in the near IR £15,000 Final at Leopardstown the following month, the pair conceding weight all round. Cahervillahow had been under pressure when falling four out in a modest novice handicap at Gowran Park on his only subsequent outing and started co-second favourite at Leopardstown, behind The Committee who received 6 lb. For a long way the betting looked likely to prove an accurate guide, The Committee disputing the lead virtually from the start until taking it up two out, Cahervillahow having to be ridden to stay in touch at halfway. But staying on under pressure Cahervillahow took second place after the second last, gained the upper hand going to the final fence and kept on so strongly as to win by twelve lengths.

Cahervillahow (b.g. 1984)	Deep Run (ch 1966)	Pampered King (b 1954)	Prince Chevalier
			Netherton Maid
		Trial By Fire (ch 1958)	Court Martial
			Mitrailleuse
	Bargara (b 1972)	Bargello (b 1960)	Auriban
			Isabelle Brand
		Borgotara (b 1956)	Precipitation
			Musardise

Cahervillahow is a stayer who needed a strong gallop and testing conditions to win over two and a half miles at Leopardstown and is well worth a try over extreme distances. By contrast none of the unraced Bargara's other three produce to have won over hurdles or in steeple-chases, including Cahervillahow's full brother Bosphorus, have shown their form beyond two and a half miles, though the promising Mossgara (by Le Moss) shapes as though he'll stay further. The next two dams were both winners, Borgotara in a two-runner race over eleven furlongs, Musardise as a two-year-old in France and also in a two-mile novice chase in Britain seven years later. A light-bodied gelding, Cahervillahow was bought for IR 22,000 guineas at Ballsbridge as a three-year-old. He showed fair winning form over hurdles and, still relatively young and lightly raced, is sure to improve further over fences. Cahervillahow would be a likely contender for the Jameson Irish Grand National at Fairyhouse granted give in the ground—though not discredited, he looked ill at ease on the good to firm going at Liverpool. *M. F. Morris, Ireland.*

CAIRNCASTLE 5 b.g. Ardross–Brookfield Miss (Welsh Pageant) [1989/90
16g a20g^{6} 24d^{4} 20f^{5}] small, leggy gelding: modest winning stayer on Flat: sold out 103
of R. J. R. Williams' stable 7,000 gns Newmarket Autumn Sales: easily best effort in novice hurdles on third start: stays 3m. *J. White.*

CAJUN DANCER 6 ch.g. Cajun–Gay Folly (Wolver Hollow) [1989/90 16f 16f^{3}
16f^{5} 16f^{4} 16g^{5} a20g^{6} 16m^{3} a16g^{2} a16g^{3} a16g^{3} a16g^{3} a16g^{5}] lengthy gelding: novice 78
selling hurdler: placed numerous times: form only at 2m on a sound surface: visored last 4 outings: has looked reluctant under pressure. *J. L. Harris.*

CALABRESE 5 ch.g. Monsanto (FR)–Salsafy (Tudor Melody) [1989/90
20s^{3} 24g* 24g* 24s^{2} 24g^{3}] 147 p

Calabrese made great strides in his second season over hurdles and developed into a smart stayer. With only eight races over hurdles behind him, there is good reason to anticipate he'll improve further, and he should be a worthy replacement in the leading staying events for stable-companion Rustle, the 1989 Waterford Crystal Stayers' Hurdle winner who seems likely to be sent chasing. Calabrese's season began in December and ended in February. His best performances came in defeat on his last two outings. At Ascot on his penultimate start he confirmed himself a cut above an ordinary handicapper with a three-length second to Ryde Again in the Daily Telegraph Hurdle. Ryde Again had been beaten three lengths by Calabrese in the quite valuable Munns Electrical Handicap on the same course in January on their previous starts, and reopposed on a stone better terms in the Daily Telegraph Hurdle. Calabrese made Ryde Again pull out all the stops. After making his ground approaching the third last, he had closed right up behind Ryde Again going to the last. Dunwoody seemed to allow Calabrese to drift to his right in search of better ground after jumping that flight, but despite keeping on strongly, the horse couldn't quicken in the last hundred yards. Calabrese faced a stiff task in the R.O.A. Rendlesham

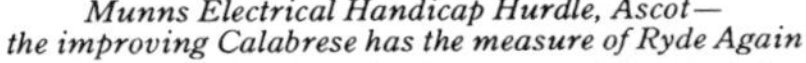

*Munns Electrical Handicap Hurdle, Ascot—
the improving Calabrese has the measure of Ryde Again*

Hurdle at Kempton towards the back-end of February, giving upwards of 4 lb to the likes of Slalom, Sprowston Boy, Miss Nero and Old Dundalk. He ran an excellent race to finish five and a half lengths third, unable to quicken at the last, behind Old Dundalk and Sprowston Boy, with the rest of the field ten lengths and more further back. Calabrese, a leggy, lengthy sort, always shaped like long distances would be his forte, never more so than when third to Propero in the two-and-a-half-mile Racing International Hurdle at Chepstow on his reappearance. Asked to tackle three miles for the first time on his next start, Calabrese easily justified favouritism in a modest handicap at Cheltenham. Calabrese has yet to race on top-of-the-ground and acts well on soft going.

Calabrese (ch.g. 1985)	Monsanto (FR) (b 1972)	Breton (b or br 1967)	Relko
			La Melba
		Moonmadness (ch 1963)	Tom Fool
			Sunset
	Salsafy (br 1972)	Tudor Melody (br 1956)	Tudor Minstrel
			Matelda
		Beetroot (ch 1965)	Psidium
			Beta

A 4,000-guinea yearling, Calabrese developed into a modest performer on the Flat, managing a single success in a mile-and-a-half maiden at Folkestone as a three-year-old. Bought out of Morley's stable for 21,000 guineas at the Newmarket Autumn Sales of that year, he won two of his three races as a juvenile hurdler for his new connections. Calabrese is the fourth winner out of the fair mile-and-a-half winner Salsafy, the others being Baz Bombati (by Sun Prince) who was very useful on the Flat and quite useful over hurdles, Macmillion (by So Blessed) a winner on the Flat and over hurdles, and Mashhur (by Homing), winner of two races as a two-year-old here and subsequently successful in America. Salsafy is a half-sister to two Flat winners and closely related to Marie Cath, a fair performer at up to a mile and a half in Britain and also a winner in France. Their dam Beetroot was a fair stayer on the Flat and is a daughter of the Royal Lodge winner Beta. *N. J. Henderson.*

CALAHONDA BAY 5 b.h. Bay Express–Bauhinia (Sagaro) [1989/90 16g a16g 16d^{4} 17f] sturdy horse: winning plater on Flat, stays 1m: poor form over hurdles, including in sellers: tailed off on firm ground final start: barely stays 2m: claimer ridden. *A. P. James.* 68

CALAHONDA SONG 4 ch.c. Song–Obergurgl (Warpath) [1989/90 16g] plating-class maiden at up to 9f on Flat, has run blinkered and visored: behind in selling hurdle at Market Rasen in October. *N. Bycroft.* —

CALAMITY JOE 7 ch.g. Gay Palm–Calamint (Punchinello) [1989/90 c21f^{ur} c20m^{pu}] smallish, workmanlike gelding: appears of little account: blinkered last 2 starts over hurdles. *R. J. Hodges.* c— —

CALAMOOR 8 br.g. Indiaro–Inez (Lower Boy) [1989/90 c24f^{6}] winning point-to-pointer: well beaten in hunter chase at Kelso in April. *Miss M. Bruce.* c—

CALAPAEZ 6 gr.g. Nishapour (FR)–Charter Belle (Runnymede) [1989/90 16d^{2} 16g^{4}] big, leggy, workmanlike gelding: smart hurdler: in frame in HSS Hire Shops Hurdle at Ascot (5 lengths second to Forest Sun) and Top Rank Christmas Hurdle at Kempton (17½ lengths fourth to Kribensis) in December: best form at further than 2m (won moderately-run race over 3m): yet to race on very soft going but acts on any other: game and genuine. *Miss B. Sanders.* 151

CALDER BRIDGE 9 b.g. Merrymount–Royal Kate (Royal Trip) [1989/90 c25g^{6} c24d^{ur} c25m^{3} c22g^{pu} c24d^{pu}] sturdy gelding: modest point-to-pointer/hunter chaser: well below form in 1989/90: stays 25f: best form with give in the ground. *C. F. Forty.* c83 —

CALEDONIAN LAD 5 b.g. Cragador–Carriemear (Averof) [1989/90 c24f] workmanlike gelding: poor novice hurdler: tailed off in hunter chase at Kelso in April: won a point-to-point later in month: blinkered third start in 1988/9. *A. M. Thomson.* c— —

CALICON 4 ch.g. Connaught–Calgary (Run The Gantlet (USA)) [1989/90 16f* 16s^{5} 16d* 16g^{2}] tall, angular gelding: winning stayer: very useful juvenile hurdler: held up when winning at Newbury in November and February (beat Fair Prospect 130

2½ lengths): easily best effort when 5 lengths second to Philosophos in Tote Placepot Hurdle at Kempton later in month: will be suited by further than 2m: acts on firm and dead ground. *I. A. Balding.*

CALIRA 11 ch.m. Coliseum–Salira (Double Jump) [1989/90 c30gpu] wiry mare: winning hurdler/chaser: was well suited by a good test of stamina: seemed to act on any going: dead. *Miss M. J. Benson.* c— —

CALLAGHAN 5 b.g. Cut Above–Super Restless (USA) (Restless Wind) [1989/90 17m4 16f* 27f3] workmanlike gelding: first sign of ability when winning conditional jockeys selling hurdle at Sedgefield in September (no bid), making most (pulled hard, almost refused at the first): looked none too keen when remote third on same course later in month: acts on firm going: claimer ridden: visored or blinkered: sold 650 gns Doncaster March Sales. *S. E. Kettlewell.* 86 §

CALL A TRUCE 5 b.g. Hard Fought–Celestial Star (So Blessed) [1989/90 a18g] close-coupled gelding: winning hurdler: better for race, behind in claimer in December: acts on dead going: suited by a sharp 2m and waiting tactics: claimer or amateur ridden in 1988/9: probably none too genuine. *F. J. O'Mahony.* —

CALL COLLECT 9 ch.g. Ballymore–Regal Bell (Princely Gift) [1989/90 c20d2 c24v* c24d* c26f* c36f] c**142** —

Call Collect confirmed himself a leading hunter chaser, but failed in his bid to become the first from that field to capture the Grand National since Grittar in 1982. Prominent in the betting at Aintree following easy victories at Ayr and Kelso and a more hard-fought success in the Christies Foxhunter Challenge Cup at Cheltenham, Call Collect finished seventh behind Mr Frisk, beaten around sixty lengths. He would almost certainly have been much better served by easier ground, and had the National not been his objective all season it's doubtful whether he'd have run. Before the Cheltenham Festival, doubts were reported about Call Collect's participation in the Foxhunter because of the ground—he'd been withdrawn at a meeting on the same course the previous year for such a reason. However, he eventually lined up the 7/4 favourite, ahead of Whitsunday, previous winner Three Counties, West Tip, Old Nick and Fudge Delight with the nine other runners 16/1 or higher. The gallop was a good one from the outset, with Whitsunday, Old Nick and Border Burg forcing the pace in turn.

Christies Foxhunter Challenge Cup, Cheltenham—Call Collect (right) about to take the lead from Old Nick; West Tip is third

After a circuit the field had become strung out, and the favourite looked to have it all to do back in tenth place after jumping none too fluently and looking to be taken off his legs. Warming to his task though, Call Collect steadily improved down the back straight and, despite a mistake three out, was disputing the lead with Old Nick and West Tip approaching the second last, where Whitsunday and Three Counties were finding only the same pace. Travelling the best from that point, Call Collect put in the best jump at the final fence which took him into the lead, and, running on strongly up the hill, won by two lengths from Old Nick, with West Tip three lengths away in third and fifteen lengths back to Three Counties and Whitsunday. Call Collect was generally quoted at 14/1 for the National the day after the Foxhunter, and steady support up until a few days before the big race made him as short as 8/1 co-favourite. On the day of the National he had drifted back to 14/1 because of the conditions. It's one thing running against hunter chasers on firm going, quite another against National horses. Call Collect was unable to go the pace. Soon a long way behind, he looked destined to be one of the last to complete with only two behind him at second Becher's, but he began to stay on from the third last and passed several horses in the straight. Call Collect has always struck us as an ideal type for the National, and we still believe he's one for the short list for the next running.

Call Collect (ch.g. 1981)	Ballymore (b 1969)	Ragusa (b 1960)	Ribot
			Fantan II
		Paddy's Sister (b 1957)	Ballyogan
			Birthday Wood
	Regal Bell (ch 1963)	Princely Gift (b 1951)	Nasrullah
			Blue Gem
		Bellatrix II (ch 1948)	Victrix
			Fille de Soleil

Call Collect is the second winning jumper out of the useful staying two-year-old Regal Bell, French hurdler Beau Regard (by Charlottesville) being the other. Regal Bell has bred numerous winners on the Flat, notably the 1978 Irish Sweeps Derby second Exdirectory, a full brother to Call Collect, and the smart French middle-distance stayer Royal Land (by Linacre). Since Call Collect, the dam has produced Local Belle, also by Ballymore, who was successful over a mile and a half in Ireland.

Call Collect, a medium-sized, rather sparely-made gelding, is an unimpressive mover. He is a thorough stayer who is likely to prove ideally suited by forcing tactics as well as plenty of give in the ground. With only eight races over regulation fences behind him, Call Collect still has something to learn about jumping, but is certain to remain among the top hunters in the next season or two. *J. Parkes.*

CALL ME LATER 6 br.m. Callernish–Miss Madam (Black Tarquin) [1989/90 F16f^{2} F16s^{3} 16s* 21s* 18d* 18v^{3}] eighth reported foal: half-sister to fair hurdler/ 130
chaser Monsieur Esclave (by Arctic Slave): dam maiden Irish hurdler: won 2 of 3 starts in point-to-points and NH Flat race at Clonmel in 1988/9: successful over hurdles in maiden event at Clonmel and minor contest at Limerick in December and in novice hurdle at Fairyhouse (put up a smart performance for a novice when short-heading Stevie Jay, pair well clear) in February: 10½ lengths third behind Scally Owen in valuable event at Punchestown later in month: will stay beyond 21f: acts on soft going: amateur ridden at Fairyhouse. *P. J. Flynn, Ireland.*

CALLOPE (USA) 6 b.m. Recitation (USA)–Caramba (FR) (Red Lord) [1989/90 16d^{pu} 24s^{pu}] lengthy, robust mare: modest novice over hurdles in —
1988/9: stays 2½m: acts on dead going. *M. Oliver.*

CAL MAL 12 b.g. Charlie's Pal–Semona (Seminole II) [1989/90 c25m^{pu}] c—
lengthy, angular gelding: one-time fair chaser: lightly raced nowadays: odds on, —
pulled up lame in hunter chase in May: stays well: seems to act on any going. *M. C. Pipe.*

CALMATA 9 br.m. Dubassoff (USA)–Raging Calm (Salvo) [1989/90 24d] lengthy mare: poor novice hurdler: amateur or claimer ridden. *Lady Ann Bowlby.* —

CAMBRIDGE GRADUATE 6 ch.g. Sunotra–Sparkation (Communication) [1989/90 F16g aF16g] third foal: dam won 9f seller: tailed off in NH Flat races: yet to race over hurdles or fences. *O. Brennan.*

CAMDEN BELLE 8 gr.m. Camden Town–Haut Lafite (Tamerlane) [1989/90 21g 20dpu] tall, workmanlike mare: poor hurdler: stays 21f: best form on a sound surface: has worn tongue strap: amateur or claimer ridden. *Miss L. Bower.* —

CAMDEN KNIGHT 5 b.h. Camden Town–Motionless (Midsummer Night II) [1989/90 16s6] leggy horse: modest middle-distance handicapper on Flat: no worthwhile form over hurdles: jumps none too fluently. *N. Bycroft.* —

CAMDORE BOY 10 b.g. Anax–Paddy's Daughter (St Paddy) [1989/90 16m 16f4 16g 17g a16g5 a20g3 a16g] compact gelding: selling hurdler: stays 2½m: acts well on top-of-the-ground: pulls hard. *J. M. Bradley.* 60

CAME DOWN 7 gr.g. Nearly A Hand–Bellentina (Rugantino) [1989/90 22m 16f5 16mpu 16d5 c16dF] big gelding: chasing type: poor form in novice hurdles (found little under pressure fourth start): in third place and beaten when falling last in novice event won by Elfast at Warwick in March on chasing debut: should stay further than 2¼m: acts on soft going: amateur or claimer ridden: usually wears a crossed noseband: will improve over fences. *N. R. Mitchell.* c93 p 74

CAMIONNAGE 9 b.g. Take A Reef–Nasty Niece (CAN) (Great Nephew) [1989/90 c24g4 c24v4 c24g3 c24vF c20d4 c22f c24d4 c24g3 c24m2 c24g* c24f2 c24g*] sparely-made, angular gelding: winning hurdler: placed in point-to-points: successful late in season in novice chase at Perth and 4-runner handicap chase at Market Rasen: stays 3m: acts on any going: has run well for an amateur and a claimer. *A. M. Crow.* c98 —

CAMPSEA-ASH 6 gr.g. Rusticaro (FR)–Lady d'Arbanville (FR) (Luthier) [1989/90 c16g* c16d3 c16g2 c17gF c17f2 c17d3 c20g3 c16f* c16m5 c20m* c16f3] big, lengthy gelding: carries condition: modest winning hurdler: better over fences: successful in novice chases at Fakenham in October and Chepstow in April (3-runner event) and handicap at Sandown in between (beat Mandray 5 lengths): sweating, creditable third behind With Gods Help in handicap at Ascot final start: best at 2m on a sound surface: tends to wander under pressure. *G. A. Hubbard.* c125 —

CAMPSTONE 8 ch.g. Push On–Arctic Moon (Arctic Slave) [1989/90 c22mpu] placed in point-to-points in Ireland: poor form in similar events in Britain: behind when pulled up in novice hunter chase in May. *Miss S. E. Cook.* c—

CAMROC 10 b.g. Vivadari–Milady Luck (Royal Highway) [1989/90 c20dpu c25fpu] winning chaser: tailed off when pulled up in hunter chase and handicap chase in March: suited by 3m+: acts on any going: claimer ridden: poor jumper. *A. J. Wilson.* c— x

CANBRACK COTTAGE 4 ch.f. Gorytus (USA)–Cottage Style (Thatch (USA)) [1989/90 16f 16g 16g] smallish, sturdy filly: first foal: dam, 1½m winner on Flat, runner-up in a novice event from 3 outings over hurdles: behind in 1m minor event on Flat in October: no form in juvenile hurdles: not raced after January: jumps none too fluently. *W. A. Stephenson.* —

CANDLEBRIGHT 6 ch.m. Lighter–Arctic Ander (Leander) [1989/90 22d 17g2 17g* 16v3 24gpu 16d* 17d 22g2 16d 20g2 16d* 16f*] sparely-made, angular mare: handicap hurdler: had a good season and showed progressive form: won at Doncaster (conditional jockeys) in January, Edinburgh (made all) in February and Perth (conditional jockeys) and Hexham in May: effective at 2m and stays 2¾m (saddle slipped when tried at 3m): acts on any going. *G. Richards.* 117 p

CANDY CONE 10 b.g. New Brig–Boundary Tale (Border Legend) [1989/90 c24gpu] strong, compact gelding: handicap chaser: behind when pulled up and dismounted in November: stays well: possibly unsuited by heavy going, acts on any other. *R. Brewis.* c— —

CANESTRELLI (USA) 5 b.g. Native Royalty (USA)–Princess Amelia (Viceregal (CAN)) [1989/90 16f2 16h2 16g3 22f2 16f3 16g5 20g4 16f 22f3 16mpu 16fro 17f4] smallish, sturdy gelding: novice selling hurdler: seems best at 2m: acts on hard ground: occasionally blinkered: seems best forcing pace: ran out before fifth on eleventh outing. *P. A. Blockley.* 67

CANEY RIVER 7 ch.g. Over The River (FR)–Hightown Jackie (David Jack) [1989/90 c24d6 c20g2 c24v3 c24g2 c24m2 c27f*] lengthy, angular gelding: won a point-to-point in Ireland in 1988: novice hurdler: all out to land the odds by 2 lengths from Parson's Cross in novice chase at Sedgefield in April: stays well: probably acts on any going. *J. J. O'Neill.* c93 —

CANFORD PALM 9 b.g. Nearly A Hand–Little Tot (Flush Royal) [1989/90 c20sur c20m3 c21g2 c24d6 c26v2 c24g2] angular, sparely-made gelding: tends to c122 —

look rather dull in coat: handicap chaser: ran creditably most starts in 1989/90 but faltered close home penultimate one: stays 3¼m, but doesn't need a test of stamina: yet to race on very firm ground, acts on any other: best on a right-handed track. *C. P. E. Brooks.*

CANNIE'S CASTLE 7 b.m. Gypsy Castle–Cannes Beach (Canadel II)
[1989/90 24m^{pu}] half-sister to winning point-to-pointer/steeplechaser Lauder- —
dale Lad (by Politico): pulled up all starts in point-to-points: tailed off when pulled
up in amateur riders novice event at Wetherby in April on hurdling debut. *Mrs S. J.
Gospel.*

CANNON LAD 8 b.g. Rajen–Miss Sovereign (Lucky Sovereign) [1989/90 c**92**
c25g^{4} c24g^{2} c24f^{3} c24f] winning point-to-pointer: placed in hunter chases at
Kelso in March and April: tailed off final start: stays 3m. *A. J. Barnett.*

CANNON'S WAY 4 b.c. Young Generation–Lady of Ireland (Be My Guest
(USA)) [1989/90 16m^{3}] sturdy colt: fair performer at up to 7f on Flat at his best 72
(claimed out of J. Berry's stable £10,001 in August): carrying condition, tired from
2 out when third in juvenile hurdle at Warwick in September: likely to prove
suited by a sharp 2m: sold 2,000 gns Ascot November Sales. *G. A. Pritchard-
Gordon.*

CANON CLASS 9 b.g. The Parson–Pallatess (Pall Mall) [1989/90 c24f^{3} c20m^{3} c**94**
c20d^{6} c25m^{ur} c26f^{4} c21f^{3} c25m^{4} c24m] medium-sized gelding: winning hurdler/ —
chaser: finds 2½m on short side and stays 3m: acts on any going: sometimes
amateur ridden. *D. Nicholson.*

CANONESS 9 b.m. St Paddy–Sea Fable (Typhoon) [1989/90 16g] small, leggy,
close-coupled mare: handicap hurdler: tailed off in December: form only at 2m: —
acts on good to firm ground: retained by trainer 3,200 gns Ascot November Sales.
P. Hayward.

CANON'S COURT 5 b.g. Main Reef–My Fawn (Hugh Lupus) [1989/90 17m^{2}
16g 20m^{pu}] half-brother to winning hurdler Raise A Hand (by Auction Ring): bad 94
maiden on Flat: second in novice hurdle at Devon & Exeter in September: off
course 7 months afterwards and showed little on return. *M. Madgwick.*

CANTACORNER 6 b.g. Sit In The Corner (USA)–Cantapet (Cantab) [1989/90
20g 20g^{2} 22d^{6} 20d] leggy, close-coupled gelding: poor novice hurdler: will be 77
suited by return to 3m: sweating badly first start. *Mrs S. M. Austin.*

CANTAMEGA 6 b.g. Deep Run–Una's Pride (Raise You Ten) [1989/90 22d*]
rangy, rather unfurnished gelding: ridden by 7-lb claimer, showed improved form 103 p
when winning novice hurdle at Stratford in December: not seen out again: will
stay 3m: acts on soft going. *Mrs J. Pitman.*

CANT GRUMBLE 5 b.m. Taufan (USA)–Luan Causca (Pampapaul) [1989/90
16g 16g^{pu}] ex-Irish mare: second foal: dam 2-y-o 5f winner: runner-up over 5f at 2 —
yrs (little form in 3 outings as 3-y-o): tailed off in novice hurdle in December: in
touch when pulled up 2 out in claimer 4 months later. *D. Dutton.*

CANTORIAL 9 ch.g. Cantab–Signal Melody (Bleep-Bleep) [1989/90 16m^{6} c**87** x
19h^{2} 16m c16m^{4} c21v^{3} 16s 19f c16f* c16f^{6} c20g^{2} c17m^{3} c20m^{4}] sturdy gelding: 87
handicap hurdler: frequently let down by his jumping over fences but won
conditional jockeys handicap at Worcester in April: tailed off final start: best form
at up to 2½m: seems to act on any going: sometimes blinkered 1987/8. *C. L.
Popham.*

CANTUS FIRMUS 4 b.c. Lyphard's Special (USA)–Capricious (FR) (Snob II)
[1989/90 16g^{4} 16m^{2} 17g^{F}] neat colt: middle-distance winner on Flat: in frame in 89
juvenile hurdles at Plumpton and Windsor in November: dead. *P. Leach.*

CAOIMHE 8 br.m. Pollerton–Cottage View (Golden Vision) [1989/90 c16g^{3}] c**84**
good-topped mare: modest form in novice hurdles: ran an encouraging first race —
over fences when third to Gay Edition in mares novice chase at Kempton in
November, but not seen out again: stays 2½m: seems suited by top-of-the-
ground: headstrong. *D. Nicholson.*

CAORAN MONA 5 b.g. Dominion–Maddelena (Tudor Melody) [1989/90 16d^{3}
16g^{2} 16d^{3} 16g] rangy gelding: handicap hurdler: ran creditably all but third outing: 104
unlikely to stay much beyond 2m: acts on firm and dead ground: reportedly lame
final start. *P. Leach.*

CAPA 10 ch.g. New Member–Poshteen (Royal Smoke) [1989/90 16f^{2}] compact
gelding: quite useful handicap hurdler: ran well in valuable Guinness Galway 124
Handicap Hurdle in August, leading 2 out but blundering last and caught close

home by I'm Confident: not seen out again: stays 21f: acts on any going: usually held up. *O. O'Neill.*

CAPELI CONE 8 b.g. Celtic Cone–Capelena (Mon Fetiche) [1989/90 c24g* c106
c24g^{5} c24g^{4} c27s^{2} c26v^{3} c24d^{6} c26s^{2} c32g^{F}] strong gelding: winning hurdler: —
won poor novice handicap chase at Bangor in November: kept on well when going down by 2 lengths to Knight Oil in novice chase at Uttoxeter in February, last completed outing: a thorough stayer: acts on heavy going: makes the odd mistake: usually ridden by claimer. *Mrs H. Parrott.*

CAPE MANTON 9 b.m. Mandamus–Cape Thriller (Thriller) [1989/90 c16s^{ur} c—
c24v^{pu} c27v^{F}] lengthy, workmanlike, plain mare: modest novice hurdler: little —
sign of ability in novice chases. *R. J. Holder.*

CAPITAL BUILDER 4 b.g. Pas de Seul–Double Touch (FR) (Nonoalco
(USA)) [1989/90 16g 16g 16g 16d 16d^{3}] leggy, close-coupled gelding: won 1m seller 65 ?
on Flat in July, when trained by G. Moore: blinkered and dropped in class, first form over hurdles when third in conditional jockeys seller at Ludlow in March. *I. Semple.*

CAPTAIN AHAB 6 b.g. Balinger–Sea Rambler (Menelek) [1989/90 17g^{4} 17d^{3}
21v^{2} 21d^{5} 22g 21s^{2} 21d^{3} 24d 24m* 20d^{2}] lengthy gelding: won novice hurdle at 107
Worcester in April: runner-up to easy winner Straight Gold in novice handicap on same course following month: stays 3m: acts on heavy and good to firm going. *G. B. Balding.*

CAPTAIN BONKERS 4 ch.g. Jasmine Star–Royal Tip (Mount Hagen (FR))
[1989/90 16s 17d 16v] sparely-made gelding: fourth foal: dam unraced half-sister —
to a winning Swedish jumper: poor and ungenuine maiden on Flat: sold out of J. Wilson's stable 2,200 gns Ascot August Sales: no sign of ability in juvenile hurdles and a seller. *M. A. Clutterbuck.*

CAPTAIN CAVEMAN 5 gr.g. Scallywag–Canadian Pacific (Spartan General)
[1989/90 22v 20s^{5} 20d^{6} 20f^{6}] second in NH Flat race: only form in novice 75
company over hurdles on final start. *R. Earnshaw.*

CAPTAIN CUTE 5 ro.g. Absalom–Cute (Hardicanute) [1989/90 16d 16g 16d]
compact gelding: no worthwhile form over hurdles: sold out of D. Thom's stable —
1,100 gns Newmarket September Sales. *R. E. Barr.*

CAPTAIN DAWN 14 b.g. Dusky Boy–Fairlap (Fairford) [1989/90 c21m] c—
workmanlike gelding: very useful chaser in 1986/7: behind in Digital Galway Plate —
(Handicap) in August: best at distances short of 2½m: acts well on top-of-the-ground and is unsuited by very soft: races up with the pace: has won 6 times at Fontwell. *J. T. Gifford.*

CAPTAIN DIBBLE 5 b.g. Crash Course–Sailor's Will (Laurence O) [1989/90 F16m*] third foal: half-brother to winning hurdler Admiral's Leap (by Quayside): dam won at up to 21f over hurdles in Ireland: 33/1, won 17-runner NH Flat race at Sandown in March by 6 lengths from Uncle Mogy: yet to race over hurdles or fences. *N. A. Twiston-Davies.*

CAPTAIN DIMITRIS 5 ch.h. Dubassoff (USA)–Proud Gipsy (Sky Gipsy)
[1989/90 17d^{pu} 17m 22f^{6}] third foal: dam never ran: no promise in 3 outings over —
hurdles, first a seller (blinkered). *Miss J. Thorne.*

CAPTAIN FRISK 7 bl.h. Politico (USA)–Jenny Frisk (Sunacelli) [1989/90 c85 +
c20d^{ro} c25d^{3} c20g^{2}] rather leggy, tall horse: half-brother to Mr Frisk (by Bivouac): stayed on when placed in novice chases at Wincanton in February and Newbury in March, going down by 10 lengths to Comandante on latter course: will be suited by a thorough test of stamina. *K. C. Bailey.*

CAPTAIN JIM 7 b.g. Proverb–Brave Jennifer (Brave Invader (USA)) [1989/90 c—
c20s^{pu}] close-coupled, good-quartered gelding: has some scope: tailed off in —
novice hurdles: runner-up in point-to-point in 1989: tailed off when pulled up in novice hunter chase at Uttoxeter in February: sold 2,700 gns Ascot June Sales. *T. D. B. Barlow.*

CAPTAIN KRAYYAN 4 b.g. Krayyan–Cap d'Antibe's (Furry Glen) [1989/90
16m 16m^{2} 16m^{4} 16s^{6} 16m] tall, lengthy ex-Irish gelding: fourth foal: dam 78
lightly-raced Irish maiden: poor middle-distance performer on Flat: in frame in 2 juvenile hurdles in November: ran poorly final outing (January): acts on good to firm and soft going: none too fluent a jumper: trained first start by T. Kinane. *T. P. McGovern.*

CAPTAIN MANNERING (USA) 5 b.g. Tina's Pet–Independentia (Home
Guard (USA)) [1989/90 F16m 16f 16m 16f^{6} 16d^{5} 16g 16d^{6} a16g^{2} 20m^{5}] good-bodied 86

gelding: visored, second in novice handicap hurdle at Southwell in March: blinkered, ran well when fifth in novice event at Newcastle later in month: stays 2½m. *L. J. Codd.*

CAPTAIN MAY 6 b.g. Welsh Captain–Maygo (Maystreak) [1989/90 16m^{F} 16g^{pu} 16d^{pu} 16m^{6} 16s 16d 16f 16d^{pu}] sparely-made gelding: poor novice selling hurdler: seems not to stay 2m when conditions are testing: blinkered last 2 starts. *R. E. Peacock.* 65 ?

CAPTAIN MOR 8 b.g. Welsh Captain–Oona More (Straight Deal) [1989/90 16f 17f c20d^{5} c24g^{6} c16g c20d* c20d^{2} c20s^{2} c16s^{2} c20m^{F} c20f^{2} c20f c20m* c20g^{3} c20f* c20m* c21f*] lengthy ex-Irish gelding: half-brother to several jumping winners, including useful chaser Clara Mountain (by Furry Glen): dam placed over hurdles and fences in Ireland: winning hurdler: won 2 handicap chases at both Sedgefield and Wetherby and one at Cartmel after turn of the year: stays 21f: acts on any going: once blinkered: has won for an amateur: trained by J. Shearman until after fifth outing. *W. A. Stephenson.* c109 —

CAPTAINS ANSWER 11 b. or br.g. Mon Capitaine–Answer Smartly (Neron) [1989/90 c17f^{6} c16f^{4}] workmanlike gelding: won a point-to-point in 1987: novice hurdler: poor form in steeplechases, including in a seller: will probably stay 3m: probably acts on any going. *K. S. Bridgwater.* c68 —

CAPUCHON 7 ch.g. New Member–Hattie (King's Troop) [1989/90 22m^{3}] brother to a poor animal: dam showed some ability at 2 yrs: runner-up in point-to-point in 1989: 27 lengths third in amateur riders novice event at Wincanton in November on hurdling debut. *Capt. T. A. Forster.* 82

CAPULET 7 b.h. Henbit (USA)–Lady Juliet (USA) (Gallant Man) [1989/90 16g 16s^{2} 16g^{5} 16s] good-topped horse: lightly-raced handicap hurdler: head second to Doc's Coat at Worcester in January, easily best effort of season: races only at around 2m: acts on heavy going (yet to race on ground firmer than good over hurdles). *C. James.* 104

CARA MUFFIN 6 b.g. Dramatic Bid (USA)–Speedy Valley (Wolver Hollow) [1989/90 c16f^{4} c16m^{4} a16g^{6} 16d^{2} 16f] tall, angular gelding: poor novice hurdler/chaser: best form at 2m with give in the ground: has hung left and found little under pressure: sometimes blinkered: sold out of Mrs C. Postlethwaite's stable 7,400 gns Doncaster January Sales after fourth start. *J. Mackie.* c75 82

CARATELLI 5 ch.g. True Song–Tagliatelle (Straight Lad) [1989/90 F16g] fifth foal: half-brother to winning hurdler Jay-Dee-Jay (by Mljet): dam novice hurdler/chaser: behind in NH Flat race at Kelso: yet to race over hurdles or fences. *R. C. Armytage.*

CARBISDALE 4 ch.g. Dunbeath (USA)–Kind Thoughts (Kashmir II) [1989/90 16g^{3} 16g^{2} 16d* 16s^{2} 16g^{3} 16v^{4} 16m^{5}] workmanlike gelding: carries plenty of condition: half-brother to useful hurdler Penny Forum (by Pas de Seul): modest maiden on Flat, stays 1½m: ridden by 7-lb claimer, won novice hurdle at Wetherby in February: better form after, including when third to Philosophos in Tote Placepot Hurdle at Kempton in February: will stay further: acts on good to firm and heavy going: has tended to wander under pressure. *E. Weymes.* 124

CARBONATE 5 b.g. Mr Fluorocarbon–Girl On A Swing (High Top) [1989/90 16g^{F} 16d^{2} 16s^{5}] lengthy, workmanlike gelding: modest hurdler: best effort of 1989/90 when second in conditional jockeys handicap at Haydock in December: likely to prove best at 2m: best form on dead going: wears crossed noseband: sold only 1,200 gns Doncaster March Sales. *M. H. Easterby.* 104

CARBON LADY 5 ch.m. Mr Fluorocarbon–Lady Marmalade (Hotfoot) [1989/90 20f^{3} 24m] leggy, close-coupled mare: selling hurdler: not seen out after September: suited by 2½m: yet to race on heavy going, acts on any other. *J. L. Harris.* 78

CARDINAL RALPH 6 b.g. Ovac (ITY)–Alice Minkthorn (Party Mink) [1989/90 22g* 20d^{2} 21s 25g^{4}] big, rather leggy, angular gelding: will make a chaser: won novice hurdle at Fontwell in December: staying-on second to stable-companion Beau Pari at Ascot following month: not wholly disgraced in valuable 25f event at Newbury in March: possibly unsuited by very soft ground. *J. T. Gifford.* 111

CARDINAL'S OUTBURST 15 b.g. Fury Royal–Easter Speaker (Articulate) [1989/90 c20f^{4}] strong gelding: poor chaser nowadays: needed race in October: stays 3¼m: suited by a sound surface: has a tendency to jump right: has won 8 times at Ludlow. *Mrs S. Armytage.* c— —

CARDS AND KISSES (USA) 4 b.f. Wind And Wuthering (USA)–Heat Haze (USA) (Jungle Savage (USA)) [1989/90 F16m^5 F16g F16f*] first reported living foal: dam lightly-raced maiden: 25/1, won 13-runner NH Flat race at Hereford in May by a neck from Attic Wit: yet to race over hurdles. *C. A. Cyzer.*

CAREER BAY 8 b.g. Orange Bay–Career (Hotfoot) [1989/90 19m c20m* c?
c22m^{F2} c24g^{pu} 21d^{pu} 16d^{pu}] lengthy gelding: handicap hurdler: gave impression —
something amiss last 2 starts: jumped none too fluently when very fortunate winner of novice chase at Ludlow in November (remote third when leaders took wrong course on run-in): stays 2¾m: acts on any going: blinkered final outing. *D. Haydn Jones.*

CARELESS KISS 6 ch.m. Persian Bold–More Kisses (Morston (FR))
[1989/90 20m^6 a18g^2 22g^5 a20g^3 16g^2] sparely-made mare: first foal: dam winning 97
half-sister to 2 successful jumpers: poor handicapper at up to 1½m on Flat, well below her best in 1989: sold out of I. Matthews' stable 1,700 gns Newmarket Autumn Sales: 25/1, showed improved form when head second to None So Wise in 22-runner novice hurdle at Windsor in March: best at 2m. *A. Moore.*

CARELESS LAD 4 ch.g. Precocious–Mousquetade (Moulton) [1989/90 17v^4
22f^2] compact gelding: placed at up to 1½m on Flat: sold out of I. Matthews' stable 102 p
13,000 gns Doncaster November Sales: 6 lengths second to Cockstown Lad in juvenile hurdle at Wincanton in March: probably stays 2¾m: should win a race. *R. G. Frost.*

CARFAX 5 ch.g. Tachypous–Montana Moss (Levmoss) [1989/90 a20g^4 16s^2
22g^6 22s* 20s 18s^4 22g 24g] small gelding: selling hurdler: won conditional 95
jockeys handicap at Folkestone in January (bought in 4,800 gns): best effort afterwards on next start: stays 2¾m: suited by plenty of give in the ground: claimer ridden: has worn blinkers. *R. P. C. Hoad.*

CARIBBEAN SUN 12 ch.g. Midsummer Night II–Sleepy (Hereward The
Wake) [1989/90 20f^{pu}] leggy gelding: temperamental, and of little account over — §
hurdles. *Mrs B. Brunt.*

CARIBEAN CONEXION 5 b.h. Indian King (USA)–Borehard (Bonne Noel)
[1989/90 a16g 16d^6 16d^4 16f^{pu}] compact horse: won 1¼m seller on Flat at 3 yrs: 68
dropped in class, fourth in selling hurdle at Bangor (trained until after then by C. J. Bell) in March. *Miss S. J. Wilton.*

CARJUJEN 6 b.g. Tumble Wind (USA)–Baldritta (FR) (Baldric II) [1989/90 16g
16g 16g 16m^3 16d 16d^5 a16g^r 16f* 16f^6 a20g^3 16f^2 16m] close-coupled, angular 83 §
gelding: successful at up to 9f on Flat: won conditional jockeys selling handicap hurdle at Bangor in March (bought in 3,600 gns): placed in similar company in April: stays 2½m: acts on firm ground: refused to race seventh start and reluctant to race at Bangor. *B. Preece.*

CARLITA (HOL) 4 ch.f. Shamaraan (FR)–Carmona (Track Spare) [1989/90
16m a16g^4 a20g] behind in juvenile hurdle at Ostend in August on debut when —
trained by C. Guest: no worthwhile form in novice hurdles at Southwell: visored final start (tailed off). *R. Guest.*

CARL'S CHOICE 9 b.g. The Brianstan–Spartan's Girl (Spartan General) **c91** +
[1989/90 c25g^5] rangy gelding: fairly useful point-to-pointer, winner 4 times in 1990: winning hunter chaser: jumped poorly in latter stages (rider lost irons 2 out) when moderate fifth at Wolverhampton in February: stays 25f: acts on heavy going. *G. I. Cooper.*

CARL'S PRIDE 6 b.h. Shack (USA)–Costerini (Soderini) [1989/90 16f 16f^5]
smallish, quite well-made horse: poor plater over hurdles. *V. Thompson.* 61

CARLY BRRIN 5 br.g. Carlin–Bios Brrin (Pitpan) [1989/90 F16v F17d 24h^F]
second foal: dam, poor maiden hurdler in Ireland, half-sister to fairly useful Irish —
hurdler Killamonan: behind in NH Flat races in March: weakened quickly from 3 out and was behind when falling last in amateur riders maiden hurdle at Hexham. *W. A. Stephenson.*

CARMAGNOLE (USA) 4 b.c. Lypheor–La Bonzo (USA) (Miracle Hill)
[1989/90 16f^2 18m* 16d^6 16f^6] compact colt: fairly useful winner at up to 13f on 102
Flat, goes well with forcing tactics: made all in juvenile hurdle at Fontwell in December: first race for 2½ months, creditable sixth behind Swift Waters in juvenile handicap at Newbury in March on final start: will stay at least 2½m: acts on firm ground and possibly unsuited by good to soft. *G. Harwood.*

CARMELUS THE GREAT 7 gr.g. General Ironside–Our Charm (Goldhill) [1989/90 c25s^pu c24g^F] plain gelding: failed to complete in 2 point-to-points in 1988: has failed to get past the sixth in steeplechases. *G. B. Balding.* c—

CARNBREA FRED 4 b.g. Montekin–Vote Barolo (Nebbiolo) [1989/90 16f^4 a16g 16d^6 16f^3 16f^5 16m^2 16s^6 16m 27s^6 a20g^6 20g^4 16m^3 20g^5 a16g^6] small, lengthy gelding: plating-class maiden on Flat: poor novice selling hurdler: stays 2½m: acts on firm and dead going: usually visored: appears difficult ride: sold 1,400 gns Ascot July Sales. *J. L. Harris.* 70

CARNEADES 10 b.g. Homing–Connarca (Connaught) [1989/90 c24m* c24m* c24m^4 c24m*] workmanlike gelding: has been fired: one-time quite useful hurdler/point-to-pointer: jumped well in the main and made all in novice chases at Worcester in August and September and in BMW Series Chase qualifier at Newbury in November: stays 3m: acts on heavy going and good to firm: races with plenty of zest: visored last 4 starts in 1985/6, blinkered last 4 outings: amateur or claimer ridden nowadays. *N. R. Mitchell.* c**110** —

CAROGROVE 7 b.g. Rusticaro (FR)–Heather Grove (Hethersett) [1989/90 20m^4 21f^2 c24f^F 24m^2 21f* 26m*] small gelding: handicap hurdler: won at Towcester and Stratford late in season: novice chaser: stays 3¼m: suited by a sound surface and acts on hard ground: often claimer ridden over hurdles (not when successful): blinkered once in 1988/9. *J. M. Bukovets.* c82 ? 98

CAROLES CLOWN 4 gr.f. Another Realm–Show Business (Auction Ring (USA)) [1989/90 a16g^4 a16s^4 a18g* a18g^4 a16g^4 a16g^2 a16g*] plating-class 5f winner at 2 yrs, but well beaten on Flat in 1989: won selling hurdles at Lingfield (no bid) in February and Southwell (bought in 3,400 gns) in May: stays 2¼m: claimer ridden all bar debut. *M. J. Haynes.* 76

CAROLINE RANGER 9 b.m. Pony Express–Lady Hawker (The Ditton) [1989/90 c20d] leggy, lightly-made mare: poor novice selling hurdler: won a point-to-point in March: rider lost irons when tailed off in hunter chase earlier in month. *Mrs Ann Weston.* c— —

CAROLS BELLE 7 ch.m. Ballymore–Love For Money (Be Friendly) [1989/90 a18g] small, sparely-made mare: poor maiden on Flat: no form in 3 outings over hurdles, including in seller. *C. F. C. Jackson.* —

CAROUSEL CROSSETT 9 b.m. Blind Harbour–Grange Classic (Stype Grange) [1989/90 c16g^2] strong, compact mare: novice hurdler/chaser: second to comfortable winner Highfrith in mares race at Wetherby in November: stays long distances: ran poorly on firm going: amateur ridden: has worn a crossed noseband. *E. M. Caine.* c**78** —

CAROUSEL ROCKET 7 ch.g. Whistling Deer–Fairy Tree (Varano) [1989/90 c20d^3 c20s^4 c17d^4 c16v^2 c24v^2 c20d^2 c21d^pu] sparely-made gelding: lightly-raced handicap hurdler: second in 3 novice chases, showing modest form: suited by testing conditions at 2m and stays 3m: acts on heavy going and good to firm. *J. S. Wilson.* c**86** —

CAROWAG 6 b.m. Scallywag–Morgan's Mark (Pirate King) [1989/90 F16g^3] workmanlike mare: has scope: half-sister to point-to-point winner Morgan's Treasure (by Lucky Wednesday): dam, fair hurdler, best at 2m: 20 lengths third to Trefelyn Cone in NH Flat race at Ludlow in December: yet to race over hurdles or fences. *Capt. T. A. Forster.*

CARPACCIO (USA) 4 b.c. Blazing Saddles (AUS)–Reine du Nil (Relko) [1989/90 F13f F16g] 1,250 3-y-o: first foal: dam 1½m winner: tailed off in NH Flat races: sold 1,650 gns Ascot June Sales: yet to race over hurdles. *K. A. Morgan.*

CARPE DIEM 5 b.m. Good Times (ITY)–Olympic Visualise (Northfields (USA)) [1989/90 16g 16d 17v^5] compact mare: sister to novice hurdler Good Seoul and half-sister to good-class but unreliable chaser Vodkatini (by Dubassoff): modest maiden at her best on Flat, stays 1m: behind in novice hurdles. *E. A. Wheeler.* —

CARPET CAPERS (USA) 6 b.g. Dance Bid (USA)–Cofimvaba (FR) (Verrieres) [1989/90 17h^2 16h* 18f^3 20f^2 16f* 16m^3 20g^3 16m* 22g^2 18g* 18s* a20s* a16g^2] small, angular gelding: selling hurdler: improved a lot and had excellent season: successful at Plumpton (thrice, has now won there 6 times) and Fontwell (twice), prior to winning claimer at Lingfield in January: good second in handicap on last-named course following month: will probably prove best at up to 2½m: acts on any going: has won for a claimer: game and genuine. *J. Ffitch-Heyes.* 111

CARRICK HILL LAD 7 b.g. Royal Fountain–Indian Lace (Indian Ruler) [1989/90 c24d* c24g* c24g* c24s* c20v* c24s3 c24d2] c**141** —

The Carrick Hills that overlook Ayr racecourse are the inspiration behind the naming of Carrick Hill Lad, and, fittingly, the Scottish course played host to four of his seven races in his highly successful first season's chasing. Easily the most important there were the West of Scotland Pattern Novices' Chase in January and the Souter of Stirling Novices' Chase in April. Prior to the first-named, the tall, angular Carrick Hill Lad had proved himself an up-and-coming chaser with handsome victories against modest opposition in a novice event and a handicap at Ayr, and in a novice event at Haydock; and also in the John Haggas Memorial Novices' Chase, which he won from Cliffalda, at Wetherby. The four-runner West of Scotland provided Carrick Hill Lad with his stiffest task up to that time. Against him in the two-and-a-half-mile event were promising novices Antinous, Aston Express and Blazing Walker, all of whom had the speed to win at the minimum trip. In the very heavy ground, Carrick Hill Lad was sent straight into the lead to make it as stiff a test as possible. Blazing Walker, who had been jumping poorly, tried to refuse, and unseated his rider at the fifth from home, but Carrick Hill Lad's two remaining rivals had managed to keep in close company. Antinous even took the lead at the third last and, momentarily, it looked as though Carrick Hill Lad was heading for his first defeat over fences, but, galloping on strongly, he regained the lead at the last and forged clear of his tired pursuers to beat Aston Express, who stayed on better than Antinous, by eight lengths. Carrick Hill Lad started favourite for the Old Road Securities Reynoldstown Novices' Chase at Ascot eleven days later. He was a disappointment however, never travelling or jumping particularly well after completely misjudging the first, and unable to land a blow at impressive winner Royal Athlete. Afterwards his trainer reported the horse's blood to be wrong. Almost two months later, he had redeemed a good deal of his reputation with a resolute second in the Souter of Stirling Novices' Chase. Royal Athlete, who had won the Mumm Club Novices' Chase at Liverpool on his previous start, justified favouritism, but was made to fight every inch of the way by Carrick Hill Lad and Formula One. The

BMW Series Chase (Qualifier), Haydock—Carrick Hill Lad out on his own

John Haggas Memorial Novices' Chase, Wetherby—
Carrick Hill Lad has to fight harder this time; Cliffalda is the challenger

three had a tremendous tussle over the final three fences, before Royal Athlete got home by two lengths and a head from the tenacious Carrick Hill Lad and Formula One.

An ambitious programme has been mapped out for Carrick Hill Lad. The Charlie Hall Memorial Chase at Wetherby and the King George VI Rank Chase at Kempton are just two talked about as possible engagements. We share a good deal of the connections' enthusiasm, though it's a moot point whether the horse is yet up to tackling the best. Carrick Hill Lad's stamina is his chief asset, and given the very soft ground he revels in, the Welsh National at Chepstow rather than the King George would seem an ideal race for him in the first half of the next season.

Carrick Hill Lad (b.g. 1983)	Royal Fountain (br 1977)	Royalty (br 1968)	Relko
			Fair Bid
		Fountain (b 1969)	Reform
			Regal Fountain
	Indian Lace (b 1971)	Indian Ruler (b 1951)	Sayajirao
			Bright Hope
		Border Lace (b 1955)	Reynard Volant
			Selskar Lace

Carrick Hill Lad is easily the best representative of his sire. Royal Fountain was a smart performer at up to a mile and a half in the early-'eighties, winning three races, notably the Wood Ditton Stakes and the Heathorn Stakes, in the latter beating subsequent Mecca-Dante winner Hello Gorgeous. Royal Fountain has produced a handful of other jumping winners, including Super Fountain, also a thorough stayer, who was successful in the North in the latest season. Carrick Hill Lad is the second, and to date, latest foal of Indian Lace. Her first produce, by Coliseum, failed to show any ability over hurdles and showed only a little in point-to-points.

Mr A. M. Picken's "Carrick Hill Lad"

Indian Lace ran in three point-to-points herself, finishing last on two occasions and pulled up when in the lead three out on the other. Carrick Hill Lad's grandam, Border Lace, also did all her racing in the pointing arena, finishing in the frame several times. Border Lace is a daughter of Reynard Volant—a name rarely come across in pedigrees nowadays; he was a high-class stayer in the mid-'forties, winning the Ascot Stakes two years in succession. *G. Richards.*

CARRIG GLAEDE 8 br.g. Kambalda–Magic Dancer (Pumps (USA)) [1989/90 c25g c25m5] workmanlike ex-Irish gelding: first foal: dam placed in bumpers event on Flat: successful in 3 point-to-points and 2 hunter chases in 1988 when trained by E. Bolger: modest form in point-to-points in Britain: tailed off in hunter chases in February and April: stays 3m: acts on good to firm ground. *Robert Goodall.* c— —

CARROLLS GROVE 9 ch.g. Lucifer (USA)–Arcticogan (Tarqogan) [1989/90 c20m*] ex-Irish gelding: winning point-to-pointer: easily won novice chase at Perth in September: not seen out again: stays 2½m: acts on a firm surface. *D. Burchell.* c93

CARROL'S CROSS 7 b. or br.m. Decent Fellow–Sallys Wish (Proverb) [1989/90 c16vpu c24spu] good-topped mare: won a point-to-point in Ireland in 1988: modest novice hurdler (ran in snatches once): jumped none too fluently and pulled up both outings over fences: will probably stay beyond 2½m: one to treat with caution: sold out of Mrs D. Haine's stable 7,800 gns Doncaster November Sales. *Andrew Turnell.* c— —

CARRY THE CAN 6 ch.m. Deep Run–Ingenious (Indigenous) [1989/90 F16m 20g3 25m 20gpu 16mur 17g 24f6 24m5 20f5] smallish mare: eighth foal: half-sister 59 ?

to winning chasers Navaro (by Varano) and Southern Reaper (by Kambalda): dam, half-sister to smart jumper Fredcoteri, won bumpers event: failed to complete in 4 point-to-points in 1989: poor form in novice hurdles. *C. Smith.*

CARTHAGENA COTTAGE 5 b.g. Sonnen Gold–Gentle Daisy (Comefast) [1989/90 F16m^{4} F16m^{su} aF16g^{2} 16d^{pu}] plain gelding: fifth foal: half-brother to winning chaser Keldlands (by Ascertain): dam Irish maiden hurdler: second in NH Flat race at Southwell in January: jumped moderately and was tailed off when pulled up 2 out in novice hurdle at Wetherby following month. *Mrs V. A. Aconley.* —

CARTREF 4 b.f. Homing–Kentucky (Warpath) [1989/90 16g^{pu} 16g^{pu}] sparely-made filly: first foal: dam poor maiden on Flat and over hurdles: tailed off when pulled up in juvenile hurdles in first half of season: blinkered final outing. *Mrs Jill Evans.* —

CARVILL'S HILL 8 b.g. Roselier (FR)–Suir Valley (Orchardist) [1989/90 c20g^{2} c19d* c24s* c24v^{2}] c**169** —

Mention the luck of the Irish to the connections of Carvill's Hill at your peril. The best novice chaser of the previous year, and the finest Irish prospect since Dawn Run, was plagued by injury in the latest season and had a most frustrating campaign. Carvill's Hill was seldom out of the news but he made only four appearances all season, one of them in the Vincent O'Brien Irish Gold Cup at Leopardstown where, starting odds on, he suffered a five-length defeat by British challenger Nick The Brief. The task of stepping into the shoes of Dawn Run proved beyond Carvill's Hill. He missed the Tote Cheltenham Gold Cup—and, in fact, wasn't seen out again after Leopardstown, the regular disconsolate bulletins about his well-being adding to the widespread overall feeling of anticlimax. Carvill's Hill is still only eight and has plenty of time to make a lasting impact on steeplechasing but his proneness to injury—he reportedly needs treatment from a back specialist after every race and after much of his schooling work over fences—obviously undermines confidence in his future. Headlines such as 'Carvill's Hill lame again' or 'Carvill's Hill not firing, says trainer' appeared as regularly as clockwork, as plans for the horse were disrupted time after time by training set-backs.

Despite early-season training troubles, Carvill's Hill arrived at Leopardstown with his reputation still largely intact. His reappearance was delayed until December when he lost little or no caste in going down by three lengths (eased near the finish) in the Durkan Brothers EBF Punchestown Chase to that other top-class Irish novice of the previous year, the mare Maid of Money; looking short of peak fitness and handled more tenderly than his main rival who had already had two races in the current season, Carvill's Hill travelled smoothly for much of the way as he and Maid of Money dominated the eight-horse field throughout. Carvill's Hill confirmed the impression that the run at Punchestown would bring him on a good deal when following up with a clear-cut victory, conceding lumps of weight all round, in the Boyne Extended Handicap Chase at Naas in January. Carvill's Hill put up another tip-top handicap performance—carrying only a 2-lb discretionary penalty allotted by the official handicapper for a fifteen-length victory at Naas—in the Harold Clarke Leopardstown Chase in February. Carvill's Hill started odds on and won in clear-cut style but the race showed that he was still not an accomplished jumper by Gold Cup standards. Carvill's Hill had given the impression in his novice days that he would become a good jumper with more experience but he still tends to jump left and isn't always fluent. However, he looked most impressive when cruising up to deprive Barney Burnett of the lead before the last and drawing clear to win in good style by six lengths. Carvill's Hill moved like a champion for a long way in the Irish Gold Cup too. He jumped well for the most part and looked easily the best horse in the race as he sailed along in the lead, clear of the scrubbed-along Nick The Brief and the hard-ridden Maid of Money, with two fences to jump. Carvill's Hill had disputed the lead with Panto Prince until going on six from home and then seemingly asserting his superiority with a fast and fluent jump at the final open ditch, three out. But the picture changed dramatically at the second last where, challenged by Nick The Brief, Carvill's Hill jumped very slowly. He never looked like staging a fightback after surrendering the initiative and had to be ridden out to hold off Maid of Money, who made a bad mistake at the last, by two and a half lengths for second place. There's good reason to believe that Carvill's Hill wasn't quite at his best and it may be significant that his trainer wasn't able to get him to his liking for some time afterwards. Carvill's Hill remained in training right up to the end of the season, the Jameson Irish Grand National being his last objective. His trainer reported in the week of the National that 'Carvill's Hill is as good now as at any time this season', but the horse was withdrawn at the eleventh hour on account of the ground.

Carvill's Hill (b.g. 1982)	Roselier (FR) (b 1973)	Misti IV (br 1958)	Medium
			Mist
		Peace Rose (gr 1959)	Fastnet Rock
			La Paix
	Suir Valley (b 1972)	Orchardist (b 1959)	No Orchids
			Partiality
		Ann Advancer (b 1968)	Even Money
			Princess Pontet

The rangy Carvill's Hill, described by his trainer as 'no oil painting when he came here' (he fetched only IR 4,200 guineas as a yearling), has matured into a fine individual, in appearance very much most people's idea of the top-class, weight-carrying chaser. He has a jumping pedigree too: his sire the Irish-based Roselier won the French Champion Hurdle and is a rising star among the jumping stallions (Royal Athlete was another notable chaser to represent him in the latest season); Carvill's Hill is the first foal of Suir Valley, a winning point-to-pointer from the same family as the Cheltenham Gold Cup winner Bregawn and the Grand National runner-up Hard Outlook. Carvill's Hill stays three miles and acts well on heavy going (he has never run on a firm surface and it's unlikely that he'll be risked on one). Paul Green purchased a half share in Carvill's Hill at the end of the season, resolving a well-publicised dispute between the existing owners;

Harold Clarke Leopardstown Chase, Leopardstown—
Carvill's Hill gives Barney Burnett 25 lb and a five-length beating

Mrs J. McMorrow's "Carvill's Hill"

the horse will be raced in Green's colours in 1990/1 and, under an arrangement made by the new owners, Dunwoody will replace Morgan as the horse's regular jockey. *J. T. R. Dreaper, Ireland.*

CARVING KNIFE (AUS) 8 ch.g. Sharp Edge–Royal Feast (Gala Performance (USA)) [1989/90 c20dpu c26v3] close-coupled, rather sparely-made gelding: no form over hurdles: won 2 point-to-points in 1989: well-beaten third behind Royal Athlete in novice chase at Newton Abbot in January. *N. A. Gaselee.* c— —

CASBATINA 4 b.f. Castle Keep–Balatina (Balidar) [1989/90 16g2] 6f seller winner at 2 yrs: no form on Flat since: 4 lengths second to Ajalita in late-season juvenile selling hurdle at Market Rasen. *J. Pearce.* 72 p

CASH AND GOLD 12 ch.g. Bilsborrow–Gold Kelpie (Cash And Courage) [1989/90 c24d c24s3 c22f4 c25mur c25fpu] small gelding: winning point-to-pointer, though not successful since 1987 (appears temperamental nowadays): tailed off in hunter chases. *R. Lowe.* c— x

CASH CRISIS 10 ch.g. Hell's Gate–Pound Foolish (Cash And Courage) [1989/90 17h5 c16f* c19f* c21f3 c16m2 c16h4 c18g3 c16mpu c21f2 c16d3 c16g4 c21g4 c21g3 c20mpu] sparely-made gelding: winning hurdler: successful in novice chases at Worcester and Hereford in August: ran creditably on occasions afterwards: weakened quickly, pulled up and dismounted before last on final start: stays 2½m: acts on any going: has worn a brush pricker: inconsistent. *A. Barrow.* **c91** —

CASHEL PALACE 5 b.m. Sweet Monday–Sunny Maid (Ballymoss) [1989/90 F17f F13d] fifth foal: dam, behind on Flat and over hurdles: well beaten in NH Flat races: yet to race over hurdles or fences. *Miss J. Eaton.*

CASHEL QUEEN 4 b.f. Sweet Monday–Sunny Maid (Ballymoss) [1989/90 F16v F17m] sixth foal: dam behind on Flat and over hurdles: tailed off in NH Flat races: yet to race over hurdles. *Miss J. Eaton.*

CASHEW KING 7 b.g. Faraway Times (USA)–Sinzinbra (Royal Palace) [1989/90 c20fur c16f* c16m* c16g* c16s*] c130 + —

Useful hurdler Cashew King made an inauspicious start to his chasing career in a novice event at Doncaster in December. Sent off favourite, he blundered badly at the first and gave his rider no chance of staying in the saddle. That, however, was the only blemish in Cashew King's season over fences and he finished unbeaten in his four subsequent starts. His biggest success came in the three-runner PML Lightning Novices' Chase at Ascot in January on his fourth outing. Cashew King was the outsider at 12/1, with his half-brother Young Snugfit and The Proclamation co-favourites at 11/10. With The Proclamation falling at the fourth and Young Snugfit running poorly due to a back injury, Cashew King gained a bloodless victory, though he impressed in his jumping of the stiff Ascot fences. Cashew King picked up another good prize at Nottingham the following month. The Nottinghamshire Novices' Chase had its usual competitive look about it and a fitting climax looked on the cards until the leading pair, Sawdust Jack and Aston Express, and Antinous, who was a close fourth, all fell independently at the penultimate jump. This handed the initiative to Cashew King who, despite a mistake at the last, held Decided by half a length, with the only other finisher Fuego Boy eight lengths away. In our view Cashew King was an extremely fortunate winner, and would probably have finished only fourth had all the field completed. There was no hint of good fortune about Cashew King's first two victories over fences, at Warwick and Wolverhampton in December.

Cashew King is one of five winning jumpers out of Sinzinbra. Her name is very well known to jumping followers thanks to the exploits of Grand National runner-up Mr Snugfit (by Jukebox), fairly useful chaser Half Brother (a full brother to Cashew King), the aforementioned Young Snugfit (by Music Boy), the very useful novice hurdler Peanut's Pet (by Tina's Pet) and winning hurdler Snugfit's Image (also by Music Boy). Sinzinbra, a

PML Lightning Novices' Chase, Ascot—
Young Snugfit leads The Proclamation (No. 2) and Cashew King in the early stages

Nottinghamshire Novices' Chase, Nottingham—
Sawdust Jack (leading) and Antinous both fall, as does Aston Express (not in picture).
Cashew King takes full advantage

daughter of a half-sister to the Irish Derby winner Your Highness, was very useful at up to one and a quarter miles at her best, but became disappointing. She is a half-sister to several winners, including the useful hurdler Kings Parade and Flat stayer Wounded Knee, the latter the grandam of Musidora and Irish One Thousand Guineas winner In The Groove. Sinzinbra died in 1987. Her last foal, a full sister to Young Snugfit and Snugfit's Image and closely related to Mr Snugfit, is the modest five-furlong winner Snuggle who is in training with Tompkins at Newmarket.

Cashew King (b.g. 1983)	Faraway Times (USA) (b or br 1974)	Olden Times (b 1958)	Relic
			Djenne
		Farnesina (b or br 1966)	Neptunus
			Fariella
	Sinzinbra (b 1971)	Royal Palace (b 1964)	Ballymoss
			Crystal Palace
		La Lidia (ch 1964)	Matador
			Lady Grand

Cashew King, who cost 1,100 guineas as a yearling at the Newmarket Sales, is a game and genuine performer who has repaid connections handsomely. He has now won ten races, including the Victor Ludorum Hurdle at Haydock in 1986/7 and the County Hurdle at Cheltenham the following season. There should be plenty of opportunities for him to increase his tally next season too, when his sound jumping should stand him in good stead in handicaps. A tall, leggy gelding, Cashew King races mainly at around two miles, though he ran well over two and a half miles at Liverpool in 1988/9. Although a winner on firm ground, he wasn't seen out after Nottingham because of the prevailing firm conditions, and he's shown all his best form with give in the ground. He has won when sweating. *B. A. McMahon.*

CASH IS KING 6 b.g. Tug of War–Norhamina (Tyrone) [1989/90 20g* c20d* c**115** p
c20g* c22d* 25m^{6}] big, useful-looking gelding with scope: very useful hurdler: 145
won handicap at Kempton in December: good sixth to Trapper John in Waterford Crystal Stayers' Hurdle at Cheltenham in March: jumped soundly in the main when winning novice chases at Plumpton and Leicester in January and Stratford in February: suited by a strongly-run race at 2½m and stays 25f: acts on good to

Cottesmore Novices' Chase (Div. 1), Leicester—Cash Is King (left) gets the better of Erostin Floats and the weakening John's Birthday

firm and heavy going: has won for a claimer: blinkered last 2 starts: will go on to better things over fences. *Mrs J. Pitman.*

CASINO MAGIC 6 b.g. Casino Boy–Gypsy Girl (Marmont) [1989/90 20d^{pu} 16m a20g^{2} a16g^{2} a20g^{4} a18g^{3}] workmanlike gelding: poor novice hurdler: form only at Lingfield. *J. L. Spearing.* 77

CASINO RUN 7 ch.m. Deep Run–Kassina (Laurence O) [1989/90 c24d^{F}] novice hurdler/chaser: stayed 2¾m: dead. *R. F. Fisher.* c— —

CASPER 5 ch.g. Grey Ghost–Marcus Lady (Marcus Superbus) [1989/90 16f 16m^{4}] compact gelding: fourth foal: half-brother to winning point-to-pointer Mr Sponge (by Pongee): dam, fair hurdler and winning chaser, stayed 25f: tailed off in selling hurdles in first half of season. *R. R. Lamb.* —

CASPIAN FLYER 7 br.g. Persian Bold–Orapa (Aureole) [1989/90 c21m^{4}] very lightly-raced maiden on Flat: successful in a point-to-point in April: fourth to Skerry Meadow in novice hunter chase at Fakenham in May. *P. B. Doyle.* c71

CASSCA 5 b.m. Full of Hope–Miss Kuwait (The Brianstan) [1989/90 aF13g^{4} 17d^{3}] in frame in NH Flat races: ridden by 7-lb claimer, 19 lengths third behind Olveston in novice hurdle at Newton Abbot in March: should improve. *M. C. Pipe.* 81 p

CASTING TIME (NZ) 6 br.g. Drums of Time (USA)–In Haste (NZ) (In The Purple (FR)) [1989/90 22s^{6} 20f] leggy, angular gelding: showed ability when sixth in novice hurdle at Fontwell in February on debut: behind in Sun Alliance Novices' Hurdle at Cheltenham following month: should improve. *D. H. Barons.* — p

CASTLEACRE 4 ch.g. Mr Fluorocarbon–Misfired (Blast) [1989/90 16m^{5} 16f^{5} 16f^{4} 16d^{6} 16m^{4} 16f 16m] small, lightly-made gelding: maiden on Flat, placed in claimers at up to 11.5f in 1989 (claimed out of G. Balding's stable £10,105 in July): modest plater over hurdles: pulls hard and barely stays 2m: acts on firm and dead going: blinkered last 2 starts. *J. Colston.* 82

CASTLE ANDREA 12 b.g. Andrea Mantegna–Carswell (Carino) [1989/90 c26d^{pu} c25m^{2}] leggy, workmanlike gelding: hunter chaser nowadays: ½-length second to Border Burg at Towcester in April: stays well: possibly unsuited by heavy ground but acts on any other: suited by a stiff track: usually looks well. *D. Jeffries.* c98

CASTLE BANKS 6 ch.g. Proverb–In The Forest (Crowded Room) [1989/90 aF16g^{pu} 20d 20g^{5} 24g^{3} 24m^{2}] strong, lengthy, angular gelding: novice hurdler: stays 3m: acts on good to firm ground. *J. A. C. Edwards.* 84

CASTLE JESTER 5 gr.h. Castle Keep–Peters Pleasure (Jimsun) [1989/90 16g 16s^{5} 18s 16s 16d^{F} 16v^{pu} 16g 16g^{6} 16f^{F} 16m 16f^{pu}] lengthy horse: poor novice selling hurdler: found nothing under pressure eighth outing: blinkered seventh to ninth and final outings: headstrong (has worn crossed noseband). *J. P. D. Elliott.* 58 §

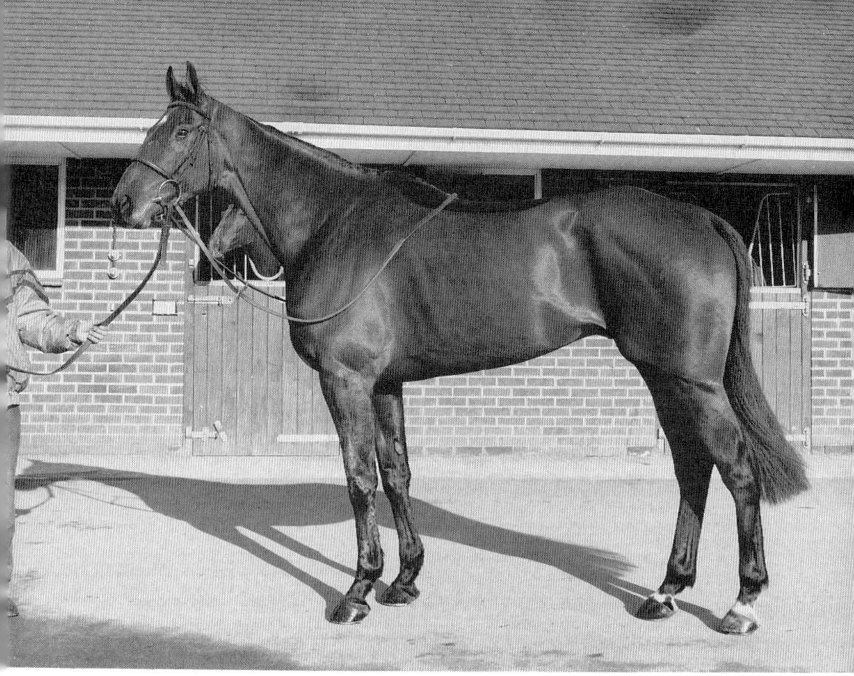

Mr Martin Myers' "Cash Is King"

CASTLEKEVIN 6 b.g. Crash Course–Theinthing (Harwell) [1989/90 16m^{2} 24m^{F}] rangy gelding: second in maiden hurdle Towcester in April: dead. *D. J. G. Murray-Smith.* 81

CASTLE OAKS 7 br.g. Strong Gale–Gillogue (Royal Orbit (USA)) [1989/90 c16g^{3} c21d* c24g^{6} c25d^{4} c25s^{pu} c26m^{pu}] angular gelding: winning hurdler: won novice chase at Towcester in December: tailed off when pulled up last 2 outings: stays 3m: acts on heavy going: usually a sound jumper. *D. R. Gandolfo.* **c91** —

CASTLE ORCHARD 6 br.g. Lepanto (GER)–Cora (Current Coin) [1989/90 F16g] fourth foal: dam won 1m seller at 5 yrs: behind in NH Flat race at Warwick: yet to race over hurdles or fences. *P. Hayward.*

CASTLE PAN 9 b.g. Pitpan–Clashdermot Lady (Shackleton) [1989/90 22g 24m c24f^{6} c16d^{5} c24g^{3}] sturdy gelding: modest winning point-to-pointer: no sign of ability over hurdles and in steeplechases (refused once): blinkered fourth start. *W. G. Reed.* c— —

CASTLERICHARDKING 5 b. or br.g. Matching Pair–Dont Rock (Rugged Man) [1989/90 F16g 16g^{4} 16m^{4}] rather unfurnished ex-Irish gelding: has scope: first foal: dam winning Irish point-to-pointer: second in NH Flat race in 1989 (trained by M. O'Connor): fourth in novice hurdles at Worcester in March and April: needs to settle. *J. A. C. Edwards.* 94

CASTLE SAINT 6 b.g. Welsh Saint–French Swallow (My Swallow) [1989/90 F17h^{4} 16g^{pu} c21g^{pu}] big, lengthy, plain gelding: second living foal: dam won over 7f at 2 yrs: fourth of 5 in NH Flat race at Carlisle in October: pulled up in a novice hurdle and a novice chase. *R. D. E. Woodhouse.* c— —

CASTLES CHOICE 8 b.g. Politico (USA)–Troy Castle (Troilus) [1989/90 c24f^{ur}] pulled up both outings over hurdles: third in a point-to-point in March: c— —

prominent when unseating rider 6 out in hunter chase at Kelso in April. *John Threadgall.*

CASTLESIDE 4 b.f. Sonnen Gold–Floor Show (Galivanter) [1989/90 16fpu] half-sister to winning hunter chaser Fred Astaire (by Be Friendly) and successful hurdler Gold Floor (by Goldhill): little sign of ability on Flat at 2 yrs: tailed off when pulled up in selling hurdle at Plumpton. *S. A. Bowen.* —

CASTLEVENNON 9 b.m. Kemal (FR)–Weaver's Fool (Weavers' Hall) [1989/90 20g 25g* 22gpu c24d3 c20g5 c20d3 c20f* c24m4 c33d4 c24g3] leggy, sparely-made mare: moderate hurdler: won at Kelso in November: fair chaser: won 3-runner handicap at Sedgefield in April, and finished very good fourth to Four Trix in William Hill Scottish National (Handicap Chase) at Ayr later in month on penultimate start: below her best final outing: stays very well: acts on any going: good mount for a claimer: usually held up. *Mrs S. A. Bramall.* c**123** ? 111

CASTLE WARDEN 13 br.g. Trombone–Tu-Ukumah (Little Buskins) [1989/90 c24spu c24gur] big gelding: useful chaser at best: tailed off when pulled up in February: stiff task and behind when unseating rider later in month: stays well: acts on any going. *J. A. C. Edwards.* c— —

CASTLE WINDOWS 7 ch.g. Le Moss–Roof Garden (Thatch (USA)) [1989/90 16g6 16m* 20g2 16v* 16g6 16g2 16g2 24d 16g 17v2 21s 21d2 20f] workmanlike ex-Irish gelding: won maiden hurdle at Tramore in August and handicap at Listowel following month: best effort in Britain when 1½ lengths second to Dwadme in novice event at Ludlow in March: travelled well until 3 out when twelfth to Regal Ambition in Sun Alliance Novices' Hurdle at Cheltenham later in month: stays 21f: acts on good to firm and heavy going: blinkered final start 1988/9: trained until after tenth outing by W. P. Mullins. *Mrs Gill E. Jones.* 123

CASUAL PASS 7 ch.g. Formidable (USA)–Pitapat (Shantung) [1989/90 24m3 16m4 20m2 16v 16d3] small, sturdy gelding: carries plenty of condition: modest hurdler: ran creditably all bar fourth start (first race for 4 months): stays 2½m: acts on any going: seems suited by racing up with the pace: blinkered once when successful in 1987/8: has looked unenthusiastic under pressure: trained until after third start by G. Richards. *T. A. K. Cuthbert.* 109

CATCHAPENNY 5 br.g. True Song–Quickapenny (Espresso) [1989/90 16v5 16m4 16g3] compact gelding: third foal: half-brother to winning hurdler/fair chaser Sneakapenny (by Levanter): dam, a useful hurdler and winning chaser, stayed well: modest form in novice hurdles: will be suited by 2½m. *M. J. Wilkinson.* 95

CATCH AT STRAWS 4 ch.g. Hayrick–Nanking (Above Suspicion) [1989/90 16f3] plain, short-legged gelding: third foal: half-brother to 7.5f seller winner Izzy Gunner (by Gunner B): dam fairly useful stayer on Flat: ridden by 7-lb claimer, third behind Sybillin in juvenile hurdle at Market Rasen in August. *J. P. Leigh.* 72

CATCH THE CROSS 4 gr.g. Alias Smith (USA)–Juliette Mariner (Welsh Pageant) [1989/90 16m 20m2 18s6 a20g* 20fsu 20f2] deep-girthed, workmanlike gelding: first foal: dam, poor staying maiden, half-sister to fairly useful sprinter Swinging Trio and granddaughter of 1000 Guineas and Oaks runner-up Spree: won novice claiming hurdle at Southwell in March: good second in novice handicap at Worcester following month: stays 2½m: acts on firm ground (stiffish task on soft): appeared not to go through with his effort on second start: blinkered last 3 outings. *Mrs D. Haine.* 102

CATHEDRAL PEAK 6 b.g. Tyrnavos–Honeypot Lane (Silly Season) [1989/90 16f] leggy gelding: quite modest handicapper on Flat, winner over 1¼m in 1989: sold out of C. Cyzer's stable 7,200 gns Newmarket Autumn Sales: well beaten in novice event at Wolverhampton on hurdling debut. *C. Spares.* —

CATHERINES PAL 9 b.g. Relko–Catherine's Plea (Petition) [1989/90 c24dpu c20dF] leggy ex-Irish gelding: quite useful hurdler at his best: lightly raced since 1986: no form in novice chases, though in lead when falling 4 out at Sligo in April. *D. J. Wintle.* c— —

CATHOS (FR) 5 b.g. Bellman (FR)–Charming Doll (Don (ITY)) [1989/90 16d2 16g5] neat gelding: plating-class novice hurdler: not raced after November: will stay beyond 2m: has been reluctant to race and carried head awkwardly: blinkered 1989/90: sold 4,900 gns Ascot May Sales. *J. A. B. Old.* 79 §

CATMAN 9 b.h. Crawter–Camina (Don Carlos) [1989/90 c18f4 c17fr] neat horse: novice selling hurdler: winning point-to-pointer: has made mistakes all starts in novice chases: not raced after August: ran out once in 1984/5 and refused final outing: has worn blinkers: sold 1,050 gns Ascot June Sales. *R. Lee.* c— x —

CAUTIOUS PETE 7 ch.g. Kambalda–Tarsilogue (Tarqogan) [1989/90 20d 16f4] workmanlike gelding: no worthwhile form in novice hurdles, though has shown ability. *W. A. Stephenson.* —

CAVALIER CROSSETT 9 b.g. Blind Harbour–Majestic Crossett (Golden Mallard) [1989/90 c20g] tall gelding: modest chaser: well below form in November: stays 2½m: best form on heavy going (ran poorly on firm): tried to run out once: amateur ridden. *E. M. Caine.* c— —

CAVALIER SPIRIT 4 ch.g. Sicyos (USA)–Cyclamen (FR) (Luthier) [1989/90 17fpu 16f6] poor maiden miler on Flat, has run blinkered: behind in novice hurdle at Huntingdon in May: sold out of J. Edwards' stable 2,200 gns Ascot October Sales after first start. *J. F. Panvert.* —

CAVARD 10 ch.g. Le Bavard (FR)–Belle Caprice (Arctic Slave) [1989/90 c16f4 25h6] sparely-made gelding: novice hurdler/chaser: little worthwhile form in Britain: ran in snatches and was dismounted immediately after passing post final start (August): seems to stay 3m: has worn a crossed noseband: has sweated. *G. A. Ham.* c— —

CAVENDISH DIAMOND 4 b.f. Decoy Boy–Tactile (Tacitus) [1989/90 16m 16f3 16spu a16g] workmanlike filly: plater on Flat, placed over 1m: third in conditional jockeys novice selling hurdle at Warwick in December: no form afterwards: acts on firm ground: sold 550 gns Ascot February Sales. *R. Simpson.* 68

CAVVIES CLOWN 10 b.g. Idiot's Delight–Cavallina (Vulgan) [1989/90 c25g* c26f4 c25m2] c**161** —

It is to be hoped Cavvies Clown doesn't go the way of that other top-class staying chaser of the recent past, Bregawn. Few who witnessed the latter's battling victories in the Hennessy Cognac Gold Cup at Newbury and the Tote Cheltenham Gold Cup in the 1982/3 season could have envisaged that temperament would get the better of him in the following campaign. Prior to 1983/4 the only sign of temperament Bregawn had shown in public was a tendency to give trouble at the start; once under way, he had been a most determined and courageous racehorse. At present that remark applies equally to Cavvies Clown who was mulish at the start and showed a

Jim Ford Challenge Cup Chase, Wincanton—
Cavvies Clown shows his well-being on his belated return

Mrs J. Ollivant's "Cavvies Clown"

reluctance to jump off in all three races in 1989/90 but who, once he got going, raced with plenty of zest. Cavvies Clown first misbehaved at the start in the previous season's Tote Cheltenham Gold Cup, in which he eventually collapsed, after a last-fence refusal when tailed off. His reappearance was delayed by the coughing which struck his stable just after Christmas. On his return to the track, Cavvies Clown showed his well-being by jumping well and making all in the Jim Ford Challenge Cup at Wincanton in February. Having set only a fairly modest pace in the early stages, he quickened approaching four out, was soon clear and finished twenty-five lengths in front of the runner-up Cool Ground. Cavvies Clown was then sent for his third attempt to lift the Gold Cup—he'd finished six lengths second to Charter Party in the 1988 running. Cavvies Clown again did extremely well to finish fourth, beaten just under twelve lengths behind Norton's Coin. In effect he lost his chance at the start, setting off at least twenty-five lengths behind his eleven opponents. The early pace was so strong that it took Cavvies Clown a long time to make inroads on the gap; and, although he'd made good headway by five out, he'd virtually shot his bolt by the final turn. It is natural to speculate on what might have happened had Cavvies Clown jumped off in touch. However, he was unable to improve significantly on his Gold Cup form in more favourable circumstances in his next and final race in the Martell Cup Chase at Liverpool three weeks later. Cavvies Clown's main rival looked to be Toby Tobias, who'd finished second, beaten three quarters of a length, in the Gold Cup and who had now to concede 4 lb. The pair had the race between them, with the three other runners left behind from the final turn. Cavvies Clown lost eight to ten lengths at the start but with no strong gallop in the early stages he quickly recovered and led after the second fence. He began to increase the pace going down the back straight for the final time and quickened appreciably four from home, but he was uable to shake off Toby Tobias. Despite running on strongly Cavvies Clown was caught after the second-last and beaten one and a half lengths at the line.

Cavvies Clown (b.g. 1980)	Idiot's Delight (b 1970)	Silly Season (br 1962)	Tom Fool
			Double Deal
		Dolphinet (b 1957)	Big Game
			Sea Gipsy
	Cavallina (br 1966)	Vulgan (b 1943)	Sirlan
			Vulgate
		Cacarina (b 1950)	Cacador
			Piper's Darling

As Cavvies Clown's dam died in 1985 there is little new to add to the details of the pedigree as given in the previous editions of *Chasers & Hurdlers*. The once-raced Cavallina, a half-sister to the top-class chaser Titus Oates, has produced two other winners, the ungenuine chaser Pikeman (by Turnpike) and the point-to-pointer Coaching Club (by New Member). Cavvies Clown is effective at twenty-one furlongs but he's ideally suited by longer distances. He is a bold jumper most of the time, suited by forcing tactics. A small, sparely-made gelding, Cavvies Clown sometimes looks dull and patchy in his coat, but he looked particularly well on his last two starts. *D. R. C. Elsworth.*

CAWSTON BAY 5 b.m. Cawston's Clown–Princess Davinia (Saintly Song) [1989/90 16f^{6} 16f^{r} 16f^{pu} 16g^{5} 16f^{ur} 16g^{4} 16m 17m^{5} a16g 20f^{bd} 20f^{2} 20g^{4}] sparely-made mare: poor novice selling hurdler: best efforts at 2½m: acts on firm going: refused to race second outing. *J. Norton.* 71

CAYMAN QUEEN 5 b.m. Tina's Pet–Harpers Girl (Crowned Prince (USA)) [1989/90 16m^{su} 16m^{2} 16s a24g^{pu}] sparely-made mare: selling hurdler: second at Towcester in December: well beaten afterwards: stays 21f: acts on any going: less than fluent jumper. *R. P. C. Hoad.* 78

CAZAUDEHORE 5 ch.g. Callernish–Clashdermot Lady (Shackleton) [1989/90 F16m^{6} F16f^{5}] IR 17,000 3-y-o: half-brother to several winning jumpers, including fair 21f winning hurdler Out The Gap (by Cheval): dam never ran: showed ability in NH Flat races at Sandown and Newbury (fifth to Norman Conqueror) in March: yet to race over hurdles or fences. *M. H. B. Robinson.*

CEDAR SHELL 5 b.h. Sharpo–Cedrella (Averof) [1989/90 16h^{2}] modest 1m winner on Flat, well below form in 1989: second to Pollock in novice hurdle at Taunton in September. *Andrew Turnell.* 84

CEETEEBEE 5 ch.m. Paddy's Stream–Bella Bambino (Bahrain) [1989/90 F16f] third foal: half-sister to useful point-to-pointer/hunter chaser Le Bambino (by Le Prince): dam winning hurdler/chaser: tailed off in NH Flat race at Ludlow: yet to race over hurdles or fences. *O. O'Neill.*

CELCIUS 6 b.g. Ile de Bourbon (USA)–Cistus (Sun Prince) [1989/90 a16g^{3} 16g^{3} a18g 16s^{4} 16v^{4} 16s^{3} 16s^{2} 17f^{2}] small, light-framed gelding: modest hurdler: often refuses to go through with his effort, and did so when second in selling handicap at Leicester in January: creditable second in non-selling handicap at Newton Abbot over 3 months later: refused third on chasing debut: stays 2¼m: acts on any going: successful for a claimer: wears blinkers over hurdles. *M. C. Pipe.* c— 110 §

CELERY RISE (NZ) 6 b.g. Palm Beach (FR)–Golden Wedding (NZ) (Sucaryl) [1989/90 17f^{5} 16f^{2} a16g^{5} 19m^{4} 21f^{5} c20g^{F} c16g^{F} 22d] unfurnished gelding: poor novice hurdler: has fallen both starts over fences: stays 19f: acts on firm going: sold 3,400 gns Ascot June Sales. *D. H. Barons.* c— 73

CELESTIAL INVADER 8 b.g. Brave Invader (USA)–Astrella Celeste (Menelek) [1989/90 24d^{pu} 16g^{F} 16d^{F}] angular gelding: very lightly raced and no sign of ability in novice hurdles: dead. *N. Miller.* —

CELTIC ASCESS 9 ch.m. Celtic Cone–Ascess (Eastern Venture) [1989/90 c19f^{2}] smallish, workmanlike mare: poor novice hurdler: wearing crossed c78 —

noseband, second in poor novice hunter chase at Hereford: will probably stay 3m. *Mrs R. C. Matheson.*

CELTIC BARD 8 b.g. Celtic Cone–Arctic Lily (Arctic Slave) [1989/90 c24gpu c24m4] compact gelding: winning hurdler/chaser: tailed off in April: stays 3¼m: best form on a yielding surface: sweated up second outing 1988/9: sketchy jumper. *T. T. Bill.* c— —

CELTIC BARLE 6 ch.g. Celtic Cone–Pelant Barle (Prince Barle) [1989/90 20d 16g 20s* 20d4] good-bodied gelding: fairly useful hurdler: successful in conditional jockeys handicap at Ascot in February: fair fourth behind Battalion at Wolverhampton later in month: will stay beyond 2½m: acts on soft going. *H. B. Hodge.* 129

CELTIC BHOY 4 b.g. Red Sunset–Nighty Night (Sassafras (FR)) [1989/90 16g a16g3 18f2 16d4 16f5] close-coupled gelding: modest handicapper on Flat, successful at up to 13f: modest juvenile hurdler: below-form fifth in handicap at Ascot final outing: stays 2¼m: acts on firm and dead ground. *P. Mitchell.* 98

CELTIC BOB 10 ch.g. Celtic Cone–Quaife Sport (Quayside) [1989/90 16g 16m2 20gF 16m4 16g 16s5 a16g* a16g3 21d 17m3 17m4 20f3 a20g2] small, robust gelding: handicap hurdler: some way below his best in 1989/90, though won at Southwell in January: didn't find a great deal under pressure penultimate outing: stays 2½m: acts on any going: good mount for a claimer: visored twice in 1985/6 and on third start. *O. O'Neill.* 105

CELTIC BOMBSHELL 6 ch.m. Celtic Cone–Birds Well (Birdbrook) [1989/90 16s 16g5] small, lengthy mare: no form over hurdles: blinkered final start. *N. Bycroft.* —

CELTIC BREEZE 7 b.g. Celtic Cone–Sipped (Ballyciptic) [1989/90 16g4] sturdy gelding: second foal: brother to useful staying hurdler Sip of Orange: dam, winning hurdler, stayed 3m: unplaced in NH Flat races: always-prominent fourth to Woodchester Glen in novice hurdle at Hexham in March: will be well suited by 2½m. *M. P. Naughton.* 81 p

CELTIC CAPRI 11 ch.g. Celtic Cone–Capelena (Mon Fetiche) [1989/90 c25g c26v5 c26v6 c25dpu] compact gelding: lightly raced but has shown ability in novice hurdles: winning point-to-pointer: poor form in steeplechases: stays 3m. *J. H. Cork.* c83 —

CELTIC CASTLE 4 b.c. Caerleon (USA)–Knighton House (Pall Mall) [1989/90 16g 16s6 24d] angular colt: half-brother to several winners, including very useful middle-distance performer Open Day (by Northfields): dam, sister to Reform, was very useful at up to 1¼m: well beaten over hurdles: blinkered second start. *J. D. Roberts.* —

CELTIC CATCH 4 br.g. Celtic Cone–Eyecatcher (Doubtless II) [1989/90 F16f] fourth foal: half-brother to 2 poor performers: dam, fair chaser, third in Grand National in 1976 and 1977: favourite, last in NH Flat race at Newbury: yet to race over hurdles. *J. R. Bosley.*

CELTIC CHIMES 6 ch.m. Celtic Cone–Dyna Bell (Double Jump) [1989/90 16f3 18gF 16m6 16f4 18g 16vsu 16g a20g4 18f3] small mare: poor novice hurdler: form only at up to 2¼m: acts on firm ground (running a fair race when slipping up after 2 out on heavy sixth outing): visored last 4 starts. *A. W. Denson.* 72

CELTIC CRACKLE 10 ch.g. Celtic Cone–Birds Well (Birdbrook) [1989/90 c17f c21f3 c24fwo c21f3 c24m2] small, lengthy gelding: poor hurdler/chaser: walked over in handicap chase at Leicester in November: not raced after December: stays 3m: probably acts on any going: blinkered once in 1985/6. *P. D. Cundell.* c79 —

CELTIC DAWN 7 b.m. Celtic Cone–Ballylaneen (Master Buck) [1989/90 c17fpu c22msu c20dpu c24vpu 20d] compact mare: poor novice hurdler: has failed to complete course in 4 races over fences: stays 2½m: has worn a tongue strap: claimer ridden. *A. B. Mactaggart.* c— —

CELTIC DOVE 7 b.m. Celtic Cone–Grey Dove (Grey Love) [1989/90 16g 17v2 21dur 16v2 21s2 22d 24m6] small, workmanlike mare: modest novice hurdler: stays 21f: acts on heavy going. *K. Bishop.* 103

CELTIC DREAM 7 ch.m. Celtic Cone–Kay's Dream (Khalkis) [1989/90 c24f2 c25g4] rangy, workmanlike mare: no form over hurdles: in frame in novice chases: not raced after November: stays 3m: moderate jumper. *T. T. Bill.* c75 x —

CELTIC FLAME 9 ch.g. Celtic Cone–Dandy's Last (Prefairy) [1989/90 c20m2 c20vur c20d4 c20gF] leggy, short-backed gelding: winning hurdler: fair chaser: c**121** x —

made several mistakes when creditable second to Private Views in handicap at Newbury in November: remote fourth on same course in February: stays 2½m: acts on dead ground: tends to sweat: moderate jumper. *P. W. Harris.*

CELTIC FLEET 9 b.g. Celtic Cone–Erica Alba (Yukon Eric (CAN)) [1989/90 c24g[3] c36g[pu]] small, sturdy gelding: good third in hunter chase at Bangor in April and was running a tremendous race a week later in quite valuable handicap at Uttoxeter (32 lb out of handicap) until pulled up lame after mistake 4 out: suited by a distance of ground: probably acts on any going: usually blinkered. *J. L. Spearing.* c88 + —

CELTIC GERTRUDE 10 ch.m. Celtic Cone–Royal Gertrude (Royal Buck) [1989/90 c24g[F] c22m[F] 25m a22g[4] a24g[2] a20g a24g[5] 24s[pu]] sturdy mare: poor novice hurdler: has failed to complete course over fences: stays 3m: blinkered nowadays. *S. R. Bowring.* c— 58

CELTIC HAMBRO 7 b.g. Celtic Cone–Ice Bird (Fighting Charlie) [1989/90 25g* 21d c25s[pu]] lengthy, workmanlike, angular ex-Irish gelding: will make a chaser: half-brother to quite useful staying jumpers Indiana Dare (by Mandamus) and Brandy Hambro (by Hot Brandy): dam, winning hurdler, is half-sister to quite useful chaser Iceman: successful in 3 point-to-points in 1989: didn't jump fluently when winning weakly-contested novice hurdle at Cheltenham in November: pulled up lame final start: will stay extreme distances. *D. Nicholson.* c— 98

CELTIC HAMLET 11 ch.g. Celtic Cone–Royal Gertrude (Royal Buck) [1989/90 c24f[3] c25g[pu] c25m[4] c21m[3] c25d[pu] a24g[3] a24g[4] c25f[6] c24m[5] c25m[3] c24m[5]] lengthy, sparely-made gelding: poor chaser/novice hurdler: stays 25f: acts on any going: sometimes blinkered. *J. E. Long.* c79 80

CELTIC KING 6 ch.g. Kinghaven–Celtic Siren (Welsh Pageant) [1989/90 16g 16f[4] 16m[4]] robust, chasing type: ex-Irish: first foal: dam poor maiden in France: placed in NH Flat race in 1988 when trained by J. Hassett: has shown ability in novice hurdles, on final start (needing race) around 17 lengths fourth to Kind'a Smart at Huntingdon in May: likely to be suited by further than 2m. *B. J. Curley.* 77

CELTIC LORD 8 ch.g. Celtic Cone–Mrs Stephens (Master Stephen) [1989/90 22m[4] 24g 21f[pu]] tall, lengthy gelding: chasing type: poor novice hurdler: only form for some time when fourth at Wincanton in October: pulled up lame final start (March). *Mrs J. G. Retter.* 80

CELTIC MANOR 7 b.g. Celtic Cone–Bell-Amys (Blandford Lad) [1989/90 16d[5]] workmanlike gelding: remote fifth in novice hurdle at Windsor in January: will be suited by longer distances. *P. J. Hobbs.* —

CELTIC MEMBER 6 ch.g. New Member–Qebir Celtice (Celtic Cone) [1989/90 F16f 16m[6] 20g] first foal: dam poor novice hurdler: well beaten in novice hurdles. *R. J. Holder.* —

CELTIC ORIGINAL 6 b.g. Celtic Cone–Ice Bird (Fighting Charlie) [1989/90 16g[5] 20d[5] 20f 20g[4]] compact, workmanlike gelding: modest form in novice hurdles: will be suited by further. *R. Lee.* 87

CELTIC PRINCE 4 ch.g. Celtic Cone–Lothian Countess (New Brig) [1989/90 F16g[4] F16m[3] F16m] leggy, workmanlike gelding: sixth foal: dam fair hurdler: in frame in NH Flat races at Kempton and Sandown: sweating and edgy, behind in well-contested event at Liverpool final start: yet to race over hurdles. *N. A. Twiston-Davies.*

CELTIC PRINCESS 10 b.m. Celtic Cone–Petal Princess (Floribunda) [1989/90 c25f[ur]] strong, sturdy mare: modest novice hurdler in 1984/5: won a point-to-point in March: jumps poorly in hunter chases: not certain to stay 2½m: acts on heavy going: blinkered last 3 outings in 1984/5. *R. T. Price.* c— x —

CELTIC REMORSE 8 b.m. Celtic Cone–Armagnac Bay (Armagnac Monarch) [1989/90 c26f[2] c26f[3] c24g[2] c27d[4] c26s[4] c32f[F] c26f* c25f[4] c26f[3]] smallish mare: winning point-to-pointer: made all in novice chase at Fontwell in March: good third in amateur riders chase on same course in May: stays 3¼m: acts on any going: has been sweating and edgy in preliminaries: has worn blinkers, best form without. *C. T. Nash.* c82

CELTIC RIFLE 6 b.h. Celtic Cone–Busted Rifle (Scottish Rifle) [1989/90 21d 20g[pu]] workmanlike horse: poor novice hurdler: form only at 2m: blinkered twice. *Mrs H. Parrott.* —

CELTIC SANDS 7 b.m. Celtic Cone–Rapenna (Straight Lad) [1989/90 20m 20s 22d 24g[pu]] small, workmanlike mare: won amateur riders maiden hurdle in 1988/9: little other form: amateur ridden nowadays. *T. L. A. Robson.* —

CELTIC SERF 6 ch.m. Celtic Cone–Branded Slave (Arctic Slave) [1989/90 16v^{pu}] sturdy, plain mare: little sign of ability over hurdles. *Capt. T. A. Forster.* —

CELTIC SHOT 8 b.g. Celtic Cone–Duckdown (Blast) [1989/90 c20g^{2} c20v* c20g* c20g* c20d^{2} c24s^{F} c16m^{6} c16d*] c**152** p —

One of the highlights of the latest season was the impressive adaptation to jumping fences of the 1988 Waterford Crystal Champion Hurdle winner Celtic Shot. The switch from hurdling to chasing is often a difficult one, even for good horses, and since the mid-'sixties only Bula, Night Nurse and Dawn Run amongst Champion Hurdlers adapted well enough to reach the top over fences. Persian War, Monksfield, Sea Pigeon, Gaye Brief and See You Then never ran in a steeplechase after their Champion Hurdle wins, nor has Beech Road so far. But like Bula, Night Nurse and Dawn Run, Celtic Shot, a strong, good-looking gelding, always had the physical appearance of a chaser. And, judged on his first season over fences, Celtic Shot looks destined to become as good as he was over hurdles.

The most pleasing aspect of Celtic Shot the chaser is his jumping. None too fluent a jumper of hurdles as a novice, falling twice, he developed into a sound rather than spectacular hurdler with experience. Celtic Shot proved a much quicker learner over fences, jumping well from the start. His only fall came, heavily, at the fourth last when out of contention in the Old Road Securities Reynoldstown Novices' Chase won by Royal Athlete at Ascot in February. Celtic Shot had created such a favourable impression previously that, at the time of that race, he was quoted at only 14/1 by the sponsors for the Tote Cheltenham Gold Cup. Celtic Shot had shown immense promise on his chasing debut when going down by a neck to the 1989 Arkle winner Waterloo Boy in a qualifier of the Arlington Premier Chase series at Chepstow in December, outjumping him for much of the way and ridden very much with an eye to the future in the latter stages. He ran another excellent race against a more experienced rival when two and a half lengths second to Sabin du Loir in the final of the series at Cheltenham in January, his jumping standing up to the strong pace set by the winner.

Novair Wayward Lad Novices' Chase, Kempton—Celtic Shot shows himself a good prospect

Celtic Shot met nothing of their calibre when completing a hat-trick in novice company in between, though he beat a fairly useful rival each time when accounting for Elfast (by twelve lengths) at Haydock in December and Nodform (comfortably by two and a half lengths) at Sandown the following month. Though less impressive in the Novair Wayward Lad Novices' Chase at Kempton in between—he was no certainty to beat Comandante when that rival's fall at the second last left him a distance clear—he'd been more conservatively ridden than usual and made a few early jumping errors as a result.

Chasing also seemed to rekindle Celtic Shot's enthusiasm. He'd looked to run lazily in the Champion Hurdle on his penultimate outing in 1988/9, but raced with plenty of zest on most starts in the latest season. Celtic Shot ran a most genuine race to win the Edinburgh Woollen Mill's Future Champion Novices' Chase at Ayr in April. Under pressure a long way out in a strongly-run race and seemingly caught flat-footed when Young Snugfit quickened to lead after the third last, Celtic Shot rallied splendidly. Jumping the last well, he stayed on strongly to catch Young Snugfit in the last fifty yards and win by a half a length, the pair ten lengths clear of Highfrith in third. Celtic Shot had finished thirteen lengths behind third-placed Young Snugfit when favourite for the Arkle Trophy at Cheltenham the previous month, never looking to be travelling particularly well on the good to firm ground. Though he won a minor hurdle on a similar surface in 1988/9, Celtic Shot, who's usually bandaged behind, has never run to within 10 lb of his best on top-of-the-ground: all his best efforts over hurdles came on very soft.

Celtic Shot (b.g. 1982)	Celtic Cone (ch 1967)	Celtic Ash (ch 1957)	Sicambre
			Ash Plant
		Fircone (ch 1959)	Mossborough
			Wood Fire
	Duckdown (b 1973)	Blast (b 1957)	Djebe
			Gale Warning
		Clay Duck (b 1966)	Dicta Drake
			Grey Rose

Although a chasing type on looks, Celtic Shot's dam the winning hurdler Duckdown showed little in four outings over fences. She's a half-sister to two good novice chasers in Clayside and Clutterbuck, however, and also to Bitter Buck, winner of a novice hurdle in the latest season. There are other good chasers further back in the family, Grey Rose notably producing the Mackeson Gold Cup winner Clear Cut, and Straight

Edinburgh Woollen Mill's Future Champion Novices' Chase, Ayr—
Celtic Shot confirms himself one of the season's best novice chasers

Mr D. E. H. Horton's "Celtic Shot"

Jet, dam of Kim Muir Memorial Challenge Cup winner Broomy Bank. Celtic Cone sires a wide variety of types—he's the sire, for instance, of the two-mile hurdler Cruising Altitude and the very useful stayer Ryde Again. Celtic Shot falls between the two extremes. He gave the impression at Ayr that he needs testing conditions to be fully effective at two miles. He stays two and a half miles well enough to suggest that three miles on a sharp course such as Kempton will be within his compass: his lasting the Gold Cup course at Cheltenham is more open to question. The revamped pattern of National Hunt racing should provide more opportunities for horses of Celtic Shot's ability, and there are new Grade 1 two-and-a-half-mile chases at Haydock and Wetherby to go for whether he turns out to stay or not. He's sure to win more races. *C. P. E. Brooks.*

CELTIC SOMERS 7 ch.g. Celtic Cone–October Fair (Will Somers) [1989/90 22d 20g 22v5 20v 16g c20gF] sturdy gelding: poor novice hurdler: behind when falling ninth in novice handicap on chasing debut. *R. H. Goldie.* c— 73

CELTIC STORM 10 br.g. Celtic Cone–Summer Camp (Varano) [1989/90 c26m3 c26mpu] plain, good-topped gelding: novice hurdler: successful in 5 point-to-points in 1990: third in hunter chase at Newton Abbot in May. *Mrs H. S. M. Ridley.* c**86** —

CELTIC SUNLIGHT 5 b.g. Celtic Cone–Hilliana (Goldhill) [1989/90 16g3 16d2 16g 22d4] compact gelding: moderate novice hurdler: not raced after December: stays 2¾m: acts on dead going: claimer ridden. *F. Jordan.* 91

CELTIC TRUST 7 ch.g. Celtic Cone–Trust Ann (Capistrano) [1989/90 c20d^F c20s^4 c22d^3] strong, workmanlike gelding: modest novice hurdler/chaser: usually makes mistakes over fences: stays well: acts on soft going. *J. C. McConnochie.* c92 x —

CELTIC WALK 6 b.g. Celtic Cone–Bushwalks Daughter (Arctic Slave) [1989/90 c20g^3 c20g* c20v^2 c20d^{pu}] compact gelding: no worthwhile form over hurdles: won novice handicap chase at Wolverhampton in January: stayed on well when 12 lengths second to Elvercone in novice event at Chepstow later in month: ran as though something was amiss final outing: will stay beyond 2½m: acts on heavy going: sound jumper. *Capt. T. A. Forster.* c92 + —

CELTIC WATERS 5 ch.m. Celtic Cone–Moonbreaker (Twilight Alley) [1989/90 F16f] half-sister to winning Irish point-to-pointer Rawyards Brig (by New Brig): dam never ran: mid-division in NH Flat race at Warwick: yet to race over hurdles or fences. *S. Christian.*

CENTAUR SONG 10 ch.g. True Song–Mid-Day Milli (Midsummer Night II) [1989/90 c22m^F c25m^{pu}] sparely-made gelding: moderate chaser: won point-to-point in March: failed to complete course in hunter chases: best form at 2m on top-on-the-ground. *D. C. O'Brien.* c— —

CENTENARY STAR 5 b.g. Broadsword (USA)–Tina's Gold (Goldhill) [1989/90 20d 16g a20g^3] sparely-made gelding: poor novice hurdler: pulls hard. *R. Hollinshead.* 68 +

CENTRE ATTRACTION 11 b.g. Little Buskins–Money For Fun (Even Money) [1989/90 c16g^2 c16d^3 c20g^{pu} c17d^4 c16v^4 c20s^5] close-coupled gelding: fair chaser: ran moderately after first 2 outings: not raced after February: has won over 2½m but is best at around 2m: probably needs give in the ground nowadays: visored once: excellent mount for a claimer: sweats on occasions: has won 6 times at Kelso. *G. Richards.* c130 d —

CEROMERE 4 b.f. Rushmere–Cerolane (Romancero) [1989/90 18v^4 20m^{pu}] third foal: dam selling hurdler: little promise in selling hurdle and novice event. *W. T. Kemp.* —

CERTAIN STYLE 7 b.g. Connaught–Nushka (Tom Fool) [1989/90 c20g* c20d^3 c20g^2 c16m c20f^2] rather leggy, useful-looking gelding: modest hurdler: successful in novice chase at Kempton in January: ran creditably in face of stiff tasks afterwards: stays 2½m: acts on firm and dead going: blinkered fourth to sixth starts. *O. Sherwood.* c113 —

CEVA PARK 5 b.g. Salluceva–South Park (Sandford Lad) [1989/90 F17m^6 F17f 20g^F 22g 25d 25g] tall, rather angular gelding: fourth foal: dam unraced: no worthwhile form in novice hurdles, but showed signs of ability fifth start. *R. Earnshaw.* —

CHACELEY LAD 5 ch.g. Creetown–Simmies Love (Record Token) [1989/90 16m^{ur} 19m^{pu}] fourth in NH Flat races: amateur ridden, pulled up fifth in novice hurdle at Hereford. *G. Price.* —

CHAGHATAI (USA) 4 ch.c. Sir Ivor–Clutch Hitter (USA) (Nodouble (USA)) [1989/90 a16g^6 a16g^4 a16g^4 16m^2 16m 16g^3] lengthy, angular colt: well beaten on Flat: sold out of Mrs L. Piggott's stable 3,000 gns Newmarket Autumn Sales: poor juvenile selling hurdler: has worn a tongue strap. *C. Spares.* 68

CHAIN SHOT 5 b.g. Pas de Seul–Burnished (Formidable (USA)) [1989/90 16s 16g 16f^2 16f^2] compact gelding: quite modest sprinter on Flat: runner-up in novice hurdles at Wolverhampton and Bangor (beaten 4 lengths by Gentleman's Jig) in March: pulls hard and will prove suited by sharp 2m and firm ground. *K. White.* 89

CHAIS DU FONDATEUR 10 ch.g. Hot Brandy–Venture More (Eastern Venture) [1989/90 c26g^{pu} c25d^F c24s^{pu} c20d^6 c25m* c24m^{pu}] small, angular gelding: only sign of ability when winning novice chase at Plumpton in 1988/9 and 4-runner handicap on same course in April: stays 25f: acts on good to firm ground. *R. Curtis.* c86 —

CHALIAND 5 ch.g. Hard Fought–Behroz (Relko) [1989/90 16d 16f^{ur} 16g 16s a16g a20g^2] leggy gelding: poor novice selling hurdler: probably stays 2½m: blinkered final start 1988/9: sold 1,550 gns Ascot April Sales: resold 1,200 gns Ascot May Sales. *S. T. Harris.* 60

CHALKHILL BLUE 5 b.m. Dunphy–Lady Probus (Shantung) [1989/90 16d^{pu} a20g^5] sparely-made mare: of little account. *D. C. Jermy.* —

CHAMPAGNE CHARLIE 13 br.g. Charlottown–The Guzzler (Behistoun) [1989/90 27g^5 20g^5 25g^5 27d^2] small, rather lightly-made gelding: handicap 92 hurdler: second at Sedgefield in January: suited by a test of stamina: probably unsuited by heavy ground, acts on any other: usually races up with the pace: has won for a claimer. *Mrs S. M. Austin.*

CHAMPAGNE LAD 4 ch.g. Hawaiian Return (USA)–Bohemian Girl (Pardao) [1989/90 16g3 16f* 16f4] short-backed, sparely-made gelding: half-brother to winning hurdlers Tinker's Trip and Traveller's Trip (both by Royal Trip): dam well beaten in 2 maidens on Flat in Ireland: won strongly-run juvenile hurdle at Cheltenham in April most impressively by 10 lengths from Good Spark, leading approaching last and quickening clear in good style: well-backed favourite, every chance 2 out, but not at all knocked about after mistake last when 8½ lengths fourth behind Ivors Guest in juvenile handicap at Ascot following month: acts on firm ground: jumps soundly: an interesting prospect who looks well worth another chance to confirm most favourable impression created at Cheltenham. *J. T. Gifford.* 123 p

CHAMPAGNE RUN 5 b.g. Runnett–Tolaytala (Be My Guest (USA)) [1989/90 20dF 18f 19fpu 22m3 25f6 22f* 21mpu 17hpu] lengthy gelding: handicap hurdler: easily best effort of 1989/90 when winning at Fontwell in May: ran poorly afterwards: stays 2¾m: ran poorly on heavy going, acts on any other: usually claimer ridden: blinkered third, sixth and seventh starts. *W. G. M. Turner.* 100

CHANCE AGAIN 7 br.m. Balinger–Chance A Look (Don't Look) [1989/90 16s 16g 22spu] sturdy mare: no promise in novice hurdles. *S. Woodman.* —

CHANCE BUY 7 b.g. Rolfe (USA)–Astonishment (Blast) [1989/90 c22sF] sparely-made gelding: only form over hurdles when third in 2½m selling handicap in 1987/8: won a point-to-point in March: sweating, soon behind and fell 2 out in novice hunter chase at Nottingham previous month. *C. T. Nash.* c— —

CHANCE REMARK (USA) 7 b.g. Elocutionist (USA)–Lucky Sway (USA) (Lucky Debonair) [1989/90 16g5 a20gpu 16g3 20g2 20d4 c20g] lengthy gelding: winning hurdler: well behind in novice chase at Carlisle in January (severed a tendon and was destroyed): stayed 2½m: blinkered fifth outing. *J. J. O'Neill.* c— 96

CHANCERY BUCK 7 ch.g. Pauper–What Vision (Golden Vision) [1989/90 c17d2 c20mpu] leggy gelding: ninth living foal: half-brother to winning Irish point-to-pointer Mr Bo Peep (by Pry): dam never ran: unplaced in a point-to-point in Ireland in 1988: 30 lengths second of 4 in novice chase at Devon & Exeter in November: made several mistakes later in month. *G. B. Balding.* c66

CHANCES PITCH 9 b.m. Saucy Kit–Minetta (Neron) [1989/90 17m] compact mare: no worthwhile form over hurdles: poor novice chaser: moderate jumper. *Mrs H. S. Wells.* c— x —

CHAN FU 5 b.g. Kafu–Chanrossa (High Top) [1989/90 20msu a18g6 16s a16g 16fpu] sparely-made gelding: little sign of ability over hurdles, including in selling company: pulled up lame final start: sold out of R. Curtis' stable 1,200 gns Ascot December Sales after second start. *J. E. Long.* —

CHANGE-ALLEY 10 ch.g. Native Bazaar–Franglars (High Perch) [1989/90 c21dpu] small, sturdy gelding: fair winning point-to-pointer: fourth in novice hunter chase in 1988 (ran in snatches): bit backward, behind until pulled up in February. *Ron Fear.* c— —

CHANGE GUARD 4 b.f. Day Is Done–Mittens (Run The Gantlet (USA)) [1989/90 16d 16mbd] sparely-made filly: third foal: half-sister to winning staying hurdler Green Archer (by Hardgreen): dam winning hurdler: modest maiden miler on Flat, tends to hang left: pulled hard when seventh in novice hurdle at Catterick in February. *Roy Robinson.* —

CHANGE THE NAME 7 ch.g. Celtic Cone–Yogurt (Saint Denys) [1989/90 24g 24g6 27g3 c24gpu 27s* 24s4 27d3 27g2 a24g2 24m2 24g*] strong gelding: won novice selling hurdle at Sedgefield in January (made all, bought in 4,400 gns) and handicap hurdle at Market Rasen in May: failed to complete in 3 point-to-points and a novice chase: stays well: acts on good to firm and soft going: visored or blinkered nowadays. *P. A. Blockley.* c— 100

CHANGE WEAR 4 b.g. Alzao (USA)–Piccadilly Lil (Pall Mall) [1989/90 16f5 16g6 16g5 16f5 20f6 20f4 16f] sparely-made gelding: only sign of ability on Flat when fourth in 1¼m minor event in 1989: poor juvenile hurdler: stays 2½m: acts on firm ground: trained first start by K. Brassey. *J. S. King.* 88

CHANTEZ-LES BAS 10 gr.m. Town Crier–Cheltenham (Connaught) [1989/90 c20s6 c27f6 c25f5] no sign of ability over hurdles in 1983/4: has since run in point-to-points, winning in March: well beaten in hunter chases. *J. N. Swinbank.* —

CHANTILLY DAWN 6 b.m. Gunner B–Liscannor Lass (Burglar) [1989/90 16s 20g[6] a22g 20f 20m] smallish, sparely-made mare: poor novice hurdler. *J. C. Haynes.* 61

CHANTILLY LACE (FR) 6 ch.m. Carwhite–Frenchouan (FR) (Jim French (USA)) [1989/90 19s[5] 17v[F] 16d 22d[5] 22g 17d 25f[5] 24g[3] 26m[5]] leggy, sparely-made mare: handicap hurdler: beaten in a seller sixth start: stays 3m: probably acts on any going. *Mrs A. Knight.* 90

CHANTRY BOY 6 b.g. Balliol–Glebe (Tacitus) [1989/90 16s 16s 16m[6]] close-coupled gelding: seemed of little account until finishing sixth in conditional jockeys novice handicap hurdle at Fakenham in March: pulls hard. *W. Holden.* 64

CHAPERALL LADY 4 br.f. Mansingh (USA)–El Chaperall (Scottish Rifle) [1989/90 F14v] fourth foal: dam Irish 1m winner: tailed off in NH Flat race at Ayr: yet to race over hurdles. *J. H. Johnson.*

CHARCOAL BURNER 5 br.g. Royal Match–Resist (Reliance II) [1989/90 16f[pu]] small gelding: third foal: dam won selling hurdles: untrustworthy handicapper on Flat, winner over 7f in 1989 (stays 1¼m): behind when pulled up last in novice hurdle at Wolverhampton in March (pulled hard). *B. R. Millman.* —

CHARDAY 5 b.m. Magnolia Lad–Charanda (Andrea Mantegna) [1989/90 16m[pu] 16m[5] 16f[6]] sparely-made mare: of little account. *Miss C. Horler.* —

CHARIOT SCENE 6 gr.g. Son of Shaka–Misty Sovereign (French Vine) [1989/90 aF16g aF16g[6] aF13g] first foal: dam of little account at 2 yrs: well beaten in NH Flat races at Lingfield: sold 1,200 gns Ascot April Sales: yet to race over hurdles or fences. *P. Howling.*

CHARLES DEVON LAD 5 br.h. Fitzwilliam (USA)–Devon Maid (Meldrum) [1989/90 17m] poor novice hurdler: well beaten in August. *N. Bradley.* —

CHARLIE BURTON 8 b.g. My Chopin–Judy Burton (Mummy's Pet) [1989/90 16f* 16m*] compact gelding: showed ability in varied company over hurdles, including selling, prior to winning novice events at Worcester and Bangor in August: best form at 2m: acts on firm ground: wears blinkers. *G. E. Jones.* 104

CHARLIE DAGG 9 br.g. Indiaro–Persian Stitch (Persia) [1989/90 16f 25g c18m[ur] 20g c16g[2] a18g c20m[pu]] workmanlike gelding: poor novice hurdler/chaser: looked none too keen when second in weakly-contested conditional jockeys selling handicap chase at Catterick in January: visored or blinkered nowadays: sold 1,000 gns Ascot June Sales. *R. Lee.* **c72** —

CHARLIE ME DARLING 6 ch.h. Sharpo–Hithermoor Lass (Red Alert) [1989/90 17f[2]] lightly-raced poor maiden on Flat: second of 4 finishers in novice event at Newton Abbot in July on hurdling debut: wore blinkers and a hood. *D. J. G. Murray-Smith.* 76

CHARLIE NOSE 7 ch.g. Stetchworth–Pride of Hatton (Gulf Pearl) [1989/90 c20s* c25d[2] c24d[6]] workmanlike ex-Irish gelding: second foal: dam of little account: winning point-to-pointer: showed ability in NH Flat races in 1988: sold out of D. Hassett's stable 34,000 gns Doncaster Spring (1988) Sales: always prominent when winning novice event at Fontwell in January on steeplechasing debut: wandered under pressure when second in similar race at Towcester in February: stiff task final outing: may prove best at around 2½m: acts on soft going. *N. J. Henderson.* **c98** +

CHARLIE PLUM 8 b.g. Laurence O–Red Pine (Khalkis) [1989/90 c16g[F]] big, strong, lengthy gelding: very lightly-raced novice hurdler/chaser: won a point-to-point in May: will probably prove suited by further than 2m: acts on any going. *D. Burchell.* c— —

CHARLIEWAM 7 ch.g. White Speck–Canute Lady (Hardicanute) [1989/90 18d 16g 16f[6]] leggy gelding: half-brother to very useful hunter chaser Beamwam (by Bing II): dam, a modest middle-distance stayer on Flat, was placed over hurdles: sixth at Hexham in March, first sign of ability in novice hurdles. *R. R. Lamb.* 62

CHARLOTTE GRAY 5 ro.m. Rolfe (USA)–Madame Russe (Bally Russe) [1989/90 F16m] fifth foal by a thoroughbred stallion: half-sister to very smart jumper The Tsarevich, fair jumper Tsarella and NH Flat race winner Tsaritsyn (all by Mummy's Pet): in rear in NH Flat race at Sandown in March: yet to race over hurdles or fences. *R. F. Johnson Houghton.*

CHARLOTTE LANE 6 ch.m. Mart Lane–Thats Char-Lotte (Virginia Boy) [1989/90 20g 19m[2] 16f[4]] sparely-made mare: first foal: dam of little account: fell 75

second in a point-to-point in March: blinkered, in frame in novice hurdles at
Hereford (better effort) and Towcester in May. *D. Burchell.*

CHARLOTTE'S GIFT 6 b.m. Welsh Captain–Mandy's Gift (Mandamus)
[1989/90 20g 16d 17g^{6} a20g a22g 22f^{5} a20g] compact, workmanlike mare: novice 73
hurdler: only form of season when moderate fifth over 2¾m. *T. Kersey.*

CHARLOTTE'S OLIVER 5 b.g. Tumble Gold–Candy Belle (Candy Cane)
[1989/90 16d 16g 17m] neat gelding: third foal: dam, unplaced in Irish NH Flat —
races, half-sister to several winners over jumps: behind in novice hurdles. *J. K. M.
Oliver.*

CHARLOU'S CHOICE 6 b.g. Maelstrom Lake–Miss Menton (Brigadier
Gerard) [1989/90 17f^{F} 16m^{6} a16g 16f^{3} 16m^{3} 16m^{4} 17m^{4} 17f^{pu} 17f^{5}] workmanlike 68
gelding: poor novice selling hurdler: best efforts at 2m on top-of-the-ground: has
looked none too keen under pressure: usually blinkered (visored fifth start):
inconsistent. *R. T. Juckes.*

CHARLTON YEOMAN 5 b.g. Sheer Grit–Bell Walks Breeze (Flaming
Breeze (CAN)) [1989/90 16m] IR 20,000 3-y-o: leggy, useful-looking gelding: fifth 89 p
foal: dam unraced half-sister to 2 winning jumpers and to dam of Lucky Vane: 22½
lengths seventh behind Tildarg in novice hurdle at Sandown in March, making
mistakes but keeping on again from 2 out: will be suited by further: sure to
improve. *J. T. Gifford.*

CHARMED KNAVE 5 b.g. Enchantment–Peerless Princess (Averof)
[1989/90 16m 16m^{6} 16g^{pu} a16g] poor sprinter on Flat: well beaten in novice —
hurdles. *E. A. Wheeler.*

CHAROSSA 5 b.m. Ardross–Charter Belle (Runnymede) [1989/90 18g^{5}]
medium-sized mare: no worthwhile form in 2 outings over hurdles, though —
showed signs of ability in mares novice event at Fontwell in November. *Miss B.
Sanders.*

CHART CROSS 4 b.c. Millfontaine–Whichcombe (Huntercombe) [1989/90
16m^{pu}] 9f seller winner on Flat: made mistakes and was pulled up reportedly —
distressed in juvenile selling hurdle at Huntingdon in September (favourite). *N.
A. Callaghan.*

CHARTER FAIR 6 b.g. Lighter–Lyndale (The Go-Between) [1989/90 F17d^{5}
F12g^{6} 16f 16g 17f^{3}] first foal: dam maiden sprint plater: showed ability in NH Flat 79
races: ridden by 7-lb claimer, third in novice event at Cartmel in May, only form
over hurdles. *D. Moffatt.*

CHARTER HARDWARE 8 b.g. Hardboy–Unsinkable Sarah (Mon **c131**
Capitaine) [1989/90 c27g^{2} c30s^{3} c30v^{4} c30v^{pu} c24m c36f] quite a useful chaser: —
15½ lengths third to Bonanza Boy in Coral Welsh National at Chepstow in
December: twelfth in Seagram Grand National at Liverpool in April: stayed very
well: acted on soft going and was unsuited by top-of-the-ground: blinkered third
start: usually jumped soundly: dead. *J. A. C. Edwards.*

CHARTER PARTY 12 b.g. Document–Ahoy There (Little Buskins) [1989/90 **c149**
c24g^{3}] big, useful-looking gelding: good mover: has been operated on for a soft —
palate and hobdayed: won Tote Cheltenham Gold Cup in 1988 and third in same
race in 1989: 11 lengths third to Golden Friend in slowly-run Edward Hanmer
Memorial Chase (limited handicap) at Haydock in November: reportedly
sustained tendon injury and not seen out again: suited by a good test of stamina:
acts on any going. *D. Nicholson.*

CHART FINDER 8 b.g. Warpath–Bubbles (Ballymoss) [1989/90 c16f^{pu} **c70**
c24m^{3} c24g^{6} c24m^{pu} 27g] sturdy gelding: winning hurdler: poor novice chaser: —
stays well: best run on good to firm ground: has given impression he has his own
ideas about the game and probably needs strong handling: often blinkered. *A.
Smith.*

CHASERS' BAR 5 ch.m. Oats–Cavo Varka (Cavo Doro) [1989/90 F16m^{3}
F17h* 17f^{2} 16f* a16g^{3} 16g 20f^{2} 20m* 20f* 20f^{5} 20f*] workmanlike mare: won NH 96
Flat race at Carlisle: successful over hurdles in novice events at Hexham and
Wetherby and handicaps at Hexham and Sedgefield: ran poorly tenth start: stays
2½m: acts on firm ground: sold out of G. Moore's stable 8,500 gns Doncaster
November Sales after fifth start. *J. E. Swiers.*

CHASE THAT DREAM 6 br.g. Track Spare–Fly Blackie (Dear Gazelle)
[1989/90 F16f] second reported living foal: dam poor novice hurdler: tailed-off last
of 7 in NH Flat race at Cheltenham in October: yet to race over hurdles or fences.
R. T. Juckes.

CHASMARELLA 5 b.m. Yukon Eric (CAN)–Miss Polly Peck (March Past) [1989/90 16m2 20g* 22g* 25gF 18s 20m3] small, sparely-made mare: selling hurdler: successful at Chepstow (hung right run-in, bought in 5,200 gns) and Folkestone (retained 1,900 gns) in December: ran moderately final start (first for 3 months): stays 2¾m: best form on a sound surface: good mount for a claimer. *A. R. Davison.* 96

CHATAM (USA) 6 b.g. Big Spruce (USA)–Cristalina (FR) (Green Dancer) [1989/90 20f2 20g2 c20vF c20d* c24f3] c139 + 146

Chatam was bought privately by present connections out of Mme Head's stable after winning a thirteen-furlong handicap at Maisons-Laffitte as a three-year-old. He turned out to be one of the best juvenile hurdlers around the following winter, winning twice and finishing third in the Daily Express Triumph Hurdle at Cheltenham from three starts. Chatam progressed into a very useful hurdler in 1988/9, winning the City Trial Hurdle (Limited Handicap) at Nottingham on his penultimate outing, but had his limitations exposed in the Champion Hurdle, finishing ninth of twelve behind Beech Road. A further two races over timber at Cheltenham on his first two starts of the latest season confirmed that Chatam is some way removed from the top of the hurdling tree. He ran as though in need of the race when fifteen lengths second to the in-form Bradbury Star in a handicap on his reappearance and was then put firmly in his place when beaten one and a half lengths by Beech Road, who gave him 12 lb, in the two-runner Spa Hurdle.

The decision to send Chatam chasing after the Spa Hurdle didn't meet with immediate success. He made several mistakes before falling four out in a novice event won by Elvercone at Chepstow. Allowing for the obvious need to improve his jumping, Chatam shaped promisingly at Chepstow and had just taken the lead still travelling strongly at the time of his departure. On his next start he jumped well, bar a mistake at the eighth, to win a qualifier of the Steel Plate And Sections Young Chasers series at Newbury in February in the style of a very promising novice. The race was run at a good gallop throughout with Chatam, taking a good hold as usual, tracking the leaders until moving smoothly to the front four from home. From there he drew further and further clear, so that at the line he was a distance ahead of second-placed Nodform. Even if the runner-up was below par, as seems likely, it was still a most impressive performance by the winner. Chatam didn't fulfil the promise he'd shown over two and a half miles on a yielding

Steel Plate And Sections Young Chasers' Novices' Chase (Qualifier), Newbury—Chatam shows himself to be a very promising novice

Dr B. Nolan's "Chatam"

surface at Newbury in the Sun Alliance Chase at Cheltenham in March on his next outing. A combination of fast conditions and the half-mile longer trip proved his undoing. Chatam made several mistakes in the Sun Alliance and had to be ridden along to hold his prominent position seven out. He still had every chance going to three from home, but could do no more from approaching the last and finished third behind Garrison Savannah and The Committee, beaten five lengths and two and a half. As ground conditions remained against Chatam in the spring the Sun Alliance proved to be his last race of the season. He certainly looked a very good prospect at Newbury, and is well worth another chance to prove it when things are in his favour in 1990/1.

Chatam (USA) (b.g. 1984)	Big Spruce (USA) (b or br 1969)	Herbager (b 1956)	Vandale II
			Flagette
		Silver Sari (b 1961)	Prince John
			Golden Sari
	Cristalina (FR) (gr 1978)	Green Dancer (b 1972)	Nijinsky
			Green Valley
		Crix (gr 1964)	Major Portion
			Covert Side

Chatam, a tall gelding, is a brother to Cristallerie, the winner of a mile selling race in France as a two-year-old. Their dam, Cristalina, was also a winner over a mile and is a half-sister to numerous French winners, including four jumpers. Chatam, a free-going sort who was raced only at two miles in his first two seasons, may prove as effective at three miles as he is at two and a half as he gets older (his sire is a strong influence for stamina), but whether he'll ever become as effective on firm ground as on soft is doubtful—he has the round action often associated with soft-ground performers. Chatam has shown a tendency to hang and jump to his left. To combat that he wears an unusual bridle, the bit being made up of three pieces, designed to prevent the horse favouring one side. On the two occasions Chatam has raced on right-handed courses over jumps he has run badly. *M. C. Pipe.*

CHATSBY 9 b.g. Sunyboy–Scotch Oats (Border Chief) [1989/90 c21s* c25s^4] c**103** deep-girthed, angular gelding: moderate chaser: won conditional jockeys — handicap at Windsor in January: ran creditably following month: stays 3m: acts on soft going: tends to sweat and be on his toes in preliminaries. *Capt. T. A. Forster.*

CHATTERIS 4 b.g. Shareef Dancer (USA)–Fenella (Thatch (USA)) [1989/90 16d 16g 16m^4] smallish gelding: sold out of P. Cole's stable 3,600 gns Newmarket 70 p Autumn Sales: first form over hurdles when 20 lengths fourth to White River in juvenile claimer at Wincanton, running on well under tender handling having never been placed to challenge: capable of better and is one to note in modest company: quite modest 1½m winner on Flat in 1990. *M. Madgwick.*

CHEADLE GREEN 13 ch.g. Saint Denys–Rathneska (Eudaemon) [1989/90 c— c21s^{pu}] robust gelding: winning chaser: poor form since 1987, including in point-to-points: stays well: acts on heavy going. *Steven Astaire.*

CHEAP METAL 5 br.g. Sonnen Gold–Economy Pep (Jimmy Reppin) [1989/90 16d^{pu} 16s^{pu} 16s 24d^{pu} 20m^{pu} 16h^3] sparely-made gelding: well beaten on Flat: 66 only form over hurdles when third (visored) in poor novice event at Hexham in April: blinkered time before: takes a good hold. *B. T. Crawford.*

CHEEKIE CHAPPIE 12 ch.g. Saucy Kit–Miller's Rood (Fable Amusant) c**77** [1989/90 c25f^3 c21m^3] lengthy gelding: fair winning point-to-pointer: lightly-raced novice hunter chaser: stays well: acts on firm ground. *H. J. H. Reynolds.*

CHEEKY FOX 4 b.g. King of Spain–Diamond Talk (Counsel) [1989/90 16f 16s^6 16d^4 16s] lengthy, angular gelding: half-brother to successful 2m hurdler Corn 86 Street (by Decoy Boy): behind both outings on Flat: fourth in juvenile event at Warwick in January, easily best effort over hurdles: ridden before halfway when well beaten on same course following month: should stay further: sold 5,000 gns Ascot May Sales. *J. R. Bosley.*

CHEEKY KING 8 b.g. Space King–Pearlyric (Eastern Lyric) [1989/90 16g^2 c— 16h* 16m^2] smallish, lightly-made gelding: won conditional jockeys selling 95 handicap hurdle at Hexham in April (no bid): good second in novice handicap hurdle at Warwick in May: poor novice chaser: ran poorly over 2½m: acts on hard ground. *H. A. T. Whiting.*

CHEERIE CHIEF 14 br.g. Barbary Chief–Shahwanna (Bahadur Shah) c**92** [1989/90 c24h^2 c20d^6 c27f*] strong, workmanlike gelding: modest hunter chaser nowadays: won at Sedgefield in May (left clear 3 out but had to be driven out after jockey almost took wrong course on run-in): stays 27f: seems to act on any going: sometimes jumps moderately. *H. Barclay.*

CHELSEA MAN 9 b.g. Idiot's Delight–River Spell (Spartan General) c**101** d [1989/90 c20m^3 c16d 22g c20g^F c16v^4 c20d c20m^4] sparely-made gelding: — winning hurdler/chaser in Ireland: no form in Britain in 1989/90: stays 2½m: blinkered fifth to seventh starts 1987/8 and last 4 outings. *Mrs L. Clay.*

CHELSEA PRINCESS 5 b.m. Ranksborough–Eaton Clown (Tycoon II) [1989/90 F16h^5] first foal: dam fair 5f winner at 2 yrs: well beaten in NH Flat races: yet to race over hurdles or fences. *Mrs J. E. Croft.*

CHELWORTH RAIDER 4 ch.g. Oats–Driven Snow (Deep Run) [1989/90 16g a16g 16s^3 16f^6 20m 16f^2] leggy gelding: first foal: dam won 2m hurdle: poor 79 juvenile hurdler: should stay beyond 2m: acts on firm and soft ground. *J. L. Spearing.*

CHEMIST BROKER (NZ) 10 b.g. Oakville–Sweet Canyon (NZ) (Headland II) [1989/90 24f^3] workmanlike gelding: fairly useful hurdler: good third of 4 at 131 Ascot in November: suited by 3m or more: acts on any going: sometimes sweating and tends to be on toes: often claimer ridden. *R. Akehurst.*

CHEMMY 6 b.m. Billion (USA)–Gambling Girl (Raise You Ten) [1989/90 16g 16g] workmanlike mare: tailed off in NH Flat races and novice hurdles. *Capt. J.* — *Wilson.*

CHERRY BRAVE 9 b.g. Le Bavard (FR)–Cherry Stack (Raise You Ten) c— [1989/90 c25f^{pu}] rangy gelding: winning hunter chaser: pulled up in handicap in — October: stays well: suited by a firm surface: blinkered final start 1987/8. *M. W. Easterby.*

CHERRY CHAP 5 b.g. Kabour–Mild Wind (Porto Bello) [1989/90 16g 16m4 16m* a16g 16g 16g a16g2 a16g4] compact, good-bodied gelding: inconsistent and probably ungenuine sprint maiden on Flat: claimer ridden, successful in selling hurdle at Nottingham in December (no bid): best effort in handicaps subsequently on penultimate start: unlikely to stay beyond 2m: acts on good to firm ground. *D. W. Chapman.* 76

CHERRY FIELD 11 gr.m. Precipice Wood–Cherish (Bargello) [1989/90 c16f3 c17g2 c20m2 c20f* c16m2 c20f* c20f2] lengthy, sparely-made ex-Irish mare: handicap chaser: won at Mallow in August and Carlisle in October: drifted right on run-in and was headed close home by Landing Board at Cheltenham later in October: stays 2½m: acts on any going: sound jumper: sold 22,000 gns Doncaster October Sales. *T. Kinane, Ireland.* c**125** —

CHERRYKINO 5 b.g. Relkino–Cherry Stack (Raise You Ten) [1989/90 F16g3] third foal: half-brother to winning hunter chaser Cherry Brave (by Le Bavard) and to novice hurdler/chaser Gaelic Cherry (by Gleason): dam, daughter of a half-sister to Arkle, won over fences in Ireland: 10 lengths third behind Trefelyn Cone in NH Flat race at Warwick in December: yet to race over hurdles or fences. *Capt. T. A. Forster.*

CHERRY SIDE 10 gr.m. General Ironside–Game Cherry (Domenico Fuoco) [1989/90 c20g c24gur c24d c24dpu c22f c24mpu] medium-sized mare: novice hurdler: winning point-to-pointer: well behind in novice chases: stays well: probably acts on any going. *J. Robinson.* c— —

CHESHIRE COVE 7 ch.g. Belfalas–Fairy (Prefairy) [1989/90 20v] behind in NH Flat race and a novice hurdle. *J. A. B. Old.* —

CHESS MISTRESS (USA) 5 b. or br.m. Run The Gantlet (USA)–Bishop's Fling (USA) (King's Bishop (USA)) [1989/90 16g 16dur 16g6 16m 19m5] sparely-made mare: plating-class middle-distance maiden on Flat: sold out of B. Hanbury's stable 6,000 gns Newmarket December Sales: easily best effort over hurdles when sixth in 2m claimer in April: resold 2,400 gns Doncaster June Sales. *J. White.* 81 ?

CHESTER PARK 8 br.g. Al Sirat (USA)–Chester's Sister (Prefairy) [1989/90 c16gpu] ex-Irish gelding: half-brother to 2 winning jumpers: dam half-sister to winning hurdler: placed in NH Flat race and over hurdles in 1986/7: won a point-to-point in 1988: tailed off when pulled up in novice chase in October. *J. R. Jenkins.* c— —

CHESWOLD 6 ch.g. Dominion–Soft Voice (Simbir) [1989/90 20dpu a16g6 16m2 16f* 16h* 20f3] close-coupled ex-Irish gelding: first foal: dam 1½m winner: placed over long distances on Flat: modest hurdler: promising second in selling handicap at Wetherby in April and subsequently won handicap hurdles at Sedgefield and Hexham: creditable third over 2½m final outing: acts on hard and dead going. *J. H. Johnson.* 96

CHEZ POLLY 4 ch.f. Homing–My Pink Parrot (Pirate King) [1989/90 18gpu] well beaten in varied events on Flat, including seller: tailed off when pulled up in juvenile hurdle at Fontwell in December. *P. R. Hedger.* —

CHIAFFA 8 b.m. Piaffer (USA)–Little Charter (Runnymede) [1989/90 22f 21f2 19g4 21f3] sparely-made mare: poor novice hurdler: probably stays 21f: acts on firm ground: blinkered on debut in 1987/8: not raced after November. *Miss C. Horler.* 69

CHIASSO FORTE (ITY) 7 b.g. Furry Glen–Cassai (FR) (Molvedo) [1989/90 16f5 16d5 c16s* c20m2 c18g* c16g4 c16s* c18v4 c20f6 c16d5] medium-sized gelding: winning hurdler in Britain: successful over fences in novice event at Listowel and 2 handicaps at Punchestown: made a few mistakes when never-dangerous sixth to Brandeston in quite valuable amateur riders novice handicap at Liverpool in April: stays 2½m: acts on any going. *A. L. T. Moore, Ireland.* c**116** —

CHICA MIA 6 b.m. Camden Town–Backwoodsgirl (Young Emperor) [1989/90 16dpu] modest winner at up to 7.6f on Flat in 1989: co-favourite, weakened approaching 2 out and pulled up last in novice hurdle at Sedgefield in January. *J. Parkes.* —

CHIC-ANITA 5 b.m. Tina's Pet–Chiquitita (Reliance II) [1989/90 16gpu] poor plater on Flat (has been blinkered): tailed off when pulled up 2 out in novice claiming hurdle at Wolverhampton in November. *T. B. Hallett.* —

CHICAS DELIGHT 4 ch.f. Rustingo–La Chica (El Cid) [1989/90 16g[pu] 19s[pu]] workmanlike filly: ninth foal: sister to fair hurdler and winning chaser Rusty Roc and half-sister to winning point-to-pointer Chica-s Beau (by Saucy Kit): dam won over 5f at 2 yrs and over hurdles: tailed off when pulled up in juvenile hurdles. *M. W. Davies.* —

CHICO VALDEZ (USA) 6 ch.g. Valdez (USA)–Lypatia (FR) (Lyphard (USA)) [1989/90 a22g c16d[pu] c16d[5] c17m[5] 17f c16m* c16g[3] c17m[2] c20f[4] c17f[ur]] close-coupled, sparely-made gelding: winning selling hurdler: won weakly-contested amateur riders novice chase at Market Rasen in April: probably stays 2½m: seems to act on any going: has looked none too keen on occasions: moderate jumper of fences. *M. C. Chapman.* c77 x —

CHIEF IRONSIDE 10 br.g. General Ironside–Killiney Lady (Lord Gayle (USA)) [1989/90 c20g[ur] c20g c20g[F] c20g[3]] big, rangy, good sort: fairly useful chaser nowadays: let down by his jumping in 1989/90: best at around 2½m on a sound surface. *J. T. Gifford.* c128 x —

CHIEF MOLE (USA) 5 gr.g. Caro–Head Spy (USA) (Chieftain) [1989/90 16f[4] 16d[2] 16g[3]] rangy gelding: novice hurdler: placed most starts, running easily best race when third in minor event at Cheltenham in November (wore net muzzle): tended to pull hard previously: will prove best at 2m. *O. Sherwood.* 127

CHIEF RUNNER 8 b.g. Arapaho–Waterhen (Deep Run) [1989/90 18f[5] 20f[F] a16g[4] 16m[5] a18g[5] a20g[5] a16g[5]] smallish gelding: poor selling hurdler: stays 2¼m: acts on good to firm ground: has won for a 7-lb claimer: found little under pressure fourth outing. *P. Howling.* 63

CHIEF'S CHOICE 5 b.g. Coquelin (USA)–Douschkina (Dubassoff (USA)) [1989/90 16m 16g 16g[pu]] half-brother to winning hurdler and novice chaser Guymyson (by Crofter): maiden on Flat: well beaten in novice hurdles: apparently lame final start. *E. H. Owen jun.* —

CHILD OF THE MIST 4 b.c. Lomond (USA)–Lighted Lamp (USA) (Sir Gaylord) [1989/90 16s[3]] lengthy colt: fairly useful middle-distance performer on Flat: sold out of B. Hills's stable 30,000 gns Newmarket Autumn Sales: staying-on 15 lengths third behind Crystal Heights in Curran Group Finale Junior Hurdle at Chepstow in December (swished tail under pressure): a promising first effort over hurdles and is sure to win a run-of-the-mill event. *O. Sherwood.* 109 p

CHILDREN'S JOIE 4 b.g. Auction Ring (USA)–Port La Joie (Charlottown) [1989/90 16f[6] 16m[5] 16g 21d[pu] 18v[pu] 20m[5] 20m[2]] close-coupled gelding: half-brother to very useful jumper Southernair (by Derrylin): plating-class middle-distance maiden on Flat: sold out of D. Arbuthnot's stable 6,200 gns Newmarket Autumn Sales: modest form over hurdles: second in juvenile seller at Chepstow in April: stays 2½m: seems suited by top-of-the-ground: visored fifth start. *S. Dow.* 88

CHILHAMPTON 8 br.g. Belfalas–Rozeen (Merry Rose) [1989/90 c22m[4]] won a point-to-point in March: well beaten in novice hunter chase at Stratford in May. *C. A. Green.* c—

CHILTON LADY 5 ch.m. Liberated–Jedhart Lass (Blandford Lad) [1989/90 aF16g[6] 16g[ur] 27f[pu]] half-sister to fairly useful staying chaser Jethart's Here (by Grangerullah): dam unraced half-sister to staying chasers Jednook and Jedheads: tailed off in NH Flat race: unseated rider when trying to refuse on hurdling debut, saddle slipped next time (blinkered): claimer ridden. *N. Miller.* —

CHINA'S WAY (USA) 4 b. or br.f. Native Uproar (USA)–China Tea (USA) (Round Table) [1989/90 a16g[pu]] placed over 1½m on Flat: tailed off when pulled up 2 out in selling hurdle at Southwell in April: sold 3,200 gns Ascot May Sales. *A. S. Reid.* —

CHIPCHASE 10 b.g. New Brig–Tillside (Lucky Brief) [1989/90 20f[2] c20m* c25f[2] c20g* c16g[4] c24g[2] c20g[2] c20f[4] 20m[4] c20g[F] c20d[5] c20f[2]] compact, good-bodied gelding: handicap hurdler/chaser: successful over fences at Perth in September and Sedgefield in November: ran well most other completed starts: stays 25f: probably acts on any going: blinkered thrice in 1986/7. *B. E. Wilkinson.* c107 99

CHIPPED METAL 11 b.g. Crash Course–Car Shine (Rise'n Shine II) [1989/90 c24m[4] c24d[4]] rangy, raw-boned gelding: tubed: winning chaser: tailed off both outings 1989/90: successful in a point-to-point in February: suited by 3m: probably acts on any going: carries head high and sometimes wears a crossed noseband: usually held up: occasionally let down by his jumping: trained by R. Francis first outing. *Sir John Barlow.* c— —

CHIROPODIST 6 b.g. Prince Tenderfoot (USA)–Corny Story (Oats) [1989/90 16m 16m 19f] compact gelding: winning hurdler in 1988/9 when trained by M. Pipe: no form in 1989/90: form only at around 2m: yet to race on heavy going, acts on any other: blinkered last 4 starts 1988/9 and final outing. *P. M. Cowley.* —

CHLOROPHYLL 7 b.m. Ballymore–Mandy Girl (Manado) [1989/90 25m6] small, plain mare: of little account over hurdles: bought for 700 gns Doncaster August Sales. *A. J. Le Blond.* —

CHOCTAW 6 gr.g. Great Nephew–Cheyenne (Sovereign Path) [1989/90 c16m2 c16m2 c20m4 c20d4 c20g* c20d2 c20f* c20m6 c20f5] strong gelding: winning hurdler: successful in novice chase at Sedgefield (made several mistakes) in February and handicap chase at Hexham (whipped round at start) in April: jumped and ran moderately last 2 outings: stays 2½m: acts on any going: blinkered sixth to ninth starts in 1988/9: difficult ride: often makes running: unreliable. *P. Beaumont.* c95 § —

CHORISTERS DREAM 7 ch.g. Song–Permutation (Pinza) [1989/90 16g 22mpu c16fpu] smallish, lengthy gelding: brother to winning hurdler Helexian: 5f winner at 2 yrs, little form on Flat since: no sign of ability in novice hurdles or a novice chase (tried to refuse eighth and pulled up 3 out): blinkered final outing: sold 1,450 gns Ascot April Sales: resold 1,200 gns Ascot May Sales. *P. N. Upson.* c— —

CHRISTMAS BASH 7 b.m. Shaab–Christmas Fun (Tangle) [1989/90 20g2] tenth foal: half-sister to winning selling hurdler Bowdens Lane (by Abergwiffy): dam unraced half-sister to two 2-y-o 5f winners: no sign of ability in point-to-points: 5 lengths second to Stroked Again in 2½m mares novice hurdle at Market Rasen in June. *R. G. Frost.* 80 p

CHRISTMAS HOLLY 9 b.g. Blind Harbour–Holly Doon (Doon) [1989/90 16f3] workmanlike gelding: fairly useful hurdler: not given a hard race when creditable last of 3 finishers behind Ryde Again in minor event at Leicester in November: effective at around 2m and stays 3m: probably acts on any going: suited by waiting tactics. *Mrs G. R. Reveley.* 126

CHRISTMAS HOLS 4 b.g. Young Generation–Foston Bridge (Relkino) [1989/90 16f 16m 16d a16g2 a16g5 a16g4 16f2 16m3 16f] compact gelding: 1¼m seller winner on Flat: sold out of C. Cyzer's stable 8,400 gns Newmarket Autumn Sales: poor juvenile hurdler: may not stay much beyond 2m: acts on firm ground: has started slowly and looked a difficult ride. *J. R. Bosley.* 79

CHRISTO (CAN) 8 ch.g. Halo (USA)–Slight Deception (USA) (Northern Dancer) [1989/90 22dpu 19s3 c26vpu 22g] heavy-topped, sturdy gelding: poor hurdler nowadays: reluctant to race and took little interest on chasing debut: suited by a test of stamina and the mud: has worn a tongue strap: seems best in blinkers (didn't wear them in 1989/90): ungenuine. *D. J. Wintle.* c— § — §

CHROEMARLIN 4 b.f. Tanfirion–Danova (FR) (Dan Cupid) [1989/90 a16g 16m4 16f4] no form on Flat: fourth in seller at Hereford in May, last and best effort over hurdles. *Mrs E. H. Heath.* 68

CHRONICLE LADY 9 b.m. Martinmas–London Spin (Derring-Do) [1989/90 26f3] leggy, close-coupled mare: poor hurdler: stays well: possibly unsuited by very soft going and goes well on top-of-the-ground: has run creditably for claimer. *I. P. Wardle.* —

CHUCKLESTONE 7 b.g. Chukaroo–Czar's Diamond (Queen's Hussar) [1989/90 20fF 20d2 24fF 24g5 24gF 22f2 24f3 22f2] neat gelding: modest novice over hurdles: stays 3m: acts on firm and dead ground: moderate jumper. *J. S. King.* 99 x

CHUFFBUTTONS 6 ch.g. Buckskin (FR)–Georgette (Neron) [1989/90 16d 16d] workmanlike gelding: half-brother to several winning jumpers, including winning hurdler/chaser Master Socks (by Harwell) and successful hurdler Pearl Prospect (by Kambalda): little sign of ability in novice hurdles. *M. Oliver.* —

CHUNKY SUPREME 6 b.g. Welsh Captain–Careg-Wen (Stephen George) [1989/90 16mpu 16m] lengthy, sparely-made, dipped-backed gelding: poor plater on Flat: of little account over hurdles. *T. J. Houlbrooke.* —

CHURCHES GREEN 11 b.g. Sassafras (FR)–Alice Johnston (Majetta) [1989/90 c17fpu] big, lengthy gelding: winning chaser: ran as though something amiss only outing of season (August): stays 2½m when conditions aren't testing: acts on any going: refused to race final outing 1986/7. *P. J. Hobbs.* c— —

CHURCH LEAP 6 b.m. Pollerton–Phaestus Sister (Seminole II) [1989/90 22d4 25d4 20g3] workmanlike mare: modest novice over hurdles: probably stays 3m: acts on dead ground. *K. C. Bailey.* 91

CILERNA'S LAD 5 b.g. Pablond–Cilerna Rock (Coliseum) [1989/90 F16v5 F16f4] half-brother to winning jumpers Cilerna Jet (by Lear Jet) and Classic Rock (by Charlottown): dam never ran: beaten over 25 lengths in NH Flat races at Haydock and Ascot (fourth of 13 to Piper's Son) in the spring: yet to race over hurdles or fences. *D. McCain.*

CIMA 12 br.g. High Top–Lemon Blossom (Acropolis) [1989/90 25gpu 26v2 21s3 21s3 25d4 21d3] smallish, short-backed gelding: modest hurdler/chaser nowadays: stays well: acts on any going: poor jumper of fences. *J. A. B. Old.* c— x 103

CINNAMON RUN 6 ch.m. Deep Run–Clarahill (Menelek) [1989/90 16g2 16s6 16m] tall mare with plenty of scope: fair hurdler: good second to Fragrant Dawn in valuable handicap at Newbury in December: given a lot to do in moderately-run race next time: will be suited by 2½m: acts on dead going (never able to challenge on good to firm final start): wears a crossed noseband: has won for a claimer. *N. A. Gaselee.* 113

CIREN JESTER 6 b.g. Cajun–Miss Africa (African Sky) [1989/90 16g2 16g] neat gelding: lightly-raced novice hurdler: sold 3,500 gns Newmarket Autumn Sales. *W. J. Musson.* 84

CISTO GIRL 5 b.m. Cisto (FR)–Tontolini (Flying Curtis) [1989/90 F13f F16f] non-thoroughbred mare: second foal: dam never ran: tailed off in NH Flat races at Hereford and Huntingdon: yet to race over hurdles or fences. *H. Jackson.*

CISTOLENA 4 ch.f. Cisto (FR)–Keep Shining (Scintillant) [1989/90 20g] sparely-made filly: third reported live foal: dam well beaten both outings over hurdles: tailed off both outings at 2 yrs: jumped slowly and always behind in novice hurdle at Bangor in April. *Miss S. J. Wilton.* —

CITY COMMENT 6 b.g. Furry Glen–Marty Mann (Tarqogan) [1989/90 20g4 17g* 20gpu 20g4 20gpu] medium-sized gelding: won novice hurdle at Carlisle in February: good fourth in novice handicap at Worcester in May (first race for 2½ months): sweating badly, looked reluctant in between: stays 2½m: has raced only on good ground. *J. A. C. Edwards.* 101

CITY ENTERTAINER 9 br.g. Tycoon II–Border Mouse (Border Chief) [1989/90 c20g4 c24g* c24d* c25fpu c33dpu] useful-looking gelding: has had a soft palate operation: fairly useful chaser nowadays: won handicaps at Wetherby in January and February (beat Travel Over 12 lengths): running well when pulled up before last and dismounted in valuable handicap at Cheltenham penultimate outing: stays 25f: acts on heavy going: tends to jump to the right. *Mrs C. Postlethwaite.* c**131** + —

CITY INDEX (USA) 4 b.g. J O Tobin (USA)–Fannie Annie (USA) (L'Enjoleur (CAN)) [1989/90 16m* 16f5 16g 16s3 a16g* 16d a16g a16gbd 16f6 16m] angular ex-Irish gelding: third foal: dam unraced: placed at up to 7f on Flat: won juvenile hurdle at Nottingham in November and novice event at Southwell in February: good sixth in novice handicap at Nottingham penultimate start: unlikely to stay much beyond 2m: acts on firm ground: found little second outing. *N. A. Smith.* 92

CITY KID 5 br.g. Black Minstrel–Glenarold Lass (Will Somers) [1989/90 16g6 16g3 21f] rather unfurnished gelding: fifth foal: half-brother to winning Irish hurdler/chaser Glen Ridge (by Golden Love): dam unraced: promising 8½ lengths third behind Forest Sun in novice hurdle at Kempton in February: well beaten on firm ground next start: should stay beyond 2m. *J. T. Gifford.* 96

CITY NATIVE 4 b.c. Be My Native (USA)–Blue Kingsmill (Roi Soleil) [1989/90 16s5] placed at up to 2m on Flat: sold out of W. Musson's stable 3,600 gns Doncaster November Sales: 50/1, around 20 lengths fifth to Regal Lake in 13-runner juvenile hurdle at Taunton in December. *L. Waring.* 76

CITY TO CITY 4 b.f. Windjammer (USA)–Beamless (Hornbeam) [1989/90 16mF a16gpu] close-coupled filly: half-sister to winning selling hurdler Beamof (by Averof): in frame in 1m sellers on Flat: no sign of ability in similar company over hurdles. *D. W. Chapman.* —

CIVILISED 5 b.h. Habitat–Dingle Bay (Petingo) [1989/90 F16f2] IR 100,000Y, 1,600 3-y-o: fourth foal: dam, Irish 1m and 1¼m winner, sister to high-class miler Pitcairn and very smart middle-distance stayer Valley Forge: 12/1, 8 lengths second of 7 to Mayfair Minx in NH Flat race at Newbury in March: yet to race over hurdles or fences. *S. Dow.*

CLANWILLIAM PRINCE 5 gr.g. Sexton Blake–Gentle Heiress (Prince Tenderfoot (USA)) [1989/90 17h3] smallish, workmanlike gelding: modest novice —

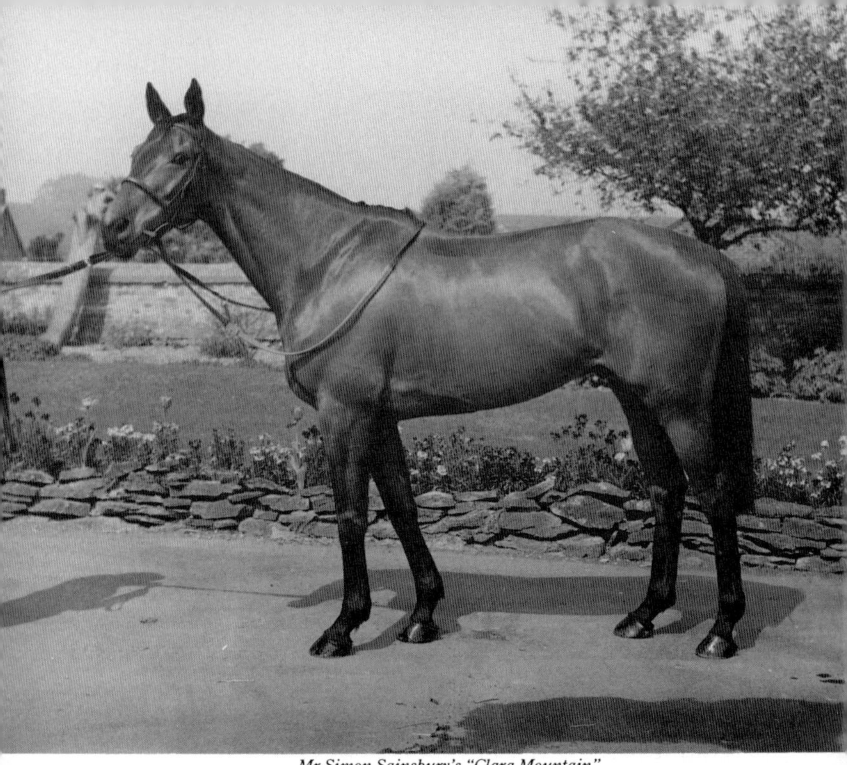

Mr Simon Sainsbury's "Clara Mountain"

hurdler: not seen out after well beaten in August: best form at around 2m: acts on firm and dead ground: blinkered last 2 starts 1988/9. *B. Smart.*

CLARA MOUNTAIN 11 b.g. Furry Glen–Oona More (Straight Deal) [1989/90 c21m5 c20f* c20g2 c20f3] workmanlike gelding: fairly useful chaser: won handicap at Newbury in November: hung badly right next time and ran a lack-lustre race final start: doesn't stay 3m on very testing ground: acts on any going: jumps boldly, though has shown a tendency to jump slightly left: usually races with plenty of zest and is suited by forcing tactics. *Capt. T. A. Forster.* c**134** —

CLARE CITIZEN 6 b.g. Black Minstrel–Kelenem (Menelek) [1989/90 16g4 21s4 24d* 22v3] lengthy, unfurnished gelding: won point-to-point in Ireland in 1988: won novice hurdle at Market Rasen in January: collapsed and died after finishing third at Folkestone later in month: stayed 3m. *J. A. C. Edwards.* 102

CLARE LAD 7 ch.g. Garda's Revenge (USA)–Sea Dike (Dike (USA)) [1989/90 16f*] handicap hurdler: won at Bangor in September: not seen out again: races only at around 2m: acts on any going: good mount for a claimer. *G. A. Ham.* 110

CLARE'S DELIGHT 5 b.m. Viking (USA)–Miss Inglewood (Dike (USA)) [1989/90 16m 16gF] sparely-made mare: winning plater on Flat, stays 7f: no form in claiming hurdles at Ludlow and Wolverhampton (sweating badly). *B. C. Morgan.* —

CLARES OWN 6 b.g. Al Sirat (USA)–Andonian (Road House II) [1989/90 c21m* c16m5 c16s4 c20g6 c20g4 c20m5 c20f3 c16f3 c20f3 c21g2] workmanlike, c87 —

rather sparely-made gelding: novice hurdler: successful in novice chase at Cartmel in August: best subsequent efforts on fourth, eighth and final starts: stays 21f: acts on firm ground, probably unsuited by heavy: blinkered last 4 outings. *J. Wade.*

CLASS ACT 4 b.g. Shirley Heights–Thespian (Ile de Bourbon (USA)) [1989/90 20g 16d] smallish gelding: winning middle-distance stayer on Flat: found little when behind in juvenile hurdles at Kempton and Warwick. *N. J. Henderson.* —

CLASSEY BOY 7 ch.g. Celtic Cone–Trespassing (Poaching) [1989/90 c24s* c25g4 c24s* c26vF c27vbd] heavy-topped gelding: won intermediate handicap chases at Bangor (tended to jump to his right) in December and Worcester in January: never travelling particularly well and was under pressure in second place when falling 2 out at Fontwell in February: suited by a thorough test of stamina, soft ground and forcing tactics. *G. A. Ham.* c106 —

CLASSICAL FLAME 7 ch.m. Belfalas–Clonaslee Baby (Konigssee) [1989/90 F16f 20f*dis 20d] leggy, sparely-made ex-Irish mare: half-sister to NH Flat race winner Lackey Hoey (by Mon Capitaine): dam never ran: in frame in NH Flat races: jumped left at the last when winning 4-runner novice hurdle at Worcester in August, and was disqualified: stayed 2½m: acted on firm ground: blinkered seventh start 1988/9: trained first start by T. Conroy: dead. *A. P. James.* 69

CLASSIC HERO 9 ch.g. Over The River (FR)–Hero's Slave (Arctic Slave) [1989/90 c26d2] big, lengthy ex-Irish gelding: winning point-to-pointer/steeplechaser: 10 lengths second to Torside in handicap chase at Newton Abbot in March: stays very well: acts on heavy going. *G. B. Balding.* c104 —

CLASSY BIRD 6 b.m. Sparkler–Slick Chick (Shiny Tenth) [1989/90 16m 16m 21s 20m3 20vF] small, lengthy mare: selling hurdler: 8 lengths third behind Patrick James in novice claiming hurdle at Leicester: looked lean next start (fell first): stays 2½m: acts on good to firm going: visored last 2 starts: sold 1,250 gns Ascot February Sales. *D. R. Gandolfo.* 67

CLAUDIA PASCAL 5 b.m. Tickled Pink–Come North (Track Spare) [1989/90 16mF 16gpu a16gpu] no worthwhile form over hurdles: sold 1,700 gns Ascot June Sales. *D. J. G. Murray-Smith.* —

CLAVERDON GIRL 6 b.m. Humdoleila–Space Beam (Space King) [1989/90 F16g] sturdy mare: second foal: half-sister to winning point-to-pointer Tudor Beam (by Mister Tudor): dam successful selling hurdler: tailed off in NH Flat race at Sandown in November: sold 2,800 gns Doncaster March Sales: yet to race over hurdles or fences. *J. Allen.*

CLAY COUNTY 5 b.g. Sheer Grit–Make-Up (Bleep-Bleep) [1989/90 16g5 16v* 16d6] well-made ex-Irish gelding: made all in novice hurdle at Ayr in February: set strong pace to 3 out and eased thereafter when sixth of 7 to Jinxy Jack in minor event at Kelso later in month: not certain to stay much beyond 2m: acts on heavy going. *R. Allan.* 110

CLAY HILL 11 ch.g. Menelek–Vul's Money (Even Money) [1989/90 c16g4 c16f3 c20mpu] workmanlike gelding: fairly useful chaser at his best: stayed 2½m: acted on any going: often made a mistake or 2: dead. *G. A. Hubbard.* c110 —

CLEANING UP 8 b.g. Carlburg–The Charwoman (Menelek) [1989/90 c21m2 c22f2] workmanlike gelding: first worthwhile form when second in early-season novice chases at Cartmel and Stratford: stays 2¾m: acts on firm going. *D. R. Gandolfo.* c86 —

CLEAN THROUGH (NZ) 5 b.g. Rapier II–Spotless (NZ) (Regalis) [1989/90 16f 16s4 16g 16spu] leggy gelding: showed promise first 2 starts in novice hurdles: ran poorly last 2 (jumped badly final one). *N. J. Henderson.* 89

CLEAR CALL (FR) 5 br.g. Bikala–Catacomb (USA) (Halo (USA)) [1989/90 16d3 18d 16g3 16g 20g 17f c20fur c16m* c20f2 c24h3 c21mF] lengthy, rather dipped-backed gelding: handicap hurdler: won 3-runner novice chase at Uttoxeter in April: stays 2½m: yet to race on very soft going, acts on any other: looked most reluctant in blinkers sixth start. *J. A. C. Edwards.* c94 111 §

CLEAR CHOICE (NZ) 8 b.g. Tierra Fuego–Flower Bird (NZ) (Fraxinus) [1989/90 c20s4 c21v2 c24gpu] good-bodied gelding: novice hurdler: winning chaser: modest form in handicaps in 1989/90: gave impression something badly amiss final start: stays 21f well: acts on heavy going. *N. R. Mitchell.* c90 —

CLEAR GIN 6 b.g. Ginger Boy–Cool Straight (Straight Lad) [1989/90 a20g4] deep-girthed gelding: poor novice selling hurdler: jumped poorly and refused ninth on chasing debut. *A. J. Taylor.* c— —

CLEARWATER BAY 4 ch.c. Creetown–Vacation (Remainder) [1989/90 16g] poor plater on Flat: tailed off in selling hurdle at Market Rasen in October. *G. R. Oldroyd.* —

CLEAR WATER DRIVE 8 ch.g. Deep Run–Rosecon (Typhoon) [1989/90 c20g^{pu} c20m^{pu}] lengthy gelding: brother to winning Irish hurdler Deep Slaney: poor form over hurdles in Ireland in 1986/7 (blinkered last 2 outings): in frame once from 5 starts in point-to-points in Britain in 1988: no form in novice chases. *R. Brotherton.* c— —

CLEASBY HILL 5 ch.g. Avocat–Strandhill (Bargello) [1989/90 F16g^{6} F17f* 16g^{4} 16d 20g 16f^{2} 20m^{2} 20g^{6} 20m^{3}] workmanlike gelding: third live foal: brother to novice hurdler Steele Justice: dam never ran: dead-heated for NH Flat race at Doncaster in December: modest novice over hurdles: stays 2½m: best form on top-of-the-ground: trained by W. A. Stephenson first start. *J. Hanson.* 90

CLEVEDON HOUSE 4 b.g. Indian King (USA)–Cereal Queen (Oats) [1989/90 16d 16g 16m^{pu}] lengthy gelding: third foal: half-brother to winning Irish hurdlers Highland Treat (by Northern Treat) and Break Fast (by Prince Tenderfoot): dam lightly-raced maiden: no worthwhile form over hurdles: dead. *B. J. Curley.* —

CLEVER CLAUDE 4 b.g. Cragador–La Mirabelle (Princely Gift) [1989/90 16g 16g a16g^{6} a16g^{5} a16g^{3}] light-framed gelding: poor plater over hurdles: races freely and unlikely to stay much beyond 2m. *W. M. Perrin.* 69

CLEVER DICK 5 b.g. Cosmo–Princess Albertina (FR) (King of The Castle (USA)) [1989/90 16g 16v^{4}] unfurnished gelding: no worthwhile form in 2 outings over hurdles. *D. M. Grissell.* —

CLEVER FOLLY 10 b.g. Idiot's Delight–Lilac Veil (Dumbarnie) [1989/90 c16m* c16g^{F} c16m^{2} c16f* c20f* c20f* c21d^{4} c20f^{5} c16f c24m^{F}] **c147** —

Clever Folly emulated his half-brother Bishops Yarn when he won the prestigious two-and-a-half-mile handicap chase, the A. F. Budge Gold Cup, at Cheltenham's December fixture. The event was known as the Glen International Gold Cup when Bishops Yarn won it in remarkable fashion in 1987. Bishops Yarn looked to have no chance of catching Clever Folly's stable-companion Music Be Magic and Gala's Image turning for home, but Gala's Image came down at the last, Music Be Magic tired up the hill and Bishops Yarn swept by to score by eight lengths. Clever Folly's success was

Charles Davis Handicap Chase, Ascot—Clever Folly justifies favouritism

Peterborough Chase, Huntingdon—Clever Folly has plenty in hand of Repington

gained in a very different manner, and unlike Bishops Yarn he did look the probable winner turning for home. Clever Folly led to the third, was back in command at the seventh and he and Dudie soon had the four other runners in trouble. Barnbrook Again and Welsh Oak were able to stay in reasonable touch, but Rusch de Farges and the Mackeson Gold Cup winner Joint Sovereignty were left trailing. Clever Folly, continuing to jump fast and fluently, took a clear advantage when Dudie made a mistake at the third last. Welsh Oak passed the weakening Dudie and flattered briefly going to the second last, but he could make no further impression on Clever Folly, who continued to run on strongly. Clever Folly won comfortably by ten lengths from Welsh Oak, with Barnbrook Again eight lengths further away in third. For long enough Clever Folly was considered best at two miles, and his first two victories of the season were gained over the trip in handicaps at Chepstow and Ascot. He didn't get off the mark over two and a half miles until his outing immediately prior to Cheltenham, when he made all in the four-runner Peterborough Chase at Huntingdon. Bishops Yarn, too, showed improved form when tackling an extra half mile late in his career, but whereas he's now ideally suited by three miles we don't expect Clever Folly

A. F. Budge Gold Cup, Cheltenham—left to right,
Dudie, Barnbrook Again and Clever Folly on the first circuit

to be quite so effective at that trip. He was beaten when falling three out on his only attempt at three miles, though he might well have been past his best for the season on that occasion and he's probably worth another chance at the distance. Bishops Yarn and Clever Folly certainly have widely differing ground requirements, the former being a mudlark whereas Clever Folly, though he has won on soft going, is ideally suited by a firm surface, as he showed at Cheltenham. Clever Folly put up easily his best performance subsequently over two and a half miles on firm ground at Newbury in March. Giving lumps of weight all round, Clever Folly finished about six lengths fifth behind Kittinger.

		Silly Season (br 1962)	Tom Fool
	Idiot's Delight (b 1970)		Double Deal
		Dolphinet (b 1957)	Big Game
Clever Folly (b.g. 1980)			Sea Gipsy
		Dumbarnie (br 1949)	Dante
	Lilac Veil (br 1966)		Lost Soul
		Big Liz (br 1957)	Le Sage
			Lisieux

Clever Folly, an angular, workmanlike individual, is the last of six foals produced by Lilac Veil, an unraced daughter of the winning hurdler Big Liz. Lilac Veil's only other winner apart from Clever Folly and Bishops Yarn (by Tycoon II) is Syringa Sam (by Saucy Kit), successful in an Irish National Hunt Flat race in 1981. The game and genuine Clever Folly is now rising eleven, but he's had only four seasons' racing (he was a fairly useful hurdler) and there's no reason to think that he won't return as good as ever in 1990/1. Given another long dry spell in the first half of the season the game and genuine Clever Folly should once again do very well. *G. Richards.*

CLEVER FOX 10 b.g. Kambalda–Leaney Escort (Escart III) [1989/90 20g^{pu}] c—
smallish gelding: lightly-raced novice hurdler/chaser/point-to-pointer: ran as though something was amiss only outing of season (March): stays 21f: acts on firm ground. *J. S. King.* —

CLEVER SHEPHERD 5 b.g. Broadsword (USA)–Reluctant Maid (Relko) [1989/90 16d 16g 16d^6 16g] leggy, workmanlike gelding: half-brother to winning jumpers Averon (by Averof) and Butlers Pet (by Mummy's Pet) and Austrian 2000 Guineas winner Lorencio (by Lorenzaccio): dam won up to 13f: poor novice hurdler: best effort on dead ground: blinkered final start. *G. Richards.* 85 ?

CLICKHAM LAD 12 ch.g. Keren–Native Queen (Native Prince) [1989/90 c17m^6 c16f^{pu} c16f^2] close-coupled gelding: poor selling chaser: best form at around 2m: acts on any going: sometimes wears blinkers: sold 1,050 gns Doncaster October Sales: won 2 point-to-points in March. *N. Chamberlain.* c— —

CLIFFALDA 7 ch.g. Young Man (FR)–Hampsruth (Sea Hawk II) [1989/90 c24g^2 c24g^2 c24g^3 c20s^{pu} 25m^{pu}] smallish, dipped-backed gelding: useful hurdler at his best: modest form in novice chases: stays 3m: acts on soft going: blinkered sixth to eighth starts 1988/9 (raced with little zest final outing): has won for a claimer. *J. A. C. Edwards.* c**112** —

CLIFTON CHAPEL 5 b.g. High Line–Britannia's Rule (Blakeney) [1989/90 16s^3 16g^3 20g*] smallish, sparely-made gelding: one-time useful middle-distance stayer on Flat: seemed suited by longer trip and jumped better than previously when winning novice hurdle at Worcester in March pushed out by 10 lengths from Cockstown Lad: will stay beyond 2½m: acts on soft going: will progress further. *H. Candy.* 117 p

CLINT NA GOOLAN 6 gr.g. Scallywag–Major Money (Current Coin) [1989/90 a16g] tall, unfurnished gelding: seems of little account. *B. Byford.* —

CLIPPERS DREAM 7 b.g. Heroic Air–Robbies Girl (Rubor) [1989/90 16d^4 16f^2 20h^2 20h^3 16m* 20d 16s^3 16d^6 16g^2 16d* 16s^2 17d 16f^2 17m^4] stocky gelding: won selling handicap hurdle at Catterick in December (bought in 3,200 gns) and novice hurdle on same course in February (edged right last): best at 2m: below form on heavy ground, acts on any other. *J. M. Jefferson.* 96

CLIVE HOUSE 6 b.g. Nearly A Hand–Royal Dialogue (Royal Buck) [1989/90 20s^3 21f^4 20f^6] big, leggy gelding: third foal: brother to a poor novice hurdler: dam twice-raced daughter of sister to top-class jumpers Salmon Spray and Larbawn: no worthwhile form over hurdles: dead. *G. B. Balding.* —

CLONBROCK BOY 4 b.g. Stanford–Kellys Risc (Pitskelly) [1989/90 a20g^{5}]
poor form on Flat, mainly in sellers (often blinkered or visored): tailed-off last in
amateur riders juvenile hurdle at Southwell in February. *T. Laxton.* —

CLONDROHID 9 ch.g. Lord Ha Ha–White Deer (My Swanee) [1989/90 c25f^{2} c—
c24g^{3} c24d^{pu} 25d^{5} c24f^{pu} 20f^{5} 24m] leggy ex-Irish gelding: fairly useful hurdler —
and moderate chaser at his best: well beaten in 1989/90 (blinkered last 2 starts):
stays 3m: acts on heavy going: sold 1,600 gns Doncaster Spring Sales. *P. A.
Blockley.*

CLONELLON GIRL 4 b.f. Millfontaine–Party Dancer (Be My Guest (USA))
[1989/90 16d^{6} 16m^{4} 16s 16g] no form on Flat: little worthwhile form over hurdles:
has been tried in blinkers and visor: trained first 2 starts by K. Morgan. *M.* —
Hourigan, Ireland.

CLONEY GRANGE 11 br.g. Bargello–Pampas Wind (Copernicus) [1989/90 c**137**
c16s^{3} c20g^{2} c24g^{2} c22d^{4} c24g^{2} c21v^{3} c20v^{5} c26v* c24m c28m^{4} c25g^{5}] leggy —
gelding: useful chaser: 25/1-winner of Ladbrokes Trial (Handicap Chase) at
Punchestown in February: sweating, tailed off in Kim Muir Memorial Challenge
Cup at Cheltenham in March: good fourth to Desert Orchid in Jameson Irish
Grand National at Fairyhouse following month: stays well: acts on good to firm
and heavy going: sometimes blinkered. *J. J. O'Connor, Ireland.*

CLONMACOGUE 9 br.g. Mandalus–Elusive Dream (Majority Blue) [1989/90
16g^{pu}] won point-to-point in Ireland in March: pulled up after fifth in novice event —
at Perth in May on hurdling debut. *B. Stevens.*

CLONROCHE GAZETTE 10 ch.g. Pauper–Clonrochess (London Gazette) c**103**
[1989/90 c26d^{2} c26g^{2} c22m^{F}] lengthy, angular gelding: quite a modest chaser:
second in hunter chases at Stratford in February and March: tailed off when
hampered and fell 4 out in Seagram Fox Hunters' Chase at Liverpool in April:
stays 3½m: probably acts on any going: has broken blood vessels: has worn a
tongue strap: inconsistent. *Peter Jones.*

CLONROCHE STREAM 11 br.g. Paddy's Stream–Clonroche Lady c—
(Charlottesvilles Flyer) [1989/90 c21g^{4} c27f^{2} c24m] workmanlike gelding: poor —
chaser: stays 27f: possibly unsuited by very firm ground, acts on any other:
usually amateur ridden: blinkered final outing 1988/9: inconsistent. *V. Thompson.*

CLOPTON 6 ch.g. General Assembly (USA)–Senthia (Parthia) [1989/90 16f* c—
16f^{2} 16m 16g^{2} 16s a16g^{4} 16m^{4} 16m 16g c17m^{3}] medium-sized gelding: 90
inconsistent selling hurdler: bought in 1,900 gns after winning conditional jockeys
handicap at Huntingdon in August: third of 4 finishers in novice handicap on same
course on chasing debut: best form over a sharp 2m: acts on firm ground: often
ridden by 7-lb claimer. *G. A. Hubbard.*

CLOS DU BOIS (FR) 4 b.g. High Top–Our Shirley (Shirley Heights)
[1989/90 17f^{2} a16g* a16g^{4}] placed over 1½m on Flat: sold out of R. J. R. Williams' 73
stable 7,000 gns Newmarket Autumn Sales: won novice hurdle at Southwell in
January: fair fourth on same course following month (pulled hard, ran wide on
bend after third). *Mrs N. Macauley.*

CLOSE ESCAPE 7 b.g. Sunyboy–Tarquann (Elegant Stephen) [1989/90 16m^{2} c92 p
17d* c20s^{2} 21d^{6}] angular gelding: won novice handicap hurdle at Devon & Exeter 92
in January: finished strongly after being hampered and losing his place 6 out when
12 lengths second to Okeetee in novice chase at Sandown in March: stays 2½m:
acts on soft going: should win a novice chase. *P. J. Hobbs.*

CLOUD BASE 4 br.g. Another Realm–A-Bye (Abernant) [1989/90 16f^{6} 16f^{5}
16f^{pu} a16g] leggy gelding: of little account: visored third start. *O. O'Neill.* —

CLOUD CHASER 7 ch.g. Hardgreen (USA)–Tudor Zara (Tudor Melody) c—
[1989/90 c17h^{4} 17f^{5} c26f^{F} c24f^{6} c20g c17v a20g^{4}] sparely-made gelding: novice 64
selling hurdler: poor novice chaser: best form at about 2m on a sound surface:
looked none too genuine once in 1988/9: usually blinkered or visored. *B. Forsey.*

CLOUGHTANEY 9 b.g. Quayside–Coadys Fancy (No Time) [1989/90 21v* c**124**
22d^{3} c19d^{4} c16g^{4} c18s 22v^{5} 25m] rather sparely-made gelding: good hurdler on 142
his day: won amateur riders hurdle at Navan in December (for second year
running): ran poorly afterwards (ran in snatches in Waterford Crystal Stayers'
Hurdle at Cheltenham final start): fourth in novice chases at Naas and
Leopardstown in January: well beaten last outing over fences: needs testing
conditions to be seen to best advantage at 2m and should stay beyond 2¾m:
suited by plenty of give in the ground: seems suited by a strongly-run race.
Patrick Mullins, Ireland.

CLOVEN ROCKS 10 gr.g. Scallywag–Jenny Owen (Counsel) [1989/90 c25m4 c26g2 c25gpu] modest novice hurdler: handicap chaser: not seen out after running poorly at Wincanton in January: dyed-in-the-wool stayer: acts on heavy going: jumps none too fluently. *Capt. T. A. Forster.* c93 —

CLOVER SONG 8 ch.m. True Song–Spartan Clover (Spartan General) [1989/90 c21fF c20fF c20spu c20g5 25dpu a24g] small, sturdy mare: novice hurdler/chaser: little promise: blinkered last 3 starts. *Mrs P. Townsley.* c— —

CLUB FOUR 4 ch.c. Absalom–Montana (Mossborough) [1989/90 16f 16m 16gpu] plain, dipped-backed colt: half-brother to winning jumpers Alabama (by Warpath) and Iowa (by So Blessed): dam poor maiden on Flat and over hurdles: little sign of ability in early-season juvenile hurdles, last a seller. *N. Tinkler.* —

CLYFFE HAZE 8 ch.g. Bonne Noel–Hazelwel (Deep Run) [1989/90 c25dpu c26vpu c20f] tall, workmanlike gelding: shows traces of stringhalt: no worthwhile form over hurdles and fences: sold 1,300 gns Ascot May Sales. *J. H. Baker.* c— —

CNOC AN OIR 6 br.m. Goldhill–Castlegannon (Perspex) [1989/90 19g 25g3 22spu 24m2 25d 24d5 28f2] sturdy ex-Irish mare: fourth foal: dam won 2¾m chase in Ireland: no form in NH Flat races and point-to-points: modest novice hurdler: thorough stayer: acts on firm and dead ground. *C. D. Broad.* 90

CNO CAPILL 6 ch.g. Lucifer (USA)–Innocent Laura (Laurence O) [1989/90 17m] fourth foal: dam unraced: tailed off in amateur riders maiden hurdle at Carlisle in April. *J. H. Johnson.* —

COBBLERS CROSS 5 ch.m. Hasty Word–Stormation (Compensation) [1989/90 F16m F17f] third in NH Flat race in 1988/9: behind in similar events in 1989/90: yet to race over hurdles or fences. *R. E. Peacock.*

COBO BAY 5 ch.g. General Assembly (USA)–Top Hope (High Top) [1989/90 16m2] strong, compact gelding: first form when second in novice hurdle at Chepstow in April: will stay further than 2m: acts on good to firm ground: should improve further and win a race. *Mrs J. Pitman.* 106 p

COCK-A-DOODLE-DO 4 b.g. Petorius–Bertida (Porto Bello) [1989/90 16d3 16d3 16g* 16g5 16g 17d6 16g3 16g2 17f6] smallish, angular gelding: maiden miler on Flat: won novice claiming hurdle at Edinburgh in January (claimed out of C. Thornton's stable £6,300): ran creditably on occasions afterwards: suited by sharp 2m: best form on good ground: blinkered final start (tailed off): usually ridden by claimer. *J. A. Hellens.* 84

COCK A LEEKIE (NZ) 7 b.g. Mayo Mellay (NZ)–Summermayo (NZ) (Summer Magic II) [1989/90 18f*] rather leggy, angular gelding: won novice hurdle at Fontwell in October: failed to get past the fifth in 2 novice chases: may prove best at distances short of 21f: acts on firm ground (ran poorly on heavy): good mount for a claimer. *D. H. Barons.* c— 99

COCKSTOWN LAD 4 b.g. Main Reef–Pasadena Girl (Busted) [1989/90 16s 16g 16g 16d2 16g4 16g4 16g 20g2 22f* 22g2] rather angular ex-Irish gelding: second foal: dam unraced: little form in 2 outings on Flat: won juvenile hurdle at Wincanton in March: ran well final outing: will stay 3m: acts on firm ground: trained until after fourth start by K. Prendergast. *R. Akehurst.* 108

CODDINGTON VILLAGE 5 b.g. Bonnova–Hidden Melody (Melodic Air) [1989/90 F16f3] second foal: dam never ran: pulled up all outings in point-to-points: 3 lengths third behind True Magic in NH Flat race at Warwick in May: yet to race over hurdles or in a steeplechase. *R. G. Brazington.*

CODENAME NIGHTJAR 7 b.g. Coded Scrap–Miss Leverdale (Great Heron (USA)) [1989/90 20gpu] leggy, lengthy gelding: no sign of ability in NH Flat races and over hurdles. *J. Townson.* —

CODGER 10 b.g. Kinglet–Oca (O'Grady) [1989/90 c21spu c22mpu] poor novice chaser: winning point-to-pointer. *Mrs H. Mobley.* c— —

COE 4 b. or br.g. Coquelin (USA)–Gully (Dike (USA)) [1989/90 16g* 16g2 16f2 16d3 16d3 16f3 18f*] sparely-made ex-Irish gelding: half-brother to a winner on Flat in Italy and a winner over jumps in France: dam won at up to 2m on Flat in Ireland: successful 3 times at up to 1½m on Flat in 1989 when trained by J. Oxx: won juvenile hurdles at Sandown in November and Fontwell in April: best efforts when placed in fair juvenile company third, fourth and sixth starts: unlikely to stay beyond 2¼m: acts on firm and dead ground. *R. Akehurst.* 110

COEURETTE 4 b.f. Nicholas Bill–Take To Heart (Steel Heart) [1989/90 19fr 20gpu] of little account and temperamental to boot: blinkered last start: bought for 725 gns Ascot February Sales. *D. Burchell.* — §

COGENT 6 b.g. Le Bavard (FR)–Cottstown Breeze (Autumn Gold) [1989/90 16f*] rangy, useful-looking gelding: has scope: half-brother to very useful staying chaser Another Breeze (by Deep Run): dam won at 2m over hurdles: won novice hurdle at Leicester in November on debut comfortably by 1½ lengths from The Illywhacker: looked sure to improve but wasn't seen out again. *J. A. Glover.* 93 p

COGNIZANT 5 b.m. Known Fact (USA)–Alia (Sun Prince) [1989/90 16f*] didn't have to be at her best to win 4-runner novice hurdle at Plumpton in August: not certain to stay much beyond 2m: probably acts on any going. *J. Ffitch-Heyes.* 71 +

COINAGE 7 gr.g. Owen Dudley–Grisbi (Grey Sovereign) [1989/90 17f3 18f2 24m4 21m2 16f6 21g 18f5] leggy gelding: has run tubed: handicap hurdler: ideally suited by around 2½m: acts on firm ground and possibly unsuited by soft: amateur ridden at not less than 10-1. *R. F. Johnson Houghton.* 96

COIRE VANNICH 6 b.m. Celtic Cone–Deepness (Deep Run) [1989/90 20sF 17d 16g* 16g3 16d4 c16g3 c20dF] small, workmanlike mare: handicap hurdler: won at Windsor in January: ran well next start: third in novice event at Wincanton on chasing debut: stays 2½m: best form on good ground: tends to sweat. *P. J. Hobbs.* c**84** p 103

COIS NA HABHNA 5 ch.g. Over The River (FR)–Arctic Lou (Arctic Slave) [1989/90 16m c16s5 c16m] big, rather unfurnished gelding: no worthwhile form in 2 outings over hurdles and 2 over fences. *R. Champion.* c– –

COKENNY BOY 5 b.g. Abednego–Northern Push (Push On) [1989/90 F16m4 F16m] third foal: half-brother to a poor novice hurdler by Torus: dam unraced half-sister to Browne's Gazette: odds on, fourth in NH Flat race at Towcester in January: mid-division in similar event at Sandown in March: yet to race over hurdles or fences. *Mrs J. Pitman.*

COLCOMBE CASTLE 7 gr.g. Persian Plan (AUS)–Vet's Bill (Hardraw Scar) [1989/90 c21d* c25g2 c25mr c24mF c26f4] lengthy gelding: fair winning point-to-pointer: made a couple of mistakes when winning hunter chase at Wincanton in February: clear when refusing 2 out at Devon & Exeter in April: every chance when falling at the last at Chepstow later in month: ran poorly final outing: stays 25f: acts on good to firm and dead ground. *B. F. W. Rendell.* c**108**

COLD MOSS 5 ch.g. Le Moss–Cold Arctic (Bargello) [1989/90 F17m] second foal: half-brother to novice hurdler Travelling Matt (by Le Bavard): dam placed in a point-to-point: behind in NH Flat race at Carlisle in April: retained by trainer 6,000 gns Doncaster Spring Sales: yet to race over hurdles or fences: sold 4,200 gns Ascot July Sales. *J. J. O'Neill.*

COLLEGE MASTER 6 b.g. Balliol–Poosie Nansie (Combat) [1989/90 F17d 27fpu] half-brother to quite useful hurdler Miss Fanackapan (by Colonist II), smart hurdler Silver Tycoon (by Tycoon II) and fair hurdler The Jolly Beggar (by Royalty): dam, of little account, is half-sister to useful staying chaser Loyal Fort: unplaced in NH Flat race at Carlisle and novice hurdle at Sedgefield (behind when pulled up 3 out): sold 6,000 gns Ascot June Sales. *T. P. Tate.* –

COLLEGE SILK 8 b.g. Balliol–Cheb's Honour (Chebs Lad) [1989/90 16s 16d] leggy gelding: novice hurdler: no form for a long time: amateur ridden: sold 2,300 gns Doncaster March Sales. *D. McCain.* –

COLLISTO 9 ch.g. Lombard (GER)–Colinetta (Alba Rock) [1989/90 21mpu] sparely-made gelding: winning hurdler: pulled up lame last 2 starts: stays 2½m: acts on any going. *D. J. Bell.* –

COLNE VALLEY KID 5 ch.g. Homing–Pink Garter (Henry The Seventh) [1989/90 16g 16s* 16g 16d] won selling handicap hurdle at Plumpton in December easily by 15 lengths (bought in 2,600 gns): no form in non-sellers otherwise. *A. Moore.* 84

COLNEY HEATH LAD 6 ch.g. Import–Pass-A-Deaney (Connaught) [1989/90 17m 16mpu 16d5 16g 16d 16g 16g 16h6] smallish, workmanlike gelding: poor novice selling hurdler: blinkered fifth and final starts: sold 900 gns Ascot June Sales. *T. W. Cunningham.* –

COLOCRACY 8 b. or br.g. Aristocracy–Coloressa (Le Tricolore) [1989/90 16dpu] lengthy gelding: tailed off when pulled up both outings in novice hurdles. *C. J. Bell.* –

COLOMBIERE 5 ch.g. Sallust–Shere Beauty (Mummy's Pet) [1989/90 16m5 16gF 16m* 16g6 a16g* 16f4 a16g] workmanlike gelding: 1m winner on Flat (probably ungenuine): won selling hurdles at Catterick in December (no bid) and Southwell (retained 3,200 gns) in February: ran well following month, but 94

moderately final start (finished lame): seems best at a sharp 2m: acts on firm ground. *G. Moore.*

COLONEL ARTHUR 6 ch.g. Politico (USA)–Selborne Lass (Deep Run) [1989/90 20d 16m] useful-looking gelding: placed in NH Flat races: behind in novice hurdles. *G. Richards.* —

COLONEL CHINSTRAP 5 ch.g. Milford–Deep Blue Sea (Gulf Pearl) [1989/90 18f^{2} 16f^{6} 16g^{4} 18g^{2} 18s^{2} 22d^{pu} 22f^{5}] bought 2,800 gns after winning 1½m selling handicap on Flat in 1989: novice selling hurdler: stays 2¼m: acts on firm and soft ground: visored fourth to sixth starts: looks difficult ride. *A. Moore.* 86

COLONEL HEATHER 15 ch.g. Laurence O–Slippaville (Trouville) [1989/90 c26g^{5} c25m^{4}] workmanlike gelding: winning point-to-pointer/hunter chaser: well beaten in 1990: suited by a good test of stamina: acts on any going: makes mistakes. *Capt M. Watson.* c— x

COLONEL JAMES 8 br.g. Captain James–Faraday Girl (Frigid Aire) [1989/90 20s^{3} 24s^{pu} 20d 21s 16d^{pu}] close-coupled gelding: poor handicapper over hurdles nowadays: only form in 1989/90 at 2½m: acts on heavy going: seems best with strong handling: pulled up lame final start. *Mrs N. S. Sharpe.* 86

COLONEL O'KELLY (NZ) 6 br.g. Kirrama (NZ)–Gold Coast (NZ) (Palm Beach (FR)) [1989/90 16g 21d 17m] lengthy gelding: no form in novice hurdles. *D. H. Barons.* —

COLONEL POPSKI 8 ch.g. Niniski (USA)–Miss Jessica (Milesian) [1989/90 17m* 17m^{5} 16f^{4} 20f^{2} 16m^{6} 22m^{4} 20f 16g 16d a16g^{5} a24g^{4} 16g c20f^{3} c20f^{4} c16m^{5} 23f^{pu}] small, lightly-made gelding: former selling hurdler: won handicap at Cartmel in August: lost his form after sixth start: poor novice chaser: stays 2¾m: acts on firm going and is unsuited by heavy: blinkered twelfth start. *Miss G. M. Rees.* c**77** 89 d

COLONEL ROSE 13 b.g. Fez–Rose Maroc (Derring-Do) [1989/90 c17g] small, sturdy gelding: moderate hurdler: novice chaser: best form at up to 2½m with give in the ground: has been tried in blinkers: usually amateur or claimer ridden. *T. Goldie.* c— —

COLONIAL LORD 4 ch.g. Milford–Miss Fanackapan (Colonist II) [1989/90 F17f] fourth foal: half-brother to poor novice hurdlers Golden Summer (by Balinger) and Raggyman (by Raga Navarro): dam, quite a useful hurdler, stayed 3m: mid-division in NH Flat race at Doncaster in March: yet to race over hurdles. *Mrs S. A. Bramall.*

COLONIAL OFFICE (USA) 4 ch.g. Assert–Belles Oreilles (CAN) (Nentego) [1989/90 21f^{5} 19h^{2} 16h^{2}] leggy gelding: staying maiden on Flat, claimed out of B. Hills's stable £8,055 in 1989: modest juvenile hurdler: will be suited by good test of stamina: blinkered final start. *P. J. Hobbs.* 92

COLONNA (USA) 4 b.g. Run The Gantlet (USA)–Evolutionary (USA) (Silent Screen (USA)) [1989/90 16g 16m 16d^{pu}] leggy, sparely-made gelding: claimed out of H. Cecil's stable £10,898 after second in 1½m seller on Flat in 1989: well beaten in juvenile hurdles: blinkered final start (jumped poorly): sold 2,100 gns Doncaster June Sales. *C. R. Beever.* —

COLOURFUL DANCER 7 ch.m. Dance In Time (CAN)–Barlow Fold (Monet) [1989/90 16h^{5} 16g^{pu}] sparely-made mare: tubed: won NH Flat race and second in maiden hurdle in Ireland in 1987/8: no worthwhile form since, including in sellers: headstrong. *William Price.* —

COLTOWN BOY 5 b.h. Town And Country–Miscontent (Bivouac) [1989/90 c16s^{pu} c16g] rangy horse: tailed off in juvenile hurdle and a novice chase. *M. Madgwick.* c— —

COLWALL PARK 5 br.g. Furry Glen–Regent's Gina (Prince Regent (FR)) [1989/90 21d] has scope: fourth foal: half-brother to Janquelle (by Red Alert), placed over hurdles in Ireland: dam Irish 1½m winner: better for race, in rear in novice hurdle at Newbury in February on debut. *Mrs H. Parrott.* —

COMANDANTE 8 b.g. Candy Cane–Meakstown (Ossian II) [1989/90 c20g^{F} c20v* c20g* c16m* c20f^{2}] c**141** —

Josh Gifford's stable had an unusually quiet spring, only seven out of an overall total of fifty winners coming after Deep Sensation's Tote Gold Trophy at Newbury on February 10th. There was one major achievement during the period, of course, Comandante's win in the Arkle Challenge Trophy at Cheltenham in March; but even he ended the season under a

Arkle Challenge Trophy, Cheltenham—
Comandante (centre) and Kiichi are set to pounce on Young Snugfit

cloud. Not that his thirty-length second to the improving Sword Beach in the Bollinger Champagne Novices' Handicap Chase at Ascot next time is anything other than useful form at the weights (he was giving Sword Beach 29 lb). Nevertheless his behaviour there was odd. He played up at the start, and when the runners set off he began bucking, continuing to do so intermittently almost up to the second fence, so that he lost considerable ground. He didn't jump so well as he can, either, and had little chance with front-running Sword Beach from before the home turn. No reason for Comandante's out-of-character display has been revealed. Hopefully he'll put everything behind him when he returns: he may not reach the top flight, but all being well should have a future in good handicap chases at up to two and a half miles.

The Arkle Challenge Trophy brought together again Comandante and the former champion hurdler Celtic Shot, three months after their first meeting in the Novair Wayward Lad Novices' Chase at Kempton. Comandante, quite a useful hurdler, had run a promising first race over fences at Kempton—he was pressing the eventual winner Celtic Shot closely when falling two out—and had won easily on both his other starts, at Folkestone and Newbury, at the latter course jumping particularly well and with plenty of zest. Even so, Celtic Shot had outstandingly the best form of the fourteen Arkle runners, and the fact that he started only half a point ahead of Comandante and Young Snugfit as 4/1 favourite was attributable mainly to the firmish going. Unfortunately, fears about Celtic Shot's effectiveness on the going proved well founded; he finished a moderate sixth, leaving a below-par Arkle by its own high standards. At least the event was run at a sound gallop. As usual Young Snugfit made the running. For much of the way he seemed the one most likely to succeed, especially when he quickened three lengths clear of Kiichi round the final turn and produced yet another good jump at the last. Celtic Shot was one of the first to be pushed along, and was being outpaced at the third last by which time Comandante, having been settled in mid-field taking a keen hold, was himself being chased along. Into the straight Comandante began to stay on in third; he deprived Kiichi of second place by outjumping him at the last, then continued to progress to lead near the line, Kiichi just getting the better of Young Snugfit for second, a length down. The three didn't have the finish to themselves: Antinous, who'd made a mistake when closing at the second last, came back to be fourth, beaten just over two lengths behind the winner.

It has been said that Comandante will be aimed at the Gold Cup in 1991. At this stage Comandante is a long way off Gold Cup standard; furthermore, his stamina is in some doubt. Possibly he has more improvement in him as he's been lightly raced so far. Because of intermittent unsoundness he's had only seventeen starts since he began in 1985/6, and the latest season was easily his busiest since 1986/7. Comandante has never run like a horse who'll stay well, though it's true he's becoming more amenable to restraint with age.

Comandante (b.g. 1982)	Candy Cane (b 1965)	Crepello (ch 1954)	Donatello II
			Crepuscule
		Candy Gift (b 1959)	Princely Gift
			Kandy Sauce
	Meakstown (b 1963)	Ossian II (b 1952)	Royal Charger
			Prudent Polly
		Tackler (ch 1944)	Pactolus
			Bibs

Comandante's breeding holds out some hope that he'll stay. His sire Candy Cane, whose best runner over the sticks has been the stable's Kybo, got an Irish Grand National second in Candy Well VI; the unraced dam Meakstown is a half-sister to the Irish Grand National winner Splash. Meakstown's three winners before Comandante were all minor ones over two miles or thereabouts: Auto Stop (by Lone Star) won twice over fences in Britain, the other two, Scotspree (also by Lone Star) and Splash Tackle (by Bluerullah), won bumpers events in Ireland. The second dam Tackler and third dam Bibs were both winning two-year-olds in their day, in the latter's case as long ago as 1939. Tackler went on to show quite useful winning form over hurdles at two miles; Bibs, also a winner on the Flat as a three-year-old, is the third dam of that game mare Sandy Sprite, who broke down when on the verge of success in the 1971 Grand National. Although he's had more than his share of training set-backs Comandante has shown his form on all types of going. A tall, lengthy gelding, he is usually a good jumper of fences. *J. T. Gifford.*

COMBE HAY 8 br.g. Rhodomantade–Safeguard (Wolver Hollow) [1989/90 c— c22d^{5} c24g^{pu}] leggy, angular gelding: no sign of ability. *P. Hayward.* —

COMBERMERE 6 b.g. Absalom–Queen's Parade (Sovereign Path) [1989/90 c**125** 16g^{3} 22m^{2} 20f^{3} 26d^{4} c25d* c24g^{2} c20g* c24d*] sturdy gelding: useful hurdler: 136 ran creditably in first half of season: won novice chases at Devon & Exeter in January, Kempton in February and Chepstow (unimpressively) in March: stays 25f: has won on top-of-the-ground but best form with give: jumps soundly and will win more races over fences. *R. G. Frost.*

COMBINED EXERCISE 6 br.g. Daring March–Dualvi (Dual) [1989/90 16g^{pu} 16s 16m 16g] lengthy, leggy gelding: handicap hurdler: ran poorly in — 1989/90, giving impression something amiss: probably stays 2¼m: acts on heavy going: probably best with strong handling: has worn a tongue strap. *R. Akehurst.*

COMBO (CZE) 6 b.g. Behistoun–Coca Cola (CZE) (Detvan) [1989/90 c20m^{2} c75 c20f^{wo} c25f^{2}] leggy, rather close-coupled gelding: no form over hurdles: modest — form over fences: walked over in novice event at Huntingdon in August: finished lame last start: stays 3m: acts on hard ground: sold 2,300 gns Ascot October Sales. *D. Nicholson.*

COMEDY BASIN 7 b.g. Comedy Star (USA)–Porcupine Basin (Lucifer c88 (USA)) [1989/90 18d 16s^{pu} c20g c16g c25f^{2} c24f* c25m^{pu} c26g^{pu} c24f^{pu}] — workmanlike gelding: novice hurdler: won novice chase at Worcester in March:

made mistakes next time: suited by a test of stamina: acts on firm ground: blinkered last start. *R. J. Holder.*

COMEDY FUN 6 b.g. Comedy Star (USA)–Get Involved (Shiny Tenth) [1989/90 c16h^F3 c16g^ur c16f^3 c17f^pu] deep-girthed gelding: no sign of ability over hurdles: poor novice chaser: let down by his jumping: sold 2,000 gns Doncaster March Sales. *N. Bycroft.* c**67** ? —

COMEDY LANE 11 b.g. Comedy Star (USA)–Border Lane (Border Legend) [1989/90 c25m c25g^5 c28g^2 c25f^4 c26m^4] big, strong, rangy gelding: moderate chaser: probably stays 3½m: acts on any going: blinkered once in 1987/8. *D. H. Barons.* c**106** —

COMEDY ROAD 6 br.g. Old Jocus–Blue Flash (Blue Lightning) [1989/90 20f* 16f^5 24g 20g^ur 17f 16d 16g c24g^2 c25g*] sturdy gelding: won novice hurdle at Wetherby in October and novice chase at Catterick in March: stays 3m: acts on firm ground: trained until after eighth start by J. Hanson. *R. Lee.* c**100** 90

COMEDY SPY 6 br.g. Scallywag–Ida Spider (Ben Novus) [1989/90 F17f^3] half-brother to 3 winning jumpers, including very useful chasers Ardent Spy (by Saucy Kit) and Ida's Delight (by Idiot's Delight): dam unraced: 16 lengths third behind Saskia's Pride in NH Flat race at Doncaster in March: yet to race over hurdles or fences. *Mrs A. R. Hewitt.*

COME HALLEY (FR) 4 b.g. Crystal Glitters (USA)–Edition Nouvelle (FR) (New Chapter) [1989/90 16s^F 16g 16g 16s^pu 22g 16g 16f^pu] neat gelding: plating-class 1¼m winner on Flat: no form over hurdles, including in a selling handicap: pulls hard: sold out of R. Boss's stable 1,600 gns Doncaster March Sales after fourth start. *Mrs A. Knight.* —

COME ON CLOVER 4 br.f. Oats–National Clover (National Trust) [1989/90 F13f^pu 16f 19m^pu] first foal: dam, very useful point-to-pointer, is daughter of Welsh Grand National winner Clover Bud: no sign of ability, including in a selling hurdle. *R. Lee.* —

COME ON COME ON 5 b.g. Hardboy–Precipitant Light (Precipitant) [1989/90 20s^pu] angular gelding: fourth foal: dam winning Irish point-to-pointer: tailed off when pulled up seventh in novice hurdle at Chepstow in December: dead. *Miss J. Thorne.* —

COME ON TOBY 4 b.g. Dubassoff (USA)–Pharaoh's Bride (Pharaoh Hophra) [1989/90 F16s 16g^6 17m^6] rather unfurnished gelding: fourth foal: half-brother to modest hurdlers Come On Gracie (by Hardiran) and Golden Acre (by Los Cerrillos): dam selling hurdle winner: well beaten in NH Flat race and 2 outings over hurdles. *S. N. Cole.* —

COME POINTING 4 b.c. Blakeney Point–Come North (Track Spare) [1989/90 16m 16m^pu] half-brother to novice hurdler Claudia Pascal (by Tickled Pink): dam best at up to 1m: tailed off in juvenile hurdle in October: dead. *B. R. Cambidge.* —

COMERS GATE 5 b.g. Impecunious–Opt Out (Spartan General) [1989/90 F16s aF16g] workmanlike gelding: third foal: half-brother to winning point-to-pointer General Option (by Levanter): dam won poor novice hurdle: well behind in NH Flat races at Warwick and Southwell in February: yet to race over hurdles or fences. *G. R. Prest.*

COMIC LINE 5 b.g. Old Jocus–Straight Lane (Straight Lad) [1989/90 F16g 20g] fifth foal: dam fairly useful point-to-pointer: behind in NH Flat race at Sandown in November and novice hurdle at Plumpton following month. *J. B. Sayers.* —

COMMANCHE BRAVE 7 ch.g. Royal Blend–Billie Jean (Sweet Revenge) [1989/90 17f 22g^F 19g 20v a20g^pu 22s 22f^r 21f] lengthy, angular gelding: no worthwhile form over hurdles: refused to race seventh start: sold 2,000 gns Ascot May Sales. *C. L. Popham.* —

COMMANDER CARVER 4 b.g. Owen Anthony–Carvers Corah (Easter Island) [1989/90 18h^3 18f^4 16d^4] close-coupled, leggy gelding: maiden middle-distance plater on Flat: poor juvenile selling hurdler: best run at 2m. *I. Campbell.* 69

COMME CI COMME CA 4 ch.c. Buzzards Bay–Morstons Maid (Morston (FR)) [1989/90 F16d^5 F12g^3 F16m] second foal: brother to winning selling hurdler Buzzards Maid: dam, plater, suited by 1½m: third behind Going On in NH Flat race at Market Rasen in March: edgy, behind in well-contested event at Liverpool following month: yet to race over hurdles. *B. Ellison.*

COMPENSATOR 5 b.g. Sweet Monday–Grayshott Hall (Compensation) [1989/90 16m^{su}] half-brother to Bradbury Hall (by Comedy Star), winner of 1½m seller: dam placed over 5f at 2 yrs: slipped up on bend after third in novice hurdle at Perth in August on debut. *T. W. Cunningham.* —

COMPOSER 12 ch.h. Music Boy–Contadina (Memling) [1989/90 16m^{3}] angular, workmanlike horse: lightly-raced novice selling hurdler: no form for a long time: sometimes blinkered. *M. B. James.* —

COMPTON PARK 9 ch.g. Eastwood Prince–Mighty Grand (Proud Chieftain) [1989/90 c25d^{5} c27s^{4} c25s^{5}] angular, deep-girthed gelding: winning chaser: ran creditably first start, best effort 1989/90: suited by about 3m: yet to race on very firm ground, acts on any other: sometimes blinkered: deliberate jumper. *J. S. King.* **c90** —

COMRA 11 b.g. Moulton–Armelle (Tribal Chief) [1989/90 c20s^{5} 27s c30v^{pu} c24s^{pu}] lightly-made gelding: selling hurdler: winning chaser: ran poorly in 1989/90: stays 3m: acts on heavy going: usually wears blinkers over hurdles, and also wore them final start over fences: usually bandaged nowadays. *G. A. Ham.* c— —

COMTEC PRINCE 8 b.g. Remainder Man–Moon Mirth (Comedy Star (USA)) [1989/90 17h 17f^{3} 25d^{6} 16g^{5} a16g^{4} a20g^{3} a16g^{5} c16f^{2} c17h^{3} c17m] close-coupled gelding: selling hurdler: easily best effort over fences when second in novice event at Taunton in April: best form at around 2m: acts on any going with possible exception of heavy: has run visored and blinkered. *B. Forsey.* **c81** 72

CONA GLEN (NZ) 9 ch.g. Lomond–Talento (NZ) (Saraceno) [1989/90 20d 22m c26v^{4} c24s^{ur} c26s^{2}] small gelding: one-time fair hurdler: made several mistakes when staying-on ½-length second to Dr Pepper in handicap chase at Fontwell in February: thorough stayer, well suited by long distances and plenty of give in the ground: tends to sweat, badly so on occasions. *Capt. T. A. Forster.* **c99** —

CONCERT PAPER 6 b.g. Over The River (FR)–Good Surprise (Maelsheachlainn) [1989/90 20m^{4} 20g^{6} 20s^{3} 20d^{3} 20v^{5} 22d^{2} 20m^{2} 20g^{3} 24g^{4}] leggy gelding: handicap hurdler: stays 3m, at least when conditions aren't very testing: acts on good to firm and soft going. *Miss S. J. Wilton.* 96

CONCLUSIVE 11 ch.g. Crash Course–French Cherry (Escart III) [1989/90 c26g* c28g* c30s^{pu} c24g^{F} c36f^{F}] tall, strong gelding: fairly useful chaser: jumped soundly in the main when winning handicaps at Carlisle and Haydock (quite valuable event) in November: travelling strongly in lead when falling 2 out at Kelso in March: fell at the third in Seagram Grand National at Liverpool in April: stays very well: acts on any going: races up with the pace: very well ridden by N. Doughty, though has won for an amateur. *G. Richards.* **c132** —

Save And Prosper Handicap Chase, Haydock—
Conclusive (right) is impressive in beating Mister Christian

CONDOR PAN 7 b.h. Condorcet (FR)–Ishtar Abu (St Chad) [1989/90 16f* 17g*] strong, dipped-backed, lengthy horse: very smart hurdler: easy winner under big weights of early-season handicaps at Killarney and Tralee: not seen out again: stays 2½m: acts on any going: races with plenty of zest. *J. Bolger, Ireland.* 159

CONE LANE 4 ch.g. On Your Mark–Cee Beauty (Ribero) [1989/90 16m* 18f2 a16g* a16g4 a16g4 a16g6 a16g5] workmanlike gelding: 7f winner on Flat: won selling hurdle at Worcester in September (bought in 6,800 gns) and juvenile hurdle at Lingfield in December: also ran well last 3 starts: stays 2¼m: acts on firm ground: blinkered final outing. *B. Gubby.* 82

CONEY DOVE 5 b.m. Celtic Cone–Shadey Dove (Deadly Nightshade) [1989/90 16g 21d 16f4] small mare: has shown signs of ability all outings over hurdles: tired 2 out over 21f: probably capable of better. *R. J. Price.* 73 p

CONFEDERATE 4 ch.g. Mummy's Game–Shenandoah (Mossborough) [1989/90 16f 17m] sparely-made gelding: half-brother to several winners by Warpath, including hurdlers Do Or Die and Wide Missouri: plating-class maiden on Flat: well behind in novice hurdle at Bangor and novice selling hurdle at Devon & Exeter: sold 2,000 gns Ascot July Sales. *Mrs S. Oliver.* —

CONNABEE 6 b.g. Connaught–Sera Sera (Hill Clown (USA)) [1989/90 16spu 16gF] workmanlike gelding: half-brother to several winners, including selling hurdler Willerby (by Great Nephew): seemingly of little account on Flat: little promise in 2 novice hurdles. *S. Woodman.* —

CONNAUGHT BROADS 7 b.m. Connaught–Suffolk Broads (Moulton) [1989/90 17fF 17f] small, sparely-made mare: poor novice selling hurdler: races only at around 2m: acts on good to firm ground: claimer ridden. *M. J. Charles.* —

CONNAUGHT CARD 8 b.g. Connaught–No Cards (No Mercy) [1989/90 16g 20s4 16d 20d] tall, leggy, angular gelding: novice hurdler: no form in 1989/90: carried head high and weakened quickly under pressure final start 1987/8: usually ridden by 7-lb claimer. *M. W. Ellerby.* —

CONNAUGHT CLEANERS 10 br.g. Raise You Ten–Bramble Rose (Pals Passage) [1989/90 22d5 22g 24g c22dpu 21fpu c26f3] sparely-made gelding: handicap hurdler/novice chaser: stays well: probably acts on any going: often claimer ridden: sometimes blinkered: has looked temperamental: sold out of William Price's stable 2,800 gns Ascot April Sales after fourth start. *K. G. Wingrove.* c— 88

CONNECT THREE 5 b.g. Deep Run–Inaghmose (Pitpan) [1989/90 F16g F16f 20fpu] sparely-made gelding: tubed: first foal: dam in mid-division in Irish NH Flat race on only outing: well beaten in NH Flat races: lean and sweating, tailed off when pulled up in novice hurdle at Ascot in May. *C. C. Trietline.* —

CONNEMARA DAWN 6 ch.g. Viking (USA)–Amendola (FR) (Amen (FR)) [1989/90 c16m2 c16m2 c24f4 c20gF a20g3 21d c19f2] leggy, close-coupled gelding: winning selling hurdler: modest novice chaser: probably stays 2½m: seems to act on any going: blinkered in 1988/9 and on last 2 starts: has run well when sweating. *R. J. Holder.* c94 94

CONNIE'S PET 6 br.m. National Trust–Not Often (Lauso) [1989/90 F16f5] second foal: half-sister to useful chaser Prize Asset (by Levanter): dam placed over hurdles and fences: 14/1, over 30 lengths fifth of 13 to Piper's Son in NH Flat race at Ascot in April on debut: yet to race over hurdles or fences. *P. J. Hobbs.*

CONSCRIPTION 10 ch.g. Gunner B–Needless (Petingo) [1989/90 c16g5 c24d4 c28gpu] strong gelding: winning hurdler/chaser: has run poorly since third start in 1988/9: stays 3m: acts on any going. *J. P. Leigh.* c— —

CONSTANT OFFICIAL 5 b.m. Official–Abbyrama (Abyss) [1989/90 F16f] second foal: half-sister to NH Flat race-placed Double U Dee (by Rapid Pass): dam never ran: mid-division in NH Flat race at Warwick in May: yet to race over hurdles or fences. *F. G. Hollis.*

CONTACT KELVIN 8 br.g. Workboy–Take My Hand (Precipice Wood) [1989/90 c22gpu c16g4 c17mpu c27gpu c16g2 a18g 16g] big, workmanlike gelding: shows traces of stringhalt: one-time fair hurdler: tailed off last 2 starts: best effort over fences when 5 lengths second to comfortable winner Astre Radieux in novice event at Hexham in March: stays 2½m: acts on soft going and good to firm. *N. Bycroft.* c88 —

CONTRADEAL 13 b.g. Crespino–Contrivance (Vimy) [1989/90 c24f4 c24f2 c24f5 c26f4 c25f*] tall, leggy, lengthy gelding: fair chaser nowadays: made all in c**119**

handicap at Towcester in May: suited by 3m+: acts on any going: has jumped sketchily: sometimes sweats: genuine, but suited by strong handling. *A. Barclay.*

CONWAY GROVE 10 b.g. Pongee–Sherry (King's Coup) [1989/90 c20f2 c25fpu] shallow-girthed gelding: winning chaser: stayed well: probably acted on any going: dead. *J. E. Swiers.* **c103** —

COOKS LAWN 5 ch.m. The Parson–Croom Cross (Menelek) [1989/90 16m 16g2 22dpu 16m6] medium-sized mare: third foal: sister to winning staying hurdler/chaser Parson's Cross: dam won 17f maiden hurdle in Ireland: short-head second to Stephens Pet in novice hurdle at Wincanton in January: ran poorly afterwards. *C. P. E. Brooks.* 88

COOL BREW 12 b.g. Menelek–Maximum Bonus (Wrekin Rambler) [1989/90 c24gF c24g4 c24gpu c24v4 c24g3 c24v2 c33dpu c32g2 c24dpu c24gpu] strong gelding: handicap chaser: ran moderately all bar second, sixth and eighth starts in 1989/90: stays well: suited by plenty of give in the ground: has worn a crossed noseband and a tongue strap. *R. Paisley.* c**96**

COOL CATCH 7 b.g. Patch–Coole Park (Wolver Hollow) [1989/90 20gpu] sparely-made ex-Irish gelding: fourth foal: half-brother to winning hurdler Miss Tristram (by Sir Tristram): dam showed a little ability both starts at 2 yrs: third in NH Flat race in 1987: little sign of ability over hurdles: sold 1,400 gns Doncaster Spring Sales. *J. H. Johnson.* —

COOLCOTTS 14 ch.g. Prince Hansel–Even More (Even Money) [1989/90 c20s6 c25m4 c25f3] tall gelding: winning hunter chaser: stays 3m well: acts on any going. *Lt-Col R. J. R. Symonds.* c**92**

COOL CRYSTAL 4 b.f. Dynastic–Cool Baby (Rubor) [1989/90 F16v] second foal: dam unraced: tailed-off last of 13 in NH Flat race at Ayr in January: yet to race over hurdles. *Mrs M. A. Kendall.*

COOL DI 5 b.m. Gallo Gallante–Cool Imp (Rubor) [1989/90 22gpu 17g 20d 16f4] sturdy mare: second foal: half-sister to winning hurdler Cool Andy (by Dynastic): dam moderate hurdler: first form over hurdles when fourth in maiden event at Hexham in March (amateur ridden): evidently suited by firm ground. *T. W. Rebanks.* 65

COOL DISTINCTION 7 b.g. Class Distinction–Arctic Flight (Arctic Slave) [1989/90 c24gpu c33dpu] strong gelding: poor novice chaser. *C. C. Trietline.* c— —

COOL EMM 5 b.h. Miami Springs–Wise Countess (USA) (Count Amber) [1989/90 16f 16d] poor maiden on Flat: well beaten in novice hurdles at Taunton and Stratford (blinkered) in first half of season. *D. Haydn Jones.* —

COOL FOUNTAIN 6 b.m. Royal Fountain–Cool Date (Arctic Slave) [1989/90 F16f 16g5 16fpu] no promise in NH Flat races and novice hurdles. *T. A. K. Cuthbert.* —

COOL GROUND 8 ch.g. Over The River (FR)–Merry Spring (Merrymount) [1989/90 c24s4 c30s2 c29g* c29d4 c24s4 c25g2] c**142** —

A very useful staying chaser with a good turn of foot, Cool Ground can be an exciting horse to watch. He first came to prominence with an astonishing victory in the Kim Muir Memorial Challenge Cup at Cheltenham in 1989, rallying from a seemingly-impossible position at the third last and quickening in fine style on the run-in to beat Charter Hardware by a length and a half. Cool Ground's strong finishing burst was seen to good effect again in valuable handicaps in the latest season. He ran a fine race in the Coral Welsh National at Chepstow in December, carrying 8 lb more than his original handicap mark and still looking in need of the outing. Well out of contention starting the second circuit, he stayed on strongly in the straight to take second place behind fifteen-length winner Bonanza Boy on the run-in. The benefit of that outing could be seen in Cool Ground at Sandown two weeks later, the pick of the paddock in a competitive twelve-runner field for the Anthony Mildmay, Peter Cazalet Memorial Handicap Chase. Though on this occasion able to lie up comfortably with the pace set in turn by Roll-A-Joint and Kodiak Island, Cool Ground looked to have it to do when Nick The Brief quickened a couple of lengths clear after the third last. In touch but pushed along, Cool Ground lost further impetus with a slight mistake two out, then rallied splendidly on

Anthony Mildmay, Peter Cazalet Memorial Handicap Chase, Sandown—
Nick The Brief starts up the run-in ahead of eventual winner Cool Ground (No. 7)

the run-in to get the best of a thrilling finish with Nick The Brief and Rowlandsons Jewels, the three separated by necks at the line.

Cool Ground further showed himself no sluggard by running at least as well as ever when returned to three miles on his last two starts, though he was forced into jumping errors over the shorter trip. In the slowly-run Charterhouse Mercantile Handicap Chase at Ascot in February, Cool Ground stayed on again after a bad mistake five out to finish a good fourth to Ten of Spades. He was up against it in the Jim Ford Challenge Cup at Wincanton later in the month, and Cavvies Clown beat him thirty lengths; outpaced most of the way he gave the impression he'll prove best with more give in the ground. Cool Ground acts on heavy going and has yet to show his form on ground firmer than good; he was withdrawn from his two engagements at the Cheltenham Festival—the Gold Cup and Ritz Club Handicap Chase—at the five-day stage with the going predicted to be on the firm side and wasn't seen out again. Though Cool Ground would have to improve considerably to be a serious challenger for the Gold Cup—he was generally quoted at around 50/1 at the time of his withdrawal—he's likely to continue to pay his way in the top long-distance handicaps and starts the season on a good mark.

Cool Ground (ch.g. 1982)	Over The River (FR) (ch 1974)	Luthier (b or br 1965)	Klairon
			Flute Enchantee
		Medenine (b 1967)	Prudent II
			Ma Congaie
	Merry Spring (ch 1977)	Merrymount (b 1970)	Charlottown
			Merry Mate
		Rose of Spring (ch 1971)	Golden Vision
			Springville Rose

Cool Ground was bred in Ireland, the second foal and only winner to date produced by Merry Spring. His sister Rapid Ground, an IR 16,500-guinea purchase as a four-year-old, finished in mid-division in a National Hunt Flat race at Sandown in March on her debut. Neither Merry Spring nor Rose of Spring made the racecourse. The third dam Springville Rose won twice at a mile and three quarters over hurdles in Ireland and bred the useful staying hurdler and winning chaser The Climp. Cool Ground, a leggy gelding, won a point-to-point and two steeplechases in Ireland when tained by Brassil. After the termination of Mitchell's contract at Whitcombe Stables in the spring, he's to be trained by Akehurst in 1990/1. Though more traditionally associated with Flat racers and hurdlers, Akehurst's former yard had a fair strike-rate with its few chasers in the latest season, highlighted by the success of Solidasarock in the S.G.B. Chase at Ascot. *N. R. Mitchell.*

COOL MOVE 5 br.g. Prince Tenderfoot (USA)–Tranquil Love (Ardoon) [1989/90 F16g F12g] neat gelding: second foal: half-brother to novice hurdler Nurse's Niece (by Sallust): dam won over 2m on Flat in Ireland: tailed off in NH Flat races: yet to race over hurdles or fences. *Mrs Gill E. Jones.*

COOL OPERATOR 7 ch.g. Song–Gentildonna (Pieces of Eight) [1989/90 20dpu 17v3] strong gelding: lightly-raced novice hurdler: third in selling handicap at Newton Abbot in December, first form: weakened closing stages and may do better under less testing conditions. *B. Stevens.* 65

COOL RECEPTION 9 ch.g. Decent Fellow–Arctic Daisy (Arctic Slave) [1989/90 c20d3 c24m2 c20fur c20spu c25g3 c27s4 c24m3 c27f*] big, workmanlike gelding: won 3-runner handicap chase at Sedgefield in April: carried head high and found nothing under pressure earlier in season: stays 3m: acts on any going: blinkered third and fourth outings: not one to trust. *W. A. Stephenson.* c97 § — §

COOL SEASON 6 ch.g. Vital Season–Iced Lolly (Master Stephen) [1989/90 c17dpu c16g4 c20dpu] medium-sized gelding: no sign of ability. *J. White.* c— —

COOL STRIKE 9 ch.g. Royal Match–Coolrobin (Light Year) [1989/90 c20gur c16d4 c20g2 c17d2 c16v2 c21d5 c20d4] quite a useful chaser: best efforts of season in handicaps at Newcastle and Ayr (beaten 2½ lengths by General Chandos) on third and fifth starts: effective at 2m and stays 2½m: acts on heavy going and is possibly unsuited by top-of-the-ground: visored last 3 outings over hurdles and final start over fences in 1988/9: sometimes wears a tongue strap. *G. M. Moore.* c125 —

COOL SUN 10 b.g. Deep Run–Stroll On (Vulgan) [1989/90 25dpu] good-bodied gelding: fairly useful chaser at his best: winning hurdler: pulled up lame in March: stayed 3¼m: won on soft going but best run on good ground: had been tried in blinkers: dead. *Mrs J. Pitman.* c— —

COOLSYTHE 6 ch.m. Avocat–Lindenise (London Gazette) [1989/90 20g] non-thoroughbred ex-Irish mare: second foal: half-sister to winning hurdler/point-to-pointer Knockan Boy (by Bargello): dam never ran: pulled up in 2 point-to-points in 1989: around 19 lengths seventh to Gold Haven in 17-runner maiden hurdle at Perth in April. *J. Parkes.* — p

COOL TRADE 6 ch.m. Celtic Cone–Clear Trade (Menelek) [1989/90 20sF 20dF] workmanlike mare: poor novice hurdler. *K. A. Morgan.* —

COOMBESBURY LANE 4 b.f. Torus–Nimble Rose (Furry Glen) [1989/90 F16f] third foal: dam never ran: tailed off in NH Flat race at Ludlow in April: yet to race over hurdles. *P. J. Jones.*

COPELAND LAD 8 b.g. Radical–No Dice (No Argument) [1989/90 c20g2 c27s3 c16d6 c20f2] big, workmanlike gelding: winning hurdler: placed in novice chases in February and March: stays well: probably acts on any going: usually claimer ridden over hurdles: has flashed tail under pressure. *J. H. Johnson.* c96 —

COPPER CAULDRON 8 b.m. Keren–Copper City (Even Money) [1989/90 c26mpu] well beaten both starts over hurdles: poor maiden point-to-pointer: pulled up in maiden hunter chase in April. *F. T. Walton.* c— —

COPPER FASTENER 9 b.g. Fine Blade (USA)–Fairy Temple (Bowsprit) [1989/90 c26g3 c22m] workmanlike, angular gelding: has been hobdayed: winning chaser/point-to-pointer: not disgraced when seventh in Seagram Fox Hunters' Chase at Liverpool in April: stays 3m: acts on soft going: sold out of T. Forster's stable 5,700 gns Doncaster November Sales. *R. W. Heyman.* c94 —

COPPERITE 7 b.g. Rapid Pass–Present Fantasy (Doubtless II) [1989/90
$20d^{pu}$] sturdy gelding: winning point-to-pointer/hurdler: ran poorly only outing —
1989/90: stays 2½m: probably acts on any going: has flashed tail under pressure.
G. Price.

COPPER MARKET 7 ch.g. Native Bazaar–Copper Cloud (Foggy Bell)
[1989/90 16g 16d $16f^{5}$ $16h^{5}$ $16g^{3}$ 16f $17f^{3}$] rangy, workmanlike gelding: poor novice 67
hurdler, has run in a seller: form only at around 2m on top-of-the-ground: visored
fifth start. *Mrs R. Wharton.*

COPPER STREAK 8 ch.g. Streak–Copper Cloud (Foggy Bell) [1989/90 16g c— x
22g $c16m^{pu}$ $21s^{3}$ $22m^{pu}$] compact gelding: handicap hurdler: wandered when third 93
behind Sir Crusty in conditional jockeys event at Sandown in February: ran poorly
next time: modest novice chaser (has made mistakes all outings): probably stays
2¾m: acts on soft going and good to firm: blinkered last 2 starts. *Capt. T. A.
Forster.*

COPPETT SONG 8 ch.g. Tobique–Sweet Rhythm (My Swanee) [1989/90 c**82** x
$c24m^{3}$ $c24s^{6}$ $c22d^{4}$ $c32f^{F}$] big, lengthy, plain gelding: won 2 point-to-points in
1989: has shown ability in steeplechases, but is let down by his jumping: looks a
thorough stayer. *G. Price.*

COPSE AND ROBBERS 8 b.g. Hot Grove–Pearl Star (Gulf Pearl) [1989/90
$20g^{3}$ 22m] tall, rather leggy gelding: modest and lightly-raced hurdler: third in 97 +
conditional jockeys handicap at Cheltenham in November: weakened in latter
stages when well beaten following month: stays 2½m: acts on soft going and good
to firm. *J. T. Gifford.*

COQUETA 5 ch.m. Coquelin (USA)–Clara Petacci (USA) (Crepello) [1989/90
$16m^{ur}$ 17m* 16v 16d $16f^{3}$ $20m^{4}$ $17f^{4}$] leggy mare: won novice hurdle at Carlisle in 84
November: best effort subsequently on fifth start: stays 2½m: acts on any going:
usually ridden by 7-lb claimer. *E. J. Alston.*

COQUILLAGE 5 b.h. Coquelin (USA)–Legs And Things (Three Legs)
[1989/90 $16g^{5}$] leggy horse: winning hurdler: fair fifth in handicap at Perth in 85
April: should stay 2½m: acts on heavy going: blinkered at Perth, visored previous
4 starts. *C. Weedon.*

CORAL HARBOUR 8 ch.g. Bay Express–Coralivia (Le Levanstell) [1989/90 c?
$17f^{3}$ $c16f^{2}$ $c18f^{pu}$ $16f^{5}$ 16s* $16d^{4}$ 16g $c16d^{6}$ $c17d^{F}$ $c18f^{pu}$ $17m^{pu}$ $17f^{4}$ $17h^{3}$] tall, 82 §
leggy, rather narrow gelding: poor hurdler: successful in conditional jockeys
event at Taunton in December: poor form at best in novice chases: best at around
2m: ran poorly on heavy going, acts on any other: successful with and without
blinkers: usually races up with the pace: has looked reluctant. *A. Barrow.*

CORBALLY BESS 10 br.m. Saulingo–Pretty Janey (Hardicanute) [1989/90 c—
$16s^{4}$ $16g^{2}$ $18v^{4}$ $16m^{6}$ $16g^{6}$] lengthy mare: selling hurdler/novice chaser: 82
weakened approaching last over 2¼m on third start: acts on heavy going. *Miss L.
Bower.*

CORBITT'S DIAMOND 6 b.g. Le Bavard (FR)–Diamonds Gift (Demo-
cratic) [1989/90 $F16m^{2}$ F16m* $16d^{5}$ 16g 16g] medium-sized gelding: half-brother 101
to fair 2½m chaser Stonepark (by Pals Passage or Three Dons) and winning
hurdler Current Gift (by Current Gold): dam unraced: passed post first in NH Flat
races at Worcester (hung left and demoted to second) in October and Hexham
following month: subsequently sold privately out of B. Ellison's stable 45,000 gns
Doncaster November Sales: in process of running his best race in novice hurdles
when swerving right and slipping badly on landing at the last in contest won by Air
Commander at Worcester (would have finished close second) in March, final
start: sure to win a novice hurdle. *J. T. Gifford.*

CORBITTS MILITARIA 8 ch.g. Pauper–Gurtreeva (Tanavar) [1989/90 c—
$20g^{pu}$ $24d^{su}$ 20g 20d $c24g^{ur}$ $c27f^{F}$ $c16g^{ur}$] sturdy gelding: brother to Irish NH Flat —
race winner Paupers Son and winning hurdler Son of Pauper: dam never ran: of
little account. *B. Ellison.*

CORDILLERO 4 b.g. Head For Heights–Petipa (FR) (Habitat) [1989/90 18g
18s] ex-Irish gelding: fourth foal: half-brother to 2 winners, including Bustineto —
(by Bustino), successful over 7f in Ireland: dam very useful sprinter: placed at up
to 13f on Flat when trained by D. K. Weld: behind in juvenile hurdles at Fontwell:
visored second start. *A. Moore.*

CORKED 11 b.g. Tumble Wind (USA)–Bristol Milk (Raise You Ten) [1989/90 c**104**
$c16g^{5}$ $c20f^{2}$ $c17g^{ur}$ $c16s^{4}$ $c16m^{4}$ $c16m^{4}$ $c20f^{3}$ $c20m^{3}$ c16m* $c19f^{2}$ $c16m^{pu}$]
good-bodied gelding: carries condition: moderate chaser: won handicap at
Towcester in May: ran a moody race final outing: effective at 2m and stays well:

acts on any going except very soft: pulls hard and usually races prominently: usually amateur ridden. *Mrs E. H. Heath.*

CORMAC'S 4 gr.g. Superlative–Tahoume (FR) (Faristan) [1989/90 16g 16m] leggy gelding: plating-class middle-distance maiden on Flat: well beaten in — juvenile hurdles in first half of season: needs to settle. *A. Bailey.*

CORMEEN CROSS 6 ch.g. Boreen Beag–Shenton Park (Indigenous) [1989/90 F16g] fourth foal: dam placed over hurdles in Ireland: behind in NH Flat race at Warwick in December: yet to race over hurdles or fences. *O. Brennan.*

CORNCHARM 9 b.g. Thatch (USA)–Just Larking (USA) (Sea Bird II) [1989/90 16f^{pu} a16g^{6}] well-made gelding: poor novice hurdler: sold 1,100 gns Ascot July — Sales. *D. C. Jermy.*

CORNET 4 b.g. Coquelin (USA)–Corny Story (Oats) [1989/90 16f^{6} 16m^{2} 20f^{5} 16g^{4} 16g^{3} 20g* 16d^{2} 20g* 17d* 16m^{5} 16d^{5}] compact gelding: half-brother to 122 winning hurdler Star of Oughterard (by Horage): modest form at 2 yrs, below his best both outings on Flat in 1989 (needs a lot of driving): showed improved form in a visor over hurdles, winning 2 novice events at Edinburgh (first a handicap), and a juvenile hurdle at Carlisle and finishing 13 lengths fifth behind Sybillin in Glenlivet Anniversary Hurdle at Liverpool: fair fifth to Joe Bumpas in quite valuable juvenile handicap at Ayr final start: stays 2½m: acts on dead going and good to firm: has hung and looked a difficult ride. *Denys Smith.*

CORNHILL BOY 5 b.g. Decoy Boy–Jubilee Eve (Royalty) [1989/90 16g 20g] leggy gelding: seems of little account: sold 1,250 gns Doncaster Spring Sales. *O.* — *Brennan.*

CORNISH SAWTHAN 7 gr.m. Rambler–Cornish Lady (The Ditton) c— [1989/90 c26f^{pu} c25f^{5}] winning point-to-pointer: tailed off in hunter chase at Warwick in May. *Mrs Betty Spry.*

CORN LILY 4 ch.f. Aragon–Ixia (I Say) [1989/90 16f* 16f^{2}] leggy, workmanlike filly: half-sister to several winners, including very useful hurdler Cardinal Flower 100 (by Sharpen Up) and modest chaser Trailing Rose (by Undulate): plater on Flat, successful 5 times at up to 1¾m in 1989: won juvenile hurdle at Catterick in November, making most: ½-length second to Joe Bumpas in similar event at Edinburgh following month, always prominent and keeping on well: will be suited by a stiffer test of stamina. *N. Tinkler.*

CORN MERCHANT 9 ch.g. Winden–Erra (Romany Air) [1989/90 c17g^{3} **c109** c26d^{2} c24m^{2} c26g^{2} c20m^{F} c20d^{3}] lengthy, workmanlike gelding: carries plenty of — condition: moderate chaser: ran creditably in 1989/90: likely to prove best at distances short of 3¼m: acts on any going. *R. G. Frost.*

CORONATION MARCH (USA) 6 b.g. Blushing Groom (FR)–Princess Ribot (Ribot) [1989/90 16f 16g] sparely-made gelding: no worthwhile form in — novice hurdles: sold 650 gns Ascot December Sales. *G. G. Gracey.*

CORPORAL CRUISER 8 b.g. General Ironside–Sheet Music (Monet) c— p [1989/90 c24m^{F}] half-brother to 2 winners on Flat: dam 2-y-o 5f winner: every chance when falling 2 out in hunter chase won by Rodden Brook at Chepstow in April. *J. T. Gifford.*

CORRARDER 6 ch.g. True Song–Craig Maigy (Idiot's Delight) [1989/90 **c96** p c22m*] successful in 2 point-to-points prior to winning novice hunter chase at Stratford in May by 2½ lengths from Master Eryl, pair long way clear: stays 2¾m. *J. G. Smyth-Osbourne.*

CORRAVORRIN 5 ch.g. Garda's Revenge–Pearl Creek (Gulf Pearl) [1989/90 20v^{pu}] compact, workmanlike gelding: half-brother to a poor novice hurdler/ — chaser by Al Sirat: dam twice-raced half-sister to several winners: won a point-to-point in Ireland in 1989: bought 30,000 gns Doncaster Spring (1989) Sales: bit backward, tailed off when pulled up last in novice hurdle at Leicester in February. *S. Christian.*

CORRIE LASS 8 ch.m. Funny Man–Space Project (Space King) [1989/90 20f 20f^{5} 24h*] sparely-made mare: won amateur riders maiden hurdle at Hexham in 79 May, holding off Bixio by ½ length having been left clear by Melkono's unseating his rider last: stays 3m: probably acts on any going. *T. P. Tate.*

CORRIE'S GIRL 5 ch.m. Whistling Deer–Soave (Le Tricolore) [1989/90 aF16g^{4}] third foal: dam unraced: 7½ lengths fourth of 10 behind Royal Cause in NH Flat race at Lingfield in January: yet to race over hurdles or fences. *B. Smart.*

CORRY'S CAPER 5 b.g. Mandalus–Glad Rain (Bahrain) [1989/90 F16m 16s^{F} 16s 16m^{ur} 16f] sturdy, close-coupled gelding: first foal: dam Irish NH Flat race —

winner: no worthwhile form in novice hurdles: likely to be suited by further than 2m: sold 1,550 gns Ascot June Sales. *D. Nicholson.*

CORSTON BLAZE 6 ch.g. Vitiges (FR)–Corston Lass (Menelek) [1989/90 F16d] fourth foal: half-brother to winning staying hurdler Corston Springs (by Bruni) and point-to-point winner Corston Lad (by Orange Bay): dam placed over hurdles: behind in NH Flat race at Kelso in February: yet to race over hurdles or fences. *J. K. M. Oliver.*

CORUSCATE 8 ch.g. Lucifer (USA)–Ten Again (Raise You Ten) [1989/90 c**93**
24g* c25s^F c24d^2 c24g^3 c24f^{pu}] strong, workmanlike gelding: won a point-to- 99
point in Ireland in 1988: edged left run-in when winning 19-runner novice hurdle at Wetherby in November by ½ length from My New Best Friend: 10 lengths second to Ever Hopeful in novice chase at Chepstow in March, best effort over fences: ran as though something was amiss last start: stays 3m. *J. T. Gifford.*

CORVALLINA 4 b.f. Corvaro (USA)–Carmelina (Habitat) [1989/90 16s^F 16s^{pu}
16v a18g^6 16s 16g] IR 2,200F, 6,200Y: Irish filly: first foal: dam, French 7.5f and 1m 75
winner, sister to very useful 1979 French 2-y-o Suvero: 1½m winner on Flat: poor form over hurdles, including in juvenile claimer at Southwell on fourth start. *M. J. Grassick, Ireland.*

CORVASSIO 6 b.m. Corvaro (USA)–Naas (Ballymore) [1989/90 c20g^3 c21s^2 c**103**
c20v^2 c18g^3 c20v* c18s* c18d^5 c18v* c20v^F c18g^F c16g] small, wiry Irish mare: —
fairly useful hurdler, blinkered when successful in 1988/9: won 3 of her first 4 completed starts after being fitted with blinkers over fences in 1989/90, namely novice event at Clonmel, handicap at Fairyhouse and mares chase at Navan (beat Astral River 2 lengths): behind when falling at the tenth in race won by Radical Lady at Haydock in March: stays 2½m: acts on any going: usually a front runner. *D. T. Hughes, Ireland.*

COSMIC FLIGHT 7 b.m. Cosmo–Sweet Flight (Falcon) [1989/90 16g* c—
c16v^F] lengthy, sparely-made mare: modest hurdler: returned from a year's 89
absence when winning claimer at Uttoxeter in December: fell seventh in mares novice chase at Chepstow following month: acted on dead and good to firm ground: dead. *D. Burchell.*

COSMIC RAY 5 b.g. Comedy Star (USA)–Hey Skip (USA) (Bold Skipper
(USA)) [1989/90 16g^5 a16g^5 16d^2 16s^4 20d 16f* 16f* 18h^2] smallish gelding: in 87
frame in varied company, including selling, prior to winning novice hurdles at Hexham in March and Wetherby in April: best form at 2m: acts on firm going: has looked less than keen: visored last 5 outings of 1988/9: claimer ridden. *Mrs V. A. Aconley.*

CO-TACK 5 ch.g. Connaught–Dulcidene (Behistoun) [1989/90 16f^2 16d^3 16f*
16h^3] sturdy gelding: selling hurdler: attracted no bid after winning handicap at 94
Hexham in September when trained by J. FitzGerald: reportedly finished lame there, but ran creditably when next seen out on same course in April: has raced only at 2m: acts on firm and dead ground: usually claimer ridden: sold 3,000 gns Ascot July Sales. *A. P. Stringer.*

COTEHELE 7 ch.m. Paddy's Stream–Primrose Cotton (Straight Lad) [1989/90
16m^5 a16g 16g^{pu} 26v^{pu}] close-coupled, rather unfurnished mare: lightly-raced 65
novice hurdler. *T. B. Hallett.*

COT LANE 5 ch.g. Remainder Man–Smokey Princess (My Smokey) [1989/90
20g^6 25g^3 24d^4] strong, compact gelding: plating-class middle-distance maiden 87
on Flat: poor novice hurdler: stays well: claimer ridden. *F. J. Yardley.*

COTTAGE RUN 10 b.g. Deep Run–Cottage View (Golden Vision) [1989/90 c—
c17f^{pu}] big, strong, lengthy gelding: one-time useful chaser: close up when pulled —
up 5 out (broke a blood vessel) in race won by Barnbrook Again at Newbury in November: stays 2½m but best form at around 2m: acts on any going: free runner, but is usually held up nowadays: has worn severe bridle: usually jumps well: also broke blood vessel once in 1986/7. *D. Nicholson.*

COUGAR 4 ch.g. Song–Flying Milly (Mill Reef (USA)) [1989/90 a16g^6 16g 16g^2
18s^{pu} a16g^6 a18g^3 a16g^2 16m 16m^2 16f^4 a20g^4 16m^4 19f^2 16g^4] small, sturdy 77
gelding: maiden plater on Flat: in frame in varied company over hurdles, including selling: ran poorly in blinkers final start: stays 19f: acts on firm ground (possibly unsuited by soft): claimed out of C. Thornton's stable £3,100 after third start. *A. S. Reid.*

COULD BE CLOUDY 4 b.g. Coded Scrap–Grecian Cloud (Galivanter)
[1989/90 16f a16g^{pu}] probably of little account on Flat: no sign of ability in juvenile —

hurdle in August and seller in May: sold out of J. Jenkins' stable 1,150 gns Doncaster September Sales. *Miss L. C. Siddall.*

COULD BE GOLD 5 ch.g. Ovac (ITY)–My Gold (St Xavier) [1989/90 F16g] sixth living foal: dam lightly-raced maiden: behind throughout in NH Flat race at Market Rasen in April: yet to race over hurdles or fences. *W. A. Stephenson.*

COUNTERPUNCH 6 b.g. Torus–Candy Belle (Candy Cane) [1989/90 16d^{pu}
16g^{pu}] well-made gelding: has pulled far too hard in 2 NH Flat races and 2 novice —
hurdles: taken early to start in 1989/90. *J. T. Gifford.*

COUNTER TENOR 4 ch.g. Absalom–Divine Penny (Divine Gift) [1989/90
16v^{pu}] compact, good-quartered gelding: half-brother to fairly useful hurdler —
Divine Charger (by Treboro): no promise in 2 outings on Flat or in Folkestone juvenile hurdle. *B. J. Curley.*

COUNTESS BLAKENEY 4 ch.f. Baron Blakeney–Waterside (Shackleton)
[1989/90 16d 16d^{ur} 16f^{pu}] sparely-made filly: fifth foal: dam, poor novice —
hurdler/chaser, sister to winning hurdler Damside and half-sister to useful hurdler Red Vase: little sign of ability in novice hurdles. *J. D. Czerpak.*

COUNTESS CROSSETT 8 b.m. Blind Harbour–Majestic Crossett (Golden c—
Mallard) [1989/90 20g 22g 20g^{2} 20d^{pu}] plain mare: poor novice hurdler: blinkered 61 ?
second and third starts. *E. M. Caine.*

COUNT FREDERICK 10 b.g. Rheingold–Miss Pinkie (Connaught) [1989/90 c—
c20s^{5} c20d^{3} c21m^{6}] big, angular gelding: poor novice hurdler/chaser: collapsed —
and died after race at Fakenham in March: stayed 3¼m: acted on heavy going. *S. Dow.*

COUNT ME OUT 5 ch.g. Vaigly Great–Balatina (Balidar) [1989/90 16s^{pu}]
smallish, sturdy gelding: plating-class handicapper on Flat, winner over 7f in —
January (wears blinkers): tailed off when pulled up 3 out in quite valuable novice hurdle at Ascot in February. *R. P. C. Hoad.*

COUNTRY CARNIVAL 7 b. or br.m. Town And Country–Fairabunda
(Floribunda) [1989/90 16g 16g 16d 17f^{pu}] small, sparely-made mare: winning —
hurdler: well beaten in handicaps in 1989/90: unlikely to stay much beyond 2m: acts on dead going. *J. H. Johnson.*

COUNTRY DAMSEL 6 b.m. Town And Country–Dusky Damsel (Sahib)
[1989/90 16m^{5} 16d 17d^{pu}] unfurnished mare: lightly-raced novice hurdler: best 78
form on a sound surface. *J. A. B. Old.*

COUNTRY DIARY 7 b.m. Town And Country–Royal Dialogue (Royal Buck)
[1989/90 21d^{pu} 17m^{2}] workmanlike mare: novice hurdler: always prominent when 87
¾-length second to Hortondale in 14-runner maiden event at Newton Abbot in April: stays 2¾m: acts on good to firm and dead going. *M. McCourt.*

COUNTRY LIFE (USA) 4 br.g. Key To Content (USA)–Roseliere (FR) (Misti IV) [1989/90 F16g^{6} F16f] 3,000 3-y-o: half-brother to several good Flat winners, including Rose Bowl (by Habitat) and Ile de Bourbon (by Nijinsky): dam, top-class middle-distance winner, is sister to good jumping sire Roselier: little sign of ability in NH Flat races in the spring: yet to race over hurdles. *R. Simpson.*

COUNTRY SINGER 7 b.m. Town And Country–Song Without Words
(Spartan General) [1989/90 22g^{pu} 24d 24f^{pu}] lengthy mare: poor novice hurdler: —
blinkered last start (sweating). *E. A. Wheeler.*

COUNTRY SPARK 12 b. or br.g. Country Retreat–Changolita (Remainder) c—
[1989/90 c21m] rather sparely-made gelding: poor maiden point-to-pointer: —
novice hunter chaser: needs a test of stamina: visored last 2 starts in 1986/7. *Gary Brown.*

COURAGEOUS BIDDER 5 b.g. Known Fact (USA)–Hysterical (High Top)
[1989/90 16f^{5} a18g^{5}] angular, workmanlike gelding: 1m winner on Flat: fifth in 77
novice hurdle at Southwell in October, first and better effort. *M. H. B. Robinson.*

COURSE HUNTER 12 b.g. Crash Course–Miss Hunter (Buckhound) c—
[1989/90 c24f^{3} c20f^{5} c36f] stocky gelding: fairly useful chaser at his best: tailed —
off all starts in 1989/90: stays 25f: possibly needs give in the ground nowadays: takes a strong hold: let down by his jumping on occasions. *D. J. G. Murray-Smith.*

COURT APPEAL 8 b.g. Star Appeal–Londonderry Air (Ballymoss) [1989/90 c—
17d^{2} 20d 22g 16d 17m^{6} 17m^{6} c17m^{pu} 19f* 20f* 20d^{F} 18f^{pu}] small gelding: former 93
selling hurdler: won novice handicaps at Taunton (by 30 lengths) and Chepstow (by 3 lengths from Tri Folene) in the spring: would have finished creditable second but for falling 2 out in similar event at Worcester in May: beaten when

pulled up reportedly lame 2 out final start: tailed off when pulled up on chasing debut: stays 19f: acts on firm and dead going: has run creditably in blinkers and when claimer ridden. *C. L. Popham.*

COURTBROOK 9 b.g. Hard Fact–Donington Queen (Grit) [1989/90 c20f4 c16m3 c16m* c17m* c17g5 c16d4] rangy gelding: poor novice hurdler: won novice chases at Leicester in December and Doncaster (handicap, stayed on strongly to beat Boutzdaroff 6 lengths) following month: ridden by 7-lb claimer, pulled too hard last outing: likely to prove best at 2m: acts on good to firm ground: carries head high. *R. Lee.* c**91** — §

COURT CHARMER 4 b.c. Enchantment–Abercourt (Abernant) [1989/90 a16gpu] well beaten on Flat, including in sellers: sold out of C. C. Elsey's stable 725 gns Ascot February Sales: tailed off when pulled up 2 out in selling hurdle at Southwell in May. *A. S. Reid.* —

COURTLANDS GIRL 8 ch.m. Crimson Beau–Queen's Treasure (Queen's Hussar) [1989/90 21f4] leggy, sparely-made mare: modest hurdler: finished lame in August and wasn't seen out again: stays at least 2½m: acts on any going: has run creditably when sweating. *W. E. Fisher.* —

COURT RAPIER 8 ch.g. Pardigras–Weepers Laura (Weepers Boy) [1989/90 c18s6 c20d5 c16m* c16f* c16g* c17f2] leggy gelding: poor hurdler: successful in 2 handicap chases at Wincanton in April and one at Worcester (beat Sandmoor Prince ¾ length) in May: best at 2m: probably acts on any going: claimer ridden fourth and fifth starts. *Mrs H. Parrott.* c**96** —

COURT RULER 7 b.g. Rolfe (USA)–Sanandrea (Upper Case (USA)) [1989/90 16f5 16g3 20dur 16m5 16g4 a16g2] neat gelding: handicap hurdler: good second to Celtic Bob at Southwell in January: set strong pace and was beaten when unseating rider 2 out over 2½m: yet to show his form on very soft going, acts on any other: blinkered once 1987/8. *Miss S. J. Wilton.* 93

COURT SHORT 6 b.g. Derring Rose–Court Fancy (Little Buskins) [1989/90 20f6] tailed-off last in 2 novice hurdles. *W. A. Stephenson.* —

COUSIN FLO 5 ch.m. True Song–Dream Isle (Indian Ruler) [1989/90 16g 16sbd 16gpu 19mF 20d] workmanlike mare: sixth foal: half-sister to good jumper Townley Stone (by Legal Tender), useful chaser/fair hurdler Auntie Dot (by Hallodri) and NH Flat race winner Sister Brown (by Murrayfield): dam winning hurdler/chaser: no worthwhile form in novice hurdles. *J. Webber.* —

COUTURE COLOR 7 br.g. Wolver Hollow–Home Sweet Home (Royal Palace) [1989/90 c20spu c22d4 c20g2 c16d2 c26d* c32g3] sparely-made, close-coupled gelding: winning point-to-pointer: showed improved form when winning handicap chase at Carlisle in March by 15 lengths from Weirpool: stays 3¼m, probably not 4m: acts on good to soft ground. *J. Mackie.* c**102** —

COUTURE STOCKINGS 6 b.g. Free State–Miss Couture (Tamerlane) [1989/90 20f*] small gelding: handicap hurdler: won conditional jockeys event at Uttoxeter in September by 2 lengths from Leon: stays 2½m: acts on firm ground: suited by forcing tactics. *J. Mackie.* 109

COUTURE TIGHTS 5 b.g. Mummy's Game–Miss Couture (Tamerlane) [1989/90 20m 16f5 20g5] sparely-made gelding: lightly raced and seems of little account on Flat: fifth in novice claiming hurdles at Leicester and Wolverhampton (finished tired and will be suited by a return to 2m). *J. Mackie.* 80

COVA CAILE 6 br.m. Ovac (ITY)–La Campesina (Arctic Slave) [1989/90 20spu 16g 21d] lengthy mare: tailed off in novice hurdles. *T. N. Bailey.* —

COVENT GARDEN (USA) 12 ch.g. Stage Door Johnny–Rock Garden (Roan Rocket) [1989/90 c24g3 c26m6 c24g5 c26g4 c25m4 c28g c26mpu] sturdy gelding: poor chaser nowadays (pulled up lame last outing): suited by a test of stamina: acts on any going: best in blinkers nowadays: still makes the odd mistake. *W. Clay.* c83 —

COVER INN 7 ro.m. Tachypous–Greyburn (Saintly Song) [1989/90 16gpu] no form over hurdles, including in sellers: visored final start 1987/8: usually claimer ridden. *G. Ripley.* —

COVER WITH HARTS 5 b.g. Indian King (USA)–Roscrea (Ballymore) [1989/90 F16g3] half-brother to Irish Harvest, Irish 1½m winner, and South Harvest (both by Oats), winner of NH Flat race and placed over hurdles: dam unraced: 4 lengths third of 17 behind Mr Woodcock in NH Flat race at Catterick in March: yet to race over hurdles or fences. *N. Bradley.*

COWDEN COTTAGE 6 ch.g. Connaught–Forty Lines (Fortino II) [1989/90
16g^4] strong, workmanlike gelding: chasing type: first outing for over a year and 84
bit backward, 19 lengths fourth to Fifth Amendment in novice hurdle at Wincanton
(kept on despite being hampered last) in January: will stay beyond 2m. *Dr D.
Chesney.*

COWGATE FOUNTAIN 4 b.f. Royal Fountain–Cowgate Lady (Most
Secret) [1989/90 F16g^3] fourth foal: dam poor novice hurdler/chaser: just over 12
lengths third behind Forget The Rest in 12-runner NH Flat race at Kelso in
March: yet to race over hurdles. *Mrs G. R. Reveley.*

COWLEY 5 gr.h. Kalaglow–Loralane (Habitat) [1989/90 16d^5 16d^4 16f^2]
close-coupled horse: quite useful middle-distance performer on Flat: sold out of 101
G. Wragg's stable 26,000 gns Newmarket Autumn Sales: in frame in novice
hurdles at Towcester in February and Newcastle (blinkered, beaten 3 lengths by
Shamirani) in March: worth a try over further: should win a novice hurdle. *J. A.
Glover.*

COWORTH PARK 5 gr.g. Wolver Hollow–Sparkling Time (USA) (Olden
Times) [1989/90 21s* 21d* 20g^4 21d^6 20g^{pu} 21m^2] rangy gelding: improved 120
hurdler in 1989/90: won novice handicaps at Fakenham and Sandown: good
second to Battalion in handicap on former course in March: stays 21f: acts on soft
going and good to firm: suited by waiting tactics. *P. Mitchell.*

COXANN 4 b.g. Connaught–Miss Nelski (Most Secret) [1989/90 16g 16d^5 16s
16s^4 16d^6 a16g^2 20g 16m^4] compact gelding: quite modest maiden on Flat: poor 78
form over hurdles: stiff task over 2½m: blinkered last 3 starts. *J. C. McConnochie.*

CRACK-A-JIM 8 ch.g. Slim Jim–Tullykeneye (Blast) [1989/90 c20f^3 24m^{pu}] c75
small, lengthy, sparely-made gelding: poor novice hurdler/chaser: suited by —
further than 2m and stays 3m: probably acts on any going: suitable mount for a
claimer. *P. J. Jones.*

CRACK A JOKE 11 b.g. Funny Man–Spin A Yarn (Doubtless II) [1989/90 c20f^4 c—
c24m^{pu} c24d^{pu} c24g^{pu} c26m^{pu}] strong, compact gelding: one-time quite useful —
chaser: no form in 1989/90: suited by a test of stamina: used to go well on a sound
surface: has won 5 times at Uttoxeter. *T. T. Bill.*

CRACKER D'OR 6 ch.g. Le Coq d'Or–Little Cracker (Blast) [1989/90 16g
20v^F 16d 17d] angular, workmanlike gelding: selling hurdler: showed a little —
ability second start: sold 1,800 gns Ascot June Sales. *A. J. Wilson.*

CRACKERJACKIE GEE 5 ch.g. Rymer–Song Without Words (Spartan
General) [1989/90 F14v] first foal: dam sister to winning point-to-pointer General
Sandy: mid-division in NH Flat race at Ayr in April: yet to race over hurdles or
fences. *S. Mellor.*

CRACKERMAC 5 b.m. Sparkler–Mac's Melody (Wollow) [1989/90 16g^F 22g]
lengthy, sparely-made mare: maiden 1¼m plater on Flat: jumped moderately —
when tailed off in novice hurdle at Wincanton in January. *Mrs Barbara Waring.*

CRACKIT 7 b.g. Jellaby–Ginger Puss (Worden II) [1989/90 18d^{pu}] very
lightly-raced and no sign of ability: sold 1,900 gns Doncaster January Sales: resold —
1,650 gns Ascot June Sales. *D. McCain.*

CRACKLE MOOR 5 b.m. Don–Carol Day (Tudor Melody) [1989/90 16g 16g
16g 16g^2 16d 16d] sturdy mare: winning hurdler: poor form in 1989/90, including in 78
sellers: found little and jumped left at last 2 on fourth start: likely to stay further
than 2m: acts on dead going: blinkered last 3 outings. *M. W. Easterby.*

CRADLE OF JAZZ (USA) 10 b.g. Verbatim (USA)–Louisiana (Nadir) c—
[1989/90 16m c16m^{pu}] smallish gelding: has been fired: handicap chaser: no form —
for a long time: stays 2½m: acts on any going. *J. A. B. Old.*

CRAFTY STYLE 7 b.g. Crafty Codger–Hi Style (Tarkhun) [1989/90 24g c22d] c—
lengthy gelding: lightly-raced novice hurdler/chaser: stays 3m: sold 2,200 gns —
Ascot June Sales. *J. A. C. Edwards.*

CRAIGMORE 6 br.g. Prince Regent (FR)–Carraig More (Escart III) [1989/90
17d 16s 16s^{pu}] compact gelding: little sign of ability in novice hurdles. *P. G. Bailey.* —

CRAIG'S QUEEN 11 b. or br.m. Quayside–Clougher Queen (Skyros) c—
[1989/90 c20v^5] ex-Irish mare: placed in point-to-points: no sign of ability in 3
hunter chases. *G. J. C. Bingham.*

CRAMMER 10 b.g. Crash Course–Miss Hunter (Buckhound) [1989/90 c24d* c**123**
c22m^2] strong gelding: winning hurdler/chaser: lightly raced of late: won hunter —
chase at Nottingham in February by 25 lengths from Water Wagtail: outpaced 3

Dingley Dell Hunters' Chase, Nottingham—
Crammer (right) is about to assert his superiority over Water Wagtail

out but stayed on again approaching the last when 7 lengths second to Lean Ar Aghaidh in 2¾m Seagram Fox Hunters' Chase at Liverpool in April: suited by a test of stamina: acts on heavy going and good to firm. *D. J. G. Murray-Smith.*

CRANCHETER 6 br.h. Red Sunset–French Cracker (Klairon) [1989/90 16d^{pu}
16d^{2} 16d 16m^{5} 16m] leggy, workmanlike horse: second to River Kingdom in 83
novice handicap hurdle at Warwick in January, best effort: unlikely to stay much beyond 2m: suited by give in the ground: blinkered final start. *T. J. Etherington.*

CRASH CALL 9 br.m. Crash Course–Lady Piersfield (Mugatpura) [1989/90 c—
c25m^{6} c25g^{pu}] lengthy, rather sparely-made mare: winning chaser: no worthwhile form for a long time: pulled up reportedly lame last outing (December): stays 25f: acts on soft going. *P. Butler.*

CRASH GARDINER 11 ch.g. Crash Course–Bella Vista Lady (Continuation) c—
[1989/90 c21m^{F}] behind in maiden hurdle and novice chase in Ireland in 1983/4: —
winning point-to-pointer in Ireland (placed in similar event in Britain in 1990): tailed off when falling at the tenth in novice hunter chase at Fakenham in May. *Mrs C. N. Weatherby.*

CRASHING BORE 6 ch.g. Boreen (FR)–Ware Princess (Crash Course) c—
[1989/90 16g^{3} 16s^{2} 21d^{6} c16d^{pu} 22d^{ur}] workmanlike gelding: novice hurdler: 88
behind when pulled up on chasing debut: dead. *S. Mellor.*

CRASH MARKET 8 b.g. Crash Course–Anail (Hill Gail) [1989/90 c16g* **c105**
c16g*] long-backed, plain gelding: made all in novice hurdle at Bangor in 1988/9 —
and in novice chase on same course and minor chase at Carlisle (jumped left, clear throughout when beating Lothian General by 20 lengths) in November: stays 2½m: acts on any going: has run well for 7-lb claimer. *R. F. Fisher.*

CRAWFORDSTOWN 10 ch.g. Dalesa–Dante's Ghost (Arctic Slave) c**61**
[1989/90 c20f^{2}] workmanlike gelding: well beaten over hurdles: won 2 point- —
to-points in May: 25 lengths second to Ponteus Pilot in novice hunter chase at Folkestone later in month. *D. C. O'Brien.*

CREAM AND GREEN 6 b.g. Welsh Chanter–Jumana (Windjammer (USA))
[1989/90 16m 16s 16g 16f 16f^{5}] sparely-made gelding: unreliable plating-class 71
handicapper at up to 1m on Flat: novice hurdler: showed ability second and fourth starts: barely stays 2m and will prove suited by a sharp track. *K. White.*

CREAM BY POST 6 b.m. Torus–Lady Manta (Bargello) [1989/90 F16g 17m 18f*] fourth foal: half-sister to winning hurdler/chaser Lislary Lad (by Gala Performance): dam, unraced half-sister to useful jumper Gallaher, from family of Arkle: won 5-runner novice event at Fontwell in April by 4 lengths from below-form Pollock, making all: stays 2¼m: acts on firm ground: should improve. *P. J. Hobbs.* 85 p

CREATIVE ILLUSION 4 br.f. Creative Plan (USA)–San Estrella (Star Gazer) [1989/90 F16g F16f3] half-sister to 3 NH Flat race winners and fair staying hurdler Whistling Tiger (by Whistling Deer): dam maiden Irish sprinter: 12 lengths third of 8 behind Doctor Syntax in NH Flat race at Hexham in May: yet to race over hurdles. *G. M. Moore.*

CREDIT CUT 8 b.g. Fine Blade (USA)–Vul's Money (Even Money) [1989/90 c20mpu c25dpu] useful-looking gelding: showed plenty of ability in novice hurdles in 1986/7 and a little in novice chase second start: sold 1,400 gns Ascot April Sales. *O. Sherwood.* c— —

CREDORA BAY 6 b.m. Orange Bay–Credo's Daughter (Credo) [1989/90 20mpu 18s a20gpu 22s] compact mare: poor novice hurdler: visored second and third starts. *S. Woodman.* —

CREEAGER 8 b.g. Creetown–Teenager (Never Say Die) [1989/90 16g3 16d4 c16g5 c16d3 c16m6 16g4] strong, compact gelding: fair hurdler: modest form, tending to make mistakes, in novice chases (best effort on fourth outing): worth a try at further than 2m: probably acts on any going: in good form on Flat in 1990. *J. Wharton.* **c94** 121

CREECH WOOD 5 b.h. Record Run–Flyweight (Salvo) [1989/90 17g3] leggy, angular horse: novice hurdler: remote third at Devon & Exeter in October. *M. Madgwick.* —

CREEPING JANE 11 b.m. Rustingo–Moving Target (Salvo) [1989/90 c25f4] fair point-to-pointer, winner in May: nearly 30 lengths fourth to As You Were in hunter chase at Warwick later in month. *Owen J. Lewis.* c**70**

CREETOWN SALLY 7 b.m. Creetown–Brocton Queen (Supreme Sovereign) [1989/90 16g 16g 16spu] good-topped mare: little sign of ability over hurdles, including in sellers. *Miss A. L. M. King.* —

CREOLE BAY 6 b.m. Kind of Hush–Creolina (Quorum) [1989/90 16f3 16f5 20f4 20g6 16g] sparely-made mare: won a point-to-point in April: novice selling hurdler: best at 2m with give in the ground: pulls hard: has worn a crossed noseband. *R. J. Eckley.* 68

CRESTED 6 b.g. Bustino–Seasurf (Seaepic (USA)) [1989/90 22dF] medium-sized, rather sparely-made gelding: winning hurdler: fell eighth only outing in 1989/90 (April): should be suited by long distances: acts on heavy going. *G. M. Moore.* —

CRESTINA CROSSETT 8 b.m. Gracious Melody–Cresta Crossett (Ebnalben) [1989/90 22gpu 16gpu 25mpu 20dpu 16g 16dpu 20f6] small mare: of little account, and probably temperamental to boot: usually blinkered nowadays. *E. M. Caine.* — §

CRETAN BOY 5 b.g. Beldale Flutter (USA)–Haida (Astec) [1989/90 16spu 16g] small, lengthy gelding: no form in selling hurdles: looks headstrong: has worn a crossed noseband and a tongue strap: sold out of C. Trietline's stable 1,950 gns Newmarket Autumn Sales. *Miss J. A. Blakeney.* —

CREVE COEUR 5 b.h. Aragon–Friths Folly (Good Bond) [1989/90 16g5 16g 16g a18sF] compact, workmanlike horse: poor maiden on Flat, stays 11.7f (has appeared headstrong): best effort in novice hurdles on debut: will prove suited by sharp 2m. *S. Dow.* 86

CRIME BUSTER 8 b.g. Crimson Beau–Laurel Wreath (Sassafras (FR)) [1989/90 18m] lengthy, rather leggy gelding: no form over hurdles. *C. D. Broad.* —

CRIMSON LADY 9 b.m. Crimson Beau–Lanzerac (Firestreak) [1989/90 c17f6 c21fpu 16h3 a16g5 a24g6] leggy, close-coupled mare: poor novice hurdler (has been beaten in selling company): behind all outings over fences: form only at around 2m: acts on firm ground: often claimer ridden: has worn a tongue strap. *P. R. Rodford.* c— 62

CRISP HEART 6 b.m. Dominion–Persevering (Blakeney) [1989/90 21hF 17h3 22f4 17g 25d4] small mare: won 1½m seller on Flat in July: close third in novice 69

selling hurdle at Devon & Exeter in August: below that form subsequently: seems not to stay 25f: acts on hard going. *C. P. Wildman.*

CRISP NOTE 6 ch.g. Kris–Airgead Beo (Hook Money) [1989/90 20v 22gpu 19sF] lengthy gelding: bit backward, in process of showing first form when falling last in novice selling hurdle at Hereford in March. *J. A. B. Old.* — p

CROCK-NA-NEE 9 b.g. Random Shot–Saucy Slave (Arctic Slave) [1989/90 c24m3 c20s* c20m4 c20d* c22m5] workmanlike ex-Irish gelding: handicap hurdler/chaser: won over fences at Bangor in December and March: creditable fifth to Wont Be Gone Long in 2¾m John Hughes Memorial Trophy Chase (Handicap) at Liverpool in April: suited by around 2½m: acts on good to firm and soft going: sold privately out of M. Murray's stable 16,500 gns Doncaster August Sales. *O. Sherwood.* c**111** —

CROESONEN 6 ch.m. Balinger–Rock Rose (Rockavon) [1989/90 F12m] fifth foal: dam won a 2m hurdle: behind in NH Flat race at Bangor in October: yet to race over hurdles or fences. *Mrs A. R. Hewitt.*

CROFTER'S COURT 4 ch.c. Crofthall–Northgate Lady (Fordham (USA)) [1989/90 16gpu 16fpu] modest 1m plater on Flat, not an easy ride (often blinkered) when trained by M. Brittain: tailed off when pulled up in selling hurdle at Market Rasen and claimer at Kelso (visored) in the spring. *Mrs J. L. Robson.* —

CROFTER'S NEST 5 ch.g. Crofter (USA)–Precious Egg (Home Guard (USA)) [1989/90 16f 16f* 17gF 17f2 16f5 16h2 19hF] neat ex-Irish gelding: second foal: half-brother to winning selling hurdler Fox Path (by Godswalk) and 1m winner Easter Glory (by Dalsaan): dam poor half-sister to Cork and Orrery Stakes winner Kearney: placed at up to 1½m on Flat: won maiden hurdle at Wexford in June: second in handicaps at Newton Abbot and Taunton in September: ran in snatches fifth outing: unlikely to stay much beyond 2m: acts on firm ground: trained by Mrs J. Harrington until after third start: sold 700 gns Ascot February Sales. *M. C. Pipe.* 94 ?

CROFT GILL 5 b.g. Crofthall–Gill Breeze (Farm Walk) [1989/90 16h4 16f] leggy, compact gelding: poor form over hurdles. *N. Bycroft.* 75

CROFTHALL BLINDER 5 ch.m. Crofthall–Blinder (Bing II) [1989/90 a16gur 16m4] leggy, sparely-made mare: first reported foal: dam in frame in novice hurdles: poor maiden on Flat: tailed-off last of 4 in selling hurdle at Leicester in December: claimer ridden. *T. Kersey.* —

CROGHAN ROSE 5 b.m. Croghan Hill–Rose Gaujard (Electrify) [1989/90 F16f2 F16f*] first foal: dam poor Irish point-to-pointer: odds on, won 11-runner NH Flat race at Huntingdon in May by short head from Sunlight Express, making virtually all: yet to race over hurdles or fences. *G. Harwood.*

CROGHAN STAR 9 br.m. Furry Glen–Star Treasure (Levmoss) [1989/90 c27f2 c24f3 c30m2 c28gpu c25f* c27d4 c24spu c25f4] leggy, lengthy mare: modest form over fences: won 2-runner novice event at Doncaster in December: stays well: acts on firm going: inconsistent. *J. Dooler.* c**91** ? —

CROIX DE GUERRE 9 b.g. Proverb–Josephine (Tamerlane) [1989/90 c20s c25m6 c24g2 c24mur] tall, useful-looking gelding: one-time quite useful hurdler: modest novice chaser: suited by 3m, a galloping track and give in the ground: blinkered last 3 starts. *Mrs J. Pitman.* c**88** —

CROMACH 8 b.g. Crozier–Frello (Bargello) [1989/90 c21m6 c24h3 c22f5] leggy, good-topped gelding: little sign of ability over hurdles or in steeplechases, but has won a point-to-point: blinkered last 5 outings: sold privately 3,900 gns Doncaster November Sales. *C. Parker.* c— —

CROMWELL POINT 4 gr.c. Another Realm–Miss Eliza (Mountain Call) [1989/90 16d 16f5] good-topped colt: poor form in maidens at 2 yrs: still bit backward, over 20 lengths fifth to Miss Tristram in selling hurdle at Catterick in November. *C. W. Thornton.* 59

CROSSETT CRUISADER 10 b.g. Gracious Melody–Portavia (Darling Boy) [1989/90 c27gur c20gF c16d c27gpu c27spu c16d c20mur] workmanlike gelding: thoroughly temperamental and no form: usually blinkered. *E. M. Caine.* c§§ §§

CROSSGLEN 6 gr.g. Bybicello–Sister Chatters (I Say) [1989/90 F13d 16g 16g 20f4 24dpu] half-brother to novice hurdler Drumoak (by Dubassoff): dam poor hurdler: no form over hurdles, including in selling handicaps. *W. A. Stephenson.* —

CROSSLAND LEISURE 5 b.g. Torus–Kathleen Beag (Vulgan) [1989/90 22m] compact gelding: little sign of ability over hurdles. *C. Weedon.* —

CROSS MASTER 13 ch.g. Master Owen–Swift Mayo (Dual) [1989/90 c24m^{2} c25m* c24m* c25m^{2}] smallish, sparely-made gelding: fair chaser: won handicaps at Wolverhampton and Nottingham in November: jumped none too fluently, hampered 3 out when going down by 3 lengths to Fib in similar race at Warwick later in month: suited by a test of stamina: acts on any going: suitable mount for a claimer. *T. T. Bill.* c**122** —

CROSSROAD LAD 4 b.g. Beldale Flutter (USA)–Croda Rossa (ITY) (Grey Sovereign) [1989/90 17f* 16f* 16f* 16f* 16d^{4} 16g 16m 16f^{2} 16f^{4}] leggy, lengthy, sparely-made gelding: no form on Flat: sold out of G. Wragg's stable 4,600 gns Ascot 2nd June Sales: won early-season juvenile hurdles at Newton Abbot, Plumpton and Cheltenham (2): easily best effort afterwards when second to Toad Along in novice handicap at Worcester in March: may prove best at around 2m at present: acts on firm going and probably unsuited by dead: tends to be mulish in preliminaries (withdrawn under orders sixth appearance): trained until after fifth start by T. Thomson Jones. *Miss K. M. George.* 109

CROWECOPPER 11 b.g. Netherkelly–Cammy (Sing Sing) [1989/90 c24m^{2} c24d^{pu} c20s^{4} c21s c24d^{3} c25f^{2} c26m* c26f^{4}] leggy gelding: handicap chaser: won at Newton Abbot in April: ran moderately final start: stays 25f: has won on soft going but is better on a sounder surface and acts on firm: has won for an inexperienced rider. *B. Preece.* c**110** —

CROWN AND HORNS 6 b.h. Song–Dash On (Klairon) [1989/90 17f^{3} 17f^{6} 16m^{3} 16f 17v^{5} 16d^{3} 16s^{3} 17m 16f^{5} 21f^{pu}] leggy, lengthy horse: poor novice hurdler, has run in a seller: likely to stay beyond 2m: probably acts on any going. *Mrs J. G. Retter.* 81

CROWN CROSSETT 8 ch.g. Blind Harbour–Guide's Ambition (Guide) [1989/90 c16g c20d c25g^{bd}] big gelding: of little account. *E. M. Caine.* c— —

CROWNED FAIR 7 b.g. Imperial Crown–Perfume Ali (Baba Ali) [1989/90 c24f^{pu}] behind in NH Flat race in 1988: sold 1,450 gns Doncaster August (1988) Sales: modest form in point-to-points in 1990 (walked over once and twice refused): jumped poorly and was tailed off when pulled up in maiden hunter chase at Hexham in April. *R. Bewley.* c—

CROWNEGO 8 br.m. Abednego–Crown Rights (Right Royal V) [1989/90 20m] compact mare: poor maiden point-to-pointer: bit backward, tailed off in novice event at Huntingdon in April on hurdling debut. *Miss K. M. George.* —

CROWN GREEN 8 b.g. Busted–Sally Bowles (Blakeney) [1989/90 c24s^{ur} c24g^{pu} c26g^{6}] compact gelding: winning hurdler: no form over fences in 1989/90 (reluctant to race second start): suited by 3m: acts on firm and dead ground (possibly unsuited by heavy). *T. Laxton.* c— —

CROWTHERS 4 gr.g. Mandrake Major–Milnsbridge (Dragonara Palace (USA)) [1989/90 16m] quite modest performer on Flat, stays 1m well: changed hands 8,200 gns Newmarket Autumn Sales: well beaten in juvenile hurdle at Catterick in December. *E. Weymes.* —

CRUDEN BAY 10 bl.g. Lucky Wednesday–Floragold (Floribunda) [1989/90 c20g^{4} c20m^{F}] leggy, close-coupled gelding: winning hurdler: novice chaser: stays 3m: seems to act on any going: has worn a crossed noseband. *Mrs T. J. McInnes Skinner.* c**76** —

CRUISING ALTITUDE 7 ch.g. Celtic Cone–Carmarthen Honey (Eborneezer) [1989/90 21g* 16f* 16f* 16g^{3} 16m^{F}] 160

Any doubts that connections of Cruising Altitude might have had about their decision to keep the horse to hurdling for another season would have been dispelled quickly. Cruising Altitude showed high-class form and by the turn of the year had won all three of his starts, earning over £28,000 in prize money. And there's time enough yet for this lightly-raced seven-year-old to make his mark over fences, despite an injury sustained when falling in the Waterford Crystal Champion Hurdle. Cruising Altitude broke a bone at the back of a knee, and while it's expected that he'll make a full recovery he won't be seen out in the first half of the 1990/91 season.

Cruising Altitude's performances in his first season over hurdles, when he was one of the leading novices, led us to believe that he'd prove best over two miles on a sound surface, even though he'd been in the

Gerry Feilden Hurdle, Newbury—Cruising Altitude impresses

process of running a good race when falling at the last over two and a half miles on soft ground. Cruising Altitude didn't run on a soft surface in the latest season; and the only occasion on which he tackled two and a half miles was in a slowly-run race for the Tom Masson Trophy at Newbury, when he easily landed the odds. Nevertheless, his victories in the Gerry Feilden Hurdle at Newbury and the Charles Heidsieck Champagne Bula Hurdle at Cheltenham, both of which were run over two miles on firm ground, suggest that such conditions suit him ideally. The Gerry Feilden featured none of the established top hurdlers, but Cruising Altitude faced quite strong opposition from some of the previous season's other leading novices, notably Morley Street. With no-one particularly keen to lead in the early stages, Cruising Altitude was allowed to pull his way to the front after the first and stride on. Quickening early in the home straight, Cruising Altitude soon had the race sewn up and was pushed out to score by six lengths and four lengths from Morley Street and Nomadic Way, who were making their seasonal reappearances. Cruising Altitude also had a fitness advantage over the champion hurdler Beech Road when they met in the Bula, and with the ground considered unsuitable for Beech Road, Cruising Altitude was sent off at odds on. Cruising Altitude looked likely to win smoothly when moving through to lead at the last, but he didn't quicken as anticipated and had to be hard driven to hold on by a head from Nomadic Way, with the strong-finishing Beech Road a length and a half back in third. In our opinion Cruising Altitude, who'd looked hard in condition, didn't quite run up to his Newbury form, and his trainer said afterwards that he felt the horse had just gone a bit over the top. It was two and a half months before Cruising Altitude was in action again, when he contested the Kingwell Hurdle at Wincanton. Not fully wound up, he wasn't given a hard race once beaten, and finished nine lengths third behind Kribensis. Cruising Altitude left the impression that he'd give a better account of himself in the Waterford

Charles Heidsieck Champagne Bula Hurdle, Cheltenham—
Cruising Altitude heads Floyd at the last; Nomadic Way is just behind

Crystal Champion Hurdle, for which he started fourth favourite at 9/1. Unfortunately, normally a quick and accurate jumper, he got no further than the second.

Cruising Altitude (ch.g. 1983)	Celtic Cone (ch 1967)	Celtic Ash (ch 1957)	Sicambre
			Ash Plant
		Fircone (ch 1959)	Mossborough
			Wood Fire
	Carmarthen Honey (b 1971)	Eborneezer (b 1955)	Ocean Swell
			Priory Princess
		Farani (b 1958)	Tenerani
			Fair Profit

Cruising Altitude, a medium-sized, rather angular gelding, takes a good hold and requires firm handling, but he's apparently more tractable than was his dam Carmarthen Honey, a fairly useful though rather wayward point-to-pointer. Carmarthen Honey, a half-sister to the winning hurdler Suviel, has bred one other winner. Her first foal Cockpit Crew (by Rymer), also trained by Sherwood, won a two-mile novice hurdle at Chepstow in the 1986/7 season. Cruising Altitude's grandam Farani was placed over hurdles; his third dam Fair Profit, who won on the Flat, is also the third dam of the 1977 Windsor Castle Stakes winner Tardot. *O. Sherwood.*

CRUMBS OF COMFORT 5 b.m. Castle Keep–Foil (Bleep-Bleep) [1989/90 16m^{pu}] leggy, workmanlike mare: no sign of ability over hurdles, including in a seller. *Miss J. Thorne.* —

CRUNCH 9 ch.g. Whistlefield–Windfall VI (Master Owen) [1989/90 c32f^{pu}] strong, lengthy gelding: winning point-to-pointer: well beaten in hunter chases. *C. Marriott.* c—

CRUSH ON YOU 9 br.g. Golden Love–Osbertstown Mill (Nice Guy) [1989/90 c25f^{pu}] ex-Irish gelding: half-brother to a winning point-to-pointer by Pry: dam unraced half-sister to useful staying chaser Bawnogues: well beaten in NH Flat races, maiden hurdle and a hunter chase: winning point-to-pointer in Britain. *K. F. Clutterbuck.* c— —

CRYMLYN SWING 6 ch.m. Swing Easy (USA)–Royal Tactic (Right Tack) [1989/90 20f^{2} 16f^{2} 17m^{2} 22f 16m^{2} 16m] leggy, lengthy, sparely-made mare: placed 67 in novice hurdles: best effort at 2m (tailed off over 2¾m): acts on firm ground: blinkered final start (well beaten in lady riders handicap). *William Price.*

CRYSTAL BALL 6 b.g. Formidable (USA)–Clouded Vision (So Blessed) [1989/90 c26s^{pu} c24d^{pu} c25m^{pu} c20m^{F} c20g^{pu}] angular, good-bodied gelding: of little account: has worn blinkers: bought for 2,200 gns Ascot September Sales. *J. D. Thomas.* c— —

CRYSTAL BEAR (NZ) 5 b.g. Veloso (NZ)–Euphemia (NZ) (Piccolo Player (USA)) [1989/90 F16g^{2} 16d* 17d^{2}] leggy gelding: half-brother to Brief Encounter (by Foreign Affair), placed in NH Flat race: second in NH Flat race at Ludlow in December: won novice hurdle at Stratford 2 months later by 5 lengths from Royal Borough: 4 lengths second to Olveston at Newton Abbot following month: ridden by claimer: will progress further. *Capt. T. A. Forster.* 107 p

CRYSTAL COMET 6 gr.m. Cosmo–Neezerbel (Eborneezer) [1989/90 F16g^{6} 17v^{2} 18s*] tall, rather unfurnished non-thoroughbred mare: first foal: dam poor maiden point-to-pointer: well beaten in NH Flat race in November: won mares novice hurdle at Fontwell in January by 25 lengths from Rosie Marchioness with remainder well strung out: will stay 2½m: acts on heavy going: should improve further. *R. G. Frost.* 105 p

CRYSTAL HAWK (USA) 6 b.g. Silver Hawk (USA)–Jury's Out (USA) (Judger (USA)) [1989/90 a16g^{4}] angular gelding: well beaten most outings over hurdles, including in sellers: acts on good to firm going: visored last outing 1988/9. *S. Woodman.* —

CRYSTAL HEIGHTS 4 ch.g. Wolver Heights–Crystal's Solo (USA) (Crystal Water (USA)) [1989/90 16g^{3} 16f^{5} 17g^{2} 16s* 17d^{3} 16f^{F} 22f^{3}] angular gelding: 7f winner on Flat at 2 yrs, placed over 1½m in 1989 when trained by G. Cottrell: 33/1, easily best performance when winning 10-runner Curran Group Finale Junior Hurdle at Chepstow in December by 10 lengths from Gay Ruffian: acts well on soft ground (moderate third over 2¾m on firm final start, though would have finished closer but for being hampered 2 out). *Mrs J. G. Retter.* 123

CRYSTAL PARK 4 b.f. Head For Heights–So Precise (FR) (Balidar) [1989/90 a16g^{6} 16g^{5} 16f^{5}] smallish filly: won 11f claimer on Flat in January: poor form over hurdles, including in a seller. *J. Wharton.* 72

CUCKOO IN THE NEST 7 br.g. Imperial Fling (USA)–Nest Builder (Home Guard (USA)) [1989/90 16f^{6} 16f^{2} 16f^{5} 16m^{4} 16m c25d^{pu} c20m^{3} c20f^{pu} 20m 16g a20g^{5} a18g^{3} a16g^{3} 16f] good-topped gelding: poor hurdler: tailed off both completed outings over fences (poor jumper): stays 2¼m: yet to race on heavy going, acts on any other: usually wears blinkers (did so when successful) or visor and has also worn a hood. *P. D. Connors.* c— x 73

CUCKOO MILL 11 b.g. Genuine–Arctic Lily (Arctic Slave) [1989/90 c20s^{4} c25g^{pu}] big, angular gelding: winning point-to-pointer: novice hurdler/chaser: blinkered once: dead. *R. J. R. Williams.* c— —

CUDDY DALE 7 b.g. Deep Run–Verbana (Boreen (FR)) [1989/90 c20f^{3} c16f^{4} c20g^{6}] long-backed gelding: useful chaser: travelled strongly in lead until weakening approaching last when under 9 lengths sixth to Joint Sovereignty in Mackeson Gold Cup at Cheltenham in November: stays 25f at least when conditions aren't testing: has won on firm going but best form with more give in the ground: headstrong, but has won for a claimer: blinkered fourth start 1987/8: has shown tendency to jump to his right. *F. Murphy.* c**138** —

CUILEANN 5 b. or br.h. Caerleon (USA)–Manfilia (Mandamus) [1989/90 20m^{pu} 16s^{6} a18g^{3} 21d^{4} 21d 24f* 24m^{pu} 24g^{3} 26m^{pu}] neat ex-Irish horse: half-brother to numerous winners, notably high-class performer at up to 1¼m Kilijaro (by African Sky): dam won at up to 1¼m: won twice at up to 1¾m on Flat in 1988, when trained by L. Browne: ridden by 3-lb claimer, won novice hurdle at Bangor in March: stays 3m (seemingly not 3¼m): acts on firm and dead going: inconsistent: sold out of R. Juckes's stable 3,500 gns Doncaster October Sales after first start. *P. M. Cowley.* 106

CULLODEN 7 gr.g. Warpath–Jasmin (Frankincense) [1989/90 16s 16g^{5} 16f 17m 20f^{pu}] brother to winning jumpers Marjoram and Red Fescue: poor novice hurdler: best efforts at around 2m on a sound surface. *Mrs B. K. Broad.* 60

CULM SOVEREIGN 10 b.g. Sovereign Bill–Copper Plate II (Spiritus) [1989/90 c17f^{3} c17f^{2}] behind only completed outing over hurdles: won a point-to-point in 1988: placed in early-season novice chases, showing poor form. *C. J. Down.* c73 —

CUMLODEN 4 ch.g. Creetown–Melinda Jane (Compensation) [1989/90 16f^6 18m] workmanlike gelding: no worthwhile form on Flat, including in a seller, — when trained by R. Hannon: tailed-off last in juvenile hurdles. *C. P. Wildman.*

CURAHEEN BOY 10 b.g. Tepukei–Curraheen Lady (Master Buck) [1989/90 **c100** c25g^2 c24g^2] lengthy gelding: top-class point-to-pointer: in frame in hunter chases in 1989 and handicap chases in October and November: stays 25f. *Miss H. C. Knight.*

CURIOUS FEELING 4 gr.f. Nishapour (FR)–Noirima (Right Tack) [1989/90 16s 18s 16v 18v^2 16g^2 16f^2 17m^3 17m*] sparely-made filly: half-sister to winning 80 hurdler Asticot (by Posse): poor maiden on Flat: sold out of C. Cyzer's stable 2,000 gns Newmarket Autumn Sales: attracted no bid after winning selling handicap hurdle at Newton Abbot in April by a length from Ragtime Solo: stays 2¼m: probably acts on any going. *J. R. Bosley.*

CURRAGH CADET 5 ch.g. Sandhurst Prince–Dunstells (Saint Crespin III) [1989/90 16m 20f 20m^{pu}] sparely-made ex-Irish gelding: half-brother to several — winners, including useful hurdler Everseal (by Patch): lightly-raced maiden on Flat, placed over 9.5f: novice hurdler: little show in 3 outings in Britain (blinkered last) in 1989/90: acts on firm and dead going. *D. R. Gandolfo.*

CURRANT OFFER 4 ro.f. Sayf El Arab (USA)–Raise The Offer (Auction Ring (USA)) [1989/90 17v^{pu}] no sign of ability on Flat: sold out of K. Brassey's — stable 1,050 gns Ascot October Sales: tailed off when pulled up 3 out in novice hurdle at Newton Abbot in January. *Mrs C. M. Budd.*

CURRY EXPRESS 7 br.g. Pony Express–Gypsy Curry (Romany Air) c94 [1989/90 20g^{pu} 22g c16g c24d^{pu} c20f^2 c24f^{ur}] compact gelding: showed first form — when 5 lengths second to What A Wally in novice chase at Ludlow in March, despite jumping none too fluently: stays 2½m: acts on firm ground: blinkered last 2 starts. *R. J. Hodges.*

CURVET (USA) 5 b.m. Ack Ack (USA)–Jingle Jan (USA) (In Reality) [1989/90 16f^4 16m* 16m^6 16m^3 a16g^4 16m^4 16g^5 16m^2 16m^3] small mare: selling hurdler: 74 jumped right when winning handicap at Worcester in September (no bid): best effort penultimate start: unlikely to stay much beyond 2m: acts on good to firm ground. *K. A. Morgan.*

CUSHINSTOWN 7 ch.g. Callernish–Bean An Ti (Festive) [1989/90 c18g **c130** c22s* c20s^{ur} c20v* c20v* c32f^6 c28m] medium-sized, rather sparely-made gelding: sixth live foal: dam unraced half-sister to a winning hurdler: runner-up in a point-to-point in 1989: won novice chase at Limerick in December, and handicap at Clonmel and Red Mills Trial Chase at Gowran Park (beat Aughanvilla 12 lengths) in February: held up and well behind until staying on in latter stages when remote sixth of 16 finishers behind Topsham Bay in National Hunt Challenge Cup Chase at Cheltenham in March: should stay beyond 2¾m: acts well on heavy going. *David J. McGrath, Ireland.*

CUT ABOVE AVERAGE 5 br.g. Mcindoe–Adroit (Ritudyr) [1989/90 16d^{pu} 16s^{pu} 16m^{pu}] sturdy gelding: second foal: dam, half-sister to 2 winning hunter — chasers, behind in novice hurdles and point-to-points: tailed off when pulled up in novice hurdles. *M. J. Wilkinson.*

CUT ABOVE THE REST 8 b.m. Indiaro–Towpath (Henry The Seventh) [1989/90 21v^{pu} 22d^{ur}] leggy mare: half-sister to winning point-to-pointer Water — Crescent (by No Mercy): runner-up once from 3 outings in point-to-points in 1989: little promise in mares novice hurdles. *N. R. Mitchell.*

CUT A CAPER 8 b.g. Gay Fandango (USA)–Brilliant Gem (Charlottown) [1989/90 16f^5 16m 16m 16s^6 a16s^6 a16g^6] small, lightly-made gelding: winning — hurdler: well below form in 1989/90: races only at 2m to 2¼m: acts on firm and dead going (seems unsuited by very soft): ridden by claimer. *R. J. O'Sullivan.*

C U TECHNIMECH 4 b.f. Chukaroo–Karyobinga (So Blessed) [1989/90 16g^{pu}] poor maiden sprint plater on Flat: behind when pulled up 3 out in claiming — hurdle at Uttoxeter in December. *M. W. Eckley.*

CUTE RYME 9 ch.m. Rymer–Christy Cute (Twilight Alley) [1989/90 c24f^2 c87 c24f* c24g^{ur}] lengthy mare: fairly useful point-to-pointer, successful in April: won 3-runner hunter chase at Ludlow earlier in month by 20 lengths from Pajanjo: hung left run-in first start: stays 3m: acts on firm ground. *Mrs A. Jones.*

CUT'N DRY 10 b.g. Dubassoff (USA)–Dissipation (USA) (Disciplinarian) [1989/90 21f] smallish, rather lightly-made gelding: poor hurdler: has been beaten —

in a seller: stays 25f: probably unsuited by heavy going, acts on any other. *J. C. Fox.*

CWM GWAUN 6 ch.g. Le Bavard (FR)–Glenbawn Lady (Orchardist) [1989/90 16d] sparely-made gelding: second in NH Flat race in 1988/9: well beaten in novice hurdle at Market Rasen in January, but eased from 2 out and better than position suggests: will be suited by further. *J. A. C. Edwards.* — p

CYNTHIA MAY 8 b.m. Totowah–Rouge El Noire (Game Rights) [1989/90 16d 16spu 19spu] rather leggy mare: of little account: blinkered final start. *P. Burgoyne.* —

CYPHRATE (USA) 4 b. or br.g. Saint Cyrien (FR)–Euphrate (FR) (Royal And Regal (USA)) [1989/90 16s* 16f] tall, rather angular gelding: half-brother to 1¼m seller winner Catherine Schratt (by General Assembly) and to a winner in Italy: dam, half-sister to Grand Prix de Paris winner Galiani, won over 6f at 2 yrs: won 1¼m maiden on Flat in France in 1989, when trained by Mme C. Head: highly-impressive all-the-way winner of juvenile hurdle at Haydock in January by 25 lengths: moved poorly down when well beaten on firm ground in Daily Express Triumph Hurdle at Cheltenham in March, showing up until 2 out: well worth another chance on softer going. *M. C. Pipe.* 115 p

CYTHERE 6 gr.g. Le Soleil–Vinotino (Rugantino) [1989/90 20g4 c18g2 c21f2] medium-sized gelding: moderate hurdler: clear second in novice chase at Fontwell in October and minor chase at Wincanton (beaten neck by Night Session) in November, despite jumping moderately: better suited by 2¾m than shorter distances and will stay 3m: acts on any going: needs to improve his jumping but has the ability to win a race over fences. *J. T. Gifford.* c**100** p 110

D

DACANI'S GUEST 5 ch.h. What A Guest–Dacani (Polyfoto) [1989/90 16f3] ex-Irish gelding: middle-distance maiden on Flat: 10 lengths third of 5 behind Rokala in 4-y-o selling hurdle at Market Rasen in August. *C. C. Trietline.* 65

DADDY'S DARLING 5 b.m. Mummy's Pet–Annie Get Your Gun (Blakeney) [1989/90 16m3] small, leggy mare: lacks scope: middle-distance handicapper on Flat, in good form in 1990: just over 2 lengths third behind Kosciosko in 20-runner selling hurdle at Leicester in December: will stay 2½m. *J. T. Gifford.* 79

DAILY QUEST 5 br.g. Sandalay–Sunquest (Great White Way (USA)) [1989/90 F16h4 16dpu] sparely-made gelding: ninth foal: dam modest maiden plater on Flat: tailed-off last of 4 finishers in NH Flat race at Hexham in October: jumped poorly and tailed off when pulled up fourth in selling hurdle on same course in December. *W. A. Stephenson.* —

DAILY SPORT SOON 5 b.h. Star Appeal–Pritillor (Privy Councillor) [1989/90 16f* 16f2 16g2 20f4 20g3 16g5 16d a18s2 16m*] small, stocky horse: won novice hurdle at Uttoxeter in October and handicap at Stratford (seemed suited by strongly-run race and showed improved form) in May: worth another try over further than 2m: acts on firm going: consistent. *J. R. Jenkins.* 111

DAINSBURY 5 b.m. Decoy Boy–Chiltern Lass (High Hat) [1989/90 16spu 16spu 16g] sturdy, lengthy mare: half-sister to several winners, including useful hurdler and fairly useful chaser Withy Bank (by Blakeney): no worthwhile form on Flat: no sign of ability in novice hurdles: looks headstrong. *Mrs A. E. Lee.* —

DAIRA FORT (USA) 4 b.c. Nureyev (USA)–Lady B Gay (USA) (Sir Gaylord) [1989/90 16g3 16v2 16gpu] workmanlike colt: has scope: fair stayer on Flat: sold out of A. Stewart's stable 29,000 gns Newmarket Autumn Sales: placed in juvenile hurdles at Wolverhampton and Leicester (beaten short head by Spring Hay) in February: ran poorly in useful company only subsequent outing: will be suited by further. *K. C. Bailey.* 111

DAISY MILLER 5 b.m. Daring March–Holiday Season (Silly Season) [1989/90 16g 16s 16m 16spu a18g6] workmanlike mare: second in 1m claimer at 3 yrs, but no other form on Flat: seems of little account as a hurdler: sold 1,800 gns Ascot April Sales. *M. Castell.* —

DAISYS DELIGHT 4 ch.g. Sandhurst Prince–Dunstells (Saint Crespin III) [1989/90 17h5] half-brother to 2 winning hurdlers, including useful Everseal (by Patch): no sign of ability on Flat: tailed-off last of 5 in juvenile hurdle at Devon & Exeter in August. *J. White.* —

DAKYNS BOY 5 ch.g. Deep Run–Mawbeg Holly (Golden Love) [1989/90 F14v*] first foal: dam never ran: 25/1, won 20-runner NH Flat race at Ayr in April by 1½ lengths from Glen Morvern: yet to race over hurdles or fences. *J. A. C. Edwards.*

DALBURY 12 b.g. Royal Palace–Tikki Tavi (Honeyway) [1989/90 c16s4 c20gpu] lengthy, rather shallow-girthed gelding: modest chaser nowadays: still backward, pulled up at the second after rider lost irons second outing 1989/90: better suited by 2½m than shorter distances: best with give in the ground: suitable mount for a claimer: best held up. *A. Moore.* c— —

DALBY DASH 5 ch.g. Bustiki–Wensum Girl (Ballymoss) [1989/90 F16g* F16gro F16m5] third foal: brother to Dalby Dancer, a winner from 1¼m to 2m on Flat and half-brother to winning selling hurdler Dalby Girl (by Young Man): dam ran twice: won NH Flat race at Uttoxeter in December: in lead when running out entering straight in similar event at Edinburgh following month: yet to race over hurdles or fences. *B. A. McMahon.*

DALBY GIRL 7 b.m. Young Man (FR)–Wensum Girl (Ballymoss) [1989/90 c16d4 c20m4 c20g5] workmanlike mare: won 2 selling hurdles in 1987/8: has shown a little ability in novice chases: stays 2½m (bit backward when well beaten over 2¾m): acts on soft going. *B. A. McMahon.* **c78** —

DALE PARK 4 b.c. Kampala–Coshlea (Red Alert) [1989/90 16g* 16s* 16v*] sparely-made colt: half-brother to novice hurdler Glamgram's Best (by Taufan): won 13f claimer on Flat in October: took well to hurdling, and won juvenile event at Ayr in November and novice event and a juvenile event on same course in January: will stay further: acts on heavy going: should continue on the upgrade. *N. Tinkler.* 108 p

DALKEY SOUND 7 gr.m. Crash Course–Silver Doll (Sovereign Gleam) [1989/90 c21m* c21d* c24d2 c16dF c20d* c20g2 c20vF c24gur] workmanlike ex-Irish mare: sister to winning Irish jumper Crash Bar and half-sister to fair hurdler Penalty Double (by Deep Run): dam winner at up to 2m on Flat and 2½m over hurdles in Ireland: winning hurdler: won novice chases at Market Rasen in September and November and Sedgefield in December: ran poorly final outing: stays 3m: acts on heavy going and good to firm: jumps well in the main, although rather low. *Mrs G. R. Reveley.* **c108** —

DALMORE 4 b.g. Runnett–Fade To Grey (Gay Fandango (USA)) [1989/90 16f6 16f] close-coupled gelding: first foal: dam, winner at up to 7f, sister to the dam of high-class hurdler Grabel: poor plater on Flat at 2 yrs, took little interest final 3 starts: jumped poorly in juvenile hurdles in October. *F. Watson.* 64 x

DALTMORE 12 br.g. Pauper–Zaleg (Zabeg) [1989/90 c24d] lengthy, shallow-girthed gelding: hunter chaser nowadays: bit backward, tailed off only outing in 1990: stays 3m well (some way below form over further): best form with give in the ground and acts on heavy going: suitable mount for an amateur: has run moderately in blinkers. *W. Jenks.* c— —

DALTON DANDY 8 b.g. Dubassoff (USA)–Donna Sight (Crosby Don) [1989/90 c20dpu c20s4 c25gF c27m3 c24f5 c26mro c25m2 c25f2 c16g2] strong, workmanlike gelding: won a point-to-point in April: inconsistent novice hurdler/chaser: in frame in 4 hunter chases and a novice chase in 1989/90: stays well: acts on any going. *V. Hall.* **c84** —

DAMANOUR (USA) 4 gr.g. Lypheor–Damana (FR) (Crystal Palace (FR)) [1989/90 16g 16mF 16g 16dbd 16g 16g 20g] small gelding: first foal: dam won from 1m to 1¾m on Flat in France: showed ability in 1m maiden on Flat in September: sold out of L. Cumani's stable 13,500 gns Newmarket September Sales: no form over hurdles, though has shown signs of ability: weakened 3 out over 2½m: needs to brush up his jumping. *G. Richards.* —

DAMERS CAVALRY 7 b.g. Stanford–Margery (FR) (Cadmus II) [1989/90 c25d3 c26m* c26g* c25m* c26g* c25f2] lengthy, workmanlike gelding: novice hurdler: won novice chases at Fontwell in December (2, second a handicap) and Doncaster following month and handicap on latter course in February: no impression from 4 out when creditable second to Topsham Bay in quite valuable novice handicap at Cheltenham in April: stays well: probably acts on any going: blinkered once in 1987/8: front runner: jumps well. *R. Lee.* **c121** —

DAMIEN'S BEAU 8 ch.g. Beau Charmeur (FR)–Riggin Banks (Ossian II) [1989/90 16f5 16f6 17m4 27f6] ex-Irish gelding: thirteenth foal: dam won in Ireland at up to 9f: showed ability in novice hurdles: favourite, weakened quickly after 73 +

mistake 3 out when remote sixth in 27f selling handicap at Sedgefield in April. *W. A. Stephenson.*

DAMIENS FELLOW 9 b.g. Decent Fellow–Betton's Folly (Immortality) [1989/90 F16f F16s^{4} F16g 16g 16m 16g 16f^{4}] leggy ex-Irish gelding: half-brother to useful staying chaser The Ellier (by Menelek) and fair staying hurdler/chaser Randomly (by Random Shot): showed a little ability in NH Flat races (trained until after third start by E. Kearns) and in novice hurdles, not at all knocked about final start: pulls hard: may do better. *W. A. Stephenson.* —

DANCE THE BLUES (USA) 10 b.g. Dance Spell (USA)–Plum Happy (USA) (Round Table) [1989/90 c20f^{2} c22f^{3}] handicap chaser: placed in small fields at Worcester in August and Stratford in September: stays 2½m: acts on firm ground: best in blinkers. *J. Webber.* **c90**

DANCING BALLERINA 7 b.m. Record Run–Glanfield (Eborneezer) [1989/90 c20s^{4} c16g^{3} c20d^{2} c20s^{5} c21g^{5} c20f^{2} c20m*] leggy mare: novice hurdler: won handicap chase at Plumpton in April by 5 lengths from Palmerston Boy: suited by 2½m: acts on any going. *M. J. Bolton.* **c83 +** —

DANCING EYES 5 b.m. Jester–Le Chat (Burglar) [1989/90 16h^{6} 16m^{5} 20m^{3} a18g^{5} 20g] leggy, sparely-made mare: selling hurdler: ran poorly last 2 starts: stays 2½m: blinkered fourth start. *M. C. Pipe.* 81

DANCING NORTH 5 b. or br.g. Shareef Dancer (USA)–Icena (Jimmy Reppin) [1989/90 aF13g^{2}] fifth foal: half-brother to 2¼m Flat winner Teevano: dam won Lowther Stakes: 20/1, 15 lengths second of 8 to Greenhills Warrior in NH Flat race at Lingfield in March: yet to race over hurdles or fences. *C. J. Benstead.*

DANCING RIVER 4 b.g. Niniski (USA)–River Chimes (Forlorn River) [1989/90 16f 16f^{5} 16g 16g* 16g* 16m^{6} 16f* 16f* 16f^{2} 17f*] leggy gelding: fifth foal: half-brother to very speedy 1984 2-y-o Absent Chimes (by Absalom): dam poor sister to high-class sprinter Rapid River: gaining fifth win over hurdles when beating Gold Service 4 lengths in novice event at Cartmel in May: successful earlier in 2 novice handicaps at Catterick, a juvenile event at Wetherby and a juvenile handicap at Haydock: suited by sharp 2m: acts on firm going: game. *W. A. Stephenson.* 116

DANCING SPY 5 b.g. Bali Dancer–Ida Spider (Ben Novus) [1989/90 F12f F16f] half-brother to 3 winning jumpers, including very useful Ardent Spy (by Saucy Kit) and Ida's Delight (by Idiot's Delight): dam unraced: well beaten in NH Flat races at Bangor (whipped round start) and Uttoxeter in the spring: yet to race over hurdles or fences. *Mrs A. R. Hewitt.*

DAN D'OR 12 br.g. Le Coq d'Or–Sweet Fanny (Bitter Sweet) [1989/90 c24g c24d^{4}] big, strong gelding: won a point-to-point in March: winning steeplechaser: well beaten in hunter chases in March and April: stays well: probably acts on any going: has won for an amateur: blinkered twice: deliberate jumper. *Mrs G. D. H. Armitage.* **c79** —

DANDY MINSTREL 6 br.g. Black Minstrel–Julanda (Tarboosh (USA)) [1989/90 c19g^{2} c17d^{F} c20m^{2} c20m^{su} c20g^{F} 21s^{5} c20f* c19f^{ur}] useful-looking gelding: handicap hurdler: held up when winning novice chase at Plumpton in March: stays 2½m: acts on firm and dead going (seemed unsuited by soft on sixth outing): blinkered fourth to sixth outings: poor jumper at present. *Mrs J. Pitman.* **c97 x** —

DANE ROSE 4 b.f. Full of Hope–Roella (Gold Rod) [1989/90 16f 16d^{pu} 16f^{pu}] sparely-made filly: no form on Flat or over hurdles (including in a seller): sold out of O. O'Neill's stable 1,550 gns Ascot December Sales after first start: resold 825 gns Ascot April Sales. *M. B. James.* —

DANGAN SHOON 8 b.g. Green Shoon–Paramatta (Pardal) [1989/90 c24f^{F} c25h^{ur} 20f^{pu} 17m^{3} 21m^{pu}] sparely-made gelding: poor form in novice hurdles: has failed to complete course over fences: sold 1,350 gns Ascot October Sales, resold 1,000 gns Ascot July Sales. *D. R. Gandolfo.* c— 70 ?

DANIEL MARTIN 11 br.g. Pamroy–Tyrone Typhoon (Typhoon) [1989/90 22g^{pu} c25m^{4} c26s^{F} c25s^{4} a24g c24g^{5} c36g^{pu}] compact, workmanlike ex-Irish gelding: fair hurdler: no form in 1989/90: made numerous mistakes when about 25 lengths fourth in novice chases at Wolverhampton and Towcester: very stiff task last start: stays 3m: acts on heavy going: blinkered fifth outing. *R. T. Juckes.* c88 —

DANISH CHIEF 9 b.g. Brave Invader (USA)–Just Darina (Three Dons) [1989/90 22d 24m^{pu} 27g c20d^{F} c21d^{5} c24m^{pu} c24g^{pu} 24g^{6} 24g] leggy, c— —

Mrs Shirley Robins' "Danny Harrold"

sparely-made gelding: winning hurdler: no form in 1989/90, including in a seller: no sign of ability in novice chases: stays 3m: acts on heavy going: has run blinkered (looked none too keen under pressure on one occasion) and visored. *K. A. Ryan.*

DANISH FOLLY 8 b.g. Floriferous–Denny's Folly (Saint Denys) [1989/90 20g 22d^{ur} 20g^{pu}] workmanlike gelding: poor novice hurdler. *M. P. Naughton.* —

DANNY HARROLD 6 b.g. Deep Run–Chillaway (Arctic Slave) [1989/90 20g^{5} 20v* 20s^{2} 16m^{2}] 133 p

Danny Harrold ran an excellent race when two and a half lengths second to Forest Sun in the Waterford Crystal Supreme Novices' Hurdle at Cheltenham in March. Well positioned on the inside of the field throughout, he disputed the lead with Rakes Lane from the home turn; then, having got the better of that rival, he was unable to match the winner's turn of foot on the run-in. Danny Harrold's starting price of 20/1 reflects his earlier less-than-smooth progress in Britain. He'd been bought privately out of Walsh's stable in Ireland after winning two point-to-points and two National Hunt Flat races in the spring of 1989 on his only starts. His reputation preceded him to the racecourse in Britain—in three outings prior to Cheltenham he started first or second favourite each time. Yet Danny Harrold won only one of those races, a run-of-the-mill novice hurdle at Chepstow in January in which he wandered and tended to carry his head awkwardly. On his hurdling debut in a quite well-contested novice event at Wolverhampton in November, Danny Harrold jumped deliberately and was beaten almost from halfway. In the Golden Miller Novices' Hurdle at Leicester in January, he ran as though something was amiss when twenty-five lengths second to the eased Regal Ambition—never going particularly well, Danny Harrold had to be pushed out to hold off the seemingly-modest Queen's Chaplain on the run-in and finished very tired.

How to explain the transformation, then? A large part must be put down to physical improvement. Unimpressive in appearance at Leicester, Danny Harrold looked in tremendous shape at Cheltenham, far and away the pick of the paddock. But it's also probable that the conditions at Cheltenham—a half-mile shorter trip and much firmer ground than he'd previously encountered—suited a horse who'd looked slightly headstrong and lacking in stamina in his previous outings. Not all Irish point-to-point winners turn out to be thorough stayers in steeplechases, as the ill-fated two-milers Wolf of Badenoch and Slieve Felim exemplify.

Danny Harrold (b.g. 1984)	Deep Run (ch 1966)	Pampered King (b 1954)	Prince Chevalier
			Netherton Maid
		Trial By Fire (ch 1958)	Court Martial
			Mitrailleuse
	Chillaway (b 1972)	Arctic Slave (b 1950)	Arctic Star
			Roman Galley
		Freezeaway (b 1961)	Vulgan
			Skateaway

At this stage Danny Harrold reminds us very much of his dam's half-brother Golden Freeze. When trained by Walsh, Golden Freeze was a fairly useful but headstrong novice over hurdles and fences who only just stayed two and a half miles. Transferred to Mrs Pitman's stable, it took time for him to become tractable enough to be considered a valid Gold Cup contender. Provided Danny Harrold settles better as he gets older, he also should stay well. The unraced Chillaway is a half-sister to three other winners over jumps, including the staying chaser Tom Miller. Her dam Freezeaway won twice over four miles over fences. Danny Harrold is Chillaway's sixth live foal and first winner. A rangy, good-quartered though rather angular gelding, Danny Harrold is to be sent chasing in 1990/1: he's an exciting prospect in a stable which traditionally does well with its novice chasers. Though he looked a difficult ride on occasions—particularly at Cheltenham, where he hung badly left on the run-in—Danny Harrold is likely to improve with age and with experience. He's won on heavy going but easily his best effort was on good to firm at Cheltenham. *Mrs J. Pitman.*

DANNY'S LUCK (NZ) 8 b.g. St Puckle–Kiss Girl (NZ) (Palm Beach) c84 x
[1989/90 c21f^{2} c17f^{3} c19f^{ur}] lengthy, workmanlike gelding: winning hurdler: —
novice chaser: stays 2½m: seems to act on any going: has won for a 7-lb claimer: badly let down by his jumping on occasions: sold privately 3,000 gns Ascot June Sales. *D. H. Barons.*

DAN O'TULLY 11 b.g. Danjovan–The Bird O'Tully (The Padisha) [1989/90 c—
c22f^{ur}] tall gelding: behind in a novice hurdle and has failed to complete course in —
steeplechases, but is a winning point-to-pointer. *C. N. Nimmo.*

DAN RAISE 9 b.g. Raise You Ten–Arctic Cut (Arctic Slave) [1989/90 25g^{6} c—
20s* 20m] rangy gelding: swerved right on run-in when winning conditional 104
jockeys handicap hurdle at Chepstow in December: seemed unsuited by much firmer ground next time: second in novice chase in 1988/9 (fell next time): suited by 2½m + : acts on heavy going. *Mrs J. Pitman.*

DANRIBO 7 b.g. Riboboy (USA)–Sheridans Daughter (Majority Blue) [1989/90 c—
17f^{5} 20f^{4} c17d^{F} 17v 16s^{pu} a16g^{pu}] strong, lengthy gelding: selling hurdler: has 77
shown little aptitude for chasing: form only at 2m: best form on top-of-the-ground: blinkered fifth outing: usually claimer ridden: sold 2,100 gns Ascot June Sales. *C. L. Popham.*

DAPPING 6 b.m. Beldale Flutter (USA)–Sass-Go (Sassafras (FR)) [1989/90
22m^{6} 24m^{2} 24g^{F} 20g^{6} 24s 20s^{4} 16s 20v 16f 25m 22d] smallish ex-Irish mare: first 100
foal: dam useful 1½m winner: winning stayer on Flat: successful hurdler: not disgraced in face of stiff task in quite valuable event at Liverpool tenth start, best effort in Britain: stays 3m: acts on good to firm ground: trained by H. de Bromhead until after eighth outing. *A. P. James.*

Aga Handicap Hurdle, Worcester—
Dare Say (left) heads Penalty Double at the last

DARA DOONE 4 b.g. Dara Monarch–Lorna Doone (USA) (Tom Rolfe) [1989/90 18h4] medium-sized gelding: half-brother to several winners on Flat, including Christian Schad (by Tumble Wind) who was also very useful novice hurdler: poor middle-distance maiden on Flat: soundly-beaten fourth of 6 behind Rislan in juvenile hurdle at Fontwell in August. *P. J. Jones.* —

DARA KING 7 ch.g. Posse (USA)–Sardara (Alcide) [1989/90 20dpu] sparely-made gelding: half-brother to Irish 2000 Guineas winner Dara Monarch (by Realm): dam staying half-sister to St Leger winner Intermezzo: little show in Irish NH Flat races in 1987: tailed off when pulled up before 4 out only outing over hurdles: dead. *K. A. Ryan.* —

DARC HANSEL 12 ch.g. Prince Hansel–Ribble (Bitter Sweet) [1989/90 c32fur] big gelding: useful chaser at best, lightly raced of late: won a point-to-point in April: a thorough stayer: probably acts on any going. *Mrs James Daly.* c— —

D'ARCY SPICE 13 ch.g. Harwell–Vulcarla (Bowsprit) [1989/90 c24mpu c26fpu] compact gelding: winning point-to-pointer: maiden hunter chaser: stays well. *Brian Clifford.* c—

DARE SAY 7 b.g. Kris–Pampered Dancer (Pampered King) [1989/90 16g* 18d* 16mF 18m5 16g 16mpu 20f5 16g] tall, leggy, close-coupled gelding: won handicaps at Sandown and Worcester in November, showing useful form, but ran poorly last 5 starts: stays 2¼m: yet to race on very soft ground, acts on any other. *J. T. Gifford.* 135 d

DARING CLASS 4 b.f. Class Distinction–Darymoss (Ballymoss) [1989/90 16gpu a16g a16g4 16h3 16f3 16h4] second foal: half-sister to winning hurdler Phelioff (by Dubassoff): showed ability in second of 2 outings at 2 yrs: placed in juvenile hurdles at Taunton in April (first a conditional jockeys seller): best efforts over a sharp 2m on very firm ground. *P. R. Rodford.* 68

DARK DEB 5 b.m. Black Minstrel–Prospective Lady (Kabale) [1989/90 F16f F16f] half-sister to quite useful staying chaser Cerimau (by Beau Chapeau) and winning chaser Two Buttons (by Boreen): well beaten in NH Flat races in the spring: yet to race over hurdles or fences. *I. G. Blair.*

DARK DESIRE 4 b.g. Alzao (USA)–Treble Cloud (Capistrano) [1989/90 17d2 18s* 16v3 16s* 16g* 16f] stocky gelding: sixth in 1¼m maiden on Flat in 1989: won juvenile hurdles at Fontwell, Sandown (made all) and Newbury (gamely by 1½ lengths from Ivors Guest) after turn of the year: always behind in Daily Express Triumph Hurdle at Cheltenham: will stay 2½m: acts on soft going (possibly unsuited by firm): useful juvenile. *M. E. D. Francis.* 126

DARK EMPEROR 9 br.g. Park Spirit–Pin Up Girl (Workboy) [1989/90 20d² 20d⁵ 20m² 22d] good-bodied gelding: second in handicap hurdles at Sedgefield in December and Newcastle in March: first race for 2 months and wearing tongue strap, looked sure to win approaching last but faded run-in and was beaten 2½ lengths by Armagret on latter course: modest novice over fences: best efforts at 2½m: acts on heavy going and good to firm: has raced with head high. *W. Storey.* c— 108

DARK GISELLE 5 b.m. King of Spain–Giselle (Pall Mall) [1989/90 17g] modest 7f plater on Flat: amateur ridden, last of 7 finishers in selling hurdle at Devon & Exeter in December. *R. J. Hodges.* —

DARK HERITAGE 7 b.g. Scorpio (FR)–Mother of The Wind (Tumble Wind (USA)) [1989/90 20f² c20g² c16fF] workmanlike gelding: modest hurdler/chaser: went down narrowly to Patenier in amateur riders event over hurdles at Southwell in August: good second to Serious Man in handicap over fences at Plumpton in November: stays 2½m: acts on any going, except perhaps heavy: has won 6 times at Plumpton: fell heavily final outing. *D. J. G. Murray-Smith.* c**106** 106

DARK HONEY 5 b.g. Marechal (FR)–Caillou (Owen Anthony) [1989/90 16d² 16s⁵ 20v² 21d³] sturdy, workmanlike gelding: fair form in novice hurdles: gave impression he'll be suited by further when going down by 1½ lengths to Young Ty at Leicester in February, penultimate start: should win a run-of-the mill novice event. *S. Dow.* 111

DARK JESTER 5 b.g. Jester–Chilcombe (Morston (FR)) [1989/90 20f³] leggy, unfurnished gelding: first form over hurdles 9 lengths third of 4 finishers behind Aldra Bond in 2½m novice event at Hexham in September: claimer ridden in 1988/9. *M. O'Neill.* 81

DARK RECORD 7 br.g. Black Minstrel–Bonny Prepack (Gala Performance (USA)) [1989/90 c16dur] second foal: dam well beaten in Irish NH Flat race: well beaten in maiden hurdles and a novice chase, but won a point-to-point in 1988/9, when trained in Ireland by P. Madden: unseated rider fifth in December on British debut. *Mrs S. A. Bramall.* c— —

DARK ROSAAN 6 br.m. Dalsaan–Miss Robust (Busted) [1989/90 17v] leggy mare: novice selling hurdler: no worthwhile form. *N. G. Ayliffe.* —

DARK SIRONA 7 b.m. Pitskelly–Step You Gaily (King's Company) [1989/90 16m 20d⁵ 20s 22spu 21f⁶ 26m³] workmanlike mare: novice hurdler: best efforts of season in handicaps on second and final starts, though seemed not to stay 3¼m on latter occasion: acts on good to firm and dead ground. *D. W. P. Arbuthnot.* 87

DARKTOWN STRUTTER 4 ch.g. Pas de Seul–Princess Henham (Record Token) [1989/90 17dpu 17fpu] behind in varied company, including selling, at 2 yrs: tailed off when pulled up fifth in novice selling hurdles in January and May. *R. W. Pincombe.* —

DARRINGTON DEAL 9 ch.m. Rymer–Chukka (Tiepolo II) [1989/90 c24m⁴] neat mare: won point-to-points in February and May: moderate fourth in novice hunter chase at Southwell in between: stays 3¼m: acts on firm ground. *Mrs Beryl Lockey.* c**75** —

DARTEL 10 ch.g. Maystreak–Valiant Victress (Nulli Secundus) [1989/90 16gpu] lengthy gelding: no sign of ability in 2 outings over hurdles: has failed to complete course in novice chases: tends to sweat. *P. N. Upson.* c— —

DARTON RI 7 b.g. Abednego–Boogie Woogie (No Argument) [1989/90 c24spu c24s⁵ c25spu c20d c25m³] rather leggy, good-topped gelding: novice hurdler: won a point-to-point in Ireland in 1988: novice steeplechaser: not disgraced when third behind easy winner The Argonaut in amateur riders event at Sandown in March: stays 3m: best run on dead ground. *D. Nicholson.* c**78** —

DART OVER 14 ro.g. Hardraw Scar–Selstone (Counsel) [1989/90 c25g⁶ c25g] angular gelding: quite a useful chaser at his best: no worthwhile form for a long time: suited by extreme distances: acts on heavy going. *R. J. Hodges.* c—

DASHALONG 8 b.g. Crash Course–Lucky You (Dalesa) [1989/90 c25s* c19fpu c25m*] lengthy, lightly-made gelding: novice hurdler: fairly useful point-to-pointer, successful in April: made several mistakes when winning maiden hunter chase at Hereford in March by 2 lengths from Wally Wrekin: finished alone on same course in May: jumped poorly in between: stays 25f: acts on soft going and possibly unsuited by very firm. *H. Morris.* c**86** ? —

DASHING DOMINOE 5 ch.g. Sweet Monday–Autumn Dream (Polacca) [1989/90 16d² 16m 16m 16d⁶] leggy gelding: hung left run-in when second in novice hurdle at Stratford in November: creditable sixth behind Abbots View in 85 novice handicap at Warwick in January: well beaten on firmer ground in between: will be suited by further than 2m: bought for 4,100 gns Doncaster September Sales. *A. Barrow.*

DAT TRAIN 6 b.g. Mandalus–Early Start (Wrekin Rambler) [1989/90 16m* 16g4 22d* 21s3 20dpu] well-made gelding: chasing type: successful in novice hurdles at Leicester in December and Windsor (handicap) following month: good third behind Aristos in novice handicap at Sandown in February: ran moderately final outing: should stay further than 2¾m: acts on good to firm and soft going. *Mrs J. Pitman.* 111

DAUNOU (FR) 4 b.c. Fabulous Dancer (USA)–Dourdan (Prudent (USA)) [1989/90 16d3 16s4 16f3 16m4] rather leggy colt: quite modest middle-distance maiden on Flat: in frame all outings over hurdles, showing modest form: claimer ridden. *S. Christian.* 87

DAUNTING PROSPECT 6 b.g. Formidable (USA)–Acquire (Burglar) [1989/90 17m 26f4 c21mpu c24gpu c26gpu 21g5 16s 17fpu 20m5 23fF] workmanlike gelding: selling hurdler: little form since winning twice in 1988/9: no sign of ability in novice chases: stays 2½m: acts on soft going: has been blinkered and visored. *M. C. Chapman.* c— —

DAUPHIN BLEU (FR) 4 b.g. Direct Flight–Shabby (FR) (Carmarthan (FR)) [1989/90 F16g F16f] French-bred gelding: mid-division in NH Flat races at Perth and Hereford in May: yet to race over hurdles. *J. Parkes.*

DAVIDS LOS 6 b.g. Los Cerrillos (ARG)–Juno Baby (Kalimnos) [1989/90 16hpu 22gF] small gelding: second foal: dam unraced: no sign of ability in 2 novice hurdles in October: amateur ridden. *B. Venn.* —

DAVID'S TREASURE 10 b.g. Pitskelly–Cecilia's Will (Crocket) [1989/90 c20spu c24gpu 20d4] rangy gelding: winning hurdler/chaser: no form for a long time: best form at 2½m: acts on heavy going: has worn blinkers: let down by his jumping on occasions. *Mrs N. S. Sharpe.* c— —

DAVY'S WEIR 10 ch.g. Paddy's Stream–Tevie (Le Levanstell) [1989/90 c20fur c24g4 c20g4 21m2 c20g5 c20s2 21s] dipped-backed gelding: handicap chaser: relegated to second after beating only other finisher Faaris a neck at Folkestone (made mistakes and jumped left) in January: good second in handicap hurdle at Sandown in December: stays 2¾m: unsuited by heavy ground but seems to act on any other: blinkered fourth and fifth outings: has won when sweating: successful 4 times at Fontwell: sold 5,400 gns Ascot June Sales. *J. T. Gifford.* c**112** 107

DAWN BELL 5 b.m. Belfort (FR)–Dobrina (FR) (Our Mirage) [1989/90 16f3 16s] small, sparely-made mare: third of 4 finishers in novice selling hurdle at Taunton in December: unlikely to stay much beyond 2m. *J. D. Roberts.* 69

DAWN BLADE 7 b.m. Fine Blade (USA)–Watch The Birdie (Polyfoto) [1989/90 18d 24s6 20d5] leggy mare: runner-up in a point-to-point in Ireland early in 1987: won 2 NH Flat races in 1988/9: led until 3 out when fifth in novice hurdle at Carlisle in March: races keenly and doesn't stay 3m. *J. J. O'Neill.* 82

DAWN BUSTER 5 b.g. Dawn Johnny (USA)–Amber Palace (Sallust) [1989/90 16m 16f* 16f6] workmanlike gelding: made all in selling handicap hurdle (no bid) at Uttoxeter in September despite jumping to his right in straight: eased once beaten in non-selling handicap following month: has raced only at around 2m: acts on firm ground. *T. J. Houlbrooke.* 70

DAWN COYOTE (USA) 7 ch.g. Grey Dawn II–Beanery (USA) (Cavan) [1989/90 16g 16g 16g6] medium-sized ex-Irish gelding: half-brother to 4 winners in USA, including high-class Rockhill Native (by Speak John): dam won 8 races in USA: won over 9f on Flat (blinkered when successful): winning hurdler: no form in 1989/90: has raced only at 2m: acts on soft going: blinkered fourth start 1988/9: sold out of J. Burns's stable 2,200 gns Doncaster August Sales. *S. J. Leadbetter.* —

DAWN LOVE 7 b.m. He Loves Me–Fog (English Prince) [1989/90 17f* 16h3 16f 16g5] sparely-made mare: won handicap hurdle at Newton Abbot in August: ran moderately after: will prove best at 2m: usually claimer ridden: needs holding up as long as possible: sold 5,800 gns Doncaster January Sales. *R. Hollinshead.* 95

DAWN PRINCE 7 b.g. King of Spain–The Dupesdawn (Jukebox) [1989/90 16d5 21s6 a16g* 17m5 c24f* c25mF c26mr c24fF] sturdy, close-coupled gelding: handicap hurdler: successful at Southwell in March: won novice chase at Taunton later in month, but failed to complete course last 3 starts: stays 3m: acts on any going: blinkered and didn't find much under pressure second start 1988/9. *M. C. Pipe.* c**96** § 98

DAWN QUEST 6 gr.m. Nadjar (FR)–Invery Lady (Sharpen Up) [1989/90 c16d6 c16v c24d c20m] lengthy, rather sparely-made ex-Irish mare: half-sister to winning hurdler Reggae Beat (by Be My Native): dam placed over 5f at 2 yrs: placed in NH Flat race: has shown a little ability over hurdles: behind in novice chases: finished lame last outing: has been tried in blinkers: sold out of M. Hourigan's stable 5,100 gns Doncaster August Sales. *M. Scudamore.* c— —

DAWN STREET 12 br.g. Dawn Review–Regent Street (Autre Prince) [1989/90 c24gpu] good-topped gelding: useful point-to-pointer: pulled up lame in hunter chase in February: stays 2½m: well suited by heavy going: usually blinkered. *Mrs J. R. Cooper.* c— —

DAYBROOK'S GIFT 7 b.g. Daybrook Lad–Current Gift (Current Coin) [1989/90 c20f6] angular gelding: no sign of ability in novice hurdles when trained by J. Jenkins: won 3 point-to-points in the spring: favourite when well beaten in novice hunter chase at Folkestone in May. *J. M. Turner.* c— —

DAYBROOK VERB 8 ch.g. Proverb–Daybrook Lass (Daybrook Lad) [1989/90 c21f2 c20m3 c24spu c24gF] angular ex-Irish gelding: fourth foal: brother to modest staying hurdler The Pike: dam maiden hurdler/chaser in Ireland: winning point-to-pointer: placed in novice chases at Thurles and Gowran Park very early in season: no form in 2 outings in Britain: trained by M. Browne until after second start. *J. Honeyball.* **c86** ?

DEADLINE 7 br.g. Strong Gale–Countess Charmere (Chamier) [1989/90 c24gpu c24spu c20g* c20m3 c24mpu c24g2] sturdy gelding: winning hurdler/ point-to-pointer: still carrying plenty of condition, rallied to lead close home when winning conditional jockeys handicap chase at Wetherby in January: jumped badly and to his right fourth start: stays 2½m. *J. W. Blundell.* **c92** —

DEADLY CHARM (USA) 4 b. or br.f. Bates Motel (USA)–Certain Something (Solinus) [1989/90 16m2 16d5 16g4 17g2 a16g2 16f5 16h2] useful-looking filly: has scope: modest middle-distance maiden on Flat when trained by J. Gosden: variable form over hurdles, best efforts first and fourth starts. *D. Nicholson.* 96 ?

DEAR APOLLO 9 ch.g. Cleon–Dear Lady (Dear Gazelle) [1989/90 c18gpu] strong, stocky gelding: lightly-raced poor maiden point-to-pointer: no sign of ability in novice chases. *R. J. O'Sullivan.* c—

DEAR BOB 7 ch.g. Malinowski (USA)–Regal Step (Ribero) [1989/90 16fpu 16f3 19f c16m a20g4 a20gpu] leggy, angular gelding: winning selling hurdler: in frame in non-sellers in 1989/90: jumped moderately on chasing debut: best form at around 2m: acts on any going: has won with and without blinkers: trained until fourth start by M. Scudamore. *J. Colston.* c— 69

DEAR MIFF 5 ch.m. Alias Smith (USA)–Dear Jem (Dragonara Palace (USA)) [1989/90 16g a16g 16f4 16f3 18f3 16hpu] sparely-made mare: poor novice selling hurdler: not disgraced over 2¼m: blinkered third start: acts on firm ground. *M. R. Channon.* 62

DEAR SARAH 4 ch.f. Dublin Taxi–Pardina (Pardao) [1989/90 F16g] half-sister to several winners here and abroad, including fair 1979 2-y-o 5f winner Swinford Rose (by Upper Case): dam won from 6f to 1¼m: last of 14 finishers in NH Flat race at Edinburgh in January: yet to race over hurdles. *T. N. Dalgetty.*

DEBDEN 5 b.g. Electric–Affection (Compensation) [1989/90 16d 16g] compact, sparely-made gelding: modest 1m winner on Flat (has looked a difficult ride): jumps none too fluently and no sign of ability over hurdles. *J. B. Sayers.* —

DEBLINS' DOUBLE 7 b.g. Kinglet–Royal Russe (Bally Russe) [1989/90 20v 20gpu] smallish, rather sparely-made gelding: poor novice hurdler: stays 2½m: possibly unsuited by very soft ground. *J. Colston.* —

DEB'S BALL 4 b.f. Glenstal (USA)–De'b Old Fruit (Levmoss) [1989/90 16g2 16m 16g5 17f*] half-sister to winning hurdler King Retain (by Cut Above): lightly-raced maiden on Flat, placed over 7f: ridden by 7-lb claimer when winning 5-runner novice hurdle at Cartmel in May by 10 lengths from No More The Fool: acts well on firm going. *D. Moffatt.* 91

DECCAN PRINCE 6 b.g. Decoy Boy–Queen's Herald (King's Leap) [1989/90 16m] leggy, lengthy gelding: novice selling hurdler. *R. J. Hodges.* —

DECENT MAN 7 b.g. Derring Rose–Addies Lass (Little Buskins) [1989/90 20m5] well-made gelding: shows traces of stringhalt: winning hurdler: sweating and edgy, made numerous mistakes and eventually pulled up on chasing debut: stays 3m: acts on good to firm and dead ground. *P. Beaumont.* c— 90

Richard Green (Fine Paintings)'s "Decided"

DECIDED (CAN) 7 b.g. Affirmed (USA)–Expediency (USA) (Vaguely Noble) c**129** +
[1989/90 16g^2 16f^5 c17g* c16g* c16s^2 c16m^3] well-made gelding: useful hurdler: 135
short-headed by Aldino in Ring & Brymer Hurdle at Kempton in October: held up when winning novice chases at Newbury in December and Kempton (beat Another Coral 3 lengths) in January: raced with little zest when ½-length second of 3 finishers to Cashew King in Nottinghamshire Novices' Chase at Nottingham following month: has a good turn of foot and is likely to prove best at distances short of 2½m when conditions are testing: acts on soft going and seems unsuited by top-of-the-ground: broke blood vessel fourth start 1988/9. *Miss H. C. Knight.*

DECIDING BID 4 ch.c. Valiyar–Final Call (Town Crier) [1989/90 16f 16m^6
16f] placed over 6f at 2 yrs, but well beaten on Flat in 1989: sold out of A. Ingham's —
stable 2,400 gns Ascot July Sales: seems of little account as a hurdler: blinkered final start. *J. E. Long.*

DECRETO 9 ch.h. Touch Paper–Tacora (Cernobbio) [1989/90 20m a16g 16m c—
25g^{pu} 16g^{ur} c16g c16d^{ur}] angular horse: maiden plater on Flat: behind in novice —
hurdles and a novice chase: unlikely to stay 3m. *C. A. Horgan.*

DEE JAY PEE 4 ch.g. Electric–Lady Gaston (Pall Mall) [1989/90 16d^2 16d^4
a16g^3] workmanlike gelding: has scope: no worthwhile form on Flat: stayed on 97
when in frame in juvenile hurdles at Wincanton and Ludlow: ran moderately at Lingfield final start: will stay beyond 2m. *B. Preece.*

DEEMSTER WILLOW 4 b.f. Ballacashtal (CAN)–Sprightly Willow (Native
Bazaar) [1989/90 17d^{ur} 16m^3 16f^4 16f^3 16d^6 17d a20s^4 a18g^4 a18g* a20g^3 17m^F 69 §
16h^{pu}] angular, plain filly: well beaten on Flat: in frame in selling hurdles prior to winning 4-runner juvenile claimer at Lingfield in February: stays 2¼m: best form on a sound surface: blinkered third start, visored eighth (ran respectably both times): usually ridden by 3-lb claimer: ungenuine. *G. B. Balding.*

DEEP AND EVEN 10 ch.g. Deep Run–Drop Even (Even Money) [1989/90 c— x
c24d^F 24g^5 24g* 26m^{pu}] lengthy gelding: handicap hurdler: won at Uttoxeter in 102

May, making most: ran as though something was amiss final start: winning chaser (makes mistakes): stays 3¼m but doesn't need a test of stamina: acts on any going with possible exception of heavy: blinkered 3 times in 1987/8: somewhat faint-hearted. *C. P. E. Brooks.*

DEEP AUBURN 11 b.g. Deep Run–Auburn (Arctic Slave) [1989/90 c20mpu 24spu] tall, lengthy, plain gelding: novice hurdler/chaser: lightly raced and no form: makes mistakes over fences. *M. J. Wilkinson.* c— x —

DEEP CLIFF 8 ch.g. Deep Run–Woodcliffe (Harwell) [1989/90 c20g3 c24g3 c24dpu c24spu c25g2 c24gpu c24m* c24gpu] workmanlike gelding: winning point-to-pointer: below best when hard-ridden winner of maiden chase at Southwell in May: stays 25f: acts on dead ground. *J. J. O'Neill.* c90 —

DEEP COLONIST 8 ch.g. Deep Run–New Colonist (Colonist II) [1989/90 c20d* c20d2 c24spu] big, workmanlike gelding: made running when winning 3 novice hurdles in 1988/9: made highly encouraging chasing debut when winning Arlington Premier Series Chase qualifier at Worcester in November, jumping particularly well, leading 2 out and holding on, despite tiring and hanging left on run-in, to score by 2 lengths from Waterloo Boy: ran a lack-lustre race next outing and jumped badly on final start (February): stays 3m: acts on soft going: possibly suited by left-handed track: races quite freely: wore crossed noseband over hurdles. *J. T. Gifford.* c**120** —

DEEP CREEK 6 ch.m. Deep Run–Bramble Lane (Boreen (FR)) [1989/90 16m] behind in NH Flat race at Perth in 1988/9 and a novice hurdle at Newcastle in November. *A. H. Mactaggart.* —

DEEP CREVASSE 5 ch.m. Rolfe (USA)–Cala Conta (Deep Run) [1989/90 F13f F16f] third foal: half-sister to winning jumper Point Made (by Tycoon II): dam showed a modicum of ability over hurdles and fences: well beaten in NH Flat races: yet to race over hurdles or fences. *M. H. B. Robinson.*

DEEP DARK DAWN 5 ch.g. Deep Run–Swinging Sovereign (Swing Easy (USA)) [1989/90 F16m3 F16g 16g 16g6 16d5 16d 16f3 21f4] workmanlike gelding: first foal: dam won NH Flat race and placed over hurdles in Ireland: in frame in novice handicap hurdle at Towcester and novice event at Ludlow (weakened 2 out): may prove best at distances short of 21f: acts on firm ground: blinkered last 2 starts. *John R. Upson.* 80

DEEP DASH 9 b.g. Deep Run–Dancing Doe (Royal Buck) [1989/90 c25f5 c24mpu] sturdy, compact gelding: novice hurdler: won a point-to-point in April: tailed off in novice hunter chase at Towcester previous month. *E. F. Astley-Arlington.* c— —

DEEP FLASH 7 b.g. Deep Run–Sirrahdis (Bally Joy) [1989/90 c16f* c16m* c16gF c16gpu c16mur] winning hurdler/point-to-pointer: made all in novice chases at Windsor in November and Sandown following month: in second place, about 10 lengths behind wide-margin winner Young Snugfit, when falling last in quite valuable event at Kempton later in December: reluctant to race fourth outing: taken steadily to post next time (led until running wide turning into back straight): stays 2½m: acts on any going: broke blood vessel fourth start 1988/9: retained by trainer 10,500 gns Doncaster Spring Sales: not one to trust implicitly. *J. A. C. Edwards.* c**130** ? —

Henry VIII Novices' Chase, Sandown—Deep Flash beats Wink Gulliver

DEEP IMPRESSION 11 b.g. Deep Run–Harmonet (Monet) [1989/90 22d 22g c20dpu c20g3] close-coupled, smallish gelding who carries plenty of condition: handicap hurdler/chaser: finished badly lame final start: stays 2¾m, at least when conditions aren't testing: acts on heavy going and good to firm: usually jumps soundly. *M. Bradstock.* **c118** ? —

DEEP KASH 5 ch.g. Deep Run–Beatrix (Escart III) [1989/90 16g 16g] half-brother to several winning jumpers, including fair chaser Killegar Kim (by Lucifer): dam, from a good jumping family, placed several times over hurdles: behind in novice hurdles at Wolverhampton (showed signs of ability) and Kempton in February. *C. G. Roach.* —

DEEP LEGEND 5 b.g. Deep Run–Hansel's Trouble (Prince Hansel) [1989/90 F16d] sixth foal: half-brother to Garryduff Mover (by Rarity), a winner over hurdles and in NH Flat race in Ireland: dam won over 2m on Flat and over hurdles in Ireland: mid-division in NH Flat race at Kelso in February: yet to race over hurdles or fences. *W. A. Stephenson.*

DEEP N' DANGEROUS 4 b.f. Balinger–Deepness (Deep Run) [1989/90 17g3] fifth living foal: half-sister to winning hurdler Coire Vannich (by Celtic Cone): dam unraced: distant third of 6 finishers in juvenile hurdle at Newton Abbot in November. *C. T. Nash.* —

DEEP PROSPECT 11 b.g. Deep Run–Tudor Gello (Bargello) [1989/90 c20dF c26dpu c24d3 c26fpu] lengthy, robust gelding: winning point-to-pointer/hunter chaser: refused on chasing debut in 1986/7: pulled up after attempting to refuse second outing 1989/90: made mistakes next 2 outings: stays 3¼m: acts on firm going. *Mrs Gill E. Jones.* c— § —

DEEP RIDGE 12 b.g. Deep Run–Bright Record (Royal Record II) [1989/90 c16f2 c17f4] attractive gelding: poor chaser: best at around 2m: probably acts on any going: has won in blinkers (hasn't worn them for a long time): suitable mount for a claimer: inconsistent and has looked none too keen under pressure. *R. J. Hodges.* **c79** § —

DEEP SENSATION 5 ch.g. Deep Run–Bannow Bay (Arctic Slave) [1989/90 16d4 20f2 16g3 16d* 16m 16d5] 148

It can sometimes take a while to adapt to a change in the title of a race, especially if that title is the original one and the race has become firmly established in the racing calendar over many years. The Tote must have been aware of this when in 1987 they took over sponsorship of the valuable two-mile handicap hurdle run at Newbury in February. The race had been known as the Schweppes Gold Trophy since its inauguration in 1963, and for many the habit of referring to the Tote Gold Trophy as 'the Schweppes' proved difficult to break. If the sponsors thought that they were well on the way to laying the ghost of the old name when they promoted the race for the fourth time they were to be very much mistaken. The race was won by Deep Sensation who happened to be trained by Josh Gifford, and as the newspapers were quick to remind everyone, it was Gifford who'd ridden all four of the Ryan Price-trained winners of the Schweppes Gold Trophy. The combination had had much to do with putting the race on the map in its early days, especially through Hill House's controversial win in 1967 which gave the sponsors tremendous value for money. The Tote will get their money's worth, too, if they persevere, for this is a race which will always generate great interest, especially amongst the betting public. The latest running was no exception, with an ante-post market being formed as soon as the weights were published in January and the betting interest being sustained right up to the off. Deep Sensation, quoted as high as 20/1 when the weights came out, was sent off the 7/1 third favourite in the seventeen-runner field, having improved his prospects in the meantime by finishing a good third behind Atlaal in the Bic Razor Lanzarote Handicap at Kempton. Deep Sensation, who impressed with his jumping, was ridden to good advantage in the Tote Gold Trophy, cutting out the running with Imperial Brush in a race run at a modest gallop. The pair quickened the pace early in the straight, and going to the second last they'd shaken off all bar Joyful Noise. Joyful Noise joined issue between the last two, and he and Deep Sensation jumped the last upsides, just ahead of Imperial Brush who was unable to quicken further. Deep Sensation and Joyful Noise were locked together up

Tote Gold Trophy Handicap Hurdle, Newbury—
a good battle between Deep Sensation (left) and Joyful Noise

the run-in, and only a head separated them at the line, where they were four lengths clear of Imperial Brush. Deep Sensation carried 11-3 in the Tote Trophy, 7lb less than top-weight Royal Derbi. Although on the upgrade Deep Sensation needed to improve substantially if he were to figure prominently in the Waterford Crystal Champion Hurdle, his next race. In finishing ninth behind Kribensis, beaten around twenty-one lengths, Deep Sensation ran right up to his Newbury form; and he'd have finished closer but for being eased once his chance had gone. Deep Sensation also performed with credit on his final start, in the Scottish Champion Hurdle at Ayr. Moving smoothly into the lead two out, he was unable to quicken going to the last and finished ten lengths fifth behind Sayparee.

Deep Sensation (ch.g. 1985)	Deep Run (ch 1966)	Pampered King (b 1954)	Prince Chevalier
			Netherton Maid
		Trial By Fire (ch 1958)	Court Martial
			Mitrailleuse
	Bannow Bay (ch 1969)	Arctic Slave (b 1950)	Arctic Star
			Roman Galley
		Honeytown (ch 1954)	Fortina
			Sanvina

Deep Sensation cost 29,000 guineas at the Doncaster Sales in May, 1988, and is beginning to look quite a bargain at that price. He's already earned over £47,000 in two seasons' racing over hurdles, and he can be expected to leave that total well behind when he starts his chasing career in the next season. Deep Sensation's long-term future has always lain over fences. Not only does he look the part for the job—he's a rangy individual with plenty of scope—but he's bred for it, too. His dam, the fair hurdler/chaser Bannow Bay, is a sister to the fairly useful hurdler Ballyowen and to the very smart chaser The Benign Bishop; and she's a half-sister to the very useful chaser Chandigar. The second dam Honeytown, a useful hurdler and winning chaser, is a daughter of the Scottish Grand National winner Sanvina. Sanvina was ridden to victory in the 1950 Scottish National by Ken Oliver, who has enjoyed such great success with Sanvina's offspring, not only as a breeder but as an owner and trainer. No doubt Oliver will be regretting not having kept Deep Sensation, whom he bred. He did retain Bannow Bay's first foal and only other winner Bannow Burn (by New Brig). Bannow Burn, successful in a maiden event

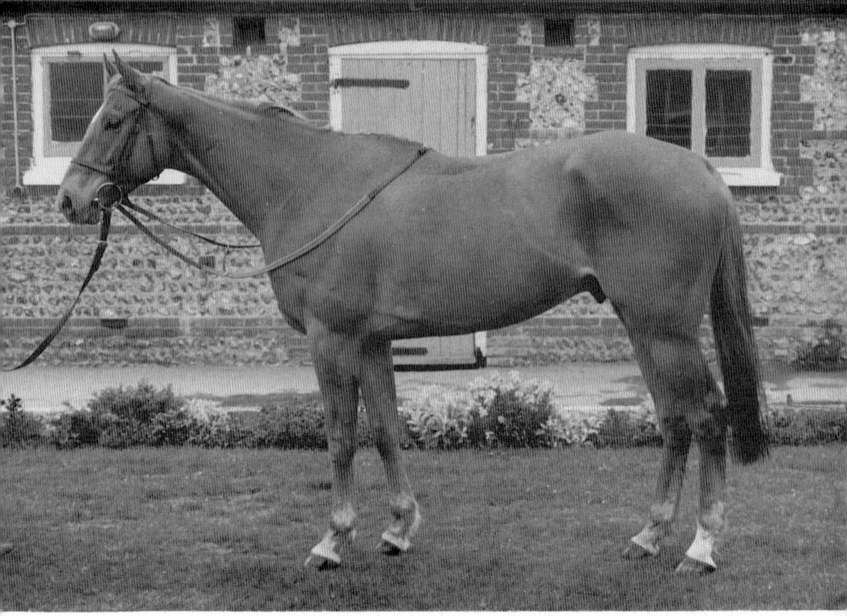

Mr R. F. Eliot's "Deep Sensation"

over hurdles, would have won a novice chase at Sedgefield but for being brought down approaching the last when holding a clear lead, sustaining injuries which led to her being put down. Bannow Bay herself died in 1987, shortly after producing a colt by Le Bavard. Deep Sensation, who acts on good to firm and dead ground, has done all his racing over two miles, apart from when finishing second to the impressive Morley Street over two and a half miles in the Mercury Communications Hurdle at Cheltenham. A strong-running type, lacking an instant turn of foot, Deep Sensation may well prove better suited by two and a half miles than two miles over fences. However, Deep Sensation will be capable of winning races over fences at either distance, and he's very much one to watch out for. *J. T. Gifford.*

DEEP SWELL 6 ch.g. Deep Run–Elsea Wood (Eborneezer) [1989/90 16gpu] tailed off in 2 NH Flat races in 1988/9: led until fifth, but weakened quickly and pulled up last in novice hurdle at Stratford in March. *B. Smart.* —

DEEP WATER BAY 6 b.g. Lochnager–Cateryne (Ballymoss) [1989/90 16dpu a16g3 16dF 16s 16g2 a16g5 16m* 16g*] close-coupled gelding: modest performer at best on Flat: attracted no bid after winning selling handicap hurdles at Fakenham in March and April: suited by sharp 2m: acts on good to firm ground: has worn net muzzle. *B. J. McMath.* 83

DEERCAL DANCER 4 ch.g. Ballacashtal (CAN)–Lookslike Reindeer (Bonne Noel) [1989/90 16g 16fpu] small, angular gelding: plater at up to 7f on Flat: behind in selling hurdle at Windsor in March: pulled up around halfway in similar event later in month: sold 875 gns Ascot April Sales. *R. Simpson.* —

DEER CREST 10 b.g. Deep Run–Skiporetta (Even Money) [1989/90 c21m2 c24f* c24g2] sturdy, short-legged gelding: winning hurdler: won a point-to-point in February and a novice hunter chase in March, holding off Gibraltar Girl by a neck in latter at Ascot: second to impressive winner Perroquet in hunter chase at c**99** —

Fakenham final start: stays 3m when conditions aren't testing: acts on any going: suited by forcing tactics: often sweats. *Capt. W. H. Bulwer-Long.*

DEERHURST 5 b.g. Swing Easy (USA)–Bonzolena (Air Trooper) [1989/90 F16g] first foal: dam of little account on Flat: tailed off in NH Flat race at Warwick in December: yet to race over hurdles or fences. *Mrs H. Parrott.*

DEERNESS SPOOK 7 ro.g. Grey Ghost–Part Rum (Parthian Star) [1989/90 16g[5] 16f[5] 20s a20g[5] a16g[ur] c16g[6] c17d[pu]] lengthy, plain gelding: poor novice hurdler: beaten long way but showed ability when sixth in novice event at Wincanton on chasing debut: likely to prove best at 2m at present: possibly unsuited by heavy ground: visored fifth start. *T. Thomson Jones.* c78 78

DEFIANTLY 5 b.m. Bold Lad (IRE)–Corona Bay (Targowice (USA)) [1989/90 F16g] second foal: half-sister to a poor Flat maiden by Godswalk: dam, winner over 2m in Ireland, half-sister to several winners, notably smart staying hurdler Ravaro: never dangerous when in mid-division in NH Flat race at Catterick in March: yet to race over hurdles or fences. *G. M. Moore.*

DEHAR BOY 4 b.g. Buzzards Bay–Nahawand (High Top) [1989/90 16g 16g[4]] compact gelding: plating-class maiden on Flat, stays 1¼m: jumped none too fluently when 17¾ lengths fourth behind Royal Wonder in novice claiming hurdle at Nottingham in October. *P. J. Feilden.* 71

DEIRDRES DREAM 6 b. or br.m. The Parson–Deirdre's Joy (Cadmus II) [1989/90 22d 25d[pu]] strong mare: half-sister to useful chaser Aughavogue (by Golden Love): remote seventh to Trefelyn Cone in 21-runner mares novice hurdle at Wincanton in February. *K. C. Bailey.* —

DELIUS 12 ch.g. The Parson–More Melody (Menelek) [1989/90 c24g[2] c25m[5]] tall, rather leggy, close-coupled gelding: high-class chaser at his best: has been difficult to train over the years: looked as though he'd be better for race when 8 lengths second to Desert Orchid in Racing Post Chase (Handicap) at Kempton in February: showed up well until 2 out but finished lame when remote last of 5 to Toby Tobias in Martell Cup Chase at Liverpool in April: stays 25f: acts on soft going (behind when pulled up on heavy): usually a fine jumper. *R. Lee.* c**152** —

DELPIOMBO 4 br.g. Lochnager–Precious Petra (Bing II) [1989/90 16m 16g 16g 16s 16v[4] 16d[4]] good-quartered gelding: fourth foal: half-brother to winning hurdler Whoknowsthebowler (by Cawston's Clown): dam winning plater on Flat and over hurdles: first sign of merit when 15½ lengths fourth behind Nearctic Bay in novice handicap hurdle at Wetherby in February on final start. *R. D. E. Woodhouse.* 79

DELTIC (USA) 4 b.c. Far North (CAN)–Moon Delta (USA) (Delta Judge) [1989/90 16f* 16f* 16f[3] 17f* 17h*] leggy, sparely-made ex-French colt: sixth foal: half-brother to 3 winners in USA, including Moon Star Miss (by Star Envoy), a minor stakes winner at up to 7f: dam placed once from 3 starts in USA: successful 3 times at up to 1½m on Flat in 1989 (claimed out of G. Collet's stable 168,820 francs (approx £17,104) in November): fair front-running juvenile hurdler who won 4 of his 5 starts, namely novice event at Wolverhampton, juvenile event at Ludlow, 2-runner handicap at Newton Abbot and another juvenile event at Devon & Exeter: jumped deliberately when soundly beaten, facing stiffer task, on his other outing: acts on hard ground: sold 7,800 gns Ascot June Sales. *M. C. Pipe.* 110

DEMI CHEVAL 12 ch.g. Menelek–Miss Hilliary (Hill Clown (USA)) [1989/90 c27f[3]] workmanlike gelding: modest point-to-pointer and maiden hunter chaser: blinkered only outing 1987/8. *R. A. May.* c— —

DEMI JOHN 8 br.g. Alias Smith (USA)–Indian Wells (Reliance II) [1989/90 16g 25g[4] 24f[3] 24g[pu] 25f 24f] lengthy gelding: modest handicap hurdler: made numerous mistakes when third in novice chase in 1988/9: suited by 2½m or more: acts on heavy going: blinkered once in 1987/8, visored tenth outing 1988/9 and last 2 starts. *P. Howling.* c— 104

DEMOCRATIC BOY 8 b.g. Free State–Klaire (Klairon) [1989/90 c20g[pu] c24g[pu] 22d[pu] c16f[3] c20f[5] c25m[ur]] close-coupled, workmanlike gelding: handicap chaser: in clear lead when saddle slipped and rider unseated on bend approaching last at Hereford in May: stays 3m: suited by a sound surface: unreliable. *J. S. King.* c88 § — §

DEMOKOS (FR) 5 ch.g. Dom Racine (FR)–Eagletown (FR) (Dictus (FR)) [1989/90 16f*] leggy, sparely-made gelding: jumped soundly when landing the odds by 2 lengths from Tajroba in conditional jockeys novice hurdle at Southwell in October: subsequently won 4 times at up to 1¾m on Flat: will stay beyond 2m: should improve. *J. G. FitzGerald.* 93 p

DENBERDAR 7 b.g. Julio Mariner–Penumbra (Wolver Hollow) [1989/90 17f* 18f4 17f*] leggy, lightly-made gelding: won handicap hurdles at Newton Abbot in July and August (ridden by 7-lb claimer): best at 2m: acts on firm ground. *A. P. James.* 99

DENBOY 8 ch.g. On Your Mark–Petal (Whistler) [1989/90 16m 16m 16d 16g2 16g] strong, compact gelding: novice selling hurdler: dead. *B. Stevens.* 79

DENITZ (FR) 8 ch.g. Sharpman–Djerba (My Swallow) [1989/90 a16g5 16d] compact, good-bodied gelding: no worthwhile form over hurdles or fences: placed 4 times on all-weather on Flat early in 1990. *C. Holmes.* c— —

DENNING (USA) 8 b. or br.h. Advocator–Sunbeam Sal (USA) (On-And-On) [1989/90 17f6] won twice over middle-distances in French Provinces as a 3-y-o, when trained by M. Zilber: led to fifth when 23 lengths sixth behind Pomatum in novice event at Newton Abbot in August on hurdling debut. *Mrs J. Wonnacott.* —

DENROSS 9 b.g. Pauper–Teryak (Red God) [1989/90 c17mF c16hur 16d c16m c16spu c16g5 c20dpu a20g3] smallish, workmanlike gelding: selling hurdler/novice chaser: let down by his jumping over fences and ran poorly when returned to hurdling: below his best over 2½m: probably acts on any going: has worn a crossed noseband: retained by trainer 1,050 gns Ascot November Sales. *J. P. D. Elliott.* c— x —

DEN'S SONG 4 ch.g. Sallust–Princess Ru (Princely Gift) [1989/90 a16g6] half-brother to several winners, including hurdler Double Rum: dam, maiden, half-sister to a winning jumper: modest 7f winner on Flat: 13 lengths sixth of 12 to Cone Lane in juvenile hurdle at Lingfield in December. *W. Carter.* 64

DEPLETE 7 b.g. Deep Run–Elite Lady (Prince Hansel) [1989/90 16g2 16s 22d4 16g3 16g5] good-bodied, workmanlike gelding: type to make a chaser: handicap hurdler: placed at Haydock in November and Wetherby in January: found nothing final start: takes good hold and probably doesn't stay 2¾m: yet to race on a firm surface. *J. W. Blundell.* 94

DE PLUVINEL 17 b.g. Arrigle Valley–dam's pedigree unknown [1989/90 c26g4 c25m2 c25f* c25m] grand old performer: third success in race when winning Royal Artillery Gold Cup at Sandown in March, leading 3 out and running on gamely to beat Roscoe Harvey 3 lengths: reportedly finished lame next start: stays 3¼m: acts on any going: good mount for an amateur. *G. R. Prest.* c**102**

DE PROFUNDIS 6 ch.g. Deep Run–Men's Fun (Menelek) [1989/90 F16g 20v 16s] strong, sturdy gelding: third in NH Flat race in 1988/9: bought out of M. Bradstock's stable 27,000 gns Doncaster August Sales: well beaten in 2 novice hurdles in January. *P. G. Bailey.* —

DEPUTY GOVERNOR 7 b.h. Tower Walk–Come On Girl (Sheshoon) [1989/90 20g6] half-brother to winning selling hurdler Town Special (by Town Crier): poor maiden on Flat: distant sixth of 7 finishers in novice hurdle at Wolverhampton in November. *D. J. Bell.* —

Royal Artillery Gold Cup Chase, Sandown—seventeen-year-old De Pluvinel wins the race for the third time

DERBY DAY 9 b.g. Shirley Heights–L'Anguissola (Soderini) [1989/90 21f^{6} 20s 27s^{pu} 24g a20g^{3}] sparely-made gelding: handicap hurdler: first form since 1986/7 when 8 lengths third behind Bahrain Bridge at Lingfield in February: stays 2½m: acts on firm going: blinkered once in 1984/5 and last 3 starts. *Miss J. A. Blakeney.* 86

DERCANDER 8 br.g. Derek H–Canny's Tudor (Tudor Cliff) [1989/90 c24d^{3} c26s^{4} c26g* c30v^{2} c29d c28g^{F}] tall, leggy gelding: fair chaser: won at Folkestone in December: stayed very well: acted on heavy going: dead. *Lady Herries.* c**115**

DEREKS DAUGHTER 10 bl.m. Derek H–Maunby Princess (Painters Boy) [1989/90 c20f^{3} c24m^{3} c24f^{4}] sparely-made mare: third in handicap chases at Uttoxeter and Perth (better effort) in August: tailed off following month and not seen out again: stays 3m, at least when conditions aren't testing: acts on firm ground: suitable mount for a claimer. *R. Tate.* c82

DERRYMORE BOY 8 br.g. Bonne Noel–Sweet Melody (Alcide) [1989/90 c21s^{F} c22m* c16s^{F} c19d c18s^{5} c18v* c16s^{3} c22g^{4}] Irish gelding: very useful hurdler: won novice chase at Fairyhouse in December and Diners Club 40th Anniversary Chase at Punchestown in February, latter by a neck from Blitzkreig: stays 2¾m: ideally suited by plenty of give in the ground. *P. Mullins, Ireland.* c**133** —

DERRY RHYTHM 5 b. or br.g. Derrylin–French Music (French Beige) [1989/90 16g 20m^{5} 16m 16s^{2}] neat gelding: poor handicapper on Flat, stays 1¼m: best effort over hurdles when 6 lengths second to Mottram's Gold in seller at Towcester in February: likely to be suited by a return to further than 2m. *P. Burgoyne.* 76

DERWENT MIST 4 b.f. Majestic Streak–Minimist (Bilsborrow) [1989/90 F16g] third foal: dam modest staying hurdler: tailed off in NH Flat race at Kelso in March: yet to race over hurdles. *D. W. MacDonald.*

DESERT DANCER 4 ch.g. Enchantment–Crimson Queen (Crimson Beau) [1989/90 16f^{pu}] well beaten on Flat: blinkered, behind when pulled up last in juvenile selling hurdle at Southwell in August. *J. J. O'Neill.* —

DESERT ORCHID 11 gr.g. Grey Mirage–Flower Child (Brother) [1989/90 c25m* c16m^{2} c24g* c21d* c24g* c26f^{3} c28m*] c**187** —

'Uneasy lies the head that wears a crown.' Desert Orchid added further in the latest season to his glittering list of achievements, winning the King George VI Rank Chase for a record-equalling third time and crowning a fine campaign with a twelve-length victory, conceding lumps of weight all round, in the Jameson Irish Grand National. In between he produced another top-notch display in the Racing Post Chase at Kempton where his breathtaking victory under 12-3 (conceding between 28 lb and 34 lb to his seven rivals) was, by our reckoning, the best performance for many a season in a steeplechase, over any distance. Desert Orchid's tally made his fourth successive National Hunt Horse Of The Year award a foregone conclusion. To win the Horse Of The Year award three times is a rarity—only triple Champion Hurdle winner Persian War achieved the feat before Desert Orchid—and to win four times was without precedent. But the voting for the award—decided by an end-of-season poll of a selected Press panel—was surprising, to say the least, and seemed to indicate that, in the eyes of some, Desert Orchid's magnetism is becoming less powerful. On each of the first three occasions Desert Orchid gained a majority of the votes, receiving sixteen out of twenty-six in 1986/7 (the year See You Then won his third Champion Hurdle), twenty-one out of twenty-five in 1987/8, and all twenty-eight in 1988/9. In the latest season, however, Desert Orchid won with only twelve out of twenty-seven votes. Six of the panel voted for Mr Frisk, four for Kribensis, three for Norton's Coin and two for Barnbrook Again. Notwithstanding the strong claims of these horses, especially Mr Frisk, whose Grand National and Whitbread victories provided some of the most memorable images of the racing season, Desert Orchid's testimonial surely spoke for itself. He is the best National Hunt horse for a long time, in our view the best since the heyday of Arkle and his brilliant contemporaries Flyingbolt and Mill House in the 'sixties: and his exploits have captured the imagination of the general public more than any other since Arkle, with the possible exception of Red Rum. Desert Orchid is racing's most resounding name and, as we have said before, he is a symbol of so much that is good about National Hunt racing and provides a magnificent image for the game.

He's tough, versatile, courageous and durable and a joy to watch, his supremely quick and accurate jumping making him a splendid sight out in front in full flow. Could any sport want a more accomplished standard-bearer?

Desert Orchid's defeat in the Tote Cheltenham Gold Cup, a defeat which many considered unthinkable beforehand, almost certainly influenced the voting. No serious challenge to Desert Orchid's supremacy among the staying chasers had emerged by Cheltenham-time, and conditions were considered likely to be more in his favour than the previous year when Desert Orchid had struggled home from Yahoo in conditions of extreme meteorological misery. The fine weather and the prospect of Desert Orchid's becoming only the sixth horse to win the Gold Cup more than once—following Golden Miller (five wins), Arkle and Cottage Rake (three each) and Easter Hero and L'Escargot (dual winners)—drew a crowd of 56,884, thought to be the biggest assembled at Cheltenham. Expectations were high, but, starting at odds on in a field of twelve, Desert Orchid ran about a stone and a half below his best—and, by our reckoning, about 7 lb below his winning performance of the previous year. The 100/1-shot Norton's Coin, an ex-point-to-pointer from a 'one-horse stable', provided the biggest shock in Gold Cup history, holding off Toby Tobias by three quarters of a length to win in record time for the race with Desert Orchid, whose chance had gone before the last, four lengths further back. For whatever reason, Desert Orchid's running was too bad—by his own very high standards—to be true. There's no doubt, however, that his defeat in what is regarded as steeplechasing's blue riband event diminished his worth in the eyes of both the general public and of some in racing. Some days, though, are best forgotten. Why dwell on one particular defeat when there are some splendid victories to recall?

As in previous years, Desert Orchid was trained in the first part of the season for a crack at the King George VI Rank Chase at Kempton on Boxing

Silver Buck Chase, Wincanton—Desert Orchid makes his reappearance

King George VI Rank Chase, Kempton—a third King George; Barnbrook Again holds on to second place

Day. He won the race in 1986, was surprisingly beaten by the French challenger Nupsala in 1987, and resumed winning ways in 1988, leaving him one short of equalling Wayward Lad's three victories. Desert Orchid's preparation in the latest season followed a familiar pattern, though he was held up in his work for some time because of the prevailing firm ground. He reappeared in a minor event at Wincanton—cantering over a single opponent in the Silver Buck Chase in November—and then, for the third year in a row, reverted to two miles in the Tingle Creek Handicap ('a good, tough little race, once round Sandown, and an ideal prep-race for the King George', according to his trainer). The Gold Cup and the Tingle Creek Handicap were the only races Desert Orchid lost during the season. Each of Desert Orchid's three opponents at Sandown was officially rated further below him than the 28-lb weight range for the race and Desert Orchid's two-and-a-half-length defeat by Long Engagement (who beat him in the same race on similar terms in 1987) raised doubts in some quarters about whether the horse might be on the decline. However, trainer Elsworth said in a *Timeform Interview* that Desert Orchid (who had had two races before the Tingle Creek the previous year) was 'short of a race' which almost certainly explains why Dunwoody set no more than a moderate gallop over a trip that isn't ideal for Desert Orchid nowadays (Long Engagement quickened the better from the last after stalking Desert Orchid all the way). 'We really got stuck into Desert Orchid between the Tingle Creek and the King George', Elsworth told us. 'We had to be more severe with his preparation than one likes to be but he took it well.' Desert Orchid faced five opponents at Kempton and, starting at 6/4 on, led throughout to win virtually unchallenged by eight lengths from his stable-companion Barnbrook Again, who was attempting three miles for the first time; Yahoo came seven lengths further back in third, ahead of Bob Tisdall, the second-favourite Pegwell Bay and Norton's Coin (33/1, beaten thirty-nine lengths by the winner). The early gallop was fairly slow and Desert Orchid's jumping wasn't so fluent as usual but, after making a bad mistake at the ditch after the water second time round, his jumping began to improve and he kept up a tremendous gallop all the way up the straight after his rider had gradually increased the tempo from about a mile out. Desert Orchid took the last three fences in typically dashing style, and came home with tremendous gusto to a rousing reception. His trainer incidentally was the first since Cazalet in 1956 to saddle first and second in the King George in the same season.

Desert Orchid's popularity was as great as ever—he was voted National Hunt 'Horse of the Eighties' by readers of the *Racing Post* at Christmas (polling twice as many votes as his nearest rival Dawn Run)—but his followers had to wait for over six weeks before he was seen out again. Desert Orchid was side-lined by coughing, as were a good number of his stable-mates at around this time, but news in January that Desert Orchid was to be entered for the Seagram Grand National became one of the main topics on the racing pages in the face of a public outcry which must have been unprecedented in advance of a race. A protracted debate ensued about whether the horse should or should not be 'risked' at Aintree. Four of the popular daily papers conducted polls of their readers, all of which were overwhelmingly in the negative. The *Daily Mail* poll, for example, brought in 9,000 votes against and only 48 for. One of Desert Orchid's owners had said at the start of the season that he would never dare to enter Desert Orchid because 'every time the National is mentioned we get a stack of hate-mail'. Desert Orchid was allotted 12-2 in the original handicap, 3 lb less than Burrough Hill Lad had been given in the race in 1985 (these are the only two horses since Mill House—a non-runner with 12-3 in 1965—to be given more than 12-0 in a National). As with Burrough Hill Lad, the handicapper assessed Desert Orchid more favourably—to the tune of 6 lb to be precise—than he would have done at the time for a handicap on a park course, which displeased some of the connections of other leading Grand National candidates. Not to put too fine a point on it, the handicapper leant over backwards to attract Desert Orchid to Aintree. But the strength of the concern of a section of the public—no-one suggested conducting opinion polls when the charismatic Red Rum was appearing year after year in the National—proved too much. Desert Orchid was withdrawn at the first forfeit stage in mid-February. His trainer took the opportunity in his *Timeform Interview* to clear the air:

> 'As everyone knows, this year's Grand National was a possibility at one time. I discussed it with Richard Burridge and he agreed that we should enter him and see what weight he got. I went on record as saying I thought he'd get 12-2—I said that was as much as we'd want him to get to consider running him. I didn't feel the handicapper could justifiably give him less than 12-2, and lo and behold that's what he got. Now I never said he was going to run because he got 12-2. My interpretation of the conversation with Richard Burridge was that if Desert Orchid got 12-2 we would see how things were after Cheltenham. I certainly thought we ought to consider the National because, for all that it's a marvellous race, a great feature and a great spectacle, it's not always that good a race class-wise, and most years—in theory at least—it's probably not as difficult to win as the Whitbread. And I thought it would be great for the horse if he could win it. I wouldn't run him at Aintree for fun and obviously I thought he had the credentials to win. But I think all the pressure from everybody—should he run or shouldn't he—finally got to Richard and his father. So we withdrew him at the first forfeit. If it was going to cause that much concern and anxiety to the owners, it didn't seem fair to prolong the agony. You can see the point of view of Richard and his father. They are in the game for fun but, of course, owning a good horse brings its pressures and problems. It's a once-in-a-lifetime experience having a horse like Desert Orchid, and it must be very difficult to cope with things logically sometimes. It's difficult enough for me to cope with it—I have never trained a horse like this before—and I can understand any owner reacting to the sort of

pressure that was put on Richard. I suppose you might say why the hell didn't we all work that out beforehand and avoid all the controversy. Well, it's like saying you're going to jump off the top diving board at the swimming pool, and when you actually get up there and look down you realise you're not so sure. Obviously with hindsight, if I'd known the way things were going to turn out, I wouldn't even have entered Desert Orchid for Aintree.'

There's reportedly some prospect of Desert Orchid's contesting the Grand National in the next season and, given similarly favourable treatment from the handicapper, he'd surely start a firm favourite. Public opinion might be brought to bear once again but we hope Desert Orchid's owners will take their decision on the merits of the case and not be influenced by a section of the general public's perception of the dangers of Aintree. There probably isn't a tougher race anywhere than the National, and there's no denying that the risks are almost certainly greater than in any other race, but it is only a matter of degree. Risks are inseparable from steeplechasing, at Aintree or anywhere else, and, in our view, the severity of the National isn't a good enough reason in itself to avoid the race. No-one knows Desert Orchid better than his trainer and those who work with him at Whitsbury. We share the view that Desert Orchid has sound credentials for the National and it would be regrettable if the sport was denied what could be one of its greatest sights, because of a fear of exposing such a popular horse to dangers which are, for an experienced and accomplished campaigner like Desert Orchid, in all probability not very much greater than those which he faces every time he sets foot on a racecourse.

An announcement about Desert Orchid's intended defection from the Grand National field was made the day he returned to action with a bloodless victory in a minor race, the Racing In Wessex Chase, at Wincanton in February. It was Desert Orchid's third trip to the races in six days. It had been intended that he would reappear in the Agfa Diamond Chase (formerly the Gainsborough) at Sandown,which was lost to the weather, and he had been withdrawn from the Charterhouse Mercantile Handicap at Ascot the

Racing In Wessex Chase, Wincanton—
Mzima Spring makes a brave attempt to hang on

Racing Post Chase (Handicap), Kempton—an exceptional performance even by Desert Orchid's standards

day before Wincanton when the going became heavy after overnight rain. Desert Orchid had little more than an exercise gallop at Wincanton—he won by twenty lengths from Bartres—but he faced a stern test in the Racing Post Chase at Kempton a little over a fortnight later. Only three of the eight runners—Desert Orchid (12-3), Delius (10-3) and Ballyhane (10-1)—were in the handicap proper, but Desert Orchid's weight included a 3-lb penalty for winning at Wincanton and he had a stiffer task on the form-book than was generally appreciated (he started odds on). Desert Orchid produced a performance to savour, taking command before the home turn after leading or disputing the lead from the start and running on strongly—putting in a blemish-free round of jumping highlighted by a brilliant leap at the second last—to win by eight lengths and the same from Delius and Seagram, with the rest strung out. Desert Orchid was cheered up the home straight and received another thoroughly-deserved ovation after crossing the line. The way we read the form-book, Desert Orchid gave an outstanding performance, his finest to date (represented by his rating of 187); puzzlingly, the official handicapper rated Desert Orchid 182 and Seagram 140 after their performances here, which underestimated Desert Orchid's merit, as it allowed Seagram only 11 lb for the sixteen lengths by which he was beaten (we allowed him the full 16 lb) and raised Desert Orchid only to the mark—including a 3-lb penalty—that he ran off at Kempton. Still more puzzling was the fact that when Seagram went on to run very well for the remainder of the season (earning an official rating of 145) the handicapper chose not to remedy the situation. What price would Desert Orchid have been if he had carried top weight off this mark against the same or similar opposition in his next race?

Desert Orchid's only appearance in a handicap after the Racing Post Chase was under 12-0 in the Jameson Irish Grand National at Fairyhouse on Easter Monday when he gained another memorable victory, conceding between 26 lb and 28 lb to thirteen rivals after the late withdrawals of Carvill's Hill (11-4 in the original handicap) and Yahoo (10-6). Desert Orchid showed no ill-effects from his hard battle with Norton's Coin and Toby Tobias at Cheltenham, outclassing the opposition to win going away by a dozen lengths after surviving a bad last-fence blunder. Barney Burnett outstayed Have A Barney, Cloney Grange, Riska's River and The Committee to take second but never looked like posing a threat to Desert Orchid whose fluent jumping allowed his rider Dunwoody—whose partnership with Desert Orchid strengthened as the season went on—to control the race almost throughout; the second favourite Bold Flyer was allowed the lead on sufferance at various stages but once Desert Orchid was sent into a clear lead approaching the second last the race was over, or rather that for first place was, barring accidents. Desert Orchid was only the third British-trained winner of the Irish National, following Don Sancho in 1928 and Rhyme 'N' Reason in 1985 (trained at the time by Murray-Smith, and subsequently transferred to Desert Orchid's trainer for whom he won the Grand National).

The Irish Grand National, which incidentally sets nowhere near so severe a test as its counterpart at Aintree, brought Desert Orchid's record earnings for a British- or Irish-based jumper to £476,739. He has now won thirty-two of his sixty-two races, his victories coming on eight different courses including Ascot and Sandown, on both of which he has won eight times, and Kempton and Wincanton, on both of which he has gained six victories. Desert Orchid's record at Cheltenham isn't so outstanding. His victory in the Gold Cup—on form an around-average Gold Cup winning performance—is the only one he has gained in seven successive appearances at the Festival meeting where his record also includes two poor runs in the Champion Hurdle, a third in the Arkle Challenge Trophy and two placings in the Queen Mother Champion Chase. There's no doubt that Desert Orchid isn't so effective at Cheltenham as he is on some of the other major courses, though it's hard to say for certain why this should be. Cheltenham is left-handed and Desert Orchid's most outstanding performances—judged strictly on the form-book—have been put up going the other way. But it's going too far to say of a horse that has won a Gold Cup (he's also won at left-handed Liverpool) that he is unsuited by a left-handed course. Desert Orchid's superb jumping technique and his excellent stamina are tailor-made for Cheltenham's stiff fences and track; his jumping

Jameson Irish Grand National, Fairyhouse—that last-fence mistake

Mr R. Burridge's "Desert Orchid"

stood him in good stead when he won his Gold Cup—he outjumped his rivals—and his stamina and gameness were illustrated by his tremendous rally that day at the end of a race which had a shattering effect on some of his opponents (there were only four finishers). Desert Orchid's trainer believes that the firm going may have contributed to the horse's performance in the latest Gold Cup. 'We know Dessie can go on it but his superior jumping wasn't such a great advantage this year, with all his rivals jumping well on the faster ground', said Elsworth. Perhaps there's something in the theory, though such explanations offered for disappointing performances are always a matter for conjecture. It's worth pointing out that ground conditions were similar for the Irish National. Report has it that Desert Orchid may be aimed at the Queen Mother Champion Chase at the next Festival, rather than at the Gold Cup. If so, he'll have to be ridden more enterprisingly than he was in the latest Tingle Creek Chase; he is vulnerable at two miles nowadays unless there's an end-to-end gallop. Desert Orchid stays extremely well and has good prospects of getting the Grand National distance.

The sturdy Desert Orchid, who sometimes sweats up, was turned out in superb condition for his races in the latest season, a credit to his trainer. As we have said, Desert Orchid has a long suit in stamina, something that couldn't have been predicted in his early days from a study of his pedigree (which has been thoroughly examined in earlier Annuals). Desert Orchid's sire Grey Mirage never won beyond seven furlongs and most of his best offspring over jumps have shown their best form at up to two and a half

		Double-U-Jay (ch 1963)	Major Portion
	Grey Mirage (gr 1969)		Renounce
		Fair Inez (gr 1958)	Prince Chevalier
Desert Orchid (gr.g. 1979)			Floria Tosca
		Brother (br 1959)	Nearula
	Flower Child (br 1967)		Aunt Agnes
		Grey Orchid (gr 1952)	No Orchids
			Harbour Lights

miles; Desert Orchid's dam the poor winning chaser Flower Child, by the sprinter Brother, gained her only victories at two miles and two and a half. Flower Child has bred two other winners, the fair hurdler and winning chaser Ragged Robin (by Baragoi) who stayed two and a half miles, and the six-year-old mare Peacework (by Workboy) who was successful in a two-mile novice handicap chase at Southwell in April. Desert Orchid's main target in the first part of the season will again be the King George VI Rank Chase. If Desert Orchid wins the King George he'll set a record of four victories in the race which may never be beaten; if he also goes on to win the Grand National he may well achieve the eminence of an Incitatus, the horse whom the Roman Emperor Caligula made a senator! *D. R. C. Elsworth.*

DESERT PALM 5 b.m. Palm Track–Diascia (Dike (USA)) [1989/90 16m*
22m^{pu} 16f^{3} 16m^{6} 17d^{5} 16d^{5} 17m^{5} 17m* 16m^{2} 20f^{2}] angular mare: won novice 83
handicap hurdle at Taunton in November and novice seller at Newton Abbot (very
easily, no bid) in May: best at 2m: acts on firm going and is unsuited by dead:
blinkered last start 1988/9. *R. J. Hodges.*

DESIGN WISE 6 b.g. Prince Bee–Wollow Princess (Wollow) [1989/90 20f^{pu}]
small gelding: 20-length winner of 2 selling hurdles in 1987/8 when trained by N. —
Tinkler: tailed off when pulled up in non-seller in April: suited by sharp 2m: acts
on hard ground. *M. T. Bowker.*

DETAILS GALORE 9 ch.h. Octavo (USA)–Barefoot Contessa (Homeric) c—
[1989/90 c16g^{pu}] sturdy horse: poor hurdler: has failed to complete course over —
fences. *W. John Smith.*

DEVASTATION 6 br.g. Strong Gale–Lady Beg (Continuation) [1989/90 22g
16f^{5} 16f^{4}] medium-sized, sparely-made ex-Irish gelding: fifth foal: half-brother to 84
winning point-to-pointer Pitbeg (by Pitpan): dam unraced: unplaced in NH Flat
races in Ireland: showed ability in novice hurdles, on last start 22 lengths fourth
behind Kharif in conditional jockeys event at Cheltenham in April, leading briefly
2 out. *D. R. C. Elsworth.*

DEVILS ELBOW 6 ch.g. Remezzo–Spartan's Legacy (Spartan General) c—
[1989/90 16m* 21d c17d^{F} c20d^{F} c16d 22f^{4} 16m^{3} 16f^{F}] leggy gelding: claimer 91
ridden, won novice handicap hurdle at Warwick in November: no sign of ability in
novice chases: takes good hold (wears crossed noseband) and suited by sharp 2m:
acts on good to firm going and soft. *N. A. Gaselee.*

DEVIL'S VALLEY 7 ch.g. Lucifer (USA)–Barrowvale (Valerullah) [1989/90
22m^{2} 20s* 20v^{2} 21d* 20f^{6}] rangy gelding: won novice hurdles at Huntingdon in 125
December and Newbury (beat Duntree comfortably by 2½ lengths in February:
blinkered, around 19 lengths sixth to Regal Ambition in Sun Alliance Novices'
Hurdle at Cheltenham, travelling well and looking main danger going to 2 out but
finding little under pressure: worth another try over 2m: acts on any going: tends
to hang and may prove suited by waiting tactics. *Mrs J. Pitman.*

DEVON ZIPPER 5 b.g. Brianston Zipper–Salmon Spirit (Big Deal) [1989/90
17h^{2} 17h^{6}] second foal: dam unraced half-sister to 2 winning point-to-pointers: 84 ?
second in 3-runner novice hurdle at Devon & Exeter in May: well beaten on same
course later in month: claimer ridden. *W. G. Turner.*

DEWSPRY BOY 10 b.g. Pry–Dewstone (Double-U-Jay) [1989/90 c19f^{3}] c**78** x
strong, rangy gelding: winning point-to-pointer: novice hurdler/steeplechaser: —
makes mistakes, often pulls hard and is a weak finisher: tired badly in closing
stages when third in novice hunter chase at Hereford in April: best at 2m: tends to
sweat up. *William R. Gaskins.*

DEXTEROUS LADY 4 b.f. Vital Season–Skilla (Mexico III) [1989/90 F16g]
half-sister to 2 minor winners on Flat: dam won over 11f: blinkered, mid-division
in NH Flat race at Kempton in February: yet to race over hurdles. *C. James.*

DIADEM DANCER 4 b.g. Solford (USA)–Pure Music (FR) (Pure Flight (USA)) [1989/90 16f3 18f2] winning plater on Flat: staying on at finish of early-season juvenile hurdles at Plumpton and Fontwell (claimer): will be suited by stiffer test of stamina. *J. E. Long.* 72

DIAMOND BOY 4 b.g. Sparkling Boy–Haddon Anna (Dragonara Palace (USA)) [1989/90 16dpu 16dpu 16f] of little account. *Miss A. L. M. King.* —

DIAMOND DIGGER 8 ch.g. Lepanto (GER)–Priceless Gem (Roi Soleil) [1989/90 c16d3 c16m6] good-bodied gelding: fair chaser: bit backward, creditable third of 4 finishers at Worcester in November: ran moderately soon afterwards and not seen out again: races only at around 2m: acts on firm and dead going: sold to B. Preece 12,200 gns Ascot July Sales. *R. J. Hodges.* c**123** —

DIAMONDING (USA) 4 b.c. Diamond Shoal–Gwynn (USA) (Native Dancer) [1989/90 16d 16g a16g5 16g2 24f 16f6 16gur 16m3 16m] smallish, good-quartered ex-French colt: half-brother to several winners in USA: dam ran twice: maiden on Flat: poor novice selling hurdler: blinkered third start: sold out of C. Elsey's stable 1,750 gns Ascot February Sales after then: resold 3,000 gns Doncaster June Sales. *N. Tinkler.* 64

DIAMOND PRINCESS 4 ch.f. Horage–Finesse (Miralgo) [1989/90 16s3] half-sister to winning jumpers Zarzaitine (by Murrayfield) and Ghosting (by Take A Reef): modest 1½m winner on Flat: made a couple of mistakes, including one at the last, when 17 lengths third behind The Widget Man in juvenile hurdle at Folkestone in December: looked likely to improve but wasn't seen out again. *P. F. I. Cole.* 81

DIAMONDS HIGH 9 ch.g. Diamonds Are Trump (USA)–Easy Path (Swing Easy (USA)) [1989/90 24m4 25fF] close-coupled gelding: winning hurdler: fell fatally at Cheltenham in October: pulled up only outing over fences: stayed 3m: best form on firm ground. *B. Forsey.* c— 105

DIANA DEE 4 b.f. Blakeney–Deep River (FR) (Val de Loir) [1989/90 16g a16g2] modest maiden on Flat, stays 1½m: sold out of B. Hills's stable 8,600 gns Newmarket December Sales: claimer ridden, second to easy winner Rocquaine in 5-runner juvenile hurdle at Lingfield in March. *P. G. Bailey.* 79

DIANES DESTINY 6 b.g. Kambalda–Kinsella's Choice (Middle Temple) [1989/90 22g2 21g3 22g* 21s 22g3 c24m3 c24s4 c25dpu c20f5 c24m3 c24f2 c26fF] smallish, workmanlike gelding: won conditional jockeys novice hurdle at Wolverhampton in November: modest form when in frame in novice chases: stays 3m: best form on ground no softer than good. *J. R. Upson.* c**94** 94

DIAPHANTINE 8 b.m. Octavo (USA)–Andara (Hugh Lupus) [1989/90 17fF 17f4 21m4 16h c17f3 c17d3 c17g3 c17gF c21vur c18s* c20d c16f c16fF] rather lightly-made mare: front-running selling hurdler: attracted no bid after winning selling handicap chase at Fontwell in February: stays 2¼m: acts on any going: trained until after ninth outing by F. Gorman. *C. L. Popham.* c**80** 73

DI BRAVURA 4 b.g. Noalto–Diorina (Manacle) [1989/90 18f5 16f6 16g4] leggy gelding: plating-class maiden on Flat: claimer ridden, best effort over hurdles when fourth in juvenile event at Kempton in October: sold 700 gns Ascot May Sales. *W. G. R. Wightman.* 80

DICEY TIME 8 br.g. Major Point–Maria di Leuca (Falcon) [1989/90 c20f3 c20f3 c24gpu] lengthy gelding: poor novice chaser (makes mistakes): won point-to-point in February. *J. R. Jenkins.* c— x —

DICKENS AND BROWNE 5 b. or br.g. Vayrann–Ravela II (Tanerko) [1989/90 16f a20g5] smallish gelding: half-brother to several winners, including very useful 6f and 1m French 2-y-o winner Riyahi (by Red God): dam, half-sister to high-class sprinter Fortino II, won at up to 13f: tailed off in novice hurdles at Newbury and Lingfield: sold 540 gns Ascot April Sales. *J. D. Czerpak.* —

DICKIE'S GIN 6 b.g. Mr Fordette–Gin An Tonic (Osprey Hawk) [1989/90 F16g4 F13d*] half-brother to winning jumpers Well Honey and Sir's At The Gin (both by Al Sirat) and modest novice hurdler Sunday For Monday (by Pal's Bambino): made virtually all to win NH Flat race at Kelso in January by 2½ lengths from Arpal Breeze: yet to race over hurdles or fences. *T. P. Tate.*

DICK KNIGHT 9 ch.g. Owen Dudley–Illumination (St Paddy) [1989/90 16g 16s5 a16g 16g] short-coupled, rather leggy gelding: winning hurdler: well beaten in sellers last 3 starts: best at around 2m: acts on any going. *P. B. Allingham.* —

DICK'S FOLLY 11 b.g. Martinmas–No Princess (Prince Regent (FR)) [1989/90 16mur] sturdy gelding: handicap hurdler: led until unseating rider 3 out —

at Chepstow in April: races only at around 2m: probably unsuited by very soft ground, acts on any other: sometimes wears blinkers: has been ridden by a claimer and an amateur. *M. C. Pipe.*

DICK THE SHEPHERD 7 b.g. Workboy–Shepherd Valley (Arrigle Valley) [1989/90 c20s^ur] first foal: dam, a twin, poor maiden point-to-pointer: won a point-to-point in March: unseated rider first in maiden hunter chase at Sedgefield previous month: sold 3,600 gns Doncaster Spring Sales. *Miss C. M. Bolitho.* c—

DICTIVE 13 b.g. Hardiran–Motif (St Elmo) [1989/90 c20d^6] big, rangy, workmanlike gelding: won a point-to-point in 1989: winning hurdler, novice chaser: stays 2½m: acts on heavy ground. *Andrew Wilson.* c— —

DIDISEEIT 10 gr.g. Grey Mirage–Golden Wine (Old Wine) [1989/90 c20v^2] won a point-to-point in 1989: collapsed and died after finishing second in maiden hunter chase at Folkestone in February. *Colin Kemball.* c78

DIE BROKE 6 b. or br.g. Pollerton–Gillogue (Royal Orbit (USA)) [1989/90 c21d^pu c24g^2 c24v^F c24d^4 c25s* c32f^4 c21d^pu] big, workmanlike gelding: novice hurdler: won novice chase at Towcester in February by 15 lengths from John's Birthday: weakened 2 out when over 25 lengths fourth to Topsham Bay in 4m National Hunt Chase Challenge Cup at Cheltenham in March: stays 25f: acts on soft ground: ran as though past his best for season final outing: should win more races over fences. *Andrew Turnell.* c108 —

DIEGO RIVERA 6 b.g. Shirley Heights–Brazen Faced (Bold And Free) [1989/90 16g^6 16d^2 16s^5 16d^4 16v*] robust gelding: 1¼m winner on Flat: won 4-runner novice handicap hurdle at Ayr in February by length from Norquay, leading close home: may not stay much beyond 2m: acts on heavy going: best in blinkers: sold 2,100 gns Doncaster Spring Sales. *M. W. Easterby.* 99

DIE IN THE SKY 9 ch.g. Welsh Pageant–Heaven And Earth (Midsummer Night II) [1989/90 c16f*] workmanlike gelding: winning point-to-pointer: behind all outings over hurdles: made virtually all, despite looking backward, to win poor novice chase at Southwell in October by 20 lengths: stays 21f: acts on any going. *Mrs T. J. McInnes Skinner.* c79 + —

DIENAU'S TROVE 9 b.g. Hot Grove–Dienau (Connaught) [1989/90 c20m^pu 16m^5] lengthy gelding: lightly-raced handicap hurdler: jumped none too fluently on chasing debut: best at sharp 2m with forcing tactics: acts on any going: usually wears blinkers. *H. J. Collingridge.* c— —

DIMENSION 8 b.g. Dominion–Airy Queen (USA) (Sadair) [1989/90 18h^3 16f^3] strong, sturdy gelding: poor hurdler: easily better effort of season on second start (September): best at 2m: acts on firm and good to soft going: blinkered nowadays: none too keen under pressure and seems suited by waiting tactics. *D. M. Grissell.* 80 §

DINGLE JACK 6 b.g. Hard Frost–Roman de La Rose (Fable Amusant) [1989/90 c20m^2 c24g^6 c26v^pu c24d^6 c20d^6 c24f^ur c26g^pu] sturdy gelding: third foal: dam unraced: winning point-to-pointer: well beaten in steeplechases. *R. J. Shail.* c—

DINSDALE LAD 4 ch.g. Sweet Monday–Forgets Image (Florescence) [1989/90 16g^pu 16g^pu 16g 16g 16d^pu 16m] angular gelding: half-brother to winning hurdler Excavator Lady (by Most Secret): placed in 5f sellers at 2 yrs: sold out of G. Moore's stable 900 gns Doncaster June Sales: no sign of ability over hurdles: sweated up last start. *M. A. Barnes.* —

DIPYN BACH 8 br.g. Welsh Pageant–More Or Less (Morston (FR)) [1989/90 16g^3 20g^2 16m* 16m 16s^3 20s* 16s* 16g^6 16m^pu] sparely-made gelding: won handicap hurdles at Towcester in November and Plumpton in December and claimer at Market Rasen in January: stays 2½m: acts on heavy going and good to firm: blinkered nowadays. *T. P. McGovern.* 104

DIRECT 7 b.g. The Parson–Let The Hare Sit (Politico (USA)) [1989/90 24g 21d 24v^4 25f^3] tall, rather leggy gelding: returned to form when 2½ lengths third behind Henry Mann in Coral Golden Hurdle Final (Handicap) at Cheltenham in March, keeping on under strong pressure (finished lame): stays 3m: acts on any going: has won for an amateur. *J. A. C. Edwards.* 134

DIRECT INTEREST 7 ch.g. Al Sirat (USA)–Honey Come Home (Timobriol) [1989/90 20d 25f^F c16m c27g^pu c16g^2 c16s^pu c16g* c16g^4 c20m^6 c24g^F c21f^2 c21f^3] strong, dipped-backed gelding: poor novice hurdler: won 4-runner novice handicap chase at Edinburgh in January: best subsequent efforts when placed in novice events at Cartmel in May: stays 21f: acts on firm going. *Denys Smith.* c80 —

DIRECTLY 7 b.g. Bay Express–Veracious (Astec) [1989/90 18d 16g^{4} 16g^{5} 20v^{4} 21d 20m] leggy gelding: has been hobdayed: handicap hurdler: best efforts on third and fourth starts, but weakened noticeably over 2½m on latter occasion and is likely to prove better at shorter distances: acts on heavy going (probably unsuited by top-of-the-ground). *G. B. Balding.* 116

DIRECTOR PLEASE 7 ch.g. Whealden–Dyna Bell (Double Jump) [1989/90 c20s^{pu} c20s^{F} c20d^{4} c22f^{ur} c20m^{pu}] sturdy gelding: poor novice chaser: stays 2½m: poor jumper of fences. *Mrs Gill E. Jones.* c**74** x —

DIRECTORS' CHOICE 5 b.g. Skyliner–Hazel Gig (Captain's Gig (USA)) [1989/90 16f^{5} 16g^{3} 16f^{4} 16g* 16s^{6} 16g^{3}] leggy gelding: quite useful at 2 yrs on Flat but has deteriorated and become ungenuine: won handicap hurdle at Plumpton in December: looked ungenuine when well beaten next time and found little under pressure last start: unlikely to stay beyond 2m: blinkered last 3 starts: one to be wary of. *W. Carter.* 92 §

DIRECT RESPONSE 6 b.g. Black Minstrel–Tulladuff (Golden Love) [1989/90 20g^{F} 20v^{pu}] leggy, shallow-girthed gelding: third in NH Flat race: only sign of ability over hurdles in novice handicap at Wetherby in November, holding slight advantage when falling last. *Mrs C. Postlethwaite.* 84

DIRTY DIANA 5 br.m. Boreen (FR)–Sesetta (Lucky Brief) [1989/90 20s^{4} F17g^{2} 16s^{2} 16v^{2} F16s* 18d* 16s^{2} 20v^{3} 20f] small, angular Irish mare: second foal: half-sister to useful Irish hurdler Atteses (by Smooth Stepper): dam fair Irish hurdler, half-sister to Super Furrow: successful in NH Flat race at Limerick in December and handicap hurdle at Thurles following month: ran well next 2 starts: always behind in Sun Alliance Novices' Hurdle at Cheltenham final outing: stays 2½m: acts on heavy going. *Capt D. G. Swan, Ireland.* 108

DISCIPLINE 5 b.m. Roman Warrior–Steadily (Whitstead) [1989/90 16m^{pu}] first foal: dam, out of half-sister to More Light and Shoot A Line, ran once: tailed off when pulled up 2 out in maiden hurdle at Towcester in April. *M. J. Wilkinson.* —

DISCO DUKE 5 b.g. Record Token–Grandgirl (Mansingh (USA)) [1989/90 16g^{4} 18g* 16m^{2} 22m^{4} 16s^{2} 16v^{2} 16d^{6} 16f] lengthy, workmanlike gelding: won selling handicap hurdle at Fontwell (no bid) in October: ran well when placed in non-sellers subsequently: stays 2¼m: probably unsuited by firm going, acts on any other. *A. Moore.* 96

DISCO TRIX 8 b.g. Pitpan–Blue Trix (Blue Chariot) [1989/90 c24d^{pu}] strong gelding: no sign of ability over hurdles or in steeplechases, but is a winning point-to-pointer. *P. Garner.* c— —

DISCREET CHARM 5 ch.m. Moorestyle–La Meme (Pall Mall) [1989/90 18d^{4} 16m^{4} 22g^{F}] angular mare: one-time fair stayer on Flat: poor novice hurdler: behind when falling 5 out over 2¾m. *Miss J. Thorne.* 72

DISCUS THROWER 8 b.g. Relkino–Broken Record (Busted) [1989/90 c21s^{pu}] big gelding: won a point-to-point in 1989: tailed off when pulled up in hunter chase in February. *Steven Astaire.* c—

DISK MAKER 5 b.g. Crooner–Sirette (Great Nephew) [1989/90 16f^{2}] medium-sized gelding: 66/1, first form over hurdles when 1½ lengths second to Le Chat Noir in 16-runner novice event at Plumpton in March: evidently suited by firm ground: 1½m winner on Flat in 1990. *R. Curtis.* 94 +

DISNEYLAND (POL) 6 ch.g. Dixieland (POL)–Dzungaria (POL) (Antiquarian) [1989/90 17f^{3} 17f^{3} 16f^{4} 16h* 17f^{4} 16h* 16m* 16d a16g* a16g* a16g^{2} a16s^{2} a16g* a16g^{2} a16g^{2} 16f^{5} 16m^{5} 16m^{4}] sturdy gelding: had a most successful season, winning novice selling hurdle (bought in 4,800 gns) and novice hurdle at Taunton, handicap at Wincanton and 3 handicaps at Lingfield: unlikely to stay much beyond 2m: acts on hard ground: tough, genuine and consistent: good mount for a claimer. *Mrs J. Pitman.* 105

DISTANT CHIMES 8 ch.g. London Bells (CAN)–Vaguely Related (Pall Mall) [1989/90 16m 16m] placed at up to 2m on Flat at 3 yrs: behind in novice hurdles. *G. Thorner.* —

DISTANT RELATION 5 b.m. Great Nephew–Perchance (Connaught) [1989/90 16m^{2} 22f^{2} a16g^{2} 16m* a16g* a16g^{3} a18s^{pu} a16g a16g* 16d a16g*] rather sparely-made mare: successful over hurdles at Wincanton and Lingfield (3 times), best effort when beating Brunoni 3 lengths in novice handicap on latter course in March on final start: stays 2¾m: acts on firm going: wears blinkers. *K. O. Cunningham-Brown.* 98

Mr M. L. Oberstein's "Dis Train"

DIS TRAIN 6 ch.g. Deep Run–Bunkilla (Arctic Slave) [1989/90 16g^{4} 18d^{6} 20s^{4}
16g^{2} 16m 16f^{3} 16d^{6}] rangy gelding: chasing type: useful hurdler: ran well when 141
½-length second to Redundant Pal in The Ladbroke at Leopardstown in January
and when 10½ lengths third behind Jubail in quite valuable handicap at Liverpool
in April: not knocked about when 18 lengths sixth behind impressive Sayparee in
Scottish Champion Hurdle (limited handicap) at Ayr on final start: probably stays
2½m: seems to act on any going: takes a good hold and wears a crossed noseband.
Mrs J. Pitman.

DISTRESS CALL 9 b.m. Saucy Kit–Jolly Pigeon (Jolly Jet) [1989/90 c22d^{pu}] c—
workmanlike mare: of little account. *S. N. Cole.* —

DISTRICT NURSE 4 b.f. Country Retreat–Furious Babs (Fury Royal)
[1989/90 aF16g F16g 16m^{pu} 19f^{pu}] leggy filly: first foal: dam temperamental —
maiden point-to-pointer: behind in NH Flat races and when pulled up in novice
hurdles. *R. J. Weaver.*

DIVINE PROBLEM 8 gr.g. Roselier (FR)–Group Problem (Divine Gift) c—
[1989/90 c20g^{ur}] lengthy, angular gelding: won amateur riders novice hurdle and —
a novice chase in 1988/9: burly, close up when unseating rider 5 out in handicap
chase at Wetherby in November: suited by a test of stamina: probably acts on any
going: needs to improve his jumping of fences: to be trained by Miss H. Knight. *W.
A. Stephenson.*

DIWAN-I-KHAS 6 b.m. Majestic Maharaj–Ovington Court (Prefairy) c82
[1989/90 18f* 16h^{4} c24m^{3} c24m^{F}] small, leggy mare: won selling hurdle at 67
Fontwell in September (no bid): 16 lengths third behind Teaplanter in novice
hunter chase at Southwell in April: probably stays 3m: acts on firm ground:
trained first 2 starts by T. Forster. *C. R. F. Ward Thomas.*

DIXTON HOUSE 11 b.g. Cantab–Bird of Honour (Dark Heron) [1989/90 c24s^pu] sturdy gelding: smart chaser: won Ritz Club National Hunt Handicap Chase at Cheltenham in 1988/9: fell first Becher's in Seagram Grand National at Liverpool next outing: pulled up lame only outing of 1989/90 (January): stays 25f: acts on heavy going (yet to race on top-of-the-ground): sound jumper. *J. A. C. Edwards.* c— —

DIZZY DORA 10 b.m. Rubor–Little Dora (Bounteous) [1989/90 c24m c26m^F c27f^pu] workmanlike mare: poor novice hurdler/chaser: pulled up lame last start: sometimes blinkered. *Miss Z. A. Green.* c— —

DJLAH 5 b.m. Glenstal (USA)–Sipapu (Targowice (USA)) [1989/90 16h^F] lengthy, sparely-made mare: in lead when falling 2 out in poor novice hurdle at Taunton in October: dead. *F. Gray.* —

DO BE BRIEF 5 ch.g. Le Moss–Right Performance (Gala Performance (USA)) [1989/90 16g* 20d^pu 16v* 16g² 20d²] IR 15,000 3-y-o: strong, chasing type: second foal: dam lightly-raced half-sister to very useful staying chaser Omerta: won from large fields of novice hurdlers at Towcester in December and Chepstow in February: ran very good race when neck second to King's Curate in quite valuable novice handicap at Ayr on final start, rallying splendidly in latter stages: better suited by 2½m than 2m, and will stay further: acts on heavy going: on the upgrade. *Mrs J. Pitman.* 126 p

DOCK BRIEF 9 br.g. Pauper–Flying Lady (Charlottesvilles Flyer) [1989/90 c26m⁴ c24d c27g c27s^F c28g⁶ c27v⁴ c20d^ro c25f⁵ c25f² c25m^pu] small, sparely-made gelding: poor winning chaser: stays well: acts on any going: visored fourth and fifth outings: makes mistakes. *R. Lee.* **c81** x —

DOCKLANDS EXPRESS 8 b.g. Roscoe Blake–Southern Moss (Sea Moss) [1989/90 c20m* c21s² c25g* c25g³ c24m* c26g* c24f² c19f* c26m*] smallish gelding: winning hurdler: had an excellent first season over fences, and was gaining sixth win when scoring by 25 lengths in handicap at Stratford in June: earlier successful in novice events at Plumpton, Warwick (handicap), Southwell and Stratford (2, beating Knight Oil ¾ length in quite valuable novice handicap on second occasion): effective at 19f and stays 3¼m: acts on any going: game and genuine: suitable mount for a claimer: jumps soundly: useful handicap chaser in the making. *K. C. Bailey.* c**126** p —

DOCKSIDER 7 ch.g. Hotfoot–Tanara (Romulus) [1989/90 16d a20g⁵ 16f⁴ 20m* 20m²] smallish, sturdy gelding: has seemed unreliable but did nothing wrong when winning novice hurdle at Huntingdon in April: stays 2½m: probably acts on any going. *Mrs E. H. Heath.* 94

DOC LODGE 4 b.f. Doc Marten–Cooling (Tycoon II) [1989/90 16g 16g⁵ 16g⁵ 16d³ 16g² 16g⁴ 16g] leggy filly: modest maiden on Flat, suited by 7f: poor juvenile hurdler: races freely and will prove suited by sharp 2m: put head in air under pressure second start: blinkered sixth outing. *R. D. E. Woodhouse.* 74

DOC'S COAT 5 b.g. Tower Walk–Gold Loch (Lochnager) [1989/90 17g 16d 16g⁴ a18g² a16g² 17v* 16s* a20s² 16s² a20g^pu 16f 17m* a18g⁶ 17m* 21m³] stocky gelding: handicap hurdler: had good season, winning at Worcester, Devon & Exeter and Newton Abbot (twice) in 1989/90: stays 2½m: acts on any going: tough and genuine. *C. P. Wildman.* 108

DOCTOR RHYTHM 5 ch.g. Cure The Blues (USA)–Mombones (Lord Gayle (USA)) [1989/90 16g^F] medium-sized gelding: won both starts in juvenile hurdles in 1988/9: fell first on reappearance: acted on firm ground: dead. *F. Jordan.* —

DOCTOR'S REMEDY 4 br.c. Doc Marten–Champagne Party (Amber Rama (USA)) [1989/90 16f⁵ 16m 16d 16d 16d⁶ a16g⁵ a16g* a20g⁵] smallish, good-quartered colt: half-brother to poor novice hurdler Champagne Mandy (by Mandrake Major): sprint maiden on Flat: bought in 3,000 gns after winning selling hurdle at Southwell in April: unlikely to stay much beyond 2m: blinkered third and fourth starts. *M. Tate.* 81

DOCTOR SYNTAX 4 b.g. Ring Bidder–Fair Sara (McIndoe) [1989/90 F17m⁵ F16f*] second foal: dam winning hurdler: won 8-runner NH Flat race at Hexham in May by 10 lengths: yet to race over hurdles. *E. J. Alston.*

DODGY DECISION 9 b.m. Rymer–Done Over (Road House II) [1989/90 c22m] showed more temperament than ability over hurdles in 1986/7: poor maiden point-to-pointer: tailed off in novice hunter chase in May: one to leave alone. *Miss C. Derryman.* c— §§

DODINGTON BELLE 6 b.m. Homing–K-Sera (Lord Gayle (USA)) [1989/90 16m^{pu}] smallish, leggy mare: no worthwhile form over hurdles. *P. R. Rodford.* —

DOLITINO 6 gr.m. Neltino–Sandoli (Sandford Lad) [1989/90 16m 20f^4 20m 16g 16g 27f^4 17m 16f^3 20m^{ur} 16g^6 17f^5 17f^4] small, sparely-made mare: novice selling hurdler: form only at around 2m on a sound surface. *Miss Z. A. Green.* 61

DOLLY PRICES 5 b.m. Silly Prices–Miss Friendly (Status Seeker) [1989/90 aF16g^5] well beaten in NH Flat races: yet to race over hurdles or fences. *W. J. Smith.*

DOLLY WARDANCE 7 gr.m. Warpath–April (Silly Season) [1989/90 16m^4 20g 16g^6 20d 16d^5] sturdy mare: creditable fifth in novice handicap hurdle at Wetherby in February: gives impression should be suited by good test of stamina. *T. W. Donnelly.* 80

DOM EDINO 7 b.g. Dominion–Edna (Shiny Tenth) [1989/90 c16m* c24f^4 c20g^6] rangy gelding: has been hobdayed: one-time useful hurdler: won novice event at Perth in September on chasing debut by short head: jumped moderately when last in 2 similar events (not seen out after November): successful over 2¾m but best form at up to 2½m: acts well on heavy going and probably unsuited by very firm: suitable mount for a claimer: has flashed tail under pressure. *M. Avison.* c**90** —

DOMINION TREASURE 5 b. or br.h. Dominion–Chrysicabana (Home Guard (USA)) [1989/90 17d 17v^4 21d* 21d* 17m^2 26f^3] small horse: successful in claiming hurdle at Towcester in February and conditional jockeys handicap at Newton Abbot in March: good second in handicap at Devon & Exeter in April: stays 21f, probably not 3¼m: acts on any going: usually ridden by claimer. *J. H. Baker.* 101

DONATE 5 ch.g. High Line–Charites (Red God) [1989/90 16m^{pu}] neat gelding: of little account. *T. P. McGovern.* —

DONATIST 4 b.c. Dominion–Kaftan (Kashmir II) [1989/90 16d 16d 16m^6] medium-sized, sturdy colt: won 9.2f claimer on Flat in August (claimed out of H. Candy's stable £9,060): dropped in class, sixth of 9 finishers in selling handicap hurdle at Fakenham in March (automatic top weight), leading to 2 out: barely stays 2m. *Miss L. Bower.* 85

DONFIL 5 ch.g. Don–Philanderess (Philemon) [1989/90 16d^F 16m] workmanlike gelding: poor plater on Flat: blinkered, tailed off in selling hurdle at Uttoxeter in November. *P. D. Evans.* —

DON KEYDROP 6 b.g. Don–Tomrousse (FR) (Diatome) [1989/90 a20g* a24g* a24g*] leggy gelding: unbeaten in 3 races over hurdles at Lingfield in 1989/90, namely novice event and handicap in January and another handicap (beat Lesbet easily by 8 lengths) following month: stays 3m: should progress further. *Miss B. Sanders.* 106 p

DONNA DEL LAGO 4 b.f. Kings Lake (USA)–Cannon Boy (USA) (Canonero II (USA)) [1989/90 16g^F 16m^6 16f^3 16m^4 16f* 20f 16f^4 20f^2 19f* 20g 22m^3] angular filly: no form on Flat: sold out of R. Hannon's stable 5,400 gns Newmarket July Sales: successful in conditional jockeys novice selling hurdle at Warwick in December (bought in 2,000 gns) and novice handicap at Hereford in April (claimer ridden): also ran well final start: stays 2¾m: acts on firm ground. *T. Casey.* 93

DONNA'S TOKEN 5 br.m. Record Token–Lyricist (Averof) [1989/90 F16m^3 16v^F 16g 16f^5] sparely-made mare: second foal: dam never ran: third in NH Flat race at Towcester in January: no worthwhile form in novice hurdles: ridden by 7-lb claimer. *M. Brown.* —

DONOSA 5 ch.m. Posse (USA)–Love Supreme (Sallust) [1989/90 16s a16g^6] sparely-made mare: of little account on Flat: behind in novice hurdle at Nottingham and claimer at Southwell. *B. Richmond.* —

DONOSTI 6 b.g. Rusticaro (FR)–Blue Flame (USA) (Crimson Satan) [1989/90 16s 16g^5 16m 16m c16h^{ur} 16m^2 c16g 16f^3 16m* 22f^4] strong, workmanlike gelding: bought in 5,800 gns after winning conditional jockeys selling hurdle at Warwick in May (trained until after then by Miss L. Bower): well beaten only completed outing over fences: probably doesn't stay 2¾m: acts on firm and dead ground. *R. Lee.* c— 78

DONPERRY 10 b.g. Don Enrico (USA)–Perry's Poppet (Easter Island) [1989/90 c16d^{pu} c16g^{pu}] big, plain gelding: very lightly raced and of little account. *W. H. Taylor.* c— —

DON'T ANNOY ME 10 b.g. Manado–Embarrassed (Busted) [1989/90 c20m^{F}] leggy gelding: winning hurdler: moderate form in novice chases: suffered a fatal fall at Huntingdon in December: probably stayed 2½m: acted on any going. *R. M. Whitaker.* c— —

DON'T-BE-CARELESS 5 b.g. Dubassoff (USA)–Careless K (Don Carlos) [1989/90 17d^{F} 16f^{pu}] second thoroughbred foal: dam unraced: tailed off when pulled up 2 out in novice hurdle at Taunton in March. *G. A. Ham.* —

DON'T BE LATE 8 ch.m. Pollerton–Miss Soundly (Maelsheachlainn) [1989/90 c20f^{ur} c25h* c24h* c21f*] leggy, rather sparely-made mare: poor hurdler: won novice handicap chases at Devon & Exeter and Taunton and a novice event at Cartmel (by 5 lengths from Direct Interest) in May: stays 3m: best form on very firm going: blinkered final start 1987/8 (ran creditably): should win more races. *M. C. Pipe.* c**106** p —

DON'T DESPAIR 8 b.m. Amboise–Seacona (Espresso) [1989/90 c24g^{pu}] small mare: half-sister to modest middle-distance handicapper Rapid Lad (by Rapid River): lightly-raced point-to-pointer: backward, tailed off when pulled up after eighth in novice hunter chase at Market Rasen in May. *T. R. Beadle.* c—

DON'T TELL RUTH 8 b.g. Miami Springs–Mount of Light (Sparkler) [1989/90 20d^{pu} 20g^{pu} 16g^{4} 16d^{5} c20d^{F} c20g^{3}] sturdy gelding: carries plenty of condition: poor novice hurdler: heavily bandaged in front, 12 lengths third to Comandante in novice chase at Newbury in March: stays 2½m. *F. Walwyn.* c**83** + 80

DON VALENTINO 5 ch.g. Don–Hells Mistress (Skymaster) [1989/90 16d 16s^{2} 16m 16d^{2} 16g^{2}] big, rangy, chasing type: useful hurdler: not seen out until second half of season: runner-up in limited handicaps at Nottingham (hung left when beaten 7 lengths by Royal Derbi) and Ayr (beaten 6 lengths by impressive Sayparee in Scottish Champion Hurdle), and in quite well-contested handicap at Uttoxeter (went down by 4 lengths to Kadan): takes a good hold and will prove best at 2m for the time being: acts on heavy going and good to firm: still a slightly sketchy jumper: blinkered last 4 starts. *Mrs J. Pitman.* 144

DOODLE DANDY 4 b.g. Prince Tenderfoot (USA)–Peggy Dell (Sovereign Gleam) [1989/90 16f^{pu} 17g^{pu}] plating-class middle-distance maiden on Flat: behind when pulled up in juvenile hurdles at Southwell (seller) and Devon & Exeter: sold out of Ronald Thompson's stable 1,000 gns Doncaster October Sales in between. *R. T. Juckes.* —

DOOLIN 4 ch.g. Krayyan–Blunted (Sharpen Up) [1989/90 16d 16m 22f^{ur}] lengthy, sparely-made ex-Irish gelding: fourth reported living foal: half-brother to French sprinter Hellisharp Run (by Runnett) and 1m winner Apatlal (by Ahonoora): dam poor maiden: placed at up to 9f on Flat when trained by A. McNamara: always behind both completed outings over hurdles. *D. R. Gandolfo.* —

DOOR LATCH 12 ch.g. Cantab–Kelly's Door (Bowsprit) [1989/90 c26g^{5} c24d c25m] rangy, useful-looking gelding: usually impresses in paddock: very smart chaser at his best: reportedly injured a tendon final start 1986/7: having only second outing since when remote fifth of 7 in sponsored event at Newbury in December, showing prominently to 4 out: tailed off both subsequent starts: stays 3¼m: acts on any going: inclined to make the odd bad mistake: usually bandaged nowadays. *J. T. Gifford.* c—

DORANS HILL LAD 6 ch.g. Orchestra–Madrilon (FR) (Le Fabuleux) [1989/90 F16g^{4} F17d* F16g^{2} F16d^{2} 16g^{3} 16g* 18d 16v* 20f^{5} 19d^{3} 16g] tall Irish gelding: half-brother to fairly useful hurdler Vino Festa (by Nebbiolo) and to a 2-y-o 1m winner by Bold Lad (USA): dam unraced: won NH Flat race at Tipperary in October: successful over hurdles in maiden event at Punchestown and handicap at Navan: ran a very good race when around 18 lengths fifth to Regal Ambition in Sun Alliance Novices' Hurdle at Cheltenham in March, coming from long way off pace and staying on strongly in latter stages: below that form afterwards, giving impression needs more of a test of stamina: will be suited by further than 2½m: acts on any going: has won for an amateur. *Anthony Mullins, Ireland.* 126

DOREEN'S PRIDE 4 ch.f. Celtic Cone–Quae Supra (On Your Mark) [1989/90 16s^{4} 16g^{3}] medium-sized filly: first foal: dam 5f winner: shaped as though she'll be suited by longer trip when staying-on 13 lengths third behind Fifth Amendment in novice hurdle at Wincanton in January: should improve further. *R. J. Holder.* 83 p

DORE RIVER 5 br.g. Cruise Missile–Cagaleena (Cagirama) [1989/90 19m^{ur} 16m^{ur}] small gelding: yet to complete course in novice hurdles (tried to refuse and unseated rider last time out). *G. J. Powell.* —

DORNVALLEY LAD 9 ch.g. Anax–Lovely Diana (Supreme Sovereign) [1989/90 c16f⁴ c25m³ c25f²] medium-sized gelding: former selling chaser: poor handicapper nowadays: probably best at around 2m: seems to need a firm surface: wears a severe bridle. *P. A. Pritchard.* c**75** ? —

DORONICUM 11 ch.g. Deep Run–May Foliage (Barman II) [1989/90 c20m² c16m* c20m* c20g⁴ c20g² 24m⁵ c16g⁶ c20dbd c25d⁶ 20m 24g c21g⁶] strong, deep-girthed gelding: modest hurdler/chaser nowadays: won claiming chases at Perth in September and October: ran moderately last 5 completed outings (kicked at start and withdrawn under orders tenth appearance): stays 3m: best form over fences on a sound surface: reportedly broke blood vessel final outing 1987/8: claimer ridden nowadays. *G. Richards.* c**107** d 97

D'OR'S GEM 7 b.g. Brigadier Gerard–Siraf (Alcide) [1989/90 c26g c21gpu c24gur c20d c26sur 20ssu 24d 16m* 16m⁶ 16f] workmanlike gelding: selling hurdler: attracted no bid after winning handicap at Sedgefield in March: poor jumper and no form over fences: stays 2½m: acts on good to firm and soft going: blinkered third outing 1987/8: sold 1,050 gns Doncaster June Sales. *P. A. Blockley.* c— x 79

DORVER (USA) 6 b. or br.g. Irish River (FR)–Tudor Gleam (USA) (Globemaster) [1989/90 16f⁶ 16g 20s³ 21g³ 20v⁴ 22g⁴ 20f⁵ 22m² 22f*] smallish, angular gelding: well beaten in 2 races on Flat: modest hurdler: won 5-runner novice handicap hurdle at Wincanton in April: stays 2¾m: acts on any going. *S. Dow.* 100

DOUBLE LIGHT 8 b.g. Lighter–Salira (Double Jump) [1989/90 24spu 21mpu] half-brother to winning hurdler/chaser Calira (by Coliseum): dam won 6f seller at 2 yrs: lightly-raced maiden point-to-pointer: tailed off when pulled up in 2 races over hurdles. *M. A. Johnson.* —

DOUBLE OPTION (USA) 9 b.g. Quack (USA)–Swagger (Prominer) [1989/90 c20f⁴] leggy gelding: selling hurdler: well-beaten fourth in hunter chase at Folkestone in May: will probably stay 2½m: acts on firm going. *N. Munday.* c— —

DOUBLE TURN 9 b.g. Comedy Star (USA)–Pearl River (NZ) (Bourbon Prince) [1989/90 c24f² c20dpu] compact, good-bodied gelding: carries plenty of condition: poor chaser: ran as though something was amiss last outing: stays 3m: acts on any going. *Mrs E. H. Heath.* c— —

DOUBLE U DEE 7 b.g. Rapid Pass–Abbyrama (Abyss) [1989/90 F16f³ F16f 25gpu] workmanlike gelding: first foal: dam never ran: under 2 lengths third of 7 in NH Flat race at Cheltenham in October: several mistakes and tailed off when pulled up 3 out in novice hurdle on same course in November: sold 4,600 gns Ascot December Sales. *C. L. Popham.* —

DOUBLE UP (NZ) 13 b.g. Double Speed (USA)–Sun Deck (NZ) (Dogger Bank) [1989/90 c24fpu c25m⁵ c20mpu] robust, deep-girthed gelding: winning chaser: broke down badly final outing (November): stays 3¼m: acts on any ground. *Mrs P. A. Hargreaves.* c— —

DOUBTFUL PACT 11 ch.g. Scallywag–Treaty Girl (Pardal) [1989/90 c26fpu] no form in novice hurdle and novice hunter chases: winning point-to-pointer. *J. C. Newman.* c— —

DOUBTLESS 8 b.g. Nonoalco (USA)–Consistent (Connaught) [1989/90 20g⁵] leggy gelding: novice hurdler: placed 5 times in 1987/8: well beaten only outing since (January): stays 3m: acts on heavy going: has run well for a 7-lb claimer. *C. J. T. Alexander.* —

DOUGLAS BRIG 12 gr.g. New Brig–Bala Raftan (Master Rocky) [1989/90 c24d³ c24m] workmanlike gelding: winning point-to-pointer/hunter chaser: bit backward, third of 4 behind very easy winner Call Collect at Kelso in February: suited by a thorough test of stamina and forcing tactics. *N. E. H. Hargreave.* c**94** —

DOVE GREY 5 gr.g. Belfort (FR)–Turtle Dove (Gyr (USA)) [1989/90 16g⁴] half-brother to 4 jumping winners by Warpath, including very useful hurdler Path of Peace: staying maiden on Flat: made much of running to 2 out when 14 lengths fourth to Sally's Dove in novice claiming hurdle at Wolverhampton in November: sold 12,000 gns Doncaster Sales later in month. *C. W. Thornton.* 81

DOVER 10 ch.g. Deep Run–Imelda (Dual) [1989/90 c24g*] neat gelding: successful in 4 point-to-points prior to making all in 5-runner hunter chase at Bangor in May (beat Sunday School 1½ lengths): stays 3m: acts on any going: often visored over hurdles: formerly unreliable. *Mrs T. Ritson.* c**94** + —

DOWN FLIGHT 10 ch.g. Run The Gantlet (USA)–Feather Bed (Gratitude) [1989/90 22m⁵ 20d 22g] small, good-bodied gelding: won 4 handicap hurdles in —

1988/9: lightly raced and no worthwhile form since: stays 3m: acts well in the mud: blinkered in 1985/6, visored tenth to thirteenth outings in 1988/9 (best efforts). *T. H. Caldwell.*

DOWNHILL RUN 9 b.g. Deep Run–Money Spinner (Even Money) [1989/90 c16f* c25m^{2} c16f^{5} c18f^{3} c17m^{ur} c16g^{4} c16d^{4} c16g^{2} c16h* c16g* c21f^{3} c21f^{pu}] tall, rather sparely-made gelding: modest chaser: won at Worcester in August and at Hexham and Uttoxeter in May: takes a good hold and best at around 2m: probably acts on any going: has shown a tendency to jump left and has won only on left-handed tracks over jumps: sold out of J. White's stable 12,000 gns Doncaster October Sales after fourth start. *J. J. Birkett.* c99 —

DO YOUR OWN THING 7 b.g. Oats–Favoured (Pampered King) [1989/90 16g 16v] good-topped gelding: lightly raced and no worthwhile form over hurdles. *B. J. Curley.* —

DRACAN HILL 5 b.g. Barley Hill–Dracandale VII (pedigree unknown) [1989/90 F16f] first foal: dam never ran: behind in NH Flat race at Cheltenham in April: yet to race over hurdles or fences. *Mrs J. E. Croft.*

DRAGONADE 9 b. or br.g. Dragonara Palace (USA)–La Sarmate (FR) (Hard Sauce) [1989/90 c25m^{F}] leggy gelding: won 4 point-to-points in 1990: novice selling hurdler/chaser: fell third in hunter chase at Devon & Exeter in April: form only at 2m: acts on heavy going: sometimes blinkered or visored: has worn a dropped noseband. *B. R. J. Young.* c— —

DRAGONS LAIR 4 b. or br.g. Homing–Dragonist (Dragonara Palace (USA)) [1989/90 16g^{2}] big, good-bodied gelding: modest middle-distance handicapper on Flat, winner twice at 3 yrs: 3 lengths second to Native Friend in juvenile hurdle at Wetherby in November: looked sure to improve but wasn't seen out again. *M. J. Camacho.* 98

DRAKE'S DRUM 5 b.g. Palm Track–Pim (Game Warden) [1989/90 16m^{F}] rather leggy gelding: no worthwhile form over hurdles. *D. Moffatt.* —

DRAMATIC EVENT 5 b.g. Kind of Hush–Welsh Jane (Bold Lad (IRE)) [1989/90 16g^{F} 16d^{pu}] neat gelding: fair 1m winner on Flat: in need of race, jumped badly and was tailed off when pulled up 2 out in novice hurdle at Windsor in January: headstrong. *J. Etherington.* —

DRAW LOTS 6 b.g. Ela-Mana-Mou–Raffmarie (Raffingora) [1989/90 17f^{ur} 16f^{3} 16h^{2} 17h^{ro} 17f^{2} 16h^{5} a16g^{3}] smallish, sparely-made gelding: novice hurdler/chaser/maiden point-to-pointer: form only at around 2m: acts on hard going: has worn pricker on near-side: ran out on fourth start (twice refused in point-to-points in 1989): not one to trust. *P. R. Rodford.* c— 72 §

DRAW POKER 5 b.g. Uncle Pokey–Hejera (Cantab) [1989/90 F16m F16f^{6}] fourth foal: brother to winning hurdler Men of Yorkshire and novice hurdler Plat Reay: dam once-raced sister to winning hurdler/chaser Old Head and half-sister to useful chaser Marnik: 26½ lengths sixth behind Driver in NH Flat race at Cheltenham in April: yet to race over hurdles or fences. *O. Sherwood.*

DRAW THE LINE 11 b.g. High Line–Minibus (John Splendid) [1989/90 16f] leggy, close-coupled gelding: selling hurdler: soundly beaten only outing of season (March): races only at around 2m: acts well on top-of-the-ground. *B. Richmond.* —

DR CORNELIUS 9 b.g. Condorcet (FR)–Auntie Molly (Wishing Star) [1989/90 c25f^{pu} c25f^{2}] small, lightly-made gelding: poor maiden hurdler/point-to-pointer: 12 lengths second of 3 to Ponteus Pilot in novice hunter chase at Hereford in May: wears blinkers: sometimes sweats. *Nick Saville.* c73 —

DREADNOUGHT 10 gr.g. Rugantino–Thwarted (The Ditton) [1989/90 a20g 20m 16g^{6} 16m a22g^{3} a20g^{3} 16m] rather leggy, shallow-girthed gelding: poor hurdler: unseated rider both outings over fences: stays 2¾m: probably acts on any going: often owner ridden at overweight. *J. Carden.* c— 62

DREAM ACADEMY 7 b.m. Town And Country–Figurehead (Seaepic (USA)) [1989/90 16g 16g^{6} 16m] sparely-made mare: winning hurdler in 1987/8: no worthwhile form since, including in selling handicap final start: has raced only at 2m: acts on soft going and is possibly unsuited by firm: trained first 2 starts by T. Caldwell. *J. Dooler.* —

DREAMCOAT (USA) 9 gr. or ro.g. Jig Time (USA)–Restless Polly (USA) (Restless Wind) [1989/90 c16m^{5}] leggy gelding: selling hurdler and novice chaser: suited by 2½m: acts on any going: has worn a tongue strap. *K. Bishop.* c— —

DREAMING STAR 5 br.g. Star Appeal–Yea Misty (USA) (Forli (ARG)) [1989/90 16g^4 20g 16m^5 16s^2 22s^5 16m^2 16s 16s^5 a18g^4] leggy, narrow gelding: inconsistent novice selling hurdler: claimer ridden, ran well in non-seller at Southwell final start: best form at up to 2¼m: acts on good to firm and soft going: blinkered third and last starts 1988/9, visored last 7 outings: has looked reluctant under pressure. *P. J. Anderson.* — 80 §

DREAM MERCHANT 8 ch.g. Welsh Pageant–Waladah (Thatch (USA)) [1989/90 c17f^{pu} c16h* 18f^5 c25f^{pu} 25d^{pu} a20g^6 c20m^{pu} 16f^{pu}] sparely-made gelding: winning hurdler: poor jumper of fences but was only runner to put in a clear round in novice chase at Plumpton in August: stayed 2½m: acted on any going: tried in blinkers and a visor: inconsistent: sold privately out of R. O'Sullivan's stable 2,500 gns Ascot November Sales after sixth start: dead. *Mrs S. M. Austin.* — c? —

DREAM TEAM 4 b.f. Dara Monarch–H R Micro (High Award) [1989/90 16f] no form at 2 yrs: tailed-off last of 11 finishers in juvenile hurdle at Southwell in August. *A. Fowler.* — —

DRESS UP 6 b.g. Cajun–Prink (USA) (Stage Door Johnny) [1989/90 17m^{ur} 16f^3 16d 16d^6 24d^5] good-bodied gelding: poor novice hurdler: not knocked about once beaten when fair fifth to Duntree in 3m novice hurdle at Chepstow following month (form previously only at around 2m): acts on soft going and is possibly unsuited by firm: blinkered third to fifth starts 1988/9, visored third outing 1989/90. *N. G. Ayliffe.* — 83

DRIVER 4 b.f. Motivate–Owen's Hobby (Owen Anthony) [1989/90 F16f* F16f^6] second foal: dam placed in point-to-points: 33/1, won 22-runner NH Flat race at Cheltenham in April by 2½ lengths from Ascot Lad: sixth in similar event at Ludlow later in month: yet to race over hurdles. *M. Brown.*

DRIVERS BUREAU 6 ch.m. Proverb–Pal Alley (Pals Passage) [1989/90 aF16g^4 aF16g^3] first foal: dam, well beaten both starts in Irish NH Flat races, is half-sister to several winning jumpers: over 30 lengths third behind Kerfuffle in NH Flat race at Lingfield in February: yet to race over hurdles or fences. *P. Mitchell.*

DROMINA STAR 9 b.g. Pauper–Kitty The Hare (Hardicanute) [1989/90 20s^F c20g^{pu}] sturdy, plain ex-Irish gelding: won 3 point-to-points in 1989: bought 10,000 gns Doncaster August Sales (privately): jumped moderately and tailed off when pulled up twelfth in novice chase at Newbury in March. *J. A. B. Old.* — c— —

DROMIN JOKER 10 b.g. Proverb–Shamrock Gem (Orchardist) [1989/90 c25m^3] rather sparely-made gelding: smart point-to-pointer, successful in February: winning hunter chaser: ran with little zest when over 20 lengths third to Father Brady at Sandown in March: stays 25f: acts on any going: has worn a crossed noseband. *D. Naylor-Leyland.* — **c81**

DROMORE CASTLE 10 b.g. Tepukei–Glen Rambler (Wrekin Rambler) [1989/90 c24d* c22m^6] workmanlike gelding: usually looks well: quite useful point-to-pointer: held up, quickened to lead run-in when winning hunter chase at Newbury in March going away by 5 lengths from Rodden Brook: well-beaten sixth to Lean Ar Aghaidh in Seagram Fox Hunters' Chase at Liverpool in April: stays 25f: seems to act on any going. *R. Waley-Cohen.* — **c110**

DROPSHOT 15 br.g. Town Crier–Lunawood (Blast) [1989/90 24m^{pu}] moderate hurdler in 1986/7: tailed off when pulled up in September: pulled up in a novice chase in 1983/4: suited by 2½m or more: acts on any going: successful with and without blinkers. *M. J. Wilkinson.* — c— —

DROVERS ROAD 9 br.m. Netherkelly–Bally Mitty (Arctic Slave) [1989/90 16m 17g 17g] stocky mare: novice selling hurdler: form only at 2m: acts on firm and dead going: sometimes amateur ridden. *N. Waggott.* — —

DROWSY 8 b.g. Mississippi–Siesta (Ribero) [1989/90 20d^6 22g^4 21d^2 22s^6 25m^6 22d^6 25m] angular, sparely-made gelding: handicap hurdler: looked most reluctant when runner-up at Warwick in January: ran in snatches when fair sixth in quite valuable event at Liverpool in April on fifth start: stays well: acts on heavy going and good to firm: wears blinkers or a visor: ridden by 7-lb claimer: one to be wary of. *O. Sherwood.* — 114 §

DR PEPPER (NZ) 13 b.g. Old Soldier–Duchess Dare (NZ) (High Rank) [1989/90 c26s* c26d^3] workmanlike gelding: modest chaser: won handicap at Fontwell in February: not disgraced when third at Newton Abbot following month: well suited by a test of stamina: acts well on heavy going and is possibly — **c101** —

unsuited by firm: blinkered third start 1986/7: has looked a difficult ride. *D. H. Barons.*

DR ROCKET 5 b.g. Ragapan–Lady Hansel (Prince Hansel) [1989/90 16g 16g
16m] leggy gelding: eighth foal: brother to Sweeps Hurdle winner Hansel Rag and —
half-brother to 3 winners, including Green Menelek (by Menelek), successful
over hurdles and fences: dam won point-to-point and placed over hurdles after
birth of second foal: behind in novice hurdles. *R. Dickin.*

DRUMSTICK 4 ch.g. Henbit (USA)–Salustrina (Sallust) [1989/90 16f^{5} 16f^{3}
17g^{5} 16g^{2} 16m 16f^{4} 16m^{2}] leggy gelding: placed over 1m on Flat: in frame 4 times 88
over hurdles: acts on firm going: trained until after third start by R. Smyly. *K. C. Bailey.*

DRU RI'S BRU RI 4 b.g. Kafu–Bru Ri (FR) (Sir Gaylord) [1989/90 16f^{6} 16f^{5}
17h^{pu} 16f 16g^{3} 16f^{4} 20g a16g* a16g^{pu}] neat gelding: poor selling hurdler: bought in 73
2,400 gns after winning at Southwell in January: reportedly lame next time: well
beaten over 2½m: acts on firm ground: has had tongue tied down. *W. Bentley.*

DRUSO (USA) 6 b.g. Raise A Cup (USA)–Pretty Pride (USA) (Kentucky
Pride) [1989/90 F16f^{3} F16g^{3} F16g^{6} a20g* 16m^{2} 21m^{2}] rangy gelding with scope: 96
half-brother to several winners on Flat in USA: dam never ran: placed in NH Flat
races: won novice hurdle at Southwell in May by 20 lengths: creditable second to
Alaoui in amateur riders hurdle at Fakenham final start: better suited by 2½m
than shorter: acts on good to firm ground: blinkered over hurdles. *R. F. Marvin.*

DRY GIN 7 ch.g. Grundy–Karajinska (USA) (Nijinsky (CAN)) [1989/90 24g^{6} c—
22g 21g^{pu}] leggy, plain gelding: won 3 novice chases in 1988/9: well beaten over —
hurdles in 1989/90: stays 3m (stiff task over 4m): acts on any going: has worn
visor, but better without. *M. C. Chapman.*

DUAL CAPACITY (USA) 6 b.g. Coastal (USA)–Fenney Mill (Levmoss)
[1989/90 16f* 16m^{3} 16g^{6} a18g] angular gelding: first form over hurdles for some 94
time when winning handicap at Stratford in September: off course nearly 6
months prior to final start (not knocked about): stays 19f: acts on any going. *W. J. Musson.*

DUAL VENTURE 8 ch.g. Brigadier Gerard–Selham (Derring-Do) [1989/90 c87
16m^{3} 16m^{4} 22d 20g^{4} 20g^{5} c21d^{F} c20m^{3}] compact, workmanlike gelding: handicap 110
hurdler: showed ability both starts in novice chases: seems best at 2m on a sound
surface over hurdles: has won for a claimer: visored fifth and last starts: sold
2,000 gns Doncaster Spring Sales. *J. G. FitzGerald.*

DUART 10 b.g. Saunter–Traverser (Spiritus) [1989/90 c18f^{3}] tall, shallow- c—
girthed gelding: winning hurdler/chaser: tailed-off last only outing of season —
(December): stays 2¾m: acts on heavy going: takes a strong hold and difficult
ride: tends to jump to the right. *J. D. Roberts.*

DUBALEA 7 b.g. Dubassoff (USA)–Thirkleby Kate VII (Bivouac) [1989/90 c95
22d^{pu} c16g^{4} c24d^{2} c22d^{ur} c25g^{5}] tall, close-coupled gelding: winning hurdler: 10 —
lengths second to Radical Lady in novice chase at Kelso in February: best at up to
3m: acts on soft going and good to firm: jumps boldly, though to his right. *J. S. Haldane.*

DUBIOUS JAKE 7 b.g. Dubassoff (USA)–Coliemore (Coliseum) [1989/90 c89
c24g^{4} c20g^{3} c24m*] smallish, sparely-made gelding: winning hurdler: odds on, —
won 4-runner novice chase at Hexham in November by 15 lengths: stays well: acts
on heavy going and good to firm: ran creditably when blinkered last 4 starts
1988/9: claimer ridden in 1989/90. *R. D. E. Woodhouse.*

DUBLIN SAGA 5 ch.m. Sagaro–Dublin Express (Tycoon II) [1989/90 F16g^{5}
16d 16g] smallish, workmanlike mare: fourth foal: half-sister to winning hurdler —
Free Travel (by Royalty): dam useful hurdler/chaser: fifth in mares NH Flat race
at Hereford in November: well beaten in novice event and a claimer over hurdles.
Mrs I. McKie.

DUBOMILOVE 7 b.g. Dubassoff (USA)–Lilmi Love (Miralgo) [1989/90 16f
20f^{4} 16f^{3} 20g^{3} 20f^{pu}] tall, close-coupled gelding: poor form in early-season novice 75
hurdles: dead. *J. P. Leigh.*

DUCKHAVEN 7 b.g. Duky–Fair Haven (Fair Seller) [1989/90 25g^{3} 24s^{2}
26v^{ur}] leggy gelding: handicap hurdler: placed at Newbury and Bangor (sweating 111
and edgy, found little): behind when refusing and unseating rider last final outing
(January): stays 3m: suited by give in the ground and acts on heavy: has won for a
claimer: blinkered last 2 starts. *J. H. Baker.*

DUDIE 12 b.g. Karabas–En Clair (Tarqogan) [1989/90 c20g^{3} c20f^{4} c20g^{3} c24m^{3} c**129**
c26f^{F} c22m^{4}] leggy, narrow gelding: fairly useful chaser: just over 3 lengths third —
behind Joint Sovereignty in Mackeson Gold Cup at Cheltenham in November, best effort of season: in frame on same course on next 3 starts: 6 lengths third behind Master Bob in 3m Kim Muir Memorial Challenge Cup: best form at 2½m: acts on any going: sometimes sweats. *R. Akehurst.*

DUDLEY 7 ch.g. Owen Dudley–Altruist (Above Suspicion) [1989/90 16v* 16m
20g] workmanlike gelding: chasing type: first foal: dam won 1¼m maiden: only 95
form over hurdles when 12/1-winner of 10-runner novice event at Folkestone in February: acts well on heavy going. *F. Walwyn.*

DUHALLOW BOY 10 b.g. Ardoon–Mallow Isle (USA) (Young Emperor) c**100**
[1989/90 c25d c20m c21d^{2} c20d^{5} c16d^{3} c19s^{3} c16g^{3} c25f^{pu}] small, strong gelding: —
carries plenty of condition: one-time quite useful hurdler: modest handicap chaser nowadays: pulled up lame final outing: stays 21f: acts on any going: suitable mount for amateur or claimer. *J. R. Upson.*

DUKE OF ABSON (NZ) 6 ch.g. Lakenheath (USA)–Moon Goddess (NZ) c—
(Greek God) [1989/90 a20g^{3} 22m 20g c25d^{ur} c26v] workmanlike gelding: behind 69
in NH Flat races in 1987/8: third in novice hurdle at Southwell in November: well beaten subsequently, including in a novice chase. *D. H. Barons.*

DUKE OF DOLLIS 11 b.g. Condorcet (FR)–Evening Primrose (Varano) c— §
[1989/90 24h^{6} 20m 20g^{pu}] small, rather shallow-girthed gelding: winning hurdler: — §
showed no aptitude for chasing: stayed 23f: acted on any going: ran freely when tried in blinkers: looked to have his own ideas about the game: dead. *W. Storey.*

DUKE OF HAZARD 7 b.g. Royal Palace–Hotlips Moll (Firestreak) [1989/90 c**84**
c16g^{4} c20f^{pu}] well-made gelding: novice hurdler: over 20 lengths fourth to —
Mallypha in novice event at Wincanton in February on chasing debut: every chance when pulled up lame 3 out at Ascot 2½ months later: may prove best at around 2m: has worn a crossed noseband. *N. A. Gaselee.*

DUKE OF PLUMSTEAD 5 gr.g. Alanrod–Natalgo (Native Admiral (USA))
[1989/90 16g^{5}] second in poor juvenile hurdle in 1988: tailed off in selling handicap —
in August: claimer ridden: sold 800 gns Ascot October Sales. *W. T. Kemp.*

DUKE'S WHISTLE 7 gr.g. Whistling Deer–Ruemaro (Peacock (FR)) c**108**
[1989/90 c20g^{F} c20s^{pu} c20m^{3} c25m* c25f*] smallish, good-quartered gelding: —
winning hurdler: successful in novice chases at Wincanton and Wolverhampton in March, landing the odds by 2½ lengths from Comedy Basin on latter course: stays 25f: acts on firm ground and is probably unsuited by soft: tends to be on toes in preliminaries: jumps soundly in the main. *D. Nicholson.*

DUMFRIES 10 b.g. Scottish Rifle–Dashing Diana (Silver Shark) [1989/90 c20s c—
c20v^{F}] robust gelding: won 3 point-to-points in 1987: bit backward when behind in novice chase at Warwick in February. *J. L. Dunlop.*

DUNARUNNA 9 b.g. Hawaiian Return (USA)–Lady Lesa (Dalesa) [1989/90 c— x
17m c27h^{pu} c24m^{pu} c24m] lengthy, dipped-backed gelding: tubed: novice selling —
hurdler: won slowly-run novice chase early in 1988/9: little worthwhile form since: stays 3¼m: acts on firm going: moderate jumper: sold 875 gns Ascot July Sales. *B. Forsey.*

DUNBAR LAD 7 b.g. Tamariscifolia–Pal Greta (Palestine) [1989/90 17m^{pu}]
ran out in NH Flat race in 1988/9: sold out of R. Allan's stable 1,600 gns Doncaster —
August Sales: failed to complete course in point-to-points (ran out once) and a novice hurdle. *T. A. K. Cuthbert.*

DUNCAN IDAHO 7 b.g. Busted–Riboreen (Ribero) [1989/90 16s^{3} 16g^{pu} 16g^{F}
17d 17m^{2} 16m^{4} 20m* 22m^{F}] tall gelding: staying maiden on Flat: attracted no bid 84
after winning selling handicap hurdle at Uttoxeter in May: will stay beyond 2½m: acts on good to firm ground. *R. Callow.*

DUNCIAD 5 b.h. Indian King (USA)–Dame Foolish (Silly Season) [1989/90
16m^{pu} 16f^{pu}] leggy, sparely-made horse: eighth foal: half-brother to 6f winner —
Strapless (by Bustino): dam at her best at 2 yrs when second in Cheveley Park Stakes: tailed off when pulled up in novice event and a seller over hurdles. *Mrs C. M. Budd.*

DUNCLIFFE DANCER 9 b.g. Tachypous–Klondyke Fire (Klondyke Bill) c—
[1989/90 19m^{pu} c21d] of little account. *N. B. Thomson.* —

DUNCTON HILL 4 ch.f. Formidable (USA)–Hazel Bush (Sassafras (FR))
[1989/90 16f^{4} 16s a20g* a20g^{2} a20g^{4} 16g] leggy filly: placed at up to 11f on Flat: 82
beat only other finisher in juvenile hurdle at Lingfield in January: ran creditably

next and last starts: stays 2½m: well beaten on soft ground: trained until after fourth start by J. White. *S. N. Cole.*

DUNGANNON 4 ch.f. Hays–Fairham (Porto Bello) [1989/90 aF14g] second foal: dam, plater, successful at up to 1m: tailed off in NH Flat race at Southwell in February: yet to race over hurdles. *T. Casey.*

DUNLORING 7 b. or br.g. Dunphy–Blessingtonia (So Blessed) [1989/90 **c102**
c16g^{su} c16g^{3} c16g^{3} c16g^{2} c16d* c16m* c16m^{2} c16d^{pu}] leggy, sparely-made —
gelding: fair 2m hurdler: won novice chases at Edinburgh (handicap) in February and Newcastle in March: destroyed after being pulled up at Ayr in April: acted on good to firm and good to soft ground. *G. M. Moore.*

DUNRAVEN ROYAL 7 b.g. Le Bavard (FR)–Vulstar (Vulgan) [1989/90 c—
c20m^{2} c26g^{co}] tall, leggy gelding: fair point-to-pointer, winner twice in 1989: beaten a distance by only other finisher Campsea-Ash in novice chase at Chepstow in April. *R. Curtis.*

DUN ROLFE 10 ch.g. Rolfe (USA)–Dunslipper (Solar Duke) [1989/90 c27f^{5}] c— x
smallish, sparely-made gelding: winning point-to-pointer (has run out and —
refused): poor novice hurdler/steeplechaser: stays 2¾m: blinkered fifth start 1986/7: makes mistakes. *W. A. Crozier.*

DUNSANY PLAYBOY 6 ch.g. Salluceva–Lagore Lady (John John) [1989/90
16s^{pu} 16g^{pu} 16f^{pu}] sparely-made ex-Irish gelding: half-brother to a poor novice —
hurdler by Brave Invader: dam of little account: behind in NH Flat race in 1988/9: tailed off when pulled up in novice hurdles: has sweated. *P. Butler.*

DUNSBROOK LAD 8 ch.g. Be Friendly–Dunsbrook Lass (Daybrook Lad) c—
[1989/90 c24d] big gelding: half-brother to a poor winning point-to-pointer: dam won several point-to-points: backward and ridden by 7-lb claimer, jumped rather sketchily but in touch until after 3 out in novice chase at Leicester in January. *O. R. Prince.*

DUNSTALL 13 b. or br.g. Bivouac–Phillopene (Wilwyn) [1989/90 c20m^{3} c20d^{4} c83 x
c22g^{4} c20g^{3} c20f^{2} c21m^{3}] big, workmanlike gelding: poor chaser: probably stays —
2¾m and acts on any going: usually held up: has won for a 7-lb claimer: jumps badly on occasions. *B. C. Morgan.*

DUNTREE 5 ch.g. Day Is Done–Bay Tree (FR) (Relko) [1989/90 16s^{5} 16g*
21d^{2} 21s^{4} 24d* 22d^{5}] tall ex-Irish gelding: will make a chaser: half-brother to 121 p
numerous winners, notably smart staying hurdler Ravaro (by Raga Navarro): dam won over 1½m in Ireland: won 2 point-to-points and a NH Flat race in 1989 when trained by J. Crowley: progressive hurdler who won novice events at Wolverhampton in January and Chepstow (beat Whats The Crack 1½ lengths) in March: stiff task, creditable fifth of 23 behind Auk Eye in handicap at Ayr in April (made a couple of mistakes): stays well: acts on soft going. *D. Nicholson.*

DUO DROM 5 ch.m. Deep Run–Lady Dromara (Lord of Verona) [1989/90 16s^{5}]
non-thoroughbred mare: half-sister to winning jumper Drom Lady (by Royalty) 78 p
and NH Flat race winner Dromakelly Lad (by Netherkelly): dam never ran: 33/1,

Hare And Hounds Novices' Hurdle, Chepstow—
Duntree (left) stays on from Whats The Crack

promising fifth to Ri-Na-Rithann in 22-runner novice hurdle at Warwick in February, leading sixth until weakening as lack of condition told from 2 out (not knocked about): should improve. *Mrs D. Haine.*

DURATIVE 5 gr.h. Moorestyle–Zedative (FR) (Zeddaan) [1989/90 17f6] leggy, sparely-made horse: plating-class sprint maiden on Flat: 50/1 and amateur ridden, tailed off in novice hurdle at Newton Abbot in August: sold 1,000 gns Ascot September Sales. *W. G. Turner.* —

DURHAM EDITION 12 ch.g. Politico (USA)–Level Stakes (Even Money) [1989/90 c24g* c26f4 c25f2 c24g* c36f2 c29f2] c**155** —

The media is rarely stuck for copy about the Grand National winner. It wasn't in 1990, and certainly wouldn't have been had the first two positions been reversed. The runner-up Durham Edition had finished second and fifth on his two previous appearances in the National, one of the few big steeplechases to have eluded Arthur Stephenson in his thirty-one years as a trainer. In the latest race—run on his seventieth birthday—Stephenson sent out three runners of which Durham Edition was easily the shortest-priced at 9/1 third favourite. Patiently ridden on the first circuit as usual, Durham Edition moved into the first six shortly after halfway and was travelling strongly from second Becher's. He was sent on into second at the penultimate fence, jumped the last going well two lengths behind Mr Frisk and drew almost upsides the eventual winner at the elbow. But if the stage was set for the perfect finale Mr Frisk remained unaware of the script. Despite jockey Grant's powerful urgings Durham Edition was unable to produce the kind of rattling finish with which Rhyme N'Reason had denied the partnership victory two years earlier. Through the last hundred yards Durham Edition was always held, though he had drawn twenty lengths clear of third-placed Rinus at the line. Durham Edition thus became the fourth horse since the war to finish second in the National at least twice without also winning it, following Tudor Line, Freddie and Greasepaint—all runners-up in consecutive years—and Wyndburgh, the only horse to have suffered the fate three times. For Grant it was the third time in five years that he had finished second; he also partnered Young Driver, second to West Tip in 1986. The exceptionally firm ground at Liverpool probably provided Durham Edition with his best chance of victory in the National as it disadvantaged many of the other contenders. He'll be fortunate to have as good an opportunity again. And age is not on his side—not since Sergeant Murphy in 1923 has a thirteen-year-old won the race.

Charlie Hall Memorial Wetherby Pattern Chase, Wetherby—Durham Edition makes a winning reappearance at 33/1

Rowland Meyrick Handicap Chase, Wetherby—Durham Edition is challenged by Ballyhane

Although the Grand National was once again the principal target of Durham Edition's season his slightly shorter than usual campaign was more ambitious, and included two notable victories. On his reappearance in November he won the Charlie Hall Memorial Wetherby Pattern Chase (at odds of 33/1) by eight lengths from Ballyhane and when returned to Wetherby on Boxing Day he got the best of a tight finish with Nick The Brief and Ballyhane in the Rowland Meyrick Handicap Chase. In both races Grant chose to ride a stable-companion, Sir Jest on the first occasion and The Thinker on the second. Durham Edition also gave a good account of himself on his other starts. He finished an eight-length fourth to Ghofar in the Hennessy Cognac Gold Cup and went down by two and a half lengths, wandering under pressure, to Royal Cedar in the Ferrero Rocher Chase at Cheltenham. Kept in training after Liverpool he once again finished second to Mr Frisk, this time in the Whitbread Gold Cup at Sandown. The issue was settled much earlier than in the National with Durham Edition off the bridle three out and never landing a blow, eventually going down by eight lengths.

Durham Edition (ch.g. 1978)	Politico (USA) (b 1967)	Right Royal V (br 1958)	Owen Tudor
			Bastia
		Tendentious (b 1959)	Tenerani
			Ambiguity
	Level Stakes (ch 1969)	Even Money (br 1955)	Krakatao
			Vendome
		Bonne Foi (b 1957)	Vulgan
			No Trust

Durham Edition's sire, the St Leger third Politico, is still going strong, standing at the Busk Hill Stud in Yorkshire at an advertised fee of £100 + £400 (Oct 1). Politico's reputation as a sire of staying chasers, built upon the likes of Political Pop, Allerlea and Stearsby as well as Durham Edition, was upheld in the latest season by the useful novice Party Politics. The dam's side of Durham Edition's pedigree is undistinguished. Neither his dam Level Stakes nor her dam Bonne Foi showed any worthwhile form over jumps. Both Level Stakes's other reported foals were by Saucy Kit, and both were poor performers, although White House Lad got his head in front in a weakly-contested novice hurdle at Ayr. Durham Edition is a tall, leggy gelding. Though a poor mover, he acts on any going and, as his performances at Liverpool underline, he jumps well and stays well. He is usually held up. *W. A. Stephenson.*

DURZI 5 b.g. High Line–Sookera (USA) (Roberto (USA)) [1989/90 16f2 16m 16s 16m2 16f] rangy gelding: modest novice hurdler: second at Wincanton in November and Fakenham (beaten a head in conditional jockeys novice handicap) in March: takes good hold and suited by sharp 2m: yet to race on heavy going, acts on any other. *C. C. Elsey.* 85

DUSKY'S SPIRIT 11 b.m. Master Spiritus–Dusky Princess II (Lord Fox) [1989/90 c27sF c24vpu] rather sparely-made mare: no sign of ability over hurdles and in steeplechases: won a point-to-point in 1989. *Mrs A. B. Appleyard.* c— —

DUST CONQUERER (USA) 9 b.g. Dust Commander (USA)–Ivory Star (USA) (Sir Ivor) [1989/90 c21dpu c25mpu] neat gelding: poor novice hurdler/chaser: stays 2¾m: acts on good to firm ground: has worn blinkers: wore a tongue strap last outing. *Mrs J. Bettles.* c— —

DUSTY DIPLOMACY (USA) 7 b.g. Run Dusty Run (USA)–Faithful Diplomacy (USA) (Diplomat Way) [1989/90 c17f3 c17h2 c16mF c21gr c18f4 c18m] leggy gelding: winning hurdler/chaser: has been beaten in sellers, including on final start (December): refused second in valuable event in Belgium fourth outing: stays 19f: acts on hard going: wears blinkers or a visor. *M. C. Pipe.* **c96** —

DUSTY MILLER 4 b.g. Current Magic–Royal Barb (Barbin) [1989/90 F16g3] fourth foal: half-brother to winning point-to-pointer Riverboat Queen (by Rapid River): dam poor maiden point-to-pointer: 50/1, 7 lengths third of 15 behind Solo Cornet in NH Flat race at Edinburgh in February: sold 16,000 gns Doncaster Spring Sales: yet to race over hurdles. *J. S. Wilson.*

DUTCH AUCTION 6 b.g. Taufan (USA)–Mock Auction (Auction Ring (USA)) [1989/90 16m] 6f winner at 2 yrs in Britain: placed over hurdles in Ireland as a juvenile: finished lame when well beaten in seller at Uttoxeter in November. *Mrs P. A. Barker.* —

DUTCH CALL 7 br.g. Callernish–Castle-Lady (Little Buskins) [1989/90 20gur 20v*] medium-sized, useful sort: will make a chaser: won 3 completed starts in point-to-points in Ireland in 1988: improving hurdler: won handicap at Haydock in January in good style by 8 lengths from Nodforms Dilemma, leading 4 out and quickening clear before last: will stay 3m: acts well on heavy going: has won for an amateur and a claimer. *J. J. O'Neill.* 134 p

DUTCH MAJESTY 4 b.f. Homing–Dutch Princess (Royalty) [1989/90 16m6 16f3 20g 18s3 a18g* a20g2] small filly: half-sister to Tote Cesarewitch winner Double Dutch (by Nicholas Bill): well beaten on Flat: made most to win 4-runner juvenile hurdle at Lingfield in February by 12 lengths: ridden by 7-lb claimer, held up when second of 4 on same course later in month (gave impression she'll be suited by return to stronger handling): stays 2½m: acts on any going: visored last 3 starts. *Miss B. Sanders.* 86

DUTCH SCHULTZ 4 b.g. Uncle Pokey–Double Duchess (Connaught) [1989/90 F12g F14v] second foal: dam, poor maiden at 2 yrs, half-sister to winning selling hurdler Airlanka: behind in NH Flat races in March and April: yet to race over hurdles. *I. Semple.*

DWADME 5 b.g. High Top–Durun (Run The Gantlet (USA)) [1989/90 16s2 21d* 17m* 25m* 20d3] 130 p

As was to be expected of one well suited by a test of stamina on the Flat, Dwadme showed much improved form when stepped up in distance over hurdles. Successful in run-of-the-mill novice company at Ludlow and Devon & Exeter, he went on to complete his hat-trick by accounting for much stronger oppositition in the twenty-five-furlong White Satin Novices' Hurdle at Liverpool in April. The third running of the White Satin Hurdle was widely expected to fall to Miinnehoma, a twelve-length winner of the Philip Cornes Saddle of Gold Final at Newbury on his previous start. He started at odds on, with only Tinryland and Dwadme seriously backed to beat him. Miinnehoma made the running, as he usually does, but he set only a steady pace and turning for home he was under pressure and being strongly pressed by The Illywhacker, the pair followed in turn by Dwadme, Tinryland and Whats The Crack. Dwadme was travelling ominously well at this point, and after moving through smoothly to take up the running at the second last he quickly put the issue beyond doubt. Clear jumping the last,

White Satin Novices' Hurdle, Liverpool—Dwadme stays on best

Dwadme was kept up to his work until the line, where he had four lengths to spare over Whats the Crack, who stayed on much the best of the remainder. Dwadme, who'd raced only on a sound surface on the Flat, acted well on the good to firm ground at Liverpool. But he went on to show himself to be effective on good to soft in a two-and-a-half-mile novice handicap at Ayr on his final start. Staying on well over a distance short of his best, Dwadme finished just under two lengths third behind King's Curate. Dwadme will improve further when returned to three miles, and he has the makings of a very useful handicapper.

Dwadme (b.g. 1985)	High Top (b 1969)	Derring-Do (b 1961)	Darius
			Sipsey Bridge
		Camenae (b 1961)	Vimy
			Madrilene
	Durun (b 1979)	Run The Gantlet (b 1968)	Tom Rolfe
			First Feather
		Duboff (br 1972)	So Blessed
			Proper Pretty

Dwadme, a compact gelding, cost his present connections 29,000 guineas at the Newmarket Autumn Sales. He won twice on the Flat for trainer Henry Candy, as did his year older half-brother Durbo (by Bustino), who also stayed well. They were the first two foals of Durun, a fairly useful winner at up to a mile and a half. She, too, was trained by Candy. Durun's third foal, Dutch Interior (by Formidable), is a winner in Italy. The second dam Duboff was one of the toughest fillies in training in the 1970's, when her eleven victories included one in the Extel Stakes and another in the Sun Chariot Stakes. Duboff is daughter of Proper Pretty, a winning half-sister to the very useful staying fillies Ticklish and Miba. *O. Sherwood.*

DWALE (USA) 5 b.h. Bates Motel (USA)–Chip O'Chocolate (USA) (Cornish Prince) [1989/90 21s^{pu} 16m^{6} 16m 24f^{3} 19f^{F} 20m 19m 22m^{4} 24m^{pu}] lengthy, angular horse: poor novice hurdler: stays 3m: acts on firm going: visored sixth and seventh starts (well beaten). *R. J. Eckley.* 70

DYFED 5 b.h. Daring March–Regency Brighton (Royal Palace) [1989/90 20g^{pu} 16g^{pu}] sparely-made horse: of little account: pulls hard. *M. Tate.* —

DYNAMIC STAR 6 b.g. Lord Gayle (USA)–Stellarevagh (Le Levanstell) [1989/90 16v^{pu} 16s^{4} 16d] workmanlike gelding: only sign of ability over hurdles when fourth in novice handicap at Uttoxeter in February. *C. C. Trietline.* 59

DYNAVON 4 b.f. Dynastic–Avon Melody (Bilsborrow) [1989/90 F17m F16f] first foal: dam poor novice hurdler: well behind in 2 NH Flat races in April: yet to race over hurdles. *D. W. MacDonald.*

E

EAGLE MOSS 8 br.g. Legal Eagle–Septett (Levmoss) [1989/90 16f^{2} 18f* 16f^{3} c16g^{ur}] sturdy gelding: handicap hurdler: won at Fontwell in October: had just taken lead when unseating rider at the last in novice event at Fakenham in October on chasing debut: stays 2¼m: acts on firm ground and dead going: blinkered last 6 starts 1987/8: sold 500 gns Ascot November Sales. *A. Moore.* c84 ? 84

EAMONS OWEN 13 br.g. Master Owen–Clerihan (Immortality) [1989/90 c16m^{5} 24g c16d^{4} c16d^{2} c25f^{6} c21g^{4} c24m^{2} c24m^{3}] poor chaser nowadays: effective at 2m and stays 25f: acts on heavy and good to firm ground: blinkered first start: usually a front runner. *J. P. Leigh.* c82 —

EARL HANSEL 9 b.g. Hardboy–Cool Amanda (Prince Hansel) [1989/90 24f* 20m^{3} 24m^{3} 25f^{pu} c24m^{4} c27g* c24g^{pu} c27d^{3} c24g^{pu} c26g^{pu} c24m^{pu}] workmanlike gelding: won conditional jockeys handicap hurdle at Uttoxeter in August and modest novice chase at Sedgefield (jumped right last 2 fences) in December: ran poorly afterwards: stays well: acts on any going: front runner: has worn a crossed noseband: seems best when fresh: sold privately 5,750 gns Ascot June Sales. *R. D. E. Woodhouse.* c93 83

EARL SOHAM 7 ch.g. Alias Smith (USA)–Lavenham Rose (Floribunda) [1989/90 20f^{5} c20f^{2} c20m^{5} c20s^{3} c20v^{3}] big, rangy gelding: modest novice/hurdler chaser: stays 2½m: best form on top-of-the-ground. *J. T. Gifford.* c100 82 +

EARLY BREEZE 4 b.g. Tumble Wind (USA)–Dawn Hail (Derring-Do) [1989/90 16g 16d^{6} 16d^{3} 16f^{3}] small gelding: fair handicapper on Flat, stays 7f (ideally suited by give in the ground): modest juvenile hurdler: reportedly broke blood vessel final start: likely to prove best at a sharp 2m. *M. McCourt.* 103

EARTH BEAM 4 b.c. Kampala–Amore Mare (Varano) [1989/90 16v^{6} 16g^{pu}] small colt: no worthwhile form in 2 outings on Flat at 2 yrs: well beaten in juvenile claiming hurdle at Leicester in February: pulled up in a seller following month. *P. J. Makin.* —

EARTH WOOD 5 ch.m. Glenstal (USA)–Faiblesse (Welsh Saint) [1989/90 16f 17g^{6} 20d 17g^{5}] small, lengthy, sparely-made mare: in frame at up to 2m on Flat in Ireland when trained by J. Bolger: poor form over hurdles, including in sellers. *T. B. Hallett.* —

EASTEND BLAKE 6 b.h. Blakeney–Dalmally (Sharpen Up) [1989/90 c16f^{pu}] small, close-coupled horse: novice selling hurdler: bit backward, tailed off when pulled up seventh in novice handicap chase at Bangor in March: stays 2½m: possibly unsuited by very soft ground, acts on any other. *C. C. Trietline.* c— —

EASTER FESTIVAL 9 b.g. Tycoon II–Arctic Festival (Arctic Slave) [1989/90 c20g^{6} c21d^{pu} c21g^{3}] tall, close-coupled gelding: poor novice hurdler/chaser: moderate jumper of fences: stays 2¾m: acts on dead going: tends to hang left under pressure: one to treat with caution. *Mrs P. Sly.* c86 x — §

EASTER LASS 4 b.f. Workboy–Cuenca (Woodville II) [1989/90 F17f F12f 16h^{pu} 16g 16m^{5}] non-thoroughbred filly: second foal: dam won 2m selling hurdle: behind in NH Flat races and selling hurdles: blinkered fourth outing. *Mrs A. E. Ratcliff.* —

EASTERN CHANT 8 b. or br.g. Shantung–Maranatha (Le Prince) [1989/90 c24m^{2} c25f* c26m^{4}] neat gelding: tailed off in juvenile hurdle in 1985 (jumped badly): point-to-pointer, successful in April: won novice hunter chase at Towcester in May by 10 lengths from Hawksmoor: stays 3m: acts on firm going. *Miss I. Dady.* c94 —

EASTERN DESTINY 12 gr.g. Gay Baron–Eastern Faith (Crown Again) [1989/90 c20s* c20s* c20d* c22m^{5} c24g*] tall, close-coupled gelding: winning point-to-pointer: useful hunter chaser: won at Warwick in February (twice) and March and at Bangor (beat Oakley House ½ length) in April: spoilt his chance with a couple of bad mistakes when 30 lengths fifth to Lean Ar Aghaidh in c118

Seagram Fox Hunters' Chase at Liverpool: stays 25f: best form with give in the ground: genuine. *Mrs J. G. Griffith.*

EASTERN EVENING 5 gr.g. Runnett–Sacola (Busted) [1989/90 16f 16s
a16g a16g^{3} a16g 16m^{5} 16m^{6}] medium-sized gelding: poor and inconsistent novice 70
hurdler: usually amateur ridden. *J. E. Long.*

EASTERN MINSTREL 6 ch.g. Black Minstrel–Shackle Walk (Little
Buskins) [1989/90 16m 20m^{5} 25m^{5} 20d^{5} 20d^{pu} 20g^{pu}] big, angular gelding with 74
scope: second foal: dam unraced: showed ability in novice hurdles second to
fourth starts: ran poorly afterwards. *W. A. Stephenson.*

EASTERN OASIS 7 b.g. Anax–Casbar Lady (Native Bazaar) [1989/90 20m^{4}
22s^{ur} 24g^{2} 22v^{4} 24g^{5} 24f^{2} 25m 22d 20g^{5} 20g^{3}] small, short-backed gelding: 109
handicap hurdler: best effort of season on third start: ran moderately last 3
outings: stays 3m: seems to act on any going: has won for an amateur and a
claimer: jumps well. *J. Andrews.*

EASTERN PLAYER 7 ch.g. Royal Match–Cigarette (Miralgo) [1989/90 c16f^{4} c**82** x
25m^{5} c20d^{pu} c21d^{pu} c21s^{pu} c21g^{5} c16d^{5} c21s^{3} c24d^{4} c20d^{4} c25g c24g^{4} c21d^{3} —
c21g^{2} c21g^{4}] neat gelding: poor handicap hurdler/novice chaser: ideally suited by
around 2½m: probably acts on any going: sometimes claimer ridden: has worn
blinkers. *Miss G. M. Rees.*

EASTERN WAY 5 ch.g. Mansingh (USA)–Kate Kimberley (Sparkler)
[1989/90 16g 22d 20m^{pu} 24g^{2}] medium-sized gelding: no worthwhile form on Flat: 89
second in poor novice event at Edinburgh in January, only sign of merit over
hurdles: stays 3m. *J. S. Wilson.*

EASTER RAMBLER 8 b.g. Scott Joplyn–Victory Corner (Sit In The Corner c—
(USA)) [1989/90 16f^{4}] workmanlike gelding: winning hurdler: novice chaser: form 61
only at 2m: acts on firm going: sometimes visored. *P. Butler.*

EAST LIMERICK 7 b.g. Sexton Blake–Shonna (USA) (Carlemont) [1989/90
16f^{2} 16f^{6} 16g^{5}] lightly-raced novice hurdler: second in conditional jockeys selling 68
handicap at Hexham in October, best effort. *W. W. Haigh.*

EAST PARK 10 b.g. Some Hand–Bally Mitty (Arctic Slave) [1989/90 16f 16g^{6}] c—
workmanlike gelding: novice hurdler: winning chaser: little form since 1986/7: —
best at around 2m: possibly unsuited by very soft ground, acts on any other:
sometimes blinkered. *N. Waggott.*

EAST RIVER 6 b.g. Midland Gayle–French Note (Eton Rambler) [1989/90
16g^{5} 16s^{2} 16s 16f] leggy, sparely-made gelding: second in novice hurdle at 102
Warwick in February: below that form afterwards: acts on soft going. *G. B.
Balding.*

EASTSHAW 8 b.g. Crash Course–What A Duchess (Bargello) [1989/90 c20s^{4} c**111** x
c20g^{4}] lengthy gelding: lightly-raced chaser, often let down by his jumping: better —
effort of season on first start: should stay beyond 2½m: acts on soft going. *Capt.
T. A. Forster.*

EASY MATCH 4 b.f. Royal Match–Flying Easy (Swing Easy (USA)) [1989/90
17v^{pu}] first foal: dam well beaten: tailed off when pulled up 3 out in juvenile selling —
hurdle at Newton Abbot (made mistakes) in January. *N. G. Ayliffe.*

EASY OVER (USA) 4 ch.g. Transworld (USA)–Love Bunny (USA)
(Exclusive Native (USA)) [1989/90 16g^{2} 16g* 16g^{5} 16v^{3} 17g] leggy, workmanlike 96
gelding: won over 1m and ran well over 1¼m on heavy ground on Flat: sold out of
S. Norton's stable 11,000 gns Newmarket Autumn Sales: won juvenile hurdle at
Edinburgh in January: bit below form afterwards, shaping as though he'll be suited
by stiffer test of stamina. *G. M. Moore.*

EASY STEED 12 b.g. Sheshoon–Kentucky Blues (Royal Record II) [1989/90 c—
c25m^{5} c32f^{6}] medium-sized gelding: winning point-to-pointer/chaser: no —
worthwhile form in steeplechases since 1987, but won a point-to-point in April:
finished lame final start. *Major S. Ellwood.*

EASY TIME (GER) 5 b.g. High Line–Easily (Swing Easy (USA)) [1989/90
20v 16d] lengthy, rather sparely-made gelding: won twice over 1½m on Flat in —
1989: tailed off in novice hurdles. *P. F. I. Cole.*

EAT YOUR HAT 6 br.g. Fine Blade (USA)–Honey's Queen (Pals Passage)
[1989/90 22v^{pu} 16g 24d^{pu}] leggy gelding: third reported foal: half-brother to 6f to —
1m winner Irish Passage (by Welsh Captain): dam never ran: no sign of ability in
novice hurdles. *P. A. Blockley.*

EBONY SWELL 9 b.g. Eborneezer–Jenysis (Compensation) [1989/90 c24dpu] rather unfurnished gelding: winning point-to-pointer: successful in 2 hunter chases in 1989: looked and ran as though in need of race in February: stays 3m: acts on any going. *S. W. Campion.* c—

EBORACUM 12 ch.g. Sheshoon–Swift Fire (Firestreak) [1989/90 c20g c24d3 25f5] stocky gelding: one-time fairly useful hurdler: winning chaser: lightly raced nowadays and no form for long time: stays well: needs give but seems unsuited by very soft ground: ran out once in 1985/6. *B. E. Wilkinson.* c— —

EBORNEEZER'S DREAM 7 ch.g. Eborneezer–Portate (Articulate) [1989/90 a16g2 a16g] workmanlike gelding: poor novice hurdler: not raced after running poorly in November: should be suited by further than 2m: ridden by 7-lb claimer. *Mrs S. Lamyman.* 81

EBRO 4 ch.g. Aragon–Caribbean Blue (Blue Cashmere) [1989/90 16f5] placed at up to 1¼m on Flat: odds on, fifth in juvenile hurdle at Huntingdon in August. *Mrs L. Piggott.* —

ECHO BEACH 9 b.g. Cidrax (FR)–Crest Aston (Steeple Aston) [1989/90 16g] compact gelding: winning point-to-pointer: modest novice hurdler, lightly raced: no sign of merit in novice chases (refused on debut): probably stays 2½m but not 3m. *Denys Smith.* c— —

ECHO ONE 4 b.g. Ercolano (USA)–Miss Monte Carlo (Reform) [1989/90 16m 18m] medium-sized gelding: first foal: dam placed over 6f at 2 yrs: successful 4 times at up to 1½m on Flat in Belgium: tailed off in juvenile hurdles in first half of season: bolted before start final outing: races freely and jumps moderately: sold 2,600 gns Ascot February Sales. *R. J. O'Sullivan.* —

ECHO SOUNDER 11 ch.g. Deep Run–Indicate (Mustang) [1989/90 c25d2 c24gF] tall, rangy gelding: fair chaser: fell fatally at Windsor in January: suited by 3m+: acted on heavy going. *Capt. T. A. Forster.* c**114** —

ECOSSAIS DANSEUR (USA) 4 ch.c. Arctic Tern (USA)–Northern Blossom (CAN) (Snow Knight) [1989/90 17g6 16v4] small, angular colt: fair performer on Flat, stays 1¼m: modest form in juvenile hurdles: has joined T. Stack in Ireland. *B. W. Hills.* 90

EDBERG 6 b. or br.g. Strong Gale–White Shoes (Tiepolo II) [1989/90 20g 22d] lengthy ex-Irish gelding: seventh foal: half-brother to fair hurdlers The Black Sack (by Kemal) and Bigee (by Windjammer): dam never ran: won NH Flat race at Naas and maiden hurdle at Leopardstown in 1988/9: sold out of M. O'Toole's stable 4,200 gns Doncaster October Sales: weakened quickly from 3 out in handicaps in January and April: may prove best at around 2m. *J. H. Johnson.* —

EDDIE KYBO 5 ch.g. Cidrax (FR)–Claragh Run (Deep Run) [1989/90 16f* 20g4 18v3 18f4 18f3 16m] first foal: dam poor Irish maiden: won novice hurdle at Plumpton in October: in frame in similar events on same course and at Fontwell: likely to stay 3m. *J. T. Gifford.* 83

EDDIES FELLA 5 b.g. New Member–Daniel's Fancy (Cheveley Lad) [1989/90 16g5 16f6 20gpu] tall, leggy gelding: second in juvenile hurdle in 1988/9: well beaten in novice events in first half of 1989/90: possibly needs soft ground: has sweated up. *R. J. Holder.* —

EDENBURT 12 ch.m. Bargello–Rockwood Lady (Aeolian) [1989/90 c28gpu c24fpu] small, sparely-made mare: poor novice hurdler/chaser: stays well: moderate jumper: blinkered final start in 1988/9. *Miss A. J. Aitkin.* c— x —

EDENSPRING 11 b.g. Pitpan–Velocity's Gift (Babur) [1989/90 c27m* c22mpu c24f* c26f* c26m2] well-made, deep-girthed, good-looking gelding: developed into a very useful hunter chaser and made all at Sedgefield, Southwell and Cheltenham (beat Polar Glen 8 lengths in Audi Champion Hunters' Chase) in the spring: ran another good race when 25 lengths second to Mystic Music in Horse And Hound Cup at Stratford in June: pulled up before halfway in Seagram Fox Hunters' Chase at Liverpool: stays 3½m: acts on any going: has worn blinkers: has looked temperamental, but did little wrong in 1989/90. *C. J. Lumsden.* c**127** —

EDGE O' BEYOND 5 ch.m. Monksfield–Bright Society (Choral Society) [1989/90 F16g3 21f3 a24g5] leggy, light-framed mare: fifth foal: dam unraced: third in mares NH Flat race at Hereford in November and mares novice hurdle at Warwick in December: weakened 2 out when well beaten over 3m 2½ months later. *P. J. Hobbs.* 76

EDGE OF THE WIND 8 b.g. Arapaho–Chammyville (Chamier) [1989/90 16f 20f[ro]] angular gelding: winning point-to-pointer: has shown signs of ability over hurdles and in steeplechases but is very headstrong (ran out in October): sold 1,000 gns Doncaster January Sales. *C. W. Thornton.* c— —

EDOZIEN 11 ch.g. Sun Prince–Lady Mouse (Sir Ivor) [1989/90 16s[pu] 20s[pu] 20s] leggy gelding: poor hurdler: no form for some time (well beaten in selling handicap final start): probably stays 2¾m (tailed off over 3m): acts on heavy going. *M. Dickinson.* —

EDWARD'S CORNER 12 b. or br.m. Sit In The Corner (USA)–Guid Tassie (French Beige) [1989/90 25g[F]] lightly-made mare: winning hurdler/chaser: fell sixth in November: stays well: suited by give in the ground: good mount for a claimer: has won 4 times at Sedgefield. *J. Dooler.* c— —

EDWARDS LAST 6 b.g. Edwards Hill–Jolly Pigeon (Jolly Jet) [1989/90 aF14g[6] 16s[pu]] workmanlike gelding: fifth foal: dam placed over hurdles: well beaten in NH Flat race and when pulled up in novice hurdle. *R. E. Peacock.* —

EDWARDS VISION 9 ch.g. Pollerton–Comeragh Vision (Golden Vision) [1989/90 c20d* c20d[6]] rangy, good sort: winning hurdler: fair chaser: having first race for nearly 2 years when winning handicap at Ayr in January, making most: never travelling well later in month: will prove best at around 2½m: acts on heavy going: has wandered under pressure, and looks a difficult ride: jumps well. *T. P. Tate.* **c121** —

EGYPT MILL 5 b.g. Deep Run–Little Dipper (Queen's Hussar) [1989/90 16g* 16d*] strong, sturdy gelding: half-brother to 4 winning jumpers, including very useful Irish performer Royal Dipper (by Royal Captive), very smart staying hurdler Henry Mann (by Mandalus) and winning hurdler/very useful novice chaser Formula One (by Ardoon): dam lightly-raced winning stayer on Flat: impressive winner of novice hurdles at Towcester in December and Ascot (by 1½ lengths from Whatever You Like) following month: dead. *Mrs J. Pitman.* 130

EIGHT SPRINGS 9 b.g. Le Bavard (FR)–Happy Adventure (Credo) [1989/90 c16m[3] c22m[4] c29f c21m[3]] lengthy gelding: winning point-to-pointer/hurdler/chaser: creditable fourth to Wont Be Gone Long in John Hughes Memorial Trophy Chase (Handicap) at Liverpool in April: very stiff task next outing, ran moderately final start: stays 3m: acts well on firm ground and seems unsuited by heavy. *J. R. Jenkins.* **c112** —

EILLIE ON 7 ch.m. Spur On–Flaming Onions (Hot Brandy) [1989/90 16g 18d 17g 16g[pu] 16d 17d 17m[5] 20f[5] 16h*] small, workmanlike mare: poor hurdler: made all when easy winner of 3-runner handicap at Kelso in May: best at around 2m: acts on hard and dead going: has worn crossed noseband: sometimes claimer ridden. *J. L. Goulding.* 79

EJAY HAITCH 5 b.h. Be My Native (USA)–Miss Spencer (Imperial Fling (USA)) [1989/90 20g[6] 24m[6] 20g[ur] 20d 24d[6]] rather sparely-made horse: poor novice hurdler: stays 2½m: claimer ridden: usually wears a crossed noseband. *T. Kersey.* —

EJREE 5 b.g. Runnett–Carntino (Bustino) [1989/90 16m 16g 16d[3] 16m[2] 19g 16g 16d[pu]] smallish, workmanlike gelding: poor novice hurdler: form only at 2m: acts on good to firm and dead going: never going well final start. *R. G. Brazington.* 76

ELA-AYABI-MOU 4 ch.f. Absalom–Fairfields (Sharpen Up) [1989/90 16m[3] 16m[3] a16g[2] a16s[3] a16g[5] a16g[5] 16m[4] 16f[3]] leggy, sparely-made filly: quite modest performer on Flat, suited by 7f: sold out of J. Payne's stable 3,200 gns Newmarket Autumn Sales: poor form over hurdles, including in a seller: reportedly finished lame final start: takes a good hold and unlikely to stay much beyond 2m: claimer ridden: has looked a difficult ride. *A. S. Reid.* 75

ELDER PRINCE 4 ch.g. Final Straw–Particular Miss (Luthier) [1989/90 16d[6] 16m* 16g[3]] sparely-made gelding: fair 5f winner and in frame at 1m on Flat: quickened well run-in when winning novice hurdle at Newcastle in March: fair third of 4 to Old Virginia in juvenile handicap at Stratford following month: likely to prove best at 2m: acts on good to firm ground. *M. H. Easterby.* 105

ELEANOR CROSS 5 br.m. Kala Shikari–Ribofleur (Ribero) [1989/90 16s[pu] 16g 16m[2] 16g[2]] big, leggy mare: runner-up in selling handicap hurdle at Fakenham in March and amateur riders maiden at Market Rasen in May: evidently suited by a sharp 2m and a sound surface. *B. Richmond.* 74

ELECTRIC DANCER 4 br.g. Electric–Chicory (Vaigly Great) [1989/90 16g] rather sparely-made gelding: first foal: dam twice-raced half-sister to 3 winning —

jumpers, including Baz Bombati and Calabrese: placed over 1½m on Flat: tailed off in juvenile hurdle at Kempton in January. *C. A. Horgan.*

ELECTRIC MONEY 4 b.c. Kafu–Silver Bullion (Silver Shark) [1989/90 17vpu 16m 16fur] sparely-made colt: modest 6f winner on Flat: sold out of G. Pritchard-Gordon's stable 2,700 gns Ascot September Sales: no sign of ability over hurdles, including in a seller. *W. G. Turner.* —

ELEGANT BAR 7 b.m. Latest Model–Evening Bar (Pardigras) [1989/90 F17h2 22mpu] first foal: dam unraced: pulled up in point-to-point in 1988: second in NH Flat race at Devon & Exeter in October: tailed off when pulled up 2 out in amateur riders novice hurdle at Wincanton following month. *P. J. Hobbs.* —

ELEGANT GUEST 7 ch.g. Be My Guest (USA)–Countess Eileen (Sassafras (FR)) [1989/90 20f2] lengthy, angular gelding: handicap hurdler: very lightly raced: walked back feelingly when second of 3 at Sedgefield in September: stays 2½m: best form on top-of-the-ground: suited by a strongly-run race: looks a hard ride and needs strong handling. *Denys Smith.* 114

ELEGANT MARY 6 gr.m. Grey Ghost–Mary Mcquaker (Acer) [1989/90 16g4 16g 20d] strong mare: won 2m novice hurdle at Sedgefield in 1987 on debut: shaped as though retaining ability when fourth in handicap at Catterick when next seen out over 2 years later, but tailed off afterwards: acts on soft going. *B. E. Wilkinson.* —

ELEGANT STRANGER 5 b.g. Krayyan–Tumvella (Tumble Wind (USA)) [1989/90 16d2 16m* 16m* 16s* 18g3 16d2] smallish, workmanlike gelding: won handicap hurdles at Windsor (conditional jockeys) in November and Wolverhampton (4-y-o event) and Fakenham in December: best effort when second at Ascot in January: best at 2m: yet to race on extremes of going, acts on any other. *M. H. Tompkins.* 117

ELEMENTARY 7 b.g. Busted–Santa Vittoria (Ragusa) [1989/90 16d2 16g 16s2 16m] 160

Owner Paul Green had two horses quoted in the ante-post betting on the Waterford Crystal Champion Hurdle in the first half of the latest season. One-time useful Flat performer Lemhill entered some lists at around 20/1 after winning by twenty lengths at Newton Abbot in August on his first outing for Pipe. Elementary, a leading Irish novice in 1988/9, ran well on the Flat in the summer and was generally available at around 12/1 immediately prior to his reappearance over hurdles in December. Neither horse gave a return to his backers. Lemhill wasn't seen out again and is evidently difficult to train nowadays. Elementary made it to Cheltenham fit and well and looked to be running a good race when moving up to be in touch with the leaders approaching the third last, but his run petered out from the next. Failing to quicken with the top two-milers in the fast conditions, he finished tenth, around twenty-four lengths behind Kribensis.

Elementary actually started at 22/1 in a field of nineteen at Cheltenham, having been available at 33/1 on the morning of the race. Though he had shown high-class form in his previous races, to some eyes Elementary had flattered to deceive—travelling smoothly on the bridle for a long way but finding less than expected under pressure in the closing stages. As he's a thoroughly genuine sort on the Flat, we're prepared to give Elementary the benefit of the doubt. He probably needed the race when narrowly beaten in the Bookmakers Hurdle at Leopardstown in December on his first run for two and a half months: having looked the probable winner when taking up the running in the straight he was worn down on the run-in by the ultra-game Grabel and beaten a head. Elementary lost no caste in defeat by Nomadic Way, who was receiving 3 lb, in the Wessel Cable Champion Hurdle on the same course the following month. Travelling well on the heels of the leaders turning into the straight, his jockey delayed his effort until before the last; when ridden, the horse kept on at only one pace to be beaten six lengths at the finish. Elementary didn't quicken either in the latter stages when nineteenth behind Redundant Pal under top-weight of 12-0 in The Ladbroke at Leopardstown in between: having moved up from last place to threaten briefly two out, he could make no further impression in the straight. Whether he will stay beyond two and a quarter miles is open to doubt. Though he stays a mile and a half on the Flat, Elementary is at

Mr Paul Green's "Elementary"

least as effective over shorter distances—he narrowly failed to beat the very useful Just Three over a mile at Phoenix Park in May—and has plenty of speed.

Elementary (b.g. 1983)	Busted (b 1963)	Crepello (ch 1954)	Donatello II
			Crepuscule
		Sans Le Sou (b 1957)	Vimy
			Martial Loan
	Santa Vittoria (b 1966)	Ragusa (b 1960)	Ribot
			Fantan II
		Running Blue (ch 1957)	Blue Peter
			Run Honey

Elementary has the pedigree of a good Flat-racer. Though Santa Vittoria was retired a maiden, she was capable of useful form and finished fourth in the Irish One Thousand Guineas. The next two dams showed plenty of ability, Running Blue finishing third in the One Thousand Guineas and Run Honey third in the Cherry Hinton Stakes, and both have left their mark at stud, notably as the grandams of the sires Persian Bold and Lord Gayle respectively. Elementary is a half-brother to several winners, including Indispensable (by Glenstal), successful in a selling handicap hurdle at Hexham in May, and the very useful Irish middle-distance filly Santa Roseanna (by Caracol). The latter has already bred three winners, including useful sprinter King's College; her foal of 1989 by Green Desert was sold for 185,000 guineas at Newmarket in December. Elementary continued to run well on the Flat in 1990, and won a mile-and-a-quarter listed race at Phoenix Park in May. He should also continue to give a good account of himself in good company over hurdles. Elementary, a strong, angular gelding, acts on any going on the Flat but gives the impression he'll prove best with give in the ground when racing at two miles over hurdles. He wore a tongue strap at Cheltenham. *J. S. Bolger, Ireland.*

ELEVEN LIGHTS (USA) 6 ch.g. Lyphard (USA)–Eleven Pelicans (USA) (Grey Dawn II) [1989/90 16f3 20f* 17h* 20f* 16fpu 20f4 20g6] sparely-made gelding: poor top-of-the-ground middle-distance maiden on Flat (usually held up): successful in novice hurdles at Sedgefield and Carlisle in September and novice handicap on former course in October: ran moderately final start (December): saddle slipped fifth start: stays 2½m: has raced only on a sound surface over hurdles. *Mrs G. R. Reveley.* 98

ELFAST 7 b.g. Neltino–Niagara Rhythm (Military) [1989/90 c16m* c20v2 c16g2 c16g2 c20s4 c16d* c20m2 c16m3 c20f* c19m* c22m2 c16m*] **c133 p** —

After finishing second in two of the qualifiers in the Steel Plate And Sections Young Chasers' Series, Elfast went one better in the Final itself, earning over £14,000 in the process. It was easy money. The tenth running of this event, which takes place at Cheltenham in April, had a very disappointing turn-out numerically, Elfast being opposed only by Espy and Certain Style. Espy had beaten Elfast by half a length at level weights in the Uttoxeter qualifier, but the latter looked to have excellent prospects of turning the tables in receipt of 7 lb. The pair shared favouritism at 11/10, with Certain Style priced at 9/1. Jumping played a big part in the outcome. Both Certain Style and Espy made mistakes, whereas Elfast never put a foot wrong. In our opinion Elfast was already travelling like a winner when Espy, who was just behind him, fell three out, leaving Elfast to come home unchallenged, thirty lengths ahead of Certain Style. This was the highlight of Elfast's busy and very successful first season over fences. On the go from early-November until the penultimate day of the season, Elfast had twelve races and finished in the frame in each of them. He kept his condition really well and very much took the eye before his final start, a credit to his trainer. Prior to Cheltenham Elfast had won novice events at Uttoxeter and Warwick; and he was successful afterwards in similar events at Hereford and Stratford. Three of Elfast's defeats are worth mentioning. He ran very well when three lengths second to On The Other Hand in a nine-runner event at Leopardstown on his fourth start; and but for a bad mistake three out he'd have been involved in the finish of the Perrier Jouet Novices' Chase at Liverpool. Elfast finished thirteen and a half lengths fourth to Boutzdaroff at Liverpool, later moved up a place on the disqualification of Blazing Walker. Elfast is equally effective at two miles and two and a half miles when the ground is on the fast side, but he appears not quite to stay the

Steel Plate And Sections Young Chasers' Final, Cheltenham—a bloodless victory for Elfast

Mr John Webber's "Elfast"

latter trip under very testing conditions. He ran slightly below his best when tried over two miles and six furlongs, going down by six lengths to Night Session in a two-runner race at Stratford.

Elfast (b.g. 1983)	Neltino (gr 1978)	Bustino (b 1971)	Busted
			Ship Yard
		Flying Nelly (gr 1970)	Nelcius
			Flying By
	Niagara Rhythm (br 1973)	Military (b 1963)	Milesian
			Burp
		Acacallis (b 1964)	Red God
			Sens Unique

Elfast hung right and carried his head high under pressure once over hurdles, but he's done nothing wrong over fences and is a much more reliable racehorse than was his dam. Niagara Rhythm, a half-sister to the quite useful jumper Master Davenport, had plenty of ability and won two-mile hurdle races at Southwell and Hereford. But Niagara Rhythm, who wore blinkers, also had more than her share of temperament, and she refused to race on a couple of occasions. The second dam Acacallis, a half-sister to numerous winners, showed modest form over six furlongs at two years; and the third dam Sens Unique was successful in a five-furlong seller at the same age. Neltino, the sire of Elfast, had his racing career curtailed by a training accident shortly after finishing unplaced in the 1981 King George V Handicap at Royal Ascot. He'd put up his best performance when winning a handicap over one and a half miles on soft ground at Kempton. Elfast, the best of Neltino's representatives to date, looks sure to continue to do well over fences. A good jumper with a turn of foot, he could well pick up a valuable handicap—the Mackeson Gold Cup would be an ideal target in the first half of the season. Elfast acts on good to soft going but he goes particularly well on a firm surface. *J. Webber.*

ELFIE'S SON 6 b.h. Sonnen Gold–Elf Trout (Elf-Arrow) [1989/90 20s5] sturdy horse: little promise in novice hurdles. *T. Thomson Jones.* —

EL GALILEO 8 b.g. Comedy Star (USA)–Spanish Sail (Matador) [1989/90 c21f3 c22gpu c24m4 c19dF c20g* c20sF c21d2 c20s3 c20mpu] sparely-made gelding: one-time fair hurdler: won handicap chase at Folkestone in January: gave impression something may have been amiss eighth outing and was pulled up next time: stays 2½m: acts on soft going: sometimes blinkered: jumps none too fluently: sold 7,200 gns Doncaster Spring Sales. *O. Sherwood.* c**107** —

ELITE BOY 8 ch.g. Deep Run–Elite Lady (Prince Hansel) [1989/90 c16d2 c20m* c20m* c20d3 c20f2 c20f2] lengthy, shallow-girthed gelding: novice hurdler: wandered approaching last, but made most to win novice chases at Wolverhampton (jumped right) and Ludlow (mulish in preliminaries) in November: ran creditably afterwards, going down by 8 lengths to Sword Beach in Racing Post Novice Chasers Series Final (Handicap) at Newbury in March on final start: stays 2½m: acts on firm and dead going: claimer ridden: sound jumper. *M. Oliver.* c**111** —

ELITE ETOILE 5 b.m. Gorytus (USA)–Antipol (Polyfoto) [1989/90 aF13g6 aF16g] half-sister to several winners on Flat, including Kars (by Karabas) who went on to win over fences: has shown ability in NH Flat races: yet to race over hurdles or fences. *B. Preece.*

ELITE LEO 5 b.g. Longleat (USA)–Abielle (Abwah) [1989/90 16v] sturdy gelding: well beaten over hurdles. *D. R. C. Elsworth.* —

ELIZA DOOLITTLE 12 b.m. Master Spiritus–Tantaliser II (Tenterhooks) [1989/90 c26fpu c18h* c16f4] failed to complete course in 2 point-to-points in 1987: won novice chase at Fontwell in April: 15 lengths fourth to Gay Edition in similar event at Taunton later in month: stays 2¼m: acts on hard ground. *G. G. Gracey.* c**81**

EL LA MONCHIQUE 5 b.m. Lochnager–Lady of Elegance (Blast) [1989/90 F12g] second reported foal: dam won selling hurdle: mid-division in NH Flat race at Market Rasen: yet to race over hurdles or fences. *C. B. B. Booth.*

ELLA ROSA 9 ch.m. Le Bavard (FR)–High School (Even Money) [1989/90 19f3 17m4] leggy mare: winning hurdler and novice chaser in Ireland: poor form in Britain: stays 2½m: acts on hard ground: blinkered final start 1988/9. *W. E. Fisher.* c— 76

ELLTEE-ESS 5 ch.g. Lighter–Verosina (Lord of Verona) [1989/90 20d5 21m5 a22g* 20d a20g6 21g4 a20g* a20g4 25m 25fpu] close-coupled gelding: handicap hurdler: successful at Southwell in December (off the bridle throughout and hung badly right run-in) and April (claimer ridden): stays 2¾m: blinkered fourth and last 4 outings. *R. J. Weaver.* 86

ELMLEY GAYLE 7 br.m. Midland Gayle–French Note (Eton Rambler) [1989/90 20dpu 16d3 20s6 21mpu] smallish, leggy mare: poor form in novice hurdles: pulled up lame final start (January): stays 21f: acts on soft going. *J. Eaton.* 80

ELOOT BRIGADE 12 b.g. Light Brigade–Diana Harwell (Harwell) [1989/90 c21f5 c26f4 c26gpu c26sbd] strong, good-bodied gelding: poor point-to-pointer/ novice chaser. *Mrs J. R. French.* c—

EL PADRINO 5 ch.g. Good Times (ITY)–Kirsova (Absalom) [1989/90 20fpu] strong gelding: plater on Flat, stays 1¼m: tailed off when pulled up lame in novice hurdle at Southwell in September. *J. R. Bostock.* —

EL-PAYASO 4 b.c. Cure The Blues (USA)–Baroness (FR) (Captain's Gig (USA)) [1989/90 16m 16mpu] neat colt: poor maiden on Flat: no sign of ability in juvenile hurdles in first half of season: sold 550 gns Ascot November Sales. *A. Moore.* —

EL POLITICASTRO 6 b.g. Politico (USA)–Jedhart Lass (Blandford Lad) [1989/90 16m 16gpu 16mr 16m 21m 20dr] rather leggy gelding: very highly-strung novice hurdler: one to leave alone. *M. J. Wilkinson.* — §

ELVERCONE 9 b.g. Celtic Cone–Capelena (Mon Fetiche) [1989/90 c16v2 c20v* c20vpu c20d3] lengthy gelding: winning hurdler: won novice chase at Chepstow in January (would have finished second if clear leader hadn't fallen at c99 — §

the last): stays 2½m: acts well on heavy going and seems unsuited by firm: best in a visor: no battler. *A. J. Wilson.*

ELVER PANTO 6 br.g. Lepanto (GER)–Capelena (Mon Fetiche) [1989/90 17vpu 17vpu 21dpu 22g] sparely-made gelding: fifth foal: half-brother to 3 winning jumpers by Celtic Cone, namely Celtic Capri, Elvercone and Capeli Cone: dam useful point-to-pointer and winning hunter chaser: no sign of ability in novice hurdles. *J. H. Cork.* —

ELYSIAN WARRIOR 5 b.g. Full of Hope–Paddock Princess (Dragonara Palace (USA)) [1989/90 16gpu 16f a18g5] workmanlike gelding: no sign of ability over hurdles: blinkered second start. *E. A. Wheeler.* —

EMBARKATION 4 ch.g. Main Reef–Pointe de Grace (FR) (Dapper Dan (USA)) [1989/90 16d4 16m] compact gelding: fair stayer on Flat when trained by L. Cumani: fourth to Silver King in Stroud Green Hurdle at Newbury in February: staying-on tenth behind Sybillin in Glenlivet Anniversary Hurdle at Liverpool 2 months later: sure to win a race over hurdles. *F. Jordan.* 106 p

EMERALD ROYALE 6 b.m. Skyliner–Miss Royal (King's Company) [1989/90 16gpu] half-sister to fairly useful sprinter Royal Fan (by Taufan): dam never ran: tailed off when pulled up in novice selling hurdle at Sedgefield in December. *R. O'Leary.* —

EMERALD SUNSET 5 b.g. Red Sunset–Kelly's Curl (Pitskelly) [1989/90 16g5 16m 16d3 16m2] sparely-made gelding: novice selling hurdler: better for race, good second to Yuan Princess in handicap at Stratford final start (first for 4 months): best form at 2m: acts on good to firm ground: edged right run-in third outing. *A. R. Davison.* 70 +

EMERKALA 6 b.m. Kala Shikari–Emerglen (Furry Glen) [1989/90 20g 16g 16gpu] leggy mare: selling hurdler: no worthwhile form since 1987/8: best at 2m on a sharp track: acts on dead going. *Miss G. M. Rees.* —

EMINENCE VERTE 5 ch.m. High Line–Greenfly (USA) (What A Pleasure (USA)) [1989/90 16gpu] lengthy, sparely-made mare: 1½m claimer winner on Flat: no sign of ability in 2 races over hurdles, latter a seller. *Mrs P. Sly.* —

EM-KAY-EM 4 ch.f. Slim Jim–Topazolite (Hessonite) [1989/90 aF16g6] first foal: dam unraced: remote sixth in NH Flat race at Southwell: yet to race over hurdles. *Miss M. K. Milligan.*

EMMADILL 10 b.m. New Member–Em Gee Bee (Ben Hawke) [1989/90 c17v6 c24dF c24g5] sturdy mare: poor novice hurdler/chaser: should stay beyond 2¼m. *C. C. Trietline.* c69 —

EMMA PEPPER 8 b.m. Latest Model–Miss Pepper (Arctic Chevalier) [1989/90 c17d4 c16m c17fpu 17mpu] lengthy, workmanlike mare: poor novice hurdler/chaser: trained until after second start by K. Bishop (subsequently off course 5½ months). *C. L. Popham.* c— —

EMMA TOM BAY 5 b.g. Bay Express–Counsel's Verdict (Firestreak) [1989/90 16d 16g 16m] placed over 7f on Flat: no form over hurdles: dead. *Mrs Barbara Waring.* —

EMMET STREET 10 ch.g. Avocat–Carnival Beauty (Carnival Dancer) [1989/90 c21f* c16m3] smallish gelding: modest chaser: won handicap at Market Rasen in August: tailed off later in month: stays 21f: acts on any going. *N. Miller.* c99 —

EMPIRE BLUE 7 b.g. Dominion–Bold Blue (Targowice (USA)) [1989/90 16g3 16gF 20g2] small, lengthy gelding: half-brother to poor novice hurdler Blue Wizard (by Enchantment): useful middle-distance handicapper on Flat (goes well fresh): placed in novice hurdles at Kempton in December and Doncaster in February (4 lengths second to Remittance Man, going left in closing stages): was slightly below his best at 2m: has pulled hard and worn a severe bridle. *P. F. I. Cole.* 113 +

EMPLOYMENT LAW 6 ch.g. Import–Pepin (Midsummer Night II) [1989/90 16dpu] big, strong, chasing type: half-brother to winning jumpers Havenwood (by Relko) and Longcliffe (by Mandamus): dam poor maiden: tailed off when pulled up in novice hurdle at Windsor in January. *Miss H. C. Knight.* —

EMRYS 7 ch.g. Welsh Pageant–Sun Approach (Sun Prince) [1989/90 16g6 16g 16d6] sparely-made gelding: winning hurdler: no form for some time: suited by sharp 2m: acts on firm ground: pulls hard (has worn severe bridle) and looks a difficult ride: sold 1,700 gns Ascot February Sales. *D. Nicholson.* —

EMSALCLA 5 ch.g. Ballacashtal (CAN)–Miss Times (Major Portion) [1989/90 16sF] poor maiden on Flat: behind when falling fifth in selling hurdle at Bangor: dead. *R. O'Leary.* —

EMSEE-H 5 b.g. Paddy's Stream–Kincsem (Nelcius) [1989/90 16d 16s 16g] workmanlike gelding: brother to useful chaser Socks Downe and half-brother to useful chaser Travelowen (by Master Owen) and quite useful chaser Travel Over (by Over The River): dam unraced: novice hurdler: showed signs of ability second start: ran as though something was amiss final start. *G. A. Hubbard.* —

EMSLEYS CHOICE 4 ch.g. Windjammer (USA)–Derrygold (Derrylin) [1989/90 16d5] modest 1m winner on Flat: fifth in juvenile hurdle at Market Rasen in August: sold 3,200 gns Ascot November Sales: dead. *T. Fairhurst.* 76

ENBORNE LAD 6 gr.g. Celtic Cone–Blue Delphinium (Quorum) [1989/90 20d* 22g2 20gF] sturdy, lengthy gelding: won quite valuable handicap hurdle at Worcester in November: stayed on strongly under pressure when going down by ¾ length to Auction Law at Haydock later in month: made mistakes but was disputing third place when falling 3 out at Kempton in December (looked lean): will stay 3m: acts on dead going (yet to race on ground firmer than good): genuine. *G. P. Enright.* 113

ENBYAR DAN 10 ch.g. Porto Bello–Alleyn (Alcide) [1989/90 c20v] small, workmanlike gelding: novice selling hurdler: tailed off both outings over fences. *Miss P. O'Connor.* c— —

ENCHANTED COURT 6 b.g. Enchantment–Abercourt (Abernant) [1989/90 16f4 20fpu 16mbd 20d6 16g 16g 16f3] workmanlike gelding: poor novice hurdler: form only at around 2m: usually blinkered or visored nowadays: trained until after fourth start by G. Oldroyd. *R. R. Lamb.* 68

ENCHANTED CROSS 5 b.m. Enchantment–Nevilles Cross (USA) (Nodouble (USA)) [1989/90 16g 17gpu 16s] tall mare: seems of little account. *D. J. Wintle.* —

ENCHANTED GODDESS 4 ch.f. Enchantment–Song God (Red God) [1989/90 16mpu 16m5 16spu] smallish, workmanlike filly: poor maiden on Flat: little promise in selling hurdles. *M. Castell.* —

ENCHANTED MAN 6 b.g. Enchantment–Queen's Treasure (Queen's Hussar) [1989/90 19f*] leggy gelding: former selling hurdler: won 3-runner claiming event at Hereford in August: not seen out again: stays 2½m: acts on firm and dead ground: best in a hood: claimer ridden. *D. Burchell.* 108

END RESULT 5 b.g. Salluceva–Patricia Brant (Reverse Charge) [1989/90 20s6 22d5 21d] sturdy non-thoroughbred ex-Irish gelding: half-brother to NH Flat race winner Kirower (by Master Buck) and novice hurdler/chaser Random Charge (by Random Shot): dam unraced sister to a winning point-to-pointer: won a point-to-point in 1989: bought 20,000 gns Doncaster Spring (1989) Sales: showed signs of ability in novice hurdles first 2 starts: bit backward, tailed off final outing (first for 2 months). *G. B. Balding.* —

ENERGIA 4 gr.f. Alias Smith (USA)–Ermione (Surumu (GER)) [1989/90 16dpu 16d 20f 22f] small filly: staying maiden on Flat: no worthwhile form over hurdles: jumped moderately final start (claimer ridden). *P. A. Blockley.* —

ENGLISH RIVER (USA) 6 b.g. Irish River (FR)–Belle Sorella (USA) (Ribot) [1989/90 16fr 17f 17fur] small gelding: thoroughly temperamental novice hurdler: blinkered second start: one to leave severely alone. *R. J. Weaver.* §§

EN GOUNASI THEON 9 ch.g. New Member–Vidi's First (Vidi Vici) [1989/90 c24g6 c26g4 c25g* c27spu c25m2 c27h* c29f] leggy, lengthy gelding: moderate chaser: won handicaps at Devon & Exeter in December and Taunton in April: very stiff task final outing: stays well: acts on any going: has won for a claimer: has worn a crossed noseband. *G. C. Doidge.* **c110** —

ENTERPRISE PRINCE 4 b.g. Lucky Wednesday–Avona (My Swallow) [1989/90 16g 16g a16g 16m6] half-brother to winning hurdler Lady Firepower (by Gunner B): winning plater on Flat, stays 7f: poor novice plater over hurdles: sold 1,700 gns Ascot May Sales. *Ronald Thompson.* 61

ENTIRE 6 ch.g. Relkino–Tactless (Romulus) [1989/90 16f 16g* 16f3] workmanlike gelding: won amateur riders maiden hurdle at Market Rasen in May: good third behind Mirage Dancer in novice event at Sedgefield later in month: form only at 2m: possibly needs a sound surface: takes a good hold: has worn a tongue strap. *R. E. Barr.* 93

ENVOPAK TOKEN 9 ch.g. Proverb–Luck Token (Festive) [1989/90 c21m^2 c143
c24d^5 c24d* c29g^F c33d^{pu}] strong, rangy gelding: useful chaser: had simple task —
when winning 3-runner handicap chase at Huntingdon in December: in touch but
ridden along when falling 5 out in Anthony Mildmay, Peter Cazalet Memorial
Handicap Chase at Sandown in January: pulled up in William Hill Scottish National
(Handicap Chase) at Ayr when next seen out in April, but was prominent for a long
way: suited by a test of stamina: acts on soft going and good to firm: tends to idle in
front but is game. *J. T. Gifford.*

EQUATOR 7 ch.g. Nijinsky (CAN)–Sound of Success (USA) (Successor)
[1989/90 16v 16v 16d^5 20d^4] tall gelding: modest hurdler: best effort of 1989/90 on 95
third start: best form at 2m: acts on heavy going: blinkered final start 1987/8. *J. S.
Haldane.*

ERADICATE 5 b.h. Tender King–Pushkar (Northfields (USA)) [1989/90 16d^3
16f^3] useful at up to 1¼m on Flat, in excellent form in 1990: third in maiden hurdle 101 p
at Edinburgh (amateur ridden) and novice event at Newcastle (beaten 3 lengths
by Shamirani): well capable of winning over hurdles. *P. Calver.*

ERICA MAY 8 b.m. Streak–Ulrica (Cacador) [1989/90 16m c25d^{pu} c22d^F] c—
lengthy mare: half-sister to winning point-to-pointer Bishops Bell (by Crozier): —
dam poor winning chaser: never placed to challenge in novice hurdle in
December: hasn't got beyond the ninth in novice chases: tends to sweat slightly
and be on her toes in preliminaries. *C. C. Elsey.*

ERIC'S WISH 10 b.g. Cawston's Clown–Sirette (Great Nephew) [1989/90 c—
c24m^{pu}] leggy, sparely-made gelding: selling hurdler: has failed to complete —
course in steeplechases: form only at around 2m: acts on firm going: blinkered
once in 1984/5. *D. W. Jagger.*

ERINS DANCER 9 b.g. Brave Invader (USA)–Geisha Dancer (Hul A Hul) c—
[1989/90 c25m^{pu}] leggy gelding: no sign of ability: pulled up lame in March. *Mrs J.* —
E. Croft.

ERNIES CHOICE 8 ch.g. Manor Farm Boy–Grade Well (Derring-Do) c—
[1989/90 c20s^{pu}] rather sparely-made gelding: well beaten in novice hurdles: —
third in a point-to-point in 1989: tailed off when pulled up ninth in hunter chase at
Warwick in February. *E. A. Lee.*

EROSTIN FLOATS 6 ch.g. Paddy's Stream–Zeta's Daughter (Master Owen) c95
[1989/90 c20m^4 c24m^6 c20g^2 c24d c20d^4 c20m^3 c24f* c24m* c24m* c25f^3] tall —
gelding: no worthwhile form in novice hurdles: won novice chases at Bangor in
March and Huntingdon and Market Rasen in April: beaten when unseating rider
last (remounted) in handicap final start: stays 3m: acts on firm going: sketchy
jumper. *J. R. Upson.*

ESCAPE PATH 5 b.m. Wolver Hollow–Keep Right (Klairon) [1989/90 16f^6]
maiden on Flat: no worthwhile form in novice hurdles: sold 1,700 gns Ascot —
November Sales. *K. A. Morgan.*

ESCRIBANA 5 b.m. Main Reef–Amorak (Wolver Hollow) [1989/90 16m*
16m^4 22f^3 21m^4 20g^2 16m a20g* 22v^4 a20g^5 22f^3 24m^F 24f^5] workmanlike mare: 102
of little account on Flat: won mares novice hurdle at Huntingdon in September
and handicap at Lingfield (3-runner event) in January: creditable third in mares
novice handicap at Nottingham in March: suited by further than 2m, and should
stay 3m: acts on firm ground: claimer ridden. *J. R. Jenkins.*

ESHA NESS 7 b.g. Crash Course–Beeston (Our Babu) [1989/90 20g^5 20d^4
20g^3] rangy gelding: will make a chaser: fair hurdler: in frame in handicaps at 119
Ascot (amateur riders) and Kempton in December: stays 2½m: yet to race on
very firm ground, acts on any other. *Mrs J. Pitman.*

ESKIMO MITE (USA) 6 b.g. Northern Baby (CAN)–Astania (GER) (Arratos
(FR)) [1989/90 21d 21d 21s 21m 24m 20m^2 25f^2] winning hurdler: only form in 103
1989/90 when runner-up twice at Huntingdon in May (2 ran on second occasion):
probably stays 25f and acts on any going: sold 4,200 gns Doncaster Spring Sales. *J.
R. Jenkins.*

ESPECIALLY BOLD 4 b.f. Lyphard's Special (USA)–Bold Design (Bold Lad
(IRE)) [1989/90 16g 16m 19s] close-coupled filly: well beaten on Flat, including in —
sellers: behind in claiming hurdles and seller. *Miss H. C. Knight.*

ES-PORT 5 b.g. Mummy's Game–Bella Lisa (River Chanter) [1989/90 24g^{pu}
22g 21d 20g^6 20s^5 25g^4 24m] smallish, sparely-made gelding: modest handicap 102
hurdler nowadays: ran poorly final start (wandered under pressure): stays 25f:
unsuited by very soft ground. *J. A. C. Edwards.*

ESPRIT DE FEMME (FR) 4 b.f. Esprit du Nord (USA)–Bustelda (FR) (Busted) [1989/90 a16g^{5} 16g 16v^{4} 20d^{6} a20g] modest 1½m winner on Flat, when trained by P. Kelleway: poor juvenile hurdler: fourth in seller in January. *V. Young.* 61

ESPY 7 b.g. Pitpan–Minorette (Miralgo) [1989/90 c16f^{F} c16m* c16m* c24g* c20m* c25m^{F} c20f^{F3}] c**134** p —

Espy is a smart chaser in the making, provided he learns to jump consistently well: his lapses in that department as a novice were costly. Unfortunately he usually came to grief in the better events. The time he got round in one he picked up the quite valuable Peter Ross Novices' Chase at Ascot in January. His jumping there was not without fault, but he made no serious errors in a slowly-run race. After leading at the second last he soon put daylight between himself and his rivals, and had twenty lengths to spare over Mighty Fine at the line. Espy had shown himself to be a talented chaser with earlier victories in ordinary novice events at Nottingham and Uttoxeter, but had fallen at the last when disputing the lead with eventual winner Young Snugfit in the Hurst Park Novices' Chase, also at Ascot, on his chasing debut. Almost two months after his winning performance at Ascot, Espy contested a qualifier of the Steel Plate And Sections Young Chasers' Novices' Chase at Uttoxeter. He and the equally promising Elfast had the race to themselves, pulling a distance clear of the remainder. Though again not impressing with his jumping, tending to fiddle the fences, Espy raced prominently from the start and took up the lead at the sixth from home. Elfast was never far away though and moved up to dispute the lead at the fourth last. The pair were virtually inseparable until the last fifty yards where Espy got the upper hand and held off his determined opponent by half a length. On this form Espy had a fair chance in the Mumm Club Novices' Chase at Liverpool the following month. He jumped well in the main but just as he'd begun to close on the leaders he fell at the fourth last. Espy fell again thirteen days later at the tricky third last at Cheltenham in the three-runner Steel Plate And Sections Young Chasers' Novices' Final, when again in with a definite chance (though not going so well as the eventual winner Elfast). The horse obviously has lots of ability, and so long as his jumping doesn't prevent him realising his full potential he should be well worth following. Espy has a turn of foot and is effective at the minimum trip, but his best form has been at two and a half to three miles. He's suited by a sound surface, and has raced only once on ground softer than good in the last two seasons (he was reportedy found to be suffering from a heart irregularity after being pulled up on that occasion).

Espy (b.g. 1983)	Pitpan (b 1969)	Pampered King (b 1954)	Prince Chevalier
			Netherton Maid
		Pitter Patter (br 1953)	Kingstone
			Rain
	Minorette (b 1968)	Miralgo (ch 1959)	Aureole
			Nella
		Quatre Bras (b 1961)	Mossborough
			Fouri

Espy is only the fifth foal of Minorette, a mare who has been at stud since the mid-'seventies. She was successful on the Flat and over hurdles and fences in France, and has produced three other winners, the best of them Observe (by Rheffic), a high-class chaser belonging to the same connections as Espy, and trained by Fred Winter. Minorette's other winners were trained in Ireland—Sub-Editor (by Super Slip) won on the Flat and over jumps there and the promising Minorettes Girl (by Strong Gale) won two bumpers events in the latest season prior to finishing third in the Seagram Supreme National Hunt Flat race at Liverpool. *C. P. E. Brooks.*

ESS-JAY-ESS 7 b.g. Bay Express–Shirwani (Major Portion) [1989/90 16d^{pu}] very lightly raced and of little account over hurdles. *Miss J. E. Blakeney.* —

ESS-KAY-DEE 5 b.g. Jasmine Star–Theft (Princely Gift) [1989/90 17m^{ro} 17f 17g] close-coupled gelding: poor novice selling hurdler: headstrong. *D. Williams.* —

ESTONIA 4 b.f. Kings Lake (USA)–Paddy's Joy (Run The Gantlet (USA)) [1989/90 16g^{6} 20g^{2} 16g* 16f^{3} a16g^{4} 16g^{3}] IR 56,000Y: sparely-made ex-Irish filly: 76

fourth foal: half-sister to useful Irish hurdler Bikaloy (by Bikala): dam unraced half-sister to Ballymore: won over 11f on Flat in 1989 when trained by T. Stack: bought in 4,000 gns after winning juvenile selling hurdle at Catterick in March: hung left in straight when third on firm ground: reportedly suffered punctured artery in hind leg when running moderately over 2½m. *N. Tinkler.*

ETERNAL CREDIT 8 ch.g. Quayside–Fair Vic (Fair Turn) [1989/90 c24mpu c24g4 c24spu c26fpu] leggy gelding: modest novice hurdler/winning chaser: no form in 1989/90: stays at least 3m: acts on firm ground and is possibly unsuited by very soft: blinkered nowadays. *M. C. Pipe.* c— —

ETHIOPIAN KING 7 ch.g. Avocat–Meneleck Queen (Menelek) [1989/90 22vpu] strong, workmanlike gelding: no form over hurdles, though showed a little ability in 1988/9. *T. J. Etherington.* —

ETON ROUGE 11 b.g. The Parson–Rouge Shack (Shackleton) [1989/90 c20v* c24v5 c29d c20d c22mpu] well-made, good-looking sort: fair chaser at best: amateur ridden, won handicap at Haydock in December: ran moderately afterwards: stays long distances: acts on heavy going and good to firm: usually races up with pace, though tends to run in snatches: usually a sound jumper (jumped deliberately when tried in blinkers in 1987/8): has won 4 times at Chepstow. *S. Christian.* **c118** d —

EUROCON 6 b.g. Ile de Bourbon (USA)–Consistent (Connaught) [1989/90 20g3 20g*] small gelding: front-running handicap hurdler: won at Doncaster in January by a neck from Prince of Rheims, rallying well to lead again close home: stays 2½m: probably acts on any going: has won for a claimer. *T. D. Barron.* 106 +

EURODIX 7 ch.g. Touch Paper–Sun Empress (Young Emperor) [1989/90 F16f 16dpu 16d 22gpu] leggy, rather angular gelding: first foal: half-brother to a poor novice hurdler by Strong Gale: dam never ran: no sign of ability in NH Flat race and novice hurdles. *N. R. Mitchell.* —

EURODOLLAR 6 gr. or ro.h. Sparkler–Silver Berry (Lorenzaccio) [1989/90 16g5 16mpu] leggy horse: fair winner over 1m at 3 and 4 yrs, when trained by J. Holt: fifth in novice hurdle at Uttoxeter in December: weakened quickly and pulled up sixth following month: not a fluent jumper. *W. Carter.* —

EUROPA POINT 5 ch.g. Deep Run–Regal Dawn (Golden Love) [1989/90 F16g2 F16m] strong, lengthy gelding: second foal: brother to a poor animal: dam, winning Irish hurdler, in frame in a novice chase: second in NH Flat race at Kempton in February: seventh behind Going On in well-contested similar event at Liverpool: yet to race over hurdles or fences. *M. H. B. Robinson.*

EVE FROM EDEN 7 ch.m. Riboboy (USA)–Fair Saint (Bleep-Bleep) [1989/90 16g 16g 22gpu 16s] rangy mare: half-sister to useful hurdler and winning chaser Comedy Fair (by Comedy Star): no sign of ability in novice hurdles. *C. James.* —

EVENING HOUR 5 ch.m. Glenstal (USA)–Field Lady (Habitat) [1989/90 16g3 16g] 7f winner on Flat in 1989: sold out of W. Holden's stable 2,000 gns Newmarket Autumn Sales: third in poor novice hurdle at Market Rasen in December: always behind at Wolverhampton following month: subsequently sold 2,700 gns Doncaster January Sales. *P. S. Felgate.* 71

EVENING RAIN 4 b.c. Hays–Fine Form (USA) (Fachendon) [1989/90 16s 17d] quite modest performer on Flat, winner twice at around 1m in 1989 when trained by Sir Mark Prescott: well beaten in juvenile hurdles. *R. J. Hodges.* —

EVENING SUNSET 4 b.g. Red Sunset–Princess Elinor (Captain James) [1989/90 16m3 17f4] small gelding: well beaten on Flat: poor form in late-season juvenile hurdles. *Miss G. M. Rees.* —

EVENLODE 6 b.g. Netherkelly–Miss Curiso (Master Spiritus) [1989/90 16s] good-bodied gelding: behind in 2 novice hurdles: pulled hard in February. *Capt. T. A. Forster.* —

EVEN SMARTER 7 b.g. Proverb–Smart Money (Even Money) [1989/90 20m 16gpu] lengthy, angular gelding: poor novice hurdler: has looked reluctant: should be suited by further than 2m. *R. Lee.* —

EVENTIDE 4 ch.f. Red Sunset–Tagik (Targowice (USA)) [1989/90 a16g3 16f a16g 16m2] light-framed filly: in frame at up to 1¼m on Flat: sold out of A. Hide's stable 2,000 gns Ascot September Sales: poor novice selling hurdler. *D. Burchell.* 66

EVEN WAVES 9 b.g. Virginia Boy–Winning Wave (USA) (Victory Morn) [1989/90 20gpu 22mpu c22mpu] rather leggy gelding: won a point-to-point in 1989: no sign of ability over hurdles or in steeplechases. *N. S. Blatchley.* c— —

EVER A LADY 6 b.m. Boreen (FR)–Ullard Lady (Official) [1989/90 16m5 24gF 22gur] compact mare: no form over hurdles, including in a seller. *T. N. Bailey.* —

EVER HOPEFUL (NZ) 8 b.g. Kutati (NZ)–Reese's Pride (NZ) (Trelay (NZ)) [1989/90 c25dpu c24gF c24d*] lengthy, workmanlike gelding: fair hurdler: jumped soundly when winning novice chase at Chepstow in March by 10 lengths from Coruscate: stays 25f: acts on good to firm and soft going: should improve further over fences. *D. H. Barons.* **c101** p —

EVERMETT 4 ch.g. Milford–Myna Tyna (Blast) [1989/90 16fpu 17fpu] sparely-made gelding: soundly beaten at 2 yrs: sold out of J. Balding's stable 680 gns Doncaster September (1988) Sales: tailed off when pulled up in selling hurdles: blinkered. *J. D. Thomas.* —

EVESHAM BUTCHERS 8 b.g. Moulton–Welsh Carol (Singing Bede) [1989/90 16mpu] small, stocky, very heavy-topped gelding: novice selling hurdler: poor novice chaser: acts on firm ground. *J. A. Bennett.* c— —

EXCAVATOR 6 b.g. Bulldozer–Lucky Favour (Ballyciptic) [1989/90 16g] lengthy gelding: no sign of ability. *C. C. Trietline.* —

EXCELLENCY 7 b.g. Cut Above–Countess Decima (USA) (Sir Gaylord) [1989/90 16fsu 16f5 24g4 c18f3 22d a20g3 a16g* a18g3 16d a16g] lengthy, sparely-made ex-Irish gelding: half-brother to useful French sprinter Miliar (by Thatch): dam never ran: 2m winner on Flat: bought in 2,700 gns after winning selling hurdle at Southwell in January: third in novice chase at Fairyhouse in September: stayed 2½m: acted on firm ground: was tried in blinkers: trained first 4 starts by D. Hughes and next 3 outings by J. Jenkins: dead. *P. Davis.* c— 87

EXCITING PROSPECT 6 ch.g. North Summit–Hopefull Polly (Polyfoto) [1989/90 16f4 20g3 16m2 20f3 16g* 16g* 16g3] leggy, rather sparely-made gelding: has stringhalt: won maiden hurdle at Edinburgh in December and handicap at Catterick (jumped really well and made all) in January: creditable third behind Loren's Courage in novice event at Ascot later in month: may prove ideally suited by forcing pace over 2m: acts on firm ground. *J. J. O'Neill.* 114

EXCLUDER 11 b.g. Giolla Mear–Sea Sonnet (Ossian II) [1989/90 c21spu c20vpu] tall, leggy gelding: poor novice hurdler/chaser: has shown signs of temperament: won only completed start in point-to-points in 1989: stays 2¾m: has run blinkered. *Derek Mills.* c— § —

EXHAUST LADY 5 b.m. Blue Refrain–Silk Fashion (Breeders Dream) [1989/90 a16g] inconsistent 1m seller winner on Flat: well beaten both outings over hurdles: claimer ridden. *R. P. C. Hoad.* —

EXIT LAUGHING 6 b.m. Shaab–Civic Duty (Averof) [1989/90 20m5] neat mare: poor novice hurdler, lightly raced: stays 2½m: blinkered only outing of 1989/90 (September). *R. Allan.* —

EXPEDITIOUS 10 b.g. Tachypous–My Own II (El Relicario) [1989/90 c17f4 17f4 c17f* c16f* c16d5 c17m2 c17f* c17m3] tall gelding: handicap chaser: won at Newton Abbot (made all in conditional jockeys event) and Uttoxeter in October and Newton Abbot (beat Wonder Bee 8 lengths) in May: best at around 2m: goes well on firm ground: jumps none too fluently on occasions. *T. B. Hallett.* **c111** —

EXPRESS AIR 7 ch.g. Pony Express–Idle Air (Romany Air) [1989/90 22m 25g* c21f2 c24gur c24s2 c25g2 c25sF 22g4 25f*] workmanlike gelding: handicap hurdler: won at Huntingdon in November and Ludlow (beat Miss Muck 12 lengths) in April: modest form in novice chases (jumps less than fluently): suited by a good test of stamina: acts on any going. *G. B. Balding.* **c100** 108

EXPRESS REALE 5 b.g. Al Sirat (USA)–Real Path VII (pedigree unknown) [1989/90 F16d] non-thoroughbred gelding: first foal: dam never ran: well beaten in NH Flat race at Catterick: yet to race over hurdles or fences. *W. A. Stephenson.*

EXTRA SPECIAL 5 ch.g. Avocat–Cummin Hill (Wrekin Rambler) [1989/90 F16m] sixth foal: brother to winning chaser Up And Coming and half-brother to winning hurdler/chaser Wrekin Hill (by Duky): dam lightly-raced Irish maiden: seventh in NH Flat race at Hexham in November: yet to race over hurdles or fences. *W. A. Stephenson.*

EYE BEE AITCH 5 b.m. Move Off–River Petterill (Another River) [1989/90 17mF 16m2 16g 16d* 16m2 16d6 16f5 17f*] small, lengthy, lightly-made mare: sister to winning hurdler Megan's Move: plater on Flat: successful in selling hurdles at Hexham in December and Cartmel (handicap) in May: bought in 2,750 gns after showing improved form to score by 12 lengths in latter: acts on firm and dead ground. *W. Storey.* 86

EYELIGHT 13 gr.g. Roan Rocket–Pie Eye (Exbury) [1989/90 16f^{6} 16m] compact gelding: winning hurdler: no form for some time, including in sellers: form only at 2m: acts on firm going: ran out once: ran very freely when tried in blinkers. *J. Carden.* — §

EYE SIGHT 7 b.m. Roscoe Blake–Pie Eye (Exbury) [1989/90 16d^{2}] lengthy mare: lightly-raced poor novice hurdler. *R. B. Francis.* 77

EYE STUNNER 5 b.m. Sayyaf–Weaver's Love (Weavers' Hall) [1989/90 a18g^{5}] ex-Irish mare: third foal: half-sister to a winner in Belgium by On Your Mark: dam Irish 1¼m winner: behind in 2 races on Flat in 1988 when trained by P. Gilmartin: tailed off in novice hurdle at Southwell. *J. G. M. O'Shea.* —

EYETRAP 9 b.g. Lucky Bay–College Maid (Choral Society) [1989/90 c19f^{6} c16g^{F}] sparely-made gelding: poor novice hurdler/chaser: acts on soft going. *Andrew Mobley.* c— —

F

FAARIS 9 b.g. Troy–Real Snug (Realm) [1989/90 c20f* c18g* c16f^{3} c20s*] strong, workmanlike gelding: won handicap chases at Plumpton and Fontwell in October and Folkestone (bumped at the last and subsequently awarded race after going down by a neck to only other finisher Davy's Weir) in January: stays 2½m: acts on any going: has worn a severe bridle and crossed noseband: tends to sweat and to swish tail under pressure. *D. M. Grissell.* **c110** —

FAATIK 7 ch.g. Kings Lake (USA)–Piney Ridge (Native Prince) [1989/90 16g] neat gelding: maiden on Flat: no sign of ability in 2 outings over hurdles (dropped himself out on hurdling debut). *M. A. Clutterbuck.* —

FABLED ORATOR 5 b.g. Lafontaine (USA)–Brompton Rose (Sun Prince) [1989/90 16g 16g^{ro} 16g] angular, sparely-made gelding: modest handicapper on Flat, won over 7f in 1989 (suited by forcing tactics and seems best racing away from others): bought out of R. Hannon's stable 6,400 gns Newmarket September Sales: pulled hard when well beaten in novice hurdles: ran out fifth second start: has worn a crossed noseband. *G. G. Gracey.* —

FABULOUS QUEEN (FR) 7 b.m. Fabulous Dancer (USA)–Moquerie (FR) (Beaugency (FR)) [1989/90 16g^{ur}] successful over 1m on Flat in France: unseated rider third in novice hurdle in March. *J. A. Glover.* —

FACTOTUM 7 b.g. Known Fact (USA)–Blue Shark (Silver Shark) [1989/90 16m^{2} 16f* 16f* 16f* 16g* 16m^{3} 16m^{4}] compact gelding: won novice hurdles at Plumpton (3, one a handicap) and Cheltenham in first half of season: races only at 2m: acts on firm and dead going. *R. Akehurst.* 107

FAILIQ (FR) 6 b.h. Bustino–Salvationist (Mill Reef (USA)) [1989/90 16m 17f^{4} 16m^{4} 16g^{5} 16d^{3} a20g^{2}] lengthy, sparely-made horse: sold out of D. Hanley's stable 6,600 gns Doncaster September Sales: poor novice hurdler: stays 2½m: acts on firm and dead ground: claimer ridden. *T. Kersey.* 80

FAIR AGNES 6 b.m. Official–Miss Pat (Pinturischio) [1989/90 16d 20d 20v^{3} 21s^{pu}] small mare: on toes, only form over hurdles when third behind Lucky Verdict in novice event at Chepstow in January: tailed off when pulled up in novice handicap (reluctant to race, jumped moderately) following month. *S. G. Griffiths.* 85

FAIR CHILD 10 ch.g. Le Bavard (FR)–Fair People (Varano) [1989/90 c26f* c25g^{4} c29d^{pu} c24f^{ur}] Atrong, sturdy, good sort: quite a useful chaser: claimer ridden, won handicap at Folkestone in December (idled in front): held in third place when unseating rider last at Newbury in March: suited by a test of stamina: acts on any going: rather deliberate jumper. *D. J. G. Murray-Smith.* **c126**

FAIR ECHO 10 b.m. Quality Fair–Early Echo (Bleep) [1989/90 c20m^{3} c20h^{3} c24g^{pu} c24f^{pu} c24m^{5} c24h^{3}] lengthy mare: modest chaser: only worthwhile form of 1989/90 on first start: suited by 2½m and more: acts on soft going (probably unsuited by top-of-the-ground). *C. Parker.* c88 d —

FAIRFIELD LAD 5 b.g. Krayyan–Mock Auction (Auction Ring (USA)) [1989/90 16f^{3} 16g^{4} 16m^{3}] sparely-made gelding: sprinter on Flat: in frame in claiming hurdles and seller. *M. H. Tompkins.* 80

FAIRFIELD'S BREEZE 5 b.m. Buckskin (FR)–Mistic Breeze (Master Owen) [1989/90 F16f] third foal: sister to novice hurdler Winabuck: dam won twice at 2m over hurdles in Ireland: well beaten in NH Flat race at Cheltenham: yet to race over hurdles or fences. *R. Dickin.*

FAIRFIELDS CONE 7 ch.m. Celtic Cone–Bond's Best (Good Bond) [1989/90 18d 16f 16d 16g 16g5 16mF 22m3] lengthy mare: winning hurdler: modest form in 1989/90: seemed not quite to stay 2¾m final start: acts on soft going: good mount for a claimer. *R. Dickin.* 97

FAIR JANET 4 b.f. Feelings (FR)–Meg's Mantle (New Brig) [1989/90 F16f3] third foal: dam, placed over 2m on Flat on only outing, half-sister to 2 winning jumpers: 7 lengths third behind Kate O'Kirkham in NH Flat race at Hexham in April: yet to race over hurdles. *Mrs M. Stirk.*

FAIR MINSTREL 6 ch.m. Longleat (USA)–Western Vale (Milesian) [1989/90 16f 16m] smallish mare: poor novice selling hurdler: sold 525 gns Ascot November Sales. *R. Dickin.* 65

FAIR PROSPECT 4 b.c. Shirley Heights–Sans Blague (USA) (The Minstrel (CAN)) [1989/90 16g5 16g2 16v2 16d2 16g4] leggy, angular colt: showed fairly useful form when placed twice on Flat in 1989: sold out of R. Hern's stable 21,000 gns Newmarket Autumn Sales: second in 3 juvenile hurdles, best effort when beaten 2½ lengths by Calicon at Newbury in February on fourth start: will be very well suited by stiffer test of stamina: should win a race. *Miss H. C. Knight.* 108

FAIRSAY 13 gr.g. Sayfar–Fair Enough (Dual) [1989/90 c26fpu] winning chaser: stayed well: acted on firm going: dead. *C. White.* c— —

FAIR SEAS 4 b.f. General Assembly (USA)–Seven Seas (FR) (Riverman (USA)) [1989/90 16dpu 16dpu 16f5 16fpu 16m* 16fpu 20g5] neat filly: placed over 1¼m on Flat: sold out of G. Wragg's stable 5,000 gns Newmarket December Sales: first form over hurdles when winning 3-runner juvenile handicap at Huntingdon in May: not discredited over 2½m: acts on good to firm going. *D. R. Wellicome.* 70

FAIRWAYS ON TARGET 4 b.g. Billion (USA)–Aileen's Belle (The Parson) [1989/90 F12g*] half-brother to winning hurdler Butt And Ben (by Crofter): dam unraced: 11/10 on, won 17-runner NH Flat race at Hexham in March by 2½ lengths from Vimchase: yet to race over hurdles. *Mrs G. R. Reveley.*

FAITHFUL DON (USA) 11 br.g. Dawn Flight (USA)–Always Faithful (Super Sam) [1989/90 17mpu 17f5 25fpu 20f4 16g c16g6 c16mpu] lightly-made gelding: winning hurdler and novice chaser: most temperamental nowadays: often blinkered. *Mrs L. H. M. Hall.* c§§ §§

FALASHA 7 b.m. Milford–Somalia (Alcide) [1989/90 21m 16dpu 22gF] compact mare: novice hurdler: showed nothing in 1989/90: blinkered once in 1986/7 (showed signs of ability in seller), visored final start. *B. Palling.* —

FALCON FLIGHT 4 ch.g. Tampero (FR)–Kemoening (Falcon) [1989/90 16f4 16d 16d2 16m4] smallish, close-coupled gelding: half-brother to Daily Express Triumph Hurdle winner Saxon Farm (by Hittite Glory) and to another winning hurdler by Our Mirage: fair form at up to 7f on Flat: sold out of J. Berry's stable 13,000 gns Doncaster September Sales: poor juvenile hurdler: likely to prove suited by a sharp 2m. *J. Mackie.* 84

FALLEN HERO 5 br.g. Tumble Gold–Santa Luna (Saint Crespin III) [1989/90 F12g] ninth foal: brother to novice hurdler/chaser Chancellorsville and half-brother to very smart hurdler/chaser Boreen Prince and winning chaser/point-to-pointer Loanan (both by Boreen): dam unraced half-sister to useful hurdler Never Lit Up: tailed off in NH Flat race at Hexham: yet to race over hurdles or fences. *W. A. Stephenson.*

FALLING FOSS 6 br.g. Workboy–Lorna Dell (Forlorn River) [1989/90 16g6 a16g a24g6 c16gpu] close-coupled gelding: poor plater over hurdles: tailed off when pulled up third on chasing debut: looks a difficult ride: sold to T. Kersey 1,100 gns Doncaster June Sales. *C. I. Ratcliffe.* c— —

FALLOPOLIS (FR) 5 b.g. Persepolis (FR)–Fancy's Child (USA) (Nijinsky (CAN)) [1989/90 16d6 16g 16g a16g] compact, rather dipped-backed ex-French gelding: placed over 11f on Flat at 3 yrs: bought out of F. Boutin's stable 68,000 francs (approx £6,300) Longchamp November (1988) Sales: only sign of ability in novice hurdles on first start (subsequently off course 2 months): sold 1,200 gns Ascot April Sales. *J. A. C. Edwards.* 77 ?

FALLOWFIELD LASS 5 ch.m. Some Hand–Gray Loch (Lochnager) [1989/90 F16f2] second foal: half-sister to 2m Flat winner Fallowfield Lad (by

Anax): dam 1m winner: second in NH Flat race at Hereford in September: yet to
race over hurdles or fences. *J. Joseph.*

FALSE ECONOMY 5 ch.g. Torus–Vulvic (Vulgan) [1989/90 F16g 16d^5 20d*
20d] rangy, rather unfurnished ex-Irish gelding: has scope and will make a chaser: 103
half-brother to very useful staying chaser Cavity Hunter (by Above Suspicion)
and winning Irish jumper Dromakeal (by No Argument): dam unplaced in Irish NH
Flat races: won novice hurdle at Carlisle in March by 6 lengths from Tribal Ruler:
disputed lead until weakening quickly from 3 out when behind in quite valuable
novice handicap at Ayr following month: will be suited by 3m: acts on dead
ground. *J. A. C. Edwards.*

FALWORTH (USA) 6 b.g. Sir Ivor–Real Wisdom (USA) (In Reality) [1989/90
21s^{pu} 22d 16f* 16m^3] compact, well-made gelding: modest hurdler: won handicap 95
at Towcester in March easily by 5 lengths from Murhaf: creditable third on same
course following month: stays 2¾m: acts on firm ground: wears blinkers. *F.
Walwyn.*

FAME AND GLORY 5 b.h. Shareef Dancer (USA)–Oh So Fair (USA)
(Graustark) [1989/90 a20g^3 24g^5 a20g^{pu} 16d] smallish, sparely-made horse: 72
remote third in poor novice event at Lingfield in January, only form over hurdles:
has had tongue tied down. *J. Parkes.*

FAMILIAR SPIRIT 4 b.c. Pitskelly–Witch of Endor (Matador) [1989/90 16m
17f] leggy colt: half-brother to several winners, including fairly useful 2m hurdler —
High Old Time (by Mount Hagen): placed over 1¼m on Flat: sold out of J.
Dunlop's stable 9,000 gns Newmarket Autumn Sales: no form in juvenile hurdle
and a seller in first half of season. *N. Tinkler.*

FAMILY PRIDE 5 b.g. Shareef Dancer (USA)–Our Home (Habitat) [1989/90
20g^{pu} 16g] sparely-made gelding: in frame in 3 middle-distance races in 1988, only — p
starts on Flat: sold out of H. Cecil's stable 2,100 gns Newmarket Autumn (1988)
Sales: weakened between last 2 when seventh in novice hurdle at Wolverhampton
in January (gave impression needed race): may win a seller. *P. J. Bevan.*

FAMOUS FLASK 8 ch.g. New Member–Regal Bristol (Le Dieu d'Or)
[1989/90 16f] rangy gelding: no sign of ability in 2 outings over hurdles. *A. Moore.* —

FAMOUS LAD 7 b.g. Bold Lad (IRE)–Famous Band (USA) (Banderilla (USA)) c**101**
[1989/90 c20v^{bd} c16d* c16s^2 c21d^{pu}] compact ex-Irish gelding: novice hurdler: —
travelled well long way when winning novice chase at Catterick in February: lost
chance with mistake last when going down by 2½ lengths to New Halen in similar
race at Hereford in March: bad mistake tenth and tailed off when pulled up final
start: may prove best at around 2m: acts on soft going. *R. Lee.*

FAMOUS RUN 10 ch.g. Deep Run–Milwaukee Famous (Blue Lightning) c75
[1989/90 c16f^5 c16f^2 c16f^4 c24g^2 c16g^F c21d^{pu} c17g^{pu}] strong, angular gelding: —
carries plenty of condition: poor novice hurdler/chaser: rather sketchy jumper of
fences: stays 3m, at least in a slowly-run race: acts on hard ground: trained by J.
Bostock first start. *B. Richmond.*

FANDANGO BOY 7 b.g. Last Fandango–African Doll (African Sky) [1989/90 c—
21d 20v a24g^3] smallish, sparely-made gelding: one-time fairly useful hurdler: —
little form in 1989/90: winning chaser: stays 21f: acts on any going: blinkered final
start 1988/9 and second outing: good mount for a claimer: often makes running.
Mrs J. G. Retter.

FANDANGO KISS 7 ch.m. Gay Fandango (USA)–Bridewell Belle (Saulingo)
[1989/90 16f^5 24f^5] sparely-made mare: awarded selling handicap hurdle in —
1987/8: little form since: form only at 2m: suited by a sound surface: ridden by 7-lb
claimer. *T. Kersey.*

FANDANGO LIGHT 9 ch.g. Gay Fandango (USA)–Crystal Light (Never Say
Die) [1989/90 a16g] compact, well-made gelding: winning hurdler: no form for a —
long time: sold 525 gns Ascot May Sales. *A. Moore.*

FANILLE 4 b.c. Top Ville–Flying Fantasy (Habitat) [1989/90 16m^5 16f^4 16m
16v^{pu} a18g^2 16m^6 16f] small, workmanlike colt: behind in 2 races on Flat: sold out 71
of P. Walwyn's stable 1,400 gns Newmarket July Sales: poor juvenile hurdler: ran
poorly in a seller third outing. *D. J. Bell.*

FANMAN 5 b.h. Taufan (USA)–Courreges (Manado) [1989/90 16g^{pu}] lightly-
raced maiden on Flat: pulled up after 3 out in novice event at Newcastle on —
hurdling debut. *C. Parker.*

FANNY DILLON 6 b.m. Orchestra–Sunshot (Candy Cane) [1989/90 22m 24v
21s^5 25d 25f] leggy mare: handicap hurdler: best efforts of 1989/90 on third and 108

fourth starts: jumped appallingly and always struggling final outing: should be suited by a test of stamina: acts on soft going. *D. R. C. Elsworth.*

FANTASIE IMPROMPTU 5 gr.m. Ballad Rock–Gay Nocturne (Lord Gayle
(USA)) [1989/90 16f* 16f^{2}] small mare: won maiden hurdle at Market Rasen in 82
July: second to easy winner Homer City in conditional jockeys novice hurdle on same course following month: has raced only at 2m: acts on firm ground. *K. A. Morgan.*

FARE LOVE 11 ch.g. Grey Love–Katie Fare (Ritudyr) [1989/90 c16m^{3} c16m^{6} c**85** x
c16m^{5}] compact gelding: poor chaser: stays 2½m when conditions aren't testing: —
acts on any going: makes mistakes. *Mrs S. M. Johnson.*

FAREWELL TO ALMS 8 b.g. Pauper–Cracked Bell (Cracksman) [1989/90 c—
c16g^{pu}] leggy, workmanlike gelding: modest form in novice hurdles: tailed off —
when pulled up in novice chase in December: should be well suited by further than 2m. *P. J. Jones.*

FARINA STREAM 6 ch.g. Paddy's Stream–Farina (Raise You Ten) [1989/90
20m 16g^{4}] tall, leggy gelding: poor novice hurdler: best form at 2m: acts on good 77
to firm going: blinkered 3 times in 1988/9: sold 1,900 gns Doncaster March Sales. *M. Avison.*

FARMCOTE AIR 8 ch.m. True Song–Mandy Lou (Spartan General) [1989/90
21m 22d^{5} 25d 20m] small, strong mare: poor novice hurdler: likely to prove suited —
by forcing tactics when racing at 2½m and should stay further: acts on heavy going (probably unsuited by a firm surface). *Mrs H. Parrott.*

FARMER BRYAN 4 ch.g. Deep Run–Erra (Romany Air) [1989/90 17d^{4}]
half-brother to 3 winning jumpers, including useful hurdler Farmer and staying 74 p
chaser Corn Merchant (both by Winden): dam selling hurdler: ridden by 7-lb claimer, around 30 lengths fourth to Olveston in novice hurdle at Newton Abbot in March: will improve over longer distances. *N. A. Gaselee.*

FARMER CHRIS 6 b.g. Official–Honey Harfat (Right Tack) [1989/90 F16f^{5}] first foal: dam novice selling hurdler: in frame in a point-to-point in May: fifth in NH Flat race at Hexham later in month: yet to race over hurdles or in a steeplechase. *R. W. Dods.*

FARMER'S FUN 4 b.f. Broadsword (USA)–Mishabo (Royalty) [1989/90 F12f^{6}] sixth foal: half-sister to winning jumpers Super Brat (by Shiny Tenth) and Beachamwell (by Record Run): dam never ran: well-beaten sixth in NH Flat race at Bangor in March: yet to race over hurdles. *Mrs A. E. Ratcliff.*

FARMER'S TOAST 8 b.g. True Song–Zanetta (Tiger) [1989/90 20d^{pu} 22v^{pu}
20v] lengthy, rather sparely-made gelding: no sign of ability over hurdles: —
headstrong. *M. J. Wilkinson.*

FARMLEA BOY 10 ch.g. Kemal (FR)–Nessie B (Star Gazer) [1989/90 c21d^{6} c**112**
c21m^{F} c25m c24m^{F} c20g^{2} c21g^{3} c16m^{2}] workmanlike gelding: handicap chaser: —
only modest form in 1989/90: suited by around 2½m: probably acts on any ground: reportedly difficult to train. *G. B. Balding.*

FAR MORE 4 ch.g. Gorytus (USA)–Demare (Pardao) [1989/90 16m^{4} 16f^{3}]
leggy gelding: modest middle-distance maiden on Flat: showed ability in 2 90
juvenile hurdles in December: has worn a crossed noseband: changed hands 11,000 gns Doncaster March Sales. *F. Durr.*

FARM WEEK 8 gr.g. General Ironside–News Letter (London Gazette) c**110** x
[1989/90 c27g^{3} c25d^{3} c24g^{6} c30v^{F} c24s^{6} c25m^{3} c24m^{2} c24m^{4} c24g^{3}] strong, —
compact gelding: handicap chaser: placed several times in 1989/90, on final occasion 10 lengths third behind Trusty Friend at Worcester: stays well: acts on heavy going and good to firm: makes mistakes. *G. B. Balding.*

FAR OUT 4 b.g. Raga Navarro (ITY)–Spaced Out (Space King) [1989/90 16s^{pu}
16d 20g 16d*] sparely-made gelding: first foal: dam winning jumper: tailed off only 85
outing on Flat: 20/1 and ridden by 3-lb claimer, won 13-runner juvenile maiden hurdle at Perth in May by a length from Smoke despite wandering under pressure: showed first sign of ability over 2½m on previous start: acts on dead going. *T. Bailey.*

FARRANRORY 6 br.m. Mandalus–Caisepuca (Lucky Guy) [1989/90 aF16g^{6} c**86**
22d c20d^{6} c24m^{2} c24d^{pu}] small ex-Irish mare: second foal: dam, lightly raced, —
showed a little ability on Flat and over hurdles in Ireland: won a point-to-point in 1989: well beaten in NH Flat race and novice hurdle: second of 3 finishers at Fakenham in March, easily best effort in novice chases: made numerous mistakes final outing. *O. O'Neill.*

FARRIERS LAD 5 b.g. Smackover–Kirkmaiden (Sea Wolf) [1989/90 F12f^{2}
F16m] rangy gelding: second reported foal: dam poor selling hurdler: second to
Yougotit in NH Flat race at Bangor in March: tailed off in well-contested event at
Liverpool following month: yet to race over hurdles or fences. *B. A. McMahon.*

FASHION FOUNTAIN 7 br.m. Royal Fountain–Royal Fashion (Salvo)
[1989/90 16f^{ur}] of little account. *K. G. Wingrove.* —

FASHION PRINCESS 4 gr.f. Van Der Linden (FR)–Pendle's Secret (Le
Johnstan) [1989/90 17fF^{3} 17h^{3} 17f^{4} 16h^{3} 17g^{2} 17d^{5} 16f^{4} 16f^{pu} 16g^{pu}] small filly: 60
half-sister to fair hurdler Rivers Secret (by Young Man): poor plater on Flat: poor
juvenile selling hurdler: broke blood vessel third outing. *Mrs A. Knight.*

FAST APPROACH 4 br.f. Daring March–Honest Opinion (Free State)
[1989/90 16f^{2} 16f^{3} 16g^{4} 16f 16f^{4} 16f^{F}] small filly: 1¼m seller winner on Flat (tends 70
to hang and pull hard): poor form over hurdles: has wandered and carried head
high: trained until after fourth start by A. Robson. *J. Dooler.*

FAST CRUISE 5 b.m. Cruise Missile–Speeder (Space King) [1989/90 F16m
F16m] third foal: dam, poor hurdler, half-sister to a winning selling chaser: behind
in NH Flat races: yet to race over hurdles or fences. *Miss B. Sykes.*

FAST FREEZE 4 b.g. Vision (USA)–Gohar (USA) (Barachois (CAN)) [1989/90
F17d 16f^{5} 17m^{4} 20f* 20f^{4}] IR 7,000F, 2,000Y: half-brother to 2 minor winners in 90
Austria and USA: dam, 5f claimer winner at 2 yrs, half-sister to good North
American performer Par Excellence, dam of very smart 1984 2-y-o stayer
Khozaam: won novice hurdle at Sedgefield in May by 15 lengths: below form in
handicap on same course later in month: stays 2½m: acts on firm going: claimer
ridden. *R. Earnshaw.*

FAST MARKET 4 gr.f. Petong–Sweet Candice (African Sky) [1989/90 17f^{2}
16h^{2}] leggy, dipped-backed filly: won 1¼m seller on firm ground on Flat in July: 62
sold out of M. Blanshard's stable 4,000 gns Newmarket July Sales: poor form in
early-season juvenile hurdles: finished lame in seller final start. *J. H. Baker.*

FAST REALM (USA) 7 b.g. Tromos–Fast Ride (FR) (Sicambre) [1989/90
16m] workmanlike gelding: made all in novice hurdle in 1988: weakened before 3 —
out all starts since, including in a seller: strong puller, unlikely to stay much
beyond 2m: suited by firm ground. *D. R. Wellicome.*

FAST STUDY 5 b.g. Crash Course–Mary May (Little Buskins) [1989/90
F16s^{su} 16m^{6}] second foal: dam winner on Flat and over hurdles in Ireland: slipped 88 p
up at halfway in NH Flat race in February: promising sixth to Fifth Amendment in
novice hurdle at Wincanton following month, staying on from 2 out without being
knocked about: sure to improve. *D. Nicholson.*

FATHER BRADY 11 b.g. The Parson–Mrs Brady (Ossian II) [1989/90 c21s^{4} c**102**
c26d^{3} c25m* c22m^{F} c26f^{4}] strong, workmanlike gelding: quite useful point-to-
pointer/hunter chaser: won at Sandown in March: close up when falling 5 out in
Seagram Fox Hunters' Chase at Liverpool in April: ran moderately final start:
stays 25f: acts on any going: usually jumps soundly: tends to sweat. *J. E. Greenall.*

FATHER FLINN 5 b.h. Wolver Hollow–Trouble Pocket (USA) (In The
Pocket) [1989/90 24g^{pu}] leggy horse: of little account: has run blinkered. *Mrs V.* —
C. Ward.

FATHER JOHN 6 ch.g. Viking (USA)–Theban Queen (Pindari) [1989/90 22g^{5}
22g 22g 21f^{pu} 16f^{5} 17m*] strong gelding: ridden by 7-lb claimer, led close home to 76 §
win poor maiden hurdle at Newton Abbot in May, having seemed reluctant when
first put under pressure: ran creditably over 2¾m on first start when trained by J.
Baker: acts on good to firm going: inconsistent. *Mrs J. Wonnacott.*

FATHER PADDY 8 b.g. Mandamus–Dream Isle (Indian Ruler) [1989/90 c—
c16g^{3} c26m^{5} c21d^{6} c25g c16d] strong gelding: poor novice hurdler/chaser: well —
beaten in 1989/90: suited by sharp 2m and top-of-the-ground: pulls hard: has worn
a crossed noseband and a net muzzle: usually taken early to post. *J. Webber.*

FATHER TIME 6 ch.g. Longleat (USA)–Noddy Time (Gratitude) [1989/90
16d^{2} 16g 16s^{3} 20s* 20g^{3} 20s] workmanlike gelding: modest handicapper on Flat 116
nowadays, won over 8.3f in 1989: successful in novice handicap hurdle at Market
Rasen in January by 30 lengths: good third behind Black Moccasin in novice event
at Doncaster later in month: well beaten in handicap at Ascot in February: stays
2½m: acts on soft going: jumps deliberately. *M. H. Tompkins.*

FAUX PAVILLON 6 ch.g. Alias Smith (USA)–Beech Tree (Fighting Ship)
[1989/90 20f^{pu} 21m^{pu} 16m^{2}] big gelding: 1½ lengths second to Frendly Fellow in 83

handicap at Uttoxeter in May, first form over hurdles: none too fluent a jumper: sold out of A. Hide's stable 8,600 gns Ascot November Sales. *Mrs J. G. Retter.*

FAVOSKI 4 b.c. Niniski (USA)–Favoletta (Baldric II) [1989/90 17g^{2} 16m^{2} 16d*
16d^{4} 16m^{pu} 22f^{F} 17m^{5}] smallish, sparely-made colt: half-brother to disappointing 108
novice hurdler Favourite Guest (by Be My Guest): fair maiden on Flat, suited by 1¼m: sold out of G. Wragg's stable 11,500 gns Newmarket Autumn Sales: won juvenile hurdle at Wincanton in February: best form on good to soft going: dead. *I. P. Wardle.*

FAVOURITE GUEST 6 b. or br.g. Be My Guest (USA)–Favoletta (Baldric
II) [1989/90 16m^{3} 16g] small, sparely-made gelding: disappointing novice hurdler: — §
never travelling well when tailed off in selling handicap in October: has looked none too keen under pressure: unlikely to stay beyond 2m: sometimes blinkered: retained by trainer 950 gns Ascot June Sales. *Miss S. J. Wilton.*

FAX ME 4 b.g. Red Sunset–Hill of Howth (Sassafras (FR)) [1989/90 F16f^{6}] second foal: dam won over 11f in Ireland: well beaten in NH Flat race at Hereford: yet to race over hurdles. *R. Simpson.*

FAYADPOUR 6 b.g. Dalsaan–Fille du Tonnerre (FR) (Faraway Son (USA))
[1989/90 16d^{pu} 16v 16g] strong, compact gelding: 1¼m winner on Flat at 3 yrs: no —
sign of ability over hurdles: blinkered last 2 starts. *E. A. Wheeler.*

FAYE'S DELIGHT 5 ch.m. Swing Easy (USA)–English Silver (Son of Silver)
[1989/90 16g^{pu}] angular mare: winning 2m selling hurdler: acted on firm ground: —
blinkered last 4 starts: ridden by 7-lb claimer: dead. *R. T. Juckes.*

FEARLESS FIGHTER 5 b.g. Formidable (USA)–Wild Asset (Welsh
Pageant) [1989/90 17h^{2} 16m^{4} 16s 18s 18v^{3} 16v 18f 16m^{6}] sturdy, angular gelding: 83 §
poor novice hurdler: stays 2¼m: acts on heavy going: unreliable. *G. P. Enright.*

FEARLESS NATIVE 4 br.g. Final Straw–Nativity (USA) (Native Royalty
(USA)) [1989/90 16m 17v 16v] medium-sized gelding: 1¼m claimer winner on —
Flat: sold out of J. Berry's stable 10,000 gns Doncaster September Sales: well beaten in juvenile hurdles: sold 3,700 gns Ascot April Sales. *R. J. Manning.*

FEARLESS STAND 4 ch.c. Import–Glendyne (Precipice Wood) [1989/90
16m^{ro} 16f^{2} 16f^{4}] plating-class maiden on Flat, stays 1¼m: in frame in early-season 69
selling hurdles at Sedgefield: ran out fifth on debut: sold 4,400 gns Doncaster October Sales. *S. E. Kettlewell.*

FEARSOME 4 gr.g. Formidable (USA)–Seriema (Petingo) [1989/90 16g 16g^{6}
16g] modest form at up to 1¼m on Flat, has run blinkered: poor form in juvenile 74
hurdles. *K. M. Brassey.*

FEASIBLE 6 b.g. Kampala–Rajang (Sharpen Up) [1989/90 16d* a16g^{4} 17f
a16g^{2} a16g^{3}] leggy, quite good-topped gelding: 33/1-winner of 5-runner novice 84
handicap hurdle at Market Rasen in August: ran well when placed in similar events at Southwell: will be suited by further than 2m: acts on dead going: has worn a tongue strap. *S. B. Avery.*

FEDERAL TROOPER 9 ch.g. Ascertain (USA)–Rough Crossing (Deep c**101**
Run) [1989/90 c17g^{3} c16f^{2} c17d* c16g^{4} c17m^{pu}] smallish, close-coupled gelding: —
winning hurdler: ridden by claimer when winning novice handicap chase at Huntingdon in December: has jumped none too fluently most other starts over fences: reportedly broke blood vessel final outing: likely to prove best at around 2m: acts on good to soft and firm ground: wears a crossed noseband. *Mrs J. Pitman.*

FEELING BETTER 4 b.g. Cure The Blues (USA)–La Mortola (Bold Lad
(IRE)) [1989/90 16g^{pu} 16g^{4} 16s^{4} 16d^{pu} 16f^{2}] smallish, lengthy ex-Irish gelding: 79
first foal: dam unraced half-sister to quite useful French 2-y-o Polifontaine, very useful performer Millfontaine and high-class miler Katies: placed at up to 1¼m on Flat: ridden by claimer, second in novice event at Worcester in April, best effort over hurdles: acts on firm ground. *F. Jordan.*

FEELING ROSEY 8 b.m. Uncle Pokey–Rose's Code (True Code) [1989/90
22d 20g^{6} 22d^{6} 24s a22g^{5} a20g^{4} 20f^{2}] compact, good-quartered mare: poor 82
hurdler: stays 3m: acts on any going: usually ridden by claimer. *D. T. Todd.*

FEILE NA HINSE 7 b.g. Cidrax (FR)–Hildamay (Cantab) [1989/90 c24g* c**113**
c20v^{3} c24f^{2}] workmanlike gelding: modest chaser: jumped well and made all in —
handicap at Fakenham in February: ran well in Timeform Chase at Haydock and handicap at Newbury in March: stays 3m: probably acts on any going. *R. Champion.*

FELL CLIMB 10 ch.g. Levanter–Rambling (Wrekin Rambler) [1989/90 c25g^{pu} **c103** x
c24d^{6} c24s^{5} c26s^{pu}] leggy, lightly-made gelding: winning hurdler/chaser: modest —
form over fences in 1989/90: stays well: best form on soft ground: best in blinkers:
usually amateur ridden: moderate jumper of fences. *P. G. Bailey.*

FELLOW'S NIGHT 7 ch.g. Deep Run–Chihuahua (Mustang) [1989/90 16g^{pu}
16f 20m^{pu} 19m* 19m^{4}] good-bodied, workmanlike gelding: won novice hurdle at 83
Hereford in April by 20 lengths: creditable fourth in novice handicap on same
course following month: stays 19f: acts on good to firm ground. *K. C. Bailey.*

FENCE JUDGE 8 b.g. Green Shoon–Bramble Belle (Vulgan) [1989/90 c24d^{4} c**97**
c25f^{2} c27s^{6} c25g^{3}] compact gelding: handicap chaser: suited by around 3m: acts —
on firm and dead ground: tends to sweat: deliberate jumper. *Capt. T. A. Forster.*

FENCHURCH COLONY 9 b.g. Tachypous–Katebird (Birdbrook) [1989/90 c—
c16f] big, good-topped gelding: lightly-raced novice hurdler/chaser: blinkered —
final start 1985/6. *L. C. Corbett.*

FENFIRE 4 b.f. Trojan Fen–Upanishad (Amber Rama (USA)) [1989/90 16s
16s^{3}] compact filly: modest, not entirely reliable handicapper on Flat, suited by 9f: 72
sold out of G. Wragg's stable 12,000 gns Newmarket December Sales: third
behind 25-length winner Cyphrate in juvenile hurdle at Haydock in January:
jumps none too fluently. *N. Tinkler.*

FENKIN 12 b. or br.g. Swing Easy (USA)–Path of Pride (Sovereign Path) c— x
[1989/90 c25m^{pu}] tall, leggy gelding: of little account over hurdles and in —
steeplechases (has jumped badly), but is a winning point-to-pointer: blinkered
only outing 1989/90. *Miss T. Brown.*

FERENTINO 5 b.g. Sparkler–Sa Fille (Mon Fils) [1989/90 F16m 16s^{pu} 17m]
leggy gelding: second in NH Flat race in 1989: no form in 2 outings over hurdles. —
P. Leach.

FERNANDO (CZE) 6 b.h. Silvaner (CZE)–Felos (HUN) (Lions) [1989/90 c—
c16g c20s 16s 21d] winning hurdler in Czechoslovakia: fourth in juvenile hurdle in —
Britain in 1987/8: no form in 1989/90, including in novice chases. *Andrew Turnell.*

FERNANDO REYES 5 ro.g. Morston (FR)–Setmark (Sharpen Up) [1989/90
16g^{6} 16d 16g^{3} 16f* 16h^{2}] close-coupled, angular gelding: poor maiden on Flat: 96
progressed with his races and in March won novice hurdle at Hexham, making
most: good second in handicap on same course following month: races keenly and
will prove best at 2m: acts on hard going. *J. I. A. Charlton.*

FEROCIOUS KNIGHT (USA) 11 b.g. Fearless Knight–Fallaha's Love c**98**
(USA) (Our Love) [1989/90 c26f*] sturdy gelding: lightly-raced handicap chaser: —
made mistakes when winning 4-runner event at Newton Abbot in August: stays
3¼m: probably needs a sound surface and acts on hard going. *Miss J. Thorne.*

FERODA 9 b.g. Ashmore (FR)–Dedham Vale (Dike (USA)) [1989/90 c**156**
c16d^{2} c16g^{2} c17d* c16f^{3} c16f c25d^{3}] —

Chasers & Hurdlers has often commented on the relatively poor choice of races in Britain for a good two-mile chaser out of the novice stage. The top two-milers in Ireland had even fewer worthwhile opportunities. Between the festival meetings at Galway in August and Punchestown in April in the latest season, only four open two-mile chases in Ireland were worth more than IR £3,000 to the winner—the most valuable an IR £5,520 race won by Have A Barney at Navan in November. Feroda, a leading Irish novice in 1988/9 when successful on successive days in the Perrier Jouet Novices' Chase and Captain Morgan Aintree Chase at Liverpool, again spent much of the latest season chasing the bigger British prizes. After going down by six lengths to the race-fit Wolf of Badenoch in a handicap at Leopardstown in December, Feroda ran four times in Britain, picking up over £28,000 in prize money and developing into a smart chaser.

Feroda's racing character has quickly become familiar to British racegoers. Though thoroughly genuine, he tends to race lazily and needs a deal of driving. Odds on for the Game Spirit Handicap Chase at Newbury in February, Feroda looked beaten when coming under pressure four fences out as The Dragon Master was sent for home. But gradually closing from the second last, he stayed on to lead early on the run-in and win by three quarters of a length, driven out after seeming to idle in front. Feroda had also stayed on strongly after coming under pressure a long way out when a length-and-a-half second to Meikleour in the Victor Chandler Handicap

Game Spirit Handicap Chase, Newbury—
Feroda (right) challenges The Dragon Master at the last

Chase at Ascot the previous month. Forced into slight mistakes at the fourth-last and third-last fences at Ascot, but for which he might well have won, Feroda was again let down by his jumping in the Queen Mother Champion Chase at Cheltenham in March. He'd lost all chance with a bad mistake three out in the Arkle Challenge Trophy on the same course the previous year, and lost ground through none-too-fluent jumping in the Champion Chase. But he rallied under strong pressure in the latter stages to finish an excellent staying-on seven-and-a-half-lengths third behind Barnbrook Again. Feroda couldn't get back into the race after getting behind early in the Captain Morgan Aintree Chase over Liverpool's sharper two-mile course the following month. Most probably he was unsuited by the very firm ground. That's more likely than that he was feeling the effects of several hard races. As we know, Feroda is very tough; he came a respectable third behind On The Other Hand in the Punchestown Festival Handicap Chase over twenty-five furlongs around three weeks later. He looked well beforehand at Punchestown, and his weakening in the latter stages having travelled strongly for a long way suggests he failed to stay a trip almost a mile further than he'd previously tackled.

<table>
<tr><td rowspan="8">Feroda
(b.g. 1981)</td><td rowspan="4">Ashmore (FR)
(b 1971)</td><td rowspan="2">Luthier
(b or br 1965)</td><td>Klairon</td></tr>
<tr><td>Flute Enchantee</td></tr>
<tr><td rowspan="2">Almyre
(b 1964)</td><td>Wild Risk</td></tr>
<tr><td>Ad Gloriam</td></tr>
<tr><td rowspan="4">Dedham Vale
(ch 1976)</td><td rowspan="2">Dike
(ch 1966)</td><td>Herbager</td></tr>
<tr><td>Delta</td></tr>
<tr><td rowspan="2">Valley Farm
(ch 1967)</td><td>Red God</td></tr>
<tr><td>Flatford Mill</td></tr>
</table>

Feroda's pedigree provides conflicting pointers as to his stamina potential. Though the sire Ashmore, who died in 1989, was a very good stayer on the Flat, none of his best produce to race over jumps, such as The Reject, Ash King and Big Ash, stayed much beyond two and a half miles. The dam Dedham Vale, a middle-distance winner on the Flat, is a half-sister to the useful stayer Ragabash but also to two hurdlers who won only at up to two and a half miles in Cooch Behar and Princes Arcade. There's plenty of speed further back in the family. Valley Farm and Flatford Mill both won over sprint distances. The latter also produced The Country Lane, a six-furlong winner and the dam of useful sprinter Bumpkin and prolific winning miler On Edge. Judged on his style of racing, Feroda should stay two and a half miles; indeed he may prove well suited by it. A lengthy, powerful gelding who shows traces of stringhalt, he acts on any going. He is sure to win more races. *A. L. T. Moore, Ireland.*

FERRYSTREAM 4 b.c. Niniski (USA)–River Call (FR) (Riverman (USA)) [1989/90 16g^{2} 16f^{4} 16m] leggy colt: fair 11.7f winner from 3 starts on Flat: sold out of G. Harwood's stable 10,500 gns Newmarket Autumn Sales: easily best effort in juvenile hurdles on first outing, in February: will stay beyond 2m: ridden by 3-lb claimer. *J. H. Baker.* 93

FESTIVE FLING 5 b.g. Last Fandango–Pandomyne (Pandofell) [1989/90 16g^{4} 16f^{4} 16m^{3} 20f^{3} 16d* 16g^{2} 16g 20d^{3} 17d^{5} 16g^{3} 16h* 16h^{2} 16d] angular, workmanlike gelding: won novice claiming hurdle at Sedgefield in December and handicap at Hexham in April: good second in handicap on latter course in May: best form at 2m on hard ground. *Denys Smith.* 94

FETTUCCINE 6 ch.g. Bybicello–Reel Keen (Firestreak) [1989/90 16f^{pu} 17f^{F} 16f^{3} 16f 20f^{6} 20s 25d^{2} 24m^{3} 25h*] compact gelding: first foal: dam placed in 7f seller at 2 yrs: finished lame when easily landing the odds in 3-runner amateur riders novice hurdle at Kelso in May: seems suited by a good test of stamina: acts on hard and dead ground: has sweated. *W. A. Stephenson.* 90

FIB 8 br.g. Sagaro–Ruskaja (Red God) [1989/90 c25m* c25f^{2} c25m^{5} c24g^{3} c25m^{6} c26v^{5}] compact, workmanlike gelding: handicap chaser: won at Warwick in November: ran moderately last 2 starts: stays 25f: acts on any going: blinkered last 5 outings in 1987/8: moderate jumper. *T. R. Greathead.* c**101** x —

FIBREGUIDE TECH 7 b.g. Uncle Pokey–Starcat (Avocat) [1989/90 c20s^{2}] lengthy, plain gelding: novice hurdler: successful in 3 point-to-points in 1990: 12 lengths second to Asigh in novice hunter chase at Uttoxeter in February: wears a crossed noseband: jumped well in the main at Uttoxeter and should improve. *Mrs T. R. Kinsey.* c**81** p —

FICTION WRITER 6 ch.g. Quayside–Chapter Four (Shackleton) [1989/90 20f^{6} 22g^{3} 25f^{4}] rangy gelding with scope: poor form in novice hurdles, best effort over 2¾m. *T. T. Bill.* 68

FIDDLE A LITTLE 5 b.g. Deep Run–Brideweir (Chandra Cross) [1989/90 20d^{pu} 16s] unfurnished gelding: sixth foal: brother to 2 poor animals and half-brother to modest hurdler Digby (by Arapaho): dam never ran: little sign of ability in 2 outings over hurdles. *G. A. Hubbard.* —

FIDDLERS THREE 7 ch.g. Orchestra–Kirin (Tyrant (USA)) [1989/90 c20d^{3} c20s^{6} c20d^{4}] tall, good-bodied gelding: winning hurdler: modest novice chaser, best effort in 1989/90 on final start: will be suited by 3m: acts on soft going. *Capt. T. A. Forster.* c**98** —

FIDDLE STRING 8 b.m. Plenty Spirit–Fiddlers Too (Neron) [1989/90 18m^{pu}] sturdy mare: half-sister to several winners, including fairly useful 1975 2-y-o Carburton (by Runnymede): dam won at 7f to 1½m: tailed off when pulled up 3 out in novice hurdle at Worcester in September on debut. *B. Preece.* —

FIDWAY 5 b.g. Fidel–Galway Maid (Jimmy Reppin) [1989/90 16g^{ur} 16m^{6} 16f* 16m*] 135 p

Retirement from the saddle is surely still some way off for thirty-five-year-old Steve Smith Eccles. He was riding as well as ever in the latest season and, as a freelance, finished in eighth place in the jockeys' table with fifty-six victories, the most notable of which was gained on Fidway in the Seagram 100 Pipers Top Novices' Hurdle at Liverpool in April. The partnership had got off to an inauspicious start at Kempton in February. Fidway, who'd pulled hard and jumped moderately, was towards the rear when apparently hampered at the fourth flight, which resulted in Smith Eccles being unseated. Scudamore was on board when Fidway finished a promising sixth at Sandown two weeks later, but Smith Eccles and Fidway were reunited in a novice event at Nottingham later in March, the champion jockey having been claimed to ride Abbotts View, who started at 4/1 on. It was Fidway, racing keenly, who looked the odds-on shot for most of the

Seagram 100 Pipers Top Novices' Hurdle, Liverpool—Fidway has quickened clear; Rakes Lane (centre) and Philosophos lead the pursuit

way. Jumping quickly, he moved smoothly past the front-running Abbotts View after the last on the far side and went on to win easily by seven lengths. Fidway ran very green once he'd hit the front, tending to dive left at the hurdles, and we thought his lack of experience might count against him at Liverpool. The majority of his fourteen opponents there had had plenty of racing both on the Flat and over hurdles, and they included three horses who'd figured prominently in Cheltenham's Waterford Crystal Supreme Novices' Hurdle, notably third-placed Rakes Lane. However, it was another relatively-inexperienced horse in My Young Man, unbeaten in two starts over hurdles, who was made favourite at 4/1. Fidway, who looked tremendously well and had clearly thrived since his run at Nottingham, started at 16/1. With the free-running My Young Man setting a very strong gallop Smith Eccles was able to settle Fidway while also keeping the horse well in touch, disputing third place. The tiring My Young Man was headed by Regal Lake on the home turn, but Regal Lake held the lead only briefly. Fidway, produced on the outside, stormed to the front at the third last and quickly drew away from his hard-ridden rivals. Around six lengths clear going to the last, Fidway began to tire and had to be kept right up to his work on the run-in, but he never looked in danger of being caught. Rakes Lane, staying on strongly, was three lengths behind him at the line, and then there was a further one and a half lengths back to third-placed Philosophos who did much the best of the four-year-olds. Of the previous five winners of the Seagram Novices' Hurdle only Convinced has so far added to that success. It's to be hoped that Fidway remains free from injury and is able to complete a full second season. If he does and he's kept to hurdling Fidway is sure to win more races, probably in handicap company. A lengthy, rather unfurnished gelding, his long-term future lies in steeplechases. Fidway has already shown an aptitude for jumping the bigger obstacles, for he

Mr A. R. Coley's "Fidway"

reportedly cleared a fence on three occasions when accompanying his wayward stable-companion Pukka Major on a starting test at Sandown.

Fidway (b.g. 1985)	Fidel (b 1968)	Relko (b 1960)	Tanerko
			Relance III
		Cuba (ch 1953)	Hyperion
			Nassau
	Galway Maid (ch 1975)	Jimmy Reppin (ch 1965)	Midsummer Night II
			Sweet Molly
		Night Lark (ch 1967)	Larkspur
			Parnava

Galway Maid, the dam of Fidway, has produced five foals to date, all by Fidel. Fidway, the third of them, is the only winner. Galway Maid, who raced without success on the Flat, over hurdles and in point-to-points in Ireland, is a daughter of the twice-raced maiden Night Lark. The third dam Parnava, a winner at up to a mile and a half in France, is a half-sister to the smart stayer Tanavar, and to Ranavalo, dam of the good sprinter Fortino II. Fidway's sire, a one-eyed horse, was a useful stayer on the Flat. The best of his offspring to date, the smart chaser Ashley House, also stayed well, but speed rather than stamina is Fidway's long suit, and we think two miles will prove to be his optimum trip. Fidway won on heavy ground on the second of two starts in Irish National Hunt Flat races in the 1988/9 season, when trained by J. Cosgrave. He acts on firm going and has yet to race on soft surface over hurdles. *T. Thomson Jones.*

FIEFDOM 10 ch.g. Home Guard (USA)–Eastwood Bounty (Bounteous)
[1989/90 16f* 16g^{pu} 16m^{6} 22d] strong, angular gelding: won 3-runner Ekbalco 118
Hurdle at Newcastle in October: never going well when sixth in handicap on same

course following month: best at 2m: seems to act on any going: has worn a tongue strap. *W. Storey.*

FIELD CHANCE 9 b.m. Whistlefield–Last Chance II (Armagnac Monarch) [1989/90 c25m3 c22g2] small mare: novice hurdler: winning point-to-pointer: placed in hunter chases at Devon & Exeter (novice) and Stratford (25 lengths second to Sanballat, better effort) in April. *F. G. Tucker.* c90 —

FIELD CONQUEROR 9 b.g. Busted–Divine Thought (Javelot) [1989/90 c20g4 c20d c24d2 c20vpu] compact ex-Irish gelding: useful chaser: best effort in Britain when neck second to Steeple View in handicap chase at Newbury in February: pulled up lame next outing: stays 3m: acts on heavy going: has been blinkered when successful. *D. R. C. Elsworth.* c141 —

FIERY SUN 5 b.g. Sexton Blake–Melanie Jane (Lord Gayle (USA)) [1989/90 16m* 16g4 25f4 16g5 20g3 16g5 16g* a16g3 a20g 17f2 16m* 16g2] neat gelding: selling hurdler: bought in 4,000 gns after winning handicaps at Market Rasen in September, Catterick in January and Market Rasen in April: needs plenty of use made of him over 2m and stays 2½m: acts on firm ground: wears a visor: claimer ridden. *G. R. Oldroyd.* 95

FIESTA DANCE 7 b.g. Record Token–Presumptuous (Gay Fandango (USA)) [1989/90 c21f2 c24f* c16f2] rangy gelding: novice hurdler: jumped none too fluently when winning 5-runner novice chase at Market Rasen in August: beaten 5 lengths by sole opponent Leon in similar event on same course later in month: stays 3m: acts on firm ground: races freely. *J. P. Leigh.* c82 —

FIFTH AMENDMENT 5 b.g. The Parson–Biowen (Master Owen) [1989/90 16g 16g* 16s* 16s3 16m*] 32,000 3-y-o: workmanlike gelding: has scope: brother to very useful hurdler/chaser Mixed Blends and half-brother to National Hunt Chase winner Topsham Bay (by Proverb) and winning hurdler Pollen Bee (by Pollerton): dam unraced sister to one winning jumper and half-sister to several others: won novice hurdles at Wincanton (2, hung left on second occasion) and Leicester in second half of season: creditable third at Sandown in between: will be suited by further than 2m: acts on good to firm and soft ground: tends to carry head high: will make a chaser. *Mrs J. Pitman.* 118

FIFTH ATTEMPT 8 b.g. Vulgan Slave–Dingle Poke (Even Money) [1989/90 c21gF c20mpu a20g3 a20g3 a20g5 21d* 21f* 25f] lengthy gelding: handicap hurdler: won twice at Ludlow in March: ran poorly final start: tailed off when pulled up after fifth in novice chase (jumped badly): seems to stay 3m: acts on firm and dead ground. *P. S. Felgate.* c— 99

FIGHTER COMMAND 4 ch.g. Milford–Olga Wagner (ITY) (Sharpen Up) [1989/90 F16m5 aF14g* aF13g*] second foal: half-brother to useful Italian winner Sesin (by Dance In Time): dam won 5 races in Italy: won NH Flat races at Southwell and Lingfield in February: dead. *J. A. Glover.*

FIGHTING DAYS (USA) 4 ch.g. Fit To Fight (USA)–August Days (USA) (In Reality) [1989/90 16f 16g 16m 16m3 16g3 16v3 16m* 16f* 18f2 16m4 16m] sparely-made, plain gelding: well beaten on Flat: won juvenile hurdles at Plumpton (maiden) and Taunton in April: good second in novice handicap at Fontwell in May, leading until run-in: reluctant to race when running moderately in lady riders handicap final outing: stays 2¼m: acts on firm ground (seems unsuited by heavy). *A. Moore.* 91

FIGHTING FINISH 6 ch.g. Lucky Mickmooch–Fighting Sal (Gail Star) [1989/90 16g6 16g3] second foal: half-brother to maiden point-to-pointer/novice chaser Pea Sal (by Peacock): dam never ran: third in novice hurdle at Newcastle in May: will be suited by further. *W. A. Stephenson.* 83

FIGHTING GORYTUS 5 b.h. Gorytus (USA)–Stella Urbis (GER) (Upper Case (USA)) [1989/90 16v4 16spu] compact horse: modest middle-distance performer on Flat: no worthwhile form in 2 novice hurdles. *C. C. B. Booth.* —

FIGHTING WORDS 4 ch.g. Prince Bee–How Hostile (Tumble Wind (USA)) [1989/90 16d3] IR 12,000 (privately) 3-y-o: workmanlike gelding: fourth foal: dam, poor Irish maiden, half-sister to smart stayer Barley Hill: green and carrying condition, staying-on 15 lengths third behind Regal Lake in Swish Hurdle at Chepstow in March on debut: will stay beyond 2m: sure to improve and win a race. *J. T. Gifford.* 108 p

FILE CONCORD 6 br.g. Strong Gale–Lady Reporter (London Gazette) [1989/90 20s* 20g*] rangy, useful-looking gelding: has scope and will make a chaser: won novice hurdles at Huntingdon (beat Remittance Man by 8 lengths) in 115 p

December and Kempton (easily, by 10 lengths from Nicknavar) following month: stays 2½m: acts on soft going: likely to improve further. *Mrs J. Pitman.*

FILI FOLIA 6 b.m. Majestic Current (USA)–Owenansea (Owen Anthony) [1989/90 20f^{F} 16g 16s 16d 16g^{F} 16f^{5} 16f^{4}] compact mare: poor form over hurdles, including in selling handicap: best run at 2m on firm ground. *R. W. Swiers.* 63

FILL THE JUG 9 br.m. Derrylin–Fleur d'Amour (Murrayfield) [1989/90 16m^{6} 17d^{2}] close-coupled mare: modest novice hurdler, lightly raced: yet to race much beyond 2m: acts on heavy going. *P. R. Rodford.* 82

FILM LIGHTING GIRL 4 ch.f. Persian Bold–Mey (Canisbay) [1989/90 a18g^{4} a20g^{2} a20g^{6}] placed over 13f on Flat: in frame in juvenile hurdle and seller at Southwell: ran moderately final start: probably stays 2½m. *J. L. Harris.* 62

FILS-DE-ROI 9 b.g. Roi Soleil–La Caline (Soderini) [1989/90 c17f^{2} c16f^{2}] sparely-made gelding: selling hurdler/chaser: stays 2½m: acts on any going: blinkered once in 1987/8: failed to complete in 2 point-to-points in the spring. *Mrs S. Oliver.* c**82** —

FILS DU PARC 7 b.g. Politico (USA)–Merry Leap (Stephen George) [1989/90 20s^{5} 22d 21d c24g^{6}] workmanlike gelding: second foal: brother to winning point-to-pointer Polly Verry: dam winning selling hurdler/point-to-pointer: well beaten in a point-to-point in 1989: strong-finishing sixth in novice event at Bangor in December, only form over hurdles: under 12 lengths fifth to Trusty Friend in novice event at Perth in April on chasing debut: trained by T. Forster until after third start. *C. Parker.* c**87** 79

FINAL ALMA 7 b.g. Final Straw–Alma Ata (Bustino) [1989/90 22g 24g 20s c24g^{4} c20v^{F} c20f^{r}] sturdy, compact gelding: handicap hurdler: let down by his jumping over fences (tailed off when trying to refuse and running out seventh on final start): stays 2½m: acts on any going. *P. Mitchell.* c— x —

FINAL CHANT 9 br.g. Joshua–Chantfour (Chantelsey) [1989/90 c24f* c24f^{F}] very useful point-to-pointer: successful in hunter chase at Hexham in March on steeplechasing debut by 15 lengths from Oh Why: odds on, every chance when falling 5 out in novice hunter chase at Wetherby following month: stays 3m: acts on firm ground. *D. A. D. Brydon.* c**105** p

FINAL FLUTTER 5 b.m. Beldale Flutter (USA)–Star Story (Red God) [1989/90 16m 16g^{F} 16g* a16g^{6} 16v 20f^{6} 16h^{2} 16m^{6} 16f^{6} 22f 16m^{6}] leggy, lightly-made mare: sold out of F. J. Houghton's stable 3,300 gns after winning selling handicap hurdle at Windsor in January: runner-up at Plumpton in March, only subsequent form: best at around 2m: probably unsuited by heavy going, acts on any other: amateur ridden when successful: often blinkered: trained by T. Kemp on fourth and fifth starts. *A. Moore.* 94 d

FINAL MADNESS 4 ch.f. Final Straw–Summer Madness (Silly Season) [1989/90 17f^{3} 16h^{5}] lengthy filly: maiden on Flat: sold out of K. Brassey's stable 1,250 gns Ascot July Sales: little promise in 2 juvenile hurdles, second a seller: dead. *C. L. Popham.* —

FINAL PLAYER 4 gr.c. Absalom–Oakwoodhill (Habat) [1989/90 16g^{pu} 16d 16d^{6} 16s 16g^{3}] stocky colt: maiden plater on Flat: juvenile selling hurdler: best effort on third outing: saddle slipped first start. *M. W. Easterby.* 70

FINAL PRESENCE 10 ch.g. El-Birillo–Final Answer (Honour Bound) [1989/90 c25g^{4} c24d^{pu}] big, lengthy gelding: fairly useful point-to-pointer and winning hunter chaser: needed race first outing: pulled up lame next time: stays 25f. *W. J. Evans.* c**85**

FINAL SELECTION 7 ch.g. Final Straw–Contralto (Busted) [1989/90 17f] robust, good-topped gelding: of little account as a hurdler: visored once. *J. White.* —

FINAL SOUND 5 b.g. Final Straw–Sound Type (Upper Case (USA)) [1989/90 16s^{4} 16g^{5} 16g^{4} 16v^{6} a16g^{5}] sturdy gelding: plating class on Flat, successful at up to 1¼m: modest form in novice and claiming hurdles: best form on good ground: visored fourth start: sold J. H. Baker 3,500 gns Ascot June Sales. *P. J. Feilden.* 83

FINAL SPRING 6 b.g. Hubble Bubble–Final Answer (Honour Bound) [1989/90 c20d^{pu}] non-thoroughbred gelding: half-brother to winning chasers Final Clear (by Clear Run) and Final Presence (by El-Birillo): dam from good pointing family: pulled up in a point-to-point in 1989: made mistakes and was tailed off when pulled up twelfth in novice chase at Warwick in January. *Mrs G. E. Jones.* c—

FINAL TOP 5 ch.g. Chaparly (FR)–Peg Top (Star Moss) [1989/90 16g 22m^{pu} 22m^{F}] tall, plain gelding: of little account: often blinkered. *H. Willis.* —

FINAL TRIP 5 ch.m. Final Straw–Tripolitaine (FR) (Nonoalco (USA)) [1989/90 16g 17m^{pu} 16f 22g^{pu} c16g^{4} c16g^{pu}] sparely-made mare: of little account. *F. Jestin.* c— —

FINBARR 8 b.g. Amboise–Anndamus (Mandamus) [1989/90 c26m^{5}] leggy gelding: no form over hurdles and in steeplechases: blinkered last 2 outings: runner-up in 2 point-to-points in 1990. *Miss D. Harris.* c— —

FINCHGLOW 7 ch.g. Some Hand–Lartway (Lauso) [1989/90 16f^{2} 16g^{6} 20m^{ur} 22m^{ur} 21m^{3} 16s^{5} 16g^{3} 22s 20m^{4}] dipped-backed gelding: poor novice hurdler: likely to prove best at 2m: acts on firm ground: makes mistakes. *J. T. Gifford.* 86 x

FINE TUDOR 4 b.g. Jimsun–Mill Haven (Mannion) [1989/90 16f 20f^{4} 16m^{4} 16f^{4}] close-coupled gelding: won 7f seller at 2 yrs but below form on Flat in 1989: sold out of M. Tompkins' stable 6,000 gns Newmarket July Sales: poor juvenile hurdler. *Mrs E. H. Heath.* —

FINGERS CROSSED 6 b.m. Touching Wood (USA)–La Pythie (FR) (Filiberto (USA)) [1989/90 20f 22d 16f^{5} 20f^{4} 20m^{3} 20g] neat mare: poor handicap hurdler: stays 2½m: goes well on top-of-the-ground: often claimer ridden. *K. A. Ryan.* 84

FINGEST 7 b.g. Imperial Fling (USA)–Derry Daughter (Derring-Do) [1989/90 c20s^{F} c24g^{4} c24d* c21s^{ur} 21d c20s^{4} c21d* c20d^{F} c24d^{6} c20d*] leggy, close-coupled gelding: fair handicap hurdler/chaser: won over fences at Market Rasen in January and March and Ayr (second race in consecutive days, led close home to beat Foyle Fisherman by 2 lengths) in April: stays 25f: acts on any going: has been blinkered. *P. D. Evans.* c**122** —

FIRE AT WILL 7 br.g. Random Shot–Kindly (Tarqogan) [1989/90 22d^{5}] close-coupled, angular gelding: novice hurdler: modest fifth only outing of season (December): will stay 3m: has raced only on a soft surface. *Capt. T. A. Forster.* —

FIRE EXPRESS (DEN) 4 gr.g. Another Realm–Fiji Express (Exbury) [1989/90 16f] leggy, rather sparely-made gelding: eighth foal: half-brother to 3 winners on Flat, including Misty Rocket (by Roan Rocket), also successful over hurdles: dam won over 7f and 1¼m in Ireland: behind in juvenile hurdle at Catterick in November: dead. *R. Guest.* —

FIREMAN'S LIFT 5 b.m. Balidar–Watch Lady (Home Guard (USA)) [1989/90 F16f] half-sister to 1983 2-y-o 5f winner Magdolin Place (by Dublin Taxi): dam ran twice: behind in 11-runner NH Flat race at Huntingdon: yet to race over hurdles or fences. *J. R. Jenkins.*

FIREWORK WILLIAM 5 ch.g. Sparkler–Spreading Sunset (Amber Rama (USA)) [1989/90 16g 17d^{pu} 17m^{2}] novice selling hurdler: races only at around 2m: best run on good to firm ground: visored third and fourth starts 1988/9. *G. A. Ham.* 85

FIRIONS LAW 5 b.g. Tanfirion–Agio (Aglojo) [1989/90 21s^{2} 16g* 20d^{2} 18d* 16g 18d^{4} 22v^{3}] lengthy, workmanlike Irish gelding: won maiden hurdle at Naas in November and minor event at Leopardstown (beat sole opponent Redundant Pal 10 lengths) following month: good third behind Trapper John in 2¾m Boardsmill Stud Boyne Hurdle at Navan in February: acts on heavy going. *Victor Bowens, Ireland.* 130 ?

FIRM FOUNDATIONS 13 br.g. Pieces of Eight–Streetcar (Crocket) [1989/90 20f^{6} 24f^{pu} c18m c21s^{pu}] leggy, rather lightly-made gelding: winning hurdler and novice chaser: has been beaten in selling chases: suited by 2½m+: appears to act on any going: usually wears blinkers: a difficult ride. *B. J. McMath.* c— § — §

FIRM POLICY 4 ch.f. Miami Springs–Matin (Rheingold) [1989/90 16g 16g] leggy, rather sparely-made filly: plating-class maiden on Flat: poor form in juvenile hurdles in November. *J. C. Haynes.* 68

FIRM PRICE 9 b.g. Our Mirage–Strip Poker (Raise You Ten) [1989/90 22m^{3} c26g^{2} 20d^{5} c25f* c24m^{4} c26d* c25g^{F} c27g^{2} c25f* c24m^{2} c24d^{2}] tall, sparely-made gelding: fair hurdler nowadays: won intermediate chase at Wolverhampton in November and handicaps at Stratford in December and Doncaster (made virtually all) in March: ran well in handicaps last 2 starts: stays 25f: acts on firm and dead going: has edged left under pressure: has a turn of foot: blinkered fourth and fifth outings: suited by a left-handed track. *J. A. C. Edwards.* c**121** 114

FIRST ADMIRAL 4 b.c. Lord Gayle (USA)–Grecian Blue (Majority Blue) [1989/90 17v 16v^{4} 16s 20d a16g^{4} 20m^{6}] angular colt: plating-class maiden on Flat: poor form over hurdles: best effort over 2m on heavy going (well beaten in seller on good to firm). *D. J. Wintle.* 66

FIRST BOUT 9 b.g. Nishapour (FR)–Right Swinger (USA) (Forward Pass) [1989/90 c20g^{3} c21d^{3} c20g* c20m c20m^{pu}] rangy gelding: one-time high-class hurdler and smart novice chaser: lightly raced of late: won handicap chase at Kempton in February: ran poorly afterwards: stays 2½m: probably acts on any going: blinkered last 3 starts. *N. J. Henderson.* **c124** —

FIRST CRACK 5 b.m. Scallywag–Furstin (Furry Glen) [1989/90 F16f^{3} F16h* 16g^{5} 16g^{ur} 16g* 16s^{2} 16f^{2} 16g^{3} 16g*] compact, workmanlike mare: won NH Flat race at Ludlow in September and novice hurdles at Warwick in December and Perth (beat Times Are Hard easily by 20 lengths) in May: races only at 2m: acts on soft ground: claimer ridden. *F. Jordan.* 114

FIRST FASTNET 5 b.m. Ahonoora–Jolie Brise (Tumble Wind (USA)) [1989/90 16m^{F}] 5f winner on Flat: no promise in 2 outings over hurdles, latest a seller: sold 3,400 gns Doncaster January Sales. *F. Durr.* —

FIRST HAND 5 b.g. Manor Farm Boy–Fairies First (Nulli Secundus) [1989/90 F16f] fifth live foal: half-brother to winning jumper Gay Rascal (by Scallywag) and fair hurdler Harry's Double (by Double Jump): dam of little account: behind in NH Flat race at Warwick in May: yet to race over hurdles or fences. *O. Sherwood.*

FIRST LORD 4 b.g. Lord Gayle (USA)–Touquaise (FR) (Takawalk II) [1989/90 16g 20s^{bd} 20f 20f] close-coupled ex-Irish gelding: eighth foal: half-brother to 5f winner Susan's Way (by Red God): dam behind in 2 races at 2 yrs: little sign of ability on Flat or over hurdles. *Mrs V. A. Aconley.* —

FIRST RANK 7 b.g. Ranksborough–Streetcar (Crocket) [1989/90 16h^{4} 16g 16m^{3} 16m^{5} 16g] tall, workmanlike gelding: novice hurdler, best effort on fourth start: unlikely to stay much beyond 2m: acts on firm ground: takes a good hold and usually makes running. *Mrs J. E. Croft.* 77

FIRST REVIEW 7 b.m. Dawn Review–Opening Order (Menelek) [1989/90 F16g 16d 20d 21d^{5} 22f^{6} 24m 24m^{5}] small, angular mare: first foal: dam, poor Irish maiden hurdler, half-sister to fairly useful Irish jumper Turloughmore Lad: poor form in novice hurdles, best effort over 21f. *M. J. Wilkinson.* 75

FIRST TOWER 4 ch.f. Tower Walk–Gluhwein (Ballymoss) [1989/90 16f^{pu}] behind in poor company on Flat: pulled up lame after 3 out in selling hurdle at Market Rasen in July. *A. M. Robson.* —

FIRST WHIP 4 ch.g. Dublin Taxi–Whip Finish (Be Friendly) [1989/90 16s^{pu} a18g^{4}] close-coupled gelding: poor form in 2 starts on Flat: sold out of J. Etherington's stable 4,200 gns Doncaster August Sales: tailed-off last of 4 in juvenile hurdle at Lingfield in February (pulled hard). *J. D. Thomas.* —

FIRTH OF FORTH 7 ch.g. Deep Run–Belle Mackay (Even Money) [1989/90 a16g^{pu} 16d^{pu} 21f^{pu}] lengthy, angular gelding: winning 2m hurdler: ran badly in 1989/90: dead. *C. J. Bell.* —

FIR TRADING 6 gr.g. Tachypous–Melfio Miss (Town Crier) [1989/90 20d^{pu}] close-coupled, sparely-made gelding: novice hurdler: ran poorly only outing in last 2 seasons: suited by 2½m. *D. L. Williams.* —

FISHERMAN'S COVE 6 b.g. Celtic Cone–Clifton Fair (Vimadee) [1989/90 20s^{pu}] second foal: behind in NH Flat race and when pulled up in a novice hurdle: dead. *Mrs S. D. Williams.* —

FISHERMAN'S CROFT 4 b.c. Dunbeath (USA)–Russeting (Mummy's Pet) [1989/90 16m^{3} 16g* 16f* 16d* 16m* 16m* 16d^{3} 16d* 16g* 16g^{2} 16d^{2} 16m 16g* 16g^{2} 16f^{F}] sparely-made colt: 1m winner on Flat: retained by trainer 3,500 gns Newmarket Autumn Sales: had a very successful first season over hurdles, winning sellers at Market Rasen, Uttoxeter, Stratford, Hexham and Nottingham (bought in 11,000 gns), claimers at Ayr and Perth and handicap at Catterick: likely to prove best at around 2m: acts on dead going and good to firm (below his best on very firm). *N. Tinkler.* 106

FISHERMANS FRIEND 4 ch.c. Pal O Mine–Sardine (Saritamer (USA)) [1989/90 16f^{pu} a16g] workmanlike colt: first foal: dam won 2m selling hurdle: tailed off in novice hurdle at Southwell. *C. F. Wall.* —

FISHERMAN'S TALE 7 b.g. Deep Run–Spin A Yarn (Doubtless II) [1989/90 c17g^{4} c16s^{F} 16g^{6} 16g] good-quartered gelding: modest novice hurdler: ran as though something amiss final start: jumped deliberately and to the left on occasions when remote fourth in novice chase at Huntingdon (will do better on left-handed track): will be suited by longer distances: sold 6,000 gns Ascot May Sales. *Andrew Turnell.* c— 82

FISHING SEASON 5 ch.g. Vital Season–Golden Mullet (Star Moss) [1989/90 21m^4 21m^5 16m c16m^F 16s a18g^{ur} a20g^5 16f 20m] angular gelding: poor novice hurdler: has been beaten in selling company: fell first on chasing debut: stays 2½m: best form on good to firm ground: has worn a crossed noseband. *Mrs A. E. Ratcliff.* c— 64

FISHING SMACK 7 b.m. Bustiki–Shell Fish (Hard Ridden) [1989/90 c20m^{ur} c24g^3 c20f^3 c16f^3 c21s^F c20s^2 c20g^3 c20d^3 c17d^5 c16d^4 c16f^F c20f^{ur} 16m^5 a20g^2 25m^6 21m] leggy mare: poor winning hurdler/novice chaser: stays 2½m but seemingly not 3m: acts on any going: pulls hard: usually claimer or amateur ridden: sketchy jumper. *B. Byford.* c83 83

FISH QUAY 7 ch.g. Quayside–Winkle (Whistler) [1989/90 c20m^F c21d^F c20g^3 c21g^2 c24d* c24d^5] lengthy, workmanlike gelding: winning hurdler: jumped better than previously over fences when winning novice chase at Kelso in January: ran as though something was amiss next outing: stays 3m: probably acts on any going: blinkered fifth outing in 1988/9: has broken blood vessel. *M. H. Easterby.* c96 —

FISTFUL OF BUCKS 4 b.g. Lochnager–Crimson Ring (Persian Bold) [1989/90 16g^6 16d* 16d 18s* 16d^4 16g*] sparely-made gelding: modest form at up to 1¼m on Flat (blinkered when successful): won claiming hurdles at Ayr (by 30 lengths) and Fontwell prior to winning juvenile handicap at Perth in April by a distance: stays 2¼m: acts on soft going. *C. Weedon.* 108

FIT FOR COUNSEL 4 b.f. Hotfoot–Rose of Shenfield (Upper Case (USA)) [1989/90 16d 16v^3 16g^4 16f* 16h^2 16f^2 16h^3 16m* 20f*] angular filly: modest winner on Flat, claimed £6,000 after finishing fourth over 10.6f in 1989: won selling hurdles at Wolverhampton (despite carrying head high and looking less than keen) in March and Stratford and Hexham (sold 6,200 gns) in May: found nothing on fifth start: best form at 2m: seems suited by firm ground: blinkered seventh outing. *M. C. Pipe.* 90 §

FIT FOR FIRING (FR) 6 b.m. In Fijar (USA)–Elizabeth Wales (Abernant) [1989/90 c20f^3 c20s* c20v^6] tall, leggy mare: winning hurdler: won mares novice chase at Folkestone in December: well beaten final outing in March: suited by around 2½m: acts on any going: claimer ridden over hurdles (jumps well). *D. R. C. Elsworth.* c95 —

FIVE LAMPS 10 b.g. Paddy's Stream–Ballinarose (Arctic Slave) [1989/90 c16m^{ur} 17d^6 18s 16m 20m^5 16m^F] rangy gelding: handicap hurdler: only modest form in 1989/90: hasn't got beyond the second in 2 outings over fences: probably stays 2½m: acts on good to firm and heavy going: usually makes running. *O. Sherwood.* c— 101

FIVE QUARTERS 7 gr.m. Native Bazaar–Pippaluk (FR) (Admiral's Boy) [1989/90 17g 17g 16s] small mare: poor novice selling hurdler: form only in blinkers. *Mrs A. Knight.* —

FLAG 5 b.g. Shirley Heights–Gallic Pride (USA) (Key To The Kingdom (USA)) [1989/90 F16f^{bd}] third foal: dam, moderate maiden, is daughter of Ribblesdale Stakes winner Gallina: brought down in NH Flat race at Catterick: dead. *Mrs P. A. Barker.*

FLAG OF TRUCE 10 b.g. Arapaho–Darling Smile (Star Signal) [1989/90 c16d^5 c16m^5] tall gelding: winning hurdler/chaser: no worthwhile form for a long time: usually blinkered nowadays. *S. Christian.* c— —

FLAIRY LAD 6 b.g. Flair Path–War Queen (Yrrah Jr) [1989/90 18f^6 17d 16d 16g 16s^6 16d 17g 19m^4] ex-Irish gelding: seventh foal: half-brother to winning Irish jumper Queen Alda (by Kambalda) and NH Flat race winner Round The Block (by Push On): dam ran twice: poor maiden hurdler: blinkered seventh start (trained until after then by M. Byrne). *R. Lee.* —

FLAKEY DOVE 4 b.f. Oats–Shadey Dove (Deadly Nightshade) [1989/90 F16m* F16v^2 F13f^2] non-thoroughbred filly: second foal: half-sister to novice hurdler Coney Dove (by Celtic Cone): dam, from good jumping family, showed useful form over hurdles: won NH Flat at Ludlow in January: second in similar events at Haydock and Hereford: yet to race over hurdles. *R. J. Price.*

FLAMING TIDE 12 b.g. Quayside–Up First (Phalorain) [1989/90 c20g c22m^F c19m c24d^{pu} c25h^5] leggy, close-coupled gelding: novice hurdler/chaser: poor form in point-to-points: seems best at around 2m: seems to act on any going: usually wears blinkers: tried to run out and unseated rider on first outing 1987/8. *R. E. Bailey.* c— —

FLAREY SARK 13 br.g. Flair Path–Sark (Chamier) [1989/90 c20d^{4} c20d] c—
strong, lengthy gelding: one-time fair chaser: no worthwhile form in hunter —
chases in 1990: stayed 3m: acted well in the mud: genuine: dead. *Mrs A. T. Pollard.*

FLASHING SILKS 5 b.m. Kind of Hush–Hit The Line (Saulingo) [1989/90
20g 18s^{pu} 16g] workmanlike mare: seems of little account. *A. Moore.* —

FLASHY DANCER 5 ch.g. Young Man (FR)–Gem-May (Mansingh (USA)) [1989/90 F16h^{2} aF16g^{5}] first foal: dam, maiden middle-distance plater, sister to a winning hurdler and half-sister to another: hung left in latter stages when second in NH Flat race at Hexham in October: reportedly finished lame in similar event at Southwell following month: yet to race over hurdles or fences. *R. W. Dods.*

FLAXEN KING 8 ch.g. Carnival Night–Doravaun (Chinatown) [1989/90 c**107**
c24g^{F} c25g* c25f*] lengthy, workmanlike gelding: novice hurdler: successful in —
novice chases at Hereford (made several mistakes) in November and Wincanton in April, easily better effort when beating Last House 8 lengths in latter: stays well: acts on firm ground: sold only 2,800 gns Ascot June Sales. *M. C. Pipe.*

FLEET ACTION 9 b.g. Heres–Indigold (Indigenous) [1989/90 c21f c20f^{6} c—
c25g^{pu}] rangy gelding: probably of little account. *R. G. Brazington.* —

FLEET COMMANDER 7 b.g. Alleged (USA)–Rule Formi (USA) (Forli
(ARG)) [1989/90 16f^{3} 16g 24s* 24s^{pu} 20s^{pu} 24m^{pu}] tall, leggy gelding: handicap 120
hurdler: won conditional jockeys event at Haydock in January: collapsed and died at Uttoxeter in March: stayed 3m: acted on any going: tried in blinkers and a visor. *M. Meade.*

FLEET FOOTED 7 b.g. Tachypous–More Or Less (Morston (FR)) [1989/90
16m 16g^{3} 16m* 16g 16d* 17d^{6} 16g 16f] neat gelding: won selling hurdle at Ludlow 93
in November (bought in 2,000 gns) and conditional jockeys claimer at Catterick in February: ran moderately last 2 starts: form only at around 2m: acts on dead and hard ground: blinkered twice in 1986/7: retained by trainer 3,200 gns Doncaster Spring Sales. *Mrs G. R. Reveley.*

FLEETING PASSION 11 br.g. Golden Love–Rambling Gift (Wrekin c—
Rambler) [1989/90 c29s^{pu} c28g c29d^{pu} c25m^{pu}] lengthy, strong-quartered gelding: winning point-to-pointer/hunter chaser: showed little in handicaps in 1989/90: stays 29f. *R. Waley-Cohen.*

FLEET SPECIAL 8 gr.g. High Top–Rockney (Roan Rocket) [1989/90 16g
16g] sparely-made gelding: lightly-raced novice hurdler: no form, pulls hard: has —
worn a tongue strap. *P. Monteith.*

FLEET SPIRIT 4 b.g. Ranksborough–Gin And Lime (Warpath) [1989/90
16m^{pu} 18s^{pu} 16d 16s^{4}] leggy gelding: second foal: dam winning stayer on Flat: —
refused to enter stalls only intended outing on Flat: no worthwhile form over hurdles (tried to refuse at the third on debut). *E. A. Wheeler.*

FLEETWOOD LASS 6 b.m. Lochnager–Lively Lassie (Never Say Die) c—
[1989/90 c20s^{pu} c16g^{pu} 20g^{F}] angular mare: winning hurdler: blinkered, behind —
when falling 2 out in seller final start: tailed off when pulled up in novice chases: form only at 2m: acts on soft going. *J. Ffitch-Heyes.*

FLEMING 10 ch.g. Royalty–Zulaika (Worden II) [1989/90 c24d^{ur} c25m^{2} c**117**
c25m^{2}] tall, workmanlike gelding: fair chaser nowadays: jumped none too fluently when second in handicaps at Catterick in December and Doncaster (stayed on when going down by 5 lengths to Man O'Magic in William Hill Golden Spurs Chase) in January: stays 3m: acts on soft going and good to firm: sketchy jumper. *P. Beaumont.*

FLEMINGTON 11 b.g. Bargello–Leuze (Vimy) [1989/90 c24g^{4} c26s^{pu} c26g^{5} c—
c26s^{5} c24g 21s] close-coupled gelding: seems of little account nowadays. *W. M.* —
Perrin.

FLEMISH FUDGE 8 b.g. Candy Cane–Leuze (Vimy) [1989/90 c21d^{pu} c24m^{F} c**100**
c24d c25s^{3} c25m^{pu}] rangy ex-Irish gelding: half-brother to several winning —
jumpers, notably Grand National winner Rubstic (by I Say) and high-class staying chaser Kildimo (by Le Bavard): dam unraced: poor maiden hurdler: novice chaser: best efforts in Britain at around 3m with plenty of give. *Miss H. C. Knight.*

FLEURCONE 8 ch.g. Celtic Cone–Little Fleur (Tudor Wood) [1989/90 21d
21f^{3} 25f^{pu}] smallish gelding: winning hurdler: failed to find his form in 1989/90: —
stays 21f: acts on heavy going (ran poorly on top-of-the-ground): usually held up: found nothing third start 1987/8. *K. White.*

FLEXIBLE FRIEND 10 br.g. Lord Gayle (USA)–My Bonnie (Highland Melody) [1989/90 16gpu 16spu] tall, lengthy gelding: novice hurdler: has shown no aptitude for chasing: seems best at around 2m: form only on a soft surface: blinkered last 5 outings. *M. J. Charles.* c— —

FLIGHT HILL 6 br.g. Relkino–Firella (Firestreak) [1989/90 16g 16d 16s4 16s6] leggy gelding: modest novice hurdler: has raced only at 2m: best form on soft ground. *D. R. C. Elsworth.* 88

FLIGHT OF STEEL 5 ch.g. Le Moss–Mary Deen (Avocat) [1989/90 F16f5] second foal: dam unraced sister to winning jumper Urbi Et Orbi and half-sister to 3 winners, including fair jumper Yiragan: around 12 lengths fifth of 7 to Mayfair Minx in NH Flat race at Newbury in March: yet to race over hurdles or fences. *O. Sherwood.*

FLOATING LOVER 11 ch.g. Crawter–Floating Dreams (Bonheur) [1989/90 c21f c21f3 c26m2 c21vpu] plain gelding: winning hurdler: poor novice chaser: pulled up lame final outing (December): probably needs at least 2½m: acts on any going. *C. W. Mitchell.* c86 —

FLODDEN FIELD 7 b.g. New Brig–Tillside (Lucky Brief) [1989/90 20m* 22d6 25m4 17g3] lengthy gelding: looks a chaser: handicap hurdler: won at Perth in October: ran well afterwards: stays 3m: acts on good to firm and dead ground. *B. E. Wilkinson.* 95

FLOLINE 6 b.g. Floriferous–Marline (Captain James) [1989/90 19d] workmanlike, rather sparely-made gelding: behind in 2 novice hurdles. *M. H. B. Robinson.* —

FLORA LOUISA 5 b.m. Rymer–Star Ruler (Indian Ruler) [1989/90 25g 24d c25d 21f2 24m 21f3] unfurnished mare: novice hurdler: well beaten on chasing debut: stays at least 21f: form only on top-of-the-ground. *Mrs I. McKie.* c— 78

FLOREAT REGINA 9 br.m. Rolfe (USA)–Rock Speedwell (Shoolerville (USA)) [1989/90 c21g5 c26d5 c20d] compact mare: winning chaser: poor form in 1989/90: stays 2½m: acts on firm going. *N. Thomas.* c79 —

FLORENCE MAY 11 ch.m. Grange Melody–Florrie Green (Florescence) [1989/90 c28gpu c25g4 c25f5] sparely-made, angular mare: winning point-to-pointer/steeplechaser: suited by a test of stamina: has shown a tendency to jump to her right. *Mrs S. Richardson.* c76

FLORIDA ISLAND 4 b.f. Miami Springs–Honiara (Pitcairn) [1989/90 17f4 16f3 16f4] third foal: dam 2-y-o 5f winner: fourth in 5f seller at 2 yrs, only outing on Flat: bought for 1,800 gns Ascot June (1989) Sales: poor form in early-season selling hurdles: claimer ridden. *W. G. M. Turner.* 53

FLOWING RIVER (USA) 4 b.c. Irish River (FR)–Honey's Flag (USA) (Hoist The Flag (USA)) [1989/90 F16g* aF16g* F16m] rather leggy colt: first foal: dam once-raced daughter of CCA Oaks second Cathy Honey: won NH Flat races at Edinburgh in January and Southwell in March: behind in well-contested event at Liverpool following month: yet to race over hurdles. *R. Allan.*

FLOYD 10 ch.g. Relko–Honey Palm (Honeyway) [1989/90 20f2 16m4 16f4 16g3 16g4 25m] useful-looking gelding, though rather sparely made: high-class hurdler in his prime: best effort of season when around 2 lengths fourth to Cruising Altitude in slowly-run Charles Heidsieck Champagne Bula Hurdle at Cheltenham on third start: around 16 lengths tenth to Trapper John in 25f Waterford Crystal Stayers' Hurdle at Cheltenham final outing (one pace in straight): stays 2½m: probably acts on any going: blinkered third to fifth outings: usually makes running: has won when sweating. *D. R. C. Elsworth.* 151

FLUTTER BLUE 4 ch.f. Blue Refrain–Kivulini (Hotfoot) [1989/90 17g6 16g] leggy filly: second reported foal: dam never ran: tailed-off last in juvenile hurdles at Newton Abbot in November and Wolverhampton following month. *J. L. Spearing.* —

FLUTTERBY BELLE 4 b.f. Beldale Flutter (USA)–Briar (Brigadier Gerard) [1989/90 16f 16f 16d a18g6] third foal: dam, 7f winner at 2 yrs, is half-sister to high-class 1¼m colt Morcon: no form over hurdles: reluctant to go down second outing, unseated rider and bolted before third appearance: makes mistakes: trained until after second start by J. Dooler. *Miss P. Hall.* —

FLUTTER MONEY 6 b.g. Beldale Flutter (USA)–Berthe Manet (Crepello) [1989/90 22d4] winning hurdler: first promise for some time when fourth at Stratford in February, travelling well to 2 out: previously raced only at 2m: acts on soft going and possibly unsuited by firm. *Miss G. Dollar.* — p

FLYAWAY (FR) 5 ch.h. Touching Wood (USA)–Flying Sauce (Sauce Boat (USA)) [1989/90 a16g* 18d4 16m2] lengthy horse: sold out of N. Tinkler's stable 3,400 gns Newmarket Autumn Sales: won handicap hurdle at Southwell in November: good second at Newcastle later in month (wore tongue strap): should stay beyond 2m: acts on good to firm ground and possibly unsuited by ground softer than good. *J. L. Harris.* 120

FLY CONCORDE (USA) 5 b.g. Northjet–Moralisme (USA) (Sir Ivor) [1989/90 16f] lengthy, sparely-made gelding: novice selling hurdler: little form since debut: blinkered second start, visored last in 1988/9. *O. O'Neill.* —

FLYING 4 b.f. Head For Heights–Pine (Supreme Sovereign) [1989/90 16m5 16g 16m* a16g5 16mbd] smallish, sparely-made filly: middle-distance maiden on Flat: sold out of R. Hern's stable 7,000 gns Newmarket Autumn Sales: bought in 8,200 gns after winning conditional jockeys selling hurdle at Ludlow in January: no form in non-sellers afterwards: acts on good to firm ground. *R. J. Manning.* 78

FLYING ACE 14 ch.g. Saucy Kit–Flying Eye (Vulgan) [1989/90 c24g4] leggy, sparely-made gelding: prolific winning point-to-pointer/hunter chaser: on the downgrade: stays very well: acts on any going: suited by forcing tactics: thoroughly game and genuine. *A. Calder.* c—

FLYING DANCER 8 b.g. Niniski (USA)–Topbird (Royalty) [1989/90 c20g2 c20mF c20msu c22gF 20d* 20g 24g2 25mpu 24f* 24f] tall, leggy, narrow gelding: won handicap hurdles at Sedgefield in January and Wetherby in April: modest form in novice chases earlier: stays 3m: probably acts on any going. *B. McLean.* c97 122

FLYING FAITH 5 b.m. Rymer–Jacqueline Jane (David Jack) [1989/90 F16f3 F16d4] half-sister to quite useful hurdler/chaser Silver Wind (by Broxted): dam unraced sister to fair chaser Dawn Breaker: in frame in NH Flat races at Newbury and Ayr (21 lengths fourth of 7 to Ruling in well-contested event) in the spring: yet to race over hurdles or fences. *Mrs Gill E. Jones.*

FLYING FERRET 9 b.g. Le Bavard (FR)–Slaney Valley (Even Money) [1989/90 c17h* c16f6] leggy ex-Irish gelding: fair chaser: long odds on when beating one opponent by a distance in amateur riders handicap at Devon & Exeter in August: behind in valuable handicap at Ascot in October: best form at around 2m: probably acts on any going: has worn severe bridle and looked headstrong. *M. C. Pipe.* c**121** ? —

FLYING FINISH 5 gr.g. Junius (USA)–Blue Alicia (Wolver Hollow) [1989/90 18f4 20fpu] leggy gelding: second living foal: dam lightly-raced maiden on Flat: no sign of ability in novice hurdles at Fontwell and Ascot. *D. M. Grissell.* —

FLYING FREEHOLD 5 b.g. Callernish–Flying Music (Little Buskins) [1989/90 16mpu 20d] useful-looking gelding: fourth foal: dam unraced: still in need of race, well beaten in novice hurdle at Market Rasen in November. *John R. Upson.* —

FLYING HYDE 4 b.f. Petong–Campagna (Romulus) [1989/90 16spu] half-sister to several winners, including hurdler Hot Company (by Hotfoot): dam won over 1¼m on Flat in France: jumped poorly and was well behind when pulled up third in juvenile hurdle at Market Rasen in January on debut. *J. Norton.* —

FLYING IRISH 9 b.g. Furry Glen–Suparoli (Super Sam) [1989/90 c24mpu] rangy, good-topped gelding: winning hurdler/chaser: no form for a long time: stays 3m: acts on dead going: has worn blinkers. *Lawrence Wells.* c— —

FLYING JUNCTION 4 ch.g. Burslem–Windy City (Windjammer (USA)) [1989/90 16d2 16g 17dF 16m4 21d 22g4 20g] lengthy gelding: sprint maiden on Flat: modest juvenile hurdler: made mistakes when running poorly final outing: ran creditably over 2¾m (weakened after leading to 3 out): acts on good to firm and dead going: ran in snatches second start (blinkered). *J. S. King.* 91

FLYING LION 5 b.g. Flying Tyke–Comedy Spring (Comedy Star (USA)) [1989/90 F16g 25h2] in rear in NH Flat races: finished lame when second of 3 behind easy winner Fettuccine in amateur riders novice hurdle at Kelso in May. *Miss S. Williamson.* ?

FLYING MESSENGER 11 b.g. Giolla Mear–Bee Flight (Airborne) [1989/90 c24mpu] big, rangy gelding: won a point-to-point from 3 starts in 1986 (ducked out at the last first outing): jumped none too fluently and was well beaten when pulled up and dismounted approaching 5 out in novice chase at Newbury in November. *P. R. Hedger.* c—

FLYING OATS (USA) 10 b.g. Empery (USA)–Kelly Keim (USA) (Needles) [1989/90 24gpu 24f5 25m 24m6 22d] tall, good-topped gelding: unreliable winning c— — §

hurdler: no worthwhile form in 1989/90: suited by a test of stamina: probably needs heavy going nowadays: sometimes blinkered (wasn't when successful in 1987/8): poor jumper: pulled up only outing over fences (jockey lost reins). *W. G. Reed.*

FLYING PHEASANT 4 b.f. Balliol–Partridge (Mossborough) [1989/90 16f] no form on Flat, including in sellers: amateur ridden, behind in juvenile hurdle at Huntingdon in August: sold 1,000 gns Newmarket September Sales. *D. T. Thom.* —

FLYING ROOFER 4 b.f. Jester–Forest Glen (Tarqogan) [1989/90 16gpu 17dpu 16fpu 16h6] sparely-made filly: has shown more temperament than ability on Flat: poor form over hurdles, including in sellers. *J. D. Roberts.* —

FLYING TREAT 5 b.m. Dutch Treat–Flying Question (pedigree unknown) [1989/90 16gpu] non-thoroughbred mare: bit backward, tailed off when pulled up 3 out in novice hurdle at Fakenham in February on debut. *M. Skinner.* —

FLYING-X-RAY 11 ch.g. New Member–Mayfly X (Flying Colours) [1989/90 c20f5 c24dpu] tall, angular gelding: won a point-to-point in May: novice hurdler/chaser: tailed off in novice hunter chase at Cheltenham in April: stays well: sold out of R. Manning's stable 1,700 gns Ascot August Sales. *D. W. Parker.* c— —

FLYING ZIAD (CAN) 7 ch.g. Ziad (USA)–Flying Souvenir (USA) (Flying Relic) [1989/90 16g4 16f*] tall, workmanlike gelding: maiden on Flat: unseated rider in a point-to-point in 1989: 66/1, appeared to show very much improved form when 3 lengths fourth of 6 behind Aldino in Ring & Brymer Hurdle at Kempton in October: won handicap at Newbury 6 days later by a head from Midnight Strike: best at around 2m: probably acts on any going: made running both times in 1989/90. *R. Curtis.* 116 +

FLY THE WIND 5 b.m. Windjammer (USA)–Eagle's Quest (Legal Eagle) [1989/90 16f 16m2 17m2 16m4 16d3 16m6 17g* 17d 17m 17m 25mpu 17f2 17m2] close-coupled mare: won selling hurdle at Devon & Exeter in December (bought in 4,500 gns): easily best subsequent effort on penultimate start: unlikely to stay much beyond 2m: yet to show her form on very soft going, acts on any other: blinkered fifth start, visored eleventh. *F. G. Hollis.* 78

FOCUS ON FOSTER 8 ch.g. Warpath–April (Silly Season) [1989/90 c24fpu c25m2 20fro c20h* c24f2 c20f2] close-coupled, good-quartered gelding: carries plenty of condition: handicap chaser: jumped rather deliberately but made virtually all when successful at Carlisle in October: ran out in lady riders hurdle earlier: stays well: probably acts on any going: visored nowadays: not seen out after October. *C. J. Bell.* c**98** —

FOGGY SCOTCH 6 br.g. Chantro–Sirene River (Another River) [1989/90 F16m2 F13d4 16s2 16g4 16g 20m5] first foal: dam poor novice hurdler/chaser: second in novice hurdle at Sedgefield in February: bit below that form afterwards: weakened 2 out over 2½m: acts on soft ground. *Mrs R. Wharton.* 80

FOLIGNO 5 ch.m. Crofter (USA)–Alpine Morn (Mourne) [1989/90 20gpu 16f6 16g 18s 16v 16g] sparely-made ex-Irish mare: half-sister to 2 winners in France and to a poor jumper: dam won over 11f in French Provinces: 1½m winner on Flat: seems of little account as a hurdler: blinkered third outing: trained until after fifth start by B. Stevens. *D. J. Wintle.* —

FOLK DANCE 8 b.g. Alias Smith (USA)–Enchanting Dancer (FR) (Nijinsky (CAN)) [1989/90 24m2 22mpu c21f3 c20m* c24f2 c24m3 c20f* c22d2 c20f4 c20g*] sparely-made, rather dipped-backed gelding: useful hurdler: won novice chases at Warwick in November, Doncaster in December and Huntingdon (handicap) in April, best effort when beating Pells Close 6 lengths on last-named course: stays 3m: probably acts on any going: winner visored and without: hasn't always gone through with his effort and isn't one to trust implicitly. *G. B. Balding.* c**112** 141

FOLLOW THAT TAXI 4 b.f. Dublin Taxi–Arkengarthdale (Sweet Story) [1989/90 17f 16spu] sparely-made filly: dam winning jumper: poor maiden on Flat: tailed off in selling hurdle at Doncaster in December: dead. *N. Bycroft.* —

FOLLOW THE DRUM 5 b.g. Daring March–Pretty Miss (So Blessed) [1989/90 a16g a20g* a18g2] winner at up to 1¼m on Flat: sold out of J. Bethell's stable 10,000 gns Newmarket Autumn Sales: made all in novice hurdle at Southwell in February: stayed 2½m: dead. *Mrs D. Haine.* 100

FOLLY HILL 10 b.g. Moulton–Molly Polly (Molvedo) [1989/90 16f6 20fpu] rangy, rather sparely-made gelding: fair hurdler at his best and winning chaser: stayed 2½m: best form on a sound surface: blinkered once, visored once: dead. *T. H. Caldwell.* c— —

FOOL'S PLEASURE 9 b.m. Idiot's Delight–Evada (Eborneezer) [1989/90 c— c25g^{pu} c25g^{pu} c20v^{6} c21g^{pu}] tall mare: winning point-to-pointer/hunter chaser: — no form in handicaps in January and February: stays well: acts on firm going. *R. J. Hodges.*

FOOT STICK 14 b.g. Tarqogan–Troon (Sheshoon) [1989/90 c26f^{2} c25h* c92 x c26f^{3}] stocky, workmanlike gelding: carries plenty of condition: poor chaser: — made most to win 5-runner handicap at Devon & Exeter in August: ran poorly at Newton Abbot later in month: stays very well: acts on any going: blinkered final outing in 1987/8: amateur ridden nowadays: moderate jumper. *R. Dickin.*

FORBES SPIRIT (USA) 5 b.m. Bold Forbes (USA)–Hasty Viento (USA) (Gallant Man) [1989/90 a18g^{F}] sparely-made mare: half-sister to useful hurdler — Lyphento (by Lyphard's Wish): poor 1¼m winner on Flat: tubed, fell fifth in claiming hurdle at Lingfield in December: dead. *P. Howling.*

FORCED MARCH (FR) 6 b.g. Direct Flight–Rambling (Wrekin Rambler) [1989/90 F16f^{3} 17d^{2} 16g^{5} 16g^{5} 16m 20m^{2}] leggy, close-coupled gelding: 91 half-brother to winning jumpers Tarn (by Deep Run) and Fell Climb (by Levanter): dam won novice hurdle: third in NH Flat race at Newbury in October: modest form in novice hurdles: stays 2½m: acts on good to firm and dead ground. *G. B. Balding.*

FORCELLO (USA) 7 b.g. Forli (ARG)–Heavenly Bow (USA) (Gun Bow) [1989/90 16g^{pu} a16g^{4} a16g^{2}] smallish, strong gelding: poor hurdler: stays 2¼m: 86 acts on heavy going. *D. Burchell.*

FOREIGN KNIGHT (CAN) 6 b. or br.g. Snow Knight–Demurely (USA) c— (Majestic Prince) [1989/90 20f^{3} 18m^{2} 22f^{pu} 24g^{3dis} 16g^{4} 25d 16s^{pu} 18m^{3}] small 67 ? gelding: poor selling hurdler: tailed off when pulled up on chasing debut: stays 23f: acts on firm going and probably unsuited by soft: usually blinkered nowadays: has worn a tongue strap: sold out of R. Juckes's stable 1,400 gns Doncaster January Sales after seventh start, not disgraced in handicap at Downpatrick in May, only subsequent outing. *J. P. Byrne, Ireland.*

FOREMAST 7 br.g. Forli (ARG)–Hey Skip (USA) (Bold Skipper (USA)) c— [1989/90 c26f^{pu} c21m^{pu}] tall, angular gelding: poor handicap hurdler: yet to — complete in steeplechases, but won a point-to-point in May: stays 2½m: probably acts on any going. *J. M. Turner.*

FOREST BREEZE 7 b.m. Strong Gale–Come Aboard (Whistler) [1989/90 20d 27s^{pu} 24s 20d^{5}] lengthy mare: poor novice hurdler. *D. J. Wintle.* —

FORESTDALE 12 b.g. Furry Glen–Silver Heights (Even Money) [1989/90 c99 c18h* c18f^{ur} c20m^{6} c17m^{4} c16h^{2} c18f^{2} c16f^{4} c20f^{F} c18f^{4}] tall, leggy gelding: — handicap chaser: won 2-runner race at Fontwell early in season: seems to stay 3m: best on top-of-the-ground: has won when sweating, but ran poorly when sweating badly seventh outing: usually jumps soundly. *C. S. Wates.*

FOREST FAWN (FR) 5 b. or br.m. Top Ville–Red Deer (FR) (Kirkland Lake) [1989/90 16g^{4} a18g^{2} 16m^{6} a16g^{4} 16s^{5} 16g 17m^{6}] sparely-made mare: 90 d modest novice hurdler: claimed out of C. Wildman's stable £9,125 after second start: below form afterwards: gives impression she'll prove best at 2m. *E. A. Wheeler.*

FOREST FLAME (USA) 5 ch.g. Green Forest (USA)–Flavia Miss (USA) (His Majesty (USA)) [1989/90 16h* 16f^{2}] rather sparely-made gelding: fair 115 hurdler: won handicap at Ludlow in May: ran well next start: not sure to stay beyond 2m: ran poorly on heavy going but seems to act on any other: blinkered nowadays: hung and looked none too keen when winning first time in 1988/9: suited by waiting tactics. *M. C. Pipe.*

FOREST LORD 6 br.g. Lord Gayle (USA)–Heart 'N' Soul (Bold Lad (IRE)) [1989/90 16d^{pu} 16m] workmanlike, good-quartered gelding with plenty of scope: — second foal: half-brother to a winning Belgian jumper by Final Straw: dam useful 5f winner in Ireland: placed in 3 Irish NH Flat races: sold out of J. Shanahan's stable 33,000 gns Doncaster Spring (1989) Sales: sweating, raced freely when well beaten in novice hurdle at Leicester: bolted before first appearance. *D. McCain.*

FOREST NYMPH (NZ) 5 b.m. Oak Ridge (FR)–Lively Lass (NZ) (Lionhearted) [1989/90 16m 16g^{6}] compact mare: showed signs of ability in novice — p hurdles at Wincanton in December and Wolverhampton (kept on steadily without being at all knocked about when sixth to Duntree) following month. *Mrs S. Oliver.*

FOREST RAIN 7 b.g. Paico–Super Money Fan (Super Slip) [1989/90 F16f* 16f5 20f5] well-made ex-Irish gelding: carries plenty of condition: first foal: dam placed in NH Flat races and a point-to-point: won NH Flat race at Roscommon in June (trained by T. Bergin): moderate novice hurdler: takes quite a good hold but has run creditably at 2½m. *N. A. Gaselee.* 93

FOREST RANGER 8 b.g. The Parson–Nora Grany (Menelek) [1989/90 c26s6 c24v3 c29d3] strong, close-coupled gelding: fair chaser: third at Haydock and Warwick (weakened 2 out) in January: stays 3¼m: acts on any going: has shown a tendency to edge right under pressure. *J. A. C. Edwards.* c**118** —

FOREST SUN 5 ch.g. Whistling Deer–Sun Spray (Nice Guy) [1989/90 16g5 16d* 21g* 16d* 16g* 16m* 20f5] 142

Few horses have had as good a first season over jumps as Forest Sun. A winner of two National Hunt Flat races in 1988/9, he went on to five successive wins over hurdles in the latest season culminating in the Waterford Crystal Supreme Novices' Hurdle at Cheltenham in March. And his total of over £52,000 in first-place money is the highest for a novice hurdler in a single season since Gaye Chance in 1980/1. Which isn't to say that Forest Sun was a novice of the calibre of Gaye Chance. The eighteen-runner field for the Supreme Novices' Hurdle was below its usual standard in quality and quantity. Though all bar three runners were winners over hurdles, only Forest Sun, Bitter Buck, Man of The West, Riverhead and Whatever You Like had shown better than fairly useful form. Atlaal, Keep Hope Alive and Sudden Victory were notable absentees, the last-named acting as pacemaker for Nomadic Way in the Champion Hurdle later in the afternoon. The Irish, who dominated the race in the 'seventies and early-'eighties, were represented solely by 50/1-shot Art Trail. Forest Sun looked to have comfortably the best form and started a well-backed 7/4 favourite, ahead of Bitter Buck (11/2) and Man of The West (6/1). But he won with little in hand. Held up within striking distance of the modest early pace set by Art Trail and then Stratford Ponds, Forest Sun moved up to join the leaders at the top of the hill. He stayed on strongly, after pecking on landing two out and jumping the last flight slightly awkwardly, to catch the hanging Danny Harrold on the run-in and beat him two and a half lengths, with 33/1-shot Rakes Lane half a length further back in third. Olnistar and Re-Release stayed on without threatening, to take fourth and fifth places respectively. Stratford Ponds, who lost his chance with a bad mistake three out, finished seventh. Art Trail was destroyed after breaking a leg. Bitter Buck, Man of The West and Whatever You Like failed to give their running on the good to firm ground.

Forest Sun's workmanlike success and his subsequent modest fifth to Vazon Bay on very firm ground in the Mumm Prize Novices' Hurdle at

H.S.S. Hire Shops Hurdle, Ascot—the novice Forest Sun joins the grey Calapaez at the last

Baring Securities Tolworth Hurdle, Sandown—
Forest Sun has quickened past Atlaal and Tinryland (hidden)

Liverpool (when looking slightly lean), suggest that he is likely to prove best with plenty of give in the ground. On a yielding surface earlier in the season he'd run up a sequence in impressive fashion and put up two performances by our reckoning several pounds better than his win at Cheltenham. At Ascot in December, Forest Sun became only the third novice, after Grand Canyon and Walnut Wonder, to win the H.S.S. Hire Shops Hurdle. Though, again, the race was less strongly contested than usual it took a very useful performance for Forest Sun to win by five lengths from Calapaez (who conceded a stone), coming from behind after Nodform and the runner-up had set a strong pace. Forest Sun shaped as though he needs testing conditions when racing at two miles when winning the Baring Securities Tolworth Hurdle at Sandown the following month. Having been under pressure to improve his position leaving the back straight, he picked

Waterford Crystal Supreme Novices' Hurdle, Cheltenham—
Forest Sun challenges Rakes Lane and Danny Harrold (No. 3) on the outside

Salehurst Paper Co. Ltd's "Forest Sun"

up well after the home turn and recovered from a mistake at the second last to win by six lengths from Atlaal. Forest Sun hadn't needed to be at his best when justifying favouritism by ten lengths in the Challow Hurdle over an extended two and a half miles at Newbury in between, Stirrup Cup and Arden both running as though something was amiss. He faced only run-of-the-mill opposition when trotting up at Kempton in a Cheltenham warm-up in February.

	Whistling Deer (ch 1973)	Whistling Wind (ch 1960)	Whistler
			Good As Gold
		Lindear (ch 1964)	Vigo
Forest Sun (ch.g. 1985)			Clearing Sky
	Sun Spray (ch 1969)	Nice Guy (ch 1957)	Democratic
			Prudent Polly
		Sunbow (ch 1961)	Beau Sabreur
			Saturnia

Forest Sun is easily the best jumper sired by Whistling Deer, a smart Irish middle-distance winner who was exported to Zimbabwe in 1988. The distaff side of his pedigree is more distinguished. Sun Spray showed little in three outings on the Flat but bred four winners at up to two and a half miles over jumps prior to Forest Sun, most notably the fairly useful Young Lover and Infielder (both by Pry) and Bright Intervals (by Condorcet). Her three foals since Forest Sun, by Tanfirion, Deep Run and Le Bavard respectively, are all in training with Harty in Ireland. The next dam Sunbow, a modest maiden on the Flat, also bred several winners, including the fair chaser Mr Midshipman, and is a half-sister to a winning hurdler out of the extended one-mile winner Saturnia. Bought for 20,000 guineas at Doncaster as a three-year-old, Forest Sun is a workmanlike gelding, at present still rather unfurnished and open to physical improvement. Whilst he will need to progress a good deal to trouble the best at two miles, Forest Sun is still relatively unexposed over longer distances. Though he tends to sweat and has been edgy in the preliminaries, he settles well in his races and should stay beyond twenty-one furlongs. It bears repetition that Forest Sun has shown his best form with plenty of give in the ground. *G. B. Balding.*

FOREVER ASTON 5 b.g. Le Moss–Go Mays (Realm) [1989/90 F16g2 16f3 16g2 22v2 20d] strong, lengthy gelding with plenty of scope: modest form in novice hurdles: stays 2¾m: seems to act on any going. *G. M. Moore.* 92

FOREVER BLUE 7 b.g. Buckskin (FR)–Blue Zeta (Bluerullah) [1989/90 24m c24g2 c16g3] handicap hurdler: placed in novice chases: probably stayed 3m: acted on heavy going: dead. *W. A. Stephenson.* **c90** —

FOREVER TINGO 8 ch.g. Evertingo–September Sal (Ritudyr) [1989/90 16fpu 16f] sparely-made, angular gelding: no form over hurdles: tailed off in a selling handicap final start: sold 1,300 gns Doncaster October Sales. *C. R. Beever.* —

FOREVER TOGETHER 4 ch.f. Hawaiian Return (USA)–Lightfoot Lady (Tekoah) [1989/90 17g5] third foal: half-sister to Irish NH Flat race winner Our River (by River Beauty): dam won 2m maiden hurdle in Ireland: soundly beaten in juvenile hurdle at Newton Abbot in November on debut. *W. T. Kemp.* —

FORGE CLOSE 9 b.g. Swing Easy (USA)–Sweet Relief (Sweet Revenge) [1989/90 19spu 16gpu] of little account. *P. R. Rodford.* —

FORGET THE BLUES 5 b.h. Blue Refrain–Regency Wood (Prince Regent (FR)) [1989/90 16g 16g 20gpu] leggy horse: third foal: dam won over hurdles: well beaten in 2 races on Flat in 1988: little promise in novice hurdles. *S. Dow.* —

FORGET THE REST 5 ro.g. Palm Track–Precipienne (Precipice Wood) [1989/90 F16g*] first foal: dam, modest staying hurdler, sister to Cheltenham Gold Cup winner Forgive'N Forget: 3/1, won 12-runner NH Flat race at Kelso in March by 12 lengths from The Wrens Den, staying on strongly: yet to race over hurdles or fences. *J. G. FitzGerald.*

FOR HEAVEN'S SAKE (FR) 5 br.g. Be My Guest (USA)–Woolf (FR) (Roi Dagobert) [1989/90 18m6 16g3] angular gelding: won 2 NH Flat races in 1988/9: first outing for 5 months, easily better effort over hurdles when 9 lengths third behind Riverhead in novice event at Wincanton in February (tended to edge left and carry head awkwardly). *C. D. Broad.* 95

FORMULA ONE 8 b.g. Ardoon–Little Dipper (Queen's Hussar) [1989/90 c20vF c20v2 c20v2 c24d3] **c136** —

Formula One ended his first season of chasing still a novice, despite showing some good form. A strong, lengthy type, he always looked the sort to do well over fences and was most unfortunate not to win over them at the very first time of asking. Comfortably in command, some eight to ten lengths clear, he fell at the last in a novice event won by Elvercone at Chepstow in January. Though beginning to tire, there is no doubt Formula One would have been a clear winner. He confirmed his potential in the quite valuable Weathercall Rising Stars Chase on the same course the following month when a length second to the much more experienced Wingspan. Formula One had jumped well in the main on his chasing debut, but tended to jump deliberately in his second race; he still held every chance however, but was unable to quicken on the flat. His jumping also left something to be desired over the stiff fences in a substandard Timeform Chase at Haydock in March: it was sketchy, and slow on occasions, though he again ran a good race, this time finishing four lengths second to Tartan Takeover. Formula One's final outing came in the quite valuable Souter of Stirling Novices' Chase at Ayr in April. He put up his best performance so far in the three-mile contest, and seemed to find the Ayr fences easier, though a bad mistake at the second last when holding a narrow lead cost him his chance. Despite rallying well he could do no more in the closing stages and finished third, well clear of the remainder, behind top novices Royal Athlete and Carrick Hill Lad, beaten just over two lengths. Formula One needs to brush up his jumping, but looks virtually assured a winning sequence in novice chases in 1990/1. He'll be making up for lost time, too. He's had very little

Mr D. A. Davies' "Formula One"

racing in his three seasons, and has probably had his training troubles. His only success to date was when amateur ridden in a novice hurdle at Market Rasen in 1988/9, following a promising first season when trained by Mrs Sykes. Formula One stayed the three miles at Ayr well, and he is capable of winning at around two and a half miles. He has yet to race on ground faster than dead.

Formula One (b.g. 1982)	Ardoon (b 1970)	Track Spare (b 1963)	Sound Track
			Rosy Myth
		Sweet Jewel (b 1963)	Will Somers
			Diamond Deuce
	Little Dipper (b 1969)	Queen's Hussar (b 1960)	March Past
			Jojo
		Swallow Falls (b 1950)	Combat
			Procne

Formula One is one of five winning jumpers out of Little Dipper; Henry Mann (by Mandalus) and the very useful Irish performer Royal Dipper (by Royal Captive) are the most notable of the rest. The ill-fated Egypt Mill (by Deep Run), winner of both his starts over hurdles in 1989/90, was Little Dipper's latest progeny to race. The distaff side of the pedigree shouts stamina. Little Dipper was a winner over fifteen furlongs; the second dam Swallow Falls won five times at up to seventeen furlongs, and Procne, the third dam, won the Ebor. Besides Little Dipper, Swallow Falls produced three other winning staying fillies, including Water Wings who was twice runner-up in the Ebor and was dam of useful jumper King Neptune. *J. A. C. Edwards.*

FOR NOTHING 5 gr.h. Bay Express–Flitterdale (Abwah) [1989/90 16d 16g] angular horse: won twice over 7f on Flat in 1990: changed hands 6,200 gns —

Mr H. J. Joel's "For The Grain"

Doncaster October Sales: behind in novice hurdles at Haydock and Catterick. *J. A. Glover.*

FORT HALL 11 b.g. Raise You Ten–Cherry Tart (Vulgan) [1989/90 c21m^4 c24f*] strong gelding: fairly useful point-to-pointer, winner twice in February and once in May: won 4-runner novice hunter chase at Huntingdon in May by a length from Shedid: stays 3m: acts on firm going: sketchy jumper. *Brigadier I. C. Lambie.* **c90**

FORTH AND TAY 8 b.g. New Brig–Shine Bright (Scintillant) [1989/90 25g 24g^6] close-coupled gelding: poor novice hurdler: should stay beyond 2½m: best run on heavy going. *Mrs J. C. Weir.* —

FOR THE GRAIN 6 b.g. Nishapour (FR)–Some Dame (Will Somers) [1989/90 c16g^2 c20g^2 c17d* c16m^{pu} c16d^4] tall, leggy gelding: fairly useful hurdler: won novice chase at Newbury in February easily by 7 lengths from Royal Pavilion: every chance until bad mistake 3 out and pulled up before next in Arkle Challenge Trophy at Cheltenham in March: couldn't recover after stumbling leaving back straight when 12½ lengths fourth to Celtic Shot in Edinburgh Woollen Mill's Future Champion Novices' Chase at Ayr in April: likely to prove best at around 2m: acts on dead going: tends to sweat and be on his toes: should make useful handicap chaser if brushing up his jumping. *D. Nicholson.* **c130 p** —

FORTLIMON (FR) 4 b.c. Cimon–Crenis (FR) (Blinis (FR)) [1989/90 15g c15.5g^F 15g^2 c18.5g^F 16g* 16g^3 16.5g^3 15.5g* 17.5g* 18g* 17.5g* 16f^{pu} 16m^6 17h^5] ex-French colt: fifth foal: half-brother to French jumping winner Crissoo (by Sissoo): dam never ran: successful in claiming hurdles at Pau, Bordeaux (2), Durtal and Auteuil (claimed out of J. Ortet's stable 86,052 francs (approx £9,253)): well beaten in Britain: fell both starts over fences: stays 2¼m. *M. C. Pipe.* c— ?

FORT LINO 7 ch.g. Bustino–Forliana (Forli (ARG)) [1989/90 21d 25gpu 21d] big, strong gelding: handicap hurdler: no form in 1989/90, weakening quickly as though something was amiss final outing: stays 2½m (seems not to stay 25f): blinkered final start 1988/9 and 1989/90: has found little: sold 2,600 gns Ascot June Sales. *D. H. Barons.* —

FORT NOEL 7 br.g. Bonne Noel–Fortellina (Fortino II) [1989/90 22v* 18v* 20f 20d] rangy, rather angular ex-Irish gelding: has scope and will make a chaser: half-brother to fair staying hurdler/chaser Harvest Fortune (by Oats): dam, placed on Flat in Ireland, half-sister to smart performer at up to 1m Supreme Sovereign: successful on only start in point-to-points in 1988: won NH Flat race at Navan in 1988/9: highly impressive when winning novice hurdle at Haydock in January virtually on bridle by 15 lengths from Montagnard, and trotted up from 2 modest rivals at Fontwell following month: failed to confirm that promise in Sun Alliance Novices' Hurdle at Cheltenham (seemed unsuited by firm ground) and novice handicap at Ayr: stays 2¾m: acts well on heavy going. *J. T. Gifford.* 127

FORTOLD (USA) 12 ch.g. Forli (ARG)–Royal Rafale (USA) (Reneged) [1989/90 18g2 18m a18g 18s 18fF 16f4] strong, close-coupled, smallish gelding: handicap hurdler: well beaten after second outing: stays 2½m: acts on any going. *G. Wareham.* 85 d

FORT SUMTER 7 b.g. Belfalas–Coniscliff Bell (Rise'n Shine II) [1989/90 c20d3 c20m4 c24vpu] lengthy gelding: lightly raced and no worthwhile form over hurdles or fences (poor jumper). *P. W. Harris.* c— x —

FORTUNE AND GLORY 4 b.f. Rusticaro (FR)–Souza Rose (Songedor) [1989/90 a16g] leggy ex-Irish filly: half-sister to useful middle-distance performer Meadow Monarch (by Meadow Mint): dam, a sprint plater, is half-sister to high-class sprinter Abergwaun: runner-up 3 times over 1½m on Flat: co-favourite, amateur ridden, tailed off in juvenile selling hurdle at Southwell in December. *Pat Mitchell.* —

Mr Geoff Meadows' "Fort Noel"

FORT WAPPING 6 b.g. Ile de Bourbon (USA)–Hot Press (Hotfoot) [1989/90 16f^2 20m^3 16g^4 20s 24g^6 c24s^{pu} a20g^{pu} 22g^3 20f* 18f^2 20m^4] angular gelding: former selling hurdler: won handicap at Plumpton in March: ran well afterwards: tailed off when pulled up on chasing debut: stays 2¾m: acts on any going: has worn a tongue strap: has run well with and without blinkers: has looked none too keen. *A. Moore.* c— 103 §

FORT WORTH 6 ch.g. Stanford–Prosperity (Sovereign Path) [1989/90 c16g^{ur} c16g^F c16m c20f^6 c20d^{pu} c16d^{ur} 20d^3] medium-sized gelding: poor novice hurdler/chaser: stays 2½m: acts on firm and dead ground: usually wears a tongue strap and a crossed noseband: sold 1,550 gns Ascot May Sales. *G. R. Oldroyd.* **c73** 92

FORTY NOW 5 ch.g. Torus–Diplomat's Tam (Tamariscifolia) [1989/90 F16f^F] first foal: dam never ran: behind when collapsed and fell over 1f out in NH Flat race at Hereford: yet to race over hurdles or fences. *W. A. Stephenson.*

FORWARD MARCH (NZ) 8 b.g. March Legend (NZ)–Naughty Marie (NZ) (Wandering Eyes) [1989/90 16g* 22g 16m a20g^4 c16f^2] workmanlike gelding: 33/1-winner of novice hurdle at Hereford in November: bit backward, jumped none too fluently but stayed on strongly closing stages when 12 lengths second to Spirited Holme in novice handicap chase at Bangor in March (finished lame): stays 2½m. *Mrs S. Oliver.* **c80** p 88

FOSSWAY MERCHANT 5 b.g. Arapahos (FR)–Super Valu (Golden Love) [1989/90 F17f^5] first foal: dam unraced sister to fair staying chaser Priest's Rock: fifth of 6 in NH Flat race at Carlisle in October: yet to race over hurdles or fences. *P. Liddle.*

FOSTON 7 br.g. Sonnen Gold–Gay Ribbon (Ribero) [1989/90 c24s* c20d^3 c24v^3 c24s^3 c21d^5] big, strong gelding: has scope: fair hurdler: won amateur riders novice chase at Market Rasen in January despite jumping slightly sketchily: made numerous mistakes when moderate fifth on final start (blinkered and heavily bandaged in front): will stay beyond 3m: acts on soft going. *M. W. Easterby.* **c97** —

FOUJITA (USA) 5 b.h. Tap Shoes (USA)–Ivory Smooth (USA) (Sir Ivor) [1989/90 16g 16m^4 16g^2 16m 16g* 16g* 16s 17f* 16f^2 16f^4 16g^5] leggy, sparely-made horse: fairly useful hurdler: won at Wolverhampton in December and January and Doncaster in March: in frame in races won by Jubail at Newbury (conditional jockeys) and Liverpool (ridden by 5-lb claimer) next 2 starts: ran as though feeling effects of his long season final outing: likely to prove best at around 2m: has won on soft going but best form on a sound surface: has worn a tongue strap (including when successful): whipped round start third outing 1988/9. *Miss S. J. Wilton.* 127

FOUNTAIN VALLEY 11 ch.g. Red Regent–Lovely Season (Silly Season) [1989/90 c20d^{pu} c16f^4 c16m] sturdy, workmanlike gelding: has run tubed: novice selling hurdler/steeplechaser: winning point-to-pointer, lightly raced since 1987. *R. Lee.* c— —

FOURACRE 6 br.g. Frigid Aire–Mezlam Queen (Terrific (NZ)) [1989/90 F12g^6 F16m 16g] behind in NH Flat races and a conditional jockeys novice hurdle. *W. Hackett.* —

FOUR ALLS LADY 4 b.f. Broadsword (USA)–Hazeldean (St Paddy) [1989/90 16f 16f^6 a16g 16g^6] sparely-made filly: second foal: dam won on Flat and over hurdles: seems of little account. *J. S. Wainwright.* 66

FOURCEES 5 b.g. Balidar–Star Duchess (Duke of Ragusa) [1989/90 F16g 16g 16d^{pu}] compact gelding: has a round action: fourth foal: brother to fair 6f to 1m winner Balindalloch: dam poor maiden: behind in NH Flat race at Sandown in November and in novice hurdle at Cheltenham in January. *A. J. Chamberlain.* —

FOUR COUNTIES 7 br.g. Balinger–Elmcharm (St Elmo) [1989/90 20d^{pu}] compact, workmanlike gelding: winning 2m hurdler: bit backward and on toes, showed little only outing of season (December): acts on firm going: takes a good hold. *J. Mackie.* —

FOUR POSTER 14 b.g. Golden Love–Eva Dodd (Orchardist) [1989/90 c25m^{pu} c26f^2] big, strong gelding: winning point-to-pointer/hunter chaser: 12 lengths second to York Royal at Folkestone in May: shapes like a thorough stayer: acts on firm going. *K. J. White.* **c85** —

FOURSHOON 4 b.g. Stanford–Haunting (Lord Gayle (USA)) [1989/90 17m 16f^3 20m] half-brother to useful hurdler/chaser Biloxi Blues (by Blue Refrain): quite modest maiden at best on Flat, stays 1m: sold out of Mrs N. Macauley's 78 stable 4,000 gns Ascot October Sales: best effort over hurdles in seller at Taunton on second start. *W. G. M. Turner.*

FOUR SPORT 8 ch.m. Swing Easy (USA)–Kingsfold Flash (Warpath) [1989/90 18f5 c18f3 c16f2] smallish, lengthy mare: poor hurdler: modest chaser: takes a good hold and barely stays 2½m: acts on any going: blinkered twice in 1985/6: has reportedly broken blood vessels: started slowly first outing: not raced after October. *J. Ffitch-Heyes.* c**102** —

FOUR STAR LINE 5 ch.g. Capricorn Line–Florida Girl (Owen Dudley) [1989/90 16m5 20f4] workmanlike gelding: winning hurdler: better effort in handicaps in 1989/90 on reappearance: should stay beyond 2m: best run on dead going. *W. G. M. Turner.* 92

FOURTH LAD 6 gr. or ro.g. Rarity–Ginkgo (Green God) [1989/90 24m 22d6] rather sparely-made, close-coupled gelding: winning hurdler: tailed off both outings 1989/90: stays 21f: well suited by the mud: has looked a difficult ride but ran well for lady rider: has been tried in blinkers. *M. Henriques.* —

FOURTH OF JULY 6 b.g. Rymer–Wayward Pam (Pamroy) [1989/90 16g 24d4 16s4 25m 19m2 20m*] workmanlike Irish gelding: useful hurdler: ran a very good race when 19 lengths fourth to Nomadic Way in Wessel Cable Champion Hurdle at Leopardstown in February on third start: didn't have to be at his best to win minor event at Fairyhouse in April: creditable seventh in Waterford Crystal Stayers' Hurdle at Cheltenham fourth start: probably stays 3m: may be ideally suited by plenty of give in the ground. *M. A. O'Toole, Ireland.* 138

FOURTH PROTOCOL 6 ch.g. Gay Fandango (USA)–Miss Golightly (Jimmy Reppin) [1989/90 16d 16m 17g4 24f5 16s5 17d c17v3 c20spu a20g 17dF] leggy, rather sparely-made gelding: poor novice selling hurdler: third in selling handicap chase at Newton Abbot in January (trained until after then by G. Cottrell): stayed 3m: acted on any going: once blinkered: dead. *J. E. Forte.* c**72** 75

FOURTH TUDOR (USA) 8 ch.g. Horatius (USA)–Fourth Dimension (USA) (Time Tested (USA)) [1989/90 16g5 c24spu c20mpu 20d 21d 24m5] sparely-made, angular gelding: winning hurdler: poor form in 1989/90: jumped none too fluently in novice chases in December: probably stays 3m: acts on any going: wears blinkers: suitable mount for a claimer. *A. W. Jones.* c— 83

FOUR TRIX 9 gr. or ro.g. Peacock (FR)–Merry Chariot (Blue Chariot) [1989/90 c20d4 c20g2 c20mpu c33d* c29f3] c**139** —

Twenty-eight runners lined up for the William Hill Scottish National at Ayr in April, the biggest field ever assembled for the race. The presence of the good-class chaser Bonanza Boy left twenty-two on the minimum 10-0 with only Four Trix among them able to carry his original allotted weight. Most of those out of the handicap proper had little chance of winning, and in testing conditions only eight of the field managed to complete; they were strung out a long way from home. Following the departure of long-time leader Macroom six out, Four Trix was one of the group still in contention. At that point he looked to be travelling no better than the others, but turning for home he suddenly came back on the bridle and led approaching the third last. His remaining opponents then began to fall by the wayside and Four Trix stayed on strongly to win by fifteen lengths from his shorter-priced stable-companion Tartan Takeover who got the better of a desperate struggle with Birling Jack by a neck. Bonanza Boy was one of eighteen pulled up, running as though past his best for the season. Four Trix turned in another fine effort on his only subsequent outing to finish third to Mr Frisk in the Whitbread Gold Cup at Sandown only a week later. Niggled along in last place passing the stands with a circuit to go, he stayed on strongly from three out and was beaten only ten lengths by the winner. Four Trix had run three times prior to the Scottish National, his reappearance having been delayed until February by a minor leg injury sustained in finishing a creditable third to Roll-A-Joint in the 1989 running. Four Trix's best performance in those earlier races was to come second to Gembridge Jupiter in the Geoffrey Gilbey Memorial Handicap Chase at Newbury on his second start when still looking in need of the outing. Four Trix travelled strongly for a long way in the two-and-a-half-mile Geoffrey Gilbey, but could do no more as lack of peak fitness told in closing stages. The race served to emphasise that Four Trix is by no means a one-paced plodder; and his astute trainer has a much wider range of options when planning Four Trix's programme for 1990/1 than he would have with most other Scottish National winners.

Four Trix (gr. or ro.g. 1981)	Peacock (FR) (gr 1968)	Devon (ch 1958)	Worden II Sees
		Peace Rose (gr 1959)	Fastnet Rock La Paix
	Merry Chariot (ro 1968)	Blue Chariot (ch 1949)	Blue Train Lanai
		Merry Trix (gr 1959)	Ossian II Little Trix

Four Trix is a half-brother to two winners, Moll of Kintire (by Politico), a winner on the Flat before going on to success over hurdles and fences in Ireland, and Super Trix (by Bonne Noel) who won novice hurdles at Wetherby and Stratford for Richards' stable in May. Four Trix's dam, the lightly-raced maiden Merry Chariot, is out of a half-sister to several winning jumpers including the very useful staying chaser Vultrix. Four Trix usually jumps soundly and seems to act on any going. A neat gelding, he is sometimes bandaged, either on both hind legs or just on his off-hind. *G. Richards.*

FOXBOROUGH LAD 11 ch.g. Some Hand–Liza Paul (Ron) [1989/90 c24v^{6} c21g^{pu}] strong, workmanlike gelding: useful point-to-pointer: winning hurdler: novice chaser: no form in 1989/90: should stay beyond 19f: possibly unsuited by heavy ground. *D. R. C. Elsworth.* c— —

FOXCOPSE 7 b.g. Healaugh Fox–Belinka (Spartan General) [1989/90 c24f^{3} c21d^{pu} c20m^{6} c24g^{pu} c16f^{pu}] lengthy gelding: poor novice hurdler/chaser: stays 2½m. *J. Webber.* c— —

FOXE'S CASTLE 10 b. or br.g. Little Buskins–Heather Lady (Space King) [1989/90 c21d^{pu} c24m^{4} 25f c24m^{4} c21m^{pu} 21m^{6}] tall, sparely-made gelding: c78 —

William Hill Scottish National Handicap Chase, Ayr— Four Trix wins from the largest field ever assembled for the race

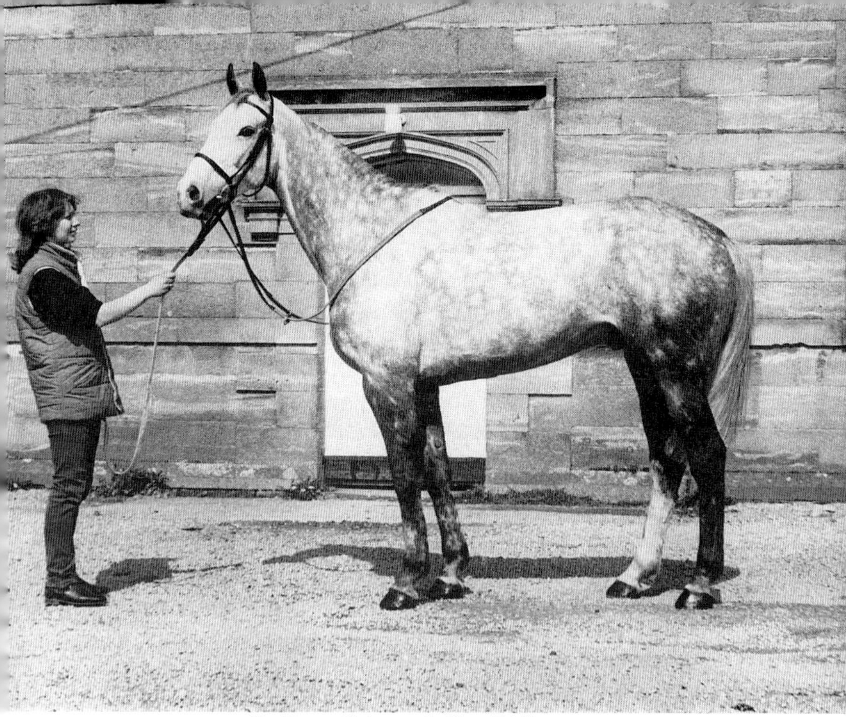

Mrs Stewart Catherwood's "Four Trix"

winning hurdler and poor novice chaser: suited by 2½m and more: probably acts on any going: has run well for a 7-lb claimer: sometimes blinkered: sold 1,550 gns Ascot July Sales. *A. S. Reid.*

FOX PATH 6 b.g. Godswalk (USA)–Precious Egg (Home Guard (USA)) [1989/90 16s* a16g^{3} 16f 16f^{F}] small, lightly-made gelding: won selling hurdle at Bangor in December (bought in 2,000 gns): close up and travelling well when falling 2 out at Ludlow in April: gave impression something possibly amiss third start: unlikely to stay much beyond 2m: seems to act on any going: ridden by claimer. *F. Jordan.* 88

FOX'S FROLIC (NZ) 5 b.g. Solaboy (USA)–Fox Mondo (NZ) (El Mondo (NZ)) [1989/90 16f^{ur} 16g^{pu} 16m^{pu}] smallish, leggy gelding: no sign of ability over hurdles: sold J. Baker 4,000 gns Ascot June Sales. *N. J. Henderson.* —

FOXTREE 7 b.g. Dubassoff (USA)–High Value (Forlorn River) [1989/90 c16s c20d^{pu} c24s^{pu}] big, leggy, close-coupled gelding: little worthwhile form over hurdles or fences. *R. C. Spicer.* c— —

FOXY BOY 7 b.g. Chantro–La Sirene (Pinturischio) [1989/90 22v^{pu} 16d^{3} 16g^{3} 16s 20d^{4} 20g] strong, workmanlike, chasing type: in frame in novice hurdles (didn't handle bends well at Catterick third start): probably stays 2½m: seemed unsuited by very soft ground when tailed off fourth outing. *J. W. Blundell.* 91

FOYLE FISHERMAN 11 b.g. No Argument–Cute Peach (Hardicanute) [1989/90 c20g^{F} c24d^{pu} c20g^{pu} c20d^{2}] big gelding: useful chaser nowadays: left clear 2 out but made a very bad mistake at the last and was headed on run-in when going down by 2 lengths to Fingest in handicap at Ayr in April: seems best forcing c**140** —

the pace at around 2½m: ideally suited by give in the ground: tends to race with
his head rather high, sometimes pulls hard and is best with strong handling. *J. T.
Gifford.*

FRAGRANT DAWN 6 br.g. Strong Gale–Aridje (Mummy's Pet) [1989/90
16g^{3} 16g^{4} 16g* 16g^{3}] close-coupled gelding: useful hurdler: well-backed 137
favourite, showed improved form when winning L'Oreal Handicap Hurdle at
Newbury in December by 4 lengths from Cinnamon Run, quickening clear in
tremendous style (eased close home): 4/1 favourite in a field of 27, 3½ lengths
third behind Redundant Pal in The Ladbroke at Leopardstown following month:
will stay beyond 2m: acts on dead going: jumps well: bandaged at Newbury. *J. G.
FitzGerald.*

FRAMFIELD 8 br.g. Monksfield–Framboise (Nasram II) [1989/90 c21d^{F} c—
c20g^{F} 24d] neat, strong gelding: winning point-to-pointer: well beaten in NH Flat —
race and a novice hurdle (blinkered): has fallen both starts in novice chases. *Mrs I.
McKie.*

FRAMPTON HOUSE 8 b.g. Fine Blue–Frampton Close (Punchinello) c—
[1989/90 22g^{pu} 22d^{3} 20d^{5} 21m^{3} c20m^{pu} c16v^{F} 22g^{5} a20g^{2} a20g^{5}] lengthy, 82
sparely-made gelding: novice hurdler: yet to complete course over fences:
probably stays 2¾m: best with give in the ground: often sweats: sometimes
ridden by 7-lb claimer. *M. J. Charles.*

FRANCESCA-BELLE 5 ch.m. Shaab–Orvotus (pedigree unknown)
[1989/90 aF16g 17m^{F}] leggy mare: behind in NH Flat races: fell fourth in novice —
selling hurdle at Devon & Exeter in April. *P. Leach.*

FRANCIS ROSE 4 ch.f. Salmon Leap (USA)–Brief Agenda (Levmoss)
[1989/90 16g 16g] small ex-Irish filly: half-sister to Irish 1¼m winner Bold And
Brief and 6f winner Ladenda (both by Bold Lad (IRE)) and novice hurdler Briefing —
(by Rusticaro): dam, placed in 9.5f race in France, daughter of 1000 Guineas
winner Pourparler: placed over 7f when trained by J. Bolger: behind in juvenile
hurdles: dead. *B. Stevens.*

FRANKTON 9 ch.g. Extra–Quadrilette (Quadriga) [1989/90 c16d c16m^{4} c16f] c—
strong, lengthy gelding: modest novice hurdler: poor form in novice chases —
(jumped none too fluently penultimate outing): best form at 2m: acts on good to
firm and soft going: sometimes sweats. *M. J. Wilkinson.*

FRAUD SQUAD 11 ch.g. Gambling Debt–Jostling (Clear Run) [1989/90 17g^{3} c—
17d^{4} c25g^{pu} c19d] smallish, workmanlike gelding: winning chaser: has shown 84
ability over hurdles: stays 2½m: acts on heavy going (well beaten on top-of-the-
ground). *P. Leach.*

FREDDIE SWALLOW 5 ch.h. Swing Easy (USA)–Rose Bridges (Calpurnius) [1989/90 F16f] fifth foal: half-brother to a prolific winner in Italy by Town
Crier: dam, plater, stayed 1¼m: tailed off in NH Flat race at Cheltenham in April:
yet to race over hurdles or fences. *P. S. Davies.*

FREDDIE TEAL 12 b.g. Bivouac–Moonfleeter (Border Legend) [1989/90 **c93**
c32f^{2} c24f^{2}] big, workmanlike gelding: quite useful point-to-pointer, winner 3
times in 1990: winning hunter chaser: neck second at Cheltenham and Wetherby
(to Bay Bridge) in May: stays very well: acts on any going. *Mrs M. F. Strawson.*

FREDS HEAD 8 ch.g. Callernish–Dreamwell (Harwell) [1989/90 c24m^{pu} **c83** +
c26s^{pu} c24g^{3}] big, angular, raw-boned gelding: first foal: dam winning
point-to-pointer in Ireland: 9 lengths third to Glass Mountain in novice chase at
Market Rasen in March: will stay beyond 3m. *G. A. Hubbard.*

FRED SPLENDID 7 b.g. Piaffer (USA)–How Splendid (John Splendid)
[1989/90 16g^{6} 16v^{3} 16d^{2} 17g 16m^{3} 16f^{5} 16m^{3}] strong, good-bodied gelding: placed 77
in 4 novice hurdles, including handicaps, in second half of season: will stay beyond
2m: acts on any going. *R. J. Hodges.*

FRED THE TREAD 8 br.g. Radetzky–Sun Queen (Lucky Sovereign) c—
[1989/90 16d^{pu}] tall gelding: handicap hurdler: burly, tailed off when pulled up 2 —
out only outing of season (January): won Hurst Park Novices' Chase at Ascot in
1988/9: best at 2m on top-of-the-ground: sometimes blinkered. *T. Casey.*

FREDWEL 15 ch.g. Fred Morris–Renwell (Renwood) [1989/90 c20s^{3}] small, c— §
sturdy gelding: hunter chaser: was suited by a good test of stamina: possibly —
unsuited by very firm going but acted on any other: dead. *Terence Brady.*

FREE AGENT 7 b.g. Glen Quaich–Vul's Money (Even Money) [1989/90 16s]
tall, good-topped gelding: won a point-to-point from 2 starts in Ireland in 1987: —
behind in 3 novice hurdles. *J. T. Gifford.*

Mr Irving Struel's "Freeline Finishing"

FREE HILL BOY 6 b. or br.g. Free Boy–Hilariana (Floriana) [1989/90 17f] angular, workmanlike gelding: second thoroughbred foal: brother to poor novice hurdler Free Jamboree: dam, 5f winner on Flat, poor novice hurdler: won a point-to-point in April: pulled hard when well beaten in novice event at Newton Abbot in October on hurdling debut. *Mrs R. Fell.* —

FREE JUSTICE 6 br.g. Impecunious–Old Brief (Lucky Brief) [1989/90 16s^{3} 16s^{6} 16s* 17m] leggy gelding with scope: won novice handicap hurdle at Hereford in March: always behind in handicap at Devon & Exeter later in month: will stay 2½m: acts on soft going and is possibly unsuited by good to firm. *A. J. Wilson.* 86

FREELANCE 11 b.g. Free Boy–Princess Fortina (Fortina) [1989/90 22d^{pu} 22d a24g^{4} a24g^{5}] sparely-made, plain gelding: only sign of ability fourth in novice hurdle at Southwell in February. *J. Pearce.* c— 78

FREELINE FINISHING 6 b.g. Furry Glen–Superday (Straight Deal) [1989/90 16g* 20d^{3} 16g* 16m] leggy, close-coupled gelding: won novice hurdles at Chepstow in December and Windsor in March: ran well when 26 lengths eighth behind Forest Sun in Waterford Crystal Supreme Novices' Hurdle at Cheltenham later in March, travelling well until 3 out, but fading quickly: good third over 2½m, though finished tired: on the upgrade. *N. J. Henderson.* 110 p

FREEMASON 9 b.g. Free State–Red Velvet (Red God) [1989/90 c16m^{3} c16m^{5} c16g^{pu}] rangy gelding: carries plenty of condition: useful hurdler at his best: just over 3 lengths third to In The Breeze in novice chase at Catterick in December: jumped none too fluently under pressure and found nil next outing: takes a good hold and is unlikely to stay much beyond 2m: best form on firm going: sometimes wears a tongue strap. *H. Alexander.* c**82** —

FREE MINX 4 b.g. Free State–Musical Minx (Jukebox) [1989/90 16g^{3} 16f^{F}] compact gelding: quite modest maiden on Flat, stays 11f: showed promise both starts in juvenile hurdles and was travelling quite well just behind leaders when falling 2 out in race won by Joe Bumpas at Edinburgh (taken early to post) in December: looked sure to win a similar race but wasn't seen out again. *M. J. Camacho.* — 91 p

FREERACER 8 b.m. Free State–Go Gracefully (Jolly Jet) [1989/90 c16f^{5}] small, lightly-made mare: poor hurdler: has shown no aptitude for chasing: stays 3m: acts on firm going: blinkered eighth and last 2 starts in 1988/9. *R. G. Frost.* — c— —

FREE SANDY 12 ch.g. Free Boy–Sandy's Ellie (Coup de Myth) [1989/90 c26f^{4}] good-topped gelding: selling hurdler/chaser: poor point-to-pointer: stays 2½m (well beaten over 25f+): seems to act on any going: looks a rather difficult ride: has been blinkered. *L. R. Vine.* — c— —

FREESTONE 5 b.h. Great Nephew–Free Dance (FR) (Green Dancer (USA)) [1989/90 16m 21m^{4} 20d 22s^{pu} 24f^{4}] rangy, rather sparely-made horse: moderate hurdler: creditable fourth at Sandown in December and Ascot (faded run-in when beaten 3¾ lengths by Alphasonic) in May: likely to prove best at around 2½m: best form on a sound surface: jumps well. *N. J. Henderson.* — 113

FREE TRAVEL 8 ch.m. Royalty–Dublin Express (Tycoon II) [1989/90 16f^{5}] tall, sparely-made mare: handicap hurdler: stays 2¼m: has won on softish ground but best form on good: has run creditably when sweating. *Capt. T. A. Forster.* — —

FREE TWIST 7 b.m. Free Boy–No More Twist (Laurence O) [1989/90 22g^{F} a16g^{5} a24g^{F}] leggy, sparely-made mare: of little account: visored last 2 starts. *S. Dow.* — —

FRENCH AGGRESSION 9 ch.g. Flandre II–Aggress (Aggressor) [1989/90 17h^{5} 20f^{5} 16f c20g c16g^{2} c16g^{3} c16v^{F} c16d^{ur} 17d 16f 24g 23f^{pu}] lengthy, plain gelding: seventh living foal: brother to winning hurdler Ingress: dam plating class on Flat: little worthwhile form: pulls hard, and is a poor jumper of fences. *Mrs D. F. Culham.* — c— x —

FRENCH CASTLE 4 b.g. Millfontaine–La Chamelle (Mount Hagen (FR)) [1989/90 16m 17g^{4} a16g^{5} 16d 16m^{pu} a20g^{5}] small, angular gelding: third foal: half-brother to 2-y-o 6f winner Runnettforfun (by Runnett): dam unraced: poor form over hurdles: has run in sellers: whipped round start fifth outing: sold 1,250 gns Ascot February Sales. *N. A. Smith.* — 58

FRENCH DADDY (USA) 5 b.h. Al Nasr (FR)–Surgical Suite (USA) (Clem) [1989/90 17f^{4} 17f^{5} 16f^{4} 17g 16f^{pu} 16d 17m^{pu}] good-topped horse: novice hurdler: ran poorly in selling company last 4 starts: barely stays 2m: acts on firm ground: blinkered fifth outing. *J. H. Baker.* — 64

FRENCH GOBLIN 7 b.g. Beau Charmeur (FR)–Straight Sprite (Three Wishes) [1989/90 c20g* c20f^{F} c24g* c24g^{pu}] deep-girthed gelding: very useful hurdler: won novice chases at Newbury in November and Kempton (quite valuable Butlins Feltham Novices' Chase comfortably by 4 lengths from The Nigelstan) following month: stayed 3¼m: acted on any going: jumped well in the main: dead. *J. T. Gifford.* — c**122** —

FRENCH HABITAT (NZ) 8 br.g. Le Fripon (NZ)–Abode (NZ) (Habitation) [1989/90 c20g^{pu} c24m^{F} c24m^{4} c25g^{pu} c20d^{pu} 21d^{pu}] tall gelding: winning hurdler: no sign of ability over fences: stays at least 2¾m: has worn visor and blinkers (wore neither when successful): often claimer ridden. *P. Davis.* — c— —

FRENDLY FELLOW 6 b.g. Grundy–Relfo (Relko) [1989/90 16f^{2} 16f* 16f* 16f^{2} 16f* 16g^{2} 16g* 18d^{3} 16f^{3} 16g 19f 16g 16f^{4} 16m* 16m^{3}] small, rather dipped-backed gelding: handicap hurdler: won at Bangor, Hereford, Plumpton and Bangor again (idled in front) in first half of season and at Uttoxeter in May: best form at up to 2¼m on ground no softer than dead: blinkered nowadays: good mount for a claimer: consistent. *F. Jordan.* — 109

FRERE HOGAN (FR) 8 b.g. Matahawk–Hantelle (FR) (Rose Laurel) [1989/90 c24g^{3}] ex-French gelding: winning hurdler/novice chaser: won 2 point-to-points prior to finishing 5½ lengths last of 3 behind Teaplanter and Some Obligation in novice hunter chase at Huntingdon in April: stays 3m. *P. A. D. Scouller.* — c**97** —

FRESH-MINT 6 b.g. Giacometti–What A Mint (Meadow Mint (USA)) [1989/90 16g 17d^{4} 19m^{2} 17g^{2} 16s^{6}] winning hurdler: close second in handicaps at Taunton and Devon & Exeter: ran poorly final outing (December): pulls hard and unlikely to stay beyond 19f: acts on hard going: blinkered last 4 starts. *P. J. Hobbs.* — 91

Butlins Feltham Novices' Chase, Kempton—a final success for the ill-fated French Goblin

FRIARY COURT 5 ch.g. Monksfield–Honours Bless (Straight Deal) [1989/90 16g] rather sparely-made gelding: half-brother to good chaser Straight Accord (by No Argument) and useful hurdler/winning chaser Another Shot (by Random Shot): dam won at 11f and 1½m: jumped sketchily and was struggling when slipping badly on home turn in novice hurdle at Wolverhampton in January. *F. Walwyn.* —

FRIDAY CLUB 6 b.g. Blue Cashmere–Balidium (Psidium) [1989/90 c17d^{F}] medium-sized gelding: little worthwhile form over hurdles: fell fourth on chasing debut. *I. P. Wardle.* c— —

FRIDAY JANE 10 b.m. Lepanto (GER)–Gretchen (Gallant Phoenix) [1989/90 c19f^{pu}] angular mare: no sign of ability. *W. D. Leach.* c— —

FRIENDLY BANKER (AUS) 6 b.g. Old Crony (USA)–Doubly Bold (AUS) (Home Guard (USA)) [1989/90 16g^{4} 16d] leggy, workmanlike gelding: poor form in novice hurdles: will be well suited by further. *Capt. T. A. Forster.* 85

FRIENDLY COAST 4 b.g. Blakeney–Noreena (Nonoalco (USA)) [1989/90 a16s^{2} a16g* a20g^{2}] half-brother to novice hurdler Yamanouchi (by Hard Fought): seemingly unreliable handicapper on Flat, winner twice at up to 2m in 1990: easy winner of juvenile hurdle at Lingfield in February: beaten 20 lengths by Druso in 2½m novice event at Southwell over 2 months later. *D. T. Thom.* 89

FRIENDLY HENRY 10 ch.g. Be Friendly–Henrys Lady (Henry The Seventh) [1989/90 24g^{pu} 17g^{5} 20s c24g c28g^{4} c25g 25d 24m] strong, workmanlike gelding: poor novice hurdler: winning chaser: creditable fourth in handicap at Nottingham in January: stays well: acts on soft going: has been tried in blinkers: inconsistent. *J. C. Fox.* c92 § —

FRIENDLY VENTURE 6 b. or br.m. Young Man (FR)–Melash (Meldrum) [1989/90 17m^{4} 16g] leggy, angular, sparely-made mare: little worthwhile form over hurdles: sold 1,100 gns Doncaster June Sales. *S. G. Payne.* —

FRISKNEY DALE LAD 5 b.g. Side Track–Midi Run (Deep Run) [1989/90 F16f* 16g^{F} 16d 16d^{6}] first foal: dam never ran: won NH Flat race at Hereford in September: poor form over hurdles. *Mrs G. R. Reveley.* 83

FRISKY FORT 5 ch.g. Fingora–Fortissimaid (Fortissimo) [1989/90 20g] half-brother to winning selling hurdler Montefiaso (by Monsanto): of little —

account on Flat: tailed off in amateur riders event at Market Rasen in August on hurdling debut. *A. Smith.*

FROME BOY 5 ch.g. New Member–Groundsel (Reform) [1989/90 F13f^{4} F16f] fifth foal: half-brother to winning hurdler Frome Girl (by Balinger): dam third over 9f at 2 yrs: well beaten in NH Flat races: yet to race over hurdles or fences. *R. J. Holder.*

FROME GIRL 6 b.m. Balinger–Groundsel (Reform) [1989/90 a16g^{4} 19m*]
small, light-framed mare: won handicap hurdle at Taunton in November by short 89
head from Fresh-Mint: stays 19f: acts on soft and good to firm going. *R. J. Holder.*

FROME LASS 4 br.f. Oats–Groundsel (Reform) [1989/90 21f^{4}] half-sister to
winning hurdler Frome Girl (by Balinger): dam third over 9f at 2 yrs: claimer 68 p
ridden, 22 lengths fourth of 5 finishers behind Richard's Hill in novice hurdle at Newton Abbot in May on debut: should improve. *R. J. Holder.*

FROSTY RECEPTION 5 ch.g. What A Guest–Stormy Queen (Typhoon)
[1989/90 22m^{6} 16m 20g 16f^{3} 21f^{3}] leggy, workmanlike gelding: novice hurdler: 95
easily best form at 2m on firm going: blinkered last 2 starts. *J. H. Baker.*

FROZEN ASSET 12 b.g. Arctic Kanda–Clear Rain (Raincheck) [1989/90 c—
c25f^{4}] winner of 4 point-to-points, latest in March: behind in novice hurdles in —
1982/3 and a hunter chase in May. *M. A. J. Anthony.*

FUDGE DELIGHT 11 ch.g. Little Buskins–Slippaville (Trouville) [1989/90 c**112**
c26g* c26f^{ur}] big gelding: one-time useful chaser: useful point-to-pointer —
nowadays: easy winner of hunter chase at Stratford in March: blundered fifteenth and behind when unseating rider nineteenth in Christies Foxhunter Chase at Cheltenham (returned lame) later in month: effective at 2½m and stays 3m in all except very testing conditions: probably acts on any going: has shown tendency to wander under pressure: suited by forcing tactics. *Robert Goodall.*

FUEGO BOY (NZ) 10 b.g. Tierra Fuego–Silver Melody (NZ) (Silver Fish) c**116** §
[1989/90 c16m^{3} c17g^{5} c16s* c16s^{5} c16s^{3} c16v* c17d^{5} c16m c16m^{5}] rangy gelding: —
shows traces of stringhalt: inconsistent over fences, but won novice events at Haydock in January and March: didn't go through with his effort fourth start and ran poorly last 2: best at 2m: acts on heavy going and good to firm: takes a good hold: suited by forcing tactics: isn't one to trust. *A. J. Wilson.*

FULL MONTY 4 ch.g. Raga Navarro (ITY)–Miss Quay (Quayside) [1989/90
16f^{3} 16f^{2} 16g^{2} 16f^{2} 16m^{F} 16m^{4} 16f^{ur} 16h^{2} 16m^{ur} 16d^{3} 16f* 17f^{3}] leggy, 88
lightly-made gelding: fifth foal: half-brother to winning hurdlers Billilov (by Anax) and Milford Quay (by Milford), latter very useful: dam, half-sister to unbeaten juvenile hurdler The Grey Bomber, fairly useful staying hurdler: maiden miler on Flat: easy winner of 3-runner juvenile hurdle at Hexham in May: ran moderately 2 days later: likely to prove best at 2m: best form on a sound surface: has looked a difficult ride. *Denys Smith.*

FULL OF DREAMS 9 ch.g. Maystreak–Panda's Gambol (Richboy) [1989/90 c—
18h^{3} 18f^{6}] dipped-backed gelding: poor novice selling hurdler: finished lame in 53
August and wasn't seen out again: usually blinkered or visored. *G. G. Gracey.*

FULL OF PORT 4 ch.f. Krayyan–Galva (Gulf Pearl) [1989/90 16d 16d 16d^{5}
16g^{4}] smallish, lengthy filly: poor maiden on Flat and over hurdles. *T. W.* 62
Donnelly.

FULL STRENGTH 7 b.g. Strong Gale–Richest (Richboy) [1989/90 16d^{6} 20g c**114** p
c16g* c16g* c16d* c16f*] rangy gelding with scope: fourth foal: dam won over —
1½m in Ireland: beaten fair way in novice hurdles in November: much better over fences and made all in novice events at Market Rasen, Bangor, Perth and Hexham (handicap, very easily by 2½ lengths from Lingham Duke) in the spring: should stay 2½m: acts on firm and dead going: sure to improve further and win more races over fences. *G. Richards.*

FUNNY MADAM 12 b.m. Funny Man–Head Madam (Border Chief) [1989/90
20f* 20g] small mare: has shown signs of ability in point-to-points, lightly raced: 73 ?
first outing over hurdles for 5 years, won amateur riders novice event at Sedgefield in April: well beaten at Market Rasen in June: stays 2½m: acts on firm ground. *T. P. Tate.*

FUNTRIX 6 gr.m. Funny Man–Annaghmore (Yrrah Jr) [1989/90 21v^{pu} 24m]
sparely-made mare: little promise in novice hurdles at Newton Abbot (mares) in —
January and Worcester in April. *K. Bishop.*

FURLANA WONDER 8 b.g. Miami Springs–Furlana (Fortino II) [1989/90 c**103**
c16g^{5} c16d^{6} c20s^{4} c24m^{pu}] tall, close-coupled ex-Irish gelding: winning hurdler: —

won novice chase at Leopardstown in 1988/9: fairly stiff tasks when soundly beaten in handicap chases in February: lost a shoe final outing: stays 2¼m: acts on heavy going and is possibly unsuited by firm. *J. J. O'Neill.*

FURNACE MILL 5 b. or br.g. Tumble Wind (USA)–Jane Bond (Good Bond) [1989/90 16m^{4} 16s^{4} 16s^{2} 16d^{5} 17g^{5}] poor novice hurdler: raced only at 2m: acted on soft going: dead. *A. P. Stringer.* 84

FURRY KNOWE 5 b.g. Furry Glen–I Know (Crespino) [1989/90 20g 20f^{4}] rangy gelding: has scope: second foal: brother to maiden Irish point-to-pointer Furryway: dam behind in Irish NH Flat race: behind in NH Flat races in 1988/9: showed ability in fair novice hurdles at Doncaster in January and Ascot in May: jumps none too fluently and may do better when brushing up his jumping. *F. Walwyn.* — p

FURRY PATH 5 b.g. Furry Glen–Troubled Heart (Prefairy) [1989/90 20f^{pu} 16m 20m^{3} 22d 20g^{su} 16s^{2} 16d^{3} 16v^{4} 20d 16g^{6}] leggy, sparely-made gelding: novice hurdler: has run in a seller: best effort when runner-up at Ayr in December: seems suited by 2m and give in the ground (though well beaten on heavy): trained until after second start by T. Craig: changed hands 6,000 gns Doncaster March Sales. *J. S. Wilson.* 89

FURRY QUEEN 4 b.f. Furry Glen–Release Record (Jukebox) [1989/90 16d^{pu}] angular filly: half-sister to poor novice hurdler Di's Delight (by Captain James): dam once-raced half-sister to a winning jumper and to the dam of Badsworth Boy: placed in 1¾m claimer on Flat in July: tailed off when pulled up before last in juvenile hurdle at Hexham in December: sold 1,800 gns Doncaster January Sales. *M. H. Easterby.* —

FURRY VENTURE 5 b.m. Furry Glen–Multeen (Deep Run) [1989/90 F16m^{2}] fourth foal: half-sister to Irish NH Flat race winner and poor novice hurdler Good Samaritan (by Fine Blade): dam never ran: length third (later promoted a place) behind The Fax Man in NH Flat race at Huntingdon in April: yet to race over hurdles or fences. *N. J. Henderson.*

FURY MANOR 12 ch.g. Fury Royal–Manor Lady (Eastern Venture) [1989/90 c25m^{pu}] big, lengthy gelding: winning point-to-pointer/hunter chaser: no form for a long time: stays 21f well: acts on firm going. *G. B. Tarry.* c—

FURZEN HILL 11 b.g. Jimsun–Lady Maggie (Distinctive) [1989/90 c24d c28g^{3} c29d^{pu}] tall gelding: handicap chaser: creditable third at Nottingham in January: very stiff task next outing: stays well: probably acts on any going: tends to sweat: blinkered final outing 1987/8. *J. S. King.* c**93** —

FU'S LADY 8 b.m. Netherkelly–Cindyr (Ritudyr) [1989/90 c20v^{F} c20g^{3} c20d* c19s* c16m^{F} c16f c20f^{5}] tall, leggy mare: useful chaser: recovered from a mistake 2 out to win handicap at Newbury in February by ½ length from One More Knight: landed the odds very easily in minor event at Hereford following month: well beaten last 2 outings: stays 2½m: has won on top-of-the-ground but is suited by plenty of give: front runner. *M. C. Pipe.* c**137** —

FUTURE REFERENCE 6 b.g. Ardoon–Melanie Jane (Lord Gayle (USA)) [1989/90 aF14g] first living foal: dam bad plater: behind in 12-runner NH Flat race at Southwell in November: yet to race over hurdles or fences. *R. Brandon.*

G

GAASID 5 ch.h. Kings Lake (USA)–Le Melody (Levmoss) [1989/90 16g^{2} 16d^{4} 16g^{2}] medium-sized horse: fair middle-distance stayer on Flat (ran well in 1990): has shown plenty of ability in useful novice company over hurdles, on last 2 starts around 14 lengths fourth to Forest Sun at Sandown and length second to Stratford Ponds at Kempton (carrying condition on first outing for 7 weeks, stayed on well): will stay 2½m: sure to win a race over hurdles. *R. Akehurst.* 124 p

GABISH 5 b.g. Try My Best (USA)–Crannog (Habitat) [1989/90 18h^{4} 16f^{4} 16f^{6} 18g^{3} 16g^{2} 16m^{2} 16g^{2} 16s^{3} 18g a16g^{5} a16g 16h^{F} 16m^{4}] small gelding: poor novice selling hurdler: stays 2¼m when conditions are fast: acts on firm ground (not disgraced on soft): blinkered final start 1988/9: trained until after first outing by R. Hoad. *J. Ffitch-Heyes.* 67

GADBROOK 8 b.g. Rymer–Quelles Amours (Spartan General) [1989/90 c24m^{2} c24g^{4} c25m* c24d^{3} c24d c20d^{2} c36g^{pu}] lengthy, plain gelding: modest chaser: won handicap at Wolverhampton in December: placed at Nottingham c99 —

(made several mistakes) and Bangor subsequently: stays 3m: probably acts on any going: visored third to fifth and final starts, blinkered in between. *R. Lee.*

GAELGOIR 6 gr.g. Godswalk (USA)–Sagosha (Irish Love) [1989/90 16s 16d] compact gelding: 1¼m winner on Flat: no worthwhile form over hurdles. *C. F. C. Jackson.* —

GAELIC CHERRY 7 b.g. Gleason (USA)–Cherry Stack (Raise You Ten) [1989/90 c24g^{F} c25d^{pu} c16v^{3} c16g] lengthy, angular gelding: poor novice hurdler/chaser: blinkered final start in 1988/9: races freely. *R. B. Francis.* c— —

GAELIC FROLIC 7 ch.g. Connaught–Frivolity (Varano) [1989/90 21f 24g*] tall, leggy, angular gelding: won amateur riders handicap hurdle at Chepstow in December, making most: reluctant to start first outing: stays 3m: best run on good ground. *P. D. Cundell.* 105

GAELIC ISSUE 5 ch.g. Lord Gayle (USA)–Tissue Paper (Touch Paper) [1989/90 20g^{F} 16g^{3} 24d^{4} 20s^{ur} 22v^{3} 20d^{4} 20f^{pu}] smallish, sparely-made gelding: modest novice hurdler: stays 2¾m but seemingly not 3m: acts on heavy going, possibly unsuited by firm. *C. Tinkler.* 90

GAELIC LOVER 6 b.g. He Loves Me–Argalie (USA) (Ace of Aces (USA)) [1989/90 16m^{4} 16f^{pu}] lengthy, sparely-made gelding: selling hurdler: races only at 2m: acts on good to firm and dead going: ridden by 7-lb claimer: blinkered final start 1987/8. *B. Richmond.* —

GAILAN'S MAGIC 4 b.g. Montekin–Densidal (Tanfirion) [1989/90 a16g] poor and inconsistent maiden on Flat: tailed off in novice hurdle at Southwell in January. *C. N. Williams.* —

GAINSAY 11 br.g. Tepukei–Swift Response (No Argument) [1989/90 24f^{6} c36f^{F}] strong, compact gelding: very useful chaser at his best: bit backward, tailed off in Keith Prowse Long Distance Hurdle at Ascot in March: possibly still needed race, behind when falling at the fourteenth in Seagram Grand National at Liverpool in April: suited by around 3m (well beaten over further): goes well in the mud: suited by strong handling and forcing tactics: usually wears blinkers: usually impresses in paddock. *Mrs J. Pitman.* c— —

GALADINE 8 gr.g. Gaberdine–Spring Gala (Ancient Monro) [1989/90 c20g c16v^{4}] lengthy gelding: has been operated on for a soft palate: winning hurdler/chaser: no form in 2 outings since 1988: stays 2½m: acts on heavy going. *M. H. Easterby.* c— —

GALA LOCH 6 br.m. Lochnager–Spring Gala (Ancient Monro) [1989/90 c21g^{pu} c16g c16d* c16s c20g^{pu}] strong, good-bodied mare: no sign of ability over hurdles: left in lead last when winning novice handicap chase at Hexham in December: no other form in 1989/90: gives impression she'll stay beyond 2m: acts on heavy going. *S. G. Payne.* c**82** —

GALALOE GLEN 6 b.g. Furry Glen–Miss Macfee (Forlorn River) [1989/90 c20m c16s^{pu} c25f] leggy, lengthy gelding: tubed: novice hurdler/chaser: little worthwhile form: blinkered fourth start 1987/8. *J. C. McConnochie.* c— —

GALA PRINCE 13 b.g. Gala Performance (USA)–Zarabanda (Kibenka) [1989/90 c24d^{pu}] modest chaser in 1987/8: tailed off when pulled up only outing in 1989/90: stays well: acts on heavy going: blinkered once in 1985/6. *T. D. Barron.* c— —

GALA'S IMAGE 10 br.g. Gala Performance (USA)–Chilita (Tarqogan) [1989/90 c24g^{3} c26f c20g^{pu} 21d c36f^{F} c24g^{5} c22m^{2}] compact, robust gelding: fair chaser: ran poorly most starts in 1989/90 (including over hurdles) though finished 5 lengths second to Auntie Dot in handicap at Stratford in May: stays 25f: acts on any going with possible exception of very firm: sometimes looks dull in coat: deliberate jumper. *J. C. McConnochie.* c**119** x —

GALLANT BUCK 10 ch.g. Derrylin–Petite Gazelle (Star Gazer) [1989/90 16h^{6} 16m^{6}] small gelding: poor hurdler nowadays: stays 3m: probably acts on any going: usually blinkered (visored first start): tends to make mistakes: ungenuine. *Mrs C. M. Budd.* — §

GALLANT GESTURE (USA) 5 ch.g. Miswaki (USA)–Bold Flourish (USA) (Bold Lad (USA)) [1989/90 16d^{6} 20f 20g^{pu}] smallish gelding: winning hurdler: best form at 2m: acted on good to soft ground: visored final start: dead. *K. A. Morgan.* —

GALLEY SONG 8 ch.m. True Song–Galley Light (Sailing Light) [1989/90 16g 16m 20s^{pu} c16f] sparely-made, angular mare: fourth foal: sister to winning hurdler Light Song and half-sister to winning hurdler Fused Light (by Fury Royal): dam, c— —

winning chaser, from family of Spanish Steps: little sign of ability in novice
hurdles and a novice chase. *K. S. Bridgwater.*

GALLIC AIR 6 ch.g. Le Moss–Country Tune (Prince Hansel) [1989/90 22d^{pu}]
24,000 4-y-o: lengthy gelding: third foal: half-brother to 1988 Sun Alliance —
Novices' Hurdle winner and successful chaser Rebel Song (by Tug of War): dam,
winning Irish hurdler, from a successful jumping family: bit backward, jumped
poorly and was tailed off when pulled up 3 out in novice hurdle at Nottingham in
January: sold 1,600 gns Doncaster Sales later in month. *O. Sherwood.*

GALLIC BELLE 4 b.f. Roman Warrior–Belle Lutine (Relkino) [1989/90 F16m
16s^{pu} 16d^{pu} 16d 16f] lengthy filly: third foal: dam never ran: mid-division in NH —
Flat race in January: no form over hurdles, including in sellers: blinkered fourth
start: sold 1,700 gns Ascot May Sales. *J. S. King.*

GALLIC PRINCE 11 b.g. Kinglet–Camargue (Combat) [1989/90 c29d^{3} c29g^{2} c**122**
c26v^{5} c30v c24m^{6} c36f] sparely-made gelding: fair chaser: second to Midnight —
Madness in handicap at Worcester in December, easily best effort in 1989/90:
always behind in Seagram Grand National at Liverpool in April: stays extremely
well: best form on ground no softer than dead: genuine: suitable mount for an
inexperienced rider. *P. J. Hobbs.*

GALLOPADE 7 ch.g. True Song–Galley Light (Sailing Light) [1989/90 18d c—
21f^{3} 24m^{pu} a20g c16f^{F}] angular, sparely-made gelding: only form over hurdles 62
third of 4 in 21f handicap at Warwick in December: jumped moderately and was
tailed off when falling at the tenth on chasing debut. *K. S. Bridgwater.*

GALLOPING CLAUDE (NZ) 8 b.g. Claudio Nicolai (USA)–Ahi Ua (NZ) c—
(Darnley) [1989/90 c16g^{4} c24m^{pu}] lengthy, sparely-made gelding: no worthwhile —
form over hurdles: of little account over fences. *R. Champion.*

GALLOWAY BREEZE 5 b.h. Day Is Done–Whispering Breeze (Caliban)
[1989/90 16m^{5} 16f^{4} 16m] strong, lengthy horse: poor novice hurdler: likely to be —
suited by a stiffer test of stamina. *Denys Smith.*

GALLOWAY LAD 7 ch.g. Domitor (USA)–Galloway Lass (Fez) [1989/90 16f]
lengthy, angular gelding: poor novice hurdler: headstrong. *D. Burchell.* 73

GALLOWAY RAIDER 6 br.g. Skyliner–Whispering Breeze (Caliban)
[1989/90 16v^{ur} 16d^{6} a20g^{6}] leggy, short-backed, sparely-made gelding: winning —
hurdler: below form in 1989/90: should stay beyond 2½m: acts on dead going:
needs to brush up his jumping: won over 2m on Flat in June. *Denys Smith.*

GALMOY 11 b.g. Flair Path–In My Time (Levmoss) [1989/90 21v^{3} 22d^{6} 22v^{2} c—
25m 24d] workmanlike, good-bodied Irish gelding: high-class hurdler at his best 134
and winning chaser: won Waterford Crystal Stayers' Hurdle at Cheltenham in
1987 and 1988 and second in race in 1989: not nearly so good in latest season, and
finished only eleventh in 1990 running of that event in March (looked in
tremendous shape, off bridle from third): best previous effort of season on third
start: well suited by around 3m: acts on heavy going. *J. E. Mulhern, Ireland.*

GALTERIO (USA) 8 b. or br.g. Christopher R (USA)–Oyace (ITY) (Hogarth c**64**
(ITY)) [1989/90 c20g c26v^{pu} c24m^{pu} c21s^{4} c20d^{4} c21g c26m^{4}] rather sparely- —
made gelding: winning hurdler: poor novice chaser: stays 2½m well, but not
3¼m: probably acts on any going: often visored: has won for a claimer: sold
privately 2,500 gns Ascot June Sales. *A. J. Wilson.*

GALWEX LADY 4 gr.f. Mendez (FR)–Shadiliya (Red Alert) [1989/90 16f^{4} c—
17g* a16g* 16m^{F} 20m* a16g^{2} a18g* 20f^{pu} 20m^{F} 16g^{pu}] small, sparely-made filly: 97
in frame in 1¼m sellers on Flat: won juvenile hurdles at Devon & Exeter (seller),
Uttoxeter and Southwell (2 claimers): claimed out of M. Pipe's stable £8,345 after
seventh start: pulled up in 2 of 3 races subsequently, giving impression
something amiss: stays 2½m: acts on good to firm ground: front runner. *C. R.
Beever.*

GAMBLING ROYAL 7 ch.g. Royal Match–Chance Belle (Foggy Bell) c89 +
[1989/90 c17d* c20f^{2}] leggy, rather sparely-made gelding: winning hurdler: —
jumped well and made most to win novice event at Devon & Exeter in November
on chasing debut by 30 lengths: clear second to Rolling Dice in similar race at
Wolverhampton later in month (finished lame and wasn't seen out again): stays
21f: acts on any going. *C. G. Roach.*

GAMESMANSHIP 9 b.g. Lepanto (GER)–Silly Games (Siliconn) [1989/90 c88
c24d^{2} c24m^{4} c24g* c28g^{4} c33d c25f^{3} c26f^{6} c36g^{5}] rather leggy gelding: novice —
hurdler: modest point-to-pointer: ridden by 7-lb claimer when winning novice

claiming chase at Edinburgh in January: very stiff task final start: suited by 3m: probably acts on any going: blinkered only outing of 1984/5. *R. W. Hartop.*

GAME TRY 5 gr.g. Mummy's Game–Pariscene (Dragonara Palace (USA))
[1989/90 17m^{pu} 17f^{4}] of little account on Flat: sold out of J. Dunlop's stable 600 —
gns Newmarket Autumn Sales: distant last of 4 finishers in selling hurdle at
Newton Abbot in September. *M. C. Chapman.*

GANARO 8 ch.g. Sagaro–Nicky's Vulgan (Vulgan) [1989/90 c17d^{pu} c20g^{F} c— x
c16d^{F} c20d^{pu} 16m^{pu}] rangy, workmanlike gelding: winning hurdler: has made —
mistakes and failed to complete course over fences: pulled up when returned to
hurdling: stays 2¼m: appears to act on any going. *G. B. Balding.*

GAN ON LAD 9 ch.g. On Your Mark–Fado (Ribero) [1989/90 20g^{pu} 16d 16m
22d 20d^{5} a22g^{4} 16f* 20f^{F} 20g^{6} 16m^{3} 20f^{pu} 24g^{4} 16f^{5} 20g^{3}] smallish, sturdy 84
gelding: selling handicap hurdler nowadays: made most when winning at Hexham
in March (no bid): claimer ridden and blinkered, ran creditably in non-seller final
start: stays 3m: acts on firm ground. *K. A. Morgan.*

GANOON (USA) 7 ch.g. Northern Baby (CAN)–Tropical Island (USA) (Raise
A Native) [1989/90 16d^{2} 16g* 16d* 16s* 16g 20m^{2} 22f^{4}] rangy gelding: front- 121
running fair hurdler: won handicaps at Wincanton and Windsor (impressively by
10 lengths) in January and Warwick following month: good second at Plumpton in
April: best at up to 2½m: acts on good to firm and heavy going: visored eleventh
start 1988/9: mounted on track and unseated rider at start at Warwick, taken down
early next time. *P. R. Hedger.*

GARCIA 6 b.g. Thatching–Song Grove (Song) [1989/90 16m 16d] sturdy
ex-Irish gelding: first foal: brother to 2-y-o 5f winner Call of The Wild and —
half-brother to a winner in Malaysia: dam won over 5.8f in Ireland: won NH Flat
race in 1987/8: runner-up twice at 2m over hurdles in 1988/9: well beaten both
starts in Britain: acts on heavy going. *D. L. Williams.*

GARDA'S GOLD 7 b.g. Garda's Revenge (USA)–Mielee (Le Levanstell) c—
[1989/90 16m 16d 16g 17v 16d c16s^{pu} 16m^{4}] smallish, sparely-made gelding: —
handicap hurdler: no form in 1989/90 (visored final outing): jumped moderately
and was tailed off when pulled up on chasing debut: best at 2m with plenty of give
in the ground: has worn a crossed noseband and a tongue strap. *R. Dickin.*

GARDENERS CHOICE 10 b.g. Mossberry–Salvo's Grace (FR) (Salvo) c80
[1989/90 c20m^{3}] leggy, shallow-girthed gelding: winning hurdler/chaser: having —
first outing since August, 1988, when third in handicap chase at Plumpton in April:
probably better suited by 2½m than 2m: acts on firm going. *D. W. Browning.*

GARGAMEL 9 b.g. Pitskelly–My Showboat (USA) (Run The Gantlet (USA)) c— p
[1989/90 c21d^{4}] leggy gelding: won over hurdles in Ireland early in 1985/6: looked —
and ran as though in need of race when over 25 lengths fourth to Colcombe Castle
in hunter chase at Wincanton in February: successful in a point-to-point following
month: has worn a crossed noseband: should do better in due course. *M. H. Dare.*

GARGOOR 4 ch.c. Kris–Icena (Jimmy Reppin) [1989/90 16g^{4} a16g*] workmanlike colt: poor maiden on Flat: won 3-runner juvenile hurdle at Southwell in 85
January by a length from Basic Fun, making virtually all: jumped sketchily on
hurdling debut (pulled hard). *N. A. Callaghan.*

GARRELGUM 7 b.g. Deep Run–Toombeola (Raise You Ten) [1989/90 22m^{5}
16m 24d 20g^{2}] good-quartered gelding: first worthwhile form over hurdles when 81
2½ lengths second to Okaz in novice handicap at Worcester in May. *Miss H. C.
Knight.*

GARRISON PARK 7 b.g. Sagaro–Olympic Visualise (Northfields (USA)) c—
[1989/90 c20g^{4} c20d^{pu}] leggy, close-coupled gelding: no worthwhile form over —
hurdles or fences: dead. *B. R. Cambidge.*

GARRISON SAVANNAH 7 b.g. Random Shot–Merry Coin (Current c**145** p
Coin) [1989/90 c24s^{3} c24g^{5} c25g^{2} c25d* c25s^{2} c24f*] —

The Sun Alliance Novices' Chase took much less winning than usual in 1990. The field of nine was the smallest since Killiney beat eight opponents in 1973, and the season's top staying novice chaser and 5/4 favourite Royal Athlete fell at the ninth before the race had begun in earnest. Royal Athlete's stable-companion the 12/1-shot Garrison Savannah proved a capable understudy. In touch in a slowly-run race, Garrison Savannah was under pressure to maintain his position starting down the hill, but he stayed on strongly after the second from home, led at the last and drew clear on the

Sun Alliance Novices' Chase, Cheltenham—everything to play for at the last where the blinkered Garrison Savannah challenges Chatam (left) and The Committee (noseband); Toureen Prince is weakening in fourth place

run-in to win by five lengths from The Committee with Chatam a further two and a half lengths away in third. In common with most Sun Alliance Chase winners Garrison Savannah is a thorough staying type who jumps soundly, and those attributes will stand him in good stead in his long-term objective, the Grand National. Good long-distance handicaps rather than the top staying chases is where we see Garrison Savannah's future. He'll need to improve a lot to be up to troubling the best staying chasers at anywhere near level weights.

The Sun Alliance was Garrison Savannah's last outing. He's not been over-raced in the last two seasons. In 1988/9 he'd looked to be progressing well over hurdles, but wasn't seen out again after winning a handicap at Cheltenham in December. Twelve months on he made his chasing debut in a novice event at Haydock, a tough course for a novice, especially first time out. Garrison Savannah took well to jumping the larger obstacles from the outset and shaped with plenty of promise in finishing third to Highfrith, looking a bit backward beforehand. Afterwards, apart from when he was run off his feet round Kempton when probably still not fully fit on his next start, Garrison Savannah improved with racing. His five-length second to Knight Oil at Towcester in January was good enough to suggest that he would be hard to beat in an ordinary novice chase. In just such a contest at Wincanton in February Garrison Savannah disposed of eighteen opponents in style, scarcely coming off the bridle and passing the post twenty-five lengths clear of second-placed Mandraki Shuffle. In his only race between then and Cheltenham, Garrison Savannah confirmed himself still on the upgrade in the quite valuable Highfield Road Novices' Chase at Warwick. Although he had to give best to Party Politics in the closing stages he looked the more likely to win for most of the way and in finishing a distance clear of the remainder earned his place in the Sun Alliance line-up.

		Pirate King (b 1953)	Prince Chevalier
	Random Shot (b 1967)		Netherton Maid
		Time And Chance (b 1957)	Supreme Court
Garrison Savannah (b.g. 1983)			Foxtrot
		Current Coin (b 1963)	Hook Money
	Merry Coin (br 1969)		Frances
		Lendy (b 1963)	Preciptic
			Lendal

Garrison Savannah, a leggy, quite good-topped gelding who invariably impresses in the paddock, was led out unsold as an unbroken three-year-old at the same Ballsbridge Derby Sale at which Mrs Pitman bought Royal Athlete; Mrs Pitman obviously had second thoughts about Garrison Savannah, for she later purchased him privately. Garrison Savannah is a half-brother to four winning jumpers, namely Big Apple and Susan's Mistake (both by Fine Blade), Ikeathy (by Be Friendly) and Diamond Merchant (by Ete Indien). Their dam, Merry Coin, a six-furlong winner as a three-year-old, is a half-sister to several winners, including the useful chaser Zongalero who will probably be best remembered for finishing second to Rubstic in the 1979 Grand National. Garrison Savannah has yet to race beyond twenty-five furlongs, but he'll stay extreme distances. He acts on any going. He was blinkered on his last four starts. *Mrs J. Pitman.*

GARRY ODDER 6 ch.g. Garryowen–Deceptive Boy (Master Buck) [1989/90
22d^{4} 20g^{5} 22d^{3} 25g* 27g^{pu} 22d^{2} 25g^{2} 20f^{2}] leggy ex-Irish gelding: first foal: dam, 97
Irish maiden, half-sister to winning jumpers Experimenting and useful Tonights The Night: won NH Flat race in 1988/9: sold out of J. Byrne's stable 15,000 gns Doncaster August Sales: won novice hurdle at Catterick in January: ran creditably most other starts: stays 25f: acts on dead going and possibly unsuited by firm: ran as though something was amiss fifth outing. *J. H. Johnson.*

GARRY PIERRO 5 b.g. Pauper–Mrs Cafferty (Brave Invader (USA)) [1989/90 F16m] half-brother to Determined Angel (by Normandy), winner on Flat and over hurdles in Ireland: dam never ran: seventh of 15 in NH Flat race at Worcester in October: yet to race over hurdles or fences. *D. R. Gandolfo.*

GARVENISH 5 b.m. Balinger–Wayward Pam (Pamroy) [1989/90 18s^{pu} 16f^{4}]
second foal: half-sister to useful Irish hurdler Fourth of July (by Rymer): dam — p
never ran: 22 lengths fourth of 6 behind No Bonus in novice hurdle at Wincanton in April: will be well suited by further. *N. A. Gaselee.*

GATTERSTOWN 7 ch.g. Over The River (FR)–Larkins Mills (Master Owen) c**100** ?
[1989/90 22d^{ur} 25g 20v c20d^{2} c20s^{pu} c20f^{2}] compact gelding: second foal: dam — p
unraced: runner-up in a point-to-point in Ireland in 1989: showed promise in novice hurdles: close second in novice chases won by Astre Radieux at Warwick in January and by Short List at Ascot in May: tended to hang left and race with his head in the air in between: will stay 3m: acts on good to firm and dead ground. *M. Oliver.*

GAULSTOWN LAD 11 br.g. Pitpan–Russian Fun (Zabeg) [1989/90 F18g^{2} c—
F16f^{3} c21d^{pu} c24m^{5}] strong, stocky ex-Irish gelding: maiden hurdler: prolific —
winner in point-to-points: well beaten in novice chase at Leicester in December: trained by P. Berry until after second start: dead. *T. Casey.*

GAVENNY GIRL 5 b.m. Rustingo–Stiperstones (Dumbarnie) [1989/90 F16g
16g] plain, angular mare: half-sister to winning hurdler Ocean Cruise (by —
Normandy): dam won over 5f at 2 yrs: tailed off in mares NH Flat race at Hereford in November: behind in novice hurdle at Ludlow following month (still bit backward). *J. Parfitt.*

GAVOMATIC 7 b.m. Pragmatic–Gavotte (Queen's Hussar) [1989/90 22d^{pu}
a20g^{pu}] sparely-made mare: no sign of ability in novice hurdles: sold 1,100 gns —
Doncaster Spring Sales. *Miss J. E. Blakeney.*

GAV'S DELIGHT 12 b.g. Furry Glen–Lauch Berg (Faberge II) [1989/90 c**121** d
c17g^{3} c20m^{3} c21g^{4} c20g^{3} c26f^{pu} 20d^{6} 27d^{pu} c16g^{pu} c20m^{3} c24m^{r}] smallish, —
angular ex-Irish gelding: winning hurdler/chaser: effective at 2m and stayed 3m: acted on any going: trained by M. Cunningham until after third start: dead. *N. Miller.*

GAY CRISELLE 7 b.m. Decoy Boy–Giselle (Pall Mall) [1989/90 c20d^{pu}] big, c—
leggy mare: winning hurdler: novice chaser: no form for a long time: sometimes —
unruly in paddock. *P. J. Hobbs.*

Steel Plate And Sections Young Chasers Novices' Chase (Qualifier), Ascot—Gay Edition (right) takes the measure of Vincanto and Palmrush (centre)

GAY EDITION 8 b.m. New Member–Gay Park (Pardigras) [1989/90 c17h* c**110**
c17f* c17h* c20f* c16f* c17d^{ur} c16g* c20m c20d^{F} c16h* c16f* c16h^{ur}] rather —
sparely-made mare: winning hurdler: most successful over fences in 1989/90 and won novice events at Devon & Exeter (3), Fontwell, Ascot and Kempton in first half of season and handicap and novice event at Taunton in April: stays 2½m: acts on hard ground (tailed off on heavy): has worn a crossed noseband: jumps soundly: genuine and consistent, and a credit to her trainer. *P. J. Hobbs.*

GAY GUNNER 9 b.g. Gunner B–Gay Ribbon (Ribero) [1989/90 c20g^{pu} c21g^{2} c**94**
c20f^{3}] big, strong gelding: modest novice hurdler/chaser: stays 21f: acts on heavy —
going, seems unsuited by firm: takes a good hold (has worn crossed noseband) and usually makes running: jumps boldly. *Miss H. C. Knight.*

GAY MELODY 8 br.m. Choral Society–Burly Try (Burlington II) [1989/90 c—
18m^{4} c21m^{pu}] ex-Irish mare: third foal: sister to winning jumper High Blend: dam —
behind in NH Flat race and maiden hurdle: winning point-to-pointer (placed in Britain in 1990): amateur ridden when winning maiden hurdle at Down Royal in 1988/9: tailed off when pulled up in novice hunter chase at Fakenham in May: stays 3m: sold out of M. Cunningham's stable 10,000 gns Doncaster August Sales after first start. *Bruce Andrews.*

GAY MOORE 9 b.g. Raise You Ten–Knockaville (Crozier) [1989/90 c24v* c**106**
c26s* c26v^{4} c24m] lengthy, workmanlike gelding: poor novice hurdler: better —
over fences and won amateur riders handicaps at Haydock and Fontwell in January: stiff task final start: stays 25f: acts on heavy going: usually held up: sweating and reluctant to start fifth outing in 1988/9: jumps soundly. *M. H. B. Robinson.*

GAY RHYTHM 10 b.m. Quiet Fling (USA)–Gay Jennie (Lord Gayle (USA)) c**69**
[1989/90 c19f^{ur} c22m c20f^{3}] workmanlike mare: of little account over hurdles: —
point-to-pointer, winner in April: just over 6 lengths third to Tricky Business in novice hunter chase at Folkestone in May. *R. H. Till.*

GAY RUFFIAN 4 b.g. Welsh Term–Alcinea (FR) (Sweet Revenge) [1989/90
16m^{2} 16m* 16g^{2} 16v* 16s^{2} 16d^{3} 16d^{2} 16s^{2} 16d^{F} 16m] sparely-made gelding: 121
middle-distance winner on Flat: won juvenile hurdles at Perth in September and Haydock in December: placed subsequently in useful company, including second to Silver King in Stroud Green Hurdle at Newbury and to Royal Derbi in 3-runner minor event at Hereford on seventh and eighth starts: will be suited by further than 2m: acts well with plenty of give in the ground: will win more races. *D. Burchell.*

GAY TICKET 6 ch.m. New Member–Gay Park (Pardigras) [1989/90 25g^{2}
21v^{pu}] angular mare: bit backward and sweating, led until close home (mistakes 92
last 2 flights) when neck second to Celtic Hambro in weakly-contested novice

hurdle at Cheltenham in November: stays well: possibly unsuited by heavy ground. *P. J. Hobbs.*

GAZETTALONG 4 b.f. Taufan (USA)–Albeni (Great Nephew) [1989/90 16m] claimed out of M. Tompkins' stable £8,300 after winning 1m claimer on Flat in September (stays 1¼m): ridden by 7-lb claimer, behind in juvenile hurdle at Perth later in month. *J. C. Gillen.* —

GEARYS COLD ROLLED 13 b.g. Kambalda–Vetsera (Hopeful Venture) [1989/90 c24m² c24g² c26dpu] poor chaser nowadays: pulled up lame final outing (November): stays 3¼m when conditions aren't testing: acts on any going but goes well on a sound surface: has run creditably for 7-lb claimer: usually sweats: moderate jumper. *C. Weedon.* **c91** x —

GEE-A 11 br.g. Arapaho–Arctic Daisy (Arctic Slave) [1989/90 20d c20g c21g³ c20f⁶ c36f c21g⁵] workmanlike, rather sparely-made gelding: fair chaser nowadays: third to The Demon Barber at Market Rasen in March, best effort of season: eighteenth in Seagram Grand National at Liverpool in April: stays 3m: probably acts on any going: sometimes blinkered: suited by racing up with pace: suitable mount for a claimer. *G. A. Hubbard.* c**122** —

GEEANTEE 5 ch.g. Abednego–Covette (Master Owen) [1989/90 F16g 17g] first foal: dam placed in 2m novice hurdles: tailed off in NH Flat race in November: in need of race, 16 lengths seventh behind City Comment in novice hurdle at Carlisle in February. *B. McLean.* —

GEE DOUBLE YOU 4 ch.g. Tap On Wood–Repicado Rose (USA) (Repicado (CHI)) [1989/90 16m 16s² 16g²] leggy gelding: quite a modest handicapper on Flat, stays 1¼m: second in juvenile hurdle at Hereford in December and novice hurdle at Wolverhampton (blinkered, went down by 3 lengths to Obeliski) in January. *D. Haydn Jones.* 90

Geoffrey Gilbey Memorial Handicap Chase, Newbury—
Chief Ironside leads eventual winner Gembridge Jupiter over the water

GEE SHARP 4 ch.c. Sharpo–Rahesh (Raffingora) [1989/90 16g^{pu}] poor form in varied company, including selling, on Flat: sold out of T. Fairhurst's stable 1,050 gns Doncaster November Sales: tailed off when pulled up in juvenile claiming hurdle at Market Rasen in April. *C. R. Beever.* —

GEE UP 7 b.g. Buckskin (FR)–Sarah Gee (Goldhill) [1989/90 16s 20d c16h^{2} c20m^{3} c18f^{4} c20f^{2}] leggy, shallow-girthed gelding: has a round action: poor novice hurdler/chaser: stays 2½m: acts on hard ground. *D. R. Greig.* c79 —

GEMBRIDGE JUPITER 12 b.g. Jupiter Pluvius–Some Ana (Neron) [1989/90 c22g^{2} c20f^{2} c20m^{2} c20d^{pu} c20g* c24m^{4} c22m] lengthy gelding: fairly useful chaser: led after 5 out and ran on resolutely to win Geoffrey Gilbey Memorial Handicap Chase at Newbury in March by 6 lengths from Four Trix: best form at around 2½m: acts on any going: usually a sound jumper, but made a few mistakes when behind in John Hughes Memorial Trophy at Liverpool on final start: races freely and is taken steadily to post: suited by a strongly-run race: genuine. *C. C. Trietline.* **c127** —

GEMTINO 7 gr.g. Neltino–Dolben Gem (Mandamus) [1989/90 16f^{F} 16m 21s^{6}] tall, workmanlike gelding: poor novice hurdler: acts on heavy going. *J. L. Harris.* 85

GENAIR (FR) 5 ch.h. General Assembly (USA)–Metair (Laser Light) [1989/90 16g* 17m^{3} 16g] angular, workmanlike horse: has been operated on for a soft palate: won novice hurdle at Kelso in November: good third at Carlisle 5 days later, but ran poorly in handicap at Haydock final start: may stay beyond 17f: acts on good to firm ground (ran poorly on heavy): winner at around 1m on Flat in 1990. *G. M. Moore.* 95

GENERAL ADVANCE 10 b.g. Push On–En Gal (Vulgan) [1989/90 c20f^{4} c17m^{pu} 20g c17f^{3} c20f^{2} 22g^{pu} c20d^{pu} c24g^{pu} c16m c20f^{F}] lengthy, workmanlike gelding: poor novice hurdler and winning chaser: stayed 2½m: probably acted on any going: dead. *Mrs S. A. Bramall.* **c94** —

GENERAL BEE 8 ch.g. Decent Fellow–Arctic Daisy (Arctic Slave) [1989/90 c21m^{5} c20f^{4}] close-coupled, deep-girthed gelding: novice hurdler/chaser: best run at around 2½m: tried to run out on 2 occasions final start 1988/9. *G. A. Hubbard.* c73 § —

GENERAL BILLY 12 ch.g. Spartan General–Dainty (Epaulette) [1989/90 c24d^{ur}] sturdy gelding: winning hurdler: fair point-to-pointer: prominent when unseating rider at the tenth in hunter chase at Bangor in March: should stay further than 21f: acts on good to firm going. *Mrs J. F. Taylor.* c— —

GENERAL CHANDOS 9 ch.g. Glen Quaich–Kitta (Spartan General) [1989/90 c20g^{ur} c20g^{4} c24f* c16v* c16s^{3} c20f^{3} c22m c20d^{5} c24g^{2} c20g^{2}] strong, lengthy gelding: fair chaser: made most to win handicaps at Edinburgh in December and Ayr in February: creditable second last 2 starts: stays 3m at least when conditions aren't testing: acts on any going: usually amateur ridden nowadays: jumps well in the main. *Mrs S. C. Bradburne.* **c122** —

GENERAL CHRYSON 10 gr.g. General Ironside–Tropical Gold (Perspex) [1989/90 c24m^{F} 25g^{5} 24g^{3} 24g^{2} 24g^{5} 21s^{4} 25d^{5}] small, strong gelding: has been fired: modest chaser: performed creditably when placed in handicap hurdles at Chepstow (amateur riders) and Kempton (ran in snatches) in December: ran moderately last 3 outings: stays 3m: yet to race on very firm ground, acts on any other: blinkered final start: moderate jumper: sold to join P. Hobbs 4,000 gns Ascot June Sales. *J. T. Gifford.* c— x 105 x

GENERAL GLORY 6 ch.g. General Ironside–Kilkileen's Glory (Arctic Slave) [1989/90 16g* 16f*] rangy gelding: improving hurdler who won 2 novice events at Newbury in November, latter by ¾ length from Holtermann: will be suited by further than 2m: acts on firm ground. *J. T. Gifford.* 100 p

GENERAL HIGHWAY 7 b.g. General Ironside–Highway Mistress (Royal Highway) [1989/90 16g^{6} 20d^{4} 20g* 20d 20f^{3}] strong, good-bodied gelding: carries condition: will make a chaser: won novice hurdle at Uttoxeter in December very easily by 25 lengths: off course 2 months afterwards, and below form on return: stays 2½m. *J. Chugg.* 114

GENERAL HINTON 6 b.g. General Assembly (USA)–Cherry Hinton (USA) (Nijinsky (CAN)) [1989/90 20g^{pu}] leggy, workmanlike gelding: eighth of 22 finishers in NH Flat race in 1988: sold out of N. Henderson's stable 4,100 gns Ascot November (1988) Sales: bit backward, behind when pulled up last in novice event at Wolverhampton in November on hurdling debut. *J. P. Price.* —

GENERALISE 8 ch.g. Young Generation–Miss Petard (Petingo) [1989/90 20s^bd 20m^pu] sparely-made gelding: winning hurdler/chaser: ran as though something was amiss final start (December): stays 2½m: acts on heavy going and is possibly unsuited by firm: has worn a tongue strap: poor jumper of fences. *G. Thorner.* c– x —

GENERAL JAMES 7 ch.g. General Ironside–Royal Bonnet (Beau Chapeau) [1989/90 F16g 21g^3 16g 22g 20g^pu c16m^4 c16f^3] rangy, good sort: ex-Irish: chasing type: dam unraced half-sister to Cheltenham Gold Cup winner Davy Lad: won NH Flat race in 1989: well beaten all starts over hurdles: promising 7 lengths third to Go West in novice chase at Towcester in March, easily better effort over fences: pulls hard but worth another chance beyond 2m: acts on firm going: should improve further over fences. *J. T. Gifford.* c89 p —

GENERAL LEE 10 b.g. Brave Invader (USA)–Miss Orleans (Panaslipper) [1989/90 16f 16d^pu 20m^ur] small, sparely-made gelding: very lightly-raced novice hurdler. *R. Wilding.* —

GENERALLY JUST 5 b.g. Golden Love–Petite Star (Super Seer) [1989/90 F16f] fifth foal: dam never ran: well beaten in NH Flat race at Hexham in April: yet to race over hurdles or fences. *Miss A. L. M. King.*

GENERALLY RIGHT 8 b.g. Fine Blade (USA)–Nire's Pride (Beau Tudor) [1989/90 c16g* c16g* c16g^3 c16v* c20f^5 c20d^pu] rangy gelding: travelled well long way and jumped soundly in the main when winning handicap chases at Worcester in December and Wincanton in January and novice chase at Chepstow (edged right on run-in) in February: under 8 lengths fifth to Brown Windsor in Cathcart Challenge Cup at Cheltenham in March: jumped none too fluently and didn't go through with effort third outing: pulled up lame final start: stays 2½m: acts on any going. *D. Nicholson.* c**125** —

GENERAL MERCHANT 10 br.g. Legal Tender–Elissa Cheng (Chinese Lacquer) [1989/90 c20d^pu c26f^pu c19m^4 c24d^6 c25h^4] tall, workmanlike gelding: winning point-to-pointer/hunter chaser: finished lame final outing: suited by a test of stamina: acts on soft going (below form on firm): usually blinkered: looked unenthusiastic first start. *G. M. Tate.* c82

GENERAL MOSS 5 b.g. Le Moss–Merendas Sister (Pauper) [1989/90 16g^pu 16s] first foal: dam unraced: well beaten in novice hurdle won by Bourbon Spirit at Sandown in February, but gave impression he has ability: broke blood vessel first outing. *O. Sherwood.* —

GENERAL PERSHING 4 br.c. Persian Bold–St Colette (So Blessed) [1989/90 16g^3 16s* 16d^F4 16d^2 16g^5] leggy, sparely-made colt: modest middle-distance performer on Flat, when trained by D. Morley: impressive winner of juvenile hurdle at Hereford in December: soon clear and around 20 lengths ahead when falling last in similar event at Sandown following month (remounted to finish fourth): ran respectably afterwards: races freely and likely to prove best at around 2m for time being: acts on soft going: claimer ridden. *F. Jordan.* 117 +

GENERALS BOY 8 b.g. General Ironside–Even More (Even Money) [1989/90 18f^4 16m^2 20f^4 25f 16g 20d 16g^3 16g^4 16g^6 c16d* c16m* c20f^3 c17f^2 c16m* c24g* c20g* c24g*] compact ex-Irish gelding: half-brother to fairly useful chaser Man of Leisure (by Prince Hansel) and winning chaser Profound (by Deep Run): winning hurdler/chaser: had a good season and won handicap chases at Sedgefield (2), Carlisle, Perth (2) and Newcastle, including 2 amateur riders events: stays 3m: acts on any going with possible exception of heavy: has been tried in blinkers: usually amateur ridden: trained by F. Flood until after second start. *J. J. O'Neill.* c**117** p 102

GENERAL SILKY 5 ch.g. General Assembly (USA)–Silky (USA) (Nijinsky (CAN)) [1989/90 a16g^2 a16g^2 a16g^2 a18g^3 16f] rather sparely-made gelding: runner-up in selling hurdle at Southwell third start (claimed out of N. Callaghan's stable £6,050): best form at 2m: ran poorly on firm going: bolted and withdrawn before intended fourth outing. *P. Davis.* 79

GENERAL TINKER 7 br.g. Cleon–Tinkers Lane (Border Chief) [1989/90 16v 16s* 21d 20d] compact gelding: won novice handicap hurdle at Nottingham in February: well beaten in similar events afterwards (stiff task last time): stays 2¾m: acts on soft going: sometimes sweating. *J. Colston.* 93

GENERAL TROY 4 ro.c. General Ironside–Silly Twit (Deep Run) [1989/90 F16g^6] first foal: dam never ran: around 23 lengths sixth of 17 to Storm Island in NH Flat race at Perth in May: yet to race over hurdles. *M. O'Neill.*

GENERAL WREKIN 10 ch.g. Peter Wrekin–Spartan Madam (Spartan c77
General) [1989/90 c25m^{4}] quite useful point-to-pointer: fourth of 5 finishers
behind easy winner Sanballat in hunter chase at Towcester in April. *J. G.
Nicholson.*

GENEROUS PASSION 4 b.f. Ya Zaman (USA)–Generous Thought
(Compensation) [1989/90 16f] well beaten in sellers at 2 yrs: tailed off in selling —
hurdle at Ludlow in April. *M. F. Barraclough.*

GENEROUS SCOT 6 b.g. Rarity–Galloping Santa (Santa Claus) [1989/90
F16g 16g^{6} 16g^{3} 16m^{su} 16d^{3} 22g^{ur} 17g^{2} 21s 20g^{5} 24m^{3}] leggy gelding: modest 93
novice hurdler: stays 3m: seems unsuited by soft going, acts on any other. *Mrs S.
Oliver.*

GENE'S ROGUE 13 b.g. Saint Denys–Pamaway (Kabale) [1989/90 c24d^{pu}] c—
ex-Irish gelding: winning hurdler/chaser: modest point-to-pointer nowadays: —
probably stays 3m: acts on heavy going: has worn blinkers. *R. D. Griffiths.*

GENIAL (NZ) 6 b.g. San Mellay (NZ)–Aladdin's Lass (NZ) (My Aladdin)
[1989/90 F17m] New Zealand-bred gelding: behind in NH Flat race at Carlisle in
April: yet to race over hurdles or fences. *P. F. Craggs.*

GENNARO 10 gr.g. Dance In Time (CAN)–Landed Lady (Realm) [1989/90 16f^{F} c69 x
a20g^{6} 16m^{6} c16f^{5} c16g^{4} c16d^{2} c20d^{6} c16m^{F} c16g^{pu} c20d 20f^{F}] lengthy, — §
workmanlike gelding: poor hurdler/novice chaser: stays 2½m: possibly suited by
give in the ground nowadays: finds little off bridle and has turned it in on
occasions: has worn blinkers and a visor: makes mistakes over fences: sold 1,250
gns Doncaster June Sales. *P. A. Blockley.*

GENOBRA 6 b.g. Young Generation–Dobra Star (FR) (Right Royal V) [1989/90
16g 16s^{pu} 16g 16v^{2} 16d] smallish, sparely-made gelding: modest hurdler: best 103
effort of season when second in conditional jockeys handicap at Ayr in February:
appears not to stay 2½m: acts well on heavy ground: finished lame first start and
moved badly down next outing. *D. McCain.*

GENTLEMAN'S JIG (CAN) 5 gr.g. Jig Time (USA)–Sunny Season (USA)
(Haveago (USA)) [1989/90 16g^{5} 16g^{4} 16f* 20g^{2} 16g^{2} 17f^{2}] strong, workmanlike 100
gelding: fair 1½m handicapper on Flat: won novice hurdle at Bangor in March: ran
creditably when runner-up in novice event and handicap on same course, and in
novice event at Cartmel afterwards: should stay beyond 2½m: acts on firm
ground: retained by trainer 10,500 gns Doncaster Spring Sales. *J. A. C. Edwards.*

GENUINE GIFT (CAN) 5 ch.h. Blushing Groom (FR)–Barb's Bold (USA)
(Bold Forbes (USA)) [1989/90 16f^{6}] leggy, good-topped horse: lightly-raced —
novice hurdler: has shown signs of ability: sold 850 gns Ascot December Sales. *C.
P. E. Brooks.*

GEORGE BUCKINGHAM 5 b.g. Royal Palace–Flying Idol (Acrania)
[1989/90 19m^{F} 16f^{r}] lengthy gelding: tried to refuse and fell first on hurdling §§
debut: refused first next time. *W. E. Fisher.*

GEORGE GREY 4 gr.c. Runnymede–Miss Moritz (Majority Blue) [1989/90
16g^{pu}] fourth foal: dam 1m winner and successful point-to-pointer: tailed off when —
pulled up fifth in juvenile hurdle at Wolverhampton in December. *W. G. Morris.*

GEORGIAN BAY 10 b.g. Laurence O–Georgette (Neron) [1989/90 c26g^{pu} c—
c26v^{pu} c24s^{pu} c26v^{pu} c25s^{pu} 24g^{4} 24d*] big, workmanlike gelding: attracted no 86
bid after winning selling handicap hurdle at Perth in May: seems to have lost his
way over fences: stays 3m: acts on heavy going: blinkered last 2 starts. *B. Stevens.*

GEORGIAN QUICKSTEP 5 b.m. Dubassoff (USA)–Fair Georgina (Silver
Cloud) [1989/90 20v^{pu} a18g^{pu} 16f 16h^{5} 19m^{pu}] sparely-made mare: poor novice 61
hurdler: tried to refuse and was pulled up seventh first outing. *A. J. Chamberlain.*

GEORGIC 7 b.m. Tumble Gold–Miss Pet Tina (Choral Society) [1989/90 c16d^{3} c**104** §
c16m^{4} c16v^{4} c16s* c16g^{2} c16d^{2} c16f^{2} c16f^{2} c16m^{2} c16g^{3} c17f*] workmanlike — §
mare: modest hurdler (whipped round start when successful): won novice chases
at Leicester in February and Huntingdon in May: easily best form at 2m with give
in the ground: has worn a crossed noseband: reluctant and started slowly second
outing and didn't go through with her effort on third: blinkered last 2 outings:
sweating and unruly when mounted fifth and tenth starts: temperamental. *Mrs J.
Pitman.*

GEOSTAR 6 b.g. Runnett–Oriental Star (Falcon) [1989/90 20m* 24g* 21g*
24g^{3} 24g^{5} 20d 20g^{5} 25m 24g] useful-looking gelding: won novice hurdles at Perth 108
(amateur riders) and Market Rasen and an amateur riders hurdle at Fakenham in

first half of season: stays 3m, and is as effective at around 2½m: acts on good to firm going: usually amateur ridden. *J. P. Leigh.*

GERAGHTY AGAIN 7 b.g. Hard Fought–Ottoline (Brigadier Gerard) [1989/90 16g 16g 16d] smallish, leggy gelding: poor novice hurdler: sold 625 gns Ascot April Sales. *B. Stevens.* —

GERAMI 10 gr.g. Grey Mirage–Psidette (Psidium) [1989/90 c26f* c24fwo c26m4 c26g2 c25m3] tall, lengthy gelding: fair handicap chaser: won 4-runner race at Newton Abbot in July: walked over at Market Rasen following month: stays 3¼m: yet to show his form on very soft going, acts on any other: usually on toes in preliminaries: blinkered final outing in 1988/9 and first 4 in 1989/90: often let down by his jumping nowadays: retained by trainer 13,500 gns Doncaster August Sales. *J. A. C. Edwards.* **c119** x —

GERYON 9 b.g. Exdirectory–Floreat Salopia (Pieces of Eight) [1989/90 16d 20d 16g6] leggy, quite good-topped gelding: modest novice hurdler: needed race first 2 starts and out of his depth third: should be suited by further than 2m. *L. Waring.* —

GET AWAY 8 ch.g. Posse (USA)–Dash On (Klairon) [1989/90 c25hr c26fpu c21mr c20dr] sparely-made gelding: novice selling hurdler: maiden point-to-pointer/hunter chaser: stays well: has worn blinkers: has refused in 3 of his last 4 starts and is one to leave severely alone. *S. F. Turton.* c§§ §§

GET STEPPING 4 ch.g. Posse (USA)–Thanks Edith (Gratitude) [1989/90 aF14g6] half-brother to several winners, including quite useful jumper Grateful Heir (by Malacate): dam a maiden: 24 lengths sixth of 13 to Fighter Command in NH Flat race at Southwell in February: yet to race over hurdles. *D. W. Browne.*

GEX (USA) 7 b.g. Exceller (USA)–Gentle Thoughts (USA) (Bold Lad (USA)) [1989/90 21gbd 20dF c21gpu c20fpu] compact gelding: poor novice hurdler: tailed off when pulled up in novice chases: not certain to stay 2½m: acts on soft going. *Miss L. Bower.* c— —

GHADBBAAN 6 b.h. Kalaglow–Firework Party (USA) (Roan Rocket) [1989/90 20g5 16m* 16s 16f4] leggy, angular horse: one-time fairly useful performer on Flat, stays 1¼m: sold out of R. Hern's stable 17,500 gns Newmarket September Sales: easily landed the odds in novice hurdle at Warwick in November: ran well afterwards: keen type, likely to prove best at 2m: acts on good to firm and soft ground. *N. Tinkler.* 92

GHOFAR 7 ch.g. Nicholas Bill–Royale Final (Henry The Seventh) [1989/90 16g c20m2 c26f* c30s4 21d4 c20gur c20f3 c36f] c**136** 114 +

Ghofar's early efforts over fences during the first half of the 1988/9 season suggested that he wouldn't have much of a future as a chaser, but the application of blinkers brought about a dramatic improvement. Ghofar, jumping with much more fluency, won three of his five starts in the second half of 1988/9; and he developed into a useful handicapper in the latest season, when he became the first six-year-old since Bright Highway in 1980 to win the Hennessy Cognac Gold Cup.

With the ground riding very firm at Newbury in November only eight lined up for the Hennessy, the first time the field had been reduced to single figures since Approaching had accounted for seven opponents under similar conditions eleven years earlier. Four of the field had been successful on their previous outing, including the 1989 Whitbread Gold Cup winner Brown Windsor who was sent off the 7/4 favourite. Durham Edition, apparently leniently treated following his victory in the Charlie Hall Memorial Wetherby Pattern Chase earlier in the month, and Ghofar came next in the betting, both priced at 5/1. Ghofar, who'd run a cracking race when second to Man O'Magic in the H & T Walker Gold Cup at Ascot the previous Saturday, wasn't immediately confirmed as a definite runner for Newbury. By the time he was, his regular partner Powell had accepted the ride on the previous season's Scottish National winner Roll-A-Joint. So Hywel Davies came in for the mount. Davies, like his colleague Steve Smith Eccles, has been in the top flight of National Hunt jockeys for many years and was riding as well as ever in the latest season. In a thrilling race Davies' experience and strength more than made up for the 2 lb overweight Ghofar had to carry for his services. Ghofar, who gave a sound display of jumping, was always prominent as Mr Frisk cut out the running, but he needed to be pushed along early in the home straight as the race began in earnest.

Hennessy Cognac Gold Cup, Newbury—winner Ghofar is partially hidden behind Mr Frisk. Brown Windsor is the other in contention at the last

Responding to pressure, he was still within a length of Mr Frisk at the last but he'd been joined by Brown Windsor, this trio now clear of the remainder headed by Durham Edition. Brown Windsor got to the leader first, and halfway up the run-in he looked likely to win. But Davies was now asking his mount for everything and Ghofar, running on gallantly, caught Brown Windsor about fifty yards out. Ghofar, setting a new course record in the very fast conditions, had a neck to spare over Brown Windsor at the line, and there was a further two and a half lengths back to Mr Frisk. Ghofar didn't manage to add to his Hennessy success, but he wasn't totally disgraced when fourth behind the impressive winner Bonanza Boy in the Coral Welsh National at Chepstow; and he ran quite well when returned to two and a half miles in the Cathcart Challenge Cup at Cheltenham, staying on to finish two and a half lengths third behind Brown Windsor. Rather surprisingly, in view of his relative inexperience, Ghofar was aimed at the Seagram Grand National. The youngest horse in the field, Ghofar made mistakes and was well behind after being badly hampered by a faller at the third, finishing in fourteenth place. There wasn't much promise in his performance, but in view of his inexperience we wouldn't want to write off his future National prospects just yet.

Ghofar ran only once on the Flat, finishing behind in a claiming race as a three-year-old. A sparely-made individual at that time, he hardly looked the type to make a jumper, and though he's strengthened up Ghofar is still by no means an impressive individual, being leggy and workmanlike. Still, handsome is as handsome does, and Ghofar has certainly proved a bargain, having cost a mere 1,000 guineas as a yearling. He's also shown useful form over hurdles, and gained one of his two victories over the smaller obstacles in the 1986 Daily Express Triumph Hurdle Trial at Cheltenham; he showed he'd retained ability in that sphere, never dangerous, in two runs in

Sir Hugh Dundas' "Ghofar"

Ghofar (ch.g. 1983)	Nicholas Bill (ch 1975)	High Line (ch 1966)	High Hat
			Time Call
		Centro (b 1966)	Vienna
			Ocean Sailing
	Royale Final (ch 1976)	Henry The Seventh (ch 1958)	King of The Tudors
			Vestal Girl
		Bleue Horizon II (b 1961)	Mourne
			Bleue Royale

handicaps in the latest season. Ghofar is the second foal and only winner produced by the twice-raced Royal Final, herself a half-sister to several winners. The second dam Bleue Horizon II, also a lightly-raced maiden, is a daughter of the very useful French mare Bleue Royale. Ghofar, who tends to sweat up, acts on any going. *D. R. C. Elsworth.*

GIANTS CASTLE 6 b.g. Great Nephew–Our Home (Habitat) [1989/90 $16d^{pu}$ $16g^{F}$ 16d a$16g^{6}$] sturdy gelding: poor novice hurdler: has run in a seller: pulls hard. *Mrs G. S. Plowright.* —

GIBBOT 5 b.g. Taufan (USA)–Gaychimes (Steel Heart) [1989/90 16g] rather sparely-made gelding: quite a modest handicapper on Flat, stays 1¼m: jumped none too fluently when behind in novice event at Huntingdon in November on hurdling debut. *P. Howling.* —

GIBBOUS MOON 8 gr.g. Red Alert–Kathinka (Sovereign Path) [1989/90 16g $16f^{F}$ 16g $16g^{pu}$] leggy gelding: lightly-raced novice hurdler: sold out of D. Elsworth's stable 3,400 gns Doncaster August Sales: dead. *P. Liddle.* —

GIBRALTAR GIRL 9 br.m. True Song–Malaria (Cheetah Peter) [1989/90 c25f* c24f2] rather sparely-made mare: won a point-to-point and novice hunter chase in March, scoring by 10 lengths from Moor Scope in latter at Towcester: will stay further than 25f: acts on firm ground. *J. T. Bailey.* c100

GIDDY BRIG 9 b.g. New Brig–Giddy Goat (Hill Clown (USA)) [1989/90 c24gpu c24fF] lengthy gelding: of little account. *S. T. Harris.* c— —

GIFT VOUCHER 13 ch.g. Gift Card (FR)–Karmala (FR) (Tanerko) [1989/90 a16g c20mpu 16mpu] sturdy, lengthy gelding: of little account. *H. E. Peachey.* c— —

GILDED YOUTH 5 ch.g. Young Generation–Woodwind (FR) (Whistling Wind) [1989/90 17f2 16f2 17f* 16m2 16m2 16m 17mpu 16f2 16mpu] smallish, sparely-made gelding: won novice hurdle at Newton Abbot in October: ran well when second subsequently: unlikely to stay much beyond 2m: acts on firm ground (yet to race on a yielding surface over hurdles): has worn a crossed noseband: trained by T. Thomson Jones until after sixth start. *Miss K. M. George.* 87

GILD THE LILY 5 b.m. Ile de Bourbon (USA)–Meliora (Crowned Prince (USA)) [1989/90 16fF] leggy mare: won 9f minor event on Flat at 3 yrs (trained by H. Cecil), and not discredited in 3 races at up to 2m in October and November: led to 3 out and was close up though under pressure when falling last in novice hurdle won by General Glory at Newbury in November: won over 1½m in Ireland for J. Bolger in 1990. *M. Madgwick.* 81 p

GILLANBONE 8 ch.g. Baptism–Joplin (Sandford Lad) [1989/90 16f 20g5 20m 20g 16m 17g4 20s6 c24d c24f3 c24m c27fF c24h4] plain, angular gelding: poor novice selling hurdler: third to Border Oak in novice chase at Hexham in March, best effort over fences: stays 3m: acts on any going: often amateur ridden: moderate jumper. *Mrs M. A. Kendall.* c77 x 61

GILLY'S COMET 6 b.m. Daring March–Moulton Star (Moulton) [1989/90 18h5 c20mpu] leggy mare: novice selling hurdler: tailed off when pulled up in novice chase at Bangor in August: blinkered second start 1988/9 and final outing. *R. T. Juckes.* c— —

GILSAN GREY 7 gr.m. Grey Ghost–Noble Hart (Dear Gazelle) [1989/90 c22f3 c24mpu c20f*] compact mare: selling hurdler: won mares novice chase at Hexham in April by 2½ lengths from Alistairs Girl: stays well: acts on firm going. *G. M. Moore.* c84 —

GINA'S CHOICE 4 b.f. Ile de Bourbon (USA)–Modern Romance (Dance In Time (CAN)) [1989/90 16f5 16d5 16f6 16m2 16g4] angular filly: well beaten on Flat, including in sellers: placed in selling hurdles in April: will stay beyond 2m. *J. Wharton.* 71

GINGA JAM 7 ch.g. Leander–Ginseng (Jock Scot) [1989/90 c16g3 c20dpu] workmanlike gelding: no worthwhile form in novice hurdles: last of 3 finishers in novice chase at Southwell in November. *W. Clay.* c68 —

GINGEMBRE 4 ch.f. Mr Fluorocarbon–Doyles Folly (Rheingold) [1989/90 16d] third foal: dam poor Flat maiden: well behind in selling hurdle at Market Rasen in November. *J. Dooler.* —

GINGERLAND 7 ch.g. Bustino–Zerbinetta (Henry The Seventh) [1989/90 c20g c21gpu] big, lengthy gelding: winning hurdler: no worthwhile form in 2 outings over fences, but showed signs of ability. *N. J. Henderson.* c— —

GINGER WINGS 6 ch.m. Ginger Boy–Sticky Wings (Heswall Honey) [1989/90 16s 18spu 16mpu] sparely-made mare: first foal: dam won a point-to-point: little promise in novice hurdles. *A. Moore.* —

GIOLLA PADRAIG 12 b.g. Giolla Mear–Barrettstown Belle (Twilight Alley) [1989/90 c20g6 c27m6 c22m3 c20g3 c20gF c20f4 c20f* c17f2 c21f5] big, rangy gelding: made all in handicap chase at Sedgefield in May: creditable second to Stan's Folly in amateur riders handicap at Cartmel later in month: third in Seagram Fox Hunters' Chase at Liverpool on third start: suited by around 2½m: yet to race on heavy ground, acts on any other: blinkered sixth start. *Denys Smith.* c115

GIOLLA WAY 11 b.g. Giolla Mear–Tina's Toi (Fortina) [1989/90 c25m* c25gpu] lengthy gelding: point-to-point winner: successful in handicap chase at Cartmel in August: pulled up after mistake 2 months later (sweating): stays 3¼m: probably acts on any going. *D. R. Gandolfo.* c89 ? —

GIPSY RAMBLER 5 gr.g. Move Off–Gipsy Silver (Pongee) [1989/90 16dpu 16g] smallish, angular gelding: no sign of ability over hurdles. *N. Chamberlain.* —

GIPSY'S TOKEN 5 b.h. Silly Prices–Gipsy Silk (Pongee) [1989/90 16g^{ro} 16g 16g 17m] angular, sparely-made horse: poor novice hurdler. *N. Chamberlain.* 62

GIRL IN GREEN 6 b.m. Connaught–Hindu Flame (Shiny Tenth) [1989/90 20d 16d] strong, lengthy mare: novice hurdler: behind both starts in 1989/90. *F. Jordan.* —

GIRTON LADY 4 b.f. Uncle Pokey–Gay Twenties (Lord Gayle (USA)) [1989/90 16m^{su}] second foal: dam winning hurdler: 33/1 and ridden by claimer, tailed off when slipped up after third in juvenile hurdle at Catterick in December. *R. M. Whitaker.* —

GISSMO 5 ch.h. Native Bazaar–Torlonia (Royal Palace) [1989/90 16v 16g 24d^{pu}] big, leggy horse: no sign of ability over hurdles: tends to sweat. *C. James.* —

GIVE ALL 4 b.g. Try My Best (USA)–Miss Spencer (Imperial Fling (USA)) [1989/90 16s 16s^{pu} a16g] workmanlike gelding: second foal: half-brother to Ejay Haitch (by Be My Native), a winning stayer on Flat and placed over hurdles: dam never ran: little worthwhile form over hurdles. *C. Spares.* —

GIVE ME A BREAK 9 b.g. Green Shoon–Carrigello (Bargello) [1989/90 c21d^{2} c20v^{4} c25f^{3}] lengthy gelding: won 4 point-to-points and in frame both starts in hunter chases in Ireland, when trained by P. Hogan: has since won 2 point-to-points in Britain, latest in March: just over 10 lengths third to Moor Scope in novice hunter chase at Plumpton later in month: suited by a test of stamina: probably acts on any going. *Robert Goodall.* c**102**

GIVUS A BUCK 7 br.g. Buckskin (FR)–My Pet (Phalorain) [1989/90 21d 21d 25f^{5}] strong, rangy, good sort: chasing type: good walker: fairly useful hurdler: easily best effort of season when good fifth behind Henry Mann in valuable handicap at Cheltenham in March: stays 25f: acts on any going. *D. R. C. Elsworth.* 128

GLADSTONIAN 12 b.g. Cantab–Ice Folly (Arctic Slave) [1989/90 c22s^{pu} c24d^{pu}] sturdy gelding: poor point-to-pointer/maiden hunter chaser: has worn tongue strap. *Richard Benson.* c—

GLADYS PUGH 4 b.f. Comedy Star (USA)–Nylon Pirate (Derring-Do) [1989/90 16d^{3} 16m] sparely-made filly: plating-class maiden on Flat: ridden by 3-lb claimer, third in novice selling hurdle at Stratford in November: favourite, tailed off in similar company at Taunton later in month: needs to improve her jumping: has joined M. Channon. *G. B. Balding.* 67

GLAMIS 7 b.g. Pollerton–Raise A Queen (Raise You Ten) [1989/90 20v] useful-looking gelding: mid-division in NH Flat race in 1988: 14/1 and edgy, soon behind and not knocked about when in mid-division in 20-runner novice hurdle at Chepstow in January won by Danny Harrold: will do better in due course. *C. P. E. Brooks.* — p

GLANMOORE 6 b.g. Amboise–Michaelmas Daisy (Royalty) [1989/90 24d 20g^{4} 22d^{5} 24f^{5} 25h^{3}] leggy, angular gelding: second foal: dam placed in varied company over hurdles, including selling: poor novice hurdler: will be suited by a thorough test of stamina: seems unsuited by hard ground: sold 5,000 gns Ascot June Sales. *T. P. Tate.* 85

GLASS MOUNTAIN 8 gr.g. Scallywag–Miss Maskin (Sikandar) [1989/90 c21d^{4} c24g* c24f^{4} c24f*] strong gelding: carries plenty of condition: successful in 2 novice hurdles in 1988/9: won novice chases at Market Rasen in March and Southwell (dismounted after passing post) in April: very bad mistake second when below form in between: stays 3m: acts on any going: bandaged in 1988/9 (broke blood vessel final start). *G. M. Moore.* c**105** p —

GLASTONBURY GROVE 8 b.g. Alias Smith (USA)–Ile de France (French Beige) [1989/90 c17m^{4} c16m^{pu}] leggy gelding: probably of little account over hurdles: poor novice chaser. *V. Thompson.* c— —

GLASTONDALE 4 b.g. Beldale Flutter (USA)–Glastonbury (Grundy) [1989/90 16d^{5}] quite modest middle-distance performer on Flat: sold out of F. Lee's stable 14,000 gns Newmarket Autumn Sales: 16½ lengths fifth behind Non Permanent in novice hurdle at Sedgefield in January: won on Flat afterwards, and should improve over hurdles. *T. D. Barron.* 83 p

GLAZEPTA AGAIN 11 ro.g. Gay Fandango (USA)–Grande Promesse (FR) (Sea Hawk II) [1989/90 c25m^{pu} c24f^{3} c26m^{3} c17m^{pu} c24m^{4}] sturdy, very dipped-backed, plain gelding: carries plenty of condition: has been tubed: winning hurdler/point-to-pointer: in frame in steeplechases: reportedly finished lame when 7½ lengths fourth to Turn Blue in hunter chase at Fakenham in May: stays 3m: seems to act on any going: found little fourth outing in 1988/9. *O. J. Carter.* c87 —

GLEBE PRINCE 10 b.g. Brave Invader (USA)–Once More (Even Money) c—
[1989/90 c16g^{F3}] in frame in 2 hunter chases in Ireland in 1986/7: modest winning form in point-to-points in Britain since: had just been headed when falling 2 out in poor novice chase at Fakenham in October (remounted): stays 3m. *T. P. McGovern.*

GLEBE SPINNEY 8 b.g. Netherkelly–My Darling (Arctic Slave) [1989/90 c98
c16m* c16m^{2} c24m^{3} c20d^{2} c16g^{3} c16d^{pu} c16m^{6}] tall, leggy gelding: poor novice —
hurdler: quite modest chaser: won handicap at Towcester in November: ran creditably next 4 outings: best up to 2½m: probably acts on any going: blinkered nowadays: has tended to go left in latter stages. *J. Wharton.*

GLENBURY 5 ch.h. Morston (FR)–Glenside Lady (So Blessed) [1989/90
16g^{pu} 16d] close-coupled horse: seemingly of little account on Flat: no promise in —
novice hurdle at Wincanton and seller at Ludlow. *J. D. Roberts.*

GLENCOE BOY 7 b.g. Pry–Rainella (Bahrain) [1989/90 18m* 20f*] compact
gelding: won selling handicap hurdle at Worcester in August (bought in 2,400 90
gns): improved on that when beating Kimacero a neck in novice handicap at Bangor following month: stays 2½m: acts on firm going: has been tried in blinkers and in visor, but is better without. *J. G. M. O'Shea.*

GLENDERRY 8 br.g. Derrylin–Summer Mist (Midsummer Night II) [1989/90
20g^{3} 16g^{5} 16s^{6} 16m^{2} 16f^{4} 20g^{2} 20m^{2} 23f^{pu}] small, rather sparely-made gelding: 92
novice hurdler: has run in sellers: looked none too resolute seventh start: stays 2½m: acts on good to firm and soft ground: visored on first outing, blinkered previously: trained by S. Muldoon until after first start. *D. Dutton.*

GLEN FINTAIG 5 b.g. Furry Glen–Nega (St Xavier) [1989/90 20g 20s^{3} 16s^{2}
20f] workmanlike gelding: first worthwhile form over hurdles ½-length second to 79
General Tinker in novice handicap at Nottingham in February, making much of running: ran well for a long way at Doncaster following month: races keenly and doesn't stay 2½m: blinkered last outing 1988/9. *A. Bailey.*

GLENFORRES 5 ch.g. Callernish–Clever Noel (Bonne Noel) [1989/90 16g^{6}
20g^{5} 16s^{5}] strong, stocky gelding: second foal: dam unraced: well beaten in —
novice hurdles: dead. *J. Webber.*

GLEN GEORGE 10 b.g. Furry Glen–Paiukiri (Ballyciptic) [1989/90 16f^{4} c102
c20v^{pu} a20g^{5} c19s^{pu} c25m^{pu} c20f^{4} c21m^{3} c24d^{pu}] rangy gelding: has been —
hobdayed: handicap hurdler/chaser: only form of season seventh start: stays 21f: goes well on firm ground. *G. A. Ham.*

GLENGOOLE 7 b.g. Glen Quaich–Blush (Twice Worthy (USA)) [1989/90 21f]
well-made gelding: half-brother to Aubaine (by Belfalas), a winner on Flat and — p
placed over hurdles in Ireland: placed in point-to-points in Ireland in 1989: 50/1 and carrying condition, over 30 lengths eighth behind Theo's Fella in novice hurdle at Newbury in March, weakening in straight and not knocked about: may do better. *B. Smart.*

GLENJARMI 8 b.g. Al Sirat (USA)–Railstown (Escart III) [1989/90 c24f] c—
ex-Irish gelding: well beaten in maiden hurdles in 1987/8: placed in point-to- —
points in Britain since: well beaten in maiden hunter chase at Hexham in April: has been tried in blinkers. *J. P. Henderson.*

GLENLAW 7 b.m. Pitpan–Glenreeba (Cappagh Boy) [1989/90 F13m^{5} F17f^{6}] fifth foal: half-sister to modest winning chaser Perfect Glen (by Kemal): dam never ran: last in NH Flat races at Perth and Carlisle in first half of season: yet to race over hurdles or fences. *T. A. K. Cuthbert.*

GLENMERE PRINCE 4 b.g. Prince Tenderfoot (USA)–Ashbourne Lass
(Ashmore (FR)) [1989/90 a16g^{2} a16g] plating-class maiden on Flat, in frame at up 80
to 7f: 8 lengths second to Friendly Coast in juvenile event at Lingfield in February, better effort over hurdles. *P. J. Feilden.*

GLEN MORVERN 4 ch.f. Carlingford Castle–Why Ask (Deep Run) [1989/90 F16g^{6} F14v^{2}] half-sister to winning hunter chaser Oh Why (by Laurence O): dam behind only outing over hurdles: 1½ lengths second to Dakyns Boy in NH Flat race at Ayr in April: yet to race over hurdles. *W. H. Crawford.*

GLEN OAK 5 b.g. Glenstal (USA)–Neeran (Wollow) [1989/90 21d^{2} 24s 25f
20f^{4}] leggy gelding: much improved hurdler in 1989/90, good second in handicap 130
at Warwick in January: below form after, but showed up well long way next 2 starts: suited by about 2½m and give in the ground: tailed off when visored on hurdling debut: fairly useful. *J. D. Roberts.*

GLEN RIDGE 9 b. or br.g. Golden Love–Glenarold Lass (Will Somers) [1989/90 c20m4 c16m5 c16h3] sturdy gelding: winning hurdler/chaser: moderate third behind Market Leader over fences at Ludlow in September: stays 2½m: acts on heavy going. *P. J. Hobbs.* c86 —

GLENRUE 13 ch.g. Carnival Night–Naomi (Golden Gorden) [1989/90 c20f4 c25gur] big, close-coupled gelding: useful chaser at his best, but no form for a long time. *G. G. Gracey.* c— —

GLENSIDE JERRY 10 b.g. Chas Sawyer–Ruckinge Girl (Eborneezer) [1989/90 21m* c24f3 c25m2 c29d2 c25m2 c29g5 c32gF c30vco c26g3 c29g*] workmanlike gelding: fair chaser: won handicap at Worcester in March by 1½ lengths from Lakefield: won novice event at Devon & Exeter in September on hurdling debut: stays well: acts on any going: usually held up: visored last 2 outings: moderate jumper of fences. *G. B. Balding.* c122 x 102

GLENSTAL ABBEY (USA) 4 ch.g. Gregorian (USA)–Full Delivery (USA) (Irish Ruler (USA)) [1989/90 16g 16f6 16v 16d6 a20g2 20m4 16m2 16m*] good-topped ex-Irish gelding: seventh foal: half-brother to 4 winners in USA: dam won at around 1m in USA: third over 1¼m on Flat in 1989: bought in 4,900 gns after winning novice selling handicap hurdle at Huntingdon in May: looked most reluctant fifth start: probably stays 2½m: acts on good to firm ground: wears blinkers. *R. Akehurst.* 85

GLENTINO 5 b.g. Glenstal (USA)–Grizabella (Bustino) [1989/90 16fpu] no sign of ability either outing over hurdles. *P. J. Hobbs.* —

GLENVALE 4 b.g. Hays–Deira (Bold Lad (IRE)) [1989/90 16m 16f] workmanlike gelding: plating-class maiden on Flat: tailed off in juvenile event and a seller (blinkered) over hurdles in first half of season. *P. Burgoyne.* —

GLEN WEAVING 6 b.g. Furry Glen–Weaving (Weavers' Hall) [1989/90 17m 16h4 16g4 21f3 c19gbd] smallish, sparely-made gelding: winning hurdler: failed to complete course over fences: was best at around 2m on a sound surface: visored once: dead. *L. J. Codd.* c— 76

GLORIOLE 6 b.g. Indian King (USA)–Escorial (Royal Palace) [1989/90 16m5] tailed off in juvenile hurdle in 1987: fifth in novice event at Perth in August, better effort over hurdles. *R. Allan.* 73

GLORY HILL 5 br.m. Cleon–Mezel Hill (Tarqogan) [1989/90 16spu a18g6] close-coupled mare: poor maiden on Flat: no sign of ability in seller and a claimer over hurdles. *P. R. Hedger.* —

GLOSS 5 b.g. Town And Country–Star Display (Sparkler) [1989/90 17h2 17fF 16hpu a16g] workmanlike gelding: headstrong and no worthwhile form over hurdles: ran out after trying to refuse on first start 1988/9: wore net muzzle in 1989/90: visored last start: subsequently sold 1,000 gns Ascot November Sales: resold 3,000 gns Ascot May Sales. *M. B. James.* — §

GLOVER'S NEEDLE 6 b.m. Dubassoff (USA)–Busy Buskins (Little Buskins) [1989/90 F13f5 F16f] non-thoroughbred mare: half-sister to 2 poor jumpers: dam in frame over hurdles and fences in Ireland: well beaten in NH Flat races in April: yet to race over hurdles or fences. *J. Colston.*

GLOWING DARKNESS 5 gr.m. Kalaglow–Guama (Gulf Pearl) [1989/90 aF14g] sixth living foal: half-sister to winning stayers Powersaver Lad (by Jaazeiro) and Rocas (by Ile de Bourbon): dam 2-y-o 7f winner: tailed off in NH Flat race at Southwell in February: yet to race over hurdles or fences. *A. P. Stringer.*

GLOW OF KHOBAR 5 gr.g. Kalaglow–Mary of Modena (Crowned Prince (USA)) [1989/90 17v] leggy gelding: poor novice selling hurdler: blinkered last outing 1988/9. *R. Callow.* —

GLYMPTON 5 b.g. Blakeney–Particular Miss (Luthier) [1989/90 16m 16spu] angular gelding: no sign of ability over hurdles: blinkered last start. *C. Tidmus.* —

GO CRAZY 8 ro.g. Pongee–Petoria (Songedor) [1989/90 16g3 16dpu] workmanlike gelding: winning selling hurdler: good third in handicap at Ayr in November: raced only at around 2m: acted on heavy going: dead. *Mrs D. F. Culham.* 93

GODDARD'S GIRL 4 b.f. Martinmas–Ready Steady Go (On Your Mark) [1989/90 a16g] small, plain filly: little worthwhile form on Flat: jumped none too fluently when behind in juvenile hurdle at Southwell in November. *M. W. Eckley.* —

GODERSMISTAKE 7 b.g. New Member–Lafitte (Lucky Sovereign) [1989/90 c20f^{ur}] rangy gelding: placed in point-to-points: behind when unseating rider tenth in novice hunter chase at Cheltenham in May. *Roger Lane.* c—

GODIVA BEARINGS 8 b.g. Martinmas–Belle Fillette (Beau Chapeau) [1989/90 16g 16m^{5}] rangy gelding: modest novice hurdler: one-paced fifth behind Tildarg at Sandown in March. *J. C. Fox.* 92

GODLORD 10 gr.g. Godswalk (USA)–Gay Pariso (Sir Gaylord) [1989/90 16f^{3} 16f] poor novice hurdler. *P. J. Bevan.* —

GODOUNOV 7 b.g. Godswalk (USA)–Grilse Run (Stupendous) [1989/90 16f^{ur} a16g 17g^{5} 16g 16g 16f^{6} 16m c21g^{4} c20f^{4} c17f^{3} c21g^{pu}] close-coupled gelding: winning hurdler: poor novice chaser: stays 2½m: acts on good to firm and soft going: has run visored, blinkered sixth start: has shown signs of temperament. *T. Fairhurst.* c73 73

GODS FOX 8 b.g. Paico–Lilgarde (Hugh Lupus) [1989/90 20d 17v^{4} 16g 16g 20v* 20s c20v^{pu}] tall, close-coupled gelding: ridden by 5-lb claimer, first worthwhile form since 1987/8 when winning handicap hurdle at Plumpton in January: tailed off when pulled up in valuable event at Chepstow on chasing debut: stays 2½m: acts on heavy going and possibly unsuited by firm. *N. R. Mitchell.* c— 112

GODS LAW 9 gr.g. Godswalk (USA)–Fluently (Ragusa) [1989/90 c16f^{3} 20f^{4}] short-coupled, lightly-made gelding: handicap hurdler: took little interest last start (September): jumped moderately when third of 4 in novice event at Hexham in September on chasing debut: unlikely to stay much beyond 2m: acts on any going: takes a good hold and is usually held up: mulish in preliminaries last 2 starts: one to treat with caution. *Mrs G. R. Reveley.* c73 — §

GO FORUM 5 ch.g. Tumble Wind (USA)–Devine Lady (The Parson) [1989/90 a16g*] small, sturdy gelding: one-time fair firm-ground performer on Flat, stays 1¾m: made much of running when successful in novice hurdle at Lingfield in November, beating Distant Relation 10 lengths. *J. Sutcliffe.* 103 +

GO GIPSY 8 br.m. Move Off–Gipsy Silver (Pongee) [1989/90 c16g^{pu} c20g^{pu} c27d^{pu}] small, lightly-built mare: lightly raced and little sign of ability. *N. Chamberlain.* c— —

GO GO GORGEOUS 4 b.g. Hello Gorgeous (USA)–Go Mays (Realm) [1989/90 16m^{4} 16d^{ro} 16f^{2} 19s^{3} 16s 16v*] angular ex-Irish gelding: fourth foal: half-brother to Mango May Sing (by Mansingh), a fairly useful 2-y-o plater, and Forever Aston (by Le Moss), placed over hurdles: dam of no account: second over 1¾m on Flat: claimer ridden, won slowly-run juvenile claiming hurdle at Leicester in February by 8 lengths: stays 19f: acts on any going: jumps none too fluently: trained first 2 starts by A. Mullins. *F. Jordan.* 97

GO-GO-SAM 6 b.g. Golden Shields–Flying Westward (Priory Prince) [1989/90 16f 16g 16d] sparely-made gelding: no form over hurdles. *P. Wakely.* —

GOING GETS TOUGH 7 ch.g. Maystreak–Cham-Ol Bazaar (Native Bazaar) [1989/90 16g^{2} c20g^{4} c16f^{2} c20f* c20f^{F2} c20m^{3} c16g^{3} c20f^{2} c20f^{ur}] workmanlike gelding: fair novice hurdler: made a couple of mistakes and drifted right on run-in when winning Hopeful Chase at Newbury in November by ¾ length from Earl Soham: 3 lengths second of 3 to Okeetee in Golden Eagle Novices' Chase at Ascot in March, eighth outing: stays 2½m: acts on firm ground, probably unsuited by heavy: has sweated up. *G. B. Balding.* c**110** 110

GOING ON 4 ch.g. Move Off–Young Lamb (Sea Hawk II) [1989/90 F12g* F16m*]

The Seagram Supreme National Hunt Flat race reinstated at Liverpool in April was an interesting contest, as were its two predecessors won by Black Moccasin and Rustle. Most National Hunt Flat races, with their fields of inexperienced, mainly slow, backward four-, five- and six-year-olds ridden by conditional or amateur jockeys, have a very limited appeal for Joe Public. Doubtless more attention would be paid if, as often advocated by trainers (and in the pages of these Annuals), top professionals were allowed to ride in them. However, at Liverpool the qualifying conditions are stiffer than normal and the prize money higher, with the result that the race attracts better-than-average fields and looks like developing into a recognised annual 'bumpers' championship. Of the twenty runners in 1990 ten were winners, nine of them unbeaten. Their breeding took a fascinatingly wide range, from classic Flat (represented by the 9/4 favourite

Ruling, by Alleged out of a winning Northern Dancer mare) to the honest-to-goodness jumping pedigrees of the majority. The second favourite Minorettes Girl was a half-sister to Observe and Espy, while also present was a half-brother to Pearlyman (Poetic Gem, from the stable of the 1988 runner-up Morley Street). The race put a premium on that quality least conspicuous in the average National Hunt Flat horse, that of speed. But some showed it in fair measure, including, surprisingly perhaps, Minorettes Girl whose two wins had been gained in much more testing conditions in Ireland. She finished a good third, behind Going On and Ruling. That Going On possessed sufficient speed to make his presence felt at Liverpool seemed on the cards from the way he'd left his eighteen opponents behind over the last two furlongs of a mile-and-a-half race on good going at Market Rasen the previous month. Both he and Ruling were held up behind a strong pace and set plenty to do at Liverpool, Ruling even more than Going On. In the end, having made sustained progress from the turn out of the back straight to take the lead running into the last furlong, Going On won convincingly by three quarters of a length.

Going On (ch.g. 1986)	Move Off (ch 1973)	Farm Walk (ch 1962)	Kribi
			Monastery Garden
		Darling Do (b 1967)	Derring-Do
			Akimbo
	Young Lamb (gr 1969)	Sea Hawk II (gr 1963)	Herbager
			Sea Nymph
		Beau Co Co (ch 1950)	Ballyogan
			Touch And Go

There's no reason to suppose that the latest Seagram Supreme National Hunt Flat race field won't again contain several horses who'll do well over obstacles, maybe down among the also-rans, not all of whom are likely to have been seen at their best under the conditions. Going On, a shade over sixteen hands according to the catalogue, was sold the following month at the Doncaster Sales as a potential jumper for 58,000 guineas. He is to be trained with that in mind by another northern-based trainer Howard Johnson. Going On's family has had some success under both codes. The dam Young Lamb, retained for 2,500 guineas after an undistinguished career on the Flat, has produced three other winners—Burns (by Midsummer Night II), Caroline Lamb (by Hotfoot) and Miss Lamb (by Relkino), all of whom won on the Flat and over hurdles. Burns was very useful over hurdles at two miles and won twice at the Liverpool fixture; Caroline Lamb is also the dam of the unbeaten chaser Master Lamb. The second and third dams were two-year-old winners, and Beau Co Co, beaten a neck in the Irish One Thousand Guineas, produced the smart sprinter Spark. *Miss S. E. Hall.*

GOING SOLO 6 ch.g. Rarity–Go-It-Alone (Linacre) [1989/90 22g] behind in NH Flat race and a novice hurdle: dead. *S. Woodman.* —

GOING UP 5 b.g. Henbit (USA)–Mill Hill (USA) (Riva Ridge (USA)) [1989/90 16g^{5} a18g^{4} 22g^{pu} 17h^{ur} 17m^{pu} 17h^{pu}] tall, leggy gelding: of little account: blinkered last outing: sold out of M. Madgwick's stable 2,000 gns Ascot February Sales after third start. *W. G. Turner.* —

GOLD BEARER 10 b.g. Golden Love–Gina Rose (Prince Hansel) [1989/90 c20s^{3} c20d^{pu}] rangy, deep-girthed gelding: useful chaser in 1987/8: needed race when just over 3 lengths third to Hitchcock in minor event at Folkestone in January: tailed off when pulled up facing much stiffer task next time: stays 3m: acts on soft ground. *C. P. E. Brooks.* c**112** —

GOLD CHILD 7 b.g. Goldhill–Aggvus (Aggressor) [1989/90 16d 22m^{pu}] plain, workmanlike gelding: winning point-to-pointer: fell second in maiden chase in 1988/9: poor form in novice and maiden hurdles. *D. L. Williams.* c— —

GOLD COLLAR 5 ch.m. Sayyaf–Colonial Line (USA) (Plenty Old (USA)) [1989/90 18g^{pu}] lightly-raced novice hurdler: pulled up and dismounted in selling handicap in December. *A. Moore.* —

GOLDEN ACRE 8 b.g. Los Cerrillos (ARG)–Pharaoh's Bride (Pharaoh Hophra) [1989/90 16g 20s^{F} 16g] lengthy, sparely-made gelding: won twice over —

hurdles in 1987/8: well beaten in 1989/90 (blinkered last start): form only at around 2m: acts on any going with possible exception of heavy. *S. N. Cole.*

GOLDEN ANN 4 b.f. Absalom–Polly Oligant (Prince Tenderfoot (USA)) [1989/90 16g² 16s⁴ 16s⁵ 16v⁵ 16d⁴] sparely-made filly: placed over 1¼m on Flat in 1989: stayed on without being knocked about when 15 lengths second to Coe in juvenile hurdle at Sandown in November, and when around 20 lengths fourth to Calicon in similar event at Newbury in February: bit below form on softer ground in between. *G. B. Balding.* 91

GOLDEN ASSET 8 b.g. Golden Love–Mehitabel (Cantab) [1989/90 21s 20m] workmanlike gelding: handicap hurdler: jumped badly in early stages on reappearance: stiff task next start: stays 3m: acts on soft going. *Mrs G. R. Reveley.* —

GOLDEN AZELIA 7 b.m. Jimsun–Persian Swallow (My Swallow) [1989/90 16g 16g 16s 20s a22g] small, sparely-made mare: selling hurdler: well beaten in 1989/90: races freely. *Miss S. J. Wilton.* —

GOLDEN BAVARD 9 ch.g. Le Bavard (FR)–Tamer Island (Tamer Park) [1989/90 a20g⁵ 25f³ 20g] stocky gelding: poor novice hurdler/chaser (beaten in seller over fences): looked reluctant last start: stays 2½m: acts on hard ground: occasionally blinkered: ridden in spurs last 2 outings: sold 1,000 gns Doncaster Spring Sales. *C. C. Trietline.* c— —

GOLDEN CASINO 12 ch.g. Olympic Casino–Cousin Kate (Coliseum) [1989/90 c24dᵘʳ] tall, strong gelding: runner-up in a point-to-point in February: very useful hunter chaser at his best: bit backward, unseated rider eighth at Market Rasen in March: suited by 3m: acts on any going but goes particularly well on firm. *M. Barthorpe.* c—

GOLDEN CELTIC 6 b.g. Rare One–Cooleen (Tarqogan) [1989/90 19d* 22s* 22v⁶ 22g*] workmanlike gelding: progressive hurdler who won novice events at Hereford in November and Folkestone in December and 19-runner handicap at Windsor (jumped superbly and showed much improved form to beat War Child 121 p

Mrs H. Brown's "Golden Celtic"

gamely by 1½ lengths) in March: unruly in preliminaries when well beaten at Haydock: stays 2¾m: acts on soft going: has shown a tendency to idle in front: wore crossed noseband at Windsor. *Miss H. C. Knight.*

GOLDEN COMPANION 6 b.g. Torus–Carrigart (Bargello) [1989/90 a18g6 16m] lengthy, good-quartered gelding: no form in novice hurdles: blinkered third outing and ran out next start in 1988/9. *J. C. McConnochie.* — §

GOLDEN CROFT 7 ch.g. Crofter (USA)–Rossian (Silent Spring) [1989/90 c16gF c16g c20mpu 24d6 23f*] leggy gelding: former selling hurdler: has looked temperamental, but did nothing wrong when winning amateur riders handicap at Cartmel in May: no sign of ability in novice chases: stays 23f: acts on any going: sometimes blinkered (not when successful). *D. McCain.* c— 85

GOLDEN DELICIOUS (NZ) 10 ch.g. Sugar Apple–Ima Sweetie (NZ) (Showoff) [1989/90 c26m2 c26f2] sturdy gelding: winning hurdler/chaser: second to Marshlander over fences at Bangor and Newton Abbot in August: stays 3¼m: acts on firm going and is probably unsuited by heavy: moderate jumper. *J. M. Bukovets.* c**106** x —

GOLDEN FANCY 13 ch.g. Gold Form–Our Edith (Will Somers) [1989/90 c16m4 c16m3 c24f4 c20g3 c16d5 c20f3 16g c20gF c24g4 c16g c20dpu c16g4] big gelding: handicap hurdler/chaser: on the downgrade: stays 2½m: acts on any going with possible exception of hard: has won 7 times at Perth. *C. J. T. Alexander.* c**95** d —

GOLDEN FARE 5 ch.g. Scallywag–Katie Fare (Ritudyr) [1989/90 F12m2 aF13g3] half-brother to winning chaser Fare Love (by Grey Love) and fairly useful hurdler Space Fair (by Space King): dam, a modest hunter chaser, stayed long distances: placed in NH Flat races at Bangor in October and Lingfield in December: yet to race over hurdles or fences. *R. J. Eckley.*

GOLDEN FOX 8 b.g. Tyrnavos–Red Spider (Red God) [1989/90 c21s5 c20m2 c24g4 c20m3 c24f2 c24f*] sturdy gelding: handicap hurdler: in frame in steeplechases (notably head second to Bizage Motors in valuable maiden at Ascot) prior to winning novice handicap at Ascot by 30 lengths from Ha'penny Bridge: stays 3m: suited by a sound surface: sometimes blinkered (was last 2 starts) or visored: changed hands 1,050 gns Ascot November Sales. *G. P. Enright.* c**102** —

GOLDEN FREEZE 8 b.g. Golden Love–Freezeaway (Vulgan) [1989/90 c20g2] c**162** —

Golden Freeze's season began most promisingly when he went down by only a neck, giving the race-fit Joint Sovereignty 16 lb, in the Mackeson Gold Cup at Cheltenham. He'd looked the probable winner when quickening to lead after the second last, then tired and was run out of it up the hill. Two features of his performance which boded particularly well for Golden Freeze's future were his jumping—gaining him ground at the fences on a course where he'd got no further than the sixth in the previous season's Gold Cup—and his greater amenability to restraint. Golden Freeze had looked headstrong on several occasions in 1988/9 and was usually equipped with a severe bridle. At Cheltenham, wearing only the stable's normal dropped noseband, he settled well, travelling comfortably in behind until produced to challenge approaching the third last. Thus Golden Freeze looked a serious contender for the season's leading staying chases—quoted as low as 16/1 for the Tote Cheltenham Gold Cup in some lists. But he wasn't seen out again. A leg injury sustained in preparation for the King George VI Rank Chase at Kempton on Boxing Day flared up again in mid-February and he was retired for the season. Golden Freeze's enforced rest didn't come out of turn—the Mackeson had been his twenty-eighth race in a career spanning only two and a half years. Granted a full recovery, Golden Freeze must again be on any short list for the Gold Cup. As a point of interest—no more—the same stable's Burrough Hill Lad wasn't seen out after November in the season immediately prior to his Gold Cup success.

Golden Freeze (b.g. 1982)	Golden Love (b 1967)	Above Suspicion (b 1956)	Court Martial
			Above Board
		Syncopation (b 1958)	Infatuation
			Dinkie Melody
	Freezeaway (b 1961)	Vulgan (b 1943)	Sirlan
			Vulgate
		Skateaway (br 1947)	Foroughi
			Zazzaway

Before the latest season, Golden Freeze had seemed barely to stay three miles when conditions were at all testing. Now that he settles better, he's likely to make the stayer his pedigree suggests. The sire Golden Love showed smart form over long distances on the Flat, notably in finishing second to Rock Roi in the 1971 Goodwood Cup. Grandam Skateaway won two steeplechases over four miles. The pick of her lightly-raced, now-deceased daughter Freezeaway's three previous winning foals was the staying chaser Tom Miller (by Menelek). Another foal, Chillaway, is the dam of Danny Harrold, runner-up in the Waterford Crystal Supreme Novices' Hurdle in the latest season and very much a chaser on looks. Golden Freeze, a big, rangy gelding, invariably impresses in appearance. He acts on heavy going—on his only outing on a firm surface to date Golden Freeze was pulled up after his saddle slipped early on. *Mrs J. Pitman.*

GOLDEN FRIEND 12 ch.g. Deep Run–Lady Laurel (El Gallo) [1989/90 c24g* c24s^pu c26g^6 c24d^3 c25g^3 c25f^4 c25m^4 c26f^2 c25m^3] workmanlike, rangy gelding: usually impresses in paddock: very useful chaser at his best: won slowly-run Edward Hanmer Memorial Chase (limited handicap) at Haydock in November by a length from The Thinker: creditable second to Royal Cedar in quite valuable limited handicap at Cheltenham in April: showed little interest third and fifth starts: suited by 3m +: acts on any going: blinkered once in 1984/5: moody and sometimes runs in snatches. *J. C. McConnochie.* c**145** § —

GOLDEN GIANT 5 ch.g. True Song–Catherine Rose (Floribunda) [1989/90 aF16g^2] half-brother to winning hurdler/chaser Infinity Rules and 3 Flat winners (all by Mandamus): dam won over hurdles: 12 lengths second of 7 finishers to Rocktor in NH Flat race at Southwell in November: dead. *P. D. Cundell.*

GOLDEN IMAGE 4 ch.f. Bustino–Kingston Rose (Tudor Music) [1989/90 16d^6 17g^5 a16g^3 a20g* a20g^3 a16g^2 a16g^4 20f^4] sparely-made filly: in frame over 1m on Flat: sold out of R. Smyly's stable 5,000 gns Newmarket Autumn Sales: won selling hurdle at Southwell in February (no bid): in frame in varied company afterwards: stays 2½m: acts on firm going: visored last 5 starts: consistent. *R. W. Dods.* 73

GOLDEN JUNE 8 ch.m. Undulate (USA)–Irene Louise (Match III) [1989/90 c20g^pu] selling hurdler and novice chaser: stays 2½m: acts on heavy going (has run moderately on firm). *D. C. Tucker.* c— —

Edward Hanmer Memorial Chase (Limited Handicap), Haydock— Golden Friend (No. 4) chases Charter Party over the last open ditch

GOLDEN LANTERN 7 b.g. Smartset–Swanee Mistress (My Swanee) [1989/90 16m5 16m 16d2 16d2 16f c16fur c17f3 c17mF] workmanlike gelding: poor novice hurdler/chaser: made numerous mistakes final start: will stay beyond 2m: found little fifth outing: blinkered third to sixth starts. *Mrs J. Pitman.* c86 x 88

GOLDEN LINK 12 ch.g. Golden Shields–Madame Rochas (Midsummer Night II) [1989/90 c26mpu] robust gelding: fairly useful point-to-pointer, winner 3 times in 1990: winning hunter chaser: pulled up lame in June: looks a thorough stayer: acts on soft going. *J. F. Symes.* c—

GOLDEN MADJAMBO 4 ch.c. Northern Tempest (USA)–Shercol (Monseigneur (USA)) [1989/90 16f4] leggy, sparely-made colt: maiden on Flat, stays 1¾m: wearing crossed noseband, around 5 lengths fourth to Gentleman's Jig in novice hurdle at Bangor in March, tending to edge left under pressure: should improve. *B. A. McMahon.* 86 p

GOLDEN MINSTREL 11 ch.g. Tudor Music–Ethel's Delight (Tiepolo II) [1989/90 c24f2 c24f3 c24g3 c26f2 c25d6 c25g* c24d3 c24m2 c22m3 c36gpu] useful-looking gelding: fair chaser nowadays: won conditional jockeys handicap at Cheltenham in January: ran creditably next 3 starts, including when third to Wont Be Gone Long in 2¾m John Hughes Memorial Trophy Chase (Handicap) at Liverpool: suited by around 3m: acts on any going: jumps none too fluently nowadays. *J. T. Gifford.* c124 —

GOLDEN MOSS 5 ch.g. Le Moss–Call Bird (Le Johnstan) [1989/90 16g3 16g6 16g6 20d6 16mpu a18g] lengthy, unfurnished gelding: modest novice hurdler: well beaten in valuable handicap at Southwell final start: free-going sort who'll prove best at 2m. *J. Ffitch-Heyes.* 99

GOLDEN OZY 9 br.g. Golden Love–Ozyett (Ozymandias) [1989/90 c24spu c26gur c26vpu c21spu c20m4 c25fpu c17f] big, strong gelding: second foal: dam never ran: placed in point-to-points in Ireland: no form in steeplechases: blinkered third, fourth and last outings: sold 3,000 gns Ascot June Sales. *C. L. Popham.* c—

GOLDEN REDEEMER 12 ch.g. Gold Rod–Second Redeemer (Menelek) [1989/90 c20g4 c20g4 c16g4 c20spu c25mpu] sturdy gelding: poor chaser: usually let down by his jumping: stays 25f: acts on heavy going: has won for a claimer. *R. B. Francis.* c83 x —

GOLDEN ROOTS 11 ch.g. National Trust–Opal Princess (Reverse Charge) [1989/90 c24d4] workmanlike gelding: fair winning point-to-pointer: novice hunter chaser: stays 25f. *Roger Lane.* c85 —

GOLDEN SAMPHIRE 5 b.m. Hays–Sea Shrub (Ballymore) [1989/90 16mpu 16g 20g 16d] small mare: has run poorly, including in sellers, since winning novice handicap hurdle in 1988/9: reluctant to race in 1989/90: sometimes visored: one to avoid. *M. C. Chapman.* — §

GOLDEN SCALLY 6 b.m. Scallywag–Tuneful Queen (Queen's Hussar) [1989/90 16gpu] compact, workmanlike mare: no sign of ability over hurdles, including in seller in October (sweating): headstrong: sold 1,300 gns Ascot November Sales. *C. J. Bell.* —

GOLDEN SHOON 6 ch.g. Green Shoon–Marigold (High Perch) [1989/90 20s3 20gpu 22fpu] big, lengthy gelding: brother to winning hurdler/chaser Richardstown and half-brother to novice hurdler Tudor Tulip (by Tudor Rhythm): dam half-sister to fair chaser Liscartan: no worthwhile form in novice hurdles: pulls hard. *Mrs S. Richardson.* —

GOLDEN SONATA 5 ch.g. Star Appeal–Song of Gold (Song) [1989/90 20f2 20m6 20f4 21gur 25gbd 21f4 21s3 24m] close-coupled gelding: jumped none too fluently when good third in moderately-run novice handicap hurdle at Fakenham in December: ran badly following month and not seen out again: stays 21f: best form on soft going. *S. Dow.* 102

GOLDEN SOUND 6 b.g. Goldhill–Regal Sound (Royal Palace) [1989/90 16m 17v4 16s4 22gpu] well-made, good sort: best effort over hurdles when fourth in novice handicap at Nottingham in February on third start: unlikely to stay beyond 2m: acts on soft going: trained by Mrs J. Pitman until after reappearance: sold 3,500 gns Doncaster Spring Sales. *O. Sherwood.* 85

GOLDEN STANDARD 5 ch.g. Ashford (USA)–Precious Mite (Tambourine II) [1989/90 16m4] rangy gelding: modest novice hurdler: sold out of M. Bradstock's stable 12,500 gns Doncaster August Sales: below-form fourth at Huntingdon in October: possibly unsuited by soft ground. *M. H. B. Robinson.* 82

GOLDEN SUMMER 7 ch.m. Balinger–Miss Fanackapan (Colonist II) [1989/90 16s^{ur} 16g 16m 18f^{5}] behind in NH Flat race in 1987: poor form in novice hurdles. *P. R. Hedger.* 77

GOLDEN TOPAZ 6 br.h. African Sky–Lochboisdale (Saritamer (USA)) [1989/90 16g 24d] leggy horse: poor novice hurdler: weakened 3 out in 3m selling handicap at Perth in May. *J. Parkes.* —

GOLDEN VEST 6 b.g. Sonnen Gold–Key Harvest (Deep Diver) [1989/90 16f^{5} 16g* 16m^{5} 16g] medium-sized gelding: has been hobdayed: showed much improved form when winning novice handicap hurdle at Bangor in November: creditable fifth in handicap next time, but well beaten last start (December): best at 2m: acts on good to firm going: sketchy jumper: ungenuine. *J. Mackie.* 93 §

GOLDEN VIEW (USA) 8 b.g. Mr Prospector (USA)–Sweeping View (USA) (Reviewer (USA)) [1989/90 16f^{pu} 16f^{pu}] tall, leggy gelding: ungenuine novice hurdler: failed to complete course in point-to-points in 1990. *H. Jackson.* §§

GOLDEN VINTAGE 4 ch.g. Glint of Gold–Boissiere (High Top) [1989/90 16g^{F} 16g^{F} 16f 17g 16v^{F} 16v^{4} 16d a16g^{pu}] sparely-made gelding: middle-distance maiden on Flat: easily best effort over hurdles when fourth in juvenile event at Plumpton in January: likely to stay beyond 2m: seems suited by plenty of give in the ground. *S. Dow.* 92 ?

GOLDEN WAVE 5 b.h. Glint of Gold–Grecian Sea (FR) (Homeric) [1989/90 16g 16s 20g] rather sparely-made horse: useful 1½m performer on Flat at 3 yrs, when trained by R. Hern: no sign of ability over hurdles. *R. D. E. Woodhouse.* —

GOLDEN WINGS 9 br.g. Goldhill–Great Lark (Great Captain) [1989/90 c24g^{5}] sturdy gelding: winning point-to-pointer: needed race when behind in hunter chase at Kempton in February: stays 3m: has worn blinkers. *S. N. Wilshire.* c— —

GOLDFIELDS 6 ch.g. Northfields (USA)–Laurier d'Or (Sassafras (FR)) [1989/90 20f^{5} 22g^{5} 20f^{4} 19g 21m^{3}] sparely-made gelding: poor novice hurdler: not raced after December: stays 21f: acts on hard ground: has worn crossed noseband. *Mrs T. Cuthbert.* 81

GOLDFINGER 7 ch.g. Billion (USA)–Old Hand (Master Owen) [1989/90 16g^{3} c16g^{3} c17g^{3}] angular, workmanlike gelding: poor novice hurdler: under a length third to Tom Caxton in handicap chase at Uttoxeter in December: good third to Decided in novice chase at Newbury later in month (eased once chance had gone run-in): takes good hold and likely to prove best at up to 2½m: sure to win a run-of-the-mill novice chase. *J. Pilkington.* c**102** 83

GOLD HAND 6 ch.g. Nearly A Hand–Way of Life (Homeric) [1989/90 16g 16d 20v 16m] neat gelding: well beaten in novice hurdles, though showed signs of ability second start: retained by trainer 2,000 gns Ascot June Sales. *K. C. Bailey.* —

GOLD HAVEN 6 ch.g. Pollerton–Coolbawn Lady (Laurence O) [1989/90 22s 20s 16g^{6} 21f^{4} 20g*] rather unfurnished gelding: first foal: dam behind in 2 NH Flat races in Ireland: showed ability over hurdles prior to winning maiden event at Perth in April by 4 lengths from Glenderry: stays 21f: acts on firm going. *K. C. Bailey.* 96

GOLD JUSTICE 6 b.g. Taufan (USA)–Nordic Maid (Vent du Nord) [1989/90 16g 16g 16g 16h^{3} 16m^{3} 17f^{5}] compact gelding: poor novice selling hurdler: races only at 2m: acts on hard going. *P. J. Makin.* 69

GOLD MIRAGE 11 b.g. Gold Rod–Ishka (Tribal Chief) [1989/90 c21m^{F} c16f^{4} c27g^{3}] well-made gelding: half-brother to 5f seller winners Handy Gray (by Grey Mirage) and Bloxwich Beauty (by Humdoleila): dam best at 5f: well beaten in novice chases: jumped badly second start. *Roy Robinson.* c—

GOLD 'N SOFT 6 br.m. Whistling Deer–Wine Lake (Guillaume Tell (USA)) [1989/90 16g^{4} 16g^{5} 20v^{pu} a18g^{5} 16s 17d* 16m^{4} 24g] small, workmanlike mare: won selling handicap hurdle at Newton Abbot in March (bought in 3,600 gns): stays 2½m: probably acts on any going: suitable mount for a claimer: has worn blinkers (did so at Newton Abbot) and was visored last 3 starts 1988/9. *J. G. O'Shea.* 89

GOLD OPTIONS 8 ch.g. Billion (USA)–Foggy Park (Foggy Bell) [1989/90 c16d* c16g^{F} c17m^{4} c16m^{3} c20m c16g^{2}] medium-sized gelding: fair hurdler: useful chaser: quickened well under pressure to regain lead on line when winning handicap at Ayr in December by a short head from Masnoon: clear when falling last at Market Rasen later in month (race won by High River): creditable third to Katabatic in Cheltenham Grand Annual Chase in March (jumped deliberately): c**139** —

best at 2m: acts on any going: suitable mount for inexperienced rider: usually blinkered nowadays. *J. G. FitzGerald.*

GOLD PROFIT 10 ch.m. Rubor–Night Profit (Carnival Night) [1989/90 24g^{pu} c—
22v^{pu} 24d 24h^{pu}] sturdy, lengthy mare: poor novice hurdler/chaser: stays well: —
acts on firm ground: blinkered third start: has looked temperamental. *W. G. Young.*

GOLD SERVICE 5 b.g. Glint of Gold–House Maid (Habitat) [1989/90 16d*
16s^{2} 16g^{3} 16g^{5} 21f^{2} 17h* 21f^{2} 17f^{2}] 8,400Y: tall, leggy, rather sparely-made 106
gelding: third foal: half-brother to Mona Lisa (by Henbit), awarded Princess Elizabeth Stakes: dam 7f winner at 2 yrs: won over 1½m on Flat in France in 1988 when trained by A. Fabre (behind in 1¼m race in Switzerland in February): made running to win novice hurdles at Haydock in December and Devon & Exeter in May: finished lame when 4 lengths second to Dancing River at Cartmel on final outing: soon beaten once headed fourth and fifth starts: best form at 2m: probably acts on any going: blinkered fifth outing, visored subsequently. *M. C. Pipe.*

GOLD SHAFT 7 b.g. Kambalda–Golden Goose (Prince Hansel) [1989/90 c20f^{4} c92 §
c20f^{2} c24g^{5} c25m^{3} c21m^{2}] leggy gelding: winning hurdler: modest chaser: stays —
2½m: suited by a sound surface: blinkered last 3 outings: faint-hearted. *J. T. Gifford.*

GOLDSPIC 7 ch.g. Spanish Gold–Spic And Span (Crisp And Even) [1989/90
21m^{pu}] second foal: dam half-sister to good Italian performer De Hooch: 100/1, —
tailed off when pulled up 2 out in novice hurdle at Devon & Exeter in September on debut. *N. H. Davis.*

GOLD STRATA 4 b.g. Gold Song–French Strata (USA) (Permian (USA))
[1989/90 16s^{pu}] lengthy gelding: no sign of ability on Flat: tailed off when pulled —
up 3 out in juvenile hurdle at Plumpton: sold 1,000 gns Ascot April Sales. *J. White.*

GOLD TINT 5 b.g. Glint of Gold–Doobie Do (Derring-Do) [1989/90 20f* 16g^{2}
17g^{2} a20g* 22g^{5} 20d^{pu} a20g^{5} 16s^{pu} 20m^{3} a20g^{pu}] smallish, leggy gelding: 107
front-running handicap hurdler: successful at Plumpton in August and Southwell in November: ridden along from before halfway when 3 lengths third to Haddon Lad at Plumpton in April: gives impression will prove best at up to 2½m: probably acts on any going: usually blinkered. *T. P. McGovern.*

GOLD TOUCH 7 b.g. Strong Gale–Nordic Maid (Vent du Nord) [1989/90 16d]
lightly-raced maiden on Flat: pulled hard when tailed off in novice hurdle at —
Windsor in January: sold 3,100 gns Ascot May Sales. *P. J. Makin.*

GOLD VALLEY 8 ch.g. Goldhill–Billy's Beauty (Arapaho) [1989/90 c16g^{5} c70
c26f^{5}] ex-Irish gelding: won a point-to-point in March: novice hurdler/chaser: —
poor form in hunter chases in April and May: sold out of J. J. Gordon's stable 3,000 gns Doncaster August Sales. *Mrs N. Bolingbroke-Kent.*

GOLFER'S SUNRISE 5 b.g. Red Sunset–Miss Stradavinsky (Auction Ring
(USA)) [1989/90 16m^{3} 16m^{6} 16g 16m 16d* 16g^{5} 16f^{5}] small gelding: finds little 74 §
under pressure and was well ridden by A. Charlton when winning conditional jockeys selling hurdle at Ludlow in March (bought in 3,400 gns): withdrawn lame intended last outing: not sure to stay further than 2m: acts on dead going: pulls hard and has worn crossed noseband: inconsistent. *K. White.*

GOMEZ 6 b. or br.g. Formidable (USA)–Alpine Niece (Great Nephew) [1989/90
25m^{pu}] compact gelding: of little account. *R. W. Dods.* —

GO MILETRIAN 6 b.g. Sonnen Gold–Chestnut Hill (Sassafras (FR)) [1989/90
16g 16d 22d^{pu}] compact, workmanlike gelding: first foal: half-brother to winning —
sprinter in Italy by Vaigly Great: dam, winning staying hurdler, half-sister to several winners, including smart hurdler/winning chaser Major Thompson: behind in novice hurdles: unlikely to stay 2¾m: sold 1,650 gns Ascot April Sales. *D. R. Gandolfo.*

GONE ASTRAY 5 ch.m. The Parson–Merry Missus (Bargello) [1989/90 16g
20m^{6} 22d^{3} 20m] close-coupled mare: only worthwhile form in novice hurdles 75
when third at Kelso in February. *F. T. Walton.*

GO NOBLEY 4 b.g. Gorytus (USA)–Noblanna (USA) (Vaguely Noble)
[1989/90 16s^{pu} 18g^{6} 16m^{6} 16d^{5} a20g* a20g* a18g* a20g* 20f^{F} a20g^{3}] small 115
gelding: well beaten on Flat: easy winner of 4 novice hurdles at Lingfield (claimer ridden on third occasion): also claimer ridden when showing much improved form to finish third in handicap at Southwell in April (was running well when falling previous start): likely to stay beyond 2½m. *T. Thomson Jones.*

GONZO'S PET 9 b.m. Rymer–Sweet Sensation (Menelek) [1989/90 16fpu 22gF 20g 20gur 20d 17d 16f] sparely-made mare: first foal: dam unplaced in novice hurdles: little sign of ability over hurdles, including in sellers: sold 1,500 gns Doncaster Spring Sales. *T. D. Walford.* —

GOODASNEW 7 b.g. Godswalk (USA)–Fast Motion (Midsummer Night II) [1989/90 20g6 c20vpu 21d 20gpu 20vpu] sparely-made, close-coupled gelding: shows traces of stringhalt: modest form in 2 novice hurdles in 1987/8: well beaten in 1989/90: jumped poorly and was tailed off when pulled up on chasing debut: probably stays 2½m: blinkered last 3 starts. *P. J. Hobbs.* c— —

GOOD CAUSE 6 ch.h. Kris–Goodwin Sands (USA) (Vaguely Noble) [1989/90 20f5 21f* 22mbd 20dpu 20m 22g 18s* 20d 18f4 a18gF] sparely-made horse: inconsistent handicap hurdler: won at Ludlow in October and Fontwell in January: creditable fourth on latter course in March: stays 21f (reportedly broke blood vessel over 23f): acts on any going. *Miss S. J. Wilton.* 107

GOODFELLOW'S FOLLY 12 br.m. New Brig–Thrupence (Royal Highway) [1989/90 20h3 c20h2 24g5] small, lightly-made mare: modest chaser and novice hurdler: first run for 7½ months, well beaten last start: needs at least 2½m and stays well: acts on any going: sold out of I. Jordon's stable 8,000 gns Doncaster August Sales. *P. F. Craggs.* c96 73

GOOD FOR THE ROSES 4 b.g. Kampala–Alleyn (Alcide) [1989/90 16f4 a16g4] leggy gelding: plating class at up to 1¼m on Flat: fourth in juvenile hurdles at Leicester in November and Lingfield in December. *G. A. Pritchard-Gordon.* 74

GOOD HOLIDAYS 4 b.f. Good Times (ITY)–Mistress Bowen (Owen Anthony) [1989/90 16g] small filly: plating-class maiden on Flat, stays 7f: sold out of M. James's stable 1,050 gns Ascot October Sales: well beaten in claiming hurdle at Wolverhampton in February. *D. Burchell.* —

GOOD MOOD 5 b.g. Jalmood (USA)–Key of The Kingdom (Grey Sovereign) [1989/90 16m* 17m2 16f3 16g3 16gpu 16g 16g 16g3] smallish, rather sparely-made gelding: hung under pressure when winning novice hurdle at Perth in August: fair third in novice handicap at Sedgefield final start (December): will stay further than 2m: acts on soft and good to firm going: claimer ridden: blinkered sixth start. *I. Semple.* 87

GOOD MORROW JACK 5 br.g. Ballymore–Rifflealp (Sterling Bay (SWE)) [1989/90 F16g 22dpu c21dpu] smallish, angular ex-Irish gelding: second foal: dam won over 6f and 7f in Ireland: failed to complete course in 3 point-to-points in 1989 (twice slipped up): behind in NH Flat race in September when trained by T. Walshe: tailed off when pulled up in novice hurdle at Kelso in February and novice chase at Market Rasen in March. *L. J. Codd.* c— —

GOOD N SHARP 9 br.g. Mummy's Pet–Sharp Lady (Sharpen Up) [1989/90 16f3 16f3 16f3] leggy, sparely-made gelding: won over 1m on Flat in 1989: lightly-raced novice hurdler: placed in sellers early in season: best form at 2m on firm ground: seems none too genuine: sold 1,600 gns Doncaster January Sales. *Mrs G. R. Reveley.* 85

GOOD POINT 6 b.g. Try My Best (USA)–Point Gammon (USA) (Bold Lad (USA)) [1989/90 16m 16d 16s a16g6 20d6 a20gpu] neat gelding: very useful plater over hurdles in 1988/9 (reportedly broke blood vessel final start): poor form in non-selling handicaps in 1989/90: successful on good to firm going but best run at 2m on soft: usually held up. *R. W. Hartop.* 90

GOOD SAILING 6 b.m. Scorpio (FR)–Mother of The Wind (Tumble Wind (USA)) [1989/90 21m 21fpu 16f] lengthy, robust mare: novice hurdler: well beaten in 1989/90: takes a good hold: sold 8,200 gns Doncaster January Sales. *Mrs D. Haine.* —

GOOD SEOUL 6 b.g. Good Times (ITY)–Olympic Visualise (Northfields (USA)) [1989/90 17g] workmanlike gelding: poor form in novice hurdles (backward, tailed off in January): pulled up in 3 point-to-points. *Miss C. J. E. Caroe.* —

GOODSHOT RICH 6 b.g. Roscoe Blake–Hunter's Treasure (Tudor Treasure) [1989/90 16f4 20g* 22mpu] well-made, chasing type: brother to winning jumper Roscoe Harvey and half-brother to NH Flat race winner Snow Bounder (by Broxted): dam, 1m winner, very useful hurdler: showed promise in novice hurdle in November and 5 months later won similar event at Perth by 12 lengths: stiffish task, ran poorly final outing: stays 2½m. *C. P. E. Brooks.* 117

GOOD SPARK 4 b. or br.g. Good Times (ITY)–Bright Spark (White Fire III) [1989/90 16m2 16m* 16m 16g* 16s2 16g* 16d* 16d2 16f2] compact ex-Irish 121 gelding: eighth foal: half-brother to winners in Belgium and Norway: dam poor half-sister to smart animals Ovaltine and Guillotina: won over 1½m on Flat (has run blinkered): took well to hurdling and won juvenile events at Windsor and Folkestone, novice event at Plumpton and quite valuable juvenile race at Warwick (beat General Pershing 1½ lengths): also ran well afterwards: unlikely to stay much beyond 2m at present: probably acts on any going: jumps well in the main: usually forces pace: claimer ridden: trained first start by N. Meade. *R. Akehurst.*

GOOD TONIC 7 b.g. Goldhill–Quinine's Girl (Deep Run) [1989/90 16m c20s[2] c16g* c16g[4] c18v[F] c16s[4] c17g* c16m*] workmanlike gelding: winning hurdler: successful over fences in novice events at Windsor, Kelso and Towcester, best effort when beating Georgic by 8 lengths on last-named course in April: effective at 2m and stays 2½m: acts on heavy and good to firm going: goes well with forcing tactics: usually jumps well: should win more races. *T. J. Etherington.* c**109** p —

GOOD TO SEE YOU 12 ch.g. Deep Run–Our Dream (Chamier) [1989/90 20d[3] 20s[3]] sturdy gelding: carries plenty of condition: winning hurdler/chaser: third in selling handicap hurdles at Sedgefield in January and February: off course over 2 years previously: suited by a thorough test of stamina: acts on any going: moderate jumper of fences. *Mrs S. M. Austin.* c— x 91

GOOD WATERS 10 b. or br.g. Paddy's Stream–Good Surprise (Maelsheachlainn) [1989/90 c24d[pu] c25g c25f c24d] close-coupled gelding: won 2 novice chases in first half of 1988/9: has shown nothing since: stays well: acts on dead going: amateur ridden: jumps soundly in the main. *S. Christian.* c—

GOOD WORD 8 ch.g. Proverb–Good Calx (Khalkis) [1989/90 24d] lengthy, workmanlike gelding: modest novice hurdler: backward when tailed off in March: brought down in novice chase in 1988/9: should stay beyond 2¾m. *Mrs S. Armytage.* c— —

GOODWYNS LAD 6 b.g. Homing–Someone Talked (USA) (Barbizon) [1989/90 19m[pu] 16f 24g 22m 17d c20d[4] c16v[pu] c24d[5] c17m[pu]] small, sparely-made gelding: fair hurdler as a juvenile: little recent form: poor novice chaser: form over hurdles only at 2m: acts on soft going: visored final outing 1987/8 and on eighth start 1988/9. *A. Barrow.* c74 —

GO RABALL GO 4 br.g. All Systems Go–Rabeeb (Home Guard (USA)) [1989/90 16f[ur]] small, sparely-made gelding: inconsistent winner at up to 7f on Flat: in rear when unseating rider second in novice hurdle at Wolverhampton in March: sold to race in Scandinavia 2,100 gns Doncaster March Sales. *C. N. Allen.* —

GORSE HUNTER 7 ch.g. Bivouac–Joyous Day (Lord of Verona) [1989/90 F16g[6] a20g[2] a24g[4] 21f[3] 24g*] lengthy gelding: seventh foal: dam, novice hurdler, comes from a successful jumping family: in frame in novice hurdles prior to winning amateur riders handicap at Perth in April by 2½ lengths from Bonnie Dundee: stays 3m: acts on firm going. *P. J. Hobbs.* 93

GO SILLY 4 b.g. Silly Prices–Allez Stanwick (Goldhill) [1989/90 F16d] second reported foal: brother to poor and probably temperamental novice hurdler Willie Butt: dam won on Flat and over jumps: behind in NH Flat race at Catterick in February: yet to race over hurdles. *Miss S. Williamson.*

GO SOUTH 6 b.g. Thatching–Run To The Sun (Run The Gantlet (USA)) [1989/90 20m* 20f[3]] medium-sized gelding: won novice hurdle at Worcester in September: would have finished second but for mistake 2 out in race won by Picador at Cheltenham following month: won twice at up to 2m on Flat subsequently: stays 2½m: probably acts on any going: usually blinkered: has looked none too keen on occasions (including at Worcester). *J. R. Jenkins.* 96 §

GOSPEL ROCK (NZ) 6 br.g. Church Parade–Leopard Rock (NZ) (Rocky Mountain (FR)) [1989/90 20g[ro]] big, workmanlike gelding: bit backward, pulled hard and in lead when running out fourth in novice hurdle at Wetherby in January. *P. Calver.* —

GOULD'S DELIGHT 4 b.f. Deep Roots–Brun's Toy (FR) (Bruni) [1989/90 a16g[F]] little sign of ability on Flat: fell second in selling hurdle at Southwell in May. *R. F. Marvin.* —

GOWAN HOUSE 11 gr.g. Pongee–Carbia (Escart III) [1989/90 c22f[4] c16m[5] c20f* c20f* c20g[3] c20g[ur] c20g[5] c20s[4] 16m c20m[6] c20h[2] c18h[ur]] small, sturdy gelding: fair chaser: won at Cheltenham and Newcastle in October: was effective from 2m to 21f: acted on any going: was sometimes claimer or amateur ridden: moderate jumper: trained until after fifth outing by W. A. Stephenson: dead. *N. A. Gaselee.* c**124** x —

GO WEST 6 b.g. Akarad (FR)–Western Goddess (Red God) [1989/90 c16g c24v3 c16v2 c17d* c20d5 c17d* c16f*] workmanlike gelding: fair hurdler: won novice chases at Newbury, Newton Abbot and Towcester, beating Georgic 6 lengths on last-named course in March: best form at around 2m: acts on any going: visored fourth start, blinkered all other outings: jumps soundly and should win more races over fences. *M. C. Pipe.* c**110** p —

GO WIN GOLD 5 b.m. Sonnen Gold–Gowyn (Goldhill) [1989/90 16spu 16d] workmanlike mare: placed in juvenile hurdles: no form in novice events in January (blinkered second start): likely to prove best at 2m. *M. H. Easterby.* —

GRAAL LEGEND 5 br.h. Cosmo–Lysippe (Spartan General) [1989/90 F16g5] second foal: dam poor novice hurdler/chaser: over 20 lengths fifth of 17 to Storm Island in NH Flat race at Perth in May: yet to race over hurdles or fences. *W. A. Stephenson.*

GRABEL 7 b.m. Bold Owl–Gay Dawn (Gay Fandango) [1989/90 16f4 20g* 19d* 16d* 16v* 22f*] 161

The Irish mare Grabel became one of jumping's biggest money winners, more than doubling her career earnings at a stroke, when she rounded off a magnificent season by taking the first running of the Dueling Grounds International Hurdle in April. The race, offering a total purse of 620,000 dollars, with 300,000 dollars (around £184,000) to the winner and prizes down to seventh, was the most valuable put on to mark the opening of the new turf track in south-west Kentucky. Despite the absence of one-time probables Barnbrook Again and Beech Road, the European challenge was a strong one and outnumbered the home contingent five to four—Grabel, Nomadic Way, Regal Ambition, the ex-New Zealand Valrodian and the French horse Collins against the Grade 1 Flat winner Uptown Swell, Polar Pleasure, Summer Colony and the ex-British Peer Prince. On his second in the Champion Hurdle Nomadic Way would almost certainly have started favourite had the race been run in Britain and he did so, at 22/10, under American conditions with the brush obstacles, a cross between hurdles and fences; Grabel was fifth in the betting at 78/10. Grabel arrived late at the course after a much-delayed journey and had her first school only the day

Bookmakers Hurdle, Leopardstown—
Grabel (right) loses the lead to Elementary at the last,
but she fights back on the run-in

before the race. In the race they went too fast for her to lie up in third early on as planned, but she was able to move forward going down the far side on the last circuit and was well in contention on the final turn, where the long-time leader Regal Ambition still led. It was on this turn that Regal Ambition broke down badly and Grabel burst to the front with two fences left. Challenged strongly by Uptown Swell soon after, she held on gamely under pressure to win by a little over two lengths. The going took its toll. Nomadic Way, the next European finisher in a distant sixth, sprained a near-fore joint badly, while Regal Ambition broke down on both forelegs. Collins, also pulled up lame, was found to have rapped himself.

Grabel has been near the top of the tree over hurdles in Ireland ever since her juvenile days, when she finished third in the Daily Express Triumph Hurdle. If she had a superior there in 1989/90 it was Elementary, whom she came back well to beat narrowly, receiving the 5-lb mares' allowance, in the Bookmakers Hurdle at Leopardstown late in December. That race marked the end of a long year in which she'd had her summer break postponed in order to go for a couple of good prizes on the Flat (she finished fourth in the Queen Alexandra Stakes on the first occasion) and the Guinness Galway Handicap Hurdle (she finished fourth in that, too). Between Galway and Leopardstown she went unbeaten through a less-exacting stayers' Flat race at Gowran Park, the Morgiana Hurdle at Punchestown and a handicap hurdle at Naas. Grabel's first big target in the new year was the Waterford Crystal Champion Hurdle. However, shortly after a very easy victory at 4/1 on in the S. P. Graham Ulster Champion Trial at Down Royal in mid-February she was found to have a blocked sinus and couldn't be made ready in time for Cheltenham. In fact, she had no further outing before Kentucky.

Grabel (apparently the name should have been Grable, after the 'forties film star Betty) fetched only 1,000 guineas as a two-year-old at the Doncaster Sales. She's the first foal and only winner of the unraced Gay Dawn, a daughter of the useful Irish middle-distance filly Slap Up. The third

Mr P. F. Kehoe's "Grabel"

Grabel (b.m. 1983)	Bold Owl (b 1976)	Bold Lad (b 1964)	Bold Ruler
			Barn Pride
		Tawny Owl (ch 1968)	Faberge II
			Owlet
	Gay Dawn (ro 1978)	Gay Fandango (ch 1972)	Forli
			Gay Violin
		Slap Up (gr 1972)	Gala Performance
			Immaculate

dam, a maiden raced only as a two-year-old, produced eleven winners spread over half the world's horse-racing countries, one of that eleven being the hurdler/chaser Star Performance, quite useful at his best who won over jumps in Britain and Ireland. Grabel is workmanlike in appearance and performance, very versatile as far as distance, ground and track are concerned. She's effective at two miles to two and three quarter miles, acts on any going and, though she's a prolific winner at Punchestown, clearly acts on any type of track. She's genuine, too—all in all a credit to the stable who not so long ago had the cruel luck to lose that other grand mare Dawn Run. *P. Mullins, Ireland.*

GRACE BECK 5 b.m. Tepukei–Kalrosa (Kalydon) [1989/90 20g 20g4 16g 20gF a20gsu 16dpu 16mF] smallish, workmanlike mare: no sign of ability in novice hurdles: blinkered fifth and sixth starts. *P. Beaumont.* —

GRACE CARD 4 b.g. Ela-Mana-Mou–Val de Grace (FR) (Val de Loir) [1989/90 aF16g* F16g4] half-brother to several winners, including Gracefully, dam of Prix de Diane winner Lypharita: dam, 10.5f winner, from good French family: won NH Flat race at Southwell in February: around 11 lengths fourth to General Idea in quite valuable similar event at Phoenix Park in May: runner-up in 2m maiden on Flat in between: yet to race over hurdles. *R. Hollinshead.*

GRACE MOORE 6 b.m. Deep Run–Super Cailin (Brave Invader (USA)) [1989/90 17m4 17h* 22f5 16h3 16g3 19g2 21f2 21v3 21v5 22d 22g] small mare: won novice handicap hurdle at Devon & Exeter in October: placed 5 times afterwards: should stay beyond 21f: acts on any going: blinkered fourth and fifth starts: jumps none too fluently: unreliable and probably ungenuine. *K. Bishop.* 85 §

GRACIE JAY 7 ch.m. Amboise–Song of Grace (Articulate) [1989/90 20g3] third foal: dam lightly-raced daughter of a winning hurdler/chaser: unseated rider first and refused first in 2 point-to-points in April: 6½ lengths third to Stroked Again in mares novice hurdle at Market Rasen in June. *T. Thomson Jones.* 79 p

GRAFTON MAISEY 11 br.m. Jimsun–Amore (ITY) (Kashmir II) [1989/90 c24dpu 20s 26v6 a24g5 22g 22mur] sturdy mare: winning hunter chaser (sometimes let down by her jumping): handicap hurdler: well beaten in 1989/90: suited by a good test of stamina: acts on heavy going: wears a crossed noseband: has won when sweating: seems best ridden up with the pace. *A. J. Mason.* c— —

GRANARY GRAIN 4 b.g. Deep Run–Poula Scawla (Pollerton) [1989/90 F16d3] second foal: dam unraced half-sister to 3 winning jumpers, notably useful hurdler/chaser Mac's Chariot: 15 lengths third behind Cab On Target in NH Flat race at Kelso in February: yet to race over hurdles. *J. S. Wilson.*

GRANDANGUS 7 b.g. Creetown–Woolcana (Some Hand) [1989/90 16gpu 16dpu] workmanlike gelding: behind in novice hurdle in 1987/8 and when pulled up in similar events in 1989/90. *Mrs A. Knight.* —

GRAND CELEBRATION (USA) 8 ch.g. Monteverdi–Blackfly (USA) (Mount Marcy) [1989/90 a20g3 a20spu] small, close-coupled, sparely-made gelding: poor novice hurdler: blinkered third outing 1988/9: dead. *P. R. Dunstan.* —

GRAND CHANCE 7 ch.g. Vaigly Great–Queen Maeve (Connaught) [1989/90 16m] workmanlike, good-quartered gelding: second in novice hurdle 1988: bit backward, weakened from 2 out in January: form only at 2m. *Grenville Richards.* —

GRAND EDOUARD 7 ch.g. Rare One–Lady Mobile (Cracksman) [1989/90 F16m6 c25dF c16fF 22spu 22s] big, angular gelding: no sign of ability: sold 1,450 gns Ascot April Sales. *J. P. D. Elliott.* c— —

GRAND HARBOUR 10 br.g. Dragonara Palace (USA)–Top of The Tree (Lorenzaccio) [1989/90 16spu] one-time fairly useful performer around 1m on Flat: tailed off when pulled up 4 out in novice event at Nottingham in February on hurdling debut. *R. Champion.* —

GRAND INQUISITOR 8 b.g. Pry–Sassenach Girl (Sassafras (FR)) [1989/90 20m⁶ c24gpu c25m⁴ c32f c24f] rather leggy ex-Irish gelding: poor maiden hurdler/chaser: won point-to-point in 1989: should be suited by a thorough test of stamina: tends to sweat: trained by E. Harty until after reappearance. *G. B. Balding.* c75 —

GRAND LOU 4 b.f. Joshua–Grand Melody (Song) [1989/90 16gpu] fifth foal: half-sister to a winning point-to-pointer by Gambling Debt: dam showed no ability: tailed off when pulled up fifth in novice hurdle at Plumpton in January. *G. Ripley.* —

GRAND OCCASION 8 b.m. Great Nephew–All Hail (Alcide) [1989/90 a16g a20g² a16g] plating-class maiden on Flat in 1985: best effort over hurdles when 1½ lengths second to Rose of Peace in 2½m seller at Lingfield in February. *D. T. Thom.* 65

GRAND PARTY 5 ch.m. Revlow–Grand Melody (Song) [1989/90 16gur] sparely-made mare: half-sister to winning point-to-pointer Unbeatable Tipp-Ex (by Gambling Debt): very lightly-raced maiden on Flat: 100/1 and in need of race, unseated rider second in conditional jockeys claimer at Worcester in December on hurdling debut. *J. M. Bradley.* —

GRAND VALUE 7 ch.g. Kambalda–Candy Slam (Candy Cane) [1989/90 c24m⁴ c20f* c24h* c26g³ c24f* c26m* c24mF] leggy gelding: won handicap chases at Uttoxeter and Carlisle in September, Ludlow (amateur riders) in October and Uttoxeter in November: beaten when falling heavily at the last in November: not seen out again: stays well: acts on firm going. *D. McCain.* c**110** —

GRANEMORE 4 br.c. Millfontaine–Polyxo (Polyfoto) [1989/90 a16g] small, lightly-made colt: plating-class maiden on Flat, stays 7f: blinkered, tailed-off last in juvenile hurdle at Southwell in November. *P. A. Blockley.* —

GRANGE EXPRESS 6 b.m. Buckskin (FR)–Grange Hansel (Prince Hansel) [1989/90 16g 22dpu] rather leggy, lengthy mare: fourth reported foal: half-sister to winning hurdler/chaser Lord Laurence (by Laurence O): dam won 2 point-to-points in Ireland: no sign of ability in 2 novice hurdles. *D. R. Gandolfo.* —

GRANGE OF GLORY 9 ch.g. Hittite Glory–Neptune's Daughter (Neptunus) [1989/90 c25mur c27f* c24fr 24d 20d 24dpu] small gelding: novice hurdler: pulled up in seller final start: won handicap chase at Sedgefield in September (remounted after straddling last fence and unseating rider): refused first on next outing: stays 27f: acts on firm and dead going: has run creditably for a claimer: isn't one to trust implicitly. *J. A. Hellens.* c83 ? —

GRANGE RUN 10 b.g. Deep Run–Ballyfin Perpetual (Milan) [1989/90 c26mF] angular gelding: behind in 2 novice hurdles in 1984: has since won a point-to-point: behind when falling fifth in hunter chase in June. *M. Stephenson.* c— —

GRANNY PRAY ON 8 ch.m. Proverb–My Copper (Sunacelli) [1989/90 c17dbd c16gF c17g⁴ c22d c26vpu 21dbd c21s² c18s c21g³] sparely-made, angular mare: winning hurdler: poor novice chaser: should stay beyond 21f: acts on heavy going: tends to sweat. *N. R. Mitchell.* c83 —

GRANNY'S BAY 7 b.g. Tycoon II–Lorien Wood (Precipice Wood) [1989/90 c16m²] sparely-made gelding: modest hurdler: shaped well when going down by a length to Espy in novice event at Nottingham in November on chasing debut, leading 3 out until close home: best over hurdles at around 2½m under testing conditions: has run well for a claimer: looked sure to improve and win a race over fences, but wasn't seen out again. *D. McCain.* c99 —

GRANNY'S PRAYER 9 br.g. Boreen (FR)–Ace Blue (Pardal) [1989/90 c20mur c24gpu c24gpu c22d⁴ c24d⁵] big, workmanlike gelding: tubed: one-time useful hurdler: fourth at Kelso in February, easily best effort in novice chases: stays 2¾m: acts on any going. *J. J. O'Neill.* c93 —

GRANVILLE PARK 9 b.g. Giolla Mear–Cherry Leaf (Vulgan) [1989/90 c20d* c20g c20d⁶] leggy gelding: modest hurdler: won hunter chase at Newbury in February by 1½ lengths from Hand Over: ran moderately afterwards: stays 25f, at least when conditions aren't testing: yet to show he acts on extremes of going: sometimes sweats and tends to be on toes. *Robert Goodall.* c**110** —

GRANYTE PALACE 6 b.g. Royal Palace–Aequanimitas (Infatuation) [1989/90 16g⁵ 20f⁵] good sort: third in NH Flat race in 1987/8: lightly-raced novice over hurdles: first outing for 2½ months, weakened 3 out over 2½m. *J. T. Gifford.* 80

GRATIFICATION 13 br.g. Gala Performance (USA)–Bright Record (Royal Record II) [1989/90 c25m c24fur] lengthy, deep-girthed gelding: won a point-to-point in April: very useful hunter chaser/fair handicapper on his day, but c— § —

is temperamental and best left alone: stays 25f: acts on any going: has won with and without blinkers. *C. J. R. Sweeting.*

GRAVITY FORCE 6 ch.g. Henbit (USA)–Gradiva (Lorenzaccio) [1989/90 16f^4 16d^5 a16g^3 a16g 16f 16g^6 16m^6] sparely-made gelding: poor novice hurdler: variable form: finished lame in selling handicap last start. *J. L. Harris.* 86 d

GRAYROSE DOUBLE 7 b.m. Celtic Cone–Mangro (Mandamus) [1989/90 20f* 20m* 19f* 20f^3 25h^3 25f*^{dis} 20f^5 c16d^5 c20m a24g^5 21f 24g^6 19m^2 20g^4] smallish, workmanlike mare: passed post first in early-season novice hurdle at Bangor and handicaps at Bangor, Hereford and Cheltenham (showed improved form but disqualified due to prohibited substance): jumped to her right when well beaten in novice chases in December (will be suited by further): stays 3m: acts on any going: good mount for a claimer. *E. H. Owen jun.* c— 93

GREAT ASPECT 6 b. or br.g. Great Nephew–Broad Horizon (Blakeney) [1989/90 16f] compact, sturdy gelding: has been fired: won 2 novice hurdles in 1988/9: ran well long way but finished lame when well beaten in valuable handicap at Cheltenham in March: will stay 2½m: probably acts on any going. *K. White.* —

GREAT AUNT SALLY 9 ch.m. Scallywag–Auntie Grace (Great Nephew) [1989/90 22m 24g^{pu} 20d^{pu} 21d 24g] workmanlike mare: novice hurdler: well beaten in 1989/90: stays 21f: acts on any going: has worn a crossed noseband: often claimer ridden 1986/7. *T. N. Bailey.* —

GREAT LAW 5 b.g. Glint of Gold–Bedfellow (Crepello) [1989/90 F16f^5 F17m 16f^4 16g^6 16g^4 16d^3 17m 16h* 16f^3 16g^2 17f^5] big, rangy, chasing type with plenty of scope: sixth foal: closely related to 17f Flat winner Bedhead (by Shirley Heights) and half-brother to useful Italian winner Blood King (by Silly Season) and 13f winner Major Setback (by Brigadier Gerard): dam, half-sister to Oaks winner Polygamy and Cheshire Oaks winner One Over Parr, stayed at least 1½m: all out to land the odds in poor novice hurdle at Hexham in April: creditable second at Newcastle 2 outings later: will be very well suited by further than 2m: best form with give in the ground: type to progress. *W. A. Stephenson.* 91 p

GREAT MORNING 6 b.g. Ovac (ITY)–Topsider (Windjammer (USA)) [1989/90 22m c20v^{ur} c24g^6] rangy ex-Irish gelding: fourth foal: dam showed little at 2 yrs: won handicap hurdle at Down Royal in 1988/9: behind in similar event at Wincanton in December: tailed off in novice chase at Worcester in March: stays 2¾m: acts on soft going. *Miss E. Sneyd.* c— —

GREAT POKEY 5 b. or br.g. Uncle Pokey–Mekhala (Menelek) [1989/90 F16d^6 F16g] fifth foal: half-brother to novice hurdler Kiri's Song (by True Song): dam won 2m novice chase: well beaten in NH Flat races in second half of season: yet to race over hurdles or fences. *A. S. Corner.*

GREAT SCOTT (FR) 8 b.g. Bolkonski–Agostina (USA) (Delta Judge) [1989/90 16f^{pu}] tall, close-coupled gelding: 9f winner on Flat at 3 yrs: behind when pulled up 2 out in novice event at Catterick in October on hurdling debut. *A. D. Brown.* —

GREAT STANDS BY 6 br.g. Welsh Captain–Same Date (Mandamus) [1989/90 18g^{pu} c20m^F 16g^{pu} a20g^5] smallish, plain gelding: probably of little account. *P. Butler.* c— —

GREAT WATER 8 br.g. Lochnager–Maxie's Melody (Tudor Melody) [1989/90 20g^{pu} 16v^{pu}] of little account: sold 1,050 gns Doncaster January Sales. *D. T. Garraton.* —

GREAT WISHFORD 10 br.m. Laggards Lane–Last Bequest (Bounteous) [1989/90 c17g^{pu} 21f^{pu}] pulled up all 3 outings over jumps. *G. C. Doidge.* c— —

GRECIAN JOS 6 b.g. Joshua–Grecian Cloud (Galivanter) [1989/90 20f 24m^2 24m^{pu}] compact, workmanlike gelding: only form over hurdles second in 3m handicap at Worcester in September: dead. *R. J. Eckley.* 71

GREEK LOVER 5 b.g. Mandalus–Smashing Lady (Ballyciptic) [1989/90 F16h^{su} F16f^5 16g] good-bodied gelding: third foal: dam poor Irish maiden: pulled hard when fifth of 7 in NH Flat race at Wetherby in October: always behind in novice hurdle on same course in December. *W. A. Stephenson.* —

GREENACRES LAD 7 ch.g. Billion (USA)–Moon Lady (Cash And Courage) [1989/90 20f^6] leggy, sparely-made gelding: won novice hurdle in 1988/9: behind in handicap at Doncaster only outing of 1989/90 (December): likely to prove best at around 2m for time being: acts on dead going. *B. A. McMahon.* —

GREEN ARCHER 7 b.g. Hardgreen (USA)–Mittens (Run The Gantlet (USA)) [1989/90 c20g^4 c24d^5 20d^2 22s] smallish gelding: handicap hurdler: good c86 117

second at Sedgefield in January: not fluent but showed ability in novice chases at Hexham in November and December: stays 3m: yet to race on very firm ground, acts on any other. *Mrs J. R. Ramsden.*

GREENBANK PARK 13 ch.g. Twilight Alley–Rustella (Silver Kumar) [1989/90 c26m* c24g4 c25g5 c29spu c27vpu c25m4 c36gpu] lightly-made, angular gelding: moderate chaser nowadays: won amateur riders handicap at Uttoxeter in December: well beaten most subsequent outings: very well suited by a good test of stamina: acts on good to firm and heavy going: has run creditably in blinkers: tends to jump to the right: has twice run out. *R. A. H. Perkins.* c**108** —

GREEN BRAMBLE 13 b.g. Green Shoon–Bardicate (Bargello) [1989/90 c24g3 c20dur c25mpu c24mur c24mpu] big gelding: one-time very useful chaser: needed race when third in hunter chase at Kempton (jumped left throughout) in February: well clear when unseating rider at the last in similar race at Huntingdon in May, fourth outing: needs further than 2m and stays 25f: probably acts on any going: probably best on left-handed tracks. *N. J. Henderson.* c**100** ? —

GREEN DOORS 6 b.g. Swing Easy (USA)–Rouge Song (Saintly Song) [1989/90 aF16g 16f5 a16g] sparely-made gelding: no sign of ability: sold 1,000 gns Ascot July Sales. *P. A. Pritchard.* —

GREEN GORSE 10 br.g. Green Shoon–Gorteen (Straight Deal) [1989/90 c25g c24g3 c24dpu] sturdy, good-bodied gelding: winning chaser: creditable last of 3 finishers at Kelso in March: suited by 3m: probably acts on any going: jumps boldly and well in the main: claimer ridden nowadays. *C. W. Thornton.* c**101** —

GREENHEART 7 br.g. Green Shoon–Giollaretta (Giolla Mear) [1989/90 c20f2 c16f* c20f* c16f* c16f2 c17m* c16g* c16g* c17fF4 c16m* c16d6 c16f* c16m2] c**139** —

Greenheart might not have turned up at the big meetings of Cheltenham and Liverpool, but, make no mistake, he was one of the best novice chasers of the season, a horse who could well have gone close in the Arkle Trophy and the Perrier Jouet Novices' Chase (both run under fast conditions) had he been fit at the time. That's always assuming, of course, that he'd have coped with the fences, a fairly large assumption where Cheltenham is concerned. A bold, sometimes reckless jumper, Greenheart was absent for much of the season after he'd come a cropper at the second-last fence in the Freebooter Novices' Chase at Doncaster early in December. At the time he seemed to have the measure of Antinous (who conceded 4 lb) and looked set for victory by some four or five lengths, but he simply overjumped the fence, one of the easier of the none-too-demanding obstacles at Doncaster, and buckled on landing. He was remounted some time later to claim fourth. Even by that stage of the season it was clear that Greenheart had the potential to go far as a novice chaser. His wins at Southwell, Kelso and four times at Sedgefield from eight previous starts, though numerous, do not sound the stuff that Arkle Chase winners are made of. However, he'd won the majority of those races in little more than a canter, with his victory under 12-6 against seasoned handicappers at Sedgefield on his most recent outing particularly impressive. The exception was when he'd tried two and a half miles on the same course in September, for on that occasion he'd had to be driven right out after pulling hard for much of the way. When Greenheart finally did reappear he quickly added two more wins in handicap company, carrying big weights to victory at Wetherby in April and Newcastle in May and putting up decidedly useful performances into the bargain. In between he had a crack at some of the other good novice chasers in the Edinburgh Woollen Mill's Future Champion Novices' Chase at Ayr. Unfortunately for Greenheart's connections, the ground was on the soft side for once, probably not ideal for Greenheart and much more in the favour of the likes of the ex-champion hurdler Celtic Shot. All the same, Greenheart led his rivals a merry dance for a long way. He had been headed, but was by no means out of it, when brought almost to a standstill by a blunder at the second last, the final open ditch. Greenheart kept on to finish a respectable sixth, beaten nearly twenty lengths by Celtic Shot. Never one to allow his horses to rest on their laurels, trainer Stephenson kept Greenheart on the go until the end of the season. After his Newcastle win (gained at the sole expense of the in-form Vulrory's Clown),

Greenheart turned up at Stratford in June on the second-last day of the season. Despite the presence of the useful novice Elfast, Greenheart looked set to provide his trainer with his record-breaking one-hundred-and-fifteenth winner of the term. But it was not to be. Greenheart was subdued in the preliminaries and ran a lack-lustre race, capitulating quickly from the second last. Hopefully he'll be back to his best in the next season, for he's still quite an exciting prospect, and a relatively untested one, for two-mile chases when conditions are fast.

Greenheart (br.g. 1983)	Green Shoon (b 1966)	Sheshoon (ch 1956)	Precipitation
			Noorani
		Chrysoprase (gr 1957)	Arctic Star
			Emerald Green
	Giollaretta (b 1979)	Giolla Mear (b 1965)	Hard Ridden
			Iacobella
		Countess Charmere (br 1963)	Chamier
			Marennes

Greenheart was bred in Ireland, the second foal of winning chaser Giollaretta, a half-sister to the useful chaser Earthstopper and two-year-old sprinter Mark Jason. Earthstopper won the 1983 Bradstone Mandarin Handicap Chase, but the following year collapsed and died after finishing fifth in Hallo Dandy's Grand National. Giollaretta has had only one reported foal since Greenheart, a filly in 1988 by Ore; she was barren to Oats the following year. Greenheart cut little ice in five races (one of them a chase) in his native country as a four- and five-year-old prior to being put into training in Britain with John Costello by owner John Upson. His early performances in this country, in chases, were characterised by odd bad jumping errors. On one occasion at Hereford he stayed down for several minutes after falling at the final fence, but was apparently only badly winded. At the end of the 1988/9 season he was acquired by his present owners, the Morley Stud. The decision to part with Greenheart must be one that Upson, now an up-and-coming trainer in his own right, rues, for this is a horse who should add plenty more successes to his already-impressive record. *W. A. Stephenson.*

GREENHILLS PRIDE 6 b.g. Sparkling Boy–Soheir (Track Spare) [1989/90 16g 17g^{2} 16g 16s 17f^{6}] good-topped gelding: handicap hurdler: good second in conditional jockeys event at Doncaster in January: fair sixth on same course in March: likely to prove best at 2m: acts on dead going (possibly unsuited by heavy). *H. J. Collingridge.* 95

GREENHILLS WARRIOR 4 ch.g. Tina's Pet–Soheir (Track Spare) [1989/90 aF13g^{2} aF13g* aF13g^{2}] fourth living foal: half-brother to winning hurdlers Greenhills Joy (by Radetzky) and Greenhills Pride (by Sparkling Boy): landed the odds by 15 lengths in NH Flat race at Lingfield in March: 10 lengths second to Barnsdale in similar event on same course later in month: yet to race over hurdles. *M. J. Ryan.*

GREEN ISLAND (USA) 4 b.g. Key To The Mint (USA)–Emerald Reef (Mill Reef (USA)) [1989/90 16f^{6} 17m^{ur} 16f^{4} 16f a16g^{2} 16s^{pu}] small gelding: behind in maiden at 2 yrs: poor juvenile hurdler: second at Lingfield in December: ran poorly 6 days later: whipped round and unseated rider on second outing: pulls hard (has worn a crossed noseband). *A. J. K. Dunn.* 70

GREEN LALEEK (USA) 6 b.h. Fluorescent Light (USA)–Rock Garden (Roan Rocket) [1989/90 16f*] half-brother to winning hurdler/chaser Covent Garden (by Stage Door Johnny): maiden miler at 3 yrs in Britain, runner-up over 11f in France since: always travelling strongly and led run-in when winning conditional jockeys selling hurdle at Sedgefield in October (bought in 5,400 gns and looked up to making his mark in better company): sold only 700 gns Ascot November Sales. *J. G. FitzGerald.* 87

GREEN LONNEN 4 ch.g. Topsin (FR)–Whiffenretz (Whiffenpoof) [1989/90 17g^{pu}] smallish, workmanlike gelding: behind in a seller at 2 yrs: tailed off when pulled up 4 out in juvenile hurdle at Carlisle in January. *J. N. Beck.* —

GREEN MARBLE 8 bl.g. Green Shoon–Ten-Cents (Taste of Honey) [1989/90 c20d^{ur} c16d^{5} c16f^{3} c16g^{2} c16s* c16d^{4} c16v^{3} c21g^{ur} c21m^{5} c26m^{3}] workmanlike gelding: handicap hurdler/chaser: won weakly-contested condi- c88 x —

Halloween Novices' Chase, Newbury—the winner Green Willow

tional jockeys chase at Plumpton in December: finished lame final outing: stays 2½m: acts on heavy going and is possibly unsuited by hard: claimer or amateur ridden: moderate jumper of fences: trained by R. Mitchell until after penultimate start. *R. Akehurst.*

GREENORE PRIDE 13 b. or br.g. Menelek–Nenagh Belle (Dalesa) [1989/90 c20s5 c22g2 c24g6 c20v5 c25f c20mur c24mpu] strong, compact gelding: handicap chaser: well beaten after second start: effective at 2m and stays 25f: possibly needs give in the ground nowadays: sometimes jumps moderately. *P. Burgoyne.* **c83** —

GREEN RIDGE 11 br.g. Green Shoon–Amazakove (Giolla Mear) [1989/90 c20s4 c24g5 c26v3 c20d c25m6] big, workmanlike gelding: poor chaser: seems suited by 2½m: acts on soft ground: jumps none too fluently. *S. Mellor.* c— —

GREEN'S COLLECTION 4 b.f. High Top–Gauloise (Welsh Pageant) [1989/90 16m2 18g] quite modest performer on Flat, winner twice over 2m in 1989: second in juvenile hurdle at Plumpton in November: pushed along when mistake 3 out and eased when ninth in similar event at Fontwell following month. *P. F. I. Cole.* 91

GREEN'S FINE ART 4 ch.g. Kind of Hush–L'Hawaienne (USA) (Hawaii) [1989/90 16f*] modest middle-distance maiden on Flat when trained by W. Haggas: odds on, made all in juvenile hurdle at Worcester in August, being left clear by Sayyure's falling 3 out and scoring by 25 lengths: looked sure to improve but wasn't seen out again. *M. C. Pipe.* 107 p

GREEN SILVER 8 gr.g. Hardgreen (USA)–Spring Silver (Palestine) [1989/90 18m2 20mpu] half-brother to 2 winners on Flat in Ireland and to useful middle-distance performer and winning hurdler Spring Hay (by Wassl): dam, placed in Irish NH Flat races, is half-sister to several winners, notably Lanzarote: won NH Flat race in 1988: second of 4 in minor event at Leopardstown in June on hurdling debut: sold out of K. Connolly's stable 10,000 gns Doncaster August Sales: tailed off when pulled up 2 out in amateur riders novice event at Perth in September. *G. Richards.* ?

GREEN SPUR 8 b.g. Status Seeker–Arctic Goose (Arctic Slave) [1989/90 20f* 25g4] sturdy, good sort: type to make a chaser: lightly raced over hurdles: 81

won novice event at Carlisle in October: weakened approaching last when fair fourth of 6 in handicap at Kelso following month: best form at 2½m: acts on firm going. *J. T. Gifford.*

GREEN TOPS 8 ch.g. Green Shoon–Gone (Whistling Wind) [1989/90 c24g* c99
c24d^3 c24g^2 c25m^2 c22d^2 c32g^4 c21d^{pu} c26g^F c26m^3] compact, workmanlike —
gelding: modest hurdler: won novice chase at Southwell in November: ran moderately after fifth start: stays well: ideally suited by give in the ground: suitable mount for a claimer: rather deliberate jumper: has worn brush pricker on near-side. *M. Avison.*

GREEN WILLOW 8 ch.g. Callernish–Kilwillow (Fray Bentos) [1989/90 c**120** p
c17g* c16g^2] big, rangy, angular gelding: one of the best novice hurdlers of —
1988/9: won novice event at Newbury in November on chasing debut by a distance from only other finisher Tinto Hill: jumped none too fluently and was outpaced after mistake 2 out when going down by 10 lengths to Antinous in similar race at Market Rasen later in month (not knocked about once beaten): will stay 3m: has won on softish ground but is best on a sound surface: has run well when sweating: races with plenty of zest: needs to brush up his jumping over fences. *J. T. Gifford.*

GREENWOOD LAD 13 b.g. Menelek–Rathcolman (Royal Buck) [1989/90 c**114**
c24f* c20d^{pu} c24d^6 c21m^6] big, good-topped gelding: very useful chaser at his —
best: won 3-runner handicap at Market Rasen in July: stayed 3m: acted on any going: twice bolted to start: was usually amateur ridden: sometimes jumped sketchily: dead. *C. Sporborg.*

GREY ADMIRAL 5 gr.g. Alias Smith (USA)–Beech Tree (Fighting Ship)
[1989/90 a20g 16f 20g^2 20g* 20f* 20g^5] close-coupled gelding: half-brother to 84
numerous winners, including several over jumps: quite modest maiden at up to 1½m on Flat: won selling handicap hurdles at Market Rasen (bought in 3,600 gns) and Huntingdon (no bid) in May: below his best in non-seller final start: stays 2½m: acts on firm going: visored last 3 outings: sold 6,000 gns Ascot July Sales. *K. A. Morgan.*

GREY CLOUD 5 gr.g. Warpath–Alexandra (Song) [1989/90 22d^{ur} 20d 16f^5
27f^{pu}] workmanlike gelding: sixth foal: brother to 3 winning jumpers: dam placed 63
over 6f and 7f at 2 yrs: poor form in novice hurdles: blinkered last 2 outings: sold privately 5,000 gns Doncaster Spring Sales. *G. M. Moore.*

GREY DANUBE 6 gr.g. Derring Rose–Deep Grey (Deep Run) [1989/90 18g^{pu}
18v 20s* 19d^F 16g^2 19s^3 18s^3 18v^2 16d*] second foal: half-brother to novice 131

Irish Life Assurance EBF Johnstown Hurdle, Naas—
a close race between Grey Danube and Bally Rue (left)

chaser Sheringham House (by Crash Course): dam won a 2½m maiden hurdle and
at up to 2¾m over fences in Ireland: successful in 3 NH Flat races in 1988/9: won
maiden hurdle at Leopardstown in December and quite valuable Irish Life
Assurance EBF Johnstown Hurdle at Naas (by short head from Bally Rue, getting
up close home) in March: 8 lengths second to easy winner Scally Owen in Irish
National Hunt Novice Hurdle Series Final at Punchestown on eighth start: will
stay 3m: acts on heavy going. *J. E. Mulhern, Ireland.*

GREY FELLOW 4 gr.c. Absalom–Follow The Brave (Owen Anthony)
[1989/90 16f* 16f^{2}] half-brother to winning hurdler Bright Fellow (by Shiny 87
Tenth): sold out of Sir Mark Prescott's stable 6,400 gns after winning 1m seller on
Flat in August: won juvenile hurdle at Plumpton later in month by 8 lengths: 3
lengths second to Crossroad Lad in similar event on same course in September:
unlikely to stay much beyond 2m. *J. Ffitch-Heyes.*

GREYFRIARS BOBBY 4 ch.g. Hard Fought–Victorian Pageant (Welsh
Pageant) [1989/90 16d^{pu} 16m^{5} 19m^{pu}] sparely-made gelding: brother to —
Merchants Dream and Heavy Brigade, both winners on Flat and novices over
hurdles: placed over 1m on Flat: showed signs of ability when fifth in juvenile
claiming hurdle at Wincanton in March. *Mrs J. G. Retter.*

GREY GATE 13 gr.g. Grey Mirage–Contentment (Nulli Secundus) [1989/90 c—
c16m^{pu}] lengthy gelding: winning hurdler: no worthwhile form in novice chases. —
W. J. L. Paul.

GREYSBY 8 gr.g. General Ironside–Kiskadee (Seven Bells) [1989/90 16g^{3} 24d
16d* 16s 20g^{5} 16g^{2} 16f^{5}] workmanlike gelding: won novice hurdle at Towcester in 99
February: ¾-length second to Last 'o' The Bunch in similar event at Catterick
following month: best at 2m: acts on dead ground (ran poorly on very soft and on
firm). *O. Brennan.*

GREY TARQUIN 18 gr.g. Tarqogan–Tinker Belle III (Star of The Forest) c—
[1989/90 c26f^{pu}] lengthy, narrow gelding: poor chaser: suited by a test of stamina: —
acts on any going. *J. J. Bridger.*

GREY TORNADO 9 ro.g. Rugantino–Tornadora (Typhoon) [1989/90 c20m^{4} c**108**
c16h* c16f^{5} c20f* c20f^{2} c19g^{2} c16g^{3} c17m^{2}] small, compact gelding: successful in —
handicap chase at Taunton and Leisure Thinking Sink Chase at Newbury (beat
sole opponent Gold Shaft 10 lengths) in October: creditable second at Newbury
and Hereford following month, and at Newton Abbot in May: best form at up to
2¾m: acts on any going: front runner: has worn a crossed noseband. *C. L.
Popham.*

GREY WHISKERS 7 gr.g. Scallywag–Happy Returns (Saucy Kit) [1989/90
16g] smallish, workmanlike gelding: first foal: dam, fair point-to-pointer and —
winning hunter chaser, stayed well: showed ability in novice hurdles at Warwick
in 1988 and Wolverhampton (bit backward) in January. *C. J. Hitchings.*

GRIDGER 8 b.g. Lepanto (GER)–Native Wings (Indigenous) [1989/90 16f^{F} c—
c20m^{F} 16d a18g^{pu} 20m^{pu}] leggy, sparely-made ex-Irish gelding: third foal: —
brother to very smart chaser Panto Prince: dam placed over hurdles and fences:
sold out of M. Scott's stable 8,000 gns Doncaster August Sales: seems of little
account. *R. W. Hartop.*

GRIFFEEDS 8 b.g. Owen Dudley–Lidmoor (Caerdeon) [1989/90 c24f* c24g^{F} c**88**
c24d^{pu}] compact gelding: placed in juvenile hurdle and in point-to-points: won —
poor hunter chase at Worcester in April by 20 lengths: tailed off when falling
thirteenth in much better race at Bangor: stays 3m: acts on firm going. *Miss I.
Dady.*

GRINGO (HUN) 11 br.g. Seebirk (EG)–Guanabara (HUN) (Imperial) [1989/90 c**96** x
c21f^{5} c24m^{3} c24m^{5} c24h* c21f^{4} c27h^{pu}] tall, lengthy, wiry gelding: poor chaser: —
odds on when winning 3-runner handicap at Taunton in September: pulled up and
dismounted on same course in April: stays 3m: acts well on firm or hard going and
possibly unsuited by soft: blinkered last 8 starts: takes a good hold and needs
strong handling: moderate jumper. *J. Honeyball.*

GROCER JACK 7 br.g. Derrylin–Kessella (Le Levanstell) [1989/90 20v
24v^{pu}] small, stocky gelding: no worthwhile form over hurdles. *C. G. Roach.* —

GROGAN 8 b.g. Sapsford–Clear Speech (Articulate) [1989/90 c20g] won novice c—
hurdle in 1987/8: behind in novice chase in January: form only at 2m: probably —
acted on any going: dead. *K. C. Bailey.*

GROOM PORTER (USA) 4 ch.c. Blushing Groom (FR)–Maurita (NZ) (Harbor Prince (USA)) [1989/90 17m] fair 1¾m winner from 3 starts on Flat: sold out of G. Harwood's stable 30,000 gns Newmarket July Sales: around 15 lengths eighth to Proud Crest in novice hurdle at Devon & Exeter in March: should improve. *S. N. Cole.* 87 p

GROOM STAR (USA) 4 ch.c. Blushing Groom (FR)–Guiding Star (SWE) (Reliance II) [1989/90 16m3 16m* 16g* 16m3 16g2 17g4] lengthy, rather leggy colt: won 2 handicaps at up to 13.6f on Flat in October (has worn net muzzle, takes keen hold and carries head high): sold out of G. Harwood's stable 15,500 gns Newmarket Autumn Sales: won juvenile hurdles at Newcastle in November and Edinburgh in December: moderate fourth final start (January): will stay further than 2m: has raced only on a sound surface over hurdles. *N. Tinkler.* 105

GROSSEN 6 gr.g. Bustomi–Novina (Connaught) [1989/90 16mpu 16g 16gpu 16m] lengthy, sparely-made gelding: won novice hurdle in 1988/9: well beaten since: unlikely to stay much beyond 2m: acts on a soft surface: visored final outing 1988/9. *Miss P. Hall.* —

GROTIUS 6 ch.h. Ardross–Tudor Whisper (Henry The Seventh) [1989/90 18d5] very lightly-raced novice hurdler: remote fifth of 16 at Worcester in November. *G. A. Ham.* —

GROUND MASTER 13 b.g. Master Owen–Background (Black Tarquin) [1989/90 c16g2 c20g4 c16d5 c16f* c17f*] deep-bodied gelding: won handicap chases at Hexham in March and Kelso in April: stays 21f: acts on any going: has worn blinkers: amateur or claimer ridden. *Major W. N. Sample.* c84 —

GROUSE MOOR 11 b.g. Wabash–Jyppy (Phebus) [1989/90 c25mpu] lightly-raced winning point-to-pointer: behind when pulled up 2 out in hunter chase at Towcester in April. *R. R. Collier.* c—

GROVELANDS 8 ch.g. Balinger–Oca (O'Grady) [1989/90 24m4 c24s5 c24dpu] small, deep-girthed gelding: winning hurdler: ran well in handicap on reappearance: well beaten in novice chases (out of his depth on second occasion): stays well: possibly unsuited by soft going. *R. Curtis.* c— 106

GROVETON (USA) 8 b.g. Big Spruce (USA)–Vatican (USA) (Bold Bidder) [1989/90 20fpu 20m 20v] leggy, workmanlike gelding: lightly raced and little sign of ability: sold 1,300 gns Ascot June Sales. *T. Casey.* —

GROWING PHASE 5 b.h. Hays–Lovely Linan (Ballylinan) [1989/90 F12f4] half-brother to several winners on Flat, including fairly useful middle-distance winner Spin of A Coin (by Boreen): dam never ran: around 8 lengths fourth behind Yougotit in NH Flat race at Bangor in March: yet to race over hurdles or fences. *J. M. Bukovets.*

GROWING POWER 6 b.g. Red Sunset–Margaree (Energist) [1989/90 22d] leggy ex-Irish gelding: won 1½m handicap on Flat in 1987: no form in 4 races over hurdles. *A. W. Denson.* —

GRUNDY LANE 8 b.g. Grundy–Tamilian (Tamerlane) [1989/90 c16g c16dpu] small, sparely-made gelding: poor handicap hurdler nowadays: no sign of ability in novice chases: will stay 2½m: acts on any going: sometimes blinkered or visored. *B. C. Morgan.* c— —

GUARENA (USA) 5 b.g. Run The Gantlet (USA)–Trenton North (USA) (Herbager) [1989/90 17f3 19hpu 21m5 22g 24d] leggy, close-coupled gelding: novice hurdler: pulled hard but ran well when eighth to Babil over 3m at Chepstow in March: visored final start in 1988/9: often claimer ridden. *D. Holly.* 86

GUERNSEY GIRL 5 ch.m. Deep Run–Falcade (Falcon) [1989/90 16s5 16gF] lengthy mare: half-sister to Badsworth Boy (by Will Hays): third in NH Flat race in 1988/9: 25/1, third and beaten when falling last in novice hurdle at Catterick in March. *J. G. FitzGerald.* —

GUIBURN'S NEPHEW 8 ch.g. National Trust–Arran Sunset (Miracle) [1989/90 c16m* c16mF c16f3 c17g2 c16g* c16mF c17m3] rangy gelding: carries plenty of condition: modest form in novice hurdles: won novice chase at Windsor in November and intermediate handicap chase at Wolverhampton (made all to beat Random Romance 7 lengths) in February: jumped none too fluently in between, and when poor third on final start: suited by forcing tactics at 2m, and is worth another try over further: acts on good to firm ground. *P. J. Hobbs.* c**121** —

GUICI'S RAG 7 b.g. Ragapan–Barradan Lass (Deep Run) [1989/90 c20g3 c24h2 c24fur] sparely-made gelding: won 2 point-to-points in 1988: poor novice c83 —

hurdler/chaser: stays 3m: has run moderately on heavy going, acts on any other: sold 10,500 gns Ascot December Sales. *J. A. C. Edwards.*

GUILTY SPARKLE 5 br.m. Roc Imp–Mayo Melody (Highland Melody) [1989/90 aF13g aF13gpu] no sign of ability in NH Flat races: yet to race over hurdles or fences. *J. M. Bradley.*

GUINEA FEATHER 8 b.m. Over The River (FR)–Halcyon Years (Royal Highway) [1989/90 16mF] sparely-made mare: lightly-raced novice hurdler: well behind when falling last only outing of season (April). *J. C. McConnochie.* —

GUN HAPPY 6 b.g. Formidable (USA)–Naughty One Gerard (Brigadier Gerard) [1989/90 16g6 16g3 16dpu] workmanlike gelding: only form in novice hurdles third at Wolverhampton in January: destroyed after breaking leg on same course. *R. J. Holder.* 88

GUNNER JIM 6 b.g. Gunner B–Well Lined (Straight Lad) [1989/90 21d] rangy gelding with scope: first living foal: dam, modest hurdler/chaser, stayed 3m: better for race, in rear in novice hurdle at Newbury in February. *K. C. Bailey.* —

GUNNER MAC 7 ch.g. Gunner B–Take My Hand (Precipice Wood) [1989/90 22g 24s3 22s 27dpu 27g6 20s4 22d2] big, workmanlike, lengthy gelding: handicap hurdler: returned to form when 6 lengths second to Auk Eye at Ayr in April: won novice chase in 1988/9: suited by a good test of stamina: suited by give in the ground and acts on heavy: visored fifth start: needs strong handling. *N. Bycroft.* c— 118

GUNNERS BEST 6 b.g. Gunner B–Swakara (Porto Bello) [1989/90 20mpu 20g] strong, compact gelding: brother to 2 winners on Flat, including Son of A Gunner, a useful juvenile hurdler: bad maiden on Flat: no sign of ability in novice hurdles. *R. J. Holder.* —

GUNNEWIN 11 ch.g. Regular Guy–Loughehoe Star (Sandyman Star) [1989/90 16gpu c24hpu] winning point-to-pointer: placed in 3m hunter chase in 1987: tailed off when pulled up in novice hurdle and a novice chase in 1990. *D. Scott.* c— —

GURTEEN BOY 8 ch.g. Tickled Pink–Joie d'Or (FR) (Kashmir II) [1989/90 a16g 20m 16d 16s* 16v6 16spu 17d* 16d] small, sturdy gelding: handicap hurdler: won at Haydock in January and Carlisle (conditional jockeys) in March: effective at 2m and stays 2¾m: acts on soft going: usually claimer ridden. *J. J. O'Neill.* 109

GURTEEN WOOD 10 b.g. The Parson–Castlejane (Signa Infesta) [1989/90 c24d5 c25mpu 24gpu] rangy gelding: winning hurdler/chaser: creditable fifth behind Tarville in handicap chase at Worcester in November: stays 3m: acts on soft going. *O. Sherwood.* c**105** —

GUSHY 4 ch.c. Hard Fought–Be Gustful (Ballymore) [1989/90 16gpu 16d6 16d4 16gpu] dipped-backed colt: modest performer on Flat, successful at up to 1m: best effort over hurdles fourth in novice claimer at Ayr in January: blinkered last 2 starts. *M. W. Easterby.* 76

GUSTAVUS ADOLPHUS 12 ch.g. Gala Performance (USA)–Realma (Realm) [1989/90 c17m5 c16m4] lengthy gelding: selling hurdler/novice chaser: races only at around 2m: acts on firm going: has worn a crossed noseband: sold out of P. Jones's stable 1,200 gns Ascot August Sales: resold 800 gns Ascot April Sales. *B. Scriven.* c69 —

GUTE NACHT 7 ch.g. Laurence O–Cherry Branch (Menelek) [1989/90 F16g] fourth foal: brother to a winning point-to-pointer and half-brother to 2 others by Proverb, including successful steeplechaser Inch Lass: dam unraced half-sister to several winners, including useful chaser Ice Plant: won a point-to-point and finished sixth in NH Flat race in Ireland in 1989: sold out of K. Woods's stable 9,000 gns Doncaster Spring (1989) Sales: behind in NH Flat race at Uttoxeter in December: yet to race over hurdles or in a steeplechase. *O. Brennan.*

G W SUPERSTAR 7 ch.m. Rymer–Miss Lara (Master Owen) [1989/90 22mpu 21v3 20s4 22g6 22s] leggy, good-topped mare: poor form in novice hurdles: stays 2¾m: acts on heavy going. *N. R. Mitchell.* 88

GYMCRAK DAWN 5 b.g. Rymer–Edwina's Dawn (Space King) [1989/90 F17d2 F16m] sparely-made gelding: fifth foal: half-brother to 2 poor animals: dam unraced daughter of a successful staying chaser: 1½ lengths second of 21 to Padaventure in NH Flat race at Carlisle in March: tailed off in well-contested event at Liverpool following month: yet to race over hurdles or fences. *M. H. Easterby.*

H

HABANNE 10 gr.g. Habat–Sister Anne (Mourne) [1989/90 16m 20m 19g[bd]] workmanlike gelding: of little account. *P. J. Anderson.* —

HADDON LAD 7 b.g. Dragonara Palace (USA)–Gresham Girl (Right Tack) [1989/90 19s[pu] 22d 21d 20g[3] 20m 20m*] small gelding: quite a moderate hurdler: won handicap at Plumpton in April by 1½ lengths from Ganoon: stays 2½m: acts on any going. *Miss A. L. M. King.* 98

HAGLER 7 br.g. Silly Prices–Reigate Head (Timber King) [1989/90 16f 22v[pu] 25g[pu] 16g 20d 20m] small, workmanlike gelding: no sign of ability: poor jumper: has worn crossed noseband. *B. Bousfield.* — x

HAILEY'S RUN 6 b.g. Runnett–Faa Paa (Skymaster) [1989/90 16f[pu]] sparely-made gelding: no form over hurdles: dead. *C. White.* —

HAIRY HAT 7 ch.g. Deep Run–Arctic Rhapsody (Bargello) [1989/90 c16d[F] c16m[5] c20g[3] 22g c20d[ur] c21m[2]] plain, rather sparely-made gelding: winning hurdler: modest novice chaser: barely stayed 2½m: acted on good to firm and soft going: sometimes found little: dead. *J. T. Gifford.* c88 —

HAJJI BABA 6 ch.g. Persian Bold–Merry Yarn (Aggressor) [1989/90 16f] workmanlike gelding with scope: carried head high under pressure when placed in novice hurdles and amateur riders selling handicap hurdle in second half of 1988/9: ran moderately only outing in 1989/90: has raced only at 2m: acts on firm ground. *J. R. Bostock.* — §

HAKEDMA 4 ch.c. Van Der Linden (FR)–Duty Watch (Import) [1989/90 16h[F] 16h[4] 16g] placed over 2m on Flat: pulled hard when remote fourth of 5 in selling hurdle at Hexham in May. *N. Waggott.* —

HALCANOR 6 ch.g. Irish River (FR)–Princess Gayle (Lord Gayle (USA)) [1989/90 16m[3] 16g* 22d[5] 20m[3] 22g[4] 16s* 16s[3] 16f[4]] leggy, rather sparely-made gelding: quite useful 2m winner on Flat at 3 yrs: sold 2,600 gns Doncaster Spring Sales: successful in handicap hurdles at Ayr in October (novice event, automatic top weight) and January (conditional jockeys race): best run at 2m on soft going. *P. Monteith.* 108

HALCYON LASS 6 b.m. Lighter–La Chunga (Queen's Hussar) [1989/90 F14v] tailed off in 2 NH Flat races: yet to race over hurdles or fences. *A. M. Crow.*

HALE'S MELODY 5 b.m. Dubassoff (USA)–Hale Lane (Comedy Star (USA)) [1989/90 aF13g[4] aF13g] second foal: dam poor plater: tailed-off last in NH Flat races at Lingfield in December and February: yet to race over hurdles or fences. *Mrs P. Townsley.*

HALEY OF APPLETON 11 br.m. The Ditton–Halo of Appleton (My Lord) [1989/90 c18f[pu]] non-thoroughbred mare: third foal: dam never ran: pulled up in a point-to-point in 1988: tailed off when pulled up ninth in novice event at Fontwell in May on steeplechasing debut. *T. Reid.* c—

HALF BROTHER 8 br.g. Faraway Times (USA)–Sinzinbra (Royal Palace) [1989/90 c21m[4]] leggy, angular gelding with plenty of scope: winning hurdler: fairly useful chaser at his best: tailed off in November, only outing in 1989/90: needs testing conditions at 2m and stays 2½m: acts on heavy going: suited by forcing tactics: has worn a dropped noseband: jumps soundly. *Mrs J. Pitman.* c— —

HALF DECENT 7 b.g. Decent Fellow–Lumer Legend (Neron) [1989/90 c20g* c22m[F]] tall gelding: won 2 novice hurdles at Sedgefield in 1988/9: sucessful in novice event at Sedgefield in November on chasing debut: suffered a fatal fall at Nottingham following month: stayed 2½m: was probably unsuited by very firm ground. *T. P. Tate.* c104 —

HALF FREE 14 b.g. Deep Run–Broken Union (Soldado) [1989/90 c20s[5] c26f[2]] lengthy gelding: high-class chaser at best: hunter chaser nowadays: ideally suited by a strongly-run race at 2½m: best form on ground no softer than dead: suited by waiting tactics: has won 8 times at Cheltenham: jumps well: appeared to try to duck out second start and hung left under pressure on third in 1988/9. *C. P. E. Brooks.* c97 —

HALF OILED 6 b.g. Forties Field (FR)–One Pint (Major Portion) [1989/90 20f] rather leggy, angular gelding: has been hobdayed: no worthwhile form in novice hurdles but gave strong indication that he possesses ability in 1988/9. *J. G. FitzGerald.* —

HALLBOROUGH 5 ch.g. Warpath–Bargain Line (Porto Bello) [1989/90 aF16g^{2} F17d] 7 lengths second to Flowing River in NH Flat race at Southwell in March: yet to race over hurdles or fences. *J. G. FitzGerald.*

HALLCROSS 6 br.g. Junius (USA)–Time To Leave (Khalkis) [1989/90 c16f^{5} c16g 16d 22g^{pu} 16m^{3}] close-coupled, sparely-made gelding: winning hurdler: no worthwhile form in 1989/90: jumped sketchily when well beaten in novice chases: will stay beyond 2m: acts on heavy going: usually visored or blinkered: sold out of O. Sherwood's stable 4,000 gns Ascot April Sales after fourth start. *J. Ffitch-Heyes.* c— —

HALLO MATEY 9 b.g. Al Sirat (USA)–Vulgan's River (Vulgan) [1989/90 c20f^{5}] sparely-made gelding: novice hurdler: winning chaser: bit backward, always behind only outing in 1989/90: stays 2½m: probably acts on any going but best on a sound surface: claimer ridden: sometimes blinkered: rather deliberate jumper. *G. A. Hubbard.* c— —

HALLO POLI 8 ch.g. Politico (USA)–Artlight (Articulate) [1989/90 c24g^{pu} c20d^{pu} c24g^{pu} c24f^{6} c25f^{ur} c21f^{pu} c16g^{3}] angular gelding: half-brother to winning hurdlers Hallo Cheeky (by Flatbush) and Hallo River (by Rapid River): of little account: visored last start. *D. L. Williams.* c—

HALLOWED 8 br.m. Wolver Hollow–Saintly Angel (So Blessed) [1989/90 c16f^{2} c16f^{5}] leggy, narrow mare: winning selling hurdler: went down narrowly to Red Procession after making a bad blunder at the last in novice chase at Southwell in August: ran moderately next time: stays 2½m: acts on firm ground: successful with and without a visor. *P. A. Pritchard.* c75 —

HALMAJOR 9 b. or br.g. Mandrake Major–Counter Coup (Busted) [1989/90 20g^{pu} c21d c24g^{5} c26s^{2} c24d^{3} c25g^{F} c25s^{pu} c24d^{pu}] close-coupled gelding: has been pin-fired: one-time fairly useful hurdler: placed in novice chases: let down by his jumping next 2 appearances: pulled up lame final start: suited by a good test of stamina and by plenty of give in the ground: claimer ridden over hurdles. *G. B. Balding.* c100 —

HALS LASS 10 ch.m. Halsall–Gay Lass III (pedigree unknown) [1989/90 c24d c24d^{pu}] lengthy mare: placed in a point-to-point in 1987: no worthwhile form in steeplechases. *C. D. Broad.* c—

HAMMER 5 b.g. Green Shoon–Woodland Lass (Perspex) [1989/90 c24v^{pu}] tailed off in NH Flat race in 1988/9: backward, tailed off when pulled up in novice chase at Chepstow in January. *K. Bishop.* c—

HAMPER 7 ch.g. Final Straw–Great Care (Home Guard (USA)) [1989/90 17d 16f^{3} 18m 17g^{6} 16g 16g^{4} 16g 18v* 21s 16m] close-coupled gelding: carries plenty of condition: still below his early-season form when winning handicap hurdle at Fontwell in February: ran moderately last 2 starts: every chance when falling 3 out in novice chase in 1988/9: stays 2¼m: acts on any going: has looked a difficult ride, but is usually amateur or claimer ridden. *N. R. Mitchell.* c— 117 d

HAMPTON GRANGE 6 br.m. Boreen (FR)–Wild Deer (Royal Buck) [1989/90 F16f^{5} 19g^{F} 22m^{pu} c16f^{4} c19f^{5}] tall, rather unfurnished mare: no form in novice hurdles: 24 lengths fourth of 6 finishers behind Minim in mares novice event at Wincanton in March on chasing debut: tailed off next start. *L. J. Codd.* c69 —

HAND OVER 11 ch.g. Quayside–Three Dieu (Three Dons) [1989/90 c20d^{2} c20s* c24d^{F} c25m^{pu}] deep-bodied gelding: fair hurdler/chaser at his best: impressive 20-length winner of hunter chase at Sandown in February: tended to jump rather low on occasions, in lead but ridden when falling 2 out in similar race won by Dromore Castle at Newbury in March: pulled up lame later in month: stays 2½m: probably acts on any going: tail swisher: usually jumps well. *J. C. Harley.* c108 —

HANDSOME JINKO 5 ch.h. Some Hand–Nelodor (Nelcius) [1989/90 17f^{2} 18f^{4} 16m 16f^{pu}] small, dipped-backed horse: half-brother to winning chaser Kate's Girl (by Lighter): dam winning hurdler: won 1¼m seller on Flat in August: second in novice selling hurdle at Newton Abbot later in month: ran poorly afterwards. *B. Stevens.* 71 ?

HANDY JENNY 5 ch.m. Nearly A Hand–Polo Pam (Tiepolo II) [1989/90 F17h] third reported foal: dam winning hurdler: backward, tailed-off last of 7 in NH Flat race at Devon & Exeter in October: yet to race over hurdles or fences. *R. J. Hodges.*

HANDY LADY 5 ch.m. Nearly A Hand–Lady London (London Gazette) [1989/90 16g] non-thoroughbred mare: fifth foal: half-sister to winning hurdler/useful point-to-pointer/hunter chaser Archie's Nephew (by Roybén): dam, —

lightly-raced hurdler, comes from a prolific winning family and is half-sister to Artifice: tailed off in selling hurdle at Windsor in March. *R. J. Hodges.*

HANDY LANE 9 b.m. Nearly A Hand–Border Lane (Border Legend) [1989/90 c20m* c20m2 c25g3 21m5 c17g2 c16mbd] smallish, sparely-made mare: won conditional jockeys handicap chase at Worcester in August: placed in similar company afterwards: blinkered, brought down first final outing (December): struggling from some way out in handicap hurdle on fourth start: stays 2¾m: acts on any going: good mount for a claimer. *D. H. Barons.* c90 —

HANKIR 10 ch.g. Avocat–Miss Ballyhill (Diritto) [1989/90 c21dF c24gpu] lengthy gelding: winning point-to-pointer/hunter chaser: stays 3m: acts on a yielding surface. *N. R. Mitchell.* c—

HANKLEY DOWN 7 ch.g. Scorpio (FR)–All Ours (Northfields (USA)) [1989/90 22m6 c16fF] strong, rangy, workmanlike gelding: poor novice hurdler: fell first in novice chase: dead. *J. T. Gifford.* c— —

HANNAH MILLIE NICK 5 b.m. Balinger–Saucy Eater (Saucy Kit) [1989/90 22d] third foal: dam winning staying hurdler: always behind in novice hurdle at Stratford in December on debut. *L. J. Codd.* —

HANSEL'S RUN 9 ch.g. Deep Run–Biddy Hansel (Prince Hansel) [1989/90 c24gpu c24dpu] big, angular gelding: lightly-raced novice hurdler: tailed off when pulled up in novice chases: takes a good hold. *Miss E. Sneyd.* c— —

HA'PENNY BRIDGE 7 br.g. Tanfirion–Lost Path (Sovereign Path) [1989/90 16d 20d6 c21vpu c25mpu c26f3 c25mpu c24f2] leggy, close-coupled gelding: poor novice hurdler/chaser: stays 3¼m: acts on firm ground and is possibly unsuited by dead. *N. G. Ayliffe.* c74 —

HA'PENNY NAP 12 br.g. Simbir–Strip Poker (Raise You Ten) [1989/90 a20g6 25g3 20g4 24g2 22s6 a18g* 24d* 16fur 17m3 24g* 24d2 23f2] plain gelding: winning chaser: attracted no bid after winning selling hurdles at Southwell in January and Perth (conditional jockeys handicap) in April: also won claimer at Edinburgh in between: stays well: acts on any going: good mount for a claimer. *C. R. Beever.* c— 99

HAPPY BREED 7 b.h. Bustino–Lucky Realm (Realm) [1989/90 16dF] lengthy horse: handicap hurdler: fell third only outing in 1989/90: best at 2m: acts on soft going: takes a good hold: has found little under pressure on occasions. *J. W. Blundell.* —

HAPPY CAVALIER 5 b.g. King of Spain–Happy Donna (Huntercombe) [1989/90 16gpu 16d 16m 16f 20g 16f4] compact gelding: of little account. *R. E. Barr.* —

HAPPY DEAL 4 b.c. Mon Cheval–Straight Look (Don't Look) [1989/90 16m5 16m] compact colt: seventh foal (fifth by Mon Cheval): dam unraced: jumped none too fluently and finished well beaten in juvenile hurdles at Ludlow (claimer) and Leicester (still bit backward) in first half of season. *A. W. Jones.* —

HAPPY HARRINGTON 4 br.c. Dara Monarch–Forlorn Chance (Fighting Don) [1989/90 16h6] angular colt: plating-class maiden on Flat: last of 6 finishers in novice selling hurdle at Hereford in August: sold 1,850 gns Ascot Sales later in month. *J. A. C. Edwards.* —

HAPPY HIGGINS 6 b.g. Strong Gale–Quayville (Quayside) [1989/90 20spu 16mF 16f3 16m5 16g] rangy gelding: best form over hurdles when 4¾ lengths third behind Sulli Boy in maiden event at Newbury in March: races freely: blinkered fourth outing: sold 8,800 gns Ascot June Sales. *N. J. Henderson.* 86

HAPPYOATS 5 b.g. Oats–Gay Nipper (Aggressor) [1989/90 F12g2 aF16g* F16g] half-brother to 2-y-o 6f winner Gayonara (by Dragonara Palace): dam won over 9f: won NH Flat race at Southwell in December: yet to race over hurdles or fences. *J. G. FitzGerald.*

HAPPY PERCY 5 ch.g. Deep Run–Purcella (Straight Lad) [1989/90 F12g5 F16g5] brother to novice hurdler Annicombe Run and half-brother to winning hurdler Tarqa (by Tarqogan) and fair hurdler/winning chaser Macusla (by Lighter): dam won over hurdles: fifth in NH Flat races at Market Rasen in the spring: yet to race over hurdles or fences. *N. J. Henderson.*

HAPPY WONDER 10 ch.m. Levanter–Gretna Wonder (Elopement) [1989/90 17g] lengthy mare: maiden point-to-pointer/steeplechaser. *G. A. Ham.* c— —

HARBINGER 5 b.g. Mandalus–Harvull (Harwell) [1989/90 16spu] second foal: dam, Irish point-to-point winner, showed little in NH Flat races and a novice —

chase: tailed off when pulled up 2 out in novice hurdle at Sandown in February. *J. T. Gifford.*

HARBOURS WELL 5 b.m. Pitpan–Palmers Well (Proverb) [1989/90 F16g5] lengthy mare: first foal: dam unraced half-sister to several winning jumpers, including Spider's Well and The Dragon Master: edgy and needing race when fifth of 16 to Trefelyn Cone in NH Flat race at Ludlow in December: yet to race over hurdles or fences. *B. Smart.*

HARBOUR WALK 7 ch.g. Quayside–Shuil Alainn (Levanter) [1989/90 16g3 22d* 20s* 24s* 22v4] medium-sized, angular gelding: battled on well when winning novice hurdles at Nottingham and Worcester in January and Uttoxeter following month: ran moderately final start: suited by a good test of stamina: acts on soft going. *Capt. T. A. Forster.* 107

HARD HOLLOW 5 b.g. Hard Fought–Boudoir (Klairon) [1989/90 16fpu 16f5 21gpu 20dpu] smallish, leggy gelding: seems of little account: blinkered first outing. *B. Smart.* —

HARD STUFF 6 ch.g. Hardboy–Spritestown (Bowsprit) [1989/90 16d* 16d 16g6] rangy gelding: won slowly-run novice handicap hurdle at Hereford in November: not disgraced when sixth behind Lissahane Lass in slowly-run race at Leicester in January: will stay beyond 2m: acts on dead going (yet to race on ground firmer than good). *D. Nicholson.* 95

HARD TO HOLD 7 b.g. He Loves Me–Run Swift (Run The Gantlet (USA)) [1989/90 18f* 20f* 20f* 18f3 24mur 20f5 a20g5 c16m5 c20m2] shallow-girthed gelding: handicap hurdler/chaser: in fine form over hurdles in August, winning at Worcester, Bangor (jumped to the right) and Huntingdon: jumped boldly when second over fences at Wincanton in November: best at up to 2½m: acts on firm and dead going: takes a good hold and has worn a severe bridle: usually amateur ridden. *D. T. Thom.* c90 102

HARD TO LIVE 8 b.g. Monksfield–Barby Road (Tin Whistle) [1989/90 16g 16f] rather leggy ex-Irish gelding: half-brother to several winners: dam poor maiden: won maiden hurdle at Downpatrick in 1986/7: shaped well in face of stiff task in handicap at Newbury in March, but ran poorly at Towcester later in month: showed some ability in novice chases early in 1987/8: seems best at around 2m: acts on firm going. *J. T. Gifford.* c— —

HARD UP 9 br.g. Impecunious–Anagola (Queen's Hussar) [1989/90 c20dF a16g5] rangy gelding: lightly-raced winning point-to-pointer: maiden steeplechaser: fifth in novice event at Southwell in March on hurdling debut (will be suited by a return to further). *Mrs F. E. White.* c— —

HARDY LAD 13 ch.g. Spartan General–Barton Wood (Woodcut) [1989/90 c28gpu] good-topped gelding: very useful out-and-out staying chaser in 1987/8: lightly raced and no form since: acts on any going: sometimes jumps rather sketchily. *Miss M. K. Milligan.* c—

HARKEN PREMIER 5 gr.g. Hard Fought–Maraquiba (FR) (Kenmare (FR)) [1989/90 16g2 a16g3 16f 16gF 16f6 16f4] sturdy gelding: plating-class middle-distance handicapper on Flat: placed in novice hurdles in November: has found little. *J. R. Jenkins.* 85

HARLEY 10 ch.g. Cranley–Harmony Rose (Drumbeg) [1989/90 c20g4 c20d c24v3 c25fpu c24dpu] strong, useful-looking gelding: ungenuine handicap hurdler (tried in blinkers once): fairly useful chaser: still carrying plenty of condition, made most until 3 out when 11 lengths third to Rinus in Greenall Whitley Gold Cup (Handicap Chase) at Haydock in March, easily best effort of season: stays 3m: acts on heavy going: usually jumps soundly. *Miss J. Eaton.* c125 — §

HARLEY STREET MAN 9 b.g. Maris Piper–Poppy-Jill (Normandy) [1989/90 c20spu c16g4 c16s* c16d3 c20d4 c16m3 c24mpu] tall, good-bodied, plain gelding: made all, despite several mistakes, in 3-runner handicap chase at Haydock in January: spoilt his chance with mistakes next outing: below his best subsequently: best form at 2m: probably acts on any going: trained first 5 starts by M. Pipe. *C. F. C. Jackson.* c106 —

HARMONEY JANE 11 b.m. Hardboy–Money (Mon Capitaine) [1989/90 c22fpu] strong, plain mare: last in juvenile hurdle in 1982/3: backward, tailed off when pulled up in hunter chase at Nottingham in March. *Mrs Trisha Dunbar.* c— —

HARP OF GOLD 4 b.g. Chief Singer–Blue Queen (Majority Blue) [1989/90 16fpu 16d] workmanlike gelding: has scope: fourth on second of 2 outings over 6f —

at 2 yrs when trained by R. Hern: no form in 2 outings over hurdles: blinkered first start: sold 3,000 gns Ascot May Sales. *Miss H. C. Knight.*

HARREEK 5 ch.g. Tap On Wood–Footway (Sovereign Path) [1989/90 20g 18v^{2} 16s 22m^{pu}] leggy, good-topped gelding: modest inconsistent winning stayer on Flat (has worn visor): sold out of P. Cole's stable 8,000 gns Newmarket Autumn Sales: little promise over hurdles: visored, looked ungenuine last outing. *M. Madgwick.* ?

HARRINGWORTH 15 br.g. Country Retreat–Dark Parting (Parting Shot) [1989/90 c24g^{pu}] compact, well-made gelding: winning point-to-pointer: let down by his jumping most outings in steeplechases: stays well: acts on heavy going. *J. R. Millington.* c—

HARRY LIME 5 b.g. Beldale Flutter (USA)–Zither (Vienna) [1989/90 16v* 16s^{2} 17m^{4}] sturdy gelding: impressive winner of novice handicap hurdle at Chepstow in January: ran creditably afterwards: should stay beyond 2m: best run on soft going. *M. C. Pipe.* 104

HARVEST BLUES 6 ch.g. Free State–Harvest Reap (Majority Blue) [1989/90 20g^{pu}] sparely-made gelding: fair hurdler at his best: pulled up seemingly lame in December and wasn't seen out again: races keenly and likely to prove best in strongly-run races at around 2m: acts on heavy going and has yet to race on top-of-the-ground. *C. R. Beever.* —

HARVEST FAIR 5 br.m. Oats–Breamish Belle (Bing II) [1989/90 F16f^{6}] third foal: dam stoutly-bred novice hurdler: around 25 lengths sixth of 12 to Bollinger in NH Flat race at Ascot in April: yet to race over hurdles or fences. *R. J. Weaver.*

HASCOMBE HILL 6 b. or br.g. Smartset–Cullen Castle (Dear Gazelle) [1989/90 16f^{2} 22g^{2} 20d^{2}] lengthy gelding: moderate novice hurdler: best form at up to 2½m: acts on firm and dead going: ran in snatches second start. *J. T. Gifford.* 94

HASTY DIVER 9 ch.g. Crash Course–Tara Babu (Garland Knight) [1989/90 c25m^{pu} c25d^{2} c24g^{2} c25g c25s^{ur} c25m^{6}] workmanlike gelding: poor chaser: stays 25f: acts on good to firm and heavy going. *J. A. B. Old.* c**83** —

HASTY GAMBLE 10 ch.g. Hasty Word–Stormation (Compensation) [1989/90 21g^{2} 20g a20g^{5} a20g* a24g^{3}] close-coupled gelding: won selling handicap hurdle at Lingfield (no bid) in December: well beaten in non-seller only subsequent start: poor novice chaser: stays 3¼m: acts on any going: has won for an amateur: sketchy jumper of fences: blinkered third start: sold 1,300 gns Ascot May Sales. *A. Moore.* c— 92

HASTY IMPORT 11 ch.g. Import–Isis Rapide (I Say) [1989/90 18d^{pu}] workmanlike gelding: winning hurdler: stays 2¾m: best form on a sound surface: tried to run out once: amateur ridden. *T. L. A. Robson.* —

HASTY SALVO 6 ch.m. Hasty Word–Salvo's Grace (FR) (Salvo) [1989/90 16m^{4} 16m^{3}] in frame in novice hurdles at Warwick and Stratford (mares event) in September, showing poor form. *K. Bishop.* 70

HATAAM 4 b.c. Shirley Heights–Nophe (USA) (Super Concorde (USA)) [1989/90 16f 17d^{4} 16v^{3} 18v* 16s^{4} 16d^{3} 17d^{pu}] workmanlike colt: plating-class form on Flat (trained in Ireland in 1989 by J. Oxx): attracted no bid after winning juvenile selling hurdle at Fontwell in February: stays 2¼m: seems suited by the mud: blinkered and claimer ridden last 5 starts. *E. A. Wheeler.* 84

HATS HIGH 5 b.g. High Top–Peculiar One (USA) (Quack (USA)) [1989/90 16g^{2} 16d^{5} 21s^{pu} 16g* 16m^{4}] lengthy, lightly-made gelding: sold out of R. Akehurst's stable 5,200 gns after winning selling hurdle at Windsor in March: hung left and didn't run on under pressure second start: should stay further than 2m: acts on heavy going (well beaten in non-seller on good to firm final outing): often visored (wasn't at Windsor): trained until after second start by J. Jenkins: not one to trust. *F. Gray.* 102 §

HATSU-GIRIE 9 b.m. Ascertain (USA)–Mrs Bear (Romancero) [1989/90 c27f^{3} c24g^{pu}] lengthy mare: quite modest chaser: stays well: acts on good to firm and soft going: usually amateur or claimer ridden: usually jumps moderately: ran poorly when blinkered once in 1987/8. *R. W. Swiers.* c— x —

HAVE A BARNEY 9 ch.g. Laurence O–Barney's Girl (My Smokey) [1989/90 c16s* c24d^{F} c20d^{F} c25v c28m^{3} c16g^{2} 20g] Irish gelding: smart chaser/fairly useful hurdler: won Fortria Handicap Chase at Navan in November: 13½ lengths third behind Desert Orchid in Jameson Irish Grand National at Fairyhouse in April: effective at 2m and stays well: best form on soft going: genuine. *A. L. T. Moore, Ireland.* c**150** 132

HAVE A BREEZE 4 ch.f. Coquelin (USA)–Courreges (Manado) [1989/90 16g^F 16d^pu] sparely-made filly: seems of little account. *C. Spares.* —

HAVERTHWAITE 8 ch.g. Palm Track–Goldwis (Golden Cloud) [1989/90 16d a16g*] useful-looking gelding: has found little and run in snatches but did nothing wrong when successful in conditional jockeys novice hurdle at Southwell (blinkered) in November: pulled up when tried at 2½m: sold 1,050 gns Doncaster January Sales. *M. H. Easterby.* 98 §

HAVON AIRCO 4 b.g. Lafontaine (USA)–Sunland Park (Baragoi) [1989/90 16f] strong, lengthy, dipped-backed gelding: fair 7f winner at 2 yrs but well beaten on Flat in 1989, trained by D. Morley: tailed-off last of 10 in juvenile hurdle at Ascot in October. *G. H. Yardley.* —

HAWAIIAN HEIR (USA) 11 b.g. Hawaii–Madam Fox (USA) (Rising Market (USA)) [1989/90 16m a18g] lightly-made gelding: handicap hurdler: tailed off in 2 outings in March: unseated rider fourth on chasing debut: best at around 2m: yet to race on heavy going, acts on any other: usually blinkered: claimer ridden. *W. Clay.* c— —

HAWAIIAN PRINCE 6 b.g. Hawaiian Return (USA)–Wrong Decision (No Argument) [1989/90 F16m 16m^pu 24d^pu] leggy, sparely-made gelding: highly-strung novice hurdler: sold out of J. J. O'Neill's stable 4,000 gns Doncaster August Sales. *Brian Thomas Crawford.* —

HAWKES BAY (NZ) 7 b.g. Balak–Floreat (NZ) (Better Honey) [1989/90 16d 16g^6 16s^co 16m 21d 16f^2 16m^F 16f^5] leggy gelding: poor novice hurdler: well beaten over 21f: acts on firm going. *R. J. Hodges.* 78

HAWKES DALE 6 ch.g. Hard Fought–Bird Reserve (Blakeney) [1989/90 22g^pu 16g c16m c20m^ur c18h^3 c16m^F] lengthy, workmanlike gelding: no worthwhile form in novice hurdles or novice chases: has worn crossed noseband: blinkered last outing. *Mrs E. H. Heath.* c— —

HAWKSMOOR 7 b.g. Certingo–Lefkara (Steeple Aston) [1989/90 c26m^F c25f^2] big, workmanlike gelding: no form over hurdles: winning point-to-pointer: 10 lengths second to Eastern Chant in hunter chase at Towcester in May: probably stays 3m: acts on firm ground: blinkered final start in 1987/8 and last outing. *J. A. C. Edwards.* c86 —

HAWTHORN JACKS 10 b.g. Paddy's Stream–Strawberry Mess (Pardal) [1989/90 c20m^5 c20s c25d^3 c24s^pu c20v] big, rangy gelding: lightly raced and poor form: rather headstrong. *G. Ripley.* c65 —

HAZEL BANK 11 gr.m. Pongee–Petoria (Songedor) [1989/90 c16d^2 c16g^3 c17g^4 c20d^3] small, sturdy mare: poor chaser: stays 2½m: acts on heavy going: sometimes wore blinkers over hurdles: wears a tongue strap. *P. Monteith.* c81 —

HAZELEELS DELIGHT 10 b.g. Raga Navarro (ITY)–Aibrean (Amber Light) [1989/90 25h^2 25g^4 c20s a20g] smallish, sparely-made gelding: novice hurdler: has run in a seller: ran creditably first 2 outings: tired last of 7 finishers in novice event at Bangor on chasing debut: stays well: acts on any going. *P. S. Davies.* c— 85

HAZY SUNSET 13 br.g. Menelek–Sunset Queen (Arctic Slave) [1989/90 c21f* c21f^F* c21f^2 c24m* c24f^su c21f* c20m* c24d^2 c20d^4 c24m^ur] strong gelding: useful front-running chaser, in good form in 1989/90: successful at Newton Abbot (twice) and Market Rasen (twice) early in season and at Wolverhampton in December (amateur ridden): destroyed after breaking a leg at Cheltenham in March: stayed 3m, at least when conditions weren't testing: best form on a sound surface. *C. P. E. Brooks.* c**137** —

HEADBEE 4 b.f. Head For Heights–Plaits (Thatching) [1989/90 16f^5 16s^bd 16m] small, sparely-made filly: plating-class maiden on Flat, stays 1½m (trained by R. Hannon): fifth of 8 in selling hurdle in December: visored last outing (jumped poorly). *M. Castell.* —

HEAD FOR HOME 5 gr.m. Grey Ghost–Reigate Head (Timber King) [1989/90 F16d F16g F17m] fifth foal: half-sister to useful staying chaser Whats What and winning hurdler Hows Tony (both by Pongee): dam poor novice hurdler: behind in NH Flat races: yet to race over hurdles or fences. *B. Bousfield.*

HEADIN' ON 10 b.g. Headin' Up–Olisa (Bally Russe) [1989/90 c17f^2 c20f^3 c20m^2 c21f^ro c17m^3 c20g* c20f^3 c24f* c24g^pu] lengthy gelding: modest chaser: won handicaps at Uttoxeter (made all) and Ascot (Bagshot Chase, left in lead when third at the last) in October: ran moderately in between and final start (November): probably stays 3m: acts on hard going: jumps untidily on occasions: has broken blood vessels. *K. White.* c**108** —

Bagshot Handicap Chase, Ascot—
Headin' On is presented with the race by Sir Jest's last-fence refusal,
after the clear leader Huntworth had run out

HEAD LAD 7 ch.g. Headin' Up–Authors Daughter (Charlottown) [1989/90 20s^{pu} 22v^{pu} a20g^{3} 20m^{pu} 16f^{pu} 16m^{4} 16m^{4}] workmanlike gelding: poor novice hurdler: blinkered last start. *R. E. Peacock.* 63

HEADLEYS BRIDGE 8 b.g. Artaius (USA)–Gale Bridge (USA) (Vaguely Noble) [1989/90 16m^{6} 16d^{pu} c20s^{pu} 16g^{5} 20g 16d 16f^{pu} 20m] good-topped, lengthy gelding: poor novice hurdler: behind when pulled up 2 out on chasing debut: races keenly and will do best at around 2m: usually ridden by claimer. *Miss J. Eaton.* c— 83 ?

HEAD OF DEFENCE 5 ch.h. Tachypous–Headliner (Pampered King) [1989/90 16m 17m^{pu} 17h^{3} 16h^{3}] sparely-made, rather dipped-backed horse: poor form on Flat: little sign of ability over hurdles: trained until after third outing by B. Palling. *J. V. Criddle.* —

HEARD IT BEFORE (FR) 5 b.h. Pharly (FR)–Lilac Charm (Bustino) [1989/90 16m^{3} 16s] small horse: modest performer at up to 1¼m on Flat, winner twice in 1989: ridden by 7-lb claimer, jumped none too fluently when third in selling hurdle at Nottingham in November (claimed out of R. Hollinshead's stable £6,115): behind in novice hurdle at Folkestone following month. *R. P. C. Hoad.* 83

HEART OF KINGS 6 ch.g. Proverb–Biowen (Master Owen) [1989/90 16g 16m^{4} 21d 20f^{3}] angular gelding: brother to fairly useful staying chaser Topsham Bay and half-brother to staying handicap hurdler/novice chaser Pollen Bee (by Pollerton) and useful Irish jumper Mixed Blends and winning hurdler Fifth Amendment (both by The Parson): dam unraced sister to staying hurdler/chaser Just Owen: poor form in novice hurdles: will stay beyond 21f. *J. T. Gifford.* 75

HEART OF STONE (USA) 8 ch.h. Dust Commander (USA)–Grankie (USA) (Nashua) [1989/90 17d 19m 24g 16g 17m^{6}] neat horse: fairly useful hurdler at best: poor performer nowadays (ran in a seller final start): suited by a strongly-run race at 2m: acts on any going. *P. Leach.* 91

HEART OF YORKSHIRE 7 ch.g. Laurence O–Royal Liatris (Ragapan) [1989/90 22v^{pu}] well behind in 2 NH Flat races and when pulled up in novice hurdle at Haydock in December. *N. Bradley.* —

HEATHER MOTH 8 b.g. Candy Cane–Rumdora (Rum (USA)) [1989/90 c24m^{4} c21m c20g^{5} c20g^{F} c20g c16d^{3} c16v^{6} c25g^{pu} c24d^{pu} c16g] rangy gelding: poor novice hurdler/chaser: blinkered last start. *T. W. Cunningham.* c64 —

HEAVENLY BROTHER 7 b.g. Baptism–High Above (Aureole) [1989/90 c20m c16d^F c16g^3 c20d^F c20d^3 c20s^{pu} c21g] leggy gelding: winning selling hurdler: poor novice chaser: gives impression he needs forcing tactics when racing at around 2m and should stay beyond 2½m: acts on heavy going (won NH Flat race on good to firm): often claimer ridden nowadays. *N. R. Mitchell.* c81 —

HEAVENLY HOOFER 7 b.g. Dance In Time (CAN)–Heavenly Chord (Hittite Glory) [1989/90 17m^6 16f^5 16f* 16m* 16f^4 16g^2 16g^6 16d^4 16g 16f 20f^6 17m^3 16f^2 16f^2 16g* 16f^4 17f^3] smallish, workmanlike gelding: made all in handicap hurdles at Sedgefield and Perth in September and at Newcastle in May: form only at around 2m: acts on hard ground. *W. Storey.* 77

HEAVY BRIGADE (FR) 7 ch.h. Hard Fought–Victorian Pageant (Welsh Pageant) [1989/90 17m^{pu} 16g^{pu}] smallish horse: winner at up to 1m on Flat: no form over hurdles: blinkered last start: dead. *A. Barrow.* —

HEIGHT O'BATTLE 4 b.c. Shirley Heights–Light O'Battle (Queen's Hussar) [1989/90 17f^3] half-brother to 2 winners, including fair hurdler Lobric (by Electric): claimed out of P. Calver's stable 13,050 gns after winning 1¼m claimer on Flat in June: remote third of 4 behind Shadeux in juvenile hurdle at Newton Abbot in August. *Mrs S. Oliver.* 69

HEIGHT OF FUN 6 b.g. Kambalda–Moongello (Bargello) [1989/90 16g^2 20f^5 25g^4 22v^5 20g^3 20f*] leggy, good-topped ex-Irish gelding: half-brother to winning point-to-pointer Pusharda (by Push On): dam unraced: variable form: won 8-runner novice hurdle at Cheltenham in April by 4 lengths from Turpin's Green, leading run-in having been held up (drifted left in closing stages): stays 2½m: acts on firm ground, ran poorly on heavy: blinkered fifth start (found nothing): one to treat with caution. *O. Sherwood.* 104 §

HEIR OF EXCITEMENT 5 b.g. Krayyan–Merry Choice (Yankee Gold) [1989/90 16m^3 16f^2 16f^3 16g^F 16g] angular gelding: modest novice hurdler: has raced only at around 2m: visored second outing 1988/9: has hung in latter stages and looks to have his own ideas about the game. *A. P. Stringer.* 88 §

HE IS GREADY 9 b.g. Shackleton–Mcgready Rose (Royal Buck) [1989/90 c24g^3 c24s^3 c24v] close-coupled gelding: winning hurdler: novice chaser: stays well: acts on heavy going. *R. O'Leary.* c71 ? —

HELEN BOY 7 b.g. Swing Easy (USA)–Tassel (Ragusa) [1989/90 c20f^F] leggy, close-coupled gelding: poor novice hurdler/chaser: wore blinkers or a visor: moderate jumper of fences: dead. *Ronald Thompson.* c— x —

HELEN HOTEL 5 ch.g. High Line–Orange Sensation (Floribunda) [1989/90 16g 16g a16g] smallish gelding: half-brother to winning hurdler Pink Sensation (by Sagaro): poor maiden on Flat (has been blinkered and visored): little sign of ability over hurdles, including in sellers: sold 1,300 gns Doncaster Spring Sales. *M. Johnston.* —

HELEN RED 4 b.f. Trojan Fen–Spindle Berry (Dance In Time (CAN)) [1989/90 16m 16d^F 16s^6 a16g^6] lengthy, plain filly: won 6f seller at 2 yrs, no form on Flat at 3 yrs: well beaten over hurdles: trained until after third start by A. Hide. *G. H. Eden.* —

HELLBRUNN 4 ch.c. Hotfoot–Midnight Music (Midsummer Night II) [1989/90 16m^5 20m^3 16g 16f^4 20g^6 20g] lengthy colt: has scope: modest 17f winner on Flat when trained by C. Brittain: close fourth behind Snugfit's Image in juvenile event at Uttoxeter in April, best effort over hurdles: should be suited by at least 2½m: acts on firm ground: ridden by 7-lb claimer. *W. Clay.* 95

HELLCATMUDWRESTLER 9 b.g. Tumble Wind (USA)–Fairy Books (King's Leap) [1989/90 c27f^F] lightly-made gelding: winning point-to-pointer: favourite, clear until falling 3 out in hunter chase won by Cheerie Chief at Sedgefield in May: acts on firm ground and a yielding surface: blinkered last start 1988/9: sold out of W. McGhie's stable 800 gns Doncaster August Sales: has looked temperamentally unsatisfactory. *Henry Bell.* c96 § — §

HELLENIC PRINCE 4 b.c. Ela-Mana-Mou–Pipina (USA) (Sir Gaylord) [1989/90 a16g* a16s* 16d^4 16m^4 a20g^3] workmanlike colt: half-brother to novice hurdler Youthful Pip (by Young Generation): modest maiden on Flat, stays 1¼m: sold out of G. Wragg's stable 4,200 gns Newmarket Autumn Sales: held up when winning maiden hurdle and juvenile hurdle at Lingfield in January: ran creditably next 2 outings: races keenly (wears crossed noseband) and will prove suited by sharp 2m. *J. Pearce.* 95

HELLION 11 ch.g. Hell's Gate–Solwyn (Soletra) [1989/90 20f^{5} 20m^{5} 21g^{F}] winning hurdler: seems of little account nowadays. *J. G. Thorpe.* —

HELLO GEORGIE 7 b.g. Hello Gorgeous (USA)–Celina (Crepello) [1989/90 c24g^{F} c24d^{5} c24g^{ur} c25g^{5} c27s^{pu} 20m] compact gelding: winning hurdler and poor novice chaser: suited by a test of stamina: acts on good to firm and dead going: blinkered last 2 outings over fences: sometimes runs in snatches: trained until after fifth start by M. H. Easterby. *T. Craig.* **c84** § —

HELLO ROCKY 9 b.g. Menelek–Fourteen Carat (Sterling Bay (SWE)) [1989/90 a22g^{5} a20g^{2}] short-backed, smallish gelding: novice hurdler: second in selling handicap in December: has jumped poorly both outings over fences (tailed off when refusing last on first occasion): stays 2¾m: acts on firm ground. *Miss E. Sneyd.* c— x 74

HELLO SAM 7 ch.g. Hello Gorgeous (USA)–Samra (Welsh Saint) [1989/90 20g c21s^{6} c24s^{ur} c27d^{F} c24g^{ur} 21d^{pu} 24g^{4}] leggy gelding: winning hurdler: clear when unseating rider 4 out in novice handicap chase at Taunton in December: close up when falling 6 out in similar race at Sedgefield following month: stays 3m: probably acts on any going: needs to improve his jumping of fences. *J. A. Bennett.* c— x 93

HELLO SPARKLER 5 b.h. Hello Gorgeous (USA)–Rheinsparkle (Rheingold) [1989/90 16f^{pu} 16m^{6}] successful at up to 1m on Flat (well below his best in 1989): claimer ridden, around 12½ lengths sixth behind Hot Company in novice hurdle at Perth in September. *R. D. E. Woodhouse.* 78

HELLO STEVE 5 b.h. Final Straw–Head First (Welsh Pageant) [1989/90 21g^{3} 20m^{2} 24g c20f* c20g*] medium-sized horse: moderate hurdler: won minor chase at Newbury and amateur riders handicap at Uttoxeter (hung right initially under pressure when beating Kingswood Kitchens 4 lengths) in the spring: should stay beyond 21f: acts on firm ground: blinkered nowadays: should improve further and win more races over fences. *C. P. E. Brooks.* c**114** p 106

HELLO SWEETIE 4 ch.f. Hello Gorgeous (USA)–My Sweetie (Bleep-Bleep) [1989/90 17g 17v^{3} 16s^{3} 16v^{4} 16g^{pu}] smallish, sparely-made filly: half-sister to 3 winners, including selling hurdler Arena Auction (by Relko): plater on Flat, placed over 7.5f: sold out of M. H. Easterby's stable 1,900 gns Doncaster June Sales: third in selling hurdle at Taunton in January and claimer at Uttoxeter in February. *Mrs A. Knight.* 75

HELLOVASTATE 5 ch.g. Enchantment–Brandenbourg (Le Levanstell) [1989/90 17f^{4} 17f^{2} 17m* 17m^{6} 16g a16g^{2} a16g^{3}] workmanlike gelding: won conditional jockeys novice hurdle at Devon & Exeter in September: wasn't seen out after November: likely to stay beyond 17f: acts on firm ground: claimer ridden. *D. H. Barons.* 89 ?

HELMAR (NZ) 4 b.g. Gay Apollo–War Field (NZ) (War Hawk) [1989/90 F16g] New Zealand-bred gelding: in mid-division in 18-runner NH Flat race at Market Rasen in April: yet to race over hurdles. *F. Jordan.*

HELOONIUM 5 br.g. Green Shoon–Helenium (Khalkis) [1989/90 20s^{pu} c16v^{pu} 16m^{pu}] leggy, close-coupled ex-Irish gelding: sixth living foal: half-brother to Norval (by King's Equity), winning hurdler at up to 2½m: dam won 4 races at around 2m over hurdles in Ireland: little sign of ability: formerly trained by J. Brassil. *N. R. Mitchell.* c— —

HENISKI 7 b.g. Henbit (USA)–Noble Girl (Be Friendly) [1989/90 16f^{5} 16m] sturdy, good-quartered gelding: novice hurdler: has run in a seller. *J. R. Fort.* —

HENNESSY HOUSE 13 b.g. Reformed Character–Daybrook Venture (Daybrook Lad) [1989/90 c20f^{6} c26f^{4}] small gelding: winning chaser: poor point-to-pointer/hunter chaser nowadays: stays 2¾m: seems to act on any going. *Mrs G. M. Gladders.* c— —

HENRIETTA PLACE 6 b.m. Sayyaf–Gilana (Averof) [1989/90 a16g a18g^{4}] small, workmanlike mare: poor form in varied company over hurdles, including selling. *G. A. Pritchard-Gordon.* 62

HENRY GEARY STEELS 10 br.g. Connaught–Halkissimo (Khalkis) [1989/90 16g] small, close-coupled gelding: selling hurdler: in need of race only outing of season (February): successful in 2 novice handicap chases in 1988/9: appears to stay 2½m when conditions aren't testing: acts on any going: tends to make the odd bad mistake. *W. Holden.* c— —

HENRY MAJOR 6 ch.g. Roman Warrior–Pretty Girl (Double-U-Jay) [1989/90 aF13g^{6} F16f] fourth foal: dam placed at up to 1¼m: well beaten in NH Flat races in the spring: yet to race over hurdles or fences. *Mrs F. E. White.*

HENRY MANN 7 br.g. Mandalus–Little Dipper (Queen's Hussar) [1989/90 21d6 22s 25f*] 158

A new trainer was in charge at Kinnersley stables in the latest season, Simon Christian having taken over on the retirement of Mercy Rimell. Kinnersley had become strongly associated with the name of Rimell down the years. Mercy's husband Fred, who trained there from 1945 until his death in 1981, was leading National Hunt trainer on five occasions, on the last of them, in 1975/6, achieving the rare feat of saddling a Gold Cup winner, Royal Frolic, and a Grand National winner, Rag Trade, in the same year. Rag Trade was his fourth Grand National winner, following E.S.B., Nicolaus Silver and Gay Trip, and he's the only person to have sent out as many as four. Rimell also won the Gold Cup with Woodland Venture, and two Champion Hurdles with Comedy of Errors. The big-race wins continued when Mercy took over the licence. Two of her best horses were the full brothers Gaye Chance and Gaye Brief, the latter another Champion Hurdle winner in 1983; six years later Celtic Chief came close to being another. The Rimells, to use a well-worn show-business expression, will be a hard act to follow. Although Christian made just a steady start in his first season at Kinnersley, he had the satisfaction of adding to the stable's list of big-race successes when sending out Henry Mann to win the Coral Golden Hurdle Final at the Cheltenham Festival, the first time that this highly competitive handicap had fallen to a horse trained there.

The intention had been to send Henry Mann chasing in the latest season, but those plans were shelved when the horse contracted a virus which kept him off the course until January. Reappearing in a qualifier of the Coral Golden Hurdle series at Warwick Henry Mann caught the eye of the stewards in finishing a promising sixth behind Qannaas, and his trainer and rider were each fined £125 for schooling in public. Henry Mann failed to confirm the promise in another qualifier at Nottingham the following month, and when he lined up for the Final he was wearing blinkers. He'd worn them only once previously, when winning the George Duller Handicap at Cheltenham in April, 1989. Though his usual partner Mulholland claimed the 5-lb allowance Henry Mann still had to concede weight to all twenty-six of his opponents in the Coral Golden Hurdle Final. Those opponents included two previous winners of the race, Taberna Lord and Rogers Princess, the latter having scored by twelve lengths from Henry Mann a year earlier. Rogers Princess started favourite for the latest running at 11/2, while Henry Mann, following his disappointing run at Nottingham, was sent off at 20/1. Three of the field, including Taberna Lord, came down at the first flight, and it soon became apparent that Rogers Princess, ill at ease on the firm ground, wasn't going to win it for a second time either. Henry Mann, who has a good turn of foot for one who stays so well, was ridden with

Coral Golden Hurdle Final (Handicap), Cheltenham—Maelkar leads over the last from Henry Mann (left) and Direct

restraint and jumped the third-last flight in fifth place. He'd moved into third on the home turn but was being ridden along at this point and looked held by both Maelkar and Direct, the former moving particularly strongly in the lead. Henry Mann produced the best finishing speed, though. Overtaking Direct at the last, he swept past Maelkar in the last hundred yards to score by two lengths in course-record time. Henry Mann wasn't seen out again, which was unfortunate. Using Maelkar as a yardstick he'd probably have been too good for Battalion in the Keith Prowse Long Distance Hurdle at Ascot later in March.

Henry Mann (br.g. 1983)	Mandalus (b or br 1974)	Mandamus (br 1960)	Petition
			Great Fun
		Laminate (gr 1957)	Abernant
			Lamri
	Little Dipper (b 1969)	Queen's Hussar (b 1960)	March Past
			Jojo
		Swallow Falls (b 1950)	Combat
			Procne

Henry Mann's full pedigree details can be found in the essay on his half-brother Formula One (by Ardoon). Suffice to say here that their dam Little Dipper, a lightly-raced winning stayer on the Flat, has bred three other winning jumpers. They include the ill-fated Egypt Mill (by Deep Run), winner of both his starts over hurdles in 1989/90; and the very useful Irish performer Royal Dipper (by Royal Captive). Henry Mann, who fetched IR 8,000 guineas as a yearling, was purchased two years later by his trainer for IR 15,000 guineas at the Tattersalls Derby Sale. A good-topped individual, he should make his mark as a staying chaser, and he could well be a leading contender for the Sun Alliance Novices' Chase come the next Cheltenham Festival. Henry Mann acts on any going. *S. Christian.*

HENSHAW 6 ch.g. Crofter (USA)–Jabula (Sheshoon) [1989/90 17f[ur] 17d[pu] 21v[F] 21m[5] 21f[pu]] compact ex-Irish gelding: lightly-raced maiden on Flat: modest form over hurdles in Ireland in 1988/9: no worthwhile form in Britain: often amateur or claimer ridden. *T. B. Hallett.* —

HERBERT UNITED 11 b.g. Sir Herbert–Anglo United (Le Tricolore) [1989/90 c16m[3] c20m[4] c25m[F] c18m* c20s[pu] c20g[3] c16g[4] c21g* c20d] lengthy, good-bodied, workmanlike gelding: has been pin-fired: fair chaser: passed post first in handicaps at Fontwell, Warwick (amateur riders, demoted to third after jumping right and causing interference at the last) and Towcester (beat Canford Palm 2½ lengths): finished lame final outing (January): stays 21f: acts on any going: usually held up: sometimes sweating and on his toes: sketchy jumper of fences. *G. B. Balding.* **c121** —

HERCLE (FR) 4 b.c. Fabulous Dancer (USA)–L'Exception (FR) (Margouillat (FR)) [1989/90 16g[pu] 16d[pu]] successful at up to 1¼m in France when trained by R. Collet, but only modest form on Flat in Britain: pulled up in juvenile hurdles at Haydock (appeared lame) in November and Newcastle in February: winner over 1m in 1990. *N. Tinkler.* —

HERE COMES CHARTER 5 b.g. Le Moss–Windtown Fancy (Perspex) [1989/90 F16g] sixth foal: half-brother to winning Irish hurdler Bishopswood Girl (by Reformed Character): dam never ran: behind in NH Flat race at Market Rasen in April: yet to race over hurdles or fences. *J. A. C. Edwards.*

HERE HE COMES 4 b.g. Alzao (USA)–Nanette (Worden II) [1989/90 16s[5] 16g[6]] neat gelding: fair maiden on Flat, in frame at up to 1¼m: showed fair ability both starts over hurdles: 18 lengths sixth of 8 finishers to Philosophos in Tote Placepot Hurdle at Kempton in February: should win a race over hurdles. *R. Akehurst.* 113 p

HERON'S JAKE 6 ch. or gr.g. Humdoleila–Heron's Mirage (Grey Mirage) [1989/90 F16f[6] aF16g[4] aF13g 16f[pu]] third foal: half-brother to winning Irish point-to-pointer Quick Vision (by Hasty Word): dam lightly-raced sister to useful chaser Repington: unplaced in NH Flat races: tailed off when pulled up in selling hurdle at Ludlow in April: sold out of J. Edwards' stable 2,900 gns Ascot December Sales after first start: resold 1,600 gns Ascot May Sales. *R. J. O'Sullivan.* —

HERON'S SAM 5 b.g. Proud Knight (USA)–Heron's Mirage (Grey Mirage) [1989/90 F16v 16f[4] a20g[6]] smallish gelding: fourth foal: half-brother to winning 61

point-to-pointer Quick Vision (by Hasty Word) and 6-y-o Heron's Jake (by Humdoleila): dam lightly-raced sister to useful chaser Repington: poor form in novice hurdles. *E. J. Alston.*

HERON VALLEY 6 b.m. Remezzo–Garbally Girl (Mugatpura) [1989/90 16g 20g 16s a16g] small mare: third foal: dam, half-sister to useful chaser Red Candle, won two 3m chases: well beaten over hurdles. *W. M. Perrin.* —

HETTA LOUISE 5 gr.m. Comedy Star (USA)–Ruetina (Rugantino) [1989/90 16g 22gpu 20gpu] workmanlike mare: sixth foal: sister to Comedian, successful on Flat and over jumps: dam ran 3 times: no sign of ability in novice hurdles and a seller. *J. P. D. Elliott.* —

HETTINGER 10 b.g. Maximilian–Fawnamore (Menelek) [1989/90 20h3 c16g4] sparely-made, workmanlike gelding: winning hurdler/chaser ideally suited by slightly shorter distances than 3m: has won on hard ground but best form on heavy: has worn a hood: poor jumper of fences. *J. Ffitch-Heyes.* c— x —

HE WHO DARES WINS 7 b.g. Le Bavard (FR)–Brave Air (Brave Invader (USA)) [1989/90 20g] tall, lengthy gelding: lightly-raced novice hurdler: has shown a little promise: will stay 3m. *W. A. Stephenson.* —

HEY BOSS 6 b.g. Furry Glen–Clarrie (Ballyciptic) [1989/90 16mpu] big, rangy gelding with plenty of scope: has shown ability in novice hurdles: saddle slipped only outing in 1989/90: tends to sweat, pulls hard and jumps none too fluently. *B. J. Curley.* —

HEY COTTAGE 5 ch.g. Pablond–Cottage Myth (Rhythmic) [1989/90 16f3 16g* 20m* 20s* 22v5 17g4 16d3 16f4] rather sparely-made, angular gelding: won novice hurdles at Bangor (2) and Carlisle in first half of season: in frame in useful novice company at Chepstow and Cheltenham (9 lengths fourth to Vazon Bay in handicap) last 2 starts: stays 2½m (seemed not to stay 2¾m in testing conditions): acts on firm and soft ground: has won for an amateur and when sweating. *D. McCain.* 112 +

HEYFLEET 7 b.g. Tachypous–Heyford (Blakeney) [1989/90 c20g2] smallish, workmanlike gelding: fair hurdler/chaser: jumped none too fluently when 7 lengths second of 3 finishers behind Repington in handicap at Huntingdon in November: stays 21f: best form with give in the ground: likely to prove ideally suited by strongly-run race: often amateur or claimer ridden. *Mrs J. Pitman.* c**110** —

HEY RAWLEY 5 b.g. Sagaro–Silly Games (Siliconn) [1989/90 F17f3 22vpu 17g* 18d 24f4 24m2] workmanlike gelding: won novice hurdle at Carlisle in January despite tending to carry head high: in frame, running creditably, in amateur riders events afterwards: stays 3m: acts on firm ground: needs to brush up his jumping. *Mrs G. R. Reveley.* 97

HEYSHOTT (USA) 6 b.g. Persepolis (FR)–Agujita (FR) (Vieux Manoir) [1989/90 a18g6] smallish, sparely-made gelding: has shown more temperament than ability over hurdles and is best left alone. *J. White.* — §

HI BOOTS 5 ch.m. Deep Run–Highlight Lady (Carnival Night) [1989/90 16m 20gF] neat mare: second foal: dam unraced half-sister to a winning point-to-pointer: little sign of ability in novice hurdles. *P. J. Jones.* —

HICKLETON BOY 8 b.g. Candy Cane–Casadonna (London Scottish) [1989/90 c24gpu] big, rather leggy gelding: winning hurdler: destroyed after being pulled up in novice chase at Newcastle in December: stayed 3¼m: best form on heavy ground. *C. R. Beever.* c— —

HICKORY RUN 4 b.g. Seymour Hicks (FR)–Ardent Runner (Runnymede) [1989/90 16dF] neat gelding: modest maiden on Flat: jumped moderately and was tailed off when falling 3 out in juvenile hurdle at Newbury in February. *G. B. Balding.* —

HIDDEN BEAUTY 4 ch.f. Vaigly Great–Phoebe Ann (Absalom) [1989/90 a16g] in frame in sellers at up to 1m on Flat: sold out of K. Ivory's stable 1,450 gns Ascot November Sales: tailed-off last of 7 finishers in claiming hurdle at Southwell in February. *D. Burchell.* —

HIDDEN PLANET 5 ch.g. Star Appeal–Neptune's Treasure (Gulf Pearl) [1989/90 16g] plating-class middle-distance stayer on Flat: no form in 2 outings over hurdles: dead. *Capt. J. A. George.* —

HIGH ALOFT 6 b.h. Cut Above–Think Ahead (Sharpen Up) [1989/90 16f 16g 16m3 a18g3 21s 17f* 16m* 16f3 18f3] small, sparely-made horse: won handicap hurdles at Doncaster (seller, no bid) and Wolverhampton in March: best at up to 93

2¼m: acts on any going, except possibly heavy: has looked irresolute but did little wrong when successful: usually blinkered nowadays. *T. Casey.*

HIGH BID 5 b.m. Auction Ring (USA)–High Move (High Top) [1989/90 19m 19s4 16g4 16d5 a16g4 21d 24m] sparely-made, angular mare: winning selling hurdler: fair fourth on third start, easily best effort in non-selling handicaps in 1989/90: will do best at distances short of 21f: acts on any going, except possibly heavy. *William Price.* 93

HIGH CHATEAU 6 b.g. Amboise–High Seeker (Hotfoot) [1989/90 21f4 22g a20g2 a20g2 21m4 a20g2 a18s4 a20g6] close-coupled, lightly-made gelding: in frame numerous times over hurdles: ran badly last 2 starts: will stay beyond 2¾m: acts on good to firm and soft going. *J. L. Spearing.* 85

HIGH CLASS AGENT (USA) 12 ch.g. Executioner (USA)–Welsh Garden (Welsh Saint) [1989/90 c17f5 c20f3 c25h2 c19f2 c21f5 c26f* c24m3 c26fpu c25f5 c25m* c25fpu c25h2] compact gelding: won novice chases at Newton Abbot in September and Devon & Exeter (despite hanging left) in April: variable form otherwise: stays 3¼m: seems to act on any going: amateur ridden: sometimes blinkered (not when successful in 1989/90): looks a difficult ride and seems to have his own ideas about the game. *M. R. Churches.* c83 § — §

HIGH DEAL 6 gr.g. Warpath–Royal Handful (Some Hand) [1989/90 16g 16g 16f] rangy, unfurnished gelding: behind in novice hurdles. *A. J. Wilson.* —

HIGH EDGE GREY 9 gr. or ro.g. Precipice Wood–China Bank (Wrekin Rambler) [1989/90 c24f3 c24g4 c20g4 c24d5 c24s4 c24m5] big, workmanlike gelding: very useful chaser at his best: showed only fair form in 1989/90, giving impression something amiss at times: stays 3¼m: acts on any going. *J. K. M. Oliver.* c**123** —

HIGH FAITH 4 ch.c. Adonijah–Faith Lift (USA) (Nearctic) [1989/90 16f 16f3 16f* 16g2 17msu 16m 16g 20g6] small, angular colt: has shown ability at up to 1½m on Flat: bought in 1,900 gns after winning juvenile selling hurdle at Worcester in August: ran moderately last 3 starts: acts on firm ground: trained until after sixth outing by W. Bissill. *O. Brennan.* 77

HIGHFIELD PRINCE 4 b.g. Prince Tenderfoot (USA)–Parler Mink (Party Mink) [1989/90 16f2 16f3 17m2 16f* 16m6 19f 16m2 16m5 16f2 17f4] sparely-made gelding: useful middle-distance plater on Flat (suited by top-of-the-ground): made most when winning juvenile hurdle at Sedgefield in September: easily best efforts subsequently when second at Wetherby and Sedgefield in May: unlikely to stay much beyond 2m: acts on firm going. *R. O'Leary.* 97

HIGH FINANCE 5 ch.g. Billion (USA)–Miss Plumes (Prince de Galles) [1989/90 16f2 16f6 21fpu a20g* 22m3 a20g4 a20g* a20g2] leggy, sparely-made gelding: handicap hurdler: won at Southwell in November and January: stays 2¾m: acts on firm ground. *R. J. Weaver.* 88

HIGHFIRE 8 b.g. High Top–Home Fire (Firestreak) [1989/90 c17dF c17d2 c17d4 c17m* c16mpu c16m3] lengthy, workmanlike gelding: winning hurder: jumps none too fluently over fences, but won novice handicap at Devon & Exeter in March by 10 lengths from Romany King: ran very well long way in useful company next time: not sure to stay much beyond 2m: acts on good to firm going. *O. O'Neill.* c**98** + —

HIGHFLYING 4 br.g. Shirley Heights–Nomadic Pleasure (Habitat) [1989/90 16g 16s 16g2] quite good-topped gelding: sold out of B. Hills's stable 6,200 gns Newmarket Autumn Sales: clear 2 lengths second to Ambuscade in juvenile hurdle at Catterick in January: will stay beyond 2m: gives impression unsuited by soft ground: jumps none too fluently: won twice over middle distances on Flat in June for R. A. Harrison, and should improve over hurdles. *S. J. Muldoon.* 93 p

HIGHFRITH 7 ch.m. Deep Run–Lulu's Daughter (Levanter) [1989/90 c16g* c24g* c24s* c22g* c24g* c22d* c20f4 c16d3] c**130** —

Gordon Richards enjoyed another fine season in 1989/90, ending up in fourth place in the trainers' table with win prize money totalling more than £300,000 to his credit from seventy-eight winners. Around three quarters of his victories came with chasers, and a large number of those were provided by novices. The likes of Carrick Hill Lad (five wins), Full Strength (four out of four), Share A Friend (four) and The Antartex (three) did more than their share to bolster the total. But no horse illustrated Richards' astute placing of his novice chasers better than Highfrith, who won the first

Edinburgh Woollen Mill Novices' Chase, Kelso—Highfrith makes it six out of six

six of her eight starts without once having to put up a performance much out of the ordinary. Highfrith *is* a well-above-average performer, that much became apparent in due course, but she impressed much more with her gameness and jumping prowess than with the level of her ability early on. Wins in two novice events at Wetherby in November, and others at Haydock, Kelso and Newcastle in December and Kelso in February, were gained at the expense of largely modest opposition. Her best performance in that time undoubtedly came on soft going at Haydock, where she defeated Rifle Range and Garrison Savannah (both making their chasing debuts) by three quarters of a length and three lengths. Highfrith put up a characteristic display that day, jumping clearly the best of the ten runners and showing plenty of resolution to last home after taking up the running two out. Highfrith faced much stiffer tasks on her final two appearances and acquitted herself very well indeed, finishing five lengths fourth to Brown Windsor in the Cathcart Challenge Cup at Cheltenham and ten and a half lengths third to Celtic Shot in the hotly-contested Edinburgh Woollen Mill's Future Champion Novices' Chase at Ayr. In both races she was rather outpaced (being forced into a couple of minor jumping errors over the minimum trip at Ayr) but stayed on determinedly. While she's quite a versatile mare, we imagine Highfrith will generally be raced over longer distances in 1990/1.

Highfrith comes from an established jumping family. The best performer amongst her closer relations is her dam's half-brother, I'm A Driver, who was a high-class two-mile chaser with Tony Dickinson about a decade ago. I'm A Driver was at his best on a sound surface and could set a tremendous pace under such conditions. Sadly, he was struck down in his prime by a disease in his off-fore. Highfrith is the third of eight reported foals out of the unraced Lulu's Daughter. All but one of those foals have been fillies, the exception Highfrith's brother The Rapids, winner of a

Mr Hugh Cavendish's "Highfrith"

Highfrith (ch.m. 1983)	Deep Run (ch 1966)	Pampered King (b 1954)	Prince Chevalier
			Netherton Maid
		Trial By Fire (ch 1958)	Court Martial
			Mitrailleuse
	Lulu's Daughter (ch 1977)	Levanter (ch 1968)	Le Levanstell
			Tenebre
		Lulu Dee (ch 1962)	Straight Deal
			Lady Dee

National Hunt Flat race in 1987. Highfrith also has sisters in the shape of the poor novice hurdler Thunder Flower (also in training with Richards) and the unraced four-year-old Audley Lady (in training with Mrs Pitman). Highfrith was placed in National Hunt Flat races and won three times at up to two and three quarter miles over hurdles in her first three seasons of racing. A sparely-made mare, she tends not to impress in appearance, sometimes looking starey in her coat, and she seemed rather light in condition when winning for the second time at Kelso. Tough, genuine and a good jumper, Highfrith starts the season on a fair handicap mark and is just the sort her trainer should continue to place to best advantage. *G. Richards.*

HIGHGATE MILD 5 br.g. Homeboy–Lady Jewel (Kibenka) [1989/90 F17f] seventh foal: dam never ran: behind in NH Flat race at Doncaster in December: yet to race over hurdles or fences. *L. J. Codd.*

HIGH HAGBERG 4 b.g. Cree Song–Persian Breakfast (Deep Diver) [1989/90 F16m aF13g] fifth foal: half-brother to fair 1985 2-y-o Calixtus (by

Whitbread White Label Handicap Hurdle, Cheltenham—
stable-companions Highland Bounty (noseband) and Nahar lead Imperial Brush over the last

Sonnen Gold): dam plater: last in NH Flat races: yet to race over hurdles. *J. E. Long.*

HIGH HAM BLUES 8 b.g. White Prince (USA)–Gwentello (Cock of The **c127**
North) [1989/90 c26g* c25g* c24m* c24f* c25g* c25m* c25s^{pu} c25m* c25f^{4}] —
lengthy, sparely-made gelding: modest hurdler: unbeaten in first 7 completed starts over fences, gaining seventh success in handicap at Devon & Exeter in March by 6 lengths from En Gounasi Theon: successful earlier in novice events at Stratford, Plumpton and Wolverhampton and handicap chases at Taunton (2) and Plumpton: stays 3¼m: acts on any going: occasionally blinkered: sometimes sweating: usually makes running: has looked a difficult ride: makes the odd mistake: sold 25,000 gns Ascot June Sales. *D. H. Barons.*

HIGH HOLBORN 4 b.c. Electric–Beira's Gift (Dominion) [1989/90 16m^{6}
16v^{pu} a16g^{pu}] good-bodied colt: modest maiden on Flat: sold out of P. Walwyn's 80
stable 5,600 gns Ascot July Sales: sixth in juvenile hurdle at Market Rasen in September. *J. Joseph.*

HIGH IMP 10 ch.g. Import–High Walk (Tower Walk) [1989/90 c16m* c16g^{3} **c109**
c16g^{2} c17g^{5} 16v^{pu} c16g^{5} c16d^{5}] leggy gelding: moderate chaser and novice —
hurdler: made virtually all to win at Bangor in October: ran moderately last 4 outings: takes a good hold and is suited by a sharp 2m: probably acts on any going: has won when sweating: successful with and without blinkers: has worn a tongue strap and a crossed noseband: good mount for a claimer. *P. Leach.*

HIGH KABOUR 4 b.f. Kabour–High Walk (Tower Walk) [1989/90 16g 16g^{pu}]
workmanlike filly: fourth living foal: half-sister to moderate 2m chaser High Imp —
(by Import): dam plater on Flat: behind in novice claiming hurdle at Nottingham in October. *R. D. E. Woodhouse.*

HIGHLAND BOUNTY 6 b.g. High Line–Segos (Runnymede) [1989/90 16f^{5}
16g* 16m^{6} 16f 16g^{3}] narrow, plain gelding: has a round action: fairly useful 127
hurdler: ridden by claimer, won moderately-run Whitbread White Label (Handicap) at Cheltenham in November: below his best subsequently (out of his depth fourth start): probably needs forcing tactics and give in the ground when racing at 2m and stays 21f: acts on any going. *S. Dow.*

HIGHLAND CHAIN 5 b.m. Furry Glen–Keep The Link (Takawalk II) [1989/90 F16f^{4} F16f^{3} F16f^{4}] second foal: sister to Irish novice chaser Fact 'N Fancies: dam moderate staying chaser: in frame in NH Flat races at Newbury, Ludlow and Hereford in the spring: yet to race over hurdles or fences. *J. A. C. Edwards.*

HIGHLAND LAIRD 6 b.g. Kampala–Bonny Hollow (Wolver Hollow)
[1989/90 16s 20m 16s^{6} 16d^{2} 20f^{pu} 20m^{pu}] well-made gelding: novice hurdler: 74

dropped in class, only form of season when second to in seller at Bangor in March: best form at 2m: acts on firm and dead ground. *J. Ringer.*

HIGHLAND PARK 4 ch.g. Simply Great (FR)–Perchance (Connaught) [1989/90 16f] workmanlike gelding: won 1½m claimer on Flat in July (has been visored): tailed-off last of 15 in juvenile hurdle at Catterick in November, making mistakes and trying to refuse sixth. *F. Watson.* —

HIGHLAND TREAT 6 b.g. Northern Treat (USA)–Cereal Queen (Oats) [1989/90 c20m4 c20g3] compact gelding: 2m winner on Flat in 1988: won handicap hurdle at Roscommon in August, 1988: in frame in 2½m novice chases at Leicester and Carlisle in January, giving impression he'll be suited by a return to shorter distances when 12 lengths third to Share A Friend on latter course: acts on any going: has won with and without blinkers. *J. A. C. Edwards.* c**89** —

HIGH LAWS 6 b.g. Royal Fountain–Dunlean (Leander) [1989/90 20m6 19g3 19d2 19gpu a24g5 22g 17dpu] workmanlike gelding: novice hurdler: has run in a seller: stays 19f (well beaten over 3m): acts on dead going: sometimes blinkered: has been reluctant to race. *William Price.* 86 §

HIGHLY DECORATED 5 b.g. Sharpo–New Ribbons (Ribero) [1989/90 16f2 16g4 20g3 16gur] workmanlike gelding: modest novice hurdler: in frame at Catterick (swished tail and edged left), Kelso and Wetherby (didn't find a great deal) in 1989/90: stays 2½m: acts on any going: ran moderately when blinkered final start 1988/9. *J. H. Johnson.* 92

HIGHMOOR LADY 6 ch.m. Slim Jim–Highmoor Lass (Rubor) [1989/90 17g6] smallish, workmanlike mare: well beaten in NH Flat races: claimer ridden, raced too freely when 17½ lengths sixth behind Hey Rawley in novice hurdle at Carlisle in January: will be suited by a less testing track. *A. Eubank.* 75

HIGH NODDY 5 b.m. Tom Noddy–High Lee (Will Hays (USA)) [1989/90 16mF 16dpu a16gpu 16f 16f 16f5] novice selling hurdler: blinkered third and final outings. *C. L. Popham.* 64

HIGH OFFICE 8 b.g. Roselier (FR)–Digynia (Dignitary) [1989/90 c24dpu c24fpu] medium-sized gelding: modest novice hurdler: failed to complete course in point-to-points and hunter chases: was suited by a test of stamina: blinkered last 2 starts over hurdles: dead. *Noel Athey.* c— —

HIGH POKEY 4 b.f. Uncle Pokey–High Seeker (Hotfoot) [1989/90 16g] sparely-made filly: behind all outings on Flat and in conditional jockeys selling hurdle at Ludlow in December. *J. L. Spearing.* —

HIGH POPPA 11 b.g. Mummy's Pet–Two For Joy (Double-U-Jay) [1989/90 c21gpu] smallish, workmanlike gelding: won selling hurdle in 1982/3: quite a useful winning point-to-pointer: modest form in hunter chases: ran too freely only outing in 1990: stays 21f: acts on soft going (ran moderately on heavy). *Tim Tarratt.* c— —

HIGH REEF 9 br.g. Take A Reef–Hi Tess (Supreme Court) [1989/90 20m6] small, lightly-made gelding: novice selling hurdler: has run blinkered. *P. Leach.* 61

HIGH RIDGE 11 b.g. High Top–Naughty Party (Parthia) [1989/90 c20s c25m6 c25f6] neat gelding: poor hurdler/chaser: stays 3m: suited by the mud: makes mistakes: best form in blinkers: visored last 3 starts in 1988/9: has won for a claimer. *Major J. C. Simison.* c— x —

HIGH RIVER 8 br.m. Joshua–High Value (Forlorn River) [1989/90 c16f3 c16g4 c16g* c16d* c16dwo c17m2 c16dur c16g3 c16mpu] slightly dipped-backed mare: modest chaser: won handicaps at Market Rasen in December and Warwick in January: walked over at Nottingham later in January: destroyed after breaking a leg at Uttoxeter in March: was best at around 2m: probably acted on any going. *B. C. Morgan.* c**111** —

HIGHRYMER 6 gr.m. Rymer–On High (Town Crier) [1989/90 24m4] strong mare: of little account as a hurdler: won a point-to-point in April: ran out in NH Flat race in 1987/8. *J. E. Brockbank.* —

HIGH SHOON 9 b. or br.g. Green Shoon–High Town Jackie (David Jack) [1989/90 c24d5] ex-Irish gelding: winning hurdler/chaser: won a point-to-point in April: moderate fifth behind easy winner Mystic Music in hunter chase at Perth following month: stays 3m: probably acts on any going. *J. A. C. Edwards.* c**93** —

HIGH STOY 4 br.g. My Top–Dorcetta (Condorcet (FR)) [1989/90 20s* 16g3 24d3] ex-Irish gelding: first foal: dam, French 1½m winner, half-sister to a winning hurdler: placed over 1½m on Flat: sold out of P. Mullins' stable 5,000 gns 90

Doncaster November Sales: won 4-runner juvenile claiming hurdle at Sedgefield in February: stayed 3m: acted on soft going: dead. *P. Monteith.*

HIGH TENSION 8 ch.g. Vitiges (FR)–Montania (Mourne) [1989/90 16f^{4}] compact gelding: one-time fair middle-distance handicapper on Flat: bit back- 82 p
ward, staying-on 18 lengths fourth of 6 to Run For Free in quite valuable novice event at Cheltenham in December on hurdling debut: will stay beyond 2m. *D. L. Williams.*

HIGH TILT 4 b.f. My Dad Tom (USA)–Torlonia (Royal Palace) [1989/90 16f^{pu}
16g^{pu}] sparely-made filly: well beaten on Flat: pulled up in conditional jockeys —
selling hurdles in December. *C. James.*

HIGH TOBY 7 ch.g. Tobique–Nant Celynen (Jimmy Reppin) [1989/90 F16g c—
c21g^{F} c26g^{pu} c24d^{F} c24m^{ur} 24m] strong, workmanlike gelding: won point-to- —
point in 1988: no other sign of ability: whipped round start fifth outing. *N. A. Twiston-Davies.*

HIGHWAY EXPRESS 9 ch.g. Pony Express–Hilda's Way (Royal Highway) c**123**
[1989/90 c21d^{4} c25s* c24v^{5} c24m c21f* c25m^{2}] strong, workmanlike gelding: —
usually impresses in appearance: fair chaser: won handicap at Sandown in February: long odds on, all out to win 3-runner minor event at Wincanton in March by ¾ length from Pernickety: soundly beaten in between: stays well: probably acts on any going: good jumper, suited by forcing tactics. *R. J. Hodges.*

HIGHWAYTRUCKRENTAL 9 bl.g. Dawn Review–Walshaw Minnie (Nice
Music) [1989/90 a18g] in rear in 2 NH Flat races in 1986/7 and a conditional —
jockeys selling hurdle at Southwell in January: lightly-raced maiden point-to-pointer. *Roy Robinson.*

HIGHWOOD LAD 4 b.g. Pia Fort–Happy Lizzie (Hapanui) [1989/90 16s^{pu}
16v^{pu}] workmanlike gelding: second foal: dam failed to complete in point-to- —
points: behind when pulled up in juvenile hurdles at Taunton and Chepstow (pulled hard): claimer ridden. *R. J. Hodges.*

HI HIGH 9 ch.g. High Line–Denosa (Worden II) [1989/90 c16m^{3} c16g^{pu}] c**109**
sparely-made gelding: poor hurdler/moderate chaser: made a bad mistake 3 out —
and was pulled up after next on final start (January): takes a strong hold and form only at around 2m: acts on firm and dead going. *R. J. Hodges.*

HILARION (FR) 6 br.g. Gay Mecene (USA)–Helvetie II (Klairon) [1989/90 c**90**
c16g^{3} c16m^{3} c16m^{2} c16m^{3} c17g^{2} c16m^{pu}] leggy gelding: walked over in novice —
hurdle in 1988/9: placed in novice chases: possibly unsuited by soft going: has looked none too keen under pressure and is one to have reservations about. *J. A. C. Edwards.*

HILDA 4 b.f. Ile de Bourbon (USA)–Palovna (FR) (Lyphard (USA)) [1989/90 F16m^{4} aF16g*] fourth foal: half-sister to 1½m Flat winners Veronica Ann (by Henbit) and Top Cut (by Cut Above): dam middle-distance maiden: won 8-runner NH Flat race at Southwell in January by 5 lengths from Pop Abroad: yet to race over hurdles. *R. Hollinshead.*

HILL BEAGLE 10 b.g. Goldhill–Beagle Bay (Deep Run) [1989/90 c16g^{F} c—
a16g* a16g* 16g^{6} a16g* a16g^{3} a16g^{3} a16g* a16g^{3} 17f a18g 16f^{3} 16m^{6} 16g^{3} 16m^{4}] 100
small, sturdy gelding: moderate hurdler: gaining fourth course win of the season when winning at Southwell in February: also ran creditably most starts afterwards: poor novice chaser: stays 2½m: seems to act on any going: pulls hard (has worn severe noseband): has won for a claimer: tough and consistent. *W. Clay.*

HILL OF BARRA 12 ch.g. Pieces of Eight–Red Sea (Zimone) [1989/90 c24g] c—
sturdy gelding: winning point-to-pointer: poor novice chaser: stays 25f: probably —
unsuited by heavy ground: sometimes blinkered. *A. P. Jones.*

HILL'S HALO 4 b.g. Kampala–Clanjingle (Tumble Wind (USA)) [1989/90 16s]
workmanlike gelding: modest middle-distance maiden on Flat: jumped none too —
fluently when tailed off in juvenile hurdle at Hereford in December. *J. A. C. Edwards.*

HILL'S PAGEANT 11 b.g. Welsh Pageant–Reita (Gilles de Retz) [1989/90 c—
c21m^{5}] compact gelding: one-time useful hurdler/fair chaser: stiffish task, last of —
5 in minor event over fences at Wincanton in December: takes a good hold and best at around 2m: acts on heavy going: wears bandages in front. *F. Walwyn.*

HILL-STREET-BLUES 12 b.g. White Prince (USA)–Crendle Hill (French
Beige) [1989/90 24g 20v 20s 21d] tall gelding: fair hurdler at his best: well beaten —
in 1989/90: stays 3m but better at slightly shorter trips when conditions are testing: acts on any going: suitable mount for a claimer. *A. S. Ridout.*

HILL STREET (FR) 8 b.g. Grandchant (FR)–Tetlin (FR) (Apollo Eight) [1989/90 20g* 16d 20m] sparely-made, angular gelding: quite a useful hurdler/chaser: very easy winner of handicap hurdle at Market Rasen in December: weakened quickly after last when moderate eighth in valuable handicap at Liverpool in April, last start: broke blood vessel in between (off course 2 months subsequently): needs stiff track and testing conditions when racing at 2m and stays 21f: acts well on heavy going: bandaged in 1989/90: needs to brush up his jumping of fences. *J. G. FitzGerald.* c— 132

HILL-WAY BLUES 5 b.g. Uncle Pokey–Carnation (Runnymede) [1989/90 aF13g^{2} a18g] second of 4 in NH Flat race at Lingfield in December: tailed-off last of 7 in novice hurdle on same course in March. *A. S. Ridout.* —

HINDERENDS 6 br.g. The Brianstan–Gleaning (Sovereign Gleam) [1989/90 aF16g F16v] second foal: half-brother to a poor novice hurdler by Remainder Man: dam winning staying hurdler: behind in NH Flat races: yet to race over hurdles or fences. *P. S. Felgate.*

HIRAM B BIRDBATH 4 b.g. Ragapan–At The King's Side (USA) (Kauai King) [1989/90 16g 16m 16g^{2} a16g* 16v^{5} 20m^{3}] smallish, close-coupled gelding: brother to Irish 1½m winner King Ragapan and fair hurdler The Irish Rhine: dam won at up to 1¼m in USA: won novice hurdle at Southwell in February: good last of 3 finishers in similar event at Sedgefield following month: had stiff task in between: stays 2½m: blinkered and claimer ridden last 4 starts. *J. A. Glover.* 102

HITCHCOCK 7 b.g. Beau Charmeur (FR)–Laurabeg (Laurence O) [1989/90 c22g*dis c20g^{F} c20m^{pu} c24s^{3} c25m^{ur} c20s* c20m^{2} c20s* c20v^{4}] rather leggy gelding: fairly useful chaser: first past post at Stratford in October (disqualified for hampering runner-up on final turn), Folkestone in January and Uttoxeter in February: best form at 2¾m: acted on heavy going: made mistakes: dead. *J. A. C. Edwards.* c**126** x —

HITCHENSTOWN 7 b.g. Town And Country–Veinarde (Derring-Do) [1989/90 c20s^{pu} c16s] rather leggy gelding: winning hurdler: has jumped none too fluently and shown no sign of ability in novice chases: stays 2½m: acts on heavy going: visored final start in 1988/9. *M. J. O'Neill.* c— —

HI-TECH BOY 8 ch.g. Tickled Pink–Jetwitch (Lear Jet) [1989/90 a16g^{pu}] lightly-made gelding: winning selling hurdler: lightly raced and no form since 1985/6: doesn't stay much beyond 2m: acts on soft going. *T. B. Hallett.* —

HIT ME AGAIN 12 ch.g. Quayside–Nell (Gilles de Retz) [1989/90 c16g^{4}] stocky gelding: won a point-to-point in February: 17 lengths fourth to Wise Gambol in hunter chase at Fakenham in April. *Russell G. Abrey.* c83

HIT THE BOX 5 ch.g. Quayside–Three Dieu (Three Dons) [1989/90 F13d^{5} aF16g^{3} aF16g^{6}] fifth foal: brother to fair hurdler/chaser Hand Over and half-brother to winning selling hurdler Top Pryal (by Prominer): dam, unraced, closely related to high-class hurdler Dondieu: third in NH Flat race at Southwell in February: sold 6,200 gns Doncaster Spring Sales: yet to race over hurdles or fences. *J. G. FitzGerald.*

HIT THE CEILING 7 br.g. Buckskin (FR)–Star of Hope (Laurence O) [1989/90 c20m^{2} c18m^{2} c24f^{su} c26g^{pu} c25f^{2} c30m^{3} c26m^{3}] big, lengthy, plain gelding: first foal: dam winning point-to-pointer: won a point-to-point in Ireland in 1989: placed in novice chases and amateur riders handicap chase: thorough stayer: jumped soundly: trained by J. Brassil until after second outing: dead. *J. J. O'Neill.* c83

HI' UPHAM 8 ch.m. Deep Run–Highly Acceptable (Immortality) [1989/90 c20s^{ur} c25d^{F} c25d^{F} c22d^{ur} c26g^{F}] lengthy mare: novice hurdler/chaser: let down by her jumping in 1989/90: stays well: acts on soft going. *D. R. Gandolfo.* c— x —

HI WALLIE 8 b.g. Fidel–Donnarabella (Bluerullah) [1989/90 16m 20m^{5} c16f^{3} c16f^{3} c16g^{4} c16g^{3} c17g^{4} c22f^{5} c17h^{2}] tall, leggy, close-coupled gelding: winning hurdler and poor novice chaser: stays 2¾m: acts on any going: has worn a tongue strap. *R. Allan.* c78 —

HIXON GIRL 7 ch.m. St Columbus–Hillvale (Narrator) [1989/90 16m^{4} 17m^{3} 16f c16d^{F} a20g^{5} a16g a20g^{4}] sparely-made mare: poor novice hurdler: fell heavily at the eighth in mares novice event on chasing debut. *W. Clay.* c— 64

HJANI 9 b.g. Tanfirion–Ikatina (Tower Walk) [1989/90 16g^{4} a20g^{3} a18g^{3} 22g a16g a16g^{pu}] good-bodied gelding: poor novice hurdler, seemingly on downgrade: pulled up lame final start: fell in a point-to-point in 1988. *P. Butler.* 78 d

HODDAM BRIG 11 b.g. New Brig–Starry Grey (Starry Halo) [1989/90 c16f* c24m4 c20g6 c24dpu c22d6 c24d c16g c20h3] sturdy gelding: novice hurdler: point-to-point winner: won 3-runner novice chase at Hexham in October: poor form afterwards: probably stays 2½m: acts on hard going. *D. Scott.* c80 —

HOGAN'S RUN 5 br.h. Tender King–Moment To Remember (USA) (Assagai) [1989/90 16f2 16f* 16f2 16f* 16f2 16f* 16m 16m 20gpu 16f2] compact, workmanlike horse: successful early in season in novice claiming hurdle at Stratford and novice hurdles at Kelso and Catterick (made all): best effort subsequently when 3 lengths second to Candlebright in handicap at Hexham in May: unlikely to stay much beyond 2m: acts well on firm ground: pulled too hard in lady riders event eighth outing (trained until after then by C. Tinkler). *Mrs S. C. Bradburne.* 99

HOGMANAY (CAN) 8 b.g. Halo (USA)–Annie Laurie (CAN) (Kennedy Road (CAN)) [1989/90 c20g2 c20m5 c16m4 c20g3 c16g* c16f2] tall, leggy, sparely-made gelding: useful chaser: made all to win handicap at Sandown in January by 1½ lengths from Broad Beam: 2 lengths second to With Gods Help at Ascot next outing, 4 months later: stays 21f, probably not 3m: acts on firm ground: game: usually makes running and jumps well: trained fourth and fifth starts by P. Feilden. *R. F. Casey.* c136 —

HOISTED 6 ch.g. Posse (USA)–Miss Petard (Petingo) [1989/90 16mbd 16f 16m3 16s 16s 17g a16gpu c16m2 16gpu] sparely-made, angular gelding: poor novice hurdler: beaten a distance by only other finisher Chico Valdez in amateur riders novice chase at Market Rasen in April: blinkered sixth start: sold to Mrs A. Knight 3,200 gns Ascot July Sales. *C. Smith.* c— 66

HOLDENBY 5 b.h. Henbit (USA)–Isadora Duncan (Primera) [1989/90 16m4 16g* a16g4] leggy, close-coupled horse: won 4-runner handicap hurdle at Sedgefield in November: finished seemingly lame when well beaten at Southwell later in month: races only at 2m: acts on hard ground: usually claimer ridden. *T. Fairhurst.* 94

HOLD ON TIGHT 5 ch.m. Battlement–Holdmetight (New Brig) [1989/90 aF13g6 16f 17f4] second foal: sister to maiden point-to-pointer Hold And Fort: dam poor novice hurdler/chaser: first sign of ability when 16 lengths fourth to Straw Blade in novice selling hurdle at Newton Abbot in May. *R. G. Frost.* 67

HOLLIST 7 b.g. Pollerton–Inagh's Image (Menelek) [1989/90 c16d5] big, strong gelding: modest novice hurdler/chaser: bit backward, sweating and on toes, always well behind only outing in 1989/90: should stay 2½m: tends to pull hard and has worn a crossed noseband: broke a blood vessel final outing in 1988/9. *Capt. T. A. Forster.* c— —

HOLLOW WONDER 8 b.m. Revlow–Honey Beam (Heswall Honey) [1989/90 16spu] sparely-made mare: seems of little account. *Mrs N. Macauley.* —

HOLLY BUOY 10 b.h. Blind Harbour–Holly Doon (Doon) [1989/90 c20gr] small, lightly-made horse: moderate hurdler/chaser at his best, but has become thoroughly temperamental (refused to race last 2 starts) and is one to leave alone. *Mrs G. R. Reveley.* c§§ §§

HOLLY KING (USA) 6 b.g. Key To The Kingdom (USA)–Chargealero (USA) (Native Charger) [1989/90 16m c16m5 c16gF c16d5 c24f5 c16gpu] rather sparely-made gelding: well beaten both completed outings over hurdles: only form over fences when 9½ lengths fifth behind Queen's Bay Lad in novice event at Sedgefield in March, fourth outing: sold 1,950 gns Ascot June Sales. *J. A. C. Edwards.* c79 —

HOLTERMANN (USA) 6 b.g. Mr Prospector (USA)–Royal Graustark (USA) (Graustark) [1989/90 16f4 16m3 16f2 16f5 16g5 21d c20g3 a20g] rangy, rather unfurnished gelding: novice hurdler: over 25 lengths last of 3 in novice chase won by Combermere at Kempton in February: takes a good hold and is likely to prove best at 2m: acts on firm and dead going: has worn crossed noseband: sold out of D. Elsworth's stable 4,000 gns Newmarket Autumn Sales after first start: has looked faint-hearted. *M. J. Haynes.* c? 99 §

HOLT PLACE 7 b.g. Be My Guest (USA)–Ya Ya (Primera) [1989/90 19g 20fF 20gF a20g6] smallish, good-bodied gelding: novice hurdler: well below form in 1989/90: should stay 2½m: ran moderately on very soft ground but seems to act on any other: suitable mount for a claimer. *N. A. Smith.* —

HOLY JOE 8 b.g. The Parson–Doonasleen (Deep Run) [1989/90 16d* 21s2 20d* 25m6] leggy ex-Irish gelding: third foal: dam, 2m winner on Flat, well beaten over hurdles: won 2 point-to-points and a NH Flat race in Ireland in 1987: sold out of C. Kinane's stable 25,000 gns Doncaster Spring Sales: won handicap hurdles at 116

Wincanton (novice event) in February and Chepstow in March: one-paced 19½ lengths sixth behind Dwadme in quite valuable novice event at Liverpool in April: probably stays 3m: acts on soft and good to firm going: has run well for an amateur. *A. J. Wilson.*

HOLY WAR 6 b.g. Northfields (USA)–Bella Carlotta (FR) (Charlottesville) [1989/90 16m 16hpu] close-coupled, rather leggy gelding: poor maiden hurdler: has been blinkered. *A. Barrow.* —

HOME COMMAND 10 ch.g. Home Guard (USA)–Fleurie (Reliance II) [1989/90 17f5 17f5] smallish, sturdy gelding: selling hurdler/chaser: stays 21f: acts on hard going: sometimes blinkered over hurdles: good mount for a claimer: sold 800 gns Ascot October Sales. *J. M. Bradley.* c— 80

HOME ON SUNDAY 6 b.g. Camden Town–Faddle (St Paddy) [1989/90 20spu] behind in NH Flat races in 1987/8: tailed off when pulled up in novice hurdle at Chepstow (bolted before start and took strong hold in race) in December. *R. Brotherton.* —

HOME OR AWAY 7 b.g. Homing–Tagik (Targowice (USA)) [1989/90 19f3] leggy, lightly-made gelding: one-time useful plater over hurdles: having first outing for 18 months, around 16 lengths third behind Ardbrin in non-selling handicap at Taunton in March: stays 19f: acts on any going: blinkered third start 1988/9. *J. H. Baker.* 88

HOMEPATH 10 b.g. Homing–Path of Pride (Sovereign Path) [1989/90 16f c20f3] angular gelding: poor form over hurdles: has shown nothing over fences: has been tried in blinkers. *J. R. Jenkins.* c— —

HOME POOL 5 ch.h. Habitat–Rossitor (Pall Mall) [1989/90 17f 19dpu] angular, sparely-made horse: poor one-paced maiden on Flat: jumped moderately and showed little promise in 2 novice hurdles. *D. J. Wintle.* —

HOMER CITY 5 b.g. Homing–Navarino Bay (Averof) [1989/90 16f* 16f4] sparely-made gelding: won conditional jockeys novice hurdle at Market Rasen in August: acted on firm ground: dead. *J. G. FitzGerald.* 87 +

HOMERIGG LAD 6 b.g. Spur On–Most Kind (Tudenham) [1989/90 F 17m 20g 22d4 20m6 20f] leggy, rather unfurnished gelding: first living foal: dam, poor plater on Flat, half-sister to 3 winners: remote fourth only completed outing in point-to-points in 1989: poor novice hurdler: probably stays 2¾m: wears crossed noseband. *Miss Z. A. Green.* 79

HOMER'S NOD 7 b.g. Quayside–Gilded Empress (Menelek) [1989/90 20g 16v 20fpu 19m5] angular ex-Irish gelding: first foal: dam behind in NH Flat race and when falling in maiden hurdle: in frame in NH Flat races: no form over hurdles but is a point-to-point winner. *C. J. Hitchings.* —

HOME STRAIGHT 4 b.g. Homing–Fast Asleep (Hotfoot) [1989/90 16g 16f3] half-brother to 2 winners on Flat: dam maiden half-sister to a winning jumper: plating-class maiden miler on Flat: sold out of M. Brittain's stable 1,600 gns Doncaster November Sales: 12 lengths third to Fernando Reyes in novice hurdle at Hexham in March: ran in seller on debut. *W. Storey.* 81

HOME TO ROOST 10 b. or br.g. Peacock (FR)–La Belle Dame (Super Sam) [1989/90 26d6 22d 27s 24g 27gpu 17d 16gsu 16f6 22f3 24m 24g2 24d4 23f4] compact gelding: winning point-to-pointer: poor jumper and no form in steeplechases: handicap hurdler: only poor form in 1989/90, including in a seller: suited by a good test of stamina: acts well on heavy going: has won for a claimer. *F. Jestin.* c— x 85

HOME TO TARA 6 b.g. Prince Tenderfoot (USA)–Gayshuka (Lord Gayle (USA)) [1989/90 16g a16g2] leggy, rather sparely-made gelding: first sign of a little ability 12 lengths second of 4 to Hill Beagle in slowly-run handicap hurdle at Southwell in November. *Mrs J. E. Croft.* 60

HO MI CHINH 8 ch.g. Homing–Fiordiligi (Tudor Melody) [1989/90 c16gur] lengthy gelding: sprint handicapper on Flat: seems not to have taken to jumping. *J. M. Bradley.* c— —

HOMME D'AFFAIRE 7 br.g. Lord Gayle (USA)–French Cracker (Klairon) [1989/90 20d3 18g 16s 16m] smallish, workmanlike gelding: fair hurdler: good third in handicap at Haydock in December: below form subsequently: stays 2½m: acts on heavy going: jumps boldly and well. *R. J. O'Sullivan.* 115

HONEYBEER MEAD 8 ch.g. Le Bavard (FR)–Midnight Oil (Menelek) [1989/90 20d c20dpu c24gpu] leggy, lengthy gelding: third in a 2m novice hurdle in 1988/9: tailed off when pulled up in novice chases. *B. J. M. Ryall.* c— —

HONEYMAN 8 gr.g. Remainder Man–Pure Honey (Don (ITY)) [1989/90 c17f2] close-coupled, rather sparely-made gelding: fair hurdler at best: modest chaser: jumped none too fluently when second in handicap at Newton Abbot in August: unlikely to stay much beyond 2m: acts on hard ground and a yielding surface: used to wear blinkers: front runner. *J. Mackie.* c**106** —

HONEY SAINT 5 b.g. Welsh Saint–Hunea (Hornbeam) [1989/90 16fF 16m5 16m4 20g 16mur 16m*] workmanlike gelding: half-brother to several winning jumpers, including fairly useful chaser Katmandu (by Yellow God): dam ran 3 times at 2 yrs: tailed off only outing on Flat: won novice handicap hurdle at Towcester in November: should stay further than 2m: acts on good to firm ground. *T. P. McGovern.* 76

HONORARY CONSUL 9 b.g. Bruni–Isadora Duncan (Primera) [1989/90 16dpu 16g6] lightly raced and of little account. *T. Craig.* —

HONOURS GRADUATE 4 br.g. Petorius–Princess Virginia (Connaught) [1989/90 16dpu] workmanlike gelding: first foal: dam, non-thoroughbred 6f and 7f winner, became thoroughly temperamental: tailed off in 5f maiden on Flat in 1988: pulled very hard, weakened quickly 3 out and pulled up before next in juvenile hurdle at Ludlow in March. *L. J. Codd.* —

HONOUR THE WIND 4 ch.c. Ahonoora–Mill Wind (Blakeney) [1989/90 16m] half-brother to novice hurdler Starwind (by Star Appeal): modest maiden on Flat, stays 9f: sold out of R. Hannon's stable 2,600 gns Newmarket Autumn Sales: tailed off in juvenile hurdle at Stratford in May. *P. R. Hedger.* —

HOOK HEAD 6 ch.g. Pollerton–Deep View (Deep Run) [1989/90 c21gpu] robust gelding: tailed off when pulled up in novice hurdle and a novice chase (jumped appallingly): sold 2,700 gns Ascot May Sales. *Andrew Turnell.* c— x —

HOPE AGAINST HOPE 4 b.f. Mansingh (USA)–Hopeful Ann (Abwah) [1989/90 16m] sparely-made filly: soundly beaten in sellers at 2 yrs: jumped poorly when tailed-off last of 9 finishers in selling hurdle at Nottingham in November. *T. H. Caldwell.* —

HOPEA (USA) 4 ro.f. Drone–Hope So (USA) (Tudor Grey) [1989/90 a16g] won over 11f on Flat in February: seventh of 10 to Mehtab in juvenile hurdle at Southwell in March. *D. T. Thom.* —

HOPE COVE (NZ) 8 b.m. Mayo Mellay (NZ)–Bundoran (NZ) (Bally Royal) [1989/90 c20dpu c24g4 c16vF c21gpu c16f3 c25mpu c26m4] lengthy, rather lightly-made mare: winning hurdler/chaser: only poor form in 1989/90: stays 2¾m: best form with plenty of give in the ground: blinkered fourth start: sold 3,400 gns Ascot June Sales. *N. A. Gaselee.* c**90** —

HOPE DIAMOND 7 b. or br.g. Sparkler–Canaan (Santa Claus) [1989/90 c19d* c20v3 c20v3 c20d2 c25f3] sparely-made gelding: fair hurdler: moderate chaser: won handicap at Devon & Exeter in January: placed in similar races subsequently, running creditably: probably stays 3m: best form with give in the ground: blinkered nowadays: rather deliberate jumper. *N. A. Gaselee.* c**111** —

HOPE END 12 br.g. Politico (USA)–Katebird (Birdbrook) [1989/90 c16d5 c20d c25m6] leggy, lightly-made gelding: modest chaser at his best: well behind all outings in 1989/90: best form at around 2m on an easy surface: blinkered once. *Mrs H. Parrott.* c— —

HOPEFUL KYBO 10 ch.g. Candy Cane–You Fell (Raise You Ten) [1989/90 24mpu c24mpu] leggy, close-coupled gelding: modest novice hurdler/chaser: very lightly raced and little form of late: stays 2½m (tailed off over 25f): probably acts on any going. *A. J. Williams.* c— —

HOPEFULL LADY 4 ch.f. Full of Hope–Frimley's One Oak (Pieces of Eight) [1989/90 16f5 16f5 17m6 16h5] probably of little account on Flat: seems little better as a hurdler: ridden by 7-lb claimer. *R. J. Hodges.* —

HOPING FOR GLORY (USA) 4 b.c. L'Emigrant (USA)–Hope For All (USA) (Secretariat (USA)) [1989/90 16g4 16g4 16d2] compact colt: modest form in 2 races over 6f on Flat in 1989 when trained by H. Cecil: modest form over hurdles: has pulled hard (taken quietly to post first and last outings): looked less than keen under pressure on final start: sold K. Morgan 5,200 gns Doncaster Spring Sales. *D. Nicholson.* 103

HOPPING AROUND 6 b.g. Prince Tenderfoot (USA)–Wurli (Wolver Hollow) [1989/90 16g2 20s* a20g2 a20g4] neat gelding: poor mover: won over 15f on Flat in 1989 (often doesn't find great deal under pressure): won novice hurdle at Sedgefield in January: second to all-the-way winner Follow The Drum at 98

Southwell in February: ran poorly last start: stays 2½m: acts on heavy going. *C. W. Thornton.*

HOP THE TWIG 5 b.m. Full of Hope–Two Shots (Dom Racine (FR)) [1989/90
16m^{3} a16g* a16g^{pu} 20g^{pu}] first foal: dam ran twice at 2 yrs: won novice hurdle at 85
Southwell in March: ran poorly afterwards. *B. Preece.*

HORATIAN 5 b.g. Horage–Assurance (FR) (Timmy Lad) [1989/90 16s^{4} 17v
a16g* a16g^{2}] rather sparely-made gelding: claimed out of Mrs J. Wonnacott's 89
stable £4,207 after winning novice claiming hurdle at Lingfield in February
(amateur ridden): clear ¾-length second to The Lighter Side on same course
following month. *A. W. Denson.*

HORTONDALE 5 ch.g. Tickled Pink–Jamaya (Double-U-Jay) [1989/90 17m*]
compact gelding: claimer ridden, won 14-runner maiden hurdle at Newton Abbot 93
in April by ¾ length from Country Diary: will stay further than 17f: acts on good to
firm and dead ground (seems unsuited by very soft): has worn pricker. *R. J. Holder.*

HOSTILE ACT 5 b.g. Glenstal (USA)–Fandetta (Gay Fandango (USA))
[1989/90 16g] close-coupled gelding: lightly-raced novice hurdler. *Miss P. Hall.* —

HOT COMPANY 5 ch.g. Hotfoot–Campagna (Romulus) [1989/90 16m* 16g^{2}
16m^{2} 16g^{3} a16g^{5} a20g^{4} 17f^{4} 16f^{3} 16f 16f^{3}] leggy, rather sparely-made gelding: won 91
novice hurdle at Perth in September: in-and-out form afterwards: best run at 2m
on good to firm ground: has found little under pressure: blinkered final start
1988/9: sold out of G. Pritchard-Gordon's stable 7,000 gns Ascot August Sales:
claimed out of D. Burchell's stable £8,401 after winning 1½m claimer on Flat in
January before fifth outing. *P. J. Bevan.*

HOT GIRL 8 b.m. Hot Grove–Gloria Maremmana (King Emperor (USA))
[1989/90 16m^{5} 18m^{2} 16m 16d^{F}] compact mare: novice hurdler: ran as though 81
something amiss last 2 starts (off course 3 months in between): will stay beyond
2¼m: acts on soft going and good to firm. *K. Bishop.*

HOT HANDED 9 ch.m. Nearly A Hand–Fiery Sol (Firestreak) [1989/90 24m^{6} c— x
18f^{3}] leggy, sparely-made mare: poor hurdler: well beaten over fences: stays 80
2¾m: acts on hard and dead going: often blinkered: usually amateur ridden. *C. T. Nash.*

HOT HOSTESS 9 b.m. Silly Season–Clever Pin (Pinza) [1989/90 c21m^{5}] c—
placed in 2 point-to-points in 1989: soundly beaten in novice hunter chase at
Fakenham in May. *Miss C. Saunders.*

HOTPLATE 7 ch.g. Buckskin (FR)–Pencil Lady (Bargello) [1989/90 c16g* c**103**
c24s^{F} c16m^{5} c16g* c20s^{3} c16d* c25m^{pu} c21d^{pu}] sparely-made gelding: winning —
hurdler: successful in novice chase at Haydock in November and in handicap
chases at Carlisle in February and March (intermediate event): effective at 2m
and stays well: acts on any going: sweating and on toes final outing. *D. McCain.*

HOUGHTON 4 b.g. Horage–Deirdre Oge (Pontifex (USA)) [1989/90 16g*
16g*] rangy, good sort: fair maiden on Flat, placed at up to 1¾m: hard ridden to 112 p
win juvenile hurdles at Wetherby and Hexham (flashed tail under pressure but
showed improved form to beat Stay Awake 1½ lengths) within 8 days in
November: will stay further than 2m: wanders under pressure. *M. W. Easterby.*

HOUNSTOUT 10 b.g. Bargello–Queen of The Bay (King's Leap) [1989/90 c**74**
c22h^{2} c26f^{F} c17f^{4} c26f^{2} c26f* c25m* c25m^{pu} c24h^{2} a20g c21m c25h^{F}] small —
gelding: selling hurdler: winning point-to-pointer: won handicap chase at Newton
Abbot (2 ran) and poor novice chase at Devon & Exeter in September: stayed
3¼m: acted on firm ground: sometimes blinkered or visored: sold privately out of
T. Hallett's stable 3,600 gns Ascot November Sales after eighth start: dead. *W. T. Kemp.*

HOWARDS WAY 5 ch.g. Touch Boy–Canty Day (Canadel II) [1989/90 F16g
F16f a16g^{5}] small, close-coupled gelding: half-brother to a 2-y-o 1¼m winner by —
Cawston's Clown and to a poor 13f winner by Crooner: dam 2-y-o 5f winner: well
beaten in NH Flat races: tailed off in novice event in November on hurdling debut.
J. Norton.

HOWDY 5 gr.m. Aragon–Infelice (Nishapour (FR)) [1989/90 16m^{6}] small, leggy
mare: novice selling hurdler: dead. *W. Storey.* —

HOWGILL 4 b.g. Tower Walk–In Form (Formidable (USA)) [1989/90 16d 16f
16f^{3} 16g^{3} 16f^{5}] workmanlike gelding: has scope: first foal: dam winning half-sister 78
to successful hurdler Daffodil: modest maiden miler on Flat: sold out of J. W.
Watts's stable 16,500 gns Doncaster August Sales: third in novice hurdles at

Manor La Touche Cup, Punchestown—
Howyanow (hoops) clears the bank on his way to winning this hunter chase under 13-0

Worcester and Bangor (handicap) in April, showing poor form: stiff task last start: unlikely to stay beyond 2m: takes good hold and has worn crossed noseband. *R. B. Francis.*

HOWJAL (USA) 5 b.h. Conquistador Cielo (USA)–Taylor Park (USA) (Sir Gaylord) [1989/90 16f 21s 16d 16m5 16g4 20gpu 16m*] leggy horse: bought in 3,400 gns after winning amateur riders selling handicap hurdle at Fakenham in May: best at 2m: acts on good to firm going. *J. R. Bostock.* 79

HOW MAJESTIC 6 b.m. Majestic Streak–Wits End (Salerno (USA)) [1989/90 20g5 21v2 24dur 22d] useful-looking mare: only worthwhile form in novice hurdles when ½-length second to Miss Muck in mares event at Newton Abbot in January: stays 21f: acts well on heavy going. *S. Christian.* 89

HOW NOW 9 b.g. Pollerton–Tape Mary (Even Money) [1989/90 c16d2 c20m2 c25g c16g* c22mF c17m4] rangy gelding: winning hurdler: moderate chaser: won by 3 lengths from Noble Eyre at Stratford in March: ran badly last start: seems ideally suited by a strongly-run race over 2m: probably acts on any going: has run well for a claimer: usually blinkered: sold to P. Hobbs 7,200 gns Ascot June Sales. *Mrs J. Pitman.* c**106** —

HOWS TONY 9 gr. or ro.g. Pongee–Reigate Head (Timber King) [1989/90 c21mF c25m c21m2] neat gelding: winning selling hurdler/point-to-pointer: 10 lengths second to Skerry Meadow in novice hunter chase at Fakenham in May: stays 2½m: acts on dead and good to firm ground (ran poorly on hard): blinkered once in 1987/8 and at Fakenham: has worn a crossed noseband: sold 7,200 gns Doncaster Spring Sales. *M. Bloom.* c**77** + —

HOW'S YER FATHER 4 b.g. Daring March–Dawn Ditty (Song) [1989/90 16f6] quite modest sprint maiden on Flat: well-beaten sixth in 13-runner juvenile hurdle at Newbury in October. *P. D. Cundell.* —

HOWYANOW 9 b.g. Deep Run–Flighty Daphne (Brave Invader (USA)) [1989/90 c24m3 c34d* c25g*] strong, good sort: a leading Irish hunter who was successful at Punchestown in April and Down Royal (long odds on) in May: c**118** +

blinkered, jumped well under 13-0 in Manor La Touche Cup on former course, beating Wolfies Delight comfortably by 4 lengths: stays extremely well: acts on any going: genuine: sure to win more races, and would be an interesting proposition against best British hunters. *Pat P. Hogan, Ireland.*

HUBLI 10 br.g. Kinglet–Perrytate (Brother) [1989/90 22g c24dpu] good-topped gelding: winning hurdler/chaser: no form for a long time: stays 3¼m well: probably acts on any going. *G. A. Ham.* c— —

HUMDECOLA 5 ch.g. Humdoleila–Nicola Lisa (Dumbarnie) [1989/90 16m 16m5 16s4 16d 16dpu 16m] lengthy, sparely-made gelding: fourth in novice hurdle at Leicester in January: well below that form subsequently: likely to prove best at sharp 2m: acts on soft going. *B. Preece.* 90 d

HUNGARY HUR 11 ch.g. Prince Hansel–Fortinette (Fortina) [1989/90 c19d* c20g6 c24d5 c20g2 c24vpu c36fpu] big, good-bodied gelding: smart Irish chaser: won handicap at Naas in November: destroyed after breaking a leg in Seagram Grand National at Liverpool in April: stayed 3m: probably acted on any going but best form in the mud: tended to wander under pressure. *J. E. Mulhern, Ireland.* c**150** —

HUNMANBY GAP 5 ch.g. Flying Tyke–Another Mufsie (Tehran Court) [1989/90 F16m aF14g2 aF16g3 16g 20g] lengthy, angular gelding: first foal: dam unraced: placed in 2 NH Flat races at Southwell: little sign of ability in novice hurdles. *A. Smith.* —

HUNTERS FEN 8 b.g. Bonne Noel–Positioned (Status Seeker) [1989/90 17dpu] leggy gelding: winning 2m hurdler: acted on good to soft going: blinkered when successful: dead. *J. S. King.* —

HUNTWORTH 10 ch.g. Funny Man–Tamorina (Quayside) [1989/90 c24fpu c24fro c29d* c28gpu c25f* c24g3 c24s* c29d c36fF c26fur c26f* c25m*] big, plain gelding: won mid-season handicap chases at Devon & Exeter, Warwick and Worcester and similar event at Newton Abbot and minor chase at Warwick (by 2½ lengths from Joint Sovereignty) in May: clear when running out after last at Ascot second start: fell at the fifteenth in Seagram Grand National at Liverpool: stays well: acts on any going: usually makes running: jumps boldly and well in the main: has won for an amateur. *M. C. Pipe.* c**125** +

HURRY ON HARRY 6 b.g. Workboy–Merry Marion (Goldengazer) [1989/90 16g 16g] big, unfurnished gelding: seems of little account. *M. J. Wilkinson.* —

HURRY UP HENRY 11 b. or br.g. Bargello–Lucille (Master Owen) [1989/90 c26s* c25g c24m* c24d*] sparely-made gelding: winning hurdler/point-to-pointer: fair chaser: won handicaps at Folkestone in December and Worcester in April and May: raced with little zest second start: stays well: acts on soft and good to firm going: amateur ridden. *G. Harwood.* c**124** —

HYDE 13 b.g. Royalty–Impatience (Kibenka) [1989/90 25dpu] tall gelding: winning point-to-pointer: fell in hunter chase in 1984/5: successful hurdler: behind when pulled up in seller in November: stays at least 2½m: acts on any going: good mount for a claimer. *I. Anderson.* c— —

HYDEONIUS 5 b.g. Crystal Palace (FR)–Razannda (FR) (Labus (FR)) [1989/90 16m* 16g* 16g* 21g6 16dpu 16s4 a16g4] neat gelding: successful in selling hurdle at Uttoxeter (bought in 8,000 gns) and novice claimer at Huntingdon and conditional jockeys claimer at Worcester in December: below form in handicaps last 3 starts: will prove ideally suited by 2m on a sharp track: acts on good to firm ground: winner over middle distances on Flat in 1990 for C. Tinkler, and should win more races over hurdles. *J. A. Glover.* 104

HYDRO-ELECTRIC 5 b.m. Electric–Lady Spey (Sir Gaylord) [1989/90 20f2 19hpu 20f5 24g3] small, sparely-made mare: poor novice selling hurdler: visored last 3 starts. *K. G. Wingrove.* 58

HYPERBOLE 5 ch.g. Bali Dancer–Third Lady (Bonne Noel) [1989/90 F16g5 a16g 16m3] workmanlike, rather sparely-made gelding: second foal: dam winning Irish hurdler: fifth of 10 in NH Flat race at Market Rasen in October: tailed off in maiden hurdle at Lingfield in January and amateur riders hurdle at Fakenham in May. *C. P. E. Brooks.* —

HYPNOSIS (USA) 11 ch.g. Unconscious (USA)–Puzzesca (Law And Order) [1989/90 c16f4 16g c17dF] strong, good-bodied gelding: carries plenty of condition: fairly useful chaser at his best: no form in 1989/90, including in handicap hurdle: best form at 2m: acts on any going: front runner: game: tends to sweat: has won only at Kempton (3 times) and Wincanton (6 times). *D. R. C. Elsworth.* c— —

HYPNOTIC 10 b.g. Royben–Magic Mountain (Menelek) [1989/90 20g^{pu} 16m^{2}] c—
big, rangy gelding: fair hurdler: creditable second to Lynemore in amateur riders 115
handicap at Sandown in March: beat one other finisher in novice chase at
Newbury (jumped deliberately) in 1988/9: best at around 2m: probably acts on any
going: usually on his toes beforehand and tends to sweat. *F. Walwyn.*

HYTHE 4 b.c. Teenoso (USA)–Full Dress II (Shantung) [1989/90 16f 16f^{3} 18f^{5}
20f^{3}] no sign of ability on Flat: sold out of G. Wragg's stable 1,800 gns Newmarket 76
Autumn Sales: poor form in juvenile hurdles: stays 2½m: acts on firm going:
blinkered last 3 starts. *P. A. Blockley.*

I

IAMA PRINCESS 7 gr.m. Miami Springs–Aughalion (Pals Passage) [1989/90 c85
c24m^{ur} c22f c21f c25m^{5} c21f^{3} c21m^{pu} c16d^{2} c16s^{pu} c20m*] lengthy, angular —
mare: plater over hurdles: won novice chase at Plumpton in April by 4 lengths
from Matta Mia Flyer: stays 21f: acts on firm ground. *Mrs J. Pitman.*

IAMA ZULU 5 ch.g. Son of Shaka–Quick Sort (Henry The Seventh) [1989/90
17v^{4} 16g^{ro} 16m^{4} 16m* 17m* 16f^{F}] rangy gelding with scope: will make a chaser: 100
half-brother to Double Discount (by Double-U-Jay), a winner on Flat and over
hurdles: won novice hurdles at Wolverhampton (made running) in March and
Devon & Exeter (better effort) in April: in process of running a fair race when
falling last in quite valuable novice handicap at Cheltenham last start: races
keenly but may well stay further than 17f: acts on good to firm ground. *P. J. Hobbs.*

IBN MAJED 8 gr.g. Godswalk (USA)–La Meme (Pall Mall) [1989/90 c20g^{F} **c126**
c20g* c21d* c20g^{5} c21d^{2}] angular, lengthy, sparely-made gelding: one-time —
smart front-running hurdler: fairly useful chaser: won handicaps at Newcastle in
December and Market Rasen (jumped deliberately in conditional jockeys event)
in January: let down by his jumping and ran moody races last 2 starts: suited by a
strongly-run race at 2½m and is worth another try over further: acts on any going:
blinkered final outing 1987/8: occasionally rather reluctant at start. *J. G.
FitzGerald.*

IBN ZAMAN (USA) 4 b.c. Graustark–Wake Robin (Summer Tan) [1989/90
16d 16g 16g 19f^{3}] medium-sized colt: slow maiden on Flat: sold out of A. Scott's 70
stable 2,400 gns Newmarket Autumn Sales: 8 lengths third behind Ultra Violet in
juvenile event at Hereford in May, first form over hurdles: blinkered third start:
sold out of C. C. Elsey's stable 900 gns Ascot May Sales after third outing. *D. N.
Carey.*

ICARUS (USA) 4 b.g. Wind And Wuthering (USA)–Cedar Waxwing (USA)
(Tom Fool) [1989/90 16g 20f^{2} 16d^{2} 16g^{2} 16g^{4}] compact gelding: modest maiden on 95
Flat (stays 1¼m) when trained by S. Norton: in frame in 4 juvenile hurdles,
showing modest form: will be suited by return to 2½m: acts on firm and dead
ground. *M. H. Easterby.*

ICE BREAKER (FR) 7 b.h. Arctic Tern (USA)–Figure de Proue (FR)
(Petingo) [1989/90 16m] poor middle-distance handicapper on Flat: tailed off in —
novice hurdle at Catterick in December. *J. S. Haldane.*

ICE VALLEY 8 b.g. Bronze Hill–Ice Blossom (Spartan General) [1989/90 c20g c—
c24g^{pu} c27d^{F} 24g 16s^{5}] well-made gelding: poor novice hurdler: no form in 3 —
novice chases: possibly doesn't stay 3m: blinkered last start. *J. G. FitzGerald.*

ICKWORTH 8 ch.g. Northfields (USA)–Syrsanta (FR) (Santa Claus) [1989/90 c—
c24s^{4} c25g^{6} 21g^{6} 24g^{6}] angular, close-coupled gelding: winning hurdler/chaser: 98
only modest form in 1989/90: stays 3m: suited by give in the ground, though
possibly not at his best on heavy. *Mrs D. Haine.*

IDA'S DELIGHT 11 br.g. Idiot's Delight–Ida Spider (Ben Novus) **c146**
[1989/90 c16f^{2} c16m^{4} c16f^{2} c16g* c16s^{3} c16f^{5} c20f* c20f^{3}] —

Southern racegoers have seen a good deal more of the Northumberland-trained Ida's Delight than their northern counterparts. In fact, he has raced only four times north of the Trent in the past two seasons. A dearth of better races for the two-mile chasers in the North over the past few seasons has meant Ida's Delight and the likes of Nohalmdun and Meikleour (these three comprised the entire field for a handicap at Cheltenham in December) have had to be campaigned almost exclusively at

Castleford Chase (Limited Handicap), Wetherby—
Nohalmdun just leads over the last from Pearlyman and Ida's Delight (black cap)

courses such as Ascot, Cheltenham and Sandown. Just how unbalanced the race programme is can be seen in the following illustration: of the sixteen most valuable two-mile handicap chases in the first half of the season, only two, both at Wetherby, were staged north of Cheltenham. In the two months prior to Christmas, only five two-mile races in the North were open to horses rated over 125, three in the space of five days in early-November and two, at Ayr and Edinburgh, in the week before Christmas. This extraordinary situation seems set to continue.

Ida's Delight made a total of seven long trips in the latest season, three times to both Ascot and Cheltenham and one to Sandown. The first-named course has provided Ida's Delight with two victories, in the Frogmore Handicap in 1988/9 and the Peregrine Handicap in March. The Peregrine Handicap looked a very competitive event beforehand, and, indeed, it provided one of the best finishes of the season. After the outsiders Numerate and Course Hunter had dropped away on the home turn, the remainder of the field battled it out hammer and tongs. Ida's Delight took a narrow advantage approaching the second last, put in a fine jump at the final fence and held on to win by a neck from Welsh Oak, with Biloxi Blues three quarters of a length away in third and long-time leader Rusch de Farges a further two lengths away in fourth. Ida's Delight was also involved in a dramatic conclusion to the Castleford Chase, a limited handicap at Wetherby in December, which provided him with his first victory of the season. Uncharacteristically forcing the pace, he looked destined for only third place when Nohalmdun and Pearlyman held a slight lead at the last jump, but, fighting back with utmost gameness, he regained the advantage close home to beat Nohalmdun and the considerately-handled Pearlyman half a length and the same. The £19,124 first prize gave trainer Charlton his biggest success. Ida's Delight ran with credit on each of his six other starts, notably when fifth, though never a threat, behind Barnbrook Again in the Queen Mother Champion Chase at Cheltenham on his sixth outing and when third behind the same horse in the South Wales Showers Caradon Mira Silver Trophy Chase on the same course on his last start.

Ida's Delight is the fourth foal out of Ida Spider, a mare who has produced two other winners, namely Ardent Spy (by Saucy Kit), a very useful staying chaser, and Sikera Spy (by Harvest Spy), a winning hurdler/chaser. A four-year-old brother to Ida's Delight named Spy's Delight is in training with Mrs Hewitt. Ida Spider, unraced herself, is a half-sister to the quite useful staying hurdler Snaggle Puss.

Ida's Delight (br.g. 1979)	Idiot's Delight (b 1970)	Silly Season (br 1962)	Tom Fool Double Deal
		Dolphinet (b 1957)	Big Game Sea Gipsy
	Ida Spider (br 1970)	Ben Novus (bl 1962)	Ben Hawke Novelty
		Laura Simmons (b 1956)	Ridge Wood Fair Lesley

Ida's Delight, a leggy gelding, has proved to be a real money-spinner for his owner/trainer, winning thirteen of his forty-six races and around £75,000 in win and place prize money. He seems to have lost a little of his speed nowadays, is well suited by the enterprising tactics employed at Wetherby, and could prove best at two and a half miles eventually—a distance which would give him more opportunities closer to home. He seems to act on any going and usually jumps well. Ida's Delight is as game and consistent as any in training. Northern racegoers deserve to see more of him! *J. I. A. Charlton.*

IDIOT'S BEAUTY 9 b.m. Idiot's Delight–Oyston Beauty (Prince Tenderfoot (USA)) [1989/90 20d 24s a20g* a20g a20g^{6}] leggy mare: won a point-to-point in 1987: successful in conditional jockeys novice hurdle at Southwell in April: ran poorly on same course afterwards: stays 2½m: acts on heavy going. *B. J. McMath.* 80

IDIOT'S RUN 5 b.m. Idiot's Delight–Credo's Run (Deep Run) [1989/90 16g^{pu} a16g] novice hurdler: no form. *R. Brotherton.* —

IDLEIGH'S RUNON 7 gr.g. Deep Run–Zion (Palestine) [1989/90 16m^{3}] easily better effort in novice hurdles when third of 5 in poor event at Uttoxeter in May: pulled up in point-to-point in April: sold out of J. Burbidge's stable 9,000 gns Doncaster August Sales. *R. B. Francis.* 70

IDOL KNIGHT 9 b.g. Tin God–Just Musk (Rose Knight) [1989/90 16g c22g^{pu}] big, well-made non-thoroughbred gelding: third foal: dam winning point-to-pointer: tailed off in novice hurdle at Market Rasen in December: jumped none too fluently and was tailed off when pulled up in novice chase at Nottingham in January. *O. Brennan.* c— —

IDREASE 6 b.g. Dunphy–Moonscape (Ribero) [1989/90 20g^{pu} 21d c20m^{pu} c26g^{pu}] leggy, good-topped gelding: no sign of ability over hurdles or fences (jumped moderately last start). *Mrs Jill Evans.* c— —

I HAVENTALIGHT 11 b.g. Pauper–Lovely Colour (Shantung) [1989/90 c24s^{F}] sturdy gelding: carried plenty of condition: very useful chaser at his best: was best at around 3m: acted on any going: blinkered first 3 starts 1988/9: suited by forcing tactics: usually made a mistake or 2: didn't always give his running: dead. *C. P. E. Brooks.* c— —

IHRA HAYES 8 ch.g. Don–Finesse (Miralgo) [1989/90 c24d^{pu}] sturdy, lengthy gelding: novice selling hurdler: winning poor point-to-pointer: backward, jumped moderately after a mistake at the tenth and was tailed off when pulled up in maiden hunter chase at Leicester in March. *A. G. Price.* c— —

IKDAM 5 b.h. Glint of Gold–Run To The Sun (Run The Gantlet (USA)) [1989/90 20m* 20f^{3} 20s^{5} 24s^{4} 21d* 25m^{4} 20f^{3}] compact, good-bodied horse: useful hurdler: ran a very good race when under 3 lengths fourth to Trapper John in Waterford Crystal Stayers' Hurdle at Cheltenham on sixth start, staying on well having been given a lot to do: creditable third behind 15-length winner Morley Street in Sandeman Aintree Hurdle at Liverpool next time (moved short to post): successful earlier in minor event at Worcester and handicap at Newbury: stays 25f: probably acts on any going: ridden by 5-lb claimer (unable to draw allowance last 2 outings). *R. J. Holder.* 147 +

I KID YOU NOT 7 ch.g. Laurence O–Miss Kilbride (Aberdeen) [1989/90 20m 20s 16g*] rather leggy, close-coupled gelding: won 11-runner handicap at Wetherby in January comfortably by ¾ length from One For The Pot: should stay 109

Cricklade Handicap Hurdle, Newbury—
Ikdam (far side) comes to challenge Sprowston Boy

2½m: acts on heavy going: looked likely to progress further, but reportedly injured himself at Wetherby and wasn't seen out again. *J. J. O'Neill.*

I LIKE IT A LOT 7 ch.g. Proverb–Jupiters Jill (Jupiter Pluvius) [1989/90 16f* 16m4 c20m c20g* c20mF c16g c20m4] lengthy, sparely-made, angular gelding: won novice handicap hurdle at Ludlow in October: made all and was eased from last when winning novice handicap chase on same course in December: disqualified for taking wrong course previous start: ran poorly last 2 outings: stays 2½m: acts on firm ground: will probably prove best on a right-hand track. *R. Lee.* c**103** 90

I'LL TAKE YOU HOME 4 b.g. Ile de Bourbon (USA)–Dancing Kathleen (Green God) [1989/90 F16g2] fourth foal: half-brother to poor novice hurdler Headley Hall (by Ahonoora): dam poor maiden: favourite, length second of 18 to Le Bucheron in NH Flat race at Market Rasen in April: yet to race over hurdles. *C. W. Thornton.*

IL TROVATORE (USA) 4 b.c. Chief Singer–Last Flair (Busted) [1989/90 16g* 16g* 16s2 16vF 16f] $37,000F, 15,000Y: small Irish colt: first foal: dam unraced half-sister to several winners including Poule d'Essai des Pouliches winner Ukraine Girl, Prix du Jockey-Club third Flair Path and a successful French jumper: won 3 times at up to 13f on Flat: won juvenile hurdles at Punchestown in October and Leopardstown (quite valuable event) following month: under pressure when falling 3 out in race won by On Deposit at Punchestown in February: well beaten in Daily Express Triumph Hurdle at Cheltenham following month: best form on good ground: useful. *N. Meade, Ireland.* 128

IMADYNA (NZ) 8 b.g. Frassino–Volidrill (NZ) (Ward Drill) [1989/90 17f2 21f* c20m* c20mur c20f* c20d3 c20f5 c20f2] tall, leggy gelding: fair hurdler: won handicap at Newton Abbot in August: successful in novice chases at Worcester following month and Cheltenham (only one to put in a clear round in valuable Charterhouse Mercantile Leisure Novices' Chase) in December: 4 lengths second to Brandeston in quite valuable amateur riders novice handicap at c**119** 119

Charterhouse Mercantile Leisure Novices' Chase, Cheltenham—the second last, where Imadyna is over safely and French Goblin is about to fall

Liverpool in April: takes good hold but stays 21f: acts on firm and dead going: broke blood vessel third start 1988/9. *D. H. Barons.*

I'M ALERT 5 b.h. Kampala–Last Trip (Sun Prince) [1989/90 16m $20f^{pu}$] seems of little account: blinkered final start. *J. C. Gillen.* —

I'M A MONKEY 5 b.g. Monksfield–Vulyere (Vulgan) [1989/90 $20m^{pu}$ $25g^{pu}$] half-brother to fairly useful point-to-pointer Eagle Moonday (by Indian Ruler or Ritudyr) and Tyere (by Tycoon II), runner-up in 3m novice hurdle: tailed off when pulled up in novice hurdles. *R. Tate.* —

I'M EXCEPTIONAL (USA) 8 b.g. Clev Er Tell (USA)–Rare (USA) (Rambunctious) [1989/90 $16s^{pu}$ $a24g^{6}$] smallish, sparely-made gelding: modest novice hurdler in 1986/7: tailed off in January: stays 21f: best form on a firm surface: sweats up: has made mistakes on occasions: visored once. *T. Rollingson.* —

I'M FINE 5 b. or br.m. Fitzwilliam (USA)–Quick Thinking (Will Somers) [1989/90 $16g^{su}$ $a16g^{6}$ $16g^{3}$] sparely-made mare: first sign of merit when staying-on third in selling hurdle at Catterick in February, giving impression she'll be suited by further. *P. Beaumont.* 77

IMMORTAL IRISH 5 b.g. Lord Gayle (USA)–Royal Meath (Realm) [1989/90 16g* $19g^{4}$] narrow gelding: won novice handicap hurdle at Market Rasen in October: creditable fourth in similar event at Hereford in November: beaten in seller previously: stays 19f. *D. R. Gandolfo.* 89

IMPAGE 12 br.g. Enbrage–Swift Imp (Swift Flight) [1989/90 $c16h^{3}$ c16f* $c17m^{4}$ **c92** d
$c17g^{5}$ $c16g^{3}$ $c16f^{4}$ $c17f^{3}$ $c16m^{6}$ $c16h^{2}$ $c20f^{2}$] big gelding: poor chaser: won —

handicap at Carlisle in October: lost his form afterwards: stays 2½m when conditions aren't testing: possibly unsuited by heavy ground, acts on any other: takes a strong hold and usually helps force the pace: sometimes let down by his jumping. *S. J. Leadbetter.*

IMPALE 6 b. or br.g. Crash Course–Show Rose (Coliseum) [1989/90 20g4 22v2 20s5 c24gF] close-coupled, leggy ex-Irish gelding: first foal: dam, winner over hurdles and fences suited by 2½m, is sister to very useful chaser Cancello: placed in NH Flat races when trained by J. Maxwell: in frame in novice hurdles at Haydock in first half of season: beaten when falling at the last in novice chase at Newbury in March: stays 2¾m: acts on heavy going. *G. Richards.* c— 96

IMPANY 11 br.g. Parasang–Swift Imp (Swift Flight) [1989/90 c16m* c17m6 c20mF c16m4 c20f3 c16g2 c16g3 c16g4 c17d c17mpu c22m c16m5 c16m4 c17f3] strong, compact gelding: won handicap chase at Worcester in August: mainly disappointing afterwards, usually finding little: best form at 2m on a sound surface: blinkered twice, including third start (running well when falling): usually a sound jumper: unreliable: trained by T. Forster until after fourth start. *J. J. O'Neill.* **c110** d — §

IMPECCABLE TIMING 7 ch.g. Paddy's Stream–Wynchy Comby (Royal Buck) [1989/90 c16g c16d c16f3 c20m2] big, lengthy gelding: winning hurdler: claimer ridden, best effort over fences when 6 lengths second to Sikera Spy in novice handicap at Worcester in April: stays 2½m: acts on good to firm and dead going. *O. O'Neill.* c**81** —

IMPERIAL BOLT (NZ) 6 b.g. Imperial Guard–Alan's Girl (NZ) (Charicles) [1989/90 24g6 20d 20spu] angular gelding: winning hurdler: sixth in 3m amateur riders handicap at Chepstow in December, only form in 1989/90: ran as though something was amiss final start: may prove ideally suited by around 2½m. *M. H. B. Robinson.* 106

IMPERIAL BRUSH 6 b.g. Sallust–Queen of The Brush (Averof) [1989/90 16g3 16f4 16g3 16d3 16g4 16f6] small, leggy, sparely-made gelding: fairly useful hurdler: best effort when just over 4 lengths third behind Deep Sensation in moderately-run Tote Gold Trophy at Newbury in February on fourth start: fair sixth behind Sybillin in Swinton Insurance Trophy at Haydock on final outing: stays 2½m: seems to act on any going: blinkered last 3 outings: has won for a claimer. *D. R. C. Elsworth.* 130

IMPERIAL CHAMPAGNE 10 gr.g. Imperial Crown–Blue Champagne (Raffingora) [1989/90 c21d5 c25mpu] leggy, lightly-made gelding: one-time fair chaser: over 25 lengths fifth of 6 finishers to Desert Orchid in minor event at Wincanton in February: stays 25f: probably acts on any going. *Miss J. Thorne.* c— —

IMPERIAL FLIGHT 5 b.g. Pampabird–Queen of Time (Charlottown) [1989/90 16m2] close-coupled, rather leggy gelding: winning hurdler: creditable second to By Line in handicap at Worcester in September: not seen out again: bred to stay beyond 2m: acts on good to firm ground: looked a bit reluctant on 2 occasions in 1988/9. *P. G. Bailey.* 107

IMPERTAIN 10 br.g. Ascertain (USA)–Swift Imp (Swift Flight) [1989/90 c16m2 c17f2 c16m3 c16f3 c20f* c20g2 c20m3 c20m6 c20g2 c16d2 c16f c20g 16g] big, lengthy gelding: carries plenty of condition: sweating, won handicap chase at Wetherby in October: variable form afterwards: tailed off in novice hurdle final start: stays 2½m: acts on any going: usually amateur or claimer ridden. *T. W. Cunningham.* c**94** —

IMPETULENCE 4 ch.f. Kind of Hush–Longgoe (Lorenzaccio) [1989/90 16mur 16dpu] maiden on Flat, has shown signs of ability but appears somewhat temperamental: awkward start, pulled hard in lead to third and behind when pulled up in juvenile hurdle in December. *R. Dickin.* —

IMPORTED SCRAP 5 gr.m. Coded Scrap–Award For Export (Abwah) [1989/90 16g 16d 17m] long-backed mare: third foal: dam, of little account at 2 yrs, behind in 2 novice hurdles: always behind in novice hurdles. *D. G. Swindlehurst.* —

IMPUNITY 5 b.g. Blakeney–Lantern Light (Le Levanstell) [1989/90 20f5 27f2 a20gpu] small, sparely-made gelding: modest form over hurdles: remote second in selling handicap at Sedgefield in September (subsequently off course 3½ months): probably stays 2½m: best form on a soft surface: usually claimer ridden: jumped moderately in 1989/90. *R. M. Whitaker.* 83

IMSHI WAHEED 5 b.g. Escapism (USA)–Shadytoo (Chingnu) [1989/90 16gpu] probably of little account. *C. D. Broad.* —

I'M STILL STANDING 5 b.g. Blue Refrain–Kikalong (Runnymede) [1989/90 27f4 20d 24mpu] tall, leggy gelding: of little account: dead. *J. Dooler.* —

I'M UNFORGETTABLE 6 b.m. Dublin Taxi–Pink Streamer (Birdbrook) [1989/90 a16g6] well beaten on Flat at 3 yrs: ridden by 5-lb claimer, never dangerous when sixth in conditional jockeys novice event at Lingfield in March on hurdling debut. *D. J. G. Murray-Smith.* 67 p

INAFIX 9 br.g. Lighter–Verona's Inn (Lord of Verona) [1989/90 c20sur c20spu] workmanlike gelding: has scope: dam, winning jumper, stayed 3m: jumps moderately and no sign of ability over hurdles: failed to complete course in 4 point-to-points in 1989 and 2 hunter chases. *David Pearson.* c— — x

IN A NUTSHELL 9 ch.g. Crimson Beau–Concisely (Connaught) [1989/90 c20m3] sparely-made gelding: winning selling hurdler: poor novice chaser: best at 2m: acts on hard going: often blinkered over hurdles (visored once): front runner, best when able to dominate. *K. A. Morgan.* c— —

INCAMELIA 9 br.m. St Columbus–Indamelia (Indian Ruler) [1989/90 c24m* c21m* c24f*] close-coupled mare: modest chaser: made all in small fields in handicaps at Nottingham in October and Towcester and Huntingdon in November, doing well to recover from a mistake on last 2 courses: stays well: acts on firm going. *N. J. Henderson.* c**108** —

INCANDESCE 11 b.g. Wolver Hollow–Lavington (Ratification) [1989/90 c20f2 c20mpu c20spu] lengthy, robust gelding: winning hurdler/chaser: best effort first start, ran as though something amiss final one: best up to 2½m: possibly unsuited by heavy ground, acts on any other. *J. A. C. Edwards.* c**102** —

INCENSE 10 b.g. Martinmas–Cabochard (Nelcius) [1989/90 c20g] plain gelding: only worthwhile form for some time when winning selling chase in 1988/9: backward in February: stays 2¾m: possibly needs give in the ground and acts on heavy going: best in blinkers. *D. G. Swindlehurst.* c— —

INCIDENTAL 5 br.g. Swing Easy (USA)–Luckley Brake (Quiet Fling (USA)) [1989/90 16g 16g5 16m 16f] leggy, rather angular gelding: first foal: dam unraced: behind in novice hurdles: looks headstrong. *Miss H. C. Knight.* —

IN CONTENTION 7 b.g. Hittite Glory–Blakes Lass (Blakeney) [1989/90 c24sF 27dF 27g3 c24dF] compact, workmanlike gelding: handicap hurdler: has fallen in his 3 starts over fences: stays well: acts on heavy going and possibly unsuited by firm: blinkered last 3 starts 1988/9: sold 3,200 gns Doncaster Spring Sales. *I. P. Wardle.* c— 88

INCREDIBLE LADY 5 gr.m. Rusticaro (FR)–Lady d'Arbanville (FR) (Luthier) [1989/90 16g 16d a16s4 a16g4] small mare: poor novice hurdler: has run in a seller. *A. W. Denson.* 69

INDALUTION 8 ch.g. Solution–Mui Linda (Mon Fils) [1989/90 c20d3 c25m2 c24f4 c21fro] sturdy, workmanlike gelding: novice selling hurdler: placed in 2 point-to-points in 1989: in frame in hunter chases: ran out early on final start: stays 25f. *N. A. Whittle.* c**82** —

INDAMU 5 b.h. Indian King (USA)–Kilfenora (Tribal Chief) [1989/90 16g 20m6 20dpu 22g] leggy horse: winning hurdler: poor form in 1989/90: takes a good hold and unlikely to stay much beyond 2m: acts on soft going. *J. L. Spearing.* 79

INDEMNITY 6 ch.g. Stanford–Tyran (Tyrant (USA)) [1989/90 16m 16m 20d] poor novice hurdler: sold 2,100 gns Doncaster August Sales. *Miss S. Williamson.* 56

INDE PULSE 8 b.g. Troy–Divine Thought (Javelot) [1989/90 22s 25d 25fF 25m 24g] neat, strong gelding: moderate hurdler: stays 25f: best form with give in the ground (well beaten on heavy): blinkered final start 1988/9 and last 3 outings: has worn a tongue strap. *N. J. Henderson.* 110

INDIAN 10 ch.g. Great Nephew–Ardneasken (Right Royal V) [1989/90 c16f2 c21f2 c17f6 c18f2 c17m5 c16m* c16h2 c16f2 c16f2 c16f5 c16m3 c16m3 c16m3 c16f* c17f4] small, close-coupled gelding: handicap chaser: won at Market Rasen in September and Towcester in May: would have won at Carlisle in October but for jockey dropping hands close home (jockey fined £525): best at 2m: acts on any going: sometimes ridden by 7-lb claimer: rather deliberate jumper: takes a strong hold: blinkered or visored nowadays. *O. Brennan.* c**91** —

INDIAN BABA 5 b.g. Indian King (USA)–Norfolk Bonnet (Morston (FR)) [1989/90 16fpu 16f5 20f] leggy gelding: fairly useful hurdler in 1988/9 (swerved badly left on run-in once): ran moderately in 1989/90: should stay beyond 2m: form only on good ground: temperamentally unsatisfactory. *G. P. Enright.* — §

INDIAN CRUISE 5 b.m. Cruise Missile–Indian Diva (Indian Ruler) [1989/90 18s 22dF] shallow-girthed mare: half-sister to NH Flat race winner Peter Piper (by True Song): dam fair hunter chaser: behind in mares novice hurdle at Fontwell and when falling 3 out in similar event at Wincanton (making a little headway when coming down). *N. J. Henderson.* —

INDIAN FIGHTER 4 b.g. Indian King (USA)–Condoree (Condorcet (FR)) [1989/90 F12g4 F14v] third foal: dam never ran: fourth in NH Flat race at Hexham in March: co-favourite, tailed off in similar event at Ayr following month: yet to race over hurdles. *M. P. Naughton.*

INDIAN MAESTRO 4 b.g. Music Maestro–Indian Wells (Reliance II) [1989/90 16f 16f3] sparely-made gelding: half-brother to quite useful staying chaser Solares (by Free State) and winning hurdler Demi John (by Alias Smith): modest at up to 1¼m on Flat: third in juvenile hurdle at Huntingdon in August: sold 4,000 gns Doncaster November Sales. *R. Guest.* 74

INDIAN RETREAT 11 ch.m. Country Retreat–Daintylet (Indian Ruler) [1989/90 c22fpu c26f3 c21m5 c20h3 c16g3 c24h3 c21mpu c24m2 c22sur] leggy mare: of little account over hurdles, but has shown a modicum of ability in point-to-points and steeplechases: sold out of D. Williams' stable 1,500 gns Doncaster November Sales after eighth start. *M. Castell.* c**67** —

INDIAN SET 6 b.m. Windjammer (USA)–Bourges (FR) (Luthier) [1989/90 16s] leggy, sparely-made mare: poor novice hurdler: barely stayed 2m: dead. *J. A. C. Edwards.* —

INDIAN SOVEREIGN 6 br.h. Indian King (USA)–Sovereign Dona (Sovereign Path) [1989/90 16gF] workmanlike horse: quite modest sprint maiden on Flat: sold out of B. Preece's stable 3,200 gns Ascot October Sales: wearing crossed noseband, well behind when falling 2 out in novice hurdle at Windsor. *J. D. Thomas.* —

INDIAN SPIRIT 4 ch.g. Mansingh (USA)–Funny-Do (Derring-Do) [1989/90 16gpu] small gelding: poor maiden on Flat: very much in need of race, pulled hard until losing place third and pulled up fifth in juvenile hurdle at Catterick. *M. W. Ellerby.* —

INDIAN STREAM 6 b.m. Royal Boxer–Wesley Boat (Forlorn River) [1989/90 16d4 16m2 17v5 16g2 a16g* a16g 17d6] leggy mare: has a round action: runner-up in selling handicap hurdles prior to winning poor non-selling handicap at Lingfield in February: races only at around 2m: acts on dead ground: has sweated up. *J. M. Bradley.* 76

INDIAN SUNRISE 9 ch.m. Gambling Debt–Indian Whistle (Rugantino) [1989/90 22m 16m 17g6 16s 26vpu 17m 17m 26fpu] small mare: poor novice selling hurdler: pulled up reportedly lame final start. *J. R. Payne.* —

INDIAN UPRISING 4 b.g. Indian King (USA)–Infanta (USA) (Intrepid Hero (USA)) [1989/90 16g 17g] strong gelding: only form on Flat when third over 6f in 1989 (virtually bolted when blinkered once): tailed off in novice and juvenile event (had tongue tied down) over hurdles in January: appears not to stay 2m. *J. W. Blundell.* —

INDISPENSABLE 5 ch.g. Glenstal (USA)–Santa Vittoria (Ragusa) [1989/90 16f3 16f2 16f5 16f 16dpu 17gpu 16f 20gpu 16h4 16g4 16f*] angular, sparely-made ex-Irish gelding: half-brother to several winners, notably Elementary (by Busted) a very useful performer on Flat and very smart hurdler: 1¼m winner on Flat: finished lame after winning selling handicap hurdle at Hexham in May: form only at 2m: acted on firm ground: visored 4 starts prior to Hexham: trained until after fourth start by J. Bolger: dead. *W. Storey.* 83

IN DREAMS 7 b.g. High Line–Blissful Evening (Blakeney) [1989/90 25fur 24d 20d 20gpu 20g] rather sparely-made gelding: half-brother to very useful hurdler Inlander (by Ile de Bourbon): one-time fair staying handicapper on Flat (no form in 1989): of little account over hurdles. *T. Kersey.* —

INFIELDER 11 b.g. Pry–Sun Spray (Nice Guy) [1989/90 c20f6] sparely-made gelding: winning hurdler/chaser: no form since 1986/7. *Mrs S. Clarke.* c— —

INFINITY RULES 9 b.g. Mandamus–Catherine Rose (Floribunda) [1989/90 c16d3 c16d* c16d2 c20d*] compact gelding: winning hurdler: won handicap chases at Towcester in February and Leicester (by ¾ length from Pernoic in amateur riders handicap) in March: stays 2½m: acts on good to firm and dead going: jumps soundly and likely to improve further over fences. *S. Mellor.* c**100** p —

INGLEBY STAR 11 b.g. Derek H–Miss Prim II (Brocade Slipper) [1989/90 c88
c20s*] fairly useful point-to-pointer: made most and finished very tired when
successful in maiden hunter chase at Sedgefield in February by 3 lengths from Par
Kelly. *Mrs S. Frank.*

IN GLORY 6 b.m. Dalsaan–Indigine (USA) (Raise A Native) [1989/90 16g 16g]
lengthy mare: half-sister to Below Zero (by Northfields), a winner on Flat and —
over hurdles: fair 7f winner on Flat (well below form in 1989): sold out of Miss S.
Hall's stable 950 gns Doncaster October Sales: behind in maiden and novice
hurdle at Edinburgh. *Mrs P. A. Barker.*

INHERIT 8 ch.g. Homing–Royal Descent (FR) (Run The Gantlet (USA))
[1989/90 16g 18g] lengthy gelding: handicap hurdler: below his best in 1989/90: —
stays 2½m (never placed to challenge over 2¾m): acts on heavy going: has won
when amateur ridden. *R. Curtis.*

INISHPOUR 8 b.h. Nishapour (FR)–Miss Britain (Tudor Melody) [1989/90
16m^{r}] fair handicapper around 1m on Flat at his best: favourite, refused to race in — §
novice event at Perth in August on hurdling debut. *Mrs R. Wharton.*

IN-KEEPING 4 b.f. Castle Keep–Primmy (Primera) [1989/90 16m^{2} 17h^{F} 16f*
16d* 16m^{2} 16s* 16g 16f 16m*] sparely-made filly: behind in minor event at 2 yrs: 109
made all in juvenile hurdles at Wincanton (claimer), Kempton and Market Rasen
and novice handicap at Hereford: well beaten in Daily Express Triumph Hurdle at
Cheltenham (looking lean, dropped herself out before third): pulls hard and is
likely to prove best at around 2m at present (has worn severe bridle): acts on any
going: drifted left and flashed tail under pressure fifth start: often claimer ridden.
M. C. Pipe.

INKPEN LADY 6 ch.m. Sharpman–Bourton Downs (Philip of Spain) [1989/90
16g^{F} 20m^{F} 22m^{pu} 22g^{pu} 16g 16v] strong, lengthy mare: no sign of ability: has run —
blinkered. *D. Welsh.*

INK SPLASH 6 b.g. Relkino–Galosh (Pandofell) [1989/90 20g^{4} 16m 27g* 22d]
strong, good sort: modest hurdler: won handicap at Sedgefield in November: 108
better for race, modest seventh at Ayr 5 months later (will be suited by return to
3m or more): stays well: acts on firm ground (well beaten on soft): has run well for
a claimer. *W. A. Stephenson.*

INKY BAY 9 b.g. Proverb–Straight Heiress (Straight Lad) [1989/90 c22g^{pu}] c—
tall, leggy, narrow gelding: winning point-to-pointer: in frame in hunter chases in
1988: behind when pulled up in similar race in April. *D. J. Shorey.*

IN MY DREAMS 7 ch.m. Belfalas–Wichita (Chamier) [1989/90 c20s^{F} c25g^{F}] c—
compact mare: poor form in novice hurdles: bit backward and was behind when —
falling in hunter chases in February: should stay 3m. *J. R. Weston.*

INNOVATOR 4 ch.g. Relkino–Gunnard (Gunner B) [1989/90 16m^{6} 16g^{pu} 16f^{3}]
small gelding: modest 1½m winner in 1989 when trained by Mrs J. Ramsden: has 81
shown a modicum of ability over hurdles: claimer ridden. *F. Jordan.*

IN ORBIT 5 b.g. Habitat–Aryenne (FR) (Green Dancer (USA)) [1989/90 16g^{pu}]
tailed off when pulled up in novice hurdle in November: won 1¼m handicap on —
Flat in 1990. *A. P. Stringer.*

IN ORDER 7 ch.g. Relkino–Expansive (Exbury) [1989/90 20s^{pu} 22d^{pu}] big,
lengthy gelding: chasing type: poor novice hurdler. *M. McCourt.* —

IN SEPTEMBER 4 b.f. Head For Heights–Maylands (Windjammer (USA))
[1989/90 16d^{pu}] angular, shallow-girthed filly: plating-class maiden on Flat when —
trained by J. Spearing (has worn blinkers): weakened quickly 3 out and was pulled
up and dismounted flat in conditional jockeys selling hurdle at Ludlow. *K. G.
Wingrove.*

INSIGHT STAR 6 b.g. Record Run–Talahache Bridge (New Brig) [1989/90
22s 20v 21d] unfurnished gelding: first foal: dam winning point-to-pointer/hunter —
chaser: well beaten in novice hurdles. *N. A. Gaselee.*

INSPECTOR BEN 11 br.g. Bold As Brass–Christmas Gorse (Woodcut) c92
[1989/90 c24m^{3} c20f^{3} c21m* c20s^{F} c20m^{5} c24g] sparely-made gelding: novice —
hurdler: has been beaten in a seller: made virtually all to win handicap chase at
Towcester in December: soundly beaten last 2 outings: suited by around 2½m:
acts on soft and good to firm ground: seems suited by forcing tactics. *J. P. Smith.*

INSTANT TAN 6 b.g. Tanfirion–Instanter (Morston (FR)) [1989/90 22d 20v
24d 22v^{3} 16f^{pu} 16d*] leggy ex-Irish gelding: fairly useful hurdler in 1988/9 when 123
trained by P. Mullins: little form in 1989/90 other than when 20/1-winner of
16-runner handicap at Ayr in April, making early running and regaining advantage

close home to score by ½ length from Sherwood Gunner: suited by 2m and give in the ground: has worn a tongue strap: jumped none too fluently at Ayr. *J. J. O'Neill.*

INSURE 12 b.g. Dusky Boy–Shady Tree (Three Wishes) [1989/90 c21spu c24g6] small, lengthy, sparely-made gelding: won 3 point-to-points in April and one in May: poor hunter chaser nowadays: jumped moderately in 1989/90: stays extreme distances: well suited by very soft ground: suitable mount for an inexperienced rider: sometimes blinkered. *Mrs E. M. R. Ludlow.* c— x —

INTARSIA 6 b.g. Smartset–London Fancy (London Gazette) [1989/90 c20g4] rangy gelding: behind in novice hurdles: fourth to Blazing Walker in novice event at Wetherby in November on chasing debut. *J. K. M. Oliver.* c86 —

INTERIM LIB 7 b.g. Lighter–Ballinew (New Brig) [1989/90 c24g2 c20m4 c16g4 c22g4 c24d3 c24v* c32f c16d5 c24g] tall, leggy gelding: had a soft palate operation after fifth start: winning point-to-pointer: novice hurdler: in frame several times over fences prior to winning novice event at Ayr in February: showed much improved form when 17½ lengths fifth to Celtic Shot in Edinburgh Woollen Mill's Future Champion Novices' Chase on same course in April: ran badly next outing: at least as effective at 2m as at 3m: suited by give in the ground and acts on heavy: takes a good hold and has worn a crossed noseband: amateur ridden: jumps well in the main. *Mrs S. C. Bradburne.* c125 ? —

INTERPLAY 5 ch.g. Be My Guest (USA)–Intermission (Stage Door Johnny) [1989/90 18g3 20g* a20g* 20sF 20s3 a20g2] quite well-made gelding: handicap hurdler: more reliable after being gelded in summer and won at Plumpton and Lingfield in November: good third in December, but long odds on when beaten 5 lengths by sole opponent on latter course following month: likely to stay beyond 2½m: suited by give in the ground: blinkered 4 times in 1988/9: front runner. *R. J. O'Sullivan.* 99

IN THE BREEZE (FR) 9 ch.g. Mount Hagen (FR)–Starval (FR) (Val de Loir) [1989/90 17f6 c16f5 c16g2 c16f5 c16m* c16g3 c16m4 c16g3 c16g5 c20d6 c16g2 c16d2 c16mpu c16g4 c20f2] workmanlike gelding: selling hurdler: won novice chase at Catterick in December: generally below that form in varied company afterwards: finished lame final start: best at 2m previously: acts on any going: has been tried in blinkers and a visor and has worn a tongue strap: sold out of T. Cunningham's stable 3,000 gns Doncaster March Sales after thirteenth start: temperamental. *P. A. Blockley.* c78 § — §

IN THE FASHION 8 br.g. Never Slip–Smashing Style (Harwell) [1989/90 c24g* c25g* c25g* c24d*] leggy, close-coupled gelding: third foal: half-brother to quite useful hurdler Kameo Style (by Kambalda): dam novice hurdler/chaser and winning point-to-pointer, is half-sister to very useful chaser Prominent Artist and daughter of very good Irish chaser Height O'Fashion: former eventer: won 3 point-to-points in 1989: jumped very well when impressive winner of novice chases at Market Rasen in December and Catterick (2) in January, and survived a couple of bad mistakes when winning similar event at Edinburgh (tended to jump left) in February comfortably by 8 lengths from Ambergate: stays 25f: will make a useful handicapper. *J. G. FitzGerald.* c122 p

IN THE KNOW 7 b.g. Known Fact (USA)–Brilliantine (USA) (Stage Door Johnny) [1989/90 c20vpu] lengthy, angular gelding: poor novice hurdler: tailed off when pulled up in maiden hunter chase in February. *D. Curtis.* c— —

IN THE ZONE 5 b.g. Martinmas–Modom (Compensation) [1989/90 21d] behind in NH Flat races: pulled hard and jumped none too fluently when well beaten in novice hurdle at Newbury (wore crossed noseband) in February. *W. G. R. Wightman.* —

INTO THE MYSTIC 8 br.g. Kemal (FR)–Rochetta (Varano) [1989/90 24m6 26d5 c20g5 c24g4 c24d6 c27dur c24g6 c27s* c25g c24g2 c24dpu c24g c24g3] leggy gelding: handicap hurdler: won novice chase at Sedgefield in February: ran creditably when placed in similar event at Hexham in March and handicap at Perth in May: suited by a test of stamina: acts on any going: has won for an amateur. *B. McLean.* c98 —

INTO THE RED 6 ch.g. Over The River (FR)–Legal Fortune (Cash And Courage) [1989/90 16d2 16s2 22d2 21d4 18d* 21s 21d4 16g2 25mF] medium-sized gelding: won moderately-run novice hurdle at Kelso in February: staying-on second to Kharif at Hexham in March: should stay beyond 2¾m: acts on heavy going: usually edgy in paddock, and has sweated: consistent. *C. C. Trietline.* 97

INTO THE TREES 6 b.g. Over The River (FR)–Diana's Flyer (Charlottes-villes Flyer) [1989/90 22dpu 19m 22m 17v] rather unfurnished gelding: ducked left —

and wandered badly approaching last when winning 2m novice hurdle in 1988/9: well beaten in handicaps in 1989/90: acts on soft going (ran poorly on hard): looks a difficult ride: blinkered final start. *N. R. Mitchell.*

INTREPID LAD 8 ch.g. Hot Grove–Mountain Rescue (Mountain Call)
[1989/90 22g 16m] sturdy, compact gelding: winning hurdler: has run in a seller: —
no form in 1989/90: unlikely to stay beyond 2¼m: seems suited by give in the
ground. *M. McCourt.*

INTREPID SON 4 ch.g. Battle Hymn–Apritina (Ivotino (USA)) [1989/90 $16f^{pu}$
a16g] sparely-made gelding: poor form in varied races at 2 yrs, including sellers: —
sold out of G. Blum's stable 360 gns Ascot August (1988) Sales: tailed off in selling
hurdle. *J. S. King.*

INTREPID WORLD (USA) 4 b.g. Transworld (USA)–Intrepid Mary Ann
(USA) (His Majesty (USA)) [1989/90 16g $a18g^{5}$ $16g^{5}$ $16m^{6}$ $16m^{6}$] compact gelding: 67 x
plating-class maiden on Flat, probably stays 15f: sold out of S. Norton's stable
4,800 gns Newmarket Autumn Sales: poor plater over hurdles: jumps moderately.
J. W. Walmsley.

INTROVERT 6 b.h. Niniski (USA)–Consister (Burglar) [1989/90 20g $25m^{4}$ c86 §
$20d^{4}$ $20g^{4}$ $c16g^{2}$ $c22d^{pu}$ $c17g^{pu}$ 16d $a20g^{2}$] leggy horse: poor novice hurdler: has 81 §
run in a seller: clear second to Mr Quick at Catterick in January, only form in
novice chases: probably stays 3m: acts on any going: sometimes blinkered or
visored: ungenuine. *A. Smith.*

INTRUM BOY 5 b.g. Boreen (FR)–Ullard Lady (Official) [1989/90 $17v^{F}$ 16d
16g] workmanlike gelding: second foal: brother to poor novice hurdler Ever A —
Lady: dam placed in Irish point-to-point: no worthwhile form in novice hurdles:
likely to stay beyond 2m. *S. Mellor.*

INVASION 6 b.g. Kings Lake (USA)–St Padina (St Paddy) [1989/90 $20g^{2}$ $20g^{2}$
20g* $22v^{4}$ $24d^{2}$ 22s* 25g*] rather leggy, close-coupled gelding: improving 130 p
hurdler who won novice event at Uttoxeter in December, handicap at Nottingham
in February (best effort, beating Prince of Rheims 25 lengths in 22-runner event)
and novice event at Kelso (landed the odds by 12 lengths) in March: stays 25f: acts
on soft going: has wandered under pressure: has won for a claimer. *J. A. Glover.*

INVISIBLE THIEF 8 ch.g. Proverb–Ballyea Jacki (Straight Lad) [1989/90 c—
$c27f^{pu}$] lengthy, angular gelding: poor chaser: destroyed after breaking a leg when
in lead approaching the last in handicap at Sedgefield in September: stayed well:
acted on firm ground and an easy surface: ran out once. *W. A. Stephenson.*

INVOLVED AGAIN 5 b.g. Ballacashtal (CAN)–Get Involved (Shiny Tenth)
[1989/90 $a16g^{5}$ $16m^{F}$] leggy, close-coupled gelding: winning 2m selling hurdler: —
well beaten in December: best run on soft going: blinkered last 3 starts 1988/9. *F.
J. O'Mahony.*

IORWERTH 4 b.c. Rymer–Wicker Basket (Pamroy) [1989/90 F16m $16d^{F}$
$16f^{pu}$] compact, rather angular colt: second foal: dam of little account over jumps: —
tailed off in NH Flat race and when pulled up in novice hurdle. *E. H. Owen jun.*

IOWA 11 br.g. So Blessed–Montana (Mossborough) [1989/90 $17g^{6}$ $c16m^{5}$ c91
$c16m^{4}$] leggy, lengthy gelding: poor hurdler/chaser: best at around 2m: acts on —
soft going and is possibly unsuited by hard: blinkered once in 1985/6. *G. C. Doidge.*

IRENE'S DAUGHTER 8 ch.m. Al Sirat (USA)–Aunt Irene (Paddy's c—
Birthday) [1989/90 $21m^{pu}$] leggy, sparely-made mare: won NH Flat race in 1987/8: —
poor form in novice chases: no form over hurdles in Britain, including in sellers:
sold 5,000 gns Doncaster August Sales. *J. P. Smith.*

IRISH DILEMMA 7 b.g. Jaazeiro (USA)–Southern Swanee (My Swanee)
[1989/90 $20m^{pu}$ $20s^{5}$ $16g^{ur}$ 16m $20m^{4}$ $27f^{4}$] leggy, sparely-made gelding: novice 74
selling hurdler: stays 27f: acts on firm going: claimer ridden. *T. Kersey.*

IRISH DITTY 4 ch.f. Derrylin–Falcrello (Falcon) [1989/90 a16g*] quite
modest maiden on Flat: ridden by 5-lb claimer, short-headed Sonar in juvenile 79 +
hurdle at Lingfield in November. *R. V. Smyth.*

IRISH GUEST 9 b.g. Northern Guest (USA)–Laikipia (St Paddy) [1989/90 c— x
$c20f^{5}$ $c16s^{pu}$] rather good-topped, workmanlike gelding: maiden hurdler/chaser/ —
point-to-pointer: best run at 2m on a sound surface: was tried in blinkers: jumped
moderately: dead. *N. R. Mitchell.*

IRISH LORD 9 b.g. Jaazeiro (USA)–Plight (Pieces of Eight) [1989/90 $c29d^{pu}$ c98
$c20f^{5}$] rangy gelding: one-time fair hurdler: won a novice chase in 1986/7: stiff —
task when last of 5 in handicap at Warwick in May: stays 25f: acts on heavy going.
M. C. Pipe.

IRISH NOBLE 15 ch.g. Crepello–Miss Ireland (Grey Sovereign) [1989/90 17f pu] sparely-made gelding: selling hurdler: poor maiden point-to-pointer: has been tried in blinkers: ungenuine. *R. W. Pincombe.* — §

IRISH RED 8 ch.g. Trombone–Smiling Diplomat (Dual) [1989/90 c24f* c26f* c24f* c24f* c24s3 c24g* c25m] leggy, rather angular gelding: easy winner of 2 handicap chases at Southwell, minor chase at Uttoxeter and BMW Series Chase qualifier at Wetherby (tended to jump left) in the autumn: first race for 3 months and amateur ridden, won handicap at Kelso in March by 2 lengths from J-J-Henry: made mistakes and tailed off in quite valuable handicap at Liverpool in April: stays 27f: acts on any going: has sweated up and often wears ear plugs: finds little off bridle on occasions. *W. A. Stephenson.* c**114** —

IRON GRAY 8 gr.g. General Ironside–Yvonne's Delight (Laurence O) [1989/90 c16d4 c16d pu c16m pu c16g3] strong, workmanlike gelding: lightly-raced chaser: shaped well when fourth at Stratford in November: subsequently gave impression something amiss: stays 2½m: acts any going. *D. Nicholson.* c**113** ? —

IRON PRINCE 4 gr.g. General Ironside–Pry Princess (Pry) [1989/90 16d6] workmanlike gelding: third foal: dam unraced half-sister to a winning hurdler: bit backward, led after third until 2 out and weakened quickly when well beaten in juvenile hurdle at Kelso. *J. K. M. Oliver.* —

ISLAND JETSETTER 4 ch.g. Tolomeo–Baridi (Ribero) [1989/90 16m3 16d4 16g ur 16g3 16g* 16f 16g2 16m2] rangy, workmanlike gelding with plenty of scope: maiden on Flat, best at around 1m: won juvenile claiming hurdle at Market Rasen in March: good second in similar race on same course following month and in handicap at Wetherby (put head in air and edged right between last 2 when beaten a neck by Stumble) in May: pulls hard and unlikely to stay much beyond 2m: acts on good to firm ground: has looked a difficult ride: usually held up. *M. H. Easterby.* 100

ISLAND LOCKSMITH 6 b.g. Brigadier Gerard–Lake Naivasha (Blakeney) [1989/90 a24g6 a20g6 a16g] half-brother to winning hurdler/chaser Lakino (by Relkino): modest maiden on Flat in Britain at 3 yrs, successful in Belgium in 1989: poor form in novice hurdles. *M. J. Ryan.* 68

ISLAND PEARL 10 ch.g. Gulf Pearl–Island Woman (King's Troop) [1989/90 c24m3] leggy, lightly-made gelding: winning hurdler/poor novice chaser: stays 2¾m (weakened closing stages over 3m): acts on firm and dead ground. *W. T. Kemp.* c— —

ISLAND SET (USA) 8 b.h. Hawaii–Desk Set (USA) (Tom Rolfe) [1989/90 16s5 16g2 16s2 16m 20f5] well-made horse: poor mover: put up smart performance when 4 lengths second to Kribensis (gave 10 lb) in Kingwell Hurdle at Wincanton in February, staying on well having been under pressure long way out: subsequently below that form in slowly-run White Rabbit Hurdle at Haydock, Waterford Crystal Champion Hurdle at Cheltenham (around 20 lengths seventh to Kribensis) and Sandeman Aintree Hurdle at Liverpool (finished lame): should stay beyond 2m: has run well on top-of-the-ground but gives impression will prove best with give: usually bandaged nowadays. *K. A. Morgan.* 153

ISLAND WONDER 8 gr.g. Algora–Island Joy (Easter Island) [1989/90 c25f F c25f3] won a point-to-point in April: last of 3 in novice hunter chase at Hereford. *Malcolm W. Davies.* c—

ISLE ORNSAY 13 ch.g. Bivouac–Woringo (Worden II) [1989/90 c21d pu c25m c25m ur c27f3] medium-sized gelding: winning point-to-pointer: poor hunter chaser. *G. Searle.* c—

ISN'T HE GORGEOUS 6 ch.g. Maystreak–Maud Gonne (Laser Light) [1989/90 16f4] first living foal: dam won over hurdles: useful 1¼m winner in Ireland at 3 yrs when trained by K. Connolly, successful in USA in 1988: odds on, beaten about a length when fourth in novice event at Taunton in December on hurdling debut (disputed lead most of way): looked sure to improve, but not seen out again. *M. C. Pipe.* 78 p

ISOBAR 4 b.g. Another Realm–Lady Eton (Le Dieu d'Or) [1989/90 16h* 16f* 16f* 16m* 16m2 17h2 16f F 16f a16g4 16m5 19s2 16g5 16d 21d4 16m5 16g 20g4 23f5 17f5] neat gelding: winning plater at 2 yrs: successful early in season in 3 selling hurdles at Hereford (bought in each time, for 4,000 gns on last occasion) and one at Huntingdon (no bid): ran moderately most starts afterwards: stays 19f: probably acts on any going: usually wears visor or blinkers: looks a difficult ride: trained until after fourteenth outing by S. Muldoon. *M. C. Chapman.* 92 d

IS REG IN 6 b.g. Liboi (USA)–Torlonia (Royal Palace) [1989/90 20s6 22d 24d 21fpu] leggy, angular gelding: poor novice hurdler: visored in 1988/9. *Miss E. Sneyd.* —

ISTHATAFACT 9 ch.g. Camden Town–Abbe's Realm (Realm) [1989/90 c18dur c16s* c21d2 c18s4 c18d4 c16v* c16s2 c16m] fairly useful Irish hurdler: won novice chase at Limerick in December and minor chase at Navan in February: outpaced from a long way out in valuable Perrier Jouet Novices' Chase at Liverpool in April: stays 21f: acts on heavy going and is probably unsuited by top-of-the-ground: has won when amateur ridden. *C. Kinane, Ireland.* c**132** —

ITALIAN TOUR 10 ch.g. Coliseum–Follow Me (Guide) [1989/90 22f5 20f6 25f4 20gF 20d 22g2 20g a20g3 a20g* a20g2] big, lengthy gelding: handicap hurdler: won at Southwell in February: creditable second on same course following month: stays 2¾m: best turf form on good ground: departed at the second both outings over fences: game front runner. *Mrs G. S. Plowright.* c— 110

ITMA 7 b.g. Nicholas Bill–Civic Duty (Averof) [1989/90 20mF 16g 20g6 16gsu c16fpu] leggy gelding: novice hurdler: pulled up seventh on chasing debut: dead. *R. Allan.* c— —

ITS A CAPPER 12 b.g. Perhapsburg–Skyvan (Skyros) [1989/90 c16g4 c24f2 23f5] winning hurdler/point-to-pointer/steeplechaser: no form for a long time. *J. R. Turner.* c— —

IT'S AFTER TIME 5 b.g. Newski (USA)–Lavenanne (Tacitus) [1989/90 F16f2] sixth foal: brother to fair hunter chaser It's Nearly Time: dam quite a useful hurdler: second favourite, clear second to Raido in NH Flat race at Uttoxeter in April: yet to race over hurdles or fences. *D. H. Barons.*

ITS ALL VERY FINE 9 ch.g. Deep Run–Flat Refusal (Raise You Ten) [1989/90 c26mF c25s6 c21gF c20v3 c24m] lengthy, good-quartered gelding: prolific winner in point-to-points in Ireland: won 2 hunter chases in Britain in 1988/9: well below his best in handicaps in 1989/90: stays 3¼m: acts on soft going: usually makes running: usually jumps well: amateur ridden. *Miss H. C. Knight.* c—

IT'S A LONG WAY 7 b.g. Le Moss–Bellejolais (Arctic Slave) [1989/90 24g3 24m* 24s 25d6 21d5] small, workmanlike gelding: handicap hurdler: won at Leicester in January: ran creditably last 2 starts: suited by a distance of ground: best form on a sound surface. *W. Carter.* 100

IT'S A PRY 9 b.g. Pry–Clogga Girl (Levanter) [1989/90 c21d3 c20fF c21spu c21g a20g4 a24g3 22g 24mF 21g3 25f4] workmanlike gelding: poor handicap hurdler/novice chaser, let down by his jumping over fences: quite headstrong and will probably prove best at up to 21f: acts on good to firm and soft going: has worn a crossed noseband. *Mrs E. H. Heath.* c**86** x 95

ITS NEARLY TIME 7 br.g. Newski (USA)–Lavenanne (Tacitus) [1989/90 c20dF c22gF] workmanlike gelding: fourth foal: dam quite a useful hurdler: successful in 2 point-to-points in 1989: showed plenty of ability in novice hunter chase won by Brockhill Boy at Ludlow, starting slowly but coming through strongly to dispute lead and looking certain winner when falling at the last (pulled hard and jumped sketchily earlier): tailed off when falling at the eighth next time: likely to prove best at around 2½m. *Mrs R. Brackenbury.* c**97**

IVEAGH HOUSE 4 b.c. Be My Guest (USA)–Waffles (Wollow) [1989/90 16v2 20g4 16g* 16f 16m 16g2] leggy colt: third foal: closely related to Irish 6f winner Great Shearwater (by Storm Bird): dam, Irish 9f winner, is daughter of 1000 Guineas winner Night Off: well beaten in minor event on Flat in November: won juvenile maiden hurdle at Wincanton in February: odds on, 1½ lengths second to Kowza in juvenile event at Uttoxeter in April (reluctant to race, led approaching last but hung right and no extra): around 21 lengths fourteenth to Rare Holiday in Daily Express Triumph Hurdle at Cheltenham on fourth start: seems not to stay 2½m. *Mrs J. Pitman.* 101 §

IVORDALE 5 b.g. Beldale Flutter (USA)–Ivoronica (Targowice (USA)) [1989/90 a16g] quite a modest handicapper around 7f on Flat when trained by M. H. Easterby (best form when blinkered): behind in novice hurdle in February. *W. G. Mann.* —

IVORDOLL 5 ch.m. Ivotino (USA)–Come On Doll (True Song) [1989/90 16g a16g4 a20g* 16m2 a16g3 20gF] sparely-made mare: unreliable winning plater on Flat (no form since 1988): favourite, easily won selling handicap hurdle at Lingfield in March (no bid): placed in non-selling novice handicaps later in month and in April: reluctant to race, made several mistakes and fell sixth in novice hurdle final start: stays 2½m: acts on good to firm going. *D. Burchell.* 82

IVORS GUEST 4 b.g. Be My Guest (USA)–Ivor's Date (USA) (Sir Ivor) [1989/90 16m5 16d2 16g 16g2 16f 16m* 16f* 16m2] leggy gelding: lightly-raced maiden on Flat: won maiden hurdle at Towcester in April and juvenile handicap at Ascot following month: ran well final outing: wandered under pressure third start and looked reluctant next time: acts on firm ground: blinkered last 4 outings. *Mrs J. Pitman.* 120

IVYCHURCH (USA) 4 ch.c. Sir Ivor–Sunday Purchase (USA) (T V Lark) [1989/90 16m 16f4 20g4 20g5 16g3 20s 16d 16m5] strong colt: carries condition: lightly-raced fair 2m winner on Flat: sold out of G. Harwood's stable 17,000 gns Newmarket September Sales: 15 lengths third behind Major Inquiry in Steel Plate Trial Hurdle at Cheltenham in January (led until after 2 out): poor form otherwise: likely to prove suited by forcing tactics when racing at 2m, and should stay 2½m: seems unsuited by soft ground. *J. Joseph.* 90 ?

I WONDER WHEN 9 ch.g. Levanter–Gretna Wonder (Elopement) [1989/90 16m 21d6 16f6] sturdy gelding: handicap hurdler: no worthwhile form in 1989/90: stays 2¾m: acts well on heavy going: has worn blinkers but not for a long time: good mount for a claimer. *G. Price.* —

IXOR (FR) 6 ch.g. Yours–Brouette (FR) (Makalu) [1989/90 22m 21fpu 20gpu 21d] lengthy gelding: no sign of ability: blinkered final start: sold 2,000 gns Doncaster Spring Sales. *R. Simpson.* —

IZADYAR 6 b.h. Akarad (FR)–Ilyaara (Huntercombe) [1989/90 16v4 16d 22d] rather leggy, good-topped horse: has been hobdayed: former selling hurdler: well beaten in 1989/90: unlikely to stay beyond 2m: acts on heavy going: visored final start 1987/8, blinkered final outing. *I. Semple.* —

J

JAAEZ 6 b.h. Ela-Mana-Mou–Almagest (Dike (USA)) [1989/90 16fF 16d 16g5 16m 16s5 20g4 16f4 20m5 20f4 20f2] leggy horse: poor novice hurdler: probably stays 2½m: best form on a sound surface: ran creditably in blinkers final start. *Mrs S. A. Bramall.* 78

JABARABA (USA) 9 b.g. Raja Baba (USA)–Time To Step (USA) (Time Tested (USA)) [1989/90 20f3 16g 20f] workmanlike gelding: winning hurdler: ran creditably in August: off course 6 months afterwards and well below form on return: stays 2½m: acts on hard going: sold 2,400 gns Ascot May Sales. *J. A. Bennett.* 91

JABRUT 5 b.g. Young Generation–Migoletty (Oats) [1989/90 20dpu 18v6 16f] smallish, sparely-made gelding: won 2m juvenile hurdle in 1988/9: off course over a year afterwards and ran poorly in handicaps in 1989/90: sold only 950 gns Ascot May Sales. *M. C. Pipe.* —

JACK AND JILL 10 gr.g. Scallywag–Royal Cottage (Prince Hansel) [1989/90 c18f4 c20s4 c20f c20s5 c20f4] leggy, plain ex-Irish gelding: maiden hurdler: won 2½m handicap chase on firm ground in 1987/8: always behind in 2 hunter chases in Britain: has run blinkered: trained until after third start by G. O'Donovan. *Mrs Gill E. Jones.* c76 —

JACK BILLMEIR 10 b.g. Filiberto (USA)–Charline (Charlottesville) [1989/90 c16h4 c17h2 c16m6 c16dF c21f4 c19dpu] leggy gelding: winning selling hurdler/poor chaser: pulled up lame final outing: stays 21f: acts on hard and dead going. *S. C. Davis.* c76 —

JACK DWYER 6 br.g. Mr Fordette–Daraheen Gate (Arcticeelagh) [1989/90 16f 24g 27g5 c27gur c24dur] angular, close-coupled gelding: half-brother to useful staying hurdler/chaser Rising Forest (by Precipice Wood): dam unraced half-sister to several winning jumpers: fourth in a point-to-point in Ireland: bought for 6,400 gns Doncaster August Sales: poor novice hurdler: poor jumper and has unseated rider both outings over fences: sold 1,800 gns Doncaster January Sales. *N. Tinkler.* c— x 66

JACK LAPPER 6 br.g. Swing Easy (USA)–Seaknot (Perhapsburg) [1989/90 22spu] big, leggy gelding: of little account. *R. P. C. Hoad.* —

JACK OF CLUBS 10 b.g. Kinglet–Laughing Stock (Woodcut) [1989/90 c24mpu] leggy, lightly-made gelding: fair chaser in 1987/8: having first race for 18 months, led until pulled up lame around halfway at Perth in September: suited by a test of stamina: acts on soft going: front runner. *B. McLean.* c— —

JACKO'S FUN 10 br.g. Funny Man–Scarlet Jackie (David Jack) [1989/90 22d^{pu}
20v^{pu} 22g^{pu} 19s] smallish, good-quartered gelding: third foal: dam placed over —
hurdles in Ireland: of little account. *Miss B. Sykes.*

JACKSCON WARRIOR 6 ch.g. Doctor Wall–Mary Mile (Athenius) [1989/90 c—
c24h^{4}] strong, compact gelding: no worthwhile form in novice hurdles: made —
mistakes when tailed off in novice event in October on chasing debut (blinkered).
Mrs J. Pitman.

JACK THE HIKER 7 b.g. Rare One–Royal Dress (Perspex) [1989/90 17f* c**78** +
c16h^{F} c16f^{4} c16f^{3} c16m^{3} c20m^{6} c16h^{pu}] big, close-coupled, workmanlike gelding: 78 +
won selling handicap hurdle at Newton Abbot in September (bought in 5,250 gns):
poor novice over fences: keen-running sort, not certain to stay much beyond 17f:
acts on firm ground: reportedly has broken blood vessels: claimer ridden: sketchy
jumper. *J. H. Baker.*

JACK THE SCAMP 10 gr.g. Commando–Swindon Lady (Danger) [1989/90 c—
c24m^{F} 16m] neat ex-Irish gelding: fell second in novice chase on jumping debut: —
tailed-off last in novice hurdle in September. *A. P. James.*

JACQUELINE'S GLEN 4 b.f. Furry Glen–June's Slipper (No Argument)
[1989/90 F16g] half-sister to winning jumpers June's Juke (by Jukebox) and
Rockbarton (by Lord Gayle): dam unraced half-sister to very useful stayer
Tamerslip: behind in NH Flat race at Perth (slowly away): yet to race over
hurdles. *J. Parkes.*

JADEBELLE 4 b.f. Beldale Flutter (USA)–Precious Jade (Northfields (USA))
[1989/90 16f^{3} 16m 16m 16m^{3} 16m^{4} 16v^{2} 16d^{5}] sparely-made, dipped-backed filly: 73
quite a modest performer on Flat (claimed out of M. Jarvis' stable £12,000 after
second in 1½m claimer in 1989): novice selling hurdler: well worth a try over
further than 2m: acts on any going: blinkered fifth outing. *W. G. M. Turner.*

JAGAN SOMBONG 7 b.g. Thatch (USA)–Welsh Pride (Welsh Saint) c**91**
[1989/90 c16g^{6} c16m^{3} c26m* 16m] sturdy gelding: selling hurdler: won 4-runner —
claiming chase at Uttoxeter in May: stays 3¼m: acts on dead and good to firm
going. *J. M. Bradley.*

JAKE MORGAN 5 b.g. Battlement–Bally Morgan (Zingari) [1989/90 F16g]
non-thoroughbred gelding: dam well beaten in juvenile hurdles: last in NH Flat
race at Edinburgh: yet to race over hurdles or fences. *J. S. Wilson.*

JALEES 4 b.c. Precocious–Walladah (USA) (Northern Dancer) [1989/90 16f
16g^{pu} 16m^{pu}] close-coupled colt: no worthwhile form on Flat (has been —
blinkered): little promise in juvenile hurdles in first half of season: blinkered last
2 starts. *G. G. Gracey.*

JAMAICA BAY (USA) 5 b.g. Lypheor–Flighting (Pitcairn) [1989/90 17f^{2}
18g* 20f* 20f^{6} 20s^{6}] leggy gelding: first foal: dam won Princess Royal Stakes: ?
winner on Flat: winner over jumps in USA, including in Queen Mother Supreme
Hurdle at Percy Warner Park in November: made a lot of the running when
around 20 lengths sixth in sponsored event at Cheltenham (saddle slipped early
on in race won by Morley Street) and Chepstow (race won by Propero) in
December: stays 2½m: acts on firm ground: wears crossed noseband: would be
rated only 126 on British form. *Jonathan E. Sheppard, USA.*

JAMALEY 4 b.g. Relkino–Clatter (Songedor) [1989/90 16g 17d^{pu} 16g] sturdy
gelding: always behind in a claimer on Flat: sold out of P. Howling's stable 1,650 —
gns Ascot July Sales: no sign of ability over hurdles, including in claimers. *S. C.
Davis.*

JAMES MY BOY 10 ch.g. Jimmy Reppin–College Brief (Lucky Brief) [1989/90
22d^{6} 20g^{5} 20v^{6} 21d* 20g* 20g 22s^{pu} 20g^{2} 20s^{F} 20g^{2}] strong, workmanlike 119
gelding: handicap hurdler: won at Warwick (claimer ridden) and Kempton within a
week in January: only form afterwards when runner-up at Kempton and Market
Rasen: suited by 2½m: acts on heavy going: has looked quite a hard ride and
suited by strong handling. *M. Dickinson.*

JAMES RIVER 4 ch.c. Star Appeal–Yorktown (Charlottown) [1989/90 16g^{pu}]
sparely-made colt: in frame at up to 1½m on Flat: sold out of J. Dunlop's stable 900 —
gns Ascot February Sales: raced freely and tailed off when pulled up in claiming
hurdle at Worcester. *Mrs A. Knight.*

JAMES STANLEY 6 b.g. Bold Lad (IRE)–Kathinka (Sovereign Path)
[1989/90 16h^{pu}] workmanlike gelding: middle-distance maiden on Flat at 3 yrs —
when trained by C. Brittain: placed once from 3 outings at around 2m over hurdles

in Ireland in 1987/8 when trained by P. Matthews: pulled up lame in seller in August: blinkered final start 1987/8. *M. J. Bolton.*

JANE CRAIG 7 b.m. Rapid Pass–Pride of Towy (Sayfar) [1989/90 22g 16f^{2} 20f^{5} 19f^{pu}] leggy mare: modest novice hurdler: pulls hard and tends to find little under pressure: stays 2½m: seems to act on any going: has been tried in blinkers: trained until after first start by R. Dickin. *N. A. Twiston-Davies.* 87 §

JANE MARPLE 6 b.m. Alias Smith (USA)–Parthia's Image (Parthia) [1989/90 a20g^{6}] successful on Flat in Belgium: behind in novice event at Lingfield on hurdling debut. *C. R. Wood.* —

JANE'S BRAVE BOY 8 b.g. Brave Shot–Jane Merryn (Above Suspicion) [1989/90 16g^{pu} 16s 16d] smallish, sparely-made gelding: poor handicapper on Flat, winner over 7f in 1989: no form over hurdles, including in selling company: trained by D. Chapman until after first outing. *T. Craig.* —

JANE'S DELIGHT 6 b.g. Royal Palace–Violate (Continuation) [1989/90 c16m^{4} c21g^{F} c20g^{pu}] strong, compact gelding: winning hurdler: modest novice chaser: jumped none to fluently final start (January): stays 2½m: acts on good to firm and dead ground (possibly unsuited by heavy): claimer ridden over hurdles: sold 2,700 gns Doncaster Spring Sales. *J. G. FitzGerald.* c**95** —

JANE'S JAUNT 7 ch.m. Move Off–Jaunty Jane (Con Brio) [1989/90 aF14g^{4} 20s^{4}] in frame in NH Flat races: fourth to Hopping Around in novice hurdle at Sedgefield in January. *Mrs G. R. Reveley.* 76

JANE'S JOY 5 ch.g. Move Off–Jaunty Jane (Con Brio) [1989/90 F16m^{2} F16f* F16f^{2} 16m* 16g^{6} 16g^{3} 17g^{5} 20f^{4} 20f* 20f^{2}] leggy, wiry gelding: third living foal: brother to novice hurdler Jane's Jaunt: dam won 1975 BMW Championship Hunter Chase: won NH Flat race at Sedgefield in October: successful over hurdles in novice events at Catterick and Sedgefield (handicap): good second to Chasers' Bar in handicap at latter course in May: stays 2½m: acts on firm ground. *Mrs G. R. Reveley.* 102

JANES STAR 6 br.g. Reformed Character–Janes Jet (Another River) [1989/90 16f^{pu}] first foal: dam plating-class maiden on Flat and over hurdles: pulled up in a point-to-point: saddle slipped before halfway and pulled up in conditional jockeys event at Market Rasen in August on hurdling debut. *G. P. Kelly.* —

JANEYS DELIGHT 9 b.m. New Henry–Keep Shining (Scintillant) [1989/90 c24f* c20f^{2} c24m^{2} c26f^{3} c25f^{pu}] workmanlike mare: won novice chase at Southwell in August: placed in similar events afterwards, jumping none too fluently on last 3 occasions (pulled up lame in November): stays 3m: acts on firm ground. *Miss S. J. Wilton.* c**85** —

JANIE-O 7 ch.m. Hittite Glory–Tweezer (Songedor) [1989/90 16g^{3} 16g* 16d 27f^{pu}] smallish, angular mare: quite modest mile handicapper on Flat (usually visored): won selling hurdle at Wetherby in November (bought in 5,000 gns): unlikely to stay 27f: trained until after third start by M. Tompkins. *J. Dooler.* 88

JANILLE 5 b.m. Takachiho–Dessert Moon (Nulli Secundus) [1989/90 F16g 24f^{ur}] half-sister to winning point-to-pointer Kyme Warrior (by Privy Seal): dam never ran: behind in NH Flat race and when unseating rider ninth in amateur riders maiden hurdle. *P. Liddle.* —

JAN-RE 6 ch.g. Deep Run–Khalketta (Khalkis) [1989/90 F16s^{4} 25d] tall, workmanlike gelding: brother to fair hurdler/chaser Deep Sound and to winning jumpers Scotsman Ice and Chesnut Fire, and half-brother to a winning selling hurdler: dam never ran: fourth in NH Flat race at Warwick in February: still bit backward, weakened quickly after mistake 4 out when in rear in novice hurdle at Huntingdon later in month. *G. A. Hubbard.* —

JANUS 12 ro.g. Ragstone–January (FR) (Sigebert) [1989/90 20f^{4} 22d^{4} 19m^{5}] smallish, lengthy gelding: useful hurdler at his best: best effort of 1989/90 on first start: runner-up only outing over fences (1985/6): stays 2¼m: acts on any going. *P. R. Hedger.* c— 88

JAPLING 12 gr.g. Brittany–Dalcius (Nelcius) [1989/90 c26g^{pu} c24g^{pu} c26f^{5} 26f^{pu}] small, rather dipped-backed gelding: winning hurdler/point-to-pointer: poor novice steeplechaser: stays 27f: acts on firm going: suitable mount for a claimer: ran creditably in blinkers once: has worn a pricker on near-side: often jumps fences poorly. *J. D. Thomas.* c**72** x —

JARPEE 4 ch.g. Bay Express–Romancing (Romulus) [1989/90 17g^{pu} 16m^{6}] small gelding: quite a modest maiden at his best on Flat: claimed out of R. —

Whitaker's stable £6,100 after finishing behind in a claimer in June: well beaten in juvenile selling hurdle in November. *N. G. Ayliffe.*

JARRAS 5 b.g. Touching Wood (USA)–Hilary's Hut (Busted) [1989/90 16g4 21s5 21fpu] sturdy gelding: handicap hurdler: bit backward, respectable fourth at Wolverhampton in December: seemed not quite to stay 21f in testing conditions next time: acts on soft going (moved poorly down, pulled up lame and dismounted on firm in March). *F. Jordan.* 94

JASMIN PATH 5 ro.m. Warpath–Jasmin (Frankincense) [1989/90 16g4 20g5 16g* 16d 16g* a16g 16g2] leggy, lengthy mare: won selling hurdles at Catterick (no bid) in February and Market Rasen (bought in 3,500 gns) following month: good second to Fisherman's Croft in claimer at Perth in April: best form at 2m on good ground: has worn a crossed noseband. *J. W. Blundell.* 85

JASON'S QUEST 6 gr.g. Golden Fleece (USA)–Carose (Caro) [1989/90 17gr] strong gelding: fairly useful juvenile hurdler in 1987/8: refused to race final start that season and in December (blinkered): sold 5,400 gns Ascot February Sales: resold 3,000 gns Ascot April Sales. *J. H. Baker.* §§

JAUNTER 10 ch.g. St Columbus–Jaunting (Jolly Jet) [1989/90 c24g3dis c24spu c22g3 c20f4 c25fpu c24f* c24m c24dpu] lightly-made gelding: modest chaser: won handicap at Worcester in April: ran poorly afterwards: stays 3m: acts on any going: usually held up: tends to jump rather slowly and drop himself out in early stages on occasions: usually claimer ridden. *W. Holden.* c95 § —

JAUNTY GIG 4 b.g. Dunphy–Hazel Gig (Captain's Gig (USA)) [1989/90 16f 16d3 16f4 16f3 20g4 20g2 20gF 17f6 24g3] leggy gelding: maiden plater at 2 yrs: selling hurdler: looked a difficult ride when good third in handicap at Edinburgh in December on final start: suited by a test of stamina: acts on firm ground. *W. A. Stephenson.* 99

JAY-DEE-JAY 7 b.m. Mljet–Tagliatelle (Straight Lad) [1989/90 26f6 21h3 20s5 16f4 24m4] smallish mare: handicap hurdler: stays well: seems to act on any going: suitable mount for a claimer. *J. D. J. Davies.* 90

JAY DOUBLE YOU 9 b.g. Free State–Touch of Dutch (Goldhill) [1989/90 24m3 c24f4 24f3 a20g2] big, rangy gelding: winning point-to-pointer: poor novice hurdler/chaser: finished lame final outing (November): stays 3m: sometimes blinkered or visored: poor jumper of fences. *N. Miller.* c75 x 79

JAYELLS DREAM 8 b.m. Space King–Sam's Song (Narrator) [1989/90 20s 22d6] leggy, lightly-made mare: modest hurdler: well beaten both starts in 1989/90: gives impression she needs further than 2m nowadays and stays 2¾m: acts on any going: usually wears blinkers: has wandered under pressure. *P. Hayward.* —

JAY JAY'S VOYAGE 7 b.h. Saunter–Traverser (Spiritus) [1989/90 16s 17d] close-coupled horse: novice hurdler: no worthwhile form. *J. D. Roberts.* —

JAYLAND 4 ch.c. Kings Lake (USA)–Santarelle (Jim French (USA)) [1989/90 16m4 16m] smallish, compact colt: placed at up to 1¾m on Flat, when trained by R. Hannon: fourth in moderately-run juvenile hurdle at Windsor in November: needed race when next seen out 2 months later (pulled hard, weakened after 3 out). *P. J. Jones.* 86

JAY-ZEE BOY 8 b.g. Moulton–Latakia (Morston (FR)) [1989/90 17mpu c20g4 c20f2 c26m* c26m2] leggy gelding: poor novice selling hurdler: poor chaser: won handicap at Uttoxeter in May: made several mistakes final outing: stays 3¼m: acts on any going. *J. M. Bradley.* c87 —

JAZETAS 7 ch.h. Jaazeiro (USA)–Mil Pesetas (Hotfoot) [1989/90 16m4 16f4 18m2 c21g* c16mF c24gpu 21m 16f3 20d3 16m2] workmanlike horse: moderate hurdler nowadays: went down by a short head to Valtaki in amateur riders handicap at Fakenham in May: jumped well when winning novice chase at Market Rasen in December, but was let down by his jumping next 2 starts: stays 21f: acts on any going: usually blinkered (wasn't on chasing debut): has shown signs of temperament and is not one to trust. *N. A. Callaghan.* c97 § 108 §

JAZZY JUMPER 8 b. or br.g. Smooth Stepper–Choralgina (Choral Society) [1989/90 c20dur c24m3 c16v* c18v2] leggy gelding: won handicap chase at Plumpton in January: went down by 2½ lengths to Never A Penny in novice event at Fontwell in February: best form at up to 2½m: acts on heavy going: jumps none too fluently over fences. *D. J. G. Murray-Smith.* c95 —

JEAN DUKE'S LAD 4 ch.g. Bay Express–Pounakha (USA) (Shecky Greene (USA)) [1989/90 16mur 16g 16m6 16s a16g] small, strong gelding: won 5f seller at 2 —

yrs, but little worthwhile form on Flat in 1989: no sign of ability over hurdles: blinkered final start: claimer ridden. *T. Kersey.*

JEASSU 7 b.g. Whistlefield–Menhaden (Menelek) [1989/90 16s4 17d 16s* 16s2 16d3] leggy gelding: won novice handicap hurdle at Nottingham in February: showed further improvement when clear 15 lengths second to Bitter Buck in novice hurdle at Haydock following month: jumped none too fluently when moderate third final start: should stay 2½m. *A. J. Wilson.* 112

JEDFOREST QUEEN 6 ch.m. Rouault–Mystic Queen (Golden Vision) [1989/90 F16f F16f] third foal: dam, novice hurdler, stayed 3m: showed a little ability in NH Flat races: yet to race over hurdles or fences. *D. W. P. Arbuthnot.*

JEFFREY GRAHAM 9 b.g. Mandrake Major–Lanchard (Space King) [1989/90 16g] workmanlike gelding: poor novice hurdler/chaser: strong puller. *F. Jordan.* c— —

JELBLEND 8 b.g. Jellaby–Just Janie (John Splendid) [1989/90 c16d3 c16m5 c20s] big, workmanlike gelding: won a point-to-point in Ireland: fell in similar event in February: poor novice chaser and behind only outing over hurdles in Britain: takes a good hold (wears a crossed noseband). *V. Thompson.* c67 —

JELLY JILL 7 ro.m. Jellaby–Petoria (Songedor) [1989/90 c16g5 c20f5 c20d c24g6 c16d3 c16g4 24dF] angular, sparely-made mare: poor novice selling hurdler/novice chaser: races freely and best at around 2m: has been tried in blinkers. *R. Allan.* c73 —

JELUPE 8 ch.g. Timber King–Lights of London (London Scottish) [1989/90 c24g4 c27d* c24d4 c28d* c33d* c24m c33d] medium-sized gelding: fairly useful point-to-pointer/hunter chaser: successful in handicaps at Sedgefield, Kelso and Newcastle: led 6 out and stayed on strongly to beat The Langholm Dyer 7 lengths in Tote Eider Chase on last-named course in February: ran poorly afterwards: needs a thorough test of stamina: probably acts on any going: trainer ridden. *R. P. Sandys-Clarke.* c126

JEMMA BELLE 4 b.f. Legal Tender–Kandy Belle (Hot Brandy) [1989/90 aF13g] first foal: dam winning hurdler: tailed off in NH Flat race: yet to race over hurdles. *P. B. Allingham.*

JENNY'S JOY 5 ch.m. Le Bavard (FR)–Blackrath Girl (Bargello) [1989/90 aF16g 16d] second foal: half-sister to maiden Irish point-to-pointer Majestic Player (by Torus): dam unraced: well beaten in NH Flat race and novice hurdle. *J. Parkes.* —

JENOOD (USA) 4 ch.c. Diamond Shoal–Rajput Princess (Prince Taj) [1989/90 16s5 16fpu] lengthy, workmanlike colt: half-brother to winning hurdler Plaza Gizon (by Little Current) and smart 1985 French 2-y-o 7f winner Rayonnante (by Tilt Up): dam, winner 5 times at around 1¼m in France, is half-sister to high-class middle-distance stayer Esprit du Nord and Irish Oaks —

Tote Eider Handicap Chase, Newcastle—Jelupe and owner/rider Mr Sandys-Clarke keep their concentration despite the loose horse, Sam da Vinci

winner Regal Exception: little promise in 2 outings over hurdles in March. *A. Moore.*

JERRY'S WISH 9 ch.g. Owen Anthony–Zena (Raoul) [1989/90 c25f[pu]] rather sparely-made gelding: no form over hurdles: winning point-to-pointer: placed in hunter chases in 1989: tailed off when pulled up in similar event in March. *Mrs J. A. C. Lundgren.* c— —

JERSEY PEARL 5 b.m. Last Fandango–Snow Chief (Tribal Chief) [1989/90 16f 16m[6] 22d[pu] 16g[pu]] leggy, angular mare: poor novice hurdler: trained until after second start by Miss P. O'Connor. *B. Stevens.* —

JESTERS PROSPECT 6 b.g. Idiot's Delight–Miss Prospect (Sweet Story) [1989/90 16f 20g[2] 22d* 20d[3] 20m[2]] won slowly-run novice hurdle at Kelso in January: ran well afterwards: stays 2¾m: best form on an easy surface. *Mrs J. D. Goodfellow.* 103

JEVINGTON GEM 4 ch.c. Vrondi–Nusaro (Sun Prince) [1989/90 16g[pu] 16g 16m[6] 16f[pu]] sparely-made colt: fifth foal: dam 5f winner at 2 yrs: poor form in juvenile hurdles: pulled up lame final start: trained by D. Grissell first 2 starts. *A. Moore.* 68

JEZAIL 10 b.g. Tarqogan–Durham Downs (Royal Buck) [1989/90 c19f* c24m[ur]] tall, good-topped gelding: carries plenty of condition: won novice hunter chase at Hereford in April: stays 21f: acts on any going: sometimes jumps none too fluently. *James Charlton.* c**89** —

JILLY WOOD 6 gr.m. Pragmatic–Bartlemy Fair (Town Crier) [1989/90 17m[2] 16h[5] 24g[F] 16f* 18g[5] 24g 19f 19f[6] 16d 21f[6]] plain, close-coupled mare: selling hurdler: won at Plumpton in October (no bid): little form afterwards: best effort at 2m: acts on firm ground and unsuited by a soft surface: has won for a claimer: sold out of Mrs J. Retter's stable 2,400 gns Ascot October Sales after third outing: trained next 2 starts by W. Kemp. *Dr P. L. J. Pritchard.* 60

JIMBALOU 7 b.g. Jimsun–Midnight Pansy (Deadly Nightshade) [1989/90 20g[5]] tall, leggy, rather plain gelding: useful hurdler: ran creditably in December: not seen out again: seems best at up to 2½m: acts on heavy going (had stiff task only start on firmer than good): has a turn of foot. *R. G. Brazington.* 135

JIM BOWIE 7 b.g. Yukon Eric (CAN)–Mingwyn Wood (Pirate King) [1989/90 c16m[F] 22s[4] c26s[pu] c26v[3] c25m[4]] sparely-made gelding: selling hurdler: third in handicap chase at Folkestone in February, only form over fences: stays 3¼m: acts on any going. *A. R. Davison.* c**88** —

JIM BRIDGER 5 ch.g. Little Wolf–Candid Queen (Good Bond) [1989/90 16g[ur] a16g[4] a16g[6] a16g[5] a16g[3] 16m[2] 16m*] sparely-made gelding: plating-class staying handicapper on Flat: landed the odds in 3-runner selling handicap hurdle at Huntingdon (bought in 2,300 gns) in April: suited by a strongly-run race over 2m and will stay further: acts on good to firm going. *P. J. Feilden.* 79

JIM HAWKINS 9 b.g. Jimsun–Booked (Counsel) [1989/90 21f] third foal: half-brother to a poor animal by March Past: dam never ran: tailed off in novice hurdle at Ludlow: sold 900 gns Ascot June Sales. *R. Lee.* —

JIM MCCRACKEN 5 b.h. Tachypous–Merchantmens Girl (Klairon) [1989/90 16f[pu] c19m[4] c20d[pu] c22m[pu]] sturdy horse: no form. *A. G. L. Taylor.* c— —

JIMMY BRIG 8 b.g. New Brig–Woodburn Kizzie (pedigree unknown) [1989/90 c24d[5] c25s[ur] c24d[6]] tall gelding: won twice and ran out twice in point-to-points in 1989: modest novice chaser: may prove suited by shorter distances than 3m: tends to jump left. *T. W. Donnelly.* c**100**

JIMMY MIFF 18 br.g. Nos Royalistes–Lark-About (Rose Knight) [1989/90 c25h[4]] lightly-made gelding: poor chaser nowadays: stays long distances: acts on any going except heavy: often makes running: has been tried in blinkers: successful at Uttoxeter 6 times: not one to trust. *I. P. Wardle.* c— § — §

JIMMY TWIST 7 br.g. My Eagle–Twist (Doudance) [1989/90 c16g c20d[pu]] angular gelding: no sign of ability in novice chases: jumps moderately. *K. Bishop.* c— x

JIMSIDIAN 8 ch.g. Porto Bello–Prime Thought (Primera) [1989/90 16g[pu]] leggy, sparely-made gelding: seems of little account. *Mrs S. C. Bradburne.* —

JIM'S MUSHROOM 6 b.m. Skyliner–Red Rose (Saint Denys) [1989/90 F16g] ninth foal: half-sister to Irish bumper winner Dane-Jor's (by Take A Reef): dam unraced: tailed off in NH Flat race in November on debut: yet to race over hurdles or fences. *J. R. Jenkins.*

JIM'S NEPHEW 4 b.g. Connaught–Grandgirl (Mansingh (USA)) [1989/90 16f 18f^5dis 16m 16f^6 16s^6] small gelding: second foal: dam unraced daughter of Lancashire Oaks runner-up Grandma: poor form over hurdles, including in sellers, in first half of season: ran poorly on soft ground: sold 1,050 gns Ascot February Sales. *A. Moore.* 63

JIMSTER 8 b.g. Jimsun–Merry Minuet (Trumpeter) [1989/90 c20g^3] big, good-topped gelding: winning hurdler: in frame in novice chases, showing modest form: stays 3m: acts on soft going. *C. T. Nash.* c93 —

JIM'S TOP 7 ch.g. Lucifer (USA)–Betty Sue (Menelek) [1989/90 20s^pu 16m^3 17g^pu a18g^pu] strong gelding: poor novice hurdler. *J. G. FitzGerald.* 77 ?

JIMSTRO 5 b.g. Jimsun–Bistro Blue (Blue Streak) [1989/90 16g 16s^4] workmanlike gelding: 100/1, first sign of ability over hurdles when fourth to Stay Awake in novice handicap at Warwick in February, running on well having been given a lot to do (made a couple of mistakes). *D. J. Wintle.* 72

JINXY JACK 6 b.g. Random Shot–True Or False (Varano) [1989/90 16g* 16g^2 16m^2 16d* 16d^5 16d* 16m^6 16d^F] 156

This horse is improving with age, and the Jinxy Jack of 1989/90 was very different from Jinxy Jack the juvenile hurdler of 1987/8. Purchased for 100,000 guineas at the 1987 Doncaster November Sales after winning three times at up to one and three quarter miles on the Flat, he just wouldn't settle after winning on his hurdling debut, jumped poorly as a consequence and gained a reputation for unreliability. But you'd not in all fairness say anything derogatory about him nowadays, though he still tends to want to get on with things early in the race. In 1989/90 he progressed to the stage where he earned himself a place in the field for the Waterford Crystal Champion Hurdle at Cheltenham in March. He travelled strongly in the rear for much of that race, but a mistake at the third from home when beginning to make ground soon saw him under pressure. Jinxy Jack stuck to his task though, and stayed on most determinedly on the stiff run to the line to finish an excellent twelve-and-a-half-length sixth behind Kribensis. Jinxy Jack finished ten lengths closer to that horse when the pair met in the Food Brokers And Primula 'Fighting Fifth' Hurdle at Newcastle in November.

Ayr New Year Hurdle (Limited Handicap), Ayr—Jinxy Jack wins very easily

Morebattle Hurdle, Kelso—Champion Hurdle contenders Jinxy Jack and Past Glories

Kribensis, looking on the backward side on his seasonal reappearance, duly landed the odds, but was made to fight hard by Jinxy Jack who was having his third outing, having won a quite valuable handicap at Wetherby on his reappearance. Jinxy Jack went on to gain a second victory, in a limited handicap at Ayr in early-January. He looked to have a stiff task in conceding 3 lb to Vicario di Bray, but the outcome could hardly have been more decisive. Always travelling supremely well, Jinxy Jack took the lead off the front-running Vicario di Bray two out and went smoothly clear to win by twelve lengths. Following a respectable fifth behind Deep Sensation under 11-8 in the Tote Gold Trophy at Newbury in February, when he gave the impression he'd have done even better ridden closer to the pace in a moderately-run race, he picked up his third race of the season in the Morebattle Hurdle at Kelso later in February. Looking in tremendous shape, Jinxy Jack led approaching the third from home and seemed to be well in command when two lengths clear of Past Glories at the last. The latter then stayed on very strongly on the long run-in and Jinxy Jack had to be ridden right out to hold on by a head, the pair thirty lengths clear. Jinxy Jack's last race of the season was as favourite for the Scottish Champion Hurdle at Ayr in April. He'd been favourite the year before when falling at the second. This time he was close up, travelling comfortably, when falling heavily at the fifth.

Jinxy Jack (b.g. 1984)	Random Shot (b 1967)	Pirate King (b 1953)	Prince Chevalier Netherton Maid
		Time And Chance (b 1957)	Supreme Court Foxtrot
	True Or False (br 1973)	Varano (b 1962)	Darius Varna II
		True (b or br 1964)	Straight Lad Parkadotia

Given that Jinxy Jack remains tractable, there is a good chance he will eventually stay two and a half miles. On breeding he should stay at least that. Sired by the smart stayer Random Shot, who has been responsible for several good horses over jumps, including Sun Alliance Novices' Chase winner Garrison Savannah, he is the second foal out of True Or False, a

Mrs B. M. McKinney's "Jinxy Jack"

mare successful in NH Flat races and over hurdles at up to two and a half miles in Ireland and also placed over three miles. True Or False's first produce, Real Swell (by Le Bavard), has made just one appearance to date, unseating his rider in a point-to-point in 1988. True Or False is one of two winning jumpers out of successful Irish hurdler/chaser True. Jinxy Jack has yet to race on very firm ground and fell on his only start in heavy conditions, but acts on any other. A big, rangy, good sort, he is to be sent chasing in the next season. Jim Thorpe, Music Be Magic and, of course, the much-lamented Noddy's Ryde, are all well known two-mile chasers to race for Richards. As Jinxy Jack is considerably better over hurdles than any of those were, he must have the potential to go right to the top over fences, and is an exciting prospect for 1990/1. *G. Richards.*

J-J-HENRY 11 b. or br.g. Ascertain (USA)–Gofton Burn (Drumbeg) [1989/90 c20g2 c20f2 c24g c25mpu c24g2 c22m c24g2 c24g2] tall gelding: fairly useful chaser: runner-up 5 times in 1989/90, on final start going down by 2½ lengths to Sir Jest at Newcastle: effective at 2½m to 3m: suited by a sound surface: usually jumps well: has worn a crossed noseband: usually looks well. *P. Beaumont.* c**128**

J M OWEN (USA) 4 ch.c. Plugged Nickle (USA)–Charmina (FR) (Nonoalco (USA)) [1989/90 16f2 16g3 a16gF 20g5] leggy, narrow colt: of little account on Flat and probably ungenuine: edged left when placed in selling hurdles: well beaten over 2½m: claimer ridden. *C. Spares.* 74

JOCK'S PERIL 5 b.g. Mljet–Lower Peril (Lower Boy) [1989/90 20fur 16m 16fpu 16d 16s] leggy, quite good-topped gelding: behind in novice hurdles. *W. D. Fairgrieve.* —

Seagram 100 Pipers Championship Final (4-Y-O Handicap Hurdle), Ayr—left to right, the much-improved Joe Bumpas, Rambo Castle and Stay Awake

JODAMI 5 b.g. Crash Course–Masterstown Lucy (Bargello) [1989/90 F16g* F16m[5] F16d[2]] angular, deep-girthed gelding: second foal: dam sister to winning jumpers Rugged Lucy and Hurry Up Henry: won NH Flat race at Kelso in March: 8 lengths second to Ruling in well-contested similar event at Ayr following month: saddle slipped in between: yet to race over hurdles or fences. *P. Beaumont.*

JODY'S BOY 9 b.g. Full of Hope–Miss Casanova (Galivanter) [1989/90 20f[3] 16f[4] c20f[3] c16g[F] c16g[5]] leggy, workmanlike gelding: fair chaser at best: broke blood vessels towards the end of 1988/9 and no form since, including over hurdles: effective at 2m and stays 27f: acts on any going: wears blinkers: sometimes on toes in preliminaries: amateur or claimer ridden. *R. W. Swiers.* c— —

JOE BUMPAS 4 b.c. Noalto–Montana Moss (Levmoss) [1989/90 16g[5] 16f* 16g[5] 16g[2] 16m[6] 16d*] strong colt: fourth living foal: half-brother to winning selling hurdler Carfax (by Tachypous): dam winning hurdler: winning middle-distance stayer on Flat: showed improved form when winning Seagram 100 Pipers Championship Final (handicap hurdle) at Ayr in April by 3 lengths from Stay Awake: earlier won juvenile event at Edinburgh: will stay beyond 2m: seems suited by plenty of give in the ground: needs strong handling (has run in snatches). *T. D. Barron.* 111

JOES BABY 7 b.m. Deep Run–Kilmorna II (Anthony) [1989/90 c24g[3] c24d[pu]] ex-Irish mare: second foal: dam behind in Irish NH Flat race: fourth in NH Flat race in 1987/8: behind in maiden hurdle in same season: won a point-to-point in 1989: remote third in novice chase in December: made mistakes following month. *P. Beaumont.* c— —

JOEY BLACK 6 br.g. Welsh Saint–Rue Del Peru (Linacre) [1989/90 16h[4] 16f[3] 16f a16g[pu]] small gelding: novice selling hurdler: suited by sharp 2m: headstrong: saddle slipped when running out once: sold 800 gns Doncaster January Sales. *P. A. Blockley.* 65

JOFEN 5 b.m. Sonnen Gold–Ensign Steel (Majority Blue) [1989/90 F16f] 1,800 4-y-o: half-sister to 3 winners (all by Lochnager), including fair sprinter and fairly useful hurdler Benfen: dam, placed over 6f, is half-sister to 3 very useful sprinters: tailed off in NH Flat race at Ascot (in touch until weakening 3f out): yet to race over hurdles or fences. *B. Smart.*

JOFF 4 br.g. Move Off–Jane's Tan (Queen's Hussar) [1989/90 16g $20g^{pu}$] ninth
reported foal: dam lightly-raced half-sister to Quorum: no sign of ability in 2 —
selling hurdles. *Mrs G. R. Reveley.*

JOGALOT 4 b.g. Lochnager–Key Harvest (Deep Diver) [1989/90 F17d F14v]
4,200Y: fifth foal: brother to a poor maiden and half-brother to 1¼m winner
Golden Vest, also a successful hurdler, and to fair 1985 2-y-o 6f winner
Aitchandoubleyou (both by Sonnen Gold): dam never ran: well beaten in NH Flat
races: yet to race over hurdles: sold 2,800 gns Ascot July Sales. *J. J. O'Neill.*

JOHN CORBET 7 b.g. Ascertain (USA)–Sweet Clare (Suki Desu) [1989/90 c85
c20f*] leggy, workmanlike gelding: novice hurdler (no worthwhile form): placed —
in point-to-points prior to winning novice hunter chase at Uttoxeter in May by 20
lengths: stays 2½m: acts on firm ground: wears a crossed noseband. *J. F.
Thompson.*

JOHN FEATHER 11 b.g. Gulf Pearl–Galtee Princess (Varano) [1989/90 c—
$16m^{ur}$ 20m] leggy, good-topped gelding: winning hurdler/chaser: lightly raced and —
no form for some time, including in a seller: best form at 2m: acts on any ground:
often ridden by claimer: often wore blinkers or a hood in 1986/7. *William Price.*

JOHN NORTH 10 b.g. Pongee–Norgill (Keren) [1989/90 $c25g^{3}$] one-time c88
modest staying hurdler: useful point-to-pointer at best (lightly raced nowadays): —
third in novice chase at Catterick in March. *Miss S. J. Turner.*

JOHNNY DANGEROUSLY 5 ch.g. Don–Absuleno (Above Suspicion)
[1989/90 16f $16s^{pu}$] neat gelding: no promise in selling hurdles: sold out of B. —
Cambidge's stable 2,000 gns Doncaster August Sales. *P. J. Anderson.*

JOHNNY SHARP (USA) 6 ch.g. Sharpen Up–Crimson Flame (USA) (Stage
Door Johnny) [1989/90 $22m^{6}$ $24f^{6}$ $21d^{F}$ $21d^{pu}$] small, leggy, close-coupled gelding: —
handicap hurdler: little worthwhile form in 1989/90: stays 3m: acts on any going
with possible exception of heavy: usually claimer ridden. *Miss S. J. Wilton.*

JOHNNY TARQUIN 17 br.g. Tarqogan–Fanny O'Dea (Sadler's Wells) c—
[1989/90 $a16g^{5}$] leggy gelding: poor selling chaser/hurdler nowadays: stays 2¼m: —
acts on hard going: has worn blinkers: amateur ridden. *R. Ledger.*

JOHNNY WILL 5 b.g. Salluceva–Hellfire Hostess (Lucifer (USA)) [1989/90
16g] sturdy, useful-looking gelding: second foal: dam winning hurdler/chaser in — p
Ireland: backward and green, made good late headway under tender handling
when eighth to None So Wise in novice hurdle at Windsor in March on debut:
capable of better, particularly granted stiffer test of stamina. *Miss H. C. Knight.*

JOHN O'DEE 7 b.g. Kambalda–Lady Parkhill (Even Money) [1989/90 20f* c**112**
$c20m^{3}$ c24f* c24g* $c24m^{pu}$ $a20g^{4}$ $c21m^{2}$ c25f* c22m $c20m^{3}$] lengthy, rather 84 +
sparely-made gelding: won novice hurdle at Huntingdon and handicap chases at
Cheltenham (amateur riders) and Fakenham early in season and quite valuable
handicap at Sandown (by ½ length from Torside) in March: effective at 2m and

VSEL Alanbrooke Memorial Handicap Chase, Sandown—
John O'Dee (left) survives earlier mistakes to beat Torside

stays 3¼m: acts on any going: makes mistakes: has won when blinkered: has worn a tongue strap: usually amateur or claimer ridden: swished tail under pressure second outing. *G. A. Hubbard.*

JOHN SAM 9 b.g. High Season–Reine d'Armagnac (Armagnac Monarch) [1989/90 c20f[ur] c26f* c26f[3] c24d[2] c26m[5]] leggy gelding: winning hurdler: fairly useful point-to-pointer: waited with, quickened clear run-in to win hunter chase at Cheltenham in April by 20 lengths from Half Free: went down by 8 lengths to Sanballat in similar race at Worcester in May: stays 3¼m: acts on any going. *G. W. Penfold.* c**109** —

JOHN'S BIRTHDAY 8 ch.g. True Song–Polaris Missile (Woodcut) [1989/90 c20g[3] c25s[2] c26g* c26g[3]] lengthy, angular gelding: brother to a poor animal and half-brother to several winning jumpers, including top-class hunter chaser Spartan Missile (by Spartan General): dam useful chaser: won his only start in a point-to-point in 1988: confirmed earlier promise when winning novice chase at Stratford in March by 5 lengths from Sooner Still, making a lot of the running and jumping really well: good third behind Docklands Express in novice handicap on same course following month: will stay extreme distances: should progress further. *N. J. Henderson.* c**102** p

JOHNS PRESENT 12 b.g. Gift Card (FR)–Kirmeen (FR) (Charlottesville) [1989/90 c20s[6] c21v* c24s[3]] rather dipped-backed gelding: made virtually all to win handicap chase at Newton Abbot in January: stayed 3m: acted well on heavy going: was suited by forcing tactics: well beaten when blinkered: good mount for a claimer: dead. *R. J. Holder.* c**117** —

JOHNSTED 4 ch.g. Red Johnnie–Busted Love (Busted) [1989/90 16g[5]] modest and inconsistent 1¾m winner on Flat: sold out of C. Brittain's stable 11,000 gns Newmarket Autumn Sales: tailed off in juvenile hurdle. *W. Clay.* —

JOINT SOVEREIGNTY 10 b.g. Status Seeker–Sovereign's Choice (Sovereign Path) [1989/90 c20f* c20g* c20f[pu] c21d[6] c36f[ur] c24g[ur] c25m[2]] c**147** d —

The useful chaser Joint Sovereignty was sold out of J. FitzGerald's stable for 14,000 guineas at the Doncaster August Sales. Three months later he'd repaid his new connections' faith in him with prize money of over £30,000 from wins in the Glynwed International Handicap Chase at Newbury and the Mackeson Gold Cup at Cheltenham. In both those events Joint Sovereignty had looked sure to be beaten as the race entered the latter stages. Approaching the last in the Glynwed International the smooth-travelling leader Vodkatini held a three- to four-length advantage over the hard-ridden Joint Sovereignty. The race changed dramatically at the last

Mackeson Gold Cup, Cheltenham—
Golden Freeze leads Joint Sovereignty and Dudie (left) over the last

though, where a bad blunder by Vodkatini handed the initiative to Joint Sovereignty, who ran on strongly to win by a length and a half with the only other runner Numerate a further thirty lengths behind. In the fifteen-runner Mackeson, Cuddy Dale set a strong pace. Joint Sovereignty, tracking the leaders initially, was under pressure to hold his position soon after halfway and as the field ran round towards the third from home at the top of the hill, he'd dropped back to seventh place. He began to stay on again approaching two out, after which Golden Freeze cruised into the lead on the bridle as Cuddy Dale dropped away. Joint Sovereignty continued to make headway but still had two to three lengths to make up approaching the final obstacle, which he hit hard. The mistake lost Joint Sovereignty little momentum, and, with Golden Freeze tiring in his first race of the season, Joint Sovereignty ran on strongly under a determined ride from McCourt to get in front close home and win by a neck, with Dudie a further three lengths away third. The only further prize money Joint Sovereignty earned during the season came from a below-par second to Huntworth in the minor event at Warwick in May that provided the record-breaking two-hundred-and-ninth winner of the season for Huntworth's trainer Martin Pipe. Joint Sovereignty had four races between the Mackeson and Warwick. In the first two of them he ran as though something was seriously amiss, despite looking well. In the other two, his proneness to the odd mistake found him out and he unseated his rider before the race had begun in earnest—at the nineteenth after never being dangerous in the Seagram Grand National at Liverpool on the first occasion. He'd been advertised for sale in the run-up to the National, and indeed he changed hands for the second time inside nine months in the end.

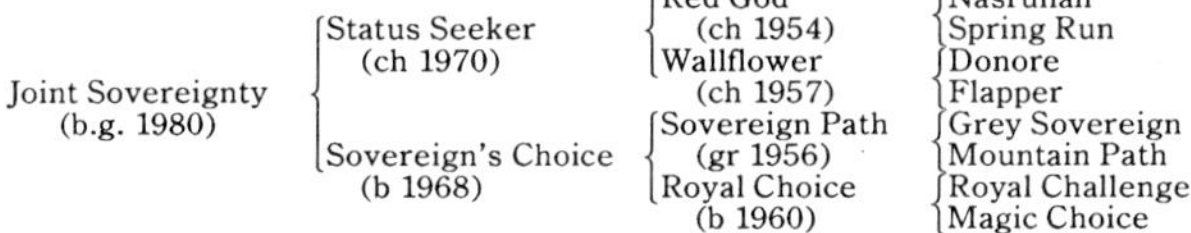

Joint Sovereignty (b.g. 1980)	Status Seeker (ch 1970)	Red God (ch 1954)	Nasrullah
			Spring Run
		Wallflower (ch 1957)	Donore
			Flapper
	Sovereign's Choice (b 1968)	Sovereign Path (gr 1956)	Grey Sovereign
			Mountain Path
		Royal Choice (b 1960)	Royal Challenger
			Magic Choice

Joint Sovereignty, a winner over hurdles in his younger days, is a half-brother to Kingly Sway (by St Alphage), who won over five furlongs as a two-year-old in Ireland. They are the only winners from nine foals produced by their dam. Sovereign's Choice, a half-sister to three fair winners at up to a mile, including Height of Himalaya who was later successful over hurdles, showed a little ability as a two-year-old. The next dam, Royal Choice, a very useful sprinter as a two-year-old, comes from the same family as the very smart chaser Balinese and the Welsh Champion Hurdle winner Frozen Alive. Joint Sovereignty, a tall, close-coupled gelding, hardly ever races at any other distance than two and a half miles, but is worth another try over further. He seems to act on any going. He was blinkered on his last three outings of the 1988/9 season, winning on the first of them. Whether he'll come back to his best remains to be seen; when he next runs it will be a long time since he showed his best form. He is to be trained by J. S. Wilson. *P. J. Hobbs.*

JOIST 8 ch.g. Malinowski (USA)–Junella (Midsummer Night II) [1989/90 c26f^2 25h^3 26f^3 26f^2 c24f* c24m* c25g^4 c24m] close-coupled gelding: handicap hurdler/chaser: successful over fences at Cheltenham and Bangor in October: ran moderately afterwards (not raced after November): stays well: acts on firm ground: has worn blinkers: looks a difficult ride (ridden in spurs at Cheltenham). *Mrs J. Wonnacott.* c**102** 102

JOKER JACK 5 ch.g. Garryowen–Deceptive Day (Master Buck) [1989/90 F16m 16v^{ur} 16m] small gelding: second foal: brother to winning hurdler Garry Odder: dam, Irish maiden, half-sister to winning jumpers Experimenting and the useful Tonights The Night: behind in NH Flat race and a novice hurdle. *R. D. Townsend.* —

JOLEJESTER 5 b.m. Relkino–Mirthful (Will Somers) [1989/90 16d^5] workmanlike mare: second foal: half-sister to useful 2m hurdler State Jester (by Free State): dam, successful at around 1¼m on Flat, was placed over hurdles: won NH 86

Flat race in 1988/9: jumped slightly deliberately but stayed on well when fifth behind Gold Service in novice hurdle at Haydock in December: in frame at 2m on Flat in 1990. *C. W. C. Elsey.*

JOLESIAN 4 b.g. Le Johnstan–Levandale (Le Levanstell) [1989/90 16g^{5} 16g^{3}
16m^{2} 18fF^{4}] sparely-made gelding: no form on Flat: sold out of Ronald 86
Thompson's stable 1,250 gns Doncaster September Sales: placed in novice hurdle at Windsor in March and juvenile maiden hurdle at Plumpton in April: every chance when falling 2 out (remounted) in novice handicap at Fontwell: acts on good to firm ground: wears crossed noseband: trained by T. Walford first start. *Mrs L. Clay.*

JOLIE GAZELLE 8 b.g. Panco–Spring Gazelle (Dear Gazelle) [1989/90 c25g^{3} c—
c27g^{5} c26m^{ur} c25d c26s^{5} c32f^{ur} c24f c25f^{pu}] leggy gelding: first foal: dam poor novice hurdler: won point-to-point in 1989: well beaten in steeplechases: blinkered last 4 starts. *P. Davis.*

JOLLIENNE 6 ch.m. Absalom–Bourienne (Bolkonski) [1989/90 18f^{3} 22f*
18g^{4} 22m^{5} a22g^{4} 20m^{pu} 22f^{6} 21f^{4}] smallish, good-bodied mare: won mares novice 85
hurdle at Wincanton in October: good sixth in handicap at Fontwell in May but below form when well backed for selling handicap at Towcester later in month: will stay beyond 2¾m: acts on firm ground and is possibly unsuited by soft surface. *S. Woodman.*

JOLLY MAC 12 br.g. Sir Herbert–Candy Puss (Candy Cane) [1989/90 c24f* c104
c24m^{F}] rather lightly-built gelding: winning hurdler: won point-to-point in 1988: —
showed only worthwhile form in steeplechases when winning handicap at Southwell in August: destroyed after breaking a shoulder at Nottingham in October: stayed 3m: acted on any going. *P. Burgoyne.*

JOLLY SURPRISE 5 b.h. Jolly Me–Madame Decoy (Decoy Boy) [1989/90
16g^{pu}] small, plain horse: fourth foal: dam winning sprinter: jumped poorly and —
was tailed off when pulled up 3 out in conditional jockeys claimer at Worcester in December on hurdling debut. *A. W. Denson.*

JOMANA 4 ch.f. Roman Warrior–Tina's Magic (Carnival Night) [1989/90 16g^{pu}
16s] second foal: half-sister to poor novice hurdler Tina's Pearl (by Old Jocus): —
dam never ran: quite modest sprinter on Flat: well beaten in juvenile hurdle at Sandown. *J. C. Fox.*

JONJO'S SON 4 b.g. Song–Speed The Plough (Grundy) [1989/90 18f^{pu}]
plating-class maiden on Flat, no form in 1989: behind when pulled up last in —
juvenile event at Fontwell in October. *W. Carter.*

JOPAJUSCHA 11 b.g. Young Emperor–Little Dipper (Queen's Hussar) c81
[1989/90 c24g^{3}] workmanlike gelding: winning point-to-pointer/hunter chaser: —
moderate third in hunter chase at Bangor in May: stays 3m: acts on any going. *Mrs R. G. Swindells.*

JOPANINI 5 b.g. Homing–Honeybuzzard (FR) (Sea Hawk II) [1989/90 16f*]
compact, good-bodied gelding: fair front-running hurdler: made all to beat Daily 115 +
Sport Soon 4 lengths in Flavel-Leisure 4-y-o Hurdle at Newbury in October: not seen out again: will be suited by further than 2m: yet to race on very soft going, probably acts on any other: jumps well. *D. T. Thom.*

JORDENS SCALLYWAG 6 ch.m. Scallywag–Paddy's Delight (Paddy's
Birthday) [1989/90 20f^{pu}] useful-looking mare: third foal: dam quite moderate —
front-running staying chaser: tailed off when pulled up 4 out in mares novice event at Huntingdon in November on hurdling debut. *Mrs P. Townsley.*

JORO 13 ch.g. Spartan General–Sassy Lady (Philemon) [1989/90 c24d^{pu}] plain c—
gelding: no worthwhile form over hurdles and in steeplechases, but is a point- —
to-point winner. *M. J. Footer.*

JOSEPH KNIBB 11 b.g. Golden Love–Green Sea (Black Tarquin) [1989/90 c—
c22m^{F}] medium-sized Irish gelding: winning hurdler/chaser: won a point-to-point —
in February: close up when falling heavily at the seventh in Seagram Fox Hunters' Chase at Liverpool in April: probably stays 3m: acts on soft going. *T. Carberry, Ireland.*

JOSEY WALES 8 b.g. Carnival Night–Graceful Grange (Prefairy) [1989/90 c75 x
c24m^{4} c26m^{pu} c28g^{pu}] leggy, angular gelding: novice hurdler: poor chaser: stays —
well: possibly unsuited by hard ground: has worn a severe bridle: makes mistakes over fences. *B. Smart.*

JO VERDI 5 ch.g. Music Boy–Green Chartreuse (French Beige) [1989/90
a16g] plain, dipped-backed gelding: well beaten over hurdles. *R. Brandon.* —

JOYFULNESS (FR) 5 b.m. Cure The Blues (USA)–Jermaric (Great Nephew) [1989/90 16f* 16g^{6} 16m 16g a16g^{3} a16g^{3} a16g^{5} 16m^{F} 16m^{2} 16h^{4} 16f^{5}] 79
sparely-made mare: finished lame after winning novice hurdle at Southwell in August: variable form afterwards: likely to prove best at 2m: acts on firm ground: blinkered last 3 starts. *P. J. Bevan.*

JOYFUL NOISE 7 b.g. Lighter–Roadway Mistress (Mandamus) [1989/90 16g 16d* 16g^{4} 16d^{2} 16m^{3} 20f^{2} 21g^{2} 25s] 150

The smart Irish hurdler Joyful Noise ran more times abroad than he did at home in the latest season. Indeed, he wasn't seen out in Ireland after finishing three and a half lengths fourth behind Redundant Pal in The Ladbroke at Leopardstown in mid-January. Joyful Noise, one of the best-backed horses in the race, ran even better than his position suggests, for he still had a wall of horses in front of him turning for home, having been held up and given plenty to do. Weaving his way through, he stayed on strongly and was closing at the finish. On his previous outing Joyful Noise had taken up the running turning for home when winning a five-runner handicap over the same course and distance. Joyful Noise's next three races after The Ladbroke all took place in England, and he was the sole Irish challenger in each of them. Joyful Noise came very close to lifting the Tote Gold Trophy Handicap at Newbury in February, going down by only a head to Deep Sensation in a driving finish. Racing off a mark 3 lb lower in the William Hill Imperial Cup at Sandown the following month, Joyful Noise was unable to produce his Newbury running under much faster conditions and was beaten fourteen lengths into third place behind Moody Man. Two miles is too sharp for Joyful Noise when the ground is on the firm side. He's effective on a firm surface over two and a half miles, though, as he showed when finishing fifteen lengths second to the high-class performer Morley Street at level weights in the Sandeman Aintree Hurdle at Liverpool. Having moved through smoothly to lead three out, Joyful Noise was comprehensively outpaced by the winner on the run-in but kept on to finish three lengths clear of third-placed Ikdam. Joyful Noise ended the season racing in France. He was beaten a length when second to Ma Puce in the Prix La Barka at Auteuil in June, but a month later he could finish only

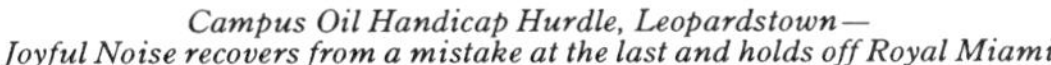

Campus Oil Handicap Hurdle, Leopardstown—
Joyful Noise recovers from a mistake at the last and holds off Royal Miami

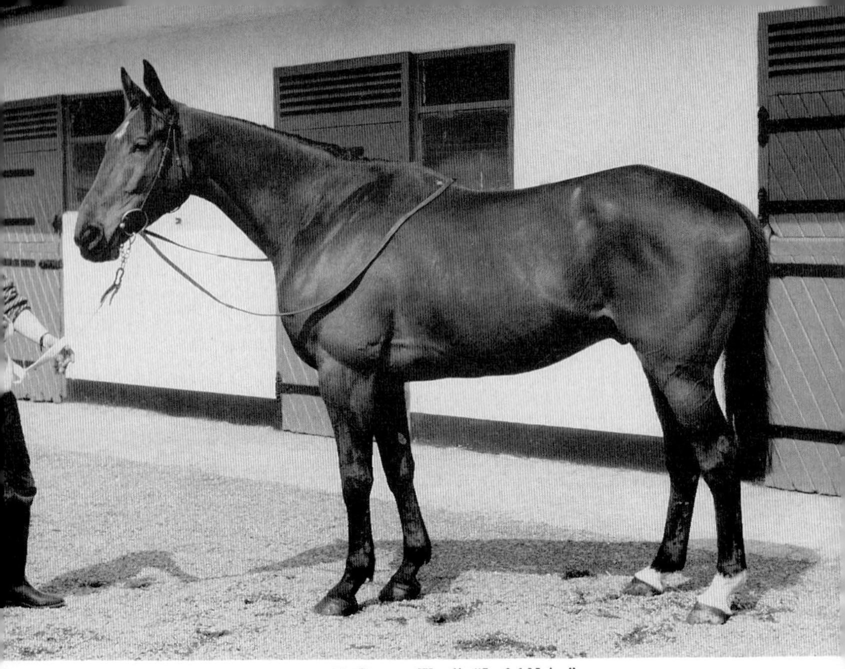

Mr Spencer Wood's "Joyful Noise"

seventh of eight behind Tongan—Ma Puce was third—in the Grande Course de Haies d'Auteuil. Joyful Noise possibly found the extended three miles beyond him on the latter occasion, but he's certainly worth another chance at such a trip under less testing conditions.

Joyful Noise (b.g. 1983)	Lighter (b 1973)	Aureole (ch 1950)	Hyperion
			Angelola
		Raft (b 1966)	Ragusa
			Kyak
	Roadway Mistress (br 1977)	Mandamus (br 1960)	Petition
			Great Fun
		Miss Soundly (ch 1964)	Maelsheachlainn
			Soundly

Joyful Noise is yet another example of how good jumpers can be picked up cheaply, for he fetched a mere 400 guineas when sold as a yearling at Doncaster in November, 1984. By the Waterford Crystal Stayers' Hurdle winner Lighter, Joyful Noise is the first foal of Roadway Mistress, a half-sister to the winning hurdler/chaser Kilroe's Calin. Roadway Mistress showed no worthwhile form in novice hurdles, but her dam Miss Soundly was a fair chaser, effective from two miles to three miles, and her grandam Soundly was a winning hurdler. This is the outstanding Arab Maid family. Soundly is a sister to the Grand Annual Chase winner Rose & Crown and a granddaughter of a sister to the dual Cheltenham Gold Cup winner Easter Hero. Joyful Noise, a good-topped gelding who carries condition, will make a chaser. He acts on any going. *A. L. T. Moore, Ireland.*

JOY'S TOY 4 ch.f. Wolverlife–Tanzanite (Marino) [1989/90 16g a16g] inconsistent 1m seller winner on Flat: well beaten in selling company over hurdles. *Pat Mitchell.* —

Kestrel Handicap Hurdle, Ascot—Jubail (right) wins cleverly from Ambassador

J-TEC BOY 4 gr.g. Orange Reef–Fotostar (Polyfoto) [1989/90 16f^{pu} 16m^{6} 17m^{F} 16g 16f 16d a16g] close-coupled gelding: little worthwhile form, including in sellers, on Flat: well beaten in juvenile hurdles and a novice claimer: saddle slipped on hurdling debut: trained until after fifth start by J. Gillen. *I. Semple.* —

JUBAIL 5 b.g. Sandhurst Prince–Fluella (Welsh Pageant) [1989/90 16m^{4} 16m^{2} 16f^{2} 16d 16f* 16f* 16f*] workmanlike gelding: useful hurdler: in excellent form in the spring following a 4½-month lay-off and won at Newbury (conditional jockeys), Ascot and Liverpool: quickened well from rear to lead flat and beat 135 p

Janneau Armagnac Handicap Hurdle, Liverpool—Jubail completes his hat-trick at the chief expense of Persillant

Persillant by ½ length in Janneau Armagnac Handicap Hurdle on last-named course: unlikely to stay much beyond 2m: acts well on firm ground: has a good turn of foot. *K. A. Morgan.*

JUBILEE MONDAY 4 b.c. Sweet Monday–Jubilee Joy (Burglar) [1989/90 16f^{pu}] lightly-raced maiden on Flat: jumped badly and was tailed off when pulled — up in juvenile hurdle at Worcester in August: sold 1,300 gns Ascot September Sales. *B. Preece.*

JUDGES FANCY 6 b.g. Monksfield–Knollwood Court (Le Jean) [1989/90 16g^{2} 20g^{3} 20g* 22v^{3} 20d^{F} 20f^{2}] compact gelding: successful in novice hurdle at 132 Newcastle in December: 66/1, showed improved form when 12 lengths second to Regal Ambition in 22-runner Sun Alliance Novices' Hurdle at Cheltenham in March, staying on well: will probably stay 3m: well suited by a sound surface: useful. *C. C. Trietline.*

JUDGMENT DAY 8 b.g. Mandamus–Vimaday (Vimadee) [1989/90 c16m^{3} c**76** x c20s^{F} c20d^{F} c16f^{6} c20m^{pu}] compact, workmanlike gelding: lightly-raced novice — hurdler/chaser: let down by his jumping most starts over fences: may prove best at around 2m. *J. W. Payne.*

JUDYS LINE 6 b.m. Capricorn Line–Gold Braid (Martial) [1989/90 22m^{3} 21g^{4} 25g^{6} 26v* 21d^{ur}] tall, workmanlike mare: won handicap hurdle at Newton Abbot 105 in January by ½ length from Cima: stays well: acts on heavy and good to firm going: trainer ridden. *Miss S. Waterman.*

JUMP 5 gr.g. General Ironside–Maroon Well (Wrekin Rambler) [1989/90 16s 16g] lengthy, good-bodied gelding: ninth foal: half-brother to 2 poor animals: dam 73 half-sister to winning jumpers Henry The Fifth and Some Surprise: better effort in novice hurdles when seventh at Wincanton in January final start. *S. Mellor.*

JUNAC 6 b.m. Cajun–Be In Touch (Windjammer) [1989/90 20d 16m^{5} 21f^{5} c16g^{ur} c— 21d^{pu} c20f^{6}] sturdy ex-Irish mare: second foal: dam showed ability on Flat: 69 maiden point-to-pointer: bought for 7,000 gns Doncaster August Sales: poor form over hurdles and in steeplechases: best at 2m: tailed off final start. *Mrs S. Minns.*

Mr J. C. de C. Scott's "Judges Fancy"

JUNEAU 11 bl. or br.m. Yukon Eric (CAN)–Articul Pat (Articulate) [1989/90 c20v⁶] winning point-to-pointer: tailed off in maiden hunter chase at Folkestone in February. *Mrs A. E. Dawes.* c—

JUNE'S FANCY 4 ch.f. Mr Fluorocarbon–Havaneza (Simbir) [1989/90 16m² 17g 19s a18g⁶] small, angular filly: poor plater on Flat, suited by 1½m: second in juvenile claiming hurdle at Ludlow in November (wore crossed noseband): well beaten afterwards, including in a seller. *D. R. Tucker.* 56

JUNGLE KNIFE 4 b.g. Kris–Jungle Queen (Twilight Alley) [1989/90 16f⁶] strong, angular gelding: half-brother to useful hurdler Jungle Jim (by Hotfoot): modest maiden on Flat, stays 1m: sold out of C. Brittain's stable 13,000 gns Doncaster October Sales: carrying plenty of condition, raced freely and weakened 2 out when sixth in juvenile hurdle at Edinburgh in December. *K. A. Morgan.* — p

JUNIOR LANCASTER 5 b.m. Dubassoff (USA)–Lancaster Rose (Canadel II) [1989/90 aF16g 21vpu] lightly-made mare: fourth foal: half-sister to winning hurdler/point-to-pointer Henry Lancaster (by Oh Henry): dam never ran: behind in NH Flat race and when pulled up in mares novice hurdle. *T. B. Hallett.* —

JUNIOR PARKER 6 br.g. Al Sirat (USA)–Black Zeta (Black Tarquin) [1989/90 22m⁶ 22s² 20v² 24d³ 22s² 20d* 22dpu] deep-girthed ex-Irish gelding: brother to winning chaser Simark and fair hurdler Mr Parker and half-brother to winning Irish jumpers Hainey's Machine (by Golden Vision) and Blue Zeta (by Bluerullah): dam unraced half-sister to very useful staying chaser Zeta's Son: won 2 point-to-points in 1989: placed in 4 novice hurdles prior to winning one at Sedgefield (long odds on) in March, making all: weakened quickly after 3 out and pulled up before last in handicap following month: probably stays 3m: acts on heavy going: best with forcing tactics. *J. A. C. Edwards.* 107

JUPITER EXPRESS 12 ch.g. Jupiter Pluvius–La Perla (Majority Blue) [1989/90 c20gpu 20m] sparely-made gelding: selling hurdler nowadays: behind when pulled up last in selling handicap on steeplechasing debut: failed to complete in 3 point-to-points in 1988: stays 2½m: acts on firm and dead going: often blinkered and claimer ridden (wasn't when successful). *R. E. Peacock.* c— —

JUPITER PRINCE 11 ch.g. Jupiter Pluvius–Lady Rois (Prince Rois) [1989/90 20gpu] leggy, lightly-built gelding: poor novice hurdler/chaser: stayed 21f: possibly needed plenty of give in the ground: dead. *R. Johnson.* c— —

JUPITER'S GLORY 6 b.g. Derring Rose–The Blazing Star (Proverb) [1989/90 F16f² 22g² 22d² 27g* 22g⁵ 25g³ 24m 24f² 27f² 24m⁴ 24gF] neat gelding: second foal: dam winning Irish point-to-pointer: won novice hurdle at Sedgefield in November: ran well most starts afterwards: stays well: acts on firm ground: ran poorly when sweating seventh outing. *W. A. Stephenson.* 100

JURANSTAN 5 b.h. Furry Glen–Atlantic Hope (Brave Invader (USA)) [1989/90 F16g 20vpu 16m] leggy horse: second foal: dam unraced: little sign of ability in a NH Flat race and novice hurdles. *C. C. Trietline.* —

JURISPRUDENCE (USA) 7 b.h. Alleged (USA)–Leliza (USA) (Gallant Romeo (USA)) [1989/90 16gpu 20m 16s³ a18g⁴ a20g³ 16mpu] smallish, angular, sparely-made horse: selling hurdler: below his best in 1989/90: stays 2½m: acts on firm going: wears crossed noseband. *P. J. Bevan.* 76

JUSSOLI 6 b.m. Don–Torino (Firestreak) [1989/90 16fur 16g³ 16g⁶ 16g⁴] small, sturdy mare: modest novice hurdler: races only at 2m: probably unsuited by heavy ground: visored first 2 and last starts: often finds little. *Miss S. E. Hall.* 90

JUST A BOOZER 6 b.g. Just A Monarch–Vineyard (pedigree unknown) [1989/90 22sF a16gpu 16vpu c16hF] lengthy, sparely-made gelding: first reported foal: dam never ran: failed to get past the sixth in novice hurdles and a maiden chase. *D. M. Grissell.* c— —

JUST A GHOST 14 gr.g. Rugantino–Just Snuff (Manicou) [1989/90 c25m⁴ c26f² c24mF c26f* c26f³] compact gelding: winning chaser/point-to-pointer: won hunter chase at Folkestone in May by 25 lengths: 21 lengths third behind Polar Glen at Fontwell a week later: stays well: acts on hard going. *Mrs J. R. French.* c82 —

JUST A HALF 8 ch.g. Most Secret–Alentejo (Privy Councillor) [1989/90 c16sF] big, good-bodied gelding: winning hurdler: modest novice chaser: close up when falling 2 out at Haydock in January: takes a good hold and is likely to prove best at around 2m: acts on heavy going (never dangerous on firm): jumps fences well in the main. *D. McCain.* c? —

JUST ANOTHER SIP 6 b.m. Lochnager–Sipped (Ballyciptic) [1989/90 16g 20g 20g] close-coupled mare: poor novice hurdler: dead. *J. G. FitzGerald.* —

JUST AS HOPEFUL (NZ) 6 b.g. In The Purple (FR)–Bighearted (NZ) (Better Honey) [1989/90 21g² 24g² 20g⁶ 24v*] tall gelding: fairly useful hurdler: won handicap at Chepstow in January by ¾ length from What About Me: suited by a thorough test of stamina: acts on heavy going: blinkered last 2 starts: has won for a claimer but idled when winning and has wandered under pressure. *D. H. Barons.* 130

JUST A TRIFLE 8 br. or gr.m. Jellaby–Just Jolly (Jolly Jet) [1989/90 22mpu] has been hobdayed: placed in point-to-points: tailed off when pulled up in amateur riders novice event at Wincanton in November on hurdling debut. *G. Stickland.* —

JUST A WHISPER 4 ch.f. Humdoleila–Salvo's Grace (FR) (Salvo) [1989/90 16m 16g 16dpu a16gpu] lengthy, rather dipped-backed filly: half-sister to winning hurdler/chaser Gardeners Choice (by Mossberry): dam won twice over hurdles after birth of first foal: no sign of ability in juvenile hurdles: pulled up lame final start. *R. Wilding.* —

JUST BLAKE 9 b.g. Blakeney–Just A Dutchess (USA) (Knightly Manner (USA)) [1989/90 c20fur c21f³ c20f³ c20mr 20f* 20f³ 20f²] useful-looking gelding: gaining fourth course win when making most to win handicap hurdle at Plumpton in September: ran creditably following month: jumped deliberately when third in 2 novice chases: stays 21f: best form on a firm surface. *J. D. Roberts.* c77 93

JUST BROOK 11 b.g. Country Retreat–Rissole (Woodcut) [1989/90 c25f⁶] sparely-made, angular gelding: poor maiden point-to-pointer: little show in hunter chases. *Dennis Hutchinson.* c—

JUST CHARLES 5 b.g. Tepukei–Easter Tinkle (Hot Brandy) [1989/90 F12g 16fpu 20gpu] fifth foal: half-brother to high-class hunter chaser Sweet Diana (by Bivouac): dam winning hurdler: mid-division in NH Flat race in March: pulled up both outings over hurdles following month. *J. W. Blundell.* —

JUST CRACKER 5 ch.g. Monsanto (FR)–Pertune (Hyperion's Curls) [1989/90 17m 17fpu 17m⁵ 18f⁴] poor novice selling hurdler. *F. G. Hollis.* 62

JUST CRUISE 4 ch.g. Milford–Glenside Lady (So Blessed) [1989/90 a16g 16m 18v⁵ a18g] sparely-made colt: seems of little account: sold 1,000 gns Ascot July Sales. *K. T. Ivory.* —

JUST FOR JOHN 7 b.m. Domitor (USA)–Farm Consultation (Farm Walk) [1989/90 16m³] lengthy mare: poor novice hurdler: will be suited by a stiffer test of stamina. *J. I. A. Charlton.* 89

JUST FOR THE CRACK 12 ch.g. The Parson–Rosesong (Kabale) [1989/90 c24fpu c24g* c24m⁶ c20m* c24d⁶] smallish, sturdy gelding: fair chaser nowadays: won handicaps at Southwell in November and Wolverhampton (by 2½ lengths from How Now) in January: ran moderately in between and on final start (first race for 4 months): stays 3m: acts on any going: claimer ridden last 4 starts. *K. C. Bailey.* **c118** —

JUST GREAT 4 br.g. Simply Great (FR)–Bourton Downs (Philip of Spain) [1989/90 a18g⁵ a16g²] won 11f handicap on Flat in January (inconsistent): favourite, short-head second to Caroles Clown in selling hurdle at Southwell in May (claimed by R. Juckes £6,101). *D. T. Thom.* 77

JUST HILLGAR 5 b.g. Royal Auction (USA)–Cairngrove (Knotty Pine) [1989/90 F16f 20fpu] workmanlike gelding: first foal: dam placed in a point-to-point in Ireland: tailed off in NH Flat race and when pulled up in a novice hurdle at Ascot. *A. Moore.* —

JUSTICE LEA 10 b.g. Kinglet–Evada (Eborneezer) [1989/90 20g c20gur 24g 24d⁶ 20f⁶ 17m³ 24m* 20f⁴ 27f* 23f² 25f²] lengthy gelding: winning point-to-pointer: behind in 2 maiden hunter chases: won handicap hurdles at Carlisle in April and Sedgefield in May: runner-up twice at Cartmel afterwards: suited by long distances and firm going: usually claimer ridden (including when successful). *T. A. K. Cuthbert.* c— 94

JUST INCREDIBLE 4 b.g. Auction Ring (USA)–Elated (Sparkler) [1989/90 aF14g⁵] IR 4,000Y, 7,000 2-y-o: fifth foal: brother to 1m winner Auchinate, later successful in Italy, and half-brother to fairly useful 7f and 1m winner Monetarist (by Monseigneur): dam won over 1m at 2 yrs: 21½ lengths fifth of 13 to Fighter Command in NH Flat race at Southwell in February: yet to race over hurdles. *J. P. Leigh.*

JUST MEASURE 5 b.m. Broadsword (USA)–Fair Measure (Quorum) [1989/90 16m 22d] lengthy mare: no worthwhile form over hurdles. *D. R. C. Elsworth.* —

JUST MICK 9 b.g. Tycoon II–Vulrory (Vulgan) [1989/90 c20m[F] c19g[3] c21d c22g c20m[4] c20g[5] c20d c20f] smallish, sturdy gelding: winning point-to-pointer: poor novice steeplechaser: stays 2½m. *Mrs H. B. Dowson.* c**71**

JUST ONE KISS 5 ch.m. Tower Walk–Mistress Royal (Royalty) [1989/90 16g a24g[5] a20g[4] 16d[5] a20g[4]] sparely-made mare: poor form over hurdles, including in sellers last 3 starts. *W. Wilson.* 66

JUST PATRIMONY 6 br.g. Petrassi (GER)–Quilpee Mai (Pee Mai) [1989/90 16g 16g[4] 16g 16f 20m[6]] close-coupled, good-quartered gelding: has scope: novice hurdler: easily best effort on second start: jumped badly final outing (blinkered): should stay beyond 2m. *O. Sherwood.* 92

JUST PERKINS 5 ch.g. Bold Owl–Buckenham Belle (Royben) [1989/90 18d[pu] 16m c16s[6] c16g[6] c24m[2] c25s[F] c20d[pu] c20f[F] c20f[4] c20m[pu]] lengthy gelding: no sign of ability over hurdles: poor form in novice chases: jumped moderately final outing: front runner who's well worth another try over 2m. *P. J. Anderson.* c**81** + —

JUST PRETEND 6 b. or br.m. Sayyaf–Lovely Pretense (USA) (Pretense (USA)) [1989/90 16g] lengthy, sparely-made mare: novice selling hurdler: needed race only outing of season (November): should stay beyond 2½m: possibly needs give in the ground: visored last 2 starts 1988/9. *C. J. Bell.* —

JUST PULHAM 5 b.g. Electric–Lady Acquiesce (Galivanter) [1989/90 16s[4] 16g*] medium-sized gelding: lightly raced on Flat, well beaten in 1989: fourth in novice hurdle at Folkestone in January and week later landed gamble in seller at Wetherby in good style (bought in 8,200 gns): claimer ridden. *G. A. Huffer.* 89 p

JUST ROSE 6 ch.m. Legal Eagle–Gambling Rose (Game Rights) [1989/90 20d 24g] angular mare: winning hurdler: no worthwhile form in 1989/90: much better suited by 2½m than shorter distances and should stay 3m: acts on soft going. *M. C. Pipe.* —

JUST SEYMOUR 4 ch.g. Seymour Hicks (FR)–Pennycress (Florescence) [1989/90 a16g[pu] 16g[pu]] neat gelding: placed over 6f at 2 yrs, well beaten on Flat since: tailed off when pulled up in novice handicap hurdle at Lingfield and juvenile hurdle at Windsor (still better for race). *B. Gubby.* —

JUST SO 7 br.g. Sousa–Just Camilla (Ascertain (USA)) [1989/90 c24f[F] c24g[bd] c25d[3] c24v* c25d[4] c32f] tall, workmanlike gelding: behind in NH Flat race in 1986/7: winning point-to-pointer: showed himself well suited by a test of stamina when winning novice chase at Chepstow in January, jumping soundly in the main and staying on strongly: didn't reproduce that form under less testing conditions: acts on heavy going: sweating final start: amateur ridden. *J. D. Roberts.* c**106**

JUST SUSANNA (USA) 4 b.f. Master Willie–Whose Broad (USA) (Hoist The Flag (USA)) [1989/90 16d[F]] placed over 1m on Flat in 1989: sold out of H. Candy's stable 2,000 gns Newmarket December Sales: behind when falling last in juvenile hurdle at Bangor: dead. *J. L. Spearing.* —

JUST THE TICKET 7 gr.m. Faraway Times (USA)–Rum Year (Quorum) [1989/90 16g* 18d*] small, sparely-made mare: won novice hurdles at Hereford (handicap) in October and Worcester following month, staying on strongly to lead flat despite swishing tail for latter success (ridden by 3-lb claimer): will stay 2½m: acts on dead going (ran poorly on good to firm). *J. H. Baker.* 100

JUSTTHEWAYYOUARE (CAN) 7 ch.g. Ziad (USA)–Helen Dickerman (Joe Price) [1989/90 c24m[F] c26g[ur] c24g* c28g[F] c32g[pu] c24m[F]] workmanlike gelding: poor novice hurdler: made mistakes when winning handicap chase at Leicester in January: stays 3m: blinkered last 3 starts in 1986/7: sold 2,200 gns Ascot June Sales: needs to improve his jumping. *R. Curtis.* c**85** x —

JUST TOO BRAVE 7 b.g. Beldale Flutter (USA)–Georgina Park (Silly Season) [1989/90 20v 16s[pu] 18f[pu] 16f 16m[5] 16m 20m[3]] strong gelding: winning hurdler: only form of 1989/90 in selling handicap final start: stays 2½m: probably unsuited by soft ground: usually blinkered or visored nowadays: has sweated: trained until after sixth start by M. McCourt. *M. J. Ryan.* 74

K

KACERE 6 ch.g. Stanford–Arodstown Tan (Atan) [1989/90 16g[pu] 16d[pu]] lengthy, light-framed gelding: winning selling hurdler: unlikely to stay much beyond 2m: acts on firm going: suitable mount for a claimer: has sweated. *William Price.* —

Champagne de Venoge Handicap Hurdle, Uttoxeter—
Kadan is about to quicken clear of the blinkered Don Valentino

KADAN (GER) 6 b.g. Horst-Herbert–Ling Lady (GER) (Marduk (GER))
[1989/90 16m* 16f* 18m* 16g 16g* 16f^{pu}] angular, sparely-made gelding: 137
improved hurdler who won handicaps at Ascot, Huntingdon and Fontwell (quite
valuable Coomes Handicap Hurdle) in first half of season and at Uttoxeter (beat
Don Valentino comfortably by 4 lengths) in April: pulled up reportedly lame final
outing: unlikely to stay much beyond 2¼m: best form on a sound surface (acts on
firm ground): usually held up: useful. *M. H. Tompkins.*

KADESH 9 b.g. Hittite Glory–Siraf (Alcide) [1989/90 16f^{pu}] sparely-made
gelding: winning hurdler: very lightly raced in recent seasons: not certain to stay —
much beyond 2m: probably acts on any going: has won for a 7-lb claimer. *R. J.
Eckley.*

KAFARMO 7 b.g. High Line–Fashion Club (Tribal Chief) [1989/90 16m 21f^{pu}]
sturdy, close-coupled gelding: novice hurdler: ran moderately in handicaps in
November: stays 2½m: found nothing fifth start 1988/9. *J. R. Jenkins.* —

KAIM PARK 7 b.g. Ovac (ITY)–Liffey's Choice (Little Buskins) [1989/90 c**79** ?
c27f* c24f^{4} c26g^{3} c24g^{F} c24f^{4} 24g^{6} c24g^{5} c32g^{pu} c24f^{5}] workmanlike gelding: 79
novice selling hurdler: won 2-runner handicap chase at Sedgefield in October:
well beaten after next start: suited by a test of stamina: best form on a sound
surface and acts on firm ground: blinkered eighth outing. *I. Semple.*

KALA FAIR 5 gr.h. Kalaglow–Fair Head (High Line) [1989/90 21f^{pu}] winning
hurdler: clear and looking certain winner when pulled up lame before 2 out in 113
handicap at Newton Abbot in August: will stay at least 21f: acts on firm going:
claimer ridden. *J. H. Baker.*

KALAHARI 4 gr.f. Kalaglow–Hot Case (Upper Case (USA)) [1989/90 16d^{pu}]
half-sister to fairly useful 7f and 1m winner Aitch N'Bee (by Northfields): dam fair —
performer, best at 7f: behind only outing on Flat when trained by J. Hills: behind
when pulled up in juvenile hurdle at Nottingham. *L. J. Codd.*

KALAKATE 5 gr.g. Kalaglow–Old Kate (Busted) [1989/90 16d^{6}] leggy gelding:
useful 1½m performer at 3 yrs (best form on top-of-the-ground): sold out of G. —
Wragg's stable 16,500 gns Newmarket Autumn Sales: pulled hard, lost touch
when jumping slowly third and finished tailed-off sixth of 7 behind Forest Sun in
quite valuable novice event at Sandown on hurdling debut. *R. Simpson.*

KALAURA 4 b. or br.f. Kala Shikari–Il Regalo (Meadow Mint (USA)) [1989/90
16f^{4}] tall, leggy filly: maiden plater on Flat, stays 1¼m: around 23 lengths fourth 67
to Sybillin in juvenile hurdle at Market Rasen in August. *A. Smith.*

KALEIDOSCOPE 5 gr.g. Kalaglow–Pot Pourri (Busted) [1989/90 16g 16g 20g] has shown more temperament than ability over hurdles and is one to leave alone: blinkered final start (saddle slipped). *T. Goldie.* §§

KALSHAN 6 b.g. Lightning (FR)–Carota (FR) (Caro) [1989/90 17v2 16m* 17f* 17f*] made all when wide-margin winner of novice hurdles at Wincanton in April and Newton Abbot and Cartmel in May, best effort when beating Gentleman's Jig 20 lengths on last-named course: not sure to stay beyond 2m: acts on firm ground: on the upgrade. *M. C. Pipe.* 121 p

KAMADOOR 7 b.g. Kambalda–Dirimage (Diritto) [1989/90 16f6 20f3 c20d6 c24v4 c25dur c25s6 c21g c21m] leggy, close-coupled gelding: winning point-to-pointer: fairly useful hurdler: held slight advantage over eventual winner Uncle Raggy when unseating rider last in novice chase at Towcester in February: jumped none too fluently and never dangerous subsequently: stays 2¾m: best form with give in the ground. *G. B. Balding.* c**94** 126

KAMAL SIDDIQI 10 b.g. Proverb–Arctic Sue (Arctic Slave) [1989/90 c20d6 c25gpu c24g4] stocky gelding: handicap chaser: ran well in amateur riders event final start: stays very well: seems to act on any going: blinkered when successful over hurdles: sometimes visored over fences, including when successful. *A. P. Stringer.* c**91** —

KAMAROCK 8 b.h. Kampala–Hey Dolly (Saint Crespin III) [1989/90 16mpu 16gpu] small horse: poor novice selling hurdler: wears blinkers. *C. Spares.* —

KAMBA LAD 7 b.g. Kambalda–Kylenora (Dusky Boy) [1989/90 20s 22gF 24m6 24g4 23f2] tall, workmanlike gelding: poor novice hurdler: stays 23f: acts well on firm ground. *J. A. C. Edwards.* 77

KAMBALDA RAMBLER 6 b. or br.g. Kambalda–Stroan Lass (Brave Invader (USA)) [1989/90 F16g4 F17d4 F16g6 16f5] first foal: dam placed in maiden hurdle in Ireland: fourth in NH Flat races: ridden by 3-lb claimer, around 18 lengths fifth of 6 to Stags Fell in novice hurdle at Kelso in April. *R. Earnshaw.* —

KAMEO STYLE 7 b.g. Kambalda–Smashing Style (Harwell) [1989/90 19g2 16d* 16g2 16g* 19g* 19s* 21d2 21s6] compact, good-topped gelding: improved hurdler who won novice handicaps at Stratford, Wolverhampton and Hereford in November and a handicap (by 30 lengths) on last-named course in December: clear 2 lengths second to Coworth Park in novice handicap at Sandown (quickened clear aproaching last, headed near finish) in January: ran as though something was amiss final start: modest form in novice chases in 1988/89: stays 21f: acts on soft going: claimer ridden: usually blinkered prior to latest season: jumps hurdles well. *F. Jordan.* c— 132

KAMI KING 4 gr.c. Kings Lake (USA)–Karafa (Nishapour (FR)) [1989/90 16d2 16g6 16m*] leggy, angular ex-French colt: first foal: dam won 4 times at up to 1½m on Flat in France: fifth over 1½m on Flat in 1989 when trained by A. de Royer-Dupre: won juvenile hurdle at Towcester in January despite jumping with little fluency: will stay beyond 2m: acts on good to firm and dead ground. *C. P. E. Brooks.* 102 p

KAMRISE 8 br.g. Kambalda–Riseaway (Raise You Ten) [1989/90 24f4 24g6 20dpu 25g6 c24g4 c24g3 c24g5 c24mF3] angular, workmanlike gelding: handicap hurdler: below his best in 1989/90: modest novice chaser: stays 3m: suited by plenty of give in the ground: has run well for a 7-lb claimer: inconsistent. *G. B. Balding.* c**96** —

KAMSEL 7 b.g. Kambalda–My Hansel (Prince Hansel) [1989/90 c17fF c16g3 c20g2 c16g* c20s3] lengthy gelding with scope: winning hurdler: won novice handicap chase at Sedgefield in December: jumped none too fluently over fences previously and ruined his chance with a bad mistake 2 out on final appearance (ran well nonetheless) in December: stays 2½m: acts on any going: reluctant to race fourth outing 1988/9: sometimes amateur ridden, including when successful over hurdles. *W. A. Stephenson.* c**94** + —

KANGAROO COURT 4 br.g. Tumble Wind (USA)–Wild Justice (Sweet Revenge) [1989/90 F14v6] half-brother to 2 minor winners on Flat: 23 lengths sixth behind Dakyns Boy in NH Flat race at Ayr in April: yet to race over hurdles. *J. J. O'Neill.*

KARAKA 4 ch.f. Good Times (ITY)–Buff Beauty (Mossborough) [1989/90 20fpu] neat filly: half-sister to winning stayer Cavalier's Blush (by King's Troop), the dam of Sprowston Boy and Young Benz: well beaten in 2 maidens on Flat: better for race, behind when pulled up in novice hurdle at Worcester in March. *R. J. Eckley.* —

KARAKTER REFERENCE 8 br.g. Reformed Character–Windtown Beauty (Laser Light) [1989/90 c20m* c21d^{bd} c25m* c24m^{2} c25s^{4} c25g^{3} c20s^{pu} 20f^{6} c22f^{2} c24m* c21m^{4}] short-backed gelding: winning point-to-pointer: modest novice hurdler: won novice chases at Huntingdon in October and Towcester in November and handicap chase at Huntingdon in April: ran poorly final outing: stays 25f: possibly suited by a sound surface nowadays: usually jumps well: sold R. O'Sullivan 21,000 gns Ascot June Sales. *L. C. Corbett.* c**103** 88

KARENOMORE 12 b.g. Karabas–Leomor (Raisin) [1989/90 c16g^{4} c16g* c16f^{F}] robust gelding: fairly useful chaser on his day: won handicap at Wetherby in November (seventh course win): close up and travelling well when falling 3 out in conditional jockeys handicap won by Yank Brown at Cheltenham in December: stays 2½m: acts on any going. *M. H. Easterby.* c**134** —

KARFIA 4 b.f. Royal Match–Kasarose (Owen Dudley) [1989/90 16m 16f^{bd} 19s^{pu}] small, angular filly: no sign of ability on Flat: sold out of A. Ingham's stable 1,000 gns Ascot July Sales: no promise over hurdles, including in sellers: wore blinkers first 2 starts: looks temperamental. *William Price.* — §

KARLOVAC 4 ch.g. Stanford–Croatia (Sharpen Up) [1989/90 16g^{pu} 16g 16f 19s^{6} 16d 16g 17m^{3} 17m 20m] leggy gelding: poor novice selling hurdler: best efforts at around 2m: blinkered 4 of last 5 starts. *C. D. Broad.* 67

KARNATAK 9 b.g. Artaius (USA)–Karera (Kalamoun) [1989/90 c21f^{2} c17h* c20f* c17f^{3} c22f^{2} c16m c22m* c20f^{pu} c20f^{2} c16d c20m^{6} c20g^{4} c16m^{3} c16f^{2} c20f* c20f^{3} c20f* c20m^{2}] small, lightly-made gelding: handicap chaser: won at Devon & Exeter, Bangor and Stratford early in season, and at Worcester and Ludlow in the spring: stays 2¾m when conditions aren't testing: suited by top-of-the-ground: blinkered when successful over hurdles (hasn't worn blinkers over fences): saddle slipped eighth outing: ridden by 7-lb claimer last 6 starts: good jumper. *K. S. Bridgwater.* c**110** — §

KARYBABY 5 b.m. Humdoleila–Karyobinga (So Blessed) [1989/90 F12f F16f^{6} 16m^{ur} 16g^{3}] first foal: dam of little account over hurdles: claimer ridden, 4 lengths third behind Sleepline Royale in claiming hurdle at Uttoxeter in May. *M. W. Eckley.* 71

KASHILL 12 b.g. Gulf Pearl–Wolver Hill (Wolver Hollow) [1989/90 c25f^{2} c20g^{3} c24m^{3} c17v c21m] sturdy gelding: winning chaser: poor form in 1989/90, including in a selling handicap: stays 3m: possibly needs give in the ground nowadays: blinkered final outing: has run well for an inexperienced rider. *Mrs J. G. Retter.* c**90** —

KATABATIC 7 br.g. Strong Gale–Garravogue (Giolla Mear) [1989/90 c16d* c16d* c16g* c20g^{2} c16m* c16f^{3}] c**141** p —

Katabatic has improved with virtually every one of his fourteen races. The winner of the last of three outings over hurdles in 1987/8, he has won six of his ten completed steeplechases in the last two seasons, gradually raised in grade so that by the end he started joint favourite when taking on some of the best two-milers in the Captain Morgan Aintree Chase, a limited handicap at Liverpool in April. Katabatic ran up to the best of his previous form in finishing six lengths third behind Nohalmdun at Liverpool, staying on well having never been able to land a blow at the leaders under the fast conditions. There are good grounds for thinking that Katabatic has further improvement in him, and he should again pay to follow in the coming season.

Katabatic's deceptive style of running should see him one step ahead of the handicapper for a while at least. Katabatic is usually held up for a late run and has tended to idle in front, thereby understating the ease of his victory. In the Cheltenham Grand Annual Challenge Cup Chase in March Katabatic, let in quite lightly considering his record, looked likely to win decisively after the second last, where he'd produced a good jump then quickened well on the inside to take a lead of two or three lengths. A mistake at the last fence seemed not to check him, but on the run-in he started to idle, drifted slightly to his right and had to be driven right out by Davies close home to hold off the strong-finishing Tresidder by a length, with Gold Options a length further back in third place.

Katabatic may also improve when campaigned again over two and a half miles. He gave the strong impression two miles would not be the limit of his stamina when winning a handicap at Worcester in November and an

Grand Annual Challenge Cup Handicap Chase, Cheltenham — fourth win of the season for Katabatic

intermediate chase at Nottingham the following month in good style. Which isn't to say that Katabatic lacks a turn of foot: he quickened well from off the pace in a moderately-run race when winning a handicap at Cheltenham in January. When tried for the first time over two and a half miles in the Fulwell Handicap Chase at Kempton later in the month, Katabatic lost no caste in a three-quarter-length defeat by subsequent Liverpool winner One More Knight, who had first run on him.

Katabatic (br.g. 1983)	Strong Gale (br 1975)	Lord Gayle (b 1965)	Sir Gaylord
			Sticky Case
		Sterntau (br 1969)	Tamerlane
			Sterna
	Garravogue (b 1973)	Giolla Mear (b 1965)	Hard Ridden
			Iacobella
		Fashion's Frill (b 1962)	Black Tarquin
			Dress Parade

Smart middle-distance performer Strong Gale had the speed to finish second in the Irish Two Thousand Guineas and has sired some two-mile specialists over jumps, such as Fragrant Dawn, as well as stouter stayers like Daily Express Triumph Hurdle winner Alone Success. Katabatic is a half-brother to two winning two-mile hurdlers, notably the useful novice Whatever You Like (by Deep Run) who promises to stay further. There is plenty of stamina further back in the family of the unraced Garravogue, who was sold for only IR 1,500 guineas at Fairyhouse in November. The poor maiden Fashion's Frill bred several winners over jumps, including William Hill Yorkshire Chase winner Get Out of Me Way. Winning hurdler Dress Parade is the dam of the very good Irish staying chaser Height O'Fashion, runner-up in two Irish Grand Nationals, to Arkle in 1964 and to Flyingbolt in 1966. Katabatic, a rangy gelding, well bought for IR 8,000 guineas at Ballsbridge as a three-year-old, has won over £35,000 in first prize money. He's sure to win more races in the coming season, which he starts on a fair mark in the handicap—dropped a pound after Liverpool. Below his best when winning on heavy going, on his first run for three months, Katabatic has shown he acts on any other. *Andrew Turnell.*

KATE BROOK 4 b.f. Nicholas Bill–Petrinella (Mummy's Pet) [1989/90 16m 16g 16mpu] workmanlike filly: fifth foal: half-sister to two 2-y-o winners: dam 2-y-o 6f winner: little promise over hurdles: claimer ridden. *A. P. James.* —

KATE KELLY 9 b.m. Netherkelly–Spring Offer (Sporting Offer) [1989/90 c20gpu] angular, dipped-backed mare: lightly-raced winning point-to-pointer: bit backward, made mistakes and was eventually pulled up in novice event on steeplechasing debut. *Mrs Gill E. Jones.* c—

KATE O'KIRKHAM 4 ch.f. Le Bavard (FR)–Kate's Wish (Wishing Star) [1989/90 F17m2 F16f*] third foal: half-sister to a winner in Belgium: dam a plater on Flat, stayed 1m: won NH Flat race at Hexham in April by short head from Levy Free: yet to race over hurdles. *Mrs V. A. Aconley.*

KATES FLING (USA) 7 b.m. Quiet Fling (USA)–Dancers Fairlight (USA) (Dancing Dervish) [1989/90 20f4 24h* 20f4 25fpu c20g3 c20gF 20s 24g5 25fpu] rather sparely-made mare: handicap hurdler: won moderately-run 3m race at Hexham in October: 5 lengths third to Sword Beach in novice chase at Sedgefield in November, only completed outing over fences: acts on hard ground (ran moderately on soft). *R. F. Fisher.* c**79** 90

KATES STAR 10 gr.g. Amazon–Sweet Imelda (Menelek) [1989/90 c20spu c16d c21m5 c20fpu c21m6] compact ex-Irish gelding: third in novice chase in 1985: poor form in hunter chases since, but won a point-to-point in April. *W. F. Caudwell.* c—

KATHIES CHOICE 7 b.m. Bribe–Montana Queen (Pinzari) [1989/90 17v 22s3] leggy, angular mare: poor plater over hurdles: seemed not quite to stay 2¾m final start (January): no worthwhile form over fences (moderate jumper). *J. M. Bradley.* c— x 66

KATHIES LAD 13 br.g. Forlorn River–Rollicking Rachael (Will Somers) [1989/90 c22g3 c21m3] leggy, lightly-made gelding: modest chaser nowadays: dull in coat, jumped none too fluently when just over 8 lengths third behind Panto Prince in minor event at Wincanton in October, final start: best at up to 2½m: acts on any going. *J. R. Jenkins.* c? —

KATHTEEN 4 b.f. Teenoso (USA)–Kath (Thatch (USA)) [1989/90 16gpu] workmanlike filly: only form on Flat when third in 1m seller: tailed off when pulled up fifth in juvenile hurdle at Catterick. *D. H. Topley.* —

KATHY COOK 5 b.m. Glenstal (USA)–Belmont Blue (Kashmir II) [1989/90 20v5] compact mare: novice selling hurdler: needs very testing conditions when racing at 2m and probably stays 2¾m. *R. Hollinshead.* 76

KATICA 4 b.f. Jester–Gwen Somers (Will Somers) [1989/90 16s6 16sur 16gur 16spu 16f4 16g6 16d5 17f3] sparely-made filly: best efforts over hurdles on last 2 starts (final one a seller): likely to prove best at around 2m: acts on firm and dead ground. *D. McCain.* 72

KATIE SCARLETT 4 b.f. Lochnager–Final Request (Sharp Edge) [1989/90 16s5 16g 16g6] close-coupled filly: inconsistent 1¼m winner on Flat: poor form in juvenile hurdles: may have difficulty in staying 2m: acts on firm going. *J. J. Bridger.* 74

KATY LOU 4 gr.f. Nishapour (FR)–Emmylou (Arctic Tern (USA)) [1989/90 16f6 18f* 16g6 a20g6] poor maiden on Flat: won juvenile selling hurdle at Fontwell in October (bought in 2,500 gns): off course 3½ months before running poorly final start: stays 2¼m. *Miss B. Sanders.* 74

KATY QUICK 9 b.m. Saucy Kit–Tesco Maid (Tesco Boy) [1989/90 c16m5] small mare: winning hurdler/chaser: raced too freely only outing 1989/90 (September): best at 2m: acts on any going: sound jumper: good mount for a claimer: sold 3,800 gns Doncaster January Sales. *T. W. Donnelly.* c— —

K C'S DANCER 5 ch.g. Buckskin (FR)–Lorna Lass (Laurence O) [1989/90 F16g 16g 24m] workmanlike gelding: first foal: dam never ran: no sign of ability. *R. Dickin.* —

KEELBY 5 b.g. Kemal (FR)–Peter's Pet (Bahrain) [1989/90 F16f] fourth foal: dam winning Irish point-to-pointer: eighth of 16 behind Raido in NH Flat race at Uttoxeter in April: yet to race over hurdles or fences. *J. G. FitzGerald.*

KEEL (GER) 6 b.h. Horst-Herbert–Kadmeia (GER) (Priamos (GER)) [1989/90 16m 16m] smallish, sparely-made horse: poor hurdler: well beaten in —

seller final start (December): races keenly and is unlikely to stay much beyond 2m: visored final start 1987/8 (successful) and first 3 starts 1988/9. *K. S. Bridgwater.*

KEELLEB 5 ch.g. Gorytus (USA)–Miss Upward (Alcide) [1989/90 16dpu 16d] stocky gelding: of little account. *T. Kersey.* —

KEEP BIDDING 4 br.g. Hays–Keep Chanting (Auction Ring (USA)) [1989/90 16m6 16g 16g6 16g] big gelding: plating-class 1½m winner on Flat: best effort over hurdles when sixth at Wetherby in January, third outing. *M. W. Easterby.* 78

KEEP HOPE ALIVE 6 b.g. Corvaro (USA)–Widschi (GER) (Dschingis Khan) [1989/90 16g* 16d3 16g2 16mpu] rangy, well-made gelding with scope: quickened clear in tremendous style between last 2 flights when winning novice hurdle at Wolverhampton in January: well-backed favourite, travelled strongly and looked likely winner 3 out but less than fluent at last 3 flights and couldn't catch length winner Voyage Sans Retour when second in handicap at Newbury in March (2 lb out of handicap and carrying 2 lb overweight): reportedly broke blood vessel final outing (co-favourite for valuable novice event at Fairyhouse): will stay 2½m: useful novice. *B. J. Curley.* 130

KEEP IT NEAT 10 br.g. Tack On–Contessa Von Oebis (Rusticate) [1989/90 c20f3] rangy, workmanlike gelding: lightly-raced point-to-pointer, winner in May: little sign of ability in steeplechases. *L. J. Bowman.* c—

KEEP STRAIGHT 4 b.g. Castle Keep–Straight To Bed (Dominion) [1989/90 16f4 16f2 a16g* 20f 16dsu a18gF a16gpu 16d6 16m 16f3 16m 16g 16g2 16h3] sparely-made gelding: ungenuine maiden on Flat: claimer ridden, won selling hurdle at Southwell in November (sold out of W. Carter's stable 2,500 gns): best subsequent effort on final start: best form at 2m: acts on hard going: visored twelfth and thirteenth starts: whipped round start first outing, slowly away twelfth start: unreliable and has looked a difficult ride. *K. A. Ryan.* 72 §

KEEP TALKING 5 b.g. Le Bavard (FR)–Keep Faith (Raise You Ten) [1989/90 21d] good sort, with scope: will make a chaser: fifth in NH Flat race in 1988/9: carrying condition, showed promise when over 30 lengths seventh to Devil's Valley in novice hurdle at Newbury in February: will be suited by long distances: will do better. *B. Smart.* — p

KEEP WALTZING 4 b.f. Castle Keep–Viennese Waltz (High Top) [1989/90 F12f 16gF 16f 16gpu] first foal: dam suited by a test of stamina: no sign of ability in selling hurdles. *N. A. Smith.* —

KELLYANN 7 b.m. Jellaby–Queen's Treasure (Queen's Hussar) [1989/90 19m6 22m c16s c16sbd 21d c24f2 c24f] sturdy mare: winning hurdler: modest novice chaser: stays 3m: acts on any going: sometimes claimer ridden (wasn't when successful): wore blinkers and a tongue strap twice in 1986/7. *S. M. Fisher.* c88 —

KELLYS AND COHENS 10 ch.g. Goldhill–Insouciante (No Worry) [1989/90 20f4 20f3 17m3 19f3] compact gelding: poor novice hurdler: yet to complete in a novice chase (fell first) and point-to-points: blinkered nowadays: sold 1,250 gns Doncaster September Sales: resold 1,000 gns Ascot May Sales. *W. Clay.* c— 68

KELLY'S DARLING 4 b.g. Pitskelly–Fair Darling (Darling Boy) [1989/90 16m 16f 16g4] lengthy, light-framed gelding: ungenuine middle-distance maiden on Flat: sold out of R. J. R. Williams' stable 2,700 gns Newmarket Autumn Sales: no sign of ability in juvenile claiming hurdle and sellers. *D. Roderick.* —

KELLY'S INSURANCE 6 b.g. Official–Get Set (Stupendous) [1989/90 c21dpu c19mF c27fur] workmanlike gelding: poor novice hurdler: yet to complete in hunter chases. *Mrs S. Kavanagh.* c— —

KELLYS PAL 7 b.g. Netherkelly–Paladore (St Paddy) [1989/90 21mpu a20g5 a22g2] sturdy gelding: first sign of ability in novice hurdles at Southwell on last 2 starts: stays 2¾m. *Mrs E. M. Andrews.* 82

KELLY'S STORY 10 br.m. Netherkelly–Fixby Story (Sweet Story) [1989/90 c25mpu c25mpu] small mare: winning point-to-pointer: novice hunter chaser. *Mrs E. J. Richards.* c— —

KELLY'S TWILIGHT 5 b.m. Netherkelly–Flirt (Twilight Alley) [1989/90 16f 21mpu] well behind in NH Flat races and a novice hurdle. *Mrs A. Holman.* —

KELPIE 12 b.m. Import–River Moy (Niagara Falls) [1989/90 c16mpu] strong mare: winning hurdler: of no account over fences: has broken blood vessels: best at 2m: acts on firm going. *Mrs A. E. Ratcliff.* c— —

KEMBERTON CORACLE 6 br.g. Lighter–Evelith (Dumbarnie) [1989/90 F17f5 20g] lengthy, angular gelding: second foal: dam unraced: fifth in NH Flat race at Doncaster in December: tailed off in novice hurdle at Sedgefield 2 months later. *J. A. C. Edwards.* —

KEMCROSS 10 ch.m. Kemal (FR)–Crossacres (Spiritus) [1989/90 c24gpu] sparely-made mare: second in novice chase in 1987/8, only sign of ability: evidently suited by a test of stamina and plenty of give in the ground. *R. Layland.* c— —

KEMYS COMMANDER 5 ch.g. Monksfield–Rockwood Lady (Aeolian) [1989/90 F16g2] half-brother to poor novice hurdler/chaser Edenburt (by Pitpan): dam never ran: 10 lengths second to stable-companion The City Minstrel in NH Flat race at Fakenham in April: yet to race over hurdles or fences. *J. A. C. Edwards.*

KENILWORTH CASTLE 4 b.c. Dunbeath (USA)–Ravenshead (Charlottown) [1989/90 20g3 16m* 16m 16g4 a16g* a20g2] leggy colt: half-brother to ungenuine novice hurdler/chaser Amrullah (by High Top): 13f winner on Flat: successful in juvenile hurdle at Nottingham (made all) in December and novice event at Southwell (led from third) in January: good second in handicap on latter course in February: stays 2½m: acts on good to firm ground: claimer ridden: blinkered last 2 starts. *R. Hollinshead.* 98

KEN LAKE 17 ch.g. Appiani II–Lake Constance (Star Gazer) [1989/90 21f2 17h4 21f3] winning point-to-pointer, placed in April: bad hurdler: stays 21f: acts on firm ground. *R. W. Pincombe.* 48

KEN SAUCE (FR) 7 gr.g. Kenmare (FR)–Sauce Royale (Royal Palace) [1989/90 17f4] placed at up to 1m at 2 yrs in French Provinces: well-beaten fourth to 30-length winner Kalshan in novice event at Newton Abbot in May on hurdling debut. *H. Willis.* —

KENTISH PIPER 5 br.g. Black Minstrel–Toombeola (Raise You Ten) [1989/90 16g 16d 16m] sturdy, close-coupled gelding: seventh foal: brother to winning hurdler Reggae Yeoman: dam fairly useful Irish hurdler: showed ability all starts in novice hurdles: gives impression he'll do better over further. *N. A. Gaselee.* 88

KENTUCKY CALLING 10 ch.m. Pry–Sun Spray (Nice Guy) [1989/90 c20fpu] small, close-coupled mare: winning selling hurdler: poor novice chaser: best at around 2m: acts on firm going. *Miss C. J. E. Caroe.* c— —

KEONI 5 ch.m. Vaigly Great–Stockingful (Santa Claus) [1989/90 20d] third in NH Flat race in 1989: well beaten in novice hurdle at Sedgefield in March. *G. M. Moore.* —

KERFUFFLE (USA) 5 ch.h. Irish River (FR)–Women's Wear (USA) (Groton) [1989/90 F16g aF16g2 aF16g*] $250,000Y: fifth foal: half-brother to 3 stakes winners: dam 2-y-o winner in North America: won 7-runner NH Flat race at Lingfield in February by 8 lengths from Work To Win: soundly beaten on Flat afterwards: yet to race over hurdles or fences. *G. Harwood.*

KERICHO 6 b.g. Joshua–Miss Jeroco (Hot Brandy) [1989/90 c20spu] smallish gelding: little sign of ability in novice hurdles and novice chases. *S. F. Turton.* c— —

KERRIS MELODY 6 br.m. Furry Glen–Slaves Melody (Arctic Slave) [1989/90 a18g5 a16g] sparely-made mare: of little account: has run blinkered. *Mrs S. Oliver.* —

KERSIL 13 b.g. Keren–Queen's Silk (Pongee) [1989/90 c16d3 c16s* c20g5 c16d3 c27g4 c16d5 c16m2 c16f2 c16m4] lengthy, lightly-made gelding: handicap chaser: won 3-runner event at Sedgefield in January: best up to 2½m: acts on any going: blinkered once in 1988/9: good mount for a claimer. *J. E. Swiers.* c85 —

KERSTELLA 9 b.m. Comedy Star (USA)–Kerstina (Coronation Year) [1989/90 c20s3] workmanlike mare: novice hurdler/chaser: won a point-to-point in April: visored, third in maiden hunter chase at Sedgefield in February, staying on well: stays 3m: ran poorly on very firm ground. *J. D. Jemmeson.* c77 —

KESWOOD JACK 7 b.g. The Parson–Petite Bally (Ballyciptic) [1989/90 16dpu 20g6 16m 16mpu] rather sparely-made gelding: poor form over hurdles: ran creditably over 2½m second start: broke blood vessel final start 1988/9. *M. J. Wilkinson.* 77

KETTI 5 br.m. Hotfoot–Nigrel (Sovereign Path) [1989/90 16mpu 18g4 18s6 20v4 16s5 18f* 16f4] small, lightly-made mare: handicap hurdler: won at Fontwell in March: ran well next time: stays 2¼m: acts on any going: usually wears blinkers (not on last 3 starts). *D. M. Grissell.* 112

KEVIN EVANS 11 ch.g. Super Slip–Court Moss (Ballymoss) [1989/90 c25m[ur]] strong, workmanlike gelding: one-time fair hurdler: novice chaser: unseated rider when trying to refuse in March: suited by a test of stamina: best form on a sound surface: poor form in point-to-points nowadays. *C. A. H. Barker.* c— —

KEVINSFORT 12 b.g. Will Somers–Hinemoa (Connaught) [1989/90 c16d[3] c16d[4] c16f[pu] c16g[pu]] strong, good-bodied gelding: has been hobdayed and operated on for a soft palate: one-time useful chaser: no worthwhile form in 1989/90: took little interest third start: best at around 2m: acts on any going: visored twice in 1987/8: has had tongue tied down. *J. G. FitzGerald.* c— § —

KEYNES 10 ch.g. Relkino–Rheola (Welsh Pageant) [1989/90 16s[4] 20s[2]] rather leggy, close-coupled gelding: handicap hurdler: better effort of season on second start (December): stays 2½m but seemingly not 3m: ran moderately on heavy going, acts on any other: has won for a claimer. *J. R. Jenkins.* 106

KHARIF 6 b.g. Formidable (USA)–Pass The Rulla (USA) (Buckpasser) [1989/90 16f[2] 20g[5] 16m* 16m 20f[2] 22g* 16d* 16g* 16f*] sturdy gelding: formerly irresolute: much improved and had a good season, winning 5 races over hurdles, namely novice events at Newcastle, Catterick, Hexham and Cheltenham (beat Walk of Life 4 lengths for final win) and handicap at Kelso (awarded race): effective from 2m to 2¾m: yet to show his form on heavy going, acts on any other: good mount for a claimer. *R. Allan.* 115

KHETA KING 7 b.g. Hittite Glory–Matala (FR) (Misti IV) [1989/90 16d[6] 22v[pu] 16v 24d[pu]] rangy gelding: sixth foal: dam winning hurdler: one-time fair middle-distance stayer on Flat: poor form in novice hurdles: ran as though something amiss final start. *D. R. C. Elsworth.* 78

KIELYCROFT 4 ch.g. Longleat (USA)–Long Drop (Tower Walk) [1989/90 F16v F17f] fifth living foal: dam, 2-y-o winner, probably stayed 1m: well beaten in NH Flat races: sold 2,100 gns Doncaster Spring Sales: yet to race over hurdles. *N. Bycroft.*

KIICHI (USA) 5 b.g. Perrault–Kahaila (Pitcairn) [1989/90 c16g[3] c16s* c16m[2] c18m[2]] c**135** —

Five-year-olds racing over fences by March are uncommon, five-year-olds competing in the two-mile novices' championship are rare. The

Irish Life Assurance EBF Nas Na Ri Chase, Naas—Kiichi (right) collars Isthatafact at the last

Irish-trained Kiichi became the first of his age to contest the Arkle Challenge Trophy at Cheltenham since 1985 and the first to complete since 1973; altogether only seven five-year-olds have run in the race. Chatham won the inaugural running in 1969 and Soloning also won the following year. Exactly twenty years later Kiichi became the next to reach a place. It looked to be asking a lot of him beforehand, with just seven races over jumps behind him, of which only two were over fences, but he fared the best of the three Irish challengers, finishing three places in front of Blitzkreig and five in front of The Musical Priest. Kiichi's lack of experience wasn't evident: indeed he jumped the demanding fences like an old hand and travelled strongly from the outset. He moved smoothly through to join the leaders approaching the third last and, although under pressure in third at the next, kept on most gamely on the run-in and caught long-time leader Young Snugfit on the post to take second a length behind Comandante. It was the second year running Kiichi had given a good account of himself at the Festival, for he'd finished sixth to Ikdam in the Daily Express Triumph Hurdle. That performance might have earned him another season over hurdles but he was chasing when next seen out at Leopardstown in January. He began with a promising third behind On The Other Hand and Elfast, and almost two months later—ten days before Cheltenham—he justified favouritism in the quite valuable Irish Life Assurance EBF Nas Na Ri Chase at Naas by ten lengths from Isthatafact. Kiichi's fourth and final race of the season came in the EBF Power Gold Cup Chase at Fairyhouse in April. Blitzkreig, who had finished just over seven lengths behind Kiichi at Cheltenham and reopposed on almost identical terms, was a different horse at Fairyhouse, leading from the fifth and always in command. Kiichi could never land a blow and was beaten three lengths by the winner who was easing up.

Kiichi (USA) (b.g. 1985)	Perrault (ch 1977)	Djakao (b 1966)	Tanerko
			Diagonale II
		Innocent Air (ch 1962)	Court Martial
			Aldousa
	Kahaila (b or br 1977)	Pitcairn (b 1971)	Petingo
			Border Bounty
		Chaldea (b 1973)	Tamerlane
			Charity Concert

Kiichi is sired by the top-class middle-distance performer Perrault, and is the third offspring and first to race of Kahaila, an American-based mare who did most of her racing in Britain and showed very useful form at up to a mile and a half. Kiichi's two-year-younger half-brother Delta Dreamer (by Tyrant) won over seven furlongs in Ireland as a two-year-old and has been placed at up to a mile since. Kahaila is the only winning produce of the unraced Chaldea, a half-sister to numerous Flat winners, notably useful miler Wild Root, and two winning jumpers, including Stegsman, successful over hurdles in 1987/8. Their dam Charity Concert, a fair mile-and-a-quarter winner, is a half-sister to the good 1956 two-year-old Skindles Hotel. Kiichi, a leggy, sparely-made gelding, has plenty of time on his side, though he probably lacks the scope ever to trouble the best, and his future would appear to lie in handicaps. Kiichi has yet to race beyond two and a quarter miles, but gave the impression at Cheltenham he would stay two and a half. He has yet to race on very firm ground, seems unsuited by heavy but has shown he acts on any other. *D. K. Weld, Ireland.*

KILBREEDY 7 b.m. The Parson–Fawnamore (Menelek) [1989/90 22m 22g a24g[3] a24g[pu]] rather leggy mare: fourth foal: dam unraced: no form in novice hurdles: blinkered second start. *J. Ffitch-Heyes.* —

KILBRITTAIN CASTLE 14 ch.g. Dike (USA)–Now Or Never (Never Say Die) [1989/90 c20f[3] c20g[3] c20s c16m[4] c20f[2]] strong, good-bodied gelding: has been fired: one-time very useful chaser, but is on the downgrade nowadays: stays 2½m: probably acts on any going: usually strong-pulling front runner who races with plenty of zest: jumps boldly: suited by a right-handed course and has won 11 times at Sandown. *F. Walwyn.* c117 —

KILCLOONEY FORREST 8 b.g. King's Equity–Carrig-an-Neady (Orchardist) [1989/90 c24s[2] c24d[pu]] sturdy gelding: winning point-to-pointer: made a c94 few mistakes but stayed on well when second in novice chase at Wetherby in February: tailed off when pulled up in good company next outing: will be suited by a thorough test of stamina. *O. Brennan.*

KILCONNEY PRINCE 8 br.g. Martinmas–Dark Gold (Raise You Ten) [1989/90 16dpu 16m5 16vF 20dpu] lengthy gelding: poor novice hurdler. *E. A. Wheeler.* 77

KILCORVINO 5 br.g. Corvaro (USA)–Kilboy Concorde (African Sky) [1989/90 F16m F12g] third foal: half-brother to Irish 1m winner Father Phil (by Kampala): dam poor Irish Flat maiden: unplaced in NH Flat races in second half of season: yet to race over hurdles or fences. *C. C. Trietline.*

KILDIMO 10 b.g. Le Bavard (FR)–Leuze (Vimy) [1989/90 c25gF c19s4 c26fF c29f] big gelding: one-time high-class chaser: only worthwhile form of 1989/90 when around 25 lengths seventh to Mr Frisk in Whitbread Gold Cup at Sandown on final start: stays well: has won on heavy going but is best on ground no softer than dead: suited by strong handling (takes a good hold and has wandered under pressure): usually held up: one to treat with caution. *G. B. Balding.* c**146** —

KILFORD 10 b.g. Northfields (USA)–Ashaireez (Abernant) [1989/90 c20g c16d6 c20d3 c20d] compact gelding: poor novice chaser: stays 2½m: acts on any going. *P. Ransom.* c**70** —

KILFRANCIS LAD 13 b.g. Milan–Wandering Princess (Prince Hansel) [1989/90 c25mur c24f* c24f* c20f3] sturdy gelding: fairly useful hunter chaser: made all when wide-margin winner at Ludlow in March and April: good third behind Buckhorn at Ascot later in April: stays 3m: acts on hard ground: jumps well. *Mrs S. M. Johnson.* c**110** —

KILKILANNE 9 b.m. Brave Invader (USA)–Arctic Minx (Arctic Slave) [1989/90 c20sF] workmanlike mare: novice hurdler/chaser: maiden point-to-pointer. *G. G. H. Adcock.* c— —

KILKILMARTIN 8 b.g. Rarity–Kilkilwell (Harwell) [1989/90 c18s3 c20dF c21dF 20d6] lengthy, deep-girthed ex-Irish gelding: novice hurdler/chaser: gave impression he'd have gone close to winning had his finishing effort started earlier on first outing: fell next 2 starts and was returned to hurdling (shaped promisingly when in mid-division in novice handicap): effective at 2¼m and should stay 3m: has raced only on an easy surface over jumps: needs to improve his jumping over fences. *P. R. Hedger.* c**106** x — p

KILLARY BAY 8 b.g. Connaught–Dutchess of Man (Petingo) [1989/90 c16d] small, sturdy, workmanlike gelding: selling hurdler: novice selling chaser (tends to make mistakes): pulled up in a point-to-point in March: best at 2m: best form on soft going: usually visored. *P. J. King.* c— —

KILLBANON 8 b.g. Imperius–Flail (Hill Gail) [1989/90 16g* 16f2 16d3 16s* 16g5 16d6 16g 16d3 16g4 16m] tall, strong, lengthy ex-Irish gelding: will make a chaser: half-brother to fair hurdler L O Broadway (by Crash Course): dam moderate hurdler: won maiden hurdle at Galway and minor event at Listowel early in season: showed ability all starts in Britain, including when twelfth behind Forest Sun in Waterford Crystal Supreme Novices' Hurdle at Cheltenham in March on final start: will be well suited by further than 2m: probably acts on any going: trained by P. Prendergast until after fifth start. *C. C. Trietline.* 107

KILLELAN LAD 8 br.g. Kambalda–Dusky Glory (Dusky Boy) [1989/90 c25m c20fur] rather sparely-made ex-Irish gelding: behind only outing over hurdles: won a point-to-point in April: would probably have finished second but for unseating rider 2 out in hunter chase won by Summons at Sandown in March: stays 3m: acts on any going. *J. H. Wingfield Digby.* c**88** ? —

KILLERTON 6 b.m. Raise You Ten–Soave (Le Tricolore) [1989/90 21d] leggy mare: second foal: dam never ran: bit backward, tailed off in novice hurdle at Newbury in February on debut. *N. A. Gaselee.* —

KILLINICK DUKE 9 b.g. Giolla Mear–Rosantus (Anthony) [1989/90 c21mur] winning hurdler in Ireland: sweating, pulled hard and unseated rider at the fourth in novice chase at Market Rasen in September: probably stays 21f: acts on any going: sold 2,000 gns Ascot October Sales. *R. D. E. Woodhouse.* c— —

KILLONE ABBEY 7 b.g. The Parson–Michelle's Fancy (Fidel) [1989/90 c20g2 c26g2 c24s2 c33v* c33dur c25m3 c33d] workmanlike gelding: fairly useful chaser: won at Ayr in January: good third to One More Knight in quite valuable handicap at Liverpool in April, keeping on well: stays very well: acts on any going. *W. A. Stephenson.* c**126** —

KILMOND WOOD 5 ch.g. Monsanto (FR)–River Belle (Divine Gift) [1989/90
$17m^{*}$ $16m^{*}$ $16f^{pu}$ $16f^{3}$] compact, workmanlike gelding: successful in novice 93
hurdles at Cartmel in August and Perth (2 ran) in October: first outing for over 6
months and claimer ridden, creditable third at Hexham in April: retained by
trainer 2,100 gns Doncaster November Sales: sold 6,000 gns Doncaster Spring
Sales. *G. M. Moore.*

KILRONAN 6 gr.h. Rusticaro (FR)–Firdosa (Relic) [1989/90 $16g^{6}$ $16m^{4}$ 16g
16f] small ex-Irish horse: won 6f handicap at 4 yrs: fourth in selling hurdle at 65
Ludlow in November: sold out of R. Curtis' stable 1,700 gns Ascot Sales later in
month: tailed off in non-sellers afterwards: races freely and barely stays 2m. *N.
Waggott.*

KILSYTH 11 b.m. Jolly Good–Harmony Thyme (Sing Sing) [1989/90 $c20f^{*}$ c89
c20m $c20m^{pu}$] small, sparely-made mare: modest chaser: first outing for over a —
year, won claimer at Edinburgh in December despite jumping left: no form
subsequently: stays 3m: acts on any going: tried in blinkers over hurdles: good
mount for a claimer: heavily bandaged in front in 1989/90. *Miss S. J. Wilton.*

KILTED SCOT 9 b.g. Le Bavard (FR)–Royal Intrigue (Royal Highway) c—
[1989/90 $c20s^{6}$] rather sparely-made, close-coupled gelding: novice hurdler: poor —
form in point-to-points: jumped moderately when tailed off in hunter chase at
Warwick in February: needs a test of stamina. *M. J. M. Evans.*

KILTON PARK 8 b.g. Jimsun–Park End (Weensland) [1989/90 $c19f^{4}$] c—
workmanlike gelding: placed in point-to-points: no sign of ability over hurdles and —
in steeplechases: has worn a crossed noseband. *R. E. Pocock.*

KIMACERO 12 b.g. Tycoon II–La Macera (Thunder Road) [1989/90 $16m^{6}$ $20f^{2}$ c—
$20m^{4}$ 25d] small, sturdy gelding: novice hurdler: placed in varied company, 80
including selling: stays 2½m, seemingly not 25f: acts on any going: usually
amateur or claimer ridden: not raced after November. *W. Clay.*

KIMSWA 9 b.g. Politico (USA)–Messalina (Pirate King) [1989/90 $c24m^{5}$ c—
$c20m^{pu}$ $c20g^{pu}$] leggy gelding: lightly-raced novice hurdler/steeplechaser: —
winning point-to-pointer. *L. C. Corbett.*

KIND ANSWER 4 ch.f. Hasty Word–Minetta (Neron) [1989/90 F16g F13d]
sister to novice hurdler Whitwood, half-sister to winning Irish hurdler Delvin
Prince and a winner in Hong Kong (both by Saucy Kit): dam won over hurdles:
behind in NH Flat races in Scotland: yet to race over hurdles. *Mrs E. Slack.*

KIND'A SMART 5 ch.g. Kind of Hush–Treasure Seeker (Deep Diver)
[1989/90 $16m^{2}$ $16f^{3}$ $16m^{*}$ $16g^{2}$ $16f^{5}$ $16g^{ur}$ $16m^{*}$ $16f^{4}$] smallish, lengthy geld- 109
ing: won lady riders novice handicap hurdle at Nottingham in November and
novice hurdle at Huntingdon in May: unlikely to stay much beyond 2m: acts on
firm ground: seems suited by waiting tactics and a strongly-run race. *K. A.
Morgan.*

KIND OF MAGIC 5 b.g. Record Token–Gay Twenties (Lord Gayle (USA))
[1989/90 16g 21g $a16g^{4}$] first foal: dam winning hurdler: poor maiden on Flat: well —
beaten over hurdles: blinkered final start. *A. P. Jones.*

KING BOO 4 b.c. Van Der Linden (FR)–Star Bella (Star Appeal) [1989/90 F12g
$F16g^{5}$ $17m^{r}$] first foal: dam novice selling hurdler: unplaced in NH Flat races: —
refused to race in amateur riders maiden hurdle at Carlisle. *G. P. Kelly.*

KING CAP 5 ch.h. Kinglet–Mandycap (Mandamus) [1989/90 F16g F16f] first
foal: dam won 2 point-to-points: well beaten in NH Flat races: yet to race over
hurdles or fences. *J. W. Blundell.*

KING CREDO 5 b.g. Kinglet–Credo's Daughter (Credo) [1989/90 $F16g^{3}$
$F16m^{2}$] sixth foal: half-brother to fair hurdler/winning chaser Cresun, fairly useful
hurdler Have Faith (both by Sunyboy) and novice hurdler Unique New York (by
Balinger): dam useful staying chaser: placed in NH Flat races at Kempton and
Sandown (beaten ½ length by Ascot Lad) in the spring: yet to race over hurdles or
fences. *S. Woodman.*

KINGFISHER BAY 5 b.h. Try My Best (USA)–Damiya (FR) (Direct Flight)
[1989/90 $17g^{3}$ $16s^{3}$ $20g^{2}$ $21m^{6}$ 16v $a20g^{*}$ $a24g^{*}$ $a24g^{*}$] leggy horse: much 93
improved on all-weather surface: won selling handicap hurdle at Lingfield
(no bid) and novice events at Southwell (handicap) and Lingfield: stays 3m. *B.
Palling.*

KING KANDA 12 br.g. Arctic Kanda–Red Satin (Articulate) [1989/90 $c24m^{4}$ c90
$c24f^{2}$ $c24f^{2}$ $c30m^{4}$ $c24g^{5}$] lengthy, sparely-made gelding: handicap chaser: stays

very well: acts on any going: visored fourth outing: not raced after November. *Mrs J. D. Goodfellow.*

KING KAS 8 b.g. Pollerton–Lady Dikler (Even Money) [1989/90 c24d^{pu} c25m c—
c20d c25f] strong, rangy gelding: handicap chaser: has lost his form: stays 25f: —
suited by ground no softer than dead: blinkered last 2 starts: sold 4,000 gns Ascot May Sales. *D. R. Gandolfo.*

KING MENELAOS 5 b.g. Ile de Bourbon (USA)–Be Sweet (Reform) [1989/90 a24g^{pu}] 13.3f winner on Flat (well beaten in 1989): sold out of P. Cole's stable 8,000 gns Newmarket Autumn Sales: broke blood vessel and pulled up —
before sixth on hurdling debut. *J. Pearce.*

KINGMON'S GIRL 13 b.m. Saucy Kit–Just-A-Honey (Track Spare) [1989/90 c—
c21m^{pu}] lengthy, rather leggy mare: winning chaser: pulled up only outing in last —
2 seasons: form only at around 2m: acts on hard going: best in blinkers: sometimes makes mistakes. *J. F. Panvert.*

KING NEON 10 b.g. Kinglet–Ditchling Beacon (High Line) [1989/90 c21g^{2} **c108**
c24g*] lengthy, rather angular gelding: useful hunter chaser: won at Kempton in February (dismounted after passing post and not seen out again): stays 3¼m: acts on any going. *G. F. Cook.*

KING OF ARAGON 5 b.g. Aragon–Selina Fair (Hugh Lupus) [1989/90 16g^{6} 16d 16d^{5} 16g 16d^{6}] leggy gelding: ungenuine novice selling hurdler: often 70 §
blinkered, wore visor final start: usually ridden by claimer. *R. Brotherton.*

KING OF SAILORS 6 br.g. King of Spain–Found At Sea (USA) (Pieces of Eight) [1989/90 20m a16g^{3} 17f] tall, leggy, angular gelding: only sign of ability 64 §
over hurdles when third in seller at Southwell in January: looked a difficult ride and most reluctant final outing. *R. Thompson.*

KING OF SPEED 11 b.h. Blue Cashmere–Celeste (Sing Sing) [1989/90 16s^{pu}] leggy horse: poor performer on Flat nowadays: well beaten in 2 novice hurdles. *B. J. Wise.* —

KING OF STEEL 4 b.g. Kemal (FR)–Black Spangle (Black Tarquin) [1989/90 F13d] half-brother to 3 winning jumpers, including Cheltenham Gold Cup winner Little Owl (by Cantab): dam lightly raced: around 18 lengths eighth behind Solo Cornet in NH Flat race at Kelso in January: yet to race over hurdles. *Mrs S. A. Bramall.*

KING OF THE LOT 7 br.g. Space King–Nicola Lisa (Dumbarnie) [1989/90 **c128**
c20g^{2} c20d^{2} c20m* c20f^{3} c20m^{3} c21f^{3}] tall, rather leggy, sparely-made gelding: —
fairly useful chaser: won 4-runner handicap at Doncaster in January in good style by 15 lengths: good third in Mildmay of Flete Challenge Cup Handicap Chase (won by New Halen) at Cheltenham and quite valuable event (won by Sure Metal) at Liverpool next 2 starts: stays 2½m: acts on any going: has run well for a claimer and when sweating and looking lean. *R. Lee.*

KING OF THE RING 5 b.g. Rusticaro (FR)–Coumfea (Gulf Pearl) [1989/90 c**87** p
20m 16d^{pu} c16m^{2} 16m^{ur} 16g^{6} 16m^{3} 19fF] smallish, good-bodied gelding: winning 87
hurdler: 8 lengths second of 3 finishers to Royal Greek in novice chase at Hereford in April: form only at 2m: acts on good to firm and dead going: has looked none too keen. *J. D. Thomas.*

KING OF THE WOOD 5 br.g. Chukaroo–Amore (ITY) (Kashmir II) [1989/90 F12m aF14g F12g] sixth foal: half-brother to winning jumper Grafton Maisey (by Jimsun): dam ran once: well beaten in NH Flat races: yet to race over hurdles or fences. *J. A. Bennett.*

KING RETAIN 7 b.g. Cut Above–De'b Old Fruit (Levmoss) [1989/90 17v^{pu} 16d a16g^{6} 16f^{4} 16h^{3}] compact, workmanlike gelding: handicap hurdler: only form 110
of season on last 2 starts: suited by forcing tactics when racing at around 2m: acts on any going: retained by trainer 2,100 gns Ascot June Sales. *C. L. Popham.*

KING'S ADVOCATE 8 ch.g. Avocat–Wesleyan (Great Nephew) [1989/90 c84
c16m^{ur} c20g^{4} c20g^{2} c25m^{pu}] lengthy gelding: novice hurdler: in frame in —
mid-season novice chases: best form at 2½m on a sound surface. *Andrew Turnell.*

KINGS ASH 4 gr.f. Hill Farmer–Mentone-Lillie (Saunter) [1989/90 16g^{pu} a16g^{pu}] good-topped filly: maiden on Flat: tailed off when pulled up in claiming —
hurdle and juvenile event in February. *R. M. Whitaker.*

KINGS BILL 11 ch.g. Sovereign Bill–Royal Heath (Langton Heath) [1989/90 c94
c25f* c25f^{3} c26m^{pu}] leggy, good-topped gelding: won a point-to-point in April:

successful in a novice hunter chase at Wincanton later in month, jumping well and scoring by 10 lengths: good third behind Sweet Rascal at Cheltenham in May: stays 25f: acts on firm going. *M. P. Fear.*

KINGSBRIDGE FLYER 8 ch.g. Pony Express–River Chant (River Chanter) [1989/90 16m 17m 20g4 20m5 22g6 25d3 21m2 21fpu] close-coupled gelding: poor novice hurdler/chaser: has been beaten in a seller: stays 25f: acts on good to firm and dead going. *A. J. Chamberlain.* c— 68

KINGSBROOK 8 b.g. Kinglet–Miss Bubbly (Track Spare) [1989/90 c20f* c16mF c24f5 c18hur c16f6] leggy gelding: novice hurdler: won slowly-run 2½m novice chase at Plumpton in October: let down by his jumping afterwards: acts on firm ground: tends to get on his toes and needs to settle. *W. G. R. Wightman.* c**83** x —

KING'S CRUSADE 7 ch.g. Reform–Crusader's Dream (St Paddy) [1989/90 17f2] smallish, rather angular gelding: selling hurdler: fair second at Newton Abbot in August: doesn't stay 2½m: probably acts on any going. *D. J. Wintle.* 69

KING'S CURATE 6 b.g. King's Ride–Parnessa (The Parson) [1989/90 16s 16s3 20v* 20d*] big, good-topped gelding: type to make a chaser: third foal: half-brother to fairly useful Irish hurdler All The Fools (by Reformed Character): dam never ran: progressive hurdler who won Scottish Farm Dairy Foods Novices' Handicap Hurdle at Ayr in April, quickening impressively to come from well off pace 3 out to lead before last, and holding off Do Be Brief by a neck after tending to idle: won novice event at Haydock previous month: stays 2½m well: acts on heavy going: amateur ridden at Ayr: promising, and sure to win more races. *S. Mellor.* 118 p

KING SEAR 8 br.g. Dubassoff (USA)–Noble Device (El Cid) [1989/90 c16d3 c20m5 c20d2 c20g2] compact gelding: well beaten in novice hurdles: won 2 point-to-points in 1989: modest novice chaser: stays 2½m: acts on good to firm and dead ground: has run well for an amateur and a claimer. *Mrs H. Parrott.* c**84** —

KINGS FOLLY 8 b.g. Hillandale–Sovereign's Folly (Sovereign Bill) [1989/90 16m4 20d3 18d5 21f*] angular, lightly-made gelding: handicap hurdler: has looked irresolute but did nothing wrong when winning conditional jockeys event at Newbury in November: stays 2½m, at least when conditions aren't very testing: acts on any going. *William Price.* 112

KING'S HARVEST 7 ch.g. Oats–Sovereign Court (Sovereign Path) [1989/90 26d4 c24gpu] lengthy, rather sparely-made gelding: useful hurdler at his best: poor fourth at Ayr in November: tailed off when pulled up on chasing debut c— —

Scottish Farm Dairy Foods Novices' Handicap Hurdle, Ayr—
King's Curate makes rapid progress to lead at the last; Dwadme (far side) finishes third

following month: suited by a good test of stamina: acts on heavy going (won NH
Flat race on good to firm). *G. M. Moore.*

KING'S IMAGE 5 b.g. Indian King (USA)–Cooliney Dancer (Dancer's Image
(USA)) [1989/90 F16d] half-brother to quite useful 1983 2-y-o 6f winner Straw (by
Thatch), winner subsequently in USA: dam Irish 2-y-o 5f winner: behind in NH
Flat race at Kelso in February: yet to race over hurdles or fences. *J. S. Haldane.*

KING SPRING 5 br.g. Royal Fountain–K-King (Fury Royal) [1989/90 F16g
F17m] brother to novice hurdler Kings Fountain and half-brother to 4 winning
jumpers, including stayers King's Brig and Easter Brig (both by New Brig): well
beaten in NH Flat races in November and April: yet to race over hurdles or fences.
C. Parker.

KINGS QUEST 5 ch.g. Touch Paper–Leapallez (Hallez (FR)) [1989/90 17m^{2}
16f* 16f^{2} 16s 16g^{F} 18d 16g^{4} 16h^{3} 16g^{pu}] neat gelding: won novice hurdle at 88
Sedgefield in September: best effort later in season on penultimate outing: likely
to prove best at around 2m at present: suited by firm ground: ridden by claimer:
ran poorly when blinkered final start. *J. J. O'Neill.*

KINGS RANK 5 br.g. Tender King–Jhansi Ki Rani (USA) (Far North (CAN)) c—
[1989/90 21h* 18h^{4} 25h^{4} c18f^{3} 19m^{4} 16g^{5} 24f^{2} 20v* 20s^{4} 24s^{2} 21s^{2} 24f^{F} 25f^{3}] 117
sparely-made gelding: won conditional jockeys hurdle at Devon & Exeter in
August and claimer at Haydock in December: ran well in handicaps in the spring:
well beaten on chasing debut: stays 3m: acts on any going: sometimes jumps none
too fluently: blinkered last 7 starts: has shown signs of temperament. *M. C. Pipe.*

KINGS VICTORY 6 ch.g. What A Guest–Directrice (GER) (Zank) [1989/90
16s^{5} 16g^{pu} 16s 16g 16m^{2}] medium-sized gelding: handicap hurdler: returned to 102
form when second at Wincanton in March: races only at around 2m: acts on good
to firm and heavy going. *M. D. I. Usher.*

KINGS WILD 9 b.g. Mandalus–Queens Trip (Mon Capitaine) [1989/90 c20g **c92**
c17v a16g^{2} c16g^{3} c16f* c16f^{2} c16f^{4} c16h^{3} c17m^{pu} c17f*] workmanlike gelding: 67
handicap chaser: soon well clear when winning at Worcester in March (broke
blood vessel closing stages) and Huntingdon in May: second of 5 in poor handicap
at Lingfield in February on hurdling debut: best at around 2m: acts on firm going:
continued after running out seventh on eighth start: blinkered next time. *A. P.
Jones.*

KINGSWOOD (BEL) 5 b.g. Tadj (FR)–Kicking Girl (FR) (Faraway Son
(USA)) [1989/90 a20g^{4} a16g^{3} a20s^{2}] second foal: dam unraced half-sister to 2 76
winners, including By The River, a prolific winner at up to 1½m in France and
USA: poor form in maiden hurdles and a claimer at Lingfield: stays 2½m. *Claude
Cuvelier, Belgium.*

KINGSWOOD KITCHENS 10 b.g. General Ironside–Tyrone Typhoon c**115**
(Typhoon) [1989/90 c21f^{2} c20f* c25g* c26m^{F} c19d^{3} c25g^{2} c26s^{3} c25s^{pu} c16m^{4} 115
c20g^{2} 26f* c21m^{2}] workmanlike, rather angular gelding: handicap chaser: won at
Ludlow (tended to carry head high) and Devon & Exeter in October: won amateur
riders handicap hurdle at Newton Abbot in May: stays well: possibly best on a
sound surface nowadays: blinkered once in 1985/6: sometimes amateur ridden,
but is well suited by stronger handling: has been bandaged off-hind. *R. G. Frost.*

KINGSWOOD RESOPAL 6 br.g. Comedy Star (USA)–Solhoon (Tycoon II)
[1989/90 20f 17m^{5} 21g^{4} 24g 20d 27s^{5}] leggy gelding: none-too-resolute selling 75 §
hurdler: poor form in non-selling amateur riders events in first half of season,
running creditably in slowly-run race over 27f: acts on any going: sometimes
blinkered. *A. Moore.*

KING TOH-TOH 4 b.c. Simply Great (FR)–Chrisanthy (So Blessed) [1989/90
16g^{pu} 16m^{pu}] sparely-made colt: placed over 1m at 2 yrs but well beaten on Flat in —
1989: tailed off when pulled up in juvenile hurdles: dead. *P. Howling.*

KINGTOR (NZ) 9 b.g. Amyntor (FR)–Sobina (NZ) (Sobig) [1989/90 c24s^{pu} c— x
c26g^{5}] workmanlike gelding: modest chaser: needed race both outings of season: —
stays 25f: acts on any going except possibly very soft: moderate jumper. *D. H.
Barons.*

KING UNIVERSE 9 b.g. Kinglet–Miss Universe (Reverse Charge) [1989/90
16g 16s 19s] sparely-made gelding: lightly-raced novice hurdler: no form in —
1989/90 (tailed off in seller final start): best effort over 17f on firm ground. *S. M.
Fisher.*

KING WILLIAM 5 b.g. Dara Monarch–Norman Delight (USA) (Val de L'Orne
(FR)) [1989/90 16g^{3} 16m^{3} 16g^{5} 16d^{2} 16g^{3} a16g^{2} a16g 16f^{F}] novice hurdler: had just 84

taken lead when falling at the last at Huntingdon in May: headstrong and not certain to stay much beyond 2m: acts on firm ground: needs to improve his jumping: sold out of Denys Smith's stable 7,400 gns Doncaster January Sales after fifth start. *J. L. Spearing.*

KINNESTON 6 b.g. Night Porter–Dysie Mary (Apollonius) [1989/90 20m6 c21dF 24gpu] well beaten in novice hurdles: fell sixth on chasing debut. *C. J. T. Alexander.* c— —

KIRAM (USA) 5 b.h. Gold Stage (USA)–Alight (FR) (Habitat) [1989/90 19gpu 16f 16g 16v 16g6 a16g a20g 24dpu] small, angular horse: successful over 1m in Ireland at 2 yrs, but has since lost his form: no form over hurdles, including in sellers: has pulled hard and made mistakes: blinkered second outing: sold out of W. Brooks's stable 1,000 gns Ascot December Sales after then. *J. E. Long.* —

KIRI'S SONG 7 b.m. True Song–Mekhala (Menelek) [1989/90 20m2 24fF] leggy, sparely-made mare: modest novice hurdler: short-headed by Go South at Worcester in September: running another good race when falling at the last at Uttoxeter following month: will stay 3m: acts on firm and dead ground. *J. L. Needham.* 91

KIRKBY FLYER 6 b.m. Gay Pilot–Impatience (Kibenka) [1989/90 16f* 16f2 16g4 16m5 16s3 16g a16g] small mare: selling hurdler: bought in 3,300 gns after winning handicap at Southwell in September: ran creditably next 4 starts: should stay beyond 2m: yet to race on heavy going, probably acts on any other: suitable mount for a claimer. *R. M. Whitaker.* 86

KIRKLAND GREEN 5 b.m. Lochnager–Spring Gala (Ancient Monro) [1989/90 F16fsu F17m 16g 20g] rather leggy mare: third foal: half-sister to winning hurdler/chaser Galadine (by Gaberdine): dam tailed-off last only start: not knocked about when in rear in novice hurdles at Ayr and Newcastle in first half of season. *M. H. Easterby.* —

KIRSTY'S BOY 7 b.g. Majestic Streak–Cute Peach (Hardicanute) [1989/90 24m* 16g4 25f2 22g4 22d3 22s5] small gelding: handicap hurdler: won at Perth in September: ran creditably next 4 starts (not raced after January): stays 3m: probably acts on any going: has been tried in blinkers and a visor (not when successful): has wandered under pressure and looked a difficult ride. *J. S. Wilson.* 117

KIRTLINGTON 5 b.g. Gay Mecene (USA)–Cley (Exbury) [1989/90 16d 16m 16g] sparely-made gelding: well beaten in 2 races on Flat: sold out of F. J. Houghton's stable 1,800 gns Ascot July Sales: no form in selling hurdles and a claimer (showed signs of ability on first start): retained by trainer 550 gns Ascot May Sales. *K. A. Morgan.* —

KISSANE 9 br.g. Kemal (FR)–Chamowen (Master Owen) [1989/90 c20gpu] strong, rangy gelding: very useful chaser at his best: behind when pulled up in handicap at Ayr in November: suited by 2½m+ and give in the ground: usually jumps particularly well. *C. D. Broad.* c— —

KISSING THE PINK 4 b.f. Runnett–Naughty One Gerard (Brigadier Gerard) [1989/90 16d 16dpu] leggy filly: half-sister to novice hurdler Gun Happy (by Formidable): behind only race at 2 yrs (unseated rider twice in preliminaries and refused to enter stalls only subsequent intended outing): bought for 1,350 gns Doncaster Spring Sales: no form in juvenile hurdles, and looks temperamental to boot. *R. J. Holder.* — §

KITANGO 9 ch.g. Saucy Kit–La Tango (Sailing Light) [1989/90 c24d4 c24f2 c24fF] leggy gelding: fairly useful winning point-to-pointer: clear ¾-length second to Mademist Susie in novice hunter chase at Newcastle in March: stays well: acts on any going. *David Kennedy.* c85

KITCHI KOO 6 b.m. Imperial Fling (USA)–Hard To Follow (Roi Lear (FR)) [1989/90 F17f4 16g 20sF 16g2 20d 21dpu 17m2] rangy mare: has scope: modest form in novice hurdles: should stay further than 17f: acts on good to firm going. *A. J. Wilson.* 85

KITTINGER 9 b.g. Crash Course–Mandaloch (Mandamus) [1989/90 20m* 22s5 c20m* c25m5 c20dpu c20g4 c21m* c20f* c22m6 c21g2] lengthy, workmanlike gelding: fairly useful chaser: won at Leicester in December and Wincanton (amateur riders event) and Newbury in March: jumped deliberately when over 20 lengths sixth to Wont Be Gone Long in John Hughes Memorial Trophy at Liverpool in April: won novice hurdle at Worcester in September: stays 3m: best form on ground no softer than dead: has won for a claimer: tends to idle. *Andrew Turnell.* c**125** 106

Delby Services Handicap Chase, Newbury—Kittinger leads from General Chandos (blaze), Gee-A (far side), Biloxi Blues (grey) and Matric

KITTY BLAKE 7 b.m. Roscoe Blake–Fair Kitty (Saucy Kit) [1989/90 20g^{6} 27g^{pu}] small mare: no sign of ability over hurdles, including in sellers: blinkered second start 1988/9. *B. M. Temple.* —

KITTY'S DAUGHTER 5 ch.m. Le Moss–Kitty Killowen VII (Avocat) [1989/90 16g^{F} 16g^{pu}] sparely-made non-thoroughbred mare: first foal: dam won bumpers race in Ireland: amateur ridden, tailed off when pulled up 2 out in novice selling hurdle at Sedgefield in December. *J. Parkes.* —

KIWI TAUKA (NZ) 7 br.g. Auk (USA)–Talama (NZ) (Oakville) [1989/90 F 17f] weakened early in straight when behind in 18-runner NH Flat race at Doncaster in December on debut: yet to race over hurdles or fences. *M. H. B. Robinson.*

K JOHN 10 b.g. Legal Eagle–Ask For Roger (Menelek) [1989/90 c19f^{pu}] sparely-made gelding: lightly raced and of no account: dead. *Mrs W. B. Beynon Brown.* c— —

KLEMZIG 4 gr.f. Buzzards Bay–Mary Crooner (Crooner) [1989/90 18f^{pu}] half-sister to winning hurdler The Grifter (by Treboro): tailed off on Flat: ridden by 7-lb claimer, tailed off when pulled up last in juvenile hurdle in October. *M. Madgwick.* —

KNIFEBOARD 4 b.c. Kris–Catalpa (Reform) [1989/90 17d^{4} 16d^{6}] useful-looking colt: lightly raced but useful 1½m winner on Flat: sold out of H. Cecil's stable 12,500 gns Newmarket Autumn Sales: showed ability in mid-season juvenile hurdles at Devon & Exeter and Warwick: will be suited by longer distances. *T. B. Hallett.* 84

KNIGHT IN SIDE 4 ch.g. Tachypous–Miss Saddler (St Paddy) [1989/90 F 16s F 12g] leggy gelding: second reported living foal: half-brother to useful jumper Teletrader (by Nearly A Hand): dam won 2¾m hurdle: seventh of 19 behind easy winner Going On in NH Flat race at Market Rasen in March: yet to race over hurdles. *R. Callow.*

KNIGHT OF PEACE 11 b. or br.g. Random Shot–True Lightning (Blue Lightning) [1989/90 c16h^{F2} c24f^{pu}] workmanlike ex-Irish gelding: maiden point-to-pointer: well beaten over hurdles and in steeplechases. *W. D. Fairgrieve.* c— —

KNIGHT OIL 7 b.g. Miner's Lamp–Fair Argument (No Argument) [1989/90 c21f* c21d^{2} c25g* c26s* c25s^{ur} c24f^{F} c25m c26g^{2}] sturdy, good sort: useful hurdler: took well to chasing and won novice events at Windsor in November, Towcester in January and Uttoxeter in February: ridden by 7-lb claimer, good c**136** —

Resort Hotels Novices' Chase, Windsor—Knight Oil leads Prize Command over the water

second to comfortable winner Docklands Express in novice handicap at Stratford in April: stays well: probably acts on any going: blinkered last 3 starts. *O. Sherwood.*

KNIGHTON LAD 9 gr.g. Peacock (FR)–Buscarina (Little Buskins) [1989/90 c— x
20d^{pu} 26d^{F} 21d 22s 21s^{4} 25f^{pu} 24m^{5}] rangy, rather plain gelding: handicap 112
hurdler: ran poorly other than on fifth start 1989/90: has shown some ability in novice chases, but jumped badly on last occasion and is best left alone over fences until his jumping improves: stays 2¾m: acts on soft going: sold only 3,100 gns Doncaster Spring Sales. *O. Sherwood.*

KNOBI OBI 11 ch.g. Le Bavard (FR)–Scotch Polly (Right Tack) [1989/90 24f^{4}
a20g^{3} a20g^{5}] compact, sturdy gelding: novice hurdler: third in seller at Lingfield 70
in February: stays 3m: acts on firm and dead ground. *Miss E. Sneyd.*

KNOCK AGAIN 6 ch.g. Floriferous–Santimwen (Cassim) [1989/90 F16g
aF16g^{5} 20g^{pu}] half-brother to 2 winning hurdlers, notably top-class performer —
Aonoch (by Deep Run): dam won at up to 2½m over hurdles in Ireland: well beaten in NH Flat races: tailed off when pulled up 3 out on hurdling debut. *J. P. Leigh.*

KNOCKAN BOY 8 b.g. Bargello–Lindenise (London Gazette) [1989/90 c—
20m^{ur} 20f^{2} 20f 20g^{pu} a20g^{5} a20g^{F}] leggy, workmanlike gelding: winning 90
point-to-pointer: winning hurdler: failed to complete course in 2 steeplechases: stayed 2½m: best form with give in the ground: claimer ridden: dead. *C. R. Beever.*

KNOCKBRACK 10 b.g. Pitpan–Highway Mistress (Royal Highway) [1989/90 c**114**
c16g* c16m^{4} c16v^{5} c16g^{6} c16v^{5} c17d* c16g* c16f] sturdy gelding: won handicap —
chases at Plumpton in December and Newbury and Worcester (despite a few mistakes and idling on run-in) in March: very stiff task final outing: has won over 19f but best at around 2m: probably acts on any going: front runner. *G. A. Ham.*

KNOCK HARD 11 b.g. Hardboy–Precipitant's Pet (Precipitant) [1989/90 c—
c25f^{F}] lengthy gelding: winning point-to-pointer/steeplechaser: poor form in —
1990: pulls hard. *W. J. Bryan.*

KNOCK THRICE 8 b.g. Ballynockan–Quibba (Bandolier) [1989/90 c16f* c92
c16f* c16f^{2} c16g^{6} c16g^{4} c16g^{5} c17g c16m^{2}] workmanlike gelding: won novice
chases at Catterick in October and November (jumped boldly, made most): good
second in handicap at Market Rasen in April, final start: best at 2m: acts on firm
going: jumps soundly in the main: game. *B. E. Wilkinson.*

KNOCKUMSHIN 7 ch.g. Kambalda–Vina's Last (Royal Buck) [1989/90 16m^{2} c101 ?
c21d^{4} c20g c20m^{2} c20m^{5} c16s^{pu} c20d^{ur} c25f a16g] workmanlike gelding: won 2 ?
Irish point-to-points in 1988: showed signs of ability in minor hurdle at
Huntingdon in October: hung right when going down by a length to Mountebor in
novice chase at Ludlow in January: every chance when unseating rider last at
Bangor in March: no other form over fences: stays 2½m (beaten a long way out
over 25f): acts on dead going and good to firm: blinkered last 3 starts: ran as
though something possibly amiss final outing. *J. R. Upson.*

KNOWAFENCE 4 b.f. Idiot's Delight–Master Suite (Master Owen) [1989/90
F16f^{5} F16f] first foal: dam successful point-to-pointer: fifth to Wessex Warrior in
NH Flat race at Wincanton in March: behind in similar event at Cheltenham
following month: yet to race over hurdles. *M. Henriques.*

KNOWETOP 4 ch.f. Sayyaf–Heirline (Great Nephew) [1989/90 16h^{3} 16g a16g^{5}
16m a16g a18g^{pu}] small, dipped-backed filly: sprint plater on Flat: of little account —
over hurdles: visored second start: sold out of S. Muldoon's stable 650 gns
Doncaster November Sales after third start. *F. M. Barton.*

KNOWSTONE 7 ch.g. Reassurance–Miss Moritz (Majority Blue) [1989/90
22g 16g 16v] sparely-made, dipped-backed gelding: no sign of ability. *C. L.* —
Popham.

KODIAK ISLAND 8 br.g. Green Shoon–Poker Face (SWE) (Borealis) c119
[1989/90 c25d* c29g] robust gelding: winning hurdler: fair chaser: won handicap —
at Towcester in December by 3 lengths from Echo Sounder: moderate eighth to
Cool Ground in valuable handicap at Sandown in January: suited by a thorough
test of stamina and give in the ground: blinkered last 6 starts. *O. Sherwood.*

KOFFI (GER) 8 b.g. Horst-Herbert–Kalliope (GER) (Obermaat) [1989/90 c—
24s^{pu} 27g^{pu} c25f^{ur}] small, lightly-built gelding: winning hurdler and novice —
chaser: lightly raced since 1985/6. *F. J. Yardley.*

K O ISLAND 7 b.g. Garda's Revenge (USA)–Tudor Story (Henry The
Seventh) [1989/90 17m^{3}] sturdy, compact gelding: winning hurdler: third in 93
selling handicap at Newton Abbot in May: gives impression he'll prove best at
distances short of 2½m: acts on any going: wears blinkers. *M. C. Pipe.*

KOKO QUEEN 4 ch.f. Noalto–Witchingham Lass (Sweet Revenge) [1989/90
16m^{5}] smallish, sparely-made filly: 6f claimer winner on Flat: sold out of P. —
Rohan's stable 1,900 gns Ascot August Sales: distant last of 5 finishers in juvenile
hurdle at Warwick in September. *William Price.*

KOKOSCHKA 8 gr. or ro.g. Alias Smith (USA)–Opinion (Great Nephew) c—
[1989/90 16g a24g 22v^{pu} 20d 20f 19f^{6} 20m^{pu}] stocky gelding: poor novice —
hurdler/chaser: stays 19f: acts on heavy ground: occasionally blinkered. *G. Roe.*

KOLA HILL 5 b.g. Croghan Hill–Akola (Hard Tack) [1989/90 16f^{pu}] leggy
gelding: sixth foal: dam unraced: badly hampered in early stages of novice hurdle —
at Leicester (suffered injury and destroyed). *Mrs V. C. Ward.*

KOO 4 b.f. Crofter (USA)–Sue's Dolly (Quorum) [1989/90 16f* 16f* 16f a16g^{pu}]
small, strong filly: placed over 6f on Flat: won juvenile selling hurdle at Southwell 80
(bought in 6,300 gns) and novice selling hurdle at Bangor (sold out of N. Tinkler's
stable 10,000 gns) in August: ran poorly in non-sellers following month (trained
by G. Roe) and January. *R. W. Hartop.*

KOO-MING 5 b.m. Mansingh (USA)–Jenny Splendid (John Splendid) [1989/90
20f 17d^{6}] light-framed mare: poor form over hurdles: has looked headstrong and is —
unlikely to stay beyond 2m. *C. L. Popham.*

KORITSAKI 5 br.m. Strong Gale–Grecian Tan (Tantivy) [1989/90 24m^{5}]
sparely-made mare: novice hurdler: won 2 point-to-points in 1990: gives 79
impression will prove best at around 2½m: acts on firm ground: ridden by claimer.
Miss H. C. Knight.

KOSCIOSKO (USA) 4 b.c. Arctic Tern (USA)–Ancient Jewel (USA) (Hail To
Reason) [1989/90 16d^{4} 16m* 16g^{6} 16g^{2} 20m^{3} 20g* 16h^{2} 20g^{5}] tall, leggy colt: 96

modest maiden on Flat: sold out of L. Cumani's stable 8,000 gns Newmarket Autumn Sales: won selling hurdles at Leicester in December (bought in 7,000 gns) and Market Rasen in April (bought in 4,400 gns): stays 2½m: best form on good ground: blinkered last 3 starts, found little last 2: sketchy jumper. *N. Tinkler.*

KOSEY RUN 7 b.m. Deep Run–Kosey Kitchen (Golden Love) [1989/90 16m^{6} 16m 16s^{pu} 17v^{pu}] smallish, lengthy ex-Irish mare: first reported foal: dam unplaced in 2 point-to-points: seems of little account. *J. R. Bosley.* —

KOURON 6 b.m. Pauper–Little Chance (Master Owen) [1989/90 F16m F16g] second foal: half-sister to winning Irish point-to-pointer Every Chance (by Over The River): dam never ran: in rear in NH Flat races at Huntingdon and Market Rasen: yet to race over hurdles or fences. *O. Brennan.*

KOWZA 4 ch.f. Young Generation–Follow The Stars (Sparkler) [1989/90 16g^{3} 16g^{5} 16s^{5} 16g^{5} 16m^{2} 16g^{2} 16d 16f 16g^{2} 16g* 16m^{3}] leggy, lengthy filly: well beaten on Flat: sold out of M. Jarvis' stable 2,400 gns Newmarket July Sales: won juvenile hurdle at Uttoxeter in April by 1½ lengths from reluctant Iveagh House: suited by a sound surface and a sharp 2m: best form forcing pace. *Mrs A. Knight.* 97

KRAYBOURNE 5 ch.g. Krayyan–Chadora (St Chad) [1989/90 16g] angular, rather unfurnished gelding: behind both outings over hurdles. *D. W. Browning.* —

KRAYMARK 4 ch.g. Krayyan–Caroline's Mark (On Your Mark) [1989/90 16m^{pu} 16g^{F}] lengthy, sparely-made gelding: plating-class maiden on Flat: no sign of ability over hurdles: jumps moderately: sold 1,200 gns Ascot April Sales. *R. Curtis.* — x

KREMLIN GUARD 5 ch.m. Home Guard (USA)–Laurel Wreath (Sassafras (FR)) [1989/90 a18s* a16g a16g^{3} 21g] modest handicapper on Flat, probably best at short of 1¼m: won novice hurdle at Lingfield in January: third in claimer on same course in March, only subsequent form: stays 2¼m. *M. H. Tompkins.* 88

KRIBENSIS 6 gr.g. Henbit (USA)–Aquaria (Double-U-Jay) [1989/90 16m* 16g* 16g* 16m*] 169

Another light season saw a stronger, better Kribensis extend his record over jumps to ten wins from eleven starts, a strike-rate befitting the Champion Hurdler. There's more to come. Very likely he'll be campaigned in exactly the same way in future: that is, in non-handicaps where nothing less than a top-class performance will suffice to beat him. And there aren't too many top-class two-milers around at present. Looking ahead to the next Champion Hurdle—which will be substantially increased in value as a result of sponsorship by the Bank of Ireland—unless Nomadic Way comes back from injury it's difficult to see beyond Kribensis and Beech Road for the race, Kribensis definitely the favoured of the pair if the going is anywhere near firm, far from a lost cause if the going is anywhere near soft.

Kribensis ran a much better race in Beech Road's Waterford Crystal Champion Hurdle than his twelve-length seventh might indicate. He'd been able to lie up from the start, and he'd held the lead from the home turn until tiring approaching the last. Thus, as the 1989/90 season got under way he stood as favourite or second favourite for the renewal at 6/1 or 7/1 in the ante-post lists. Kribensis' main objective in the first half of the season was

Food Brokers And Primula 'Fighting Fifth' Hurdle, Newcastle—
Kribensis takes the measure of Jinxy Jack (No. 2), Past Glories and Osric

the Top Rank Christmas Hurdle at Kempton, a race he'd won from older horses as a four-year-old. He was given a run before then, which was probably just as well since he looked decidedly rusty, carrying condition, on his come-back in the Food Brokers And Primula 'Fighting Fifth' Hurdle at Newcastle in November. Held up as usual, he jumped indifferently early on but eventually warmed to his task, landed running in front after a fine jump at the last and was driven out to win by two and a half lengths and three from Jinxy Jack and Past Glories, form which looked better at the end of the season than at the time. Kribensis' winning margin in the Christmas Hurdle the following month was identical, but he impressed much more than at Newcastle and he and the runner-up, Osric, finished clear of the rest of the usual single-figure field. Osric, the winner in 1987, is a good test when conditions are as right for him as they were at Kempton, and he brought the best out of Kribensis. In a strongly-run race Kribensis travelled well, jumping soundly. When the pacemaker Beldale Star began to weaken going to the second last Kribensis and Osric quickened on, Osric showing slightly ahead at first. But Kribensis measured each of the last two flights perfectly and found the better pace under pressure to settle the issue on the flat. In 1988/9 the Christmas Hurdle turned out to be Kribensis' last race before the Champion Hurdle. In the latest season he was given a run two thirds of the way through that eleven-week period in the Kingwell Hurdle at Wincanton, a race dominated by Bula and Lanzarote in the first six years, then not won by another champion hurdler since. The odds-on Kribensis kept himself right in the Cheltenham picture by beating a field which included four other big-race probables with something to spare. Island Set, receiving 10 lb, finished four lengths down in second place having had difficulty going the pace; next came a shade-burly Cruising Altitude, beaten nine lengths at level weights with the winner.

Good as this latest performance was—probably the best of Kribensis' career up to then—Beech Road remained a solid favourite for the Champion Hurdle, following his excellent second to Vagador at Fontwell, until the ground began to dry up. On the day they bet 2/1 Beech Road, 95/40 Kribensis, 8/1 bar; with just the improving Nomadic Way, Cruising Altitude, Morley Street and Vagador of the others in the field of nineteen shorter than 22/1. Besides the two favourites Vagador was the only horse to have taken part the previous year. The firmish ground faced most of the runners with conditions they'd not been used to racing on regularly (at seven years of age

Top Rank Christmas Hurdle, Kempton—
Kribensis wins the race for the second year running; Osric makes him work hard

Waterford Crystal Champion Hurdle, Cheltenham—four in line at the last; from left to right, Beech Road, Past Glories, Kribensis and Nomadic Way

the Irish challengers Elementary and Redundant Pal had one run between them over hurdles on the ground), and placed some at a disadvantage. Nomadic Way's connections, apprehensive that he might not get a stiff enough test of stamina, did their best to see he had one by putting in a pacemaker, the very useful novice Sudden Victory. The pace was a strong one from the start. Sudden Victory lasted until the top of the hill, giving way quickly to Nomadic Way, who'd tracked him closely, and 150/1-shot Past Glories, regarded as suited by soft ground prior to the race. At this stage the field, minus Persian Style, Bank View and Cruising Altitude who'd all fallen early on, was quite tightly grouped with Kribensis creeping through towards the outside. Nomadic Way could not shake off the best of his pursuers down the hill but still had the lead under pressure on the home turn, pressed by Past Glories, Kribensis and Beech Road, the last-named having come from last place. In the end, as expected in the conditions, it all boiled down to a test of speed. Kribensis lost no momentum through jumping the last very big; he soon showed ahead of the other three, and kept on strongly to win by three lengths from Nomadic Way with Past Glories and Beech Road close up in third and fourth respectively. Then came a gap of eight lengths to Morley Street and Jinxy Jack, and another seven to Island Set. At that, Kribensis was retired for the season.

Kribensis (gr.g. 1984)	Henbit (USA) (b 1977)	Hawaii (b 1964)	Utrillo II
			Ethane
		Chateaucreek (ch 1970)	Chateaugay
			Mooncreek
	Aquaria (gr 1969)	Double-U-Jay (ch 1963)	Major Portion
			Renounce
		Sea Imp (br 1958)	Abernant
			Murray Bay

Victory—in course-record time—took Kribensis' earnings over hurdles past the 125,000 guineas he cost as a foal, and he has now won almost £175,000. As an advertisement for his sire as a sire of jumpers he stands out from the rest, though coming along behind is the top juvenile Sybillin. The Derby winner Henbit nowadays stands as a dual-purpose stallion at Sandville Stud in Cork, having made little impact with his progeny on the Flat. Kribensis, a good third under 9-6 in the King George V Handicap at Royal Ascot is also one of the best of them in that department, behind the 1989 Grand Prix de Deauville winner Borromini. The dam Aquaria ran unplaced in an early-season maiden at Leopardstown as a three-year-old. She's had a productive career at stud and is the dam of six winners so far, including the Windsor Castle Stakes winner Cooliney Prince (by Tumble Wind) and another by the same sire called Tumble Rita who showed useful form, by that country's standards, in Belgium. Aquaria's foal of 1988, a gelded brother to Kribensis, fetched IR 41,000 guineas at the Fairyhouse November Sales in 1989. The next two dams ran on the Flat, Sea Imp with some success for Peter Easterby's stable: she was a speedy two-year-old who seemingly failed to train on.

Sheikh Mohammed's "Kribensis"

We must not leave Kribensis before giving further consideration to his defeat in the Champion Hurdle—the main piece of evidence, when contrasted with his win twelve months later, for the case that he's better suited by a sound surface than a soft one. Maybe he is, but the evidence is inconclusive. On the Flat Kribensis acted on any going (that Royal Ascot run came on soft); furthermore, he won the Daily Express Triumph Hurdle on dead, admittedly against less exacting opposition. Possibly the real significance of the ground to Kribensis in 1989 lay in that it imposed a test of stamina on a horse not then grown to full strength who'd been off the course for eleven weeks. Now that he's stronger, the ground may not be so important. We shall see. Kribensis has raced only at two miles and isn't likely to be asked to tackle much further as long as he remains in the top class. Almost certainly one reason for the early end to his season was that the big hurdle at Liverpool is run over two and a half. A lengthy gelding, Kribensis jumps hurdles very well and is thoroughly reliable. *M. R. Stoute.*

KRISFIELD 5 b. or br.g. Anfield–Kristallina (Homeric) [1989/90 16g^{F} 16d^{5}] small, sparely-made gelding: first sign of ability over hurdles when fifth in claimer at Ayr in January: sold 5,400 gns Ascot February Sales. *M. Brittain.* 83

KRISTEN 11 ch.m. Sheshoon–Sweet Boronia (Mandamus) [1989/90 a24g^{pu}] lightly-made mare: winning selling hurdler: has run once since 1983/4 (has been to stud): stays 2½m: seems to act on any going: once blinkered. *Mrs J. Wonnacott.* —

KRISTENSON 13 b.g. Menelek–Chantry Bay (Marshal Pil) [1989/90 c20s^{4} c24g^{F} c24g^{2} c24v^{5} c24v^{3} c24d^{F} c24g^{6}] strong, sturdy gelding: winning hurdler: c**80** —

poor novice chaser nowadays: stays well: best form on an easy surface: suitable mount for an amateur or a claimer. *R. F. Fisher.*

KRUSAVITCH 4 ch.f. Sunley Builds–Dipsicato (Music Maestro) [1989/90 16v 16s4 16v] angular filly: temperamental maiden on Flat: easily best effort in juvenile hurdles when staying-on fourth at Plumpton in December: will be suited by further than 2m. *R. Curtis.* 93

KRYPTON KNIGHT 5 ch.g. Star Appeal–Bold Pioneer (Wolver Hollow) [1989/90 20d 20g5 17g4 16s3 16s2 17d2 16v3 a20g6] small, lightly-made gelding: novice selling hurdler: best form at around 2m: acts on heavy going: blinkered final start, visored previous three. *D. R. Tucker.* 81

KRYSTLE SAINT 9 ch.m. St Columbus–Clear Thinking (Articulate) [1989/90 c21dur c21s5 c21d5 c25s6 c20d5 c24f3] rangy, rather leggy mare: winning chaser: poor form in 1989/90: stays 3m: acts on any going: headstrong, has tended to jump right and run in snatches: not one to trust. *K. A. Morgan.* c**82** §

KUMAKAS NEPHEW 7 ch.g. Push On–Darling's Double (Menelek) [1989/90 c24sF4 22g2] smallish, lengthy gelding: fairly useful hurdler: good second to Big White Chief in handicap at Wolverhampton in December: in lead when falling seventeenth in National Hunt Challenge Cup at Cheltenham in 1989: beaten when falling last (remounted) in novice chase won by Highfrith at Haydock in December: stays well: acts on heavy going: tends to hang markedly left. *M. C. Pipe.* c— p 131

KUMASI 5 b.g. Runnett–Ashanti (Yankee Gold) [1989/90 16mF] big, lengthy ex-Irish gelding: first foal: dam Irish 7f and 1m winner: behind in maiden at 2 yrs: successful in NH Flat race in 1989: fell fatally in novice hurdle at Ascot in November. *D. R. C. Elsworth.* —

KUSHBALOO 5 b.h. Kambalda–Cushla (Zabeg) [1989/90 F14v F16g F16f] half-brother to winning Irish jumpers Clonmullen and Graiguemore (both by Three Wishes) and winning jumper Dennis Auburn (by Dusky Boy): behind in NH Flat races: yet to race over hurdles or fences. *C. Parker.*

KUWAIT LEEL 8 b.g. Ile de Bourbon (USA)–Love And Care (USA) (Ballymoss) [1989/90 22d 22gpu] small, well-made gelding: winning hurdler: no worthwhile form in 2 outings in December: stays 25f: acts on heavy going. *F. Jordan.* —

KUWAIT MUTAR 8 b.g. Martinmas–Willowy (Mourne) [1989/90 16m a20g2 a20g5] workmanlike gelding: novice hurdler: second in handicap at Southwell in January: little other form, including in a seller: stays 2½m: has reportedly broken blood vessels. *R. Guest.* 85

KUWAIT STAR 7 ch.g. Balidar–Kadsai (Lorenzaccio) [1989/90 c18f4 c25m3 c20fF c20mpu] stocky gelding: poor novice hurdler/chaser: was best at around 2m on soft going: blinkered once: dead. *N. B. Thomson.* c— —

KWACHA 4 b.c. Reesh–Madame Quickly (Saint Crespin III) [1989/90 16f2 16m5] close-coupled, workmanlike colt: half-brother to modest chaser Bolt The Gate (by Bustino): no worthwhile form on Flat: poor form in 2 outings over hurdles early in season, second a seller: sold 5,200 gns Doncaster October Sales. *J. Mackie.* 69

KWI 4 b.g. Krayyan–Angevin (English Prince) [1989/90 16f 16f 16fpu 17dpu 20g6] angular gelding: plating-class maiden on Flat (looks a difficult ride): sold out of M. Tompkins' stable 4,000 gns Newmarket July Sales: no form over hurdles, including in sellers: blinkered over 2½m (unlikely to stay trip). *F. Gray.* —

KYLE PRINCE 11 ch.g. Prince Hansel–Ceol An Ghra (Patrick) [1989/90 c24m5] lengthy, rather sparely-made gelding: novice hurdler: winning chaser: no form since 1986/7 (looked very much in need of race only outing 1989/90): should stay beyond 2m: blinkered once in 1986/7. *P. Ransom.* c— —

KYLE WOOD 11 ch.g. Daybrook Lad–Ten-Cents (Taste of Honey) [1989/90 c22fF c22fF c20m6 c24hur c24hpu 22m 20fpu] workmanlike gelding: winning point-to-pointer in Ireland: little worthwhile form in Britain: dead. *P. J. Jones.* c— —

KYOTO 12 b.g. Averof–Klondyke Fire (Klondyke Bill) [1989/90 c21g2 c19f2 c20mr c24gpu] tall, workmanlike gelding: modest front-running chaser nowadays: stays 3m: best on a sound surface and acts on hard going: has looked ungenuine on occasions (refused after being remounted third start): visored third outing 1988/9: takes good hold and needs strong handling. *J. R. Jenkins.* c**101** § —

L

LA BELLE OF SANTO 7 b.m. Monsanto (FR)–Henrietta Belle (Irish Ball (FR)) [1989/90 22g^{pu} a16g a18g 16f^{6} 17m] neat mare: selling hurdler: form only at 2m on firm ground. *B. K. Wells.* 68

LA BOEUF 14 bl.g. Bing II–True Grit (Klairon) [1989/90 c24g^{ur} c24d c24m^{5}] rather sparely-made gelding: poor chaser nowadays: stays well: acts on any going. *R. R. Lamb.* c83 —

LA CASTANA 4 ch.f. Dunbeath (USA)–Din Brown (USA) (Tom Rolfe) [1989/90 16g^{6} 16m* 16g^{2} 16g* a20g* a16g* a16s^{4} a16g^{3} 16m 20g] sparely-made filly: 1½m seller winner on Flat: improved after winning conditional jockeys selling hurdle at Huntingdon (bought in 5,200 gns) in December and won claimer at Market Rasen and 2 juvenile hurdles at Lingfield: well below her best last 2 outings: stays 2½m: acts on good to firm ground. *C. R. Beever.* 100 ?

LACE PAROSOL 4 ro.f. Neltino–Anglophil (Philemon) [1989/90 aF13g^{4}] fifth living foal: dam, 2-y-o 6f winner, behind in selling hurdles: 31 lengths fourth of 7 to Barnsdale in NH Flat race at Lingfield in February: yet to race over hurdles. *M. J. Charles.*

LACIDAR 10 b. or br.g. Radical–No Dice (No Argument) [1989/90 c21m c20f^{2} c20m^{pu} c20g* c20g^{2} c20g* c20g* c20f^{2} c24m*] useful-looking gelding: carries plenty of condition: fairly useful chaser: won at Sedgefield (twice) and Newcastle prior to winning quite valuable handicap chase at Wetherby in April by a length from Stay On Tracks: good second to New Halen in valuable event at Cheltenham penultimate outing: stays 3m: acts on any going with possible exception of heavy: has won for a claimer: usually ridden up with the pace: genuine. *J. H. Johnson.* **c126** —

LAD LANE 6 b. or br.g. Proverb–Quarry Lane (Bargello) [1989/90 16d] unfurnished gelding: seventh foal: half-brother to 2 poor animals: dam never ran: reluctant to post and soon tailed off in novice hurdle at Towcester in February. *T. Casey.* —

LADY BARNETT 6 br.m. Daring March–Skilla (Mexico III) [1989/90 c16g^{F} c24f^{2} c22f^{F} 24m] poor novice hurdler: jumped none too fluently when going down by 10 lengths to Border Oak in novice chase at Hexham in March: stays 3m: acts on firm ground. *B. Ellison.* c72 x —

LADY BE BRAVE 7 b.m. Laurence O–Miss Argument (No Argument) [1989/90 22g^{pu}] ex-Irish mare: well beaten in novice chase and a novice hurdle: won a point-to-point in 1989. *R. Dickin.* c— —

LADY BLUES SINGER 4 ch.f. Chief Singer–Moaning Low (Burglar) [1989/90 16f^{pu}] half-sister to winning hurdler Sunley Spirit (by Wolver Hollow): poor sprint maiden on Flat: weakened 3 out and pulled up before next in juvenile hurdle at Ludlow in March. *J. Perrett.* —

LADY CATCHER 8 b.m. Free Boy–Eyecatcher (Doubtless II) [1989/90 17v 22d^{bd} a20g^{4}] light-framed, close-coupled mare: poor novice hurdler/chaser: best form at around 2m. *J. R. Bosley.* c— 62

LADY ELLERTON 6 br.m. Java Tiger–Kenny (Royal Pennant) [1989/90 F16f 16m^{pu}] small mare: second foal: dam showed little sign of ability: tailed off in NH Flat race: broke down and destroyed in novice hurdle. *R. W. Swiers.* —

LADY KHADIJA 4 b.f. Nicholas Bill–Chenkynowa (Connaught) [1989/90 16m 16d 16g^{pu} 16g^{5} a18g a16g 16g] plain filly: little sign of ability on Flat: headstrong juvenile selling hurdler: saddle slipped third start (sweating): trained first 4 starts by G. Kelly. *N. Tinkler.* —

LADY LAX 6 ch.m. Henbit (USA)–Spoilt Miss (USA) (Riva Ridge (USA)) [1989/90 16f^{2} 16h^{2} 16f^{6} 16g^{5} 16d^{4} 16m 16h^{3}] sturdy mare: novice selling hurdler: may not stay much beyond 2m: acts on hard ground: broke a blood vessel fourth start 1988/9. *P. M. Cowley.* 73

LADY LONGMEAD 9 ch.m. Crimson Beau–Jester's Girl (Will Somers) [1989/90 17m^{4} 16m^{5}] sparely-made mare: winning 17f selling hurdler: tailed off both outings in May: fell at the seventh on chasing debut: acts on firm going. *W. G. M. Turner.* c— —

LADY MING 7 b.m. Flatbush–Mingside (Shackleton) [1989/90 16g 20g^{pu}] third foal: dam unraced sister to fairly useful Irish chaser Smartside: little promise in 2 outings over hurdles. *R. H. Goldie.* —

LADY NIGHTSHADE 6 b. or br.m. Newski (USA)–Rayles Amanda (Aban) [1989/90 F17h3 22f4] good-bodied non-thoroughbred mare: first foal: dam never ran: won a point-to-point in April: third in NH Flat race at Devon & Exeter in October: remote fourth in mares novice hurdle at Wincanton later in month (led to 3 out). *M. C. Pipe.* —

LADY NOEL 6 ch.m. Bonne Noel–Raheen Lady (Candy Cane) [1989/90 c24gpu] first foal: dam unraced daughter of a fair winning sprinter: amateur ridden, tailed off when pulled up in novice chase at Southwell (pulled hard) in November on debut: sold 3,000 gns Doncaster Spring Sales. *C. R. Saunders.* c—

LADY OF BALDWIN 9 b.m. Decent Fellow–Star O'Solway (Star Moss) [1989/90 c20s c24s4 c24g c17g4 c16f c20f4 c25fpu] rangy mare: poor novice chaser: stays 2½m: acts on firm going: visored last 3 outings: moderate jumper. *A. J. Wilson.* c80 x

LADY PAY 4 b.f. Hubble Bubble–Princess Pay (Kadir Cup) [1989/90 19sbd 20vpu 16fpu] fourth reported foal: half-sister to winning jumper Ragens Boy (by Rajen): dam never ran: seems of little account. *Mrs Jill Evans.* —

LADY PRY 7 ch.m. Pry–Like Now (Cracksman) [1989/90 c21fF] unfurnished mare: no form over hurdles: pulled up in 2 point-to-points and fell in novice hunter chase in 1990: blinkered last 2 starts 1988/9 (ran out on first occasion). *Peter Morris.* c— —

LADY ROSABELLE 4 ch.f. Broadsword (USA)–T V Star (St Columbus) [1989/90 16m 16g] angular, workmanlike filly: first living foal: dam won over hurdles: tailed off only outing on Flat and in 2 juvenile hurdles. *Miss A. L. M. King.* —

LADY ROSANNA 5 b.m. Kind of Hush–Rosaceae (Sagaro) [1989/90 16g2 16m* 16d5 16d4 16g 17m*] rangy mare: fair handicapper on Flat, suited by around 1¾m: landed the odds in novice hurdle at Wincanton in December (led from third) and in mares novice handicap at Devon & Exeter (made all) in April: unlikely to stay much beyond 17f: seems suited by a sound surface: suited by racing up with pace. *I. A. Balding.* 102 p

LADY RUN 8 b.m. Deep Run–Abbeylands Lass (Royal Highway) [1989/90 22m] sparely-made ex-Irish mare: poor novice hurdler/chaser: claimer ridden, tailed off at Windsor in November on British debut. *Mrs P. Townsley.* c— —

LADY STOCK 4 ch.f. Crofter (USA)–Millingdale (Tumble Wind (USA)) [1989/90 16g] half-sister to winning chaser Out of Stock (by Neltino): modest 7f winner at 3 yrs when trained by G. Cottrell: tailed off in claiming hurdle at Uttoxeter in May. *J. White.* —

LADY TOKEN 6 b.m. Roscoe Blake–Princess Token (Khalkis) [1989/90 F16m 20g 20d3 27g3 27gpu 24d 20d3 20g5] sturdy, close-coupled mare: first foal: dam useful point-to-pointer and novice steeplechaser: poor form in novice hurdles: thorough stayer who'll be suited by a return to 3m+: usually ridden by Mrs A. Farrell. *H. J. Gill.* 86

LADY TRISSIE 7 gr.m. Politico (USA)–Jane Again (Spartan General) [1989/90 F16f 20dpu 25g 20d c22fF c24mF c24mpu 20f3] leggy, plain mare: sister to winning hurdler Treble Trouble and half-sister to novice selling hurdler Easter Jane (by Palm Track): dam fair hurdler: of little account: blinkered seventh outing. *P. Beaumont.* c— —

LADY WESTGATE 6 b.m. Welsh Chanter–Church Bay (Reliance II) [1989/90 c20spu c25mur] leggy mare: novice hurdler/hunter chaser: tried to refuse and unseated rider final outing: successful over long distances on Flat in 1990 for G. B. Balding. *R. P. Shepherd.* c— —

LADY WESTOWN 6 b.m. Town And Country–Hay-Hay (Hook Money) [1989/90 24f* 24d3 21m* 24fF 24g 24f2] neat mare: idled run-in when winning handicap hurdles at Uttoxeter and Warwick (mares) in first half of season: first outing for 4½ months, neck second to Lapiaffe at Chepstow in May (left in lead last, caught near finish): stays 3m: yet to show her form on very soft going, acts on any other: ridden by claimer third, fourth and final starts. *R. J. Holder.* 108

LAFOSSE 9 b.g. Status Seeker–Meelgarrow (Raise You Ten) [1989/90 20s 21d] heavy-topped gelding: has been tubed: winning hurdler: tailed off both starts of season: runner-up 4 times over fences in 1987/8: stays well: acts on heavy going and seems unsuited by firm. *Mrs J. Pitman.* c— —

LA FRITE 4 b.f. John French–Saratoga Chip (USA) (Plenty Old (USA)) [1989/90 16m 17gpu 16spu] small, sparely-made filly: second foal: dam, winner of —

7f seller, of little account over hurdles: seems little better over hurdles herself: sold 1,250 gns Ascot February Sales. *D. R. Tucker.*

LAID BACK 9 ch.g. Bonne Noel–Babu Saar (Battle Burn) [1989/90 c26g^5 22g c— x
25d^3] sparely-made, plain gelding: winning hurdler/chaser: poor form in 1989/90: 83
suited by 3m and more: acts on heavy ground (fell only outing on top-of-the-
ground): poor jumper of fences: visored final start. *G. M. Moore.*

LAKEFIELD 11 b.g. Pitpan–Chamspex (Perspex) [1989/90 c22g^5 c24g^6 c25g^3 c**93**
c28g^4 c29g^2] big, plain gelding: quite a modest chaser: suited by a thorough test
of stamina: acts on soft going: usually jumps soundly: sometimes ridden by 7-lb
claimer. *J. M. Bukovets.*

LAKE MISSION 5 b.g. Blakeney–Missed Blessing (So Blessed) [1989/90
16m^3 16g^6 16s 16m* 16d a16g^5] sturdy, good-bodied gelding: won novice handicap 89
hurdle at Wincanton in December: bit below form subsequently (not seen out
after February): races only at 2m: seems suited by a sound surface. *D. Nicholson.*

LAKESIDE LASS 4 b.f. Import–Celtic Love (Irish Love) [1989/90 16f^{pu} 16s]
leggy filly: second reported foal: dam winning hurdler: behind in maiden and —
minor events on Flat: tailed off in juvenile hurdle at Plumpton in December. *G. G.
Gracey.*

LAKE TEEREEN 5 ch.g. Callernish–Gusserane Lark (Napoleon Bonaparte)
[1989/90 16s^3 16m^2] lengthy, unfurnished gelding: second foal: brother to winning 83
point-to-pointer/novice chaser Bit of A Clown: dam placed in an Irish point-
to-point: placed in novice hurdles at Folkestone and Wincanton: off course 4
months in between: will stay further. *J. T. Gifford.*

LAKE VALENTINA 9 br.g. Blakeney–La Levantina (Le Levanstell) c**90**
[1989/90 24m^3 c24g^{pu} c27d^3 c25g^2 c27s^5 c25g c24g* c24f^F] small gelding: fairly 111
useful hurdler at his best: won slowly-run novice chase at Hexham in March: fell
fatally on same course later in month: was suited by 3m: acted on any going: found
nothing once in 1987/8: trained until after fifth outing by M. W. Easterby. *J. E.
Swiers.*

LAKMON 4 br.g. Final Straw–Tanagrea (Blakeney) [1989/90 F16s F17f^6] first
foal: dam unraced sister to Irish Derby winner Tyrnavos and half-sister to several
other high-class performers: well beaten in NH Flat races: yet to race over
hurdles. *Mrs E. H. Heath.*

LA MOLINILLA 7 b.m. Lochnager–Celtic Tara (Welsh Saint) [1989/90 18h*
16m 22f*] small, close-coupled mare: selling hurdler: won handicaps at Fontwell 70
(novice event, bought in 2,100 gns) in August and Stratford (conditional jockeys,
sold 3,800 gns) following month, not having to be at best on latter course: ran
poorly in between: probably stays 2¾m: acts on hard ground: has run creditably
for a 7-lb claimer. *Miss S. J. Wilton.*

LAMPASS 6 b. or br.g. Never Got A Chance–Annagh Delight (Saint Denys) c**77** x
[1989/90 22v^{pu} c26s^{pu} c26s^4 c24d^{ur} c24f^5 c26f^{ur} c24m^F] workmanlike gelding: —
novice hurdler/chaser: clear when unseating rider 4 out in race won by Deep Cliff
at Southwell in May on final outing: has given impression he'll prove best at
distances short of 3m: blinkered fifth start: makes mistakes over fences. *J. A. C.
Edwards.*

LANACRE BRIDGE 13 b.g. Langton Heath–So Gay (Peter-So-Gay) c— x
[1989/90 c26d^5] tall, rather leggy gelding: handicap chaser: frequently let down by —
his jumping: stays 25f: acts on any going: sometimes blinkered. *P. J. Hobbs.*

LANAVOE 11 b.g. Tudor Rocket–Ballincanty (Le Prince) [1989/90 c18f^2 c22d^3 c**126**
c17g* c21g^F c20s^2 c16g* c16d^4 c17s^{ur} c16d^2 c20d^3 c18d^3 c22m* c36f^F] Irish —
gelding: handicap chaser: successful at Galway in September, Roscommon in
October and Limerick in March: fell first Becher's in Seagram Grand National at
Liverpool in April: stays 2¾m: acts on good to firm and heavy going. *F. J. Lacy,
Ireland.*

LANDA'S TIPPLE 6 b.m. Jimsun–Beychevelle (Sir Herbert) [1989/90 20v c—
c26s^F c25d^{pu}] compact mare: no worthwhile form over hurdles or fences: visored —
final outing: sold 1,350 gns Ascot April Sales. *D. R. Gandolfo.*

LANDING BOARD 12 ch.g. Deep Run–High School (Even Money) [1989/90 c**118**
c22m^3 c20f* c20d^2 c20g^F] workmanlike gelding: fair chaser: sweating, won —
4-runner handicap at Cheltenham in October: had a cut on his near-hind prior to
running moderately next 2 starts (not raced after November): stays 3m: ran
moderately on hard going, probably acts on any other: claimer ridden: sometimes
jumps sketchily: has won 5 times at Huntingdon. *P. W. Harris.*

LANDMARK 7 b.h. Mill Reef (USA)–Christchurch (FR) (So Blessed) [1989/90 16s 16v^4 17g* 16s 16g^3] angular, workmanlike horse: sold out of P. Howling's stable 1,400 gns Newmarket Autumn Sales: won selling handicap hurdle at Carlisle in February (bought in 3,100 gns): raced only at around 2m: easily best form on good ground: dead. *J. D. J. Davies.* — 76

LANDSKER OATS 4 b.f. Oats–Gemmerly Jane (Bally Russe) [1989/90 aF16g^6 16s^{ur} a16g] leggy filly: first foal: dam quite a useful point-to-pointer and winning hunter chaser: sixth of 12 in NH Flat race at Southwell in February: tailed off in novice hurdle on same course in April. *Mrs A. E. Ratcliff.* — —

LANDSKI 7 b.g. Niniski (USA)–Misacre (St Alphage) [1989/90 16m* 16m^5 20g a16g^3 16g*] well-made gelding: handicap hurdler: showed improved form each time when winning at Huntingdon in September and Wetherby (ridden halfway when beating Sweet City a neck) in December: should stay 2½m (sweating, ran badly when tried at trip): probably acts on any going: has run creditably for an amateur: trained until after fourth outing by J. Jenkins. *J. Parkes.* — 116

L'ANE ROUGE 9 b.g. Deep Run–Imperial Leather (Coronation Year) [1989/90 c25f^4 c29d^F c24d c30v^{ur} 22g^6 c25f^{pu}] big, workmanlike ex-Irish gelding: fairly useful chaser at his best: makes mistakes and seems to have lost his way: stays 3m: acts on heavy going and unsuited by firm. *M. C. Pipe.* — c— x / —

LANGROVE 6 b.g. Cleon–Dear Lady (Dear Gazelle) [1989/90 16f^6 20h^4 16f^3 16m c20g^{pu} c20d^{pu} a22g* 20f] workmanlike gelding: ridden by 5-lb claimer, won handicap hurdle at Southwell in March, despite starting slowly and looking rather reluctant when first put under pressure: ran poorly final outing: tailed off when pulled up in novice chases: stays 2¾m: acts on hard ground: blinkered last 2 starts. *Mrs V. A. Aconley.* — c— / 75

LANGSHOTT MANOR 8 ch.g. Celtic Cone–Be Spartan (Spartan General) [1989/90 c16f^{pu}] workmanlike gelding: third in NH Flat race in 1986/7: tailed off in similar event in 1987/8: jumped deliberately and was tailed off when pulled up ninth on chasing debut in December. *C. S. Wates.* — c—

LANGTON MIST 5 b.g. Grey Ghost–La Raine (Majority Blue) [1989/90 F16g] brother to 5f winner Grey Tan, half-brother to 5f seller winner Jimmy Raine (by Jimmy Reppin) and winning 2m chaser Barn Brae (by Derek H): dam 2-y-o 5f winner, seemed later to need further: well beaten in NH Flat race at Catterick in March: yet to race over hurdles or fences. *Mrs V. A. Aconley.*

LAPIAFFE 6 b.g. Piaffer (USA)–Laval (Cheval) [1989/90 22m 19m^3 22m* 22d^5 22m^{pu} 25g* 21d^{ur} 25g^6 22m^5 24m^4 21m^2 24f*] leggy, sparely-made gelding: handicap hurdler: won at Nottingham and Newbury (conditional jockeys) in December and Chepstow in May: stays 3m: probably acts on any going: edged left when successful in 1988/9, hung right fourth start 1989/90: inconsistent. *R. J. Hodges.* — 102

LAPIERRE 5 b.h. Lafontaine (USA)–Lucky Omen (Queen's Hussar) [1989/90 16s 16s^6] medium-sized, lengthy horse: smart performer at up to 1¼m at 3 yrs but well below his best on Flat since: travelled quite well until weakening in latter stages of novice hurdles at Ascot and Sandown in February: likely to do better. *C. E. Brittain.* — — p

LA PLUME 9 b.g. Whistling Deer–Air Queen (Vulgan's Air) [1989/90 c20g^3 c20f^4 c18f* c24m^3 c21g^6 c25g^2 c20g^2 c25g^2 c24g^3 c28d^4 c32g^{pu} c20f^3 c27f^2 c27f^2] workmanlike ex-Irish gelding: winning hurdler: successful in novice chase at Wexford in August: in frame in handicaps in Britain subsequently, showing only modest form: stays well: acts on firm and dead going: blinkered first 2 and final starts: trained by F. Flood until after third outing. *P. Beaumont.* — **c90** / —

L'AQUINO 5 ch.m. Kings Lake (USA)–Willowy (Mourne) [1989/90 22v 20m^2 a20g^2 a24g^2 19s* a20g^3 20g^2] sparely-made mare: half-sister to winning hurdlers Low Quay (by Quayside) and Willow Gorge (by Hello Gorgeous): dam half-sister to very smart hurdler Sea Tale: placed at up to 1½m on Flat: won novice selling hurdle at Hereford in March (bought in 6,000 gns): placed in non-sellers otherwise: should be suited by further than 2½m: acts on soft going. *M. A. Jarvis.* — 100

LARCHWOOD 9 b.m. Precipice Wood–Last Alliance (Honour Bound) [1989/90 c25m^5 c20d^{pu}] lengthy, deep-girthed mare: winning hurdler/chaser: well beaten in December (favourite) and January: suited by 2½m+: acts on good to firm and soft going: pulls hard (has worn crossed noseband): tends to be on toes and sweat in preliminaries: said to have broken blood vessels. *S. Christian.* — c— / —

LARKAWAY 5 b.m. Furry Glen–The White Lark (Great White Way (USA)) [1989/90 16m] leggy, angular mare: fifth foal: half-sister to fair Irish jumping — —

winner Slyguff (by Kambalda): dam winner on Flat and over hurdles in Ireland: tailed off in novice hurdle at Sandown in March. *C. V. Bravery.*

LARKSMORE 5 br.m. Royal Fountain–Newtonmore (Game Rights) [1989/90
22d 16s^{5} 21d] medium-sized mare: fifth foal: dam unraced: fifth behind Rositary in 81
mares novice hurdle at Towcester in February, only form. *Miss D. J. Baker.*

LARKSPUR LASS 7 b.m. Maori King–Kitbag (Galivanter) [1989/90 16f^{5}]
second foal: dam never ran: well beaten in novice hurdle at Towcester in May. *K.* —
C. Bailey.

LARLOCH 6 br.g. Young Generation–Black Fire (Firestreak) [1989/90 16m^{6}
16m] workmanlike gelding: poor form over hurdles. *G. Richards.* 75

LARRY HILL 15 b.g. Laurence O–Must Run (Mustang) [1989/90 24m^{5} 25f c— x
25g^{5}] lengthy gelding: winning hurdler/point-to-pointer and poor novice chaser 75
(sketchy jumper): not seen out after November: suited by a good test of stamina:
acts on a firm surface, but ideally suited by plenty of give. *Mrs J. D. Goodfellow.*

LARRY-O 10 ch.g. Laurence O–Penthouse Pet (Deep Run) [1989/90 c24g^{pu} c—
c21m^{pu} c24s^{5}] big, rather sparely-made gelding: fair chaser in 1987/8: let down by —
his jumping first 2 outings and ran too freely final start 1989/90: stays 25f: acts on
any going: successful with and without blinkers. *C. P. E. Brooks.*

LARRY'S BOTTLE 13 ch.g. Golden Love–Breaking Point (Breakspear II) c—
[1989/90 c16f^{pu}] tall gelding: winning hurdler/chaser: stayed 2½m: acted on any —
going: sometimes blinkered: dead. *Mrs I. McKie.*

LA SHAKA 7 b.m. Son of Shaka–Lady Sylvania (Hornbeam) [1989/90 18g^{pu}]
workmanlike, lengthy mare: novice hurdler: no worthwhile form since 1987/8: —
suited by testing conditions at 2m and stays 2½m: acts on heavy going. *A. Moore.*

LAST BRANDY 7 b.g. The Brianstan–Escargot (Escart III) [1989/90 20m^{pu}
21f^{pu}] lengthy, rather dipped-backed gelding: of little account: sold 1,900 gns —
Ascot July Sales. *Mrs S. M. Johnson.*

LAST BUCK 10 br.g. Master Buck–Last Wish (Three Wishes) [1989/90 c18h^{4} c— x
21f^{5} 16f^{3} c18f^{r}] sparely-made gelding: maiden point-to-pointer: poor novice over 61 ?
hurdles and in steeplechases: visored nowadays: poor jumper of fences. *J. J.
Bridger.*

LAST EXTRAVAGANCE 9 b.g. Bluerullah–Queen Hansel (Prince Hansel) c—
[1989/90 c25m^{ur}] workmanlike gelding: no worthwhile form over hurdles and in —
steeplechases: sold out of D. Gandolfo's stable 3,000 gns Ascot October Sales:
won a point-to-point in February. *M. R. Churches.*

LAST GRAIN 8 b.g. Remainder Man–Wheatley (Town Crier) [1989/90 c20s*] c**101**
tall, close-coupled gelding: has been fired: moderate hurdler: jumped well when —
winning novice chase at Ayr in December easily by 5 lengths from Viking Rocket:
stayed 2½m: acted well on soft ground: broke down badly at Ayr and reportedly
has been retired. *J. S. Wilson.*

LAST HOUSE 7 ch.m. Vital Season–Parkhouse (Spartan General) [1989/90 c**133**
22d* 25g c21v^{2} c26v* c26v^{2} c24s^{2} c25s^{4} c26m* c25f^{2}] close-coupled, sparely- 117
made mare: handicap hurdler: won at Stratford in November: always prominent
when winning novice chases at Newton Abbot in January (by 20 lengths) and April
(by 25 lengths): second to Royal Athlete in similar race on same course and in Old
Road Securities Reynoldstown Novices' Chase at Ascot in between: well below
her best final start: stays very well: probably unsuited by very firm ground, and
goes well in the mud: jumps soundly: useful. *Mrs M. Easton.*

LASTING MEMORY 4 b.f. Ardross–Irreprochable (Mount Hagen (FR))
[1989/90 17d^{2} 17d a18g* 17m* 17f^{2} 16m^{2} 16m] leggy, sparely-made filly: no form 93
on Flat: sold out of D. Chapman's stable 1,800 gns Doncaster June Sales: won
claiming hurdle at Lingfield in February and juvenile event at Newton Abbot 2
months later: will stay 2½m: best form on a sound surface (beaten in a seller on
good to soft). *R. G. Frost.*

LASTOFTHEBROWNIES 10 b.g. Giolla Mear–Another Rose (Trouville) c**130**
[1989/90 c25g c24d c20g^{4} c24d^{2} c20g^{5} c25v^{4} c24s^{3} c26v^{pu} c36f^{5}] sturdy, —
good-bodied gelding: fairly useful Irish chaser: in frame, running creditably, in
handicaps in 1989/90, on last occasion 14 lengths third behind Carvill's Hill in
Harold Clarke Leopardstown Chase: ran well in race for third year in succession
when staying-on remote fifth to Mr Frisk in Seagram Grand National at Liverpool
in April: stays very well: acts on heavy going. *M. F. Morris, Ireland.*

LAST OF THE FLIES 9 ch.g. Kemal (FR)–Gledswing (Reynard Volant) c86
[1989/90 c24g^{5} c24m^{3}] rangy, workmanlike gelding: placed in point-to-points in

1987: placed in novice chases, showing modest form: not seen out after November: stays 3m: acts on soft going: amateur ridden. *A. H. Mactaggart.*

LAST 'O' THE BUNCH 6 ch.h. Meldrum–Golden Royalty (Royalty) [1989/90 F16g 16d3 20s2 20g 17g5 16d* 16g* 16m] workmanlike horse: claimer ridden, made running when successful in maiden hurdle at Edinburgh in February and novice event at Catterick in March: best effort when staying-on 28 lengths eighth behind Fidway in Seagram 100 Pipers Top Novices' Hurdle at Liverpool on final start: withdrawn after unseating rider and running loose before intended third start: will prove best at 2m: acts on good to firm and dead ground: has worn crossed noseband. *E. Weymes.* 106

LATCHMOSS 4 ch.f. Telsmoss–Laveche (Cheval) [1989/90 F16f] sister to poor novice selling hurdler Cullen's Pet: dam never ran: well beaten in NH Flat race at Ascot in April: yet to race over hurdles. *Mrs A. Knight.*

LATE DELIVERY 8 b.g. Pony Express–La Merlette (Balidar) [1989/90 c25gF c20f2] tall, leggy gelding: novice hurdler: maiden point-to-pointer: 15 lengths second to Rectory Boy in novice hunter chase at Cheltenham in May. *David Kench.* c83 —

LATENT TALENT 6 b.g. Celtic Cone–Fra Mau (Wolver Hollow) [1989/90 16gF 16g* 20g* 20spu] big, rangy, chasing type: has plenty of scope: first foal: dam fairly useful hurdler/novice chaser, stayed at least 2½m: always prominent and jumped well when winning novice hurdles at Newbury and Haydock (drifted left closing stages when beating Invasion by 4 lengths) in November: weakened quickly 3 out and pulled up in similar event at Chepstow in December: has won over 2½m, but may prove best at shorter for time being. *O. Sherwood.* 113 +

LATERAL 6 b.g. Tina's Pet–Wounded Knee (Busted) [1989/90 16m 16g 16g2] leggy, close-coupled gelding: novice selling hurdler: second at Hereford in October: likely to prove best at around 2m: acts on firm ground. *J. M. Bradley.* 71

LATE SESSION 6 ch.g. Enchantment–Treatise (Bold Lad (IRE)) [1989/90 c24m2 c24f*] small, sturdy gelding: novice hurdler: maiden point-to-pointer: promising second to Rodden Brook in hunter chase at Chepstow in April and following month won 2-runner similar event on same course by 25 lengths from Tom Penny: stays 3m: acts on firm ground: should win more hunter chases. *R. W. Savery.* c**105** p —

LATE TROOPER 8 ch.g. Soldier Rose–Out Late (Fury Royal) [1989/90 24mpu] of little account over hurdles: in frame in point-to-points in 1990. *P. A. Pritchard.* —

LATIN AMERICAN 13 b.g. Genuine–Samba (Sammy Davis) [1989/90 c25m6] won a point-to-point in April: fair chaser in his day, but has deteriorated considerably: stays 3m: acts on any going: excellent mount for an inexperienced rider: probably best in blinkers nowadays. *Michael J. Moore.* c— —

LATTIN GENERAL 8 b.g. General Ironside–Lattins Lady (Happy New Year) [1989/90 c17f2 c19m*] neat, stocky gelding: winning hurdler: made most when winning 5-runner novice chase at Devon & Exeter in September by 25 lengths: races freely but stays 21f: acts on firm ground. *C. P. E. Brooks.* c87 —

LAUDERDALE LAD 8 b.g. Politico–Cannes Beach (Canadel II) [1989/90 c20d* c24g3 c24gF c25dF c24g3 c24s3 c20d c20d5 c25f2 c26m2] workmanlike gelding: first foal: dam, well beaten in a novice hurdle and a novice chase, is a half-sister to staying chaser Pongee Boy and daughter of very useful hunter chaser Bright Beach: successful once from 2 starts in point-to-points in 1988: bought for 19,000 gns Doncaster August Sales: won novice chase at Worcester in November: placed several times subsequently, including in handicaps: best form at 3m: acts on any going. *J. S. King.* c**102**

LAUGHING GRAVY 10 b.g. Monsanto (FR)–Poppy Time (Hook Money) [1989/90 16m] stocky gelding: tailed-off last in novice hurdles: dead. *Mrs Barbara Waring.* —

LAUGHTERINPARADISE 4 b.c. Cry No More–New Farm Lady (Native Bazaar) [1989/90 16f] well beaten at 2 yrs: behind in selling hurdle at Ludlow in April. *D. W. P. Arbuthnot.* —

LAUNDRYMAN 7 b.g. Celtic Cone–Lovely Laura (Lauso) [1989/90 16mur 16g3 16g2] lengthy gelding: modest novice hurdler: well-backed favourite, 10 lengths second to Fifth Amendment at Wincanton in January: may prove best at 2m on a sharp track: acts on soft going: tends to make mistakes. *S. Mellor.* 93 x

LAURA MARY 6 b.m. Foggy Bell–Fleur-Babu (Babu) [1989/90 16g^{pu}]
sparely-made mare: fourth reported foal: sister to winning hurdler/novice chaser —
Snow Babu: dam pulled up in 2 point-to-points: behind when pulled up 3 out in
novice hurdle at Windsor in March. *M. J. Wilkinson.*

LAURENBEL 9 b.g. Dublin Taxi–Betbellof (Averof) [1989/90 c16f c21f^{pu} c**87**
c16m^{F} c16g a16g^{pu} 17m c17m^{4} c16f^{F} c18f^{ur} c16h^{2} c18f^{3}] compact gelding: poor —
novice hurdler/chaser: best form at around 2m: acts on hard going: blinkered last
start in 1986/7 and last 2 outings (best efforts in 1989/90): has worn a crossed
noseband. *N. R. Mitchell.*

LAURIE-O 6 b.g. Deep Run–Eight of Diamonds (Silent Spring) [1989/90 F16f^{3}
20g^{F} 16f^{4} 20g 20f^{3} 20m] tall, lengthy gelding with scope: in frame in NH Flat 82
races and novice hurdles: stays 2½m: acts on firm going. *Mrs G. R. Reveley.*

LAVA FALLS (USA) 4 b. or br.c. Riverman (USA)–In Triumph (USA) (Hoist
The Flag (USA)) [1989/90 16s 16d^{6} 16f^{5} 16g^{3} 16f* 16m^{2}] angular, sparely-made 92
colt: modest performer around 1m on Flat: sold out of W. Hastings-Bass's stable
17,000 gns Newmarket December Sales: won novice handicap hurdle at
Towcester in May: good second in handicap on same course 9 days later: unlikely
to stay much beyond 2m: acts on firm going. *M. C. Banks.*

LAVROSKY (USA) 6 b.g. Nijinsky (CAN)–Just A Game (Tarboosh (USA)) c**98** +
[1989/90 c17g* c16g^{ur}] lengthy, rather sparely-made gelding: winning hurdler: —
led from fifth when winning novice chase at Huntingdon in November: jumped
none too fluently when ridden with more restraint following month (moderate
fourth when unseating rider last): will stay 2½m: acts on soft going: sold 2,700
gns Doncaster Spring Sales. *B. Stevens.*

LAWDON BRAVE 5 b.g. The Parson–Hill Invader (Brave Invader (USA))
[1989/90 16m] third foal: brother to a poor animal: dam lightly-raced sister to very —
useful hurdler Kilwarren: always behind in novice hurdle at Worcester in April. *S.
Christian.*

LAWLEY 8 br.g. Humdoleila–Cloudari (Pindari) [1989/90 c20s^{3} c20d^{4} c24m^{pu}] c**94**
lengthy gelding: selling hurdler: winning hunter chaser: 24 lengths third to Hand —
Over at Sandown in February: should stay beyond 2½m: acts on heavy going:
blinkered last 2 starts 1986/7. *Mrs Angus Campbell.*

LAWSON PRINCESS 6 b. or br.m. Latest Model–Calamity (Haven)
[1989/90 22d^{pu}] small, sparely-made mare: sister to winning chaser Upstanding: —
dam winning point-to-pointer: fell in a point-to-point in 1989: pulled up lame in
mares novice hurdle in February. *N. H. Davis.*

LAZY RHYTHM (USA) 4 gr.c. Drone–Ritual Dance (Godswalk (USA))
[1989/90 16f^{4}] leggy colt: fair winner over 1m on Flat in 1989: sold out of J. 86
Dunlop's stable 27,000 gns Newmarket Autumn Sales: 19 lengths fourth of 7
finishers to Calicon in juvenile hurdle at Newbury in November: raced freely and
needs to learn to settle. *R. Akehurst.*

L C MONRO 10 br.m. Ancient Monro–Way Up (Three Wishes) [1989/90 c—
c25g^{pu}] lengthy mare: winning point-to-pointer, gained latest success in March:
has failed to complete course in hunter chases. *Mrs J. A. Skelton.*

LEACROFT 6 b.g. Domitor (USA)–Whitmarsh (Hessonite) [1989/90 16f^{F} 16m
16d* 16g^{2} 16m] smallish, compact gelding: won conditional jockeys selling 86
handicap hurdle at Sedgefield in March (no bid): good second in non-selling
conditional jockeys handicap at Hexham later in month: races only at 2m: acts on
dead going. *W. W. Haigh.*

LEADING ARTIST 15 b.g. Menelek–Suvonne (Cacador) [1989/90 c25h^{3}] c**79**
lightly-made gelding: winning hurdler/chaser: poor point-to-pointer/hunter —
chaser nowadays: stays well: acts on any going: has run creditably in blinkers:
suitable mount for a claimer. *Mrs Judith Young.*

LEADING SUPPLIER 4 b.f. Leading Man–Dunoon Court (Dunoon Star)
[1989/90 F16m aF16g 16m^{5}] small filly: half-sister to winning jumpers Warren —
Gorse (by Lucky Sovereign) and Pamrina (by Pamroy): dam novice hurdler: tailed
off in NH Flat races and a novice hurdle. *P. J. Anderson.*

LEAMLARA LAD 10 b. or gr.g. Antwerp City–Beths' Bermudas (Brilliant c**88** x
Pil) [1989/90 c24g^{2} c25d^{pu} c22g^{F}] lengthy gelding: winning hurdler/chaser: —
jumped better than usual when second of 3 at Market Rasen in November: stays
3m: acts on heavy going and good to firm. *Mrs P. Sly.*

LEAN AR AGHAIDH 13 ch.g. Proverb–Carry On Jackie (David Jack) c**129**
[1989/90 c24d^{4} c26d* c20d^{3} c22m*] tall, rangy gelding: one-time smart chaser: —
hunter chaser nowadays: won Seagram Fox Hunters' Chase at Liverpool in April

in good style by 7 lengths from Crammer, jumping well and making most from the ninth: had made virtually all to win at Stratford (idled on run-in) in February: outpaced run-in over an inadequate trip in between: stays very well: acts on any going but goes particularly well on top-of-the-ground: suited by forcing tactics: bold jumper. *S. Mellor.*

LEANDER LAD 5 b.g. Paico–Miss Leander (Leander) [1989/90 16m^2 16g 20s 16g^3 16g^4 16d^4 16g 16f^2] leggy, workmanlike gelding: modest novice hurdler: barely stays 2m: best efforts on good going. *D. McCain.* 87

LEAN ORT 12 ch.g. Proverb–Carry On Jackie (David Jack) [1989/90 c24g^3 c26g^4 c28m^3 c24d^4 c26d^4 c25m^{pu} c24m c25f^2] workmanlike gelding: poor chaser: stays 3½m: acts on any going: moderate jumper. *J. Mackie.* c73 x —

LEARNED STAR 5 b.h. Bustiki–Learned Lady (Crozier) [1989/90 F16m F17f] first foal: dam winning hurdler/steeplechaser/point-to-pointer: mid-division in NH Flat races in October and March: yet to race over hurdles or fences. *J. L. Eyre.*

LEAVE IT TO BALLY 10 ch.g. Ballymore–Time To Leave (Khalkis) [1989/90 24f^4 c26f^F c25m^4 c25g^3 a22g^{pu} c20m^{pu}] compact gelding: novice selling hurdler: poor novice over fences: stays 3m: probably acts on any going: has been tried in blinkers: has run well for a 7-lb claimer: tends to carry his head to the left: ran poorly on all-weather fifth start, pulled up lame next. *P. J. Bevan.* c**79** 79

LEAVENWORTH 6 ch.g. Bustino–Hide The Key (USA) (Key To The Mint (USA)) [1989/90 25g*] workmanlike gelding: showed improved form when winning quite valuable handicap hurdle at Cheltenham in November by ½ length from Sketcher: not seen out again: stays 25f: acts on soft going: blinkered last 2 starts 1987/8: often sweats. *R. J. Holder.* 119 +

LE BLEU 10 b.m. Levanter–Chelwood Blue (Blue Streak) [1989/90 16g^{pu}] poor novice hurdler. *W. E. Fisher.* —

LE BUCHERON 4 b.g. Vaigly Great–Couteau (Nelcius) [1989/90 aF14g^4 F16g*] sixth reported foal: half-brother to Canif (by Saritamer), successful at up to 1m: dam won on Flat and over hurdles: well backed, won 18-runner NH Flat race at Market Rasen in April: yet to race over hurdles. *M. J. Ryan.*

LECALE LADY 6 ch.m. Torus–Lucy's Pal (Random Shot) [1989/90 16m^4 18f^6 17f^5 16g 22g 16d^{pu} 18d 20s^{pu}] plain, sturdy ex-Irish mare: first foal: dam unraced: —

Seagram Fox Hunters' Chase, Liverpool—Lean Ar Aghaidh gives a bold display of jumping; the weakening Giolla Padraig finishes third

Murphy's Handicap Hurdle, Cheltenham—
Sketcher and Pokeree (grey) lead eventual winner Leavenworth over the last

poor novice hurdler: no form in Britain, including in seller: trained by F. Flood until after third start. *J. Parkes.*

LE CAROTTE 8 ch.g. Balinger–Camargue (Combat) [1989/90 21f* 26f* 21f^{2} c19m^{F} 25f^{4} 21d 21d^{pu}] lengthy, workmanlike gelding: fairly useful hurdler at his best: won twice within 3 days at Newton Abbot in July: ran poorly last 2 starts: runner-up in novice chase early in 1988/9 (subsequently let down by his jumping): stays 3¼m: best form on a sound surface: broke blood vessel fifth start: sold out of P. Hobbs's stable only 1,100 gns Ascot November Sales after fifth start (off course over 3 months afterwards). *A. Barrow.* c— x 126 d

LE CHAT NOIR 7 br.g. Paico–June (Pendragon) [1989/90 20d^{3} 16f^{3} c16f^{4} c20g^{F} 16d^{2} 16v^{2} 16f* 16h^{2}] tall ex-Irish gelding: fifth foal: dam Irish 2m winner on Flat and 21f winner over hurdles: placed several times over hurdles (best efforts fifth and sixth starts) prior to winning novice event at Plumpton in March: 5/1 on when beaten on hard ground there later in month: well beaten on chasing debut: should be suited by further than 2m: successful on firm going but best form with plenty of give. *D. M. Grissell.* c— p 106

LEDSHAM 5 b.g. Gorytus (USA)–Concert (Appiani II) [1989/90 16d^{4}] compact, good-bodied gelding: plating-class middle-distance maiden on Flat: bit backward, tended to wander under pressure but kept on to finish 11 lengths fourth of 25 behind Lissahane Lass in novice event at Leicester in January on hurdling debut: should improve. *M. J. Camacho.* 90 p

LEFT HANDED 7 br.g. Strong Gale–Gleann Buidhe (Pampered King) [1989/90 c24f^{pu} 20g 20f^{6} 16f 16f^{4}] lengthy, rather sparely-made gelding: poor novice hurdler: behind when pulled up on chasing debut: sold 4,200 gns Doncaster November Sales: ran poorly in point-to-points afterwards. *J. Norton.* c— 66

LEGAL COIN 6 ch.m. Official–Anxious Coin (Prince Silver) [1989/90 16s 20g^{5} 21m 16s 16f^{6} 16d^{5} 20m] small, workmanlike mare: novice selling hurdler: should stay beyond 2m: probably acts on any going. *K. White.* 66

LEGAL SUGAR 12 b.g. Legal Eagle–Sugar Sugar (Midsummer Night II) [1989/90 c17h^{3} c16h^{su} c20m^{F}] leggy gelding: winning selling chaser: no worthwhile form for a long time: stays 2½m: acts on soft going and good to firm. *P. J. Jones.* c— —

LEGAL TINA 5 ch.m. Ballacashtal (CAN)–Pitapat (Shantung) [1989/90 16f^{4} 18g^{3} 16m^{4} 19g^{pu} 16s^{F} 16v^{3} 16m] leggy mare: half-sister to fair hurdlers Pat 89 p

Wollow (by Wollow) and Casual Pass (by Formidable): plating-class maiden on
Flat: poor form over hurdles, shaping well, given lot to do by 7-lb claimer,
penultimate outing: likely to prove best at 2m: acts on good to firm and heavy
going: gives impression capable of better. *S. Dow.*

LE GRAND MAITRE 9 ch.g. Over The River (FR)–Cora Swan (Tarqogan) c**101** ?
[1989/90 c26m* c26g* c20f^{F} c24f^{pu} c26g c26d^{pu}] sturdy, dipped-backed gelding: —
handicap chaser: successful at Stratford (sweating) and Uttoxeter early in season:
ran poorly last 3 starts: stays well: probably acts on any ground: claimer ridden. *G.
Roe.*

LEG UP 11 ch.g. Quality Fair–Early Echo (Bleep) [1989/90 c26v^{pu} c17v a24g c—
c26d^{pu}] angular, rather plain gelding: winning chaser and novice hurdler: well —
beaten in 1989/90, including in a seller: suited by a test of stamina: acts on firm
and dead going. *Mrs J. Wonnacott.*

LEIA MECENE (FR) 4 b.g. Gay Mecene (USA)–Dekeleia (Exbury) [1989/90
16g a16g a16g^{2} a16g^{3} a16g^{pu}] small, sparely-made gelding: half-brother to a 72
winning French jumper: well beaten on Flat in 1989: second in selling hurdle at
Lingfield in January: no worthwhile form in non-sellers otherwise: trained first
start by Miss P. O'Connor. *J. P. D. Elliott.*

LEIGH BOY (USA) 4 b.g. Bates Motel (USA)–Afasheen (Sheshoon) [1989/90
16d* 16s* 16g* 16d^{pu} 16d^{5}] compact gelding: winning middle-distance stayer on 107
Flat: sold out of R. J. R. Williams' stable 22,000 gns Newmarket Autumn Sales:
successful in juvenile hurdle at Hexham in December and in novice events at Ayr
and Newcastle following month: ran moderately last start: likely to need testing
conditions to be seen to best advantage at 2m, and will be well suited by 2½m. *G.
M. Moore.*

LEISURETIME SMILE 9 b.g. Arapaho–Darling Smile (Star Signal) c—
[1989/90 20g^{6}] lengthy, good-quartered, dipped-backed gelding: novice hurdler/ —
winning chaser: well beaten in seller in November: form only at around 2m: best
form on top-of-the-ground: headstrong and tends to sweat up: usually ridden by
claimer: sold 400 gns Ascot December Sales. *N. Bradley.*

LEMHILL 8 b.g. He Loves Me–Moonscape (Ribero) [1989/90 17f*] compact
gelding: has shown plenty of ability over hurdles, notably when third behind 104 +
Grabel in Sean P Graham Memorial Hurdle at Leopardstown in 1988/9 (trained in
Ireland by K. Connolly): long odds on, 20-length winner of novice hurdle at
Newton Abbot in August: not seen out again: likely to stay beyond 2m: acts on soft
going: has broken blood vessels. *M. C. Pipe.*

LEMON BALM 4 b.f. High Top–Applemint (USA) (Sir Ivor) [1989/90 16s^{F}
a16g^{4} a18g] sparely-made filly: soundly beaten on Flat: fourth in novice hurdle at 77
Southwell in February. *J. C. McConnochie.*

L'ENCHERE 5 b.m. Lafontaine (USA)–Lady Bidder (Auction Ring (USA)) c—
[1989/90 18f^{3} 16f^{2} 16g 16g^{3} 16m^{3} 16m* 16g* 16s^{5} c16g^{5} c16g^{pu} a16g] selling 76
hurdler: attracted no bid after winning handicaps at Warwick in November and
Plumpton (conditional jockeys) in December: remote fifth in novice event at
Windsor in January on chasing debut: suited by a sharp 2m and sound surface:
ridden by claimer or amateur: takes a good hold and has worn a crossed noseband.
G. G. Gracey.

LENDING HAND 5 gr.g. Tina's Pet–Spanish Chestnut (Philip of Spain)
[1989/90 a16g a16g^{4} 17m^{4} 16m^{3} 16m^{2} 16f^{4}] leggy gelding: novice selling hurdler: 78
races only at around 2m: best form on top-of-the-ground: has run creditably for a
claimer. *J. Joseph.*

LENINGRAD (USA) 6 ch.g. Nureyev (USA)–Diorama (USA) (Secretariat c—
(USA)) [1989/90 c17d^{pu} c20f c24f^{co} c25m^{pu} c20g^{3}] workmanlike ex-French —
gelding: half-brother to a winner in USA: lightly raced and no form on Flat: placed
once from 3 starts over hurdles in France: won a point-to-point in Britain in 1989:
no sign of ability in steeplechases. *P. R. Rodford.*

LEON 8 gr.g. Niniski (USA)–Lorelene (FR) (Lorenzaccio) [1989/90 c16f* c16f^{F} c**96**
c24m* 19f^{2} c24m^{ur} 20f^{2} 20m^{4} a20g 22d^{pu} a18g^{2} 16m^{3} c24f^{2} 20m 24g^{5} c26m^{2}] 92
smallish, sparely-made gelding: winning hurdler: successful in poor novice
chases at Market Rasen and Perth (jumped moderately) in August: second in
claiming chase at Uttoxeter final outing: stays 3¼m: ran poorly on very soft going,
probably acts on any other: blinkered last 2 outings of 1988/9 and seventh start:
has raced with tongue tied down: sold out of N. Tinkler's stable 7,000 gns
Doncaster September Sales after seventh start. *W. Clay.*

LE PICCOLAGE 6 b.g. The Parson–Daithis Coleen (Carnival Night) [1989/90 16g 16d4 21d5] rangy, rather unfurnished gelding: has scope and will make a chaser: third foal: dam never ran: modest form in novice hurdles: will be suited by a good test of stamina. *N. J. Henderson.* 93

LEPUS 7 b.g. French Vine–Spectra (Mandamus) [1989/90 c17f4 c21f6 17h3 c21f4 c19m2 c17m5 c26f] smallish, workmanlike gelding: poor novice hurdler: won a point-to-point in 1989: poor form in steeplechases, including in a selling handicap. *W. G. Turner.* c70 —

LE RELISH 5 ch.g. Relkino–Light And Shade (High Line) [1989/90 F16g 22gpu] smallish, angular gelding: first foal: dam 1¾m winner: behind in NH Flat race and pulled up in a novice hurdle: dead. *K. Bishop.* —

LE ROUGE 10 ch.g. Crespin Rouge–Fair Pandora (Quality Fair) [1989/90 c21m] poor maiden point-to-pointer/novice hunter chaser. *N. J. Pomfret.* c—

LESBET 5 b.m. Hotfoot–Remeta (Reform) [1989/90 17hF 26f3 24m5 22gpu 28g2 24g4 a22g* 27s6 a24g* a24g4 a24g2 a24g* a20g5 24m6] small, workmanlike mare: handicap hurdler: won at Lingfield in December, January and February: ran creditably, stiffish task, final outing: suited by a test of stamina: acts on any going: usually ridden by claimer or an amateur. *C. P. Wildman.* 98

LESCYN 5 ch.m. Wolverlife–Nature's Way (Zamindar) [1989/90 16d 16gF] sparely-made, angular mare: poor maiden on Flat, stays 1m: jumped poorly when well beaten in novice selling hurdle at Stratford in November: sold 850 gns Ascot December Sales. *J. A. C. Edwards.* —

LES PARVENUS 6 b.g. Smartset–Entry Hill (Menelek) [1989/90 c20d2 c32fF] smallish Irish gelding: second foal: half-brother to winning Irish jumper Corpse Reviver (by Quayside): dam unraced half-sister to West Tip: no form over hurdles: won a point-to-point in February: second in maiden hunter chase at Fairyhouse following month: behind when falling 3 out in National Hunt Chase Challenge Cup at Cheltenham: should stay well: sold 25,000 gns Doncaster Spring Sales. *M. A. O'Toole, Ireland.* c79 + —

LETHAL WEAPON 6 b.g. Prominer–Hammer And Tongs (Politico (USA)) [1989/90 c25fpu] first foal: dam winning point-to-pointer in Ireland: placed in point-to-points: tailed off when pulled up in maiden hunter chase at Cartmel in May. *W. A. Stephenson.* c—

LET ME THINK 6 b.g. Pollerton–Miss Cathy (Tobrouk (FR)) [1989/90 16spu a16g 20g 21f5] smallish, rather sparely-made gelding: showed ability in novice hurdles in 1988/9: well beaten in 1989/90: should stay well. *L. C. Corbett.* —

LETRIC 9 ch.g. King Sitric–Scarlet Letch (New Brig) [1989/90 c24dF] strong gelding: behind in NH Flat race and novice hurdle: suffered a fatal fall in novice chase in February. *R. Brewis.* c— —

LETS GO ALLEGRO 5 b.m. Le Johnstan–Fanny Keyser (Majority Blue) [1989/90 17f4 16hF] sparely-made mare: moderate jumper and no form over hurdles. *D. Holly.* — x

LET'S MOVE 4 ch.f. Move Off–Let's Dance (Mansingh (USA)) [1989/90 17h2] leggy filly: no sign of ability on Flat: easily beaten by sole opponent Builders Gold in juvenile hurdle at Carlisle in October. *Mrs G. R. Reveley.* ?

LETTEREWE 4 b.f. Alias Smith (USA)–Princess Nefertiti (Tutankhamen) [1989/90 16f* 16mur] angular, sparely-made filly: half-sister to several winners on Flat, including Any Business (by Music Maestro), also successful over hurdles: lightly-raced maiden on Flat: won juvenile hurdle at Leicester in November, leading from fifth and soon clear: had just been headed but still travelling well when unseating rider fifth on same course following month: likely to stay 2½m. *G. A. Pritchard-Gordon.* 96

LEVANTINE ROSE 10 br.m. Levanter–Gambling Rose (Game Rights) [1989/90 24m6 25d* 20g6 c20f5 c26fpu] smallish, workmanlike mare: handicap hurdler/novice chaser: only form for some time when winning selling hurdle at Hereford (no bid) in November: stays 25f: acts on firm and dead ground. *M. C. Pipe.* c— 93

LEVISHAM 5 ch.r. Valiyar–Bridestones (Jan Ekels) [1989/90 20f3 24f6 20g] poor novice selling hurdler: stayed 2½m: seemed to act on any going: sold out of Mrs D. Haine's stable 1,550 gns Ascot September Sales: resold 800 gns Ascot November Sales: dead. *R. D. E. Woodhouse.* 84 d

LEVY FREE 5 ch.g. Kinglet–Metaxa (Khalkis) [1989/90 F17m3 F16f2] brother to winning hurdler Cheerful Days and half-brother to winning jumpers Met

William Hill Handicap Hurdle, Sandown—
Liadett (No. 5) keeps on too well for Protection (far side) and Afaristoun

Officer (by Sunyboy) and Blue Rainbow (by Balinger): dam half-sister to very smart hunter chaser False Note and fair staying chaser Napoleon Brandy: placed in NH Flat races in April: switched in closing stages when short-head second to Kate O'Kirkham at Hexham: yet to race over hurdles or fences. *Mrs G. R. Reveley.*

LEXDEN 4 b.c. Blakeney–Annabella (Habitat) [1989/90 16g^6 16s^2 16v^3 16d^6]
small, sturdy colt: fair middle-distance maiden on Flat: sold out of G. Wragg's 91
stable 13,000 gns Newmarket Autumn Sales: placed in juvenile hurdles at Warwick and Leicester in February: jumped with little confidence final start. *W. M. Perrin.*

LEY LINE 6 ch.m. Lighter–Hyaline (High Line) [1989/90 F16f F12g] sparely-made mare: has shown a little ability in NH Flat races: yet to race over hurdles or fences. *Dr J. F. Robinson.*

L FOREVER 7 ch.g. Laurence O–Immortal Queen (Immortality) [1989/90
22g] close-coupled, good-topped gelding: behind in NH Flat races in 1988/9 and a —
novice hurdle in January (bit backward). *Mrs S. Richardson.*

LIADETT (USA) 5 b.g. Lydian (FR)–Provincia (CHI) (Balconaje (ARG))
[1989/90 16d^2 16g^4 16m* 20v^5 22s 16f 16f^5] leggy, sparely-made gelding: fairly 134
useful hurdler: won William Hill Handicap Hurdle at Sandown in December gamely by ¾ length from Protection: ran moderately next time and poorly last 3 starts: should stay beyond 2¼m: acts on any going: usually a front runner: jumps none too fluently. *M. C. Pipe.*

LIANE BEAUTY 4 b.f. Castle Keep–Princess Fair (Crowned Prince (USA))
[1989/90 17f^F] poor plater at up to 1m on Flat: beaten when falling 2 out in juvenile —
hurdle at Newton Abbot in September. *Mrs S. Armytage.*

LIBERTY SQUARE 9 ch.g. Al Sirat (USA)–Tide Gate (Dike (USA)) [1989/90 c—
c26f^3] close-coupled gelding: winning 2m hurdler: modest point-to-pointer, —
winner in April: remote third of 4 in hunter chase at Folkestone in May: acts on heavy going: ran out final start 1985/6, blinkered second outing. *Dr D. B. A. Silk.*

LIBILLARY (USA) 7 b.g. Liloy (FR)–Nobiliary (USA) (Vaguely Noble) c—
[1989/90 16m 16m 16s c20d^{pu} c20s^{pu} c18s^{pu}] lengthy gelding: poor novice —
hurdler: of little account over fences: sold 1,550 gns Ascot June Sales. *N. R. Mitchell.*

LICKY BEG 10 b.g. Flower Robe–Laurentum Rose (Golden Years) [1989/90 c—
c24f^{ur}] point-to-pointer, winner in March: unseated rider fourth in maiden hunter chase at Hexham following month. *Mrs S. Fenwick.*

LIE IN WAIT 7 ch.h. Mill Reef (USA)–Pitiless Panther (No Mercy) [1989/90 17f2 16f] medium-sized horse: good second in novice hurdle in 1988/9 (ran poorly in blinkers final start): well below that form, jumping poorly, in 1989/90, blinkered on second occasion. *P. D. Connors.* 83 x

LIEUTENANT GENERAL 4 gr.g. Sandhurst Prince–Miscellaneous (Lord Gayle (USA)) [1989/90 16f4 16d4 16m5 16fpu] sparely-made gelding: maiden plater on Flat and over hurdles: sold out of C. Thornton's stable 1,500 gns Doncaster August Sales after first start: dead. *S. B. Avery.* 73

LIFE PEERAGE (USA) 5 b.g. Roberto (USA)–Countess Tully (Hotfoot) [1989/90 16f2 16m3 16d2] workmanlike gelding: maiden on Flat (has broken blood vessels): in frame all 5 outings over hurdles, on last occasion going down by ½ length to Feasible in novice handicap at Market Rasen in August: won a point-to-point in March. *J. Mackie.* 94

LIFE'S A LARK 5 ch.g. Wolverlife–Red Lark (Larkspur) [1989/90 16f3 20f2 20g3] workmanlike gelding: handicap hurdler: not seen out after running moderately in November: stays 2½m: acts on firm going. *T. D. Barron.* 86

LIGHT BIDDER 5 b.m. Auction Ring (USA)–Foudre (Petingo) [1989/90 F12m5 F16f] fourth living foal: half-sister to temperamental Light Thatch (by Thatch): dam won over 1¼m: behind in NH Flat races in October: yet to race over hurdles or fences. *L. J. Codd.*

LIGHT DANCER 4 ch.g. Niniski (USA)–Foudre (Petingo) [1989/90 16d6 16mpu] leggy, angular gelding: no worthwhile form on Flat: well-beaten sixth in juvenile hurdle at Market Rasen in March, jumping none too fluently. *L. J. Codd.* —

LIGHT DEMON 13 br.g. Lucifer (USA)–Menloe (Charlottesville) [1989/90 c22m] big gelding: winning point-to-pointer/hunter chaser: always behind in Seagram Fox Hunters' Chase at Liverpool in April: stays 3m: acts on soft going: has worn blinkers. *C. Holmes.* c—

LIGHTFALL (USA) 6 b.g. Forli (ARG)–Flood Light (USA) (Bold Lad (USA)) [1989/90 22g 16s4 c16v4 c16g4] workmanlike gelding: poor novice hurdler: no worthwhile form in novice chases: stays 2½m. *R. Allan.* c— 73

LIGHT GENERAL 6 ch.g. Lighter–Spartan Anna (Spartan General) [1989/90 F16f c21s5 c25sur c25f4] leggy gelding: third foal: dam won a point-to-point: behind in NH Flat race at Newbury when trained by B. Forsey: fifth of 8 finishers in hunter chase at Towcester in February, jumping moderately: tailed off final start. *Mrs S. Kavanagh.* c75

LIGHTNING WIND 7 b.g. Windjammer (USA)–Grace Note (Parthia) [1989/90 16g6 16m2 16m* 16g5 16m] lengthy, rather sparely-made gelding: handicap hurdler: won at Huntingdon in December: below that form afterwards: keen type, races only at around 2m: acts on firm going and possibly unsuited by a soft surface: has won when sweating: reluctant to race first outing 1988/9. *N. A. Gaselee.* 103

LIGHT TRAVELLER 10 gr. or ro.g. Roan Rocket–Balidium (Psidium) [1989/90 c17f* c16g4] sturdy, workmanlike gelding: carries plenty of condition: poor hurdler: won novice chase at Kelso in October by 20 lengths (task made easier when challenging Kamsel fell at the last): ran lack-lustre race following month and not seen out again: stays 3m: acts on any going: sometimes amateur ridden, including when successful. *R. E. Barr.* c86 —

LIGHTWATER AGAIN 8 ch.g. Celtic Cone–Charmer's Girl (Pappatea) [1989/90 c20gpu c16s2 c20d5 c20dF c25g c20d3 c16mF c16fF c16mur 16gpu c16g6] strong, lengthy gelding: carries condition: winning hurdler and novice chaser: stays 2½m: acts on heavy going. *C. R. Beever.* c88 ? —

LIHAR 4 ch.g. Lomond (USA)–Mpani (Habitat) [1989/90 17gpu 16dpu a22g5 17d 16f3 16f 18m 16m 20g4] strong, angular gelding: maiden on Flat: sold out of G. Wragg's stable 3,400 gns Newmarket Autumn Sales: selling hurdler: stays 2½m: acted on firm ground: often blinkered: dead. *R. W. Dods.* 78

LIKEABLE LADY 6 gr.m. Piaffer (USA)–Lady Andrea (Andrea Mantegna) [1989/90 16m a18gpu] smallish, close-coupled mare: lightly-raced novice hurdler (has been beaten in a seller): blinkered, pulled up and dismounted at Lingfield in December. *Miss P. O'Connor.* —

LILAC TIME 4 b.f. Town And Country–Harp Strings (FR) (Luthier) [1989/90 16m3 16f4 19s5 a18g2 16d a20g5 a16g2 a16g 16f3] sparely-made filly: inconsistent juvenile hurdler: fair third in seller final start: best form at 2m: acts on firm ground. *R. Hollinshead.* 75

LIMAVADY 11 b. or br.g. Quayside–Tender Eyes (Raise You Ten) [1989/90 c24s^pu c20m^pu] stocky gelding: winning chaser: often let down by his jumping: stays 25f: probably acts on any going: looks a difficult ride. *Mrs E. H. Heath.* c— x —

LINDANJAN 6 b.m. Radetzk -Cherio Honey (Macherio) [1989/90 17g 25d^pu] sparely-made mare: of little acco. *N. Kernick.* —

LINDEAN PERIL 5 b.g. Mljet–ı ılly Peril (Politico (USA)) [1989/90 16m^2 16f^su 16g^4 16f^pu] non-thoroughbred gelding: second foal: dam unraced: poor novice hurdler: trained until after third outing by W. Fairgrieve. *D. McCaskill.* 70

LINDEN BRIG 8 br.m. New Brig–Velvet Cap II (Moyrath Jet) [1989/90 c24d^pu c24g^pu c24v^4 c28d^6 c32g^pu] neat mare: placed in point-to-points in 1988: well beaten in steeplechases. *B. McLean.* c—

LINDSEY DOYLE 4 ch.f. Stanford–Sans Blague (Above Suspicion) [1989/90 16d^5 16g^4] lengthy, workmanlike filly: maiden plater at 2 yrs, best effort over 1m: showed ability in novice claiming hurdle at Sedgefield in December and juvenile seller at Catterick in January: claimer ridden. *Mrs S. A. Ward.* 67

LINEBACKER 6 b.g. High Line–Gay Trinket (Grey Sovereign) [1989/90 16f 17f 17m^6 16g^6 16g] sturdy gelding: 1¾m winner on Flat: poor novice hurdler: well beaten in seller last start: subsequently sold 1,400 gns Doncaster October Sales: resold 1,250 gns Ascot February Sales: placed in point-to-points. *M. C. Chapman.* —

LINE OF GOLD (USA) 8 ch.g. Main Reef–Princess Parthia (Parthia) [1989/90 c21f^3 24m^6 c21f^4] good-bodied gelding: winning hurdler/chaser: in frame in small fields at Newton Abbot in July and August: stays 3m: acts on any going. *C. Weedon.* **c105** —

LINGHAM BRIDE 8 b.m. Deep Run–Bride View (Chinatown) [1989/90 c20f^2 c24f^2 c16f^4 c27g* c27g^F2 c20g^3 c27d^3 c27s^3 c28g^3 16g c24f* 24f^3 c27f^3] small, lightly-made mare: handicap hurdler: creditable third at Wetherby in April: won handicap chases at Sedgefield (third course win) in November and Hexham in March: stays well: acts on any going: usually amateur or claimer ridden: genuine. *J. E. Swiers.* **c96** 96

LINGHAM DUKE 9 ch.g. Duc d'Orleans–Soya (Silnet) [1989/90 c20g^ur c16g^6 c16d^3 c16g^F c16m c16s^ur c24g^ur c16d^6 c20g^3 c16g c16d^ur c24s c16d^4 c16g^co c16f^4 c16f^4 c16m^6 c16f* c16m^F c20f^2 c16f^2] big, angular gelding: well beaten over hurdles: won by 8 lengths from only other finisher Peacework in novice handicap chase at Sedgefield in May: stays 2½m: acts on firm going: sometimes jumps none too fluently: usually amateur or claimer ridden nowadays. *J. E. Swiers.* **c83** —

LINGHAM MAGIC 5 b. or br.m. Current Magic–Old Mill Lady (Royal Goblin) [1989/90 20g^pu 16d^pu 16d 16f^3 16f^3 16f^4] smallish, workmanlike mare: poor novice hurdler: amateur ridden. *J. E. Swiers.* 62

LINKSIDE 5 b.g. Good Thyne (USA)–Laurel Wood (Laurence O) [1989/90 F16g^4] second foal: dam never ran: around 9 lengths fourth of 17 to Storm Island in NH Flat race at Perth in May: yet to race over hurdles or fences. *M. O'Neill.*

LINLITHGOW PALACE 8 ch.g. Royal Palace–Moonbreaker (Twilight Alley) [1989/90 c21d^pu c20g^4 c16d^4 c20f^3] leggy, workmanlike non-thoroughbred gelding: no sign of ability. *A. M. Crow.* c— —

LINN FALLS 5 br.m. Royal Fountain–Border Gloria (Border Chief) [1989/90 F17d^3 F16g 20g] half-sister to successful staying jumpers Pitcruivie (by Saucy Kit) and Border Spark (by Lighter): dam, quite a modest chaser, stayed 3m: third in NH Flat race at Carlisle in March: claimer ridden, held up and always behind in novice hurdle at Perth following month. *G. Richards.* —

LINPAC WEST 4 b.c. Posse (USA)–North Page (FR) (Northfields (USA)) [1989/90 16g^F] leggy, sparely-made colt: useful winner at up to 10.6f on Flat (well suited by the mud): favourite, close second when edging left and falling last in juvenile hurdle won by Rustino at Wetherby in December: sure to win a race over hurdles. *C. W. C. Elsey.* 94 p

LIONOR 7 ch.g. Billion (USA)–Hazor (Joshua) [1989/90 21f^pu] behind in NH Flat race in Ireland in 1987: placed in point-to-points in 1990: tailed off when pulled up 2 out in novice hurdle at Newton Abbot in May. *Mrs J. Wonnacott.* —

LIOSEAN 4 gr.g. Silly Prices–Manche (Palestine) [1989/90 F12g F14v] brother to fair sprinter Not So Silly: dam second in three 5f races at 2 yrs: weakened some way out when behind in NH Flat races: yet to race over hurdles. *N. Chamberlain.*

LIRCHUR 4 b.f. Lir–Amberush (No Rush) [1989/90 16f2 18f* 16f6 18f3 18f2 a16g 16s4 20g4] sparely-made filly: first reported foal: dam winning hurdler: maiden plater on Flat: won juvenile claiming hurdle at Fontwell in September: in frame in selling company afterwards: stays 2¼m (soundly beaten over 2½m): seems to act on any going. *A. Moore.* 74

LISAHANE LAD 4 b.g. Daring March–Puff Pastry (Reform) [1989/90 F16m 21fpu] second foal: dam, 2-y-o 5f winner, stayed 1½m at 3 yrs: well beaten in NH Flat race in March: soon tailed off and pulled up 2 out in novice hurdle following month. *N. A. Smith.* —

LISALEEN LADY 5 b.m. Miner's Lamp–Chestnut Fire (Deep Run) [1989/90 18d 16g5 16m2 22g 16s4] smallish, well-made mare: produced a foal in 1988: won point-to-point and NH Flat race in 1988/9: in frame in novice hurdles at Wincanton in December and Towcester in February: should be suited by further than 2m. *D. Nicholson.* 89

LISARDA 11 b.g. Moulton–Alisarda (Aureole) [1989/90 c19m6 c25f2] close-coupled, good-topped gelding: winning hurdler/point-to-pointer: 15 lengths second to Park Shade in hunter chase at Cheltenham in May (finished lame): probably acts on any going: has worn blinkers: trained first start by Mrs S. Pearson. *A. R. Porter.* c69 + —

LISFENNELL 8 ch.g. Deep Run–Inneen Alainn (Prince Hansel) [1989/90 16d 16g 16f] strong gelding: novice hurdler/chaser: very headstrong and one to leave alone: has been tried in blinkers: sold 1,400 gns Doncaster Spring Sales. *P. A. Blockley.* c— § — §

LISGAYLE 7 br.m. Midland Gayle–Lis Ghorran (Anthony) [1989/90 16gpu 16gpu 16mF 17g 16gpu] lightly-made mare: of little account: blinkered last start: sold 900 gns Doncaster March Sales. *R. E. Barr.* —

LISLARY LAD 10 br.g. Gala Performance (USA)–Lady Manta (Bargello) [1989/90 c26f2 c25m3 c26m3 c25g2 c20fF c20dur c21m2 c20d* c25mur c26h2] close-coupled gelding: winning point-to-pointer: won amateur riders handicap chase at Chepstow in March: stays 3m: acts on any going: blinkered last 3 starts over hurdles: tends to make mistakes over fences: trained until after fifth start by M. Bradley. *J. D. Roberts.* c109 —

LISSAHANE LASS 4 b. or br.f. Daring March–The Suestan (Ballyciptic) [1989/90 16f2 16s2 16g* 16d* 16mpu] sparely-made filly: has shown signs of ability on Flat: won 2 novice hurdles at Leicester in January in good style: subsequently off course 10 weeks and was always behind and pulled up in Glenlivet Anniversary Hurdle at Liverpool on her return. *P. R. Hedger.* 107

LITTLE BAVARD 10 ch.g. Le Bavard (FR)–Kathleen Beag (Vulgan) [1989/90 c26mpu] winning point-to-pointer: lightly raced and no form recently: should stay 3m: acts on soft going. *Mrs Andrea Fisher.* c— —

LITTLE BIGHORN 5 b.h. Blakeney–Nip In The Air (USA) (Northern Dancer) [1989/90 16g3 16g2 16d* 16m* 16g6] quite useful at around 1¼m on Flat: won maiden hurdle at Navan and Jameson Gold Cup Hurdle at Fairyhouse in April, latter by 6 lengths from North To Alaska: reportedly broke blood vessel final start (wore blinkers): best run on good to firm ground. *N. Meade, Ireland.* 131

LITTLE CAMDORE 5 ch.m. Cruise Missile–Paddy's Daughter (St Paddy) [1989/90 aF13g6] fourth reported foal: half-sister to winning selling hurdler Camdore Boy (by Anax): dam of little account: sixth of 8 in NH Flat race at Lingfield in March: yet to race over hurdles or fences. *J. M. Bradley.*

LITTLE CHANTER 5 b.m. Welsh Chanter–Armandia (Alcide) [1989/90 16f 16g] winning selling hurdler: well beaten in non-selling handicaps in July and October: acts well on soft going. *J. R. Bostock.* —

LITTLEDALE (USA) 4 b.c. Lypheor–Smeralda (Grey Sovereign) [1989/90 16g] leggy, sparely-made colt: half-brother to fairly useful hurdler Jorge Miguel (by Welsh Pageant) and winning Irish hurdler Battle Hero (by Miami Springs): placed at around 1m on Flat: sold out of L. Cumani's stable 15,000 gns Newmarket Autumn Sales: well beaten in juvenile maiden hurdle at Wincanton in February. *D. J. G. Murray-Smith.* —

LITTLE DICKENS 8 b.g. Great Expectations (USA)–Welsh Spear (Welsh Saint) [1989/90 c20f3 c18gpu] lengthy gelding: of little account. *E. L. Beever.* c— —

LITTLE GENERAL 7 ch.g. General Ironside–Coolentallagh (Perhapsburg) [1989/90 c18g5 c26vpu c25spu c25m5 c26f2 c24f c25m* c24g c26f*] stocky, c92

compact gelding: won novice chases at Plumpton in April and Uttoxeter (by 25
lengths) in May: stiff task in between: stays well: acts on firm going: trained until
after reappearance by G. Gregson. *C. Weedon.*

LITTLEGO 5 b.g. Croghan Hill–Iamstopped (Furry Glen) [1989/90 16d^2 16s^2
16s^4 a18g^2 16m* 19f^2 16f^2 16f^2] leggy ex-Irish gelding: second foal: half-brother to 92
winning 2m hurdler Murphy (by Touch Paper) and winning 2¼m selling hurdler
Waverley Girl (by Seymour Hicks): dam placed at up to 1m in Ireland: second over
1½m on Flat in 1989: won novice handicap hurdle at Plumpton in April: ran well
last 2 starts: best form at 2m: acts on any going: blinkered final outing: has found
little: trained until after first start by P. Griffin. *J. R. Jenkins.*

LITTLEGOOD GAMBLER 7 ch.g. Doctor Wall–Littlegood Lass (Ron) c—
[1989/90 20g^6 20g 22d c20v c16d^5] lengthy gelding: well beaten in novice hurdles —
and novice chases: races freely: blinkered last 2 outings. *T. R. Greathead.*

LITTLE GOOSE GIRL 4 ch.f. Alias Smith (USA)–Mother Goose (Absalom)
[1989/90 a16g 16v 16v] no sign of ability on Flat and in selling hurdles. *C. P.* —
Wildman.

LITTLE GUY 4 b.g. Regular Guy–Little White Dove (Lucky Guy) [1989/90
F16v^{pu} 16d^6 17f] small gelding: first reported foal: dam won 6f seller at 2 yrs: 69
pulled up in NH Flat race at Navan in February: amateur ridden, never-dangerous
sixth in juvenile maiden hurdle at Perth in May: well beaten in seller later in
month. *J. Parkes.*

LITTLE HANNAH 7 b.m. Chantro–Hannah's Song (Saintly Song) [1989/90
16d^{pu} 16g 16d^{pu}] compact mare: seems of little account: has been blinkered. *W. J.* —
Smith.

LITTLE HORMEAD 5 b.m. Cruise Missile–Ballygoman (Little Buskins) c—
[1989/90 16d^{pu} c20m^{pu}] compact mare: well behind in NH Flat race in 1988/9: —
pulled up in novice hurdle and a novice chase. *M. A. Johnson.*

LITTLE KATRINA 9 b.m. Little Buskins–Bowess (Bowsprit) [1989/90 c—
c20m^{pu}] strong mare: winning hurdler/chaser: very lightly raced and no worth- —
while form for a long time: stays 3m: acts on any going. *W. T. Kemp.*

LITTLE KEV 6 b.g. Frimley Park–Brandenbourg (Le Levanstell) [1989/90 c—
c17m c26f^6] workmanlike gelding: novice hurdler/chaser: no worthwhile form. *D.* —
H. Barons.

LITTLE KHAN 11 b.m. Maystreak–Escargot (Escart III) [1989/90 20m^{pu}]
lightly-made, shallow-girthed mare: poor novice hurdler: lightly raced and no —
form recently. *Mrs S. M. Johnson.*

LITTLE LONDON 11 br.g. Pieces of Eight–Whistler's Princess (King c83
Emperor (USA)) [1989/90 24m 24f^4 21f^5 c25f^3 c25m^4 c24m 24f 25f^5] small, —
lengthy gelding: handicap hurdler (no worthwhile form in 1989/90): poor chaser:
stays 25f: acts on any going: usually blinkered. *T. Morton.*

LITTLE MAN 6 br.g. Mandalus–Time Ago (Bargello) [1989/90 16g 17v c16g^{ur} c—
a20g] neat ex-Irish gelding: fourth foal: dam unraced: no form over hurdles: —
jumped none too fluently and unseated rider sixth in novice chase at Wolverhampton in January: tends to sweat. *R. G. Frost.*

LITTLE MYND 11 b.m. Space King–Lady Mynd (Straight Deal) [1989/90 c83
c22d^5 c16v^3 c24v^{pu} c20g^6 c20v] smallish, workmanlike mare: winning hurdler: —
novice chaser: stayed on when third in mares event at Chepstow in January:
appears not to stay beyond 2¾m: blinkered fourth outing. *R. Lee.*

LITTLE-NIPPER 5 ch.g. Derrylin–Emily Kent (Royal Palace) [1989/90 F16g
16g 20s 20g^6 16d*] rangy gelding: has scope: won novice handicap hurdle at 91 p
Cheltenham in January by 5 lengths from Los Buccaneros (ridden approaching 2
out, stayed on to lead flat): prominent long way over 2½m in better company
previous start: acts on dead going. *D. Nicholson.*

LITTLE POLVEIR 13 b.g. Cantab–Blue Speedwell (Escart III) [1989/90 c—
c28g^5 c24g^5 c30s c29g^{pu}] strong, lengthy gelding: useful chaser at his best: won —
1989 Seagram Grand National: well beaten all completed outings in 1989/90: very
well suited by a thorough test of stamina: best on an easy surface: suited by
forcing tactics and strong handling: wore blinkers eighth start 1988/9: has been
retired. *G. B. Balding.*

LITTLE RED FLOWER 4 b.f. Blakeney–Roda Haxan (Huntercombe)
[1989/90 16v^{pu} 16f^5 16f^5 16g^2 16m 16f^2] small, workmanlike filly: behind both 72
outings on Flat in Britain at 3 yrs: sold out of J. Dunlop's stable 1,150 gns

Newmarket July Sales: showed nothing in 2 starts in Ireland when trained by M. McCausland: resold 950 gns Doncaster October Sales: runner-up in selling hurdles at Stratford in April and Hereford following month: acts on firm going. *F. Jordan.*

LITTLE SAIL 4 ch.f. Little Wolf–Sarasail (Hitting Away) [1989/90 F13f* F16f* F16f] half-sister to numerous winners, majority over jumps, including smart chaser Sea Merchant (by Idiot's Delight): dam, maiden, best at 1m: won NH Flat races at Hereford and Ludlow in April: eighth of 21 in similar event at Warwick following month: yet to race over hurdles. *R. J. Holder.*

LITTLE TOM 5 b.g. Nearly A Hand–Lost In Silence (Silent Spring) [1989/90
16g 16v^{ur} 16g^5 20g^5] useful-looking gelding: has scope: sixth living foal: brother 79
to winning jumpers Silent Surrender and Tom Caxton and half-brother to winning jumper Silent Twirl (by Piaffer): dam never ran: poor novice hurdler: best form at 2m. *J. S. King.*

LITTLE TORO 8 b.g. Torus–Little Echo (Little Buskins) [1989/90 16g 16g c—
18m^6 20d 18g c20s^6 20v^3 20s^5 16s 16g 21m^3 20m^2 20f^2 20m^5] leggy, 111 §
sparely-made gelding: modest and inconsistent hurdler: runner-up in claimer at Chepstow and handicap at Cheltenham in April: tailed off in novice event on chasing debut: stays 2¾m: seems to act on any going: has worn blinkers but is usually visored nowadays: has run well for a claimer: took little interest second start and has run in snatches. *G. B. Balding.*

LITTLE TUGBOAT 6 br.m. Duky–Loobagh Bridge (River Beauty) [1989/90
F16g 21f^6 20m^{pu}] IR 2,200 4-y-o: lengthy mare: first foal: dam poor maiden —
hurdler: no sign of ability in novice hurdles in December and March. *N. A. Smith.*

LIVE IN HOPE 8 b.g. Condorcet (FR)–Hopefull Polly (Polyfoto) [1989/90
16h^4 16m^2 16f* a20g^{pu} 19f*] sparely-made gelding: lightly-raced hurdler: won in 107
small fields in handicaps at Wincanton in April and Hereford following month: stays 2½m: acts on firm and good to soft ground. *D. J. G. Murray-Smith.*

LIVERTON LAD 6 ch.g. Palm Track–Persian Silver (Cash And Courage)
[1989/90 18d^{pu}] sixth in 2 NH Flat races in 1988/9: pulled up last in novice hurdle —
at Worcester in November: dead. *Mrs A. R. Hewitt.*

LIVING FIRE 11 b.g. Le Bavard (FR)–Lovely Pine (Woodville II) [1989/90 c85
c20m^2 c20g^2 c20g^3 c20f^{ur}] leggy, sparely-made gelding: won novice hurdle and —
novice chase in 1985/6: successful in point-to-points since: placed in handicap chases in November: should be suited by further than 2½m: acts on soft going and good to firm. *G. M. Moore.*

LIZAWAY 6 ch.m. Casino Boy–Mahogany Lady (Renwood) [1989/90 22s^{pu}]
non-thoroughbred mare: tailed off in NH Flat race in 1988/9: tailed off when pulled —
up eighth in novice hurdle at Folkestone in December. *Miss B. Sanders.*

LIZZIES LASS 5 br.m. Sandalay–Kiltegan (Charlottesvilles Flyer) [1989/90
22g 21f^5 20m] plain mare: behind in NH Flat race and novice hurdles. *F. Gray.* —

LIZZY LONGSTOCKING 8 br.m. Jimsun–Darling Emma (Dairialatan)
[1989/90 16f* 16m^3 17d^4 16f^2 16s a16g^4 16f^4 17h^3 16f^3] lightly-made mare: 90
handicap hurdler: won at Wincanton in October: returned to form last 2 outings: best at around 2m: acts on any going: takes good hold and usually makes running: suitable mount for a claimer. *Mrs J. Wonnacott.*

LLANGWARREN 4 br.g. Penmarric (USA)–Young Mistress (Young Emperor) [1989/90 16m^{pu}] of little account on Flat (has worn blinkers and a hood): —
behind when pulled up in juvenile hurdle in May. *B. J. Wise.*

LOADPLAN LASS 4 b.f. Nicholas Bill–Strathclair (Klairon) [1989/90 16m^4
16m^2 16s^3 16d 16f 16m^5] leggy, light-framed filly: half-sister to useful hurdler and 78
winning chaser Strathline (by High Line): in frame over 6f at 2 yrs, but well beaten on Flat in 1989: juvenile selling hurdler: best effort on second start: sold out of C. Booth's stable 3,700 gns Doncaster January Sales after third outing. *A. P. James.*

LOADSAMONEY 4 b.g. Gypsy Castle–Ladyville (Lord Nelson (FR))
[1989/90 22g^5] no worthwhile form on Flat: well-beaten fifth of 7 in juvenile —
hurdle at Stratford in April. *D. J. G. Murray-Smith.*

LOANINGDALE 5 ch.g. Lomond (USA)–Aliceva (Alcide) [1989/90 16g^4 16s^4
16d 21f* 24m^5 20f* 20f*] well-made ex-Irish gelding: half-brother to several 133
winners, notably Irish 2000 Guineas winner Nikoli (by Great Nephew), very smart Captain James (by Captain's Gig) and Coronation Stakes winner Sutton Place (by Tyrant): dam won over 1¼m and is half-sister to dam of Levmoss, Sweet

Mimosa and Le Moss: 1¼m winner on Flat when trained by R. Nevin (has run blinkered): successful in novice hurdles at Newbury in March and at Ascot and Haydock (handicap) in May, best efforts when blinkered on last 2 courses: quickly recovered from mistake last when beating Paco's Boy 6 lengths at Haydock: should stay beyond 21f: acts well on firm ground: looks a difficult ride (carries head high and tends to hang right). *R. Akehurst.*

LOBRIC 5 b.g. Electric–Light O'Battle (Queen's Hussar) [1989/90 18f^{4} 16g^{3}
20v^{2} 20g^{2} a20g* 24g^{2} 20v^{2}] workmanlike gelding: won handicap hurdle at 107
Lingfield in January: good second at Kempton (ran in snatches) and Plumpton subsequently: didn't find a great deal on second start: stays 3m: acts on any going: reluctant to race fifth appearance 1988/9. *J. R. Jenkins.*

LOCALITY 5 b.m. Lochnager–Declamation (Town Crier) [1989/90 16d^{4} 16m]
workmanlike mare: has scope: poor maiden on Flat: 14 lengths fourth behind Last 85
'o' The Bunch in maiden hurdle at Edinburgh in February: never dangerous on faster ground next start. *N. Tinkler.*

LOCAL WHISPER 6 b.g. Deep Run–Dream Toi (Carlburg) [1989/90 16f^{4}
21g^{5} 20s] tall, workmanlike gelding: will make a chaser: first foal: dam fair staying 96
chaser: won 2 point-to-points in Ireland in 1989: bought 61,000 gns Doncaster Spring Sales: 20 lengths fifth to Forest Sun in moderately-run Challow Hurdle at Newbury in December: 11/8 on, beaten some way out in novice hurdle at Worcester following month (hung right after 3 out): possibly unsuited by soft ground. *D. R. C. Elsworth.*

LOCHAR BRIG 11 b.g. Bilsborrow–Lochar Lass (Drumbeg) [1989/90 20f^{2} c—
24m 22f^{4} 27f^{3} 20g^{6} 24m^{6} c20f^{pu} 16g 20d^{pu} 24m^{pu}] rangy gelding: winning 66
point-to-pointer: poor novice hurdler/chaser: blinkered third outing 1988/9. *D. McCaskill.*

LOCHERRE 6 gr.g. Lochnager–Chemin de Guerre (Warpath) [1989/90 16g
16s* 16d 16s 17g^{F}] workmanlike gelding: made all in slowly-run novice hurdle at 94
Nottingham in January (jumped badly left on occasions): prominent when falling 4 out in novice handicap at Doncaster in February: well beaten in between: acts on soft going. *O. Brennan.*

LOCHOICH 6 b.m. Bybicello–Fanny Adams (Sweet Ration) [1989/90 20m^{F}
20g 20d] compact mare: well beaten in novice hurdles. *Mrs G. L. Simpson.* —

LOCKWOOD PRINCE 7 b.g. Tanfirion–Mink Fur (CAN) (Victoria Park) **c119**
[1989/90 c25f* c25g^{3} c25f^{4} c25m c25f*] small, sturdy gelding: fair hurdler/ —
chaser: won handicaps over fences at Wincanton in October (sweating, jumped deliberately on occasions but made virtually all) and March (held up, led 3 out to score by 4 lengths from Lauderdale Lad): well beaten in between: stays 3¼m: acts on firm and dead going: has won when sweating: inconsistent. *R. G. Frost.*

LOFTINESS 4 ch.g. High Line–Waltz (Jimmy Reppin) [1989/90 F16g^{6} F16m^{5}] second foal: dam 1m maiden race winner: showed ability in NH Flat races at Kempton and Sandown, finishing 13½ lengths fifth of 19 behind Will I Fly in latter in March: yet to race over hurdles. *N. J. Henderson.*

LOGAMIMO 4 br.c. Lord Gayle (USA)–Miss Morgan (Native Prince) [1989/90
16g^{4} 16g^{5} 16g* 16g* 16g^{4} 16f* 16g* 16g^{2}] neat colt: fair performer on Flat, 105
successful 5 times at up to 12.2f in 1989 (usually blinkered): retained by trainer 19,000 gns Doncaster November Sales: won maiden hurdle at Edinburgh and claimers at Market Rasen (2) and Kelso: long odds on, second in juvenile seller at Worcester in May (claimed by J. Hellens £9,000): will stay beyond 2m: acts on firm ground: wears blinkers: has worn tongue strap: changed hands 10,000 gns Doncaster January Sales. *N. Tinkler.*

LOG CABIN 9 b.g. Connaught–Haida (Astec) [1989/90 c16g^{4}] lengthy gelding: c79
winning selling hurdler: fourth of 5 finishers in minor event at Carlisle in —
November on chasing debut: effective at 2m and stays well: acts on any going: suitable mount for a claimer: blinkered once in 1986/7. *B. Ellison.*

LOLLYS PATCH 10 b.g. Carlburg–Coolgreen Lolly (Blue Chariot) [1989/90 c88
c25m^{3} c32f^{4}] sturdy gelding: fairly useful point-to-pointer: creditable third of 5 —
finishers behind easy winner Sanballat in hunter chase at Towcester in April: stays 3m (beaten a long way over 4m): has worn blinkers. *C. M. T. Main.*

LOMBARDY STAR 13 b.g. Milan–Stellar Lady (Star Signal) [1989/90 c20g] c—
big, rangy gelding: novice hurdler/chaser: tailed off only outing of season —
(February): stays 3m: acts on heavy going. *David Pritchard.*

LONDON EXPRESS 6 ch.m. True Song–Loophole (London Gazette) [1989/90 16f 16h3] fourth foal: sister to 2¾m hurdle winner True Loop: dam, winning hurdler, half-sister to Dramatist: third of 6 finishers in novice hurdle at Taunton in April: will be suited by further. *P. J. Hobbs.* 73

LONDON LEADER 8 ch.g. London Bells (CAN)–Stop Thinking (Divine Gift) [1989/90 c16d2 c16f* c16m3 c17g c20gur] lengthy, rather sparely-made gelding: won novice chase at Leicester in November: destroyed after breaking a leg at Wolverhampton in January: was best at 2m: probably acted on any going. *R. Lee.* c**91** —

LONDON WINDOWS 8 b.g. Balliol–Chebs Lass (Chebs Lad) [1989/90 20f4 16m 16f3 16m4 16d5 a20g3 c20m* c20f5 c20gpu a16g5 c16g5 a20g2 c16f5 c20m5 c16f* c17m6 c20f3 c20f6 c16f2] leggy gelding: poor novice hurdler: has been beaten in a seller: won novice handicap chase at Huntingdon in December and 2-runner novice chase at Towcester in May: has run poorly most other starts over fences: stays 2½m when conditions aren't testing: acts on firm going: tends to make mistakes: changed hands 2,300 gns Newmarket September Sales: sold out of D. Thom's stable 4,200 gns Doncaster November Sales after sixth start. *D. L. Williams.* c**80** 77

LONELLA 4 b.c. Lomond (USA)–Actinella (Thatch (USA)) [1989/90 16dpu] 64,000F, IR 260,000Y: leggy, good-topped ex-Irish colt: fourth foal: dam, 6f winner, sister to Thatching and Golden Thatch: lightly-raced maiden on Flat: sold out of J. Bolger's stable 4,000 gns Newmarket Autumn Sales: bit backward, tailed off when pulled up in juvenile claiming hurdle at Stratford in February. *J. H. Baker.* —

LONELY REEF 5 b.h. Pas de Seul–Merriment (USA) (Go Marching (USA)) [1989/90 16h* 17h* 16m3 16m3 a20g2] small, sparely-made horse: second foal: half-brother to a winner in France: dam sister to high-class French miler Brinkmanship: winner at up to 1¼m on Flat in Belgium in 1988: made all in novice hurdles at Taunton and Devon & Exeter: good third in lady riders novice handicap at Nottingham fourth start: creditable second in 2½m novice event at Lingfield in December: acts on hard ground: wears blinkers and a tongue strap. *M. C. Pipe.* 109

LONELY SAILOR 5 ch.g. Pas De Seul–Marine Life (Deep Diver) [1989/90 F16f6] brother to fairly useful middle-distance performer Marine Diver and half-brother to a winner in France: dam, 6f winner in Ireland, is half-sister to high-class 1m to 1½m performer Dickens Hill: well beaten in NH Flat race at Huntingdon in May: yet to race over hurdles or fences. *N. A. Smith.*

LONG ENGAGEMENT 9 b.g. Mandalus–Selk Fly (Selko) [1989/90 c16m2 c16m* c16gpu c16g c17d3 c16m c25fpu] leggy, quite good-topped gelding: has been hobdayed: smart 2m chaser at his best: quickened to lead approaching last when winning Tingle Creek Chase (limited handicap) at Sandown in December by 2½ lengths from Desert Orchid: ran poorly third outing and moderately on next 3: c**146** ? —

Tingle Creek Handicap Chase, Sandown—
Long Engagement (spots) makes the most of his weight concession from Desert Orchid.
They're followed by Prideaux Boy and Hogmanay

pulled up lame final start: probably acts on any going: ran poorly when blinkered eighth outing 1988/9: usually looks well. *D. Nicholson.*

LONGGHURST 7 b.g. Camden Town–Olanrose (Kythnos) [1989/90 22g 22m^{4} 22m 16g^{4} 16s* 16g a20g^{4} a20g^{2}] leggy, sparely-made gelding: selling hurdler/novice chaser nowadays: claimer ridden, won at Taunton in December (bought in 3,200 gns): best at short of 3m when conditions are very testing: acts on any going: sometimes blinkered nowadays (wasn't last 4 starts): poor jumper of fences. *B. Forsey.* c— x 94

LONGIRL SISTER 4 ch.f. Longleat (USA)–Refectory (Reform) [1989/90 16m^{5}] won 4 times in Belgium at 2 yrs, including in listed company (no worthwhile form on Flat in Britain): over 20 lengths fifth to Fighting Days in juvenile maiden hurdle at Plumpton in April. *J. Ffitch-Heyes.* 64 p

LONG JOHN SILVIA 9 ch.m. Celtic Cone–Hidden Treasure (Tudor Treasure) [1989/90 c24f^{3} c27f* c27f* c24h*] lengthy mare: wide-margin winner of poor novice chases at Sedgefield (2) in September and Carlisle in October: stays well: acts on hard going: makes the odd mistake. *Mrs G. R. Reveley.* c**99**

LONGRIVER LADY 7 b.m. Town And Country–Peggy Wig (Counsel) [1989/90 c24d*] neat, deep-girthed mare: winning hurdler: fair chaser: made all and stayed on gamely to win handicap at Worcester in November by 3 lengths from Warner's End: stays 3m: acts on soft going and good to firm: sound jumper. *R. J. Holder.* c**116** —

LONG TALL SALLY 4 b.f. Adonijah–Double Shuffle (Tachypous) [1989/90 18g^{4} 22g a20s^{bd}] leggy filly: in frame at up to 1¼m on Flat: poor juvenile hurdler: dead. *R. Curtis.* 75

LOOK AT ME NOW 4 b.f. Blushing Scribe (USA)–Shortigal (Galivanter) [1989/90 16m^{pu} 16g] leggy filly: half-sister to North Light (by Northern Flash), winner of a 2-runner selling hurdle: dam unraced half-sister to a fair hurdler: little sign of ability on Flat: always behind in claiming hurdle at Market Rasen in December. *B. Richmond.* —

LOOK LIVELY (USA) 5 b.g. Smarten (USA)–Danseuse (USA) (Jig Time (USA)) [1989/90 20f^{2}] rather leggy, sparely-made gelding: won twice over hurdles in 1988/9: creditable second of 3 finishers to Hard To Hold at Huntingdon on only 113

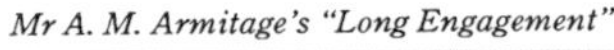

Mr A. M. Armitage's "Long Engagement"

outing of 1989/90 (August): stays 2¾m: acts on firm ground: has run well for a claimer. *J. T. Gifford.*

LOOSE FLING 5 b.h. Imperial Fling (USA)–In Leiu (Tutankhamen) [1989/90 20g^{6}] smallish horse: poor novice hurdler: should be suited by 2½m (always behind at trip in January): tends to be on edge in paddock. *Mrs B. Butterworth.* —

LOOSE RUCK 6 b.g. Runnett–Where Is It (Wolver Hollow) [1989/90 16m^{F} 16m^{pu} 16g^{pu} a16g^{pu} a20g] close-coupled, sparely-made gelding: 2m selling hurdler: no form since 1986/7: blinkered third start: sold 1,100 gns Ascot June Sales. *J. E. Long.* —

L'ORAZ 6 b.m. Ile de Bourbon (USA)–Oraza (GER) (Zank) [1989/90 16m^{F} 20s^{5}] rangy mare with scope: third in NH Flat race in 1988/9: in touch when falling 3 out in novice hurdle at Leicester in December: still carrying condition, travelled comfortably long way and eased once losing touch before 3 out in Golden Miller Novices' Hurdle at Leicester following month. *Mrs S. Lamyman.* — p

LORD ADMIRAL (USA) 8 b.g. Topsider (USA)–Tumbling Dancer (USA) (Dancer's Image (USA)) [1989/90 18f^{2} 18m* 16d c16f c20m^{3} c21f^{4} c20g^{3} c16g* c16m* c16f^{2}] strong, well-made ex-Irish gelding: has scope: won novice hurdle at Worcester in September on British debut (trained by P. Finn previously): successful in 2 handicap chases at Windsor in January: never-nearer 4 lengths second to Kings Wild in similar race at Worcester in March: best at up to 2¼m: probably acts on any going. *Mrs S. Armytage.* c91 87

LORD CAPILANO 7 ch.g. Busted–Finbay (ITY) (Canisbay) [1989/90 20g^{4} 25g 16s^{ur} 20g] lengthy, workmanlike gelding: lightly-raced novice hurdler: stays 2½m. *R. J. Holder.* 85

LORD IT OVER (USA) 7 b.g. Best Turn (USA)–Idle Hour Princess (USA) (Ribot) [1989/90 16g c25f^{pu}] compact gelding: winning selling hurdler: pulled up lame on chasing debut: stays 2¼m: suited by firm going: has worn a crossed noseband: often sweating: sold out of L. Wordingham's stable 900 gns Doncaster January Sales after first outing. *M. C. Chapman.* c— —

LORD KILGAYLE 6 b.g. Lord Gayle (USA)–Kilfenora (Tribal Chief) [1989/90 16d^{6} 20d 21m^{6} 24m 16s] small, sparely-made gelding: poor novice hurdler: form only at around 2m. *A. J. Chamberlain.* 72

LORD LAURENCE 11 ch.g. Laurence O–Grange Hansel (Prince Hansel) [1989/90 24g^{pu} c25f^{3}] lengthy, workmanlike gelding: winning hurdler/chaser: was suited by 3m and more: acted well on a sound surface: blinkered once: dead. *D. R. Gandolfo.* c— —

LORD LENEY 12 b. or br.g. Deep Run–Dame Leney (Arctic Chevalier) [1989/90 c24g^{pu} c27d^{pu} c16g^{3}] winning hurdler/chaser in Ireland: no form in Britain: stayed 2½m: acted on heavy going: dead. *D. McCaskill.* c— —

LORD MUSTARD 7 ch.g. Lord Ha Ha–Royal Cloak (Hardicanute) [1989/90 c25d* c24g^{pu}] smallish, sturdy gelding: has a round action: winning hurdler: bit backward, led 2 out when winning minor event at Hereford in November on chasing debut: would have finished clear second to Carrick Hill Lad in BMW Series Chase qualifier at Haydock later in month but for breaking down badly approaching last: stays well: acts on heavy going. *J. A. C. Edwards.* c**106** —

LORD PURNA 8 ch.g. Sir Mago–Lady Annapurna (High Perch) [1989/90 c24d^{pu}] sparely-made gelding: won a point-to-point in March and walked over in one in April: won hunter chase at Sedgefield in 1988/9: suited by 3m or more: acts on hard ground and possibly unsuited by a yielding surface. *A. W. Johnson.* c—

LORD ROLFE 4 ch.c. Rolfe (USA)–Stepout (Sagaro) [1989/90 16m^{pu} 16g^{pu} 20g*] lengthy colt: half-brother to ungenuine selling hurdler Raspberry Copse (by Riboboy): placed over 2m on Flat: won selling hurdle at Plumpton in January by 15 lengths (bought in 4,400 gns): pulled up in non-sellers previously: seems suited by 2½m: claimer ridden. *J. D. J. Davies.* 87

LORDSHIP 5 b.g. Lord Gayle (USA)–All Gold Rose (Rheingold) [1989/90 16d^{5} 16m^{5} 17m 16f^{F}] smallish, lightly-made gelding: novice hurdler: bought 5,100 gns Doncaster November Sales: poor form afterwards. *M. A. Barnes.* 90

LORD SOLENT 11 b.g. Smokey Rockett–Mill Court (Damremont) [1989/90 c20v^{4} c26f^{6}] won a point-to-point in May: poor form in novice hurdles (has run in a seller) and in hunter chases. *Mrs P. A. Tetley.* c70 —

LORD'S WAY 9 b.m. Lord Nelson (FR)–Craigie Way (Palm Track) [1989/90 16h^{F}] smallish, deep-girthed mare: first foal: dam point-to-point winner and daughter of useful hunter chaser Miss Craigie: failed to complete course in 3 —

point-to-points in 1988: backward, tailed off when falling last in novice hurdle at Hexham in October. *T. A. K. Cuthbert.*

LORD TORENAGA 7 b. or br.g. Ballymore–Tudor Bay (FR) (Canisbay) [1989/90 c20s3 c16g c24s2 c25dpu c27v5 c25m5] deep-girthed gelding: tubed: winning point-to-pointer: fair hurdler at his best: poor form in novice chases: needs strongly-run race at 2½m and stays 3m: acts on soft going. *F. Walwyn.* c85 —

LORD WINDERMERE 5 b.g. Taufan (USA)–Repercussion (Roan Rocket) [1989/90 16f 16f 16d] leggy gelding: no sign of ability: blinkered last start: dead. *J. M. Bradley.* —

LOREN'S COURAGE (USA) 5 ch.g. Solford (USA)–Roman Luster (USA) (Proudest Roman (USA)) [1989/90 16m6 16g*] compact, good-bodied gelding: fairly useful on Flat, winner twice over 1½m in 1989 (best on a sound surface): jumped better than on hurdling debut earlier in month when winning novice event at Ascot in January by 2 lengths from Stratford Ponds, pair well clear: will be suited by stiffer test of stamina: should improve and win more races. *G. Harwood.* 130 p

LORENTEGGIO (USA) 5 b.g. Al Nasr (FR)–Clairvoyance (USA) (Round Table) [1989/90 20m5 16f5] plating-class stayer on Flat, successful 3 times in 1989: sold out of D. Chapman's stable 5,800 gns Doncaster October Sales: beaten over 25 lengths when fifth in novice hurdles at Plumpton in November and Taunton following month: will be suited by return to 2½m. *T. B. Hallett.* 84

LORIOT 13 ch.g. Lord Gayle (USA)–Golden Moss (Sheshoon) [1989/90 c20f6 c26d4 c24m c28gpu] smallish, rather leggy gelding: staying handicap chaser. *N. K. Thick.* c— —

LOR MOSS 10 ch.g. Mossberry–Lor Darnie (Dumbarnie) [1989/90 c22gF c24d5 c20g6 c20m3 c20d c21m4] tall, leggy gelding: modest and inconsistent chaser nowadays: seems best at around 2½m: acts on any going: blinkered last outing. *A. F. Leighton.* c**101** —

LOS BUCCANEROS 7 br.g. Neltino–Pirella (Pirate King) [1989/90 16g6 16d2 17g* 16f* 16f6] useful-looking gelding: will make a chaser: very good mover: won novice hurdles at Doncaster (handicap) in February and Ludlow (beat sole opponent First Crack by 25 lengths) in March: around 10 lengths sixth to Vazon Bay in quite valuable novice handicap at Cheltenham on final start (no extra closing stages): unlikely to stay much beyond 2m: acts on firm ground. *S. Christian.* 106

LOST ART 7 ch.g. Artaius (USA)–Flosshilde (Rheingold) [1989/90 22d 18d 20m a20s4 a20g5 21spu a24g2 a20g2 a20gur] neat ex-Irish gelding: poor winning hurdler: stays 2½m, apparently not 3m: seems to act on any going: sometimes wears blinkers (did so when successful): has run well for an amateur. *M. J. Charles.* 85

LOST FORTUNE 7 ch.g. Nearly A Hand–Opt Out (Spartan General) [1989/90 16m 19dpu] workmanlike gelding: second foal: half-brother to winning point-to-pointer General Option (by Levanter): dam won poor novice hurdle: fell and refused in point-to-points in 1989: no sign of ability in novice hurdles. *A. J. Silvester.* —

LOST PRIDE 7 b. or br.g. Flatbush–Half Moon Bay (Behistoun) [1989/90 16spu] failed to complete course in novice hurdles: dead. *A. J. Chamberlain.* —

LOTHARIO 5 ch.g. Hello Gorgeous (USA)–Fairy Footsteps (Mill Reef (USA)) [1989/90 16f] workmanlike gelding: little sign of ability on Flat: sold out of H. Cecil's stable 6,800 gns Newmarket July (1988) Sales: resold 1,400 gns Ascot September (1988) Sales: jumped moderately when tailed-off last in novice hurdle at Uttoxeter in September. *B. Byford.* —

LOTHIAN ADMIRAL 8 b.g. Roscoe Blake–Lothian Lady (New Brig) [1989/90 c16g2 c20g2 c16v3] close-coupled gelding: winning hurdler: placed in novice chases, showing modest form: will be suited by a return to further (stays 25f): acts on heavy going. *G. Richards.* c**90** —

LOTHIAN CAPTAIN 5 b.g. Roscoe Blake–Lothian Lady (New Brig) [1989/90 F16g 22dpu 16d 18d 16v3 16d5 16g6 20d 20g5] workmanlike gelding: poor novice hurdler: stays 2½m: acts on heavy going. *W. H. Crawford.* 86

LOTHIAN ROSE 4 b.f. Roscoe Blake–Lothian Lady (New Brig) [1989/90 F12g] sister to winning hurdlers Lothian Admiral and Lothian Sultan and half-sister to winning hurdler/chaser Spartan Prince and to successful point-to-pointer Lothian General (both by Spartan General): dam lightly-raced sister to several winners: never-dangerous eighth of 17 to Fairways On Target in NH Flat race at Hexham in March: yet to race over hurdles. *W. H. Crawford.*

LOTHIAN SULTAN 6 b.g. Roscoe Blake–Lothian Lady (New Brig) [1989/90 16d* 16g 16g] workmanlike gelding: has scope: unplaced in NH Flat races in 1987/8: sold out of W. Crawford's stable 15,000 gns Doncaster August (1988) Sales: won novice hurdle at Chepstow in November comfortably by 6 lengths from Chief Mole: ran as though something was amiss next time (subsequently off course 5 weeks) and below his best final start: will be suited by 2½m: acts on dead going. *J. T. Gifford.* 99

LOTSCHEN LADY 6 b.m. Prince Regent (FR)–Irish Aunt (Tyrone) [1989/90 20v^{pu} 16g^{F} 16d a16g^{3} a18g^{3} 17m^{3} 24m* 21f^{6}] small mare: poor form in varied company over hurdles, including selling, prior to winning handicap at Towcester in April: suited by 3m: acts on good to firm going. *D. R. Gandolfo.* 88

LOTTIE'S FURY 6 br.g. Furry Glen–Sneem (Rum (USA)) [1989/90 c16f^{2} c20f*] leggy, workmanlike gelding: handicap hurdler: won 3-runner novice chase at Uttoxeter in September: stayed 2½m: possibly unsuited by very soft ground, acted on any other: dead. *W. A. Stephenson.* c**83** —

LOTUS ISLAND 6 gr.h. Ile de Bourbon (USA)–Be Easy (Be Friendly) [1989/90 16f^{5} 16f^{2} 16m* 16f^{3}] smallish, lightly-made horse: bought in 4,400 gns after winning selling hurdle at Stratford in September: finished lame next time: races only at 2m: acts on any going: tends to find little: wears blinkers. *N. Tinkler.* 97 §

LOUGH ROAD 8 ch.g. Laurence O–Vixen's Red (Bargello) [1989/90 c20d^{pu} c21d^{2} c20f c24g^{F} c24m^{2} c21d^{F} c26m^{2}] sparely-made, angular gelding: winning point-to-pointer: novice hurdler: runner-up in 3 novice chases in the spring: stays 3¼m: acts on any going: visored last start. *Mrs G. E. Jones.* c**89** —

LOVE ABOVE 7 ch.g. Cut Above–Romantic Love (Sovereign Path) [1989/90 c25f^{ur} c20f c25f] good-topped gelding: seems of little account. *Mrs Gillian A. Russell Holmes.* c— —

LOVE AND LIFE 4 b. or br.f. Lyphard's Special (USA)–Miss Olympus (Sir Gaylord) [1989/90 18m^{ur}] lengthy, angular filly: poor form at up to 1¼m on Flat (claimed out of C. Cyzer's stable £6,010 in June): chased leaders until unseating rider fourth in juvenile hurdle at Fontwell in December. *W. G. M. Turner.* —

LOVE ANEW (USA) 5 b.g. Sensitive Prince (USA)–Armure Bleue (FR) (Riverman (USA)) [1989/90 16d^{pu} 16m 16m*] sturdy ex-Irish gelding: first foal: dam unraced half-sister to French 1m and 9f winner Albertine: in frame at up to 1½m on Flat in 1988 when trained by D. K. Weld: well beaten in novice hurdle in November (trained by B. McMath): won similar event at Chepstow 5 months later by short head from Cobo Bay, rallying after mistake at the last: acts on good to firm going: should win more races. *O. Sherwood.* 106 p

LOVELY LIZZIE 7 ro.m. Anax–Lizzie Eustace (Firestreak) [1989/90 a20g 16g 16d^{F} 16f^{3}] close-coupled mare: poor novice selling hurdler: refused to race in a point-to-point in March: probably stays 2½m: acts on hard ground: sold out of I. Jordon's stable 1,900 gns Doncaster August Sales. *B. R. Cambidge.* 64

LOVELY WONGA 4 b.g. Tanfirion–Teala (Troy) [1989/90 16h* 16f^{5} 18f^{4} 17h* 16f^{5} 16f^{pu} 16s 16m^{5} 16g^{2} 20g^{2} 16m^{3} 18f^{2}] small gelding: maiden plater on Flat: temperamental over hurdles, but won juvenile events at Plumpton in August and Devon & Exeter (seller, looked none too keen) in October (no bid): placed in sellers afterwards: stays 2½m: acts on hard ground: isn't one to trust. *D. A. Wilson.* 83 §

LOVE ON THE ROCKS 5 b.m. Martinmas–Love Is Blind (USA) (Hasty Road) [1989/90 20g^{3} 24d a24g^{4}] leggy, close-coupled mare: novice hurdler: third at Wolverhampton in December: well below form afterwards: stays 2½m: best form on good ground. *P. D. Evans.* 84 ?

LOVER BILL 8 b.g. Golden Love–Billeragh Girl (Normandy) [1989/90 c24g^{4} c20m^{4} c25g^{2} c25g^{2} c24m^{2} c25s^{3} c32f c24f] workmanlike gelding: novice hurdler/chaser: found little under pressure seventh outing: stays 3m: acts on good to firm and soft ground: blinkered final start in 1988/9 and last 6 outings. *M. J. Wilkinson.* c**78** —

LOVER COVER (USA) 8 b.g. Screen King (USA)–Gallant Courtship (USA) (Gallant Romeo (USA)) [1989/90 16f^{4} 17m 16f] leggy, narrow gelding: novice selling hurdler: jumped poorly and eventually refused only outing over fences (1986/7): should stay beyond 2m: acts on any going: blinkered fifth outing in 1986/7: not one to trust. *A. J. Wilson.* c— § 71 §

LOVE TO DANCE 5 b.h. Dominion–Atoka (March Past) [1989/90 16g] leggy gelding: no worthwhile form over hurdles: claimer ridden. *R. P. C. Hoad.* —

LOVING 5 b.m. Good Times (ITY)–Exquisite (Exbury) [1989/90 16f[6] 16f] small mare: poor plater over hurdles: visored second outing and blinkered third in 1988/9. *G. Blum.* 75

LOVING BROTHER SID 4 b.g. Prince Tenderfoot (USA)–Full of Flavour (Romulus) [1989/90 16d[pu]] leggy gelding: half-brother to winning hurdler Arrowroot (by Warpath): well beaten on Flat: jumped badly and was tailed off when pulled up in selling hurdle at Market Rasen in November: sold 1,400 gns Doncaster Sales later in month. *C. W. Thornton.* —

LOWCROSS VENTURE 8 ch.g. Rymer–Winning Venture (Eastern Venture) [1989/90 c20d[6]] rangy gelding: placed in point-to-points in 1989: jumped none too fluently when behind in novice hunter chase at Ludlow in March. *R. G. Corbett.* c—

LOW RATION 7 ch.m. Revlow–Adoration (FR) (Dancer's Image (USA)) [1989/90 c21f[pu]] lengthy, lightly-made mare: poor novice selling hurdler: tailed off when pulled up in novice chase in July: tailed off over 2¾m: sometimes blinkered. *W. M. Perrin.* c— —

LUBUS 8 b.m. Fordham (USA)–Candescent (USA) (Buckpasser) [1989/90 27g 25m[pu]] of little account over hurdles. *V. Hall.* —

LUCAYAN GOLD 6 br.g. Ardross–Lucayan Lady (Swing Easy (USA)) [1989/90 16f[2]] sparely-made gelding: very lightly-raced novice hurdler: 33/1, 3 lengths second of 4 to Shu Fly at Hereford in May. *K. Bishop.* 90 ?

LUCIFER LIGHT 7 b.g. Salluceva–Boyne Light (Light Thrust) [1989/90 22v[pu]] workmanlike gelding: fourth foal: half-brother to Manasota Key (by Brave Invader), a winner of a 3m hurdle: dam unraced half-sister to dam of Corbiere: failed to complete course in 5 point-to-points in 1989: jumped poorly and tailed off when pulled up in novice hurdle at Folkestone in January. *J. Ringer.* —

LUCKACTIVE 4 ch.c. Lucky Wednesday–Swakara (Porto Bello) [1989/90 F12f[5] F16f F16f] half-brother to 2 winners, including useful hurdler Son of A Gunner (by Gunner B): dam fairly useful sprinter: behind in NH Flat races in the spring: yet to race over hurdles. *G. H. Jones.*

LUCKSIN 8 br.g. Lucky Wednesday–Galivanter Girl (Galivanter) [1989/90 c20m[3]] smallish, sparely-made gelding: novice hurdler/chaser: little worthwhile form: sometimes blinkered. *R. Akehurst.* c— —

LUCKY BLAKE 7 b.g. Blakeney–Lucky Omen (Queen's Hussar) [1989/90 c16d] small, sturdy gelding: selling hurdler and novice chaser: tailed off in hunter chase in March: won a point-to-point following month: stays 2½m: acts on any going: has been visored and blinkered (not when successful). *C. W. Cooper.* c— —

LUCKY FEN 10 br.g. Lucky Wednesday–Ensign Steel (Majority Blue) [1989/90 16d c16g[pu] c16g c20d[pu] c24d[F] c24f[5]] big, lengthy gelding: poor handicap hurdler/novice chaser: stays 19f: acts on any going: blinkered twice over hurdles: sold 1,050 gns Ascot July Sales. *B. Forsey.* c— —

LUCKY GROVE 5 b. or br.m. Lucky Wednesday–Saran (Le Levanstell) [1989/90 16f] half-sister to winning hurdler Thrucham Lad (by Double-U-Jay): winning plater on Flat, stays 1¼m: tailed-off last of 9 in novice hurdle at Southwell in August. *S. R. Bowring.* —

LUCKY HELMET 6 b.g. Riot Helmet–Lucky Pace (Lucky Brief) [1989/90 24g[4] 16d 17g* 20f[3]] ex-Irish gelding: first foal: dam maiden point-to-pointer in Ireland: won point-to-point in 1989: 20/1-winner of maiden hurdle at Tipperary in November: 12 lengths third behind Paco's Boy in 5-runner novice event at Uttoxeter 6 months later: not disgraced over 3m: trained until after third start by J. Sheahan. *W. G. McKenzie-Coles.* 88

LUCKY HUMBUG 7 ch.g. Lucky Wednesday–Be My Sweet (Galivanter) [1989/90 16g 27s[pu]] rather leggy gelding: poor novice hurdler: pulled up, reportedly lame, in January. *W. J. Pearce.* —

LUCKY JORDON 7 ch.g. Bybicello–Sister Chatters (I Say) [1989/90 16f 24g 22d 25d] workmanlike gelding: fourth foal: dam a poor hurdler: no sign of ability over hurdles: dead. *W. A. Stephenson.* —

LUCKY LANDERS 5 ch.g. Ascendant–Chetsford Water (Sir Lark) [1989/90 F16m F16f[2] F16d[5]] second foal: dam lightly-raced hurdler/chaser: neck second to Wessex Warrior in NH Flat race at Wincanton in March: 28 lengths fifth of 7 to Ruling in well-contested similar event at Ayr following month: yet to race over hurdles or fences. *M. C. Pipe.*

Richard Green (Fine Paintings)'s "Lucky Verdict"

LUCKY LANE 6 b.g. Mart Lane–O Token (Laurence O) [1989/90 20gpu] smallish, close-coupled gelding: first foal: dam unraced: burly, tailed off when pulled up 2 out in novice handicap at Wetherby in November on hurdling debut. *H. J. Gill.* —

LUCKY LENA 10 b.m. Leander–Quiet Sailing (Dumbarnie) [1989/90 16g 20gpu a16g 16s 16d 16m3 16g 16d4 16f2 16f] lengthy mare: novice selling hurdler: ran well last 2 starts: acts on firm going: blinkered third start. *S. A. Torr.* 74

LUCKY OAK 4 ch.g. Tap On Wood–Zalinndia (FR) (Brigadier Gerard) [1989/90 16d6 a16g6 16g6] leggy gelding: plating-class maiden on Flat, suited by 1¼m: bought out of P. Cole's stable 10,000 gns Newmarket July Sales: well beaten in juvenile hurdles. *R. P. C. Hoad.* —

LUCKY RETURN 8 b.g. Hawaiian Return (USA)–Dryrot (Barnie's Image) [1989/90 F20d6 F16s c22dpu 22g6 c20gpu] big, workmanlike ex-Irish gelding: first foal: dam winning Irish hurdler: won a point-to-point in 1989: unplaced in NH Flat races: behind when pulled up in novice chases and well beaten in novice hurdle: trained until after third start by T. Bergin. *T. P. McGovern.* c— —

LUCKY RHUMBA 7 b.g. Rambah–Old Currency (Lucky Brief) [1989/90 F16m F16g 20gpu c25gpu c21dF] rather sparely-made gelding: third foal: dam plating-class maiden on Flat: seems of little account. *R. D. E. Woodhouse.* c— —

LUCKY ROMANY 8 b.g. High Season–Romany Lone (Romany Air) [1989/90 17g3] medium-sized non-thoroughbred gelding: placed in 2 point-to-points in 1988: 14 lengths third behind Madame Ruby in novice event at Devon & Exeter in October on hurdling debut (tended to wander under pressure): seemed sure to improve but wasn't seen out again. *P. J. Hobbs.* 90

LUCKY VERDICT 4 b.g. Touching Wood (USA)–Noor (Mill Reef (USA)) [1989/90 16m2 17d* 20v* 16d2 16s3 16f5] neat gelding: half-brother to quite useful hurdler Karajan (by Kalaglow): fairly useful top-of-the-ground stayer on Flat: sold 134 p out of J. Hills's stable 29,000 gns Newmarket Autumn Sales: won juvenile hurdle at Devon & Exeter and novice hurdle at Chepstow in January: ran very well to finish just over 2 lengths fifth to Rare Holiday in Daily Express Triumph Hurdle at Cheltenham in March, staying on well: let down by his jumping fourth and fifth outings: suited by a good gallop when racing at 2m and will stay beyond 2½m: successful on heavy ground, but best run on firm: wears blinkers: in good form on Flat in 1990: should do well when returned to hurdling. *M. C. Pipe.*

LUCY KING 9 b.m. Kinglet–Elucidation (Specific) [1989/90 a16g a16g] c—
sparely-made mare: probably of little account. *Mrs J. E. Croft.* —

LUCY LASTIC 6 b.m. Tycoon II–Nikancy (Castlenik) [1989/90 17m^4 16f^5 20f^3
16m a20g^2 a20g^3 a22g^2 a16g^4 a18g^2 a24g* a24g* a22g^3] close-coupled mare: 95
handicap hurdler: showed improved form each time when winning twice at Southwell in February, gaining latter success by 10 lengths from The Pike: good third behind Langrove on same course following month: stays 3m: acts on firm and dead going. *W. Clay.*

LUCY'S BRIG 6 b.m. New Brig–Tumbeleena (Blandford Lad) [1989/90 16d^{pu}
16f^{pu}] half-sister to point-to-pointer Hartside Hill (by Bronze Hill): dam won —
novice chases at 2m and 3m: backward, tailed off when pulled up in novice hurdles. *T. D. C. Dun.*

LUDA LADY 7 b.m. Red Regent–Crepine (Roan Rocket) [1989/90 c20h^2] c?
rangy mare: behind in novice hurdles: sold out of K. Morgan's stable 2,300 gns —
Doncaster August (1988) Sales: won a point-to-point in 1989: beaten 1½ lengths by very easy winner Waltingo in 2-runner novice chase at Carlisle in September. *S. G. Payne.*

LUDERMAIN 5 ch.m. Oats–Peacock Vain (Shiny Tenth) [1989/90 16g^F 16f^6
24m^{pu}] sturdy mare: little sign of ability in 2 completed outings over hurdles. *J. W. Walmsley.* —

LULA BLAKE 5 b.m. Roscoe Blake–Ablula (Abwah) [1989/90 16s 20f^4] rather
sparely-made mare: poor novice hurdler: stays 2½m: acts on any going. *F. Jordan.* 77

LULAV 12 br.g. Prince Regent (FR)–Scarletta (Red God) [1989/90 26f^{pu} 16f^3] c— §
neat gelding: poor selling hurdler/chaser nowadays: stays 2½m: probably acts on 65 §
any going: has worn blinkers and a visor: sketchy jumper: no battler: sold 440 gns Ascot December Sales. *J. J. Bridger.*

LUMBERJACK (USA) 6 b.g. Big Spruce (USA)–Snip (Shantung) [1989/90
20d^3 16m^4 16s^4 16d^{pu}] close-coupled, sparely-made gelding: useful hurdler: good 136
third in valuable handicap at Chepstow in November, giving impression would be suited by return to 2m, but ran moderately at that trip in similar contests afterwards: acts on soft going: has won for a claimer. *J. G. FitzGerald.*

LUMLEY LAKE 7 ch.g. Le Bavard (FR)–Penthouse Girl (Stubbs Gazette) c75
[1989/90 c16s^6 c17d^F c24f^6] big, rangy gelding: has shown signs of a little ability in —
novice hurdles and chases. *J. T. Gifford.*

L'UOMO PIU 6 b.g. Paddy's Stream–Easter Vigil (Arctic Slave) [1989/90 16f^3
16g^5 16g* 16d^3 16g^3 16s^3 a18g^4] workmanlike gelding: handicap hurdler: won at 119
Wolverhampton in December: in frame all subsequent outings, on last of them creditable fourth to Whitewash in valuable event at Southwell: will prove best at around 2m: acts on soft going (ran poorly on heavy): has worn a crossed noseband: hung left fifth start, found little next time. *Mrs J. Pitman.*

LUPY MINSTREL 5 br.h. Black Minstrel–Lupreno (Hugh Lupus) [1989/90 F17m F16g] leggy horse: half-brother to fairly useful hurdler/very useful chaser Alkepa (by The Parson): dam poor maiden on Flat: behind in NH Flat races at Carlisle in November and Kelso in March: yet to race over hurdles or fences. *C. Parker.*

LUREX GIRL 6 ch.m. Camden Town–Klairelle (Klairon) [1989/90 16d 20d
20v^5 16v 17d^2 20m] small, workmanlike mare: novice selling hurdler: ran well 73
fifth start: best form at around 2m: acts on a soft surface (well beaten on good to firm). *D. R. Tucker.*

LUREX STAR 4 b.g. Thatching–Stellarevagh (Le Levanstell) [1989/90 16s
a16g^6 a20s^3 a18g] plating-class maiden on Flat: soundly beaten over hurdles, —
including in a seller: acts on dead going: blinkered last 3 starts. *Miss P. O'Connor.*

LUSTY LAD 5 b.g. Decoy Boy–Gluhwein (Ballymoss) [1989/90 16h* 18f^{pu}]
small, sparely-made gelding: modest handicapper on Flat, stays 7f: won novice 92
hurdle at Plumpton in August: reportedly broke a blood vessel later in month and

A. F. Budge (Equine) Limited's "Lumberjack"

not seen out again: unlikely to stay much beyond 2m: acts on hard going. *M. J. Haynes.*

LUTINETTE 5 b.m. Swing Easy (USA)–Belle Lutine (Relkino) [1989/90 16s^{pu} 17d 17m 19h^{pu}] sparely-made mare: no worthwhile form in selling hurdles: pulled up and dismounted last start. *N. G. Ayliffe.* —

LUXULYAN LAD 7 b.g. Idiot's Delight–Sarasail (Hitting Away) [1989/90 20g 21f^{5}] angular gelding: brother to smart 2m chaser Sea Merchant: very lightly raced and no sign of ability. *C. G. Roach.* —

LYNDEN LASS 4 ch.f. Say Primula–Fishermans Lass (Articulate) [1989/90 16g 16d 16g 24g] sturdy, lengthy filly: third foal: half-sister to winning hurdler Royal Invader (by Silly Prices): dam, well beaten in 2 selling hurdles, is sister to useful hurdler/chaser Fisherman's Cot: no sign of ability over hurdles, including in sellers. *R. W. Dods.* —

LYNEMORE 8 ch.m. Nearly A Hand–Freuchie (Vulgan) [1989/90 16m*] strong, good-bodied mare: has been fired: will make a chaser: favourite, prominent throughout when beating Hypnotic 2½ lengths in amateur riders handicap hurdle at Sandown in March (hung right closing stages): free-going sort, likely to prove best at 2m: acts on good to firm going and has run moderately on a soft surface: claimer ridden in 1988/9. *Capt. T. A. Forster.* 112

LYNKIMGEM 4 ch.g. Royal Match–Sweet Millie (Methane) [1989/90 17m 17f^{4} 16g 16d^{pu} 16g] of little account. *M. C. Chapman.* —

LYNWOOD LAD 9 ch.g. Precipice Wood–Lyns Legend (Marengo) [1989/90 c20s^{3} c25g^{3} c24d c26f^{3} c32f^{pu}] lengthy, shallow-girthed, angular gelding: well beaten over hurdles: fair point-to-pointer: placed in hunter chases, jumping c90 —

slowly on occasions fourth start: broke down last outing: stays 3¼m: acts on firm
going. *G. M. Price.*

LYPHARD'S CANDY 4 ch.c. Lyphard's Wish (FR)–What A Candy (USA)
(Key To The Mint (USA)) [1989/90 16v] lengthy colt: second foal: half-brother to —
5f winner Fine A Leau (by Youth): dam useful French 2-y-o 7f winner, later won at
up to 9f in USA: fair performer on Flat, winner at up to 11f when trained by J. Oxx:
2/1 co-favourite but looking to need race, scratched to post and was never going
well in race when behind in juvenile hurdle at Chepstow in January: has been
returned to Ireland. *D. R. C. Elsworth.*

LYPHEORIC (USA) 5 b.h. Lypheor–Fabulous Salt (USA) (Le Fabuleux)
[1989/90 20g* 16d^{3} 20g* 21d^{2} 20d^{pu}] leggy, useful-looking horse: most 113
impressive all-the-way winner of novice handicap hurdles at Newcastle in January
and Kempton following month: clear length second, leading until flat, to Tug of
Gold in similar event at Newbury in March: stays 2½m: acts on dead going: has
worn a tongue strap. *Mrs J. R. Ramsden.*

LYPH (USA) 4 b.g. Lypheor–Scottish Lass (Scotland) [1989/90 16g^{F} 16g 16f^{2}
16f^{4} 16m* 16f 16m^{3} 16m] well beaten in 2 races on Flat in 1989: sold out of J. 73
Gosden's stable 4,700 gns Newmarket Autumn Sales: won selling handicap
hurdle at Plumpton in April (bought in 3,600 gns): acts on firm ground: ran poorly
when blinkered last outing. *P. R. Hedger.*

LYREEN RIVER 6 b.g. Rusticaro (FR)–Mehudenna (Ribero) [1989/90 16f^{3}
16f* 17f* 16f* 16f^{pu}] leggy gelding: successful in selling hurdle at Southwell 104
(bought out of B. Curley's stable 7,800 gns) and novice hurdles at Carlisle and
Kelso in October: broke leg at Newcastle later in month: raced only at around 2m:
acted on firm ground: blinkered once. *C. R. Beever.*

LYSANDER 8 br.g. Ile de Bourbon (USA)–Helcia (Habitat) [1989/90 20g 21d
24d] workmanlike gelding: novice hurdler: dead. *M. Tate.* —

M

MACANJAC 11 b. or br.g. Random Shot–Moonraker VI (Giolla Mear) [1989/90
16g^{F}] leggy, good-topped gelding: winning point-to-pointer: bit backward and —
amateur ridden, behind when fell 2 out in novice event at Huntingdon in
November on hurdling debut. *M. J. Jerram.*

MACARTHUR 5 b.g. Ardross–Polly Peachum (Singing Strand) [1989/90 16d
16g^{4} 16g^{3} 16d 17f^{3} 16g] workmanlike gelding: handicap hurdler: creditable third at 100
Edinburgh in January and Doncaster in March: stays 2½m: acts on firm and dead
ground: suited by forcing tactics: has raced with tongue tied down: good mount for
a claimer: jumps hurdles well and should make a chaser. *M. W. Easterby.*

MACHO MAN 5 br.g. Mummy's Game–Shoshoni (Ballymoss) [1989/90 16m
16g 20g 17g^{5} 16v^{4} 16d 16g^{3} 20g^{4}] smallish, sparely-made gelding: handicap 96
hurdler: in frame at Ayr in February and Perth in April on fifth and seventh starts:
ran moderately most others: best at 2m: best form on a soft surface: suited by
forcing tactics: blinkered last outing of 1988/9. *J. J. O'Neill.*

MACINTYRE 5 b.g. Morston (FR)–Walk By (Tower Walk) [1989/90 F16f]
half-brother to fair sprinter Scintillo (by Hot Spark) and a winner in Belgium by
Sharpen Up: dam sprinter: tailed-off last in NH Flat race at Newbury: yet to race
over hurdles or fences. *S. Dow.*

MACLENNAN 11 b.g. Helluvafella–Gratora (Gratitude) [1989/90 c24f^{5} c—
c26m^{4}] point-to-point winner: well beaten in hunter chases. *P. B. Hall.*

MACNAB'S QUEST 12 b.g. Laggards Lane–Last Bequest (Bounteous) c95
[1989/90 c26f^{F} c25f^{2}] workmanlike gelding: fair point-to-pointer, successful in
March and April: winning hunter chaser: spoilt his chance by jumping deliberately
when fast-finishing 2½ lengths second to Sweet Rascal at Cheltenham in May: in
lead when falling 2 out at Uttoxeter previous month: stays well: acts on hard and
dead ground. *Mrs Judith Young.*

MACROOM 8 b.g. Furry Glen–Crashing Juno (Crash Course) [1989/90 c24g^{4} c128
c24g* c24g^{3} c24d^{F} c25s^{2} c33d^{F}] sturdy, workmanlike gelding: won handicap —
chase at Newbury in December, showing much improved form: led until suffering
a fatal fall 6 out in William Hill Scottish National at Ayr in April: stayed well: acted
on heavy going: usually jumped well. *S. Mellor.*

MADAM CHEVALIER 9 b.m. Kinglet–Chanter Mark (River Chanter) [1989/90 17h² 17f] smallish, workmanlike mare: winning hurdler: has raced only at Carlisle: second of 3 to easy winner Magic At Dawn in handicap in October: last 11 days later: will stay 2½m: acts on dead going: has worn crossed noseband. *T. A. K. Cuthbert.* 79

MADAME MINT 5 b.m. Raga Navarro (ITY)–What A Mint (Meadow Mint (USA)) [1989/90 17g⁵] small, compact mare: poor novice hurdler: remote fifth in selling handicap in November. *R. J. Holder.* —

MADAME RUBY (FR) 6 br. or gr.m. Homing–Strathdearn (Saritamer (USA)) [1989/90 17h* 17g* 21fpu] 6,200Y, 500 2-y-o: small, workmanlike mare: second foal: half-sister to quite useful hurdler Might Move (by Town And Country): dam won over 12.2f: held up when winning novice hurdles at Devon & Exeter in August and October: challenging when pulled up lame before 2 out in mares event at Warwick in December: jumps soundly. *M. C. Pipe.* 108

MADAM MELODY (FR) 4 b. or br.f. Big John (FR)–Infanta (FR) (Prince Regent (FR)) [1989/90 20mpu 16vpu] close-coupled filly: poor maiden on Flat: sold out of T. Barron's stable 1,100 gns Doncaster August Sales: behind when pulled up in juvenile hurdle at Uttoxeter (mulish in preliminaries) and novice event at Chepstow (bandaged, sweating). *R. Williams.* —

MADAM TAYLOR 5 b.m. Free State–Hourglass (Mansingh (USA)) [1989/90 16g 16g 16g⁵ 16g] rather angular, dipped-backed mare: plating-class handicapper on Flat: poor form in novice hurdles. *H. J. Collingridge.* 65

MADE FOR LIFE 8 b.m. Billion (USA)–Safe Passage (Charlottown) [1989/90 c20sur c25gpu c21m] leggy mare: no sign of ability over hurdles: won a point-to-point in April: behind in novice hunter chase at Fakenham in March. *R. Burridge.* c— —

MADEMIST SUSIE 9 br.m. French Vine–Ginger Fury (Fury Royal) [1989/90 c22s² c24d* c24f* c24f²] rangy, rather angular mare: useful point-to-pointer: won hunter chases at Leicester (maiden) and Newcastle (novice, by ¾ length from Kitango after being waited with) in March: 6 lengths second to Waverley Mill in novice hunter chase at Wetherby following month: stays well: acts on any going. *M. J. Hill.* c**106**

MADJDEC 8 b.g. Roscoe Blake–Chukka (Tiepolo II) [1989/90 c17f²] strong, good-bodied gelding: poor form over hurdles: 20 lengths second of 4 finishers in novice chase at Kelso in October: seems to stay well. *C. Parker.* c**69** —

MADONIJAH 4 ch.f. Adonijah–Linda's Design (Persian Bold) [1989/90 16d 16g] quite modest but inconsistent maiden on Flat: behind in novice claiming hurdle and juvenile seller: dead. *W. Storey.* —

MAELKAR (FR) 6 b.g. Maelstrom Lake–Karabice (Karabas) [1989/90 22spu 25f² 24f²] tall, leggy, narrow gelding: lightly-raced hurdler: put up useful performance when 2 lengths second to Henry Mann in Coral Golden Hurdle Final (Handicap) at Cheltenham in March, travelling strongly from start and leading approaching last until drifting left and headed near finish: ran creditably when 6 lengths second to Battalion in Keith Prowse Long Distance Hurdle at Ascot later in month: stays 25f, but gives impression he'll prove just as effective at 2½m: acts on any going: jumps well. *J. J. O'Neill.* 145

MAGICAL MORRIS 8 ch.g. Balinger–River Spell (Spartan General) [1989/90 c20f³ c24f c20fF] lengthy gelding: pulled up in 2 point-to-points in 1989: poor form in hunter chases. *W. R. Hacking.* c**66**

MAGIC AT DAWN (USA) 5 ch.g. Diamond Prospect (USA)–Implicit (Grundy) [1989/90 16mpu 17h* 16f* 17f* 16f⁴] strong, compact gelding: in fine form in October, winning handicap hurdles at Carlisle (2) and Kelso: ran creditably at Wetherby later in month: unlikely to stay much beyond 2m: acts on hard going. *G. M. Moore.* 110

MAGIC BAY 8 b.g. Current Magic–Tweed (Haris II) [1989/90 c17mpu c20dpu c24s²] leggy, close-coupled non-thoroughbred Belgian gelding: third reported foal: dam never ran: successful in a handicap hurdle in Belgium in 1986, and won 5 handicap chases there, including in May, 1989: made mistakes all 3 starts in Britain, in February 30 lengths second to sole opponent Tartan Takeover at Nottingham: stays 2¾m. *Allan Smith, Belgium.* c? —

MAGIC ISLAND 8 b.g. Manado–Skhiza (Targowice (USA)) [1989/90 c25sur] lengthy, rather sparely-made gelding: maiden on Flat: tailed off only outing over c— x —

hurdles: won point-to-point in February: behind when unseating rider 5 out in maiden hunter chase at Hereford in March. *Dennis Bell (Cwmbran).*

MAGIC MELISSA 8 ch.m. New Member–Cape Mandalin (Mandamus) [1989/90 c20dF c16dF 22dF 17d 22gpu 22spu] angular, sparely-made mare: poor novice hurdler/chaser: sold 1,000 gns Doncaster March Sales. *R. J. Holder.* c— —

MAGIC MILLION 4 b.g. Gorytus (USA)–Beach Light (Bustino) [1989/90 16g6 16g 16g2dis 16g* 16g2 16s* 16s* 16f] lengthy, sparely-made Irish gelding: has a round action: successful twice over 1¼m on Flat in 1989: won juvenile hurdles at Fairyhouse, Punchestown and Leopardstown (beat Rare Holiday 5 lengths in Stillorgan Hurdle in February): travelled strongly long way but wandered under pressure when around 5½ lengths seventh to Rare Holiday in Daily Express Triumph Hurdle at Cheltenham in March: acts on any going: has won for an amateur. *M. A. O'Toole, Ireland.* 131

MAGIC OATS 4 b.f. Oats–Duckdown (Blast) [1989/90 16v6 16g] rather sparely-made filly: fifth foal: half-sister to Celtic Shot (by Celtic Cone): dam winning hurdler from good jumping family: soundly beaten in juvenile hurdles at Haydock and Newbury in December: sent to race in Ireland. *C. P. E. Brooks.* —

MAGIC QUEST 4 ch.f. Posse (USA)–Satina (Pall Mall) [1989/90 16f 16f a18g] lightly-made, plain filly: well beaten in claimer on Flat when trained by Dr J. Scargill: tailed off in selling hurdles: sold 640 gns Doncaster March Sales. *R. Hollinshead.* —

MAGIC SOLDIER 5 br.g. Mandrake Major–Dior Queen (Manacle) [1989/90 16g2 16g* 20m 16s 16g5] rangy gelding: has scope: made virtually all to win novice hurdle at Wetherby in November: best effort afterwards on final start (first for over 4 months): carried head rather high first outing: form only at 2m. *G. Richards.* 85

MAGNOLIA DANCER 6 b.g. Magnolia Lad–Storm Dancer (Carnival Dancer) [1989/90 a20g a18s5] seems of little account: blinkered final start. *M. J. Charles.* —

MAGNOX 9 ch.g. Keren–So Blue (Espresso) [1989/90 c20gpu] lightly-built gelding: poor novice hurdler: tailed off when pulled up in novice event on chasing debut (November): stays well. *N. Chamberlain.* c— —

MAGNUS PYM 5 b.g. Al Nasr (FR)–Full of Reason (USA) (Bold Reason) [1989/90 16f 16d 16s] good-topped gelding: very useful juvenile hurdler in 1988/9: behind in good company in 1989/90: will be suited by further than 2m: acts on heavy going and good to firm: blinkered final start. *D. R. C. Elsworth.* —

MAGWOOD 10 b.g. Precipice Wood–Big Maggie (Master Owen) [1989/90 c16m c33dpu c24gpu] workmanlike gelding: winning hurdler/chaser: stays well: acts on heavy going and seems unsuited by firm: has worn a brush pricker on near-side. *C. Parker.* c— —

MAHANA 6 b.g. Tepukei–Easby Saint (Saintly Song) [1989/90 20g 20g 20g3] compact gelding: poor novice hurdler: probably stays 2½m. *J. G. FitzGerald.* 80

MAID MARINER 8 br.m. Julio Mariner–Molly Polly (Molvedo) [1989/90 16f6 16f3 24m2 24m* 24mF 24f 24g 24g3 25m3 20g*] small mare: won handicap hurdles at Worcester in September and Market Rasen in June: stays 3m: form only on a sound surface: has been tried in blinkers and a visor: has won for a claimer but looks a difficult ride: inconsistent. *Miss G. M. Rees.* 91 §

MAID OF MONEY 8 b.m. Crash Course–Hansel Money (Prince Hansel) [1989/90 c20d* c20g* c20g* c20d* c25d2 c24v3 c26f6] **c155** —

The 1989 Jameson Irish Grand National winner Maid of Money came through her final season unscathed and is now in foal to Orchestra. She'll be sorely missed by Irish jumping, but at least as a mare she, unlike the vast majority of her opponents, still has the chance of making a further contribution via the paddocks. Maid of Money had put up an outstanding performance for a novice carrying 11-6 in the Irish National, and hopes were high that she and fellow novice Carvill's Hill would go on and revitalize the local chasing scene after it had endured a lack-lustre period. The pair met in the Durkan Brothers International EBF Punchestown Chase in December. Maid of Money, with a couple of easy victories in lesser races on the same course in the autumn already in the bag, started favourite ahead of Carvill's Hill who was making his reappearance. Maid of Money beat him very gamely by three lengths. The trip was generally regarded as short of her

*Durkan Brothers International EBF Punchestown Chase, Punchestown—
Maid of Money jumps the last more fluently than Carvill's Hill*

best but she was kept to two and a half miles for one more race. The policy paid off handsomely, for although she seemed set to be relegated to third by Waterloo Boy and Super Furrow when they caught up with her at the last in the valuable Black And White Whisky Champion Chase at Leopardstown later in December, she rallied to get back up and justify favouritism by half a length and three quarters of a length; it was her second win in the race.

Maid of Money started favourite yet again in the Charterhouse Mercantile Chase at Cheltenham in January, just ahead of Toby Tobias in a four-horse race. However, the improving Toby Tobias beat her by ten lengths, decisively enough to suggest that she'd have great difficulty in turning the tables in the Tote Cheltenham Gold Cup even if she jumped better than here (where she'd hit the eighth and ninth) or at Leopardstown (where she'd tended to brush through the fences at top pace). Maid of Money's next run in the Vincent O'Brien Irish Gold Cup at Leopardstown in February further suggested she wouldn't quite be good enough to win the Gold Cup. Nevertheless she put up a typically genuine performance in finishing third to Nick The Brief and Carvill's Hill, rallying as Carvill's Hill threatened to run away down the back straight and still sticking on though outpaced from the home turn and blundering at the last. In receipt of the 5-lb mares' allowance, she went under by five lengths and two and a half lengths. The curtain came down on Maid of Money's racing career in the Tote Cheltenham Gold Cup. For the first time she was faced with firm going, and the going might well have been responsible for her performing below her best. She couldn't go the pace, and it was mainly her gameness that earned her sixth place, about twenty-five lengths behind Norton's Coin.

Maid of Money (b.m. 1982)	Crash Course (b 1971)	Busted (b 1963)	Crepello
			Sans Le Sou
		Lucky Stream (b 1956)	Persian Gulf
			Kypris
	Hansel Money (ch 1972)	Prince Hansel (ch 1961)	The Phoenix
			Saucy Wilhelmina
		Clonmoney (ch 1962)	Even Money
			Luckibash

Maid of Money's dam Hansel Money had the distinction of providing two runners in the same Gold Cup: she is also the dam of Ten of Spades (by Raise You Ten). Though neither was able to pull off victory in 1990, the

Black And White Whisky Champion Chase, Leopardstown—
Waterloo Boy holds a slight advantage over Maid of Money at the final fence

family can boast a Gold Cup winner—the second dam Clonmoney's half-sister Glencaraig Lady who won in 1972. Clonmoney herself won on the Flat and at up to three miles over hurdles in Ireland. Maid of Money, a lengthy, workmanlike mare, stayed well but hadn't the need of a thorough test of stamina that many Irish Grand National winners have had. Maid of Money acted well on an easy surface. She was commendably consistent. *J. R. H. Fowler, Ireland.*

MAINTOWN 9 ch.m. Remainder Man–Copstown (Sovereign Gleam) [1989/90 c16m* c16g* c17g^{3} c17g^{3}] sparely-made, dipped-backed mare: winning selling hurdler: won novice chase at Nottingham in October and handicap chase at Southwell in November: remote third in handicaps later in November and December: races only at around 2m: acts on firm going: has worn blinkers (not when successful): jumps very well in the main over fences. *M. C. Pipe.* c98 —

MAITREDEE 11 b.g. Le Patron–No Cert (Tycoon II) [1989/90 c18f* c16m^{6} c18f^{ur} c18g^{5} c16m^{5} c16d^{pu}] leggy gelding: handicap chaser: beat one other finisher at Fontwell in September: well beaten afterwards: best at up to 2½m: acts on any going: wears a crossed noseband: suited by forcing tactics: usually jumps well: usually amateur ridden. *N. R. Mitchell.* c93 ? —

MAJESTIC BRUNO 6 b.g. Majestic Maharaj–Palestine Fairey (Pal O Mine) [1989/90 c25g^{pu} c20g^{5} c16g^{3} c20g^{3} c20d c16h^{3} c16m^{4} c17f^{4} c24h^{2}] lengthy, sparely-made gelding: poor novice hurdler/chaser: probably stays 3m: has run in snatches: blinkered second outing: has had tongue tied down. *N. A. Gaselee.* c78 —

MAJESTICIAN (GER) 7 b.g. Honduras (GER)–Marlova (FR) (Salvo) [1989/90 16m 20g] compact gelding: one-time fair stayer on Flat (lazy type): sold out of G. Pritchard-Gordon's stable 9,500 gns Ascot Autumn Sales: poor form in novice hurdles: will be suited by long distances. *B. Llewellyn.* —

MAJESTIC MASK 9 br.g. Majestic Streak–Newmaskin (New Brig) [1989/90 c16m c16d a22g] lengthy, dipped-backed gelding: well beaten over hurdles: winning point-to-pointer: behind in novice chases. *B. Gee.* c— —

MAJESTIC MISS 6 ch.m. Majestic Current (USA)–Moette (Mossy Face) [1989/90 20m4 20m] lengthy, sparely-made mare: poor novice hurdler: well suited by a test of stamina: usually claimer ridden. *R. B. Francis.* 73

MAJESTIC PLAYER 6 ch.m. Torus–Blackrath Girl (Bargello) [1989/90 F16g F16d] ex-Irish mare: first foal: dam unraced: maiden point-to-pointer: in rear in NH Flat races: yet to race over hurdles or in a steeplechase. *Denys Smith.*

MAJESTIC RIDE 6 b.g. Palm Track–Lakeland Lady (Leander) [1989/90 16f 20m6 c20spu c24dpu c20spu 17m 16g5 16g5] tall, angular gelding: poor novice hurdler (best effort final outing): has jumped poorly and been pulled up all starts over fences. *J. K. M. Oliver.* c— x 80

MAJESTIC RING (CAN) 8 b.g. Majestic Prince–Savage Call (USA) (Jungle Savage (USA)) [1989/90 20f2 c16d3 c16g3 25g6 c16m2] neat gelding: novice hurdler/chaser: has plenty of ability but is faint-hearted: stays 2½m: possibly unsuited by heavy going: sketchy jumper of fences: has worn a tongue strap: blinkered last 6 outings 1988/9: suited by strong handling: sold privately out of P. Kelleway's stable 6,000 gns Doncaster August Sales. *P. Monteith.* c**87** § 87 §

MAJESTIC RUN 5 b.m. Deep Run–Brickeendown (Bargello) [1989/90 F16f2 F16f5] fifth foal: half-sister to Irish NH Flat race winner Clara Girl (by Fine Blade): dam won 2m hurdle in Ireland: second in NH Flat race at Ludlow in April: fifth to Cards And Kisses at Hereford following month: yet to race over hurdles or fences. *M. C. Pipe.*

MAJESTIC SILVER 4 gr.f. Majestic Maharaj–Doon Silver (Doon) [1989/90 F16f F16f] first foal: dam selling hurdler: behind in NH Flat races: yet to race over hurdles. *P. R. Rodford.*

MAJOR DON 10 ch.g. Mandrake Major–Kindling (Psidium) [1989/90 16fF] big, strong gelding: useful on Flat at best: fell both starts over hurdles: dead. *E. Weymes.* —

MAJOR EFFORT 5 ro.g. General Ironside–Julie's Gi-Gi (Brave Invader (USA)) [1989/90 16m2 16g3 21f2 16m2 c16sF c16m6 c20dF 16m 20m*] rather sparely-made gelding: half-brother to 4 winners, including selling hurdler/poor chaser Broughty Pier (by Simbir) and selling hurdler Rowley Lodge (by Northern Guest): dam poor Irish maiden: showed ability all starts prior to winning novice hurdle at Huntingdon in April by 2 lengths from Brave Setanta: let down by his jumping over fences (would have won 4-y-o novice chase at Chepstow in December on chasing debut but for falling 2 out): stays 21f: acts on firm ground: edged left under pressure third start. *G. B. Balding.* c**94** 94

MAJOR FREDIE 4 ch.g. Major Petingo (FR)–Piber (Saintly Song) [1989/90 16d3 16g 20f a16g* a16g4 a18g2] compact gelding: plater on Flat, placed over 1¼m: blinkered, made virtually all to win juvenile selling hurdle at Southwell in December (bought out of K. Ryan's stable 6,200 gns): ran well both subsequent starts: pulls hard and seems not to stay beyond 2¼m: trained until after second outing by A. Brown. *T. Kersey.* 92

MAJORIAN 12 b.g. Majority Blue–Tinker Lass (Tin Whistle) [1989/90 16m c17mF4 c17f4] compact gelding: novice selling hurdler and poor novice chaser: blinkered second outing. *M. J. Collins.* c— —

MAJOR INQUIRY (USA) 4 b.g. The Minstrel (CAN)–Hire A Brain (USA) (Seattle Slew (USA)) [1989/90 16g* 16m* 16g* 16f] lengthy, rather sparely-made gelding: fairly useful performer at up to 1¾m on Flat in Ireland, when trained by D. K. Weld (ran well at up to 2½m on Flat in Britain in 1990): quickened well to lead in closing stages when winning juvenile hurdles at Cheltenham and Ascot (Aurelius Hurdle) in November and Steel Plate Trial Hurdle (beat Stage Player 8 lengths) at Cheltenham in January: looking in tremendous shape, unable to quicken from 2 out when twelfth behind Rare Holiday in Daily Express Triumph Hurdle at Cheltenham in March (reportedly broke blood vessel): will stay at least 2½m: has raced only on a sound surface over hurdles: should continue on the upgrade. *D. R. C. Elsworth.* 123 p

MAJOR MATCH (NZ) 8 b.g. Frassino–Burks Rainbow (NZ) (Weyand (USA)) [1989/90 c21f* c21f2 c20m2 c22g* c21m2 c20g* c21g4] rather sparely-made gelding: won handicap chase at Newton Abbot (sweating) in August and awarded similar events at Stratford and Warwick: ran a moody race final outing (January): stays 2¾m: best form on a sound surface: blinkered last 2 starts: not one to rely on. *Capt. T. A. Forster.* c**112** § —

MAJOR PLAYER 5 ch.m. Some Hand–Fursena (Fury Royal) [1989/90 F16g4 F16f] third foal: half-sister to Arrow Valley (by Lighter), placed in a novice hurdle:

dam winning point-to-pointer/hunter chaser: fourth in NH Flat race at Fakenham in April: well beaten at Hereford following month: yet to race over hurdles or fences. *R. J. Weaver.*

MAJOR ROUGE 8 ch.g. Mandrake Major–Red Form (Reform) [1989/90 c27f^{5} **c84**
c24h^{2} c24f* c24f^{3} c24m^{2} c24g^{ur} c24f^{3} c24g^{6} c24g^{2} c24m^{5}] deep-girthed, angular —
gelding: poor hurdler: won 3 point-to-points in 1989: finished alone in 3-runner chase at Carlisle in October: first race for over 3 months, soundly beaten final start: stays 3m: acts on firm going: takes a good hold: usually blinkered (was when successful): good mount for a claimer. *J. I. A. Charlton.*

MAJOR ROW 10 b. or br.g. Kambalda–Vina's Last (Royal Buck) [1989/90 **c89**
c26d^{3} c24m^{2} c24g* c28m^{F}] sparely-made gelding: maiden hurdler: handicap —
chaser: won at Southwell in November: fell heavily following month (lame): stays well: acts on heavy going: blinkered second and third outings: sold 5,400 gns Doncaster Spring Sales. *J. G. FitzGerald.*

MAJOR THORN 11 b.g. Soldier Rose–Sweet Judy (Sweet Story) [1989/90 c—
c20f^{4} c24m^{pu} c26g^{pu}] rangy, rather plain gelding: very lightly-raced maiden point-to-pointer/steeplechaser: *P. J. Anderson.*

MAJOR TOM 13 b.g. Cantab–Ice Folly (Arctic Slave) [1989/90 c24g^{6} c18m^{3} c77
c20s c26s^{pu} c20v^{4} c26s^{pu} c25f c26h^{3} c26f^{6} c25m^{4}] compact gelding: poor chaser: —
suited by 3m and more: acts on any going: suitable mount for amateur or claimer. *H. Willis.*

MAJUBA ROAD 10 ch.m. Scottish Rifle–Cleo Baby (Dicta Drake) [1989/90 **c90**
c16s^{3} c16d^{6} a20g^{pu} c20h^{ur} c16m^{3}] sparely-made mare: winning hurdler/chaser: —
pulled up in selling hurdle third start: best form at up to 2½m: seems suited by a sound surface: blinkered final outing 1987/8. *J. Ffitch-Heyes.*

MAKE MY NIGHT 7 ch.g. Lepanto (GER)–Lady Vulgan (Vulgan) [1989/90 c—
21f^{pu} 16f^{co} 16h^{6} c16f^{F} c17f^{6}] compact ex-Irish gelding: ninth foal: half-brother to —
poor novice hurdler/chaser Lewis Built (by Henry The Seventh): dam sister to smart Irish chaser Corrie-Vacoul: no promise over hurdles and in steeplechases: maiden point-to-pointer: trained on reappearance by J. Davies: sold 675 gns Ascot June Sales. *W. G. M. Turner.*

MALACANANG 6 b.m. Riboboy (USA)–Gold Spangle (Klondyke Bill)
[1989/90 16m^{pu} 16f 16m 16f^{5} 16m^{2} 16f^{pu}] leggy, narrow mare: winning hurdler: 71
second in conditional jockeys handicap seller at Hereford in May: pulled up and dismounted next time: unlikely to stay much beyond 2m: acts on firm going and unsuited by soft ground: tends to sweat. *J. P. Smith.*

MALAMUTE SALOON (USA) 4 ch.c. Arctic Tern (USA)–Square
Generation (USA) (Olden Times) [1989/90 16v^{2} 16d^{F} 16v^{3}] small colt: placed at up 98 +
to 1½m on Flat: sold out of H. Cecil's stable 30,000 gns Newmarket Autumn Sales: 10 lengths second to Man For All Season in juvenile hurdle at Chepstow in January (pulled hard and jumped slowly in early stages): fell fifth next time and jumped with little confidence when moderate third in February. *M. C. Pipe.*

MALICHO 7 b.g. Malicious–Brava (Gala Performance (USA)) [1989/90 c16g^{3} **c87**
c19g^{4} c16f^{5}] leggy, angular gelding: winning hurdler: novice chaser: not raced —
after November: stays 2½m: suited by a sound surface: sold 5,000 gns Ascot February Sales. *G. B. Balding.*

MALISTRANO 9 b.g. Malinowski (USA)–Kilistrano (Capistrano) [1989/90 c— x
c16f^{2} c20f^{pu} c17m^{pu} c16d^{5} c16g^{ur} c20m^{5} c20g^{6} c16f^{3} c16f^{ur} c20m^{pu}] compact —
gelding: modest hurdler/chaser: let down by jumping and ran badly in 1989/90: usually blinkered. *J. R. Upson.*

MALLYPHA (FR) 6 b.g. Bellypha–Marzala (USA (Honest Pleasure (USA)) c**105**
[1989/90 16m* 16d 16d^{3} c16g* c20g^{4}] good-bodied gelding: best effort over 120
hurdles when winning handicap hurdle at Windsor in November: led from the fifth when winning novice chase at Wincanton in February: reluctant to start and made a bad mistake at the ninth when fourth to Comandante at Newbury in March: likely to prove best at around 2m: acts on firm and dead ground: blinkered final start 1988/9 (ran creditably). *D. R. C. Elsworth.*

MALTBY BOY 7 b.g. Royal Palace–Assel Zawie (Sit In The Corner (USA)) c78
[1989/90 c24f^{3}] successful in a point-to-point in April: 16 lengths last of 3 finishers to Fort Hall in novice hunter chase at Huntingdon in May. *Miss A. Salmon.*

MALYA MAL 11 gr.g. Precipice Wood–Replete (Rapace) [1989/90 18f^{5} c16g^{5} c89 ?
c20g^{3} c20f^{ur} c20s^{F} 20v^{pu} c26d^{pu} c20m^{6} c20m^{ur}] tall, rather light-framed gelding: —
has run tubed: formerly useful chaser: poor form in 1989/90: stays 2½m: acts on

any going: takes a good hold: tends to sweat: inclined to make mistakes and sometimes jumps to the right. *J. J. Bridger.*

MAMAMERE 6 b.m. Tres Gate–Baidedones (Welsh Pageant) [1989/90 17h^{F3} c—
17d^{2} 16f^{6} 17d c17d c16f^{6} c21m^{3} c25f^{5}] leggy mare: former selling hurdler: good 86
second in handicap at Devon & Exeter in November: poor form in novice chases: best form at around 2m: good mount for claimer: acts on hard and dead going. *S. N. Cole.*

MA MIGHT NOT 6 b.m. Kinglet–Argosa (No Argument) [1989/90 F16f F16f^{5}] second foal: dam, daughter of a winning Irish hurdler, pulled up in 2 novice hurdles: behind in NH Flat races in May: yet to race over hurdles or fences. *W. G. M. Turner.*

MANCHESTERSKYTRAIN 11 b.g. Home Guard (USA)–Aswellas (Le Lev- c—
anstell) [1989/90 c26v^{pu} c20d^{F} c25m^{pu} c17d^{pu} c18f^{F} c16h^{5} c16m^{ur}] workmanlike —
gelding: poor novice hurdler/chaser: ridden by 7-lb claimer. *Mrs C. M. Budd.*

MANDALAY PRINCE 6 b.g. Nishapour (FR)–Ops (Welsh Saint) [1989/90
24g^{pu}] angular gelding: novice hurdler: showed fairly useful form once in 1988/9: —
pulled up, reportedly lame, in November: suited by test of stamina: best form on dead going: ridden by 7-lb claimer. *T. Kersey.*

MANDAVI 9 b.g. Mandalus–Kimin (Kibenka) [1989/90 c20s^{F}] compact, c**113** ?
good-quartered gelding: useful hurdler in 1986/7: having only second outing —
since, jumped rather deliberately, ridden to challenge eventual 25-length winner Redgrave Devil when falling at the last in novice event at Bangor in December on chasing debut: stays 3m: yet to race on heavy ground, acts on any other: good mount for a claimer: has won when sweating: genuine: seemed sure to win a race over fences, but wasn't seen out again and sold only 2,600 gns Ascot June Sales. *N. J. Henderson.*

MANDER'S WAY 5 b.g. Furry Glen–Art Mistress (Master Owen) [1989/90
16s* 16s^{3} 16m^{pu}] 35,000 3-y-o: angular, useful-looking gelding: has scope: sixth 102

Lord Vestey's "Mander's Way"

foal: half-brother to 2 winning hurdlers: dam, winning hurdler up to 2½m in Ireland, sister to Artifice: gambled-on favourite, won novice hurdle at Folkestone in January on debut in good style: odds on, moderate third at Warwick 4½ weeks later: soon struggling and tailed off when pulled up in valuable novice event at Liverpool: will stay beyond 2m: acts on soft going. *Miss H. C. Knight.*

MANDRAKI SHUFFLE 8 b.g. Mandalus–Indictment (Desert Call) [1989/90 c20g4 c25d4 c24s2 c24s2 c25d2 c21g4 c24d5] strong, workmanlike gelding: novice hurdler/chaser: tried to run out paddock bend and hung left afterwards final outing: stays 3m: acts on soft going: usually blinkered nowadays: unreliable. *O. Sherwood.* **c94** § —

MANDRAY 7 br.g. Mandalus–Kimin (Kibenka) [1989/90 c20d3 c16m* c16f2 c16f* c20dF c16f6 c16m*] strong, rangy gelding: carries plenty of condition: won handicap chases at Uttoxeter, Southwell and Stratford (made all to beat Broad Beam 7 lengths) in the spring: found little third and sixth starts: best in strongly-run race around 2m: probably acts on any going. *J. R. Upson.* **c125** —

MANDY'S TINO 5 b.g. Neltino–Mandy's Melody (Highland Melody) [1989/90 16g 16f5 a16g4 20m5 a20g 16m5 16f4] leggy, sparely-made gelding: poor form at 2m in novice hurdles: unseated rider going to post, unruly at start and tried to refuse at fourth on sixth outing: visored final start. *J. L. Harris.* 69 §

MAN FOR ALL SEASON (USA) 4 b.c. Sir Ivor–Val de Val (FR) (Val de Loir) [1989/90 16s4 16v* 16d5 16g5 16f 22g3] tall, workmanlike colt: has plenty of scope: half-brother to a winning French jumper by My Swallow: middle-distance maiden on Flat: sold out of R. J. R. Williams' stable 16,000 gns Newmarket Autumn Sales: stayed on strongly to win juvenile hurdle at Chepstow in January by 10 lengths from Malamute Saloon: best effort afterwards when 2½ lengths third behind Mr Dormouse at Stratford: will stay 3m: needs give in the ground (acts well on heavy). *J. H. Baker.* 107 +

MANGROVE 6 b.g. Mandalus–Pine Princess (Neron) [1989/90 17d6 20m5 22d c20g3] lengthy, good-quartered gelding: modest hurdler: settled better than usual and was prominent until weakening 2 out when over 25 lengths third to Pendennis in novice event at Leicester in January on chasing debut (jumped soundly): best form at 2m: acts on soft going. *P. G. Bailey.* c85 —

MANHATTAN BEACH 6 b.g. Tepukei–Open House (Road House II) [1989/90 19mpu 22spu 20v 19sF] leggy gelding: no sign of ability. *G. Thorner.* —

MANHATTAN BOY 8 b.g. Oats–Into Harbour (Right Tack) [1989/90 16f5 16f* 16f2 16f5] neat gelding: a standing dish at Plumpton: gained ninth course win in selling hurdle in August (bought in 2,500 gns): dropped out tamely final start (October): stays 2½m: acts on any going: good mount for a claimer: visored once in 1986/7. *J. Ffitch-Heyes.* 98

MANHATTAN CHASE 7 b.g. Deep Run–Price Rise (Raise You Ten) [1989/90 22d4 17g 24dpu] lengthy, workmanlike gelding: novice hurdler: jumped and ran poorly final start: should stay beyond 2¾m. *G. Richards.* 84

MANHATTAN RIVER 4 ch.g. Gorytus (USA)–East River (FR) (Arctic Tern (USA)) [1989/90 16g 16gpu] smallish, good-quartered gelding: 7f winner on Flat: little promise in novice claimer and a juvenile event over hurdles: sold 4,500 gns Doncaster January Sales. *N. Bradley.* —

MAN IN THE MOON 7 b.g. Mansingh (USA)–Lady Antonia (Owen Anthony) [1989/90 16f3 21gpu c16f c20gpu] sparely-made gelding: selling hurdler: no promise in novice chases: stays 2½m: acts well on firm ground: suitable mount for claimer: often blinkered nowadays. *Miss L. Bower.* c— 72

MANIX 9 b.g. Manado–Ixee (FR) (Breton) [1989/90 16f 16m5] poor novice hurdler: has run in a seller: blinkered third outing 1988/9 and both starts in 1989/90. *P. Monteith.* —

MANJANIQ 6 b.g. Kings Lake (USA)–Ivory Home (FR) (Home Guard (USA)) [1989/90 16m5 16m a20g4 16f a18g] lengthy gelding: poor novice hurdler: looked most reluctant when tailed off in seller fourth start: should stay 2½m: sometimes blinkered or visored: jumps less than fluently: one to leave alone: changed hands 1,050 gns Doncaster March Sales. *J. R. Jenkins.* — §

MANNA REEF 12 b.g. Menelek–Homewrecker (Wrekin Rambler) [1989/90 c24dpu c22mr] well-made gelding: has been hobdayed: hunter chaser nowadays: tailed off when refusing 4 out in Seagram Fox Hunters' Chase at Liverpool: stays 2¾m: acts on heavy and good to firm going: has won for a claimer. *B. H. Lenaghan.* c— —

MANNYS CHOICE 5 br.g. Netherkelly–Sporting Image (Vulgan) [1989/90 16f^pu] workmanlike gelding: poor novice hurdler: behind when pulled up lame before 2 out in November. *A. Moore.* —

MAN OF FUN (USA) 5 b. or br.g. Mickey Mcguire (USA)–Philandering (USA) (Handsome Boy) [1989/90 20g² 16m* 16g³ 18g* 16m* 16s 24f⁴ 22m] sturdy, plain ex-Irish gelding: won handicap hurdles at Gowran Park (amateur riders), Kilbeggan and Tramore early in season and was also successful over 1¾m on Flat in between: no form in Britain on final 2 starts: probably stays 2½m: acts on firm ground and is possibly unsuited by soft: usually blinkered nowadays: sold out of M. O'Toole's stable 6,500 gns Doncaster October Sales after sixth start. *Miss A. L. M. King.* 100 ?

MAN OF MAUM 5 ch.h. Stanford–Kitty Ellis (Le Levanstell) [1989/90 16f^F 16d^pu 16g 16g 16m^F] sparely-made horse: third foal: dam won over hurdles in Ireland: poor maiden on Flat and over hurdles: has run in a seller: will do best at sharp 2m: has worn a tongue strap. *R. Earnshaw.* 69 +

MAN OF THE WEST 7 b.g. Mandalus–Belle of The West (Royal Buck) [1989/90 20d* 20m² 16g* 16d* 16s² 16m 16m^pu] sturdy, lengthy, good sort: will make a chaser: landed the odds in novice hurdles at Market Rasen in November, December and January: showed improved form when ½-length second to Whatever You Like (rec 10 lb) in quite valuable A F Budge Novices' Hurdle at Ascot in February (drifted right): said by trainer to be suffering from virus when below form in Waterford Crystal Supreme Novices' Hurdle at Cheltenham in March and Seagram 100 Pipers Top Novices' Hurdle at Liverpool following month: pulls hard and will prove best at 2m at present: suited by give in the ground: usually wears crossed noseband. *J. G. FitzGerald.* 134

MAN O'MAGIC 9 br.g. Manado–Garrucha (Prince Taj) [1989/90 c20m* c21m* c21m² c25m* c24s³ c26f* c25m³ c24g*] c**147** —

There couldn't have been a more appropriate winner of the Paul Croucher Memorial Trophy Handicap Chase at Newbury in March than Man O'Magic. Croucher, killed in a car crash in August, 1988, rode Man O'Magic in most of his races over hurdles and played a major role in the horse's development. The partnership was successful on four occasions, during which time Man O'Magic progressed from a moderate novice to a fairly useful handicapper. We doubt if even his former rider could have guessed that Man O'Magic would go on to such good things over fences. The leggy, lightly-made Man O'Magic hardly looked the type for steeplechasing but he soon showed himself to be a very sound jumper, much more adept than many of the more robust opponents that took him on in novice company in his first season over fences. And his jumping was to stand him in good stead when he took on more experienced rivals in his second season.

There are few chasers around with a better record than Man O'Magic. In sixteen starts he's won ten times and been placed on the others, picking up over £88,000 in prize money. The most important race Man O'Magic won in his first season over fences was the Bollinger Champagne Novices' Chase at Ascot, and he went on to be successful in an even more prestigious event on the same course on his reappearance. This was the H & T Walker Gold Cup, a limited handicap run in November restricted to horses that hadn't won a steeple chase before July 30th, 1988. For the second time in its short history the number of horses taking part in the H & T Walker Chase reached double figures, but the closing stages of the race concerned just two of them. Ghofar and Hogmanay forced the pace from the start, but no sooner had the former got the better of the duel early in the straight than he was faced with the challenge of Man O'Magic, who was travelling strongly. A good jump at the second last took Man O'Magic upsides Ghofar, and he produced the better finishing speed to win by a length and a half. Following an easy win in a two-runner race at Towcester, Man O'Magic was put in his place by the subsequent Cheltenham Gold Cup runner-up Toby Tobias in a minor event at Wincanton, being beaten twelve lengths into second place. Man O'Magic had had his limitations exposed following a run of five victories, but he remained a formidable opponent in handicap company, and on his next start he defied top weight in the William Hill Golden Spurs Chase at Doncaster in January. Man O'Magic, who hadn't been raced beyond two and three quarter miles previously, stayed the extended three miles well at Doncaster, where the ground placed the emphasis more on speed than stamina. Mark Perrett, who has ridden Man O'Magic in the majority of his races over fences, appeared to have no doubts about his mount's stamina and gave him an enterprising ride. Having travelled strongly under restraint from the start, Man O'Magic was allowed to stride on in the lead approaching the sixth-last fence, and turning for home he had all his rivals bar Rowlandsons Jewels in trouble. Mistakes at the next two fences put paid to Rowlandsons Jewels' chances and allowed the hard-ridden Fleming to move into second place. Man O'Magic, still travelling comfortably, had his task made easier when Fleming hit the second last, and he needed only to be pushed along to maintain his advantage. At the line he had five lengths to spare over Fleming. Man O'Magic's four remaining races were all at three miles or more, and he won two of them. Besides his two-length victory over Sam da Vinci in the Paul Croucher Memorial, Man O'Magic had a win in a minor event at Perth on his final start, landing the odds by twenty lengths. The Whitbread Gold Cup had been a possible target for Man O'Magic, but his trainer took the horse to Perth for the better ground. Apparently Man O'Magic became jarred up in finishing thirteen and a half lengths third to Toby Tobias in the Martell Cup Chase at Liverpool on his previous outing. Man O'Magic certainly looked ill-at-ease on the firm going that day and his jumping suffered as a result, but prior to that he'd acted very well on top-of-the-ground. Man O'Magic has shown his form on good to soft going but he ran a little below his best on soft ground when third to Ten of Spades in the Charterhouse Mercantile Handicap at Ascot.

Judged on his breeding Man O'Magic should have turned out to be best at up to a mile. His sire Manado won the Prix de la Salamandre and the Grand Criterium as a two-year-old, while his dam Garrucha was a very speedy performer in France, where she won three races and also finished in the frame in the Prix d'Arenberg, Prix Eclipse and Prix Morny. The best of Garrucha's numerous winners on the Flat possessed plenty of speed.

H & T Walker Gold Cup, Ascot—
Man O'Magic makes a winning reappearance at the expense of Ghofar

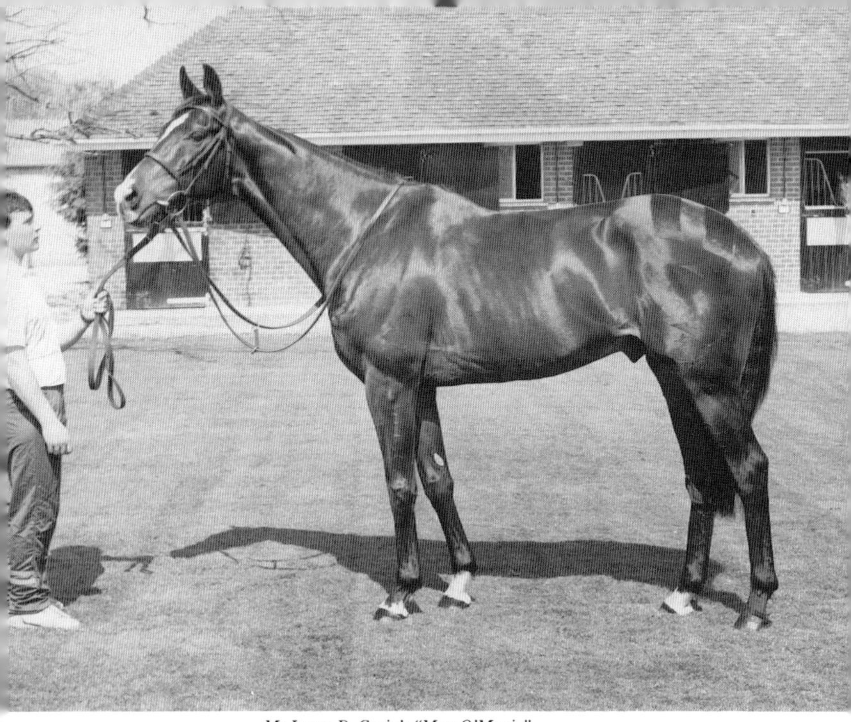

Mr James D. Greig's "Man O'Magic"

Man O'Magic (br.g. 1981)	Manado (b 1973)	Captain's Gig (b 1965)	Turn-To Make Sail
		Slipstream (gr 1967)	Sing Sing Palestream
	Garrucha (br 1961)	Prince Taj (b 1954)	Prince Bio Malindi
		Gibellina (ch 1952)	Clarion III Feria

Northern Spring (by My Swallow), the top two-year-old in Italy in 1975, was subsequently a useful winner over a mile in Britain, while Peranka (by Klairon or Palestine) showed useful form over sprint distances. Man O'Magic, on the other hand, gained his only win on the Flat in a mile-and-a-half maiden event at Warwick in 1984, and at the end of that season he was bought by his present trainer for 2,900 guineas at the Newmarket Autumn Sales. Man O'Magic wore blinkers for the first time at Warwick, and they've become an integral part of his equipment over jumps. Thoroughly genuine and consistent, Man O'Magic looks sure to continue to do well. *K. C. Bailey.*

MAN ON THE LINE 7 ch.g. Whistling Deer–Black Tulip (Pals Passage) [1989/90 20g5] compact, workmanlike gelding: fairly useful hurdler in 1988/9: tailed off in handicap in October: stays 21f: acts on good to firm and dead going. *R. Akehurst.* —

MANOR PARK CRUMPET 6 ch.m. True Song–Madge Spartan (Spartan General) [1989/90 16m] compact mare: sister to fair hurdler True Spartan: dam —

winning hunter chaser: last in mares novice hurdle at Stratford in September. *R. J. Weaver.*

MANOR PARK LASS 6 b.m. Torus–Evening Primrose (Varano) [1989/90 a20gpu 16m a24gpu 16fur 16gpu 16f5 20f3] small, close-coupled mare: little sign of ability: blinkered fifth and sixth outings. *R. J. Weaver.* —

MANOSA MILL 5 b.g. Red Sunset–Egyptian Moon (Kalamoun) [1989/90 16dpu 16d] sparely-made, angular gelding: second reported foal: dam, second over 1m on only start at 2 yrs, is half-sister to Circus Plume: last in minor event in June, only outing on Flat: last in novice claiming hurdle at Sedgefield in December. *Roy Robinson.* —

MANOUSHKA 5 b.m. Ile de Bourbon (USA)–Gilwanigan (Captain's Gig (USA)) [1989/90 16f2 16f 16f a16g5] neat mare: poor novice selling hurdler: form only at 2m on firm going: visored final start 1988/9. *P. Butler.* 68

MANS NO ANGEL 5 b.g. Aragon–No Halo (Aureole) [1989/90 16m 17m5 16f6 16f3 16g5 16f6 16m] small gelding: plater on Flat, in frame at up to 1¼m: poor novice over hurdles (ran in seller third start): headstrong. *T. Craig.* 76

MANSTON MARAUDER 14 b.g. Dubassoff (USA)–Smokey's Sister (Forlorn River) [1989/90 c20spu c24d4] neat gelding: poor hunter chaser nowadays: best form at much shorter distances than 25f: best with give in the ground and acts well on heavy going: suited by waiting tactics. *Mrs L. E. Pile.* c— —

MANTINIK 5 b.g. Sayyaf–Bonny Rand (USA) (Hillary) [1989/90 16g 16g 16g 16v 17m5 16m2] small gelding: novice selling hurdler: visored, second to Western Divide in handicap at Towcester in April, best effort: tried to refuse and unseated rider 2 out only outing 1988/9. *J. D. J. Davies.* 74

MANTINOLAS 11 b.m. Mandamus–Happy Tino (Rugantino) [1989/90 c22sur] lengthy mare: useful winning point-to-pointer: jumped well when second in novice chase in 1987: unseated rider fifth in novice hunter chase in February: stays 3m. *Mrs K. R. J. Nicholas.* c—

MANTON MARK 7 b.g. On Your Mark–Sindy's Sister (Fidalgo) [1989/90 c16gF] tailed off in novice hurdle in 1988/9: fell fatally second in novice chase at Kempton in December. *P. R. Hedger.* c— —

MAPLE HAYES 4 b.f. Pas de Seul–Sweet Eliane (Birdbrook) [1989/90 16d6 17d6 16m 16g6 16g 16f5 17m5 16g3 16m5 16m4] compact filly: poor maiden on Flat: sold out of R. Hollinshead's stable 3,000 gns Doncaster September Sales: poor juvenile selling hurdler: barely stays 2m. *Mrs A. Knight.* 69

MARACAS BAY 11 b.g. Simbir–Valiretta (USA) (Go Marching (USA)) [1989/90 27s c20gpu] compact gelding: novice hurdler: has run in a seller: no form over fences: seems to stay 3m: acts on soft going: usually wears blinkers or a visor: usually amateur ridden. *N. Waggott.* c— —

MARCELLINA 8 ch.m. Welsh Pageant–Connarca (Connaught) [1989/90 16g5 16m6 20m* 20g6 24s6 17g* 24g3 20d 17d2] handicap hurdler: won at Carlisle in November (amateur riders) and January: ran well when placed on same course afterwards: tailed off when pulled up on chasing debut in 1987/8: effective at around 2m and stays 3m: acts on good to firm and dead ground: usually claimer ridden. *E. J. Alston.* c— 107

MARCH AMADEUS 8 ch.g. Sousa–Dotted Swiss (Super Slip) [1989/90 c25g*] big, workmanlike gelding: winning point-to-pointer: jumped none too fluently in early stages, but stayed on strongly to lead approaching 2 out when winning slowly-run hunter chase at Wolverhampton (finished lame) in February by 20 lengths: stays 25f. *Mrs H. E. North.* **c100**

MARCH FOLLY 4 gr.f. Daring March–Creme de La Creme (Saritamer (USA)) [1989/90 16gpu 18fpu] sparely-made filly: third foal: dam ran 3 times: behind when pulled up in novice hurdle and juvenile event: pulls hard. *P. R. Hedger.* —

MARCHMAN 5 b.g. Daring March–Saltation (Sallust) [1989/90 16g c16s 16f* 16m* 18f* 18f* 16m4] rangy, workmanlike gelding: in good form in spring and won novice hurdle at Newbury, novice handicaps at Uttoxeter and Fontwell and handicap on last-named course: tailed off on chasing debut: takes good hold and unlikely to stay much beyond 2¼m: acts on firm going. *J. S. King.* c— 100

MARCH ON 4 b.g. Daring March–Dualvi (Dual) [1989/90 16g* 16spu 16g] tall, leggy gelding: brother to 2 winners on Flat, including Combined Exercise who has also won over hurdles: well beaten only outing on Flat: jumped well in main when 99 winning juvenile hurdle at Kempton in November: failed to confirm that promise afterwards: possibly unsuited by soft ground. *R. V. Smyth.*

MARCOMTE 7 ch.g. Vicomte–Marcus Lady (Marcus Superbus) [1989/90 16m 20f5] strong gelding: no sign of ability in novice hurdles. *D. A. Lamb.* —

MARDOOD 5 b.h. Ela-Mana-Mou–Tigeen (Habitat) [1989/90 16g 16m3] lengthy horse: placed in juvenile hurdle in 1988/9 and claimer at Ludlow (didn't go through with effort) in January. *J. P. Price.* 90

MARDY'S MARIGOLD 6 ch.m. Vrondi–Linbury Lady (Royal Palace) [1989/90 16d] angular, sparely-made mare: evidently of no account on Flat or over hurdles. *F. G. Hollis.* —

MAREJO 9 ch.m. Creetown–Sarona (Lord of Verona) [1989/90 c17m3 c16g4 c17g2 c16g2 c17d* c16g3 c16d* c16m3 c16g2 c16g3] sturdy mare: handicap chaser: won at Kelso in January and Catterick in February: ran creditably most other starts: best at around 2m in a strongly-run race: acts on any going: usually held up: usually jumps well. *F. T. Walton.* **c113** —

MARICAMA 7 b.h. Julio Mariner–Cama (FR) (Pardao) [1989/90 16h*] blinkered, won 6-runner novice handicap hurdle at Taunton in May by 2 lengths from Sporting Idol: stays 2¾m: acts on hard going (tailed off when pulled up on heavy only outing 1987/8). *M. C. Pipe.* 87

MARIE'S VALENTINE 7 b.m. Piaffer (USA)–Tavuto (Pitcairn) [1989/90 16f 16m] poor maiden miler on Flat when last ran at 4 yrs: has since been to stud, producing foals in 1988 and 1989: well beaten in novice and maiden hurdle. *W. G. Mann.* —

MARIE SWIFT 5 b.m. Main Reef–Sarus (Amber Rama (USA)) [1989/90 F16s5 16dpu 16m] lengthy, sparely-made mare: fourth foal: half-sister to 2 poor animals: dam stayed 1½m: fifth in NH Flat race at Warwick in February: no sign of ability in novice hurdles. *R. Dickin.* —

MARIE ZEPHYR 6 b.m. Treboro (USA)–Thimothea (FR) (Timmy My Boy) [1989/90 16g 16v6 a20gpu 20g 20s] angular mare: novice hurdler: well beaten in 1989/90, including in a seller: should stay beyond 2m: ran poorly on very firm ground: ran in snatches once. *C. W. C. Elsey.* —

MARINA MEDE 6 b.m. Runnymede–Bodicea (King's Troop) [1989/90 16m 16sF 16s 16d] smallish, good-quartered mare: behind in novice hurdles and a seller. *C. D. Broad.* —

MARINERS DREAM 9 br.g. Julio Mariner–My Ginny (Palestine) [1989/90 c17mpu c25hur c26fur c24hpu] neat gelding: poor hurdler/novice chaser: let down by his jumping over fences: stayed 3m: acted on any going: tried in blinkers and a visor: dead. *N. R. Mitchell.* c— x —

MARINER'S LAD 8 ch.g. Julio Mariner–Sorebelle (Prince Tenderfoot (USA)) [1989/90 16m 16m c20m6 c16m3] workmanlike gelding: winning hurdler: no worthwhile form for some time: let down by his jumping when well beaten in novice chases: has run respectably over 2½m: probably acts on any going: often blinkered nowadays. *A. P. James.* c— x —

MARINERS LAW 7 b.g. Julio Mariner–Gallic Law (Galivanter) [1989/90 16g 20f 20f 16g] neat gelding: twice runner-up over hurdles in 1988/9 (didn't find a great deal under pressure in amateur riders event on one occasion): well beaten subsequently: stays 2½m: blinkered final start 1988/9 and last 2 outings: sold out of J. FitzGerald's stable 1,700 gns Doncaster November Sales. *Miss G. M. Rees.* —

MARINERS PET 4 b.f. Julio Mariner–Fullstop (Salvo) [1989/90 F16m4 F16m4] third foal: half-sister to winning hurdler Assumtion (by Jimsun): dam poor maiden on Flat and over hurdles: close fourth in NH Flat races at Huntingdon and Sandown: yet to race over hurdles. *R. G. Brazington.*

MARINERS SECRET 4 b.f. Julio Mariner–Midnight Pansy (Deadly Nightshade) [1989/90 16g 16s3] neat filly: fourth reported foal: half-sister to 3 winning hurdlers, including useful performers Jimsintime and Jimbalou (both by Jimsun): dam placed over hurdles: behind in minor event on Flat in October: remote third behind General Pershing in juvenile hurdle at Hereford in December. *R. G. Brazington.* 83

MARINER'S STAR 8 b.g. Julio Mariner–Falling Gold (USA) (High Echelon) [1989/90 21vpu 16d c16g5 c20f4 c24fpu c20g4] leggy gelding: modest novice hurdler/chaser: better suited by 2½m than 2m, and will stay further: acts on firm and dead going (has run moderately on heavy). *J. R. Bosley.* c82 —

MARK AIZLEWOOD 5 b.h. Nicholas Bill–Lunar Queen (Queen's Hussar) [1989/90 16f 16g^F 24d^pu 20f^2] compact horse: poor mover: modest and none-too-genuine handicapper on Flat: clear of remainder when 2 lengths second to Regent Cross in novice handicap at Newcastle in March, first form over hurdles: stays 2½m: acts on firm going: visored last 2 starts: took little interest on hurdling debut. *R. M. Whitaker.* 82

MARK-EDEN 7 b.g. On Your Mark–Dainty Eden (Orbit) [1989/90 16g 16g^4 16g^3 16g^pu] leggy, good-topped gelding: poor sprint maiden on Flat: in frame in maiden hurdle and novice event: dead. *G. M. Moore.* 90

MARKET FORCES 7 b.g. Soldier Rose–Cover Your Money (Precipice Wood) [1989/90 c21d^5 c24g^F c24g^5 c24d] leggy, good-topped gelding: winning hurdler: showed some ability on chasing debut, but subsequently let down by his jumping: stays 21f: acts on heavy going: tends to sweat: has worn a crossed noseband: has run well when claimer ridden. *N. A. Gaselee.* **c86** x —

MARKET LEADER 10 b. or br.g. Kala Shikari–Natflat (Barrons Court) [1989/90 16m^6 c16m^2 c16h* c16m^5 c16d* c19g^ur c17m^2 c16g* c16g^3 c16g* c16f*] lengthy gelding: winning hurdler/chaser: had good season and won handicap chases at Ludlow (3), Hereford and Market Rasen: best form at 2m: acts on firm and dead going: consistent. *R. Lee.* **c115** —

MARKET MAKER 4 b.c. Kafu–One Rose (Pall Mall) [1989/90 16h^5] poor maiden firm-ground miler on Flat, usually blinkered: sold out of F. J. Houghton's stable 4,200 gns Ascot September Sales: resold 1,500 gns Doncaster November Sales: remote last of 5 in selling hurdle at Hexham. *F. S. Storey.* —

MARKET PRICES 4 b.g. Silly Prices–Cathro (Appiani II) [1989/90 16g^pu] sixth foal: dam bad plater: pulled up 2 out in juvenile hurdle at Uttoxeter: dead. *Mrs S. M. Johnson.* —

MARKET SPIRIT 6 ch.g. Kind of Hush–Derraillia (Derring-Do) [1989/90 16f] neat gelding: winning hurdler: raced only at around 2m: best form on a sound surface: claimer ridden: took a good hold: dead. *P. Liddle.* —

MARK KYBO 6 b.g. Niels–Raglan Lane (Allangrange) [1989/90 16d^5 16f] medium-sized gelding: second foal: dam ran twice at 2 yrs: claimer ridden, promising fifth in novice hurdle at Towcester in February on debut: mid-division in similar contest at Plumpton following month. *J. T. Gifford.* 90

MARLBOROUGH LADY 4 gr.f. Rusticaro (FR)–Noir Afrique (African Sky) [1989/90 16m 16m^3 16s^3 16g^4 16m^6 17m 19f^4 16m^5] small filly: plater on Flat, probably stays 1¼m: sold out of D. Thom's stable 1,800 gns Doncaster September Sales: in frame in juvenile hurdles and a claimer: ran moderately on top-of-the-ground last 4 starts (including in selling company): likely to prove best at around 2m: easily best form on soft going. *Mrs A. Knight.* 68 ?

MARLEFIELD 8 ch.g. Le Bavard (FR)–Ballyowen (Arctic Slave) [1989/90 c16g^pu c22g^5 c20d^ur c16g^6 c22f^4] tall, leggy gelding: ungenuine novice hurdler/chaser: probably stays 2¾m: broke blood vessel final start. *J. K. M. Oliver.* **c80** § —

MARLEY MONARCH 6 ch.g. Dara Monarch–Sea Dog (Sea Hawk II) [1989/90 16h^3 c20f^ur c16d^pu] stocky gelding: lightly-raced novice hurdler: disputing lead when unseating rider 5 out in novice event at Plumpton in October on chasing debut: well behind when pulled up and dismounted 3 out in similar race following month: stays 2¼m: probably acts on any going. *D. M. Grissell.* c— 86

MARLIN DANCER 5 b.g. Niniski (USA)–Mullet (Star Appeal) [1989/90 16g^2] close-coupled, rather sparely-made gelding: winning hurdler: jumped none too fluently but finished distance clear of remainder when second in conditional jockeys seller at Bangor in November: will stay 2½m: acts on heavy going. *J. D. J. Davies.* 86 +

MARMION 5 b. or br.g. Sweet Monday–Parrot Fashion (Pieces of Eight) [1989/90 16g 22g 18s] sturdy gelding: well beaten over hurdles. *J. V. Redmond.* —

MAROUAT 5 ch.g. Torus–El Reine (Bargello) [1989/90 16f 16g^5 16m^co] leggy, workmanlike gelding: sixth foal: half-brother to Irish 2½m bumpers winner Regal Quest (by Le Bavard): dam won bumpers race and placed over hurdles in Ireland: showed some ability in novice hurdle at Cheltenham in January on second start: badly hampered and crashed through wing at third later in month. *C. P. E. Brooks.* 82

MARQUEE CAFE 6 ch.g. Sallust–Royal Sensation (Prince Regent (FR)) [1989/90 19m 22d^2 22d* 24g 22s^pu] smallish, angular gelding: handicap hurdler: won moderately-run race at Nottingham in January: beaten a long way afterwards: 98

stays 2¾m: acts on dead going and good to firm: has won for a 7-lb claimer. *Miss G. Dollar.*

MARRADONG BROOK 5 ch.g. Giacometti–Freuchie (Vulgan) [1989/90
16d^{2} 17d^{3} 21m*] workmanlike gelding: has scope: showed ability over hurdles 102 +
prior to winning novice handicap at Ludlow in most impressive fashion by 20
lengths from Tribal Mascot, leading 2 out, quickening clear in tremendous style
and eased considerably run-in: looked certain to win more races, but wasn't seen
out again: better suited by 21f than 2m and should stay further: acts on good to
firm going. *Capt. T. A. Forster.*

MARSDALE 5 b.m. Royal Palace–Jamuna (Canisbay) [1989/90 16m^{pu}] half-
sister to 1978 2-y-o 5f and 6f winner Royal Connection (by Royalty): dam placed
over 1m in France: tailed off in NH Flat races: behind when pulled up in novice —
handicap on hurdling debut. *Mrs P. Townsley.*

MARSH KING 9 b.g. Kinglet–Camargue (Combat) [1989/90 c20d^{F}] sparely- c—
made gelding: fairly useful hurdler at his best: lightly raced: fell eighth in novice —
event in November on chasing debut: stays 3m: possibly unsuited by heavy
ground, acts on any other: often sweats and gets very much on toes: good mount
for an inexperienced rider: sometimes bandaged. *P. J. Hobbs.*

MARSHLANDER 11 b.g. Sheshoon–Dinamarsh (Nelcius) [1989/90 c26m* **c110**
c26f* c24m* c24m^{2} c24f^{2} c24f^{2} c28m^{2} c25m* c25m^{2} c25g^{3} c24g^{4} c26m^{2}] tall
gelding: had a good season and won handicap chases at Bangor, Newton Abbot,
Worcester and Towcester: ran creditably most other starts: stays 3¼m: acts on
firm ground. *D. R. Gandolfo.*

MARSH MINK 8 b.m. Our Jimmy (USA)–Swinging Mink (Swing Easy (USA)) c—
[1989/90 16g 17v 22d^{6} 22g c24f^{F}] lengthy, unfurnished mare: has shown a little 78
ability in novice hurdles: beaten when falling at the fourteenth in novice event on
chasing debut: will be suited by a stiff test of stamina. *P. J. Hobbs.*

MARSIR 7 b.g. Sir Mago–National Day (Marcus Brutus) [1989/90 c16g^{F} c20g^{ur} c80 x
c20g^{4} c16g^{5} c20d^{5} c27d^{2} c25g^{4} c24g^{F} c24m^{3}] sturdy gelding: poor novice —
hurdler/chaser: stays well: often let down by his jumping. *Roy Robinson.*

MARTIAL COMMANDER (USA) 10 b.g. Bold Commander (USA)– c80
Mijanou (USA) (Gallant Romeo (USA)) [1989/90 c26m^{4} c24s^{5} c26g^{5} c26g^{2} c26v^{4}] —
small gelding: winning hurdler/poor novice chaser: needs long distances: acts on
heavy going: blinkered last 2 starts. *G. P. Enright.*

MARTINELLI 11 b.g. Martinmas–Panetta (USA) (Pantene) [1989/90 17h^{3}
16f^{pu} 16g a16g^{6} 16d^{5}] small, workmanlike gelding: selling hurdler nowadays: ran 64
poorly in 1989/90: best form at 2m: acts on any going: occasionally blinkered. *C. R. Beever.*

MARTIN O'SHAUNESSY 7 b.g. Martinmas–O'Shaunessy (Charlottesville)
[1989/90 22d 22v^{pu} 22d^{pu}] lengthy, workmanlike gelding: no sign of ability in —
2¾m novice hurdles. *A. Fowler.*

MARTINSBURG 7 b.g. Sir Nulli–Lady Fleur (Golden Merle) [1989/90 F16h^{4}
24g^{F} 20f^{pu}] workmanlike, close-coupled gelding: no sign of ability, including in a —
selling handicap. *W. G. Morris.*

MARTIN'S FRIEND 7 br.g. Noble Imp–Indian Madness (Indian Ruler)
[1989/90 F16g 20s^{pu} 24m^{pu}] leggy, sparely-made gelding: third foal: half-brother —
to useful staying chaser Midnight Madness (by Genuine): dam never ran: well
beaten in NH Flat race: tailed off when pulled up in novice hurdles. *D. Bloomfield.*

MARTINSMOON 5 ch.m. Homeboy–Moonvein (New Member) [1989/90 26f^{5}
20h^{2} 17h^{3} 21m^{3} 21m^{4} 22m^{5} 20m^{2} 21f^{2} 20f^{3} a20g^{2} a22g^{3} a24g^{3} a24g^{3} 20m^{6}] 91
smallish, workmanlike mare: handicap hurdler: placed 10 times in 1989/90
(trained until after thirteenth start by W. G. M. Turner): stays 2¾m: acts on firm
going and is possibly unsuited by soft: blinkered once in 1988/9: has run well for a
claimer but looks a difficult ride. *J. L. Spearing.*

MARTIN THOMAS 7 br.g. Auction Ring (USA)–Canelle (Sassafras (FR)) c82
[1989/90 c24g^{pu} c24f^{3} c25f^{pu} c26g^{pu}] angular ex-Irish gelding: poor novice —
hurdler/chaser. *J. D. Thomas.*

MARY ANGUS 5 b.m. Oats–March Maid (Marmaduke) [1989/90 16m^{pu}]
fourth foal: half-sister to novice hurdler Frans Girl (by Take A Reef): dam never —
ran: amateur ridden, soon tailed off and pulled up 2 out in mares novice event at
Stratford in September. *L. J. Righton.*

MASCALLS LADY 5 b.m. Nicholas Bill–Whisper Gently (Pitskelly) [1989/90
a16g^{pu} 16g^{pu} 17m^{F}] sparely-made mare: only form on Flat when winning 1m seller —

at 3 yrs: failed to get past fourth in all-weather selling hurdle (trained by W. G. Turner) and 2 novice events. *N. B. Thomson.*

MASHUM 4 br.g. Humdoleila–Masami (King Log) [1989/90 F12g^{5} F16g] fifth foal: half-brother to a winner in Austria by Mister Tudor: dam of no account: fifth in NH Flat race at Hexham in March: well beaten in similar event at Kelso later in month: yet to race over hurdles. *A. C. Batey.*

MASNOON (USA) 7 ch.g. Sharpen Up–A Twinkling (USA) (Prince John) **c131**
[1989/90 c20g c16d^{2} c16d* c16g* c16s^{3} c16v^{3} c16d^{3} c16m^{4} c16f^{6} c20f^{pu}] tall —
gelding: useful chaser: landed the odds in small fields at Sedgefield in December and Catterick in January: creditable fourth to Katabatic in valuable handicap at Cheltenham in March and creditable sixth to Nohalmdun in similar race at Liverpool in April: ran poorly final start: would have won but for taking wrong course on run-in at Sedgefield on first outing: best form at 2m: unsuited by very soft going, acts on any other: amateur ridden except sixth start: to be trained by J. Eyre. *Denys Smith.*

MASONS AVENUE 5 b. or br.h. Taufan (USA)–Line of Reason (High Line)
[1989/90 16f^{3} 16f* 16h^{5}] medium-sized horse: quite a modest handicapper on Flat: 95
won novice hurdle at Uttoxeter in August: acted on firm ground: dead. *N. Tinkler.*

MASSINGHAM 6 ch.g. Deep Run–Ballygirl (Ballyciptic) [1989/90 16d 20g^{6}
16g^{6} 24m^{pu}] workmanlike gelding: fourth foal: half-brother to 1m winner Tudor 81
Chief (by Tudenham): dam never ran: poor form in novice hurdles: raced too freely to stay 2½m. *C. P. E. Brooks.*

MASTER ATTORNEY 8 b.g. General Ironside–Miss Leap Year (Cantab) c83
[1989/90 c20g c16m^{4} c24s^{5} c20g^{4} c20f c20f c16m^{6} c21f^{F}] workmanlike gelding: —
poor novice hurdler/chaser: destroyed after falling at Cartmel in May: stayed 3m: was sometimes blinkered. *D. McCain.*

MASTER BARN 10 ch.g. Celtic Cone–Rummara (Quorum) [1989/90 c25f* c94
c20d^{ur} c21v^{pu} 21m c17m^{F} c24f^{2} 24f^{4} 24f^{2}] big, lengthy gelding: fairly useful 126
hurdler: ran well last 2 starts, making most at Ascot in April and May: usually let down by his jumping over fences, but won novice chase at Wolverhampton in October: stays 25f and effective at shorter: acts on firm ground and is unsuited by soft: blinkered sixth start: needs to improve his jumping to progress over fences. *R. G. Frost.*

MASTER BLACKSMITH 13 br.g. Vivify–Another Knother (Premonition) c—
[1989/90 c24d^{pu}] strong, workmanlike gelding: lightly-raced point-to-pointer,

Kim Muir Memorial Challenge Cup, Cheltenham—Master Bob is clear of Golden Minstrel

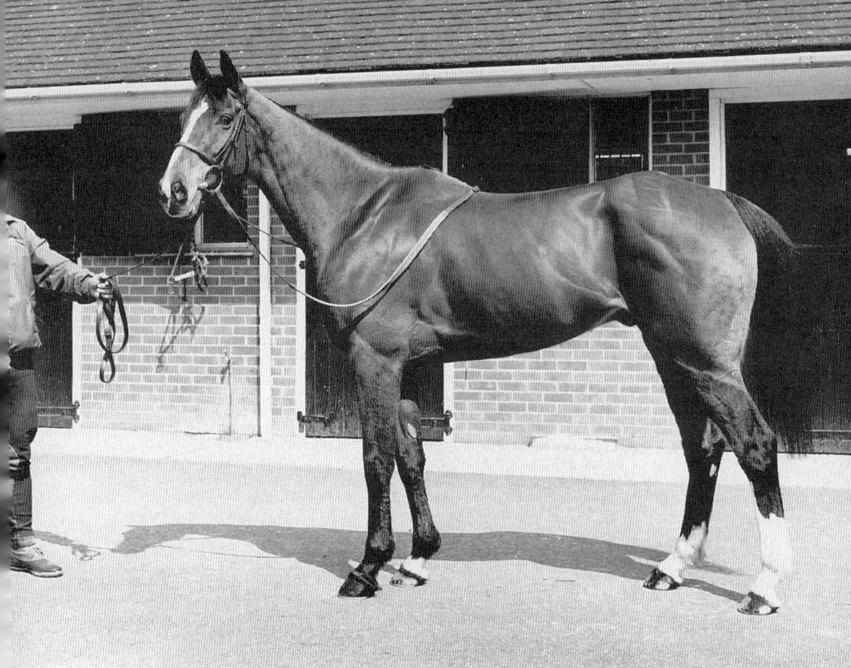

Mr Ian Wills's "Master Bob"

winner in March and April: tailed off when pulled up in maiden hunter chase at Leicester in March. *C. W. Cooper.*

MASTER BOB 10 b.g. Pitpan–Good Calx (Khalkis) [1989/90 c24g^{2} c24m^{3} c25d^{pu} c24m* c26f^{3}] leggy, rather sparely-made gelding: fair chaser: 20/1, won 17-runner Kim Muir Memorial Challenge Cup Handicap Chase at Cheltenham in March by 3 lengths from Golden Minstrel, leading at the last and idling run-in: let down by his jumping previous 2 starts and didn't go through with his effort final outing: suited by a test of stamina: acts on any going: sometimes blinkered (was at Cheltenham) or visored. *N. J. Henderson.* c**127** § —

MASTER BOON 11 b.g. Sagaro–Miss Boon (Road House II) [1989/90 c20d^{pu}] neat gelding: novice selling hurdler: winning chaser: poor point-to-pointer: bit backward and jumped badly in March: seems suited by a good test of stamina: form only on soft ground over fences: has worn blinkers (didn't when successful). *Tyrone Stratton.* c— —

MASTER COMEDY 6 b.g. Comedy Star (USA)–Romardia (Romulus) [1989/90 22s^{pu} c20v^{2} c24g^{2} c18s^{2} c17d^{6}] leggy, sparely-made gelding: poor novice selling hurdler: runner-up in 3 races over fences, showing modest form: needs further than 2m and stays 3m, at least when conditions aren't testing: acts on heavy going: has worn crossed noseband. *Miss L. Bower.* c97 —

MASTER CORNET 5 ch.g. Celtic Cone–Yogurt (Saint Denys) [1989/90 25g 20g 24d] workmanlike gelding: brother to winning staying hurdler Change The Name and half-brother to fairly useful staying chaser Masterplan (by Master Owen): dam winning Irish hurdler: well beaten in novice hurdles. *P. A. Blockley.* —

MASTER ERYL 7 ro.g. Anax–Blackberry Hill (Sovereign Path) [1989/90 c20g* c25f^{2} c24g^{F} c25f^{F} c22m^{2} c26m^{pu}] tall gelding: fifth live foal: dam 7f c99 x winner: fairly useful point-to-pointer: hunter chaser: hung right run-in when winning at Doncaster in February: second on same course following month (swerved badly right after 2 out) and at Stratford in May (hampered near finish when going down by 2½ lengths to Corrarder): stays 3m: has worn a crossed noseband: makes mistakes. *Mrs Roger Guilding.*

MASTER FRENCH 10 b.g. Ancient Monro–Miss French (Sunny Brae) c—
[1989/90 c24g^{pu} c24s^{pu} c25g c24g^{pu}] rangy gelding: useful point-to-pointer: no —
sign of ability over hurdles or in steeplechases. *B. T. Crawford.*

MASTER GLEASON 7 br. or ro.g. Gleason (USA)–Mesena (Pals Passage) c87
[1989/90 20d^{pu} c16g^{F} c20m^{3} c24f^{F}] useful-looking gelding: poor novice hurdler/ —
chaser: will stay beyond 2½m: acts on good to firm going. *D. J. G. Murray-Smith.*

MASTER HARDY 11 b.g. Lord Nelson (FR)–Elf's Bow (Elf-Arrow) [1989/90 c74 +
c21d^{5} c25m^{6} c25f^{ur} c25m^{4}] lengthy, sparely-made gelding: fairly useful point-to-pointer, successful twice in March: would probably have finished third but for unseating rider 4 out in hunter chase won by Park Shade at Cheltenham in May. *P. J. Hunt.*

MASTER LAMB 7 gr.g. Absalom–Caroline Lamb (Hotfoot) [1989/90 c17m*] c119
well-made gelding: winning hurdler: unbeaten in 6 steeplechases: jumped well in —
main and showed improved form when winning handicap at Cartmel in August: not seen out again: stays 21f: has won on firm going but will probably prove ideally suited by more give: has worn a tongue strap: front runner. *J. J. O'Neill.*

MASTER MARRON 5 b.g. Hotfoot–Sally Conkers (Roi Lear (FR)) [1989/90
16g 20v 24d^{pu} 24s^{pu} 22g 25g 25m] lengthy gelding: well beaten in NH Flat races —
and novice hurdles. *D. J. Wintle.*

MASTER MARTIN 12 b.g. Martinmas–Princess Irmgard (Delirium) c77 x
[1989/90 17h^{6} 17f c17h^{F} 21f^{3} c17m^{4} c17h^{ur} c17f^{ur} a18g^{5} a16g c17m^{F} 17h^{6}] smallish 63
gelding: poor novice hurdler/chaser: poor jumper of fences. *W. R. Williams.*

MASTER MAYO 7 b.h. Argentinos–Mayo Lassie (Arctic Slave) [1989/90 c89
c24m^{2}] big, workmanlike horse: winning hurdler: 12 lengths second to Bonnie —
Artist in novice chase at Newcastle in November: suited by 3m: acts on firm and dead ground: good mount for an amateur. *J. I. A. Charlton.*

MASTER MERLIN 6 b.g. Straight Knight–Salmon Spirit (Big Deal) [1989/90
24m^{pu}] first foal: dam unraced half-sister to 2 winning point-to-pointers: behind —
until pulled up 2 out in novice hurdle at Uttoxeter on debut. *R. Dickin.*

MASTER MUCK 7 b.g. Sagaro–Emperor's Gift (Menelek) [1989/90 20d^{pu}] c— x
rather leggy gelding: winning hurdler: always behind in December: yet to com- —
plete course over fences: seems suited by a test of stamina. *N. A. Twiston-Davies.*

MASTER OF LYRIC 8 br.g. Grange Melody–Miss Goodyear (Trouville) c—
[1989/90 c20m] big, workmanlike gelding: carries plenty of condition: modest —
novice hurdler: winning chaser: burly only outing of 1989/90 (January): will stay long distances: acts on good to firm ground and is possibly unsuited by very soft: blinkered last 5 outings in 1988/9. *R. Akehurst.*

MASTER OF PARIS (USA) 6 b.g. Master Willie–Woman of Paris (FR) (Sir c71 +
Ribot) [1989/90 c18g^{F} 16g^{6} c20g^{3}] tall, angular ex-Irish gelding: won a point- —
to-point in 1989: maiden hurdler: seemed not to stay 2½m in selling handicap chase at Bangor in April: bolted going to start second start: trained first start by N. McGrath. *P. Burgoyne.*

MASTER OF SHANE 11 b.g. Cantab–Miss Goodyear (Trouville) [1989/90 c— x
c20m c24h^{2} c16m^{pu} c22g^{pu} c20s^{pu}] lengthy gelding: winning hurdler/chaser: —
stays 2¾m: acts on soft going: makes mistakes: trained by Mrs N. Sharpe until after third start. *J. R. Jenkins.*

MASTERPLAN 13 b.g. Master Owen–Yogurt (Saint Denys) [1989/90 c20d^{3}] c—
leggy gelding: fair chaser: ran as though needing race when remote third in —
hunter chase at Newbury in February: effective at 2½m and stays 3m well (tired third when falling last over 4m): yet to race on very firm ground, acts on any other: bold jumper. *W. Jenks.*

MASTER PLAN (FR) 4 b.g. Carwhite–Manene (FR) (Tapioca (FR)) [1989/90
16g] claimed out of R. Boss's stable £20,500 after winning 9f claimer on Flat in — p
October: 4/1, around 21 lengths eighth behind Southend Scallywag in 10-runner juvenile hurdle at Kelso in November: won again at 9f on Flat in 1990. *J. S. Wilson.*

MASTER RAJH 6 b.g. Majestic Maharaj–Miss Medina (St Elmo) [1989/90 c115 p
c16g^{2} c16d* c16g* c16f* c16g*] leggy, workmanlike gelding: novice hurdler: took —
very well to chasing and won novice events at Nottingham, Wolverhampton (2)

and Bangor: just got up to beat below-par Boutzdaroff in sponsored event on
last-named course: takes a keen hold and is likely to prove best at around 2m on a
sound surface: on the upgrade and should win more races. *J. Chugg.*

MASTER REDWOOD 6 ch.g. General Ironside–Chammyville (Chamier)
[1989/90 16f $16g^{pu}$ $16g^{pu}$] IR 6,000 4-y-o: leggy gelding: half-brother to smart —
chaser Villierstown (by Giolla Mear) and to 2 winning point-to-pointers: dam
unraced: no sign of ability over hurdles: visored and wore tongue strap in claimer
final start. *T. T. Bill.*

MASTER SALESMAN 7 b.g. Torenaga–Madam Milan (Milan) [1989/90 c88
$c16g^{4}$ $c20d^{pu}$ c16d $c16m^{2}$ $c16f^{2}$ $c16d^{pu}$ $16f^{pu}$] sturdy gelding: winning hurdler: in —
frame in novice chases: should stay beyond 2m: acts on firm ground. *F. T. Walton.*

MASTER SOUTH LAD 6 b.g. Shrivenham–Miss Rosewyn (Wynkell) c94
[1989/90 $c16f^{2}$] tall gelding: has shown ability in novice hurdles: 25/1 and claimer —
ridden, long way clear of remainder when 4 lengths second to Night Session in
6-runner novice chase at Wincanton in October. *R. J. Hodges.*

MASTER THATCHER 4 b.g. Thatching–Mistress Vyne (Prince Tenderfoot
(USA)) [1989/90 16s $16d^{pu}$] IR 16,000F, 38,000Y, 2,500 3-y-o: half-brother to 2 —
winners, including 1m seller winner Trailfinder (by Fordham), later successful
abroad: dam placed over 5f: split pastern and destroyed after pulling up in juvenile
hurdle at Warwick. *A. J. Chamberlain.*

MASTER TIM 6 ch.g. Timolin (FR)–Straight Beauty (Straight Lad) [1989/90
$16m^{pu}$] good-topped, lengthy gelding: fourth foal: dam, of no account, is half-sister —
to winning Irish hurdler Mr Sandman: fifth in NH Flat race: tailed off when pulled
up 2 out in novice hurdle at Leicester in December. *B. Smart.*

MASTER TREASURE 8 ch.g. Fair Turn–Real Treasure (Master Owen) c—
[1989/90 $c25m^{ur}$] ex-Irish gelding: little sign of ability over hurdles: yet to com- —
plete course in steeplechases, but won a point-to-point in April: has been tried in
blinkers. *P. H. Shakespeare.*

MASTER TYKE 5 gr.g. Flying Tyke–Habatashie (Habat) [1989/90 a16g a16g]
plater on Flat (won 7f claimer in 1990) : tailed off in a novice event and a seller —
over hurdles. *R. P. C. Hoad.*

MASTER VINCE 12 b.g. Menelek–Oh Babe (Javelot) [1989/90 $a16g^{4}$ $c16d^{3}$ c96 x
$c16s^{F}$ $c16g^{6}$ $c16g^{3}$ $c17f^{ur}$] small, sparely-made, close-coupled gelding: winning —
hurdler/chaser: creditable third in handicaps at Stratford in February and
Uttoxeter in May: stays 2¼m: probably suited by give in the ground nowadays:
suitable mount for a claimer: found little off bridle once in 1986/7: often let down
by his jumping over fences. *J. White.*

MASTER VULGAN 11 br.g. Master Buck–Kathleen Beag (Vulgan) [1989/90 c86
c20d $c24g^{2}$] leggy, narrow gelding: winning chaser: still needed race when —
runner-up at Carlisle in February (sweating): stays well: acts on good to firm and
soft going: sometimes claimer ridden: sound jumper: acts well on sharp tracks:
held up: sold 4,000 gns Doncaster Spring Sales. *Mrs G. R. Reveley.*

MASTER WILLIAM 6 b.g. Pollerton–Ballyea Jacki (Straight Lad) [1989/90
22d $20s^{F}$ 20v $22g^{2}$ $20m^{3}$] smallish, workmanlike gelding: first form over hurdles 90
when placed in novice events at Stratford (handicap) and Huntingdon (3 lengths
third behind Major Effort) in the spring: will be suited by 3m: seems suited by a
sound surface. *J. A. C. Edwards.*

MATCHING WOOD 6 b.g. Touching Wood (USA)–Matloch (Matador)
[1989/90 $20g^{pu}$ $24d^{F}$ $25f^{pu}$] rangy gelding: tailed off in maiden at 2 yrs: failed to —
complete in novice hurdles: unlikely to stay 3m. *R. J. Holder.*

MATCHPLAY 12 b.g. Ribero–Cut And Thrust (Pardal) [1989/90 $c20s^{pu}$ $c20s^{4}$ c—
$c16m^{pu}$] big, strong gelding: useful hunter chaser at his best: ran poorly in
1989/90: stays 2½m: acts on any going: blinkered and wore a tongue strap second
outing (trained until after then by G. Pidgeon). *R. Lee.*

MATRACE 5 ch.m. Mummy's Game–Sospirae (Sandford Lad) [1989/90 16m
16d 22d $20g^{6}$] poor maiden on Flat, in frame at up to 13f: little sign of ability in —
novice hurdles. *J. S. Haldane.*

MATRIC 9 b. or br.g. Mandalus–Bel Arbre (Beau Chapeau) [1989/90 c21s* c119
c20d $c20f^{4}$ $c20f^{4}$] good-topped gelding: fair chaser: won handicap at Market Rasen
in January: good fourth to Kittinger at Newbury in March on third start: ran poorly
otherwise: best form at up to 21f: acts on any going. *J. W. Blundell.*

MATTA MIA FLYER 5 br.m. Boreen (FR)–Wild Deer (Royal Buck) [1989/90 c77
$18s^{pu}$ $c20m^{2}$ $c18f^{3}$] second foal: dam won point-to-point in Ireland: tailed off when —

pulled up 3 out in mares novice hurdle at Fontwell in January: placed in novice chases at Plumpton (2½m, better effort) and Fontwell in the spring: likely to stay 3m: evidently suited by top-of-the-ground. *P. Butler.*

MATWAPA (USA) 5 ch.m. Valdez (USA)–Mattan (USA) (Tentam (USA))
[1989/90 16m^4] leggy mare: poor form over hurdles: dead. *Mrs D. Haine.* 68

MAUDLINS CROSS 5 ch.h. Vaigly Great–Pepin (Midsummer Night II) c—
[1989/90 16d a16g c16s c16g^5 c16m^3] half-brother to winning hurdler Havenwood —
(by Relko): well beaten on Flat, and over hurdles and fences: trained by M. W. Easterby first 2 starts. *J. H. Johnson.*

MAUJENDOR 10 b.g. Rose Laurel–Mark My Word (On Your Mark) [1989/90
20m 24f 25f^2] neat gelding: handicap hurdler: 3 lengths second to Tommys Dream 91
at Hereford in May, only form of 1989/90: suited by a test of stamina: acts on any going: has run creditably for a claimer. *M. Tate.*

MAUNDY BOY 9 b.g. True Song–Steal-A-Look (Don't Look) [1989/90 c22s^F] c84 ?
close-coupled, rather sparely-made gelding: winning hurdler: poor form in —
steeplechases: suited by plenty of give in the ground. *B. Finch.*

MAUREEN'S CAVALIER 6 ch.g. Saher–Aethelflaed (Realm) [1989/90
16g^{ur}] small, deep-girthed gelding: of little account. *P. Burgoyne.* —

MAVERICK'S CREEK (NZ) 4 ro.g. Kutati (NZ)–Lady Nella (NZ) (Lord Kearsey) [1989/90 F17m] behind in NH Flat race at Carlisle: yet to race over hurdles. *D. Moffatt.*

MAW BROON 7 b.m. Silly Prices–Brown's Babu (Top Hat) [1989/90 20m c—
27g^4 20d^3 20s] leggy mare: selling hurdler: jumped moderately when tailed off in 79
novice event on chasing debut: stays 3m: acts on heavy going (no form on firm): good mount for a claimer. *Miss A. J. Aitkin.*

MAXIMUM MAN 4 b.g. Sweet Monday–Wyn-Bank (Green God) [1989/90
16g^{pu}] sturdy gelding: fourth foal: dam fair handicapper when in the mood on Flat, —
won a 2m hurdle: modest maiden on Flat: 33/1 and ridden by 3-lb claimer, tailed off when pulled up 3 out in 21-runner juvenile event at Wetherby on hurdling debut. *M. W. Easterby.*

MAYBE BABY 5 b.g. Don–Treasure Ship (Sovereign Lord) [1989/90 16g 16g
16g 16d 16d^{pu}] leggy, workmanlike gelding: poor novice hurdler. *D. H. Barons.* —

MAYBOURNE 6 ch.g. Deep Run–Easy Can (Tudor Music) [1989/90 16g^{pu}]
workmanlike gelding: fourth in NH Flat race: bit burly, tailed off when pulled up 2 —
out in quite valuable novice hurdle at Kempton in December: dead. *D. M. Grissell.*

MAYFAIR MINX 6 b.m. St Columbus–Belgrave Queen (Sheshoon) [1989/90 F16f* F16m^6 F16f^4] half-sister to 2 winning jumpers, including fairly useful staying chaser Vulgan Warrior (by Vulgan Slave): dam of little account: won NH Flat race at Newbury in March: fourth behind Little Sail at Ludlow following month: sixth behind Going On in well-contested event at Liverpool in between: yet to race over hurdles or fences. *S. Christian.*

MAYFAIR MOSS 5 b.g. Telsmoss–Fair Frederica (Crawter) [1989/90 16m^{pu}]
small, sturdy gelding: tailed off when pulled up in novice and selling hurdles. *Mrs* —
H. Fullerton.

MAYORAN (NZ) 6 b.g. Mayo Mellay (NZ)–Bundoran (NZ) (Bally Royal)
[1989/90 17g^2 17d* 20g^2 21v^{ro} 20v^3 20d^3 21d^3 21m*] leggy, angular gelding: won 126
novice hurdle at Devon & Exeter in November and handicap at Newton Abbot (beat Lapiaffe 4 lengths) in April: will be suited by further than 21f: acts on good to firm and heavy going: visored fifth, sixth and final starts: disputing lead when running out fourth outing. *D. H. Barons.*

MAZANO (USA) 5 ch.g. Vaguely Noble–Itsamaza (USA) (Limit To Reason
(USA)) [1989/90 a16g^{pu}] won over 1½m from 2 starts on Flat at 3 yrs: sold out of —
G. Harwood's stable 5,200 gns Ascot December (1988) Sales: behind when pulled up before last in maiden hurdle at Lingfield in January: dead. *P. Mitchell.*

MCCALLUN 6 b.g. Hittite Glory–Queen Kate (Queen's Hussar) [1989/90
21f^{pu}] leggy, close-coupled gelding: winning selling hurdler: best at around 2m: —
acts on any going. *P. R. Rodford.*

MCCARTNEY 4 b.g. Tug of War–Red Cross (Pitpan) [1989/90 F16d] fourth foal: dam unraced half-sister to several jumping winners, notably smart chaser Our Greenwood and high-class hunter chaser Atha Cliath: well-beaten seventh in NH Flat race at Kelso: yet to race over hurdles. *G. M. Moore.*

MCGUIGAN 6 b.m. True Song–Kitengi (Elf-Arrow) [1989/90 F16m aF14g 20f4 a20g 16m] tall, leggy mare: second foal: dam won her only 2 completed outings in point-to-points: no sign of ability: blinkered last 2 starts. *B. Byford.* —

MEADOW LAD 11 ch.g. Foggy Bell–Ruby Sherry (Straight Cut) [1989/90 c25h4 c26fF c25m2 c25hF c22spu c25mpu c25m5] big gelding: failed to complete course in 2 novice hurdles in 1984/5: maiden point-to-pointer: bad novice chaser: poor jumper: trained until after fourth start by B. Forsey. *David Dicey.* c71 x —

MEADOW MOOR 7 b.h. Comedy Star (USA)–Miss Golightly (Jimmy Reppin) [1989/90 16g 16fpu] smallish horse: winning hurdler: best at 2m: probably acted on any going: dead. *R. R. Lamb.* —

MEADOW TERRACE 6 br.g. Young Man (FR)–Rebecca Sarah (Mansingh (USA)) [1989/90 a16gpu c22mpu c27dpu] leggy gelding: lightly raced and no sign of ability (jumped badly on chasing debut). *T. Kersey.* c— —

MEANIE MINNA 4 b.f. Derrylin–Pirate Maid (Auction Ring (USA)) [1989/90 a16g 16d 16g] small filly: modest maiden on Flat, stays 7f: sold out of P. Walwyn's stable 1,900 gns Doncaster November Sales: well beaten over hurdles: jumped poorly final outing. *J. Norton.* —

MEAN TO ME 4 b.f. Homing–Mac's Melody (Wollow) [1989/90 16f] sparely-made filly: lightly-raced maiden on Flat, placed over 1¼m in February: sweating, pulled hard and led to fourth when remote seventh in juvenile fillies selling hurdle at Wolverhampton. *Mrs Barbara Waring.* —

MEAT THE FOULKES (NZ) 9 b.g. Sea Anchor–Divinity (NZ) (Holy Smoke II) [1989/90 c24gpu] lengthy gelding: lightly-raced novice hurdler/chaser: had just moved smoothly into lead when breaking down and pulled up 2 out in handicap at Bangor in November: should stay 3m. *G. A. Ham.* c92 ? —

MEDES 9 b.g. Artaius (USA)–Close Relation (Levmoss) [1989/90 19f6] workmanlike gelding: winning hurdler: always behind in September: in frame in 2 point-to-points subsequently: stays 25f: seems to act on any going: has been tried in blinkers but is better without: has won for a 7-lb claimer. *W. Price.* —

MEDIA LEADER 10 br.m. True Song–Black Baize (Black Tarquin) [1989/90 c25mpu c24mpu] workmanlike mare: won 2 point-to-points in May (first a walk over): poor novice hurdler/maiden hunter chaser. *David Ladhams.* c— —

MEDITATOR 6 ch.g. High Line–Thoughtful (Northfields (USA)) [1989/90 18spu 21s4 25gF] close-coupled gelding: handicap hurdler: looked probable winner when falling 2 out at Doncaster in February: will stay 3m: acts on dead going. *W. M. Perrin.* 111

MEDUCK 5 b.g. Connaught–Wheatley (Town Crier) [1989/90 F13d2] half-brother to winning jumpers Tommy Tudor (by Tudor Rhythm) and Last Grain (by Remainder Man): dam of no account: second in NH Flat race at Kelso in January: dead. *M. H. Tompkins.*

MEGA BLUE 5 gr.m. Scallywag–Town Blues (Charlottown) [1989/90 F16g] first foal: dam poor plater on Flat and over hurdles: tailed off in NH Flat race at Warwick: yet to race over hurdles or fences. *Miss L. C. Siddall.*

MEGABUCKS 5 b.m. Buckskin (FR)–Floater (Brave Invader (USA)) [1989/90 16dF 17g* 16d* 16g3 16g* 16g 16g 16g5 16d5 a18g] neat ex-Irish mare: third foal: half-sister to fair Irish hurdler Over The Seas (by North Summit): dam ran in 2 Irish NH Flat races: winner 4 times at up to 1½m on Flat (occasionally blinkered, including when successful): won maiden hurdle and minor event at Tralee in August and valuable handicap at Leopardstown in October: best effort in Britain when 15 lengths fifth to Sacre d'Or in Crown Berger Hurdle at Chepstow on ninth outing: should be suited by further than 2m: trained until after seventh start by J. Bolger. *W. J. Musson.* 118

MEGABYTE KING 5 b.g. King's Ride–Lawless Secret (Meadsville) [1989/90 16mpu 16g4 16dur] leggy, close-coupled gelding: poor novice hurdler: dead. *B. Stevens.* 61

MEGADYNE 7 b.m. Balidar–Tots (Dual) [1989/90 a16g 16m5 16f*] poor maiden on Flat: 33/1 and claimer ridden, won novice hurdle at Huntingdon in May by 2 lengths from Mr Kewmill: acts on firm going: has looked a difficult ride. *C. F. Wall.* 67 ?

MEGANAIRE 5 ch.m. Song–Lady of Wales (Welsh Pageant) [1989/90 16f6] novice hurdler: tailed off in August. *P. A. Blockley.* —

MEGAN'S MOVE 7 ch.m. Move Off–River Petterill (Another River) [1989/90 20g*] sparely-made mare: modest hurdler: won handicap at Sedgefield in November by 6 lengths from Stepauli: not seen out again: unlikely to stay beyond 2½m: acts on any going. *W. Storey.* 93

MEGAWATT 6 gr.m. Scallywag–Big Maggie (Master Owen) [1989/90 16m^{pu}] strong mare: second in NH Flat race: no sign of ability in novice hurdles: dead. *Mrs A. R. Hewitt.* —

MEGIDDO 9 b.g. Welsh Saint–Great Aunt (Great Nephew) [1989/90 c22h* c25h^{3} c26f^{pu}] workmanlike gelding: winning point-to-pointer: beat only other finisher in novice chase at Devon & Exeter in August: jumped deliberately and ran in snatches final start, later in month: should stay beyond 2¾m: acts on hard ground: thrice blinkered, including last 2 starts. *Mrs J. Wonnacott.* c**78** —

MEHTAB 4 b.f. Touching Wood (USA)–Zaheen (Silver Shark) [1989/90 16s^{5} 17g^{5} a16g^{5} a16g*] leggy, rather angular filly: unreliable 1m winner on Flat: sold out of B. Hanbury's stable 5,400 gns Newmarket Autumn Sales: makes mistakes over hurdles, but won juvenile event at Southwell in March (blinkered) by 2 lengths from Burkes Progress: claimer ridden previously. *Mrs P. Sly.* 79

MEIGLE STREET 5 b.m. Balgaddy–Golden Owen (Master Owen) [1989/90 F16g] behind in NH Flat races: yet to race over hurdles or fences. *J. S. Haldane.*

MEIKLEOUR 11 b.g. Reliance II–Videmanette (High Perch) [1989/90 c16m^{3} c16m* c16f^{3} c16g*] c**154** —

The Victor Chandler Handicap Chase at Ascot in January has quickly become established as a highlight in the jumping calendar. Originally framed to replace the final of the Embassy Premier Chase series, discontinued after 1986, the intended first two runnings were both lost to the weather. But the two editions since, each the most valuable two-mile handicap chase of the season, have been well worth the sponsor's money. In 1989 Desert Orchid gave Panto Prince 22 lb and beat him in a thrilling finish. The next running had a very competitive field, even after the overnight withdrawal of Barnbrook Again. Established good-class two-milers such as Pearlyman and Panto Prince were set to concede plenty of weight to progressive sorts such as Blueberry King, Feroda and Nohalmdun. Betting took a wide range, with only Norton's Coin of the ten runners starting at longer than 14/1 and almost £50,000 in big bets wagered on seven different

Manicou Handicap Chase, Ascot—Meikleour makes all

Victor Chandler Handicap Chase, Ascot—second course win of the season for Meikleour; the grey Star's Delight gives chase

contenders according to the returns published in *The Sporting Life*. The 7/2 favourite Blueberry King, a winner at Ascot and Newbury the previous month, could finish only sixth behind Meikleour, a 10/1-shot who had run well below his best when last of three to Nohalmdun at Cheltenham on his most recent outing. Meikleour tends to go well fresh—that run at Cheltenham was his third in a month, and on top of that he'd reportedly been suffering from a blood disorder. Looking bright and well after a five-week lay-off, Meikleour raced with plenty of zest at Ascot, duelling up front with Star's Delight. The pair set a strong pace, stretching the field so that when Star's Delight, 12 lb out of the handicap, began to weaken after the second last, Meikleour was left clear. He ran on well to hold off the strong-finishing Feroda by a length and a half, the pair seven lengths clear of Panto Prince, who caught Star's Delight for third place near the finish, with Pearlyman five lengths further back in fifth. The subsequent performances in the Queen Mother Champion Chase at Cheltenham of Feroda (third) and Pearlyman (going well until breaking down after three out) underlined the merit of Meikleour's win. Meikleour himself was withdrawn at the five-day stage of that race and, in fact, wasn't seen out after the Victor Chandler. Though relatively lightly raced, Meikleour has been a good servant to connections, winning twelve of his twenty-nine races over jumps, spread over seven seasons. He'd picked up another valuable prize in winning the Manicou Handicap Chase at Ascot in November, when, after setting a modest pace, jumping left, he'd quickened steadily from Swinley Bottom and run on strongly to hold off Long Engagement by five lengths.

Meikleour (b.g. 1979)	Reliance II (b 1962)	Tantieme (b 1947)	Deux Pour Cent
			Terka
		Relance III (ch 1952)	Relic
			Polaire II
	Videmanette (b 1966)	High Perch (ch 1956)	Alycidon
			Phaetonia
		Cheveley Lass (b 1948)	Precipitation
			Borolys

Before being sent chasing in 1986, Meikleour was campaigned on the Flat, winning six handicaps at up to two miles. His owner Mrs Leggat has bred two other successful stayers out of the fairly useful hurdler Videmanette, namely Mountain Cross (by French Beige), winner of the Ascot

Stakes and Queen Alexandra Stakes within three days in 1978, and Chester Cup-third Almond Valley, subsequently successful in Australia. The next dam Cheveley Lass, third foal of the unraced Borolys, ran only once. But she bred several winners, including Sally Stream, fourth in the Irish One Thousand Guineas and Irish Oaks, and Bastille, 33/1-winner of a division of the Gloucestershire Hurdle at Cheltenham in 1960. Meikleour, a free-running sort, has been raced only at around two miles over jumps. A strong, compact, good-bodied gelding who carries plenty of condition, Meikleour has shown his form on ground ranging from heavy through to good to firm. Better than ever as an eleven-year-old, he should win more races whilst he retains his enthusiasm. *J. G. FitzGerald.*

MEINE VONNE LADY 5 br.m. Jalmood (USA)–Gold Rupee (Native Prince (USA)) [1989/90 16d^pu 16d^pu] sturdy mare: modest 1m plater on Flat: pulled up in novice hurdle at Catterick and seller at Bangor: sold 2,000 gns Doncaster Spring Sales. *D. McCain.* —

MEISTER 10 b.g. Monseigneur (USA)–Matitcha (FR) (Bold Lad (IRE)) [1989/90 c26m*] small gelding: winning hurdler: favourite, won hunter chase at Newton Abbot in May by 12 lengths from Ballyneety: had won 2 point-to-points earlier: suited by a test of stamina: probably acts on any going: has worn a crossed noseband: moderate jumper of fences. *A. E. S. Nuttall.* c**100** x —

MELARKA 5 b.m. Dara Monarch–Melka (Relko) [1989/90 16m] 1m winner and placed at up to 1½m on Flat: placed at 2m over hurdles in Ireland: well beaten both outings in Britain: acts on heavy going and is possibly unsuited by top-of-the-ground. *D. R. C. Elsworth.* —

MELEAGRIS 6 b.g. True Song–Fritillaria (Bargello) [1989/90 F16g³ 16s⁴ 17g 20m³] rather leggy gelding: in frame in NH Flat races and novice hurdles: will be suited by 3m. *R. C. Armytage.* 90

MELENDEZ (USA) 7 ch.g. Le Fabuleux–Touch of Midas (USA) (Majestic Prince) [1989/90 24d⁴ 25g] sturdy gelding: fair but ungenuine hurdler: stays 25f: acts on firm going: suited by strong handling: not a proficient jumper: one to treat with caution. *M. C. Pipe.* 117 §

MELICUS (USA) 5 b.h. Providential–Melodina (Tudor Melody) [1989/90 20s^pu 16g⁶] sparely-made, angular horse: half-brother to triple Champion Hurdle winner See You Then (by Royal Palace): fair 2m winner on Flat at 3 yrs: weakened after being prominent long way in novice hurdles at Chepstow in December and Windsor in March. *P. F. I. Cole.* —

MELISSA GOLD 9 ch.m. Deep Run–Imelda (Dual) [1989/90 c25g^pu] workmanlike mare: winning point-to-pointer: of little account over hurdles and in steeplechases. *G. R. Bebbington.* c— —

MELKONO 6 br.g. Meldrum–Ivory Coast (Poaching) [1989/90 17m³ 24h^ur] sturdy gelding: disputing lead when unseating rider last in 3m amateur riders maiden hurdle at Hexham won by Corrie Lass in May: acts on hard ground. *E. Weymes.* 84

MELLOTTIE 5 b. or br.g. Meldrum–Lottie Lehmann (Goldhill) [1989/90 F16m* F13m* 16f* 16g²] rangy gelding: has scope: first foal: dam winner on Flat and over hurdles: won NH Flat races at Market Rasen and Perth: impressive winner of novice hurdle at Newcastle in October: jumped none too fluently when 1½ lengths second to Magic Soldier in similar event at Wetherby following month: 9f winner on Flat in 1990: will improve over hurdles. *Mrs G. R. Reveley.* 88 p

MELLOW LIGHT 7 b.g. Wolver Hollow–Mellifont (Hook Money) [1989/90 c20v^pu c20m c16d^ur] of little account. *R. C. Armytage.* c— —

MELODY GILL 4 br.f. Tudor Rhythm–Gill Breeze (Farm Walk) [1989/90 16m^pu 16f a16g³ 20g] lengthy, sparely-made filly: ninth foal: dam unraced sister to fairly useful staying hurdler Tree Breeze and to winning hurdlers Gay Walk and Meadow Walk: no worthwhile form on Flat at 2 yrs: remote third in selling hurdle at Southwell in November: finished lame next time. *Mrs P. A. Barker.* 52

MELODY LANE 5 b. or br.m. Horage–Melody Ryde (Shooting Chant) [1989/90 16f³ 16m 16g 16f^F 16s⁴ a16g^pu] small, sturdy mare: modest handicapper on Flat, successful at up to 1m: poor form in selling company over hurdles: pulled up and dismounted final start: blinkered last 3 starts. *R. J. Hodges.* 62

MELODY RUN 8 b.g. Grange Melody–Carnbane Princess (Record Run) [1989/90 20m 21f⁵] stocky ex-Irish gelding: first foal: dam unraced: unplaced in —

NH Flat races: behind in maiden and novice hurdles: poor maiden point-to-pointer: has been blinkered. *Mrs V. Teal.*

MELSONBY 8 br.g. Politico (USA)–Melmin (Comandeer) [1989/90 c22g3 c24d4 c24vpu c24f5] won a point-to-point in 1989: poor form in novice chases. *E. H. Robson.* c75

MEL'S ROSE 5 ch.g. Anfield–Ragtime Rose (Ragstone) [1989/90 16g2 16s2] moderate 7f winner on Flat: runner-up in novice hurdles at Warwick (to First Crack) in December and Nottingham (jumped poorly and below form) in January. *G. A. Huffer.* 97

MELWAY BOY 9 b.g. Celtic Cone–Thirlestane (Hill Clown (USA)) [1989/90 20g c20d c21d6 c22f3 c17m* c17f2] strong, sturdy gelding: no worthwhile form over hurdles: jumped better than previously when winning novice handicap chase at Huntingdon in May: ran creditably next start: likely to prove best at around 2m: acts on firm going. *J. Twibell.* c81 —

MEMBERSHIP 9 ch.g. New Member–Spick And Span (Smartie) [1989/90 c26f5] half-brother to a poor point-to-pointer by Rugantino: dam, 6f winner, placed over hurdles and in point-to-points: modest maiden point-to-pointer: bit backward, jumped none too fluently when well beaten in novice chase at Newton Abbot in October. *R. J. Hodges.* c—

MEMBERS MERLIN 10 b.g. New Member–Quarry Hill (Drumbeg) [1989/90 c26f2] lengthy gelding: modest point-to-pointer, winner in April and May: in frame in novice chases and a hunter chase (8 lengths second to Shedid at Folkestone in May): stays 3¼m: acts on firm ground and is probably unsuited by the mud: blinkered third start 1988/9. *J. A. Pearce.* c86

MEMBERS METTLE 5 ch.m. New Member–Armagnac Spirit (Armagnac Monarch) [1989/90 F16g 16mr] half-sister to poor animal Ash Water (by Pipers Wait): dam never ran: behind in mares NH Flat race at Hereford in November: behind when refusing and unseating rider second in novice hurdle at Wincanton following month (amateur ridden). *R. J. Hodges.* — §

MEMBERSON 12 ch.g. New Member–Miss Stalbridge (Eastern Venture) [1989/90 c24fpu c25fur c32v4 c32g3 c24g c29d c29s6 c25s4 c24d6 c25m* c25f3 c121

Food Brokers Royal Game Handicap Chase, Sandown—a close thing at the second last. Baies leads Swardean, Memberson and Tarconey

c26f^ur c29f] strong, rangy gelding: fair chaser nowadays: ran best race for a year when winning handicap at Sandown in March by 2½ lengths from Tarconey: very stiff task and not disgraced on same course final start: suited by long distances: acts on any going: sometimes runs in snatches: suitable mount for an amateur: inconsistent. *P. Dufosee.*

MEMBERS' REVENGE 9 b.g. New Member–Aileens Revenge (Sweet Revenge) [1989/90 c16d3 c16d2 c16f* c17h* c16f2] lengthy gelding: won maiden chase at Southwell in April and novice handicap at Devon & Exeter following month: good second in handicap at Towcester final start: races only at around 2m: probably acts on any going. *S. Christian.* c99 —

MENDICK ADVENTURE 9 b.m. Mandrake Major–Open House (Road House II) [1989/90 16v6 16g] fourth foal: half-sister to 3 poor novice hurdlers: plating-class sprint handicapper on Flat (has worn blinkers): poor form in novice hurdles. *B. Mactaggart.* —

MENICO 6 b.h. Politico (USA)–My Seer (Menelek) [1989/90 F14v 16gpu] first foal: dam no sign of ability in 2 novice hurdles: mid-division in NH Flat race at Ayr in April: behind when pulled up last in novice hurdle at Perth following month. *R. Allan.* —

MENINGI 9 ch.g. Bustino–Miss Filbert (Compensation) [1989/90 c17g c20d* c20dur c16g2 c16m] leggy, rather narrow gelding: modest chaser nowadays: won handicap at Huntingdon in February: stays 2½m: probably needs give in the ground nowadays and acts on heavy going: blinkered once in 1985/6: sometimes amateur or claimer ridden. *Mrs H. Parrott.* c**102** —

MENINGIS PAL 7 b.m. Tanfirion–Glen Swilly (Prince Tenderfoot (USA)) [1989/90 16g] ninth in NH Flat race in 1988: always behind in novice event at Worcester in December on hurdling debut. *A. J. Wilson.* —

MEN OF YORKSHIRE 7 b.g. Uncle Pokey–Hejera (Cantab) [1989/90 a16g* a16g2 16d a16g* a20g*] good-quartered, deep-girthed gelding: raced up with pace when winning handicap hurdles at Lingfield in December and February (2): stays 2½m: refused to race second outing 1987/8. *D. M. Grissell.* 121

MERALTO 4 ch.f. Noalto–Miss Merlin (Manacle) [1989/90 16f 18f5] half-sister to winning hurdler Uncle Oliver (by Monsanto): winning plater on Flat, stays 7f: sold out of P. Rohan's stable 1,450 gns Ascot July Sales: well beaten in juvenile hurdles at Plumpton and Fontwell. *H. Willis.* —

MERANO (FR) 7 ch.g. Tip Moss (FR)–Association (FR) (Margouillat (FR)) [1989/90 16s3 16d6 20dF 24d*] workmanlike gelding: one-time fair handicapper at up to 15f on Flat: showed plenty of ability in novice hurdles prior to winning one at Market Rasen in March, making virtually all: stays 3m: acts on dead going. *M. W. Easterby.* 108 p

MERCIA GOLD 7 ch.g. Roman Warrior–Maygold (High Line) [1989/90 16d 17g 16f 17m6] small, lengthy gelding: novice hurdler: well beaten of late, including in sellers: blinkered last 3 starts. *T. A. K. Cuthbert.* —

MERCURIUS 8 ch.g. Roman Warrior–Just Splendid (John Splendid) [1989/90 c16gpu c16g5 c16d* c16v* c16v* c16dpu] rangy gelding: won novice handicap chases at Ayr in January (2) and February: out of his depth final start: unlikely to stay much beyond 2m: acts on heavy going: jumps well. *D. Robertson.* c97 —

MERCURY MOON 5 gr.g. Belfort (FR)–Tringa (GER) (Kaiseradler) [1989/90 20m4] good-bodied gelding: well beaten over hurdles. *M. McCourt.* —

MEREWOOD MAGIC 4 b.f. Skyliner–Sicova (Sicilian Prince) [1989/90 F16g F13d] fourth foal: dam lightly-raced Irish maiden: behind in NH Flat races in Scotland: yet to race over hurdles. *E. Weymes.*

MERITMOORE 7 b.g. Moorestyle–More Treasure (Ballymore) [1989/90 16g 16g 16g2 16g6 16d2 16d3 16d5] rangy gelding: handicap hurdler: placed at Edinburgh (twice) and Newcastle: suited by strongly-run race at 2m: acts on dead going (finished lame on good to firm): usually ridden by 7-lb claimer. *G. M. Moore.* 107

MERRYACRES 7 b.g. Homing–Joking (Ribero) [1989/90 c16f2 c20f3 c21gpu] workmanlike gelding: winning hurdler: placed in novice chases: not seen out after running poorly in December: gives impression he'll prove best at around 2m: acts on firm ground. *R. M. Whitaker.* c83 —

MERRY JUNIOR 7 ch.g. Rymer–Jane Junior (Guide) [1989/90 22mF] lengthy, workmanlike gelding: useful hurdler: was suited by 2½m: acted on soft going and good to firm: dead. *E. H. Owen jun.* —

MERRY MARIGOLD 4 b.f. Sonnen Gold–Manna Green (Bustino) [1989/90 16s^{3} 17v^{3} 16g^{3} 16d 16d] rather sparely-made filly: won at up to 7f at 2 yrs, but well beaten on Flat in 1989: poor form on first 3 starts in juvenile hurdles. *J. D. Roberts.* 76

MERRY MASTER 6 br.g. Le Coq d'Or–Merry Missus (Bargello) [1989/90 F16g^{2} F16g^{6} F17m*] first foal: half-brother to novice hurdler Gone Astray (by The Parson): dam winning chaser, best at around 2m: won 24-runner NH Flat race at Carlisle in April by 2 lengths from Kate O'Kirkham: yet to race over hurdles or fences. *R. C. Armytage.*

MERRY MATIC 6 gr.g. Pragmatic–Victor's Valley (Deep Run) [1989/90 F16f* F16f^{2} 16m] good-topped ex-Irish gelding: first foal: dam winning Irish hurdler: successful in NH Flat race at Roscommon in June: sold out of E. Bolger's stable 20,000 gns Doncaster August Sales after second outing: jumped none too fluently when behind in novice event at Huntingdon in October on hurdling debut. *F. Gray.* —

MERRYMOLES 7 b.g. Tyrnavos–Sovereign Help (Sovereign Lord) [1989/90 20g 20d 16m 16f^{F}] small gelding: well beaten over hurdles, including in a seller. *Miss C. J. E. Caroe.* —

MERYETT (BEL) 6 b.m. Le Grand Meaulnes–Maji (Preciptic) [1989/90 25g^{4} 24g^{3} c20s^{3} 27s^{3} c24m^{F} c20v^{F}] lengthy, sparely-made mare: poor novice hurdler/chaser: stays well: acts on heavy going. *J. White.* **c82** 76

MESA KID (USA) 11 b.g. Jig Dancer (USA)–Double Princess (USA) (Prince Blessed) [1989/90 16m 20m] small gelding: lightly-raced hurdler nowadays: behind in selling handicap final outing: stays 2½m: acts on firm going: sometimes visored (wasn't when successful). *G. Barnett.* —

MESEMBRYANTHEMUM 5 br.m. Warpath–Delphinium (Tin King) [1989/90 aF16g a24g 24f^{pu} 20g^{pu}] angular mare: no sign of ability over hurdles. *A. J. Rumsey.* —

MESHRARF 4 gr.g. Rusticaro (FR)–Lady Wise (Lord Gayle (USA)) [1989/90 16g^{5} 16g 16f^{2} 16g 16d^{3} a16g^{4} a16s^{5} a18g^{3} a20g^{3} 17f 16f 16g^{6} 20g^{pu}] smallish, lengthy gelding: behind in 2 maidens on Flat: didn't go through with effort when second in selling hurdle at Catterick (claimed out of J. Czerpak's stable £6,256) in November: claimed out of C. Beever's stable £6,121 after ninth start: subsequently lost his form: blinkered seventh to ninth and last 3 outings. *Miss S. J. Wilton.* 71 §

METCALFE FLEET 9 ch.g. Wollow–Time Was (Crowned Prince (USA)) [1989/90 c19f^{5} c20f^{3}] workmanlike gelding: no sign of ability over hurdles or in steeplechases, but won a point-to-point in May. *P. F. J. Duckett.* c— —

METHANO 4 b.c. Alzao (USA)–Gulf Bird (Gulf Pearl) [1989/90 20g^{3}] lengthy colt: won over 15.3f on Flat in 1989: sold out of C. Brittain's stable 13,000 gns Newmarket Autumn Sales: collapsed and died after finishing third in juvenile hurdle at Kempton. *R. Akehurst.* 96

METRO LINER 4 br.g. Zino–Bellinzona (Northfields (USA)) [1989/90 16m] placed over 7f in Ireland at 3 yrs, well beaten in Britain: tailed-off last of 7 in juvenile hurdle at Stratford in May. *R. Akehurst.* —

METROPOLIS DANCER 5 b.g. Hard Fought–Reliant Nell (Reliance II) [1989/90 F13d^{4} 20d^{pu}] fifth living foal: half-brother to French winners Tamatave and Reliquaire (both by Northfields): dam won at up to 15.5f in France: fourth in NH Flat race at Kelso in January: tailed off when pulled up 2 out in novice hurdle at Newcastle following month. *J. S. Wilson.* —

MET STATION 7 b.g. Royal Fountain–Lido Light (Good Light) [1989/90 21f 16f] lengthy, shallow-girthed gelding: poor novice hurdler: stays 2¾m. *M. J. Wilkinson.* —

MEZIARA 9 b.g. Dominion–Abertywi (Bounteous) [1989/90 24g^{5} 22m 24g^{2} 26v^{4} 24v 21d 21m^{4}] small, good-bodied gelding: handicap hurdler: ran poorly after third start: fell only outing over fences: stays well: acts on heavy going and possibly unsuited by top-of-the-ground: sometimes wears blinkers or visor: has looked a difficult ride. *D. R. Tucker.* c— 115 d

MIAMI BAY 6 b.g. Miami Springs–Symposium (Bold Lad (IRE)) [1989/90 16f^{5}] sparely-made gelding: of little account over hurdles: blinkered, finished lame in August. *S. B. Avery.* —

MIAMI BEAR 4 b.g. Miami Springs–Belinda Bear (Ragstone) [1989/90 17m^{6} 16f^{3} a16g^{2} 17g* a16g] good-bodied gelding: half-brother to Pooella (by Porto Bello), winner of a 25f selling hurdle: in frame at up to 1½m on Flat (best effort on 90

Bournstream '7''s "Midfielder"

soft going): won juvenile hurdle at Carlisle in January: behind in novice event at Southwell later in month: will stay 2½m. *J. Berry.*

MIAMI PRIDE 4 b.f. Miami Springs–Gwynpride (Val de L'Orne (FR)) [1989/90 17hro 16mpu 16h6 16g] sparely-made filly: first foal: dam poor plater over hurdles: sprint plater on Flat: ran out in juvenile selling hurdle at Carlisle in September (put back in race and finished remote third): tailed off in similar company following month: headstrong and wears severe bridle. *M. B. James.* —

M I BABE 5 ch.m. Celtic Cone–Cover Your Money (Precipice Wood) [1989/90 16m* 16m2 16g3 16s5 16m3 16m2 16m* 16fF] lengthy mare: won novice hurdle at Huntingdon in December and handicap at Towcester in April: likely to stay beyond 2m: acts on good to firm ground. *Mrs I. McKie.* 101

MICKEY CINDERS 12 ch.g. Little Buskins–Jennifer Gentle (London Gazette) [1989/90 c20s] angular, rather sparely-made gelding: point-to-point winner: modest form in novice chases: behind in maiden hunter chase at Sedgefield in February. *Peter Dowson.* c— —

MICKLEHAM 5 ch.g. Ahonoora–Cliona (FR) (Ballymore) [1989/90 16d 16m] workmanlike gelding: fourth foal: half-brother to French 10.5f winner Nanuma (by Bold Lad (IRE)): dam, useful French 1¼m winner, is out of Kew, a very useful sister to Floribunda: behind in selling hurdle (tubed) and novice event in March. *B. Forsey.* —

MICKLEY TREASURE 10 b.g. Gold Rod–Treasure Trail (Takawalk II) [1989/90 c26fpu] point-to-pointer, successful in April: pulled up and dismounted before second-last in hunter chase at Newton Abbot in May. *W. Bush.* c—

MICK'S STAR 10 br.g. Orange Bay–Starboard Belle (Right Tack) [1989/90 c26fF c36f c33dpu] tall, narrow, leggy gelding: one-time useful chaser: lightly c— —

raced: nineteenth in Seagram Grand National at Liverpool in April: suited by a good test of stamina: best with plenty of give in the ground: usually jumps well: wears bandages. *Mrs J. Pitman.*

MIC-MAC EXPRESS 7 ch.g. Pony Express–Nipperkin (Worden II) [1989/90 c20f* c22gpu c22m5 c20f4] placed in a point-to-point in 1989: won hunter chase at Fontwell in March: creditable fourth at Folkestone in May: stays 2½m: acts on firm ground. *Mrs L. A. Syckelmoore.* c**74**

MIDDLE HALF 5 b.g. Formidable (USA)–Moiety Bird (Falcon) [1989/90 16f4] maiden on Flat: 8 lengths fourth behind Akdam in novice hurdle at Worcester in April. *P. F. I. Cole.* 74

MIDDLEWICK 5 b.g. Ballacashtal (CAN)–Thunder Bay (Canisbay) [1989/90 16g3 16m] sturdy gelding: half-brother to winning hurdler Storm of Plenty (by Billion): dam stayed 1½m: jumped better as race progressed when third in novice hurdle at Wincanton in January: mid-division at Worcester 3½ months later. *S. Christian.* 89

MIDFIELDER 4 ch.g. Formidable (USA)–Pampas Flower (Pampered King) [1989/90 16f4 16v3 16s* 17v2 16d* 16gF 16f 16m2] neat gelding: fairly useful miler on Flat, when trained by P. Walwyn: won juvenile hurdle at Taunton in December and novice hurdle at Windsor following month: ran well in Daily Express Triumph Hurdle (eighth to Rare Holiday) at Cheltenham and Glenlivet Anniversary Hurdle (never-nearer 8 lengths second to Sybillin) at Liverpool last 2 completed starts: likely to prove best at a sharp 2m: best form on top-of-the-ground. *P. J. Hobbs.* 130

MIDLAND EXPRESS 7 ch.g. Midland Gayle–Queens County (Harwell) [1989/90 16g4 16m2 22g c16g2 c20d4 c17gF 20m 22d] sparely-made, angular gelding: fair hurdler: ran well first 2 starts, well below his best last 2: in frame in novice chases: gives impression he'll prove best at up to 2½m: acts on any going: seems best on a galloping track: has won for a 7-lb claimer. *Denys Smith.* c**100** 119

MIDLAND GLENN 6 ch.g. Midland Gayle–Dawn Dreamer (Avocat) [1989/90 16f5 16m* 16m* 20g* 20m* 22d* 20d* 20f] angular, sparely-made gelding: progressive hurdler who won novice hurdles at Huntingdon, Uttoxeter, Wetherby (handicap) and Newcastle (2) and handicap at Ayr: in touch going well until fading from 2 out when around 22 lengths eighth to Regal Ambition in Sun Alliance Novices' Hurdle at Cheltenham in March (reportedly sustained serious injury): stays 2¾m: acts on firm and dead ground: amateur ridden apart from seventh start: jumps well: has a turn of foot. *J. L. Eyre.* 123

Coral Golden Handicap Hurdle (Qualifier), Ayr—the progressive Midland Glenn wins easily

MIDLAND LAD 5 br.g. Midland Gayle–Dikaro Lady (Dike (USA)) [1989/90 16d 16d 17g] compact, good-quartered gelding: first foal: dam fairly useful 2m chaser: showed ability all starts in novice hurdles: may do better. *J. L. Eyre.* 82

MIDNIGHT BUTLER 10 b.g. Rhett Butler–Midnight Canter VI (Prince Hansel) [1989/90 c20s[F] c19m[pu]] angular ex-Irish gelding: won point-to-point and 2¼m novice chase in 1986: tailed off when pulled up in hunter chase at Hereford in April: acts on firm ground: has worn a crossed noseband. *J. N. Cochrane-Barnett.* c—

MIDNIGHT COUNT 10 b.g. Lauso–Rising Prices (Royal Record II) [1989/90 c16g[4] c20v[2] c20d[ur] c20s[3]] big, imposing gelding: carries plenty of condition: lightly-raced chaser, high class at his best: placed in quite valuable handicaps at Haydock in January and Warwick (best effort of season) in February: probably stays 2½m: has a markedly round action, and needs give in the ground (acts well on soft): has run well when sweating: sometimes bandaged in front. *J. T. Gifford.* c**144** —

MIDNIGHT MADNESS 12 b.g. Genuine–Indian Madness (Indian Ruler) [1989/90 c24m[pu] c29d[4] c26g* c29g* c26v[4] c32g[2] c29d* c33d[3] c29d[F] c36g[pu]] sparely-made gelding: useful chaser: won handicaps at Newton Abbot in November, Worcester in December and Warwick (beat Mister Christian a neck in quite valuable event) in January: fell heavily at the second on ninth outing and ran poorly when next seen out 7 weeks later: thorough stayer: possibly not at his best on heavy going, acts on any other: suited by forcing tactics: genuine: goes well for 7-lb claimer R. Greene. *D. Bloomfield.* c**143** —

MIDNIGHT MISS (NZ) 6 br.m. Princes Gate–Princess Jane (NZ) (Head Hunter) [1989/90 16d[6] 16g 24d] leggy mare: shaped promisingly first 2 starts in novice hurdles, on second occasion running-on seventh to Stratford Ponds at Kempton: seemed not to stay 3m final start (may prove best at up to 2½m). *M. H. B. Robinson.* 94

MIDNIGHT RUN 11 ch.g. Deep Run–Night Spot (Midsummer Night II) [1989/90 24m[pu] 24m 16g c20d[pu] c20d[F] c16s[5] c22g[3] c20d[4] c16s[4] c17m[4]] leggy, workmanlike gelding: NH Flat race winner: poor form in varied company over hurdles and fences (jumps moderately): best effort at 2m on good ground over hurdles: keen type: has worn a crossed noseband. *R. Dickin.* c**75** x —

Sky Blue Handicap Chase, Warwick—Midnight Train continues on the upgrade

Mr M. L. Oberstein's "Midnight Train"

MIDNIGHT STORM 6 br.g. Strong Gale–Gala Noon (Gala Performance (USA)) [1989/90 c22m* c20g^{pu}] lengthy gelding: winning hurdler: made all in novice chase at Nottingham in December, winning by a distance: stayed 2¾m: acted on good to firm and heavy going: dead. *O. Sherwood.* c? —

MIDNIGHT STRIKE (USA) 6 b.g. Topsider (USA)–Revels End (Welsh Pageant) [1989/90 17h* 17f* 18f* 16f^{3} 16f^{2} 16g^{3} 16m 16m^{3} 16f* 17h^{5}] close-coupled, rather sparely-made gelding: improved hurdler: won handicaps at Devon & Exeter (2) and Fontwell early in season and Taunton in April: stays 2¼m: easily best form on top-of-the-ground: blinkered nowadays: found little fourth to sixth starts and isn't one to trust. *J. H. Baker.* 130 §

MIDNIGHT TRAIN 9 b.g. Oats–Gail Borden (Blue Chariot) [1989/90 c16m* c20d^{F} c20g^{3} c20m^{pu} c20d^{4} c20s* c20s*] leggy, rather close-coupled gelding: progressive chaser: won handicap at Wincanton in November and minor event at Leicester and handicap at Warwick (beat Multum In Parvo 8 lengths) in February: will stay beyond 2½m: acts on heavy going and good to firm: broke blood vessels third and fourth starts: useful. *Mrs J. Pitman.* c**143** p —

MIDSUMMER WALK 8 b.m. Buckskin (FR)–Midnight Dancer (Midsummer Night II) [1989/90 22g^{6} 28g^{pu} a16g^{pu} a20g^{4} a20g^{pu} c24f^{F} 27f^{pu}] lengthy, good-quartered mare: winning selling hurdler: poor form in 1989/90: started slowly and fell fifth on chasing debut: stays 25f. *R. T. Juckes.* c— 69

MIDWEEK MELODY 4 br.f. Lucky Wednesday–Even Song (Falcon) [1989/90 F16f^{5} F16f 20g] half-sister to 3 winners, including fair 7f to 9f winner —

Barrie Baby (by Import): dam showed little ability: fifth in NH Flat race: started slowly when tailed off in mares novice hurdle at Market Rasen in June. *C. D. Broad.*

MIG 5 b.m. Sagaro–Lady Gaylord (Double Jump) [1989/90 16f^{ur} 16f] leggy,
lengthy mare: lightly-raced staying maiden on Flat: well beaten in novice hurdle —
at Uttoxeter in September: whipped round and unseated rider at start on hurdling
debut. *A. D. Brown.*

MIGHT MOVE 7 gr. or ro.g. Town And Country–Strathdearn (Saritamer
(USA)) [1989/90 16g^{6} 16d] smallish, lengthy gelding: quite a useful hurdler at his —
best: not discredited first outing: best form at around 2m: acts on heavy going: has
won for a claimer: tends to get behind early. *M. C. Pipe.*

MIGHTY FALCON 5 b.g. Comedy Star–Lettuce (So Blessed) [1989/90 16m
16f 22g^{6} 24d 22g^{3} 21s* 21d 22m^{pu}] tall, leggy gelding: brother to Lincoln 95
Handicap and Royal Hunt Cup winner Mighty Fly and half-brother to Derby third
Mighty Flutter: dam half-sister to Rubstic and Kildimo: behind in maidens on
Flat: won novice handicap hurdle at Towcester in February: ran in snatches next
time: should stay beyond 2¾m: acts on soft going and seems unsuited by
top-of-the-ground: blinkered last 3 starts. *D. R. C. Elsworth.*

MIGHTY FINE 9 b.g. Crash Course–Aggvus (Aggressor) [1989/90 c21d* c**108**
c24g^{2} c25d^{5} c25m^{bd}] big, strong gelding: won novice chase at Towcester in —
December: stayed 3m: acted on soft going: amateur ridden: dead. *S. Christian.*

MIGHTY GLOW 6 gr.g. Kalaglow–Faridetta (Good Bond) [1989/90 20f* 22f^{2}
20f^{3} 21g^{3} 20m] leggy, narrow, sparely-made gelding: won handicap hurdle at 110
Sedgefield in September: ran moderately in amateur riders events last 2 starts:
stays 2¾m: acts on firm and dead going: visored fourth start: usually ridden by
Mrs A. Farrell (wasn't last 2 outings): won 2 handicaps over 1¾m on Flat in 1990.
C. Tinkler.

MIGHTY MARK 11 b.g. Rebel Prince–White Net (Monet) [1989/90 c17d c—
c20d^{F} c33d^{pu}] tall gelding: won William Hill Scottish National at Ayr in 1988: —
unraced in 1988/9: showed signs of retaining ability on reappearance: failed to
complete subsequently: stays very well: acts on any going: usually amateur
ridden. *F. T. Walton.*

MIGHTY PRINCE 5 ch.g. Pharly (FR)–Anne Stuart (FR) (Bolkonski) c**99**
[1989/90 17v 16s* 16d^{2} 16m^{2} 20h^{6} c17m* c16f^{3}] rather sparely-made gelding: 106
made all in claiming hurdle at Nottingham in February: won novice chase at
Newton Abbot in April: best at around 2m: looked none too keen when well beaten
on heavy ground, acts on any other: usually blinkered over hurdles. *M. C. Pipe.*

MIGHTY SUPREMO (USA) 9 b.g. Raja Baba (USA)–Glut's Kin (USA)
(Water Prince) [1989/90 17f^{4} 17m 16g 16f 16h^{2} 16h^{4} 16f^{5} 17f^{4}] novice selling 66
hurdler: form only at around 2m: acts on hard going: usually ridden by 7-lb
claimer. *T. A. K. Cuthbert.*

MIINNEHOMA 7 b. or br.g. Kambalda–Mrs Cairns (Choral Society)
[1989/90 22m* 22v* 25g* 25g* 25m^{4}] 138

We didn't see the best of front-running Miinnehoma at Liverpool. A weak odds-on shot for the White Satin Novices' Hurdle, he never threatened to dominate as he usually does: the pace was only steady, he was taken on on the final circuit and finally collared three out, eventually being relegated to fourth place behind Dwadme, Whats The Crack and Tinryland, beaten twelve lengths by the winner. Prophetically, Miinnehoma's trainer had said after he had won the Philip Cornes Saddle Of Gold Final at Newbury four weeks earlier 'You don't realize how much a race like this takes out of a horse'. It seems probable that despite being kept away from the Cheltenham Festival in order to give him more time to recover, Miinnehoma's races had taken their toll.

Up until Liverpool Miinnehoma's season had been one of all-conquering progress, and he'd started at even money for the Final in a small field of promising staying novices. He came to hurdling in a roundabout way. He began his career in point-to-points in Ireland as a five-year-old, winning his first race by a distance and just failing to get up in the other. In May of 1988 he appeared at the Doncaster Sales, was bought by his present owner for 35,000 guineas and sent to be trained by Owen Brennan, for whom he won first time out in the 1988/9 season in a National Hunt Flat race at

Philip Cornes Saddle Of Gold Hurdle (Final), Newbury—
Miinnehoma leads throughout

Uttoxeter (at 25/1) and was placed in both subsequent runs in similar company. By the time he made a winning hurdling debut at Fontwell in December 1989, Miinnehoma had changed stables again. Although that first form didn't amount to much, by the end of the month he'd established himself as a good prospect, a particularly resolute galloper who stayed all day, in the course of stringing out sizeable fields at odds on in novice events at Haydock and Newbury. In the latter, a Philip Cornes Qualifier, his jockey went to great pains to ensure a thorough test and really pressed on from four out, in the end leaving all except Sunninghill Celtic well behind. While small, the field for the Final was also select. Black Moccasin, Remittance Man and Beau Pari had all, like Miinnehoma, won their most recent race; and the two other runners, Strong Gold and Cardinal Ralph, had won a race during the season. Miinnehoma beat them very convincingly, though with bludgeon rather than rapier. He jumped off in front, stepped up the pace on the second circuit, and from the cross hurdle began to grind his four remaining opponents into submission. Strong Gold had fallen early on. Black Moccasin dropped away first; by the second last only Remittance Man, who'd raced closest to the leader throughout, was still in touch; soon even he was left struggling as Miinnehoma galloped on and on and jumped the last like a fresh horse. Twelve lengths was the winning margin, another fifteen to third-placed Beau Pari.

Miinnehoma's form in the Final puts him up with most of the novices who ran at Cheltenham, though it's doubtful whether he would have been a match there for his stable-companion the Sun Alliance Novices' Hurdle winner Regal Ambition, especially over two and a half miles. In point of fact, there is no suitable race in the three days of the Cheltenham Festival for an out-and-out staying novice like Miinnehoma. It is asking a great deal of

Mr Freddie Starr's "Miinnehoma"

Miinnehoma (b. or br.g. 1983)	Kambalda (b 1970)	Right Royal V (br 1958)	Owen Tudor
			Bastia
		Opencast (br 1957)	Mossborough
			Coal Board
	Mrs Cairns (b or br 1974)	Choral Society (b 1959)	Pinza
			Tessa Gillian
		Arctic Mint (b 1962)	Arctic Slave
			Ballinagre Walk

such a horse to run him in either the Stayers' Hurdle Championship or the Coral Golden Handicap. In time Miinnehoma would probably improve enough to be able to take on the top staying hurdlers; he'd have to, or else be at the mercy of a handicapper very likely to take him to task for past achievements. However, Miinnehoma probably goes chasing. If so, his early grounding in Ireland should stand him in good stead. Physically he is not a particularly imposing individual, though he was described in the Doncaster catalogue as 16.1½ hands, which is plenty big enough. The catalogue contained little of interest about his breeding, for there wasn't a lot to tell. Miinnehoma is the second and last foal of a mare who was pulled up in an Irish National Hunt Flat race on her only outing. The next dam Arctic Mint ran for three seasons over hurdles in Ireland without reaching a place, the third dam never ran. Arctic Mint, the dam of a minor hurdles winner, was a sister to two winning jumpers herself. Miinnehoma has won on ground ranging from heavy to good to firm. His win on good to firm came at Fontwell; he was beaten under similar conditions at Liverpool so there's a possibility that an easier surface suits him better. *M. C. Pipe.*

MIKES BOYS 6 ch.g. Record Run–Our Denise (Bend A Bow (USA)) [1989/90 16g[F] 16m[5]] big, angular gelding: seems of little account. *J. B. Sayers.* —

MIKE'S DIAMOND (NZ) 6 b.g. Trictrac (FR)–Subdue (NZ) (Celtic Park) [1989/90 16g 16m[5]] sturdy gelding: better effort in novice hurdles at Wincanton when around 11 lengths fifth to Fifth Amendment in March: likely to stay further: ridden by 7-lb claimer. *Andrew Turnell.* 97

MIKEY'S MONKEY 7 b.m. Monksfield–Just Darina (Three Dons) [1989/90 c22mpu c20f2] poor maiden hurdler/point-to-pointer: hampered 2 out when 20 lengths second to John Corbet in novice hunter chase at Uttoxeter in May: stays 2½m: visored nowadays. *Rodger Farrant.* c65 —

MILE END 5 b.g. Camden Town–Lady of Primrose (He Loves Me) [1989/90 16dpu 16g 16f a20gpu a16g6] lightly-made gelding: of little account. *A. S. Ridout.* —

MILESIAN DANCER 10 ch.g. Godswalk (USA)–Yavana (Milesian) [1989/90 25dpu 16v3 20s] smallish, sparely-made gelding: poor hurdler/chaser nowadays: beaten in a seller final start: best form at distances short of 2¾m: acts on any going: has been tried in blinkers: suitable mount for a claimer. *J. J. O'Neill.* c— 72

MILFORD QUAY 7 ch.h. Milford–Miss Quay (Quayside) [1989/90 21f* 21m* 16f* 20d2 16f2 16g* 16s3 16s* 16f 24f4] sparely-made horse: front-running hurdler: much improved in 1989/90 and put up a very useful performance to win White Rabbit Hurdle at Haydock in March on eighth start by 12 lengths from Island Set, quickening in good style approaching last: successful earlier in handicaps at Huntingdon, Warwick and Cheltenham (2): ran moderately in valuable handicap at Cheltenham and in Keith Prowse Long Distance Hurdle at Ascot later in March: stays 21f, not 3m: has won on firm going but seems ideally suited by plenty of give: has wandered under pressure and tended to carry his head rather high: sketchy jumper. *M. C. Pipe.* 146

MILINETTA 5 b.m. Milford–Golden Linnet (Sing Sing) [1989/90 17f6 22fpu 20v* 16m5] sparely-made mare: first worthwhile form over hurdles when winning conditional jockeys selling handicap at Chepstow in January despite looking none too keen run-in (no bid): tailed off next time: stays 2½m: acts on heavy going: visored last 2 starts. *M. C. Pipe.* 82

MILITARY BAND (FR) 12 b.g. Sassafras (FR)–Melody Hour (Sing Sing) [1989/90 24d2 22m2 24f4 24g4 24g3 21s2 22m2 25mpu] tall, leggy, narrow gelding: handicap hurdler: generally ran well in 1989/90: runner-up in novice chase in 1988/9: stays well: probably unsuited by heavy going, acts on any other: sometimes blinkered. *Mrs J. G. Retter.* c— 108

MILITARY BLAZE 4 ch.g. Sandhurst Prince–Echo Repeating (Ballymore) [1989/90 F13d5 aF16g 16d] angular gelding: third foal: dam unraced half-sister to very smart middle-distance performer Fingal's Cave: showed ability in 13f NH Flat race: jumped none too fluently when behind in juvenile hurdle at Market Rasen in March. *J. Parkes.* —

MILITARY EXPRESS 7 b.g. Pony Express–Millstar (Military) [1989/90 17vpu 22g 16m 24d] rather sparely-made gelding: poor form in novice hurdles. *R. J. Hodges.* 83

White Rabbit Hurdle, Haydock—Milford Quay quickens on from Sayparee

MILITARY HONOUR 5 b.g. Shirley Heights–Princess Tiara (Crowned Prince (USA)) [1989/90 16g 20g* 24s] rather sparely-made gelding: won novice handicap hurdle at Wetherby in December: stays 2½m: possibly unsuited by soft ground. *M. W. Easterby.* 103

MILITARY SALUTE 5 b.g. Sandhurst Prince–Wavetree (Realm) [1989/90 18d^ur 16g 16m 16g 16g^4 16f^2 20f^2 16h^2 16f*] leggy, angular gelding: poor middle-distance maiden on Flat: ridden by 3-lb claimer, won selling hurdle at Hereford in May by 20 lengths (bought in 5,200 gns): suited by 2m and firm going. *R. Brotherton.* 90

MILK QUOTA 7 br.g. Healaugh Fox–Gina (Teme Valley) [1989/90 c24f^3] modest point-to-point winner: well beaten in poor novice hunter chase at Worcester in April. *Mrs J. H. E. Eckley.* c—

MILLADY 7 b.m. Chas Sawyer–Laydoney (Even Money) [1989/90 22m^pu 16m 16g 16s] sparely-made mare: no sign of ability: sold 1,300 gns Ascot April Sales. *J. P. D. Elliott.* —

MILLBECK LAD 4 b.g. Millfontaine–Miss Damus (Mandamus) [1989/90 a16g^ur] small gelding: poor form in sellers and claimers at around 1m on Flat: bumped and unseated rider second in juvenile selling hurdle at Southwell in December. *D. Burchell.* —

MILL DE LEASE 5 b.h. Milford–Melting Snows (High Top) [1989/90 16f* 16g^3 16f^3 16m 16m^5 17f^5 20d* 20s^2] leggy, rather sparely-made horse: won novice hurdle at Uttoxeter in September and handicap at Sedgefield in December: good second in handicap on latter course in January: stays 2½m well: acts on any going: has won for an amateur. *J. Dooler.* 95

MILLEONE 4 b.g. Milford–Mama Leone (Young Emperor) [1989/90 16f 16f^pu 16g* 16h^2 16g^2 16f* 16g^2] leggy gelding: plating-class form at 2 yrs: tended to carry head high when winning selling handicap hurdle at Market Rasen (wandered run-in, bought in 2,500 gns) in August and seller at Kelso (no bid) in October: hung left run-in when good second in juvenile claimer at Nottingham later in month: acts on firm ground. *W. A. Stephenson.* 82 §

MILLER'S GILT 5 b.h. Glint of Gold–Hecalene (FR) (Sir Gaylord) [1989/90 17h 17m^3 17m^3 16h 16g^3 20f^6 17m^F 16m] small horse: poor plater on Flat (possibly ungenuine) and over hurdles: remounted after whipping round and unseating rider at start fourth outing: found little next time: has worn a crossed noseband: trained until after sixth outing by W. G. M. Turner. *J. A. B. Old.* 63

MILL FOLLY 8 b.g. Pry–Browngello (Bargello) [1989/90 c20s^pu c20f^pu] compact, deep-girthed gelding: third foal: half-brother to a poor animal: dam never ran: no promise in 2 novice chases. *J. Eaton.* c—

MILLFORD HAVEN 5 b.g. Welsh Saint–Flute (FR) (Luthier) [1989/90 16f^ro] leggy gelding: novice hurdler: close up when running out 3 out in poor race at Huntingdon in May: ran poorly on soft ground final start in 1988/9. *Dr J. D. Scargill.* ?

MILLIE BELLE 4 ch.f. Milford–Charter Belle (Runnymede) [1989/90 18f* 16f^3 16f^3 16g^4] leggy filly: half-sister to 4 winning hurdlers, including smart Calapaez (by Nishapour): dam won 1¼m seller: placed at up to 2m on Flat: won juvenile hurdle at Fontwell in August: modest form when in frame subsequently: will be suited by further than 2¼m: acts on firm ground: looked reluctant final start (November). *Miss B. Sanders.* 90

MILLIE'S SECRET 6 ch.m. Dynastic–Sweet Millie (Methane) [1989/90 F16f^5 F16m] first foal: dam moderate staying hurdler/chaser: unplaced in NH Flat races in first half of season: yet to race over hurdles or fences. *J. H. Johnson.*

MILL KNOCK 8 b.g. Park Row–Barlocco Bay (Cantab) [1989/90 c24f^ur c24f 24f^5] well beaten over hurdles: won a point-to-point in February: unplaced in maiden hunter chase and amateur riders maiden hurdle at Hexham. *J. D. Thompson.* c— —

MILLMERRAN 5 b.m. Jimsun–Sarah's Joy (Full of Hope) [1989/90 16m 16m 16d a20g^pu] neat mare: well beaten over hurdles: has worn tongue strap. *C. D. Broad.* —

MILL MINSTREL 7 br.g. Black Minstrel–Red Cross (Pitpan) [1989/90 c16g^pu] tall, angular gelding:second foal: dam never ran: tailed off when pulled up eighth in novice chase at Bangor. *Mrs S. J. Smith.* c—

MILLPOND BOY 6 ch.g. Connaught–Nonsensical (Silly Season) [1989/90 16g 17d 16g] lengthy, sparely-made gelding: novice hurdler: failed to find his form —

in 1989/90: will prove best at up to 2½m at present: possibly unsuited by heavy going: ridden by claimer. *R. J. Hodges.*

MILL RELIC 7 br.g. Gay Fandango (USA)–Sweet Reproach (Relic) [1989/90 16g 20gpu c22dF c20dpu c25f] rangy gelding: seems of little account: blinkered last 2 outings. *J. Eaton.* c— —

MILLSTREAK 10 b.g. Majestic Streak–Just Millie (pedigree unknown) [1989/90 c25fF] neat gelding: novice selling hurdler: poor novice chaser: successful in point-to-points in 1990: probably stays 2½m: sometimes blinkered: sometimes amateur ridden: poor jumper. *Miss A. S. Ross.* c— x — x

MILL TERN 8 ch.g. Milford–Mitsuki (Crowned Prince (USA)) [1989/90 16g*] leggy, narrow gelding: claimer ridden, won 18-runner selling handicap hurdle at Market Rasen in November: bought in 5,200 gns afterwards: races only at 2m: wears blinkers. *A. W. Potts.* 68

MILLTOWN BRIDGE 6 b.g. Pitpan–Just Killiney (Bargello) [1989/90 F16g 16mpu] tall gelding: second foal: half-brother to poor novice hurdler Justakin (by Buckskin): dam showed some ability over hurdles in Ireland: behind in NH Flat race at Kempton in February: blundered badly second and eventually tailed off when pulled up 2 out on hurdling debut. *R. J. Hodges.* —

MILLTOWN LADY 6 ch.m. Deep Run–Elite Lady (Prince Hansel) [1989/90 F16m4 F16v 16gpu 20dpu 16d 16g] angular mare: no sign of ability over hurdles. *J. I. A. Charlton.* —

MILO PLASCHY 6 b.g. Abednego–Ice Folly (Arctic Slave) [1989/90 F16g] sixth live foal: brother to modest novice hurdler Joe's Folly and half-brother to winning chaser Major Tom and successful point-to-pointer Gladstonian (both by Cantab): dam never ran: behind throughout in NH Flat race at Market Rasen in April on debut: yet to race over hurdles or fences. *M. W. Easterby.*

MILS MIJ 5 br.g. Slim Jim–Katie Grey (Pongee) [1989/90 22v 22s3] compact gelding: won 3 times over hurdles as a juvenile: below form in handicaps in 1989/90, but gave impression retains ability: needs stiff track and testing conditions to be seen to best advantage at 2m and should stay beyond 2½m: acts on any going. *J. J. O'Neill.* — p

MILTON BRYAN 5 ch.g. Red Sunset–Priddy Moun (Kalamoun) [1989/90 16f5 16f* 20m4 20s a20s* a20g* a20g* a20g4 20mpu 22fpu] smallish, plain gelding: former selling hurdler: won handicaps at Leicester (conditional jockeys) and Lingfield (3): pulled up last 2 starts (dismounted final one): stays 2½m: probably acts on any going: blinkered last 3 starts 1988/9: below form when sweating: very well suited by all-weather track. *J. Ffitch-Heyes.* 105 ?

MIND YOUR BACK 7 b.g. Random Shot–Cant Pet (Cantab) [1989/90 c22gpu c24g4 c16dF 20gpu] tall, leggy gelding: winning hurdler: showed ability first and third starts over fences: races freely up with the pace and may prove best at 2m for time being: acts on good to firm and dead going: jumps well in the main and should do better over fences. *J. G. FitzGerald.* c— p —

MINERAL DUST 7 ch.g. Callernish–Magnesium (Khalkis) [1989/90 20f4 22g3 24g* 24spu 25d2 25m 25m] leggy, sparely-made gelding: won handicap hurdle at Kempton in January: second at Newbury in March: out of his depth in between and on last 2 starts: stays 3m: acts on soft going: ran out third start 1988/9: usually held up: inconsistent. *Mrs G. E. Jones.* 109

MINIM 7 b.m. Rymer–Court Circles (Flush Royal) [1989/90 16f6 c16s5 c18s c17d4 c17m3 c16f*] rather leggy mare: novice hurdler: won mares novice chase at Wincanton in March by 10 lengths from Georgic: should stay beyond 2m: acts on firm ground and probably unsuited by very soft. *D. R. C. Elsworth.* c**92** —

MINIMUM RISK 5 b. or gr.g. Kris–Bare Minimum (Bustino) [1989/90 16fF c16spu c16m 16d] sturdy, close-coupled gelding: appears of little account: blinkered final start. *P. R. Hedger.* c— —

MINORETTES GIRL 5 b.m. Strong Gale–Minorette (Miralgo) [1989/90 F16s* F16d* F16m3] deep-girthed Irish mare: half-sister to high-class chaser Observe (by Rheffic) and quite useful hurdler/chaser Espy (by Pitpan): dam, 1m winner on Flat, winning jumper in France and Italy: won NH Flat races at Naas in January (by 15 lengths) and March (by 12 lengths): always prominent, racing wide, when 3¾ lengths third of 20 behind Going On in well-contested similar event at Liverpool in April: yet to race over hurdles or fences. *Patrick Mullins, Ireland.*

MINSK 4 ch.f. Kabour–Wedded Bliss (Relko) [1989/90 16gpu] second foal: dam won on Flat and over hurdles: poor maiden on Flat: behind when pulled up 3 out in claiming hurdle at Market Rasen in December. *D. W. Chapman.* —

MINT-MASTER 5 ch.g. Deep Run–Bold Penny (Beau Chapeau) [1989/90 F16f 16m2] first foal: dam winning hurdler at up to 21f in Ireland: seventh in NH Flat race at Cheltenham in April: 8 lengths second of 5 to Arsonist in novice hurdle at Towcester following month: will be suited by longer distances. *Mrs I. McKie.* 84 p

MIRACLE WORKER 4 b.g. Saher–Divine Dilly (Divine Gift) [1989/90 17d 16g 16g 16g] compact gelding: little sign of ability on Flat or in juvenile hurdles. *G. B. Balding.* —

MIRAGE DANCER 7 b.g. Ile de Bourbon (USA)–Come Dancing (CAN) (Northern Dancer) [1989/90 20g 17m2 16m 20d2 20g2 22fco 20m3 20f2 20f4 16f*] smallish gelding: won novice hurdle at Sedgefield in May: stays 2½m: acts on firm and dead ground: has hung under pressure and found little. *Miss C. J. E. Caroe.* 95

MIRAMAC 9 b.g. Relkino–Magical (Aggressor) [1989/90 20g4 22m* 20dpu] compact, sturdy gelding: handicap hurdler: won at Wincanton in March: favourite, ran poorly next start: stays 3m: probably acts on any going: has run well in visor. *R. G. Frost.* 104

MIRANDINHA 6 ch.g. Nicholas Bill–Matsui (Falcon) [1989/90 22g 22v 24d 21d3] workmanlike gelding: winning hurdler: modest form in handicaps in 1989/90: stays 2¾m: acts on dead going: has sweated: edged left final start. *B. Ellison.* 95

MIRIAM'S FANCY VI 6 b.g. The Parson–Deep Sea (pedigree unknown) [1989/90 16g 16g F20d2 F16d* 18d 18v* 20v*] non-thoroughbred Irish gelding: won NH Flat race at Thurles in January: successful over hurdles subsequently in maiden at Navan (made all) and Red Mills Trial Hurdle at Gowran Park (beat Dozing Bull 15 lengths): stays 2½m: acts on heavy going: amateur ridden at Gowran Park: useful and is sure to win more races. *E. J. O'Grady, Ireland.* 131 p

MIRIYOUN 5 b. or gr.h. Dalsaan–Minourika (FR) (Zeddaan) [1989/90 16d2 16s4 17v3] sparely-made ex-French horse: third foal: half-brother to 2 winners, including Manndesh (by Thatching), successful over 9f in France: dam won at up to 10.5f in France: successful over same trip himself at 3 yrs (placed at up to 1½m in 1989) when trained by A. de Royer-Dupre: modest form in mid-season novice hurdles: gives impression he'll be suited by return to less testing conditions. *C. P. E. Brooks.* 96

MIRPUR 8 b.g. Leander–Malina (Astec) [1989/90 20f3 25f5] leggy, sparely-made gelding: handicap hurdler: novice chaser: suited by further than 2m and stays 23f: acts on any going: takes quite a good hold. *Mrs G. R. Reveley.* c— 101

MISHY'S STAR 8 b.m. Balliol–Conte Bleu (Jan Ekels) [1989/90 21m3 22mpu] tall mare: poor novice hurdler: failed to complete both outings over fences: probably stays 3m: has looked less than an easy ride. *J. E. Forte.* c— § 75

MISS ARK ROYAL 5 b.m. Broadsword (USA)–Starboard Belle (Right Tack) [1989/90 16s 16dF 18s 24m6 18f*] small, sparely-made mare: half-sister to several winners, notably useful staying chaser Mick's Star (by Orange Bay): quite modest middle-distance maiden on Flat: dropped in class and ridden by 7-lb claimer, justified favouritism in selling handicap hurdle at Fontwell in May, making all (bought in 3,500 gns): should stay well (showed promise at 3m): acts on firm ground. *A. R. Davison.* 79

MISS A TURN 4 b.f. Tyrnavos–Misacre (St Alphage) [1989/90 16g 18v6 16s6 a16g4 18fbd] lengthy filly: seventh reported foal: half-sister to useful 6f to 1m performer Amarone (by Realm) and fair hurdler Landski (by Niniski): dam plating class: poor selling hurdler: has been reluctant to race: blinkered second to fourth outings: trained until after fourth start by R. Simpson. *A. W. Denson.* 52 §

MISS BLIZARD 8 br.m. Vitiges (FR)–Snow Damsel (Mandamus) [1989/90 c20fpu] showed ability in NH Flat races in 1987: poor maiden point-to-pointer: tailed off when pulled up in novice hunter chase at Folkestone in May. *Mrs V. O'Brien.* c—

MISS CELEBRITY 4 b.f. Skyliner–Lady O'Grady (Paddy's Stream) [1989/90 17h2 16f6] 1¼m seller winner on Flat (not one to trust): second in juvenile hurdle in August: well-beaten favourite for seller later in month: wears blinkers. *D. J. G. Murray-Smith.* 67

MISS CHALK 4 ch.f. Dominion–Stoney (Balidar) [1989/90 16s* 16g 16d* 16f 17m4] angular filly: plater on Flat, winner over 1¼m in 1990: sold out of M. 82

Blanshard's stable 3,000 gns Newmarket Autumn Sales: successful in selling hurdle at Bangor in December (made all, bought in 5,000 gns) and juvenile claimer at Stratford (led from third) in February: ran moderately in selling company last 2 starts: likely to prove best at around 2m: possibly needs give in the ground: reportedly broke blood vessel at Stratford. *M. C. Pipe.*

MISS CHEERFUL 5 ch.m. Last Fandango–Meadow Nymph (Meadow Court) [1989/90 F17h4 16g 16s 17m6 17mpu] lengthy, rather sparely-made mare: in frame in NH Flat races: little sign of ability in novice hurdles. *P. Leach.* —

MISS CHIKARA 6 b.m. Majestic Maharaj–Miss Gazelle (Dear Gazelle) [1989/90 F12f3 F16f] third reported foal: dam unraced daughter of a winning hurdler: third in NH Flat race at Bangor in March: tailed-off last of 12 at Ascot following month: yet to race over hurdles or fences. *R. J. Hodges.*

MISS CLUB ROYAL 7 b.m. Avocat–Miss Leap Year (Cantab) [1989/90 c24m3 c27g2 c27gF* c28gpu c24g2 c24gpu c24d2 c24fur c26m* c24h* c24g2 c24f*] lengthy, workmanlike mare: successful in handicap chases at Sedgefield, Uttoxeter and Hexham (2): she and sole rival Lingham Bride fell and were remounted at fourth last at Sedgefield: ran creditably on her other completed starts: suited by a test of stamina: acts on any going. *J. G. FitzGerald.* c**107** —

MISSELFORE 7 b.m. Reform–Chalke Valley (Ragstone) [1989/90 16f] poor novice hurdler, lightly raced: sold 1,000 gns Doncaster November Sales. *M. F. Barraclough.* —

MISS ENRICO 4 b.f. Don Enrico (USA)–Mill Miss (Typhoon) [1989/90 F16f2] third foal: half-sister to winning point-to-pointer Miss Cone (by Celtic Cone): dam of no account: 33/1, 7 lengths second of 10 to Norman Conqueror in NH Flat race at Newbury in March: yet to race over hurdles. *C. D. Broad.*

MISS EUTOPIA 5 b.m. Dunphy–Fair Colleen (King Emperor (USA)) [1989/90 F16g] sixth live foal: dam unraced half-sister to top-class 2-y-o Double Jump and top-class middle-distance horse Royalty: well beaten in NH Flat race at Edinburgh in January: yet to race over hurdles or fences. *R. Brandon.*

MISS EXAMINER 4 ch.f. Absalom–Buttermilk Sky (Midsummer Night II) [1989/90 16f] won 1¼m seller on Flat in 1989: sold out of M. Tompkins' stable 4,600 gns Newmarket July Sales: tailed off in juvenile selling hurdle at Southwell in August. *W. H. Bissill.* —

MISS FERN 5 b.m. Cruise Missile–Fernshaw (Country Retreat) [1989/90 16m 16g 16m 16dbd 16v5 16s 22f4 20g] leggy, sparely-made mare: poor novice hurdler: never dangerous over 2¾m: stiffish task next time. *R. Dickin.* 74

MISS HADDON 7 b.m. Free Boy–River Dance (Runnymede) [1989/90 16gpu 16g 16g] workmanlike mare: has a round action: tailed off in novice hurdles. *J. R. Bosley.* —

MISSILE MAGGIE 5 b.m. Cruise Missile–Big Maggie (Master Owen) [1989/90 17gpu] smallish, good-quartered mare: tailed off in NH Flat race and when pulled up 4 out in novice hurdle: sold 1,550 gns Ascot April Sales. *M. B. James.* —

MISSING MAN 10 ch.g. Proverb–Castle Treasure (Perspex) [1989/90 c20g c20s2 c25fpu c24m5] big, strong, workmanlike gelding: winning chaser: second in handicap at Sandown in February, easily best effort of season: stays 3m: acts on soft going and is possibly unsuited by top-of-the-ground: tends to be rather edgy and on his toes in preliminaries. *J. T. Gifford.* c**116** —

MISS KAMSY 6 b. or br.m. Kambalda–Daisy Owen (Master Owen) [1989/90 20f* 20m5] smallish, sparely-made mare: won 4-runner conditional jockeys novice handicap hurdle at Sedgefield in September: ran poorly in November and not seen out again: stays 2½m: acts on firm going: has looked a difficult ride. *R. F. Fisher.* 81

MISS KILPATRICK 4 ch.f. Noalto–Ann Wilson (Tumble Wind (USA)) [1989/90 16spu 16s 17v5] leggy, rather sparely-made filly: no form on Flat and over hurdles, including in sellers: ridden by claimer. *D. C. Jermy.* —

MISS LAMB 6 ch.m. Relkino–Young Lamb (Sea Hawk II) [1989/90 21d3] leggy, rather sparely-made mare: fair hurdler: good third behind Qannaas in handicap at Warwick in January (no extra from last): stays 21f: acts on heavy going: jumps well. *J. J. O'Neill.* 120

MISS LAWSUIT 6 b.m. Neltino–Bella Rosetta (Willowick (USA)) [1989/90 c16f* c20fpu] good-bodied mare: winning selling hurdler: jumped left, but made all to beat only opponent in novice chase at Uttoxeter in August: tailed off when c? —

pulled up 3 out at Plumpton later in month: acts on any going: pulls hard (has worn
a crossed noseband). *J. White.*

MISS MAGIC 5 b.m. Cruise Missile–Magic Mountain (Menelek) [1989/90
16g^{F} 16f 22g^{3} 16m^{4} 22d a20g^{3} 16f^{3}] leggy mare: fifth foal: half-sister to useful 76
hurdler/winning chaser Hypnotic (by Royben): dam useful staying hurdler: placed
in novice hurdles: should stay beyond 2¾m: best form on a sound surface: sold
5,600 gns Ascot July Sales. *F. Walwyn.*

MISS MANGAROO 4 b.f. Oats–Mangro (Mandamus) [1989/90 F16g^{4} F16f^{2}]
fourth foal: sister to novice hurdler Watermead and half-sister to winning staying
hurdler Grayrose Double (by Celtic Cone): dam, well beaten in NH Flat race and
novice hurdles, is from a very good jumping family: 10 lengths second to Doctor
Syntax in NH Flat race at Hexham in May: yet to race over hurdles. *Mrs G. R.
Reveley.*

MISS MAREVA 4 b.f. Skyliner–Tinterne (Tin King) [1989/90 16s^{pu}] smallish,
good-quartered filly: little worthwhile form on Flat: tailed off when pulled up 4 out —
in selling hurdle at Bangor in December. *J. Mackie.*

MISS MARJORIE HILL 4 ro.f. Royal Match–Overseas (Sea Hawk II)
[1989/90 F16f^{pu} 17f^{pu}] half-sister to 2 winners, including staying hurdler Harbour —
Bazaar (by Native Bazaar): dam poor maiden: tailed off when pulled up in NH Flat
race at Warwick and a novice hurdle at Cartmel, both in May. *M. C. Chapman.*

MISS ME NOT 8 br.m. Tycoon II–Khotso (Alcide) [1989/90 a18g* a18g^{3}] neat
mare: former selling hurdler: won claiming hurdle at Lingfield in December: 99
stayed 2½m: acted on hard and good to soft going: dead. *B. J. Wise.*

MISS MUCK 5 b.m. Balinger–Emperor's Gift (Menelek) [1989/90 16d 21v*
22d^{5} 20d^{6} 22g^{6} 25f^{2}] workmanlike mare: half-sister to smart hurdler/winning 96
chaser Mrs Muck (by Air Trooper) and winning hurdler Master Muck (by Sagaro):
dam fairly useful hurdler: won mares novice hurdle at Newton Abbot (wandered in
straight) in January: ran creditably afterwards: suited by test of stamina: acts on
heavy going: jumps none too fluently. *N. A. Twiston-Davies.*

MISS NEPTUNE (NZ) 6 b.m. Rapier II–All At Sea (NZ) (Man The Rail)
[1989/90 22d^{2} 22g^{3}] leggy mare: modest novice hurdler: will be well suited by 91
further than 2¾m: acts on dead going. *D. H. Barons.*

MISS NERO 9 br.m. Crozier–Romany Miss (Master Owen) [1989/90 24s 24g^{4}
25m] small, rather lightly-built mare: very useful hurdler at her best: placed in 129
Waterford Crystal Stayers' Hurdle in 1988 and 1989 (well beaten in latest running
in March): around 15 lengths fourth to Old Dundalk in ROA Rendlesham Hurdle at
Kempton, best effort of season: stays very well: has won on firm going but much
better form with plenty of give: jumps well: genuine. *R. Lee.*

MISS PATDONNA 4 b.f. Starch Reduced–Karousa Girl (Rouser) [1989/90
16m 16m^{F} 16m^{4} 16d] small, workmanlike filly: won 7f seller at 2 yrs, well beaten in —
1989: poor plater over hurdles: amateur ridden second start. *B. Palling.*

MISS PATINO 7 gr.m. Neltino–Pamsam (Constable) [1989/90 16f^{pu} 16m^{2}
16m^{pu}] small, plain mare: novice hurdler: not seen out after September: best form 71
at 2m on soft going. *M. J. Wilkinson.*

MISS POKEY 4 b.f. Uncle Pokey–Silken Swift (Saulingo) [1989/90 16g 16g^{6}
16g^{6} 19s* 21s 20f^{5} 20m* 20g^{pu}] small, sparely-made filly: modest 1½m winner on 110
Flat: claimer ridden, won claiming hurdles at Hereford in December and
Chepstow in April: stays 2½m: acts on good to firm and soft going: visored second
and third (ran in snatches) starts. *R. J. Holder.*

MISS QUIZZIE 7 b.m. Quizair–Bluebottle II (Happy Monarch) [1989/90 16h^{su}
20f^{pu} 16m^{pu}] sturdy non-thoroughbred mare: dam won 2 point-to-points: tailed —
off when pulled up in novice hurdles. *R. Champion.*

MISS RANOVA 5 ch.m. Giacometti–Miss Casanova (Galivanter) [1989/90 16g
16s] small, wiry mare: pulled hard when well beaten in 2 novice hurdles. *J. M.* —
Bradley.

MISS RELSUN 6 ch.m. Le Soleil–Relax (Seminole II) [1989/90 16f* 16f^{2}]
leggy mare: won 3 times on Flat at up to 1¼m in 1989 and made a successful 103
reappearance over hurdles in handicap at Southwell in August: fair second at
Sedgefield following month: likely to prove best at around 2m: acts on firm going.
Mrs G. R. Reveley.

MISS RUGHILL 7 b.m. New Member–Gamlingay (Rosyth) [1989/90 c25f^{pu}] c—
third foal: dam poor novice hurdler/chaser: won point-to-point in May: tailed off
when pulled up in hunter chase at Warwick later in month. *Mrs Greta Edwards.*

MISS SHERBROOKE 6 b.m. Workboy–Miss Kadir (Kadir Cup) [1989/90 16f[3] 16m[2] 16g[4]] small mare: poor novice hurdler: made running, racing freely, when in frame in varied company (including selling) at Catterick in 1989/90: likely to prove best at 2m. *M. W. Ellerby.* 76

MISS STOCKIN 6 b.m. Balinger–Reine d'Armagnac (Armagnac Monarch) [1989/90 20s[pu]] workmanlike mare: no worthwhile form in novice hurdles: pulled up lame only outing of season. *F. J. Yardley.* —

MISS SWALLOW 5 br.m. Strong Gale–Therene (Levanter) [1989/90 16m[5] 16g[3] 16m[pu]] lengthy, rather sparely-made mare: third in novice hurdle at Bangor in November: dead. *I. Semple.* 87

MISS TIMBER TOPPER 6 b.m. Liberated–Tacitina (Tacitus) [1989/90 24g[4] 24g[pu] 25f* 22g[3] a24g[3]] rather unfurnished mare: first form over hurdles when making all in novice event at Doncaster in December: good third in mares event at Kelso following month but ran a lack-lustre race at Southwell final start (January): stays well: acts on firm ground. *Miss L. C. Siddall.* 90

MISS TRISTRAM (NZ) 5 b.m. Sir Tristram–Coole Park (Wolver Hollow) [1989/90 16f* 16m[2] 16m 16m[2] 16d[4] 16f* 16m[4] 16m[5] 16d] small mare: middle-distance maiden on Flat: won selling hurdles at Southwell in August (bought in 4,400 gns) in August and Catterick (no bid) in November: unlikely to stay much beyond 2m: acts on firm ground and possibly unsuited by dead: ridden by 7-lb claimer: blinkered final start: sold privately 2,250 gns Ascot May Sales: in foal to Meldrum. *J. Parkes.* 86

MISS VAL 4 gr.f. Nishapour (FR)–Light Opera (FR) (Vienna) [1989/90 16m[pu] 20g[pu]] tailed off only outing on Flat: sold out of W. Pearce's stable 2,500 gns Doncaster September Sales: blinkered, tailed off when pulled up in novice hurdles. *T. Kersey.* —

MISS VICTORIA REES 10 b.m. Rhodomantade–Golden Silhouette (Twilight Alley) [1989/90 c21m[F]] eighth foal: half-sister to winning hurdler Golden Murray (by Murrayfield): dam well beaten in maiden races on Flat: fell fifth in novice event on chasing debut. *Miss J. Thorne.* c—

MISS WESLEY 5 b.m. Raga Navarro (ITY)–Balcanoona (Cawston's Clown) [1989/90 16h[pu]] sparely-made mare: poor sprint plater on Flat: tailed off when pulled up in novice seller on hurdling debut. *P. A. Pritchard.* —

MISS WRENSBOROUGH 7 b.m. Buckskin (FR)–Brieflet (Lucky Brief) [1989/90 22s 22d 20v[6] 22f[2]] small mare: won a point-to-point and a NH Flat race in 1989: first worthwhile form over hurdles when second in novice handicap at Nottingham in March, running on from 2 out having been given a lot to do: will stay 3m: acts on firm ground (won NH Flat race on soft). *D. R. Gandolfo.* 86 +

MISTER BOOT 11 b.g. Arapaho–Nevada-Credo (Credo) [1989/90 22d 26v[pu] 20s[3] 25d[pu]] good-bodied, workmanlike gelding: handicap hurdler: modest form at best in 1989/90, giving impression something possibly amiss: modest novice chaser: suited by 3m: best form on a soft surface: usually amateur or claimer ridden over hurdles: has run creditably in a visor: blinkered final start: sold 1,000 gns Ascot June Sales. *O. Sherwood.* c— 100

MISTER BUTLER 11 b.g. Menelek–Golden Number (Goldhill) [1989/90 c21f[2] c21f[5] c24h* c25f* c24f[pu] c24m[4] c25m[2] c24m[2] c25f[4]] sturdy gelding: handicap chaser: wide-margin winner at Ludlow (2 ran) in September and Plumpton (3 ran) in October: below form afterwards: stays 25f: possibly unsuited by very soft ground, acts on any other: sometimes let down by his jumping. *P. J. Jones.* c**101** —

MISTER BYBLOS 4 b.g. Lomond (USA)–Current Jargon (USA) (Little Current (USA)) [1989/90 16d[6] a16g[2] a18g[3] 16m[pu]] small, sparely-made gelding: fifth foal: half-brother to Irish Flat winners No Jargon (by Nonoalco) and Capricorn Son (by Northern Baby): dam, placed at up to 1¼m in Ireland, out of half-sister to Fort Marcy and Key To The Mint: little form on Flat (usually blinkered): sold out of D. K. Weld's stable 6,400 gns Newmarket Autumn Sales: poor form in juvenile hurdles in January: blinkered, pulled up (rider lost irons) in seller final outing: best form at 2m: sold to J. H. Baker 3,600 gns Newmarket July Sales. *Dr J. D. Scargill.* 78

MISTER CHRISTIAN (NZ) 9 b.g. Captain Jason (NZ)–Grisette (NZ) (Arctic Explorer) [1989/90 c25g* c28g[2] c29g[3] c26v[2] c30v[3] c29d[2] c29d[2]] leggy, shallow-girthed gelding: fair chaser: won handicap at Hereford in October: ran well afterwards: stays very well: acts on heavy going and good to firm (ran in snatches when well beaten on very firm ground): successful with and without c**121** —

blinkers: visored once in 1987/8: sometimes jumps none too fluently. *D. H. Barons.*

MISTER ED 7 ch.g. Monsieure Edouarde–Are You Poaching (Poaching) [1989/90 c25g[F3] c26s[F] c25s[pu] c36g[pu]] sparely-made gelding: winning chaser: jumps moderately and failed to put in a clear round in 1989/90: never going well last 2 starts (off course 4 months in between): stays 25f: acts on dead going: retained by trainer 5,600 gns Ascot June Sales. *R. Curtis.* c— x

MISTER FEATHERS 9 b.g. Town And Country–Nikali (Siliconn) [1989/90 c20d[ur] c20g* c16d* c19d[2] c21m[2] c20m[6] c20f* c20f[2] c16g[2] c20f*] robust, compact gelding: won handicap chases at Kempton (conditional jockeys, made several mistakes and edged left run-in) in November, Towcester in December, Bangor in March and Uttoxeter in May: stays 2½m: acts on firm and dead ground: has been blinkered and also hooded thrice in 1986/7: game and consistent. *J. S. King.* c**111** —

MISTER GEBO 5 b.g. Strong Gale–Miss Goldiane (Baragoi) [1989/90 F16g F16g] sparely-made gelding: third living foal: brother to fairly useful hurdler Strong Gold: dam unraced half-sister to Artiste Gaye, dam of numerous winners including Gaye Brief and Gaye Chance: behind in NH Flat races at Ludlow and Catterick: yet to race over hurdles or fences. *J. A. C. Edwards.*

MISTER HALF-CHANCE 4 b.g. Nearly A Hand–Lavilla (Tycoon II) [1989/90 F16s[6] F16v] fourth foal: half-brother to Irish NH Flat race winner Some Madam (by Some Hand): dam, from an excellent jumping family, showed no worthwhile form: sixth in NH Flat race at Warwick in February: yet to race over hurdles. *D. R. C. Elsworth.*

MISTER HARTIGAN 10 b.g. Menelek–Fortrition (David Jack) [1989/90 c26g* c28g[2] c24d[5] c27v[pu] c24d*] strong, good-bodied gelding: has been fired: fair chaser: won handicaps at Uttoxeter (conditional jockeys) in December and Ayr in April, latter by 2 lengths from Rich Remorse: stays 3½m: acts on heavy going. *J. A. C. Edwards.* c**119** —

MISTER JOLLY 4 b.g. Le Moss–Santimwen (Cassim) [1989/90 F16f[4] F16f[3]] half-brother to 2 winning hurdlers, notably top-class performer Aonoch (by Deep Run): dam won at up to 2½m over hurdles in Ireland: in frame in NH Flat races at

George Graham Memorial Handicap Chase, Ayr—
Mister Hartigan takes full advantage of Rich Remorse's mistakes

Uttoxeter and Hereford (around 10 lengths third behind Cards And Kisses) in the spring: yet to race over hurdles. *Mrs S. Oliver.*

MISTER LAWSON 4 ch.g. Blushing Scribe (USA)–Nonpareil (FR) (Pharly (FR)) [1989/90 a16g3 a16g* a16g2 a16g* a16gF 16f6] fairly useful winner over 5f at 2 yrs, no form on Flat in 1989: won novice hurdle at Lingfield in February and 3-runner juvenile handicap on same course following month: creditable sixth at Uttoxeter final start: always likely to be best at a sharp 2m: acts on firm ground: sold 4,400 gns Ascot June Sales. *Mrs J. Pitman.* 101

MISTER MARCH 7 b.g. Marching On–Jetwitch (Lear Jet) [1989/90 16f3 16d 16g 16gpu 16gpu] leggy, sparely-made gelding: half-brother to winning selling hurdler Hi-Tech Boy (by Tickled Pink): poor handicapper on Flat, stays 7f: novice selling hurdler: unlikely to stay much beyond 2m: acts on firm and dead ground. *D. W. Chapman.* 70

MISTER MOODY (FR) 5 ch.h. Mister Thatch–Moonly (FR) (Lionel) [1989/90 16m2 20g6 20s 16g6 16g] leggy, plain ex-French horse: fifth foal: half-brother to Flat winners Miss de Proville (by Iron Duke) and Danly (by Kamaridaan): dam won at up to 12.5f: placed at up to 15f on Flat: claimed out of P. Costes' stable 41,000 francs (approx £3,992) in October: second in selling hurdle at Uttoxeter in November (claimed out of M. Pipe's stable £6,600): bit below that form subsequently: should stay beyond 2m: acts on good to firm ground. *J. A. Hellens.* 84

MISTER ODDY 4 b.g. Dubassoff (USA)–Somerford Glory (Hittite Glory) [1989/90 16g3 16dpu 16g2 16d 16dpu] leggy gelding: modest maiden on Flat, stays 7f: placed in juvenile hurdles at Kempton in November and Windsor in January: ran poorly on softer ground otherwise. *J. S. King.* 90

MISTER PETARD 8 b.g. Sandy Creek–Miss Upward (Alcide) [1989/90 16g c16gpu] neat gelding: of little account. *B. Ellison.* c— —

MISTER POINT 8 ch.g. Ahonoora–Rozmeen (FR) (Relko) [1989/90 c20gF c20m3 c20m2 c16g* c16g* c16g* c20d* c16mpu] rather angular, sparely-made gelding: fairly useful hurdler at his best: won mid-season chases at Ayr, Edinburgh, Wetherby and Newcastle: behind when pulled up in Arkle Challenge Trophy Chase at Cheltenham in March: stays 2½m: acts on soft going and good to firm: still has something to learn about jumping fences. *M. H. Easterby.* c**111** —

MISTER TICKLE 5 b.g. Deep Run–Desert Maid (Proverb) [1989/90 16g 16dpu 16s 16s 16s] sturdy, workmanlike gelding: first foal: dam unraced half-sister to several winning jumpers, notably very smart staying chaser Everett: little sign of ability in novice hurdles. *R. Dickin.* —

Bobby Renton Memorial Novices' Chase, Wetherby—Mister Point dominates

MISTER TUFTIE 5 b.g. Black Minstrel–Articinna (Arctic Slave) [1989/90 F16g 16g 22vpu 16g] workmanlike gelding: has shown a little promise over hurdles. *G. Richards.* —

MISTOSH 6 b.m. White Speck–Keyvaca (Master Owen) [1989/90 16fpu] sparely-made mare: fourth foal: sister to a poor hurdler: dam of little account: in need of race and very green, jumped poorly and was tailed off when pulled up fifth in novice hurdle at Edinburgh in December on debut. *R. R. Lamb.* —

MISTRAL STORY 5 b.g. Pitpan–Flashy Flake (Candy Cane) [1989/90 16g2 16d] tall, leggy gelding: fifth foal: half-brother to winning hurdler Mad About Ya (by Fine Blade) and novice selling hurdler Poro Boy (by Whistling Deer): dam won over hurdles: promising 2½ lengths second to easy winner Forest Sun in 21-runner novice hurdle at Kempton in February on debut: tailed off in Crown Berger Hurdle at Chepstow following month (prominent to fourth, soon under pressure): worth another chance. *J. T. Gifford.* 102

MISTRESS ROSS 7 b.m. Impecunious–Rostresse (Rosyth) [1989/90 20g5 21f3 c20s] sparely-made mare: poor novice hurdler: always behind on chasing debut: stays 21f: ran creditably in blinkers on second outing. *G. Thorner.* c— 62

MISTS OF TIME 7 gr. or ro.g. Grey Dawn II–Hyroglyph (USA) (Northern Dancer) [1989/90 20f 16g 20m 22d2 24g 20g c20f3 c22f* c24f4] big, workmanlike gelding: handicap hurdler: won novice chase at Nottingham in March: jumped none too fluently, but had every chance when slipping on final bend in similar race at Ludlow in April: stays 2¾m: acts on firm and dead ground (possibly unsuited by very soft): blinkered second outing 1988/9. *C. J. Vernon Miller.* c**96** 99

MISTY JOY 5 gr.m. General Ironside–Darjoy (Darantus) [1989/90 16m5 16m 16f3 20d] workmanlike mare: bad novice hurdler. *W. T. Kemp.* 59

MISTY LEA 5 b.g. Royal Boxer–Misty Glen (Leander) [1989/90 aF16g6] leggy gelding: first foal: dam winning hurdler who stayed 3m: well beaten in NH Flat races: yet to race over hurdles or fences. *J. M. Bradley.*

MISTY MIRAGE 10 b.g. Grey Mirage–Will She Win (Arcticeelagh) [1989/90 16gpu c16m3 c16g6 c20gpu] sturdy gelding: lightly-raced winning selling hurdler: no form for some time: makes numerous mistakes and no form in novice chases: best form at 2m: acts on heavy going: blinkered twice in 1983/4: claimer ridden. *S. A. Torr.* c— x —

MITHRAS 12 b.g. Centaurus–Timidora (Timimi) [1989/90 c25g3 c30m5 c29g4 c26g3 c36g4 c26g3] rangy gelding: fair chaser nowadays: suited by a thorough test of stamina and give in the ground: has won for a claimer: usually races up with the pace. *B. Preece.* c**115** —

MITILINI 10 ch.g. Julio Mariner–Charming Thought (USA) (Stage Door Johnny) [1989/90 c26mpu] small, short-backed gelding: carries plenty of condition: winning point-to-pointer: poor novice hurdler/steeplechaser: has been beaten in sellers: stays 3m: acts on any going: moderate jumper. *Christopher Shankland.* c— x —

MITRE HOUSE 10 b.g. Bonne Noel–Gormla (Vulgan) [1989/90 c20fpu] tall gelding: type to carry condition: no sign of ability over hurdles and in steeplechases, but won a point-to-point in March. *Mrs A. Price.* c— —

MIXED BLENDS 8 b.m. The Parson–Biowen (Master Owen) [1989/90 c20dF c18d2 c21s* c18g* c16s5 c20s3 c24s4 c24f5 c25m4 c22g3 c25g*] c**136** —

Mixed Blends was covered by Carlingford Castle during the season and has been retired to the paddocks. She was a useful hurdler at her best, runner-up to Vagador in the Waterford Crystal Supreme Novices' Hurdle at Cheltenham in 1988. Sent chasing in the latest season, Mixed Blends won the IR £11,500 EBF Tattersalls Gold Cup Novices' Handicap Chase over three miles at Punchestown in April on her final appearance. Superior stamina won her the day at Punchestown. She jumped untidily early on and lay some way off the strong pace set by Blitzkreig from halfway. But Mixed Blends stayed on strongly in the latter stages, overcame mistakes at the third- and second-last fences to head Blitzkreig approaching the last, and went on to win driven out by eight lengths. Though Mixed Blends had won novice chases over shorter trips at Navan and Punchestown (the latter by two lengths from Toureen Prince) in the first half of the season, she showed her best form at three miles. She ran a good race when around eighteen lengths fourth to Royal Athlete in the Old Road Securities Reynoldstown

EBF Tattersalls Gold Cup, Punchestown—
Mixed Blends stays on better than Blitzkreig

Novices' Chase at Ascot in February, staying on and giving the impression she might have finished third but for a mistake at the last. Mixed Blends ran below that form in two subsequent outings under much faster conditions in Britain. She dropped out quickly from the top of the hill when over eighteen lengths fifth to Garrison Savannah in the Sun Alliance Novices' Chase at Cheltenham and could never reach the leaders when over twenty-five lengths fourth to Royal Athlete in the Mumm Club Novices' Chase at Liverpool three weeks later.

Mixed Blends (b.m. 1982)	The Parson (b 1968)	Aureole (ch 1950)	Hyperion
			Angelola
		Bracey Bridge (b 1962)	Chanteur II
			Rutherford Bridge
	Biowen (br 1974)	Master Owen (b 1956)	Owen Tudor
			Miss Maisie
		Own Blend (br 1955)	Monsieur L'Amiral
			Sailors Maid

If her breeding is anything to go by, Mixed Blends should make her mark as a jumping broodmare. The Parson has made the top ten National Hunt sires in Britain in terms of money won in each of the last five seasons. His best runners in the latest season included Trapper John and Wont Be Gone Long. The Parson has been a strong influence for stamina at stud, and most of those on the distaff side of Mixed Blends's pedigree have been stayers too. Topsham Bay (by Proverb), winner of the National Hunt Chase Challenge Cup over four miles at Cheltenham in the latest season, was the unraced Biowen's fourth foal. She has also produced Pollen Bee (by Pollerton), a winning hurdler who stayed well, Mixed Blends's full brother Fifth Amendment, a winner three times over hurdles in 1989/90 who shapes as though he'll be suited by further than two miles, and the poor novice Heart of Kings (by Proverb). Own Blend, only foal of the unraced Sailors Maid, was placed in a point-to-point on her only outing. She produced several winners, including staying hurdler/chaser Just Owen and Munster National Chase winner Owenius. No surprise, then, that Mixed Blends was

Mr John Spearman's "Mixed Blends"

better suited by three miles than shorter distances and ran as if she would probably have stayed further. A smallish, workmanlike mare, she was suited by give in the ground. *M. F. Morris, Ireland.*

MIXED BLESSING 6 b.m. Confused–Bovey Bells (Supreme Sovereign) [1989/90 16f4 16mF 16g 16mpu 16g4] leggy, sparely-made mare: poor novice hurdler: pulled hard in a selling handicap final start: best run at 2m on firm ground. *L. Wordingham.* 66

MIZAJ 6 ch.g. Thatching–Stickpin (Gulf Pearl) [1989/90 16m* 16gpu 16g5 16g3 c16dpu] rather leggy gelding: won handicap hurdle at Newcastle in November (edged left run-in): below form subsequently (reportedly finished lame second start and gave impression something was amiss next time): jumped badly on chasing debut: will prove best at around 2m: acts on soft going and good to firm: trained until after fourth outing by G. Moore. *G. Richards.* c— 110

MOCK LORD 7 ch.g. Lord Ha Ha–Bella Abzug (Karabas) [1989/90 20fpu 21gur 16m] small, sturdy gelding: third foal: dam modest maiden: brother to 2m hurdle winner Forty Grand: pulled up in 3 point-to-points in 1989: no sign of ability in 3 outings over hurdles in October: sold 1,300 gns Ascot December Sales. *J. R. Millington.* —

MODESTINO (USA) 4 b. or br.c. Fappiano (USA)–Demitasse (USA) (Young Emperor) [1989/90 16f5 17m3 16f2] brother to useful Irish hurdler Demon Fate: placed over 1¼m and 1½m on Flat: sold out of J. Gosden's stable 6,200 gns 83

Newmarket Autumn Sales: poor form over hurdles in the spring: worth a try over further. *N. Miller.*

MOD SQUAD 4 ch.f. Montekin–Fauchee (Busted) [1989/90 16g] ex-Irish filly: fifth foal: half-sister to Star of Dulargy (by Burslem), placed on Flat and over hurdles in Ireland: dam lightly-raced 1½m winner in Ireland: maiden on Flat: always behind in novice hurdle at Kelso in March. *W. Storey.* —

MOE GREENE 10 b.g. Corawice–Seabring Lass (Three Dons) [1989/90 c24dF c24v6 c24m] leggy, close-coupled gelding: handicap chaser: unraced in 1988/9: no worthwhile form in 1989/90: stays well: acts on any going: suitable mount for a claimer. *J. C. McConnochie.* c— —

MOHAMMED EL-SAHN 4 b.g. Trojan Fen–Hoonah (FR) (Luthier) [1989/90 16f2] useful but unreliable 1¼m plater on Flat (has looked ungenerous): sold out of D. Morley's stable 6,000 gns Newmarket Autumn Sales: 5 lengths second to Deltic in juvenile hurdle at Ludlow in March: can win a small race over hurdles. *J. G. M. O'Shea.* 97 p

MOHARABUIEE 4 b.f. Pas de Seul–Clonavee (USA) (Northern Dancer) [1989/90 a16g 16g] inconsistent maiden plater on Flat, stays 1¼m (has found little): behind in selling hurdles: sold 1,400 gns Ascot May Sales. *R. Hollinshead.* —

MO ICHI DO 4 b.g. Lomond (USA)–Engageante (FR) (Beaugency (FR)) [1989/90 16m 16s 16g 16d 20f 18f* 16f* 16mF 16g 16f4] small gelding: fair middle-distance maiden on Flat: sold out of B. Hills's stable 11,500 gns Newmarket Autumn Sales: won selling handicap hurdle at Fontwell (bought in 6,000 gns) and novice handicap at Ludlow in the spring: good fourth in novice handicap at Uttoxeter final outing: will stay beyond 2¼m: acts on firm going. *Miss S. J. Wilton.* 92

MOIETY 5 gr.g. General Ironside–Pry's Delight (Pry) [1989/90 16g 16s 16d c16g c24gpu] lengthy, dipped-backed gelding: brother to modest staying hurdler Whiskey Grain (by Laurence O): little sign of ability. *J. K. M. Oliver.* c— —

MOLE BOARD 8 br.g. Deep Run–Sharpaway (Royal Highway) [1989/90 16gF 16s3] close-coupled, sparely-made gelding: high-class hurdler at his best, but difficult to train: niggled along from some way out when well-below-form last of 3 behind Royal Derbi in minor event at Hereford in March: has won over 2½m but is best at 2m: best form with plenty of give in the ground: sometimes sweated in 1987/8, edgy in preliminaries last 2 outings: difficult to assess nowadays. *J. A. B. Old.* ?

MOLISE 4 b.f. Town And Country–Quaint (St Paddy) [1989/90 16g 17mpu] sparely-made filly: second foal: dam disappointing maiden on Flat: no promise in 2 outings over hurdles (pulled up before halfway last time). *S. F. Turton.* —

MOLOCH 7 b.g. Godswalk (USA)–Carthagian (Thatch (USA)) [1989/90 16m 16g3 a18g6] compact gelding: novice selling hurdler: form only at 2m: acts on good to firm ground: has looked none too keen: blinkered once in 1987/8. *Mrs S. M. Austin.* 63

MOMENT OF TRUTH 6 b.g. Known Fact (USA)–Chieftain Girl (USA) (Chieftain II) [1989/90 16s 16g 16d4 16g* 16d4 16m2 16f* 16dF 16g* 16g] compact gelding: maiden on Flat: won novice handicap hurdle at Sedgefield in February, handicap hurdle at Hexham in March and novice hurdle at Newcastle in May: gives impression he'll prove best at 2m: acts on firm and good to soft going: has worn crossed noseband: claimer ridden last 4 starts. *P. Monteith.* 106

MOMENTS JOY 4 ch.f. Adonijah–My Own II (El Relicario) [1989/90 16f 18gpu] smallish, lengthy filly: half-sister to several winners, including modest 2m chaser Expeditious (by Tachypous): placed over 1½m on Flat: no sign of ability in juvenile hurdles. *J. W. Hills.* —

MONANORE 13 ch.g. Prefairy–Mouskouri (Will Somers) [1989/90 c24spu c30gF c29dpu c33v4 c28g5 c25gpu c36fro] big, lengthy ex-Irish gelding: fairly useful chaser at his best: well beaten in 1989/90: ran out in Seagram Grand National at Liverpool (completed course in race on 3 previous occasions): stays well: acts on heavy going. *N. Tinkler.* c— —

MONARU 4 b.g. Montekin–Raubritter (Levmoss) [1989/90 17d* 16f* 18g2 21m3 16s2 22g 22f5 25m2] smallish, angular gelding: staying maiden on Flat: successful in juvenile hurdles at Devon & Exeter (seller, retained 11,500 gns) and Leicester in November: second in varied events after, on final start (blinkered) bit below form: should stay beyond 2¼m: acts on any going: usually visored: usually a front runner: moderate jumper: has looked none too keen. *M. C. Pipe.* 100 x

*William Hill Novices' Handicap Hurdle, Sandown—
this quite valuable prize goes to Montalino*

MONASIRA 5 ch.m. Lord Ha Ha–Westburn VII (pedigree unknown) [1989/90 F16g 16m 24m^{pu}] workmanlike non-thoroughbred mare: no sign of ability in novice hurdles. *R. Dickin.* —

MONASTIC CALM 6 b.g. Majestic Maharaj–Cantabrae (Cantab) [1989/90 20s^{pu} c22d^{F} a20g 21d^{F} a20g^{5} 22m^{pu}] angular gelding: poor novice hurdler: fell third on chasing debut: stays 2½m. *P. Davis.* c— 64

MONDAY CLUB 6 ch.g. Remezzo–Jena (Brigadier Gerard) [1989/90 F16g^{6} c16g^{ur} c16d^{pu} c25m^{F} 24d] leggy, angular gelding: fifth foal: dam showed little: let down by his jumping in novice chases and a novice hurdle but has shown signs of ability. *G. B. Balding.* c— x —

MONDRIAN (USA) 4 ch.g. Sir Ivor–Turban (USA) (Bagdad) [1989/90 16g^{F}] small gelding: little show in 2 maidens on Flat: sold out of H. Cecil's stable 4,000 gns Newmarket July Sales: behind until falling last in juvenile hurdle at Wetherby: dead. *K. A. Morgan.* —

MONETARY FUND 6 br.g. Red Sunset–Msida (Majority Blue) [1989/90 20g] compact gelding: winning hurdler: behind only outing of season: should stay beyond 2m: acts on heavy going: ran moderately when sweating slightly. *R. Akehurst.* —

MONKEY HUNTER 7 b.g. Monksfield–Miss Hunter (Buckhound) [1989/90 20g^{pu} 20m 20d 22d^{5} c24v^{F} c20d^{6} c24v^{pu} c24s^{6} c24d c24m^{4} c27f^{4}] lengthy gelding: poor novice hurdler/chaser: stays 27f: acts on firm and dead going: claimer or amateur ridden: sold 6,800 gns Doncaster Spring Sales. *Mrs S. A. Bramall.* c**78** 77

MONKSANDER 4 b.g. Monksfield–Maudie's Choice (Nebbiolo) [1989/90 F16m^{5}] second foal: dam poor Irish maiden: fifth of 11 in NH Flat race at Huntingdon in April: yet to race over hurdles. *G. B. Balding.*

MONKS IMAGE 8 b.g. Monksfield–Wallie Girl (Right Tack) [1989/90 25m^{pu}] compact, dipped-backed gelding: poor novice over hurdles: jumped moderately and fell 5 out on chasing debut. *J. Akehurst.* c— —

MONK'S MISTAKE 8 ch.g. Monksfield–Hardyglass Lass (Master Owen) [1989/90 16d^{6} 16s^{3} 16d* 16d^{2} 16g^{4} 16d* 16d] compact, rather sparely-made gelding: handicap hurdler: won at Warwick in January (conditional jockeys) and March (idled in front): stays 2¼m: acts on firm and dead ground. *R. Lee.* 112

MON REGRET 5 ch.g. Record Token–Charlotte's Image (Towern) [1989/90 16m 16g^{pu} c16s^{pu} 16s] workmanlike gelding: no worthwhile form over hurdles: well behind when pulled up 5 out in novice chase at Chepstow: blinkered final start. *J. A. B. Old.* c— —

MONRITA 8 b.g. Monksfield–Narita (Narrator) [1989/90 16g6 a20g3 16g2 20m 16g 24s6 a18g2 22dpu] sturdy, workmanlike gelding: winning 2m hurdler: well beaten over fences: acted on soft going: occasionally visored: dead. *C. J. Bell.* c— 85

MONSIEUR TOURBIERE 4 ch.g. Le Moss–Miss Nelly (Saulingo) [1989/90 16fpu 16g] sparely-made gelding: no promise in 2 selling hurdles. *M. Castell.* —

MONTAGNARD 6 b.g. Strong Gale–Louisa Stuart (FR) (Ruysdael II) [1989/90 20g2 22v2] smallish, sparely-made gelding: lightly-raced novice hurdler: runner-up at Uttoxeter and Haydock (kept on gamely when going down by 15 lengths to impressive winner Fort Noel) in mid-season: will be suited by 3m: acts on heavy going. *M. Bradstock.* 115

MONTALINO 7 gr.g. Neltino–Montage (Polyfoto) [1989/90 20d 22m3 16m* 16gur] workmanlike gelding: won quite valuable William Hill Novices' Handicap Hurdle at Sandown in December: beaten in second place behind eventual 20-length winner Acre Hill when unseating rider last in novice hurdle at Cheltenham following month: best form at 2m: acts on good to firm ground. *J. T. Gifford.* 104

MONTEVIOT 6 b.m. Scallywag–Mikadora (Cavo Doro) [1989/90 18d 20d 16g5] modest novice hurdler: form only at around 2m: acts on heavy going (yet to race on ground firmer than good): has worn crossed noseband: sold 12,000 gns Doncaster Spring Sales. *S. J. Leadbetter.* —

MONTGOMERY 9 b.g. Push On–Mirror Back (Master Owen) [1989/90 c26d* c24m c24m* c25m2 c26gpu c28g c24d2 c24m4 c24f2] lengthy, workmanlike gelding: won handicap chases at Stratford (conditional jockeys) and Windsor in November: good second in novice events at Chepstow on seventh and final starts: stays 3¼m: acts on heavy going: blinkered twice in 1986/7: sometimes jumps moderately. *W. G. McKenzie-Coles.* c93 —

MONTOOBI 5 b.g. Tickled Pink–Marlotte (Mosquito II) [1989/90 F16m 20mpu] sturdy gelding: second foal: dam won a point-to-point: pulled up and dismounted 3 out in novice hurdle in April: dead. *T. Casey.* —

MONUMENTAL LAD 7 ro.g. Jellaby–Monumental Moment (St Paddy) [1989/90 c16g2 c20gF] leggy, workmanlike gelding: winning hurdler: hung left when 3 lengths second of 5 finishers to Crash Market in novice event at Bangor in November on chasing debut: fell fourth next time: stays 2½m: acts on soft going: claimer ridden last 5 outings. *Mrs H. Parrott.* c99 —

MOODY MAN 5 b.g. Ela-Mana-Mou–Princess Redowa (Prince Regent (FR)) [1989/90 16d* 17v* 16d6 16d4 16m* 16f*] 144

Former jumps jockey Philip Hobbs has quickly established himself as a trainer, and has now sent out one-hundred-and-four winners since North Yard provided his stable with its first winner from its first runner at Devon & Exeter on August 22nd, 1985. Each season has seen an increase in winners for Hobbs, and the forty-five totalled in the latest season was easily his best tally. Though perhaps still remembered as Bonanza Boy's first trainer—the horse won him the Challow Hurdle at Newbury, the Persian War Novices' Hurdle at Chepstow and the Peter Cox Novices' Chase at Ascot—Hobbs has enjoyed plenty of other notable successes with horses such as Gallic Prince, Joint Sovereignty, Prize Asset, Gay Edition, winner of eight races over fences in her novice season, and the much improved Moody Man. On his last two outings of the season the last-named pulled off a big handicap double in the William Hill Imperial Cup at Sandown and the County Hurdle at Cheltenham, a double achieved previously by only Floyd in the same season (1985); Flaming East won the County Hurdle in 1957 and the Imperial Cup the following year. Before Sandown Moody Man had usually been held up in his races and had raced on ground no faster than good over hurdles, including when successful in handicaps at Haydock and Newton Abbot in December, the former a conditional jockeys event. When he showed improved form at Sandown then improved again at Cheltenham five days later, he was ridden up with the pace in races that took place under fast conditions. In the Imperial Cup Moody Man was left in a clear lead at the second last when second-placed Bradbury Star fell, bringing down two horses and hampering others, and he went on to draw away on the flat and win by ten lengths from Penny Forum. Had they all stood up he would probably still have won. Penalized 7 lb at Cheltenham, he had to fight hard for a narrow win from Smart Performer and Persillant.

Moody Man (b.g. 1985)	Ela-Mana-Mou (b 1976)	Pitcairn (b 1971)	Petingo
			Border Bounty
		Rose Bertin (ch 1970)	High Hat
			Wide Awake
	Princess Redowa (b or br 1976)	Prince Regent (br 1966)	Right Royal V
			Noduleuse
		Ballydowa (ch 1971)	Ballymoss
			Redowa

Moody Man, a useful winning plater on the Flat, was bought out of M. H. Easterby's stable for 5,000 guineas at the 1988 Doncaster August Sales. A rare bargain, obviously. He changed hands again, privately, shortly after Cheltenham and is now in training in the USA. A rangy gelding, Moody Man is the fourth foal out of useful mile winner Princess Redowa. She has produced two other winners, namely Ladoisko (by Gay Mecene), a winning hurdler in Ireland and subsequently successful in Germany, and Princely Estate (by Northfields), a modest mile-and-a-quarter winner. The second dam, winning sprinter Ballydowa, a half-sister to the good middle-distance colt Red Regent, produced one other winner, the quite useful Flat horse and fair hurdler Ballytop. Her dam Redowa was a winning sister to the top-class sprinter/miler Yellow God. *P. J. Hobbs.*

MOON RUN 7 ch.h. Deep Run–Etoile de Lune (Apollo Eight) [1989/90 F16g 22g 16s c17m^{pu}] leggy, rather angular horse: third foal: half-brother to winning staying chaser Samsun (by Sunyboy): dam half-sister to useful staying chaser Scroggy: won 2 point-to-points in Ireland in 1989: well beaten in NH Flat race and 2 novice hurdles (took a good hold and tended to hang left on second occasion): well behind when pulled up on chasing debut: wears a crossed noseband. *G. A. Ham.* c— —

MOONS QUADRILLE 14 b.g. Quadriga–Tailor Don (Fighting Don) [1989/90 c27d^{pu} c27s^{5} c28g^{5} c16d^{4} c27g] strong gelding: winning point-to-pointer/hunter chaser: poor form in 1989/90: suited by a test of stamina: acts on any going. *Mrs S. J. Gospel.* c73

MOON WARRIOR 5 b.h. The Brianstan–Brigannie Moon (Brigadier Gerard) [1989/90 16m^{pu}] poor maiden on Flat: tailed off when pulled up last in novice hurdle at Windsor in November. *D. A. Wilson.* —

William Hill Imperial Cup, Sandown—Moody Man shows improved form

County Handicap Hurdle, Cheltenham—
Persillant leads Moody Man and Smart Performer over the last

MOORE STYLISH 7 b. or br.m. Moorestyle–Coralivia (Le Levanstell) [1989/90 16g3 16s 16m4 16m*] lengthy mare: handicap hurdler: won at Huntingdon in April: unlikely to stay much beyond 2m: acts on soft going and good to firm. *J. Ringer.* 100

MOORFIELD LADY 6 ch.m. Vicomte–Aberklair (Klairon) [1989/90 16d5 16mpu 16g 16d6 17g5 20g 16g4 16f3 16m* 16f2] lengthy mare: made most when winning novice hurdle at Market Rasen in April in game fashion: good second at Newcastle following month: tends to race freely and is likely to prove best at around 2m: acts on firm ground: has sweated. *B. E. Wilkinson.* 93

MOOR FROLICKING 4 ch.f. Morston (FR)–Woodland Frolic (Hittite Glory) [1989/90 16d a16g] plating class on Flat, winner twice over 1m in 1990: behind in juvenile hurdles: seems to have difficulty in staying 2m. *T. M. Jones.* —

MOORLANDER 5 b.g. River Knight (FR)–Lady Perrin (Merrymount) [1989/90 16g6 16dpu 16d 16g 16d] leggy, sparely-made gelding: novice selling hurdler: pulls hard and races only at 2m: best run on good ground. *W. H. Tinning.* 69

MOOR SCOPE 8 ch.g. Whistlefield–Horoscope (Romany Air) [1989/90 c21s2 c20s2 c25f* c25f2] lengthy, workmanlike gelding: winning point-to-pointer: jumped soundly in the main when winning novice hunter chase at Plumpton in March: good second at Towcester later in month: stays 25f: acts on any going. *J. F. F. White.* c**102**

MOORSTOWN RAMBLER 7 ch.g. Push On–Miss Moorstown (Master Owen) [1989/90 c24f4] workmanlike gelding: winning hurdler: well-beaten last of 4 in novice event at Leicester in November on chasing debut: better suited by 21f than shorter distances and should stay further: acts on dead going: has won for a claimer. *M. Oliver.* c— —

MORE ACTION 8 b.g. Deep Run–Una's Pride (Raise You Ten) [1989/90 c20s4 c25g4 c24d4] big, rangy gelding: successful in 2 point-to-points and in 2 hunter chases in Ireland in 1988: modest form in hunter chases in Britain: stays well: acts on heavy going. *Miss H. C. Knight.* c88

MORE BY LUCK 4 ch.g. Miami Springs–La Miranda (Miralgo) [1989/90 16spu] placed in 1¼m sellers on Flat in 1989: tailed off when pulled up last in juvenile hurdle at Hereford in December. *R. J. Holder.* —

MORE DISTINCT 6 b.m. Class Distinction–Coliemore (Coliseum) [1989/90 20g5 22d 24s3 24s3 22v4 c20dF] lengthy, workmanlike mare: handicap hurdler: fell fatally on chasing debut: stayed 3m: acted well on heavy going. *J. M. Jefferson.* c— 104

Mercury Communications Hurdle, Cheltenham—
Morley Street takes over from Ikdam at the last

MORE FOOL YOU 8 gr.g. Funny Man–Annaghmore (Yrrah Jr) [1989/90 c24s^{6}] smallish, sturdy gelding: winning hurdler: jumped sketchily in early stages when tailed off in novice chase at Windsor in January: effective at 2½f in testing conditions and stays 3m: acts on heavy going (yet to race on top-of-the-ground). *K. Bishop.* c— —

MORE ONE WAY 9 b. or br.g. Arapaho–Safe Return (Canisbay) [1989/90 c25m^{6} c25g c25g^{pu}] good-topped gelding: poor hurdler/chaser: no form in 1989/90 (pulled up lame final start): stays 3m: acts on any ground: often claimer ridden over hurdles. *N. R. Mitchell.* c— —

MORETON'S MARTHA 5 b.m. Derrylin–Kissimmee (FR) (Petingo) [1989/90 16m 16g] sparely-made mare: little sign of ability over hurdles: tailed off in seller final start. *Andrew Turnell.* —

MORLEY STREET 6 ch.g. Deep Run–High Board (High Line) [1989/90 16f^{2} 20f* 20s^{2} 16m^{5} 20f*] 162 p

Toby Balding began the latest season with two of the leading candidates for the Champion Hurdle in Beech Road and Morley Street. In the event, Beech Road finished fourth behind Kribensis, with Morley Street fifth a further eight lengths back. It's doubtful whether Morley Street will get another chance to prove himself the hurdler he's promised to be on occasions, but he remains a terrific prospect. He's still relatively lightly

Sandeman Aintree Hurdle, Liverpool—Morley Street is too quick for Joyful Noise

Michael Jackson Bloodstock Ltd's "Morley Street"

raced, with only ten starts over hurdles and three in National Hunt Flat races to his name, and for the second season in succession his performance at the Grand National meeting showed him to be a horse with still untapped potential.

The field for the Sandeman Aintree Hurdle wasn't so strong as usual, almost certainly on account of the prevailing firm ground, and Morley Street, who looked spot on in terms of condition, was sent off 5/4-on favourite. His main rivals in the betting were two more of the Champion Hurdle runners, Vagador (eighth) and Island Set (seventh). The Tote Gold Trophy runner-up Joyful Noise, Stayers' Hurdle fourth Ikdam, and one-time smart stayer Taberna Lord were the only other starters. The winner could be named a long way from home. Morley Street crept closer in the back straight, joined the leader Joyful Noise still on the bridle at the final flight then sprinted clear when nudged along on the run-in, quickly putting fifteen lengths between himself and the runner-up. While Morley Street's task wasn't so difficult as it could have been—both Vagador and Island Set ran as though ill at ease on the ground—it was hard not to be impressed by the speed he showed throughout the race. He had seemed beaten for pace, however, in the Champion Hurdle three weeks earlier, struggling to quicken from the third last and coming back just over twelve lengths behind Kribensis. Nonetheless, that was as good a performance as any he'd put up previously, and probably encouraged his trainer who'd reportedly been of the opinion that the horse wasn't at his peak following eleven weeks off the track because of a minor viral infection. Morley Street's previous races in the latest season had resulted in a win and two seconds. He was a tenderly-handled runner-up to Cruising Altitude in the Gerry Feilden

Hurdle on his reappearance, and then confirmed the promise of that effort when easily landing the odds from Deep Sensation in the Mercury Communications Hurdle at Cheltenham, once again displaying a fine turn of foot. That turn of foot was missing, however, in the Racing International Hurdle, the second leg of the Sport of Kings Challenge, at Chepstow two weeks later, where Morley Street went down by three quarters of a length to Propero having moved to the front with three to jump. Morley Street left the impression there that he might have done better with his finishing effort delayed longer, but in all probability he just wasn't quite right on the day and he's much better judged on his last two appearances.

Morley Street (ch.g. 1984)	Deep Run (ch 1966)	Pampered King (b 1954)	Prince Chevalier
			Netherton Maid
		Trial By Fire (ch 1958)	Court Martial
			Mitrailleuse
	High Board (b 1977)	High Line (ch 1966)	High Hat
			Time Call
		Matchboard (br 1963)	Straight Deal
			Royal Alliance

There was talk of Morley Street's being sent chasing early in the latest season; nothing came of it, but it's now highly likely that he'll be chasing in 1990/1. It's difficult to put forward a better prospect. There won't be many other novices around with the speed to trouble him at the minimum trip, and yet he could just as easily be campaigned over longer distances should connections so desire. He has the advantage of being able to act on any going, too. Morley Street is a good jumper of hurdles, although that is by no means a guarantee of a successful transition to larger obstacles as we saw with Beech Road. Provided he does take to jumping fences, Morley Street could get even closer to the top of the tree than he did over hurdles. On make and breeding the rangy Morley Street should be well on the way to becoming a chaser. His unraced dam is a daughter of the top-notch hunter chaser/point-to-pointer Matchboard, sixteen times a winner over fences and a three-parts sister to that good Irish chaser Royal Bond. *G. B. Balding.*

MORNING COFFEE 4 b.f. Kabour–Underbarrow Rose (Andrea Mantegna) [1989/90 F16g 16s 17h^{4} 17m^{3}] sparely-made filly: third foal: dam novice selling hurdler: first form over hurdles when third of 5 in juvenile event at Newton Abbot in May. *R. G. Frost.* 63

MORNING CRY 6 ch.g. Royal Match–Gay Seeker (Status Seeker) [1989/90 17d^{pu} 16g^{pu} a16g] no sign of ability: dead. *C. G. Roach.* —

MORNING EXCHANGE 10 b.g. Deep Run–Brideweir (Chandra Cross) [1989/90 22f^{5}] lengthy gelding: of little account over hurdles: fell first on chasing debut: has worn blinkers. *N. B. Thomson.* c— —

MORNING RUN 8 b.m. Deep Run–Brideweir (Chandra Cross) [1989/90 c16g^{pu} c26g^{pu} 22f^{pu}] sparely-made mare: of little account: has worn blinkers: headstrong. *N. B. Thomson.* c— —

MORNING TIDE 5 ch.m. Dubassoff (USA)–Tinatwo (Fortina) [1989/90 F16g^{6} F16m] half-sister to a poor animal: dam won 2m hurdle: sixth in mares NH Flat race at Hereford in November: yet to race over hurdles or fences. *J. E. Forte.*

MORPION 8 b.m. Scallywag–Greenfield Girl (Pendragon) [1989/90 17d^{2} 16d 22g^{4} c20g^{F}] leggy, workmanlike mare: lightly-raced novice hurdler: in lead when falling 3 out in novice event won by Over The Firs at Uttoxeter in May on chasing debut: stays 2¾m: acts on firm and dead ground. *A. J. Wilson.* c— p 81

MORVERN 11 b.g. Thatch (USA)–Sleat (Santa Claus) [1989/90 20m^{5} 28g^{pu} a20g] winning hurdler/chaser: no form for a long time: usually blinkered or visored. *Mrs Jill Evans.* c— —

MO'S CHORISTER 4 b.g. Lir–Revelstoke (North Stoke) [1989/90 16d] leggy gelding: first foal: dam of little account: tailed-off last of 16 finishers in juvenile hurdle at Wincanton in February on debut. *D. H. Barons.* —

MOSOF 9 b.g. Oats–Hail To Vail (USA) (Hail To Reason) [1989/90 c18f^{pu}] tall, leggy gelding: lightly-raced handicap chaser: pulled up lame in September and not seen out again: best form at up to 2¼m: acts on any going. *J. T. Gifford.* c— —

MOSSAL BAY 9 ch.g. Goldhill–Kortisso (Wrekin Rambler) [1989/90 c19spu c24dbd] robust ex-Irish gelding: successful point-to-pointer: no form in steeplechases. *J. A. B. Old.* c— —

MOSS CONNELL 8 ch.g. Carnival Night–Doon Mist (Golden Vision) [1989/90 c21m5 c24s6 c20d c20d] lengthy gelding: novice chaser: no form in 1989/90: seems not to stay 3¼m: ran moderately on good to firm final start 1987/8: blinkered second and final outings: jumps none too fluently. *Mrs I. McKie.* c—

MOSSGARA 5 b.g. Le Moss–Bargara (Bargello) [1989/90 20m2 20g2 21d* 20g*] IR 26,000 3-y-o: rangy, useful-looking, chasing type: half-brother to several winning jumpers, including useful chaser Cahervillahow (by Deep Run): dam, unraced, from a successful jumping family: won novice hurdles at Warwick in March (by 15 lengths) and Uttoxeter (handicap) following month, latter by 2½ lengths under top weight: will stay beyond 21f: acts on dead going: wears crossed noseband: will progress further. *Mrs J. Pitman.* 118 p

MOST INTERESTING 5 b.m. Music Boy–Quick Glance (Oats) [1989/90 16s6 16v4 16g 16d* 16m6] smallish mare: won novice selling hurdle at Worcester in May (no bid): good sixth in novice handicap at Stratford following month: given plenty to do both starts: has raced only at 2m: acts on good to firm and dead ground. *G. H. Jones.* 89 +

MOTALEE 12 br.g. Raise You Ten–Background (Black Tarquin) [1989/90 c24fpu] sparely-made gelding: modest point-to-pointer, winner in February: pulled up in hunter chases. *Mrs S. Taylor.* c—

MOTOR BIKE MAN 14 b.g. Spartan General–Princess Hippolyte (Aggressor) [1989/90 c26f4] big gelding: winning point-to-pointer: novice chaser: seems well suited by a test of stamina. *D. C. Robinson.* c73

MOTOR CLOAK 4 b.c. Motivate–Cavalry Cloak (Queen's Hussar) [1989/90 16g4] small colt: sixth foal: half-brother to 2 poor performers: dam never ran: staying-on 20 lengths fourth to Iveagh House in juvenile maiden hurdle at Wincanton in February: should improve. *M. Brown.* 84 p

MOTTRAM'S GOLD 5 ch.g. Good Times (ITY)–Speed The Plough (Grundy) [1989/90 19dpu 16g 16s 16v2 16s* 16sur 16d] smallish, angular gelding: ridden by 7-lb claimer, won selling hurdle at Towcester in February (bought in 4,600 gns): always behind in novice handicap following month: should stay beyond 2m: acts on heavy going. *R. Dickin.* 82

MOU-DAFA 10 br.g. Mugatpura–Fanny O'Dea (Sadler's Wells) [1989/90 c16g2 c17m* c18f*] small, narrow gelding: fairly useful chaser: made virtually all when winning handicaps at Newton Abbot and Fontwell (beat Palace Yard 6 lengths) in May: stays 2¼m (weakened from 4 out when tried at 2½m): goes very well on top-of-the-ground: genuine. *M. C. Pipe.* c**133** —

MOULTON BULL 4 ch.g. Chabrias (FR)–Welsh Cloud (Welsh Saint) [1989/90 F17m] third foal: dam won over 5f and 7f at 2 yrs: tailed off in NH Flat race at Carlisle in April: yet to race over hurdles. *S. J. Leadbetter.*

MOUNTAICO 8 b.g. Paico–Mount Rainier (Danjovan) [1989/90 21f2 20m6 c22d4 c20g3 c25f3 c26vpu c25g c21gur c25v* c26v2 c26s6 c32fpu] leggy, close-coupled gelding: novice hurdler: won novice chase at Plumpton in January: claimer ridden, made most when clear 4 lengths second to Bumbles Folly in handicap at Fontwell following month: stays 3¼m: probably suited by give in the ground nowadays (acts well on heavy): blinkered final start 1988/9 and on last 4 outings. *N. R. Mitchell.* c**92** 82

MOUNTAIN CABIN 8 ch.g. Patch–Sweet Mountain (Whistling Wind) [1989/90 c24d2 c24gF] leggy gelding: successful on both starts in point-to-points in Ireland in 1988: let down by his jumping in steeplechases: looked a difficult ride, hanging left on run-in, when going down by 3 lengths to Tartan Trix in novice event at Leicester in January: stays 3m. *D. J. G. Murray-Smith.* c**104** x

MOUNTAIN CRASH 10 b.g. Crash Course–Cross Pearl (Pearl Orient) [1989/90 c25d c21d3 c20g6 c20gF c20g5 c24g4] smallish, lengthy gelding: handicap hurdler/chaser: below his best in 1989/90: effective at 2½m and stays 3m: probably acts on any going, but best form over hurdles on ground no softer than dead: blinkered final start: sold 4,600 gns Ascot June Sales. *J. A. C. Edwards.* c**95** —

MOUNTAIN LIFE 4 b.g. Wolverlife–Stramenta (Thatching) [1989/90 16vpu 16g 17mpu] first foal: dam unraced: tailed off in selling hurdle. *R. J. O'Sullivan.* —

MOUNTAIN MAN 14 b.g. Wolver Hollow–Beck (St Paddy) [1989/90 16m3 16m5 17g* 20s 16g2 16gpu 16d 17m5 a20g6] leggy, lengthy, lightly-made gelding: c— 83

has stringhalt: poor hurdler nowadays: won at Devon & Exeter in December: ran creditably on same course penultimate start: no form in 2 races over fences: stays 2½m, at least when conditions aren't testing: acts on any going: ran poorly on all-weather final outing: takes a strong hold: claimer ridden. *R. Dickin.*

MOUNTAIN MUSE 6 b.m. Sunyboy–Royal Pam (Pamroy) [1989/90 16s] sturdy, workmanlike mare: second living foal: dam, unraced, comes from a successful jumping family: better for race, behind in mares novice hurdle at Towcester in February. *N. A. Gaselee.* —

MOUNTAIN RETREAT 4 br.g. Top Ville–Tarrystone (So Blessed) [1989/90 16mpu] rather leggy gelding: modest performer on Flat when trained by L. Cumani, successful in 1¾m maiden in 1989: tailed off when pulled up in Seagram 100 Pipers Top Novices' Hurdle at Liverpool in April. *Mrs D. Haine.* —

MOUNTAIN RUN 6 b.g. Deep Run–Palaska (Mountain Call) [1989/90 17h3 17fF 18f5 16d c16gF c16f5 a16g6] plain gelding: poor novice hurdler: always well behind but wasn't knocked about in novice chase at Warwick in December: has worn a crossed noseband: has looked temperamentally unsatisfactory. *R. G. Frost.* c— — §

MOUNTAIN SHADOW 5 b.h. Tyrnavos–Follow Me Follow (Wollow) [1989/90 c16d6 c16f3] workmanlike horse: no sign of ability over hurdles: ran as though still not fully fit when 12½ lengths third behind Spirited Holme in novice handicap chase at Bangor in March, and may improve further. *M. Scudamore.* c**75** —

MOUNT ARGUS 8 ch.g. Don–Pendula (Tamerlane) [1989/90 c26f*] novice hurdler: fairly useful point-to-pointer: left in lead 2 out when landing the odds by ½ length from Toffee Apple in hunter chase at Uttoxeter in April: stays 3¼m: acts on firm going. *Mrs H. J. Clarke.* c**92** p —

MOUNT EATON FOX 7 b.g. Buckskin (FR)–Town Fox (Continuation) [1989/90 20g 22spu 20m4] tall, lengthy gelding: has scope: first form over hurdles when 7 lengths fourth to Docksider in novice event at Huntingdon in April: will stay beyond 2½m: seems suited by top-of-the-ground. *D. R. Greig.* 88

MOUNTEBOR 6 b.g. Prince Regent (FR)–Land (Baldric II) [1989/90 16g* 16g6 16g5 c20m* c24g* c21g2 c20m* c24g3] lengthy gelding: won handicap hurdle at Hereford in October: successful in novice chase at Ludlow in January and handicap chases at Edinburgh in February and Huntingdon in April: stays 3m, at least when conditions aren't testing: probably acts on any going. *J. A. C. Edwards.* c**109** 114

MOUNT EREBUS 8 ch.g. Quayside–Well Mannered (Menelek) [1989/90 16g 16m 16dF 16f] close-coupled, deep-girthed gelding: novice hurdler: raced keenly and was close up when falling 4 out in handicap won by Rusty Roc at Chepstow in March: well beaten next time. *Lord Head.* —

MOUNT FALCON 8 br.g. Paico–Lady Mell (Milan) [1989/90 c20f c18fF c16f4 c18g4 c16m* c16gur c22d6] sturdy ex-Irish gelding: second foal: dam won 2m hurdle in Ireland: poor maiden hurdler: benefited from mishaps to 3 opponents when winning 7-runner novice chase at Tramore in August: tailed off in similar race at Stratford in February: acts on good to firm ground (won NH Flat race on heavy): occasionally blinkered, including when successful: trained by T. Lacy until after fifth outing. *F. Sheridan.* c**86** —

MOUNT OLIVER 12 b.g. No Argument–Bayview Rambler (Wrekin Rambler) [1989/90 c24d* c26g2 c25g2 c24g2] strong, workmanlike gelding: modest chaser: won at Nottingham in December: second in conditional jockeys events at Uttoxeter later in month and at Cheltenham and Kempton in January: stays extreme distances: acts on any going: has run well for an amateur and a claimer: has worn blinkers: visored nowadays. *R. Dickin.* c**107** —

MOUNT PARSON 10 ch.g. The Parson–Salwood (Woodville II) [1989/90 c20f3 c26g4 c24s5] well-made gelding: very useful hurdler: one of the best novice chasers in Ireland in 1987/8: fair form when in frame in handicaps in Britain: best at around 2½m: acted well in the mud: dead. *Andrew Turnell.* c**124** —

MOUNT PATRICK 6 b.g. Paddy's Stream–Hills of Fashion (Tarqogan) [1989/90 16g 16g] workmanlike gelding: behind in NH Flat race: showed a little ability in novice hurdle at Ludlow in December: tailed off at Wolverhampton (still bit backward) following month: sold 9,000 gns Doncaster Spring Sales. *Capt. T. A. Forster.* —

MOUNT TORUS 6 br.g. Torus–Mountview Lady (Master Buck) [1989/90 16d 16g 16m3] medium-sized gelding: first form over hurdles when 4½ lengths third 82 behind Northern Barry in 8-runner novice handicap at Stratford: acts on good to firm ground: claimer ridden. *S. Christian.*

MOUNT WOOD 7 gr.m. Rupert Bear–Injaka (Right Boy) [1989/90 16s 24d^{pu}] leggy mare: behind in claimer and seller on Flat in 1986: no promise in novice hurdles at Nottingham and Market Rasen (still bit backward). *H. J. Collingridge.* —

MOVE ABOUT 6 ch.g. Move Off–Toadpool (Pongee) [1989/90 16g 16g^{4} 16g^{3} 16m^{2} 19g^{6} 16f^{2} a16g^{5} c16m 16f^{6} 16m] leggy, close-coupled gelding: novice selling hurdler: tailed off in novice handicap chase: best form at around 2m: blinkered last start 1988/9 and on first outing: claimer ridden. *Mrs H. Parrott.* c— 67

MOVE AHEAD 6 ch.m. Move Off–Reigate Head (Timber King) [1989/90 16f^{pu}] small, lengthy mare: mid-division in NH Flat races: little sign of ability in novice hurdles. *B. Bousfield.* —

MOVING TIME 5 ch.g. Move Off–Ribera (Ribston) [1989/90 16f^{pu} 16f 16f^{5} 16g 17f^{pu} 16g 16g 20g^{pu}] small, plain gelding: poor novice hurdler: pulled up and dismounted final start (January). *N. Chamberlain.* —

MOWTHORPE 5 ch.g. Ballad Rock–Simeonova (Northfields (USA)) [1989/90 16g^{4} 16d^{bd} 16d* 20s^{4} 16g^{2} 16g^{6}] dipped-backed gelding: ridden by 7-lb claimer, won handicap hurdle at Sedgefield in December: good second at Catterick in January: below form final start (February): seemed not to stay 2½m in testing conditions: acts on good to firm and dead going. *M. W. Easterby.* 94

MOYA MOWA 13 b.m. My Swallow–La Mariposa (USA) (T V Lark) [1989/90 17f^{5} 17f^{4} 17d a20g 26f^{pu}] moderate winning hurdler at her best: has been to stud: seems of little account nowadays. *J. E. Forte.* —

MOYA'S GIRL 6 ch.m. Prince Titian–Moya's Star (Top Star) [1989/90 16d^{pu} 16m^{6} 20m^{6}] small mare: first reported foal: dam useful point-to-pointer: only sign of ability when sixth in novice hurdle at Ludlow in January on second start. *K. R. Owen.* 67

MOYSPRUIT 11 br.g. Import–River Moy (Niagara Falls) [1989/90 c20f^{4}] strong gelding: point-to-pointer, winner in March and April: maiden hunter chaser: finished lame when well beaten at Cheltenham in May: suited by 21f+: possibly unsuited by heavy ground, acts on any other. *W. H. Bissill.* c— —

MOZE TIDY 5 b.g. Rushmere–Church Belle (Spartan General) [1989/90 16d^{2} 16s^{2} 20f 20d] rather leggy gelding: has scope: third foal: half-brother to maiden point-to-pointer Easter Princess (by Cleon): dam winning staying hurdler: runner-up in novice hurdles at Towcester and Sandown (beaten 2 lengths by Bourbon Spirit) in February: should be suited by 2½m: acts on soft going (out of his depth on firm). *J. T. Gifford.* 103

MR ACACIA 4 b.g. Enchantment–Lightening Blue (Roan Rocket) [1989/90 20g^{5} 17d^{6}] sturdy gelding: little sign of ability on Flat: poor form in juvenile hurdles at Haydock and Devon & Exeter: claimer ridden. *R. J. Holder.* 75

MR AVENGER 9 br.g. Sweet Revenge–Particella (Parthia) [1989/90 16s 16v^{5} 21s^{pu} a16g^{2} a16g 24m 17m* 20m^{2}] small, strong, workmanlike gelding: bought in 2,750 gns after winning conditional jockeys selling handicap hurdle at Newton Abbot in May easily by 15 lengths: stays 2½m: acts on good to firm ground: blinkered last 7 starts: trained until after fifth outing by J. Elliott. *G. A. Ham.* 79

MR BOSTON 5 b.g. Halyudh (USA)–Edith Rose (Cheval) [1989/90 16g^{su} 20m^{4} 16d^{2} 16m^{3} 16g^{5} 17g^{2} 17g 22d* 24d] angular, workmanlike gelding: chasing type: claimer ridden, won novice hurdle at Kelso in February comfortably by 10 lengths from Garry Odder: ran poorly at Market Rasen following month: stays 2¾m: acts on good to firm and dead going. *R. D. E. Woodhouse.* 96

MR BRISKET 8 ch.g. Import–Argostone (Rockavon) [1989/90 c21m^{pu} c16f c24g^{4} c20g] workmanlike gelding: poor novice hurdler/chaser. *R. Tate.* c— —

MR CARACTACUS 9 b.g. Hittite Glory–Carol Service (Daring Display (USA)) [1989/90 20d 22g 24g^{F} a20g 18f^{6} 20h^{3} 17m^{3} 27f* 20f*] leggy, narrow gelding: won selling handicap hurdles at Sedgefield in April (amateur ridden, attracted no bid) and May (conditional jockeys, bought in 6,000 gns): stays 27f: suited by top-of-the-ground: suitable mount for a claimer: blinkered fourth start. *G. G. Gracey.* 95

MR CHRIS 11 ch.g. Lucifer (USA)–Dalliance (Royal Highway) [1989/90 c22m^{pu}] well-made gelding: winning chaser and novice hurdler: pulled up after 3 fences of Seagram Fox Hunters' Chase at Liverpool in April: seems to stay 27f: acts on heavy ground: visored fifth start and blinkered sixth in 1986/7: sold out of M. Naughton's stable 5,700 gns Doncaster October Sales. *S. Gormley.* c— —

MR DIBBS 9 ch.g. Random Shot–Hopestown (Bahrain) [1989/90 c20g^{pu} c20f^{F} c80
c21s^{4} c20m^{ur} c20g^{6} c20d^{F}] tall gelding: winning hurdler: novice chaser: stays —
3m: acts on soft going: blinkered last 2 outings of 1986/7: temperament under
suspicion. *M. Oliver.*

MR DORMOUSE 4 b.g. Comedy Star (USA)–Tea-Pot (Ragstone) [1989/90
16v^{4} 16g^{6} 16s^{5} 20d^{3} 20f^{2} 22g*] sparely-made gelding: half-brother to winning 103
hurdler One For The Pot (by Nicholas Bill): dam fair hurdler at up to 21f: poor
maiden on Flat: won juvenile hurdle at Stratford in April by a length from
Cockstown Lad: shapes like a stayer and will be suited by 3m: acts on firm and
dead ground: visored last 2 starts. *C. W. C. Elsey.*

MR DUDLEY 5 b.g. Riboboy (USA)–Arctic Jewel (Mandamus) [1989/90 16m
24g^{6} 20s^{4} 16m] leggy gelding: poor novice selling hurdler: best effort over 2½m 54
on soft ground. *F. S. Storey.*

MR DYNAMIC 8 b.g. Over The River (FR)–Rita's Star (Star Gazer) [1989/90 c81
c26v^{pu} c20d^{3} c20d c22f^{5} c20m^{2} c20m^{4} c26g^{5}] medium-sized gelding: won a —
point-to-point in 1987: has shown a little ability in novice company over hurdles
and in steeplechases: stays 2½m: acts on any going: has worn blinkers: trained
until after first start by O. O'Neill. *P. M. Cowley.*

MR ENTERTAINER 7 gr.g. Neltino–Office Party (Counsel) [1989/90 c20g^{5} c105
c20d^{2} c20g* c20d* c20m*] useful-looking gelding: modest novice hurdler: —
successful in novice chases at Worcester (2, first a handicap) and Uttoxeter
(landed the odds unchallenged by 12 lengths from Roy Prince) in May: stays 2½m:
acts on dead and good to firm ground. *N. A. Gaselee.*

MR FAGIN 9 ch.g. Lucifer (USA)–Ballycashin (Vulgan) [1989/90 c19m^{2} c16g c77 §
c25f^{pu}] tall gelding: behind only outing over hurdles: poor novice chaser: has —
seemed to take little interest on occasions: stays 3m: acts on firm ground:
blinkered nowadays: isn't one to trust. *M. Oliver.*

MR FENWICK 6 ch.g. Domitor (USA)–Topsey Lorac (St Columbus) [1989/90
24f^{4}] good-topped, workmanlike gelding: will make a chaser: fair hurdler: needing —
race, soon clear but was headed 2 out and finished very tired in handicap at
Uttoxeter in October: suited by 3m: acts on good to firm and dead going: genuine.
J. L. Eyre.

MR FFITCH 4 b.g. Hays–Lady Topknot (High Top) [1989/90 16s^{pu} 16s 18s^{pu}]
medium-sized gelding: second foal: brother to French 1¼m winner Lady Hays: —
dam ran once: jumped moderately when tailed off in juvenile hurdle at Plumpton
in December. *J. Ffitch-Heyes.*

MR FINNLEE 8 gr.g. Roselier (FR)–Samosata (Super Sam) [1989/90 c20d^{5} c—
c20f^{F}] compact gelding: novice hurdler: winning point-to-pointer: poor novice —
steeplechaser: effective at 2m on soft going and will stay 3m. *J. J. Whelan.*

MR FOG PATCHES 8 ch.g. Patch–Cashelgarran (Never Say Die) [1989/90 c—
c24g^{F} c24g^{F} 22g] tall gelding: fair hurdler in 1986/7: still carrying condition, well —
beaten last start: bit backward, well behind when falling in novice chases: stays
3m: probably acts on any going: has won for a claimer. *T. M. Jones.*

MR FRISK 11 ch.g. Bivouac–Jenny Frisk (Sunacelli) [1989/90 c24g^{4} c153
c24f* c26f^{3} c26f^{3} c24g^{5} c24m^{4} c36f* c29f*]

The theory of 'man-made' climatic change has never been so prevalent as nowadays. It seems fashionable to blame 'global warming'—caused by 'the greenhouse effect'—for nearly all unusual or freak weather conditions. Storm-force winds; torrential rain and flooding; heatwaves; and mild winters and long periods of dry weather alike seem to be explained by the effects of 'global warming'. The latest winter was an extraordinary one in some parts of the country for extremes of weather, but the impression given by stories in some sections of the national Press illustrated the dangers of jumping to premature conclusions. The currently-fashionable theories were given prominent coverage but there seemed little recognition of the naturally-occurring fluctuations in climate which have produced similarly extreme conditions in past decades, even centuries—when concern about such things as the emissions of carbon dioxide (the main 'greenhouse' gas causing 'global warming') and the exploitation of the Earth's fossil fuel resources wasn't so justified. The very dry spell which ended the latest winter was reflected in the exceptionally firm going at the season's two major festivals, Cheltenham and Liverpool. Such conditions occur rarely but are not unique. On going ideal for the setting up of fast times no fewer than ten new records were created at the three-day Cheltenham meeting, six on the old course over the first two days and four on the new course on the final day, including one which bettered a new mark earlier in the afternoon. The lay-out of the Mildmay course at Liverpool, over which the hurdle races and conventional steeplechases are run, was altered prior to the 1990 meeting, but the time records were broken for both distances used for races over the Grand National fences. The winners of the John Hughes Memorial Trophy (Wont Be Gone Long) and the Seagram Fox Hunters' Chase (Lean Ar Aghaidh) were both inside the previous record for the two-and-three-quarter-mile course, set by Inch Arran in 1973. Red Rum's time record for the Grand National course and distance, also set in 1973, was smashed by the Grand National winner Mr Frisk who completed the course in 8m 47.8sec, more than fourteen seconds faster than Red Rum. At least eight in the National bettered Red Rum's winning time, illustrating the unseasonably fast conditions. The going on the National course was officially returned as 'firm' for the first time since Nicolaus Silver's year, 1961.

Of all the factors that can influence the performance of a racehorse the going is generally the most critical. Only a small proportion of the racehorse population can be said to 'act on any going'; some horses are much more effective with give in the ground (lightly-made individuals with comparatively little body-weight to lift out of the ground often seem to be well suited by a soft surface); others are particularly well suited by firm going. The outcome of nearly every race is influenced to some extent by the state of the ground, the influence sometimes being to a marked degree. The fact that the latest Seagram-sponsored Grand National was run on very firm going almost certainly made all the difference to the result. The race went to the confirmed top-of-the-ground front-runner Mr Frisk, a resolute galloper and a bold jumper who had looked for some time an ideal National type, given suitable conditions. Mr Frisk had been taken out on the eve of the 1989 Grand National because of the soft ground. In the weeks leading up to the latest race, there seemed little prospect of soft ground. Such conditions would have suited the three top weights Bonanza Boy (11-9), Hungary Hur (11-2) and the tried and tested Grand National campaigner West Tip (10-11), along with two other fancied horses who had shown their aptitude for Aintree's big, unusual fences, the good hunter Call Collect, impressive winner of the previous year's Seagram Fox Hunters' and straight from a victory in the Christies Foxhunter Chase at the Cheltenham Festival (from which there had at one time been talk of his withdrawal because of the ground), and Lastofthebrownies who had run well in the two previous Grand Nationals. Rain on the Sunday before the National improved ground conditions a little but the effect was short-lived and the prevailing firm ground finally ruled out the previous year's third The Thinker (who had been set to carry 11-9); The Thinker's withdrawal left Durham Edition, second in 1988 and fifth in 1989, as the principal hope to give trainer Stephenson, who saddled three runners, what would have been an extremely popular Grand National triumph on his seventieth birthday. Durham Edition had run out of steam the previous year after travelling like a winner between the last two fences, and the prevailing firm ground seemed likely to be much more in his favour. The going was also certain to suit the favourite Brown Windsor and the second favourite Bigsun. Bigsun had revelled in the firm ground conditions at Cheltenham when winning the Ritz Club National Hunt Handicap and Brown Windsor, winner of the Cathcart over two and a half miles at the Festival meeting, had won the previous season's Whitbread Gold Cup on a sound surface. Brown Windsor was from a stable with a good recent record in the National and was ridden by White who had completed the course on all his six rides in the National. The consistent Brown Windsor had an unblemished jumping record, being among those in the field—who also included Call Collect, Polyfemus (who had beaten Brown Windsor narrowly in the Mandarin Handicap at Newbury in December) and the Maryland Hunt Cup winner Uncle Merlin—who had never fallen or unseated their riders over hurdles or fences. Uncle Merlin, following in the footsteps of Jay Trump and Ben Nevis, both Maryland Hunt

Seagram Grand National Handicap Chase, Liverpool—the third fence; Uncle Merlin has taken an early lead from the grey Star's Delight, Gee-A and Mr Frisk (No. 6)

Cup winners successful in the National, only joined the top forty handicapped horses—the permitted maximum number of starters—when some of those above him in the original handicap were withdrawn at the five-day stage. Uncle Merlin's trainer had saddled three National winners, including Ben Nevis. Trainer Richards was seeking his third success in the race with the well-fancied Greenall Whitley Gold Cup winner Rinus and the useful handicapper Conclusive. A new handicap qualification, which barred horses officially assessed below 105 from the National, had no effect on the number of original entries which, at one hundred and two, was actually six higher than in 1989. The presence among the original entries, however, of Desert Orchid—withdrawn at the first forfeit stage after being given 12-2—led to the compressing of the weights and only fifteen of the eventual thirty-eight starters ran off the mark given to them in the original long handicap; the

The third again—where Conclusive falls in front of Bartres

First Becher's—the leader puts in a very long jump; No. 25 is Polyfemus

remainder were set to carry between 2 lb and 16 lb more than the weight originally given. As usual, a good number of the runners at or near the foot of the handicap carried overweight—fourteen in all including, among those prominent in the betting, Bigsun (2 lb over), Rinus (4 lb over), Uncle Merlin (3 lb over) and Polyfemus (2 lb over) all of whom were already 'out of the handicap', as was another leading fancy the Hennessy Cognac Gold Cup winner Ghofar, Desert Orchid's stable-companion and the youngest horse in the field, who had been allotted 9-11 in the original handicap. The betting took its usual wide range, with Brown Windsor and Bigsun starting at 7/1 and 15/2 respectively, ahead of Durham Edition 9/1, Rinus 13/1, Ghofar and Call Collect (the one-time co-favourite) 14/1, Mr Frisk, Uncle Merlin and Bonanza Boy (who headed the betting when the weights came out, ignoring Desert Orchid) 16/1, Polyfemus 18/1, West Tip and Lastofthebrownies 20/1, and 25/1 bar.

The Chair—Uncle Merlin and Mr Frisk safely negotiate this daunting obstacle

Like the latest Tote Cheltenham Gold Cup winner Norton's Coin, Mr Frisk graduated to steeplechasing from point-to-points. Bought for 15,500 guineas at the Doncaster Sales in May 1986, Mr Frisk had a splendid first season over fences, winning seven of his nine races and showing virtually continous improvement until managing only fifth behind Kildimo and Playschool in the Sun Alliance Novices' Chase at Cheltenham. He ended that first campaign for his present connections with a superb display against handicappers in a valuable event at Wetherby, showing the dashing style of jumping and the gameness that have become the hallmark of his best performances. Mr Frisk continued his smooth transition to handicap company the next season, paying his way with two victories (in the second of which he was ridden for the first time by the amateur Mr Armytage) and coming a creditable third to the subsequent Grand National winner Rhyme 'N' Reason in the very valuable Racing Post Handicap at Kempton. Even better was to follow in the 1988/9 season when the Anthony Mildmay, Peter Cazalet Memorial Trophy Handicap at Sandown provided Mr Frisk with his biggest victory up to that time. It was his third of the season, following all-the-way wins in handicaps at Ascot (partnered for the second time, again the only occasion during the season, by Mr Armytage) and at Doncaster. Mr Armytage, the Newmarket correspondent of the *Racing Post*, was Mr Frisk's jockey for most of the latest season, riding him on all his outings except his first and fifth, and partnering him to a repeat victory at Ascot in November in the Punch Bowl Amateur Riders' Handicap. Mr Frisk didn't win again before the National but he finished third in the Hennessy for the second successive year, running right up to his best in ideal conditions when beaten a neck and two and a half lengths by Ghofar and Brown Windsor, only giving best on the run-in after leading or disputing the lead nearly all the way. Mr Frisk wasn't ridden to best advantage conceding lumps of weight all round in a small field for the Constant Security Handicap at Doncaster on his next appearance after the Hennessy; starting 11/10 favourite after winning the corresponding race in each of the two previous seasons Mr Frisk was outpaced after being ridden with much more restraint than usual, managing only third of four. Mr Frisk ran moderately in his next race, after being off the course for a month, and then came a fair fourth to Master Bob under top weight in the Kim Muir Memorial Handicap at the Cheltenham Festival. Judged on his best form Mr Frisk was very well handicapped in the National: carrying 10-6, he was a stone better off with the Hennessy winner Ghofar at the weights carried, met Brown Windsor on terms 9 lb better than at Newbury, and was 9 lb better off with Durham Edition who had finished five lengths behind Mr Frisk when fourth in the Hennessy.

The late withdrawal of the declared runners Sacred Path and Why So Hasty left the latest National field two short of its permitted maximum; ten horses had been compulsorily eliminated overnight, prompting discussion about allowing a list of reserve runners to be drawn up for future Nationals. Except that the farrier had to be called to Polyfemus, the Grand National parade and other preliminaries were largely incident-free—the rather excitable Mr Frisk was sweating as usual—and the field was dispatched promptly. It was supposedly Reg Hobbs, sending out his son Bruce to ride Battleship in the 1938 National, who first gave the now-commonplace advice 'Just hunt him round the first time, then when you've jumped the water, if you're still in with a chance, you can start riding a race'. The riders who adopted that policy in the latest National soon found themselves well behind. The pace was fast and furious from the start with Uncle Merlin showing ahead before the third and jumping fluently as he blazed the trail with Mr Frisk, Polyfemus and Brown Windsor among those closest in the chasing group. Uncle Merlin put in a spectacular leap at first Becher's by which time the field was well strung out with such as Call Collect, West Tip, Ghofar and Bonanza Boy already well down the field unable to go the pace. The scorching pace was maintained throughout the first circuit but all the best-fancied horses were still standing as Uncle Merlin and Mr Frisk matched strides several lengths clear going out into the country for the final time, Mr Frisk having briefly shown in front passing the stands. There were

Onto the second circuit—beyond the fence
Rinus (hooped cap) and Durham Edition (seams) come into the picture

twenty-seven survivors in all at halfway, though Polyfemus—eventually pulled up at second Valentine's when no longer in contention—had ruined his chance with a very bad mistake at the Chair. Rinus moved into the first four going down to Becher's for the second time and the patiently-ridden Durham Edition also moved up, travelling smoothly. The sensible changes made to Becher's since the previous year had the desired effect of reducing the casualties at that fence, though, as so often in the past, it produced an incident that changed the whole complexion of the race. Uncle Merlin, still going well in front and steered closer to the inside than first-time round, seemed to be caught out by the drop, landed awkwardly, and parted

Second Becher's—end of the race for Uncle Merlin, as he lands awkwardly

Second Valentine's—Mr Frisk now has the advantage

company with his rider. Mr Frisk was left six lengths clear of Rinus and Brown Windsor, with the stable-companions Durham Edition and Sir Jest just behind. Mr Armytage, who rode a commendable race throughout on the exuberant Mr Frisk, showed particularly fine judgement once out in front, continuing to ride into the fences to make full use of Mr Frisk's bold jumping but keeping some reserves in hand while maintaining the lead presented to him. Brown Windsor began to drop back after Valentine's but Durham Edition, moving with eye-catching ease from second Becher's, looked a very big danger to Mr Frisk after being sent past Rinus into second place before the penultimate fence. Mr Frisk jumped the last fence two lengths in front and was soon pressed by Durham Edition who almost drew upsides at the elbow. Mr Armytage took his whip twice to Mr Frisk just inside the final furlong, to remind him a final effort was needed, and then rode him out with hands and heels to hold off the strongly-ridden Durham Edition by three quarters of a length in a stirring finish. Mr Frisk and Durham Edition both finished in great style, Durham Edition, who now joins Tudor Line, Wyndburgh, Freddie and Greasepaint, in finishing second in at least two Nationals in the post-war era without winning, drawing twenty lengths clear of third-placed Rinus. Brown Windsor kept on at one pace to hold off Lastofthebrownies narrowly for fourth, a further twelve lengths behind; Bigsun, never in the hunt, managed sixth, ahead of Call Collect, the outsiders Bartres and Sir Jest, and West Tip. There were twenty finishers (Ghofar came fourteenth and Bonanza Boy sixteenth). Sadly, the race was marred by two fatalities: the smart Irish chaser Hungary Hur broke a leg early on the second circuit and the 1989 Scottish National winner Roll-A-Joint broke his neck at the first Canal Turn. Five other horses were killed at the three-day meeting, four of them in hurdle races, which served as a reminder—in the wake of the remodelling of Becher's—that no amount of course reconstruction can remove all the hazards from jumping. The Grand National deaths could have occurred in any race.

Mr Frisk's triumph and the prominent showing of Uncle Merlin maintained the long-standing North American connection with the Grand National. Mr Frisk's octogenarian owner Mrs Duffey, whose father bred Battleship, lives in Maryland. Mr Frisk provided Lambourn trainer Kim

Bailey with far and away his biggest victory and Bailey deserves a lot of credit for his handling of the horse. Mr Frisk used to be such a handful at home that in his early days he had to do much of his training riderless, led by his trainer's wife on her hunter. The horse has calmed down considerably since, and is now ridden out (his trainer's wife rides him in his serious work). Mr Frisk suffered no ill-effects from his tough race at Aintree and earned a special place in the record books by adding the Whitbread Gold Cup to the Seagram Grand National, becoming the first horse to complete the double, going one better than Nicolaus Silver, runner-up to Pas Seul at Sandown after winning at Aintree. Lean Ar Aghaidh, who won the 1987 Whitbread after coming third to Maori Venture in the National, is the only other horse to finish in the first three in both the National and the Whitbread in the same season. The latest Whitbread field wasn't one of the strongest assembled for the race—the loss of Desert Orchid to the Jameson Irish Grand National was a big blow for the sponsors and the Sandown executive—but Mr Frisk couldn't have won in more impressive style. There are no penalties in the Whitbread after the publication of the weights, which come out before the National. Mr Frisk carried 10-5 and met the National runner-up Durham Edition on terms 1 lb better than at Aintree; Mr Frisk started 9/2 favourite, ahead of the consistent Seagram at 5/1, the previous year's runner-up Sam da Vinci at 11/2, Durham Edition at 13/2, Wont Be Gone Long at 7/1, and the William Hill Scottish National winner Four Trix at 15/2. Five of the first six in the betting filled the first five places in the race, Durham Edition coming eight lengths second, never getting in a blow at Mr Frisk who made all, jumped superbly throughout and steadily increased his lead in the final straight to win unchallenged to a great reception. Four Trix finished two lengths behind Durham Edition in third, with Wont Be Gone Long fourth and Sam da Vinci fifth. A feature of the finish of the Whitbread was that the first three had all had gruelling races over long distances in the weeks immediately beforehand. Their performances, in particular, were a

The last—Durham Edition begins to challenge . . . . .

. . . . . but Mr Frisk holds him to the line

marvellous advertisement for National Hunt racing, as well as for their own toughness and resilience, and the skill of their trainers.

Both the sire and the dam of the tall, rather sparely-made Mr Frisk are now dead. His sire Bivouac was a very useful miler at his best who was raced for four seasons; he was retired to his owner-breeder Lord Rosebery's Mentmore Stud but lasted there only a short time before being transferred to the Low Hall Stud near York where he covered fewer than two hundred thoroughbred mares in eight seasons. Bivouac has met with some success as a sire of jumpers—both under rules and in point-to-points—but he stood at a fee of only £100 when Mr Frisk's dam Jenny Frisk visited him in 1978. Jenny Frisk won two point-to-points and produced six foals at stud. Mr Frisk, who won four point-to-points for his breeder, Yorkshire farmer Ralph Dalton, is the only winner so far out of Jenny Frisk, but Captain Frisk (by Politico, sire of Durham Edition) may become another in the next season. Seven-year-old Captain Frisk, a stable-companion of Mr Frisk sold to his trainer in a private deal, was placed in novice chases at Wincanton and Newbury in 1989/90, jumping soundly. Jenny Frisk's last foal, four-year-old Master Frisk (by Broadsword), passed through the ring in May—unsold at 16,500 gns at the Doncaster Spring Sales. Jenny Frisk's pedigree is undistinguished: her sire the stoutly-bred Sunacelli was a good

Whitbread Gold Cup, Sandown—Mr Frisk beats Durham Edition again

Mrs Harry J. Duffey's "Mr Frisk"

Mr Frisk (ch.g. 1979)	Bivouac (b 1961)	Darius (b 1951)	Dante
			Yasna
		Camp Fire (br 1948)	Big Game
			Blue Smoke
	Jenny Frisk (ch 1971)	Sunacelli (ch 1962)	Botticelli
			Astrid Sun
		Bygot Bug (ch 1963)	The Bug
			Amour Light

horse in the North—he topped the Northern Free Handicap in 1964—but made hardly any impression at stud, and her dam the sprint-bred Bygot Bug, who achieved her only placings on the Flat in poor maiden events at Stockton and Catterick as a two-year-old, was subsequently raced without success over hurdles and in point-to-points. *K. C. Bailey.*

MR GEE 5 b.g. Crooner–Miss Desla (Light Thrust) [1989/90 22g^{3} 21s^{pu} 24d^{4}] rangy gelding, slightly unfurnished: novice hurdler: sweating and blinkered, good fourth to Duntree at Chepstow in March: collapsed after race previous start (first for 3 months): seems suited by a test of stamina. *R. Curtis.* 90

MR GOSSIP 8 b.g. Le Bavard (FR)–Regency View (Royal Highway) [1989/90 c21d* c20d^{4} c24s^{pu} 22s 25f 22d] leggy gelding: useful hurdler at his best: no worthwhile form over hurdles in 1989/90: jumped left throughout when winning novice chase at Towcester in December: ran poorly in similar events following month: out-and-out stayer, likely to prove suited by testing conditions: has won **c96** —

for a claimer but gives impression suited by strong handling: blinkered last 4
starts: tends to run in snatches and idle in front. *N. J. Henderson.*

MR JERSEY 8 b.m. Crash Course–Belle Mackay (Even Money) [1989/90 c—
c16g^{F} c21f^{pu} 20f^{2} 21f^{pu}] rangy mare: poor novice hurdler: jumped moderately 73
when failing to complete course both outings over fences. *J. R. Jenkins.*

MR KEWMILL 7 b.g. Homing–Muninga (St Alphage) [1989/90 16g^{5} 16m^{3}
17g^{6} 17v^{6} 16m^{4} 16h^{4} 16f^{2} 22m^{pu}] small, leggy, close-coupled gelding: novice 70 ?
selling hurdler: stiff task when tried at 2¾m: acts on firm ground: visored first
outing. *J. A. Bennett.*

MR KEY (USA) 9 b.g. Key To The Kingdom (USA)–Funny Diplomat (USA) **c131**
(Diplomat Way) [1989/90 c17f^{F} c17d^{2} c16m^{pu}] good-topped gelding: fairly useful —
chaser: still needed race when going down by 2½ lengths to Knockbrack at
Newbury in March: best form at 2m: acts on heavy and good to firm going: visored
once in 1986/7: suited by forcing tactics: has been mulish in preliminaries and is
led in at start nowadays. *D. J. G. Murray-Smith.*

MR KIRBY 8 b.g. Monksfield–Mayfield Grove (Khalkis) [1989/90 c21d^{3} c24g^{4} c88
c20v^{pu} c24s^{pu} c20d^{2} c21g^{pu} c22f^{pu}] tall, rather leggy gelding: handicap hurdler: in —
frame in novice chases: probably stays 3m: acts on soft going: ran poorly in
blinkers final start 1988/9: tends to sweat: inconsistent. *A. P. Jones.*

MR LION 8 ch.g. Windjammer (USA)–Polly Darling (Darling Boy) [1989/90
25g] leggy, quite good-topped gelding: very lightly-raced novice hurdler: evid- —
ently difficult to train. *N. R. Mitchell.*

MR MACGROO 10 b.g. Copper Man–Zita III (sire unknown) [1989/90 c24m^{3}] c— p
small, strong non-thoroughbred gelding: third foal: dam unraced: backward,
showed definite signs of ability, weakening after jumping and travelling quite well
until home straight, when 25 lengths third of 4 finishers to Assaglawi in novice
chase at Worcester in October. *G. B. Balding.*

MR MAJINTY 6 gr.g. Formidable (USA)–Boule de Suif (Major Portion)
[1989/90 20v^{3} 18s^{5} 21d 17d^{pu} 20m^{ro}] strong gelding: selling hurdler: probably —
needs further than 2m and stays 21f but seemingly not 3m: acts on firm ground:
blinkered fourth start: ran out second final appearance. *Mrs H. Fullerton.*

MR MAYFAIR 7 b.g. The Parson–Doe Royale (Royal Buck) [1989/90 20g^{pu}]
lengthy, workmanlike gelding: winning hurdler: broke down at Kempton in —
November: stays 21f. *J. A. C. Edwards.*

MR MCGREGOR 8 b.g. Formidable (USA)–Mrs Tiggywinkle (Silly Season)
[1989/90 18h^{2}] smallish, workmanlike, lengthy gelding: selling hurdler: good 67
second to La Molinilla in novice handicap at Fontwell in August: seems to stay
2½m: acts on hard ground. *K. R. Supple.*

MR MURDOCK 5 b.g. Last Fandango–Moss Pink (USA) (Levmoss) [1989/90
17m 17h^{2} 20m^{3} 25g^{4} 17f^{3} 16h^{2} 17m^{4} 18f^{3}] angular, sparely-made gelding: novice 80 §
selling hurdler: ran moderately last 2 starts, looking none too keen on first
occasion: stays 25f: probably acts on any going: blinkered fifth to seventh outings:
has run creditably for a claimer. *P. Leach.*

MR PANACHE 8 ch.g. Dublin Taxi–Becalmed (Right Tack) [1989/90 c16f^{3} c81
c21m^{4} c16h* c16m^{pu} c17h^{3} c17f^{4}] compact, good-bodied gelding: novice selling —
hurdler: only one to put in a clear round in novice chase at Hexham in October:
finished lame and not seen out again until April: best form at 2m on top-of-
the-ground. *J. S. Hubbuck.*

MR PARKER 8 br.g. Al Sirat (USA)–Black Zeta (Black Tarquin) [1989/90 c16d c—
c20d^{pu}] big, rangy, good sort: winning hurdler: novice chaser, ran poorly in —
1989/90: probably stays 3m: acts on soft going. *G. A. Hubbard.*

MR PINKERTON 11 ch.g. Pauper–Chalk Slipper (Panaslipper) [1989/90 c95
c26g* c24d^{2} c28g c24d^{4} c26m^{pu}] big, workmanlike gelding: modest novice —
hurdler: won handicap chase at Folkestone in January: ran poorly last 3 outings:
stays 3m: acts on good to firm and dead going: blinkered last 2 starts. *N. A.
Gaselee.*

MR POD 4 b.g. Grey Ghost–Forlorn Lady (Forlorn River) [1989/90 17m^{pu}
16g^{pu}] third foal: half-brother to a poor animal by Pongee: dam moderate hurdler: —
behind when pulled up in juvenile hurdles in April. *R. R. Lamb.*

MR PRESLEY 4 b.g. Tender King–Theda (Mummy's Pet) [1989/90 a16g^{6}
a16g^{4} 20g^{pu} a20g^{2} a20g^{4} a20g^{4} 18f^{4}] leggy gelding: no sign of ability on Flat: poor 65
form in selling hurdles: stays 2½m: blinkered last 4 starts: front runner: makes
mistakes. *W. Wilson.*

MR QUICK 11 b.g. Saucy Kit–Tesco Maid (Tesco Boy) [1989/90 c21g⁴ c16d* c16g* c20m⁶ c16g⁴ c20d⁵ c16g² c16mF c16m* c16f³ c16m²] good-topped gelding: one-time fair hurdler: won novice chases at Market Rasen and Catterick in January and handicap chase at Market Rasen in April: also ran creditably last 2 outings: barely stays 2m: suited by top-of-the-ground: tends to make the odd mistake: usually races up with the pace. *J. Wharton.* c**102** —

MR REX 8 b.g. Bowling Pin–Fortina Lass (Schomberg) [1989/90 c20m⁴ c26m c20g⁴ c21dpu 27spu c26sF] workmanlike gelding: winning hurdler: well beaten in novice chases: destroyed after falling at Folkestone in January: stayed 2¾m: form only on a sound surface: blinkered once: was a poor jumper. *J. E. Long.* c— x —

MR ROBINSON 6 b.g. Cawston's Clown–Viduli (Firestreak) [1989/90 F16m] rangy, good-bodied gelding: fifth foal: half-brother to a poor novice hurdler by Gay Fandango: dam unraced: tailed off in 15-runner NH Flat race at Worcester in October: yet to race over hurdles or fences. *Mrs A. R. Hewitt.*

MR RUMPOLE 6 b.g. Whistlefield–Mighty Nice (Vimadee) [1989/90 16mpu c20gpu c20g⁶] tall gelding: no sign of ability in NH Flat race, novice hurdle and in novice chases. *J. Chugg.* c— —

MRS DODD 4 br.c. Petorius–Standing Ovation (Godswalk (USA)) [1989/90 F16m] second foal: dam 1½m winner in Ireland: mid-division in NH Flat race at Ludlow in January: yet to race over hurdles. *F. Jordan.*

MR SEAGULL 12 ch.g. Deep Run–Marsa (Roi de Navarre II) [1989/90 21hpu] workmanlike gelding: handicap hurdler/chaser: pulled up lame in August and wasn't seen out again: effective at 2m and stays 25f: acts on any going. *Mrs S. J. R. Hembrow.* c— —

MRS GIDDY 9 b.m. Royalty–Bright Performance (Gala Performance (USA)) [1989/90 c24d³] sparely-made mare: tailed off in 2 races over hurdles in 1986: winning point-to-pointer: 6½ lengths third behind Dromore Castle in hunter chase at Newbury in March, leading and mistake last, bumped soon after and no extra: stays 3m. *Mrs M. Bealing.* c**100** —

MRS JENNIFER 5 bl.m. River Knight (FR)–Wreck-Em-All (Wrekin Rambler) [1989/90 F16g 22g 18d] sparely-made mare: well beaten in NH Flat races and novice hurdles. *R. Allan.* —

MRS MEYRICK 9 b.m. Owen Dudley–Social Bee (Galivanter) [1989/90 c16d² c16m⁶ c20fF 20dpu] workmanlike mare: poor performer on Flat, winner 3 times at up to 15f in 1989: no sign of ability in point-to-points or a novice hurdle: runner-up in novice chase at Market Rasen in August. *R. M. Whitaker.* c82 —

MRS MUCK 9 b.m. Air Trooper–Emperor's Gift (Menelek) [1989/90 26d² 24s* 24s⁵] small, compact, rather sparely-made mare: very useful hurdler: won c— x 150

Mandor Flexible Doors Premier Long Distance Hurdle, Haydock—Mrs Muck forges clear

Mandor Flexible Doors Premier Long Distance Hurdle at Haydock in January comfortably by 12 lengths from Trapper John: moderate fifth to Ryde Again in Daily Telegraph Hurdle at Ascot following month (under pressure some way out): jumped none too fluently when winning novice chase early in 1987/8, and was let down by her jumping subsequently: stays well: probably acts on any going: genuine. *N. A. Twiston-Davies.*

MRS MUDDLE 7 b.m. Gleason (USA)–Cathy Mont (Woodville II) [1989/90 22g^{4} 16g] compact mare: novice selling hurdler: tailed off when refusing 3 out on chasing debut: stays 2¾m: acts on firm ground. *R. E. Barr.* c— 78

MRS PEOPLEATER 7 b.m. Ancient Monro–Flea Pit (Sir Lark) [1989/90 16g^{6} 21g^{4} 22g 18s a16g^{4} c18h^{4} 16f^{pu}] rangy mare: winning selling hurdler: well beaten in novice chases: stays 2¾m: acts on soft going. *P. Howling.* c— 81

MRS PEPPERPOT 7 b.m. Kinglet–Nostra (Javelin) [1989/90 21f^{2} 25g^{F} 22d a24g] leggy mare: novice hurdler: second in mares event at Warwick in December: well beaten subsequently: winning point-to-pointer: stays 2¾m: acts on firm going. *Mrs I. McKie.* 83

MR STRIDER 6 b.g. Charlaw–Queen of Myshal (Majetta) [1989/90 16g 16g 20v 24d^{pu} a16g] compact gelding: sixth foal: dam unraced: behind in novice hurdles: sold 2,000 gns Doncaster March Sales. *M. J. Wilkinson.* —

MR THERM 5 gr.g. Kalaglow–Yole Tartare (Captain's Gig (USA)) [1989/90 c16s^{ur} c16d c16d^{2} c16d^{2}] small, sparely-made gelding: novice chaser: good staying-on second at Catterick in February, final start (jumped soundly): has worn a tongue strap. *M. W. Easterby.* c93 —

MR WINKLE 5 gr.g. Royal Blend–Kefhalik (Precipice Wood) [1989/90 F13d^{6} 20d^{ro} 16d 17g 24d] small gelding: third foal: half-brother to winning hurdler Minature Miss (by Move Off): dam, successful at up to 2½m over hurdles, half-sister to The Wilk: well beaten in novice hurdles and a claimer: reins broke and ran out on hurdling debut: sold 2,700 gns Doncaster Spring Sales. *W. A. Stephenson.* —

MR WOODCOCK 5 b.g. Sit In The Corner (USA)–Grey Bird (Eastern Venture) [1989/90 F16g^{6} F16g^{2} F16g* 16g^{2}] fifth foal: dam fair staying hurdler: won NH Flat race at Catterick in March: favourite, 1½ lengths second to Woodchester Glen in novice hurdle at Hexham later in month: should improve and win a novice hurdle. *Mrs G. R. Reveley.* 87 p

MSHAHARA 12 ch.g. Beau Chapeau–Immortal Queen (Immortality) [1989/90 16f 20g^{2} 22m^{2} c16f^{2} c20f^{2} c18m* c20s* c17d^{2} c16m 16m^{6} c20f^{F} 16f* c21m^{4} 20f^{pu}] sturdy gelding: winning point-to-pointer in Ireland: won novice selling hurdle at Towcester (no bid) and conditional jockeys chases at Fontwell (seller, no bid) and Folkestone (handicap): stayed 2¾m: acted on any going: front runner: dead. *P. R. Hedger.* c96 82

MUBAARIS 7 ch.g. Hello Gorgeous (USA)–Aloft (High Top) [1989/90 25f^{3} 25g 25f* 24f^{ur} 25m^{3} a20g^{5} 25g^{3} 25f] compact gelding: ungenuine handicap hurdler: won slowly-run event at Catterick in November: stays well: acts on any going: ridden by claimer: blinkered last start: hangs and difficult ride: trained until after sixth start by M. Skinner. *B. Richmond.* 106 §

MUCHGRANGE 8 ch.m. Sweet Revenge–Millgrange (Sallymount) [1989/90 22d^{pu} 27s^{3} c24s^{4} c27d^{ur} c27g^{5} c27v^{2} c24d c32g^{5} c24m^{pu}] smallish, sturdy mare: second foal: dam won on Flat and over hurdles: won a point-to-point in Ireland in 1989: bought for 4,200 gns Doncaster August Sales: blinkered, first form over hurdles third in novice seller at Sedgefield in January: best effort over fences when going down by ½ length to The Quohee, pair long way clear, in amateur riders handicap at Chepstow in February: needs long distances and plenty of give in the ground. *P. J. Bevan.* c83 73

MUCK OR MONEY 6 b.g. Slim Jim–Karena III (Rubor) [1989/90 F17f^{4} 16f^{r} 16g^{6} 16m 20g 20d^{6} 17g c24f^{4} c22f^{bd} 24f] compact, angular gelding: poor novice hurdler/chaser: probably stays 3m: refused third on hurdling debut, reared start on fourth outing and whipped round at start on fifth. *J. I. A. Charlton.* c73 79

MUDAHIM 4 b.g. Shareef Dancer (USA)–Mariska (FR) (Tanerko) [1989/90 F16m^{3} F16d* F16g^{3}] brother to Triple Kiss, successful over 1m in Ireland, and half-brother to 4 other winners: dam twice-raced sister to Relko: won NH Flat race at Catterick in February: yet to race over hurdles. *C. D. Broad.*

MUGONI BEACH 5 b.g. Equal Opportunity–Cuckoo Flower (Murrayfield) [1989/90 F16f^{3}] third foal: half-brother to winning point-to-pointer and Irish NH

Flat race winner Foxy Games (by New Member): dam ran twice at 2 yrs: 7½ lengths third behind Driver in NH Flat race at Cheltenham in April: yet to race over hurdles or fences. *M. C. Pipe.*

MUGWUMP 8 b.g. Mugatpura–San Rullagh (Bluerullah) [1989/90 c20d^F c18v^3 c20f^{pu}] sturdy gelding: showed a little ability on second of 3 starts in 2m novice hurdles in 1987/8: no form in novice chases in 1989/90. *R. J. Hodges.* c— —

MUIRFIELD VILLAGE 4 b.c. Lomond (USA)–Ukelele (USA) (Riva Ridge (USA)) [1989/90 16f^5 16f^6 18g* 18s^2 16d] small colt: 1¼m winner on Flat (not genuine): sold out of B. Hills's stable 3,600 gns Newmarket Autumn Sales: won juvenile hurdle at Fontwell in December: clear of remainder when 10 lengths second to Dark Desire on same course following month: stays 2¼m: acts on soft ground: has carried head high: pulled too hard second start. *S. Dow.* 102

MULLAUN 6 b. or br.m. Deep Run–Quadro (Dusky Boy) [1989/90 20s] ex-Irish mare: first foal: dam winning Irish 2m hurdler: runner-up in 3 NH Flat races: well beaten over hurdles. *Miss A. L. M. King.* —

MULLED WINE 9 b.m. Bivouac–Lady Mede (Runnymede) [1989/90 20g 27s^{pu} 17g] small mare: first foal: dam showed some ability at 2 yrs: of little account. *M. W. Ellerby.* —

MULLION COVE 7 ch.g. Deep Run–News Letter (London Gazette) [1989/90 24d^{pu} 16s] IR 7,300Y: angular, plain gelding: fourth foal: half-brother to fair chaser Farm Week (by General Ironside): dam won Irish NH Flat race: behind in novice hurdle at Warwick (raced freely) in February. *J. Honeyball.* —

MULTUM IN PARVO 7 b.g. Proverb–Kova's Daughter (Brave Invader (USA)) [1989/90 c16d^2 c16m^2 c16g^2 c16g* c20v* c20s^2 c20f^2 c20m^5] lengthy, rather unfurnished gelding: winning hurdler: runner-up in 3 novice chases prior to winning handicap chases at Towcester and Plumpton in January: ran well next 2 starts, particularly on second occasion when going down by a short head to Brown Windsor in Cathcart Challenge Cup Chase at Cheltenham in March: found nothing off bridle last outing: will stay 3m: acts on any going: claimer ridden fifth and sixth starts. *J. A. C. Edwards.* **c131** —

MUMMY'S CHANCE 6 b.g. Mummy's Game–Kalopia (Kalydon) [1989/90 16f 16g 22g^{pu}] robust gelding: won 5f selling handicap on Flat in 1989 (acts on hard going, usually blinkered): sold out of J. Berry's stable 5,800 gns Doncaster September Sales: no sign of ability in novice hurdles: sold 1,150 gns Ascot April Sales. *R. J. Manning.* c— —

MUMMY'S SONG 5 b.g. Mummy's Pet–Welsh Miniature (Owen Anthony) [1989/90 16h^5 16g^3 16d^{pu} 16m^{pu} 16m* 16f^5] angular, sparely-made gelding: 50/1, finished distressed when winning conditional jockeys selling handicap hurdle at Hereford in May (not offered for auction): last of 5 finishers in similar company on same course later in month: barely stays 2m: best on a sound surface: sold out of J. White's stable 1,600 gns Ascot September Sales after first outing. *J. Harriman.* 72

MUMMY'S TOY BOY 4 br.c. Mansingh (USA)–Easterly Gael (Tudor Music) [1989/90 16f^3 16m^5 16f^{pu}] first foal: dam successful on Flat and on all 6 completed starts over hurdles: behind in 6f maiden auction event at 2 yrs: third in juvenile hurdle at Bangor in September. *R. J. Eckley.* 65

MUNDY MOON 5 b.m. Nearly A Hand–Lake Victoria (Stupendous) [1989/90 F16g 16f 16m 16g^{ro}] rather sparely-made mare: half-sister to 2 minor winners on Flat: dam winning sprinter: well beaten in NH Flat race and novice hurdles: behind when running out fourth on last start. *R. J. Hodges.* —

MUNJARID 5 ch.h. Habitat–Connaught Bridge (Connaught) [1989/90 20d 22g^2 21s^5 22s^4 16d^4 21f^2] leggy horse: won twice at up to 1¼m on Flat in France in 1988 (modest form in Britain in 1989): novice hurdler: ran best race when staying-on 9 lengths fourth to Sacre d'Or in 2m Crown Berger Hurdle at Chepstow in March, and would probably have finished second but for being badly hampered 2 out: beaten short head by stable-companion Theo's Fella at Newbury later in month: probably stays 2¾m: visored last 4 outings. *G. B. Balding.* 106 +

MURHAF (USA) 7 br.g. Sharpen Up–Noble Legion (CAN) (Vaguely Noble) [1989/90 16m 16g^2 a16g^3 16g a16g* a16g^2 a20s^6 a16g^2 a16g^4 16f^2 17m^F 16m^{pu}] sturdy gelding: front-running handicap hurdler: won at Lingfield in January: ran creditably on occasions afterwards, on last completed start 5 lengths second to Falworth at Towcester: best at around 2m: acts on hard ground: blinkered sixth start 1988/9: has shown signs of temperament. *J. Joseph.* 93

MURPHY 6 ch.g. Touch Paper–Iamstopped (Furry Glen) [1989/90 16m^{3} 16m^{4} 16g 16m 16f^{F} 16s a16g^{3} a16g* 16f* 16f^{6} 17f^{3}] neat gelding: modest hurdler: won handicaps at Lingfield and Wincanton in March: ran moderately last 2 starts: best at a sharp 2m on a sound surface: found little second start: blinkered tenth outing. *O. Sherwood.* 100

MURPHY'S CHOICE 7 ch.g. Crash Course–Purlane (FR) (Kashmir II) [1989/90 24m^{5} 27f^{5} 16g^{pu} c24d c24v^{pu}] showed signs of ability in novice hurdles in 1987/8: well beaten since, including in a novice chase. *T. W. Cunningham.* c— —

MURPHY'S MAN 6 b.g. Belfalas–Speckled Leinster (Prefairy) [1989/90 16s^{5} 22s^{3}] well-made gelding: will make a chaser: seventh foal: brother to novice hurdler Bonanza Rebel: dam won at 1¾m on Flat and 2m over hurdles in Ireland: beaten 14 lengths in novice hurdles at Folkestone (won by Mander's Way) in January and Fontwell (behind Stately Lover) following month: should stay 2¾m: still bit backward at Fontwell and should do better. *J. T. Gifford.* 101 p

MUSCLETON 5 gr.g. Le Moss–Countless (Super Sam) [1989/90 16m^{6} 17m^{3}] rangy gelding with scope: favourite, close third of 14 behind Hortondale in maiden hurdle at Newton Abbot in April: will be suited by further. *D. R. C. Elsworth.* 92

MUSHERA MOUNTAIN 9 b.g. Bluerullah–Ballynos (Kythnos) [1989/90 c16d^{6}] leggy, sparely-made gelding: no form in novice hurdles and in a hunter chase: dead. *R. A. Bethell.* c— —

MUSICAL MOMENTS 4 b.f. Vision (USA)–Miami Melody (Miami Springs) [1989/90 16h^{4} 17d^{4} 17g^{4} 19s^{4} 20v 17v^{2}] small, sparely-made filly: little worthwhile form on Flat, including in a seller: sold out of Sir Mark Prescott's stable 1,250 gns Newmarket September Sales: in frame in selling hurdles: best effort in blinkers final outing (January): claimer ridden previously: visored time before. *J. D. Roberts.* 80

MUSICAL MYSTERY 8 ch.g. Orchestra–Last Trip (Sun Prince) [1989/90 16v 20g 16g^{4} 16d* 17d^{4} 16g^{4} 16d] good-bodied gelding: modest hurdler nowadays: won handicap at Newcastle in February: best form at 2m: acts on heavy going and is possibly unsuited by top-of-the-ground: good mount for a claimer. *M. Avison.* 98

Telecom Eireann Thyestes Handicap Chase, Gowran Park—
Mweenish makes light of testing conditions

Mr Peter S. Thompson's "Mweenish"

MUSIC BE MAGIC 11 b.g. Brave Invader (USA)–Forgello (Bargello) [1989/90 16m^{4} c16f^{3} 20f^{3} c16m^{3}] good-topped, workmanlike gelding: useful chaser and fair hurdler at his best, but seems to have his own ideas about the game nowadays: stays 2½m: seems to act on any going: sometimes jumps none too fluently: has shown a tendency to go left when tired: blinkered twice in 1987/8 and visored last start. *G. Richards.* c— § — §

MUSSEL BED 13 ch.g. Deep Run–Artella (Tartan) [1989/90 c25m^{F}] compact gelding: winning point-to-pointer/hunter chaser: stays well: acts on heavy going: has worn blinkers: ran out first outing 1985/6. *Mrs J. V. Wilkinson.* c— —

MUST BE MAGIC 6 b.m. Comedy Star (USA)–Jinja (St Paddy) [1989/90 16s 17g^{F} 16f^{3} 16f^{5} 16m 16h^{4}] sparely-made mare: novice selling hurdler: was best over sharp 2m on a sound surface: pulled hard: visored final outing: dead. *T. H. Caldwell.* 78

MUTCH LARK 5 b.m. Crested Lark–Mutchkin (Espresso) [1989/90 aF13g^{3} F13f^{6} a16g^{5}] half-sister to 2 poor novice hurdlers: dam won 1¼m seller on Flat: showed ability in NH Flat races: 18½ lengths fifth behind Shirley Ann in novice hurdle at Southwell in April. *P. Davis.* 68

MWEENISH 8 b.g. Callernish–No Trix (No Argument) [1989/90 c20f^{3} c26d^{2} c25v* c24s^{F} c30v^{pu} c24m^{pu} c25m] rangy gelding: jumped better than previously and showed improved form when winning quite valuable Telecom Eireann Thyestes Handicap Chase at Gowran Park in January by 12 lengths from Lanigans Wine: failed to reproduce that form: stays 3¼m: acts well on heavy going. *J. Webber.* c**130** —

MY BID 6 b.m. Cleon–Pleasure Bid (Mon Plaisir) [1989/90 F16s F17d^{6} F16g^{5}] first foal: dam, winning 2m hurdler, half-sister to top-class chaser Charlie

Potheen and daughter of a fairly useful point-to-pointer: 16 lengths fifth behind The City Minstrel in NH Flat race at Fakenham in April: yet to race over hurdles or fences. *W. J. Musson.*

MY BOY STAN 6 b.g. Dalsaan–My My Marie (Artaius (USA)) [1989/90 16g^{pu}]
workmanlike gelding: lightly-raced novice hurdler: dead. *R. Callow.* —

MY BROTHER CLIFF 4 ch.g. Brotherly (USA)–Tudor Primrose (Tudor
Sam) [1989/90 16f^{4}] second foal: dam unraced: well-beaten fourth of 6 finishers in —
juvenile hurdle at Bangor in September. *P. D. Connors.*

MY BROTHER JAKE 4 b.g. My Dad Tom (USA)–Silken Sheba (Royalty)
[1989/90 18m] leggy gelding: plating-class middle-distance maiden on Flat (tends —
to hang): tailed off in juvenile hurdle at Fontwell in December. *J. M. Bradley.*

MY CUP OF TEA 7 b.g. Porto Bello–Aravania (Rarity) [1989/90 c17f*] **c125**
angular, sparely-made gelding: had an excellent first season over fences in —
1988/9, winning 7 novice chases and a handicap chase: successful in another handicap at Newton Abbot in July: not seen out again: unlikely to stay much beyond 2m: acts very well on top-of-the-ground, and has yet to race on a yielding surface: genuine. *M. C. Pipe.*

MY DARK ROSALEEN 4 br.f. King of Spain–Irish Holiday (Simbir)
[1989/90 16d^{pu} 17v^{F}] sparely-made filly: modest sprint maiden on Flat, has run —
blinkered: little promise in juvenile hurdle at Sandown (jumped moderately) and novice event at Newton Abbot: pulls hard. *Mrs A. Knight.*

MY DOMINION 8 b.g. Dominion–Madge (Tudor Melody) [1989/90 21g^{F} 16s
20s 27s] lightly-made gelding: one-time fairly useful hurdler: plater nowadays: —
seems to stay well: probably acts on any going: suitable mount for a claimer: sold 1,400 gns Ascot February Sales. *W. T. Kemp.*

MYFOR 4 ch.g. Be My Guest (USA)–Forliana (Forli (ARG)) [1989/90 16d^{2} 16m]
half-brother to winning hurdler Fort Lino (by Bustino): dam, middle-distance 94
winner, half-sister to winning chaser Mosof: fair but irresolute maiden on Flat, stays 1¼m: sold out of B. Hills's stable 25,000 gns Newmarket Autumn Sales: odds on, pushed along some way out when 12 lengths second to Welshman in juvenile hurdle at Bangor in March: blinkered, slowly away second outing: very coltish on debut. *M. C. Pipe.*

MY GOLDEN WONDER 6 b.g. Gunner B–Presumptuous (Gay Fandango (USA)) [1989/90 F16f] behind in 2 NH Flat races: maiden point-to-pointer: yet to race over hurdles or in a steeplechase. *M. C. Pipe.*

MY GREY PHANTOM (USA) 5 gr.m. Vigors (USA)–Inreality Star (USA)
(In Reality) [1989/90 16m^{4}] angular mare: in frame at up to 1½m on Flat: first form 63
over hurdles when fourth behind Fiery Sun in selling handicap at Market Rasen in September: may do better over further. *D. J. Wintle.*

MY IMPRESSION 4 b.g. Lomond (USA)–Wish You Were Here (USA) (Secretariat (USA)) [1989/90 F16f^{5}] first foal: dam, modest 7f and 1¼m winner, is out of top-class middle-distance mare Summer Guest: 11½ lengths fifth behind Driver in NH Flat race at Cheltenham in April: yet to race over hurdles. *H. Candy.*

MY LADY MINSTREL 4 ch.f. Brotherly (USA)–Lady Peggy (Young Nelson)
[1989/90 a16g] poor and inconsistent sprint maiden on Flat: behind in selling —
hurdle at Southwell in March. *J. L. Spearing.*

MYLIEGE 6 b.h. Lord Gayle (USA)–My Natalie (Rheingold) [1989/90 16m 25g
24g 20v^{pu} 17v* 18g^{3} 25m^{3}] leggy horse: won selling handicap hurdle (no bid) at 89
Newton Abbot in December: below form last 2 outings: stays 3m: acts on heavy going and good to firm: blinkered last 3 starts 1987/8: usually ridden by 7-lb claimer. *G. A. Ham.*

MY LUCKY STAR 4 gr.f. Ballacashtal (CAN)–La Comedienne (Comedy Star
(USA)) [1989/90 16f^{5}] won 7f seller on Flat at 3 yrs: ridden by 7-lb claimer when —
11½ lengths fifth to Megadyne in novice hurdle at Huntingdon in May. *Andrew Turnell.*

MY MELLOW MAN 7 ch.g. Malicious–Mincy (No Mercy) [1989/90 c25m^{4} c**78**
c24m^{4}] compact gelding: fairly useful point-to-pointer: fourth to Pardi's Gift in novice hunter chase at Devon & Exeter in April, first and better effort. *W. G. Gooden.*

MY MERLIN 4 b.g. My Chopin–Miss Rubor VII (pedigree unknown) [1989/90 F13d] non-thoroughbred gelding: second foal: dam unraced: tailed off in NH Flat race at Kelso in January: yet to race over hurdles. *Mrs M. A. Kendall.*

MY MOYALE 7 b.m. Grandiose–Moya Mowa (My Swallow) [1989/90 21f^{4}] lengthy, lightly-made mare: of little account. *J. E. Forte.* —

MYNAH KEY 9 ch.g. Kemal (FR)–Galah Bird (Darling Boy) [1989/90 22s 22g] lengthy gelding: quite a useful hurdler at his best: shaped as though retaining ability when eighth to Invasion at Nottingham in February: well beaten on a sounder surface only subsequent start: unseated rider second on chasing debut: suited by a good test of stamina: acts on heavy going: good mount for a claimer. *R. A. H. Perkins.* c— —

MY NEW BEST FRIEND 6 b.g. Prince Bee–Tender Song (Pretendre) [1989/90 17f^{5} 27f* 24g* 24g^{2} 22g 24g^{pu} a24g^{2} a24g*] leggy, angular ex-Irish gelding: fifth living foal: half-brother to Mr Juicy (by The Brianstan), a winner on Flat and over hurdles: dam unraced half-sister to high-class Noble Dancer: lightly-raced staying maiden on Flat when trained by J. Bolger (has worn blinkers): successful in early-season selling handicap hurdles at Sedgefield and Uttoxeter (attracted no bid on both occasions) and 7-runner novice handicap at Southwell (made all) in January: stays well: acts on firm going: seems best visored: has won for a claimer. *R. Lee.* 108

MY PILOT 6 b.g. Al Sirat (USA)–Dandyville (Vulgan) [1989/90 c21d^{pu} 21d^{3}] robust, workmanlike gelding: lightly raced novice hurdler, creditable third at Newbury in March: tailed off when pulled up last in novice chase: will stay beyond 21f. *G. B. Balding.* c— 95

MY PRAYER 6 ch.m. Buckskin (FR)–Yellow Idol (Yellow God) [1989/90 17g^{ur} 16d^{pu} 16f^{pu}] leggy, angular mare: poor novice hurdler: blinkered last start. *Mrs Jill Evans.* —

MY PURPLE PROSE 9 b.m. Rymer–Lady Marcia (Arctic Slave) [1989/90 17d^{5} c16v^{F}] compact, workmanlike mare: handicap chaser: poor novice hurdler: seems best at 2m with plenty of give in the ground. *J. A. B. Old.* c— —

MY REEF 5 ch.h. Main Reef–Lassalia (Sallust) [1989/90 16f 16f^{ur} 16g^{4} 16f^{5} 16g^{6} 16s] sparely-made horse: poor novice selling hurdler. *J. R. Bostock.* —

MY SERENADE (USA) 6 b.m. Sensitive Prince (USA)–Mau Mae (USA) (Hawaii) [1989/90 16f^{F} 16h^{6} 16g^{6} 16g^{pu}] sparely-made mare: winning sprint plater on Flat: poor novice hurdler: has been beaten in a seller. *P. J. Bevan.* —

MY SKIWAY 7 b.g. Newski (USA)–Good Way (Good Apple) [1989/90 c20d^{3} c20d^{3}] stocky gelding: winning hurdler/chaser: still looked in need of race and ran accordingly when 8½ lengths third to Lislary Lad in amateur riders handicap at Chepstow in March: stays well: acts on any going: usually a bold jumper. *T. W. Donnelly.* c**107** —

MY SON JOHN 7 ch.g. Plenty Spirit–Lady Keeper (Worden II) [1989/90 22d^{bd} 24s^{pu}] lengthy gelding: sixth live foal: dam, poor novice hurdler, is half-sister to 1978 Cheltenham Gold Cup winner Midnight Court: bit backward, tailed off when pulled up 3 out in novice hurdle at Uttoxeter in February. *B. Preece.* —

MYSTERY'S NIECE 7 b.m. Belfalas–Place Pigalle (Pals Passage) [1989/90 16g 20d] lengthy, quite good-topped mare: always behind in novice hurdles. *R. Layland.* —

MYSTIC MONKEY 5 ch.g. Royal Match–Thorganby Melody (Highland Melody) [1989/90 20v^{pu} 17f^{pu}] of little account and apparently temperamental on Flat: probably no better over hurdles: blinkered second outing. *T. B. Hallett.* —

MYSTIC MUSIC 11 b.m. Hansel's Nephew–Mystic Mintet (King Log) [1989/90 c24g* c24d* c26m*] c**143**

Mystic Music put up the best performance by a hunter chaser in 1990 when she won the Horse And Hound Cup at Stratford on the last day of the season. Good performances by hunters were a rare occurrence, partly due to prevailing firm ground, during the four-month hunters' season. The most notable efforts prior to Stratford had come from the first three home in the Cheltenham Foxhunters, Call Collect, Old Nick and West Tip, from Lean Ar Aghaidh at Aintree and from Ah Whisht at Punchestown. Mystic Music herself had had a fairly quiet season until Stratford. She had gained an easy win at Edinburgh in February—her rivals included the redoubtable Flying Ace running his last race—but then suffered a blood irregularity which caused her to miss Cheltenham; and a slip up on a bend in a point-to-point on Grand National day kept her off until Perth in mid-May. Mystic Music showed her well-being there with an impressive fifteen-length win from

Secret Brae at odds of 9/4 on. Mystic Music was also odds on at Stratford with only two of her eight opponents, the progressive Sanballat and the Audi Champion Hunters Chase winner Edenspring, starting at less than 20/1. Mystic Music's performance was a joy to watch. Always handy, travelling strongly and jumping well, she outjumped John Sam and Edenspring to lead three out, sprinted clear, gained another five lengths with an outstanding leap at the next and continued to pull clear on the bridle until being eased on the run-in by her regular partner Mr Anderson. Mystic Music still finished twenty-five lengths clear—it could have been well over thirty—of Edenspring with a further twenty back to the outsider Brookside King and a below-form Sanballat.

Mystic Music, who is unbeaten in her last nine completed starts, was winning the Horse And Hound Cup for the second time. She became the seventh horse to win the race more than once, not the sixth as reported in the racing Press. The previous six were Bantry Bay, three-time winner Baulking Green, Credit Call, who won four times, Rolls Rambler, Otter Way, who gained his wins at the ages of eight and fifteen, and Three Counties, successful in the two years prior to Mystic Music's first victory. Mystic Music has a third Stratford win as her main target for 1991. Connections will consider Cheltenham, though they regard her jumping as too extravagant for Aintree. Provided she retains her ability at the age of twelve she'll be the one they have to beat at Cheltenham (with Call Collect aiming at the Gold Cup) and Stratford. 'They' are likely to be headed by the very promising Teaplanter.

Mystic Music (b.m. 1979)	Hansel's Nephew (b 1965)	Fidalgo (b 1956)	Arctic Star Miss France
		Princess Gretel (ch 1960)	The Phoenix Saucy Wilhelmina
	Mystic Mintet (b 1975)	King Log (br 1962)	Relic Queen's Beast
		Bontet (ch 1968)	Bounteous Miss Hooka

Mystic Music is a leggy, sparely-made mare who wears an off-side brush pricker. Her breeding was dealt with in detail in *Chasers & Hurdlers 1988/89*. She stays three and a quarter miles, acts on any going and is thoroughly dependable. *Miss H. Wilson.*

MYSTIC PALACE (NZ) 7 ch.g. Double Nearco (USA)–Mystic Light (NZ) (Lomond) [1989/90 17v^{6} 22g c20g^{pu} c17d^{2} c17m^{2} c16m^{F}] compact gelding: raced freely and showed little in novice hurdles: ridden by 7-lb claimer when runner-up in novice chases at Newton Abbot in March and April: should win a novice chase. *D. H. Barons.* c**101** —

MY TATA 4 b.c. Hasty Word–Oujarater (Adropejo) [1989/90 20d^{pu}] compact, deep-girthed colt: third foal: dam winning hurdler: backward, well behind when pulled up in novice hurdle at Wolverhampton in February. *B. Palling.* —

MY VALENTINE CARD (USA) 4 ch.f. Forli (ARG)–Super Valentine (USA) (Super Concorde (USA)) [1989/90 16g 16g 16m 16g 16d* 16g^{2} 16g^{3}] angular filly: plating-class maiden on Flat (has looked temperamental): first form over hurdles when winning selling handicap hurdle (bought in 2,400 gns) at Market Rasen (tended to idle on run-in) in January: placed in claimers subsequently: unlikely to stay beyond 2m: acts on dead going: visored and claimer ridden last 3 starts: pulls hard and wears severe bridle (has also worn brush pricker). *S. G. Norton.* 80

MY VIEW 6 ch.g. Buckskin (FR)–Fairy Rath (Indigenous) [1989/90 16v^{2} 16g^{4} 19d* 18d* 19d^{F} 17v^{3} 18v^{6} 20f 16m^{3}] tall, rather angular Irish gelding: fifth foal: half-brother to a poor novice hurdler/chaser by Fine Blade: dam won a 2m novice hurdle: won novice hurdles at Naas in November and Leopardstown (quite valuable event) in December: good third in handicap sixth start: given plenty to do, stayed on one pace after mistake 3 out when around 20 lengths seventh to Regal Ambition in Sun Alliance Novices' Hurdle at Cheltenham penultimate start: should stay 2½m: acts on good to firm and heavy going. *Miss Emer Purcell, Ireland.* 131

MY WILLIE MAN 7 b.g. Young Man (FR)–Preference (Sky Gipsy) [1989/90 16m 16g^{pu}] second foal: dam poor maiden on Flat: tailed off in novice hurdle at —

Royal Borough Novices' Hurdle, Windsor—
My Young Man makes a winning debut over jumps

Sedgefield in March and when pulled up 3 out in similar race at Market Rasen in April: sold 3,200 gns Ascot July Sales. *J. L. Harris.*

MY YOUNG MAN 5 b.g. Young Man (FR)–Hampsruth (Sea Hawk II) [1989/90 F16g* 16m* 16f* 16m] leggy, useful-looking gelding: brother to very useful hurdler Cliffalda: successful in NH Flat race at Sandown in November: most impressive all-the-way winner of novice hurdles at Windsor later in month and Wolverhampton in March: raced too freely when seventh behind Fidway in Seagram 100 Pipers Top Novices' Hurdle at Liverpool (dropped out tamely once headed 3 out) in April: acts on firm ground: jumps boldly and well: needs to become more tractable, but should make up into a useful handicapper. *C. P. E. Brooks.* 115 p

MZIMA SPRING 11 gr. or ro.m. Scallywag–Lady Colonist (Colonist II) [1989/90 c17g² c16g² c21d³] angular mare: winning hurdler: fairly useful chaser: led or disputed lead for a long way, but weakened run-in when 21½ lengths third to Desert Orchid in minor event at Wincanton in February: stays 2¾m: acts on any going: jumps well: reportedly slipped a tendon at Wincanton and wasn't seen out again. *Mrs J. G. Retter.* c**129** —

N

NAATELL (USA) 7 b. or br.g. Cox's Ridge (USA)–Lisanninga (Whodunit) [1989/90 16f⁵ 16f⁴ c20g^ur 16s² 16g*] leggy gelding: won conditional jockeys handicap hurdle at Wincanton in January cleverly by ¾ length from Squadron: unseated rider eighth on chasing debut: form only at 2m: acts on any going: trained until after first outing by S. Dow. *N. R. Mitchell.* c— 85

NABIL 9 ch.g. Malinowski (USA)–Clara Petacci (USA) (Crepello) [1989/90 20g^pu 19s^pu 16d^pu] sparely-made gelding: of little account. *C. A. Horgan.* —

NAE BOTHER 6 b.g. Neltino–Pirella (Pirate King) [1989/90 16s⁴ 16g*] small gelding: showed improved form when winning selling handicap hurdle at Fakenham in February: finished lame and attracted no bid afterwards: likely to prove best at 2m. *J. Wharton.* 96

NAEVOG 7 br.m. Ela-Mana-Mou–Gale Bridge (USA) (Vaguely Noble) [1989/90
22d* 16s^{6} 25m^{2}] small, sparely-made Irish mare: useful hurdler: won Findus 143 +
Hurdle at Leopardstown in December by 2½ lengths from Trapper John (gave 10
lb): 1½ lengths second to same horse (gave 5 lb) in Waterford Crystal Stayers'
Hurdle at Cheltenham in March: stays 25f: acts on good to firm and heavy going.
L. Browne, Ireland.

NAFUAT 6 b.g. Taufan (USA)–Jerusalem (Palestine) [1989/90 16s^{pu} 16f 16g]
leggy, close-coupled gelding: modest and unenthusiastic handicapper on Flat —
nowadays, stays 7f: sold out of J. W. Watts's stable 4,000 gns Doncaster January
Sales: no sign of ability in novice hurdles. *Mrs P. A. Barker.*

NAHAR 5 b. or br.h. Known Fact (USA)–Muznah (Royal And Regal (USA))
[1989/90 16m^{3} 18f^{2} 16f^{F} 16g^{2} 16g^{2} 20f^{F} 20g^{4} 16m^{bd} a20g*] neat horse: fairly 133
useful hurdler: jumped very well when winning Builder Group Gold Cup
(Handicap Hurdle) at Lingfield in March easily by 15 lengths from Regal Lake:
placed in quite valuable handicaps earlier: stays 2½m: below form on heavy going,
seems to act on any other: looked ungenuine fifth start. *S. Dow.*

NA LA GIRI 4 b.c. Nishapour (FR)–Les Sylphides (FR) (Kashmir II) [1989/90
16m^{2} 16f* 16g^{3} 20g^{6} 21d^{pu} 16s 18s] small, close-coupled colt: useful winning 79
plater on Flat, stays 1¼m: successful in selling hurdle at Towcester in November
(bought in 7,500 gns): hampered and forced out fourth on sixth start: best at
around 2m: acts on firm going: blinkered on final outing: jumps well. *R. Simpson.*

NAMELOC 6 ch.g. Deep Run–Kitty Cullen (Pollerton) [1989/90 16g^{2}] sturdy
Irish gelding: useful stayer on Flat: made mistakes in early stages and had a lot to 112 P
do 2 out, but stayed on well when going down by 8 lengths to Vestris Abu in BMW
Champion Novice Hurdle at Punchestown in April: will stay further: sure to
improve and will win races over hurdles. *J. E. Kiely, Ireland.*

NAMOOS 9 br.g. Thatching–Little Firefly (USA) (Bold Ruler) [1989/90 c21s^{6}] c—
good-bodied gelding: winning selling hurdler/point-to-pointer: well beaten in —
novice chases and a hunter chase: stays 2¾m: acts on any going: has worn
blinkers but not for a long time. *Mrs D. H. McCarthy.*

NANCY ARDROSS 4 b.f. Ardross–Classy Nancy (USA) (Cutlass (USA))
[1989/90 16g^{6} 16g^{F} 16d 20s^{3} a16g* a16g] lightly-made filly: little worthwhile form 82
on Flat: showed improved form when making all in selling hurdle at Southwell in
March: sold out of J. Hetherton's stable 8,000 gns afterwards: ran poorly in novice
event on same course following month: wears crossed noseband. *A. S. Reid.*

NARANA 6 b.g. Don–Broccoli (Welsh Saint) [1989/90 c24d^{5} c32g^{pu}] well-made c—
gelding: winning chaser: ran badly in 1989/90: stays 2¾m: acts on soft going and
good to firm. *W. A. Stephenson.*

NARCONE 9 b.m. Kambalda–Lady Coleman (Master Owen) [1989/90 c25f^{3} c—
c20f^{ur} c20f^{3}] leggy mare: poor chaser: stays 2½m: acts on soft going and good to —
firm: sold 4,600 gns Ascot February Sales. *W. T. Kemp.*

NARE POINT 5 ch.g. Floriferous–Rather Grand (Will Somers) [1989/90 16g]
well-made gelding: fifth live foal: dam placed over 6f and 7f in Ireland: behind in —
novice hurdle at Kempton in February. *Mrs J. Pitman.*

NARROWWATER CASTLE 7 br.g. Tanfirion–Rachel Ruysch (Skymaster)
[1989/90 22d^{pu} 24d 16f^{4} 16g^{4} 20g] sturdy ex-Irish gelding: half-brother to Derby 84
runner-up Carlingford Castle (by Le Bavard) and fairly useful sprinter/miler
Exhilarate (by Wolverlife): dam showed ability at 2 yrs, but only plating class at 3
yrs: won point-to-point in 1988: novice hurdler: best effort at 2m on firm ground:
blinkered last 3 starts: sold 2,600 gns Ascot June Sales. *M. Avison.*

NATHAN BLAKE 5 gr.g. Sexton Blake–Nana (Forlorn River) [1989/90
F16m^{3} 16g 20g^{4} 16m* 21s 21f* 19m* 21f^{pu}] close-coupled ex-Irish gelding: 106
half-brother to Welsh River (by Welsh Saint), successful over sprint distances at 2
yrs: dam 2-y-o 5f winner: won NH Flat race at Roscommon in 1989: sold privately
out of M. Quaid's stable 28,000 gns Doncaster August Sales after first start:
successful in novice hurdles at Ludlow in January and April and Hereford in May:
ran poorly final outing: stays 21f: acts on firm ground and is unsuited by soft:
blinkered last 5 starts. *K. C. Bailey.*

NATHIR (USA) 4 b.c. Diesis–As You Would (USA) (Fleet Nasrullah) [1989/90
16s 16g 16f^{5}] lengthy colt: plating-class maiden on Flat, stays 1¼m: sold out of J. —
Benstead's stable 4,100 gns Newmarket September Sales: little worthwhile form
in juvenile hurdles and a seller. *P. Butler.*

NATIVE FRIEND 4 b.g. Be My Native (USA)–Wet Powder (Above Suspicion) [1989/90 16f2 16m* 16f2 16f* 16g* 16v3 16f3 16mF] leggy, close-coupled gelding: half-brother to very useful hurdler Seldom Dry (by Rarity): modest staying handicapper on Flat: successful in juvenile hurdles at Perth, Kelso and Wetherby in first half of season: subsequently off course 4 months but returned much better than before, finishing 2 lengths third to Ninja in Victor Ludorum Hurdle at Haydock and 1½ lengths third to Rare Holiday in Daily Express Triumph Hurdle at Cheltenham: disputing lead with eventual winner, stable-companion Sybillin, when falling fatally at the last in Glenlivet Anniversary Hurdle at Liverpool: acted on any going: usually jumped well. *J. G. FitzGerald.* 135

NATIVE RIVER 5 ch.g. Deep River–Native Love (Native Prince) [1989/90 16mpu 16m] half-brother to several winners, including hurdler Eileen Mary (by Furry Glen): poor sprint maiden on Flat: behind in selling hurdle at Catterick in December. *W. Bentley.* —

NATIVE ROMANCE 5 br.m. Be My Native (USA)–Linda's Romance (USA) (Restless Restless (USA)) [1989/90 16h 16gF 16m] leggy mare: 7f winner at 3 yrs when trained by R. Armstrong: little sign of ability over hurdles: headstrong. *J. Joseph.* —

NATIVE ROSE 6 ch.m. Gone Native–One To Rose (Huntercombe) [1989/90 16m 16m 16g] light-framed mare: seems of little account. *J. M. Bradley.* —

NATIVE SCOT 4 ch.f. Be My Native (USA)–Bunduq (Scottish Rifle) [1989/90 16g2 16s2 16d2 16d3] leggy filly: plating-class maiden on Flat, stays 1¼m: placed in juvenile hurdles and a novice event: wandered under pressure first start and hung run-in on third: gives impression she'll do best at sharp 2m. *F. H. Lee.* 80

NATURALLY AUTUMN 6 ch.m. Hello Gorgeous (USA)–Allotria (Red God) [1989/90 c25g3 c27f* c24mF c24g3] leggy, angular mare: winning hurdler: overcame mistakes when winning poor hunter chase at Sedgefield in April by 7 lengths from Sister Sam: stays well: acts on firm ground: has looked none too keen and is one to treat with caution. *A. R. Boocock.* c84 — §

NAUGHTS N' CROSSES 5 b. or br.m. Connaught–Criss Cross (Clever Fella) [1989/90 16f3] workmanlike mare: poor plater over hurdles: has run creditably for a claimer: sold 3,000 gns Doncaster November Sales: no form in point-to-points in 1990. *Capt J. Wilson.* 69

NAUTICAL JOKE 11 b.g. Sea Catch–Carnival Jest (Carnival Dancer) [1989/90 c24f* c30m* c28g3 c24d6 c25d3 c24m2 c36fur c24g4 c24g3] tall, leggy gelding: fairly useful chaser: easily landed the odds in small fields in handicaps at Newcastle in October and November: ran creditably on occasions afterwards: ran well for a long way but behind when unseating rider 4 out in Seagram Grand National at Liverpool: stays well: acts on any going: sometimes jumps none too fluently: good mount for an amateur. *W. A. Stephenson.* c**133** —

NAVARESQUE 5 b.m. Raga Navarro (ITY)–Esquinade (Silly Season) [1989/90 16d 16m4 16f4 16fbd 16m 16fpu] leggy, close-coupled mare: poor novice selling hurdler: winner at up to 1m on Flat in 1990. *R. J. Hodges.* 68

NEARBRIDGE 10 b.g. Nearly A Hand–Miss Stalbridge (Eastern Venture) [1989/90 c16gpu c24gpu] sturdy, workmanlike gelding: very lightly raced and no sign of ability over hurdles: tailed off when pulled up in novice chases. *P. Dufosee.* c— —

NEARCTIC BAY (USA) 4 b.g. Explodent (USA)–Golferette (USA) (Mr Randy) [1989/90 16f 16g6 16s4 17g 16d* 16d 20mpu 16gpu] big, stocky gelding: lightly-raced maiden on Flat: sold out of R. Casey's stable 3,000 gns Doncaster September Sales: won novice handicap hurdle at Wetherby in February: no form afterwards: should stay beyond 2m: acts on dead ground (behind when pulled up 2 out on good to firm): wears tongue strap. *Mrs P. A. Barker.* 89

NEARLY MEDINA 8 ch.m. Nearly A Hand–Miss Medina (St Elmo) [1989/90 c17g* c17g* c16g4 c24g3 c16dF] leggy mare: poor novice hurdler: won handicap chases at Newton Abbot in November and Devon & Exeter in December: suffered a fatal fall at Warwick in January: was best at around 2m: acted on soft going and seemed unsuited by firm: was usually claimer or amateur ridden. *R. J. Hodges.* c**104** —

NEARLY READY 7 br.g. Matching Pair–Orcatina (Orchardist) [1989/90 c19gF c20g5 c16g2 c16d2 c16m2 c16f5 c16f6 c20m* c16g2 c16m2 c17m* c20f* c17f3] very big ex-Irish gelding: third foal: half-brother to winning Irish point-to-pointer O Catina (by Laurence O): dam, half-sister to 3 winning chasers, never ran: winning point-to-pointer: won maiden chase at Southwell in March and novice handicaps at Huntingdon and Warwick in May: stays 2½m: yet to race on c**100**

very soft going, acts on any other: raced much too freely in blinkers seventh start. *John R. Upson.*

NEARLY TIME 7 gr.m. Nearly A Hand–Half A Minute (Romany Air) [1989/90 F16g] sister to novice hurdler King of Diamonds and half-sister to point-to-point winner Wait A Minute (by Crozier): dam and grandam (Another Minute) prolific point-to-point winners: behind in NH Flat race at Warwick in December: yet to race over hurdles or fences. *B. Smart.*

NEAT STYLE 5 b.m. Sweet Monday–Octavia (Sallust) [1989/90 16f 16m5] lengthy mare: won 3 times at up to 1¼m in 1989, including in a seller (claimed out of R. Hollinshead's stable £14,502): fifth in novice hurdle at Huntingdon in October: dead. *T. T. Bill.* 67

NEBECHAL 7 ch.m. Native Bazaar–Stanegate (Coliseum) [1989/90 16g 22f4] smallish mare: poor novice hurdler: sold 1,400 gns Doncaster January Sales. *Miss Z. A. Green.* 62

NECOCHEA 6 b.m. Julio Mariner–Mar Del Plata (Crowned Prince (USA)) [1989/90 25g* 24g4 25g5 24g4 22s 26m4] leggy, close-coupled mare: moderate hurdler: made all in conditional jockeys event at Newbury in November: ran a moody race third and last 2 starts: suited by a test of stamina: possibly unsuited by very soft going: needs a strongly-run race and is probably suited by a galloping track: sometimes blinkered: not one to trust. *N. A. Gaselee.* 116 §

NEEDWOOD LEADER 9 b.g. Averof–The Doe (Alcide) [1989/90 c24dpu] sparely-made gelding: novice selling hurdler: has shown little aptitude for steeplechasing, jumping moderately, but won a point-to-point in March: best at around 2m on top-of-the-ground: usually blinkered over hurdles. *Dr P. L. J. Pritchard.* c– x —

NEEHA 4 b.g. Nishapour (FR)–Acantha (Prince Tenderfoot (USA)) [1989/90 16m2 16s 16g 16d 16mpu] angular gelding: placed at up to 1m on Flat: second in juvenile hurdle at Nottingham in December: trained until after third start by I. Matthews: dead. *R. Simpson.* 87

NELION'S LASS 5 b.m. Sonnen Gold–Nelion (Grey Sovereign) [1989/90 F16v F16g] half-sister to several winners here and abroad, notably high-class stayer Recupere (by Reliance II): dam won over 6f and 1m at 2 yrs: tailed off in NH Flat races at Ayr in January and Kelso in March: yet to race over hurdles or fences. *D. Robertson.*

NELSON RIVER (USA) 5 br.g. Green Forest (USA)–Maple River (USA) (Clandestine) [1989/90 16g5 17f2] leggy, rather lightly-made gelding: moderate handicapper around 1m on Flat: sold out of I. Balding's stable 10,500 gns Newmarket Autumn Sales: odds on, beaten a head by Stroked Again in novice hurdle at Cartmel in May: saddle slipped on debut (wore crossed noseband and pulled hard). *M. C. Pipe.* 88

NELSONS BEACH 12 ch.g. Lord Nelson (FR)–Bright Beach (Little Cloud) [1989/90 c26mF c24f*] strong, compact gelding: point-to-point winner: won hunter chase at Hexham in May by ¾ length from Sister Sam: suited by a test of stamina: probably acts on any going. *J. M. Dun.* **c84** —

NELSONS DOCKYARD 9 ch.g. Thatching–Be Gyrful (Gyr (USA)) [1989/90 c20vpu] poor novice hurdler: made mistakes and tailed off when pulled up in maiden hunter chase at Folkestone in February: won a point-to-point following month. *L. R. Vine.* c— —

NEM CON 6 b.g. Buckskin (FR)–Summerfield Gold (Cracksman) [1989/90 16m 20gpu] leggy, close-coupled gelding: little sign of ability in novice hurdles. *C. R. Beever.* —

NENNI (FR) 11 ch.g. Urf (FR)–Carentonne (FR) (Dark Tiger) [1989/90 c32f3] chunky gelding: winning point-to-pointer/hunter chaser: 4 lengths third behind close finishers Tartevie and Freddie Teal at Cheltenham in May: stays very well: acts on firm ground. *Mrs Phyl Robertson.* **c89**

NERAK SENGA 8 ch.g. Crimson Beau–Ballinkillen (Levmoss) [1989/90 20d5 21f c21s c20g4 c24g3 c24m* c21m3] workmanlike gelding: no form on Flat at 3 yrs: won 3 point-to-points from 4 starts in 1989: promising fifth in novice hurdle at Worcester in November but well beaten next start: won 5-runner novice chase at Fakenham in March by ½ length from Farranrory: likely to need a good test of stamina: amateur ridden. *Mrs J. Bloom.* **c92** 94

NESAGA 6 ch.m. Sagaro–Netley (Major Portion) [1989/90 F16g 16gpu 16spu] leggy, quite good-topped mare: half-sister to winning hurdler Harvester Solar (by —

Porto Bello): dam won over 1½m on Flat in France: mid-division in mares NH Flat
race: tailed off when pulled up in novice hurdles. *M. J. Wilkinson.*

NESSFIELD 4 b.f. Tumble Wind (USA)–Ceiling (Thatch (USA)) [1989/90 16g^{F}
16d^{5} 16s^{2} 16g^{3} 16f^{2} 20m^{4} 16d] sparely-made, angular filly: second foal: dam, 85
maiden, half-sister to 2 winning jumpers: second in 1¼m claimer on Flat in
September: sold out of W. Haggas' stable 1,100 gns Newmarket Autumn Sales:
poor form over hurdles: has given impression she barely stays 2m when
conditions are testing (weakened in latter stages of slowly-run race over 2½m):
acts on any going. *K. A. Morgan.*

NET CALL (USA) 4 b.f. Quack (USA)–Sarcenet (USA) (Inverness Drive
(USA)) [1989/90 16g^{3} 16d^{3} 21m] poor maiden plater on Flat (has run visored and 66
blinkered): third in 2 selling hurdles at Worcester in May. *N. A. Smith.*

NETHERBRIDGE 12 b.g. Netherkelly–Bream Bridge (Manicou) [1989/90 c–
c24d] small, lengthy, lightly-made gelding: poor chaser: stays 3m: acts on any –
going. *C. Smyth.*

NEVER A PENNY 7 b.g. Nearly A Hand–Pilicina (Milesian) [1989/90 c20g c**92**
c20s^{2} c25v^{2} c18v* c25s^{4} c16f^{F} c20m^{F}] workmanlike gelding: modest novice –
hurdler: won novice chase at Fontwell in February: leading by about 2 lengths
when falling at the last in handicap at Plumpton in April, final start: best form at up
to 2½m: acts on heavy going: blinkered sixth outing: usually amateur or claimer
ridden in 1988/9. *J. P. D. Elliott.*

NEVER EVER 5 gr.g. Bradbury Master–Gillian Rosemary (John Splendid)
[1989/90 F13f] first foal: dam winning point-to-pointer: tailed off in NH Flat race at
Hereford in April: yet to race over hurdles or fences. *R. Lee.*

NEVER IN 4 b.g. Aragon–Recent Events (Stanford) [1989/90 16f^{pu}] fair plater
at up to 7f on Flat: sold out of C. Tinkler's stable 3,000 gns Doncaster September –
Sales: ridden by 7-lb claimer, behind when pulled up in juvenile selling hurdle at
Uttoxeter (jumped badly) in October: sold 2,300 gns Doncaster Spring Sales. *T.
H. Caldwell.*

NEVER LEARN 7 ch.g. Shack (USA)–Belle Fillette (Beau Chapeau) [1989/90 c–
c17d^{r}] fourth foal: half-brother to modest novice hurdler Godiva Bearings (by
Martinmas): dam won NH Flat race in Ireland: backward and ridden by 7-lb
claimer, tailed off and very tired when refusing 5 out in novice chase at Newbury
in March. *B. Stevens.*

NEVILLE'S-DELIGHT 11 b.g. Golden Love–Mehitabel (Cantab) [1989/90 c–
c20m^{pu} c24h^{2} c24m^{pu}] strong, lengthy gelding: winning point-to-pointer/
steeplechaser: little worthwhile form for some time: stays well: acts on any going.
Michael Berrow.

NEW ARRANGEMENT 4 b.g. Trojan Fen–Cariole (Pardao) [1989/90 16g
16d* 17g] medium-sized gelding: won 1¼m maiden on all-weather in October, 104
when trained by B. Hanbury: fortunate winner of juvenile hurdle at Sandown in
January, benefiting from fall of clear leader General Pershing at the last: ran
moderately next time: will be suited by a stiffer test of stamina. *J. R. Jenkins.*

NEW ASSET 5 b.g. Newski (USA)–Rose Cottage (Rose Knight) [1989/90 F16f]
fifth foal: half-brother to 2 poor animals: dam quite modest hurdler: mid-division
in NH Flat race at Warwick in May: yet to race over hurdles or fences. *P. J. Hobbs.*

NEW BABY 6 b.g. Sallust–Lagolette (Green God) [1989/90 16m 20g^{pu} 16m]
close-coupled gelding: winning 2m hurdler: broke a leg in seller at Catterick in –
December and was destroyed: blinkered second start. *D. Yeoman.*

NEWBAWN DALE 7 ch.g. Ovac (ITY)–Hunea (Hornbeam) [1989/90 c20s^{ur} c**91**
c24f^{ur} c24f^{3}] workmanlike gelding: novice hurdler: walked over in a point-to- –
point in April: 33/1, 6½ lengths third of 12 behind Blue Ravine in maiden hunter
chase at Hexham later in month: stays 3m: refused on chasing debut: blinkered
last 3 starts. *P. Pittendrigh.*

NEW BLUE 6 ro.g. Silly Prices–Blue Haze (pedigree unknown) [1989/90 16m^{6}
16d^{pu} 16g^{pu}] workmanlike, good-quartered gelding: well beaten in novice hur- –
dles: dead. *T. D. Barron.*

NEW FARMER 8 ch.g. New Member–Erra (Romany Air) [1989/90 c22s^{pu} c**94**
c25f^{2}] neat gelding: modest hurdler: placed in novice chases and a novice hunter –
chase: extremely well suited by a good test of stamina: acts on any going:
sometimes visored: needs chasing along and none too easy ride: sold out of O.
Brennan's stable 6,600 gns Doncaster August Sales. *R. M. Billing.*

NEW GAME 8 b.m. New Member–Rare Game (Raise You Ten) [1989/90 18g^{pu} c16g^{6} c20m^{4} c20s^{pu} 22s a20g^{4} a20g^{3} a20g 22f 19f^{3} c24h^{3} c26f*] lengthy mare: poor maiden point-to-pointer: poor selling hurdler: won novice chase at Fontwell in May: stays 3¼m: acts on firm ground. *P. J. Jones.* c74 58

NEW GOLD DREAM 9 b.g. Abednego–Cottage Venture (Faust) [1989/90 c22s^{pu} c25f^{F}] stocky gelding: winning hurdler: poor form in novice chases: tailed off when pulled up in novice hunter chase in February: best run at 2½m: acts on hard going: usually wears a crossed noseband: has found little under pressure and courage under suspicion. *I. Bareham.* c— —

NEW HALEN 9 br.g. Dikusa–Miss Pear (Breakspear II) [1989/90 c26f^{3} c20f* c20f^{2} c16f^{2} c21f^{3} c22f^{3} c16m^{2} c16f^{2} c20f* c19d* c19g^{ur} c16s* c20f* c22m^{ur}] c**126** —

New Halen: a delightful story of metamorphosis. Prior to the latest season this horse, though placed numerous times, was still a maiden after a total of thirty-six races on the Flat, over hurdles and over fences. As a jumper he'd run on ground ranging from heavy to firm over distances ranging from two miles to twenty-five furlongs, showing himself to be none too fluent a jumper and, worse, inclined to find little off the bridle. In short, he looked a thoroughly exposed, moderate performer not to be trusted. A season on, New Halen had won five races including the last four he completed, had been placed on his seven other completed starts and had risen well over two stone in the handicap. Although New Halen managed to win a novice chase at Worcester in the early weeks of the season, it wasn't until a change of riding tactics were employed after his sixth start that he started to show significant improvement in form and attitude. Allowed to make the running, he ran out a wide-margin winner of handicap chases at Wolverhampton in October and Hereford in November. After unseating his rider at the last when held by the improving Thar-An-Bharr at Hereford later in November New Halen was absent from the racecourse for over

Mildmay of Flete Challenge Cup Handicap Chase, Cheltenham—
66/1-shot New Halen wins on merit

three months. On his return he took advantage of a last-fence blunder by Famous Lad to win a run-of-the-mill novice event, also at Hereford, before being sent to the Cheltenham Festival for the Mildmay of Flete Challenge Cup. Despite his improvement New Halen looked a forlorn hope. Even after the weights rose he was still set to carry 18 lb more than his allotted weight of 8-10, reduced 7 lb by the claim of his regular rider Eamon Tierney. New Halen, who looked particularly well and was beautifully turned out, started at 66/1 in a fourteen-strong field and won entirely on merit. In doing so he gave trainer and rider respectively their first Festival winner with their first runner and ride. Always to the fore in a race run at a good gallop, New Halen led at the tenth, quickened clear in tremendous style after the second last and was driven out to win by eight lengths from Lacidar. On his only subsequent outing New Halen was in the course of running another good race when a leather broke and he unseated his rider four out, close up, in the John Hughes Memorial Trophy at Liverpool in April.

New Halen (br.g. 1981)	Dikusa (b 1973)	Dike (ch 1966)	Herbager
			Delta
		Miss Upward (b 1964)	Alcide
			Aiming High
	Miss Pear (br 1968)	Breakspear II (br 1961)	Bold Ruler
			Pocket Edition
		Miss California (gr 1958)	Djebelilla
			Icone d'Or

New Halen's sire, Dikusa, a half-brother to the Ribblesdale Stakes winner Miss Petard, was a fairly useful performer at up to a mile and three quarters. The dam Miss Pear, who died in 1985, won at up to a mile and a half on the Flat in Ireland. She has produced one other winner, namely Glenviggan (by Be Friendly) successful in a two-mile maiden hurdle in Ireland. The next dam, Miss California, won on the Flat, over hurdles and fences. New Halen, a leggy, rather sparely-made gelding, stays at least two and three quarter miles and acts on any going. It will be interesting to see what he brings us in 1990/1. *A. P. James.*

NEW KINGSGROVE 11 b.g. Kinglet–Maidensgrove (Canadel II) [1989/90 24m^{2} 25m^{2} 24m^{2} 24h^{3} 25f^{3} 20m^{6} 27g^{2} c16f^{3} 24g^{5} 24g^{4}] lengthy, lightly-made gelding: modest hurdler: runner-up 5 times in 1989/90: ran poorly ninth start, and below his best on last: has jumped poorly and shown no form over fences: stays well: acts on any ground: blinkered once in 1985/6, usually visored nowadays (wasn't on ninth start): good mount for amateur or claimer. *P. Monteith.* c— x 102

NEWLAR 11 br.g. Dominion Day–Star Strip (Star Signal) [1989/90 20g^{4} c27g] workmanlike gelding: moderate hurdler/chaser: suited by a test of stamina: acts on any going: has run well for a claimer: blinkered last 7 starts 1988/9. *S. Mellor.* c— 98

NEW MILL HOUSE 7 ch.g. Tobique–Ascess (Eastern Venture) [1989/90 20g 17v 18d^{2} 16d^{3} 16g] Irish gelding: eighth foal: half-brother to a winning hurdler by Celtic Cone: dam, poor hurdler/chaser, half-sister to several winning jumpers: fairly useful hurdler: placed in handicap at Fairyhouse and sponsored event at Naas (just over 6 lengths third behind Grey Danube) fifth and sixth starts: best form at up to 2¼m: acts on heavy going. *A. L. T. Moore, Ireland.* 131

NEWNHAM 13 ch.g. Cantab–Ribon Perfume (Sale Time) [1989/90 c22m^{4} c32f^{F} c24m^{3}] compact gelding: has done most of his racing in point-to-points, but put up high-class performance by hunter-chase standards when 50/1-winner of 1988 Seagram Fox Hunters' Chase at Liverpool: stayed on again after the last when 18 lengths fourth to Lean Ar Aghaidh in latest running of that event in April: fell fourth in Maryland Hunt Cup later in month: modest third at Fakenham in May: should stay extreme distances: best run on good ground: sound jumper: genuine. *M. A. Johnson.* **c114**

NEW OUTLOOK 6 ch.g. Tumble Gold–Goldfoot (Prince Tenderfoot (USA)) [1989/90 22d 20g 16g^{5} 16m 20g^{3} 16g 16g 20d c24s c20g^{F} c22m^{pu}] rangy ex-Irish gelding: seventh foal: half-brother to a winner in Belgium: dam never ran: winning hurdler: third in handicap at Tipperary in October, but well beaten over hurdles subsequently: every chance when falling last in novice handicap chase won by Folk Dance at Huntingdon in April: stays 2½m: acts on firm ground: trained until after ninth start by S. O'Farrell. *P. D. Cundell.* c— ?

NIAD 6 b.g. Lighter–Taxi Freight (Brave Invader (USA)) [1989/90 16g4 20d4 20m4 20g4] big, lengthy gelding: will make a chaser: first foal: dam, little worthwhile form in 3 hurdle races, sister to fair hurdler Ali Forever and half-sister to fair jumper Royal Thrust: modest novice hurdler: best effort on second start: likely to stay beyond 2½m. *J. H. Johnson.* 96

NICE DYNASTY (FR) 6 ch.g. Nice Havrais (USA)–Danesta (USA) (Majestic Prince) [1989/90 16dpu] rather leggy gelding: winning hurdler: broke down at Ascot in January: unlikely to stay much beyond 2m: acts on dead going. *O. Sherwood.* —

NICE WORK 4 b.f. Workboy–Pandorana (Pandofell) [1989/90 16mpu] half-sister to fair staying hurdler Crammond Brig (by New Brig): dam winning staying hurdler: tailed off only outing on Flat and when pulled up 3 out in juvenile hurdle at Perth in September. *C. J. T. Alexander.* —

NICHOLAS GOLD 6 b.g. Tumble Gold–Nicky's Guess (Three Dons) [1989/90 16fpu] leggy gelding: of little account: sold 1,600 gns Doncaster October Sales. *L. Wordingham.* —

NICHOLCONE 7 b.m. Celtic Cone–Candy Stripe (Wrekin Rambler) [1989/90 16d 22gpu 20d5] smallish, workmanlike mare: second in NH Flat race in 1987/8: soundly-beaten fifth in novice hurdle at Sedgefield in March. *J. G. FitzGerald.* —

NICKEL SILVER (FR) 6 ch.g. Son of Silver–Dana's Return (USA) (Turn-to) [1989/90 16g6] well-made gelding: novice hurdler: first run for 18 months, stayed on in latter stages when never-nearer sixth to 20-length winner First Crack at Perth in May: has given impression he's worth a try at 2½m: acts on good to firm going: tends to sweat and be on toes. *G. Richards.* 80 +

NICKNAVAR 5 ch.g. Raga Navarro (ITY)–Bay Girl (Persian Bold) [1989/90 16d4 16g 16s 20v5 20g2 22s5 21d 20h2] small, angular gelding: no longer of any account on Flat: sold out of J. Wharton's stable 5,200 gns Ascot October Sales: runner-up in novice hurdle at Kempton (amateur ridden) and an amateur riders handicap at Plumpton in second half of season: seems suited by 2½m: acts on any going. *Mrs P. A. Tetley.* 98

NICK THE BRIEF 8 b.g. Duky–Roman Twilight (Romulus) [1989/90 c20s3 c24g2 c29g2 c24s* c24v* c26fpu] c**166** —

As expected, the big, strong, lengthy Nick The Brief, one of the leading staying novice chasers of the 1988/9 season and with the scope to continue to improve, developed into a high-class performer in the latest campaign. Trained under permit by his owner nowadays, having been handled by John Costello as a novice, Nick The Brief progressed at such a rate that by the time the Cheltenham Gold Cup came to be run in March only three of the fourteen-strong field were preferred to him in the betting. Nick The Brief's odds of 10/1 looked to represent fair value judged on his performance in his previous race in the Vincent O'Brien Irish Gold Cup at Leopardstown in February. His five opponents in the Irish Gold Cup included Panto Prince and the leading Irish staying chasers Carvill's Hill—winner of the race in 1989—and Maid of Money. The pace was strong enough to result in the outsiders, Candy Well VI and Hungary Hur, dropping well behind from the first fence in the back straight for the final time and Panto Prince being beaten a distance at the finish. It was Panto Prince who made the running with Carvill's Hill until beginning to tire six out, where the latter went on by about five lengths from Nick The Brief and Maid of Money. The chasing pair closed up under pressure four out, but when Carvill's Hill, who had still to be asked for his effort, outjumped them at the next, he looked the likely winner. The picture changed dramatically at the second last, though, where a slow jump by the leader resulted in Nick The Brief's landing in front, after which Nick The Brief stayed on the strongest from the turn into the straight and drew clear on the run-in. At the post he was five lengths in front of Carvill's Hill with Maid of Money a further two and a half lengths away third. Nick The Brief, a thorough stayer for whom the stiffer the test of stamina the better, was ideally suited by the heavy ground at Leopardstown. Unfortunately for his supporters the going was firm at Cheltenham on Gold Cup day. Nick The Brief looked ill-at-ease under the conditions and was behind when pulled up starting the final circuit. So, Nick The Brief's season ended on a low note, but, granted plenty of give in the ground and provided all goes well with him, he should give a much better account of himself in the next Gold Cup. Whatever his fate at Cheltenham he seems sure to win more good-class races.

Nick The Brief's performance in the Irish Gold Cup is easily his best. His record in four races earlier in the campaign was that of an improving chaser, and his jumping, which had given cause for concern on occasions in his days as a novice, had become sound and dependable. Following a pipe-opener, when looking very much in need of the race, in a qualifier of the Arlington Premier Series Chase at Haydock in December, Nick The Brief failed only narrowly to win valuable handicaps at Wetherby on Boxing Day and Sandown in January. At Wetherby, in the Rowland Meyrick Chase, he made most of the running after being left in front at the sixth and kept on very gamely, coming under pressure some way out, only to give best close home and be beaten half a length by Durham Edition. At Sandown, in the Anthony Mildmay, Peter Cazalet Memorial Chase, Nick The Brief looked the likely winner after quickening a few lengths clear three out, but was overhauled in the last fifty yards and beaten a neck by Cool Ground. Another valuable handicap seemed about to escape Nick The Brief approaching the last fence of the Peter Marsh Chase at Haydock later in January. Having again been pushed into a lead of a few lengths approaching the third from home he looked like he might be beaten as Bishops Yarn, attempting to win the race for the second year in succession, touched down in front over the last. However, as usual Nick The Brief rallied in fine style under pressure on the run-in, and this time regained the lead close home and beat Bishops Yarn half a length.

Nick The Brief (b.g. 1982)	Duky (ch 1974)	Midsummer Night II (ch 1957)	Djeddah Night Sound
		Frondia (ch 1969)	Parthia French Fern
	Roman Twilight (br 1967)	Romulus (b 1959)	Ribot Arietta
		Miss Crepello (b 1959)	Crepello Iskandaria

Nick The Brief fetched IR 9,000 guineas as an unbroken three-year-old at the Ballsbridge Derby Sale. He is the fourth winner of his dam Roman

Peter Marsh Chase (Limited Handicap), Haydock—
little between Nick The Brief (No. 5) and Bishops Yarn

Vincent O'Brien Irish Gold Cup, Leopardstown—
Nick The Brief puts up a high-class performance to beat Carvill's Hill (right) and Maid of Money

Twilight, who was placed over five furlongs in Ireland as a two-year-old. All Roman Twilight's other winning produce were successful on the Flat, including the sprinters Sellbob (by Red God) and General Nero (by King

Mr J. R. Upson's "Nick The Brief"

Emperor). The next dam Miss Crepello, a winner over a mile and a half, is a daughter of a half-sister to Imprudence, winner of the One Thousand Guineas, Oaks and Poule d'Essai des Pouliches. Nick The Brief's sire Duky was a dour French stayer who finished second to Buckskin in the 1978 Prix du Cadran. From limited opportunities at the beginning of his stud career Duky's first crop included the very useful staying chaser Handy Trick. Demand for Duky's services has grown in recent years and through the exploits of Nick The Brief and others he should figure more prominently in the sires' list in the near future. *J. R. Upson.*

NICK THE DREAMER 5 ch.g. Nicholas Bill–Dream of Fortune (Barbary Pirate) [1989/90 F16m* F16m[2] a16g* 16g 16d[bd] 20d*] smallish, angular gelding: second foal: dam never ran: won NH Flat race at Warwick in September: ridden by 3-lb claimer, successful in novice hurdle at Southwell in November and novice handicap at Huntingdon in February: better suited by 2½m than 2m: acts on dead going. *W. G. M. Turner.* 100

NICKY'S JOY 14 b.g. Beau Lavender–Slippery Della (Blue Chariot) [1989/90 c25f[3] c18m[6] c20d[F] c20g[pu] c20m[pu] c20m[pu]] smallish gelding: handicap chaser: poor form in 1989/90: tailed off when pulled up on hurdling debut: stays 3m: acts on any going: sometimes jumps sketchily: best with strong handling. *P. R. Hedger.* c84 —

NICOLAKI 5 gr.g. Busted–Nicholas Grey (Track Spare) [1989/90 16m[5] 16g 22g[pu]] half-brother to winning hurdler/chaser Young Nicholas (by Young Generation): modest 1½m winner on Flat (soundly beaten in 1989): only a little sign of ability in novice hurdles: sold 1,700 gns Doncaster Spring Sales. *T. M. Jones.* —

NICOLA NICKLEBY 4 b.f. Homeboy–Time of Your Life (Mount Hagen (FR)) [1989/90 16f[5] 16f 16g] small, workmanlike filly: half-sister to winning hurdler Charlie Dickins (by Homeboy): no form on Flat and over hurdles: tends to sweat. *R. Hollinshead.* —

NICORIDGE 8 b.g. Riva Ridge (USA)–Nicoletta (Busted) [1989/90 16f[ur] 16g 16m 16m[5]] leggy, lightly-made gelding: poor novice hurdler: pulls hard and seems none too genuine: trained until after third start by C. Bell. *V. Thompson.* 71 §

NIDD BRIDGES 4 br.f. Grey Ghost–Bargello's Lady (Bargello) [1989/90 16g 20d[6]] third foal: half-sister to quite useful chaser Sword Beach (by Scallywag): dam winning staying hurdler/chaser: well beaten in novice hurdles. *R. D. E. Woodhouse.* —

NIGHT ATTACK 14 ch.g. Midsummer Night II–Surfacing (Worden II) [1989/90 c18h[3] c20f[F] c20f[2] c24h[3]] workmanlike gelding: poor novice hurdler/chaser, winning point-to-pointer: little form for a long time: blinkered nowadays. *J. P. D. Elliott.* c— —

NIGHT BLOOMER (USA) 5 b.m. Told (USA)–Ms Bloomers (USA) (Carlemont) [1989/90 21f[pu] 16h[F] 17f 17g] sparely-made mare: lightly-raced maiden on Flat (has looked headstrong): little sign of ability over hurdles: saddle reportedly broke third start (seller): trained first start by M. Pipe: sold 2,100 gns Ascot November Sales. *Mrs J. Wonnacott.* —

NIGHT CHARMER 4 b.f. Burslem–Wind Shadow (Windjammer (USA)) [1989/90 16m[5] 16f[2] 16g[3] 16g 20g[pu] 16g[5]] sparely-made filly: fourth foal: dam unplaced on Flat and over hurdles in Ireland: poor form at best on Flat: placed in seller and juvenile hurdle at Kelso: ran poorly last 3 starts: should be suited by stiffer test of stamina. *J. S. Wilson.* 67

NIGHT GUEST 8 br.g. Northern Guest (USA)–Night Rose (Sovereign Gleam) [1989/90 c16m* c16f* c17f[3]] tall, close-coupled gelding: winning hurdler: won 3-runner novice chase at Perth in August and 4-runner novice chase at Hexham in September: seems best at around 2m: form only on a sound surface. *P. Monteith.* c87 —

NIGHT PRY 9 b.m. Pry–Night Spot (Midsummer Night II) [1989/90 c22g[6]] ex-Irish mare: in frame in NH Flat races in 1986: won a point-to-point in March: well beaten in hunter chase won by Sanballat at Stratford in April. *Miss S. Pilkington.* c—

NIGHT SAFE 9 b.g. Pollerton–Safe And Happy (Tudor Melody) [1989/90 c21s c20g[3] c24d* c24f[4]] rangy gelding: winning hurdler/point-to-pointer: led from the seventh when winning hunter chase at Bangor in March by 8 lengths from Turn c92 —

Mill: stays 3m: best on an easy surface, but possibly unsuited by very soft ground: blinkered first start in 1987/8. *Mrs J. G. Griffith.*

NIGHT SESSION 7 ch.g. Roselier (FR)–Love The Irish (Irish Love) [1989/90 c16h* c16f* c22d* c21f* c19f* c20mF c22m* 21mF c22m4] leggy, angular gelding: winning hurdler: won his first 6 completed starts over fences, namely novice events at Taunton, Wincanton, Stratford (2) and Hereford and minor event at Wincanton: creditable fourth to Sir Jest in minor event at Stratford in June: will stay 3m: acts on hard and dead ground: should win more races over fences. *O. Sherwood.* c**131** —

NIGHT TIME GIRL 7 ch.m. Aure-U-Lupi–Night Profit (Carnival Night) [1989/90 16vpu 25gpu 24fpu 16hF 24gF 16fpu] little promise over hurdles, including in a selling handicap. *W. G. Young.* —

NIJANNA 9 br.m. Quiet Fling (USA)–Lindera (Linacre) [1989/90 c24g3] strong, compact mare: useful point-to-pointer: winning hunter chaser: well-beaten third of 4 finishers behind Mystic Music at Edinburgh in February: suited by 3m: acts on any going. *T. N. Dalgetty.* c— —

NIKLAS ANGEL 4 b.g. Petorius–The Woodbird (Tudor Melody) [1989/90 16h3] lengthy gelding: plater on Flat, successful at up to 1m: odds on, moved poorly to post and jumped none too fluently when tailed off in juvenile hurdle at Plumpton in August. *C. N. Allen.* —

NINE CORNERS 6 ch.g. Legal Tender–Yoriet (Hornet) [1989/90 16mpu] big, rangy gelding: chasing type: second foal: brother to winning staying chaser Warner's End: dam never ran: green and in need of race, jumped poorly and tailed off when pulled up 3 out in novice hurdle at Uttoxeter in December. *J. Webber.* —

NINEOFUS 4 b.g. Lochnager–Mountain Child (Mountain Call) [1989/90 16g6 16g 16f4 16g3 16g2 16d6 16g* 16dpu 16f2] leggy gelding: half-brother to winning jumpers Grange Hill Girl (by Workboy) and Uptown Randb's (by Uncle Pokey): no worthwhile form at 2 yrs: won novice hurdle at Kelso in March: good head second to Zucchini at Wetherby in May: acts on firm going (has run moderately on dead). *M. H. Easterby.* 96

NINJA 4 ch.g. Niniski (USA)–Buckhurst (Gulf Pearl) [1989/90 16g5 16sF 16g* 16g2 16d2 16s* 16v* 16f2] 136

No winner of the Victor Ludorum Hurdle has gone on to success in the Daily Express Triumph Hurdle since Coral Diver in 1969, and prior to the latest season none since Rathconrath in 1977 had reached the frame. Little surprise then, perhaps, that the general reaction to the latest running, with a five-runner field the smallest in the race's history and only two lengths separating the first three home, should be unenthusiastic. Press comment ranged from *The Sporting Life* correspondent's '(the race) possibly was not a relevant Triumph Hurdle trial' to 'the early pace made the race pointless' from the *Pacemaker Update International* reporter. Certainly Ninja's suc-

Victor Ludorum Hurdle, Haydock—Native Friend leads Ninja over the last

cess at Haydock owed some part to a good tactical ride from Dunwoody in a slowly-run race. Always well positioned, Ninja was produced to lead early on the run-in and held off the strong-finishing Vestris Abu, who had been given plenty to do, by half a length, the pair a length and a half clear of third-placed Native Friend who was conceding 6 lb. But there looked to be some reasons for taking a positive view of the form in a season that had seen no outstanding performances by a juvenile. Though Ninja had shown only modest form in winning at Wolverhampton (awarded the race on the technical disqualification of Sartorius) and Warwick from six previous outings over hurdles, he'd seemed likely to be suited by the very testing conditions at Haydock. And he impressed in appearance and demeanour in the preliminaries. Vestris Abu, a fairly useful Flat performer, had run an excellent race against the older Bank View on similarly heavy ground at Leopardstown on his most recent outing. Native Friend had shown fair form in winning three times on a sound surface early in the season; and the first three had quickly drawn well clear of fourth-placed Carbisdale, third behind Philosophos at Kempton a week previously. Nearly all the signs were that the trio were at least useful.

The trio proved the point when making the frame behind Rare Holiday in the Triumph Hurdle twelve days later. Ninja, a 50/1-shot on the firm ground at Cheltenham, ran an excellent race to finish second, beaten a length. Always in touch, he could be seen travelling strongly in behind the leaders on the home turn, and stayed on well despite tending to edge slightly left, to finish a length clear of Native Friend, hampered by the winner on the run-in, who turned the tables on Vestris Abu, a further half length back in fourth. Vestris Abu went on to win the valuable BMW Champion Novice Hurdle at Punchestown, and Native Friend was alongside the eventual winner Sybillin when falling fatally at the last in the Glenlivet Anniversary Hurdle at Liverpool. Ninja wasn't seen out again. He was sold

Mr H. R. Mould's "Ninja"

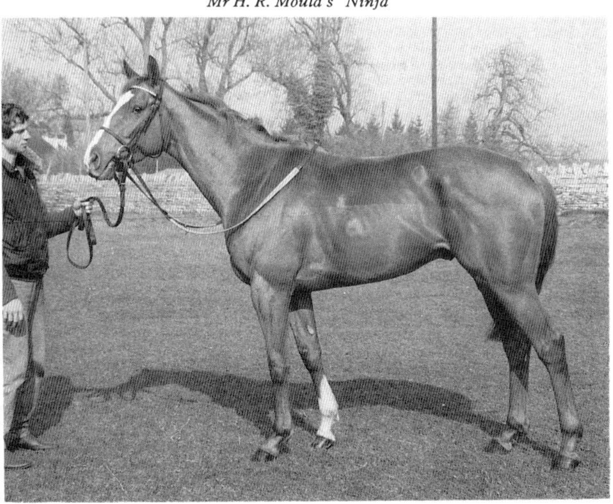

privately after Cheltenham and is to be trained in the United States by F. Raquet. Nicholson's Daily Express Triumph Hurdle runner-up of 1989, Highland Bud, bought two months later for 105,000 guineas, won the Breeders' Cup Steeplechase and Colonial Cup for Sheppard in the latest season, so demand from the States for this type of horse seems likely to continue.

Ninja (ch.g. 1986)	Niniski (USA) (b 1976)	Nijinsky (b 1967)	Northern Dancer
			Flaming Page
		Virginia Hills (b 1971)	Tom Rolfe
			Ridin' Easy
	Buckhurst (ch 1976)	Gulf Pearl (ch 1962)	Persian Gulf
			Nan
		Last Flutter (ch 1959)	Stephen Paul
			Poker Dice

Bought for 23,000 guineas at Newmarket as a foal and resold for 20,000 guineas at the same venue a year later, Ninja has the pedigree of a Flat racer. He is brother to the useful miler Ininsky and a half-brother to Tregeagle (by Treboro), a winner in Switzerland. Their dam, the seven-furlong-placed Buckhurst, is a sister to the useful two-year-old of 1977 Beldale Lark. The unraced Last Flutter bred several other winners and was a half-sister to the fairly useful sprinter Game Chip, out of the five-furlong winner at two years Poker Dice. Ninja's best effort on the Flat was third place in a seven-furlong maiden won by Scenic at Chester as a two-year-old when trained by Pritchard-Gordon. He showed little in three outings in 1989 and was sent to Nicholson and subsequently gelded. Close coupled and sparely made, Ninja lacked some of the obvious physical scope of some of his contemporaries and might have been difficult to place if remaining in Britain. However, his form is only a few pounds short of that shown by Highland Bud as a juvenile and he should win races in the States if adapting to conditions. *D. Nicholson.*

NIPPER SMITH 7 b.g. Chantro–Alice Springs (Coronation Year) [1989/90 c16s5 c16gpu c16dpu 16f5 16mpu] small, sparely-made gelding: selling hurdler: no form in 1989/90: has shown nothing in novice chases: best form at 2m: acts on soft going and is possibly unsuited by top-of-the-ground: blinkered twice in 1987/8 and last 2 outings. *J. Skelton.* c— —

NITE OF SPRING 12 ch.g. Hessonite–Hazel Spring (Drumbeg) [1989/90 c24f3 c20f5 c24m2 c21m] small gelding: novice selling hurdler: poor form in novice and handicap chases, usually making mistakes: barely stays 3m: sometimes blinkered over hurdles. *Miss Z. A. Green.* c**70** x —

NOBBANOKKER 8 br.g. Milan–Irish Aunt (Tyrone) [1989/90 c20dpu c25g2 c24d* c26f] big, workmanlike gelding: winning point-to-pointer: won hunter chase at Leicester in March by 2 lengths from West Tip: beaten a long way but not at all disgraced when eighth of 10 finishers behind Call Collect in Christies Foxhunter Chase at Cheltenham: stays well: acts on any going. *J. E. Greenall.* c**99** +

NOBBY 4 b.c. Dalsaan–Parkeen Princess (He Loves Me) [1989/90 16gbd 16m 16g5 a16g2 a16g4 16f] leggy, sparely-made colt: fair performer on Flat in 1989 when trained by Sir Mark Prescott, winner 4 times at up to 1¼m (best at 1m): second to Softly in juvenile hurdle at Lingfield in February, easily best effort. *J. Ffitch-Heyes.* 87 ?

NOBLE BID 6 b.h. Kings Lake (USA)–First Round (Primera) [1989/90 16m6 16f4 16m2 16m* 16m* 16m3 16s 20g* 16f5 16f4 16m4] sturdy horse: won selling hurdle at Worcester (no bid), novice handicap at Ludlow (made virtually all) and novice claimer at Wolverhampton in first half of season: stays 2½m: acts on firm ground and seems unsuited by soft: successful with and without blinkers (didn't wear them when successful at 2½m): has worn bandages: jumps well. *Miss S. J. Wilton.* 89

NOBLE EYRE 9 br.g. Aristocracy–Jane Eyre (Master Buck) [1989/90 16m3 22g 17d3 c16g3 c16d2 c16d* 17v6 c16d5 c16g2 c16f5 c16m3 c16g4] smallish, workmanlike gelding: modest hurdler/chaser: won amateur riders handicap chase at Stratford in December: effective at 2m and stays 3m: probably acts on any going. *D. R. Gandolfo.* c**89** 86

NOBLE FLYER 10 ch.g. Pry–Osbertstown Mill (Nice Guy) [1989/90 c26gpu c20dbd c20m6 c20gpu c26spu c20fpu] sparely-made gelding: lightly-raced novice hurdler/chaser: little form. *C. V. Bravery.* c— —

NOBLE PROSPECT 6 b.m. Tall Noble (USA)–Prosper Lion (Regret) [1989/90 20m 16g2 16d 16d] rangy mare: second in novice selling handicap hurdle at Sedgefield in November, best effort: blinkered then and on last start. *J. J. O'Neill.* 74

NOBLE RAIDER 6 b.g. Sir Mordred–Clonroche Hawk (Arctic Slave) [1989/90 F16g4 aF16g* aF16g2 16g3] fifth living foal: half-brother to quite useful staying chaser Master Tercel (by Master Owen) and fairly useful hurdler/chaser Yeoman Broker (by Pauper): dam poor performer over hurdles and fences in Ireland: won NH Flat race at Southwell in January: outpaced soon after halfway when remote third of 5 in novice hurdle at Catterick in March: should do better given a stiffer test of stamina. *J. G. FitzGerald.* — p

NOBLE SCAMP 5 gr.m. Scallywag–Gouly Duff (Party Mink) [1989/90 F16m5 F17h2 F16mpu 20g 16g4 25m2 24d 24f3 27f* 24m*] unfurnished mare: dam placed in point-to-points: won novice hurdles at Sedgefield (ridden by 7-lb claimer) and Wetherby (amateur riders, beat Hey Rawley 7 lengths) in April: stays well: suited by top-of-the-ground: tried to run out in NH Flat race third start. *J. Parkes.* 98 p

NOBLE STORM 8 b.g. Morston (FR)–Brave Ballard (Derring-Do) [1989/90 16m 20m 24fpu] leggy, sparely-made gelding: handicap hurdler: ran well in face of stiff task in valuable event at Liverpool second start: pulled up lame next time: stays 2½m: acts on good to firm and dead ground. *P. J. Jones.* 102

NOBLE VIKING 7 ch.g. Viking (USA)–Lepello (Le Levanstell) [1989/90 20dro] lengthy, workmanlike gelding: handicap hurdler: looked none too keen under pressure once in 1987/8: pulled hard and ran out fifth in March: stays 3m: best on top-of-the-ground: has worn blinkers. *Mrs J. Pitman.* — §

NO BONUS 6 ch.g. Baragoi–Lillytip (Tepukei) [1989/90 16g6 16m 16f* 16h2 16f* 16h3] lengthy, unfurnished gelding: 4-length winner of novice hurdles at Taunton in March and Wincanton following month: ran creditably in between but poorly otherwise: quite stoutly bred but takes a good hold and may prove best at around 2m at present: acts on hard ground. *D. J. G. Murray-Smith.* 97

NO CREDIBILITY 8 ch.g. Ahonoora–Karlaine (Tutankhamen) [1989/90 16f2 16g2 16m2 16g4 16g3 16g* 20spu 16d 20g4 16f 16m4 16g 24g6 20g6] sparely-made gelding: made virtually all when winning poor novice hurdle at Market Rasen in December: beaten in sellers previously: stays 2½m (well beaten over 3m): acts on good to firm ground: blinkered once: hangs under pressure and seems a difficult ride: often ridden by claimer. *B. Richmond.* 81 §

NOD AND A WINK 5 b.m. Casino Boy–Regal Nod (Tom Noddy) [1989/90 F16v] first foal: dam placed over hurdles after birth of foal: mid-division in NH Flat race at Haydock in March: yet to race over hurdles or fences. *B. A. McMahon.*

NODDY'S DAUGHTER 5 b.m. Tom Noddy–Spanish Eyes (Eborneezer) [1989/90 F16fro 19mpu] non-thoroughbred mare: second foal: dam a bad point-to-pointer: ran out in NH Flat race at Ludlow: tailed off when pulled up in novice hurdle at Hereford. *B. Palling.* —

NO DEFECT 11 ro.g. No Mercy–Ruby's Chance (Charlottesville) [1989/90 c16hF c16h4] sparely-made, long-backed gelding: of little account over hurdles: let down by his jumping over fences in August. *M. Bradstock.* c— —

NODFORM 6 b.g. Good Thyne (USA)–Matriarch (Martinmas) [1989/90 20d 20f* 16d3 c20g2 c24g* c20d2] c**126** + 147

Bought for 70,000 guineas at the Doncaster Spring Sales in 1988 shortly after impressive successes in National Hunt Flat races at Ayr and Market Rasen, the then-four-year-old Nodform, a medium-sized, good sort in appearance, looked to have the potential to do well over jumps. He made a good start to his hurdling career the following winter, winning an ordinary novice event at Newbury in good style on his debut and then showing progressive form, though failing to win again, against the better novices. In the latest season Nodform showed further improvement over hurdles and embarked on a chasing career that promises a bright future. He put up a very useful performance to win the valuable Racecall Ascot Hurdle on the second of his three starts over timber before the turn of the year. Having run as though badly in need of the race when well beaten on his re-appearance two weeks earlier, Nodform started at 12/1 in a field of five behind the odds-on Sabin du Loir, who was attempting to win the race for the third year in succession. Sabin du Loir set a tremendous gallop, closely

Racecall Ascot Hurdle, Ascot—Nodform shows much improved form to beat Floyd

attended by Nodform who was also racing with plenty of enthusiasm. When Sabin du Loir began to drop out of contention shortly after the fourth from home Nodform took command and, running on gamely in the straight, won convincingly by six lengths from Floyd. The going had been firm for the two-and-a-half-mile Ascot Hurdle and Nodform didn't show quite the same zest on a yielding surface when returned to Ascot for the two-mile H.S.S. Hire Shop Hurdle in December. Nevertheless he wasn't totally disgraced in finishing thirteen lengths third to Forest Sun.

Nodform had his attentions switched to fences in the New Year. He made his chasing debut in the six-runner Fairlawne Novices' Chase at Sandown which looked beforehand to be virtually a match between himself and the former champion hurdler Celtic Shot, a wide-margin winner of novice chases on his previous two starts. Celtic Shot and Nodform dominated the race throughout. Both jumped well and Nodform showed plenty of promise. Though outpaced in the closing stages and beaten two and a half lengths, he wasn't given an unduly hard race once the winner had taken his measure. Nodform followed up that effort by landing the odds in the Hampton Novices' Chase at Kempton later in January easily by three lengths from Combermere, with the remainder well beaten. Again jumping well, Nodform set a modest pace from the third, gradually increased the tempo from eight out and quickened decisively approaching the last. Similar tactics were employed in his next race, a qualifier of the Steel Plate And Sections series at Newbury in February. He soon had most of his opponents in trouble after increasing the tempo from the fifth but couldn't shake off Chatam, was readily outpaced from four out and eventually beaten a distance. Nodform seemed to be labouring in the closing stages and gave the impression that all was not well with him. Possibly he was suffering from the coughing that had struck his stable at the time. The Steel Plate And Sections Qualifier turned out to be Nodform's last race of the season. Hopefully he'll return to the racecourse fit and well in 1990/1 when he should make up into a good handicap chaser at least.

Nodform (b.g. 1984)	Good Thyne (USA) (br 1977)	Herbager (b 1956)	Vandale II
			Flagette
		Foreseer (b or br 1969)	Round Table
			Regal Gleam
	Matriarch (b 1978)	Martinmas (b 1969)	Silly Season
			Calvine
		Lintola (br 1963)	Constable
			Another Exile

Mr H. J. Joel's "Nodform"

Nodform is from the first crop of the Irish St Leger runner-up Good Thyne, a half-brother to two other sires in Caerleon and Vision. He is the second foal of Matriarch, unplaced from four starts on the Flat in Ireland. The 1985 produce, Efemkay (by Aliyoun) won over six furlongs as a two- year-old. The next dam, Lintola, a half-sister to the fair hurdler Vital Exile, was a useful five-furlong winner. Nodform, a free-going type, showed at Kempton that he stays three miles, in a moderately-run race at any rate. Whether he'll prove as effective at the trip in a race run at a strong gallop throughout remains to be seen. Everything points to Nodform's being ideally suited by a firm surface, but he's not so ill-suited by a yielding one that he can be dismissed out of hand on it. *J. T. Gifford.*

NODFORMS DILEMMA (USA) 7 ch.g. State Dinner (USA)–Princess Jo Jo (Prince John) [1989/90 c16g^4 c20s^{pu} 20v^2 20g^5 22s 21m^4 24f^5] rather leggy gelding: fair hurdler: bought out of D. Eddy's stable 30,000 gns Doncaster August Sales: good second at Haydock in January: ran moderately or worse afterwards: jumped deliberately both starts over fences: stays 3m: acts on any going: blinkered fifth start: sold 8,600 gns Doncaster Spring Sales. *O. Sherwood.* c— 123

NO EXPECTATIONS 4 b.f. Strong Gale–Newland's Bloom (Lucifer (USA)) [1989/90 F16f] non-thoroughbred filly: first foal: dam unraced: tailed off in NH Flat race at Ludlow in April: yet to race over hurdles. *K. C. Bailey.*

NO GRANDAD 6 br.m. Strong Gale–Blue Beep VII (pedigree unknown) [1989/90 c18g^2 c20g^4 c17g^2 c16s^2 c20g^3 c24g^3 c21s* c18g^4 c24g* c24d* c26v^{pu} c32f] angular Irish mare: maiden hurdler: won novice chase at Galway in October and handicaps at Fairyhouse and Thurles within 4 days in January: stays 3m: acts on soft going (ran moderately on firm at Cheltenham): has won for an amateur. *Mrs Pauline Gavin, Ireland.* c**108** —

NOHALMDUN 9 b.g. Dragonara Palace (USA)–Damsel (Pampered King) [1989/90 c16f* c16d3 c16g2 c16g c16m c16f* c16f* c16f5] **c148** —

The Captain Morgan Aintree Chase, now established as the curtain raiser on Grand National day, once again fell to a horse who was out of the handicap, namely Nohalmdun. He carried 4 lb more than his mark in the long handicap in a race where the statutory minimum weight is 10-7. Only four of the twelve runners raced off their proper mark, including Waterloo Boy and the previous year's winner Feroda, second and third respectively in the Queen Mother Champion Chase at Cheltenham. Waterloo Boy, who carried top weight of 11-12, shared favouritism with Katabatic, the winner of the Grand Annual Chase at Cheltenham. Nohalmdun, seven lengths behind Katabatic at Cheltenham, now re-opposed on terms 7 lb better and looked to have fair prospects of turning the tables. The Grand Annual Chase had been Nohalmdun's first race for two months and, along with Prideaux Boy, winner of the Captain Morgan Chase in 1988, and Prize Asset, the runner-up in 1989, he came to Aintree a relatively fresh horse. With the ground decidedly on the firm side, the Mildmay course, despite having undergone alterations designed to make it less sharp, still rode very fast, and several of the runners were unable to go the strong pace set by Knockbrack. Knockbrack gave way to Clever Folly at the seventh, where the slow-starting Private Views fell fatally, and Clever Folly held the advantage until turning for home. Prize Asset now took over, pressed by The A Train, but none was travelling better than the patiently-ridden Nohalmdun, who'd made smooth and steady progress to take third place. Joining Prize Asset at the second last, Nohalmdun quickly drew clear and was driven out to score by five lengths from Prize Asset. Katabatic lacked the pace to reach a challenging position but stayed on to finish third, six lengths behind Nohalmdun, with Waterloo Boy, hampered and checked early in the straight, a further three quarters of a length away in fourth place. Nohalmdun's other wins during the season were both gained at Cheltenham. For the fifth time in six seasons' racing Nohalmdun was successful first time out, on this occasion beating Ida's Delight three quarters of a length in a three-runner

Captain Morgan Aintree Chase, Liverpool—the strongly-run two miles suits Nohalmdun

handicap in December; and he won a similar event on his first outing after Aintree, comfortably accounting for the only other finisher Pantomime Prince by two lengths.

Nohalmdun (b.g. 1981)	Dragonara Palace (USA) (gr 1971)	Young Emperor (gr 1963)	Grey Sovereign
			Young Empress
		Rubys Princess (b 1962)	Fidalgo
			Persian Ruby
	Damsel (b 1969)	Pampered King (b 1954)	Prince Chevalier
			Netherton Maid
		Damara (ch 1962)	Aggressor
			Petronella

Nohalmdun is one of only two winners produced by Damsel, the other being Mummy's Delight (by Mummy's Pet), a sprinting two-year-old. Damsel, a half-sister to the Prix Kergorlay and Prix Gladiateur winner Marson, won over a mile as a two-year-old. The leggy, workmanlike Nohalmdun, who acts on any going, can produce a good turn of foot at the end of a strongly-run race at two miles, and waiting tactics suit him ideally. Although not quite so good over fences as he was over hurdles—he finished in the frame in two Champion Hurdles—Nohalmdun is nevertheless a very useful performer and has won seven of his fourteen starts in steeplechases. He should go on winning races for some time yet. *M. H. Easterby.*

NO INTERFERENCE 5 b.m. Silly Prices–Ereka Oak (Derek H) [1989/90 F16h^{3} F16f^{3} F16m^{6}] second foal: sister to a poor animal: dam never ran: showed a little ability in early-season NH Flat races: yet to race over hurdles or fences. *F. Taylor.*

NOIRE SMALL (USA) 8 b.m. Elocutionist (USA)–Small Indulgence (USA) (Fast Hilarious (USA)) [1989/90 c21m^{3} c21f^{pu} a20g^{3}] tall, lengthy mare: poor novice hurdler: sweating, travelled strongly until mistake 4 out when 14 lengths third to Bronze Final in novice chase at Wincanton in October: stays 2½m: acts on firm going: visored final outing 1988/9, blinkered last time out. *P. R. Hedger.* c**82** 72

NOMADIC WAY (USA) 5 b.h. Assert–Kittyhawk (Bustino) [1989/90 16f^{3} 16f^{2} 16s* 16m^{2} 22f^{6}] 166

Nomadic Way emulated Flash Imp when he took second place in the Waterford Crystal Champion Hurdle two years after winning the Cesarewitch. Flash Imp, beaten eight lengths by Comedy of Errors in the 1975 Champion Hurdle, went on to finish third behind Night Nurse and Bird's Nest in the following year's race. Though injured on his final start Nomadic Way should be back in action in 1990/1; if he comes back all right we'd certainly expect him to play a prominent part in the 1991 Champion Hurdle, and he may even improve enough to win it. Nomadic Way, a five-year-old, was having only his eighth outing over hurdles at Cheltenham. He'd shown plenty of ability as a juvenile, winning at Sandown and Ascot and finishing second to Royal Derbi in the Tote Placepot Hurdle at Kempton. His only moderate run came in the Daily Express Triumph Hurdle at Cheltenham, where he was blinkered for the first time over hurdles. Blinkers had brought out the best in Nomadic Way on the Flat, and they were to do so over hurdles in the latest season.

That Nomadic Way was a much improved performer soon became apparent. On ground considered likely to be too lively for him at the trip, Nomadic Way finished a promising third behind Cruising Altitude in the Gerry Feilden Hurdle at Newbury in November; and the following month he was beaten only a head by the same horse in the Charles Heidsieck Champagne Bula Hurdle at Cheltenham. If such a stout stayer could acquit himself so well when the emphasis was on speed, what would he be capable of given more testing conditions? Nomadic Way provided the answer in the Wessel Cable Champion Hurdle in February, an event which was postponed six days following the abandonment of the original fixture at Leopardstown due to gale-force winds. In a very strongly-run race on soft ground, Nomadic Way put up a high-class performance to win by six lengths from the favourite Elementary. Nomadic Way raced in second place as Toranfield cut out the running, being poised to challenge at the second last where Island Set, the only other British challenger, and Elementary were on his heels.

Wessel Cable Champion Hurdle, Leopardstown—
a high-class performance from Nomadic Way

Nomadic Way was still travelling strongly as he took the lead turning into the straight, though not, apparently, so strongly as Elementary who was still being heavily restrained. Nomadic Way's rider Powell then seized the initiative by kicking on, and Nomadic Way responded immediately to gain a clear advantage. Nomadic Way had first run on Elementary, but in the end it turned out not to matter. Though Elementary drew well ahead of the remainder he was unable to make much impression on Nomadic Way who ran on very strongly all the way to the line. It was a performance which suggested that Nomadic Way would be one to reckon with in the Champion Hurdle, particularly given similar conditions. As it turned out the ground at Cheltenham was on the firm side and Nomadic Way, ridden close to the pace and kicked on coming down the hill, couldn't muster the speed to get away from his rivals. A length up but flat out turning for home, Nomadic Way was joined at the last by Kribensis, Past Glories and Beech Road. Kribensis produced the best pace and went on to win by three lengths from Nomadic Way, who battled on gamely to hold off the other two. Instead of going for the two-and-a-half-mile Sandeman Aintree Hurdle with Nomadic Way, connections adventurously sent him to the USA for the Dueling Grounds International Hurdle, run over two and three quarter miles. The gamble didn't pay off, Nomadic Way trailing in lame, sixth of the seven finishers behind the Irish-trained mare Grabel. It's worth recalling that Flash Imp stayed nothing like so well over hurdles as might have been expected from his performances on the Flat. He showed much better form at two miles than two and a half, and didn't stay three miles. We'd be very surprised if Nomadic Way didn't prove as effective at two and a half miles as he is at two, but it seems likely that he'll continue to be campaigned mainly at the shorter distance.

By the French and Irish Derby winner Assert out of the Lowther Stakes winner Kittyhawk, Nomadic Way might have been expected to make

Nomadic Way (USA) (b.h. 1985)	Assert (b 1979)	Be My Guest (ch 1974)	Northern Dancer
			What A Treat
		Irish Bird (b or br 1970)	Sea Bird II
			Irish Lass II
	Kittyhawk (b 1978)	Bustino (b 1971)	Busted
			Ship Yard
		Sky Fever (b 1969)	Skymaster
			Harlequinade

up into a good middle-distance performer on the Flat, but it soon became apparent that he lacked a turn of foot and that long distances were required to bring out the best in him. Nomadic Way's success in the Tote Cesarewitch was his fifth as a three-year-old, and he was to win once more the following year before going on to finish fourth in the Gold Cup at Royal Ascot. Nomadic Way's owner acquired Kittyhawk mid-way through her second season. She soon repaid part of her purchase price by winning the seven-furlong Kiveton Park Steel Stakes at Doncaster, and then went on to finish third behind To-Agori-Mou and Cracaval in the Queen Elizabeth II Stakes at Ascot, subsequently moved up a place on Cracaval's disqualification. Kittyhawk's other winning produce include the fair middle-distance performer Storm Force (by Storm Bird) and the smart 1985 French two-year-old maiden With Hope (by Irish River), the latter subsequently successful in the States. Kittyhawk's fifth foal Kitty Russe (by Nureyev) has shown enough to suggest that she'll win a small race on the Flat. Nomadic Way's grandam Sky Fever, a useful winner over five furlongs, is a half-sister to the 1974 Portland Handicap winner Matinee. Their dam Harlequinade, who won over a mile and a quarter, comes from the same family as the 1962 Champion Hurdle winner Anzio. Nomadic Way, a small, lengthy horse, acts on any going. *B. W. Hills.*

NOM DE FORT 5 gr.g. Belfort (FR)–French Strata (USA) (Permian (USA)) [1989/90 16m^{6} 16f 20m^{6}] sparely-made gelding: poor novice hurdler: acts on firm and dead going. *R. C. Spicer.* 78

NOMELAP 5 b.g. Palemon–Coronation Heath (Coronation Year) [1989/90 17m a16g^{pu} 16f^{pu} 16h^{5} 16m^{pu} 18f^{pu}] lengthy, shallow-girthed gelding: of little account: has whipped round at start. *P. Butler.* —

NO MORE THE FOOL 4 ch.g. Jester–Prima Bella (High Hat) [1989/90 17f^{3} 17f^{2}] fair middle-distance performer on Flat, winner several times in 1990: made much of running when 10 lengths second to Deb's Ball in 5-runner juvenile hurdle at Cartmel in May: reportedly finished lame 2 days earlier. *J. Berry.* 87

NON CONSTAT (USA) 6 b.h. Vaguely Noble–Jamila (Sir Gaylord) [1989/90 16d 17f a18g a20g^{5}] lightly-raced winning hurdler: best effort of season on second start: refused to race third outing (trained until after then by T. Kersey): visored in 1988/9, blinkered last time out. *R. Thompson.* — §

NONE SO WISE (USA) 4 ch.g. Believe It (USA)–Nonesuch Bay (Mill Reef (USA)) [1989/90 16g 16g* 16f^{3}] workmanlike gelding: placed over 1¾m on Flat: always prominent when winning novice hurdle at Windsor in March by a head from Careless Kiss: fair third behind Deltic at Wolverhampton later in month: takes a good hold. *R. Akehurst.* 101

NONE TOO DEAR (USA) 8 gr.g. Caro–Service Compris (USA) (Real Value (USA)) [1989/90 16d 16d 20g^{6} 20d^{2}] leggy, sparely-made gelding: inconsistent handicap hurdler: 6 lengths second to Holy Joe at Chepstow in March: stays 2½m: best form with give in the ground: suited by waiting tactics: looks a difficult ride: blinkered last 3 outings in 1985/6, usually visored nowadays. *G. B. Balding.* 112

NON PERMANENT 4 b.g. Niniski (USA)–Perma Fina (Nonoalco (USA)) [1989/90 16m^{4} 16d* 16s^{6} 20g^{2} 16d^{3} 16d^{pu}] leggy, sparely-made gelding: won 1¼m selling handicap on Flat in October: sold out of A. Scott's stable 16,000 gns Newmarket Autumn Sales: won novice hurdle at Sedgefield in January: placed at Edinburgh and Market Rasen afterwards: stays 2½m: acts on dead going: claimer ridden all bar fourth and last starts. *P. A. Blockley.* 98

NONSTOP 11 ch.g. Nonoalco (USA)–Fast Motion (Midsummer Night II) [1989/90 c16m^{pu}] big gelding: poor chaser: pulled up only outing of season (September): form only at around 2m: goes well on top-of-the-ground: sometimes wears blinkers. *T. W. Donnelly.* c— —

NONSUCH HERO 6 ch.m. Leander–Karella (FR) (Salvo) [1989/90 19m^2]
well beaten in NH Flat race: 33/1, never dangerous when 15 lengths second to Our 77
Survivor in 12-runner novice event at Taunton in November on hurdling debut. *P. J. Jones.*

NONSUCH PALACE 6 b.g. Glint of Gold–Starlight Roof (USA) (Northern
Dancer) [1989/90 18f^3 22m^{pu} 20v^4 18s] stocky gelding: selling hurdler: should 82
stay beyond 2½m: probably acts on any going: sold 750 gns Ascot February Sales.
N. R. Mitchell.

NO ONE TO BLAME 8 gr.g. Roselier (FR)–San Remi (Chamier) [1989/90 **c120**
c25s* c25d^F c25m^4 c24d* c26m^2 c24g* c22m^3 26m^{pu}] leggy, lengthy gelding: —
fair chaser: won handicaps at Plumpton in December, Ludlow in March and
Market Rasen in April: broke down in handicap hurdle in June: stays 25f: acts on
heavy going and good to firm. *N. J. Henderson.*

NO PAY RISE 7 b.g. Faraway Times (USA)–Melfio Miss (Town Crier)
[1989/90 20d^{pu} 16f] big, leggy, plain gelding: second foal: half-brother to a winner —
in Belgium by Music Boy: dam, poor plater, stayed 7f: no sign of ability 2 novice
hurdles in March. *E. J. Alston.*

NO POLITICS 10 b.m. Politico (USA)–Frockham Brae (No Argument) c73
[1989/90 c20g^4 c24m^{pu}] sparely-made mare: poor novice hurdler/chaser and —
winning point-to-pointer. *Capt. T. A. Forster.*

NO RANSOM 10 ch.g. Royal Captive–Crepitus (Suki Desu) [1989/90 c20g^{pu} c—
21s] lengthy, workmanlike gelding: winning hurdler: very stiff task last time out —
(February): pulled up in novice chases: acts on any going. *D. J. Wintle.*

NO REBASSE 8 b.g. Over The River (FR)–Good Surprise (Maelsheachlainn) c—
[1989/90 18d^6 c21d c25g c25d^6 25d] compact, workmanlike ex-Irish gelding: —
brother to staying hurdler Concert Paper and half-brother to winning staying
chaser Good Waters (by Paddy's Stream): dam winning Irish hurdler/point-to-pointer: poor novice hurdler/chaser: ran in snatches fourth start. *Mrs S. Armytage.*

NORE HILL 5 ch.g. Town And Country–Hat Hill (Roan Rocket) [1989/90 16g^F
16s^{pu} 16m 16f^2 16m 16m^5 16f* 16m^6 19h^3 17h^2] small, lightly-made gelding: 81
selling hurdler: bought in 3,800 gns after winning at Taunton in April: best at
around 2m: probably acts on any going: visored last 4 starts, usually blinkered
previously. *R. Brotherton.*

NO RESPONSE 5 ch.m. Connaught–Ritratto (Pinturischio) [1989/90 F12g
16g^{pu} 20d^{pu}] small mare: ninth foal: half-sister to a winner on Flat by Workboy —
and a winner in Algeria by Mandrake Major: dam never ran: no sign of ability:
blinkered in selling hurdle second start. *G. P. Kelly.*

NORFOLK WIND 5 b.m. Windjammer (USA)–Mabella (Julio Mariner)
[1989/90 20g] first foal: dam, of little account on Flat, half-sister to several —
winners: backward, tailed off in novice hurdle at Sedgefield in February. *E. R. Heseltine.*

NORHAM CASTLE 7 b.g. Scott Joplyn–Gay Amanda (Counsel) [1989/90
18f^{pu} 16f^{pu} 16f^2 16m^{pu}] tall, workmanlike gelding: only sign of ability over hurdles 59
when second of 3 finishers in selling handicap at Plumpton in October (amateur
ridden): maiden point-to-pointer. *R. R. Ledger.*

NORMAN CONQUEROR 5 br.g. Royal Fountain–Constant Rose (Confusion) [1989/90 F16f* F16m^4] workmanlike gelding: third foal: half-brother to 2
poor animals: dam won 4 times over 1¼m at 4 yrs: favourite, won NH Flat race at
Newbury in March by 7 lengths from Miss Enrico: stayed on steadily when 9¾
lengths fourth of 20 behind Going On in well-contested similar event at Liverpool
following month: yet to race over hurdles or fences. *T. Thomson Jones.*

NORMHURST 4 ch.g. Lucky Wednesday–Bronze Princess (Hul A Hul)
[1989/90 16d^{pu} 16d 16v^{pu}] sparely-made gelding: half-brother to winning hurdler —
Boschendal (by Orange Bay): modest performer on Flat, winner over 11f in
September: no worthwhile form in novice hurdles: has looked none too keen. *C. Tinkler.*

NORQUAY (USA) 5 ch.g. Arctic Tern (USA)–Godetia (USA) (Sir Ivor)
[1989/90 16f^3 16d* 16g^2 16m* 16s^F 16g 16v^2 16v^2] close-coupled, rather 106
lightly-made gelding: moderate miler on Flat: won selling hurdles at Market
Rasen in November (bought in 8,000 gns) and Uttoxeter in December (handicap,
bought in 12,000 gns): runner-up subsequently in claimer at Haydock and novice
handicap at Ayr: likely to prove best at around 2m: best form on heavy going:
suited by waiting tactics. *N. Tinkler.*

NORSE IMP 4 b.f. Impecunious–Norsemen's Lady (Habat) [1989/90 17g^{pu}]
fourth foal: half-sister to fair staying hurdler Norstown (by Town And Country): —
dam poor maiden: tailed off when pulled up in juvenile hurdle in November. *R. J.
Holder.*

NORTHANTS 4 b.g. Northern Baby (CAN)–Astania (GER) (Arratos (FR))
[1989/90 16m^{2} 16d^{3}] compact gelding: brother to winning hurdler Eskimo Mite: 116
fair but temperamental middle-distance performer on Flat: length second to
Sartorius, pair well clear, in juvenile hurdle at Leicester in January: eased once
beaten when distant last of 3 finishers to Sayyure in quite valuable juvenile event
at Cheltenham later in month. *Mrs L. Piggott.*

NORTH BRIGADE 10 ch.g. Northfields (USA)–Brigata (Brigadier Gerard) c—
[1989/90 c22m c26f^{ur}] rather angular ex-Irish handicap hurdler/chaser: modest —
form in point-to-points in Britain: tailed off in Seagram Fox Hunters' at Liverpool
in April: stays 3m: probably acts on any going: broke blood vessel fourth start
1988/9. *J. C. Collett.*

NORTHERN ALLIANCE 6 ch.g. Northfields (USA)–Plight (Pieces of
Eight) [1989/90 16s 20v 16v* 16v^{4} 21d] sparely-made gelding: quite modest stayer 87
on Flat (has looked a difficult ride): sold out of G. Lewis' stable 2,700 gns
Newmarket September Sales: won conditional jockeys selling hurdle at Plumpton
in January (no bid): creditable fourth in novice handicap at Folkestone following
month: form only at 2m: acts on heavy going. *A. Moore.*

NORTHERN BARRY 6 ch.g. Northfields (USA)–Yankee Lady (Lord Gayle
(USA)) [1989/90 16m 16m* 16m] workmanlike gelding: won novice handicap 90 §
hurdle at Stratford in May: sweating, ran moderately next time: best form at 2m:
acts on good to firm ground: usually blinkered prior to last 2 starts: has looked
ungenuine. *J. C. McConnochie.*

NORTHERN BRAVE 4 ch.c. Mill Reef (USA)–Sharpina (Sharpen Up)
[1989/90 16g^{2} 16d^{3} 16g^{2} 16d^{4}] close-coupled, rather sparely-made colt: modest 94
1½m maiden on Flat: sold out of H. Thomson Jones's stable 15,000 gns
Newmarket Autumn Sales: modest form in juvenile hurdles: seemed unsuited by
slowly-run race last outing: likely to stay beyond 2m: blinkered last 2 starts. *N.
Tinkler.*

NORTHERN HALO 9 ch.g. Northfields (USA)–Halomata (Hallez (FR))
[1989/90 16f 21m^{6} 18g^{pu} 16f 16f 18f^{6} 16f^{5}] small, lightly-made gelding: handicap —
hurdler: has lost his form (favourite for seller final outing): stays 2½m: acts on
hard going (well beaten on heavy): best visored: trained until after sixth start by
A. Chamberlain. *G. A. Ham.*

NORTHERN IMAGE 4 ch.f. Northern Tempest (USA)–Charlotte's Image
(Towern) [1989/90 17f^{pu} 16h^{F} 16d^{ur} 16f^{pu} a16g] small, plain filly: of little account. —
R. G. Frost.

NORTHERN LION 7 br.g. Northfields (USA)–Pride of Kilcarn (Klairon)
[1989/90 16d 16g 16s^{pu} 18g^{5} 18v^{6} 18d a18g* 18f^{2}] half-brother to several winners, 104
including staying chaser Bold Acclaim (by Persian Bold): dam lightly-raced
half-sister to St Leger and Irish Derby winner Sodium: won over 1½m on Flat in
1987: won novice hurdle at Southwell in February by 25 lengths: second of 8 in
handicap at Kilbeggan in May: stays 2¼m: trained until after sixth start by J.
Fowler. *M. J. Grassick, Ireland.*

NORTHERN MEADOW 9 b.g. Northern Value (USA)–Babaville c**104** +
(Meadsville) [1989/90 c27f^{4} c24f^{2} c26m* c24h* c24d^{4} c24f^{ro} c26m^{6}] angular, —
workmanlike gelding: won point-to-point in March, and hunter chases at Carlisle
in April (maiden event by 20 lengths from Bay Bridge) and Kelso in May (beat sole
opponent Cheerie Chief 2½ lengths): would also have won at Hexham on sixth
start but for taking wrong course approaching last: raced too freely final outing:
stays well: acts on hard going (ran moderately on good to soft). *S. Chadwick.*

NORTHERN RAIN 4 ch.g. Ballacashtal (CAN)–Summer Rain (Palestine)
[1989/90 16f^{F} a16g^{6} 16g] neat gelding: plating-class performer at up to 1m on Flat: —
little sign of ability over hurdles, including a seller: sold 1,600 gns Ascot May
Sales. *C. N. Allen.*

NORTHERN RULER 8 br.g. Rolfe (USA)–Sanandrea (Upper Case (USA))
[1989/90 24m 25g 24d^{pu} a22g^{6}] small, lightly-made gelding: handicap hurdler: no —
worthwhile form in 1989/90: stays 3m: acts on heavy going: has worn blinkers. *R.
Thompson.*

NORTHERN SOCIETY (USA) 7 b.g. Norcliffe (CAN)–Te Ve Society c—
(USA) (Te Vega) [1989/90 c20d^{pu}] leggy gelding: modest staying maiden on Flat:

fair point-to-pointer in 1989: bit backward when pulled up in hunter chase at Newbury in February, but raced prominently for some way and gave indication of possessing ability. *Peter Scott.*

NORTHERN WARRIOR 4 b.c. Tender King–Dance Away (Red God) [1989/90 16g3 16fpu] compact colt: placed at 7f on Flat: third in juvenile hurdle at Kempton in October: dead. *Mrs J. Pitman.* 81

NORTH HOLLOW 5 b.g. Tyrnavos–Philigree (Moulton) [1989/90 16g 16g4] leggy gelding: poor maiden on Flat: easily better effort in claiming hurdles when 4 lengths fourth behind Sleepline Royale at Uttoxeter in May. *D. McCain.* 82

NORTHLANDS WAY 5 ch.g. Orchestra–Nessie B (Star Gazer) [1989/90 aF16g4 16g 16v 16s 16g] leggy, lengthy gelding: half-brother to winning chaser Farmlea Boy (by Kemal): dam maiden on Flat and over hurdles in Ireland: fourth in NH Flat race at Southwell in December: of little account over hurdles. *D. J. Wintle.* —

NORTH LANE 13 b.g. Dusky Boy–Carlow Smile (Sunny Streak) [1989/90 c26m3 c24m3 c25g2 c27s3 c30v* c30vur] medium-sized gelding: fair chaser nowadays: won handicap at Chepstow in January by 2½ lengths from Dercander: looked likely winner until unseating rider 2 out in John Hughes Grand National Trial (Handicap Chase) on same course in February: suited by a test of stamina: acts on firm going but revels in the mud: suited by forcing tactics: makes a mistake or two. *M. C. Pipe.* **c119** —

NORTHUMBRIA 11 b.g. High Line–By Command (March Past) [1989/90 25m] tall, workmanlike gelding: poor novice hurdler: winning chaser: needs testing conditions at 2½m and stays well: probably acts on any going. *H. Alexander.* c— —

NORTON'S COIN 9 ch.g. Mount Cassino–Grove Chance (St Columbus) [1989/90 c24g6 c16g c20d2 c20d3 c26f*] **c168**

'Racing's a funny old game', some never tire of telling us. But the legions of supporters and admirers of Desert Orchid must have been among those who found it hard to see the joke as the 100/1-outsider Norton's Coin pulled off the biggest surprise in Cheltenham Gold Cup history, beating odds-on Desert Orchid into third place in front of a record crowd that had assembled in expectation of that horse's winning steeplechasing's blue riband event for the second successive year. The victory of ex-point-to-pointer Norton's Coin—he won by three quarters of a length from Toby Tobias with Desert Orchid four lengths further back—was achieved in record time for the course and distance. The Gold Cup was run at a blistering gallop throughout on abnormally firm ground for the time of year and the winner's time of 6m 30.90sec was more than four seconds inside the previous best, set by Dawn Run on firmish ground in the same race four years earlier. The first six in the latest Gold Cup all finished inside Dawn Run's time. Regular readers will know that we don't regard a course-record time as having any particular significance—a fast time usually means no more than conditions were ideal for the setting up of a fast time. That

Tote Cheltenham Gold Cup Chase, Cheltenham—
Norton's Coin (centre) is almost up with Toby Tobias, as Desert Orchid can do no more

certainly applies to the latest Gold Cup. Norton's Coin's time was fast, very fast, but most of the times at the Festival meeting were fast. Ten of the eighteen winners set time records, some of them by exceptional margins including the National Hunt Challenge Cup winner Topsham Bay (over seventeen seconds inside the four-mile chase record on the old course), the Coral Golden Hurdle winner Henry Mann (over nine seconds under the three-mile-one-furlong record for the old hurdle course), the Ritz Club National Hunt Handicap Chase winner Bigsun (over eight seconds below the new-course record for three miles one furlong) and the Sun Alliance Novices' Hurdle winner Regal Ambition (almost six seconds below the old-course record for two and a half miles). As in the Gold Cup a number of other runners in most of the events won by the record setters finished the course inside the previous best time, indicating the exceptionally fast conditions.

Norton's Coin made dramatic improvement in the second half of the 1988/9 season, putting up his two best performances at Cheltenham where he pulled off a surprising victory in the South Wales Showers Mira Silver Trophy, a conditions event, at the April meeting after coming eight lengths second to the 66/1-shot Observer Corps on heavy ground in the Cathcart at the Festival meeting. The Cathcart was Norton's Coin's only defeat in his last four races that season, his other victories coming in handicaps at Bangor and Newbury. He was summed up in *Chasers & Hurdlers 1988/89* thus: 'He has a good turn of foot which should see his winning more races in handicap company in 1989/90—he begins the season on a fair mark'. In an unorthodox campaign, Norton's Coin reappeared in the King George VI Rank Chase on Boxing Day (finishing thirty-nine lengths last of six to Desert Orchid at 33/1), then reverted to two miles in the Victor Chandler Handicap at Ascot (ninth of ten). His best run of the season before the Gold Cup came at Cheltenham at the end of January when he ran Willsford (received 10 lb) to a length in the Lechlade Handicap Chase over two and a half miles, jumping soundly and staying on strongly. Norton's Coin started favourite for the Harwell Handicap at Newbury in February on his only subsequent outing before the Festival meeting but managed only third, beaten quickly in the home straight, to Fu's Lady and One More Knight. He was reported by his trainer to have returned slightly amiss. Apparently, the Cathcart Challenge Cup had been earmarked as Norton's Coin's long-term Cheltenham objective and by the time his connections realised that the horse wasn't qualified (the race is restricted to first- and second-season chasers nowadays) the most obvious alternative, the Mildmay of Flete Handicap, had closed.

So it was that Norton's Coin lined up against Desert Orchid and a field that also included the dual Welsh National winner Bonanza Boy, the up-and-coming Toby Tobias, the Irish Gold Cup winner Nick The Brief and two horses who had finished second in a Cheltenham Gold Cup, Yahoo and Cavvies Clown. Cavvies Clown gave a moody display at the start and was very slowly away, jumping the first twenty-five lengths or more adrift. Desert Orchid made the running, pressed nearly all the way by the 20/1-shot Ten of Spades who ran a fine race and was in the lead at the last open ditch, six from home, from Desert Orchid, with Toby Tobias and the patiently-ridden Norton's Coin both close up and moving well; just behind, Pegwell Bay, Yahoo and Bonanza Boy were starting to feel the pace, but Cavvies Clown was beginning to get into the picture, staying on well, though still with a lot to do. Desert Orchid was back in front again at the third last but when he was forced wide by the tiring Ten of Spades on the home turn Toby Tobias seized the initiative and held a narrow lead over Desert Orchid and Norton's Coin at the second last where the beaten Ten of Spades fell. The writing was on the wall for Desert Orchid jumping the final fence which Norton's Coin took almost upsides Toby Tobias, both jumping it well. The very forcefully-ridden Norton's Coin produced a strong burst on the flat to overtake the similarly game Toby Tobias in the closing stages, the victory soured a little by the fact that the winner returned badly marked, his rider McCourt receiving a three-day suspension for using his whip 'with a degree of severity which injured his horse'. The other finishers were well strung

Mr S. G. Griffiths' "Norton's Coin"

out behind third-placed Desert Orchid: Cavvies Clown came fourth (less than twelve lengths behind the winner), Pegwell Bay fifth, the only Irish-trained challenger Maid of Money sixth, Yahoo seventh and Bonanza Boy eighth (Nick The Brief was pulled up after a circuit).

Norton's Coin (ch.g. 1981)	Mount Cassino (b 1970)	Varano (b 1962)	Darius
			Varna II
		Fusilade (b 1961)	High Treason
			Arquebuse
	Grove Chance (ch 1977)	St Columbus (ch 1967)	Saint Crespin III
			Lovely Lady II
		Spotty Bebe (ch 1967)	Credo
			Bebe Royale

The general amazement with which Norton's Coin's Gold Cup victory was greeted was shared by his owner-trainer Sirrell Griffiths, a three-horse permit trainer from Nantgaredig near Carmarthen—'Like anyone else I thought Desert Orchid would win. Milking the cows this morning, I worked out that with a bit of luck we might be third'. At a time when the upper echelons of Flat-racing in particular seem increasingly to be the almost-exclusive domain of a number of wealthy owners, Norton's Coin's success should give hope to everyone who is in racehorse ownership, or breeding, in a small way. If Norton's Coin's Gold Cup victory itself strained credulity to the limits, then the same thing can surely be said of his breeding. He is the product of a mating arranged by his owner-trainer who stood the sire Mount Cassino and owned the unraced dam Grove Chance. Mount Cassino, no better than a fairly useful handicapper from a mile to a mile and a quarter, was operated on for a wind infirmity and was sold as a five-year-old at the end of his racing days for only 700 guineas at the Newmarket Autumn Sales: he covered mostly ponies and cobs during a fairly short career at stud (he was put down because of laminitis in 1983). Griffiths' mare Grove Chance—'Was it £425 or £475 I paid for her? Not very much anyway'—was one of only a few thoroughbred mares covered by Mount Cassino. She was sold, carrying Norton's Coin, to a neighbouring farmer Mr G. P. Thomas, who is officially credited with breeding Norton's Coin. Norton's Coin, the only foal produced by Grove Chance, a daughter of the top-flight hurdler St Columbus (sire of Grand National winner Maori Venture), was bought back by Mr Griffiths—reportedly for £4,800—after he had developed into a useful performer 'between the flags' for Mr Thomas, winning four point-to-points and a hunter chase, improving in each of his three seasons' racing. The game Norton's Coin is usually held up to make the most effective use of his turn of foot but he needs strong handling in a finish and showed marked improvement once he started to receive professional assistance (Dunwoody rode him in four of his last five races in 1988/9 and Davies was on board in the Cathcart). The lengthy Norton's Coin acts on any going. He appeared to walk away feelingly after the Gold Cup and wasn't seen out again, reportedly being confined to his box for several weeks afterwards. *S. G. Griffiths.*

NORTON WARRIOR 7 gr.g. King of Spain–Sylvanecte (FR) (Silver Shark) [1989/90 c16g3 c16g5 c16m5] workmanlike gelding: quite a useful hurdler: modest novice chaser: jumped deliberately when soundly beaten last 2 starts: stays 2½m: acts on heavy going. *M. H. Easterby.* c98 —

NORWICH CASTLE (USA) 6 b.m. Sir Ivor–Raininsky (USA) (Nijinsky (CAN)) [1989/90 16g6 16dF 16s 16s6 16f] leggy, sparely-made mare: novice hurdler: below her best in 1989/90: acts on soft going. *F. Jordan.* 83

NOSTRESS 5 b.g. Camden Town–Not To Worry (USA) (Stevward) [1989/90 a20gpu] sparely-made gelding: first foal: dam poor staying maiden on Flat: jumped sketchily, tailed off when pulled up 2 out in novice hurdle at Southwell in November: sold privately 1,900 gns Doncaster January Sales. *R. Brandon.* —

NO SWEAT 11 b.g. Ashmore (FR)–Phantasmagoria (Le Haar) [1989/90 c26fpu] rather sparely-made gelding: winning hurdler/point-to-pointer: no sign of ability in steeplechases: pulled up, reportedly lame, in May: should stay 2½m: acts on any going with possible exception of heavy. *Miss S. Barraclough.* c— —

NOTA-PENNYLESS 8 b.m. New Member–Penny-A-Look (Don't Look) [1989/90 16d 21vpu] sparely-made mare: second foal: dam won point-to-point: no sign of ability in novice hurdles. *R. J. Hodges.* —

NOT EASY 10 ro.m. Warpath–Virginia (Pirate King) [1989/90 c24f3 c21g5] workmanlike mare: selling hurdler and novice chaser: placed in point-to-points prior to finishing well beaten in novice handicap chases: stays well: best form with plenty of give in the ground: sometimes ridden by 7-lb claimer: inconsistent: sketchy jumper of fences. *W. A. Stephenson.* c— —

NOT QUITE A LADY 11 b.m. Ascertain (USA)–Really True (Metropolis) [1989/90 c24f5 c27fro c24f3 c25f6] point-to-pointer, winner 6 times in 1990: well beaten in hunter chases: ran out after iron broke second start. *C. Heaton.* c—

NOTRE CHEVAL 11 b.g. Weavers' Hall–Polar Point (Arctic Prince) [1989/90 c25gpu c25s5 c27spu c25dF c24g c28g c26dpu] neat gelding: winning hurdler/chaser: no worthwhile form for a long time. *J. Honeyball.* c— —

NOT SO SHY 5 b.m. Star Appeal–Nanushka (Lochnager) [1989/90 16d5 16g 16g3] workmanlike mare: modest middle-distance performer at 3 yrs: best effort over hurdles when 1¾ lengths third behind Logamimo in maiden event at Edinburgh in January: headstrong and likely to need a sharp 2m: claimer ridden. *Miss L. C. Siddall.* 88

NOTTA POPSI 9 ch.g. Nearly A Hand–Swaynes Lady (St Alphage) [1989/90 24mpu] leggy, narrow, short-coupled gelding: winning hurdler: successful in novice chase in 1988: pulled up lame when next seen out in October: suited by 2½m and more: best form on a sound surface. *J. L. Spearing.* c— —

NOUGAT RUSSE 9 b.g. Sweet Story–Natasha VI (Blue Cliff) [1989/90 c21dpu c26vpu c25mpu c25f3 c24f3] tall, workmanlike gelding: placed in 2 point-to-points in 1988: blinkered and ridden by 7-lb claimer when third in novice chases at Wolverhampton and Worcester in March: stays 25f: acts on firm ground. *N. A. Twiston-Davies.* c84

NOVA LAD 6 ch.g. Andy Rew–Safe 'n' Sound (Good Investment (USA)) [1989/90 a16g^{2} a16g^{3} a16g^{3} a16g* a20g^{3}] leggy gelding: won novice handicap hurdle at Southwell in April: ran creditably over 2½m on same course later in month. *P. J. Bevan.* **97**

NOW AND THEN 5 ch.g. Over The River (FR)–Lady Rois (Prince Rois) [1989/90 F16d F17d] half-brother to winning hurdlers Anois Is Aris (by Frisky Ruler) and Skygrange (by Al Sirat), latter also successful over fences: dam well beaten in 2 maiden hurdles in Ireland: behind in NH Flat races in February and March: yet to race over hurdles or fences. *Mrs S. A. Bramall.*

NO WAY BWANA 7 b.g. Hasty Word–Stormation (Compensation) [1989/90 16f^{pu}] strong, close-coupled gelding: poor form in novice hurdles: stays 2½m: blinkered last 2 starts (pulled up each time). *M. C. Pipe.* —

NO WAY JOSE 6 b.m. Sunyboy–Metaxa (Khalkis) [1989/90 18g^{6} a18g^{5}] close-coupled, sparely-made mare: no worthwhile form over hurdles. *D. M. Grissell.* —

NUMBER CRUNCHER 5 ch.g. Orchestra–I'm No Saint (St Chad) [1989/90 F16s^{3}] half-brother to 1982 Irish 2-y-o 9f winner Saint Simbir (by Simbir) and winners in France and Italy: dam poor Irish maiden: backward, moved poorly to post prior to finishing 5½ lengths third of 25 behind Cache Fleur in NH Flat race at Warwick in February: yet to race over hurdles or fences. *S. Mellor.*

NUMERATE 11 b.g. Paddy's Stream–Flying Music (Little Buskins) [1989/90 c24m^{ur} c24f^{3} c22m^{5} c27f^{2} c20f^{3} c20f^{2} c20m^{3} c21m^{ur} c20s^{5} c20g^{4} c20d^{5} c24f^{4} c20f^{6} c20m^{pu}] tall, close-coupled gelding: winning chaser: very much on the downgrade nowadays: unlikely to stay 25f in testing conditions: acts on any going: suited by waiting tactics: isn't one to trust. *P. Davis.* **c94** d —

NUNS JEWEL 4 ch.f. Julio Mariner–Nunswalk (The Parson) [1989/90 16g^{6} 17g^{3} 17d^{3} 20g^{3} 20m^{4} 20v 17v^{ur} a20g] small, compact filly: third foal: half-sister to winning selling hurdler Nuns Royal (by Royal Boxer): dam, winning hurdler/chaser, stayed at least 2½m: modest plater over hurdles: stays 2½m: seems unsuited by heavy ground: often claimer ridden: swerved and unseated rider seventh start. *J. M. Bradley.* 75

NUNS LITTLE ONE 5 ch.m. Celtic Cone–Nunswalk (The Parson) [1989/90 F12m^{3} 16g^{5} 22g^{2} 22m^{6} 20g^{F} 17d^{3} 20g^{2} 16v^{6} a20g^{4}] small, angular mare: novice selling hurdler: creditable fourth in non-seller at Lingfield in February: best form at 2½m to 2¾m on good ground: blinkered eighth start. *J. M. Bradley.* 72

NUNS ROYAL 6 ch.m. Royal Boxer–Nunswalk (The Parson) [1989/90 16s^{pu} a24g^{pu}] sparely-made mare: selling hurdler/novice chaser: no form for a long time: acts on heavy going: claimer ridden: sometimes blinkered. *R. T. Juckes.* c— —

NURSE'S NIECE 6 b.m. Sallust–Tranquil Love (Ardoon) [1989/90 17v^{pu} 16v 17d] compact mare: seems of little account. *Mrs J. G. Retter.* —

NUTT'S CORNER 8 b.m. Cantab–Welcome Corner (Welcome News) [1989/90 c20s^{F}] workmanlike ex-Irish mare: fourth foal: sister to an Irish point-to-point winner: dam, runner-up in 2 point-to-points, behind in NH Flat race and both outings over hurdles: winning point-to-pointer: slipped up only outing over hurdles: led until falling seventh in novice hunter chase at Uttoxeter in February. *Mrs A. B. Garton.* c— —

O

OAKEN 9 b.g. Connaught–Syringa (Set Fair) [1989/90 c24m^{2} c24d^{F} c25f* c24g^{2} c25g^{F} c24d^{2}] tall, close-coupled gelding: fair chaser: won 2-runner race at Catterick in November: stayed 3½m: acted on any going: made mistakes: dead. *Denys Smith.* **c117** x —

OAKGROVE 8 gr.g. Hot Grove–Blades (Supreme Sovereign) [1989/90 c20d^{5} c24d^{5} c26f^{2}] robust, good-bodied gelding: novice hurdler: winning point-to-pointer/steeplechaser: good second to Polar Glen in hunter chase at Fontwell in May, leading to 2 out: stays 27f: probably acts on any going: inconsistent: moderate jumper. *E. Knight.* **c88** x —

OAKHURST LAD 9 b.g. Paper Cap–Flying Court (Pallard Court) [1989/90 c20v^{2} c25f^{pu}] very lightly-raced winning point-to-pointer: 15 lengths second to Wheel Tapper in maiden hunter chase at Folkestone in February. *Roy Trigg.* c85

OAKLANDS GREY 8 gr.m. Grey Ghost–Sweet Vixen (Derek H) [1989/90 c20dF c25gpu c20sur c16d c25g c20f5] plain mare: novice hurdler/chaser: no worthwhile form. *Miss S. Williamson.* c— —

OAKLEY HOUSE 11 b.g. Menelek–Arctic Rock (Arctic Slave) [1989/90 c21spu c24s* c22mF c24g2] strong gelding: winning hurdler/chaser/point-to-pointer: led from the second, setting slow pace and quickening after last to win hunter chase at Haydock in March by 2½ lengths from Ready Steady: ½-length second to Eastern Destiny in similar event at Bangor following month: stays 3m: acts on any going: has worn blinkers. *C. Coxen.* c**108** —

OASIS 4 ch.f. Valiyar–Emaline (FR) (Empery (USA)) [1989/90 16fsu 16m6 18m5 16spu a16gpu 16f2 17h3 17m* 17h2] rather leggy filly: well beaten on Flat: bought out of R. Smyth's stable 2,100 gns Ascot July Sales: won maiden hurdle at Newton Abbot in May by 12 lengths: second to easy winner Deltic in juvenile event at Devon & Exeter later in month: best at around 2m on a firm surface: sold out of J. Baker's stable 1,800 gns Ascot April Sales after fifth start. *Mrs J. Wonnacott.* 88

OBAS GIRL 5 b.m. Mansingh (USA)–Chinese Princess (Sunny Way) [1989/90 16mF 16f 20g 16m4 16gpu] small mare: poor novice selling hurdler: pulled up lame last start: best form in blinkers. *J. C. Fox.* 63

OBEE FAST 6 ch.m. Dubassoff (USA)–In Confidence (Most Secret) [1989/90 a16g6] smallish, good-quartered mare: poor novice selling hurdler: form only on top-of-the-ground. *N. R. Mitchell.* —

OBELISKI 4 b.g. Aragon–Pasha's Dream (Tarboosh (USA)) [1989/90 16g4 16d6 16g* 17g* 16d3] angular, rather sparely-made gelding: won 1¼m seller and good second in 1½m handicap in 1989 (goes well on soft ground): successful in novice hurdle at Wolverhampton and juvenile event at Doncaster in January: eased once beaten when good third behind Royal Square in Chatteris Fen Hurdle at Huntingdon following month: will stay 2½m: looks a difficult ride. *M. H. Tompkins.* 116

O B JOYFUL 4 b.f. Jester–Our Bernie (Continuation) [1989/90 17h4] leggy filly: fifth living foal: half-sister to sprint winners Tauber (by Taufan) and Camps Heath and Kreigspiel (both by Ahonoora): dam runner-up 3 times at up to 1m in Ireland: remote fourth in juvenile selling hurdle at Devon & Exeter in October: sold 2,500 gns Ascot May Sales. *J. H. Baker.* —

OBSERVER CORPS 9 b.g. Celtic Cone–Listen Here (No Argument) [1989/90 c20spu c20mpu c20dF] strong, close-coupled gelding: put up a very useful performance when winning Cathcart Challenge Cup Chase at Cheltenham on only start in 1988/9: burly first 2 outings of 1989/90: claimer ridden, led 3 out but fell next in handicap won by Fingest at Ayr in April: stayed 2½m: acted on heavy going: dead. *J. A. C. Edwards.* c— —

OCCAMIST (USA) 5 ch.g. Diesis–Solo Naskra (USA) (Naskra (USA)) [1989/90 16m6 16g* 16g5 a16g6 16m 17m6 16m] small, sparely-made gelding: won selling hurdle at Hereford in November (bought in 5,200 gns): ran poorly last 4 starts. *C. C. Elsey.* 84 d

OCEAN LINK 6 gr.g. Cunard–La Chatelaine (Border Chief) [1989/90 F16g 16m 21fF 24m 22m2] leggy, sparely-made gelding: second foal: dam, poor maiden point-to-pointer, sister to top-class chaser The Laird and half-sister to useful point-to-pointer Sir Kay: 50/1, first sign of ability over hurdles when 2 lengths second to Super Trix in conditional jockeys novice handicap at Stratford in May. *G. R. Prest.* 79

OCEAN ROGUE 9 b. or br.g. Scallywag–Ocean Rock (Rockavon) [1989/90 c20sF c20mpu a24gF 24dpu a24g3 a24g3 20m 24f5] rangy gelding: poor novice hurdler: well beaten last 2 starts: stays 3m: blinkered final outing. *W. Clay.* c— 77

OCEAN THIEF 5 b.g. Zambrano–Tillside Brig (New Brig) [1989/90 22dpu] lengthy gelding: well beaten in NH Flat races: tailed off when pulled up after seventh in novice hurdle at Stratford in December. *C. F. Grant-Ives.* —

OCEANUS 9 b.g. Julio Mariner–Princess Zena (Habitat) [1989/90 c20gpu c24d c21d c24m* c24g4] leggy, lightly-made gelding: handicap hurdler: first form in novice chases when beating Camionnage 5 lengths in 4-runner event at Wetherby in May: suited by a distance of ground: best form on top-of-the-ground: blinkered final outing 1985/6. *J. Mackie.* c89 —

OCHEEKOBEE 11 b.g. Dubassoff (USA)–Bay Rambler (Wrekin Rambler) [1989/90 c20f4 c20f6] ex-Irish gelding: won NH Flat race in 1986 and point- c— —

to-point in 1988: poor novice hurdler/steeplechaser: has worn a tongue strap: trained by H. Cleary until after first outing. *G. A. Ham.*

OCKLEY 4 ch.g. Tolomeo–Santita (Charlottown) [1989/90 16m*] compact gelding: showed some ability at 2 yrs but well beaten on Flat in 1989: led 2 out and 86 p
mistake last when winning juvenile hurdle at Market Rasen in September by a head from Watershed: looked likely to improve but wasn't seen out again. *N. A. Gaselee.*

OCKY'S FLIER 6 bl.g. Aban–Ceile (Galivanter) [1989/90 17m^{ur} 17g^{5} 16d^{3}] c—
leggy gelding: best effort over hurdles when close third in novice event at 84 ?
Stratford in November: no worthwhile form over fences: has been blinkered: sweated up second start. *N. Kernick.*

ODYN PRINCE 4 br.g. Andy Rew–Silver Water (Wolver Hollow) [1989/90 17f^{pu} 16m^{4} 17f^{2} 16f^{pu}] angular gelding: maiden on Flat: second in juvenile selling 71
hurdle at Newton Abbot in October: ran poorly when next seen out 7 weeks later: races keenly: sold 900 gns Ascot February Sales. *B. Stevens.*

OF COURSE 5 b.g. Crash Course–Blue Bleep VII (pedigree unknown) [1989/90 18d^{6} 20d 16d] angular non-thoroughbred ex-Irish gelding: has scope: 89
fourth foal: half-brother to winning Irish chaser No Grandad (by Strong Gale): dam unraced: successful in point-to-point and NH Flat race in 1988/9, when trained by P. Madden: favourite, sixth in novice event at Kelso in February on hurdling debut: well beaten subsequently, jumping none too fluently last start. *W. A. Stephenson.*

OFF AND ON 4 b.f. Touching Wood (USA)–Off The Reel (USA) (Silent Screen (USA)) [1989/90 16d^{4} 16g] small, workmanlike filly: half-sister to fairly useful —
hurdler Urizen (by High Line): appears of little account on Flat: sold out of W. Jarvis' stable 950 gns Newmarket Autumn Sales: little sign of ability in juvenile hurdle and a novice event at Kelso. *I. Semple.*

OFFICER GROWLER 6 br.g. Mandalus–Deep Cristina (Deep Run) [1989/90 16g^{pu} 16f^{F} 16m^{5} 16m^{pu}] lengthy gelding: winning hurdler: below his best 83
only completed start of 1989/90: acts on dead going: blinkered final outing: wore brush pricker on near-side second start. *Mrs D. Haine.*

OFFICER'S GLORY 12 b.g. Ragapan–Officer's Fort (Even Money) [1989/90 c—
c25f^{4}] sturdy gelding: winning hunter chaser in Ireland: successful in 3 point-to-points in Britain in 1990: finished lame when well beaten in hunter chase at Cheltenham in May. *Mrs J. P. Mayes.*

OFFICIAL LADY 6 b.m. Official–Kick About (Rugantino) [1989/90 20v] lengthy, sparely-made mare: behind in NH Flat races: sweating, tailed off in —
novice hurdle at Chepstow in January. *S. G. Griffiths.*

OFFICIAL RECEPTION (USA) 4 b.g. State Dinner (USA)–Petals 'n Lace (USA) (Restless Native) [1989/90 16g* 16v^{6} 16f] workmanlike, good-quartered 126

Golden Eagle Novices' Chase, Ascot—
Okeetee (breastgirth) and Power Punch dispute the lead at the last open ditch, ahead of the only other runner Going Gets Tough

Irish gelding: sixth foal: half-brother to 4 winners in USA: dam won 10 races at up to 9f in USA: 1½m winner on Flat: won quite valuable juvenile hurdle at Fairyhouse in December by 1½ lengths from Dail Eireann: sixth of 8 to Bank View in minor hurdle at Leopardstown 2½ months later: well beaten in Daily Express Triumph Hurdle at Cheltenham (blinkered). *M. A. O'Toole, Ireland.*

OFF THE BRU 5 b.g. General Ironside–Amelieranne (Daybrook Lad)
[1989/90 F13d F16v 20m 20g 24g^{6}] strong, workmanlike gelding: will make a 73
chaser: brother to Claim To Fame and half-brother to Annabrook Lass (by Laurence O), both winning hurdlers in Ireland: dam winning chaser at up to 3m in Ireland: ninth in 2½m maiden hurdle at Perth in April, only worthwhile form: pulled hard when well beaten over 3m next time. *Mrs S. C. Bradburne.*

OF THAT ILK 10 b. or br.m. Dynastic–Shine Bright (Scintillant) [1989/90
22g^{4} 20g 24g 24d^{F}] small mare: selling hurdler: best effort of season when fourth 81 ?
in non-seller in March: stays 2¾m but seemingly not 3m: probably acts on any going: suitable mount for a claimer. *Mrs J. C. Weir.*

OGENDEBA 10 b.g. Abednego–Shady Tree (Three Wishes) [1989/90 c24d c**100**
c29g^{pu} c25s^{2} c26g^{3} c30v^{pu} c26v^{pu}] sturdy gelding: carries condition: handicap —
chaser: best effort of season when third of 4 finishers at Folkestone in December: suited by stiff test of stamina: acts on heavy going. *P. G. Bailey.*

OH DEAR 8 b.m. Paico–Coniscliff Bell (Rise'n Shine II) [1989/90 24s 22v^{6}
20s^{pu}] rather leggy mare: runner-up in Irish NH Flat races: has shown ability in —
novice hurdles, but was well beaten in 3 handicaps in 1989/90: blinkered last start. *J. J. O'Neill.*

OH FATHER 8 b.g. The Parson–Dial-A-Bird (Falcon) [1989/90 c21f^{3} 18h^{pu} c—
c20m^{5} c25g^{pu}] leggy gelding: poor novice hurdler/chaser: looked none too keen — §
on occasions: sometimes blinkered, and was visored once: dead. *T. P. McGovern.*

OHILL SKY 6 b.g. Skyliner–Royal Inheritance (Will Somers) [1989/90 c16m^{pu} c—
c27d^{pu} c16m^{F} c16m^{r} c16g^{5} c21g^{6}] workmanlike gelding: poor plater over hurdles —
in 1987/8: of little account over fences. *T. Kersey.*

OH MOTHER 5 b. or br.m. Uncle Pokey–Chumolaori (Indian Ruler) [1989/90 c—
F16m 16d 16d 20g 20g c17g] lengthy mare: no sign of ability in novice hurdles —
(visored last 2 starts) and a novice chase. *R. Tate.*

OH SO NIPPY 4 b.g. Martinmas–Listen To Me (He Loves Me) [1989/90 17g^{pu}
20g^{pu}] leggy, sparely-made gelding: third foal: half-brother to winning selling —
hurdler Out On A Flyer (by Comedy Star): dam best at 5f: behind when pulled up in juvenile hurdles. *C. L. Popham.*

OH SO RIPE 5 ch.m. Deep Run–Perished (Arctic Chevalier) [1989/90 16m^{pu}
16d 16m] second reported foal: dam unplaced in Irish NH Flat races: tailed off in —
novice hurdles. *P. J. Jones.*

OH WHY 8 ch.g. Laurence O–Why Ask (Deep Run) [1989/90 c24v^{2} c24d^{pu} c**102**
c22f* c24f^{2} c24f^{2} c25f*] workmanlike gelding: won hunter chases at Nottingham —
in March and Hereford (by 5 lengths from Walk In Rhythm) in May: stays well: acts on any going. *W. A. Stephenson.*

OIL FEVER 10 ch.g. Deep Run–Ivernia (Golden Vision) [1989/90 17g c21v^{F} c—
17d^{pu} c17v^{F} 26v^{pu} a20g^{pu}] rangy gelding: winning hurdler in Ireland: no sign of —
ability in Britain, including over fences: blinkered last 2 starts: dead. *Mrs J. Wonnacott.*

OISINS CASTLE 11 b.g. Bluerullah–Japonica (Vic Day) [1989/90 c16g^{3} c20d* c**87**
c20d^{4} c16d^{pu}] leggy ex-Irish gelding: novice hurdler: handicap chaser: jumped —
well and made all at Hexham in December: stays 2¾m: acts on dead going: has worn a crossed noseband: sold 1,200 gns Doncaster Spring Sales. *J. H. Johnson.*

OKAZ (USA) 5 b.g. Temperence Hill (USA)–She Is Gorgeous (USA) (Drop
Volley) [1989/90 16g 20g 20g 16m^{5} 16f* 19m* 20g*] sparely-made gelding: no 103 p
worthwhile form on Flat at 3 yrs when trained by R. Hannon: in good form late in season and won selling hurdle at Ludlow (bought in 5,000 gns) and novice handicaps at Hereford and Worcester: stays 2½m: acts on firm ground: claimer ridden last 2 starts: has further improvement in him. *G. B. Balding.*

OKEETEE 7 b.g. Raise You Ten–Peppardstown (Javelot) [1989/90 16g* 22v^{5} c**113** p
20d^{4} c20m* c20s* c20m* c20f*] leggy gelding: won novice hurdle at Kempton in 103
November: made all in novice chase at Doncaster in January, and made most when successful in similar events at Sandown in February (jumped left) and March and in 3-runner Golden Eagle Novices' Chase at Ascot later in March: jumped slightly to his right throughout when beating Going Gets Tough 3 lengths at Ascot: stays

Coot Handicap Chase, Newcastle—Old Applejack dominates throughout

2¾m: acts on firm and dead going: has won when sweating: should win more races over fences. *C. P. E. Brooks.*

O K KID 5 b.g. Sonnen Gold–Jeldi (Tribal Chief) [1989/90 16m^{pu} 17g^{pu}] lengthy gelding: quite modest form over 5f at 2 yrs: tailed off when pulled up in selling hurdle at Worcester and novice hurdle (blinkered) at Devon & Exeter early in season. *W. G. M. Turner.* —

O K NURSE 6 gr.m. Mandrake Major–Grisma (Grisaille) [1989/90 17h^{3} 20g^{6} 16m] workmanlike mare: seems of little account. *J. Mulhall.* —

R.O.A. Rendlesham Hurdle, Kempton—33/1-shot Old Dundalk (No. 2) starts to get the better of Sprowston Boy

O K SON 11 b.g. Oaksam–Dear Liz II (Dear Gazelle) [1989/90 c16h2 c21f4 c16fpu c18g3 c16dpu c18m2 c16g3] workmanlike gelding: poor winning chaser: headstrong and best at up to 2¼m: probably acts on any going: usually jumps boldly: has run well for inexperienced rider: sold 1,150 gns Ascot February Sales. *M. J. Bolton.* c85

OLD APPLEJACK 10 ch.g. Hot Brandy–Windfall VI (Master Owen) [1989/90 c20g3 c24m* c24g4 c25g* c28g3 c20d* c24m3 c22m c20f*] lengthy, angular gelding: quite a useful chaser: had a good season and won handicaps at Newcastle (2), Catterick and Wetherby, beating Blazing Walker by 4 lengths on last-named course in April: effective at 2½m and stays well: acts on firm and dead going: has won for a claimer: jumps well: genuine. *J. H. Johnson.* c**127**

OLD DEER PARK 4 b.c. Blakeney–Hurry On Honey (Be Friendly) [1989/90 16g5 a16g4 16g2 16s4 20v6] sparely-made colt: maiden on Flat: in frame in juvenile hurdles, showing poor form: favourite when well beaten in 2½m seller: ridden by claimer. *D. H. Barons.* 79

OLD DUNDALK 6 b.g. Derrylin–Georgiana (Never Say Die) [1989/90 24g* 25m 24f3] workmanlike gelding: lightly-raced hurdler, evidently difficult to train: showed much improved form when 33/1-winner of 7-runner ROA Rendlesham Hurdle at Kempton in February, quickening run-in to beat Sprowston Boy 2½ lengths: well beaten in Waterford Crystal Stayers' Hurdle at Cheltenham but finished creditable third behind Battalion in Keith Prowse Long Distance Hurdle at Ascot, both in March: suited by 3m: seems to act on any going: looked none too keen first start 1988/9, blinkered next outing. *D. J. G. Murray-Smith.* 148

OLD DUTCH HOLBORN 5 ch.g. Derrylin–Gay City (Forlorn River) [1989/90 16d5 16g3 16g* 16m6 16d2 16d2 a20g3 a18s3 16g 16m5 a16gpu] sturdy gelding: won claiming hurdle at Wolverhampton in November: below that form in 105 d

Mr M. V. Walsh's "Old Dundalk"

varied company, including selling, subsequently: pulled up lame last start: unlikely to stay much beyond 2m: trained first 2 starts by K. Cunningham-Brown, third by Miss S. Wilton and next 6 by C. Beever. *Miss S. J. Wilton.*

OLDE CYDER 5 b.g. Royal Boxer–Cider Drinker (Space King) [1989/90 17m 17m4] small gelding: of little account. *J. M. Bradley.* —

OLD KILPATRICK 5 b. or br.g. Touching Wood (USA)–Mother Brown (Candy Cane) [1989/90 16s] short-backed gelding: fair form over hurdles in 1988/9: stays 2½m: acts on heavy going: wore blinkers after first start in 1988/9: ran poorly without blinkers on reappearance in January. *M. C. Pipe.* —

OLD MALTON 8 ch.g. Whitstead–Bridestones (Jan Ekels) [1989/90 20g 25g] compact gelding: fairly useful hurdler at his best: showed little in 1989/90: stayed 25f: acted on soft going: dead. *M. H. Easterby.* —

OLD MORTALITY 4 b.g. Uncle Pokey–Speed Trap (Pontifex (USA)) [1989/90 F16g] fourth foal: dam fair but inconsistent sprinter: behind in NH Flat race at Perth in May: yet to race over hurdles. *R. Allan.*

OLD NICK 9 ch.g. Goldhill–Madam Nick (Espresso) [1989/90 c24vur c25g* c26f2] c**140** —

Old Nick was a rare 'find' in a somewhat humdrum hunter chase season. He ran a tremendous race on only his third outing over steeplechase fences to divide Call Collect and West Tip in the Christies Foxhunter Chase at Cheltenham in March, beaten only two lengths. On previous displays there seemed a strong possibility that Old Nick wouldn't get very far round Cheltenham—he'd dived through the first fence at Ayr then taken chances in winning unchallenged at Catterick. However, he jumped boldly and, in the main, accurately there. He set a good pace on the outside for a long way, came back strongly when Border Burg made an attempt to dominate the race, and battled it out with the two other principals from the third last (where he made a mistake). When hard pressed at the last he went badly left across West Tip, losing ground to Call Collect in the process, but he kept on well in pursuit of the winner up the hill. In view of his inexperience over fences Old Nick should have further improvement in him if he keeps sound. Reportedly Old Nick's hurdling career was ended by his breaking down. He raced for Arthur Stephenson and Jack Hanson in his younger days, winning three novice events for the latter in the 1985/6 season. For his present stable he has also done well in point-to-points: he won two in 1989, including the Grimthorpe Gold Cup at the Middleton, and another in February in the latest season.

Old Nick (ch.g. 1981)	Goldhill (br 1961)	Le Dieu d'Or (bl 1952)	Petition
			Gilded Bee
		Gilded Rose (b 1950)	Midas
			Lovely Rosa
	Madam Nick (ch 1966)	Espresso (ch 1958)	Acropolis
			Babylon
		Nicky B (ch 1959)	Rockefella
			Coastal Star

Old Nick's dam Madam Nick was a small, Flat-racing mare; she won twice over seven furlongs as a two-year-old and was placed numerous times at up to a mile and a half in the next two years. She was nothing out of the ordinary as winners go, and she produced nothing out of the ordinary apart from Old Nick, unless the Belgian listed winner Slidam (by Super Slip) counts as one; another of her foals, Corbitts For Gold (by Al Sirat), is a point-to-point winner. The next two dams were both minor Flat winners who also produced winners, a couple out of Nicky B—Young Nick and Bam Bam—over hurdles. Old Nick, a strong, short-backed gelding, stays three and a quarter miles well. He went to Cheltenham with a reputation for being a soft-ground performer (all his hurdling wins were on soft or heavy), but he obviously acts on firm. *Mrs H. Bell.*

OLD VIRGINIA 4 ch.g. Burslem–Molly's Party (Be My Guest (USA)) [1989/90 16m 16d3 16gur 16m* 18m3 16g* 16f4] sparely-made ex-Irish gelding: 103
second foal: dam unraced: poor maiden on Flat (has been tried in blinkers): won juvenile hurdle at Plumpton in November and 4-runner juvenile handicap at

Stratford in April: stays 2¼m: acts on good to firm ground: trained first 2 starts by K. Prendergast. *R. Akehurst.*

OLIVERS HILL 7 b.g. Decent Fellow–Walnut Hill (Pry) [1989/90 16f^{3} 16f^{2} 20m^{4}] close-coupled, workmanlike ex-Irish gelding: third foal: half-brother to 80
winning Irish hurdler/chaser Wheeler Dealer (by Little Buskins): dam won over hurdles in Ireland: won NH Flat race in 1988/9: successful in 1½m amateurs event on Flat in 1989: placed behind Cosmic Ray in novice hurdles at Hexham in March and Wetherby (led until close home) in April: seems not to stay 2½m: acts on firm ground. *T. P. Tate.*

OLLIE-P 5 ch.g. Red Sunset–Rosemary's Rhythm (Gala Performance (USA)) [1989/90 18f^{pu} 16f 20g^{pu} 16v^{pu}] workmanlike gelding: of little account. *M. J.* —
Haynes.

OLNISTAR (FR) 4 b.f. Balsamo (FR)–Star Light (FR) (Val De Loir) [1989/90 16g^{ur} 16g^{2} 16d* 20g^{2} 16d^{3} 16s* 16m^{4} 20f] small, leggy, lightly-made filly: 118
half-sister to several winners, notably good hurdler/chaser Sabin du Loir (by Go Marching): dam French 11f winner: won juvenile hurdles at Nottingham in December and Hereford (unimpressive) in March: put up improved performance to finish 10 lengths fourth to Forest Sun in Waterford Crystal Supreme Novices' Hurdle at Cheltenham later in March, staying on very strongly: tailed off in quite valuable novice event at Liverpool final start: stays 2½m: best form on a sound surface. *D. Nicholson.*

OLVESTON (NZ) 6 b.g. Sea Anchor–Statira (NZ) (Imperial March (CAN)) [1989/90 F16f* 20d^{3} 16g^{4} 16g^{2} 21d^{pu} 16m^{3} 17d* 17m^{2} 17m^{2}] workmanlike 116
gelding: unbeaten in 3 NH Flat races, including one at Newbury in October: won novice hurdle at Newton Abbot in March by 4 lengths from Crystal Bear, leading from third: ridden by 7-lb claimer, excellent second to Doc's Coat in handicap on same course final start: best at around 2m: acts on good to firm and dead ground: has pulled hard. *D. H. Barons.*

Mrs Claire Smith's "Olnistar"

Heidsieck Dry Monopole Handicap Chase, Liverpool—
One More Knight (left) finishes strongly to catch Seagram.
Between them are Rapier Thrust (noseband) and Killone Abbey

OLYMPIC CHALLENGER 6 b.g. Anfield–Calibina (Caliban) [1989/90 16f*
17f^{3} 16s a18g^{4}] neat ex-Irish gelding: quite modest handicapper on Flat, probably 91
stays 11f: won novice claiming hurdle at Leicester in November: ran creditably
next outing, moderately last 2: stays 2¼m: acts on any going: wears blinkers. *J.
Mackie.*

OLYMPUS REEF 5 b.g. Main Reef–Elizabethan (Tudor Melody) [1989/90
16h^{4} 16m 16m^{2} 16g^{6} 16d^{2} 20g^{4} 16m^{4} 20g^{3} a16g* a20g^{2} a24g* a20g* a20g^{3} 20f^{pu} 90
16m] good-topped gelding: no worthwhile form on Flat: won novice hurdles at
Southwell (handicap) and Lingfield prior to winning handicap on latter course in
February: showed ability in sellers previously: stays 3m: yet to race on very soft
going, acts on any other: claimed out of B. Curley's stable £5,405 after first start,
out of J. Colston's stable £5,400 after fifth. *P. Davis.*

ON DEPOSIT 4 b.g. Gorytus (USA)–Papsie's Pet (Busted) [1989/90 16g 16g
16s^{5} 16d* 16s^{3} 16s* 16v* 16f] leggy Irish gelding: third foal: brother to a winner in 129
Sweden: dam, lightly-raced 9f winner in Ireland, half-sister to numerous winners,
including Irish hurdler Taurean: placed over 1½m on Flat: won juvenile hurdles at
Naas, Thurles and Punchestown (beat Stigon ½ length in Baltinglass Hurdle) in
second half of season: well beaten in Daily Express Triumph Hurdle at
Cheltenham: acts on heavy going: blinkered last 5 starts. *E. J. O'Grady, Ireland.*

ONEFACE 6 b.m. General Ironside–Green Face (Green Shoon) [1989/90 16s^{pu}
16s^{pu} 16f 24m 19m^{pu}] smallish ex-Irish mare: first foal: dam placed in —
point-to-point in Ireland: dead-heated for fourth in NH Flat race in 1988/9: no sign
of ability in novice hurdles: blinkered last 2 starts. *M. Oliver.*

ONE FOR THE NORTH 5 b.g. Old Jocus–Coach Tour (News Item) [1989/90
F16d^{4} F16v F16g^{2}] half-brother to 2½m hurdle winner Cigarillo (by Royal
Smoke): dam never ran: 7 lengths second to Jodami in NH Flat race at Kelso in
March: retained by trainer 12,000 gns Doncaster Spring Sales: yet to race over
hurdles or fences. *J. G. FitzGerald.*

ONE FOR THE POT 5 ch.g. Nicholas Bill–Tea-Pot (Ragstone) [1989/90 16g^{2}
16s* 16g^{2} 16v* 20s^{3}] small gelding: improved hurdler, winner of handicaps at Ayr 108 p
in December (novice event) and February: found little in between and on last start

(caught close home and finished around 2 lengths third behind Big White Chief at Haydock): suited by a strongly-run race at 2m but seems barely to stay 2½m in testing conditions: acts on heavy going: suited by waiting tactics: won 3 times at around 1½m on Flat in spring. *Mrs J. R. Ramsden.*

ONE FOR THE ROAD 7 gr.m. Warpath–Eternally (Ballymoss) [1989/90 c22f[ur]] ex-Irish mare: fifth living foal: sister to winning jumpers Auld Lang Syne and End of The Road: dam needed long distances: won NH Flat race and third in 2 maiden hurdles in 1988/9: would probably have finished second but for unseating rider 3 out in hunter chase at Nottingham in March: usually blinkered (including when successful). *Graham Burton.* c— p —

ONE GOOD TURN 4 b.g. Tyrnavos–Musical Princess (Cavo Doro) [1989/90 16g[5] 16g[6] 20g[F]] compact gelding: runner-up in 11f seller on Flat: poor juvenile hurdler. *D. Moffatt.* 74

ONE MORE KNIGHT 7 b.g. Roselier (FR)–Ballyadam Lass (Menelek) [1989/90 c20s[F] c20g[ur] c20g* c20d[2] c25m*] tall, close-coupled gelding: useful chaser: kept on well to beat Katabatic ¾ length in Fulwell Handicap Chase at Kempton in January: jumped sketchily, ridden entering straight but stayed on strongly to lead run-in when winning quite valuable Heidsieck Dry Monopole Chase (Handicap) at Liverpool in April by a length from Seagram: stays 25f: acts on heavy going and good to firm: takes a good hold: has worn a crossed noseband and a tongue strap. *Mrs I. McKie.* c**136** —

ONE OF THE LADS 8 ch.g. Decent Fellow–Medford Lady (Kabale) [1989/90 20f* 20f[pu]] smallish, workmanlike gelding: won 4-runner lady riders handicap hurdle at Sedgefield in September: pulled up, reportedly lame, following month: poor novice chaser: stays 2½m: acts on firm going: visored final outing 1988/9: usually amateur or claimer ridden. *B. R. Cambidge.* c— 76

ONE TO MARK 7 b. or br.g. He Loves Me–Markon (On Your Mark) [1989/90 20s[pu] 16g 16g 16d[pu]] lengthy, rather sparely-made gelding: winning hurdler: no worthwhile form in 1989/90: best at around 2m: acts on soft going: not a fluent jumper: headstrong and looks no easy ride. *R. A. Bennett.* —

ONEUPMANSHIP 5 ch.g. Derrylin–Lucky Janie (Dual) [1989/90 19m[F] 16s[3] 16d[2] 16s[bd]] smallish, leggy gelding: won NH Flat race in 1988/9: in lead and travelling best when falling 2 out in novice hurdle at Taunton in November: placed in similar events at Plumpton in December and Windsor in January (well clear of remainder when 3 lengths second to Midfielder): will stay 2½m: should win a novice hurdle. *D. R. C. Elsworth.* 110

ONE UP ONE DOWN 7 b.m. Shack (USA)–Good Opportunity (USA) (Hail To Reason) [1989/90 24m[pu]] half-sister to 1m winner Northern Chance (by Northfields) and winners in Italy and France: dam twice-raced half-sister to Bold And Brave, a very smart winner at up to 1m: tailed off when pulled up 3 out in novice hurdle at Chepstow in April. *J. D. Czerpak.* —

ON HIS OWN 7 br.g. Paico–Luvvy Duvvy (Levmoss) [1989/90 24m[2] 24m[5] 25f[2] 24d[pu] 22m[4] c25m[4] c24s[pu] a20g* a20g[2]] tall, leggy gelding: winning point-to-pointer: amateur ridden, made all in handicap hurdle at Lingfield in February: fourth in novice event at Towcester in November on chasing debut: stays 3m: acts on firm and dead going: has won for a 7-lb claimer. *N. R. Mitchell.* c73 98

ONLY FOR ME (USA) 7 b.g. Accipiter (USA)–Precious (USA) (Bold Lad (USA)) [1989/90 16g[pu] 16g[pu]] sturdy gelding: showed signs of ability in juvenile hurdle in 1986, but none in 2 novice events in 1989/90 (wore crossed noseband): jumps none too fluently: has failed to complete in point-to-points. *P. J. Hobbs.* —

ONLY JOKING 6 b.m. Balinger–Comical (Comedy Star (USA)) [1989/90 21f[6] 22f[4] 25m[pu] 21f] sparely-made mare: poor form over hurdles: blinkered last 3 starts. *Mrs A. Knight.* 55

ONLY TROUBLE 9 b. or br.m. Trasi's Son–Kadella (Kadir Cup) [1989/90 c20g[4] c20s[3] c25g[3] c20v[F] c24m c24m[6]] lengthy, rather plain mare: novice hurdler: modest chaser: very good seventh to Master Bob in valuable handicap at Cheltenham in March: well beaten final start: stays 3¼m: acts on heavy going and good to firm: sometimes amateur ridden, invariably at overweight: sometimes sweating and edgy in paddock: tends to make mistakes. *T. J. Houlbrooke.* c**100** + —

ON REFLECTION 8 b.g. Golden Love–Ballygannon (Light Thrust) [1989/90 c28m[4] c24g[5] c28g* c24d*] big, rather sparely-made gelding: has a round action: winning point-to-pointer: won 2 handicap chases at Nottingham in January, scoring by 12 lengths on second occasion: stays 3½m: yet to race on very firm c**102**

ground, acts on any other: blinkered last 2 starts: tends to jump to his left, and jumped none too fluently final outing. *K. C. Bailey.*

ON TAP 6 ch.g. Tap On Wood–Joshua's Daughter (Joshua) [1989/90 16g^2 16m* 16g^4 16f] strong, workmanlike gelding: will make a chaser: fair hurdler: made most when winning sponsored handicap at Newcastle in November: first race for 2½ months and favourite, well-beaten tenth of 17 finishers in valuable handicap at Cheltenham in March (lost place quickly at halfway but stayed on towards finish): unlikely to stay much beyond 2m: acts on good to firm ground. *M. H. Easterby.* 122

ON THE FIDDLE 7 br.g. Orchestra–Speed Writer (Saulingo) [1989/90 c20s] ex-Irish gelding: second living foal: dam unraced: runner-up only completed start in point-to-points: second of 4 in hunter chase at Downpatrick in 1989: soon well behind in maiden hunter chase at Sedgefield in February. *J. P. Seymour.* c–

ON THE HOOCH 5 ch.m. Over The River (FR)–Bit of Fashion (Master Owen) [1989/90 F13m^4 16g^{ur} 16m 16f^5 22g^5 18d^2 20d* 21f 20g^3 16f* 16g^3] close-coupled mare: second foal: half-sister to winning Irish jumper Aherlow Glen (by Le Bavard): dam behind in maiden hurdle in Ireland: won novice hurdles at Newcastle in February (mares race) and May (made most): should stay beyond 2½m: acts on firm and good to soft going: amateur ridden. *Mrs S. C. Bradburne.* 96

ON THE OTHER HAND 7 b.g. Proverb–Saltee Star (Arapaho) [1989/90 c16d^2 c18g^5 c22d^2 c19d^3 c16g* c18s* c20v^{pu} c22g c25d*] Irish gelding: first foal: dam unraced half-sister to dam of good staying chaser Righthand Man: fair winning hurdler: made all in novice chases at Leopardstown in January (beat Elfast 3 lengths) and February (Arkle Perpetual Challenge Cup): won Punchestown Festival Handicap Chase in April by short head from The Committee: stays 3m well: acts on soft going (possibly unsuited by heavy): quite useful. *J. E. Mulhern, Ireland.* c**132** –

ON THE ROCKS 4 ch.f. Julio Mariner–Cool Spirit (Hot Brandy) [1989/90 16s 20g^{pu}] half-sister to fairly useful stayer on Flat and over hurdles Wait And See (by Biskrah) and to winning staying chaser Rich Nickel (by Celtic Cone): dam never ran: well beaten in juvenile event and a seller over hurdles. *J. B. Sayers.* –

Arkle Perpetual Challenge Cup Chase, Leopardstown—On The Other Hand makes all

ON THE TWIST 8 b.g. Callernish–Irish Beauty (Even Money) [1989/90 c24g^2 c30s^{pu} c20d^5] angular gelding: winning chaser: bit backward, below his best when second in conditional jockeys handicap at Huntingdon in November (jumped sketchily): tailed off final start (December): suited by 3m and soft ground: reluctant to race second start in 1987/8: ridden by 7-lb claimer when successful. *G. A. Hubbard.* **c101** —

ONWARD AND UPWARDS 5 ch.g. Le Bavard (FR)–Westford (Hereford) [1989/90 F16g^3] second foal: dam, behind in point-to-point and a hunter chase in Ireland, is sister to a winning Irish point-to-pointer and half-sister to a winning hurdler: weak 10/1-chance, 11 lengths third of 18 to Le Bucheron in NH Flat race at Market Rasen in April: yet to race over hurdles or fences. *Mrs D. Haine.*

OOLAJAY 4 b.f. Sandhurst Prince–Airy Queen (USA) (Sadair) [1989/90 16f^{ur}] compact filly: half-sister to 4 winners, including fairly useful Irish 2-y-o winner Okanango (by Homeric): dam won at 2 yrs and 3 yrs in Italy: wearing crossed noseband, jumped badly (almost refused fourth) and was tailed off when pulled up between last 2 in juvenile hurdle at Sedgefield in September. *B. Gee.* —

OORAIN LASS 7 b.m. Lord Nelson (FR)–Little Shewalton (Fez) [1989/90 16g 22d^{pu} 16v^5 16d^{pu}] sparely-made mare: little form over hurdles. *T. Goldie.* —

OPAL GLEN 8 b.g. Kampala–Greek Opal (Furry Glen) [1989/90 c16d^{pu} c24s^{pu} c16g^{pu} c16d^5] smallish, plain gelding: seems of little account: jumped badly last 2 starts: blinkered last 3 outings. *B. Byford.* **cxx** —

OPAL SURPRISE 4 b.f. Royal Boxer–Opal Lady (Averof) [1989/90 16f a16g^6 16g^6 17d^{pu}] sparely-made filly: well beaten in seller at 2 yrs, only outing on Flat: only form in selling hurdles when sixth in conditional jockeys event at Ludlow third start. *J. M. Bradley.* 67

OPEN ALL HOURS 8 b.g. Martinmas–Land (Baldric II) [1989/90 16v^{pu}] compact gelding: winner over 1¼m on Flat: no sign of ability over hurdles, lightly raced. *R. Akehurst.* —

OPENING OVERTURE (USA) 4 b.f. At The Threshold (USA)–Rhine Queen (FR) (Rheingold) [1989/90 16f 16g] medium-sized filly: modest middle-distance maiden on Flat (claimed out of W. Jarvis' stable £8,568 in November): showed a little ability in juvenile hurdle at Warwick in December, but well beaten in claimer at Wolverhampton (favourite) following month. *C. R. Beever.* —

OPERATIC SCORE 6 ch.g. Kind of Hush–Grand Opera (Great Nephew) [1989/90 16f^3 16m^2 16f* 16m^4 22g a16g^2 a16g* a20s^5 16g* 16g 16m^2 16f^4 16m* 16f^3] compact gelding: improved handicap hurdler: won at Towcester in November, Lingfield in January, Fakenham in February and Plumpton in April: fair third at Taunton final start: best at around 2m: acts on firm ground and seems unsuited by very soft: runs the odd moderate race. *J. R. Jenkins.* 121

OPTIMISM FLAMED 7 b.g. Malinowski (USA)–Sea Swallow (FR) (Dan Cupid) [1989/90 16f^3 17f^3] close-coupled gelding: novice hurdler: 4½ lengths third behind Mill de Lease at Uttoxeter in September: visored, found nothing from 3 out following month: not one to trust. *C. J. Bell.* 82 §

OPTIMISTIC LADY 5 ch.m. Full of Hope–Red Lady (Warpath) [1989/90 16g^4 16g] leggy mare: poor novice selling hurdler: usually claimer ridden. *J. H. Johnson.* 57

OPTIMOSA 8 ch.g. Full of Hope–Wimosa (Mossborough) [1989/90 a18g c17d^{pu} c17f^{pu} 17h^{pu}] sparely-made gelding: of little account: blinkered last 2 starts. *J. E. Forte.* c— —

OPTIONAL CHOICE (USA) 6 b.g. Northern View–Muchisma (USA) (El Macho (USA)) [1989/90 16f^3 20f^2 20m^{pu} a20g^5 22g^{pu}] smallish gelding: novice hurdler: good second at Southwell in September: ran poorly afterwards: suited by 2½m: acts on firm ground: blinkered third start. *R. C. Spicer.* 90 ?

ORANGE KING 6 ch.g. Kings Lake (USA)–Jaffa (Right Royal V) [1989/90 16g 20m c20d^{pu}] tall, strong gelding: no worthwhile form over hurdles: tailed off when pulled up in hunter chase: sometimes blinkered: sold out of M. Naughton's stable 2,100 gns Doncaster November Sales after second start. *Mrs Sandra C. Oliver.* c— —

ORANGEY 6 br.g. Orange Bay–Venshoon (Hopeful Venture) [1989/90 25d 22g c20f^4 c25m^{pu}] sparely-made, angular gelding: placed in point-to-points in 1989: behind in novice hurdles and a hunter chase. *Mrs L. Clay.* c— —

ORBIS (USA) 4 b.c. Conquistador Cielo (USA)–Nicole Mon Amour (USA) (Bold Bidder) [1989/90 16s^{4} 16d^{4} 16s^{5} 16v^{2} 16v^{4} 20f 20m* 19d* 16m^{2} 135
16m^{4} 16d* 16g]

The Sun Alliance Novices' Hurdle at Cheltenham was a watershed in Orbis' first season over hurdles. Previously unsuccessful in five races in Ireland and apparently just a modest performer, Orbis, the only four-year-old in the field, showed much improved form to finish ninth of twenty-two behind Regal Ambition, beaten around twenty-five lengths. Orbis continued his progress when returned to Ireland. Within ten days of running in the Sun Alliance Hurdle he'd won a minor event at Leopardstown and a handicap at Naas, and a month later he was successful in the Guinness Trophy Champion Four-Year-Old Hurdle at Punchestown. The 1989 Guinness Hurdle had attracted four challengers from Britain including Royal Derbi, who in winning it put up the best performance by a juvenile that season. The latest running not only failed to attract any British challenger, it also failed to attract the top Irish juvenile Rare Holiday, who wasn't seen out over hurdles after winning the Daily Express Triumph Hurdle. Of those to have run in the Triumph Hurdle only Orbis' stable-companion Bally Rue, who'd finished ninth, was in the line-up at Punchestown. Bally Rue and the improving Rocket Dancer looked the chief dangers to Orbis who was sent off favourite at 7/4. Orbis, the pick of the paddock, unlike at Cheltenham where he'd been edgy and coltish, set such a strong gallop that he had most of his rivals in trouble a long way from home. Rocket Dancer was being ridden along when falling three out, which left the struggling Bally Rue in third place. At this stage only Pas de Mot threatened to make a race of it with the leader, but he began to come to the end of his tether soon after turning for home. Orbis was also beginning to tire, which wasn't surprising considering the gallop he'd set. However, responding most gamely to hard driving from the second last, Orbis never looked likely to be caught and he won by three lengths and the same from Jennycomequick and Only Great.

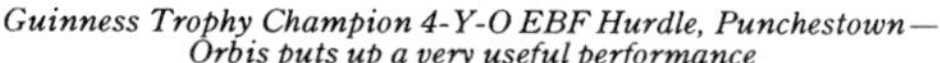

Guinness Trophy Champion 4-Y-O EBF Hurdle, Punchestown—
Orbis puts up a very useful performance

Mrs Catherine Shubotham's "Orbis"

The second and third, having been well outpaced, stayed on past tiring rivals in the straight and were almost certainly flattered by their finishing positions. Orbis had a stiffer task and ran a long way below his best in a handicap shortly afterwards, and it's reasonable to assume that he hadn't fully recovered from his hard race at Punchestown.

Orbis (USA) (b.c. 1986)	Conquistador Cielo (USA) (b 1979)	Mr Prospector (b 1970)	Raise A Native
			Gold Digger
		K D Princess (b 1971)	Bold Commander
			Tammy's Turn
	Nicole Mon Amour (USA) (b 1979)	Bold Bidder (b 1962)	Bold Ruler
			High Bid
		Kennelot (b 1974)	Gallant Man
			Queen Sucree

Orbis is the third foal of Nicole Mon Amour, who won twice at up to a mile and a quarter in the USA. Nicole Mon Amour, a half-sister to the Kentucky Derby and Belmont Stakes runner-up Stephan's Odyssey and to the Grade 1 Acorn Stakes winner Lotka, has produced two other winners by the Belmont Stakes winner Conquistador Cielo. Samerkand has been successful several times in the USA, while Cielamour has won over seven furlongs in Britain and at up to a mile and a half in Ireland, showing very useful form. Nicole Mon Amour's fourth foal Batzushka (by Danzig), has shown useful form at up to a mile over here. Orbis, successful himself over nine furlongs and eleven furlongs on the Flat as a three-year-old, and placed at up to a mile and a half since, has the makings of a smart handicapper over hurdles. A compact colt, he stays two and a half miles and acts on good to firm and dead ground. He was amateur ridden when gaining his first two wins over hurdles. *J. S. Bolger, Ireland.*

ORCHIPEDZO 5 ch.g. Le Moss–Jupiters Jill (Jupiter Pluvius) [1989/90 16s] angular gelding: tailed off in NH Flat races: took a good hold and made a couple of mistakes when behind in novice hurdle at Warwick in February. *R. Lee.* —

ORDER OF MERIT 5 b.g. Cut Above–Lady Habitat (Habitat) [1989/90 16h4 17h5 16gur 16fpu a16gpu] small, sturdy gelding: won 1¼m seller on Flat in 1989 (sold out of D. Elsworth's stable 6,400 gns): no sign of ability over hurdles, including in seller: pulled up feelingly in early stages of final start. *D. A. Wilson.* —

ORDER PAPER 5 b.g. Taufan (USA)–Lady of Surana (Shirley Heights) [1989/90 16s3 16g4 16v2] modest middle-distance handicapper on Flat, suited by plenty of give in the ground: in frame in novice hurdles, at Ayr in February finishing 15 lengths second to Clay County: suited by testing conditions at 2m and will stay further. *J. S. Wilson.* 97

OREGON TRAIL 10 b.g. Auction Ring–Oriental Star (Falcon) [1989/90 c19s3 c20gpu c20fpu c24d c20g4] sturdy gelding: smart and thoroughly game chaser in 1986/7: very lightly raced since: well below his best in 1989/90, jumping none too fluently: effective from 2m to 3m: probably acts on any going. *S. Christian.* **c111** —

ORIENTAL DREAM 6 ch.g. Northfields (USA)–Jenny (Red God) [1989/90 16m 16d5 16m3 21f6 16g 16g6 16m5 a18g6 a20g 17d4 17m3] sturdy gelding: novice hurdler: third in selling handicap at Newton Abbot final outing: swished tail and looked none too keen sixth start: form only at around 2m: acts on good to firm and soft going: has been tried in blinkers. *W. G. Morris.* 68 §

ORIENTAL EXPRESS 7 b.g. Whitstead–Miss Argyle (Mountain Call) [1989/90 20f 16g 16v 16s 16g6 16g 20s 16d5] leggy, lightly-made gelding: selling hurdler: poor form in 1989/90: suited by a good gallop over 2m and probably stays 3m: possibly unsuited by very firm ground, acts on any other. *Ronald Thompson.* —

ORIENTESSA 5 b.m. Don Roberto (USA)–Green Bay (FR) (Great Nephew) [1989/90 16f4] poor novice selling hurdler. *J. E. Long.* 58

ORIGAMI 5 ch.g. Horage–Demeter (Silly Season) [1989/90 16d5 16m] plain, sparely-made, dipped-backed gelding: fair fifth in slowly-run novice handicap hurdle at Hereford in November: ran moderately later in month and not seen out again. *William Price.* 87

ORLEANS SOUND 6 b.g. Duc d'Orleans–What A Performance (Gala Performance (USA)) [1989/90 16sF 16d 16g] angular, sparely-made gelding: well beaten on Flat and in novice hurdles. *S. Mellor.* —

ORPHAN FRANK 7 ch.g. Barley Hill–Franked (On Your Mark) [1989/90 c16gur 21g5 16g c16d c19f] small gelding: of little account: moderate jumper: trained until after third start by P. Allingham. *David Pritchard.* c— x —

ORSETT (USA) 4 ch.g. Our Native (USA)–Ornamental (USA) (Triple Crown (USA)) [1989/90 16d 16s a18g3 16m* 16g2 16g6] lengthy gelding: maiden on Flat: sold out of B. Hills's stable 10,500 gns Newmarket Autumn Sales: won conditional jockeys selling handicap hurdle at Huntingdon in April (bought in 3,900 gns): good second in novice handicap at Bangor later in month: best form at 2m: acts on good to firm going: sold 7,500 gns Ascot May Sales. *Dr J. D. Scargill.* 76

ORTY 5 b.g. Wolverlife–Diana's Choice (Tudor Music) [1989/90 16g] lightly-made gelding: lightly-raced novice selling hurdler: amateur ridden. *D. McCain.* —

ORWELL OPINION 8 gr.g. Roselier (FR)–Brief Summary (Lucky Brief) [1989/90 16s4 20d 20v] smallish ex-Irish gelding: first foal: dam unraced half-sister to several winners, including useful jumper Orwell Times: placed in NH Flat race in 1986: showed signs of ability all starts over hurdles, never placed to challenge final one. *R. O'Leary.* 78

OSRIC 7 b.g. Radetzky–Jolimo (Fortissimo) [1989/90 16m4 16fF 16g2 16g 16g2] sparely-made gelding: good hurdler: best effort of season when 2½ lengths second to Kribensis in Top Rank Christmas Hurdle at Kempton: subsequently ran respectably in The Ladbroke at Leopardstown (seventh behind Redundant Pal) and Bic Razor Lanzarote Handicap Hurdle at Kempton (led 2 out, caught near finish by Atlaal): easily best form at 2m with give in the ground: usually bandaged in front: takes a good hold. *M. J. Ryan.* 158

OTHET 6 b.g. Thatch (USA)–Hot Pad (Hotfoot) [1989/90 16gpu 16g 18s] medium-sized gelding: swished tail under pressure when successful in novice hurdle in 1988/9: no worthwhile form in 1989/90: likely to prove best at around 2m: acts on firm going. *M. D. I. Usher.* —

OTI (USA) 4 ch.c. Far North (CAN)–Shay Sheery (USA) (A Dragon Killer) [1989/90 19h* 17f*] workmanlike colt: brother to St Leger fourth Norwick: modest form at up to 1m at 2 yrs: sold out of G. Harwood's stable 10,000 gns Newmarket Autumn (1988) Sales: made most when winning novice hurdle at Taunton in April and selling hurdle at Cartmel (bought in 11,500 gns) in May: 99

easily better effort when beating Colonial Office 8 lengths in former: stays 19f. *M. C. Pipe.*

OTTERBURN HOUSE 6 b.g. Proverb–High Energy (Dalesa) [1989/90 F17m* 20g3 20d] rather leggy gelding: has scope: half-brother to winning jumpers Telemeter Gem (by Decent Fellow) and Button Your Lip (by Le Bavard), both of whom stay well: dam won over hurdles in Ireland: won NH Flat race at Carlisle in November: staying-on 6½ lengths third behind Remittance Man in novice hurdle at Doncaster in February: seemed unsuited by softer ground next time (eased once beaten and worth another chance): will stay 3m. *J. G. FitzGerald.* 95

OTTERBURN (USA) 4 b.c. Raise A Man (USA)–Summertime Lady (USA) (No Robbery) [1989/90 16s 16gF 16s 16mF 18f4] sparely-made colt: modest temperamental maiden on Flat: sold out of W. Haggas' stable 7,600 gns Newmarket Autumn Sales: poor novice over hurdles (well beaten in seller final outing): blinkered last 2 starts (reluctant to race on first occasion). *R. J. O'Sullivan.* 74 §

OUBLIER L'ENNUI (FR) 5 b.m. Bellman (FR)–Cassowary (Kashmir II) [1989/90 18f3 16m2 18f5 20g4 18g2 a16g* a20g2] leggy mare: handicap hurdler: won at Lingfield in January by 3 lengths from Disneyland: creditable second on same course following month: stays 2½m: acts on firm and dead ground: often ridden by claimer. *Miss B. Sanders.* 105

OUR DEADLY 5 b.g. Official–Miss Posy (Pitskelly) [1989/90 F16v* F16g 16gpu] ex-Irish gelding: first foal: dam won 6f seller at 2 yrs and placed in similar company over hurdles: placed in 2 point-to-points in 1989: won NH Flat race at Ayr in January: destroyed after pulling up in novice hurdle in March. *Mrs H. S. Wells.* —

OUR DESSA 7 br.m. Derek H–Jeanne du Barry (Dubassoff (USA)) [1989/90 c27gur 20g 25gpu] well beaten over hurdles: unseated rider fourth on chasing debut. *J. H. Johnson.* c— —

OUR FANDANGO 8 b.g. Gay Fandango (USA)–Azucena (Queen's Hussar) [1989/90 c20mpu c16fpu] sparely-made gelding: winning hurdler/chaser: no form in steeplechases in 1989/90, though won a point-to-point in May: acts on any going: best in blinkers: sold 2,500 gns Ascot May Sales. *R. Brotherton.* c— —

OUR FELLOW 8 br.g. Boreen (FR)–Suspicious Vulvic (Above Suspicion) [1989/90 c24gF c20g2 c26s* c20m2 c25dpu c32fpu] big, rangy ex-Irish gelding: fifth foal: dam unraced sister to very useful chaser Cavity Hunter: maiden point-to-pointer: jumped soundly when winning novice chase at Folkestone in January: made a couple of mistakes but finished clear of remainder when going down by 3 lengths to Okeetee in similar race at Doncaster in January: ran as though something amiss next outing: stays 3¼m: acts on soft and good to firm going. *D. J. G. Murray-Smith.* c**104**

OUR GINGER 6 ch.m. Le Johnstan–Summersoon (Sheshoon) [1989/90 a16g4] sparely-made mare: 2m novice selling hurdler: best effort when second on soft ground in 1988/9: never dangerous at Southwell in November. *Ronald Thompson.* 65

OUR HERO 7 ch.g. Posse (USA)–Blonda (Exbury) [1989/90 24mpu] leggy, sparely-made gelding: no form over hurdles. *P. Liddle.* —

OUR NOBBY 8 br.g. McIndoe–Fair Arctic (Bally Russe) [1989/90 c16g4 c20s* c20g6 c22mF] rather leggy, workmanlike gelding: led 2 out when winning handicap chase at Sandown in February by 2 lengths from Missing Man: ran poorly next outing: best form at up to 2½m: acts on any going: visored once. *M. Madgwick.* c**116** —

OUR PHIL 12 ch.g. Sandford Lad–Four Queens (Quorum) [1989/90 22d c27gpu] sturdy, dipped-backed ex-Irish gelding: poor maiden hurdler: won point-to-point in 1983 and third in hunter chase in 1984, but has run poorly since. *J. Parkes.* c— —

OUR SURVIVOR 6 b.g. Trimmingham–Lougharue (Deep Run) [1989/90 F16f* 20dpu 19m* 22d c20gur c21g 25m 24m 24mF] rangy ex-Irish gelding: will make a chaser: third foal: dam unraced: won 2 point-to-points and a NH Flat race in 1989: won novice hurdle at Taunton in November: no other worthwhile form over hurdles: in touch when unseating rider 5 out in novice handicap chase at Wolverhampton in January: tailed off in similar event next start: stays 19f (stiff tasks both completed starts over 3m): acts on good to firm ground: blinkered eighth start: has been mounted on track. *Miss H. C. Knight.* c— 94

OUR TILLY 7 b.g. Grundy–Chiparia (Song) [1989/90 18m4 16m] sparely-made, dipped-backed gelding: winning selling hurdler: lightly raced and little form of late: blinkered final outing (started slowly). *J. Colston.* —

OUR WHITE HART 10 br.g. Manado–Valiretta (USA) (Go Marching (USA)) [1989/90 21d 16f4 18f2 25f 21m* 19f2] small gelding: handicap hurdler/chaser: won over hurdles at Warwick in May: stays 21f (always behind over 3m): acts on any going: sometimes wears a hood or blinkers: takes a good hold: not one to trust implicitly. *K. C. Bailey.* c— 95 §

OUTCAST 6 b.g. Final Straw–Persian Market (Taj Dewan) [1989/90 16d3 16g3 a16g4 16g4 16s3 c16spu 20m2 16m4 18fpu] workmanlike gelding: poor novice hurdler: jumped none too fluently and was tailed off when pulled up in novice chase in March: probably stays 2½m and acts on any going: blinkered eighth outing: inconsistent. *A. Moore.* c— 88

OUTLAW 11 ch.g. Morston (FR)–Heathfield (Hethersett) [1989/90 c16dur] sturdy gelding: fairly useful chaser at his best: blundered sixth and unseated rider next only outing of season (December): best at 2m: probably acts on any going: successful with and without blinkers: sometimes jumps none too fluently: has done all his winning on left-handed courses: none too consistent. *J. A. C. Edwards.* c— —

OUT OF RANGE 7 b.m. Faraway Times (USA)–Namur (Amber Rama (USA)) [1989/90 16g6 16g 16d 16m6 20m2 16fur] leggy mare: quite a useful hurdler: best effort of season when length second to Sayparee in Martell Hurdle (Handicap) at Liverpool in April, leading briefly run-in: stays 2½m: acts on heavy going and good to firm: suited by waiting tactics: has won when sweating. *D. R. C. Elsworth.* 128

OUT ON A FLYER 6 b.m. Comedy Star (USA)–Listen To Me (He Loves Me) [1989/90 16f6 16f5 16m6 17mF 16f2 16f4 17h* 16h* 16m4] workmanlike mare: sprint handicapper on Flat: sold out of D. Elsworth's stable 2,000 gns Doncaster November (1988) Sales: attracted no bid after winning selling hurdles at Carlisle and Hexham in October: fourth in novice handicap on former course following month: pulls hard and suited by a sharp 2m: acts on hard ground: claimer ridden. *J. J. O'Neill.* 92

OUT RUN 4 gr.g. Nishapour (FR)–Shalara (Dancer's Image (USA)) [1989/90 17f*] successful at up to 1m at 2 yrs, but below form on Flat at 3 yrs when trained by R. Hannon (has worn blinkers): 6/5 favourite, very easy 20-length winner of 7-runner juvenile hurdle at Newton Abbot in July, drawing clear from 3 out: not seen out again. *M. C. Pipe.* 82 p

OUTSIDE EDGE 9 b.g. Kemal (FR)–Smooth Lady (Tarqogan) [1989/90 c30spu c30v c29s4 c24dpu] angular gelding: fair chaser: only worthwhile form of season when fourth behind Woodgate at Warwick in February: made mistakes and took little interest in second half of race next time: stays well: acts on heavy going: tends to edge left and race with his head rather high under pressure: bandaged all round second outing: to join M. Pipe. *D. J. G. Murray-Smith.* c**120** —

OUTSTANDING BILL 4 ch.g. Nicholas Bill–Hardwick Amber (Tanfirion) [1989/90 16g* 16m4 16g4 16m2 16g3 16g3] sparely-made gelding: has shown ability at up to 1½m on Flat: won juvenile hurdle at Sedgefield in November: in frame in similar events subsequently: will stay further: acts on good to firm ground: no battler. *J. M. Jefferson.* 95

OUTWOOD LASS 12 br.m. Most Secret–Birgeen (Bing II) [1989/90 19f4 16gpu 20gF 19gpu] sparely-made mare: lightly raced and no worthwhile form for a long time over hurdles: well beaten in 2 novice chases: usually wears blinkers. *B. K. Wells.* c— —

OUT YONDER 7 ch.g. Air Trooper–Modom (Compensation) [1989/90 20g] sturdy, angular gelding: winning hurdler: pulled up and dismounted only outing of season (November): evidently best at 2m (doesn't stay 3m): acts on heavy going: best in blinkers: has worn a severe bridle: looks a difficult ride. *W. G. R. Wightman.* —

OVERHEREOVERTHERE 7 ch.g. Green Shoon–Cool Madam (Master Owen) [1989/90 c21d4 c24g] big, rangy ex-Irish gelding: third living foal: half-brother to winning Irish hurdler Run Madam (by Deep Run): dam useful 2-y-o 6f winner in Ireland: winner of 4 point-to-points in Ireland when trained by T. Costello: in need of race and claimer ridden, not knocked about from 2 out when 15 lengths third behind Mr Gossip in novice chase at Towcester (carried head high) in December: tailed off in similar race later in month. *John R. Upson.* c**84**

OVER THE FIRS 7 ch.g. Over The River (FR)–Kincone Wexford VI (Shackleton) [1989/90 c16m3 c16g* c17h* c20g* 24g* c21g*] ex-Irish gelding: c**122** p 96 p dam placed in point-to-points in Ireland: second in point-to-point in 1987: won NH Flat race in 1988/9: not seen out until mid-April but had tremendous season: won amateur riders novice hurdle and a maiden chase at Perth, novice chase at Kelso and novice handicap chases at Uttoxeter and Market Rasen: best effort when beating Clares Own 12 lengths under 11-13 on last-named course: stays 3m: acts on hard ground: has further improvement in him and will go on to better things. *W. A. Stephenson.*

OVER THE ROAD 9 ch.g. Over The River (FR)–Legal Fortune (Cash And Courage) [1989/90 c24g c29d c29s3 c30v3 c29d6] workmanlike gelding: fair chaser: 11 lengths third to Sandicliffe Boy in John Hughes Grand National Trial (Handicap Chase) at Chepstow in February, fourth and best effort of season: very well suited by a good test of stamina: acts on heavy going: jumps none too fluently. *J. R. Upson.* **c120** —

OVER THE STYX 5 br.g. Over The River (FR)–My Dear Good Woman (Lucifer (USA)) [1989/90 F13d3 F16d2 F16v4 17m] first foal: dam never ran: in frame in NH Flat races: never-dangerous seventh in novice hurdle at Carlisle in April. *G. Richards.* — p

OVERT (USA) 5 b.m. Ben Fab (CAN)–Lady More Friendly (USA) (Villamor (USA)) [1989/90 20f 20m4 21m 20g 20g2 a20g5 21d2 20fF] angular, sparely-made mare: runner-up in claiming hurdles at Wolverhampton in December and Towcester (outstayed by Dominion Treasure) in February: has run in sellers: likely to prove best at distances short of 21f: acts on dead going. *Miss S. J. Wilton.* 75 +

OWEN 6 b.g. Pollerton–Princess Charmere (Tepukei) [1989/90 16m 16g6 16s5 c20fF 16m2 16m 22f5] handicap hurdler: second at Chepstow in May, easily best effort in 1989/90: still close up but beginning to weaken when falling 2 out in novice chase won by Dandy Minstrel at Plumpton in March: best form at around 2m: acts on heavy going and good to firm. *B. Smart.* c— 108

OWEN DUFF 11 ch.g. Paddy's Stream–Boolaben (Arctic Slave) [1989/90 c24m c24f5 c26f5] strong, compact gelding: winning point-to-pointer/hunter chaser: poor form in 1989/90: stays 3m: suited by top-of-the-ground. *Miss M. Furness.* **c81** —

OWEN SHERRY 13 b.g. Master Owen–Miss Raheeina (Kabale) [1989/90 c24g4] strong gelding: winning point-to-pointer: novice hunter chaser. *Mrs T. H. Hayward.* c—

OWEN SOMER 5 b.g. Tudorville–Floral Somer (Will Somers) [1989/90 F16m 16s] sparely-made gelding: first foal: dam winning hunter chaser: tailed off in NH Flat race in October when trained by J. Wales: behind in novice hurdle at Plumpton in December. *W. T. Kemp.* —

OWL CASTLE 7 b.h. Bold Owl–My Duty (Sea Hawk II) [1989/90 22m4] close-coupled horse: lightly-raced novice hurdler: stays 2¾m. *K. O. Cunningham-Brown.* 102

OWNERS VISION 10 ch.g. Owen Anthony–Proviso (Golden Vision) [1989/90 c20v5 c24fpu] leggy gelding: point-to-point winner: well beaten in hunter chases: pulled up and dismounted final start. *Mrs T. C. Betts.* c—

OXALIS 6 b.m. Connaught–Phlox (Floriana) [1989/90 16d 16f4 16gpu 16f] sturdy mare: second in NH Flat races and placed at up to 13f on Flat: sold out of G. Huffer's stable 1,300 gns Newmarket September Sales: only form over hurdles when fourth in minor event at Catterick in November: claimer ridden. *R. W. Dods.* 68

OXFORD PLACE 6 br.g. Derrylin–Garden Party (Reform) [1989/90 c20v3 c20d c20v3 c24g6] workmanlike gelding: winning hurdler: no worthwhile form over fences: doesn't stay 2½m: acts on dead going: heavily bandaged in front third outing. *Ronald Thompson.* c— —

OXNEAD 6 ch.m. Balinger–Blades (Supreme Sovereign) [1989/90 16m 16g 20f3] compact, workmanlike mare: third foal: half-sister to winning chaser Oakgrove and winning point-to-pointer Not So Sharp (both by Roan Rocket): dam, maiden plater, ran only at 2 yrs: last in a point-to-point: well beaten in novice hurdles. *M. Skinner.* —

OXSTALL'S LADY 6 b.m. The Brianstan–Charlotte Mary (Lauso) [1989/90 19s] small, sturdy mare: seems of little account as a hurdler. *M. F. Barraclough.* —

OXYMERON (USA) 6 ch.h. Temperence Hill (USA)–Luv Luvin' (USA) (Raise A Native) [1989/90 22m 20m a20g2 a20g2 a20g* a20gF a24g6] sparely-made horse: handicap hurdler: tenderly handled to lead close home when winning amateur riders event at Lingfield in January: stays 2½m (weakened 2 out 87 §

when tailed off over 3m): best form on good ground: often blinkered nowadays: usually amateur or claimer ridden: no battler. *K. C. Bailey.*

OYDE HILLS 11 br.g. Night Sky–My Affair (Hollybush Wonder) [1989/90 22v c26gpu] sturdy, close-coupled gelding: winning point-to-pointer/steeplechaser: has become very unreliable, and is as likely to refuse as not. *G. Richards.* c— § —

OYSTER POND 13 b.g. Martinmas–Masai Princess (USA) (Assagai) [1989/90 c20dpu c22mF] sturdy gelding: poor chaser/point-to-pointer nowadays: saddle slipped and rider lost irons on reappearance: appears to stay 25f: acts on any going: has worn visor: strong-pulling front runner: often let down by his jumping. *R. J. Brown.* c— x —

P

PACIFIC SOUND 7 b.g. Palm Track–Pacific Dream (Meldrum) [1989/90 20g 20g 20g5 20g] good-bodied gelding: has scope: modest novice hurdler: ran poorly final start (February): will be suited by a return to 3m: acts on good to firm ground. *Miss L. C. Siddall.* 95

PACO'S BOY 5 b.g. Good Thyne (USA)–Jeremique (Sunny Way) [1989/90 F17f* 20g3 22v* 20d5 20f2 20g2 20f*] good-topped gelding: won NH Flat race at Carlisle in October and novice hurdles at Ayr in February and Uttoxeter (made all to win by 10 lengths from 4 poor opponents) in May: will stay 3m: acts on any going. *J. J. O'Neill.* 119

PACTOLUS (USA) 7 b.h. Lydian (FR)–Honey Sand (USA) (Windy Sands) [1989/90 16s 16g 16f3 20m4] rather sparely-made horse: lightly-raced winning hurdler: ran well when 4½ lengths fourth behind Sayparee in valuable handicap at Liverpool in April (9 lb out of handicap): stays 2½m: acts on any going. *S. Christian.* 114

PADAVENTURE 5 b.g. Belfalas–Cardamine (Indigenous) [1989/90 F17d* F16d6] sixth foal: dam won NH Flat race and maiden hurdle in Ireland: won NH Flat race at Carlisle in March by 1½ lengths from Gymcrak Dawn: well-beaten sixth of 7 at Ayr following month: yet to race over hurdles or fences. *Mrs G. R. Reveley.*

PADDYBORO 12 ch.g. Paddy's Progress–Kellsboro (Coxcomb) [1989/90 c20g* c24s2 c25f5 c20m] rangy, good sort: very useful chaser: led on bridle approaching 2 out but idled and had to be ridden on run-in when winning quite valuable handicap at Cheltenham in January by 1½ lengths from Private Views: 5 lengths second to Ten of Spades in slowly-run 3m Charterhouse Mercantile Chase (Handicap) at Ascot in February: well beaten afterwards: suited by around 2½m and give in the ground: has a good turn of foot and is usually held up: has broken blood vessels. *J. T. Gifford.* c**144** —

PADDY BUCK 10 ch.g. Caribo–Buck's Rose (Royal Buck) [1989/90 c25g5] rangy gelding: winning point-to-pointer/steeplechaser: made numerous mistakes when tailed off in October: stays 3¼m (tailed off when pulled up in valuable event over 4m): acts on heavy going. *J. Honeyball.* c—

PADDY HAYTON 9 br.g. St Paddy–Natenka (Native Prince) [1989/90 c24gpu c27spu c24g6 c27s2 c24g3 c28d3] good-topped gelding: handicap chaser: ran well on fourth and final starts: stays well: acts on any going: blinkered last 2 outings in 1986/7 and fourth and fifth starts. *S. J. Leadbetter.* c95 + —

PADDY IN PARIS 7 ch.g. Paddy's Stream–Wrekin Rose (Master Owen) [1989/90 20f] workmanlike gelding: behind in NH Flat race and novice hurdle. *J. L. Needham.* —

PADDY MURPHY 9 b.g. Pollerton–Gone Too (Perspex) [1989/90 c24g6] strong, lengthy gelding: winning hunter chaser: stayed well: acted on any going: dead. *Tony Lapping.* c—

PADDY O'BRIEN 10 gr.g. Scallywag–Penrith (Nulli Secundus) [1989/90 17gpu c17hur c17mpu c17h2] big, robust gelding: winning hurdler: poor novice chaser: best form at around 2m: acts on dead going: needs to brush up his jumping: trained on reappearance by P. Rodford. *Mrs J. Wonnacott.* c**81** ? —

PADDY'S DREAM 10 b.g. Paddy's Stream–Fairyslave (Arctic Slave) [1989/90 c25dpu] lengthy gelding: winning hurdler: jumps deliberately and no sign of ability over fences: refused once: one to leave alone. *Miss P. O'Connor.* c— x —

PADDY'S GLEN 13 br.g. Furry Glen–Tricia (St Paddy) [1989/90 c21m c20f4 c27f6 c24m2 c20f2 c16f c22m5 c20g c20f2 c21g3] has stringhalt: winning point-to-pointer: tailed off only race over hurdles: poor novice chaser: stays 2½m: acts on firm ground. *Mrs P. A. Barker.* c70 —

PADDY'S OWEN 8 b.m. Paddy's Stream–Ellerslie Owen (Master Owen) [1989/90 20fr] compact mare: of little account: sold 1,650 gns Doncaster October Sales: resold 2,400 gns Ascot December Sales. *P. Davis.* —

PADDYS OYSTER 7 b.g. Tanfirion–Kaly Queen (Queen's Hussar) [1989/90 16gpu c20mF c20m4 c16gpu] leggy, sparely-made ex-Irish gelding: first foal: dam middle-distance maiden: maiden point-to-pointer: bought 6,000 gns Doncaster Spring (1988) Sales: no form over hurdles and in steeplechases: blinkered final outing (jumped poorly): sold 2,300 gns Doncaster Spring Sales. *O. Brennan.* c— —

PADDY'S POND 12 ch.g. Paddy's Stream–Clerihan (Immortality) [1989/90 17g6 c25f4 c20m2 c26m2 c24gF c24m5] tall gelding: made several minor errors when placed in novice chase at Warwick in November and amateur riders handicap chase at Uttoxeter in December: ran moderately in January on final start: stays well: acts on good to firm ground. *G. A. Ham.* c87 —

PADDY WILL 6 b.m. Dublin Taxi–Polygon (Tarboosh (USA)) [1989/90 16m 16g2 20m6] tall, leggy mare: selling hurdler: second in handicap at Stratford in October: ran poorly later in month: ran a moody race third start 1988/9: best form at 2m: acts on soft going: blinkered nowadays. *F. Jordan.* 72 §

PAGEANT LINE 8 ch.m. Balinger–Clothes Line (High Line) [1989/90 20dpu] lengthy mare: poor novice hurdler: visored once in 1986/7 (ran well). *J. L. Spearing.* —

PAGE OF GOLD 10 b.m. Goldhill–Chapter Four (Shackleton) [1989/90 c20gpu c24s2 c26d3 c24s2] sturdy mare: has shown ability over hurdles: modest chaser: placed in handicaps in December (2) and January: suited by a test of stamina: acts on soft going: gives impression she'll be suited by a galloping track. *D. R. Gandolfo.* c105 —

PAILIN 4 b.f. Blue Refrain–Petploy (Faberge II) [1989/90 17h3 17m3 17m5 17h5] leggy filly: seems of little account as a hurdler. *W. G. Turner.* —

Captain F. Tyrwhitt-Drake's "Paddyboro"

PAJANJO 11 ch.g. Northern Flash (CAN)–Quick Draw (Kalydon) [1989/90 c79
c24f^{2}] workmanlike gelding: modest 2m hurdler in 1985/6: won a point-to-point in —
April: 20 lengths second of 3 to Cute Ryme in hunter chase at Ludlow later in
month, every chance when mistake last: acts on any going. *Dr A. Thomas.*

PALACE GARDENS 6 b.g. Royal Boxer–Privy Court (Adropejo) [1989/90
16m 17v 20v 20s 20m] sparely-made gelding: poor novice hurdler. *J. M. Bradley.* —

PALACE YARD 8 ch.g. Town And Country–Escorial (Royal Palace) [1989/90 c93 x
c16h^{ur} c17f^{3} c20m^{3} c22m^{2} c20g^{2} c16m^{3} c20m* c20m* c20f^{3} c18f^{2} c24g^{2}] tall, —
workmanlike gelding: handicap chaser: won twice at Huntingdon in May: ran
creditably after: probably stays 3m: acts on any going: moderate jumper. *K. G.
Wingrove.*

PALAIS DE DANSE 6 ch.h. Dance In Time (CAN)–Dunfermline (Royal
Palace) [1989/90 16g 16d^{4} 17g^{3} 16s] leggy, sparely-made horse: novice selling 70 §
hurdler: tried to refuse third and hung left thereafter first start: has had tongue
tied down: claimer ridden. *A. W. Potts.*

PALAIS ROSE (FR) 9 gr.g. Crystal Palace (FR)–Texan Belle (FR) (St
Paddy) [1989/90 16f 20m^{pu} 16f^{3} 19f^{3}] 10.5f winner on Flat in France: only sign of 64 ?
ability over hurdles when third in minor event at Warwick in May on third start:
tailed off in seller on hurdling debut. *C. J. Vernon Miller.*

PALANQUIN 8 ch.g. Royal Palace–Duresme (Starry Halo) [1989/90 c16g^{bd} c— x
c24g c22f^{6} c24g^{pu}] leggy gelding: poor novice hurdler/chaser: jumps moderately. —
Miss M. J. Benson.

PALE STAR 8 b.m. Kampala–Kimstar (Aureole) [1989/90 c16h^{2} 16f^{6}] small c—
mare: no worthwhile form over hurdles, including in a seller: unseated rider fifth —
and slipped up approaching eighth but went on to complete course in novice chase
at Plumpton in August (2 finished). *J. White.*

PALMAHALM 8 b.m. Mandrake Major–Dame Connaught (Connaught) c— p
[1989/90 c25g^{F}] fairly useful point-to-pointer, winner 4 times in 1990: in third
when falling thirteenth in novice hunter chase won by Old Nick at Catterick in
March. *K. Anderson.*

PALMER'S GOLD 9 b.g. Palm Track–Golden Pinelopi (Sovereign Lord) c88
[1989/90 c20f^{4} c26m^{3} c24f^{3} 24f^{4} 21f^{3} 24m^{4} 19m^{3} 20g^{5} 25f^{4}] sturdy gelding: poor 75
chaser/novice hurdler: stays 25f: acts on firm going. *E. H. Owen jun.*

PALMERSTON BOY 7 b.g. Tickled Pink–Silver Swallow (My Swallow) c77
[1989/90 c16g^{4} c20g^{F} c18v^{4} c17d c20m^{2} c20f^{F}] workmanlike gelding: winning —
selling hurdler: poor novice chaser: stays 2½m: acts on good to firm and dead
going. *A. Moore.*

PALM HOUSE 5 ch.g. Coquelin (USA)–Kew Gift (Faraway Son (USA))
[1989/90 24m^{6} 16m^{4} 20g^{3} 20m^{2} 16m 20v^{6} 20g^{2} 16g* 16g^{5}] leggy, angular gelding: 111
handicap hurdler: won at Edinburgh in January: ran poorly in claimer at Perth
nearly 4 months later: stays 2½m: acts on good to firm and dead going. *G.
Richards.*

PALM LAD 7 b.g. Palm Track–Captain Frances (Captain's Gig (USA)) c90
[1989/90 c16m^{3} c20m^{2} c16g^{5} c16d^{ro} c16d^{F} c16g^{3} c25g^{pu} c16f* c20g^{pu}] strong, —
lengthy gelding: novice hurdler: made most when winning novice chase at
Hexham in March: unfortunate in novice handicap on same course on fourth start,
following loose horse out at the last when looking likely winner: well behind when
pulled up 2 out final start: likely to prove best at 2m: acts on firm and dead ground:
has worn crossed noseband. *G. Richards.*

PALM REEF 6 b.g. Main Reef–Fingers (Lord Gayle (USA)) [1989/90 16d^{pu}
a18g^{bd} 20g] small, sturdy gelding: maiden on Flat, well beaten in 1989: little —
promise in 3 outings over hurdles (visored first): sold 1,600 gns Ascot February
Sales. *M. Madgwick.*

PALMRUSH 6 b.g. Tepukei–Vulrusika (Vulgan) [1989/90 c16g* c16f^{3} c16f^{4}] c95
rather unfurnished gelding: winning hurdler: made most when winning amateur —
riders novice chase at Market Rasen in October: creditable last of 3 finishers
behind Gay Edition at Ascot later in month: made a bad mistake at the sixth and
ran moderately following month: races freely and may prove best at 2m for the
present: acts on firm ground (ran poorly on dead ground final start 1988/9). *C. W.
Thornton.*

PALM SWIFT 4 b.f. Rabdan–Swiftsand (Sharpen Up) [1989/90 16g^{pu} 16m^{4}
16m^{6}] sparely-made filly: lightly raced and no worthwhile form on Flat: poor form 76
over hurdles. *A. J. Chamberlain.*

PALS GALORE 8 b. or br.g. Paddy's Stream–Ballygoman Maid (Light Thrust) c—
[1989/90 c20v^{pu} c16d^{pu} c16v^{F}] leggy, close-coupled gelding: modest novice —
hurdler: failed to complete in novice chases: stayed 2½m: dead. *D. McCain.*

PALVIC GREY 6 gr.m. Kampala–Ambient (Amber Rama (USA)) [1989/90 16g
17f^{6}] leggy mare: poor novice hurdler. *Miss G. M. Rees.* —

PAMBER PRIORY 7 b.g. Balinger–Miset (Right Royal V) [1989/90 20g^{3}]
rather leggy gelding: winning hurdler: fair third in handicap at Kempton in 109
October: will stay beyond 2½m: acts on soft going. *B. Smart.*

PAMELA'S LAD 4 ch.g. Dalsaan–La Margarite (Bonne Noel) [1989/90 F16g]
first foal: dam, lightly raced, placed in novice hurdles at 2½m: remote seventh in
NH Flat race at Market Rasen: yet to race over hurdles. *D. J. Wintle.*

PAMEVA 5 br.g. Decent Fellow–Alhamdulillah (Pry) [1989/90 F16v* F16d^{3}]
fourth foal: brother to NH Flat race-placed Show Out Sunday: dam, winning
hurdler, stayed 3m: won NH Flat race at Haydock in March: dead. *J. A. C.
Edwards.*

PAMPAROID 10 gr.g. Polaroid–Pampas Maid (Chou Chin Chow) [1989/90 c—
c20f^{pu} c20f^{pu} c26f^{pu}] neat gelding: winning hurdler: pulled up all starts in chases: — §
stays 2¾m: acts on any going: not resolute. *Mrs Karen Rowe-Shepherd.*

PAMPERING 9 b.g. Pamroy–Crosswise (Firestreak) [1989/90 c28g^{6} c27s^{3}] c**123**
sparely-made gelding: fairly useful chaser: creditable third to Bluff Knoll in —
handicap at Ayr in December: suited by a thorough test of stamina: acts on heavy
going: tends to sweat and be on his toes in preliminaries, but is more settled
nowadays. *J. E. Brockbank.*

PAMROY'S DAUGHTER 9 b.m. Pamroy–Laydoney (Even Money) [1989/90 c—
c27f^{4} c22m^{pu}] winning point-to-pointer: well beaten in hunter chases. *W. Allcock.*

PAN ARCTIC 11 b.g. Pitpan–Arctic Sue (Arctic Slave) [1989/90 c20s^{pu} c20d^{pu} c**87** §
c16m^{4} c20f^{F} c22m c20f^{4} c24m* c24d^{5} c24f^{3}] modest chaser nowadays: best —
effort of 1989/90 when winning at Huntingdon (claimer ridden) in May: stays 3m
when conditions aren't testing: acts on any going: well suited by a strongly-run
race: blinkered once in 1988/9: has run well for an amateur: finds little off bridle on
occasions and isn't one to trust. *T. T. Bill.*

PANAVISTA 10 b.g. Cheval–Vista Vision (Don't Look) [1989/90 c25g^{5}] c—
lengthy, dipped-backed gelding: winning point-to-pointer: maiden hunter chaser. —
Mrs V. J. Dungait.

PANEGYRIST 15 b.g. Sweet Story–Pandorana (Pandofell) [1989/90 c24v^{3} c**85** ?
c32g^{pu}] workmanlike gelding: poor chaser: stays 25f: acts on heavy going:
amateur or claimer ridden. *C. J. T. Alexander.*

PANSONG 4 b.c. Absalom–Sea Chant (Julio Mariner) [1989/90 16f^{2} 16f^{5} a16g^{3}
a16g^{2} 16d^{6} 16d^{6} a16g^{5} 16g 16f^{F}] small, good-quartered colt: winning plater on 68
Flat, stays 9f: poor form over hurdles, including in sellers: jumps none too
fluently: blinkered eighth start (raced too freely): claimer ridden: sold 1,800 gns
Doncaster March Sales. *T. Fairhurst.*

PANTECHNICON 10 b.g. Pitpan–Avatea (Arctic Slave) [1989/90 c16m^{4} c16f^{2} c**116**
c16f^{pu} c18g^{ur} c19d^{2} c16d^{3} c17g^{2} c18f^{2}] big, rangy gelding: handicap chaser: ran —
creditably when placed in first half of season: best at distances short of 2½m: acts
on any going: pulls hard: successful for a claimer: tends to make the odd mistake.
A. Barrow.

PANTO LADY 4 br.f. Lepanto (GER)–Dusky Damsel (Sahib) [1989/90 16m^{6}
16f^{5} 16m^{3} 16g^{6} 16g 16v^{5} 17m 16g^{6}] leggy filly: half-sister to several poor 61
performers over jumps: lightly-raced maiden on Flat: poor novice selling hurdler:
blinkered last 2 starts: trained until after fourth outing by J. Johnson. *Mrs S. C.
Bradburne.*

PANTOMIME PRINCE 7 b.g. Lepanto (GER)–Annie Louise (Parthia) c**119**
[1989/90 c16f^{3} c16m^{F} c16g^{3} c16f^{2} c20g^{pu}] strong, workmanlike gelding: winning —
hurdler: fair chaser: ran creditably when placed in 1989/90: pulled up lame final
outing (only start beyond 2m): acts well on a firm surface: makes mistakes. *C. W.
Thornton.*

PANTO PRINCE 9 br.g. Lepanto (GER)–Native Wings (Indigenous) c**156**
[1989/90 c21m* c17g* c16m* c20g^{2} c24d^{2} c20g^{2} c16g^{3} c24v^{4} c16f^{6} c20m^{6} —
c16f*]

What's the betting that the Terry Biddlecombe South West Pattern
Chase and the Plymouth Gin Haldon Gold Cup Chase will be early-season

targets for Panto Prince in 1990/1? He won those events on consecutive days in October, when the former had £6,000 in added prize money and the latter had £10,000. In the new pattern for 1990/1 both races will be worth £25,000 and there'll be twelve days between them. The considerable increase in prize money for these races could be a mixed blessing for Panto Prince's connections, for Panto Prince will surely face much stronger opposition than he did in 1989. Panto Prince started at 9/2 on when accounting for five opponents in the Terry Biddlecombe Chase at Wincanton, taking so little out of himself that he was able to hand out similar treatment to four rivals in the Haldon Gold Cup at Devon & Exeter less than twenty-four hours later. Seagram, easily the best horse that Panto Prince met in those events, was racing over a distance very much on the short side for him at Devon & Exeter, and Panto Prince had his measure from a long way out. Panto Prince was also to start at odds on when gaining his other two victories. At Uttoxeter in November he beat Clever Folly eight lengths in a sponsored four-runner race; and at Chepstow in May he won a two-mile minor event, the Coinmaster Chase, for the second year in succession, beating the only other runner Wingspan by two and a half lengths. Panto Prince's best performances in defeat came on his fifth, sixth and seventh starts, performances which show how versatile he is regarding distance. He finished five lengths second to Solidasarock in the three-mile SGB Handicap at Ascot in December and eight and a half lengths third to Meikleour in the two-mile Victor Chandler Handicap on the same course the following month; and in between he was beaten two and a half lengths by Pukka Major in a quite valuable two-and-a-half-mile handicap at Kempton. It's possible that Panto Prince found the three miles beyond him in the Vincent O'Brien Irish Gold Cup at Leopardstown, which was run in very testing conditions. However, he also ran moderately on his next two starts, including in the Queen Mother Champion Chase, and he may have been feeling the effects of some hard races.

Mrs L. M. Warren's "Panto Prince"

Panto Prince (br.g. 1981)	Lepanto (GER) (bl 1973)	Priamos (br 1964)	Birkhahn
			Palazzo
		Promised Lady (ch 1961)	Prince Chevalier
			Belle Sauvage
	Native Wings (b 1971)	Indigenous (ch 1956)	Mustang
			Silver Thistle
		Flying Wings (b 1953)	Pappageno II
			Lovely Wings

Panto Prince is the only winner produced by Native Wings, a mare who had a chequered career in Ireland and Britain in bumpers events, hurdle races, steeplechases and point-to-points. Placed on numerous occasions, Native Wings was still a maiden when she was retired in 1978. Each of the next two dams, Flying Wings and Lovely Wings, were Irish Flat and jumping winners. Panto Prince, a leggy, sparely-made gelding, acts on any going. Thoroughly genuine, he's normally a fine jumper and has completed the course without mishap in all thirty-four of his starts over fences. *C. L. Popham.*

PANTOUR 10 b.g. Pitpan–Touralou (Giolla Mear) [1989/90 c25g^{3}] strong, lengthy gelding: winning point-to-pointer and poor novice chaser: probably stays 3m: tends to sweat. *Mrs Pat Mullen.* c93

PAPAJOTO 5 b.g. Ahonoora–Papukeena (Simbir) [1989/90 18m^{4} 16g^{3} 20d^{pu} 16g 16f^{6} 16s 16d* 16d^{4} 20m 16d^{2} 16f* 16m^{2}] angular gelding: made running to win novice handicap hurdles at Wolverhampton in February and Uttoxeter in May: good second in novice handicap at Stratford final start: stays 2¼m: acts on any going: blinkered fourth start: trained until after fifth outing by G. Pritchard-Gordon. *M. O'Neill.* 100

PAPER BOY 4 b.c. Montekin–Another Deb (African Sky) [1989/90 17h^{4}] poor form, including in sellers, on Flat: tailed off in juvenile hurdle at Devon & Exeter in August. *A. P. James.* —

PARADISE PARK 6 b.h. Nicholas Bill–Pandoras Gold (Wishing Star) [1989/90 16g^{5} 16g^{6} 16f] rangy horse: no sign of ability on Flat: poor novice hurdler. *J. T. Gifford.* 70

PARANG 9 b.g. Sharpen Up–Parmelia (Ballymoss) [1989/90 c16g^{3}] useful-looking gelding: winning hurdler/modest novice chaser: jumped soundly in main when third behind Blazing Walker in novice handicap at Newcastle in January: likely to prove best at around 2m: best form on top-of-the-ground. *P. T. Walwyn.* c90 —

PARAVEL 8 b.g. Whitstead–Rosehill (Stupendous) [1989/90 c24f^{6}] fourth live foal: dam ran only 3 times: won a point-to-point in April: well beaten in novice hunter chase at Newcastle in March. *R. W. Green.* c—

PARDI'S GIFT 8 ch.g. Pardigras–Olive's Gift (Native Bazaar) [1989/90 c25m* c26m^{6} c25h^{2}] workmanlike gelding: winning point-to-pointer: won novice hunter chase at Devon & Exeter in April: better effort afterwards when 25 lengths second on same course: will stay extreme distances: acts on hard ground. *Mrs Betty Spry.* c92

PARENTUS 7 b.g. Derrylin–Flaxen Hair (Thatch (USA)) [1989/90 16m^{pu} 16s 27s a20g* a20g a20g* a20g^{4} a20g^{2} 24m^{pu} a20g^{pu}] stocky, compact gelding: won handicap hurdles at Lingfield in January (seller, no bid) and February (ridden by 5-lb claimer): finished lame final start: stays 2½m: seems suited by a sound surface. *J. E. Long.* 81

PARHAM 7 b.g. Pauper–Clonrochenell (Harwell) [1989/90 c20m c24m^{5} c21s^{ur} c24m^{4} 24m c20f^{3}] lengthy, workmanlike gelding: has scope: jumped better than previously and showed only sign of ability when fourth in novice chase at Huntingdon in April: blinkered last 3 outings. *G. A. Hubbard.* c79 —

PARISH RIGGED 12 b.g. Master Buck–Very Very (Vulgan) [1989/90 c24f^{2} c24f^{F} c25m* c24m* c26m^{5} c25f^{3} c20d c27m^{pu} c19m^{2} c32f^{5}] tall gelding: won handicap chases at Warwick and Worcester in September: second in hunter chase at Hereford in April: broke down final start: suited by a test of stamina: acts well on firm going: successful with and without blinkers: inconsistent. *D. R. Bloor.* c97 § —

PARISIAN 5 b.h. Shirley Heights–Miss Paris (Sovereign Path) [1989/90 17g a16g^{5} 20g 17d^{pu} a16g^{5} a24g^{6}] neat horse: unplaced in 6f maiden at 2 yrs, only outing on Flat: sold out of G. Wragg's stable 700 gns Newmarket Autumn (1988) Sales: poor form over hurdles. *J. A. Bennett.* —

PARIS MATCH 8 b. or br.g. Bold Lad (IRE)–Miss Paris (Sovereign Path)
[1989/90 16m* 17m* 16m^{6} 16m^{3} 16f^{3} 16g 16h^{2} 16d 16f^{2} 17f*] lengthy gelding: 89
attracted no bid after winning selling handicap hurdles at Perth and Cartmel
(finished lame) in August: blinkered, beat Roscoe The Brave a length in
non-selling handicap on latter course in May: races only at around 2m: acts on
firm ground: claimer ridden nowadays: has appeared to break blood vessels. *G. M.
Moore.*

PARKBHRIDE 4 b.g. Wolver Hollow–Gulistan (Sharpen Up) [1989/90 16f^{3}
16f^{F} 16m^{4} a16g^{4} a20g^{3} 16f 20m^{5}] rather sparely-made gelding: no form on Flat: 75
poor form in juvenile hurdles, including in a seller: stays 2½m: acts on firm going:
blinkered second and third starts: sold 1,500 gns Ascot June Sales. *C. A. Horgan.*

PARK DRIFT 4 ch.g. Say Primula–Kerera (Keren) [1989/90 F12g F17m 24h^{3}
16d] third foal: dam, half-sister to a winning hurdler, of little account: well beaten 67
in NH Flat races: weakened in latter stages when third in 3m amateur riders
maiden hurdle at Hexham in May. *J. H. Johnson.*

PAR KELLY 10 b.g. Le Johnstan–Dunreekann (Fidalgo) [1989/90 c20s^{2} c24d^{5}] **c85**
compact gelding: fair point-to-pointer: maiden hunter chaser: second at
Sedgefield in February: gave impression he'll be suited by a return to shorter
distances over 3m. *Mrs J. Sowersby.*

PARKLANDS BELLE 6 b.m. Stanford–Kelly's Curl (Pitskelly) [1989/90
16s^{6} 16s] small mare: poor and inconsistent 1m winner on Flat: no worthwhile —
form in 2 selling hurdles in December. *R. J. Hodges.*

PARK PRINCE 9 b.g. Shackleton–Proud Rain (pedigree unknown) [1989/90 c—
c24d^{pu}] compact, good-quartered gelding: novice hurdler: successful in 2 novice —
chases in 1988/9: stayed well: acted on heavy going: dead. *W. A. Stephenson.*

PARK SHADE 11 b.g. Jupiter Pluvius–Shady Tree (Three Wishes) [1989/90 **c80** ?
c26d^{6} c25f* c26m^{pu}] rangy gelding: novice hurdler: won a point-to-point in April: —
won hunter chase at Cheltenham following month despite trying to run out at
second last (had been tailed off until 3 leaders came to grief 4 out): made mistakes
next outing: stays 3m: acts on firm ground. *Robin Mathew.*

PARK SLAVE 8 b.g. Park Row–Cool Date (Arctic Slave) [1989/90 16f^{2} 16m^{6} **c81**
c16s^{3} 20m^{pu}] strong, sturdy gelding: chasing type: poor form in novice hurdles: 81
first race for 2 months, weakened approaching last when third in novice event at
Sedgefield in January on chasing debut: best run on good ground over hurdles:
takes good hold and has worn a severe bridle: trainer ridden. *Mrs V. S. Jackson.*

PARK STREET 5 b.g. Runnett–Chieftain Girl (USA) (Chieftain II) [1989/90
16m* 16d 16d 16h^{2} 17f^{2} 16f^{3}] rangy gelding: 1m winner on Flat: easy winner of 107 ?
novice hurdle at Warwick in November: variable form after, best effort when
second in handicap at Taunton fourth start: likely to prove best at sharp 2m: has
been tried in blinkers: not one to trust. *O. Sherwood.*

PARKWAY EXPRESS 4 ch.f. Sagaro–Parrot Fashion (Pieces of Eight)
[1989/90 F16m] fifth foal: dam fair performer on Flat, best at 1¼m: tailed off in NH
Flat race at Sandown: yet to race over hurdles. *B. Stevens.*

PARLEZVOUSFRANCAIS 6 b.g. Blakeney–Oula-Ka Fu-Fu (Run The **c96**
Gantlet (USA)) [1989/90 c16m^{2} 24f^{ur} 25g^{3} c26v^{r} 24v 25f 25m 24f^{5} 24f^{3} 26f^{2} 115
21m^{2}] lengthy, sparely-made gelding: fair hurdler: second twice at Newton Abbot
in May: second in novice chase at Uttoxeter in November: very tired when
refusing last final outing over fences: stays well: probably acts on any going: ran
poorly when blinkered sixth and seventh starts: usually a front runner, but held
up last 4 starts. *M. C. Pipe.*

PARSONIFY 5 b.g. The Parson–Kosey Kitchen (Golden Love) [1989/90 16v^{6}
16g 20m^{pu}] leggy, close-coupled gelding: well beaten in novice hurdles. *G. P.* —
Enright.

PARSON'S CROSS 6 b.g. The Parson–Croom Cross (Menelek) [1989/90 **c97**
c27g^{2} c24g* c24d^{4} c24v^{F} c27s^{4} c24d^{3} c27f^{2} c27f* c24f^{F} c24g^{pu}] well-made —
gelding: winning hurdler: won novice handicap chase at Ayr in December (jumped
badly right last 2 fences) and 3-runner handicap at Sedgefield in May: stays well:
acts on firm and dead going: needs to brush up his jumping. *W. A. Stephenson.*

PARSONS GREEN 6 b.g. The Parson–Move Along Gypsy (Menelek)
[1989/90 21d^{3} 20g^{3} 21d^{3} 25g^{2} 25m^{3}] tall gelding: has scope: fairly useful hurdler: 122
placed all starts 1989/90, including good 12½ lengths third behind Sip of Orange in
Oddbins Hurdle (Handicap) at Liverpool on final outing: suited by test of stamina:
acts on dead and good to firm ground: sweating at Liverpool. *N. J. Henderson.*

PARSONS LAW 7 ch.m. The Parson–Wrekalong (Wrekin Rambler) [1989/90 24f³ c20g⁴] smallish, sparely-made mare: fair hurdler at her best: staying-on fourth in novice chase at Wolverhampton in February: stays 2¾m (well below his best both attempts at 3m): acts on good to firm and dead going: has won for an amateur: should improve over fences. *J. A. C. Edwards.* c— p —

PARSONS PLEASURE 7 b.g. Pry–Will Preach (Will Somers) [1989/90 16g⁶ c16dF c16g⁵] workmanlike gelding: modest novice hurdler: jumped none too fluently when remote fifth in intermediate handicap chase at Wolverhampton in February: will stay 2½m. *M. J. Wilkinson.* c— 84

PARTRIDGE FLATT 5 ch.g. Known Fact (USA)–Castleisland (Deep Diver) [1989/90 16g⁵ 16g 20g 16f⁶] workmanlike gelding: poor novice hurdler. *B. E. Wilkinson.* 84

PARTY BOY 7 b.g. Pardigras–Guyana (Lucky Guy) [1989/90 16s 16s] sparely-made gelding: novice hurdler: best effort on first start. *P. J. Hobbs.* 81 +

PARTY PERIL 5 ch.g. Mljet–Gentle Peril (Rebel Prince) [1989/90 16mpu 16fur 16fpu 16g a16gpu] workmanlike gelding: poor and temperamental novice hurdler: dead. *N. Miller.* — §

PARTY POLITICS 6 br.g. Politico (USA)–Spin Again (Royalty) [1989/90 c20gF c20mpu c20s* c25s* c20m⁴] c**144**

It's already possible to draw two firm conclusions from Party Politics' seven races to date. The first is that he's a more-than-useful recruit to steeplechasing. Runner-up on the second of two outings in point-to-points in 1989, Party Politics was sent to be trained by Gaselee in the latest season and showed form which, at best, entitles him to be regarded as one of the leading novice chasers. He belied a starting price of 40/1 when spread-eagling a sixteen-runner field at Warwick in February, leading from five out to beat Romany King pushed out by ten lengths, the pair twenty lengths clear. Stepped up in class, Party Politics dented a few reputations when the 25/1-winner of the quite valuable Highfield Road Novices' Chase on the same course two weeks later. Always prominent behind the pace set by High Ham Blues, seeking his seventh straight win, and the fairly useful Knight Oil, Party Politics stayed on strongly to lead on the run-in and win by seven lengths from subsequent Sun Alliance Novices' Chase winner Garrison Savannah who finished a distance clear of the remainder. Knight Oil had looked to be travelling only third best when unseating his rider three out.

The second conclusion to be drawn is that Party Politics is beholden to the state of the ground. It was soft on both occasions at Warwick. On good to firm he was tailed off when pulled up in a run-of-the-mill novice chase at Leicester in January and ran way below his best when fourth to Okeetee at Sandown in March. On good ground at Uttoxeter on his chasing debut in January, Party Politics was in touch when falling at the ninth.

Party Politics (br.g. 1984)	Politico (USA) (b 1967)	Right Royal V (br 1958)	Owen Tudor
			Bastia
		Tendentious (b 1959)	Tenerani
			Ambiguity
	Spin Again (br 1975)	Royalty (br 1968)	Relko
			Fair Bid
		Spin A Yarn (br 1967)	Doubtless II
			Spinning Coin

Party Politics shapes like a thorough stayer, taking after the best of Politico's jumping produce such as Durham Edition, Political Pop and Stearsby. The distaff side of his pedigree, a successful jumping one, is less strong an influence for stamina. The three dams on the bottom line, all successful chasers, never won beyond twenty-one furlongs in steeple-chases, the distance of Spin Again's longest victory, though Spinning Coin won over three miles in point-to-points. However, Spin A Yarn is a sister to two winning three-mile chasers, including the useful High Havens, and is the dam of useful staying chaser Crack A Joke. Spin Again has had two live foals by Celtic Cone since Party Politics; the first of them Celtic Showman, a twin, is the only one to have run to date, finishing well beaten in a National

Hunt Flat race in 1989. Party Politics is sure to win races in handicap company. He didn't contest the top novice events and was well beaten on his final start which means he starts the season quite well treated. A big, rangy gelding, and still relatively young, he may well have further improvement in him, too. Granted a test of stamina and plenty of give in the ground, Party Politics should make a very useful chaser, and he's one to watch out for. *N. A. Gaselee.*

PASS THE PLATE 12 b.g. The Parson–Putcha (USA) (Hunters Moon IV) c—
[1989/90 c24g] compact gelding: winning hurdler/chaser: fair point-to-pointer: —
stays 3m: acts on heavy going. *P. L. Southcombe.*

PAST GLORIES 7 b.h. Hittite Glory–Snow Tribe (Great Nephew)
[1989/90 16m^{3} 16f^{5} 16g 16s^{5} 16d^{2} 16m^{3}] 165

Past Glories became the latest in the recent series of long-priced placed horses in the Waterford Crystal Champion Hurdle when he finished an excellent third to Kribensis. In the past decade a number of 'no-hopers' have run the race of their lives in the race, starting with Boreen Prince (50/1) in 1983 who turned out to be the first of three successive big-priced seconds when going down to Gaye Brief; Cima (66/1) came next in Dawn Run's year, then Robin Wonder (66/1) chased home See You Then in 1985 with Stan's Pride (100/1) in third. Four years on Beech Road (50/1) joined Kirriemuir as the longest-priced winner of the race. At 150/1 Past Glories is the longest-priced horse to reach a place in the Champion Hurdle. His odds reflected the fact he'd had training troubles after winning the Welsh Champion Hurdle at Chepstow and the Swinton Insurance Trophy at Haydock in 1987/8 and had failed to recover that form. Furthermore, the

Mr N. Hetherton's "Past Glories" (J. J. Quinn)

firm ground was widely considered against him. However, so strongly did he travel through the race you'd have thought he was one of the leading fancies. Racing prominently from the outset, he moved up to dispute the lead with eventual second Nomadic Way at the fourth last and maintained his position until the run to the last. Though passed by Kribensis and Nomadic Way and joined by Beech Road on the run-in, Past Glories wouldn't be denied a place and stayed on very strongly to hold off Beech Road for third, three and three quarter lengths behind the winner. Although there wasn't sufficient promise in his races prior to Cheltenham to suggest Past Glories would play a significant part in the Champion Hurdle, he had run creditably on all but his fourth start of the season, notably when third to Kribensis in the Food Brokers And Primula 'Fighting Fifth' Hurdle at Newcastle in November on his reappearance and when a close second, running on very strongly from the last, to Jinxy Jack, who was conceding 6 lb, in the Morebattle Hurdle at Kelso in February.

Past Glories (b.h. 1983)	Hittite Glory (b 1973)	Habitat (b 1966)	Sir Gaylord
			Little Hut
		Hazy Idea (b 1967)	Hethersett
			Won't Linger
	Snow Tribe (b 1972)	Great Nephew (b 1963)	Honeyway
			Sybil's Niece
		Cold Storage (b 1965)	Never Say Die
			Snow Court

Past Glories, a fairly useful stayer on the Flat in 1988, is the fourth home-bred foal of Snow Tribe, who was also a fairly useful stayer. Her first three offspring all won on the Flat, the most notable being Line Slinger (by High Line) who won the Yorkshire Cup; another, Snow Blessed (by So Blessed), subsequently showed quite useful form over jumps. Snow Tribe's three foals since Past Glories have achieved little. Snow Tribe is a half-sister to the fair middle-distance performer Misnomer, the dam of several winners, including fair hurdlers York Cottage and Half Asleep. Past Glories' grandam Cold Storage finished third in the 1968 St Leger and since being exported to Argentina in 1974 has produced Tangaroa, winner of the Group 1 Gran Premio Seleccion. Past Glories has been raced only at two miles over hurdles, but gives the impression he'll stay two and a half miles. Clearly he acts just as well on a firm surface as he does on a soft one. Past Glories was tried in blinkers on the second of his two disappointing starts in 1988/9. *J. Hetherton.*

PAST MIDNIGHT 4 ch.f. Longleat (USA)–Fearless Felon (USA) (Bailjumper (USA)) [1989/90 16s^{pu} 17d^{pu} 16f^{pu}] placed over sprint distances at 2 yrs: sold out of C. Cyzer's stable 1,500 gns Newmarket July Sales: tailed off when pulled up in juvenile hurdles and a seller. *D. N. Carey.* —

PAT ALASKA 7 br.g. Ovac (ITY)–Indicate (Mustang) [1989/90 F16f^{5} F17g c27f*] behind in maiden hurdles and NH Flat races (blinkered) in Ireland: won a point-to-point in April and later in month won hunter chase at Taunton by 1½ lengths from Saleapolo: stays well: acts on firm ground. *Mrs Nerys Dutfield.* c**86** p —

PATAUDI (USA) 10 b.h. Apalachee (USA)–Bonavista (Dead Ahead) [1989/90 16f^{pu}] rather dipped-backed horse: tailed off when pulled up both outings over hurdles. *P. Howling.* —

PATCHOULI'S PET 7 b.m. Mummy's Pet–Primage (Primera) [1989/90 26f^{2} 24f^{3} 25h^{5} 24m^{5} 24m 25f^{3} 24f^{5} 28g^{5} a20g 28f^{3} 17m 27f^{3} 24g] small, lightly-made mare: plating-class handicap hurdler: stays very well: acts on firm going and unsuited by soft: blinkered final outing: unreliable. *W. G. Morris.* 84 §

PAT CULLEN 5 b.g. The Parson–Duhallow Hazel (Major Point) [1989/90 22m^{5} 22s^{ur} 21d^{pu}] leggy ex-Irish gelding: first foal: dam unraced: won NH Flat race in 1988/9: has shown ability in maiden and novice hurdles, including when unseating rider 3 out at Folkestone in December (travelling well and would have gone close): weakened quickly 3 out and pulled up last in novice handicap at Newbury 2 months later. *D. J. G. Murray-Smith.* 92

PATENIER (USA) 5 ro.h. Sassafras (FR)–Absaretch (CAN) (Dancer's Image (USA)) [1989/90 20f* 16f*] rangy horse: won early-season amateur riders hurdle at Southwell and handicap at Plumpton (beat Manhattan Boy 2 lengths): stayed 102

2½m: acted on firm and dead ground: refused to race once in 1988/9: dead. *V. Young.*

PATRICIA BRIDGET 4 ch.f. Sagaro–Tinted Blonde (USA) (Charles Elliott (USA)) [1989/90 F16g] first reported foal: dam, sister to 3 winners and half-sister to several others, showed little in 4 outings on Flat: tailed off in NH Flat race at Fakenham: yet to race over hurdles. *J. Ringer.*

PATRICK JAMES 5 b.g. Kampala–Up The Gates (Captain James) [1989/90
16g^{6} 16g^{2} 16s^{6} 20m* 16m* 16s* 16s^{3} 16g^{3}] close-coupled gelding: won claiming 101
hurdles at Leicester (2) and Ludlow: below-form third in similar events at
Nottingham and Perth: stays 2½m: acts on good to firm and soft going. *F. Jordan.*

PATROCLUS 5 b.g. Tyrnavos–Athenia Princess (Athens Wood) [1989/90
22g^{4} 22m 22v] workmanlike gelding: poor novice hurdler: refused on debut and — §
tried to do so several times on final start: one to leave well alone. *R. Voorspuy.*

PATROL LEADER 5 br.g. Trimmingham–Arctic Actress (Arctic Slave)
[1989/90 F16g^{4} 16g 16g^{3}] workmanlike, rather sparely-made gelding: half-brother 95 p
to smart hurdler and useful chaser Snowtown Boy (by Town Crier): dam very
useful staying chaser: in frame in NH Flat race at Ludlow and novice hurdle at
Stratford (5½ lengths third behind Sound of Islay): should improve sufficiently to
win over hurdles. *Mrs J. Pitman.*

PATS MINSTREL 5 b.g. Black Minstrel–Lohunda Park (Malinowski (USA))
[1989/90 22g^{6} 16g^{3} 16g*] workmanlike ex-Irish gelding: first foal: dam showed a 89
little ability over sprint distances in Ireland: won point-to-point in 1989: made all
when successful in novice hurdle at Fakenham in February: should stay further
than 2m (bit backward when tried over 2¾m). *R. Champion.*

PAT WOLLOW 8 b.g. Wollow–Pitapat (Shantung) [1989/90 c22d^{F} c20d c— x
c24s^{pu} c24g^{pu}] tall, lengthy gelding: winning hurdler: jumps moderately and no —
worthwhile form in novice chases: stays 2½m: acts on heavy going. *G. M. Moore.*

PAUL PRY 10 b.g. Pry–Slave Light (Arctic Slave) [1989/90 c22g^{F} c16d] big, c—
close-coupled gelding: winning chaser: no form for some time: should stay 2½m: —
form only on good ground. *Miss T. A. White.*

PAYLINS 6 ch.g. Crash Course–Game Sunset (Menelek) [1989/90 16g^{ur} 16d^{bd}
16v] rangy gelding: has scope: third foal: dam, sister to Western Sunset, won over —
2½m on Flat and up to 17f over hurdles in Ireland: no worthwhile form in novice
hurdles: has looked headstrong: sold 2,500 gns Ascot May Sales. *Capt. T. A. Forster.*

PEACEFUL LANE 12 b.g. Crozier–Denmead (Cagire II) [1989/90 c16d^{pu}] c—
rather plain gelding: winning point-to-pointer: little sign of ability in hunter
chases. *M. A. Johnson.*

PEACEWORK 6 br.m. Workboy–Flower Child (Brother) [1989/90 16g 25g^{pu} c83
16g^{6} c16f* c16f^{2}] leggy, close-coupled mare: no form over hurdles: made all in —
3-runner novice handicap chase at Southwell in April: odds on, beaten 8 lengths
by only other finisher Lingham Duke in novice handicap at Sedgefield following
month: headstrong, best at 2m: acts on firm ground. *Mrs G. R. Reveley.*

PEACH LEAF 9 b.g. Brave Invader (USA)–Cant Pet (Cantab) [1989/90 c24d^{6}] c—
chunky, plain ex-Irish gelding: useful point-to-pointer/hunter chaser in Ireland: —
tailed-off last in maiden hunter chase at Leicester in March. *N. J. Pewter.*

PEAJADE 6 b.g. Buckskin (FR)–Kaminaki (Deep Run) [1989/90 F16g^{2} 16g^{3}
16d^{pu} 20d] leggy, workmanlike gelding with scope: won NH Flat race in 1988/9: 98 ?
third in novice hurdle at Chepstow in December: ran poorly on softer ground
afterwards (blinkered final start). *M. H. B. Robinson.*

PEAK DISTRICT 4 b.c. Beldale Flutter (USA)–Grand Teton (Bustino)
[1989/90 16s^{F}] smallish colt: in frame at up to 1¼m on Flat: sold out of G. Wragg's —
stable 13,000 gns Newmarket Autumn Sales: fell first in juvenile hurdle at
Warwick (moved poorly to post) in February. *K. S. Bridgwater.*

PEALLA 5 b.g. Dara Monarch–Nofertiti (FR) (Exbury) [1989/90 20v^{6}] leggy,
shallow-girthed gelding: winning hurdler: best at 2m: acted on soft going: dead. *R.* —
J. O'Sullivan.

PEANUTS PET 5 b.h. Tina's Pet–Sinzinbra (Royal Palace) [1989/90 16g*
16d* 16g 17g* 16s^{3} 16m^{5} 20d^{4} 16f] close-coupled horse: won decisively in large 128
fields of novice hurdlers at Worcester and Haydock in December but wandered
and was ridden out when winning Rossington Main Novices' Hurdle at Doncaster
in January by length from Rakes Lane: fourth, weakening run-in, to King's Curate
in quite valuable novice handicap at Ayr in April: may prove ideally suited by

Rossington Main Novices' Hurdle, Doncaster—
Peanuts Pet (right) gets the better of Rakes Lane

strongly-run races at around 2m: suited by plenty of give in the ground. *B. A. McMahon.*

PEARL PROSPECT 7 br.g. Kambalda–Georgette (Neron) [1989/90 16f* 16d* 16g5] leggy, workmanlike gelding: won novice handicap hurdles at Wincanton in November and Nottingham following month: most impressive on latter course, quickening clear run-in to beat Marradong Brook 12 lengths: well beaten in useful novice company at Kempton in January: stays 2¼m: possibly unsuited by very soft going, acts on any other. *Miss H. C. Knight.* 104 +

PEARL RUN 9 ch.g. Gulf Pearl–Deep Down (Deep Run) [1989/90 20d6] small gelding: fairly useful hurdler at his best: bit backward, well beaten in February: best form at up to 2½m: acts on soft going: claimer ridden nowadays. *G. Price.* —

PEARL WHITE 4 ch.f. Star Appeal–Pearling (Ribero) [1989/90 17fur a20g 16gpu] placed at up to 1m on Flat, showing poor form: sold out of M. Bell's stable 1,600 gns Newmarket Autumn Sales: tailed off in selling hurdle. *K. A. Ryan.* —

PEARLY KING (USA) 7 b.g. Tromos–Perfect Mix (USA) (The Pie King) [1989/90 16g] tall, leggy gelding: unreliable handicap hurdler: backward in December: edged left when fourth in novice chase in 1988/9: seems not to stay 2½m: acts on heavy going: tends to sweat: has won for a claimer: blinkered last start 1988/9: sold 4,800 gns Ascot May Sales. *S. Christian.* c— — §

PEARLYMAN 11 b.g. Mandamus–Pearlyric (Eastern Lyric) [1989/90 c16g3 c16g5 c16fpu] c**163** —

After the latest season it's tempting to conclude that come-backs should be left to Frank Sinatra. High-class performers See You Then, Playschool, River Ceiriog, The West Awake and Pearlyman all returned after injury and failed to win a race between them. But going to the third-last fence in the Queen Mother Champion Chase at Cheltenham, the last-named, winner of the race in 1987 and 1988, looked like handsomely rewarding his connections' perseverance. Waited with initially, Pearlyman had improved his place steadily from halfway and could be seen travelling strongly in a close fourth place behind Sabin du Loir, Barnbrook Again and Waterloo Boy. But just as the race was hotting up, Pearlyman hit the third last and was immediately pulled up. He was subsequently found to have aggravated an old injury on his near-fore, and was retired. The way Barnbrook Again had to be hard ridden to hold off Waterloo Boy by half a length, with Feroda coming from some way off the pace to finish only seven lengths further back in third, suggests that Pearlyman would have taken some beating but for breaking down. Pearlyman had started 6/1 third favourite for the race, two previous runs under big weights in handicaps having suggested that even if he didn't retain all of his ability he certainly warranted serious consideration in a non-vintage year. At Wetherby in December in the Castleford Chase, Pearlyman just got the worst of a battle with Ida's Delight and Nohalmdun, each receiving 24 lb. Pearlyman wasn't at all disgraced when fourteen lengths fifth to Meikleour in the well-contested Victor Chandler Chase at Ascot the following month, the stiffness of his task illustrated by his giving 24 lb to subsequent Queen Mother Champion Chase third Feroda. Indeed, Pearlyman did well to finish so close, having got behind through jumping less well than usual early on.

Pearlyman (b.g. 1979)	Mandamus (br 1960)	Petition (b 1944)	Fair Trial
			Art Paper
		Great Fun (br 1945)	Big Game
			Merry Devon
	Pearlyric (b 1965)	Eastern Lyric (gr 1943)	Taj Ud Din
			Cossor Song
		Pearl Smoke (b 1960)	My Smokey
			Arctic Pearl

Pearlyman's dam Pearlyric has bred two other winners, the modest hurdler/chaser Pearlyking and the selling hurdler Cheeky King (both by Space King). Her last two foals, both by Rymer, were sold at the Doncaster Spring Sales in 1989; her three-year-old joined Mrs Bramall for 16,000 guineas; the four-year-old, now named Poetic Gem, was bought for 21,000 guineas and finished third in a National Hunt Flat race at Sandown in March for G. B. Balding. Pearlyman is easily the best jumper sired by Mandamus. Indeed, at his peak we rated Pearlyman behind only Badsworth Boy amongst specialist two-mile chasers since Dunkirk in the 'sixties. In winning the Queen Mother Champion Chase he accounted both times for Very Promising and Desert Orchid—two horses well up to winning the race in an average year. The most valuable of Pearlyman's three other wins at Cheltenham came in the Grand Annual Challenge Cup as a novice in 1985/6—a season which also saw his winning quite valuable novice events at Ascot and Liverpool. The stocky Pearlyman put up some good weight-carrying performances in other handicaps, most notably when trouncing his field in the Castleford Chase at Wetherby in December, 1987, under 12-7.

A free runner with a good turn of foot, Pearlyman never raced beyond seventeen furlongs. He acted on good to firm and soft ground. Cheltenham was the first time he'd been risked on really firm. A difficult horse to train almost throughout his career—he raced only twenty-eight times in eight seasons—Pearlyman was fired after winning a novice hurdle at Wincanton on his only outing of 1984/5, and missed the whole of the 1988/9 season due to a tendon strain. Though bandaged in front on each outing in his final season, Pearlyman invariably impressed in condition, in particular at Wetherby, looking in tremendous shape for his first outing in twenty months. *J. A. C. Edwards.*

PEA SAL 7 b.g. Peacock (FR)–Fighting Sal (Gail Star) [1989/90 c24s c25g c25d^3 c26s^3 c20d] tall gelding: carries plenty of condition: placed in point-to-points in Ireland: novice hurdler/chaser: best effort when third to Knight Oil over fences at Uttoxeter in February, fourth outing: suited by at least 3m and plenty of give in the ground. *M. Oliver.* **c101** —

PEATY GLEN 5 b.g. Furry Glen–June's Slipper (No Argument) [1989/90 F 16f] half-brother to winning jumpers Shanbally Boy (by Random Shot), June's Juke (by Jukebox) and Rockbarton (by Lord Gayle): dam unraced half-sister to very useful stayer Tamerslip: favourite, well-beaten seventh in NH Flat race at Ascot: yet to race over hurdles or fences. *G. B. Balding.*

PECCAVI 6 ch.g. Hard Fought–Princess Sinna (Sun Prince) [1989/90 c24dpu c16fF] apparently of little account on Flat: tailed off when pulled up in hunter chase at Worcester in May: disputing lead when falling last in novice chase won by Blue Rainbow at Hereford later in month. *V. R. Bishop.* **c80**

PECHE D'OR 6 ch.g. Glint of Gold–Fishermans Bridge (Crepello) [1989/90 24mpu 16mpu 16g6 16m] sparely-made gelding: winning hurdler: no form in 1989/90, finding nothing under pressure when well beaten in seller final start: stays 21f: acts on any going: blinkered in 1987/8 and on final start: subsequently sold 1,550 gns Ascot December Sales. *D. Burchell.* —

PEERGLOW 6 br.m. Raga Navarro (ITY)–Go Perrys (High Hat) [1989/90 16g3 a16g2 16s4 a16g2 a18g3 a16g5 16m a20g5] smallish, leggy mare: novice selling hurdler: stays 2¼m: blinkered nowadays: has looked less than keen. *C. N. Williams.* 72

PEER PRINCE (USA) 5 br.h. Vaguely Noble–Sweet Maid (USA) (Proud Clarion) [1989/90 18f* 16m* 16m* 16g5 16m2 22f4] smallish, well-made horse: made running when successful over hurdles at Fontwell, Warwick and Chepstow (Timeform Hurdle) early in season: sold privately out of G. Pritchard-Gordon's stable after fifth start: appeared to show much improved form when around 13 lengths fourth to Grabel in very valuable Dueling Grounds International Hurdle when next seen out in April: stays 2¾m: acts on hard ground and is possibly unsuited by a soft surface: races with plenty of zest: jumps very well. *C. Fenwick, USA.* 153 ?

PEGASUS HEIGHTS 4 ch.g. Air Trooper–Confetti Copse (Town And Country) [1989/90 16g 16m] lengthy, angular gelding: tailed off in minor event on Flat: no sign of ability in juvenile hurdles at Wincanton. *R. J. Hodges.* —

Timeform Hurdle, Chepstow—Peer Prince holds off Jubail and Nahar

Major A. K. Barlow's "Pegwell Bay"

PEGMARINE (USA) 7 b.g. Text (USA)–Symbionese (USA) (Bold Reason) [1989/90 25gpu] compact gelding: lightly-raced maiden on Flat: sold out of M. Jarvis' stable 1,700 gns Ascot 2nd June (1986) Sales: jumped badly and tailed off when pulled up 4 out in novice hurdle at Newbury in December. *Mrs A. M. Woodrow.* —

PEG'S GEM 5 b.m. Sparkler–Eastern Air (Levanter) [1989/90 F12g3] second foal: dam won at 1½m and 13f: staying-on third behind Fairways On Target in NH Flat race at Hexham in March: yet to race over hurdles or fences. *P. Monteith.*

PEGWELL BAY 9 b.g. Tobique–Multigrey (Eastern Lyric) [1989/90 c20g* c24g5 c21g2 c26f5 c20f2] c**160** —

Until he was pulled up when behind in very testing conditions in the Tote Cheltenham Gold Cup on his final start Pegwell Bay did nothing but improve in 1988/9. Success in the Glynwed International Handicap Chase at Newbury and the Mackeson Gold Cup and A. F. Budge Gold Cup at Cheltenham was followed by his running Desert Orchid to three quarters of a length when in receipt of 18 lb in the Racecall Gainsborough Handicap Chase over twenty-five furlongs at Sandown. There was reason to think that the eight-year-old Pegwell Bay would progress further after his first race of the latest season, which came in the quite valuable C & L Murphy Trial Handicap Chase at Kempton in November. The outsider of three behind the Queen Mother Champion Chase winner Barnbrook Again and the in-form Panto Prince, Pegwell Bay pulled his way into the lead after the fourth, made the rest of the running and won by four lengths from Panto Prince;

Barnbrook Again ran a lifeless race and was tailed off when falling six out. Despite the small field the form looked sound when Panto Prince went on to finish a creditable second in the SGB Handicap Chase at Ascot on his next start. Pegwell Bay's next race was in the King George VI Rank Chase at Kempton on Boxing Day and he started second favourite behind the eventual winner Desert Orchid in a field of six. Fine jumping and an enthusiastic approach to the job on hand had been a feature of Pegwell Bay's performance as he stretched Desert Orchid down the far side second time round in the previous season's Gainsborough, but, ridden with more restraint, he ran a lack-lustre race in the King George and trailed in a well-beaten fifth; he made several jumping errors and was already having difficulty staying in touch when a further mistake five out effectively put paid to what chance he had.

Pegwell Bay's jumping was again not so bold as usual, despite a return to forcing tactics, in the John Bull Chase at Wincanton in January. Setting a steady pace in the early stages, he quickened six out but couldn't shake off his only serious opponent Toby Tobias, who took command three from home and won by eight lengths. Subsequent events showed that Pegwell Bay faced a very stiff task in conceding 8 lb to the rapidly-improving winner, who went on to finish a close second to Norton's Coin in the Tote Cheltenham Gold Cup. Pegwell Bay also ran in the Gold Cup but spoiled his effort with a couple of mistakes. Travelling strongly in third place starting the final circuit, he looked in trouble before the top of the hill, was beaten before three out and finished fifth, twenty-three lengths behind Toby Tobias. On his only subsequent start Pegwell Bay was returned to Cheltenham for the South Wales Showers Caradon Mira Silver Trophy. Unfortunately for him a back-to-form Barnbrook Again produced an exceptional performance—the best of the season by any chaser apart from Desert Orchid—and gave him 10 lb and a ten-length beating. In a strongly-run race, Pegwell Bay was struggling after a mistake at the tenth of the seventeen fences, but he stuck to his task and stayed on to go into second place two out, though with no chance of catching Barnbrook Again.

Pegwell Bay (b.g. 1981)	Tobique (ch 1974)	Connaught (b 1965)	St Paddy
			Nagaika
		Ship Yard (ch 1963)	Doutelle
			Paving Stone
	Multigrey (gr 1963)	Eastern Lyric (gr 1943)	Taj Ud Din
			Cossor Song
		Maiden Wrangler (br 1945)	Quadrangle
			Kennel Maid

Pegwell Bay is a half-brother to two winners, Intersport (by Deadly Nightshade), the winner of a two-and-a-half-mile novice hurdle, and Berulia (by Track Spare), who won over six furlongs as a two-year-old. Their dam, Multigrey, was a fair staying hurdler as was the next dam Maiden Wrangler. With the notable exception of the Gainsborough Chase, Pegwell Bay's best performances over fences have been at two and a half miles. He acts on heavy going but has shown better form on a sounder surface. *Capt. T. A. Forster.*

PELHAM SUITE 5 ch.g. Ovac (ITY)–Treasured Gift (Vivadari) [1989/90 16s^{ur}] sturdy gelding: second foal: dam unraced sister to winning staying chaser Camroc: backward, jumped moderately and was tailed off when unseating rider 2 out in novice hurdle at Sandown on debut. *J. T. Gifford.* —

PELLS CLOSE 7 gr.g. He Loves Me–Seriema (Petingo) [1989/90 c17h^{2} c18f^{3} c20f* c20f^{F} c22m^{4} c20f^{2} c21f^{3} c24s c20m^{2} c20g^{2} c25m^{pu}] plain gelding: winning selling hurdler: won novice chase at Plumpton in August: let down by his jumping and looked to have his own ideas about the game on several occasions afterwards though good second at Huntingdon twice in April: stays 2¾m: acts on any going: often visored (was when successful) or blinkered: looks a difficult ride but has won for a 7-lb claimer: one to treat with caution. *S. Dow.* c81 § —

PELOTA 4 gr.f. Petong–Lucky Deal (Floribunda) [1989/90 16f^{6} 16m^{4} 16f] angular filly: seems of little account on Flat and over hurdles: blinkered final start: sold 1,150 gns Newmarket September Sales. *A. N. Lee.* —

PEMBROKESHIRE LAD 9 ch.g. Nearly A Hand–Lady Columbus (St Columbus) [1989/90 c25g^{F} c25d^{4} c24g^{3} c36g^{2}] useful-looking gelding: fair chaser nowadays: staying-on 15 lengths second to Willsford in Taylorsteel Midlands Grand National at Uttoxeter in April: stays well: best form with give in the ground: jumps soundly in the main. *R. Lee.* **c118**

PENALTY DOUBLE 6 b.g. Deep Run–Silver Doll (Sovereign Gleam) [1989/90 16g* 18d^{2} 16f* 18m^{4} 17d^{4} 16s 16m* 16g^{6}] rather unfurnished gelding: won handicap hurdles at Stratford in October, Wincanton in November and Chepstow (beat Owen 2 lengths) in April: moderate sixth final outing: will stay 2½m: acts on firm and dead going (possibly unsuited by very soft): none too fluent a jumper: tends to be on toes in preliminaries. *C. P. E. Brooks.* 118

PEN BAL QUEEN 4 b.f. Record Run–Dazzling Hue (Double Jump) [1989/90 aF13g^{5}] half-sister to 2½m hurdle winner Blues Bank (by Malicious): dam never ran: well-beaten fifth in NH Flat race at Lingfield in February: yet to race over hurdles. *R. Curtis.*

PENDENNIS 7 ch.g. Pollerton–Lady Reporter (London Gazette) [1989/90 c20g^{F} c20g* c20d^{pu} c16m^{2} c20f^{3} c16m^{2}] big, lengthy, good sort with plenty of scope: winning hurdler: won novice chase at Leicester in January by 1½ lengths from Western Legend, pair long way clear: ran well when placed in useful company afterwards, going down by 7 lengths to Al Hashimi at Chepstow in April on final start: stays 2½m: acts on firm and dead going: should make a useful handicapper. *N. J. Henderson.* **c120** p —

PENDLE LYRIC 8 b.m. Roscoe Blake–Penny Princess (Normandy) [1989/90 24d^{pu} 18s^{pu} 22g^{pu}] lengthy mare: second foal: dam, poor novice hurdler, is daughter of a poor sister to Pendil: tailed off when pulled up in novice hurdles. *W. A. Wales.* —

PENDLE ROYAL 14 ch.g. Royal Duet–Pennis Pearl (Pendragon) [1989/90 c25f^{5}] sturdy gelding: winning point-to-pointer: lightly-raced novice hurdler/chaser. *Mrs Corrina Hirst.* c**67** —

PENDLEY GOLD 9 ch.g. Le Bavard (FR)–Angel's Song (Ragusa) [1989/90 16g^{6} 16g^{4} 16g^{2} 16s 16d^{4} 17d 16g^{5} 22g^{6}] workmanlike gelding: handicap hurdler: good second at Ayr in December: ran moderately afterwards: stays 2½m: acts on heavy going (yet to race on a firm surface): suitable mount for a claimer: usually visored nowadays. *M. P. Naughton.* 93 d

PENHILL 5 b.g. Ballacashtal (CAN)–Midnight Mistress (Midsummer Night II) [1989/90 17m^{ur} 17m^{3} 16f* 20f* 20f^{ur} 20f^{3}] medium-sized gelding: handicap hurdler: made most to win in small fields at Hexham and Southwell within a week in September: creditable third later in month: stays 2½m: seems to act on any going. *G. M. Moore.* 111

PENLLYNE'S PRIDE 9 ch.g. Tachypous–Fodens Eve (Dike (USA)) [1989/90 21h^{2} 16f^{2} 17f^{3} 17f^{4} c20m^{4} c17h* c16m^{3} c16f^{F} c16f^{F} 16g a16g^{3} a16g^{4} a18g* a16g^{6} a16g* a20g^{3} a16g] long-backed gelding: bought in after winning selling handicap hurdles at Southwell (2,500 gns) and Lingfield (2,200 gns) in February: jumped deliberately but made all in handicap chase at Devon & Exeter in October (2 finished): has been reluctant to race: seems to stay 21f when conditions are fast: probably acts on any going: has been blinkered (including all 3 times when successful in 1989/90) and visored often: has won for a claimer. *R. T. Juckes.* c**72** 80

PENNILESS IMP 5 br.m. Impecunious–Munlochy (Allangrange) [1989/90 F16m] third foal: dam of no account: tailed off in NH Flat race at Ludlow: yet to race over hurdles or fences. *L. Waring.*

PENNY DREADFUL 7 ch.m. Nickel King–Catherine Street (Pall Mall) [1989/90 F16m 16g^{pu}] third live foal: dam poor maiden: behind in NH Flat race in October and tailed off when pulled up 3 out in novice hurdle in December. *T. Casey.* —

PENNY FORUM 6 b.g. Pas de Seul–Kind Thoughts (Kashmir II) [1989/90 16g 16g^{6} 16m^{2}] smallish, sparely-made gelding: useful hurdler: showed improved form when staying-on 10 lengths second to Moody Man in William Hill Imperial Cup (Handicap) at Sandown in March: takes a good hold: stays 2½m: acts on top-of-the-ground and seems unsuited by heavy: usually bandaged near-fore: wears blinkers: in good form over long distances on Flat in 1990. *J. Sutcliffe.* 140

PENNY KING 9 br.g. Pauper–Kiltegan (Charlottesvilles Flyer) [1989/90 c20s^{4}] rather sparely-made ex-Irish gelding: has been hobdayed: won a point-to-point in 1986 and NH Flat race in 1987: placed 3 times over hurdles: c**91** —

winning steeplechaser: sold out of T. Bergin's stable 13,000 gns Doncaster August Sales: gave impression he'd be suited by a return to further when fourth in hunter chase at Sandown in February: subsequently placed in point-to-points: stays 3m: acts on heavy going: has worn a crossed noseband: reportedly broke a blood vessel penultimate outing of 1988/9. *Glenn Humphrey.*

PENNY LOVER 6 gr. or ro.g. Sonnen Gold–Continental Divide (Sharp Edge) [1989/90 16s4 a20g3 a24g4] smallish, lengthy gelding: poor novice hurdler: suited by 2½m: blinkered last 2 starts of 1987/8, visored final outing 1988/9. *P. S. Felgate.* 85

PENNY ROSE 9 b.m. Whistlefield–Gambling Rose (Game Rights) [1989/90 16s3 21d 21fpu] sparely-made mare: won NH Flat race in 1985/6: third in mares novice hurdle at Towcester in February: didn't stay 21f after, and jumped with no confidence on firm going final start. *M. C. Pipe.* 93

PENNYSAVER 5 b.m. Le Johnstan–Bonitass (Shiny Tenth) [1989/90 16gpu 16g] smallish mare: of little account. *S. C. Davis.* —

PENSIONER PATCH 8 ch.g. Grey Ghost–Final Edition (Derek H) [1989/90 22f3 20m2 16m 22m] stocky gelding: modest novice hurdler: stays 2½m: acts on good to firm going. *J. T. Gifford.* 87

PENSIVE BEAUTY 5 b.m. Penmarric (USA)–Guanabara (GER) (Sigebert) [1989/90 16fpu] well beaten in modest company on Flat: behind when pulled up fifth in novice selling hurdle at Taunton in December. *W. G. Turner.* —

PENTHOUSE C (USA) 9 b.g. Cannonade (USA)–Poundcake (USA) (Hail To Reason) [1989/90 16g 16s 16g] big gelding: lightly-raced maiden on Flat: behind in novice hurdles. *A. R. Davison.* —

PENTINO 10 gr.m. Rugantino–Penandlou (High Perch) [1989/90 c24f c22mpu] rangy mare: winning point-to-pointer and poor novice chaser: best at up to 2¾m: best form on top-of-the-ground: has worn a tongue strap. *B. W. Holmes.* c—

PENYGROES 7 b.g. Welsh Pageant–Wolver Valley (Wolver Hollow) [1989/90 16gpu 16gF] small gelding: no form in 4 outings over hurdles (has only once got past the second). *G. H. Yardley.* —

PEOPLE'S CHOICE 5 br.g. Strong Gale–Carrig-An-Neady (Orchardist) [1989/90 16m 20g 16g 20s 16d 16s c16fF c21g3 c20f* c21f*] small gelding: half-brother to winning staying chaser Welfare (by Carlburg), winning Irish hurdler Run For Silver (by Proverb) and winning point-to-pointer Kilclooney Forrest (by King's Equity): dam unraced: well beaten in novice hurdles: won maiden chase at Wetherby and novice chase at Cartmel (by a neck from Walk of Life) in May, both 4-runner races: will stay beyond 21f: acts on firm ground: likely to progress further. *W. A. Stephenson.* c**86** p —

PERCHCOURT 5 b.g. Red Sunset–Faddle (St Paddy) [1989/90 20gpu] plating-class staying maiden on Flat: behind when pulled up last in novice hurdle at Wetherby in November: sold 1,000 gns Doncaster January Sales. *R. M. Whitaker.* —

PERENNELLA 4 ch.f. Kind of Hush–Oranella (Orange Bay) [1989/90 F17f] first foal: dam, daughter of a useful winner in Italy, winner at up to 2¼m on Flat: tailed off in NH Flat race at Doncaster: yet to race over hurdles. *T. T. Bill.*

PERFECT GLEN 10 ch.g. Kemal (FR)–Glenreeba (Cappagh Boy) [1989/90 c24fpu] big, workmanlike gelding: poor chaser nowadays: fourth in a point-to-point in March: tailed off when pulled up in hunter chase at Wetherby in May: best form at around 2m: goes well on top-of-the-ground: sometimes sweats up: usually makes mistakes. *P. J. Harle.* c— x —

PERFECT STRANGER 6 b.g. Wolver Hollow–Mrs Walmsley (Lorenzaccio) [1989/90 16f 17g4 22m3 24gpu] leggy, sparely-made gelding: handicap hurdler: good third at Wincanton in December: stays 2¾m (tailed off when pulled up and dismounted run-in over 3m): acts on firm going and is possibly unsuited by soft. *T. B. Hallett.* 109

PERISTYLE 4 br.f. Tolomeo–Persevering (Blakeney) [1989/90 16f2 17m* 17m* 16g* 16m*] leggy filly: half-sister to a novice selling hurdler by Dominion: dam winning half-sister to useful hurdler Pueblo: plating-class maiden on Flat, best form at 1½m: sold out of R. Hollinshead's stable 5,200 gns Newmarket Autumn Sales: made running when easily landing the odds in juvenile selling hurdles at Devon & Exeter in March and Stratford (bought out of M. Pipe's stable 13,000 gns) in April and novice selling hurdle on first-named course in between: made most to win handicap at Stratford in May by 1½ lengths from Bumptious Boy: will stay further: acts on firm ground. *R. Lee.* 100 p

PERMANENTLY PINK 4 b.g. Auction Ring (USA)–Hawaiian Joss (USA)
(Hawaii) [1989/90 17f^{F} 16m 16d^{pu}] sparely-made gelding: won 7f seller at 2 yrs —
(little worthwhile form on Flat since when trained by H. O'Neill): seems of little
account over hurdles: changed hands 800 gns Ascot February Sales. *R. J. Hodges.*

PERNICKETY 10 b.g. Proverb–Royal Rally (Royal Record II) [1989/90 c25g^{3} **c80**
c27v^{ur} c26s^{5} c26d^{4} c25m^{pu} c21f^{2} c27h^{2} c24m c19f^{3}] workmanlike gelding: novice —
hurdler: winning point-to-pointer/hunter chaser: sold out of J. Greenall's stable
3,200 gns Ascot October Sales: in frame several times in 1989/90: stays 25f: acts
on any going. *C. L. Popham.*

PERNOIC 10 b.m. Peter Wrekin–Pernel (Space King) [1989/90 c25m^{2} c24m^{pu} **c95**
c28g^{pu} c27v^{su} c20d^{2} c24m* c24g^{2} c26m^{2}] small, lengthy mare: handicap chaser —
nowadays: left clear last when winning at Chepstow in April: close second
afterwards at Worcester and Uttoxeter (to Jay-Zee Boy): didn't go through with
her effort fifth start: stays 3¼m: acts on firm going: trained by J. Dalton until after
third start. *R. Lee.*

PERROQUET 10 gr.g. Precipice Wood–Verosina (Lord of Verona) [1989/90 **c123**
c21g* c20d* c24g*] sturdy gelding: very useful point-to-pointer/hunter chaser: —
has won 6 times at Fakenham, including in February and April (beat Deer Crest
impressively by 10 lengths): successful at Leicester in between: effective at 2½m
and stays 3m: probably acts on any going: suited by forcing tactics. *G. Vergette.*

PERRY WELL 6 b.g. Maculata–Magic Minstrel (Pitpan) [1989/90 22s^{4} 22v^{pu}
24m^{3} 20d^{5}] compact gelding: modest novice hurdler: stays 3m: acts on soft and 95
good to firm ground. *K. C. Bailey.*

PERSIAN LUCK 4 br.g. Persian Bold–Ansedonia (Captain's Gig (USA))
[1989/90 16g 16f 16h* 18f^{4} 16m^{2}] angular gelding: half-brother to winning 91
Franco-Belgian jumper Wathaab (by Wolver Hollow): modest handicapper at up to
7f on Flat when trained by P. Cole: made most when winning 5-runner novice
hurdle at Plumpton in March: length second of 3 to Fair Seas in juvenile handicap
at Huntingdon in May: pulls hard and likely to prove best over sharp 2m: acts on
hard ground: has been taken early to post: amateur ridden. *D. Welsh.*

PERSIAN MONARCH 4 gr.c. Persepolis (FR)–Aristata (Habitat) [1989/90
16m^{6} 16m 16f^{pu}] leggy colt: third in 1m seller in 1989: no form in juvenile hurdles —
in first half of season: sold 1,200 gns Doncaster January Sales. *R. Hollinshead.*

PERSIAN STYLE 6 br.g. Persian Bold–Marcela (Reform) [1989/90 16g*
16m^{F} 16m^{pu}] small, strong, close-coupled gelding: stayed on well after a mistake 129
at the last when winning minor hurdle at Cheltenham in November by 2 lengths
from Jinxy Jack: subsequently off course 4 months: broke blood vessel final start:
should be suited by 2½m (in lead when falling 3 out over trip in 1987/8): acts on
heavy going. *J. T. Gifford.*

PERSIAN SWORD 4 b.g. Broadsword (USA)–Sorraia (El Ruedo) [1989/90
16m 16g 16d 16f] rather sparely-made gelding: seventh reported foal: dam never —
ran: novice hurdler: no form: claimer ridden. *D. Nicholson.*

PERSILLANT 6 b.h. Persian Bold–Gauloise (Welsh Pageant) [1989/90 16m
16d^{4} 16g^{2} 16d 16d 16f^{3} 16f^{2} 16f^{4} 16f*] compact horse: useful hurdler: long odds on, 138
well below his best when beating Strike A Chord a short head (originally adjudged
to have dead-heated) in minor event at Warwick in May: in frame on previous 3
starts in County Hurdle at Cheltenham (length third behind Moody Man), Janneau
Armagnac Hurdle at Liverpool (½-length second to Jubail) and Swinton Insurance
Trophy at Haydock (2½ lengths fourth behind Sybillin): will stay 2½m: acts on
firm and dead going. *N. Tinkler.*

PERTEMPS NETWORK 6 br.g. Touching Wood (USA)–No Relation (Klai- **c100**
ron) [1989/90 c16g^{F} c20m* c20m^{2} 24g^{4} 24s^{3} 21s^{5}] compact gelding: leading 146
novice hurdler in 1988/9: ran in snatches when 22 lengths third behind Mrs Muck
in valuable sponsored event at Haydock in January: 11/4 on and blinkered, tailed
off, finishing distressed, in minor event at Warwick following month: jumped
rather deliberately when winning 2-runner novice chase at Leicester in December: none too fluent when 20 lengths second to Rynode in similar race at
Wolverhampton later in month: stays 3m: well suited by soft ground and forcing
tactics: probably best with strong handling: needs to improve his jumping of
fences: has joined R. Lee. *M. C. Pipe.*

PETALOUDA 6 ch.m. Avgerinos–Normandy Velvet (Normandy) [1989/90 16f
16h^{5} 20m 16m 21f^{5} 18f^{su}] lengthy, sparely-made mare: lightly-raced novice 59
hurdler: has run in a seller. *P. Howling.*

PETER PIPER 6 ch.g. True Song–Indian Diva (Indian Ruler) [1989/90 16g5 21d5 21fpu] rangy gelding: will make a chaser: won NH Flat race in 1988/9: modest form in novice hurdles: beaten when pulled up lame 2 out final start: will be suited by 3m. *N. J. Henderson.* 97

PETE'S SAKE 5 b.g. Scorpio–Pete's Money (USA) (Caucasus) [1989/90 c20s4] good-bodied gelding: first foal: half-brother to 1m winner Yuno Why (by Horage): dam unraced sister to a winner in USA and half-sister to a stakes winner by Top Command: placed in a point-to-point in 1989: bought for 24,000 gns Doncaster Spring (1989) Sales: made a couple of mistakes and weakened from 3 out when remote fourth to Party Politics in novice chase at Warwick in February. *F. Walwyn.* c**86** p

PETORINO 4 b.c. Petorius–Torino (Firestreak) [1989/90 16f3 16fpu] quite a modest sprint maiden on Flat: third in selling hurdle at Market Rasen in July: pulled up lame when next seen out 8 weeks later: has worn a tongue strap. *R. O'Leary.* 78

PETTICOAT POWER 4 b.f. Petorius–Red Realm (Realm) [1989/90 16g3 16d4] small, sparely-made filly: second foal: dam, won over 8.5f and 9.5f in Ireland, half-sister to useful hurdler Old Dundalk: modest 7f winner on Flat: changed hands 4,200 gns Newcastle Autumn Sales: ridden by 7-lb claimer when in frame in juvenile hurdle and a novice hurdle (remote fourth) at Windsor in January: headstrong and will prove best at 2m. *G. B. Balding.* 84

PETTY BRIDGE 6 b.g. Weavers' Hall–Royal Cup (Politico (USA)) [1989/90 22d2 22g4] leggy gelding: modest novice hurdler: stays 2¾m: acts on dead going. *A. P. James.* 92

PHAISTOS (FR) 5 gr.h. Bellypha–Sainte Gemme (FR) (Dancer's Image (USA)) [1989/90 F12m F16g] third foal: brother to French 8.5f winner Saint Hermine and half-brother to another winner by Akarad: dam French provincial 8.3f winner: ninth in NH Flat race at Bangor in October: visored, tailed off in similar event at Ayr following month: yet to race over hurdles or fences. *M. P. Naughton.*

PHALIES FOLLY 8 ch.g. Pauper–Lucy Ladybird (Menelek) [1989/90 24spu c20dpu 24f3 22m5] leggy, close-coupled gelding: poor novice hurdler: pulled up on chasing debut. *M. F. Barraclough.* c— 66

PHANTOM SINGER 4 ch.f. Relkino–Grace Note (Parthia) [1989/90 16sF 16d5 a16g] angular filly: half-sister to several winners over hurdles: modest 11f winner on Flat: sold out of Sir Mark Prescott's stable 15,000 gns Newmarket Autumn Sales: jumped none too fluently when around 19 lengths fifth of 6 to Royal Square in Chatteris Fen Hurdle at Huntingdon in February: well beaten at Lingfield 8 days later: sold P. Monteith 8,600 gns Doncaster Spring Sales. *N. A. Callaghan.* 87 ?

PHARAMINEUX 4 ch.g. Pharly (FR)–Miss Longchamp (Northfields (USA)) [1989/90 16f 16dur] strong gelding: modest 1¾m winner on Flat: behind in juvenile hurdle at Huntingdon in August and when unseating rider last at Kempton in November. *W. Wilson.* —

PHAROAH'S LAEN 9 b.g. Laen–Pharaoh's Lady (Pharaoh Hophra) [1989/90 c26v* c25d* c25fpu] tall, leggy gelding: fair hurdler: very useful chaser: showed improved form when winning handicap chase at Newton Abbot in December and Warwick Premier Chase (staying on dourly to score by 2½ lengths from Steeple View) in January, making most and jumping soundly on each occasion: led until pulled up lame after 3 out in Ritz Club National Hunt Handicap Chase at Cheltenham in March: a thorough stayer: acts on any going: suitable mount for an amateur or claimer. *M. C. Pipe.* c**145** —

PHAROAH'S SON 4 ch.g. Hello Sonny–Pharaoh's Lady (Pharaoh Hophra) [1989/90 F16f6] half-brother to very useful staying chaser Pharoah's Laen (by Laen): dam never ran: 15 lengths sixth behind True Magic in NH Flat race at Warwick in May: yet to race over hurdles. *M. C. Pipe.*

PHILIP 8 b.g. Kala Shikari–Canteen Katie (King's Troop) [1989/90 16f6 16d 16m] compact gelding: fairly useful sprinter at 5 yrs but has deteriorated on Flat since: behind in novice hurdles. *N. Tinkler.* —

PHILIPPONNAT (USA) 4 b.g. Sensitive Prince (USA)–August Bride (USA) (Chieftain II) [1989/90 16s] leggy gelding: well beaten in varied company on Flat: sold out of M. Usher's stable 2,900 gns Newmarket Autumn Sales: soon ridden and finished tailed off in juvenile hurdle at Hereford in December. *A. F. Leighton.* —

PHILOSOPHOS 4 b.g. High Top–Pacificus (USA) (Northern Dancer) [1989/90 17g* $16g^{2}$ $16d^{5}$ 16g* $16m^{2}$ $16m^{3}$ $16f^{5}$] 135

The latest crops of juvenile and two-mile novice hurdlers were less than vintage ones, notwithstanding the successes of Sybillin and Atlaal in open competition in big handicaps. There were few potentially top-notch hurdlers obvious amongst them. A contributory factor may have been the dominance of the top end of the market at the Horses In Training Sales at Newmarket in the autumn by foreign buyers. The sale is a traditional source of jumping recruits from the Flat, but in the latest season, of forty-four three-year-olds and upwards changing hands for 30,000 guineas or more, around three quarters went for export, principally to Saudi Arabia. Only eight raced over hurdles in Britain in the latest season, most notably the fairly useful novice Stratford Ponds.

There were still bargains to be found at the lower end of the market, however. Philosophos, bought out of P. Walwyn's stable for 6,500 guineas, developed into a leading juvenile. He recouped his purchase price with interest when winning the quite valuable Tote Placepot Hurdle at Kempton in February. A winner at Devon & Exeter on his hurdling debut in December, Philosophos had been a quite well-beaten fifth to New Arrangement in a well-contested event on good to soft ground at Sandown the following month—never able to get back into the race after a mistake at the third—and started at 33/1 in a field of eleven for the Tote Placepot Hurdle. Philosophos travelled comfortably from the start on the good ground at Kempton, tracking the good pace set by General Pershing and Carbisdale. Sent to the front two flights out, he ran on well to win by five lengths and six from Calicon and Carbisdale. Philosophos' dramatic improvement—seemingly a surprise to connections who had withdrawn him from the Daily Express Triumph Hurdle at the first forfeit stage earlier in the week—was confirmed in three outings on firmer ground in the spring. On each occasion he travelled strongly for a long way until beaten for a turn of speed in the latter stages. In the quite valuable Northern Champion Juvenile Handicap Hurdle at Newcastle in March, Philosophos led two out but couldn't quicken clear of Rouyan who rallied to lead at the last and beat him two and a half lengths. Philosophos kept on without being able to reach the front when four and a half lengths third behind Fidway in the Seagram 100 Pipers Top Novices' Hurdle at Liverpool and six and a half lengths fifth to Sybillin in the Swinton Insurance Trophy at Haydock, running slightly below his best on

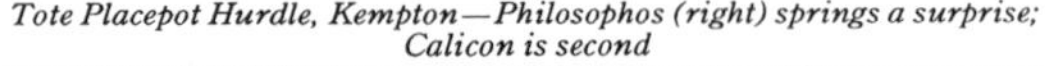
Tote Placepot Hurdle, Kempton—Philosophos (right) springs a surprise; Calicon is second

the very firm ground on the latter course. Philosophos is likely always to be suited by a good gallop when racing at two miles—forcing tactics may be worth trying—and will stay further.

Philosophos (b.g. 1986)	High Top (b 1969)	Derring-Do (b 1961)	Darius
			Sipsey Bridge
		Camenae (b 1961)	Vimy
			Madrilene
	Pacificus (USA) (b 1981)	Northern Dancer (b 1961)	Nearctic
			Natalma
		Pacific Princess (b 1973)	Damascus
			Fiji

Philosophos comes from a successful Flat family. Pacificus, a winner twice over thirteen furlongs in Britain, is the third foal out of smart American winner at up to nine furlongs, Pacific Princess, the dam also of 1990 Canadian Oaks third Tropical Sound. The next dam, Coronation Stakes winner Fiji, bred the useful mile-and-a-quarter performer Safety Match and Fleet Wahine, successful in the Ribblesdale Stakes and Yorkshire Oaks, from eight winning foals. Philosophos showed his only form on the Flat when runner-up in two handicaps at up to thirteen furlongs as a three-year-old. He should make a useful handicapper over hurdles. A leggy gelding, of medium size for a hurdler, Philosophos has run well when sweating slightly and when looking dull in his coat. He was ridden in all his races by conditional jockey McFarland, who was unable to draw his allowance at Kempton and Liverpool and lost his claim with a win at Taunton ten days prior to Haydock. *J. H. Baker.*

PHILOTAS 6 b.g. Pitskelly–Damaring (USA) (Saidam) [1989/90 16d^{4} 16g^{4} 16m 17f^{pu} 16g 17f^{5}] lightly-made gelding: novice selling hurdler: has race only at around 2m: possibly needs give in the ground: ran poorly in blinkers fourth start: has looked ungenuine. *Miss G. M. Rees.* 69

PHILS FRIEND 4 ch.g. Sunley Builds–Our Denise (Bend A Bow (USA)) [1989/90 16g^{ur} 16g a20g^{pu}] plain gelding: fourth reported foal: dam, quite modest, probably stayed 1m: no sign of ability in juvenile hurdles (tried to refuse and unseated rider debut): visored last 2 starts. *J. J. Bridger.* —

PHOEBE MERYLL 4 br.f. Marching On–Mistress Meryll (Tower Walk) [1989/90 16g 16f 16f^{pu}] sparely-made filly: plating-class maiden on Flat, in frame at up to 7f: sold out of J. W. Watts's stable 1,550 gns Doncaster November Sales: little promise over hurdles. *J. Parfitt.* —

PHOENIX GOLD 10 ch.g. Precipice Wood–Valeria (Vulgan) [1989/90 c20s^{ur} c20g*] strong, good sort: lightly raced but has developed into a very useful c**146** p —

Towton Handicap Chase, Wetherby—Phoenix Gold is an impressive winner

chaser: led approaching last and quickened clear to win handicap at Wetherby in December most impressively by 10 lengths from Villierstown: stays 2½m: acts on soft going (yet to race on top-of-the-ground): taken early to post on second start in 1988/9 and mounted on track since: usually races with enthusiasm: sure to win more races if all is well with him. *J. G. FitzGerald.*

PHOTINIA 5 b.g. Tender King–Permutation (Pinza) [1989/90 25f] leggy,
sparely-made gelding: modest hurdler: backward, tailed off in handicap at —
Catterick in October: stays well: acts on firm going (well beaten on soft going):
ridden by claimer. *T. Fairhurst.*

PHYLLIDA FOX 7 ro.m. Healaugh Fox–Fastidium (Psidium) [1989/90 16g
a20g 21s^{pu} 19s^{3} 25f^{2} 24m^{3} 25f^{pu}] leggy, plain mare: poor plater over hurdles: 79
blinkered third start. *R. J. Eckley.*

PHYLL-TARQUIN 10 b.m. Tarqogan–Purcella (Straight Lad) [1989/90
24m^{pu}] deep-bodied mare: of little account. *J. D. Roberts.* —

PHYRIAFAIR 9 b.g. Rouser–Brazen Lady (Bold As Brass) [1989/90 16h* c—
17f^{ur} 16h*] strong, sturdy gelding: led a long way out when winning novice 93
handicap hurdles at Hereford in August and Ludlow (by 25 lengths) following
month: has shown ability in novice chases: free-going sort, best at a sharp 2m:
acts on any going: has been mounted on course and was taken down early at
Ludlow. *R. Lee.*

PIA ROCKET 6 b.m. Pia Fort–Happy Lizzie (Hapanui) [1989/90 F16f] first foal: sister to novice hurdler Highwood Lad: dam failed to complete in point-to-points: tailed off in NH Flat race at Ludlow: yet to race over hurdles or fences. *R. J. Hodges.*

PICADOR 6 b.g. Piaffer (USA)–Go Gently (New Member) [1989/90 17m* 20f*
18f^{3} 20g^{pu} 20f* 24f* 24f*] angular, workmanlike gelding: improved after winning 121 p
early-season novice hurdles at Devon & Exeter and Cheltenham and was
successful in handicaps at Wolverhampton (novice event), Ascot (Alpine Meadow
Hurdle) and Cheltenham (beat Babil readily by 2 lengths in 3-runner event): stays
3m: acts on firm ground: effective with and without blinkers: should continue on
the upgrade. *P. J. Hobbs.*

PICASSO MOODS 6 b.g. Idiot's Delight–Alpogemy (Border Chief) [1989/90
21f* 21m* 20s^{2} 24s^{3} 21f* 24m^{4} 22f^{F}] rangy, angular ex-Irish gelding: fifth foal: 112
dam unraced: every chance when carried out 2 out in point-to-point in 1989:
claimer ridden, successful in novice hurdles at Towcester in November,
December and March: stayed 21f: probably acted on any going: dead. *O. Sherwood.*

PICA SWORD 4 br.c. Broadsword (USA)–Picotee (Pieces of Eight) [1989/90
16m 16f^{3} 17g^{2}] unfurnished colt: dam winning 2m hurdler: placed in juvenile 89
hurdles at Leicester and Newton Abbot (1½ lengths second to Softly) within 4
days in November. *C. P. E. Brooks.*

PIGEON ISLAND 8 b.g. General Ironside–Brown Cherry (Master Buck) c**81**
[1989/90 c24f^{2} c20m^{pu}] rather leggy gelding: lightly raced and no form in novice —
hurdles: second of 3 finishers in novice chase at Market Rasen in August, best
effort over fences: stays 3m: acts on firm ground. *P. A. Blockley.*

PIKEMAN 8 b.g. Turnpike–Cavallina (Vulgan) [1989/90 c26g^{pu} c24s^{pu} c28g^{2} c**89** §
c27v^{3} c20d c25g^{4} c25m^{5} c27f^{3}] compact gelding: winning chaser: let down by his —
jumping most outings in 1989/90, best efforts on third and sixth starts: stays 3½m
when conditions aren't testing: acts on dead going: usually visored or blinkered
nowadays: ungenuine. *R. Lee.*

PILLAR OF FIRE (USA) 5 b.g. Master Willie–As You Would (USA) (Fleet
Nasrullah) [1989/90 16s^{pu} 16g^{F} 16f^{5} 16g^{4} 16g^{pu}] good-bodied gelding: tempera- 78
mental 13f winner on Flat: sold out of C. Cyzer's stable 4,000 gns Newmarket
Autumn Sales: poor form in novice hurdles: dead. *M. D. I. Usher.*

PIN CUSHION 4 ch.f. Blue Cashmere–Tribal Princess (Tribal Chief) [1989/90
16m^{pu} 16f^{pu}] lengthy, angular, plain filly: sister to poor maiden How Blue and —
half-sister to a winner in Belgium: pulled up both outings over hurdles (saddle
slipped on debut). *D. J. Bell.*

PINE CODGER 5 gr.m. Legal Eagle–Precious Love (Precipice Wood)
[1989/90 16f 17m] good-bodied mare: fourth live foal: half-sister to winning selling —
hurdler Terrys Town (by Creetown): dam never ran: tailed off only outing on Flat
at 3 yrs: tailed off in novice hurdles. *C. Parker.*

PINEMARTIN 7 b.g. Pry–Sassenach Girl (Sassafras (FR)) [1989/90 c20m^{F} c—
17m^{2} 20g] rangy gelding: modest novice hurdler: close up when falling 4 out in 88

Tote Silver Trophy Handicap Hurdle, Chepstow—the winner Pipers Copse (No. 8) is upsides Milford Quay (No. 1) and Lumberjack at the last

novice chase at Perth in September: best at around 2m: acts on good to firm and dead ground. *G. Richards.*

PINEY POINT 5 ch.g. Buzzards Bay–Rockaway (Siliconn) [1989/90 18f^{4} 16g 16m^{5}] compact gelding: poor novice selling hurdler: stays 2¼m: best form on firm ground: blinkered last 2 starts. *G. Ripley.* —

PINISI 5 ch.g. Final Straw–Bireme (Grundy) [1989/90 16d^{pu} 24d] angular gelding: half-brother to winning hurdler Dhoni (by Bustino): maiden on Flat: sold out of R. Hern's stable 18,000 gns Ascot August Sales: little promise in novice hurdles: jumps none too fluently. *G. M. Moore.* —

PINK PANTHER 10 ch.g. Moulton–Pink Moss (Ballymoss) [1989/90 c16d c20s^{pu} 20g^{pu}] big, workmanlike gelding: novice hurdler/chaser: stays 3m: acts on dead going: sold 1,400 gns Doncaster June Sales. *D. McCain.* c— —

PIPERS COPSE 8 ch.g. Celtic Cone–Tarqoretta (Tarqogan) [1989/90 20g* 20d* 24g] leggy gelding: improved and won handicap hurdles at Kempton in October and Chepstow (valuable Tote Silver Trophy by 4 lengths from Milford Quay) following month: first outing for 3½ months, ran in snatches when well beaten in ROA Rendlesham Hurdle on former course in February: should be suited by 3m: acts on dead going. *G. Harwood.* 130

PIPER'S SON 4 b.g. Sagaro–Lovely Laura (Lauso) [1989/90 F16f*] half-brother to 2 winners, including 2m hurdle race winner Laureppa (by Jimmy Reppin): dam placed over 6f in France at 2 yrs: 4/1 from 12/1, won 13-runner NH Flat race at Ascot by 15 lengths from Cache Fleur with remainder well strung out: yet to race over hurdles. *M. Bradstock.*

PIRACY 6 gr.g. Rusticaro (FR)–All At Sea (Sea Hawk II) [1989/90 16m^{ur}] big, plain gelding: modest hurdler: unseated rider first in December: stays 2½m: moderate jumper. *Mrs D. Haine.* — x

PITCHCOTT HILL 5 b. or br.g. Pollerton–Khalice (Khalkis) [1989/90 F16s F16m] third foal: half-brother to winning Irish hurdler Wangantang (by Deep Run): dam winning hurdler/chaser in Ireland: behind in NH Flat races: yet to race over hurdles or fences. *D. Nicholson.*

PITHY 8 ch.g. Orange Bay–Pranky (Bold Lad (IRE)) [1989/90 c16d4 c20g4 c25m2] close-coupled, angular gelding: novice hurdler: modest chaser: 10 lengths second to Rymer King in handicap at Wolverhampton in December: stays 25f: acts on good to firm and dead ground but is possibly unsuited by heavy: has run well for a claimer over hurdles but gives impression he needs stronger handling over fences. *G. H. Yardley.* c**101** —

PIT PIECE 4 b.g. Pumps (USA)–On The Wing (Danger) [1989/90 16g 16gpu] smallish gelding: third reported foal: dam won on Flat and over hurdles in Ireland: well beaten at 2 yrs: tailed off in juvenile hurdle at Kelso in November: jumped poorly later in month. *J. S. Wilson.* —

PIT PONY 6 b.g. Hittite Glory–Watch Lady (Home Guard (USA)) [1989/90 16m6 16g5 16gpu 16g4 16g6 16d3 18d2 17g4 16gbd 16d6 16g4] small, compact gelding: inconsistent handicap hurdler: found nothing after being left clear 2 out eighth outing: stays 2½m: suited by plenty of give in the ground: sometimes visored (including when successful): one to have reservations about. *J. S. Wilson.* 86 §

PLAGUE O' RATS 6 b.g. Pitskelly–Hillbrow (Swing Easy (USA)) [1989/90 21v6 c20g c24gF 17d3 20f4 17h* 22m3] workmanlike, angular gelding: made all in 3-runner novice hurdle at Devon & Exeter in May: made much of running when creditable third in novice handicap at Stratford final start: always behind only completed outing over fences: stays 2¾m: seems to act on any going (possibly not heavy): has looked none too keen. *R. G. Frost.* c— 89

PLAIN JIM 13 b.g. Jimmy Reppin–Sidam (Psidium) [1989/90 c26fpu c26f6] big, rangy gelding: poor novice hurdler/chaser: has run in a seller: stays 3m: poor jumper: won a point-to-point in May. *Jamie Poulton.* c— x —

PLASTIC SPACEAGE 7 b.g. The Parson–Chestnut Fire (Deep Run) [1989/90 20v c20g c17d4 c17dur] tall, leggy gelding: first sign of ability when fourth in novice chase at Newbury in February: every chance when unseating rider 3 out in similar race on same course following month: gives impression he'll be suited by stiffer test of stamina. *J. A. B. Old.* c**89** —

PLATONIC AFFAIR 9 b.g. Kemal (FR)–Deep Shine (Deep Run) [1989/90 22m2 20f6 18f2 20m2 20f3 20d2 20gur 20g2 21f3 20d 16g] small, sturdy gelding: modest hurdler: showed ability in novice chase in 1987/8: stays 2¾m: acts on hard ground and dead going: has won for a claimer: trained by J. J. O'Neill until after first start. *D. A. Wilson.* c— 101

PLAUSIBLE 5 b.h. Neltino–False Evidence (Counsel) [1989/90 16g2 17vpu 16g a18g4] small horse: modest middle-distance stayer on Flat, usually blinkered or visored (claimed out of A. Hide's stable £9,350 after winning claimer in September): always-prominent second in novice hurdle at Warwick in December: only form afterwards (blinkered) moderate fourth in novice handicap at Lingfield in March: trained until after second start by K. Brassey. *K. O. Cunningham-Brown.* 94

PLAYFIELDS 16 b.g. Northfields (USA)–Windo (Derring-Do) [1989/90 c18m c16dpu c17v] small gelding: selling chaser: needs a test of stamina: acts on any going: sometimes wears blinkers. *P. Burgoyne.* c— —

PLAYPEN 6 b.g. Sit In The Corner (USA)–Blue Nursery (Bluerullah) [1989/90 16g 21s3 a24g2 17m2 21m3] small gelding: poor novice hurdler: probably stays 3m: acts on good to firm and soft going. *R. G. Frost.* 82

PLAYSCHOOL (NZ) 12 b.g. Valuta–Min Tide (NZ) (Harleigh) [1989/90 c24spu c29spu] sparely-made gelding: top-class chaser at his best: ran as though in need of race both starts in 1989/90: stays well: acts on any going. *D. H. Barons.* c— —

PLAY TO WIN 5 b.g. Runnett–Fair Or Foul (Patch) [1989/90 16g 16f] sparely-made gelding: no form over hurdles, including in sellers. *F. Gibson.* —

PLAZA GIZON (USA) 5 ch.g. Little Current (USA)–Regal Endeavour (USA) (Roberto (USA)) [1989/90 16m* 16g4 20m3 a20g* a18g* a24g2 a20g*] leggy, rather sparely-made gelding: won twice over middle distances on Flat in France in 1988, when trained by A. de Royer-Dupre: successful over hurdles in novice event at Huntingdon and 2 novice events and a handicap at Lingfield: not raced after January: stays 3m: acts on good to firm ground. *J. R. Jenkins.* 112

PLAZA TORO 11 ch.g. Ashmore (FR)–Duke Street (USA) (Lorenzaccio) [1989/90 21f4 26fpu 17f4 21f* 26f* 24f* 25h2 25f*] sparely-made, shallow-girthed gelding: front-running handicap hurdler: successful early in season at Newton Abbot (twice, has now won 6 times there) and Uttoxeter and was awarded race at 106

Cheltenham on technical disqualification of first past post: suited by long distances: acts on any going: good mount for a claimer. *W. G. Turner.*

PLEATED (USA) 8 b.g. Grey Dawn II–Kick Pleat (Windy Sands) [1989/90 c26f*] lengthy, sparely-made gelding: has been tubed: modest novice hurdler: jumped well when winning 3-runner intermediate chase at Uttoxeter in October very easily by 15 lengths: stays 3m: acts on firm going: blinkered third outing (jumped deliberately). *J. S. King.* c92 —

PLEDGDON GREEN 10 gr.g. Broxted–Lynn Regis (Ballymoss) [1989/90 c17m2 c16f4 c27fur] workmanlike gelding: poor hurdler/novice chaser: best at 2m: probably acts on any going: has pulled hard and worn a crossed noseband: usually amateur ridden. *V. Thompson.* c71 —

PLICATE (USA) 6 b.m. Buckfinder (USA)–Plie (USA) (Raja Baba (USA)) [1989/90 20spu 16g a16g 16gpu] rangy mare: poor maiden on Flat: no sign of ability in novice hurdles and a selling handicap: blinkered final start. *M. C. Banks.* —

PLUM TREE 4 ch.f. Dominion–Snow Tree (Welsh Pageant) [1989/90 16h*] sparely-made filly: first foal: dam, middle-distance winner, daughter of half-sister to smart stayer Celtic Cone: well beaten in 2 outings at 2 yrs: attracted no bid after winning juvenile selling hurdle at Taunton in October by 12 lengths from Fast Market: looked sure to improve but wasn't seen out again. *M. C. Pipe.* 73 p

POACHER'S PAL 5 br.h. Golden Love–Easter Noddy (Sir Herbert) [1989/90 16g 24d 20m 25g5 24g] sturdy horse: first foal: dam unraced: poor form over hurdles, including in sellers. *W. A. Stephenson.* —

POACHING POCKET 7 gr.g. Some Hand–Grey Bird (Eastern Venture) [1989/90 c20fF 22m 20g* 20f3 25gF] sparely-made gelding: first form over hurdles when winning novice handicap at Uttoxeter in October: good third in slowly-run novice hurdle on same course later in month: very stiff task, in lead when falling 5 out in handicap at Cheltenham in November: no form over fences: stays 2½m: acts on firm ground: has worn a crossed noseband. *P. D. Connors.* c— 85

POCKETED (USA) 4 b.c. Full Pocket (USA)–Duchess of Malfi (USA) (Prince John) [1989/90 16f* a16g 16d2 a16g* a16s3 a16g2 16m4] workmanlike colt: half-brother to useful jumpers in France and America: claimed out of Mrs L. Piggott's stable £7,056 after third in 1m claimer on Flat in August: won juvenile hurdles at Bangor following month and at Lingfield in January: creditable fourth in novice handicap at Fakenham in March: acts on firm ground. *J. R. Jenkins.* 92

POCKET JAMMER 4 b.f. Windjammer (USA)–Trouble Pocket (USA) (In The Pocket) [1989/90 16d 24fur] ninth foal: half-sister to 2-y-o 7f seller winner Late Progress (by On Your Mark) and to a winner in USA: dam never ran: tailed off in selling hurdle at Bangor in March: weakening when unseating rider 2 out in maiden event at Hexham in May: dead. *M. O'Neill.* —

POETIC GEM 5 b.g. Rymer–Pearlyric (Eastern Lyric) [1989/90 F16m3 F16m] 21,000 4-y-o: leggy, close-coupled gelding: half-brother to top-class 2m chaser Pearlyman (by Mandamus) and modest hurdler/chaser Pearlyking (by Space King): dam fairly useful hurdler: third in NH Flat race at Sandown in March: behind in well-contested event at Liverpool following month: yet to race over hurdles or fences. *G. B. Balding.*

POINT CLEAR 10 b.g. Le Bavard (FR)–Vulstar (Vulgan) [1989/90 a18g5 16m] sparely-made gelding: novice selling hurdler: maiden point-to-pointer: seems suited by 2½m: sometimes sweats up. *Mrs F. E. White.* —

POINTER MAN 9 ch.g. Major Point–Spanish Empress (Don (ITY)) [1989/90 20mpu] sturdy ex-Irish gelding: winning 2m hurdler: little form in novice chases in 1987/8: blinkered when successful: first outing for 18 months, tailed off when pulled up in December. *B. T. Crawford.* c— —

POINT MADE 7 b.g. Tycoon II–Cala Conta (Deep Run) [1989/90 16f2 c17m* c16g* c16f6 c16gF c20m2 c16gF a16g* a16g2 a20g3 c18f3 c16mwo c16m4 c21f2] close-coupled gelding: handicap hurdler: won at Lingfield in February: successful in early-season novice chase at Devon & Exeter (trained by Mrs J. Pitman) and intermediate chase at Stratford: walked over in handicap at Towcester in April: creditable second to Walnut Way in handicap at Newton Abbot final start: stays 2½m: yet to show his form on very soft going, acts on any other: good mount for a claimer: broke blood vessel second start 1988/9. *J. R. Bosley.* c104 104

POKEREE 7 gr.g. Uncle Pokey–Border Squaw (Warpath) [1989/90 25g3] lengthy gelding: handicap hurdler: jumped none too fluently when good third behind Leavenworth at Cheltenham in November: stays 3m: probably acts on any 115 +

going: claimer ridden: blinkered sixth start, visored final outing in 1988/9: won over 13f on Flat in 1990. *D. Moffatt.*

POKEY'S BELLE 6 b.m. Uncle Pokey–Belle of Sark (Daybrook Lad) [1989/90 20f 22g] workmanlike mare: well beaten in novice hurdles. *D. L. Williams.* —

POLAR DELTA 8 b.g. Polar Jinks–Delemar (Signa Infesta) [1989/90 c16m^{6} c20f^{3} c20g^{4} c21d^{pu} c20m^{F} c16f^{4} c16g c20g^{6} 22f^{ro} 20m] strong, workmanlike gelding: maiden point-to-pointer/poor novice chaser/hurdler: trained until after fourth start by P. Liddle. *D. McCaskill.* c62 —

POLAR GLEN 9 gr.g. Polaroid–Glenallen (Carnatic) [1989/90 c21d^{6} c25m^{4} c26f^{2} c25m^{3} c26f*] smallish, sparely-made gelding: fairly useful hunter chaser: won by 6 lengths from Oakgrove at Fontwell in May: suited by a good test of stamina: acts on any going: sometimes blinkered. *Jock Cullen.* **c110** —

POLAR ICE 14 b.g. Crozier–Ice C Ice (Thirteen of Diamonds) [1989/90 c16f^{5} 20s 27s^{pu} a20g a20g^{5} c22f^{pu}] compact, dipped-backed gelding: poor novice selling hurdler: novice chaser (jumped badly final outing): not certain to stay extreme distances. *J. L. Harris.* c— —

POLARIS 4 ro.g. Move Off–Toadpool (Pongee) [1989/90 aF16g F16d] third foal: brother to winning hurdler Bright Dancer: dam, sister to winning chaser Oakley Cross, well beaten in novice hurdle: tailed off in NH Flat races: yet to race over hurdles. *N. Chamberlain.*

POLAR NOMAD 9 br.g. Mandalus–Polar Lady (Arctic Slave) [1989/90 c24g^{2} c28m^{su} c30g^{2} c33d^{6} c24g^{6} c24g^{4}] big, rangy gelding: fair chaser at his best: respectable second on first start, ran moderately afterwards: suited by a thorough test of stamina: probably needs give in the ground: blinkered final outing. *W. A. Stephenson.* **c110** ?

POLAR VISION 4 b.g. Lyphard's Special (USA)–Arctic Drama (Northern Baby (CAN)) [1989/90 16g 16g^{6} 18s^{2} 16d] smallish, workmanlike gelding: middle-distance maiden on Flat (has run blinkered): sold out of C. Brittain's stable 15,500 gns Newmarket Autumn Sales: second in claiming hurdle at Fontwell in February: well below that form following month: will stay beyond 2¼m: acts on soft going: jumps none too fluently: retained by trainer 7,000 gns Ascot May Sales. *C. C. Elsey.* 96

POLDER 4 b.g. Lochnager–Dutch Girl (Workboy) [1989/90 16d 16g^{F} 17f 16g^{F} 16s 16g^{4} 17m^{2} 16f* 16g 16f*] leggy, lengthy gelding: well beaten in 2 sellers and a claimer at 2 yrs: won selling hurdles at Hereford in April (no bid) and May (bought in 2,600 gns): ran poorly in between: likely to prove best at around 2m: acts on firm going: wore a hood seventh start: claimed out of M. W. Easterby's stable £5,080 after sixth outing. *D. Burchell.* 86

POLECROFT 7 b.g. Crofter (USA)–Grange Kova (Allangrange) [1989/90 17v 21s] leggy, sparely-made gelding: selling hurdler: best form at 2m: acts on heavy going: blinkered third outing 1987/8: has run creditably for a claimer: has worn a crossed noseband. *M. W. Davies.* —

POLISH 12 gr.g. Tycoon II–Preshine (Specific) [1989/90 20s^{6} 24s^{4} 20d^{4} 27d^{bd} 22d] small, close-coupled gelding: handicap hurdler: poor form in 1989/90: has shown little aptitude for chasing: stays 3m: acts on soft going and is unsuited by top-of-the-ground: tailed off when blinkered once in 1985/6: has won for a claimer: has given impression that he has his own ideas about the game. *D. J. Wintle.* c— x 87

POLITBURO (USA) 10 b.g. Maribeau–Lovely Guinevere (USA) (Round Table) [1989/90 c24m^{ur} c21f^{2} c25f^{4}] big, good-topped gelding: of little account over hurdles: poor novice steeplechaser: won a point-to-point in March. *T. Normington.* c71 —

POLITE LADY 6 ch.m. Politico (USA)–Cowgate Lady (Most Secret) [1989/90 F16d] third foal: dam poor novice hurdler/chaser: behind in NH Flat race at Kelso in February: yet to race over hurdles or fences. *A. J. Wight.*

POLITICAL JUDGE 9 b.g. Politico (USA)–Madame Serenity (What A Man) [1989/90 c22f^{2} c20f^{4}] rangy, angular gelding: winning point-to-pointer/hunter chaser: thorough stayer: acts on firm ground: rider wears spurs. *D. C. Robinson.* c98

POLITICAL PROSPECT 8 b.m. Politico (USA)–Miss Prospect (Sweet Story) [1989/90 24m^{4} 22f^{6} c22m^{6} c24m^{F} c24f^{5} c24g^{ur} c20g^{4} c24d^{pu} 20d^{4} 25g^{pu}] compact mare: novice hurdler/chaser: held slight lead when falling 2 out over fences at Newcastle in November: also let down by her jumping next 2 starts: c84 x 78 suited by 3m: yet to show her form on extremes of going: blinkered last 2 starts (pulled up reportedly lame on final one). *Mrs J. D. Goodfellow.*

POLITICAL STORM 7 ch.m. Politico (USA)–Wrekin Fancy (Wrekin Rambler) [1989/90 16gpu] maiden point-to-pointer: tailed off when pulled up fourth in novice event at Perth on hurdling debut. *F. T. Walton.* —

POLLIBRIG 6 br.m. Politico (USA)–Taras Brig (New Brig) [1989/90 c20g6 c24dpu c24m3] workmanlike mare: second foal: dam, daughter of a useful point-to-pointer and winning hunter chaser, pulled up both outings over hurdles: poor form in novice chases, best effort over 3m on good to firm ground. *J. K. M. Oliver.* c69

POLLOCK (FR) 7 b.g. Arctic Tern (USA)–Golden Gleam (FR) (Lyphard (USA)) [1989/90 16m* 16m2 17m3 16h* 19g* 16g2 16d2 18f2 16m3 16g*] leggy, angular ex-French gelding: third foal: half-brother to 2 winners by Crystal Palace, notably good-class middle-distance performer Galla Placida: dam 1¼m winner: won twice at up to 1¼m on Flat in 1989 (claimed out of T. Clout's stable 126,000 francs (approx £12,200) after final start): won early-season novice hurdles at Worcester, Taunton and Hereford, and conditional jockeys novice event at Market Rasen in April: ran moderately eighth and ninth starts: stays 19f: has won on hard going, but best form with give in the ground: takes a good hold. *M. C. Pipe.* 120

POLLY-LOO 6 b.m. Owen Anthony–Meg Potter (Right Tack) [1989/90 16f] first foal: dam, 6f seller winner on Flat, poor plater over hurdles: tailed off in maiden hurdle at Market Rasen in July on debut. *Miss P. Hall.* —

POLO BOY 10 ch.g. Red Alert–Bermuda (Doutelle) [1989/90 c25m] close-coupled gelding: poor novice hurdler/chaser: twice attempted to refuse on only outing of season: was best at around 2m on ground no softer than dead: sometimes blinkered: dead. *G. B. Balding.* c— —

POLO PRINCE 7 gr.g. Nishapour (FR)–Tiepoless (Tiepolo II) [1989/90 c21f5 c16fro F18m3 F18f 16f c16f5] ex-Irish gelding: sixth foal: half-brother to Irish NH Flat race winner Just Sublime (by Corvaro): dam won on Flat and over hurdles: poor novice hurdler/chaser: beaten in selling handicap fifth outing: refused once in 1988/9, ran out second start: blinkered next time. *J. J. O'Neill.* c? —

POL SLAK 7 ch.g. Pollerton–Kilbrack (Perspex) [1989/90 22s2] medium-sized gelding: shaped like a thorough stayer when 12 lengths second to Senegalais in novice event at Folkestone in December on hurdling debut. *J. A. C. Edwards.* 82

POLYFEMUS 8 ch.g. Pollerton–Bardicate (Bargello) [1989/90 c27g* c26g* c29d5 c36fpu] strong, sturdy gelding: quite a useful chaser: made all at Chepstow c132 —

Save & Prosper Mandarin Handicap Chase, Newbury—eventual winner Polyfemus leads Brown Windsor (virtually obscured), Solidasarock, Door Latch (stripes) and Mount Parson in the early stages

Mr George Johnson's "Polyfemus"

and Newbury in December: prominent until a bad mistake at the Chair and was eventually pulled up in Seagram Grand National at Liverpool in April: stays well: acts on good to firm and dead going: sound jumper: races with plenty of zest. *M. H. B. Robinson.*

POLYNIXOS 4 b.g. Raga Navarro (ITY)–Whistler's Princess (King Emperor (USA)) [1989/90 16fpu] leggy, sparely-made gelding: half-brother to winning staying hurdler/chaser Little London (by Pieces of Eight): maiden plater on Flat: tailed off when pulled up fifth in juvenile hurdle at Market Rasen in August. *R. Thompson.* —

POMATUM 5 b.g. General Assembly (USA)–Pomade (Luthier) [1989/90 17f* 19hpu] neat gelding: won novice hurdle at Newton Abbot in August: pulled up lame later in month: best at around 2m: acts on firm going. *J. R. Bosley.* 82

POMMARDY 11 b.g. Hardiran–Pomme (Polic) [1989/90 c16d4 c16d4] small, strong gelding: winning chaser: stayed 2½m: acted on any going: headstrong: tended to sweat: dead. *Mrs J. H. Chadwick.* c**101** —

PONDERED BID 6 b. or br.g. Auction Ring (USA)–Ponca (Jim French (USA)) [1989/90 20fF 16s6 17v3 16s4 16d 17d3 16m6 16m5] angular gelding: handicap hurdler: form only at around 2m: acts on heavy going and seems unsuited by top-of-the-ground: has run creditably with and without blinkers. *I. P. Wardle.* 74

PONTEUS PILOT 9 ch.g. Levanter–Quelle Pas (Kelling) [1989/90 c20f* c25f*] lengthy gelding: poor novice hurdler: won a point-to-point in April: successful in novice hunter chases at Folkestone and Hereford following month: stays 3m: acts on firm ground. *R. Alner.* c**86** —

PONTEVECCHIO BELLA 4 ch.f. Main Reef–Linguist (Mossborough) [1989/90 16g3 16f2 16fF 16g3 a18gpu 16d4 16d 16m6 16g5 23f3] close-coupled, sparely-made filly: half-sister to modest chaser Freddie Bee (by Welsh Saint): placed over 1¼m on Flat: modest juvenile selling hurdler: stays 23f: acts on firm 76 ground: blinkered third and eighth outings: trained by G. Pritchard-Gordon first start. *R. T. Juckes.*

PONTEVECCHIO NOTTE 5 b.h. Blakeney–Oula-Ka Fu-Fu (Run The Gantlet (USA)) [1989/90 17v^4 17m^2 22f* 20f^2] neat horse: brother to fair staying hurdler Parlezvousfrancais and half-brother to winning hurdler/chaser Oula Owl (by Tachypous): fairly useful middle-distance handicapper on Flat (best form on firm ground): sold out of G. Pritchard-Gordon's stable 5,600 gns Ascot September Sales: progressive form in novice hurdles: won at Wincanton in March: 2½ lengths second to Stratford Ponds in slowly-run race at Ascot following month (wandered run-in): will stay 3m: acts on firm ground (possibly unsuited by heavy): ridden by 7-lb claimer. *W. G. Turner.* 115 p

POONA EXPRESS 9 b.g. Amen (FR)–Bold Strike (FR) (Bold Lad (USA)) [1989/90 24m 21f^2 22g 25d^2 25g^2 24g a22g^F 20s^{pu} a24g^3 28f^F] close-coupled, sturdy gelding: poor hurdler nowadays: suited by a test of stamina: acts on heavy going: sometimes blinkered (including last 7 starts): looked none too keen in seller fourth start. *A. S. Ridout.* 86

POP ABROAD 5 b. or br.m. Broadsword (USA)–Lady Poppy (Sahib) [1989/90 aF16g^2 aF16g^5 F17f^2 24m^5] third foal: dam, 1½m winner, showed a little ability over hurdles: second in NH Flat races at Southwell in January and Doncaster in March: tailed off in novice hurdle at Uttoxeter in April. *P. J. Bevan.* —

POPESWOOD 7 b.g. Nicholas Bill–Villarrica (FR) (Dan Cupid) [1989/90 20d 20s 20g^3 25d 22m] leggy gelding: shows traces of stringhalt: handicap hurdler: suited by further than 2m but yet to show he stays beyond 2¾m: acts on heavy going and seems unsuited by top-of-the-ground: has won for a 7-lb claimer: ran moderately when sweating final start 1988/9. *W. G. R. Wightman.* 102

POPPADOM 4 b.f. Rapid River–Poppy Day (Soleil II) [1989/90 F16d] half-sister to several winners, including hurdler Popping On (by Sonnen Gold): dam sprinter: mid-division in NH Flat race at Catterick in February: yet to race over hurdles. *J. R. Turner.*

POPPE INNE BELLE 4 b.f. Magnolia Lad–Parton Belle (Heres) [1989/90 F13f F16f] second foal: dam, winning hurdler/chaser, stayed 3m: tailed off in NH Flat races: yet to race over hurdles. *Mrs A. Knight.*

POPPING ON 6 b.m. Sonnen Gold–Poppy Day (Soleil II) [1989/90 25f 27d^{pu} 24d 16d 17d] lengthy, leggy mare: won slowly-run 2½m novice hurdle in 1988/9: little form since: acts on dead going. *J. R. Turner.* —

POPPLE 7 ch.g. Country Retreat–Poppy Lansdowne (Levmoss) [1989/90 a16g 21f^4 25f^{pu}] lengthy gelding: no sign of ability in novice hurdles. *Graeme Roe.* —

POP SONG 6 b.g. High Season–Top of The Pops II (Hanover) [1989/90 21f^3 17g^5 22m^{pu} 20s^2 25g^2 21d 22d^3] sparely-made, close-coupled gelding: handicap hurdler: stays 3m: acts on soft going. *G. L. Roe.* 96

PORKINSON BANGER 6 br.g. Golden Love–Tarabelle (Tarqogan) [1989/90 16d 20g] workmanlike gelding: second in NH Flat race: no form in 2 outings over hurdles: shapes like a stayer. *A. J. Wilson.* —

PORRIDGE OATS 5 gr.m. Oats–Bellarina (Rugantino) [1989/90 F16g 16m] small mare: first foal: dam won 2m hurdle: tailed off in mares NH Flat race and a novice hurdle. *R. J. Eckley.* —

PORTER'S SONG 9 ch.g. True Song–Spartan Clover (Spartan General) [1989/90 c22s^F c24d^{pu} c21m^{pu}] strong, good-bodied gelding: won a point-to-point in May: lightly raced and little sign of ability in hunter chases. *H. Hutsby.* c—

PORTLEMOUTH (NZ) 6 br.m. Rapier II–Fullrate (NZ) (Aureate) [1989/90 19d] workmanlike, good-quartered mare: well beaten in novice hurdles. *D. H. Barons.* —

PORT OF TIME 6 ch.g. Dance In Time (CAN)–Linguistic (Porto Bello) [1989/90 16s^{pu} 16m^4 16g 22m^6 20f^2] rangy gelding: novice hurdler: poor form in 1989/90: seemed not to stay 2½m: acted on good to soft going: trained until after third outing by J. Allen: dead. *M. F. Barraclough.* 78

PORTONIA 6 b.m. Ascertain (USA)–Hardwick Sun (Dieu Soleil) [1989/90 16g c24f^F c27f^{ur} c16m c24d] first foal: half-sister to NH Flat race winner and successful hurdler Schiehallion (by Scallywag): dam won novice hurdle: little worthwhile form over hurdles and fences. *J. M. Jefferson.* c— —

POSEIDONIA 4 ch.g. Red Sunset–Late Swallow (My Swallow) [1989/90 16m^3 16m^6 16m^{pu} a16g^6] leggy, rather sparely-made gelding: half-brother to winning 87

hurdler Spring Flight (by Captain James): sprint maiden on Flat: showed ability in juvenile hurdles first 2 starts: ran badly in sellers afterwards (broke blood vessel third outing). *J. Sutcliffe.*

POSITIVE 8 ch.g. Posse (USA)–Hello Honey (Crepello) [1989/90 16gpu 16dpu] close-coupled gelding: one-time fairly useful 2m hurdler and fair chaser: stiff task first outing, reportedly broke blood vessel on second: suited by give in the ground and acts on heavy going: visored or blinkered over hurdles nowadays, and also on last outing over fences. *K. C. Bailey.* c— —

POSITIVE WAY 6 b.g. Ardross–Abbe's Realm (Realm) [1989/90 20g6] inconsistent middle-distance handicapper on Flat: odds on, behind in amateur riders novice event at Market Rasen in August on hurdling debut: withdrawn reportedly lame at start twice subsequently. *S. J. Muldoon.* —

POSSESSED 6 b.g. Posse (USA)–Mariinsky (Nijinsky (CAN)) [1989/90 aF16g3 F16g aF16g4] fifth foal: half-brother to 2-y-o 7f winner Silver Ikon (by Godswalk), subsequently a good winner abroad, and to an Italian 10.5f winner by General Assembly: dam 1¾m winner: in frame in NH Flat races: yet to race over hurdles or fences. *R. Brandon.*

POSSETIVE PLANT 5 ch.g. Posse (USA)–Sakeena (Moulton) [1989/90 16g4 16s2 16d4] leggy, workmanlike gelding: modest maiden on Flat and over hurdles: has tended to carry head high under pressure. *J. M. Jefferson.* 92

POSSIBLE AMBITION (USA) 5 ch.g. Perrault–Its Possible (USA) (Bold Ambition) [1989/90 16gpu] lengthy, workmanlike gelding: no sign of ability over hurdles: blinkered in seller only outing of season. *J. W. Blundell.* —

POSTLEBURY 7 ch.g. New Member–Barge Mistress (Bargello) [1989/90 20sbd 24dF 16f6] lengthy gelding: second foal: dam unraced: runner-up twice in point-to-points in 1989: no form in novice hurdles. *J. A. B. Old.* —

POTATO KING 5 b.g. Hard Fought–Fenland Queen (King's Troop) [1989/90 20fF 16f5 20fur] workmanlike gelding: poor novice hurdler: appears not to stay 2½m: blinkered last start 1988/9: sold 4,000 gns Doncaster June Sales. *Denys Smith.* 75

POTIPHAR 4 br.c. Warpath–Zulaika Hopwood (Royalty) [1989/90 16m 16g a16g4 a16g5] workmanlike colt: third foal: dam 1½m winner: poor juvenile hurdler: easily best effort on third start. *P. Beaumont.* 67

POUNENTES 13 b.g. Tumble Wind (USA)–La Chanteuse (Hethersett) [1989/90 c16dpu a20g c20g6 16m] neat, strong, good-bodied gelding: formerly quite useful chaser: no worthwhile form for a long time: has won with and without blinkers: visored second start: unreliable: sold out of W. McGhie's stable 2,400 gns Doncaster October Sales. *A. Smith.* c— § — §

POWER BOAT 4 ch.g. Jalmood (USA)–Bedeni (Parthia) [1989/90 16d 16d3 a20g4] workmanlike gelding: well beaten on Flat: has shown signs of ability over hurdles, easily best effort on second start. *M. Avison.* — p

POWER HAPPY 5 ch.m. Instant Fame–Dawn Dreamer (Avocat) [1989/90 F16f4 F17m2 20v6] rangy, workmanlike mare: half-sister to fair hurdler Midland Glenn (by Midland Gayle): dam unraced: second in NH Flat race at Carlisle in November: still looked in need of race when remote sixth behind Lucky Verdict in novice hurdle at Chepstow 2 months later (prominent until early in straight). *Mrs S. Minns.* —

POWER PUNCH 6 b.g. Black Minstrel–Kellsboro Star (Coxcomb) [1989/90 16f4 20f6 16d c17gF c16m6 c26m c20s2 c24gF c26g c21g5 c18vur c20vpu c20v2 c20m2 c20fF3] big, well-made gelding: type to carry condition: modest novice hurdler/chaser: stays 2½m: probably acts on any going: moderate jumper of fences: whipped round start sixth outing. *W. T. Kemp.* c96 x 79

POWER REIGNS 5 ch.h. Star Appeal–All Risks (Pitcairn) [1989/90 16h2 16f4] rather sparely-made horse: poor novice selling hurdler: has looked less than genuine: visored twice in 1988/9. *P. Butler.* 73 ?

POWIS LASS 5 ch.m. Buckskin (FR)–Random View (Random Shot) [1989/90 F16f] non-thoroughbred mare: second foal: dam winning Irish hurdler: behind in NH Flat race at Newbury in October: sold 2,200 gns Ascot June Sales: yet to race over hurdles or fences. *N. R. Mitchell.*

POWYS 10 b.g. Busted–Caer-Gai (Royal Palace) [1989/90 20dpu c24mF 20m] strong, rangy gelding: novice hurdler: lightly raced and little form of late, including over fences. *Mrs E. H. Heath.* c— —

POWYS PRINCE 7 b.g. Roscoe Blake–Darling Eve (Darling Boy) [1989/90 16m5 16m2 16m5 16m a20g4 16sbd 16m] leggy, close-coupled gelding: handicap hurdler: should stay beyond 2m: acts on good to firm ground: sometimes blinkered: has hung under pressure. *J. A. Glover.* 93

PRAGADA 7 b.g. Pragmatic–Adare Lady (Varano) [1989/90 25g 26d3 24g5 24s4 25m] big gelding: useful hurdler nowadays: in frame at Ascot in Youngmans Long Walk Hurdle in December (15 lengths third to Royal Athlete) and Daily Telegraph Hurdle in February (7 lengths fourth to Ryde Again): fair eighth to Trapper John in Waterford Crystal Stayers' Hurdle at Cheltenham final start: ran as though something was amiss third start: stays 3m well: likely to prove suited by give in the ground. *J. T. Gifford.* 140

PRAIRIE AGENT 5 b.m. Main Reef–Regal Guard (Realm) [1989/90 16gsu 16m a20g* a20gpu a20g* a22gpu a20g6 a20g3 20g2] neat mare: sister to fairly useful point-to-pointer Aqua Verde: bad staying maiden on Flat: won selling hurdles at Southwell in January (no bid) and February (bought out of P. Felgate's stable 3,000 gns): ridden by 7-lb claimer, ran creditably in non-seller final start: will stay beyond 2½m. *T. Kersey.* 83

PRAIRIE OYSTER 7 ch.g. Northfields (USA)–Huahinee (FR) (Riverman (USA)) [1989/90 20s] sturdy gelding: fair but ungenuine handicap hurdler: took little interest only outing of season (December): needs testing conditions at 2½m and stays 3m: acts on soft going (yet to race on top-of-the-ground): blinkered fifth start and visored last outing in 1987/8. *R. Curtis.* — §

PRAIRIE STORM 6 br.g. Strong Gale–Meadow Wings (Lucifer (USA)) [1989/90 22spu 22d 24d 21d 25g4 24m] leggy, lengthy gelding: only form when fourth in novice hurdle at Kelso in March: stays well. *T. J. Etherington.* 87

PREBEN 4 b.g. Known Fact (USA)–Jokers High (USA) (Vaguely Noble) [1989/90 17fF 17h3 18f3 16m5 16f3] modest maiden at 2 yrs: sold out of P. Cole's stable 3,000 gns Doncaster February Sales: placed in varied company over hurdles, including selling: stays 2¼m: acts on firm ground. *J. Joseph.* 71

PREBEN FUR 13 b.g. Mon Capitaine–Flashing Beauty (Straight Lad) [1989/90 c21g4 c24m6 c16mpu] medium-sized gelding: poor chaser nowadays: barely stays 3m: easily best form in the mud: has worn blinkers but seems better without: no battler. *M. C. Chapman.* c**88** § —

PRECIOUS BOY 4 b.g. Taufan (USA)–Carrigeen Moss (Red God) [1989/90 16g* 16g2] fair performer on Flat, winner over 8.2f in 1989: sold out of I. Matthews' stable 22,000 gns Doncaster November Sales: won juvenile hurdle at Kelso in December easily by 8 lengths: 5/1 on, below that form when second in novice event at Catterick 11 days later. *G. M. Moore.* 102

PRECIOUS LINK 7 gr.g. Relkino–The Silver Darling (John Splendid) [1989/90 c24f3 c25m* c25g3 c25g2] tall, sparely-made gelding: handicap chaser: won at Plumpton in November: ran well next start: stays 3¼m: acts on heavy going and good to firm: raced too freely in blinkers last 2 starts of 1987/8: has worn a crossed noseband: reportedly prone to breaking blood vessels. *W. G. M. Turner.* c**98** —

PRECIOUS MEMORIES 5 br.g. Kabour–Kings Fillet (King's Bench) [1989/90 16m a16g6 a16g6] lightly-made gelding: winning hurdler: no worthwhile form in handicaps (first a seller) in 1989/90: probably stays 2½m: twice blinkered (not when successful). *D. W. Chapman.* —

PRECIPICE RUN 5 ch.g. Deep Run–Lothian Lassie (Precipice Wood) [1989/90 F12g F14v F16g4] first foal: dam lightly-raced half-sister to 3 winning jumpers: fourth of 18 in NH Flat race at Market Rasen in April: yet to race over hurdles or fences. *O. O'Neill.*

PRECIS (USA) 11 b.g. Pretense–Vaguely Familiar (USA) (Vaguely Noble) [1989/90 c24vF] lengthy, good-bodied gelding: fair hurdler/winning chaser: suffered a fatal fall at Ayr in February: stayed 2¾m: went well in the mud: usually amateur or claimer ridden. *Miss C. E. J. Dawson.* c— —

PRECOCIOUSLY 4 ch.f. Precocious–Grankie (USA) (Nashua) [1989/90 16g 16g6 16fF 16m a16g* 17m4 17h*] small filly: half-sister to fairly useful hurdler Heart of Stone (by Dust Commander): 1¼m seller winner on Flat: won claiming hurdles at Lingfield in January and Devon & Exeter in May: unlikely to stay much beyond 2m: acts on hard going: blinkered sixth outing (ran respectably): sold out of S. Dow's stable 2,400 gns Ascot May Sales after fifth start. *B. Forsey.* 73

PREDESTINE 5 b.g. Bold Owl–Combe Grove Lady (Simbir) [1989/90 18s 16g6] small gelding: modest handicapper on Flat, winner over 1½m in 1990: 70 p ridden by 7-lb claimer, keeping-on 20 lengths sixth of 21 behind Hats High in selling hurdle at Windsor in March: should improve again. *M. Madgwick.*

PREDICTABLE 4 ch.g. Music Boy–Piccadilly Etta (Floribunda) [1989/90 16m 16g] lengthy, robust gelding: won twice up to 1m on Flat in 1990: behind in juvenile hurdle at Nottingham and claimer at Market Rasen earlier. *R. M. Whitaker.* —

PREDOMINATE 9 ch.g. Thatch (USA)–Miss Noname (High Top) [1989/90 c21v^{6} c20g^{pu} 21d 21d^{pu} 25d^{pu} 20m^{pu} 22d^{pu}] strong, compact gelding: one-time fairly useful hurdler: well below form in 1989/90, giving impression something amiss: has shown little aptitude for fences: stays 2½m: acts on any going: blinkered last 3 starts. *O. Sherwood.* c— —

PREMIER CHARLIE 12 b.g. Prince de Galles–Cauldron (Kabale) [1989/90 c20f^{pu} c24m] big gelding: quite a useful chaser at his best: no form in 1989/90: suited by 2½m+: acts on good to firm and dead ground: makes mistakes. *Miss H. C. Knight.* c— x —

PREMIER PRINCESS 4 b.f. Hard Fought–Manntika (Kalamoun) [1989/90 16f^{2} 16m^{pu} 16d 16m 16g^{4} 16g^{5} 16g^{3} 20g* 20g^{6} 16m^{3} 22f* 20f* 22f^{4} 20m^{6}] sparely-made filly: poor staying maiden on Flat: won selling hurdle at Doncaster in January (no bid) and novice handicaps at Nottingham (mares) and Hexham in March: ran well penultimate start: will stay 3m: acts on firm ground. *W. Bentley.* 97

PRESAGE 4 b.c. Petong–Discreet (Jukebox) [1989/90 a16g] sparely-made colt: 7f maiden on Flat: tailed off in juvenile selling hurdle at Southwell in December: sold 1,150 gns Doncaster Spring Sales. *J. P. Leigh.* —

PRESENTE (FR) 5 br.m. Home Guard (USA)–Barratt Oak (Daring Display (USA)) [1989/90 17g] sparely-made mare: poor plater on Flat: behind after mistake second in novice hurdle at Devon & Exeter in October. *J. D. Roberts.* —

PRESENT TIMES 4 b.g. Sayf El Arab (USA)–Coins And Art (USA) (Mississipian (USA)) [1989/90 16f^{pu} 16d^{5} 16d 18f^{2}] leggy gelding: quite modest maiden at up to 7f on Flat: second in juvenile selling handicap at Fontwell in March, best effort over hurdles: sold out of K. Wingrove's stable 2,100 gns Ascot February Sales after third start. *A. Moore.* 76

PRESIDENT FREDDIE 4 ch.g. Free State–Solatia (Kalydon) [1989/90 F16g] eighth foal: dam won over 1½m: eighth of 18 to Le Bucheron in NH Flat race at Market Rasen in April: yet to race over hurdles. *J. W. Blundell.*

PRESIDENTIAL STAR (USA) 4 b.f. President (FR)–Out of This World (High Top) [1989/90 16g^{pu} a16g 18g^{pu} a16g 16v 16h^{4} 18f^{5}] sparely-made filly: poor maiden on Flat: sold out of S. Norton's stable 1,300 gns Newmarket July Sales: poor plater over hurdles: form only at 2m on hard going: visored fourth start. *P. Butler.* 70

PRESIDENT'S PUPPET 8 ch.g. Tug of War–Maggie's Leap (Fortina) [1989/90 c24m^{F} 25h] leggy, lengthy gelding: no sign of ability over hurdles: pulled hard, jumped poorly and was beaten when falling 3 out in novice chase at Worcester in August. *M. C. Pipe.* c— —

PRESIDIO 4 ro.g. Beldale Flutter (USA)–Danielle Delight (Song) [1989/90 16m^{ro} 16m a16g* a16g^{6} 16m^{2} 16h* 17f^{6}] sparely-made gelding: plating-class maiden on Flat: sold out of Miss A. Whitfield's stable 1,800 gns Ascot October Sales: successful in claiming hurdle at Lingfield (made all) in January and seller at Ludlow (led from third, no bid) in May: saddle slipped first start: unlikely to stay much beyond 2m: acts on hard ground: sold 980 gns Doncaster June Sales. *J. White.* 90

PRETTY GAYLE 8 ch.m. Midland Gayle–Pretty Damsel (Prince Hansel) [1989/90 20m^{4} 25m* 27g^{6} 24g* 20g] sparely-made mare: won amateur riders novice hurdle at Catterick in December and slowly-run handicap at Edinburgh in February: gave trouble in paddock prior to running poorly in novice event in June: stays 3m: acts on good to firm and dead going: blinkered fifth start 1988/9: amateur or claimer ridden. *J. L. Eyre.* 97

PRETTY IN PINK 4 b.f. Formidable (USA)–Londonderry Air (Ballymoss) [1989/90 F13d^{6} F16g] 2,000Y: half-sister to several winners here and abroad, including successful hurdler Hetty Green (by Bay Express): dam 5f winner at 2 yrs: behind in NH Flat races and 2 outings on Flat subsequently: yet to race over hurdles. *D. Moffatt.*

PRETTY PRECOCIOUS 4 b.f. Precocious–Siouxsie (Warpath) [1989/90 16s^{pu} 16m 17v^{pu}] leggy filly: 9f seller winner on Flat (difficult ride): sold out of F. —

Lee's stable 3,500 gns Doncaster October Sales: little promise over hurdles: pulled too hard in seller final start: has worn severe bridle. *J. L. Spearing.*

PREWSTYLE 5 b.m. Rymer–Darling Eve (Darling Boy) [1989/90 16g^{pu} 16s^{pu} 20g^{pu}] compact mare: tailed off when pulled up over hurdles: visored in sellers last 2 starts: sold 950 gns Ascot February Sales. *D. R. Gandolfo.* —

PRICELESS CITIZEN 5 b.g. Skyliner–London Spin (Derring-Do) [1989/90 17g^{pu}] seems of little account. *D. R. Tucker.* —

PRICE OF OAK 7 br.m. Silly Prices–Ereka Oak (Derek H) [1989/90 c16f^{pu}] tall, leggy mare: appears of little account. *F. Taylor.* c— —

PRICEY 6 b. or br.m. Silly Prices–Nella The Nipper (Inside Straight) [1989/90 F16d F16g^{6} 16f] fourth living foal: dam winning point-to-pointer: sixth in NH Flat race at Catterick in March: last of 8 finishers in novice hurdle at Hexham later in month. *M. S. Vernon.* —

PRIDEAUX 6 b.g. Mill Reef (USA)–Gallic Pride (USA) (Key To The Kingdom (USA)) [1989/90 c20g^{pu}] smallish, lengthy, workmanlike gelding: winning hurdler: pulled up lame on chasing debut in February: stays 2½m: acts on firm ground: sometimes blinkered, including on first and last starts 1988/9: tends to sweat. *J. Mackie.* c— —

PRIDEAUX BOY 12 b.g. Idiot's Delight–Firella (Firestreak) [1989/90 c16m^{3} c16m^{3} c16d^{5} c16f c21f^{F}] lengthy, shallow-girthed gelding: one-time high-class hurdler and useful chaser: best efforts of season on first 2 starts: never travelling well last 2 completed outings: only just stays 2m: unsuited by very soft ground: usually held up: jumps rather low and deliberately on occasions: tends to get warm in preliminaries and takes a good hold. *C. G. Roach.* **c141** d —

PRIDE HILL (NZ) 8 b.g. Diamante D–Purple Dream (NZ) (In The Purple (FR)) [1989/90 c20g^{3} c20s^{F} c22g^{ur} c24f^{pu} c24d^{4}] lengthy, smallish gelding: handicap chaser: suited by 2½m and give in the ground: tends to make the odd mistake. *F. Jordan.* **c101** —

PRIDE OF A GUNNER 7 b.g. Gunner B–Bettys Pride (Kythnos) [1989/90 16h^{3} 17f^{6}] workmanlike, angular gelding: second reported foal: dam, poor novice hurdler, stayed 21f: well beaten in novice hurdles: dead. *Mrs J. Wonnacott.* —

PRIME WARDEN 4 b.c. Blakeney–Misguided (Homing) [1989/90 18g^{ur}] modest maiden on Flat: sold out of J. Toller's stable 6,100 gns Newmarket December Sales: unseated rider second in juvenile hurdle at Fontwell later in month. *J. Ffitch-Heyes.* —

PRIMROSE STAR 5 ch.m. Le Coq d'Or–Star Attention (Northfields (USA)) [1989/90 16f^{4} 16f* 16m^{F} 16f^{2} 16m^{3} 16d^{4} 16d^{3} 16d 16d^{2} 16m^{4} 16f* 20f^{2} 16f^{2} 17m* 16f*] small, sparely-made mare: won selling hurdles at Catterick, Newcastle and Carlisle (conditional jockeys, bought in 3,200 gns) prior to winning conditional jockeys novice hurdle at Sedgefield in April: probably stays 2½m: acts on hard and dead ground: good mount for a claimer. *W. A. Stephenson.* 101

PRINCEABLE LADY 6 b.m. Saher–Douriya (Brave Invader (USA)) [1989/90 16m^{5} 16d 16g 16g a20g^{pu}] leggy, workmanlike mare: modest hurdler: best at around 2m: acted on any going: visored fourth start: dead. *D. H. Topley.* —

PRINCE BOLD (FR) 7 b.g. Rex Magna (FR)–Lady Bold (Bold Lad (IRE)) [1989/90 19s^{pu} 20m c16g^{3} c17g^{ur} c16s^{r} c16f^{pu}] workmanlike gelding: winning hurdler: third in novice chase at Wolverhampton in February: best form at 2m: acted on any going: wore blinkers: often reluctant to race: dead. *Miss S. J. Wilton.* **c103** § — §

PRINCE BUBBLY 9 b.g. Hubble Bubble–Jet Princess (Jolly Jet) [1989/90 c24f^{2} c20f^{2} c24m^{pu}] lengthy gelding: handicap chaser: pulled up reportedly lame at Perth in August: stays 3m: acts on firm going: usually blinkered over hurdles, occasionally over fences. *M. Avison.* **c89** —

PRINCE BUSKINS 15 b.g. Little Buskins–Princess Gem (Prince Hansel) [1989/90 17h^{ur} 26f^{5} c19m^{3} 17m] small gelding: poor novice hurdler/chaser: has been beaten in sellers: stays 3¼m: possibly not at his best on heavy ground: often ridden by 7-lb claimer. *F. Gorman.* c— —

PRINCE CARLTON 15 b.g. Autre Prince–Non Such Valley (Colonist II) [1989/90 c24f^{5} c24g^{2} c24s^{6} c24g c21m* c24m^{F} c21g^{3} c24m^{3} c20m^{F}] small, lightly-made gelding: poor chaser nowadays: gained tenth course win at Fakenham in March: effective at 21f and stays 3¼m: acts on any going: usually jumps well: good mount for an inexperienced rider: races with plenty of zest: goes well on sharp tracks: genuine. *Mrs J. Bloom.* **c81** —

PRINCE CELTIC 6 b.g. Celtic Cone–Kam Tsin Princess (Prince Regent (FR)) [1989/90 17f3 17h2 a18g6 a22g3 20f c20m c20mpu c26fF c26g4 c24m3 c26f2] leggy, angular gelding: poor novice hurdler/chaser: stays 3¼m: yet to race on heavy going, probably acts on any other: occasionally blinkered: usually claimer ridden. *W. Clay.* c80 75

PRINCE CEVA 5 ch.g. Salluceva–Sicilian Princess (Sicilian Prince) [1989/90 16d 16g6 20g] close-coupled, angular gelding: fourth foal: half-brother to winning hunter chaser Random Place (by Random Shot): dam winning Irish point-to-pointer: no worthwhile form over hurdles, though has shown signs of ability: should be suited by long distances. *G. Richards.* —

PRINCE ENGELBERT 5 br.g. Persian Bold–Polyester Girl (Ridan (USA)) [1989/90 16g5 16d 16g6 16mpu] leggy, close-coupled gelding: bad maiden on Flat: poor form in selling hurdles, best effort on first start: sold out of J. Parkes's stable 1,800 gns Ascot April Sales after third start. *J. Ffitch-Heyes.* 78

PRINCE GREMIN 4 gr.g. Scallywag–Tuneful Queen (Queen's Hussar) [1989/90 F16f F16f] third foal: brother to a poor animal: dam twice-raced half-sister to 2 winning hurdlers: behind in NH Flat races at Newbury and Ascot: yet to race over hurdles. *J. O'Donoghue.*

PRINCE KLENK 9 b.g. Random Shot–Delia Ross (Dalesa) [1989/90 24m3 24v5 21s] plain gelding: poor handicap hurdler nowadays: stays well: seems to act on any going: usually amateur ridden: sometimes sweats and tends to be on toes in paddock. *A. R. Davison.* 96

PRINCE LEONARDO 10 br.g. Rarity–Social Smash (USA) (Social Climber) [1989/90 20g5 a20g] big gelding: poor plater over hurdles: headstrong point-to-pointer and maiden hunter chaser: usually wears blinkers: temperamental. *D. J. Wintle.* c— § — §

PRINCE METTERNICH 9 ch.g. Tall Noble (USA)–Coloressa (Le Tricolore) [1989/90 c24f*] sparely-made gelding: fair chaser: won 4-runner handicap at Cheltenham in October by 8 lengths from Woodside Road: suited by a thorough test of stamina: acts on any going: tends to jump rather low on occasions: suitable mount for a claimer. *C. J. Bell.* c**123** —

PRINCE MOON 10 br.g. Ampney Prince–Moon Ray (Halation) [1989/90 20f] workmanlike gelding: poor hurdler/modest chaser: failed to complete in point-to-points in 1990: has refused numerous times and is one to leave severely alone. *G. B. Balding.* c§§ §§

PRINCE NEPAL 6 b.g. Kinglet–Nepal (Indian Ruler) [1989/90 c21mpu c16g2] half-brother to winning point-to-pointer Barnap (by Barolo) and staying chaser Royal Gurkha (by Royalty): dam never ran: won point-to-point in March: 7 lengths second to Wise Gambol in hunter chase at Fakenham following month. *R. Champion.* c93

PRINCE OF BABYLON 5 ch.g. Abednego–Princess Grainne (Majority Blue) [1989/90 F12g] 5,500 (privately) 4-y-o: half-brother to 2 winning point-to-pointers by Choral Society: dam unraced half-sister to several winners: mid-division in NH Flat race at Market Rasen in March: yet to race over hurdles or fences. *J. W. Blundell.*

PRINCE OF BARODA 6 b.g. Torenaga–Princess Baroda (Hardicanute) [1989/90 F16f] half-brother to winning Irish hurdler/chaser Amacart (by Milan): dam won at up to 15f in Ireland: behind in NH Flat race at Uttoxeter in April: yet to race over hurdles or fences. *J. L. Needham.*

PRINCE OF DIAMONDS 7 b.g. Remezzo–Queen's Crystal (Royal Palace) [1989/90 16f* 25g5] leggy, lengthy gelding: should make a chaser: on toes and sweating, won 6-runner novice hurdle at Ascot in October: pulled hard and finished tailed off following month: should stay beyond 2m: acts on firm ground. *P. J. Hobbs.* 105

PRINCE OF RHEIMS 5 ch.g. Sandhurst Prince–Fairmile (Milesian) [1989/90 16g 16g4 20m* 20v4 20g2 22s2 25gpu] tall, rather angular gelding: handicap hurdler: won at Leicester in December: stayed 2¾m: acted on good to firm and soft ground: looked a difficult ride: dead. *J. Mackie.* 115

PRINCE ROB 4 b.c. Robellino (USA)–Derrain (Prince Tenderfoot (USA)) [1989/90 16mpu] plating-class maiden on Flat, stays 1½m: sold out of R. Hollinshead's stable 6,600 gns Ascot August Sales: tailed off when pulled up 2 out in selling handicap hurdle at Fakenham in March (automatic top weight). *Miss L. Bower.* —

PRINCE SATIRE (USA) 7 b.h. Sensitive Prince (USA)–No Comedy (USA) (Droll Role) [1989/90 20d^{3} 24g^{6}] sparely-made horse: handicap hurdler: dropped himself out early on but stayed on strongly in latter stages when third in amateur riders event at Ascot in December: weakened quickly after leading to 2 out later in month: stays 2½m: acts well on heavy going: found little only outing 1987/8 (blinkered) and ran a moody race third start 1988/9. *R. Akehurst.* 118

PRINCE'S COURT 7 b.g. Kinglet–Court Scene (Royal Levee (USA)) [1989/90 16m^{4} 16f* 16m 22g^{F} 16f 21f* 24f* 22m^{4}] workmanlike gelding: second foal: dam quite a moderate maiden at 2 yrs: won novice hurdle at Taunton in December and novice handicap at Warwick and novice event at Uttoxeter in May: stays 3m: acts on firm ground. *F. Walwyn.* 89

PRINCE'S DRIVE 12 b.g. Sovereign Path–Fille de Fizz (Ragusa) [1989/90 22m^{F} 22g 21d 24v a20g 21d^{F}] strong, compact gelding: winning hurdler: little form since 1985/6, including in novice chases: stayed well: acted on any going: dead. *B. Palling.* c— —

PRINCE SOBUR 4 b.g. Jalmood (USA)–Ultra Vires (High Line) [1989/90 16g] leggy gelding: modest on Flat, winner over 1¾m in 1990: backward, behind in juvenile hurdle at Newbury in December. *M. Blanshard.* —

PRINCE SOL 11 b.g. Roi Soleil–Princess Story (Prince de Galles) [1989/90 c20f^{pu}] plain gelding: poor novice hurdler/chaser: has run in a seller: stays 3m: no form on very soft ground: usually amateur ridden: has worn blinkers and a crossed noseband: poor jumper of fences. *V. Thompson.* c— x —

PRINCESS FALCON 5 ch.m. Chukaroo–Coxmoore Sweaters (Wynkell) [1989/90 16s^{F} 16f 16m^{pu}] leggy, rather lengthy mare: no sign of ability. *G. Roe.* —

PRINCESS JENNY 8 b.m. Home Guard (USA)–Princess of Verona (King's Leap) [1989/90 16d^{pu}] tall, close-coupled mare: poor maiden on Flat: no form in 2 outings over hurdles. *M. Tate.* —

PRINCESS RYMER 7 b.m. Rymer–Iseult (Songedor) [1989/90 16f^{6} 16f^{2}] lengthy, sparely-made mare: novice selling hurdler: second in handicap at Uttoxeter in September (found little run-in): races only at 2m: acts on firm ground. *T. T. Bill.* 59

PRINCESS SIHAM 5 ch.m. Chabrias (FR)–Fickle Fortune (Mount Hagen (FR)) [1989/90 17h^{4} 22f^{6} 16d^{pu}] leggy, close-coupled mare: inconsistent maiden plater on Flat, suited by 1¼m: well beaten in novice hurdles: wears crossed noseband. *N. R. Mitchell.* —

PRINCESS WU 4 b.f. Sandhurst Prince–Hsian (Shantung) [1989/90 16g^{pu}] middle-distance maiden on Flat: blinkered, started slowly and was tailed off when pulled up 3 out in selling hurdle at Windsor in March: sold 850 gns Ascot May Sales. *R. W. Stubbs.* —

PRINCE VALMY (FR) 5 b. or br.g. Mill Reef (USA)–Princesse Vali (FR) (Val de L'Orne (FR)) [1989/90 16m 16g 16g 19f^{5}] lengthy, angular gelding: novice hurdler: little form since first outing 1988/9: possibly needs soft ground: none too fluent a jumper: sold out of J. Edwards' stable 5,000 gns Ascot April Sales after third start. *Mrs J. Wonnacott.* —

PRINCE VINCENNE (NZ) 5 b.g. So Bold (NZ)–Hoream's Wonder (AUS) (Horbury) [1989/90 F16m F17d] unplaced in NH Flat races: yet to race over hurdles or fences. *M. H. B. Robinson.*

PRINCE ZAMARO 6 ch.g. Sagaro–Hazelsha (Romulus) [1989/90 16h^{6}] small, dipped-backed gelding: no worthwhile form over hurdles. *M. Madgwick.* —

PRINCE ZEUS 11 br.g. Prince de Galles–Zeus Girl (Zeus Boy) [1989/90 c20s^{pu} c26f^{3}] sparely-made gelding: won novice chase in 1986/7: modest point-to-pointer: well beaten in hunter chases. *D. G. Knowles.* c— —

PRINCIPAL 8 ch.g. Deep Run–Lulu Dee (Straight Deal) [1989/90 a16g^{pu} 16m^{5} 16s^{6} 16g^{2} 16g 16g^{3} c16g^{F} 16d^{3} 16m^{2}] sparely-made, angular gelding: novice hurdler: beaten in a seller last start: fell first on chasing debut: blinkered fifth to seventh and last starts: finds nothing under pressure and wanders: sold 2,000 gns Doncaster Spring Sales: unreliable. *J. G. FitzGerald.* c— 88 §

PRINS HENDRIK 5 b.h. Town And Country–Rose of Raby (Averof) [1989/90 16s^{pu} 16f^{6} 16f^{6}] leggy horse: first foal: dam fair 5f winner at 2 yrs, modest at 3 yrs: winner at up to 1¼m in Holland in 1988: poor form over hurdles: acts on firm ground. *P. J. Feilden.* 76

United House Construction Handicap Chase, Ascot—Prize Asset returns better than ever

PRINTER 8 ch.g. Velvet Prince–Potterlane (Timber King) [1989/90 c20g4 c27g5 c16m4 c24g5 c20fpu c20mpu] compact gelding: has been hobdayed: won 2 point-to-points in 1989: modest form in novice chases: stays 2½m: acts on good to firm ground: sold 3,200 gns Doncaster Spring Sales. *S. E. Kettlewell.* c**83**

PRINTERS DEVIL 6 gr.g. Hawaiian Return (USA)–Cathy's Glory (Seminole II) [1989/90 c21dpu] leggy, quite good-topped gelding: no sign of ability over jumps: dead. *J. Wharton.* c— —

PRIORS COPPICE 8 b.g. Monksfield–Just Darina (Three Dons) [1989/90 c24gpu c20v4 c20s5 c20v5 c24dF] lengthy gelding: poor novice hurdler: modest novice chaser: gives impression he'll be suited by further than 2½m: acts on heavy going. *C. L. Popham.* c**90** —

PRIOR'S PADDOCK 8 b.g. Monksfield–Keening (Bally Joy) [1989/90 20f4 20f c26gpu] lengthy, sparely-made ex-Irish gelding: second living foal: half-brother to a maiden point-to-pointer by Menelek: dam, 21f winner on Flat, successful at up to 3m over hurdles: unplaced in NH Flat races in 1987/8: poor form in novice hurdles: tailed off when pulled up in novice chase. *L. J. Codd.* c— 76

PRIORY BAY 4 b.f. Petong–Salt of The Earth (Sterling Bay (SWE)) [1989/90 a16g] sparely-made filly: plating-class maiden on Flat: blinkered, behind in juvenile hurdle at Southwell in November. *J. R. Jenkins.* —

PRISCILLIAN 6 b.g. Runnett–Douala (GER) (Pentathlon) [1989/90 c16m4 c16dF] angular, good sort: novice hurdler: about 3 lengths behind eventual 20-length winner Master Rajh when falling at the last in novice chase at Nottingham in January: will be suited by a stiffer test of stamina. *D. Nicholson.* c**100** —

PRIVATEPERFORMANCE 8 ch.g. Gala Performance (USA)–Privee (FR) (Tarbes (FR)) [1989/90 c16d2] sparely-made, narrow gelding: winning hurdler: 6 lengths second to Some Obligation in hunter chase at Leicester in March: gives impression he'll be suited by further than 2m: suited by plenty of give in the ground: blinkered last 4 outings of 1987/8: should improve over fences. *W. J. Brown.* c**91** p —

PRIVATE VIEWS 9 b.g. Radical–Informal Vue (Royal Buck) [1989/90 c20m* c17g2 c20g2 c16f c16fF] lengthy, rather narrow gelding: very useful bold-jumping front-running chaser at his best, but temperamental and often reluctant to race: won handicap at Newbury in November: suffered a fatal fall at Liverpool in April: c**146** § — §

stayed 21f: ran moderately on hard ground but probably acted on any other: blinkered twice in 1986/7 and last 3 starts. *N. A. Gaselee.*

PRIX DU NORD (USA) 4 b.g. Northern Prospect (USA)–Bisouloun (FR) (Sharpman) [1989/90 16f 16f3 a16g6 16m 16m 16m3 16m* 16f6 16gpu] smallish, close-coupled gelding: little form on Flat (one to be wary of): won slowly-run 4-runner juvenile selling hurdle at Huntingdon in May (bought in 4,100 gns): acts on good to firm going: visored third start, blinkered fourth and fifth: usually claimer ridden: sold out of B. Preece's stable 950 gns Doncaster September Sales after second outing. *K. G. Wingrove.* 74

PRIZE ASSET 10 b.g. Levanter–Not Often (Lauso) [1989/90 c16f* c20g c16d4 c16f2 c16fur c16f4] lengthy gelding: useful chaser: won valuable United House Construction Chase (Handicap) at Ascot in October by 8 lengths from Ida's Delight: 5 lengths second to Nohalmdun in Captain Morgan Aintree Chase (limited handicap) at Liverpool in April: best at 2m: acts on any going: tends to get on toes in preliminaries: sometimes let down by his jumping: game and genuine. *P. J. Hobbs.* c**142** —

PRIZE COMMAND 13 br.g. Mandamus–Prize Catch (The Pelican) [1989/90 c21f6 c24sF c25g c26sF c25f6 c24f4 c21m*] strong, lengthy gelding: lightly-raced maiden point-to-pointer: no sign of ability in novice hurdles: finished alone in novice chase at Towcester in April: poor form over fences previously: stays 3m: acts on firm ground. *N. A. Gaselee.* c77 —

PRIZE MELODY 7 b.m. Remezzo–Prize Note (Trumpeter) [1989/90 c19f4 c20m c16f2] rather sparely-made mare: poor novice hurdler/chaser. *N. A. Gaselee.* c— —

PROA 5 gr.g. Kalaglow–Bedeni (Parthia) [1989/90 F16f 16g 16g 16g 17d] rather dipped-backed gelding: tubed: half-brother to several winners, including very useful 1976 2-y-o Sky Ship (by Roan Rocket) and smart 1¼m winner Upper Deck (by Sun Prince): dam disappointing member of a good family: no worthwhile form in NH Flat race and over hurdles, including in sellers: blinkered last 2 starts. *J. P. D. Elliott.* —

Mrs C. James's "Prize Asset"

PROBLEM CHILD 7 b.g. Daring March–Lena's Girl (Never Say Die) [1989/90 c21vpu c21m4 c20s c20mpu] rangy gelding: winning hurdler/chaser: little form in 1989/90: stays 2½m: probably acts on any going: blinkered fifth start 1987/8: has won for a 7-lb claimer. *R. Simpson.* c— —

PROCURATOR (USA) 4 b.c. Alleged (USA)–Northeastern (USA) (Northern Dancer) [1989/90 16gF 16d4 16d5 16g4] lengthy colt: fair maiden on Flat, suited by 1¾m: sold out of B. Hills's stable 20,000 gns Newmarket Autumn Sales: modest form over hurdles: will be suited by further than 2m: best run on dead ground: claimer ridden. *D. Moffatt.* 88

PROGRESSIVE 11 b.g. Hot Spark–Fair Path (Javelot) [1989/90 c26f3] won point-to-points in February and April: better effort in hunter chases when 25 lengths third behind Beera Quest in novice event at Newton Abbot in May. *D. M. Kemp-Gee.* c— —

PROJECTILE 7 ch.g. Bybicello–Gillycan (Rockavon) [1989/90 16f 17mpu 17mpu 19fF 16h6] sturdy gelding: of little account: blinkered last 2 starts: sold 1,350 gns Ascot July Sales. *B. R. Millman.* —

PROMPTER 4 ch.g. Hasty Word–Trewenol (Goldhill) [1989/90 F16f F16f] third living foal: dam of no account: behind in NH Flat races at Warwick and Huntingdon: sold 2,200 gns Ascot June Sales: yet to race over hurdles. *D. Nicholson.*

PROPERO 5 b.g. Electric–Nadwa (Tyrant (USA)) [1989/90 16f3 16m 20d* 20s* 20d3 18s3] good-bodied gelding: won amateur riders handicap hurdle at Ascot and Racing International Hurdle at Chepstow in December, showing much improved form when beating Morley Street gamely by ¾ length in slowly-run race on latter course: not disgraced behind Beech Road in Bishops Cleeve Hurdle at Cheltenham and behind Vagador in National Spirit Challenge Trophy Hurdle at Fontwell (stiff task, never going particularly well) afterwards: suited by 2½m and plenty of give in the ground: very useful. *J. T. Gifford.* 145

PROPLUS 8 ch.g. Proverb–Castle Treasure (Perspex) [1989/90 c24g c24g4 c24f3 c24mF c24fur c26g* c24m* c26m*] rangy, sparely-made gelding: winning hurdler: won his last 3 races over fences, namely novice events at Uttoxeter and Stratford and (in between) handicap at Southwell: stays well: acts on dead going and firm (possibly unsuited by hard): has sweated: blinkered fourth and fifth starts: on the upgrade. *J. A. C. Edwards.* c**110** p —

PROTECTION 8 ch.g. Thatch (USA)–Fairy Fans (Petingo) [1989/90 16m2 16m2 16g3 16g2] close-coupled gelding: useful hurdler: placed in quite well contested handicaps all starts of season, on final one second of 5 to Milford Quay at Cheltenham in January (blinkered): unlikely to stay beyond 2m: acts on dead going and good to firm. *Andrew Turnell.* 135

PROUD CREST (USA) 6 gr.h. Cox's Ridge (USA)–Nancy Be Good (USA) (Burned Up) [1989/90 16g 16d* 21s3 20v2 17m* 20fpu] rangy horse: useful middle-distance stayer on Flat in 1987: successful in novice hurdles at Towcester in February and Devon & Exeter (all out, giving impression may be suited by return to stiffer test of stamina) following month: ran as though something amiss in quite valuable event at Liverpool final start (blinkered): stays 2½m: acts on good to firm and heavy going. *O. Sherwood.* 109

PROUD PATRIOT 5 ch.g. Kalaglow–Sandforinia (Sandford Lad) [1989/90 16mpu 16g] lengthy colt: winning 2m hurdler: broke blood vessel on reappearance in October and was well beaten when next seen out over hurdles in December (won over 1½m on Flat in between): probably unsuited by heavy ground. *R. Akehurst.* —

PROUD POMPEY 9 ch.g. Ragapan–Fyjia (Hul A Hul) [1989/90 a16g 20dpu a16g3 a20g6 24g a24g6 c20mpu] compact, workmanlike gelding: bad novice hurdler: tailed off when pulled up in selling handicap on chasing debut: visored last 2 starts. *R. W. Hartop.* c— 55

PROVERBIAL LUCK 6 ch.g. Proverb–Barradan Lass (Deep Run) [1989/90 c27f2] won a point-to-point in May: length-second to Cheerie Chief in hunter chase at Sedgefield in May. *W. A. Stephenson.* c**84** p

PROVERBIAL ROSE 8 b.m. Proverb–Agapantha (Pampered King) [1989/90 c16g4 c27g3 c20m3 c20spu c24dF3 c25d6] ex-Irish mare: fourth foal: half-sister to Irish bumper winner Heyn' Dad (by Straight Lad): dam, winner over 11.7f on Flat, is half-sister to very useful jumper Potentate: successful in 4 point-to-points, 2 of them in 1989: in frame in steeplechases at up to 27f, showing poor form: blinkered last 2 outings. *R. Champion.* c**66**

PROVERBIAL SESSION 9 ch.g. Proverb–Courting Session (No Alibi) [1989/90 a20g^{2} c21g^{6} a20g^{3}] sturdy, lengthy gelding: poor novice hurdler/chaser: stays 2½m: headstrong: wears blinkers. *W. G. McKenzie-Coles.* c73 77

PROVERB SON 6 ch.g. Proverb–Baobab (Bargello) [1989/90 20s^{pu} c18m^{3} c20d c18d^{4} c18g c24s^{3} c22s^{ur} 21f^{2}] ex-Irish gelding: fourth foal: dam placed in point-to-points and hunter chase in Ireland: winning point-to-pointer: in frame in novice chases at Clonmel in first half of season: first race for over 4 months, second in novice hurdle at Newton Abbot in May: stays 3m: probably acts on any going: trained until after seventh start by Mrs E. Finn. *P. J. Hobbs.* c86 86 +

PROVERITY 9 ch.g. Proverb–Calamity Jane (Never Dwell) [1989/90 c24g^{4} c29g^{pu} c25g c25m^{pu} c24g^{5} c26g^{2}] sturdy, workmanlike gelding: fairly useful chaser in 1988/9: didn't run up to his best in 1989/90: suited by 3m + and top-of-the-ground: blinkered fifth outing: dead. *J. A. C. Edwards.* c**120** —

PROVIDE 9 ch.g. Proverb–Nona Bel (Perspex) [1989/90 c24g^{2} c24g^{pu} c26f] workmanlike gelding: winning point-to-pointer: 1½ lengths second to King Neon in hunter chase at Kempton in February: tailed off in Christies Foxhunter Chase at Cheltenham following month: stays 3m: acts on soft going: jumps none too fluently. *C. R. Wood.* c**97** —

PROVIDENCE BEAU 4 b.g. Anfield–Sandra Bella (Crooner) [1989/90 16m^{pu} a16g^{4}] second foal: dam winning hurdler: always behind in minor event at 2 yrs: tailed off in 4-runner juvenile hurdle at Lingfield in March. *A. S. Ridout.* —

PROVIDENCE LODGE 8 b.m. The Parson–Pallatess (Pall Mall) [1989/90 c20m^{2} c21f^{5} c24d^{2} c25d^{F} c25s^{5} c24d^{bd}] leggy mare: winning hurdler: modest novice chaser: stays 3m: best form with give in the ground: blinkered nowadays. *F. Walwyn.* c93 —

PROVING 6 ch.g. Proverb–Golden Strings (Perspex) [1989/90 16s^{6}] rangy gelding: second foal: dam unraced: backward and green, kept on steadily when around 19 lengths sixth to Whatever You Like in quite valuable novice hurdle at Ascot in February on debut: will be suited by further: sure to improve. *J. T. Gifford.* — p

PRYING PARSONS 9 b.g. Pry–Mrs Parsons (Brave Invader (USA)) [1989/90 c19f^{3}] big, rangy gelding: one-time fair hurdler: better for race, jumped sketchily and finished tired when remote third in novice chase at Hereford in April: suited by 2½m: acts on firm and dead ground. *J. P. D. Elliott.* c— p —

PRY'S-JOY 6 b.g. Pry–Charmaines Joy (London Gazette) [1989/90 F16m 16g 20s^{pu} c24m^{pu} c26s^{ro}] big, workmanlike gelding: second foal: dam behind in Irish NH Flat races: no worthwhile form over hurdles or fences: ran out final start (January). *G. A. Hubbard.* c— —

P S P SPIRIT 7 b.g. Vital Season–Le Tequila (Lear Jet) [1989/90 c26f^{3}] workmanlike gelding: poor novice hurdler: sold out of R. Hodges' stable 3,500 gns Ascot October Sales: won a point-to-point in March: 20 lengths third to Shedid in hunter chase at Folkestone in May. *J. W. Elliott.* c77 —

PUBLIC RELATIONS 13 br.g. Sir Herbert–Gormla (Vulgan) [1989/90 c29m^{4}] little worthwhile form over hurdles and in steeplechases but is a winning point-to-pointer. *C. J. Bennett.* c— —

PUCKS PLACE 9 ch.g. Midsummer Night II–Pirate's Cottage (Pirate King) [1989/90 c20d^{4} c24d^{4} c25s c24g^{r} c24f^{r}] well-made gelding: fairly useful but unreliable staying chaser: could be rated 127 on his best form of 1989/90: refused to race third outing: refused at the second next start (blinkered) and at the first on final outing. *N. A. Gaselee.* c§§ —

PUKKA MAJOR (USA) 9 gr.g. Le Fabuleux–Pakeha (FR) (Zeddaan) [1989/90 c20g* c20g^{r} c20d^{r} c20d^{pu} c20s^{6} c36f^{ur} c24g^{pu}] tall, rather lightly-made gelding: useful chaser on his day: won 'Ghostbusters II' Handicap Chase at Kempton in December (rated 146): refused or was most reluctant to race most subsequent outings: ran well for a long way but was weakening when unseating rider 4 out in Seagram Grand National at Liverpool in April: one to leave alone. *T. Thomson Jones.* c§§ —

PULLOVER 5 ch.m. Windjammer (USA)–Woolcana (Some Hand) [1989/90 16g 16f 16m 17g a16g] sturdy mare: quite modest 7f winner on Flat: sold out of T. Barron's stable 2,300 gns Doncaster September Sales: little promise in novice company over hurdles: trained until after third start by J. O'Shea. *J. C. McConnochie.* —

PULSE 12 b.g. Duc d'Orleans–Soya (Silnet) [1989/90 c20f^{5}] rangy, angular gelding: quite useful winning point-to-pointer: novice hunter chaser: well beaten at Sandown in March. *Michael Swinburn.* c— —

PUNCHBAG (USA) 4 b.c. Glint of Gold–Cassy's Pet (Sing Sing) [1989/90 16g 17d* 17v^{2} a20g* 16m^{4} a20g] leggy colt: modest middle-distance maiden on Flat: sold out of C. Cyzer's stable 4,600 gns Newmarket Autumn Sales: won novice selling hurdle at Devon & Exeter in January (bought in 2,700 gns) and 4-runner juvenile hurdle at Lingfield following month: tailed off in novice event at Southwell final start: stays 2½m: yet to race on very firm going, acts on any other. *G. A. Ham.* 94

PUNCHING GLORY 6 b.g. Idiot's Delight–Hitting Supreme (Supreme Sovereign) [1989/90 20g 16g^{4}] sturdy gelding: first race for 9 weeks, 7 lengths fourth behind Sound of Islay in novice hurdle at Stratford in March, keeping on steadily without being subjected to a hard ride: should stay beyond 2m: may improve further. *N. J. Henderson.* 94

PUNTERS LAD 10 br.g. Home Guard (USA)–Arioza (FR) (Tambourine II) [1989/90 c20f^{2} c18f* c25f^{3} c17g^{F} c18m^{4}] tall, close-coupled gelding: has been tubed: poor chaser: 33/1 when winning 5-runner amateur riders handicap at Fontwell in October, only form of season (not raced after December): barely stays 2½m: acts on any going. *P. Howling.* **c90** ? —

PURA MONEY 8 b.g. Mugatpura–Bell Money (Even Money) [1989/90 c16m^{3} c16m^{2} c16m^{4} c16g^{3} c16d* c20d^{2} c16g^{2} c16g* c20g^{F} c16s^{4} c20d^{6} c16m^{4} c16g^{4}] strong, rangy gelding: novice hurdler: successful in handicap chases at Ayr (conditional jockeys) in November and Edinburgh in January: unlikely to stay beyond 2½m, at least when conditions are testing: probably acts on any going: suitable mount for an amateur or claimer. *G. Richards.* **c105** —

PURBECK DOVE 5 gr.g. Celtic Cone–Grey Dove (Grey Love) [1989/90 20s^{3} 21d] workmanlike gelding: has scope: unplaced in NH Flat races: better effort in novice hurdles when third at Worcester in January: will be suited by good test of stamina. *Mrs H. Parrott.* 85

PURNAGO 8 b.g. Torenaga–Purranna (Mugatpura) [1989/90 c20s^{2} c26f^{6} c20f^{2}] workmanlike gelding: winning hunter chaser: showed much improved form when sixth behind Call Collect in Christies Foxhunter Chase at Cheltenham in March: spoilt his chance with a mistake at the last and by wandering on run-in when going down by a length to Buckhorn at Ascot in April: stays 3¼m: below form on heavy going, acts on any other. *Mrs J. M. F. Dibben.* **c114**

PURPLE POINT (NZ) 5 br.g. In The Purple (FR)–Grospoint (NZ) (Sobig) [1989/90 F16g] mid-division in NH Flat race at Kempton in February: yet to race over hurdles or fences. *D. H. Barons.*

PURPLE PRINCE (USA) 7 b.g. Sensitive Prince (USA)–Roses For The Lady (USA) (Buffalo Lark (USA)) [1989/90 16g* 17g^{2} 16s^{2} 17d^{5} a24g^{pu}] selling hurdler: won handicap at Plumpton in November (no bid): ran well next start: best form at around 2m on a sound surface. *P. Leach.* 94

PURPLE SILK 6 b.m. Belfalas–Lucky Money (Even Money) [1989/90 20m^{2} 16d^{2} 20g 17g^{3} 16d^{2} 21f^{5} 16f] smallish mare: modest novice over hurdles: probably stays 21f: acts on firm and dead ground: claimer ridden. *E. H. Owen jun.* 98

PYJAMAS 9 ch.g. Lighter–Arctic Dawn (Arctic Slave) [1989/90 20m^{3} c24m^{ur} c24f^{2} c24g^{ur} c20m^{4} c20g* c24g^{F} c17g^{3} c16m* c17d^{5} c24d^{3} c20g* c20d^{2} c21f^{2}] leggy, workmanlike gelding: modest chaser and novice hurdler: won handicaps over fences at Wetherby (conditional jockeys) in November, Catterick in December and Perth in April: stays 3m and effective at much shorter distances: possibly ideally suited by a sound surface. *G. Richards.* **c106** 86

PYLEIGH COURT 8 br.g. National Trust–Langton Water (Langton Heath) [1989/90 22m] leggy gelding: poor hurdler: needed race only outing of season (March): unlikely to stay beyond 21f: acts on firm and dead ground: has run creditably for a claimer. *N. A. Gaselee.* c— —

PYLEIGH PRINCE 9 b.g. Kinglet–Langton Water (Langton Heath) [1989/90 c26d^{ur}] tall, sparely-made gelding: winning chaser and novice hurdler: no worthwhile form for a long time (in frame in 2 point-to-points in the spring): stays at least 3m: probably acts on any going. *Mrs C. L. Brittain.* c— —

PYRO PENNANT 5 b.g. Official–Courtney Pennant (Angus) [1989/90 F16s F16v] non-thoroughbred gelding: second foal: dam never ran: well behind in NH Flat races: yet to race over hurdles or fences. *D. J. Wintle.*

PYTCHLEY PRINCE 7 b.g. Tyrnavos–Athenia Princess (Athens Wood) [1989/90 16d4 16g2 20m* a20g3 20d 17gpu] good-bodied gelding: handicap hurdler: won at Leicester in December: stayed 2½m: acted on soft going and good to firm: blinkered last 2 starts 1988/9: was usually held up: ridden by claimer: dead. *R. Hollinshead.* 94

Q

QAJAR 6 gr.g. Nishapour (FR)–Gravina (Godswalk (USA)) [1989/90 20m] smallish, sturdy ex-Irish gelding: first foal: dam disappointing middle-distance maiden: middle-distance staying maiden on Flat: winning hurdler: very much in need of race, tailed off in handicap at Leicester in December on British debut: should stay beyond 2m: acts on heavy going: often blinkered (wasn't last 5 outings). *P. Ransom.* —

QANNAAS 6 br.h. Kris–Red Berry (Great Nephew) [1989/90 20m3 22m* 22g* 25g3 21d 21d* 21d 25f 20f3 20m*] sturdy horse: had a fine season and won novice hurdles at Windsor and Folkestone and handicaps at Warwick and Uttoxeter: stays 2¾m: acts on good to firm and dead ground: wears blinkers: suited by forcing tactics. *Mrs D. Haine.* 126

QUAI D'ORSAY 5 b.g. Be My Guest (USA)–Noblanna (USA) (Vaguely Noble) [1989/90 21mF a16g3 16dpu 20fF 18fF 20h* 16m2 20m6] smallish, well-made gelding: former selling hurdler: won amateur riders handicap at Plumpton in March: stays 2½m: acts on any going: tried to run out once 1988/9: blinkered last 2 outings 1988/9 and third start 1989/90. *F. J. O'Mahony.* 102 §

QUAKER BOB 5 b.g. Oats–Bobette (King Bob) [1989/90 F16f2] second foal: dam fair staying hurdler and winning chaser: keeping-on 12 lengths second of 12 to Bollinger in NH Flat race at Ascot in April: yet to race over hurdles or fences. *P. J. Hobbs.*

QUALITY PRINCE 9 b. or br.g. Prince Tenderfoot (USA)–Brig O'Doon (Shantung) [1989/90 24m*] compact gelding: first form for a long time when winning amateur riders handicap hurdle at Perth in August: stays 3m: acts on heavy going and good to firm: often ridden by claimer: blinkered once in 1985/6. *M. Avison.* 100

QUARNDON 5 ch.g. Deep Run–Dame Lucy (Prince Hansel) [1989/90 F16d] half-brother to Irish 19f hurdle race winner Lenmoss (by Laurence O): dam lightly-raced half-sister to 1972 Gold Cup winner Glencaraig Lady and to grandam of Maid of Money and Ten of Spades: behind in NH Flat race at Kelso in February: yet to race over hurdles or fences. *J. K. M. Oliver.*

QUARRY TOWN 7 b.g. Mandalus–Weary Lil (Tiepolo II) [1989/90 16g c16g c20dF c16s3 c16d2 c20m* c16m* c20dr] smallish, good-quartered gelding: second foal: dam placed in Irish NH Flat race: won 2 point-to-points in Ireland in 1989: bought for 23,000 gns Doncaster August Sales: well beaten both outings over hurdles: won maiden chase and novice handicap at Southwell in the spring: jumped badly left and was beaten when refusing at the last on final outing: stays 2½m: acts well on top-of-the-ground. *J. A. C. Edwards.* c**95** —

QUARTOFERA 5 b.m. Lucky Wednesday–Avona (My Swallow) [1989/90 16f6 17f] workmanlike mare: tailed off in NH Flat race and 2 novice hurdles: sold 975 gns Ascot October Sales. *R. J. Holder.* —

QUASSIMI 6 gr.g. Ahonoora–Silk Empress (Young Emperor) [1989/90 c20g4 c20g3 c20f* c16m* c20g2 c24gpu c17f*] sparely-made gelding: modest novice hurdler: successful in novice chases at Newcastle in March, Carlisle in April and Cartmel in May: stays 2½m: acts on any going. *G. Richards.* c**104** —

QUAY ANCHOR 7 ch.g. Quayside–Charming Girl (Sound Track) [1989/90 16d 16g 16d 16g5 16g3] novice hurdler: races only at 2m: best form on good ground: sold K. Morgan 2,000 gns Ascot June Sales. *T. P. Tate.* 78

QUAYSIDE BUOY 7 br.g. Quayside–Ivernia (Golden Vision) [1989/90 20m5] leggy gelding: novice hurdler: well beaten in September: stays 2½m: acts on firm going: not one to trust. *J. L. Needham.* — §

QUAY WALL 7 b.m. Paddy's Stream–Polar Sprite (Arctic Slave) [1989/90 c19gpu 22mF a20g3 22mpu] tall mare: modest novice hurdler: made mistakes on chasing debut: gives impression she'll prove suited by long distances: blinkered last 3 starts. *F. Walwyn.* c— 94

QUEEN MATILDA 6 b.m. Castle Keep–Daydreamer (Star Gazer) [1989/90 16h* 16g] sparely-made mare: first race for almost a year, won novice hurdle at Taunton in October: well beaten at Plumpton following month: races only at around 2m: probably acts on any going: usually claimer ridden (wasn't at Taunton). *W. G. M. Turner.* 80

QUEEN OF SPARTA 5 b.m. Idiot's Delight–Spartan's Girl (Spartan General) [1989/90 F16m F16f] fourth foal: half-sister to fairly useful point-to-pointer/winning hunter chaser Carl's Pride (by The Brianstan) and winning jumpers Roys Dilemma and Bold Spartan (both by Bold Owl): dam winning point-to-pointer: unplaced in NH Flat races at Sandown and Ascot in the spring: yet to race over hurdles or fences. *M. J. Wilkinson.*

QUEEN RUN 5 ch.m. Irish Rifle–Babs Reflection VII (pedigree unknown) [1989/90 a20gpu] non-thoroughbred mare: dam unraced: tailed off when pulled up sixth in selling hurdle at Southwell in January on debut. *Graeme Roe.* —

QUEEN'S BAY LAD 6 br.g. Faraway Times (USA)–Silk's Suggestion (Shantung) [1989/90 c20g5 c16d* c20m* c16f4 c16fF c16m c20f3] small, workmanlike gelding: poor novice hurdler (has looked reluctant): won 2 novice chases at Sedgefield in March, and in lead when falling last in similar event on same course in April: stays 2½m: acts on firm and dead going: has worn a brush pricker: claimer ridden. *G. M. Moore.* c**103** —

QUEEN'S BISHOP 7 b.g. The Parson–Lady of Desmond (Menelek) [1989/90 20g6 16s 19s5] leggy gelding: poor novice hurdler: blinkered in seller final start. *K. C. Bailey.* 66

QUEEN'S CHAPLAIN 6 b.g. The Parson–Reginasway (Flair Path) [1989/90 16g 16g3 20sbd 20s3 20v4 21d 24m3 24m2] strong, good-bodied gelding with scope: novice hurdler: in frame several times, showing modest form: stays 3m: acts on good to firm and soft ground (possibly unsuited by heavy). *D. Nicholson.* 103

QUEENS COURIER 4 ch.f. Sayf El Arab (USA)–Veneziana (Tiger) [1989/90 16s 16f] lengthy filly: little show on Flat: tailed off in novice hurdle at Nottingham (trained by Miss G. Rees) and fillies seller at Wolverhampton. *J. Balding.* —

QUEEN'S DARLING 8 ch.m. Le Moss–King's Darling (King of The Tudors) [1989/90 25g 24d2 24d2] rather sparely-made mare: lightly-raced novice hurdler: stays 3m: acts on dead ground: ran well when blinkered final start. *J. G. FitzGerald.* 98

QUEENS MAN 8 ch.g. Remainder Man–Dior Queen (Manacle) [1989/90 16f5 16m 25f2 20m3 20f* 22f*] workmanlike gelding: former selling hurdler: won non-selling handicaps at Sedgefield and Kelso (finished lame) in April: stays 2¾m, though seemingly not 25f: goes well on top-of-the-ground: visored, refused to race on hurdling debut in 1986: claimer ridden in 1989/90. *T. Fairhurst.* 99

QUEENS PALACE 12 ch.g. Altosa Palace–Melche (Menelek) [1989/90 16m 24g4 c16d4 20d4 c20m5 c20gpu] lengthy gelding: novice selling hurdler: winning selling chaser: stays 3m: seems to act on any going: usually ridden by 7-lb claimer: sometimes wears a hood: moderate jumper. *Miss S. J. Wilton.* c75 x 69

QUEENSWAY BOY 11 ch.g. Kemal (FR)–Oscillation (FR) (Honest Boy) [1989/90 c26gpu c29dpu c24m c26mpu] strong, compact gelding: formerly useful staying chaser: no worthwhile form for a long time: has been tried in blinkers. *Miss A. L. M. King.* c— —

QUEL ECLAT 5 b.g. Creetown–Coriace (Prince Consort) [1989/90 16d5 16m4 16d 16gpu 16gpu a16g 16d] leggy gelding: novice selling hurdler: races only at 2m: acts on good to firm and dead ground: blinkered fourth start. *B. Ellison.* 68

QUESSARD 6 ch.g. Ardross–Marquessa d'Howfen (Pitcairn) [1989/90 16g 25gpu] lengthy, well-made gelding: has stringhalt: winning hurdler: little promise in 2 handicaps in 1989/90: suited by forcing tactics at 2m, and stays 2½m: acts on good to firm and dead ground. *F. H. Lee.* —

QUESTION OF DEGREE 4 b.c. Known Fact (USA)–Bernice Clare (Skymaster) [1989/90 16g4 16g5 16g* 16g* 16d3 16d*] close-coupled colt: half-brother to winning hurdler Commander Robert (by Wolver Hollow): 8.2f claimer winner on Flat when trained by Miss S. Hall: won juvenile hurdles at Wetherby, Edinburgh and Newbury: quickened comfortably clear in closing stages on first 2 courses but all out to hold off Sea Buck by short head in handicap on last-named in March: will prove ideally suited by sharp 2m. *N. Tinkler.* 111 p

QUICK ADVICE 8 b.g. Potent Councillor–Carbia (Escart III) [1989/90 c21f*] half-brother to fairly useful jumpers Gowan House (by Pongee) and Sunbia (by c79 p

Sunyboy): dam won over hurdles and fences at around 2m: successful in point-to-points in February and March (refused to race once): odds on, won weakly-contested novice hunter chase at Towcester in May by 10 lengths, soon recovering from slow start. *C. K. B. Rudd.*

QUICK FLASH 10 b.g. Streak–Screen Goddess (Caliban) [1989/90 c25f^{pu} c—
25d^{pu}] workmanlike gelding: poor novice hurdler/chaser: pulled up in selling —
handicap final start: winning point-to-pointer. *W. Price.*

QUICK RAPOR 5 b.g. Rapid Pass–Dark Sensation (Thriller) [1989/90 16g
16s^{pu} 16m] tall, chasing type with scope: fourth foal: half-brother to winning —
point-to-pointer Dark Image (by Bold As Brass): dam won point-to-point: little promise in novice hurdles. *Capt. T. A. Forster.*

QUICK REACTION 7 b.g. Main Reef–Swift Response (No Argument)
[1989/90 20g^{6} 16d^{5} 20g^{4} 20m^{4} 24s^{F} a20g^{4} 28f 20m^{2} 25m^{su}] smallish, well-made 81
gelding: handicap hurdler: stays 2½m: acts on firm ground. *Mrs E. H. Heath.*

QUICK RIPOSTE 6 b.m. Comedy Star (USA)–Miss Hippolyta (High Line)
[1989/90 a18g^{pu}] rather sparely-made mare: of little account. *A. Csaky.* —

QUIDDITY 7 b.g. Pollerton–Windbush (Whistling Wind) [1989/90 16m 21s
20g^{pu}] well-made gelding: chasing type: lightly raced over hurdles: stiff tasks in 75
novice handicaps last 2 starts: best run at 2m on good to firm ground. *K. C. Bailey.*

QUIDEST 7 ch.g. Ovac (ITY)–Gothic Arch (Gail Star) [1989/90 24m^{2} 22f^{3}]
angular gelding: novice hurdler: first form in small fields at Perth and Kelso early 77
in season: stays 3m: acts on firm ground. *A. Fowler.*

QUIET RIOT 8 b.g. Hotfoot–Tuyenu (Welsh Pageant) [1989/90 16v^{3} 16v]
strong, workmanlike gelding: winner at up to 1¾m on Flat: lightly-raced novice 82
hurdler: likely to be suited by further than 2m. *J. White.*

QUIET STAR (NZ) 9 br.g. Big Hush (NZ)–Astronomy (Red Mars) [1989/90 c—
c22f^{pu} 20f^{pu}] small gelding: of little account: sometimes blinkered: sold 1,000 gns —
Doncaster October Sales: resold 610 gns Doncaster November Sales. *P. Davis.*

QUILANTARO (CHI) 9 b.g. Tantoul (USA)–Baluta (CHI) (Persaldo) c87
[1989/90 c20g c22d^{ur} c26g^{pu} c24g^{pu} c20f^{3} c24f^{pu} c20g^{pu} c24h^{2} c25f^{2}] —
workmanlike gelding: winning hurdler: modest novice chaser: stays 25f: acts on firm and dead ground: blinkered fourth and when running well last 2 starts. *C. J. Vernon Miller.*

QUINTO 4 b.g. Tumble Wind (USA)–Con Carni (Blakeney) [1989/90 16m
16g^{pu}] close-coupled gelding: plater on Flat, placed at up to 1½m: sold out of P. —
Makin's stable 5,200 gns Newmarket Autumn Sales: tailed off in juvenile hurdle at Windsor in November: pulled up lame in claimer in April. *Miss P. Hall.*

QUITE SO 6 br.m. Mansingh (USA)–Chiquitita (Reliance II) [1989/90 17f^{3} 18f^{2}
16m^{3} 16f^{3} 16f^{4} a18g^{2} a16g^{pu} 16g^{pu}] small, plain mare: novice selling hurdler: pulls 67
hard and unlikely to stay beyond 2¼m: acts on firm ground: has put head in air. *J. Pearce.*

QUIXALL CROSSETT 5 b.g. Beverley Boy–Grange Classic (Stype Grange) [1989/90 F16d] second foal: half-brother to novice hurdler/chaser Carousel Crossett (by Blind Harbour): dam novice hurdler: tailed off in NH Flat race at Catterick in February: yet to race over hurdles or fences. *E. M. Caine.*

QUOTA ONE 6 br.g. Buckskin (FR)–Sarah Gee (Goldhill) [1989/90 16g^{2} 20g^{2}
20s 20d^{5} 20m^{pu}] novice hurdler: stayed 2½m: acted on good to soft ground: dead. 90
J. W. Blundell.

R

RAAHIN (USA) 5 ch.h. Super Concorde (USA)–Bonnie Hope (USA) (Nijinsky
(CAN)) [1989/90 18f* 20f* 24g^{3}] lengthy, sparely-made horse: won Salmon Spray 120
Challenge Trophy Hurdle (limited handicap) at Fontwell and conditional jockeys handicap hurdle at Ascot in October: moderate third to Auction Law in slowly-run 3m handicap at Kempton in December (held up on that occasion, but had been best forcing pace over shorter distances): stays 2½m: has won on soft going but best form on firm: changed hands 16,000 gns Newmarket Autumn Sales after second start. *R. Akehurst.*

RABA RIBA 5 gr.g. Oats–Erica Alba (Yukon Eric (CAN)) [1989/90 F16f] half-brother to successful staying hurdler/chaser Celtic Fleet and poor novice hurdler Kerry Calluna (both by Celtic Cone): dam never ran: around 22 lengths seventh of 16 to Raido in NH Flat race at Uttoxeter in April: yet to race over hurdles or fences. *J. L. Spearing.*

RACEY NASKRA (USA) 4 b.f. Star de Naskra (USA)–Langness (USA) (Roberto (USA)) [1989/90 16s[5] 16d[r]] smallish, angular filly: modest 7.5f winner on Flat: sold out of H. Cecil's stable 10,000 gns Newmarket December Sales: no promise over hurdles (refused third on final outing): sold 3,300 gns Doncaster March Sales. *N. Tinkler.* —

RACHAN MASTER 8 b.g. Windjammer (USA)–Polygon (Tarboosh (USA)) [1989/90 c20s[4] c22g[F]] rangy, angular gelding: no form over hurdles: fell fatally in novice chase at Nottingham in January: stayed 2½m. *A. J. Wilson.* c— —

RADICAL LADY 6 b.m. Radical–Peaceful Madrigal (Blue Cliff) [1989/90 22g[2] c24d[2] c20g* c24d* c24v* c20v* c32f[pu]] sparely-made ex-Irish mare: ninth foal: half-sister to a poor animal by Reformed Character: dam never ran: won a point-to-point in 1989: second in mares novice hurdle at Kelso in December: subsequently won novice chases at Newcastle (mares), Kelso, Ayr and Haydock: beat Random Romance 5 lengths in Tattersalls Mares Only Novices' Chase Final (limited handicap) on last-named course in March: let down by her jumping final outing: stays 3m: acts on heavy going. *G. M. Moore.* c**106** 90 p

RADICAL REQUEST 7 br.g. Derring Rose–Kitty Laurence (Laurence O) [1989/90 c22m[6] c20d[4] c16g[3] c20d[5] c20v[2] c20s[pu]] close-coupled gelding: winning hurdler/chaser: modest form over fences in Britain in 1989/90: stays 2½m: suited by give in the ground and acts on heavy going: blinkered once in 1987/8: ridden by 7-lb claimer second to fifth starts. *G. Roe.* c**110** —

RADICAL VIEWS 5 b.g. Radical–Regency View (Royal Highway) [1989/90 16m[2] 20s[4] 22d[6] 20g 19f[4]] robust gelding: has scope: poor novice hurdler: probably stays 2¾m: acts on good to firm and dead ground: blinkered final start. *N. A. Gaselee.* 87

RADISH 'N' LEMON 4 b.c. Young Generation–Lady of Chalon (USA) (Young Emperor) [1989/90 16g[2] 16g[5] a16g[5] a16g 16d[4]] leggy, sparely-made colt: plater on Flat: poor form over hurdles, including in selling company: below form at Southwell third and fourth starts: unlikely to stay much beyond 2m: claimer ridden. *B. Stevens.* 78

RAGAFAN 13 ch.g. Ragstone–Hi-Baby (High Treason) [1989/90 c20d[F] c20f[ur]] sturdy gelding: hunter chaser/point-to-pointer nowadays: every chance when falling 2 out at Warwick in March: won a point-to-point following month: stays 21f: acts on any going: blinkered once. *C. R. Wood.* c? —

RAGALOO 4 ch.g. Ragapan–Tangmalangaloo (Laurence O) [1989/90 F16g] fourth foal: dam, poor Irish point-to-pointer, half-sister to 2 winning jumpers: mid-division in NH Flat race at Kempton in February: yet to race over hurdles. *C. D. Broad.*

RAGENS BOY 9 b.g. Rajen–Princess Pay (Kadir Cup) [1989/90 c20g[bd] c20g c20s[pu]] sturdy gelding: carries plenty of condition: winning chaser: no form in 1989/90: ran in snatches second outing: suited by 2½m: acts on soft going. *Mrs Jill Evans.* c— —

RAGESCA 11 ch.m. Ragstone–Queen Francesca (Frankincense) [1989/90 20d] very lightly-raced novice hurdler: very stiff task in amateur riders handicap at Ascot in December. *Mrs B. Dukes.* —

RAGLAN ROSE 7 b.m. Roselier (FR)–Shady Shadow (Ragapan) [1989/90 19f[pu]] lightly-made mare: no form over hurdles (pulled up after saddle slipped when dropped to selling company). *T. W. Donnelly.* —

RAGLAN STREET (USA) 4 b.c. Sassafras (FR)–Welsh Maiden (Welsh Pageant) [1989/90 16d] leggy colt: poor form on Flat, including in sellers: sold out of T. Barron's stable 2,000 gns Doncaster August Sales: tailed off in juvenile hurdle at Warwick in January. *K. C. Bailey.* —

RAG TIME BELLE 4 ch.f. Raga Navarro (ITY)–Betbellof (Averof) [1989/90 16d 16m[F] a16g] leggy, lightly-made filly: little form on Flat: sold out of P. Jones's stable 1,450 gns Ascot 2nd June Sales: no promise over hurdles, including in a seller. *M. W. Eckley.* —

RAGTIME SOLO 6 b.g. Raga Navarro (ITY)–Solentown (Town Crier) [1989/90 17v 17d 20g[5] 16s 22d 16m 17d 17m 17m[2] 16f[3] 16f[pu]] leggy, close-coupled gelding: selling hurdler: poor form in 1989/90: has run respectably over 2¾m: acts on heavy going: has won with and without blinkers. *R. J. Hodges.* 83

Tattersalls Mares Novices' Handicap Chase (Final), Haydock—together early on are, from left to right, Corvassio, Rondeau, Random Romance, Meryett, the winner Radical Lady and Blue Rainbow

RAHEEN NA MORE 10 ch.g. Push On–Raheen Angel (Tarqogan) [1989/90 c16f^5 c17f^5 c24h^4 c25f^3] sturdy gelding: no form over hurdles: placed in point-to-points: poor novice steeplechaser: probably stays 3m. *R. G. Frost.* c**67** —

RAHIIB 8 b.g. Final Straw–Head First (Welsh Pageant) [1989/90 c26m^3 c26m^3] strong, compact gelding: has a round action: lightly-raced chaser: stays 3¼m: acts on any going: front runner: successful 3 times at Newton Abbot. *M. C. Pipe.* c**100** —

RAIDO 5 ch.g. Black Minstrel–Fair Songstress (Compensation) [1989/90 F16f*] half-brother to French Flat winner Scapuccio and 1½m winner Mister Lucky (both by Royalty): dam useful at up to 1m: won 16-runner NH Flat race at Uttoxeter in April by 4 lengths from It's After Time: yet to race over hurdles or fences. *J. A. C. Edwards.*

RAINBOW BRITE (FR) 5 b.g. Maelstrom Lake–Orfila (FR) (Margouillat (FR)) [1989/90 16d 16s 19m^2 20d 16m*] lengthy, workmanlike gelding: won 5-runner novice hurdle at Uttoxeter in May: stays 2¼m: acts on firm ground: visored in 1988/9 and on fourth start. *G. H. Jones.* 81

RAIN MARK 9 b.g. Politico (USA)–Rightful Ruler (Sovereign Lord) [1989/90 c20m^3 c24g^3 c24g^{bd} c24g^5 c16s^2 c20g c20s^3 c20m^5] rather sparely-made gelding: no form over hurdles: winning point-to-pointer: poor novice chaser: made a few mistakes last start: stays 3m: acts on good to firm and soft going: sold 10,500 gns Doncaster Spring Sales. *J. S. E. Turner.* c**84** —

RAIN-N-SUN 4 gr.g. Warpath–Sun Noddy (Tom Noddy) [1989/90 16f 16f^4 16m 16d^{pu} 16m] angular, plain gelding: well beaten on Flat: no worthwhile form over hurdles: visored last 2 starts. *J. L. Harris.* —

RAISABILLION 8 b.g. Billion (USA)–Small Problem (Songedor) [1989/90 c25d^F c25g^6 c24g^F c20d^{pu}] leggy gelding: winning hurdler/chaser: little form in 1989/90: stays well: probably acts on any going: good mount for an inexperienced rider: trained until after third start by G. Moore. *M. O'Neill.* c— —

RAISE AN ARGUMENT 11 b.g. No Argument–Ten Again (Raise You Ten) [1989/90 c20g^{pu} c20g^3 c17d* c20s^4 c16m c22m c20d^3] workmanlike, good-bodied gelding: fair chaser: won slowly-run minor event at Kelso in February by ½ length from Cool Strike: below that form subsequently: best at up to 2½m: acts on heavy going: suited by waiting tactics: sometimes let down by his jumping nowadays: found little under pressure second start. *J. J. O'Neill.* c**118** —

RAISE A STAR 5 b.g. Red Sunset–Hill's Realm (USA) (Key To The Kingdom (USA)) [1989/90 16g 16v 16v^{pu}] poor maiden on Flat, stays 1¼m: well beaten in novice claiming hurdle and a seller: changed hands 1,250 gns Ascot February Sales. *R. Akehurst.* —

Mr John Livock's "Rakes Lane"

RAISE MEMORIES 4 b.f. Skyliner–Really (Sovereign Gleam) [1989/90 16s^{6} 16s^{pu}] angular, deep-girthed filly: half-sister to winning hurdler Erostin Ruler (by — Fordham): plating-class maiden at 2 yrs: well beaten in juvenile hurdle at Haydock in January: sweating, virtually refused at the fourth following month. *B. A. McMahon.*

RAJIV'S DEBT 6 ch.h. Stanford–Morcal (Dragonara Palace (USA)) [1989/90 18f^{pu}] poor plater on Flat in 1987: blinkered, tailed off when pulled up 2 out in — selling hurdle in September. *H. Willis.*

RAKES LANE 5 b.g. Pitskelly–Mrs Cullumbine (Silly Season) [1989/90 16g 16m* 16g^{3} 17g^{2} 16g^{4} 16m^{3} 16m^{2} 20f^{2}] leggy gelding: fairly useful middle-distance 132 performer at 3 yrs: sold out of S. Norton's stable 30,000 gns Newmarket Autumn (1988) Sales: won novice hurdle at Leicester in January: in frame all subsequent outings, easily best efforts on sixth and seventh starts when 3 lengths third behind Forest Sun in Waterford Crystal Supreme Novices' Hurdle at Cheltenham and 3 lengths second to Fidway in Seagram 100 Pipers Top Novices' Hurdle at Liverpool: finished lame final outing: likely to prove best at 2m: acts on good to firm ground: bandaged in front fifth to seventh starts. *J. R. Jenkins.*

RAMAKIED 13 b.g. Deep Run–Tudor Gello (Bargello) [1989/90 c20d^{3} c20g^{F}] c— lengthy, workmanlike gelding: winning chaser: lightly raced nowadays and no — worthwhile form for a long time. *Miss L. Bower.*

RAMBLING ECHO 9 b.g. Rymer–Tarquann (Elegant Stephen) [1989/90 c89 x c21d^{2} c26s^{6} c25s c20v^{5} c24g* c25m^{2} c24m] sparely-made gelding: winning — hurdler: jumped better than previously over fences when winning novice chase at Worcester in March: whipped round start and took no part third outing: stays 3m: acts on any going: blinkered twice in 1987/8 and visored twice in 1988/9. *O. Sherwood.*

RAMBLING MONK 7 ch.g. Monksfield–Merry Rambler (Wrekin Rambler) [1989/90 16f 20m^{pu}] lengthy, workmanlike gelding: fourth foal: half-brother to winning hurdler Aisling Geal (by Brave Invader): dam unraced sister to useful Irish jumper Fair Rambler: won NH Flat race in Ireland in 1988: well beaten in novice hurdles at Uttoxeter in October and Sedgefield in March. *J. J. Birkett.* —

RAMBLING SONG 10 ch.g. True Song–Tenella (Wrekin Rambler) [1989/90 c20g^{2}] strong gelding: carries plenty of condition: fairly useful chaser: creditable second to Mister Feathers in conditional jockeys handicap at Kempton in November: best form at 2½m: acts on heavy ground: amateur ridden in 1986/7: usually jumps well. *Capt. T. A. Forster.* c**127**

RAMBLING WILD 9 ch.g. Deep Run–Rockaway Rose (Stormpoint) [1989/90 16m c16d^{2} c16f^{6} c16g^{pu} 16m^{2}] strong, lengthy gelding: novice hurdler: moderate chaser (frequently let down by his jumping): probably acted on any going: trained until after fourth start by B. Preece: dead. *K. White.* c**104** x 92

RAMBO CASTLE 4 b.g. Castle Keep–Rampage (Busted) [1989/90 16d* 16s^{4} 17d^{3} 16d^{3} 16h*] angular, sparely-made gelding: half-brother to fairly useful hurdler Rampallion (by Riboboy): dam, winner from 11f to 1¾m, half-sister to fairly useful hurdler/chaser Dumper: quite useful at up to 2¼m on Flat: won juvenile hurdles at Nottingham in December and Hexham in April: best effort when just over 3 lengths third behind Joe Bumpas in quite valuable juvenile handicap at Ayr fourth start: will be well suited by further: best run on dead ground: sold out of S. Norton's stable 16,500 gns Doncaster March Sales after third outing. *N. Tinkler.* 120

RAMBO WARRIOR 5 ch.h. Roman Warrior–Military Queen (Military) [1989/90 22g^{pu} a20g^{6}] angular horse: second foal: dam won over 5f at 2 yrs and was later a poor novice chaser: behind in a seller at 2 yrs: tailed off in novice claiming hurdle at Southwell in February. *M. H. Weston.* —

RAMILIE 8 b.m. Rambah–Millipede (Military) [1989/90 16g* 20f^{2} 16d^{pu} 16g^{4}] rather narrow mare: handicap hurdler: won at Hexham in November: good second next start and ran creditably on final outing (January): stays 2¾m: best run on firm ground, though has won on good to soft: blinkered once in 1986/7. *Mrs G. R. Reveley.* 100

RAMPALLION 7 b.g. Riboboy (USA)–Rampage (Busted) [1989/90 16g^{4} 16d 16g] lengthy gelding: handicap hurdler: promising fourth at Wolverhampton in January: behind in Tote Gold Trophy at Newbury (hampered fourth) and race won by Kadan at Uttoxeter (bandaged on first outing for 2½ months): best at 2m: yet to race on very firm going, seems to act on any other: has worn a crossed noseband: has a turn of foot. *B. Smart.* 122

RAMPANT 11 br.g. Reliance II–Glimmer of Hope (Never Say Die) [1989/90 c22m^{4} c16g^{4} c27g] leggy, sparely-made gelding: modest hurdler in 1986/7: poor form in novice chases: effective at 2m and stays well: acts on good to firm and dead going: amateur or claimer ridden. *R. E. Barr.* c**85** —

RAMPSBECK LAD 5 b.g. Davout–Story Writer (Sweet Story) [1989/90 20m 20s 20d^{pu}] half-brother to poor novice hurdler/chaser Copy Writer (by Copte): dam 11f winner: well beaten in novice hurdles: amateur ridden. *S. G. Payne.* —

RAMROD 5 ch.g. Giacometti–Come On Girl (Sheshoon) [1989/90 17h^{4} 16m 16h^{2} 16g^{4} 16g* 16d^{4} 16f^{2} 22m^{F} 16m 17d^{6} 16g^{3} 16m^{5} 16f* 22m^{6} 16f^{5}] tall gelding: has found little under pressure but looks more resolute nowadays and won novice handicap hurdle at Nottingham in October and novice seller at Taunton (bought in 4,800 gns) in March: seems best at around 2m: seems to act on any going: wears blinkers. *R. J. Hodges.* 88

RAMSDELL 8 ch.g. Paddy's Stream–Strawberry Mess (Pardal) [1989/90 c20m* c20g^{2} c24m* c25m^{3} c24g^{3} c25f^{ur} c25f] leggy, workmanlike gelding: novice hurdler: jumped well in main when winning novice chases at Warwick in September and Leicester in December: fair third in handicaps afterwards: suited by 3m: acts on good to firm going: blinkered last 3 outings of 1988/9, and on last 2 starts: claimer ridden at Warwick. *B. Smart.* c**90** —

R AND B UPDATE 4 b.g. Longleat (USA)–Neringulla (African Sky) [1989/90 16m] workmanlike gelding: sprint maiden on Flat: blinkered, tried to refuse at first 2 flights and finished tailed off in selling hurdle at Leicester in December: one to leave alone. *G. A. Huffer.* — §

RANDOLPH CRESCENT 7 br.g. Le Bavard (FR)–Cailin Meireach (Prince Hansel) [1989/90 c24g c25g^{3} c24g^{2} c24m^{2} c24g^{pu} c21g] lengthy gelding: novice hurdler/chaser: creditable second over fences at Ludlow (to Tennfores) in c99 —

Drumjohn Handicap Chase, Ayr—Randolph Place puts in a better round of jumping. Villierstown is second

December and Leicester (to Royal Athlete) in January: stays well: acts on good to firm and soft ground: gives impression he'll be suited by forcing tactics: broke a blood vessel fifth outing. *D. Nicholson.*

RANDOLPH PLACE 9 br.g. Pitpan–French Cherry (Escart III) [1989/90 c24g^ur c20g* c24g^ur c20g^6 c20d^ur 25g^5 22d^3] big, good-topped gelding: fairly useful chaser but is frequently let down by his jumping: jumped better than usual when winning handicap at Ayr in December: good third behind Auk Eye in handicap hurdle on same course in April: stays 25f: acts on heavy going. *G. Richards.* c**137** x 131

RANDOMLY 11 ch.g. Random Shot–Betton's Folly (Immortality) [1989/90 c25f^wo c20g^pu c28g^6 c20s c26d^F c24m] sparely-made, close-coupled gelding: handicap chaser: walked over at Towcester in November: well beaten subsequently: stays well: suited by plenty of give in the ground: suitable mount for an amateur or claimer: rather a deliberate jumper nowadays. *C. J. Bell.* c— —

RANDOM PLACE 8 ch.g. Random Shot–Sicilian Princess (Sicilian Prince) [1989/90 c24d c28g^pu c26m^5 c22g^5 c26m^5] compact gelding: winning hunter chaser: poor form in 1989/90 (jumped badly left on reappearance): stays 3m: acts on soft going. *R. Callow.* c**78**

RANDOM ROMANCE 7 b.m. Eric–Embuscade (Random Shot) [1989/90 16d^4 16d^pu c16s* c16g^2 c16s^2 c20v^2 c25f^3 c20m] compact mare: novice hurdler: won mares novice chase at Worcester in January: kept on gamely when going down by 5 lengths to Radical Lady in Tattersalls Mares Only Novices' Chase Final (limited handicap) at Haydock on sixth start: stays 2½m: acts on soft and good to firm ground: keen sort. *D. Nicholson.* c**97** —

RANDOM TIME 10 b.g. Random Shot–Sowing Time (Arctic Time) [1989/90 c20v*] strong gelding: no form over hurdles: won a poor point-to-point in 1987: finished lame when winning maiden hunter chase at Folkestone in February by 1½ lengths from Didiseeit: will stay 3m: acts on heavy going. *W. R. Hacking.* c**80** —

RANDOM WARRIOR 6 b.g. Random Shot–Regency Cherry (Master Buck) [1989/90 16d 20g^pu 24g* 20g^5 25d^4 20d 24d^4 c25g^pu 24g^5 20f^2 16f^4] small gelding: won selling handicap hurdle at Edinburgh (no bid) in December: made mistakes, tailed off when pulled up on chasing debut: stays 3m: acts on firm and dead going. *J. Parkes.* c— 89

RANDOM WIND 9 ch.m. Random Shot–Hulava Time (Hul A Hul) [1989/90 c21f^4 c18f^2 c20m^F c19m^F 17m^6 c26f^pu c20m^4 c20f^2 c21m^pu] rather leggy mare: winning hurdler and poor novice chaser: stays 2½m: acts on firm going: sold 5,700 gns Ascot June Sales. *N. R. Mitchell.* c**71** —

RANDYBAY 5 b.g. Bay Express–Kiara (Great Nephew) [1989/90 F16f5 F16g5] sixth foal: dam of little account: around 15 lengths fifth in NH Flat races at Uttoxeter (16 ran) and Market Rasen (18 ran) in April: yet to race over hurdles or fences. *J. Mackie.*

RAPIDARIS 4 b.g. Rapid River–Stellaris (Star Appeal) [1989/90 16f5 16f3 16g 16f3] small gelding: poor maiden on Flat and over hurdles: sold 1,150 gns Ascot December Sales. *T. Fairhurst.* 67

RAPID BOY 6 b. or br.g. Rapid River–Silver Thread (Sayfar) [1989/90 F16m F16g aF16g] workmanlike, plain gelding: first living foal: dam never ran: behind in NH Flat races: yet to race over hurdles or fences. *Mrs E. B. Scott.*

RAPID GROUND 5 ch.m. Over The River (FR)–Merry Spring (Merrymount) [1989/90 F16m] IR 16,500 4-y-o: sister to useful staying chaser Cool Ground: dam unraced: about 20 lengths ninth of 17 behind Captain Dibble in NH Flat race at Sandown in March: yet to race over hurdles or fences. *D. J. G. Murray-Smith.*

RAPID SLANE 6 ch.g. Rapid River–Slane Lady (Escart III) [1989/90 16f4 16fbd 20g] leggy, rather dipped-backed gelding: poor novice hurdler: made virtually all until brought down 2 out at Newcastle in October: in mid-division at Wetherby following month and not seen out again: sweated up first 2 starts: needs to settle. *D. Lee.* 76 +

RAPIER THRUST 8 ch.g. Fine Blade (USA)–Zoom Zoom (Bargello) [1989/90 22s4 c25m5] leggy, angular gelding: useful hurdler at his best: better for race, showed he retains much of his ability when remote fourth in handicap at Nottingham in February, travelling strongly until weakening in straight (not at all knocked about): also useful over fences, and finished creditable fifth to One More Knight in quite valuable handicap at Liverpool in April: stays 3m when conditions aren't testing: acts on any going: suited by forcing tactics: tends to jump to his right. *J. G. FitzGerald.* c**133** — p

RAPPAHANNOCK 8 ch.g. Deep Run–Dangle (Beau Tudor) [1989/90 c16f5 c16g4 c16gur] lengthy gelding: modest novice hurdler: tailed off both completed outings over fences: pulls hard: sometimes claimer ridden. *P. W. Harris.* c— —

RARE BID (NZ) 7 br.g. Balak–So Rare (NZ) (Sobig) [1989/90 c16mF c16f* c24f2 c24s4 c20gF c21g6 c16g c16v5 c17m5 c21m* c24hpu] leggy, sparely-made gelding: poor novice hurdler: won 3-runner chases at Wincanton in November and April: effective at 2m and stays 3m, at least when conditions aren't testing: acts on firm ground: usually claimer or amateur ridden. *R. J. Hodges.* c**94** ? —

RARE FIRE 6 ro.g. Rarity–El Diana (Tarboosh (USA)) [1989/90 c24fpu] workmanlike gelding: of little account over hurdles: sold out of R. Earnshaw's stable 3,500 gns Doncaster August Sales: third in a point-to-point in March: pulled up in novice hunter chase following month. *Mrs J. N. Askew.* c— —

RARE FISH 4 b.g. Salmon Leap (USA)–Excellent Fun (USA) (Exceller (USA)) [1989/90 18g 16d 16m5 17m2 16fro 16mpu] sparely-made gelding: first foal: dam unraced: poor juvenile hurdler: dead. *G. B. Balding.* 73

RARE HOLIDAY 4 ch.g. Caerleon (USA)–Temporary Lull (USA) (Super Concorde (USA)) [1989/90 16s6 16s5 16s2 16f*] 137 p

To hear some people talk, Irish jump racing is just about on its last legs, overrun by soft-ground plodders not good enough to be part of the well-publicized drain overseas. Nevertheless, while undoubtedly short of top-class performers, particularly chasers, Irish stables managed to win two of the races at a firm-ground Cheltenham Festival, the Waterford Crystal Stayers' Hurdle with Trapper John and the Daily Express Triumph Hurdle with Rare Holiday. And there was further cause for Irish satisfaction in the two races in Naevog's second to Trapper John, and in the prominent showing of Vestris Abu (fourth), Magic Million (seventh) and Bally Rue (ninth) behind Rare Holiday. The Irish have a good record in the Stayers' Hurdle and an improving one in the Triumph—they've now won two Triumph Hurdles in six years, three in thirteen, having gone almost thirty years before they won one. Meladon and Northern Game were Rare Holiday's predecessors.

The Triumph Hurdle has a deserved reputation for producing shock results. On the face of things, the latest was true to tradition, with Rare Holiday at 25/1 winning from Ninja at 50/1, Native Friend at 20/1 and Vestris Abu at 33/1; the 5/1 favourite Stone Flake came only twenty-seventh of

Daily Express Triumph Hurdle, Cheltenham—little to choose at the last between, from right to left, Rare Holiday, Native Friend, Vestris Abu and Ninja. Sayyure and Lucky Verdict are just behind them.

twenty-nine finishers. However, there's no doubt that there was plenty of confidence behind Rare Holiday despite the fact that he'd not won a race over hurdles (Heighlin in 1980 had been the last maiden to succeed). That confidence stemmed partly from his improving form, but more from his being a proven firm-ground horse on the Flat, useful at a mile and a half upwards. Rare Holiday had just three races over hurdles in the winter, all on soft going; he'd made the frame for the first time in the third of them, in the quite well-contested Stillorgan Hurdle at Leopardstown in February, where he'd run through the field to finish five lengths second to Magic Million after being held up until three out. Magic Million, who'd gone clear between the last two and was never challenged, started the shortest-priced of the Irish challengers at 14/1. Critics of the Triumph Hurdle are unlikely to have been persuaded by anything they saw in the latest running that the race does not impose too stiff a test on an inexperienced youngster. On the contrary. The race was a very keenly-contested affair—once the starter had managed to get the runners into line—with a large bunch of horses jostling and bumping their way round, some of them eventually subjected to severe punishment, some of it crudely administered, up the hill in search of a place. Bally Rue made much of the running at a good pace but couldn't slip the pack, and was just one of a dozen who rose almost together at the second last. Rare Holiday was on the premises there despite having been hampered at the previous one; on the way round he'd been tucked in just behind the leaders, travelling well. By the last turn the leaders had hardly begun to sort themselves out, and even going to the last flight it's fair to say at least eight held chances, with perhaps the Victor Ludorum winner Ninja looking strongest. The accompanying photograph illustrates the state of play. The outcome remained in doubt to the line and beyond, for Rare Holiday had to survive a stewards inquiry before the race was his. Under strong pressure on the run-in he first squeezed out Native Friend then slightly interfered with Vestris Abu before getting up very gamely by half a length. A total of two and a half lengths covered the first six home, little more than eleven lengths covered the first ten. Supporters of the race could point to there being only one faller—Crystal Heights when towards the rear at the last. It transpired that the favourite had been kicked at the long-delayed start. The blanket finish called into question the value of the Triumph Hurdle form. By the close of the season the evidence pointed to the race's being non-vintage, but the subsequent running of Native Friend, Vestris Abu, Sayyure (sixth), Midfielder (eighth) and Bally Rue indicated that it still represented, as usual, some of the best juvenile form of the season. Several in the field look likely to go on, among them four who weren't raced over hurdles again: Lucky Verdict, Silver King, Rare Holiday's former stable-companion Major

Inquiry and Rare Holiday himself. For Rare Holiday it was back to the Flat afterwards, and in July he won a listed race over a mile and three quarters at Tipperary.

Rare Holiday (ch.g. 1986)	Caerleon (USA) (b 1980)	Nijinsky (b 1967)	Northern Dancer
			Flaming Page
		Foreseer (b or br 1969)	Round Table
			Regal Gleam
	Temporary Lull (USA) (ch 1980)	Super Concorde (br 1975)	Bold Reasoning
			Prime Abord
		Magazine (b 1970)	Prince John
			Day Line

The leggy, good-topped Rare Holiday has a Flat-racing pedigree. He is quite closely related to a top jumper, though, as his grandam the CCA Oaks winner Magazine is three parts sister to Barnbrook Again's dam Single Line. Rare Holiday's dam Temporary Lull, an unraced sister to the 1987 Nell Gwyn Stakes winner Martha Stevens, made a good start at stud. Her first foal Wait Till Monday (by Maelstrom Lake) showed useful form for Weld as a two-year-old and two years later won the Grade 2 Bay Meadows Handicap in the United States. The next foal failed to win, but then came Rare Holiday, followed by Monumental Gesture (by Head For Heights) who won over a mile and a half at Mallow in May. One wouldn't expect the French Derby winner Caerleon to be making much of a show in the jumping statistics at this early stage of his career though he's prominent on the Flat. However, he's also the sire of a useful jumper in France called Swinging Home. *D. K. Weld, Ireland.*

RARE LUCK 7 b.m. Rare One–Silly Millie (Menelek) [1989/90 16m^4 21v^4 c16s^6 c22d^5 c20v^{pu} 21f^3 22m* 22f^2 25m] smallish, sturdy mare: won 2 point-to-points in Ireland in 1988: won handicap hurdle at Wincanton in April: ran creditably next outing: poor form, let down by her jumping, in novice chases: stays 2¾m: acts on any going. *P. J. Jones.* c**78** x 95

Dr Michael Smurfit's "Rare Holiday"

RARELY AT ODDS 6 b.g. Tyrnavos–Carol Service (Daring Display (USA)) [1989/90 20f5 22g5 22m 22f3] stocky gelding: novice hurdler: good third behind True Loop at Fontwell in May (first outing for 6 months): should stay 3m: acts on firm ground: trained until after third start by G. Gracey. *J. T. Gifford.* 82

RARE TOPAZE (USA) 4 b.g. Green Forest (USA)–Pink Topaze (Djakao) [1989/90 16gpu] medium-sized gelding: half-brother to Poule d'Essai des Poulains and Prix Lupin winner Fast Topaze (by Far North) and very useful French 1¼m performer Peak Value (by Blushing Groom): dam maiden half-sister to Poule d'Essai des Poulains winner Blue Tom: unplaced both outings at 2 yrs when trained by F. Boutin: favourite, in mid-division when pulled up before last in juvenile hurdle at Kempton in November. *D. R. C. Elsworth.* —

RASPBERRY COPSE 5 b.m. Riboboy (USA)–Stepout (Sagaro) [1989/90 16g 16mr 16mpu] small, leggy mare: novice selling hurdler: reluctant nowadays and is best avoided. *Miss G. M. Rees.* §§

RASTANNORA (USA) 5 b.m. Al Nasr (FR)–Fabled Land (USA) (Graustark) [1989/90 19f5 16h* 17m3 16f2 19hF] leggy, lightly-made mare: former selling hurdler: won non-selling handicap at Taunton in April: good second there later in month, and was in clear lead when falling 2 out in 19f race on same course in May: probably acts on any going. *M. C. Pipe.* 99 +

RATHBAWN DAN 7 b.g. Homeboy–Last Trick (Acer) [1989/90 c20fpu 21m2] workmanlike, good-bodied gelding: first form in novice hurdles when 5 lengths second of 5 to Slightly Gone at Towcester in December: always behind and eventually pulled up in minor event at Newbury on chasing debut. *M. McCormack.* c— 87

RATHER GORGEOUS 5 br.m. Billion (USA)–Fair Sara (McIndoe) [1989/90 F17m F16f] first foal: dam winning hurdler: little sign of ability in NH Flat races: yet to race over hurdles or fences. *Capt. J. Wilson.*

RATHNAGEERA CASTLE 7 b.m. Paddy's Stream–Rocks Rose (Little Buskins) [1989/90 c16d* c16m* c20fF c16hur] selling hurdler: made all in novice chases at Market Rasen and Worcester (made a few mistakes): would have won similar event over 2½m at Bangor in September but for falling last: takes a good hold and may prove best at around 2m: seems to act on any going. *K. C. Bailey.* c94 —

RATH WONDER 9 b.g. Golden Love–Ardglass Belle (Carnival Night) [1989/90 c25g4 c26g6] big, workmanlike gelding: novice hurdler: jumped boldly and made all in poor novice chase in 1988/9: well beaten both starts in 1989/90: stays 25f: acts on firm ground: sold 4,200 gns Doncaster March Sales. *R. B. Francis.* c— —

RAUSAL 11 b.g. Lauso–Aur (Aureole) [1989/90 c28g4 c29g6 c32v5 c30v6 c29d c33dpu] workmanlike gelding: handicap chaser: gave impression something amiss final outing: needs long distances and plenty of give in the ground: blinkered last 2 starts: sketchy jumper, but has run creditably for claimer. *T. N. Bailey.* c**113** —

RAVELSTON 7 b.g. Anax–Jinja (St Paddy) [1989/90 26v 21spu c21gF c24gur 17m 26f6 16g4 21m4] leggy, short-backed gelding: poor novice selling hurdler: hasn't got beyond sixth in novice chases: headstrong: has worn crossed noseband: blinkered last 3 starts. *J. Honeyball.* c— x —

RAVENSDALE ROAD 7 br.g. Malinowski (USA)–Tulchan Bird (Santamoss) [1989/90 22m 20m c22d6 25g c20m2 c16d4 c16m2 c20m c20fF c20m6 c19fpu] medium-sized gelding: poor novice hurdler/chaser: stays 2¼m: best form on good ground: sometimes blinkered. *A. P. James.* c**78** —

RAVENTURA 7 b.m. Harris–Furious Heights (Bey Shadow) [1989/90 F16m 16h5] lengthy, sparely-made non-thoroughbred mare: fifth foal: dam unraced: well beaten in NH Flat race at Warwick in September and novice hurdle at Hexham (jumped poorly in lead to fourth) following month. *E. J. Alston.* —

RAVEN VENTURE 10 b.g. Le Coq d'Or–Bride's Burn (Bishop's Move) [1989/90 c20mpu c25fpu c20g* c20d* c24d4 c20fpu c20g2 c20d* c24f4] rangy, rather plain gelding: has been hobdayed: point-to-point winner: won handicap chases at Edinburgh and Leicester in January and Perth (made most) in May: stays 2½m: acts on firm and dead going: blinkered third start in 1988/9, visored nowadays. *D. Lee.* c**109**

RAWHIDE 6 ch.g. Buckskin (FR)–Shuil Eile (Deep Run) [1989/90 16s3 17d2 20d3 24g* 24v3 24d* 24g* 22s4 25f] small, sturdy Irish gelding: first foal: dam won twice over hurdles at up to 2½m: won handicap hurdle at Thurles in November and quite valuable handicaps at Leopardstown in December and January: second favourite, struggling halfway in valuable handicap at Cheltenham 113 in March (finished lame): suited by 3m: acts on heavy going, possibly unsuited by firm. *M. F. Morris, Ireland.*

RAWLSBURY 5 b.g. Comedy Star (USA)–Princess Charybdis (Ballymoss) [1989/90 aF13g* aF16g3] third foal: dam behind in 7.6f maiden at 3 yrs on only outing: won NH Flat race at Lingfield in December: third on same course following month: yet to race over hurdles or fences. *A. Csaky.*

RAWTHEY BANK 8 b.g. Roscoe Blake–Cordon Rouge (Never Say Die) [1989/90 c20gpu] workmanlike gelding: novice hurdler/chaser: has shown some ability over fences, but jumped moderately and was pulled up only outing of season (November). *A. D. Brown.* c— —

RAZEEN 5 ch.g. Be My Guest (USA)–Fast Motion (Midsummer Night II) [1989/90 16dF 16gr] sparely-made gelding: half-brother to winning chaser Nonstop (by Nonoalco): jumped none too fluently and was beaten when falling last in novice hurdle at Stratford in November: badly hampered second and refused fifth in similar event at Huntingdon later in month (put back in race): winner on Flat in Scandinavia. *J. G. FitzGerald.* —

RAZZLE DAZZLE BOY 8 ch.g. Some Hand–Fair Georgina (Silver Cloud) [1989/90 c20fpu c21mpu c20m6 c21f4 c17m* c16m5] compact gelding: winning hurdler: won novice handicap chase at Newton Abbot in May by a short head from Strictly Business: stays 21f: acts on firm going: occasionally amateur ridden. *W. R. Williams.* c**81** —

REACH ME DOWN 6 b.m. Cheval–Tangmalangaloo (Laurence O) [1989/90 F17h* 18g2 22m* 20f* 20spu 22d4 21s6 21d 21f* 24f3] medium-sized mare: 111

Hoechst Panacur EBF Mares Novices' Handicap Hurdle Final, Newbury— Reach Me Down stays on strongly

second foal: dam unraced: won point-to-point in Ireland in 1989: bought for 7,000
gns Doncaster August Sales: won NH Flat race at Devon & Exeter in October:
successful over hurdles in novice events at Wincanton (amateur riders) and
Huntingdon (mares) and in Hoechst Panacur Mares Only Novices' Hurdle Final
(Handicap) at Newbury, beating Trefelyn Cone 4 lengths in last-named: stayed
well: acted on firm and good to soft going: dead. *G. B. Balding.*

READ ALL ABOUT IT 9 ch.g. London Gazette–Pet Jackdaw (Vulgan) c—
[1989/90 c24h^{4} 24g^{3} 27f^{2} 28g^{3} 24g^{pu} 27g^{6} c17f^{F}] lengthy, rather sparely-made 77
gelding: maiden point-to-pointer: poor novice hurdler/chaser: stays well: acts on
firm going: claimer ridden: blinkered fourth and last 2 starts. *R. D. E. Woodhouse.*

READY STEADY 8 ch.g. Bivouac–Very Merry (Lord of Verona) [1989/90 c**105**
c24s^{2} c24m* c22m] workmanlike gelding: useful point-to-pointer, winner 3 times
in February: led from twelfth when winning hunter chase at Newcastle in March
by 4 lengths from Straight Pilot: well beaten in Seagram Fox Hunters' Chase at
Liverpool following month: stays 3m: acts on any going: headstrong and has worn
a crossed noseband: jumps sketchily: amateur ridden. *Mrs P. M. Shrubsole.*

READY WIT 9 br.g. Bay Express–Brevity (Pindari) [1989/90 a16g^{4} 16d^{F}]
modest performer on Flat in 1986 (lightly raced and little form since): showed 82
signs of ability in novice hurdles at Southwell in November and Windsor
(weakening when fell 2 out) in January. *M. P. Muggeridge.*

REAL CLASS 7 b.g. Deep Run–Our Cherry (Tarqogan) [1989/90 c16g^{pu} c**91**
c26g^{2}] rangy gelding: winning hurdler: staying-on 10 lengths second to Proplus in —
novice chase at Uttoxeter in April: stays well: acts on dead going: trained first
start by D. Elsworth (off course 4 months afterwards). *R. Lee.*

REALISM 5 b.g. Known Fact (USA)–Miss Reasoning (USA) (Bold Reasoning
(USA)) [1989/90 a16g^{2} 16d^{6} a16g^{5}] compact gelding: won 1½m handicap on Flat in 89
February: handicap hurdler: runner-up at Lingfield in November: tailed off in 2
races in spring: acts on heavy going. *K. O. Cunningham-Brown.*

REALLY NEAT 4 gr.f. Alias Smith (USA)–Tiddley (Filiberto (USA)) [1989/90
18f^{3} 16f^{4} a16g^{6} a16g^{6} 17m^{pu}] sparely-made filly: third foal: dam, lightly raced, best 65
effort over 11f: juvenile selling hurdler: well beaten when blinkered third and
fourth starts: should stay beyond 2m: sold out of D. Gandolfo's stable 1,650 gns
Ascot February Sales after fourth outing. *L. Waring.*

REASON TO LAUGH 4 b.g. Comedy Star (USA)–Legal Sound (Legal Eagle)
[1989/90 16g^{6}] little worthwhile form on Flat: tailed-off last in selling handicap —
hurdle at Market Rasen in August. *J. Balding.*

REBEL SONG 8 b.g. Tug of War–Country Tune (Prince Hansel) [1989/90 c**115** §
c24m^{pu} c25g^{4} c25m^{F} c24d^{pu}] useful hurdler: usually let down by deliberate —
jumping over fences: didn't go through with his effort when fourth to Rubika in
handicap chase at Wolverhampton in February: stays 25f: acts on soft going: takes
a good hold: blinkered last 5 starts in 1988/9 and last in 1989/90: has his own ideas
about the game. *O. Sherwood.*

RECHARGEABLE 4 b.g. Music Boy–Ciliata (So Blessed) [1989/90 a16g*
16m^{F} a16g^{5}] angular gelding: modest maiden on Flat, stays 7f: claimer ridden, led 91
after first when winning juvenile selling hurdle at Southwell in December (bought
in 2,200 gns): well beaten on same course in May: sold 6,200 gns Newmarket July
Sales. *A. S. Reid.*

RECIDIVIST 4 b.f. Royben–On Remand (Reform) [1989/90 16m* 16s 16s^{2}
16g^{3} 16m] workmanlike filly: plating-class maiden on Flat: easy winner of juvenile 87
selling hurdle at Taunton in November (bought in 6,200 gns): placed in
non-sellers subsequently: acts on good to firm and soft ground: twice amateur
ridden. *R. J. Hodges.*

RECOLLECT 8 b.g. Vaigly Great–Archaic (Relic) [1989/90 16m* 16g] close-
coupled gelding: handicap hurdler: won at Worcester in October: well beaten later 92
in month and not seen out again: unlikely to stay beyond 17f: acts on good to firm
ground: has won when sweating. *Miss J. Thorne.*

RECORD DANCER 10 b.g. Dancer's Image (USA)–Treacle (Hornbeam) c—
[1989/90 21f^{pu}] rather leggy gelding: handicap hurdler: capable of fair form but is — §
ungenuine: little worthwhile form over fences: stays 3m: probably acts on any
going: has run well for a claimer: pulled up lame in November. *N. A. Gaselee.*

RECORD FLIGHT 6 ch.m. Record Token–Lady Relka (Relko) [1989/90 16f^{2}
21g* 20d^{5} 20g 17d^{2} 16d^{3} 21s^{2} 21m^{6} 21d^{2} 21f^{2} 24f] lengthy, lightly-made mare: 113
handicap hurdler: won amateur riders event at Newton Abbot in November: ran

creditably on occasions afterwards: suited by around 2½m: acts on any going with exception of very firm: has run creditably when sweating. *R. J. Hodges.*

RECORD TROUT 9 ch.g. Record Run–Elf Trout (Elf-Arrow) [1989/90 c20v^{F}] c—
poor novice hurdler: won a point-to-point in April: beaten when falling 5 out in —
hunter chase in February. *J. C. S. Hickman.*

RECORD WING 12 b.g. Record Run–O'Flynn (Prince Regent (FR)) [1989/90
16g^{pu}] small gelding: poor hurdler nowadays, lightly raced: sold 625 gns Ascot —
April Sales. *M. Scudamore.*

RECTORY BOY 7 b.g. Rustingo–Ron's Girl (Ron) [1989/90 c25s^{ur} c20f* c95
c25f^{ur} c26m^{3}] angular gelding: novice hurdler: successful point-to-pointer: won —
novice hunter chase at Cheltenham in May by 15 lengths: weakened approaching
last when third in similar race over 3¼m at Stratford in June, giving impression he
didn't stay: acts on firm going. *B. Llewellyn.*

REDALLY 7 b.g. Ballymore–Red Aster (St Alphage) [1989/90 c25g^{2} c24s^{pu} c89
c17v^{2} c26v^{5} c20v^{pu}] sparely-made gelding: no form over hurdles: placed in a —
point-to-point in 1988: in lead when breaking leg and pulled up approaching last in
conditional jockeys chase at Fontwell in February: blinkered first 2 outings,
visored last three. *M. C. Pipe.*

RED BOLT 8 ch.g. Stanford–Amy Jane (Guillaume Tell (USA)) [1989/90 18f^{6} c72
c16f^{3} 16f^{5}] small, sturdy gelding: selling hurdler: novice chaser: seems best at —
2m: suited by top-of-the-ground: wears bandages: sold privately 1,500 gns Ascot
September Sales. *P. D. Evans.*

RED BREWSTER 4 b.g. Burslem–Red Magic (Red God) [1989/90 17f^{2} 16g^{5}]
plating-class maiden on Flat: showed ability in juvenile hurdles at Newton Abbot 75
(remote second to Shadeux) and Kempton in October: jumped none too fluently in
latter. *Mrs A. Knight.*

RED COLUMBIA 9 ch.g. St Columbus–Red Tan (Crespin Rouge) [1989/90 c**103**
c24d^{ur} c26g^{6} c30v c24d^{4} c28g^{3} c29d^{pu} c29g^{3}] tall, good-bodied gelding: carries —
plenty of condition: handicap chaser: ran creditably when in frame at Wetherby
and Wolverhampton in February and Worcester in March: stays very well: needs
give in the ground. *M. J. Wilkinson.*

RED DUSK 6 ch.m. Deep Run–Bannow Bay (Arctic Slave) [1989/90 20f]
medium-sized mare: poor form in novice hurdles: stays 2½m. *J. K. M. Oliver.* —

RED FESCUE 8 gr.g. Warpath–Jasmin (Frankincense) [1989/90 c17f^{ur} c17f^{pu} c—
c20f^{4}] dipped-backed gelding: carries plenty of condition: no form over hurdles: —
winning chaser: tailed off only completed start in 1989/90: stays 21f: acts on firm
going: visored last 5 starts. *J. J. Bridger.*

REDGRAVE DEVIL 8 ch.m. Tug of War–Be A Devil (Arctic Slave) [1989/90 c**120**
c17g* c20s* c22g^{pu}] leggy, sparely-made mare: fair hurdler at her best: made all —
in mares novice chase at Newton Abbot and virtually all in novice chase at Bangor
(still travelling strongly when the challenging Mandavi fell at the last): looked set
to win similar race at Nottingham in January until breaking down and being pulled
up late on: stays 21f: acts on any going: blinkered twice 1986/7: sometimes hangs
left under pressure, though was good mount for a 7-lb claimer over hurdles: sound
jumper. *M. C. Pipe.*

REDGRAVE ROSE 10 b.m. Tug of War–Lady Ashton (Anthony) [1989/90 c99
c24m^{2} c24m^{F} c26m^{2}] tall, lengthy, workmanlike mare: handicap hurdler/chaser: —
second over fences at Worcester (made mistakes) and Stratford in September:
stays well: probably acts on any going: has won for a claimer. *K. Bishop.*

RED HACKLE 5 b.g. Beldale Flutter (USA)–Tartan Pimpernel (Blakeney)
[1989/90 16s 24m^{3} 21m^{5} 22f^{2}] workmanlike gelding: shows traces of stringhalt: 108
handicap hurdler: ran well second and fourth starts, poorly (blinkered) in
between: stays 3m: acts on any going: has carried head high. *M. C. Pipe.*

RED HOOD 5 b.m. Wolverlife–Dab Chick (Cavo Doro) [1989/90 F13f F16f 16d]
second foal: dam placed at up to 1¼m on Flat in Ireland: tailed off in NH Flat races: —
behind in novice selling hurdle at Worcester. *R. Lee.*

RED HOT LADY 4 b.f. Red Sunset–Breezy Answer (On Your Mark) [1989/90
16f^{4} 18f^{5}] plating-class maiden on Flat: fourth in juvenile hurdle in August: 65
destroyed after severing a tendon in seller in October. *R. Voorspuy.*

RED INDIAN 4 ch.g. Be My Native (USA)–Martialette (Welsh Saint) [1989/90
16d 16g^{2} a16g^{4}] lengthy colt: placed at up to 1¼m on Flat: 5 lengths second to La 95
Castana in 19-runner claiming hurdle at Market Rasen in December (would have

gone close but for mistake 2 out): found little under pressure when well beaten next time. *W. W. Haigh.*

REDMARLEY 8 ch.g. Malinowski (USA)–Meadow Rhapsody (Ragusa) [1989/90 19gpu] rather sparely-made gelding: modest form in novice hurdles in 1987/8: tailed off when pulled up in November: stays 2¾m: best run on firm ground: visored third start 1987/8 (well beaten): sold 1,000 gns Ascot December Sales. *M. Oliver.* —

RED MATCH 5 ch.g. Royal Match–Hi Mary (High Line) [1989/90 aF16g4] workmanlike gelding: second foal: dam moderate hurdler: 10 lengths fourth behind Flowing River in NH Flat race at Southwell in March: yet to race over hurdles or fences. *R. E. Pocock.*

REDMINT 6 ch.m. Lucifer (USA)–Quefort (Quayside) [1989/90 aF16g5 25gpu a20g3] smallish, angular mare: second foal: dam unraced: well beaten in NH Flat race: beaten 30 lengths when third in novice hurdle at Southwell in January. *A. S. Reid.* —

RED MORGAN 13 ch.g. Fireprince–Bally Morgan (Zingari) [1989/90 c20s6] lengthy gelding: maiden point-to-pointer: tailed off in hunter chases. *J. Tredwell.* c—

RED PLANET 5 b.g. Sir Ivor–Miss Mars (Red God) [1989/90 a20g6 20s5 16d5 16dpu] workmanlike gelding: winning hurdler: ran poorly in 1989/90, including in sellers: stays 2½m: best form on good to firm ground: blinkered last 2 outings 1988/9, visored on reappearance: sold 1,700 gns Doncaster March Sales. *Denys Smith.* —

RED PROCESSION 6 ch.g. Red Sunset–Procession (Sovereign Path) [1989/90 c16f* c16m2 c16d4 16m 17f3 c16fF 16m 16m4 c16fpu 16fpu 16f3 16d6 16f3] leggy gelding: handicap hurdler: third in seller final start: won novice event at Southwell in August on chasing debut: best at around 2m: acts on any going except possibly very soft: sometimes visored. *P. Liddle.* c**78** + 78

RED RAMBO 9 ch.g. Mossberry–Red Squaw (Tribal Chief) [1989/90 20gpu] compact, workmanlike gelding: modest novice hurdler: tailed off when pulled up in December: stays 2¾m: acts on dead going: has run creditably for claimer: wears a crossed noseband. *R. Dickin.* —

RED RONDO 6 ch.g. Rontino–Ivy Hill (Cantab) [1989/90 F17d F16g] half-brother to Ivanter (by Levanter), placed over hurdles and a winning point-to-pointer: dam won a point-to-point: successful in 3 point-to-points in Ireland in 1989: mid-division in NH Flat races at Carlisle and Market Rasen in spring: yet to race over hurdles or in a steeplechase. *J. A. C. Edwards.*

RED RUDDEL 7 b.g. Proverb–Mountain Bell (Pyrenean) [1989/90 16f* 20g* 24f* 20f5 24g 20f4 16m6 25m] lengthy, sparely-made gelding: hobdayed: retained 20,000 gns Doncaster August Sales: fair hurdler: successful in handicaps at Wetherby (2) and Ascot (idled in front) in first half of season: off course 4 months after fifth start: shaped as though retaining plenty of ability next 2 outings but ran a lifeless race when favourite on final start: jumped none too fluently in novice chases in 1988/9: stays well: yet to show his form on heavy going but probably acts on any other: has hung under pressure. *J. Hanson.* c— 119

RED SAILS 4 b.f. Town And Country–Helm (Royal Palace) [1989/90 16dF 17gpu] unfurnished filly: half-sister to winning hurdler Hawser (by Dominion): dam lightly-raced 1¼m winner: tailed off when pulled up in juvenile hurdle at Doncaster in January. *F. Walwyn.* —

RED TIMBER 6 ch.g. Nishapour (FR)–Welsh Miniature (Owen Anthony) [1989/90 16f 16m c16f c16m* c16d3 c17m c16f6 c16m5 c16m 16h3 16m] good-topped gelding: poor hurdler: well beaten in seller final start: jumped soundly in the main when winning conditional jockeys handicap chase at Wolverhampton in December: looked none too keen subsequently, finding nothing seventh start: races only at around 2m: acts on hard ground: usually held up: blinkered last 7 starts: moody: sold 3,300 gns Ascot June Sales. *D. Nicholson.* c**80** § 80 §

REDUNDANT PAL 7 ch.g. Redundant–Palesa (Palestine) [1989/90 16g 16g* 18d2 16g* 16m 16f] 149

Redundant Pal seems a difficult horse to weigh up, even to his closest connections. When winning The Ladbroke at Leopardstown in 1989, he started the longest price (16/1) of three runners trained by Mullins, who would apparently have preferred the horse to have run in a novice event at the same meeting. When winning the same race under a much stiffer weight

The Ladbroke, Leopardstown—Redundant Pal challenges between Fragrant Dawn (left) and Dis Train at the last

in the latest season, Redundant Pal started at 20/1, having been beaten ten lengths by the novice Firions Law when 5/1 on for a two-runner minor event at Leopardstown two weeks earlier. Though Redundant Pal was reported to be suffering from cramp after that race, his trainer was unable to offer an explanation for his improved form at a stewards' inquiry after The Ladbroke. Without presuming to tell the trainer his job, one or two facets of the horse's racing character suggest themselves as pointers towards a possible explanation. Firstly Redundant Pal is a confirmed two-mile specialist, over which trip he won the Newbridge Hurdle at Naas in November. His match with Firions Law was over two and a quarter miles on good to soft going. Redundant Pal, at one time a very hard puller, also gives the impression he needs holding up for as long as possible—in the Seagram 100 Pipers Novices' Hurdle at Liverpool in 1989 he led over the last but edged right on the run-in and finished third. Against Firions Law, Redundant Pal had to make much of the running and could find no extra in the closing stages. There was no problem in holding up Redundant Pal behind the strong pace set by Royal Derbi and Toranfield in the twenty-seven-runner field for the latest Ladbroke. When asked to move up he made relentless progress from halfway, came through to challenge at the last, took the lead from Dis Train on the run-in and held on by half a length. The pair drew three lengths clear of 4/1 favourite Fragrant Dawn and the strong-finishing pair Joyful Noise and the Mullins-trained Sayparee, the latter the choice of principal stable-jockey Tony Mullins. Firions Law, reapposing on terms 6 lb better than when beating Redundant Pal, finished twentieth.

The subsequent performances of those who finished close up, most receiving weight, in The Ladbroke suggested that Redundant Pal was worth a crack at the best two milers. Joyful Noise and Vicario di Bray (sixth at Leopardstown) finished second in the Tote Gold Trophy at Newbury and the Daily Mail Racecall Champion Hurdle Trial at Haydock respectively. Toranfield (eighth) and Derrinore (tenth) drew twenty lengths clear of the remainder when fighting out the finish of quite a valuable handicap at Naas. And Osric (seventh) was narrowly beaten in the Bic Razor Lanzarote Handicap Hurdle at Kempton. However, Redundant Pal, a 33/1-shot, was never able to challenge in the Waterford Crystal Champion Hurdle at Cheltenham, finishing over thirty lengths behind Kribensis in fourteenth place. He had also run below his best in the Waterford Crystal Supreme Novices' Hurdle on the same course on each of the two previous seasons and is possibly unsuited by such a testing, undulating track. Redundant Pal fared slightly better when seventh to Jubail in the Janneau Armagnac Handicap Hurdle over Liverpool's easier course, though still never threatening on the very firm ground.

Redundant Pal (ch.g. 1983)	Redundant (ch 1969)	Busted (b 1963)	Crepello
			Sans Le Sou
		Sucu Sucu (ch 1960)	Tudor Jinks
			Tory Victory
	Palesa (b 1967)	Palestine (gr 1947)	Fair Trial
			Una
		Va Beni (b 1962)	Infatuation
			Rosie V

There is plenty of speed in Redundant Pal's pedigree. The French seven-and-a-half-furlong winner Palesa is a half-sister to the useful sprinter I Don't Mind, dam of high-class hurdler Swingit Gunner. Their dam, mile-and-a-quarter winner Va Beni, was a half-sister to useful miler Nicois out of the unraced Rosie V. Redundant Pal is a half-brother to the Belgian Group 3 winner Sea Bomb (by Bruni) and to the successful Irish jumpers Twilight God (by Yellow God) and Davbaton (by Royal Captive). He was bought for IR 5,000 guineas at Ballsbridge as a three-year-old and won three National Hunt Flat races before being sent hurdling. A plain gelding, still leggy, he should make a chaser when the time comes. If kept to hurdling he should win more races, though he's likely to be set a stiff task by the handicapper if attempting to become the first horse to win The Ladbroke three times. Fredcoteri carried 11-13 into fourth place when attempting to complete a hat-trick in 1984/5 when the race was known as the Sweeps Handicap Hurdle. Comedy of Errors had no luck in running when fourth, subsequently promoted to third, on his attempt at a third win in 1975/6, in the days before the race became a handicap. *Patrick Mullins, Ireland.*

REEDLING (USA) 5 b.g. Riverman (USA)–Mary Biz (USA) (T V Lark) [1989/90 16h^4 16f* 18f^4 16f^5 16f^2 19h^4] angular, sparely-made gelding: won conditional jockeys novice hurdle at Hereford in August: ran well fourth and fifth (seller) outings, moderately final one (blinkered): stays 2¼m: acts on firm and good to soft ground. *G. P. Enright.* 81

REEF PATRICK 5 b.g. Main Reef–Dooneena (Welsh Pageant) [1989/90 16d^2 16f* 16f^2 17g^2 16s 16s 17f 20m^6] small, angular gelding: won selling hurdle at Leicester in November (no bid): well below form last 4 starts: likely to prove suited by 2m: acts on firm ground and possibly unsuited by very soft: usually a front runner: trained by M. Tompkins until after fifth outing. *J. Dooler.* 93 d

REFFOLDS 7 ch.g. Green Shoon–Penthouse Pet (Deep Run) [1989/90 c20g^{pu}] lengthy, good-topped gelding: no sign of ability. *T. J. Etherington.* c— —

REFRAIN NO MORE 5 ch.m. Blue Refrain–More Rheola (Morston (FR)) [1989/90 F12g^5] second foal: dam behind in NH Flat race and a novice hurdle: around 14 lengths fifth behind Teddy Bruere in NH Flat race at Market Rasen in November: yet to race over hurdles or fences. *C. Smith.*

REGAL AMBITION 6 b.g. Royal Palace–Quick Aim (Pardal) [1989/90 20d* 20f^2 20s* 20s* 20f* 22f^{pu}] 151

The extraordinary achievements of Pond House stables leave no room to doubt that as a trainer of National Hunt horses Martin Pipe has no equal. His feat of saddling 208 winners in 1988/9 was hailed as 'a record that will never be beaten'; but Pipe confounded the prophecy by sending out 224 in 1989/90. Pipe achieves a remarkably high ratio of winners to runners—35% in the latest season—and makes training winners look easy, which is the mark of a genius. His renowned ability to make a silk purse out of a sow's ear was illustrated once again in the latest season through the big-race successes of such as Milford Quay, Run For Free and Regal Ambition. The transformation brought about in the last-named was remarkable. A modest mile-and-a-quarter winner on the Flat as a three-year-old when trained by Shaw, Regal Ambition looked to be on the downgrade the following season, hanging badly left on one occasion and seeming not to have an ideal attitude. Subsequently off the course for a year, he was transferred to Pipe who commented that 'he must have had a few problems' in a *Timeform Interview*.

Golden Miller Novices' Hurdle, Leicester—Regal Ambition is unchallenged

Yet, sent hurdling, Regal Ambition strolled home by thirty lengths at Worcester on his debut in November. And he went on to win three of his next four starts, putting up the best performance of the season by a novice when winning the Sun Alliance Novices' Hurdle at Cheltenham in March by a margin exceded only by Ten Plus in seventeen runnings of the race.

Regal Ambition had looked a very exciting prospect prior to Cheltenham. Ridden from the front in customary stable fashion, he showed no signs of shirking the issue over hurdles. Indeed, he looked ready to go round again after winning at Worcester and also after spreadeagling a large field in a qualifier of the Philip Cornes series at Chepstow the following month. Regal Ambition was particularly impressive at Chepstow where he

Sun Alliance Novices' Hurdle, Cheltenham—
Regal Ambition is just ahead of stable-companion Run For Free in the early stages

drew clear from the fourth-last without being at all hard pressed to win by fifteen lengths from Strong Gold, with the well-regarded novices Black Moccasin and Beau Pari each beaten a further fifteen lengths in third and fourth places respectively. He was equally impressive in following up in the Golden Miller Novices' Hurdle at Leicester in January, scoring, eased virtually to a walk on the run-in, by twenty-five lengths from Danny Harrold who gave the impression something was amiss with him.

Regal Ambition's starting a well-backed 3/1 favourite for the twenty-two-runner Sun Alliance well illustrated the kind of impression he had created. Though the choice of stable jockey Scudamore, he seemed, on form, to have tough opponents in stable-companion and impressive Warwick winner Run For Free (who started at 6/1) and Irish National Hunt Novice Hurdle Series Final winner Scally Owen (9/1), Fort Noel (5/1), most impressive when winning at Haydock, Midland Glenn (8/1) seeking his seventh successive victory and Tinryland (12/1). None of the horses to finish behind Regal Ambition at Chepstow and Leicester reopposed him at Cheltenham. Our chief doubt as to Regal Ambition's prospects concerned the ground. His best run had been on soft and he'd been some way below that form when short-headed by Remittance Man on firm at Cheltenham in December. However, Regal Ambition had been less forcefully ridden than usual and beaten for finishing speed on the latter occasion. Regal Ambition had no problems with the ground in the Sun Alliance. He was soon travelling strongly in the lead, and, though challenged briefly in the early stages by Run For Free, quickened decisively before the fourth last and began to draw well clear before the straight. He stayed on strongly to win by twelve lengths and three quarters of a length from Judges Fancy and Tom's Little Bet, both of whom also kept on well in the latter stages. Run For Free, a further three lengths back in fourth place, fared best of those who raced close up from the start. Devil's Valley had looked the main danger to the winner going to the second last but found little under pressure, finishing sixth. Fort Noel (thirteenth) and Scally Owen (pulled up) ran as though unsuited by the ground.

Sold privately to American owners after Cheltenham, Regal Ambition was sent to Kentucky to contest the valuable Dueling Grounds International Hurdle. He was still in the lead when breaking down badly on both forelegs three out. He's reportedly to be trained by J. Elliot in Pennsylvania, and granted a full recovery is sure to win races in the States.

Regal Ambition (b.g. 1984)	Royal Palace (b 1964)	Ballymoss (ch 1954)	Mossborough
			Indian Call
		Crystal Palace (b 1956)	Solar Slipper
			Queen of Light
	Quick Aim (b 1966)	Pardal (b 1947)	Pharis II
			Adargatis
		Steady Aim (b 1943)	Felstead
			Quick Arrow

Regal Ambition is from a distinguished family. His grandam Steady Aim won the Oaks in 1946 on the last of three appearances. Retired after injury whilst in preparation for a clash with Airborne in the St Leger, Steady Aim bred five winners, including the smart miler Immortal and Sure Shot, a useful winner at up to one and three quarter miles. Steady Aim was a half-sister to six winners out of the successful mile-and-a-half performer Quick Arrow. Quick Aim, who died in 1984, had done little to improve the family's record until the arrival of Regal Ambition. Seemingly of little account on the Flat and over hurdles, she'd produced just one winner, the modest Irish hurdler Shanbally (by Lucky Brief), from eight previous live foals. Royal Palace, retired from stud in 1986, left his mark on National Hunt racing principally as the sire of champion hurdler See You Then and Sinzinbra, the dam of Mr Snugfit, Cashew King and Young Snugfit. Regal Ambition looked a top-class staying hurdler in the making when winning at Cheltenham. He should have few problems with the bigger American hurdles—a leggy, angular, plain gelding, he tended to jump British hurdles more like a chaser. Though he has a round action, Regal Ambition showed he acts at least as well on firm ground as he does on soft. *M. C. Pipe.*

REGAL BEE 7 br.m. Royal Fountain–Brown Bee III (Marcus Superbus) [1989/90 24m 20g] workmanlike mare: won novice hurdle in 1988/9: tailed off in handicaps in November and April: stays 3m: best form on good ground: may be worth trying in blinkers. *W. G. Reed.* —

REGAL BRASS 6 gr.h. Royal Palace–Two Friendly (Be Friendly) [1989/90 16m 16f3 16g 16g6 16g2 20g4 16g 16s2 16s5 20fpu] sparely-made horse: novice hurdler: has run in a seller: moved badly to post when running poorly on firm ground final start (probably needs an easier surface nowadays): will prove best at around 2m: has run well for a 7-lb claimer: trained until after eighth outing by P. Blockley. *B. A. McMahon.* 77

REGAL CASTLE 7 b.g. Tachypous–Right Mall (Pall Mall) [1989/90 16g6 16d c20v3 c18s 20f5] leggy, sparely-made gelding: handicap hurdler: below form in 1989/90: left clear at the last but weakened quickly run-in when third to Elvercone in 2½m novice event at Chepstow in January on chasing debut: jumped moderately next outing: likely to prove best at around 2m: acts on soft going: ridden by claimer in 1987/8: blinkered last 3 starts. *N. J. Henderson.* c**85** 109

REGALCROFT 6 b.g. Crofter (USA)–Regal Ray (Prince Regent (FR)) [1989/90 16spu] leggy gelding: maiden on Flat (probably ungenuine): little sign of ability over hurdles, including in a seller. *D. Haydn Jones.* —

REGAL ESTATE 6 ch.g. Royal Palace–Salira (Double Jump) [1989/90 16g5 20g6 16d3 18d5 16s] tall gelding: won NH Flat race in 1988/9: modest novice hurdler: likely to be suited by forcing tactics when racing at 2m: acts on heavy going: has worn pricker on near-side: usually claimer ridden, but gives impression he's none too easy a ride and will be suited by stronger handling: needs to brush up his jumping. *D. Moffatt.* 95

REGAL FLAME 7 b.m. Royalty–Firella (Firestreak) [1989/90 F16g] won NH Flat race at Hereford in November, 1988: tailed off in similar event at Warwick in December: yet to race over hurdles or fences. *R. G. Frost.*

REGAL LAKE 4 b. or br.c. Kings Lake (USA)–Thistlewood (Kalamoun) [1989/90 16s* 16g2 16g2 16g2 16d* a20g2 16m6] sparely-made colt: middle-distance maiden on Flat: sold out of M. Stoute's stable 22,000 gns Newmarket Autumn Sales: won juvenile hurdle at Taunton in December and Swish Hurdle at 122

Swish Hurdle, Chepstow—Regal Lake's final victory

Chepstow in March: destroyed after fracturing a cannon bone in valuable novice event at Liverpool: stayed 2½m: acted on soft going. *Mrs J. Pitman.*

REGAL SALUTE 4 br.f. Dara Monarch–Forelock (Condorcet (FR)) [1989/90 16v5 16g] placed at up to 1¼m on Flat: sold out of W. Haggas' stable 9,000 gns Newmarket Autumn Sales: soundly beaten in juvenile hurdles at Haydock and Wolverhampton in December. *P. J. Bevan.* —

REGAL TIGER 5 gr.h. On Your Mark–Regal Doll (Sovereign Path) [1989/90 17fF 17fpu] lengthy horse: lightly-raced maiden on Flat: pulled very hard and was tailed off when pulled up fifth in novice hurdle at Newton Abbot in August (wore severe bridle). *Miss J. Thorne.* —

REGARDLESS 8 b.g. Quayside–Bel Arbre (Beau Chapeau) [1989/90 20f6 c22g* c25g2 c22d4 c24s c20fpu] close-coupled gelding: winning point-to-pointer: winning hurdler: left clear at the last when winning weakly-contested Nottingham Champion Novices' Chase in January by 30 lengths: ran a lack-lustre race next start: let down by his jumping afterwards: stays 3m when conditions aren't testing: acts on soft going: has won for a 7-lb claimer. *J. W. Blundell.* c**97** ? —

REGENT CROSS 5 b.g. Prince Regent (FR)–Holy Cross (Arcticeelagh) [1989/90 16d 16g 16g6 20g 20f* 22f 16f3] strong, good-bodied gelding: first foal: dam, maiden hurdler/winning point-to-pointer in Ireland, half-sister to several winning jumpers including top-class hunter chaser Eliogarty: won novice handicap hurdle at Newcastle in March: 4 lengths third behind Zucchini in novice event at Wetherby in May: ran poorly in between: stays 2½m: acts on firm going: claimer ridden when successful. *W. A. Stephenson.* 93

REGGAE BEAT 5 b.g. Be My Native (USA)–Invery Lady (Sharpen Up) [1989/90 16m 16g* 16d 16m2 16g 16d 16m] leggy gelding: showed improved form when winning handicap hurdle at Fakenham in October: second at Huntingdon in December and not disgraced next time, but ran moderately last 2 starts: suited by a sharp 2m and a sound surface. *I. Campbell.* 108

REGGAE YEOMAN 6 b.g. Black Minstrel–Toombeola (Raise You Ten) [1989/90 18g* 18g* 21d 21m] workmanlike gelding: will make a chaser: handicap hurdler: won at Fontwell in October and December (made all): well beaten over 21f, running in snatches on second occasion: stays 2¼m: acts on heavy going. *J. T. Gifford.* 121

REGIMENTAL MARCH (USA) 4 b.c. Diamond Shoal–Slow March (Queen's Hussar) [1989/90 17m 16fF] small colt: half-brother to novice hurdler Silent Journey (by Nearly A Hand): lightly-raced maiden on Flat: tailed off in juvenile hurdle at Cartmel in August: bumped and fell fourth at Sedgefield following month: sold 600 gns Doncaster October Sales. *D. Yeoman.* —

REGULAR VULGAN 7 b.g. Regular Guy–Vulgan's Law (Vulgan) [1989/90 c21dF 22g 21f3 16m 19mpu] ex-Irish gelding: eighth foal: brother to winning hurdler High Viscosity and half-brother to winning staying hurdler Woodland (by Mad For Money): dam unraced: runner-up in point-to-points in 1989: novice hurdler/chaser: twice blinkered: dead. *N. A. Twiston-Davies.* c— 78

REHAB VENTURE 6 ch.g. Deep Run–Hansel's Princess (Prince Hansel) [1989/90 16g c16m c20v6 c24gpu] leggy, rather sparely-made ex-Irish gelding: eighth foal: half-brother to winning Irish hurdler Foxborough (by Laurence O): dam unraced: runner-up in NH Flat races: well beaten over hurdles and fences, but has shown signs of a little ability: headstrong. *J. A. B. Old.* c— —

REHEARSING (USA) 7 gr.g. Nijinsky (CAN)–Zerelda (USA) (In Reality) [1989/90 16s a16g* a16g2 a16g2 a16g* a16gpu] leggy, rather sparely-made gelding: held up when winning conditional jockeys handicap hurdle at Southwell in January and novice handicap on same course (showed improved form) in March: pulled up lame final outing: will stay further: ran creditably when visored final start 1988/9 (seller): trained until after third outing by T. Thomson Jones. *Miss K. M. George.* 89

REINDEER WALK 8 gr.g. Godswalk (USA)–Carcajou (High Top) [1989/90 16s 16s 16g a16g] robust gelding: seems of little account: pulls hard. *W. M. Perrin.* —

REIN DE TOUT 7 b.g. Al Sirat (USA)–Not At All (Royal Highway) [1989/90 18m2 c26fur c25f* c26f* c25h* c26f2 26vpu 21s6 c24f2] small, lengthy, angular ex-Irish gelding: first foal: dam winning hurdler/chaser in Ireland: maiden hurdler: second at Limerick in July, when trained by Mrs J. Harrington: jumped moderately when winning early-season novice chases at Plumpton, Fontwell and Devon & Exeter: second of 3 in novice handicap at Hexham in May on final start: stays 3¼m: acts on firm ground and is possibly unsuited by heavy. *M. C. Pipe.* c**88** x 88

REIVER'S LAD 9 b.g. Dynastic–Reiver's Lass (David Jack) [1989/90 c24m^{pu} c27s^{pu} c20g* c24g* c28d^{pu} c16d^{2} c20f^{pu} c24m^{2} c24g^{5}] angular gelding: fair point-to-pointer: won handicap chases at Carlisle in January and February (benefited from mishaps to his 3 rivals 2 out): creditable second twice on same course: jumped none too fluently and ran a moody race in amateur riders handicap fifth outing: stays 3m: acts on good to firm and dead ground: suited by strong handling. *F. T. Walton.* **c95**

REJOINUS 5 ch.g. Blue Refrain–Teesdale (Aggressor) [1989/90 20g^{6} 20g^{3}] big, workmanlike gelding: will make a chaser: won NH Flat race in 1988/9: 9 lengths third behind Young Ty in slowly-run novice hurdle at Wetherby in January, one pace from 2 out: gives impression may do better at 2m. *A. P. Stringer.* 87

RELATED SOUND 4 b.c. Uncle Pokey–Darling June (Midsummer Night II) [1989/90 16g^{pu} 16g 16m 16m 16d 16m^{6} 16g 21m^{5}] angular, plain colt: probably of little account: blinkered third and fourth starts. *M. F. Barraclough.* —

RELATIVELY EASY 7 b.m. Relkino–Linguistic (Porto Bello) [1989/90 c24d] rangy mare: successful in 2 novice chases in 1988/9: ran as though very much in need of race only outing of 1989/90 (December): stays well: acts on any going: usually a sound jumper. *D. Nicholson.* c— —

RELIVE 4 ch.f. Last Fandango–Garraun (North Stoke) [1989/90 17m^{pu} 16h^{ur} 16g^{5} 18f^{pu}] small filly: second foal: dam ran only once: fifth in juvenile seller at Stratford, only completed start over hurdles: looks ungenuine. *J. P. D. Elliott.* 58 §

REMEDY THE MALADY 9 br.g. Crash Course–Promiscuous (Tower Walk) [1989/90 c32v* c30s^{F} c29d c33d^{pu}] big, strong, workmanlike gelding: made a few mistakes including one at the last (rider lost irons) when winning handicap chase at Haydock in December by 12 lengths from Tarconey: in second place when falling 6 out in Coral Welsh National at Chepstow later in month: ran poorly in valuable handicaps afterwards: stays very well: acts on heavy going and good to firm: front runner who races with plenty of zest. *M. H. B. Robinson.* c**126** —

REMEMBER DEWY 9 gr.m. New Member–Dewy's Quince (Quorum) [1989/90 20v] tall, leggy mare: won 3 point-to-points in 1989: better for race, tailed off in novice hurdle at Chepstow in January: sold 3,000 gns Ascot July Sales. *Grenville Richards.* —

REMEMBER JOSH 6 gr.g. Rusticaro (FR)–Viable (Nagami) [1989/90 F16g F16f F12g 16g^{6} 24d^{6} 25g^{4} 24s^{pu} c22f^{ur} c24m^{pu} c24m^{ur} c21g^{pu}] leggy, angular gelding: seventh live foal: dam placed in NH Flat race: amateur ridden, fourth in novice hurdle at Catterick in January: showed nothing on soft ground next start: poor jumper and has yet to complete course in novice chases: suited by test of stamina. *R. Tate.* c— x 82 ?

Ronnie Johnston Memorial Trophy (Handicap Chase), Haydock— Remedy The Malady's rider loses his irons at the last

REMEMBER NODDY 5 ch.g. Tom Noddy–Member's Lady (New Member) [1989/90 F16f] non-thoroughbred gelding: first foal: dam of little account over hurdles and in point-to-points: tailed-off last of 9 in NH Flat race at Wincanton in March: yet to race over hurdles or fences. *J. D. Roberts.*

REMEMBER THE ALAMO 4 b.g. Scorpio (FR)–Chelsea Charmer (Ballymore) [1989/90 16s4 16d 20g] workmanlike ex-Irish gelding: third foal: dam Irish 1m winner: placed over 1½m when trained by M. Corbett: one-paced fourth behind 25-length winner Cyphrate in juvenile hurdle at Haydock in January: well beaten subsequently, but not knocked about final outing. *J. J. O'Neill.* 75 +

REMITTANCE MAN 6 b.g. Prince Regent (FR)–Mittens (Run The Gantlet (USA)) [1989/90 20f2 20f* 20s2 20g2 20g* 25g2 20f2] compact gelding: successful in novice hurdles at Cheltenham (short-headed Regal Ambition) and Doncaster: runner-up all other starts, on last 2 beaten 12 lengths by Miinnehoma in Philip Cornes Saddle Of Gold Hurdle (Final) at Newbury in March and 1½ lengths by Vazon Bay in Mumm Prize Novices' Hurdle at Liverpool in April: stays 25f: suited by a sound surface and acts on firm ground. *N. J. Henderson.* 129

REMULA 7 gr.m. Remezzo–Consula (Privy Councillor) [1989/90 16g 22s c20dpu] sturdy mare: tenth foal: half-sister to a minor winner in France and fairly useful 1978 2-y-o maiden Sahibson (by Sahib): dam fair miler: always behind in novice hurdles at Towcester and Folkestone (jumped poorly): tailed off when pulled up on chasing debut. *D. R. Gandolfo.* c— —

RENAGOWN 7 b.g. Pragmatic–Midnight Oil (Menelek) [1989/90 F17g5 c22d* c16g* c22s4 c18m* c22g2 c25gF] third foal: half-brother to smart Irish hurdler Shannon Spray and novice hurdler Honeybeer Mead (both by Le Bavard): dam sister to Lough Inagh, a very useful hurdler and high-class chaser: took well to chasing and won novice events at Limerick and Tipperary (quite valuable event) and handicap at Leopardstown (beat Belsir 10 lengths): 5 lengths second to All Jeff in quite valuable novice event at Fairyhouse in April: stays 2¾m: acts on good to firm and dead ground: usually makes running. *Enda Bolger, Ireland.* c**133** —

RENO'S JEM 4 b.f. Starch Reduced–Miss Purchase (Sterling Bay (SWE)) [1989/90 16vpu 16mpu] sparely-made filly: first reported foal: dam won over hurdles: of little account: sold 1,550 gns Ascot June Sales: resold 1,050 gns Ascot July Sales. *A. J. Rumsey.* —

RENO'S QUEST 7 gr.g. Roscoe Blake–Auto Sam (Even Say) [1989/90 20spu 24spu] good-bodied gelding: tailed off in NH Flat race and novice hurdles. *A. J. Rumsey.* —

RENSHAW WOOD 10 b.m. Ascertain (USA)–Annamanda (Tycoon II) [1989/90 20m2 c24f3 21m2 a20g2 a24g3 a24g4 24f* 22f6] close-coupled, workmanlike mare: poor chaser: won amateur riders novice hurdle at Hexham in March: stays 3m: acts on firm going: amateur ridden: moody. *P. Beaumont.* c**82** 88

RENTAGHOST 12 ro.g. Grey Ghost–Rosamond (Spiritus) [1989/90 c16f* c16f3 c16dpu c17m2 c16gur] very big gelding: fair chaser: lightly raced and c**116** —

Flamborough Head Novices' Hurdle, Doncaster—
Remittance Man draws clear of Empire Blue and Otterburn House

evidently difficult to train: having first race for 3 years, didn't have to be anywhere near his best to beat sole opponent Malistrano very easily in handicap at Southwell in October: ran creditably when placed both other completed outings: free-running front runner, best at around 2m: needs a sound surface: normally a fine jumper. *T. D. Barron.*

RENTATENT 10 br.g. Boreen (FR)–St Mary's Square (Acropolis) [1989/90 c26g^ur] won a point-to-point in Ireland in 1986 (poor form in similar events in Britain): showed ability in a hunter chase in 1989. *Mrs F. A. Lockwood.* c—

REPALDO 4 b.g. Lighter–Snodland (Amber Light) [1989/90 16d^pu 16d^pu 16m 17m^4] leggy gelding: third foal: dam unplaced over hurdles: poor juvenile selling hurdler: blinkered last start. *R. J. Hodges.* 64

REPEAT THE DOSE 5 b.g. Abednego–Bahia de Palma (No Argument) [1989/90 16m^4 16d^3 20g^2 16g^2 20m*] lengthy ex-Irish gelding: has scope: first foal: dam won 2 steeplechases and several point-to-points in Ireland: won 5-runner novice handicap hurdle at Huntingdon in April: better suited by 2½m than 2m, and may well stay further: acts on good to firm ground. *T. J. Etherington.* 102

REPINGTON 12 br.g. Grey Mirage–Heron's Dolly (Combat) [1989/90 c20f^3 c20f^su c20g* c20g* c20f^2 c20v^2 c20m^pu c20f^2 c20m^4 c20f^3 c22m^pu] strong gelding: moody in 1988/9: has since changed stables and raced with zest when winning handicap chases at Bangor (made all) and Huntingdon in November: ran well next 3 completed starts, moderately last 3: stays 3m: acts on any going: sometimes blinkered: often sweats: has broken blood vessels. *T. T. Bill.* c**116** —

RE-RELEASE 5 ch.m. Baptism–Release Record (Jukebox) [1989/90 16s* 16s^3 16m^5 16m] workmanlike mare: half-sister to 2 poor novice hurdlers: dam once-raced half-sister to a winning jumper and to the dam of Badsworth Boy: fair handicapper at up to 1½m on Flat: won novice hurdle at Nottingham in February (made most), and ran very well when 12½ lengths fifth behind Forest Sun in Waterford Crystal Supreme Novices' Hurdle at Cheltenham in March: bumped after the third and never travelling particularly well subsequently in good novice company at Liverpool following month: will stay beyond 2m: best form on good to 118 §

Charnwood Novices' Hurdle, Nottingham—Re-Release makes a winning debut over hurdles

firm going: wore a visor first 2 starts, blinkered last 2: has plenty of ability, but is moody and best treated with caution. *M. C. Pipe.*

RESIDENCY 6 b.g. Dominion–Restive (Relic) [1989/90 16g^{pu} 16g] workmanlike gelding: half-brother to fairly useful chaser Restless Shot (by Salvo): placed —
at up to 7f on Flat: tailed off in novice hurdle at Wolverhampton in January: pulls hard. *J. Webber.*

RESPRAY 4 gr.f. Rusticaro (FR)–Nye (FR) (Sanctus II) [1989/90 16f] in frame
at up to 9f on Flat (has run tubed): 33/1, tailed-off last of 11 in juvenile hurdle at —
Huntingdon in August. *M. Johnston.*

RESTANDBETHANKFUL 8 b.m. Random Shot–Quetta's Dual (Dual)
[1989/90 a16g a20g^{3}] close-coupled mare: handicap hurdler: reportedly finished 87
lame when creditable third at Southwell in November: stays 2½m: acts on any going: claimer ridden. *Mrs S. Lamyman.*

RESTLESS RHAPSODY 7 ch.g. Young Generation–Bohemian Rhapsody
(On Your Mark) [1989/90 16g^{6} 16m] sturdy gelding: winning sprint handicapper —
on Flat (effective with or without blinkers): sold out of W. Haggas' stable 2,400 gns Ascot September Sales: bandaged, little promise in 2 selling hurdles in November: sold 975 gns Ascot April Sales. *K. White.*

RETAIL RUNNER 5 b.g. Trimmingham–Deep Rose (Deep Run) [1989/90
16g^{4} 16s^{4} 16g] tall, close-coupled gelding: seventh foal: half-brother to winning 96
Irish point-to-pointer Mendon Rose (by Arapaho): dam unraced: modest form when fourth in novice hurdles at Kempton and Folkestone: on toes, pulled hard and weakened 2 out final start (February). *J. T. Gifford.*

RETSOF MISSILE 4 b.g. Cruise Missile–Arctic Surprise (Rugged Man)
[1989/90 16f^{pu}] fourth foal: half-brother to winning hurdler Driven Snow (by Deep —
Run): dam well beaten in Irish maiden hurdle: behind until pulled up 3 out in juvenile hurdle at Bangor in September. *Mrs H. Parrott.*

RETTINO 5 ch.g. Revlow–Nuttino (Rugantino) [1989/90 aF16g] third foal: dam lightly-raced novice hurdler/chaser: behind in NH Flat race at Lingfield in January: dead. *C. C. Trietline.*

RETURN TO ROMANCE 4 b.f. Trojan Fen–Honest Penny (USA) (Honest
Pleasure (USA)) [1989/90 16f^{2} 16f* 16g^{4} 16f^{2} 16g^{3} 22g^{3} 21s] leggy filly: winning 98
plater at up to 12.5f on Flat (sold out of C. Horgan's stable 6,000 gns in October): won juvenile hurdle at Ascot in October despite swerving approaching last: good third in novice event at Wincanton in January on sixth start: stays 2¾m: acts on firm ground (ran poorly on soft): ridden by claimer: has swished tail under pressure. *F. Jordan.*

REVARO 4 b.g. Corvaro (USA)–Quick Dream (Crepello) [1989/90 16g^{4} 16g^{5}]
workmanlike gelding: half-brother to winning Irish hurdler Dreamy Gent (by 85
Ahonoora): modest soft-ground handicapper on Flat, winner twice over 1¼m early in 1989: just over 9 lengths fourth to Dale Park in juvenile hurdle at Ayr in November: moderate fifth at Hexham later in month. *Mrs J. R. Ramsden.*

REVILLER'S GLORY 6 b.g. Hittite Glory–Zulaika Hopwood (Royalty)
[1989/90 20g 22d 20g^{5} 20g] tall, rather unfurnished gelding: poor novice hurdler: 74
may do better at distances short of 2½m: has worn crossed noseband: sweating and edgy third start. *P. Beaumont.*

REWBELL 4 ch.f. Andy Rew–Miss Bell (Young Christopher) [1989/90 F16m] first foal: dam, half-sister to a winning staying chaser, showed signs of a little ability both outings over hurdles: saddle slipped and finished tailed off in NH Flat race at Ludlow in January: yet to race over hurdles. *P. J. Anderson.*

RHODBRIDGE 8 b.g. Rhodomantade–Fossebridge (Straight Lad) [1989/90 c— x
c16d^{6} c17g^{6} c20f^{ur} c20m^{4} c20g^{6} c22g c20d^{pu}] rangy, workmanlike gelding: no —
worthwhile form over hurdles or fences (sometimes jumps moderately): should be suited by further than 2m. *G. B. Balding.*

RHODE ISLAND RED 7 ch.g. Henbit (USA)–Embarrassed (Busted) c83 §
[1989/90 20f^{6} c26f^{ur} c20f^{F} c25f^{pu} 25g 21m^{6} c26m^{6} c26g^{2} c24m^{pu} c24s^{pu} a20g^{4} 83 §
a24g^{4} c26f^{6}] sturdy, close-coupled gelding: poor winning hurdler/novice chaser: stays 3¼m: possibly unsuited by heavy ground, acts on any other: visored and ridden in spurs once in 1986/7: unreliable. *A. Moore.*

RHUM BAY 5 ch.h. Buzzards Bay–Czar's Diamond (Queen's Hussar) [1989/90
16s^{pu}] lengthy, dipped-backed horse: well beaten on Flat: little promise in 2 —
outings over hurdles: changed hands 800 gns Ascot February Sales. *H. J. Collingridge.*

RHYMING KATE 5 b.m. Rymer–Gokatiego (Huntercombe) [1989/90 F16m^{su}
16s^{pu}] second foal: dam unraced: in lead when slipping up 6f out in NH Flat race at —
Hexham in November: tailed off when pulled up 3 out in novice hurdle at Ayr in
January. *J. S. Wilson.*

RHYTHM DANCER 7 b.m. Rarity–Party Dancer (Be My Guest (USA))
[1989/90 F12m^{6} 17g^{pu} a20g a18g 16d^{pu} 16m 16h^{4}] no sign of ability over hurdles,
including in selling company: blinkered fifth start: sold out of J. O'Shea's stable —
650 gns Ascot April Sales after sixth start. *William Price.*

RIBOKEYES BOY 8 b.g. Riboboy (USA)–Molvitesse (Molvedo) [1989/90
16d* 16m^{4} 16v 16m^{3} 16m^{pu}] sparely-made gelding: won novice handicap hurdle at 86
Kempton in November: creditable third at Plumpton in April: ran poorly final
outing: stays 2¼m: acts on good to firm and heavy going: claimer ridden bar
fourth start. *A. R. Davison.*

RIBO MELODY 7 b.m. Riboboy (USA)–Sovereign Melody (Fortino II) c93
[1989/90 16f^{4} 16m* c16f^{2}] smallish, sparely-made, angular mare: made running 100
when successful in handicap hurdle at Perth in August (ridden by 7-lb claimer):
odds on, led until run-in when going down by 1½ lengths to Smart In Black in
novice chase at Southwell in September (jumped boldly but to the right, and made
the occasional mistake): best at around 2m: acts on firm going. *B. McLean.*

RIBOT STAR 11 b.g. Star Appeal–Ribo Pride (Ribero) [1989/90 20f 20h 17m c—
17m^{5} 16m^{6}] lightly-made gelding: winning hurdler: well beaten in 1989/90, in —
sellers last 3 starts: maiden point-to-pointer: no form in hunter chases: stays
2½m: acts on any going: blinkered fourth outing. *J. E. Long.*

RICARDO BOOTS 4 ro.g. Remainder Man–Mountainette (Peter Wrekin)
[1989/90 16s^{pu} 16d^{2} 16f] workmanlike gelding: carries condition: third foal: dam
half-sister to a winning hurdler: well beaten in 2 races at 2 yrs: staying-on 30 71
lengths (looked less) second to White River in conditional jockeys selling hurdle
at Ludlow in March. *B. Preece.*

RICHARDS BAY 9 b.g. Record Run–Gowyn (Goldhill) [1989/90 c20g^{5} c16d^{3} c89
c20d^{pu} c17d^{pu} c16v^{2} c20g] angular, workmanlike gelding: poor chaser: stays —
2½m: needs give in the ground and acts on heavy going: usually races up with
pace. *I. Semple.*

RICHARD'S HILL 7 br.g. Fidel–Baroness Vimy (Barrons Court) [1989/90
24m^{6} 21f* 21m* 24m* 22m*] leggy gelding: brother to winning hurdler Richards 119 p
Kate: dam very lightly-raced maiden Irish hurdler, daughter of winning hurdler:
placed in a NH Flat race in Ireland in 1987 and a point-to-point in Britain in
February: progressive hurdler who won novice event and handicap at Newton
Abbot, novice handicap at Uttoxeter (made all) and minor event at Stratford (by 5
lengths from Alaoui) late in season: stays 3m: acts on firm going. *T. B. Hallett.*

RICHARD'S LAD 5 b.g. Magnolia Lad–Parton Queen (Charlottown) [1989/90
F16m^{6}] third foal: brother to a bad maiden: dam seemed of no account: staying-on
sixth of 17 finishers behind Thatcher Rock in NH Flat race at Huntingdon in
October: sold 2,100 gns Ascot April Sales: yet to race over hurdles or fences. *G. P.
Enright.*

RICHARDS PET 4 ch.g. Noalto–Whipalash (Stephen George) [1989/90 16g
16d 16m^{4} 16g^{5} 16d^{3}] close-coupled gelding: placed at up to 9f on Flat, when 81
trained by G. Cottrell: around 10 lengths third behind Miss Chalk in juvenile
claiming hurdle at Stratford in February, eased once beaten. *Miss G. Dollar.*

RICH HILL 11 b.g. Giolla Mear–Fugitive (Sadler's Wells) [1989/90 c18f^{ur} c—
c20f^{pu}] lengthy ex-Irish gelding: handicap chaser: winner 6 times in 1986: has run
only 4 times since: stays 21f: acts on any going: sold privately out of E. Mitchell's
stable 4,700 gns Doncaster August Sales. *Capt. J. A. George.*

RICH NEPHEW 5 b. or br.g. Great Nephew–Strike It Rich (FR) (Rheingold)
[1989/90 16g* 16f^{5} 16m^{2} 16g* 16g* 16f] lengthy, good-bodied gelding: won novice 108
hurdle at Uttoxeter in October (carried head high) and handicaps at Edinburgh in
December and Leicester in January: edgy, hampered 2 out when well beaten in
valuable event at Cheltenham final start: unlikely to stay much beyond 2m: acts
on good to firm ground. *C. Weedon.*

RICH REMORSE 11 b.g. Tycoon II–Kero Code (Straight Lad) [1989/90 c25s* **c116** x
c24d^{4} c24d^{2}] strong, compact gelding: fair chaser: won handicap at Towcester in
February gamely by 1½ lengths from Bronze Effigy: 2 lengths second to Mister
Hartigan at Ayr in April: suited by a test of stamina and plenty of give in the
ground: makes mistakes. *R. Curtis.*

RICKESTON LAD 7 b.g. Piaffer (USA)–Jolly Smooth (Jolly Jet) [1989/90 16g
16g a16g^{2} a16g^{2}] sparely-made, plain gelding: handicap hurdler: runner-up at 91
Lingfield and Southwell (beaten a neck by only other finisher Dawn Prince) in
second half of season: likely to prove best at around 2m: acts on soft going. *B.
Palling.*

RIDDLEMEROO 5 b.g. Chukaroo–True Melody (Pardigras) [1989/90 F16m^{5}
aF16g^{4}] small, leggy gelding: second foal: dam, third in a NH Flat race, behind
both completed outings over hurdles: unplaced in NH Flat races at Worcester in
October and Southwell following month: yet to race over hurdles or fences. *J.
Colston.*

RIDE THE WIND 6 ch.g. Windjammer (USA)–Madam Clare (Ennis) [1989/90
16g^{pu}] leggy gelding: behind in NH Flat race, and when pulled up in novice hurdle —
in March: sold 2,200 gns Ascot May Sales. *Mrs D. Haine.*

RIDGEFIELD 12 br.g. Firestreak–Chebs Lass (Chebs Lad) [1989/90 c21m^{pu}] c—
close-coupled gelding: very lightly raced of late: placed in novice hurdles: yet to —
complete course over fences. *J. Foulds.*

RIESENER 4 ch.g. Touching Wood (USA)–Sharp Run (Sharpen Up) [1989/90
16m^{3} 16m^{4} 16f 16g 16m^{6} 17f^{3} 16d^{5} 16g a16g^{5} 16d^{pu}] smallish, close-coupled 70 ?
gelding: little form on Flat: juvenile selling hurdler: easily best effort on sixth
start: visored fifth to eighth and last outings: seems suited by firm ground: races
freely: trained first start by R. Hollinshead. *Mrs P. A. Barker.*

RIFLE RANGE 7 b.g. Torus–Miss Bavard (Le Bavard (FR)) [1989/90 c24s^{2} c**117**
c24g^{F} c24s* c27d* c20s* c24f^{pu}] rangy, sparely-made gelding: quite a useful —
hurdler: won novice chases at Haydock and Sedgefield in January and Haydock
again in March: in lead and still travelling strongly, bad mistake 5 out and pulled
up after another bad error at the next in Sun Alliance Novices' Chase at
Cheltenham later in March: stays well: acts on soft going: headstrong and has
worn a crossed noseband: taken early to post third outing: jumps none too fluently
and to his left. *T. P. Tate.*

RIGHT CARD 12 br.g. Gift Card (FR)–Toranquine (FR) (Right Royal V) c**118**
[1989/90 c25m^{3} c25f^{pu} c24g^{pu} c24d^{ur} c24d^{pu} c25f^{ur}] lengthy, sparely-made
gelding: lightly-raced winning chaser: only form of season on first start, but was in
lead when unseating rider at the fourteenth final one: suited by a test of stamina:
acts on firm and dead ground: blinkered last 3 starts. *P. G. Bailey.*

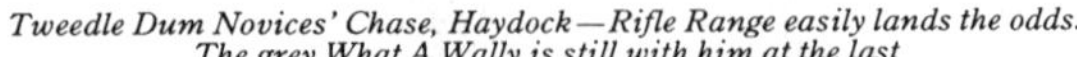

*Tweedle Dum Novices' Chase, Haydock—Rifle Range easily lands the odds.
The grey What A Wally is still with him at the last*

RIGHT FORMULA 8 b.m. Monseigneur (USA)–Stradey Park (Murrayfield) [1989/90 a20g a16g^{pu}] sturdy, close-coupled mare: lightly raced and no sign of ability. *B. Preece.* —

RIGHT ON CUE 4 b.g. Taufan (USA)–Cigarette (Miralgo) [1989/90 20g^{pu} 16d^{pu} 16g 20f] small gelding: half-brother to winning hurdler Eastern Player (by Royal Match): of little account: visored last 2 starts. *M. C. Chapman.* —

RIGHT PATH 5 b.g. Ya Zaman (USA)–Our Ena (Tower Walk) [1989/90 16f 16f^{4} 16m^{pu}] small, sparely-made gelding: poor plater over hurdles. *N. Tinkler.* 61

RIGHT STEP (FR) 5 ch.g. Noalcoholic (FR)–Right Dancer (Dance In Time (CAN)) [1989/90 16m^{3} 20f^{2} 20f* 18f^{ur} 22g* 22m] leggy gelding: successful in novice hurdles at Southwell and Fontwell: well beaten last start (November): stays 2¾m: acts on any going: has won for a claimer: ran poorly when blinkered fourth start 1988/9: trained by G. Moore first 3 starts. *R. J. O'Sullivan.* 95

RIG STEEL 10 ch.g. Welsh Pageant–Fir Tree (Santa Claus) [1989/90 c25m* c27g^{4} c25d^{4} c24v^{2} c25g^{2} c20d c24m^{5} c26m^{3}] lengthy, workmanlike gelding: won 3-runner handicap chase at Warwick in November: ran creditably most subsequent starts, including when fifth to Master Bob in Kim Muir Memorial Challenge Cup Handicap Chase at Cheltenham in March: suited by a test of stamina: acts on any going. *J. M. Bukovets.* c**113** —

RIKISGIRL 5 gr.m. Baron Blakeney–Rikis (Town Crier) [1989/90 F16f] fifth foal: half-sister to novice hurdler Red Desiree (by Piaffer): dam ran 3 times: tailed off in 23-runner NH Flat race at Newbury in October: yet to race over hurdles or fences. *M. C. Pipe.*

RIM OF PEARL 7 b.m. Rymer–Pearl Smoke (My Smokey) [1989/90 20g^{pu} a16g^{6}] leggy mare: poor novice hurdler: showed a little ability final start (April). *B. R. Cambidge.* 66

RI-NA-RITHANN 5 b.g. Deep Run–Casacello (Punchinello) [1989/90 16g^{3} 16s* 16m* 16s* 16d^{2} 20f^{4} 16f^{2}] rangy, good sort: every inch a chaser: progressive hurdler who won novice events at Plumpton, Towcester and Warwick: went right in latter stages when in frame behind stable-companion Vazon Bay in Mumm Prize Novices' Hurdle at Liverpool (4 lengths fourth) and EBF Novices' Hurdle Final (Handicap) at Cheltenham (2 lengths second): stays 2½m: acts on any going: should pay to follow. *Mrs J. Pitman.* 127 p

RING ME BACK 5 b.m. Ring Bidder–Snippet (Ragstone) [1989/90 16f] leggy, sparely-made mare: novice selling hurdler: tailed off only outing of season (August): sold 1,075 gns Ascot November Sales. *G. R. Bebbington.* —

RINGMORE 8 ch.g. Porto Bello–Dirrie Star (Dunoon Star) [1989/90 16m^{2} c17m^{2} c16d^{3} c16g^{2} c16g* c16m^{2} c16g^{2} c16g* 16g c16d^{3} c16m^{2} c16m^{2} c20g^{4} c16g^{3}] strong, good-bodied gelding: handicap hurdler: won handicap chases at Edinburgh in December and Catterick following month: ran creditably most subsequent starts: form only at around 2m: acts on any going: excellent mount for a claimer: sound jumper. *J. Parkes.* c**101** 96

RING RUSSELL 7 ch.g. Belfalas–Ring Twice (Prince Hansel) [1989/90 20s 16s 21d] compact gelding: behind in 2 NH Flat races in 1988: well beaten in novice hurdles: sold 1,500 gns Ascot May Sales. *Andrew Turnell.* —

RINGYBOY 5 b.g. Runnett–Graunuaile (Proud Chieftain) [1989/90 16g^{3} 16g 18s 16s^{4} 16d^{3}] rather leggy gelding: handicap hurdler: ran respectably when in frame, though didn't find much in closing stages final start: not sure to stay much beyond 2m: acts on heavy going. *R. Akehurst.* 101

RINUS 9 br.g. Netherkelly–Pirella (Pirate King) [1989/90 c20g^{5} c24s^{3} c24v* c36f^{3}] c**139** —

A bout of coughing restricted Rinus to just four races in the latest season—a light schedule for one who had clocked up almost seventy miles and ten victories in twenty-two starts during his two previous seasons over fences. Though brief, his campaign included a notable, if fortunate, victory in the Greenall Whitley Gold Cup at Haydock in March. Although Rinus quickened well entering the straight there, the leader Willsford appeared to have his measure until knuckling on landing at the last. Rinus kept on well to beat The Thinker, who was conceding 21 lb, by four (officially three) lengths; The Thinker had beaten him by four lengths on terms 17 lb better in the Tommy Whittle Chase at the same course in December when the pair had finished second and third behind Baies. It was the Grand National for

Greenall Whitley Handicap Chase, Haydock—the leader Willsford is about to fall at the last, leaving Rinus to go on and win

Rinus after the Greenall Whitley. Despite being 3 lb out of the handicap, and with his rider Doughty putting up 4 lb overweight, Rinus started a well-fancied 13/1 fourth favourite at Liverpool. Some were probably influenced by his trainer's and jockey's excellent record in the race. Doughty had completed the course on each of his six previous attempts at the National, giving Richards his second winner after Lucius in 1978 when partnering Hallo Dandy in 1984. Apart from sharing a trainer and jockey, however, Rinus and Hallo Dandy don't have much in common as Grand National horses. Hallo Dandy's jumping at Aintree was zestful, occasionally breath-taking. Rinus, never a particularly fluent jumper, was sketchy at times in the race. He was kept just behind the leading group on the first circuit, moved into the first four at second Becher's, but had no chance with the eventual first and second from two out. Rinus plugged on gamely for third, twenty lengths behind Mr Frisk and Durham Edition, twelve lengths clear of Brown Windsor in fourth. It was a tremendous effort, particularly in view of his interrupted season. Rinus is reportedly to be trained with the Grand National in mind in 1990/1; granted a trouble-free preparation, and with the experience of Aintree's fences to stand him in good stead, Rinus looks sure to give another good account of himself in the race. That he stays very well and acts on any going is clearly in his favour. It's also worth noting, in view of the tactics employed successfully on Mr Frisk in the National, that Rinus goes very well with forcing tactics.

Rinus (br.g. 1981)	Netherkelly (br 1970)	Le Levanstell (b 1957)	Le Lavandou
			Stella's Sister
		Princess Quay (br 1962)	Babur
			Hunter's Quay
	Pirella (b 1967)	Pirate King (b 1953)	Prince Chevalier
			Netherton Maid
		Tudora (b 1957)	King of The Tudors
			Lovely Day

Rinus' dam Pirella has produced several winners, including in the latest season Los Buccaneros and the selling hurdler Nae Bother, both by Neltino. Further back, both Rinus' grandam Tudora and great-grandam Lovely Day were minor winners on the Flat, the latter being a full sister to Grand Weather, winner of the Irish Two Thousand Guineas. *G. Richards.*

Mr A. M. Proos's "Rinus"

RIOT ISLAND 8 b.g. Riot Helmet–Clyda Valley (Titango) [1989/90 c24d2] lengthy gelding: has run tubed: winning point-to-pointer: second in hunter chases: bit backward, not knocked about once winner had taken his measure when going down by 8 lengths to Call Collect at Kelso in February: stays well: acts on any going. *A. C. Whillans.* c91

RIPSTER 6 b.g. Ahonoora–Goirtin (Levmoss) [1989/90 17f3] neat gelding: selling hurdler: modest third at Newton Abbot in July: races only at around 2m: acts on firm ground: usually blinkered. *Miss S. J. Wilton.* 74

RISATINA 4 ch.f. Sallust–Saga's Humour (Bustino) [1989/90 17h6 17gpu 16g] small filly: maiden on Flat: no sign of ability over hurdles, including in sellers: blinkered first start, visored last. *Mrs A. Knight.* —

RISK ANOTHER 7 ch.g. Hot Spark–Speadon (Eudaemon) [1989/90 24f6 24m5 c27fpu c24g2 c25f3 c24f3 c24gpu] lengthy, workmanlike gelding: poor novice hurdler/chaser: placed in hunter chases in 1989/90: stays well. *Mrs W. R. Tullie.* c78 —

RISKA'S RIVER 8 b.g. Over The River (FR)–Meelgarrow (Raise You Ten) [1989/90 c17s2 c24g c24d c18g2 c20s* c24s4 c24m* c28m5] Irish gelding: fairly useful hurdler/chaser: successful in 4-runner chases at Punchestown in January and Leopardstown in March, latter a handicap: about 14 lengths fifth behind Desert Orchid in Jameson Irish Grand National at Fairyhouse: stays well: acts on heavy and good to firm ground: prone to breaking blood vessels. *F. Flood, Ireland.* c137 —

RISK FACTOR 4 b.g. Auction Ring (USA)–Flying Anna (Roan Rocket) [1989/90 16g 16s6 17g4] close-coupled, good-topped gelding: modest maiden on Flat: poor juvenile hurdler. *D. Moffatt.* 72

RISLAN (USA) 4 b.c. Diesis–Sanctum Sanctorum (USA) (Secretariat (USA)) [1989/90 18h* 16f* 16f] neat colt: placed over 1m on Flat: sold out of P. Cole's 94 stable 9,000 gns Newmarket July Sales: won juvenile hurdles at Fontwell and Huntingdon in August: every chance until mistake last and virtually pulled up at Ascot 2 months later: stays 2¼m: acts on hard ground. *G. P. Enright.*

RIVA ROSE 9 b.g. Caribo–Rose of The West (Royal Buck) [1989/90 c20m* c24m* c20m^{ro} c22g^{2} c20m^{3}] tall, close-coupled, good sort: usually impresses in appearance: one-time very useful hurdler: won novice chases at Warwick in November and Huntingdon in December: every chance when running out last in race won by Rynode at Wolverhampton later in December: appeared ungenuine final start: stays 3m: acts on good to firm and heavy ground: broke blood vessel second start 1987/8: usually jumps soundly: blinkered fourth outing: sold 4,700 gns Ascot June Sales: resold 3,400 gns Ascot July Sales: one to treat with caution. *Mrs J. Pitman.* **c116** § —

RIVER BED (FR) 6 ch.g. Sharpman–River Craft (Reliance) [1989/90 c21g^{F}] angular, sparely-made gelding: winning hurdler/chaser: in touch when falling 6 out in handicap at Fakenham in April: stays 2½m: acts on firm and dead going. *J. A. C. Edwards.* c— —

RIVER CEIRIOG 9 ch.g. Broxted–Quarry Wood (Super Sam) [1989/90 c16g^{ur}] tall, plain, sparely-made gelding: one-time high-class hurdler: pushed along when unseating rider tenth in novice chase at Kempton in January: best form in strongly-run races at around 2m on a sound surface, and doesn't stay 21f: jumped moderately most outings 1986/7: suited by racing up with the pace. *N. J. Henderson.* c— —

RIVER FLY 5 ch.g. Over The River (FR)–Diana's Flyer (Charlottesvilles Flyer) [1989/90 F16g] second living foal: brother to winning hurdler Into The Trees: dam unplaced in NH Flat races and point-to-points in Ireland: well beaten in NH Flat race at Sandown in November: yet to race over hurdles or fences. *C. C. Trietline.*

RIVERHEAD (USA) 6 b.h. Riverman (USA)–Tertiary (USA) (Vaguely Noble) [1989/90 16g^{4} 16s* 16g^{2} 16s^{4} 16s* 16g* 16m^{6} 16m^{4}] strong, good-bodied horse: very useful novice hurdler: won at Folkestone in January and Sandown and Wincanton in February: bit below his best in good company on fast ground subsequently, being held up and given a lot to do when 7 lengths fourth behind Fidway in Seagram 100 Pipers Top Novices' Hurdle at Liverpool: will prove best at 2m: acts on soft going: bandaged all round last 2 starts (previously bandaged in front): tends to be on toes in preliminaries: suited by exaggerated waiting tactics. *D. R. C. Elsworth.* 131

Village Novices' Hurdle, Sandown—Riverhead is in pursuit of Bitter Buck

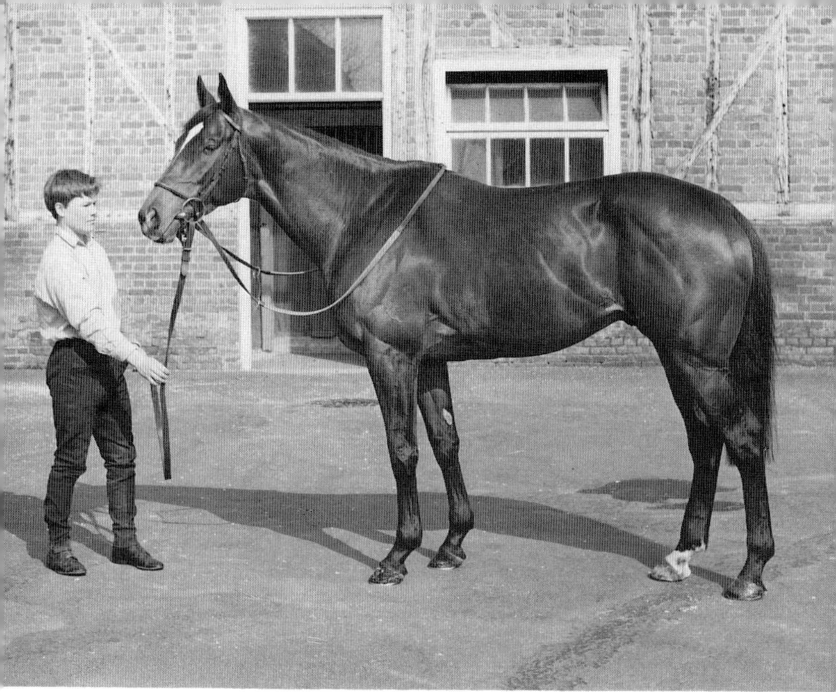

White Horse Racing Ltd's "Riverhead"

RIVER HOUSE 8 ch.g. Over The River (FR)–Kinsella's Choice (Middle Temple) [1989/90 c20g⁶ c20g* c24d³ c24gF c24dpu c27d² c24d c20d⁶ c22f³ c24m³ c20f*] angular ex-Irish gelding: half-brother to winning hurdler Dianes Destiny (by Kambalda) and 2 NH Flat race winners: dam unraced sister to quite moderate hurdler/chaser Advocate and half-sister to 3 winning jumpers: placed in 2 point-to-points in 1989: won novice chases at Hexham in November and Sedgefield (beat Lingham Duke 10 lengths) in May: in-and-out form in between: stays 27f: acts on firm and dead ground. *W. A. Stephenson.* **c105** ?

RIVER KINGDOM 7 b.g. Riverman (USA)–Victory Kingdom (CAN) (Viceregal (CAN)) [1989/90 16fF 16g 16d* 16dbd 16g³ 16gpu] angular gelding: showed ability over hurdles prior to winning novice handicap at Warwick in January: first race for 2 months, ran poorly final outing: has raced only at about 2m: acts on firm and dead going. *J. V. Redmond.* 80

RIVERNOT 8 br.g. Over The River (FR)–Tabithatouchmenot (Master Buck) [1989/90 c33v³ c24gF3 c28d² c26d³ c24dpu c24g⁴ c25f³] smallish, workmanlike gelding: winning hurdler/chaser: hung right when second in amateur riders handicap chase at Kelso in February: stays 3½m: acts on heavy ground: sometimes blinkered: tends to sweat: unreliable. *W. A. Stephenson.* c**110** § —

RIVER PEARL 5 b.m. Oats–Dark Pearl (Harwell) [1989/90 22v⁴ 20m] second foal: dam fair staying jumper: 21 lengths fourth behind Paco's Boy in novice hurdle at Ayr in February, not knocked about after weakening 2 out: always behind and not knocked about at Newcastle following month. *J. S. Wilson.* 70

RIVERS EDGE 12 b.g. Sharpen Up–Ebb And Flo (Forlorn River) [1989/90 c16m⁵ c22hwo c20dpu] rather narrow, leggy gelding: handicap chaser: walked c98 —

over at Kelso in May: destroyed after breaking a leg at Perth later in month: stayed 2½m: acted on any going. *Denys Smith.*

RIVERSIDE DRIVE 11 b.g. Country Retreat–Taxi (Phebus) [1989/90 c25m^{pu}] tall, lengthy, sparely-made gelding: no worthwhile form over hurdles since winning early in 1987/8: won a point-to-point in May: behind when pulled up in hunter chase at Towcester same month: stays well: acts on firm ground. *K. J. Phelps.* c— —

RIVERSTICK 8 ch.g. Full of Hope–Home In Pasadena (Home Guard (USA)) [1989/90 c20s^{F} c20d^{5}] compact, good-quartered gelding: poor novice hurdler in Ireland: blinkered last 2 starts 1987/8: remote fifth in novice hunter chase at Ludlow in March: won a point-to-point later in month: sold 8,200 gns Ascot June Sales. *E. G. Dilworth.* c— —

RIVERTINO 6 ch.g. Ivotino (USA)–River Damsel (Forlorn River) [1989/90 c16g^{F} 20f^{5} 25g^{3} 22g^{2} 22d^{2} 20s^{3} 22v^{2}] leggy, sparely-made gelding: placed in novice events and handicaps over hurdles: unable to quicken closing stages when 2 lengths second to Admiral's Leap in novice event at Folkestone in February on final start: fell first on chasing debut: out-and-out stayer who'll be suited by return to 3m: acts on heavy going. *P. Mitchell.* c— 108

RIVER TROUT 9 ch.g. Le Bavard (FR)–Lovely Ana (Tit For Tat II) [1989/90 c20f^{2}] leggy, sparely-made gelding: has stringhalt: winning chaser and novice hurdler: second in hunter chase at Folkestone in May: won point-to-point earlier in month: stays 2¾m: acts on soft and good to firm going: tends to sweat. *Alan Hill.* c75 —

RIVERVALE 7 ch.g. Over The River (FR)–Sweetville (Charlottesvilles Flyer) [1989/90 c20m^{5} c25m^{pu}] sparely-made, angular gelding: no sign of ability. *J. Webber.* c— —

RIVER WARRIOR 12 b.g. Forlorn River–Wounded Knee (Busted) [1989/90 c21f^{3}] small, lightly-made gelding: selling chaser: creditable third in non-selling handicap at Newton Abbot in September: stays 3¼m: acts on any going: ran out once: inconsistent. *J. M. Bradley.* c86 § —

RIX WOODCOCK 9 br.g. Lord Gayle (USA)–Silk Lady (Tribal Chief) [1989/90 16m^{5}] small, lightly-built gelding: handicap hurdler: stayed on from 2 out without being knocked about when fifth at Perth in September: best at around 2m: acts on any going: good mount for an inexperienced rider. *J. C. Gillen.* —

RIYADH LIGHTS 5 b.g. Formidable (USA)–Rivers Maid (Rarity) [1989/90 22h* 20f* 24m^{6} 21m^{pu}] neat gelding: successful in novice hurdles at Fontwell (handicap, 2 ran) and Worcester (awarded race after going down by a length to Classical Flame) in August: pulled up lame in September and not seen out again: probably stays 2¾m: acts on hard ground. *J. B. Sayers.* 80

R LAD 6 b.g. Rushmere–Brismaid (Flandre II) [1989/90 18f^{4} c21d c20g^{pu} c18s c24g c26f^{F}] big, plain gelding: poor novice hurdler/chaser: form only at up to 2¼m: acts on heavy going: visored final outing 1988/9. *M. Madgwick.* c— 78

ROADSTER 14 b.g. Streetfighter–Malin (Beau Sabreur) [1989/90 c20s^{2} c20d^{3} c24g^{5}] strong, stocky, good-bodied gelding: carries plenty of condition: useful chaser at his best: on the downgrade: best at distances short of 3m: probably acts on any going but goes well in the mud: makes the odd mistake. *C. T. Nash.* c90 ? —

ROAD UP 4 ch.c. Smackover–Road To Somewhere (Gilded Leader) [1989/90 16g^{pu}] leggy, good-topped colt: second foal: dam unraced: bad mistake fourth and tailed off when pulled up 2 out in juvenile hurdle at Wolverhampton in December. *B. A. McMahon.* —

ROARS OF APPLAUSE 8 ch.g. Funny Man–Jacqui Owen (Master Owen) [1989/90 c21m* c24g^{2}] workmanlike gelding: winning hurdler: successful in a point-to-point in March, and later in month won novice hunter chase at Fakenham (finished strongly to lead close home and beat Deer Crest ¾ length): went down by a short head to Bay Bridge in similar race at Market Rasen in May: suited by 2½m and more: acts on soft going and good to firm. *Colin Fitch.* c98 —

ROBBIE BURNS 4 br.c. Daring March–Gangawayhame (Lochnager) [1989/90 16f^{2} 16g^{6} 16g^{2} 16d] useful-looking colt: maiden on Flat: runner-up in juvenile hurdle at Newbury in November and novice event at Plumpton in January: well beaten final start: acts on firm ground. *R. V. Smyth.* 100

ROBCOURT HILL 5 br.g. Callernish–Cooney Island (Distinctly (USA)) [1989/90 F14v^{4}] third foal: dam unraced half-sister to several winners, notably fairly useful Irish chaser Garrynagree: 16½ lengths fourth behind Dakyns Boy in NH Flat race at Ayr in April: yet to race over hurdles or fences. *J. A. C. Edwards.*

ROBERT HENRY (NZ) 14 br.g. Ribotlight–Quake (NZ) (Pictavia) [1989/90 c73 x
c24g^{3} c25m^{pu}] big, strong gelding: winning point-to-pointer: poor novice chaser: stays 3m: makes mistakes: sometimes ridden in spurs nowadays. *Mrs P. A. Hargreaves.*

ROBIN GOODFELLOW 9 b. or br.g. Decent Fellow–Paperchain (Articulate) [1989/90 17d^{F}] sturdy gelding: useful novice hurdler in 1986/7: lightly raced —
subsequently: stayed 2½m: went well on soft going: dead. *G. B. Balding.*

ROBINSON'S CLASSIC 6 ch.m. Ashbro Laddo–Hasty Arrow (No Comment) [1989/90 F16d^{pu} 16h^{pu}] sixth foal: half-sister to 3 poor animals: dam —
fair hurdler and winning chaser: saddle slipped and pulled up halfway in NH Flat race at Catterick (trained by W. A. Stephenson): jumped poorly and tailed off when pulled up 2 out in novice hurdle at Hexham in April. *R. W. Dods.*

ROBIN WONDER 12 b.g. Dawn Review–Rainbow Wonder (Runnymede)
[1989/90 16g^{5} 24g] useful hurdler at his best: well beaten both starts of 1989/90: — §
best at up to 2¾m: acts on any going: usually claimer ridden nowadays: sometimes runs in snatches, and doesn't always give his running: blinkered once. *D. R. C. Elsworth.*

ROBSIM 8 br.g. Garda's Revenge (USA)–Aunty Peg (Rustam) [1989/90 c24d^{4} c79
c27g^{6} c24g^{3} c27d c20m^{3} c24f^{pu}] tall gelding: poor novice hurdler/chaser: best —
effort at 2½m: sometimes sweats: trained until after fourth start by G. Moore. *Mrs S. J. Smith.*

ROBUSTI 8 ch.g. Bustino–Juliette Marny (Blakeney) [1989/90 20g] good-bodied gelding: winning stayer on Flat (has been tried in blinkers): showed plenty —
of ability over hurdles in 1987/8, and on final start won Grande Course de Haies de Printemps at Auteuil: no form in 2 outings in Britain (tailed off when automatic top weight for handicap at Kempton in December): stays 2½m: acts on dead going. *J. A. B. Old.*

ROC DE PRINCE (FR) 7 br.g. Djarvis (FR)–Haute Volta II (FR) (Beau Fixe) c136
[1989/90 c16d^{2} c21g^{2} c20g c24g^{2} c24s* c24s* c24s* c26v^{5} c26d^{2} c24m^{2} c22m* —
c25d^{4}] tall, close-coupled, sparely-made gelding: behind in novice hurdles in Britain: won a chase at Auteuil in 1987/8: in fine form over fences in Ireland in second half of season and won handicaps at Punchestown, Fairyhouse (2) and Naas, twice making all: stays 3¼m: acts on good to firm and soft going: useful. *Ruby Walsh, Ireland.*

ROCHALLOR 4 ch.g. Dara Monarch–Ballymaloe Girl (Nonoalco (USA)) [1989/90 17f^{F} 16g* 16g^{5}] lightly-made, angular gelding: claimed out of R. 102
Hannon's stable £12,300 after winning 1¼m claimer on Flat in June: made all in juvenile hurdle at Kempton in October: good fifth, beaten around 8 lengths, behind Major Inquiry at Cheltenham following month: blinkered last 2 starts. *M. C. Pipe.*

ROCHE 4 b.g. Balliol–Pink Stripes (Pyjama Hunt) [1989/90 16f^{5} 16m^{3} 17m^{ur}
16m 17h^{2} 16f 16g^{pu} a16g^{5}] small gelding: little worthwhile form, including in 61
sellers, on Flat: poor form in selling company over hurdles: has run blinkered: trained until after first outing by N. Callaghan. *J. L. Spearing.*

ROCHE ROSIE 6 b.m. Mossberry–Quiet Sailing (Dumbarnie) [1989/90 16g^{pu} 16m^{5}] sixth reported foal: half-sister to novice selling hurdler Roche Girl (by
Mujon): dam winning hurdler: last of 5 in novice hurdle at Uttoxeter in May. *S. A. Torr.* —

ROCHES ROOST 7 b.m. Pauper–Okie (Connaught) [1989/90 17m^{2} 16f^{3} 16m^{5} c—
c20f^{4} 20m^{pu}] neat mare: selling hurdler: jumped poorly on chasing debut: best 66
form at up to 2¼m: acts on firm going: blinkered last start. *B. Ellison.*

ROCKARIA 5 b.g. Ballad Rock–Grazia (Aureole) [1989/90 17g^{2} 16m^{5} a16g]
sturdy gelding: successful at up to 1m on Flat: clear second in 4-y-o novice hurdle 95
at Devon & Exeter: subsequently sold out of G. Balding's stable 10,000 gns Newmarket Autumn Sales: ran moderately afterwards. *M. C. Pipe.*

ROCKCLIFFE 11 b.g. Owen Anthony–Colonian Queen (Colonist II) [1989/90 c96
c24m* c21m^{3} c24m* c24g* c26g^{3} c24g^{5} c24g^{2} c24g^{2}] lengthy, shallow-girthed —
gelding: of little account over hurdles: winning point-to-pointer: successful in early-season novice chases at Huntingdon, Perth and Market Rasen: second in handicaps at Edinburgh in January and February: stays 3m: acts on good to firm ground: ridden by 7-lb claimer. *R. Tate.*

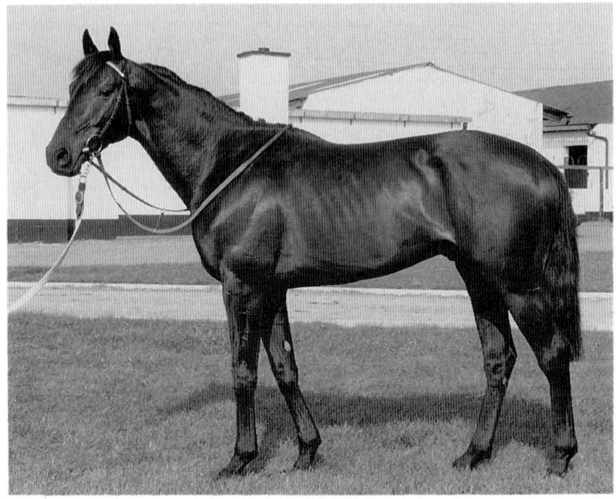

Mr P. Garvey's "Rocket Dancer"

ROCKET DANCER 4 b.c. Niniski (USA)–Dora's Rocket (Roan Rocket)
[1989/90 16v^5 16d^6 16m* 16m* 16d^F 17f^2] second foal: dam, placed over 6f at 2 132
yrs, sister to very useful sprinter Rory's Rocket and half-sister to several
winners: won juvenile hurdles at Naas and Fairyhouse in April: beaten short head
by Vestris Abu in sponsored handicap at Dundalk following month: seems suited
by a firm surface: won over 2m on Flat in 1990. *N. Meade, Ireland.*

ROCKMARTIN 8 b.g. Fair Season–Aunt Eva (Great Nephew) [1989/90 16f* c93
a16g^2 a20g^2 a20g^2 c16d^4 20d 16f^4 c25f^4 c20m^2 c24h^F] strong, deep-bodied 100
gelding: won conditional jockeys selling handicap hurdle at Hexham in October
(no bid): ran creditably most subsequent starts, on last completed outing finishing
2 lengths second to Captain Mor in handicap chase at Wetherby: stays 3m: below
his best on very soft going, acts on any other: blinkered seventh and eighth starts:
doesn't always go through with his effort: sold out of C. Thornton's stable 7,200
gns Doncaster November Sales after second start. *J. H. Johnson.*

ROCK OF AGES 6 ro.m. Blakeney–Rockery (FR) (Roan Rocket) [1989/90
22g^4 21d^5] sturdy mare: lightly-raced novice hurdler: moderate fourth at 77
Wincanton in January: well beaten in claimer following month: will prove best at
distances shorter than 21f. *M. C. Pipe.*

ROCK ON KELLY 6 b.g. Netherkelly–Escallop (Kabale) [1989/90 F16g 16g]
strong, workmanlike gelding: second foal by a thoroughbred stallion: half-brother —
to winning point-to-pointer Sea Challenger (by Seaepic): dam winning point-to-
pointer/hunter chaser: tailed-off last in NH Flat race and novice hurdle. *J. White.*

ROCK SAINT 13 ch.g. St Columbus–Moon Venture (Eastern Venture) c**107**
[1989/90 c24m^5 c24m^2 c21m^4 c25g c20v c21g*] big, lengthy, workmanlike —
gelding: has a round action: jumped well in main and ran on gamely to win
handicap chase at Wincanton in February by 7 lengths from Tidal Stream: stays
25f: acts on any going: sometimes amateur ridden: has won 6 times at Lingfield.
G. G. A. Gregson.

ROCK SALT 8 ch.g. Ballad Rock–Sea Music (Atan) [1989/90 17m^{pu}] leggy
gelding: no sign of ability. *P. Butler.* —

ROCKTOR (NZ) 5 b.g. Shy Rambler (USA)–Sobina (NZ) (Sobig) [1989/90 F16g* aF16g* F16m^{4}] close-coupled, workmanlike gelding: half-brother to winning staying chaser Kingtor (by Amyntor): won NH Flat races at Market Rasen and Southwell in first half of season: 12½ lengths fourth of 19 behind Will I Fly in similar event at Sandown in March: yet to race over hurdles or fences. *D. H. Barons.*

ROCKY PIT 8 b.g. Pitpan–Prellgo (El Gallo) [1989/90 16g 24g^{pu} c20d^{5} c25v^{3} c25s^{F} c20v^{6} c26f^{5}] leggy, quite good-topped gelding: poor novice hurdler/chaser: stays 2½m: acts on soft going. *J. V. Redmond.* c— —

ROCKY REEF 5 b.m. Diamond Shoal–Gohar (USA) (Barachois (CAN)) [1989/90 17f^{3} 17f^{2}] poor novice hurdler: blinkered, 1½ lengths second of 4 finishers to Thats Nice in seller at Newton Abbot in September. *R. J. Manning.* 71

ROCQUAINE 4 ch.g. Ballad Rock–Lola Sharp (Sharpen Up) [1989/90 16g^{4} 16f^{5} a16g*] angular gelding: quite modest 6f winner on Flat: favourite, won 5-runner juvenile hurdle at Lingfield in March easily by 10 lengths from Diana Dee: suited by sharp 2m. *Mrs J. Pitman.* 93

RODCHENKO (USA) 5 b.h. Run The Gantlet (USA)–Golden Jolie (USA) (Royal Serenade) [1989/90 a16g^{3} 16m^{2} 16s^{5} a20g* a20g^{ur} a20g^{4} a20g^{2} 24m*] small horse: won handicap hurdles at Southwell in January and Uttoxeter in March: stayed 3m: acted on good to firm ground: usually a front runner: visored last 2 starts: dead. *T. H. Caldwell.* 109

RODDEN BROOK 8 ch.g. Pablond–Ronadeen (Aberdeen) [1989/90 c21d^{3} c25g* c24d^{2} c26f^{pu} c24m* c24d^{3} c26m^{pu}] workmanlike gelding: successful point-to-pointer: won hunter chases at Wolverhampton in February and Chepstow in April: 15 lengths third to Sanballat in similar race at Worcester in May: stays 25f: acts on good to firm and dead going. *Mrs H. Tutte.* **c116**

RODDEN FARM 6 b.h. Comedy Star (USA)–Polly Toodle (Kabale) [1989/90 16f^{4}] second foal: dam fairly useful hurdler: amateur ridden when last of 4 behind Eddie Kybo in novice event at Plumpton in October on hurdling debut. *R. J. Hodges.* —

RODELINDA 4 br.f. Ranksborough–Frimley Grove (Tower Walk) [1989/90 F16g^{pu}] fourth foal: half-sister to winning sprinter Frimley Parkson (by Frimley Park): dam never ran: behind when pulled up 5f out in NH Flat race at Kempton in February: sold 1,300 gns Ascot April Sales: yet to race over hurdles. *D. M. Grissell.*

RODERICK ANTHONY 12 ch.g. Owen Anthony–Royal Writ (Bowsprit) [1989/90 c24f^{pu}] tall, angular, sparely-made gelding: has been hobdayed: fair point-to-pointer: novice hunter chaser: pulled up lame in March. *R. E. Dance.* c— —

RODOMONT 6 b.g. Shirley Heights–Louise Moulton (Moulton) [1989/90 16d^{5}] compact, workmanlike gelding: placed over 1m at 2 yrs, but very lightly raced on Flat since: bit backward, promising 28 lengths fifth behind Kharif in novice hurdle at Catterick in February, taking good hold in rear and running on strongly towards finish: will prove capable of better. *J. G. FitzGerald.* 75 p

ROGERS PRINCESS 8 b.m. Owen Anthony–Ask For Roger (Menelek) [1989/90 22g 24g^{4} 21s* 24g^{5} 25f^{co} 24f] sturdy mare: fairly useful hurdler: easily best effort in 1989/90 when fifth of 7 to Old Dundalk in quite valuable event at Kempton: earlier won minor event at Warwick: suited by 3m: best form with give in the ground: has won for an amateur. *M. Tate.* 130

ROGGAN HALL 4 br.f. Balidar–Star of The Arctic (Arctic Chevalier) [1989/90 16f^{3} 16m^{bd} 16d 16f^{6}] leggy filly: fourth foal: dam fair winning jumper: behind in 2 maidens at 2 yrs: no worthwhile form over hurdles: claimer ridden. *R. Earnshaw.* —

ROKALA 5 b.m. Kalaglow–Romantiki (USA) (Giboulee (CAN)) [1989/90 16f^{2} 16f* 16f*] leggy mare: selling hurdler: won handicap at Worcester and 4-y-o event at Market Rasen in August: acted on any going: often blinkered: dead. *N. Tinkler.* 95

ROKER ROYALE 4 ch.f. Dara Monarch–Simbella (Simbir) [1989/90 16d] lengthy, rather leggy filly: half-sister to winning Irish hurdler Class Apart (by Martinmas): fair maiden plater on Flat, stays 1m (wears blinkers and possibly ungenuine): showed signs of ability in selling hurdle at Market Rasen in November: sold 1,700 gns Doncaster Sales later in month. *M. H. Easterby.* —

ROLIAD 6 br.g. Rolfe (USA)–Clear Whistle (Tin Whistle) [1989/90 16m^{2} 17m* 20f^{pu}] angular, rather sparely-made gelding: bought in 6,500 gns after easily landing the odds in selling hurdle at Cartmel in August: favourite, close up and 92

going well when pulled up lame 3 out in novice event at Carlisle in October: should stay beyond 17f: acts on good to firm going: claimer ridden. *J. J. O'Neill.*

ROLL-A-JOINT 12 ch.g. Take A Reef–Sark (Chamier) [1989/90 c25m^{2} c26f^{6} c32v^{pu} c30s^{5} c29g^{6} c29s^{2} c30v^{2} c24d c26m^{4} c36f^{F}] leggy, lightly-made gelding: quite a useful chaser: won 1989 William Hill Scottish National at Ayr: runner-up in quite valuable handicaps at Wincanton, Warwick and Chepstow in 1989/90: suffered a fatal fall in Seagram Grand National at Liverpool in April: needed further than 3m when ground was firm, and stayed long distances: probably acted on any going: usually jumped soundly. *C. L. Popham.* **c131** —

ROLLAWAY 9 b.g. Barolo–Doozle (Combat) [1989/90 c22f^{4} c24m^{2}] modest winning point-to-pointer: 11½ lengths fourth to Royal Craftsman in novice chase at Stratford in September: beaten a distance by only other finisher Rockcliffe in similar event at Huntingdon later in month. *J. Webber.* c80

ROLLING DICE 7 b.m. Balinger–Imperial Stake (Sovereign Lord) [1989/90 c16d^{F} c16m^{2} c20f* c16m^{F} c20m c16m^{3} c20m^{3}] strong mare: novice hurdler: poor form in point-to-points in 1989: won novice chase at Wolverhampton in November: should stay beyond 2½m: acts on firm ground. *Mrs I. McKie.* c90 —

ROMAN CHARIOT 8 b.m. Roman Warrior–Goldmine (Goldhill) [1989/90 c26f^{4}] workmanlike mare: behind in novice hurdles: poor point-to-pointer/hunter chaser. *E. Cook.* c— —

ROMAN CRACKSHOT 6 b.g. Roman Glory–Ogeno (Rugantino) [1989/90 16g^{F} 16g 16d 16g 16f^{6}] workmanlike gelding: bandaged all round, pulled hard when 13½ lengths sixth behind Marchman in slowly-run novice hurdle at Newbury in March, best effort. *J. O'Donoghue.* 79

ROMAN DART 6 b.g. Roman Warrior–Angodeen (Aberdeen) [1989/90 c16g* c16s* c16s^{5} c16g^{3} c16s^{3} c16g^{4}] lengthy gelding: no worthwhile form over hurdles: jumped soundly when winning novice chase at Southwell in November and novice handicap chase at Hereford in December: barely stays 2m under testing conditions. *M. Scudamore.* c85 —

ROMAN DUSK 10 b.g. Beatic–Half Moon Bay (Behistoun) [1989/90 16f^{2} 16g] big, plain gelding: quite a modest hurdler: good second of 4 to Magic At Dawn at Kelso in October: out of his depth in minor event at Ayr a week later: no sign of ability over fences: stays 3m: acts on any going: good mount for a claimer. *B. E. Wilkinson.* c— 94

ROMAN NAUT 4 b.g. Connaught–Green Menelek (Menelek) [1989/90 16g 16g^{pu}] sturdy, close-coupled gelding: chasing type: first foal: dam, successful over hurdles and fences, half-sister to Sweeps Hurdle winner Hansel Rag: little promise in juvenile hurdles. *B. E. Wilkinson.* —

ROMAN SEA 9 b. or br.g. High Season–Dignity (Romany Air) [1989/90 c24g^{pu}] compact gelding: modest point-to-pointer: poor form in steeplechases. *H. W. Wheeler.* c—

ROMANTIC MELODY 4 ch.f. Battle Hymn–Love Patrol (Green God) [1989/90 16f 16g 16m] leggy, sparely-made filly: placed at up to 1m on Flat: first sign of a little ability over hurdles when seventh in claimer at Ludlow in January, final start. *K. S. Bridgwater.* — p

ROMANTIC PLAYBOY 5 b.g. Balliol–Bils Romance (Bilsborrow) [1989/90 a16g 16m 16m] first foal: dam unraced: tailed off in novice hurdles. *J. Ringer.* —

ROMANY KING 6 br.g. Crash Course–Winsome Lady (Tarqogan) [1989/90 20d^{6} c20d^{bd} c20s^{2} c18s* c20d^{2} c20d* c17m^{2} c21d^{2}] workmanlike gelding: winning hurdler: won novice chases at Fontwell in February and Chepstow (handicap) in March: didn't take eye in paddock (rather light in condition and dull and patchy in coat) but nevertheless ran creditably when second to Astre Radieux in novice handicap at Ayr in April on last start: suited by around 2½m: probably acts on any going. *G. B. Balding.* **c109** —

ROMANY SPLIT 5 b.h. Official–Romany Park (Romany Air) [1989/90 F16m^{ro} F16f] third foal: dam, point-to-point winner, half-sister to 2 winning hurdlers: in fifth place when swerving badly left and running out over 2f out in NH Flat race at Sandown in March: mid-division in similar event at Cheltenham following month: yet to race over hurdles or fences. *N. A. Twiston-Davies.*

ROMERHOF 9 b.g. Orchestra–Ghana's Daughter (Sallust) [1989/90 c16s c16s^{5} c16f^{5} c16f^{2}] close-coupled, good-bodied gelding: moderate hurdler: placed in novice chases, showing poor form: stays 19f: probably acts on any going. *T. W. Donnelly.* c79 —

ROMFUL PRINCE 7 b.g. White Prince (USA)–Romfultears (Romany Air) [1989/90 17g4 17g3 20dpu] lengthy, sparely-made gelding: modest hurdler: creditable third at Devon & Exeter (amateur ridden) in December: ran poorly later in month: stays 2½m: acts on heavy going: wears crossed noseband. *C. W. Mitchell.* 103

ROMULEX 12 gr.g. Roman Warrior–Complex Girl (Entanglement) [1989/90 c21dpu] big, lengthy gelding: fair point-to-pointer nowadays, successful twice in April and once in May: winning hunter chaser: let down by his jumping in 1988 and in February: well suited by a test of stamina: acts on any going: blinkered once. *Mrs J. A. Baimbridge.* c— —

RONALDS CAROLE 10 b.g. Sheshoon–Robert's Carol (Sing Sing) [1989/90 c24d5] strong, sturdy gelding: moderate staying chaser in 1987/8: soundly beaten only outing since: acts on soft going: usually blinkered nowadays. *Andrew Wilson.* c— —

RONANS BIRTHDAY 8 b.g. Furry Glen–Mountain Sedge (Goldhill) [1989/90 22gpu c16g2 c20g5 c25g3 c24gF c25spu c16sur c20d] big, lengthy gelding: winning point-to-pointer: poor novice hurdler/chaser: jumped moderately and was pulled up after trying to refuse sixth start: stays 25f. *Mrs S. Oliver.* c86 —

RON CANELLO 14 b.g. Can-Can–Hasty Rondo (Cacador) [1989/90 c26mpu] workmanlike gelding: winning point-to-pointer/hunter chaser: very lightly raced since 1988: stays well: acts on firm ground. *R. Astle.* c—

RONDEAU 7 ch.m. Orchestra–Sunshot (Candy Cane) [1989/90 c16sF 21s c24g5 c20v5] plain mare: modest hurdler: well beaten second start: well beaten in novice chases, making a couple of mistakes and running in snatches on third start: stays 2¾m: acts on soft ground (ran moderately on firm): has won for a claimer: has been blinkered. *P. J. Jones.* c78 —

RONNIE WILL 7 b.g. Balinger–Donna May (Nerium) [1989/90 16g2 25g6 21m4] small, sturdy gelding: jumped moderately when second to easy winner Kameo Style in novice handicap hurdle at Wolverhampton in November: ran creditably next time: blinkered last start. *N. A. Twiston-Davies.* 78

RONOCCO 8 ch.g. Baptism–Kilteelagh Lady (King's Leap) [1989/90 17fpu 17f c16h3 c16m c17vpu c17m6 c16m4 c16f5] leggy, sparely-made gelding: poor hurdler/novice chaser: stays 2¼m: acts on firm and dead going: front runner: sold out of G. Stickland's stable 500 gns Ascot December Sales after fourth outing. *Mrs S. D. Williams.* c— —

ROODLE DOODLE 10 ro.m. Rugantino–Jolly Music (Money Business) [1989/90 c25mur c24dpu] strong, compact mare: fairly useful point-to-pointer: novice hunter chaser: suited by 2½m+: acts on firm going: usually amateur ridden. *O. J. Carter.* c— —

ROOF GHOST 6 b.g. Thatching–Vital Spirit (Tachypous) [1989/90 16gpu 16dpu a20g a16g4 a16g5] workmanlike gelding: plating-class at up to 1m on Flat (none too genuine): sold out of J. Wilson's stable 4,200 gns Doncaster September Sales: of little account over hurdles. *R. A. Bennett.* —

ROONEY 4 b.g. Glen Quaich–Dashing Bird (Dominion) [1989/90 F17m F16g 16d] first foal: dam showed promise at 2 yrs, only outing: well beaten in NH Flat races: 13/2, never near to challenge when around 16 lengths seventh to Far Out in 13-runner juvenile maiden hurdle at Perth in May. *N. Bradley.* 69

ROOSTERS TIPPLE 4 b.g. Henbit (USA)–Amiel (Nonoalco (USA)) [1989/90 16g 16g 16d] big, workmanlike gelding: placed over 1m at 2 yrs, best effort on Flat: changed hands 4,600 gns Newmarket Autumn Sales: behind in juvenile events and a novice event over hurdles. *M. W. Easterby.* —

ROPE 4 b.g. Rolfe (USA)–Mountain Rescue (Mountain Call) [1989/90 F16f5] half-brother to winning hurdler Intrepid Lad (by Hot Grove): dam 2-y-o 6f winner: 12½ lengths fifth behind True Magic in NH Flat race at Warwick in May: yet to race over hurdles. *F. Walwyn.*

ROSCAM LADY 5 ch.m. Cruise Missile–Willmon (Willipeg) [1989/90 F16f 20g] fourth foal: dam of no account: behind in NH Flat race in September: better for race and green, ran on steadily having been held up when eighth behind Judges Fancy in novice hurdle at Newcastle in December: may do better. *Mrs G. R. Reveley.* — p

ROSCOE HARVEY 8 br.g. Roscoe Blake–Hunter's Treasure (Tudor Treasure) [1989/90 c20g* c20gF c20m* c19dpu c20g2 c25mur c18f4 c25f2 c21gpu] strong gelding: fair chaser: won handicaps at Sandown in November and Uttoxeter (jumped to his right) in December: creditable second to First Bout in c121 —

similar race at Kempton in February: stays 21f (below form when second over 25f): acts on soft and good to firm going: takes a good hold and usually makes running. *C. P. E. Brooks.*

ROSCOE SPATE 8 b.g. Roscoe Blake–Minibus (John Splendid) [1989/90 21fur 26fpu] workmanlike gelding: winning point-to-pointer: maiden hunter chaser: beaten when trying to run out and unseating rider at second last in novice event at Newton Abbot in August on hurdling debut: blinkered, tailed off when pulled up in a handicap 8 days later. *T. B. Hallett.* c— —

ROSCOE THE BRAVE 6 br.g. Roscoe Blake–My Plucky Lady (Cash And Courage) [1989/90 16g2 16g5 16m6 16d a16g2 a16g4 16h6 16m5 16m2 17f2] leggy gelding: modest hurdler: should stay beyond 17f: acts on firm and dead going: ran moderately when blinkered eighth start: weak finisher. *S. E. Kettlewell.* 96

ROSCOFF 8 b.m. Roscoe Blake–Kaminaki (Deep Run) [1989/90 c16dur c16g4 c17g2 c16s3 c16v5 c16s3 c20vpu c16d3 c16f3 c25m3] sparely-made, angular mare: no worthwhile form in novice hurdles: in frame in novice chases, showing poor form: seems best at around 2m: usually claimer or amateur ridden. *P. J. Hobbs.* c77 + —

ROSEATE LODGE 4 b.g. Habitat–Elegant Tern (USA) (Sea Bird II) [1989/90 16f] smallish, leggy gelding: fair performer on Flat, winner 3 times at around 1m in 1989: jumped none too fluently and eased after mistake 2 out when seventh behind My Young Man in novice hurdle at Wolverhampton in March: sure to improve. *M. H. Tompkins.* — p

ROSE FESTIVAL 4 br.f. Ile de Bourbon (USA)–Vendemmia (Silly Season) [1989/90 16g3 16v6] leggy filly: quite modest maiden on Flat: sold out of Sir Mark Prescott's stable 6,000 gns Newmarket Autumn Sales: always-prominent 6½ lengths third behind Good Spark in 14-runner novice hurdle at Plumpton in January: blinkered, well beaten on heavy going only subsequent outing: sent to race in Ireland. *R. J. O'Sullivan.* 81

Withington Handicap Chase, Sandown—Roscoe Harvey makes all

ROSE GARDENIA 5 ch.m. Henbit (USA)–Royal Descent (FR) (Run The Gantlet (USA)) [1989/90 $16f^2$] sparely-made, angular mare: novice selling hurdler: blinkered nowadays: usually ridden by claimer: moderate jumper. *W. Clay.* 66 ?

ROSEHIP 5 b.g. Derring Rose–Fairy Island (Prince Hansel) [1989/90 $F16f^6$ F16g] third foal: brother to fair hurdler The Red One and half-brother to winning hurdler Wayward Singer (by The Parson): dam lightly raced and little form: pulled up in a point-to-point in Ireland in 1989: unplaced in NH Flat races in the spring: yet to race over hurdles or in a steeplechase. *R. Hollinshead.*

ROSE LAWN 10 b.g. Celtic Cone–Brumelle (Brightworthy) [1989/90 $c20s^F$] workmanlike gelding: lightly-raced winning point-to-pointer: bit backward, tailed off when falling at the sixth in novice chase at Uttoxeter in February. *Mrs S. M. Newell.* c—

ROSE MASTER 7 b.g. Derring Rose–Toy Mistress (Milan) [1989/90 $17v^F$ 20v $16s^{bd}$] rather leggy gelding: tailed off in novice hurdles. *G. A. Ham.* —

ROSE OF PEACE 6 b.m. Tug of War–Rosecon (Typhoon) [1989/90 17f $22m^5$ a20g* a20g] sparely-made mare: dropped in class and ridden by 7-lb claimer, showed only worthwhile form over hurdles when winning selling hurdle at Lingfield in February (no bid): stays 2½m. *T. B. Hallett.* 67

ROSE OF THE GLEN 4 ch.f. Respighi–Ruckinge Girl (Eborneezer) [1989/90 $F16f^4$] half-sister to fairly useful staying chaser Glenside Jerry (by Chas Sawyer): dam of little account over hurdles: 14½ lengths fourth of 12 to Bollinger in NH Flat race at Ascot in April: yet to race over hurdles. *G. G. Gracey.*

ROSE ORCHARD 8 b.m. Rouser–Darling Rose (Darling Boy) [1989/90 $c25s^r$ $c29m^2$] strong mare: well beaten in novice hurdles: won point-to-points in February and March: made mistakes and was very tired when refusing at the last in maiden hunter chase at Hereford in between: 4 lengths second to Thames Air in novice hunter chase at Warwick in May. *Mrs M. P. Marfell.* c**89** ? —

ROSE'S PRIDE 4 b.f. Ballacashtal (CAN)–Tropingay (Cawston's Clown) [1989/90 $16g^6$ $16g^6$ $16f^{pu}$] sparely-made filly: placed over 1¼m on Flat: sold out of R. Smyly's stable 2,400 gns Ascot December Sales: no sign of ability in juvenile claiming hurdles. *R. W. Dods.* —

ROSE TABLEAU 7 ch.m. Ballymore–Princess Pageant (Welsh Pageant) [1989/90 $17h^2$ $22f^2$ $20g^6$ $24m^4$ $20g^4$ $20d^3$ $22d^2$ $24g^3$] leggy, sparely-made, plain mare: novice hurdler: looked none too keen when 1½ lengths second to Springvale Crusade at Ayr in January, penultimate start: stays 3m: best form on an easy surface: has worn a tongue strap and blinkers. *Mrs H. S. Wells.* 92

ROSGILL 4 ch.c. Mill Reef (USA)–Speedy Rose (On Your Mark) [1989/90 $16g^5$ 16d] medium-sized colt: middle-distance winner on Flat: sold out of A. Fabre's stable 10,500 gns Newmarket Autumn Sales: 33 lengths fifth of 13 behind Royal Square in juvenile hurdle at Kempton in January: still bit backward, well beaten at Newbury following month. *P. Mitchell.* 88

ROSIE CONE 8 ch.m. Celtic Cone–Arctic Festival (Arctic Slave) [1989/90 $24s^5$ $a24g^2$ 28f] small, sparely-made mare: 6 lengths second to Lucy Lastic in 6-runner handicap hurdle at Southwell in February: probably stays 3m: acts on heavy going (well beaten on firm last start): sketchy jumper: visored fourth and fifth starts 1986/7, usually blinkered since: sometimes claimer ridden. *Mrs P. Sly.* 99

ROSIE MARCHIONESS 7 br.m. Neltino–Maid of Honor II (Honour Bound) [1989/90 $18s^2$ 22d 20d 18f*] medium-sized mare: won 6-runner novice hurdle at Fontwell in March: acts on firm ground: gives impression she'll do best at distances short of 2¾m. *F. Walwyn.* 85

ROSIE MAY DICKINS 4 b.f. King of Spain–Gipsy Scott (Sky Gipsy) [1989/90 16d] half-sister to winning selling hurdler Blackheath (by Track Spare): well beaten at 2 yrs when trained by J. Berry: carrying condition, always behind in juvenile hurdle at Nottingham in December. *S. Mellor.* —

ROSIE'S JUMPER 7 br.g. Rhodomantade–Coxmoore Sweaters (Wynkell) [1989/90 $20d^{pu}$ c16g] compact gelding: of little account: refused to race on hurdling debut: dead. *G. Roe.* c— — §

ROSIE'S MEMBER 9 b.g. New Member–Pinzarose (Pinzan) [1989/90 20d $20m^2$] tall, angular gelding: has been hobdayed: lightly-raced novice hurdler: stays 2½m: acts on good to firm and soft going: tends to hang left under pressure: sold 2,000 gns Doncaster Spring Sales. *Mrs C. Postlethwaite.* 101

ROSITARY (FR) 7 b.m. Trenel–Houri V (FR) (Vieux Chateau) [1989/90 $F16g^2$ 22g $18s^3$ 16s* 25d* 22d $20g^2$] sparely-made mare: won novice hurdles at 109

Towcester (mares) and Huntingdon within a week in February: second race in 4 days, creditable second to Goodshot Rich at Perth in April: stays 25f: acts on soft going. *S. Mellor.*

ROSOGLIO (FR) 6 ch. or br.g. Roi de Carreau (FR)–Salopette (FR) (Dapper c—
Dan (USA)) [1989/90 c22h^{r} c21f^{pu} 17f* 17h* 21f^{5} 17f^{3} 17m* 16h^{3}] leggy, rather 79
narrow gelding: won 3 early-season novice selling hurdles (first conditional jockeys) at Devon & Exeter: reportedly finished lame final outing (September): ran out at the second on chasing debut: has looked headstrong and best form at around 2m on very firm ground: usually blinkered: trained by P. Hobbs until after third start. *T. B. Hallett.*

ROSSA PRINCE 12 br.g. Pitpan–Santa Belle (Delirium) [1989/90 c20f^{2}] c74
ex-Irish gelding: winning point-to-pointer: novice hurdler/chaser: 6 lengths —
second to Tricky Business in novice hunter chase at Folkestone in May. *Ian M. McGready.*

ROSSHELM 5 ch.h. Ardross–Ice Cream Soda (Tumble Wind (USA)) [1989/90 F17f] first foal: dam lightly-raced maiden: last of 18 in NH Flat race at Doncaster in December: yet to race over hurdles or fences. *W. A. Stephenson.*

ROSSMICHAEL 5 ch.g. On Your Mark–Sea Dike (Dike (USA)) [1989/90 16d
20d^{pu} 16g 20g^{4} 22g^{pu}] workmanlike ex-Irish gelding: fifth foal: half-brother to 84
winning jumpers Seatell (by Guillaume Tell) and Clare Lad (by Garda's Revenge): dam won over 1¼m in Ireland: little form on Flat: poor form over hurdles. *G. A. Ham.*

ROSSVILLE 5 ch.g. Kemal (FR)–Golden Ingot (Prince Hansel) [1989/90 F16m
20g 20m] rangy ex-Irish gelding: has plenty of scope: sixth foal: dam unraced: —
seventh in NH Flat race at Dundalk in 1988/9: behind both outings over hurdles. *Mrs S. A. Bramall.*

ROSTHERNE 8 ch.g. Crimson Beau–Correct Approach (Right Tack) [1989/90
16d^{2}] sturdy gelding: very lightly-raced novice hurdler: 4 lengths second, clear, to 98
Kharif at Catterick in February: withdrawn after bolting before start at Perth 2 months later: should stay beyond 2m: jumps sketchily. *J. G. FitzGerald.*

ROSTOVOL 5 b.g. Vaigly Great–Emerin (King Emperor (USA)) [1989/90
16g^{6}] leggy gelding: half-brother to winning Irish hurdler Lucky Knight (by 77
Rarity): modest winner on Flat, stays 1m: bit backward and amateur ridden, jumped sketchily, weakened run-in and eased when 23½ lengths sixth behind Sacre d'Or in novice event at Huntingdon in November on hurdling debut. *D. H. Topley.*

ROSTREAMER 7 b.g. Paddy's Stream–Tarqogan's Rose (Tarqogan) [1989/90 c76 §
22g 20d^{5} 22m c26m^{3} c24s^{pu} c26g^{pu} c24f] leggy, short-backed gelding: winning —
hurdler: not a fluent jumper of fences, and refuses to do his best: stays well: acts on soft and good to firm ground: blinkered last 2 starts. *C. V. Bravery.*

ROSTUILE 12 b.g. Tepukei–Buxom Filly (Bargello) [1989/90 c24d] sturdy c—
gelding: poor novice hurdler/chaser: fair winning point-to-pointer: stays 3m: —
blinkered in 1984/5. *G. H. Wagstaff.*

ROTATE 10 ch.g. Roman Warrior–Waterbeck (Weathercock) [1989/90 25f^{pu} c—
c24d^{F}] workmanlike gelding: poor novice hurdler: winning point-to-pointer/ —
hunter chaser: stays 27f: acts on firm ground. *W. M. Nelson.*

ROTTEN FOR DAPHNE 4 b.f. Beldale Flutter (USA)–Canadian Charisma (Supreme Sovereign) [1989/90 aF13g^{3} aF13g^{5} aF13g^{5}] third foal: dam lightly-raced maiden: beaten over 20 lengths in NH Flat races at Lingfield: yet to race over hurdles. *E. A. Wheeler.*

ROUGE ROI 5 b.g. Hays–Restless Morn (Morston (FR)) [1989/90 16s^{pu}]
leggy, sparely-made gelding: poor novice selling hurdler: visored only outing in —
1989/90. *P. D. Evans.*

ROUGH CUT 5 ch.g. Krayyan–Angelic Appeal (Star Appeal) [1989/90 19s^{pu}
16d^{pu}] angular, sparely-made gelding: showed ability over hurdles in 1988/9: —
tailed off when pulled up in 2 races in December: best at 2m: acts on good to firm and heavy going: blinkered 3 times in 1988/9: ridden by 7-lb claimer. *R. T. Juckes.*

ROUGH SAILING 6 ch.g. True Song–Galley Light (Sailing Light) [1989/90
F16s^{su} 16f^{6} 16f^{pu}] rather unfurnished gelding: brother to winning hurdler Light 67
Song and half-brother to winning hurdler Fused Light (by Fury Royal): dam, winning chaser, from family of Spanish Steps: slipped up halfway in NH Flat race in February: last of 6 finishers to Fidway in novice hurdle at Nottingham following month. *K. S. Bridgwater.*

ROULADE 6 ch.m. True Song–Cartwheel (Escart III) [1989/90 c16gF 21fpu c16m] narrow mare: no form over hurdles or fences: blinkered last 2 starts. *J. Webber.* c— —

ROUNDSTONE 12 b.g. Vivify–True Pardal (Pardal) [1989/90 c20gF c16gpu] big gelding: winning hurdler/chaser: failed to get beyond the ninth both outings in 1989/90: won slowly-run race at 2½m: suited by give in the ground. *J. T. Gifford.* c— —

ROUND THE WREKIN 7 ch.m. Peter Wrekin–Iona Flyer (Le Tricolore) [1989/90 16g 22gF 22d 20d] lengthy mare: second foal: dam of no account: of little account. *I. Anderson.* —

ROUSSE DE POMME 7 ch.m. Fine Blue–Pomme (Polic) [1989/90 16g 20dur 16gpu 16gpu] smallish mare: half-sister to useful hurdler/chaser Applalto and winning hurdler/chaser Applante (both by Alto Volante): dam never ran: no sign of ability in novice hurdles: blinkered last start (jumped slowly). *Mrs J. H. Chadwick.* —

ROUTE MARCH 11 ch.g. Queen's Hussar–Wide of The Mark (Gulf Pearl) [1989/90 a20g 20g a22g6 a20g5 a20g6 a20g6 20m5 20m5] small, lightly-made gelding: poor hurdler: has run in sellers: stays 3m: acts on any going: has been tried in blinkers and a visor. *P. A. Pritchard.* 67

ROUYAN 4 b.g. Akarad (FR)–Rosy Moon (FR) (Sheshoon) [1989/90 16d6 17g3 16d3 16g 16d2 16m* 16dpu] leggy, lengthy gelding: fairly useful 1¾m winner on Flat: sold out of F. J. Houghton's stable 28,000 gns Newmarket Autumn Sales: showed plenty of ability over hurdles prior to winning quite valuable juvenile handicap at Newcastle in March (carried head rather high under pressure) by 2½ lengths from Philosophos: ran poorly next start: will stay 2½m: acts on dead going and good to firm: wore bandages and boots in front at Newcastle. *R. Simpson.* 124

ROVIGO 9 br.g. Great Nephew–Zantedeschia (Zimone) [1989/90 24g 24dpu 23f4] compact gelding: winning selling hurdler: no form in 1989/90: stayed 3m: acted on any going: dead. *W. A. Stephenson.* —

ROVING GLEN 9 b.g. Proverb–Glenosheen (Menelek) [1989/90 c16d6 c20gur c24s c28gpu] leggy, workmanlike gelding: modest hurdler/novice chaser: stays 21f: acts on firm going and is possibly unsuited by heavy: has run well for an amateur: sold 3,600 gns Ascot May Sales. *Mrs S. Armytage.* c— —

ROVING SEAL 8 br.m. Privy Seal–Roving Belle (Wrekin Rambler) [1989/90 c25mr c19fr c25mur c25f4 c26f2] workmanlike mare: first form when neck second to Beera Quest in novice hunter chase at Newton Abbot in May: had seemed thoroughly temperamental previously: stays well: acts on firm ground. *W. G. M. Turner.* c**72** § —

Northern Champion Juvenile Handicap Hurdle, Newcastle—
Rouyan takes over from Philosophos, Bescaby Boy and Carbisdale (blaze)

ROWAN LEAF 7 ch.g. Dynastic–Young Ash Leaf (New Brig) [1989/90 16d]
rangy gelding: no worthwhile form in novice hurdles. *R. McDonald.* —

ROWAN VILLE 5 b.m. Sexton Blake–Hello Stranger (Milesian) [1989/90
16f^{r}] sparely-made, dipped-backed ex-Irish mare: won 11f handicap on soft going — §
on Flat at 3 yrs: yet to get to halfway in 2 outings over hurdles (slowly away and
refused third on British debut in September). *T. W. Donnelly.*

ROWDY 4 bl.g. Lucky Wednesday–Angel Row (Prince Regent (FR)) [1989/90
16g^{pu} 16f^{5} 16m^{5}] rather sparely-made gelding: brother to novice hurdler Vendredi —
Treize: dam, 1m winner, half-sister to winning chaser Park Row: poor maiden 1m
plater on Flat: sold out of S. Bowring's stable 1,400 gns Doncaster August Sales:
amateur ridden, soundly-beaten last of 5 finishers in 2 juvenile hurdles at
Wetherby in the spring. *R. E. Barr.*

ROWHEDGE 4 ch.c. Tolomeo–Strident Note (The Minstrel (CAN)) [1989/90
16d 17g 16f^{4}] lightly-made colt: first foal: dam maiden half-sister to Teenoso: third 75
in 6f maiden at 2 yrs, only outing on Flat: sold out of G. Wragg's stable 6,200 gns
Newmarket Autumn Sales: 6½ lengths fourth behind Basic Fun in juvenile
claiming hurdle at Sedgefield in April: wears crossed noseband. *W. M. Perrin.*

ROWLANDSONS JEWELS 9 br.g. Avocat–Coolavane (David Jack) [1989/90 c**135**
c25g* c20m c26f^{2} c25m* c29g^{3} c25m^{3}] leggy gelding: won handicap chases at —
Sandown in November and Wincanton in December: close third behind Cool
Ground and Nick The Brief in Anthony Mildmay, Peter Cazalet Memorial Handicap Chase at Sandown in January: let down by his jumping final start: suited by
3m+: acts on any going: usually bandaged nowadays: tends to sweat. *D. J. G.
Murray-Smith.*

ROWLANDSONS TROPHY 5 b.g. Vaigly Great–Queen's Parade (Sove-
reign Path) [1989/90 21m^{3} 22m^{5} 24s] robust, dipped-backed gelding: moderate 106
hurdler: probably stays 2¾m (never going particularly well when tried at 3m):
acts on good to firm and heavy going. *K. O. Cunningham-Brown.*

ROXALL CLUMP 6 b.g. Neltino–Wyn-Bank (Green God) [1989/90 16g^{3}
20s^{ur} 16s^{ro} 20d^{6}] well-made gelding: has shown some ability in novice hurdles: 86
close up when running out 4 out third outing. *P. G. Bailey.*

*Babcock & Brown (KW) Handicap Chase, Sandown—
Rowlandsons Jewels is just behind Seagram in the early stages*

ROYAL ASTRONAUT (USA) 6 ch.g. Grey Dawn II–Short Stanza (USA) (Verbatim (USA)) [1989/90 22d4] compact gelding: moderate hurdler: ran much better than position suggests when just over 20 lengths fourth behind Auk Eye in 2¾m handicap at Ayr in April, quickening clear after 3 out but being headed at the next and finishing tired: likely to prove best at up to 2½m: has raced only in testing conditions over hurdles. *R. Akehurst.* 106 +

ROYAL ATHLETE 7 ch.g. Roselier (FR)–Darjoy (Darantus) [1989/90 26d* c24m* c26v* c24s* c24gbd c24fF c25m* c24d*] c**151** p 151 p

A fall at the ninth when a short-priced favourite for the Sun Alliance Novices' Chase at Cheltenham in March was the only blemish on Royal Athlete's season. The fall merely delayed confirmation of Royal Athlete's dominant place amongst the staying novices by three weeks, until he won the Mumm Club Chase at Liverpool giving weight all round. He'll go on to make the top class over a distance of ground in 1990/1. He still has something to learn about jumping fences, which isn't surprising since he's had only four months' chasing and five full chases so far (he was brought down early on at Kempton in his race prior to Cheltenham). At present he errs on the side of boldness, an abundant zest for the game as a whole being an attractive part of his racing make-up.

Royal Athlete made his chasing debut in January at Leicester, a course at which Mrs Pitman is not only by a long way the leading trainer over the last five years but also one at which she has a high winner-to-runner ratio; down the years many of the stable's good horses have been on view there. Beforehand the race looked above average for the track. Royal Athlete himself was a way-above-average recruit, for the previous month he'd won the Youngmans Long Walk Hurdle at Ascot by three lengths from Mrs Muck, giving a performance which would have put him in line for a shot at the long-distance hurdling championship had he not made a success of chasing; and he duly won at Leicester with a lot in hand after a beginners' mixture of a round finished off with a fine leap at the last. Just one more outing for experience at Newton Abbot, then he was regarded as ready to tackle the Ascot fences in the valuable Old Road Securities Reynoldstown Novices' Chase in February. The confidence in his readiness for Ascot proved well placed, but his supporters had a nasty moment to endure when he completely missed out the fourth last, coming desperately close to unseating his rider. Royal Athlete held a lead of some eight to ten lengths at the time, with both his supposed main rivals Carrick Hill Lad and Celtic Shot struggling. He'd taken such a keen hold that he'd been given his head six out and had quickly stretched the field of seven. It's a measure of how much the horse had in reserve that nothing remotely threatened to take

*Old Road Securities Reynoldstown Novices' Chase, Ascot—
Royal Athlete (No. 5) shows the way to Carrick Hill Lad*

Mumm Club Novices' Chase, Liverpool—
Royal Athlete (left) gets the better of the much improved Arctic Call

advantage of his mistake. He was in full stride again by the third last, met the last two correctly and galloped on in tremendous style to win by fifteen lengths from Last House, the mare who'd also finished second to him at Newton Abbot.

Souter of Stirling Novices' Chase, Ayr—another big prize for Royal Athlete, who disposes of Formula One (centre) and Carrick Hill Lad in game fashion

Mr L. Johnson's "Royal Athlete"

The Mumm Club Chase seemed no easy way back to the winner's enclosure for Royal Athlete following his two mishaps, and though he started favourite it was at 5/2 as opposed to 5/4 at Cheltenham. The race nowadays is an important part of the staying novices' programme and attracted a field of eleven which also included the improving pair Espy and Arctic Call, the leading Irish novice Cahervillahow, like Royal Athlete unbeaten in all completed outings over fences, and two who'd run in the Sun Alliance, Mixed Blends and Knight Oil. Royal Athlete had to concede weight, of course; on top of that it's a sharp three miles at Liverpool, especially on firmish going, and so far Royal Athlete had been giving the impression he was an out-and-out stayer suited by testing conditions. To his credit he managed to cope. He settled in behind as Arctic Call and The Nigelstan set a strong pace, tending to jump flatter than at Ascot and not to stand off. Though there were moments when Arctic Call threatened to get away from his opponents Royal Athlete moved up steadily on the final circuit and was well placed to challenge in second on the final turn. The challenge seemed to spur Arctic Call on; as one quickened so did the other, Arctic Call still in front, the pair drawing clear of the others once Espy fell at the fourth last when moving past The Nigelstan into third. Not until the run-in did Royal Athlete wear Arctic Call down. He rallied to go almost level at the last from three lengths down at the second last, lost ground to Arctic Call over the last, then gradually got on top, going half a length up near the finish. The runner-up received 6 lb; third-placed Cahervillahow, who looked a good horse in the making but made a couple of bad mistakes, received 3 lb. Royal Athlete had one more race before being put away for the season, in the Souter of Stirling Novices' Chase at Ayr. There he found Carrick Hill Lad (at levels) a much tougher proposition than before and had to call on all his reserves to get up in a close finish with that horse and Formula One. Actually he won going away in the end, by two lengths and a head, but had come under pressure to stay in touch with the other two turning for home. Some of his jumping hadn't been entirely convincing in a moderately-run affair and it was as well that he saved as good a jump as any he'd produced for the last, where the three rose almost in line.

Royal Athlete (ch.g. 1983)	Roselier (FR) (b 1973)	Misti IV (br 1958)	Medium
			Mist
		Peace Rose (gr 1959)	Fastnet Rock
			La Paix
	Darjoy (br 1976)	Darantus (b 1960)	Buisson Ardent
			Duranta
		Our Joy (b 1957)	Vulgan
			Jess Figaro

Royal Athlete could be a Grand National fancy one day. If he ever won the race he would be the second from the family to do so, following West Tip whose dam Astryl was a sister to Royal Athlete's grandam Our Joy. Our Joy won point-to-points and was placed over hurdles. To Darantus she first produced Darantus Joy, a winner over fences in Ireland, then Royal Athlete's dam, the unraced Darjoy. Darjoy has been responsible for another winner in Dis Fiove (by Le Bavard), successful in Ireland on the Flat as well as over hurdles and fences. Her five-year-old Misty Joy (by General Ironside) so far shows none of their ability. *Mrs J. Pitman.*

ROYAL BANNER 5 b.m. Royal Palace–Pink Streamer (Birdbrook) [1989/90 aF13g^{3} F16f^{6} F16f] half-sister to poor plater Patsy's Taxi (by Dublin Taxi): dam of little account: third of 8 in NH Flat race at Lingfield in March: yet to race over hurdles or fences. *D. J. G. Murray-Smith.*

ROYAL BATTERY (NZ) 7 br.g. Norfolk Air–All At Sea (NZ) (Man The Rail) [1989/90 c19g^{bd} c25d^{4} c24g^{3} c25d^{2} c25d^{F} c25g^{ur} c24d^{F} c32f^{2} c24f^{4} c36g^{F}] rather unfurnished gelding: novice hurdler/chaser: long way clear of remainder when 4 lengths second to stable-companion Topsham Bay in National Hunt Chase Challenge Cup at Cheltenham in March, eighth outing: running very well when falling five out in valuable contest at Uttoxeter final outing: suited by extreme distances: acts on any going: tried to run out and unseated rider 2 out on sixth start: sweats: has run well for a 7-lb claimer: inconsistent. *D. H. Barons.* c**121** § —

ROYAL BEE 6 br.g. Royal Fountain–Brown Bee III (Marcus Superbus) [1989/90 c24g^{pu} 20d 20d 20m] strong, lengthy, useful-looking gelding: second foal: brother to winning 2½m hurdler Regal Bee: dam winner over hurdles and in a point-to-point: jumped badly and was behind when pulled up sixth in novice chase at Carlisle in February: behind in novice hurdles subsequently. *W. G. Reed.* c— —

ROYAL BEQUEST (CAN) 4 b.c. Mill Reef (USA)–Regal Heiress (English Prince) [1989/90 16s^{5} 16d] neat colt: fair form at best in middle-distance maidens on Flat: sold out of M. Stoute's stable 19,000 gns Newmarket Autumn Sales: well beaten in novice hurdles at Nottingham (odds on, jumped poorly) and Wetherby (jumped none too fluently). *N. Tinkler.* —

ROYAL-BLUE BELLE 4 b.f. Castle Keep–Pat Pong (Mummy's Pet) [1989/90 16m^{6} 16m 16s a16g a16g] leggy filly: seems of little account. *T. Kersey.* —

ROYAL BOROUGH 5 b.g. Bustino–Lady R B (USA) (Gun Shot) [1989/90 16d^{4} 16s 16d^{2} 16f^{4}] rather sparely-made gelding: fairly useful middle-distance performer on Flat: fourth in well-contested novice hurdle at Ascot (slowly run) in January: failed to confirm that promise: races freely. *Miss H. C. Knight.* 102 ?

ROYAL BOWLER 11 b.g. Beau Chapeau–Royal Inquisitor (Royal Buck) [1989/90 c24g^{pu}] workmanlike gelding: handicap chaser: pulled up lame in January, and wasn't seen out again: stays well: probably acts on any going. *J. I. A. Charlton.* c— —

ROYAL BRUSH 5 b.m. King of Spain–Broomstick Corner (USA) (Bustino) [1989/90 22g^{pu} 16g^{pu}] lengthy, workmanlike mare: showed signs of ability in maiden at 2 yrs: behind when pulled up in novice hurdles at Wolverhampton in January and Windsor in March. *G. P. Enright.* —

ROYAL BUSKINS 11 ch.m. White Prince (USA)–Mini Buskins (Little Buskins) [1989/90 c25m^{6}] lengthy mare: no form over hurdles in 1984/5: useful point-to-pointer: tailed off in hunter chase at Towcester in May. *J. Sprake.* c— —

ROYAL CASINO 13 ch.g. Gambling Debt–Pickled Walnut (Hornbeam) [1989/90 c25hpu] smallish gelding: fairly useful point-to-pointer/hunter chaser at best: poor form in 1990: stays well: suited by give in the ground. *A. J. Sendell.* c— —

ROYAL CAUSE 6 ch.m. Le Bavard (FR)–Rosina Royal (Skyros) [1989/90 F16g aF16g* aF16g] sister to fair staying chaser Abba Lad and half-sister to winning jumpers Scroggy and Buck Royale (both by Master Buck) and Lonach (by Deep Run): dam never ran: won NH Flat race at Lingfield in January: yet to race over hurdles or fences. *N. J. Henderson.*

ROYAL CEDAR 9 br.g. Celtic Cone–Petal Princess (Floribunda) [1989/90 c24gF c24f* c28g* c25f* c29gur c25mpu c25m c26f*] well-made gelding: fairly useful chaser: won handicaps at Newbury in October and Cheltenham in November, December and April: won Champagne Piper Heidsieck Golden Miller Chase (limited handicap) by a length from Golden Friend for last success: stays 3½m: acts on any going: often races up with pace: makes the odd mistake. *J. C. McConnochie.* c**129** —

ROYAL CELT 6 ch.m. Celtic Cone–Doubly Royal (Royal Buck) [1989/90 F17m] first living foal: dam, fair hurdler/chaser, stayed 25f: backward, behind in NH Flat race at Carlisle in November: yet to race over hurdles or fences. *R. B. Francis.*

ROYAL CHARGE (USA) 9 b.g. King Pellinore (USA)–Reload (FR) (Relko) [1989/90 21dF 24d 25g*] leggy, close-coupled gelding: handicap hurdler: only form of season when winning by a neck from Parsons Green at Doncaster in February: stays well: acts on any going. *D. R. Wellicome.* 101

ROYAL COURSE 5 ch.g. On Your Mark–Debnic (Counsel) [1989/90 a16gpu] very lightly-raced novice hurdler: pulled up in a seller in February. *J. S. Wainwright.* —

ROYAL CRACKER 9 b.g. He Loves Me–French Cracker (Klairon) [1989/90 c17m4 c16g* c16f2 c17f* c16g2 c16g2 c17m3] sparely-made gelding: won handicap chases at Southwell in November and Doncaster (conditional jockeys event, despite hanging right run-in) following month: good second in similar races at c**114** —

Champagne Piper Heidsieck Golden Miller Handicap Chase, Cheltenham— Royal Cedar (right) shows more resolution than eventual third Master Bob

City Trial Handicap Hurdle, Nottingham—Royal Derbi returns to form

Uttoxeter and Cheltenham subsequently: best form at around 2m: acts on any going: usually races to the fore: often visored. *T. T. Bill.*

ROYAL CRAFTSMAN 9 b. or br.g. Workboy–Royal Huntress (Royal Avenue) [1989/90 c22f* c24m² c24g⁴] strong gelding: fair hurdler: won novice chase at Stratford in September: didn't go through with his effort when going down by ½ length to Carneades in similar race at Worcester later in month: looked as though he'd be better for race at Kempton 5 months later: stays 3m: acts on firm going: sometimes blinkered or visored prior to 1988/9. *A. J. K. Dunn.* c**107** —

ROYAL CRUSADER 7 b.m. Welsh Chanter–Taurette (Major Portion) [1989/90 c24fpu] leggy, sparely-made mare: seems of little account. *B. Preece.* c— —

ROYAL DERBI 5 b.g. Derrylin–Royal Birthday (St Paddy) [1989/90 16g⁵ 16f⁶ 16g 16d⁶ 16s* 16s* 16m² 16g* 16f] 151

Once again Royal Derbi was the only British-trained winner at the three-day Punchestown Festival meeting in April. He'd put up the best performance by a juvenile during the season when winning the Guinness

Waterford Castle Hotel Handicap Hurdle, Punchestown—the game Royal Derbi runs on too strongly for Glamorous Gale

Mr M. Tabor's "Royal Derbi"

Trophy Champion Four-Year-Old Hurdle there in 1989; and on his latest visit to the course Royal Derbi defied top-weight of 12-0 in the Waterford Castle Hotel Handicap Hurdle. Royal Derbi, who'd made almost continuous progress during a very busy first season over hurdles, also improved with racing in his second season. Following three moderate runs Royal Derbi showed clear signs of a return to his best when sixth behind Deep Sensation in the Tote Gold Trophy at Newbury in February, and a week later he got off the mark in the City Trial Hurdle, a limited handicap run at Nottingham. The race attracted a lot of attention as it featured the triple champion hurdler See You Then, making his first appearance for two years. His presence resulted in six of the eight runners carrying more than their weight in the long handicap, Aldino being the only other one to race off his proper mark. Royal Derbi was only a couple of pounds out though, and whereas See You Then and Aldino both ran a long way below their best he showed himself to be better than ever. In a truly-run race Royal Derbi led three out and ran on strongly to score by seven lengths from Don Valentino, with the remainder well strung out. Royal Derbi faced only two opponents in the Fred Rimell Hurdle at Hereford on his next start, and without being impressive he landed the odds readily enough from the juvenile Gay Ruffian and a below-par Mole Board. Royal Derbi, who hadn't been entered for the Champion Hurdle, wasn't seen out again for six weeks. Reappearing in the Huzzar Handicap Hurdle at Fairyhouse, he tried to make all the running but was worn down near the finish by Athy Spirit, who was receiving 28 lb. Royal Derbi turned the tables on Athy Spirit on terms 4 lb better at Punchestown the following week. On this occasion Royal Derbi didn't take up the running until the sixth and, running on gamely under pressure, he always looked like holding on in the straight, a good jump at the last clinching matters. At the post Royal Derbi had two and a half lengths to spare over Glamorous Gale, with Athy Spirit a further length away in third. Royal Derbi's season ended with a defeat in the Swinton Insurance Trophy at Haydock, where the ground rode very firm. Although he'd won on a similar surface early on in his juvenile career Royal Derbi has yet to prove that he's fully effective on it. However, his mistake at the third could also have proved his undoing, for he was never going well afterwards and his jockey accepted the situation fully three flights from home. As to Royal Derbi's going requirements it can safely be said that he's effective on ground ranging from good to firm through to heavy.

Royal Derbi (b.g. 1985)	Derrylin (b 1975)	Derring-Do (b 1961)	Darius
			Sipsey Bridge
		Antigua (ch 1958)	Hyperion
			Nassau
	Royal Birthday (b 1976)	St Paddy (b 1957)	Aureole
			Edie Kelly
		Laroyso (ch 1967)	Lauso
			Royal China

Royal Derbi is the third foal of Royal Birthday, a stoutly-bred mare who showed no sign of ability in three outings on the Flat. Royal Birthday's first two foals, Quinn West Flyer (by Tudor Rhythm) and Hawkes Hill Flyer (by Nicholas Bill), were both lightly raced and apparently of little account. The second dam Laroyso, a fair winning stayer on the Flat, is responsible for the Norwegian One Thousand Guineas and Norwegian Oaks winner Laminia. Royal Derbi has raced only at two miles over hurdles and it seems likely that he'll prove best at around this distance. Given a strong gallop he's effective coming from off the pace, as he showed at Nottingham; otherwise forcing tactics probably suit him best. A small, workmanlike gelding who jumps well, Royal Derbi is thoroughly genuine. *N. A. Callaghan.*

ROYAL EFFIGY 7 b.g. Henbit (USA)–Queen's Penny (Queen's Hussar) [1989/90 16f^{2} 16f* 17f^{4}] close-coupled, workmanlike gelding: handicap hurdler: 89 easily landed the odds in 3-runner event at Uttoxeter in August: carried head high and found little on run-in previous month: moved badly to post final start (August): best at around 2m: acts on any going: has been successful for a claimer: usually bandaged. *R. J. Weaver.*

ROYAL ESTIMATE 4 br.g. Tender King–Nistona (Will Somers) [1989/90 16g^{3} 16d 16d^{3} 16m^{2}] neat gelding: half-brother to winning selling hurdler Lover's 102 Secret (by Skyliner): fair performer on Flat, winner 3 times at up to 1m in 1989 (usually blinkered): placed in juvenile hurdles and a novice hurdle, showing moderate form: best effort third start. *M. W. Easterby.*

ROYAL FAME 6 ch.g. Instant Fame–Royal Chanter (Virginia Boy) [1989/90 20s^{pu}] compact, workmanlike gelding: second foal: dam never ran: no sign of — ability in Irish NH Flat races in 1988/9: sold out of D. McNeilly's stable 2,000 gns Doncaster August Sales: bit backward, pulled up 4 out in novice hurdle at Bangor in December. *Mrs S. Minns.*

ROYAL FOREST 4 b.f. Royal Fountain–Princess Davinia (Saintly Song) [1989/90 16f^{pu} a18g] third foal: half-sister to 2 poor animals: dam bad plater: tailed — off in selling hurdle: dead. *J. Norton.*

ROYAL GOSSIP 8 ch.g. Le Bavard (FR)–Royal Intrigue (Royal Highway) c— [1989/90 20g*] compact, workmanlike gelding: type to carry condition: moderate 107 hurdler: won 5-runner event at Market Rasen in March by 2 lengths from James My Boy: modest novice chaser: stays well: acts on soft going. *Mrs I. McKie.*

ROYAL GREEK 8 ch.g. Royal Captive–Greek Empress (Royal Buck) c**107** [1989/90 c16g^{2} c16f^{ur} c16m* c16g^{3} c16v^{F} c20d c16m* c16g^{2}] strong, workmanlike — gelding: winning hurdler: won novice chases at Catterick in December and Hereford in April: should stay beyond 2m: acts on good to firm and soft going: broke a blood vessel fourth start: trained by G. Moore until after fifth outing. *M. C. Pipe.*

ROYAL GROOM 5 b.g. Coquelin (USA)–Adorable Princess (Royal Palace) [1989/90 16g] leggy gelding: poor maiden on Flat (pulled up lame in a seller in — 1989): sold out of I. Balding's stable 1,050 gns Ascot November Sales: bit backward, tailed off in novice hurdle at Kempton in January. *C. A. Horgan.*

ROYAL GURKHA 10 b.g. Royalty–Nepal (Indian Ruler) [1989/90 c25h^{2} c24m^{2} c24m^{3} c21m^{4} c24g^{3} c26m c26f^{3} c24d^{3} c25f^{2} c24g^{4}] tall, plain gelding: novice hurdler: poor chaser: stays 3¼m: acts on any going: races up with the pace. *R. G. Frost.* c97 —

ROYAL HALO (USA) 9 b.g. Halo (USA)–Lady Gordon (USA) (Royal Levee (USA)) [1989/90 16g^{F} 16f 16g^{pu} 18f^{3} 16m] workmanlike gelding: 5 lengths third behind Ketti in handicap at Fontwell in March, only form over hurdles. *J. V. Redmond.* 83

ROYAL HERO 9 b. or br.g. Heres–Royal Rondo (Prince Barle) [1989/90 21d^{5} 24m^{3} 24g^{4}] leggy, close-coupled gelding: winning hurdler: in frame in handicaps at Chepstow and Perth (amateur riders event) in April: suited by 2½m: acts on heavy going. *P. Leach.* 98

ROYAL ILLUSION 6 b.g. Creative Plan (USA)–Semper Fi (Above Suspicion) [1989/90 16g 16d^{pu} 16g] leggy, narrow gelding: smart juvenile hurdler in 1987/8: little show in handicaps in 1989/90: will stay beyond 2m: acts on soft going but best run on good ground: jumps well. *G. M. Moore.* —

ROYAL INVADER 6 b.g. Silly Prices–Fishermans Lass (Articulate) [1989/90 20g 18d 20g* 22d^{4} 20d^{4} 20m] angular gelding: showed ability over hurdles prior to winning novice event at Sedgefield in February: will prove best at up to 2½m: form only on a yielding surface. *R. W. Dods.* 87

ROYAL JESTER 6 b.g. Royal Fountain–Tormina (Tormento) [1989/90 22d] workmanlike non-thoroughbred gelding: first foal: dam unraced: needing race, pulled hard when behind in novice hurdle at Ayr in November. *R. McDonald.* —

ROYAL LIFE LINE 5 ch.g. Royal Match–Total Line (High Line) [1989/90 16f^{F} 17f^{pu}] small gelding: has failed to complete course in 4 races over hurdles, latest a seller. *A. Barrow.* —

ROYAL LYRIC 7 b.g. Royal Palace–Spanish Harpist (Don Carlos) [1989/90 16m^{5}] rangy gelding: well beaten all outings over hurdles. *Capt. J. A. George.* —

ROYAL MARENGO 7 b.h. Royal Boxer–Lady Zeta (Marengo) [1989/90 c20m^{ur} c20m^{3} c18m^{F}] workmanlike horse: no sign of ability. *J. M. Bradley.* c— x

ROYAL MEETING 6 b.m. Dara Monarch–Press Luncheon (Be Friendly) [1989/90 17h^{3}] tall, sparely-made mare: poor hurdler: not sure to stay much beyond 2m: acts on hard going. *D. J. G. Murray-Smith.* 69

ROYAL MERE 13 ch.g. Duc d'Orleans–Shady Venture (Eastern Venture) [1989/90 c20g] strong gelding: winning chaser: modest point-to-pointer nowadays: stays 2½m: acts on any going. *Mrs P. A. Rigby.* c— —

ROYAL MIAMI 5 b.m. Miami Springs–Royal Cup (Politico (USA)) [1989/90 16d^{4} 16g* 16d^{2} 18g* 16d 19s^{F} 16v^{F} 16d* 16f 19d^{pu}] small, lengthy mare: half-sister to winning hurdlers Curragh Breeze and Strike A Point (both by Furry Glen): dam never ran: successful over 9f on Flat: won handicap hurdles at the Curragh in November, Fairyhouse in January and Naas in March: well beaten in valuable handicap at Cheltenham later in March (took keen hold and hung left): stays 2¼m: acts on soft going (probably unsuited by firm). *Victor Bowens, Ireland.* 122

ROYAL MILE 5 b.g. Tyrnavos–Royal Rib (Sovereign Path) [1989/90 20g* 20f^{4} 20f^{2} 20h* 24g^{2} 24g^{5} 24m^{2} 25g^{2} 27d* 24g^{4} 20m* 22g^{5} 24f^{5} 27f^{2} 23f^{4}] tall, leggy gelding: won novice hurdles at Market Rasen (amateur riders) and Hexham in first half of season and handicap and novice event at Sedgefield: stays well: acts on hard ground and good to soft. *W. A. Stephenson.* 119

ROYAL NORMAN 14 b.g. Normandy–Ensign's Last (Dumbarnie) [1989/90 c25m c28g^{pu}] big gelding: poor chaser nowadays: wears blinkers. *A. H. Brisbourne.* c— —

ROYAL PAVILION 7 ch.g. Royalty–Manushi (Crozier) [1989/90 16g^{3} c16f c17d^{2} c18s^{4}] rangy gelding: novice hurdler: 7 lengths second to For The Grain in novice chase at Newbury in February: should stay beyond 2m: acts on soft going and good to firm. *F. Walwyn.* c92 92

ROYAL REFRAIN 5 ch.g. True Song–Polaris Royal (Fury Royal) [1989/90 16g] rangy, workmanlike gelding: has scope: will make a chaser: fourth foal: dam lightly-raced half-sister to 3 winners, notably top-class hunter chaser Spartan Missile: bit backward, behind in novice hurdle at Wincanton in January on debut. *Capt. T. A. Forster.* —

ROYAL RELIANCE 7 b.m. Rymer–Last Alliance (Honour Bound) [1989/90 20d^{pu} 20g^{pu}] rangy mare: chasing type: seventh in NH Flat race in 1988: tailed off —

Chatteris Fen Hurdle, Huntingdon—Royal Square jumps his way into favouritism for the Daily Express Triumph Hurdle

when pulled up 3 out in novice hurdles at Wolverhampton and Worcester. *S. Christian.*

ROYAL ROSCOE 7 b.g. Roscoe Blake–Normandy Sign (Normandy) [1989/90 16gpu 20g] robust gelding: lightly raced and no sign of ability. *A. H. Brisbourne.* —

ROYAL ROUSER 7 b.g. He Loves Me–Royal Sensation (Prince Regent (FR)) [1989/90 16gpu] leggy, sparely-made gelding: winning hurdler: well behind over fences: has been visored and worn a hood: has looked none too keen and isn't one to rely on: sold 1,100 gns Doncaster April Sales. *J. R. Fort.* c— § — §

ROYAL RUFFIN (USA) 6 ch.h. Snow Knight–Rubye Brooks (USA) (Bold Hour (USA)) [1989/90 20sF 16h2 16f*] angular ex-French horse: half-brother to 3 winners in USA: dam won at around 1m in USA: successful at up to 11f on Flat in France, including in 1989 (claimed out of C. Lerner's stable 41,000 francs (approx £3,992)): blinkered, landed the odds in 4-runner novice hurdle at Hexham in May: sold 3,400 gns Ascot June Sales. *M. C. Pipe.* 80 p

ROYAL SHEPHERD 7 br.g. Red Regent–Shepherds Bush (Shooting Chant) [1989/90 20f5 20d 22d5] smallish, leggy gelding: modest hurdler: below his best in 1989/90: probably stays 2¾m: acts on heavy going and has run creditably on hard: has worn blinkers. *G. B. Balding.* —

ROYAL SQUARE (CAN) 4 ch.c. Gregorian (USA)–Dance Crazy (USA) (Foolish Pleasure (USA)) [1989/90 16g* 16d* 16f] lengthy, good sort with scope: useful 2m winner on Flat: jumped well in the main when winning juvenile hurdle at Kempton in January and Chatteris Fen Hurdle at Huntingdon (made all to beat Good Spark 8 lengths) following month: outpaced approaching last when around 11 lengths tenth to Rare Holiday in Daily Express Triumph Hurdle at Cheltenham (gave impression he'll prove suited by further when conditions are fast): acts on firm and dead going: useful. *G. Harwood.* 126 p

ROYAL STING 4 b.g. Prince Bee–Dolly-Longlegs (Majority Blue) [1989/90 16f2 17f2 16d 16m3 16m3 20g3] sparely-made, angular gelding: half-brother to winning hurdler The Mississippian (by Tumble Wind): little worthwhile form on Flat: sold out of M. Fetherston-Godley's stable 2,200 gns Ascot July Sales: placed in varied company over hurdles, including selling: probably stays 2½m: acts on firm going: blinkered last 3 outings. *M. H. B. Robinson.* 77

ROYAL SUMMIT 5 b.g. Thatching–Hill of Tara (Royal Palace) [1989/90 16m] ex-Irish gelding: placed over sprint distances when trained by M. O'Toole: always behind in novice hurdle at Worcester in April. *N. A. Smith.* —

ROYAL TAFI 4 b.g. Tanfirion–Queen's Pet (Pall Mall) [1989/90 a18g^{pu}] poor maiden on Flat: pulled up lame in juvenile claiming hurdle at Southwell in March. *B. Richmond.* —

ROYAL TOM 13 b.g. Fury Royal–Nitty (Galliot) [1989/90 c21f^{F}] lightly-raced maiden point-to-pointer: little worthwhile form over hurdles: yet to get round in steeplechases. *C. W. Loggin.* c— —

ROYAL TREATY 6 ch.g. Tower Walk–Covenant (Good Bond) [1989/90 16g] leggy, close-coupled gelding: won 2m selling hurdle in 1987/8: sold out of E. Eldin's stable 700 gns Newmarket Autumn (1988) Sales: backward, well beaten in non-seller in October: acts on good to firm ground. *R. E. Peacock.* —

ROYAL TRIBUTE 5 ch.h. Ribdale–Dizzy Day (My Boy Willie) [1989/90 20m^{pu} 20g a24g c16g^{ur} c22d^{5} c20m c20h^{2}] big, lengthy horse: poor novice hurdler/chaser: stays 2½m: acts on hard ground: blinkered third start. *N. Chamberlain.* **c82** —

ROYALTY BAY 7 b.g. Royalty–Warham Trout (Barolo) [1989/90 24m^{4} 22v c20s^{5} c20d^{bd} c20d^{pu}] rangy gelding: poor novice hurdler/chaser: probably best at up to 21f. *J. L. Spearing.* c— 87

ROYAL UPHAM 5 b.g. Royal Boxer–Saucy Upham (Saucy Kit) [1989/90 F16g] second living foal: dam, half-sister to several winning jumpers, modest hurdler who stayed 3m: behind in NH Flat race at Kempton in February: yet to race over hurdles or fences. *Mrs H. Parrott.*

ROYAL VICTORY 5 ch.g. Abednego–Manister Lady (Carlburg) [1989/90 F16g] second foal: dam unraced: tailed off in NH Flat race at Market Rasen in April: dead. *J. J. Birkett.*

ROYAL WONDER 4 b.f. Welsh Saint–Collectors' Item (Run The Gantlet (USA)) [1989/90 18f^{2} 17f* 18f* 16g* 20g* 16f* 16s^{4} 16d^{2} 16f 20m 16g^{4} 18f*] leggy filly: claimed out of M. Ryan's stable £6,111 after winning 1¾m claimer on Flat in 1989: showed signs of temperament and variable form, but won juvenile hurdles at 110 §

Northern Junior Hurdle, Haydock—the blinkered Royal Wonder is accompanied by Valiant Dash in the early stages

Newton Abbot, Fontwell, Haydock and Cheltenham and novice claimer at Nottingham in first half of season and seller at Fontwell (bought in 7,400 gns) in May: suited by strongly-run race at 2m and stays 2½m: best form on firm ground: blinkered nowadays: sold 8,600 gns Ascot June Sales. *M. C. Pipe.*

ROYLE SPEEDMASTER 6 ch.g. Green Shoon–Cahermone Ivy (Perspex) [1989/90 19d4 20s 20d5] lengthy, workmanlike gelding: 5¾ lengths fifth behind Nick The Dreamer in novice handicap at Huntingdon in February, best effort over hurdles: claimer ridden. *J. A. C. Edwards.* 91

ROY PRINCE 7 b.g. Royal Blend–Kam Tsin Princess (Prince Regent (FR)) [1989/90 c17f* c17h3 c16f3 c20m3 c16m3 c20d2 c20m2] close-coupled, angular gelding: winning hurdler: won novice chase at Newton Abbot in July: ran creditably most subsequent starts: stays 2½m: probably acts on any going: claimer ridden. *W. Clay.* c84 —

ROYS DILEMMA 8 b.m. Bold Owl–Spartan's Girl (Spartan General) [1989/90 24mpu 20spu] leggy, sparely-made mare: winning hurdler: poor novice over fences: best form at around 2½m: acts on heavy going and good to firm: usually claimer ridden. *W. R. Sheedy.* c— —

ROY'S DREAM 7 b.g. Down The Hatch–Promising Dream (Dreamy Eyes) [1989/90 16g 20f5 17m*] rangy gelding with scope: second favourite, won 15-runner amateur riders maiden hurdle at Carlisle in April by 10 lengths from Stormseal Boy: stays 2½m: acts on good to firm going. *S. J. Leadbetter.* c— 95

ROZEL GAMBLE 9 b.g. Sunyboy–Gallic Counsel (Vulgan) [1989/90 22mpu 20m 22g5 25d] angular gelding: little sign of ability. *T. Casey.* —

RUADH ADHAR 4 b.f. Heroic Air–Rosemarkie (Goldhill) [1989/90 16g 17g] workmanlike, shallow-girthed filly: little form on Flat: jumped moderately when tailed-off last in juvenile hurdles. *J. S. Wilson.* —

RUBIE'S CHOICE 9 gr.g. Goldhill–Mini Vada (Menelek) [1989/90 c24d4] compact gelding: useful point-to-pointer, winner in February: fourth to 30-length winner Teaplanter in maiden hunter chase at Leicester in March. *M. G. Sheppard.* c92

RUBIKA (FR) 7 b.g. Saumon (FR)–Eureka III (FR) (Vieux Chateau) [1989/90 c16g2 c26m4 c24d5 24d5 c20v5 c25g* c28d* c32g* c22m] angular gelding: novice hurdler: much improved over fences in 1989/90 (formerly looked none too keen): made running when successful in handicaps at Wolverhampton, Kelso (amateur riders event) and Hexham (amateur ridden): suited by a good test of stamina: acts on heavy going: blinkered last 4 outings in 1988/9 and fourth and fifth starts: usually jumps well. *S. Mellor.* c112 —

RUBINS BOY 4 ch.g. Riberetto–Gaie Pretense (FR) (Pretendre) [1989/90 F16m F16f] second reported foal: dam French 1½m winner: unplaced in NH Flat races in March: yet to race over hurdles. *B. Smart.*

RUBY DAVIES 4 b.f. Ya Zaman (USA)–Tarpon Springs (Grey Sovereign) [1989/90 16dpu 16f4 16g*] light-framed filly: half-sister to a winning German jumper by Sea Hawk II: little form in poor company on Flat: sold out of J. Wilson's stable 1,600 gns Ascot August Sales: first worthwhile form over hurdles when winning 7-runner juvenile selling hurdle at Worcester (no bid) in May. *D. Burchell.* 87

RUBYDORA 6 b.m. Buckskin (FR)–Superdora (Super Slip) [1989/90 20g4 20d2 16g2 a20g2 20g3 c20gF c17m6 16g2 a20g* a20g2] rangy mare: placed several times in novice hurdles prior to winning novice claimer at Southwell in February: reportedly finished lame following month: no form in 2 novice chases, jumping slowly and taking little interest on latter occasion: will stay 3m: acts on good to firm and dead ground: has been visored, blinkered last 3 outings: has been mulish in preliminaries and is no battler. *M. H. Easterby.* c— § 94 §

RUBY SHOES 4 b.f. Day Is Done–Very Seldom (Rarity) [1989/90 16d 16gpu] smallish, sparely-made filly: first foal: dam placed over hurdles in Ireland: 1m winner on Flat: well beaten in novice claiming hurdle at Sedgefield in December. *R. Bastiman.* —

RUDDA STAR 5 b.m. General David–Glaven (Blakeney) [1989/90 F16d] third foal: dam poor novice hurdler: behind in NH Flat race at Catterick in February: yet to race over hurdles or fences. *Roy Robinson.*

RUDOLPH MOLE 7 ch.g. Takachiho–Hidden Best (Don't Look) [1989/90 c16g6 c16f4 c20fF] small, leggy gelding: modest form in point-to-points: winning hunter chaser: best form at 2m on a sound surface. *Capt M. Watson.* c83 —

Mr Trevor Hemmings' "Rubika"

RUE DE CHAILLOT 4 b.g. Al Nasr (FR)–Heidi Badgett (USA) (Raise A
Native) [1989/90 $18s^{pu}$] first foal: dam minor 6f winner at 2 yrs in USA: tailed off —
when pulled up fifth in juvenile hurdle at Fontwell in January: sold 1,250 gns Ascot
February Sales. *N. J. Henderson.*

RUE ST JACQUES 7 b.g. Chukaroo–Solsbury Hill (Firestreak) [1989/90 **c79**
c$16m^{3}$ c$17m^{pu}$ 16h $16f^{pu}$] lengthy, sparely-made gelding: winning hurdler: pulled —
up reportedly lame in selling handicap final start (October): 10 lengths third of 5
behind Rathnageera Castle in novice chase at Worcester in September: races only
at around 2m: acts on hard going: blinkered first 2 starts 1987/8 and last outing. *B.
Smart.*

RUGESSTINO 9 b.g. Rugantino–Bay Princess (Bay King) [1989/90 c$20s^{pu}$] c—
sturdy gelding: poor maiden point-to-pointer: behind when pulled up in hunter
chase in February. *A. G. Sanderson.*

RUGGED BARON 9 b.g. Rugged Man–Burlington Miss (Burlington II) c—
[1989/90 c$24f^{4}$] tall gelding: in frame in point-to-points and novice hunter chases: —
seems of little account over hurdles: sold 3,000 gns Ascot June Sales. *V.
Thompson.*

RUGGED SPIRIT 10 gr.g. Rugantino–Express Spirit (Pony Express) c—
[1989/90 c$17h^{2}$] compact gelding: winning hurdler/chaser: reportedly finished —
lame when beaten a distance by sole opponent in amateur riders handicap chase at
Devon & Exeter in August and wasn't seen out again: stays 3¼m: acts on hard
ground and is possibly unsuited by soft. *S. F. Turton.*

RULER'S GOLD 6 b.g. Majestic Maharaj–Treasury (Henry The Seventh)
[1989/90 F16g 16g] lengthy, unfurnished gelding: seventh foal: half-brother to a —
poor animal by Streak: dam of little account: behind in NH Flat race at Uttoxeter
in December: blinkered, tailed off in novice hurdle at Wincanton following month:
sold 1,050 gns Ascot February Sales. *P. J. Hobbs.*

RULING DYNASTY 6 br.g. Ile de Bourbon (USA)–Bahariva (FR) (Sir c99
Gaylord (USA)) [1989/90 c17f* c20f* c16m^{3} 16f^{3} 17g*] small gelding: fair hurdler: 115
returned to his best when winning easily at Devon & Exeter in October, but
wasn't seen out again: landed the odds in 3-runner novice chases at Newton Abbot
(jumped deliberately) and Plumpton (jumped to the right and made mistakes) in
September: best form at up to 2¼m: has run moderately on heavy ground, acts on
any other: blinkered nowadays: seems best held up. *M. C. Pipe.*

RULING (USA) 4 b.c. Alleged (USA)–All Dance (USA) (Northern Dancer)
[1989/90 F16g* F16m^{2} F16d*] compact colt: second foal: half-brother to novice
hurdler Arctic Cider (by Arctic Tern): dam winner over 1m in France and later
placed in USA: won NH Flat races at Kempton in February and Ayr (well-contested event) in April: strong-finishing ¾-length second to Going On in
Seagram Supreme NH Flat Race at Liverpool in between: yet to race over
hurdles. *R. J. Holder.*

RUN AGAIN 5 br.h. Runnett–Bee Hawk (Sea Hawk II) [1989/90 16g^{2} 16m^{4}]
compact horse: sixth foal: brother to 2m chase winner Telemachus: dam quite a 91
useful stayer: won over 9f and placed over 1½m on Flat in Ireland in 1988: in frame
in novice hurdles at Cheltenham (wandered) and Ludlow (carried head high) in
January: jumps none too fluently. *M. Bradstock.*

RUN AND BECOME 5 b.h. Niniski (USA)–Gone Gay (Crepello) [1989/90
F16f F16g] tall horse: has scope: half-brother to useful 7f and 1m winner
Ganimede and winning hurdler Ruby Wine (both by Red God): dam stayed 1½m:
well beaten in NH Flat races at Newbury and Sandown in first half of season: yet
to race over hurdles or fences. *A. R. Davison.*

RUN AND SKIP 12 b.g. Deep Run–Skiporetta (Even Money) [1989/90 c28g^{4} **c137**
c24g^{2}] lengthy gelding: useful front-running chaser nowadays: still carrying —
condition, led until 5 out and stayed on when going down by 10 lengths to Bonanza
Boy in limited handicap at Chepstow in December: stays well: acts on any going:
tends to make mistakes and has shown a tendency to jump to his right: game and
genuine. *J. L. Spearing.*

RUNAWAY TRAIN 7 ch.g. Deep Run–Apair (Red Slipper) [1989/90 c16m^{pu} c70 x
c16d^{5} c16s^{4} c16g^{pu} c16g^{5} c16f^{ur}] lengthy, workmanlike gelding: modest novice —
hurdler and poor novice chaser: dead. *R. J. Hodges.*

RUN BY 6 br.g. Runnett–Losenger (Wolver Hollow) [1989/90 16g 16g] medium-sized gelding: modest maiden miler on Flat (probably none too genuine): in rear in —
novice hurdles. *D. R. C. Elsworth.*

A. F. Budge Novices' Hurdle, Cheltenham—Run For Free (right) is too good for Xhai

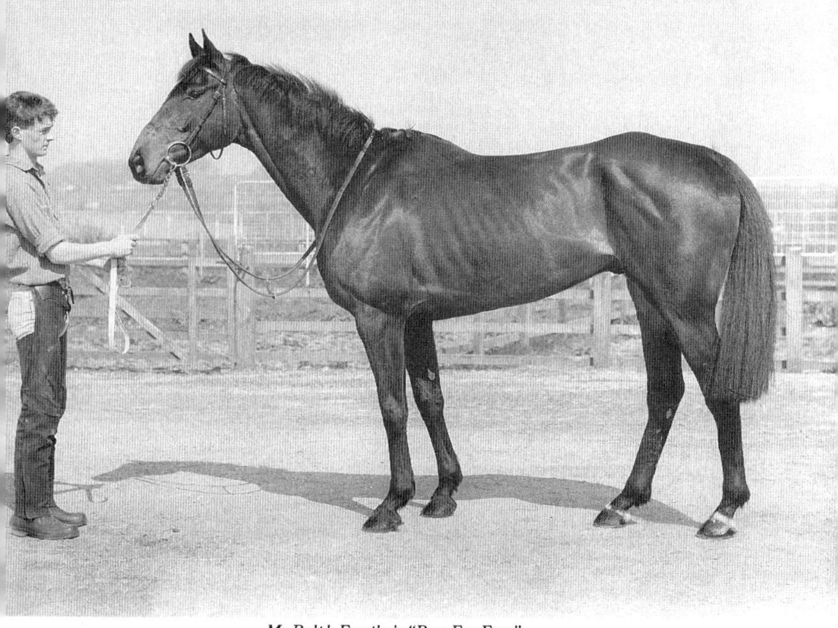

Mr Ralph Freethy's "Run For Free"

RUNCIBLE 6 ch.g. Deep Run–Lady Dromara (Lord of Verona) [1989/90 c17gur c24m c20g6 c20m5] strong, good-bodied gelding with scope: poor novice chaser. *Andrew Turnell.* c**72** —

RUN ETOILE 6 ch.m. Deep Run–Etoile de Lune (Apollo Eight) [1989/90 17m] sturdy mare: lightly-raced novice hurdler: no form. *J. A. Hellens.* —

RUN FOR FREE 6 b.g. Deep Run–Credit Card (Current Coin) [1989/90 c20g2 a20g* 16f* 20g* 21s* 20f4 20f6] c**110** p 137

All-weather jumps racing came to Britain in 1989/90. More precisely, hurdle racing on an all-weather surface came to two courses, Lingfield with its Equitrack and Southwell with its Fibresand; as yet there's been no attempt to stage a chase, nor has there been a serious test of the surface from the elements. The all-weather wasn't popular with the racegoer. Attendances at both courses were extremely low during the winter, and those who made the effort saw a plethora of low-grade cards. The best horse on view outside the Lingfield March 17th meeting, which was of necessity switched from turf, was Run For Free, winner of a novice hurdle at Southwell in November. He possesses ability way above that normally found there and went on to extend his winning run to four in two visits to Cheltenham and another to Warwick. The Coventry City Novices' Trial Hurdle at Warwick in February, which he took by twenty lengths from Holy Joe, is quite a valuable race. It had been won in the previous two years by Sayfar's Lad and Rebel Song, both winners afterwards of the Sun Alliance Novices' Hurdle at the Cheltenham Festival. Run For Free put up a creditable performance in the same race at the Festival in finishing fourth to his stable-companion the favourite Regal Ambition, beaten just under sixteen lengths. On that form he had a better chance than most in the Mumm Prize

Novices' Hurdle at Liverpool three weeks later, but he failed to take any advantage of odds-on shot Forest Sun's lack-lustre showing and didn't make the frame. He drifted to 7/1 from half the price, and was probably past his best.

Run For Free (b.g. 1984)	Deep Run (ch 1966)	Pampered King (b 1954)	Prince Chevalier
			Netherton Maid
		Trial By Fire (ch 1958)	Court Martial
			Mitrailleuse
	Credit Card (b 1971)	Current Coin (b 1963)	Hook Money
			Frances
		Tarkita (br 1966)	Black Tarquin
			Nikita

It's not clear where Run For Free's future lies, although he's now too good to run in most races on the all-weather. His one and only race over fences, at Newbury in November on his first outing for his present stable (he was formerly with Turnell), produced a curate's egg of a performance. He held out promise of beating French Goblin until he hit the second last hard; then, not for the first time, he hung markedly left on the run-in, and didn't go through with his effort. He had a reputation for being untrustworthy at that stage of his career but put that behind him when returned to hurdling, his run at Liverpool the only slight blemish on his subsequent record. It was thought he needed to be able to dominate to produce his best, yet in the Sun Alliance he hung on well behind Regal Ambition after that horse had thwarted him early on. If Run For Free does remain over hurdles he starts the season on a favourable mark. A lengthy, sparely-made gelding, he stays at least twenty-one furlongs and acts on any going. He wears a severe bridle, presumably to help the jockey prevent his hanging. On a couple of occasions the manner in which Run For Free has finished the course suggested that a distance of twenty-one furlongs may not be the limit of his stamina. On the pedigree side there's plenty of encouragement for stamina—his dam finished third in the Irish Grand National and his half-brother Bankers Benefit (by Le Bavard) finished second. *M. C. Pipe.*

RUN FREE 5 b.g. Julio Mariner–Lucky Appeal (Star Appeal) [1989/90 16g^{F}] sparely-made gelding: won selling hurdle in 1988/9: changed hands 4,400 gns Doncaster November Sales: very stiff task, in process of running good race when falling 2 out in L'Oreal Handicap won by Fragrant Dawn at Newbury in December: will stay beyond 2m: acts on heavy going. *R. Guest.* —

RUN HIGH 7 b.g. Thatch (USA)–Fleet Noble (USA) (Vaguely Noble) [1989/90 16s 16s 16m] good-bodied gelding: modest middle-distance stayer on Flat: fair hurdler: not at all knocked about once beaten in handicaps on first 2 starts but ran moderately on good to firm going in William Hill Imperial Cup at Sandown on third: will be suited by further: acts on heavy going. *P. Mitchell.* 114

RUN LEAH RUN 11 b.g. Deep Run–Thrifty Pat (Even Money) [1989/90 c24d^{pu}] strong gelding: winning hurdler/chaser: needing race, tailed off when pulled up in hunter chase in February: stays well: acts on any going: has run well for a claimer: suited by forcing tactics. *John R. Wilson.* c— —

RUNNER DUCK 4 ch.g. On Your Mark–Khaki Campbell (USA) (Quack (USA)) [1989/90 16f 16f^{6} 16m^{6}] small gelding: plating-class maiden on Flat and over hurdles: sold 875 gns Ascot April Sales. *G. B. Balding.* 78

RUNNETT FOR CASH 4 b.f. Runnett–Melissa Claire (Camden Town) [1989/90 16f^{5}] small, light-framed filly: plating class and none too genuine performer on Flat, dead-heated over 1m in August (has been blinkered): jumped poorly and well beaten in selling hurdle at Leicester in November: sold 1,100 gns Doncaster January Sales. *Mrs J. R. Ramsden.* —

RUNNING FORTUNE 5 b.m. Goldhills Pride–Kingdom Come (Klondyke Bill) [1989/90 16m 27s^{5} 20g^{5}] poor novice hurdler: has run in a seller: best effort at 2m on top-of-the-ground. *G. M. Moore.* 68

RUNNING SANDS 6 b.g. Record Run–Sirette (Great Nephew) [1989/90 16f^{6} 20g^{5} 16g^{6} c18s^{5} c20m^{F} c20f^{3} c24f^{5}] rangy gelding: poor hurdler: has shown plenty of ability in novice chases: ran better than position at finish indicates when fifth in Royal Fern Novices' Chase at Ascot in April, leading from the third until tiring significantly after 3 out: stays 2½m: acts on any going: should win a novice chase when returned to distances short of 3m. *J. T. Gifford.* c**100** —

RUN 'N SEEK 6 ch.g. Deep Run–Gift Seeker (Status Seeker) [1989/90 17g2 16f3 16m6 16f3 a20g2] angular, workmanlike ex-Irish gelding: first foal: dam winner on Flat and over hurdles in Ireland: novice hurdler: jumped moderately and finished lame when second at Southwell in November: best form at around 2m: acts on firm ground: trained until after third outing by A. Moore. *N. Miller.* 88

RUN OF GOLD 5 ch.m. Deep Run–The Ceiriog (Deep Diver) [1989/90 F12m] third foal: sister to winning hurdler Run of Weld: dam won several races over hurdles at up to 23f, notably Swedish Champion Hurdle: tailed off in NH Flat race at Bangor in October: yet to race over hurdles or fences. *W. G. Morris.*

RUN OF WELD 7 ch.g. Deep Run–The Ceiriog (Deep Diver) [1989/90 16g4 16m3 16f4 22m5 17g5] lengthy, dipped-backed gelding: poor hurdler: best form at 2m: acts on soft going and possibly unsuited by hard: usually races freely. *W. G. Morris.* 81

RUN ON STIRLING 6 b.m. Celtic Cone–Night Action (Dusky Boy) [1989/90 16m3 16f3] lengthy, unfurnished mare: poor novice hurdler: races only at around 2m: acts on firm ground. *C. P. E. Brooks.* 79

RUN PET RUN 5 ch.m. Deep Run–Tierna's Pet (Laurence O) [1989/90 16g 22g 22d 16s4 16g 16g] workmanlike mare: poor novice hurdler. *J. N. Beck.* 59

RUN ROUND THE PARK 5 ch.g. Deep Run–Miel Crepe (Counsel) [1989/90 F16m] half-brother to winning hurdler Rose of The Sea (by Diamonds Are Trump): dam lightly raced and little sign of ability on Flat in Ireland: tailed off in NH Flat race at Towcester in January: yet to race over hurdles or fences. *D. Nicholson.*

RUN TO FORM 5 br.g. Deep Run–Let The Hare Sit (Politico (USA)) [1989/90 16g* 16s2 20d* 16d6 20d] compact, workmanlike gelding: successful in novice hurdles at Ludlow in December and Wolverhampton in February: no impression from 3 out when modest sixth to Sacre d'Or in Crown Berger Hurdle at Chepstow in March: lost all chance when badly hampered after 3 out last start: suited by 2½m: acts on soft going. *Mrs J. Pitman.* 117

RUNUN 4 br.c. Sharpo–Silent Movie (Shirley Heights) [1989/90 16s6 16gpu] rather sparely-made colt: first foal: dam maiden half-sister to smart middle-distance horse and winning hurdler Rhyme Royal: fairly useful but inconsistent 7f winner on Flat: sold out of C. Brittain's stable 16,000 gns Newmarket Autumn Sales: showed a little ability when sixth in novice hurdle at Haydock in January, but never travelling well later in month: jumps none too fluently. *N. Tinkler.* —

RUN WEST 9 b.g. Record Run–Lush Gold (Goldhill) [1989/90 c24m5] workmanlike gelding: winning point-to-pointer, walked over in May: well-beaten fifth behind Teaplanter in novice hunter chase at Southwell in April. *Mrs M. D. Rebori.* c—

RUSCAROFF 4 gr.g. Rusticaro (FR)–Fair Or Foul (Patch) [1989/90 16m5 16d4 16g6 16g6 a16g4] quite modest maiden on Flat, stays 1½m: sold out J. Hills's stable 11,000 gns Newmarket Autumn Sales: poor form over hurdles: set too strong a pace and looked a difficult ride fourth start. *G. M. Moore.* 78

RUSCH DE FARGES (FR) 7 ch.g. Italic (FR)–Bielly (FR) (St Paddy) [1989/90 c20f5 c24s4 c24s6 c20f4 c20m] rangy gelding: winning hurdler: smart chaser, but is frequently let down by his jumping: weakened after 2 out when just over 9 lengths fourth to Nick The Brief in Peter Marsh Chase (limited handicap) at Haydock in January, second and best effort in 1989/90: stays 25f: acts on heavy going (not disgraced when fourth to Ida's Delight on firm ground at Ascot on fourth start). *M. C. Pipe.* c**150** x —

RUSHBEDS 11 b.g. Ercolano (USA)–Lichen Lady (Pardao) [1989/90 c24f3] angular gelding: modest winning point-to-pointer: novice hunter chaser: best form at 2m: acts on any going. *J. S. Payne.* c78 —

RUSHLUAN 6 gr.g. Kalaglow–Labista (Crowned Prince (USA)) [1989/90 16g 20g4 16g3 16v 17d*] sparely-made gelding: showed ability, including in a seller, prior to winning novice handicap hurdle at Newton Abbot in March by 1½ lengths from Fill The Jug: never dangerous on heavy ground previous start: races freely and may prove best at 2m: middle-distance winner on Flat in 1990. *R. J. Hodges.* 93

RUSINGA ISLAND 4 ch.f. Oats–Gretta's Girl (Arctic Kanda) [1989/90 16g 16fpu] small filly: fifth reported foal: dam won over hurdles: no promise over hurdles, including in fillies seller. *C. James.* —

RUSTIC COMEDY 5 br.g. Comedy Star (USA)–Cecilia Gallerani (Pinturischio) [1989/90 17d 19m 17d* 20s4 16sF 16f4] useful-looking gelding with some scope: fair hurdler: successful in handicap at Devon & Exeter in January: credit- 117 able fourth behind Moody Man in County Handicap Hurdle at Cheltenham in March, final outing: best at 2m: seems to act on any going: sometimes blinkered, including when successful: usually claimer ridden (not at Devon & Exeter). *D. R. C. Elsworth.*

RUSTINO 4 ch.c. Bustino–Miss Britain (Tudor Melody) [1989/90 16g 16g^{3} 20f^{3}
16g* 17g^{3} 17g 24d^{3}] workmanlike colt: half-brother to 2 winners, including 95
winning hurdler Yozzer Hughes (by Tumble Wind): modest stayer on Flat, winner in 1990: won juvenile hurdle at Wetherby in December: ran creditably when placed afterwards: needs plenty of use making of him at 2m and stays 3m: acts on dead going: unseated rider going down third start. *A. M. Robson.*

RUSTSTONE 10 b.h. Rustingo–Newstown (London Gazette) [1989/90 c16d^{2} c**117**
c20m c24g^{F} c19s* c20d^{6} 24v^{3} c20s^{3} c19s^{2} c20d^{4} c25m^{pu} c25f^{F4} c20m^{2} 25f] 117
leggy, lightly-made, plain horse: fair chaser: won at Hereford in December: looked probable winner when falling last on same course in April: tailed off in handicap hurdle last start: best form at around 2½m: ideally suited by give in the ground and acts on heavy: ridden by 7-lb claimer: suited by forcing tactics: tends to jump none too fluently and to his right on occasions: genuine. *R. L. Brown.*

RUSTY LAW 8 gr.g. Rusticaro (FR)–La Loie Fuller (FR) (Rheffic (FR))
[1989/90 16s^{3} 22g^{4}] lengthy, lightly-made gelding: modest hurdler: in frame in 103
handicaps at Huntingdon in December and Windsor (still bit backward) in January: stays 2¾m: acts on good to firm and dead going: claimer ridden. *M. C. Banks.*

RUSTY ROC 9 b.g. Rustingo–La Chica (El Cid) [1989/90 16g 20d 16f 16g* 17v^{3} c—
16s^{4} 16d*] lightly-made gelding: fair hurdler: won at Ludlow (hung left flat) in 124
December and Chepstow in March: front runner, suited by around 2m: acts on any going: has run creditably when sweating: game and genuine. *M. W. Davies.*

RUSTYS SPECIAL 8 ch.m. Rustingo–Newstown (London Gazette) [1989/90 c—
17m] sparely-made mare: novice selling hurdler: jumped poorly and was tailed off —
when falling 4 out in mares novice event on chasing debut: will prove best at 2m on a sharp track: acts on dead going. *M. Brown.*

RUTHS PRIDE 5 ch.m. Amboise–Ruths Image (Grey Love) [1989/90 F16g] small mare: fourth foal: half-sister to winning hurdlers Ruths Magic (by Current Magic) and Ruths Love (by Barbaro): dam poor novice hurdler: soon tailed off in NH Flat race at Ludlow in December: yet to race over hurdles or fences. *G. M. Price.*

RUTH'S STAR 7 br.m. Uncle Pokey–Cool Vixen (Shackleton) [1989/90 16f^{2}
16f a16g^{6} 16f^{pu}] poor novice hurdler. *C. R. Beever.* 57 ?

RU VALENTINO 6 ch.g. Deep Run–Tape Mary (Even Money) [1989/90 20m^{5}
25d^{5} 20m* 24m*] leggy, rather angular gelding: will make a chaser: favourite, 105 p
won novice hurdles at Uttoxeter in March and April: stays 3m: yet to race on extremes of going, acts on any other. *J. A. C. Edwards.*

RYDE AGAIN 7 ch.g. Celtic Cone–Rydewell (Blast) [1989/90 16f* c20v^{F} c—
16g^{3} 24g^{2} 24s* 25m^{F}] 146

There were few more misleading performances during the season than the one put up by Ryde Again in a minor event at Leicester in November on his reappearance. Having looked a stayer when third in the 1989 Coral Golden Hurdle Final at Cheltenham, Ryde Again at first glance gave the impression at Leicester that he still had prospects of winning a good race at two miles over hurdles, sprinting ten lengths clear of the odds-on Milford Quay in the closing stages. Ryde Again could hardly have been more impressive in the manner of his victory but Milford Quay, who was conceding 10 lb, looked to run some way below his best and by our reckoning Ryde Again had improved only marginally on his previous form at the trip. So it was no surprise that Ryde Again's limitations at two miles should be exposed in the New Year's Day Hurdle at Windsor, in which he finished third behind Aldino, and that he should then be returned to racing at three miles. Ryde Again put up two very useful performances at the longer trip, both of them at Ascot. In the Munns Electrical Hurdle in January Ryde Again was the only one to make a race of it with Calabrese. The latter looked a handicap snip running off the same mark as when successful by fifteen lengths at Cheltenham on his previous start, and he started at odds on. Ryde Again pressed Calabrese strongly in the home straight and was still in with a

Daily Telegraph Hurdle, Ascot—a gutsy display from Ryde Again (foreground) to turn the tables on Calabrese

chance at the last, but Calabrese, in receipt of a stone from Ryde Again, held the latter's challenge by three lengths. Ryde Again took his revenge when the pair met at level weights in the Daily Telegraph Hurdle the following month. Held up, as he usually is, Ryde Again stayed on strongly under pressure to lead approaching the last, and he went on to win by three lengths from Calabrese. Crimson Embers and Rose Ravine, two previous winners of this Ascot race, had gone on to take the Waterford Crystal Stayers' Hurdle at Cheltenham, Ryde Again's next race. Ryde Again, who started favourite, was just behind the leaders but being scrubbed along when he fell at the second last. This was Ryde Again's second fall of the season. The first occurred on his chasing debut in a novice event at Haydock in December. Ryde Again gave the first fence plenty of daylight but hardly rose at the next, taking a crashing fall and bringing down another runner. If he's seen out over fences again it won't be before the turn of the year, his trainer having earmarked him for some valuable hurdle races in the first half of the season, notably the Youngmans Long Walk Hurdle at Ascot in December which will have £40,000 in added prize money.

Ryde Again (ch.g. 1983)	Celtic Cone (ch 1967)	Celtic Ash (ch 1957)	Sicambre
			Ash Plant
		Fircone (ch 1959)	Mossborough
			Wood Fire
	Rydewell (ch 1964)	Blast (b 1957)	Djebe
			Gale Warning
		Arceeno (ch 1953)	Arciere
			Avageeno

Ryde Again, bred by his owner, is the eighth of ten living foals produced by the splendid broodmare Rydewell, who was put out of stud in 1986. Apart from Ryde Again, Rydewell is best known as the dam of Celtic Ryde (a full brother to Ryde Again) and Noddy's Ryde (by Tom Noddy), two of the most popular jumpers of the 'eighties. The former, also trained by Cundell, was a top-class hurdler who could produce a telling burst of speed in the closing stages after being ridden with restraint, the latter a good chaser who blazed the trail. They were both best at two miles, while their half-sister Private Well (by Privy Seal) gained her only successes over hurdles at that trip. Rydewell, herself a useful two-mile juvenile hurdler, is a daughter of the fair staying hurdler Arceeno, the latter a half-sister to the smart staying chaser Bowgeeno. Rydewell's last two foals are stable-companions of Ryde Again's. Rydewells Daughter, also by Celtic Cone, has shown only poor form in novice hurdles, while the four-year-old filly Broad Ryde (by Broadsword) has yet to race. The consistent Ryde Again, a lengthy, workmanlike gelding, is suited by strong handling.He acts on any going. *P. D. Cundell.*

RYDENE 7 b.m. Rymer–Deepness (Deep Run) [1989/90 20m^{pu} 16f^{6}] sturdy mare: yet to complete course in point-to-points (refused once): little promise in novice hurdles at Huntingdon (trained by J. King) and Towcester in the spring. *Dr P. Pritchard.* —

RYDEWELLS DAUGHTER 5 ch.m. Celtic Cone–Rydewell (Blast) [1989/90 16f^{3} 16g 21v^{6} 16s 22f^{pu}] lengthy, unfurnished mare: has scope: sister to high-class 2m hurdler Celtic Ryde and very useful staying hurdler Ryde Again, and half-sister to several other winners, notably high-class 2m chaser Noddy's Ryde (by Tom Noddy): dam quite a useful hurdler: only form in novice hurdles when third at Leicester on debut: seemed not to stay 21f. *P. D. Cundell.* 78

RYDWELLS-STAR 11 ch.m. Precipice Star–Rydwell (Never Dwell) [1989/90 21h^{F} 21f* 21f* 21f^{2}] workmanlike mare: poor maiden point-to-pointer: won novice hurdles at Devon & Exeter (handicap) and Newton Abbot in August: beaten a distance when second to Waafi in novice handicap on latter course in September: fell second on steeplechasing debut: stayed 21f: acted on firm ground: in foal to Sula Bula. *B. Forsey.* c— 89

RYECROFT 12 b.g. Condorcet (FR)–Moonlight Story (Narrator) [1989/90 c21g^{ur} c20f^{pu}] sparely-made gelding: winning hurdler: modest novice chaser: probably stays 2¾m: probably acts on any going: sometimes wears a tongue strap: blinkered twice in 1986/7: has won for a claimer: sometimes makes mistakes. *B. Ellison.* c— x —

RYE SPIRIT 4 b.c. Meldrum–Bath Miss (Appiani II) [1989/90 16f] brother to moderate hurdler Albert The Great: dam won over 7f at 2 yrs: slow-starting last of 8 in juvenile hurdle at Hexham in September. *Mrs P. A. Barker.* —

RYMER KING 8 b.g. Rymer–Belinda Pocket (Pampered King) [1989/90 20d^{pu} c25m* c25g* c25d^{4} c24d^{3}] leggy, workmanlike gelding: has been operated on for soft palate: modest hurdler: won handicap chases at Wolverhampton in December and January: made a few mistakes and ridden from some way out when moderate third at Huntingdon in February: out of his depth penultimate outing: stays 25f: probably acts on any going. *J. Chugg.* **c114** + —

RYMING JACK 4 gr.g. Rymer–Jack's Love (Grey Love) [1989/90 F16g] second foal: dam never ran: well-beaten seventh in NH Flat race at Kelso in March: yet to race over hurdles. *T. D. Barron.*

RYMOLBREESE 5 gr.m. Rymer–Moll (Rugantino) [1989/90 a20g^{4} a16g^{4} 16f] angular mare: poor novice hurdler: probably stays 2½m. *Mrs S. Oliver.* 70

RYMSTER 7 b.g. Rymer–Funny Baby (Fable Amusant) [1989/90 c16g^{6}] tall, rather sparely-made gelding: useful hurdler: made a few mistakes, including a bad one at the eighth, and wasn't knocked about afterwards when behind in novice chase won by Decided at Kempton in January: unlikely to stay beyond 2m: acts on dead going. *N. J. Henderson.* c— —

RYNODE 7 b.m. Rymer–Pernel (Space King) [1989/90 c20m*] angular mare: placed in a point-to-point: left well clear as Riva Rose ran out at the last when winning novice chase at Wolverhampton in December by 20 lengths from Pertemps Network: stays 2½m: acts on good to firm going: takes a keen hold and jumps rather low on occcasions: looked sure to win more races over fences, but wasn't seen out again. *R. Lee.* **c106**

RYTON GUARD 5 br.g. Strong Gale–Gardez Le Reste (Even Money) [1989/90 16g 16g 16m^{4}] rather sparely-made gelding: sixth foal: half-brother to winning Irish hurdler Announcement (by Laurence O) and winning Irish point-to-pointer First Attempt (by Proverb): dam won over hurdles and fences: poor form in novice hurdles. *S. Christian.* 78

RYTON RUN 5 b.g. Deep Run–Money Spinner (Even Money) [1989/90 16m 16g^{2} 21f 16g^{2}] lengthy gelding: brother to winning chaser Downhill Run: dam winning hurdler: runner-up in novice hurdles at Fakenham in February and Uttoxeter in May: well beaten over 21f: sold 16,000 gns Doncaster Spring Sales. *Mrs D. Haine.* 86

S

SAADOUN (FR) 7 br.g. Grandchant (FR)–Rose Valery (FR) (Carvin) [1989/90 16g4 16g] ex-French gelding: third foal: half-brother to Blue Mink (by Jefferson), French winner at up to 1¼m: dam French 1½m winner: little form in 5 races on Flat when trained by F. Palmer: poor form in novice hurdles. *Mrs P. Sly.* 71

SABAKI RIVER 6 br.g. Idiot's Delight–Keen Lass (Andrea Mantegna) [1989/90 16gF 16g4] leggy, unfurnished gelding: has scope: second foal: dam, bad plater on Flat, behind only outing over hurdles: closing on eventual winner General Glory when falling last in novice hurdle at Newbury in November: better for race, not knocked about when 10 lengths fourth to Villa Recos at Windsor 2½ months later: withdrawn after bolting before start on intended hurdling debut in October (taken down early at Windsor): takes good hold and wears crossed noseband. *Mrs J. G. Retter.* 92 p

SABDABEANI 5 b.h. Good Times (ITY)–Canvas Shoe (Hotfoot) [1989/90 16g 16mur 17g 16h5 16f] compact horse: winning selling hurdler: no form in 1989/90: likely to prove best over sharp 2m on a sound surface: edged left and found little final start 1988/9: trained until after second start by J. H. Johnson. *N. Waggott.* —

SABIN DU LOIR (FR) 11 b.g. Go Marching (USA)–Star Light (FR) (Val de Loir) [1989/90 20f4 c20s* c20s* c20d* c16f4 c20f4] c155 —

In his second season over fences Sabin du Loir showed form very nearly the equal of his best over hurdles. Which is to say he developed into a good-class chaser. He is still the same bold-jumping front runner and continues to race with plenty of zest. Sabin du Loir ran his rivals into the ground when winning a qualifier of the Arlington Premier Chase series at Haydock in December by twenty lengths from Blazing Walker and when successful in a three-runner intermediate chase on the same course the following month by fifteen lengths from Swardean. He had to work harder to pick up one of the biggest prizes for first- and second-season chasers in the final of the Arlington series at Cheltenham in January. Going downhill from the fourth-last fence, Sabin du Loir looked to have taken the measure of the useful handicapper Midnight Train and Waterloo Boy, who had beaten him into third place in the Arkle Challenge Trophy over a half mile shorter trip the previous season. But the novice Celtic Shot, favourite and ridden by Scudamore in preference to Sabin du Loir, looked far from done with as he moved up to take the advantage with a good jump at the third from home. Switched to the outside after a mistake at that fence, Sabin du Loir rallied strongly. He regained a narrow lead after the next and stayed on very well

Arlington Premier Series Chase (Final), Cheltenham—
Sabin du Loir (left) proves too good for leading novice Celtic Shot

Mr B. A. Kilpatrick's "Sabin du Loir"

despite hanging left up the hill to win driven out by two and a half lengths, the pair twenty-five lengths clear. Sabin du Loir finished a good fourth to Barnbrook Again on two subsequent appearances at Cheltenham in conditions previously considered less than ideal for him. Over two miles on firm ground in the Queen Mother Champion Chase in March he was beaten just over eight lengths. Having led until three out he was outpaced only after a mistake at the last. Sabin du Loir ran up to his best when beaten around twenty lengths in the South Wales Showers Caradon Mira Silver Trophy Chase the following month, conceding 10 lb to second and third Pegwell Bay and Ida's Delight.

Sabin du Loir (FR) (b.g. 1979)	Go Marching (USA) (b 1965)	Princequillo (b 1940)	Prince Rose
			Cosquilla
		Leallah (br 1954)	Nasrullah
			Lea Lark
	Star Light (FR) (b 1966)	Val de Loir (b 1959)	Vieux Manoir
			Vali II
		Star Vixen (ch 1955)	Borealis
			Bronze Vixen

The French-bred Sabin du Loir is a half-brother to two winning jumpers in his native country and to the four-year-old Olnistar (by Balsamo), a fair hurdler who finished fourth to Forest Sun in the Waterford Crystal Supreme Novices' Hurdle at Cheltenham. Star Light won over eleven furlongs on the Flat in France. The next two dams won on the Flat in Britain, Star Vixen at up to two miles. Sabin du Loir won twice at up to a mile and three quarters in the French provinces as a three-year-old. Though no longer eligible for the Arlington series, Sabin du Loir should not lack suitable targets in the coming season thanks to the creation of several new valuable two-and-a-half-mile chases. Most of his best wins have been at two and a half miles, notably in the Sun Alliance Novices' Hurdle at Cheltenham in 1983 and in the Ascot Hurdle, currently sponsored by Racecall, in 1987 and 1988. Bidding for a hat-trick in the last-named event in the latest season, Sabin du Loir ran a rare moderate race—taken on in front, he dropped out once headed after the fourth last and finished a remote fourth to Nodform. Sabin du Loir seemed not to stay the trip when tried over three and a quarter miles in 1987/8. A rather lightly-made gelding with a very round action, he seems unsuited by heavy going but acts on any other. *M. C. Pipe.*

SABRE STAR 5 b. or br.m. Broadsword (USA)–Mexican Star (Master Buck) [1989/90 aF14g] first foal: dam, poor hurdler, half-sister to 3 winners, including useful staying chaser Zongalero: tailed-off last of 12 in NH Flat race at Southwell in November: yet to race over hurdles or fences. *J. Webber.*

SACRED GEM 5 b.g. Mr Fluorocarbon–Skerne Springs (Canadel II) [1989/90
16g* 16g^{bd} 16s^{3} 16f 16f^{pu}] leggy, workmanlike gelding: sixth foal: dam placed at 95
up to 1½m: successful in novice hurdle at Catterick in January: good eighth to Vazon Bay in quite valuable novice handicap at Cheltenham in April: dead. *M. J. Camacho.*

SACRE D'OR (USA) 5 b.g. Lemhi Gold (USA)–Dedicated To Sue (USA) (Su
Ka Wa) [1989/90 16g* 16d^{3} 17g^{3} 16d^{2} 16d* 16d^{4}] workmanlike gelding: looking 134
very well, won Crown Berger Hurdle at Chepstow in March by 7 lengths from Ri-Na-Rithann, leading 2 out and running on well: showed further improvement to finish 9 lengths fourth behind Sayparee in Scottish Champion Hurdle (limited handicap) at Ayr following month: successful earlier in novice event at Huntingdon: likely to prove best at around 2m: has raced only on an easy surface over hurdles: a very useful novice. *J. Mackie.*

SACRED PATH 10 b.g. Godswalk (USA)–Crepe Rose (FR) (Crepello) c**122**
[1989/90 c28g^{5} c29d^{pu} c33d^{pu}] fair chaser: lightly raced nowadays: showed he'd —
retained ability when fifth at Wolverhampton in February: pulled up next 2 outings, but was prominent for a long way on second occasion: well suited by a thorough test of stamina: acts on heavy going: blinkered final outing: jumps soundly in the main: front runner. *O. Sherwood.*

SADDIQUE 5 b.g. Skyliner–Danova (FR) (Dan Cupid) [1989/90 16m^{5}] small,
lightly-made gelding: won 17f juvenile selling hurdle early in 1988/9: well beaten —
since: blinkered final start 1988/9: sold 425 gns Ascot November Sales: resold privately 600 gns Doncaster January Sales. *S. N. Cole.*

SADDLER'S CHOICE 5 b.g. Buckskin (FR)–Lady Perry (David Jack)
[1989/90 20g^{4}] strong gelding: will make a chaser: sixth foal: dam winning 2m 85 p
hurdler/chaser in Ireland: claimer ridden, showed plenty of promise when around 13 lengths fourth behind Wise Customer in novice hurdle at Bangor in April, travelling strongly until lack of condition told 2 out: sold 25,000 gns Doncaster Spring Sales: sure to improve. *N. A. Gaselee.*

SAFE DISTANCE 5 ch.g. Lord Gayle (USA)–Our Sarah (Pampapaul)
[1989/90 21g^{pu} 16g^{pu}] smallish, good-quartered ex-Irish gelding: second foal: —
half-brother to winning Irish hurdler Son of Sarah (by Corvaro): dam showed a little ability at 2 yrs in Ireland: little sign of ability on Flat: behind when pulled up in minor hurdle at Newbury in December and novice event at Plumpton following month. *Miss P. O'Connor.*

SAFELY AWAY 7 ch.g. Politico (USA)–Carbia (Escart III) [1989/90 c27d^{pu}] c—
runner-up only completed start from 6 outings in point-to-points in 1989: no sign —
of ability over hurdles or in a steeplechase. *Miss S. J. Turner.*

SAFFRON PALM 6 b.g. Palm Track–New Saffron (New Member) [1989/90
16d 16s] rangy, useful-looking gelding: has scope and will make a chaser: no — p
worthwhile form over hurdles but has shown signs of ability: likely to be suited by return to further: sweating badly final start. *F. Walwyn.*

SAGAMAN (GER) 4 b.g. Solo Dancer (GER)–Scholastika (GER) (Alpenkonig
(GER)) [1989/90 16d 16g* 16g 16d^{2} 16m^{3} 16m] angular gelding: quite modest 106
middle-distance staying maiden on Flat (has been blinkered): always prominent when winning juvenile hurdle at Newcastle in December: looked a most difficult ride when second at Kelso in February, jumping badly right and hanging: visored, very stiff task final start: one to have reservations about. *L. J. Codd.*

SAGARO SUN 4 b.g. Sagaro–Star Alert (Red Alert) [1989/90 F16f] fourth foal: brother to a poor performer: dam a maiden: behind in NH Flat race at Huntingdon in May: yet to race over hurdles. *P. R. Hedger.*

SAGART AROON 10 b.g. The Parson–Mountain Bell (Pyrenean) [1989/90 c16d^{6}] small, sturdy gelding: novice hurdler/chaser: variable form, including in selling company: stays 2¾m: acts on dead going: moderate jumper of fences: sometimes blinkered or visored. *O. Brennan.* c— x — §

SAILING AROUND 5 b.m. Viking (USA)–Spinning Jenny (Timmy My Boy) [1989/90 18m^{F} 16m 19g 16g^{5} 16d^{pu}] neat mare: lightly raced and little form on Flat since 2 yrs: poor form over hurdles, including in selling handicap: visored first 2 outings, blinkered last 2: moderate jumper. *P. D. Evans.* 60 x

SAILOR BOY 4 b.c. Main Reef–Main Sail (Blakeney) [1989/90 16g] fair stayer on Flat: sold out of R. Hern's stable 30,000 gns Newmarket Autumn Sales: in need of race, jumped left, made mistakes and weakened after sixth having raced freely when well-beaten eighth behind Royal Square in juvenile hurdle at Kempton in January: should improve. *R. Akehurst.* — p

SAILORS BANK 7 b.g. Owen Anthony–Sylv (Calpurnius) [1989/90 16g 22d] little sign of ability: dead. *R. Brotherton.* —

SAILOR'S DELIGHT 6 b.g. Idiot's Delight–Sarasail (Hitting Away) [1989/90 20f^{2} 16d 16g 20g^{3} 20g^{3} c16m^{3} c17g^{3} c16f^{2}] close-coupled gelding: type to carry condition: novice hurdler/chaser: stays 2½m: acts on firm ground. *W. A. Stephenson.* c88 84

SAILORS GIRL 4 ch.f. Julio Mariner–Miss Colleen (Joshua) [1989/90 F13f 16g^{pu} 16f^{pu}] first foal: dam never ran: tailed off in NH Flat race and when pulled up in selling hurdles. *Mrs A. Knight.* —

SAILORS LUCK 5 b.g. Idiot's Delight–Sarasail (Hitting Away) [1989/90 16g^{4} 16g^{2} 21g 16g^{2}] sparely-made gelding: retained by trainer 13,000 gns Ascot August Sales: runner-up in novice hurdles at Towcester in December and Windsor (to Villa Recos) following month: races freely and is likely to prove best at 2m. *S. Dow.* 95

SAINTLY LAD 8 b.g. Derrylin–Saintly Miss (St Paddy) [1989/90 a20g^{4}] strong gelding: blinkered, first form in novice hurdles when fourth at Southwell in November. *P. D. Cundell.* 67

SAINTLY PATH 7 ch.g. Deep Run–Shuil Le Dia (Kabale) [1989/90 22d^{pu} 16s 16d c16v^{F} c16s c17g^{5}] strong ex-Irish gelding: chasing type: half-brother to useful Irish hurdler Gortnalee (by Menelek): dam, closely related to useful Irish hurdler/chaser Shuil Donn, won a bumpers event on Flat: won 2 NH Flat races in 1988: behind in novice hurdles and chases, being let down by his jumping over fences. *J. K. M. Oliver.* c— x —

SAINT SYSTEMS 4 b.f. Uncle Pokey–Fire Mountain (Dragonara Palace (USA)) [1989/90 16s^{pu}] workmanlike filly: poor sprinter on Flat, winner in 1990: bit backward, tailed off when pulled up in juvenile hurdle at Hereford in December. *R. J. Hodges.* —

SAINT TRISTAN 6 b.g. Tyrnavos–Greyburn (Saintly Song) [1989/90 16g] half-brother to winning hurdler and novice chaser Tremar Lad (by Monsanto): little worthwhile form on Flat: tailed-off last in novice event at Catterick in January on hurdling debut (wore crossed noseband). *W. W. Haigh.* —

SAIYYAAF 7 b.g. Thatching–Nana's Girl (Tin Whistle) [1989/90 16g 16d^{pu}] strong gelding: lightly raced and of little account. *A. W. Potts.* —

SAIZANO 8 b.g. Tyrant (USA)–Voir Tout En Beau (USA) (Cloudy Dawn (USA)) [1989/90 16g] leggy, lightly-made gelding: winning selling hurdler: behind in October: novice chaser: stays 2½m: yet to race on very firm ground, probably acts on any other: sold privately 3,675 gns Ascot May Sales. *J. C. Gillen.* c— —

SAKR 8 ch.g. Hotfoot–Grande Fille (Fortino II) [1989/90 17f* 17f^{2} 19h^{2} 17f* 17f* 16h* 16m* 17v a16g^{3} a16g 16s 19f^{6} 19f^{3}] lightly-made gelding: winning point-to-pointer and novice chaser: front-running hurdler who won 3 races at Newton Abbot (novice event, novice handicap and a handicap) and handicaps at Taunton (started slowly) and Bangor (reportedly sustained skinned leg): subsequently off course 2½ months, and only form afterwards on last 2 starts (found little final outing): stays 19f: acts on hard ground: visored once: sometimes taken early to post: very mulish in preliminaries on third outing. *Mrs J. Wonnacott.* c— 104

SALAMANDER JOE 5 br.g. Salluceva–Fast And Clever (Clever Fella) [1989/90 F16m^{6} 16g] workmanlike non-thoroughbred gelding: fifth foal: dam of little account on Flat in Ireland: sixth in NH Flat race at Ludlow in January: eighth in novice hurdle at Wolverhampton following month, looking green and not knocked about: should improve. *D. Nicholson.* — p

SALAMART 7 br.g. Aban–Hespera (Good Apple) [1989/90 19m^{ur} c20g^{pu}] rangy, rather sparely-made gelding: well beaten in NH Flat races: behind when unseating rider 2 out in novice event on hurdling debut and jumped poorly and tailed off when pulled up on chasing debut in first half of season. *Miss J. Thorne.* c— —

SALAR'S SPIRIT 4 ch.c. Salmon Leap (USA)–Indigine (USA) (Raise A Native) [1989/90 16g^{5}] medium-sized colt: closely related to winning selling hurdler Below Zero (by Northfields): lightly-raced maiden on Flat: sold out of W. Jarvis' stable 2,100 gns Newmarket Autumn Sales: looked and ran as though needing race when remote fifth in juvenile maiden hurdle at Wincanton in January: should do better. *C. C. Elsey.* — p

SALCOMBE (NZ) 8 b.g. Amyntor (FR)–Lilium (NZ) (Oncidium) [1989/90 c20d^{pu}] workmanlike gelding: novice hurdler: first outing for 17 months, pulled up before fourth in novice chase in March: will be suited by 3m: possibly unsuited by heavy ground: sold 1,750 gns Ascot May Sales. *D. H. Barons.* c— —

SALEAPOLO 6 ch.m. Leander–Polo Pam (Tiepolo II) [1989/90 c27f^{2} c20f^{F}] second reported foal: half-sister to a poor point-to-pointer by New Member: dam winning hurdler: tailed off when pulled up only outing over hurdles: successful in 2 point-to-points in March and one in April: clear 1½ lengths second to Pat Alaska in hunter chase at Taunton later in April: stays well. *Miss V. L. Dibben.* c79 p —

SALEHURST 10 b.g. Scallywag–Snare (Poaching) [1989/90 c25f*] tall, good sort: handicap chaser: won by short head from Crowecopper at Wolverhampton in March: stays very well: acts on any going: moderate jumper. *G. B. Balding.* c**115** x —

SALES PROMOTER 7 b.h. Tower Walk–The Danstan (The Brianstan) [1989/90 20s^{pu} 16s^{6}] workmanlike horse: poor maiden on Flat: poor novice hurdler: has worn a crossed noseband. *R. C. Price.* 60

SALFORD RAPHAELLA 6 ch.m. Deep Run–Hazeldean (St Paddy) [1989/90 20m^{pu}] lengthy, lightly-made mare: of little account: blinkered final outing in 1987/8. *G. Price.* —

SALINE 5 ch.m. Sallust–Silk Rein (Shantung) [1989/90 16s^{6} 16d] workmanlike, plain mare: in frame at up to 1¼m on Flat: only sign of a little ability over hurdles when sixth in claimer at Market Rasen in January: blinkered final start. *J. Mackie.* —

SALLY FORTH 4 b.g. Sallust–Sally Knox (Busted) [1989/90 16g^{pu} a16g^{5} a16g^{3} a20g^{2} a16g^{5} 16g] good-topped gelding: claimed out of G. Pritchard-Gordon's stable £10,561 after finishing second in 1m claimer on Flat in 1989: poor form in juvenile hurdles at Lingfield: behind in selling handicap final start. *J. R. Bostock.* 69

SALLY'S DOVE 5 ch.m. Celtic Cone–Nimble Dove (Starch Reduced) [1989/90 16m^{6} 16g* 16g 16s^{6} 16d* 16f^{2} 18f^{5} 20m^{5}] small, good-quartered mare: first foal: dam fair staying hurdler: won novice claiming hurdle at Wolverhampton in November and seller at Bangor (bought out of G. Price's stable 7,250 gns) in March: good second in handicap at Worcester later in March, but well below form afterwards: should stay beyond 2m: acts on firm and dead going: has won for a claimer. *P. J. Anderson.* 90

SALLY'S GEM 5 b.g. Hasty Word–China Bank (Wrekin Rambler) [1989/90 16s 16m 16d 20g^{pu}] leggy, good-topped gelding: third foal: half-brother to useful staying chaser High Edge Grey (by Precipice Wood): dam useful stayer on Flat and won at up to 3m over hurdles: novice hurdler: only worthwhile form on second start. *J. White.* 70

SALMAN 12 gr.g. Comedy Star (USA)–Lovely Beak (Counsel) [1989/90 c19m^{pu}] compact, well-made gelding: lightly-raced winning hurdler and novice chaser: poor point-to-pointer nowadays: tailed off when pulled up seventh in hunter chase in April. *Mrs Sandra C. Oliver.* c— —

SALMON STREAM (USA) 5 b.m. Irish River (FR)–Mary Deva (Dhaudevi (FR)) [1989/90 21f^{4} 16h^{5}] winning hurdler: soundly beaten early in season (blinkered final start): should stay 2½m: has raced only on very firm ground over hurdles: amateur ridden when successful: sold 1,400 gns Newmarket December Sales. *O. Sherwood.* —

SALTY FARE 6 b.g. Furry Glen–Royal Account (Henry The Seventh) [1989/90 16s 16m] rangy gelding with scope: behind in NH Flat races and novice hurdles. *Capt. T. A. Forster.* —

SALUBRIOUS 5 ch.m. Sallust–Now Then (Sandford Lad) [1989/90 16f] lengthy ex-Irish mare: second foal: dam placed at up to 1¼m on Flat in Ireland: won over 1½m on Flat in 1988: blinkered and bit backward, tailed off in novice hurdle at Uttoxeter (jumped moderately) in October. *T. B. Hallett.* —

SALVAGER 6 b.g. Balinger–Mahnaz (Deep Diver) [1989/90 F16m] first foal: dam never ran: in rear in NH Flat race at Sandown: yet to race over hurdles or fences. *F. J. O'Mahony.*

SAMBRIAN 5 b.g. The Brianstan–Stolen Halo (Manacle) [1989/90 20f3 24g 16g 27g 25fpu 16g 21mpu] leggy gelding: first foal: dam third in 2m selling hurdle: well beaten both outings at 2 yrs: sold out of P. Blockley's stable 1,000 gns Ascot December (1988) Sales: little form in novice hurdles: blinkered fifth start (trained until after then by J. Dooler). *P. B. Allingham.* —

SAMBRIDGE 8 ch.g. New Member–Miss Stalbridge (Eastern Venture) [1989/90 c26spu] rangy gelding: no sign of ability: makes mistakes over fences. *P. Dufosee.* c— x —

SAM DA VINCI 11 ch.g. Saucy Kit–Fortilage (Fortina) [1989/90 c24f4 c29d c33dur c25fpu c26f2 c24m3 c29f5] tall gelding: useful chaser: best effort of 1989/90 when 2 lengths second to Man O'Magic in handicap at Newbury in March: ran creditably on other occasions, including Whitbread Gold Cup (fifth to Mr Frisk): stays well: acts on any going: usually impresses in appearance. *J. W. Blundell.* **c136** —

SAMFEN 8 ro.g. Sonnen Gold–Ensign Steel (Majority Blue) [1989/90 c27s2 c24s3 c24d] lengthy gelding: fair chaser: creditable second to Bluff Knoll in handicap at Ayr in December: ran moderately afterwards: stays well: has run moderately on heavy going, acts on any other: usually visored or blinkered nowadays: tends to make the odd mistake. *M. H. Easterby.* **c119** —

SAMHAAN 8 ch.h. Niniski (USA)–Mai Pussy (Realm) [1989/90 16f2] workmanlike horse: modest form in novice hurdles: short-head second at Worcester in August: worth a try over further than 2m: probably acts on any going: seems best in blinkers. *M. McCormack.* 97

SAMMY THE SHAMMY 7 ch.g. Manor Farm Boy–Barca Dorata (Cavo Doro) [1989/90 a16g6] leggy, workmanlike gelding: poor novice hurdler, lightly raced. *J. R. Jenkins.* —

SAMOAAN CHARGER 4 b.g. Aragon–Sea Charm (Julio Mariner) [1989/90 16spu] leggy gelding: modest maiden on Flat (placed over 1m), when trained by R. J. R. Williams: carrying a lot of condition, jumped appallingly and was tailed off when pulled up 3 out in juvenile hurdle at Plumpton in December. *R. Voorspuy.* —

SAMONIA 10 b.m. Rolfe (USA)–Nevilles Cross (USA) (Nodouble (USA)) [1989/90 20gpu 20d 22f5 24gF 20f3 20g4 20f5] angular, lightly-built mare: handicap hurdler: stays 25f: acts on any going: claimer ridden when successful. *T. W. Cunningham.* 69

SAMOVAR 5 b.m. Moorestyle–Restful (Ribero) [1989/90 17f3 18f4 19f2 16m3 16f* 16g6 a16g2 16m3 16m a16g2 16d 16f* 17m4] angular mare: won selling hurdle at Plumpton in October (made all, bought in 5,600 gns) and novice handicap hurdle at Towcester (idled in front when beating Smiley 2 lengths) in March: ran creditably when placed in between: stays 19f: acts on firm ground and seems unsuited by a soft surface. *J. Joseph.* 78

SAM SHORROCK 8 b. or br.g. Vivadari–To Windward (Hard Tack) [1989/90 F16f c20m2 c24gpu c25g5 c25dpu c27vbd c32f] chunky non-thoroughbred ex-Irish gelding: first foal: dam unraced: winning point-to-pointer: second in novice chase at Sligo in June (trained until after then by V. O'Brien): no worthwhile form in Britain. *G. Thorner.* **c92** d

SAMSON-AGONISTES 4 b.c. Bold Fort–Hello Cuddles (He Loves Me) [1989/90 16f] quite a modest performer on Flat, winner over 5f in 1990: behind in juvenile selling hurdle at Worcester in August. *B. Preece.* —

SAMSUN 8 b.g. Sunyboy–Etoile de Lune (Apollo Eight) [1989/90 c26m4 c26m2 c24m2] leggy, angular gelding: modest chaser: creditable second in handicaps at Uttoxeter and Nottingham in November: will stay extreme distances: acts on good to firm ground and is probably unsuited by a yielding surface: ran in snatches once in 1988/9. *J. Webber.* c92 —

SANAMAR 6 ch.g. Hello Gorgeous (USA)–Miss Markey (Gay Fandango (USA)) [1989/90 16dF 16d3 21d 16g5] angular gelding: fair stayer on Flat in 1988, unraced in 1989: sold out of J. Hills's stable 5,200 gns Ascot June Sales: third in novice hurdle at Stratford in February: well beaten afterwards: claimer ridden. *T. R. Greathead.* 101 ?

SANBALLAT 8 b.g. Hunters Fort–Brown Shackel (Shackleton) [1989/90 c20dur c20sF c20dur c25m* c22g* c24d* c26m4] lengthy ex-Irish gelding: half-brother to winning selling hurdler Tim's Brief (by Avocat): dam behind in **c119** +

Irish NH Flat race: unplaced in 3 NH Flat races in 1987: smart point-to-pointer: won maiden hunter chase at Down Royal in 1988/9 by a distance when trained by I. Ferguson: let down by his jumping first 3 starts in 1990, but won hunter chases at Towcester and Stratford in April and Worcester (by 8 lengths from John Sam) in May: stays 25f: acts on soft and good to firm going: takes a good hold and is usually dropped out early on: sure to win more hunter chases. *D. Nicholson.*

SAN CARLOS 8 b.g. Formidable (USA)–Omentello (Elopement) [1989/90 20m3 21g] rather leggy, close-coupled gelding: handicap hurdler: fourth in 2 novice chases in 1988/9: best at up to 2¼m: acted on any going: won for a 7-lb claimer: wasn't one to rely on: dead. *K. A. Morgan.* c— § 110 §

SAN CARLOS BAY 9 ch.g. Julio Mariner–Mimika (Lorenzaccio) [1989/90 26dF] sparely-made gelding: winning hurdler: fell fatally at Ayr in November: stayed 2½m: acted on dead going: usually wore visor. *R. R. Lamb.* —

SAND CASTLE 9 ch.g. Tap On Wood–Pacific Sands (Sandford Lad) [1989/90 16m2 20m* 25m*] compact, workmanlike gelding: modest hurdler/chaser: claimer ridden, won 2 handicap hurdles at Huntingdon in May, gaining latter success comfortably by 5 lengths from Boschendal with remainder well strung out: stays 3m: acts on any going: blinkered last 5 outings in 1986/7. *M. J. Ryan.* c— 108

SANDICLIFFE BOY 9 b.g. Jaazeiro (USA)–Almost (Levmoss) [1989/90 c25s* c30v5 c24s5 c30v*] tall, sparely-made gelding: moderate chaser: won handicaps at Hereford in December and Chepstow (John Hughes Grand National Trial) in February: stayed on well to lead approaching last and score by 3 lengths from Roll-A-Joint in latter: below form in between: stays well: acts on heavy going. *R. Lee.* **c114**

SANDMOOR PRINCE 7 b.g. Grundy–Princesse du Seine (FR) (Val de Loir) [1989/90 c25dur c16g2 c16g6 c25g5 c24dpu c20m c16f2 c16g2 c16m2 c16g*] leggy gelding: winning point-to-pointer: no form over hurdles: won maiden chase at Market Rasen in June: best at 2m: acts on firm going: trainer ridden. *Dr P. L. J. Pritchard.* c88 —

SANDYMOUNT HOUSE 10 br.g. Young Emperor–Musette (Tudor Music) [1989/90 c20d] tall gelding: winning hunter chaser: poor form at best in recent seasons: stays 3m: acts on any going: blinkered final start 1987/8: takes a good hold. *Miss Margaret Angell.* c—

SAN FRANCISCO JOE (USA) 6 b. or br.g. Plum Bold (USA)–Destacion (USA) (Decimator (USA)) [1989/90 16gF a18gF 20sro a20g2 a18g* 17m6 16m2] compact gelding: won handicap hurdle at Southwell in March: ½-length second to Northern Barry in novice handicap at Stratford in May: stays 2½m: acts on good to firm and dead going: has looked less than keen under pressure and ran out at third last on third outing: often claimer ridden. *A. W. Denson.* 89 §

SAN OVAC 7 b.g. Ovac (ITY)–Sanvitalia (Right Tack) [1989/90 c17m6 c16h2 c20m2 c24h* c25f* c24g4 c24mpu c25m2 c20dpu c20fF c20g3] workmanlike gelding: poor novice hurdler: made all in novice chases at Taunton and Plumpton in October: creditable second to easy winner The Argonaut in amateur riders event at Sandown in March: took little interest next outing: stays 25f: acts on hard and dead ground: usually blinkered nowadays: tends to make mistakes. *C. P. E. Brooks.* c89 —

SANSOOL 4 b.g. Dominion–Young Diana (Young Generation) [1989/90 16f6] placed over 1½m on Flat (has swished tail under pressure): over 25 lengths sixth in juvenile selling hurdle at Southwell in August: sold 3,200 gns Newmarket September Sales: resold 3,000 gns Doncaster November Sales. *N. A. Callaghan.* —

SANTAC 5 b.g. Tachypous–Sandy Keerie (Sandy Creek) [1989/90 16f6 17hF4] workmanlike gelding: winning selling hurdler: gives impression he needs further than 2m nowadays and stays 23f: probably acts on any going. *D. McCain.* —

SANTARAY 4 ch.c. Formidable (USA)–Stockingful (Santa Claus) [1989/90 F12g4 F16m] good-topped colt: half-brother to several winners, including winning hurdler Kasu (by Try My Best) and NH Flat race winner Velda (by Thatch): dam half-sister to smart miler Richboy: fourth behind Going On in NH Flat race at Market Rasen in March: wearing crossed noseband, always behind in well-contested event at Liverpool following month: yet to race over hurdles. *J. Mackie.*

SANTELLA BOBKES (USA) 5 b.h. Solford (USA)–Ambiente (USA) (Tentam (USA)) [1989/90 16m 22m* 26dpu 24s 25d] good-topped horse: put up useful performance when winning minor event at Wolverhampton in October by 6 lengths from Combermere: failed to confirm that improvement, never travelling well when soundly beaten final start: stays 2¾m: yet to race on extremes of 143 ?

going, acts on any other: blinkered in 1989/90: sold only 6,000 gns Ascot 2nd July Sales: best treated with caution. *G. Harwood.*

SANTELLA BOY 8 b.h. Sparkler–Hors Serie (USA) (Vaguely Noble) [1989/90 16d⁶ 22m 16g] lengthy horse: modest novice hurdler in 1985/6: behind all starts when next seen out in 1989/90: acts well on heavy going: visored final start. *J. R. Jenkins.* —

SANTELLA PAL (USA) 9 b.g. Effervescing (USA)–Hempens Pal (USA) (Hempen) [1989/90 a16g⁴ 16m] rather leggy, good-topped gelding: has been operated on for a wind infirmity: winning hurdler: well beaten in 1989/90: stays 2¼m well: best form on ground no softer than dead: claimer ridden. *D. R. C. Elsworth.* —

SANTIETOWN 8 ch.g. Bonne Noel–Irish Ville (Meadsville) [1989/90 c25dpu c24s c24g] tall gelding: second once from 2 starts in point-to-points in 1988: no sign of ability in novice chases (poor jumper). *C. Sporborg.* c— x

SANTO BOY 7 b. or br.g. Monsanto (FR)–Mandrian (Mandamus) [1989/90 16m³ 16m⁵ 16s* 16m* a18g] smallish, good-bodied gelding: carries condition: won novice handicap hurdles at Uttoxeter (ridden by 7-lb claimer) in February and Fakenham in March (conditional jockeys): stiff task in valuable handicap at Southwell later in March: suited by sharp 2m when conditions are testing: acts on good to firm and soft going. *J. A. Glover.* 97

SANTOPADRE 8 gr.g. Welsh Saint–Shanty (Sea Hawk II) [1989/90 c16g c16sF c16dF c16g⁵] lengthy gelding: fairly useful hurdler: showed ability in February on chasing debut: fell on next 2 starts and finished tailed off final outing: suited by 2m and sound surface: good mount for a claimer. *O. O'Neill.* c**91** —

SAPPHIRE FLIGHT 5 gr.m. Scallywag–Last Flight (Saucy Kit) [1989/90 F16m F16f] angular, sparely-made mare: half-sister to winning hurdler/chaser Celtic Flight and to useful staying hurdler Ruby Flight (both by Celtic Cone): dam unraced daughter of very useful hurdler Flight's Orchid: unplaced in NH Flat races: yet to race over hurdles or fences. *R. J. Eckley.*

SARAH'S WROATH 5 b.g. Morston (FR)–All Our Yesterdays (Jimsun) [1989/90 16m 16g 16v 20m] small, angular gelding: first foal: dam winning hurdler at up to 23f: only sign of ability when seventh in novice hurdle third start: should stay beyond 2m. *M. Scudamore.* 88

SARA LANE 6 ch.m. Sagaro–Maypole Lane (Grundy) [1989/90 20d 21v⁴ 17d 21s⁶] lengthy mare: modest novice hurdler: will be suited by further than 21f: possibly needs testing conditions: edged left on flat final start 1988/9. *N. G. Ayliffe.* 88

SARATOGA SOL 7 ch.m. Sunyboy–Sailor's Sol (The Bo'sun) [1989/90 18s⁶ 22v⁵ 22g⁴ 20m⁵ 22mpu] small mare: poor form in novice hurdles: best efforts over 2¾m: seems unsuited by good to firm. *J. Ffitch-Heyes.* 81

SARDAR 8 ch.g. Ardoon–Si (Ragusa) [1989/90 20gpu] compact gelding: no sign of ability over hurdles: has worn crossed noseband and a tongue strap: refused in a point-to-point in February. *R. E. Peacock.* —

SARNIA SOUND 5 ch.g. Music Boy–St Pauli Girl (St Paddy) [1989/90 16gpu 16d⁶ 16gpu 16g a18gpu 16g* 20f² 17f⁶] sturdy gelding: half-brother to smart jumper Major Thompson (by Brigadier Gerard): poor middle-distance maiden on Flat (has looked a difficult ride): sold out of W. Musson's stable 1,900 gns Ascot November Sales: first form over hurdles when winning claimer at Perth in April (claimed out of Mrs P. Barker's stable £4,577): ran in sellers afterwards: best form at 2m on good ground. *C. R. Beever.* 69 +

SARTORIUS 4 b.c. Henbit (USA)–Salvationist (Mill Reef (USA)) [1989/90 16g*dis 16m* 20g³] rather sparely-made colt: 10.6f winner on Flat in August: sold out of H. Cecil's stable 13,000 gns Newmarket Autumn Sales: passed post first in juvenile hurdles at Wolverhampton (subsequently disqualified on technical grounds) and Leicester (beat Northants cleverly by a length): mistake 3 out and wasn't knocked about in straight when 24 lengths third behind Sayyure at Ascot in January: should stay beyond 2m: acts on good to firm ground: possibly capable of better. *P. G. Bailey.* 117 p

SARYAN 7 b.g. Try My Best (USA)–High Fidelyty (FR) (Hautain) [1989/90 20m²] leggy, good-topped gelding: modest hurdler, lightly raced: second in selling handicap at Wolverhampton in October (hung right and found little): best form at 2m: acts on a firm and dead going: needs holding up for as long as possible and looks a difficult ride: won over 11f in 1990. *B. J. Curley.* 86 §

SASKIA'S PRIDE 4 ch.f. Giacometti–Anjamadi (Buff's Own) [1989/90 F17f*] fifth foal: sister to 1½m seller winner on Flat and winning hurdler at up to 2½m Saskia's Reprieve: dam never ran: co-favourite, won NH Flat race at Doncaster in March by 15 lengths from Pop Abroad: yet to race over hurdles. *J. F. Bottomley.*

SASKIA'S REPRIEVE 6 ch.g. Giacometti–Anjamadi (Buff's Own) [1989/90
16f^{2} 20f^{3} 20g^{3}] small, sparely-made gelding: handicap hurdler: ran creditably all 3 106
starts in first half of season: suited by galloping track at 2m and stays 2½m: unsuited by very soft going, acts on any other: claimer ridden: visored nowadays. *J. F. Bottomley.*

SASPRING 15 b.g. Sassafras (FR)–Belitis (Tudor Melody) [1989/90 c25f] c—
smallish gelding: selling chaser: poor point-to-pointer nowadays: stays 3m: acts —
on any going: sometimes wears blinkers (didn't when successful) and has also been visored. *Mervyn G. Evans.*

SASSANOCO 9 b.g. Nonoalco (USA)–Sassanian (Sassafras (FR)) [1989/90 c— x
c16g^{F}] leggy gelding: modest hurdler/chaser: best form at up to 2½m: acted on —
firm and dead going: sometimes made mistakes: occasionally visored (not when successful): didn't always go through with his effort: dead. *J. White.*

SASSY BONNE 4 ch.f. Good Thyne (USA)–Saucy Slave (Arctic Slave) [1989/90 F17m^{6}] IR 13,000 3-y-o: half-sister to several winning jumpers: dam, twice a winner over hurdles at around 2m in Ireland, is half-sister to smart hurdler Troyswood: 20 lengths sixth behind Merry Master in NH Flat race at Carlisle: yet to race over hurdles. *G. Richards.*

SATIN D'OR 4 ch.f. Le Coq d'Or–Super Satin (Lord of Verona) [1989/90 F16g] seventh foal: half-sister to winning staying chasers Super Tony (by Owen Anthony) and Super Fountain (by Royal Fountain): dam placed over hurdles: tailed off in NH Flat race at Perth: yet to race over hurdles. *F. T. Walton.*

SATURN MOON 5 ch.m. Monsanto (FR)–Ritruda (USA) (Roi Dagobert)
[1989/90 21m] poor novice hurdler: visored last 2 outings 1988/9: sold out of J. S. —
Wilson's stable 3,400 gns Doncaster August Sales. *Mrs A. Knight.*

SAUCY MINSTREL 6 b.m. Black Minstrel–Billeragh Girl (Normandy) c—
[1989/90 c25d^{pu} c26v^{F} 24d 20f 24m] unfurnished ex-Irish mare: second foal: —
half-sister to modest novice hurdler/chaser Lover Bill (by Golden Love): dam half-sister to 2 winning hurdlers, notably smart Troyswood: runner-up in a point-to-point in 1989: no worthwhile form in novice events over hurdles and fences. *Miss J. Thorne.*

SAUCY TOUCH 4 ch.g. Touch Boy–Saucy Bridget (Hard Sauce) [1989/90
F16g^{4} F16d F16f^{5} 16f^{5}] seventh foal: half-brother to a poor animal by Joshua: dam —
half-sister to Sunlit Spar, quite useful at up 1¾m on Flat: has shown a little ability in NH Flat races: tailed off in novice hurdle at Sedgefield. *R. W. Swiers.*

SAULIRE 5 b.g. High Top–Strathoykel (Aberdeen) [1989/90 16d^{5} 16m 16g 22d]
leggy, angular gelding: plating-class maiden on Flat: poor form in novice hurdles: 79
dead. *S. Dow.*

SAUNDERS LASS 6 b.m. Hillandale–Portella (Porto Bello) [1989/90 16g^{4}
16f^{F} a16g^{2} 16f*] lengthy mare: placed in varied company over hurdles prior to 82
winning selling handicap (no bid) at Wetherby in May by 5 lengths from Paris Match: likely to prove best over a sharp 2m: acts on any going. *P. J. Bevan.*

SAUNTERSON 5 b.g. Saunter–Rosepic (Seaepic (USA)) [1989/90 F17f] first reported foal: dam unraced: behind in NH Flat race at Doncaster: yet to race over hurdles or fences. *O. Brennan.*

SAVERLEY-GREEN 5 br.h. Ballacashtal (CAN)–Zakushki (Royal Palace) [1989/90 F16f F12m] second foal: dam twice-raced half-sister to several winners: well beaten in NH Flat races in first half of season: blinkered final start: yet to race over hurdles or fences. *W. Clay.*

SAWDUST JACK 6 b.g. Rarity–Ribero's Overture (Ribero) [1989/90 c16s* c**120** p
c16s^{F} c16s^{F} c16d] tall, sparely-made gelding: fair hurdler: won poor novice chase —
at Sedgefield in January: in process of running an excellent race when falling 2 out in Nottinghamshire Novices' Chase won by Cashew King at Nottingham third start, holding slight advantage and giving impression would have finished second: ran well until weakening approaching 3 out when behind in valuable event won by Celtic Shot at Ayr in April: likely to prove best at 2m in testing conditions: blinkered last 3 starts 1988/9 and last 2 outings: sure to win more races over fences. *M. W. Easterby.*

SAWYER'S SON 11 b.g. Chas Sawyer–Perkelater (Right Honourable Gentleman) [1989/90 c24gpu] small, sturdy, plain gelding: former selling hurdler/steeplechaser: won 2-runner point-to-point in 1990: stays 3m: probably acts on any going: poor jumper. *Mrs P. A. Rigby.* c— x —

SAYALOT 4 b.g. Sayyaf–Lottie's Charm (Charlottesville) [1989/90 16m a16g] winning middle-distance plater on Flat: sold out of M. Bell's stable 1,400 gns Newmarket Autumn Sales: little sign of ability in 2 outings over hurdles, first a seller. *K. A. Ryan.* —

SAYANT 5 b.g. Sayyaf–Bodnant (Welsh Pageant) [1989/90 16g6 16m5 a16g3 16m4 a16g*] sturdy gelding: won claiming hurdle at Southwell in February by 10 lengths from Basic Fun: placed in sellers previously: worth a try over further than 2m: acts on good to firm going. *W. Clay.* 91

SAYMORE 4 ch.g. Seymour Hicks (FR)–Huahinee (FR) (Riverman (USA)) [1989/90 16dpu 16gpu] smallish, sparely-made gelding: half-brother to ungenuine winning hurdler Prairie Oyster (by Northfields): fairly useful 1m winner on Flat (stays 1¼m): sold out of M. Francis' stable 40,000 gns Newmarket Autumn Sales: pulled up in juvenile hurdles at Sandown in January and Fairyhouse (broke blood vessel) in April. *C. P. E. Brooks.* —

SAYPAREE 5 b.g. Saher–Parijatak (Pardao) [1989/90 16s2 16g 16g 16d3 16g5 16s3 16f 20m* 16d* 16fpu] 143 p

A change proved even better than a rest for Sayparee. He raced for three different stables in the latest season and showed his best form for the last of them. When trained in Ireland by Mullins, Sayparee won twice on the Flat and four times over hurdles, but five outings in his second season as a hurdler failed to yield a victory and he was then sent to England to be trained by Jonjo O'Neill. Following two more defeats—after which the official handicapper dropped him by 9 lb—he was moved to Pipe's stable, and within five weeks Sayparee had won the Martell Handicap Hurdle at Liverpool and the Scottish Champion Hurdle at Ayr. On his last outing for Mullins Sayparee had finished strongly to take fifth place behind his stable-companion Redundant Pal in The Ladbroke at Leopardstown in January, and he ran a promising first race for O'Neill when third behind Milford Quay in a minor event at Haydock in March. However, after finishing tailed off in the County Hurdle at Cheltenham later that month Sayparee was on the move again. Sayparee, raced only at two miles over hurdles, and apparently best on a soft surface, had his first outing for Pipe's stable in the Martell Hurdle run over two and a half miles on good to firm ground. He came back to form to win it by a length from Out of Range,

Martell Handicap Hurdle, Liverpool—eventual winner Sayparee (left) is disputing third place behind Artful Abbot (No. 18) and Out of Range at the last

Scottish Champion Handicap Hurdle, Ayr—
more comfortable this time for Sayparee (armlets);
Don Valentino (foreground) finished second

leading in the last half furlong having been held up. Although Sayparee had twice made the running when successful in Ireland waiting tactics suit him much better, for he's capable of producing a good turn of foot in the closing stages, as he was to show to great effect in the Scottish Champion Hurdle. Sayparee, confidently ridden by Lower in place of the injured Scudamore, was last of the thirteen runners turning for home at Ayr, but he made swift progress through the field and was poised to challenge when Deep Sensation quickened into the lead at the second last. Still hard on the bridle, Sayparee jumped to the front at the last and, with only the minimum of encouragement from his rider, sprinted away to win by six lengths from Don Valentino. Sayparee raced off bottom weight in this limited handicap and was receiving 7 lb from Don Valentino, who on his previous start had finished only eleventh behind Kribensis in the Waterford Crystal Champion Hurdle. Nevertheless, Sayparee could not have been more impressive and at the time we were of the opinion that he could well be on the verge of top class within twelve months and a strong contender for the Champion Hurdle. Our enthusiasm was to be tempered by what happened to him on his final outing. A short-priced favourite for the Swinton Insurance Trophy at Haydock, Sayparee struck into himself and had to be pulled up three out. We understand that Sayparee's injury was quite serious and that it will be Christmas-time at least before he's back in action. It's to be hoped that Sayparee does make a full recovery and that he'll be seen out at some stage in 1990/1, for he looked a very good prospect at Ayr.

Sayparee, by the Diomed Stakes winner Saher, is the fourth foal of the fair Irish hurdler Parijatak, who won five races at up to two and a half miles when trained by Mullins. Mullins also had success with Parijatak's first and third foals, respectively named Pariglit (by Lock Diamond) and Par Pry (by Pry). The former won three hurdle races at up to two and a quarter miles, the latter won a two-mile National Hunt Flat race and a seventeen-furlong maiden hurdle. Sayparee's grandam Tongue Twister, placed over a mile and

Sayparee (b.g. 1985)	Saher (b 1976)	Great Nephew (b 1963)	Honeyway
			Sybil's Niece
		Another Chance (b 1967)	Romulus
			Recount
	Parijatak (ch 1971)	Pardao (ch 1958)	Pardal
			Three Weeks
		Tongue Twister (ch 1966)	Twilight Alley
			Word Perfect

a quarter, comes from the same family as the very smart milers Royal Charger and Tessa Gillian. Sayparee, a small, leggy gelding, has run in a crossed noseband. Despite his success at Liverpool we expect him to prove best at around two miles on an easy surface. *M. C. Pipe.*

SAY SHANAZ 4 b. or br.f. Tickled Pink–Wild Pumpkin (Auction Ring (USA)) [1989/90 16s 16d 16f^{6} 16h^{4} 17f* 17h^{4}] sparely-made filly: poor maiden on Flat: sold out of G. Harwood's stable 4,250 gns after winning conditional jockeys selling handicap hurdle at Newton Abbot in May: well beaten in non-seller next time: acts on firm going: trained first 3 starts by J. Czerpak. *B. Preece.* 70

SAY YOU 6 b.g. Sayyaf–Braida (FR) (Tissot) [1989/90 18f^{3} 16f] neat gelding: poor novice hurdler: form only on reappearance. *P. Howling.* 71

SAYYURE (USA) 4 b.c. Lydian (FR)–Periquito (USA) (Olden Times) [1989/90 16f^{F} 16m^{4} 16f* 16g^{5} 20g^{2} 20f* 20g* 20g* 16d* 16f^{6} 16m^{6}] 134

Sayyure's season as a juvenile hurdler can be divided roughly into two parts. The first—August to early-December, encompassing six starts—yielded victories at Wetherby and Doncaster, and no reason to believe Sayyure was anything very much out of the ordinary. The second—late-December to April—revealed a marked improvement in him and brought victories at Kempton, Ascot and Cheltenham and highly creditable performances in two valuable juvenile championship races. Little more needs to be said now about the first section, except that he had broken a blood vessel when turning in a moderate performance on his fourth start, and had shown a tendency to flash his tail under pressure—a trait subsequently proved to be nothing that should be held against him. His wins at Kempton and Ascot showed him to be on the upgrade, and by the time he contested the four-runner Food Brokers 'Finesse' Hurdle at Cheltenham in January he was clearly one of the best juveniles around. Sayyure is a battler, and his performance at Cheltenham was typical of him. After making the running until after the second last he looked beaten when headed by chief rival and

Food Brokers Finesse Hurdle, Cheltenham—
Sayyure (left) puts up a very useful performance to beat Lucky Verdict

odds-on favourite Lucky Verdict, but Sayyure stayed on so strongly under pressure that he regained the lead after a good jump at the last and drew clear towards the finish to put two and a half lengths between himself and Lucky Verdict; Northants, the only other finisher, was a further thirty lengths away. Sayyure looked a likely type for the Daily Express Triumph Hurdle on the same course two months later and turned in a most commendable effort in finishing sixth to Rare Holiday, beaten only two and a half lengths, at the same time giving the impression he'd be suited by a return to further. Sayyure ran below his best when fifteen and a half lengths sixth behind Sybillin in the Glenlivet Anniversary Hurdle at Liverpool the following month, but wasn't knocked about or disgraced, and again looked as though two miles was on the short side when running against the best.

Sayyure (USA) (b.c. 1986)	Lydian (FR) (ch 1978)	Lyphard (b 1969)	Northern Dancer
			Goofed
		Miss Manon (b 1970)	Bon Mot III
			Miss Molly
	Periquito (USA) (b 1976)	Olden Times (b 1958)	Relic
			Djenne
		Bold Aunt (b 1970)	Bold Lad
			Aunt Tilt

Sayyure is by the very smart French-trained middle-distance horse Lydian, who'll be remembered by some for his refusal to enter the stalls in Shergar's Derby. Lydian has sired other winning hurdlers, notably the fairly useful Liadett. Sayyure is the fifth winning foal of Periquito who ran just four times. Three of her offspring have been successful abroad, whilst the other Primitive Rising (by Raise A Man) was a very useful stayer in the late-'eighties. The second dam Bold Aunt, a winner in the USA, is a half-sister to the dam of the smart seven-furlong to one-and-a-quarter-mile performer Over The Ocean. Their dam Aunt Tilt, a stakes-placed winner, is a half-sister to Damascus. Sayyure, still a maiden on the Flat, cost IR 84,000 guineas as a yearling and began his career as a two-year-old with Cecil in Newmarket. He ran once that season before being sold to present connections for 9,200 guineas at the Newmarket Autumn Sales and developing into a modest out-and-out stayer as a three-year-old. As Sayyure, a lengthy, sturdy colt, thrived on his racing in his first season over hurdles, it could well be the same story next term, when he should give a good account of himself in handicaps, particularly over two and a half miles and more. He has shown his form on ground ranging from firm to dead (he has yet to race on any softer over hurdles). *N. Tinkler.*

SCALE MODEL 8 b.m. Latest Model–Ruby Sherry (Straight Cut) [1989/90 c16dpu c20m3 c24d c25m c28g5 c24spu c24d c25m c25f5 c24m2 c20fpu c26mF] stocky, compact mare: poor handicapper over fences: suited by long distances: possibly suited by give in the ground nowadays: ridden by 7-lb claimer when successful: tends to make mistakes and get behind in early stages: inconsistent. *J. Roper.* **c77** § —

SCALLYMERE 7 b.m. Scallywag–Penny Queen (Space King) [1989/90 16m 16f 16g 16g] smallish, workmanlike mare: no sign of ability over hurdles, including in a seller. *A. H. Brisbourne.* —

SCALLY OWEN 6 br.g. Scallywag–Owen Belle (Master Owen) [1989/90 21sF 16s* 21s4 20d* 19d* 18d 18v* 18v* 20fpu] 145

The latest National Hunt season in Ireland was enlivened by the institution of two series of races for novice hurdlers and novice chasers. Both series consisted of a number of qualifying races—each worth IR £6,900 to the winner thanks to the support of an anonymous sponsor—run over distances ranging from two miles to two and a half miles on eleven different courses, leading to a valuable final in February. One of the chief beneficiaries of this laudable scheme was the Irish racegoer, able to see the best novices racing regularly against each other prior to their challenging for the top British events later in the season. In the chase series, Cahervillahow and Welcome Pin put up two of the best performances of the

Mrs P. Mullins' "Scally Owen"

season by Irish novices when winning the qualifiers at Naas and Fairyhouse respectively in January, prior to the former's hard-fought success over The Committee in the final at Leopardstown. The hurdle series featured a number of good races, notably Call Me Later's short-heading Stevie Jay, the pair twenty lengths clear of a fairly useful field, in the Fairyhouse qualifier in February. But the IR £12,500 Final at Punchestown later in the month was turned into a procession by Scally Owen, a well-beaten eighth, never placed to challenge, at Fairyhouse. An all-the-way winner of a run-of-the-mill novice event at Leopardstown in the interim, Scally Owen soon led at Punchestown. Gradually extending his advantage from the third last, Scally Owen turned into the straight well clear and was eased considerably on the run-in to win by eight lengths from Grey Danube, with third-placed Call Me Later a further two and a half lengths back.

No stewards inquiry was held into Scally Owen's improved showing compared with Fairyhouse. When ridden from the front previously, Scally Owen had shown progressive and fairly useful form. He'd won a maiden hurdle at Navan and a minor event at Leopardstown in the first half of the season and the Slaney Hurdle at Naas in January, though his task in the last-named was simplified by the falls of My View and Grey Danube in the early stages. When waited with, as at Fairyhouse, Scally Owen had fared less well. He was behind until falling five out at Galway on his hurdling debut and was never able to challenge when a well-beaten fourth at Navan in November. Scally Owen couldn't get the lead when disappointing in the Sun Alliance Novices' Hurdle at Cheltenham in March. Prominent in the chasing group behind Regal Ambition at halfway, he gradually dropped out and was behind when pulled up before the second last. Scally Owen was probably unsuited by the firm ground at Cheltenham. He had shown his best form previously with plenty of give—the going at Punchestown was very heavy after a blizzard earlier in the afternoon.

Scally Owen (br.g. 1984)	Scallywag (gr 1973)	Sea Hawk II (gr 1963)	Herbager
			Sea Nymph
		Scammell (b 1956)	Dante
			Always
	Owen Belle (br 1976)	Master Owen (b 1956)	Owen Tudor
			Miss Maisie
		Nidee (ch 1962)	Ossian II
			Rosbrin Rose

The first foal of the unraced Owen Belle, Scally Owen is from one of the best jumping families in Ireland not listed in the *General Stud Book*. The third dam Rosbrin Rose, a winner twice over two miles on the Flat on successive days as a six-year-old, was a sister to 1956 Champion Hurdle winner Doorknocker and to Door Girl, the grandam of high-class staying chaser Door Latch. Rosbrin Rose bred several winners over jumps, notably the useful chaser Exhibit B. The unraced Nidee produced two winners over jumps and Slave De, the dam of Queen Mother Champion Chase winner Buck House. Owen Belle's yearling of 1989, a sister to Scally Owen, was sold privately for 5,000 guineas at Doncaster in November. Scally Owen was bought for 7,000 guineas at the same venue as a three-year-old. Including two successes in National Hunt Flat races, he has since won almost IR £29,000 in two seasons' racing. A close-coupled, workmanlike gelding, Scally Owen will probably be kept over hurdles for the time being. His best prospects for further success look to be as a stayer. He should have little problem in staying three miles. Granted little more than normal improvement and plenty of give in the ground, Scally Owen could be a live contender to follow up recent Irish successes in the Stayers' Hurdle at Cheltenham. *Patrick Mullins, Ireland.*

SCAMPERED 6 b.m. Scallywag–Quick Worker (Workboy) [1989/90 18g 16g 16g 18s^{4} 22d 22g^{6}] lengthy mare: poor novice hurdler: well beaten over 2¾m: pulls hard. *J. T. Gifford.* 72

SCAMPEROO 6 b.m. Chukaroo–Scamper (Abwah) [1989/90 16m^{6}] angular, sparely-made mare: little sign of ability. *Mrs Gill E. Jones.* —

SCAMPI 5 b.g. Fine Blade (USA)–Lady Piersfield (Mugatpura) [1989/90 F16f^{2} F16f^{6}] neat gelding: fourth foal: half-brother to winning chaser Crash Call (by Crash Course): dam won 2¾m novice chase in Ireland: second in NH Flat race at Wetherby in October: dead. *J. Hanson.*

SCANNER LAD 4 br.g. Mansingh (USA)–Immodest Miss (Daring Display (USA)) [1989/90 16h^{pu} 17f^{2} 16f^{pu} 17m^{2} 17m^{4}] sparely-made gelding: little worthwhile form on Flat: poor early-season form over hurdles, including in a seller: wears blinkers. *J. A. Bennett.* 59 ?

SCAN THE VIEW 7 br.m. Shrivenham–Brief Scandal (Counsel) [1989/90 a16g^{pu}] tailed off when pulled up in novice hurdles and a selling handicap: has been tried in blinkers. *P. R. Rodford.* —

SCARLET DYMOND 8 b.m. Rymer–Eight of Diamonds (Silent Spring) [1989/90 16d 22m 17d c16s c21g c25d^{6} c25m^{3} c24g^{4} c25m^{2} c17f*] sparely-made mare: poor novice hurdler: won maiden chase at Newton Abbot in May by ¾ length from Tabacos: seemed not quite to stay 25f previous start: acts on firm ground: tends to sweat: reportedly has dehydration problems and has twice collapsed after race. *G. A. Ham.* c82 —

SCARLET LEGEND 4 b.g. Legend of France (USA)–Orillia (Red God) [1989/90 16d^{ur} a16g^{3}] round-barrelled gelding: no worthwhile form on Flat: led until unseating rider fifth in juvenile hurdle at Warwick in January: distant last of 3 in similar event at Southwell later in month: dead. *Mrs L. Piggott.* —

SCARNING DALE 7 b.g. Cawston's Clown–Within Bounds (Canisbay) [1989/90 F17m^{4} 16g^{pu} 20g 16s^{5} 16d* 17g^{3} 18d^{3}] lengthy, good-bodied gelding: showed improved form to win novice hurdle at Kelso in January: ran creditably afterwards: stays 2¼m: acts on dead going. *P. Monteith.* 100

SCATTERBUCK 9 br.g. Kambalda–Dusky Glory (Dusky Boy) [1989/90 22d^{pu} 19m 20s^{5}] close-coupled, lightly-made gelding: lightly-raced winning hurdler: stays 2¾m: acts on good to firm going: usually amateur ridden: blinkered final start. *M. Bradstock.* —

SCATTERSHOT 5 ro.g. General Ironside–At Random (Random Shot) [1989/90 F16g^{4}] non-thoroughbred gelding: first foal: dam placed in point-to-points in Ireland: fourth behind Schiehallion in NH Flat race at Ayr in November: yet to race over hurdles or fences. *Mrs S. C. Bradburne.*

SCHIEHALLION 5 ch.m. Scallywag–Hardwick Sun (Dieu Soleil) [1989/90
F16g* 20g* 22d^{5} 20d^{2} 20d] angular mare: successful in 2 NH Flat races at Ayr, 97
including in November: won novice hurdle on same course in December: showed improved form when 7 lengths second to On The Hooch in mares novice event at Newcastle (tried to make all) in February: ran moderately in quite valuable novice handicap at Ayr in April: stays 2½m, but races keenly and may prove as effective at 2m. *J. M. Jefferson.*

SCHLEMMER 8 br.g. London Bells (CAN)–Lacemaker (Astec) [1989/90 c—
c20d^{4}] lengthy, sparely-made gelding: modest chaser: poor fourth to Perroquet in —
hunter chase at Leicester in March: stays 2½m: acts on good to firm and dead going: takes a good hold: visored last 6 starts 1988/9: ran a moody race final start of that season. *M. E. Goode.*

SCOBIE DOUGH 4 br.g. Over The River (FR)–Clerihan Miss (Tarqogan)
[1989/90 16m^{pu} 16m 16m^{ro} 16m^{pu} 16s^{pu}] small gelding: behind in claimer and a —
seller on Flat: headstrong novice selling hurdler: ran out 4 out third start. *Miss S. J. Wilton.*

SCOLE 5 b.g. Deep Run–Verbana (Boreen (FR)) [1989/90 F16g] brother to useful chaser Cuddy Dale and half-brother to winning hurdler Glide On (by Le Bavard): dam well beaten on Flat: behind in NH Flat race at Kempton: yet to race over hurdles or fences. *G. A. Hubbard.*

SCORCH MAN 5 b.g. Ya Zaman (USA)–Cailin Oir (Sallust) [1989/90 16f] neat
gelding: no worthwhile form over hurdles, including in selling company. *G. A.* —
Ham.

SCOTCH DOUBLE (USA) 4 b.g. Duns Scotus (CAN)–Role Twice (USA)
(Droll Role) [1989/90 16d^{pu}] fair 2m winner on Flat (blinkered when successful): —
sold out of M. Francis' stable 13,000 gns Newmarket Autumn Sales: pulled up before fourth in juvenile hurdle at Kelso in February: dead. *N. Waggott.*

SCOTGAVOTTE (FR) 4 b.f. Dunbeath (USA)–French Minuet (FR) (Jim
French (USA)) [1989/90 16f^{4}] plating-class maiden at up to 1¼m on Flat, has run 69
visored: tired approaching last when fourth in juvenile hurdle at Wetherby in October: sold 4,700 gns Doncaster November Sales. *M. J. Camacho.*

SCOTLANDWELL 5 b.g. Royal Fountain–Dysie Mary (Apollonius) [1989/90
20g^{pu} 24g^{pu}] fifth foal: half-brother to winning point-to-pointer/hunter chaser —
Lillies Brig (by New Brig): dam of little account: tailed off when pulled up in novice hurdles at Perth. *C. J. T. Alexander.*

SCOTS GAP 5 b.g. Relkino–Suffolk Broads (Moulton) [1989/90 16g^{5} 20m^{pu}
16s 20s^{2} a20g^{6} 24f*] leggy gelding: reportedly finished lame when winning 72
amateur riders maiden hurdle at Hexham in May, leading close home: stays 3m: acts on firm ground. *A. P. Stringer.*

SCOTS LAD 9 b.g. Lochnager–Marbella II (Match III) [1989/90 16s 22s^{2} 21m c—
c25g^{pu} a24g^{4}] rangy gelding: novice selling hurdler: winning chaser: stays 25f: 65
acts on firm going: changed hands 1,000 gns Doncaster September Sales. *D. C. Jermy.*

SCOTTISH EXPRESS 5 b.g. Celtic Cone–Travellers Cheque (Kibenka)
[1989/90 F17f 16s] leggy gelding: fourth foal: half-brother to a poor novice by —
Panco: dam lightly-raced daughter of fair staying chaser Lira: in rear in NH Flat race in December and novice hurdle (blinkered) following month. *P. R. Hedger.*

SCOTTISH GOLD 6 b.g. Sonnen Gold–Calaburn (Caliban) [1989/90 22g*]
successful in amateur riders maiden hurdle at Kelso in November, beating 90 +
Jupiter's Glory 4 lengths: stays 2¾m: acts on firm going. *J. S. Wilson.*

SCRABBLE MASTER 4 ch.g. Sunley Builds–Quorum's Diajem (Thesauros)
[1989/90 aF13g 16h^{pu} 16m 18f^{pu}] leggy gelding: first foal: dam unraced: appears of —
little account. *Miss L. Bower.*

SCRUM HALF 7 br.g. Gleason (USA)–Full of Game (Arctic Chevalier)
[1989/90 18f^{pu}] fourth foal: half-brother to a winning point-to-pointer by Record —
Run: dam, placed in bumpers events in Ireland, showed no form over hurdles: tailed off when pulled up in novice event at Fontwell in October on hurdling debut: subsequently sold 1,700 gns Ascot October Sales. *Mrs L. Clay.*

SCYLLA'S CHIP 8 b.g. Armagnac Monarch–Just Scylla (Jock Scot) [1989/90 27s* 22d 25d 25m] leggy, close-coupled gelding: successful in amateur riders handicap hurdle at Folkestone in December: ran well next outing: out of his depth final start: fell first on chasing debut: stays well: acts on soft going and is possibly unsuited by top-of-the-ground: sometimes amateur ridden at overweight. *N. J. Wheeler.* c— 88

SEA ARROW 5 gr.m. Sagaro–Seajan (Mandamus) [1989/90 F16g² aF16g⁴] lengthy mare: first foal: dam, daughter of useful hurdler Sea Empress, won once on Flat and 3 times over hurdles (well suited by good test of stamina): in frame in NH Flat races at Market Rasen in October and Southwell (hung left in latter stages) in January: yet to race over hurdles or fences. *J. P. Leigh.*

SEA BUCK 4 b.g. Simply Great (FR)–Heatherside (Hethersett) [1989/90 16f³ 16g* 16d² 16s⁶ 16d² 16f] leggy gelding: quite modest maiden on Flat: won juvenile hurdle at Wolverhampton in December: stayed on well when second in similar event at Sandown following month and in juvenile handicap at Newbury (short-headed by Question of Degree) in March: will be suited by further: acts on dead going (well beaten on firm in Daily Express Triumph Hurdle at Cheltenham): visored last 3 starts. *G. B. Balding.* 106

SEA CHALLENGER 9 ch.m. Seaepic (USA)–Escallop (Kabale) [1989/90 c25f² c25g⁴ c24f³ c26f³ c26g⁴ c24g⁵] leggy, rather plain mare: won a point-to-point and second in a hunter chase in 1988: well beaten in steeplechases since (has looked a difficult ride): stays 3m: usually amateur ridden. *R. R. Ledger.* c—

SEA DEVIL 4 gr.g. Absalom–Miss Poinciana (Averof) [1989/90 16g 16d 16g] lengthy gelding: modest sprinter: well beaten in juvenile hurdles. *M. J. Camacho.* —

SEA EXPRESS 10 b. or br.g. Seaepic (USA)–Expresso (Roan Rocket) [1989/90 c20m² c20gpu] rangy gelding: lightly-raced point-to-pointer/hunter chaser: second in handicap chase at Perth in September: stays 25f: acts on hard ground. *D. Burchell.* c**94** —

SEA FLOWER (NZ) 8 ch.m. Sea Anchor–Golden Flower (NZ) (Tip The Bottle) [1989/90 24m* 20f² 24gF] lengthy, workmanlike mare: won handicap hurdle at Chepstow in October: first outing for 10 weeks and heavily bandaged near-hind, in process of running a creditable race when falling 2 out in contest won by Calabrese at Cheltenham in January: behind in novice handicap chase in 1988/9: suited by 3m: acts on any going. *D. H. Barons.* c— 117

SEAGRAM (NZ) 10 ch.g. Balak–Llanah (NZ) (Bally Royal) [1989/90 c24m* c24g* c17g² c25g² c24m* c25f³ c24dpu c24g³ c25f² c25m² c29f] c**148** —

Apart from when he was pulled up on going that doesn't suit him on his seventh outing and when running below form, probably past his best for the season, in the Whitbread Gold Cup on his final start, Seagram was a model of consistency. He finished no worse than third in his ten other races—mostly in good-class handicaps—and earned over £40,000 for his connections. Seagram won three races, all in the first half of the season. Having progressed into a useful chaser in the previous campaign, he showed himself still to be on the upgrade with impressive wide-margin successes in the Mercedes Benz Chase at Chepstow and the Charisma Gold Cup at Kempton on his first two starts. Both those handicaps were over three miles and on each occasion Seagram was given a similar tactical ride, racing prominently until sent to the front around seven from home. Six days after the Charisma Gold Cup, he showed his versatility by running Panto Prince to three lengths when conceding 3 lb in the seventeen-furlong Plymouth Gin Haldon Gold Challenge Cup at Devon & Exeter, having had little difficulty staying close up in a strongly-run race. As a consequence of those performances, Seagram faced a stiffer task when he was returned to handicaps, but at Ascot in November he won the race named after the Queen Mother's smart chaser of the 'sixties, The Rip. Seagram showed tremendous battling qualities, after making mistakes three out and at the last, to get back up on the line and beat Black Spur a short head. In the second half of the season, Seagram failed only narrowly to gain further successes in both the Ritz Club National Hunt Handicap Chase at Cheltenham and the Heidsieck Dry Monopole Handicap Chase at Liverpool. In the Ritz Club, he was worn down close home and beaten a head by Bigsun after leading three out and looking the likely winner when quickening on

The Rip Handicap Chase, Ascot—top-weight Seagram (right) gives two stone to Black Spur

the final turn. In the Heidsieck Dry Monopole, he set a sedate gallop in the early stages, repelled several challengers from three out, but had no answer to the strong finishing effort of One More Knight and was beaten a length. The Heidsieck Dry Monopole was Seagram's last race before the Whitbread Gold Cup. He should return refreshed after a summer's rest and continue to give a good account of himself.

Seagram (NZ) (ch.g. 1980)	Balak (b 1971)	Busted (b 1963)	Crepello
			Sans Le Sou
		Schonbrunn (b 1957)	Blue Peter
			Marie Therese
	Llanah (NZ) (b 1973)	Bally Royal (b 1960)	Ballymoss
			Code Militaire
		Llanis Castle (b 1956)	Llanstephan
			Castle Moat

Seagram was bred in New Zealand, and was one of the first of many potential chasers brought over from there by his trainer. The distaff side of the pedigree brings a reminder of another good ex-New Zealand chaser Royal Mail, the 1980 Whitbread Gold Cup winner who was by the useful top-of-the-ground stayer Bally Royal out of a mare by the exported Llanstephan. The sire Balak, another British-bred, won numerous races in Italy before being retired to New Zealand. Seagram is suited by a sound surface. Apart from in the Whitbread he was ridden by the 3-lb claimer Nigel Hawke, who was unable to draw the allowance in the Haldon Gold Cup. A smallish, workmanlike gelding, Seagram looked extremely well throughout his busy season and is a credit to his trainer. *D. H. Barons.*

SEAL PRINCE 9 b.g. Eastwood Prince–China Seal (Chinese Lacquer) c—
[1989/90 21d^{pu} 24g c24d^{pu}] tall, leggy, plain gelding: little form over hurdles or fences. *Major R. H. Dening.* —

SEA PENNANT 14 b.g. Angus–Le Pennant (Le Jacobin) [1989/90 20s^{pu} 16v 16d^{4} a16g^{4} 17g] lengthy gelding: fair hurdler at his best: only form for long time 72
when fourth in seller fourth start: best at around 2m: acts on any going: usually ridden by claimer. *I. R. Jones.*

SEARCHER 5 br.g. Furry Glen–Pollys Flake (Will Somers) [1989/90 F12m* F16g F12g] first foal: dam won 3 times over hurdles and was placed over fences in Ireland: odds on, won NH Flat race at Bangor in October: mid-division in similar events in February and March: yet to race over hurdles or fences. *D. H. Barons.*

SEA SHADOW 5 ch.g. Hello Gorgeous (USA)–Marie Antoinette (Habitat) [1989/90 16h* 16m^6 16f^2 16g^{pu} a16g* a18g* a16g^F a18g^4 a16g^5 16g^{pu} 19f] 105 ? compact, sparely-made gelding: won selling hurdles at Ludlow (no bid) and Southwell (bought in 6,000 gns) and a novice handicap hurdle at Lingfield: looked likely winner when falling 2 out in handicap at Southwell seventh outing: below form afterwards, finishing reportedly lame final start: stays 2¼m: acts on hard ground: usually blinkered: has broken blood vessels: trained until after ninth outing by E. Wheeler. *A. Barrow.*

SEASON'S AHEAD 7 ch.m. Politico (USA)–Early Echo (Bleep) [1989/90 c— c24g^4 c24g^{F4} c24v^F] workmanlike mare: novice hurdler: winning chaser: under — pressure when falling 2 out (remounted to finish fourth) at Carlisle in February: well suited by a test of stamina: acts on heavy ground. *S. G. Payne.*

SEATON GIRL 6 b.m. Ovac (ITY)–Forest Music (Tudor Music) [1989/90 17f^6 c— 16m^4 17g c16m 17v^2 18s^4 a20g^2 a16g^3 17m^4 21f^2 16m^F] small, sparely-made mare: 80 selling hurdler: novice chaser: seemed not quite to stay a stiff 21f penultimate start: acts on any going: rather inconsistent. *R. G. Frost.*

SEATTLE PRIDE (CAN) 4 b.g. Seattle Song (USA)–Minstrelsy (USA) (The Minstrel (CAN)) [1989/90 a16g* 16g^6] quite modest maiden on Flat at his 91 + best (has worn blinkers): won 4-runner juvenile hurdle at Lingfield in March without coming off bridle: favourite, well beaten in novice handicap at Fakenham following month. *M. H. Tompkins.*

SEA VALE 6 ch.g. Vital Season–Valeria (Vulgan) [1989/90 16s^{pu}] half-brother to winning jumpers Tompion (by Crozier), Meldon Lady (by Ballymoss) and very useful Phoenix Gold (by Precipice Wood): dam, poor NH performer, is sister to — very smart Corrie-Vacoul: tailed off when pulled up 2 out in novice hurdle at Sandown. *N. A. Gaselee.*

SEBEL HOUSE 7 b.g. Buckskin (FR)–Lulu Dee (Straight Deal) [1989/90 16d^4 20g^3] leggy, sparely-made gelding: won NH Flat race in 1988/9: in frame in novice 99 hurdles: may stay beyond 2¾m: acts on dead going. *D. McCain.*

SECOND AWARD 5 ch.m. Cruise Missile–Cash Award (Cash And Courage) [1989/90 16g^4 a16g^5 16g^F] tall mare: poor form in novice hurdles. *J. P. Leigh.* 70

SECOND MORTGAGE 9 gr.g. Tack On–Gables Grey (Colonist II) [1989/90 16v^{ro} a18g^6] leggy, angular gelding: no form over hurdles: has twice run out in §§ early stages: blinkered final start: one to leave alone. *J. Ffitch-Heyes.*

SECRET BRAE 10 b.g. Secret Ace–Fezanmac (Fez) [1989/90 c24d^5 c24d^2] c**103** strong, compact gelding: successful in 5 point-to-points in 1990: fair hunter chaser: collapsed and died after finishing second to easy winner Mystic Music at Perth: stayed 3m: acted on any going. *H. Barclay.*

SECRET CONTRACT 5 b.g. Caruso–Sealed Contract (Runnymede) [1989/90 16f^3 16f^6 16g^4 16m^F] sparely-made gelding: poor plater at up to 1m on 76 Flat: third in novice hurdle at Sedgefield in September: every chance when falling heavily 2 out in selling hurdle at Catterick in December. *Mrs G. R. Reveley.*

SECRET DANCER 4 ch.g. Last Fandango–Secret Isle (USA) (Voluntario III) [1989/90 16g^6 16g^6 20f 16d^5 24d] strong, lengthy gelding: in frame in 1¼m seller 75 on Flat (tends to race with head high and often looks none too keen): poor novice hurdler: form only at 2m: sold 1,250 gns Doncaster March Sales: resold 1,250 gns Ascot July Sales. *R. M. Whitaker.*

SECRET FINALE 11 ro.g. Warpath–Fox Covert (Gigantic) [1989/90 25g 20g^{pu} 25d* 27g^4 24d^5 20f^{pu}] compact gelding: carries a lot of condition: modest 102 ? hurdler nowadays: won conditional jockeys claimer at Kelso in February: ran as though something amiss last 2 starts: stays well: acts on any going: good mount for a claimer: has won 6 times at Sedgefield. *J. R. Fort.*

SECRET FOUR 4 b.g. My Top–Secret Top (African Sky) [1989/90 17v 16f^{ur} 16m^2] rather sparely-made ex-Irish gelding: fifth foal: half-brother to 1984 2-y-o 87 Irish 5f winner Fringe of Heaven (by Godswalk), later successful in Italy: dam ran once: modest middle-distance handicapper on Flat: behind in juvenile hurdle at Gowran Park in January (trained by A. Redmond): close up when unseating rider 2 out in maiden event at Newbury in March: never a factor when beaten 20 lengths by front-running Kalshan in novice hurdle at Wincanton following month. *R. Akehurst.*

SECRET FRIEND 4 b.g. Relkino–Aunt Eva (Great Nephew) [1989/90 F16g[5] F16g[6]] half-brother to 3 winners, including successful hurdler and novice chaser Rockmartin (by Fair Season): dam, winner over 1m and 1¼m, half-sister to Cesarewitch winner Centurion: unplaced in NH Flat races: yet to race over hurdles. *C. W. Thornton.*

SECRET LIFE 5 b.g. Corvaro (USA)–Intriguing (Lypheor) [1989/90 F16g[3] 16g 20g 16m] compact, dipped-backed gelding: second foal: dam poor Irish Flat maiden: third in NH Flat race at Uttoxeter in December: well beaten in novice hurdles. *W. A. Stephenson.* —

SECRET MEMBER 6 ch.g. Peacefull Member–Ennis Rose (Ennis) [1989/90 F16f F16g[ur] 16g[co] 20s[pu] 22g[pu]] sixth foal: half-brother to winning hurdler Silver Peace (by Gallup Poll or Silver Cloud): dam unraced: no sign of ability: saddle slipped fourth start. *R. J. Hodges.* —

SECRET RITE 7 ch.g. Kambalda–Deepdecending (Deep Run) [1989/90 c20g[3]] workmanlike gelding: winning hurdler: placed in novice chases, last of 3 only outing of 1989/90, facing stiff task: stays 2½m, but probably not 3m: best form over hurdles on a sound surface: needs to improve his jumping over fences. *J. T. Gifford.* c? —

SECRET SIN 13 b.m. Most Secret–Sugar Maple (Sweet Story) [1989/90 24g[pu]] strong, compact mare: won novice hurdle in 1982: very lightly raced and little form since, including in novice chases and point-to-points. *P. F. Craggs.* c— —

SECRET SUMMIT (USA) 4 b.c. Diamond Shoal–Ygraine (Blakeney) [1989/90 16m a16g 18g 16s[pu] 16m[3]] ex-Irish colt: third foal: dam unraced: poor maiden on Flat (has been blinkered): third to Fighting Days in maiden event at Plumpton in April, best effort in juvenile hurdles: trained by T. Kinane first start. *T. P. McGovern.* 80

SECRET VALE 9 b.m. Most Secret–Hillvale (Narrator) [1989/90 19h[pu]] strong, lengthy, dipped-backed mare: lightly-raced novice hurdler/chaser: sketchy jumper: dead. *P. A. Blockley.* c— —

SECURITY ALERT 4 b.c. Head For Heights–Wise Blood (Kalamoun) [1989/90 16f[pu]] tall, unfurnished colt: third foal: half-brother to a winner in USA by Auction Ring: dam behind in maiden at 2 yrs: wearing hood and eyeshield, pulled hard and beaten when blundering badly 3 out (eventually pulled up last) in juvenile hurdle at Newbury in November. *D. J. G. Murray-Smith.* —

SEDGEWELL LAD 8 ch.g. Proud Challenge–Meadow Nymph (Meadow Court) [1989/90 c16m[2] c16g[F] c16s c17m[5] c17f[4]] tall gelding: modest chaser: ran poorly after first start: free-running sort, best form at around 2m (stiff task over 21f): acts on any going. *P. Leach.* c96 —

SEDGEWELL ORCHID 5 gr.m. John de Coombe–Lyn Affair (Royal Palace) [1989/90 21m[pu] 16m] no sign of ability over hurdles. *P. Leach.* —

SEE YOU BOY 7 ch.g. Whiffenpoof–L's Girl (Sovereign Bill) [1989/90 F16m 16h[6]] strong gelding: second foal: dam unraced: behind in NH Flat race and novice hurdle at Taunton in October: dead. *C. L. Popham.* —

SEE YOU THEN 10 br.g. Royal Palace–Melodina (Tudor Melody) [1989/90 16s[6] 16g[F] 16m 16d] rangy, rather angular gelding: poor mover with a round action: former top-class hurdler who won Waterford Crystal Champion Hurdle at Cheltenham in 1985, 1986 and 1987: well beaten in latest running of that event in March (blinkered) and in Scottish Champion Hurdle at Ayr following month: close up, though beaten, when falling 2 out in race won by Kribensis at Wincanton earlier: suited by 2m on fast ground: had a fine turn of foot and was suited by waiting tactics: jumped well: bandaged all round in 1989/90: has been retired. *N. J. Henderson.* —

SEE YOU THERE 8 ch.g. Prominer–Mariner's Leap (King's Leap) [1989/90 c26m[F] c24d[3] c25m* c24g[3] c25m[pu] c25d[2] c26d[pu]] sturdy, good-topped gelding: moderate novice hurdler: moderate chaser: won handicap at Catterick in December: ran as if something amiss final start: stays 3m: acts on any going: suited by a strongly-run race: blinkered twice in 1988/9. *J. G. FitzGerald.* c112 —

SEISMIC LINE 5 br.g. Ardoon–Too Soon (Sheshoon) [1989/90 F16g 16m[ur] 20g[pu] 16s[pu] 16d[pu] 16s 20d[pu] 16g] smallish gelding: half-brother to 4 winners by Sterling Bay, including useful Irish 9f winner Bolton Tom, and to 1m to 9f winner Tender Bender (by Prince Tenderfoot): dam stayer: of little account. *B. Stevens.* —

SELF AID 7 b.m. Fine Blade (USA)–Laurolin (Laurence O) [1989/90 21f^{4} 21m^{6} 17g* 16f^{4} 21v^{pu} 22g^{5}] leggy, lightly-made mare: winning point-to-pointer: novice chaser: won selling handicap hurdle at Newton Abbot in November (bought in 3,800 gns): saddle slipped fifth outing: effective at around 2m and stays well: acts on any going. *J. D. Roberts.* c— 87

SELF IMPROVEMENT (USA) 4 b.c. Sharpen Up–Imaflash (USA) (Reviewer (USA)) [1989/90 16d] modest 1¼m winner on Flat in 1989 (trained by J. Gosden), soundly beaten since (found little when visored once): eighth in juvenile maiden hurdle at Perth in May. *N. Tinkler.* 64

SELF RAISING 5 ch.g. Boreen (FR)–Just Image (Saidam) [1989/90 16m^{5} 25m^{pu} 16s] stocky gelding: no worthwhile form over hurdles, including in a seller: blinkered sixth start 1988/9. *B. Preece.* —

SEMINOFF (FR) 4 b.g. In Fijar (USA)–Borjana (USA) (To The Quick (USA)) [1989/90 16m 16g^{F} 16g 16g^{F} 16d^{pu} 16m] leggy gelding: well beaten in 2 outings on Flat: poor juvenile hurdler: poor jumper: trained until after third outing by R. Champion. *T. Craig.* — x

SENEGALAIS (FR) 6 b.g. Quart de Vin (FR)–Divonne (FR) (Vieux Chateau) [1989/90 16g^{6} 22s* 24g^{pu} 21d^{6}] leggy gelding: easily best effort over hurdles when winning novice event at Folkestone in December: needed race final start: should stay 3m: acts on soft going. *S. Mellor.* 92

SENOJOJ 5 b.g. Tachypous–Merency (Meldrum) [1989/90 16m 16g^{6} 16s^{2} 18s^{5} 16g^{pu}] medium-sized gelding: selling hurdler: ran creditably in non-selling handicaps third and fourth starts: pulled up lame final outing: stays 2¼m: acts on soft going: sometimes visored (including when successful): has looked none too keen: trained by J. Jenkins until after third start. *J. P. D. Elliott.* 90

SENOR TOMAS 7 b.g. Sparkler–Pearlemor (Gulf Pearl) [1989/90 20g^{6}] good-topped gelding: one-time fair handicapper at up to 1¾m on Flat: third in novice event in 1988/9 on hurdling debut: better for race, not knocked about unduly at Kempton in January. *O. Sherwood.* —

SEQUESTRATOR 7 b.g. African Sky–Miss Redmarshall (Most Secret) [1989/90 16f^{4} 16m 16f^{2} 16h^{F}] smallish gelding: poor handicapper on Flat, suited by 7f and firm ground: best effort in novice hurdles when second at Uttoxeter in September (made most): well beaten when falling at Taunton following month: pulls hard and may prove suited by forcing tactics and 2m. *P. D. Evans.* 85

SEREMO 4 gr.g. Morston (FR)–Serenata (Larrinaga) [1989/90 16v^{5}] angular, lightly-made gelding: quite modest 1¼m winner on Flat: well beaten in slowly-run juvenile claiming hurdle at Leicester in February, pulling hard and weakening quickly 3 out: sold 2,700 gns Ascot May Sales. *Mrs N. Macauley.* —

SERGEANT AT ARMS 5 b.h. Shirley Heights–Sunningdale Queen (Gay Fandango (USA)) [1989/90 21m^{4} 20s 22s^{6} a24g^{pu}] angular horse: half-brother to Unpaid Member (by Moorestyle), a winner on Flat and over hurdles: poor staying maiden on Flat: poor novice hurdler: stays 2¾m. *J. E. Long.* 81

SERGEANT SILVER 5 gr.g. General Ironside–Coolentallagh (Perhapsburg) [1989/90 F16m F17m] fifth foal: brother to winning staying chaser Little General, novice hurdler/chaser Whynot Wingetts and NH Flat race-placed Loch Bran Lass: dam winning 2m hurdler/chaser in Ireland: seventh in NH Flat races at Sandown and Carlisle: yet to race over hurdles or fences. *R. J. Eckley.*

SERGEANT SPRITE 10 gr.g. General Ironside–Miss Sprite (Bowsprit) [1989/90 c25f^{4} c25g^{5} c24d^{5} c28g c26m^{6} c24g^{6} c26m^{5}] sturdy gelding: winning hurdler/chaser: little worthwhile form in 1989/90: stays 3m: seems to act on any going: blinkered final outing: trained until after fourth outing by P. Ransom. *Mrs J. Pitman.* c— —

SERIOUS MAN 7 b.g. Sexton Blake–Lorna Doone (USA) (Tom Rolfe) [1989/90 c20g* c20f* c20g c16f^{pu} c25h^{F}] workmanlike gelding: novice hurdler: won handicap chases at Plumpton and Folkestone in first half of season: blinkered, fell fatally on former course in March: stayed 2¾m: acted on any going. *D. M. Grissell.* c**105** —

SERIOUS MONEY 6 b.m. Silly Prices–Derigold (Derek H) [1989/90 27f^{4}] smallish, workmanlike mare: no sign of ability: dead. *C. C. Trietline.* —

SERIOZHA 7 b.g. Cut Above–Anna Karenina (Princely Gift) [1989/90 c25v^{pu} c20s^{F} c26f^{pu}] half-brother to Irish 9f winner Anna Mill (by Mill Reef): showed ability over hurdles in 1987/8: failed to complete course in hunter chases. *R. Curtis.* c— —

SETTER COUNTRY 6 b.m. Town And Country–Top Soprano (High Top) c94
[1989/90 c17g^{F} c16d* c16m^{2} c16v^{2} c16s^{2} c16g* c16s^{4} c20v^{3} c17d^{6}] sparely-made —
mare: modest hurdler: successful in mares novice chase at Nottingham in
December and handicap chase at Wincanton following month: creditable fourth to
Wink Gulliver in Daniel Homes Novices' Chase at Ascot in February: best at
around 2m: yet to race on very firm ground, acts on any other: suited by forcing
tactics: claimer ridden (unable to draw allowance at Ascot). *R. J. Hodges.*

SEVENS OUT 8 ch.g. Touch Paper–Rosie Probert (Captain's Gig (USA)) c98
[1989/90 c20s^{F} c16g^{4} c21g^{F} 16m^{6}] leggy gelding: modest form in novice hurdles: —
winning chaser: will stay beyond 2m: acts on dead going: visored second and third
outings. *A. J. Wilson.*

SEVERN INVADER 5 b.g. Al Sirat (USA)–Wunder Madchen (Brave Invader
(USA)) [1989/90 F16s 16d 21d 17d^{6}] IR 6,000 3-y-o: second foal: dam, Irish NH —
Flat race winner, half-sister to a winning hurdler: seventh in NH Flat race in
February: behind in novice hurdles. *R. Dickin.*

SEVERN SOUND 12 b.g. Manacle–Octroi (Ocarina) [1989/90 c20m^{4} c16m^{6} c78
c20g^{5} c20f^{4}] neat gelding: selling hurdler and modest chaser: gives impression —
ideally suited by 2m: best form on a sound surface: placed in point-to-point in
April (ran out in similar event earlier). *J. M. Bradley.*

SEW HIGH 7 b.g. Nicholas Bill–Sew Nice (Tower Walk) [1989/90 17f^{F} 17g]
small, angular gelding: quite modest sprint handicapper on Flat: sold out of B. —
McMahon's stable 1,900 gns Ascot September Sales: tailed off in novice hurdle in
October: likely to have difficulty in staying 2m. *Mrs J. Wonnacott.*

SEXTON 5 b.h. Beldale Flutter (USA)–Be Tuneful (Be Friendly) [1989/90 16s^{4}
20v] smallish, compact horse: novice selling hurdler: form only at 2m. *N. G.* —
Ayliffe.

SEXTON ASH 8 b.g. Sexton Blake–Golden Ash (Skymaster) [1989/90 20g 21g c—
c26g^{6} 26v^{pu} 24g 24f^{2}] sturdy gelding: handicap hurdler: only form of 1989/90 79 §
when second of 4 at Uttoxeter in May: made mistakes when well beaten on
chasing debut: stays 25f: acts on hard going: best in blinkers: trained until after
fourth start by M. Pipe: has looked most reluctant. *Miss S. J. Wilton.*

SEXTON BOY 6 gr.g. Sexton Blake–Honey May (Artaius (USA)) [1989/90
16m 16h^{5} 16m^{6}] ex-Irish gelding: first foal: dam placed over sprint distances in —
Ireland: 7f winner on Flat: poor form in novice hurdle and sellers: blinkered last 2
starts. *C. C. Trietline.*

SHACKIN BRIG 13 b.g. New Brig–Tillside (Lucky Brief) [1989/90 c24g^{5}] c81 §
compact, good-topped gelding: winning hunter chaser/point-to-pointer: ran
moody races last 2 starts of 1988/9: not disgraced in hunter chase in March: stays
3m: acts on heavy going: usually wears blinkers: isn't one to trust. *Mrs C. M.*
Gisborne.

SHACKMAN 4 ch.g. Shack (USA)–Peperonia (Prince Taj) [1989/90 16m 16f^{3}
16m 16f^{4} 16f^{2} 16f 20g] sturdy gelding: half-brother to winning point-to-pointer 72
Saddam (by Persian Bold): little worthwhile form on Flat: poor selling hurdler:
dead. *J. H. Johnson.*

SHADES OF RED 10 ch.g. Whistling Deer–Positioned (Status Seeker) c—
[1989/90 c24g^{ur}] unreliable maiden plater on Flat at 3 yrs: unseated rider fifth in
novice event on chasing debut. *C. B. B. Booth.*

SHADEUX 4 ch.g. Valiyar–A Deux (FR) (Crepello) [1989/90 17f* 17v* 16d^{ur}]
claimed £15,530 after winning 1½m claimer on Flat in June: made running when 120 ?
impressive winner of juvenile hurdles at Newton Abbot in August and January:
never travelling particularly well and was behind when unseating rider 3 out in
quite valuable event at Warwick later in month: should stay further than 17f: acts
on any going: blinkered last 2 starts: sold 4,600 gns Ascot May Sales. *M. C. Pipe.*

SHADING 6 gr.g. Homing–Silver Shadow (Birdbrook) [1989/90 F16f^{4} F16f]
fourth foal: dam very useful and thoroughly genuine hurdler: won NH Flat race in
1988/9: fourth in similar event at Catterick in October: tailed-off last at Ascot in
April: yet to race over hurdles or fences. *M. H. Easterby.*

SHADY BLADE 6 b. or br.m. Tanfirion–Fashion Shade (Fine Blade (USA))
[1989/90 20g^{4} 20m^{pu}] poor hurdler: dead. *D. McCaskill.* —

SHADY ROAD 8 b.g. Laurence O–Aprils End (Star Signal) [1989/90 18d^{3} 20d^{2} c103 p
20g^{4} 16m^{5} a20g^{4} c20d*] lengthy, workmanlike gelding: winning point-to-pointer 103
in Ireland: modest novice hurdler: made successful steeplechasing debut in
novice event at Ludlow in March, quickening well to lead flat and beat Romany

King 2 lengths (jumped slightly low): stays 2½m: acts on dead going: should improve over fences. *O. O'Neill.*

SHAHEAT 9 b.g. Parole–Golden Grove (Roan Rocket) [1989/90 c20g c20s^{6} c20d^{pu} c22g c20s^{ur} c21s^{3} c25m^{F}] neat gelding: maiden point-to-pointer: poor chaser: stays 21f: acts on good to firm and soft going: visored last 4 outings. *D. R. Gandolfo.* c73

SHAHRAYAR (MOR) 4 b.f. Happy Lord (FR)–Bellinga (FR) (Violon d'Ingres) [1989/90 16m 16g 16f^{6}] angular, sparely-made filly: behind both outings on Flat: sold out of G. Lewis' stable 1,400 gns Doncaster August Sales: no worthwhile form over hurdles in first half of season, including in seller. *K. A. Morgan.* —

SHAKIRA BLEND 5 br.g. Royal Blend–High Seeker (Hotfoot) [1989/90 16f^{pu}] of little account on Flat: well beaten in selling hurdle in 1988: visored, saddle slipped in May: sold 1,900 gns Ascot July Sales. *R. Dickin.* —

SHALBANEY 6 br.h. The Brianstan–Aldbury Girl (Galivanter) [1989/90 16g 16d 16g] medium-sized horse: ninth in NH Flat race in 1988: well beaten in 3 novice hurdles at Windsor. *C. A. Horgan.* —

SHALBOOD 4 b.c. Runnett–Deer Park (FR) (Faraway Son (USA)) [1989/90 16d a16g^{6}] lengthy, robust colt: has scope: dam maiden half-sister to 2 winning French jumpers: 7f winner at 2 yrs, well below form on Flat in 1989 (looks ungenuine): sold out of Mrs L. Piggott's stable 7,500 gns Newmarket Autumn Sales: well beaten in juvenile claimer and a novice event over hurdles: sold 1,500 gns Doncaster January Sales. *C. Spares.* —

SHALCHLO BOY 6 gr.g. Rusticaro (FR)–Mala Mala (Crepello) [1989/90 17d* 16f^{6} 17g* 17d^{4} 26v^{5} 16g^{5} 16m^{F} 16f^{2} 17m* 21m^{4} 17h^{2} 17h*] small, sturdy gelding: gaining fourth course victory of season when comfortably winning handicap hurdle at Devon & Exeter in May, showing improved form: successful in 3 handicaps (first 2 novice events) earlier: best at around 2m: acts on hard and dead going: blinkered first outing: has won for an amateur: usually a front-runner. *Mrs J. Wonnacott.* 112

SHALYMYRRH 6 b.m. Rymer–Shahzadeh (Menelek) [1989/90 16m 22d^{pu} 16m 20g] smallish, workmanlike mare: well beaten in novice hurdles: has worn crossed noseband. *J. Webber.* —

SHAMIRANI 4 gr.g. Darshaan–Sharmada (FR) (Zeddaan) [1989/90 17g^{pu} 16d* 16f* 16m 16f^{2} 16f^{3}] tall, leggy gelding: fourth foal: dam, 5f winner at 2 yrs, half-sister to 3 winning French jumpers: useful form in 3 outings at up to 11.5f on Flat: sold out of M. Stoute's stable 40,000 gns Newmarket Autumn Sales: successful at Newcastle in juvenile hurdle (swished tail) in February and novice event in March: ran creditably behind Dancing River at Wetherby and Haydock (handicap, none too fluent) last 2 starts: acts on good to soft and firm going: takes a good hold: has worn a crossed noseband. *J. H. Johnson.* 113

SHAMROCK MASTER 12 br.g. Menelek–Gypsy Miss (Master Owen) [1989/90 c20s^{ur} c22s^{5}] close-coupled, sparely-made gelding: novice hurdler/chaser: winning point-to-pointer: no form in 1989/90, blinkered final outing (soon ridden): stays well. *Miss Mary Hamilton Ellis.* c— —

SHAMROCK STAR 4 ch.g. Horage–Alfarouse (Home Guard (USA)) [1989/90 16d^{pu}] lengthy gelding: first foal: dam never ran: bit backward, tailed off when pulled up 2 out in juvenile hurdle at Warwick: sold 2,500 gns Ascot May Sales. *R. Curtis.* —

SHANBALLY BOY 9 b.g. Random Shot–June's Slipper (No Argument) [1989/90 c26s^{3} c25s^{F} c24m^{3} c24m^{3}] smallish, workmanlike gelding: handicap chaser: stays well: acts on heavy going and good to firm: has joined N. Henderson. *D. J. G. Murray-Smith.* c**106** —

SHANGOSEER 9 b.g. Record Token–Fly For Home (Habitat) [1989/90 c16d^{5} c20s^{pu} c16f^{2} c16m^{2} c20g] compact gelding: handicap chaser: co-favourite, ran moderately in selling handicap final outing: stays 2½m and is worth another try at 3m: acts on any going. *J. White.* c**90** —

SHANKHOUSE GIRL 6 gr.m. General Ironside–Truly Fair (Gulf Pearl) [1989/90 16f^{4} 16f 22g^{pu}] medium-sized mare: fifth foal: half-sister to winning Irish point-to-pointer Irish Road (by Choral Society): dam a maiden: little sign of ability in novice hurdles. *J. I. A. Charlton.* —

SHANNAGARY 9 ch.g. Deep Run–Farranfore (Fortina) [1989/90 c21m^{3} c16m^{2} c19d^{pu} c21g^{5} c21m^{2}] dipped-backed gelding: handicap chaser: best form of c**108** —

season on first 2 starts: stays 21f: acts on good to firm and soft going: has tended to hang right, and looked none too keen second start. *J. A. B. Old.*

SHANNON PRINCE 8 b.g. Pollerton–Milkmaid (Astec) [1989/90 16dpu 16m 16m6 a20g 19s6 24d 20g] lengthy ex-Irish gelding: 1½m winner and placed at up to 2m on Flat: poor novice hurdler: tailed off in seller fifth start. *A. P. James.* —

SHARE A FRIEND 9 ch.m. Ascertain (USA)–Gilly's Folly (Sikandar) [1989/90 22s6 c20g* c20gur c24g* c24s* c24m* c24gpu] tall, sparely-made mare: winning hurdler: jumped soundly in main and was impressive each time when winning novice chases at Carlisle (3) and Wetherby in second half of season: out of her depth final start: stays 3m: acts on good to firm and heavy going. *G. Richards.* **c110** —

SHARON'S ROYALE 7 ch.g. Royal Match–Rose Amber (Amber Rama (USA)) [1989/90 16d2 16g 16m 16g a16g4] sturdy, workmanlike gelding: modest form in novice hurdles: will prove best at around 2m: best form with give in the ground: blinkered final start (ran moderately): sold out of R. Whitaker's stable 9,200 gns Doncaster October Sales. *A. P. Jones.* 96

SHARPALONG (USA) 8 ch.g. Sharpen Up–Caroglen Jo (CAN) (Victoria Park) [1989/90 22m] workmanlike gelding: novice hurdler: only form over 25f on firm going. *Mrs T. Cuthbert.* —

SHARP CHARTER 4 ch.c. Kris–Centrocon (High Line) [1989/90 16gpu] workmanlike colt: half-brother to fairly useful hurdler Larchmont (by Home Guard): fair staying maiden on Flat, looks a difficult ride and probably best visored: sold out of M. Stoute's stable 19,000 gns Newmarket Autumn Sales: pulled up after second in juvenile maiden hurdle at Wincanton in February. *K. White.* —

SHARPFORD 5 ch.g. Milford–Sharp And Sweet (Javelot) [1989/90 16s 20g a20g4] leggy gelding: poor novice selling hurdler: best form at 2m on dead going: blinkered final start. *D. W. Browning.* —

SHARPGUN (FR) 4 ch.c. Sharpo–Whitegun (FR) (Carwhite) [1989/90 16m 16m4 16g2 16s3 16v* 16v3 16d] leggy colt: placed at up to 1m on Flat: sold out of P. Kelleway's stable 10,000 gns Newmarket Autumn Sales: showed plenty of ability over hurdles prior to winning juvenile event at Folkestone in January: clear 1½ lengths third behind Badrakhani at Plumpton later in month: may not stay much beyond 2m: seems to need the mud. *V. Young.* 107

SHARP JEWEL 9 ch.g. Fine Blade (USA)–Regent Ruby (Pyrenean) [1989/90 c20m4 c24m3] strong, close-coupled gelding: handicap chaser: sweating and below form both starts 1989/90: stays 3m: acts on any going. *W. F. Caudwell.* **c113** —

SHARP JUSTICE 4 ch.c. Sharpo–Lady Justice (Status Seeker) [1989/90 16s4 16g4] close-coupled colt: useful but inconsistent performer at up to 7f on Flat: showed ability both starts, on second 15 lengths fourth, no extra from 2 out, to Philosophos in Tote Placepot Hurdle at Kempton in February: unlikely to stay beyond 2m: can win a race over hurdles. *M. J. Ryan.* 116 p

SHARP KING (FR) 7 ch.g. Sharpman–Princesse Kay (FR) (Roi Lear (FR)) [1989/90 22d 20d 21m3] angular gelding: winning hurdler: stays 2½m: possibly needs a sound surface. *K. A. Morgan.* 94

SHARP'N SHINE (USA) 4 b.g. Sharpen Up–Repetitious (Northfields (USA)) [1989/90 16g 16g 16d a16g5] medium-sized gelding: 1m winner at 2 yrs, but became temperamental on Flat in 1989: sold out of M. Stoute's stable 13,500 gns Newmarket Autumn Sales: poor novice hurdler: blinkered final start. *C. James.* —

SHARP ORDER 5 ch.g. Sharpo–Cardinal Palace (Royal Palace) [1989/90 16gpu 16m 16s4 16m6 17g3] leggy, sparely-made gelding: winning selling hurdler: poor form in varied company in 1989/90: likely to prove best at around 2m: acts on good to firm ground: has worn crossed noseband and raced with tongue tied down: has carried head high. *Miss S. J. Wilton.* 79

SHARPRIDGE 6 ch.g. Nearly A Hand–Maria's Piece (Rose Knight) [1989/90 16g 16m 16fF 17m] rangy gelding: has scope: no worthwhile form over hurdles. *J. S. King.* —

SHARP ROSE 6 ch.m. Steel City–Red Rose III (St Elmo) [1989/90 17h4 16g4 20f] small, sparely-made mare: poor novice hurdler: best form at 2m. *J. L. Goulding.* 65

SHARP SHAPE (USA) 5 ch.h. Sharpen Up–Love That Girl (USA) (High Echelon) [1989/90 16g5 16g 20s5 a16g6 16s 24m] sparely-made horse: maiden on Flat: sold out of R. Hannon's stable 2,900 gns Newmarket July Sales: poor novice 81

hurdler: well beaten last 3 starts: probably stays 2½m: acts on soft going: blinkered final outing. *D. J. Bell.*

SHARP SONG 9 ch.g. Sharpen Up–Mixed Melody (Alcide) [1989/90 c20f^{pu} c—
c20f^{pu} c16g^{ur} c20f^{pu}] workmanlike gelding: fair chaser at his best: ran badly in —
1989/90: stays 2½m: suited by a sound surface: sometimes blinkered, visored final outing: inclined to make the odd mistake. *T. Fairhurst.*

SHASTON 5 ch.g. Rolfe (USA)–Nicaline (High Line) [1989/90 22m^{2} 22g^{4} 24s^{2} 25d^{3} 21d* 22f^{3}] smallish, sparely-made gelding: won maiden hurdle at Warwick in 99
March: good third in novice event at Wincanton later in month: stays 3m: acts on any going: seems best in blinkers: often amateur ridden (not at Warwick): has found little. *W. G. M. Turner.*

SHAY 5 b.g. Hays–Barefoot Contessa (Homeric) [1989/90 16d^{pu}] small gelding:
modest 5f winner at his best on Flat: sold out of M. Brittain's stable 2,500 gns —
Doncaster June (1989) Sales: behind when pulled up in novice hurdle at Stratford (pulled hard). *A. J. Chamberlain.*

SHEAN LAD 10 b.g. Deep Run–Shean Lass (Black Rock) [1989/90 c16g^{2} c79 x
c24g^{5} c16g^{5} c16m^{6} 17g^{pu}] lengthy, well-made gelding: winning hurdler: poor —
novice chaser (let down by his jumping most outings): suited by 2m and top-of-the-ground over hurdles: blinkered final outing: broke a blood vessel last start of 1988/9: trained until after second outing by G. Richards. *Miss L. C. Siddall.*

SHEDARBO 5 ch.g. Sagaro–Song of Grace (Articulate) [1989/90 F17m 16s^{6}]
sturdy gelding: fourth foal: half-brother to modest novice hurdler House of Lords —
(by Politico): dam lightly-raced daughter of a winning hurdler/chaser: mid-division in NH Flat race in November: well beaten in novice hurdle at Sedgefield 3 months later. *D. McCain.*

SHEDID 9 ch.m. St Columbus–Shewill (Evening Trial) [1989/90 c26f* c24f^{2}] c88
first foal: dam point-to-point winner: modest winning point-to-pointer: won novice hunter chase at Folkestone in May: good second at Huntingdon later in month: stays 3¼m: acts on firm ground. *Mrs P. Rowe.*

SHEER STEEL 10 ch.g. Precipice Wood–Flora Finching (Fortina) [1989/90 c102 x
c24d^{pu} c28g^{ur} c21d* c27v^{F} c28g^{3}] leggy, angular gelding: handicap chaser: won —
at Towcester in February: ran creditably final start: effective at 21f and stays well: acts on soft going: well beaten in blinkers once in 1987/8: moderate jumper. *J. M. Bukovets.*

SHEER WATER 7 br.m. Vital Season–Irene Louise (Match III) [1989/90 16g^{pu}] successful in point-to-points in March and April: of little account over
hurdles: sold 3,600 gns Ascot December Sales. *D. C. Tucker.* —

SHELBOURNE 8 br.g. Shirley Heights–Super Dancer (Taj Dewan) [1989/90 16g 22d^{pu} 20g] tall, close-coupled gelding: one-time fairly useful hurdler: little —
sign of retaining ability in 1989/90: should be suited by further than 2m: acts on good to firm and soft going (possibly unsuited by heavy). *J. S. Haldane.*

SHELLY'S FOLLY 5 b.h. Music Boy–Gay Maria (Tacitus) [1989/90 16m^{6}] small, close-coupled horse: maiden plater over hurdles: unlikely to stay much
beyond 2m: acts on dead going. *Mrs G. E. Jones.* —

SHENDAR 8 b.g. Rymer–Miss Starworthy (Twilight Alley) [1989/90 c25m* c82
c24f^{2}] big, workmanlike gelding: winning point-to-pointer: won novice hunter chase at Wolverhampton in March: creditable 20 lengths second at Worcester in April: will stay beyond 25f: acts on firm ground. *W. R. J. Everall.*

SHENYOUP 9 ch.g. Sandy Creek–Roanoke (Charlottesville) [1989/90 17f*
18h^{2} 20f^{pu}] workmanlike gelding: has been fired: selling hurdler: attracted no bid 83
after winning handicap at Newton Abbot in July: ran as though something was amiss final start (September): stays 2½m: suited by firm ground: has worn a visor, and run blinkered (did first 2 starts 1989/90). *J. Ffitch-Heyes.*

SHEPPIE'S DOUBLE 7 b.m. Scallywag–Quadrille II (Quadriga) [1989/90
16f^{6} 21f^{pu}] well beaten only completed start over hurdles. *G. B. Barlow.* —

SHERALAM 11 b.g. Carvin–Sursum Corda (FR) (Le Haar) [1989/90 c20m^{6} c—
a16g^{5}] sturdy gelding: winning point-to-pointer: poor novice hurdler/chaser: —
possibly unsuited by soft ground. *N. J. Wheeler.*

SHERINGHAM HOUSE 7 b.g. Crash Course–Deep Grey (Deep Run) c—
[1989/90 c16f^{3} c16g^{4} c20d^{pu} c17f^{F} c21f^{3}] robust gelding: no worthwhile form in novice chases: sold 4,000 gns Doncaster June Sales. *J. White.*

SHERMAGO 8 b.m. Humdoleila–Tartarbee (Charlottesville) [1989/90 16m3 16f2] rather sparely-made mare: poor novice hurdler: form only at 2m: acts on firm ground. *Mrs J. D. Goodfellow.* 76

SHERMAN WAY 8 ch.g. Proverb–Helens Tower (Dual) [1989/90 c20v6] winning point-to-pointer (has refused once): tailed off in maiden hunter chase at Folkestone in February. *J. C. S. Hickman.* c–

SHERPAMAN 8 b.g. Northfields (USA)–McCoy (USA) (Hillsdale) [1989/90 25mpu 16g a16g6] smallish, round-barrelled gelding: poor novice selling hurdler: sometimes blinkered: sold 750 gns Ascot May Sales. *G. P. Kelly.* –

SHERRY GO GO 5 b.m. The Brianstan–My Nan (Pampered King) [1989/90 21dpu] lengthy, workmanlike mare: no sign of ability in NH Flat race and 2 novice hurdles. *Miss R. J. Hamar.* –

SHERWOOD GUNNER 8 ch.g. Gunner B–Wheel Grace (Gulf Pearl) [1989/90 16g3 20dpu 16g 16g* 16s5 17f2 16d2 16m3 16f*] workmanlike gelding: fair hurdler: won handicaps at Catterick in February and Wetherby (beat Dancing River 4 lengths) in May: best at 2m: acts on any going. *O. Brennan.* 123

SHERZINE 4 br.f. Gorytus (USA)–Tableline (USA) (Round Table) [1989/90 16f2 17g6] won 1½m seller on Flat in 1989: second in juvenile selling hurdle at Southwell in August: well beaten in non-seller at Devon & Exeter 4 months later: sold out of M. H. Easterby's stable 3,900 gns Doncaster October Sales in between. *Mrs J. G. Retter.* 73

SHESHELLS 5 b.m. Zino–Sandy Doll (Thatching) [1989/90 17m2 16h* 16f4] leggy mare: won novice hurdle at Hexham in October: broke down in seller later in month. *G. M. Moore.* 84

SHEVAJI 4 br.g. Indian King (USA)–Brave Ivy (Decoy Boy) [1989/90 F14v5] first foal: dam, sprint maiden, is half-sister to smart miler Young Runaway: 19 lengths fifth behind Dakyns Boy in NH Flat race at Ayr in April: yet to race over hurdles. *Miss S. E. Hall.*

SHIFNAL 5 ch.g. Tower Walk–Leitha (Vienna) [1989/90 17hpu] compact gelding: novice selling hurdler: pulled up lame at Devon & Exeter in August. *A. P. James.* –

SHIFTY ALBERT 4 ch.g. Morston (FR)–Miss Shifter (Realm) [1989/90 16f3] no sign of ability on Flat: ridden by 3-lb claimer, remote third of 4 in selling hurdle at Hereford in September: sold 750 gns Ascot October Sales. *R. Simpson.* –

SHIKABELL 6 br.m. Kala Shikari–Betbellof (Averof) [1989/90 c17f4 c16f3] leggy mare: winning hurdler: poor form in 2 outings over fences early in season: will prove best at around 2m: suited by a sound surface. *P. J. Jones.* c70 –

SHILGROVE PLACE 8 ch.g. Le Bavard (FR)–Petmon (Eudaemon) [1989/90 20g* 24sF 24d4 22v2] useful-looking gelding: will make a chaser: fair hurdler: won moderately-run handicap at Newcastle in January: creditable second at Ayr in February: stays 2¾m, seemingly not 3m: acts on any going: claimer or amateur ridden: genuine. *Mrs S. A. Bramall.* 123

SHIMONI 6 ch.g. Swing Easy (USA)–Ramuk's Queen (Queen's Hussar) [1989/90 20vF 16m 17m 20m] leggy, sparely-made gelding: novice selling hurdler: no worthwhile form in 1989/90. *F. G. Hollis.* –

SHINING ART 5 ch.g. Artaius (USA)–Moonlight Sonata (So Blessed) [1989/90 24g2] leggy gelding: novice hurdler: good second in amateur riders event at Perth in May: stays 3m: acts on heavy going: has sweated. *D. McCain.* 89

SHINING DEEP 6 ch.g. Deep Run–Ever Shining (Indigenous) [1989/90 20gpu] big, rather angular gelding: seventh foal: half-brother to Axial Flow (by Pitpan), winner of NH Flat race and placed over hurdles in Ireland: dam winning Irish hurdler: bit backward, well behind when pulled up in novice hurdle at Wetherby in January. *J. Mackie.* –

SHIONA ANNE 6 b.m. Royal Fountain–Miss Craigie (New Brig) [1989/90 16d 16s5 18d] unfurnished mare: tried to run out and unseated rider on third start in NH Flat races: poor form in novice hurdles. *R. H. Goldie.* 71

SHIP OF STATE 7 b.g. Troy–Sea Venture (FR) (Diatome) [1989/90 19mpu] lightly-raced novice hurdler: pulled up only outing in last 3 seasons. *M. C. Pipe.* –

SHIPWRIGHT 9 br.g. Hotfoot–Ripeck (Ribot) [1989/90 c26f2 c24g* c26v4 c21gF] big, deep-girthed gelding: carries plenty of condition: handicap hurdler: won poor novice chase at Cheltenham in November by 20 lengths: well-beaten c81 –

fourth behind Royal Athlete at Newton Abbot in January: stays 3¼m: acts on any going. *R. G. Frost.*

SHIRLEY ANN 7 ch.m. Buckskin (FR)–Doone Gate (Arctic Slave) [1989/90 21m a16g4 a20g4 a20g4 a20g3 16gpu 16gro a16g* a20g] tall, leggy mare: claimer ridden, won novice hurdle at Southwell in April: ran out second on previous start: stays 2½m: blinkered third start: unreliable. *R. J. Weaver.* 86 §

SHIRYON 5 b.h. Tickled Pink–Assel Zawie (Sit In The Corner (USA)) [1989/90 16g] leggy horse: novice selling hurdler: never dangerous only outing of season (November): best run at 2m on dead ground. *P. J. Bevan.* —

SHOCK ABSORBER 6 b.g. Old Jocus–Please Go (Tangle) [1989/90 17d] little sign of ability in 2 novice hurdles at Devon & Exeter. *J. H. Baker.* —

SHOKRAN 5 b.g. Top Ville–Celtic Twilight (Varano) [1989/90 20g a16g5] seems of little account over hurdles: blinkered first outing: sold 1,050 gns Ascot February Sales. *R. Simpson.* —

SHOOLER PRINCE 13 b.g. Shoolerville (USA)–Winning Venture (Eastern Venture) [1989/90 c24mpu] sturdy gelding: poor chaser: stays 3m: best form with give in the ground and acts on heavy going: sometimes makes mistakes. *Miss S. Pilkington.* c— —

SHOON HILL 6 br.g. Green Shoon–Carrig-An-Neady (Orchardist) [1989/90 20g 22d 20d] half-brother to 4 jumps winners, including staying chaser Welfare (by Carlburg) and modest chaser People's Choice (by Strong Gale): dam never ran: tailed off in novice hurdles. *W. A. Stephenson.* —

SHOON WIND 7 b.g. Green Shoon–Gone (Whistling Wind) [1989/90 22g3 24g 20v 25g* 20g 24g4 25g 25f 24gpu] workmanlike gelding: handicap hurdler: raced wide throughout when winning at Catterick in January: lost his way over fences after winning novice chase in 1988/9: stays well: acts on heavy going: inconsistent and has looked a difficult ride. *C. R. Beever.* c— 109

SHOPWELL 6 b.g. The Parson–Zitas Toi (Chinatown) [1989/90 22g 20g 17d5 21mpu] ex-Irish gelding: first foal: dam, winning point-to-pointer and placed over hurdles in Ireland, half-sister to 3 jumping winners: won point-to-point in 1989: poor form in novice hurdles: should be suited by further than 2m. *D. R. Gandolfo.* 69

SHOREHAM LADY 5 br.m. Strong Gale–Tarpon Springs (Grey Sovereign) [1989/90 16m 17vF 16g 21d6] lengthy mare: half-sister to winning 2m hurdler Gouldswood (by Mr Fluorocarbon): poor middle-distance maiden on Flat: sold out of P. Rohan's stable 6,800 gns Ascot August Sales: first sign of ability in novice hurdles when sixth behind Mossgara at Warwick in March, travelling strongly until losing place after 4 out and not knocked about thereafter: gives impression capable of better and is one to keep an eye on in modest company. *S. N. Cole.* — p

SHORE LIGHT 6 br.g. Sparkler–Cabotage (Sea Hawk II) [1989/90 c16g] big, workmanlike gelding: novice hurdler: made mistakes when tailed off on chasing debut. *S. Dow.* c— —

SHORT LIST 7 b.g. Octavo (USA)–Allitess (Mugatpura) [1989/90 c16d5 c20mpu c20fpu c16g5 c24m3 c25m3 c20f* c24m3] lengthy gelding: won novice chase at Ascot in May, jumping well and leading from sixth but only just holding on: ran poorly all other starts of season: stays 3m: acts on any going: tends to sweat and be on toes in preliminaries: sold 10,000 gns Ascot June Sales. *J. T. Gifford.* **c101** ? —

SHORT MEASURE 5 ch.m. Arkan–Gambling Princess VII (pedigree unknown) [1989/90 F12g F16f3] non-thoroughbred mare: first reported foal: dam never ran: around 15 lengths third of 9 behind Wessex Warrior in NH Flat race at Wincanton in March (swerved left start): yet to race over hurdles or fences. *Mrs Gill E. Jones.*

SHORT SHOT 4 b.g. Young Generation–Blessed Damsel (So Blessed) [1989/90 16m] workmanlike gelding: half-brother to novice hurdler Bustamente (by Busted): placed over 1¼m on Flat: sold out of W. Hastings-Bass's stable 16,500 gns Newmarket Autumn Sales: not knocked about after losing touch 3 out in juvenile hurdle at Windsor in November. *J. R. Jenkins.* —

SHOT AND SHELL (USA) 5 b.g. Damascus (USA)–Leap Lively (USA) (Nijinsky (CAN)) [1989/90 16f3 18f2 16f4 18g4 20g 16s2 a20g 16v] leggy, light-framed gelding: novice selling hurdler: stays 2¼m: acts on firm and soft ground (well beaten on heavy): blinkered in 1989/90. *G. P. Enright.* 73

SHOTINGO 10 b.g. Rustingo–Pennyshot (Big Shot) [1989/90 c20spu] lengthy, shallow-girthed gelding: winning chaser: made numerous mistakes only outing of c— —

season (December): stays 2¾m: acts on good to firm and soft going: usually claimer ridden. *W. R. Sheedy.*

SHOWDOWN 4 ch.g. Final Straw–Sideshow (Welsh Pageant) [1989/90 16f^5 16m 18m 18g^5] sturdy gelding: half-brother to fair hurdler Arbitrage (by Monsanto): modest winning miler on Flat: fifth in juvenile hurdles at Ascot in October and Fontwell in December. *A. Moore.* 78

SHOW US GLORY 4 b.f. Show-A-Leg–Transonic (Continuation) [1989/90 16f^{ur} 16f^{pu}] no sign of ability on Flat or in selling hurdles. *R. Thompson.* —

SHREWD INVESTOR 8 ch.g. Proverb–Buckstown Lass (Dual) [1989/90 20f^{pu}] workmanlike gelding: lightly-raced novice hurdler: pulled up lame at Sedgefield in September. *Miss L. C. Siddall.* —

SHRRAAR 4 b.g. Lomond (USA)–Cairnfold (USA) (Never Bend) [1989/90 20m 18g^{pu}] leggy, angular gelding: soundly beaten in 3 outings on Flat: sold out of A. Stewart's stable 6,000 gns Newmarket Autumn Sales: no sign of ability in juvenile hurdles: sold 1,600 gns Doncaster January Sales. *B. Stevens.* —

SHU FLY (NZ) 6 ch.g. Tom's Shu (USA)–Alycone (NZ) (Philoctetes) [1989/90 16s a16g* 16m a18g 16f^4 16m^2 16g* 16f* 16m^2] smallish gelding: won novice hurdles at Lingfield (conditional jockeys) in March and Uttoxeter and Hereford in May: sweating, very good second in lady riders handicap at Stratford final start (idled run-in): best form at 2m: acts on firm ground. *Mrs S. Oliver.* 115

SHUTTLE HILL 5 b.g. Green Shoon–Shinaro (Straight Deal) [1989/90 F16g^2 F16g^4] brother to very smart hurdler and winning chaser Miller Hill and half-brother to quite useful hurdlers Marshell Key (by Deep Run) and Without A Doubt (by Prominer): dam of little account: second in NH Flat race at Catterick in March: bolted and unseated rider before start of similar event at Kelso later in month: yet to race over hurdles or fences. *T. P. Tate.*

SHY HIKER 7 ch.m. Netherkelly–High Seeker (Hotfoot) [1989/90 16d 16m 21m^{pu} a20g^5 a16g^2 a16g^2 a20g* 16g^5 20g^3 24m^3 22m^2] workmanlike mare: ridden by 7-lb claimer, won novice handicap hurdle at Southwell in April: ran creditably last 3 starts: barely stays 3m: acts on good to firm ground. *R. Dickin.* 86

SHY MISTRESS 7 b.m. Cawston's Clown–Shy Talk (Sharpen Up) [1989/90 20s^F 16s^{pu} 21d] leggy mare: successful over 6f on Flat in 1989: sold out of A. Jones's stable 900 gns Doncaster November Sales: no form over hurdles (in touch when falling seventh on first start): unlikely to stay 2½m. *G. A. Ham.* —

SIBTON ABBEY 5 b.g. Strong Gale–Bally Decent (Wrekin Rambler) [1989/90 20m^3 20f^4 16s 16g^2 16d 16s^2 20d^2 16m^3 20f*] lengthy gelding: has scope: runner-up in 3 novice hurdles prior to winning poor contest at Worcester in March very easily by 15 lengths: stays 2½m: acts on any going: has run well for a claimer. *G. A. Hubbard.* 94

SICILIAN ANSWER 13 b.g. No Argument–Sicilian Girl (Sicilian Prince) [1989/90 c16g^F c24v^6 c30g* c28d^4] well-made gelding: won handicap chase at Newcastle in January from one other finisher: made a few mistakes when soundly beaten next outing: seems not to stay extreme distances when conditions are testing: acts on any going: good mount for an amateur or claimer. *G. Richards.* **c111** —

SICILIAN PASSAGE 8 gr.g. Pals Passage–Hiriwa (Diritto) [1989/90 c17d^6 c16m* c20m^3] rather dipped-backed gelding: winning hurdler: having only third race since 1986/7 when winning novice handicap chase at Wolverhampton in January: good third in handicap on same course in March: stays 2½m: acts on good to firm ground: has won for a claimer. *D. Nicholson.* c**103** —

SICILIAN SWING 5 b.g. Swing Easy (USA)–Mab (Morston (FR)) [1989/90 16g 17f 16g^2 16v 16g] tall, leggy gelding: half-brother to winning hurdler Brampton Lyn (by Derrylin): dam, maiden, half-sister to a winning chaser: little sign of ability on Flat: second in conditional jockeys selling hurdle at Towcester in December, best effort: may be worth a try over further than 2m: seems unsuited by heavy ground. *W. Holden.* 79

SICILIAN VESPERS 5 b.m. Mummy's Game–Orange Silk (Moulton) [1989/90 17h* 17m a18g^3] neat mare: 7f seller winner on Flat: bought in 5,500 gns after winning novice selling hurdle at Devon & Exeter in August from one other finisher: raced freely and finished tired in handicap at Southwell in November. *J. White.* 73 ?

SIDBURY HILL 14 br.g. Cheval–Watermark II (Sadler's Wells) [1989/90 c27s^5 c30v c26s^2 c26v^{pu} c29g^4] big, strong gelding: modest chaser: out-and-out c97

stayer: probably needs give in the ground nowadays: blinkered once in 1987/8:
needs plenty of driving. *S. Pike.*

SIDE BRACE (NZ) 6 gr.g. Mayo Mellay (NZ)–Grey Mist (NZ) (Karayar)
[1989/90 17h^3 21f^3 20m^4 19g^5 a20g^2 25g a20g^3 17d^6] neat gelding: novice hurdler: 81
races freely, stays 2½m: acts on firm ground (ran moderately on dead final start).
D. H. Barons.

SIDVIC 11 b.g. Harvest Spirit–Olisa (Bally Russe) [1989/90 c16s^{pu} c16d^{pu} c16g^5 c— x
c16v^5 c16g^{ur} c28g^{pu} c16g^{pu} c16f^6] very tall gelding: winning chaser: well below —
his best in 1989/90: best form at 2m with give in the ground: usually claimer
ridden nowadays: has worn a crossed noseband: moderate jumper: sold 1,500 gns
Ascot June Sales. *R. D. E. Woodhouse.*

SIEGERIN 6 b.m. Wolver Hollow–Sigtrudis (Sigebert) [1989/90 16f^2 16g^5 20g^3 c**86**
20m^6 c16g^5 c20s^3 c20d^4 c20m^{pu}] leggy, sparely-made mare: handicap hurdler: 98
modest novice chaser: ran in snatches seventh start: stays 2½m: acts on any
going: pulled up lame final outing (March). *M. E. D. Francis.*

SIGNORE ODONE 8 b.g. Milford–Duchy (Rheingold) [1989/90 c16f* c**106**
c16m^{pu}] workmanlike gelding: winning hurdler: made all in novice chase at —
Market Rasen in August: raced only at around 2m: acted on firm ground and good
to soft: dead. *M. H. Easterby.*

SIKERA 4 b.f. Decoy Boy–Cider With Kathy (Relko) [1989/90 aF13g^2 16f 16g^4
17m^{pu}] sparely-made filly: first foal: dam placed in selling hurdles at up to 2½m: 72
second in NH Flat race at Lingfield in February: best effort over hurdles when
fourth in juvenile event at Perth in April: ran poorly in blinkers final start. *P. J.
Hobbs.*

SIKERA SPY 8 b.m. Harvest Spirit–Ida Spider (Ben Novus) [1989/90 16m c**99** p
c16m^3 c16g^2 c20f^3 c20m*] winning hurdler: won novice handicap chase at —
Worcester in April by 6 lengths from Impeccable Timing, making all: stays 2½m:
best form on top-of-the-ground. *Mrs A. R. Hewitt.*

SILENT CHANT 6 br.g. Smooth Stepper–Florimell (Shooting Chant)
[1989/90 F16m^2 16s^5 21d 20m* 21f^{3dis}] IR 9,000 4-y-o: smallish, angular gelding: 89 +
half-brother to fair Irish hurdler/chaser Trimar Gold (by Goldhill) and to a winner
in Italy by Mount Hagen: dam unraced half-sister to several winners: showed best
form when blinkered on last 2 starts, winning novice hurdle at Plumpton in April
on first occasion: disqualified for failing to draw correct weight next time: will stay
3m: acts on firm ground. *D. J. G. Murray-Smith.*

SILENT HARMONY 8 ch.m. Nearly A Hand–Song Without Words (Spartan
General) [1989/90 17m^4 22f^{pu} 16m] small, plain mare: no sign of ability: blinkered —
first outing. *N. B. Thomson.*

SILENT PRINCESS 4 b.f. King of Spain–Silent Dancer (Quiet Fling (USA))
[1989/90 17h^2 16m^{pu} 18f^{pu} 16g 16d a20g* a20g^3 a20g^2 a22g^4 16f a20g* 20f^4] 88 §
sparely-made filly: poor maiden on Flat: bought in 3,000 gns after winning selling
hurdles at Southwell in January and April: stays 2½m: best form on fibresand: has
worn blinkers, visored last 2 starts: claimer ridden: has looked ungenuine, and is
thoroughly inconsistent: sold out of P. Walwyn's stable 2,500 gns Ascot
November Sales after third start. *J. L. Harris.*

SILENT RING (USA) 4 b. or br.g. Silent Cal (USA)–Rafters Ring (USA)
(Delta Judge) [1989/90 16f^5 16f^2 16m* 18m^6 16d^4 22d^6 20g^{pu} 16d^4 16f^6] leggy 86
gelding: poor maiden on Flat: won juvenile hurdle at Towcester in November: ran
creditably on occasions afterwards: probably stays 2¾m: acts on firm and dead
ground: visored third outing, blinkered sixth to eighth: jumped badly right on
occasions eighth start. *P. R. Hedger.*

SILENT TOM 8 b.g. Tom Noddy–Silent Sleeves (Dumbarnie) [1989/90 16d]
big, lengthy gelding: no worthwhile form over hurdles: headstrong. *S. Christian.* —

SILENT TWIRL 7 b.m. Piaffer (USA)–Lost In Silence (Silent Spring) c**106**
[1989/90 c19g*] sparely-made mare: winning hurdler: jumped soundly when —
winning novice chase at Hereford in October: stays 19f: possibly unsuited by
heavy going, acts on any other: has run well when sweating. *J. S. King.*

SILENT WISH (USA) 4 ch.g. Silent Screen (USA)–Petita (USA) (Nashua)
[1989/90 16s^F] third foal: dam, placed at up to 1½m, half-sister to a minor winner: —
fell second in juvenile hurdle at Taunton in December. *Miss A. J. Whitfield.*

SILK DYNASTY 4 b.g. Prince Tenderfoot (USA)–Mountain Chase (Mount
Hagen (FR)) [1989/90 16f^F 16f^3 16s 16g^5] small gelding: 1½m winner on Flat in 83

January: modest form in juvenile hurdles earlier: below form on soft ground: needs to improve his jumping. *M. E. D. Francis.*

SILKEN SONG 7 b.g. Taufan (USA)–Courreges (Manado) [1989/90 20g 20v 16gpu a20g6] close-coupled, rather sparely-made gelding: novice selling hurdler: blinkered third start (trained until after then by D. Burchell). *P. Davis.* —

SILKS DOMINO 5 ch.g. Dominion–Bourgeonette (Mummy's Pet) [1989/90 20fur 16m a24g*] leggy, sparely-made gelding: plating-class stayer on Flat: won novice hurdle at Southwell in February by a length from Banker's Gossip: stays 3m: ridden by 5-lb claimer. *M. J. Ryan.* 90 p

SILLIAN 8 ch.g. Billion (USA)–Celtic View (Celtic Cone) [1989/90 16s5 16g3 16f] rather leggy, good-topped gelding: will make a chaser: has been hobdayed: fair hurdler: ridden by 3-lb claimer, good third behind Kadan at Uttoxeter in April, running on well: stiff task, tailed off in Swinton Insurance Trophy Hurdle at Haydock following month: suited by a sharp 2m: possibly unsuited by firm ground. *Mrs A. R. Hewitt.* 120

SILLY BEGGAR 7 b.m. Silly Prices–Netherby Maid (Derek H) [1989/90 24m4 25m3] workmanlike mare: handicap hurdler: finished lame when third at Cartmel in August: stays 3m: probably acts on any going. *J. Sunter.* 97

SILLY JUDGE 7 b.g. Silly Prices–Rookery Judge (Arctic Judge) [1989/90 16d 16g 18d 20m] leggy gelding: no worthwhile form over hurdles. *J. K. M. Oliver.* —

SILLY SAUSAGE 5 ch.m. Silly Answer–Scale The Peak (Scallywag) [1989/90 aF16g5 F16m3] length second, demoted a place, to The Fax Man in NH Flat race at Huntingdon in April: yet to race over hurdles or fences. *J. C. McConnochie.*

SILVER AGE (USA) 4 b.c. Silver Hawk (USA)–Our Paige (USA) (Grand Revival (USA)) [1989/90 17dpu] no form on Flat: tailed off when pulled up 2 out in juvenile hurdle at Devon & Exeter. *J. M. Bradley.* —

SILVER ARCH 5 b.h. Starch Reduced–Slightly Saucy (Galivanter) [1989/90 17f2 20gF 20f4] small, lightly-made horse: novice hurdler: best form at up to 17f: acts on hard going: ridden by 7-lb claimer: blinkered, found nothing under pressure fourth outing 1988/9: not seen out after October. *R. Hollinshead.* 78

SILVER CANNON (USA) 8 gr.g. Lot O'Gold (USA)–So High (USA) (Sea Bird II) [1989/90 c16f2 c18f* c16f3 c18g2 c16m3 c18s c16g c18f2 c18h* c16f5 c20f*] sparely-made gelding: winning selling hurdler: won handicap chases at Fontwell in October, April and May, making all in small fields on last 2 occasions: stays 2½m: acts on any going: pulls hard: tends to jump to his left: blinkered once in 1987/8: suited by a sharp track. *R. Voorspuy.* c96 —

SILVERCROSS LAD 7 gr.g. Sayfar–Steep Bit (Precipice Wood) [1989/90 16m 16f 18f3 25f3] plain gelding: failed to complete in 2 point-to-points: third in 2¼m novice event at Fontwell in March, first worthwhile form over hurdles: failed to stay 3m next time: acts on firm ground. *R. T. Juckes.* 78

SILVERHILLS 7 ch.g. Touch Paper–Rosie Probert (Captain's Gig (USA)) [1989/90 20vpu 20g] strong, chasing type: brother to Irish NH Flat race winner Sevens: dam won point-to-point in Ireland: in frame in 2 Irish NH Flat races in 1987/8: little promise in novice hurdles in January: sweats and pulls hard. *G. A. Ham.* —

SILVERINO 4 gr.g. Relkino–Silver Tips (High Top) [1989/90 16g 21f5] lengthy, shallow-girthed gelding: fifth foal: half-brother to 1½m winner Taylor Cares (by Good Times) and winning hurdler Sterling Silver (by Star Appeal): dam won at 7f and 1m: no worthwhile form in 2 outings over hurdles at Newbury in March, though showed signs of ability on first occasion. *A. Moore.* —

SILVER KING (FR) 4 ch.g. Son of Silver–Lakara (USA) (Le Fabuleux) [1989/90 16g2 17v* 16d* 16f] lengthy, sparely-made ex-French gelding: second foal: half-brother to French 1¼m winner Fairlane (by Fabulous Dancer): dam won at around 11f in France: successful over 1½m on Flat when trained by M. Papoin: made all in juvenile hurdles at Newton Abbot in January (won by a distance) and Newbury following month, beating Gay Ruffian 8 lengths in Stroud Green Hurdle on latter course: jumped moderately when well beaten in Daily Express Triumph Hurdle at Cheltenham (well worth another chance on easier going): will be well suited by 2½m: acts on heavy going. *M. C. Pipe.* 129 p

SILVER PALE 9 ch.g. Carnival Night–Doon Mist (Golden Vision) [1989/90 c20f* c20g5 c20sF c20g4 c20m2 c25g5 c24dF] sturdy ex-Irish gelding: winning point-to-pointer: jumped soundly when easy winner of handicap chase at Lei- **c114**

cester in November: ran well fourth and fifth starts: seems suited by 2½m: acts on any going. *M. Oliver.*

SILVER PATROL 5 gr.g. Rusticaro (FR)–Goccia d'Oro (ITY) (Bolkonski) [1989/90 16g^F 16s] smallish, angular gelding: no form over hurdles: sold C. Popham 2,900 gns Ascot July Sales. *A. P. Stringer.* —

SILVER'S GIRL 5 b.m. Sweet Monday–Persian Silver (Cash And Courage) [1989/90 17m^{pu}] sparely-made mare: 1¼m winner on Flat: no form in 2 outings over hurdles. *D. Moffatt.* —

SILVER SKYLARK 6 ch.g. True Song–Silver Spartan (Spartan General) [1989/90 20d 25g^{pu}] leggy, rather angular gelding: third foal: brother to winning hurdler Competitive Bid: dam sister to useful hunter chaser Spartan Rambler: backward, no form in 2 novice hurdles in first half of season. *P. J. Hobbs.* —

SILVER SNOW 12 gr.m. Abwah–Silver Yarn (Peter's Yarn) [1989/90 a20g a20g 21f c20m^2 c20m^3 c21g] long-backed mare: poor hurdler/novice chaser: needs further than 2m nowadays and stays 3m: yet to show her form on very soft ground: moderate jumper. *Mrs E. B. Scott.* c**67** x —

SIMASCALA 4 b.g. Electric–Elegida (Habitat) [1989/90 16f^4 16f^3 16f^4 16d^5] rather dipped-backed gelding: poor performer on Flat nowadays: poor form in juvenile hurdles in first half of season: worth a try over further than 2m: acts on firm ground (well beaten on dead): visored last 3 starts. *W. Wilson.* 80

SIMBAD 14 b.g. Simbir–Amsterdam Lassie (Arctic Storm) [1989/90 16s] strong, good sort: quite a useful staying hurdler in 1984/5: very lightly raced since: tailed off only outing 1989/90 (January). *D. Moffatt.* —

SIMILE 4 b. or br.f. Silly Prices–Millisles (Pongee) [1989/90 F13d 16g^F 16d^{pu} 16d^{pu}] small filly: first foal: dam of little account: seems no better herself. *N. Chamberlain.* —

SIMMIE 5 b.g. Buckskin (FR)–Miss Dunbrody (Le Prince) [1989/90 16s 16g] has scope: third living foal: dam, won NH Flat race and placed over hurdles in Ireland, half-sister to several winners, notably very useful chaser Green Bramble and quite useful chasers Deviner and Polyfemus: showed signs of ability when ninth to Forest Sun in novice hurdle at Kempton in February on second start: likely to improve further. *G. A. Hubbard.* — p

SIMON BOLIVAR 11 ro.g. Grey Mirage–Penview (Pendragon) [1989/90 c20f^{pu}] smallish, lengthy gelding: poor handicap chaser: stayed 21f: acted on any going: was usually claimer or amateur ridden: dead. *S. G. Payne.* c— —

Stroud Green Hurdle, Newbury—Silver King looks a good staying hurdler in the making

Oddbins Handicap Hurdle, Liverpool—Sip of Orange (near side) gets the better of a stirring battle with Trapper John

SIMON DAMIAN 7 ch.g. Roman Warrior–Our Polly (Henry The Seventh) [1989/90 22g* 22m* 24f] big gelding: won conditional jockeys handicap hurdle at Stratford and novice hurdle at Wincanton within 6 days in October: tailed off when next seen out 6 weeks later: stays 2¾m: acts on good to firm ground. *W. G. M. Turner.* 93 +

SIMPLE PLEASURE 5 b.g. Idiot's Delight–Kirkham Lass (Parasang) [1989/90 F17f3 16f5] compact gelding: first foal: dam unraced sister to a poor novice: third of 6 in NH Flat race at Carlisle in October: carrying condition, remote fifth in novice hurdle at Newcastle later in month. *Mrs M. Stirk.* —

SIMPLY PERFECT 4 b.g. Wassl–Haneena (Habitat) [1989/90 16d2 16d3 17d5 a16g5] smallish, sparely-made gelding: modest maiden on Flat, probably stays 1¾m: sold out of H. Thomson Jones's stable 8,000 gns Newmarket July Sales: best efforts over hurdles on first 2 starts: will be suited by 2½m. *M. Johnston.* 93

SINGALETTO 6 b.m. Neltino–Sweet Singer (Roan Rocket) [1989/90 20spu a18g4] smallish, angular mare: lightly-raced novice hurdler: remote fourth in a selling handicap in February. *B. A. McMahon.* —

SINGING FLAME 8 b.g. Royal Match–Pilots Row (Tanavar) [1989/90 16d 20m 20d 16s c16g c24mF c20g] compact ex-Irish gelding: half-brother to winning Irish hurdler Vita Veritas (by Linacre): novice hurdler: no form, including in a seller, in Britain: prominent when falling 6 out in maiden chase in May: well beaten in selling handicap next time: best form at 2m on soft ground: usually blinkered. *J. G. M. O'Shea.* c— —

SINGING GOLD 4 b.c. Gold Claim–Gellifawr (Saulingo) [1989/90 a16gF a16gpu] won 8.3f selling handicap on Flat for J. Pearce in May: no form in 2 outings over hurdles earlier (blinkered). *R. Guest.* —

SINGING HILLS 9 b.m. Crash Course–Purcella (Straight Lad) [1989/90 16dpu 16s] lengthy mare: novice hurdler: no form since 1987/8. *J. S. Allen.* —

SINGING SEAL 9 ch.g. Privy Seal–Blue Song (Majority Blue) [1989/90 c24dF c24fpu] leggy gelding: fairly useful winning point-to-pointer: jumped rather deliberately, but would have finished third but for falling at the last in novice chase at Chepstow in March: never going well when favourite for similar race at Southwell following month: possibly unsuited by firm ground. *R. Curtis.* c?

SINGLE SHOOTER (USA) 5 b.g. Nodouble (USA)–Irish Sister (USA) (Needles) [1989/90 16h2 18f* a16g6] leggy, workmanlike gelding: made all when 97

30-length winner of novice hurdle at Fontwell in August: well beaten at Lingfield in November: stays 2¼m: yet to race on ground softer than good. *R. J. O'Sullivan.*

SINGLESOLE 5 ch.g. Celtic Cone–Milly Kelly (Murrayfield) [1989/90 16m^{2} 20d^{4} 16s^{2} 16s] small gelding: novice hurdler: should be suited by further than 2m: acts on good to firm and soft ground. *Mrs P. Sly.* 87

SING THE BLUES 6 b.g. Blue Cashmere–Pulcini (Quartette) [1989/90 a16g* 16m^{F} a16g* a16g* a16g* a18g* a20g^{3}] rangy, rather sparely-made gelding: successful in novice handicap hurdles at Lingfield in December, January, February (2) and March: good third behind Nahar in quite valuable handicap on same course later in March: stays 2½m: goes well on equitrack. *C. J. Benstead.* 107

SIP OF ORANGE 8 ch.m. Celtic Cone–Sipped (Ballyciptic) [1989/90 20d 24g* 24s^{F} 21d 25f^{4} 25m*] workmanlike mare: put up useful performance when winning 21-runner Oddbins Hurdle (Handicap) at Liverpool in April by ½ length from Trapper John, holding on well run-in: earlier successful at Wetherby and good fourth in Coral Golden Hurdle Final (Handicap) at Cheltenham: stayed 3m: not at her best on very soft ground but acted on any other: stud. *J. G. FitzGerald.* 135

SIR ANDREW LEWIS 4 br.g. Petorius–Spooning (Ashmore (FR)) [1989/90 16f] lightly-made gelding: poor maiden at up to 7f on Flat: sold out of C. Allen's stable 1,000 gns Newmarket September Sales: tailed-off last of 12 in juvenile selling hurdle at Uttoxeter in October. *D. R. Wellicome.* —

SIR BADSWORTH 12 b.g. Tarboosh (USA)–High Reserve (Young Emperor) [1989/90 c17m^{3} c20m^{2} c16g^{3} c21f^{4} c21f^{3}] angular gelding: handicap chaser: stays 21f, but not 3m: well suited by top-of-the-ground: usually held up: moody: has won 5 times at Cartmel. *T. Laxton.* c**107** —

SIR BRENDON 4 b.g. Don–Brenda Girl (Tarboosh (USA)) [1989/90 F16g 16g^{pu}] third foal: dam unraced: behind in NH Flat race and when pulled up around halfway in conditional jockeys novice hurdle at Market Rasen. *W. T. Kemp.* —

SIR COSMO 4 b.c. Simply Great (FR)–Singing Away (Welsh Pageant) [1989/90 16g^{F} 16m^{pu} 20g^{pu} 16d 18v^{pu} 16d^{pu} 18f^{5}] sparely-made ex-Irish colt: seventh foal: half-brother to 1¾m winner Jazzy Lady (by Persian Bold): dam, from excellent family, ran only at 2 yrs: poor form over hurdles. *B. Stevens.* 60

SIR CRUSTY 8 br.g. Gunner B–Brazen (Cash And Courage) [1989/90 21d^{pu} 21s* 25f^{6}] compact gelding: handicap hurdler: won conditional jockeys event at Sandown in February (wandered and looked none too keen): fair sixth behind Henry Mann in Coral Golden Hurdle Final at Cheltenham following month: stays 3m: acts on any going. *R. J. Holder.* 118

SIR DUBEL 9 br.g. Al Sirat (USA)–Killanny Bridge (Hallez (FR)) [1989/90 a20g^{6} a16g^{4} a20g a20g^{3} a20g^{5} 16d] angular gelding: novice hurdler/chaser: in frame in selling hurdle and novice claimer at Southwell in 1989/90: probably stays 2½m: acts on firm ground: blinkered fifth start 1988/9, visored last 2 outings. *J. L. Harris.* c— 69

SIR EDWARD 5 b.g. Formidable (USA)–Pearl Wedding (Gulf Pearl) [1989/90 16f^{ur} 16f^{4} 16f^{5} 20f^{6}] sparely-made gelding: poor novice selling hurdler: best form at 2m on firm ground: jumps poorly. *T. Kersey.* 56 x

SIRE NANTAIS (FR) 6 br.g. Meisir (FR)–Farala (Faunus (FR)) [1989/90 c17.5g^{3} 19.5d c18v* c20m* c20g* c21v* c21d* c16m c20f^{F}] leggy, workmanlike ex-French gelding: third foal: half-brother to winning French jumper Prince Nantais (by Dammar): dam placed over 1¼m in France: winning hurdler: bought out of R. Cherruau's stable 96,700 francs (approx £9,797) after winning claiming chase at Auteuil in November: made all in novice chases at Leicester, Uttoxeter, Newton Abbot and Market Rasen (despite mistakes): outpaced after a mistake at the ninth when over 17 lengths last of 8 finishers behind Comandante in Arkle Challenge Trophy at Cheltenham in March: stays 21f: acts on heavy going and good to firm: needs to brush up his jumping. *M. C. Pipe.* c**124** + —

SIRGAME 4 b.c. Thatching–Vaunt (USA) (Hill Rise) [1989/90 16f^{pu}] sturdy colt: half-brother to 2¾m hurdle winner Eye Flasher (by Sexton Blake): no worthwhile form on Flat (once visored): tailed off when pulled up 3 out in juvenile hurdle at Warwick. *Mrs N. Macauley.* —

SIR GYPSY (USA) 6 ch.g. Sir Ivor–Highland Gypsy (USA) (Our Native (USA)) [1989/90 24g] leggy, workmanlike gelding: poor novice hurdler: blinkered last 2 starts 1987/8. *J. Mackie.* —

SIR HUMPHREY 10 ch.g. High Line–Greek Money (Sovereign Path) [1989/90 16g^{6}] sparely-made gelding: winning hurdler: needed race only outing in —

last 2 seasons: races only at 2m: acts on firm and dead going: has won for a claimer. *I. Campbell.*

SIR JAMESTOWN (USA) 6 b.g. Pleasant Colony (USA)–Magnificent Lady (Nonoalco (USA)) [1989/90 16g^{6} 16d^{4} 16m^{6} a16g^{3} 16f^{2} 16m* 17h^{2} 16m^{3} 18f^{2} 16m^{5}] 92 robust gelding: won maiden hurdle at Towcester in April: ran creditably next 3 starts, moderately in lady riders handicap final outing (gave impression something amiss): will prove best at around 2m: acts on firm going: has found little. *N. J. Henderson.*

SIR JEST 12 b.g. Sea Catch–Carnival Jest (Carnival Dancer) [1989/90 c24m* **c142** c24fr c24g^{F} c27s^{F} c28d* c36f c24g* c22m*] strong, lengthy gelding: useful — chaser on his day: won handicaps at Perth in September, Sedgefield in March and Newcastle in May and minor event (by 6 lengths from Walnut Way) at Stratford in June: ninth of 20 finishers behind Mr Frisk in Seagram Grand National at Liverpool in April: stays well: acts on any going: usually held up: ran out once in 1988/9, and refused at the last on second start in 1989/90. *W. A. Stephenson.*

SIR KENWIN 12 b.g. Sir Nulli–Cute Smokey (My Smokey) [1989/90 c21s^{F} **c71** c20f^{3}] compact, workmanlike gelding: winning point-to-pointer: poor chaser: — third in hunter chase at Folkestone in May: stays 25f: acts on soft going: seems unsuited by sharp track: has been blinkered: inconsistent: trained first start by C. Stratford. *C. Holmes.*

SIR LESTER 14 b.g. Bend A Bow (USA)–Treaty Girl (Pardal) [1989/90 c16d^{pu} **c75** c17v c16f^{5}] leggy, narrow gelding: poor chaser nowadays: best at around 2m: acts — on firm ground: sometimes makes mistakes: usually amateur ridden nowadays. *C. T. Nash.*

SIR NODDY 7 ch.g. Tom Noddy–Pinzarose (Pinzan) [1989/90 F17f 20s^{pu} 20s^{pu} 21d 20g 25f* 20g^{3} 20g^{6}] big, workmanlike gelding: will make a chaser: 99 fourth living foal: half-brother to novice hurdler Rosie's Member (by New Member): dam never ran: won 3 point-to-points in 1989: won novice hurdle at Hereford in April, leading from second: better subsequent effort on next start: stays 3m: acts on firm ground. *C. J. Vernon Miller.*

SIROCKO BAY 6 b.g. Royal Blend–Trapalanda (Warpath) [1989/90 16m^{3} 16g^{F} 16g^{5} 16m^{3} 16m^{6} a16g^{4} 20g a16g^{3} a16g^{2} a20g* a20g^{pu}] leggy, lightly-made 77 gelding: won novice handicap hurdle at Southwell in February: stayed 2½m: blinkered once: dead. *M. F. Barraclough.*

McEwans Best Scotch Durham National Handicap Chase, Sedgefield— the second of four wins in another good season for Sir Jest

SIR PERCY 7 b.h. Blakeney–Nicoletta (Busted) [1989/90 16d^{pu}] workmanlike
horse: one-time fairly useful 1¾m performer on Flat: showed promise in a novice —
hurdle in 1986/7: pulled up in a claimer in February. *Mrs N. Macauley.*

SIRRAH JAY 10 b. or br.g. Tug of War–Dellasville (Trouville) [1989/90 c21f^{pu} **c102**
c20s^{pu} c24g^{5} c20v^{4} c20d* c20d^{4}] compact, workmanlike gelding: handicap
chaser: won at Warwick in March, despite hanging left approaching the last: stays
3m: acts on heavy going: has worn a crossed noseband and a brush pricker (on
near-side): blinkered eighth start in 1988/9: inconsistent. *N. R. Mitchell.*

SIR'S AT THE GIN 9 ch.g. Al Sirat (USA)–Gin An Tonic (Osprey Hawk) **c103**
[1989/90 24d^{6} c17g^{2} c20d* c20g^{3} c20d* c25f^{2} c21m^{2} c24f^{ur}] lengthy, workman- —
like gelding: tends to look dull in coat: winning hurdler: won handicap chase and
novice event at Huntingdon in mid-season: ran well last 2 completed starts: stays
3m: unsuited by soft ground, acts on any other: best with forcing tactics: raced
with little zest when blinkered final start 1988/9: found nothing on first outing. *J.
T. Gifford.*

SIR SPEEDY 7 b.g. Owen Anthony–Fair Georgina (Silver Cloud) [1989/90
16f^{2}] leggy, good-topped gelding: winning selling hurdler: ran creditably only 88
outing of season (August): best form at around 2m: acts on any going: suitable
mount for a claimer. *A. D. Brown.*

SIR VAYLORD (FR) 4 ch.g. Vayrann–Miss Gaylord (FR) (Sir Gaylord
(USA)) [1989/90 17s^{3} 16d 16s* 16f^{6}] ex-French gelding: won twice over 7f at 2 yrs, ?
failed to reach frame at 3 yrs: claimed out of X. Guigand's stable 86,647 francs
(approx £9,317) after winning claiming hurdle at Enghien in April: 9/4 on, over 30
lengths sixth to Fighting Days in 8-runner juvenile event at Taunton later in
month (finished lame): acts on soft going and possibly unsuited by firm. *M. C.
Pipe.*

SIR WAGER 9 b.g. Immortal Knight–Fine Flutter (Flush Royal) [1989/90 **c88**
c26s^{pu} c25s^{3} c25d^{5} c20v^{su} c20d] small, rather sparely-made gelding: handicap —
chaser: only form of season on second start: stays 25f: best form with give in the
ground: sometimes blinkered or visored. *Mrs L. Clay.*

SISTER CHABRIAS 5 b.m. Chabrias (FR)–Ginger Tart (Swing Easy (USA))
[1989/90 16f^{4} 16m^{F}] modest handicapper on Flat, stays 7f: pulled hard but showed 89
ability in novice hurdles at Worcester and Bangor (beaten when fell last) in
August: needs to settle. *M. C. Pipe.*

SISTER CHERYL 5 ch.m. Vaigly Great–Miss Merlin (Manacle) [1989/90
16m^{pu} 16h^{pu}] rather leggy, plain mare: little sign of ability over hurdles, including —
in a seller. *R. G. Frost.*

SISTER-IN-LAW 7 ch.m. Legal Tender–Sister Brown (Murrayfield)
[1989/90 25g 16g^{4} 18s^{5} 22g^{2} 22d 20g^{5} 21d^{3}] compact mare: modest novice over 89
hurdles: stays 2¾m: acts on dead going. *W. G. R. Wightman.*

SISTER SAM 10 ch.m. Pamroy–Fortilage (Fortina) [1989/90 c25g^{bd} c27m^{5} **c78**
c27f^{2} c27f^{4} c24f^{2}] modest winning form in point-to-points: second in hunter
chases at Sedgefield and Hexham: stays well: acts on firm ground. *T. D. Smith.*

SIT IN THE DARK 7 br.g. Sit In The Corner (USA)–Bromosa (Brother) c—
[1989/90 c24m^{6}] tall, workmanlike gelding: novice selling hurdler: well beaten on —
chasing debut: blinkered once in 1986/7: ridden by 7-lb claimer: has looked less
than resolute under pressure: sold 1,700 gns Ascot December Sales: resold 2,000
gns Ascot July Sales. *O. O'Neill.*

SIX SHOT 10 b.g. Cornuto–Miss Bewildered (Master Stephen) [1989/90 20g^{pu} **c80** ?
c21g^{F} c24d^{4} c20f^{4} c25f^{3} c20d^{pu} c17h^{3}] tall, good-topped gelding: quite a useful —
hurdler at his best: poor novice over fences: stays 2¾m: acts on any going:
blinkered final start (stiff task, tailed off). *R. J. Hodges.*

SIZZLING SUN 5 b.m. Sunyboy–Royal Blast (Royal Palm) [1989/90 F16m
aF13g] second foal: dam winning selling hurdler: tailed off in NH Flat races in
January and February: yet to race over hurdles or fences. *J. Honeyball.*

SKERRY MEADOW 6 b.g. Anfield–Mi Tia (Great Nephew) [1989/90 c26m^{4} **c85**
c21m*] tailed-off last in claimer on Flat in 1987: won a point-to-point and a novice
hunter chase in May, latter at Fakenham: stays 21f. *O. J. Carter.*

SKETCHER (NZ) 7 b.g. Candyboy (NZ)–Jezebel (NZ) (Ardistaan) [1989/90
25g^{2} 25g^{2} 24g^{2} 22m^{2} 24g^{5} 25d*] tall, leggy gelding: useful hurdler: showed 139
improved form when winning handicap at Newbury in March by 10 lengths from
Mineral Dust, making much of running and drawing clear under strong pressure
run-in: stays well: best form on ground softer than good: game. *D. H. Barons.*

SKIDDY LAD 8 ch.g. Music Maestro–Skiddy River (Saratoga Skiddy) [1989/90 16s6] workmanlike gelding: poor winning hurdler: stiff task only outing 1989/90 (January). *S. G. Smith.* —

SKIMMING 5 b.h. Mill Reef (USA)–Mighty Fly (Comedy Star (USA)) [1989/90 16m4 17m4 16m4 16f 16d6] leggy, rather sparely-made horse: novice hurdler: ran poorly in sellers last 2 starts: trained first 3 outings by G. Moore, fourth by J. Gillen: dead. *I. Semple.* 80

SKINNHILL 6 b.g. Final Straw–Twenty Two (FR) (Busted) [1989/90 c20g2 c20m* c20s4 c20g* c22d2 c24d3 c20f5 c20g3 c20f*] close-coupled gelding: handicap hurdler: won novice chases at Leicester in January and Wolverhampton in February and handicap chase at Warwick in May: probably stays 2¾m: acts on any going: usually blinkered nowadays (visored third start 1988/9): has run well for an amateur. *T. Thomson Jones.* c**107** —

SKIPLAM WOOD 4 b.f. Cree Song–Mab (Morston (FR)) [1989/90 16m 16gpu 17g 16gur 16g5 16g2 16d] small, sparely-made filly: plating-class maiden on Flat, stays 7f: only form over hurdles when second in claimer at Perth in May: races keenly (wears crossed noseband) and unlikely to stay much beyond 2m. *D. Lee.* 63 +

SKIPPING TIM 11 b.g. Deep Run–Skiporetta (Even Money) [1989/90 c17f* c17f2 c26f* c25f* c25m* c20f* c21f2 c20mF c20v3] lengthy, dipped-backed gelding: ridden by 7-lb claimer, made all in selling handicap chase at Newton Abbot in July (bought out of P. Hobbs's stable 5,500 gns): successful afterwards in novice chases on same course and at Hereford and Cheltenham, and in handicap chase at Devon & Exeter: stays 3¼m: best form on top-of-the-ground: takes a good hold and races with plenty of zest. *M. C. Pipe.* c**102** —

SKITTLE ALLEY 4 b.g. Adonijah–Skittish (USA) (Far North (CAN)) [1989/90 aF16g3 F16d4] second foal: dam lightly-raced 1½m winner: in frame in NH Flat races at Southwell and Kelso: yet to race over hurdles. *S. Mellor.*

SKOLERN 6 b.g. Lochnager–Piethorne (Fine Blade (USA)) [1989/90 16m* 16g* 16g 17g6 17f] close-coupled, angular gelding: modest 7f and 1m performer on Flat: sold privately out of R. Whitaker's stable 5,000 gns Doncaster October Sales: won novice hurdles in large fields at Catterick and Ayr in December: well beaten next 2 starts, but ran respectably in handicap at Doncaster in March: will prove best at a sharp 2m: acts on firm ground. *Mrs P. A. Barker.* 101

SKRAGGS PLUS TWO 6 ch.h. Owen Anthony–Carvers Corah (Easter Island) [1989/90 18f2 16h4] poor novice selling hurdler: stays 2½m. *Mrs A. Knight.* 69

SKYGRANGE 9 b.g. Al Sirat (USA)–Lady Rois (Prince Rois) [1989/90 c24gpu] tall, lengthy, rather sparely-made gelding: winning chaser: runner-up in point-to-point in February: made mistakes in hunter chase at Fakenham in April: stays well: seems to act on any going: blinkered final start in 1987/8 and on last 2 outings 1988/9: moody. *J. M. Turner.* c— § — §

SKYLANDER 11 b.g. African Sky–Lagosta (USA) (Ragusa) [1989/90 c16h3 c16m4 c20mpu] leggy, lightly-made gelding: poor chaser: form only at around 2m: suited by firm going: sometimes blinkered: has looked none too keen under pressure: sold 725 gns Ascot June Sales: one to treat with caution. *P. S. Davies.* c**91** § —

SKY WATCHER 4 b.g. Skyliner–Holernzaye (Sallust) [1989/90 16m 16fur 16gro 16f6 16g3 16g5] smallish, angular gelding: plater on Flat, stays 1¼m: poor juvenile selling hurdler: makes mistakes: saddle slipped third start: blinkered fifth start (trained until after then by D. Smith, subsequently off course over 6 months). *J. Dooler.* 67 x

SLALOM 9 ch.g. Deep Run–Arctic Nook (Arctic Slave) [1989/90 c20d3 26dpu 20d2 24g6 25mpu] big, rangy, workmanlike gelding: very smart hurdler: not subjected to a hard ride when 15 lengths second to Beech Road in Bishops Cleeve Hurdle at Cheltenham in January: ran as though something amiss both subsequent starts (blinkered last): won 4 novice chases in 1988/9: wasn't knocked about after hampered 2 out when third at Worcester in November: stays 3m: yet to race on very firm ground, acts on any other: tends to idle in front and is suited by waiting tactics: broke a blood vessel fifth start 1988/9: has made a couple of mistakes each outing over fences. *M. H. B. Robinson.* c— 155

SLANEY PRINCE 10 b.g. Sassafras (FR)–Pastina (March Past) [1989/90 17f5 21hF 24f5 c24mur 20f 16m2 16f5 16m 16g 16mpu c20g] good-quartered gelding: handicap hurdler: poor form in 1989/90, including in sellers: poor novice chaser: best form at 2m: acts on any going: successful with and without blinkers. *P. D. Connors.* c— 68

SLANEY RAMBLER 9 ch.g. Tepukei–Difoolish (Dionisio) [1989/90 c20f] ex-Irish gelding: novice hurdler/chaser: winning point-to-pointer: visored, tailed off in hunter chase at Folkestone. *C. Holmes.* c— —

SLATYFORD LANE 9 ch.m. Le Bavard (FR)–Kathleen Beag (Vulgan) [1989/90 22d] sparely-made mare: lightly-raced maiden point-to-pointer: well beaten over hurdles: unruly in paddock and withdrawn once. *T. W. Cunningham.* —

SLAVE KING 11 b.g. Kinglet–Slavetown (Arctic Slave) [1989/90 20g4 21f 24g5 22mpu] lightly-made gelding: modest front-running handicap hurdler, lightly raced: stays 2¾m: probably acts on any going. *Mrs N. S. Sharpe.* 94

SLAVE TIME 8 ch.g. Vulgan Slave–Rakene (Welsh Rake) [1989/90 c24d4 c24f4] 6,200 6-y-o: strong, workmanlike gelding: half-brother to 2 winners on Flat: dam unraced sister to winning hurdler Jack Jiggs: winning point-to-pointer: well-beaten last of 4 finishers in hunter chases. *D. Gill.* c—

SLEEPERS 6 br.m. Swing Easy (USA)–Jenny's Rocket (Roan Rocket) [1989/90 16dpu] second foal: dam winning hurdler: unreliable plating-class sprinter on Flat: sold out of C. Booth's stable 1,350 gns Ascot November Sales: started slowly and was tailed off when pulled up 2 out in seller at Bangor on hurdling debut. *G. H. Jones.* —

SLEEPLINE ROYALE 4 ch.g. Buzzards Bay–Sleepline Princess (Royal Palace) [1989/90 16d3 16dpu 16g* 16g* 16g* 16s2 16mF 16d 16f* 16g* 16f3 16f] leggy, close-coupled gelding: quite modest performer on Flat, stays 1¼m: took well to hurdling and won claimers at Wolverhampton (2), Wincanton (idled in front), Chepstow and Uttoxeter (second race in 3 days) after turn of the year: good third in handicap at Warwick in May: not sure to stay much beyond 2m: yet to race on heavy going, acts on any other: has sweated and been on toes: has won for a claimer. *R. J. Holder.* 105

SLICE OFTHE ACTION 7 b.g. Random Shot–Tangle Tut (Tangle) [1989/90 16m] angular gelding: half-brother to very smart 2m chaser Danish Flight (by Pitpan) and moderate 2m chaser Outlaw Man (by Knotty Pine): dam last in maiden hurdle on only outing: bit backward, always behind in novice hurdle at Ludlow on debut. *C. G. Roach.* —

SLIEVE FELIM 10 ch.g. Deep Run–Wine List (Frigid Aire) [1989/90 16f4 c16m* c16m* c16fF] leggy, lengthy gelding: smart front-running 2m chaser on his day who won 12 of his 25 races over fences, including handicaps at Perth in August and September: fell fatally at Ascot in October: acted on any going: was very headstrong: jumped to the right. *W. A. Stephenson.* c**148** —

SLIGHTLY GONE 5 b.g. Balinger–Nearly Straight (Straight Lad) [1989/90 17d3 21m* 22g 22f5] workmanlike gelding: first foal: dam won 21f hurdle: won novice hurdle at Towcester in December: well beaten afterwards (stiff task third start, subsequently off course 2½ months): stays 21f: acts on good to firm and dead going. *F. Walwyn.* 93

SLIP DANCER 6 b.g. Treboro (USA)–Fire Dance (FR) (Habitat) [1989/90 16g 16s 24gpu] medium-sized gelding: no worthwhile form over hurdles: pulled up and dismounted in selling handicap final start. *R. Allan.* —

SLIPPERY MAX 6 b.g. Nicholas Bill–Noammo (Realm) [1989/90 16f4 16m2 16f2 16f* 16f* 16h3 16g* 16g* 16d* 16g2 17f6 a16g6 16m6 16m4 16g 17f2] leggy, sparely-made gelding: successful in selling hurdles at Bangor (2, retained 6,500 gns on second occasion), Sedgefield and Fakenham, and a novice hurdle at Market Rasen in first half of season: claimed £7,101 after second in seller at Cartmel final start: will stay beyond 2m: has won on firm going but best with give in the ground: has worn crossed noseband: found little in front on tenth start, slowly away on thirteenth: claimed out of D. Nicholson's stable £8,376 after third start. *C. R. Beever.* 95

SLIP UP 10 b.g. Quiet Fling (USA)–Artemis (King Emperor (USA)) [1989/90 20f2 25h* 24m 28g4 a20g5 24g] small, sparely-made gelding: well ridden when winning amateur riders handicap hurdle at Hereford in August: ran moderately afterwards: stays well: acts on hard ground. *F. Gray.* 80

SLOCHD 12 ch.g. Bing II–Fanny Adams (Sweet Ration) [1989/90 16fpu] moderate winning point-to-pointer: no form in hunter chase and a maiden hurdle. *Mrs G. L. Simpson.* c— —

SLOSHED 6 b.g. Tug of War–Lager (Prince Hansel) [1989/90 16m] lengthy, chasing type: little worthwhile form over hurdles. *T. W. Cunningham.* —

SLOTAMATICS 7 b. or br.g. Royal Fountain–Sardan (Lauso) [1989/90 16f^{6}
20g^{pu}] third reported foal: half-brother to winning jumper Worthy Heiress (by —
Richboy) who stayed very well: dam placed in a novice chase: little sign of ability
in novice hurdles at Wetherby and Perth. *G. Richards.*

SMACK ON TARGET 5 gr.m. Smackover–Albine (Amber X) [1989/90 16g
21s^{pu} 16d^{6} 16d] good-bodied mare: novice selling hurdler: no form in 1989/90: — §
swished tail and didn't run on on sixth start 1988/9: has worn blinkers and a visor.
P. J. Anderson.

SMALLWOOD WILLET 10 ch.g. Funny Man–Miss Fleece All (Tangle) **c90**
[1989/90 c25f^{2} c16f^{2} c20f*] lengthy gelding: won hunter chase at Folkestone in
May very easily by 15 lengths: earlier successful in 2 point-to-points: stays 3m:
acts on firm going: jumped badly right and tried to run out twice on second start
1987/8: wears a crossed noseband. *T. J. Swaffield.*

SMART BROAD 5 b.m. Broadsword (USA)–Mary Mod (El Cid) [1989/90
16s^{pu} 16g] compact mare: little sign of ability over hurdles, including in sellers: —
sold 1,600 gns Ascot April Sales. *J. P. D. Elliott.*

SMARTIE EXPRESS 8 b. or br.g. Pony Express–Spick And Span (Smartie)
[1989/90 24f^{3} 22m 24g^{3} 22m^{4}] close-coupled gelding: fair hurdler: ran creditably 116
when in frame in 1989/90: needs a stiff track or testing conditions when racing at
around 2m and stays 3m: acts on hard and dead going: good mount for a claimer. *R.
J. Hodges.*

SMART IN BLACK 8 b. or br.h. Roscoe Blake–Cool Down (Warpath) c**100**
[1989/90 16f* 20f* 20m^{2} 16f^{3} c16f*] small horse: won handicap hurdles at Market 105
Rasen and Southwell and novice chase on latter course early in season: stayed
2½m: acted on hard ground: sometimes wore blinkers (not when successful):
dead. *G. Richards.*

SMART IN TWEED 4 gr.f. Castle Keep–Cool Down (Warpath) [1989/90 17m
16g^{F}] third foal: half-sister to winning hurdler/chaser Smart In Black (by Roscoe —
Blake): dam of no account: tailed off in juvenile hurdle at Carlisle in April: beaten
when falling 3 out next time (started slowly). *G. Richards.*

SMART JACK 9 b.g. Pollerton–Smart Money (Even Money) [1989/90 20d^{pu}
16g^{F} 16v a20g^{2}] compact gelding: winning hurdler: lightly raced nowadays: first 84
form for some time when second at Southwell in February: stays well: probably
acts on any going: has won when sweating. *R. F. Fisher.*

SMART MART 11 ch.g. Jimmy Reppin–Fochetta (Fortino II) [1989/90 16g] c—
compact gelding: poor novice hurdler/chaser: lightly raced and little form of late. —
J. M. Bradley.

SMART PERFORMER 5 b.g. Formidable (USA)–Brilliant Rosa (Luthier)
[1989/90 16g 16s^{2} 16v^{5} 16s^{4} 16g^{3} 16f^{2} 16f^{2}] good-bodied gelding: fairly useful 130
hurdler: runner-up in County Handicap Hurdle at Cheltenham and Trillium
Handicap Hurdle at Ascot (hung right from 2 out and dismounted after post when
going down by 1½ lengths to Ambassador) on last 2 starts: will prove best at 2m:
acts on any going except heavy. *N. Tinkler.*

SMART PILOT 11 ch.g. Sir Mago–Saucy Polly (Blue Lightning) [1989/90 c—
c24d^{pu}] rather sparely-made gelding: very lightly-raced point-to-pointer, winner
in April: needing race, tailed off when pulled up in hunter chase at Nottingham in
February. *A. W. Johnson.*

SMART SLAVE 7 b.g. Smartset–Slave Trade (African Sky) [1989/90 16f 20d^{pu} c**78**
c16m^{4} c16m^{4} a18g^{2} c16f^{pu}] sparely-made gelding: novice hurdler/chaser: 78
probably stays 2¼m: acts on firm ground: usually amateur ridden. *Miss L. Bower.*

SMART TAR 9 b.g. Seaepic (USA)–I'm Smart (Menelek) [1989/90 c24d^{6} c26g] c—
strong, workmanlike gelding: very useful chaser: successful notably in Mildmay
of Flete Challenge Cup (Handicap) at Cheltenham in 1987/8 and in Piper
Champagne Golden Miller Chase (limited handicap) on same course in 1988/9:
also close up and travelling strongly when unseating rider twentieth in Seagram
Grand National at Liverpool in 1988/9: behind both outings in 1989/90: stayed
3¼m: was well suited by plenty of give in the ground: sweated on occasions: dead.
M. J. Wilkinson.

SMAYMAN 6 br.g. Touching Wood (USA)–Monaco Melody (Tudor Melody)
[1989/90 22v 20m^{6}] angular gelding: first worthwhile form in novice hurdles when 80
around 17 lengths sixth to Docksider over 2½m at Huntingdon in April (might
have finished closer but for saddle slipping). *F. Walwyn.*

SMILE AGAIN 7 b.g. Sagaro–Heckley Surprise (Foggy Bell) [1989/90 16d5 c16s c16dF] big, workmanlike gelding: poor novice hurdler: showed promise on first of 2 starts in novice chases: should stay beyond 2m (struggling a long way out over 2½m). *Miss H. C. Knight.* c— —

SMILEY 5 b.h. Blakeney–Laughing Girl (Sassafras (FR)) [1989/90 20vpu 16s* 16d3 16f2 20m2 24g] smallish, workmanlike horse: 100/1-winner of slowly-run novice handicap hurdle at Wetherby in February: ran well when runner-up twice afterwards: stays 2½m, probably not 3m: acts on firm and soft ground. *J. W. Blundell.* 89

SMILING BEAR (USA) 7 b.g. Nikoli–Share A Smile (USA) (Hagley (USA)) [1989/90 16f 16f5 17fpu] handicap hurdler: soundly beaten in 1989/90: best at 2m: acts on any going: visored last start: sold 850 gns Doncaster August Sales: subsequently placed in point-to-points. *M. C. Chapman.* —

SMITH COLLEGE 6 gr.g. Pragmatic–Mid-Way Model (Royal Highway) [1989/90 16s 20fpu] close-coupled gelding: third foal: half-brother to winning Irish point-to-pointer/hunter chaser What A Mistake (by Duky): dam maiden Irish hurdler: no worthwhile form in 2 novice hurdles. *J. T. Gifford.* —

SMITHONIAN 6 ch.g. Stetchworth (USA)–Inkflash (Hul A Hul) [1989/90 22d 24g* 25fbd] lengthy, workmanlike gelding: won conditional jockeys handicap hurdle at Carlisle in February: destroyed after being brought down at Cheltenham following month: stayed 3m: acted on heavy going. *Mrs G. R. Reveley.* 112

SMITH'S CRACKER 4 ch.g. Derrylin–Festal Spirit (Jimmy Reppin) [1989/90 F16v2 F16d3 aF16g3] first foal: dam fair stayer on Flat: placed in NH Flat races at Ayr, Catterick and Southwell: yet to race over hurdles. *M. H. Easterby.*

SMITH'S LAD 8 b.g. Normandy–Scrahan (Wily Trout) [1989/90 c16dpu c16dpu c16s] rangy gelding: poor novice hurdler/chaser: blinkered fifth start in 1987/8. *Roy J. Smith.* c— —

SMITHS VENTURE 5 b.g. Bustineto–April Shade (Harwell) [1989/90 16d4 20d2 20d2 24d] leggy, lengthy gelding: won 2 NH Flat races in 1988/9: in frame in novice hurdles in 1989/90, showing moderate form: stays 2½m: jumps none too fluently. *M. H. Easterby.* 101

SMITHY BEAR 8 b.g. Rupert Bear–Avonteous (Rockavon) [1989/90 c19d4 c20s5 c24spu c16vpu 21d 16m5 c16m4] small, close-coupled gelding: poor hurdler/novice chaser: possibly needs further than 2m when ground is on firm side, and stays 2½m: acts on any going: often blinkered or visored nowadays: jumps soundly. *William Price.* c85 86

SMOKE 4 gr.f. Rusticaro (FR)–Fire-Screen (Roan Rocket) [1989/90 16d2 16f4] ex-Irish filly: half-sister to 3 winners, including fairly useful 1981 2-y-o 7f winner Marquessa d'Howfen (by Pitcairn): dam won over 1¼m: runner-up over 7.5f on Flat when trained by C. Collins: in frame in juvenile maiden hurdle at Perth and novice hurdle at Wetherby (blinkered) in May: ridden by 5-lb claimer. *J. Parkes.* 79

SMOKEY TRACK 5 b.m. Uncle Pokey–Malmar (Palm Track) [1989/90 16g] sturdy, workmanlike mare: no form over hurdles. *K. A. Morgan.* —

SMOOTH ESCORT 6 b.g. Beau Charmeur (FR)–Wishing Trout (Three Wishes) [1989/90 16m6 22d2 20d6 20m3 24m2] sparely-made, close-coupled gelding: placed in novice hurdles, showing moderate form: suited by 2¾m +: acts on dead and good to firm going. *Mrs D. Haine.* 97

SMOOTH FLIGHT 4 ch.f. Sandhurst Prince–Female Mudwrestler (Ahonoora) [1989/90 16g] leggy, workmanlike filly: fair front-running miler, in good form in 1990: jumped none too fluently when well beaten in juvenile hurdle at Kempton in November. *R. W. Stubbs.* —

SMOOTH START 5 b.g. Smooth Stepper–Ardmoyne (Le Bavard (FR)) [1989/90 16f6 16m* 16d5 22d2 16g 16d 16s 20f 20g] compact, workmanlike ex-Irish gelding: first foal: dam behind in NH Flat race and maiden hurdle in Ireland: won point-to-point in 1989: won maiden hurdle at Clonmel in September: tailed off all starts in Britain: stays 2¾m: acts on good to firm and dead going: trained by P. Finn until after fourth start. *A. P. James.* 104 d

SMULLYAN 8 b.g. Faraway Times (USA)–Wounded Knee (Busted) [1989/90 c21spu c20g5 c24d3 c24m4 c24fF] lengthy, sparely-made gelding: won 2 point-to-points in 1988: winning hunter chaser: in frame at Leicester and Newcastle in March: stays 3m: acts on firm ground and is possibly unsuited by soft: blinkered once. *T. A. Hughes.* c93 —

SNAKE EYE 5 b.g. Tina's Pet–Dingle Belle (Dominion) [1989/90 16g 16g^{3}] small, strong gelding: poor novice hurdler: third in selling handicap at Fakenham 85
in April: barely stays 2m. *J. Wharton.*

SNAPPIT 8 b.g. Billion (USA)–Snippet (Ragstone) [1989/90 20s 20s] big, workmanlike gelding: winning hurdler: behind in handicaps, first a seller, in —
1989/90 (stiff task second outing): stays 3m: acts on any going. *D. McCain.*

SNAPPY DATE (USA) 4 ch.c. Blushing Groom (FR)–Mystery Mood (USA) (Night Invader (USA)) [1989/90 16g^{5} 16m^{2} 16m^{3}] placed over 1m on Flat: sold out 90
of M. Stoute's stable 7,400 gns Newmarket Autumn Sales: placed in juvenile hurdles at Stratford in May: visored on second occasion: started slowly on debut. *K. A. Morgan.*

SNAPSHOT BABY 6 br.m. Faraway Times (USA)–Firecat (Run The Gantlet (USA)) [1989/90 17f^{pu} 16m 22f^{pu}] probably of little account on Flat: seems little —
better as a hurdler. *R. Voorspuy.*

SNEAKAPENNY 8 ch.g. Levanter–Quickapenny (Espresso) [1989/90 c20g^{6} c**121**
c25d^{pu} c24s^{ur} c26v* c25m^{4} c26m^{pu} c33d^{pu}] strong, workmanlike gelding: fair —
chaser: returned to form when winning handicap at Folkestone in February by 4 lengths from Canford Palm: made a couple of mistakes next 2 outings: stays well: acts on heavy going and good to firm. *M. J. Wilkinson.*

SNEVES 5 b.g. Bali Dancer–Tuneful Queen (Queen's Hussar) [1989/90 F12g^{6} F17f 16g 20d 20m^{pu}] lengthy gelding: second foal: dam twice-raced half-sister to 2 —
winning hurdlers: well beaten in novice hurdles. *J. Mackie.*

SNIGGY 4 b.f. Belfort (FR)–Firey Kim (CAN) (Cannonade (USA)) [1989/90 a16g^{6}] poor and ungenuine maiden on Flat: 16 lengths sixth behind Kenilworth 64
Castle in novice hurdle at Southwell in January, swishing tail under pressure. *D. W. Browne.*

SNITTERFIELD 12 b.g. Royal Match–Mile Cross (Milesian) [1989/90 c18h^{2} c**93**
17m^{3} c16m^{4} c18s^{4} c16f* c18f^{3} c20h^{3}] small, lightly-made gelding: modest chaser: 78
won amateur riders handicap at Plumpton in March: third in amateur riders handicap hurdle at Devon & Exeter in September: stays 21f: acts on any going: has been tried in blinkers, but is better without: let down by his jumping on occasions: good mount for an amateur or claimer. *M. Madgwick.*

SNITTON LANE 4 b.f. Cruise Missile–Cala di Volpe (Hardiran) [1989/90 F16g* F16g^{3}] third living foal: dam never ran: won NH Flat race at Market Rasen in April: third of 17 in similar race at Perth following month: yet to race over hurdles. *J. A. C. Edwards.*

SNOOKER TABLE 7 b.g. Ballymore–Northern Twilight (English Prince) [1989/90 16m* 16d 16m^{5}] leggy gelding: quite a modest hurdler: won conditional 103
jockeys selling hurdle at Uttoxeter in March (no bid): good seventh behind Instant Tan in non-selling handicap at Ayr next start, but ran poorly final outing: stays 2½m (well beaten over further): acts on good to firm and dead going: claimer ridden. *K. White.*

SNOW BABU 8 b.h. Foggy Bell–Fleur-Babu (Babu) [1989/90 20m c16g^{5} c**75**
c20v^{ur} c20s^{F} c20g 25d^{ur} 24g c20g^{3}] tall, sparely-made horse: winning hurdler: —
poor novice chaser: suited by a test of stamina: acts well on heavy going. *D. Moffatt.*

SNOW BLESSED 13 br.g. So Blessed–Snow Tribe (Great Nephew) [1989/90 c— §
c16d c16v^{3} c16v^{pu} c16g] poor chaser nowadays: best at up to 2½m: acts on any —
going: blinkered once: usually ridden by 7-lb claimer nowadays: sketchy jumper: inconsistent. *C. J. T. Alexander.*

SNOWFIRE CHAP 7 ch.g. Salluceva–Fainne Nua (Paddy's Birthday) c**102**
[1989/90 20g c20g^{5} c24g^{F} c24m^{5} c27d* c24g^{F} c27s^{2} c24s^{5} c24g^{4} c24d^{pu}] lengthy —
gelding: winning hurdler: won novice handicap chase at Sedgefield in January: generally ran poorly afterwards: well suited by a test of stamina: acts on good to firm and soft going: usually claimer ridden: blinkered once in 1986/7 and last 2 starts 1988/9: rather sketchy jumper of hurdles and tends to jump to his right over fences. *Mrs R. Wharton.*

SNOW HALL 7 b.g. Smokey Rockett–Another Roseberry (Grey Ghost) [1989/90 25g^{pu}] mid-division in 2 NH Flat races early in 1988/9: sold out of T. —
Walford's stable 1,900 gns Ascot October Sales: tailed off when pulled up in novice hurdle at Catterick in January. *R. D. E. Woodhouse.*

SNOW RHAPSODY 5 ch.m. Be My Guest (USA)–La Paille (Thatch (USA)) [1989/90 17f^{pu} 16d] workmanlike mare: poor maiden on Flat: tailed off in novice —

hurdle in November: subsequently sold 750 gns Ascot November Sales. *S. N. Cole.*

SNOW ROBIN 6 b.g. Panco–Moon Glow (Right Royal V) [1989/90 16f] leggy gelding: of little account. *Miss G. M. Rees.* —

SNOW ROSE 5 ch.m. Deep Run–Kilmanahan (Arctic Slave) [1989/90 20m 22gpu 16d] dipped-backed, sparely-made mare: no sign of ability: sold 2,200 gns Doncaster Spring Sales. *B. McLean.* —

SNOWY AUTUMN 6 ch.m. Deep Run–Autumn Queen (Menelek) [1989/90 21v 20dpu 16s 22s] smallish, lengthy mare: poor form in novice hurdles. *J. A. B. Old.* 76

SNOWY BONDLAIR 11 ch.g. Czarist–Gora Gully (Hot Brandy) [1989/90 c16g2 c16g5 c16h2 c16g3 c16m* c16h* c16m4] leggy, lightly-made gelding: handicap chaser: won at Worcester in April and Ludlow in May: pulls hard and best at around 2m: probably acts on any going: sometimes wears a crossed noseband: claimer ridden. *D. J. G. Murray-Smith.* c**113** —

SNUGFIT'S IMAGE 4 b.g. Music Boy–Sinzinbra (Royal Palace) [1989/90 16g2 16d 16d6 19f2 16f* 16g3 16m3] robust gelding: brother to useful hurdler/chaser Young Snugfit, closely related to Grand National runner-up Mr Snugfit (by Jukebox) and half-brother to 2 fairly useful jumpers by Faraway Times, including Cashew King: poor maiden sprinter on Flat (trained by J. Berry in 1989): won juvenile hurdle at Uttoxeter in April: broke blood vessel final start: stayed 19f: acted on firm going: ridden by 7-lb claimer fourth and fifth starts: dead. *O. Sherwood.* 96

SOBRIETY 5 b.h. Noalcoholic (FR)–Sacred Mountain (St Paddy) [1989/90 16m3 16gpu] workmanlike horse: quite modest performer on Flat, stays 1¼m (won over 7.6f in 1990): ridden by 7-lb claimer, 8 lengths third behind Big Red in 19-runner novice hurdle at Wincanton in November: acts on good to firm ground. *G. B. Balding.* 93

SOCA DANCER 6 b.g. Julio Mariner–Dancing Kathleen (Green God) [1989/90 16m 17m5] smallish, angular gelding: novice selling hurdler: well beaten in August: best at around 2m on top-of-the-ground: visored once: has worn a crossed noseband. *V. Thompson.* —

SOCIABILITY 14 b.g. Pieces of Eight–Limerick Queen (Whistling Wind) [1989/90 c24fpu] seems of little account, including in point-to-points. *A. M. Crow.* c— —

SOCIAL CIRCLE 5 b.m. Henbit (USA)–Princesse Anglaise (Crepello) [1989/90 18g a16g5 16g6 16g* 16d6 a20g 16s] smallish, sparely-made mare: sweating, won conditional jockeys selling hurdle at Towcester in December (bought in 3,800 gns): beaten fair way in novice company subsequently: yet to race on top-of-the-ground. *N. A. Smith.* 77

SOCIAL CLIMBER 6 b. or br.g. Crash Course–What A Duchess (Bargello) [1989/90 16g5 22g* 21s4] strong, lengthy gelding: won novice hurdle at Wincanton in January by 5 lengths from Ask Moss despite hanging left and looking inexperienced in closing stages: good staying-on fourth to Aristos in novice handicap at Sandown following month: will stay 3m. *Capt. T. A. Forster.* 112 p

SOCIETY GUEST 4 ch.g. High Line–Welcome Break (Wollow) [1989/90 16g6 16m] strong, workmanlike gelding: modest middle-distance maiden on Flat: sold out of I. Matthews' stable 24,000 gns Doncaster November Sales: first race for 3 months, 29 lengths ninth, blundering badly 4 out and never dangerous, behind Fidway in Seagram 100 Pipers Top Novices' Hurdle at Liverpool in April: showed some promise on debut. *Andrew Turnell.* 104

SOCKS DOWNE 11 b. or br.g. Paddy's Stream–Kincsem (Nelcius) [1989/90 c16d5 c20g2 c20m6] useful-looking gelding: quite a useful front-running chaser on his day in 1986/7: having only third outing since when second in handicap at Fontwell in December: jumped deliberately and ran poorly next time: probably stays 3m: acts well in the mud: has worn a crossed noseband: has looked reluctant on occasions. *Mrs J. Pitman.* c**112** —

SODA FOUNTAIN 4 b.f. Lafontaine (USA)–Sugar Lump (Candy Cane) [1989/90 aF16g*] fourth foal: sister to novice hurdler The Vatman Cometh and half-sister to Strong Fancy (by Royal Match), a NH Flat race winner and placed over hurdles: dam won at 2¼m and 21f over hurdles in Ireland: won NH Flat race at Lingfield in January: yet to race over hurdles. *Miss B. Sanders.*

SOFTLY 4 b.c. Beldale Flutter (USA)–Soft Pedal (Hotfoot) [1989/90 17g* 16f6 16g a16g* 16f2] unfurnished colt: half-brother to 2 winners, including modest 106

1986 2-y-o winner Summer Sky (by Skyliner): dam won 5 times at around 6f: won juvenile hurdles at Newton Abbot in November and Lingfield (amateur ridden) in February: pulls hard (wore dropped noseband last start) and unlikely to stay much beyond 2m: acts on firm going. *P. J. Hobbs.*

SO GIFTED 4 b.f. Niniski (USA)–Maybe So (So Blessed) [1989/90 16f 16m 16g a18g 16f] leggy, angular filly: one-time modest performer on Flat, stays 7f (once blinkered): sold out of J. W. Watts's stable 3,000 gns Doncaster September Sales: behind in juvenile hurdles and selling handicaps. *J. Norton.* —

SOHAIL (USA) 7 ch.g. Topsider (USA)–Your Nuts (USA) (Creme Dela Creme) [1989/90 16f^{3} 17m^{3} c17m^{2} c16f* c16f* c16m^{pu} c16s^{ur} c16s^{2} c16d^{3} c20h* c20m^{4} c16h^{2} c21f^{4}] leggy, good-topped gelding: winning hurdler/chaser: successful over fences at Stratford and Plumpton (twice) in 1989/90: stays 2½m: acts on any going: rather sketchy jumper: occasionally sweating: pulls hard. *J. White.* **c105** 93

SOLAR BREEZE 4 b.f. Tom Noddy–Space Miss (Space King) [1989/90 16m 20m] sparely-made filly: third foal: dam unraced: tailed off in juvenile hurdles, trying to run out 3 out last start: poor jumper: sold 500 gns Ascot February Sales. *J. M. Bradley.* — x

SOLAR CLOUD 8 ch.g. Northfields (USA)–Passing Fancy (USA) (Buckpasser) [1989/90 c22g^{4} c20g^{3} c21m^{3} c21f* c20m^{4} c20m^{3} c22g^{6} c21m^{3} c22m^{pu}] short-coupled, light-framed gelding: modest chaser nowadays: won handicap at Towcester in November, despite hanging left and looking none too keen on run-in: ran a moody race seventh outing: best at up to 21f on top-of-the-ground: visored twice and has also worn blinkers: faint-hearted. *M. J. Charles.* **c97** § —

SOLARES 10 br.g. Free State–Indian Wells (Reliance II) [1989/90 c32v^{pu} c24s^{4} c28d^{F} c36f] workmanlike gelding: carries plenty of condition: has been operated on for a soft palate and hobdayed: quite useful front-running chaser at his best: tailed off at Ayr in January and Liverpool (seventeenth in Seagram Grand National) in April: stays well: goes well in the mud: good mount for a claimer: sold out of J. Berry's stable 18,000 gns Doncaster March Sales after third start. *J. L. Eyre.* c— —

SOLAR GREEN 5 ch.g. Green Shoon–Solaranda (Green God) [1989/90 F13f F16f^{ro}] fifth foal: dam never ran: tailed off in NH Flat race at Hereford in April: ran out after 4f in similar event at Cheltenham later in month: yet to race over hurdles or fences. *L. J. Codd.*

SOLAR MASTER 6 b.g. Old Lucky–Space Miss (Space King) [1989/90 16f^{5} 16s^{pu} a16g^{4} a16g^{4} a16g^{6} 20g^{pu}] sparely-made, angular gelding: poor novice hurdler: form only at 2m: acts on firm ground and possibly unsuited by soft. *J. D. Thomas.* 64

SOLAR TIME 9 br.g. Another River–Solar Glory (Kabale) [1989/90 24h^{2} 22m^{4}] sparely-made gelding: winning chaser in Ireland: won selling hurdle in 1988/9: in frame in non-selling handicaps at Hexham in October and Nottingham in December: seems suited by further than 2m and stays 3m: seems to act on any going. *C. R. Beever.* c— 88

SOLDIER BRAVE 4 b.g. Persian Bold–Gilwanigan (Captain's Gig (USA)) [1989/90 16m^{2} 16m^{4} 17g^{5} a16g 16d^{F} 16m 16h* 17m^{pu} 16f^{5} 16h* 16f^{2}] close-coupled gelding: 1m seller winner on Flat (trained by I. Balding): selling hurdler: won at Taunton in April (conditional jockeys, retained 4,600 gns) and May (bought in 3,400 gns): unlikely to stay much beyond 2m: acts on hard ground: saddle slipped eighth start. *R. J. Manning.* 85

SOLEIL EXPRESS 4 b.g. Bay Express–Peters Pleasure (Jimsun) [1989/90 16d^{pu} 16f^{pu}] sparely-made gelding: fourth foal: half-brother to 2-y-o 5f seller winner Steel Cavalier (by Dublin Taxi): dam showed form only at 2 yrs: tailed off when pulled up in claiming hurdle and a seller: sold 2,500 gns Ascot May Sales. *J. D. Czerpak.* —

SOLENT LAD 7 b.h. Undulate (USA)–River Palace (Royal Palace) [1989/90 16g c20g^{ur} c20m^{F} c18f^{pu} c20s^{pu} c16g^{2} c16m^{3} c16d^{6} c16g^{ur} 20m^{pu} c16g^{5}] lengthy, workmanlike horse: handicap hurdler/chaser: runner-up over fences at Windsor in January, only form in 1989/90: should stay 2½m: acts on any going: good mount for a claimer: thoroughly untrustworthy. *B. Stevens.* **c95** § —

SOLENT STEEL 5 gr.m. Undulate (USA)–Tavaro (Gustav) [1989/90 16g^{4}] sparely-made mare: poor plater over hurdles. *A. J. Chamberlain.* —

SOLENT SUN 5 b.g. Undulate (USA)–River Palace (Royal Palace) [1989/90 16g] leggy gelding: poor novice selling hurdler: form only at 2m on heavy. *B. Stevens.* —

SOLICITOR'S CHOICE 7 b.g. Cagirama–Girostar (Drumbeg) [1989/90 16d 20g^{ur} 16g^{5} 16d^{pu} c16d^{2} c20m^{4} c17g^{ur} c16f^{3} c20m^{3} c24h^{2} c24g^{3}] lengthy, good-quartered gelding: winning hurdler: modest novice chaser: stays 3m, at least when conditions aren't testing: acts on any going. *Mrs R. Wharton.* c93 —

SOLIDASAROCK 8 ch.g. Hardboy–Limefield Rita (Mon Capitaine) [1989/90 c24f^{2} c24g* c26f^{F} c24d* c26g^{3} c24g^{5} c20f^{6}] c136 —

Solidasarock, winner of early-season novice chases at Worcester and Taunton in 1988/9 when trained by Murray-Smith, progressed into a useful chaser for his new stable in the latest campaign. Leg trouble had kept Solidasarock off the track for a year by the time he ran in a handicap at Newbury in October. A promising second to Royal Cedar there, Solidasarock won his next two completed races, the Curridge Handicap Chase at Newbury in November and the very valuable SGB Handicap Chase at Ascot in December. The handicapper had the opportunity to take into account Solidasarock's two-length success over Master Bob in the Curridge when framing the weights for the early-closing SGB and allotted him 8-11 in the original handicap. Despite a rise in the weights at the five-day declaration stage, Solidasarock still ran in the SGB with 11 lb more than his proper mark after his weight had been raised to the minimum 10-0. Solidasarock, who was sweating profusely beforehand, started at 33/1 in a field of twelve. In the race he showed no ill effects from the crashing fall he'd taken at the first in the Hennessy Cognac Gold Cup on his previous start, jumping well and racing prominently as the top-weight Panto Prince set only a modest pace. When the leader increased the tempo six from home Solidasarock was good enough to go with him and the pair quickly opened up a four- to five-length gap. Solidasarock jumped to the front three out and, after measuring the last accurately, drew clear on the run-in. At the line he was five lengths ahead of a tired Panto Prince who held on to second place by three quarters of a length from Brown Windsor. Solidasarock met Brown Windsor on terms 13 lb worse in the Save & Prosper Mandarin Handicap Chase at Newbury later in December. A combination of that and an extra quarter of a mile proved to be Solidasarock's undoing. Always close up, he looked the likely winner when taking a narrow advantage shortly after three out, but he edged left afterwards, was outstayed on the run-in and finished third behind Polyfemus and Brown Windsor, beaten a neck and three lengths. He was returned to three miles for the Racing Post Chase at Kempton in February. The presence of Desert Orchid in the eight-strong field meant Solidasarock was

SGB Handicap Chase, Ascot—33/1-shot Solidasarock jumps the last clear of Panto Prince

a stone out of the handicap. After vying for the lead with that horse down the far side for the last time, Solidasarock weakened quickly in the finishing straight and passed the post a well-beaten fifth. In his only subsequent race Solidasarock ran below form when sixth to New Halen in the strongly-run two-and-a-half-mile Mildmay of Flete Challenge Cup at Cheltenham in March. A strongly-run race over two and a half miles probably isn't ideal for Solidasarock; we think he'll prove best at three. He jumps well for one of his relative inexperience over fences but may have further improvement in him. He acts on any going and should win more races in 1990/1.

		Hard Ridden (b 1955)	Hard Sauce
	Hardboy (b 1968)		Toute Belle II
		Signal Hill II (b 1954)	Hill Prince
Solidasarock (ch.g. 1982)			Highway Code
		Mon Capitaine (ch 1952)	Wild Risk
	Limefield Rita (ch 1969)		Cappella
		Christy's Bow (b 1960)	Bowsprit
			Christy Cut

Solidasarock, an angular, useful-looking gelding, fetched IR 8,400 guineas as an unnamed three-year-old at Goffs April Sales. He is a half-brother to the useful chaser Poyntz Pass (by Gail Star), who showed his best form at up to two and a half miles. Their dam Limefield Rita, a sister to Captain Christy, was unraced. The Cheltenham Gold Cup and dual King George VI Chase winner Captain Christy was also a top-class hurdler before his attentions were turned to the bigger obstacles. He won the Irish Sweeps Hurdle in scintillating style in the 1972/3 season, when he was also a good third to Comedy of Errors and Easby Abbey in the Champion Hurdle. Solidasarock, the winner of a point-to-point in Ireland as a four-year-old, managed one success over timber, in a maiden hurdle at Wincanton in 1986/7. *R. Akehurst.*

SOLINSKY 5 ch.m. Bali Dancer–Sailor's Sol (The Bo'sun) [1989/90 18f^{5} 16m^{4}] half-sister to winning hurdlers Ashbury Lad (by Andrea Mantegna) and Soldier Sahib (by Sahib): dam, half-sister to winning jumpers Soho Sol, Ozandels and Golden Sol, was placed over 1½m: in frame once from 2 starts over 1¼m on Flat in 1989: tailed-off last in selling hurdle at Fontwell in October and amateur riders novice hurdle at Fakenham in May. *Miss L. Bower.* —

SOLITAIRE 10 br.m. Warpath–So Precious (Tamerlane) [1989/90 20f^{pu} 20g a20g c18m^{r} 20s^{pu} 22g^{pu} 21d] small mare: appears of no account nowadays: sometimes wears blinkers or a visor: trained until after sixth start by P. Butler. *J. H. Baker.* c— —

SOLITARY REAPER 5 b.g. Valiyar–Fardella (ITY) (Molvedo) [1989/90 20d^{5} 22m 18g^{6} a16g* a16s^{5} a16g^{2} a16g^{3} a16g^{2} a16g^{3}] leggy gelding: no bid after winning selling hurdle at Lingfield in January: placed in non-sellers on same course subsequently: probably stays 2¾m. *Miss B. Sanders.* 89

SOLO CORNET 5 br.g. Furry Glen–Royal Willow (Royal Buck) [1989/90 F16g^{5} F13d* F16g*] IR 2,400F, IR 5,400Y: third foal: dam, maiden hurdler, half-sister to winning staying chaser Dickwyn: won NH Flat races at Kelso in January and Edinburgh following month: yet to race over hurdles or fences. *J. G. FitzGerald.*

SOLOMON LAD 7 ch.h. Chinese Kung Fu–Lookslike Reindeer (Bonne Noel) [1989/90 17h^{6}] first foal: dam won over 5f at 2 yrs in Ireland and stayed 1½m: second over 1½m on Flat at 3 yrs: well beaten in novice seller at Devon & Exeter in August on hurdling debut. *B. Forsey.* —

SOLO PLAYER 7 b.m. Blue Refrain–Abercorn Flyer (Silly Season) [1989/90 16m^{su} 18m^{5}] leggy mare: poor novice hurdler: stays 19f: suited by firm ground: has been tried in blinkers and visored: sold 3,200 gns Doncaster January Sales. *L. J. Codd.* 71

SOLSTICE BELL 8 br.m. Record Token–Nasty Niece (CAN) (Great Nephew) [1989/90 21f^{2} 17f^{2} 17h^{2} 18h* 20f^{4}] leggy mare: former selling hurdler: having fourth race in 2 weeks when winning handicap hurdle at Fontwell in August by 10 lengths: behind in novice chases (poor jumper): stays 2½m: best on very firm ground: blinkered nowadays: usually a front runner. *R. Voorspuy.* c— x 94

SOMBRERO GOLD 6 ch.g. Miami Springs–Alleyn (Alcide) [1989/90 24g] lengthy, angular gelding: poor novice hurdler. *N. Bradley.* —

SOMEBODY 6 b.h. Bustino–Kashmir Lass (Kashmir II) [1989/90 20d 21d 21s* 20s] round-barrelled horse: amateur ridden, won handicap hurdle at Warwick in 121 February by a length from Telemeter Gem: will stay 3m: acts on heavy going: blinkered 5 of last 6 starts (was at Warwick). *J. White.*

SOME CONCERN (NZ) 6 b.g. Aythorpe–Alcirur (NZ) (Alcimedes) [1989/90 16d^{pu} 16g^{ur} 16g] sparely-made gelding: no sign of ability, including in a selling — hurdle. *Capt. T. A. Forster.*

SOME DO NOT 6 b.g. Maculata–Ballynavin Money (Even Money) [1989/90 c**104** 22g^{6} 21m* 22s^{pu} c24s^{F} c25m^{F} c24g^{2} c21g^{F}] sturdy gelding: half-brother to 81 + winning chasers King's Crest (by Prince Hansel) and Milanessa (by Milan): dam unraced half-sister to several winners, including smart chaser Tacroy and Bunkilla, the dam of Dis Train: won a point-to-point in Ireland in 1989: bought 20,000 gns Doncaster Spring (1989) Sales: won 5-runner novice hurdle at Warwick in November: has fallen in 3 of his 4 chases but has shown plenty of ability too, and was a couple of lengths clear of eventual winner Spritebrand when departing at the last in handicap at Market Rasen in April, last start: probably stays 3m: should win over fences, but needs to improve his jumping. *N. J. Henderson.*

SOME FINGERS 5 ch.g. Some Hand–Salira (Double Jump) [1989/90 F12g F14v] half-brother to 3 winners, including staying hurdler/chaser Calira (by Coliseum): dam won 6f seller at 2 yrs: behind in NH Flat races: yet to race over hurdles or fences. *Miss M. J. Benson.*

SOME HERO 6 b.g. Boreen Beag–Tipperary Star (Arcticeelagh) [1989/90 16g^{6} 17m 20g 20g^{5}] lengthy, rather unfurnished gelding: poor form in novice 74 hurdles: dead. *W. A. Stephenson.*

SOME MACHINE 11 b. or br.g. Prominer–Peking (Le Prince) [1989/90 27g^{3} c— § 20g* 27g* 24d 24m] strong, heavy-topped gelding: moderate hurdler and novice 114 § chaser: successful in handicaps at Hexham (seller, attracted no bid) in November and Sedgefield following month: stays 27f: acts on dead going: blinkered last 2 starts 1986/7 and last 4 outings: has appeared ungenuine in the past and took little interest last 2 starts. *J. G. FitzGerald.*

SOME OBLIGATION 5 b.g. Gleason (USA)–Happy Lass (Tarqogan) c**111** p [1989/90 c20g^{F} c16d* c25f* c24g^{2}]

Around a hundred and forty hunter chases are run each year, approximately eighty per cent of them over three miles or more, the rest over distances ranging from two miles to two and three quarter miles. The latter group help vary the programme and give speedier hunters an extra option, but are the three annual two-mile hunter chases necessary or even desirable? After all, hunters aren't supposed to be two-mile chasers; in theory they should be capable of carrying big weights over long distances in the field. Whether or not, one of the two-mile races in 1990 served to provide the promising Some Obligation with his first success. It came at Leicester in March. Well fancied following a most encouraging steeplechase debut at Doncaster the previous month—he was travelling very well when falling four out—Some Obligation could scarcely have been more impressive in winning by six lengths from Privateperformance. Always moving strongly, he led on the bridle at the second last and soon went clear under little encouragement from the rider. Five days later he contested a three-mile event back at Doncaster and again showed himself to be one of the best young hunters to emerge, and also put up an amazing performance in beating Master Eryl two lengths. Held up to the degree that at one point he was in the region of a furlong off the pace, he'd reduced that deficit somewhat by the time they swung into the straight, but he was still fifteen lengths behind the leader Master Eryl at the second last. As that horse began to hang badly right, Some Obligation went by to lead at the last and was ridden out on the flat to maintain the advantage. Some Obligation tasted defeat for the first time in completed hunter chases when going down by five lengths to the highly-promising Teaplanter in a four-runner event at Huntingdon in April.

Some Obligation is the ninth foal of Happy Lass, a winner at up to a mile and a half in Ireland. The dam has produced three other winning

Some Obligation (b.g. 1985)	Gleason (USA) (b 1976)	Nijinsky (b 1967)	Northern Dancer
			Flaming Page
		Gleam (br 1967)	Spy Well
			Glamour
	Happy Lass (br 1968)	Tarqogan (br 1960)	Black Tarquin
			Rosyogan
		Never On Time (b 1961)	Arctic Time
			Never Venture

jumpers, namely Dunabunk (by Brave Invader), The Go Boy (by Rarity) who was a quite useful hurdler, and Girseach (by Furry Glen). Happy Lass, daughter of the unraced Never On Time, is a sister to a two-mile Flat winner and half-sister to three other winners, including Winds of Time a heavily-backed winner of a selling hurdle at Liverpool in 1980. Some Obligation started his career in Ireland, running in three point-to-points in 1989. He failed to show any ability, being pulled up on heavy ground twice and finishing a well-beaten fifth on the other start. In steeplechases he's yet to race on ground softer than dead and acts on firm going. Though a winner over the minimum trip, his best form has been at three miles. A workmanlike gelding, he has plenty of improvement to come and could win a string of races if kept to hunter chases. If switched to handicaps he might do well in those too. *J. R. Upson.*

SOME POSSE 8 b.g. Posse (USA)–Some Dame (FR) (Vieux Manoir) [1989/90 c25spu] well beaten both outings on Flat at 3 yrs: modest maiden point-to-pointer: sweating, tailed off when pulled up in maiden hunter chase at Hereford in March. *P. G. Watkins.* c—

SOMETHING SIMILAR 7 b.g. Artaius (USA)–Alice Kyteler (Crepello) [1989/90 16g4] compact, good-bodied gelding: lightly-raced novice hurdler: first form when 28 lengths fourth to First Crack at Perth in May: gives impression he barely stays 2m. *W. A. Stephenson.* 86

SONALTO 4 br.c. Noalto–Sanandrea (Upper Case (USA)) [1989/90 16f5 16m 16m 16d 16g2 a16g3 16d6 16f2 16m4 16f3 16f2 17m5 16f* 16f3] half-brother to Northern Ruler (by Rolfe), winner at up to 3m over hurdles: modest maiden on Flat, suited by 1m: attracted no bid after winning selling handicap hurdle at Sedgefield in May: unlikely to stay much beyond 2m: acts on firm ground: suitable mount for claimer: trained until after eighth outing by D. Smith. *D. L. Williams.* 82

SONAR 4 b. or br.c. Pitskelly–Diana's Choice (Tudor Music) [1989/90 16g2 a16g2 a16g3 a16g] sparely-made colt: temperamental maiden on Flat, stays 13f (has been blinkered): placed in juvenile hurdles, over a sharp 2m, showing modest form: may be suited by stiffer test of stamina. *Pat Mitchell.* 84

SONEETO 4 b.g. Teenoso (USA)–Flying Bid (Auction Ring (USA)) [1989/90 16g a16g* 18g3 16d 16g] tall, leggy gelding: temperamental maiden on Flat, when trained by R. Hannon: won juvenile hurdle at Lingfield in December: probably stays 2¼m. *S. Woodman.* 88

SONIC LORD 5 b.h. Final Straw–Lucent (Irish Ball (FR)) [1989/90 18spu a16gr] sturdy horse: unreliable on Flat but won twice over 1¼m in 1989 (visored on first occasion, blinkered on second): has shown more temperament than ability over hurdles: wears blinkers: one to leave alone. *R. Voorspuy.* §§

SONNENDEW 7 br.g. Sonnen Gold–Bally-Do (Ballymoss) [1989/90 c20v3 c25f4] leggy, sparely-made gelding: won a point-to-point in March: 3½ lengths third to Random Time in maiden hunter chase at Folkestone previous month. *Miss P. Russell.* c76 —

SONNY HILL LAD 7 ch.g. Celtic Cone–Honey Dipper (Golden Dipper) [1989/90 24m*] small, sturdy gelding: gained third course win when running on gamely to beat On His Own 1½ lengths in handicap hurdle at Worcester in September: stays 3m: acts on any going: good mount for an amateur or claimer. *R. J. Holder.* 114

SONNY ONE SHINE 9 b.g. Mandalus–Wreck-Em-All (Wrekin Rambler) [1989/90 22dpu] smallish gelding: one-time fair hurdler: bit backward only outing in 1989/90: stays 2½m: acts on heavy going. *R. Allan.* —

SONSIE MO 5 b.g. Lighter–Charlotte Amalie (No Mercy) [1989/90 16v2 16d4 20d5 16f6 20g 16f* 16d4 16f6] sparely-made gelding: won 4-runner handicap hurdle at Newcastle in May: best at 2m: acts on any going: wears a crossed noseband. *Mrs S. C. Bradburne.* 94

SOONER STILL 6 b.g. Tachypous–Sooner Or Later (Sheshoon) [1989/90 c22d2 c24g3 c25d* c20v c26s3 c26g2 c26f*] sparely-made, angular gelding: quite useful hurdler: 15-length winner of handicap chase at Plumpton in January and novice chase at Uttoxeter in April: suited by a thorough test of stamina: acts on any going: blinkered last 2 starts 1987/8: good mount for an amateur or claimer. *J. A. C. Edwards.* c**114** —

SOPHARME 4 b.c. Pharly (FR)–Concert (Appiani II) [1989/90 20vpu 16vpu 16d] small, sturdy colt: sixth live foal: half-brother to quite useful 1¼m winner Boccioni (by Welsh Pageant) and a winner abroad: dam unraced half-sister to very useful stayer Fortissimo: well beaten in selling hurdle at Bangor in March. *R. J. Holder.* —

SOPRINELA 10 b. or br.m. Foggy Bell–Solent Princess (Prince Barle) [1989/90 c24d*] workmanlike mare: won 2 point-to-points in February and one in March: also won a hunter chase at Market Rasen in March, despite jumping slowly at last 2 fences: stays 3m: wears blinkers. *B. Belchem.* c**90**

SOROPTIMISTER 5 br.g. Swing Easy (USA)–Cora (Current Coin) [1989/90 16gpu 16f] leggy, good-topped gelding: little sign of ability on Flat: tailed off in novice hurdle at Newbury in November: sold 950 gns Ascot February Sales. *P. Hayward.* —

SOSPIRANDO 5 b.g. Music Boy–Andalucia (Rheingold) [1989/90 16s 16d 16g 16s] leggy gelding: has shown a modicum of ability over hurdles: takes a good hold and barely stays 2m. *J. Ringer.* —

SOULFUL STRUT 9 ch.g. Derrylin–Russellia (Red God) [1989/90 c16m c17gpu c16g2 c16g2 c16s5 c16g] big, strong, good-topped gelding: moderate chaser: runner-up twice at Wincanton in January: well beaten subsequently (reluctant to race first time): stays 2½m: acts on firm and dead ground: bold jumper: wore pricker on near-side last start. *N. R. Mitchell.* c**103** —

SOUND OF ISLAY 5 b.g. Deep Run–Sharpaway (Royal Highway) [1989/90 16g*] useful-looking gelding, unfurnished at present: fourth foal: brother to top-class hurdler Mole Board and winning staying Irish hurdler Deep Dawn: dam Irish NH Flat race winner: 33/1, made impressive hurdling debut when winning 17-runner novice event at Stratford in March by 4 lengths from Do Be Brief, travelling strongly, leading approaching last and quickening clear despite looking green: will stay 2½m: looks an exciting prospect. *Capt. T. A. Forster.* 100 P

SOURCE OF MAGIC 8 b.g. Golden Love–Ballinlonig Lass (Diritto) [1989/90 20g*] sturdy gelding: showed improved form when winning novice handicap hurdle at Bangor in May comfortably by 8 lengths from L'Aquino: beaten in sellers previously: stays 2½m. *A. W. Denson.* 84

SOUTH BAR 5 gr.m. Scallywag–Erra (Romany Air) [1989/90 21dpu] plain mare: half-sister to 3 winning jumpers, including useful hurdler Farmer and staying chaser Corn Merchant (both by Winden): dam selling hurdler: needing race, tailed off when pulled up last in maiden hurdle at Warwick in March. *A. P. Jones.* —

SOUTH CROSS (USA) 5 ch.g. Valdez (USA)–Blue Cross Nurse (USA) (Needles) [1989/90 20g 16m* 16g 20g6 16s5 c16gF c17g2 c22f* c20gF] sturdy gelding: well-backed favourite, won novice handicap hurdle at Hexham in November: ran poorly over hurdles subsequently: won novice chase at Kelso in April by 2 lengths from Border Oak: stays 2¾m: acts on any going: visored last start over hurdles. *G. M. Moore.* c84 104

SOUTHDOWN SPIRIT 14 b.g. Sir Nulli–Blue Ivy (Fleche Bleu) [1989/90 c26g3] strong gelding: winning chaser: was suited by a thorough test of stamina and the mud: blinkered last 5 outings: dead. *Miss L. Bower.* c— —

SOUTHEND SCALLYWAG 4 b.f. Tina's Pet–By The Lake (Tyrant (USA)) [1989/90 17m 16f* 16m3 16m* 16g* 16g 16f3 20g6 20f*] leggy filly: 1m winner on Flat: successful in juvenile hurdles at Hexham, Perth and Kelso, and in a 3-runner handicap at Hexham: stays 2½m: acts on firm ground: suited by forcing tactics. *G. M. Moore.* 110

SOUTHERNAIR 10 b.g. Derrylin–Port La Joie (Charlottown) [1989/90 c20g2 c20m c20f3 c20g* c20s2 c20sF c18g c17v4 c22mur c22m5] neat gelding: fair chaser nowadays: won handicap at Fontwell in December: led 4 out until hampered and unseated rider 2 out (pushed along at the time and would probably have finished second) in John Hughes Memorial Trophy Chase (Handicap) won by Wont Be Gone Long at Liverpool in April: didn't go through with his effort fifth start: stays 2½m: acts on heavy going and good to firm: blinkered third to sixth c**123** —

Mr S. Powell's "Southernair"

and last outings: sometimes dull in coat: usually jumps soundly: has won 7 times at Fontwell. *J. R. Jenkins.*

SOUTHERN HERMIT 10 b.g. Monsieure Edouarde–Motif (St Elmo) [1989/90 c17m3] big, workmanlike gelding: poor novice chaser: stays 21f: acts on firm going: blinkered last 2 starts 1986/7 (refused on first occasion and tried to do so on second). *Mrs J. G. Retter.* c79 —

SOUTHERN REAPER 8 ch.g. Kambalda–Ingenious (Indigenous) [1989/90 c20m* c20gbd c20fpu] tall, workmanlike gelding: novice hurdler: claimer ridden, jumped better than previously when winning novice chase at Chepstow in October: brought down at the eighth next outing and pulled up lame on last: stays 2½m: acts on good to firm going. *J. R. Upson.* c92 x —

SOUTHERNS 8 ch.g. Lord of Arabia–Londoretta (London Gazette) [1989/90 c20f4 c16h5 c16f3 c20dpu c22mF] strong gelding: poor chaser: stayed 2½m: seemed suited by top-of-the-ground: blinkered last 4 outings: dead. *F. M. Barton.* c— —

SOUTHERN SUPREME 7 b.g. Dunphy–Miss Etta (King's Troop) [1989/90 16f 16m3 16m5] big, useful-looking gelding: will make a chaser: half-brother to several winners, including modest hurdlers Erminia (by Gulf Pearl) and Shumard (by Sweet Revenge): dam never ran: poor form in novice hurdles: will stay beyond 2m. *J. T. Gifford.* 81

SOUTHOVER LAD (NZ) 7 b.g. Frassino–Tarea (NZ) (Balios) [1989/90 20m2 16g* 16g2] lengthy gelding: jumped badly but made most of running when winning novice hurdle at Stratford in October by 25 lengths: jumped better and showed improved form when head second to General Glory on stiffer track at Newbury following month: stays 2½m: races keenly. *D. H. Barons.* 104

SOUTH POOL (NZ) 6 ch.g. Harbor Prince (USA)–Romany Robe (Sky Gipsy) [1989/90 17d 20mpu c20gur c20d c21g c17d3 c16m3] wiry gelding: poor novice hurdler: 6¾ lengths third to Go West at Newton Abbot in March, penultimate start and easily best effort in novice chases: blinkered 4 of last 5 outings over hurdles and last 2 starts over fences: has looked unenthusiastic and isn't one to trust. *D. H. Barons.* c95 § — §

SOUTHROP 4 b.c. Auction Ring (USA)–Giovinezza (FR) (Roi Dagobert) [1989/90 16g] workmanlike colt: modest sprint handicapper on Flat: took a good —

hold when tailed off in 17-runner juvenile hurdle at Wolverhampton in December. *M. Blanshard.*

SOUTH STACK 4 b.g. Daring March–Lady Henham (Breakspear II) [1989/90 16gpu] plater on Flat, successful over 7f in 1989: tailed off when pulled up 2 out in juvenile hurdle at Wetherby in November. *Ronald Thompson.* c— —

SOUTHSTONE ROCK 7 b.g. Don Enrico (USA)–Sunstreak Girl (Right Flare) [1989/90 c24f5 c20f5] tall, plain gelding: blind near eye: no sign of ability. *R. D. Taylor.* c— —

SOUTIEN 5 b.m. Dubassoff (USA)–Soumark (Weatherbird) [1989/90 18f3 16f 16f] leggy mare: seems of little account. *J. P. D. Elliott.* —

SOVEREIGN STEPS 8 b.g. Royal Palace–Aequanimitas (Infatuation) [1989/90 c20m5] leggy, workmanlike gelding: no form in novice hurdles and novice chases. *K. A. Morgan.* c— —

SOVEREIGN STREAM 6 b.g. Paddy's Stream–Noble Lynn (Brave Invader (USA)) [1989/90 16mpu 22mpu] leggy, workmanlike gelding: winning hurdler: pulled up both outings in 1989/90: stays 19f: acts on dead going: needs to improve his jumping. *A. Barrow.* —

SOYBEAN 6 gr.h. Ardross–Meanz Beanz (High Top) [1989/90 17m 16g 20d 22d6 20g3 25g5 25g] smallish, workmanlike horse: poor novice hurdler: gives impression will need a thorough test of stamina: blinkered final start 1988/9: amateur or claimer ridden. *A. C. Batey.* 73

SPACE CHASER 7 b.g. Space King–Bow Baby (Bowsprit) [1989/90 16g 19d6 24gpu] lengthy gelding: no sign of ability over hurdles: dead. *F. Jordan.* —

SPACE FAIR 7 b.g. Space King–Katie Fare (Ritudyr) [1989/90 16m 20m] leggy, workmanlike gelding: useful hurdler, winner of 5 of his 7 races in 1988/9: ran a very good race when twelfth to Kribensis in Waterford Crystal Champion Hurdle at Cheltenham in March, but poorly when favourite in valuable handicap at Liverpool following month: stays 21f: possibly unsuited by heavy going, acts on any other: races freely: claimer ridden (unable to draw allowance at Cheltenham): ran out fourth start and hung left on run-in when winning once in 1988/9. *R. Lee.* 140 ?

SPACE GEM 9 b.g. Space King–Nicola Lisa (Dumbarnie) [1989/90 c20d5 c20g5] sparely-made gelding: poor novice hurdler/chaser: stays well. *R. E. Peacock.* c**78** —

SPACE LAB 5 b.g. Tanfirion–Marzooga (Bold Lad (IRE)) [1989/90 22h2 18f2] stocky gelding: poor form in novice hurdles: stays 2¾m: tailed off both outings on heavy going. *Mrs L. Clay.* 79

SPACE PRINCE 9 b.g. Space King–Queens Purse (Lucky Sovereign) [1989/90 c24d3] lengthy, rather sparely-made gelding: winning point-to-pointer: maiden hunter chaser: stays 3m: acts on firm and dead ground. *R. A. Phillips.* c**96**

SPACIAL (USA) 6 b.h. Star Appeal–Abeer (USA) (Dewan (USA)) [1989/90 c16d* c20m2 c16f*] tall, useful-looking horse: moderate hurdler: won novice chases at Kempton in November and Folkestone (jumped rather deliberately) in December: stays 2½m: well beaten on heavy ground and yet to race on hard, acts on any other: suited by a right-handed track: has run well for a 7-lb claimer: needs to brush up his jumping. *N. A. Gaselee.* c**110** —

SPANGO VALLEY 4 b.g. Tom Noddy–Nordan Enterprise (Rapid River) [1989/90 F16m aF14g] first foal: dam poor Flat maiden: tailed off in NH Flat races at Towcester and Southwell: yet to race over hurdles. *D. J. Wintle.*

SPANISH CAVALIER 10 ch.g. Grundy–Escorial (Royal Palace) [1989/90 17f5] very lightly-raced novice hurdler: dead. *J. H. Baker.* —

SPANISH LOVE 4 b. or br.f. Precocious–San Marguerite (Blakeney) [1989/90 16d 16f6] small filly: placed at up to 1m on Flat: poor form over hurdles, including in a seller. *M. McCormack.* 61

SPANISH MOU 5 b.m. King of Spain–Baggage (Zeus Boy) [1989/90 16m 16s5 16sr] small mare: poor plater on Flat and over hurdles: reluctant to race, tailed off when refusing last start. *M. W. Eckley.* — §

SPANISH PRINCESS 6 b.m. King of Spain–Doogali (Doon) [1989/90 16f5 20f3] leggy, sparely-made mare: poor novice hurdler: best form at 2m: acts on firm going: has worn a crossed noseband. *G. P. Enright.* 76

SPANISH REEL 8 b.g. Gay Fandango (USA)–De Nada (Ragusa) [1989/90 16f3 16g2 16m* 16g3 a16g2 a16g2] close-coupled gelding: fair but irresolute hurdler: did nothing wrong when winning at Wolverhampton in October: raced only at 119 §

around 2m: best form on top-of-the-ground: had a turn of foot: dead. *J. A. C. Edwards.*

SPANISH SERVANT 5 ch.g. Don–Please Oblige (Le Levanstell) [1989/90 16d4] good-bodied, workmanlike gelding: useful hurdler: ran well when fourth behind Instant Tan in handicap at Ayr in April: needs testing conditions when racing at 2m and will stay 2½m: yet to race on top-of-the-ground. *R. Akehurst.* 135

SPANISH SONG 5 br.g. King of Spain–Rock Concert (Star Appeal) [1989/90 a16g 16g] rangy gelding: no form over hurdles. *M. C. Chapman.* —

SPARKLER GEBE 4 b.c. Be My Native (USA)–Siliferous (Sandy Creek) [1989/90 16g 16spu] sparely-made colt: placed over 1½m on Flat: tailed off in juvenile hurdles. *P. G. Bailey.* —

SPARKLING CINDERS 6 b.m. Netherkelly–Cindyr (Ritudyr) [1989/90 aF16g3 aF16g a24g6 20f2 16m3] sparely-made mare: fourth foal: sister to useful 2½m chaser Fu's Lady: dam, modest novice hurdler and poor point-to-pointer, half-sister to 2 winning hurdlers: beaten over 20 lengths in NH Flat races: forced pace when placed in novice hurdle at Worcester in March and maiden hurdle at Towcester in April: stays 2½m. *N. A. Twiston-Davies.* 76

SPARKLING JUDY 6 b.m. Sparkling Boy–Welcome Sara (Lucky Brief) [1989/90 17hpu] small mare: poor plater over hurdles. *D. N. Carey.* —

SPARKLING LORD 12 gr.g. Lord Nelson (FR)–Grey Sparkle (Pongee) [1989/90 c20fpu] lengthy, sparely-made gelding: of little account over hurdles: winning point-to-pointer: no sign of ability in hunter chases, jumping poorly. *B. A. James.* c— x —

SPARK OF PEACE 8 ch.g. Royal Match–Geneva (Linacre) [1989/90 22dpu 20g3 20s* 18d* 24g* 25g4 24d5] sturdy gelding: in fine form in first half of January and won handicap hurdles at Sedgefield, Kelso and Edinburgh (conditional jockeys event): ran moderately last 2 starts: fifth in novice handicap in 1988/9, easily better effort over fences: has won over 3m, but best run at 2¼m: appears unsuited by hard going but probably acts on any other: ridden by 7-lb claimer. *P. A. Blockley.* c— 100

SPARK OF WIT 4 b.g. Comedy Star (USA)–Rekindle (Relkino) [1989/90 17fF] first foal: dam, poor maiden, is half-sister to smart hurdler and useful chaser No Bombs: well beaten in varied company on Flat: behind when falling 2 out in juvenile hurdle at Newton Abbot in July: sold 3,400 gns Ascot August Sales. *R. J. Holder.* —

SPAR LADY 7 b.m. Tanfirion–Royal Reserve (Royal Palace) [1989/90 16g 17d c16vF 21m 17m 16f3] lengthy, sparely-made mare: poor novice hurdler: tailed off when falling 5 out in mares novice event on chasing debut: blinkered fourth start. *J. D. Roberts.* c— 75

SPARRING 5 b.m. Sagaro–Parabems (Swing Easy (USA)) [1989/90 19dpu 16gpu 16m 16vpu] sparely-made mare: no sign of ability on Flat or over hurdles, including in sellers: trained until after second start by G. Yardley. *R. G. Brazington.* —

SPARTAN CHIEF 9 ch.g. True Song–Silver Spartan (Spartan General) [1989/90 c20m3] lengthy gelding: poor novice hurdler: best effort over fences when just over 3 lengths third to Imadyna in novice event at Worcester in September: stays 2½m: acts on good to firm going. *Mrs G. E. Jones.* c**74** + —

SPARTAN FLASHBACK 11 b.g. Flashback–Spartan Lass (Spartan General) [1989/90 16m4] close-coupled gelding: winning hurdler: well beaten in amateur riders selling handicap in May: stays 2¼m: acts on soft going: sometimes claimer ridden, and was when successful: modest point-to-pointer. *G. H. Barber.* —

SPARTAN LEMON 7 ch.m. Spartan Jester–Port'N Lemon (Hot Brandy) [1989/90 c25spu c25fpu] rangy mare: won a point-to-point in April: pulled up in hunter chases in March and May. *D. G. L. Llewellin.* c—

SPARTAN RAFT 9 ch.g. Lighter–Tanaway (Spartan General) [1989/90 25fpu 24fpu 20mpu] strong gelding: winning hurdler: pulled up all starts in 1989/90: suited by 2½m + : form only on top-of-the-ground. *G. R. Prest.* —

SPARTAN RAMBLER 13 ch.g. Spartan General–Hay Bag (Ritudyr) [1989/90 c26d4] small gelding: won hunter chase in 1986: lightly raced and modest form since: needs a thorough test of stamina and give in the ground. *H. Hutsby.* c— —

SPARTONA 6 ch.m. Cisto (FR)–Dorothy May (Spartan General) [1989/90 F17f 16m2 24d3 20gF 20d5 16g2 20f5] lengthy mare: first foal: dam winning point-to-pointer: placed in novice hurdles: stays 3m: ran moderately on firm ground. *M. W. Easterby.* 89

SPEAKERS CORNER 7 ch.g. Politico (USA)–Gusty Lucy (White Speck) c**102**
[1989/90 c25d^{2} c24g^{4} c25g* c24m^{4} c24d c32f] lengthy gelding: modest novice —
hurdler: won 3-runner novice chase at Cheltenham in January: stays 25f (stiff
task at 4m): acts on soft going: usually takes good hold: jumps deliberately on
occasions: tends to sweat. *M. J. Wilkinson.*

SPECIAL PANSY 6 b.m. Mart Lane–Pansy Rock (Roxy (FR)) [1989/90 F12f
20g^{pu}] leggy mare: first foal: dam, daughter of a fair hurdler, well beaten in novice —
hurdles: tailed off in NH Flat race at Bangor: destroyed after pulling up in novice
hurdle on same course. *Mrs N. S. Sharpe.*

SPECIAL PRICE 5 ro.g. Silly Prices–Manche (Palestine) [1989/90 17m^{r}]
poor and ungenuine maiden on Flat: bit backward and edgy, refused to race in — §
novice hurdle at Carlisle in November. *N. Chamberlain.*

SPECIAL RESERVE 5 b.g. Auction Ring (USA)–Grande Madame (Monseigneur (USA)) [1989/90 16g 16g^{5} 16f 17m^{pu} 16m^{4} 16f^{4} 17f^{3} 17m^{3}] sparely-made 73
gelding: poor 1m seller winner on Flat: sold out of P. Feilden's stable 2,000 gns
Ascot December Sales: novice selling hurdler: best efforts on second and seventh
starts: unlikely to stay much beyond 2m: yet to race on a yielding surface over
hurdles: amateur ridden. *G. Stickland.*

SPECIAL SETTLEMENT (USA) 9 b.h. Riva Ridge (USA)–Laura Bell c84
(USA) (Jacinto) [1989/90 c16m^{4} c20m^{2} c16f* c16f c20m^{6} c20f^{4} c16g^{5} a20g* a16g^{2} 88
a20g^{6}] smallish, rather lightly-made horse: handicap hurdler/chaser: won over
fences at Hexham in October and over hurdles at Southwell in March: stays 2½m
but not 3m: acts on any going: sometimes claimer ridden (including when
successful): often has tongue tied down. *R. Allan.*

SPECIAL VENTURE 9 b.m. Giolla Mear–Winsome Lady (Tarqogan) c—
[1989/90 c16d^{F} c20f^{F}] lengthy, good-quartered mare: winning hurdler/chaser: has —
won over 2½m but best form at around 2m: acts on soft and good to firm going:
visored last 3 starts 1988/9 and on first outing: usually claimer ridden. *O. O'Neill.*

SPECKYFOUREYES 7 b.m. Blue Cashmere–Sprightly Sprite (Babur)
[1989/90 20g^{F} 21m^{2} 20f^{pu} a20g^{6}] smallish mare: moderate hurdler: runner-up in 106
handicap at Warwick in November: best in strongly-run races at around 2½m:
acts on good to firm and dead going: sold 3,100 gns Ascot April Sales. *J. Pearce.*

SPECULATION 8 ch.g. New Member–Stockley Crystal (Dairialatan) c—
[1989/90 c24g^{5} c25f^{F}] leggy gelding: point-to-point winner in April: tailed off in
hunter chase later in month. *M. H. Gingell.*

SPEECH 7 ch.g. Salluceva–Malone (Politico (USA)) [1989/90 c16g^{3} c20f^{2} c**97**
c20s^{F} c25g^{2} c20d^{2} c25g^{3} c25g^{6} c24f^{ur} c24d c20h* c20d^{4} c24f*] strong ex-Irish —
gelding: fourth foal: half-brother to winning point-to-pointer The Dub (by Brave
Invader) and winning Irish jumpers Island Bridge (by Mandalus) and Tokay Lady
(by Furry Glen): dam tailed off in maiden hurdle on only outing: poor maiden
hurdler: jumped better with experience over fences and won 2 novice events at
Hexham in May, second a handicap: stays 3m: acts on hard and dead going:
blinkered first outing in 1988/9. *W. A. Stephenson.*

SPEEDY BOY 8 ch.g. Tachypous–Grandpa's Legacy (Zeus Boy) [1989/90 20g c—
24m^{pu} c21g c26f^{4} 24m^{pu} 20m^{3} 25m^{4} 20m] workmanlike gelding: winning hurdler 83
and novice chaser: behind in selling handicap last start: stays 2¾m (seems not
quite to stay 3m): acts on firm ground (has run moderately on heavy): best visored
or blinkered: has run creditably for an amateur. *G. P. Enright.*

SPEEDY SNAPS LAD 5 b.g. Magnolia Lad–Parton Gold (The Go-Between)
[1989/90 16f^{6}] leggy gelding: poor novice selling hurdler: blinkered only outing in 60
1989/90. *P. M. Cowley.*

SPENT FORCE 5 gr.g. Mummy's Pet–Tamer Grange (Saritamer (USA))
[1989/90 a16g 16g^{pu}] seems of little account: sold 900 gns Doncaster March Sales. —
Ronald Thompson.

SPHINX 6 b.g. Auction Ring (USA)–The Yellow Girl (Yellow God) [1989/90
16g^{5} 16m^{3} 16g^{pu}] sturdy gelding: only worthwhile form over hurdles when third 69
behind Deep Water Bay in selling handicap at Fakenham in March. *J. R. Bostock.*

SPIANZI 8 ch.m. Funny Man–Tamorina (Quayside) [1989/90 c20f^{4}] third foal: c—
sister to a poor animal: dam unraced daughter of fair chaser Tamoretta, a
half-sister to Spanish Steps: won a point-to-point in May: made a couple of
mistakes when tailed off in novice hunter chase at Folkestone later in month. *Mrs
R. W. Farrant.*

SPINNEY LIGHT 7 b.g. Seaepic (USA)–Sara's Light (Precipice Wood)
[1989/90 22d^{pu} 16d a16g^{3} 16s^{pu} 21f^{pu}] robust gelding: first foal: dam, lightly-raced 81

maiden point-to-pointer, daughter of a winning hurdler/chaser: 6½ lengths third to Kenilworth Castle in novice event at Southwell in January, only sign of merit over hurdles. *W. G. Mann.*

SPIRESLAKE 7 ch.g. Paddy's Stream–Hero's Slave (Arctic Slave) [1989/90 20s pu] leggy gelding: fourth foal: half-brother to winning chasers Tar Knight (by Tarqogan) and Classic Hero (by Over The River) and to winning hurdler Hero's Hill (by Abednego): dam half-sister to fair staying chaser Coolishall: unbeaten in 3 point-to-points in 1988, showing fair form: 50/1 and very much in need of race, behind when pulled up 3 out in Golden Miller Novices' Hurdle at Leicester in January. *A. J. Wilson.* —

SPIRITED HOLME (FR) 5 b.g. Gay Mecene (USA)–Lyphard's Holme (Lyphard) [1989/90 16d pu 16g 16m c16s 4 c16s 2 c16v 5 c16d c16f 4 c16f 4 c16f* c16m 3 c16f* c20f 3 c20f 6 16g 4] sturdy ex-Irish gelding: middle-distance maiden on Flat: winning hurdler: no form over hurdles in Britain: won novice chases at Bangor (handicap) in March and Sedgefield (left clear last) in April: best at 2m: acts on any going: usually visored nowadays (wasn't when gaining last win): sometimes claimer ridden. *D. L. Williams.* c96 —

SPIRIT OF KIBRIS 5 ch.g. Quayside–Golden Shuil (Master Owen) [1989/90 16d 6 16g 4 21f] rather leggy, close-coupled gelding: modest form in novice hurdles: possibly unsuited by firm ground: should be suited by further than 2m. *Mrs J. Pitman.* 85

SPIRIT OF YOUTH 5 b.m. Kind of Hush–Bustle (Busted) [1989/90 F16f] third foal: dam lightly raced and no form: behind in NH Flat race at Warwick in May: yet to race over hurdles or fences. *M. D. I. Usher.*

SPIRITUALIST 4 ch.c. Simply Great (FR)–Parima (Pardao) [1989/90 16g] angular colt: placed at up to 2m on Flat: sold out of S. Norton's stable 11,000 gns Newmarket Autumn Sales: well beaten in juvenile hurdle at Wetherby in December, looking very headstrong. *Dr J. D. Scargill.* —

SPITE AND MALICE 8 b.g. Hot Grove–La Mirabelle (Princely Gift) [1989/90 20g pu a18g 6] very lightly raced and no sign of ability in novice hurdles. *Mrs P. Townsley.* —

SPITTIN MICK 6 b.g. The Brianstan–La Fille (Crooner) [1989/90 16g pu] small, lengthy gelding: half-brother to novice hurdler New Forest Lad (by Palm Track): plating-class handicapper on Flat, stays 7f: tailed off when pulled up 2 out in seller at Wetherby in November on hurdling debut. *G. M. Moore.* —

SPLASHMAN (USA) 4 ch.c. Riverman–L'Extravagante (Le Fabuleux) [1989/90 16f 5 16m 5] rangy colt: fair maiden at best on Flat, stays 15f: sold out of L. Cumani's stable 36,000 gns Newmarket Autumn Sales: no worthwhile form in juvenile hurdles: blinkered second start. *J. R. Jenkins.* —

SPLENDID FELLOW 9 br.g. Decent Fellow–Forest Fun (Pardao) [1989/90 20g 16s 16s c20g F c18s ur a20g] sparely-made gelding: selling hurdler: no form for some time: tailed off when falling last in novice chase at Kempton in January: blinkered last start: has worn a brush pricker: sold 700 gns Ascot April Sales. *G. G. Gracey.* c— —

SPLITTHEDIFFERENCE 6 br.g. Pollerton–Glen Rambler (Wrekin Rambler) [1989/90 c16g F c16g 2 c20m F c21g 3 c20f* c20g 6] rangy gelding: carries plenty of condition: novice hurdler: won novice chase at Wolverhampton in March going away by 5 lengths from Elite Boy, pair well clear: ran poorly following month: will stay 3m: acts on firm ground: tends to sweat. *D. Nicholson.* c**104** —

SPONSOR LIGHT 6 ch.g. Lighter–Sponsorship (Sparkler) [1989/90 F17m] first foal: dam 2-y-o 6f seller winner: yet to complete course in point-to-points: well beaten in NH Flat race at Carlisle in April: yet to race over hurdles or in a steeplechase. *J. L. Gledson.*

SPOOKY 9 ch.m. Grey Ghost–Hatton Bridge (Rydon Bridge) [1989/90 c20f pu] lengthy, angular mare: runner-up in a point-to-point in 1987: well beaten over hurdles and in a steeplechase. *M. S. Vernon.* c— —

SPORTING CHALLENGE 5 b.g. Artaius (USA)–Karissima (Kalamoun) [1989/90 20m pu 16f 4 16g 5] sturdy gelding: little worthwhile form on Flat: poor form in selling hurdles in first half of season: sold 700 gns Doncaster January Sales. *P. A. Blockley.* 68

SPORTING IDOL 5 b.g. Mummy's Game–Village Idol (Blakeney) [1989/90 17v 3 16d 16v 6 17d 5 17m 5 16f 2 16f 3 16h 2] leggy gelding: half-brother to winning hurdler Hickling Squires (by Tachypous): winning plater on Flat, probably best at up to 1m: sold out of T. Jones's stable 3,000 gns Ascot December Sales: second in 89 ?

novice handicap hurdles at Ludlow in April and Taunton (claimer ridden, swerved left between last 2) in May: acts on any going: blinkered fifth start. *C. L. Popham.*

SPORTING LEADER 7 ch.g. Laurence O–Arun River (Runnymede) [1989/90 16d 22d] workmanlike ex-Irish gelding: sixth foal: dam useful 2-y-o 5f — winner in Ireland: fell all 3 starts in point-to-points in 1989: well beaten in novice hurdles: still bit backward second start. *Miss M. K. Milligan.*

SPORTSNEWS 8 b.g. New Member–Dicopin (Deauville II) [1989/90 c24sF c90 x c26v6 c25d c27vF c32fpu c24dpu c24g3] workmanlike gelding: novice hurdler: — unfortunate in amateur riders handicap chase at Chepstow in February, leading 5 out and staying on strongly when falling 2 out: also let down by his jumping on his other starts: stays well: acts on heavy going: blinkered second and third starts: trained first 5 outings by P. Hobbs and next by P. Monteith. *Mrs S. C. Bradburne.*

SPRING COTTAGE 10 b.g. Rouser–Flying Florrie (I Say) [1989/90 a20g6 16m5 24g4 22m6 22d a20g6 a16g4 20m3 a20g4] small gelding: poor novice hurdler: 74 probably stays 3m: possibly best with give in the ground. *W. Hardy.*

SPRINGFIELD MATCH 5 b.m. Royal Match–Petoria (Songedor) [1989/90 16m] small mare: half-sister to winning jumpers Gray Heat (by Ribston) and Hazel — Bank (by Pongee): poor maiden on Flat: beaten over 30 lengths in seller at Catterick in December on hurdling debut. *P. Wigham.*

SPRING HAY 4 gr.c. Wassl–Spring Silver (Palestine) [1989/90 16g3 16dF 16v* 16f] well-made colt: half-brother to 3 winners in Ireland, including NH Flat race 124 p winner and moderate novice hurdler Green Silver (by Hardgreen): dam, placed in Irish bumpers, is half-sister to Lanzarote: useful middle-distance maiden on Flat: won juvenile hurdle at Leicester in February: outpaced throughout but showed further improvement when around 13 lengths eleventh to Rare Holiday in Daily Express Triumph Hurdle at Cheltenham (jumped none too fluently) in March: will be suited by 2½m. *D. Nicholson.*

SPRINGHOLM 8 br.g. Mandalus–Lady Hiltop (Prince Hansel) [1989/90 c**129** c16g2 c17f2 c16d2 c16g3 c16g4 c16m* c16f3] strong gelding: fairly useful chaser: —

Brigadier C. B. Harvey's "Springholm"

led from the second to win amateur riders handicap at Sandown in March by 7 lengths from Ringmore: found little under pressure fourth outing: best form at around 2m: probably acts on any going: takes a good hold. *D. Nicholson.*

SPRINGLAKE'S LADY 4 b.f. Music Boy–North Pine (Import) [1989/90 16h
17g 17d 17vpu a16g a20g*] sparely-made filly: first foal: dam poor half-sister to 63
several winning jumpers: plater on Flat, stays 9f: sold out of W. Pearce's stable
2,000 gns Doncaster September Sales: benefited from irresolution of her opponents when winning 3-runner juvenile claiming hurdle at Lingfield in March:
seemed of little account previously. *J. E. Forte.*

SPRINGMAN 6 b.g. Young Man (FR)–Spring Secret (USA) (Hillary) [1989/90
16mF] angular gelding: lightly-raced novice hurdler, best effort over 2½m. *A.* —
Smith.

SPRING PAUPER 9 b. or br.g. Pauper–Spring Campaign (Vic Day) [1989/90 c—
c21spu c24s c25gpu 24m] lengthy gelding: winning hurdler/chaser: no form in —
1989/90: stays 3m: acts on heavy going. *D. McCain.*

SPRING PLAY 6 ch.g. Hard Fought–Spring Snow (Reliance II) [1989/90 16spu
18g4 18s 20d* a16g3 21m2] never off bridle when winning selling handicap hurdle 95
at Sedgefield (bought in 7,800 gns) in January: placed in handicap hurdles at
Lingfield in February and Warwick in May: stays 21f: acts on good to firm and dead
going: visored at Sedgefield. *A. W. Denson.*

SPRING RAG 4 b.g. Raga Navarro (ITY)–Spring Music (Silly Season)
[1989/90 16f4 16g 16d* 16d4 16mpu 20g5 20g] sparely-made gelding: brother to 98
winning hurdler Springing Sidney and half-brother to 2 other winning jumpers: no
worthwhile form on Flat: claimer ridden, successful in juvenile hurdle at Warwick
in January: seemed to run very well next time but only poor form subsequently:
best form at 2m: acts on dead going: visored last start. *G. B. Balding.*

SPRING TIDE 6 b.m. Take A Reef–Spring Kingdom (Supreme Sovereign)
[1989/90 16dpu 16g 20d] very lightly raced and no sign of ability over hurdles. *M.* —
Skinner.

SPRING TIME PEARL 7 br.m. Black Minstrel–Autumn Pearl (Autumn c—
Gold) [1989/90 c25dpu c27spu] ex-Irish mare: half-sister to winning chaser The
Buckwheat (by Golden Love): dam never ran: second in 2 point-to-points in 1989:
tailed off when pulled up in novice chases in February. *C. D. Broad.*

SPRINGVALE CRUSADE 7 b.g. Callernish–Harlem Lady (Arctic Slave)
[1989/90 22d*] small gelding: showed ability prior to winning novice hurdle at Ayr 96
in January: stays 3m: acts on heavy going. *R. F. Fisher.*

SPRING WEDDING 5 ch.m. Tudorville–St Lucian Breeze (Vivify) [1989/90
F16m a20gF a16gpu] leggy mare: first foal: dam once-raced half-sister to useful —
hurdler/fair chaser Rutley and to Topham Trophy winner Canit: in rear in NH Flat
race: made most until falling 2 out in poor novice hurdle at Southwell in April. *J.*
Webber.

SPRITEBRAND 10 br.g. Workboy–Benedetta da Castello (St Paddy) c**124**
[1989/90 c21dpu c16d* c17m5 c20d5 c24g4 c21g*] strong gelding: fair chaser: won —
claiming chase at Sedgefield in January and handicap at Market Rasen in April:
best at around 2½m: probably acts on any going, but seems ideally suited by a
sound surface: sketchy jumper. *M. H. Easterby.*

SPROWSTON BOY 7 ch.g. Dominion–Cavalier's Blush (King's Troop)
[1989/90 21d2 24g2 a20gpu] close-coupled, sparely-made gelding: tends to look 145
dull and hard in condition: very useful hurdler: made much of running when
second to Ikdam in handicap at Newbury and to Old Dundalk in ROA Rendlesham
Hurdle at Kempton in February: stays 3m: acts on any going: usually jumps well:
good mount for a claimer: game. *W. M. Perrin.*

SPRUCER 5 b.g. Prince Regent (FR)–Knollwood Court (Le Jean) [1989/90
F12g2 F16f4 F16m] tall gelding: half-brother to winning hurdlers Judges Fancy
and Mary's Gift (both by Monksfield): dam placed several times over hurdles in
Ireland: in frame in NH Flat races at Market Rasen and Newbury in March: yet to
race over hurdles or fences. *Mrs I. McKie.*

SPS CREATIVE 4 gr.f. Petong–Rosalina (Porto Bello) [1989/90 16g 16f]
half-sister to winning hurdler Duneany (by Free State): poor sprint maiden on —
Flat: sold out of M. Brittain's stable 750 gns Doncaster November Sales: little
sign of ability in juvenile hurdle in December and novice hurdle in March. *M. A.*
Barnes.

SQUADRON (CAN) 7 ch.g. Vice Regent (USA)–Quadrillion (USA) (Quadrangle (USA)) [1989/90 16g 16m 18g^6 16g^2 16d^4 16s 21g^5 20g^3 16m^3] smallish, plain gelding: quite a modest hurdler: stays 2½m: acts on heavy going and good to firm: blinkered last outing: sold 8,500 gns Ascot June Sales. *C. Weedon.* 95

SQUEEZE PLAY 5 b.g. Gleason (USA)–Cherry Leaf (Vulgan) [1989/90 16f^2 16g^5 16g 16m^3 16g^3 20g^4] useful-looking gelding with scope: modest novice hurdler: likely to prove suited by 2½m. *Andrew Turnell.* 93

SQUIRE JIM 6 b.g. Jimsun–Squiffy (Articulate) [1989/90 19f* 20f^3 20m^3 19d^3 22m^2 25g* 19f^2] close-coupled, rather leggy gelding: won novice hurdles at Hereford in September and November: always-prominent ¾-length second to Ardbrin in handicap at Taunton in March: stays 3m: seems suited by a sound surface and acts on firm ground. *R. G. Brazington.* 117

SQUIRE LAMB 5 gr.g. Absalom–Caroline Lamb (Hotfoot) [1989/90 16g^3] strong, compact gelding: placed in 2 NH Flat races in 1988/9: ran on strongly in latter stages having been given plenty to do when 4 lengths third of 17 behind Run To Form in novice hurdle at Ludlow in December. *N. A. Gaselee.* 94 +

SQUIRSKY 4 b.c. Tina's Pet–Targos Delight (Targowice (USA)) [1989/90 16g 16m] sturdy colt: half-brother to winning selling hurdler Miami Holiday (by Miami Springs): placed over sprint distances at 2 yrs, but well beaten on Flat since: behind in juvenile hurdle and a seller: sold 1,350 gns Ascot February Sales. *R. Hollinshead.* —

STAFFORD LAD 4 b.c. Tachypous–Frizzante (Varano) [1989/90 16m^{pu}] rather leggy colt: no worthwhile form on Flat: sold out of T. Fairhurst's stable 1,450 gns Ascot August Sales: tailed off when pulled up 2 out in juvenile hurdle at Ascot in November. *P. R. Rodford.* —

STAG DINNER 7 ch.g. Le Bavard (FR)–Ethel's Delight (Tiepolo II) [1989/90 c24g^{ur} 24g 22m^4] medium-sized gelding: one-time fair hurdler: no worthwhile form in 2 outings late in season: jumped badly right and unseated rider at the second on chasing debut: suited by 3m: acts on firm going: tends to sweat. *C. P. E. Brooks.* c— —

STAGE PLAYER 4 b.g. Ile de Bourbon (USA)–Popkins (Romulus) [1989/90 16m* 16g^2 16f] smallish, workmanlike gelding: fairly useful 1¼m winner on Flat: won juvenile hurdle at Leicester in December impressively by 10 lengths: 8 lengths second of 6 to Major Inquiry in Steel Plate Trial Hurdle at Cheltenham following month (trained until after then by I. Matthews): looking lean, well beaten in Daily Express Triumph Hurdle on latter course in March: will prove suited by 2m: acts on good to firm ground. *R. Simpson.* 105

STAGE QUEEN 4 br.f. Dawn Johnny (USA)–Queen of The Kop (Queen's Hussar) [1989/90 16f] placed in 1¼m seller on Flat (tends to wander): ridden by 7-lb claimer, remote seventh of 11 finishers in juvenile selling hurdle at Southwell in August. *F. Jordan.* —

STAGHOUND 8 gr.g. Buckskin (FR)–Blue Delphinium (Quorum) [1989/90 21m^5 24f] lengthy gelding: moderate hurdler/chaser: first form over hurdles for some time when staying-on fifth behind Battalion at Sandown in March: stays 3m: acts on hard and dead going. *J. T. Gifford.* c— 111

STAG HUNTER 6 b.g. Royal Fountain–Scarlet Letch (New Brig) [1989/90 16f^2 22d^2 24g^3] strong, sturdy gelding: novice hurdler: stayed 3m: best form with give in the ground: dead. *R. Brewis.* 94

STAGS FELL 5 gr.g. Step Together (USA)–Honey's Queen (Pals Passage) [1989/90 18d 20d 16g^3 16f^2 16f* 16f*] leggy, rather angular gelding: won novice hurdles in small fields at Sedgefield and Kelso in April: should stay beyond 2¼m (patchy in coat, well beaten over 2½m): acts on firm and dead ground. *G. M. Moore.* 91

STAGSHAW BELLE 6 b.m. Royal Fountain–Besciamella (Foggy Bell) [1989/90 16f] leggy, rather unfurnished mare: in rear in NH Flat race at Catterick in 1988/9 and in novice hurdle at Kelso in October. *J. I. A. Charlton.* —

STAINCLIFFE LAD 5 gr.h. Sonnen Gold–Poly Negative (Polyfoto) [1989/90 17m^{pu} 17m] leggy, lengthy horse: of little account: blinkered last start 1988/9: sold out of V. Hall's stable 1,350 gns Doncaster November Sales. *R. G. Frost.* —

STAMPY 9 ch.g. Sallust–Caer-Gai (Royal Palace) [1989/90 a18g^{pu} c20d c25v^{ur} c20v^{ur} c18s^{pu} c20f^{pu}] tall, angular gelding: poor novice hurdler/chaser: best at 2m: acts on any going. *J. J. Bridger.* c— —

STAND AT EASE 5 b.g. The Brianstan–Plush (Lombard (GER)) [1989/90 16g a16g] close-coupled gelding: plating-class maiden on Flat (acts well in the mud): behind in novice hurdles at Ayr (handicap) in October and Southwell following month. *P. Liddle.* —

ST ANDREW'S BAY 10 b.g. Rymer–Raise The Standard (Distinctly (USA)) [1989/90 c21g*] rangy gelding: winning hurdler: moderate jumper of fences, but won 6-runner handicap at Fakenham in April: better suited by 2½m than shorter distances (well beaten over 3m): acts on soft going. *C. Weedon.* c94 x —

ST ANLO 8 b.m. Sir Nulli–Bridport (Porto Bello) [1989/90 19d 16g6] leggy, sparely-made mare: poor novice hurdler: has been beaten in a seller. *B. K. Wells.* 65

STAN'S FOLLY 9 b.g. Lighter–Cumbria Lass (Marine Corps) [1989/90 c21m3 c16m4 c20gF c16g5 c20g c20s5 c20d5 c16v4 c16g5 c16m5 c16g3 c20g3 c17f*] workmanlike gelding: won amateur riders handicap chase at Cartmel in May: stays 2½m: acts on firm going. *S. G. Payne.* c85 —

STANS JOY 6 b.g. Buckskin (FR)–Just Our Luck (London Gazette) [1989/90 16d6 20v c17gF] tall, workmanlike gelding: novice hurdler: no worthwhile form: bit backward, tailed off when falling 3 out in novice event on chasing debut: tends to be on toes, and was reluctant to line up first start. *Miss A. L. M. King.* c— —

STANSTED FLYER 4 b.g. Rabdan–Maputo Princess (Raga Navarro (ITY)) [1989/90 16f] maiden plater on Flat: tailed-off last of 8 finishers in juvenile hurdle at Leicester in November. *J. F. Bottomley.* —

STANTON QUEEN 8 br.m. Most Secret–Castle Rough (Counsel) [1989/90 19dpu 20dpu 16m 16dpu a16g a20g] sparely-made mare: no form in novice hurdles or a seller (has worn a crossed noseband): fell in 2 point-to-points in 1989. *K. White.* —

STANWICK MONUMENT 5 ch.m. Grey Ghost–Stanwick Gold (Goldhill) [1989/90 F16d F17d] second foal: dam winning point-to-pointer: well beaten in NH Flat races in February and March: yet to race over hurdles or fences. *Miss S. Williamson.*

STAPEHILL 4 b.c. Bon Sang (FR)–Native Bride (Native Prince) [1989/90 16fF 16m 16f4] leggy colt: maiden on Flat: poor juvenile selling hurdler: visored final start: dead. *S. J. Muldoon.* 59

STARARCHY 4 b. or br.g. Starch Reduced–Good Sport (True Song) [1989/90 aF16g] first reported foal: dam placed once in selling hurdle: seventh of 10 in NH Flat race at Lingfield: yet to race over hurdles. *R. Lee.*

STAR BLEND 8 ch.g. Royal Blend–Star Speaker (Philemon) [1989/90 a16g c26f4] placed in point-to-point in 1989: behind in novice hurdle at Southwell and novice chase at Fontwell in the spring. *J. Ffitch-Heyes.* c— —

STARCHY BLAKE 5 b.g. Starch Reduced–Pem Pem (Blakeney) [1989/90 16g5 16d3 18d3] sturdy gelding: novice selling hurdler: good third in non-selling handicap at Kelso final start: stays 2¼m: acts on dead going: blinkered last 2 outings. *T. E. Jeffrey.* 77

STAR COVER 4 b.f. Starch Reduced–Rosey Covert (Sahib) [1989/90 a16gpu 16sur] second foal: dam winning selling hurdler: placed at up to 7f on Flat: no sign of ability in 2 juvenile claiming hurdles. *S. R. Bowring.* —

STARDUST ROC 7 br.h. Roc Imp–Mayo Melody (Highland Melody) [1989/90 c16m c19dpu c20m5 c25f5 c20f2 c20m6 c24f2 c24mpu c25m*] tall, close-coupled horse: poor chaser: reportedly finished lame when winning at Hereford in May (left in lead by Democratic Boy's unseating rider before last when clear): in and out of form previously: stays 3m: acts on firm ground. *J. M. Bradley.* c94 —

STARJESTIC 12 b.g. Majestic Streak–Star Sheba (Pampered King) [1989/90 c16m4 c17d3 c16g c16s3 c16f3 c16m* c16m2 c20dpu] big, strong gelding: inconsistent handicap chaser: won at Southwell in April: unruly at start next time: unlikely to stay much beyond 2m: acts on any going: has won for amateur: usually held up: blinkered last 3 starts. *N. Bradley.* c91 —

STAR LANE 7 br.g. Comedy Star (USA)–Border Lane (Border Legend) [1989/90 21dpu 24dpu] workmanlike gelding: type to carry condition: no sign of ability in NH Flat race and 2 novice hurdles. *P. J. Hobbs.* —

STARLIGHT ROCKY 14 b.g. This Above All–Anna Star (Reynard Volant) [1989/90 24h5 17f2 25f 20m] strong gelding: selling hurdler and novice chaser: not seen out after November: stays 2½m: acts on any going. *Miss Z. A. Green.* c— 66

STARLIGHT WONDER 4 ch.f. Star Appeal–My Lady Muriel (USA) (Visible (USA)) [1989/90 16m 17g6 16g 16g6 16f 16fF] small, sparely-made filly: fourth in 6f claimer on Flat in October: sold out of E. Eldin's stable 1,050 gns Newmarket Autumn Sales: poor plater over hurdles. *R. E. Barr.* —

STAR MAESTRO 8 br.g. Music Maestro–Maryland Star (I Say) [1989/90 17f3 16f5 c16g4 c16g2] lightly-made gelding: novice selling hurdler: jumped poorly when well beaten in novice chases in October: pulls hard and barely stays 2m: acts on firm going: has worn a crossed noseband. *O. Brennan.* c— 67

STAR MOON 4 b.c. Tyrnavos–Lady of The Manor (Astec) [1989/90 20gpu 16g 16s 16dpu] small, plain colt: no sign of ability: blinkered third start. *N. Bycroft.* —

STAR OATS 4 ch.g. Oats–Starproof (Comedy Star (USA)) [1989/90 16m 16m5] fourth foal: half-brother to Hollia (by Touch Boy), 5f winner at 2 yrs: dam, plater, stayed 7f: well beaten in early-season juvenile hurdles at Perth. *G. Richards.* —

STAR OF A GUNNER 10 ch.g. Gunner B–Starkist (So Blessed) [1989/90 16m3 16m6 16g5 18s6 16s 17v6 16s6] neat gelding: handicap hurdler: ran creditably first 2 starts, moderately afterwards: barely stays 2m: acts on soft and good to firm going: blinkered third and last outings: trained until after third outing by R. Holder (subsequently off course 2 months). *M. A. McCullagh, Ireland.* 101 d

STAR OF ESK 8 b.g. Bybicello–Simprim Lady (Cantab) [1989/90 20f4 20g c20gF c20gpu 25gpu] big, workmanlike gelding: only form when fourth in novice hurdle at Carlisle in October: soon tailed off and eventually pulled up in novice chase at Edinburgh in January. *G. Richards.* c— 73

STAR OF IRELAND 10 b.g. Star Appeal–Belligerent (Roan Rocket) [1989/90 16gpu 16gpu 16dpu] narrow, rather lightly-built gelding: fair hurdler at his best: pulled up all outings in 1989/90: stays 2¼m: probably acts on any going: blinkered last start. *W. R. Sheedy.* —

STAR OF KUWAIT 6 b.m. Crooner–Miss Kuwait (The Brianstan) [1989/90 18s3 16g] leggy, sparely-made mare: winning hurdler: first outing for 15 months, third in handicap at Fontwell in January: ran poorly later in month: stays 2¼m: acts on any going. *M. C. Pipe.* 93

STAR OF OUGHTERARD 5 b.g. Horage–Corny Story (Oats) [1989/90 24mF 24m6] leggy gelding: winning hurdler: stays 2¾m: acts on hard going: blinkered final outing (September). *T. P. McGovern.* —

STAR OF ROMANY 10 b.m. High Season–Romany Lone (Romany Air) [1989/90 17f 22m] workmanlike mare: sister to a maiden point-to-pointer: tailed off only completed start in point-to-points and in 2 novice hurdles in October. *P. J. Hobbs.* —

STAR OF SCREEN (USA) 10 b.g. Vaguely Noble–Slip Screen (USA) (Silent Screen (USA)) [1989/90 c29dpu] leggy gelding: one-time useful though inconsistent handicap chaser: won 3 point-to-points in 1989: tailed off when pulled up in January: well suited by a thorough test of stamina: acts on any going: moderate jumper: has worn blinkers over hurdles. *G. Harwood.* c— x — x

STAR OF THE GLEN 4 b.c. Glenstal (USA)–Bamstar (Relko) [1989/90 16m 16g* 20g4 16d6 16d4 16d5 16f] lengthy colt: half-brother to winning hurdler Benisa Ryder (by Stanford): maiden on Flat: 50/1, beat Silver King ¾ length in moderately-run juvenile hurdle at Newbury in December: best efforts subsequently in Stroud Green Hurdle on same course and in Chatteris Fen Hurdle at Huntingdon on fourth and fifth starts: bit below form over 2½m: acts on dead going (probably unsuited by firm). *C. A. Horgan.* 107

STAR PLAYER 4 ch.c. Simply Great (FR)–Star Girl (Sovereign Gleam) [1989/90 16m3 16d3] rather leggy, sparely-made colt: half-brother to winning hurdler Star Regal (by Royal And Regal): runner-up in 1¾m maiden in 1989, only outing on Flat: sold out of G. Harwood's stable 9,000 gns Newmarket Autumn Sales: ridden by claimer, third in juvenile hurdle at Towcester in January and novice event on same course following month. *J. H. Baker.* 98

STAR REEF 5 ch.g. Main Reef–Star Girl (Sovereign Gleam) [1989/90 17mur 17m] small gelding: no form over hurdles, including in sellers: blinkered final start 1988/9: sold out of P. Bailey's stable 1,700 gns Ascot November Sales: resold 1,500 gns Ascot June Sales. *Miss T. J. Turner.* —

STAR'S DELIGHT 8 gr.g. John de Coombe–Vanity Surprise (Blakeney) [1989/90 c16d* c16g* c20g* c16g* c16s* c16g4 c36fpu] leggy, lightly-made gelding: had an excellent season, developing into a useful chaser: made all in handicaps at Chepstow, Cheltenham and Haydock (2) in November and Haydock c**144** —

John Seyfried Mickleton Handicap Chase, Cheltenham—second win in a week for much-improved Star's Delight

again in January: raced with plenty of zest when very good fourth to Meikleour in Victor Chandler Handicap Chase at Ascot: pulled up thirteenth in Seagram Grand National at Liverpool: stays 2½m, at least when conditions aren't testing: acts on heavy going and good to firm: suitable mount for a claimer: usually jumps well: genuine and consistent. *M. C. Pipe.*

STAR SEASON 6 b.g. Newski (USA)–Silly Moo (Silly Season) [1989/90 17v[2] 16s* 16d[3]] workmanlike, angular gelding: handicap hurdler: won at Sandown in February by 4 lengths from Doc's Coat, coming from some way off pace in moderately-run race: stayed on when very close fourth behind Instant Tan at Ayr 2 months later, giving impression worth a try over further: acts on heavy going. *R. J. Holder.* 111

STAR SHINER (USA) 7 ch.g. Screen King (USA)–Poteen (Cavan) [1989/90 c20s[ur] c18f[5] c20f[F] c26f[pu]] angular gelding: novice selling hurdler: poor novice chaser: every chance when falling 2 out in novice hunter chase at Folkestone in May: behind when pulled up, reportedly lame, next time: blinkered first 2 starts 1988/9: trained by Mrs J. Fogarty first start: ungenuine. *P. R. Hedger.* c78 § — §

START BAY (NZ) 8 b.g. Kutati (NZ)–Suzy Que (NZ) (Copsale) [1989/90 c22m[6]] leggy, rather sparely-made gelding: no sign of ability in novice hurdles and novice chases (jumps badly), but won a point-to-point in April. *R. A. Goddard.* c— x —

STATE CASE 12 br.g. Shackleton–Miss Pindado (Pinzari) [1989/90 c20d[pu] c19m*] stocky gelding: carries plenty of condition: hunter chaser nowadays: won at Hereford in April: stays 2½m when conditions aren't testing: acts well on a sound surface: usually a front runner. *Miss Scarlett J. Crew.* c89 —

STATED CASE 5 b.g. Beldale Flutter (USA)–High Point Lady (CAN) (Knightly Dawn (USA)) [1989/90 16d* 16g[6]] rather sparely-made gelding: impressive winner of juvenile hurdle on only start in 1988/9 and of handicap at Chepstow (quickened clear from 2 out when beating Liadett 7 lengths) in November: dropped out quickly, as though something amiss, later in month: not seen out again: will probably prove best at 2m: acts on soft going. *M. H. Easterby.* 124

STATE JESTER 7 b.g. Free State–Mirthful (Will Somers) [1989/90 16f[6]] workmanlike gelding: quite a useful hurdler: won Swinton Insurance Trophy Handicap at Haydock in 1988/9: favourite, around 14 lengths sixth, never dangerous, behind I'm Confident in valuable Guinness Galway Handicap Hurdle —

on only outing of 1989/90 (August): will prove best at around 2m: best form on good ground: wears a crossed noseband. *C. W. C. Elsey.*

STATE LAD 6 b.g. Free State–Lady Bess (Straight Lad) [1989/90 16g^4 16d
20g^3 24g* 25g^3] workmanlike gelding: chasing type: 10-length winner of novice 96
hurdle at Edinburgh in January: good third behind Invasion in similar event at Kelso in March, leading until last: suited by around 3m. *R. C. Armytage.*

STATELY LOVER 7 b.g. Free State–Maid In Love (Sky Gipsy) [1989/90 22g^4
22v* 22s* 20f] big, rangy gelding with scope: chasing type: won a point-to-point 120
in 1989: progressive form first 3 starts and was successful in novice hurdles at Folkestone in January and Fontwell (beat Junior Parker 8 lengths despite swerving left run-in) following month: well beaten on firm ground in Sun Alliance Novices' Hurdle at Cheltenham in March: will stay 3m: acts on soft going. *D. M. Grissell.*

STATFOLD PAM 7 gr.m. Pamroy–Statfold Pride (Precipice Wood) [1989/90
20g 21d 20g] angular, sparely-made mare: no worthwhile form over hurdles: failed —
to complete in 2 point-to-points in 1988. *B. C. Morgan.*

ST ATHANS LAD 5 b.g. Crooner–Greasby Girl (John Splendid) [1989/90 21d
20d^{pu} 20m^3] showed plenty of ability over hurdles in 1988/9: poor form in 85
1989/90: stays 2½m: acts on soft and good to firm going: races freely. *R. Curtis.*

STATIONERS DREAM 5 b.g. Enchantment–Just Janie (John Splendid) [1989/90 F16f^5 F16m^5 F16m] 2,100F, 3,800Y, 7,000 2-y-o: lengthy, rather plain gelding: brother to novice selling hurdler Just Enchanting and half-brother to a winner in Belgium: dam sprinter: unplaced in NH Flat races in September and October: yet to race over hurdles or fences. *J. D. Roberts.*

STAY AWAKE 4 ch.g. Anfield–Djimbaran Bay (Le Levanstell) [1989/90 16m
16m 16g^5 16g^2 16m* 16g^3 16s 16d* a16g^2 16d 16s* 17g^F 17d^{pu} 16d^2 16f^2] lengthy, 110
good-topped gelding: will make a chaser: has been hobdayed: half-brother to winning hurdler Bettyknowes (by Satingo): winner at up to 9f on Flat, including in 1990: successful over hurdles in juvenile event at Catterick and novice handicaps at Sedgefield and Warwick: good second in juvenile handicaps at Ayr and Warwick

Executive Box Novices' Handicap Hurdle, Warwick— two of the season's leading conditional jockeys R. Supple and N. Mann fight out the finish on Stay Awake (near side) and Sleepline Royale respectively

final 2 starts: unlikely to stay much beyond 2m: probably acts on any going: blinkered fifth and sixth starts. *J. J. O'Neill.*

STAYHAR GOLD 8 br.g. Dubassoff (USA)–Arctic Fern (Arcticeelagh) c—
[1989/90 16g 17d 21d^{pu} c21g^{F} c17d^{pu}] leggy, quite good-topped gelding: winning —
hurdler: no form for some time, including over fences (sketchy jumper): should stay further than 2m: acts on soft going: sold 3,300 gns Ascot May Sales. *J. H. Baker.*

STAY ON TRACKS 8 gr.g. Roselier (FR)–Bee In Bonnet (Track Spare) c**137**
[1989/90 c20g* c20g^{4} c20g^{F} c24g* c20g^{4} c20d^{pu} c20m^{4} c24m^{2} c24f* c20f^{3}] —
compact, rather sparely-made gelding: useful chaser: won at Ayr and Edinburgh in first half of season, and at Newcastle in May: amateur ridden, beat only other finisher Biloxi Blues a head on last-named course: jumped moderately last start: stays 3m: acts on any going: genuine. *W. A. Stephenson.*

ST COLEMAN'S WELL 7 br.g. Callernish–Divided Loyalties (Balidar)
[1989/90 16m^{2} 16d^{2} 16s^{2} 16d^{6} 17d 16g^{5} 16g^{3} 18s^{3} 16d^{5} 16g 16m* 16f 16m 16g^{4}] 119
Irish gelding: fair hurdler: won minor event at the Curragh in March: stiffish task, eighth to Jubail in quite valuable handicap at Liverpool next start (off bridle throughout): ran creditably final outing: stays 2¼m: acts on soft going and good to firm. *John Crowley, Ireland.*

STEARSBY 11 br.g. Politico (USA)–Lucky Sprite (Galivanter) [1989/90 c32v^{pu} c—
c30s^{pu} c29g] big, workmanlike gelding: has been hobdayed: invariably impresses —
in appearance: high-class chaser at his best: useful form in 1988/9 but tailed off only completed start in 1989/90 (January): suited by a good test of stamina: yet to show form on extremes of ground, acts on any other: wears a crossed noseband: suited by forcing tactics: tends to jump to the right and make the occasional mistake: to rejoin Mrs J. Pitman in 1990/91 season. *G. A. Ham.*

STEEL CYGNET 7 gr.g. Taufan (USA)–Swan Girl (My Swanee) [1989/90
16f^{6}] small gelding: poor novice hurdler: blinkered only outing of season (April): —
sold 1,000 gns Ascot July Sales. *G. P. Enright.*

STEEL PROGRESS 7 b.g. The Brianstan–Highland-Orchid (Highland c—
Melody) [1989/90 c21d^{pu}] workmanlike gelding: lightly raced and no worthwhile —
form. *Mrs A. M. Gough.*

STEEPLE VIEW 9 b.g. The Parson–Deep View (Deep Run) [1989/90 c24g^{2} c**139**
c20m^{pu} c24g^{2} c25d^{2} c24d* c25f^{pu}] rangy, good sort: useful chaser: quickened —
clear 3 out and ran on well to win quite valuable handicap at Newbury in February by a neck from Field Conqueror: pulled up lame next outing: stays 25f: suited by give in the ground: visored second outing: sound jumper. *O. Sherwood.*

STEFFI 4 ch.f. Precocious–Western Gem (Sheshoon) [1989/90 16v^{pu}] smallish,
good-quartered filly: quite modest handicapper on Flat, best at up to 1¼m: never —
travelling particularly well and tailed off when pulled up last in juvenile hurdle at Leicester in February (jumped none too fluently). *G. A. Pritchard-Gordon.*

STEGSMAN 8 b.g. Fordham (USA)–Charity Concert (Vimy) [1989/90 c20s^{pu} c—
c24g^{5}] rangy gelding: winning hurdler: moderate novice chaser at best: well —
beaten in December: should stay 3m: acts on heavy going and possibly unsuited by firm. *J. W. Blundell.*

STELLAJOE 4 b.f. Le Dauphin–Right Shady (Right Tack) [1989/90 16m^{6} 20g^{3}
16v^{5} 16v^{6} a18g^{2} a16g*] poor maiden plater on Flat: selling hurdler: ridden by 7-lb 69
claimer, won juvenile event at Lingfield (no bid) in February by 10 lengths: stays 2½m: seems unsuited by heavy going. *A. R. Davison.*

ST ELMO'S FIRE 5 b.g. Electric–Sealady (Seaepic (USA)) [1989/90 16d 16f
16f^{4} 16g^{2}] smallish, sparely-made gelding: fair handicapper on Flat, stays 9f: sold 92
out of Sir Mark Prescott's stable 18,000 gns Newmarket Autumn Sales: in frame in novice hurdles at Newbury and Fakenham (handicap): found little in latter stages on first 2 starts: likely to prove best at 2m: best run on good going: blinkered second and third outings: claimer ridden at Fakenham. *C. P. E. Brooks.*

STEPAULI 8 b.g. Le Bavard (FR)–Charming Ways (Master Buck) [1989/90 c— x
c21f^{pu} c25h^{F} 20f^{4} 20f^{5} 16f^{5} 16f^{3} 25f^{2} 20g^{2} 25g^{3} 25f^{3} 20f^{3} 24m^{pu} 27f^{2} 20g^{pu}] 84 x
workmanlike, sparely-made gelding: selling hurdler: no worthwhile form over fences: stays very well: acts on firm going: usually blinkered or visored: poor jumper. *P. A. Blockley.*

STEPDAUGHTER 4 b.f. Relkino–Great Dancer (Great Nephew) [1989/90
16f] angular filly: first foal: dam unraced: tailed off in selling hurdle at Kelso in —
October. *Mrs S. C. Bradburne.*

STEPFASTER 5 gr.m. Step Together (USA)–Pollyfaster (Polyfoto) [1989/90 F16m 16h^{2} 16f^{bd} 16g^{3} 20g*] unfurnished mare: second foal: dam unraced: won amateur riders novice hurdle at Sedgefield in November by 30 lengths (left well clear when close challenger Briefing unseated rider at the last): stays 2½m: jumps well. *W. A. Stephenson.* 82

STEPHENS PET 7 ch.g. Piaffer (USA)–Mrs Stephens (Master Stephen) [1989/90 16g 16g* 16v^{6} 21d^{pu} 20g 17m] sturdy gelding: won novice hurdle at Wincanton in January: ran moderately afterwards: form only at 2m: acts on heavy going: sweating first 2 starts. *O. O'Neill.* 93

STEPPEY LANE 5 b.m. Tachypous–Alpine Alice (Abwah) [1989/90 16d^{2} 16s*] leggy mare: moderate staying handicapper on Flat: stayed on strongly from last to lead close home and beat Gold Service 2 lengths in novice hurdle at Haydock in January: will stay 2½m: acts on soft going: mounted on track: likely to progress. *W. W. Haigh.* 97 p

STEP TO STARDOM 5 ch.g. Julio Mariner–Starbright (Petingo) [1989/90 16f^{pu} 16g^{pu}] fourth in 1¾m maiden on Flat in 1988: sold out of C. Brittain's stable 1,200 gns Newmarket Autumn Sales same year: pulled up in novice hurdles at Wincanton and Kempton. *T. Reid.* —

STERLING SILVER 5 b.h. Star Appeal–Silver Tips (High Top) [1989/90 16g^{5} 16d^{2}] angular, sparely-made horse: winning hurdler: good second to Va Lute in handicap at Wincanton in February: races freely, but should stay further than 2m: acts on soft going: still a slightly sketchy jumper: claimer ridden. *J. H. Baker.* 103

STERLING VIRTUE (USA) 9 b.g. Silver Series (USA)–Virgin (FR) (Zeddaan) [1989/90 c16m^{3} c17f^{5} c16m^{6}] neat gelding: winning hurdler: selling chaser: not seen out after September: best at up to 2¼m: acts on any going: hard puller. *K. G. Wingrove.* c— —

Fairview New Homes Handicap Chase, Newbury—Steeple View clears the last

STERNE (FR) 8 b.g. Arctic Tern (USA)–Cesarine (Royal Palace) [1989/90
25g^{4} 24g^{3} 24v^{6} 24s^{pu}] rangy, sparely-made gelding: fair hurdler on his day: 50/1, 119 §
staying-on third behind Calabrese at Ascot in January: well beaten next time and
out of his depth final start: stays 3m: acts on heavy going: blinkered final outing
1986/7 (jumped moderately): not one to trust. *Miss E. Sneyd.*

STEVEYVUL 6 ro.h. Whistlefield–Persian Water (Waterfall) [1989/90 16g^{5}
16d a16g] lengthy, workmanlike horse with scope: claimer ridden, poor form in 81
novice hurdles: well beaten on good to soft ground. *O. O'Neill.*

STEVIE JAY 5 b.g. Rontino–Oakland Rose (Pyrenean) [1989/90 F16s^{3} F16v^{3}
F16d^{2} F17g* 16v* 16d* 18d^{2} 16v 18v 16d^{pu}] third foal: dam behind in 2 NH Flat 136
races: successful in NH Flat race at Tipperary, maiden hurdle at Clonmel and
quite valuable novice hurdle at Thurles: good second to Call Me Later in quite
valuable novice event at Fairyhouse: stayed 2¼m: acted on heavy going: dead. *M.
Hourigan, Ireland.*

ST GABRIEL 9 b.g. Furry Glen–French Honey (Vulgan) [1989/90 c17g^{su} c**112** ?
c16g^{4} c16s^{F2} c16s^{3}] long-backed, angular gelding: 2 lengths behind sole opponent —
Star's Delight and travelling the better when falling 2 out (remounted) in handicap
chase at Haydock in January: looked held when bad mistake last in race won by
Harley Street Man on same course later in month: will probably stay beyond 2m:
acts on heavy going: amateur or claimer ridden over hurdles: still has something
to learn about jumping fences: sold to C. Popham 2,400 gns Ascot June Sales. *T. P.
Tate.*

ST HELENS BOY 8 b.g. Abwah–Cullen (Quorum) [1989/90 c24f^{4}] lengthy c—
gelding: winning hunter chaser: tailed off at Ludlow in April: refused in a —
point-to-point previous month: stays 3m: probably acts on any going. *J. Tudor.*

STIGON 4 ch.g. Red Johnnie–Will Tack (Will Scarlet) [1989/90 16d^{6} 16d 16s^{3}
17v* 16s^{3} 16v^{2} 16f 16m^{2} 16g^{3}] small, lengthy Irish gelding: fourth foal: dam, 125
winner over 6f in Ireland, half-sister to a winning hurdler: maiden on Flat: won
juvenile maiden hurdle at Gowran Park in January: placed 5 times, on final
occasion 4½ lengths third behind Bally Rue in quite valuable juvenile event at
Fairyhouse: blundered second and in circumstances ran well when around 19
lengths thirteenth behind Rare Holiday in Daily Express Triumph Hurdle at
Cheltenham on seventh start: will stay beyond 17f: probably acts on any going:
blinkered last 7 starts. *Daniel J. Murphy, Ireland.*

STILL WATERS 6 b.g. Deep Run–Auburn (Arctic Slave) [1989/90 16m 16m]
plain gelding: fourth foal: brother to poor novice over jumps Deep Auburn, —
runner-up in 2 bumpers: dam won over hurdles and fences: no form in 2 outings
over hurdles: dead. *M. Bradstock.*

STIRABOUT 10 b.g. Oats–Magic Light (Tarqogan) [1989/90 c19d^{5} c18m^{4}] c**71**
small, sparely-made gelding: winning hurdler/chaser: remote fourth in condit- —
ional jockeys seller at Fontwell in December: stays 2¾m: probably acts on any
going: usually blinkered nowadays. *P. Davis.*

STIRLING EXPRESS 5 ch.g. Blue Refrain–Great Aunt Ivy (Bay Express)
[1989/90 16d] lengthy, sparely-made gelding: in frame in NH Flat races: showed — p
some promise though well beaten in novice hurdle won by Man of The West at
Market Rasen in January, travelling well until 2 out and eased once chance had
gone: will do better under less testing conditions. *J. Mackie.*

STIRRUP CUP 6 b.g. Majestic Maharaj–Gold Gift (Gold Rod) [1989/90 16g*
21g] leggy, rather unfurnished gelding: won NH Flat race in 1988/9: made most 100 p
promising debut over hurdles in novice event at Haydock in November, always
travelling strongly, leading on bridle 2 out and beating Super Trix by 20 lengths
(jumped well in the main): finished lame when last of 8 in Challow Hurdle at
Newbury following month: worth another chance. *O. Sherwood.*

STISTED PARK 5 b.g. Be My Native (USA)–Up To You (Sallust) [1989/90
20f^{4}] sparely-made gelding: fairly useful 1½m plater on Flat: well beaten in juve- —
nile hurdle in 1988/9 and in novice event at Southwell in September (co-favourite,
pulled hard). *M. H. Tompkins.*

ST JAMES'S RISK 7 b.g. Captain James–Queen's Bazaar (Queen's Hussar)
[1989/90 18f^{pu}] smallish, workmanlike gelding: poor novice selling hurdler: pulls —
hard: has worn a crossed noseband. *J. J. Bridger.*

ST LOUIS BLUES 5 b.h. Cure The Blues (USA)–Flaretown (Town Crier)
[1989/90 16f^{3} 16f^{2}] smallish, good-topped horse: placed in handicap hurdles at 81
Market Rasen in July and Bangor in August: races freely and is suited by a sharp
2m and firm ground: trained by R. Curtis until after first start. *J. A. C. Edwards.*

STOKE PERO 4 ch.g. Northern Tempest (USA)–Our Mandy (Mansingh (USA)) [1989/90 16g 17m^{pu}] lengthy, sparely-made gelding: half-brother to temperamental novice hurdler Bantel Banzai (by Mandrake Major): seems of little account. *N. G. Ayliffe.* —

STOLEN STAR 6 b.m. Jasmine Star–Theft (Princely Gift) [1989/90 20g^{pu} 20m] leggy, rather sparely-made mare: half-sister to several poor animals: no sign of ability in novice hurdles. *N. A. Twiston-Davies.* —

STONEBROKER 8 ch.m. Morston (FR)–Overspent (Busted) [1989/90 16m^{r} 16f] smallish mare: lightly-raced novice hurdler: blinkered, reluctant in preliminaries and refused to race on reappearance: always behind next time. *D. Haydn Jones.* — §

STONE DRUM (USA) 4 ch.c. The Minstrel (CAN)–Mists of Time (USA) (Graustark) [1989/90 16d^{pu} 20m^{pu}] ex-Irish colt: 1½m winner on Flat: pulled up both outings over hurdles: dead. *M. Bradstock.* —

STONE FLAKE (USA) 4 ch.c. Diesis–Wyandra (So Blessed) [1989/90 16g* 16f] sparely-made colt: sixth foal: dam unraced half-sister to a winning Italian jumper: useful at his best on Flat, stays 1m: changed hands 22,000 gns Newmarket December Sales: impressive winner of 5-runner juvenile hurdle at Wolverhampton in February, leading 3 out and soon quickening clear to beat Regal Lake 15 lengths: 5/1 favourite, kicked at start and never going well in 30-runner Daily Express Triumph Hurdle at Cheltenham following month (bandaged). *P. A. Kelleway.* 132

STONE MADNESS 6 br.m. Yukon Eric (CAN)–Mingwyn Wood (Pirate King) [1989/90 20v] small mare: selling hurdler: well beaten only outing of season (January): stays 2¾m: acts on heavy going. *A. R. Davison.* —

STONEY CREEK 10 bl.g. Menelek–Black Lark (Domenico Fuoco) [1989/90 24m* 24m^{4} 20f^{4} 21f^{2} 22g^{5} 20d 28f* 24f^{4} 21f^{5} 25m^{5}] strong gelding: inconsistent hurdler/chaser: won handicap hurdles at Worcester in August and Nottingham in March: stays well: acts on any going: rather deliberate jumper of fences: usually wears blinkers: has worn a tongue strap: sometimes sweating: claimer ridden. *K. C. Bailey.* c— 106

STOP TWO 6 b.g. Buckskin (FR)–Natanya (Menelek) [1989/90 20g 20s 16g 16f^{6}] good-topped gelding: poor novice hurdler: should be suited by further than 2m: form only on heavy going. *M. Oliver.* —

STORMGUARD 7 b.g. Thatching–Silk And Satin (Charlottown) [1989/90 c16f^{6} c26g^{pu} 16g 16g^{3} a16g^{6} a16g 20g^{3} a20g^{4} c16g^{3} c20m^{3} c24m^{pu} c20g^{6} 20m 20f^{4}] leggy, close-coupled gelding: novice hurdler/winning chaser: poor plater nowadays: stays 2½m, seemingly not 3m: acts on firm going: occasionally blinkered or visored: has worn a tongue strap: has looked none too keen on occasions. *W. Clay.* **c85** 73

STORM ISLAND 5 b.g. Strong Gale–Sleemana (Prince Hansel) [1989/90 F16g^{3} F16g*] first foal: dam won several times up to 2¾m over jumps and also won on Flat in Ireland: won 17-runner NH Flat race at Perth in May by 1½ lengths from stable-companion Book of Runes: yet to race over hurdles or fences. *J. A. C. Edwards.*

STORMSEAL BOY 4 b.g. Tyrnavos–Firente (Firestreak) [1989/90 F16v^{3} 16s^{ur} 16m^{5} 17m^{2} 16g^{3}] useful-looking gelding: seventh foal: half-brother to winning hurdler Patrick's Star (by Star Appeal) and 1m and 9f winner Fond Kiss (by Young Generation): dam 1½m winner: placed in amateur riders maiden hurdle at Carlisle and claimer at Perth (good third) in April: will be suited by further than 2m. *J. M. Jefferson.* 92

STORM WARRIOR 5 b.g. Main Reef–Spadilla (Javelot) [1989/90 16f^{4} 16f^{2} 16g* 20m^{5} a18g* 16g^{6} a16g^{3} 16g a16g^{2} a20g* a18g* a16g^{3} a20g* a20g^{2} a20g^{2} a16g* a18g^{2} a24g^{2} a16g^{6} a20g* a20g^{4} a20g* c16g^{5}] leggy gelding: gaining eighth victory of season when winning handicap hurdle at Southwell in May: earlier successful in selling handicaps at Hereford (bought in 3,000 gns) and Southwell (retained 4,000 gns), 4 non-selling handicaps on latter course (one an amateur riders event) and an amateur riders handicap at Lingfield: made mistakes when over 20 lengths fifth in novice chase at Bangor in May (will be suited by further over fences): stays 3m: acts on any going: wears blinkers: good mount for a claimer. *B. Preece.* c— 110

STORMWATCH 7 b.g. Kambalda–Glenbrien Dusky (Dusky Boy) [1989/90 22d 20g^{6} 21d^{4}] smallish, close-coupled gelding: winning hurdler: only form in 101

handicaps in 1989/90 when fourth in conditional jockeys race at Newton Abbot in
March: probably best at up to 2½m for time being: acts on soft going (placed in NH
Flat races on top-of-the-ground). *D. R. Gandolfo.*

STORMY DOMAIN 5 b.h. Dunphy–Lea Landing (Meadow Court) [1989/90
F16g^{6} F16g F16v 17m^{6} 22f^{pu}] half-brother to Irish 8.6f and 1¼m winner —
Bouganville (by Gulf Pearl), French 1½m winner Pitiless (by Pitcairn) and
winning hurdler Tilbury (by Realm): dam placed from 5f to 7f: no sign of ability:
sold out of J. Parkes's stable 1,750 gns Ascot April Sales after third start. *P. Leach.*

STORMY MONARCH 9 b.g. Fordham (USA)–Stormy Queen (Typhoon) c—
[1989/90 20m 24v a20g^{6} c26g^{pu} c20f^{6} c24m^{F} 16f^{3} 20m] compact gelding: selling 85
hurdler nowadays: no sign of ability in novice chases: stays 3m: possibly unsuited
by soft going, acts on any other: has looked none too keen: visored fifth outing. *G.
H. Jones.*

STORMY PRAISE (USA) 6 ch.h. Storm Bird (CAN)–Prayers'n Promises
(USA) (Foolish Pleasure (USA)) [1989/90 16f^{F} 16g 16g a16g^{2}] quite modest ?
maiden on Flat (headstrong), effective at 6f and 7f: sold out of C. James's stable
2,500 gns Ascot October Sales: well beaten in novice hurdles prior to finishing 10
lengths second of 3 at Southwell in January. *P. R. Rodford.*

STORMY'S MAD 6 ch.g. Royal Match–Copped (Tumble Wind (USA))
[1989/90 16g 17g 16m] first foal: dam unplaced in 2 Irish NH Flat races: in frame —
over 1¼m on Flat: placed in maiden hurdles in Ireland in 1988/9: no worthwhile
form in Britain: acts on firm ground. *J. P. Leigh.*

STRADEY CASTLE 4 gr.f. Absalom–Comedy Miss (Comedy Star (USA))
[1989/90 16v^{pu} 16g 16m a18g^{5} a16g^{5} 16g^{pu} 16g^{pu}] sparely-made filly: tailed off —
only start on Flat: little form over hurdles, including in sellers: blinkered fifth
start. *K. S. Bridgwater.*

STRAIGHT BRANDY 7 b.g. Sit In The Corner (USA)–Fair Spirit (Spiritus)
[1989/90 F16m^{4} 16g 16d^{4} 16g 22d^{pu} 21d] tall gelding: fourth foal: dam poor chaser: 88 ?
fourth in NH Flat race at Worcester in October on debut and novice hurdle at
Stratford in December: ran poorly last 2 starts: sold 3,000 gns Ascot June Sales.
D. Nicholson.

STRAIGHT DOWN 13 b.g. Straight Lad–Down Memory Lane (Star Gazer) c85
[1989/90 c17m^{4} c16f^{2} c16m^{3} c16m* c16f* c16m^{4} c16g^{3} c16m^{3} c16g^{2} c16m^{3} c16g^{3} —
c16d^{4} a22g^{pu} c16f^{3} c16g^{3} c16g^{2} c21f^{2}] big gelding: front-running chaser: game
winner of handicaps at Perth and Catterick in October: good second at Cartmel in
May, final start: stays 21f: appears to act on any going: has been tried in blinkers.
Mrs P. A. Barker.

STRAIGHT GIN 9 b.m. Ginger Boy–Cool Straight (Straight Lad) [1989/90 c—
c24f^{pu} a20g^{3} a18g* a24g^{pu}] workmanlike mare: poor handicap chaser: won novice 89
hurdle at Lingfield in December by 10 lengths: suited by further than 2m (tailed
off when pulled up lame over 3m final start): acts on firm ground and seems
unsuited by soft: has won in blinkers: amateur ridden. *A. J. Taylor.*

STRAIGHT GOLD 5 ch.m. Vaigly Great–Merokette (Blast) [1989/90 16m^{4}
16m^{3} 16m* 16g^{4} 20d*] smallish, angular mare: modest middle-distance 104
handicapper on Flat: sold out of I. Balding's stable 12,500 gns Newmarket Autumn
Sales: won novice hurdles at Worcester in April (made most) and May (held up):
amateur ridden, showed improved form in handicap on second occasion: stays
2½m: acts on good to firm and dead ground. *G. A. Ham.*

STRAIGHT PILOT 8 br.g. Ascertain (USA)–Lucky Flight (Lucky Leapre- c**101**
chaun) [1989/90 c20d* c25g^{2} c24m^{2} c22m] workmanlike gelding: winning point-
to-pointer: won hunter chase at Wetherby in February by 2 lengths from
below-form Call Collect: 4 lengths second to Ready Steady in similar race at
Newcastle in March, third start: stays well: acts on good to firm and dead ground.
David Ford.

STRANDS OF GOLD 11 b.g. Le Coq d'Or–Sweet Fanny (Bitter Sweet) c—
[1989/90 c33d^{pu} c29f^{pu}] strong, compact gelding: smart chaser at his best: won —
1988 Hennessy Cognac Gold Cup: tailed off when pulled up in William Hill
Scottish National at Ayr and Whitbread Gold Cup at Sandown in April: stays very
well: probably acts on any going but is suited by testing conditions at 3m: has
shown a tendency to drift under pressure: usually held up: usually jumps soundly.
M. C. Pipe.

STRATFORD PONDS 5 b.h. High Top–Opinion (Great Nephew) [1989/90
16g^{4} 16g^{2} 16g* 16m 20f^{2} 20f* 16g^{5}] sturdy, workmanlike horse: fairly useful 128
middle-distance handicapper on Flat: sold out of J. Dunlop's stable 40,000 gns

Dovecote Novices' Hurdle, Kempton—
Stratford Ponds jumps the last clear of Gaasid (centre) and Alkinor Rex

Newmarket Autumn Sales: won novice hurdles at Kempton (always prominent) in February and Ascot (held up, led approaching last to beat Pontevecchio Notte 2½ lengths in slowly-run race) in April: around 13 lengths fifth to Vestris Abu in BMW Champion Novice Hurdle at Punchestown (jumped less well than usual): stays 2½m: acts on firm ground. *O. Sherwood.*

STRAW BLADE 4 ch.f. Final Straw–Little Niece (Great Nephew) [1989/90 16f* 16g4 18s5 16spu 17f* 17h*] sparely-made filly: claimed out of J. Dunlop's stable £12,501 after winning 10.6f claimer on Flat in 1989: made all to win juvenile hurdle at Newbury in October by 30 lengths: subsequently off course 2 months and didn't recapture that form, though won sellers at Newton Abbot (no bid) and Devon & Exeter (bought in 2,900 gns) in May: may prove best at around 2m: best run on firm ground: blinkered fourth outing: sold to G. Ham 5,200 gns Ascot June Sales. *M. C. Pipe.* 106 ?

STRAW CASTLE 5 ch.m. Final Straw–Candy Castle (Habitat) [1989/90 16f6 16d 16g 16f4] sparely-made mare: poor maiden on Flat: poor plater over hurdles: wears blinkers: jumps none too fluently. *T. B. Hallett.* 78 ?

STREAM BRIDGE 9 b.g. Carlburg–Hay Casta (Will Hays (USA)) [1989/90 c24s2 c24g* c24s3 c28g2 c24m2 c25m3 c36gF] leggy gelding: winning hurdler: won handicap chase at Windsor in January: also ran well fourth and fifth starts: stays well: acts on heavy going and good to firm: usually jumps soundly. *O. Sherwood.* c**115** —

STREAM OF BUNCLODY 9 b.g. Legal Eagle–Tutty (Hotfoot) [1989/90 c24d] winning point-to-pointer: always behind in hunter chase at Ayr in April. *Peter Henderson.* c—

STREETFIGHTER (USA) 6 b.h. Roberto (USA)–Excitable Miss (USA) (Gallant Man) [1989/90 22g c16m5 c21f5 c24s2 c26vur c24v5 c25mpu] leggy horse: winning hurdler: second in novice handicap at Taunton in December, best effort over fences: stays 3m: acts on any going: wears blinkers: has looked a difficult ride (ran moody races first and last starts). *J. H. Baker.* c**78** § —

STRICTLY BUSINESS 8 b.g. Song–Bella Lisa (River Chanter) [1989/90 16g c20gF c21m3 c17d c16d5 c18f4 17h4 c17m2] tall gelding: winning hurdler: finished c**81** —

Mrs Shirley Robins' "Strong Gold"

lame when short-head second in novice handicap chase at Newton Abbot in May: keen-going sort, likely to prove suited by a sharp 2m: seems suited by a firm surface: trained until after sixth start by C. Popham. *M. C. Pipe.*

STRIDE HOME 5 ch.m. Absalom–Another Treat (Derring-Do) [1989/90 16m 16d] small, workmanlike mare: poor novice hurdler: seems to act on any going: blinkered last 2 starts. *M. Madgwick.* —

STRIDING EDGE 5 ch.g. Viking (USA)–Kospia (King Emperor (USA)) [1989/90 16g a16g] ex-Irish gelding: in frame at up to 9.5f on Flat: seventh in maiden hurdle at Naas in November (trained by J. Murphy) and conditional jockeys novice event at Lingfield (never dangerous, around 24 lengths behind Shu Fly) in March. *J. R. Jenkins.* 77

STRIKE A CHORD 5 b.m. Song–Marguerite Gerard (Rheingold) [1989/90 16g 16f5 17mur 16m3 17f3 20d3 16f2 16f5 16m*] rather sparely-made mare: game winner of novice handicap hurdle at Stratford in June: placed second, having originally been awarded dead-heat with Persillant, in minor hurdle at Warwick previous month: stays 2½m: acts on firm ground. *Miss G. Dollar.* 93

STRIKE A POINT 8 b.g. Furry Glen–Royal Cup (Politico (USA)) [1989/90 21dur 20d2 22s5 22d* 24m2 20mF] leggy gelding: fair handicap hurdler: won at Stratford in February: stayed 3m: acted on heavy going and good to firm: dead. *P. M. Cowley.* 122

STRING PLAYER 8 ch.g. Orchestra–Ghana's Daughter (Sallust) [1989/90 22s] smallish, sparely-made gelding: useful hurdler at his best: soundly beaten only outing of 1989/90 (February): won 2 novice chases in 1988/9: suited by a strongly-run race at 2m and stays 2¾m well: probably acts on any going though best form over fences on firm ground: usually a quick jumper. *F. H. Lee.* c— —

STROKED AGAIN 5 b.m. On Your Mark–Anniversary Waltz (Carnival Dancer) [1989/90 F16f F16m* F16m6 a16g3 16g2 17f* 20g*] ex-Irish mare: third foal: dam, 2-y-o seller winner, half-sister to a winning hurdler: won NH Flat race at Sligo very early in season, when trained by Miss S. Barkley: successful very late in season in novice hurdles at Cartmel and Market Rasen (mares): better suited by 2½m than shorter: acts on firm going. *B. Richmond.* 92

STROKESTOWN LAD 6 b. or br.g. Tanfirion–Misippus (Green God) [1989/90 17f* 16s6 16d 20d5 20s] sturdy ex-Irish gelding: fourth foal: half-brother to 2 poor maidens: dam of no account: won handicap hurdle at Tipperary in June (trained by P. Mullins): off course 6 months afterwards and well below form on return: stays 2½m: acts on any going. *M. Bradstock.* 131 d

STRONG BEAU 5 br.g. Strong Gale–Red Pine (Khalkis) [1989/90 F16f4] third foal: half-brother to Irish NH Flat race winner Pinaster Bay (by Ragapan) and to modest novice hurdler/chaser Charlie Plum (by Laurence O): dam placed in a point-to-point: 9½ lengths fourth of 22 behind Driver in NH Flat race at Cheltenham in April: yet to race over hurdles or fences. *D. Nicholson.*

STRONG BREEZE 6 b.g. Strong Gale–Salty Breeze (Pitpan) [1989/90 16g] third in NH Flat race in 1988/9: well beaten in maiden event at Edinburgh in January on hurdling debut. *R. F. Fisher.* —

STRONG CALLING 5 br.g. Strong Gale–Knowing Card (Green Shoon) [1989/90 F16g 16g 20g5 20fpu] first foal: dam won on Flat and over hurdles: no worthwhile form in novice hurdles: dead. *W. A. Stephenson.* —

STRONG FANCY 7 br.g. Royal Match–Sugar Lump (Candy Cane) [1989/90 16g2 20v3 20g4] sturdy gelding: moderate novice hurdler: stays 2½m: may prove best suited by give in the ground: claimer ridden. *Mrs R. Wharton.* 102

STRONG GOLD 7 b.g. Strong Gale–Miss Goldiane (Baragoi) [1989/90 20g* 20s2 21d4 20s6 20g3 25gF 25f 24m*] strong, lengthy gelding: won novice hurdle at Plumpton in November and handicap at Chepstow in April, showing return to form when leading from fourth to beat The Shiner easily by 10 lengths in latter: stays 3m: acts on good to firm and heavy going: blinkered last 4 outings: quite useful on his day. *Mrs J. Pitman.* 129

STRONG LANGUAGE 5 ch.m. Formidable (USA)–Linguistic (Porto Bello) [1989/90 18f* 16f 16m5 17g6 16g 16m3] workmanlike mare: easy winner of selling hurdle at Fontwell in October (bought in 3,200 gns): best subsequent effort when third in handicap at Sedgefield in March: stays 2¼m: acts on firm ground: blinkered final start 1988/9: trained until after third outing by J. White. *J. L. Harris.* 75

STRUELL ROYALE 9 ch.g. Royal Captive–Greek Empress (Royal Buck) [1989/90 17d 16f c17f c21m2] ex-Irish gelding: second foal: brother to winning jumper Royal Greek: dam half-sister to several winners, notably Rathgorman: winning point-to-pointer: poor novice over hurdles (refused once) and in steeplechases: withdrawn after bolting before third intended outing: started slowly next time. *W. R. Williams.* c67 —

ST SUNDAY'S BECK 4 ch.g. Nicholas Bill–Lingdale Lady (Sandford Lad) [1989/90 F16f] third living foal: half-brother to novice hurdler Boynton (by Riboboy): dam stayed 6f: eighth of 11 in NH Flat race at Hexham in April: yet to race over hurdles. *A. Fowler.*

STUMBLE 6 ch.g. Sayyaf–Tumble Royal (Tumble Wind (USA)) [1989/90 17gpu 16d 17f4 16m* 16g* 16m*] sturdy, compact gelding: in good form late in season and won handicap hurdles at Wetherby (seller, no bid), Perth and Wetherby again: suited by 2m and a sharp track: best form on a sound surface: has a turn of foot and is invariably held up: may improve further. *J. Mackie.* 106 p

STUPID CUPID 6 b.m. Idiot's Delight–Trianqo (Tarqogan) [1989/90 16m2 16g* 16m3 20gpu 20d5] leggy, lightly-made mare: mistakes last 2 and idled in front when winning mares novice hurdle at Market Rasen in November: good fifth to King's Curate in quite valuable novice handicap at Ayr in April: stays 2½m: acts on good to firm and dead ground: off course 2 months before each of last 2 outings. *J. T. Gifford.* 100

ST WILLIAM 13 b.g. St Paddy–Lower Slade (Solar Duke) [1989/90 c21m5 c16d3 c16g4 c16m2 c18m2 c16s3 c16d* c16mpu] tall gelding: poor chaser nowadays: won amateur riders handicap at Plumpton in January: stays 19f: acts on any going: well below his best in blinkers: sometimes makes mistakes: has run well when sweating: sometimes takes little interest. *R. J. Hodges.* c87 § —

Ashford Novices' Hurdle, Kempton—Sudden Victory jumps the last well

SUASANAN SIOSANA 5 b. or br.g. Frigid Aire–Efficiency (Pardao) [1989/90 F16m 16g 21d 16m^{3} 20m] close-coupled, deep-girthed gelding: half-brother to useful Irish hurdler Ballychorus Dream (by Over The River) and winning hurdlers John McNab (by Whistling Wind) and Kilcha Girl (by Callernish): dam, lightly raced, is related to Snow Knight: no worthwhile form in novice hurdles. *John R. Upson.* —

SUBURBIA 4 b.f. Another Realm–Leaplet (Alcide) [1989/90 16d] lightly raced and no sign of ability on Flat: never going well in selling hurdle at Market Rasen in November. *F. Watson.* —

SUDBROOKE PARK 12 ch.g. Duc d'Orleans–Miss Hill (Warden of The Hills) [1989/90 22g^{pu} 25m^{2} c24s^{4} c25g^{ur} c24d^{3} c21d^{F} c24g^{5}] medium-sized gelding: poor winning hurdler/novice chaser: stays well: acts on heavy and good to firm ground: blinkered third start 1987/8: sometimes makes mistakes. *J. Parkes.* **c78** + 81

SUDDEN VICTORY 6 ch.g. Kings Lake (USA)–Shebeen (Saint Crespin III) [1989/90 16g* 16g* 16d 16m] lightly-made gelding: smart performer at up to 2m on Flat: won novice hurdles at Plumpton and Kempton in January, latter by 2 lengths from Riverhead, pair long way clear: around 14 lengths seventh, staying on, to Deep Sensation in moderately-run Tote Gold Trophy at Newbury in February: led to 4 out when thirteenth of 16 finishers in Waterford Crystal Champion Hurdle at Cheltenham following month: will stay beyond 2m: acts on soft going. *B. W. Hills.* 135

SUEDE LADY 7 b.m. Leading Man–Dunoon Court (Dunoon Star) [1989/90 c16f^{4} c21m^{ur} c16f^{pu} 16g] lengthy mare: of little account. *Mrs G. Bartle.* c— —

SUFFOLK DOWNS 8 b.g. Fine Blade (USA)–Woodford (Autumn Gold) [1989/90 c20m* c25m^{pu}] tall gelding: claimer ridden, won 3-runner handicap chase at Perth in August: pulled up lame later in month: stays 3m: acts on heavy and good to firm going: usually sweats up: sometimes bandaged near-hind. *N. Miller.* **c97** —

SUIKERBOS 12 gr.g. Immortal Love–Sugar Bush (Sagebush) [1989/90 c25f^{pu}] plain gelding: quite useful point-to-pointer at his best, winner in April: c—

won novice hunter chase in 1989: tailed off when pulled up eleventh at Cheltenham in May: stays 3m: acts on firm going. *K. Pritchard.*

SUIVEZ MOI 6 ch.g. Pas de Seul–Reparata (Jukebox) [1989/90 21g*] small, sparely-made gelding: won handicap hurdle at Fakenham in April, only outing of season: should stay beyond 21f: often amateur or claimer ridden. *C. N. Allen.* 90

SUKAAB 5 gr.g. Nishapour (FR)–Nye (FR) (Sanctus II) [1989/90 16f5 16m2 17m3] leggy gelding: novice hurdler: placed at Perth and Cartmel in August: suited by a sharp 2m: yet to race on a soft surface: to be trained by G. Richards. *B. McLean.* 84

SUKEY TAWDRY 4 gr.f. Wassl–Jenny Diver (USA) (Hatchet Man (USA)) [1989/90 17m 16mF 16g 16m5 16mpu a20sF a20g5 a18g4 16fF 16f 16m3 16f5] leggy filly: won 1m seller in 1989: poor novice selling hurdler: seems not to stay 2½m: saddle slipped fifth start: blinkered last outing: sold out of M. Chapman's stable 1,800 gns Doncaster November Sales after third outing. *J. L. Spearing.* 67

SULCIS 5 ch.g. Castle Keep–Skiboule (BEL) (Boulou) [1989/90 16g* 16g5 20m] lengthy gelding: showed improved form when making all in handicap hurdle at Wolverhampton in November: ran moderately both subsequent starts: should stay 2½m: ridden by claimer. *R. Hollinshead.* 104

SULETTE 6 br.m. Sunyboy–Aluette (Gregalach's Nephew) [1989/90 16d 16g 20gpu 16mpu] small, sparely-made non-thoroughbred mare: fourth living foal: half-sister to novice hurdler/chaser Indian Rulette (by Indian Ruler): dam unraced sister to useful staying chaser Alu Alu: has shown little aptitude for hurdling. *J. R. Bosley.* —

SULLI BOY (NOR) 5 b.g. Sparkling Boy–Lady Sullivan (Pitcairn) [1989/90 16f3 16f* 20f4] sparely-made, rather dipped-backed gelding: fourth foal: half-brother to 2 winners in Norway by Le Johnstan: dam lightly raced and well beaten on Flat: won twice over 1m in Norway in 1989: sweating slightly, won moderately -run maiden hurdle at Newbury in March by ¾ length from Bell Glass: seemed to run very well when 19 lengths fourth to Babil in 2½m novice event at Ascot a week later (weakened in straight): has raced only on firm ground over hurdles. *Miss B. Sanders.* 110 ?

SULUK (USA) 5 b.h. Lypheor–Cheerful Heart (Petingo) [1989/90 19g5 16g6 a16g* a16g* a20g* a16g* a16g* a16g* a18g5] sparely-made horse: much improved on fibresand at Southwell and won 6 times over hurdles there in second half of season (novice handicap and 5 handicaps): gained last success by 2½ lengths from Disneyland in 3-runner event: likely to prove best at around 2m: usually ridden by claimer Gary Lyons (wasn't when fair fifth final start). *R. Hollinshead.* 115

SUM INSURED 7 br.g. Mandalus–Knocklow VI (Master Owen) [1989/90 c24fF c24dpu] good-bodied gelding: novice hurdler: winning chaser: failed to complete course in 2 outings in 1989/90: stays 2½m: takes a good hold: usually jumps well. *O. Sherwood.* c— —

SUMMERHILL SALLY 4 b.f. Dunbeath (USA)–Sharper Still (Sharpen Up) [1989/90 16m 16m6 16f 16s5 a16g6] neat filly: second in 1¼m claimer on Flat in June: sold out of J. Dunlop's stable 5,400 gns Ascot August Sales: poor juvenile selling hurdler. *P. Leach.* 62

SUMMERHILL SHADOW 5 gr.g. Alias Smith (USA)–New Top (New Brig) [1989/90 16spu] workmanlike gelding: remote third in novice hurdle in 1988/9: jumped none too fluently and tailed off when pulled up last only outing of 1989/90 (January). *D. M. Grissell.* —

SUMMER PARK 5 ch.h. Ballacashtal (CAN)–Summer Rain (Palestine) [1989/90 17fpu 16f 16g] sparely-made horse: of little account: dead. *J. Joseph.* —

SUMMONS 11 ch.g. Rouser–Silk II (Counsel) [1989/90 c20s c20d5 c20f* c24mF3 c26mpu] close-coupled gelding: won a point-to-point in March: didn't have to run up to his best to land the odds in hunter chase at Sandown in March: let down by his jumping afterwards: best form at around 2½m: acts on any going with possible exception of heavy: has tended to jump to his right on occasions: usually looks rather dull in coat. *Miss A. Embiricos.* c**105** —

SUNCIA 6 br.m. Sunyboy–Ascencia (Crozier) [1989/90 16g 16d 20dur 20m5] leggy mare: poor form in novice hurdles. *M. J. Wilkinson.* 68

SUNDAY CHAMPERS 8 b. or br.m. True Song–Poppywee (Spartan General) [1989/90 c22s3 c20dur c24dpu c20fpu] workmanlike mare: fair point-to-pointer: c**82** §

third in novice hunter chase at Nottingham in February: whipped round and unseated rider at start second outing, looked temperamental next time and ran as though something amiss final outing. *Mrs Joan Tice.*

SUNDAY FOR MONDAY 7 ch.g. Pal's Bambino–Gin An Tonic (Osprey Hawk) [1989/90 21f2 21m4 24m3 25f2 c24g c24spu c20mpu c25mpu] big, lengthy gelding: modest novice hurdler: best efforts of season when placed in handicaps at Worcester and Cheltenham: has shown nothing in novice chases: stays 3m: possibly unsuited by extremes of going: often claimer ridden. *R. J. Hodges.* c— 90

SUNDAY JIM 6 b.g. Jimsun–Berkeley Belle (Runnymede) [1989/90 20f2 20f3 21fF 20m5 a22g] sturdy gelding: novice selling hurdler: placed in non-sellers in August: stays 2½m: acts on firm ground. *H. J. M. Webb.* 77

SUNDAY SCHOOL 10 b.m. Joshua–Upper Class (Double Jump) [1989/90 c24g2] big mare: quite useful winning point-to-pointer: 1½ lengths second to Dover in hunter chase at Bangor in May: stays 25f: acts on firm ground: sold 12,000 gns Ascot June Sales. *F. J. Dilworth.* c**87**

SUNDAYSPORT SCOOP 5 b.h. Great Nephew–Heaven Knows (Yellow God) [1989/90 18m3 22f3 16g 16d5 20g3] small, stocky horse: poor novice selling hurdler: moved badly to post last start (creditable third): stays 2¾m. *W. Clay.* 70

SUN FOLLOWER 4 ch.f. Relkino–Tactless (Romulus) [1989/90 16dpu] lengthy filly: brother to 1¼m seller winner and winning hurdler Entire and half-brother to 4 other winners, including very useful Padro (by Runnymede), a winner at up to 7f: dam won over 1¼m: bit backward, tailed off when pulled up 2 out in juvenile hurdle at Sandown in January. *J. J. Bridger.* —

SUN-KING JOHNNY 4 ch.g. Royal Vulcan–Dracons Girl (Cave of Dracan) [1989/90 aF16g] second foal by a thoroughbred stallion: dam of little account: tailed-off last of 10 in NH Flat race at Lingfield in January: yet to race over hurdles. *Mrs R. Murdoch.*

SUNLEY SUNSHINE 4 b.f. Sunley Builds–Brown Velvet (Mansingh (USA)) [1989/90 16m 16g4 16h3] leggy filly: maiden on Flat, stays 1¼m: poor juvenile hurdler: unlikely to stay much beyond 2m. *M. H. B. Robinson.* 82

SUNLIGHT EXPRESS 4 b.g. Homing–Princess Sunshine (Busted) [1989/90 F16f2] first reported foal: dam, well beaten in modest company, is out of half-sister to top-class Flat performers Double Jump and Royalty: clear short-head second to Croghan Rose in 11-runner NH Flat race at Huntingdon in May: yet to race over hurdles. *Mrs L. Piggott.*

SUNNINGHILL CELTIC 6 ch.g. Celtic Cone–Aunt Livia (Royalty) [1989/90 16f 25g2] lengthy, rather unfurnished gelding: finished long way clear of remainder when 1½ lengths second to Miinnehoma in novice hurdle at Newbury in December, making good headway approaching 3 out and staying on strongly: sure to improve and will win a staying novice event. *D. R. C. Elsworth.* 118 p

SUN 'N' RAYNE 9 b.g. Sunotra–Romayne (Rubor) [1989/90 c17f] angular gelding: won a point-to-point in 1988: well beaten in steeplechases, including a selling handicap: blinkered only outing of season (July): sold 1,950 gns Ascot November Sales: resold 3,800 gns Doncaster January Sales. *J. Ffitch-Heyes.* c—

SUNNY SLAVE 9 b.g. Sunyboy–Slavetown (Arctic Slave) [1989/90 c24s4] leggy gelding: moderate hurdler/chaser: first outing for nearly a year, showed signs of retaining ability when not-knocked-about fourth in handicap at Windsor in January: stays 25f: acts on heavy going. *N. J. Henderson.* c**98** —

SUN OF CHANCE 6 b.g. Sunyboy–Chance A Look (Don't Look) [1989/90 F16g F16f6] fifth foal: brother to winning hurdler Sundiata and half-brother to novice hurdler/chaser Treble Chance (by Balinger): dam, quite modest chaser, stayed well but raced mainly at up to 19f: well beaten in NH Flat races at Kempton and Ascot (sixth of 13 to Piper's Son) in second half of season: yet to race over hurdles or fences. *S. Woodman.*

SUN PEARL 5 ch.m. Le Soleil–Seed Pearl (Ben Novus) [1989/90 16m 16s 16mF] small non-thoroughbred mare: first foal: dam, quite useful hurdler/fair chaser, stayed well: behind in novice hurdles: jumps none too fluently. *J. T. Gifford.* —

SUN RISING 12 b.g. Sunyboy–Kipping Hill (Petition) [1989/90 c24dpu] medium-sized gelding: useful chaser at his best: bad mistake twelfth and pulled up and dismounted soon after, only outing of 1989/90 (December): stays 3m: seems to act on any going: wears blinkers: suited by racing up with the c— —

pace but tends to run lazily and needs plenty of driving: sometimes sweats. *F. Walwyn.*

SUNSET AGAIN 5 ch.g. Al Sirat (USA)–Noddy (Prince Hansel) [1989/90 F12g^{4} F17f 16s^{6} 16m 20f* 20m^{3} 22f^{3} 20m] 3,500 3-y-o: smallish, unfurnished gelding: fifth foal: dam ran once: won novice hurdle at Worcester in March cleverly by ½ length from Donna Del Lago: good third of 4 finishers in novice handicap at Wincanton 2 outings later: stays 2¾m: acts on firm ground. *M. H. B. Robinson.* 100

SUNSET COURT 8 ch.g. Quayside–Shamrock Penny (Flyover) [1989/90 16g^{3} 21d 16f*] angular gelding: half-brother to winning point-to-pointer Tullispark (by Menelek) and successful Irish hunter chaser Tallyman (by Pitpan): dam won over 7.5f in Ireland: made all when easy winner of 3-runner novice hurdle at Taunton in March: raced too freely to stay 2½m previous outing: acts on firm ground: sold only 2,100 gns Ascot June Sales. *C. P. E. Brooks.* 87 +

SUNSET CRUISE 5 b.g. Cruise Missile–Suntino (Rugantino) [1989/90 16g 22d^{pu} 16g] workmanlike gelding: second foal: half-brother to poor novice Sunset Vine (by French Vine): dam, half-sister to useful jumper Golden Vow, fair winning point-to-pointer: no sign of ability in novice hurdles: dead. *D. Lee.* —

SUNSET REINS FREE 5 b.h. Red Sunset–Free Rein (Sagaro) [1989/90 16m* 16g^{5} 17g^{5} 16d^{4} 16f^{3}] lengthy, angular horse: modest middle-distance handicapper on Flat, usually visored nowadays: won novice hurdle at Wolverhampton in October: in frame on same course last 2 starts (third behind impressive My Young Man in March): acts on firm and dead going: has tended to wander and is worth trying in a visor or blinkers. *E. J. Alston.* 100

SUNSET SAM 6 br.g. Dolman–Braeval (Quorum) [1989/90 18s^{3} 16s 17d 25m* 24f^{5} 26m^{2}] leggy, sparely-made gelding: selling hurdler: attracted no bid after winning at Hereford in April: ran well in non-selling handicaps last 2 starts: stays 3¼m: acts on firm ground. *R. Callow.* 92

SUNSET VINE 7 b.g. French Vine–Suntino (Rugantino) [1989/90 c24m^{pu} c25f^{3} c25d^{pu} c25g^{F} c26m^{bd} c25m^{pu} a20g^{5} c20g] workmanlike gelding: no worthwhile form over hurdles: poor novice chaser (tailed off in seller last outing): visored last 2 starts: sold 3,800 gns Ascot Junes Sales. *A. J. Wilson.* c79 —

SUNSHINE BLUES 7 b.g. Sunyboy–Fatal Hour (Fate) [1989/90 20m^{F}] tall gelding: has scope: half-brother to Rinnaga (by Larrinaga), a winning stayer on Flat and placed over hurdles: dam never ran: well behind when falling last in novice hurdle at Uttoxeter in March. *F. Walwyn.* —

SUNSTANE 6 ch.m. Sunyboy–Stanegate (Coliseum) [1989/90 aF13g^{4}] half-sister to very useful staying hurdler Atrabates (by Precipice Wood): well beaten in 2 NH Flat races: yet to race over hurdles or fences. *O. Sherwood.*

SUN STORM 5 ch.m. Sunyboy–Pacific Rush (Typhoon) [1989/90 F16m] sister to novice hurdler Summer Sun: dam won over 1½m in Ireland: 50/1, tailed off in NH Flat race at Towcester in January: yet to race over hurdles or fences. *Mrs B. Dukes.*

SUNYLYN 10 b.m. Sunyboy–Elmolyn (St Elmo) [1989/90 c25d^{pu} c26d^{pu}] big, lengthy mare: former hunter chaser: winning chaser: pulled up in December (reportedly lame on second occasion): stays 25f: suited by a yielding surface: takes a strong hold: broke blood vessel third start 1986/7. *W. N. Mawle.* c—

SUNY ZETA 6 b.m. Sunyboy–Blue Zeta (Bluerullah) [1989/90 F16g] behind in 3 NH Flat races at Ayr: yet to race over hurdles or fences. *R. H. Goldie.*

SUPER EXPRESS 9 ch.g. Hotfoot–Gwynfa (Welsh Pageant) [1989/90 c19d^{ur} c16d^{4} c25m^{2} 17v^{6} c19d^{5} c17v^{5} c25g^{pu}] lengthy, workmanlike gelding: modest chaser: tends to make mistakes and finds little under pressure: reluctant to race last start: barely stays 3m: probably acts on any going but ideally suited by plenty of give: blinkered fifth and sixth outings: not one to trust. *D. H. Barons.* **c100** § —

SUPER FOUNTAIN 7 b.m. Royal Fountain–Super Satin (Lord of Verona) [1989/90 c24d^{3} c22d^{3} c24d* c24d^{5} c24f^{3}] lengthy mare: winning point-to-pointer: successful in novice chase at Carlisle in March: thorough stayer: acts on dead going and seems unsuited by firm. *F. T. Walton.* **c91** —

SUPER FURROW 10 br.g. Super Slip–Fillo (Anthony) [1989/90 c21m^{5} c24s^{2} c20g^{3} c20d^{3}] big, workmanlike Irish gelding: smart chaser: third behind Maid of Money in Durkan Brothers International EBF Punchestown Chase and Black & White Whisky Champion Chase at Leopardstown (beaten just over a length) last 2 **c156** —

Mrs Margaret Marshall's "Super Furrow"

starts: stays 3m: acts on any going: best form in blinkers: game. *Jeremiah J. O'Neill, Ireland.*

SUPER IDEA 5 b.m. Red Sunset–Priors Mistress (Sallust) [1989/90 16m 20m^{pu} a16g 16m] neat mare: poor novice selling hurdler: seems suited by 2m and —
top-of-the-ground: wears blinkers or a visor. *K. G. Wingrove.*

SUPER JULES (FR) 5 ch.g. Trio (FR)–Silver Plate (FR) (Son of Silver) c—
[1989/90 a20g^{2} a18g^{6} a24g^{4} a20g* a20g^{3} a24g 17m 16f^{pu}] angular gelding: won 72
juvenile hurdle and fell in a steeplechase in France: poor form in Britain: won 2-runner 2½m handicap at Lingfield in January: well beaten subsequently: blinkered third to seventh starts. *J. A. B. Old.*

SUPERLASSIE 4 b.f. Superlative–Brig of Ayr (Brigadier Gerard) [1989/90 a16g 16d 16f^{pu}] sparely-made filly: bad plater on Flat: no worthwhile form in a —
claimer and 2 sellers over hurdles: pulled up lame last time. *M. Castell.*

SUPER REGAL 8 b.g. Fordham (USA)–Little Angle (Gulf Pearl) [1989/90 a20g^{3} 20g] compact gelding: modest hurdler at best: claimer ridden, tired from 72
last when third in handicap at Southwell in November: very stiff task next start: stays 2½m: probably acts on any going: blinkered last 2 starts 1987/8. *R. J. Eckley.*

SUPER RELATIVE 4 b.g. Superlative–Breton's Sister (Relko) [1989/90 16g^{6} 20g^{pu} 16m^{3} 16f 16f 16f 17f^{5} 20m^{pu}] neat gelding: poor maiden on Flat: third in 58
selling hurdle at Nottingham in December, only form: sold out of N. Tinkler's stable 1,700 gns Doncaster January Sales after fourth start. *M. F. Barraclough.*

SUPER SENSE 5 b.g. Pragmatic–Killonan Lass (The Parson) [1989/90 16s 16m^{4}] rangy gelding: fifth foal: half-brother to novice hurdler Andy Boy (by Mr 88
Fordette): dam behind in NH Flat race on only outing: never-dangerous 20 lengths fourth of 10 finishers to Love Anew at Chepstow in April, better effort in novice hurdles. *J. T. Gifford.*

SUPER SOL 6 ch.m. Rolfe (USA)–Solo Waltz (Quiet Fling (USA)) [1989/90 16f^{2} 16m^{4} 16g a18g^{5} a16g^{F} 16m^{5} 19f 16m^{4} 16h^{4} 16m^{4}] leggy, sparely-made mare: 77
winning selling hurdler: ran creditably in non-selling handicaps first 2 and eighth starts: barely stays 2½m: yet to race on heavy going, acts on any other. *K. A. Morgan.*

SUPER SUE 7 b.m. Lochnager–Annamanda (Tycoon II) [1989/90 16f^{6} 20f^{2} c— x
c21d^{4} c20g^{5} 16f^{3}] strong, compact mare: type to carry condition: poor novice 73

hurdler/chaser: best form at 2m on good to firm going: moderate jumper of fences. *P. Beaumont.*

SUPER TONY 13 ch.g. Owen Anthony–Super Satin (Lord of Verona) [1989/90 c95
c20f* c24h^{wo} c24f^{wo} c24m^{pu}] lengthy gelding: handicap chaser: gained all 7 of his —
wins at Hexham, including in September and in October (walked over twice): destroyed after severing tendon on same course: stayed well: probably acted on any going. *F. T. Walton.*

SUPER TRIX 7 gr.g. Bonne Noel–Merry Chariot (Blue Chariot) [1989/90 17m^5 c92
16g^2 c16g^4 c16g^2 c20s^3 c24g^4 17g^4 c20d^{ur} c24d^{ro} 20m^5 c16g^5 20m* 22m* 21f^4] 108
close-coupled ex-Irish gelding: half-brother to 2 winning jumpers, including useful performer Four Trix (by Peacock): won novice hurdles at Wetherby and Stratford (conditional jockeys handicap) in May: moderate novice chaser: stays 2¾m: acts on heavy going and good to firm: tends to hang left, badly so when blinkered eleventh start: found nothing when visored seventh outing. *G. Richards.*

SUPPOZE 7 br.g. Crozier–Great Supper (Slippered) [1989/90 c20s^{ur} c27d^5] c—
brother to winning hurdler Ballytigue Lad: dam unraced sister to a winning chaser —
and half-sister to useful hunter chaser Carndonagh: no form in novice hurdle, point-to-point and novice chases: sold 1,150 gns Doncaster Spring Sales. *W. A. Stephenson.*

SUPREME DEALER 5 ch.g. The Parson–Vul's Money (Even Money) [1989/90 F16f^2 16d] lengthy gelding: sixth foal: half-brother to winning
hurdler/point-to-pointer Woolly Jumper (by Pyrenean), useful chaser Clay Hill —
(by Menelek) and fairly useful novice hurdler Credit Cut (by Fine Blade): dam won 2m maiden hurdle in Ireland: neck second of 23 to Olveston in NH Flat race at Newbury in October: well beaten in novice hurdle at Towcester in February, taking good hold and weakening quickly after slight mistake 3 out. *J. T. Gifford.*

SUPREME ISSUE 4 b.f. Bustiki–Slings And Arrows (Warpath) [1989/90 F16s^2 F16v] sturdy filly: first foal: dam plating-class maiden at 2 yrs: 1½ lengths second to Cache Fleur in 25-runner NH Flat race at Warwick in February: well-beaten seventh at Haydock following month: yet to race over hurdles. *J. A. Glover.*

SUPREME WARRIOR 4 b.g. Simply Great (FR)–Sindo (Derring-Do)
[1989/90 16f^5 16f^6] small gelding: modest maiden at up to 1¾m on Flat: showed 75
ability in juvenile hurdles at Cheltenham and Ascot in October: will be suited by 2½m: ridden by claimer: has worn a crossed noseband. *P. J. Hobbs.*

SURE METAL 7 b.g. Billion (USA)–Sujini (Tycoon II) [1989/90 c20g^4 c20s^3 c**134**
c20g^3 c20v^{pu} c20m* c20f^{pu}] workmanlike, angular gelding: fair novice hurdler: —

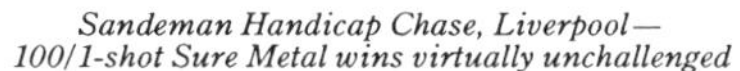

Sandeman Handicap Chase, Liverpool—
100/1-shot Sure Metal wins virtually unchallenged

showed much improved form over fences when 100/1-winner of Sandeman Chase (Handicap) at Liverpool in April: made all and clear throughout final circuit, scoring by 6 lengths from Tartan Tailor: out of his depth next outing (led until bad mistake eighth): stays 2½m: has form on heavy going, but evidently suited by top-of-the-ground: races freely and suited by forcing tactics (held up first 4 outings): has worn a crossed noseband and is taken quietly to post. *D. McCain.*

SUREST DANCER (USA) 4 b.c. Green Dancer (USA)–Oopsie Daisy (USA)
(Dewan) [1989/90 16g^{6} 16g^{5} 16g] sparely-made colt: modest staying maiden 85
on Flat: sold out of P. Walwyn's stable 8,000 gns Newmarket Autumn Sales: best effort in juvenile hurdles when fifth at Newcastle in December. *Mrs P. A. Barker.*

SURE WILL 5 b.g. Burslem–Wurli (Wolver Hollow) [1989/90 16m* 16s^{6} 20s^{4}
a16g^{4} 16d^{5}] smallish, sparely-made gelding: won handicap hurdle at Uttoxeter 98
in November: well beaten last 2 starts: seems not to stay 2½m: acts on good to firm and dead going: has worn a crossed noseband: has won for a claimer. *C. N. Allen.*

SUSAN HENCHARD 6 b.m. Auction Ring (USA)–Let Slip (Busted) [1989/90
16s 16g 16d^{4} 17f^{3} 16f^{2} 16d^{2} 16m] compact, workmanlike mare: novice hurdler: 78
placed in sellers in 1989/90: suited by a sharp 2m: acts on firm and dead going: often ridden by claimer: sold out of M. Avison's stable 2,300 gns Doncaster March Sales after fifth start. *M. F. Barraclough.*

SUSSEX OVERSEAS 8 b.g. Anax–Go Perrys (High Hat) [1989/90 a20g^{pu}]
small, sparely-made gelding: selling hurdler: no form for long time: stays 2½m —
(very stiff task at 3m): acts on soft going: has worn blinkers: has worn a tongue strap. *F. S. Jackson.*

SUVAMARVAL 8 gr.m. Suvarov–Mavala (Phebus) [1989/90 16m^{pu} 16d^{ur}]
workmanlike mare: of little account. *K. A. Linton.* —

SUZY LORENZO 5 b. or br.m. Swing Easy (USA)–Love Beach (Lorenzaccio)
[1989/90 18g a16g] big, lengthy mare: half-sister to smart 2m hurdler Jimmy —
Lorenzo (by Our Jimmy): poor maiden on Flat: tailed off in novice hurdles at Fontwell and Lingfield (blinkered): sold privately 2,000 gns Ascot February Sales. *P. R. Hedger.*

SVELTISSIMA 4 b.f. Dunphy–Night Vision (Yellow God) [1989/90 16f^{5} 16m^{3}
16g^{pu}] lengthy, workmanlike filly: half-sister to winning hurdler Tinkersfield (by 80
Tap On Wood): fair winning plater on Flat: third in juvenile hurdle at Market Rasen in September: behind when pulled up next start 6 months later. *G. R. Oldroyd.*

SVENGALIE 8 b.g. Miami Springs–Temple Queen (King Emperor (USA)) c—
[1989/90 c16d c20f^{pu}] lengthy, dipped-backed gelding: no form in point-to-points and hunter chases in Britain, though showed signs of ability on reappearance. *Lady R. Stuart-Wortley-Hunt.*

SWARDEAN 8 b.g. Le Coq d'Or–Katie Little (Nulli Secundus) [1989/90 c24d* **c129** ?
c24s^{5} c20s^{2} c28g^{4} c25m^{5}] lengthy, workmanlike gelding: fairly useful chaser: —
won handicap at Market Rasen in November by a distance, being left clear at the last: 15 lengths second to Sabin du Loir in intermediate chase at Haydock in January: stays 25f (didn't jump so fluently as usual when well beaten over 3½m): has run moderately on extremes of ground: headstrong and bolted before start 3 times in 1988/9. *R. Lee.*

SWEET BEN 5 ch.g. Sweet Monday–Oolywig (Copte (FR)) [1989/90 17g^{5}
22m] leggy gelding: well beaten in NH Flat races and novice hurdles (sweating —
final start): visored last outing 1988/9. *G. G. Gracey.*

SWEET CITY 5 ch.h. Sweet Monday–City's Sister (Maystreak) [1989/90 16g^{6}
16g^{6} 16g^{2} 20s^{2} 16s^{3}] workmanlike horse: fairly useful hurdler: ran well last 127
3 starts, on final one finishing 1½ lengths third behind Ganoon at Warwick in February: stays 2½m: acts on soft going (possibly unsuited by heavy): blinkered sixth start, visored last 4, in 1988/9: suitable mount for a claimer. *G. Richards.*

SWEET DIANA 11 b.m. Bivouac–Easter Tinkle (Hot Brandy) [1989/90 c25f^{2}] **c97**
leggy, sparely-made mare: useful hunter chaser at her best: 2 lengths second to —
As You Were at Warwick in May: stays well: acts on any going: front runner. *C. D. Dawson.*

SWEETEN GALE 4 ch.f. On Your Mark–Betty Bun (St Chad) [1989/90 16s^{pu}]
sparely-made filly: placed over 5f at 2 yrs: bandaged, tailed off when pulled up 3 —
out in juvenile hurdle at Market Rasen in January. *T. Kersey.*

SWEETING 5 b.g. Lighter–Snare (Poaching) [1989/90 F16f^{2} F16m^{5} 16d^{ro} 20f]
7,700 3-y-o: leggy, lengthy gelding: half-brother to winning hurdlers Unguarded —
(by Hasty Word) and Battue (by Precipice Wood) and to fair staying chaser
Salehurst (by Scallywag): dam poor novice hurdler: showed ability in NH Flat
races in October: always behind in novice hurdle at Doncaster in March. *J.
White.*

SWEET MARINER 4 ch.g. Julio Mariner–Sweet Bush (The Brianstan)
[1989/90 F16g] second reported foal: half-brother to novice hurdler Shernoake (by
Magnolia Lad): dam unraced: tailed off in NH Flat race at Fakenham in April: yet
to race over hurdles. *Miss A. L. M. King.*

SWEET NIAMH 7 br.m. Ovac (ITY)–Pre Shake (Prefairy) [1989/90 F16f^{3}
F17g^{3} F20d^{2} 16m^{bd} 20d^{6} 21d] sparely-made ex-Irish mare: first foal: dam winning —
Irish hurdler/chaser at up to 21f: won point-to-point in 1989: placed in early-
season NH Flat races when trained by F. O'Brien: showed a little ability in novice
hurdle at Kempton in November: tailed off at Warwick 4 months later. *F.
Sheridan.*

SWEET RASCAL 11 gr.m. Scallywag–Bitter Chimie (Bitter Sweet) [1989/90 c**93**
c26f c24m^{3} c25f* c24d^{pu}] neat mare: useful point-to-pointer, winner twice in —
March: successful in hunter chase at Cheltenham in May by 2½ lengths from
Macnab's Quest, leading 2 out: effective at 2½m and stays well: acts on any going.
M. A. Clutterbuck.

SWEET SIRENIA 8 br.m. Al Sirat (USA)–Sweet Imelda (Menelek) [1989/90 c— x
24g^{2} 22m^{5} c25g^{6} c24m a20g^{4} c22d^{pu}] leggy mare: poor novice hurdler/chaser: 73
stays well: poor jumper of fences: blinkered fourth start 1988/9. *Mrs A. E. Ratcliff.*

SWEET THURSDAY 4 ch.f. Sunley Builds–Adrift (Acrania) [1989/90 17f^{3}
16m^{6} 17g 16g^{6} 16m^{2} 20g] sparely-made filly: runner-up to very easy winner 72
Fisherman's Croft in selling hurdle at Nottingham in November, only form. *B.
Stevens.*

SWELL ROMANCE 5 b.g. Formidable (USA)–Geopelia (Raffingora)
[1989/90 a20g^{5}] smallish, lengthy gelding: bad maiden on Flat: tailed off in novice —
hurdle at Southwell in November. *J. L. Harris.*

SWIFT AFFAIR 5 gr.m. Hasty Word–Love Another (Grey Love) [1989/90
16g^{2} 16m 17f^{pu}] leggy, sparely-made mare: claimer ridden, second in selling 58
handicap hurdle at Stratford in March (trained by M. Eckley), only form: pulled up
lame last outing: blinkered last 2 starts. *D. J. Wintle.*

SWIFT ASCENT (USA) 8 b.g. Crow (FR)–Barely Flying (USA) (Fleet c**68**
Nasrullah) [1989/90 16f^{2} c16m^{5} c16f^{pu} 17m^{5} 16m^{2} 16g^{2}] tall, leggy gelding: selling 85
hurdler: good second to Atig in non-selling handicaps at Worcester in April and
May: last of 5 in novice event on chasing debut: form only at around 2m: acts on
firm going: suitable mount for a claimer. *A. Barrow.*

SWIFT CARRIAGE 4 br.f. Carriage Way–River Petterill (Another River)
[1989/90 F16g^{3} aF14g^{3} 16g^{6} 16g] fifth foal: half-sister to 3 winners by Move Off, —
including successful 2½m hurdler Megan's Move: dam fair performer at up to 9f:
third in NH Flat races at Edinburgh and Southwell: claimer ridden, showed some
promise in novice hurdle at Catterick in February: always behind in juvenile
claimer at Market Rasen following month. *J. M. Jefferson.*

SWIFT CHARLIE 5 br.g. Shua Jo–Bridport (Porto Bello) [1989/90 F16f]
second foal: half-brother to a poor animal by Sir Nulli: dam of little account: tailed
off in NH Flat race at Hereford in May: yet to race over hurdles or fences. *B. K.
Wells.*

SWIFT ENCOUNTER 11 b.g. Owen Dudley–Pop Gun (King's Troop) c— §
[1989/90 21f^{pu}] compact gelding: selling hurdler and novice chaser: stays 25f: acts — §
on any going: sometimes wears blinkers: claimer ridden nowadays: not one to
trust. *N. B. Thomson.*

SWIFT MELODY 9 b.m. Grange Melody–Spring Twilight (Panaslipper) c—
[1989/90 16f 22m^{6} 20s^{6} 16g 16m^{4} 16m^{4}] smallish, sparely-made mare: winning 87
hurdler/chaser: poor form over hurdles in 1989/90: will stay 3m: acts on heavy
going. *G. B. Balding.*

SWIFT WATERS 4 b.c. Sadler's Wells (USA)–Rapids (USA) (Head of The
River (USA)) [1989/90 16d^{3} 16g^{3} 16d* 16m* 16f* 16m] sturdy colt: maiden on 126

Spring Handicap Hurdle, Newbury—Swift Waters leads Softly over the last

Flat: won juvenile hurdles at Ludlow, Sandown and Newbury in March (last 2 handicaps), putting up a useful performance under top weight on last-named course: best form on firm ground: dead. *Mrs J. Pitman.*

SWINDLE BECK 6 ch.g. Deep Run–Castle River (Even Money) [1989/90 F16f] sixth foal: dam, half-sister to winning chaser Barony Fort, comes from successful jumping family: behind in NH Flat race at Catterick in October: yet to race over hurdles or fences. *W. A. Stephenson.*

SWINGING NOE JOE 4 b.g. Swing Easy (USA)–Palace Pet (Dragonara Palace (USA)) [1989/90 16g 16s5 17v] leggy gelding: placed at up to 7f on Flat: well beaten in juvenile hurdles: blinkered last start. *N. R. Mitchell.* —

SWING MY WAY 5 ch.h. Swing Easy (USA)–Concern (Brigadier Gerard) [1989/90 16gpu 16g 17dpu 16d] angular horse: of little account. *G. B. Balding.* —

SWING TO STEEL 8 ch.g. Most Secret–Staryllis Girl (Star Moss) [1989/90 c17f* c21f* c20fF] leggy, angular gelding: fair chaser: won at Newton Abbot in August and September: in lead when falling 2 out at Uttoxeter: stayed 21f: acted on any going: dead. *M. C. Pipe.* c**124** —

SWINHOE CROFT 8 b.g. Orange Bay–On A Bit (Mummy's Pet) [1989/90 c21s3 c24dpu] leggy gelding: winning hurdler/chaser/point-to-pointer: stayed on well when 3 lengths third to True Bloom in hunter chase at Towcaster in February: stays well: acts on heavy going: ran moderately in blinkers final start 1986/7. *J. S. Furnival.* c**106** —

SWIRL HOWE 10 ch.g. Tug of War–Couriette (Bleep-Bleep) [1989/90 c24g4] strong gelding: winning hurdler: fairly useful chaser: last of 4 finishers at Wetherby in January (collapsed and died after race): was suited by a good test of stamina: acted on soft going and probably unsuited by very firm. *W. A. Stephenson.* c— —

SWOOPING 5 b.g. Kings Lake (USA)–High Hawk (Shirley Heights) [1989/90 16g 16g3 20g3] lengthy, rather dipped-backed gelding: poor novice hurdler: fair third over 2½m at Plumpton in December. *J. R. Bosley.* 82

SWORD BEACH 6 ch.g. Scallywag–Bargello's Lady (Bargello) [1989/90 c20g2 c20g* c20m2 c20d2 c20d2 c20mF c20s* c20d* c20f* c20f* c24f3] leggy gelding: had a very good first season over fences, winning novice event and 2 c**122** —

Racing Post Novices' Chase Series Final (Handicap), Newbury—eventual winner Sword Beach (No. 4) jumps the water alongside Trigpoint Charlie

handicaps at Sedgefield, Racing Post Novices' Chase Series Final (Handicap) at Newbury and Bollinger Champagne Novices' Chase (Handicap) at Ascot: made most to beat Comandante 30 lengths in last-named event in April: suited by 2½m: acts on any going: visored sixth start in 1988/9: jumps soundly. *M. H. Easterby.*

SWORD EDGE 13 ch.g. Sharpen Up–Coulter Belle (Quorum) [1989/90 27s^{pu} c**76**
c26s^{6} c28g^{pu} c25h^{2} c25m^{3} c26f^{4} c26f^{2}] small gelding: poor novice hurdler/ —
chaser: stays 3¼m: acts on hard ground: blinkered once. *T. Reid.*

SYBILLIN 4 b.g. Henbit (USA)–Tea House (Sassafras (FR)) [1989/90
16f* 16f* 16d* 16m^{2} 18d^{5} 17g^{2} 16m 16m* 16f* 18g^{3} 20g] 138

The best juvenile hurdler award goes to Sybillin, who improved out of all recognition to win the Glenlivet Anniversary Hurdle at Liverpool in April on his eighth start and confirmed the improvement by following up in the valuable Swinton Insurance Trophy at Haydock in May. Just why Sybillin should have improved so dramatically at that stage of his career is impossible to work out from the form-book, but improve he certainly did. By Liverpool Sybillin seemed fairly well exposed. He'd started off by winning three small races at Market Rasen in August, then had been beaten four times, including in handicaps off an official mark of 96, 96 again and 105 respectively. His best effort in the handicaps had been his head second to Los Buccaneros at Doncaster in February on his sixth start. Next time he'd finished unplaced, eased when beaten going to the last, behind Rouyan in a well-contested race at Newcastle. So Sybillin started at 25/1 for the Glenlivet Anniversary Hurdle in a field of eighteen which included five horses who'd figured prominently behind Rare Holiday in the Daily Express

Swinton Insurance Trophy, Haydock—Sybillin touches down over the last ahead of Vestris Abu (right) and Windbound Lass (partially hidden)

Triumph Hurdle at Cheltenham—Sybillin's much shorter-priced stable-companion Native Friend (third), Vestris Abu (fourth), Sayyure (sixth), Midfielder (eighth) and Bally Rue (ninth). A slow gallop early on resulted in the field staying well bunched for some way. Sybillin moved up to track the leading trio of Bally Rue, Sayyure and Native Friend from halfway, and when Sayyure dropped away on the home turn he was left a close third. Shamirani, Swift Waters and Cornet all threatened briefly at the third last, but the leading trio had pulled away again by the next. Sybillin overtook the tiring Bally Rue after that flight and had just headed Native Friend at the last when the latter fell fatally. Sybillin, who was getting the better of Native Friend anyway, was left well clear on the flat and, pushed out with hands and heels, recorded an eight-length victory over Midfielder, who put in his best work at the finish, with Bally Rue a short head away in third. Incidentally, there were no pictorial records to be had of this important race—the professional photographers attending the meeting were in dispute with the track management, and staged a strike for the duration of the one event.

Four-year-olds running in the Swinton Insurance Hurdle at Haydock had been thin on the ground prior to the latest season, largely because only the best of them had been good enough to get in the handicap. In a non-vintage edition in 1990 the four-year-olds were represented by Vestris Abu, winner of the BMW Champion Novice Hurdle at Punchestown after finishing well behind at Liverpool, and Philosophos, as well as Sybillin. All three seemed to have been well treated by the handicapper and all gave a good account of themselves. Vestris Abu set a searing gallop, soon held a clear advantage, and beginning the turn out of the back straight it seemed he'd stolen the race, so far was he clear of Imperial Brush, Philosophos, Sybillin and the rest. He began to tire after jumping the third last, but still managed to hold on to his lead until the last, where he was closely followed by Sybillin, Windbound Lass, Persillant and Philosophos with the weakening Imperial Brush still well clear of the remainder in sixth. Sybillin took the lead early on the run-in and gamely held off all challengers to score by three quarters of a length from Windbound Lass, becoming the first of his age to win the event. Vestris Abu, who stuck most doggedly to his task, was a length further back in third, Persillant fourth and Philosophos fifth. Market leaders Sayparee and Kadan were never in the hunt and both were pulled up

Marquesa de Moratalla's "Sybillin"

seemingly lame. Despite the prominence of the juveniles, the result doesn't indicate that they were a particularly good bunch in 1989/90; on the contrary, it suggests they were not, as the three in the Swinton Insurance, all clearly among the best of their age, had relatively low handicap marks. Sybillin's season was far from over and he was sent to France to contest races at Auteuil at the end of May and early June. In the first of them, the two-and-a-quarter-mile Prix de Longchamp, he again acquitted himself well, finishing a close third to Bleu Roi; but when well fancied in the two-and-a-half-mile Prix Alain du Breil he finished last of twelve, reportedly pulling too hard.

Sybillin (b.g. 1986)	Henbit (USA) (b 1977)	Hawaii (b 1964)	Utrillo II
			Ethane
		Chateaucreek (ch 1970)	Chateaugay
			Mooncreek
	Tea House (ch 1980)	Sassafras (b 1967)	Sheshoon
			Ruta
		House Tie (b 1975)	Be Friendly
			Mesopotamia

A 15,500-guinea purchase as a foal, Sybillin ran seven times on the Flat, showing modest form when winning a mile maiden at Edinburgh as a two-year-old. He finished well beaten otherwise. He is the second foal of useful Irish six-furlong and one-mile winner Tea House. The dam's first foal Mr Sunday Sport (a brother to Sybillin) was successful over six and seven furlongs as a two-year-old here and subsequently won several races in Italy. Tea House is one of several winners produced by House Tie, the pick of them being the very useful French mile-to-mile-and-a-quarter performer

Academic and fairly useful sprinter Bag O'Rhythm. House Tie, an Irish one-mile winner, is a daughter of the high-class two-year-old Mesopotamia. Sybillin's sire Henbit, the 1980 Derby winner, is also responsible for Champion Hurdler Kribensis. Sybillin, like Kribensis, possesses a good turn of foot; he is unlikely to stay much beyond two and a quarter miles, so we'd be inclined not to be disappointed with his last run. Though a winner on good to soft going, he has shown much his best form on a firm surface. A rather sparely-made type in appearance, Sybillin probably lacks the scope to make up into a leading hurdler, but he jumps well and should be able to win more races in handicap company. *J. G. FitzGerald.*

SYRUS P TURNTABLE 4 b.g. King of Spain–Lizabeth Chudleigh (Imperial
Fling (USA)) [1989/90 16m] close-coupled, angular gelding: 6f winner at 2 yrs, —
placed over 1m at 3 yrs: sold out of C. Tinkler's stable 2,700 gns Ascot August
Sales: 66/1, tailed off in juvenile claimer at Ludlow in November on hurdling
debut. *M. A. Clutterbuck.*

T

TABACOS 7 ch.g. Sagaro–Shere Beauty (Mummy's Pet) [1989/90 17g 16d^{3} 20d c**86**
a16g^{5} c17m^{5} c17f^{2} c17m^{4} c16m^{3}] leggy, sparely-made gelding: poor novice 82
hurdler (has run in selling company): ridden by 3-lb claimer when placed over
fences late in season: seems to stay 21f: acts on firm ground. *W. G. Turner.*

TABELLINA 6 ch.m. Tina's Pet–Abielle (Abwah) [1989/90 c16v c20d^{6} c16v^{3} c**89**
c16d c24f^{6}] big mare: modest novice hurdler/chaser: likely to prove best at 2m: —
best form on a yielding surface: usually blinkered. *D. R. C. Elsworth.*

TABERNA LORD 9 b.g. Le Coq d'Or–Norwich Girl (Green God) [1989/90 c— x
22m 21d 25f^{bd} 25m 20f^{6}] compact gelding: smart staying hurdler at his best: no —
form in 1989/90, though well backed in valuable handicaps on third and fourth
starts: won novice chase in 1987/8: let down by his jumping over fences since:
stays 25f: has won on soft going but best form on a sound surface: visored final
outing. *A. J. Wilson.*

TACHADOR 9 ch.g. Tachypous–Adored (Aggressor) [1989/90 22m a20g 16s^{F}] c—
smallish, stocky, plain gelding: amateur ridden, slight lead when falling last in 102
selling handicap hurdle at Folkestone in December: fell third on chasing debut:
stays 3m: acts on heavy going: not a fluent jumper: has run creditably for a
claimer. *R. J. Hodges.*

TA CHANCE 4 ch.f. On Your Mark–Telstop (FR) (Fine Top) [1989/90 16f^{2} 16f^{3}
a16g^{pu}] small, lightly-made filly: placed at up to 6f at 2 yrs and in early-season 82
juvenile hurdles: pulled up lame in claimer in November. *William Price.*

TACTICO 8 b.g. Deep Run–Astereen (Brave Invader (USA)) [1989/90 c16m^{pu} c**123**
c16m^{4} c16g^{3} c16d^{4} c16g^{3} c16d^{5} c17g^{5} c17g* c20g c17d^{2} c16s^{2} c16v^{F} c16g^{2} c16d^{2} c16s* —
c16m^{ur} c16g* c16g* c16g* c16m^{3}] leggy, close-coupled gelding: fair chaser: had a
good season and won at Kelso in December, Wetherby in February, Perth in April
and Bangor and Perth in May: best at around 2m: acts on any going: has worn
bandages: best in blinkers: trained by W. Fairgrieve until after ninth outing: tough
and consistent. *J. J. O'Neill.*

TADBIR 5 b.g. Try My Best (USA)–La Grange (Habitat) [1989/90 16m^{6} 16g^{5} c§§
16s^{6} 16d^{3} 16g^{4} a16g^{5} c16g c21d^{F} c16g^{ur} c21g^{r} 17f^{r} 17f^{r}] leggy, close-coupled §§
gelding: novice selling hurdler/novice chaser: refused in early stages last 3 starts:
blinkered final outing: thorough jade: sold out of W. Musson's stable 5,700 gns
Doncaster January Sales after sixth start. *M. C. Chapman.*

TAFFY JONES 11 br.g. Welsh Pageant–Shallow Stream (Reliance II) [1989/90 c**110**
c16f* c17f^{3} c17f* c16h^{2} c16m^{2} c16m^{3} c18f^{2} c16d^{2} c16d* c16g^{F} c16g^{5} c16f^{4} c17h* 94
20g^{4}] handicap chaser: won at Market Rasen (twice) and Devon & Exeter early in
season, and at Devon & Exeter again in May: ran creditably in handicap hurdle
final start: stays 2½m: acts on hard and dead ground: tends to jump to the right:
visored seventh start 1988/9: goes well for claimer C. Maude. *M. McCormack.*

TAFTAZANI (USA) 5 b.h. Roberto (USA)–La Toulzanie (FR) (Sanctus II)
[1989/90 20f^{4} 20f] leggy horse: modest novice hurdler: better effort in March 91
on first start: stays 2½m: acts on firm and dead going: ran moderately when
blinkered once in 1988/9. *R. J. Holder.*

TAGLIO DE CHAMPFEU (FR) 5 ch.g. Pamponi (FR)–Gazelle Blonde
(FR) (Cris Kraft) [1989/90 F16m^{4} F12g 20g 16s] leggy gelding: dam won at up to 72
10.5f: fourth in NH Flat race at Huntingdon in October: poor form in novice
hurdles at Plumpton in December: sold 1,450 gns Ascot April Sales. *R. Curtis.*

TAGMOUN CHAUFOUR (FR) 5 ch.g. Pavo Real (FR)–Bien Venue (FR)
(Popof) [1989/90 20s^{pu} 16g 21d 21d 24d^{6} 21m^{pu}] small, plain gelding: poor form in 72
novice hurdles: doesn't stay 3m: possibly unsuited by top-of-the-ground. *A.
Barrow.*

TAGRED 5 b. or br.g. The Parson–Merry Memories (Anthony) [1989/90
F16v^{3}] seventh foal: brother to fair hurdler Hearn's Hotel and half-brother to
winning chaser Espeut (by March Parade): dam from successful jumping family:
12 lengths third behind Pameva in NH Flat race at Haydock in March: yet to race
over hurdles or fences. *D. J. G. Murray-Smith.*

TAIMEITUK 5 ch.g. Main Reef–Romantic Love (Sovereign Path) [1989/90
20m] smallish, workmanlike gelding: winning hurdler: tailed off only outing of
season (December): stays 3m: acts on firm ground (ran badly on soft): has run in —
snatches and looked a difficult ride. *I. P. Wardle.*

TAJROBA (USA) 5 b.g. Solford (USA)–You're So Vain (USA) (Pardallo II)
[1989/90 16f^{pu} 16f^{2} 20f* 20d* 20m^{2} 20g*] tall, leggy gelding: improved hurdler 120
who won novice events at Uttoxeter, Kempton and Wolverhampton (beat
Mayoran ¾ length in quite well-contested event) in first half of season: unlikely
to stay much beyond 2½m: possibly unsuited by very soft ground, acts on any
other: has won for a claimer and when sweating (on toes at Wolverhampton). *J. R.
Jenkins.*

TAKE A LIBERTY 5 ch.m. Aragon–Liberty Tree (Dominion) [1989/90 16g^{5}
16m^{5} 20m] small, sparely-made filly: poor novice hurdler: well beaten in 2½m 65
selling handicap. *Miss S. J. Wilton.*

TAKEAWAY 4 ch.g. Ivotino (USA)–Come On Doll (True Song) [1989/90
aF16g^{6} aF16g] second foal: brother to Ivordoll, winner on Flat and (at 2½m) over
hurdles: dam ran once: unplaced in NH Flat races at Lingfield: sold 1,000 gns
Ascot May Sales: yet to race over hurdles. *J. White.*

TAKE ISSUE 5 b.g. Absalom–Abstract (French Beige) [1989/90 16m^{5} 16d 16s
16s^{6} a16g* 18f] workmanlike gelding: won claiming hurdle at Lingfield in March: 105
probably stays 2½m: seems to act on any going: visored final start (ran moderately). *J. Sutcliffe.*

*Perthshire Memories Handicap Chase, Perth—the principals, left to right,
Straight Down (third), Tactico (winner), Pura Money (fourth) and Marejo (second)*

TAKE NO TRASH 9 b.g. Deep Run–Karolette (Konigssee) [1989/90 c24gF c24gr 27s2 24g a20g4 a20g6 21d5 24m5] sturdy, rather angular gelding: winning hurdler: no worthwhile form in steeplechases (refused 3 out second outing): stays well: acts on heavy going. *B. Byford.* c— 94

TAKES IT NEAT 5 b.g. Tachypous–Pickled (Pitcairn) [1989/90 20d] angular, workmanlike gelding: has a round action: little sign of ability on Flat: behind in novice hurdle at Worcester: sold 925 gns Ascot February Sales. *D. J. Wintle.* —

TAKE YOUR PICK 5 b. or br.m. Gorytus (USA)–Takealetter (Wolver Hollow) [1989/90 16g] sparely-made mare: no promise in 2 races over hurdles, latest a seller: sold out of P. Blockley's stable 1,150 gns Doncaster September Sales: resold 1,200 gns Doncaster January Sales. *Mrs A. Chippendale.* —

TALAB 5 b.g. Beldale Flutter (USA)–Glen Dancer (Furry Glen) [1989/90 16m 16s 16g 16v6 a16g3 16f*] leggy gelding: won selling hurdle at Plumpton in March, making much of running (no bid): other form only on previous start: acts on firm going: blinkered fourth start. *J. V. Redmond.* 75

TALATON FLYER 4 b.g. Kala Shikari–Pertune (Hyperion's Curls) [1989/90 17m2 17m* 17h4] third live foal: dam poor novice hurdler/chaser: won juvenile hurdle at Newton Abbot in May (second run in 2 days): well beaten in handicap at Devon & Exeter later in month: unlikely to stay much beyond 2m. *P. J. Hobbs.* 82

TALKING MONEY 6 ch.g. Quayside–Shuil Alainn (Levanter) [1989/90 20spu] won NH Flat race in 1989: ridden by 3-lb claimer, jumped less than fluently but travelled well for a long way in Golden Miller Novices' Hurdle at Leicester in February (eased once beaten and was eventually pulled up 2 out): should improve. *G. B. Balding.* — p

TALK NO TRASH 6 ch.g. Deep Run–Woodlore (Le Tricolore) [1989/90 c16g6 c24d c24gpu] rangy ex-Irish gelding: half-brother to winning Irish point-to-pointers Laurel Wood (by Laurence O) and Golden Ochra (by General Ironside): dam unraced: runner-up in point-to-point: no form in novice chases. *C. R. Beever.* c—

TALLAND FREESPIRIT 10 gr.g. Rugantino–My Orphaleine (Spiritus) [1989/90 c22mpu] poor maiden point-to-pointer: tailed off when pulled up in novice hunter chase at Stratford. *W. B. Hutton.* c—

TALUS 6 gr.g. Kalaglow–Helcia (Habitat) [1989/90 16m] leggy, lengthy, angular gelding: lightly-raced winning hurdler: tailed off only outing of season (November): stays 21f: acts on firm going: blinkered once in 1987/8. *J. R. Bosley.* —

TAMERTOWN LAD 9 b.g. Creetown–Gay Tamarind (Tamerlane) [1989/90 17m4 16f5 c17g5 c16m4 c16gur c16g3 c16g* c16d4 c16f c20m c16m3 c17m4] compact gelding: selling hurdler: won conditional jockeys selling handicap chase at Catterick in January (no bid): ran poorly afterwards: seems best at around 2m: acts on hard ground. *A. W. Potts.* c75 —

TAMINO 9 b.g. Tap On Wood–Pamina (Brigadier Gerard) [1989/90 c20g4 c24f4 c20dF c24g2 c21m* c21gpu c20mpu] close-coupled, rather sparely-made gelding: handicap chaser: won at Windsor in January despite hanging badly left entering straight: found little under pressure previous outing and ran in snatches second start: stays 3m: probably acts on any going: blinkered last 6 outings. *Mrs L. Clay.* c**107** —

TAM'S ARIA 8 b.g. True Song–Tamoretta (Chamossaire) [1989/90 a24g4] leggy gelding: winning point-to-pointer: well beaten in novice hurdles. *Mrs E. H. Heath.* —

TANCRED SAND 7 ch.g. Nicholas Bill–Another Move (Farm Walk) [1989/90 16g* 16d4 16g] lengthy, sparely-made gelding: quite useful hurdler: won handicap at Ayr in December: stayed 2½m: acted on heavy going: visored final start: dead. *J. M. Jefferson.* 129

TANG 5 ch.g. Mansingh (USA)–Great Blue White (Great Nephew) [1989/90 18spu 22f*] smallish, sparely-made gelding: favourite, first form over hurdles when winning 5-runner conditional jockeys selling handicap at Fontwell in April by 15 lengths, making all (no bid): formerly moderate jumper: stays 2¾m: acts on firm ground: trained first outing (January) by T. Hallett. *R. Akehurst.* 84

TANG DYNASTY 5 b.g. Artaius (USA)–Favant (Faberge II) [1989/90 20gpu 20mpu] leggy gelding: probably of little account: blinkered final start. *S. R. Bowring.* —

TANGLED STRING 6 b.g. Idiot's Delight–Heartstring (Fortissimo) [1989/90 21f6 20f6] leggy gelding: novice hurdler: variable form: stays 2½m: ran poorly on soft ground: has looked headstrong (wore dropped noseband in 1989/90). *D. R. C. Elsworth.* 99 ?

TANNINGTON 7 b.g. Deep Run–Kertina (Fortina) [1989/90 c24g^{6}] sparely-made gelding: tailed off in 2 novice hurdles and a novice chase (backward and sweating). *G. A. Hubbard.* c— —

TANTALITE 5 b. or br.m. Tanfirion–Capricorn Lady (Persian Bold) [1989/90 21f^{4}] smallish, lightly-made ex-Irish mare: first foal: dam poor Irish maiden: placed over 1½m on Flat in 1988: tailed off both outings over hurdles: sold 825 gns Ascot December Sales. *M. Oliver.* —

TANWORTH 5 ch.m. Stetchworth (USA)–Fotopan (Polyfoto) [1989/90 F16s F12g] second foal: dam winning 2m hurdler in Ireland: backward, well beaten in NH Flat races at Warwick and Market Rasen: yet to race over hurdles or fences. *Mrs V. C. Ward.*

TAP DANCING 4 ch.g. Sallust–Amorak (Wolver Hollow) [1989/90 16d^{2} 16f^{F} 16m^{3} 16m^{3} 16s a16g^{6} 16f^{3} 16m^{4}] close-coupled gelding: plating-class maiden on Flat: dropped in class, in frame in selling handicap hurdles last 2 starts: best form on top-of-the-ground: trained until after third start by R. Casey. *M. O'Neill.* 81

TAPLYCH D'AIRY (FR) 5 b.g. Lychee (FR)–Capeline (FR) (Noe) [1989/90 16f^{pu}] sturdy gelding: bit backward and wearing crossed noseband, tailed off when pulled up fifth in novice hurdle at Wolverhampton in March on debut. *J. Webber.* —

TAPSTER LAD 6 b.g. Strong Gale–Tip Your Toes (Prince Tenderfoot (USA)) [1989/90 16g] lengthy gelding: has been hobdayed: no form in novice hurdles, but showed signs of ability at Kempton in November. *N. J. Henderson.* —

TAPSTER VALLEY 7 br.m. Politico (USA)–Game Reward (Game Rights) [1989/90 16g] lengthy mare: fourth in NH Flat race in 1988: edgy in preliminaries, pulled very hard and weakened quickly from fifth in novice hurdle at Towcester in December: needs to settle. *C. C. Trietline.* —

TARA BOY 5 b.h. Rusticaro (FR)–Flosshilde (Rheingold) [1989/90 20m 19g^{6} 17m^{6} 20g^{4} 22m^{4} 16s c16m a20g^{6} c20f^{5} c24f^{4} c20g c20g^{2} c26f^{F}] leggy horse: poor novice hurdler/chaser: stays 3m: acts on firm ground: blinkered final start 1988/9. *R. B. Francis.* **c79** 90

TARAHUMARA 8 b.m. Soldier Rose–Cover Your Money (Precipice Wood) [1989/90 20m c21g^{3} c24d^{F}] leggy, sparely-made mare: winning hurdler/chaser: well beaten in 1989/90: unlikely to stay beyond 2½m: acts on heavy going: poor jumper. *J. T. Gifford.* c— x —

TARATONG 4 b.f. Bold Fort–Lucinski (Malinowski (USA)) [1989/90 16d 16d 16f 16f a16g] smallish, workmanlike filly: of little account. *K. White.* —

TARCOLA 11 b.g. Tarqogan–Game Hen (Choral Society) [1989/90 c24g^{pu}] workmanlike gelding: won a point-to-point in 1986: poor maiden hurdler/steeplechaser. *Mrs T. J. McInnes Skinner.* c— —

TARCONEY 10 ch.g. Celtic Cone–Tarqoretta (Tarqogan) [1989/90 c27g^{6} c32v^{2} c29g^{5} c20d^{6} c25s^{3} c25m^{2} c21m* c29f^{6} c25f^{3}] angular, workmanlike gelding: fairly useful chaser: won handicap at Towcester in April: most creditable sixth behind Mr Frisk in Whitbread Gold Cup (Handicap Chase) at Sandown later in month (slightly hampered 3 out): stays well: acts on any going: sometimes sweats: suited by a stiff track and has gained his 3 other wins over fences at Sandown: ran out fourth start 1988/9. *P. D. Cundell.* c**126** —

TARKOVSKY 5 b.g. Moorestyle–Fallen Rose (Busted) [1989/90 16d* 20d^{4} 20s^{3} 25g a20g^{4} 16v^{5} 16s^{5} 16f 16m^{5}] compact, workmanlike gelding: won novice hurdle at Chepstow in November: below his best in second half of season, giving impression now needs stiffer test of stamina: stays 2½m: acts on soft going. *R. Lee.* 97

TARLOGIE 4 b.g. Touching Wood (USA)–Soft Chinook (USA) (Hitting Away) [1989/90 16f^{6} 16f 16f^{5} 16m^{4} 17f 27s 16h^{2} 16h^{3} 24d 16f^{6}] smallish, angular gelding: plater on Flat, stays 1½m: selling hurdler: best efforts at 2m on hard ground: trained first 6 starts by S. Muldoon: sold to race in Ireland 2,300 gns Doncaster Spring Sales. *J. H. Johnson.* 75

TARMON LASS 4 b.f. What A Guest–Turiana (USA) (Citation) [1989/90 16g^{4} 16s^{2} 16d^{4} 16f^{4} 16g^{ur} 16g^{4}] ex-Irish filly: half-sister to winning stayer On Her Own (by Busted) and winning hurdler Turi (by Welsh Pageant): dam, winner at up to 7f, half-sister to Kentucky Derby and Preakness Stakes winner Forward Pass: placed at up to 1½m on Flat: in frame in early-season juvenile hurdles, when trained by K. Connolly: off course 5 months after fourth start: ran moderately in seller at Market Rasen final outing: blinkered fourth start. *J. Parkes.* 82 ?

TARN 12 b.g. Deep Run–Rambling (Wrekin Rambler) [1989/90 c20f^{ur} c16f^{2} c16m^{F} c20g^{5} c21m^{pu}] sparely-made gelding: has been hobdayed: fair chaser: ran moderately last 2 starts (off course 2 months before each): stays 2½m: acts on any going: races up with the pace: good mount for a claimer: usually goes well fresh. *N. A. Gaselee.* **c124** —

TARPROMISE 10 b.g. Tarqogan–Let's Compromise (No Argument) [1989/90 16m^{6} 16m^{3} 17f^{2} 21m* 21m^{5}] workmanlike, good-bodied gelding: winning chaser: won handicap hurdle at Devon & Exeter in September: well beaten in novice event a week later (started slowly): stays 21f: acts on firm ground: races freely: has worn a severe bridle. *D. J. Wintle.* c— 73

TARQOGAN'S BEST 10 bl.g. Tarqogan–Balldado (Harwell) [1989/90 c20g* 23f*] tall, leggy gelding: won selling handicap chase at Bangor (bought in 4,250 gns) and claiming hurdle at Cartmel in May: stays 3m: acts on any going: blinkered twice and visored once in 1988/9 (refused 3 times that season). *M. C. Pipe.* **c123** § 105 §

TARTAN TABARD 8 b.g. Le Bavard (FR)–Serrulata (Raise You Ten) [1989/90 c20s^{2} c24v^{6} c24v^{F} c16d^{5} c17g^{pu} c26g^{pu}] tall, leggy gelding: winning hurdler: second in novice chase at Ayr in January: let down by his jumping afterwards: pulled up and dismounted on final start: needs very testing conditions at around 2m, and probably stays 3m: acts on heavy going: below form when amateur ridden. *G. Richards.* **c93** x —

TARTAN TAILOR 9 b.g. Patch–Court Time (Arctic Time) [1989/90 16g^{3} c16g* 16g^{F} c20m^{2} c20d^{ur} c16g*] tall, close-coupled gelding: fairly useful hurdler/chaser: won over fences at Wetherby (handicap) in November and Perth (minor event) in April: 6 lengths second to Sure Metal in quite valuable handicap at Liverpool in between: stays 2½m: probably acts on any going: has found little under pressure. *G. Richards.* **c131** + 123

TARTAN TAKEOVER 8 b.g. Tycoon II–Tina Fort (Fortina) [1989/90 c24g* c27s^{pu} c24s* c20v* c33d^{2}] **c130**

The Timeform Chase at Haydock in March attracted a disappointing field. In the past the race has been a stepping-stone to Cheltenham: both Little Owl and Forgive'N Forget won the Timeform Chase and the Gold Cup in the same year, and the 1989 winner Southern Minstrel went down by half

Timeform Chase, Haydock—Tartan Takeover (left) stays on to win the latest edition of this valuable event, from Formula One (centre) and Feile Na Hinse

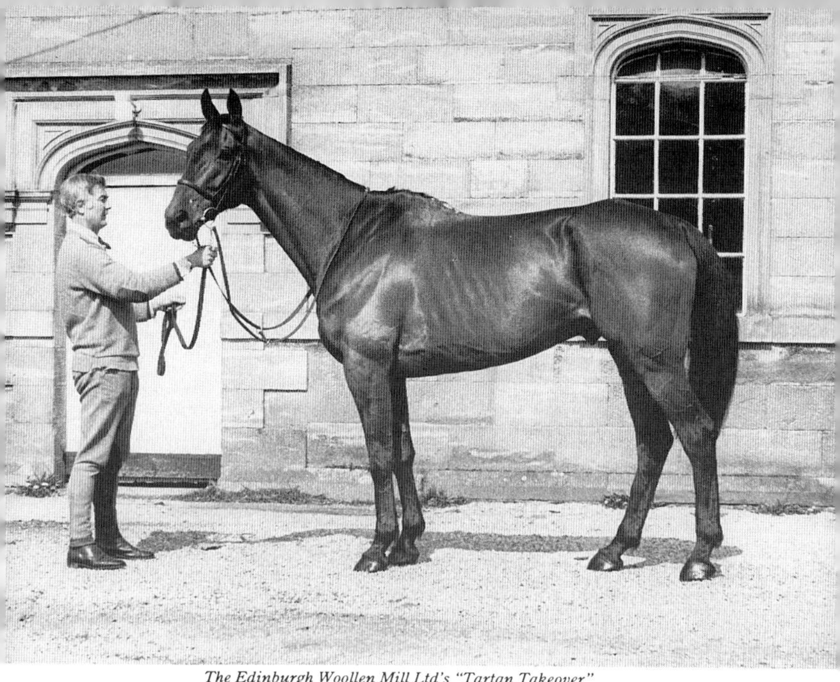

The Edinburgh Woollen Mill Ltd's "Tartan Takeover"

a length to Waterloo Boy in the Arkle. The latest edition of the Timeform Chase—won by Tartan Takeover—lost much of its significance when it suffered the major defection of Carvill's Hill. Among the other five-day entries Hennessy winner Ghofar was kept in the South for the Geoffrey Gilbey Memorial Chase at Newbury whilst Willsford tackled the Greenall Whitley Gold Cup—the next race on the Haydock card and won by Tartan Takeover's stable-companion Rinus after Willsford's last-fence fall. Of the five that went to post for the Timeform Chase the novice Blazing Walker stood out on form, but ran poorly, and Only Trouble fell having set a modest pace to the eleventh. Tartan Takeover made a number of mistakes but began to stay on strongly when niggled along entering the straight, collared Formula One and Feile Na Hinse at the last and stayed on well to win by four lengths.

Tartan Takeover's victory in the Timeform Chase was the most notable of the season for his owners the Edinburgh Woollen Mill Ltd. The firm has run horses since 1982 and a good deal of publicity has been generated by the exploits of Tartan Tailor (winner of the Waterford Crystal Supreme Novices' Hurdle), Randolph Place, The Langholm Dyer and Tartan Trader. It also maintains an extensive programme of race sponsorship. In the latest season Edinburgh Woollen Mill finished ninth in the owners' table for win prize money, sixth for total prize money won and fourth for number of races won, with eighteen victories. Prior to Haydock Tartan Takeover had contributed two successes, winning handicap chases at Ayr in November and Nottingham in February. Tartan Takeover wasn't sent on to Cheltenham. On his only subsequent outing he finished an excellent, staying-on fifteen-length second to stable-companion Four Trix in the William Hill Scottish National at Ayr, 6 lb out of the handicap.

Tartan Takeover (b.g. 1982)	Tycoon II (b 1962)	Tamerlane (br 1952)	Persian Gulf
			Eastern Empress
		Djebel Idra (b 1957)	Phil Drake
			Djebellica
	Tina Fort (b 1963)	Fortina (ch 1941)	Formor
			Bertina
		Ceylon Queen (b or br 1954)	King Hal
			Ceylon Cottage

Tartan Takeover is a big, rangy gelding. He needs give in the ground and acts well on heavy going. He reportedly suffered from sore shins after being pulled up on rain-softened ground at Ayr in December—although the going was soft his trainer claimed that the considerable bulk of the horse had taken him through to the firmer ground below the surface. Given suitable conditions he's effective at two and a half miles and he stays very well. As a novice he won for an amateur. Tartan Takeover's pedigree was fully examined in *Chasers & Hurdlers 1988/89*. He's a half-brother to three winners out of the moderate staying chaser Tina Fort. *G. Richards.*

TARTAN TEMPEST 7 br.g. Crozier–Frello (Bargello) [1989/90 c20g^{bd} **c101** x
c20g^{4} c24d* c24d^{4} c24d^{ur} c24d^{2} c21d^{4} c24g^{4}] well-made gelding: winning —
hurdler: none too fluent a jumper of fences but won novice event at Hexham in December: stays 3m: acts on heavy going. *G. Richards.*

TARTAN TORCHLIGHT 10 b.g. Brave Invader (USA)–Outdoor Girl (Blue c—
Chariot) [1989/90 c20m^{5}] lengthy gelding: winning hurdler/chaser: stays 2½m: —
acts on soft going: sketchy jumper: sold 7,000 gns Doncaster October Sales: runner-up in a point-to-point in March. *G. Richards.*

TARTAN TRADEMARK 8 ch.g. Deep Run–Golden Shuil (Master Owen) **c121**
[1989/90 c21g^{2} c20g^{5} c20g* c20d* c20s^{4} c24g* c25g* c25g^{5} c24m^{F} c20f* —
c22m^{pu} c20m^{4}] rather leggy gelding: fair front-running chaser: had fine season: won at Carlisle, Ayr, Kelso, Catterick and Hexham in 1989/90: effective at 2½m and stays 25f: acts on any going: broke blood vessel second and last 2 outings. *G. Richards.*

TARTAN TRIX 7 b.g. Pitpan–Blue Trix (Blue Chariot) [1989/90 22d c20g^{2} **c107** p
c26s^{3} c24d* c25s*] workmanlike gelding: winning hurdler: on the upgrade over —
fences: won novice event at Leicester in January and novice handicap at Sandown (finished tired) following month: best at up to 3m: acts on soft going: has worn a crossed noseband: sound jumper: should improve again. *Mrs J. Pitman.*

TARTEVIE 12 b.g. Tarqogan–Tevie (Le Levanstell) [1989/90 c25f^{5} c24f^{3} **c101**
c24d* c32f*] smallish, lengthy gelding: won a point-to-point in April: subsequently won hunter chases at Ayr (by 20 lengths) and Cheltenham (by a neck from Freddie Teal), latter event for second year running: suited by a thorough test of stamina: acts on any going: game. *Major M. W. Sample.*

TARVILLE 12 b.g. Woodville II–Stella's Art (Le Levanstell) [1989/90 20m **c95**
28g* c24d*] leggy, lightly-made gelding: fair point-to-pointer: won handicap 89
hurdle at Nottingham in October and handicap chase at Worcester following month: stays well: best on an easy surface: blinkered once in 1984/5. *J. Parfitt.*

TASAR 9 gr.g. Pongee–Foreign Bird (Lauso) [1989/90 c24f* c24f* c24m* **c122**
c24g* c24f^{2} c24d^{5} c20g^{5}] strong gelding: fair chaser: won twice at Kelso in —
October and twice at Hexham following month: first race for 4 months, well below his best final start: probably stays 3½m: acts on any going: usually wears blinkers (didn't final outing): has won for an amateur: makes mistakes on occasions. *W. A. Stephenson.*

TASHONYA 8 b.g. Grundy–Explorelka (Relko) [1989/90 16m^{5} 16g 16g 25d^{5}
16m^{2} 16g] lightly-made gelding: winning hurdler: creditable second in seller at 82
Ludlow in November: ran poorly in non-seller following month: probably stays 2½m: acts on any going except heavy: sometimes blinkered: sometimes sweats up: has seemed unreliable. *B. K. Wells.*

TASKALADY 4 b.f. Touching Wood (USA)–Damaska (USA) (Damascus
(USA)) [1989/90 17d^{5} 17v^{4} 18v^{3} 16d 18f^{6}] sparely-made filly: 11f seller winner on 55
Flat: sold out of M. Brittain's stable 2,000 gns Doncaster November Sales: poor juvenile selling hurdler: well beaten last 2 starts. *Mrs A. Knight.*

TAU 5 ch.g. Kambalda–Mystry Tour (Master Buck) [1989/90 c20f^{5}] first foal: dam lightly-raced Irish maiden: in frame in 2 point-to-points in April: well beaten in novice hunter chase at Folkestone in May. *Lady Harmsworth-Blunt.* c—

TAUREAN TYCOON 6 b.g. Octogenarian–Eastling (Tycoon II) [1989/90 16d a18g^{pu}] angular, lightly-made gelding: first foal: dam of no account over hurdles: no sign of ability in 2 races on Flat at 3 yrs: little promise in novice hurdles. *D. L. Williams.* —

TAVERN TIME 9 br.g. Pitpan–My Copper (Sunacelli) [1989/90 c20g^{pu} c17d^{6} c16f^{5} c16m] rangy, workmanlike gelding: winning hurdler/chaser in Ireland: no worthwhile form in Britain: stays 2¼m: seems best on an easy surface. *R. Paisley.* c— —

TA WARDLE 6 ch.g. Import–Zephyr Lady (Windjammer (USA)) [1989/90 16g^{ur} 16d^{pu}] big, leggy gelding: handicap hurdler: failed to complete in 1989/90: form only at 2m: acts on any going: tried to refuse second outing 1987/8. *M. J. Bolton.* —

TAXIADS 8 b.g. Radetzky–Florabette (Floribunda) [1989/90 22d^{pu} 20s^{pu} 22s^{pu} c21g^{pu} c25f c24f^{pu}] compact gelding: selling hurdler: no form in novice chases (moderate jumper): stays well: probably acts on any going: has been tried in blinkers. *S. T. Harris.* c— x —

TAXI LAD 6 ch.g. Dublin Taxi–Midnight Pansy (Deadly Nightshade) [1989/90 c16s^{2} c20g c20g^{5}] tall, strong, short-backed gelding: winning hurdler: second in novice handicap chase at Hereford in December: not discredited final start: stays 19f: acts on soft going. *R. G. Brazington.* **c80** —

TAXI ON TARGET 5 gr.g. Roselier (FR)–Violet Glade (Tarqogan) [1989/90 F16g^{5} 20g] workmanlike gelding: second in NH Flat race in 1989 (whipped round start): never placed to challenge in novice hurdle at Newcastle in December. *Mrs G. R. Reveley.* —

TAYLORMADE BOY 7 b.g. Dominion–Ash Gayle (Lord Gayle (USA)) [1989/90 20s^{5} 20g^{5} 24g^{3} 20m] leggy, sparely-made gelding: handicap hurdler: ran creditably first 3 starts: stays 3m: suited by give in the ground: ran in snatches second outing. *Denys Smith.* 109

TAYLORS PET 5 b.m. Tina's Pet–Quick Kick (Saritamer (USA)) [1989/90 16m] plating-class middle-distance maiden on Flat: behind in conditional jockeys novice hurdle at Cheltenham in November. *J. C. Gillen.* —

TAYLORS QUEEN 4 b.f. Tender King–Fenland Queen (King's Troop) [1989/90 16m^{pu} a16g] half-sister to novice hurdler Potato King (by Hard Fought): —

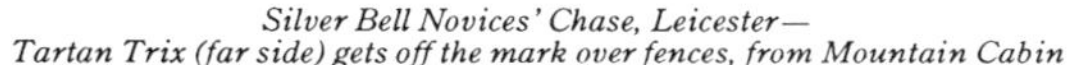

Silver Bell Novices' Chase, Leicester—
Tartan Trix (far side) gets off the mark over fences, from Mountain Cabin

won 1m claimer on Flat in 1989: little promise in 2 outings over hurdles (claimer ridden): sold out of H. Collingridge's stable 1,200 gns Newmarket December Sales in between. *B. J. McMath.*

TEACAKE 6 b.g. Deep Run–Another Adventure (Dual) [1989/90 16g 16s 16g] workmanlike, good-quartered gelding: sixth foal: brother to Trumpledor, runner-up in Irish NH Flat race: dam second in two 2m maiden hurdles in Ireland: well beaten in novice hurdles. *G. Richards.* —

TEACHER'S DRAM 4 b.f. Strong Gale–Top Marks (Breakspear II) [1989/90 16s 16d] workmanlike filly: little sign of ability on Flat: tailed off in juvenile hurdles. *R. Dickin.* —

TEACLOTH 4 br.f. Raga Navarro (ITY)–Dishcloth (Fury Royal) [1989/90 16m 16spu 16gur 16gpu] small, sparely-made filly: first foal: dam fairly useful 2m hurdler and winning chaser: little promise in selling hurdles. *R. J. Eckley.* —

TEAM APPROACH 9 ch.g. Le Bavard (FR)–Overdressed (Le Tricolore) [1989/90 c20sur c20d2 c20f2] leggy gelding: modest hunter chaser nowadays: stays 3m: acts on any going: has worn a crossed noseband. *D. R. Bloor.* c93 —

TEAM CHALLENGE 8 ch.g. Laurence O–Maid O'The Wood (Prince Hansel) [1989/90 c32v3 c30s6 c29g6 c29d6 c30v5 c36f] deep-girthed gelding: fair chaser: completing course for second year running when eleventh to Mr Frisk in Seagram Grand National at Liverpool in April: suited by a good test of stamina: probably acts on any going: has shown tendency to wander under pressure: usually blinkered or visored and has worn a hood: usually a sound jumper. *Mrs J. Pitman.* **c118** —

TEAPLANTER 7 b.g. National Trust–Miss India (Indian Ruler) [1989/90 c22sF c24d* c24g* c24m*] **c116 P**

Trying to spot the next Mr Frisk or the next Norton's Coin to come through from the point-to-point field is a fascinating game that anyone who follows the amateur sport can (and probably does) play. We can't say we've seen a horse that fits the bill yet, but we saw an exciting young prospect in 1990 who could go a long way given the opportunity. Teaplanter's his name. He made his steeplechasing debut in a novice hunter chase at Nottingham in February with the following credentials: he had the right breeding for the job, being out of a three-times winning hurdler and a half-brother to four winning point-to-pointers/hunter chasers, notably the top-class Miss Crozina (by Crozier), and he'd been successful in two point-to-points, a maiden at Guilsborough in 1989 and a restricted, very impressively, at Cottenham earlier in February. Teaplanter, a tall gelding, impressed enormously at Nottingham and was extremely unfortunate not to get off the mark over regulation fences at the first time of asking. Jumping well for a horse of such limited experience, he led from the tenth and was five lengths clear of eventual winner Brockhill Boy and cruising on the bridle when falling at the second last. Thankfully, the fall had no lasting effects and Teaplanter never looked back, recording victories in a maiden hunter chase at Leicester (by thirty lengths and more) the following month and novice hunter chases at Huntingdon and Southwell in April. He beat Some Obligation, another up-and-coming young hunter, five lengths at Huntingdon and subsequent Towcester scorer Eastern Chant eight lengths at Southwell. He gave the impression the sharp track was against him at Southwell, and the probability is that he'll prove best on a galloping one. Teaplanter stays three miles. The going at Nottingham was soft, and he subsequently raced on ground ranging

Teaplanter (b.g. 1983)	National Trust (b 1964)	Relic (bl 1945)	War Relic
			Bridal Colors
		Fortune's Darling (b 1956)	Fair Trial
			Tinted Venus
	Miss India (b 1966)	Indian Ruler (b 1951)	Sayajirao
			Bright Hope
		Miss Mimms (b 1950)	Bobsleigh
			Mimms

from dead to good to firm. Whatever Teaplanter's objectives in 1990/1, whether they be more hunter chases or something higher, his reappearance will be eagerly awaited. *R. G. Russell.*

TEARFUL PRINCE 6 b.g. White Prince (USA)–Romfultears (Romany Air) [1989/90 22m 17v^{3} 22g 16g^{pu}] brother to winning hurdler Romful Prince: dam, last on only completed outing over hurdles, is half-sister to winning jumper Lustful Lady: poor form in novice hurdles: pulled up lame final start. *C. W. Mitchell.* 76

TEBITTO 7 b.g. Derrylin–Over Beyond (Bold Lad (IRE)) [1989/90 c17m^{2} c16m* 16m^{ur} 16f^{2} 17f^{wo} 16g^{5} 18s^{2} 21d 16m^{4} 16f^{F} 16f^{6} c16m^{6}] sturdy gelding: fair hurdler: walked over at Doncaster in December: creditable fourth behind Moody Man in William Hill Imperial Cup (Handicap) at Sandown in March: won novice chase at Stratford in September: best form at up to 2¼m: acts on any going: good mount for a claimer: suited by forcing tactics: moderate jumper of fences: sold D. Wintle 10,600 gns Ascot June Sales. *Andrew Turnell.* c93 x 120

TEDDY BRUERE (FR) 5 b.g. Dom Louis (FR)–Missis Bruere (FR) (Dilettante II) [1989/90 F12g* 16f^{6} 16d^{2} 16s^{F}] leggy non-thoroughbred gelding: dam showed ability on Flat and over jumps in France: won NH Flat race at Market Rasen in November: runner-up in novice hurdle at Kelso in January: fell fatally at Nottingham. *J. G. FitzGerald.* 96

TEE QU 5 b.g. Jimsun–Stephouette (Stephen George) [1989/90 F16m* F16m^{2} 16g 16m^{6} 16s 20f^{pu}] angular gelding: awarded race after finishing second in NH Flat race at Worcester in October: poor form in novice hurdles. *J. S. King.* 75

TEETON FROLIC 4 b.f. Sunley Builds–Sunday Champers (True Song) [1989/90 24m^{pu}] first foal: dam unraced: hampered eighth and pulled up next in novice hurdle at Worcester in April on debut. *M. H. B. Robinson.* —

TEIGN SPIRIT 7 b.m. Battlement–True Spirit II (True Code) [1989/90 17h^{2}] smallish mare: maiden point-to-pointer: little promise in hunter chase and a selling hurdle. *Mrs. A. Knight.* c— —

TEL-ECHO 6 ch.h. Nishapour (FR)–Rhodante (Busted) [1989/90 16s^{4} 20d^{4}] lengthy, sparely-made horse: quite useful hurdler: 20½ lengths fourth behind Bank View in valuable sponsored event at Haydock in January, staying on well in straight having lost place after mistake fifth: made mistakes (seemed to lack confidence) when remote fourth to Beech Road in Bishops Cleeve Hurdle at Cheltenham a week later (led to approaching 2 out, outpaced thereafter): will stay 3m: acts on soft going: has joined H. Whiting. *M. C. Pipe.* 133

TELEMACHUS 6 b.g. Runnett–Bee Hawk (Sea Hawk II) [1989/90 17g 16d c16g^{3} a16g c16h* c16m^{2} c16f^{2} c16h^{3} c16m* c16f^{3}] leggy gelding: novice hurdler: won maiden chase at Plumpton in March and novice handicap at Stratford in May: pulls hard and will prove best at 2m: acts on hard ground: blinkered second start. *C. L. Popham.* c90 —

TELEMAHOS 8 b.g. Tap On Wood–The Woodbird (Tudor Melody) [1989/90 16d^{3} 20d^{3} 16f^{4} 16f^{3} 16s^{3} 22g 21f^{pu}] leggy, close-coupled, sparely-made gelding: won a point-to-point in 1988 (refused to race once): modest form in novice hurdles: stays 2½m: best form with plenty of give in the ground. *J. D. Roberts.* 98

TELEMETER GEM 9 b.m. Decent Fellow–High Energy (Dalesa) [1989/90 16s^{6} 22v^{5} 24g^{5} 21s^{2}] handicap hurdler: lightly raced: suited by a good test of stamina: acts on soft going: looked a difficult ride final start 1986/7. *R. F. Fisher.* 97

TELL ME NO MORE 6 b.m. Latest Model–Queen of The Bogs (Straight Rule) [1989/90 F17m] non-thoroughbred mare: first foal: dam winning 2m chaser: well beaten in NH Flat race at Carlisle in April: yet to race over hurdles or fences. *Mrs B. K. Broad.*

TELL'S TOWER 4 b.f. Dunbeath (USA)–Gallatin Valley (USA) (Apalachee (USA)) [1989/90 16g 16s^{pu} a16g] leggy filly: has scope: behind only outing on Flat: no sign of ability over hurdles. *R. Hollinshead.* —

TELL YOU WHAT 5 ch.g. Crested Lark–Andromeda II (Romany Air) [1989/90 F16m 16g 20m 21f^{3}] tall non-thoroughbred gelding: has scope: second foal: dam poor novice hurdler/chaser: tailed off in novice hurdles. *T. Casey.* —

TEMPERABLE 6 ch.g. Touching Wood (USA)–On Demand (Mandamus) [1989/90 24s^{5} 22g^{6} a24g^{6} c24d^{4} c24d^{ur} c24m^{F} c26f^{4}] smallish gelding: winning hurdler: poor novice chaser: suited by a good test of stamina: best form on soft going over hurdles: has worn a crossed noseband and a brush pricker: sold out of M. Tompkins' stable 4,000 gns Ascot August Sales. *J. D. Thomas.* c82 —

TEMPERED POINT (USA) 4 br.c. Temperence Hill (USA)–Parissaul (Saulingo) [1989/90 16s 16g 16v^{4} 16d^{pu}] neat colt: first foal: dam, placed over —

sprint distances at 2 yrs, is half-sister to Musidora Stakes and Yorkshire Oaks winner Condessa: little promise in juvenile hurdles. *D. R. C. Elsworth.*

TEMPLEMALEY 10 b. or br.g. Tepukei–Kilnacarriga (Baba Ali) [1989/90 c— c20g^{F}] of little account. *A. G. Price.* —

TEMPLE REEF 6 ch.g. Mill Reef (USA)–Makura (Pampered King) [1989/90 21f^{3} 26f^{4} 20f* 26f^{2}] small gelding: modest front-running hurdler: trotted up in 100 3-runner seller at Uttoxeter in August (bought in 6,100 gns): best form at up to 21f: acts on any going: visored final start, blinkered previous 5: jumps none too fluently. *M. C. Pipe.*

TEMPLE TUOHY 11 gr.g. Precipice Wood–Fairy Temple (Bowsprit) c73 [1989/90 20g^{2} c20f^{3} c24m^{F} c25g^{pu}] rangy gelding: modest novice hurdler/poor 91 novice chaser: off course 6 months prior to final start: stays 21f: best form on a sound surface: sold 3,400 gns Doncaster Spring Sales. *J. G. FitzGerald.*

TEN A PENNY 10 ch.m. Whistlefield–Ten Knots (Raise You Ten) [1989/90 c— 20m 17g c24m^{pu} c20f^{3}] sparely-made mare: of little account. *T. A. K. Cuthbert.* —

TEN DEEP 5 ch.m. Deep Run–Tendale (Raise You Ten) [1989/90 F16g^{4} 16g 16f^{3} 17m 16m] sparely-made mare: first foal: dam runner-up in Irish NH Flat race: — remote fourth in mares NH Flat race at Hereford: well beaten in novice hurdles. *K. Bishop.*

TENDER PET 10 b.g. Mummy's Pet–Tender Courtesan (Primera) [1989/90 c— c24f] lightly raced and no form over hurdles or in maiden hunter chases: modest — maiden point-to-pointer. *R. Dixon.*

TENDER WHISPER 5 b.m. Tender King–Queens Message (Town Crier) [1989/90 a16g^{3}] no sign of ability over hurdles, including in seller. *D. Burchell.* —

TENECOUNT 6 ch.g. Country Retreat–Tenella (Wrekin Rambler) [1989/90 c— c22d^{F} c16m^{pu} c20m c16m c16s^{6} c21m^{pu}] workmanlike gelding: no worthwhile — form: pulls hard and has worn a crossed noseband: whipped round start fourth outing. *C. R. Saunders.*

TENESAINT 9 ch.g. St Columbus–Tenella (Wrekin Rambler) [1989/90 c24m^{3} c134 c24m^{pu} c19s^{4} c20m^{2} c20d^{pu} c24s* c29d^{3} c26f^{3}] lengthy, rather leggy gelding: — useful chaser: won handicap at Leicester in February by 4 lengths from Willsford: ran well next start: ran in snatches fifth outing: suited by 3m and more: acts on good to firm and soft going: amateur ridden. *C. R. Saunders.*

Trial Handicap Chase, Leicester—Tenesaint and amateur rider Mr Sansome

Jock Scott Handicap Chase, Ascot—
Ten of Spades (left) makes a successful return from a long lay-off;
the other horse, Fu's Lady, finished third

TENIENTE 6 ch.g. Smooth Stepper–Ballynavin Run (Deep Run) [1989/90 16s 16v* 16d4 16v2] rangy, rather angular gelding: won novice handicap hurdle at Folkestone in January: ran quite well after: likely to prove suited by a strongly-run race over a sharp 2m: acts on heavy going: pulled hard and found little fifth outing. *J. T. Gifford.* 97

TEN IN HAND 10 b. or br.g. Raise You Ten–Sandrina (Choral Society) [1989/90 a20g4 c24f4 c25g5] big, lengthy, angular gelding: winning hurdler: modest novice chaser: out-and-out stayer: possibly unsuited by heavy going, acts on any other: visored first outing: often amateur or claimer ridden, but gives impression he'll benefit from stronger handling: sold 3,800 gns Doncaster March Sales. *M. Bradstock.* c— 86

TENNFORES 9 b.g. Raise You Ten–Coolfores IV (Above Suspicion) [1989/90 c24g* c24g3 c26s c24g* c21m] strong, stocky gelding: won novice chases at Ludlow in December and Fakenham in February: suited by a good test of stamina: acts on heavy going: visored last 2 outings 1988/9, blinkered last 2 starts 1989/90: usually jumps well. *N. J. Henderson.* c**100** —

TEN OF CLUBS 9 b.g. Raise You Ten–Sno-Cat (Arctic Slave) [1989/90 c24d c20spu c24s3 c27d5] tall, rangy gelding: chasing type: showed ability in novice chases on last 2 starts: should be suited by long distances. *M. W. Easterby.* c**81** —

TEN OF SPADES 10 b.g. Raise You Ten–Hansel Money (Prince Hansel) [1989/90 c20g* c24s* c26fF] c**157** —

The retirement of Fulke Walwyn in May brought to an end one of the longest and most distinguished careers in National Hunt racing. An involvement in the sport stretching over sixty years from his start as an amateur brought over three hundred winners in the saddle, including Reynoldstown in the 1936 Grand National, and around two thousand three hundred in fifty-one years as a trainer with five National Hunt trainers' championships on the way. The list of big-race winners sent out from Walwyn's Saxon House stables in Lambourn makes impressive reading. He won the Champion Hurdle in 1962 with Anzio and in 1965 with Kirriemuir plus numerous other hurdle races at the Festival, not to mention three Imperial Cups and a Schweppes Gold Trophy, but it is for his handling of staying chasers that he is renowned. The chasers would fill a book on their own. In brief, there were four Cheltenham Gold Cup winners—Mont Tremblant (1952), Mandarin (1962), Mill House (1963) and The Dikler (1973)—and four King George VI Chase winners—Rowland Roy (1947), Mandarin (1957 and 1959), Mill House (1963) and The Dikler (1971). Notable big handicaps won include the Grand National (Team Spirit in 1964), the Scottish Grand National (twice), the Hennessy Gold Cup (seven times) and the Whitbread Gold Cup (also seven times). Special Cargo's defeat of Lettoch and Diamond Edge by short heads in the Whitbread of 1984 must rate as one of the best finishes in jumping history. Sending out the first and third in that race was a notable training feat as well, all the more so since both horses were ex-invalids, thirteen-year-old Diamond Edge having only his second run after nearly two years off the track with leg trouble.

Walwyn's skill and patience with unsound horses was again in evidence in the latest season, most notably in the performances of the stable's leading runner Ten of Spades. Ten of Spades, a useful chaser with Mrs Rimell in 1987/8, had been kept off the course for a lengthy spell by leg trouble but was brought back in such fine fettle that he showed improved form. Ten of Spades made his reappearance in the six-runner Jock Scott Handicap Chase at Ascot in January. Sent off the outsider at 20/1, he was always to the fore, survived a bad mistake at the fourth, led at the last and won driven out by one and a half lengths from The Dragon Master. Ten of Spades continued on the come-back trail when winning the valuable Mercantile Handicap Chase on the same course the following month—a race also won by Walwyn in 1972 (Prairie Dog) and 1977 (Ghost Writer) when known as the Whitbread Trial Handicap Chase. With the late withdrawal of Desert Orchid, only Rusch de Farges and Ballyhane of the seven runners were in the handicap proper. Ten of Spades, carrying 5 lb more than his long handicap mark, made virtually all, outstaying Paddyboro, who looked the likely winner when disputing the lead three out, and beating him by five lengths, with the never-dangerous Man O'Magic two and a half lengths back in third. Connections were sufficiently impressed by Ten of Spades's performance that they let him take his chance in the Tote Cheltenham Gold Cup in March. He appeared to face a very stiff task beforehand, though he had his supporters at 20/1 and ran the race of his life. He constantly harried the front-running Desert Orchid and led from the sixteenth until the run to the second last. Though weakening under pressure approaching that fence he was still in fourth place, around two lengths ahead of eventual fourth Cavvies Clown, when falling heavily—the

Charterhouse Mercantile Handicap Chase, Ascot—Paddyboro finds Ten of Spades too strong

second successive Saxon House representative to have fallen in the closing stages of the Gold Cup. Ten Plus, Walwyn's best horse since Diamond Edge, had fallen fatally when leading at the third last in the 1989 running. Fortunately, Ten of Spades escaped unscathed and, if all remains well with him in 1990/1, this lightly-raced ten-year-old looks capable of winning more long-distance chases. He'll be in the care of N. Henderson in future. Ten of Spades, a strong, heavy-bodied gelding who carries plenty of condition, acts on any going. A genuine sort, he usually takes a strong hold and races up with the pace. He's normally a sound jumper.

Ten of Spades (b.g. 1980)	Raise You Ten (br 1960)	Tehran (b 1941)	Bois Roussel
			Stafaralla
		Visor (bl 1951)	Combat
			Eyewash
	Hansel Money (ch 1972)	Prince Hansel (ch 1961)	The Phoenix
			Saucy Wilhelmina
		Clonmoney (ch 1962)	Even Money
			Luckibash

The pedigree is of little relevance now, but, for the record, Ten of Spades is by the same sire as Ten Plus and the 1975 Cheltenham Gold Cup winner Ten Up; Raise You Ten is generally a strong influence for stamina. Ten of Spades is the second foal of the lightly-raced Hansel Money, a daughter of a half-sister to the 1972 Cheltenham Gold Cup winner Glencaraig Lady. Hansel Money has since produced the winning hurdler/chaser Lolly's Boy (by Le Bavard) and the good-class Irish chaser Maid of Money (by Crash Course), the latter sixth in the 1990 Gold Cup. *F. Walwyn.*

TENOFUS 5 ch.h. Crofter (USA)–Valley of Diamonds (Florescence) [1989/90 16g^{pu} 19m^{pu}] modest winning miler on Flat at 3 yrs: tailed off when pulled up in 2 novice hurdles at Hereford (off course 4½ months in between): sold 3,100 gns Ascot July Sales. *J. D. Thomas.* —

TENPERCENT 7 b.g. Corvaro (USA)–Schotia (FR) (Sanctus II) [1989/90 21s^{F}] fair hurdler as a juvenile: fell fatally at Fakenham: stayed 2½m: best form on a soft surface. *B. Stevens.* —

TENTER CLOSE 4 b.g. Gorytus (USA)–Love Land (FR) (Kautokeino (FR)) [1989/90 16d a16g^{6} 16d^{pu} 16f^{ur}] angular gelding: won a claimer and 2 sellers on Flat (stays 13.8f) in 1989 (sold out of R. Whitaker's stable 8,000 gns after final success): sixth at Southwell in February, only form in novice hurdles: blinkered last 2 starts (raced too freely on first occasion). *K. A. Ryan.* 75

TEPULEA 6 ch.m. Tepukei–Thirkleby Kate VII (Bivouac) [1989/90 F16d F16g^{pu}] second foal: half-sister to winning hurdler and novice chaser Dubalea (by Dubassoff): dam never ran: behind in NH Flat race in February, and pulled up in similar event following month: dead. *J. S. Haldane.*

TEPYLON 11 b.g. Maystreak–Just-A-Honey (Track Spare) [1989/90 c22m^{F} c21s^{ur} c21d^{pu} c27g^{6} c24g^{6} a20g^{5}] big, rather dipped-backed gelding: poor hurdler: moderate jumper and no form over fences: stays 3¼m: acts on soft going: has been tried in blinkers: sold out of J. J. O'Neill's stable 3,000 gns Ascot August Sales. *J. Pearce.* c— x —

TERRACOTTA ARMY 4 ch.g. Red Sunset–Xian (Sallust) [1989/90 16g^{pu} 17g^{ur}] close-coupled, sparely-made gelding: half-brother to winning Irish hurdler Opportunity (by Prince Tenderfoot): of little account on Flat at 2 yrs: sold out of D. Hanley's stable 1,100 gns Ascot October Sales: failed to get past the third in 2 outings over hurdles: sold G. Ham 2,200 gns Doncaster June Sales. *P. Liddle.* —

TERRA DI SIENA 8 ch.g. Manor Farm Boy–Paddys Tern (St Paddy) [1989/90 19s^{2} 16g^{3} 16d^{F} 26v^{3} c21g* c16d^{F} c21g^{6}] compact gelding: former selling hurdler: won novice handicap chase at Wincanton in January, jumping boldly and well and leading from eleventh: in process of running a good race when falling at the last next outing but ran moderately final start (jumped none too fluently): seems ideally suited by around 2½m: acts on any going. *P. J. Hobbs.* c96 91 +

TERRASSEUR (FR) 5 ch.g. No Lute (FR)–Grande Terre (FR) (Carvin) [1989/90 20m^{2} 22d^{3} 20m 25m] angular, workmanlike gelding: plating-class maiden on Flat: placed in novice hurdles: probably stayed 2¾m: dead. *M. H. Easterby.* 91

TERRIBLE GEL (FR) 5 b.g. Raisingelle (USA)–Ina du Soleil (FR) (Or de Chine) [1989/90 F16f^{6} F16f] half-brother to winning French chaser Rambranlt (by Reasonable Choice): unplaced in NH Flat races at Newbury and Cheltenham in the spring: yet to race over hurdles or fences. *D. J. G. Murray-Smith.*

TERRY JO 6 b.g. Royal Blend–Barby's Girl (Barbaro) [1989/90 c21f^{F} 22m **c80**
c24g^{pu} c20v^{4}] leggy gelding: poor form in novice hurdles: over 25 lengths fourth —
of 7 finishers behind Comandante in novice chase at Folkestone in February, first completed outing over fences. *R. P. C. Hoad.*

TERRY'S LAD 10 b.g. Mugatpura–Belle Tanya (Super Slip) [1989/90 c26d^{pu} **c82**
c24d^{6}] sturdy gelding: no sign of ability over hurdles: poor novice chaser: has won —
point-to-points. *C. J. Vale.*

TERRYS TOWN 4 b.g. Creetown–Precious Love (Precipice Wood) [1989/90
17f^{2} 16f^{6} 17f* 17g^{6} 16m 17f^{4}] rather sparely-made gelding: soundly beaten in 74
sellers at 2 yrs: won slowly-run juvenile selling hurdle at Newton Abbot in October (bought in 3,250 gns): first race for 5½ months when fair fourth in conditional jockeys selling handicap in May: acts on firm ground. *G. A. Ham.*

TERRYWARNER SPORTS 5 b.g. Furry Glen–Granny Knot (London
Gazette) [1989/90 17d^{4} 16g 20v^{4}] leggy gelding: first foal: dam placed over 1¾m in 78
Ireland: showed ability in novice hurdles, including when remote fourth behind easy winner Lucky Verdict over 2½m at Chepstow in January. *P. J. Hobbs.*

TEWIT CASTLE 8 b.g. Enbrage–Slane Lady (Escart III) [1989/90 16d 20s
25m 25m^{pu}] lengthy gelding: one-time useful hurdler: no form in 1989/90: suited —
by a test of stamina: acted on good to firm and soft going: dead. *D. Lee.*

TEWTRELL LAD 7 ch.g. Paddy's Stream–May Foliage (Barman II) [1989/90 **c96**
16g^{5} c24f* c25m^{F} c25s^{pu} c25m^{2} c24m^{5} c25f*] strong, workmanlike gelding: 77
handicap hurdler/chaser: won at Windsor in November and Towcester in May: suited by 3m and firm ground: sometimes on his toes in preliminaries: still has something to learn about jumping. *J. M. Bukovets.*

TEXAN COWBOY 6 b. or br.g. Prince Tenderfoot (USA)–Hy Carol (High
Hat) [1989/90 16f 20s 18f] smallish gelding: winning hurdler: no form in 1989/90 —
(took little interest first start): best at 2m: acts on soft going and possibly unsuited by firm: blinkered third outing 1988/9: looks a difficult ride. *J. T. Gifford.*

THAMES AIR 10 b.m. Crash Course–Santal Air (Ballyciptic) [1989/90 c22g **c92** ?
c29m* c26m^{pu}] lengthy mare: of little account over hurdles: won 2 point- —
to-points in 1989: won 4-runner novice hunter chase at Warwick in May: made mistakes final start: stays well: acts on good to firm ground. *Mrs S. Richardson.*

THAMESDOWN TOOTSIE 5 b.m. Comedy Star (USA)–Lizzie Lightfoot
(Hotfoot) [1989/90 16m^{5} 16v* 16v^{4} 21d 22f 21f^{4}] close-coupled mare: little sign of 87
ability on Flat: won conditional jockeys selling hurdle at Chepstow in January (sold out of S. Mellor's stable 4,200 gns): best form at 2m: acts well on heavy going (probably unsuited by firm). *A. P. Jones.*

THAMES TRADER 9 ch.g. Over The River (FR)–Fun Princess (Prince **c86**
Hansel) [1989/90 c18h^{2} c18f* c20f^{2} c18f^{2} c18h^{2} c18f^{2}] strong, compact gelding: —
poor hurdler: won novice chase at Fontwell in August: good second all subsequent outings: stays 2½m: seems to act on any going. *Mrs L. Clay.*

THANKS A MILLION 4 ch.f. Simply Great (FR)–Friendly Thoughts (USA)
(Al Hattab (USA)) [1989/90 16f^{2}] sold out of J. Hills's stable 8,200 gns after 84
winning 1¼m seller on Flat in August: hard-ridden ½-length second to Virginia's Bay in juvenile hurdle at Stratford following month. *W. G. M. Turner.*

THANK YOURSELF 6 ch.m. Le Bavard (FR)–So Called (Prince Hansel)
[1989/90 16m^{4} 18m 20g^{pu}] lengthy, sparely-made mare: in frame in Irish NH Flat 59
races: poor form in novice hurdles: pulled up and dismounted final start (December). *T. M. Jones.*

THARALEOS (USA) 10 ch.g. Junction (USA)–Right About (USA) (Citation)
[1989/90 18d^{pu} 25g^{F} 24g^{6} 20s^{2} 20m^{6}] stocky gelding: poor hurdler: second in 82
selling handicap at Sedgefield in February: stays 2½m: acts on any going: wears a tongue strap. *F. Watson.*

THAR-AN-BHARR 8 b.g. Over The River (FR)–Another Bird (Arctic Slave) **c119**
[1989/90 c16f^{3} c20f^{2} c16h* c16f^{2} c16f^{3} c16m^{2} c16g^{2} c16d* c17g* c16f* c19g* c16s*] lengthy, good-quartered gelding: has been hobdayed: thrived during a busy first half of season and won handicap chases at Hereford, Stratford, Newbury, Wolverhampton and Fakenham (conditional jockeys, under 12-7):

barely stays 2½m: acts on any going: claimer ridden nowadays: game and genuine: not seen out after December. *J. R. Upson.*

THARROS 4 b.c. Nishapour (FR)–Bold Maiden (USA) (Bold Lad (USA)) [1989/90 16m5 16m 16d5 16f 16m3] leggy, sparely-made colt: placed over 9f on Flat: modest form over hurdles: barely stays 2m: wore tongue strap fourth start: sold 5,000 gns Ascot June Sales. *M. E. D. Francis.* 88

THARSIS 5 ch.g. What A Guest–Grande Promesse (FR) (Sea Hawk II) [1989/90 16g5 20g*] smallish, workmanlike gelding: best effort over hurdles when winning novice handicap at Edinburgh in January: suited by 2½m: claimer ridden first 2 starts 1988/9. *W. Bentley.* 96

THATCHER ROCK (NZ) 5 b.g. Le Grand Seigneur (CAN)–Lady Joelyn (NZ) (Noble Bijou (USA)) [1989/90 F16m* F16g3 F16m] workmanlike gelding: won NH Flat race at Huntingdon in October: 14 lengths eighth of 20 behind Going On in well-contested event at Liverpool in April: yet to race over hurdles or fences. *D. H. Barons.*

THATS FOR SURE 9 gr.g. Idiot's Delight–Brinkwood (Precipice Wood) [1989/90 c26gpu] winning hurdler/chaser: jumped moderately and was tailed off when pulled up in hunter chase in March: stays 25f: acts on heavy going (ran moderately on good to firm). *Mrs S. Maxse.* c— —

THATS IRISH 5 br.m. Furry Glen–Kilbricken Money (Even Money) [1989/90 F16m] IR 16,000 4-y-o: fourth foal: dam winning Irish hurdler/chaser: tailed off in NH Flat race at Sandown in March: yet to race over hurdles or fences. *C. V. Bravery.*

THATS NICE 7 ch.g. Grundy–Copt Hall Realm (Realm) [1989/90 17f5 17f* 21m5 16h6 24g2 20m* 16d* 19m a16g5 21d 16f2 17m* 16f2 19h2 17m2 20m] close-coupled gelding: selling hurdler: successful at Newton Abbot (twice, retained 3,250 gns after final win), Wolverhampton and Worcester: best up to 2½m: acts on any going: usually blinkered and claimer ridden: has twice run out. *C. L. Popham.* 100

THATS THE BUSINESS 6 br.g. Milan–Laragh (Fray Bentos) [1989/90 F16g] non-thoroughbred ex-Irish gelding: second foal: dam placed in Irish point-to-points: in touch when falling 3 out in point-to-point in 1989: mid-division in NH Flat race at Kempton in February: yet to race over hurdles or in a steeplechase. *G. B. Balding.*

THE ANTARTEX 7 ro.g. Vital Season–Rue Talma (Vigo) [1989/90 24g6 c16g2 c16g* c16g* c20v* c16v2] leggy, workmanlike gelding: novice hurdler: led or disputed lead throughout when winning novice chase at Hexham in November, intermediate chase at Newcastle and novice chase at Haydock in January: stays well: has raced only on an easy surface: still has something to learn about jumping, but should improve further over fences. *G. Richards.* c107 p 82

THE ARGONAUT (NZ) 12 br.g. Showoff–Syalbi (NZ) (Sobig) [1989/90 c20m5 c20d c25m* c24gF c21m*] rangy gelding: fair chaser: won Horse and c**118** —

Horse And Hound Grand Military Gold Cup, Sandown—the one-hundred-and-fiftieth running: The Argonaut is unchallenged after his two main rivals are early casualties

Hound Grand Military Gold Cup at Sandown in March (by 15 lengths from San Ovac) and amateur riders chase at Fakenham in May: stays 3m: best form on ground no softer than dead (jumped with little confidence on heavy). *F. Walwyn.*

THE ARTFUL RASCAL 6 b.g. Scallywag–Quick Exit (David Jack) [1989/90 20s[F] 21d 16m[3]] rangy gelding: modest novice hurdler: should stay well: best run on dead ground. *J. T. Gifford.* 96

THE A TRAIN 8 b.g. Tumble Gold–Wrong Decision (No Argument) [1989/90 c16m[2] c16g* c16s* c16g* c16m c16m[2] c16f[5] c16g[4]] big, good-topped, handsome gelding: usually impresses in appearance: quite useful chaser: won at Kempton in January and Sandown and Kempton in February: good fifth to Nohalmdun in Captain Morgan Aintree Chase (limited handicap) at Liverpool in April: lost his chance with mistake at the last on final outing: races only at around 2m: ran poorly on heavy going, probably acts on any other: blinkered final start 1988/9: often sweating and edgy in preliminaries. *Mrs J. Pitman.* c**132** —

THE BAINNE GIRL 8 ch.m. Camden Town–Larkview (Supreme Sovereign) [1989/90 16g[pu] 16g[pu]] leggy, workmanlike mare: no sign of ability over hurdles. *J. M. Bradley.* —

THE BAKEWELL BOY 8 br.g. Kemal (FR)–Warham Fantasy (Barolo) [1989/90 c24g[6] c24d c26f[pu]] sturdy, workmanlike gelding: fairly useful chaser at his best: needed race first 2 starts, out of his depth final one: stays 3¼m: probably acts on any going: tends to sweat and be on toes in preliminaries. *R. G. Frost.* c— —

THE BARON GREY 4 gr.g. Baron Blakeney–I-Ching (No Mercy) [1989/90 16m[pu]] no worthwhile form on Flat, including in sellers: tailed off when pulled up last in juvenile hurdle at Towcester. *O. O'Neill.* —

THE BEAR LOVER 8 br.g. Random Shot–Miss Mouri (Domaha) [1989/90 25g[5] 21s 24m[5]] small, stocky gelding: lightly-raced novice over hurdles: stiff task and not disgraced over 3m final start: unplaced in 2 point-to-points in 1988. *M. Oliver.* 82

THE BERWICK 8 br.g. Space King–Barneo (Dumbarnie) [1989/90 16m[pu] a20g 25g[pu] a20g[5] a16g a16g[5] a16g[pu]] angular gelding: poor novice hurdler/chaser: pulled up and dismounted 2 out in seller last start: blinkered sixth outing: claimer ridden: sold 2,500 gns Doncaster Spring Sales. *W. Clay.* c— ?

THE BIRTHDAYS 6 ch.g. Salluceva–Sovereign Miss (Sovereign Path) [1989/90 c20f[F]] ex-Irish gelding: ninth foal: dam never ran: behind in NH Flat races and maiden hurdles in 1988/9: won a point-to-point in Britain in May: fell fatally in novice hunter chase later in month. *G. F. Hammond.* c— —

THE BRICHIN 9 br.g. Kambalda–Dream Kuda (Will Somers) [1989/90 17f[pu] 17h 17f[3] 16m[5] 16h[3] 21f* 21f[4] c16m[2] c16m[3] a20g[6] a16g[3] 17m 16g[4] 16h[4]] lengthy gelding: selling hurdler: won 4-runner non-selling handicap at Newton Abbot in October: poor novice chaser: successful over 21f but seems best at around 2m: c77 79

Easter Hero Handicap Chase, Kempton—The A Train is pressed by Mzima Spring

acts on hard ground: usually amateur or claimer ridden: visored tenth start 1988/9. *L. C. Corbett.*

THE BUCKWHEAT 9 b.g. Golden Love–Autumn Pearl (Autumn Gold) [1989/90 c24s^pu c24g c25g^6 c28g^pu] rangy gelding: handicap chaser: stays 3¼m: acts on soft going: moderate jumper. *C. F. C. Jackson.* c— x —

THE BUILDER 11 ch.g. Deep Run–Bramble Leaf (Even Money) [1989/90 c24d* c28d^pu] workmanlike gelding: fair chaser nowadays: won handicap at Kelso in January: pulled up lame following month: stays 3m well: acts well in testing conditions: sometimes sweats: usually races up with pace: genuine. *Mrs G. R. Reveley.* c**122** —

THE BURLEYMAN 8 br.g. Belfalas–Taitu (Menelek) [1989/90 c24d^F c24g c24f^ur] big, workmanlike gelding: tailed off in novice chase, only completed outing: broke a leg at Hexham in March. *W. A. Stephenson.* c— —

THE BUTLER 4 ch.g. Roman Warrior–Just Nicola (Eborneezer) [1989/90 F13f] non-thoroughbred gelding: half-brother to poor novice hurdler Coinridge (by Charlie's Pal): dam daughter of Grand National winner Nickel Coin: tailed off in NH Flat race at Hereford in April: yet to race over hurdles. *W. G. M. Turner.*

THE CANNY MAN 7 ch.g. Last Fandango–Easy Can (Tudor Music) [1989/90 c24f^r] of little account: has refused and run out in point-to-points, and refused third in a hunter chase. *George R. Moscrop.* c— § —

THE CHERRY MAN 8 b.g. Paddy's Stream–Bonny Wild (Vulgan's Air) [1989/90 16m^3 16m^4 20g^5 20m^2 c20g^ro c20g^5 20d^4 20f^3 20f^4 20m^4 a20g] tall gelding: modest novice hurdler: well behind in novice chase at Sandown in January: ran out second in similar race previous start: stays 2½m: acts on firm and dead ground: sometimes blinkered: has hung right under pressure. *C. F. Wall.* c— 93

THE CHOSEN ONE 16 b.g. King's Leap–Tots (Dual) [1989/90 17m] workmanlike gelding: selling hurdler and novice chaser: stays 2¾m: acts on any going: sketchy jumper of fences: blinkered last 4 starts 1986/7. *Mrs S. Lamyman.* c— —

THE CIDER AND BUN 10 b.g. Gulf Pearl–Stormy Breeze (Little Buskins) [1989/90 c16f^pu c26m^5 c21d^5] sturdy, workmanlike gelding: poor hurdler/novice chaser: stayed 2½m: seemed to act on any going: blinkered once 1986/7: dead. *Mrs L. Clay.* c**71** —

THE CITY MINSTREL 5 br.g. Black Minstrel–Miss Diga (Tarqogan) [1989/90 F16g* F16g] first foal: dam lightly-raced Irish maiden: won NH Flat race at Fakenham in April: favourite, behind in similar event at Perth following month: yet to race over hurdles or fences. *J. A. C. Edwards.*

THE COBALT UNIT 11 ch.g. Deep Run–Gorryelm (Arctic Slave) [1989/90 c16f^4 c24f* c16m^2 c24f^4 c26f^2 c24f^2 c24m^pu] workmanlike gelding: poor chaser: made all in 3-runner handicap at Southwell in August: stayed 3m: acted on firm going: blinkered once in 1985/6: won for an amateur: headstrong and made mistakes: dead. *B. Byford.* c**76** x —

THE COMMITTEE 7 b.g. Derring Rose–What A Whet (Fine Blade (USA)) [1989/90 c20d* c20g* c16g^2 c18g^F c16s^2 c18s^2 c20v^2 c24f^2 c28m^6 c25d^2] c**141** —

Derring Rose enlivened the British jumping scene in the early-'eighties. At his best he was a top-class hurdler who put up an amazing performance to win the Waterford Crystal Stayers' Hurdle at Cheltenham in 1981 by thirty lengths. But he was just as well known for his temperamental idiosyncrasies, often refusing to give of his best; he was retired to stud after pulling himself up for the third time in the Champion Hurdle of 1982. Derring Rose is now making a mark in his new sphere, and sired the winners of over £72,000 in total prize money in Britain and Ireland in the latest season. Almost half of that money was contributed by The Committee, from his first crop, a useful hurdler who developed into one of the top novice chasers in Ireland. Like his sire, The Committee is a stayer, who put up his best performances over distances of three miles or more. He ran a good race when five lengths second to Garrison Savannah in the Sun Alliance Novices' Chase at Cheltenham in March; having been slightly hampered at the fifth last he stayed on well until finding no extra on the run-in. In the Punchestown Festival Handicap Chase the following month The Committee was beaten a short head, giving 7 lb to the winner On The Other Hand. He stayed on resolutely in the latter stages, and might have got

Corcrain Enterprises Ltd's "The Committee"

up in different circumstances—his conditional jockey, unable to draw an allowance due to the value of the race, dropped his whip after the last. The Committee was far from disgraced over three and a half miles in the Jameson Irish Grand National at Fairyhouse in between, weakening only in the straight to finish around fourteen and a half lengths sixth to Desert Orchid from 18 lb out of the handicap. Held up in each of those races, The Committee was more forcefully ridden when campaigned over shorter distances earlier in the season. He made much of the running when successful in run-of-the-mill novice events at Down Royal and Punchestown in November. Campaigned against the best of the Irish novices subsequently, The Committee ran some good races, notably when runner-up to Blitzkreig over two miles in the Dennys Gold Medal Novice Chase at Leopardstown in December and to Welcome Pin in a qualifier of the Irish National Hunt Novice Chase series over an extra quarter of a mile at Fairyhouse the following month, on each occasion leading until the third last. When favourite for the final of the novice chase series at Leopardstown in February, The Committee was taken on in front by On The Other Hand and eventually beaten twelve lengths by the impressive Cahervillahow.

The Committee (b.g. 1983)	Derring Rose (b 1975)	Derring-Do (b 1961)	Darius
			Sipsey Bridge
		Bandi Rosa (b 1968)	Relko
			Bubunia
	What A Whet (br 1976)	Fine Blade (b 1968)	Fortino II
			Cursorial
		Concerto (br 1970)	Sing Sing
			Mahal

What A Whet was one of the less distinguished mares in Derring Rose's first book. A poor maiden hurdler, she is a sister to the modest two-mile hurdle winner Cornelius Kelly out of the sprint maiden Concerto.

The next dam Mahal, however, was a useful winner at up to a mile and a quarter, and a half-sister to the very smart one-mile to mile-and-a-quarter performer Tesco Boy. The Committee is the second of What A Whet's three reported foals and her only winner. A rather sparely-made, still leggy gelding, The Committee has been kept busy since being placed in a point-to-point on his debut as a four-year-old, and won a National Hunt Flat race and four of his nine starts over hurdles prior to being sent chasing. He holds his form well however and should win more races. The Committee acts on any going. *J. H. Scott, Ireland.*

THE DECENT THING 7 br.g. Decent Fellow–Paperchain (Articulate) [1989/90 21gpu] sturdy, workmanlike gelding: fair hurdler at his best: pulled up lame before last in Tom Masson Trophy Hurdle won by Cruising Altitude at Newbury in November: will stay beyond 21f: acts on soft going. *G. B. Balding.* —

THE DEMON BARBER 8 b.g. Fine Blade (USA)–Mingy (Della Strada) [1989/90 c20g5 c20d2 c24vpu c21g* c24d3 c24gpu] leggy, rather angular gelding: usually makes mistakes over fences but won handicap at Market Rasen in March: barely stays 3m: acts on good to firm and soft going. *G. Richards.* c**118** x —

THE DOORMAKER 8 ch.g. Balinger–Romany Queen (Romany Air) [1989/90 16d 20d c20gF c22d3 c24m4 c25vur] angular, good-bodied gelding: has shown traces of stringhalt: novice hurdler: poor form in novice chases in 1989/90: probably stays 3m: acts on good to firm and soft going. *Capt. T. A. Forster.* c80 —

THE DRAGON MASTER 8 br.g. Pollerton–Glen Rambler (Wrekin Rambler) [1989/90 c20g2 c17d2] tall, leggy gelding: useful chaser: edged left in closing stages when good second in quite valuable handicaps at Ascot (to Ten of Spades) in January and Newbury (to Feroda) in February: stays 2½m: acts on good to firm and soft going: takes a keen hold and has worn a pricker on off-side. *R. Waley-Cohen.* c**139**

THE EGG BARON 6 b.h. Revlow–Bois de Rose (Indian Ruler) [1989/90 16gpu 16g5 16s* 16g3] well-made horse: won novice hurdle at Sedgefield in February, soon clear and never challenged: well beaten at Catterick following month: acts on soft going. *C. J. Bell.* 85

THE EQUALIZER 9 ch.g. Status Seeker–Scotch Polly (Right Tack) [1989/90 c20vpu] novice hurdler: winning point-to-pointer: behind when pulled up both outings in hunter chases. *Michael Roberts.* c— —

THE FARMERSKITCHEN 8 ch.g. General Ironside–Cambrian Explorer (Shackleton) [1989/90 c20sF c20dur 19fpu] compact gelding: novice hurdler: winning chaser: no form in 1989/90: should stay beyond 2m: best form on soft going: ridden by 7-lb claimer nowadays: sold 2,100 gns Doncaster Spring Sales. *O. O'Neill.* c— —

THE FAX MAN 5 gr.g. Rusticaro (FR)–Spring Step (Tepukei) [1989/90 F16m*] first foal: dam never ran: won NH Flat race at Huntingdon in April by a length from subsequently-demoted Silly Sausage: yet to race over hurdles or fences. *B. J. Curley.*

THE FINK SISTERS 7 ch.m. Tap On Wood–Mount Hala (Mount Hagen (FR)) [1989/90 22d6 20d6 22v 16s 20f* 24d5 16f6] close-coupled, sparely-made mare: won 3-runner conditional jockeys selling hurdle at Newcastle in May (no bid): stays 2¾m: acts on any going: blinkered second start 1988/9: often claimer or amateur ridden: headstrong, and has wandered under pressure. *T. W. Cunningham.* 78 §

THE FIXER 9 ch.g. Our Mirage–Carambola (Hul A Hul) [1989/90 17gur 16d3 16f2 17m2 24g3] neat gelding: selling hurdler: seems to stay 3m: acts on dead and firm going: has worn blinkers (not in 1989/90). *P. Monteith.* 71

THE FLY BOYS 8 ch.g. Sousa–Ravenna (Celtic Ash) [1989/90 c16m3] leggy gelding: lightly-raced winning hurdler: made mistakes when remote third in novice event at Taunton on chasing debut: likely to prove best at around 2m for time being: acts on firm going. *B. Forsey.* c88 —

THE FOOTMAN 8 br.h. Hotfoot–Philogyny (Philip of Spain) [1989/90 16m3] lengthy horse: one-time fairly useful hurdler: jumped none too fluently behind easy 20-length winner Aldino in 3-runner minor event at Huntingdon in October: suited by heavy ground: wears a tongue strap. *R. W. Stubbs.* ?

THEFRIENDLYBARBER 7 gr.g. General Ironside–Aprils End (Star Signal) [1989/90 c20d2 c24f3] close-coupled gelding: maiden hurdler: winning c85 —

point-to-pointer: made mistakes in hunter chases at Ludlow in March: should stay beyond 2½m: acts on firm and dead ground. *Lady Susan Brooke.*

THE FROZEN PADRE 9 br.g. Ragapan–Arctic Brilliance (Arctic Slave) [1989/90 c24g^{pu} 25g^{5} 25g^{pu}] sturdy, workmanlike gelding: has shown signs of ability over hurdles but none over fences: wears blinkers or visor: has worn a tongue strap. *J. Webber.* c— —

THE FRUIT 11 ch.g. Kambalda–Beautiful Night (Midsummer Night II) [1989/90 c20f^{4} c21g^{3} c21m c21m^{4} c20m^{ur} c20m^{3} c20m^{3}] tall, close-coupled gelding: poor chaser: stays 2½m: acts on firm going: amateur ridden: poor jumper. *R. R. Ledger.* **c75** x —

THE GAELCHARN 6 ch.g. Prince Bee–Lady Habitat (Habitat) [1989/90 16g 16g 21d^{6} 20g^{3} 20d^{3} 24g^{2} 24f^{6}] sturdy, close-coupled gelding: handicap hurdler: stays 3m: acts on soft going, seems unsuited by heavy and firm: sweating first and sixth outings: hung left fifth start. *C. P. E. Brooks.* 108

THE GANNOCHY (USA) 4 ch.g. Coastal (USA)–Bright View (Hot Spark) [1989/90 16f^{3} 16h^{2} 16m^{5} 16f^{3} a16g^{ur} 16f* 16m 16m^{pu}] neat gelding: ungenuine middle-distance maiden on Flat: claimer ridden, made all in selling hurdle at Huntingdon in November (bought in 2,900 gns): ran poorly last 2 starts (off course 3½ months in between): didn't find much under pressure first start: wears blinkers: trained first 2 outings by N. Henderson, next 5 by D. J. Bell. *L. Wordingham.* 83 §

THE GODFATHER 7 b.g. Don–Barney Kempinski (Karabas) [1989/90 c16m^{pu} c17f^{ur} c17m^{F}] dipped-backed gelding: winning 2m chaser: acted on firm ground: was poor jumper: dead. *P. G. Bailey.* c— x —

THE GREEN STUFF 5 ch.g. Green Shoon–Cottage View (Golden Vision) [1989/90 16g^{F} 16d 16d 16g^{6} c16g^{5} c16d^{3}] big, strong gelding with scope: poor form in novice events over hurdles and fences. *J. R. Upson.* c75 80

THE GREY GUNNER 10 gr.g. Pry–Willsie's Blunder (Orchardist) [1989/90 c20m* c21f^{2} c18g* c16m^{6}] lengthy gelding: novice hurdler: won 2 point-to-points in 1989: formerly a poor jumper in steeplechases but won novice events at Bangor and Fontwell early in season: stays 2½m: acts on firm ground: has worn a crossed noseband. *Miss H. C. Knight.* **c96** —

THE GRIFTER 6 gr.g. Treboro (USA)–Mary Crooner (Crooner) [1989/90 18g 16g 20g^{pu}] strong, sturdy gelding: handicap hurdler: lightly raced and little form of late, seeming to take little interest final start: should stay beyond 2m: acts on soft going. *M. Madgwick.* —

THE HACIENDEROS 11 b.g. Deep Run–Farina (Raise You Ten) [1989/90 c20d^{6} c20m* c25d] strong, lengthy, good sort: carries plenty of condition: won handicap chase at Fairyhouse in April by ½ length from Charlie Lucky: stiff task next time: probably stays 3m: acts on good to firm and soft going. *B. J. Curley.* **c111** —

THEHELLHEIS 5 b.g. Posse (USA)–Hail To Vail (USA) (Hail To Reason) [1989/90 F16f F16g] half-brother to several winners, including fair chaser Mosof (by Oats): dam never ran: well beaten in NH Flat races at Ascot and Market Rasen: yet to race over hurdles or fences. *R. F. Marvin.*

THE HOUGH 9 b.g. Palm Track–Dunoon Twinkle (Dunoon Star) [1989/90 20f*] small, lightly-made gelding: won handicap hurdle at Sedgefield in September: second in handicap on chasing debut in 1988: stays 2½m: acts on hard ground: has worn a crossed noseband. *Mrs G. R. Reveley.* c— 89

THE HUCKLEBUCK 5 ch.g. Buckskin (FR)–Iron Star (General Ironside) [1989/90 F16s 21d^{pu} 16g c20d^{pu}] IR 7,000 3-y-o: lengthy, angular gelding: first foal: dam unraced half-sister to winning hurdler Wonderful Lily and to winning chaser Shady Road: no sign of ability in NH Flat race, 2 novice hurdles and a novice chase. *R. Dickin.* c— —

THE HUMBLE TILLER 7 b.g. Rarity–Bardicate (Bargello) [1989/90 c21d^{4} c21g* c21d^{pu}] medium-sized gelding: winning hurdler: won novice chase at Windsor in March, jumping soundly, but having to be driven out as lack of condition told (first race for 2½ months): ran as though something amiss next start: stays 2¾m: acts on heavy going: claimer ridden over hurdles. *N. J. Henderson.* **c91** + —

THE ILLYWHACKER 5 b.g. Dawn Review–Trucken Queen (Harwell) [1989/90 16f^{2} 16g 17v* 22g^{ro} 20v^{3} 22g* 20f 25m^{5}] tall, leggy gelding: successful 115

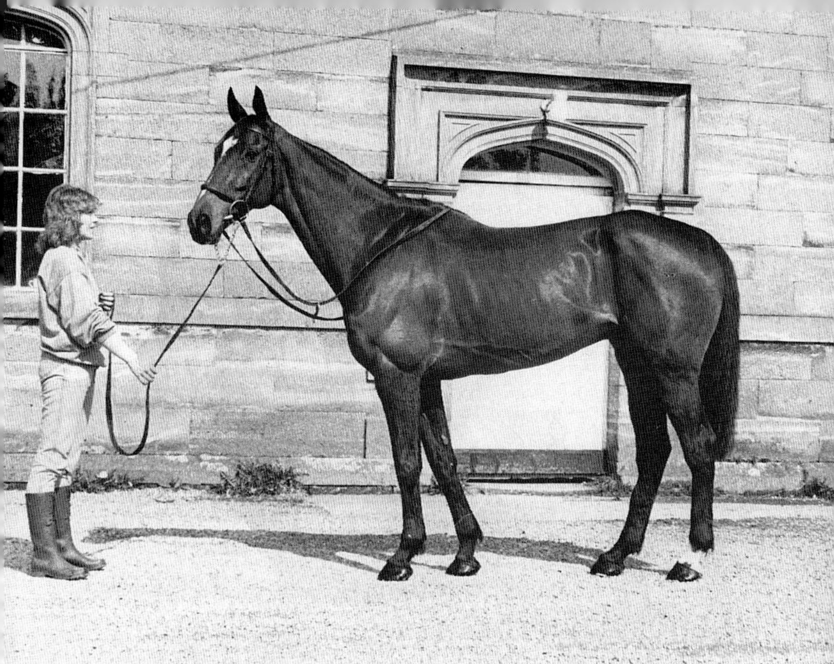

The Edinburgh Woollen Mill Ltd's "The Langholm Dyer"

in novice hurdles at Newton Abbot (amateur ridden) in December and Windsor in March: weakened quickly approaching last when 17 lengths fifth behind Dwadme in quite valuable event at Liverpool in April: races keenly (wears crossed noseband) and will prove best at around 2½m: probably acts on any going: blinkered last 3 outings: ran out fourth start: wandered and looked a difficult ride next time. *Mrs J. Pitman.*

THE JOGGER 5 b.g. Deep Run–Pollychant (Politico (USA)) [1989/90 F16m^2 F16m^5] second foal: dam, winning Irish point-to-pointer, half-sister to fair hurdler/chaser The Welder: showed ability in 2 NH Flat races at Sandown in the spring: yet to race over hurdles or fences. *O. Sherwood.*

THE KENDALIST 6 ch.g. Scallywag–Kenda (Bargello) [1989/90 16d] tall, workmanlike gelding: unplaced in NH Flat races: jumped none too fluently when behind in novice hurdle at Chepstow in November. *Capt. T. A. Forster.* —

THEKKIAN 6 ch.h. Thatching–Debian (Relko) [1989/90 16m] quite modest handicapper at up to 7f on Flat, has looked irresolute and needs exaggerated waiting tactics: sold out of R. Hollinshead's stable 3,200 gns Doncaster January Sales: tailed off in novice hurdle at Sedgefield. *P. A. Blockley.* —

THE LANGHOLM DYER 11 b. or br.g. Crash Course–Belle Artiste (Artist's Son) [1989/90 c24m^3 c24m^{pu} c28g^3 c24m^F c25m^3 c24d^3 c24g* c28g^F c33d^2 c26g^2 c28d^3 c24m* c24g* c36g^3] leggy, lengthy gelding: fairly useful chaser: made most to win handicaps at Carlisle (2) and Bangor in second half of season: stays very well: acts on any going: suited by forcing tactics: has won for a claimer: visored sixth outing. *G. Richards.* c**127** —

THE LAST BUT ONE 5 b.g. Idiot's Delight–Romany Empress (Roman Warrior) [1989/90 F16v F16f^6] first foal: dam, unraced sister to 3 poor performers, daughter of 2-y-o 5f winner: never dangerous when around 12 lengths sixth of 10 to Norman Conqueror in NH Flat race at Newbury in March: yet to race over hurdles or fences. *D. J. Wintle.*

THE LAST TUNE 6 b.m. Gunner B–Tempest Girl (Caliban) [1989/90 a16g6] angular, workmanlike mare: winning hurdler: not knocked about once beaten only outing of season (November): form only at 2m: acts on dead going (yet to race on top-of-the-ground). *J. M. Bukovets.* —

THE LATE MAN 9 ch.g. Tudor Rocket–Kytton (Kythnos) [1989/90 a20gpu 25d6 17m] smallish, workmanlike gelding: selling hurdler and novice chaser: no form since early 1988/9: stays 2½m: acts on good to firm ground: blinkered final start 1987/8: moderate jumper. *C. C. Trietline.* c— x —

THE LEGGETT 7 b.g. Faraway Times (USA)–Mrs Mcnicholas (Tudor Music) [1989/90 c18f* c20s* c16s* c16d* c16s* c21m3 c20f* c22m] leggy, sparely-made gelding: developed into a fairly useful chaser, and won handicaps at Taunton (2) and Chepstow in December, Stratford in February and Haydock and Sandown in March: tailed off when favourite for John Hughes Memorial Trophy Chase (Handicap) at Liverpool, final start: stays 2¾m: acts on any going. *M. C. Pipe.* c**126** —

THE LIDGATE STAR 7 b.g. Pitskelly–Gold Pollen (Klondyke Bill) [1989/90 16m4 16m6 16g 20f6 a20g 16m6] tall, rather sparely-made gelding: poor novice hurdler: seems not to stay 2½m. *M. Tate.* 61

THE LIGHTER SIDE 4 br.g. Comedy Star (USA)–Moberry (Mossberry) [1989/90 16f 17f* 16g a16g* a20g2 a16g* a18g* a20g2 a16g* a16g* a18g3 a16g* 16g* 16g4] compact gelding: maiden on Flat: sold out of W. Pearce's stable 7,400 gns after winning selling hurdle at Doncaster in December: much improved subsequently and won handicaps at Southwell (4), Lingfield and Bangor: best form at 2m: acts on firm going: often ridden by 7-lb claimer: genuine and consistent. *B. Preece.* 110

THE LUCKPENNY MAN 11 b. or br.g. Giolla Mear–Curraheen Lady (Master Buck) [1989/90 c18fpu c20m3 c20gur c18mF c20g6 c25g6] big, lengthy gelding: handicap chaser: ran poorly in 1989/90 (reportedly broke blood vessel first outing): stays 2½m but seemingly not 3m: seems to act on any going: tends to be on his toes and sweat in preliminaries: moderate jumper. *Mrs L. Clay.* c— x —

Carpenter Handicap Chase, Haydock—two of the season's more successful young chasers, The Leggett (left) and Astre Radieux

THE MAGUE 6 br.g. Bold Owl–Silvery Moon (Lorenzaccio) [1989/90 16f^{4} 17h^{3} 16f 16g^{2} 16m^{5}] small, well-made gelding: modest handicapper on Flat, winner twice at around 1¼m in 1990: put in mixed round of jumping, hung left and looked none too keen run-in when second in novice handicap hurdle at Nottingham in October: claimer ridden, but will be suited by stronger handling. *Miss L. C. Siddall.* 82

THE MALDIVE LADY 4 b.f. Oats–Kaotesse (Djakao (FR)) [1989/90 a16g^{pu}] half-sister to winning hurdler Blue Disc (by Disc Jockey): behind all outings on Flat: tailed off when pulled up last in juvenile hurdle at Lingfield in November. *J. R. Jenkins.* —

THE MALTKILN 7 br.g. Sonnen Gold–Kittaspec Gal (Mandamus) [1989/90 c20g^{ur} c20g^{F} c24g^{3} c24d^{r} c27s* c24d^{2} c28d^{2} c27g* c24g^{F} c32g^{F} c24d^{pu}] leggy, workmanlike gelding: handicap chaser: won at Sedgefield in January and February (idled on run-in): beaten when falling next 2 starts: well suited by long distances: acts on soft going: usually blinkered or visored nowadays. *Mrs R. Wharton.* c96 —

THE MASTER GUNNER 6 ch.g. Gunner B–Major Isle (Major Portion) [1989/90 16m] workmanlike gelding: winning hurdler: best form at 2m: acts on soft going (needing race, tailed off on good to firm in October). *P. G. Bailey.* —

THE MIGHTY BISHOP 7 b.g. Bishop of Orange–Ballynock (Belgrave) [1989/90 c24d] rangy non-thoroughbred gelding: second reported foal: brother to winning point-to-pointer Badgers Mead: dam unraced sister to winning Irish chaser/point-to-pointer King Cacador: successful in a point-to-point in Ireland in 1989: needing race, well beaten in maiden hunter chase at Leicester in March, but wasn't knocked about when beaten and gave the impression he'll do better in due course. *C. Sporborg.* c—

THE MILROY 7 b.g. Buckskin (FR)–Sno-Cat (Arctic Slave) [1989/90 16g* 20g^{2} c20g^{5}] big, leggy gelding: has been hobdayed: won novice hurdle at Newbury in November by 10 lengths from Atlaal: good second at Cheltenham 2 months later: wasn't knocked about after a bad mistake at the eleventh when tailed off in novice chase at Newbury in March: probably stays 2½m: has worn crossed noseband: likely to prove capable of better over fences. *O. Sherwood.* c— p 129

THE MISHAP 7 br.h. Tanfirion–Superspin (Tamerlane) [1989/90 16f] compact, good-bodied horse: 1¼m winner on Flat: no worthwhile form over hurdles. *Mrs I. McKie.* —

THE MOSSES 5 br.g. Kinglet–Yutoi Lady (Arctic Slave) [1989/90 16g 16d] unfurnished gelding: half-brother to winning Irish jumper Karemuchmore (by Pamroy): dam a poor chaser: well beaten in novice hurdles at Wincanton and Towcester. *Capt. T. A. Forster.* —

THE MUSICAL PRIEST 8 ch.g. Baptism–Bunch of Blue (Martinmas) [1989/90 c16d^{2} c18s c18s^{ur} c18v^{3} c16m c16g^{2}] compact, good-bodied Irish gelding: one-time useful hurdler: passed post first in novice chase at Leopardstown in December but went left in closing stages and was demoted to second: placed in Diners Club Chase at Punchestown (just over a length third behind Derrymore Boy) and novice chase at Thurles (well below form, breaking blood vessel) afterwards: ran well when around 15 lengths seventh to Comandante in Arkle Challenge Trophy Chase at Cheltenham in between: best at up to 2¼m: acts on any going: suitable mount for an amateur: tends to find little off bridle. *Miss Emer Purcell, Ireland.* c127 —

THE NATIONS WAY 8 b.g. National Trust–Lastway (The Ditton) [1989/90 c21v] big gelding: third foal: half-brother to winning point-to-pointer Gamblingway (by Gambling Debt): dam never ran: won a point-to-point in 1988: last of 8 finishers in novice chase at Newton Abbot in December. *J. H. Baker.* c—

THE NIGELSTAN 9 b.g. Fine Blade (USA)–Owenette (Master Owen) [1989/90 c20d^{ur} c24g^{3} c24g^{2} c24m^{ur} c26s^{4} c24s* c24g* c25m^{6} c25g^{pu}] leggy gelding: novice hurdler: won novice chases at Windsor in January and Kempton (by a head from Toureen Prince) in February: well beaten in valuable novice events at Liverpool and Punchestown (behind when pulled up) afterwards: should stay beyond 3m: acts on soft ground: jumps none too fluently on occasions. *P. R. Hedger.* c118 —

THE OIL BARON 4 gr.g. Absalom–Ruby's Chance (Charlottesville) [1989/90 16f^{F} 16s^{5} 16m^{pu} a16g^{6}] leggy gelding: poor middle-distance maiden on Flat: disputing third place when falling last in juvenile hurdle at Warwick in December: seemed not to stay 2m in very soft ground next time: ran poorly in seller final outing: trained until after third start by R. Akehurst. *R. P. C. Hoad.* 88

THE ONLY WAY OUT 4 ch.f. Humdoleila–Psidette (Psidium) [1989/90 16s 16d5 20f] sparely-made filly: half-sister to moderate chaser Dawn Fox (by Healaugh Fox) and fairly useful chaser Gerami (by Grey Mirage): dam lightly raced: well beaten over hurdles (still bit backward final start). *M. W. Eckley.* —

THEO'S FELLA 6 br.g. Decent Fellow–Scottish Vulgan (Vulgan) [1989/90 16g 16g 20d 21f* 25m] workmanlike gelding: 20/1, won 18-runner novice hurdle at Newbury in March by short head from stable-companion Munjarid, rallying well after a mistake at the last: not knocked about once losing place in quite valuable event at Liverpool following month: should stay 3m: acts on firm going. *G. B. Balding.* 106 +

THE OVERNIGHT MAN 5 ch.h. Smackover–Highland Rossie (Pablond) [1989/90 16g a16g*] sparely-made horse: selling hurdler: won at Southwell in April (sold 4,000 gns): probably stays 2½m: seems to act on any going: ran in snatches third start 1988/9 and looked less than keen under pressure next outing: usually blinkered (wasn't when successful). *B. A. McMahon.* 81

THE PAIN BARRIER 11 b.g. Blakeney–Vilswitch (Vilmorin) [1989/90 c26g3] compact gelding: developed into a smart hunter chaser in 1986: reportedly met with a set-back and was having only second race since that season when well beaten at Stratford in March: stays 3¼m when conditions aren't testing: suited by top-of-the-ground. *M. J. Langton.* c— —

THE PAPPARAZI 10 ch.g. Boreen (FR)–Marble Owen (Master Owen) [1989/90 22g c20gur] strong gelding: lightly-raced winning hurdler: favourite, travelling well when unseating rider ninth in novice event at Folkestone in January on chasing debut: stays 3m: acts on dead going. *B. J. Curley.* c— p —

THE PARSON'S NUN 6 ch.m. The Parson–Hill Invader (Brave Invader (USA)) [1989/90 16d4 24m 20v5 24d] lengthy, sparely-made mare: novice hurdler: not disgraced over 3m (should stay trip): has looked a difficult ride. *R. J. Eckley.* 86

THE PIKE 7 b.g. Proverb–Daybrook Lass (Daybrook Lad) [1989/90 25f* 24m* 27g4 26dpu a24g* a24g2 25g 24f4 24f2 27f3] angular gelding: handicap hurdler: successful at Catterick, Newcastle and Southwell in 1989/90: stays 27f: below his best on very soft going, acts on any other: successful when claimer ridden: has worn a crossed noseband: usually a front runner, though held up when good second on ninth outing. *Mrs V. A. Aconley.* 115

THE PIT LADDIE 5 b.g. Miner's Lamp–Diamond Panes (Lock Diamond) [1989/90 16m 20g 16m] stocky gelding: first foal: dam poor Irish maiden point-to-pointer: no worthwhile form in novice hurdles: dead. *W. A. Stephenson.* —

THE PLAIN WAIN 7 br.m. Majestic Streak–Medwyn Heiress (pedigree unknown) [1989/90 22d] no sign of ability in 2 novice hurdles. *W. A. Stephenson.* —

THE PLUMLEY FLYER 5 b.g. Prince Bee–High Fi (High Hat) [1989/90 F16s 16d 16g5 20m4] 12,000 3-y-o: strong gelding: half-brother to 4 winners, including hurdler End of Era (by Patch): dam unraced half-sister to useful hurdler Royal Illusion: modest form in novice hurdles: probably stays 2½m: sold 13,000 gns Doncaster Spring Sales. *J. C. McConnochie.* 85

THE POD'S REVENGE 5 b.g. Pollerton–Fair People (Varano) [1989/90 F17m5 16g 22v 17g] strong, lengthy gelding: chasing type: NH Flat race winner: showed signs of ability in novice hurdles: should be well suited by a stiffer test of stamina. *G. M. Moore.* 88

THE PRICE IS RIGHT 6 br.g. Rolfe (USA)–Lady Jewel (Kibenka) [1989/90 16d] tailed off in maiden race at 2 yrs and novice hurdle at Sedgefield. *G. R. Oldroyd.* —

THE PRIDE OF POKEY 6 br.m. Uncle Pokey–Vikrom (Menelek) [1989/90 c16gpu c16d3] good-topped, workmanlike mare: no sign of ability. *Mrs S. C. Bradburne.* c— —

THEPRINCEOFKINGS 6 br.g. Prince Regent (FR)–Betty Sue (Menelek) [1989/90 16d] smallish ex-Irish gelding: second foal: dam unraced sister to fair hurdler/chaser Arctic Menelek: pulled up in point-to-point in 1988: amateur ridden, eighth in novice hurdle at Towcester in February, weakening as lack of condition told 2 out and not knocked about. *S. Christian.* —

THE PROCESSOR 9 b.g. Cleon–Indian Leap (Indian Ruler) [1989/90 21m 21mF] one-time fair hurdler: fell heavily only outing over fences: stays 21f: acts on any going with possible exception of very soft. *O. Sherwood.* c— —

THE PROCLAMATION 7 br.g. Callernish–Lilquin (Hill Gail) [1989/90 c20d* c16gF] rangy, well-made ex-Irish gelding: impressive winner of BMW Champion Novice Hurdle at Punchestown in 1989: again impressive when making successful chasing debut in Peter Cox Novices' Chase at Ascot in December, beating Deep Colonist by 15 lengths: fell fourth in valuable novice event on same course following month: stayed 2½m: acted on good to soft ground: dead. *N. J. Henderson.* c**122** —

THE PROGRAMMER 5 b.g. Paddy's Stream–Arcticogan (Tarqogan) [1989/90 20g 20g2] smallish, angular gelding: fourth foal: half-brother to winning chaser/point-to-pointer Carrolls Grove (by Lucifer): dam never ran: still carrying condition, 3 lengths second to Royal Invader in novice hurdle at Sedgefield in February, hanging left and looking a difficult ride throughout: stays 2½m. *B. McLean.* 84

THE PURSEWARDEN 7 b.g. Down The Hatch–Miss Sonnet (Master Owen) [1989/90 18f* 18f2 16f5 16m4 16g5 16h* 16fpu] rather leggy, workmanlike gelding: won novice hurdles at Fontwell in October and Taunton in April: should stay beyond 2¼m: yet to race on very soft going, acts on any other. *F. Walwyn.* 99

THE PUTNEY LARK 6 b.g. Merrymount–Blue Lagoon (Forlorn River) [1989/90 20g5 22s4 20d c17d3 22f4] poor novice hurdler: 12 lengths third to Go West in novice event at Newbury in March on chasing debut (jumped soundly and should improve): gives impression he'll do best at distances short of 2¾m. *Mrs J. Pitman.* c**88** p 81

THE QUIETSTAN 7 ch.g. Gay Fandango (USA)–Viduli (Firestreak) [1989/90 16d4 16v c16sF] compact gelding: fourth in novice handicap hurdle at Wincanton in February: fell third on chasing debut: races keenly and will prove best at 2m on ground no softer than dead. *N. R. Mitchell.* c— 81

THE QUOHEE 8 b.g. Candy Cane–Canky (Cantab) [1989/90 c24m5 c25s3 c27s c27v* c25m5] rangy, angular ex-Irish gelding: third foal: brother to Irish bumpers winner Caninot: dam won 3 hunter chases and numerous point-to-points in Ireland: winning point-to-pointer: modest steeplechaser: won amateur riders handicap at Chepstow in February: stiffish task next outing: stays very well: acts on heavy going: broke blood vessel final outing 1988/9. *J. H. Baker.* c**90**

THE RANNOCH 7 b.g. Relkino–Jamelah (Grundy) [1989/90 20mpu] tall gelding: winning hurdler: pulled up lame at Perth in August: stays 2½m: acts on heavy going. *I. Semple.* —

Peter Cox Novices' Chase, Ascot—highly impressive The Proclamation

THE RECTOR 16 ch.g. Royal Cavalier–Gypsy Touch (Romany Air) [1989/90 c17h2 c21fpu c25m4 c25mpu] poor novice hurdler/chaser/point-to-pointer. *R. W. Pincombe.* c— —

THE RED ONE 6 b.g. Derring Rose–Fairy Island (Prince Hansel) [1989/90 20f* 25f3] lengthy gelding: won handicap hurdle at Sedgefield in October: reportedly finished lame when third at Catterick later in month and not seen out again: stays 2½m: acts on firm going. *J. Hanson.* 118

THE REEDCUTTER 9 b.g. Blakeney–Croda Rossa (ITY) (Grey Sovereign) [1989/90 20mpu 16h5 16mF 22m 16m6] small, good-bodied gelding: poor novice hurdler: stays 2½m: acts on any going: wears blinkers or a visor: sold 1,500 gns Doncaster June Sales. *F. Gibson.* —

THERE YOU ARE 4 b.f. Kings Lake (USA)–Occupation (Homing) [1989/90 16f2 16g a18g2 16f4 16m6 16hur 20f3] leggy, narrow filly: 1½m winner on Flat (has looked ungenuine): juvenile hurdler: best efforts on third and fourth outings (latter in a seller): stays 2¼m: acts on firm going: sold out of N. Henderson's stable 2,700 gns Doncaster October Sales after second start, out of J. Kavanagh's stable 3,400 gns Doncaster January Sales after third. *C. C. Trietline.* 73

THE SCOURGE 8 b.g. Scorpio (FR)–When The Saints (Bay Express) [1989/90 c26mpu] tall gelding: pulled up all starts in hunter chases. *R. W. Pincombe.* c—

THE SHINER 10 b.g. Julio Mariner–Wolver Valley (Wolver Hollow) [1989/90 24v 22spu 25d3 25m 24m2] short-coupled, rather lightly-built gelding: handicap hurdler: behind when pulled up on chasing debut: stays well: acts on good to firm and heavy going: usually blinkered: has also worn a hood (including when successful): has won for an amateur. *D. J. G. Murray-Smith.* c— 112

THE SHUFFLER 9 br.g. Decent Fellow–Royal Pothole (Royal Highway) [1989/90 c24g* c24g2 c20mF] lengthy gelding: easy winner of conditional jockeys handicap chase at Huntingdon in November: in lead when falling 3 out on same course in December: stays 3m: acts on heavy going: usually a sound jumper of fences: occasionally mulish in preliminaries: has reportedly broken blood vessels. *J. G. FitzGerald.* c**99** —

THE SHY CONTROLLER 5 b.g. Kind of Hush–Heyford (Blakeney) [1989/90 16g4] big, close-coupled gelding: has scope: in need of race and green, 17½ lengths fourth behind Freeline Finishing in novice hurdle at Windsor in March, keeping on steadily having been outpaced 4 out: should improve. *Mrs J. Pitman.* 80 p

THE SKIRRID 8 b.g. Pardigras–Astonishment (Blast) [1989/90 25h6 28gF] leggy, sparely-made, shallow-girthed gelding: winning point-to-pointer: no sign of ability over hurdles: usually amateur ridden. *S. C. Davis.* —

THE SLATER 5 ch.g. Town And Country–Yashama (Supreme Red) [1989/90 F16g aF14g3 aF16g5] leggy gelding: has scope: third foal: dam never ran: third of 12 in NH Flat race at Southwell in November: yet to race over hurdles or fences. *W. G. M. Turner.*

THE STAMP DEALER 7 b. or br.g. Runnett–Royal Meath (Realm) [1989/90 16m6] leggy, sparely-made gelding: poor novice selling hurdler: barely stays 2m: blinkered first start 1988/9. *A. W. Jones.* 62

THE TAN MAN 7 b.g. Tanfirion–Lady Begorra (Roi Soleil) [1989/90 19g 16fF c20d5 c20spu] rather sparely-made gelding: poor novice hurdler: just over 30 lengths fifth behind Antinous in novice event at Warwick in January on chasing debut: jumped none too fluently next outing: has worn a crossed noseband: blinkered sixth outing 1988/9: sold 1,400 gns Ascot April Sales. *Miss H. C. Knight.* c**74** —

THE TANNER (USA) 5 ch.h. Plugged Nickle (USA)–Petita (USA) (Nashua) [1989/90 17g6 17dpu 17h2 17m4 17hF] novice selling hurdler: races only at around 2m: probably acts on any going: usually claimer ridden (wasn't when in process of running a good race on final outing). *W. J. Reed.* 67

THE THINKER 12 ch.g. Cantab–Maine Pet (Light Year) [1989/90 c24g2 c24s2 c24g5 c24v2] c**157** —

The 1987 Tote Cheltenham Gold Cup winner The Thinker earned more headlines for the races he missed than those he contested in the latest season. He was withdrawn at the five-day stage from the latest Gold Cup due to a bout of coughing in the stable which caused all of Stephenson's string to miss their engagements at Cheltenham and on the eve of his

T. P. M. McDonagh Ltd's "The Thinker" (C. Grant)

reported principal target, the Seagram Grand National, due to the firmness of the ground. A gallant third under 11-10 behind Little Polveir in the race in 1989, he was generally quoted at 16/1 with a pound less to carry at the time of his withdrawal. Finally, a last-minute decision to switch from the William Hill Scottish National at Ayr, where the ground was good to soft, to the Whitbread Gold Cup a week later backfired when The Thinker was again withdrawn on the eve of the race due to the firmness of the ground.

When The Thinker made it onto the course he sometimes showed he was still capable of producing good form. In the slowly-run Edward Hanmer Memorial Handicap Chase at Haydock in November he kept on in tremendous fashion to finish a length second to Golden Friend, conceding a stone to the winner who is a very useful chaser on his day. The Thinker also stayed on strongly up the long Haydock run-in when three lengths second to Rinus in the Greenall Whitley Gold Cup Handicap Chase in March, though he had never looked likely to win, having lost a lot of ground early through sketchy jumping. The Thinker was below his best in between. He ran a lack-lustre race when beaten a short-head by Baies in the Tommy Whittle Chase at Haydock in December, looking very laboured and having to be hard ridden in the latter stages. After by-passing the Coral Welsh National—in which he'd finished third in 1988—The Thinker was soundly beaten behind stable-companion Durham Edition in the Rowland Meyrick Handicap Chase

The Thinker (ch.g. 1978)	Cantab (b 1957)	Cantaber (ch 1946)	Djebel Polaris
		Balek (bl 1946)	Mehemet Ali Balaclava
	Maine Pet (br 1965)	Light Year (ch 1958)	Chamier Spring Light
		Arklow Lass (br 1957)	Straight Deal Meadowbrook

at Wetherby on Boxing Day. Though the good ground and steady early pace there put less emphasis on stamina than would have been ideal, The Thinker had looked to be in trouble passing the stands for the first time and his subsequent ten-week absence suggests something might have been amiss.

The Thinker is a brother to two winning jumpers in point-to-pointer Go Straight and successful hurdler/chaser Heather-Can. The latter is now at stud and has produced a filly by Deep Run and a colt by Orchestra from her first two coverings. Maine Pet was an unraced sister to successful chaser Arc Lamp out of the winning hurdler Arklow Lass, in turn a half-sister to several winners including the useful staying chaser Away For Slates. At his best The Thinker, a workmanlike gelding, is a top-class chaser. He usually jumps well, though he is prone to the occasional error—he fell at the tenth in the Gold Cup in 1989 and made mistakes at second Becher's and two out when third in the Grand National. He is suited by a thorough test of stamina and probably needs give in the ground. The Thinker tends to come to hand quickly. He has won first time out in two of the last four seasons in which he raced—he missed 1987/8 through injury—and ran well on his reappearance in the latest season. *W. A. Stephenson.*

THE THIRSTY FARMER 11 b.g. Grisaille–Hooks And Eyes (Tenterhooks) **c112**
[1989/90 c28g* c25m c33d^{5} c36g^{pu}] sparely-made gelding: handicap chaser: won —
at Windsor in March: stiff tasks subsequently, and was far from disgraced when fifth to Four Trix in William Hill Scottish National (Handicap Chase) at Ayr in April: ran as though feeling effects of that hard race on next outing, a week later: a thorough stayer who needs plenty of driving: acts on heavy going and good to firm: often blinkered or visored. *M. C. Pipe.*

THE TORRIDGE 5 b.h. Busted–Red Habit (Habitat) [1989/90 16g^{pu} 16g
17m^{pu} 16m^{pu}] good-topped horse: fourth foal: dam once-raced daughter of smart —
1973 2-y-o Red Berry: well behind in claimer at 3 yrs, only outing on Flat: little sign of ability in novice hurdles. *R. Callow.*

THE UNDERGRADUATE 11 gr.g. Scallywag–Mrs Cantab (Cantab) **c74 x**
[1989/90 c24g^{3} c27g^{4} c25f^{2} c25m^{3}] rangy gelding: winning hurdler: poor novice —
chaser: stays well: acts on heavy going: makes mistakes over fences: usually blinkered nowadays. *C. C. Trietline.*

THE UNDERTAKER 6 b.g. River Knight (FR)–Nora's Choice (King's Leap) c—
[1989/90 22f^{2} 24g^{5} 22g^{3} c20g c25d^{pu}] angular gelding: novice hurdler: no form 77
over fences: blinkered once: dead. *J. B. Sayers.*

THE VATMAN COMETH 5 b.g. Lafontaine (USA)–Sugar Lump (Candy
Cane) [1989/90 21d^{6} 16m^{2}] leggy, workmanlike gelding: shaped promisingly in 106 p
novice hurdles in March, on second start 2 lengths second to Fifth Amendment at Wincanton: will be suited by return to further: will improve further and win races. *J. R. Upson.*

THE WELDER 12 b.g. Bargello–Chantarella (Typhoon) [1989/90 c16f^{2} c20f^{2} **c107**
c16d c16f^{4} c16g^{4} c16g* c16g^{4}] sparely-made gelding: handicap chaser: won —
conditional jockeys event at Ascot in January: below his best previous 3 outings, and on final start: stays 2½m: acts on any going with possible exception of heavy: suited by forcing tactics: suitable mount for a claimer: tends to jump to the left and rather low on occasions: genuine. *R. Lee.*

THE WEST AWAKE 9 br.g. Green Shoon–Ballygoman Maid (Light Thrust) **c143**
[1989/90 c24g^{3}] workmanlike gelding: has been pin fired: one of the best novice —
chasers of 1987/8, notably winning Sun Alliance Chase at Cheltenham: missed 1988/9 season due to recurring splint problem: bit backward, jumped none too fluently and ridden from halfway, when third to Bonanza Boy in limited handicap at Chepstow in December: suited by 3m: acts on soft going and yet to race on top-of-the-ground: blinkered nowadays. *O. Sherwood.*

THE WIDGET MAN 4 b.g. Callernish–Le Tricolore Token (pedigree
unknown) [1989/90 16s* 16g^{5} 16d^{3}] lengthy, angular gelding: first known foal: 102
dam unraced: won juvenile hurdle at Folkestone in December easily by 12 lengths: pulled hard when below that form in Steel Plate Trial Hurdle at Cheltenham and juvenile event at Wincanton. *J. T. Gifford.*

Peter Vaux Memorial Trophy, Catterick— course-specialist The Wilk (right) and Withy Bank

THE WILK 11 b.g. Pongee–Oh Look (Ommeyad) [1989/90 c25f* c27g³ c25m^wo c24g⁵ c25m⁴ c28g* c28g* c25d* c25g* c24m^F c24f^F] sturdy gelding: fairly useful chaser: often let down by his jumping but won 6 times at Catterick in 1989/90 (has now won 8 times there): stays very well: acts on any going: usually held up: sold 9,600 gns Doncaster Spring Sales. *W. A. Stephenson.* **c132** x —

THE WOODEN HUT 7 ch.g. Windjammer (USA)–Bunduq (Scottish Rifle) [1989/90 c20g^F c20s^F 22d^pu 16g] sparely-made gelding: inconsistent middle-distance handicapper on Flat: poor novice hurdler: has fallen both outings over fences. *R. Voorspuy.* c— 71

THE WRENS DEN 5 b.m. Le Moss–The Wren's Nest (Wrekin Rambler) [1989/90 F16d F16g² F16f⁴] third foal: half-sister to winning Irish hurdler Le Roilelet (by Le Bavard): dam won on Flat and over hurdles in Ireland: in frame in NH Flat races at Kelso and Hexham in the spring: yet to race over hurdles or fences. *Mrs S. A. Bramall.*

THE YOKEL 4 b.g. Hays–Some Dame (Will Somers) [1989/90 16f⁶ 17m⁵ 17m⁴] plating-class 1¼m maiden on Flat: poor form in juvenile hurdles, including in a seller: sold out of G. Pritchard-Gordon's stable 2,600 gns Ascot October Sales after first start. *R. J. Manning.* 59

THIMONI 5 ch.m. Ahonoora–Thimothea (FR) (Timmy My Boy) [1989/90 16m 27g^pu] lengthy mare: poor novice hurdler: stays 2½m: blinkered last 3 outings of 1988/9. *G. M. Moore.* —

THINKING CAP 9 ch.g. Bargello–Grangeclare Lady (Menelek) [1989/90 c19s⁴ c24g c24v⁵ c22s⁴ c25v⁶ c24s⁴ c26v³ c36f^F c25d] winning Irish hurdler/chaser: fell at the third in Seagram Grand National at Liverpool in April: stays well: acts on heavy going. *A. L. T. Moore, Ireland.* **c110** —

THIN RED LINE 6 b. or br.g. Brigadier Gerard–Golden Keep (Worden II) [1989/90 16s* a18g³ 16d 16g³ 17f 17h²] leggy gelding: won selling handicap hurdle at Fakenham in December (bought in 2,700 gns): placed in modest company afterwards: likely to prove best at 2m: blinkered last start 1988/9, visored 1989/90: none too genuine and not to be trusted. *J. R. Jenkins.* 80 §

THIONVILLE 10 b.g. African Sky–Mariska (FR) (Tanerko) [1989/90 20d^F 17v 17d 18s 17m^pu] smallish, sparely-made gelding: one-time fairly useful 2m hurdler: no form in 1989/90: dead. *S. F. Turton.* —

Mr R. Haggas' "Third In Line"

THIRD IN LINE 7 ch.g. Proverb–Snipkin (Straight Lad) [1989/90 c22f* c20m* c24f^F c20m^2 c20m^F c24g* c20g* c20f^4] leggy, angular, sparely-made gelding: moderate hurdler: easy winner of novice chases at Kelso and Bangor in October and Edinburgh (2) in January: led until close home when going down by ½ length to Blazing Walker in Dipper Novices' Chase at Newcastle in November: ran as though something amiss final outing: stays 3m: acts well on firm going: blinkered last start in 1988/9: jumps well in the main: sold 20,000 gns Doncaster Spring Sales. *J. G. FitzGerald.* **c119** —

THIRD SON 4 b. or br.c. Oats–Angodeen (Aberdeen) [1989/90 16g^3 16d^3 16s^2 16v^2 16s^5 17d^4 16d 16g^F] tall, leggy colt: fourth foal: half-brother to winning hurdlers Don't Shout and An-Go-Look (both by Don't Look) and winning chaser Roman Dart (by Roman Warrior): dam poor novice hurdler: modest juvenile hurdler: visored final start (in lead when falling 3 out): worth a try over further than 2m: acts on heavy going. *J. M. Jefferson.* 97

THIRTY FIRST 5 gr.g. Castle Keep–January (FR) (Sigebert) [1989/90 16d a18g^2 a20g^2] lengthy gelding: closely related to useful hurdler Janus (by Ragstone) and half-brother to several winners, including a couple of hurdlers: fair stayer on Flat (has found little under pressure): second in novice hurdles at Southwell and Lingfield (beaten 25 lengths): will stay beyond 2½m. *J. L. Dunlop.* 83

THIS NETTLE DANGER 6 b.g. Kambalda–Golden Goose (Prince Hansel) [1989/90 16f^3 25f^2 c20g^F 21s^4 20m^2 20f^3 20g^2] leggy, rather sparely-made gelding: modest novice hurdler: fell second on chasing debut: seems best at short of 3m: acts on soft going and good to firm. *J. A. Glover.* c— 93

THISTLE MONARCH 5 b.g. Rontino–Lavender Blue (Silly Season) [1989/90 F 14v^3] fourth foal: dam never ran: co-favourite, 6½ lengths third behind Dakyns Boy in NH Flat race at Ayr in April: yet to race over hurdles or fences. *J. S. Wilson.*

THORNFIELD GROVE 6 b.g. Royal Fountain–Joyous Sound (Bleep-Bleep) [1989/90 F16f 20g] fourth foal: half-brother to a poor animal by Leander: dam showed a little ability at 2 yrs: fourth in NH Flat race: in need of race, never-dangerous seventh behind Latent Talent in novice event at Haydock in November on hurdling debut. *Mrs R. Wharton.*
—

THREE BELLS 8 ch.g. Song–Triple Bar (Jimmy Reppin) [1989/90 16h^{5}] plating-class sprint maiden on Flat in Britain in 1986: subsequently won on Flat in the Channel Islands: tailed off in novice event at Taunton in September on hurdling debut. *C. P. Billot.*
—

THREE COUNTIES 13 b.g. Little Buskins–Fair Reply (Babur) [1989/90 c24g^{4} c26f^{4}] medium-sized, useful-looking gelding: high-class hunter chaser at his best: won 1989 Christies Foxhunter Chase at Cheltenham: 20 lengths fourth behind Call Collect in 1990 running: stays very well: acts on any going: sound jumper: genuine. *J. W. Blundell.*
c**126**
—

THREEOUTOFFOUR 5 b.h. Milford–Smiling (Silly Season) [1989/90 16d 16g^{5} 16s* 16d 16f] leggy, workmanlike horse with scope: dam winning hurdler: no worthwhile form at 2 yrs: won novice hurdle at Nottingham in January by 25 lengths: found little under pressure in similar event in February, and finished last when favourite for novice handicap nearly 4 months later: should stay further than 2m: acts on soft going. *O. Brennan.*
106

THREEPLAND 7 b.g. Rugged Man–Prosper Lion (Regret) [1989/90 22d c24g^{3} a20g^{3} a24g^{5} c24g^{pu} 26m^{pu}] big, rangy gelding: handicap hurdler/chaser: suited by 2½m: acts on firm ground (won NH Flat race on heavy): has sweated on occasions. *R. F. Fisher.*
c**98**
98

THUNDER FLOWER 5 ch.m. Deep Run–Lulu's Daughter (Levanter) [1989/90 F13m^{3} F17f^{2} F16m^{5} 25m^{3} 22g^{6} 16m^{4} 24g^{pu}] sturdy mare: fifth foal: sister to NH Flat race winner The Rapids and fair hurdler/useful chaser Highfrith: dam unraced half-sister to I'm A Driver: placed in NH Flat races: poor form over hurdles: best effort at 2m. *G. Richards.*
85

THUNDERING 5 b.g. Persian Bold–Am Stretchin' (USA) (Ambiorix II) [1989/90 16g^{pu} 16d^{pu}] sturdy gelding: half-brother to 2 winners over jumps abroad: pulled up 2 out in novice hurdles in first half of season: sold 1,450 gns Doncaster January Sales: subsequently won 1m seller on Flat. *A. W. Jones.*
—

THUNDERWOOD 8 ch.g. Lombard (GER)–Calibre (Caliban) [1989/90 21s^{pu} a24g^{pu}] sturdy gelding: poor novice hurdler: failed to complete course in 2 novice chases in 1988/9: should be suited by 2½m. *T. Reid.*
c—
—

THURLESTONE (NZ) 7 ch.g. Balkan Knight (USA)–Tabessia (NZ) (As Before) [1989/90 16s^{5} 16g^{6} 16g^{4}] leggy gelding: winning hurdler: best effort in handicaps in 1989/90 when fourth at Wincanton (gave impression he'll be suited by a return to further) in January: stays 2¼m: acts on firm going. *Capt. T. A. Forster.*
97

THURSBY 7 br.g. Abyssinia–Dane Hole (Past Petition) [1989/90 c20m^{F} c25d^{5} c25s] strong, compact non-thoroughbred gelding: first living foal: dam unraced: winner of 3 point-to-points, 2 of them by wide margins, in 1989: jumped none too fluently when never-nearer fifth in novice chase at Towcester in February: ran moderately later in month: will be suited by a thorough test of stamina. *Capt. T. A. Forster.*
c**83**

TIARUM 8 b.g. Tiran (HUN)–Contessa (HUN) (Peleid) [1989/90 16f^{2} 17f^{4} 17f* 17f^{2} 17m^{2} 16m* 17m 16m 16m^{3} 16m^{6} 16m^{6}] small, lightly-made gelding: selling hurdler: won conditional jockeys handicap at Newton Abbot (no bid) and lady riders non-selling handicap at Stratford very early in season: well behind in novice event on chasing debut: barely stays 2m when conditions are testing: acts on firm and soft ground: blinkered once 1987/8. *G. A. Ham.*
c—
86

TIBER MELODY 7 ch.g. True Song–Tamoretta (Chamossaire) [1989/90 24m^{pu}] brother to winning point-to-pointer Tam's Aria and half-brother to winning chaser La Gingold (by Will Somers): dam, fair chaser, half-sister to Spanish Steps: behind when pulled up in novice hurdle at Worcester. *M. J. Wilkinson.*
—

TIBER RIVER 6 b.g. Troy–River Call (FR) (Riverman (USA)) [1989/90 21f^{3} 20d 16m* 16m^{3}] sturdy gelding: won 4-runner amateur riders novice hurdle at Fakenham in May by a distance: good third in lady riders handicap at Stratford final start: stays 2½m: acts on firm ground: blinkered once in 1987/8 and on last 2 outings. *C. P. E. Brooks.*
104

TICARC 9 b.g. Push On–Arctic Calm (Arctic Slave) [1989/90 c21s^{pu}] rangy c— §
gelding: third in novice chase in Ireland in 1987: won 2 point-to-points in Britain in
1988: needing race, reluctant to race and was pulled up at the fifth in hunter chase
at Towcester in February. *S. E. W. Rea.*

TICKLE ME PINK 5 b.g. Gleason (USA)–Western Wendy (Young Emperor)
[1989/90 16h^{pu}] leggy gelding: of little account: sold 1,500 gns Ascot November —
Sales. *P. Howling.*

TICKLE YOUR FANCY 4 b.g. Tickled Pink–Florries Fancy (Breeders
Dream) [1989/90 16f^{6} 16f^{ur} 16f^{pu}] smallish, rather lightly-made gelding: probably —
of little account on Flat: no worthwhile form in selling hurdles: sold 925 gns Ascot
October Sales. *J. A. Bennett.*

TICOVER 7 b. or br.m. Politico (USA)–Evericia (Immortality) [1989/90 17m^{6}]
well beaten in NH Flat races: tailed off in early-season novice hurdle at Cartmel: —
sold 3,300 gns Doncaster October Sales. *F. S. Storey.*

TIDAL STREAM 7 b.g. Paddy's Stream–Sea Empress (Perhapsburg) **c106**
[1989/90 c16d^{4} c19d^{4} c20v* c20s^{2} c21g^{2}] good-bodied gelding: winning hurdler: —
moderate chaser: always prominent when winning handicap at Chepstow in
January: second in similar races at Uttoxeter and Wincanton in February: will stay
3m: acts on heavy going: consistent. *Capt. T. A. Forster.*

TIE BACK 4 b. or br.f. Tender King–Grattan Princess (Tumble Wind (USA))
[1989/90 16v^{pu} 16g] lengthy filly: poor maiden on Flat: pulls too hard for her own —
good over hurdles. *M. J. Camacho.*

TIEITOFF 5 b.g. Monksfield–Hypolite (Brave Invader (USA)) [1989/90 F16g]
fifth foal: half-brother to winning staying hurdler Prominent Ruler (by Prominer):
dam poor Irish maiden on Flat and over jumps: tailed off in NH Flat race at
Warwick: yet to race over hurdles or fences. *M. O'Neill.*

TIERIKI 7 b.g. Riki Lash–Tiepola (Tiepoletto) [1989/90 20d^{pu} 27g^{4} 25f^{5} 24f
24m^{4} 27f^{5}] dipped-backed gelding: poor novice hurdler: best effort over 27f on 68
good ground. *B. M. Temple.*

TIFFANYS NEDINE 4 b.g. Rymer–Gokatiego (Huntercombe) [1989/90
F16g] third foal: brother to novice hurdler Rhyming Kate: dam unraced: behind in
NH Flat race at Market Rasen: yet to race over hurdles. *R. Champion.*

TIGER CLAW (USA) 4 b.g. Diamond Shoal–Tiger Scout (USA) (Silent Screen
(USA)) [1989/90 16f* 16g^{4}] leggy, sparely-made gelding: won juvenile hurdle at 104
Newbury in November: jumped none too fluently and didn't respond to pressure
when remote fourth at Folkestone following month: visored: subsequently won
twice over 1½m on Flat with R. Hodges. *I. A. Balding.*

TIGERS PET 6 b.g. Tina's Pet–Too Do (Manado) [1989/90 16m^{5} 16m^{4} a20g
16m* 16f* 20g] sparely-made gelding: former selling hurdler: won 2 non-selling 88
handicaps at Towcester in May, better effort on second occasion: best at 2m: acts
on firm ground: has won for a claimer: reportedly broke blood vessel third start:
trained until after next outing by W. Bissill. *O. Brennan.*

TIGER TED 10 b.g. Night Thought–Linden Light (Amber Light) [1989/90 c—
c25m^{ur} c25g^{pu}] rangy gelding: modest chaser, lightly raced: stays 3¼m: best on a —
sound surface and acts on hard going. *P. G. Bailey.*

TIGER TIGER 5 ch.g. Enchantment–Fleur d'Amour (Murrayfield) [1989/90
20v^{pu} 16d 16v^{pu} 16g^{4} 16g 20d^{pu} 16g^{6} 17f^{6}] compact, sturdy gelding: poor novice 74
hurdler: only worthwhile form in 1989/90 in sellers on fourth and seventh starts:
best at 2m: has run with tongue tied down. *Ronald Thompson.*

TIGHT TURN 11 ch.g. Avocat–Rufter (Falcon) [1989/90 c17g^{4}] small gelding: c—
quite a modest hurdler: never dangerous when over 20 lengths fourth in handicap —
chase at Newton Abbot in November: stays 21f: acts on any going. *R. G. Frost.*

TIKITAMA 7 b.m. Bustiki–Tarama (Tamerlane) [1989/90 16m] half-sister to 3
winning jumpers, notably 1982 Grand National winner Grittar (by Grisaille): dam —
won 2m novice hurdle: placed in point-to-points in 1989: tailed off in novice event
at Huntingdon in December on hurdling debut. *R. J. Weaver.*

TILDARG 6 ch.g. Black Minstrel–Real Treasure (Master Owen) [1989/90 F16d
F16g* 16m* 16m^{pu}] IR 5,800 3-y-o: good-topped, lengthy ex-Irish gelding: has 110 p
scope: half-brother to winning hurdler/chaser Rockfield Boy (by Master Owen):
dam unraced: won a point-to-point in 1989 and NH Flat race at Naas in November
(trained by I. Ferguson): favourite but better for race, won novice hurdle at
Sandown in March by 3 lengths from Acre Hill, leading from third: dull in coat,
well behind when pulled up 3 out in valuable novice event at Liverpool following

month: worth another chance to confirm promise of his hurdling debut. *O. Sherwood.*

TILL IT HURTS 4 b.g. Owen Anthony–High Authority (High Award) [1989/90 16g 16fpu 16v] small, lengthy gelding: second foal: dam won twice over 5f at 2 yrs: no sign of ability over hurdles, including in a seller: has worn a tongue strap. *Mrs G. E. Jones.* —

TILSTONE LODGE 5 br.g. Try My Best (USA)–Sabirone (FR) (Iron Duke (FR)) [1989/90 16m5 16mpu a16g a16g3 16fF] leggy, shallow-girthed gelding: no form on Flat: only form over hurdles when third in novice handicap at Southwell in March: blinkered last 3 starts: sweating badly and edgy second outing. *T. H. Caldwell.* 54

TILTING WIND 7 ch.g. Windjammer (USA)–Tilting (Galivanter) [1989/90 16fF] last of 5 in maiden at 2 yrs: tailed off when falling last in selling hurdle: dead. *C. R. Beever.* —

TILT TECH FLYER 5 b.g. Windjammer (USA)–Queen Kate (Queen's Hussar) [1989/90 16s* 16g4 16v4 16v*] tall gelding: half-brother to NH Flat race winner Smiles Better (by Royalty): modest performer at up to 1m on Flat: won novice hurdles at Folkestone in December and February (handicap): unlikely to stay much beyond 2m: acts on heavy going: ridden by 5-lb claimer. *R. Akehurst.* 103

TIMBER'S BOY 5 b.g. Nemorino (USA)–Ludorum's Praise (Song of Praise) [1989/90 16dpu 24d] leggy gelding: fourth foal: dam of no account on Flat: well behind in NH Flat races and a novice hurdle. *J. Ringer.* —

TIME AFTER TIME 8 ch.m. High Award–Tide And Time (Easter Island) [1989/90 c25mF] lengthy mare: no sign of ability over hurdles: won a point-to-oint in March: fell at the third in novice hunter chase following month. *J. D. Hankinson.* c— —

TIME-BEE 9 ch.g. Manado–Alli-Bee (Violon d'Ingres) [1989/90 16f 16m 16fF 16f4] leggy, angular gelding: poor front-running handicap hurdler: has run in a seller: possibly unsuited by very soft ground, acts on any other: usually blinkered. *J. P. Smith.* 71

TIME CARRIAGE 4 br.g. Carriage Way–Harmony Thyme (Sing Sing) [1989/90 F17m] half-brother to several minor winners: dam won over 5f as a 2-y-o: tailed off in NH Flat race at Carlisle: yet to race over hurdles. *V. Hall.*

TIMELY STAR 9 b.g. Faraway Times (USA)–Star Pearl (Star Moss) [1989/90 22m6 c24gpu 24s6 c20dur c20d*] tall, good sort: useful hurdler at his best: blinkered, won novice chase at Bangor in March by 5 lengths from Autumn Sport: probably stayed 3m and acted on any going: dead. *Mrs J. Pitman.* c**103** 130

TIME MODULE 6 b.g. Latest Model–Gemini Miss (My Swanee) [1989/90 16fpu 16gpu 20d 16g 16v 21s 17d 17m3] leggy gelding: 100/1, first sign of ability over hurdles when third behind Dwadme in novice event at Devon & Exeter: evidently suited by top-of-the-ground. *D. D. Scott.* 79

TIME ON MY HANDS 4 ch.f. Warpath–Midsummer Madness (Silly Season) [1989/90 16s6 17vpu 16gpu 17d 16f3 17m2 16f*] leggy filly: won 9f seller on Flat in 1989: sold out of C. Thornton's stable 5,800 gns Doncaster October Sales: won novice handicap hurdle at Ludlow in April by 1½ lengths from Sporting Idol: seems suited by sharp 2m, top-of-the-ground and forcing tactics. *Mrs A. Knight.* 87

TIMES ARE HARD 6 b.g. Bay Express–Raffinrula (Raffingora) [1989/90 16s5 16g* 16g2] sparely-made gelding: lightly raced on Flat, won 1m and 1¼m handicaps in January: won novice hurdle at Perth in April: no chance with 20-length winner First Crack on same course following month: may not stay much beyond 2m. *D. Burchell.* 98

TIME STAR (NZ) 6 br.g. Drums of Time (USA)–Crescent Star (NZ) (Persian Garden) [1989/90 16f6 16g 22g] unfurnished gelding: no worthwhile form over hurdles, looking none too keen final start. *Capt. T. A. Forster.* —

TIMMINION 8 ch.g. Dominion–My Baby Love (Sovereign Path) [1989/90 20g4 16g 20s6 20g*] leggy gelding: fairly useful hurdler: returned to form when winning handicap at Perth in April by 12 lengths from Candlebright: will stay beyond 2½m: best form on a sound surface. *A. P. Stringer.* 127

TIMMY BOY 10 ch.g. Timolin (FR)–Cabarita (USA) (First Landing) [1989/90 16m 16h] sturdy gelding: winning hurdler: has been beaten in sellers: form only at 2m: appears to act on any going. *J. P. Smith.* —

Haven Novices' Hurdle, Kempton—Tinryland leads Gaasid over the last

TIMONTADE 8 br.g. Rhodomantade–Right On Time (Right Boy) [1989/90 21h^{pu}] medium-sized gelding: third in 2 maiden hurdles in 1986/7: no form since. *Mrs J. Wonnacott.* —

TIMSOLO 7 ch.g. Remainder Man–Miss Tehran (Manacle) [1989/90 a20g* a20g^{2} 16g^{6}] small gelding: won handicap hurdle at Southwell in November: good second on same course following day, but well below form next start: stays 2¾m: probably acts on any going: has won when sweating: won two 1¾m handicaps on Flat in January. *C. Tinkler.* 106

TIMURS DOUBLE 9 b.g. Double Form–Timur's Daughter (Tamerlane) [1989/90 c24g] rangy gelding: moderate hurdler/poor novice chaser: won 2 point-to-points in March: jumped none too fluently when tailed off in hunter chase following month: stays 2½m: acts on any going: blinkered once in 1988/9 (made a couple of bad mistakes and took little interest). *C. J. Sample.* c— § —

TINA'S BRIG 9 b.m. Majestic Streak–Cliburn New Cut (New Brig) [1989/90 16s] lightly-made, wiry mare: winning hurdler/chaser: doesn't stay 2½m under very testing conditions: probably acts on any going: usually amateur or claimer ridden: moderate jumper of fences. *T. W. Donnelly.* c— x —

TINA'S HIDEAWAY 5 b. or br.m. Kabour–Tina Glitters (Goldhill) [1989/90 F16v 17g] plain, close-coupled mare: fourth foal: half-sister to winning point-to-pointer/hunter chaser Astral Spirit (by Bivouac): dam unraced half-sister to several winning jumpers, including useful hurdler Graphics Solar: tailed off in NH Flat race and a novice hurdle: sold 1,750 gns Doncaster March Sales. *J. J. O'Neill.* —

TINAS LAD 7 b.g. Jellaby–Arbatina (Sallust) [1989/90 c16g^{2} c16g^{F} c17f^{3} c20m^{5}] workmanlike gelding: fair hurdler: modest form in novice chases: unlikely to stay much beyond 2m: acts on firm and dead ground: free-running sort, who seems suited by racing up with the pace: in good form on Flat in 1990. *J. A. C. Edwards.* c**98** —

TINGLE BROOK 6 br.g. Paddy's Stream–Yvonne's Fancy (Continuation) [1989/90 F16g F17d 20g^{pu} 16g^{pu}] fourth foal: dam never ran: behind in NH Flat races and when pulled up in novice hurdles. *G. Richards.* —

TINKERS BROOK 5 b.g. Last Fandango–Roman Spa (Young Emperor) [1989/90 F16f 19m^{5} 17v] angular gelding: half-brother to prolific winners in Belgium and Italy: dam placed over 5f: well behind in NH Flat race and novice hurdles. *A. Barrow.* —

TINKERS GOLD 8 ch.g. Levanter–Rose Cottage (Rose Knight) [1989/90 16g^{pu}] leggy gelding: fourth foal: half-brother to a poor animal by Ml Jet: dam quite modest hurdler: little sign of ability in novice hurdles. *P. J. Hobbs.* —

TINKLING STAR 6 b.g. Lepanto (GER)–Tinkling Sound (Sound Track) [1989/90 16g 16s 16s 16m 21d] leggy, quite good-topped gelding: poor form in novice hurdles. *J. C. Fox.* 72

TINK-N-TOUGHT 7 b.m. Record Token–Silver Shadow (Birdbrook) [1989/90 17m F] half-sister to NH Flat race winner Shading (by Homing): dam very useful and thoroughly genuine hurdler: weakening when falling 2 out in amateur riders maiden hurdle at Carlisle. *J. J. O'Neill.* —

TINRYLAND 6 b.g. Prince Regent (FR)–Tonduff Star (Royal Highway) [1989/90 F16m* F16m* 16g* 16d3 16s 16g6 20fF 25m3] close-coupled ex-Irish gelding: second foal: half-brother to NH Flat race winner Tunduff Glen (by Furry Glen): dam winning Irish hurdler at up to 2¾m: won 2 early-season NH Flat races when trained by P. Prendergast and Haven Novices' Hurdle (by ½ length from Gaasid) at Kempton in December: very good third behind Forest Sun in Baring Securities Tolworth Hurdle at Sandown following month and fair third behind Dwadme in White Satin Novices' Hurdle at Liverpool in April: lost his chance with a mistake all outings in between (in touch and going well when falling sixth in Sun Alliance Novices' Hurdle at Cheltenham on seventh): should prove suited by further than 2m: best form on dead going (possibly unsuited by soft). *N. J. Henderson.* 136

TINSEL ROSE 7 ch.m. Porto Bello–Love Is Blind (USA) (Hasty Road) [1989/90 17g 16spu 16spu a16g5] leggy, lightly-made mare: winning selling hurdler: no form in 1989/90: seems to act on any going: claimer ridden. *R. J. Hodges.* —

TINTO HILL 7 br.g. Mandrake Major–Chantabelle (Chantelsey) [1989/90 c16d c17g2 c16f2 c18m5 c16fF a16g5] sparely-made gelding: well beaten over hurdles, including in a seller: second in novice chase at Newbury and intermediate chase at Wincanton in November: soundly beaten fourth start: has worn a crossed noseband and severe bridle. *Miss L. Bower.* c85 —

TINY STEAL 6 b.g. Pollerton–Spray (St Chad) [1989/90 c20dur c17g6 c20mpu] big, rangy gelding with plenty of scope: tailed off in novice chase in February: moderate jumper. *W. G. Morris.* c— x

TIPP DOWN 7 ch.g. Crash Course–Caramore Lady (Deep Run) [1989/90 21d2] sturdy gelding: 15 lengths second to Mossgara in novice hurdle at Warwick in March: should improve and win a similar event. *D. J. G. Murray-Smith.* 94 p

TIPPER LAD 8 b.g. Ascendant–Seven Threes (Langton Heath) [1989/90 c22m3 c21gpu 16s c26gpu c20f6 c26mpu] lengthy gelding: of little account. *C. F. Lee.* c— —

TIPPING TIM 5 b.g. King's Ride–Jeanarie (Reformed Character) [1989/90 16dpu 20g 25dpu 21fpu] workmanlike, lengthy gelding: first foal: dam, poor Irish Flat maiden, half-sister to 2 winning jumpers, including useful chaser Bold Argument: no sign of ability in novice hurdles. *N. A. Twiston-Davies.* —

TIP-TAP 8 gr.m. Tachypous–Dashing Diana (Silver Shark) [1989/90 16mpu 16h6 16h5] smallish, short-backed mare: poor novice hurdler: has run in a seller. *M. T. Bowker.* —

TIPTONIAN 11 gr.g. Royalty–Pretty Fast (Firestreak) [1989/90 17f4 16f3 20f3 c19f2 c20m2 c20h* c16f2 c16sur c16m* c16dur c16m5 c16f5 c16f4] rather sparely-made gelding: modest hurdler: creditable third in seller second start: won novice chase at Ludlow in September and novice handicap chase at Leicester (jumped left last 2) in January: stays 2¾m: acts on hard going and possibly unsuited by soft: has run well for a claimer. *K. S. Bridgwater.* c93 86

TIS FRANK AGAIN 8 b.g. Roselier (FR)–Orwell Brief (Lucky Brief) [1989/90 21d* 24d3 24m] rangy gelding: first outing for almost 2 years, won handicap hurdle at Warwick in March: claimer ridden, creditable third behind Duntree in novice event at Chepstow later in month: stays 3m: acts on heavy going and probably unsuited by firm: blinkered last start 1987/8. *D. J. G. Murray-Smith.* 106

TITO L'EFFRONTE (FR) 5 b.g. Pamponi (FR)–Linea (FR) (Laniste) [1989/90 17d* 18d* 19v2 c22d2 c20m* c21g2 c23s* 25m c19s3 21.5g4] big, leggy, lightly-made French gelding: very useful hurdler/chaser: successful over hurdles at Auteuil in September and October, and over fences there in December and in Grand Prix de Pau in February: last of 18 finishers in Waterford Crystal Stayers' Hurdle at Cheltenham in March (prominent long way): stays 23f: yet to race on very firm going, acts on any other. *Jean Dasque, France.* c? ?

TITUS FILLE 4 b.f. Lucky Wednesday–Maiden d'Or (Songedor) [1989/90 aF16g] half-sister to stayer Shmain (by Sheshoon), winner on Flat and over hurdles, and winning hunter chaser Walk In Rhythm (by Tower Walk): dam won at up to 1m: well beaten in NH Flat race at Southwell: sold 800 gns Doncaster March Sales: yet to race over hurdles. *M. Dickinson.*

TITUS GOLD 5 b.g. Sonnen Gold–Chemin de Guerre (Warpath) [1989/90 16v5 16dur 16s* 20s4 16spu] leggy gelding: won handicap hurdle at Nottingham in January: ran poorly final start: doesn't stay 2½m: suited by plenty of give in the ground: successful only when blinkered or visored. *M. Dickinson.* 107

TITUS ROCK 4 b.g. Bay Express–La Balconne (Taj Dewan) [1989/90 F12f F16gpu] 2,000F: half-brother to 2 winners in Belgium by Dragonara Palace: dam winning hurdler: behind in NH Flat race: pulled up lame next time: yet to race over hurdles. *M. Dickinson.*

TIVIAN 10 b.g. Busted–Jovian (Hardicanute) [1989/90 21d 16s] leggy gelding: modest hurdler nowadays: third in novice event in 1988/9 on chasing debut: not disgraced over 23f: best form on heavy going. *J. White.* c— —

TOAD ALONG 5 b.g. Daring March–Fille de Phaeton (Sun Prince) [1989/90 a16g2 16f4 16f* 16m2 16m3 16h* 17m3] big gelding: won novice handicap hurdle at Worcester in March (idled run-in) and novice hurdle at Ludlow in May: stiffish task, not disgraced when third of 4 in handicap at Newton Abbot final outing: likely to prove suited by sharp 2m: acts on hard ground and seems unsuited by soft: wears a tongue strap and has worn net muzzle. *O. Sherwood.* 104

TO ASTERI (USA) 9 ch.g. Big Burn (USA)–Bridal Shower (USA) (Hail To Reason) [1989/90 c20m c20dpu c20dpu c24mpu c19f6 c16m c20fpu] lengthy gelding: winning hurdler: no form over fences: ran poorly in blinkers sixth outing 1987/8. *Miss J. Horwood.* c— —

TOBY TOBIAS 8 b.g. Furry Glen–Aurora Lady (Beau Chapeau) [1989/90 c25mur c20g* c21m* c21g* c25d* c24dur c26f2 c25m*] c**167** —

The Wincanton executive can be proud of its efforts to put on interesting conditions races, and it thoroughly deserves the recently-announced inclusion in the Pattern of the Terry Biddlecombe Chase, run in October with prize money upped from £6,000 in 1989 to £25,000. Two of Wincanton's conditions races in the latest season, the Mid Season Chase run just before the turn of the year and the John Bull Chase run just after it, were significant landmarks in the career of Toby Tobias, a good-class Irish hurdler in 1987/8 who'd since been working his way up the chasing ladder in Britain. In fact, the two races announced he'd 'arrived'. In his first season over fences Toby Tobias won twice and looked very promising but he was a trifle lacking in confidence and fell five out in the Mumm Club Novices' Chase at Liverpool, his biggest test. So he began his second season in minor handicaps, winning one at Worcester in December having unseated his rider when hampered at the third at Plumpton on his only previous outing. Then came Wincanton.

John Bull Chase, Wincanton—Toby Tobias (near side) takes a ditch with Pegwell Bay

Charterhouse Mercantile Chase, Cheltenham—
Toby Tobias, Maid of Money and Bigsun at the third last

Ending Man O'Magic's sequence of five victories most convincingly at levels in the Mid Season Chase was a smart performance; beating the high-class Pegwell Bay easily by eight lengths, receiving only 8 lb, in the John Bull Chase was an even better one and it earned him a run in the Charterhouse Mercantile Chase at Cheltenham later in January, where he came up against the leading Irish mare Maid of Money on trial for the Tote Cheltenham Gold Cup.

At this point in his career Toby Tobias was thought too immature for the Gold Cup by his trainer and had the Cathcart as a more likely target. But

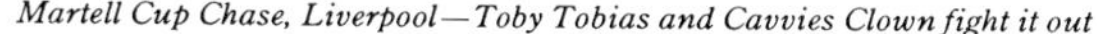

Martell Cup Chase, Liverpool—Toby Tobias and Cavvies Clown fight it out

Mrs Elizabeth Hitchins' "Toby Tobias"

he beat Maid of Money fairly and squarely by ten lengths, with Bigsun and the only other runner, the outsider Rymer King, left behind. He jumped the fences well, apart from hitting the second last hard; he moved easily under restraint most of the way, led from four out and steadily drew clear on the flat, though he gave the impression towards the end that the distance (three miles one furlong on the New Course) was plenty far enough. Although the weights favoured the winner—if he met Maid of Money at weight-for-sex he would be 6 lb worse off—it was clear he was still improving, and when Toby Tobias came out again he himself was on trial for the Gold Cup, in the Byrne Brothers Compton Chase at Newbury. He blundered and unseated his rider at the tenth in that, when a heavily-backed odds-on favourite against Barnbrook Again, Yahoo and Golden Friend. However, the race had its positive aspects. Toby Tobias came to no harm, and before he'd gone out of the contest he'd succeeded again in making a good impression, notably by the ease with which he'd moved up to dispute the lead at the previous fence with Barnbrook Again who was going a fair clip. In the end, despite this set-back Toby Tobias was sent for the Gold Cup rather than the Cathcart. Connections can't have any regrets about the decision, for he almost pulled it off. Looking in magnificent shape, he received a fine ride and responded with the best jumping of his career—a blemish-free round. He was taken round the inside, hugging the rail to save ground. Always handy, he seized the initiative as Desert Orchid was forced wide by Ten of Spades on the home turn and had a two-length lead approaching the last. He couldn't hang on though, and despite giving all he had under pressure he was run out of it near the finish by Norton's Coin; the winning distance was only three quarters of a length.

The Martell Cup Chase at Liverpool offers the chance of quick compensation for those who've run well in defeat in the Gold Cup. But under its various titles the race has seldom failed to spring a surprise—for instance, Beau Ranger won at 40/1 in 1986, Desert Orchid fell when favourite in 1989. In 1990 the Martell Cup went to the favourite for the first time in its seven-year history, as Toby Tobias confirmed Cheltenham placings with Cavvies Clown who'd finished fourth there after losing around twenty-five lengths at the start. Cavvies Clown showed ahead after the second at Liverpool despite setting off behind the four other runners. Toby Tobias, again in superb shape, was tucked in behind taking a keen hold, jumping soundly for the most part, just chancing the odd one. Having travelled really well, he had to be shaken up when Cavvies Clown pressed for home after the fourth last but he found the necessary acceleration. The pair left Delius, Golden Friend and Man O'Magic struggling as the race drew to a thrilling climax. Toby Tobias took the last two fences at some speed but so did Cavvies Clown. Toby Tobias had a slight advantage approaching the last, got away from the fence just the quicker and ran on really well to win by a length and a half; he was giving the runner-up 4 lb. Obviously, a repeat of his Liverpool and Cheltenham form will put Toby Tobias right in line for more big races in 1990/1. There must be a fair chance, though, that he'll improve a bit more yet.

Toby Tobias (b.g. 1982)	Furry Glen (b 1971)	Wolver Hollow (b 1964)	Sovereign Path
			Cygnet
		Cleftess (br 1956)	Hill Gail
			Cleft
	Aurora Lady (ch 1973)	Beau Chapeau (ch 1963)	High Hat
			Beau Co Co
		Aurora Peach (ch 1968)	Anthony
			Dotia

The leggy, useful-looking Toby Tobias is the first foal of Aurora Lady; the dam's second foal, the hurdler What About Me (by Condorcet), is also a winning stayer, albeit much lower down the scale. Neither the second dam Aurora Peach nor the third dam Dotia ran, but each was a sister to a couple of minor jumping winners. Aurora Lady did make the racecourse. A late-developer, she won an Irish National Hunt Flat race and handicap hurdles around two and a half miles at Thurles and Mallow as a seven-year-old. Her brother Portroe Prince was killed in a fall at Uttoxeter three years later, having won three chases in Britain that season. Toby Tobias' progress in the latest season has outdated the comment on his sire, the Irish Two Thousand Guineas winner Furry Glen, made in the short essay on Vicario di Bray in *Chasers & Hurdlers 1988/89* in which we said that that horse was probably the best of the sire's runners. No doubt about it now who's best, and prospective chaser Vicario di Bray will have to fulfil all he's ever promised if he's to get back into the reckoning. Toby Tobias stays three and a quarter miles well. He acts on any going. *Mrs J. Pitman.*

TOCHENKA 6 ch.m. Fine Blue–Authors Daughter (Charlottown) [1989/90 F16m^{6} 16s 22g^{5} 16m^{4} 21f^{4} 20f] strong, workmanlike mare: second foal: dam won 88
3m maiden chase: poor novice hurdler: will be suited by 3m: acts on firm ground. *Mrs J. E. Croft.*

TOCKINGTON GREEN 5 b.m. Al Sirat (USA)–Clerihan (Immortality) [1989/90 F16f] first foal: dam unraced: blinkered, tailed off in NH Flat race at Uttoxeter: yet to race over hurdles or fences. *D. H. Barons.*

TODDLIN HAME 8 br.g. Bronze Hill–Pandorana (Pandofell) [1989/90 c20d^{2}] c89
strong, stocky gelding: poor novice hurdler: poor chaser: creditable second in —
4-runner handicap at Ayr in November: stays 3m: acts on heavy going. *C. Parker.*

TOEBOARD 4 b.g. Rushmere–Ile Voleur (Burglar) [1989/90 17g^{pu} 18g^{pu} 16v^{pu}] fourth foal: dam never ran: behind when pulled up in juvenile hurdles and a —
seller (blinkered). *Miss L. Bower.*

TOFFEE APPLE 7 b.g. Comedy Star (USA)–Apple of My Eye (Silver Cloud) c91
[1989/90 c22s^{6} c25s^{3} c32f^{pu} c25m^{2} c26f^{2} c20f^{pu} c29m^{3}] sturdy gelding: placed —
twice over hurdles in 1986/7: winning point-to-pointer: placed in hunter chases: should be suited by long distances: probably acts on any going. *S. Pike.*

TOKANDA 6 ch.g. Record Token–Andalucia (Rheingold) [1989/90 16f 25m^{4}] winning plater on Flat: lightly-raced novice selling hurdler. *F. J. Yardley.* —

TOKYO JOE 7 b.g. Double Form–Moortown Lady (No Mercy) [1989/90 16m* 16s^{4} 16f] sturdy ex-Irish gelding: successful at up to 1¼m on Flat: won maiden hurdle at Roscommon in September: in need of race (first for 6 months), soundly beaten in novice hurdle at Bangor on British debut: acts on good to firm and soft going: trained by M. Halford until after second start. *P. Ransom.* 99 ?

TOM BROCK 12 b.g. Crozier–Badger Copse (Rosyth) [1989/90 c19m^{pu}] rangy gelding: winning 2m chaser: no worthwhile form for a long time, including in hunter chases: sold 1,350 gns Ascot July Sales. *Mrs J. Conway.* c— —

TOM CAXTON 9 b.g. Nearly A Hand–Lost In Silence (Silent Spring) [1989/90 c16g*] lengthy, rather sparely-made gelding: fair chaser: won handicap at Uttoxeter in December by a head from Royal Cracker: barely stays 2m: probably acts on any going: takes a strong hold: has run well for 7-lb claimer: game. *J. S. King.* **c114** —

TOM KITTY 5 b.g. Broadsword (USA)–Golden Murry (Murrayfield) [1989/90 16m^{5} 16f 20v^{pu} 16g^{F} 16g 20d^{pu}] angular gelding: well beaten over hurdles. *P. A. Blockley.* —

TOMMY ARR 4 b.g. Neltino–Promenade Concert (Tower Walk) [1989/90 16g 16s^{pu} a16g] compact gelding: behind in a seller at 2 yrs and both completed outings over hurdles: pulls hard. *M. J. Wilkinson.* —

TOMMY FARMER 8 b.g. Roselier (FR)–Fannie Farmer (Royal Avenue) [1989/90 c27g^{ur} c27g^{6} c20g c27g^{pu} c24d^{pu} c27f^{3} c24m^{2} c24g^{pu} c20f^{4}] workmanlike gelding: poor novice chaser: stays well: probably acts on any going. *D. Lee.* c87

TOMMY OWT 5 ch.g. Mr Fluorocarbon–Helping Hand (Right Boy) [1989/90 F16d^{2} F17f^{5}] third foal: half-brother to Skerne Spark (by Hotfoot), placed on Flat and over hurdles: dam winning hurdler: second in NH Flat race at Catterick in February: sold 10,000 gns Doncaster Spring Sales: yet to race over hurdles or fences. *M. J. Camacho.*

TOMMYS DREAM 7 b.m. Le Bavard (FR)–Tricia (St Paddy) [1989/90 16m* 16m* 20m^{3} 16d^{3} 21m^{3} 16m^{3} 16f^{2} 16f^{3} 17h* 25f*] smallish mare: won novice hurdles at Worcester and Warwick (made most in mares event) in September and handicaps at Devon & Exeter and Hereford (by 3 lengths from Maujendor) in May: stays 3m: acts on hard ground: has won for a claimer. *S. Christian.* 111

TOM PASCOE 5 b.g. Delamain (USA)–All Class (Laurence O) [1989/90 aF16g 16m^{pu}] IR 3,500 3-y-o: unfurnished gelding: first foal: dam unraced half-sister to a NH Flat race winner and a winning point-to-pointer: behind in NH Flat race: didn't jump well and was tailed off when pulled up 2 out in novice hurdle. *Mrs H. Parrott.* —

TOM PENNY 8 b.g. Tom Noddy–Pennyworth (Brightworthy) [1989/90 c24m^{F} c24f^{2}] half-brother to winning point-to-pointer Bright Hope (by Haven): dam won 3 point-to-points: fair winning point-to-pointer: beaten 25 lengths by Late Session in 2-runner hunter chase at Chepstow in May. *Mrs R. Harry.* **c90** ?

TOM'S LITTLE BET 6 gr.m. Scallywag–Fleet Street Fifty (I Say) [1989/90 17d 20d^{5} 22g* 21s^{6} 20f^{3} 20f^{pu}] compact mare: easy winner of novice handicap hurdle at Wincanton in January: 200/1, showed much improved form when 12¾ lengths third behind Regal Ambition in Sun Alliance Novices' Hurdle at Cheltenham in March, running on strongly from rear: pulled up lame after seventh in quite valuable event at Liverpool following month: stays 2¾m: seems well suited by a sound surface. *W. R. Williams.* 126

TOM'S LITTLE WILL 7 b. or br.g. Celtic Cone–Fleet Street Fifty (I Say) [1989/90 c22d^{ur} 17v c21g^{pu} a20g^{5} a24g^{pu} 21m^{pu}] sturdy gelding: of little account: has worn blinkers. *W. R. Williams.* c— —

TOM TOWLEY 4 b.g. Reformed Character–Darwin Tulip (Campaign) [1989/90 16g^{pu} 16g 17g 20s^{2}] lightly-made gelding: half-brother to moderate staying hurdler Radwhaw (by Abwah): finished lame when second of 4 in poor juvenile claiming hurdle at Sedgefield, first sign of ability. *A. Smith.* 85 ?

TOM TROUBADOUR 7 b. or br.g. Black Minstrel–Graceland (Golden Love) [1989/90 20m* 21g^{2} 20f* 21g^{4}] big, rangy, slightly unfurnished gelding with scope: chasing type: behind in NH Flat race in 1987/8 (trained by Mrs C. Collins): won novice hurdles at Chepstow in October and Ascot (made all) following month: set slow pace until last when 3 lengths second of 3 finishers to easy winner Cruising Altitude (gave 8 lb) in Tom Masson Trophy Hurdle at Newbury: gave 123 +

impression he'll do better with more forcing tactics when moderate fourth to Forest Sun at Newbury in December: stays 2½m: acts on firm ground. *J. T. Gifford.*

TONGSUNIAN 13 gr.g. Moulton–Queens Message (Town Crier) [1989/90 c16s4 c17v4 c18f2 c25m4 c16h4 c17hur c21m3] plain, sparely-made gelding: winning hurdler and poor novice chaser: has been beaten in sellers: probably acts on any going: has worn a crossed noseband. *J. B. Shears.* c76 —

TONIGHTS THE NIGHT 9 ch.g. Simbir–Sarejay Day (Vic Day) [1989/90 c21m* c24dpu] big, long-backed, workmanlike gelding: has been hobdayed: useful chaser: won quite valuable handicap at Wincanton in November with something in hand by 3 lengths from Envopak Token: pulled up lame following month: stays 3m but best form at around 2½m: acts on heavy going and good to firm. *O. Sherwood.* c135 —

TONY MURPHYS MAN 5 br.g. Strong Gale–Bold Aroon (Bold Lad (IRE)) [1989/90 16f5 22spu] smallish gelding: half-brother to 3 winners, including 1980 2-y-o 6f seller winner Spanish Tormenta (by Furry Glen): dam never ran: fifth in novice hurdle at Leicester in November: tailed off when pulled up last in 2¾m event at Folkestone 5 weeks later. *J. R. Upson.* 82

TOO LATE 7 b.g. Mister Tudor–Premier Bond (Good Bond) [1989/90 c16gr c20g2 c20d] sturdy, workmanlike gelding: winning hurdler: made a couple of mistakes when second in novice chase at Edinburgh in January: refused 2 out previous start: will stay beyond 2½m: acts on soft going: sold 1,700 gns Ascot May Sales. *R. C. Armytage.* c92 —

TOOLEY STREET 11 ch.g. Levanter–Be Nice (Bowsprit) [1989/90 c24mpu] rangy gelding: novice hurdler and winning 3m chaser in 1986/7: pulled up only outing since. *Sir Christopher Wates.* c— —

TOP CROWN 5 b.g. High Top–Crown Witness (Crowned Prince (USA)) [1989/90 17f* 17f3 17m* 16d] leggy, sparely-made gelding: won selling hurdles at Newton Abbot in August (bought in 3,100 gns) and Devon & Exeter (no bid) following month: ran moderately otherwise, looking a difficult ride final outing: stays 2½m: yet to race on heavy going, acts on any other: blinkered in 1989/90: sold 1,175 gns Ascot November Sales. *M. C. Pipe.* 87

'Badger Beer' Handicap Chase, Wincanton—right to left at the third last, Tonights The Night, Envopak Token and Shannagary

TOP D'OR (FR) 5 b.g. Pot d'Or (FR)–Jupe de Laine (FR) (Vieux Chateau) [1989/90 aF16g^{6} 20g^{ur} 16s 20f^{pu}] compact French-bred gelding: dam winning — French jumper: no sign of ability: wore eyeshield last 3 starts: sold 960 gns Doncaster Spring Sales. *G. M. Moore.*

TOP ENTERTAINER 4 ch.g. Be My Guest (USA)–Her Review (USA) (Reviewer (USA)) [1989/90 16g^{pu} 18s^{5} 16m^{2} 16m] leggy, light-framed ex-Irish 85 gelding: fifth foal: half-brother to Widely Known (by Ela-Mana-Mou), winner over 1¼m on Flat in Ireland: dam unraced: showed a little ability on Flat (has been blinkered) when trained by D. K. Weld: best effort over hurdles when second in juvenile claimer at Wincanton in March: not knocked about in stronger company next time: likely to prove best at 2m: acts on good to firm going. *C. Weedon.*

TOP FEATHER 8 b.m. High Top–Sipapu (Targowice (USA)) [1989/90 16m] lightly-raced novice hurdler. *Mrs S. Armytage.* —

TOPGLOW 6 ro.g. Kalaglow–Lady Gaylass (USA) (Sir Gaylord) [1989/90 a16g^{2}] 1½m winner in 1988, little worthwhile form on Flat in 1989: 15 lengths 81 second to Distant Relation in novice event at Lingfield on hurdling debut: sold 2,600 gns Newmarket July Sales. *D. M. Grissell.*

TOPHARD 4 b.g. Lyphard's Special (USA)–Tomard (Thatching) [1989/90 16f^{2} 16g 16v 21d^{4} 24d^{6}] sparely-made gelding: blinkered, won 15f claimer on Flat in 89 1989: sold out of W. Pearce's stable 6,000 gns Newmarket Autumn Sales: modest novice over hurdles: stays 3m: acts on firm and dead ground. *R. Lee.*

TOPHATTER 10 ch.g. Proverb–Calamity Jane (Never Dwell) [1989/90 c? c24m*] tall, sparely-made gelding: distant second when left in lead last, and went — on to win hunter chase at Huntingdon in May by 8 lengths from Wages of Sin: suited by a test of stamina: yet to show his form on very firm ground, acts on any other. *M. Shine.*

TOPKAPI 7 b.g. Beldale Flutter (USA)–Pithead (High Top) [1989/90 c16s c— c16g^{pu} a16g^{5} c20m^{pu}] lengthy gelding: winning hurdler: poor novice chaser: acts — on hard going: hard puller: has worn a tongue strap: looked to turn it in once over hurdles: sold 2,400 gns Doncaster June Sales. *J. White.*

TOPORI 11 br.g. High Top–Lady Oriana (Tudor Melody) [1989/90 16s] c— sparely-made gelding: selling hurdler: well beaten over fences: unlikely to stay — much beyond 2¼m: probably acts on any going. *D. J. Wintle.*

TOP O' TH' GREEN 7 b.g. Take A Reef–Fanny Green (Space King) [1989/90 c— x c24g^{F} c20g^{pu} 22s^{pu} c22f^{F}] rangy gelding with plenty of scope: modest novice — hurdler at best: has made mistakes all outings over fences: should stay beyond 2m. *J. A. C. Edwards.*

TOPSHAM BAY 7 b.g. Proverb–Biowen (Master Owen) [1989/90 20s c**124** p c21g^{pu} c25d^{pu} c24g^{4} c32f* c25f*] —

The National Hunt Chase Challenge Cup at the Cheltenham Festival meeting has averaged twenty-five runners a year in the post-war era. Considering that the race is for novice chasers ridden by amateurs and run over four miles, there have been surprisingly few form upsets. Prior to the latest running the longest-priced winners in that period were Prattler in 1946 and Reverend Prince in 1955, both at 33/1. The most recent National Hunt Chase in March attracted twenty-five runners and was won by Topsham Bay at 40/1. He'd had three starts over fences earlier in the season. In the first two of them he'd jumped none too fluently and was well behind when eventually pulled up, but in the third, at Newbury earlier in March, he'd jumped soundly apart from a mistake at the sixth, and, though a well-beaten fourth behind Arctic Call, wasn't unduly knocked about. Topsham Bay jumped the stiff fences adequately and was always handily placed as the field went along at a good gallop in the National Hunt Chase. He was under pressure when his stable-companion Royal Battery went to the front three out, but he stayed on to lead at the next, kept on the stronger afterwards and won by four lengths with Ballinhassig a further twenty lengths away in third. Topsham Bay showed further improvement when returned to Cheltenham for the Thomson's Novices' Handicap Chase in April on his only subsequent start. Again always prominent in a strongly-run race, he led five out, drew clear after the favourite Bizage Motors blundered away his chance at the next and won by twelve lengths from Damers Cavalry.

National Hunt Chase, Cheltenham—
stable-companions Topsham Bay and Royal Battery draw clear

Following an outing in a National Hunt Flat race in 1987/8, Topsham Bay showed promise in two novice hurdles the following season. He was a bit backward when behind in a qualifier of the Philip Cornes series won by one of the leading novice hurdlers of the latest campaign, Regal Ambition, at Chepstow in December before having his attentions switched to fences. The seven-year-old Topsham Bay, a big, strong gelding, has made only nine racecourse appearances and it is likely that he has further improvement in him; he seems sure to win more long-distance chases. He acts well on firm ground, conditions that frequently prevail for the Whitbread Gold Cup at Sandown in the spring; his owner won the Whitbread with Larbawn in 1969 and 1970. Though he's some way to go Topsham Bay may well improve sufficiently to get into the handicap proper in a race such as that in 1990/1.

Topsham Bay (b.g. 1983)	Proverb (ch 1970)	Reliance II (b 1962)	Tantieme
			Relance III
		Causerie (br 1961)	Cagire II
			Happy Thought
	Biowen (br 1974)	Master Owen (b 1956)	Owen Tudor
			Miss Maisie
		Own Blend (br 1955)	Monsieur L'Amiral
			Sailors Maid

Topsham Bay, a brother to the novice hurdler Heart of Kings, is a half-brother to three winners—the moderate hurdler Pollen Bee (by Pollerton) and the useful Irish hurdler/chaser Mixed Blends and Fifth Amendment (both by The Parson), the last-named successful in novice hurdles at Wincanton and Leicester in the latest season. Their dam, Biowen, is an unraced sister to the winning jumpers Just Owen and Blendmaster, and a half-sister to several other winners, including the fairly useful staying chaser Owenius. Topsham Bay is from the penultimate crop of dual Goodwood Cup and Doncaster Cup winner Proverb who died in 1984. Proverb is also the sire of the Whitbread Gold Cup winners By The Way and Lean Ar Aghaidh, the Coral Welsh National winner Righthand Man and the Sun Alliance Chase winner Envopak Token. *D. H. Barons.*

TOPSOIL 8 br.h. Relkino–Partridge Brook (Birdbrook) [1989/90 16g $20s^{6}$ $16d^{2}$ 16d $16d^{ur}$] compact horse: winning hurdler: second in conditional jockeys selling 83

Skipton Novices' Chase, Wetherby—Tort is pressed by Speech

handicap at Sedgefield in January: not disgraced over 2½m: best form with plenty of give in the ground. *D. J. Wintle.*

TOP VILLAIN 4 b.g. Top Ville–Swan Ann (My Swanee) [1989/90 16g4 16d3 16m] angular gelding: lightly-raced maiden on Flat (has shown ability as well as signs of temperament): sold out of R. Hern's stable 34,000 gns Newmarket Autumn Sales: in frame in juvenile hurdles at Newbury (hung left) and Warwick (didn't respond to pressure): ran best race when ninth behind Sybillin in Glenlivet Anniversary Hurdle at Liverpool around 3 months later, travelling well until 3 out: has the ability to win a race but looks one to be wary of. *Andrew Turnell.* 107 §

TORANFIELD 6 b.g. Monksfield–Toranquine (FR) (Right Royal V) [1989/90 18g* 22d5 16g 19s* 16s3 20m6 16g] leggy gelding: useful hurdler: made all in handicaps at Fairyhouse in December and Naas in January: ran a very good race when 18 lengths third behind Nomadic Way in Wessel Cable Champion Hurdle at Leopardstown in February: creditable sixth, prominent until 2 out, behind Sayparee in valuable event at Liverpool 2 months later: stays 2½m (not at all disgraced over 2¾m): acts on heavy and good to firm going. *F. Lennon, Ireland.* 139

TORENAGA'S TRIUMPH 4 b.g. Mummy's Game–Autumn Breeze (King's Bench) [1989/90 17m 17f3 17gpu 17m5] leggy, angular gelding: closely related to 4 sprint winners by Mummy's Pet, including fairly useful Coded Scrap and Touch of Salt: dam ran twice: seems of little account. *Mrs J. Wonnacott.* —

TORKABAR (USA) 5 ch.h. Vaguely Noble–Tarsila (High Top) [1989/90 20g2] smallish, rather sparely-made horse: modest hurdler: hung left run-in when creditable second to Auction Law in conditional jockeys handicap at Cheltenham in November: stays 2½m: acts on soft going (ran moderately on heavy last start 1988/9). *G. A. Ham.* 109 +

TORRANCE 6 br.g. Niels–Aurambre (FR) (Sicambre) [1989/90 16hpu 17gpu] quite modest at up to 9f on Flat, winner in September: sold out of D. Wilson's stable 5,000 gns Ascot September Sales: no form in novice hurdles: pulled up lame final start. *Mrs J. Wonnacott.* —

TORRE TRADER 7 b.g. Ascertain (USA)–Warham Fantasy (Barolo) [1989/90 c21f4 c21f2 c16h2] leggy, workmanlike gelding: poor novice hurdler and winning chaser: ran well in handicaps at Newton Abbot in September and Taunton c85 —

in October: sweating, made mistakes and beaten a distance in between: stays 3m: yet to show his form on heavy going, acts on any other. *R. G. Frost.*

TORSIDE 11 ch.g. Funny Man–Annaghmore (Yrrah Jr) [1989/90 21m* 22d3 c21s2 c26d* c25f2 c36fpu 26f5] leggy, plain gelding: useful chaser: made all in handicap at Newton Abbot in March: badly hampered third and pulled up shortly afterwards in Seagram Grand National at Liverpool in April: amateur ridden, easy winner of 3-runner novice hurdle at Ludlow in November: suited by a good test of stamina: best form on a yielding surface: blinkered last 4 starts. *M. C. Pipe.* c**136** 101

TORT 6 b.g. Le Moss–Steady Flow (Reliance II) [1989/90 c16m* c20d* c25mF] lengthy, rather unfurnished ex-Irish gelding: fourth foal: dam second over 1½m from 2 starts in Ireland: won NH Flat race and a point-to-point in Ireland: created a good impression when winning maiden chase at Leicester in January but wasn't so impressive when justifying favouritism in novice chase at Wetherby in February: stays 2½m: likely to prove suited by top-of-the-ground: swished his tail and was rather on his toes in preliminaries at Leicester: usually jumps soundly. *J. Mackie.* c**117** p

TORULA BRIDGE 6 b.m. Torus–Killanny Bridge (Hallez (FR)) [1989/90 17d 19m 22dur 16g] leggy mare: third foal: half-sister to Irish bumper winner Sir Dubel (by Al Sirat): dam behind in 3 bumpers races: no sign of ability in novice hurdles. *W. R. Williams.* —

TORYMORE GREEN 11 b.g. Mr Bigmore–Gretel Green (Prince Hansel) [1989/90 c26m3] novice hurdler/chaser: suited by 2¾m. *J. C. McConnochie.* c— —

TOSCANA 9 ch.m. Town And Country–Constanza (Sun Prince) [1989/90 22m a20g* 16f2 19g a18g3 20g*] lengthy mare: poor and inconsistent 1½m performer on Flat: successful over hurdles in seller at Lingfield in November (no bid) and novice claimer at Wolverhampton (comfortably) in December: stays 2½m: acts on firm ground. *D. Marks.* 83

TOTAL LINKING 6 gr.m. Prince Regent (FR)–Happy Princess (Supreme Sovereign) [1989/90 16m3 16d6 21m 16g a16g4] workmanlike mare: poor novice hurdler: doesn't stay 21f: blinkered final outing. *B. Smart.* 68

TOUCH GO GO 5 b.g. Touch Boy–Lucky Donation (Lucky Brief) [1989/90 F16g F17m F12g] smallish, lengthy gelding: fourth foal: dam, fair hurdler, stayed 2½m: behind in NH Flat races: yet to race over hurdles or fences. *J. P. Leigh.*

TOUCHING STAR 5 b.g. Touching Wood (USA)–Beaufort Star (Great Nephew) [1989/90 16d] close-coupled gelding: modest novice hurdler: looked and ran as though in need of race in February: seems suited by a sharp 2m and top-of-the-ground: won 1¼m handicap on Flat in April. *F. Jordan.* —

TOUCH ME TOUCH ME 5 ch.m. Last Fandango–Lombardia (Lombard (GER)) [1989/90 16m a20g] of little account: blinkered on debut: sold 1,000 gns Ascot April Sales. *K. G. Wingrove.* —

TOUCH OF FUN 10 ch.g. Welham–Paddy's Poppet (Paddy's Progress) [1989/90 c21dpu] tall gelding: quite useful point-to-pointer: wide-margin winner of hunter chase at Cheltenham in 1988: having first race since that season and bit backward, made mistakes and was behind when pulled up in February: stays 3¼m: acts on soft going: takes a good hold. *T. S. Warner.* c— —

TOUCH OF SPEED 6 b.g. Touch Paper–Maggie Mine (Native Prince) [1989/90 c16m2 c16m5 c16g5 c20mpu 16dpu a16g2 a20g2 16f] compact gelding: handicap hurdler: ran moderately in selling company final start (first for 4 months): second in novice chase at Worcester in September: jumped poorly over fences afterwards: unlikely to stay 2½m: acts on firm and dead ground: usually held up: has worn a crossed noseband: trained until after seventh start by D. Williams. *H. A. T. Whiting.* c**81** x 82

TOUGH COOKIE 5 gr.g. Lochnager–Jovenita (High Top) [1989/90 16g 16f5 16d4 16g5 16gpu] workmanlike gelding: poor novice hurdler: races only at 2m: best effort on dead going: pulled up lame final start. *R. Allan.* 87

TOUGH OUT 6 b.g. Tumble Wind (USA)–Ragatina (Ragusa) [1989/90 F16f F16g 16d 16spu a16gpu 16f 16fpu] small, sturdy gelding: carries condition: sixth living foal: half-brother to winning staying jumper Unicol (by Manado) and a winner in France by Double Form: dam, placed over 1m, is half-sister to very useful sprinters Rollahead and Glenturret: no sign of ability over hurdles, including in a seller (races too freely): blinkered fifth start. *N. A. Smith.* —

TOUKSHAD (USA) 7 b.g. Sir Ivor–La Toulzanie (FR) (Sanctus II) [1989/90 c20vpu c18s c20f3 c25h*] leggy gelding: winning hurdler: finished lame when c**80** + —

winning poor novice handicap chase at Plumpton in March: stays 3m: acts on any going. *R. J. O'Sullivan.*

TOUR DE FORCE 10 ch.g. Reliance II–Set To Work (Workboy) [1989/90 20s 16g 16s^F 16m^F] big gelding: one-time fair hurdler: little show in 1989/90, ran in seller final start: last in novice event on chasing debut: best at 2m: probably acts on any going: sometimes wears blinkers (not when successful). *P. J. Makin.* c— —

TOUREEN PRINCE 7 b.g. Cheval–Lauregeen (Laurence O) [1989/90 c16d* c18g² c16s³ c22d* c24g² c24f⁴] c**136** + —

Toureen Prince, a leading novice hurdler in 1988/9, was sent over fences in the latest season. He had six races in all, three in Ireland in the first half of the campaign when trained by Mullins and three in Britain in the second half for his present connections. Toureen Prince won twice and finished in the money on his four other starts. His wins came in the Bishopscourt Chase at Navan in November and an ordinary novice event at Nottingham in February. On each occasion he started at odds on and ran out an impressive winner. Toureen Prince didn't need to show the same level of form as he'd shown in Ireland to win as easily as he did at Nottingham, but he gave an excellent display of fast, accurate jumping. The Nottingham race was a slowly-run contest over two and three quarter miles; the only other time Toureen Prince had raced beyond two and a quarter miles was when tailed off in the previous season's two-and-a-half-mile Sun Alliance Novices' Hurdle at Cheltenham. His target at the latest Festival meeting was the three-mile Sun Alliance Novices' Chase, a race usually won by a thorough staying type who jumps soundly. Toureen Prince's jumping seemed unlikely to let him down, but would he stay? The question of his stamina had been left largely unanswered after he'd gone down by a head to The Nigelstan in the three-mile Manor Novices' Chase at Kempton in February; Kempton's three miles is easier than most and the race was slowly run. In the Sun Alliance Toureen Prince put up his best performance to date over fences in finishing ten and a half lengths fourth to Garrison Savannah. Travelling strongly in the front rank for a long way, Toureen Prince led from the fifteenth, was still in front over the second last, then weakened steadily and gave the strong impression that he'll be suited by a return to shorter distances. If he were ours, the seven-year-old Toureen Prince, who has further improvement in him as a chaser, would be aimed at

*Racing Post Novices' Chase (Qualifier), Nottingham—
odds-on Toureen Prince leads the field on the first circuit*

Mr Paul Stamp's "Toureen Prince"

the important two-and-a-half-mile handicaps in 1990/1. A sound jumper, he looks sure to win more races.

Toureen Prince (b.g. 1983)	Cheval (b 1965)	Javelot (b 1956)	Fast Fox
			Djaina
		Shevaun (b 1952)	Solonaway
			Gameness
	Lauregeen (b 1974)	Laurence O (ch 1965)	Saint Crespin III
			Feevagh
		Vulgeeno (b 1955)	Vulgan
			Avageeno

Toureen Prince is the third foal and first winner of his dam Lauregeen, who won two point-to-points and was unplaced in two hunter chases in Ireland. She's a half-sister to the fairly useful staying chaser Straight Vulgan. Their dam, Vulgeeno, a half-sister to two winning chasers, notably the smart stayer Bowgeeno, was lightly raced. Toureen Prince's sire Cheval was a good-class middle-distance handicapper, and a very game one too. The best of his previous produce is Crimson Embers, winner of the Waterford Crystal Stayers' Hurdle in 1982 and 1986. Toureen Prince is a good-bodied gelding, more a chaser in appearance than a hurdler. He acts on any going. *Miss H. C. Knight.*

TOURMALIEN 5 ch.g. Caerleon (USA)–Jacinth (Red God) [1989/90 16s^{pu}] lengthy gelding: lightly-raced maiden on Flat: little sign of ability in 2 novice hurdles. *R. P. C. Hoad.* —

TOUR VIEILLE 7 b.g. Bold Lad (IRE)–Noreena (Nonoalco (USA)) [1989/90 a16g^{4} a16g^{pu} c16m^{ur} c19m^{3} c16g^{F}] novice hurdler: has run in a seller: poor third in novice chase in May: has worn blinkers. *P. A. Pritchard.* c— —

TOWER SIDE 7 ch.g. Deep Run–Be Nice (Bowsprit) [1989/90 16h^{su}] workmanlike gelding: lightly-raced novice hurdler: dead. *C. S. Wates.* —

TOWER STEPS 5 b.g. Tower Walk–Rosia Steps (Red Pins) [1989/90 16g^{2} 16g^{2} 16g^{5}] strong gelding: runner-up in novice hurdles at Kelso and Ayr: usually jumped well: dead. *C. Parker.* 94

TOWER WATCH 7 b. or br.g. Tower Walk–Joan Doreen (Lucky Brief)
[1989/90 20m^{pu} 16d^{pu}] small, sparely-made gelding: poor novice selling hurdler: —
stays 2½m: probably acts on any going. *R. Brotherton.*

TOWN PATROL 4 br.g. Town And Country–Swing Gently (Swing Easy
(USA)) [1989/90 18f^{pu}] poor maiden on Flat: tailed off when pulled up last in —
juvenile claiming hurdle at Fontwell in September: sold 1,300 gns Newmarket
Autumn Sales. *M. D. I. Usher.*

TOWN PLANNER 8 gr. or ro.g. Oedipus Complex–Brigg Jinks (Tudor Jinks)
[1989/90 20g^{pu} 25m^{pu} 16g 20g^{F} 16d a16g] angular gelding: no sign of ability in —
novice hurdles. *J. G. Thorpe.*

TOWNY BOY 4 b.g. Camden Town–Serenesse (Habat) [1989/90 16s^{4} 16g^{5}]
smallish, workmanlike gelding: fair 1¼m winner on Flat: modest form in claiming 83
hurdle at Market Rasen and novice event at Hexham, on each occasion unable to
quicken in latter stages. *J. M. Jefferson.*

TOYTOWN 9 b.g. Pitpan–Sinarga (Even Money) [1989/90 c20m^{3} c22d^{pu} c—
c20d^{pu}] big, lengthy gelding: lightly raced and no sign of ability: visored fourth —
start 1988/9. *P. Ransom.*

TRACE OF IRONY (USA) 4 b. or br.f. Cannonade (USA)–Tracy L (USA)
(Bold Favorite (USA)) [1989/90 16g^{F}] plating-class maiden on Flat: sold out of C. —
Wall's stable 3,400 gns Doncaster March Sales: every chance 2 out, but beaten
when falling last in juvenile selling hurdle won by Peristyle at Stratford. *Mrs A.
Knight.*

TRAFALGAR BLUE 10 ch.g. Tug of War–Arcticanute (Hardicanute) **c105** x
[1989/90 c21g^{3} c16f^{su} c16m^{2} c16h* c20f^{3} c16f^{3} c16g^{F} c16d^{2} c17f^{F}] lengthy, —
sparely-made gelding: handicap chaser: won at Carlisle in October: stayed 2½m:
acted on any going: tended to hang and race with head in air: was usually held up:
once blinkered in 1988/9: jumped moderately on occasions: dead. *Ronald
Thompson.*

TRAFALGAR BUOY 6 b.g. Radetzky–Changan (Touch Paper) [1989/90 16g^{bd}
16m^{4}] lengthy gelding: poor form over hurdles, including in selling company: sold 67
1,700 gns Ascot April Sales. *M. Madgwick.*

TRAIN ROBBER 5 b.g. Sharp Deal–Biggsie's Bird (Even Money) [1989/90
F16f^{4} F16f^{5} 19m^{3} 20g 20g 19h^{3} 20f^{3}] leggy gelding: first foal: dam won poor 2m 77
novice hurdle: showed ability in NH Flat races: poor form in novice hurdles. *W. G.
McKenzie-Coles.*

TRANBY CROFT 6 b.h. Final Straw–Daisy Warwick (USA) (Ribot) [1989/90
21m^{2} 16f^{pu}] close-coupled horse: novice hurdler: creditable second at Devon & 100
Exeter in September: moved poorly down and was pulled up lame next time
(blinkered): stays 2½m. *M. C. Pipe.*

TRANQUIL WATERS (USA) 4 ch.c. Diesis–Ebbing Tide (USA) (His
Majesty (USA)) [1989/90 16g^{4}] leggy colt: won 1½m apprentice race on Flat in 90 p
October: sold out of H. Cecil's stable 30,000 gns Newmarket Autumm Sales:
around 10 lengths fourth behind March On in juvenile hurdle at Kempton in
November: should improve. *N. Tinkler.*

TRANSPLANT BLUE 7 b.g. Buckskin (FR)–Slave Light (Arctic Slave)
[1989/90 16g^{pu}] tall, close-coupled, plain gelding: modest novice hurdler: —
sweating and needing race, behind when pulled up 2 out in January: seems better
suited by 21f than shorter distances (never placed to challenge over 25f in 1988).
L. C. Corbett.

TRAPEZE ARTIST 9 b.h. High Line–Maternal (High Top) [1989/90 20f^{2}
20m^{3} 21f^{3}] neat horse: ungenuine staying handicapper on Flat: fair form in novice 81 §
hurdles in 1985/6: showed more temperament than ability subsequently: stayed
2½m: acted on firm going: blinkered last 3 outings (finished reportedly lame final
start): retired to Wood End Stud, fee £250 + £250. *J. M. Bukovets.*

TRAPPER JOHN 6 b.g. The Parson–Blueola (Bluerullah) [1989/90 c— p
c21s^{ur} c20v^{F} 21v^{4} 22d^{2} 24s^{2} 22v* 25m* 25m^{2}] 159

Irish-trained horses have a better recent record in the Waterford Crystal Stayers' Hurdle than in any other race at the Cheltenham Festival meeting, thanks to the victories of Galmoy in 1987 and 1988 and Trapper John in 1990. Who knows, perhaps one or the other would have been in a different race for a British stable had he shown signs of making a chaser. Both had been returned to long-distance hurdling after a brief spell of

*Waterford Crystal Stayers' Hurdle, Cheltenham—
Bluff Cove just leads Trapper John (left) over the last,
with Pragada and Cash Is King also in the picture*

racing or schooling over fences, as indeed had other winners in the last few years—Rustle, Gaye Chance and Crimson Embers. Trapper John, a good-topped gelding and very useful novice hurdler in 1988/9, looked the sort to make a chaser. But after failing to complete in novice events at Galway—eventually pulled up having been remounted after unseating his rider at the second—and Gowran Park in the first half of the season, he was returned to hurdling and developed into a smart stayer. Trapper John trounced Galmoy in the latter's customary warm-up race, the Boardsmill Stud Boyne Hurdle at Navan in February, conceding him 7 lb and beating him by twelve lengths. He had run equally good races when runner-up to Naevog in the Findus Hurdle at Leopardstown in December and to Mrs Muck in the Mandor Flexible Doors Premier Long Distance Hurdle at Haydock the following month, though he was beaten a comfortable twelve lengths on the latter course by the winner who was receiving 9 lb. In the absence of the injured Mrs Muck, Trapper John started 15/2 fourth favourite of twenty-two at Cheltenham, behind 11/2 favourite Ryde Again, Fourth of July (6/1) and the promising novice chaser Cash Is King (7/1). The openness of the betting was reflected in a tight finish to the race. Held up in mid-division as Bluff Cove, Flying Dancer and Floyd disputed the lead in the first half of the race, Trapper John made headway from the fourth last to join Brabazon and Cash Is King two flights out, just behind Bluff Cove who set up a clear lead again on the home turn. Still two lengths down jumping the last, Trapper John stayed on strongly to lead halfway up the run-in and bravely held Naevog's strong challenge by a length and a half. Just over three lengths covered Bluff Cove, Ikdam, Brabazon and Cash Is King, the next four home, eight lengths clear of Fourth of July. Ryde Again was out of the first half dozen and being pushed along when falling at the second last. Despite such a hard race—his jockey was suspended for two days for excessive use of the whip—and his looking to finish slightly lame, Trapper John put up an excellent performance under top weight of 12-0 in the Oddbins Handicap Hurdle at Liverpool three weeks later. Looking none the worse for his exertions, he stayed on strongly having been off the bridle from a long way out and failed by only half a length, giving 25 lb to Coral Golden Hurdle fourth Sip of Orange, the pair drawing twelve lengths clear.

Trapper John (b.g. 1984)	The Parson (b 1968)	Aureole (ch 1950)	Hyperion
			Angelola
		Bracey Bridge (b 1962)	Chanteur II
			Rutherford Bridge
	Blueola (ch 1973)	Bluerullah (br 1963)	Valerullah
			Windsor Blue
		Chinola (ch 1966)	Chou Chin Chow
			Merry Tola

Trapper John's dam is a sister to another game and genuine Irish jumper in Chinrullah, fourth in the Waterford Crystal Stayers' Hurdle in 1978 and first past the post in the Queen Mother Champion Chase two years later. Their dam Chinola, who ran a few times without success in bumpers races, is a half-sister to several winning jumpers and to the very useful stayer Arcticola. Trapper John's dam Blueola, placed on the Flat and over hurdles, has failed to breed a winner from five other foals of racing age. Trapper John is sure to win more races. If kept to hurdling next season—as he would be if he were ours—he would be sure to be a leading contender for another Stayers' Hurdle: of those not to have opposed him in the latest running, only Battalion, Calabrese, Lucky Verdict and Scally Owen at present look to have it in them to make top class amongst the younger staying hurdlers. A thorough stayer, Trapper John would not be affected by a change in the going at Cheltenham: he has shown his form on ground ranging from heavy through to good to firm. *M. F. Morris, Ireland.*

TRAPRAIN LAW 7 b.g. Politico (USA)–Pops Girl (Deep Run) [1989/90 c24g^{pu} c24d^{4} c24d* c24d^{3} c24g*] lengthy gelding: no worthwhile form over hurdles: better over fences, and won novice events at Ayr in January and Newcastle in May, latter by 1½ lengths from Solicitor's Choice: stays 3m: acts on dead going. *J. K. M. Oliver.* c**101** —

TRAUMATIC LAURA 5 gr.m. Pragmatic–Trim (Miralgo) [1989/90 20g 24g] workmanlike mare: poor novice hurdler: blinkered twice. *B. E. Wilkinson.* —

TRAVAIL GIRL 9 b.m. Forties Field (FR)–Ma Principaute (FR) (Misti IV) [1989/90 22g^{pu} 20s^{pu} c18s^{2} c20d c24d^{3} c24f^{pu} c20m^{2} c20g^{2}] lengthy, rather angular mare: novice hurdler: runner-up in 3 selling handicap chases: gives impression she'll prove best at around 2½m: acts on good to firm and soft going. *G. A. Ham.* c86 —

TRAVELLER'S TRIP 9 ch.g. Royal Trip–Bohemian Girl (Pardao) [1989/90 c16f^{3} c16m^{r} c16g^{2} c16d^{4} c17m^{3} c16f^{3} c16f^{ur} c16m^{2}] leggy, workmanlike gelding: modest hurdler: novice chaser: takes a keen hold and is likely to prove best at around 2m: seems to act on any going: refused 4 out second outing (trained until after then by O. Brennan). *J. Mackie.* c87 —

TRAVEL MUSIC 5 b.m. Kafu–Octet (Octavo (USA)) [1989/90 16m^{pu} 16f 16g^{4}] sturdy mare: poor novice selling hurdler. *D. R. Wellicome.* 58

TRAVEL OVER 9 b.g. Over The River (FR)–Kincsem (Nelcius) [1989/90 c24d^{2} c28g^{4} c24v c24d^{5}] big, strong, rangy gelding: quite a useful chaser on his day: good second to City Entertainer in handicap at Wetherby in February: ran poorly after: suited by around 3m: acts on heavy and good to firm going. *R. Lee.* c**134** ? —

TRAVISTOWN 8 b.g. Grange Melody–Ednamore (Vulgan) [1989/90 c19m^{ur} c25f^{6} c20f^{4}] quite good-topped gelding: no worthwhile form over hurdles in 1987/8 (blinkered fourth outing): won 2 point-to-points in 1989: tailed off in hunter chases. *Mrs M. Llewellyn.* c— —

TREASURE LORD 7 b.g. Don–Treasure Ship (Sovereign Lord) [1989/90 16g 16g a16g^{3} c20m^{pu}] sparely-made gelding: poor novice hurdler: tailed off when pulled up in novice event on chasing debut: form only at 2m on a sound surface: blinkered last 3 starts. *E. A. Wheeler.* c— 61

TREBLE CHANCE 8 b.m. Balinger–Chance A Look (Don't Look) [1989/90 c16g^{2} c17g^{6} c16m^{5} c20s^{6} c16s^{2} c16g^{pu} c25m^{4}] leggy mare: novice hurdler/chaser: turned it in fifth start: best form at up to 2¼m (bred to stay further) with give in the ground: visored fourth to sixth starts. *S. Woodman.* c85 § —

TREBLE TROUBLE 5 ch.g. Politico (USA)–Jane Again (Spartan General)
[1989/90 16d* 22v^3 21d^{pu} 24d^5 21s^F 21m^2 20d^2] rather unfurnished gelding: has 110
scope: won novice hurdle at Stratford in November: ran well second, fourth and
last 2 outings, moderately otherwise: seems suited by around 2¾m: acts on good
to firm and heavy going: jumps none too fluently: trained until after fifth start by
Mrs C. Postlethwaite. *O. Sherwood.*

TREBONKERS 6 b.g. Treboro (USA)–Sally Conkers (Roi Lear (FR)) c—
[1989/90 16m^5 20f* 22d 16s 16g^5 c20g^5 a20g^5 24d^2 20d 24f* 22g 24m 20g^6 23f^3] 97
leggy gelding: handicap hurdler: won at Edinburgh in December and Newcastle
(claimer ridden) in March: below form afterwards: well behind in novice event on
chasing debut: stays 3m, at least when conditions aren't testing: seems to act on
any going: visored tenth to thirteenth outings 1988/9. *J. S. Wilson.*

TRECAULDAH 6 b.m. Treboro (USA)–Hannie Caulder (Workboy) [1989/90
16d 16s 21m 21d] leggy, shallow-girthed mare: poor novice hurdler: blinkered —
second and third starts: sold 2,900 gns Ascot July Sales. *W. Carter.*

TREDARA 4 b.f. Dara Monarch–Bay Tree (FR) (Relko) [1989/90 16f 16m^F]
leggy ex-Irish filly: half-sister to numerous winners, notably smart staying —
hurdler Ravaro (by Raga Navarro): dam won over 1½m in Ireland: won over 1¾m
on Flat: seventh in juvenile hurdle at Leicester in November: fell fatally at
Nottingham. *Miss A. L. M. King.*

TREE DANCE 7 br.m. Sonnen Gold–Tree Breeze (Farm Walk) [1989/90 16f^{pu}
16f^2] light-framed mare: 4 lengths second to Papajoto in novice handicap at 80
Uttoxeter in May, first worthwhile form over hurdles. *D. Burchell.*

TREE POPPY 7 b.m. Rolfe (USA)–Caribs Love (Caliban) [1989/90 16s^3 16s^6
20s* 20d^5 16m^2 16g^6] workmanlike, rather sparely-made mare: fairly useful 128
hurdler: won handicap at Uttoxeter in February in good style: 8 lengths second of
3 finishers to easy winner Beech Road in Welsh Champion Hurdle at Chepstow in
April: well beaten in between and below her best in handicap at Punchestown final
start: stays 2½m: acts well on heavy going. *R. Lee.*

TREFELYN CONE 6 ch.m. Celtic Cone–Trefelyn Heather (Arctic
Chevalier) [1989/90 F16g* F16g* F16g* 22d* 20d* 21f^2] sparely-made, plain 119 p
mare: third foal: half-sister to winning hurdler Trefelyn Rose (by Tom Noddy):
dam winning point-to-pointer: won her 2 completed starts in point-to-points in
1989: won NH Flat races at Hereford, Ludlow and Warwick in first half of season:
made all in novice hurdles at Wincanton (mares event) in February and Market
Rasen (finished full of running when beating Arctic Skylight 25 lengths) following
month: odds on, set too strong a pace and headed run-in when 4 lengths second to
Reach Me Down in Hoechst Panacur Mares Only Novices' Hurdle Final
(Handicap) at Newbury: will stay 3m: acts on firm and dead ground: will win more
races. *M. C. Pipe.*

TREFELYN ROSE 7 b.m. Tom Noddy–Trefelyn Heather (Arctic Chevalier) c—
[1989/90 c25d^F 24s^4 16s 21f* 21h^{pu}] lengthy mare: maiden point-to-pointer: 93
jumped deliberately, led until falling eleventh in novice chase in February:
all-the-way winner of novice hurdle at Ludlow in April: pulled up and dismounted
2 out in 2-runner novice handicap on same course following month: stays 3m: acts
on firm ground: has worn crossed noseband: blinkered last 2 starts. *M. C. Pipe.*

TREMAR LAD 8 ch.g. Monsanto (FR)–Greyburn (Saintly Song) [1989/90 c—
c16d^{pu} a20g^6 a20g 20d^6 28f^5 19f 24f^F 18f^4 25f] lengthy, well-made gelding: 72
handicap hurdler: fourth at Worcester in April, only worthwhile form of 1989/90:
runner-up in novice chase in 1988/9: stays 2½m (well beaten over further): suited
by a firm surface: blinkered fourth to eighth starts: has worn off-side pricker. *P.
Davis.*

TREMATON 7 gr.m. Pragmatic–Bartlemy Fair (Town Crier) [1989/90 20f^{pu} c72
c25f^3] leggy mare: novice selling hurdler: won a point-to-point in May: third in —
maiden hunter chase at Cartmel same month: usually blinkered over hurdles: sold
out of R. Juckes's stable 2,300 gns Ascot September Sales after first start. *Miss A.
J. Green.*

TREMAYNE 7 b.g. Trimmingham–Beagle Bay (Deep Run) [1989/90 c16d^3 c88
c16m^2 c16d^{pu}] big, close-coupled gelding: novice hurdler/chaser: tended to hang —
fire under pressure when second to Tiptonian in novice handicap at Leicester in
January: jumped none too fluently following month: should stay 2½m. *Capt. T. A.
Forster.*

TREMMIN 5 b.m. Horage–Ballinavail (Rarity) [1989/90 16g 20d^F 18s 21d^4]
medium-sized mare: handicap hurdler: only form of 1989/90 when fourth at 95
Ludlow (amateur ridden, under pressure long way out): stays 21f. *R. J. Manning.*

TRENTSIDE VALOUR 5 b.g. Tudorville–Trent Valley (Grey Mirage) [1989/90 F16g] first foal: dam won 2m selling hurdle and stayed 3m: tailed off in NH Flat race at Catterick: yet to race over hurdles or fences. *C. Smith.*

TRESIDDER 8 b.g. Connaught–Twenty Two (FR) (Busted) [1989/90 c20g^{2} c16s^{5} c16m^{2}] leggy, sparely-made gelding: much improved chaser: finished strongly when going down by a length to Katabatic in Cheltenham Grand Annual Chase in March on final start: ideally suited by 2m: yet to race on very firm ground, acts on any other: usually held up. *M. W. Easterby.* c**132** —

TRES SPORTIF 4 br.f. Daring March–Impeccable Lady (Silly Season) [1989/90 a18g^{3} 17v* 17f^{2} 16m^{4} 16m] leggy filly: won 6f seller at 2 yrs when trained by P. Cundell: ridden by 7-lb claimer, won juvenile selling hurdle at Newton Abbot in January (no bid): ran moderately last 2 starts: unlikely to stay much beyond 2m: acts on any going: wears blinkers: sold 1,650 gns Ascot July Sales. *M. C. Pipe.* 81

TREVA 6 b.g. Treboro (USA)–Balante (Balidar) [1989/90 17m 22f^{F}] leggy gelding: poor form in novice hurdles: dead. *N. B. Thomson.* —

TREVAYLOR (NZ) 6 ch.g. Rapier II–Regal Bride (NZ) (Regalis) [1989/90 17v^{5} 16g 17d 17m^{4} 21m^{pu}] leggy gelding: poor novice hurdler: has pulled hard. *T. C. Le Grice.* 71

TREWITHIEN 6 ch.m. Air Trooper–Balitree (Balidar) [1989/90 a16g^{5} 22m a20g^{pu} 17m^{2} 16f^{3} 17m^{4} 16f^{F}] small mare: handicap hurdler: form only at around 2m: acts on hard ground: claimer ridden. *D. H. Barons.* 88

TREYFORD 10 ch.g. Deep Run–Bunkilla (Arctic Slave) [1989/90 c22f* c24m^{2} c20m^{4}] tall, short-coupled gelding: fair chaser: won handicap at Stratford in September: ran a lack-lustre race final outing (November): likely to prove best at distances short of 3m: acts on firm and dead going: suited by strongly-run race: sold 8,600 gns Ascot June Sales. *D. R. Greig.* c**121** —

TRIBAL DRUM 11 gr.g. Warpath–Enchanting (Behistoun) [1989/90 20s 18s 20v^{5} 22g] leggy, close-coupled gelding: inconsistent handicap hurdler: no form over fences: stays 2½m: suited by plenty of give in the ground: occasionally visored (not when successful). *D. W. Browning.* c— —

TRIBAL MASCOT (USA) 5 b.g. Our Native (USA)–Little Lady Luck (USA) (Jacinto) [1989/90 16f^{4} 20m* 22m^{6} 21s^{5} a20g^{3} 21m^{2}] close-coupled gelding: won novice handicap hurdle at Bangor in October: good second in similar event at Ludlow in January: stays 21f: acts on good to firm and soft going. *D. R. Gandolfo.* 90

TRIBAL RULER 5 b.g. Prince Tenderfoot (USA)–Candolcis (Candy Cane) [1989/90 16f^{6} 20g^{3} 20f^{2} 20m^{6} 20g^{2} 20d* 20v^{6} 20d^{2}] leggy, quite good-topped gelding: won novice hurdle at Sedgefield in January: stays 2½m: acts on any going, except perhaps heavy: has run well when sweating. *D. McCain.* 105

TRICKY BUSINESS 12 b. or br.g. Tycoon II–Gay Tricks (Vulgan) [1989/90 c20f*] winning hurdler/point-to-pointer: visored, made most when winning novice hunter chase at Folkestone in May by 6 lengths from Rossa Prince: stays well: acts on firm ground. *G. Evans.* c**80** —

TRIDENT TESTED 5 b.g. Cruise Missile–Coombe Valley (Ballyglitter) [1989/90 22v^{pu} 22g 17m] leggy non-thoroughbred gelding: first foal: dam unraced half-sister to a winning point-to-pointer: tailed off in novice hurdles in December (trained until after then by M. Robinson) and April (jumped none too fluently). *M. C. Pipe.* —

TRI FOLENE (FR) 4 b.f. Nebos (GER)–Jefty (FR) (Jefferson) [1989/90 16g* 16g* 16g* 16d^{5} 17m^{3} 20m* 16f^{3} 20f^{2}] angular ex-French filly: fourth foal: half-sister to Egau (by Northern Treat), placed at up to 1½m in France: dam placed over 15.5f in France: placed at up to 1½m in 1989 (claimed out of C. Lerner's stable 45,101 francs (approx £4,391) after finishing second in October): successful in conditional jockeys selling hurdle at Nottingham (bought in 10,000 gns) and juvenile events at Plumpton and Haydock in first half of season and novice event at Market Rasen in April: ran creditably afterwards in juvenile handicap at Ascot and novice handicap at Chepstow: stays 2½m: acts on firm ground: usually a front runner: has sweated up: jumps well in main. *M. C. Pipe.* 119

TRIGPOINT CHARLIE 10 b.g. Bronze Hill–Salambo II (Salmon King) [1989/90 c27f^{3} c27f^{2} c20f* c22m* c22g^{2} c24g* c24d^{4} c20f^{ur} c20g^{3} c16m* c20f* c21f*] strong gelding: won novice chases at Sedgefield in October and Kelso in November and handicaps at Edinburgh (despite jumping badly left last 2 fences) in January and Wetherby (conditional jockeys event), Hexham and Cartmel in May: c**112** —

stays 3m at least when conditions aren't testing: acts on firm and dead ground. *W. A. Stephenson.*

TRILL ALONG 4 ch.g. Longleat (USA)–Cabaletta (Double Jump) [1989/90 F16f^{4}] third foal: half-brother to winning hurdler Cabanax (by Anax): dam ran 3 times: 12½ lengths fourth behind Doctor Syntax in NH Flat race at Hexham: yet to race over hurdles. *E. Weymes.*

TRING PARK 4 b.g. Niniski (USA)–Habanna (Habitat) [1989/90 16g^{3} 16m 20f^{4}
20g^{pu}] workmanlike gelding: half-brother to novice hurdler Blue Bourbon (by Ile 98
de Bourbon): maiden on Flat, claimed by R. Curtis £7,202 after placed in 1½m claimer in January: had previously shown ability in juvenile hurdles: ran poorly in blinkers final start: stays 2½m. *M. H. Tompkins.*

TRIOMING 4 b.c. Homing–Third Generation (Decoy Boy) [1989/90 F16g] 31,000Y: second reported foal: dam sprint maiden: behind in NH Flat race at Kempton: yet to race over hurdles. *A. P. Jones.*

TRIPLE TOP 5 b.g. High Top–Dalmally (Sharpen Up) [1989/90 16m^{2} 16g*
16g^{3} 17g^{4} 16m*] lengthy, workmanlike gelding: half-brother to novice selling 108
hurdler Eastend Blake (by Blakeney) who stays 2½m: plating-class maiden on Flat, stays 9f: led soon after halfway when winning novice hurdles at Catterick in January and Sedgefield (beat Royal Estimate 6 lengths) in March: likely to stay 2½m: claimer ridden all bar fourth start. *Miss L. C. Siddall.*

TRIP THE DAISEY 4 gr.f. Touching Wood (USA)–Easymede (Runnymede)
[1989/90 16m 16d^{F} 16g 16d a20g^{3} a16g 16m] sparely-made filly: sold out of H. —
Candy's stable 4,600 gns after winning 1¼m seller on Flat in August: well beaten over hurdles, including in sellers: blinkered second start. *K. A. Ryan.*

TRISTRAM'S LAKE (NZ) 4 b.f. Sir Tristram–Coole Park (Wolver Hollow)
[1989/90 16d a16g 16g 16g 17g] small filly: sixth foal: sister to winning hurdler —
Miss Tristram: dam ran twice: of little account. *J. Parkes.*

TRIUMPHANT PURSUIT 9 ch.g. General Ironside–Mary Roe (Cracksman) c—
[1989/90 c20g^{F} c16s c20g^{5} c27s^{F} c20f^{F}] angular gelding: novice hurdler: well —
beaten in novice chases: dead. *J. Wade.*

TRIVET 7 ch.g. Thatching–Borana (Aureole) [1989/90 16f^{5} 16m 16f* 16m^{5} c80
c17m^{F} c16f^{4}] lengthy, angular gelding: lightly raced over hurdles: won minor 89
event at Catterick in November: poor form in novice chases: unlikely to stay much beyond 2m: acts on firm ground: has tongue tied down. *J. Mackie.*

TROJAN GOD 8 b.g. Tyrnavos–My Lynnie (Frankincense) [1989/90 16f^{pu} c—
16m 16m] small, close-coupled gelding: selling hurdler: no sign of ability in novice —
chases: stays 2¼m: acts on firm ground, and seems unsuited by a soft surface: has worn blinkers (better without), visored final start. *G. H. Jones.*

TROJAN ROSE 4 br.f. Decoy Boy–Firdale Rosie (Town Crier) [1989/90 19s^{F}
16d^{pu}] smallish, workmanlike filly: third foal: sister to Decoy Express, placed —
twice at 2 yrs: dam 2-y-o 5f winner, appeared not to train on: failed to get past the fifth in 2 juvenile claiming hurdles. *J. M. Bukovets.*

TROJAN SONG 6 b.g. Troy–Melody Hour (Sing Sing) [1989/90 17f^{pu} 17g 17d*
21g 17g 17v 17d^{3} 21s 22m^{6} 17m^{4}] smallish, sparely-made gelding: inconsistent 88 §
handicap hurdler: won at Devon & Exeter in November: promises to stay 21f: acts on hard and dead going: has won for a claimer: blinkered last 2 starts of 1987/8 and first 4 of 1988/9: took little interest second start: trained until after seventh outing by F. Gorman. *R. G. Frost.*

TROJAN WAR 6 b.h. Troy–Sea Venture (FR) (Diatome) [1989/90 20s^{pu}]
sturdy horse: lightly-raced novice hurdler: should stay 2½m: sketchy jumper: —
visored twice, blinkered once (looked none too keen), in 1987/8. *C. Spares.*

TROOP LEADER 11 b.g. Queen's Hussar–Lizzie Lightfoot (Hotfoot)
[1989/90 16m] strong, compact gelding: lightly-raced hurdler: well beaten in —
April: races only at around 2m: seems to act on any going. *F. Walwyn.*

TROOP THE COLOUR 10 ch.g. Soldier Rose–Clear Beat (Clear Run) c—
[1989/90 c26m^{5}] tall, lengthy gelding: behind in novice hurdles: winning chaser: —
stays well: acts on soft going: sold 1,050 gns Ascot February Sales. *D. Nicholson.*

TROPENNA 7 b.g. Bybicello–Highmoor Lass (Rubor) [1989/90 20f^{3} 25f^{5} c**76** p
20m^{5} 16f^{3} c16m^{4}] big, workmanlike gelding: chasing type: poor novice hurdler: 85
fourth in novice event at Carlisle on chasing debut: probably stays 3m: should improve over fences. *J. L. Goulding.*

TROPICAL MIST (FR) 10 b. or br.g. Faraway Son (USA)–Tropical Cream (USA) (Creme Dela Creme) [1989/90 21g^{6} c20g^{pu} c24s* c24s^{pu} a20g] leggy, narrow gelding: handicap hurdler: won novice handicap chase at Taunton in December: ran poorly afterwards: stays 3m: seems to act on any going. *G. A. Ham.* c107 —

TROPICO 7 ch.g. Hot Spark–Bella Canto (Crooner) [1989/90 16g^{5} 16d^{pu} a16g^{pu}] lightly-raced novice hurdler. *I. P. Wardle.* —

TROSTREY 6 b. or br.g. Tom Noddy–Trefair (Graig Hill Master) [1989/90 16s] big, rangy, good sort with plenty of scope: no worthwhile form in 2 novice hurdles but has shown signs of ability and looks the sort to do better in time. *R. Lee.* — p

TROUT ANGLER 9 br.g. Rarity–Gun Tana (FR) (Tanerko) [1989/90 c25f* c26s^{pu} c24g^{ur} c29s^{pu} c25s^{pu}] leggy gelding: won 3-runner handicap chase at Wincanton in November: lost his form afterwards: stays 25f: behind on hard ground but seems to act on any other: suited by forcing tactics: has won for an amateur. *Miss P. O'Connor.* c108 —

TRUBLION (FR) 5 b.g. Cherubin (FR)–Mirella II (FR) (Clairon (BEL)) [1989/90 F16v^{6}] non-thoroughbred French-bred gelding: dam poor French maiden on Flat: favourite, well beaten in NH Flat race at Haydock: yet to race over hurdles or fences. *S. Mellor.*

TRUE BLOOM 11 ch.g. True Song–Ebony Bloom (Eborneezer) [1989/90 c21s* c20s^{3} c25m^{2} c16f*] leggy, close-coupled gelding: useful point-to-pointer/ hunter chaser: won at Towcester in February and Cheltenham (beat Smallwood Willet 2 lengths) in May: best at distances short of 3m: acts on any going: tends to sweat and look rather dull in coat. *G. B. Tarry.* c109

TRUE BRIT (FR) 6 ch.h. Grundy–Charlotteen (Charlottown) [1989/90 16g] stocky horse: selling hurdler: bit backward when behind in non-seller in October: probably acts on any going. *P. Ransom.* —

TRUE CLOWN 8 b.m. True Song–Copperclown (Spartan General) [1989/90 c22d^{5} c21f] tall, close-coupled mare: novice hurdler: promising fifth in novice event at Stratford in November on chasing debut: made several mistakes and was beaten a long way out later in month. *D. Nicholson.* c— —

TRUE FAN 5 b.g. Taufan (USA)–Crepe Myrtle (Crepello) [1989/90 F16m^{2} F17m^{2} 16f^{ur} 16m 16d^{pu} 16f] rangy ex-Irish gelding: half-brother to 5 winners, including useful 1976 2-y-o Ground Cover (by Huntercombe), subsequently a stakes winner at up to 1¼m in North America: dam 1m winner: behind in maiden at 2 yrs: runner-up in NH Flat races at Roscommon and Dundalk (2 ran) in August when trained by Ruby Walsh: no sign of ability in novice hurdles: has worn dropped noseband. *T. H. Caldwell.* —

TRUE GENT (USA) 6 b.h. Lord Gaylord (USA)–Glamour Girl (ARG) (Mysolo) [1989/90 16f^{4}] leggy, lightly-made horse: tubed: poor novice selling hurdler: has run with tongue tied down. *S. J. Muldoon.* 67

TRUE HOLLOW 8 ch.g. True Song–Wilspoon Hollow (Wolver Hollow) [1989/90 c20g^{pu} c25f^{pu} c25s^{4} c25f^{6} c25m^{3} c24f^{6} c26f^{5} c32f^{pu}] big, leggy gelding: poor novice hunter chaser: poor jumper. *Mrs P. M. Pile.* c— x —

TRUE LOOP 8 ch.g. True Song–Loophole (London Gazette) [1989/90 22d^{4} 27s^{4} 21s 22f*] workmanlike, good-quartered gelding: will make a chaser: first run for 3½ months, won novice hurdle at Fontwell in May by ½ length from Chucklestone: stays well: acts on any going: well beaten when blinkered third start. *F. Walwyn.* 101

TRUELY ROYAL 6 b.g. Royal Fountain–True Friend (Bilsborrow) [1989/90 F17d] non-thoroughbred gelding: dam winning hurdler: seventh in NH Flat race at Carlisle on debut: yet to race over hurdles or fences. *A. Eubank.*

TRUE MAGIC 6 ch.g. Decent Fellow–Moyle Majic (Mon Capitaine) [1989/90 F16g^{2} F16m^{2} F16f*] third foal: half-brother to useful Irish jumper Haepenny Well (by General Ironside): dam, 2½m hurdle winner, is daughter of half-sister to Bula: won NH Flat race at Warwick in May by a length from Croghan Rose: yet to race over hurdles or fences. *D. J. G. Murray-Smith.*

TRUE SPARTAN 10 ch.g. True Song–Madge Spartan (Spartan General) [1989/90 24s^{4} 16v* 21d^{F} 20d^{4} 16s^{5} 21s^{3} 20s] sparely-made gelding: inconsistent hurdler: won claimer at Haydock in January: jumped sketchily when behind on only outing over fences: stays 21f: acts on heavy going: usually claimer or amateur ridden (not when successful). *G. Price.* c— 108

TRUISM 5 b.g. Known Fact (USA)–Great Care (Home Guard (USA)) [1989/90 16d^F 16m^6 17d^F 17f* 17m*] workmanlike gelding: won two 4-runner handicap hurdles at Newton Abbot in May, making all for an easy 10-length success over Benisa Ryder for last win: unlikely to stay much beyond 2m: acts on firm going: bolted before start once. *Mrs J. G. Retter.* 94

TRULY HOT 5 b.m. True Song–Duiker (Sovereign Lord) [1989/90 F16s 16f^5 21f^4] half-sister to winning hurdler Gemsbok (by Redundant) and to winning point-to-pointer Bontebok (by Take A Reef): dam 5f winner: tailed off in novice hurdles. *C. J. Vernon Miller.* —

TRUNDLE 4 gr.g. True Song–Pinchapenny (Scallywag) [1989/90 F16f F16f^4] first foal: dam, from an excellent jumping family, ran twice: 25 lengths fourth to Croghan Rose in NH Flat race at Huntingdon in May: yet to race over hurdles. *P. Howling.*

TRUST THE GYPSY 8 br.g. National Trust–Zingarella (Romany Air) [1989/90 c16m^4 c20m^3 c16m^6 c20g c16m^6] leggy gelding: poor novice hurdler: won both completed starts in point-to-points, though failed to put in a clear round on his other 5 outings, in 1989: in frame in early-season novice chases: well beaten afterwards (broke blood vessel final start). *R. J. Hodges.* c78 —

TRUST THE IRISH 9 b.g. Ile de Bourbon (USA)–Trusted Maiden (Busted) [1989/90 22m* 20s^{pu}] small, light-framed gelding: handicap hurdler: ridden by 7-lb claimer, won at Wincanton in November: ran poorly 3 months later: stays 2¾m: acts on good to firm and soft going. *R. J. Holder.* 119

TRUSTY FRIEND 8 b.g. True Song–Princess Camilla (Prince Barle) [1989/90 c24g^{ur} c24v^F c24g^5 c24d^4 c24g* c24g*] big, leggy gelding: handicap hurdler: successful in novice chase at Perth (made most) in April and handicap at Worcester (always prominent when beating Pernoic a short head) following month: stays 3m: acts on heavy going and is possibly unsuited by firm: jumps well in the main. *J. A. C. Edwards.* c**103** —

TRY ME NOW 4 b.g. Try My Best (USA)–Sapientia (FR) (Prudent II) [1989/90 16f^5 16g^4] claimed out of Mrs L. Piggott's stable £10,050 after finishing second in 1m claimer in July: never near to challenge when remote fourth in juvenile hurdle at Newbury in November: may have difficulty in staying 2m. *J. R. Upson.* 76

TRYUMPHANT LAD 6 gr.g. Roselier (FR)–Blackbog Lass (Le Tricolore) [1989/90 16d 22m^{su} 21m^2 22g 21d 22g 22g c20m^F c25f^4] lengthy, sparely-made gelding: poor novice hurdler/chaser: stays 21f: acts on good to firm going: has looked none too keen. *T. M. Jones.* c79 ? 80 §

TSARELLA 8 b.m. Mummy's Pet–Madame Russe (Bally Russe) [1989/90 c20f* c25m^2 c24g^3 c20m^3 c24f* c25m^{pu}] strong, good-bodied mare: fair chaser: c**115** —

*Brown Chamberlin Handicap Chase, Newbury—
the winner Tsarella (left) and Fair Child early on*

won Arlington Premier Series Chase qualifier at Newbury in November and handicap on same course in March, making most despite jumping to her right on occasions both times: jumped poorly final outing: stays 3m: acts on any going: blinkered final start in 1987/8: has looked a difficult ride on occasions. *N. J. Henderson.*

TUBBS 6 b.g. Official–Charmer's Girl (Pappatea) [1989/90 16g 21d] sturdy gelding: half-brother to very useful chaser Henry Kissinger (by New Member) and winning hurdler Lightwater Again (by Celtic Cone): dam novice hurdler: little promise in 2 outings over hurdles. *Mrs S. Armytage.* —

TUCK BOX 4 ch.g. Bustino–Sweet Hour (Primera) [1989/90 17m^{pu} 19s^{F}] small, workmanlike gelding: fair maiden on Flat: sold out of R. Hern's stable 2,500 gns Ascot July Sales: tailed off when falling last in juvenile claimer at Hereford: dead. *J. White.* —

TUDOR D'OR 7 br.m. Mister Tudor–Petit d'Or (Petit Instant) [1989/90 19d^{5} 20m^{5} 22d^{pu}] light-framed mare: poor form over hurdles: will be suited by a return to 2m. *R. J. Holder.* 85

TUDOR FUN 10 b.g. Tudor Rhythm–Coca (Levmoss) [1989/90 c25f^{ur}] workmanlike gelding: fourth in a point-to-point in April: poor novice hurdler/chaser: has run in sellers: usually blinkered. *J. A. Hewitt.* c— —

TUDOR ORCHID 5 b.m. Tudor Rhythm–Flower Child (Brother) [1989/90 F16m] half-sister to Desert Orchid (by Grey Mirage): dam winning chaser: tailed off in NH Flat race at Sandown: yet to race over hurdles or fences. *M. H. B. Robinson.*

TUDOR ROMANCE 5 b.g. Aragon–Dovey (Welsh Pageant) [1989/90 16g 16g^{pu} 16s 16d^{5}] big, workmanlike gelding: fifth in novice handicap at Bangor in March, only sign of ability over hurdles: won 1½m handicap on Flat later in month: pulls hard. *M. W. Eckley.* 76

TUDOR SUN 8 b.g. Sunyboy–Cottage Melody (Super Song) [1989/90 21v^{pu} 20g^{pu}] big, sparely-made gelding: no worthwhile form over hurdles. *B. Forsey.* —

TUFF STICK 5 b.g. Welsh Saint–Corr Lady (Lorenzaccio) [1989/90 16g c16g^{pu}] lengthy, good-bodied ex-Irish gelding: fifth foal: half-brother to 1m and 9f winner Miami Star (by Miami Springs) and 2 winners abroad: dam unraced: won over 1¼m on Flat in 1988: placed in 2 maiden hurdles in 1988/9: still carrying condition, made mistakes and was tailed off when pulled up in intermediate handicap on chasing debut: blinkered second and final starts 1988/9. *J. A. B. Old.* c— —

TUFOLI 6 b.m. Mljet–Tagliatelle (Straight Lad) [1989/90 F16f] fourth foal: sister to winning hurdler Jay-Dee-Jay: dam novice hurdler/chaser: mid-division in NH Flat race at Newbury: yet to race over hurdles or fences. *P. R. Rodford.*

TUFTY LADY 6 b.m. Riboboy (USA)–War Talk (USA) (Assagai) [1989/90 a16g^{6}] small mare: lightly-raced novice selling hurdler: sold 2,000 gns Ascot December Sales. *I. Campbell.* 62

TUGBOAT 11 ch.g. Grundy–Pirate Queen (Pirate King) [1989/90 21d^{pu}] small, lengthy gelding: fair handicap hurdler at best: suited by 2½m+: acts on any going: successful with and without blinkers. *P. J. Makin.* —

TUG OF GOLD 5 gr.g. Tug of War–Grey Squirrell (Golden Gorden) [1989/90 F16g^{4} 22v^{4} 21g 20s^{2} 21s^{pu} 21d* 24d^{3}] leggy, close-coupled gelding: first foal: dam Irish novice hurdler/chaser: won last of 4 outings in point-to-points in Ireland in 1989: won novice handicap hurdle at Newbury in March by a length from Lypheoric, leading run-in: creditable third behind Babil in novice hurdle at Chepstow later in month: reported by trainer to have choked on fifth start and wore tongue strap after: probably stays 3m: acts on soft going. *D. Nicholson.* 99

TULLOMAGRANGE 11 b.g. No Argument–Turn Back (Match III) [1989/90 c21f^{4} c25h^{3} c16f^{3} c21m^{2} c24m^{4} c25g^{6}] big, workmanlike gelding: handicap chaser: first outing for 2 months when very good second to Panto Prince at Wincanton in October: stays 3m: acts on any going but best form on firm: refused third outing in 1987/8 and ran out final start that season: sometimes jumps moderately: sold out of J. Bridger's stable 1,700 gns Ascot September Sales after third outing. *P. J. Hobbs.* c**84** x

TULUM 5 b.g. Blakeney–Inca Girl (Tribal Chief) [1989/90 16d 27s^{2} 25g^{6}] poor maiden on Flat: stayed on well having been given a lot to do when second in novice selling hurdle at Sedgefield in January: eased when well beaten in novice event at Catterick later in month: stays well. *Mrs G. R. Reveley.* 87

TUMBLED BRIDE 4 b.f. Tumble Wind (USA)–Bridewell Belle (Saulingo) [1989/90 16s 16f 18f^{ur} 16m^{pu} 16g 16m^{pu}] leggy, sparely-made ex-Irish filly: third foal: half-sister to winning selling hurdler Fandango Kiss (by Gay Fandango): dam, granddaughter of Fair Astronomer, won over 1m in Ireland: in frame at up to 1m on Flat: little sign of ability over hurdles, including in sellers. *W. T. Kemp.* —

TUMBLE JACK 8 b.g. Tumble Wind (USA)–Alli-Bee (Violon d'Ingres) [1989/90 c26g^{4} c25d^{4} c24d^{4}] tall, sparely-made gelding: behind in novice hurdle: winning chaser: stays 3m: acts on soft going: needs to improve his jumping. *B. Byford.* **c86** —

TUMBLE JIM 11 b.g. Tumble Wind (USA)–Little Rastro (Above Suspicion) [1989/90 c16f^{3} c16m^{4} c16f^{3} c16f^{6} c20d^{ur} c20f^{4} c17f^{5}] leggy gelding: poor chaser: stays 2½m: best on a sound surface: has been tried in blinkers but hasn't worn them since 1983/4: usually held up: usually ridden by 7-lb claimer. *T. W. Cunningham.* **c80** —

TUMBLE TIME 6 b.h. Tumble Wind (USA)–Odette Odile (Home Guard (USA)) [1989/90 c25f^{3}] sturdy horse: blinkered, no form over hurdles: won a point-to-point in April: 20 lengths third behind Kings Bill in novice hunter chase at Wincanton. *A. L. C. Figg.* **c78** —

TUNS HILL 8 ch.g. True Song–Aggreccles (Aggressor) [1989/90 16g 21f^{5} 20d 20s^{ur} c20g^{3} c16g^{2} c20v* c20s^{5} c16v^{3}] small, deep-girthed gelding: modest hurdler nowadays: led close home to win conditional jockeys chase at Fontwell in February: never-dangerous third to Generally Right in novice event at Chepstow later in month: stays 2½m: acts on heavy going: usually ridden by claimer: blinkered fourth start. *R. Dickin.* **c105** 101

TUNSWAY LAD 5 b.g. Cruise Missile–Ogeno (Rugantino) [1989/90 F16g] third foal: dam poor novice hurdler/chaser: tailed off in NH Flat race at Uttoxeter in December: yet to race over hurdles or fences. *D. J. Wintle.*

TURKANA 10 ch.g. Kambalda–Anthony's Lady (Anthony) [1989/90 c24d^{4}] strong gelding: modest hurdler: improved into a fair chaser in 1986/7: burly and tailed off in November: stays 2½m: probably best on ground no softer than dead: makes a mistake or 2 on occasions. *J. R. Upson.* c— —

TURKISH TOURIST 5 b.g. Busted–Kalazero (Kalamoun) [1989/90 16g 16s] rangy gelding: has plenty of scope: no worthwhile form over hurdles, but has shown signs of ability: seemed unsuited by soft ground final start: pulls hard. *D. T. Thom.* —

TURNBERRY DAWN 8 ch.g. Fair Turn–Shuil Alainn (Levanter) [1989/90 c21f^{5} c21m^{4} c24g^{2} c20m^{3} c25d^{5} c20f^{5} 24m^{pu}] leggy ex-Irish gelding: no worthwhile form over hurdles: poor form in novice chases: stays 3m: well beaten on a yielding surface. *T. B. Hallett.* **c84** —

TURN BLUE 11 ch.g. Fair Turn–Blue Birthday (Blue Chariot) [1989/90 c24g^{3} c24m*] rangy gelding: modest chaser: won a point-to-point and Fakenham hunter chase (by ½ length from Auld Jake) in May: stays 3m: acts on any going: blinkered once in 1987/8: makes mistakes. *Major E. W. O'F. Wilson.* **c94** x

TURNERS KEEP 6 b.m. Just A Monarch–Crown Reach (Impecunious) [1989/90 16m] smallish, sparely-made mare: seems of little account. *C. S. Wates.* c— —

TURN MILL 9 b.m. Latest Model–Ruby Sherry (Straight Cut) [1989/90 c25g^{5} c24d^{2}] lengthy mare: poor novice hurdler: won a point-to-point in April: stayed on when going down by 8 lengths to Night Safe in hunter chase at Bangor previous month. *Mrs S. A. Potter.* **c80** —

TURN UP THE WICK 7 b.m. Over The River (FR)–Lovely Daisy (Menelek) [1989/90 16g^{pu} 16h^{pu} 16f] smallish mare: of little account: trained by Miss A. King until after second start. *R. Lee.* —

TURPIN'S GREEN 7 b.g. Nearly A Hand–Maria's Piece (Rose Knight) [1989/90 20g^{pu} 16g^{F} 16m^{4} 20f^{2} 24m^{pu}] big, rangy gelding: has plenty of scope: in frame in novice hurdles at Sandown in March and Cheltenham (wandered) in April, on latter course 4 lengths second to Height of Fun in handicap: stays 2½m: acts on firm ground. *J. S. King.* 95

TUXFORD 10 b.g. Crozier–Dairyguard (Tynwald) [1989/90 c21f^{pu} c24f^{2}] rangy gelding: poor novice chaser: stays 3m: acts on hard ground. *O. Brennan.* **c80** —

TWENTY ONE RED 5 br.g. Dunphy–Monalda (FR) (Claude) [1989/90 16g^{5} 16d 20g^{5}] strong gelding: poor novice hurdler: not seen out after December: sold 2,300 gns Doncaster Spring Sales. *D. McCain.* —

TWICE AS VAGUE (USA) 4 b.c. Two Davids (USA)–Vaguely Sensitive
(USA) (Sensitive Prince (USA)) [1989/90 16d] stocky colt: first foal: dam —
twice-raced half-sister to Indian Skimmer: carrying condition, tailed off in
juvenile hurdle at Market Rasen in March. *N. Tinkler.*

TWIGGERS 4 gr.g. Petong–Petulengra (Mummy's Pet) [1989/90 16s^{pu} 17m
17m^{pu}] poor maiden on Flat: sold out of K. Brassey's stable 2,200 gns Ascot 2nd —
June (1989) Sales: little promise over hurdles. *J. H. Baker.*

TWIN OAKS 10 br.g. Raise You Ten–En Clair (Tarqogan) [1989/90 c24g^{6} c—
c26f^{pu}] big, rangy, good sort: smart novice chaser in 1987/8: has reportedly —
suffered leg problems since and still needed race second start in 1989/90: will stay
extreme distances: acts on dead going. *D. J. G. Murray-Smith.*

TWO REALMS 4 b.f. Another Realm–Two Shots (Dom Racine (FR)) [1989/90
16f^{4}] sparely-made filly: maiden plater on Flat (takes a keen hold): raced too —
freely in juvenile claiming hurdle at Wincanton in October. *K. O. Cunningham-Brown.*

TYCOON MOON 9 b.m. Tycoon II–Moonbreaker (Twilight Alley) [1989/90 c**90**
c20m^{3} c22f^{4} c24g^{3} c22m^{3} c24g^{4} c24g^{2} c24d^{6} c24v* c24v^{2} c28d^{5}] sparely-made, —
angular mare: won novice chase at Ayr in January by a neck from Watersign: ran a
moody race last outing: will stay extreme distances: suited by heavy going:
usually amateur ridden: blinkered last 6 starts. *Mrs D. Thomson.*

TYPHOON LUCY 6 br.m. Laurence O–Tyrone Typhoon (Typhoon) [1989/90
16m^{2} 16d^{3} 16g*] workmanlike mare: showed improved form when winning 93
14-runner novice handicap hurdle at Sedgefield in December by 4 lengths from
Yamanouchi: should stay 2½m. *Mrs G. R. Reveley.*

TYRED N'SNOOKERD 6 b.g. Le Johnstan–Dobella (Sovereign Lord)
[1989/90 21d 21s 20g* 22m 25m 20g^{pu}] leggy, workmanlike gelding: handicap 111
hurdler: won moderately-run race at Kempton in February: ran moderately
afterwards: probably stays 3m: acts on good to firm and dead going (ran poorly on
very soft): visored final start 1988/9, blinkered last 5: has won for a claimer. *P. R. Hedger.*

TYRIAN KING 5 ch.g. Royal Match–Apple Blossom (Orange Bay) [1989/90
16g 16g] neat gelding: poor novice hurdler: amateur ridden in 1989/90. *S. Christian.* —

U

UGANDAN AFFAIRS 5 b.g. Kampala–Karens Pet (Mummy's Pet) [1989/90
16d 16v^{2} 16m] workmanlike gelding: won over 1¼m on Flat at 3 yrs: 2½ lengths 106 p
second to Do Be Brief in novice hurdle at Chepstow in February: in touch and
travelling well until blundering badly 2 out in Waterford Crystal Supreme
Novices' Hurdle won by Forest Sun at Cheltenham following month: looks certain
to win races over hurdles. *P. J. Makin.*

UGLY 4 b.g. Cleon–Lammas (Manicou) [1989/90 16s^{pu} 16s] third foal: dam poor
novice hurdler/chaser: tailed off in juvenile hurdle at Plumpton in December. *A. Moore.* —

ULLSWATER 4 b.g. Wassl–Dignified Air (FR) (Wolver Hollow) [1989/90 16s
16f^{5} 16d 16g^{3} 16g^{2} 16g^{3} 19m^{3}] close-coupled ex-Irish gelding: first foal: dam, 6f 96
winner, out of a half-sister to very smart Joking Apart: behind only outing on Flat:
modest form over hurdles: stays 19f: acts on good to firm ground: claimer ridden:
trained by E. Bolger first start. *F. Jordan.*

ULTRA VIOLET (FR) 4 ch.g. Quart de Vin (FR)–Ebonite (FR) (Or de Chine)
[1989/90 17h^{ro} 16h* 19f* 16m^{3}] leggy, rather sparely-made gelding: in frame over 98 §
1¼m on Flat in France in 1989, when trained by J. H. Barbe: won juvenile hurdles
at Taunton and Hereford (long odds on, ran in snatches and looked none too
keen) in May: stays 19f: acts on hard ground: blinkered second and third outings,
visored final one (ran respectably): ran out after 2 out first start: one to have
reservations about. *M. C. Pipe.*

UMBRELLA GIRL 6 br.m. Creative Plan (USA)–Carambola (Hul A Hul)
[1989/90 18m 16g 16m 16m] lightly-made mare: behind in NH Flat race and all —
starts over hurdles. *A. P. James.*

UNCLE BUCKY 5 gr.g. Nishapour (FR)–Maellen (River Beauty) [1989/90
17h^{pu}] smallish gelding: novice selling hurdler: odds on, led until pulled up lame 2 79 ?

out in 3-runner race at Devon & Exeter in August: usually blinkered: often claimer ridden. *J. H. Baker.*

UNCLE ERNIE 5 b.g. Uncle Pokey–Ladyfold (Never Dwell) [1989/90 16d6 16g* 16g3 16d3 16m2 16g2] workmanlike gelding: modest middle-distance handicapper on Flat when trained by Mrs J. Ramsden: successful in novice hurdle at Wetherby in December: would have won at Catterick in February on fourth start but for slipping after 2 out: may stay further: acts on good to firm and dead going. *J. G. FitzGerald.* 104

UNCLE MERLIN (USA) 9 b.g. Easy Gallop (USA)–Aunt Sheila (USA) (Mystic II) [1989/90 c24d c24m2 c25g4 c25g* c24d2 c36fur] c**129** +

The departure of the 1989 Maryland Hunt Cup winner Uncle Merlin at second Becher's in the Seagram Grand National might well have influenced the outcome of the race significantly. He was in the lead going great guns when stumbling on landing and parting company with his rider. 'Make no mistake he would have won,' his jockey Davies said afterwards. 'I hadn't even had to give him a breather. That's how easily he was going.' Uncle Merlin jumped all the fences before second Becher's without serious error, leading the National field a merry dance after showing in front from early on. Mr Frisk stuck close to Uncle Merlin on the second circuit and was left six lengths clear. The result of the National can sometimes be forecast accurately soon after the field has jumped Becher's for the second time and, though too far out to say for certain whether Uncle Merlin would have beaten Mr Frisk and Durham Edition, there's no doubt Uncle Merlin was travelling like a winner before he came unstuck. Granted similar conditions and a fair weight he'll be on our short-list for the next National.

Uncle Merlin's exhilarating assault on the Grand National course on the prevailing very firm ground was partly responsible for the setting of a new time record for the race. Had Uncle Merlin won he would have emulated Jay Trump and Ben Nevis, previous Maryland Hunt Cup winners who have triumphed at Aintree. Uncle Merlin was transferred in the autumn to Forster's yard where Ben Nevis had been prepared for the National. Uncle Merlin's first taste of British steeplechase fences came at Worcester in mid-November when he carried automatic top weight—having run fewer than three times in Britain—in a handicap framed for horses rated 0-125; on his best form he obviously had a very good chance, especially when the weights for the other runners went up 5 lb because of four overnight withdrawals (the rule covering the raising of weights in handicaps ignores automatic top weights). But a backward Uncle Merlin, ridden by his American trainer the amateur Mr Neilson, wasn't given anything like a hard race and came last of eight finishers, jumping really well. With the need to qualify for a proper assessment by the handicapper for the Grand National, Uncle Merlin had two more outings in quick succession—under top weight in minor handicaps at Ludlow and Devon & Exeter, each time ridden by Mr Neilson who handled him sympathetically. Mr Neilson would have had to put up considerable overweight to take the mount at Aintree and Davies rode the horse in his two other races before the National. Uncle Merlin improved considerably on his earlier efforts when winning a small handicap at Wincanton in January and then, after the National weights had been published, put up an even better performance when second in a more competitive handicap at Ludlow in March. Uncle Merlin was given only 8-13 in the original handicap for the National, a mark low enough to make his participation in the race dependent upon a fair number of those above him being withdrawn. Only the top forty handicapped horses were permitted to run and Uncle Merlin only became a certain qualifier at the five-day stage (he carried 10-3, including 3 lb overweight).

The angular Uncle Merlin is by the now-deceased Round Table stallion Easy Gallop, a useful racehorse at around a mile and a mile and a quarter who won eight of his thirty-seven races during three seasons' racing. Uncle Merlin's dam Aunt Sheila was a moderate racemare but she was tough—running in forty-one races over six seasons—and was successful on the Flat at up to two and a quarter miles and also over jumps at around two miles; she is a half-sister to the good American jumper Uncle Edwin whose victories

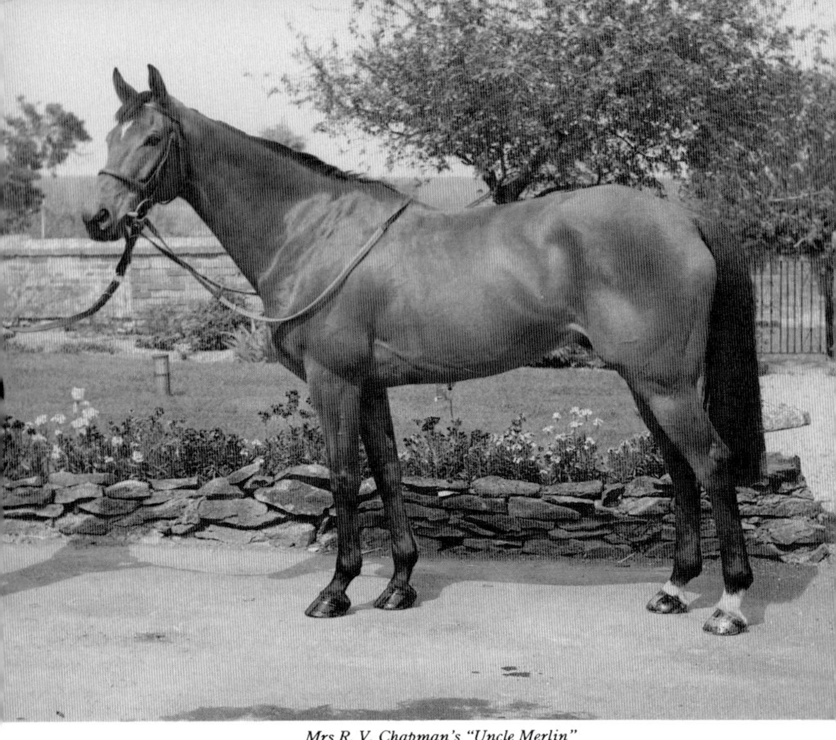

Mrs R. V. Chapman's "Uncle Merlin"

Uncle Merlin (USA) (b.g. 1981)	Easy Gallop (USA) (b 1973)	Round Table (b 1954)	Princequillo
			Knight's Daughter
		Capercaillie (b 1967)	Native Dancer
			Morning Sunrise
	Aunt Sheila (USA) (b or br 1970)	Mystic (b 1954)	Relic
			Tosca
		Cousin Yvonne (b 1963)	Besomer
			External Relations

included those in the Iroquois Steeplechase, the Bolla Hard Scuffle Steeplechase and the National Steeplechase (he also finished third in the American Grand National). Uncle Merlin is the first of six reported foals out of Aunt Sheila whose second and third foals, the fillies Gala Gaiety (by Gala Harry) and Snow Leopard (by Northern Raja), won at around a mile; Gala Gaiety was notably tough, winning ten of seventy-seven starts from three to seven years. The four-mile Maryland Hunt Cup, run over post and rails fences, is easily the most important of the victories gained by Uncle Merlin in the United States. In the tradition of Maryland Hunt Cup winners—the race is a rigorous test of stamina and jumping ability—Uncle Merlin is an out-and-out stayer and a sound jumper. He has shown form on an easy surface but the going was exceptionally firm for the Grand National and when Uncle Merlin won the Maryland Hunt Cup, and he clearly revels in such conditions. *Capt. T. A. Forster.*

UNCLE MOGY 4 ch.g. Monsanto (FR)–Primrolla (Relko) [1989/90 F16g F16m2 F16d] second foal: half-brother to fair 5f to 1m winner Primulette (by Mummy's Pet): dam won over 1¼m and also useful hurdler: 6 lengths second to Captain Dibble in NH Flat race at Sandown in March: yet to race over hurdles. *D. Nicholson.*

UNCLE OLIVER 9 b.g. Monsanto (FR)–Miss Merlin (Manacle) [1989/90 c27mur] short-backed gelding: winning hurdler: well below his best since early in 1987/8 season: unseated rider at the seventh in hunter chase at Sedgefield in March: stays 3m: seems suited by firm ground: usually amateur ridden. *V. Thompson.* c— —

UNCLE PARKS (NZ) 4 b.g. Diagramatic (USA)–Talento (NZ) (Saraceno) [1989/90 F16f] half-brother to fair staying hurdler/novice chaser Cona Glen (by Lomond): well beaten in NH Flat race at Ascot in April: yet to race over hurdles. *F. Jordan.*

UNCLE RAGGY 7 b.g. Monksfield–Lorna Doone (Raise You Ten) [1989/90 c21d c24m6 c25g4 c25d* c25s3 c32f5] rangy gelding: poor form in novice hurdles: won novice chase at Towcester in February: creditable fifth to Topsham Bay in valuable event at Cheltenham in March: needs a thorough test of stamina: acts on firm and dead going. *D. Nicholson.* c**103** —

UNCLES CHOICE 7 br.g. Warpath–Shenandoah (Mossborough) [1989/90 c25fpu] tall, angular gelding: poor novice hurdler: placed in point-to-points: tailed off when pulled up in hunter chases: has worn a crossed noseband. *Mrs A. Price.* c— —

UNDAUNTED 6 b.g. Mandalus–Inundated (Raise You Ten) [1989/90 26d5 20sro] close-coupled, workmanlike gelding: smart novice hurdler in 1988/9: every chance when running out 3 out in sponsored event won by Propero at Chepstow in December: was best at around 2½m: acted on heavy going: raced freely: dead. *Mrs J. Pitman.* 141

UNDER OFFER 9 br.g. Rhodomantade–Blue Flash (Blue Lightning) [1989/90 22d3 c24g3 c20s3 c24g] leggy, lengthy gelding: moderate hurdler: third in novice chases at Kempton and Warwick, showing modest form: suited by a test of stamina: acts on soft going and good to firm. *P. G. Bailey.* c**94** 101

UNDER THE STARS 8 ch.g. Ahonoora–Moonlight Night (Huntercombe) [1989/90 17f3 17h4 17f2 17f4 c17m] close-coupled gelding: selling hurdler: well beaten only start over fences: stays 2¼m: acts on firm ground: looked a slightly difficult ride first outing (amateur ridden): usually blinkered in 1989/90. *R. J. Hodges.* c— 75

UNEX-PLAINED 7 b.g. Last Fandango–Miss Pinkerton (Above Suspicion) [1989/90 c16g5 c17d6 c20g4 c20s5 c20d6] smallish, workmanlike gelding: fair hurdler/chaser at his best: only modest form in 1989/90: stays 2½m: acts on heavy going and is possibly unsuited by top-of-the-ground. *G. M. Moore.* c**108** ? —

UNICOL 8 ch.g. Manado–Ragatina (Ragusa) [1989/90 c24d4 c26s2 c26g2 c20d3] good-bodied gelding: winning hurdler: moderate chaser: runner-up twice at Folkestone in December: a thorough stayer: acts on heavy going: blinkered fourth start 1986/7. *S. Mellor.* c**104** —

UNITYFARM OLTOWNER 6 b.g. Le Johnstan–Ribble Reed (Bullrush) [1989/90 c17f3 17h4 c17f3] leggy, good-topped gelding: winning selling hurdler: poor novice chaser: takes a good hold and seems suited by a sharp 2m: acts on firm ground: blinkered nowadays: has joined R. Hodges. *P. J. Hobbs.* c**65** 75

UNPAID MEMBER 6 b.g. Moorestyle–Sunningdale Queen (Gay Fandango (USA)) [1989/90 16m2 16g5 c16f2 c16f6 c16g3 c20f4 16d 17f 20m* 16f3 20m4 20f3] sparely-made gelding: handicap hurdler: won at Market Rasen in April: ran moderately last 2 starts: in frame in novice chases: stays 2½m: yet to race on heavy going, acts on any other: looked irresolute under pressure fourth start 1988/9. *P. A. Blockley.* c**88** 103

UNSCRUPULOUS GENT 8 ch.g. Over The River (FR)–Even Lass (Even Money) [1989/90 c24d5 c20g4 c20d2 c24m3 c22mur c24g6 c20m2 c20d3] rangy gelding: poor novice hurdler: winning chaser: placed in hunter chase and 3 handicaps in 1989/90: effective at 2½m and stays long distances: acts on soft going and good to firm: sold 14,500 gns Doncaster June Sales. *J. Mackie.* c**96** —

UNTIED 5 b.g. Blakeney–Set Free (Worden II) [1989/90 16f 16g a16g] leggy gelding: seems of little account: blinkered second start. *P. D. Connors.* —

UNWANTED GIFT 4 b.g. Auction Ring (USA)–Carioca (Gala Performance (USA)) [1989/90 16m] rather sparely-made gelding: modest maiden at up to 7f on —

Flat: took keen hold and jumped none too fluently when tailed off in juvenile claiming hurdle at Wincanton in March: sold 1,150 gns Ascot May Sales. *D. H. Barons.*

UP AND COMING 7 b.g. Avocat–Cummin Hill (Wrekin Rambler) [1989/90 c22d* c24mpu c25f* c25m* c24fpu] strong gelding: novice hurdler: took well to chasing and won novice handicap at Stratford (amateur ridden) in December and handicaps at Towcester in March and April: ran as though something amiss last outing: stays 25f: acts on firm and dead going. *N. J. Henderson.* c**122** —

UP-A-POINT 5 gr.g. Rusticaro (FR)–Malmsey (Jukebox) [1989/90 16s6 16s 17g3 16d6 16m* 16g3] leggy gelding: made virtually all when successful in novice handicap hurdle at Uttoxeter in March: suited by sharp 2m: best form on a sound surface. *F. H. Lee.* 93

UPHAM RAINBOW 7 b.g. Pitpan–Kintrout (Little Buskins) [1989/90 c16gF 17g a22g2 a24gF a24g3 c24fF] sturdy, lengthy gelding: poor form over hurdles: held in second place when falling 3 out in novice chase won by Answers Please at Ludlow in April, last start: should stay 3m. *D. R. Gandolfo.* c84 69 +

UPHAM VIEW 5 b.m. Oats–Real View (Royal Highway) [1989/90 F16m6 22s5] rather leggy filly: sweating, sixth in NH Flat race at Worcester in October: bit backward, one-paced fifth behind Senegalais in novice hurdle at Folkestone in December: will be suited by a thorough test of stamina. *D. R. Gandolfo.* 76

UPSTANDING 8 b.g. Latest Model–Calamity (Haven) [1989/90 c20hur c25h2 c26f* c26gpu c25fpu] deep-girthed, workmanlike gelding: looked to have his own ideas about the game until making all in novice chase at Newton Abbot in October: jumped none too fluently next outing and pulled up lame on last: stays 3¼m: acts on firm ground: has worn a crossed noseband and is sometimes taken early to post: probably suited by a left-handed track. *N. H. Davis.* c**86**

UP THE CHERRIES 6 b.g. Official–Crown Bird (Birdbrook) [1989/90 aF16g2] second foal: half-brother to novice hurdler Debbies Prince (by Lighter): dam won novice hurdle: beaten a head by Royal Cause in NH Flat race at Lingfield in January: sold 2,000 gns Ascot June Sales: yet to race over hurdles or fences. *C. P. E. Brooks.*

UP THE LADDER 6 gr.g. Taufan (USA)–Magnesia (Upper Case (USA)) [1989/90 16g 16s* 16g5 20g a20g a16g2 a16g3 a16g] sparely-made, angular gelding: inconsistent selling hurdler: won conditional jockeys event at Hereford (bought in 2,500 gns) in December: jumped moderately when behind on chasing debut: form only at up to 2¼m: probably acts on any going: blinkered final outing (ran moderately). *D. J. Wintle.* c— 86

UP THE SNICKET 9 br.g. Al Sirat (USA)–Trial By Fire (Court Martial) [1989/90 c27fpu] novice hurdler: winning point-to-pointer: pulled up lame in May: dead. *R. T. Dennis.* c— —

UPTOWN BEAT 5 ch.g. Town And Country–Samba (Sammy Davis) [1989/90 20d 17m6] half-brother to winning hurdlers Bossanova Boy (by Rhodomantade) and Latin American (by Genuine), latter also a fair chaser: poor maiden on Flat when trained by D. Elsworth: poor form in novice hurdle at Worcester in November and maiden hurdle at Newton Abbot in April. *M. R. Channon.* 68

UPTOWN RANDB'S 7 b.m. Uncle Pokey–Mountain Child (Mountain Call) [1989/90 17fur 16f 20m 16fbd] won 3 times over hurdles in 1986/7: tailed off subsequent completed outings: acted on firm going: dead. *T. Kersey.* —

UPWELL 6 b.g. Tanfirion–Debnic (Counsel) [1989/90 27spu 16g 17m4 16f4 16f2] lengthy, sparely-made gelding: poor plater over hurdles: ran well last start: best at around 2m on top-of-the-ground: has worn a crossed noseband. *R. Johnson.* 77

UP WEST 4 b.g. King of Spain–Shaky Puddin (Ragstone) [1989/90 16mpu] no worthwhile form on Flat: tailed off when pulled up in novice hurdle at Catterick: dead. *S. G. Norton.* —

UP YONDER 6 ch.g. Moor House–Peggy Jet (Willipeg) [1989/90 16g4] leggy, workmanlike gelding: well-beaten fourth of 5 in novice hurdle at Newcastle in May. *B. E. Wilkinson.* —

URBAN SURFER 6 b.g. Le Bavard (FR)–Reynella (Royal Buck) [1989/90 16g 25gpu] lengthy gelding: second foal: brother to winning staying hurdler Scandalous Rumour: dam Irish NH Flat race winner: well beaten in novice hurdles at Plumpton and Newbury (backward, not fluent and pulled up 3 out) in first half of season. *D. M. Grissell.* —

URIZEN 5 ch.g. High Line–Off The Reel (USA) (Silent Screen (USA)) [1989/90 16m3 20f4 21d 25f] rather leggy, close-coupled gelding: fairly useful hurdler: fourth to Morley Street in Mercury Communications Hurdle at Cheltenham in December, best effort of season: stays 2½m: best form on a sound surface (well beaten on heavy): seems suited by forcing tactics: jumps boldly. *D. R. C. Elsworth.* 134

US AND JOE 7 b.g. Candy Cane–How Ready (Babur) [1989/90 c20d* c21gF c24d4 c20g* c18d* c20v2 c28mF c16gpu] leggy Irish gelding: useful chaser: won handicaps at Clonmel (made all) in November, Leopardstown in January and Fairyhouse in February: good second to Bonalma in P Z Mower Chase at Thurles later in February: looked lean final outing: best at up to 2½m: acts on heavy going. *Patrick Mullins, Ireland.* c**142** —

USARIO 6 ch.g. Abednego–Frozen Ground (Arctic Slave) [1989/90 20mpu] fourth foal: dam, winning hurdler, stayed 3m: 50/1, tailed off when pulled up 4 out in amateur riders novice hurdle at Perth in September. *D. McCaskill.* —

USEFUL ADDITION 8 b.m. Royalty–Facade (Double Jump) [1989/90 22mpu 20gF 24gpu 20g] small, leggy mare: modest novice hurdler at best: lightly raced and no form for a long time: stays 2½m: possibly unsuited by extremes of ground. *M. Tate.* —

USELESS MEMBER 8 ch.g. Whistling Top–Bow-Bar (Bargello) [1989/90 18h5 16f6 16s] plain gelding: selling hurdler: well beaten in 1989/90: stayed 2¼m: acted on any going: ran out in a point-to-point in 1987: dead. *A. Moore.* —

UTOPIAN 12 b.g. Radical–Tuti (Tudor Minstrel) [1989/90 16f c20f4] strong, close-coupled gelding: poor novice hurdler/chaser: possibly unsuited by soft ground: has worn blinkers: usually amateur or claimer ridden. *G. Roe.* c— —

V

VAGADOR (CAN) 7 ch.g. Vaguely Noble–Louisador (Indian Hemp) [1989/90 18s* 16m 20f4 16d] 155

Vagador hasn't quite lived up to the promise he showed in his first season over hurdles when he won all his five races, notably the Waterford Crystal Supreme Novices' Hurdle at Cheltenham. That same season Vagador was also successful in the National Spirit Challenge Trophy at Fontwell, and this event has provided him with his only victory in the last

'National Spirit' Challenge Trophy, Fontwell—
Vagador (left) turns the tables on the previous year's winner Beech Road

couple of seasons. It came in the latest running in February. Vagador, who'd been beaten twenty lengths by Beech Road in the National Spirit Trophy twelve months earlier, now met the latter on terms 25 lb better. The turnaround in the weights was just enough to enable Vagador, who was making his seasonal reappearance, to get the better of Beech Road for the first time in four attempts. Beech Road, who'd led from the third, quickened the pace after the sixth, where Vagador joined Valrodian in pursuit. Valrodian could find no more from the home turn, but Beech Road was unable to shake off Vagador and the latter proved just the stronger on the run-in after the pair had jumped the last upsides. Vagador won by a head, and there was a gap of thirty lengths to third-placed Propero. In the previous season Vagador had gone on to run well behind Beech Road in both the Waterford Crystal Champion Hurdle and the Sandeman Aintree Hurdle, finishing fifth and fourth respectively. He didn't fare so well in the latest runnings, although in the circumstances he wasn't disgraced in the Champion Hurdle. After his usual rider Perrett was taken ill at the last minute, Vagador was ridden at Cheltenham by his owner Miss Harwood, who was unable to claim her 5-lb allowance. Vagador would have benefited from stronger handling, for he doesn't have the speed to be seen to advantage over two miles on fast ground and needs plenty of driving. Well placed until four out, Vagador couldn't quicken once the race began in earnest and finished around twenty-one lengths behind Kribensis in eighth. The ground was even firmer in the Sandeman Hurdle and Vagador was never travelling well on it, coming home a well-beaten fourth of the six runners. Vagador had an easy surface to race on in the Scottish Champion Hurdle at Ayr, but this time he gave the impression that there was something wrong with him and he trailed in last of the eleven finishers. It was therefore encouraging to see Vagador run with credit when returned to Flat racing in the summer. Reportedly he may go chasing in 1990/1.

Vagador (CAN) (ch.g. 1983)	Vaguely Noble (b 1965)	Vienna (ch 1957)	Aureole
			Turkish Blood
		Noble Lassie (b 1956)	Nearco
			Belle Sauvage
	Louisador (ch 1964)	Indian Hemp (ch 1949)	Nasrullah
			Sabzy
		Louise Mason (b 1957)	Count Fleet
			Kinfolks

Vagador is a brother to two middle-distance winners, Valour and Paleocene, and closely related to another, Favorable Exchange (by Exceller). Valour won the Grosser Preis Von Baden and the Prix Jean de Chaudenay in the late-'seventies. The dam, who has produced at least seven winners, was one of the best American two-year-old fillies in 1966. She won eleven races in four seasons, none over further than six furlongs. Her dam, the unraced Louise Mason, was out of a winning sister to the Santa Anita Derby winner Chanlea. Vagador, a compact gelding, should stay beyond two and a half miles. He's ideally suited by give in the ground. *G. Harwood.*

VAGARA 5 ch.h. Vaigly Great–Habitual Beauty (Habat) [1989/90 a16g^{pu}] compact horse: bad sprint maiden on Flat: sold out of M. Brittain's stable 500 gns — Doncaster November (1988) Sales: needing race, tailed off when pulled up 2 out in novice event at Southwell in November on hurdling debut. *R. F. Casey.*

VAGOG 5 b.g. Glint of Gold–Vadrouille (USA) (Foolish Pleasure (USA)) [1989/90 21g^{2} 24f*] small, rather lightly-made gelding: fair hurdler: won handicap 122 at Cheltenham in December by 3 lengths from Ambergate: suited by a test of stamina and forcing tactics: acts on any going: has won for a claimer: game. *M. C. Pipe.*

VAGUELY ARTISTIC 8 gr.g. Vaigly Great–Roanette (Roan Rocket) c98 § [1989/90 c17f* c17m^{2} c16m* 16g c17m^{6} c16m* c17m^{3} c16s^{2} c16m^{5} c20m^{4}] tall — gelding: modest chaser: won handicaps at Huntingdon, Worcester (conditional jockeys) and Windsor in first half of season: behind in 2 races in second half: ran in snatches eighth start: best at around 2m: probably acts on any going: usually blinkered or visored nowadays: sketchy jumper: has looked faint-hearted and is suited by waiting tactics: claimer ridden. *G. A. Hubbard.*

VAIGLY BLAZED 6 ch.g. Vaigly Great–Monkey Tricks (Saint Crespin III)
[1989/90 16f^{5}] close-coupled, sparely-made gelding: no form over hurdles. *C. A.* —
Horgan.

VAIGLY PERCEPTIVE 4 b.c. Vaigly Great–Ash Gayle (Lord Gayle (USA))
[1989/90 16m 16m* 16m 16g 16d 16m^{5} 16m 16m^{3}] small colt: half-brother to 73
winning hurdler Taylormade Boy (by Dominion): placed over sprint distances:
won juvenile claiming hurdle at Ludlow in November: ran creditably in selling
handicap final start: likely to prove best at a sharp 2m: acts on good to firm ground
(ran moderately on dead). *B. Stevens.*

VAIGRANT WIND 4 ch.f. Vaigly Great–Silent Prayer (Queen's Hussar)
[1989/90 16g a16g^{5}] half-sister to winning Irish hurdler Saorstat and novice —
hurdler Primula Again (both by Free State): dam successful 2m top-of-the-ground
hurdler: won over 6f at 2 yrs but below form on Flat in 1989, when trained by R.
Hannon: no worthwhile form in juvenile hurdles in first half of season. *D. R.*
Gandolfo.

VALASSY 7 b.g. Northern Value (USA)–Plum Sassy (Prince Tenderfoot c**96**
(USA)) [1989/90 c21s* c25d^{F} c25d^{pu} c20d^{6} c21d^{6} c24g^{2}] lengthy gelding: —
successful in a point-to-point and a maiden hurdle in Ireland: won novice chase at
Fakenham in December: good second in similar event at Perth in April: let down
by his jumping most outings in between: stays 3m: acts on heavy going. *J. A. C.*
Edwards.

VALENTINOS JOY 11 b. or br.g. Master Buck–Vulady (Vulgan) [1989/90 c**97** §
c16m^{4} c24g^{3} c25f^{3} c20g^{4} c20g^{2} c17f^{2} c16g^{3}] small, sparely-made gelding: modest —
chaser nowadays: stays 3m: acts on any going: ridden by 7-lb claimer when
successful in 1988/9: visored last outing: finds little off bridle. *G. R. Oldroyd.*

VALE OF SECRECY 9 b.g. The Parson–Arctic Rhapsody (Bargello)
[1989/90 22s^{4} 21d^{5} 22v^{3} 22v* 22d 22d] rather lightly-made, close-coupled 114
gelding: moderate hurdler: won 4-runner handicap at Ayr in February comfortably
by 6 lengths from Shilgrove Place: ran poorly afterwards: should stay further than
2¾m: acts on heavy going. *R. F. Fisher.*

VALIANT BOY 4 b.g. Connaught–Irish Amber (Amber Rama (USA)) [1989/90
16g^{ro} 16g* 16g^{4} a20g^{2} a20g* a16g* a20g*] rangy gelding: lightly-raced maiden 112
on Flat: made all in novice selling hurdle at Sedgefield (bought in 6,000 gns) in
December: ridden with more restraint when winning juvenile hurdles at
Southwell in February (2, first an amateur riders event) and March: stays 2½m:
wearing blinkers and crossed noseband, ran out in early stages on hurdling debut
(trained by J. Mackie). *S. E. Kettlewell.*

VALIANT DASH 4 b.g. Valiyar–Dame Ashfield (Grundy) [1989/90 16f* 16m*
17m* 16m^{2} 16m* 16g^{4} 16m^{4} 20g^{6} 20d^{6} a18g^{4} 16d^{6} 21h* 16d^{3} 23f*] close-coupled 115
gelding: in frame at up to 1¾m on Flat: had a good first season over hurdles and
won seller at Market Rasen (bought in 5,700 gns), claimer and juvenile event at
Bangor, novice handicap at Ludlow and juvenile event and handicap at Cartmel:
stays 23f: acts on firm and dead going: usually claimer ridden: genuine and
consistent. *S. E. Kettlewell.*

VALIANT PILGRIM 10 b.g. Jimmy Reppin–Plain Pilgrim (Menelek)
[1989/90 22m* 20g^{pu}] big, good-looking, chasing type: lightly-raced hurdler: only 80
form when winning moderately-run conditional jockeys novice handicap at
Nottingham in December: stays 2¾m: acts on good to firm going. *J. G. FitzGerald.*

VALIANT STAR 4 br.g. Noalto–Duns Tew (Mandamus) [1989/90 16f 20m 16g
16g] fifth foal: half-brother to fair 2-y-o 5f winner Balcanoona (by Cawston's —
Clown): dam won over 5f at 2 yrs: tailed off over hurdles: flashed tail under
pressure second outing: blinkered second and third starts, visored last. *Mrs R.*
Wharton.

VALLEY JUSTICE 10 ch.g. Avocat–Cherry Valley (Cantab) [1989/90 c20g^{3} c—
c20v^{pu} c25g^{ur}] tall, rather sparely-made gelding: poor chaser: jumped slowly last —
start: stays 3¼m: probably acts on any ground: sometimes blinkered: sold 2,200
gns Doncaster Spring Sales. *C. C. Trietline.*

VALLEY OF DANUATA 5 b.g. Taufan (USA)–Dane Valley (Simbir)
[1989/90 16m 16g^{5} 16g^{6} 16g 16f^{6} 18f*] rather sparely-made gelding: moderate 104
hurdler: won 6-runner handicap at Worcester in April by 6 lengths from Our
White Hart: worth a try over further than 2¼m: acts on firm and dead going:
ridden by claimer. *F. Jordan.*

VALOROSO 10 b.g. Young Emperor–My Plucky Lady (Cash And Courage) c—
[1989/90 c27f^{4} c27f^{F} c17f^{ur} c16f^{6}] workmanlike gelding: won point-to-point in —

March: poor selling hurdler and novice selling chaser: stays 2½m: probably acts on any going: usually held up: blinkered last 4 starts in 1986/7. *Mrs K. J. Tutty.*

VALRODIAN (NZ) 7 b.g. Allgrit (USA)–Nyleva (NZ) (Bucentaur) [1989/90 16v* 16v* 16g^{4} 16s 18s^{5} 16s^{4} 16f 22f] compact gelding: leading hurdler in New Zealand, winner 5 times including in Waikato and Wellington Hurdles: fourth of 5 in New Year's Day Hurdle at Windsor and slowly-run White Rabbit Hurdle at Haydock: acts on heavy going (well beaten on firm last 2 outings). *M. H. B. Robinson.* 132 ?

VALTAKI 5 b.g. Valiyar–Taqa (Blakeney) [1989/90 17f* 17h^{2} 17f^{3} 16m 16g* 22m 16m 16g^{2} 16g 16g 16m 16h^{2} 16g* 16f* 16m* 16m^{6}] neat gelding: won selling hurdles at Newton Abbot (bought in 4,400 gns) and Stratford (sold out of J. Baker's stable 4,500 gns) early in season and non-selling handicaps at Bangor, Warwick and Fakenham (amateur riders) in May: ran poorly, swishing tail, final outing: should stay beyond 2m: yet to race on heavy going, seems to act on any other: has worn a tongue strap: often claimer ridden: blinkered fourth start (well beaten). *L. J. Codd.* 98

VALUED OPINION 11 ch.g. New Member–Dairi Orchid (Dairialatan) [1989/90 c20f^{pu}] leggy, angular gelding: winning point-to-pointer: novice hunter chaser. *Mrs S. S. Harbour.* c— —

VA LUTE (FR) 6 b.g. No Lute (FR)–Viverba (FR) (Sanctus II) [1989/90 16s^{4} 16s* 16g^{2} 16d* 16s 16m^{4}] small, lightly-made gelding: improved hurdler: successful in seller at Taunton (bought in 2,600 gns) in December and handicap at Wincanton (pulled hard) in February: stays 2¼m: yet to race on heavy going, acts on any other. *R. J. Holder.* 114

VALVERDE 6 ch.m. Crofter (USA)–Kindle (Firestreak) [1989/90 17f^{2} 18f^{4} 16m 18g^{6} 17g 16s^{pu} 16m^{4} a20g] small, sparely-made mare: selling hurdler: only form of season on first and seventh starts: seems barely to stay 2m in testing conditions: acts on any going: blinkered 3 times in 1987/8 and on seventh start. *A. Barrow.* 64

VANASHING TANNER 10 ch.g. Rugantino–Bridle Lane (Track Spare) [1989/90 c24m^{4} c26g^{pu}] strong gelding: well beaten over hurdles and in novice chases, but is a point-to-point winner. *S. Pike.* c— —

VANDENBERG (NZ) 9 br.h. Le Fripon (NZ)–Elana (NZ) (Trictrac) [1989/90 16g 16g^{F} 16f^{5}] workmanlike horse: won over hurdles at Baden-Baden in 1987: very lightly raced since, showing modest form: probably stays 2½m: sold 925 gns Ascot June Sales. *N. J. Henderson.* —

VARINGEN 9 b.g. Mandrake Major–Toreadora (Matador) [1989/90 c17m^{pu} c16m^{4}] big, leggy gelding: of little account: blinkered last 5 starts. *J. P. D. Elliott.* c— —

VASSAL 5 ro.g. Kalaglow–Vresia (Vitiges (FR)) [1989/90 16g^{F} a20g 20d^{pu}] angular gelding: plating-class maiden at up to 1¾m on Flat: sold out of H. Candy's stable 6,600 gns Newmarket Autumn Sales: jumped poorly and finished tailed off in novice hurdles. *M. C. Chapman.* —

VAULT (USA) 4 b.c. Golden Act (USA)–Open Gate (USA) (Dr Fager (USA)) [1989/90 16d^{4} 16g^{F} 16d^{6} 16f^{4}] compact, useful-looking colt: fairly useful 7f maiden on Flat when trained by L. Cumani: in process of running best race over hurdles when falling 2 out in juvenile event won by Dark Desire at Newbury in March: will prove suited by sharp 2m: gave impression unsuited by firm ground final outing. *O. Sherwood.* 104 +

VAYRUA (FR) 5 ch.g. Vayrann–Nabua (FR) (Le Fabuleux) [1989/90 16g^{pu}] good-topped gelding: a leading juvenile hurdler in 1988/9: carrying condition, dropped out quickly from fourth last and was pulled up 2 out in valuable handicap at Kempton in January: will stay beyond 2m: acts on heavy going. *G. Harwood.* —

VAZON BAY 6 b.g. Deep Run–Fair Argument (No Argument) [1989/90 16f* 16g^{pu} 16s^{4} 20f* 16f*] 136 p

Apparently exposed as just a run-of-the-mill novice hurdler, Vazon Bay improved dramatically in April and won both the Mumm Prize Novices' Hurdle at Liverpool and the EBF Novices' Handicap Hurdle Final at Cheltenham, recouping most of the IR 26,000 guineas paid for him at the Tattersalls Derby Sale in 1987. Vazon Bay's previous efforts had made little impression on his purchase price. In fourteen outings, two of them in National Hunt Flat races, Vazon Bay's only success had come in a novice hurdle at Leicester in November, worth £1,224 to the winner. Starting at 7/4

*Mumm Prize Novices' Hurdle, Liverpool—
Vazon Bay seems to have given the race to Remittance Man,
but recovers quickly*

on, he easily accounted for nine modest rivals. At Liverpool Vazon Bay started at 33/1, having done little to enhance his reputation in the meantime. That was due to bad luck rather than lack of ability, though. At Kempton on Boxing Day Vazon Bay was in the process of running a good race when pulled up quickly before the second last. He was found to have suffered a stress fracture on a splint, which led to his being pin-fired, and in the circumstances it was remarkable to see him back in action by mid-February; on his return he finished a respectable fourth of nineteen at Sandown, having been badly hampered early on. However, it still seemed a lot to expect of Vazon Bay to cut much ice in the Mumm Prize Novices' Hurdle, a race which looked to be at the mercy of the Waterford Crystal Supreme

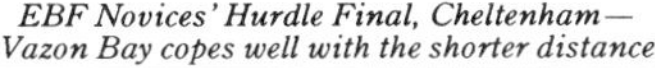

*EBF Novices' Hurdle Final, Cheltenham—
Vazon Bay copes well with the shorter distance*

Novices' Hurdle winner Forest Sun. It wasn't surprising therefore that Vazon Bay should be ignored in the betting, though significantly the stable-jockey Pitman chose to ride him in preference to Ri-Na-Rithann. Of even greater significance was the ground, which rode very firm. Vazon Bay had run only once on a similar surface, when winning at Leicester, and he was to show that he's particularly well suited by such conditions. Although Forest Sun failed to give his running, it still needed a much improved performance from Vazon Bay to win the Mumm Prize Novices' Hurdle. Held up in a race run at only a moderate gallop, Vazon Bay moved through into third place on the home turn and joined Remittance Man in the lead at the second last. The pair were still upsides at the last, which Vazon Bay met all wrong, seeming to have lost his chance. However, he recovered quickly and, staying on strongly, won going away by one and a half lengths and the same from Remittance Man and Young Ty. Ri-Na-Rithann was a further length away in fourth place. The return to two miles in the EBF Novices' Handicap Hurdle Final posed no problems for Vazon Bay; in fact, he showed further improvement. His performance in winning by two lengths under 12-0 is a good indication of the progress he'd made in twelve months. In 1989 Vazon Bay started favourite for the same Final but could finish only ninth under 10-11! Kept in close touch with the leaders from the start, Vazon Bay could be seen travelling strongly in second place as Hey Cottage stretched the field on the long run to the second-last flight, and he was the only runner still on the bridle as he moved into the lead turning for home. Shaken up approaching the last, Vazon Bay quickened a couple of lengths clear and maintained his advantage, being kept right up to his work. In second place came Ri-Na-Rithann, who was meeting Vazon Bay on terms 7 lb better than at Liverpool.

Vazon Bay (br.g. 1984)	Deep Run (ch 1966)	Pampered King (b 1954)	Prince Chevalier
			Netherton Maid
		Trial By Fire (ch 1958)	Court Martial
			Mitrailleuse
	Fair Argument (b 1976)	No Argument (b 1960)	Narrator
			Persuader
		Fair Maiden (ch 1953)	River Prince
			Miss Matilda

Vazon Bay, who takes a good hold and usually wears a crossed noseband, may prove best at up to two and a half miles for the time being, although judged on his breeding he should stay three miles. The dam Fair Argument won three times at up to two and a half miles over hurdles in Ireland, and she was leading when falling at the last in a three-mile handicap. Fair Argument also showed ability over fences, and was in the process of running a good race when falling at the second last in a steeplechase run over three miles and a furlong in very testing conditions. Vazon Bay's half-brother Knight Oil (by Miner's Lamp) is well suited by a test of stamina. Knight Oil, a very useful novice hurdler in 1988/9, was successful at up to three and a quarter miles over fences in the latest season. There's plenty of stamina to be found further back in Vazon Bay's pedigree. His grandam, Fair Maiden, is an unraced half-sister to Wheat Germ, dam of the top-class chaser Crisp. Fair Maiden produced nine winners, including the out-and-out stayer Aureate, who finished second in the Chester Cup, Brown Jack Stakes and Cesarewitch, and the fair staying hurdler/chaser Bolus Head, a full brother to Fair Argument. The next dam, Miss Matilda, was a half-sister to the Derby winner Papyrus. Vazon Bay will, no doubt, be tackling fences in the near future. A strong, rangy individual who jumps hurdles well, he's capable of making an even bigger name for himself as a chaser and he looks one to follow. Vazon Bay wore blinkers on his last eight starts. *Mrs J. Pitman.*

VELVET PEARL 7 ch.m. Record Token–Pearlinda (Gulf Pearl) [1989/90 16g $16s$ c16gpu 16g 16f4 17m2 16h3] strong mare: winning hurdler: neck second to Azusa in handicap at Carlisle in April on penultimate start, only worthwhile form of season: reportedly finished lame last outing: soon well behind and eventually pulled up on only start over fences: stays 2½m: best form with give in the ground: usually blinkered or visored: trained first start by J. Gillen. *I. Semple.* c— 79

VENDREDI TREIZE 7 b. or br.g. Lucky Wednesday–Angel Row (Prince Regent (FR)) [1989/90 16mpu a16g3] poor performer on Flat nowadays (sometimes blinkered): 22 lengths third behind Clos du Bois in novice hurdle at Southwell in January: raced too freely first start. *S. R. Bowring.* —

VERDON CANYON 6 b.g. African Sky–Windy City (Windjammer (USA)) [1989/90 18f* 16f4 16f 16g a16g] short-backed gelding: no bid after winning 3-runner conditional jockeys selling handicap hurdle at Fontwell in August: ran poorly last 3 starts: not certain to stay 2½m: acts on firm going: blinkered fourth outing: inconsistent. *G. A. Pritchard-Gordon.* 83 d

VERITATE 6 b.m. Roman Warrior–Empress of England (Constable) [1989/90 21d2 21f6 24m] lengthy, workmanlike mare: will make a chaser: 50/1 and ridden by 7-lb claimer, 2½ lengths second to Shaston in 19-runner novice hurdle at Warwick in March, best effort: stays 21f (weakened 4 out over 3m): acts on dead ground. *M. J. Wilkinson.* 91

VERONA CHIEF 7 ch.g. Viking Chief–Verona Star (Lord of Verona) [1989/90 20d c20gpu c16gF] rangy gelding: novice hurdler/chaser: no worthwhile form: dead. *B. E. Wilkinson.* c— —

VERSATILE 6 ch.g. Final Straw–Expansive (Exbury) [1989/90 17d 16d6 16s 16d4 16m3 16m5] workmanlike gelding: winning hurdler: poor form in handicaps in 1989/90: likely to prove best at 2m: acts on soft going. *N. J. Henderson.* 92

VERTIGO 5 b.h. Shirley Heights–Western Partner (USA) (West Coast Scout (USA)) [1989/90 16gF] leggy horse: tailed off in minor event at 2 yrs: backward, fell first on hurdling debut. *Mrs J. Wonnacott.* —

VERY CHEERING 7 b.g. Gleason (USA)–Cherry Joy (Bally Joy) [1989/90 F16m F16m 22vpu 17g] plain gelding: sixth foal: half-brother to winning hurdler Bell Founder (by Pry): dam, from a successful jumping family, won on Flat and over hurdles: showed a little ability in NH Flat race on second start: well beaten in novice hurdle at Carlisle in January. *J. S. E. Turner.* —

VESTAL HILLS 4 b.g. Shirley Heights–Vestal Virgin (USA) (Hail To Reason) [1989/90 16g6] rather leggy, good-topped gelding: modest handicapper on Flat nowadays (has reportedly broken blood vessels): green and needing race, prominent to 2 out and not knocked about once beaten in juvenile hurdle won by Dark Desire at Newbury in March: should improve. *I. A. Balding.* — p

VESTRIS 6 ch.h. Habitat–Aryenne (FR) (Green Dancer (USA)) [1989/90 16dpu 20dpu 17g] sparely-made horse: seems of little account. *N. Kernick.* —

VESTRIS ABU 4 b.c. Lyphard's Special (USA)–Ishtar Abu (St Chad) [1989/90 17v2 16s5 16v2 16v2 16f4 16m 16g* 16f3 17f*] 135 p

Irish trainers had a remarkably strong hand in juvenile hurdlers in the latest season, none more so than Jim Bolger, with Bally Rue, Orbis and Vestris Abu. These three have shown form of a similar standard so far, but our guess is that the strong, attractive Vestris Abu will turn out to be the best of them. Vestris Abu showed useful form on the Flat, winning over a mile as a two-year-old and over seven furlongs and eleven furlongs as a three-year-old. He wasn't seen out over hurdles until January and for long enough it seemed as though he might end the season tagged the best juvenile hurdler not to win a race, for he didn't get off the mark until his seventh start, in late-April. Vestris Abu had, for the most part, been running in good company, and he'd been running well, too. Following an excellent second to the year-older Bank View at Leopardstown, Vestris Abu finished in the frame in both the Victor Ludorum Hurdle at Haydock and the Daily Express Triumph Hurdle at Cheltenham. He looked unlucky at Haydock, finishing strongly in the testing conditions to overhaul Native Friend but failing by half a length to catch Ninja. On firm ground at Cheltenham, Vestris Abu was beaten on merit by both Ninja and Native Friend, who finished second and third respectively behind Rare Holiday. Vestris Abu, kept in closer touch than at Haydock, quickened to lead entering the straight, but he lost a bit of momentum at the last and kept on at one pace under severe pressure. He finished fourth, two lengths behind the winner. Following a below-par performance in the Glenlivet Hurdle at Liverpool Vestris Abu took full advantage of the favourable conditions in the BMW Champion Novice Hurdle at Punchestown, where not only were his main rivals heavily penalized, but he also received a maiden allowance. Vestris Abu, the one

BMW Champion Novice EBF Hurdle, Punchestown—Vestris Abu gets off the mark

four-year-old in the eight-runner field, made no mistake. Headed at the fifth, he soon regained the lead and quickened clear from the second last to win pushed out by eight lengths from Nameloc. Vestris Abu wasn't allowed to rest on his laurels. Less than two weeks later he was on his travels once again, to Haydock for the Swinton Insurance Trophy Handicap Hurdle. Vestris Abu, 2 lb out of the handicap, ran a cracking race to finish third behind another four-year-old Sybillin and Windbound Lass, beaten three quarters of a length and one length, setting a strong pace, coming under pressure two out and keeping on well once headed at the last. Vestris Abu's jumping, which had been very sketchy earlier in the season, was good in the main at Haydock, his only mistake coming at the fifth. Vestris Abu ended the season with a victory in the Carroll Trophy Handicap Hurdle at Dundalk, once again making most of the running. He looked in trouble when headed approaching the last by the other four-year-old Rocket Dancer, who was receiving 3 lb, but, rallying gamely, got back up to win by a short head, the pair twenty lengths clear. It was a thrilling finish fought out between Ireland's leading National Hunt riders Swan and Carmody. Swan came out the better here, as he did in the jockeys' championship which he won for the first time. His total of seventy-three winners in an Irish season has been bettered only once, by Martin Molony.

Vestris Abu (b.c. 1986)	Lyphard's Special (USA) (b 1980)	Lyphard (b 1969)	Northern Dancer
			Goofed
		My Bupers (b or br 1967)	Bupers
			Princess Revoked
	Ishtar Abu (b 1973)	St Chad (ch 1964)	St Paddy
			Caerphilly
		Shoubad (b 1961)	Vimy
			After The Show

Vestris Abu is from the first crop of Lyphard's Special, a good-looking individual who showed very smart form over middle distances when trained by Harwood. Lyphard's Special began his stud career in Ireland and is now in Japan. Ishtar Abu, the dam of Vestris Abu, won a mile-and-a-half maiden

Mrs Catherine Shubotham's "Vestris Abu"

on the Flat in Ireland. Four of her other foals have been successful for Bolger's stable, the best of them being Noora Abu (by Ahonoora) and Condor Pan (by Condorcet). Noora Abu, splendidly tough and genuine, won the Group 2 Pretty Polly Stakes as a seven-year-old in 1989, while Condor Pan, useful at up to two miles on the Flat, won the Bula Hurdle at Cheltenham in 1988. Kelly's Boy (by Pitskelly) and Curie Abu (by Crofter) are the dam's other winners, the former successful over hurdles and fences in Britain after scoring over middle distances on the Flat in Ireland. The second dam, Shoubad, won over a mile, while the third dam, After The Show, won the Pretty Polly Stakes thirty-two years before Noora Abu did. After The Show also finished second in the Irish One Thousand Guineas and fourth in the Irish Oaks. Vestris Abu's form is on a par with that shown by Condor Pan in his first season over hurdles, and there seems no reason why he shouldn't eventually make up into a very smart hurdler, too. Vestris Abu, who has worn a tongue strap, may well stay two and a half miles. He acts on any going. *J. Bolger, Ireland.*

VIA VERITAS 6 ch.m. Vicomte–Red Ragusa (Homeric) [1989/90 20f[3] 16m[pu]] sparely-made mare: third in novice hurdle at Bangor in August: pulled up 3 months later and wasn't seen out again: acts on firm ground. *R. Hollinshead.* 66

VICARIO DI BRAY (ITY) 7 b.g. Furry Glen–Via Del Tabacco (Ballymoss) [1989/90 16g[5] 16d[2] 16g[6] 16s[2] 25m] rangy, good sort, every inch a chaser: won Daily Mail Racedial Champion Hurdle Trial at Haydock in 1988/9: 1½ lengths second to Bank View in same race fourth outing: one pace from 2 out when ninth to Trapper John in Waterford Crystal Stayers' Hurdle at Cheltenham in March: may prove best at up to 2½m: acts on heavy going: suited by waiting tactics in a strongly-run race (well below form when making running second start): broke blood vessel final start 1988/9: to be sent chasing in 1990/1. *J. J. O'Neill.* 150

VICARS LANDING 7 b.g. Rusticaro (FR)–Rhinestone (Never Say Die) [1989/90 c20m* c20gF] big, rangy, good sort: useful chaser: won handicap at c**136** —

River Thames Novices' Hurdle, Windsor— the winner Victory Gate (No. 18) is led over the last by the runner-up Devil's Valley

Worcester in October by a neck from Major Match: close up when falling heavily 4 out (sustained injury to near-fore tendon) in Mackeson Gold Cup at Cheltenham in November: stays 2½m: acts on good to firm going: usually jumps well. *O. Sherwood.*

VICEROY JESTER 5 br.g. Jester–Midnight Patrol (Ashmore (FR)) [1989/90 16d5 16f2] lengthy, sparely-made gelding: moderate form at up to 1½m on Flat: clear 7 lengths second to Deltic in novice hurdle at Wolverhampton (pulled hard) in March: acts on firm ground. *R. J. Holder.* 105

VICEROY MAJOR 7 ch.g. Bay Express–Lady Marmalade (Hotfoot) [1989/90 16m 17g3 16s 17v4 a20g4 a16g 17m 17f] workmanlike gelding: novice hurdler/chaser: fourth in a seller at Newton Abbot, fourth and best effort in 1989/90: best at around 2m on an easy surface: blinkered once in 1986/7: trained until after fifth start by W. G. Turner. *N. B. Thomson.* c— 64

VICKI-VICKI VEE 5 ch.m. Busted Fiddle–Olymena (Royalty) [1989/90 16d] sparely-made mare: seems of little account. *R. Williams.* —

VICKSTOWN 8 b.h. Town And Country–Empress Victoria (Brave Invader (USA)) [1989/90 16g6 c16m* c16g5 c16mF4] sparely-made, dipped-backed horse: poor novice hurdler: made a few mistakes when winning novice chase at Wolverhampton in November: ran moderately next outing: tends to pull hard and barely stays 2m: acts on firm going: wore tongue strap last 3 starts over hurdles: visored twice in 1986/7. *B. C. Morgan.* c86 —

VICO EQUENSE 5 gr.m. Absalom–Miss Diaward (Supreme Sovereign) [1989/90 20g] smallish, sparely-made mare: poor novice hurdler: amateur ridden only outing in 1989/90. *S. G. Payne.* —

VICTORIA STAR 6 b. or br.m. Comedy Star (USA)–Empress Victoria (Brave Invader (USA)) [1989/90 24fpu 27fpu 24m 16m] workmanlike mare: poor plater over hurdles: looks none too keen: often blinkered. *Miss S. J. Wilton.* — §

VICTORIOUS KING 4 b.g. Petorius–Petit Secret (Petingo) [1989/90 17f4] no worthwhile form, including in sellers, on Flat: sold out of P. Cole's stable 1,600 72 gns Newmarket July Sales: blinkered and odds on when 6 lengths last of 4 behind Rosoglio in conditional jockeys novice selling hurdle at Devon & Exeter in August. *M. C. Pipe.*

VICTOR'S STAR 11 ch.g. Wishing Star–Rosantus (Anthony) [1989/90 c25fpu] poor novice chaser: winning point-to-pointer. *C. F. Grant-Ives.* c— —

VICTORY BOY 12 b.g. Lord Nelson (FR)–Three Oaks (Drumbeg) [1989/90 20hwo 24h4 25g6 20g5] strong, compact gelding: poor selling hurdler: walked over in non-selling handicap at Carlisle in September: good fourth in moderately-run race over 3m following month: well beaten last 2 starts: tailed off when pulled up only start over fences: probably acts on any going. *T. A. K. Cuthbert.* c— 69 ?

VICTORY GATE (USA) 5 b.g. Lydian (FR)–Pago Miss (USA) (Pago Pago) [1989/90 20d4 22m* 21g4 22v2] leggy, workmanlike gelding: won novice hurdle at Windsor in November: in frame subsequently in minor race at Newbury and novice event at Folkestone (neck second to Stately Lover): should stay further than 2¾m: yet to race on firm going, acts on any other. *A. Moore.* 113

VICTORY LANE 4 b.g. Valiyar–Open Country (Town And Country) [1989/90 16s 20gpu] workmanlike gelding: poor maiden on Flat, when trained by R. Hannon: behind in juvenile hurdle at Plumpton in December and when pulled up before last in similar event at Ascot (reluctant 3 out and 2 out) in January. *P. J. Jones.* —

VICTORY WIND 5 ch.g. Asdic–Cool Wind (Windjammer (USA)) [1989/90 16h3 16mur 19m3 16mur 19m4] workmanlike gelding: plater on Flat, suited by 7f: in frame over hurdles at Hereford: ran in seller first start: may prove best at 2m: ridden by claimer: trained first 2 outings by G. Price. *T. Morton.* 67

VIGANO (USA) 4 ch.g. Lyphard (USA)–Pasadoble (USA) (Prove Out (USA)) [1989/90 16d5 20gpu] leggy gelding: modest maiden miler on Flat: sold out of H. Cecil's stable 10,000 gns Newmarket Autumn Sales: pulled hard when 14 lengths fifth to Olnistar in 17-runner juvenile hurdle at Nottingham in December: behind when pulled up 2 out next time: likely to prove best at 2m. *K. C. Bailey.* 89

VIGI'S GREY 11 gr.g. Come On Grey–Vigi (Vigo) [1989/90 17f4 21fpu 26fpu] sparely-made, plain gelding: very lightly raced and seems of little account. *R. W. Pincombe.* —

VIKING ROCKET 6 ch.m. Viking (USA)–Calcine (Roan Rocket) [1989/90 20d6 26d3 c20s2 22g3 25m] sparely-made, rather plain mare: usually looks well: moderate hurdler: made a few mistakes when going down by 5 lengths to Last Grain in novice event at Ayr in December on chasing debut: stays 3m: well suited by the mud: suitable mount for a claimer: genuine: should improve over fences. *C. Parker.* c**91** p 107

VIKING VENTURE 5 ch.h. Viking (USA)–Mattira (FR) (Rheffic (FR)) [1989/90 16m6 18f3] small horse: moderate hurdler: better effort of season when third of 6 behind Raahin in quite valuable event at Fontwell in October: stays 19f: seems best on a sound surface: has won for a claimer. *D. A. Wilson.* 106

VILLAGE HERO 7 b.g. Blakeney–Thereby (Star Moss) [1989/90 a20g2 a20gpu] workmanlike gelding: very lightly-raced novice hurdler: runner-up at Southwell in April: suited by 2½m: dead. *D. J. G. Murray-Smith.* 99

VILLAGE PRINCESS 7 br.m. Rolfe (USA)–Saffron Princess (Thriller) [1989/90 16m 16f4 20m5 21g 24mpu] compact mare: poor novice hurdler: best effort over 2½m: sold out of R. Hickman's stable 12,500 gns Doncaster October Sales. *N. A. Smith.* 75

VILLA RECOS 5 b.g. Deep Run–Lovely Colour (Shantung) [1989/90 16g4 16g4 16g* 16g*] workmanlike, rather close-coupled gelding: won novice hurdles at Windsor in January and Wolverhampton following month: likely to stay beyond 2m: has raced only on good ground over hurdles: should continue to progress. *Mrs J. Pitman.* 108 p

VILLA TARANTO 5 b.m. Ashmore (FR)–Gunnard (Gunner B) [1989/90 aF14g aF16g aF16g] first foal: dam winning middle-distance plater on Flat: behind in NH Flat races at Southwell in second half of season: yet to race over hurdles or fences. *Mrs B. Brunt.*

VILLIERSTOWN 11 b.g. Giolla Mear–Chammyville (Chamier) [1989/90 c24m4 c20g* c20g2 c20g2 c20g3 c22m2 c24g4] lightly-made gelding: very useful chaser: won John Hughes Memorial Trophy Chase (Handicap) at Liverpool in 1989 and ran a game race in latest running in April, going down by 4 lengths to c**146** —

Tennents Special Handicap Chase, Ayr—
another win for the genuine front-running Villierstown

Wont Be Gone Long: successful earlier in 1989/90 season in handicap at Ayr: best at up to 2¾m: acts on any going: jumps well and usually a front runner: wears a dropped noseband: genuine. *W. A. Stephenson.*

VIMCHASE 4 ch.g. Slim Jim–Vimys Pet (Lord Nelson (FR)) [1989/90 F12g2 F16m F17m] second foal: brother to novice hurdler Trebleim: dam, who won 2 NH Flat races, showed poor form in novice hurdles: second in NH Flat race at Hexham in March: yet to race over hurdles. *Denys Smith.*

VINCANTO 8 ch.g. Orchestra–Subiacco (Yellow River) [1989/90 c18f* c16f* c16f2 c20g5 c20g2] lengthy, rather sparely-made gelding: winning hurdler: 10-length winner of novice chases at Fontwell (bolted before start) in September and Cheltenham in October: dropped out quickly 3 out when 20 lengths second in handicap at Folkestone in January, last start: stays 2½m: seems to act on any going. *J. T. Gifford.* c**101** —

VINCCI 13 br.g. Saulingo–Kazannka (FR) (Wild Risk) [1989/90 c24f2 c19m5 c24fF3 c25fur] strong gelding: useful point-to-pointer/winning hunter chaser: in touch when falling 4 out in 3-runner race won by Cute Ryme at Ludlow in April (remounted): stays 3m: acts on hard ground. *Miss C. Phillips.* c**91** —

VINO FESTA 11 ch.m. Nebbiolo–Madrilon (FR) (Le Fabuleux) [1989/90 20g 21dpu] lengthy, lightly-made mare: fairly useful hurdler in 1986/7: lightly raced and no form since: has worn blinkers but is better without. *R. A. H. Perkins.* —

VINTAGE LAD 7 b.g. Crash Course–Phaestus Sister (Seminole II) [1989/90 17m 16h c26f4 c24f3 c21v5 c21g4] lengthy, workmanlike gelding: winning hurdler: in frame in novice chases, showing poor form: probably stays 3m: blinkered second start. *R. J. Hodges.* c— —

VINTAGE VELVET 8 ch.g. Rarity–Funicular (Arctic Slave) [1989/90 24d4 24g5 20g] ex-Irish gelding: maiden hurdler: won a point-to-point in 1988: sold out of J. Hassett's stable 30,000 gns Doncaster Spring (1988) Sales: fourth to Babil in novice hurdle at Chepstow in March: below that form last 2 outings: stays 3m: acts on dead going. *K. C. Bailey.* 93

VIRGINIA PAGEANT 8 b.g. Welsh Pageant–Virginia Wade (Virginia Boy) [1989/90 20f3 25h5] tall, leggy, lightly-made gelding: winning selling hurdler: 83 §

creditable third in non-selling handicap at Plumpton in September: seemed not to stay 25f next time: stays 2½m: acts on any going: has worn blinkers: sometimes has tongue tied down: has looked none too genuine. *F. Gray.*

VIRGINIA'S BAY 4 b.g. Uncle Pokey–Carnation (Runnymede) [1989/90 16f* 16m2 16f4 16f3 a20g4 16g a16g 16fpu] sturdy, workmanlike gelding: poor handicapper on Flat, stays 7f: won juvenile hurdle at Stratford in September: off course 3 months after fourth start and didn't recapture his form: unlikely to stay much beyond 2m: acts on firm ground: front runner: visored third to sixth starts: trained until after sixth outing by Miss B. Sanders. *F. J. O'Mahony.* 90 d

VIRIDIAN 5 b.g. Green Shoon–Cahermone Ivy (Perspex) [1989/90 20g3 22d3 21d 22g3 20m* 20f4] workmanlike gelding: held up when winning novice hurdle at Newcastle in March: creditable fourth to Height of Fun in novice handicap at Cheltenham following month: stays 2¾m: acts on firm going. *Miss A. L. M. King.* 98

VISCOUNT TULLY 5 b.g. Blakeney–Cymbal (Ribero) [1989/90 16m 22m5 22g6 22d* 21d5 24v 22d] close-coupled gelding: won handicap hurdle at Nottingham in December: ran moderately subsequently: should stay 3m: acts on soft going. *C. F. C. Jackson.* 104

VISION OF WONDER 6 b.g. Tyrnavos–Valeur (Val de Loir) [1989/90 c17f5 c20f4 16f4 19f2 24m5 20f2 25h4 16m4 19h* 17h2] leggy, close-coupled gelding: handicap hurdler: won by 15 lengths at Taunton in May: let down by his jumping in 2 novice chases: stays 2½m but seemingly not 3m: acts on hard going: has won for a claimer. *J. S. King.* c— 90

VISTULE (USA) 8 ch.g. Dust Commander (USA)–Riverdance (FR) (Lyphard (USA)) [1989/90 18f4] strong, lengthy gelding: winning hurdler/chaser: well beaten in September, and wasn't seen out again: stays 2½m, at least when conditions aren't testing: acts on firm going: has won for a 7-lb claimer over hurdles. *Miss S. J. Wilton.* c— —

VISUAL STAR 4 b.g. Vision (USA)–Eternal Tam (USA) (Tentam (USA)) [1989/90 16g 16s 16d a16g] rather sparely-made gelding: plating-class maiden miler on Flat (has run blinkered): sold out of M. Brittain's stable 7,600 gns Doncaster November Sales: well beaten over hurdles. *Mrs C. Postlethwaite.* —

VITAIR 7 ch.m. Pony Express–Dancing Air (Romany Air) [1989/90 c25gpu] lengthy, angular mare: half-sister to maiden point-to-pointer Dancing Court (by Mandamus): dam winning point-to-pointer/hunter chaser: bit backward, tailed off when pulled up in hunter chase at Wolverhampton in February: won a point-to-point following month: sold 3,500 gns Ascot June Sales. *W. Bush.* c—

VITAL EXPORT 8 b.g. Vital Season–K B Export (So Blessed) [1989/90 16m c16m c21fpu c16spu] small, close-coupled gelding: of little account: has been blinkered. *B. Scriven.* c— —

VITAL SINGER 5 br.g. Vital Season–Tia Song (Acrania) [1989/90 aF16g 16dF] first foal: dam winning hurdler: tailed off in NH Flat race at Lingfield in January: fell fourth in selling hurdle at Bangor in March. *D. Burchell.* —

VITAL SPLENDID 5 ch.m. Vital Season–Pepe Lew (John Splendid) [1989/90 20m 16g] neat mare: no sign of ability: visored last start. *D. Holly.* —

VITE VITE 4 ch.g. Kind of Hush–Swiftacre (Bay Express) [1989/90 16dpu] workmanlike gelding: modest handicapper on Flat, winner over 1¼m in November: jumped none too fluently and was behind when pulled up after mistake 2 out in juvenile hurdle at Kempton earlier in month. *J. Sutcliffe.* —

VODKA FIZZ 5 ch.g. Don–Doon Royal (Ardoon) [1989/90 16g] unfurnished, workmanlike gelding: first foal: dam, poor Irish maiden, is half-sister to useful hurdler Beparoejojo: needing race, never dangerous and not knocked about when in rear in novice hurdle at Windsor in March. *J. T. Gifford.* —

VODKATINI 11 b.g. Dubassoff (USA)–Olympic Visualise (Northfields (USA)) [1989/90 c20f2 c20g c16dpu c17gur c16g c17d4 c16m] compact gelding: high-class chaser at his best: mistake last when going down by 1½ lengths to Joint Sovereignty in quite valuable handicap at Newbury in October, best effort of season: headstrong and best at up to 2½m: acts on any going: usually jumps well in main, but made a few bad mistakes sixth outing: tends to idle in front: blinkered second outing: temperamental and led in at start nowadays (refused to race twice in 1988/9, and very reluctant on third and sixth starts in 1989/90). *J. T. Gifford.* c152 § —

VON TRAPPE 13 b.g. Normandy–Sharp Awakening (King Hal) [1989/90 c24dpu c24gF c24gF c24mpu] close-coupled gelding: useful chaser in 1987/8: failed to complete course in 1989/90: effective at 2½m and stays well: acts on any c— x —

Mansion House Handicap Chase, Doncaster—Vulrory's Clown (right) leads from High River on the way to the third of six wins in the season

going with possible exception of heavy: usually held up: showed no interest fourth start 1987/8: tends to sweat nowadays: usually erratic jumper of fences. *M. Oliver.*

VOYAGE SANS RETOUR (FR) 5 ch.h. Le Nain Jaune (FR)–Mativa (FR) (Satingo) [1989/90 16g* 16f5 20f*] leggy, rather sparely-made horse: useful hurdler: won handicaps at Newbury in March (by a length from Keep Hope Alive) and Cheltenham in April (by 2½ lengths from Little Toro): battled on well when fifth to Jubail in quite valuable event at Liverpool in between: stays 2½m: acts on any going: blinkered last 5 starts. *M. C. Pipe.* 140

VOYANT 11 ch.g. Star Appeal–Vernier (High Hat) [1989/90 25g5 22d2] small, sparely-made gelding: useful hurdler: good second to easy winner Midland Glenn at Ayr in December: fell in novice chase in 1986: stays 3¼m: acts on heavy going: has idled in front and looks a difficult ride: has worn a tongue strap. *J. Mackie.* c— 135

VULGAN WARRIOR 8 b.g. Vulgan Slave–Belgrave Queen (Sheshoon) [1989/90 c21m2 c24gpu c26m3 c25m6 c29fF] tall, lengthy, rather leggy gelding: quite a useful chaser: spoilt his chance with a mistake 3 out when creditable third to Zeta's Lad in handicap at Uttoxeter in March, first outing for 3 months: made a few mistakes and didn't find a great deal from 2 out next outing: under strong pressure when falling 3 out in Whitbread Gold Cup (Handicap Chase) at Sandown in April: suited by 3m and more: acts on good to firm and dead going. *S. Christian.* c**131** —

VULMAN 11 b.g. Straight Knight–Vulgan Spirit (Salmonway Spirit) [1989/90 c25f5] tall, leggy gelding: winning point-to-pointer: tailed off in hunter chase at Wincanton in April. *Mrs A. J. Barker.* c—

VULNERABLE 9 ch.g. Le Bavard (FR)–Vulady (Vulgan) [1989/90 24gpu] close-coupled, workmanlike gelding: poor novice hurdler: won 2 chases early in 1988/9: first race for over 18 months, pulled up reportedly lame in May: stays 3m: best form with give in the ground: moderate jumper. *M. C. Chapman.* c— x —

VULRORY'S CLOWN 12 b.g. Idiot's Delight–Vulrory (Vulgan) [1989/90 c16f5 c20m* c20f3 c16g2 c16s* c17m* c20f* c16m2 c16m* c16f2 c16g*] workmanlike gelding: fairly useful chaser: had another good season and successful in handicaps at Warwick in November, Market Rasen and Doncaster (gamely by ½ length from High River in quite valuable event) in January and Doncaster, Southwell and Market Rasen in May: stays 2½m: acts on any going: c**126** —

bold jumper: suited by forcing tactics: tends to sweat: usually bandaged: has worn a brush pricker: game and genuine. *O. Brennan.*

VULUKEI 5 b.m. Tepukei–Vulrusika (Vulgan) [1989/90 F16g] sister to winning hurdler/chaser Palmrush and half-sister to successful staying chaser Titan Wood (by Sit In The Corner): dam never ran: tailed off in NH Flat race at Kelso in March: yet to race over hurdles or fences. *Mrs P. A. Barker.*

VYNZ SUPREME 10 b.g. Supreme Sovereign–High Drama (Hill Clown (USA)) [1989/90 16f 20f c16m^{pu} c16g^{pu}] lengthy, rather sparely-made gelding: winning hurdler: has lost his form: pulled up both outings over fences. *Mrs N. S. Sharpe.* c— —

W

WAAFI 8 b.g. Wolver Hollow–Geraldville (Lord Gayle (USA)) [1989/90 21f* 20f^{pu} a20g^{4}] lengthy, lightly-made gelding: had had a soft palate operation: only worthwhile form in novice hurdles when winning 4-runner handicap at Newton Abbot in September by a distance: stayed 21f: acted on firm ground: blinkered final start: dead. *K. C. Bailey.* 91

WACKERS MAGIC 6 ch.g. Celtic Cone–Jackyda (Royal Palm) [1989/90 20v^{pu} 16m] workmanlike gelding: third in NH Flat race in 1988/9: little sign of ability in 2 outings over hurdles. *M. C. Pipe.* —

WADSWICK LADY 5 b.m. New Member–Pollys Owen (Master Owen) [1989/90 16m^{5}] first foal: dam, winning hurdler/chaser, stayed well: never-dangerous fifth to Distant Relation in 13-runner novice hurdle at Wincanton in December on debut. *R. J. Holder.* —

WAGES OF SIN 11 ch.g. Hell's Gate–In For A Penny (Soletra) [1989/90 c20g c24d^{F} c27f^{F} c24m^{2} c24f^{3}] sparely-made gelding: winning hunter chaser: poor form in 1990: refused last final start (eventually completed): stays 3m: acts on firm going: makes mistakes. *R. Green.* c— x

WAGON LOAD 5 ch.g. Bustino–Noble Girl (Be Friendly) [1989/90 16d^{4} 16m^{5} 20m^{4}] small gelding: modest form over hurdles as a juvenile: below his best in 1989/90: should stay beyond 2m: acts on heavy going and possibly unsuited by top-of-the-ground: blinkered first 2 starts. *J. Ffitch-Heyes.* 87

WAHIBA 6 b.g. Tumble Wind (USA)–Lady Kasbah (Lord Gayle (USA)) [1989/90 24m^{3} 20g^{2} 20d^{4} 21m* 16g^{4} 16d^{5}] smallish, angular gelding: well ridden by claimer N. Mann when winning slowly-run 21f handicap hurdle at Sandown in December: better effort subsequently when good fifth to Ambassador in handicap at Ascot in January: stays 21f: possibly unsuited by very firm ground, acts on any other: has worn a crossed noseband. *R. J. Holder.* 129

WAIT YOU THERE (USA) 5 b.g. Nureyev (USA)–Ma Mere L'Oie (FR) (Lightning (FR)) [1989/90 16m^{4} 25m^{5} 16g* 20g^{3} 20m^{4} 16f*] leggy gelding: won novice hurdles at Catterick in February and Hexham in April: also ran creditably in slowly-run race over 3m: acts on firm ground (well beaten on heavy). *H. Alexander.* 95

WALD KONIGIN 4 ch.f. Kinglet–Nightwood (Sparkler) [1989/90 F16f] fourth foal: half-sister to Night Warrior (by Roman Warrior), successful at up to 1m: dam staying maiden: tailed off in NH Flat race at Ludlow in April: yet to race over hurdles. *J. Roper.*

WALDRON HILL 10 ch.g. Hotfoot–Ankole (Crepello) [1989/90 16h^{3} 16g^{3}] compact gelding: poor novice hurdler: has failed to complete course in point-to-points: well-beaten fourth in novice chase in 1988. *Mrs S. A. Bramall.* c— 60

WALHAN 10 b.g. Captain James–The Cosmos (Windsor Sun) [1989/90 17f* 17f^{5} c16h^{pu}] workmanlike gelding: bought in 2,000 gns after winning 4-runner selling handicap hurdle at Newton Abbot in August by 15 lengths: tailed off when pulled up on chasing debut: races only at around 2m: acts on firm and dead going (well beaten on soft): best forcing pace. *C. L. Popham.* c— 78

WALKING CANE 14 b.g. Candy Cane–Visitare (Hard Ridden) [1989/90 c26s^{pu}] strong gelding: winning hurdler/chaser: no form for a long time: probably stays 3¼m: acts on hard going and is possibly unsuited by heavy: moderate jumper. *G. Ripley.* c— x —

WALK IN RHYTHM 9 b.g. Tower Walk–Maiden d'Or (Songedor) [1989/90 c20d^{ur} c24f^{pu} c19m c22g^{4} c16f^{3} c16g^{4} c25f^{2}] well-made gelding: winning hunter chaser: 5 lengths second to Oh Why at Hereford in May: stays 25f: acts on firm and soft going: has worn a crossed noseband, and a pricker on off-side. *Mrs A. Price.* — c89 / —

WALK OF LIFE (USA) 5 b.h. Northern Baby (CAN)–Ballena Ridge (USA) (Riva Ridge (USA)) [1989/90 16h^{2} 22m* a20g* 22m^{3} c16s^{3} 19s^{2} 16g* 20f* 16f^{2} c18f* c21g* c21m* c21f^{2}] sparely-made horse: well beaten in Britain at 2 yrs when trained by G. Harwood, successful 5 times on Flat in France since, including over 1½m in October (claimed out of Y. Porzier's stable 81,000 francs (approx £7,887)): won novice hurdles at Wincanton and Southwell and a claimer and a novice handicap at Worcester: successful in novice events over fences at Fontwell, Market Rasen and Newton Abbot in May: has found little, including when second in novice seller on sixth outing: stays 2¾m: best form on a sound surface: wears blinkers: has worn a tongue strap. *M. C. Pipe.* — c93 p / 113

WALL STREET SLUMP 4 gr.g. Belfort (FR)–Running Dancer (FR) (Dancer's Image (USA)) [1989/90 16f] lengthy gelding: plating class and temperamentally unsatisfactory maiden on Flat: took very strong hold when tailed off in juvenile hurdle at Edinburgh in December: sold 1,600 gns Doncaster June Sales. *P. Monteith.* — —

WALLY WOMBAT 12 b.g. Abwah–Enlighten (Twilight Alley) [1989/90 c20s^{2} c20v^{2} c25g c20d c22m] rather lightly-made, workmanlike gelding: has been fired: quite a modest chaser: second in handicaps at Chepstow in December and January: stays 2½m well (behind when tried over further): suited by plenty of give in the ground: moody. *M. Scudamore.* — c96 / —

WALLY WREKIN 7 ch.h. Peter Wrekin–Winning Venture (Eastern Venture) [1989/90 c25s^{2} c24g^{4}] compact horse: jumped none too fluently and showed no worthwhile form over hurdles in 1987/8: won only start in point-to-points in 1989: in frame in hunter chases at Hereford (maiden) in March and Bangor following month: may prove suited by distances short of 3m. *J. A. C. Edwards.* — c84 + / —

WALNUT WAY 11 ch.m. Gambling Debt–Pickled Walnut (Hornbeam) [1989/90 c21f* c21f* c21m^{2} c16d* c20m^{2} c16d^{2} c20m* c21f* c22m^{2}] compact mare: winning point-to-pointer: successful in novice chases at Newton Abbot (2) in August and Chepstow in November and handicap chases at Chepstow and Newton Abbot in the spring: good second to Sir Jest in minor event at Stratford on final outing: stays 2¾m: acts on firm and dead going: suited by a left-handed track. *M. C. Pipe.* — c128 / —

WALTER STREET 5 b.g. Lochnager–Shady Desire (Meldrum) [1989/90 F17f F13d 16s 16d^{pu}] leggy gelding: fourth foal: half-brother to fair 6f and 7f winner Ben Jarrow (by Roman Warrior): dam won from 5f to 1m: little form in 2 NH Flat races (trained by P. Liddle) and 2 outings over hurdles. *A. J. Le Blond.* — —

WALTER THE GREAT 8 b.g. Uncle Pokey–Clouds of Gold (Goldhill) [1989/90 20s 20f] workmanlike gelding: well beaten over hurdles, including in a seller, but gave impression he has some ability last start. *Mrs B. K. Broad.* — —

WALTINGO 7 b.g. Certingo–Honeyglen (Tynwald) [1989/90 c20f* c20h* c22f^{2} c27g^{2} c24g^{2} c24g^{F} c27d^{pu} c24s^{4} c24g^{3} c24g^{5} c24f* c24f*] useful-looking gelding: winning hurdler: successful in novice chases at Bangor and Carlisle in September, and quite valuable novice handicap at Newcastle and handicap at Wetherby in May, showing much improved form on last 2 occasions: stays 27f: acts on any going: found little off bridle third start and edged right on run-in on fourth. *W. A. Stephenson.* — c119 p / —

WANTAGE 8 b.g. Relkino–Alma (Shiny Tenth) [1989/90 16d^{bd} 16s^{ur} 16d^{5}] rather leggy, close-coupled gelding: winning hurdler: very lightly raced since 1985/6: travelling well when unseating rider 3 out in handicap at Nottingham in January: moderate fifth at Windsor later in month, travelling well to 3 out, but soon beaten: should stay 2½m: acts on heavy going: broke blood vessel final start 1985/6. *Capt. T. A. Forster.* — 100 ?

WAPPING REIGN 8 b.g. London Gazette–Queen of Rheims (Raise You Ten) [1989/90 c22g^{pu} c25g^{pu} c22d^{pu}] tall, leggy, shallow-girthed gelding: won a point-to-point and second in NH Flat race in Ireland: behind when pulled up in a novice hurdle and novice chases (jumped moderately): blinkered last outing: sold 2,900 gns Ascot April Sales. *K. C. Bailey.* — c— / —

WAR CHILD 6 b.m. Welsh Chanter–Winter Sunshine (Crisp And Even) [1989/90 16g^{4} 16d^{6} 16s^{5} 22g^{2}] leggy, close-coupled mare: winning selling hurdler: — 93 seemed suited by longer trip when good second to Golden Celtic in 2¾m non-selling handicap at Windsor in March: acts on heavy going: has won for a claimer. *A. Moore.*

WAR DANCER 8 ch.g. Tug of War–Cacadors Polly (Juvenile Court) [1989/90 c21v4] rather leggy gelding: lightly-raced hurdler: jumped none too fluently when well beaten in novice chase at Newton Abbot in December: stays 21f: seems suited by a yielding surface. *D. J. G. Murray-Smith.* c— —

WARDSOFF 13 b.g. Dubassoff (USA)–Greensward II (Count Turf) [1989/90 c24h2 c20f4 c24m3 c24g5 c24hpu] leggy gelding: poor chaser: suited by 3m: acted on any going: successful with and without blinkers: often ridden by claimer: dead. *T. A. K. Cuthbert.* c**67** —

WARGAME 10 ch.g. Warpath–Sunshine Holyday (Three Wishes) [1989/90 20m3 16g3 22g3 25m* 20g 25g6 24g 20d] big gelding: moderate hurdler: won slowly-run handicap at Catterick in December: demoted to third after passing post first at Kelso previous start: ran moderately last 4 outings: stays 25f: acts on soft and good to firm going: usually amateur ridden. *A. C. Batey.* 108 d

WAR HOUSE 7 ch.m. Tug of War–Brilliant Girl (Lucifer (USA)) [1989/90 25m 16s 24gpu] smallish, lengthy mare: Irish NH Flat race winner: novice hurdler: no worthwhile form in Britain, including in selling handicap: should stay 2½m: possibly needs plenty of give in the ground. *R. R. Lamb.* —

WARLEGGAN 9 br.g. Star Appeal–Dauphiness (Supreme Sovereign) [1989/90 c24d c26m c24gpu] leggy gelding: unbeaten in 5 handicap chases in 1988/9: well beaten in March and April: stays 3¼m: acts on firm and dead going: jumps untidily on occasions: has won for an amateur. *G. A. Ham.* c— —

WARM WINTER 4 gr.f. Kalaglow–Fair Head (High Line) [1989/90 16s6 16v5 16s3 16g* 18f2 16mF] leggy, sparely-made filly: sister to winning hurdler Kala Fair: lightly-raced maiden on Flat: won selling handicap hurdle at Stratford (bought in 5,000 gns) in March: improved further when clear 5 lengths second to Royal Wonder in seller at Fontwell in May: stays 2¼m: acts well on firm ground: sold to J. H. Baker 5,500 gns Ascot June Sales. *R. Curtis.* 91

WARNER FOR FITNESS 7 b.g. Lochnager–Damsel (Pampered King) [1989/90 17m4 16f6] half-brother to high-class hurdler and very useful chaser Nohalmdun (by Dragonara Palace): fourth in maiden hurdle at Newton Abbot in April: dead. *P. J. Hobbs.* 90

WARNER FOR LEISURE 12 b.g. Jimsun–Besselsleigh Lass (Quorum) [1989/90 17m* 17h2 c16d3 20d c20gur c20g4] big, rangy gelding: moderate chaser nowadays: made all in amateur riders handicap hurdle at Devon & Exeter in September: suited by a strongly-run race at 2m and probably stays 2½m: seems unsuited by very soft ground but probably acts on any other: has worn blinkers but does just as well without: moody and isn't one to rely on. *P. J. Hobbs.* c**111** § 111 §

WARNER'S END 9 ch.g. Legal Tender–Yoriet (Hornet) [1989/90 c24d2 c24d6 c25m6 c20m*] big, rangy gelding: modest chaser: game winner of handicap at Leicester in January: stays well: acts on soft and good to firm going: takes a strong hold and is suited by racing to the fore: blinkered last 2 outings. *J. Webber.* c**92** —

WARREN BRIDGE 9 b.g. Pony Express–Blaze Away IV (pedigree unknown) [1989/90 c24d2] smallish gelding: modest point-to-pointer, winner in 1989: behind and pushed along at halfway, but stayed on well from 4 out when 30 lengths second to Teaplanter in maiden hunter chase at Leicester in March: should win a similar race when stamina is at a premium. *V. G. Greenway.* c**99**

WARRENS BOY 8 ch.g. Gladden–Divinitess (Divine Gift) [1989/90 21h* 20f4 20f5] won NH Flat races in 1987 and 1988: won novice hurdle at Devon & Exeter in August: will stay 3m: acts on hard ground. *D. J. G. Murray-Smith.* 79

WARRIORS CODE 7 ch.g. Roman Warrior–Rose's Code (True Code) [1989/90 16g6 24dpu 20sro a20g* a20g3] lengthy, workmanlike gelding: 33/1 and claimer ridden, won 12-runner novice hurdle at Southwell in January: ran creditably next time: stays 2½m: has looked most temperamental. *D. T. Todd.* 94 §

WARRIORS MOTTO 7 ch.g. Tug of War–Mikimoto (Gulf Pearl) [1989/90 22g6] sixth in NH Flat race at Bangor in 1988/9 and when well beaten in amateur riders maiden at Kelso in November on hurdling debut. *T. P. Tate.* —

WARRIOR'S PROMISE 5 ch.g. Mansingh (USA)–Pegs Promise (Tumble Wind (USA)) [1989/90 c24gur 16hr 22g 22m 20g6 16g4 27s4 a24g5 16d 16g 16f3 16f c24f3 c16f4 c25mur 24m] rather sparely-made gelding: novice selling hurdler: poor novice chaser: refused to race second start (blinkered) and very reluctant to c**79** § 68 §

race ninth outing (slowly into stride last start): best run at 2½m on good ground: one to treat with caution. *D. L. Williams.*

WARWICK SUITE 8 b.g. Orchestra–Place To Place (USA) (No Robbery) [1989/90 16g^{6} 16m 16g^{2} 16g* 16d^{5} 20g 18d^{4} 16v* 16d^{5} 16f^{pu}] sturdy, workmanlike gelding: modest hurdler: won handicaps at Haydock in November and Ayr (conditional jockeys) in February: modest novice chaser: stays 2¾m: suited by plenty of give in the ground: blinkered or visored: ran in snatches second outing: suitable mount for a claimer: has won 4 times at Ayr. *M. P. Naughton.* c— 94

WASSELNI 4 br.g. Wassl–Monongelia (Welsh Pageant) [1989/90 16g 16m^{6} 16g^{pu}] angular, sparely-made gelding: placed over 1¾m on Flat: sold out of M. Jarvis' stable 14,500 gns Newmarket July Sales and subsequently gelded: well beaten over hurdles. *K. A. Morgan.* —

WATERDALE (USA) 7 b.g. Caucasus (USA)–Green Girl (Petingo) [1989/90 c24d] big, lengthy gelding: winning hurdler: bit backward, tailed off in novice chase at Hexham in December: should stay beyond 2m: acts on dead going. *M. W. Easterby.* c— —

WATERFORD WAY 7 ch.g. Double Form–Lovettsville (Le Levanstell) [1989/90 20f^{5}] lengthy, good-quartered gelding: no worthwhile form over hurdles. *K. W. Hogg.* —

WATERHAY 7 b.g. Callernish–Crookhaven (Arctic Slave) [1989/90 22s^{pu} c20g^{6} c20d c28g^{6}] rangy, workmanlike gelding: poor novice hurdler/chaser. *S. Mellor.* c— —

WATERLOO BOY 7 ch.g. Deep Run–Sapphire Red (Red Alert) [1989/90 c20d^{2} c20g* c20d^{2} c20d^{3} c16f^{2} c16f^{4}] c**163** —

The whip and the rules about its use were again a controversial issue in the latest season. A major row broke out between the Jockeys' Association and racing's ruling body the Jockey Club after six riders received suspensions for improper use of the whip at the three-day Cheltenham Festival meeting. The Jockeys' Association strongly criticised the stewards at Cheltenham for being 'too stringent', a view shared by many observers. The suspensions imposed on Davies and Dunwoody after a stirring finish to the Queen Mother Champion Chase were particularly harsh. The pair rode magnificently, particularly from the last fence to the line, as their mounts Barnbrook Again and Waterloo Boy fought out a memorable duel. Both riders used their whips correctly but were found to have used them 'excessively' (the stewards are recommended to consider enquiring where any rider uses his whip more than ten times after the second last). Our view of the rights and wrongs of the stewards' actions after the Queen Mother Champion Chase is given in the essay on Barnbrook Again, but both the trainer and jockey of the runner-up Waterloo Boy made notable contributions to the debate at the time. 'You won't see a better race than that and Richard has certainly never ridden a better one,' said Waterloo Boy's trainer, while the horse's rider, writing in *Horse and Hound*, pulled no punches. Expressing disappointment that he and Davies had dropped their original idea of lodging an appeal, Dunwoody wrote: 'The appeal, if nothing else, would have exposed once again the inconsistencies of the decisions of Major Steveney, the advising stipendiary in charge, and the Cheltenham stewards. Major Steveney gives the impression he dislikes my style of riding, but this should not be allowed to prejudice his manner and style of questioning at an inquiry. Why also were the trainers and the vets not called upon to give evidence, as is usually the case? Guidelines . . . have done a lot of good, yet it still remains that one day we can do one thing and be applauded for it and the next day do the very same and have our living taken away . . . we have got the ridiculous case of guidelines sometimes being interpreted as rules.' The plea for consistency was echoed by others. The sometimes widely-differing interpretations of these particular rules by stewards up and down the country are unfair on jockeys and create ill-will which is damaging to racing's public image. The sooner this particular controversy is resolved the better. The guidelines themselves—originally drawn up without any consultation with jockeys or trainers—need to be examined again in the light of more than two years' experience. The specifying of a norm for the number of times the whip can be used has been

Mr M. R. Deeley's "Waterloo Boy"

at the root of much of the trouble and should be dropped. The guidelines should focus on correct use of the whip, not the frequency with which it can be used. Hitting a horse at the wrong time (out of rhythm with its stride), striking it in the wrong place, or using the whip when it has nothing more to give, is far more offensive than using it correctly a dozen or more times on a horse that is responding and running on strongly in the closing stages of a race when maximum effort is required. The whip is an essential part of race-riding, necessary, over jumps in particular, also as an aid to keeping a leg-weary horse straight as well as getting the best out of it in a finish; and any rules governing its use can only work in the best interests of racing if they are widely regarded as fair—which, at the moment, they're not.

Waterloo Boy's performance in the Queen Mother Champion Chase—he went down by half a length—was his best of the season, returning to the course and distance over which he gained the most important victory of his career to date, in the Arkle Challenge Trophy at the previous year's Festival meeting. Two miles is probably Waterloo Boy's best trip but the shortage of suitable condition-race trials leading up to the Queen Mother Champion Chase meant that his four races in the latest season before Cheltenham were all over two and a half. After a creditable second on his reappearance in the Worcester qualifier of the Arlington Premier Chase series, Waterloo Boy went on to gain his only victory in the Chepstow qualifier in the same series, being sent on from before the third last, recovering from a mistake two out and holding on gamely by a neck from Celtic Shot, first and second both giving the impression they would improve for the race. Waterloo Boy failed to confirm the form with Celtic Shot in the Final, run at Cheltenham at the end of January, when his jumping—which is usually very sound—was none too fluent and he was struggling before the home turn, eventually coming third, two and a half lengths and twenty-five lengths behind Sabin du Loir and Celtic Shot. Waterloo Boy had run much better a month earlier when sent to Ireland for the very valuable Black & White Whisky Champion Chase: he looked the winner when holding a slight lead at the last but was just run out of it on the flat by Maid of Money. Waterloo Boy's only outing after the Queen Mother Champion Chase was in the Captain Morgan Aintree Chase at Liverpool, a limited handicap in which, under top weight of 11-12, he was badly hampered and lost ground when going well in a good position approaching the third last but for which he'd have done better than his still-creditable fourth, beaten just under seven lengths, to Nohalmdun.

Waterloo Boy (ch.g. 1983)	Deep Run (ch 1966)	Pampered King (b 1954)	Prince Chevalier
			Netherton Maid
		Trial By Fire (ch 1958)	Court Martial
			Mitrailleuse
	Sapphire Red (ch 1977)	Red Alert (ch 1971)	Red God
			Ashton Jane
		Sapphire Lady (b 1968)	Majority Blue
			Sayann

There is an air of inevitability about top place in the National Hunt stallion statistics these days. Waterloo Boy's sire Deep Run was champion sire over jumps in Britain for the eleventh successive season, beating Vulgan's post-war record of ten. Deep Run gets winners over all distances but a fair proportion of his best horses possess good speed. There's not much stamina on the distaff side of Waterloo Boy's pedigree, dealt with fully in *Chasers & Hurdlers 1988/89*. Waterloo Boy's dam the unraced Sapphire Red was sprint-bred, by the Jersey Stakes and Stewards' Cup winner Red Alert out of a five-furlong winner. Sapphire Red's first four foals have all won, including the modest Tigh An Cheoil (by Goldhill), a winner over two miles on the Flat who was successful in a two-mile handicap hurdle at Tramore in the latest season. The well-made Waterloo Boy acts on any going. He's very genuine and reliable and, it bears repeating, a good jumper, altogether a grand type. Waterloo Boy could well be the one they'll all have to beat in the Queen Mother Champion Chase come Cheltenham. *D. Nicholson.*

WATERMEAD 5 b.g. Oats–Mangro (Mandamus) [1989/90 16g 16g 20g^{pu}] leggy gelding: third foal: half-brother to winning staying hurdler Grayrose Double (by Celtic Cone): dam, well beaten in NH Flat race and novice hurdles, from good jumping family: no worthwhile form in novice hurdles. *D. R. Gandolfo.* —

WATER ORCHID 5 b.g. Lafontaine (USA)–Johnnie's Lass (Menelek) [1989/90 F16g 16s^{ur} 16s^{3} 20d] big, workmanlike gelding: has scope: remote third in slowly-run novice hurdle at Nottingham in January: pulled hard and weakened 3 out over 2½m. *D. McCain.* —

WATERSHED 4 b.c. Blakeney–Anadyomene (Sea Hawk II) [1989/90 16f^{5} 16m^{2} 16m^{2}] claimed out of Mrs L. Piggott's stable 10,500 gns after winning 11.3f claimer on Flat in 1989: runner-up in 2 early-season juvenile hurdles: dead. *N. Tinkler.* 86

WATERSIGN 9 b.g. Camden Town–Larkview (Supreme Sovereign) [1989/90 c16g^{3} c24v^{2}] big, rangy ex-Irish gelding: won a point-to-point in Ireland in 1988 and a similar event in Britain in 1989: placed in novice chases at Ayr in November and January: stays 3m. *W. A. Stephenson.* c94

WATERSMEET DOWN 7 ch.g. Carlburg–Brians Vulgan (Vulgan) [1989/90 c17f^{5} c25m^{ur} c25f^{2} c24f^{3} c24f^{3} c21m^{5} c24g^{ur} c24m* c25f^{F} c24m^{pu}] workmanlike, sparely-made gelding: poor novice hurdler: won amateur riders handicap chase at Ludlow in November by 6 lengths from Uncle Merlin: ran moderately final start (January): suited by 3m and firm going: blinkered nowadays: amateur ridden last 6 outings. *P. J. Hobbs.* c95 —

WATER SPRITE 6 ch.m. Pry–Sun Spray (Nice Guy) [1989/90 F16f^{6} 16g 21f^{pu} 20m^{pu}] lengthy, sparely-made mare: sister to fairly useful jumpers Young Lover and Infielder and half-sister to fairly useful chaser Bright Intervals (by Condorcet) —

and top novice hurdler Forest Sun (by Whistling Deer): dam half-sister to fair jumper Mr Midshipman: sixth in NH Flat race at Newbury in October: little sign of ability in novice hurdles. *S. Dow.*

WATERTIGHT (USA) 5 b.g. Affirmed (USA)–Brookward (USA) (Stevward) [1989/90 16g4 24g* 20fF 20d* 22s2 22v2 24g 20v4 20d6] rather leggy, sparely-made gelding: won novice handicap hurdles at Market Rasen in November and Hexham in December: stays 3m: acts on heavy going: has run well for a claimer. *G. M. Moore.* 123

WATER WAGTAIL 9 ch.g. Over The River (FR)–What-A-Bird (Saint Denys) [1989/90 c24d2 c24sF c24m6 c24g3 c24d3 c24d6 c24f3] leggy, rather sparely-made gelding: winning hunter chaser: ran poorly after first outing in 1989/90: stays well: acts on any going: blinkered sixth outing: sometimes sweating: has looked ungenuine on occasions. *W. A. Stephenson.* c**106** d —

WAVE 7 br.h. Mississippi–Wink (Milesian) [1989/90 16f] sparely-made horse: sweating, finished lame when behind in novice hurdle at Uttoxeter in September. *M. Bradstock.* —

WAVERLEY BOY 8 br.g. Scallywag–Mansina (Mansingh (USA)) [1989/90 c16mF c16d4 c25g3 c20mF a20g4 a20g3 a20g* a20g4 a22g2] good-bodied gelding: won handicap hurdle at Southwell in February: no form over fences: stays 3m. *J. S. Wainwright.* c— 79

WAVERLEY GIRL 4 b.f. Seymour Hicks (FR)–Iamstopped (Furry Glen) [1989/90 a16gro 16d a16g4 16g2 a18g* 16gr a18g4 a20g] sparely-made filly: half-sister to winning 2m hurdler Murphy (by Touch Paper): little sign of ability on Flat: won selling hurdle at Southwell in January by a distance (bought in 2,300 gns): soundly-beaten fourth in novice hurdle on same course following month: likely to stay beyond 2¼m (saddle slipped early on when tried over 2½m): ran out on hurdling debut and refused and unseated rider first on sixth outing. *J. S. Wainwright.* 82 §

WAVERLEY MILL 9 b.g. Little Buskins–Fair Corina (Menelek) [1989/90 c24f*] tall gelding: novice hurdler: fair point-to-pointer, winner in February and April: let down by his jumping in steeplechases prior to winning novice hunter chase at Wetherby in April by 6 lengths from Mademist Susie, making most: stays 3m: acts on firm going: takes a good hold: has worn a crossed noseband. *Mrs Alix Stevenson.* c**110** p —

WAY CLEAR 7 b.m. Bulldozer–Welsh Wise (Welsh Saint) [1989/90 16g 16s6 20s 20m] leggy, sparely-made mare: poor novice hurdler: probably stays 2½m: acts on firm ground: sold 1,800 gns Doncaster Spring Sales. *C. J. Bell.* 73

WAYCROSS 5 ch.g. Deep Run–Topeka (Allangrange) [1989/90 19gpu 16spu 16dpu 20g6 21f5] sparely-made, rather angular gelding: poor form in novice handicap hurdles last 2 starts: blinkered, ran in seller third start (trained until after then by M. Oliver). *P. J. Hobbs.* 72

WAYSIDE 8 br.g. Smokey Rockett–Rosamond (Spiritus) [1989/90 c21gpu c17f4 c22m2 c24gpu] leggy, rather sparely-made gelding: poor novice hurdler/chaser: stays 25f. *P. Liddle.* c**72** —

WAYSIDE BOY 5 b.g. Deep Run–Ciotog (Varano) [1989/90 F16g F13d3] half-brother to Irish 9.5f winner Foggy Glen (by Furry Glen): dam won over 7.5f at 3 yrs in Ireland: 5½ lengths third behind Solo Cornet in NH Flat race at Kelso in January: yet to race over hurdles or fences. *G. Richards.*

WAY UNDER 10 b.g. Menelek–In The Limelight (Prince Hansel) [1989/90 c25fF c25f3 c26h* c25m5 c24mpu c26f* c26m4] good-bodied gelding: carries plenty of condition: modest chaser: won handicap and amateur riders event at Fontwell in the spring: a thorough stayer: acts on hard ground and seems unsuited by soft: sometimes gets behind in early stages. *D. H. L. Nugent.* c**109** —

WAYWARD LUKE 6 b.g. Bustiki–Lukes Lass (Hoarwithy) [1989/90 22mF c20gpu c16m c26sur 25dpu] workmanlike gelding: first foal: dam unraced: little promise in novice events over hurdles and fences. *R. Dickin.* c— —

WAYWARD SINGER 7 ch.g. The Parson–Fairy Island (Prince Hansel) [1989/90 24f2 21f4] smallish, workmanlike gelding: modest hurdler: hung left run-in when creditable second in conditional jockeys handicap at Uttoxeter in August: finished lame and off course 7½ months: behind on only start over fences: stays 3m: acts on any going: claimer ridden nowadays: blinkered fifteenth start 1988/9. *J. R. Upson.* c— 94

WEBBS WONDER 5 b.g. Latest Model–Gay Park (Pardigras) [1989/90 16g^{2} 16g* 21d^{4} 20f] leggy, angular gelding: has scope: third foal: half-brother to 99 successful hurdler/chaser Gay Edition and novice hurdler Gay Ticket (both by New Member): dam fair hurdler and quite useful staying chaser: ridden by 7-lb claimer, won novice hurdle at Warwick in December: creditable fourth to Devil's Valley over 21f at Newbury in February: out of his depth last start: wears crossed noseband. *P. J. Hobbs.*

WEDDING FEAST 5 ch.g. Oats–High Affair (High Line) [1989/90 F16f F16g] second foal: dam, tailed off in 1½m maiden, half-sister to fair 6f to 1m winner Havon Cool: mid-division in NH Flat races at Cheltenham and Market Rasen in the spring: yet to race over hurdles or fences. *J. C. McConnochie.*

WEE GHOSTIE 5 gr.g. Grey Ghost–Sandrek (Derek H) [1989/90 F16g] first foal: dam, novice hurdler/chaser, suited by 21f: tailed off in NH Flat race at Kelso in March: yet to race over hurdles or fences. *Miss F. Geddes.*

WEETMANS WAGON 6 ch.g. Welsh Chanter–Judy Green (Green God) [1989/90 22m^{2} 24s^{pu} 22g 16s^{2} 16s^{3} 16m^{4}] big, strong gelding: chasing type: 102 moderate hurdler: runner-up at Nottingham in December and Haydock (wandered under pressure) in January: stays 2¾m when conditions aren't testing: acts on soft and good to firm ground. *B. A. McMahon.*

WEE WILLIAM 13 b.g. Workboy–Obedience (Reliance II) [1989/90 c26m^{pu}] c— small, stocky gelding: poor chaser nowadays: stays 25f: best form on a sound — surface: good mount for a claimer: jumps rather deliberately: usually held up. *B. G. Hicks.*

WEFFIE 4 ch.f. On Your Mark–Catch Crop (Capistrano) [1989/90 16f^{5} 18s^{pu} 16d^{4} 16f] sparely-made filly: winning plater on Flat, suited by 1m: poor novice 66 selling hurdler: sold out of R. O'Leary's stable 2,000 gns Doncaster September Sales after first start: resold 1,200 gns Ascot April Sales. *B. Stevens.*

WEIGHT PROBLEM 13 ch.g. Proverb–Queen of Killonan (Ossian II) c89 [1989/90 c20f^{3} c20s^{pu} c20d^{3} c24f^{4}] sturdy gelding: quite modest chaser: stays — 3m: probably acts on any going: usually held up: usually blinkered nowadays. *P. J. Bevan.*

WEIRPOOL 8 ch.g. Le Bavard (FR)–Vulplume (Vulgan) [1989/90 c17m* c115 c20g^{6} c20g^{F} c20d^{3} c24g* c25g* c24d^{5} c26d^{2} c22m] rangy gelding: won handicap — chases at Huntingdon in October and Kempton (made virtually all) and Wincanton in January, last 2 conditional jockeys events: stays 3¼m: acts on good to firm and dead going: jumps well: ridden by claimer: trained until after third start by W. T. Kemp. *M. H. B. Robinson.*

WEISS ROSE (FR) 5 b.m. Pilgrim (USA)–Seul (Faberge II) [1989/90 16f^{3} 16g^{3} 17g^{2} a16g*] smallish, workmanlike mare: won 6-runner mares novice 81 handicap hurdle at Lingfield in January: beaten in a seller last start 1988/9: claimer ridden nowadays: sold out of C. Holmes's stable 2,700 gns Ascot September Sales. *W. G. Turner.*

WELCOME PIN 9 b.g. Bowling Pin–Welcome Tangle (Welcome News) c142 [1989/90 c18m* c16s^{6} c19d^{2} c18s* c18v^{5} c16s^{6}] —

The story of Welcome Pin is one of success against the odds. His unraced sire Bowling Pin has produced live foals from only just over one in three of the mares he has covered since being retired to stud in 1978; the dam Welcome Tangle bred only one living foal in her first seven years in the paddocks. And Welcome Pin himself has been beset by problems since showing very useful form as a novice hurdler in 1986/7. He showed little in the next two seasons, falling at the third in a novice chase on his only outing in 1987/8, and was off the course for ten months after finishing well beaten in a handicap hurdle in January, 1989. However, returned to chasing in the latest season, Welcome Pin put up two performances which entitle him to be regarded as one of the best novices in Ireland. Carrying a 6-lb penalty as a result of a comfortable neck defeat of On The Other Hand in the Drinmore Chase at Fairyhouse the previous month, Welcome Pin went down by only a length to Cahervillahow in a qualifier of the Irish National Hunt Novice Chase series at Naas in January. He led from the final turn until late on the run-in and finished fifteen lengths clear of the remainder. Welcome Pin put up an equally good performance to win a similar contest at Fairyhouse in January. Having made smooth headway to join front runner The Committee at the third last, he didn't have to be hard pressed to establish a two-length advantage at the line.

Welcome Pin ran poorly on his two subsequent appearances, on the first occasion when favourite for the Diners Club Chase at Punchestown in February. He was soon beaten after a mistake four out and finished over twenty lengths behind Derrymore Boy; an examination by the Turf Club veterinary officer ordered by the stewards, reportedly could detect nothing wrong with him. In the Irish Life Assurance Nas Na Ri Chase at Naas a week later Welcome Pin weakened quickly from four out to finish a remote last of six behind Kiichi. It's to be hoped that Welcome Pin can be brought back to his best. From what we know of him as a hurdler he is suited by a test of stamina and would be sure to improve over fences granted the opportunity to race over further than nineteen furlongs.

Welcome Pin (b.g. 1981)	Bowling Pin (b 1975)	Run The Gantlet (b 1968)	Tom Rolfe
			First Feather
		Belaying Pin (b 1968)	Iron Peg
			Lay In
	Welcome Tangle (b 1974)	Welcome News (ch 1959)	Three Cheers
			Last Port
		Cantangle (b 1968)	Cantab
			Spangle

The winning point-to-pointer Welcome Tangle has improved her stud record of late, producing a colt in 1988—sold for IR 17,500 guineas as a foal at Fairyhouse—and a filly the following year, both by Bowling Pin again. Her dam Cantangle showed ability in maiden hurdles and bred two other winners by Avocat, including two-mile chaser Avocan. She is a sister to the winning staying chaser Mourneview out of the successful hurdler/chaser Spangle, the latter grandam of Little Owl. Welcome Pin won two National Hunt Flat races and three races over hurdles when trained by P. Mullins. He was sold privately immediately prior to finishing seventh in the Waterford Crystal Supreme Novices' Hurdle at Cheltenham in 1987. A medium-sized gelding, Welcome Pin has won on good to firm ground but has shown his best form with plenty of give. *J. E. Mulhern, Ireland.*

WELCOME TIDINGS 6 b.m. Record Run–Glanfield (Eborneezer) [1989/90 18s^{pu} 16d^{pu}] tall, leggy mare: very lightly raced and no sign of ability. *M. J. Bolton.* —

WELL COVERED 9 b. or br.g. Thatch (USA)–Tirana (Ragusa) [1989/90 20f^{F} 20m^{2} 19f^{4} 20f* 25f^{bd} 25g c20f^{3} c20m^{2}] leggy, close-coupled gelding: usually looks well: modest hurdler: won slowly-run conditional jockeys event at Cheltenham in October: poor form in novice chases: stays 3m: unsuited by very soft ground but probably acts on any other: blinkered third start: finds little off bridle and needs exaggerated waiting tactics. *R. Hollinshead.* c73 107 §

WELL INFORMED 8 ch.g. Sallust–Ladys View (Tin Whistle) [1989/90 20g^{pu} a16g c16d^{pu} a16g^{5}] leggy, sparely-made gelding: poor novice hurdler: tailed off when pulled up on chasing debut: stays 2¼m. *F. Coton.* c— —

WELLINGTON BROWN 6 b.g. Faraway Times (USA)–Chevulgan (Cheval) [1989/90 c25m*] leggy, good-topped gelding: of little account as a hurdler: won point-to-points in February and April (2) and hunter chase in between: jumped better as race progressed when scoring comfortably by 8 lengths from Abbotsham in latter at Wincanton: stays 25f: acts on good to firm going: will improve. *J. R. Vail.* c92 p —

WELLS O'WEARIE 14 ch.g. Cheval–Little Dora (Bounteous) [1989/90 c25m^{pu}] poor hurdler: moderate jumper in steeplechases: winning point-to-pointer: dead. *D. F. Gillard.* c— —

WELSH BARD 6 b.g. Welsh Saint–Songorella (Song) [1989/90 16f^{pu} 16g^{4} 16g* 16g 18v^{2} 16m 16d^{4}] leggy, quite useful-looking Irish gelding: fourth foal: half-brother to a modest maiden by Shack: dam 5f winner at 2 yrs: very useful hurdler: won handicap at Leopardstown in November: 2½ lengths second to Bright Note at Navan in January: unlikely to stay much beyond 2¼m: acts on heavy going (ran poorly on firm). *T. F. Lacy, Ireland.* 145

WELSH COLUMN 4 b.f. Welsh Captain–Bally's Step (Ballynockan) [1989/90 16s 16d] sparely-made filly: quite modest handicapper around 1m on Flat, needs —

the mud: sold out of R. Whitaker's stable 3,100 gns Ascot November Sales: tailed off in juvenile hurdles in December and January. *Grenville Richards.*

WELSH COMMANDER 7 b.g. Welsh Chanter–Black Barret (Bargello) [1989/90 20m^5 c25d^F c24g^F] workmanlike gelding: successful in NH Flat race in 1988/9: showed a little ability when fifth in novice hurdle at Worcester in September: behind when falling both outings over fences: sold 1,500 gns Ascot June Sales. *K. C. Bailey.* c— 76

WELSH FLUTE 4 b.f. Welsh Captain–Spanish Flute (Philip of Spain) [1989/90 16m^5 16m 16g^4 16g^5 16g^F a18g^5] small, lightly-made filly: plating class on Flat and over hurdles. *R. Thompson.* 63

WELSH GUARD 8 br.g. Welsh Pageant–Mariinsky (Nijinsky (CAN)) [1989/90 16f^2 20g^2 16g*] leggy, lengthy, plain gelding: claimer ridden, won novice selling handicap hurdle at Sedgefield in November by 15 lengths (no bid): probably stays 2½m. *Ronald Thompson.* 99

WELSHMAN 4 ch.g. Final Straw–Joie de Galles (Welsh Pageant) [1989/90 16v^6 16d^5 16d*] compact gelding: fourth foal: dam, 1½m winner, half-sister to 2 winning hurdlers, including fairly useful Reclaim: modest 1½m winner on Flat, goes well in the mud: showed ability over hurdles prior to winning 12-runner juvenile event at Bangor in March by 12 lengths: acts on dead going. *M. Blanshard.* 105

WELSHMAN'S CREEK 4 ch.g. Orchestra–Malibu Lady (Ragapan) [1989/90 F16f] second foal: half-brother to maiden hurdler Welshman's Gully (by Jasmine Star): dam lightly-raced maiden: mid-division in NH Flat race at Cheltenham in April: yet to race over hurdles. *D. M. Grissell.*

WELSH MANSION 4 b.g. Longleat (USA)–La Gallia (Welsh Saint) [1989/90 16f 16g a16g^5 20s^{pu}] angular, sparely-made gelding: sixth reported live foal: dam won over hurdles: won 2 claimers at around 1m on Flat in 1989: no form over hurdles: visored last 3 starts: sold privately 10,000 gns Doncaster Spring Sales. *P. Davis.* —

WELSH OAK 10 gr.g. Jimsun–Besselsleigh Lass (Quorum) [1989/90 c21f* c24f* 22m* c20f^2 c20g^4 c20f^2 c24g^{pu}] compact gelding: modest hurdler and useful chaser: won 2-runner handicap chases at Newton Abbot and Bangor (fourth course win) and slowly-run handicap hurdle at Stratford early in season: creditable second in A F Budge Gold Cup at Cheltenham (to Clever Folly) in December and quite valuable handicap at Ascot (to Ida's Delight) in March: probably stays 3m: acts on any going: has worn blinkers but better form without. *D. R. Gandolfo.* c**136** 111 +

WELSH PAGEANTRY 7 b.m. Welsh Pageant–Sacred Mountain (St Paddy) [1989/90 16s] smallish, lengthy mare: middle-distance winner on Flat: not unduly knocked about when seventh in novice event won by Riverhead at Sandown in February, only second outing over hurdles: will improve. *M. E. D. Francis.* — p

WENSLEYDALEWILLIAM 4 ch.g. Tudorville–Kingsfold Flash (Warpath) [1989/90 F16g^5] fourth foal: half-brother to useful Flat performer Kingsfold Flame (by No Loiterer): dam plater: 17 lengths fifth of 17 behind Mr Woodcock in NH Flat race at Catterick in March: yet to race over hurdles. *C. W. Thornton.*

WE'RE IN THE MONEY 6 ch.m. Billion (USA)–Fandance (Gay Fandango (USA)) [1989/90 20f^4 20f^3 24f^F 22m^F] workmanlike mare: poor hurdler: stays 2¾m: acts on firm ground and is possibly unsuited by very soft: blinkered once in 1987/8: often visored, including when successful: reluctant to go down final start 1988/9. *G. Roe.* —

WESSEX 8 b.h. Free State–Bonandra (Andrea Mantegna) [1989/90 20g^2 24g* 20d^2 22s^3 20g 24d] small horse: handicap hurdler: won at Worcester in December: ran well next 2 starts, but poorly last 2: stays 3m: acts on soft going (yet to race on top-of-the-ground over hurdles): successful with and without blinkers. *N. Tinkler.* 127

WESSEX MILORD 5 ch.g. Stanford–Miss Osprey (Sea Hawk II) [1989/90 16m^{pu} 17m] of little account. *J. A. Bennett.* —

WESSEX WARRIOR 4 b.g. Anfield–Achiever (Tarqogan) [1989/90 F16f* F16f^5] 1,200Y: third foal: dam, daughter of a winning hurdler, showed little ability in 2 races over hurdles: won 9-runner NH Flat race at Wincanton in March: yet to race over hurdles. *M. R. Channon.*

WEST ENDER 7 gr.g. Pongee–Three Oaks (Drumbeg) [1989/90 24g^4 20m^2] lengthy, workmanlike gelding: winning chaser: poor novice hurdler: stays 3m: c— 94

acts on good to firm and heavy ground: has worn a brush pricker and a severe bridle: has tended to carry head high. *J. M. Jefferson.*

WESTERN COUNTIES 11 ch.g. True Song–Gay Air (Romany Air) [1989/90 17h^{4} c20f* c17f^{3} c20m* c20m*] lightly-built gelding: novice hurdler: won handicap chases at Worcester in August and September (2): made a couple of mistakes when well beaten third start: stays 2½m: acts on any going: ridden by claimer: wears a crossed noseband: has done all his winning on left-handed courses. *R. J. Holder.* c**113** 73

WESTERN DANDY 7 b.g. The Parson–Whisht Lassie (Menelek) [1989/90 c16m* c16f^{2} c17g^{6} c16s^{2} c16m^{pu} c16m^{3} c20m*] big gelding: winning hurdler: won novice chases at Warwick in November and May (3-runner handicap, blinkered): jumped rather deliberately and ran in snatches when going down by 5 lengths to Wink Gulliver in Daniel Homes Novices' Chase at Ascot in February, fourth outing: found little from 3 out third start: probably stays 2½m: seems to act on any going. *N. A. Gaselee.* c**109** —

WESTERN DIVIDE (USA) 5 b.g. Sharpen Up–River Nile (USA) (Damascus (USA)) [1989/90 16f^{3} 16g 16g^{4} 16d 16d^{5} 16f 16m*] small gelding: poor maiden on Flat: sold out of B. Hills's stable 6,200 gns Newmarket Autumn (1988) Sales: won selling handicap hurdle at Towcester (no bid) in April: acts on firm ground: has looked a difficult ride: blinkered fifth start: none too consistent. *J. Perrett.* 85

WESTERN GUN (USA) 5 b.h. Lypheor–Fandangerina (USA) (Grey Dawn II) [1989/90 16g^{2}] smallish, sparely-made horse: useful performer at up to 1m on Flat when trained by R. Armstrong: promising 4 lengths second to Duntree in novice hurdle at Wolverhampton in January, pulling hard and putting in a mixed round of jumping but quickening well approaching last until outstayed by winner on run-in: should improve enough to win a small race over sharp 2m. *S. Christian.* 89 p

WESTERN LEGEND 6 ch.g. Proverb–Calamity Jane (Never Dwell) [1989/90 c20g* c20g^{2} c20d* c20g*] workmanlike gelding: winning hurdler: took very well to chasing in 1989/90 and won novice events at Folkestone, Huntingdon and Bangor: easily best performance on last-named course in April, jumping well and scoring impressively by 15 lengths from King Sear: will stay 3m: acts on dead going: a useful chaser in the making and is one to follow. *J. A. C. Edwards.* c**122** p —

WESTERN REVIVAL 8 ch.g. Alias Smith (USA)–Resurgence (Runnymede) [1989/90 c20g c16d^{4} c20d c16d c20f^{2} c24f^{pu} c27f^{pu}] lengthy, angular gelding: winning hurdler and poor novice chaser: pulled up lame last start (April): suited by long distances and top-of-the-ground. *W. H. Tinning.* c72 —

WESTERN WOLF 5 ch.h. Wolverlife–Sweet Kate (Slippered) [1989/90 16g^{pu}] ex-Irish horse: half-brother to Irish NH Flat race winner Christmas Kate (by Bonne Noel): dam placed over hurdles in Ireland: fair miler on Flat (has run blinkered): showed some ability over hurdles in Ireland in 1988/9: broke blood vessel only outing in 1989/90. *W. Carter.* —

WESTGATE 8 ch.g. New Member–Pirate's Mate (Barbary Pirate) [1989/90 c20f^{2} c22d^{pu}] lengthy, angular gelding: maiden point-to-pointer: poor novice chaser: dead. *J. Webber.* c82

WEST LODGE LADY 5 ch.m. Crooner–Rose of France (Grand Roi) [1989/90 22m^{pu} 16m 16m 16g 16d a20g^{pu} 16g 17m 17h^{3} 16h^{pu}] angular mare: seventh foal: dam won over 1¼m and 11f: seems of little account: blinkered last start. *N. B. Thomson.* —

WEST PALM BEACH 8 br.m. Our Jimmy (USA)–Somerton Princess (My Swanee) [1989/90 c25f^{pu}] won point-to-points in April and May: well behind when pulled up in hunter chase later in May. *L. Harkins.* c—

WEST TIP 13 b.g. Gala Performance (USA)–Astryl (Vulgan) [1989/90 c24d^{3} c28g^{6} c24d^{2} c26f^{3} c36f c33d^{pu}] big, strong gelding: very smart chaser at his best: won 1986 Seagram Grand National: in frame in next 3 Grand Nationals, and finished tenth in latest running: easily best effort of 1989/90 when 5 lengths third behind Call Collect in Christies Foxhunter Chase at Cheltenham in March on fourth start: took little interest final outing: needs a thorough test of stamina and give in the ground: suited by strong handling: usually a sound jumper: tends to idle in front. *M. Oliver.* c**137** —

WESTWARD DRIFT 5 ch.g. Paddy's Stream–Quay Blues (Quayside) [1989/90 F13d 16f^{5} 20g^{pu}] second foal: dam won NH Flat race in Ireland: little sign of ability in NH Flat race and 2 novice hurdles. *G. Richards.* —

Mr A. M. Ennever's "Whatever You Like"

WESTWAY 7 br.g. Paddy's Stream–Halcyon Years (Royal Highway) [1989/90 22s 22g5 24m 20m4] good-topped gelding: handicap hurdler: best effort of season when fifth to Golden Celtic at Windsor in March: jumped poorly when tailed off on only start over fences: should stay further than 2¾m: acts on heavy going and seems unsuited by firm surface: has worn blinkers, including when successful: seems suited by forcing tactics. *G. A. Ham.* c— 109

WHAAT FETTLE 5 br.g. Strong Gale–Double Century (Double-U-Jay) [1989/90 F17d F12g] fourth foal: half-brother to a poor animal by Tamariscifolia: dam successful at up to 1½m on Flat in Ireland: mid-division in NH Flat races at Carlisle and Hexham in March: yet to race over hurdles or fences. *G. Richards.*

WHARF BRIDGE 5 ch.g. Nickel King–Princes' Tale (Gambrinus) [1989/90 aF14g] half-brother to winning hurdler Bravo of Venice (by Rugantino): dam unraced: behind in NH Flat race at Southwell in November: yet to race over hurdles or fences. *M. Bradstock.*

WHARRY BURN 9 b.g. Gunner B–Sarum Lady (Floribunda) [1989/90 c24s4 c24spu] compact gelding: one-time fair hurdler: winning chaser: bit backward, 6 lengths fourth behind Huntworth at Worcester in January: pulled up and dismounted later in month: probably stays 3m: probably acts on any going: has run creditably for a claimer. *Capt. T. A. Forster.* c99 —

WHAT A BEWT 7 b.g. Anax–Mantavella (Andrea Mantegna) [1989/90 20fF] compact gelding: well beaten in NH Flat races: beaten when falling 2 out in novice hurdle at Worcester in March: dead. *P. D. Evans.* —

WHAT ABOUT ME 7 ch.g. Condorcet (FR)–Aurora Lady (Beau Chapeau) [1989/90 20g6 20g 22d4 24g5 24s5 24v2 24d6 22g*] lengthy gelding: handicap hurdler: made most when winning by length from Candlebright at Kelso in March: stays 3m: acts on heavy going: claimer ridden. *Mrs S. A. Bramall.* 118

WHAT A LINE 8 ch.g. High Line–Something To Hide (Double-U-Jay) [1989/90 16f* 16f2 20f* 20f*] lightly-made gelding: former selling hurdler: won 109 early-season handicap hurdles at Southwell (2) and Sedgefield: stayed 2½m: acted on firm and good to soft going: dead. *Mrs G. R. Reveley.*

WHAT A SNIP (USA) 5 b.g. Water Bank (USA)–Snip (Shantung) [1989/90 20f^{pu} 20f^{pu}] sparely-made gelding: novice selling hurdler: pulled up in non-sellers early in season (looked reluctant first occasion): acts on dead going: visored all bar first outing 1988/9. *D. H. Topley.* —

WHAT A TO DO 6 b.g. Le Bavard (FR)–Alfie's Wish (Three Wishes) [1989/90 16g^{6} 20v^{6} c20s^{pu}] close-coupled gelding: seventh in NH Flat race in 1988/9: carrying condition, showed promise in novice hurdles at Towcester and Chepstow: made a couple of mistakes and was tailed off when pulled up in novice chase at Warwick in February: should stay 2½m: tends to sweat. *Capt. T. A. Forster.* c— 87 p

WHAT A WALLY 8 gr.g. General Ironside–Saint Malva (Welsh Pageant) [1989/90 F17m^{5} F17g^{3} 16d^{6} 17d^{4} c16g^{2} c16s^{5} c20g^{4} c16m^{3} c24g c20s^{2} c24d^{F} c20f* c20f^{wo} c25m^{2} c24m^{6}] tall ex-Irish gelding: second foal: dam never ran: maiden hurdler/point-to-pointer: won novice chase at Ludlow in March: walked over in handicap on same course later in month: stays 25f: probably acts on any going: lost interest once headed on eighth outing: suited by strongly-run race: trained first 4 starts by W. Burke. *M. Oliver.* c99 ?

WHATEVER YOU LIKE 6 b.g. Deep Run–Garravogue (Giolla Mear) [1989/90 16d^{2} 16s* 16m] tall, unfurnished gelding: half-brother to 2 winning jumpers, notably useful chaser Katabatic (by Strong Gale): dam unraced half-sister to William Hill Yorkshire Chase winner Get Out of Me Way: confirmed promise shown on hurdling debut when winning quite valuable A F Budge Novices' Hurdle at Ascot in February by ½ length from Man of The West: sweating slightly and unimpressive in paddock, travelled well for a long way, but dropped out quickly approaching 2 out and eased thereafter when around 26 lengths ninth behind Forest Sun in Waterford Crystal Supreme Novices' Hurdle at Cheltenham in March: will be suited by 2½m: acts on soft going. *N. J. Henderson.* 125

WHAT IF 6 ch.m. Nicholas Bill–Starproof (Comedy Star (USA)) [1989/90 16f 20f^{4} c16g^{F} c16m^{F} 16m* 16f^{3} 17f^{6}] leggy, close-coupled mare: changed hands 2,600 gns Doncaster October Sales: bought in 3,400 gns after winning selling hurdle at Towcester in May: good third in handicap at Hexham later in month: showed promise but fell both starts in novice chases: best form at 2m on top-of-the-ground: has reportedly broken blood vessels. *O. Brennan.* c— p 88

WHAT'S A GUINEA 6 ch.m. Crofter (USA)–Key Note (Kythnos) [1989/90 16m^{5} 16g] smallish mare: poor hurdler: finished lame last time out (October): worth a try over 2½m: acts on heavy going and seems unsuited by firm. *S. C. Davis.* 79

WHATS THE CRACK 7 b.g. The Parson–Mighty Crack (Deep Run) [1989/90 20s^{6} 25d^{2} 24d^{2} 25m^{2}] angular ex-Irish gelding: first foal: dam unraced sister to winning pointer-to-pointer/hurdler and useful chaser Good Crack: won a point-to-point in 1989: runner-up in novice hurdles at Huntingdon, Chepstow and Liverpool: showed improved form on last-named course in April, going down by 4 lengths to Dwadme in White Satin Novices' Hurdle, staying on well under pressure in straight: stays 3m: best form on good to firm going: sure to win races over hurdles. *Miss H. C. Knight.* 126

WHATS WHAT 11 gr.g. Pongee–Reigate Head (Timber King) [1989/90 c20f^{4} c24g^{pu}] smallish, good-quartered gelding: useful chaser at his best: in need of race, never placed to challenge and not knocked about when last of 4 at Newcastle in October: pulled up lame following month: stays 25f: acts on any going: whipped round start final outing 1988/9: looks a difficult ride (tends to hang), but has won for an amateur. *B. Bousfield.* c— —

WHATS YOUR PROBLEM 7 b.g. Buckskin (FR)–Laurenca (Laurence O) [1989/90 c24g^{ur} c20s^{pu} c24g^{6}] lengthy, good sort: placed in point-to-points in Ireland in 1988: won both starts in similar events in Britain in 1989: ran well until tiring approaching 2 out and was eased afterwards when well-beaten sixth to Arctic Call in novice chase at Newbury in March: may prove best at distances shorter than 3m. *Miss H. C. Knight.* c— p

WHAT'S YOURS 13 b.g. New Member–Romany Serenade (Romany Air) [1989/90 c24d^{pu}] tall, workmanlike gelding: winning point-to-pointer: second in hunter chase in 1988/9: needed race only outing 1989/90 (March): stays 3¼m: acts on any going: refused once over hurdles. *G. W. Giddings.* c— —

WHEAL PROSPER 5 b.g. Strong Gale–Kells Bay (Deep Run) [1989/90 17v^{6} 17m^{pu}] third foal: dam, placed over hurdles in Ireland, sister to a winning hurdler —

and half-sister to a winning hurdler: no sign of ability in 2 races over hurdles at Newton Abbot. *C. G. Roach.*

WHEELIES NEWMEMBER 7 ch.g. New Member–Idyll-Liquor (Narrator) [1989/90 c20m^F c16g^{ur} c20s^6 c24f c20h^4] leggy gelding: no sign of ability: sold out of J. White's stable 3,400 gns Doncaster October Sales after second start. *Mrs A. Hamilton.* c— —

WHEEL TAPPER 6 ch.g. True Song–Spartan Clown (Spartan General) [1989/90 c20v*] well beaten in NH Flat races: made most from eighth and survived mistake at the last when winning maiden hunter chase at Folkestone in February easily by 15 lengths from Oakhurst Lad: will stay 3m: sure to improve. *H. Hutsby.* c**97** p

WHETCOMBE DEE-CEE 6 ch.g. Cheval–What A Vision (Golden Vision) [1989/90 F16m 17g] smallish gelding: half-brother to Irish maiden hurdler Leon Lorac (by Beau Chapeau): dam unraced: eighth of 15 in NH Flat race at Worcester in October: tailed off in novice hurdle at Devon & Exeter later in month. *T. B. Hallett.* —

WHICH WAY NOW 9 b.g. Mandamus–Manimay (Manicou) [1989/90 c24m^6 c24g^2 c24g^3] rangy ex-Irish gelding: winning point-to-pointer/hunter chaser: second of 3 to Bishopdale in handicap at Market Rasen in October: ran poorly later in month: stays 3m: possibly unsuited by heavy going, acts on any other. *R. Champion.* c**96**

WHIFFLER 8 b.g. Whiffenpoof–China Seal (Chinese Lacquer) [1989/90 16g] workmanlike gelding: third foal: half-brother to a poor animal: dam, half-sister to winning chaser Seal-Sprite, tried to refuse and was pulled up on only outing: started slowly, jumped deliberately and was always tailed off in novice hurdle at Wincanton in January (running subject of stewards inquiry): sold 2,700 gns Ascot July Sales. *Major R. H. Dening.* —

WHISKEY BLUES 5 b.g. Cure The Blues (USA)–Ozone (Auction Ring (USA)) [1989/90 16g^F 16m 16g 16g* 16f^3] leggy gelding: first sign of ability when winning novice handicap hurdle at Fakenham in April: creditable third in similar event at Ludlow later in month: will prove best at around 2m: acts on firm going: usually claimer ridden. *M. Skinner.* 80

WHISKEY GRAIN 8 b.g. Laurence O–Pry's Delight (Pry) [1989/90 24m^3 25f*] small, well-made gelding: handicap hurdler: claimer ridden, pushed along some way out and left in lead 2 out when winning at Cheltenham in October: not seen out again: suited by 3m: probably acts on any going. *G. A. Ham.* 112

WHISKEY MAC 7 gr.g. Roselier (FR)–San Remi (Chamier) [1989/90 16d 16s F20d 24v^F 16s^4 16v 22f^2 24g^3] ex-Irish gelding: sixth reported foal: brother to fair hurdler/chaser No One To Blame: dam winning hurdler: maiden hurdler: placed in handicaps at Kelso and Perth (amateur riders) in April: stays 3m: acts on any going: blinkered third, fifth and sixth starts: trained until after sixth start by F. Flood. *N. Miller.* 95

WHISPERING KNIGHT 12 b.g. Rugged Man–Reynoldstown Maid II (Blue Chariot) [1989/90 c24d^{ur}] lightly-raced novice hurdler/chaser: no worthwhile form. *R. H. Goldie.* c— —

WHISTLE BLOWER 5 ch.g. Le Bavard (FR)–Grangeclare Lady (Menelek) [1989/90 16g 16m] good sort: ninth foal: half-brother to fair 2m chaser Royal Radar (by Propeller) and fair hurdler/chaser Thinking Cap (by Bargello): dam never ran: jumped badly (and violently left at last 2 flights) but stayed on well without being knocked about when eighth in novice hurdle at Kempton in February: jumped better when well beaten at Wincanton following month. *Miss H. C. Knight.* —

WHISTLING EDDY 6 ch.g. Whistling Deer–Silver Tongue (Salvo) [1989/90 16m 20g^{pu}] rangy, unfurnished gelding: has scope: first foal: dam, of little account, from excellent jumping family: behind in NH Flat races: showed signs of ability in novice hurdle at Uttoxeter in December: pulled up when next seen out over 4 months later: sold 5,400 gns Ascot June Sales. *N. J. Henderson.* —

WHISTLING EDGE 7 ch.m. Whistling Deer–Seaville (Charlottesvilles Flyer) [1989/90 16f c19g^5 c16g^4 c20m^5 c20f^5 c16m^5] compact mare: winning hurdler: poor novice chaser: best form on a sound surface: was sometimes blinkered: dead. *K. S. Bridgwater.* c— —

WHISTLING TIGER 5 b.h. Whistling Deer–San Estrella (Star Gazer) [1989/90 16g^2 24g^3 21d 20s 20s^5 24m^5] leggy, lightly-made horse: fair hurdler: 116

best effort when third at Worcester in December: stays 3m: acts on good to firm and dead ground (seems unsuited by very soft). *D. Burchell.*

WHITCOMBE WARRIOR 4 b.g. Tina's Pet–Minuetto (Roan Rocket) [1989/90 16s ur 17v6 16d] compact gelding: lightly-raced maiden on Flat: behind in juvenile hurdles at Newton Abbot and Wincanton in second half of season. *N. R. Mitchell.* —

WHITE CITY BOY 9 br.g. Arapaho–Field Money (Even Money) [1989/90 c24f4] workmanlike gelding: poor walker: behind in NH Flat race and a maiden hurdle: fairly useful point-to-pointer, winner in March: kept on one pace when 16 lengths fourth behind Deer Crest in novice hunter chase at Ascot in March (finished lame): will be suited by a thorough test of stamina. *J. R. Newton.* c88 —

WHITEHOUSE GEM 7 ch.m. Amboise–Golden Pinelopi (Sovereign Lord) [1989/90 16f3 16f3 19h3] smallish, workmanlike mare: poor novice hurdler: beaten before 3 out when well below form over 19f in August: acts on firm going. *Miss S. J. Wilton.* 86

WHITE LINEN 4 ch.f. Nishapour (FR)–In The Clover (Meadow Mint (USA)) [1989/90 16v 16g 16d3 16g ur 16d5 16s a16g] ex-Irish filly: half-sister to 4 winners, including fairly useful 6f to 1¼m winner Music Lover and useful miler Santella Mac (both by Gay Fandango): dam won over 7f at 2 yrs in Ireland: placed over 11f on Flat: poor juvenile hurdler: blinkered sixth start (trained until after then by M. O'Toole). *N. A. Smith.* 87

WHITE RIVER 4 ch.c. Pharly (FR)–Regain (Relko) [1989/90 16g2 16g 16d* 16m* 16f] compact colt: won conditional jockeys selling hurdle at Ludlow (bought in 4,600 gns) and a juvenile claimer at Wincanton in March: ran poorly final start: will stay beyond 2m: acts on good to firm and dead ground: jumps well in the main: successful twice over extended 15f on Flat in July. *D. Haydn Jones.* 91

WHITERIVER GROVE 10 b.g. Tarqogan–Annaly's Last (Choral Society) [1989/90 24m3] poor winning hurdler: poor novice chaser: stays 3m: acts on any going: has worn blinkers and a visor: sold 2,200 gns Ascot November Sales. *P. J. Hobbs.* c— 73

WHITEWASH (USA) 5 ch.h. Majestic Light (USA)–Clear Ceiling (USA) (Bold Ruler) [1989/90 16m2 21s2 16m2 a20g* a20g* a20g* a20g* a18g* 20f pu] leggy, workmanlike horse: has been hobdayed: much improved hurdler: successful in 2 novice events and 2 handicaps at Southwell prior to winning valuable Fibresand Handicap Hurdle there in March by 4 lengths from Alaoui, leading from third: jumped none too fluently and was pulled up after mistake 3 out final start: gives impression he'll prove best at distances short of 21f: acts on good to firm and soft going: blinkered all bar first 2 starts of season: has raced with tongue tied down. *Mrs D. Haine.* 129

WHITSUNDAY 11 ch.g. Sunyboy–Boxing Day II (Doubtless II) [1989/90 c26f5 c22m F] tall, lengthy gelding: useful point-to-pointer (winner twice in February) and hunter chaser: prominent until 3 out when 21 lengths fifth behind Call Collect in Christies Foxhunter Chase at Cheltenham in March: close up when falling eleventh in Seagram Fox Hunters' Chase at Liverpool following month: stays 3m: acts on any going: usually jumps very well: reportedly broke blood vessel final start 1988/9. *M. E. Chamberlayne.* c**125**

WHITSUN EEL 4 br.g. Chukaroo–Jalna (Free Boy) [1989/90 F16f] first foal: dam novice selling hurdler: in rear in NH Flat race at Huntingdon in May: yet to race over hurdles. *J. A. Bennett.*

WHITWOOD 5 b.g. Hasty Word–Minetta (Neron) [1989/90 F16m 16d] strong gelding: half-brother to winning Irish hurdler Delvin Prince and a winner in Hong Kong (both by Saucy Kit): dam won over hurdles: eighth in NH Flat race at Market Rasen in September: bit backward, never dangerous when seventh behind Man of The West in novice hurdle on same course over 3 months later: will be suited by further. *C. J. Bell.* 75

WHOEVER 8 b.g. Flashback–Sealac (Sea Wolf) [1989/90 20d 22s 16g F a16g3 a20g5 a16g* 16g] leggy, lightly-made gelding: selling hurdler: won at Lingfield in March (no bid): well beaten in novice chase in 1988/9: form only at around 2m: acts on heavy going: usually blinkered in 1986/7: suitable mount for a claimer. *J. D. J. Davies.* c— 73

WHO IS HE 6 b.g. Smooth Stepper–Ross Lady (Master Buck) [1989/90 20g pu 20d 18d 20d 20g pu] tall, leggy gelding: second foal: half-brother to winning Irish point-to-pointer Far Senior (by Al Sirat): dam well beaten in Irish NH Flat races: —

bought for 16,000 gns Doncaster August (1988) Sales: tailed off in novice hurdles: sold 4,100 gns Doncaster Spring Sales. *D. Lee.*

WHO'LL SIOUX WHO 5 b.g. Rapid Pass–Susanella (Eborneezer) [1989/90
17v^{pu} 16s^{su}] no form in NH Flat race and 2 novice hurdles: dead. *R. J. Hodges.* —

WHYBROWS 4 b.g. Star Appeal–Haida (Astec) [1989/90 17m^{5}] half-brother to
winning selling hurdler Log Cabin (by Connaught): modest maiden on Flat, placed 77
over 12.3f: favourite, around 12 lengths fifth in juvenile hurdle at Cartmel in
August: sold 13,000 gns Doncaster September Sales. *D. Smith.*

WHY NOT FLOPSY 5 b.m. Quayside–Realinda (Realm) [1989/90 16g^{pu} 16d^{4}
16g^{pu}] workmanlike mare: little sign of ability: sold 1,700 gns Ascot February —
Sales. *Miss A. L. M. King.*

WHY SO HASTY 9 b.g. Proverb–Well Caught (Golden Vision) [1989/90 c24g^{2} c**125**
c20g^{4}] leggy, sparely-made ex-Irish gelding: third foal: dam placed in a point-
to-point in Ireland: winning point-to-pointer/hunter chaser: 3 lengths second to
Zuko in handicap at Kempton in December: last of 4 finishers behind Ten of
Spades at Ascot following month: stays 3m: acts on any going: tends to be on his
toes and rather edgy in preliminaries: sold to M. Chapman 4,200 gns Doncaster
March Sales. *N. J. Henderson.*

WHYTEMOUNT STAR 11 b.g. Jupiter Pluvius–Nashala (Sanctus II) c—
[1989/90 c21s^{F}] rather sparely-made ex-Irish gelding: in frame in NH Flat races —
and maiden hurdles: winning point-to-pointer: in frame in 2 hunter chases in 1988:
fell third in similar event in February. *A. L. C. Figg.*

WICINGA 4 ch.g. Viking (USA)–Lazy Belle (USA) (Drone) [1989/90 F16g 16d^{5}
16g^{pu}] leggy gelding: first foal: dam showed some ability on Flat: eighth in NH —
Flat race: bit backward, held up and never placed to challenge in juvenile hurdle at
Kelso in February: jumped right at third and pulled up before next at Hexham
following month. *J. S. Wilson.*

WICKET 5 b.m. Deep Run–Knock Off (Arctic Slave) [1989/90 F16s 16g 16m] IR
13,000 3-y-o: rather unfurnished non-thoroughbred mare: half-sister to several —
winners over jumps: dam, placed over hurdles, from good jumping family:
mid-division in novice hurdles at Kempton in February and Worcester in April. *M.
J. Wilkinson.*

WICKFIELD LAD 7 gr.g. Owen Anthony–Dumbella (Dumbarnie) [1989/90
16g 17m^{3} 20g 21f^{F} 19m^{6}] sturdy gelding: half-brother to winning hurdler Celtic 72
Bell (by Celtic Cone): dam won on Flat and over hurdles in April: poor novice
hurdler: best efforts at around 2m. *P. M. Cowley.*

WICK POUND 4 b.c. Niniski (USA)–Hors Serie (USA) (Vaguely Noble)
[1989/90 16s^{pu} 16g] sparely-made colt: brother to winning hurdler Cock Sparrow: — p
fair 1½m winner on Flat: sold out of R. Hern's stable 23,000 gns Newmarket
Autumn Sales: better for race, good headway from 4 out then eased once beaten
before second last when seventh to Dark Desire in juvenile hurdle at Newbury in
March: capable of better. *J. A. B. Old.*

WIDE RECEIVER 5 ch.g. Posse (USA)–Red Partridge (Solinus) [1989/90
17m 16g^{3} 16d] leggy gelding: placed in selling hurdle in 1988/9, and in novice 85
event at Catterick in January: found little and finished tired final start (gave
impression something possibly amiss). *Mrs S. A. Ward.*

WIGFORD LAD 6 ch.g. Charlie's Pal–Golden Festival (Naucetra) [1989/90
20f^{pu} 20m 17g 25g^{pu} 19m^{6} 17m^{pu}] workmanlike gelding: sixth foal by a thorough- —
bred stallion: dam won 2m chase: no sign of ability over hurdles, including in
seller: blinkered fifth start. *G. L. Roe.*

WIGGBURN 11 ch.g. Dalesa–Rayvox (Rise'n Shine II) [1989/90 c20g^{F} c20s^{pu} c**94**
c20d^{5} c22m c20f^{4} c26g^{5} c26m^{4}] close-coupled, rather lightly-built gelding: fairly —
useful chaser at his best: modest form in 1989/90, giving impression something
was amiss fourth start: suited by 2½m to 2¾m: seems best on ground no softer
than dead: has won 5 times at Ludlow. *Mrs A. R. Hewitt.*

WIGTOWN BAY 7 br.g. Young Nelson–Bonnie Bladnoch (Lord of Verona) c**125** p
[1989/90 c20f* c20g* c20g^{2} c20f* c20m^{F} c20f*] plain gelding: progressive chas- —
er: won handicaps at Uttoxeter (2), Wetherby and Doncaster in 1989/90: gained
last success on first-named course in April, beating Auntie Dot by 15 lengths:
suited by 2½m: acts on firm and dead going: has worn a crossed noseband. *J.
Mackie.*

WILD ARGOSY 11 ch.g. Lucifer (USA)–Mountain Sedge (Goldhill) [1989/90 c**92** x
c20m^{5} c20m^{4} c20m* c20g^{5} c20g c20m^{5} c20f^{ur}] workmanlike gelding: won selling —

handicap chase at Uttoxeter in April (no bid): ran poorly afterwards: stays 2½m but not 3m: seems to act on any going with possible exception of heavy: makes mistakes: blinkered last 2 outings: inconsistent. *T. T. Bill.*

WILD GEESE 12 b.g. Kashmir II–Ring Rose (Relko) [1989/90 16f^{pu} a20g^{pu}] small, lightly-made gelding: selling hurdler and poor novice chaser: stays 19f: probably acts on any going: makes mistakes. *D. C. Jermy.* c— x —

WILDNITE 6 b.g. Whealden–Melinite (Milesian) [1989/90 16s^{pu} 16d 21d^{pu}] compact gelding: brother to winning point-to-pointer Early Nite: no sign of ability in novice hurdles. *Mrs S. Oliver.* —

WILDWOOD 10 gr.g. Yankee Gold–Hop Step (Double Jump) [1989/90 c20v^{F} c20g^{4} c24g^{pu}] ex-Irish gelding: winning hurdler/chaser/point-to-pointer: 18½ lengths fourth to Southernair in handicap chase at Fontwell in December: stays 2½m: acts on heavy going and good to firm. *R. Curtis.* c**101** —

WILDWOOD MOSS 11 b.m. Ballymoss–Sylvan Path (Sovereign Path) [1989/90 c19f^{3} c16m^{6}] big, rangy mare: no worthwhile form over hurdles: poor maiden point-to-pointer/novice chaser: ran out second start 1988/9. *Mrs S. D. Williams.* c— —

WILL COWAN 5 b. or br.g. Tudor Diver–Pemrock (Saulingo) [1989/90 F16v^{5} F17d 16f 17m^{pu} 24g] third foal: dam ran once: no sign of ability over hurdles. *Miss M. K. Milligan.* —

WILLESDON (USA) 6 ch.h. Master Willie–Dona Maya (USA) (Reviewer (USA)) [1989/90 16f^{3} 17h*] sparely-made horse: has been hobdayed: reportedly finished lame when winning conditional jockeys handicap hurdle at Devon & Exeter in August: races only at around 2m: yet to race on heavy going, acts on any other. *A. Barrow.* 90

WILLIAM CRUMP 9 b.g. Guillaume Tell (USA)–Red Rag (Ragusa) [1989/90 26f* 25g^{F}] fair hurdler: won amateur riders handicap at Newton Abbot in August: winning chaser: stayed 3¼m: acted on any going: dead. *K. C. Bailey.* c— 119

WILLIAMSFIELD 5 gr.g. Kafu–Royal Bundle (Crowned Prince (USA)) [1989/90 16g 16d^{pu}] rather leggy, lengthy gelding: third living foal: half-brother to fairly useful 9f winner/novice hurdler Chance Ina Million (by Rarity): dam placed over 1m in Ireland: no sign of ability in novice hurdles at Kempton and Leicester. *M. Bradstock.* —

WILLIE BUTT 5 b.g. Silly Prices–Allez Stanwick (Goldhill) [1989/90 16f 16m 16f^{6}] sturdy gelding: poor form over hurdles: refused on debut (1988/9): tried to do so second outing 1989/90: wears crossed noseband. *Miss S. Williamson.* 64 §

WILLIE MCGARR (USA) 5 ch.g. Master Willie–Pay T V (USA) (T V Commercial (USA)) [1989/90 17h^{5} 16f^{2} 17f^{4} 16m^{3} 16h^{4} 16m^{3} 16f^{2} 16d^{4} 16g a20g^{6} 17m^{4} 16f 16f^{r}] sparely-made gelding: novice selling hurdler: left at start twelfth outing (visored), refused to race next time: form only at around 2m: acts on firm and dead going. *B. Palling.* 78 §

WILL I FLY 4 b.c. What A Guest–Monalda (FR) (Claude) [1989/90 F16m* F16m F16m^{3}] fourth living foal: half-brother to a winner in Italy by Persian Bold and fair 1½m winner/novice hurdler Twenty One Red (by Dunphy): dam won in Italy and is half-sister to Italian Derby winner Marracci: 25/1, won 19-runner NH Flat race at Sandown in March by 10 lengths: close third of 5 behind Ascot Lad on same course following month: yet to race over hurdles. *K. C. Bailey.*

WILLILOV 4 ch.g. Rabdan–Miss Love (Ragstone) [1989/90 16f] compact gelding: second foal: dam winning hurdler: little worthwhile form on Flat: in need of race, last of 9 finishers in juvenile hurdle at Kelso in October (eased once chance had gone). *Denys Smith.* —

WILL JAMES 4 ch.g. Raga Navarro (ITY)–Sleekit (Blakeney) [1989/90 16m 16d 16d 16d* 16f 16m* 17m^{2} 22f^{5}] strong gelding: won novice hurdles at Bangor (handicap) in March and Wincanton (amateur ridden) in April: good second at Newton Abbot in May: ran poorly over 2¾m: acts on good to firm and dead ground (well beaten on very firm): blinkered last 5 starts: trained until after second start by A. Turnell. *M. C. Pipe.* 95

WILLOWESQ 7 ch.g. Octogenarian–Tenon Saw (Songedor) [1989/90 20d^{pu} c16m^{3} c16m^{6} c16s^{3} c16s^{4} c16d c20f^{4} c24f 16f] lengthy, sparely-made gelding: poor novice hurdler/chaser: probably doesn't stay 3m: has worn a crossed noseband. *D. L. Williams.* c**74** —

WILLOW GORGE 7 ch.g. Hello Gorgeous (USA)–Willowy (Mourne) [1989/90 21m^{3} 22m^{F} 25f^{4} 24d^{5}] sparely-made gelding: modest hurdler: not seen out after November: probably stays 3m: acts on any going. *Miss B. Sanders.* 101

WILLOW HOLDING 5 b.g. Some Hand–Catherines April (Fez) [1989/90 F16d F17d] first living foal: dam winning point-to-pointer: mid-division in NH Flat races at Kelso and Carlisle: yet to race over hurdles or fences. *T. W. Donnelly.*

WILLOWSON 9 b.g. Vulcott–Goldie's Willow (Julia's Hamlet) [1989/90 20f^{3} 21f^{2} 20d^{4} 24m^{4}] leggy gelding: poor novice hurdler: no sign of ability in novice chases: stays 25f: acts on firm and good to soft going. *K. White.* c— 86

WILL'S BOUNTY 7 b.g. Tudor Treasure–Silva (Spartan General) [1989/90 F16m^{4} F16f* F16f 16g 20g^{pu} 16m 16m^{pu}] sparely-made gelding: first live foal: dam poor novice hurdler: won NH Flat race at Cheltenham in October: has shown some ability in novice hurdles: keen type, will prove best at 2m. *J. Colston.* —

WILL'S DREAM 6 b.g. Asdic–Quick Walk (Farm Walk) [1989/90 16g 16d 16d^{pu}] tall, leggy gelding: of little account. *J. Colston.* —

WILLSFORD 7 b.g. Beau Charmeur (FR)–Wish Again (Three Wishes) [1989/90 c20m^{4} c20d* c20d* c24s^{2} c24v^{F} c25f^{pu} c36g*] c**141** —

Mrs Pitman has picked up several bargains at Ballsbridge in recent years: Cash Is King, Dis Train, Royal Athlete, Vazon Bay and Willsford between them cost a total of only just over IR 80,000 guineas as three-year-olds. The last-named has proved particularly well bought for IR 6,000 guineas at the November Sale in 1986. Willsford showed useful form over hurdles, notably when winning the Racegoers Club County Handicap Hurdle at Cheltenham in 1989. The winner of five of his eight completed races over fences, he picked up another valuable prize in the Taylorsteel Midlands Grand National over four and a half miles at Uttoxeter in April. Always prominent, Willsford quickened clear with Royal Battery approaching the final turn and looked to be going the better when that rival's fall at the fifth last left him with a commanding advantage. Willsford maintained a fifteen-length lead over runner-up Pembrokeshire Lad to the line, the latter eight lengths clear of The Langholm Dyer and two other finishers. However, he had been pushed along from halfway up the straight, giving the

Taylorsteel Midlands Grand National, Uttoxeter—
Willsford (foreground) lands this quite valuable prize

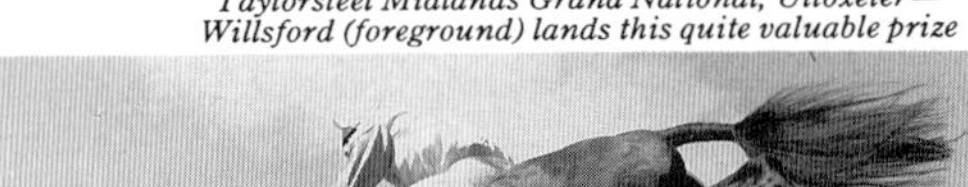

impression he might have been coming to the end of his tether. Willsford had not previously shaped as though he would necessarily be suited by extreme distances. He had been campaigned principally at two miles both over hurdles and as a novice chaser. And two successes in two-and-a-half-mile handicap chases in January had shown his turn of speed to good effect. At Warwick, Willsford had quickened into a clear lead from the fourth last for an easy fifteen-length win over King of The Lot. In a quite valuable event at Cheltenham a fortnight later he was always travelling strongly, quickened well when asked for his effort approaching the second last and prevailed by a length from Norton's Coin. The longer trip couldn't be blamed for Willsford's lack of success when moved up to three miles. He never looked to be travelling well enough to challenge when a below-form second at Leicester in February. And he was beaten soon after halfway and eventually pulled up in the Ritz Club National Hunt Handicap Chase at Cheltenham the following month, seemingly unsuited by the firm ground and having reportedly broken a blood vessel too. In between, Willsford was a most unfortunate loser in the Greenall Whitley Gold Cup Chase at Haydock. Having made smooth headway through the field to jump into the lead at the second last, he was two lengths clear when knuckling over on landing over the final fence. Though Rinus ran on strongly to hold off The Thinker we doubt he would have caught Willsford who had looked to be travelling strongly when coming to grief.

Willsford (b.g. 1983)	Beau Charmeur (FR) (b 1968)	Le Fabuleux (ch 1961)	Wild Risk
			Anguar
		Cymbale (br 1963)	Soleil Levant
			Blue Kiss
	Wish Again (b or br 1972)	Three Wishes (ch 1957)	Straight Deal
			Fairy Queen
		Winged Sprite (b 1954)	The Phoenix
			Sprite

Willsford's two-year-younger brother, now named Vicompt de Valmont, was bought for IR 40,000 guineas at Fairyhouse in 1989 and is in training with Henderson. No doubt his purchase price was influenced by Willsford's recent success in the County Hurdle and that of French Goblin, first foal of a winning sister to his dam, in the Youngmans Long Walk Hurdle at Ascot earlier in that season. The unraced Wish Again's only foal prior to Willsford, Doctor Busby, also by Beau Charmeur, was a fair winner over hurdles and fences in Ireland. Wish Again is a half-sister to several winners out of the staying maiden Winged Sprite, notably the fairly useful chaser Sandy Sprite, runner-up in the Welsh Grand National in 1971. Two-mile winner Sprite bred several winners, including the very useful stayer Avril Spirit, and was a half-sister to the successful hurdler Tackler, dam of the 1965 Irish Grand National winner Splash. Willsford looks sure to enhance the family's record further. He has the makings of a smart chaser and his good turn of foot should see his winning more races in all but the best company. His seeming effectiveness at two and a half miles to four and a half miles will make Willsford easier than most to place, though he probably needs give in the ground. A workmanlike gelding, he wore blinkers for the first time when winning the County Hurdle and has worn them ever since. *Mrs J. Pitman.*

WILLY MAC 9 b.g. Ancient Monro–Minny Mouse (Comandeer) [1989/90 16v 17g] compact gelding: no form in novice hurdles: pulled hard when visored once. *J. E. Dixon.* —

WILSARUTH 8 ch.g. Winden–Spanish Ruler (Indian Ruler) [1989/90 c26f^4] c— leggy, close-coupled gelding: selling hurdler: won a point-to-point in 1989: over — 30 lengths fourth to John Sam in hunter chase at Cheltenham in April: stays 3m in slowly-run race: acts on soft going: sweated up second start 1987/8. *B. A. Hall.*

WILTSHIRE YEOMAN 10 ch.g. Derrylin–Ribo Pride (Ribero) [1989/90 **c90** c16d^4 c16g^6 16g c17d^3 c17d^5 c16g^3 c20g^4] leggy, angular gelding: handicap — hurdler: moderate novice over fences, best effort in 1989/90 when third in handicap at Stratford in March on sixth start: best form at around 2m: acts on heavy going: has won for an amateur and a claimer. *P. Hayward.*

WILY YEOMAN 11 b.g. Little Buskins–Scrahan (Wily Trout) [1989/90 c26g^ur] strong, good-looking gelding: carries plenty of condition: fairly useful chaser in 1987/8: has since won 7 point-to-points, including 2 in 1990: unseated rider sixth in hunter chase in March: better suited by 2½m than 2m and should stay 3m: acts on any going: seems best forcing the pace. *Mrs S. N. J. Embiricos.* c— —

WIMBLEBALL 10 b. or br.h. Sunrising–Polly Wall (Live Spirit) [1989/90 c24m^ur c24m^ur c25g^pu c16s^6 c19d^6 c21v^ro c17v^2 c21s^pu c27v^pu c25m^4 c18f* c16h^3 c21m^4 c26f^2 c26m^ur] small horse: handicap chaser: won at Taunton in March: made running and was 2 lengths clear of eventual wide-margin winner Biloxi Blues when unseating rider last at Newton Abbot in May: effective at 2m and stays 3¼m: acts on any going: has worn a tongue strap: ran out sixth outing. *J. R. Payne.* c91 + —

WIMBLEBALL LASS 5 b.m. Wimbleball–Idson Lass (Levanter) [1989/90 17m^ur] first foal: dam winning hurdler: behind when unseating rider second in novice hurdle at Devon & Exeter in March. *J. R. Payne.* —

WIMBORNE 5 ro.h. What A Guest–Khadija (Habat) [1989/90 17m 16m^6 16g^4] leggy, workmanlike horse: won two 1m sellers on Flat in 1989: best effort over hurdles fourth in maiden at Edinburgh in December (pulled hard). *R. Bastiman.* 84

WINABUCK 7 ch.g. Buckskin (FR)–Mistic Breeze (Master Owen) [1989/90 22d^ur 20g^5 16v^5 16s^4 20g^3] rangy, workmanlike, chasing type: good third in novice handicap hurdle at Uttoxeter in April: will stay beyond 2½m: best efforts of season on good ground: tends to sweat. *R. Dickin.* 88

WINART 12 br.g. Scottish Rifle–Alice (Parthia) [1989/90 20v^ur 18v^5] compact gelding: handicap hurdler: well below form in 1989/90: stays 21f: suited by give in the ground: has been tried in blinkers: good mount for a claimer: has run creditably when sweating. *P. R. Rodford.* —

WINDBOUND LASS 7 ch.m. Crofter (USA)–Nevilles Cross (USA) (Nodouble (USA)) [1989/90 17f^2 16f 16f^3 16f^3 16g 16f^2] leggy, sparely-made mare: fairly useful hurdler: best effort when ¾-length second to Sybillin in Swinton Insurance Trophy (Handicap) at Haydock in May on final start: best at 2m: acts on any going, but goes particularly well on a firm surface: usually claimer ridden nowadays. *R. J. Holder.* 133

WINDMEDE 6 gr.g. Windjammer (USA)–Easymede (Runnymede) [1989/90 16d^5 20d^pu] leggy gelding: no worthwhile form over hurdles: seems not to stay 2½m: sold 900 gns Ascot February Sales. *J. B. Sayers.* —

WINDMILL COTTAGE 6 b.g. Coded Scrap–Cuckoos Cottage (Vimadee) [1989/90 c25f^F] third foal: dam never ran: yet to complete course in point-to-points: fell second in maiden hunter chase at Cartmel in May. *T. M. Robson.* c—

WINDRUSH SONG 9 b.m. True Song–Aftab Kuh (Coronation Year) [1989/90 c25m^F] tall, sparely-made mare: selling hurdler: has failed to complete course in 3 outings in steeplechases: seems not to stay beyond 2½m: acts on good to firm going and possibly unsuited by a yielding surface: blinkered final start in 1987/8. *W. E. Dudley.* c— —

WINDSOR PARK (USA) 4 br.c. Bold Forbes (USA)–Round Tower (High Top) [1989/90 a16g^2 18g a16g^2] claimed out of W. Hastings-Bass's stable £18,000 after winning 1¼m claimer on Flat in October: won 1½m handicap later in month: modest form when runner-up in juvenile hurdles at Lingfield in December and January (2 ran): likely to prove best at 2m. *R. J. O'Sullivan.* 86

WINDWARD ARIOM 4 ch.g. Pas de Seul–Deja Vu (FR) (Be My Guest (USA)) [1989/90 16f^ur 17m^3 16f 16f^5 a16g^2 16g^3 16f^5 16m] close-coupled, light-framed gelding: plating-class maiden on Flat: poor juvenile hurdler: has run well for a claimer: usually races freely up with pace. *D. H. Topley.* 87

WINDY ASH 7 ch.m. Windjammer (USA)–Bryony Ash (Ribero) [1989/90 16f^4] leggy mare: novice selling hurdler: fourth of 5 in handicap at Hexham in May. *M. C. Pipe.* 65

WINGCOMMANDER EATS 5 b.g. Nishapour (FR)–Rhodie Blake (Blakeney) [1989/90 20g a20g^4 a16g^2 a16s* a20g^3 a16g* 16d^4] former selling hurdler: won handicap hurdles at Lingfield in January (conditional jockeys) and February (claimer ridden), latter by 20 lengths: best at around 2m: probably acts on any going. *J. Joseph.* 95

WINGED FOOT 4 b.f. Tap On Wood–Goirtin (Levmoss) [1989/90 16m^4 16g 16m^4 16g 16g^4 16d* 17g^2 20s] small, rather angular filly: maiden on Flat: won conditional jockeys selling handicap hurdle at Sedgefield in January (no bid): 82

seems not to stay 2½m: acts on dead going: usually ridden by 7-lb claimer. *J. Parkes.*

WINGETTS 14 b. or br.g. Mugatpura–Shining Blade (Sayajirao) [1989/90 c26f^wo c18g^4] strong, medium-sized gelding: poor chaser nowadays: walked over at Fontwell in October: stays 21f: acts on any going. *Miss L. Bower.* c— —

WING OF FREEDOM 6 ch.m. Troy–Marablue (Bold Lad (IRE)) [1989/90 20f^pu] staying maiden on Flat: tailed off when pulled up in novice hurdle in August. *A. P. James.* —

WINGSPAN (USA) 6 b.g. Storm Bird (CAN)–Miss Renege (USA) (Riva Ridge (USA)) [1989/90 c16d^2 c17g^F c16v^F c20v* c20m* c21m* c16f^2] c**140** —

Unlike his owner, ex-England goalkeeper Peter Shilton, the improving young chaser Wingspan is usually seen up front, dictating the pace in customary fashion for a runner from the stable. He takes some catching, too, and has won nine of his thirteen completed starts since joining Pipe midway through the 1987/8 season. A fairly useful hurdler, Wingspan has progressed well over fences, so that on his final outing at Chepstow in May he was beaten only two and a half lengths in a match at level weights by Panto Prince who looked to have little more to spare at the finish. Wingspan is a similar type to Panto Prince, a keen sort and a bold jumper. He suffered for jumping a little too boldly when falling in the lead at the fifth-last fence in a handicap at Newbury in December. However, when ridden with more restraint, seemingly to curb such extravagance, at Chepstow the following month Wingspan jumped with less fluency than usual. He made a mistake three out and eventually fell at the last when poised to challenge. Allowed to stride on once again in his later races Wingspan jumped well in the main, though slightly to his right on occasions.

At this stage of his career, Wingspan is less of a stayer than Panto Prince has turned out to be. Two and a half miles on heavy ground at Chepstow seemed to stretch his stamina to the limit in a minor event in February. Given a breather at the end of the back straight, Wingspan looked to be travelling comfortably in the lead two out but after landing slightly flat-footed over the last he had to be driven quite firmly to maintain a length advantage over Formula One to the line. Wingspan put up much better performances over a similar trip on good to firm ground subsequently. In a

Weathercall Rising Stars Chase, Chepstow—Wingspan holds off Formula One

handicap at Wolverhampton in March, he drew eight lengths clear of closest pursuer Baluchi from the second last without having to be at all hard pressed. In a similar event at Newton Abbot on Easter Monday, he strolled home fifteen lengths clear of Shannagary. Wingspan lost no caste in a six-length defeat by Katabatic over two miles in an intermediate chase at Nottingham in December, the pair finishing a distance clear.

Wingspan (USA) (b.g. 1984)	Storm Bird (CAN) (b 1978)	Northern Dancer (b 1961)	Nearctic
			Natalma
		South Ocean (b 1967)	New Providence
			Shining Sun
	Miss Renege (USA) (b 1979)	Riva Ridge (b 1969)	First Landing
			Iberia
		Allofthem (ch 1964)	Bagdad
			Gal I Love

Wingspan was originally bought for 175,000 dollars at Keeneland as a yearling, less than half the average for Storm Bird's second crop which also included Indian Skimmer and Bluebird. There are some good Flat winners in his family. Miss Renege, a five-furlong winner at two years, is a half-sister to the minor stakes winner Two Rings, dam of 1979 Champion Stakes winner Northern Baby and two stakes winners in the States. The next dam Allofthem won four races at up to a mile. She is a sister to Santa Anita Derby-second Sabre Mountain and half-sister to several winners, including Homespun, the dam of the American sire Sportin' Life. Gal I Loved is an unraced sister to Champion American two-year-old of 1957 Nadir. Miss Renege has since produced a sister to Wingspan, successful at around four furlongs as a two-year-old in 1987, and a half-brother by Dixieland Band, called Mister Dixieland, bought for 110,000 dollars as a two-year-old in 1989 and imported to Britain. Wingspan failed to live up to his purchase price or breeding on the Flat and was sold out of Douieb's stable for 9,200 guineas at Newmarket after being placed once over seven furlongs as a three-year-old. A smallish, workmanlike gelding, he has taken so well to jumping he should win more races. Though he has looked a difficult ride on occasions—he usually wore a dropped noseband in the latest season—Wingspan rarely runs a moderate race. He acts on any going. *M. C. Pipe.*

WINK GULLIVER 6 gr.g. Strong Gale–Pale Maid (Rise'n Shine II) [1989/90 c16m* c16m^{2} c17g^{4} c16s* c16m^{5} c16m] sturdy, good sort: handicap hurdler: made all, despite several mistakes, to win Daniel Homes Novices' Chase at Ascot in February gamely by 5 lengths from Western Dandy: successful earlier in novice event at Taunton: creditable fifth to Katabatic in valuable handicap at Cheltenham in March, weakening after a mistake 2 out: best form at 2m: acts on heavy and good to firm going: seemed unsuited by track at Fontwell final start 1987/8: needs to brush up his jumping. *D. R. C. Elsworth.* c**125** —

WINNIE THE WITCH 6 b.m. Leading Man–Star Ruler (Indian Ruler) [1989/90 16d^{F} 20d* 21s 21d^{2}] shallow-girthed mare: handicap hurdler: won at Leicester in January: good second at Warwick in March: stays 21f: acts on dead going: claimer ridden when successful. *K. S. Bridgwater.* 109

WINNING DANCER 7 b.g. Dance In Time (CAN)–Ravenshead (Charlottown) [1989/90 16s 16s 18g^{5} 16g^{3} 16m^{3} 16g^{4}] sparely-made gelding: winning hurdler: in frame in 2 handicaps at Fakenham and a claimer at Perth: ran in sellers earlier: best at 2m: acts on heavy and good to firm going. *Miss L. Bower.* 82

WINSOR BOND 12 ch.g. Jimmy Reppin–Romany Girl (Worden II) [1989/90 c26d^{pu} c24m^{3}] lengthy, workmanlike gelding: poor chaser: stays 3¼m: acts on good to firm and dead going: has won for an amateur. *J. M. Bukovets.* c85 —

WINTER MEASURE 10 b.g. Pamroy–Funny Baby (Fable Amusant) [1989/90 c16m* c16m^{2}] tall gelding: poor chaser nowadays: won at Worcester in September: finished lame when running creditably following month: stays 2½m: probably acts on any going: sketchy jumper: didn't go through with his effort once in 1988/9: one to be wary of. *Mrs G. E. Jones.* c95 § —

WINTERS SOVEREIGN 10 br.g. Sovereign King–Wintersbrig (New Brig) [1989/90 c25f*] strong, good-bodied gelding: poor novice hurdler: sold 2,100 gns Doncaster August Sales: won point-to-points in February and April and maiden c83 —

Daniel Homes Novices' Chase, Ascot—Wink Gulliver is clear of Western Dandy at the last

hunter chase at Hexham (by 6 lengths from Dalton Dandy) in May: stays 25f: seems to act on any going: has worn blinkers. *N. E. H. Hargreave.*

WINTER STORM 5 b.g. Formidable (USA)–December Rose (Silly Season) [1989/90 16f^{pu} 16s] sturdy gelding: seems not to have taken to hurdling: sold out of T. Barron's stable 1,600 gns Doncaster October Sales after first outing. *J. K. M. Oliver.* —

WINTER WONDER 5 b.m. Sunyboy–Chancebeg (Random Shot) [1989/90 F16f] first foal: dam, half-sister to several winners including good 2m horses Drumikill and Jabeg, behind in novice hurdles: tailed-off last of 23 in NH Flat race at Newbury in October: yet to race over hurdles or fences. *L. C. Corbett.*

WIRE LASS 6 b.m. New Brig–Anotherwire (Cagirama) [1989/90 22g^{pu} 20s^{F} 22d 20d] third foal: dam quite a moderate staying hurdler: well beaten in novice hurdles. *J. A. Hellens.* —

WISCONSIN 6 b.m. Mummy's Game–Montana (Mossborough) [1989/90 c21f^{5} 25m^{4} 21f^{4} c16g^{6} c24g^{2} c21s^{4} c27d^{4} c25m^{4} c25g c33d c21d^{pu} c25f^{5} c24f^{4} 25f* 23f^{3}] lengthy, sparely-made mare: won handicap hurdle at Cartmel in May: poor novice chaser: stays 25f: acts on firm and dead ground: sometimes visored (was when successful): tends to sweat: moderate jumper. *M. C. Chapman.* c**74** x 85

WISECOURSE (USA) 6 b.g. Irish River (FR)–Strigida (Habitat) [1989/90 a16g^{5} 16m] workmanlike gelding: poor novice selling hurdler: blinkered fourth start 1988/9: sold 1,500 gns Ascot December Sales: resold 1,450 gns Ascot June Sales. *C. C. Trietline.* 68

WISE CRACKER 9 b.g. Hittite Glory–Exquisite (Exbury) [1989/90 c16f^{pu} c17m^{5} c20f^{3} c20f^{3} c16m^{2} c21g^{pu}] lightly-made gelding: poor chaser: yet to show he stays much beyond 2m: acts on soft and good to firm going: usually blinkered or visored: has won for a claimer: changed hands 4,600 gns Doncaster September Sales: trained until after fourth outing by P. Blockley: subsequently off course nearly 7 months. *B. Richmond.* c85 —

WISE CUSTOMER 6 ch.g. Deep Run–Clontinty Queen (Laurence O) [1989/90 16g⁴ 20g*] well-made, compact ex-Irish gelding: type to make a chaser: fourth foal: brother to 2 winning jumpers, including fair staying chaser Tom Bir: dam unraced half-sister to fairly useful hurdler How Brave: won 2 point-to-points prior to finishing second in NH Flat race in 1989: sold out of P. P. Hogan's stable 50,000 gns Doncaster Spring (1989) Sales: showed promise in novice hurdle at Wincanton in February, and 2 months later won similar event at Bangor by 2½ lengths from Gentleman's Jig, quickening to lead 3 out: stays 2½m: sure to improve further and should win more races. *A. Turnell.* 97 p

WISE GAMBOL 11 b.g. Gambling Debt–Nutkin (Roan Rocket) [1989/90 c21g³ c16d⁵ c16g*] leggy gelding: winning point-to-pointer: won hunter chases at Fakenham in 1988/9 and in April (beat Prince Nepal 7 lengths): stays 3m: acts on any going. *Simon J. Stearn.* c**102**

WISE TIMES 6 b.m. Young Generation–Ballinkillen (Levmoss) [1989/90 18g 16mpu 16f 17mpu] strong, close-coupled mare: lightly-raced novice hurdler: trained until after second start by D. Elsworth (off course nearly 5 months afterwards and bit backward on return). *C. C. Elsey.* —

WISHLON (USA) 7 b.g. Lyphard's Wish (FR)–Swiss Swish (USA) (Wajima (USA)) [1989/90 16g⁵ 16f⁴ 16g] tall, leggy gelding: smart hurdler: successful 3 times in 1988/9, notably in New Year's Day Hurdle at Windsor: best effort of 1989/90 when fifth behind Dare Say in handicap at Sandown in November: gave impression next 2 starts needs stiffer test of stamina: acts on firm ground (ran moderately on soft): often claimer ridden: has been successful when sweating badly. *R. V. Smyth.* 151

WITCHES RUN 6 ch.m. Deep Run–Nora Grany (Menelek) [1989/90 18g] workmanlike mare: showed some promise over hurdles in 1988/9: second favourite but better for race, ran moderately at Fontwell in October and not seen out again: should be suited by further than 2m. *P. J. Hobbs.* —

WITERO 7 b.g. Heroic Air–Wits End (Salerno (USA)) [1989/90 24f⁶] lightly raced and no sign of ability over hurdles: placed in point-to-points in 1990. *Miss Z. A. Green.* —

WITH GODS HELP 6 br.g. Godswalk (USA)–Social Partner (Sparkler) [1989/90 c18g* c16f³ c16d² c16s* 16g⁶ c17sF c16d* c18g² c16s³ c16spu c16f⁴ c17m* c16g* c16f* c16g² c16m⁴] leggy ex-Irish gelding: first foal: dam of little account: winning hurdler: won novice chase at Kilbeggan, minor chase at Listowel and handicap at Naas in first half of season: subsequently showed fairly useful form in handicaps in Britain and won at Newton Abbot, Stratford (amateur ridden) and Ascot (beat Hogmanay 2 lengths in quite valuable event despite running in snatches and hanging badly left): stays 2¼m: successful on soft ground but best form over fences on a firm surface: trained until after tenth start by T. Carberry. *C. P. E. Brooks.* c**125** —

WITHOUT A DOUBT 8 br.g. Prominer–Shinaro (Straight Deal) [1989/90 16g⁵ 16g⁵ 16mbd] good-topped gelding who carries condition: will make a chaser: fairly useful hurdler: around 5 lengths fifth to Atlaal in Bic Razor Lanzarote Handicap Hurdle at Kempton in January, finishing best of all: close up but under pressure when brought down 2 out in William Hill Imperial Cup at Sandown in March: likely to prove best at around 2m: acts on heavy going: usually ridden by claimer. *T. P. Tate.* 127

WITHY BANK 8 b.g. Blakeney–Chiltern Lass (High Hat) [1989/90 20g⁵ 22g 24g² 24g⁶ 24d³ c28g² c25g² c24m* c33dpu] medium-sized gelding: fairly useful hurdler/chaser: won handicap chase at Newcastle in March by 10 lengths from Nautical Joke, jumping deliberately in early stages, but better after reminders at the eighth: stays well: acts on good to firm and dead going: has edged left under pressure and appeared to idle. *M. H. Easterby.* c**128** 128

WIZARD OF WAS 7 b.m. Anax–Pat's Fancy (Falcon) [1989/90 c16mur c20vbd] moderate novice hurdler: departed early both starts over fences: stays 2½m: seems to act on any going: looks a difficult ride. *Alf Watson.* c— — §

WIZZARD ARTIST 5 b.h. Electric–Polly Darling (Darling Boy) [1989/90 20m* 20g⁶] won novice hurdle at Plumpton in November: collapsed and died on same course following month: stayed 2½m: acted on good to firm ground. *M. J. Haynes.* 108

WOBBLY 7 gr.g. Billion (USA)–Guilsway (Track Spare) [1989/90 16gpu 20fpu] plain, good-bodied gelding: second foal: brother to a poor animal: dam won a —

Cara Compaq Computer Handicap Chase, Leopardstown—last win for the ill-fated Wolf of Badenoch

novice hurdle: tailed off when pulled up in 2 outings over hurdles in May. *J. Carden.*

WODEHOUSE 5 b.g. Sunnyboy–Flammula (Wrekin Rambler) [1989/90 16m^F 16g^5] rangy gelding: brother to winning chaser Pippahmint Lass and half-brother to winning chaser/point-to-pointer Trust To Luck (by Mandamus): dam fair hurdler: made mistakes when around 20 lengths fifth to Air Commander in novice hurdle at Worcester in March, staying on to be nearest at finish: should improve. *Andrew Turnell.* 82 p

WOLFHANGAR 8 ch.g. Decent Fellow–Vaguely Vulgan (Vulgan) [1989/90 c16d c16m* c16g^pu] lengthy, workmanlike gelding: fair chaser: won handicap at Nottingham in November by 6 lengths from Glebe Spinney, despite idling on run-in: pulled up lame next time: well beaten when tried over 2½m: acts on good to firm and dead going: takes a good hold: rather sketchy jumper. *C. P. E. Brooks.* c**120** —

WOLF OF BADENOCH 9 b.g. Giolla Mear–Casacello (Punchinello) [1989/90 c16s^2 c18g* c16d* 16d^3 16g c16v^3] tall, light-bodied Irish gelding: very useful hurdler: very smart front-running chaser, one of best chasers in Ireland in recent years: successful under 12-0 in handicaps at Fairyhouse and Leopardstown (beat Feroda 6 lengths) in December: best at 2m: acted on heavy going: genuine: dead. *J. E. Mulhern, Ireland.* c**161** —

WOLVER DAN 8 b.g. Wolver Hollow–Danilla (USA) (Turn-To) [1989/90 c21d^5 c24g^4 c16d^pu c25g^6 c21d^pu c24g^6 c24f^5] rangy gelding: poor novice hurdler/chaser: best effort over 3m on heavy ground: makes mistakes. *J. P. Leigh.* c**76** x —

WOLVER GEM 4 b.g. Wolver Hollow–Perle's Fashion (Sallust) [1989/90 16g 16g 16d 17m^6 18h^3] smallish gelding: maiden on Flat: poor plater over hurdles: blinkered last outing: sold privately out of Mrs G. Reveley's stable 1,000 gns Doncaster January Sales after first start. *K. A. Linton.* 67

WONDER BEE 7 ch.g. Grandiose–Honey Wonder (Winden) [1989/90 c20d^ur c16m^4 16f^5 16s^2 16m^5 16f^3 c17m^3 c17f^2] handicap hurdler/chaser: below form in amateur riders event and conditional jockeys race last 2 outings over hurdles: generally spoils his chance with mistakes over fences: should stay further than 17f: probably acts on any going: blinkered second outing. *D. R. C. Elsworth.* c**111** x 113

WONDERINE (FR) 5 br.m. The Wonder (FR)–Tarpeienne (FR) (Tarbes (FR)) [1989/90 21f* 17g* 18g* 20m* 21d^pu] tall, leggy ex-French mare: fourth 117

foal: half-sister to French Flat winners Township and Baby Ship (both by Brinkmanship): dam in frame over 9f in France: winner at up to 1¾m on Flat: made most to win novice hurdles at Ludlow, Devon & Exeter and Fontwell (mares event) in October and Uttoxeter in November: stayed 21f: acted on firm ground and was possibly unsuited by heavy: dead. *M. C. Pipe.*

WONDER MAN (FR) 5 ch.g. The Wonder (FR)–Juvenilia (FR) (Kashmir II) [1989/90 16g* 16g6 16g5 16f6 16f4 16f] tall gelding: type to make a chaser: useful hurdler: won handicap at Kempton in December: ran creditably next start, but moderately afterwards: barely stays 2m when conditions are testing: acts on soft going, possibly unsuited by a firm surface: races freely: usually jumps well: sweating and on toes fifth outing. *Mrs J. Pitman.* 134

WONT BE GONE LONG 8 b.g. The Parson–Most Seen (Mustang) [1989/90 c25f* c24g c25g4 c25mpu c22m* c29f4] leggy, sparely-made gelding: useful chaser: first race for over 2 months, won John Hughes Memorial Trophy Chase (Handicap) at Liverpool in April by 4 lengths from Villierstown: 15 lb out of handicap, ran very well when 12 lengths fourth behind Mr Frisk in Whitbread Gold Cup at Sandown later in month: successful early in season in BMW Series Final (Handicap) at Cheltenham, beating Bonnie Artist by ¾ length: stays very well: suited by a firm surface: goes well fresh: sound jumper. *N. J. Henderson.* c**136** —

WOODCHESTER GLEN 6 b.g. Furry Glen–Brave Wish (Brave Invader (USA)) [1989/90 16g 16f5 16m3 a16g2 16m2 16f* 16g4 20g* 20g2 16g* 20f a16g3] lengthy, workmanlike gelding: won novice hurdles at Edinburgh in December and January and at Hexham in March: ran creditably in handicap at Southwell final start: has won over 2½m but may prove best at around 2m: acts on firm ground: suitable mount for a claimer. *A. Fowler.* 99

WOODENBRIDGE 7 ch.g. Thatch (USA)–December Blossom (Condorcet (FR)) [1989/90 16g a20g2 17m] leggy gelding: winning selling hurdler: stayed 2½m: acted on good to soft going: occasionally blinkered, including when successful: dead. *O. O'Neill.* 82

Mrs Shirley Robins' "Wonder Man"

John Hughes Memorial Trophy, Liverpool—Wont Be Gone Long (No. 13) and Villierstown dispute the lead ahead of Golden Minstrel; New Halen is the riderless horse

WOODGATE 9 ch.g. Quayside–Owen Money (Master Owen) [1989/90 c24g5 c29d5 c29s* c30v4 c29d4] smallish, sparely-made gelding: useful chaser: led 7 out and eased close home when winning handicap at Warwick in February by 5 lengths from Roll-A-Joint, pair long way clear: better subsequent effort on same course final start: stays well: acts on heavy going. *Capt. T. A. Forster.* c**135** —

WOODKNOT 5 b.g. Tap On Wood–Sister Connie (St Paddy) [1989/90 16h3 16f3 20g4 16d* 20gF a24g4] small, angular gelding: selling hurdler: won at Stratford in December (bought in 2,600 gns): clear when falling 3 out at Plumpton following month: probably stays 2½m (well beaten over 3m): acts on firm and dead going: blinkered final start 1988/9: has looked none too keen under pressure. *F. Jordan.* 97

WOODLAND GENERATOR 11 ch.g. True Song–Dainty (Epaulette) [1989/90 c24d6 c21mpu] rather sparely-made gelding: winning hurdler/chaser: ran poorly in 2 races in November: stays 3¼m: yet to show he acts on extremes of going: poor jumper of fences: visored nowadays. *P. A. Pritchard.* c— x —

WOODLAND RETREAT 10 ch.m. Country Retreat–Woodland Wedding (Woodcut) [1989/90 21m c22mbd c21d5 c22d6 c22d2 c20d3 c16f2] long-backed, plain mare: no sign of ability over hurdles: won a point-to-point in 1987: saddle slipped at the last when 2 lengths second to Master Rajh in novice handicap chase at Wolverhampton in March on final outing: stays 2¾m: acts on firm and dead ground: ridden by 7-lb claimer last 5 starts. *J. A. Pickering.* c**85** —

WOODLANDS GENHIRE 5 ch.g. Celtic Cone–Spartella (Spartan General) [1989/90 16g 16d 25dpu 21d] leggy, workmanlike gelding: dam useful hunter chaser: no sign of ability in novice hurdles. *P. A. Pritchard.* —

WOODLANDS GENPOWER 8 b.g. Celtic Cone–April Sovereign (Lucky Sovereign) [1989/90 22g 21s4 24m c26gpu 26mpu] compact gelding: handicap hurdler and novice chaser: no form in 1989/90: stays 25f: acts on heavy going: visored last 2 outings 1988/9 (well beaten). *P. A. Pritchard.* c— —

WOODLANDS GREY 4 gr.c. Nishapour (FR)–Topling (High Top) [1989/90 16f6 16m a16gpu 16f 16m] sparely-made colt: little worthwhile form over hurdles, including in selling handicap. *P. A. Pritchard.* —

WOODLANDS LAD 15 ch.g. Jimmy Reppin–Ptelea (Psidium) [1989/90 c29s c—
c27v^{bd} c28g c28g c36g^{pu}] big, strong gelding: poor chaser: stays well: acts on —
heavy going: good mount for a claimer. *P. A. Pritchard.*

WOODLANDS LADY 4 b.f. Oats–Sand Lady (Sandford Lad) [1989/90 F16m
aF16g 16f^{pu}] light-framed filly: first foal: dam won 1m seller and placed over —
hurdles: mid-division in NH Flat races: tailed off when pulled up 2 out in juvenile
fillies selling hurdle at Wolverhampton. *Miss S. J. Wilton.*

WOODSIDE ROAD 10 ch.g. Paddy's Stream–White Trout (Bargello) c**107** §
[1989/90 c24m^{3} c24f^{2} c28m*] tall, rather sparely-made gelding: ridden by 7-lb
claimer, won handicap chase at Nottingham in December by 1½ lengths from
Marshlander, leading run-in: stays 3½m: acts on any going: best in blinkers:
temperamental and not one to trust. *D. Nicholson.*

WOOD SPOILER 9 br.g. Blue And Grey–Souriciere (Count Albany) [1989/90 c77 ?
c24g^{pu} c16f^{2} c16f^{ur} 16m] well beaten both outings over hurdles (latest a selling —
handicap): neck second to Hoddam Brig in 3-runner novice chase at Hexham in
October: sold 800 gns Ascot April Sales. *T. Fairhurst.*

WOODURATHER 4 br.g. Touching Wood (USA)–Rather Warm (Tribal
Chief) [1989/90 17m^{pu}] odds on, weakened 3 out and pulled up after next in — p
maiden hurdle at Newton Abbot in May: won 1¼m handicap on Flat 2 months
later: seems sure to do better when returned to hurdling. *M. C. Pipe.*

WOOLMANS 11 b.g. Dawn Review–Highland Night (Night Thought) [1989/90 c**81**
c24m^{2}] leggy, shallow-girthed gelding: of little account over hurdles: poor —
point-to-pointer, winner in March: 5 lengths second to Erostin Floats in novice
chase at Market Rasen following month. *B. J. McMath.*

WOOLY RAGS 4 ch.f. Raga Navarro (ITY)–Woolcana (Some Hand) [1989/90
16f^{pu}] won 6f seller at 2 yrs, but well beaten on Flat in 1989: tailed off when pulled —
up 2 out in juvenile hurdle at Leicester in November: sold 925 gns Ascot July
Sales. *P. A. Pritchard.*

WORDEL 12 b.g. Royalty–Golden Wonder (Golden Cloud) [1989/90 c26g^{4} c77
c26s^{pu} c24g^{2} c25m c21g^{2}] workmanlike gelding: carries plenty of condition: —
novice hurdler/chaser: runner-up in handicap chases at Fakenham in February
and April: suited by 3m and give in the ground. *Mrs R. Murdoch.*

WORKADAY 8 gr.m. Workboy–Courting Day (Right Boy) [1989/90 16m]
compact mare: of little account. *A. Smith.* —

WORKING SUCCESS 5 b.m. Workboy–Key To Success (Brave Invader
(USA)) [1989/90 16d 20d*] claimer ridden, showed improved form when winning 87
handicap hurdle at Sedgefield in March (held up, led last): stays 2½m: acts on soft
going. *Mrs G. R. Reveley.*

WORK ON AIR 4 ch.g. Doc Marten–Set To Work (Workboy) [1989/90 16f
a16g^{4}] compact gelding: half-brother to fair hurdler Tour de Force (by Reliance 55
II): placed at up to 1m on Flat: remote fourth in selling hurdle at Southwell in
November. *C. Tinkler.*

WORK TO WIN 5 ch.g. That's Swanee–Lady Cherry (Bargello) [1989/90
F16g^{5} aF16g^{2} F16f^{4}] half-brother to winning Irish point-to-pointer Rainbow Brite
(by Cantab): dam unraced: in frame in NH Flat races at Lingfield in February and
Warwick in May: yet to race over hurdles or fences. *O. Sherwood.*

WORLDSPORTFLYER 4 b.c. Hays–Arabian Pearl (Deep Diver) [1989/90
18f 16g^{pu} 17f a16g^{3} 16g 16d^{2} 20s^{pu} 16d 16d 16g^{3} 16m^{4}] leggy, angular, narrow colt: 71 §
plater on Flat: sold out of A. Lee's stable 1,700 gns Newmarket Autumn Sales:
poor plater over hurdles: dropped himself out seventh and ninth starts: should be
suited by further than 2m: acts on dead going. *M. C. Chapman.*

WORRELL-FRY 5 b.g. Horage–Rathcoffey Daisy (Pampapaul) [1989/90
aF16g] 500 3-y-o: first reported foal: dam never ran: tailed-off last of 10 in NH Flat
race at Lingfield in January: yet to race over hurdles or fences. *Mrs P. Townsley.*

WORTHY KNIGHT 9 ch.g. Dubassoff (USA)–Quidsworth (Trullah) [1989/90 c**127**
c20d^{2} c20m c25m c24g^{3}] neat gelding: fairly useful chaser: best effort of season —
when 21 lengths third behind Man O'Magic in minor event at Perth in April: likely
to prove best at distances short of 3¼m: acts on any going with possible exception
of heavy: takes a strong hold: makes the odd mistake. *B. McLean.*

WORTHY LIGHT 9 b.m. Lighter–Sardan (Lauso) [1989/90 c21f^{pu} c20m^{5} 21f^{4} c76 x
22g c16s c25m^{3} c25m^{pu} c25f^{5} c24f^{4} c24m^{5} c20m c24h^{4}] sturdy mare: poor novice 71
hurdler/chaser: stays 25f: moderate jumper: blinkered last outing. *C. C. Trietline.*

WORTHY PRINCE 6 b.g. Balliol–Princess Vronski (The Brianstan) [1989/90 16f2 16f] close-coupled gelding: jumped poorly when second in selling hurdle at Southwell in October: sold 1,500 gns Newmarket Autumn Sales. *C. N. Williams.* 68 ?

WOT PET 7 b.g. Crozier–Annies Pet (Normandy) [1989/90 c24d3] maiden point-to-pointer, placed twice in February: just over 20 lengths third to Tartevie in hunter chase at Ayr in April. *T. M. Gibson.* c**88** p

WREKIN HILL 8 b.g. Duky–Cummin Hill (Wrekin Rambler) [1989/90 c24g* c25mpu] big, rangy gelding: winning hurdler: bit backward, made successful chasing debut in novice event at Wetherby in January, leading 3 out and beating Comedy Road comfortably by 12 lengths: burly when next seen out at Liverpool in April (tailed off when pulled up): suited by a good test of stamina: acts on any going. *W. A. Stephenson.* c**109** —

WREKIN LAD 8 br.g. Peter Wrekin–That Space (Space King) [1989/90 c25gur c24d3] smallish, lengthy gelding: of little account as a hurdler: successful in a point-to-point in February: in frame in hunter chases, including when staying-on 5 lengths third to Mademist Susie in maiden event at Leicester in March: stays 3m: has been tried in blinkers. *Mrs Ian James.* c88 —

WREKIN MELODY 9 b.g. Peter Wrekin–Sam's Song (Narrator) [1989/90 c16mur c24dpu c25g* c25g4 c24gF c24fF] leggy, sparely-made gelding: modest novice hurdler: 100/1-winner of slowly-run novice chase at Catterick in February, beating Lake Valentina 4 lengths: creditable fourth in similar race on same course following month: stays 25f. *F. Watson.* c94 —

WREKIN WARRIOR 5 b.g. Coded Scrap–Miss Denetop (Eborneezer) [1989/90 F16v F12f 16f a16gpu] tall, leggy, lengthy gelding: half-brother to 3 winning hurdlers, including quite useful Mr Denetop (by Pongee): dam free-running novice hurdler, best at 2m: seems of little account. *B. Preece.* —

W SIX TIMES 13 b.g. Random Shot–Autumn Girl (Autumn Gold) [1989/90 24gpu] lightly-made, leggy gelding: one-time very useful chaser: very lightly raced and no form of late. *J. Parkes.* c— —

WYARDS WONDER 4 b.g. Hotfoot–Tenth Hussar (Shiny Tenth) [1989/90 16spu] well beaten on Flat: tailed off when pulled up sixth in juvenile hurdle at Folkestone in December. *Miss B. Sanders.* —

WYCOMBE LADY 6 b.m. Tachypous–Facade (Double Jump) [1989/90 16d4 16s2 16sF 22g 22d 17d] novice selling hurdler: should stay beyond 17f: acts on soft going: trained first 5 starts by K. Bishop: sold 1,600 gns Ascot May Sales. *R. Akehurst.* 69

WYTHERSTONE 4 b.g. Hotfoot–Jurassic (Grundy) [1989/90 16d5 16s 16g] workmanlike gelding: type to carry condition: third foal: dam unraced: little sign of ability in juvenile hurdles. *M. W. Easterby.* —

WYVERN 7 ch.g. Dragonara Palace (USA)–Rosalina (Porto Bello) [1989/90 20fpu c20gpu c24gpu a20gpu c20dur c20f c26fur c20g4 20mpu] sturdy gelding: winning hurdler: tailed off in novice chases: stays 2½m: acts on firm going: blinkered fifth and last 2 outings: often claimer ridden, including when successful. *W. Clay.* c— —

X

XAFU XAFU 4 b.c. Kafu–On The Road (On Your Mark) [1989/90 16fpu] behind when pulled up last in juvenile hurdle at Leicester in November: won twice in modest company at around 1m in 1990. *M. H. Tompkins.* —

XARMIL 8 b.g. Cidrax (FR)–Millbank Rose (Barrons Court) [1989/90 c24f5] ex-Irish gelding: maiden hurdler: won a point-to-point in 1988: sold out of I. Ferguson's stable 5,000 gns Doncaster August Sales: blinkered, moderate fifth in maiden hunter chase at Hexham in April. *Major M. W. Sample.* c79 —

XEROMEDE 6 b.g. Runnymede–Nervous Cough (New Linacre) [1989/90 17m 21fpu] of little account. *N. Kernick.* —

XHAI 8 b.g. Brave Shot–Wild Thyme (Galivanter) [1989/90 16m5 16f2 a16g3 18v2 16g 16f 16m*] workmanlike gelding: won lady riders handicap hurdle at Stratford in June, rallying run-in despite edging left: had run well on Flat and, at times, over hurdles earlier: stays 2¼m: acts on any going: blinkered last 5 starts. *R. Simpson.* 93

XMAS TREE 9 b.g. Flatbush–Carol H (Lucky Leaprechaun) [1989/90 c24f c24f^{6}] compact, sturdy gelding: lightly-raced novice hurdler/chaser: showed a little ability in maiden hunter chase last start: blinkered final outing in 1988/9. *Mrs R. Birtwistle.* c**79** —

XYLOPHONE 8 b.m. Tap On Wood–Cecily (Prince Regent (FR)) [1989/90 18g^{5} c16g^{F} c17g^{4} c20s^{F} c16m^{F} 16g 16m 16g^{5}] leggy, sparely-made mare: selling hurdler and poor novice chaser (moderate jumper): should stay beyond 2m: usually amateur or claimer ridden: not one to trust. *Miss L. Bower.* c**71** x 71 §

Z

YABOYAA 6 b.g. Pragmatic–Trim (Miralgo) [1989/90 16f^{2} 20g^{3} 16m^{3} 20f^{4}] rangy, unfurnished ex-Irish gelding: has plenty of scope: fifth foal: brother to Seskin Mist, placed over hurdles and fences in Ireland: poor hurdler: dam won over fences in Ireland: won NH Flat race in 1989 when trained by H. Kirk: novice hurdler: stayed on when under 6 lengths fourth to Stratford Ponds at Ascot in April: will stay beyond 2½m: acts on firm ground: takes a good hold: should win races over hurdles. *J. T. Gifford.* 112

YACHT CLUB 8 b.g. New Member–Sparflow (Spartan General) [1989/90 c16d^{F} c16g^{F} 20g^{bd} 20g^{4} 20g^{4} 20f 20f^{2} a20g] workmanlike gelding: first foal: dam pulled up in 2 point-to-points: won 2 point-to-points in Ireland in 1989: bought for 15,000 gns Doncaster August Sales: fell early on in 2 novice chases in January: poor form in novice hurdles: 7/2 on, mistakes last 2 flights when second in amateur riders event at Sedgefield in April: will be suited by 3m. *J. L. Eyre.* c— x 87 x

YAHOO 9 b.g. Trombone–Coolroe Aga (Laurence O) [1989/90 c24g^{3} c24g^{pu} c24g^{3} c24s^{3} c24d^{2} c26f c33d^{pu}] sparely-made gelding: excellent second in Tote Cheltenham Gold Cup and won Martell Cup Chase at Liverpool in 1988/9: below his best since, though wasn't disgraced when third to Nick The Brief in Peter Marsh Chase (limited handicap) at Haydock in January, fourth start: stays well: has won on firm going but is well suited by plenty of give: blinkered last 2 outings: occasionally let down by his jumping. *J. A. C. Edwards.* c**160** —

YAMANOUCHI 6 b.g. Hard Fought–Noreena (Nonoalco (USA)) [1989/90 17d^{6} 16m^{6} 20m^{4} 16g^{2} 16g^{6} 20d^{5} 20g^{4} a18g^{5}] ex-Irish gelding: second foal: dam twice-raced daughter of good 1969 French 2-y-o Vela: poor form at 2 yrs: novice hurdler: ran in seller last outing: stays 2½m: acts on good to firm going. *J. H. Johnson.* 87

YAMASHITA (USA) 5 b.g. Vaguely Noble–Princesse Aglae (FR) (Crowned Prince (USA)) [1989/90 16m^{F}] workmanlike gelding: modest middle-distance maiden on Flat: ridden by 7-lb claimer, led 3 out until headed and fell next in novice hurdle won by Pollock at Worcester in August (took a good hold): would have finished second had he completed. *F. Jordan.* 95

YA MUNA 5 ch.m. Vitiges (FR)–La Vosgienne (Ashmore (FR)) [1989/90 16h^{su}] lengthy, sparely-made mare: no worthwhile over hurdles: blinkered first 3 starts: dead. *J. Ffitch-Heyes.* —

YANBU 5 b.g. Artaius (USA)–Belle Bretonne (Celtic Ash) [1989/90 16m 16s* a20g^{3} 16s^{2} a18g 16g^{3} 16g^{5} a16g] smallish gelding: selling hurdler: won handicap at Folkestone in December (bought in 6,000 gns): stays 2½m: acts on heavy going: usually blinkered nowadays: ungenuine. *J. R. Jenkins.* 100 §

YANK BROWN 10 b.g. Giolla Mear–Lorinda (Seminole II) [1989/90 c16g^{2} c16f^{F} c16f*] fairly useful chaser, lightly raced: has been fired: always going well, beat only other finisher Tarn 1½ lengths in conditional jockeys handicap at Cheltenham in December: races only at 2m: acts on firm going: usually pulls hard and suited by racing up with the leaders. *J. G. FitzGerald.* c**129** —

YANKEE SILVER 9 gr.m. Yankee Gold–Cup Bearer (Neron) [1989/90 16m 16m^{pu} 16g] sparely-made mare: handicap hurdler: no form in 1989/90: free-running sort, best at 2m: easily best form on good ground: broke blood vessel in 1988/9. *G. G. Gracey.* —

YELLOW BEAR 8 ch.g. Gold Form–Dumb Kathy (Dumbarnie) [1989/90 16g^{pu}] winning 2m hurdler: tailed off when pulled up in claimer in April: acts on heavy going (well beaten on top-of-the-ground): blinkered last 5 starts 1986/7: refused to race once. *J. Parkes.* — §

Mr Alan Parker's "Yahoo"

YELLOW SPRING 5 b.g. Buckskin (FR)–Carrigello (Bargello) [1989/90 F16g 18f[F]] half-brother to winning point-to-pointer and novice hunter chaser Give Me A Break (by Green Shoon): dam behind in NH Flat race and maiden hurdle: eighth in NH Flat race at Kempton in February: staying-on third when falling last in novice hurdle won by Rosie Marchioness at Fontwell in March (gave impression he'd have finished second had he completed). *D. M. Grissell.* —

YEOMAN FARMER 6 br.g. Trombone–Ballykeel Owen (Master Owen) [1989/90 16g[3] 16g[6]] rangy gelding: chasing type: fourth foal: half-brother to a poor novice over jumps by Glen Quaich: dam never ran: most promising third behind Egypt Mill in novice hurdle at Towcester in December on debut: in need of race, around 22 lengths sixth behind Freeline Finishing at Windsor 2½ months later, weakening quickly 3 out: worth another chance to confirm promise shown at Towcester. *J. T. Gifford.* 96

YEOMAN METRO 6 ch.g. Pollerton–Plassey Queen (Merlin) [1989/90 16d[2] 22m[2]] angular, workmanlike gelding: second in novice hurdles at Chepstow in November and Fontwell (2 lengths behind Miinnehoma) a month later: will be suited by stiffer test of stamina: should win a race. *J. T. Gifford.* 109

YESICAN 4 gr.c. Kalaglow–Geoffrey's Sister (Sparkler) [1989/90 16s[pu]] promising fourth in 7f event on Flat in 1989: sold out of L. Cumani's stable 9,600 gns Newmarket Autumn Sales: better for race, behind when pulled up in juvenile hurdle at Haydock in January: sold 1,300 gns Doncaster March Sales. *N. Tinkler.* —

YET 5 gr.m. Last Fandango–Rana of Coombe (Moulton) [1989/90 16f 16d[2] 16g[4] 16m 16s[2] a20g[3] 22f[2] 20g[6]] smallish, sparely-made mare: poor handicapper on Flat, successful over 1¼m: novice selling hurdler: stays 2¾m: acts on any going: blinkered fourth start (ran moderately): sold out of M. Ryan's stable 1,500 gns Ascot April Sales after sixth start. *W. T. Kemp.* 81

YIMKIN GOLD 9 b.m. Sandside Bay–Double d'Or (Phidigo) [1989/90 c25m ur] workmanlike mare: appears to be of little account and temperamental to boot. *B. G. T. Pike.* c— §

YIRAGAN 8 ch.g. Cantab–Foreverusa (Poona) [1989/90 c24m2 c24g* c26v2] leggy, sparely-made gelding: fair hurdler: most impressive winner of novice chase at Newbury in December, jumping boldly and well in the main: jumped less well but wasn't discredited when 20 lengths second to Last House in similar race at Newton Abbot following month: suited by a good test of stamina: acts on heavy and good to firm going: has worn a crossed noseband: taken early to post last 2 starts: likely to continue on the upgrade. *D. H. Barons.* c116 p —

YOOHOO NAN 7 b.g. Avocat–Red Tab (Cantab) [1989/90 21m5 24mF 24fF] lengthy, angular gelding: winning hurdler: fell fatally at Uttoxeter in October: was suited by 2½m: acted on any going. *R. Lee.* —

YORKBAY 6 b.g. Hello Gorgeous (USA)–Invitation (Faberge II) [1989/90 16f4 17m3] smallish, sparely-made gelding: selling hurdler: below best in 2 races early in season: best form at 2m: acts on any going: visored last 3 starts 1987/8, blinkered last outing. *N. Tinkler.* 80

YORK GLASS 4 b.f. Ampney Prince–Lingala (Pinturischio) [1989/90 16f] small, rather lightly-made filly: poor maiden on Flat: jumped soundly, eased once outpaced from third last when seventh in selling hurdle at Catterick in November. *A. P. Stringer.* —

YORK IMPERIAL 9 br.g. Belfalas–Regency Princess (Prince Regent (FR)) [1989/90 c16d6 c20m2 c20m2] lengthy, angular gelding: second foal: dam, half-sister to 2 winning jumpers, was poor maiden on Flat: fair point-to-pointer, successful 3 times in 1989: second in novice chases at Sedgefield and Southwell in March: will be suited by further than 2½m: amateur ridden. *B. Gee.* c88

YORK ROYAL 8 ch.g. Baptism–Annagh Girl (Menelek) [1989/90 c21g4 c26f*] lengthy, rather leggy gelding: fair point-to-pointer, won 3 times in April (first a walk over) and once in May: won 6-runner hunter chase at Folkestone later in May by 12 lengths: stays 3¼m: acts on firm ground. *M. J. Jerram.* c94

YORKSHIRE HOLLY 7 br.g. Bivouac–Holly Doon (Doon) [1989/90 20d* 20g* 20v3 24d* 16fF 20m] small, rather leggy gelding: improved hurdler who won handicaps at Haydock and Wetherby in December and Wetherby again in February: every chance when falling 2 out in County Hurdle won by Moody Man 138

Waterloo Handicap Hurdle, Haydock — Yorkshire Holly, one of forty-one winners trained by Mrs Reveley in her best season

at Cheltenham in March: always behind in valuable race at Liverpool final start: stays 3m: best form on good or dead ground. *Mrs G. R. Reveley.*

YORKSHIREMAN (USA) 5 ch.g. Our Native (USA)–Queen Vega (USA) (Te Vega) [1989/90 16g3 16d* 16fF 16m 17gF] sparely-made gelding: won handicap hurdle at Market Rasen in November: every chance when falling in minor event at Leicester later in month and handicap at Carlisle (2 out, when leading) in January: may prove best at 2m: acts on soft going. *J. A. Glover.* 116

YORKSHIRE PRINCESS 5 ch.m. Junius (USA)–Magic Lady (Gala Performance (USA)) [1989/90 20gpu 16fpu] smallish, sparely-made mare: maiden plater on Flat, placed at up to 1¼m: tailed off when pulled up in selling hurdles: blinkered last start. *D. R. Tucker.* —

YORK STREET (USA) 5 ch.m. Diamond Shoal–Albany Girl (USA) (Alydar (USA)) [1989/90 17m3] poor form at 2 yrs: sold out of I. Balding's stable 775 gns Ascot November Sales: 100/1 and ridden by 3-lb claimer, just over 4 lengths third behind Proud Crest in 18-runner novice hurdle at Devon & Exeter in March: should improve. *J. H. Baker.* 92 p

YOUGOTIT 4 b.f. Orange Reef–Costerini (Soderini) [1989/90 aF16g3 F12f* F13f3] half-sister to 2 winners, including Hard About (by Right Tack), useful on Flat and over hurdles: dam 1m winner: won NH Flat race at Bangor in March by 7 lengths: 27 lengths third in similar event at Hereford following month: yet to race over hurdles. *R. O'Leary.*

YOUNG ASPIRATION 4 ch.g. Coquelin (USA)–Persian Case (Upper Case (USA)) [1989/90 17gF 16gF] sparely-made gelding: well beaten on Flat: fell both outings in selling hurdles: dead. *N. Kernick.* —

YOUNG BAVARD 9 ch.g. Le Bavard (FR)–Aranuskie (My Swanee) [1989/90 c24fF 26dpu c26g3 c24fF] rather leggy gelding: useful hurdler in 1988/9: jumped deliberately on occasions and gave impression needs stiffer test of stamina when 13 lengths third behind John's Birthday in novice chase at Stratford in March: stays well: acts on heavy and good to firm going: blinkered last outing. *D. J. G. Murray-Smith.* c88 —

YOUNG DRIVER 13 b.g. Linacre–Pepe (Taboun) [1989/90 c25m5 c36fpu] tall gelding: useful chaser at his best: second in Seagram Grand National at Liverpool in 1985/6: lightly raced and no form since (broke down in latest running of Seagram Grand National): suited by a stiff test of stamina: acts on any going: has won in blinkers and worn a visor. *D. J. Bell.* c— —

YOUNG FACT 5 b.g. Known Fact (USA)–Yelming (Thatch (USA)) [1989/90 16s 16g5 17d4] modest novice hurdler: races only at around 2m: acts on good to firm and dead going: winner over 11.5f on Flat in 1990. *D. R. C. Elsworth.* 94

YOUNG FARMER 6 ch.g. Celtic Cone–High Affair (High Line) [1989/90 F16s] sturdy, plain gelding: first foal: dam, tailed off in 1½m maiden, half-sister to fair 6f to 1m winner Havon Cool: tailed off in NH Flat race at Warwick in February: dead. *J. L. Spearing.*

YOUNG FOOL 6 br.g. Young Man (FR)–Fool 'Em (Dadda Bert) [1989/90 c21gpu c24sur c16d] neat gelding: third in 2 point-to-points in 1989: well behind in amateur riders handicap chase at Sedgefield in January. *C. Smith.* c—

YOUNG GENERAL 4 br.c. Young Generation–Amerella (Welsh Pageant) [1989/90 16m3 20f6] angular colt: half-brother to fairly useful hurdler Honest Word (by Touching Wood): fair middle-distance maiden on Flat: favourite, 9½ lengths third behind Old Virginia in juvenile hurdle at Plumpton in November: quickly lost touch turning into straight at Doncaster following month. *M. H. B. Robinson.* 94

YOUNG GERARD 5 ch.g. Brigadier Gerard–Eastern Queen (Sharpen Up) [1989/90 16h* 20f3 17f3 17f4] small gelding: first form when winning selling hurdle at Hexham (no bid) in May: not disgraced in similar company next 2 outings: stays 2½m: acts on hard ground: visored last 4 starts. *M. C. Chapman.* 82

YOUNG GHOST 5 gr.m. Grey Ghost–Young Scatt (Derek H) [1989/90 F16f6] first foal: dam unraced: blinkered, tailed-off last in NH Flat race at Sedgefield in October: yet to race over hurdles or fences. *B. E. Wilkinson.*

YOUNG LINE 4 b.c. Young Generation–Quay Line (High Line) [1989/90 16s 16f] leggy colt: fifth living foal by a thoroughbred stallion: half-brother to 3 winners on Flat, including useful 1986 2-y-o 1m winner Known Line (by Known Fact): dam won Park Hill Stakes: well beaten in juvenile hurdles at Hereford and Ludlow in March: has worn crossed noseband. *Miss H. C. Knight.* —

YOUNG MORETON 6 b.g. Young Generation–Kissimmee (FR) (Petingo) [1989/90 16m[6]] smallish, workmanlike gelding: novice hurdler: no form since 1987/8: best run at 2m on good ground. *Andrew Turnell.* —

YOUNG MURPHY 8 b.g. Proverb–Coinscraper (Current Coin) [1989/90 c25g[co] c24f[ro] c24f[ro] c16f[r]] tall, leggy gelding: most temperamental maiden point-to-pointer/hunter chaser: best left severely alone. *Tony Lapping.* c§§

YOUNG MUZZY 7 b.g. Asdic–Quick Walk (Farm Walk) [1989/90 16d[6] 16m[6]] neat gelding: behind in NH Flat race and novice hurdles: looked a difficult ride last start. *L. J. Codd.* —

YOUNG NICHOLAS 9 br.g. Young Generation–Nicholas Grey (Track Spare) [1989/90 24f[6] c20g[2] c22g* c24m*] compact gelding: poor hurdler and modest chaser nowadays: won conditional jockeys handicap at Nottingham and novice handicap at Windsor in January: stays 2¾m: acts on heavy and good to firm ground: blinkered twice in 1987/8: sometimes jumps sketchily, but did nothing wrong last 2 starts. *J. D. Roberts.* c**100** —

YOUNG PAGEANT 6 ch.h. Welsh Pageant–Young Mementa (Young Christopher) [1989/90 16g 20f[5] 16g[5] 16d[3] 18d[6] a18g[6] a18g[5] 16m c16f[ur] c16f[6] c16m c24h[ur] c20f[3]] medium-sized horse: winning selling hurdler: only form over fences when third of 4 in handicap at Sedgefield in May: best form over hurdles at 2m: acts on good to firm ground: often claimer ridden: sometimes visored. *R. W. Dods.* c**77** 75

YOUNG POKEY 5 b.g. Uncle Pokey–Young Romance (King's Troop) [1989/90 21g[5] 16g[2]] rangy gelding: won 2 NH Flat races in 1988/9: favourite, 12 lengths second to Freeline Finishing in novice hurdle at Windsor in March, unable to quicken from 3 out: weakened last but showed rather better form over 21f: may do best with forcing tactics over 2m: jumps deliberately: should win a run-of-the-mill novice hurdle. *O. Sherwood.* 107 ?

YOUNG SNUGFIT 6 ch.g. Music Boy–Sinzinbra (Royal Palace) [1989/90 c16g* c17g[F] c16f* c16g* c16g[2] c16m[3] c16m[2] c16d[2]] c**144** —

The useful hurdler Young Snugfit took well to fences and was unquestionably one of the best two-mile novices of 1989/90. A bold jumper who races with plenty of enthusiasm, Young Snugfit was an impressive winner of his first three completed starts in the first half of the season and was beaten only narrowly in three of the most important races for horses of his type in the second half. He looked an exciting recruit to the chasing ranks from the day at Kempton in October when he made his debut over the larger obstacles in a qualifier of the Steel Plate And Sections Young Chasers' series. Having pulled his way into the lead by the second, Young Snugfit jumped like an old hand, quickened almost effortlessly when chal-

Rank Motorway Services Novices' Chase, Kempton—
Young Snugfit (checks) in the air with Deep Flash; Antinous is the other in the picture

Mr John Poynton's "Young Snugfit"

lenged three out and won very easily by ten lengths from Brave Defender. If the bare form didn't amount to a great deal the manner of Young Snugfit's victory suggested that he was potentially a high-class novice. Following a fall when tracking the eventual winner Green Willow five out in the Halloween Novices' Chase at Newbury, Young Snugfit enhanced his reputation with wide-margin successes in the quite valuable Hurst Park Novices' Chase at Ascot in November and the Rank Motor Novices' Chase at Kempton in December. Showing no ill-effects from his fall at Newbury, he jumped well and set a strong pace on each occasion. His jumping was put under pressure in the Hurst Park when Espy joined him in the lead six out, but Young Snugfit measured the remaining fences well and held a slight lead over his hard-ridden rival when that horse fell at the last.

Young Snugfit ran disappointingly in his first race of the New Year, when beaten a distance by the only other finisher Cashew King in the P.M.L. Lightning Novices' Chase at Ascot. Having raced with less zest than usual, Young Snugfit made a few mistakes and reportedly sustained a back injury. Whatever the reason for his showing, he was clearly a long way below his best. Given a two-month break, he recovered from whatever had ailed him and looked well when returned to the racecourse for the Arkle Challenge Trophy at Cheltenham. It was soon apparent that Young Snugfit was back to his old self as he set a sound pace, jumping well. He looked sure to win after quickening about three lengths clear rounding the home turn, but was found out by the final hill and overhauled in the last one hundred yards, first by Comandante and then by Kiichi to be beaten a length and a neck. Over the easier two miles of the Mildmay course at Liverpool in April, Young Snugfit was generally thought likely to gain compensation in the fourteen-runner Perrier Jouet Novices' Chase and started a short-priced favourite. Always to the fore in a strongly-run race, he went a length up after the second from home only to lose out in a driving finish to Boutzdaroff, the pair well clear. It was a similar story in the Edinburgh Woollen Mill's Future Champions Novices' Chase at Ayr two weeks later. This time Young Snugfit was sent about his business in earnest three out, but was worn down close home and beaten half a length by Celtic Shot; once again the leading pair finished well clear.

A big, lengthy, slightly dipped-backed gelding, the six-year-old Young Snugfit still has room for physical improvement and should make up into a cracking two-mile chaser in 1990/1. Changes to the racing programme introduced for the coming season mean, among other things, that there will be more prize money at the top level of jump racing. In the two-mile chasing division, the Castleford Chase at Wetherby in December has become a conditions race and carries added money of £50,000 compared to half that amount in 1989 when it was a handicap. The Wetherby track with its easy turns provides a very fair test for any horse, but is ideal for the free-running individual with plenty of jumping ability. The Castleford Chase would seem the obvious target for Young Snugfit in the first half of the season.

Young Snugfit (ch.g. 1984)	Music Boy (ch 1973)	Jukebox (b 1966)	Sing Sing
			Bibi Mah
		Veronique (b 1961)	Matador
			Narcisse
	Sinzinbra (b 1971)	Royal Palace (b 1964)	Ballymoss
			Crystal Palace
		La Lidia (ch 1964)	Matador
			Lady Grand

Young Snugfit is one of eight winners from the eleven foals produced by his dam, who died in 1987. Besides Young Snugfit Sinzinbra has produced three other winners by Music Boy, namely Superb Singer, a winner over five furlongs as a three-year-old, Snugfit's Image, who won a two-mile juvenile hurdle for the stable at Uttoxeter in April, and the three-year-old Snuggle, a winner over five furlongs in 1989. Young Snugfit is closely related to the 1985 Grand National runner-up Mr Snugfit, who is by Music Boy's sire Jukebox. Sinzinbra's other winning produce are the useful jumpers Cashew King and Half Brother (both by Faraway Times) and Peanuts Pet (by Tina's Pet), a very useful novice hurdler in the latest season who won three races. Sinzinbra, a daughter of a half-sister to the Irish Derby winner Your Highness, was a very useful performer at up to a mile and a quarter. She was a half-sister to several winners, including the useful hurdler Kings Parade.

Young Snugfit, who was trained by Mick Easterby prior to the latest season, showed modest form on the Flat as a three-year-old, winning handicaps over five and six furlongs. He is most unlikely to stay beyond two miles over jumps and will prove best on a sharp track. All types of going come alike to him. *O. Sherwood.*

YOUNG TY 6 br.g. Lighter–Star of Tycoon (Tycoon II) [1989/90 F16f* F16f* 20g* 20v* 16m^{F} 16f* 20f^{3}] angular, rather sparely-made gelding: unbeaten in 3 NH Flat races: won novice hurdles at Wetherby (hung badly right run-in) in January, Leicester in February and Newcastle (long odds on) in March: staying-on 3 lengths third behind Vazon Bay in Mumm Prize Novices' Hurdle at Liverpool: stays 2½m: acts on any going: amateur ridden: races keenly: has worn a crossed noseband: has further improvement in him. *Dr J. F. Robinson.* 128 p

YOUNG VITAL 6 ch.g. Vital Season–Irene Louise (Match III) [1989/90 F16f^{6}] close-coupled gelding: well beaten in NH Flat races: dead. *D. C. Tucker.*

YOUNG WARRIOR 6 ch.g. Roman Warrior–Teenager (Never Say Die) [1989/90 c21d^{pu} c20v^{2} c21g c20d^{3}] leggy, plain gelding: winning hurdler: jumped well in main when 10 lengths second of 3 finishers to The Antartex in novice chase at Haydock in January: several mistakes and well beaten subsequently: suited by a test of stamina, plenty of give in the ground and a galloping track. *Miss H. C. Knight.* c95 ? —

YOUNG WILKIE 6 br.m. Callernish–Kincsem (Nelcius) [1989/90 F17f^{6} 16m^{4} 16g^{4}] seventh foal: half-sister to 4 winning jumpers, including useful chasers Travelowen (by Master Owen) and Socks Downe (by Paddy's Stream) and quite 82

useful chaser Travel Over (by Over The River): dam unraced: sixth in NH Flat race at Doncaster in December: better effort in novice hurdles when fourth at Catterick in February on final start. *T. D. Barron.*

YOUTHFUL PIP 5 b.g. Young Generation–Pipina (USA) (Sir Gaylord)
[1989/90 16d^{3} 16g 17f^{5} 16g^{3} 16m^{F} 16d^{4} 16g a16g] rather sparely-made gelding: in 85
frame at up to 1½m on Flat: modest novice selling hurdler: reluctant to post and found little sixth start: acts on dead going: has worn a tongue strap: blinkered fourth and seventh outings: jumps none too fluently: trained until after seventh start by M. W. Easterby. *S. B. Avery.*

YOUWAITONME 8 gr.g. The Parson–Fort Etna (Be Friendly) [1989/90 c**85**
c25g^{pu} c25m^{2} c21d^{bd} c24m^{2} c26s^{4} c32f] sparely-made gelding: has a round action: brother to Irish 1¼m to 1½m winner Etna's Princess and half-brother to winning hurdler Slatt Noble (by Tall Noble): dam, sister to a winning hurdler, 2-y-o 5f winner: won a point-to-point in Ireland in 1989: second in novice chases at Towcester and Leicester in first half of season: stays 3¼m: probably acts on any going: blinkered last outing: makes the odd mistake. *K. C. Bailey.*

YOZZER HUGHES 5 br.g. Tumble Wind (USA)–Miss Britain (Tudor Melody)
[1989/90 22g^{pu} 16d 16m 16g 16h* 17m] sparely-made gelding: heavily-backed 108
favourite, only form of season when winning selling handicap hurdle at Plumpton in March by 15 lengths (bought in 7,000 gns): again well-backed favourite in non-seller final start: best at 2m: acts on any going: ridden by 7-lb claimer. *G. A. Ham.*

YREKA BAY 8 b.g. Le Bavard (FR)–Maureens Dote (David Jack) [1989/90 c**78**
c25d^{6} c25v^{ur} c21g^{4} c20m^{5}] rangy gelding: first foal: dam lightly-raced Irish maiden: unplaced in NH Flat races in 1986: won a point-to-point in 1989: jumped soundly when fourth of 18 behind The Humble Tiller in novice chase at Windsor in March: should be well suited by 3m. *J. A. C. Edwards.*

YUAN PRINCESS 5 ch.m. Tender King–Skyey (Skymaster) [1989/90 16m
a16g 16f^{4} 16m^{5} 16m*] smallish mare: selling hurdler: sold out of D. Roderick's 65
stable 1,750 gns Ascot October Sales: sweating, won handicap at Stratford in June (bought in 3,400 gns): likely to prove suited by sharp 2m: acts on good to firm ground. *J. C. McConnochie.*

YUFFROUW ANN 5 b.m. Tyrnavos–Recline (Wollow) [1989/90 a16g^{pu} 16d^{pu}]
small, sparely-made mare: of little account: usually blinkered or visored: sold —
2,000 gns Ascot April Sales. *K. G. Wingrove.*

YUVRAJ 6 b.g. Final Straw–Never Never Land (Habitat) [1989/90 16f^{6}]
compact gelding: selling hurdler: dropped out quickly approaching last only —
outing of season (August): form only at 2m: acts on soft and good to firm going (blinkered when running poorly on heavy): has been ridden by claimer (not when successful). *B. J. McMath.*

Z

ZACTOO 4 br.g. Tycoon II–Maidensgrove (Canadel II) [1989/90 F17f] fourth thoroughbred foal: half-brother to winning hurdlers Shirley Grove (by Vulgan Slave) and New Kingsgrove (by Kinglet) and winning point-to-pointer Prohibition Boy (by Gilded Leader): dam won on Flat and over hurdles: tailed off in NH Flat race at Doncaster in March: yet to race over hurdles. *B. Preece.*

ZAGAZIG (USA) 7 b.g. Chieftain II–I'll Take It (USA) (Royal Levee (USA))
[1989/90 20g^{6} 16g^{5} 16d 18f 20h^{4}] workmanlike gelding: carries condition:
handicap hurdler: modest form in 1989/90: best form at 2m: yet to race on heavy 92
going, acts on any other: usually held up: good mount for a claimer. *G. Ripley.*

ZAMIL (USA) 5 b.g. Lyphard (USA)–Wayward Lass (USA) (Hail The Pirates
(USA)) [1989/90 16m^{5} 18f^{6} 21g^{2}] good-topped gelding: fair hurdler: first outing for 123
over 2 months, 2 lengths second to Babil in minor event at Newbury in December, staying on well: stays 21f: best form with give in the ground: sold 4,600 gns Ascot June Sales. *J. T. Gifford.*

ZAMOANA 4 b.f. Nicholas Bill–Zamandra (Foggy Bell) [1989/90 F16g] first foal: dam fair hurdler: tailed off in NH Flat race at Perth in May: yet to race over hurdles. *C. R. Beever.*

ZAMORE 4 b.g. Dominion–Jove's Voodoo (USA) (Northern Jove (CAN))
[1989/90 17h* 18h^{2} 17f* 17h* 17m* 16m^{4dis}] neat gelding: 1m seller winner on 98

First National Handicap Chase, Ascot—Zuko runs on too strongly for Ballyhane

Flat: wide-margin winner of juvenile hurdles at Devon & Exeter in August (3) and September: acted on hard ground: dead. *M. C. Pipe.*

ZAMZAM 5 b.m. High Top–Nebiha (Nebbiolo) [1989/90 16g] leggy, sparely-made mare: won 2m juvenile hurdle in 1988/9 (ridden by 7-lb claimer): well beaten since: acts on heavy going. *F. Gray.* —

ZANUSSI LINE 6 b.g. High Line–Angelica (SWE) (Hornbeam) [1989/90 16d 17g c21v] angular gelding: novice selling hurdler: showed nothing only start over fences: needs testing conditions at 2m, and should be suited by 2½m: sold 750 gns Ascot February Sales. *D. R. Tucker.* c— —

ZARIBEE 5 b.g. Prince Bee–Zariba (Home Guard (USA)) [1989/90 20h* 20f2 27f* 28g6 c27d6] lengthy gelding: successful in novice hurdles at Carlisle in September and Sedgefield in October: tailed off in novice handicap chase at Sedgefield in January: stays 3¼m: acts on hard ground. *W. A. Stephenson.* c— 89

ZEPAGAS 4 b.g. Gorytus (USA)–Wampum (Warfare) [1989/90 18f6] modest maiden on Flat, stays 8.5f: sold out of C. Brittain's stable 3,200 gns Newmarket July Sales: well-beaten sixth of 7 in juvenile hurdle at Fontwell in August: sold 1,700 gns Ascot October Sales. *J. White.* —

ZEPPELIN (GER) 7 b. or br.g. Limbo (GER)–Zandvoort (Arjon) [1989/90 16g 20g6] rather sparely-made gelding: novice hurdler: well beaten in 1989/90: races freely and is likely to prove best forcing pace at around 2m. *M. Bradstock.* —

ZETA'S LAD 7 ch.g. Over The River (FR)–Zeta's Daughter (Master Owen) [1989/90 c20d* c26m* c33dr] angular, sparely-made gelding: quite a useful chaser: won at Chepstow and Uttoxeter (by 4 lengths from No One To Blame) in March, idling on run-in each time: weakened 4 out and refused last (broke down) in William Hill Scottish National at Ayr: stays well: acts on heavy and good to firm ground. *J. R. Upson.* c**127** —

ZEUS 6 ch.g. Morston (FR)–Fodens Eve (Dike (USA)) [1989/90 18f5] lengthy, good-topped gelding: lightly-raced novice hurdler: tailed-off last at Fontwell in April: stays 2½m. *H. Willis.* —

ZINGARO BOY 6 b.g. Casino Boy–Sukhasana (Ritudyr) [1989/90 16g 22gpu a18spu] leggy, angular gelding: no sign of ability over hurdles: blinkered last 2 starts. *K. C. Bailey.* —

ZION PARK 4 b.f. Buzzards Bay–Quaife Sport (Quayside) [1989/90 F12f] fifth foal: half-sister to winning hurdler Celtic Bob (by Celtic Cone): dam never ran: mid-division in NH Flat race at Bangor in March: yet to race over hurdles. *J. Colston.*

ZIO PEPPINO 9 ch.g. Thatch (USA)–Victorian Habit (Habitat) [1989/90 16gpu] 1m winner on Flat: no sign of ability over hurdles. *J. P. Smith.* —

ZIPWITCH 5 b.m. Brianston Zipper–Moorland Spirit (The Ditton) [1989/90 F17h6 16fpu 16mpu] small, sturdy mare: fourth foal: dam never ran: seems of little account: blinkered final start. *Mrs J. G. Retter.* —

ZUCCHINI 4 ch.g. Absalom–Hot Spice (Hotfoot) [1989/90 16g2 16m* 16f*] angular, workmanlike gelding: has scope: modest 7.5f winner on Flat: none too fluent a jumper of hurdles, but won juvenile event (hung left under pressure then rallied to lead near finish) and novice event (stumbled badly after last, regained lead close home) at Wetherby in May: acts on firm ground: can improve again, especially if brushing up his jumping. *K. A. Morgan.* 96 p

ZUKO (CHI) 9 b.g. Kimono (CHI)–La Saudade (CHI) (Candaules) [1989/90 c20g3 c25m* c24g* c24g* c20g3] compact gelding: developed into a useful chaser and won at Sandown, Kempton and Ascot: led 4 out when beating Ballyhane 7 lengths in First National Chase (Handicap) on last-named course in January: gave impression he'd be suited by a return to further when 5 lengths third to First Bout in 2½m handicap at Kempton following month: injured foreleg shortly afterwards and not seen out again: stays 25f: acts on any going: sound jumper. *S. Mellor.* c**137** —

ZULU (FR) 5 b.h. Zino–Marilu (FR) (Luthier) [1989/90 17f* 17fF a16g*] smallish, angular ex-French horse: won over 9f and 1¼m on Flat in 1988 and over 1m in 1989: claimed out of P. Bary's stable 125,000 francs (approx £12,100): won novice hurdles at Newton Abbot in September and Southwell in November: dismounted after passing post on latter course and not seen out again: ran as though something amiss in between: sold only 800 gns Ascot April Sales. *M. C. Pipe.* 122 ?

ZUMMERSET (NZ) 8 b.g. Star Wolf–Homunga Miss (NZ) (Masthead) [1989/90 22gpu c20g2 c24spu c24sF c25dpu c20dF c20dpu c24fpu] compact gelding: poor novice hurdler: second in novice chase at Plumpton in December: let down by his jumping most subsequent starts: stays 2½m: has edged left closing stages: broke blood vessel first outing. *D. H. Barons.* c**88** d —

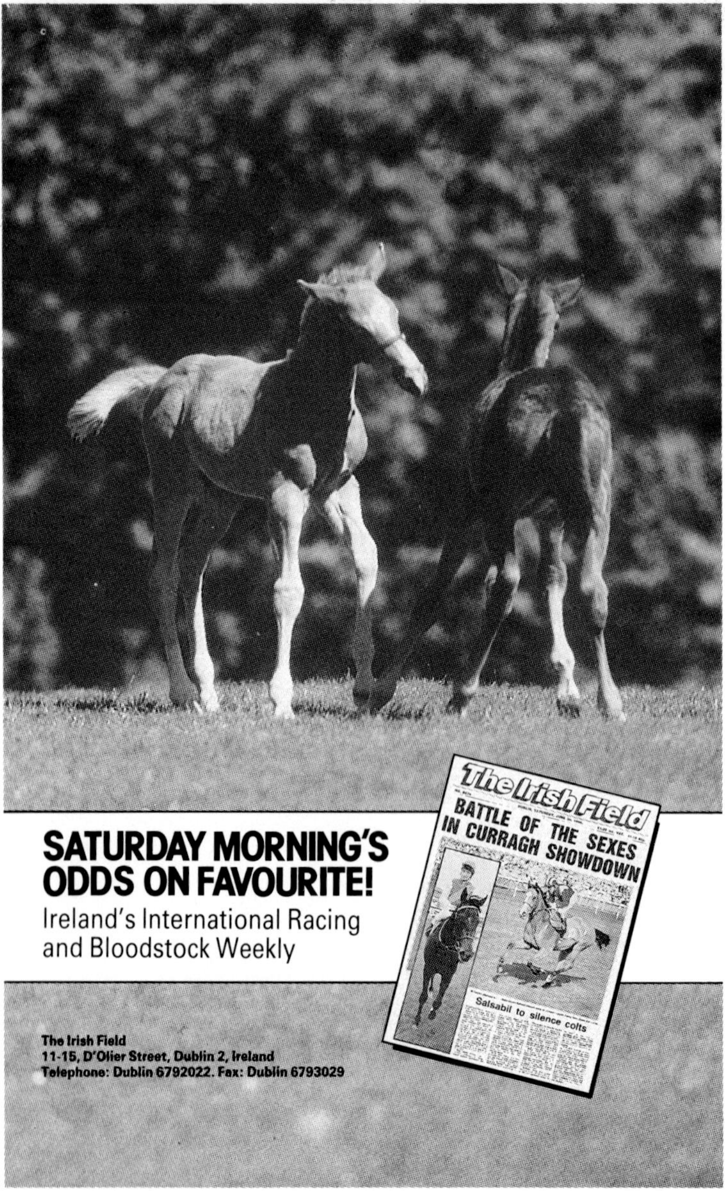

The Irish Field
BATTLE OF THE SEXES IN CURRAGH SHOWDOWN
Salsabil to silence colts
SATURDAY MORNING'S ODDS ON FAVOURITE!
Ireland's International Racing and Bloodstock Weekly
The Irish Field
11-15, D'Olier Street, Dublin 2, Ireland
Telephone: Dublin 6792022. Fax: Dublin 6793029

TIMEFORM
CHAMPION JUMPERS
1989/90

CHAMPION JUMPER
BEST TWO-MILE CHASER
BEST STAYING CHASER
(RATED AT 187)

DESERT ORCHID

11 gr.g. Grey Mirage–Flower Child (Brother)
Owner Mr R. Burridge Trainer D. Elsworth

BEST NOVICE CHASER (RATED AT 152p)

CELTIC SHOT

8 b.g. Celtic Cone–Duckdown (Blast)
Owner Mr D. Horton Trainer C. Brooks

BEST HUNTER CHASER (RATED AT 143)

MYSTIC MUSIC

11 b.m. Hansel's Nephew–Mystic Mintet (King Log)
Owner Miss H. Wilson Trainer Miss H. Wilson

BEST TWO-MILE HURDLER (RATED AT 169)

KRIBENSIS

6 gr.g. Henbit–Aquaria (Double-U-Jay)
Owner Sheikh Mohammed Trainer M. Stoute

BEST STAYING HURDLER (RATED AT 159)

TRAPPER JOHN

6 b.g The Parson–Blueola (Bluerullah)
Owner Mrs P. Fanning Trainer M. Morris

BEST NOVICE HURDLER (RATED AT 151)

REGAL AMBITION

6 b.g. Royal Palace–Quick Aim (Pardal)
Owner Skeltools Ltd Trainer M. Pipe

BEST JUVENILE HURDLER (RATED AT 138)

SYBILLIN

4 b.g Henbit–Tea House (Sassafras)
Owner Marquesa de Moratalla Trainer J. FitzGerald

THE TIMEFORM TOP CHASERS AND HURDLERS

Here are listed the 'Top 100' Chasers and Hurdlers in the annual.

Chasers

187	Desert Orchid
174	Barnbrook Again
169	Carvill's Hill
168	Norton's Coin
167	Toby Tobias
166	Nick The Brief
165	Bonanza Boy
163	Pearlyman
163	Waterloo Boy
162	Golden Freeze
161?	Beau Ranger
161	Cavvies Clown
161	Wolf of Badenoch
160	Pegwell Bay
160	Yahoo
157	Ten of Spades
157	The Thinker
156?	Ballyhane
156	Feroda
156	Panto Prince
156	Super Furrow
155	Durham Edition
155	Maid of Money
155	Sabin du Loir
154	Meikleour
153	Bishops Yarn
153	Mr Frisk
152p	Celtic Shot
152§	Vodkatini
152	Delius
151p	Royal Athlete
150	Brown Windsor
150	Have A Barney
150	Hungary Hur
150x	Rusch de Farges
149	Charter Party
148	Nohalmdun
148	Seagram
148	Slieve Felim
147	Clever Folly
147	Man O'Magic
147d	Joint Sovereignty
146p	Phoenix Gold
146?	Long Engagement
146§	Private Views
146	Ida's Delight
146	Kildimo
146	Villierstown
145p	Garrison Savannah
145§	Golden Friend
145	Pharoah's Laen
144p	Arctic Call
144	Baies
144	Belsir
144	Bigsun
144	Blueberry King
144	Midnight Count
144	Paddyboro
144	Party Politics
144	Star's Delight
144	Young Snugfit
143p	Cahervillahow
143p	Midnight Train
143	Blitzkreig
143	Envopak Token
143	Midnight Madness
143	Mystic Music
143	The West Awake
142	Call Collect
142	Cool Ground
142	Prize Asset
142	Sir Jest
142	Us And Joe
142	Welcome Pin
141p	Katabatic
141+	All Jeff
141d	Prideaux Boy
141?	Bob Tisdall
141	Carrick Hill Lad
141	Comandante
141	Field Conqueror
141	The Committee
141	Willsford
140?	Blazing Walker
140§	Bajan Sunshine
140	Boraceva
140	Foyle Fisherman
140	Old Nick
140	Wingspan
139+	Chatam
139	Antinous
139	Barney Burnett
139	Four Trix
139	Gold Options
139	Greenheart
139	Rinus
139	Steeple View
139	The Dragon Master
138	Cuddy Dale
137	Boutzdaroff

Hurdlers

169	Kribensis
168	Beech Road
166	Nomadic Way
165	Past Glories
162p	Morley Street
161	Grabel
160	Cruising Altitude
160	Elementary
159	Trapper John
158	Henry Mann
158	Osric
156	Jinxy Jack
155	Slalom
155	Vagador
153p	Battalion
153?	Peer Prince
153	Island Set
151p	Royal Athlete
151	Calapaez
151	Floyd
151	Regal Ambition
151	Royal Derbi
151	Wishlon
150	Joyful Noise
150	Mrs Muck
150	Vicario di Bray
149	Bank View
149	Redundant Pal
148	Deep Sensation
148	Old Dundalk
147p	Calabrese
147+	Ikdam
147	Bluff Cove
147	Nodform
146	Chatam
146	Milford Quay
146	Pertemps Network
146	Ryde Again
145	Aldino
145	Brabazon
145	Cash Is King
145	Maelkar
145	Propero
145	Scally Owen
145	Sprowston Boy
145	Welsh Bard
144	Don Valentino
144	Moody Man
143p	Sayparee
143+	Naevog
143?	Santella Bobkes
143	Beldale Star
142	Cloughtaney
142	Forest Sun
141	Bradbury Star
141	Dis Train
141	Folk Dance
141	Undaunted
140?	Space Fair
140	Penny Forum
140	Pragada
140	Voyage Sans Retour
139	Sketcher
139	Toranfield
138	Arctic Teal
138	Fourth of July
138	Miinnehoma
138	Persillant
138	Sybillin
138	Yorkshire Holly
137p	Rare Holiday
137	Ambassador
137	Fragrant Dawn
137	Kadan
137	Run For Free
136p	Vazon Bay
136	Combermere

136	Lumberjack	135	Bally Rue	135	Spanish Servant
136	Ninja	135	Decided	135	Sudden Victory
136	Stevie Jay	135	Jimbalou	135	Voyant
136	Tinryland	135	Native Friend	135d	Dare Say
135p	Fidway	135	Orbis	134p	Dutch Call
135p	Jubail	135	Philosophos	134p	Lucky Verdict
135p	Vestris Abu	135	Protection	134	Babil
135	Afaristoun	135	Sip of Orange		

THE TIMEFORM TOP NOVICES, JUVENILES AND HUNTER CHASERS

Here are listed the 'Top 20' Novice Hurdlers, Novice Chasers, Juvenile Hurdlers and Hunter Chasers

Novice Hurdlers

151	Regal Ambition
145	Brabazon
145	Scally Owen
142	Forest Sun
138	Miinnehoma
137	Run For Free
136p	Vazon Bay
136	Stevie Jay
136	Tinryland
135p	Fidway
135	Sudden Victory
134	Babil
134	Man of The West
134	Sacre d'Or
133p	Danny Harrold
133	Atlaal
133	Loaningdale
132	Judges Fancy
132	Kameo Style
132	Rakes Lane

Novice Chasers

152p	Celtic Shot
151p	Royal Athlete
145p	Garrison Savannah
144p	Arctic Call
144	Party Politics
144	Young Snugfit
143p	Cahervillahow
143	Blitzkreig
142	Welcome Pin
141+	All Jeff
141	Carrick Hill Lad
141	Comandante
141	The Committee
140?	Blazing Walker
139+	Chatam
139	Antinous
139	Greenheart
137	Boutzdaroff
137	Cloney Grange
136+	Toureen Prince

Juvenile Hurdlers

138	Sybillin
137p	Rare Holiday
136	Ninja
135p	Vestris Abu
135	Bally Rue
135	Native Friend
135	Orbis
135	Philosophos
134p	Lucky Verdict
134	Sayyure
132	Stone Flake
132	Rocket Dancer
131	Magic Million
130	Calicon
130	Midfielder
129p	Silver King
129	On Deposit
128	Bell Glass
128	Il Trovatore
127	Ambuscade

Hunter Chasers

143	Mystic Music
142	Call Collect
140	Old Nick
137	West Tip
129	Lean Ar Aghaidh
127	Edenspring
126+	Ah Whisht
126	Three Counties
125	Whitsunday
123	Crammer
123	Perroquet
119+	Sanballat
118+	Howyanow
118	Eastern Destiny
116P	Teaplanter
116	Rodden Brook
115	Giolla Padraig
114	Brookside King
114	Newnham
114	Purnago

1989/90 STATISTICS

The following tables show the leading owners, trainers, jockeys, amateur riders, horses and sires of winners during the 1989/90 season. Except for the lists of horses and sires of winners, which relate to racing in both Britain and Ireland, these statistics refer only to racing under Jockey Club Rules. Some of the tables are reproduced by permission of *The Sporting Life*.

OWNERS

		Horses	*Races Won*	*Stakes £*
1.	Mrs Harry J. Duffey	1	3	124,230
2.	P. Piller	17	39	118,291
3.	Sheikh Mohammed	2	6	106,532
4.	Mrs E. Hitchins	5	13	87,045
5.	Mel Davies	1	4	81,693
6.	R. Burridge	1	4	74,012
7.	Salehurst Paper Co Ltd	3	7	71,389
8.	S. G. Griffiths	1	1	67,003
9.	The Edinburgh Woollen Mill Ltd	7	18	63,331
10.	N B Mason (Farms) Ltd	2	8	59,922
11.	Pell-mell Partners	7	12	59,152
12.	Maurice E. Pinto	2	5	57,628

TRAINERS

		Horses	*Races Won*	*Stakes £*
1.	M. C. Pipe	95	224	668,606
2.	Mrs J. Pitman	44	93	395,275
3.	G. Richards	32	78	324,480
4.	W. A. Stephenson	42	116	324,308
5.	D. R. C. Elsworth	12	24	245,448
6.	J. T. Gifford	34	50	243,870
7.	K. C. Bailey	16	34	241,102
8.	J. G. FitzGerald	32	58	234,071
9.	C. P. E. Brooks	26	56	211,438
10.	O. Sherwood	33	58	207,183
11.	G. B. Balding	23	42	200,276
12.	N. J. Henderson	27	41	193,428

SIRES OF WINNERS

		Horses	*Races Won*	*Stakes £*
1.	Deep Run (1966)	40	80	304,867
2.	Celtic Cone (1967)	30	54	217,963
3.	Henbit (1977)	6	14	169,729
4.	Bivouac (1961)	5	9	140,590
5.	Roselier (1973)	6	21	121,701
6.	The Parson (1968)	13	20	114,247
7.	Idiot's Delight (1970)	8	19	107,258
8.	Proverb (1970)	14	32	105,254
9.	Strong Gale (1975)	15	25	90,458
10.	Grey Mirage (1969)	4	8	86,481
11.	Furry Glen (1971)	13	21	81,579
12.	Raise You Ten (1960)	7	14	79,997

JOCKEYS

		1st	2nd	3rd	Unpl	Total Mts	Per Cent
1.	P. Scudamore	170	79	45	229	523	32.5
2.	R. Dunwoody	102	102	84	316	604	16.9
3.	G. McCourt	100	58	54	223	435	23.0
4.	C. Grant	94	68	57	206	425	22.1
5.	M. Dwyer	75	54	47	203	379	19.8
6.	H. Davies	60	52	39	255	406	14.8
7.	M. Pitman	57	38	17	79	191	29.8
8.	S. Smith Eccles	56	28	20	115	219	25.6
9.	J. Osborne	53	39	31	153	276	19.2
10.	M. Perrett	52	28	22	126	228	22.8
11.	J. Lower	49	19	16	64	148	33.1
12.	P. Niven	48	32	28	156	264	18.2

AMATEUR RIDERS

		1st	2nd	3rd	Unpl	Total Mts	Per Cent
1.	P. McMahon	15	5	10	50	80	18.8
2.	K. Johnson	14	7	8	41	70	20.0
3.	G. Upton	13	13	11	59	96	13.5
4.	S. Swiers	10	9	18	55	92	10.9
5.	D. Gray	8	1	1	8	18	44.4
6.	J. Durkan	7	5	3	27	42	16.7
7.	A. Walter	7	7	5	24	43	16.3
8.	Miss A. Harwood	6	2	1	9	18	33.3

HORSES

		Races Won	Stakes £
1.	Desert Orchid (11 yrs) gr.g. Grey Mirage–Flower Child	5	127,604
2.	Mr Frisk (11 yrs) ch.g. Bivouac–Jenny Frisk	3	124,230
3.	Kribensis (6 yrs) gr.g. Henbit–Aquaria	4	102,765
4.	Barnbrook Again (9 yrs) b.g. Nebbiolo–Single Line	4	81,693
5.	Norton's Coin (9 yrs) ch.g. Mount Cassino–Grove Chance	1	67,003
6.	Royal Athlete (7 yrs) ch.g. Roselier–Darjoy	6	64,319
7.	Nick The Brief (8 yrs) b.g. Duky–Roman Twilight	2	59,862
8.	Sybillin (4 yrs) b.g. Henbit–Tea House	5	56,782
9.	Forest Sun (5 yrs) ch.g. Whistling Deer–Sun Spray	5	52,839
10.	Man O'Magic (9 yrs) br.g. Manado–Garrucha	5	52,682
11.	Maid of Money (8 yrs) b.m. Crash Course–Hansel Money	4	48,035
12.	Four Trix (9 yrs) gr. or ro.g. Peacock–Merry Chariot	1	46,237

BIG RACE RESULTS 1989/90

Prize money for racing in Ireland has been converted to £ Sterling at the exchange rate current at the time of the race. The figures are correct to the nearest £.

1 TIMEFORM HURDLE (FREE HANDICAP) (4y) 2m
£6,017 Chepstow 7 October

Peer Prince (USA) 11-8 SSmithEccles 1
Jubail 10-1 STurner hd.2
Nahar 10-12 RGuest nk.3
Palm House 9-10 MMoloney 8.4
Zamil (USA) 10-5 RRowe 4.5
Viking Venture 10-4 JFrost .. 3.6
Valley of Danuata 10-1 JLodder 7
Santella Bobkes (USA) 11-10 MPerrett 8

11/4 PEER PRINCE, 100/30 Jubail, 5/1 Santella Bobkes, 13/2 Valley of Danuata, 7/1 Zamil, 12/1 Nahar, Viking Venture, 33/1 Palm House
C. Pick (G. Pritchard-Gordon) 8ran 3m50.12 (Good to Firm)

2 RING & BRYMER HURDLE 2m
£4,718 Kempton 21 October

Aldino 6-11-7 JOsborne 1
Decided (Can) 6-10-11 PScudamore sh.2
Combermere 5-10-11 JFrost 2½.3
Flying Ziad (Can) 6-10-11 RGoldstein ½.4
1* Peer Prince (USA) 4-11-0 DMurphy 2.5
Sir Jamestown (USA) 5-10-11 JWhite dist.6

6/4 ALDINO, 7/4 Decided, 100/30 Peer Prince, 12/1 Combermere, 66/1 Flying Ziad, 100/1 Sir Jamestown
A. Boyd-Rochfort (O. Sherwood) 6ran 3m47.25 (Good)

3 CHARISMA GOLD CUP (HANDICAP CHASE) 3m
£8,266 Kempton 21 October

Seagram (NZ) 9-11-7 NHawke 1
Steeple View 8-11-7 JOsborne 20.2
Burglars Walk 9-10-0 RGoldstein dist.3
Davy's Weir 9-10-6 RRowe . nk.4
Royal Cedar 8-10-5 RDunwoody ..... f

11/8 SEAGRAM, 15/8 Steeple View, 9/2 Davy's Weir, 8/1 Royal Cedar, 50/1 Burglars Walk
E. Parker (D. Barons) 5ran 6m06.95 (Good)

4 UNITED HOUSE CONSTRUCTION CHASE (HANDICAP) 2m
£15,140 Ascot 25 October

Prize Asset 9-11-3 SEarle 1
Ida's Delight 10-11-10 BStorey 8.2
Pantomime Prince 6-10-7 MHammond ½.3
Cuddy Dale 6-11-10 DMurphy 10.4
Grey Tornado 8-10-7 BPowell 2.5
Flying Ferret 8-10-8 PScudamore 15.6
Slieve Felim 9-12-0 RDunwoody ..... f
O K Son 10-10-7 RGoldstein ..... pu
Pantechnicon 9-10-4 WIrvine ..... pu

100/30 PRIZE ASSET, 4/1 Cuddy Dale, 9/2 Slieve Felim, 5/1 Flying Ferret, 11/2 Pantomime Prince, 7/1 Ida's Delight, 12/1 Grey Tornado, 14/1 Pantechnicon, 66/1 O K Son
Mrs C. James (P. Hobbs) 9ran 3m47.95 (Firm)

5 TOTE SILVER TROPHY (HANDICAP HURDLE) 2½m
£16,999 Chepstow 4 November

Pipers Copse 7-10-4 MPerrett 1
Milford Quay 6-11-10 PScudamore 4.2
Lumberjack (USA) 5-11-1 DByrne 4.3
Aston Express 6-11-5 MHammond 15.4
Firm Price 8-10-8 DTegg ... 1½.5
Viking Rocket 5-10-6 STurner 10.6
Nodform 5-11-5 EMurphy 3.7
Knighton Lad 8-10-6 JOsborne ..... pu

2/1 MILFORD QUAY, 7/2 Pipers Copse, 5/1 Lumberjack, 6/1 Aston Express, 10/1 Knighton Lad, Nodform, 14/1 Firm Price, Viking Rocket
Mrs P. Locke (G. Harwood) 8ran 4m52.71 (Good to Soft)

6 CHARLIE HALL MEMORIAL WETHERBY PATTERN CHASE 3m 100y
£18,695 Wetherby 4 November

Durham Edition 11-11-2 AMerrigan 1

Ballyhane 8-11-2 RRowe 8.2
Yahoo 8-11-10 NWilliamson 10.3
High Edge Grey 8-11-10 TReed 30.4
Sir Jest 11-11-2 CGrant .... f
Randolph Place 8-11-10 GMcCourt .... ur
Whats What 10-11-2 PNiven .. pu

13/8 Yahoo, 7/4 Ballyhane, 8/1 High Edge Grey, 10/1 Randolph Place, Sir Jest, 20/1 Whats What, 33/1 DURHAM EDITION

R. Oxley (W. A. Stephenson) 7ran 6m26.30 (Good)

7 WHITBREAD WHITE LABEL HANDICAP HURDLE 2m
£14,020 Cheltenham 11 November

Highland Bounty 5-10-4 STurner 1
1[3] **Nahar** 4-11-0 DMurphy 5.2
Imperial Brush 5-10-7 PHolley sh.3
Fragrant Dawn 5-10-13 DByrne 7.4
Vicario di Bray (Ity) 6-12-0 RDunwoody 2½.5
Stated Case 4-11-0 RMarley . 2.6
Tuns Hill 7-9-9 MJones 10.7
Ghofar 6-11-5 BPowell nk.8
Little Toro 7-10-7 SHodgson ... 9
Tartan Tailor 8-11-6 GMcCourt .... f

9/4 Stated Case, 7/2 Vicario di Bray, 6/1 Fragrant Dawn, 8/1 Tartan Tailor, 10/1 Nahar, 12/1 Imperial Brush, 14/1 Ghofar, HIGHLAND BOUNTY, 20/1 Little Toro, 50/1 Tuns Hill

A. Etheridge (S. Dow) 10ran 3m59.82 (Good)

8 MACKESON GOLD CUP HANDICAP CHASE 2½m
£24,395 Cheltenham 11 November

Joint Sovereignty 9-10-4 GMcCourt 1
Golden Freeze 7-11-6 MPitman nk.2
Dudie 11-10-0 LHarvey 3.3
Stay On Tracks 7-10-3 AMerrigan 5.4
Baluchi 8-10-0 GLandau sh.5
4 Cuddy Dale 6-10-4 DMurphy hd.6
Beau Ranger 11-12-0 PScudamore 1½.7
Chief Ironside 9-10-3 EMcKinley 1½.8
4* Prize Asset 9-10-4 SEarle 3.9
Vodkatini 10-11-6 RRowe 1½.10
Belsir 7-11-0 MFlynn 11
Foyle Fisherman 10-11-0 EMurphy .... f
Vicars Landing 6-10-0 JOsborne .... f
Raise An Argument 10-10-1 RDunwoody .... pu
Butlers Pet 10-10-3 PRichards .... pu

5/1 Beau Ranger, 7/1 Cuddy Dale, Prize Asset, Vicars Landing, 9/1 Vodkatini, 10/1 JOINT SOVEREIGNTY, Raise An Argument, Stay On Tracks, 11/1 Golden Freeze, 12/1 Chief Ironside, 25/1 Baluchi, 33/1 Belsir, Dudie, Foyle Fisherman, 200/1 Butlers Pet

G. Giddy (P. Hobbs) 15ran 5m05.31 (Good)

9 DIPPER NOVICES' CHASE 2½m
£10,047 Newcastle 11 November

Blazing Walker 5-11-9 CGrant 1
Third In Line 6-11-13 MDwyer ½.2
Mister Point 7-11-6 LWyer 2½.3
Interim Lib 6-11-6 MrJBradburne dist.4
Flying Dancer 7-11-6 BStorey .. f
Granny's Prayer 8-11-6 MHammond .... ur

8/11 BLAZING WALKER, 100/30 Third In Line, 15/2 Flying Dancer, 8/1 Mister Point, 16/1 Granny's Prayer, Interim Lib

P. Piller (W. A. Stephenson) 6ran 5m04.70 (Good to Firm)

10 C & L MURPHY TRIAL CHASE (LIMITED HANDICAP) 2½m
£8,766 Kempton 15 November

Pegwell Bay 8-11-7 CLlewellyn 1
Panto Prince 8-10-12 ILawrence 4.2
Barnbrook Again 8-11-10 BPowell .... f

4/6 Barnbrook Again, 7/4 Panto Prince, 7/1 PEGWELL BAY

Major A. Barlow (T. Forster) 3ran 5m07.68 (Good)

11 RACECALL ASCOT HURDLE 2½m
£14,129 Ascot 17 November

5 **Nodform** 5-10-11 RRowe 1
Floyd 9-11-7 GBradley 6.2
2[3] **Combermere** 5-10-11 JFrost 10.3
Sabin du Loir 10-10-11 PScudamore 15.4
Altountash 5-10-11 MWilliams .... pu

5/6 Sabin du Loir, 2/1 Floyd, 7/1 Combermere, 12/1 NODFORM, 50/1 Altountash

H. J. Joel (J. Gifford) 5ran 4m40.57 (Firm)

12 H & T WALKER GOLD CUP CHASE (LIMITED HANDICAP) 2½m
£23,820 Ascot 18 November

Man O'Magic 8-11-5 MPerrett **1**
7 **Ghofar** 6-11-5 BPowell 1½.**2**
Biloxi Blues 7-11-3 RBeggan 10.**3**
Herbert United 10-10-12 JFrost hd.4
Hogmanay (Can) 7-11-8 HDavies ¾.5
Impertain 9-10-7 MDwyer 10.6
Rowlandsons Jewels 8-11-1 MBowlby 20.7
Ruststone 9-11-0 JBrown 8
Southernair 9-11-8 RDunwoody 9
3² Steeple View 8-11-10 JOsborne .... pu
Hitchcock 6-10-12 TMorgan .. pu

11/4 Rowlandsons Jewels, 13/2 Hogmanay, 7/1 Hitchcock, 15/2 Biloxi Blues, 9/1 MAN O'MAGIC, 10/1 Ghofar, Steeple View, 11/1 Herbert United, 16/1 Ruststone, Southernair, 66/1 Impertain
J. D. Greig (K. Bailey) 11ran 4m45.70 (Good to Firm)

13 EDWARD HANMER MEMORIAL CHASE (LIMITED HANDICAP) 3m
£10,123 Haydock 22 November

Golden Friend 11-10-10 GMcCourt **1**
The Thinker 11-11-10 CGrant 1.**2**
Charter Party 11-11-10 RDunwoody 10.**3**
Eternal Credit 7-10-0 RMacNeice dist.4
6³ Yahoo 8-12-0 TMorgan .... pu

1/1 Yahoo, 9/4 The Thinker, 9/2 GOLDEN FRIEND, 8/1 Charter Party, 100/1 Eternal Credit
D. G. Meade (J. McConnochie) 5ran 6m33.87 (Good)

14 NORTH STREET HANDICAP CHASE 2m160y
£10,224 Newbury 25 November

10³ **Barnbrook Again** 8-12-0 BPowell **1**
Springholm 7-10-1 RDunwoody 1.**2**
Mr Key (USA) 8-10-4 MBowlby .... f
Cottage Run 9-10-1 JOsborne .... pu

5/4 BARNBROOK AGAIN, 13/8 Springholm, 7/1 Cottage Run, Mr Key
M. Davies (D. Elsworth) 4ran 3m58.13 (Firm)

15 GERRY FEILDEN HURDLE 2m100y
£10,227 Newbury 25 November

Cruising Altitude 6-11-3 JOsborne **1**
Morley Street 5-11-3 JFrost 6.**2**
Nomadic Way (USA) 4-11-0 KMooney 4.**3**
Wishlon (USA) 6-11-6 RGoldstein 1.4
2² Decided (Can) 6-11-0 PScudamore 6.5
Royal Derbi 4-11-3 HDavies . 6.6
Fairfields Cone 6-10-9 MJones 8.7
Magnus Pym 4-11-0 GBradley 10.8

6/5 CRUISING ALTITUDE, 7/2 Morley Street, 11/2 Decided, 7/1 Wishlon, 12/1 Nomadic Way, 14/1 Royal Derbi, 16/1 Magnus Pym, 66/1 Fairfields Cone
Mrs C. Heath (O. Sherwood) 8ran 3m48.47 (Firm)

16 HENNESSY COGNAC GOLD CUP HANDICAP CHASE 3¼m82y
£30,272 Newbury 25 November

12³ **Ghofar** 6-10-2 HDavies **1**
Brown Windsor 7-11-3 RDunwoody nk.**2**
Mr Frisk 10-11-8 MrMArmytage 2½.**3**
6* Durham Edition 11-11-2 AMerrigan 5.4
6² Ballyhane 8-11-10 RRowe .. 15.5
Roll-A-Joint 11-10-8 BPowell ¾.6
Gala's Image 9-10-6 JShortt 10.7
Solidasarock 7-10-0 PScudamore .... f

7/4 Brown Windsor, 5/1 Durham Edition, GHOFAR, 6/1 Ballyhane, 13/2 Roll-A-Joint, 14/1 Gala's Image, Solidasarock, 16/1 Mr Frisk
Sir H. Dundas (D. Elsworth) 8ran 6m28.29 (Firm)

17 FOOD BROKERS AND PRIMULA FIGHTING FIFTH HURDLE 2m
£13,940 Newcastle 25 November

Kribensis 5-11-9 MDwyer **1**
Jinxy Jack 5-11-0 NDoughty 2½.**2**
Past Glories 6-11-0 JQuinn 3.**3**
Osric 6-11-0 GMcCourt 2.4
Mill de Lease 4-11-0 WWorthington 30.5

4/7 KRIBENSIS, 5/2 Osric, 13/2 Jinxy Jack, 33/1 Past Glories, 250/1 Mill de Lease

Sheikh Mohammed (M. Stoute) 5ran 4m01.70 (Good to Firm)

18 ARLINGTON PREMIER SERIES CHASE (QUALIFIER) 2½m
£3,366 Chepstow 2 December

Waterloo Boy 6-11-7 JOsborne **1**
Celtic Shot 7-11-0 PScudamore nk.**2**
Midnight Train 8-11-7 MPitman 10.**3**
Pithy 7-11-4 MBosley 20.4
Salamart 6-11-0 NDawe .... pu

7/4 Celtic Shot, WATERLOO BOY, 2/1 Midnight Train, 50/1 Pithy, 150/1 Salamart
M. R. Deeley (D. Nicholson) 5ran 5m02.97 (Good)

19 REHEARSAL CHASE (LIMITED HANDICAP) 3m
£5,952 Chepstow 2 December

Bonanza Boy 8-11-10 PScudamore **1**
Run And Skip 11-10-9 HDavies 10.**2**
The West Awake 8-11-2 JOsborne 1.**3**
Ace of Spies 8-10-7 JBryan . 15.4
Little Polveir 12-10-7 JFrost 25.5
12 Ruststone 9-10-3 JBrown .... f

11/4 Run And Skip, 3/1 Ace of Spies, The West Awake, 4/1 BONANZA BOY, 16/1 Little Polveir, 33/1 Ruststone
S. Dunster (M. Pipe) 6ran 6m07.00 (Good)

20 WILLIAM HILL HANDICAP HURDLE 2m
£19,300 Sandown 2 December

Liadett (USA) 4-10-0 JLower **1**
Protection 7-10-2 RDunwoody ¾.**2**
Afaristoun (Fr) 5-10-6 TMorgan 4.**3**
11² Floyd 9-11-13 GBradley 5.4
Dare Say 6-10-3 RRowe .... f
Beldale Star 6-10-0 LHarvey .... f

9/4 Dare Say, 5/2 Beldale Star, 7/2 Protection, 4/1 Floyd, 12/1 Afaristoun, LIADETT
F. A. Farrant (M. Pipe) 6ran 3m52.18 (Good to Firm)

21 TINGLE CREEK CHASE (LIMITED HANDICAP) 2m18y
£10,040 Sandown 2 December

Long Engagement 8-10-0 BPowell **1**
Desert Orchid 10-12-0 RDunwoody 2½.**2**
Prideaux Boy 11-10-0 JShortt 2.**3**
12 Hogmanay (Can) 7-10-0 AWebb 8.4

1/2 Desert Orchid, 4/1 Prideaux Boy, 9/2 LONG ENGAGEMENT, 20/1 Hogmanay
A. M. Armitage (D. Nicholson) 4ran 3m57.00 (Good to Firm)

22 BMW SERIES FINAL (HANDICAP CHASE) 3m 1f
£10,625 Cheltenham 8 December

Wont Be Gone Long 7-11-13 RDunwoody **1**
Bonnie Artist 6-10-12 AMerrigan ¾.**2**
Mountaico 7-9-9 DSkyrme 15.**3**
Lockwood Prince 6-11-9 JFrost 25.4

7/4 WONT BE GONE LONG, 2/1 Bonnie Artist, Lockwood Prince, 16/1 Mountaico
R. Waley-Cohen (N. Henderson) 4ran 6m42.33 (Firm)

23 CHARTERHOUSE MERCANTILE LEISURE NOVICES' CHASE 2½m
£12,585 Cheltenham 9 December

Imadyna (NZ) 7-11-6 SEarle . **1**
Going Gets Tough 6-11-10 JFrost dist.**2**
French Goblin 6-11-6 RRowe ... f

4/7 French Goblin, 4/1 Going Gets Tough, IMADYNA
E. Parker (D. Barons) 3ran 5m21.40 (Firm)

24 CHARLES HEIDSIECK CHAMPAGNE BULA HURDLE 2m
£14,146 Cheltenham 9 December

15* **Cruising Altitude** 6-11-4 JOsborne **1**
15³ **Nomadic Way (USA)** 4-11-0 PScudamore hd.**2**
Beech Road 7-11-10 RGuest 1½.**3**
20 Floyd 9-11-10 GBradley hd.4
17³ Past Glories 6-11-6 JQuinn 12.5
12³ Biloxi Blues 7-10-12 BPowell 8.6
7* Highland Bounty 5-11-2 DMurphy 7
17 Osric 6-10-12 GMcCourt .... f

8/11 CRUISING ALTITUDE, 5/1 Beech Road, 7/1 Nomadic Way, 8/1 Osric, 17/2 Floyd, 20/1 Past Glories, 25/1 Biloxi Blues, 100/1 Highland Bounty
Mrs C. Heath (O. Sherwood) 8ran 3m55.34 (Firm)

25 A. F. BUDGE GOLD CUP 2½m
(HANDICAP CHASE)
£20,910 Cheltenham 9 December

Clever Folly 9-10-4
NDoughty **1**
Welsh Oak 9-10-1
RDunwoody 10.**2**
14* **Barnbrook Again** 8-12-0
BPowell 8.**3**
8³ Dudie 11-10-0 LHarvey ¾.4
Rusch de Farges (Fr) 6-11-6
PScudamore dist.5
8* Joint Sovereignty 9-10-9
GMcCourt .... pu

2/1 Barnbrook Again, 4/1 CLEVER FOLLY, Rusch de Farges, 5/1 Joint Sovereignty, 7/1 Dudie, 14/1 Welsh Oak
N. B. Mason (Farms) Ltd (G. Richards) 6ran 5m03.85 (Firm)

26 MERCURY 2½m
COMMUNICATIONS
HURDLE (SPORT OF
KINGS CHALLENGE)
£14,914 Cheltenham 9 December

15² **Morley Street** 5-11-6 JFrost . **1**
Deep Sensation 4-11-1
RDunwoody 7.**2**
Ikdam 4-11-1 NColeman . 2½.**3**
Urizen 4-11-1 BPowell ½.4
Height of Fun 5-11-6
JOsborne 10.5
Jamaica Bay (USA) 4-11-1
BMiller hd.6
Indian Baba 4-11-1
GMcCourt 25.7
7² Nahar 4-11-1 DMurphy .... f

4/7 MORLEY STREET, 11/2 Urizen, 8/1 Ikdam, 17/2 Deep Sensation, 12/1 Jamaica Bay, 20/1 Nahar, 25/1 Height of Fun, 33/1 Indian Baba
Salehurst Paper Co Ltd (G. Balding) 8ran 5m02.20 (Firm)

27 FREEBOOTER 2m150y
NOVICES' CHASE
£11,056 Doncaster 9 December

Antinous 5-11-8 LWyer **1**
Campsea-Ash 5-11-4
BMurphy 10.**2**
Tinas Lad 6-11-4
TMorgan 30.**3**
Greenheart 6-11-4
CGrant dist.4

11/10 ANTINOUS, 5/4 Greenheart, 8/1 Tinas Lad, 20/1 Campsea-Ash
Lt-Col R. Warden (M. H. Easterby) 4ran 3m58.20 (Firm)

28 DURKAN BROTHERS 2½m
INTERNATIONAL EBF
PUNCHESTOWN CHASE
£11,038 Punchestown 9 December

Maid of Money 7-11-9
APowell **1**
Carvill's Hill 7-12-0
KMorgan 3.**2**
Super Furrow 9-11-9 PGill . 3.**3**
Lastofthebrownies 9-10-9
CO'Dwyer 2.4
Bobsline 13-11-6 MrFFlood . 8.5
Hungary Hur 10-12-0
TCarmody 7.6
Abbey Glen 7-10-9 MFlynn .. 4.7
Roc de Prince (Fr) 6-10-9
BSheridan 8

2/1 MAID OF MONEY, 5/2 Carvill's Hill, 9/2 Hungary Hur, 6/1 Abbey Glen, 10/1 Super Furrow, 16/1 Bobsline, 25/1 Lastofthebrownies, 100/1 Roc de Prince
Mrs H. McCormick (J. Fowler) 8ran 5m34.90 (Good)

29 ARLINGTON PREMIER 2½m
SERIES CHASE
(QUALIFIER)
£3,980 Haydock 13 December

11 **Sabin du Loir (Fr)** 10-11-7
PScudamore **1**
9* **Blazing Walker** 5-11-7
AMerrigan 20.**2**
Nick The Brief 7-11-4
RSupple 20.**3**
Tartan Trademark 7-11-7
GMcCourt dist.4
Canford Palm 8-11-7
BdeHaan .... ur
Phoenix Gold 9-11-7
MDwyer .... ur
Stegsman 7-11-0 MBrennan .. pu

7/4 SABIN DU LOIR, 9/4 Phoenix Gold, 4/1 Nick The Brief, 5/1 Blazing Walker, 12/1 Tartan Trademark, 20/1 Canford Palm, 100/1 Stegsman
B. A. Kilpatrick (M. Pipe) 7ran 5m27.66 (Soft)

30 TOMMY WHITTLE 3m
CHASE
£8,149 Haydock 13 December

Baies 7-10-12 PScudamore **1**
13² **The Thinker** 11-11-2
AMerrigan sh.**2**
Rinus 8-10-12 NDoughty 4.**3**
Cool Ground 7-10-12
ATory 25.4
Swardean 7-11-2
BDowling hd.5
I Haventalight 10-10-12
RTeague .... f
13* Golden Friend 11-11-2
GMcCourt .... pu
Playschool (NZ) 11-11-2
HDavies .... pu
13 Eternal Credit 7-10-12
MFoster .... pu

4/5 The Thinker, 7/2 Playschool, 11/2 Golden Friend, 12/1 Swardean, 16/1 Rinus, 20/1 BAIES, 33/1 Cool Ground, 66/1 I Haventalight, 100/1 Eternal Credit

Mrs B. Samuel (C. Brooks) 9ran 6m37.92 (Soft)

31 PETER COX NOVICES' CHASE 2½m
£6,696 Ascot 16 December

The Proclamation 6-10-12 RDunwoody 1
Deep Colonist 7-11-1 RRowe 15.2
23* **Imadyna (NZ)** 7-11-11 SEarle 4.3
Amrullah 9-10-12 GMoore .. 20.4
Gay Edition 7-11-6 PHobbs ...... f
Master Barn 9-11-1 JFrost ..... ur
Get Away 7-10-12 BPowell ... ref

4/5 Deep Colonist, 5/2 THE PROCLAMATION, 7/1 Imadyna, 14/1 Gay Edition, 20/1 Master Barn, 40/1 Amrullah, 100/1 Get Away

M. Buckley (N. Henderson) 7ran 5m00.88 (Good to Soft)

32 H.S.S. HIRE SHOPS HURDLE 2m
£6,056 Ascot 16 December

Forest Sun 4-10-8 JFrost 1
Calapaez 5-11-8 MPerrett ... 5.2
11* **Nodform** 5-11-8 RRowe 8.3
Persillant 5-10-8 RDunwoody ¾.4
Bank View 4-11-4 MHill 30.5
Quai d'Orsay 4-10-8 MKinane .... pu
Touch of Speed 5-10-8 MRichards .... pu

2/1 Nodform, 3/1 Calapaez, 7/2 FOREST SUN, 5/1 Persillant, 9/1 Bank View, 66/1 Quai d'Orsay, 100/1 Touch of Speed

Salehurst Paper Co Ltd (G. Balding) 7ran 3m59.35 (Good to Soft)

33 YOUNGMANS LONG WALK HURDLE 3¼m
£10,317 Ascot 16 December

Royal Athlete 6-10-8 DGallagher 1
Mrs Muck 8-10-10 CLlewellyn 3.2
Pragada 6-10-8 RRowe 12.3
11³ Combermere 5-10-8 JFrost .. 3.4
Undaunted 5-10-8 BdeHaan . 2.5
5 Knighton Lad 8-11-1 JOsborne . f
Slalom 8-11-1 JWhite .... pu
Bluff Cove 7-10-8 RDunwoody .... pu
1 Santella Bobkes (USA) 4-10-8 MPerrett .... pu
The Pike 6-10-8 JQuinn .... pu
Young Bavard 8-10-8 MBowlby .... pu

5/4 Slalom, 4/1 Pragada, 6/1 Santella Bobkes, 9/1 Mrs Muck, 14/1 Undaunted, 16/1 Young Bavard, 20/1 Combermere, 25/1 Bluff Cove, 33/1 ROYAL ATHLETE, The Pike, 50/1 Knighton Lad

G. Johnson (Mrs J. Pitman) 11ran 6m14.64 (Good to Soft)

34 SGB HANDICAP CHASE 3m
£26,093 Ascot 16 December

16 **Solidasarock** 7-10-0 LHarvey 1
10² **Panto Prince** 8-11-10 BPowell 5.2
16² **Brown Windsor** 7-11-0 JWhite ¾.3
Bigsun 8-10-2 RDunwoody .. ½.4
Envopak Token 8-11-1 PHobbs 7.5
Smart Tar 8-11-0 CLlewellyn 20.6
8 Foyle Fisherman 10-11-5 EMurphy .... pu
3* Seagram (NZ) 9-10-10 NHawke .... pu
Sun Rising 11-10-12 KMooney .... pu
Bartres 10-10-7 MBowlby ..... pu
Tonights The Night 8-10-7 JOsborne .... pu
Von Trappe 12-10-1 MPerrett .... pu

11/4 Tonights The Night, 100/30 Brown Windsor, 7/2 Envopak Token, 12/1 Bigsun, 14/1 Panto Prince, Smart Tar, 16/1 Bartres, Foyle Fisherman, 20/1 Seagram, 25/1 Sun Rising, 33/1 SOLIDASAROCK, 50/1 Von Trappe

L. Randall (R. Akehurst) 12ran 6m22.72 (Good to Soft)

35 FROGMORE HANDICAP CHASE 2m
£9,240 Ascot 16 December

Blueberry King 6-10-0 LHarvey 1
14² **Springholm** 7-10-4 RDunwoody 15.2
Nohalmdun 8-10-7 LWyer .. 7.3
8 Prize Asset 9-10-11 SEarle . 12.4
21³ Prideaux Boy 11-11-4 JShortt 30.5
Outlaw 10-10-0 DTegg .... f
8 Vodkatini 10-11-10 RRowe .... pu

2/1 Nohalmdun, 7/2 Springholm, 11/2 Prize Asset, Vodkatini, 13/2 BLUEBERRY KING, 9/1 Prideaux Boy, 25/1 Outlaw

Pell-mell Partners (A. Turnell) 7ran 3m55.92 (Good to Soft)

36 CURRAN GROUP FINALE JUNIOR HURDLE (3y) 2m
£7,700 Chepstow 23 December

Crystal Heights 11-0 BPowell 1
Gay Ruffian 11-0 DBurchell 10.2
Child of The Mist 11-0 JOsborne 5.3

Royal Wonder 10-9 PScudamore ½.4
Calicon 11-0 JFrost dist.5
Ninja 11-0 RDunwoody f
First Whip 11-0 DTegg pu
Wick Pound 11-0 SMcNeill pu
Go Nobley 11-0 HDavies pu
March On 11-0 RGoldstein pu

15/8 Royal Wonder, 11/4 Calicon, 7/2 Gay Ruffian, 8/1 March On, 9/1 Child of The Mist, 33/1 CRYSTAL HEIGHTS, Ninja, 40/1 Go Nobley, Wick Pound, 100/1 First Whip

Mrs K. A. Stuart (Mrs J. G. Retter) 10ran 4m18.45 (Soft)

37 CORAL WELSH NATIONAL 3¾m
£21,980 Chepstow 23 December

19* **Bonanza Boy** 8-11-11 PScudamore 1
30 **Cool Ground** 7-9-13 ATory 15.2
Charter Hardware 7-9-11 NWilliamson ½.3
16* Ghofar 6-10-0 BPowell 4.4
16 Roll-A-Joint 11-10-0 RDunwoody 12.5
Team Challenge 7-10-0 BdeHaan 1.6
19 Little Polveir 12-10-5 JFrost 7
Remedy The Malady 8-10-1 JDuggan f
Stearsby 10-10-7 SMcNeill pu
Conclusive 10-10-4 NDoughty pu
Outside Edge 8-10-0 MBowlby pu
On The Twist 7-10-3 DMurphy pu

15/8 BONANZA BOY, 11/2 Ghofar, 9/1 Charter Hardware, 10/1 Conclusive, Cool Ground, 11/1 Remedy The Malady, 12/1 Little Polveir, 16/1 Stearsby, 18/1 Roll-A-Joint, 25/1 Team Challenge, 33/1 Outside Edge, 150/1 On The Twist

S. Dunster (M. Pipe) 12ran 7m59.43 (Soft)

38 RACING INTERNATIONAL HURDLE (SPORT OF KINGS CHALLENGE) 2½m
£8,940 Chepstow 23 December

Propero 4-11-1 RRowe 1
26* **Morley Street** 5-11-6 JFrost ¾.2
Calabrese 4-11-1 PHarley 10.3
Dis Train 5-11-6 MBowlby 4.4
26³ Ikdam 4-11-1 NColeman 4.5
26 Jamaica Bay (USA) 4-11-1 BMiller 3.6
Little-Nipper 4-11-1 RDunwoody 30.7
33 Undaunted 5-11-6 MPitman ro

8/13 Morley Street, 13/2 Undaunted, 7/1 Ikdam, 11/1 PROPERO, 20/1 Calabrese, 25/1 Dis Train, 33/1 Jamaica Bay, 200/1 Little-Nipper

Mrs S. A. Willis (J. Gifford) 8ran 5m17.14 (Soft)

39 HAVEN NOVICES' HURDLE 2m
£5,865 Kempton 26 December

Tinryland 5-11-10 RDunwoody 1
Gaasid 4-11-0 LHarvey ½.2
Empire Blue 6-11-0 PScudamore 1.3
Riverhead (USA) 5-11-0 BPowell 1½.4
Holtermann (USA) 5-11-0 CLlewellyn 3.5
Golden Moss 4-10-9 SMcKeever nk.6
Big Red 5-11-5 GMcCourt 20.7
Scampered 5-10-9 PHobbs 5.8
Bloodless Coup 7-10-7 SConlon 8.9
Williamsfield 4-11-0 TMorgan 10
Run By 5-11-0 GBradley 11
Roman Crackshot 5-11-0 MFurlong f
Vazon Bay 5-11-5 MPitman pu
Royal Halo (USA) 8-11-0 RGoldstein pu
Maybourne 5-11-0 HDavies pu
Morning Cry 5-11-0 JShortt pu
Step To Stardom 4-11-0 EMcKinley pu

100/30 Riverhead, 4/1 Vazon Bay, 5/1 TINRYLAND, 6/1 Empire Blue, 13/2 Gaasid, 16/1 Big Red, Run By, 25/1 Holtermann, Maybourne, 33/1 Bloodless Coup, Scampered, Williamsfield, 50/1 Golden Moss, Morning Cry, Step To Stardom, 66/1 Royal Halo, 100/1 Roman Crackshot

M. Buckley (N. Henderson) 17ran 3m51.92 (Good)

40 BUTLIN'S FELTHAM NOVICES' CHASE 3m
£11,990 Kempton 26 December

23 **French Goblin** 6-10-11 PHobbs 1
The Nigelstan 8-10-11 BPowell 4.2
Sooner Still 5-10-11 TMorgan 20.3
Speakers Corner 6-10-11 CLlewellyn 3.4
Garrison Savannah 6-10-11 MPitman 15.5
Power Punch 5-10-11 SMcKeever f
Rifle Range 6-10-11 GBradley f

15/8 FRENCH GOBLIN, 2/1 Rifle Range, 5/2 Garrison Savannah, 10/1 Sooner Still, 16/1 Speakers Corner, 25/1 The Nigelstan, 100/1 Power Punch

M. E. Pinto (J. Gifford) 7ran 6m02.75 (Good)

41 KING GEORGE VI RANK CHASE 3m
£40,986 Kempton 26 December

21[2] **Desert Orchid** 10-11-10 RDunwoody **1**
25[3] **Barnbrook Again** 8-11-10 BPowell 8.**2**
13 **Yahoo** 8-11-10 TMorgan 7.**3**
Bob Tisdall 10-11-10 PScudamore 3.4
10* Pegwell Bay 8-11-10 CLlewellyn 6.5
Norton's Coin 8-11-10 GMcCourt 15.6

4/6 DESERT ORCHID, 9/2 Pegwell Bay, 11/2 Yahoo, 13/2 Barnbrook Again, 33/1 Norton's Coin, 66/1 Bob Tisdall
R. Burridge (D. Elsworth) 6ran 6m04.25 (Good)

42 NOVAIR WAYWARD LAD NOVICES' CHASE 2½m
£9,065 Kempton 26 December

18[2] **Celtic Shot** 7-11-4 PScudamore **1**
Abbreviation 6-11-7 EMcKinley dist.**2**
Comandante 7-11-0 PHobbs ..... f
Le Chat Noir 6-11-0 HDavies .... f
Golden June 7-10-9 JShortt .... pu

3/10 CELTIC SHOT, 5/1 Comandante, 10/1 Abbreviation, 20/1 Le Chat Noir, 100/1 Golden June
D. E. H. Horton (C. Brooks) 5ran 5m16.39 (Good)

43 JOHN HAGGAS MEMORIAL NOVICES' CHASE 3m100y
£5,390 Wetherby 26 December

Carrick Hill Lad 6-11-8 NDoughty **1**
Cliffalda 6-11-1 NWilliamson 2.**2**
22[2] **Bonnie Artist** 5-11-7 AMerrigan 20.**3**
Mind Your Back 6-11-1 MDwyer dist.4
River House 7-11-1 CGrant ...... f
Snowfire Chap 6-11-1 TReed .... f
King's Harvest 6-11-1 LWyer .... pu

8/13 CARRICK HILL LAD, 4/1 Cliffalda, 7/1 Bonnie Artist, 10/1 Mind Your Back, 14/1 King's Harvest, 16/1 River House, 25/1 Snowfire Chap
A. M. Picken (G. Richards) 7ran 6m26.36 (Good)

44 ROWLAND MEYRICK HANDICAP CHASE 3m100y
£16,505 Wetherby 26 December

16 **Durham Edition** 11-10-6 AMerrigan **1**
29[3] **Nick The Brief** 7-10-5 RSupple ½.**2**
16 **Ballyhane** 8-11-0 RRowe sh.**3**
Old Applejack 9-10-0 TReed dist.4
30[2] The Thinker 11-11-10 CGrant 30.5
Birling Jack 8-9-12 NWilliamson .... ur
6 Randolph Place 8-10-5 NDoughty .... ur

2/1 Randolph Place, 100/30 The Thinker, 4/1 Ballyhane, 5/1 DURHAM EDITION, Nick The Brief, 10/1 Birling Jack, 33/1 Old Applejack
R. Oxley (W. A. Stephenson) 7ran 6m19.39 (Good)

45 RANK MOTORWAY SERVICES NOVICES' CHASE 2m
£7,765 Kempton 27 December

Young Snugfit 5-11-7 JOsborne **1**
For The Grain 5-11-0 RDunwoody 20.**2**
27* **Antinous** 5-11-7 LWyer 15.**3**
Deep Flash 6-11-4 NWilliamson .... f
Manton Mark 6-11-0 MrLFogarty .... f
Real Class 6-11-0 BPowell ..... pu

9/4 Deep Flash, 11/4 YOUNG SNUGFIT, 3/1 Antinous, 6/1 For The Grain, 10/1 Real Class, 100/1 Manton Mark
J. Poynton (O. Sherwood) 6ran 3m48.83 (Good)

46 TOP RANK CHRISTMAS HURDLE 2m
£28,348 Kempton 27 December

17* **Kribensis** 5-11-3 RDunwoody **1**
24 **Osric** 6-11-3 GMcCourt ... 2½.**2**
24 **Floyd** 9-11-3 GBradley 10.**3**
32[2] Calapaez 5-11-3 MPerrett 5.4
2* Aldino 6-11-3 JOsborne 15.5
20 Beldale Star 6-11-3 LHarvey 2.6
15 Wishlon (USA) 6-11-3 RGoldstein 4.7
Positive 6-11-3 RBeggan .... pu

4/6 KRIBENSIS, 5/1 Calapaez, 6/1 Floyd, 12/1 Osric, 20/1 Aldino, Wishlon, 25/1 Beldale Star, 50/1 Positive
Sheikh Mohammed (M. Stoute) 8ran 3m45.27 (Good)

47 BOBBY RENTON MEMORIAL NOVICES' CHASE 2m50y
£3,753 Wetherby 27 December

9[3] **Mister Point** 7-11-12 RMarley **1**
Super Trix 6-11-0 NDoughty 7.**2**

Forever Blue 6-11-0
CGrant 6.3
Contact Kelvin 7-11-0
PNiven 20.4
Shean Lad 9-10-9 AQuinn ... 10.5
Battle of Wits 8-11-0
AMerrigan dist.6
Lingham Duke 8-11-0
AOrkney .... f

1/1 MISTER POINT, 5/2 Forever Blue, 3/1 Super Trix, 25/1 Shean Lad, 50/1 Lingham Duke, 100/1 Battle of Wits, Contact Kelvin
M. Battle (M. H. Easterby) 7ran 4m03.43 (Good)

48 CASTLEFORD CHASE 2m50y
£19,124 Wetherby 27 December
4² **Ida's Delight** 10-10-7
BStorey 1
35³ **Nohalmdun** 8-10-7
RMarley ½.2
Pearlyman 10-12-3
TMorgan ½.3
Midnight Count 9-11-10
PHobbs dist.4
21* Long Engagement 8-10-7
MDwyer .... pu

8/11 Long Engagement, 9/2 Midnight Count, 13/2 Nohalmdun, 15/2 Pearlyman, 17/2 IDA'S DELIGHT
J. Charlton (J. Charlton) 5ran 3m57.30 (Good)

49 FINDUS HURDLE 2¾m
£9,952 Leopardstown 27 December
Naevog 6-10-6 TTaaffe 1
Trapper John 5-11-2
CSwan 2½.2
Cloughtaney 8-11-2
AMullins 10.3
Lucky Baloo 7-10-6
JDonnelly ½.4
Toranfield 5-10-11 FWoods 10.5
Galmoy 10-11-11 TCarmody . 8.6
Astral River 6-10-6
MrDMurphy 7

1/1 Cloughtaney, 4/1 Toranfield, 9/2 Galmoy, 8/1 NAEVOG, Trapper John, 14/1 Lucky Baloo, 33/1 Astral River
Mrs J. Byrne (L. Browne) 7ran 5m34.00 (Good to Soft)

50 BLACK AND WHITE WHISKY CHAMPION CHASE 2½m
£29,615 Leopardstown 28 December
28* **Maid of Money** 7-11-9
APowell 1
18* **Waterloo Boy** 6-12-0
RDunwoody ½.2
28³ **Super Furrow** 9-12-0
TCarmody ¾.3
Have A Barney 8-12-0 TTaaffe f

11/10 MAID OF MONEY, 6/4 Waterloo Boy, 6/1 Super Furrow, 7/1 Have A Barney
Mrs H. A. McCormick (J. Fowler) 4ran 5m38.90 (Good to Soft)

51 BOOKMAKERS HURDLE 2m
£14,784 Leopardstown 29 December
Grabel 6-11-9 AMullins 1
Elementary 6-12-0
TCarmody hd.2
Wolf of Badenoch 8-12-0
BSheridan dist.3
Bonalma 9-12-0 TTaaffe 12.4
Roark 7-12-0
MrDGeoghegan 5

8/11 GRABEL, 2/1 Elementary, 7/1 Wolf of Badenoch, 12/1 Bonalma, 16/1 Roark
P. F. Kehoe (P. Mullins) 5ran 3m50.20 (Good to Soft)

52 CHALLOW HURDLE 2½m 120y
£6,992 Newbury 29 December
36* **Forest Sun** 4-11-13 JFrost 1
Ard T'Match 4-11-8
WMorris 10.2
Dorver (USA) 5-11-8
RDunwoody 6.3
Tom Troubadour 6-11-13
EMurphy 3.4
Local Whisper 5-11-8
BPowell 1.5
Arden 5-11-13 PScudamore .. 3.6
Balvenie 5-11-8 GMcCourt 7
Stirrup Cup 5-11-8 JOsborne ... 8

6/4 FOREST SUN, 13/8 Stirrup Cup, 13/2 Arden, 8/1 Tom Troubadour, 9/1 Local Whisper, 50/1 Balvenie, 66/1 Ard T'Match, Dorver
Salehurst Paper Co Ltd (G. Balding) 8ran 5m02.23 (Good)

53 SAVE & PROSPER MANDARIN HANDICAP CHASE 3¼m82y
£6,940 Newbury 30 December
Polyfemus 7-10-5 JWhite 1
34³ **Brown Windsor** 7-11-10
RDunwoody nk.2
34* **Solidasarock** 7-10-13
LHarvey 3.3
Mount Parson 9-10-8
GMcCourt 20.4
Door Latch 11-11-5
RRowe 12.5
30 Golden Friend 11-11-10
HDavies 15.6
34 Smart Tar 8-11-8
CLlewellyn hd.7

2/1 Brown Windsor, 3/1 POLYFEMUS, 4/1 Solidasarock, 11/2 Smart Tar, 9/1 Mount Parson, 14/1 Golden Friend, 16/1 Door Latch
G. Johnson (M. Robinson) 7ran 6m40.57 (Good)

54 L'OREAL HANDICAP HURDLE 2m100y
£5,504 Newbury 30 December

7 **Fragrant Dawn** 5-11-10 MDwyer 1
Cinnamon Run 5-10-0 BPowell 4.2
7^3 **Imperial Brush** 5-10-7 PHolley 2.3
Tebitto 6-10-5 HDavies 2.4
Directly 6-10-7 JFrost 2½.5
Regal Castle 6-10-2 RDunwoody hd.6
Gods Fox 7-9-13 ATory 7
Ringyboy 4-10-0 LHarvey 8
Reggae Beat 4-10-1 RCampbell 9
Celtic Barle 5-10-3 JOsborne 10
The Gaelcharn 5-10-2 PScudamore 11
32 Bank View 4-11-10 GMcCourt 12
Penny Forum 5-11-6 DMcKeown 13
Platonic Affair 8-9-9 JCallaghan 14
One To Mark 6-9-7 PHarley 15
Run Free 4-9-9 VSmith .... f

5/2 FRAGRANT DAWN, 6/1 Imperial Brush, 7/1 Tebitto, 8/1 Celtic Barle, Directly, 10/1 Bank View, 11/1 Penny Forum, 12/1 Regal Castle, 14/1 Reggae Beat, Ringyboy, 20/1 Cinnamon Run, The Gaelcharn, 33/1 Gods Fox, Platonic Affair, 50/1 Run Free, 66/1 One To Mark
W. H. O'Gorman (J. FitzGerald) 16ran 3m53.78 (Good)

55 NEW YEAR'S DAY HURDLE 2m30y
£13,745 Windsor 1 January

46 **Aldino** 7-11-7 JOsborne 1
46 **Beldale Star** 7-11-4 LHarvey 2½.2
Ryde Again 7-11-4 RStronge 7.3
Valrodian (NZ) 7-11-4 JDuggan 6.4
Robin Wonder 12-11-4 PHolley 30.5

9/4 Ryde Again, 5/2 Beldale Star, 3/1 ALDINO, 4/1 Valrodian, 5/1 Robin Wonder
A. Boyd-Rochfort (O. Sherwood) 5ran 3m48.17 (Good)

56 SPA HURDLE 2½m
£6,832 Cheltenham 2 January

24^3 **Beech Road** 8-11-12 RGuest . 1
Chatam (USA) 6-11-0 PScudamore 1½.2

1/3 BEECH ROAD, 11/4 Chatam
T. Geake (G. Balding) 2ran 5m46.30 (Good)

57 FAIRLAWNE NOVICES' CHASE 2½m68y
£4,302 Sandown 6 January

42* **Celtic Shot** 8-11-6 PScudamore 1
32^3 **Nodform** 6-10-12 PHobbs 2½.2
7 **Tuns Hill** 8-10-12 SEarle . dist.3
31 Amrullah 10-10-12 GMoore 12.4
The Cherry Man 8-10-12 SKeightley 15.5
Rare Bid (NZ) 7-11-2 MrCMaude .... f

2/5 CELTIC SHOT, 3/1 Nodform, 33/1 Amrullah, The Cherry Man, Rare Bid, 50/1 Tuns Hill
D. E. H. Horton (C. Brooks) 6ran 5m07.95 (Good)

58 ANTHONY MILDMAY PETER CAZALET MEMORIAL HANDICAP CHASE 3m5f18y
£14,330 Sandown 6 January

37^2 **Cool Ground** 8-10-5 ATory ... 1
44^2 **Nick The Brief** 8-11-9 MLynch nk.2
12 **Rowlandsons Jewels** 9-10-9 MBowlby nk.3
30* Baies 8-11-8 PScudamore 6.4
Tarconey 10-10-0 RStronge 15.5
58 Team Challenge 8-10-0 BdeHaan ½.6
37 Roll-A-Joint 12-10-11 BPowell d-ht.6
Kodiak Island 8-10-0 JOsborne 1½.8
37 Stearsby 11-11-4 SMcNeill 9
34 Envopak Token 9-11-10 PHobbs .... f
3 Royal Cedar 9-10-8 SSmithEccles .... ur
58 Little Polveir 13-11-1 JFrost .. pu

9/2 Royal Cedar, 6/1 COOL GROUND, 13/2 Kodiak Island, 7/1 Baies, 15/2 Nick The Brief, Rowlandsons Jewels, 10/1 Envopak Token, 14/1 Tarconey, 16/1 Team Challenge, 25/1 Roll-A-Joint, Stearsby, 40/1 Little Polveir
Whitcombe Manor Racing Stables Ltd (N. Mitchell) 12ran 7m36.41 (Good)

59 BARING SECURITIES TOLWORTH HURDLE 2m
£7,280 Sandown 6 January

52* **Forest Sun** 5-11-12 JFrost 1
Atlaal 5-11-9 SSmithEccles . 6.2
39* **Tinryland** 6-11-12 JWhite .. nk.3
39^2 Gaasid 5-11-5 LHarvey 8.4
Lady Rosanna 5-11-0 EMurphy 20.5
Kalakate 5-11-5 WMorris ... 12.6
Park Street 5-11-5 JOsborne 8.7

8/11 FOREST SUN, 4/1 Tinryland, 8/1

Gaasid, 9/1 Lady Rosanna, 16/1 Atlaal, 25/1 Park Street, 33/1 Kalakate
Salehurst Paper Co Ltd (G. Balding) 7ran 4m03.16 (Good to Soft)

60 JOHN BULL CHASE 2m5f
£3,655 Wincanton 11 January

Toby Tobias 8-11-6 MPitman 1
41 **Pegwell Bay** 9-12-0 CLlewellyn 8.2
The Fruit 11-11-12 MrsNLedger dist.3
Vintage Lad 7-10-13 ILawrence 30.4

8/11 Pegwell Bay, 6/5 TOBY TOBIAS, 150/1 Vintage Lad, 200/1 The Fruit
Mrs E. Hutchins (Mrs J. Pitman) 4ran 5m16.13 (Good)

61 MUNNS ELECTRICAL HURDLE (HANDICAP) 3m
£10,264 Ascot 12 January

38^3 **Calabrese** 5-10-5 RDunwoody 1
55^3 **Ryde Again** 7-11-5 RStronge 3.2
Sterne (Fr) 8-10-0 DGallagher 10.3
Pertemps Network 6-12-0 PScudamore 1½.4
Sketcher (NZ) 7-10-5 SEarle 4.5
Withy Bank 8-10-0 RGarrity . 8.6
Derby Day 9-10-0 BPowell . 15.7
Take No Trash 9-10-0 GMartin 8
55 Robin Wonder 12-10-11 PHolley 9
Arctic Teal 6-11-2 JOsborne ..... f

4/5 CALABRESE, 6/1 Arctic Teal, 13/2 Withy Bank, 9/1 Ryde Again, 10/1 Pertemps Network, 11/1 Sketcher, 33/1 Robin Wonder, 50/1 Sterne, Take No Trash, 200/1 Derby Day
Mrs A. Fagan (N. Henderson) 10ran 5m41.24 (Good)

62 P.M.L. LIGHTNING NOVICES' CHASE 2m
£17,017 Ascot 12 January

Cashew King 7-11-5 TWall ... 1
Young Snugfit 6-11-13 JOsborne dist.2
The Proclamation 7-11-9 RDunwoody .... f

11/10 The Proclamation, Young Snugfit, 12/1 CASHEW KING
P. Moss (B. McMahon) 3ran 3m54.68 (Good)

63 FIRST NATIONAL CHASE (HANDICAP) 3m
£11,355 Ascot 12 January

Zuko (Chi) 9-10-0 MPerrett .. 1
44^3 **Ballyhane** 9-11-11 RRowe .. 7.2
Macroom 8-10-0 SCowley ... 3.3
41 Bob Tisdall 11-11-10 PScudamore 15.4
16^3 Mr Frisk 11-11-6 ATory 20.5
The Bakewell Boy 8-10-4 JFrost 2½.6
Against The Grain 9-10-9 RDunwoody 7
Memberson 12-10-6 MrGUpton 8
J-J-Henry 11-10-9 MrsAFarrell 9
34 Von Trappe 13-10-4 JRailton .... f
Burannpour 10-10-9 ACharlton .... pu

3/1 Macroom, 4/1 Ballyhane, 6/1 Bob Tisdall, ZUKO, 13/2 Mr Frisk, 8/1 The Bakewell Boy, 16/1 Against The Grain, 20/1 J-J-Henry, 50/1 Burannpour, Memberson, Von Trappe
S. Powell (S. Mellor) 11ran 6m13.41 (Good)

64 VICTOR CHANDLER HANDICAP CHASE 2m
£30,378 Ascot 13 January

Meikleour 11-10-0 DByrne ... 1
Feroda 9-10-0 JOsborne ... 1½.2
34^2 **Panto Prince** 9-10-11 BPowell 7.3
Star's Delight 8-10-0 PScudamore ½.4
64 Pearlyman 11-11-10 TMorgan 5.5
35* Blueberry King 7-10-0 LHarvey 1.6
48 Long Engagement 9-10-9 RDunwoody 1½.7
48^2 Nohalmdun 9-10-0 RMarley 1½.8
41 Norton's Coin 9-10-0 MPerrett ½.9
35 Vodkatini 11-10-9 RRowe 10

7/2 Blueberry King, 4/1 Panto Prince, 11/2 Feroda, 6/1 Pearlyman, 10/1 MEIKLEOUR, 11/1 Long Engagement, Vodkatini, 12/1 Nohalmdun, 14/1 Star's Delight, 20/1 Norton's Coin
Mrs A. C. Leggat (J. FitzGerald) 10ran 3m55.70 (Good)

65 PETER ROSS NOVICES' CHASE 3m
£7,310 Ascot 13 January

Espy 7-11-4 PScudamore 1
Mighty Fine 9-11-4 MrGUpton 20.2
Lauderdale Lad 8-11-4 HDavies 1½.3
Golden Fox 8-11-4 MPerrett 4.4
Sea Challenger 9-10-13 MrsNLedger dist.5
40* French Goblin 7-12-0 RRowe .... pu
57 Amrullah 10-11-4 GMoore ..... pu
Aristos 6-11-4 SMcNeill .... pu

Priors Coppice 8-11-4
BPowell .... pu
Timely Star 9-11-4
MBowlby .... pu

13/8 French Goblin, 3/1 Timely Star, 5/1 ESPY, Mighty Fine, 16/1 Golden Fox, 20/1 Lauderdale Lad, 33/1 Aristos, 50/1 Priors Coppice, 66/1 Amrullah, 100/1 Sea Challenger

R. E. A. Bott (Wigmore St) Ltd (C. Brooks) 10ran 6m24.72 (Good)

66 THE LADBROKE (HANDICAP HURDLE) 2m
£27,311 Leopardstown 13 January

Redundant Pal 7-11-5
CO'Dwyer 1
38 **Dis Train** 6-10-12
MPitman ½.2
54* **Fragrant Dawn** 6-10-1
MDwyer 3.3
Joyful Noise 7-10-6
TTaaffe sh.4
Sayparee 5-10-9
AMullins sh.5
7 Vicario di Bray (Ity) 7-11-4
RSupple 3.6
46[2] Osric 7-11-11 GMcCourt hd.7
49 Toranfield 6-10-8 FWoods 5.8
St Coleman's Well 7-10-0
GO'Neill 1.9
Derrinore 5-10-5 PGill ½.10
Welsh Bard 6-11-6
MrALacy hd.11
24 Past Glories 7-11-12
JQuinn sh.12
Peanuts Pet 5-10-0
TWall 2½.13
Marlion 9-10-0 LCusack ¾.14
Lough Gale 6-10-4
BSheridan ½.15
Castle Windows 7-10-1
KO'Brien hd.17
Tawkin 5-10-3 MTreacy ... sh.17
Bright Note 7-10-7
HRogers 1.18
51[2] Elementary 7-12-0
MFlynn 2.19
Firions Law 5-10-0
CBowens 2½.20
15 Royal Derbi 5-11-4
GBradley 5.21
Atteses 6-11-5 CSwan 22
Random Prince 6-10-7
DO'Connor 23
51[3] Wolf of Badenoch 9-11-6
TCarmody 24
Maiden Fair 7-10-3 APowell .. 25
51 Roark 8-11-10 KMorgan 26
Capable (USA) 8-11-4 DDoran .. f

4/1 Fragrant Dawn, 7/1 Joyful Noise, 8/1 Elementary, 10/1 Osric, 12/1 Lough Gale, 14/1 Marlion, Peanuts Pet, 16/1 Toranfield, Vicario di Bray, 20/1 Dis Train, Firions Law, REDUNDANT PAL, Royal Derbi, Sayparee, Wolf of Badenoch, 25/1 Tawkin, 33/1 Castle Windows, Past Glories, Random Prince, 40/1 Atteses, Welsh Bard, 50/1 Bright Note, Derrinore, Maiden Fair, 66/1 Capable, Roark, St Coleman's Well

P. S. O'Neill (P. Mullins) 27ran 3m47.00 (Good)

67 TELECOM EIREANN THYESTES HANDICAP CHASE 3m 170y
£13,561 Gowran Park 18 January

Mweenish 8-10-0 PGill 1
Lanigans Wine 8-10-0
CO'Dwyer 12.2
Auntie Dot 9-10-6
APowell ½.3
28 Lastofthebrownies 10-10-13
TCarmody 6.4
Attitude Adjuster 10-10-0
CSwan 10.5
Thinking Cap 9-10-1
PMalone 1.6
Amy Fairy 9-10-0 JDoyle 1.7
Fatal Hesitation 7-10-6
MrRKehoe 1.8
Barney Burnett 10-11-3
BSheridan 9
Derry Gowan 8-10-3 JTitley .. 10
50 Have A Barney 9-12-0
TTaaffe 11
Mirage Day 7-10-0 KO'Brien . 12
Feltrim Hill Lad 9-11-3
MissSCollen 13
Cranlome 12-10-0 TRyan 14
Inch Colleen 8-10-0 MFlynn .. ur
Ceolbridge Baby 9-10-0
MrACoonan .... pu

7/1 Feltrim Hill Lad, Have A Barney, Lastofthebrownies, 8/1 Auntie Dot, Barney Burnett, 10/1 Inch Colleen, 11/1 Mirage Day, 12/1 Lanigans Wine, 14/1 Fatal Hesitation, 16/1 Attitude Adjuster, Cranlome, Thinking Cap, 20/1 MWEENISH, 33/1 Amy Fairy, Ceolbridge Baby, Derry Gowan

P. S. Thompson (J. Webber) 16ran 7m09.30 (Heavy)

68 MANDOR FLEXIBLE DOORS PREMIER LONG DISTANCE HURDLE 3m
£9,620 Haydock 20 January

33[2] **Mrs Muck** 9-11-2 GBradley ... 1
49[2] **Trapper John** 6-11-11
CSwan 12.2
61 **Pertemps Network** 6-12-0
PScudamore 10.3
38 Ikdam 5-12-0 NColeman 5.4
Shilgrove Place 8-11-7
JO'Gorman .... f
Auction Law (NZ) 6-11-7
MDwyer .... pu
Fleet Commander 7-11-7
MRichards .... pu

13/8 MRS MUCK, 9/4 Trapper John, 4/1 Pertemps Network, 6/1 Auction Law,

25/1 Ikdam, 33/1 Shilgrove Place, 50/1 Fleet Commander
N. A. Twiston-Davies (N. A. Twiston-Davies) 7ran 6m18.81 (Soft)

69 DAILY MAIL RACECALL CHAMPION HURDLE TRIAL 2m
£9,500 Haydock 20 January

54 **Bank View** 5-11-8 GBradley . 1
66 **Vicario di Bray (Ity)** 7-11-11 MDwyer 1½.2
5[2] **Milford Quay** 7-11-8 PScudamore 4.3
Tel-Echo 6-11-11 TMorgan 15.4
66 Past Glories 7-11-8 JQuinn ... 4.5
Tree Poppy 7-11-3 BDowling 8.6
55 Valrodian (NZ) 7-11-8 JWhite .. 7

13/8 Vicario di Bray, 3/1 Milford Quay, 4/1 Valrodian, 5/1 Past Glories, 14/1 Tel-Echo, 20/1 Tree Poppy, 33/1 BANK VIEW
Bank View Hire Ltd (N. Tinkler) 7ran 4m06.15 (Soft)

70 PETER MARSH CHASE (LIMITED HANDICAP) 3m
£15,310 Haydock 20 January

58[2] **Nick The Brief** 8-10-9 MLynch 1
Bishops Yarn 11-11-0 RGuest ½.2
41[3] **Yahoo** 9-12-0 TMorgan 8.3
25 Rusch de Farges (Fr) 7-11-5 PScudamore ¾.4
53 Mount Parson 10-10-7 GBradley dist.5
Dixton House 11-10-11 JWhite .... pu

15/8 NICK THE BRIEF, 7/2 Bishops Yarn, 4/1 Rusch de Farges, Yahoo, 14/1 Dixton House, 16/1 Mount Parson
J. R. Upson (J. R. Upson) 6ran 6m39.19 (Soft)

71 BIC RAZOR LANZAROTE HANDICAP HURDLE 2m
£14,961 Kempton 20 January

59[2] **Atlaal** 5-10-3 RDunwoody 1
66 **Osric** 7-11-10 GMcCourt ... hd.2
26[2] **Deep Sensation** 5-10-13 RRowe 2.3
20[3] Afaristoun (Fr) 6-10-7 NWilliamson 1½.4
Without A Doubt 8-9-12 BMcGiff 1½.5
Wonder Man (Fr) 5-11-1 MPitman 5.6
Tancred Sand 7-10-6 MHill . hd.7
Kadan (Ger) 6-10-9 SSmithEccles 2½.8
Out of Range 7-10-3 AMcCabe nk.9
Austhorpe Sunset 6-9-12 PHarte hd.10
Royal Illusion 6-10-7 DMurphy 2.11
54 Gods Fox 8-10-0 LHarvey 12
Vayrua (Fr) 5-11-6 MPerrett .... pu

5/2 Wonder Man, 4/1 Osric, 11/2 Kadan, 15/2 Without A Doubt, 10/1 ATLAAL, 14/1 Vayrua, 16/1 Deep Sensation, 20/1 Tancred Sand, 25/1 Afaristoun, Austhorpe Sunset, Out of Range, 33/1 Royal Illusion, 100/1 Gods Fox
O. Donnelly (J. Jenkins) 13ran 3m49.36 (Good)

72 FULWELL HANDICAP CHASE 2½m
£8,130 Kempton 20 January

One More Knight 7-11-0 LHarvey 1
Katabatic 7-11-8 HDavies ¾.2
First Bout 9-11-3 RDunwoody 8.3
25[2] Welsh Oak 10-11-10 SSmithEccles dist.4
Bright Intervals 8-11-10 BdeHaan .... pu

6/4 Katabatic, 5/2 Welsh Oak, 4/1 ONE MORE KNIGHT, 6/1 First Bout, 14/1 Bright Intervals
R. West (Mrs I. McKie) 5ran 5m09.31 (Good)

73 RACEPHONE NATIONAL HANDICAP CHASE 3½m 180y
£6,232 Warwick 20 January

Midnight Madness 12-11-1 RGreene 1
Mister Christian (NZ) 9-10-0 SEarle nk.2
Forest Ranger 8-10-0 DTegg 20.3
58* Cool Ground 8-10-11 ATory ¾.4
Woodgate 9-10-9 CLlewellyn ¾.5
58 Team Challenge 8-10-2 DGallagher 2½.6
Rausal 11-9-9 JLodder nk.7
37 Remedy The Malady 9-10-11 JDuggan 25.8
Sam da Vinci 11-11-10 MBrennan 9
Dercander 8-10-2 TGrantham 10
Eton Rouge 11-10-0 JBryan ... 11
63 Memberson 12-10-5 MrGUpton 12
Over The Road 9-10-12 KBurke 13
L'Ane Rouge 9-11-1 JLower .... f
Monanore 13-11-1 LWyer ..... pu
Star of Screen (USA) 10-10-8 MissAHarwood .... pu

Fair Child 10-10-10
MBowlby .... pu
Furzen Hill 11-10-0 BPowell . pu

9/4 Cool Ground, 4/1 Remedy The Malady, 11/1 Mister Christian, 12/1 Woodgate, 14/1 Fair Child, Forest Ranger, L'Ane Rouge, 16/1 Dercander, MIDNIGHT MADNESS, Star of Screen, Team Challenge, 20/1 Memberson, Sam da Vinci, 25/1 Eton Rouge, 33/1 Monanore, Over The Road, 66/1 Rausal, 100/1 Furzen Hill
D. Bloomfield (D. Bloomfield) 18ran 7m32.84 (Good to Soft)

74 ROSSINGTON MAIN NOVICES' HURDLE 2m150y
£6,320 Doncaster 26 January

66 **Peanuts Pet** 5-11-0 TWall 1
Rakes Lane 5-11-0
TMorgan 1.2
Sacre d'Or (USA) 5-11-4
SO'Neill 5.3
Triple Top 5-11-0 PNiven 7.4
Sunset Reins Free 5-11-0
KDoolan 2½.5
Skolern 6-11-4 CHawkins dist.6

4/5 PEANUTS PET, 9/2 Rakes Lane, 6/1 Sacre d'Or, 8/1 Triple Top, 12/1 Skolern, 33/1 Sunset Reins Free
L. Perry (B. McMahon) 6ran 3m59.82 (Good)

75 WEST OF SCOTLAND PATTERN NOVICES' CHASE 2½m
£10,330 Ayr 27 January

43* **Carrick Hill Lad** 7-11-11
NDoughty 1
5 **Aston Express** 7-11-7
PNiven 8.2
45^3 **Antinous** 6-11-13 LWyer 8.3
29^2 Blazing Walker 6-11-13
CGrant .... ur

11/10 CARRICK HILL LAD, 13/8 Blazing Walker, 11/2 Antinous, 14/1 Aston Express
A. M. Picken (G. Richards) 4ran 5m21.20 (Heavy)

76 CHARTERHOUSE MERCANTILE CHASE 3m1f
£10,016 Cheltenham 27 January

60* **Toby Tobias** 8-11-6 MPitman 1
50* **Maid of Money** 8-11-7
APowell 10.2
34 **Bigsun** 9-11-8
RDunwoody 15.3
Rymer King 8-11-6
MLynch 10.4

1/1 Maid of Money, 5/4 TOBY TOBIAS, 9/1 Bigsun, 25/1 Rymer King
Mrs E. Hitchins (Mrs J. Pitman) 4ran 6m49.64 (Good to Soft)

77 ARLINGTON PREMIER SERIES CHASE FINAL 2½m
£20,370 Cheltenham 27 January

29* **Sabin du Loir (Fr)** 11-11-7
GMcCourt 1
57* **Celtic Shot** 8-11-7
PScudamore 2½.2
50^2 **Waterloo Boy** 7-11-7
RDunwoody 25.3
18^3 Midnight Train 9-11-7
MPitman 8.4

6/5 Celtic Shot, 9/4 SABIN DU LOIR, 3/1 Waterloo Boy, 16/1 Midnight Train
B. A. Kilpatrick (M. Pipe) 4ran 5m24.07 (Good to Soft)

78 BISHOPS CLEEVE HURDLE 2½m
£5,432 Cheltenham 27 January

56* **Beech Road** 8-12-0 RGuest ... 1
33 **Slalom** 9-12-0 JWhite 15.2
38* **Propero** 5-12-0 RRowe 12.3
69 Tel-Echo 6-11-10
PScudamore 20.4
Strokestown Lad 6-11-8
SMcNeill 20.5

1/3 BEECH ROAD, 11/2 Tel-Echo, 7/1 Propero, 14/1 Slalom, 200/1 Strokestown Lad
T. Geake (G. Balding) 5ran 5m26.39 (Good to Soft)

79 WILLIAM HILL GOLDEN SPURS HANDICAP CHASE 3m122y
£15,858 Doncaster 27 January

12* **Man O'Magic** 9-11-10
MPerrett 1
Fleming 10-10-0 PFarrell 5.2
58^3 **Rowlandsons Jewels** 9-11-6
MBowlby 12.3
No One To Blame 8-10-4
JOsborne 10.4
Kittinger 9-10-13 SO'Neill ... 2.5
Fib 8-10-0 JRailton 15.6
63 J-J-Henry 11-11-9
MrsAFarrell .... pu
Proverity 9-11-8 TMorgan .... pu
58 Royal Cedar 9-11-5 JShortt .... pu
22* Wont Be Gone Lone 8-10-13
SSmithEccles .... pu
See You There 8-10-2
MDwyer .... pu

3/1 Rowlandsons Jewels, 7/2 MAN O'MAGIC, 6/1 See You There, 7/1 Royal Cedar, 15/2 Kittinger, 8/1 No One To Blame, 12/1 Wont Be Gone Long, 16/1 Fleming, Proverity, 33/1 Fib, J-J-Henry
J. D. Greig (K. Bailey) 11ran 5m56.94 (Good to Firm)

80 GOLDEN MILLER NOVICES' HURDLE 2½m
£3,980 Leicester 30 January

Regal Ambition 6-11-13
PScudamore 1

Danny Harrold 6-11-5
MPitman 25.2
Queen's Chaplain 6-11-5
RDunwoody 1.3
Betrim 6-10-12 NMann dist.4
L'Oraz 6-10-7 DTelfer 20.5
Whats The Crack 7-11-5
RBeggan 15.6
Quota One 6-11-5 MBrennan ... 7
Sir Noddy 7-11-5 SO'Neill ..... pu
Spireslake 7-11-5 HDavies .... pu
Talking Money 6-11-2
WMcFarland .... pu

4/6 REGAL AMBITION, 13/8 Danny Harrold, 11/1 Talking Money, 20/1 Queen's Chaplain, 25/1 Betrim, Quota One, 50/1 L'Oraz, Spireslake, 66/1 Sir Noddy, Whats The Crack
Skeltools Ltd (M. Pipe) 10ran 5m03.67 (Soft)

81 A.F. BUDGE NOVICES' HURDLE 2m
£9,240 Ascot 7 February

Whatever You Like 6-11-4
JWhite 1
Man of The West 7-12-0
MDwyer ½.2
71* **Atlaal** 5-12-0 GMcCourt .. 1½.3
39 Riverhead (USA) 6-11-8
BPowell 1½.4
Dark Honey 5-11-4 RGuest 12.5
Proving 6-11-4 MLaurence .. 4.6
Lapierre 5-11-4 RDennis 8.7
59³ Tinryland 6-12-0
RDunwoody ½.8
Book of Gold 5-11-4 RRowe ... pu
Count Me Out 5-11-4
MHoad .... pu

9/4 Riverhead, 5/1 Atlaal, Tinryland, WHATEVER YOU LIKE, 11/2 Man of The West, 9/1 Lapierre, 20/1 Book of Gold, Dark Honey, 33/1 Proving, 66/1 Count Me Out
A. M. Ennever (N. Henderson) 10ran 4m13.20 (Soft)

82 DANIEL HOMES NOVICES' CHASE 2m
£11,875 Ascot 7 February

Wink Gulliver 6-11-4
RArnott 1
Western Dandy 7-11-4
BPowell 5.2
Another Coral 7-12-0
RDunwoody 12.3
Setter Country 6-10-13
WIrvine 1.4
Fuego Boy (NZ) 10-11-4
BDowling ½.5
Lumley Lake 7-11-4
RRowe 25.6
Beau Guest (Fr) 8-11-4
MDwyer .... ur

13/8 Another Coral, 4/1 WINK GULLIVER, 5/1 Fuego Boy, 8/1 Western Dandy, 9/1 Setter Country, 10/1 Beau Guest, 33/1 Lumley Lake
Mrs T. M. Moriarty (D. Elsworth) 7ran 4m15.77 (Soft)

83 DAILY TELEGRAPH HURDLE 3m
£12,538 Ascot 7 February

61² **Ryde Again** 7-11-10
GMcCourt 1
61* **Calabrese** 5-11-0
RDunwoody 3.2
Brabazon (USA) 5-11-0
BPowell 2½.3
33³ Pragada 7-11-0 RRowe 1½.4
68* Mrs Muck 9-11-5
PScudamore 5.5
65 Timely Star 9-11-0 MPitman 7.6
33 Santella Bobkes (USA) 5-11-0
MPerrett 12.7
Miss Nero 9-11-5
BDowling 2½.8
Glen Oak 5-11-0
MrGUpton 2½.9
Mineral Dust 7-11-0 JBryan ... pu
61³ Sterne (Fr) 8-11-0
DGallagher .... pu

1/1 Mrs Muck, 11/4 RYDE AGAIN, 6/1 Calabrese, 10/1 Timely Star, 12/1 Pragada, 16/1 Miss Nero, Santella Bobkes, 25/1 Brabazon, 50/1 Mineral Dust, 66/1 Glen Oak, Sterne
Mrs K. I. Hayward (P. Cundell) 11ran 6m13.02 (Soft)

84 CHARTERHOUSE MERCANTILE CHASE (HANDICAP) 3m
£25,813 Ascot 7 February

Ten of Spades 10-10-0
KMooney 1
Paddyboro 12-10-0
PHobbs 5.2
79* **Man O'Magic** 9-10-0
MPerrett 2½.3
73 Cool Ground 8-9-13 ATory ... 2.4
63² Ballyhane 9-10-0 RRowe 4.5
70 Rusch de Farges (Fr) 7-10-6
PScudamore dist.6
Castle Warden 13-10-0
BPowell .... pu

13/8 Ballyhane, 7/2 Man O'Magic, 11/2 Rusch de Farges, TEN OF SPADES, 7/1 Cool Ground, 12/1 Paddyboro, 25/1 Castle Warden
Mrs W. H. Whitbread (F. Walwyn) 7ran 6m49.77 (Soft)

85 OLD ROAD SECURITIES REYNOLDSTOWN NOVICES' CHASE 3m
£18,230 Ascot 7 February

33* **Royal Athlete** 7-11-8
MPitman 1
Last House 7-11-3
DGallagher 15.2

75* **Carrick Hill Lad** 7-11-12
NDoughty 3.**3**
Mixed Blends 8-11-7
CSwan nk.4
Buckshee Boy 8-11-12
PDever dist.5
77² Celtic Shot 8-11-12
PScudamore .... f
31² Deep Colonist 8-11-8
RRowe .... pu

11/8 Carrick Hill Lad, 5/2 Celtic Shot, 11/4 ROYAL ATHLETE, 8/1 Deep Colonist, 25/1 Last House, 33/1 Mixed Blends, 50/1 Buckshee Boy
G. Johnson (Mrs J. Pitman) 7ran 6m47.05 (Soft)

86 STROUD GREEN HURDLE (4y) 2m100y
£4,403 Newbury 9 February

Silver King (Fr) 11-0
PScudamore **1**
36² **Gay Ruffian** 11-0
DBurchell 8.**2**
Rouyan 11-0 WMorris 10.**3**
Embarkation 11-0 JLodder ... 1.4
Man For All Season (USA) 11-0
WMcFarland ¾.5
Star of The Glen 11-5
BPowell 3.6
Muirfield Village 11-0
STurner 7
Able Leader 11-0 RRowe .... pu
Leigh Boy (USA) 11-0
MDwyer .... pu

5/6 SILVER KING, 9/2 Man For All Season, 8/1 Gay Ruffian, Leigh Boy, 9/1 Able Leader, 16/1 Star of The Glen, 25/1 Embarkation, Muirfield Village, Rouyan
Pipe Scudamore Racing Plc (M. Pipe) 9ran 4m00.77 (Good to Soft)

87 GAME SPIRIT CHASE (LIMITED HANDICAP) 2m160y
£10,960 Newbury 10 February

64² **Feroda** 9-11-2 TTaaffe **1**
The Dragon Master 8-10-10
HDavies ¾.**2**
64 **Long Engagement** 9-11-10
RDunwoody 12.**3**
Hypnosis (USA) 11-10-7
GBradley .... f

10/11 FERODA, 15/8 The Dragon Master, 13/2 Long Engagement, 10/1 Hypnosis
N. McCarthy (A. Moore, Ire) 4ran 4m21.19 (Good to Soft)

88 TOTE GOLD TROPHY HANDICAP HURDLE 2m100y
£32,200 Newbury 10 February

71³ **Deep Sensation** 5-11-3
RRowe **1**
66 **Joyful Noise** 7-11-5
TTaaffe hd.**2**
54³ **Imperial Brush** 6-10-0
PHolley 4.**3**
Moody Man 5-10-5 PHobbs .. 3.4
17² Jinxy Jack 6-11-8
NDoughty 1½.5
66 Royal Derbi 5-11-10
HDavies 2½.6
Sudden Victory 6-11-2
KMooney 2½.7
Ambassador 7-10-1
PScudamore 2.8
32 Persillant 6-10-7 GMcCourt . 1.9
Hill Street (Fr) 8-10-13
MDwyer 8.10
15 Magnus Pym 5-10-13
GBradley ½.11
Badihar (USA) 6-10-5
MBowlby 2.12
71 Out of Range 7-10-6
AMcCabe nk.13
Don Valentino 5-11-8
MPitman 1½.14
71 Afaristoun (Fr) 6-10-13
TMorgan 15
Rampallion 7-10-6
RDunwoody 16
46 Positive 8-10-12 MPerrett .... pu

4/1 Hill Street, 13/2 Sudden Victory, 7/1 DEEP SENSATION, 15/2 Don Valentino, Jinxy Jack, 9/1 Ambassador, 10/1 Joyful Noise, 12/1 Moody Man, 16/1 Afaristoun, Magnus Pym, Rampallion, 25/1 Out of Range, 33/1 Badihar, Imperial Brush, Persillant, Positive, 66/1 Royal Derbi
R. F. Eliot (J. Gifford) 17ran 4m04.63 (Good to Soft)

89 BYRNE BROTHERS COMPTON CHASE 3m
£11,030 Newbury 10 February

41² **Barnbrook Again** 9-11-2
HDavies **1**
70³ **Yahoo** 9-11-12 TMorgan .. dist.**2**
53 **Golden Friend** 12-11-4
GMcCourt 20.**3**
76* Toby Tobias 8-11-6
MPitman .... ur

8/11 Toby Tobias, 11/4 BARNBROOK AGAIN, 100/30 Yahoo, 25/1 Golden Friend
M. Davies (D. Elsworth) 4ran 6m20.03 (Good to Soft)

90 HAROLD CLARKE LEOPARDSTOWN HANDICAP CHASE 3m
£10,849 Leopardstown 10 February

28² **Carvill's Hill** 8-12-2
KMorgan **1**
67 **Barney Burnett** 10-10-5
BSheridan 6.**2**
67 **Lastofthebrownies** 10-10-1
TCarmody 8.**3**
Riska's River 8-10-5
CO'Dwyer ½.4

67 Feltrim Hill Lad 9-10-5 CSwan 6.5
Rust Never Sleeps 6-10-0 GO'Neill 5.6
67 Fatal Hesitation 7-10-1 MrRKehoe hd.7
67* Mweenish 8-10-0 MLynch ...... f
Bean Alainn 8-10-0 KO'Brien .... pu

4/5 CARVILL'S HILL, 6/1 Mweenish, 8/1 Lastofthebrownies, Riska's River, 10/1 Feltrim Hill Lad, 12/1 Barney Burnett, 14/1 Rust Never Sleeps, 33/1 Bean Alainn, Fatal Hesitation

Mrs J. McMorrow (J. Dreaper) 9ran 6m36.80 (Heavy)

91 WESSEL CABLE CHAMPION HURDLE 2m
£28,160 Leopardstown 10 February

24[2] **Nomadic Way (USA)** 5-11-4 BPowell 1
66 **Elementary** 7-11-7 TCarmody 6.2
66 **Toranfield** 6-11-7 FWoods 12.3
Fourth of July 7-11-7 BSheridan 1.4
Island Set (USA) 8-11-7 DMurphy 20.5
49* Naevog 7-11-2 CSwan 6
66 Roark 8-11-7 MrDGeoghegan . 7
Dail Eirean 4-10-9 APowell ... pu

2/1 Elementary, 3/1 NOMADIC WAY, 9/2 Naevog, 11/2 Island Set, 7/1 Toranfield, 12/1 Dail Eireann, 14/1 Fourth of July, 66/1 Roark

R. E. Sangster (B. Hills) 8ran 4m00.30 (Heavy)

92 TOTE EIDER HANDICAP CHASE 4m 1f
£11,258 Newcastle 17 February

Jelupe 8-10-0 MrRSandys-Clarke 1
The Langholm Dyer 11-9-11 LO'Hara 7.2
75* **Midnight Madness** 12-11-2 RGreene 10.3
Ardesee 10-10-0 ACarroll .. 10.4
Boraceva 7-10-10 MrSMullins 20.5
Polar Nomad 9-10-1 PNiven . 1.6
Gamesmanship 9-10-1 SO'Neill 7
Wisconsin 6-10-0 WWorthington 8
73 Sam da Vinci 11-11-10 MBrennan .... ur
Killone Abbey 7-10-4 CGrant .... ur
73 Rausal 11-10-0 RSupple .... pu
Cool Brew 12-10-0 BStorey ... pu
Andrew 7-10-0 CHawkins ..... pu

5/2 Midnight Madness, 7/2 Killone Abbey, 9/2 Boraceva, 13/2 JELUPE, 12/1 Polar Nomad, Sam da Vinci, The Langholm Dyer, 25/1 Rausal, 33/1 Andrew, Ardesee, Cool Brew, 100/1 Gamesmanship, 200/1 Wisconsin

R. P. Sandys-Clarke (R. P. Sandys-Clarke) 13ran 8m52.30 (Good to Soft)

93 CITY TRIAL HURDLE (LIMITED HANDICAP) 2m
£7,505 Nottingham 17 February

88 **Royal Derbi** 5-10-7 HDavies . 1
88 **Don Valentino** 5-10-7 MBowlby 7.2
74* **Peanuts Pet** 5-10-7 TWall . 15.3
5[3] Lumberjack (USA) 6-10-7 MDwyer 5.4
55 Aldino 7-11-0 JOsborne 10.5
See You Then 10-12-0 SSmithEccles 15.6
55[2] Beldale Star 7-10-2 JLeech 7
88 Magnus Pym 5-10-4 PHolley ... 8

7/4 ROYAL DERBI, 3/1 Don Valentino, 11/2 Aldino, 8/1 Beldale Star, 9/1 See You Then, 12/1 Lumberjack, Peanuts Pet, 16/1 Magnus Pym

M. Tabor (N. Callaghan) 8ran 4m02.29 (Soft)

94 NOTTINGHAMSHIRE NOVICES' CHASE 2m
£11,230 Nottingham 17 February

Cashew King 7-11-10 TWall . 1
15 **Decided (Can)** 7-11-10 RBeggan ½.2
82 **Fuego Boy (NZ)** 10-11-5 JOsborne 8.3
75[3] Antinous 6-11-10 LWyer .... f
75[2] Aston Express 7-11-5 MDwyer .... f
Sawdust Jack 6-11-5 SSmithEccles .... f

7/4 CASHEW KING, Decided, 6/1 Aston Express, 13/2 Antinous, 20/1 Fuego Boy, Sawdust Jack

P. Moss (B. McMahon) 6ran 4m11.71 (Soft)

95 NOEL MCCABE DISTRIBUTORS HURDLE 2m
£6,509 Leopardstown 17 February

69* **Bank View** 5-12-0 GMcCourt 1
Vestris Abu 4-10-5 TCarmody 2.2
66 **Derrinore** 5-11-8 PGill 6.3
All That Crack 5-10-9 THyde ¾.4
Alleged Savage (USA) 4-10-9 BSheridan ½.5
Official Reception (USA) 4-10-6 MrJBanahan 2.6
Stevie Jay 5-11-8 KO'Brien 7
Lough Key 4-10-5 CSwan 8

2/1 BANK VIEW, 9/4 Stevie Jay, 7/2 Derrinore, 6/1 Alleged Savage, 8/1 Official Reception, 10/1 Vestris Abu, 33/1 Lough Key, 50/1 All That Crack

Date (Bloodstock) Ltd (N. Tinkler) 8ran 4m22.00 (Heavy)

96 VINCENT O'BRIEN IRISH GOLD CUP CHASE 3m
£44,552 Leopardstown 17 February

70* **Nick The Brief** 8-12-0 MLynch 1
90* **Carvill's Hill** 8-12-0 KMorgan 5.2
76² **Maid of Money** 8-11-9 APowell 2½.3
64³ Panto Prince 9-12-0 BPowell dist.4
Candy Well VI 8-12-0 JKavanagh 5
28 Hungary Hur 11-12-0 TCarmody .... pu

8/11 Carvill's Hill, 7/2 Maid of Money, 5/1 NICK THE BRIEF, 7/1 Panto Prince, 20/1 Hungary Hur, 66/1 Candy Well VI
J. R. Upson (J. R. Upson) 6ran 6m36.10 (Heavy)

96A IRISH NATIONAL HUNT NOVICE CHASE SERIES FINAL 2½m
£13,962 Leopardstown 17 February

Cahervillahow 6-11-12 CSwan 1
The Committee 7-11-6 CO'Dwyer 12.2
Larchmont 9-11-2 GMcCourt 8.3
Dutch Royal 8-11-6 BSheridan 6.4
Coursing Guy 8-11-2 TTaaffe 15.5
On The Other Hand 7-11-12 TCarmody .... f
What A Fox 8-11-6 KO'Brien .... pu

7/4 The Committee, 3/1 CAHERVILLAHOW, On The Other Hand, 4/1 Larchmont, 12/1 Coursing Guy, Dutch Royal, 14/1 What A Fox
Mrs Miles Valentine (M. Morris) 7ran 5m54.1 (Heavy)

97 NATIONAL SPIRIT CHALLENGE TROPHY HURDLE 2¼m
£5,254 Fontwell 19 February

Vagador (Can) 7-10-9 MPerrett 1
78* **Beech Road** 8-11-9 RGuest hd.2
78³ **Propero** 5-11-9 RRowe 30.3
Breakout 6-10-5 JHarris ... 2½.4
69 Valrodian (NZ) 7-10-12 JWhite hd.5

4/9 Beech Road, 11/4 VAGADOR, 10/1 Propero, 33/1 Valrodian, 200/1 Breakout
Miss Amanda Harwood (G. Harwood) 5ran 4m41.50 (Soft)

98 KINGWELL HURDLE 2m
£10,430 Wincanton 22 February

46* **Kribensis** 6-11-12 RDunwoody 1
91 **Island Set (USA)** 8-11-2 GMcCourt 4.2
24* **Cruising Altitude** 7-11-12 JOsborne 5.3
46³ Floyd 10-11-8 GBradley 5.4
Shalchlo Boy 6-11-2 BPowell dist.5
Geryon 9-11-2 MrsJWaring 6
Mole Board 8-11-2 SMcNeill ... f
93 See You Then 10-11-2 SSmithEccles .... f

4/6 KRIBENSIS, 4/1 Cruising Altitude, 10/1 Island Set, Mole Board, 12/1 Floyd, 20/1 See You Then, 500/1 Geryon, Shalchlo Boy
Sheikh Mohammed (M. Stoute) 8ran 3m37.94 (Good)

99 JIM FORD CHALLENGE CUP CHASE 3m 1f
£9,070 Wincanton 22 February

Cavvies Clown 10-11-6 GBradley 1
84 **Cool Ground** 8-11-0 BPowell 25.2
89³ **Golden Friend** 12-11-6 GMcCourt 30.3
Kildimo 10-11-6 JFrost .... f

10/11 CAVVIES CLOWN, 9/4 Kildimo, 5/1 Cool Ground, 14/1 Golden Friend
Mrs J. Ollivant (D. Elsworth) 4ran 6m32.28 (Good)

100 MOREBATTLE HURDLE 2m
£4,503 Kelso 23 February

88 **Jinxy Jack** 6-11-11 NDoughty 1
69 **Past Glories** 7-11-5 JQuinn hd.2
Casual Pass 7-11-5 CGrant 30.3
Moment of Truth 6-11-5 DNolan sh.4
Equator 7-11-5 DByrne 7.5
Clay County 5-11-5 BStorey 12.6
Tewit Castle 8-11-5 GBradley 7

4/6 JINXY JACK, 4/1 Past Glories, 6/1 Clay County, 33/1 Moment of Truth, Tewit Castle, 66/1 Casual Pass, Equator
Mrs B. M. McKinney (G. Richards) 7ran 3m54.51 (Good to Soft)

101 TOTE PLACEPOT HURDLE (4y) 2m
£10,755 Kempton 24 February

Philosophos 11-0 WMcFarland 1
36 **Calicon** 11-0 JFrost 5.2
Carbisdale 11-0 BPowell 6.3

Sharp Justice 10-10
RDunwoody 4.4
General Pershing 10-10
JLodder 2½.5
Here He Comes 10-10
LHarvey ½.6
86³ Rouyan 10-10 WMorris 20.7
Celtic Bhoy 10-10 DMurphy 8
Midfielder 11-0 PHobbs .... f
Bounden Duty (USA) 10-10
MPerrett .... ur
Daira Fort (USA) 10-10
JOsborne .... pu

11/4 General Pershing, 5/1 Sharp Justice, 11/2 Daira Fort, 6/1 Midfielder, 13/2 Calicon, 9/1 Bounden Duty, 12/1 Carbisdale, 20/1 Celtic Bhoy, Here He Comes, Rouyan, 33/1 PHILOSOPHOS

P. Slade (J. H. Baker) 11ran 3m53.32 (Good)

102 RACING POST HANDICAP CHASE 3m
£24,100 Kempton 24 February

41* **Desert Orchid** 11-12-3
RDunwoody 1
Delius 12-10-3 PHobbs 8.2
34 **Seagram (NZ)** 10-9-11
NHawke 8.3
84 Ballyhane 9-10-1 RRowe 15.4
53³ Solidasarock 8-10-0
LHarvey 4.5
Twin Oaks 10-10-0
MBowlby 1.6
84 Castle Warden 13-9-11
NWilliamson .... ur
Pucks Place 9-10-0 AAdams . ref

8/11 DESERT ORCHID, 7/2 Ballyhane, 6/1 Delius, 12/1 Solidasarock, 25/1 Twin Oaks, 33/1 Seagram, 50/1 Castle Warden, 100/1 Pucks Place

R. Burridge (D. Elsworth) 8ran 5m59.82 (Good)

103 R.O.A. RENDLESHAM HURDLE 3m
£7,059 Kempton 24 February

Old Dundalk 6-11-3
MBowlby 1
Sprowston Boy 7-11-3
DMurphy 2½.2
83² **Calabrese** 5-11-7
RDunwoody 3.3
83 Miss Nero 9-10-12
WMcFarland 10.4
Rogers Princess 8-11-2
SKeightley 3.5
78² Slalom 9-11-3 JWhite 15.6
5* Pipers Copse 8-11-3 MPerrett . 7

2/1 Slalom, 11/4 Calabrese, 7/2 Sprowston Boy, 11/2 Pipers Copse, 9/1 Miss Nero, 20/1 Rogers Princess, 33/1 OLD DUNDALK

M. V. Walsh (D. Murray-Smith) 7ran 6m08.80 (Good)

103A IRISH NATIONAL HUNT NOVICE HURDLE SERIES FINAL 2m2½f
£11,792 Punchestown 24 February

Scally Owen 6-11-12
AMullins 1
Grey Danube 6-11-6
TCarmody 8.2
Call Me Later 6-11-7
KO'Brien 2½.3
Half Set 7-11-8 TTaaffe sh.4
Anne's Buckskin 7-11-12
CSwan 5.5
My View 6-11-10 CO'Dwyer . 8.6
Dinnys Corner 6-11-2
KMorgan 5.7
Kindly King 6-11-2
LCusack hd.8
95 Stevie Jay 5-11-7
MrAMartin 12.9
Barkisland 6-11-6
BSheridan 10
Adanac 7-11-2
MrJDempsey 11
Nancy Myles 5-10-12
MrFFlood .... f
Opryland 5-11-3 FWoods .... pu

4/1 Anne's Buckskin, Call Me Later, 9/2 Nancy Myles, 7/1 SCALLY OWEN, Stevie Jay, 8/1 Opryland, 10/1 My View, 14/1 Barkisland, Grey Danube, Half Set, 25/1 Adanac, Dinnys Corner, Kindly King

Mrs P. Mullins (P. Mullins) 13ran 5m13.1 (Heavy)

104 TATTERSALLS MARES ONLY NOVICES' CHASE FINAL (LIMITED HANDICAP) 2½m
£7,440 Haydock 3 March

Radical Lady 6-10-12
MDwyer 1
Random Romance 7-10-8
RDunwoody 5.2
82 Setter Country 6-10-5
WIrvine 25.3
Blue Rainbow 7-10-13
TMorgan 1½.4
Rondeau 7-10-7 MKinane ... hd.5
Fit For Firing (Fr) 6-11-0
CGrant 12.6
Little Mynd 11-10-0 RGreene .. 7
Corvassio 6-11-10 CSwan .... f
Meryett (Bel) 6-10-0
PMcDermott .... f
Dalkey Sound 7-11-2 PNiven ... f
Rare Luck 7-10-7 RMarley .... pu
Roscoff 8-10-0 MrBClifford ... pu

5/2 RADICAL LADY, 4/1 Dalkey Sound, 9/2 Fit For Firing, 15/2 Random Romance, 17/2 Blue Rainbow, 9/1 Corvassio, Setter Country, 14/1 Rare Luck, 33/1 Little Mynd, Meryett, Rondeau, Roscoff

N. B. Mason (Farms) Ltd (G. Moore) 12ran 5m37.29 (Heavy)

105 TIMEFORM CHASE 2½m
£10,123 Haydock 3 March

Tartan Takeover 8-11-0 MDwyer 1
Formula One 8-11-0 TMorgan 4.2
Feile Na Hinse 7-11-0 JRailton ½.3
75 Blazing Walker 6-11-0 CGrant dist.4
Only Trouble 9-11-1 RDunwoody ..... f

6/4 Blazing Walker, 2/1 TARTAN TAKEOVER, 5/2 Formula One, 16/1 Feile Na Hinse, Only Trouble

Edinburgh Woollen Mill Ltd (G. Richards) 5ran 5m37.28 (Heavy)

106 GREENALL WHITLEY GOLD CUP (HANDICAP CHASE) 3m
£21,120 Haydock 3 March

30³ **Rinus** 9-10-4 RDunwoody 1
44 **The Thinker** 12-11-11 CGrant 4.2
Harley 10-9-11 NWilliamson 7.3
70² Bishops Yarn 11-11-2 RGuest 12.4
Highway Express 9-9-11 WIrvine 4.5
Moe Green 10-10-2 JRailton 20.6
Travel Over 9-10-0 BDowling 7
Willsford 7-10-0 DGallagher ..... f
Season's Ahead 7-10-0 JKinane ..... f
Bucko 13-10-8 MDwyer ..... pu
Brownhill Lass 9-9-7 GScope ..... pu

5/2 Bishops Yarn, 3/1 Willsford, 9/2 Travel Over, 11/2 RINUS, 9/1 Bucko, 10/1 The Thinker, 12/1 Highway Express, 33/1 Harley, 50/1 Brownhill Lass, Moe Green, 150/1 Season's Ahead

A. M. Proos (G. Richards) 11ran 6m40.14 (Heavy)

107 VICTOR LUDORUM HURDLE (4y) 2m
£5,141 Haydock 3 March

36 **Ninja** 11-4 RDunwoody 1
Vestris Abu 11-4 CSwan ½.2
Native Friend 11-10 MDwyer 1½.3
101³ Carbisdale 11-10 RGuest 12.4
Hiram B Birdbath 11-4 JWhite 30.5

8/11 Vestris Abu, 9/2 Carbisdale, 5/1 Native Friend, NINJA, 20/1 Hiram B Birdbath

H. R. Mould (D. Nicholson) 5ran 4m09.04 (Heavy)

108 PHILIP CORNES SADDLE OF GOLD HURDLE FINAL 3m 120y
£10,138 Newbury 3 March

Miinnehoma 7-11-5 PScudamore 1
Remittance Man 6-11-5 JWhite 12.2
Beau Pari 6-11-5 EMurphy 15.3
Cardinal Ralph 6-11-5 PHobbs 2.4
Black Moccasin 7-11-5 MBowlby 12.5
Strong Gold 7-11-5 BdeHaan ..... f

1/1 MIINNEHOMA, 9/4 Black Moccasin, 6/1 Remittance Man, 14/1 Beau Pari, Strong Gold, 33/1 Cardinal Ralph

F. Starr (M. Pipe) 6ran 6m08.44 (Good)

109 CROWN BERGER HURDLE (5y) 2m
£13,500 Chepstow 10 March

74³ **Sacre d'Or (USA)** 11-5 SO'Neill 1
Ri-Na-Rithann 11-5 DGallagher 7.2
Hey Cottage 11-5 GMcCourt 1½.3
Munjarid 11-5 JFrost ½.4
Megabucks 11-4 MPerrett 6.5
Run To Form 11-5 MPitman . 3.6
Loaningdale 11-5 LHarvey ... 8.7
Akdam (USA) 11-5 KMooney 4.8
Distant Relation 11-0 HDavies 9
Mistral Story 11-5 EMurphy .. 10
Alkinor Rex 11-5 MRichards ..... f
Belmoredean 11-5 JOsborne .. pu

7/4 Run To Form, 7/2 Mistral Story, 6/1 Alkinor Rex, 7/1 Ri-Na-Rithann, 12/1 Megabucks, 14/1 SACRE D'OR, 16/1 Belmoredean, Loaningdale, 20/1 Hey Cottage, 33/1 Akdam, Munjarid, 50/1 Distant Relation

J. W. H. Fryer (J. Mackie) 12ran 4m03.12 (Good to Soft)

110 WILLIAM HILL IMPERIAL CUP (HANDICAP HURDLE) 2m
£16,050 Sandown 10 March

88 **Moody Man** 5-10-13 PHobbs . 1
54 **Penny Forum** 6-11-7 DMcKeown 10.2
88² **Joyful Noise** 7-11-10 TTaaffe 4.3
54 Tebitto 7-10-0 RBoucher .. 2½.4
93³ Peanuts Pet 5-10-10 TWall ... 4.5
88 Out of Range 7-11-5 GBradley 2½.6
54² Cinnamon Run 6-10-3 BPowell 4.7

88 Ambassador 7-11-4 PScudamore hd.8
Run High 7-10-7 DMurphy ... 8.9
88 Afaristoun (Fr) 6-11-9 TMorgan sh.10
Midnight Strike (USA) 6-10-12 WMcFarland 11
Bradbury Star 5-11-2 TPinfield . f
26 Nahar 5-11-3 RDunwoody ..... bd
71 Without A Doubt 8-10-10 BMcGiff .... bd
20 Dare Say 7-11-8 RRowe .... pu

5/1 Joyful Noise, 6/1 Ambassador, 7/1 Without A Doubt, 8/1 Peanuts Pet, 10/1 Run High, 11/1 Bradbury Star, Midnight Strike, 12/1 Cinnamon Run, 14/1 Afaristoun, Penny Forum, 20/1 Dare Say, MOODY MAN, Nahar, Out of Range, 33/1 Tebitto

J. Burley (P. Hobbs) 15ran 3m48.30 (Good to Firm)

111 WATERFORD CRYSTAL SUPREME NOVICES' HURDLE 2m
£30,515 Cheltenham 13 March

59* **Forest Sun** 5-11-8 JFrost 1
80^2 **Danny Harrold** 6-11-8 MPitman 2½.2
74^2 **Rakes Lane** 5-11-8 TMorgan ½.3
Olnistar (Fr) 4-10-9 GMcCourt 7.4
Re-Release 5-11-3 JLower 2½.5
81 Riverhead (USA) 6-11-8 GBradley 5.6
Stratford Ponds 5-11-8 JOsborne nk.7
Freeline Finishing 6-11-8 JWhite 8.8
81* Whatever You Like 6-11-8 RDunwoody 9
Bitter Buck 7-11-3 PScudamore 10
81^2 Man of The West 7-11-8 MDwyer 11
Killbanon 8-11-8 BPowell 12
Andy Boy 6-11-8 MLynch 13
Shu Fly (NZ) 6-11-8 RHyett ... 14
Ugandan Affair 5-11-8 RGuest 15
Young Ty 6-11-8 MrSSwiers ..... f
Art Trail 6-11-8 CO'Dwyer .... pu
39 Golden Moss 5-11-8 DMcKeown .... pu

7/4 FOREST SUN, 11/2 Bitter Buck, 6/1 Man of The West, 10/1 Riverhead, Stratford Ponds, 11/1 Whatever You Like, 14/1 Freeline Finishing, 16/1 Young Ty, 20/1 Danny Harrold, 25/1 Re-Release, 33/1 Rakes Lane, 50/1 Art Trail, 66/1 Olnistar, Ugandan Affairs, 100/1 Shu Fly, 200/1 Golden Moss, Killbanon, 250/1 Andy Boy

Salehurst Paper Co Ltd (G. Balding) 18ran 3m53.72 (Good to Firm)

112 ARKLE CHALLENGE TROPHY CHASE 2m
£35,758 Cheltenham 13 March

42 **Comandante** 8-11-8 PHobbs . 1
Kiichi (USA) 5-11-0 BSheridan 1.2
45* **Young Snugfit** 6-11-8 JOsborne nk.3
94 Antinous 6-11-8 LWyer 1.4
Blitzkreig 7-11-8 TRyan 5.5
85 Celtic Shot 8-11-8 PScudamore 7.6
The Musical Priest 8-11-8 TCarmody nk.7
Sire Nantais (Fr) 6-11-8 JLower 3.8
82^3 Another Coral 7-11-8 MDwyer . f
Guiburn's Nephew 8-11-8 HDavies .... f
45^2 For The Grain 6-11-8 RDunwoody .... pu
In The Breeze (Fr) 9-11-8 LCusack .... pu
47* Mister Point 8-11-8 RMarley .... pu
82^2 Western Dandy 7-11-8 BPowell .... pu

4/1 Celtic Shot, 9/2 COMANDANTE, Young Snugfit, 8/1 Blitzkreig, 9/1 Sire Nantais, 12/1 Kiichi, 14/1 Antinous, Guiburn's Nephew, 16/1 For The Grain, 20/1 Another Coral, 25/1 Mister Point, 40/1 The Musical Priest, Western Dandy, 500/1 In The Breeze

M. E. Pinto (J. Gifford) 14ran 3m53.32 (Good to Firm)

113 WATERFORD CRYSTAL CHAMPION HURDLE CHALLENGE TROPHY 2m
£50,047 Cheltenham 13 March

98* **Kribensis** 6-12-0 RDunwoody 1
91* **Nomadic Way (USA)** 5-12-0 PScudamore 3.2
100^2 **Past Glories** 7-12-0 JQuinn ¾.3
97^2 Beech Road 8-12-0 RGuest . ½.4
38^2 Morley Street 6-12-0 JFrost . 8.5
100* Jinxy Jack 6-12-0 NDoughty nk.6
98^2 Island Set (USA) 8-12-0 CGrant 7.7
97* Vagador (Can) 7-12-0 MissAHarwood 1½.8
88* Deep Sensation 5-12-0 RRowe hd.9
91^2 Elementary 7-12-0 TCarmody 3.10
93^2 Don Valentino 5-12-0 HDavies ½.11
Space Fair 7-12-0 WMcFarland 4.12
88 Sudden Victory 6-12-0 KMooney 2.13
66* Redundant Pal 7-12-0 CO'Dwyer 2.14

98 See You Then 10-12-0 SSmithEccles 15
66^2 Dis Train 6-12-0 MPitman 16
98^3 Cruising Altitude 7-12-0 JOsborne .... f
Persian Style 6-12-0 PHobbs .... f
95* Bank View 5-12-0 GMcCourt ... f

2/1 Beech Road, 95/40 KRIBENSIS, 8/1 Nomadic Way, 9/1 Cruising Altitude, 10/1 Morley Street, 16/1 Vagador, 22/1 Elementary, 25/1 See You Then, 33/1 Deep Sensation, Redundant Pal, 40/1 Island Set, 50/1 Bank View, Don Valentino, Jinxy Jack, 100/1 Dis Train, 150/1 Past Glories, Persian Style, Space Fair, Sudden Victory

Sheikh Mohammed (M. Stoute) 19ran 3m50.70 (Good to Firm)

114 WATERFORD CRYSTAL STAYERS' HURDLE 3m1f
£39,376 Cheltenham 13 March

68^2 **Trapper John** 6-11-10 CSwan **1**
91 **Naevog** 7-11-5 TTaaffe **1½.2**
33 **Bluff Cove** 8-11-0 RDunwoody **1.3**
68 Ikdam 5-11-10 NMann nk.4
83^3 Brabazon (USA) 5-11-10 SSmithEccles 2.5
Cash Is King 6-11-10 MPitman hd.6
91 Fourth of July 7-11-10 PScudamore 8.7
83 Pragada 7-11-10 RRowe nk.8
69^2 Vicario di Bray (Ity) 7-11-10 MDwyer 2.9
98 Floyd 10-11-10 GBradley ... ½.10
49 Galmoy 11-11-10 TCarmody ¾.11
103* Old Dundalk 6-11-10 MBowlby 12.12
83 Mineral Dust 7-11-10 JBryan 3.13
103 Miss Nero 9-11-5 BDowling .. 14
100 Tewit Castle 8-11-10 JOsborne 15
Scylla's Chip 8-11-10 MrNWheeler 16
49^3 Cloughtaney 9-11-10 AMullins 17
Tito L'Effronte (Fr) 5-11-10 CAubert 18
83* Ryde Again 7-11-10 GMcCourt f
43^2 Cliffalda 7-11-10 TMorgan ..... pu
9 Flying Dancer 8-11-10 CGrant .... pu
114 Slalom 9-11-10 JWhite .... pu

11/2 Ryde Again, 6/1 Fourth of July, 7/1 Cash Is King, 15/2 TRAPPER JOHN, 9/1 Old Dundalk, 10/1 Floyd, 14/1 Galmoy, Slalom, 16/1 Naevog, Vicario di Bray, 20/1 Brabazon, Miss Nero, 25/1 Pragada, Tito L'Effronte, 33/1 Bluff Cove, Cliffalda, Cloughtaney, Ikdam, 200/1 Flying Dancer, Mineral Dust, Tewit Castle, 500/1 Scylla's Chip

Mrs P. F. N. Fanning (M. Morris) 22ran 6m28.10 (Good to Firm)

115 KIM MUIR MEMORIAL CHALLENGE CUP (HANDICAP CHASE) 3m
£16,032 Cheltenham 13 March

Master Bob 10-10-1 MrJBerry **1**
Golden Minstrel 11-9-8 MrCBurnett-Wells **3.2**
25 **Dudie** 12-9-13 MrDMcCain . **3.3**
63 Mr Frisk 11-11-10 MrMArmytage 1½.4
Rig Steel 10-10-0 MrJDempsey 7.5
Gallic Prince 11-9-7 MrCMaude 5.6
105 Only Trouble 9-11-4 MrTHoulbrooke 1½.7
37^3 Charter Hardware 8-10-7 MrPFenton 1½.8
106 Highway Express 9-10-2 MrGUpton 9
Gay Moore 9-9-9 MissCBeasley 10
92* Jelupe 8-9-10 MrRSandys-Clarke 11
106 Moe Greene 10-9-12 MrJBanahan 12
Its All Very Fine 9-10-6 MrDNaylor-Leyland 13
Cloney Grange 11-9-11 MrFFlood 14
Hazy Sunset 13-11-1 MrJDurkan .... ur
Bajan Sunshine 11-10-8 MrCFarrell .... pu
90 Mweenish 8-10-7 MrTCostello .... pu

9/2 Jelupe, 7/1 Mr Frisk, 8/1 Highway Express, 9/1 Dudie, 10/1 Golden Minstrel, 11/1 Charter Hardware, Hazy Sunset, Mweenish, 14/1 Bajan Sunshine, Cloney Grange, 20/1 Gallic Prince, MASTER BOB, 25/1 Gay Moore, Rig Steel, 33/1 Moe Greene, 66/1 Only Trouble, 100/1 Its All Very Fine

I. Wills (N. Henderson) 17ran 6m11.14 (Good to Firm)

116 CHELTENHAM GRAND ANNUAL CHASE CHALLENGE CUP (HANDICAP) 2m
£19,884 Cheltenham 13 March

72^2 **Katabatic** 7-10-8 HDavies **1**
Tresidder 8-10-2 RBeggan .. **1.2**
Gold Options 8-10-10 MDwyer **1.3**
Masnoon (USA) 7-10-5 MrPMcMahon 3.4
82* Wink Gulliver 6-10-0 RArnott 1.5
Broad Beam 10-10-0 PHobbs ½.6
64 Nohalmdun 9-11-1 RMarley ½.7

The A Train 8-10-6
BdeHaan 3.8
87[3] Long Engagement 9-11-8
RDunwoody 2½.9
8 Raise An Argument 11-10-3
BPowell 3.10
64 Vodkatini 11-11-10 RRowe 11
Fu's Lady 8-10-12
PScudamore .... f
14 Mr Key (USA) 9-11-2
MBowlby .... pu

11/4 KATABATIC, 5/1 Fu's Lady, 11/2 The A Train, Wink Gulliver, 10/1 Gold Options, 11/1 Nohalmdun, Tresidder, 16/1 Masnoon, Mr Key, Raise An Argument, 20/1 Long Engagement, Vodkatini, 66/1 Broad Beam

Pell-mell Partners (A. Turnell) 13ran 3m54.56 (Good to Firm)

117 SUN ALLIANCE NOVICES' HURDLE 2½m
£32,395 Cheltenham 14 March

80* **Regal Ambition** 6-11-7
PScudamore **1**
Judges Fancy 6-11-7
RSupple 12.**2**
Tom's Little Bet 6-11-2
DGallagher ¾.**3**
Run For Free 6-11-7 JLower . 3.4
Dorans Hill Lad 6-11-7
AMullins 2.5
Devil's Valley 7-11-7
MPitman 1½.6
My View 6-11-7 TTaaffe 1.7
Midland Glenn 6-11-7
MrPMcMahon 1½.8
Orbis (USA) 4-10-12
TCarmody 3.9
The Illywhacker 5-11-7
MBowlby 5.10
52[2] Ard T'Match 5-11-7
WMorris 4.11
66 Castle Windows 7-11-7
MrCFarrell ¾.12
Fort Noel 7-11-7 RRowe 13
Dirty Diana 5-11-2 CSwan 14
Webbs Wonder 5-11-7
PHobbs 15
Celtic Original 6-11-7
BDowling 16
Stately Lover 7-11-7
HDavies 17
Casting Time (NZ) 6-11-7
BPowell 18
Moze Tidy 5-11-7 EMurphy ... 19
81 Tinryland 6-11-7 RDunwoody .. f
Ben Oliver 5-11-7 LWyer ...... bd
Scally Owen 6-11-7
MDwyer .... pu

3/1 REGAL AMBITION, 5/1 Fort Noel, 6/1 Run For Free, 8/1 Midland Glenn, 9/1 Scally Owen, 12/1 Tinryland, 16/1 Devil's Valley, 25/1 Dorans Hill Lad, 33/1 Stately Lover, The Illywhacker, 50/1 Ben Oliver, Dirty Diana, My View, Orbis, 66/1 Castle Windows, Judges Fancy, Moze Tidy, 100/1 Ard T'Match, Webbs Wonder, 200/1 Celtic Original, Tom's Little Bet, 300/1 Casting Time

Skeltools Ltd (M. Pipe) 22ran 4m56.29 (Firm)

118 QUEEN MOTHER CHAMPION CHASE 2m
£44,820 Cheltenham 14 March

89* **Barnbrook Again** 9-12-0
HDavies **1**
77[3] **Waterloo Boy** 7-12-0
RDunwoody ½.**2**
87* **Feroda** 9-12-0 TTaaffe 7.**3**
77* Sabin du Loir (Fr) 11-12-0
PScudamore ¾.4
48* Ida's Delight 11-12-0
BStorey 10.5
96 Panto Prince 9-12-0
BPowell 2½.6
Private Views 9-12-0
KMooney 10.7
12 Impertain 10-12-0 LCusack 8
64 Pearlyman 11-12-0
TMorgan .... pu

11/10 BARNBROOK AGAIN, 4/1 Sabin du Loir, 6/1 Pearlyman, 8/1 Waterloo Boy, 9/1 Feroda, 16/1 Panto Prince, Private Views, 50/1 Ida's Delight, 500/1 Impertain

M. Davies (D. Elsworth) 9ran 3m50.77 (Firm)

119 CORAL GOLDEN HURDLE FINAL (HANDICAP) 3m1f
£23,751 Cheltenham 14 March

Henry Mann 7-11-9
AMulholland **1**
Maelkar (Fr) 6-11-3
RSupple 2.**2**
Direct 7-10-4
NWilliamson ½.**3**
Sip of Orange 8-10-7
MDwyer 4.4
Givus A Buck 7-10-11
PHolley 12.5
Sir Crusty 8-9-12 NMann ... 2½.6
83 Glen Oak 5-10-7
MrGUpton hd.7
Shoon Wind 7-9-9 BMcGiff ... 5.8
Broctune Grey 6-10-8
GMcCourt nk.9
Demi John 8-10-0 JWhite 4.10
103 Rogers Princess 8-11-2
SKeightley 6.11
108 Strong Gold 7-10-6
MBowlby 2½.12
Mubaaris 7-9-11 SWoods 13
26 Urizen 7-11-6 BPowell 14
Mr Gossip 8-11-0 PHarley 15
Alphasonic (USA) 6-10-7
MPerrett 16
Rawhide 6-10-8 CSwan 17
61 Arctic Teal 6-11-5 ASmith 18
Qannaas 6-10-9
SSmithEccles 19

Fanny Dillon 6-10-1 AMcCabe ... 20
Parlezvousfrancais 6-10-4 PScudamore ... 21
Atrabates 10-10-6 JOsborne .. 22
88 Badihar (USA) 6-10-10 PVerling ... f
Inde Pulse 8-10-7 RDunwoody f
Taberna Lord 9-10-3 LHarvey ... bd
Smithonian 6-9-7 RHodge ..... bd
33 Knighton Lad 9-10-0 MRichards ... pu

11/2 Rogers Princess, 6/1 Rawhide, 7/1 Taberna Lord, 14/1 Arctic Teal, Sir Crusty, 16/1 Broctune Grey, Parlezvousfrancais, 20/1 Alphasonic, Badihar, HENRY MANN, Smithonian, 22/1 Maelkar, 25/1 Atrabates, Inde Pulse, Knighton Lad, Sip of Orange, Strong Gold, Urizen, 33/1 Direct, Fanny Dillon, Mr Gossip, Qannaas, 40/1 Givus A Buck, Shoon Wind, 50/1 Glen Oak, 66/1 Mubaaris, 150/1 Demi John
L. Wilson (S. Christian) 27ran 6m18.72 (Firm)

120 SUN ALLIANCE CHASE 3m
£40,470 Cheltenham 14 March

40 **Garrison Savannah** 7-11-4 BdeHaan ... **1**
96A[2] **The Committee** 7-11-4 MFlynn ... 5.**2**
56[2] **Chatam (USA)** 6-11-4 PScudamore ... 2½.**3**
Toureen Prince 7-11-4 RBeggan ... 3.4
85 Mixed Blends 8-10-13 TCarmody ... 8.5
All Jeff (Fr) 6-11-4 GLandau ...... f
85* Royal Athlete 7-11-4 MPitman f
Knight Oil 7-11-4 MRichards .... f
40 Rifle Range 7-11-4 GBradley ... pu

5/4 Royal Athlete, 7/2 Chatam, 9/1 Knight Oil, Toureen Prince, 12/1 GARRISON SAVANNAH, 14/1 Mixed Blends, Rifle Range, 20/1 The Committee, 25/1 All Jeff
Autofour Engineering (Mrs J. Pitman) 9ran 6m08.64 (Firm)

121 NATIONAL HUNT CHASE CHALLENGE CUP 4m
£15,295 Cheltenham 14 March

Topsham Bay 7-12-0 MrPHacking ... **1**
Royal Battery (NZ) 7-12-0 MrGOxley ... 4.**2**
Ballinhassig 6-12-0 MrDCostello ... 20.**3**
Die Broke 6-12-4 MrGUpton ... 2½.4
Uncle Raggy 7-12-4 MrPGraffin ... 1½.5
Cushinstown 7-12-7 MrJBerry ... ½.6
40 Speakers Corner 7-12-4 MrJWrathall ... 7.7
Another Troup 8-12-0 MrDTownsend ... 8
Blue Ravine 11-12-0 MrSBell .. 9
No Grandad 6-12-2 MrFMcGrath ... 10
Youwaitonme 8-12-0 MrMArmytage ... 11
Just So 7-12-4 MrSBurrough . 12
9 Interim Lib 7-12-4 MrJBradburne ... 13
Lover Bill 8-12-0 MrWMullins ... 14
Grand Inquisitor 8-12-0 MrAHarvey ... 15
Sam Shorrock 8-12-0 MrTIllsley ... 16
Les Parvenus 6-12-0 MrJBanahan ... f
Celtic Remorse 8-11-9 MrsPNash ... f
Coppett Song 8-12-0 MrDDuggan ... f
Jolie Gazelle 8-12-0 MrGMorrow ... ur
22[3] Mountaico 8-12-4 MrTMitchell ... pu
Toffee Apple 7-12-0 MrAWalter ... pu
Sportsnews 8-12-0 MrBClifford ... pu
Our Fellow 8-12-4 MrJDurkan ... pu
104* Radical Lady 6-12-2 MrTCostello ... pu

11/2 Die Broke, Radical Lady, 6/1 Ballinhassig, Cushinstown, 11/1 Les Parvenus, 12/1 Our Fellow, 14/1 No Grandad, 16/1 Uncle Raggy, 25/1 Blue Ravine, Royal Battery, 28/1 Youwaitonme, 33/1 Grand Inquisitor, Interim Lib, Just So, Speakers Corner, 40/1 Sportsnews, TOPSHAM BAY, 50/1 Lover Bill, Toffee Apple, 100/1 Another Troup, Celtic Remorse, Coppett Song, Mountaico, Sam Shorrock, 200/1 Jolie Gazelle
M. L. Marsh (D. Barons) 25ran 8m12.73 (Firm)

122 MILDMAY OF FLETE CHALLENGE CUP (HANDICAP CHASE) 2½m
£21,720 Cheltenham 14 March

New Halen 9-9-7 ETierney ... **1**
Lacidar 10-10-7 TReed 8.**2**
King of The Lot 7-10-9 BDowling ... 2.**3**
67[3] Auntie Dot 9-11-2 MLynch ... 4.4
31[3] Imadyna (NZ) 8-10-0 SEarle . 5.5
102 Solidasarock 8-11-8 LHarvey ... 6.6
Worthy Knight 9-10-13 BStorey ... nk.7

72[3] First Bout 9-10-11 RDunwoody 8
Brookmount 8-11-6 RRowe ...... f
Observer Corps 9-11-10 TMorgan .... pu
Oregon Trail 10-11-5 RBeggan .... pu
Four Trix 9-11-8 NDoughty ... pu
Aughavogue 8-11-5 DTegg .... pu
Problem Child 7-10-0 WMorris .... pu

100/30 First Bout, 6/1 Solidasarock, 7/1 Four Trix, King of The Lot, 9/1 Lacidar, 10/1 Aughavogue, Brookmount, Worthy Knight, 12/1 Imadyna, 16/1 Auntie Dot, 25/1 Observer Corps, 33/1 Oregon Trail, 66/1 NEW HALEN, 100/1 Problem Child

Mrs S. Siviter (A. P. James) 14ran 4m58.55 (Firm)

123 DAILY EXPRESS TRIUMPH HURDLE (4y) 2m
£34,039 Cheltenham 15 March

Rare Holiday 11-0 BSheridan **1**
107* **Ninja** 11-0 HDavies ½.**2**
107[3] **Native Friend** 11-0 MDwyer 1.**3**
107[2] Vestris Abu 11-0 CSwan ½.4
Lucky Verdict 11-0 NDoughty nk.5
Sayyure (USA) 11-0 GMcCourt nk.6
Magic Million 11-0 TCarmody 3.7
101 Midfielder 11-0 PHobbs 1½.8
Bally Rue (USA) 11-0 MrEKearns 4.9
Royal Square (Can) 11-0 RRowe nk.10
Spring Hay 11-0 RDunwoody 2½.11
Major Inquiry 11-0 GBradley ¾.12
Stigon 11-0 MFlynn 5.13
Iveagh House 11-0 MBowlby 2.14
Ivors Guest 11-0 MPitman 15
On Deposit 11-0 TRyan 16
Dark Desire 11-0 MRichards . 17
Il Trovatore (USA) 11-0 TMorgan 18
86* Silver King (Fr) 11-0 PScudamore 19
Badrakhani (Fr) 11-0 JWhite .. 20
Sea Buck 11-0 JFrost 21
95 Official Reception (USA) 11-0 APowell 22
Cyphrate (USA) 11-0 JLower . 23
In-Keeping 10-9 RMacNeice . 24
86 Man For All Season (USA) 11-0 WMcFarland 25
Stage Player 11-0 WMorris 26
Stone Flake (USA) 11-0 SSmithEccles 27
36 Royal Wonder 10-9 SEarle 28
86 Able Leader 11-0 EMurphy ... 29
36* Crystal Heights 11-0 BPowell . f

5/1 Stone Flake, 11/2 Major Inquiry, 9/1 Royal Square, Sayyure, 11/1 Silver King, 14/1 Magic Million, 16/1 Cyphrate, 20/1 Dark Desire, Native Friend, Spring Hay, 25/1 RARE HOLIDAY, 33/1 Ivors Guest, Lucky Verdict, Midfielder, Royal Wonder, Vestris Abu, 40/1 Il Trovatore, 50/1 Ninja, On Deposit, Official Reception, Sea Buck, 66/1 Badrakhani, Crystal Heights, Iveagh House, 80/1 Bally Rue, 100/1 Able Leader, In-Keeping, Man For All Season, Stage Player, Stigon

Dr M. Smurfit (D. K. Weld, Ireland) 30ran 3m54.40 (Firm)

124 CHRISTIES FOXHUNTER CHASE CHALLENGE CUP 3¼m
£14,158 Cheltenham 15 March

Call Collect 9-12-0 MrRMartin **1**
Old Nick 9-12-0 MrNSmith . 2.**2**
West Tip 13-12-0 MrMArmytage 3.**3**
Three Counties 13-12-0 MissKRimell 15.4
Whitsunday 11-12-0 MrMChamberlayne 1.5
Purnago 8-12-0 MissJBarrow 15.6
Border Burg 13-12-0 MrAHill 15.7
Nobbanokker 8-12-0 MrJGreenall 4.8
Sweet Rascal 11-11-9 MrTJones 9
Provide 9-12-0 MrSClaisse ... 10
Fudge Delight 11-12-0 MrRGoodall .... ur
Deep Prospect 11-12-0 MrNJones .... pu
General Merchant 10-12-0 MrJHarley .... pu
Mitilini 10-12-0 MrCCoyne ... pu
Rodden Brook 8-12-0 MrPMacEwan .... pu

7/4 CALL COLLECT, 5/1 Whitsunday, 11/2 Three Counties, 8/1 West Tip, 12/1 Fudge Delight, Old Nick, 16/1 Nobbanokker, Rodden Brook, 20/1 Border Burg, Provide, Sweet Rascal, 66/1 Purnago, 100/1 Deep Prospect, General Merchant, Mitilini

J. Clements (J. Parkes) 15ran 6m39.23 (Firm)

125 TOTE CHELTENHAM GOLD CUP CHASE 3¼m
£67,003 Cheltenham 15 March

64 **Norton's Coin** 9-12-0 GMcCourt **1**
89 **Toby Tobias** 8-12-0 MPitman ¾.**2**
102* **Desert Orchid** 11-12-0 RDunwoody **4.3**

99 Cavvies Clown 10-12-0 GBradley 7.4
60² Pegwell Bay 9-12-0 BPowell 12.5
96³ Maid of Money 8-11-9 APowell 1.6
89² Yahoo 9-12-0 TMorgan 15.7
37* Bonanza Boy 9-12-0 PScudamore 2½.8
99 Kildimo 10-12-0 JFrost .... f
84* Ten of Spades 10-12-0 KMooney .... f
96* Nick The Brief 8-12-0 MLynch .... pu
63 The Bakewell Boy 8-12-0 SSmithEccles .... pu

10/11 Desert Orchid, 15/2 Bonanza Boy, 8/1 Toby Tobias, 10/1 Cavvies Clown, Nick The Brief, 20/1 Pegwell Bay, Ten of Spades, 25/1 Maid of Money, 40/1 Yahoo, 50/1 Kildimo, 100/1 NORTON'S COIN, 200/1 The Bakewell Boy

S. G. Griffiths (S. G. Griffiths) 12ran 6m30.90 (Firm)

126 RITZ CLUB NATIONAL HUNT HANDICAP CHASE 3m 1f
£27,585 Cheltenham 15 March

76³ **Bigsun** 9-10-11 RDunwoody .. **1**
106³ **Seagram (NZ)** 10-10-12 NHawke hd.**2**
92 **Boraceva** 7-10-9 JFrost 8.**3**
99³ Golden Friend 12-11-5 GMcCourt 20.4
84² Paddyboro 12-11-9 RRowe . 15.5
63 Bob Tisdall 11-11-10 TMorgan 20.6
92 Sam da Vinci 11-11-6 MBrennan .... pu
Pharoah's Laen 9-11-4 PScudamore .... pu
12 Steeple View 9-10-13 MRichards .... pu
106 Willsford 7-10-12 DGallagher .... pu
City Entertainer 9-10-11 MDwyer .... pu
106³ Harley 10-10-5 BPowell .... pu
73 L'Ane Rouge 9-9-11 RMacNeice .... pu
Missing Man 10-10-0 EMurphy .... pu

9/2 Boraceva, Willsford, 6/1 City Entertainer, 15/2 BIGSUN, Pharoah's Laen, 10/1 Seagram, 12/1 Paddyboro, Steeple View, 20/1 Sam da Vinci, 25/1 Harley, Missing Man, 33/1 Bob Tisdall, Golden Friend, 50/1 L'Ane Rouge

J. F. Horn (D. Nicholson) 14ran 6m13.30 (Firm)

127 CATHCART CHALLENGE CUP CHASE 2½m
£23,100 Cheltenham 15 March

53² **Brown Windsor** 8-11-3 JWhite **1**
Multum In Parvo 7-11-0 TMorgan sh.**2**
37 **Ghofar** 7-11-3 BPowell 2½.**3**
Highfrith 7-10-12 NDoughty 2½.4
Generally Right 8-11-0 RDunwoody 2½.5
64 Blueberry King 7-11-3 GMcCourt 1½.6
Lough Road 8-11-0 JBryan dist.7
Raven Venture 10-11-0 LWyer .... pu

13/8 BROWN WINDSOR, 3/1 Blueberry King, 5/1 Ghofar, 15/2 Highfrith, 10/1 Generally Right, 12/1 Multum In Parvo, 33/1 Raven Venture, 66/1 Lough Road

W. Shand Kydd (N. Henderson) 8ran 5m04.26 (Firm)

128 COUNTY HANDICAP HURDLE 2m
£19,521 Cheltenham 15 March

110* **Moody Man** 5-11-2 PHobbs ... **1**
Smart Performer 5-10-3 GMcCourt ½.**2**
88 **Persillant** 6-10-2 MHill ½.**3**
Rustic Comedy 5-9-11 PHolley 10.4
110 Ambassador 7-10-7 JLower hd.5
71 Wonder Man (Fr) 5-11-3 MPitman 10.6
Windbound Lass 7-10-9 NColeman ½.7
69³ Milford Quay 7-11-10 MFoster 4.8
Doc's Coat 5-10-7 BWright 1½.9
On Tap 6-10-5 LWyer 5.10
Rich Nephew 5-10-0 AWebb 2.11
Dapping 6-9-7 ETierney ... hd.12
Xhai 8-10-0 WMorris ½.13
Great Aspect 6-10-0 TWall hd.14
Royal Miami 5-10-1 CBowens 15
66 Sayparee 5-11-9 MDwyer 16
20* Liadett (USA) 5-11-3 PScudamore 17
Yorkshire Holly 7-11-0 RDunwoody .... f
110 Tebitto 7-9-7 RBoucher .... f
Instant Tan 6-10-0 RSupple ... pu

11/2 On Tap, 6/1 Smart Performer, 8/1 Wonder Man, Yorkshire Holly, 9/1 MOODY MAN, 10/1 Sayparee, 11/1 Milford Quay, 12/1 Liadett, 16/1 Persillant, Royal Miami, Windbound Lass, 20/1 Ambassador, Instant Tan, Rich Nephew, Rustic Comedy, Tebitto, 50/1 Great Aspect, 100/1 Dapping, Doc's Coat, Xhai

J. Burley (P. Hobbs) 20ran 3m51.20 (Firm)

129 BUILDER GROUP GOLD CUP (HANDICAP HURDLE) 2½m
£7,700 Lingfield (All-Weather) 17 March

110 **Nahar** 5-10-7 HDavies **1**
Regal Lake 4-10-0 DGallagher 15.**2**
Sing The Blues 6-10-0 DMcKeown 8.**3**
Milton Bryan 5-9-11 IShoemark 2½.4
Lesbet 5-9-9 PBarnard 12.5
Bahrain Bridge 5-9-7 SHazell 1½.6
39 Holtermann (USA) 6-10-0 RArnott ½.7
Alaoui 8-9-7 VSlattery 7.8
103[2] Sprowston Boy 7-11-9 SCurran .... pu

11/8 Regal Lake, 4/1 Sprowston Boy, 9/2 NAHAR, 6/1 Sing The Blues, 16/1 Milton Bryan, 20/1 Alaoui, Bahrain Bridge, 33/1 Lesbet

R. Cross (S. Dow) 9ran 4m40.00 (Standard)

130 NORTHERN CHAMPION JUVENILE HANDICAP HURDLE (4y) 2m
£5,900 Newcastle 17 March

101 **Rouyan** 11-1 WMorris **1**
101* **Philosophos** 11-11 WMcFarland 2½.**2**
Bescaby Boy 11-3 RGarritty 1.**3**
Ambuscade (USA) 11-10 NDoughty 2½.4
107 Carbisdale 11-3 JCallaghan . ½.5
Dancing River 10-7 CGrant 10.6
Fisherman's Croft 11-6 GMcCourt 7.7
Sybillin 11-9 MDwyer 8.8
Drumstick 9-13 ILawrence 9
Top Entertainer 10-0 AWebb 10
Favoski 11-6 BStorey .... pu

100/30 Dancing River, 9/2 Philosophos, 7/1 Ambuscade, ROUYAN, Sybillin, 8/1 Carbisdale, 11/1 Bescaby Boy, 12/1 Fisherman's Croft, 14/1 Favoski, Top Entertainer, 25/1 Drumstick

Darfam Racing (R. Simpson) 11ran 3m55.07 (Good to Firm)

131 HOECHST PANACUR EBF MARES ONLY NOVICES' HURDLE FINAL (LIMITED HANDICAP) 2½m120y
£7,298 Newbury 24 March

Reach Me Down 6-10-9 WMcFarland **1**
Trefelyn Cone 6-12-0 PScudamore 4.**2**
104 **Rare Luck** 7-10-0 MKinane 5.**3**
Tochenka 6-10-0 JRailton .. 1½.4
Purple Silk 6-10-3 SDavies . nk.5
Veritate 6-10-6 BPowell 12.6
On The Hooch 5-10-7 MrJBradburne 12.7
Grayrose Double 7-10-12 DBurchell 8.8
Bremhill Rosie 7-11-7 MRichards .... pu
Penny Rose 9-10-5 JLower .... pu
Air Streak 6-10-0 AWebb .... pu

8/11 Trefelyn Cone, 6/1 Bremhill Rosie, 7/1 REACH ME DOWN, 9/1 On The Hooch, 14/1 Purple Silk, 16/1 Veritate, 20/1 Tochenka, 33/1 Air Streak, Grayrose Double, Penny Rose, 50/1 Rare Luck

Rumble Racing Club (G. Balding) 11ran 4m59.62 (Firm)

132 KEITH PROWSE LONG DISTANCE HURDLE 3m
£15,270 Ascot 31 March

Battalion (USA) 6-11-7 BdeHaan **1**
119[2] **Maelkar (Fr)** 6-11-4 MDwyer 6.**2**
114 **Old Dundalk** 6-12-2 MBowlby 12.**3**
128 Milford Quay 7-11-7 PScudamore 15.4
Nodforms Dilemma (USA) 7-11-4 JOsborne dist.5
Gainsay 11-12-2 MPitman 6
Tremar Lad 8-11-4 Tarnya Davies .... f
Abbotsham 5-11-4 MrCBurnett-Wells .... pu

2/1 Maelkar, Milford Quay, 100/30 BATTALION, 7/1 Old Dundalk, 25/1 Nodforms Dilemma, 50/1 Gainsay, 100/1 Abbotsham, Tremar Lad

R. L. Dormer (C. Brooks) 8ran 5m29.05 (Firm)

133 PEREGRINE HANDICAP CHASE 2½m
£8,928 Ascot 31 March

118 **Ida's Delight** 11-11-2 BStorey **1**
72 **Welsh Oak** 10-10-7 RDunwoody nk.**2**
24 **Biloxi Blues** 8-10-0 BPowell ¾.**3**
84 Rusch de Farges (Fr) 7-11-10 PScudamore 2.4
Course Hunter 12-10-0 MBowlby dist.5
Numerate 11-10-0 Tarnya Davies 6

2/1 Biloxi Blues, 9/4 Welsh Oak, 11/4 IDA'S DELIGHT, 7/1 Rusch de Farges, 16/1 Course Hunter, 66/1 Numerate

J. Charlton (J. Charlton) 6ran 4m45.76 (Firm)

134 ODDBINS HURDLE (HANDICAP) 3m 1f
£9,200 Liverpool 5 April

119 **Sip of Orange** 8-10-3 MDwyer 1
114* **Trapper John** 6-12-0 CSwan ½.2
Parsons Green 6-10-0 JWhite 12.3
119 Arctic Teal 6-11-4 JOsborne . 5.4
119 Atrabates 6-10-0 MRichards 2.5
Drowsy 8-9-7 ASmith 7.6
Eastern Oasis 7-10-0 DByrne 1½.7
119 Inde Pulse 8-10-2 RDunwoody 1½.8
128 Dapping 6-10-0 SKeightley 12.9
119 Taberna Lord 9-10-0 LHarvey 10
5 Viking Rocket 6-9-9 LO'Hara 11
The Shiner 10-9-11 PVerling . 12
Bel Course 8-9-7 WMarston .. 13
114 Mineral Dust 7-10-0 JBryan .. 14
Flying Oats (USA) 10-10-2 TReed 15
Tyred N'Snookerd 6-9-11 ILawrence 16
119 Parlezvousfrancais 6-10-1 PScudamore 17
Billy Tobin 10-10-0 MrsJThurlow ..... f
114 Tewit Castle 8-10-8 LWyer ... pu
Military Band (Fr) 12-10-0 BPowell ..... pu
Brompton Road 7-9-11 CDennis ..... pu

9/2 Trapper John, 5/1 SIP OF ORANGE, 13/2 Taberna Lord, 7/1 Parsons Green, 16/1 Arctic Teal, Inde Pulse, 20/1 Brompton Road, Parlezvousfrancais, 22/1 Eastern Oasis, 25/1 Military Man, The Shiner, Tyred N'Snookerd, Viking Rocket, 33/1 Drowsy, Mineral Dust, Tewit Castle, 50/1 Atrabates, 66/1 Dapping, 200/1 Bel Course, Billy Tobin, Flying Oats
Mrs R. Haggie (J. FitzGerald) 21ran 5m58.42 (Good to Firm)

135 MARTELL CUP CHASE 3m 1f
£22,218 Liverpool 5 April

125² **Toby Tobias** 8-11-9 MPitman 1
125 **Cavvies Clown** 10-11-5 GBradley 1½.2
84³ **Man O'Magic** 9-11-5 MPerrett 12.3
126 Golden Friend 12-11-5 GMcCourt 2½.4
102² Delius 12-11-5 PScudamore 12.5

1/1 TOBY TOBIAS, 5/2 Cavvies Clown, 5/1 Delius, 17/2 Man O'Magic, 33/1 Golden Friend
Mrs E. Hitchins (Mrs J. Pitman) 5ran 6m18.64 (Good to Firm)

136 SEAGRAM 100 PIPERS TOP NOVICES' HURDLE 2m
£10,736 Liverpool 5 April

Fidway 5-11-0 SSmithEccles 1
111³ **Rakes Lane** 5-11-0 TMorgan 3.2
130² **Philosophos** 4-11-2 WMcFarland 1½.3
111 Riverhead (USA) 6-11-0 GBradley 2½.4
81³ Atlaal 5-11-8 RDunwoody 3.5
129² Regal Lake 4-10-12 MPitman 8.6
My Young Man 5-11-0 BdeHaan sh.7
Last O'The Bunch 6-11-0 LWyer 10.8
Society Guest 4-10-8 GMcCourt 9
111 Re-Release 5-10-9 PScudamore 10
123 Iveagh House 4-10-8 MBowlby 11
Mander's Way 5-11-0 RBeggan ..... pu
111 Man of The West 7-11-0 MDwyer ..... pu
Tildarg 6-11-0 JOsborne ..... pu
Mountain Retreat 4-10-8 MLynch ..... pu

4/1 My Young Man, 5/1 Riverhead, 6/1 Rakes Lane, 15/2 Man of The West, 9/1 Re-Release, Tildarg, 10/1 Atlaal, 14/1 Mander's Way, Regal Lake, 16/1 FIDWAY, 20/1 Philosophos, 50/1 Iveagh House, Last O'The Bunch, Mountain Retreat, Society Guest
A. R. Coley (T. Thomson Jones) 15ran 3m50.89 (Good to Firm)

137 JOHN HUGHES MEMORIAL TROPHY (HANDICAP CHASE) 2¾m
£18,381 Liverpool 5 April

79 **Wont Be Gone Long** 8-10-2 RDunwoody 1
Villierstown 11-11-10 CGrant 4.2
115² **Golden Minstrel** 11-10-2 RRowe 3.3
Eight Springs 9-10-3 HDavies 12.4
Crock-Na-Nee 9-10-0 JOsborne 1½.5
79 Kittinger 9-10-5 GMcCourt 2½.6
Gembridge Jupiter 12-10-7 PDever 1½.7
General Chandos 9-10-7 MrJBradburne 1.8
44 Old Applejack 10-10-8 TReed 3.9
116 Broad Beam 10-9-13 CMaude nk.10

Bad Trade 9-9-9 MrKJohnson 4.11
79 J-J-Henry 11-10-9 MrsAFarrell nk.12
116 Raise An Argument 11-10-4 RSupple 13
Weirpool 8-9-11 ILawrence ... 14
Rubika (Fr) 7-10-0 MPerrett . 15
Wiggburn 11-10-1 SO'Neill 16
122 Auntie Dot 9-10-11 MLynch .. 17
Pan Arctic 11-10-2 JRailton ... 18
Impany 11-10-0 LWyer 19
John O'Dee 7-10-13 DMurphy 20
The Leggett 7-10-4 PScudamore 21
Wally Wombat 12-10-0 DTegg 22
72 Bright Intervals 8-10-8 BdeHaan .... f
How Now 9-10-0 MBowlby ...... f
Our Nobby 8-10-0 BPowell ...... f
12 Southernair 10-10-6 SSmithEccles .... ur
122* New Halen 9-9-11 ETierney .. ur
106 Bucko 13-11-2 MDwyer .... pu
73 Eton Rouge 11-10-2 JBryan ... pu
29 Tartan Trademark 8-10-3 NDoughty .... pu

15/2 The Leggett, 10/1 Kittinger, Villierstown, 11/1 New Halen, 12/1 Tartan Trademark, 14/1 Auntie Dot, Golden Minstrel, Old Applejack, 20/1 Crock-Na-Nee, Gembridge Jupiter, Rubika, 25/1 Bad Trade, Bucko, General Chandos, J-J-Henry, Raise An Argument, Weirpool, WONT BE GONE LONG, 33/1 Bright Intervals, How Now, John O'Dee, Southernair, 40/1 Eight Springs, Eton Rouge, 50/1 Broad Beam, Our Nobby, 66/1 Pan Arctic, Wiggburn, 100/1 Impany, 150/1 Wally Wombat

R. Waley-Cohen (N. Henderson) 30ran 5m28.29 (Good to Firm)

138 MUMM CLUB NOVICES' CHASE 3m 1f

£21,036 Liverpool 5 April

120 **Royal Athlete** 7-11-9 MPitman 1
Arctic Call 7-11-3 JOsborne ½.2
96A* **Cahervillahow** 6-11-6 CSwan 10.3
120 Mixed Blends 8-10-12 TCarmody 15.4
Aughanvilla 7-11-3 GMcCourt nk.5
40² The Nigelstan 9-11-3 MPerrett 15.6
120 Knight Oil 7-11-3 MRichards ... 7
65* Espy 7-11-6 PScudamore .... f
Tort 6-11-3 SO'Neill .... f
Hotplate 7-11-3 MDwyer ...... pu
Wrekin Hill 8-11-3 CGrant .... pu

5/2 ROYAL ATHLETE, 7/2 Espy, 9/2 Cahervillahow, 7/1 Arctic Call, 10/1 Knight Oil, 14/1 Tort, 16/1 Aughanvilla, Mixed Blends, 25/1 The Nigelstan, 33/1 Wrekin Hill, 50/1 Hotplate

L. Johnson (Mrs J. Pitman) 11ran 6m11.43 (Good to Firm)

139 HEIDSIECK DRY MONOPOLE HANDICAP CHASE 3m 1f

£8,827 Liverpool 6 April

72* **One More Knight** 7-10-12 LHarvey 1
126² **Seagram (NZ)** 10-11-8 NHawke 1.2
92 **Killone Abbey** 7-9-13 MrKJohnson 1½.3
126³ Boraceva 7-11-3 JFrost ½.4
Rapier Thrust 8-11-2 MDwyer 5.5
Vulgan Warrior 8-10-7 JOsborne 5.6
79 Royal Cedar 9-10-11 LWyer 1½.7
122 Worthy Knight 9-10-8 GMcCourt hd.8
The Thirsty Farmer 11-10-1 PScudamore 1½.9
115 Mweenish 8-10-10 MLynch ... 10
Irish Red 8-10-0 CGrant 11
Tsarella 8-10-2 RDunwoody .. pu

9/2 Tsarella, Vulgan Warrior, 15/2 Seagram, 8/1 Boraceva, 9/1 Irish Red, Rapier Thrust, 10/1 ONE MORE KNIGHT, 14/1 Killone Abbey, Royal Cedar, Worthy Knight, 16/1 The Thirsty Farmer, 20/1 Mweenish

R. West (Mrs I. McKie) 12ran 6m10.36 (Good to Firm)

140 MARTELL HANDICAP HURDLE 2½m

£12,251 Liverpool 6 April

128 **Sayparee** 5-11-3 PScudamore 1
110 **Out of Range** 7-10-11 GBradley 1.2
Artful Abbot 6-10-0 MLynch 2½.3
Pactolus (USA) 7-9-11 AMulholland 1.4
119 Badihar (USA) 6-10-3 MBowlby ½.5
91³ Toranfield 6-11-9 FWoods 3.6
Noble Storm 8-10-0 MKinane 10.7
88 Hill Street (Fr) 8-11-2 MDwyer 4.8
113 Space Fair 7-10-7 WMcFarland 6.9
Midland Express 7-10-6 CGrant 10
128 Yorkshire Holly 7-11-10 PNiven 11
54 Directly 7-10-4 JFrost 12
Al Asoof (USA) 5-11-7 MRichards .... pu

Predominate 9-10-4
JOsborne .... pu

5/2 Space Fair, 15/2 Hill Street, 9/1 Directly, Toranfield, Yorkshire Holly, 10/1 SAYPAREE, 12/1 Badihar, Out of Range, 14/1 Midland Express, 16/1 Al Asoof, 20/1 Pactolus, 33/1 Predominate, 50/1 Artful Abbot, Noble Storm

E. Scarth (M. Pipe) 14ran 4m40.47 (Good to Firm)

141 GLENLIVET ANNIVERSARY HURDLE (4y) 2m
£25,800 Liverpool 6 April

130 **Sybillin** 11-0 DByrne 1
123 **Midfielder** 11-0 PHobbs 8.2
123 **Bally Rue (USA)** 11-0
MrEKearns sh.3
130 Ambuscade (USA) 11-0
NDoughty 3.4
Cornet 11-0 CGrant 2.5
123 Sayyure (USA) 11-0
GMcCourt 2½.6
123 Vestris Abu 11-0 CSwan 1½.7
Shamirani 11-0 BStorey ... 2½.8
Top Villain 11-0
RDunwoody 8.9
86 Embarkation 11-0 JLodder ½.10
Swift Waters 11-0 MPitman 6.11
86[2] Gay Ruffian 11-0 DBurchell ... 12
Sagaman (Ger) 11-0 STurner . 13
City Index (USA) 11-0
TPinfield 14
Myfor 11-0 PScudamore 15
123[3] Native Friend 11-0 MDwyer .... f
Spring Rag 11-0 JFrost .... f
Lissahane Lass 10-9
MRichards .... pu

9/4 Swift Waters, 6/1 Native Friend, Vestris Abu, 8/1 Sayyure, 9/1 Midfielder, 11/1 Shamirani, 14/1 Lissahane Lass, 16/1 Embarkation, 20/1 Ambuscade, Gay Ruffian, Myfor, 25/1 Bally Rue, SYBILLIN, 33/1 Cornet, Spring Rag, Top Villain, 66/1 Sagaman, 200/1 City Index

Marquesa de Moratalla (J. FitzGerald) 18ran 3m52.68 (Good to Firm)

142 SEAGRAM FOX HUNTERS' CHASE 2¾m
£8,774 Liverpool 6 April

Lean Ar Aghaidh 13-12-0
MrDGray 1
Crammer 10-12-0
MrJDurkan 7.2
Giolla Padraig 12-12-0
MrPMcMahon 10.3
Newnham 13-12-0
MrSAndrews 1.4
Eastern Destiny 12-12-0
MrAGriffith 12.5
Dromore Castle 10-12-0
MrNRidout 10.6
Copper Fastener 9-12-0
MrRHeyman 2½.7
Straight Pilot 8-12-0
MrSSwiers 20.8
Ready Steady 8-12-0
MrJGrossick 6.9
Light Demon 13-12-0
MrCHolmes 10
North Brigade 10-12-0
MrJPritchard 11
Border Sun 12-12-0
MrSSweeting .... f
124 Whitsunday 11-12-0
MrMChamberlayne .... f
Oakley House 11-12-0
MrJBarlow .... f
Father Brady 11-12-0
MrJGreenall .... f
Centaur Song 10-12-0
MrPHickman .... f
Clonroche Gazette 10-12-0
MrHWheeler .... f
Flaming Tide 12-12-0
MrRBailey .... f
Joseph Knibb 11-12-0
MrPCarberry .... f
Oyster Pond 13-12-1
MrCCoyne .... f
Southerns 8-12-0
MrGRobertson .... f
Unscrupulous Gent 8-12-0
MrDYearsley .... ur
Edenspring 11-12-0
MrCLumsden .... pu
Mr Chris 11-12-0 MrRFord ... pu
Manna Reef 12-12-0
MrCBarlow .... ref

5/1 LEAN AR AGHAIDH, 13/2 Crammer, 7/1 Whitsunday, 11/1 Ready Steady, 12/1 Dromore Castle, Eastern Destiny, 14/1 Joseph Knibb, Newnham, 16/1 Father Brady, Oakley House, Straight Pilot, 20/1 Border Sun, 25/1 Edenspring, Giolla Padraig, Unscrupulous Gent, 33/1 Centaur Song, Clonroche Gazette, 50/1 Copper Fastener, 661/ Mr Chris, North Brigade, 100/1 Flaming Tide, Light Demon, Manna Reef, Oyster Pond, Southerns

Mrs W. Tulloch (S. Mellor) 25ran 5m31.05 (Good to Firm)

143 PERRIER JOUET NOVICES' CHASE 2m
£11,385 Liverpool 6 April

Order of finish—Blazing Walker subsequently disqualified

Boutzdaroff 8-11-1 DByrne .. 1
112[3] **Young Snugfit** 6-11-8
JOsborne hd.2
105 **Blazing Walker** 6-11-11
CGrant 12.3
Elfast 7-11-1 MLynch 1½.4
112 Antinous 6-11-11 LWyer ... 1½.5
27[2] Campsea-Ash 6-11-5
DMurphy 1½.6
Certain Style 7-11-1
MRichards 12.7

116 Wink Gulliver 6-11-11
RArnott 10.8
Isthatafact 9-11-1 TKinane 9
94³ Fuego Boy (NZ) 10-11-5
BdeHaan 10
Mshahara 12-10-12
ILawrence 11
45 Deep Flash 7-11-5 TMorgan .... f
Highfire 8-11-5 GBradley ...... pu
Meningi 9-11-1 HDavies .... pu

11/8 Young Snugfit, 5/1 Antinous, 7/1 Elfast, 8/1 BOUTZDAROFF, 14/1 Isthatafact, 16/1 Blazing Walker, Wink Gulliver, 20/1 Deep Flash, Fuego Boy, 25/1 Certain Style, 33/1 Campsea-Ash, Highfire, 66/1 Meningi, Mshahara

Robinson Publications Ltd (J. FitzGerald) 14ran 3m46.65 (Good to Firm)

144 WHITE SATIN NOVICES' HURDLE 3m1f
£8,667 Liverpool 6 April

Dwadme 5-11-4 JOsborne 1
80 **Whats The Crack** 7-11-4
RBeggan 4.2
117 **Tinryland** 6-11-7
RDunwoody 6.3
108* Miinnehoma 7-11-10
PScudamore 2.4
117 The Illywhacker 5-11-4
MPitman 5.5
Holy Joe 8-11-4 AWebb 2½.6
Theo's Fella 6-11-4 RGuest 7
Our Survivor 6-11-4 JDuggan .. 8
Geostar 6-11-4 MrWMorgan ... 9
Into The Red 6-11-4 RSupple ... f

10/11 Miinnehoma, 4/1 Tinryland, 5/1 DWADME, 12/1 Holy Joe, 16/1 Theo's Fella, 20/1 The Illywhacker, Whats The Crack, 50/1 Geostar, 66/1 Into The Red, Our Survivor

Olympic N.H. Racing (O. Sherwood) 10ran 5m58.64 (Good to Firm)

145 CAPTAIN MORGAN AINTREE CHASE (LIMITED HANDICAP) 2m
£19,712 Liverpool 7 April

116 **Nohalmdun** 9-10-7 LWyer 1
35 **Prize Asset** 10-10-7 SEarle . 5.2
116* **Katabatic** 7-10-7 HDavies .. 1.3
118² Waterloo Boy 7-11-12
RDunwoody ¾.4
116 The A Train 8-10-7
MBowlby 4.5
116 Masnoon (USA) 7-10-7
MrPMcMahon ½.6
25* Clever Folly 10-10-11
NDoughty 2.7
118³ Feroda 9-11-5 TTaaffe 8.8
35 Prideaux Boy 12-10-7 JShortt .. 9
116 Fu's Lady 8-10-7
PScudamore 10
Knockbrack 10-10-7 BPowell 11
118 Private Views 9-10-10
KMooney .... f

4/1 Katabatic, Waterloo Boy, 5/1 Feroda, 13/2 Clever Folly, 10/1 Prize Asset, 11/1 NOHALMDUN, 14/1 Fu's Lady, Prideaux Boy, 20/1 Private Views, 25/1 Masnoon, The A Train, 100/1 Knockbrack

Ulceby Farms Ltd (M. H. Easterby) 12ran 3m45.60 (Firm)

146 SANDEMAN AINTREE HURDLE 2½m
£24,090 Liverpool 7 April

113 **Morley Street** 6-11-6 JFrost . 1
110³ **Joyful Noise** 7-11-6
TTaaffe 15.2
114 **Ikdam** 5-11-6 NMann 3.3
113 Vagador (Can) 7-11-6
MPerrett 15.4
113 Island Set (USA) 8-11-6
CGrant 25.5
134 Taberna Lord 9-11-6 LHarvey . 6

4/5 MORLEY STREET, 7/2 Vagador, 17/2 Island Set, 9/1 Ikdam, 11/1 Joyful Noise, 33/1 Taberna Lord

Michael Jackson Bloodstock Ltd (G. Balding) 6ran 4m39.62 (Firm)

147 SEAGRAM GRAND NATIONAL HANDICAP CHASE 4½m
£70,871 Liverpool 7 April

115 **Mr Frisk** 11-10-6
MrMArmytage 1
44* **Durham Edition** 12-10-9
CGrant ¾.2
106* **Rinus** 9-10-4 NDoughty 20.3
127* Brown Windsor 8-10-10
JWhite 12.4
90³ Lastofthebrownies 10-10-0
CSwan ½.5
126* Bigsun 9-10-2 RDunwoody . 25.6
124* Call Collect 9-10-5
MrRMartin 1½.7
34 Bartres 11-10-0 MBowlby .. 12.8
6 Sir Jest 12-10-0 BStorey 9
124³ West Tip 13-10-11 PHobbs 10
73 Team Challenge 8-10-0
BdeHaan 11
115 Charter Hardware 8-10-0
NWilliamson 12
115 Gallic Prince 11-10-4
MrJSimo 13
127³ Ghofar 7-10-0 BPowell 14
133 Course Hunter 12-10-4
GBradley 15
125 Bonanza Boy 9-11-9
PScudamore 16
Solares 10-10-0
MrPMcMahon 17
Gee-A 11-10-2 DMurphy 18
Mick's Star 10-10-1 SO'Neill . 19
126 Bob Tisdall 11-10-5
KMooney 20
132 Gainsay 11-10-7 MPitman .... f

67 Thinking Cap 9-10-0 PMalone . f
Lanavoe 11-10-0 PLeech .... f
37 Conclusive 11-10-4 SSmithEccles .... f
58 Roll-A-Joint 12-10-0 SMcNeill . f
16 Gala's Image 10-10-0 JShortt ... f
25 Joint Sovereignty 10-10-1 LWyer .... ur
Nautical Joke 11-10-0 MrKJohnson .... ur
Pukka Major (USA) 9-10-4 MRichards .... ur
Huntworth 10-10-9 MrAWalter .... ur
Uncle Merlin (USA) 9-10-3 HDavies .... ur
96 Hungary Hur 11-11-2 TCarmody .... pu
63 Against The Grain 9-10-0 JOsborne .... pu
53* Polyfemus 8-10-2 RRowe ...... pu
Torside 11-10-3 JFrost .... pu
64 Star's Delight 8-10-0 JLower . pu
Young Driver 13-10-4 JDuggan .... pu
73 Monanore 13-10-5 TTaaffe .... ro

7/1 Brown Windsor, 15/2 Bigsun, 9/1 Durham Edition, 13/1 Rinus, 14/1 Call Collect, Ghofar, 16/1 Bonanza Boy, MR FRISK, Uncle Merlin, 18/1 Polyfemus, 20/1 Lastofthebrownies, West Tip, 25/1 Against The Grain, 28/1 Conclusive, Roll-A-Joint, 50/1 Hungary Hur, Joint Sovereignty, Star's Delight, Team Challenge, 66/1 Bartres, Bob Tisdall, Charter Hardware, Course Hunter, Gainsay, Gala's Image, Gee-A, Huntworth, Mick's Star, Nautical Joke, Sir Jest, Torside, 100/1 Gallic Prince, Lanavoe, Monanore, Pukka Major, Thinking Cap, 150/1 Solares, Young Driver

Mrs H. J. Duffey (K. Bailey) 38ran
8m47.80 (Firm)

148 JANNEAU ARMAGNAC HANDICAP HURDLE 2m
£12,461 Liverpool 7 April

1² **Jubail** 5-10-0 RSupple 1
128³ **Persillant** 6-10-4 GMcCourt ½.2
113 **Dis Train** 6-11-2 MPitman . 10.3
Foujita (USA) 5-9-9 SDavies 1½.4
Voyage Sans Retour (Fr) 5-10-13 PScudamore ½.5
110 Bradbury Star 5-10-9 RRowe 4.6
113 Redundant Pal 7-11-10 CO'Dwyer 2.7
66 St Coleman's Well 7-10-0 GO'Neill 1½.8
128 Wonder Man (Fr) 5-10-9 MBowlby 9
97 Valrodian (NZ) 7-10-9 JDuggan 10
93 Aldino 7-11-7 JOsborne 11

11/4 JUBAIL, 9/2 Bradbury Star, 11/2 Voyage Sans Retour, 13/2 Persillant, 11/1 Aldino, Dis Train, Redundant Pal, 12/1 Foujita, 20/1 St Coleman's Well, Wonder Man, 33/1 Valrodian

V. C. Bootle (K. Morgan) 11ran
3m45.19 (Firm)

149 MUMM PRIZE NOVICES' HURDLE 2½m
£11,000 Liverpool 7 April

39 **Vazon Bay** 6-11-1 MPitman .. 1
108² **Remittance Man** 6-11-1 JWhite 1½.2
111 **Young Ty** 6-11-1 MrSSwiers 1½.3
109² Ri-Na-Rithann 5-11-1 MBowlby 1.4
111* Forest Sun 5-11-9 JFrost ... 1½.5
117 Run For Free 6-11-5 PScudamore 2½.6
111 Olnistar (Fr) 4-10-3 RDunwoody 7
36 Go Nobley 4-10-8 HDavies ...... f
Proud Crest (USA) 6-11-1 JOsborne .... pu
117³ Tom's Little Bet 6-10-10 GMcCourt .... pu

8/13 Forest Sun, 7/1 Run For Free, 8/1 Olnistar, 10/1 Remittance Man, Young Ty, 16/1 Ri-Na-Rithann, Tom's Little Bet, 28/1 Proud Crest, 33/1 Go Nobley, VAZON BAY

Mrs E. Hitchins (Mrs J. Pitman) 10ran
4m38.90 (Firm)

150 BOLLINGER CHAMPAGNE NOVICES' HANDICAP CHASE 2½m
£14,880 Ascot 11 April

Sword Beach 6-10-1 LWyer .. 1
112* **Comandante** 8-12-2 PHobbs 30.2
Spirited Holme (Fr) 5-10-2 RDunwoody 30.3
Six Shot 10-10-0 BPowell 4
San Ovac 7-10-4 PScudamore .. f
23² Going Gets Tough 7-10-4 JFrost .... ur

6/4 SWORD BEACH, 7/4 Comandante, 4/1 Going Gets Tough, 14/1 Spirited Holme, 25/1 San Ovac, 100/1 Six Shot

Mrs S. J. Mason (M. H. Easterby) 6ran
4m41.70 (Firm)

151 JAMESON IRISH GRAND NATIONAL (HANDICAP CHASE) 3½m
£53,592 Fairyhouse 16 April

125³ **Desert Orchid** 11-12-0 RDunwoody 1
90² **Barney Burnett** 10-10-0 BSheridan 12.2
67 **Have A Barney** 9-10-2 TTaaffe 1½.3

115 Cloney Grange 11-10-0 DO'Connor nk.4
90 Riska's River 8-10-0 MrFFlood nk.5
120[2] The Committee 7-10-0 CO'Dwyer ½.6
90 Feltrim Hill Lad 9-10-0 MLynch 6.7
121 Cushinstown 7-10-0 AO'Brien 8
Another Plano 9-10-0 CSwan ... f
Us And Joe 7-10-0 MFlynn .... f
Caddy 9-10-0 TRyan .... f
Bankers Benefit 7-10-0 APowell .... pu
Bold Flyer 7-10-0 MissSCollen .... pu
8 Belsir 8-10-0 TCarmody .... pu

Evens DESERT ORCHID, 6/1 Bold Flyer, 7/1 Have A Barney, 14/1 Us And Joe, 16/1 Barney Burnett, The Committee, 20/1 Another Plano, Belsir, 25/1 Riska's River, 33/1 Caddy, Feltrim Hill Lad, 40/1 Bankers Benefit, Cushinstown, 100/1 Cloney Grange
R. Burridge (D. Elsworth) 14ran 7m30.9 (Good to Firm)

152 EBF GOLD CUP CHASE 2¼m
£12,450 Fairyhouse 17 April

112 **Blitzkreig** 7-12-0 TCarmody . 1
112[2] **Kiichi (USA)** 5-11-7 BSheridan 3.2
Irish Wind (Fr) 7-11-7 MFlynn 20.3
49 Astral River 7-11-6 MrPMurphy 15.4
Shabra Boy 8-11-3 CO'Dwyer .. 5
Lord de Montfort 6-12-0 CSwan .... f

5/4 Kiichi, 6/4 BLITZKREIG, 6/1 Lord de Montfort, 16/1 Astral River, 20/1 Irish Wind, 100/1 Shabra Boy
J. McManus (E. O'Grady) 6ran 4m38.8 (Good to Firm)

153 TATTERSALLS NOVICE CHASE 2¾m
£6,764 Fairyhouse 18 April

120 **All Jeff (FR)** 6-11-13 BdeHaan 1
Renagown 7-11-10 KO'Brien 5.2
138 **Mixed Blends** 8-11-8 CSwan 8.3
Derrymore Boy 8-11-13 CO'Dwyer 8.4
Pepys 9-11-1 HRogers 4.5
On The Other Hand 7-11-13 TCarmody 4.6

7/4 ALL JEFF, 9/4 Renagown, 4/1 Mixed Blends, 5/1 Derrymore Boy, 7/1 On The Other Hand, 50/1 Pepys
Lady Joseph (C. Brooks) 6ran 5m57.3 (Good)

154 EBF NOVICES' HURDLE FINAL (HANDICAP) 2m
£11,145 Cheltenham 18 April

149* **Vazon Bay** 6-12-0 MPitman .. 1
149 **Ri-Na-Rithann** 5-11-7 MBowlby 2.2
Tommy's Dream 7-9-9 NMann 1.3
109[3] Hey Cottage 5-10-13 GMcCourt 6.4
Ballyanto 5-10-1 NDawe 1.5
Los Buccaneros 7-9-12 AMulholland nk.6
Air Commander 5-10-0 JOsborne 3.7
Sacred Gem 5-9-12 JCallaghan hd.8
East River 6-9-12 WMcFarland ¾.9
131 Purple Silk 6-9-12 SDavies 10
Abbots View 6-10-8 PScudamore .... f
Iama Zulu 5-10-1 PHobbs .... f

4/1 Abbotts View, 6/1 Los Buccaneros, 7/1 East River, Iama Zulu, VAZON BAY, 8/1 Air Commander, Ri-Na-Rithann, 10/1 Hey Cottage, 20/1 Purple Silk, Tommy's Dream, 50/1 Sacred Gem, 66/1 Ballyanto
Mrs E. Hitchins (Mrs J. Pitman) 12ran 4m01.97 (Firm)

155 SOUTH WALES SHOWERS CARADON MIRA SILVER TROPHY CHASE 2½m
£15,620 Cheltenham 18 April

118* **Barnbrook Again** 9-11-10 HDavies 1
125 **Pegwell Bay** 9-11-0 BPowell 10.2
133* **Ida's Delight** 11-11-0 BStorey 12.3
118 Sabin du Loir (Fr) 11-11-10 RDunwoody nk.4
Sure Metal 7-11-0 GMcCourt pu

6/4 BARNBROOK AGAIN, 13/8 Pegwell Bay, 4/1 Sabin du Loir, 14/1 Ida's Delight, 20/1 Sure Metal
M. Davies (D. Elsworth) 5ran 5m01.58 (Firm)

156 SOUTER OF STIRLING NOVICES' CHASE 3m110y
£8,740 Ayr 20 April

138* **Royal Athlete** 7-11-13 MPitman 1
85[3] **Carrick Hill Lad** 7-11-13 NDoughty 2.2
105[2] **Formula One** 8-11-5 NWilliamson hd.3
Camionnage 9-11-5 AOrkney 30.4
Super Fountain 7-11-5 BStorey sh.5
Charlie Nose 7-11-10 RDunwoody 15.6

Speech 7-11-5 CGrant 3.7
Border Oak 8-11-10 LO'Hara . pu
Into The Mystic 8-11-10 PNiven .... pu
43 Snowfire Chap 7-11-10 MDwyer .... pu
Grovelands 8-11-5 RGoldstein .... pu
Kilclooney Forrest 8-11-5 MBrennan .... pu
121 Sportsnews 8-11-5 DNolan .... pu
Farranrory 6-11-0 VSlattery .. pu

Evens ROYAL ATHLETE, 2/1 Carrick Hill Lad, 10/1 Formula One, 20/1 Charlie Nose, Kilclooney Forrest, 40/1 Super Fountain, 50/1 Snowfire Chap, Speech, 100/1 Farranrory, Into The Mystic, 200/1 Border Oak, Camionnage, Grovelands, 500/1 Sportsnews

L. Johnson (Mrs J. Pitman) 14ran 6m27.90 (Good to Soft)

157 SCOTTISH CHAMPION HURDLE (LIMITED HANDICAP) 2m
£16,180 Ayr 20 April

140* **Sayparee** 5-10-7 JLower 1
113 **Don Valentino** 5-11-0 MPitman 6.2
148 **Aldino** 7-11-3 JOsborne 2.3
109* Sacre d'Or (USA) 5-10-7 SO'Neill 1.4
113 Deep Sensation 5-11-6 RRowe 1.5
148^{3} Dis Train 6-10-12 MBowlby 8.6
136 Atlaal 5-10-10 RDunwoody . 10.7
109 Alkinor Rex 5-10-7 BdeHaan 4.8
113 See You Then 10-11-2 SSmithEccles 1½.9
140 Al Asoof (USA) 5-10-10 BPowell 10
146 Vagador (Can) 7-11-11 MPerrett 11
113 Jinxy Jack 6-11-10 NDoughty ... f
93 Lumberjack (USA) 6-10-10 MDwyer .... pu

9/2 Jinxy Jack, 11/2 SAYPAREE, 13/2 Deep Sensation, 7/1 Don Valentino, 8/1 Lumberjack, 10/1 Vagador, 11/1 Dis Train, 16/1 Aldino, Atlaal, Sacre d'Or, 25/1 See You Then, 33/1 Al Asoof, 40/1 Alkinor Rex

E. Scarth (M. Pipe) 13ran 3m42.80 (Good to Soft)

158 EDINBURGH WOOLLEN MILL'S FUTURE CHAMPIONS NOVICES' CHASE 2m
£13,804 Ayr 21 April

112 **Celtic Shot** 8-11-13 GMcCourt 1
143^{2} **Young Snugfit** 6-11-10 JOsborne ½.2
127 **Highfrith** 7-11-5 RRowe ... 10.3
112 For The Grain 6-11-7 RDunwoody 2.4
121 Interim Lib 7-11-7 MrRBradburne 5.5
27 Greenheart 7-11-7 CGrant . nk.6
94 Sawdust Jack 6-11-3 MPerrett 1½.7
94 Aston Express 7-11-7 PNiven . 8
Alistairs Girl 7-10-12 TReed ... 9
Mercurius 8-11-7 BStorey ..... pu
Dunloring 7-11-3 PHobbs ...... pu
Master Salesman 7-11-3 SO'Neill .... pu

5/2 CELTIC SHOT, Young Snugfit, 10/1 Greenheart, Sawdust Jack, 11/1 For The Grain, 14/1 Aston Express, Highfrith, 50/1 Dunloring, 66/1 Master Salesman, Mercurius, 200/1 Alistairs Girl, Interim Lib

D. E. H. Horton (C. Brooks) 12ran 3m50.94 (Good to Soft)

159 WILLIAM HILL SCOTTISH NATIONAL (HANDICAP CHASE) 4m 120y
£46,237 Ayr 21 April

122 **Four Trix** 9-10-0 DByrne 1
105* **Tartan Takeover** 8-10-0 RRowe 15.2
44 **Birling Jack** 9-10-0 PNiven nk.3
Castlevennon 9-9-11 JO'Gorman 10.4
139 The Thirsty Farmer 11-10-0 SEarle 20.5
121 Blue Ravine 11-9-8 MrSBell dist.6
139^{3} Killone Abbey 7-9-9 MrKJohnson 3.7
115 Jelupe 8-10-0 MrRSandys-Clarke 20.8
63^{3} Macroom 8-10-0 MPerrett ...... f
147 Bonanza Boy 9-11-10 JLower pu
Magwood 10-10-0 STurner .... pu
Backpacker 10-9-8 RMoore ... pu
Botham 10-10-2 TReed .... pu
Cool Distinction 7-10-0 PCaldwell .... pu
92 Ardesee 10-10-0 ACarroll ..... pu
Sneakapenny 8-10-0 AOrkney .... pu
125 Yahoo 9-11-3 NWilliamson .... pu
Strands of Gold 11-11-2 GMcCourt .... pu
58 Envopak Token 9-10-9 PHobbs .... pu
147 Mick's Star 10-10-3 SO'Neill . pu
147 West Tip 13-10-2 RDunwoody .... pu
139 Boraceva 7-10-3 JFrost .... pu
Mighty Mark 11-10-0 BStorey .... pu
126 City Entertainer 9-10-0 JQuinn .... pu
Sacred Path 10-10-0 JOsborne .... pu
73 Remedy The Malady 9-10-0 JDuggan .... pu

61 Withy Bank 8-10-0 LWyer ..... pu
Zeta's Lad 7-10-0 MLynch .... ref

6/1 Bonanza Boy, 7/1 Boraceva, 11/1 Withy Bank, 12/1 Envopak Token, Tartan Takeover, Zeta's Lad, 14/1 Killone Abbey, 16/1 Birling Jack, City Entertainer, Jelupe, Mighty Mark, Remedy The Malady, Yahoo, 20/1 Macroom, Mick's Star, Strands of Gold, 25/1 FOUR TRIX, West Tip, 33/1 Sacred Path, 50/1 The Thirsty Farmer, Sneakapenny, 100/1 Ardesee, Castlevennon, 200/1 Botham, Magwood, 250/1 Backpacker, 500/1 Blue Ravine, Cool Distinction

Mrs S. Catherwood (G. Richards) 28ran 8m30.54 (Good to Soft)

160 DUELING GROUNDS INTERNATIONAL HURDLE 2¾m
£184,049 Dueling Grounds 22 April

51* **Grabel** 7-10-11 AMullins 1
Uptown Swell (USA) 8-11-2 BMiller 2¼.2
Polar Pleasure (USA) 8-11-2 CRyan 8.3
2 Peer Prince (USA) 5-11-2 SSmithEccles 3.4
Summer Colony (USA) 7-11-2 BGuessford 2½.5
113² Nomadic Way (USA) 5-11-2 RDunwoody dist.6
148 Valrodian (NZ) 7-11-2 JLawrence 7
117* Regal Ambition 6-11-2 JLower .... pu
Collins (FR) 7-11-2 DMescam .... pu

22/10 Nomadic Way, 26/10 Regal Ambition, 36/10 Collins, 53/10 Uptown Swell, 78/10 GRABEL, 20/1 Summer Colony, 21/1 Polar Pleasure, 26/1 Peer Prince, 63/1 Valrodian

Mrs M. Mullins & P. F. Kehoe (P. Mullins) 9ran 5m29.00 (Firm)

161 BMW CHAMPION NOVICE HURDLE 2m
£11,509 Punchestown 24 April

141 **Vestris Abu** 4-10-5 CSwan 1
Nameloc 6-10-13 MrJFlynn . 8.2
Sweet Charmer 7-11-11 MrPFenton 2.3
Ennereilly River 7-11-8 FO'Brien ¾.4
111 Stratford Ponds 5-11-7 JOsborne 2½.5
Little Bighorn 5-11-13 TCarmody 3.6
Mass Appeal 5-11-2 CBowens . 7
117 Dorans Hill Lad 6-11-8 AMullins 8

85/40 Little Bighorn, 5/2 VESTRIS ABU, 3/1 Stratford Ponds, 10/1 Dorans Hill Lad, 12/1 Sweet Charmer, 14/1 Ennereilly River, Mass Appeal, 16/1 Nameloc

Mrs C. Shubotham (J. Bolger) 8ran 3m45.6 (Good)

162 EBF TATTERSALLS GOLD CUP (NOVICE CHASE) 3m 132y
£11,303 Punchestown 25 April

153³ **Mixed Blends** 8-11-0 CSwan . 1
152* **Blitzkreig** 7-12-0 TCarmody 8.2
Coursing Guy 8-10-7 CO'Dwyer 4.3
Aughanvilla 7-10-13 RDunwoody 20.4
151 Cloney Grange 11-10-3 HRogers 12.5
153³ Renagown 7-11-11 KO'Brien .... f
138 The Nigelstan 9-11-0 MPerrett .... pu
Livio Berruti 9-10-0 JKavanagh .... pu

6/4 Blitzkreig, 7/4 MIXED BLENDS, 5/1 Renagown, 6/1 Aughanvilla, 7/1 Cloney Grange, The Nigelstan, 14/1 Coursing Guy, 100/1 Livio Berruti

J. Spearman (M. Morris) 8ran 6m34.1 (Good)

163 WHITBREAD GOLD CUP (HANDICAP CHASE) 3m5f18y
£48,800 Sandown 28 April

147* **Mr Frisk** 11-10-5 MrMArmytage 1
147² **Durham Edition** 12-10-9 CGrant 8.2
159* **Four Trix** 9-10-1 DByrne 2.3
137* Wont Be Gone Long 8-10-0 RDunwoody 2.4
126 Sam da Vinci 11-10-7 LWyer 10.5
58 Tarconey 10-10-0 RStronge . 3.6
125 Kildimo 10-11-7 MLynch ¾.7
73 Memberson 12-9-8 PHarley 6.8
139² Seagram (NZ) 10-10-8 HDavies 8.9
137 Eight Springs 9-10-0 MPerrett 12.10
En Gounasi Theon 9-9-11 PHolley 11
139 Vulgan Warrior 8-10-0 KMooney .... f
159 Strands of Gold 11-11-3 JLower .... pu

9/2 MR FRISK, 5/1 Seagram, 11/2 Sam da Vinci, 13/2 Durham Edition, 7/1 Wont Be Gone Long, 15/2 Four Trix, 12/1 Kildimo, 16/1 Strands of Gold, 20/1 Tarconey, Vulgan Warrior, 25/1 Eight Springs, 33/1 Memberson, 100/1 En Gounasi Theon

Mrs H. J. Duffey (K. Bailey) 13ran 7m12.66 (Firm)

164 SWINTON INSURANCE TROPHY (HANDICAP HURDLE) 2m

£25,720 Haydock 7 May

141* **Sybillin** 4-10-1 DByrne 1
128 **Windbound Lass** 7-9-10 NMann ¾2
161* **Vestris Abu** 4-10-0 TCarmody 1.3
148[2] Persillant 6-10-8 GMcCourt ¾.4
136[3] Philosphos 4-10-2 WMcFarland 4.5
88[3] Imperial Brush 6-9-12 PHolley 2½.6
110 Peanuts Pet 5-10-1 TWall ... 20.7
71 Austhorpe Sunset 6-9-9 JCallaghan 8
93* Royal Derbi 5-11-10 HDavies 9
140[3] Artful Abbot 6-10-0 BDowling 10
Sillian 8-10-0 SO'Neill 11
140 Out of Range 7-10-7 GBradley .... ur
157* Sayparee 5-11-5 JLower .... pu
71 Kadan (Ger) 6-10-11 SSmithEccles .... pu

9/4 Sayparee, 5/1 Kadan, 7/1 Persillant, 8/1 SYBILLIN, Vestris Abu, 9/1 Royal Derbi, 11/1 Philosophos, 14/1 Out of Range, 16/1 Peanuts Pet, 20/1 Imperial Brush, 25/1 Windbound Lass, 33/1 Austhorpe Sunset, Sillian, 50/1 Artful Abbot

Marquesa de Moratalla (J. FitzGerald) 14ran 3m37.89 (Firm)

165 HORSE AND HOUND CUP (FINAL CHAMPION HUNTERS' CHASE) 3¼m

£5,647 Stratford 2 June

Mystic Music 11-11-9 KAnderson 1
142 **Edenspring** 11-12-0 TJackson 25.2
Brookside King 10-12-0 CFarrell 20.3
Sanballat 8-12-0 JWeatherby 5.4
John Sam 9-12-0 MArmytage ½.5
Northern Meadow 9-12-0 MrsJThurlow 6.6
Golden Link 12-12-0 PScholfield .... pu
124 Rodden Brook 8-12-0 PMacEwan .... pu
Summons 11-12-0 MissAEmbiricos .... pu

8/11 MYSTIC MUSIC, 5/2 Sanballat, 7/1 Edenspring, 20/1 John Sam, 25/1 Rodden Brook, Summons, 50/1 Brookside King, Northern Meadow, 66/1 Golden Link

Miss H. Wilson (Miss H. Wilson) 9ran 6m53.8 (Good to Firm)

INDEX TO BIG RACE RESULTS

TRAINERS

The figures in brackets are the number of winners each trainer has had in Britain over the past five seasons from 1985/86 to 1989/90 inclusive. Quarters and telephone numbers are given.

Akehurst, R. P. J. (10:23:21:43:30)
Whitcombe
Dorchester (0305) 251429
and 260724

Allan, A. R. (5:2:4:6:10)
Cornhill-on-Tweed
Crookham (089082) 581

Allen, C. N. (—:—:0:2:2)
Newmarket Newmarket (0638) 76767
and 667870
and mobilephone (0831) 271411

Allingham, P. B. (1:0:0:0:0)
Luton Offley (046276) 337

Alston, E. J. (1:4:2:0:5)
Preston Longton (0772) 612120

Anderson, P. J. (—:—:0:1:0)
Church Stretton
Longville (06943) 387

Arbuthnot, D. W. P. (1:0:0:0:0)
Newbury Newbury (0635) 578427

Armstrong, R. W. (0:0:0:0:0)
Newmarket
Newmarket (0638) 663333/4

Armytage, R. C. (16:4:7:1:2)
Middleham Wensleydale (0969) 23970

Armytage, Mrs S. (—:—:—:4:4)
Malmesbury (06667) 238

Arthur, P. J. (—:0:0:0:0)
Abingdon Abingdon (0235) 850669

Austin, Mrs S. M. (—:0:1:1:0)
Malton Burythorpe (065385) 200

Avison, M. (1:3:10:3:4)
Nawton Helmsley (0439) 71672

Ayliffe, N. G. (1:0:0:1:0)
Minehead Winsford (064385) 265

Bailey, A. (2:7:5:0:0)
Newmarket
Newmarket (0638) 661537

Bailey, K. C. (22:31:20:18:34)
Lambourn Lambourn (0488) 71483

Bailey, P. G. (6:14:10:12:2)
Salisbury
Amesbury (0980) 622964 (home)
and 622682 (office)

Bailey, T. N. (0:0:3:2:1)
Brinsop Hereford (0432) 760817

Baker, J. H. (5:5:14:15:15)
Tiverton (03985) 317

Balding, G. B. (9:57:40:59:42)
Weyhill Weyhill (026 477) 2278

Balding, I. A. (3:3:1:1:5)
Kingsclere Kingsclere (0635) 298210

Balding, J. (—:0:0:0:0)
Doncaster Doncaster (0302) 710096
and Retford (0777) 818407 (stable)

Barker, Mrs P. A. (—:—:—:2:6)
Richmond (N. Yorks)
Darlington (0325) 378266

Barnes, M. A. (—:—:—:0:0)
Penrith Langwathby (076881) 257

Barons, D. H. (21:30:29:36:40)
Kingsbridge
Kingsbridge (0548) 550326
and 550411

Barr, R. E. (2:5:1:1:2)
Stokesley Stokesley (0642) 710687

Barraclough, M. F. (0:0:0:0:1)
Claverdon Claverdon (092684) 3332

Barratt, L. J. (0:0:0:0:0)
Oswestry
Queens Head (069 188) 209

Barron, T. D. (3:2:9:6:4)
Thirsk Thirsk (0845) 587 435

Barrow, A. K. (0:0:2:4:4)
Bridgwater Bridgwater (0278) 732522

Bastiman, R. (—:—:—:0:0)
Wetherby Wetherby (0937) 63050

Beaumont, P. (—:7:0:8:4)
Brandsby Brandsby (03475) 208

Beever, C. R. (—:—:—:10:17)
Doncaster Doncaster (0302) 725939

Bell, C. J. (4:16:7:7:4)
Cleckheaton (0274) 872715
and carphone (0836) 273153

Bell, D. J. (—:0:1:0:1)
Chipping Norton
Chipping Norton (0608) 730070

Bell, M. L. W. (—:—:—:—:0)
Newmarket
Newmarket (0638) 666567

Bennett, J. A. (—:0:3:2:3)
Sparsholt Childrey (023559) 635

Bennett, R. A. (—:—:—:1:0)
Maidenhead
Maidenhead (0628) 30290

Benstead, C. J. (0:0:0:0:5)
Epsom Ashtead (037 22) 73152

Bentley, W. (0:1:0:1:5)
Middleham Wensleydale (0969) 22289

Berry, J. (5:6:1:3:1)
Lancaster Forton (0524) 791179

Bethell, J. D. W. (0:0:0:0:0)
Didcot Abingdon (0235) 834333

Bevan, P. J. (5:2:3:3:3)
Kingstone
Dapple Heath (0889) 500647 (yard)
or 500670 (home)

Bill, T. T. (15:16:8:6:8)
Ashby-de-la-Zouch
Ashby-de-la-Zouch (0530) 415881

Bishop, K. S. (9:5:16:5:1)
Bridgwater Spaxton (027867) 437

Blakeney, Miss J. E. (—:—:—:—:0)
Marlborough
Ogbourne St George (067284) 509
and 516

Blanshard, M. T. W. (0:0:0:0:1)
Lambourn Lambourn (0488) 71091

Blockley, P. A. (—:10:13:13:8)
Catwick
Hornsea (0964) 542583 (home)
and 562440 (stable)
Blundell, J. W. (8:13:12:11:6)
Grimsby Grimsby (0472) 840256
and 840494
Bolton, M. J. (5:2:2:1:1)
East Grinstead
Shrewton (0980) 621059
Booth, C. B. B. (0:0:0:0:0)
Flaxton
Whitwell-on-the-Hill (065 381) 586
Bosley, J. R. (0:4:3:2:5)
Bampton
Bampton Castle (0993) 850212
Boss, R. (0:1:0:0:0)
Newmarket
Newmarket (0638) 661335
Bostock, J. R. (—:—:—:0:2)
Swaffham Kings Lynn (0553) 765231
Bottomley, J. F. (—:—:—:—:1)
Malton
Malton (0653) 694597 (stable)
Bower, Miss L. J. (7:10:6:4:2)
Alresford Bramdean (096 279) 552
Bowker, M. T. (5:0:0:0:0)
Kendal Cartmel (05395) 60533
Bowring, S. R. (3:0:2:0:0)
Mansfield Mansfield (0623) 822451
Bradburne, Mrs S. C. (—:—:—:1:6)
Cupar Letham (Fife) (033781) 325
Bradley, J. M. (5:12:16:12:4)
Chepstow Chepstow (0291) 622486
Bradley, N. (—:—:3:3:3)
Wetherby Wetherby (0937) 63142
Bradstock, M. F. (—:—:0:1:1)
East Garston
Great Shefford (048839) 8801
Bramall, Mrs S. A. (0:0:1:11:6)
Hutton Sessay Thirsk (0845) 401333
Brassey, K. M. (—:—:—:0:0)
Lambourn Lambourn (0488) 71508
Bravery, C. V. (0:0:5:1:0)
Jevington Polegate (03212) 3662
Brazington, R. G. (4:3:5:2:2)
Redmarley, Glos.
Staunton Court (045284) 384
Brennan, O. (9:8:10:14:16)
Newark Caunton (063 686) 332
Bridger, J. J. (2:1:1:1:0)
Chichester Liphook (0428) 722528
Bridgwater, K. S. (3:1:2:3:8)
Solihull Lapworth (05643) 2895
Brisbourne, A. H. (2:0:0:0:0)
Shrewsbury Nesscliffe (074381) 360
and 536
Brittain, C. E. (—:—:—:—:0)
Newmarket
Newmarket (0638) 663739
and 664347
Brittain, M. A. (—:0:0:0:0)
Warthill
Stamford Bridge (0759) 71472
Broad, C. D. (—:—:—:—:1)
Westbury Upon Severn
Gloucester (0452) 76835 (office)
and 830015 (home)
Brooks, C. P. E. (—:—:—:41:56)
Lambourn
Lambourn (0488) 72077 (office)
and 72909 (home)
Brooks, W. G. A. (—:0:0:0:2)
Lambourn Lambourn (0488) 72140
Brotherton, R. (—:—:—:1:2)
Evesham Evesham (0386) 3023
Brown, M. L. (1:0:0:1:1)
Llandovery Llangadog (0550) 777403
Browne, D. W. P. (—:—:—:—:0)
Lambourn
Lambourn (0488) 71265 (home)
and 72078 (stable)
and carphone (0860) 398166
Budd, Mrs C. M. (—:—:—:—:0)
Bridgwater
Bukovets, J. M. (0:0:1:6:6)
Solihull
Henley-in-Arden (05642) 4631
Burchell, W. D. (8:12:14:12:11)
Ebbw Vale Ebbw Vale (0495) 302551
Burgoyne, P. V. J. P. (0:1:0:4:1)
Sparsholt Childrey (023 559) 688
Butler, P. (2:3:3:2:1)
Lewes Plumpton (0273) 890124
Bycroft, N. (2:3:4:2:0)
Brandsby Brandsby (03475) 641

Caldwell, T. H. (0:1:1:4:2)
Warrington Arley (056585) 275
Callaghan, N. A. (0:4:2:8:4)
Newmarket
Newmarket (0638) 664040
Callow, R. (—:—:—:1:2)
Somerton, Somerset
Somerton (0458) 72194
Calver, P. (3:5:1:0:0)
Ripon Ripon (0765) 700313
Camacho, M. J. C. (3:2:4:0:1)
Malton Malton (0653) 694901
Cambidge, B. R. (1:5:0:0:2)
Shifnal
Weston-under-Lizard (095 276) 249
Campbell, I. (1:3:3:5:2)
Newmarket
Newmarket (0638) 660829
Candy, H. D. N. B. (0:0:0:0:1)
Wantage Uffington (036 782) 276
Caroe, Miss C. J. E. (1:2:0:0:1)
Appleby Kirkby Thore (0930) 61818
Carter W. Y. (—:—:—:2:6)
Leatherhead
Leatherhead (0372) 377209
Casey, W. T. (5:20:17:12:4)
Lambourn Lambourn (0488) 73004
Castell, M. (0:0:0:0:0)
Knightwick
Knightwick (0886) 21538
Chamberlain, A. J. (0:1:0:1:0)
Swindon Cirencester (0285) 861347
Chamberlain, N. (0:1:2:0:0)
West Auckland
Bishop Auckland (0388) 832465
Champion, R. (5:2:4:6:2)
Newmarket
Newmarket (0638) 666546

Channon, M. R. (—:—:—:—:1)
Lambourn (0264) 810225 (home)
and (0488) 71149 (stable)
Chapman, D. W. (2:1:1:3:1)
Stillington Easingwold (0347) 21683
Chapman, M. C. (3:3:6:10:4)
Market Rasen
Market Rasen (0673) 843663
Charles, M. J. (—:0:0:0:1)
Warwick Warwick (0926) 493878
Charlton, J. I. A. (7:8:10:5:8)
Stocksfield Stocksfield (0661) 843247
Christian, S. P. L. (15:22:22:15:12)
Kinnersley
Severn Stoke (090567) 233
Chugg, J. (3:1:1:1:7)
Oxford (0993) 830219
Clay, Mrs L. (0:1:4:2:2)
Arundel Bognor Regis (0243) 551440
Clay, W. (4:12:4:14:11)
Fulford
Stoke-on-Trent (0782) 392131
Codd, L. J. (—:—:0:1:4)
Redditch Inkberrow (0386) 793263
Cole, P. F. I. (—:—:—:—:0)
Whatcombe
Chaddleworth (04882) 433 or 434
Cole, S. N. (0:0:2:0:0)
Rackenford Rackenford (088488) 205
Collingridge, H. J. (1:0:1:1:0)
Newmarket
Newmarket (0638) 665454
Colston, J. (6:0:2:1:2)
Worcester Worcester (0905) 830 252
Connors, P. D. (—:—:—:0:1)
Hednesford
Hednesford (05438) 77823
Cottrell, L. G. (1:2:2:1:0)
Cullompton Kentisbeare (088 46) 320
Cowley, P. M. (—:—:—:1:2)
Cheltenham
Cheltenham (0242) 580092
and 680298 (stable)
Craig, T. (4:4:4:0:0)
Dunbar Dunbar (0368) 62583
Crawford, B. T. (—:—:—:—:0)
Aslockton Whatton (0949) 50238
Croft, Mrs J. E. (1:0:0:0:0)
Deddington Deddington (0869) 38534
Cundell, P. D. (13:8:9:6:5)
Newbury Newbury (0635) 578267
Cunningham, T. W. (0:7:1:5:3)
Northallerton
East Harlsey (060982) 695
Cunningham-Brown, K. O. (0:0:0:0:4)
Stockbridge Andover (0264) 781611
Curley, B. J. (1:9:16:13:4)
Newmarket
Stetchworth (063876) 8251
Curtis, R. (0:3:10:11:6)
Epsom (0372) 277645
Cuthbert, T. A. K. (1:1:0:1:3)
Carlisle Carlisle (0228) 60822
Cyzer, C. A. (0:—:0:0:1)
Horsham Southwater (0403) 730255
Czerpak J. D. (—:—:—:—:0)
Farnham
Frensham (Surrey) (025125) 3505

Davies, J. D. J. (6:7:4:5:3)
Dymchurch
Folkestone (0303) 874089
Davis, P. W. (8:1:3:6:4)
Redditch
Astwood Bank (052789) 3174
Davison, A. R. (0:0:4:7:5)
Caterham Caterham (0883) 44523
Denson, A. W. (—:2:0:1:5)
Epsom Epsom (03727) 29398
Dickin, R. (—:8:10:11:6)
Dymock Dymock (053185) 644
Dickinson, M. (1:0:2:2:3)
Melton Mowbray
Whissendine (066479) 752
Dods, R. W. (0:1:0:1:2)
Darlington Darlington (0325) 374270
Doidge, G. C. (2:1:1:2:2)
Ivybridge Modbury (0548) 830 515
Donnelly, T. W. (—:—:1:0:0)
Hartshorne
Burton-on-Trent (0283) 226046
and 216965 (office)
Dooler, J. (1:0:1:1:3)
Goole Goole (0405) 861903
Dow, S. L. (0:0:5:3:6)
Guildford
Epsom (03727) 21490 (stable)
and Ashtead (03722) 75878 (home)
Dunlop, J. L. (0:0:—:—:0)
Arundel
Arundel (0903) 882194 (office)
or 882106 (home)
Durr, F. (—:0:2:0:0)
Newmarket
Newmarket (0638) 730030
Dutton, D. (—:—:—:—:0)
Malton North Grimston (09446) 364

Earnshaw, R. (—:0:1:0:1)
Harrogate Harrogate (0423) 567790
Easterby, M. H. (34:38:23:45:29)
Malton
Kirby Misperton (065 386) 566
Easterby, M. W. (9:10:18:22:10)
Sheriff Hutton
Sheriff Hutton (034 77) 368
Eaton, Miss J. M. (1:1:4:1:0)
Lancaster Hornby (0468) 21374
Eckley, M. W. (2:5:2:1:1)
Ludlow Brimfield (058 472) 372
Eckley, R. J. (0:2:2:1:0)
Kington Lyonshall (05448) 216
Eden, G. H. (—:—:—:—:0)
Newmarket
Newmarket (0638) 667938
Edwards, J. A. C. (41:54:61:78:47)
Ross-on-Wye
Harewood End (098 987) 259
and 639 (home)
Eldin, E. (0:0:1:0:0)
Newmarket
Newmarket (0638) 662036 or 663217
Ellerby, M. W. (5:1:0:0:0)
Pickering Pickering (0751) 74092
Elliott, J. P. D. (—:0:0:0:1)
Alton, Hants. Alton (0420) 63733

Ellison, B. (—:—:—:—:2)
Burythorpe Malton (0653) 600158
Elsey, C. C. (—:—:—:0:1)
Lambourn Lambourn (0488) 71242
Elsey, C. W. C. (5:7:3:4:1)
Malton Malton (0653) 693149
Elsworth, D. R. C. (37:34:47:54:24)
Fordingbridge
Rockbourne (07253) 220 (home) or 528 (office)
Enright, G. P. (2:3:5:6:6)
Haywards Heath
Lewes (0273) 479183
Etherington, J. (0:0:1:3:0)
Malton Malton (0653) 692842
Etherington, T. J. (—:—:0:3:4)
Beare Green
Newdigate (030677) 529
Evans, Mrs J. J. (0:0:0:0:0)
Llanymynech
Guilsfield (093 875) 316
Evans, P. D. (—:—:—:1:3)
Welshpool Trewern (093874) 288

Fairhurst, T. (4:3:2:5:3)
Middleham
Wensleydale (0969) 23362
Fanshawe, J. R. (—:—:—:—:0)
Newmarket
Newmarket (0638) 660153 and 664525
Feilden, P. J. (—:—:—:0:2)
Newmarket Exning (063877) 637
Felgate, P. S. (2:3:3:2:4)
Melton Mowbray
Melton Mowbray (0664) 812019
Fetherston-Godley, M. J. (0:0:1:0:0)
East Ilsley East Ilsley (063 528) 250
Ffitch-Heyes, J. R. (3:15:8:12:15)
Lewes Brighton (0273) 480804
Fisher, R. F. (17:17:8:6:8)
Ulverston Ulverston (0229) 55664 and 55819 (office)
Fisher, W. E. (5:0:2:0:0)
Chewton Mendip
FitzGerald, J. G. (28:73:49:59:58)
Malton Malton (0653) 692718
FitzGerald, Lord J. (—:—:—:0:0)
Newmarket
Newmarket (0638) 660605
Forsey, B. (5:9:6:3:4)
Crowcombe Crowcombe (098 48) 270
Forster, T. A. (47:32:38:34:23)
Letcombe Bassett
Wantage (023 57) 3092
Fowler, A. (—:—:1:2:4)
Newark
Fox, J. C. (1:1:2:3:0)
Amesbury Shrewton (0980) 620861
Francis, M. E. D. (0:2:4:7:5)
Lambourn Lambourn (0488) 71700
Francis, R. B. (8:7:6:3:0)
Malpas Tilston (082 98) 208 (office) and 515 (home)
Frost, R. G. (9:9:15:20:15)
Buckfastleigh
Buckfastleigh (03644) 2267

Gandolfo, D. R. (17:19:13:8:14)
Wantage Wantage (023 57) 3242
Gaselee, N. A. D. C. (26:18:24:13:19)
Lambourn Lambourn (0488) 71503
Gifford, J. T. (56:60:91:64:50)
Findon (0903) 872226
Glover, J. A. (1:6:4:3:13)
Worksop Worksop (0909) 475962 or 475425 (stable)
Goldie, R. H. (1:0:2:1:1)
Dundonald Troon (0292) 314323 and 317222
Goulding, J. L. (0:0:0:1:1)
Brigham Cockermouth (0900) 825393
Gracey, G. G. (3:6:6:3:7)
Winkfield
Winkfield Row (0344) 890461
Graham, N. A. (—:—:—:—:0)
Newmarket
Newmarket (0638) 665202 (office) and 667851 (home)
Green, Miss Z. A. (0:0:0:0:0)
Carlisle Low Ireby (09657) 219
Grissell, D. M. (7:6:7:14:16)
Heathfield Brightling (042 482) 241
Gubby, B. (—:0:—:0:2)
Bagshot Bagshot (0276) 63282 and 71030 (evenings)
Guest, R. (—:—:—:1:0)
Newmarket
Newmarket (0638) 661508

Haggas, W. J. (—:0:0:0:0)
Newmarket
Newmarket (0638) 667013
Haigh, W. W. (0:2:2:1:4)
Malton Malton (0653) 694428
Haine, Mrs D. E. S. (0:5:7:6:11)
Newmarket Exning (063877) 719
Haldane, J. S. (3:3:0:3:0)
Kelso Kelso (0573) 24956
Hall, Miss P. J. (0:0:2:1:0)
Grantham Grantham (0476) 860891
Hall, Miss S. E. (4:4:1:0:2)
Middleham
Wensleydale (0969) 40223
Hallett, T. B. (5:7:3:2:13)
Saltash Saltash (0752) 846829
Ham, G. A. (8:4:9:25:21)
Axbridge Edingworth (0934) 750331
Hannon, R. M. (0:0:0:0:0)
Marlborough
Collingbourne Ducis (0264) 850254
Hanson, J. (7:5:5:2:6)
Wetherby Wetherby (0937) 62841 and 66776 (yard)
Harris, J. L. (1:3:2:2:3)
Melton Mowbray Harby (0949) 60671
Harris, P. W. (8:8:7:6:4)
Berkhamsted
Hemel Hempstead (0442) 842 480
Harris, S. T. (3:0:0:0:0)
Amersham Chesham (0494) 715446
Harrison, R. A. (—:—:—:—:0)
Middleham Wensleydale (0969) 23788
Hartop, R. W. (2:2:0:0:1)
Mansfield Mansfield (0623) 883 081

Harwood, G. (0:0:5:6:19)
Pulborough
Pulborough (079 82) 3011
or 3012
Haynes, M. J. (1:0:0:1:4)
Epsom Burgh Heath (073 73) 51140
Hayward, P. A. (3:1:4:3:0)
Netheravon Netheravon (0980) 70585
Heath, Mrs E. H. (—:—:—:7:2)
Royston Royston (0763) 87345
Hedger, P. R. (4:7:9:14:13)
Arundel Eastergate (024 368) 3863
Henderson, N. J. (46:67:40:43:41)
Lambourn Lambourn (0488) 72259
Herries, Lady (1:5:0:2:1)
Arundel Patching (090 674) 421
Hetherton, J. (—:—:—:0:1)
Malton Malton (0653) 696778
Hewitt, Mrs S. A. (2:3:4:2:1)
Malpas Broxton (082 925) 314
Hide, A. G. (0:0:0:0:0)
Newmarket
Newmarket (0638) 662063
Hill, C. J. (0:0:0:0:0)
Barnstaple Barnstaple (0271) 42048
Hills, B. W. (0:0:0:3:2)
Marlborough
Marlborough (0672) 514901 (office)
and 514871 (home)
Hills, J. W. (—:0:—:0:0)
Lambourn Lambourn (0488) 71548
Hoad, R. P. C. (1:3:2:2:1)
Lewes Brighton (0273) 477124
Hobbs, P. J. (2:12:22:24:45)
Watchet Washford (0984) 40366
Hodges, R. J. (20:17:21:18:19)
Somerton
Charlton Mackrell (045 822) 3922
Holden, W. (2:6:0:4:1)
Newmarket Exning (063 877) 384
Holder, R. J. (19:15:17:25:33)
Portbury Pill (027 581) 2192 and 4185
Hollinshead, R. (7:6:7:4:15)
Upper Longdon
Armitage (0543) 490298 and 490490
Hollis, F. G. (1:0:0:0:1)
Cullompton Plymtree (08847) 342
and Kentisbeare (08846) 398
Holmes, C. J. (12:12:1:0:0)
Gerrards Cross
Chalfont St Giles (02407) 5964
Holt, L. J. (0:0:0:0:0)
Tunworth Basingstoke (0256) 463376
Honeyball, J. (0:1:0:3:1)
Taunton
Kingston St Mary (082345) 266
Horgan, C. A. (0:0:0:0:1)
Billingbear
Winkfield Row (0344) 425382
Houghton, R. F. J. (0:0:0:3:3)
Blewbury Blewbury (0235) 850480
Howling, P. (—:0:1:0:1)
Brook (0428) 794065 (stable)
Hudson, J. P. (—:—:—:0:0)
Lambourn Lambourn (0488) 71485
Huffer, G. A. (2:2:0:0:1)
Newmarket
Newmarket (0638) 667997

Ivory, K. T. (0:1:2:0:0)
Radlett (0923) 855337

Jackson, C. F. C. (6:5:4:1:1)
Malvern Malvern (0886) 880463
James, A. P. (2:0:0:2:7)
Bosbury Bosbury (053186) 264
James, C. J. (4:3:0:0:0)
Newbury
Great Shefford (048 839) 280
James, M. B. C. (0:0:0:0:0)
Whitchurch Whitchurch (0948) 4067
Jarvis, M. A. (—:—:2:0:1)
Newmarket
Newmarket (0638) 661702
and 662519
Jefferson, J. M. (7:7:9:8:6)
Malton Malton (0653) 697225
Jenkins, J. R. (35:41:24:29:31)
Royston Royston (0763) 241141
and 246611
Jermy, D. C. (0:0:1:1:0)
Warminster
Warminster (0985) 213155
Johnson, J. H. (1:6:5:14:14)
Bishop Auckland
Bishop Auckland (0388) 762113
and 730872
Johnston, M. S. (—:0:0:0:1)
Middleham Wensleydale (0969) 22237
Jones, A. P. (—:—:—:—:2)
Lambourn Lambourn (0488) 72637
Jones, A. W. (1:1:0:1:1)
Oswestry Oswestry (0691) 659720
Jones, D. H. (2:3:0:1:3)
Pontypridd Pontypridd (0443) 202515
Jones, Mrs G. E. (2:3:1:4:3)
Upton-on-Severn
Upton-on-Severn (06846) 2691
Jones, G. H. (1:0:0:1:2)
Tenbury Wells Leysters (056887) 676
and 305 (stable)
Jones, H. Thomson (0:0:0:0:0)
Newmarket
Newmarket (0638) 664884
Jones, P. J. (4:8:8:6:4)
Marlborough
Lockeridge (067286) 427
Jones, T. M. (0:1:0:1:0)
Guildford Shere (048 641) 2604
Jones, T. Thomson (—:—:—:6:17)
Lambourn Lambourn (0488) 71596
and 72933
Jordan, F. T. J. (7:10:8:16:21)
Leominster
Steens Bridge (056882) 281
Juckes, R. T. (2:2:2:3:3)
Abberley, Worcs.
Great Witley (0299) 896471

Kelleway, P. A. (1:2:1:0:1)
Newmarket
Newmarket (0638) 661461
Kelly, G. P. (—:—:0:0:0)
Sheriff Hutton
Sheriff Hutton (03477) 518

Kemp, W. T. (5:12:10:6:2)
Ashford, Kent Ashford (0233) 72525
Kernick, N. (1:1:1:0:1)
Kingsteignton (0364) 42755
Kersey, T. (0:0:2:1:1)
West Melton
Rotherham (0709) 873166
Kettlewell, S. E. (—:0:0:2:11)
Middleham
Wensleydale (0969) 40295
King, Miss A. L. M. (1:6:2:2:2)
Stratford-on-Avon
Stratford-on-Avon (0789) 205087
King, J. S. (7:14:7:16:16)
Swindon Broad Hinton (0793) 731481
Knight, Mrs A. J. (0:2:2:3:2)
Cullompton Hemyock (0823) 680959
Knight, Miss H. C. (—:—:—:—:15)
Wantage
East Hendred (0235) 833535

Lamb, R. R. (—:—:—:—:3)
Seahouses Seahouses (0665) 720 260
Leach, P. S. (—:—:—:1:2)
Taunton
Bishop's Lydeard (0823) 433249
Leadbetter, S. J. (3:1:3:2:2)
Ladykirk
Berwick-Upon-Tweed (0289) 82519
Lee, A. N. (—:—:0:1:0)
Newmarket
Newmarket (0638) 662734 (home)
and 669783 (stable)
Lee, D. (8:4:3:4:3)
Pickering Pickering (0751) 32425
Lee, F. H. (8:12:1:7:1)
Wilmslow Wilmslow (0625) 529672
and 533250 (stud)
Lee, R. A. (—:5:19:29:37)
Presteigne Presteigne (0544) 267672
and mobilephone (0836) 537145
Leigh, J. P. (5:0:3:1:4)
Willoughton, Lincs.
Hemswell (042773) 210
Lewis, G. (—:—:—:—:0)
Epsom Ashtead (03722) 77662
or 77366
Liddle, P. (2:1:1:3:3)
Chester-le-Street
Wearside (091) 410-2072
Long, J. E. (0:1:2:3:2)
Plumpton Plumpton (0273) 890244

Macauley, Mrs N. J. (0:1:0:0:1)
Sproxton Grantham (0476) 860578
and 860090 (office)
Mackie, W. J. W. (0:5:1:11:18)
Derby Sudbury (028378) 604
Madgwick, M. J. (4:1:8:4:2)
Denmead Horndean (0705) 258313
Makin, P. J. (0:5:0:1:0)
Ogbourne Maisey
Marlborough (0672) 512973
Mann, W. G. (0:2:1:0:0)
Leamington Spa
Harbury (0926) 612659

Manning, R. J. (—:—:0:1:3)
Winterbourne, Avon
Winterbourne (0454) 773274
Marks, D. (0:1:1:0:2)
Lambourn Lambourn (0488) 71767
Marvin, R. F. (—:—:—:—:1)
Newark Mansfield (0623) 822714
McCain, D. (15:4:12:13:13)
Birkdale Southport (0704) 66007
or 69677
McCauley, K. B. (—:—:—:—:0)
Melsonby Darlington (0325) 718008
McConnochie, J. C. (—:—:—:—:7)
Stratford-on-Avon
Alderminster (078987) 607
McCormack, M. (1:1:0:3:4)
Wantage Childrey (023 559) 433
McCourt, M. (3:3:3:2:0)
Letcombe Regis
Wantage (023 57) 4456
McDonald, R. (4:2:0:0:0)
Duns Chirnside (089081) 218 and 446
McGovern, T. P. (—:—:—:4:6)
Lewes Lewes (0273) 483197
McKie, Mrs V. J. (5:3:3:6:7)
Buckingham
Steeple Claydon (029673) 707
McLean, B. (2:3:7:3:4)
Morpeth Felton (0670) 787478
or 787314 (home)
McMahon, B. A. (5:11:3:8:11)
Tamworth Tamworth (0827) 62901
McMath, B. J. (—:—:0:1:3)
Timworth Culford (028484) 439
Mellor, S. T. E. (25:24:6:11:21)
Wanborough Swindon (0793) 790230
Miller, C. J. V. (2:4:2:2:2)
Shipston-on-Stour
Ilmington (0608) 82357
Millman, B. R. (—:—:—:—:0)
Cullompton (0884) 6620
and carphone (0860) 661854
Mitchell, N. R. (1:2:2:17:12)
Dorchester Cerne Abbas (03003) 651
Mitchell, P. (16:3:5:7:4)
Epsom Ashtead (037 22) 73729
Mitchell, Pat K. (0:0:0:0:0)
Newmarket
Newmarket (0638) 660013
Moffatt, D. (6:8:10:5:3)
Cartmel Cartmel (05395) 36689
Monteith, P. (2:6:5:6:10)
Rosewell Edinburgh (031) 440-2309
Moore, A. (20:9:10:5:11)
Woodingdean Brighton (0273) 681679
Moore, G. M. (16:30:47:37:53)
Middleham Wensleydale (0969) 23823
Morgan, B. C. (2:2:3:2:4)
Barton-under-Needwood
Hoar Cross (028 375) 304
Morgan, K. A. (5:8:11:20:12)
Waltham-on-the-Wolds
Waltham-on-the-Wolds (066478) 711
Morris, D. (—:—:—:—:0)
Newmarket
Newmarket (0638) 667959
Morris, W. G. (0:1:0:2:0)
Hartlebury Hartlebury (0299) 250953

Muggeridge, M. P. (—:—:—:—:0)
Marlborough
Collingbourne Ducis (0264) 850652
Mulhall, J. L. (0:2:0:0:0)
York York (0904) 706321
Murphy, M. P. F. (—:—:—:—:0)
Bury St Edmunds
Culford (028484) 8980
and Newmarket (0638) 665328
Murray, B. W. (—:—:—:—:0)
Malton Malton (0653) 692879
Murray-Smith, D. J. G.
(8:12:34:35:17)
Upper Lambourn
Lambourn (0488) 71041
Musson, W. J. (2:0:2:0:3)
Newmarket
Newmarket (0638) 663371

Naughton, M. P. (13:9:11:5:3)
Richmond, N. Yorks.
Richmond (0748) 2803
Nicholson, D. (22:42:50:39:42)
Condicote Cotswold (0451) 30417
Norton, J. (3:4:1:0:2)
Barnsley Barnsley (0226) 387633
Norton, S. G. (0:0:0:0:2)
Barnsley Wakefield (0924) 830450
and 830406 (office)

O'Connor, Miss P. (0:0:2:1:1)
Stockbridge
Stockbridge (026 481) 352
O'Donoghue, J. (0:0:0:0:0)
Reigate Reigate (073 72) 45241
Old, J. A. B. (10:8:6:9:2)
Ditcheat Ditcheat (074986) 656
and carphone (0836) 721459
Oldroyd, G. R. (0:1:2:2:3)
Malton Malton (0653) 695991 (home)
and Burythorpe (065385) 224
(stable)
O'Leary, R. M. (—:0:1:0:2)
Malton
Kirby Misperton (065386) 684
and 404
Oliver, J. K. M. (4:6:6:7:4)
Hawick Denholm (045 087) 216
Oliver, M. E. (8:5:8:3:5)
Droitwich Hartlebury (0299) 250500
and 250497
Oliver, Mrs S. (6:12:16:12:10)
Himley
Wombourne (0902) 892648 (stable)
and 892017 (home)
O'Mahony, F. J. (—:—:—:3:1)
Dormansland Lingfield (0342) 834166
O'Neill, J. J. (—:3:14:29:34)
Penrith Skelton (08534) 555
O'Neill, M. J. (—:—:—:0:2)
Lydiate
Liverpool 051-531 9616 (office),
6887 (home) and 526 9115 (evening)
O'Neill, O. (7:8:19:10:4)
Cheltenham
Bishops Cleeve (024 267) 3275

O'Shea, J. G. M. (—:—:1:3:3)
Kidderminster
Kidderminster (0562) 823160
O'Sullivan, R. J. (2:8:16:13:6)
Bognor Pagham (02432) 67563
Owen, E. H. (3:1:4:2:3)
Denbigh Llandyrnog (08244) 264
and 356

Palling, B. (2:4:1:1:3)
Cowbridge Cowbridge (044 63) 2089
Parker, C. (7:2:8:9:2)
Lockerbie Kettleholm (05765) 232
Parkes, J. E. (4:4:1:11:14)
Malton Malton (0653) 697570
Parrott, Mrs H. K. (1:0:1:2:5)
Deerhurst
Tewkesbury (0684) 292214
Payne, J. W. (0:0:0:0:0)
Newmarket
Newmarket (0638) 668675
Payne, S. G. (1:4:2:0:3)
Carlisle Aspatria (06973) 20010
Peacock, R. E. (7:8:4:2:0)
Tarporley Tarporley (0829) 732716
Pearce, J. N. (—:0:7:4:2)
Newmarket
Newmarket (0638) 664669
Pearce, W. J. (0:0:0:0:1)
Hambleton Thirsk (0845) 597373
Perrin, W. M. (1:0:1:2:0)
Buntingford Barkway (076 384) 8113
Pickering, J. A. (—:—:—:2:1)
Wigston Parva Leire (0455) 220535
Piggott, Mrs S. E. (—:—:0:0:0)
Newmarket
Newmarket (0638) 662584
Pipe, M. C. (79:106:129:208:224)
Wellington, Somerset
Craddock (0884) 40715
Pitman, Mrs J. S. (46:39:45:62:93)
Lambourn Lambourn (0488) 71714
Popham, C. L. (5:3:12:20:17)
Bishop's Lydeard
Bishop's Lydeard (0823) 432769
Potts, A. W. (0:0:0:0:2)
Barton-on-Humber
Saxby All Saints (065 261) 750
Preece, W. G. (6:12:9:10:22)
Telford Uppington (095 286) 249
Prescott, Sir Mark (0:0:0:0:0)
Newmarket
Newmarket (0638) 662117
Prest, G. R. (2:1:0:4:1)
Chieveley Chieveley (063521) 660
Price, G. H. (5:7:2:1:3)
Leominster
Steens Bridge (056 882) 235
Price, W. J. (0:1:0:2:1)
Ebbw Vale Ebbw Vale (0495) 303655
Pritchard, P. A. (2:6:0:5:0)
Shipston-on-Stour
Tysoe (029588) 689
Pritchard-Gordon, G. A. (6:1:1:5:5)
Newmarket
Newmarket (0638) 662824

Ramsden, Mrs L. E. (0:3:0:1:4)
Sandhutton Thirsk (0845) 587226
Ransom, P. B. (0:0:0:1:0)
Leominster Wigmore (056 886) 253
Redmond, J. V. (—:—:0:0:2)
Guildford Guildford (0483) 892233
Reed, W. G. (1:2:4:1:2)
Hexham Hexham (0434) 344201
Rees, Miss G. M. (2:1:3:2:3)
Scunthorpe
Scunthorpe (0724) 863347
Retter, Mrs J. G. (0:1:1:11:3)
Whitestone Exeter (0392) 81410
Reveley, Mrs M. (11:25:25:23:41)
Malton Malton (0653) 600295
Richards, G. W. (56:59:72:69:78)
Greystoke Greystoke (085 33) 392
Richmond, B. A. (1:0:2:2:3)
Wellingore Lincoln (0522) 810578
Ringer, D. J. (—:—:—:5:1)
Newmarket
Newmarket (0638) 662653
and 666021 (home)
Ripley, G. (0:0:0:0:0)
Ashford Ham Street (023 373) 2462
Roach, C. G. (5:2:4:1:1)
St Austell St Austell (0726) 812744
Roberts, J. D. (4:8:3:3:7)
Tiverton Bampton (0398) 31626
Robinson, M. H. B. (—:3:7:13:8)
Wantage Wantage (0235) 835050
Robinson, W. R. (6:1:4:0:0)
Scarborough
Scarborough (0723) 862162
Robson, A. M. (0:0:0:0:1)
Malton
Burythorpe (065385) 318 and
Malton (0653) 697768 (home)
Rodford, P. R. (1:0:2:0:0)
Martock Martock (0935) 823459
Roe, C. G. A. M. (0:3:0:4:1)
Chalford Brimscombe (0453) 885487
Ryan, K. A. (—:—:—:—:1)
Laceby Grimsby (0472) 71258
and 72561 (yard)
mobilephone (0860) 424437
Ryan, M. J. (4:5:8:8:11)
Newmarket
Newmarket (0638) 664172

Sanders, Miss B. V. J. (0:2:9:8:14)
Epsom Ashtead (03722) 78453
Scargill, Dr J. D. (—:—:0:2:1)
Newmarket
Newmarket (0638) 663254
Scudamore, M. J. (1:4:0:2:2)
Hoarwithy Carey (043 270) 253
Semple, I. (—:—:—:—:2)
Crossford
Carluke (0555) 71994 (office)
and 50910 (home) and 50660
Sharpe, Mrs N. S. A. (—:3:1:0:0)
Leominster Leominster (0568) 2673
Sherwood, O. M. C. (48:41:42:53:58)
Upper Lambourn
Lambourn (0488) 71411

Siddall, Miss L. C. (1:1:4:3:3)
York Appleton Roebuck (090484) 291
Simpson, R. (5:10:6:3:3)
Upper Lambourn
Lambourn (0488) 72688
Skinner, M. M. (1:1:4:4:2)
Snetterton
Great Hockham (0953) 605256
Sly, Mrs P. M. (5:1:3:0:1)
Peterborough
Peterborough (0733) 270212
Smart, B. (—:1:4:6:2)
Lambourn Lambourn (0488) 71632
Smith A. (3:3:3:3:0)
Beverley Beverley (0482) 882520
Smith, C. (—:—:—:—:0)
Wellingore Lincoln (0526) 833245
Smith, D. (26:32:26:20:13)
Bishop Auckland
Bishop Auckland (0388) 603317
and 606180
Smith, J. P. (1:1:0:1:1)
Rugeley Burntwood (054 36) 6587
Smith, N. A. (0:0:0:1:3)
Evesham Evesham (0386) 860131
Smyth, R. V. (2:6:1:3:2)
Epsom Epsom (037 27) 20053
Sneyd, Miss E. (1:0:0:1:0)
Pangbourne
Upper Basildon (049162) 574
Spares, C. W. (3:4:1:3:0)
Aslockton Whatton (0949) 50099
Spearing, J. L. (17:14:15:6:4)
Alcester
Bidford-on-Avon (0789) 772639
Stephenson, W. A. (73:65:93:89:116)
Bishop Auckland
Rushyford (0388) 720213
and 720432 (hostel)
Stevens, B. (5:9:8:5:5)
Winchester
Winchester (0962) 883030
Storey, W. L. (6:8:7:4:9)
Consett Edmundbyers (0207) 55259
Stoute, M. R. (0:0:3:3:4)
Newmarket
Newmarket (0638) 663801
Stringer, A. P. (—:—:1:1:2)
Carlton Husthwaite
Thirsk (0845) 401329
Stubbs, R. W. (0:1:0:0:0)
Newmarket
Newmarket (0638) 560014
Sutcliffe, J. R. E. (—:—:0:3:2)
Epsom Ashtead (037 22) 72825

Tate, F. M. (4:3:2:3:2)
Kidderminster
Chaddesley Corbett (056 283) 243
Tate, R. (0:4:0:0:3)
Thirsk Thirsk (0845) 537375
Tate, T. P. (3:2:1:5:9)
Tadcaster Tadcaster (0937) 836036
Thom, D. T. (2:2:2:1:5)
Newmarket Exning (063 877) 288
Thomas, J. D. (2:0:—:—:0)
Cowbridge Cowbridge (0446) 760815

Thompson, R. (1:0:3:3:0)
Grantham
Castle Bytham (0780) 410812
Thompson, Ronald (5:3:0:1:3)
Doncaster
Doncaster (0302) 842 857, 845904 and 840174
Thompson, V. (11:3:6:2:0)
Alnwick Embleton (066 576) 272
Thomson, N. B. (0:3:0:1:0)
Shaftesbury East Stour (074785) 262
Thorne, Miss J. C. (—:3:1:1:2)
Bridgwater Holford (027 874) 588
Thorner, G. E. (5:2:1:0:0)
Letcombe Regis
Wantage (023 57) 3003
Thornton, C. W. (5:9:8:6:4)
Middleham Wensleydale (0969) 23350
Tinkler, C. H. (1:10:7:5:5)
Malton Malton (0653) 695981
Tinkler, N. D. (5:4:16:54:49)
Malton Burythorpe (065385) 245 and 512
Tompkins, M. H. (2:3:2:7:17)
Newmarket
Newmarket (0638) 661434
Topley, D. H. (—:—:—:0:0)
Esh Wearside 091-373 5460 (office) and 0312 (home) and 091-384-0989
Townsley, Mrs P. L. (0:2:0:0:0)
Newdigate Newdigate (030 677) 492
Trietline, C. C. (7:6:9:8:4)
Welford-on-Avon
Stratford-on-Avon (0789) 750 294
Tucker, D. C. (0:2:1:0:0)
Frome Frome (0373) 62383
Tucker, D. R. (2:2:2:3:0)
Cullompton Hemyock (0823) 680 159
Turnell, A. (4:16:19:11:16)
East Hendred
East Hendred (0235 833) 297
Turner, W. G. (4:7:1:3:6)
Tavistock Mary Tavy (082 281) 237
Turner, W. (Bill) G. M. (3:6:2:10:11)
Corton Denham
Corton Denham (096322) 523
Twiston-Davies, N. A. (4:1:3:2:8)
Cheltenham
Guiting Power (04515) 278

Usher, M. D. I. (0:0:5:2:0)
East Garston
Lambourn (0488) 398953/4 (office) and 71307 (home)

Voorspuy, R. (0:0:0:5:4)
Polegate Polegate (032 12) 7133

Wainwright, J. S. (—:0:1:0:2)
Malton Burythorpe (065385) 537
Wall, C. F. (—:—:0:0:1)
Newmarket
Newmarket (0638) 661999
Walwyn, F. T. T. (30:15:26:15:18)
Lambourn Lambourn (0488) 71555
Walwyn, P. T. (1:8:1:0:0)
Lambourn Lambourn (0488) 71347
Wardle, I. P. (7:3:11:6:2)
Newmarket
Newmarket (0638) 666388
Waring, Mrs B. H. (1:0:0:0:0)
Malmesbury (0225) 742044
Watson, F. (6:4:1:0:1)
Sedgefield Sedgefield (0740) 20582
Weaver, R. J. (—:—:1:2:6)
Leicester Markfield (0530) 243105
Webber, J. H. (21:10:20:15:9)
Banbury Cropredy (0295) 750226 and 750466 (stable) and mobilephone (0836) 580129
Weedon, C. V. (—:2:3:1:11)
Chiddingfold Wormley (042879) 3344
Weymes, E. (0:0:—:1:3)
Leyburn Wensleydale (0969) 40229
Wharton, J. (—:—:1:4:6)
Melton Mowbray
Melton Mowbray (0664) 78334 (stable) and 65225 (home)
Wharton, Mrs V. R. T. (—:—:—:0:5)
Middleham Wensleydale (0969) 23173
Wheeler, E. A. (1:0:2:2:6)
Lambourn Lambourn (0488) 71650
Whitaker, R. M. (1:8:6:5:3)
Wetherby Leeds (0532) 892265 and Wetherby (0937) 62122
White, J. R. (—:—:—:14:16)
Wendover Wendover (0296) 623387
White, K. B. (1:4:6:6:8)
Craven Arms Munslow (058 476) 200
Whitfield, Miss A. J. (—:—:—:0:0)
Lambourn Lambourn (0488) 72342
Whiting, H. A. T. (0:0:—:—:1)
Broadway Broadway (0386) 858489 and 852569
Wigham, P. (0:—:—:—:0)
Malton Rillington (09442) 332
Wightman, W. G. R. (2:2:1:3:1)
Upham
Bishop's Waltham (0489) 892565
Wildman, C. P. (1:1:2:2:7)
Salisbury
Durrington Walls (0980) 52226
Wilkinson, B. E. (3:6:7:5:8)
Middleham Wensleydale (0969) 23385
Wilkinson, M. J. (—:3:6:4:2)
Chipping Warden
Chipping Warden (029586) 713
Williams, C. N. (1:0:0:0:0)
Newmarket
Newmarket (0638) 665116
Williams, D. L. (6:3:4:1:5)
Lower Broadheath
Bromsgrove (0527) 33731 and Worcester (0905) 640074 and (0836) 547894
Williams, R. J. R. (0:0:3:0:0)
Newmarket
Newmarket (0638) 663 218
Williams, W. R. (1:1:0:0:2)
Idestone Exeter (0392) 81558
Willis, H. (—:—:0:1:0)
Twyford, Hants
Twyford (0962) 712159

Wilson, A. J. (4:4:10:3:8)
Cheltenham
Cheltenham (0242) 244713

Wilson, D. A. (7:3:3:2:2)
Headley
Ashtead (03722) 78327 (office)
and 73839 (home)

Wilson, Capt. J. H. (1:2:1:0:0)
Preston Hesketh Bank (0772) 812780

Wilson, J. S. (8:12:12:9:5)
Ayr Ayr (0292) 266232

Wilson, W. T. J. (—:—:0:0:0)
Newmarket
Newmarket (0638) 661393

Wilton, Miss S. J. (—:0:12:22:17)
Stoke-on-Trent
Stoke-on-Trent (0782) 550861

Wingrove, K. G. (2:1:1:4:3)
Rugby Southam (092 681) 3958

Wintle, D. J. (11:9:15:10:5)
Westbury-on-Severn
Westbury-on-Severn (045 276) 459
and 825

Wise, B. J. (0:1:1:1:1)
Polegate Polegate (032 12) 3331
and 2505

Wonnacott, Mrs J. (0:0:3:0:16)
Tavistock
Newton Abbot (082287) 215

Woodhouse, R. D. E. (3:2:5:4:4)
York
Whitwell-on-the-Hill (065 381) 637

Woodman, S. (—:1:0:1:2)
Chichester Chichester (0243) 527136

Yardley, F. J. (2:1:0:0:0)
Ombersley Worcester (0905) 620477

Yardley, G. H. (0:1:0:1:0)
Malvern Worcester (0905) 830245

Yeoman, D. (6:1:1:1:0)
Sherburn (N. Yorks)
Sherburn (0944) 70088

The following relinquished their licence during the season

Bather, Miss S. (—:0:0:0:0)
Blum, G. (2:1:0:0:0)
Bowden, P. A. (4:4:0:0:0)
Brown, A. D. (—:1:3:3:0)
Bulgin, T. S. M. (2:1:1:0:0)
Corbett, L. C. (—:—:—:1:4)
Douglas-Home, J. T. A. (2:0:1:0:0)
Eddy, D. (0:0:8:7:0)
Fairgrieve, W. D. (3:2:4:5:1)
Gillen, J. C. (—:0:3:0:0)
Hanbury, B. (—:—:—:0:0)
Hanley, D. L. (—:—:1:0:0)
Hastings-Bass, W. E. R. H. (1:0:0:0:0)
Ingham, A. P. (1:4:2:0:0)
Jordon, I. D. (2:5:1:1:0)
Luxton, C. F. (0:2:1:0:0)
Matthews, I. V. (1:5:4:2:1)
O'Donnell, D. T. (—:—:0:0:0)
Oliver, Miss S. (—:0:2:0:0)
Painting, N. D. (0:0:0:0:0)
Postlethwaite, Mrs C. (1:3:2:0:3)
Rohan, H. P. (1:—:0:1:0)
Sayers, J. B. (3:2:2:2:2)
Smyly, R. M. (—:0:0:0:1)
Venn, B. H. (0:0:0:0:0)
Williamson, Miss S. L. (—:0:0:0:0)

The following had his licence withdrawn

Muldoon, S. J. (—:0:0:0:4)

PERMIT HOLDERS

The following is a list of permit holders. The figures in brackets are the numbers of winners each permit holder has had over the past five seasons, from 1985/86 to 1989/90 inclusive. Quarters and telephone numbers are given.

Aconley, Mrs V. A. (—:1:1:3:7)
Westow
Whitwell-on-the-Hill (065381) 594
and Malton (0653) 695042 (home)

Aitkin, Miss A. J. (—:0:0:0:0)
Yarm Eaglescliffe (0642) 780562

Alexander, C. J. T. (0:1:2:3:0)
Dollar Dollar (02594) 2482
and Falkirk (0324) 21672

Alexander, H. H. F. (0:0:1:0:2)
Lanchester Lanchester (0207) 520896

Allen, J. S. (—:—:—:0:0)
Warwick Claverdon (092684) 2026

Anderson, I. F. F. (0:2:0:0:0)
Welshpool
Guilsfield (093875) 509

Andrews, Mrs E. M. (0:0:2:2:0)
Luton Offley (046276) 263

Andrews, J. (1:0:1:4:0)
Ladybank Ladybank (0337) 30335

Appleyard, Mrs A. B. (0:0:0:0:0)
Bristol Temple Cloud (0761) 52458

Avery, S. B. (—:—:—:0:1)
Ulceby Roxton (0469) 72078
and Barnetby (0652) 680744
Aynsley, J. W. F. (2:0:0:0:0)
Rothbury Rothbury (0669) 20271

Baker, Miss D. J. (0:—:0:0:0)
Cranleigh Cranleigh (0483) 277306
Banks, M. C. (1:1:2:0:1)
Sandy Sandy (0767) 50563
Barber, G. H. (0:0:0:0:0)
Chelmsford
Malden, Essex (0621) 828213
Barclay, Mrs A. (—:—:—:1:1)
Moreton-in-Marsh
Stow-on-the-Wold (0451) 30680
Barclay, H. (1:0:2:0:1)
Lockerbie Lockerbie (05762) 2604
Barlow, G. B. (1:0:0:0:0)
Sandbach Crewe (0270) 762036
Barnett, G. W. (0:0:0:0:0)
Stoke-on-Trent
Stoke-on-Trent (0782) 316777
Bartle, Mrs G. M. (0:1:0:0:0)
Tadcaster Tadcaster (0937) 834342
Barton, F. M. (0:0:0:0:0)
Macclesfield
Prestbury (0625) 829633
Barton, R. B. (—:—:0:1:0)
Wadswick, Wilts
Hawthorn (0225) 810700
Batey, A. C. (1:2:0:0:1)
Prudhoe Stocksfield (0661) 842284
Bebbington, G. R. (—:—:0:0:0)
Norton, Salop
Craven Arms (05882) 2511
Beck, J. N. (0:0:0:0:0)
Lasswade Edinburgh 031-663-7676
Beever, E. L. (1:0:0:0:0)
Lamberhurst
Lamberhurst (0892) 890738
Bell, C. H. P. (0:0:0:0:0)
Morpeth Morpeth (0670) 760560
Benson, Miss M. J. (3:0:2:0:0)
Hexham Hexham (0434) 681203
Birkett, J. J. (—:0:0:1:2)
Workington
Workington (0900) 604189
Bishop, V. R. (1:1:1:1:0)
Hereford Clifford (04973) 221
Bissill, W. H. (0:0:0:0:2)
Newark Newark (0636) 704221
Blackmore, A. G. (0:1:2:0:2)
Hertford Cuffley (0707) 875060
Blair, I. G. (0:0:0:0:0)
Dursley Dursley (0453) 2020
Blatchley, N. S. (—:—:—:—:0)
Bloom, Mrs B. M. (2:0:0:0:2)
Wymondham, Norfolk
Wymondham (0953) 603176
Bloomfield, D. E. F. (0:6:1:1:3)
Launceston
Coads Green (056682) 232
Bloor, D. R. (0:1:1:0:2)
Nuneaton Hinckley (0455) 291739
Bousfield, B. (0:3:1:4:0)
Brough Brough (09304) 391
Bowen, S. A. (—:0:0:0:0)
Canterbury Nonington (0304) 841876
Bowlby, Lady A. L. M. (0:0:0:0:0)
Thirsk Thirsk (0845) 597331
Bowman, L. J. (0:—:0:0:0)
Pembury, Kent
Pembury (089282) 2388
Brandon, R. (—:—:—:0:0)
Doncaster Doncaster (0302) 721015
Brewis, R. (1:5:4:3:1)
Belford Belford (06683) 239
Broad, Mrs B. K. (0:0:0:0:0)
Bedale Bedale (0677) 22267
Brockbank, J. E. (6:0:0:3:0)
Wigton Wigton (0965) 42391
Brookes, N. H. (0:0:0:0:0)
Cheltenham
Bishops Cleeve (024267) 5037
Brooks, Mrs E. M. (—:—:—:0:1)
Bideford Torrington (0805) 23156
Brown, R. L. (1:1:0:3:1)
Abergavenny Cross Ash (087386) 278
Browning, D. W. (0:0:1:2:0)
Heathfield Heathfield (04352) 2425
Brunt, Mrs B. (0:0:0:0:0)
Newark Mansfield (0623) 860109
Butterworth, Mrs B. (0:0:0:0:0)
Appleby Kirkby Thore (0930) 61117
Byford, B. (—:0:1:3:1)
Colchester Colchester (0206) 240235

Caine, E. M. (0:0:0:1:0)
Middlesbrough Bilsdale (04396) 227
Carden, J. (0:0:0:0:0)
Macclesfield
Alderley Edge (0625) 829748
Carter, O. J. (2:1:0:1:1)
Ottery St Mary
Ottery St Mary (0404) 812436
Casey, R. F. (—:0:2:3:0)
Exning mobilephone (0831) 104775
Caudwell, W. F. (—:—:—:1:0)
Abingdon Abingdon (0235) 31241
Chadwick, Mrs J. D. H. H.
(—:1:4:0:0)
Kingham Kingham (060871) 345
Chesney, Dr D. (0:1:1:0:0)
Dorchester Dorchester (0305) 65450
Chippendale, Mrs A. P. (0:—:—:—:0)
Clitheroe Clitheroe (0200) 25494
Churches, M. R. (0:0:0:0:2)
Wells Glastonbury (0458) 31141
Clutterbuck, M. A. (—:—:—:1:1)
Lydney Netherend (059452) 292
Collins, M. J. (—:0:0:0:0)
Horley Smallfield (034284) 2507
Cork, J. H. (0:—:—:—:0)
Newton Abbot
Newton Abbot (0626) 4619
Corner, A. S. (0:0:0:—:0)
Richmond
Barton, Yorks (032577) 308
Coton, F. (0:—:0:—:0)
Nottingham
Nottingham (0602) 663048
Craggs, P. F. (1:0:0:0:0)
Morpeth Hartburn (067072) 260

Crawford, Lt Cdr W. H. (2:0:1:0:1)
Haddington
Haddington (062 082) 2229
Criddle, J. V. (0:—:0:0:0)
Newport, Gwent
Penhow (0633) 400401 and 400491
Crow, A. M. (—:0:0:0:2)
Linlithgow Linlithgow (0506) 842194
Csaky, A. (—:—:0:0:1)
Wolland, Dorset
Hazelbury Bryan (02586) 543
Culham, Mrs G. P. (1:0:0:2:0)
Dumfries Southwick (038778) 225
Cuthbert, Mrs B. M. (—:0:0:0:0)
Tetsworth Tetsworth (084428) 417

Dalgetty, T. N. (0:2:0:1:0)
Jedburgh Camptown (08354) 324
Dalton, J. N. (1:3:2:1:0)
ShifnalNorton (0ley Edge (0625) 861234
Davies, M. W. (0:2:3:2:2)
Abergavenny
Abergavenny (0873) 2292
Davies, P. S. (—:—:—:0:0)
Bromyard Bromyard (0885) 82567
Davis, N. H. (—:—:—:0:1)
Bridgwater
Nether Stowey (0278) 732722
Davis, S. C. (—:—:—:0:0)
Abergavenny
Abergavenny (0873) 890764
Dening, Major R. H. (0:0:0:0:0)
Cullompton
Cullompton (0884) 32275
Dingwall, C. J. (0:0:0:0:0)
Liverpool Liverpool (051) 678-1762
Dixon, J. E. (1:0:0:0:0)
Carlisle Dalston (0228) 710318
Dollar, Miss G. (—:—:—:0:2)
East Hendred
Abingdon (0235) 834537
Down, C. J. (3:1:1:0:0)
Cullompton Cullompton (0884) 33097
Dowson, Mrs P. A. (0:0:0:0:0)
Pershore Pershore (0386) 552029
Dufosee, P. (3:2:1:2:1)
Warminster
Maiden Bradley (09853) 250
Dukes, Mrs P. E. (0:—:0:0:0)
Upham, Hants
Owslebury (096274) 231
Dun, G. R. (0:0:0:0:0)
Heriot Heriot (087535) 219
Dun, T. D. C. (0:1:0:0:0)
Heriot Heriot (087535) 225
Dunn, A. J. K. (0:0:0:2:1)
Minehead Minehead (0643) 862573
Dunstan, P. R. (0:0:0:0:0)
Axminster Hawkchurch (02977) 353

Easton, Mrs M. (0:0:1:1:3)
Fordingbridge
Martin Cross (072589) 375
Eaton, J. N. (—:0:0:0:0)
Pershore
Elmley Castle (038674) 313
Edwards, G. F. (—:—:—:—:0)
Eley, N. T. (—:—:0:—:0)
East Anstey
Anstey Mills (03984) 267
Eubank, A. (0:0:0:1:0)
Cockermouth
Cockermouth (0900) 823027
Eyre, J. L. (—:—:—:—:8)
Mirfield Dewsbury (0924) 492058

Fell, Mrs R. S. (—:—:0:0:0)
Plymouth Shaugh Prior (075539) 322
Fort, J. R. (—:—:—:0:1)
Willington Wearside 091-378-2319
Forte, J. E. (0:1:0:0:1)
Teignmouth
Teignmouth (06267) 5377
French, Mrs S. (0:0:1:0:1)
Meopham Meopham (0474) 814397
Fullerton, Mrs H. J. (—:0:0:0:0)
Dorchester Dorchester (0305) 65323

Garraton, D. T. (—:—:—:0:0)
Malton Rillington (09442) 506
Garvey, P. R. (0:0:0:0:0)
Redditch Inkberrow (0386) 793115
Geddes, Miss F. M. (—:0:0:0:0)
Pickering Lastingham (07515) 235
Gee, B. (—:—:—:—:0)
Worksop Dinnington (0909) 567571
George, J. A. (0:0:—:—:0)
Stroud Painswick (0452) 813487
George, Miss K. M. (—:—:—:—:1)
Princes Risborough
Gibbon, P. F. (—:—:0:0:0)
Darlington Darlington (0325) 720399
Gibson, F. (0:0:0:0:0)
Sheffield Worksop (0909) 771591
Gill, H. J. (—:—:—:—:0)
Aberford Leeds (0532) 813273
Gill, Mrs S. A. (0:0:0:0:0)
Moreton-in-Marsh
Barton-on-the-Heath (060874) 466
Gledson, J. L. (3:1:0:0:0)
Hexham Bellingham (0660) 20218
Goldie, T. (0:0:0:0:0)
Kilwinning Torranyard (029485) 385
Goodfellow, Mrs A. C. D. (6:2:2:2:1)
Mindrum Mindrum (089085) 209
Gorman, F. T. (1:1:0:1:1)
Callington Liskeard (0579) 83451
Gospel, Mrs S. J. (—:—:—:—:1)
Kirkbymoorside
Kirkbymoorside (0751) 33219
Graham, C. (—:—:—:0:0)
Berwick-on-Tweed
Crookham (089082) 552
Graham, G. R. (0:0:0:0:0)
Wadhurst Wadhurst (089288) 2034
Grant-Ives, C. F. (0:0:0:1:0)
Towcester Blakesley (0327) 860435
Gray, F. (2:6:1:2:1)
Warninglid Warninglid (044485) 235

Greathead, T. R. (0:1:0:2:1)
Chipping Norton
Chipping Norton (0608) 2954
Gregson, G. G. A. (0:1:0:4:1)
Shepton Mallet
Greig, D. R. (0:0:1:0:0)
Cranleigh Cranleigh (0483) 272737
Griffith, Mrs J. G. (0:1:1:2:5)
Denbigh Trefnant (074574) 633
Griffiths, S. G. (0:1:0:3:1)
Carmarthen
Nantgaredig (026788) 321

Hackett, A. W. (1:0:0:0:0)
Leicester Rearsby (066474) 535
Hall, G. V. (0:0:0:0:0)
Hartlepool Hartlepool (0429) 234141
and 279511 (home)
Hall, Mrs L. H. M. (—:—:—:0:0)
Chathill Chathill (066589) 245
Hamar, Miss R. J. (0:0:0:0:0)
Clun Clun (05884) 207 and 693
Hamilton, Mrs A. (0:0:0:0:0)
Newcastle Otterburn (0830) 30219
Hardy, W. (0:0:0:0:0)
Nottingham
Burton Joyce (060231) 2519 and 3577
Hargreaves, Mrs P. A. (—:0:2:0:0)
Alresford Alresford (096273) 2749
Harper, H. C. (0:0:1:0:0)
Banbury Banbury (0295) 811223
Harriman, J. (0:0:0:0:1)
Tredegar Tredegar (049525) 3724
Harris, A. G. (—:—:—:0:0)
Compton Martin
Compton Dando (0761) 221328
Harrison, W. H. (0:0:0:0:0)
Wigton Abbeytown (09656) 231
Harry, Mrs R. L. M. (—:—:0:0:0)
Dinas Powys
Dinas Powys (0222) 512308
Haynes, H. E. (0:0:0:0:0)
Swindon Swindon (0793) 762437
Haynes, J. C. (—:—:0:0:0)
Levens Witherslack (044852) 280
Head, The Viscount (—:—0:0:0)
Salisbury
Coombe Bissett (072277) 318
Hellens, J. A. (1:0:0:0:1)
Durham Wearside (091) 388-5403
Hembrow, Mrs S. J. R. (0:0:2:1:0)
Taunton Henlade (0823) 442546
Henriques, M. R. Q. (5:4:2:1:0)
Cirencester
Fossebridge (028572) 304
Heseltine, E. R. (0:0:—:—:0)
Hicks, B. G. (0:1:0:0:0)
Newport, Gwent
Castleton (0633) 680324
Hills, T. R. (0:0:0:0:0)
Ashford Charing (023371) 2224
Hitchings, C. J. (1:2:1:0:0)
Malvern Hanley Swan (0684) 310442
Hodge, H. B. (—:2:1:0:1)
Ware Ware (0920) 3624
Holly, D. (3:0:—:0:0)
Pontyclun Llantrisant (0443) 222131

Holman, Mrs A. (0:—:—:0:0)
Norwich Aylsham (0263) 732493
Horler, Miss C. J. (—:—:0:0:0)
Bath Faulkland (037387) 216
Horwood, Miss J. E. (—:0:0:0:0)
Swerford Hook Norton (0608) 737227
Houlbrooke, T. J. (—:0:1:2:1)
Ledbury Much Marcle (053184) 368
Hubbard, G. A. (1:12:6:15:15)
Woodbridge
Worlingworth (072876) 243 and 554
Hubbuck, J. S. (0:0:0:0:1)
Hexham Hexham (0434) 602913
Hutsby, H. (1:0:0:1:1)
Stratford Stratford (0789) 740241

Jackson, F. S. (1:0:0:0:0)
Nottingham
Nottingham (0602) 663832
and 663970
Jackson, H. S. (0:0:0:0:0)
Bedford Bedford (0234) 740201
Jackson, Mrs V. S. (—:—:1:0:0)
Ponteland Whalton (067075) 388
James, Mrs M. C. (—:—:0:0:0)
Lower Slaughter
Cotswold (0451) 20288
Jeffrey, T. E. (3:0:0:1:0)
Rothbury Embleton (066576) 664
Jerram, M. J. A. (—:—0:1:1)
Aythorpe Roding, Essex
Good Easter (024531) 215
Jestin, F. (0:—:0:2:0)
Wigton Caldbeck (06998) 439
Johnson, M. A. (—:—:—:0:0)
Little Hormead
Great Hormead (076389) 372
Johnson, R. W. (1:0:0:0:0)
Newcastle Tyneside (091) 267-4464
Johnson, Mrs S. M. (—:—:—:1:2)
Madley, Hereford
Golden Valley (0981) 250214
Jones, G. E. (0:0:0:0:2)
Lampeter Llangybi (057045) 261
Jones, I. R. (0:1:4:0:0)
Cwmbran Cwmbran (06333) 2399
Jones, Mrs M. A. (—:—:0:0:1)
Lambourn Lambourn (0488) 72409
Jones, Mrs P. E. (—:1:0:0:0)
Pontyclun Llantrisant (0443) 227642
Joseph, J. (—:—:1:3:6)
Coleshill, Bucks
Chesham (0494) 722239

Kendall, Mrs M. A. (0:0:0:0:0)
Penrith Hackthorpe (09312) 318
Key, B. L. (0:0:2:2:1)
Malvern Malvern (06845) 3830

Lamyman, Mrs S. (0:0:2:0:1)
Louth Tetford [065883) 260
Laxton, T. (1:4:1:3:0)
Clitheroe Clitheroe (0200) 23719
Layland, J. R. M. (0:0:0:0:0)
Gisburn Gisburn (0200) 445490

Le Blond, A. J. (0:0:0:0:0)
Houghton-le-Spring
Wearside (091) 526-3442
Ledger, R. R. (0:0:0:0:0)
Sittingbourne
Sittingbourne (0795) 23360
Lee, Mrs A. E. (0:0:—:0:0)
Towcester Blakesley (0327) 860793
Lee, C. F. (0:0:0:0:0)
Southwell Newark (0636) 830318
Le Grice, T. C. (1:0:0:0:0)
Penzance Penzance (0736) 2750
Leighton, A. F. (2:0:2:1:0)
Worcester Worcester (0905) 640440
Linton, K. A. (—:—:—:0:0)
Ladybank, Fife
Ladybank (0337) 30764
Llewellyn, B. J. (0:1:1:1:1)
Bargoed Rhymney (0685) 841259
Love, J. (0:0:0:0:0)
Johnstone
Bridge of Weir (0505) 612135

MacDonald, D. W. (0:0:1:1:0)
Cockermouth
Cockermouth (0900) 826092
Mactaggart, A. H. (4:3:0:0:0)
Hawick
Bonchester Bridge (045086) 314
Mactaggart, B. (1:0:2:0:0)
Hawick Hawick (0450) 72322
and 72086 (home)
Mahon, J. (0:0:0:0:0)
Stratford Stratford (0789) 299029
and 296692
Mason, A. J. (—:—:—:1:0)
Bibury Bibury (028574) 266
Maundrell, G. C. (0:0:0:0:0)
Marlborough
Ogbourne St George (067284) 202
Mawle, W. N. (1:2:0:1:0)
Banbury Banbury (0295) 710367
McCaskill, D. A. (—:—:0:0:0)
Chester-le-Street
Wearside (091) 410-2938 (home)
and 488-7062 (yard)
McGarva, D. (2:0:0:4:0)
Kilmacolm Kilmacolm (050587) 2240
McInnes Skinner, Mrs C.
(—:—:0:0:0)
Melton Mowbray
Somerby (066477) 327
McKenzie-Coles, W. G. (0:0:0:1:2)
Taunton
Lydeard St Lawrence (09847) 334
Meade, C. M. (—:2:—:—:2)
Tiverton Rackenford (088488) 216
Miller, N. (—:—:—:1:2)
Ferryhill
Wearside (091) 410-9696 (office)
and Bishop Auckland (0388) 721565
Milligan, Miss M. K. (—:—:—:1:2)
Middleham Wensleydale (0969) 22990
Millington, J. R. (0:0:0:0:0)
Kilby Leicester (0533) 402375
Minns, Mrs S. A. (—:—:1:0:0)
Droitwich Droitwich (0905) 621201

Mitchell, C. W. (0:0:1:1:0)
Dorchester
Buckland Newton (03005) 276
Mobley, Mrs H. M. (—:0:0:0:0)
Banbury Banbury (0295) 710297
Morton, K. (—:0:—:—:0)
Morton, T. (2:0:1:1:0)
Leominster Kingsland (056881) 488
Murdoch, Mrs M. (1:0:0:0:0)
Maidstone Maidstone (0622) 843236

Neaves, A. S. (3:0:0:0:0)
Faversham Eastling (079 589) 274
Needham, J. L. (0:0:0:0:0)
Ludlow Ludlow (0584) 2112 and 4826
Nelson, W. M. (—:—:0:0:0)
Dumfries Collin (038775) 237
North, Mrs H. E. (—:—:0:0:1)
Withiel Florey
Brompton Regis (03987) 202
Nugent, D. H. L. (0:1:0:4:2)
Newbury Chaddleworth (04882) 209

Oseman, D. J. (—:—:—:—:0)
Owen, K. R. (—:—:—:0:0)
Denbigh Llandyrnog (08244) 266

Paisley, R. (—:—:1:2:0)
Langholm Langholm (03873) 80698
and 80308 (office)
Panvert, J. F. (—:—:0:—:0)
Hildenborough
Hildenborough (0732) 838443
Parfitt, J. (1:0:1:0:3)
Rhymney Rhymney (0685) 840137
Park, I. (—:—:0:0:0)
Eaglescliffe
Eaglescliffe (0642) 580263
Parry, Dr. L. G. (0:0:0:—:0)
Market Rasen
Market Rasen (0673) 843585
Paul, W. J. L. (—:0:0:0:0)
Tring Aylesbury (0296) 681762
Payne, J. R. (0:0:0:1:1)
Dulverton
Brompton Regis (03987) 244
Peachey, H. E. (0:0:0:0:0)
Stratford Stratford (0789) 294520
Perkins, R. A. H. (6:—:—:—:1)
Hartshorne
Burton-on-Trent (0283) 21595
and 21323
Perrett, A. C. J. (2:3:3:0:1)
Cheltenham
Andoversford (0242) 820244
and 820841
Peter-Hoblyn, G. H. (—:—:—:—:0)
Pike, S. L. (0:0:0:1:0)
Sidmouth Sidbury (03957) 485
Pile, Mrs P. M. (0:0:0:0:0)
Leamington
Farnborough, Banbury (029589) 661
Pilkington, J. (—:—:0:0:1)
Birtsmorton
Birtsmorton (068481) 580

Pilkington, Mrs J. St C. (1:0:0:0:0)
Stow-on-the-Wold
Stow-on-the-Wold (0451) 30641
Pincombe, R. W. (0:—:—:0:0)
South Molton
Bishops Nympton (07697) 331
Pitcher, D. F. (0:0:0:0:0)
Burnham, Bucks
Burnham (06286) 66177
Plowright, Mrs G. S. (0:0:1:2:1)
Sheffield Barnsley (0226) 790472
Pocock, R. E. (1:1:0:0:0)
Bridgwater Holford (027874) 236
Powell, G. J. (—:—:1:1:0)
Abbeydore
Golden Valley (0981) 240204
Price, Mrs A. (0:—:0:1:0)
Price, G. M. (0:0:0:1:0)
Brecon Llangorse (087484) 212
Price, J. P. (1:3:0:0:0)
Leominster Kingsland (056881) 264
Price, R. C. (—:—:—:—:0)
Hereford
Hay-on-Wye (0497) 820447
Price, R. J. (0:0:0:0:1)
Leominster Leominster (0568) 5638
and 2333
Price, T. J. (0:0:1:0:0)
Chepstow Caldicot (0291) 421596
Price, W. (0:1:0:2:0)
Leominster Kingsland (056881) 439
Prince, O. R. (—:—:—:0:0)
Barton-under-Needwood
Hoar Cross (028375) 229
Pritchard, P. L. J. (—:—:—:—:1)
Purton, Glos Dursley (0453) 811881
Pugh, R. C. (0:0:0:0:0)
Worcester Worcester (0905) 640547
and 640211

Ratcliff, Mrs A. E. (0:0:0:0:0)
Warwick Claverdon (092684) 2209
Ratcliffe, C. I. (—:—:—:0:0)
Saddleworth
Saddleworth (0457) 872097
Rebanks, T. W. (—:—:—:—:0)
Penrith Shap (09316) 225
Reed, W. J. (0:0:0:0:0)
Barnstaple
Chittlehamholt (07694) 292
Reid, A. S. (—:—:—:—:1)
Thurleigh (071-723-1824)
Reid, T. (—:—:—:—:0)
Haywards Heath
Haywards Heath (0444) 413914
Richards, G. (2:0:—:—:0)
Crickhowell
Ridout, A. S. (—:—:—:0:0)
Fordingbridge
Rockbourne (07253) 646
Righton, L. J. (—:—:—:0:0)
Moreton-in-Marsh
Moreton-in-Marsh (0608) 50784
Robertson, D. (0:0:1:0:3)
Kilmarnock Craigie (056386) 201
Robinson, J. (0:0:0:0:0)
Annan Annan (04612) 2792

Robinson, Dr J. F. (0:0:0:1:5)
Leeds Leeds (0532) 813252
Robson, E. H. (4:3:0:0:0)
Morpeth Morpeth (0830) 30207
Robson, Mrs J. L. (—:—:—:—:0)
Redmarshall Stockton (0642) 588069
Robson, T. L. A. (0:1:0:1:0)
Alnwick Whittingham (066574) 307
Roderick, D. (0:0:0:0:0)
Maesteg Maesteg (0656) 732780
Roe, G. L. (—:—:—:—:1)
Yelverton Yelverton (0822) 852850
Rollingson, T. (0:0:0:0:0)
Halstead Hedingham (0787) 237318
Roper, J. H. (—:0:1:0:0)
Suckley Suckley (08864) 368
Rumsey, A. J. (—:—:0:0:0)
Bobbington Bobbington (038488) 269
Ryall, B. J. M. (—:—:0:0:0)
Yeovil
Marston Magna (0935) 850222

Salkeld, Miss J. (2:—:1:0:0)
Moffat Moffat (0683) 20127
and 20028 (home)
Sample, W. N. (0:0:0:0:2)
Morpeth Scots Gap (067074) 627
Sandys-Clarke, R. P. (—:—:—:3:3)
Darlington Staindrop (0833) 60215
Saul, Mrs M. M. (0:—:0:0:0)
Spilsby, Lincs Spilsby (0790) 52034
Saunders, C. R. (0:1:3:3:2)
Northampton
Northampton (0604) 770234
Scott, D. D. (0:0:0:0:1)
Minehead Minehead (0643) 2430
Scott, D. W. (—:—:0:0:0)
Hexham Slaley (043473) 313
Scott, Mrs E. B. (0:0:0:0:0)
Keyworth
Wymeswold (0509) 880489
Scriven, B. A. (0:1:0:0:0)
Taunton North Curry (0823) 490208
Shail, R. J. (0:1:1:0:0)
Ledbury Bromesberrow (053181) 286
Shears, J. B. (—:—:0:0:0)
Chagford Chagford (06473) 2356
Sheedy, W. R. (0:—:0:2:0)
Newport, Gwent
Penhow (0633) 400646
Sheridan, F. (2:0:0:—:0)
Rowington Lapworth (05643) 2011
Shrubsole, Mrs P. M. (—:—:—:0:1)
Berwick-on-Tweed
Berwick-on-Tweed (0289) 88638
Silvester, A. J. (—:—:—:—:0)
Droitwich Worcester (0905) 620454
Simmons, J. C. (—:—:0:1:0)
Abridge, Essex
Theydon Bois (037881) 2440
Simpson, Mrs G. L. (—:—:—:0:0)
Hexham Slaley (0434) 673413
Skelton, J. (0:0:1:0:0)
Skipton Earby (0282) 842503
Slack, Mrs D. E. (1:0:1:0:0)
Appleby Appleby (0930) 51354
Smith, C. (—:—:—:—:0)

Smith, M. J. (—:0:3:0:0)
Thornaby
Middlesbrough (0642) 593198
Smith, Mrs M. M. (—:—:0:0:0)
Launceston Launceston (0566) 86221
Smith, Roy J. (1:0:—:0:0)
Loughborough
Wymeswold (0509) 880689
Smith, S. G. (2:0:0:1:0)
Grimsby Grimsby (0472) 840276
Smith, Mrs S. J. (—:—:—:—:0)
Bingley
Smith, W. J. (—:—:—:0:0)
Islip
Charlton-on-Otmoor (086733) 224
Smith, W. J. F. (0:0:2:0:0)
Richmond Richmond (0748) 2629
Spicer, R. C. (0:0:0:0:0)
Spalding
Pinchbeck Bars (077587) 444
Sporborg, C. H. (0:2:0:3:1)
Bishops Stortford
Albury, Herts (027974) 444
Stevens, S. R. (—:0:0:1:0)
Exeter Whimpole (0404) 822205
Stevens, S. T. R. (2:1:2:1:0)
South Molton
Bishops Nympton (07697) 254
Stickland, G. W. (0:0:1:0:0)
Stalbridge Stalbridge (0963) 62492
Stirk, Mrs M. K. (2:2:0:0:0)
Ripon Kirkby Malzeard (076583) 447
Storey, F. S. (2:0:0:2:0)
Carlisle Kirklinton (022875) 331
Sunter, J. (—:—:—:0:0)
Newton Aycliffe
Aycliffe (0325) 318657
Supple, K. R. (—:0:0:0:0)
Maidstone Maidstone (0622) 6516
Swiers, J. E. (1:4:2:6:8)
Helperby
Boroughbridge (0423) 322153
Swiers, R. W. (2:2:2:9:0)
Helperby
Boroughbridge (0423) 322226
Swindlehurst, D. G. (2:0:0:0:0)
Carlisle
Rockcliffe, Cumbria (022874) 289
Sykes, Miss E. (0:0:0:0:0)
Ludlow Seifton (058473) 656

Taylor, A. G. L. (—:0:0:0:0)
Worcester Worcester (0905) 352536
Taylor, A. J. (0:1:0:0:1)
Hassocks Plumpton (0273) 890156
Taylor, F. (1:0:0:0:0)
Richmond Darlington (0325) 374394
Taylor, W. H. (0:0:0:0:0)
Worcester Worcester (0905) 355065
Teal, Mrs V. J. (0:0:0:0:0)
St Clears Llanteg (083483) 694
Temple, B. M. (0:1:0:0:0)
Driffield Driffield (0377) 42321
Tetley, Mrs P. A. (—:—:—:—:0)
Cranleigh Cranleigh (0483) 274013
Thick, N. K. (—:—:0:0:0)
Dymock Dymock (053185) 453

Thompson, J. D. (0:—:0:0:0)
Hexham Bellingham (0660) 30236
Thomson, A. M. (—:—:—:—:0)
Greenlaw Greenlaw (03616) 514
Thomson, Mrs D. (0:0:0:1:1)
Kinross Kinross (0577) 63418
Thorpe, J. G. (0:1:0:0:0)
Brigg Brigg (0652) 52135
Tidmus, C. B. (0:0:1:0:0)
Wantage West Hanney (023587) 588
Tinning, W. H. (0:0:1:0:0)
Harrogate Harewood (0532) 886260
Todd, D. T. (0:1:2:0:1)
Lincoln Wragby (0673) 858242
Torr, S. A. (1:0:0:0:0)
Leek Blackshaw (053834) 266
Townsend, R. D. (0:0:1:1:0)
Charing Charing (023371) 2586
Townson, J. (—:—:—:0:0)
Blackburn Whalley (025482) 3412
Trotter, J. A. (—:—:—:—:0)
Tullie, Mrs A. F. (0:0:0:0:1)
Eyemouth Chirnside (089081) 226
Turner, J. R. (2:0:0:1:0)
Helperby
Boroughbridge (0423) 322239
Turner, J. S. E. (—:0:0:0:0)
Whitchurch, Salop
Whitchurch (0948) 3527
Turner, Miss S. J. (—:—:—:—:0)
Ripon Harrogate (0423) 324096
Turner, Miss T. J. (—:—:—:—:0)
Oakhampton
Turton, S. F. (—:—:—:1:0)
Yealmpton Plymouth (0752) 880105
Tutty, Mrs K. J. (—:—:—:—:0)
Northallerton
Osmotherley (060983) 624
Twibell, J. (0:0:0:0:1)
Dinnington
Dinnington (0909) 562338

Upson, J. R. (—:—:—:—:22)
Towcester
Upson, P. N. (0:0:0:0:0)
Ashford, Kent
Sellindge (030381) 2320

Vergette, G. M. (0:0:3:2:3)
Peterborough
Market Deeping (0778) 342226
Vernon, M. S. (—:—:—:0:0)
Darlington Darlington (0325) 300590

Wade, J. (5:0:1:—:1)
Ferryhill Sedgefield (0740) 30310
Waggott, N. (0:0:0:0:0)
Spennymoor
Spennymoor (0388) 819012
Wakely, P. (0:0:0:0:0)
Cullompton Kentisbeare (08846) 357
Wales, J. A. (0:0:0:0:0)
King's Lynn Fincham (03664) 213
Wales, W. A. (0:0:0:0:0)
Fakenham Binham (032875) 580

Waley-Cohen, R. B. (0:2:0:3:1)
Banbury Edgehill (029587) 632
Walford, T. D. (0:0:0:0:0)
Sheriff Hutton
Sheriff Hutton (03477) 382
Walmsley, J. W. (—:—:—:0:0)
Tadcaster Tadcaster (0937) 833380
Walton, F. T. (5:4:4:4:8)
Morpeth Rothbury (0669) 40253
Ward, Mrs S. A. (0:1:0:0:1)
Northallerton
East Harlsey (060982) 293

Ward, Mrs V. C. (—:—:—:0:0)
Grantham Culverthorpe (05295) 260
Wareham, G. A. (2:0:0:0:0)
Findon Findon (090671) 2774
Waring, L. E. (0:0:0:0:0)
Wellington, Somerset
Wellington (082347) 2660
Waterman, Miss S. E. (0:0:0:0:1)
Dorchester Evershot (093583) 394
Wates, C. S. (2:2:3:0:1)
Rye Northiam (07974) 2125
Watson, A. (0:0:—:—:0)
Skipton Earby (028284) 2228
Webb, H. J. M. (0:0:0:0:0)
Faringdon Faringdon (0367) 20173
Weir, Mrs J. C. (0:1:0:0:0)
Cupar Gauldry (082624) 753 and 707
Wellicome, D. R. (0:1:0:4:2)
Northampton
Northampton (0604) 740587
Wells, B. K. (0:0:1:0:0)
Kidderminster
Chaddesley Corbett (056283) 296
Wells, Mrs H. S. (—:—:—:0:1)
Lockerbie Lockerbie (05762) 4129
Welsh, D. D. G. (—:—:—:0:1)
Sevenoaks Meopham (0474) 813132
Weston, M. H. (—:—:0:0:0)
Worcester Worcester (0905) 52361
Wheeler, N. J. (0:0:0:0:1)
Battle Rushlake Green (0435) 830571
White, C. J. (0:—:—:—:0)
Steyning Steyning (0903) 816258

White, Mrs F. E. (—:—:—:0:0)
Chelmsford
Maldon, Essex (0621) 742161
White, Miss T. A. (—:—:—:0:0)
Newbury East Ilsley (063528) 608
Wight, A. J. (—:—:—:0:0)
Cockburnspath
Cockburnspath (03683) 219
Wilding, R. J. (—:—:—:0:0)
Church Stretton
Marshbrook (06946) 232
Wilkinson, Mrs J. V. (—:—:—:1:0)
Chesham
Kings Langley (09277) 65624
Williams, A. J. (—:—:0:0:0)
Newport
Gwent Magor (0633) 880255
Williams, D. (0:0:0:—:0)
Exeter Starcross (0626) 890268
Williams, Mrs F. A. W. (—:0:0:0:0)
Hitchin Hitchin (0462) 34762
Williams, M. G. (0:0:—:0:0)
Newport, Gwent
Magor (0633) 880282
Williams, R. (0:0:0:0:0)
Pontypool Talywain (0495) 772360
and 772201
Williams, Mrs S. D. (—:0:0:0:0)
Crediton Wichenford (0884) 860600
Wood, C. R. (—:—:—:0:0)
Petersfield Petersfield (0730) 61756
Woodrow, Mrs A. M. (—:—:0:0:0)
High Wycombe
Radnage (024026) 2557
Wordingham, L. W. (2:0:0:—:0)
Fakenham Binham (032875) 343

Young, B. R. J. (0:0:0:0:0)
Liskeard Liskeard (0579) 20087
Young, J. R. A. (0:0:0:0:0)
Loughborough Sileby (050981) 3567
Young, V. P. (0:0:0:1:3)
Hastings Hastings (0424) 438425
Young, W. G. (0:0:1:0:0)
Carluke Crossford (055586) 226

JOCKEYS

The figures in brackets show the number of winners each jockey has ridden in Britain during the past five seasons from 1985/86 to 1989/90 inclusive. Also included are telephone numbers and riding weights.

Akehurst, J. C. (0:1:1:3:2) 10 3
Heathfield (043 52) 4713
Armytage, Miss G. (10:18:10:4:6) .9 7
c/o East Ilsley (063528) 203 and 273

Arnott, T. R. (5:5:7:2:3) 10 0
Rockbourne (07253) 504
Ayliffe, M. G. (2:0:0:1:0) 10 4
c/o Winsford (063 385) 265

Barlow, J. (4:0:0:0:1) 10 0
Newmarket (0638) 713018
Bastard, M. H. (5:4:3:4:1) 10 0
Lambourn (0488) 72747
Beggan, R. J. (13:30:28:24:22) 10 0
Marlborough (0672) 40868 and
mobilephone (0836) 507343 or agent
Carey (043270) 460/448 and
mobilephone (0860) 394890
Bosley, M. R. (8:10:10:4:5) 10 2
Bampton Castle (0993) 850212
Bowlby, M. S. S. (9:29:14:28:25) . 10 0
Lambourn (0488) 72210 and
carphone (0831) 472211
Bradley, G. J. (39:53:37:34:30) 10 4
Stamford Bridge (0759) 71586 and
carphone (0836) 753052 (agent)
Childrey (023559) 533 (home) and
mobilephones (0860) 327649 and
722772
Brady, J. N. (—:—:—:0:0) 9 7
Downton (Wilts) (0725) 3213
Brennan, M. J. (14:21:16:17:22) .. 10 0
Newark (0636) 701207 and
carphone (0860) 550554
Brisbourne, W. M. (2:0:0:0:0) 10 2
Nesscliffe (074381) 360
Browne, D. W. (20:24:20:5:0) 10 3
Lambourn (0488) 39706 and
carphone (0860) 398166
Bryan, J. R. (14:8:2:6:3) 10 0
Ridgway Cross (088 684) 748
Burchell, D. J. (5:4:14:13:12) 10 1
c/o Ebbw Vale (0495) 302551
Burke, K. R. (7:7:2:10:5) 10 0
Fenton Claypole (0636) 84522 (home)
and 84750 and
carphone (0860) 744172
Byrne, D. C. (—:3:9:29:44) 9 10
York (0904) 647213 (agent) and
Malton (0653) 692288 (home),
mobilephone (0836) 278374
Byrne, E. M. (—:—:—:—:0) 9 12
Kingsbridge (0548) 550148
Byrne, R. (1:—:—:—:0) 9 7

Caldwell, P. H. (0:1:0:6:1) 10 0
Warrington (0925) 602679
Campbell, R. (1:5:3:5:2) 10 0
Newmarket (0638) 730638
Carroll, A. W. (10:12:17:7:10) 10 0
Newmarket (0638) 751607
Chapman, R. H. (1:4:2:0:0) 10 0
c/o Lambourn (0488) 71555 and
(0793) 825356 (afternoon and evening)
Charles-Jones, G. F. H.
(15:8:4:11:0) 10 0
Wootton Bassett (0793) 790317
Clay, Miss D. L. (1:7:5:12:3) 10 0
(0767) 260618
Coleman, N. F. (9:11:15:23:6) 10 0
Torquay (0803) 615843
Condell, D. (17:3:0:0:1) 9 7
c/o Wensleydale (0969) 22237
Corrigan, P. P. (7:2:2:4:6) 10 0
Haywards Heath (0444) 881594
Cowley, S. (—:—:12:1:5) 10 0
Cheltenham (0242) 528634
Cox, C. G. (33:18:8:3:0) 10 0
Lambourn (0488) 72418
Crank, R. W. (19:18:9:4:1) 10 2
Tattenhall (0829) 70672
Crosse, M. J. (—:—:—:3:0) 10 0
Haywards Heath (0444) 85586

Davies, G. (4:8:8:8:1) 10 0
Chepstow (029 12) 2486
Davies, H. J. (58:40:33:50:60) 10 3
Ashbury (079 371) 395
Davies, J. D. (6:8:0:0:0) 10 0
c/o Bishop's Lydeard (0823) 432769
Davis, Miss T. M. J. (7:16:7:4:3) 9 7
Lambourn (0488) 72677
Dawe, N. J. (0:0:1:1:2) 10 0
Worthing (0903) 884749 and
(0295) 68619 (agent)
De Haan, B. (22:15:16:15:29) 10 0
Lambourn (0488) 72163
Dennis, R. T. J. (4:4:0:0:1) 10 0
Newmarket (0638) 750191
Dever, P. (8:13:3:1:4) 10 0
Broadway (0386) 858988
Dicks, A. C. (1:1:1:0:0) 9 0
Bristol (0272) 519184 and
Pill (027581) 2192
Doolan, K. J. (5:4:11:1:6) 10 0
Edmundbyers (0207) 55259
Doughty, D. N. (27:11:18:33:46) .. 10 5
Penrith (0768) 67800
Dowling, B. (6:17:14:17:23) 10 0
Tewkesbury (0684) 298227 and
(056888) 460
Duggan, J. D. (13:7:3:4:3) 10 0
(023559) 533
Dunwoody, T. R.
(55:70:79:91:102) 10 1
(023559) 287 or
carphone (0836) 502290 and (agent)
Carey (043270) 460/448 or
mobilephone (0860) 394890
Dwyer, M. P. (30:81:73:93:75) 10 2
Rillington (09442) 8841,
Stamford Bridge (0759) 71586
(agent)

Earle, S. A. (3:6:21:13:22) 10 0
Bishop's Lydeard (0823) 433346 and
mobilephone (0860) 252348
Eccles, S. Smith
(65:56:30:45:56) 10 3
Newmarket (0638) 77719 and
carphone (0836) 241780
Evans, C. (4:6:1:1:3) 10 0
Tonyrefail (0443) 673630

Fahey, R. A. (—:12:0:29:18) 10 0
York (0904) 647213 (agent) and
Kirby Misperton (065386) 635 and
mobilephone (0836) 567580
Farrell, P. A. (7:6:3:6:3) 9 10
Brandsby (03475) 273 and 208
Ffitch-Heyes, Miss P. A. D.
(2:14:4:4:1) 9 10
Ashtead (0372) 276106
Forte, A. M. (—:—:—:0:1) 9 7
Teignmouth (06267) 79006

Frost, J. D. (14:14:30:41:46) 10 4
Buckfastleigh (03644) 2267
Furlong, M. J. (0:2:4:7:6) 10 0
Lewes (0273) 476515

Gallagher, D. T. (—:14:15:3:23) .. 10 0
Marlborough (0672) 40809, carphone (0836) 776937 and (agent) (0932) 243913 and carphone (0860) 234342
Goldstein, R. (12:9:20:32:21) 10 0
Lewes (0273) 476755
Gorman, A. F. (4:1:0:2:0) 10 0
Newbury (0635) 248660 and 248036
Grant, C. (41:63:80:38:94) 10 0
Bishop Auckland (0388) 710425 and mobilephone (0860) 230131
Grantham, T. O. (8:10:11:4:6) 10 0
Findon (090671) 2432
Guest, R. C. (7:20:18:19:13) 10 1
(0420) 62383, carphone (0836) 781938 and Weyhill (026477) 2278

Hansen, J. M. (5:6:4:4:1) 10 0
Selkirk (0750) 22110 and 22848 (home)
Harker, G. A. (6:16:16:5:7) 10 0
Eaglescliffe (0642) 780995 and York (0904) 647213 (office)
Harris, J. A. (4:2:1:3:2) 10 0
Harby (0949) 60671
Harris, Miss V. M. (1:3:1:0:0) 10 0
Harby (0949) 60671
Harvey, L. J. (9:19:17:11:25) 10 0
Bampton, Devon (0398) 31478 and carphone (0831) 117816
Hawke, N. J. (—:0:12:18:17) 9 7
(0804) 23891
Hawkins, C. (29:11:17:12:11) 10 3
Northallerton (0609) 748734
Hayes, Mrs J. (1:7:1:4:5) 9 7
Lambourn (0488) 72649
Hayes, W. J. (0:0:4:5:0) 9 7
Lambourn (0488) 72649
Hill, M. R. (6:6:5:0:12) 10 2
Malton (0653) 697234
Hobbs, P. D. (12:20:26:47:43) 10 1
(0903) 743928 and mobilephone (0860) 729794 and c/o Findon (090671) 2226
Hopwood, C. J. (0:3:1:0:0) 10 2
Hemyock (0823) 680959
Humphreys, W. G. (2:10:14:4:6) .9 12
Cheltenham (0242) 39531 (home) mobilephone (0836) 777100 and (agent) Carey (043270) 460/448 or mobilephone (0860) 394890
Hyett, R. G. (7:8:12:8:5) 10 2
Bosbury (053 186) 312

James, Miss S. E. (1:2:0:0:0) 9 7
Whitchurch (0948) 4067 and 2679
Jarvis, T. O. (2:3:0:—:2) 10 0
(0636) 893219 and 626325 (office)
Johnson, S. N. (6:8:6:0:2) 10 7
Whatton (0949) 50752
Jones, A. E. (4:13:3:7:2) 10 0
Great Shefford (048839) 742
Jones, G. H. (5:0:0:0:0) 10 7
Leysters (056 887) 676
Jones, K. (14:4:12:1:0) 10 4
Embleton (066576) 722

Keightley, S. L. (1:2:3:5:5) 10 0
Newmarket (0638) 666070
Kellett, C. N. (1:1:0:—:3) 10 3
Hornsea (0964) 562684
Kinane, J. K. (3:7:3:6:1) 9 7
c/o Selkirk (0750) 22110 and St Boswells (0835) 23814
Kinane, M. J. (1:10:16:8:8) 10 0
Worthing (0903) 884935
Knight, S. George (5:3:2:3:2) 9 7
Kentisbeare (0823) 680959
Knox, W. D. R. (3:3:5:2:3) 10 6
Abergavenny (0873) 6776

Laurence, M. C. G.
(—:—:—:—:0) 10 0
Leech, P. J. (—:—:—:—:3) 10 0
Lambourn (0488) 71105
Llewellyn, C. (2:7:41:20:19) 10 0
Wantage (02357) 3410 and carphone (0860) 288880 and (agent) Carey (043270) 448/460 or mobilephone (0860) 394890
Lower, J. A. (25:36:11:27:49) 10 0
Wellington (082347) 3580
Lynch, M. M. (—:—:—:12:17) 10 0
(0295) 712139

Marley, R. J. (2:11:20:21:11) 10 0
Malton (0653) 696205 and Northallerton (0609) 748749 or mobilephone (0836) 229366 (agent)

Martin, G. J. (4:3:0:0:2) 9 7
(03475) 641 and (0206) 240235
McCourt, G. M.
(38:33:68:86:100) 10 4
Childrey (023559) 501, mobilephones (0836) 749191 and 236625 and (agent) Stamford Bridge (0759) 71586 (home) and mobilephone (0836) 753052
McKeown, D. W. E.
(1:24:17:31:30) 10 0
(0372) 276106 and (0860) 718952 (agent) or carphone (0836) 672574
McKinley, E. M. (—:0:2:3:0) 9 7
c/o Findon (090671) 2226
McLaughlin, J. F. S. (4:7:10:7:4) ... 9 10
Newmarket (0638) 668115
McNeill, S. R. O. (8:18:9:22:15) ... 10 0
Great Shefford (048839) 8861
Meagher, M. G. (10:10:0:3:0) 10 0
Longton (0772) 612120 and Liverpool (051-531) 6887
Merrigan, A. T. A.
(0:5:26:28:10) 10 0
Bishop Auckland (0388) 813877 and 720213
Mitchell, S. (0:3:0:—:0) 10 0
Mansfield (0623) 823800
Mooney, J. W. (0:0:0:0:0) 10 7
(0472) 883298

Mooney, K. P. (37:18:32:22:21) ... 10 0
Lambourn (0488) 72176
Moore, G. L. (14:5:5:2:9) 10 4
Brighton (0273) 681679
Moore, J. S. (2:15:5:2:0) 10 0
Warminster (0985) 6286 and Andover (0264) 50706
Morgan, G. P. (0:0:0:1:0) 9 7
Bristol (0272) 570959
Morgan, T. W. (—:18:44:51:19) ... 10 3
Dean (0594) 544594 and mobilephone (0836) 784719
Morris, Mrs C. L. (9:6:4:3:2) 8 9
c/o Brighton (0273) 681679
Morris, D. (0:13:16:4:6) 10 0
(0883) 344893 and mobilephone (0860) 758412
Morris, W. A. F. F. (2:0:2:0:2) 10 0
Hartlebury (0299) 250686 and Kidderminster (0562) 755625
Murphy, D. J. (6:18:15:19:15) 10 0
c/o Exning (063877) 645
Murphy, E. R. (37:17:8:10:9) 10 0
Worthing (0903) 60687
Murphy, M. F. (—:—:0:0:0) 10 0
c/o Mansfield (0623) 822451

Nicholls, P. F. (9:18:18:15:0) 10 5
c/o Kingsbridge (0548) 550326 and Almondsbury (0454) 612900
Niven, P. D. (15:28:30:49:48) 10 0
York (0904) 647213 (agent) and mobilephone (0860) 260999
Nolan, D. A. (4:11:4:0:6) 10 5
Edinburgh (031-440) 2309

O'Hagan, A. T. (2:2:3:4:0) 10 0
Tenbury Wells (0584) 810627
O'Neill, S. J. (9:12:12:18:19) 10 0
Bunbury (0829) 260660
Orkney, R. A. (2:4:4:4:11) 10 0
Wensleydale (0969) 22845, mobilephone (0836) 371957 and Coxwold (03476) 482 (agent) or carphone (0836) 326084
Osborne, J. A. (1:13:21:22:53) 10 0
Lambourn (0488) 398931 (home) and carphone (0860) 533422

Perrett, M. E. (0:19:24:27:52) 9 7
Ashington (0903) 892895 (home), carphone (0836) 221273 and c/o Pulborough (07982) 3011/2423 (office)
Pitman, M. A. (28:9:27:40:57) 10 3
c/o Lambourn (0488) 71714
Powell, B. G. (45:48:38:64:48) 9 7
Swindon (0793) 782286 (home) and Radiophone (0860) 314745 and (agent) Carey (043270) 448/460 or mobilephone (0860) 394890
Price, A. J. (0:3:0:1:0) 10 0
North Grimston (09446) 370

Quinn, J. J. (10:11:5:9:10) 10 0
North Grimston (09446) 370

Reed, W. T. (14:6:16:11:14) 10 4
Hexham (0434) 344201 and Coxwold (03476) 482 (agent) or carphone (0836) 326084
Richards, M. R. (10:9:7:30:25) 10 0
c/o Swindon (0793) 782286
Richards, P. L. (15:10:5:3:3) 10 2
Holford (027874) 405 (daytime) and Nether Stowey (0278) 733203 (evening)
Robson, J. M. (1:0:0:0:0) 10 2
Swindon (0793) 740611
Rowe, R. (48:50:64:30:31) 10 0
Storrington (0903) 742871
Rowell, R. (4:13:3:1:1) 10 0
Polegate (03212) 3331

Scudamore, P. M.
(91:124:132:221:170) 10 0
Guiting Power (0451) 850741 and carphone (0836) 514820 and mobilephone (0860) 559759
Shaw, D. (5:0:4:2:6) 9 10
Mansfield (0623) 743661
Shortt, J. (—:—:—:7:11) 10 2
Stratford-on-Avon (0789) 773296
Smith, A. G. (0:2:0:2:0) 10 0
Smith, C. A. (13:10:14:12:5) 10 2
Malvern (068 45) 5900
Storey, B. (20:15:25:30:32) 10 0
Kirklinton (022 875) 331 and 376 and mobilephone (0860) 432881
Storey, Miss F. J. (1:1:1:0:0) 10 5
Edmundbyers (0207) 55259
Stronge, R. M. (16:17:4:9:2) 10 0
Supple, R. J. (—:—:5:8:34) 10 0
Northallerton (0609) 748749 or mobilephone (0836) 229366

Tegg, D. R. (1:6:23:21:12) 10 0
Hereford (0432) 352674
Townend, K. (3:5:0:0:0) 10 2
Stratton-on-the-Fosse (0761) 232705
Turner, S. (3:3:14:29:25) 10 0
(0937) 62690 or (agent) Northallerton (0609) 748749 and mobilephone (0836) 229366

Vaughan, R. R. (—:—:0:1:0) 9 7
Shrewton (0980) 624695
Vincent, Miss L. J. (0:2:4:5:5) 9 2
Swindon (0793) 782286

Wall, T. R. (4:10:4:15:15) 9 7
Cressage (095289) 743 and (0860) 256211 (carphone)
Webb, A. (23:15:20:15:10) 10 0
Stratford (0789) 68812 and (agent) Carey (043270) 448/460 and mobilephone (0860) 394890
White, J. A. (19:14:15:27:31) 10 0
Lambourn (0488) 72831
Wilkinson, D. (4:7:3:5:2) 9 7
Wensleydale (0969) 24229
Williams, Mark (—:—:—:0:0) 9 10
Longdown (Exeter) (039281) 558 and (0272) 510260
Williams, M. (3:7:27:16:2) 10 0
Wellington (0823) 665156 (home) and carphone (0836) 588690

Wonnacott, D. J. (2:0:2:0:6)......... 10 0
Tavistock (0822) 664 16
Worthington, W. M. (4:1:4:1:7)... 10 0
c/o Scunthorpe (0724) 863347
Wright, B. J. (6:1:3:3:5).................. 10 7
Lambourn (0488) 72688
Wyer, L. A. (—:33:30:36:33)......... 10 0
Malton (0653) 694776 and Northallerton (0609) 748749 or mobilephone (0836) 229366 (agent)

Youlden, S. R. (10:4:—:—:1)........ 10 0
Wetherby (0937) 844974

The following relinquished their licence during the season

Hammond, M. D. (23:36:63:33:35)
Shilston, S. R. W. (12:11:11:1:1)
Tuck, P. C. (39:59:71:23:5)

CONDITIONAL JOCKEYS

The following list shows the employer and riding weight of every conditional jockey who held a licence for the 1989/90 season. The figures in brackets show firstly the allowance claimed by each rider at the end of the season and secondly the number of winners each jockey has ridden in this country during the past five seasons, from 1985/86 to 1989/90 inclusive.

Conditional jockeys are entitled to the following allowances in steeplechases and hurdle races open to professional jockeys: 7 lb until they have won 15 races, thereafter 5 lb until they have won 25 races; thereafter 3 lb until they have won 40 races (wins in apprentice, opportunity and National Hunt Flat races not to count). The allowances could be claimed in the following races, with the exception of opportunity races: (a) all handicaps except the Grand National (b) all selling races (c) all other races with guaranteed prize money of not more than £5,000.

Adams, A. J. (1:6:14:3:8)................9 7
(N. Gaselee)
Lambourn (0488) 72238 and (0235) 819093 (agent)
Ahern, M. J. (3) (0:5:1:3:10)...........9 9
(J. Jenkins)
Royston (0763) 41141
Allen, M. (7) (—:—:—:—:0) 9 7
(J. Edwards)
Alston, M. E. (7) (0:1:0:0:3) 9 12
(E. Alston)
Arnold, S. P. (7) (—:—:—:—:0).....9 7
(R. Eckley)
Ashworth, L. R. (7)
(—:—:—:—:0) 9 7
(A. Davison)
Atkinson, J. K. (7)
(—:—:—:—:0) 10 0
(J. Ffitch-Heyes)
Ayles, W. J. (7) (—:—:—:—:0) 9 7
(W. Kemp)

Barnard, P. J. (5) (—:—:—:—:7)...9 3
(T. Thomson Jones)
Marlborough (0672) 10613 (home) and (0638) 76686 (agent)
Barry, D. J. P. (7) (—:—:—:0:1) 9 7
(G. Richards)
Bellamy, R. (5) (—:—:0:4:16)........9 7
(D. Nicholson)
Carey 043270 448/460 and carphone (0860) 394890
Bevan, R. C. (5) (—:1:4:3:8) 10 0
(W. Clay)
Billany, Miss A. L. (7)
(—:—:—:—:0) 8 8
(J. Thorpe)
Bird, W. K. (7) (—:—:—:—:0) 9 7
(J. Bukovets)
Bohane, G. (7) (—:—:—:3:1).........9 6
(J. Upson)
Bottomley, A. J. (7)
(—:—:—:0:0)........................... 10 0
(J. Bottomley)
Boucher, R. A. (7) (—:2:2:2:1).......9 7
(A. Turnell)
(02357) 70673
Bray, C. W.(7) (—:—:—:—:0) 9 7
(P. Davis)
Brennan, Miss H. F. (7)
(—:—:—:0:0)........................... 10 0
(O. Brennan)
Bridger, Miss R. J. (7)
(—:—:—:0:0)..............................9 7
(J. Bridger)
Bridgwater, D. G. (7)
(—:—:—:0:3)..............................9 0
(D. Nicholson)
Brown, J. L. (7) (4:1:1:5:2)........... 10 4
(M. Brown)

Brown, M. P. (7) (—:0:1:1:1) 10 0
(J. Davies)

Burke, J. H. (7) (—:—:—:0:0) 10 0
(T. Donnelly)

Burland, Miss D. M. (7)
(—:—:—:0:0) 9 7
(K. Bishop)

Burton, J. N. (7) (—:0:1:0:2) 9 7
(J. FitzGerald)

Byrne, C. P. (7) (—:—:—:—:0)...... 9 5
(J. Jenkins)

Caldwell, P. (Pat) A. (7)
(0:0:0:0:1) 9 7
(T. Caldwell)
Northallerton (0609) 748241 and
mobilephone (0836) 229366 (agent)

Callaghan, J. G. (3)
(—:—:0:11:24) 9 7
(G. Moore)
Northallerton (0609) 748749 and
mobilephone (0836) 229366 (agent)

Carr, P. A. (7) (—:—:—:—:0) 9 7
(D. Smith)

Carson, R. W. (7) (—:—:—:—:0) ... 9 7
(C. Spares)

Carter, M. D. (7) (—:—:—:—:0) 9 7
(J. Wainwright)

Chandler, L. E. (7) (—:—:0:0:0) 9 7
(Mrs D. Haine)

Charlton, A. (3) (1:9:14:9:9) 10 0
(G. Balding) Weyhill (026477) 2583

Clarke, J. (7) (—:0:1:3:1) 9 10
(A. Moore)

Coglan, M. V. (7) (—:—:—:0:0)...... 9 7
(J. Pearce)

Collett, M. K. (7) (—:—:—:—:0) ... 9 0
(Mrs G. Jones)

Collins, P. M. (7) (—:—:—:—:0).... 9 7
(D. Grissell)

Conlon, S. P. (7) (0:—:0:1:0) 9 7
(D. Elsworth)

Cook, G. (7) (—:—:0:1:0) 9 7
(P. Liddle)

Cooney, D. (7) (—:—:—:—:0) 9 7
(J. Czerpak)

Corkell, J. D. (7) (—:—:—:0:3) 10 0
(Mrs V. Aconley)

Courtney, A. M. (7)
(—:—:—:—:0) 9 7
(Mrs S. Oliver)

Crone, G. S. (7) (—:—:—:—:1) 9 7
(G. Harwood)

Crossman, D. R. (7) (—:0:0:5:2) 9 7
(D. Smith)

Cunningham, W. S. (7)
(3:4:0:5:3) 9 7
(T. Cunningham)

Curran, J. M. (7) (—:—:—:—:0) 9 7
(W. Perrin)

Cusack, S. P. (7) (—:0:—:0:0) 9 7
(J. McConnochie)

Cuthbert, Miss C. (7)
(—:—:—:0:3) 9 7
(T. Cuthbert)

Dace, L. A. (7) (—:—:—:—:0) 8 11
(R. Smyth)

Da Costa, J. W. (7) (—:0:0:0:0)....... 9 7
(B. Wells)

Dalton, B. P. (7) (—:—:—:—:1)..... 9 7
(J. Jefferson)

Darby, J. P. F. (7) (—:—:—:—:0) .. 9 0
(Mrs S. Piggott)

David, A. N. (7) (—:—:—:0:1) 9 7
(R. Lee)

Davies, P. W. (7) (0:0:0:0:0) 9 7
(J. Old)

Davies, S. (5) (1:4:6:8:7).................. 9 12
(Miss S. Wilton)

Davis, R. S. (7) (—:—:0:1:0) 10 4
(P. Davis)

Dempsey, C. (7) (—:—:—:0:2)....... 9 7
(C. Brooks)

Denaro, M. J. (7) (—:—:—:—:0).... 9 7
(C. Allen)

Dennis, C. P. (3) (1:6:11:11:4)......... 9 11
(K. McCauley)

Dennis, D. J. (7) (—:—:—:—:1) 9 7
(J. Pickering)

Dicken, A. R. (7) (—:—:0:0:0)........ 9 10
(S. Dow)

Dillon, J. E. (7) (—:—:1:0:0) 9 7
(W. A. Stephenson)

Donaldson, G. P. (7)
(—:—:0:0:0) 10 0
(T. Casey)

Doran, B. N. (7) (—:—:—:0:0) 9 7
(D. Williams)

Doyle, M. A. (7) (—:—:0:0:2).......... 9 7
(J. Edwards)

Driscoll, J. P. (7) (—:—:—:—:1).... 9 7
(J. Scargill)

Duffy, J. A. (7) (—:—:—:0:0).......... 9 7
(G. Thorner)

Dunne, D. (7) (—:—:—:—:1).......... 9 0
(R. Allen)

Dobson, D. G. (7)(—:—:—:0:0)...... 9 7
(C. Parker)

Donaldson, G. P. (7)
(—:—:0:0:0) 10 0
(T. Casey)

Doran, B. N. (7) (—:—:—:0:0) 9 7
(D. Williams)

Doyle, M. A. (7) (—:—:0:0:0).......... 9 7
(J. Edwards)

Driscoll, J. P. (7) (—:—:—:—:0).... 9 7
(J. Scargill)

Duffy, J. A. (7) (—:—:—:0:0).......... 9 7
(G. Thorner)

Dunne, D. (7) (—:—:—:—:0).......... 9 0
(R. Allan)

Dwan, W. J. (7) (—:—:0:1:1)........... 9 7
(J. FitzGerald)

Edwards, Miss G. (7)
(—:—:—:—:0) 8 10
(R. Swiers)

Eldredge, Miss. L. C. (7)
(—:—:—:—:0) 9 7
(R. Lee)

Fanning, J. K. (7) (—:—:—:—:1)... 9 0
(T. Fairhurst)

Farley, B. J. (7) (—:—:—:—:0)...... 9 6
(T. Thomson Jones)

Farmer, R. B. (7) (—:—:—:—:0)...9 7
(G. Balding)
Fitzgerald, M. A. (7)
(—:—:—:2:1) 10 0
(R. Hodges)
FitzGerald, M. P. (7)
(—:—:—:—:0) 9 7
(M. Bradstock)
Foster, M. R. (7) (—:—:—:2:9) 9 8
(M. Pipe)
Foster, S. J. (7) (—:—:—:2:1).........9 10
(G. Balding)
Fox, S. (7) (—:—:—:1:0)..................9 7
(J. Fox)
Fry, W. S. (7) (—:—:—:—:0) 9 7
(T. Tate)
Fuller, T. (7) (—:—:—:—:0)...........8 12
(D. Wintle)

Garritty, R. J. (3) (1:1:0:21:22) 10 0
(M. H. Easterby)
Malton (0653) 600221 and
Coxwold (03476) 482 or
carphone (0836) 326084 (agent)
Garside, D. W. (7)
(—:—:—:—:0) 9 7
(M. Camacho)
Gartland, J. J. J. (7)
(—:—:—:0:0) 10 0
(J. Czerpak)
Gibbons, C. M. (7)
(—:—:—:—:0) 9 7
(C. Trietline)
Goddings, R. W. (7) (—:—:—:1:0). 9 10
(P. Hedger)
Graham, S. J. (7) (—:—:—:—:0)....9 7
(J. Needham)
Greene, R. J. (7) (—:—:0:2:12) 9 7
(R. Lee)
Grimwood, O. T. A. (7)
(—:—:—:—:0) 10 0
(B. Stevens)

Halden, Miss R. (7)
(—:—:—:0:1) 9 7
(C. Bell)
Halls, J. I. (7) (—:—:0:0:0)..............9 10
(Miss B. Sanders)
Harley, P. M. (7) (—:0:2:3:5)..........9 7
(N. Henderson) (0932) 243913 and
carphone (0860) 234342 (agent)
Harris, S. A. (7) (0:1:1:0:2) 9 0
(J. Harris)
Harris, S. D. (7) (—:—:—:—:0) 9 3
(M. Usher)
Harte, P. G. (3) (—:—:13:16:1) 9 7
(Mrs R. Wharton)
Hay, B. T. (7) (1:0:0:0:0)................ 10 7
(T. Craig)
Hazell, M. G. (7) (0:0:0:0:1) 10 5
(N. Gaselee)
Hazell, S. F. (7) (—:—:—:—:1)......9 7
(A. Denson)
Heaver, G. R. D. (7) (1:4:1:0:1)......9 7
(R. Akehurst)
Henfrey, Miss J. M.
(7) (—:—:—:0:0)........................... 10 0
(K. Morgan)

Heywood, A. N. (7) (—:—:—:0:1) .9 7
(W. Stephenson)
Hoad, M. R. (7) (1:2:3:2:1)............. 10 0
(R. Hoad)
(0932) 243913 and
carphone (0860) 234342 (agent)
Hodge, R. J. (7) (—:0:4:0:11) 9 7
(Mrs G. Reveley)
Hodgson, S. P. (7) (0:0:0:9:6) 9 12
(G. Balding)
Holley, P. S. (3) (1:4:6:22:11) 9 11
(D. Elsworth)
Hood, D. G. W. (7) (4:2:4:4:8) 9 12
(P. Blockley)
carphone (0860) 370777 and
Worthing (0903) 208758 (agent)
Huggan, C. H. (7) (—:—:0:1:0) 9 10
(N. Henderson)
Hughes, P. (7) (—:—:—:—:0) 9 7
(T. Bailey)
Hughes, P. (7) (—:—:—:—:0) 9 7
(W. (Bill) Turner)

Irvine, W. S. (3) (1:3:15:23:14) 9 7
(R. Hodges)

Jackson, Miss A. E. (7)
(—:—:0:0:1) 9 7
(M. Dickinson)
Jenner, M. B. (7) (—:—:0:0:0)........9 7
(T. McGovern)
Jennings, M. (7) (—:—:—:—:0)... 10 0
(N. Gaselee)
Jones, K. A. (7) (—:—:—:—:0).......9 7
(M. Channon)
Jones, M. P. (5) (—:—:6:12:9) 9 2
(R. Dickin)
Juckes, A. G. (7) (—:—:—:1:11) 9 7
(B. Preece)
(0836) 694307
Judge, Miss R. M. (—:—:—:—:0)..9 7
(K. Ryan)

Kane, M. (7) (—:0:—:0:0) 9 7
(J. Fox)
Kelly, P. P. (7) (—:—:—:—:0)........9 7
(M. Wilkinson)
Kersey, Miss S. (7) (0:0:1:1:1)........9 8
(T. Kersey)
Knight, A. J. (7) (—:—:—:0:1)........9 10
(S. Dow)

Laird, A. P. (7) (—:—:—:—:0) 9 7
(M. O'Neill)
Larnach, A. A. (7) (—:—:—:—:3)..9 7
(W. Stephenson)
Lawrence, I. R. (3) (0:0:7:15:21) ...9 7
(K. Bailey)
Wantage (02357) 69671
mobilephone (0860) 823336
Leach, N. R. (7) (0:0:—:1:1)............9 7
(G. Richards)
Leech, J. P. (5) (—:—:5:10:16) 10 0
(R. Akehurst)
Lambourn (0488) 72259 and 73245
(evenings)
Leech, T. M. (7) (—:0:0:0:0) 9 7
(Miss S. Wilton)

Lees, D. W. (7) (—:—:—:—:0) 9 7
(J. Spearing)
Leese, M. (7) (—:—:—:0:0) 9 7
(Ronald Thompson)
Linton, A. (7) (—:—:—:—:0)..........9 0
(J. Wilson)
Lodder, J. D. (3) (—:—:—:10:25)...9 7
(F. Jordan) (0568) 611068 and
carphone (0831) 486302
Long, Miss L. G. (7) (1:0:0:0:1) 9 7
(J. Long)
Lyons, Gary (3) (—:—:—:8:31) ... 10 0
(R. Hollinshead)
Lyons, G. M. (3) (—:0:16:18:7).......9 11
(M. W. Easterby)
Malton (0653) 697455 and
mobilephone (0836) 747727

Mackey, S. C. (1:0:2:6:8)..............10 0
(G. Ham)
Macneice, R. J. J. (7)
(—:—:5:7:2)...................................9 7
(M. Pipe)
Madgwick D. S. (7)
(—:—:—:—:0)..............................10 3
(M. Madgwick)
Mann, N. J. W. (5) (—:—:—:3:24)..9 0
(R. Holder)
mobilephone (0831) 236034
Manson, J. P. P. (7) (—:—:—:0:1) .9 7
(J. Mackie)
Marston, W. J. (7) (—:—:—:—:1)..9 7
(D. Nicholson)
Martin, D. M. (7) (0:0:—:0:0) 9 7
(P. Liddle)
Martin, R. B. (7) (—:—:1:1:0) 10 0
(T. Etherington)
Mason, S. T. (7) (—:—:1:1:0)..........9 7
(R. Curtis)
Matthews, D. D. (7)
(—:—:—:—:0)...............................9 7
(Mrs A. Knight)
Maude, C. G. (7) (0:0:0:3:12) 9 7
(P. Hobbs) (02357) 3410
McCabe, A. J. (7) (—:—:1:2:1) 9 7
(D. Elsworth)
McCabe, J. B. (7) (—:—:—:—:0) ...9 7
(Mrs J. Pitman)
McCarthy, J. A. (7) (—:—:—:0:2)..9 7
(T. Casey)
McDermott, P. S. (7) (0:3:0:5:7)....9 7
(C. Broad)
Huntley (0452) 830251
McDougall, S. J. (7) (—:0:—:0:0) ..9 7
(B. Smart)
McEntee, P. S. (7) (—:—:0:1:0).....9 10
(W. Musson)
McFarland, W. J. (0:2:2:23:26)......9 9
(G. Balding) (02357) 65135 and
mobilephone (0836) 507631
McGiff, B. C. (5) (—:—:0:9:18) 9 7
(C. Beever) (0347) 6482 and
carphone (0836) 326084 (agent)
McGonagle, M. (7)
(—:—:—:—:1) 9 7
(S. Christian)
McLellan, A. D. (7) (0:—:—:—:1) .9 7
(R. Manning)

Meade, D. N. (7) (—:—:—:—:0) 9 7
(D. Gandolfo)
Meredith, D. (7) (—:—:—:—:2).....8 0
(R. Dickin)
Midgley, P. T. (7) (—:—:—:2:5).....9 4
(P. Blockley)
Milner, R. G. A. (7) (—:—:0:1:1)....9 7
(N. Henderson)
Moffatt, D. J. (7) (—:—:—:—:1) 9 7
(D. Moffatt)
Moloney, M. J. (5)
(—:—:—:—:8) 9 7
(G. Richards)
Moore, R. W. (7) (—:—:—:0:2) 9 7
(G. Enright)
Mulholland, A. B. (5) (2:4:11:9:7)..9 9
(S. Christian) (090567) 382 and
mobilephone (0836) 784439
Mullaney, L. A. (7) (—:—:—:0:0)..9 10
(M. H. Easterby)
Mumford, Miss H. J. (7)
(—:—:—:—:0) 9 0
(P. Jones)
Murphy, S. J. C. (7) (—:—:0:3:5) ...9 0
(A. Davison)
Murtagh, F. P. (7)(—:—:—:2:0) 9 7
(J. J. O'Neill)

Neaves, J. P. (7) (—:—:—:—:3).....9 0
(W. (Bill) Turner)
Neighbour, S. P. (7) (—:0:1:0:0) 9 10
(J. Gifford)
Nixon, A. (7) (—:—:—:0:1) 9 7
(J. Eyre)
Norledge, Miss M. J. (7)
(—:—:—:—:0) 9 7
(R. Juckes)

O'Connor, C. (7) (—:—:—:0:0) 9 7
(D. Murray-Smith)
O'Donovan, E. F. (7)
(—:—:0:0:0).................................9 7
(N. Gaselee)
O'Dowd, B. (7) (—:—:—:0:0).........9 7
(A. Wilson)
O'Dwyer, P. M. (7) (—:—:—:0:0)..9 11
(Miss A. King)
O'Gorman, J. M. (3) (3:2:6:19:4)....9 11
(Mrs S. Bramall) Thirsk (0845) 401287
O'Hara, L. S. (5) (0:0:0:21:10)........9 7
(G. Richards)
mobilephone (0860) 498107 and
Stamford Bridge (0759) 71586 or
carphone (0836) 753052 (agent)
O'Hare, L. N. P. (7)
(—:—:—:—:0) 9 0
(R. Bennett)
Oldershaw, D. B. (7)
(—:0:0:—:0).................................9 4
(M. Eckley)
Osborn, G. A. (7) (—:—:—:—:0)....9 7
(Miss S. Wilton)
O'Sullivan, D. K. (7)
(—:—:1:10:4)...............................9 12
(R. O'Sullivan)

Parker, A. (7) (—:—:—:0:0)..........9 10
(W. Stephenson)

Parker, Miss N. J. (7)
(—:—:—:—:0) 9 0
(B. Richmond)
Pearson, S. L. (7) (—:—:0:0:0) 10 0
(T. Forster)
Peill, M. A. (7) (—:—:—:0:0) 9 7
(Mrs S. Austin)
Pinfield, T. R. (5) (2:0:9:10:3) 10 0
(J. Gifford) 090 671-3984 and
mobilephone (0831) 254398 or 209874
Piper, G. E. (7) (—:—:0:0:0) 9 7
(D. Barons)
Plumridge, S. C. (7)
(—:—:—:1:0) 9 10
(S. Harris)
Poole, D. (7) (—:—:—:—:1) 9 10
(J. Wilson)
Pope, Miss L. (7) (—:—:0:0:0) 8 12
(J. Baker)
Potts, T. M. (7) (0:0:0:0:2) 9 7
(A. Potts)
Priest, C. (7) (—:—:—:0:0) 8 7
(N. Bycroft)
Prince, C. J. (7) (2:1:0:0:0) 9 7
(B. Morgan)
Pullin, J. R. (7) (—:—:—:0:0) 9 7
(J. McConnochie)

Quinn, A. J. (5) (2:2:6:7:4) 9 8
(Miss L. Siddall)

Railton, J. A. (3) (—:4:4:18:21) 10 2
(T. Forster)
Carey (043270) 460/448 or
mobilephone (0860) 394890 (agent)
and Lambourn (0488) 71890 and
mobilephone (0860) 282467
Rees, D. C. (7) (—:—:—:0:0) 9 7
(B. Palling)
Richardson, S. P. (7)
(—:—:—:0:2) 9 7
(N. Tinkler)
Richmond, D. S. (7)
(—:—:—:1:2) 9 4
(M. Pipe)
Roche, N. D. (7) (—:—:0:1:1) 10 0
(B. Ellison) (03727) 24018 (agent)
Rowe, G. T. (7) (—:—:0:—:2) 9 9
(J. Gifford)
Rudd, T. P. (7) (—:—:—:—:0) 9 0
(D. Murray-Smith)
Lambourn (0488) 71239 and 71041
Ryan, C. J. M. (7) (—:—:—:7:1) 9 12
(M. W. Easterby)
Sheriff Hutton (03477) 794 and
York (0904) 647213 agent
Ryan, J. B. (5) (6:6:2:1:11) 9 0
(M. Ryan)
Newmarket (0638) 664172

Salt, Miss V. M. (7) (—:—:0:0:0) ... 9 0
(R. Weaver)
Scope, G. J. (7) (—:—:—:0:1) 9 7
(R. Goldie)
Shoemark, I. W. (3) (2:1:15:4:11) .. 9 9
(S. Mellor)
Swindon (0793) 790230, 828054 and
carphone (0836) 638615

Skyrme, D. V. (3) (2:2:6:9:15) 9 7
(P. Harris) (0444) 2827830 (home) and
carphone (0836) 381957
Slattery, J. V. (7) (—:—:—:6:3) 9 7
(O. O'Neill)
Smith, A. S. (7) (1:—:1:4:8) 9 7
(O. Sherwood)
Smith, C. N. (5) (1:1:5:3:14) 9 7
(J. Parkes) Coxwold (03476) 482 and
carphone (0836) 326084 (agent)
Smith, V. (5) (—:0:0:0:5) 9 9
(H. Collingridge)
Newmarket (0638) 668972
Smyth, U. P. (7) (—:—:—:1:0) 10 0
(N. Henderson)
c/o Hornsea (0964) 562991
Stanford, A. M. (7) (—:0:1:1:1) 9 7
(M. O'Neill)
Stenning, J. (7) (—:—:—:—:0) 8 12
(J. Long)
Sterry, W. A. (7) (—:—:—:—:0) 9 10
(D. Tucker)
Stevens, M. (7) (0:0:1:0:0) 9 12
(B. Stevens)
Stokell, Miss A. (7) (—:—:0:0:1) ... 9 7
(M. Barraclough)
Claverdon (092684) 3332
Stone, Mrs T. (7) (—:—:—:—:1) ... 9 7
(K. Wingrove)
Sullivan, D. A. (7) (—:—:—:1:0) 9 7
(N. Tinkler)
Supple, J. A. (7) (—:—:—:—:0) 9 7
(W. Stephenson)
Sweeney, A. P. (7) (—:—:0:3:0) 9 7
(B. Curley)

Teague, R. J. (7) (—:—:0:5:1) 9 7
(C. Brooks)
Telfer, D. M. (7) (1:3:3:1:1) 10 0
(Mrs S. Lamyman)
Thomson, G. J. (7) (—:1:0:0:0) 9 7
(J. Oliver)
Tierney, E. (7)(—:—:—:0:6) 9 7
(A. James)
Tory, A. S. (3) (1:0:1:15:15) 10 0
(N. Mitchell) (0258) 840216
Townsley, Miss L. L. (7)
(—:—:—:0:0) 9 7
(Mrs P. Townsley)
Tuite, J. M.(7) (—:0:0:0:7) 10 0
(Mrs J. Pitman)
Tynan, T. A. (7) (—:0:0:—:0) 9 7
(P. Howling)

Verling, P. M. (3) (—:—:3:14:5) 9 10
(D. Murray-Smith)
Lambourn (0488) 73125 and
Worthing (0903) 208758 (agent)

Ward, D. A. (7) (—:—:—:—:0) 9 0
(D. Gandolfo)
Ward, R. J. (7) (—:—:—:—:0) 9 7
(I. Wardle)
White, T. P. (7) (—:5:9:0:0) 9 7
(W. A. Stephenson)
Whitham, A. D. (7)
(—:—:—:—:1) 9 7
(R. Earnshaw)

Whittle, F. J. (7) (—:—:0:0:2) 9 7
(J. Glover)
Williams, D. J. (7) (—:—:0:0:0) 9 7
(M. Bradley)
Williams, N. J. (7) (—:—:—:—:0)..9 7
(J. King)
Williams, P. D. (7) (—:—:—:0:0)...9 7
(F. Jordan)
Williams, S. D. (7)
(—:—:—:—:5) 9 7
(J. Mackie)
Williamson, N. (—:—:—:—:20) 9 7
(J. Edwards)
Winterbotham, J. R. (7)
(—:—:1:0:0) 9 10
(G. Moore)
Woods, A. T. (7) (—:—:—:0:0) 9 4
(J. Edwards)
Woods, S. P. C. (3) (2:6:11:2:8).......9 11
(F. Durr) Newmarket (0638) 715755

The following relinquished their licence during the season

Barry, T. P. (—:—:—:0:2)
Bates, J. M. (—:—:—:—:0)
Bellisario, M. (—:0:—:0:1)
Benneyworth, D. C. (1:0:5:2:1)
Bentley, D. B. (—:—:—:—:0)
Bowker, Miss J. (—:—:—:—:0)
Boxhall, A. P. (—:—:—:—:0)
Burden, S. J. (—:—:0:—:0)
Cloke, T. N. (—:—:—:—:2)
Collins, M. G. (—:—:—:—:0)
Davies, L. S. (—:—:—:—:0)
Dengel, D. A. (—:—:—:—:0)
Dobson, D. G. (—:—:—:0:0)
Durnin, A. (—:—:—:—:0)
Evans, Miss R. L. (—:—:0:0:0)
Hanley, B. A. (—:—:—:—:0)
Heath, L. (—:—:—:0:0)
Hickey, S. (—:—:0:0:0)
Hickson, A. G. (—:—:0:—:0)
Jackson, M. J. (—:—:—:—:0)
Johnson, P. M. (—:—:1:5:1)
Kent, T. J. (—:—:—:0:1)
Leese, A. (0:—:0:—:0)
Maher, S. J. J. (—:—:—:—:0)
McKeever, S. W. (—:—:—:8:3)
McMahon, H. I. (—:—:—:—:0)
Muggeridge, M. P. (0:1:4:1:0)
Murphy, B. J. (—:—:0:2:2)
Murray, D. (—:—:—:0:0)
Neilson, J. L. (—:—:0:0:0)
O'Connor, N. G. (—:—:—:—:0)
O'Donovan, S. H. (—:—:—:—:4)
O'Hanlan, J. (—:1:0:0:0)
O'Ware, J. (—:—:—:—:0)
Pengelly, Miss S. (—:—:—:—:1)
Perratt, W. F. (—:—:—:0:1)
Protheroe, T. S. (—:—:—:—:0)
Rolls, A. M. (—:0:1:1:0)
Roper, A. J. (—:—:—:—:0)
Sharratt, M. R. (—:0:0:0:0)
Skelton, J. A. (—:—:—:—:0)
Stone, Mrs T. (—:—:—:—:0)
Tinker, S. P. (—:—:—:0:0)
Todd, I. (—:—:—:—:0)
Urwin, W. D. (—:—:—:—:0)
Warburton, O. F. (—:—:—:—:0)
Williams, C. (0:0:0:0:0)
Woodall, C. (—:—:0:0:0)

AMATEUR RIDERS

The following is a list of 'Category B' amateur riders who hold a permit to ride in flat races, steeplechases, hurdle races and National Hunt Flat races. The figures in brackets show the numbers of winners each jockey has ridden in this country during the past five seasons, from 1985/86 to 1989/90 inclusive. Also included are their telephone numbers.

H. R. H. Princess Royal (—:0:1:0:0)
c/o (0451) 30417
Alner, R. H. (0:0:1:1:2)
(02586) 271
Anderson, K. (3:7:2:6:4)
(04615) 482
Andrews, S. R. (5:4:8:4:0)
Offley (046 276) 263
Armytage, M. D. (1:9:12:7:6)
Newmarket (0638) 730052

Bailey, E. D. (0:0:0:4:1)
(02357) 67547
Bailey, Mrs T. L. (0:0:0:0:1)
(063528) 253
Barlow, T. D. B. (—:0:2:1:0)
Barons, R. D. R. (1:0:0:0:0)
c/o (0548) 550326
Barrow, Miss J. G. (0:0:1:2:1)
(0278) 732413
Barton, J. W. (—:—0:1:0)
Batters, M. J. (—:0:0:1:0)
(07254) 609
Baxter, Miss S. E. (2:0:5:1:0)
c/o (0827) 62901
Bealby, A. J. (—:1:0:0:0)
Bealby, C. C. (1:2:0:0:0)
(0476) 72749
Beardsall, J. H. (—:—:0:2:0)
Wensleydale (0969) 24218
Beasley, Miss C. J. (1:2:2:0:2)
(0952) 460636

Belcher, Miss S. J. (1:0:1:0:0)
Ticehurst (0580) 200039
Bell, S. B. (—:0:0:0:3)
Bethell, Mrs E. A. (—:—:0:0:0)
Bethell, W. A. (0:0:0:0:0)
(0964) 562996
Billot, Miss S. A. (—:—:—:—:0)
(0488) 84285
Bissill, Mrs M. (—:—:0:0:0)
Bissill, W. H. (0:0:—:0:0)
(0949) 50226
Blackford, Miss L. A. (—:—:—:—:0)
(0964) 562996
Bloom, N. M. (1:1:0:1:1)
Wymondham (0953) 603137
Bloor, D. R. (0:0:1:0:0)
Hinckley (0455) 291739
Bowlby, Mrs A. (—:—:0:0:0)
(0488) 72210
Bowlby, A. A. (0:0:0:0:0)
Culverthorpe (05295) 242
Bradburne, J. G. (0:4:0:0:5)
Letham, Fife (033 781) 325
Bradburne, Mrs S. C. (0:1:1:1:0)
Letham, Fife (033781) 325
Brookes, N. H. (0:0:0:0:0)
Bishops Cleeve (024 267) 5037
Brookshaw, S. A. (0:0:0:0:4)
Brown, R. H. (1:5:0:0:1)
Helmsley (0439) 70026
Brunt, R. C. (0:0:0:0:0)
Bullard, S. R. (2:0:0:1:0)
Newmarket (0638) 669780
Burnett-Wells, C. P. (—:—:3:2:2)
(090671) 2226
Burrough, S. C. (—:—:0:4:5)
Bush, N. (0:0:0:1:0)
Bath (0225) 891293
Bush, S. (0:1:0:1:0)
Castle Combe (0249) 782317

Cambidge, J. R. (1:2:0:0:1)
Weston-under-Lizard (095 276) 249
Campion, S. W. (0:—:0:2:0)
Carden, J. (0:0:0:0:0)
Alderley Edge (0625) 829748
Christopher, Mrs K. M.
(—:—:—:—:0)
Claisse, S. J. (0:—:0:0:0)
Clifford, B. M. (—:—:—:—:4)
Cockram, D. D. L. (0:0:0:0:0)
Wickenby 067-35231
Conway, Mrs J. (0:0:—:—:0)
Cosgrove, G. D. (—:—:0:1:0)
(0235) 833535
Cowell, S. A. (1:0:0:0:0)
Tillingham (062187) 310
Craggs, P. F. (2:2:0:1:6)
Hartburn (067072) 260
Crawford, B. T. (1:0:0:0:0)
Whatton (0949) 50238
Crow, A. M. (0:—:0:0:0)
Linlithgow (0506) 842194
Crow, Miss L. L. (0:—:0:0:0)
Curling, Miss P. (0:1:1:0:1)
Holford (027 874) 405
Darby, M. V. (0:0:1:0:0)
Stourport (029 93) 2375

Dare, Miss A. (0:1:0:0:0)
(0454) 778778
Davies, Miss J. (—:—:0:0:2)
(0748) 4630
Davison, Miss Z. C. (0:3:1:2:3)
Lower Beeding (040 376) 700
Delve, Miss L. D. (0:0:0:0:0)
Dickin, S. (0:0:0:0:0)
Uppington (095286) 439
Downing, R. S. (0:0:0:0:0)
(0787) 61766
Dowrick, I. S. (0:0:0:0:0)
Doyle, P. J. (—:3:3:9:1)
(08533) 392
Duggan, D. G. (1:0:0:0:2)
c/o (056) 882281
Dun, J. M. (0:1:0:1:0)
Heriot (087535) 307
Dunn, N. G. H. (0:0:1:0:0)
Blagdon Hill (082342) 530
Durkan, J. P. P. (—:—:—:1:7)
Lambourn (0488) 72077

Easterby, T. D. (0:0:0:0:0)
c/o (065386) 600
Eaton, Miss L. V. (0:1:0:0:0)
(0468) 21374
Edwards, G. F. (0:0:0:0:0)
Exford (064 383) 549
Elliott, Mrs C. F. (0:0:0:0:0)
Alton (0420) 63733
Ellis, Miss K. J. (0:0:0:0:0)
Poundsgate (03643) 457
Elwell, Mrs T. M. (0:1:0:0:0)
Cropredy (029575) 758
Embiricos, Miss A. E.
(—:—:2:2:1)
Evatt, D. B. (0:0:0:0:0)
(0342) 810482

Farrant, A. J. (—:—:—:—:4)
(027581) 2192
Farrell, Mrs A. L. (1:11:2:6:3)
Brandsby (03475) 273
Farrell, C. (—:—:2:3:6)
(0488) 72909
Felton, M. J. (0:1:0:0:0)
(07255) 267
Finegan, H. P. (—:—:—:0:0)
c/o (0233) 72525
Fogarty, L. C. (0:1:0:0:0)
(0252) 332392
Ford, R. (0:0:2:0:3)
(0900) 826092
Fowler, A. (5:1:0:0:0)
Gaddesby (0664) 840203
Franks, D. R. (0:0:0:0:0)
Spennymoor (0388) 819188
French, Miss S. (0:1:1:1:2)
Meopham (0474) 814397

Gandolfo, Miss E. A. (—:—:—:1:0)
(02357) 3242
Gault, Mrs J. E. (—:—:0:0:0)
Gee, M. P. (0:0:0:0:0)
Worksop (0909) 566666
Gibbon, Mrs L. J. (0:0:0:0:0)
Colchester (0206) 250832

Gill, H. J. (0:—:0:0:0)
(0532) 813273
Gray, D. M. (—:—:—:—:8)
Greed, T. R. (0:0:0:1:0)
Green, K. A. (0:1:0:0:0)
Greenall, J. E. (3:2:7:7:6)
082 786 238
Greenway, C. E. R. (0:0:0:0:0)
(0606) 882387
Griffith, A. D. W. (0:0:0:2:1)
071-402 2572
Griffith, E. J. W. (0:1:1:0:4)
(074574) 633
Grissell, Mrs D. C. (—:0:1:0:2)
(042 482) 241
Grossick, J. (0:0:1:0:1)
(0875) 52115

Hacking, W. P. (4:5:4:5:2)
Findon (090671) 3984
Hale, R. A. (—:—:2:0:0)
Greystoke (08533) 564
Hambly, A. A. (1:0:0:0:2)
Yarpole (056885) 778 and
mobilephone (0860) 72 1081
Hamer, M. P. (0:0:1:0:0)
(0656) 860275
Hancock, C. T. C. (—:—:—:—:0)
Hanmer, G. D. (—:—:0:2:0)
(0283) 550035
Harding-Jones, P. (—:3:6:6:0)
North Weald (037882) 2183
Hargreave, N. E. H. (0:0:1:1:2)
Harley, J. C. (—:0:2:0:1)
Droxford (0489) 877207
Harwood, Miss A. J. (—:0:0:3:6)
Pulborough (079 82) 2195
Henry, Miss J. C. (1:2:1:1:0)
Hewitt, R. J. (0:0:0:0:0)
Hickman, A. D. (0:0:0:0:0)
Hill, A. (5:8:3:3:1)
Kingston Blount (0844) 51268
Hills, T. J. (0:0:0:0:0)
(023371) 2224
Hobbs, Mrs S. L. (—:0:1:0:2)
Washford (0984) 40366
Hollinshead, A. N. (0:0:0:0:0)
(0542) 490490
Holman, Mrs A. (0:—:—:0:0)
Aylsham (0263) 732493
Hosgood, P. J. (—:—:0:0:1)
(0364) 42267
Houlbrooke, T. J. (0:0:2:0:0)
Much Marcle (053 184) 268

Illsley, T. C. (0:0:0:1:0)

Jackson, T. H. (1:0:0:0:3)
Ridgeway 457
Jackson, Mrs V. S. (0:0:1:1:0)
Whalton (067075) 388
James, A. C. (—:1:0:0:1)
Jeffrey, T. E. (2:0:0:0:0)
Embleton (066 576) 664
Johnson, K. (—:—:0:14:14)
(091) 2674464
Johnson, P. (4:5:1:2:0)
Tyneside (091) 2674464
Johnson Houghton, G. F.
(0:1:0:0:0)
(0235) 850480
Jones, D. S. (—:0:0:0:0)
(026723) 6661
Jones, Miss I. D. W. (1:1:0:1:1)
(0691) 659720
Jones, T. L. (0:0:1:2:2)
(0222) 882217
Juster, Miss M. (—:—:1:0:0)
Newmarket (0638) 662915

Kendall, Mrs M. A. (1:0:0:0:0)
Hackthorpe (093 12) 318
Kinsella, D. A. (2:0:1:0:0)
East Harlsey (060982) 272

Lane, C. W. S. (0:0:1:1:0)
(082281) 477
Langton, Miss A. S. (3:3:1:0:0)
Lay, A. L. (1:2:2:0:0)
Great Tew (060883) 608
Ledger, Mrs N. (0:0:0:1:0)
Sittingbourne (0795) 23360
Litston, Mrs J. A. (—:2:0:0:0)
Llewellyn, Miss B. (—:1:1:0:0)
(0685) 841259
Love, S. (0:0:0:0:0)
(041330) 5700 and (041956) 5306
Lumsden, C. J. (0:0:0:0:0)
c/o (045388) 437105

MacEwan, A. G. P. B. (0:0:0:1:3)
Newmarket (0638) 669796
Mactaggart, D. C. (5:5:3:1:2)
Bonchester Bridge (045 086) 314
Marks, Miss A. K. (—:1:1:0:0)
(0488) 71767
Matthews, Mrs J. (0:0:0:0:0)
Wellington (082347) 2660
Maundrell, G. C. (1:1:0:1:0)
Ogbourne St George (067284) 202
McCain, D. R. (—:—:0:4:6)
c/o (0638) 665432
McCaull, Miss H. (—:—:1:0:0)
McKie, I. R. (2:2:0:1:0)
(029673) 707
McMahon, E. S. A. (2:1:0:0:0)
Tamworth (0827) 62901
McMahon, P. (—:—:—:—:15)
Millington, P. J. (0:0:0:1:0)
Great Glen (053759) 3314
Mills, Mrs J. M. (1:0:0:0:0)
(0364) 53223
Mitchell, N. R. (—:0:0:0:0)
(0305) 251429
Mitchell, T. L. J. (1:1:0:4:5)
(0305) 251429 and 68069
Monnier, F. C. P. (—:—:—:—:2)
Moore, T. W. (0:0:0:3:1)
Great Dunmow (0371) 821013
Morgan, W. G. N. (0:0:1:0:2)
Morrison, T. (0:0:0:1:0)
Morrow, G. T. (0:0:0:—:1)
(0229) 55664
Morton, Miss J. E. (0:0:—:—:0)
Mullins, S. (0:1:2:3:2)
(0264) 772600

Munro-Wilson, B. G. E. (2:3:2:1:0)
(09547) 347 (home) and
071-377 2066 (office)
Murgatroyd, Miss S. C. (—:2:3:0:0)
(0638) 751607

Nash, Mrs P. L. (—:—:—:—:0)
(036782) 510
Naylor-Leyland, D. G. E.
(4:1:2:3:0)
(0491) 680320
Noonan, Mrs H. M. (—:2:0:0:1)
Nott, W. J. (—:0:0:1:0)
Nuttall, R. E. (0:0:0:0:1)

O'Brien, J. L. C. (0:0:0:0:0)
Elham (030384) 215
O'Reilly, P. F. (0:0:0:3:0)
(0984) 40532
Oxley, J. A. G. (2:0:2:1:3)
(0488) 71556

Panvert, J. F. (—:—:0:0:0)
Pickering, J. A. (0:0:0:1:0)
Pidgeon, Miss J. (0:1:4:1:0)
(029576) 8237
Portman, J. G. B. (2:1:0:0:0)
(0235) 59205
Portman, M. H. B. (—:—:—:0:0)
Poulton, J. C. (0:0:0:0:0)
Plumpton (0273) 890244
Pritchard, J. M. (—:0:0:0:0)
(0684) 297119
Pritchard, P. L. J. (—:—:1:1:2)
(0453) 811881

Ratcliffe, C. I. (0:0:0:0:0)
Saddleworth (045 77) 2097
Rees, Mrs G. S. (1:2:0:0:0)
(077 473) 4409
Ridout, N. T. (1:0:0:0:1)
Rimell, Miss K. (—:2:3:2:0)
Severn Stoke (090 567) 233
Ringer, D. J. (0:0:1:0:0)
Newmarket (0638) 662653
Robertson, D. (0:0:0:0:0)
Craigie (056386) 201
Robinson, D. H. (0:0:0:1:0)
Chertsey (09328) 60601
Robinson, G. (0:0:2:0:1)
(04612) 2852 and 2792
Robinson, R. (0:0:0:0:0)
Annan (04612) 2852
Robson, A. W. (—:1:0:0:1)
(066 589) 276
Robson, Mrs R. A. (—:—:—:—:0)
(066574) 307
Rooney, T. P. (0:0:1:0:0)
(0633) 895878
Russell, R. G. (3:0:3:1:3)
(032736) 208

Sample, C. J. (1:1:2:2:1)
Scots Gap (067074) 245
Sample, M. W. (—:—:1:0:2)
Sandys-Clarke, R. P. (—:—:—:3:3)
Sansome, A. D. (—:—:0:—:2)
(0604) 770991
Saunders, Mrs J. A. (0:0:3:6:1)
(060124) 739
Scholfield, P. M. (0:1:2:0:0)
Starcross (0626) 890764
Scott, D. W. (—:—:0:0:1)
Slaley (043473) 313
Scott, Miss J. M. (0:0:0:0:0)
(0509) 880489
Sharp, J. C. (0:0:0:3:1)
(08012) 4578
Shiels, R. (3:1:0:0:1)
(0835) 62743
Shinton, S. N. (0:0:0:0:0)
Newport, Gwent (0633) 50489
Simpson, Mrs G. L. (—:—:0:0:0)
Slaley (043473) 413
Smith, Mrs D. A. (—:—:—:—:0)
(0684) 573830
Smith, K. H. (0:0:0:0:0)
Charing (023371) 2768
Smith, N. F. (—:0:—:1:1)
Smith, T. D. (0:1:0:0:0)
Smith, T. E. G. (1:1:1:0:0)
Wokingham (0734) 761116
Snell, S. G. (0:0:0:0:0)
Southcombe, Miss J. A.
(—:0:0:3:0)
c/o (026477) 2278
Sowersby, M. E. (1:0:0:0:0)
Beeford (026288) 212
Sporborg, W. H. (0:2:0:2:2)
Albury, Herts (0279 74) 444
Stapleton, Mrs Y. E. (0:0:—:—:0)
Stephens, D. O. (0:0:0:0:0)
Penhow (0633) 400909
Stephenson, T. M. (0:1:0:1:0)
Birtsmorton (068481) 312
Stickland, S. G. (0:0:1:0:0)
Stalbridge (0963) 62492
Stronge, A. N. (—:—:—:0:0)
Swiers, S. J. (6:0:2:12:10)
Boroughbridge (0423) 324155
Swindlehurst, D. J. (2:0:0:0:0)
Rockcliffe (022 874) 289

Taiano, P. G. (0:0:0:0:0)
Welwyn (043871) 8506
Tate, Miss F. E. (—:1:0:0:0)
Taylor, A. J. (0:0:0:0:1)
Plumpton (0273) 890156
Teal, R. A. (0:0:0:0:0)
(099421) 396
Thompson, M. (9:3:6:5:0)
Embleton (066 576) 272
Thurlow, Mrs J. (0:0:1:0:3)
(0965) 20576
Townsend, D. J. (0:0:1:0:0)
Charing (023371) 2586
Townsley, P. F. R. (0:2:0:0:0)
(030677) 492
Trice-Rolph, J. C. (—:—:0:3:1)
(0451) 32039
Tudor, J. W. (0:0:1:1:0)
Bridgend (0656) 50001
Turner, Miss A. J. (0:0:0:0:0)
Shaugh Prior (075539) 231
Tutton, A. G. (0:0:0:0:0)
Byfield (0327) 61083

Tutty, N. D. (2:0:0:0:4)
(060983) 624 and (0642) 78 1894

Upton, G. (1:1:4:7:13)
Upton-On-Severn (06846) 3710 and (036782) 710

Vaughan-Jones, O. (0:0:0:—:0)
Vergette, Mrs H. A. L. (0:0:3:0:3)
Vickery, Mrs R. A. (3:0:1:1:0)
North Cadbury (0963) 40421

Waggott, Miss T. (0:0:1:0:0)
Spennymoor (0388) 819012
Wales, W. A. (0:0:0:0:2)
Binham (032875) 580
Wallace, Miss L. (0:1:0:0:0)
(0743) 860387
Walsh, M. E. J. (—:2:0:1:0)
(05762) 2680
Walter, A. H. (0:0:2:5:7)
(045) 421751
Walton, A. E. (0:0:1:0:0)
(0400) 50531
Walton, J. B. (9:0:3:2:0)
Rothbury (0669) 40253
Waterman, Miss S. E. (0:0:0:0:1)
Evershot (093 583) 394

Watson, M. R. M. (—:0:0:1:0)
Wellings, M. (1:0:0:0:1)
Dudley (0384) 52060
Welsh, A. (0:0:0:0:1)
(0474) 813132
Whales, T. P. (—:0:0:0:1)
(0328) 701788
Wheeler, H. W. (1:0:0:0:0)
Wheeler, N. J. (0:0:0:0:1)
Rushlake Green (0435) 830571
Whitaker, S. R. (0:2:3:1:2)
Leeds (0532) 892265
White, R. (—:0:0:2:0)
(0488) 72831
Williamson, Miss S. L.
(—:—:—:0:0)
(032574) 839
Wilson, C. R. (0:0:0:0:0)
(032574) 595
Wilson, N. (—:—:—:0:4)
Wilson, Miss S. J. (0:0:0:0:0)
Newmarket (0638) 667400
Wonnacott, Mrs C. L. (—:—:0:1:5)
(0822) 616416
Wragg, G. J. D. (0:0:2:0:0)
(071-370) 0980
Wrathall, J. (8:2:0:0:0)
Market Harborough (0858) 32075

LEADING TRAINERS 1946-90

		Winning Horses	*Races Won*	*Stakes £*
1945-46	T. Rayson	2	5	9,933
1946-47	F. Walwyn	36	60	11,115
1947-48	F. Walwyn	40	75	16,790
1948-49	F. Walwyn	36	64	15,563
1949-50	P. Cazalet	29	75	18,427
1950-51	F. Rimell	24	60	18,381
1951-52	N. Crump	22	41	19,357
1952-53	V. O'Brien	4	5	15,515
1953-54	V. O'Brien	7	8	14,274
1954-55	R. Price	24	47	13,888
1955-56	W. Hall	18	41	15,807
1956-57	N. Crump	19	39	18,495
1957-58	F. Walwyn	14	35	23,013
1958-59	R. Price	29	52	26,550
1959-60	P. Cazalet	25	58	22,270
1960-61	F. Rimell	28	58	34,811
1961-62	R. Price	34	64	40,950
1962-63	K. Piggott	4	6	23,091
1963-64	F. Walwyn	30	59	67,129
1964-65	P. Cazalet	34	82	36,153
1965-66	R. Price	29	65	42,276
1966-67	R. Price	34	73	41,222
1967-68	Denys Smith	26	55	37,944
1968-69	F. Rimell	32	62	38,344
1969-70	F. Rimell	35	77	61,864
1970-71	F. Winter	29	73	60,739
1971-72	F. Winter	31	72	62,863
1972-73	F. Winter	37	85	79,066
1973-74	F. Winter	41	89	101,781
1974-75	F. Winter	39	81	74,205
1975-76	F. Rimell	30	49	111,740
1976-77	F. Winter	31	75	85,202
1977-78	F. Winter	44	90	145,915
1978-79	M. H. Easterby	24	56	150,746
1979-80	M. H. Easterby	31	75	218,258
1980-81	M. H. Easterby	34	71	235,867
1981-82	M. Dickinson	32	84	296,028
1982-83	M. Dickinson	42	120	358,837
1983-84	M. Dickinson	30	86	266,146
1984-85	F. Winter	43	85	218,978
1985-86	N. Henderson	27	46	168,234
1986-87	N. Henderson	38	67	222,949
1987-88	D. Elsworth	24	50	358,891
1988-89	M. Pipe	88	208	589,445
1989-90	M. Pipe	95	224	668,606

CHAMPION JOCKEYS 1946-90

		Winners	*Total Mts*	*Per Cent*
1945-46	F. Rimell	54	163	33.13
1946-47	J. Dowdeswell	58	232	25.00
1947-48	B. Marshall	66	237	27.85
1948-49	T. Molony	60	378	15.87
1949-50	T. Molony	95	438	21.69
1950-51	T. Molony	83	430	19.30
1951-52	T. Molony	99	438	22.60
1952-53	F. Winter	121	471	25.69
1953-54	R. Francis	76	331	22.96
1954-55	T. Molony	67	373	17.96
1955-56	F. Winter	74	346	21.39
1956-57	F. Winter	80	329	24.32
1957-58	F. Winter	82	359	22.84
1958-59	T. Brookshaw	83	423	19.62
1959-60	S. Mellor	68	429	15.85
1960-61	S. Mellor	117	608	19.24
1961-62	S. Mellor	80	485	16.49
1962-63	J. Gifford	70	375	18.67
1963-64	J. Gifford	94	408	23.04
1964-65	T. Biddlecombe	114	531	21.47
1965-66	T. Biddlecombe	102	471	21.66
1966-67	J. Gifford	122	530	23.02
1967-68	J. Gifford	82	438	18.72
1968-69	B. R. Davies	77	346	22.25
	T. Biddlecombe	77	372	20.70
1969-70	B. R. Davies	91	476	19.12
1970-71	G. Thorner	74	413	17.92
1971-72	B. R. Davies	89	487	18.28
1972-73	R. Barry	125	437	28.60
1973-74	R. Barry	94	410	22.93
1974-75	T. Stack	82	577	14.21
1975-76	J. Francome	96	392	24.49
1976-77	T. Stack	97	515	18.83
1977-78	J. J. O'Neill	149	545	27.33
1978-79	J. Francome	95	403	23.57
1979-80	J. J. O'Neill	115	517	22.24
1980-81	J. Francome	105	574	18.29
1981-82	J. Francome	120	549	21.85
	P. Scudamore	120	623	19.26
1982-83	J. Francome	106	487	21.77
1983-84	J. Francome	131	529	24.77
1984-85	J. Francome	101	374	27.01
1985-86	P. Scudamore	91	537	16.95
1986-87	P. Scudamore	123	578	21.28
1987-88	P. Scudamore	132	557	23.69
1988-89	P. Scudamore	221	663	33.33
1989-90	P. Scudamore	170	523	32.50

CHARACTERISTICS OF RACECOURSES

ASCOT—The triangular, right-handed circuit is approximately a mile and three quarters round. The turns are easy and in spite of the downhill run to the water jump in Swinley Bottom the course is galloping in nature. The sides of the triangle away from the stands have four fences each, and the circuit is completed by two plain fences in the straight of two furlongs. The finish is uphill and the course is a real test of stamina when the ground is heavy. The fences are stiff, and good jumping is essential.

AYR—The Ayr course is a left-handed circuit of one and a half miles comprising nine fences, with well-graduated turns. There is a steady downhill run to the home turn and a gentle rise to the finish. There is a run-in of 210 yards. When the going is firm the course is quite sharp.

BANGOR—Bangor has a left-handed circuit of approximately one and a half miles. Nine easy fences are jumped in a circuit and the run-in is about a furlong. The track is fairly sharp because of its many bends, and the paddock bend is very tight.

CARLISLE—The course is right-handed, pear-shaped and undulating, a mile and five furlongs in extent. The track is a particularly stiff one and the uphill home stretch is very severe. The three-mile start on the chase course is on a spur at the first bend, the horses taking the first fence only once. Normally there are nine fences to a circuit but on the final one the water jump is omitted, making a run-in of 300 yards. A long-striding galloper suited by a real test of stamina is an ideal type for Carlisle.

CARTMEL—This tight, undulating, left-handed circuit is a little over a mile round. There are six fences to a circuit and the winning post is a little over a furlong from the turn into the finishing straight, which bisects the course and which the horses enter after two circuits for races of seventeen furlongs or three circuits for twenty-five furlongs. The fences are stiff for a minor track; the run of half a mile from the last fence is the longest in the country.

CATTERICK—The Catterick course is a left-handed, oval-shaped circuit of around a mile and a quarter, with eight fences and a run-in of about 280 yards. Races over two miles and three miles start on an extension to the straight and over two miles the first fence is jumped before joining the round course. Catterick's undulations and sharp turns make it unsuitable for the long-striding galloper and ideal for the nippy, front-running type of horse.

CHELTENHAM—There are two left-handed courses at Cheltenham, the Old Course and the New Course. The Old Course is oval in shape and about one and a half miles in extent. There are nine fences to a circuit, only one of which is jumped in the final straight.
The New Course leaves the old track at the furthest point from the stands and runs parallel to it before rejoining at the entrance to the finishing straight. This circuit is a little longer than the Old Course and has ten fences, two of which are jumped in the final straight.
The most telling feature of both courses is their testing nature. The fences are stiff and the last half mile is uphill, with a run-in of just over a furlong. The four-mile and two-and-a-half-mile starts are on an extension, with five fences, which bisects both courses almost at right angles. The two-mile start is also on this extension, and two fences are jumped before reaching the main circuit.

CHEPSTOW—Chepstow is a left-handed, undulating, oval course, nearly two miles round with eleven fences to a circuit, a five-furlong home straight and a run-in of 250 yards. With five fences (four hurdles) in the straight, front runners do well here.

DEVON & EXETER—This is a tricky, hilly course. Its right-handed two-mile circuit is laid out in a long oval, with eleven fences and a run-in of over 300 yards. Only one fence is jumped twice in races of seventeen furlongs. The position of the fences varies between the summer and winter courses, the winter one having four in each straight and the summer one five in the back straight and three in the half-mile home straight which is on the rise all the way to the finish.

HAYDOCK PARK RACECOURSE

PRINCIPAL NATIONAL HUNT RACES 1990/1

WEDNESDAY, NOVEMBER 21
The Edward Hanmer Memorial Chase
The Standard Life Handicap Steeplechase
The Standard Life Handicap Hurdle
The BMW Series Chase Qualifier

THURSDAY, NOVEMBER 22
The Tim Molony Memorial Handicap Chase
The Coral Golden Hurdle Qualifier

WEDNESDAY, DECEMBER 12
The Tommy Whittle Chase
The Waterloo Pattern Hurdle
The Arlington Premier Chase Qualifier

SATURDAY, JANUARY 5
The Windowcraft Grade One Pattern Chase

SATURDAY, JANUARY 19
The Peter Marsh Chase
The Save & Prosper Champion Hurdle Trial
The Mandor Premier Long Distance Hurdle

FRIDAY, MARCH 1
The Carpenter Handicap Chase
The White Rabbit Hurdle

SATURDAY, MARCH 2
The Greenall Whitley Gold Cup Chase
The Timeform Chase
The Victor Ludorum Hurdle

N.B. The details given above are correct at time of going to press, but factors outside the control of the Haydock Park Executive may result in alterations having to be made

All enquiries to:
HAYDOCK PARK RACECOURSE, NEWTON-LE-WILLOWS, MERSEYSIDE WA12 0HQ
Phone: Ashton-in-Makerfield (0942) 727345

DONCASTER—The Doncaster course is a left-handed pear-shaped circuit of approximately two miles, and has eleven fences with a run-in of 240 yards. Only one fence is jumped twice in races over two miles. The course is flat apart from one slight hill about one and a quarter miles from the finish. This galloping track is ideal for the long-striding individual, though it would be wrong to suggest that the handy sort is unsuited by it for Doncaster is one of the fairest tracks in the country and a well-drained one too.

EDINBURGH—A right-handed oval track a little over a mile and a quarter in extent, almost flat with sharp bends, favouring the handy type of animal. There are eight fences (four in each straight) or six flights of hurdles (four in the back straight, two in the home straight) to a circuit. The two-mile start is on a spur on the last bend.

FAKENHAM—Fakenham is an undulating, sharp track, ideal for the handy, front-running type and unsuitable for the long-striding animal. The left-handed, square-shaped track has a circuit of a mile, six fences to each circuit and a run-in of 250 yards.

FOLKESTONE—The course is right-handed and approximately eleven furlongs round. The turns are easy, but the undulations can put a long-striding horse off balance. There are eight fences to a circuit, the fences relatively easy, and a run-in of about a furlong.

FONTWELL—There are two very different types of track at Fontwell, the hurdle course being left-handed, an oval about a mile in circumference with four flights, and the chase course a figure of eight with seven fences which are all in the two straight intersections linked with the hurdle course. Fontwell is not a course for the big, long-striding chaser, and despite the easy fences it can cause problems for inexperienced chasers. The unusual demands made by its layout have produced a number of track specialists over the years.

HAYDOCK—The left-handed oval-shaped circuit of a mile and five furlongs has ten fences which are spaced evenly along the back and home stretches. The fences are stiff. The last open ditch and water jump are omitted on the final circuit leaving a run-in of 440 yards. The course is flat and for chasers is of a galloping nature, as it is also for hurdlers when the old course is being used; the new hurdles course, inside the chase course, is sharp and has tight bends.

HEREFORD—Hereford's right-handed circuit of about a mile and a half is almost square and has nine fences, of which the first after the winning post has to be taken on a turn. The home turn, which is on falling ground, is pretty sharp but the other bends are easy. The fences are fairly stiff.

HEXHAM—Hexham has an undulating left-handed circuit of a mile and a half with ten fences. Although the fences are easy the course is very testing: the long back straight runs steeply downhill for most of the way but there is a steep climb from the end of the back straight to the home straight, which levels out in front of the stands. The finish is on a spur, the spur having one fence and a run-in of about a furlong.

HUNTINGDON—The course is right-handed, oval with easy bends, and is a flat, fast track about one and a half miles in length with nine fences to a circuit, some of them rather tricky. Races over two and a half miles are started on an extension of the far straight and there is a run of about a furlong to the first fence.

KELSO—The left-handed Kelso course has two tracks, the oval hurdle course of one mile 330 yards and the chase course of one mile 600 yards. There are nine fences to be jumped in a complete circuit of the chase course. The run-in, which is on an elbow, is a tiring one of 440 yards. The hurdle track is very sharp, with a particularly sharp bend after the stands.

KEMPTON—Kempton is a very fair test for a jumper; it is a flat, triangular circuit of one mile five furlongs, right-handed with a run-in from the last fence of about 175 yards. There are ten fences to a circuit.

LEICESTER—The right-handed course is rectangular in shape, a mile and three quarters in extent and has ten fences. Leicester is a stiff test and the last three furlongs are uphill. The run-in of 250 yards has a slight elbow on the chase course 150 yards from the winning post. The runners in three-mile chases miss out the first open ditch.

LINGFIELD—The new configuration at Lingfield incorporates a mile-and-a-quarter all-weather track. The original turf course, which encloses the all-weather, has been re-aligned so that the turn out of the home straight is much more gradual, but most of its characteristics remain. It is about a mile and a half in length, triangular and taken left-handed, sharp, has several gradients and a tight downhill turn into the straight. Nine fences have to be jumped in a complete circuit, while the run-in is comparatively short. The all-weather surface is Equitrack, whereas Southwell's is Fibresand.

LIVERPOOL—The Grand National course is triangular with its apex (at the Canal Turn) the furthest point from the stands. It covers two and a quarter miles and is perfectly flat throughout. Inside is the easier Mildmay course, providing a circuit of one and a half miles, which has birch fences. Despite re-alignment of the last two bends in 1989, a major feature of the Mildmay course remains its sharpness. The Grand National is run over two complete circuits taking in sixteen spruce fences first time round and fourteen the second, and the race provides one of the toughest tests ever devised for horse and rider. The run from the final fence to the winning post is 494 yards long and includes an elbow.

LUDLOW—Ludlow is a right-handed track in the shape of an oval, with a nine-fence chase circuit about a mile and a half and a run-in of 450 yards. The hurdle course, which runs on the outside of the chase course, has easier turns. Whereas the chase course is flat, the hurdle course has slight undulations but they rarely provide difficulties for a long-striding horse.

MARKET RASEN—There is a right-handed, oval circuit of a mile and a quarter, eight relatively easy fences and a run-in of 250 yards at Market Rasen. The track is sharp, covered with minor undulations, and favours the handy, nippy type of horse.

NEWBURY—The oval Newbury course is about a mile and three quarters in circumference and is set inside the Flat track, following a left-handed line. It is one of the fairest courses in the country, but the fences are stiff. The home straight is five furlongs with three plain fences, an open ditch (the water jump being omitted on the final circuit) and a run-in of 255 yards. The course is galloping in nature, with easy bends, plenty of room and few significant undulations.

NEWCASTLE—The Newcastle track is laid out inside the Flat racecourse, its left-handed circuit of one and three quarter miles containing eleven fences. There is a steady rise from the fourth last to the winning post and the course puts a premium on stamina, with the fences being on the stiff side. The ground is often testing here, too.

NEWTON ABBOT—Newton Abbot has a flat, oval, tight, left-handed circuit of about nine furlongs that favours the handy sort of horse. There are seven fences to a circuit, and a very short run-in.

NOTTINGHAM—The course has an oval circuit of about a mile and a half. The left-handed turns are easy and the home straight is over four and a half furlongs with lengthy run-ins on both hurdle and chase courses, making the track a galloping one. In races over two miles thirteen fences have to be taken.

PERTH—Perth is a right-handed circuit of one and a quarter miles, with eight fences to the circuit. The course has sweeping turns and a flat running surface. The water jump is in front of the stands and is left out on the run-in, leaving a long run from last fence to winning post.

PLUMPTON—The oblong-shaped course is only nine furlongs in circumference and has tight, left-handed bends, steep undulations, and an uphill home straight. The climb becomes pretty steep near the finish but the course is not a particularly stiff one; it favours the handy and quick-jumping types. There are seven fences to a circuit and the run-in is 200 yards.

SANDOWN—Sandown's right-handed oval course of thirteen furlongs is a testing and, for the steeplechasers, a tricky one. Of the eleven fences on a circuit seven are on the back straight, with the water jump in the middle of the line. The three fences after the water come in very quick succession and many races are won and lost here. From the home turn to 100 yards from the finish the climb is severe; there are two fences in the straight and a run-in of 220 yards. The hurdles course uses the Flat racing circuit.

SEDGEFIELD—The circuit is approximately a mile and a quarter, oval, and taken left-handed. It is essentially sharp in character and the eight fences are fairly easy, though some uphill sections of the undulating ground, notably the final 150 yards, are punishing and three-and-a-quarter-mile chases are a thorough test of stamina with a run-in of 525 yards (the water jump being left out on the last circuit of all chases). The run-in for hurdle races is 200 yards.

SOUTHWELL—The new track is laid out in a tight, level, mile-and-a-quarter oval, a spur to the three-furlong run-in providing a three-mile start. The runners go left-handed. There are two types of surface, all-weather and turf, the all-weather track being on the outside of the turf track. The all-weather surface is Fibresand whereas Lingfield's is Equitrack. The old, sharp, triangular turf track remains in a slightly modified lay-out (six fences, only one in the straight), and was used for chases in 1989/90.

STRATFORD—The sharp Stratford track is flat, triangular in shape and has a left-handed circuit of a mile and a quarter, taking in eight fences, of which only one is in the short straight before the winning post. The run-in is 200 yards.

TAUNTON—The right-handed course is a long oval, about a mile and a quarter round, and has eight fences, four in each straight. The bend after the winning post is tight and the chase run-in short.

TOWCESTER—Towcester is a right-handed course, a mile and three quarters round, and is generally against the collar. The last mile or so is very punishing with a steep climb to the home turn and a continuing rise past the winning post. Of the ten fences on the circuit, two are in the finishing straight. The run-in is 200 yards.

UTTOXETER—The course is an oval of approximately a mile and a quarter with mainly easy, sweeping, left-handed bends, and is essentially of a galloping nature, although there are minor undulations and the back stretch has slight bends. The two-mile hurdle course is among the fastest in the country. There are eight fences (the second-last seems particularly stiff), with a run-in of around 170 yards. Races of two miles, three and a quarter miles and four and a half miles are started on a spur on the last bend.

WARWICK—Warwick's left-handed course is a mile and three quarters round and there are ten fences to a circuit. The bends are rather tight and the track is a sharp one, favouring the handy horse. There is a run-in of 250 yards, the finishing straight is short and has only two fences.

WETHERBY—The course is left-handed, with easy turns and follows a long oval circuit of a mile and a half. There are nine fences, and in races over three miles all the fences are jumped twice. The slightly uphill run-in is comparatively short for the chasers. The Wetherby track provides a very fair test for any horse, but is ideal for the free-running, long-striding individual with plenty of jumping ability. The old hurdle course is much sharper in character, having a circuit of one and a quarter miles with only two hurdles in the straight.

WINCANTON—Wincanton is a galloping course with an oval, right-handed circuit of just over eleven furlongs containing nine fences. The run from the last fence is only about 200 yards.

WINDSOR—Windsor is laid out in a figure-of-eight pattern, the larger upper loop containing seven fences and the lower loop two fences. Three-mile chases take in almost two circuits. The track is flat, and sharp in nature.

WOLVERHAMPTON—The Wolverhampton course is a triangular, nine-fence circuit taken in a left-handed direction. The circuit is a mile and a half in length and is a galloping track, level throughout and with a straight of more than four furlongs. The run-in is fairly short. Hurdle races over two miles and three and a quarter miles start on a chute on the inside of the course halfway down the straight.

WORCESTER—The course is laid out in the shape of a long oval of thirteen furlongs, flat throughout with easy, left-handed turns. There are nine fences, five in the back straight, four in the home straight, and a run-in of 220 yards. The start for races over two and a quarter miles is on an extension at the beginning of the home straight and that for races over three miles is on an extension at the beginning of the back straight.

ERRATA & ADDENDA

'CHASERS & HURDLERS 1988/89'

Ben Oliver	won at Perth, not Ayr
Bonanza Boy	previous trainer Philip Hobbs
Carvill's Hill	additional form figure (at end) c25v*
Feroda	gelding, not horse
Five Lamps	won at Fontwell, not Folkestone
Greenheart	dam won twice over fences in Ireland at around 2½m
Jolejester	second foal: half-sister to useful 2m hurdler State Jester (by Free State)
Theo's Fella	dam sister to Castleruddery

'CHASERS & HURDLERS 1987/88'

Have A Barney	trainer A. L. T. Moore, Ireland

FIXTURES 1990/91

(a) Denotes all-weather jumping meeting
(aF) Denotes all-weather Flat meeting
* Denotes evening meeting

October

1 Mon. Carlisle, Fontwell, Southwell
2 Tue. Devon & Exeter
3 Wed. Cheltenham, Sedgefield
4 Thu. Cheltenham
5 Fri. Hexham
6 Sat. Chepstow, Kelso, Uttoxeter, Worcester
9 Tue. Newton Abbot
10 Wed. Plumpton, Towcester
11 Thu. Wincanton
12 Fri. Carlisle, Market Rasen
13 Sat. Ayr, Bangor, Southwell, Warwick
15 Mon. Fontwell
16 Tue. Sedgefield
17 Wed. Cheltenham, Wetherby
18 Thu. Hexham, Taunton, Uttoxeter
19 Fri. Ludlow
20 Sat. Kelso, Kempton, Southwell, Stratford
22 Mon. Fakenham
23 Tue. Plumpton
24 Wed. Ascot, Newcastle
25 Thu. Southwell, Wincanton
26 Fri. Devon & Exeter, Hereford, Newbury
27 Sat. Catterick, Huntingdon
30 Tue. Fontwell
31 Wed. Newbury, Sedgefield

November

1 Thu. Kempton, Stratford
2 Fri. Bangor, Lingfield (aF), Wetherby
3 Sat. Chepstow, Sandown, Southwell (aF), Wetherby, Worcester
5 Mon. Plumpton, Wolverhampton
6 Tue. Devon & Exeter, Hereford, Nottingham
7 Wed. Kelso, Newbury, Southwell (aF)
8 Thu. Lingfield (aF), Uttoxeter, Wincanton
9 Fri. Cheltenham, Hexham, Market Rasen
10 Sat. Cheltenham, Newcastle, Windsor
12 Mon. Carlisle, Wolverhampton
13 Tue. Sedgefield, Southwell (aF)
14 Wed. Kempton, Worcester
15 Thu. Lingfield (aF), Taunton, Towcester
16 Fri. Ascot, Ayr, Huntingdon
17 Sat. Ascot, Ayr, Catterick, Warwick
19 Mon. Bangor, Leicester, Windsor
20 Tue. Southwell (aF), Wetherby, Wolverhampton
21 Wed. Haydock, Kelso, Plumpton,
22 Thu. Haydock, Lingfield (aF), Ludlow, Wincanton
23 Fri. Leicester, Newbury, Sedgefield
24 Sat. Market Rasen, Newbury, Newcastle, Towcester
26 Mon. Catterick, Folkestone, Nottingham
27 Tue. Huntingdon, Newton Abbot, Stratford
28 Wed. Hereford, Hexham
29 Thu. Carlisle, Lingfield (aF), Taunton, Warwick
30 Fri. Bangor, Sandown, Southwell (aF)

December

1 Sat. Chepstow, Nottingham, Sandown, Wetherby
3 Mon. Kelso, Worcester
4 Tue. Fontwell, Leicester, Newcastle
5 Wed. Catterick, Huntingdon, Ludlow, Southwell (aF)
6 Thu. Lingfield (aF), Taunton, Uttoxeter, Windsor
7 Fri. Cheltenham, Devon & Exeter, Doncaster
8 Sat. Cheltenham, Doncaster, Lingfield, Towcester
10 Mon. Edinburgh, Warwick
11 Tue. Plumpton, Sedgefield
12 Wed. Haydock, Worcester
13 Thu. Haydock, Southwell (aF)
14 Fri. Catterick, Fakenham, Hereford
15 Sat. Ascot, Edinburgh, Lingfield (aF), Nottingham
18 Tue. Folkestone, Southwell (aF)
19 Wed. Bangor, Lingfield (aF)
20 Thu. Kelso, Towcester
21 Fri. Hexham, Ludlow, Uttoxeter
22 Sat. Chepstow, Edinburgh, Hereford, Lingfield
26 Wed. Huntingdon, Kempton, Market Rasen, Newton Abbot, Sedgefield, Wetherby, Wincanton, Wolverhampton
27 Thu. Kempton, Lingfield (aF), Taunton, Wetherby, Wolverhampton
28 Fri. Carlisle, Fontwell, Newbury, Stratford
29 Sat. Folkestone, Newbury, Newcastle, Southwell (aF), Warwick
31 Mon. Catterick, Cheltenham, Leicester, Plumpton, Southwell (a)

January

1 Tue. Catterick, Cheltenham, Devon & Exeter, Leicester, Lingfield (aF), Windsor
2 Wed. Ayr, Southwell (aF)
3 Thu. Ayr, Lingfield (a), Nottingham, Sedgefield
4 Fri. Edinburgh, Newton Abbot, Southwell (aF)
5 Sat. Haydock, Lingfield (aF), Market Rasen, Sandown, Worcester
7 Mon. Lingfield, Southwell (a), Wolverhampton
8 Tue. Chepstow, Leicester, Lingfield (a)
9 Wed. Kelso, Plumpton, Southwell (a)
10 Thu. Lingfield (a), Wincanton
11 Fri. Ascot, Edinburgh, Southwell (aF), Wetherby
12 Sat. Ascot, Lingfield (aF), Market Rasen, Newcastle, Warwick
14 Mon. Carlisle, Fontwell, Southwell (a)
15 Tue. Folkestone, Lingfield (a), Sedgefield
16 Wed. Ludlow, Southwell (aF), Windsor
17 Thu. Lingfield (a), Taunton
18 Fri. Catterick, Kempton, Southwell (aF), Towcester
19 Sat. Catterick, Haydock, Kempton, Lingfield (aF), Warwick
21 Mon. Leicester, Lingfield, Southwell (a)
22 Tue. Chepstow, Lingfield (aF), Nottingham
23 Wed. Sedgefield, Southwell (a), Wolverhampton
24 Thu. Huntingdon, Lingfield (a), Newton Abbot
25 Fri. Doncaster, Southwell (aF), Wincanton
26 Sat. Ayr, Cheltenham, Doncaster, Lingfield (aF)
28 Mon. Ayr, Plumpton, Southwell (a)
29 Tue. Leicester, Lingfield (a), Sedgefield
30 Wed. Nottingham, Southwell (aF), Windsor
31 Thu. Edinburgh, Lingfield (a), Towcester

February

1 Fri. Bangor, Kelso, Lingfield, Southwell (aF)
2 Sat. Chepstow, Lingfield (aF), Sandown, Stratford, Wetherby
4 Mon. Fontwell, Southwell (a), Wolverhampton
5 Tue. Carlisle, Lingfield (aF), Warwick
6 Wed. Ascot, Ludlow, Southwell (a)
7 Thu. Huntingdon, Lingfield (a), Wincanton
8 Fri. Newbury, Sedgefield, Southwell (aF)
9 Sat. Ayr, Catterick, Lingfield (aF), Newbury, Uttoxeter
11 Mon. Hereford, Plumpton, Southwell (a)
12 Tue. Lingfield (a), Newton Abbot, Towcester
13 Wed. Ayr, Folkestone, Southwell (aF), Worcester
14 Thu. Leicester, Lingfield (a), Sandown, Taunton
15 Fri. Edinburgh, Fakenham, Sandown, Southwell (aF)
16 Sat. Chepstow, Lingfield (aF), Newcastle, Nottingham, Windsor
18 Mon. Fontwell, Southwell (a), Wolverhampton
19 Tue. Huntingdon, Lingfield (aF), Sedgefield
20 Wed. Catterick, Southwell (a), Warwick
21 Thu. Folkestone, Lingfield (a), Wincanton
22 Fri. Kelso, Kempton, Southwell (aF)
23 Sat. Doncaster, Edinburgh, Kempton, Lingfield (aF), Stratford
25 Mon. Doncaster, Leicester, Lingfield, Southwell (a)
26 Tue. Lingfield (a), Nottingham
27 Wed. Plumpton, Southwell (aF), Wetherby, Worcester
28 Thu. Lingfield (a), Ludlow

March

1 Fri. Haydock, Newbury, Southwell (aF)
2 Sat. Haydock, Hereford, Lingfield (aF), Market Rasen, Newbury
4 Mon. Leicester, Southwell (a), Windsor
5 Tue. Lingfield (aF), Sedgefield, Warwick
6 Wed. Bangor, Catterick, Folkestone, Southwell (a)
7 Thu. Lingfield (a), Stratford, Wincanton
8 Fri. Carlisle, Market Rasen, Sandown, Southwell (aF)
9 Sat. Ayr, Chepstow, Doncaster, Lingfield (aF), Sandown
11 Mon. Ayr, Plumpton
12 Tue. Cheltenham, Lingfield (aF), Sedgefield
13 Wed. Cheltenham, Newton Abbot
14 Thu. Cheltenham, Hexham
15 Fri. Fakenham, Lingfield, Wolverhampton
16 Sat. Chepstow, Lingfield, Newcastle, Southwell (aF), Uttoxeter
18 Mon. Newcastle, Wolverhampton
19 Tue. Fontwell, Nottingham
20 Wed. Kelso, Southwell (aF), Worcester
21 Thu. Devon & Exeter, Towcester

22 Fri. Ludlow, Newbury
23 Sat. Bangor, Hexham, Lingfield (aF), Newbury
25 Mon. Hexham
26 Tue. Sandown
27 Wed. Worcester
28 Thu. Southwell, Taunton
30 Sat. Carlisle, Newton Abbot, Plumpton, Southwell, Towcester

April

1 Mon. Carlisle, Chepstow, Fakenham, Hereford, Huntingdon, Market Rasen, Newton Abbot, Plumpton, Towcester, Uttoxeter, Wetherby, Wincanton
2 Tue. Chepstow, Uttoxeter, Wetherby
3 Wed. Worcester
4 Thu. Liverpool
5 Fri. Devon & Exeter, Liverpool
6 Sat. Hereford, Liverpool
8 Mon. Kelso
10 Wed. Ascot, Ludlow
11 Thu. Taunton
12 Fri. Plumpton, Wincanton
13 Sat. Ascot, Southwell
15 Mon. Huntingdon
16 Tue. Fontwell, Sedgefield
17 Wed. Cheltenham
18 Thu. Ayr, Cheltenham
19 Fri. Ayr
20 Sat. Ayr, Bangor, Stratford
23 Tue. Perth
24 Wed. Perth
25 Thu. Ludlow, Perth, Wincanton*
26 Fri. Southwell, Taunton*
27 Sat. Hexham, Market Rasen, Sandown, Worcester*
29 Mon. Hexham*
30 Tue. Ascot*, Sedgefield*

May

1 Wed. Cheltenham*, Kelso
2 Thu. Newton Abbot*
3 Fri. Newton Abbot
4 Sat. Hereford, Hexham*, Uttoxeter
6 Mon. Devon & Exeter, Fontwell, Haydock, Ludlow, Newcastle, Southwell, Warwick
7 Tue. Chepstow, Sedgefield*
8 Wed. Wetherby*, Worcester*
9 Thu. Huntingdon*, Uttoxeter*
10 Fri. Stratford*, Taunton*
11 Sat. Market Rasen*, Newcastle*, Warwick*
14 Tue. Folkestone*, Newton Abbot, Towcester*
15 Wed. Hereford, Newton Abbot*, Perth*
16 Thu. Huntingdon*, Perth
17 Fri. Stratford*
18 Sat. Bangor, Warwick*
22 Wed. Worcester
24 Fri. Sedgefield, Towcester
25 Sat. Cartmel, Hexham
27 Mon. Cartmel, Devon & Exeter, Fakenham, Fontwell, Hereford, Hexham*, Huntingdon, Uttoxeter, Wetherby
28 Tue. Uttoxeter*
29 Wed. Cartmel
31 Fri. Stratford*

June

1 Sat. Market Rasen*, Stratford

BIG RACE RESULTS

GRAND NATIONAL (Liverpool, 4m 856yds)

1946 £8,805
1. **Lovely Cottage** 9-10-8 *(Capt R. Petre)*
2. Jack Finlay 7-10-2 *(W. Kidney)*
3. Prince Regent 11-12-5 *(T. Hyde)*

SP: 25/1; 100/1; 3/1 43 ran
T. Rayson 4:3

1947 £10,007
1. **Caughoo** 8-10-0 *(E. Dempsey)*
2. Lough Conn 11-10-1 *(D. McCann)*
3. Kami 10-10-13 *(Mr J. Hislop)*

SP: 100/1; 33/1; 33/1 57 ran
H. McDowell, in Ireland 20:4

1948 £9,103
1. **Sheila's Cottage** 9-10-7 *(A. Thompson)*
2. First of the Dandies 11-10-4 *(J. Brogan)*
3. Cromwell 7-10-11 *(Lord Mildmay)*

SP: 50/1; 25/1; 33/1 43 ran
N. Crump 1:6

1949 £9,528
1. **Russian Hero** 9-10-8 *(L. McMorrow)*
2. Roimond 8-11-12 *(R. Francis)*
3. Royal Mount 10-10-12 *(P. Doyle)*

SP: 66/1; 22/1; 18/1 43 ran
G. Owen 8:1

1950 £9,314
1. **Freebooter** 9-11-11 *(J. Power)*
2. Wot No Sun 8-11-8 *(A. Thompson)*
3. Acthon Major 10-11-2 *(R. J. O'Ryan)*

SP: 10/1; 100/7; 33/1 49 ran
R. Renton 15:10

1951 £8,815
1. **Nickel Coin** 9-10-1 *(J. Bullock)*
2. Royal Tan 7-10-13 *(Mr A. O'Brien)*
3. Derrinstown 11-10-0 *(A. Power)*

SP: 40/1; 22/1; 66/1 36 ran
J. O'Donoghue 6:bad

1952 £9,268
1. **Teal** 10-10-12 *(A. Thompson)*
2. Legal Joy 9-10-4 *(M. Scudamore)*
3. Wot No Sun 10-11-7 *(D. Dick)*

SP: 100/7; 100/6; 33/1 47 ran
N. Crump 5:bad

1953 £9,330
1. **Early Mist** 8-11-2 *(B. Marshall)*
2. Mont Tremblant 7-12-5 *(D. Dick)*
3. Irish Lizard 10-10-6 *(R. Turnell)*

SP: 20/1; 18/1; 33/1 31 ran
M. V. O'Brien, in Ireland 20:4

1954 £8,571
1. **Royal Tan** 10-11-7 *(B. Marshall)*
2. Tudor Line 9-10-7 *(G. Slack)*
3. Irish Lizard 11-10-5 *(M. Scudamore)*

SP: 8/1; 10/1; 15/2 29 ran
M. V. O'Brien, in Ireland nk:10

1955 £8,934
1. **Quare Times** 9-11-0 *(P. Taaffe)*
2. Tudor Line 10-11-3 *(G. Slack)*
3. Carey's Cottage 8-10-11 *(T. Taaffe)*

SP: 100/9; 10/1; 20/1 30 ran
M. V. O'Brien, in Ireland 12:4

1956 £8,695
1. **E.S.B.** 10-11-3 *(D. Dick)*
2. Gentle Moya 10-10-2 *(G. Milburn)*
3. Royal Tan 12-12-1 *(T. Taaffe)*

SP: 100/7; 22/1; 28/1 29 ran
F. Rimell 10:10

1957 £8,868
1. **Sundew** 11-11-7 *(F. Winter)*
2. Wyndburgh 7-10-7 *(M. Batchelor)*
3. Tiberetta 9-10-0 *(A. Oughton)*

SP: 20/1; 25/1; 66/1 35 ran
F. Hudson 8:6

1958 £13,719
1. **Mr What** 8-10-6 *(A. Freeman)*
2. Tiberetta 10-10-6 *(G. Slack)*
3. Green Drill 8-10-10 *(G. Milburn)*

SP: 18/1; 28/1; 28/1 31 ran
T. Taaffe, in Ireland 30:15

1959 £13,646
1. **Oxo** 8-10-13 *(M. Scudamore)*
2. Wyndburgh 9-10-12 *(T. Brookshaw)*
3. Mr What 9-11-9 *(T. Taaffe)*

SP: 8/1; 10/1; 6/1 34 ran
W. Stephenson 1½:8

1960 £13,134
1. **Merryman II** 9-10-12 *(G. Scott)*
2. Badanloch 9-10-9 *(S. Mellor)*
3. Clear Profit 10-10-1 *(B. Wilkinson)*

SP: 13/2 100/7; 20/1 26 ran
N. Crump 15:12

1961 £20,020
1. **Nicolaus Silver** 9-10-1 *(H. Beasley)*
2. Merryman II 10-11-12 *(D. Ancil)*
3. O'Malley Point 10-11-4 *(P. Farrell)*

SP: 28/1; 8/1; 100/6 35 ran
F. Rimell 5:nk

1962 £20,238
1. **Kilmore** 12-10-4 *(F. Winter)*
2. Wyndburgh 12-10-9 *(T. Barnes)*
3. Mr What 12-10-9 *(J. Lehane)*

SP: 28/1; 45/1; 22/1 32 ran
R. Price 10:10

1963 £21,315
1. **Ayala** 9-10-0 *(P. Buckley)*
2. Carrickbeg 7-10-3 *(Mr J. Lawrence)*
3. Hawa's Song 10-10-0 *(P. Broderick)*

SP: 66/1; 20/1; 28/1 47 ran
K. Piggott ¾:5

1964 £20,280
1. **Team Spirit** 12-10-3 *(G. W. Robinson)*
2. Purple Silk 9-10-4 *(J. Kenneally)*
3. Peacetown 10-10-1 *(R. Edwards)*

SP: 18/1; 100/6; 40/1 33 ran
F. Walwyn ½:6

1965 £22,041
1. **Jay Trump** 8-11-5 *(Mr C. Smith)*
2. Freddie 8-11-10 *(P. McCarron)*
3. Mr Jones 10-11-5 *(Mr C. Collins)*

SP: 100/6; 7/2; 50/1 47 ran
F. Winter ¾:20

1966 £22,334
1. **Anglo** 8-10-0 *(T. Norman)*
2. Freddie 9-11-7 *(P. McCarron)*
3. Forest Prince 8-10-8 *(G. Scott)*

SP: 50/1; 11/4; 100/7 47 ran
F. Winter 20:5

1967 £17,630
1. **Foinavon** 9-10-0 *(J. Buckingham)*
2. Honey End 10-10-4 *(J. Gifford)*
3. Red Alligator 8-10-0 *(B. Fletcher)*

SP: 100/1; 15/2; 30/1 44 ran
J. Kempton 15:3

1968 £17,848
1. **Red Alligator** 9-10-0 *(B. Fletcher)*
2. Moidore's Token 11-10-8 *(B. Brogan)*
3. Different Class 8-11-5 *(D. Mould)*

SP: 100/7; 100/6; 17/2 45 ran
Denys Smith 20:nk

1969 £17,849
1. **Highland Wedding** 12-10-4 *(E. P. Harty)*
2. Steel Bridge 11-10-0 *(R. Pitman)*
3. Rondetto 13-10-6 *(J. King)*

SP: 100/9; 50/1; 25/1 30 ran
G. Balding 12:1

1970 £14,804
1. **Gay Trip** 8-11-5 *(P. Taaffe)*
2. Vulture 8-10-0 *(S. Barker)*
3. Miss Hunter 9-10-0 *(F. Shortt)*

SP: 15/1; 15/1; 33/1 28 ran
F. Rimell 20:½

1971 £15,500
1. **Specify** 9-10-13 *(J. Cook)*
2. Black Secret 7-11-5 *(Mr J. Dreaper)*
3. Astbury 8-10-0 *(J. Bourke)*

SP: 28/1; 20/1; 33/1 38 ran
J. E. Sutcliffe nk:2½

1972 £25,765
1. **Well To Do** 9-10-1 *(G. Thorner)*
2. Gay Trip 10-11-9 *(T. Biddlecombe)*
3. Black Secret 8-11-2 *(S. Barker)*
3. General Symons 9-10-0 *(P. Kiely)*

SP: 14/1; 12/1; 40/1 42 ran
T. Forster 2:3:d.h

1973 £25,486
1. **Red Rum** 8-10-5 *(B. Fletcher)*
2. Crisp 10-12-0 *(R. Pitman)*
3. L'Escargot 10-12-0 *(T. Carberry)*

SP: 9/1; 9/1; 11/1 38 ran
D. McCain ¾:25

1974 £25,102
1. **Red Rum** 9-12-0 *(B. Fletcher)*
2. L'Escargot 11-11-13 *(T. Carberry)*
3. Charles Dickens 10-10-0 *(A. Turnell)*

SP: 11/1; 17/2; 50/1 42 ran
D. McCain 7:s.hd

1975 £38,005
1. **L'Escargot** 12-11-3 *(T. Carberry)*
2. Red Rum 10-12-0 *(B. Fletcher)*
3. Spanish Steps 12-10-3 *(W. Smith)*

SP: 13/2; 7/2; 20/1 31 ran
D. L. Moore, in Ireland 15:8

1976 £37,420
1. **Rag Trade** 10-10-12 *(J. Burke)*
2. Red Rum 11-11-10 *(T. Stack)*
3. Eyecatcher 10-10-7 *(B. Fletcher)*

SP: 14/1; 10/1; 28/1 32 ran
F. Rimell 2:8

1977 £41,140
1. **Red Rum** 12-11-8 *(T. Stack)*
2. Churchtown Boy 10-10-0 *(M. Blackshaw)*
3. Eyecatcher 11-10-1 *(C. Read)*

SP: 9/1; 20/1; 18/1 42 ran
D. McCain 25:6

1978 £39,092
1. **Lucius** 9-10-9 *(R. Davies)*
2. Sebastian V 10-10-1 *(R. Lamb)*
3. Drumroan 10-10-0 *(G. Newman)*

SP: 14/1; 25/1; 50/1 37 ran
G. Richards ½:nk

1979 £40,506
1. **Rubstic** 10-10-0 *(M. Barnes)*
2. Zongalero 9-10-5 *(B. R. Davies)*
3. Rough And Tumble 9-10-7 *(J. Francome)*

SP: 25/1; 20/1; 14/1 34 ran
S. Leadbetter 1½:5

1980 £45,595

1. **Ben Nevis** 12-10-12 *(Mr C. Fenwick)*
2. Rough And Tumble 10-10-11 *(J. Francome)*
3. The Pilgarlic 12-10-4 *(R. Hyett)*

SP: 40/1; 11/1; 33/1 30 ran
T. Forster 20:10

1981 £51,324

1. **Aldaniti** 11-10-13 *(R. Champion)*
2. Spartan Missile 9-11-5 *(Mr J. Thorne)*
3. Royal Mail 11-11-7 *(P. Blacker)*

SP: 10/1; 8/1; 16/1 39 ran
J. Gifford 4:2

1982 £52,507

1. **Grittar** 9-11-5 *(Mr R. Saunders)*
2. Hard Outlook 11-10-1 *(A. Webber)*
3. Loving Words 9-10-11 *(R. Hoare)*

SP: 7/1; 50/1; 16/1 39 ran
F. Gilman 15:dist

1983 52,949

1. **Corbiere** 8-11-4 *(B. de Haan)*
2. Greasepaint 8-10-7 *(Mr C. Magnier)*
3. Yer Man 8-10-0 *(T. O'Connell)*

SP: 13/1; 14/1; 80/1 41 ran
Mrs J. Pitman ¾:20

1984 £54,769

1. **Hallo Dandy** 10-10-2 *(N. Doughty)*
2. Greasepaint 9-11-2 *(T. Carmody)*
3. Corbiere 9-12-0 *(B. de Haan)*

SP: 13/1; 9/1; 16/1 40 ran
G. Richards 4:1½

1985 £54,314

1. **Last Suspect** 11-10-5 *(H. Davies)*
2. Mr Snugfit 8-10-0 *(P. Tuck)*
3. Corbiere 10-11-10 *(P. Scudamore)*

SP: 50/1; 12/1; 9/1 40 ran
T. Forster 1½:3

1986 £60,647

1. **West Tip** 9-10-11 *(R. Dunwoody)*
2. Young Driver 9-10-0 *(C. Grant)*
3. Classified 10-10-3 *(S. Smith Eccles)*

SP: 15/2; 66/1; 22/1 40 ran
M. Oliver 2:20

1987 £64,710

1 **Maori Venture** 11-10-13 *(S. C. Knight)*
2. The Tsarevich 11-10-5 *(J. White)*
3. Lean Ar Aghaidh 10-10-0 *(G. Landau)*

SP: 28/1; 20/1; 14/1 40 ran
A. Turnell 5:4

1988 £68,740

1. **Rhyme 'N' Reason** 6-11-0 *(B. Powell)*
2. Durham Edition 10-10-9 *(C. Grant)*
3. Monanore 11-10-4 *(T. Taaffe)*

SP: 10/1; 20/1; 33/1 40 ran
D. Elsworth 4:15

1989 £66,840

1. **Little Polveir** 12-10-3 *(J. Frost)*
2. West Tip 12-10-11 *(R. Dunwoody)*
3. The Thinker 11-11-10 *(S. Sherwood)*

SP: 28/1; 12/1; 10/1 40 ran
G. Balding 7:½

1990 £70,871

1. **Mr Frisk** 11-10-6 *(Mr M. Armytage)*
2. Durham Edition 12-10-9 *(C. Grant)*
3. Rinus 9-10-4 *(N. Doughty)*

SP: 16/1; 9/1; 13/1 38 ran
K. Bailey ¾:20

GOLD CUP (Cheltenham, 3¼m)

1946 £1,130
1. **Prince Regent** 11-12-0 *(T. Hyde)*
2. Poor Flame 8-12-0 *(F. Rimell)*
3. Red April 9-12-0 *(G. Kelly)*

SP: 4/7; 5/1; 9/2 6 ran
T. Dreaper, in Ireland 5:4

1947 £1,140
1. **Fortina** 6-12-0 *(Mr R. Black)*
2. Happy Home 8-12-0 *(D. L. Moore)*
3. Prince Blackthorn 9-12-0 *(R. Turnell)*

SP: 8/1; 3/1; 8/1 12 ran
H. Christie 10:6

1948 £1,911
1. **Cottage Rake** 9-12-0 *(A. Brabazon)*
2. Happy Home 9-12-0 *(M. Molony)*
3. Coloured School Boy 8-12-0 *(E. Vinall)*

SP: 10/1; 6/1; 10/1 12 ran
M. V. O'Brien, in Ireland 1½:10

1949 £2,817
1. **Cottage Rake** 10-12-0 *(A. Brabazon)*
2. Cool Customer 10-12-0 *(P. Murphy)*
3. Coloured School Boy 9-12-0 *(E. Vinall)*

SP: 4/6; 13/2; 8/1 6 ran
M. V. O'Brien, in Ireland 2:6

1950 £2,936
1. **Cottage Rake** 11-12-0 *(A. Brabazon)*
2. Finnure 9-12-0 *(M. Molony)*
3. Garde Toi 9-12-0 *(Marquis de Portago)*

SP: 5/6; 5/4; 100/1 6 ran
M. V. O'Brien, in Ireland 10:8

1951 £2,783
1. **Silver Fame** 12-12-0 *(M. Molony)*
2. Greenogue 9-12-0 *(G. Kelly)*
3. Mighty Fine 9-12-0 *(J. Bullock)*

SP: 6/4; 100/8; 10/1 6 ran
G. Beeby s.hd:2

1952 £3,232
1. **Mont Tremblant** 6-12-0 *(D. Dick)*
2. Shaef 8-12-0 *(F. Winter)*
3. Galloway Braes 7-12-0 *(R. Morrow)*

SP: 8/1; 7/1; 66/1 13 ran
F. Walwyn 10:4

1953 £3,258
1. **Knock Hard** 9-12-0 *(T. Molony)*
2. Halloween 8-12-0 *(F. Winter)*
3. Galloway Braes 8-12-0 *(R. Morrow)*

SP: 11/2; 5/2; 33/1 12 ran
M. V. O'Brien, in Ireland 5:2

1954 £3,576
1. **Four Ten** 8-12-0 *(T. Cusack)*
2. Mariner's Log 7-12-0 *(P. Taaffe)*
3. Halloween 9-12-0 *(G. Slack)*

SP: 100/6; 20/1; 100/6 6 ran
J. Roberts 4:4

1955 £3,775
1. **Gay Donald** 9-12-0 *(A. Grantham)*
2. Halloween 10-12-0 *(F. Winter)*
3. Four Ten 9-12-0 *(T. Cusack)*

SP: 33/1; 7/2; 3/1 9 ran
J. Ford 10:8

1956 £3,750
1. **Limber Hill** 9-12-0 *(J. Power)*
2. Vigor 8-12-0 *(R. Emery)*
3. Halloween 11-12-0 *(F. Winter)*

SP: 11/8; 50/1; 100/8 11 ran
W. Dutton 4:1½

1957 £3,996
1. **Linwell** 9-12-0 *(M. Scudamore)*
2. Kerstin 7-12-0 *(G. Milburn)*
3. Rose Park 11-12-0 *(G. Nicholls)*

SP: 100/9; 6/1; 100/8 13 ran
C. Mallon 1:5

1958 £5,788
1. **Kerstin** 8-12-0 *(S. Hayhurst)*
2. Polar Flight 8-12-0 *(G. Slack)*
3. Gay Donald 12-12-0 *(F. Winter)*

SP: 7/1; 11/2; 13/2 9 ran
C. Bewicke ½:bad

1959 £5,363
1. **Roddy Owen** 10-12-0 *(H. Beasley)*
2. Linwell 11-12-0 *(F. Winter)*
3. Lochroe 11-12-0 *(A. Freeman)*

SP: 5/1; 11/2; 100/9 11 ran
D. Morgan, in Ireland 3:10

1960 £5,414
1. **Pas Seul** 7-12-0 *(W. Rees)*
2. Lochroe 12-12-0 *(D. Mould)*
3. Zonda 9-12-0 *(G. W. Robinson)*

SP: 6/1; 25/1; 8/1 12 ran
R. Turnell 1:5

1961 £6,043
1. **Saffron Tartan** 10-12-0 *(F. Winter)*
2. Pas Seul 8-12-0 *(D. Dick)*
3. Mandarin 10-12-0 *(P. Madden)*

SP: 2/1; 100/30; 100/7 11 ran
D. Butchers 1½:3

1962 £5,720
1. **Mandarin** 11-12-0 *(F. Winter)*
2. Fortria 10-12-0 *(P. Taaffe)*
3. Cocky Consort 9-12-0 *(C. Stobbs)*

SP: 7/2; 3/1; 50/1 9 ran
F. Walwyn 1:10

1963 £5,958
1. **Mill House** 6-12-0 *(G. W. Robinson)*
2. Fortria 11-12-0 *(P. Taaffe)*
3. Duke of York 8-12-0 *(F. Winter)*

SP: 7/2; 4/1; 7/1 12 ran
F. Walwyn 12:4

1964 £8,004
1. **Arkle** 7-12-0 *(P. Taaffe)*
2. Mill House 7-12-0 *(G. W. Robinson)*
3. Pas Seul 11-12-0 *(D. Dick)*

SP: 7/4; 8/13; 50/1 4 ran
T. Dreaper, in Ireland 5:25

1965 £7,986
1. **Arkle** 8-12-0 *(P. Taaffe)*
2. Mill House 8-12-0 *(G. W. Robinson)*
3. Stoney Crossing 7-12-0 *(Mr W. Roycroft)*

SP: 30/100; 100/30; 100/1 4 ran
T. Dreaper, in Ireland 20:30

1966 £7,674
1. **Arkle** 9-12-0 *(P. Taaffe)*
2. Dormant 9-12-0 *(M. Scudamore)*
3. Snaigow 7-12-0 *(D. Nicholson)*

SP: 1/10; 20/1; 100/7 5 ran
T. Dreaper, in Ireland 30:10

1967 £7,999
1. **Woodland Venture** 7-12-0 *(T. Biddlecombe)*
2. Stalbridge Colonist 8-12-0 *(S. Mellor)*
3. What A Myth 10-12-0 *(P. Kelleway)*

SP: 100/8; 11/2; 3/1 8 ran
F. Rimell ¾:2

1968 £7,713
1. **Fort Leney** 10-12-0 *(P. Taaffe)*
2. The Laird 7-12-0 *(J. King)*
3. Stalbridge Colonist 9-12-0 *(T. Biddlecombe)*

SP: 11/2; 3/1; 7/2 5 ran
T. Dreaper, in Ireland nk:1

1969 £8,129
1. **What A Myth** 12-12-0 *(P. Kelleway)*
2. Domacorn 7-12-0 *(T. Biddlecombe)*
3. Playlord 8-12-0 *(R. Barry)*

SP: 8/1; 7/2; 4/1 11 ran
R. Price 1½:20

1970 £8,103
1. **L'Escargot** 7-12-0 *(T. Carberry)*
2. French Tan 8-12-0 *(P. Taaffe)*
3. Spanish Steps 7-12-0 *(J. Cook)*

SP: 33/1; 81; 9/4 12 ran
D. L. Moore, in Ireland 1½:10

1971 £7,995
1. **L'Escargot** 8-12-0 *(T. Carberry)*
2. Leap Frog 7-12-0 *(V. O'Brien)*
3. The Dikler 8-12-0 *(B. Brogan)*

SP: 7/2; 7/2; 15/2 8 ran
D. L. Moore, in Ireland 10:15

1972 £15,255
1. **Glencaraig Lady** 8-12-0 *(F. Berry)*
2. Royal Toss 10-12-0 *(N. Wakley)*
3. The Dikler 9-12-0 *(B. Brogan)*

SP: 6/1; 22/1; 11/1 12 ran
F. Flood, in Ireland ¾:hd

1973 £15,125
1. **The Dikler** 10-12-0 *(R. Barry)*
2. Pendil 8-12-0 *(R. Pitman)*
3. Charlie Potheen 8-12-0 *(T. Biddlecombe)*

SP: 9/1; 4/6; 9/2 8 ran
F. Walwyn s.hd:6

1974 £14,572
1. **Captain Christy** 7-12-0 *(H. Beasley)*
2. The Dikler 11-12-0 *(R. Barry)*
3. Game Spirit 8-12-0 *(T. Biddlecombe)*

SP: 7/1; 5/1; 20/1 7 ran
P. Taaffe, in Ireland 5:20

1975 £17,757
1. **Ten Up** 8-12-0 *(T. Carberry)*
2. Soothsayer 8-12-0 *(R. Pitman)*
3. Bula 10-12-0 *(J. Francome)*

SP: 2/1; 28/1; 5/1 8 ran
J. Dreaper, in Ireland 6:½

1976 £18,134
1. **Royal Frolic** 7-12-0 *(J. Burke)*
2. Brown Lad 10-12-0 *(T. Carberry)*
3. Colebridge 12-12-0 *(F. Berry)*

SP: 14/1; 13/8; 12/1 11 ran
F. Rimell 5:5

1977 £21,990
1. **Davy Lad** 7-12-0 *(D. T. Hughes)*
2. Tied Cottage 9-12-0 *(T. Carberry)*
3. Summerville 11-12-0 *(J. King)*

SP: 14/1; 20/1; 15/1 13 ran
M. O'Toole, in Ireland 6:20

1978 £23,827
1. **Midnight Court** 7-12-0 *(J. Francome)*
2. Brown Lad 12-12-0 *(T. Carberry)*
3. Master H 9-12-0 *(R. Crank)*

SP: 5/2; 8/1; 18/1 10 ran
F. Winter 7:1

1979 £30,293
1. **Alverton** 9-12-0 *(J. J. O'Neill)*
2. Royal Mail 9-12-0 *(P. Blacker)*
3. Aldaniti 9-12-0 *(R. Champion)*

SP: 5/1; 7/1; 40/1 14 ran
M. H. Easterby 25:20

1980 £35,997

1. **Master Smudge** 8-12-0 *(R. Hoare)*
2. Mac Vidi 15-12-0 *(P. Leach)*
3. Approaching 9-12-0 *(B. R. Davies)*

SP: 14/1; 66/1; 11/1 15 ran
A. Barrow 5:2½

1981 £44,259

1. **Little Owl** 7-12-0 *(Mr A. J. Wilson)*
2. Night Nurse 10-12-0 *(A. Brown)*
3. Silver Buck 9-12-0 *(T. Carmody)*

SP: 6/1; 6/1; 7/2 15 ran
M. H. Easterby 1½:10

1982 £48,386

1. **Silver Buck** 10-12-0 *(R. Earnshaw)*
2. Bregawn 8-12-0 *(G. Bradley)*
3. Sunset Cristo 8-12-0 *(C. Grant)*

SP: 8/1; 18/1; 100/1 22 ran
M. Dickinson 2:12

1983 £45,260

1. **Bregawn** 9-12-0 *(G. Bradley)*
2. Captain John 9-12-0 *(D. Goulding)*
3. Wayward Lad 8-12-0 *(J. J. O'Neill)*

SP: 100/30; 11/1; 6/1 11 ran
M. Dickinson 5:1½

1984 £47,375

1. **Burrough Hill Lad** 8-12-0 *(P. Tuck)*
2. Brown Chamberlin 9-12-0 *(J. Francome)*
3. Drumlargan 10-12-0 *(Mr F. Codd)*

SP: 7/2; 5/1; 16/1 12 ran
Mrs J. Pitman 3:8

1985 £52,560

1. **Forgive'N Forget** 8-12-0 *(M. Dwyer)*
2. Righthand Man 8-12-0 *(G. Bradley)*
3. Earls Brig 10-12-0 *(P. Tuck)*

SP: 7/1; 15/2; 13/2 15 ran
J. FitzGerald 1½:2½

1986 £54,900

1. **Dawn Run** 8-11-9 *(J. J. O'Neill)*
2. Wayward Lad 11-12-0 *(G. Bradley)*
3. Forgive'N Forget 9-12-0 *(M. Dwyer)*

SP: 15/8; 8/1; 7/2 11 ran
P. Mullins, in Ireland 1:2½

1987 £55,500

1. **The Thinker** 9-12-0 *(R. Lamb)*
2. Cybrandian 9-12-0 *(C. Grant)*
3. Door Latch 9-12-0 *(R. Rowe)*

SP: 13/2; 25/1; 9/1 12 ran
W. A. Stephenson 1½:2½

1988 £61,960

1. **Charter Party** 10-12-0 *(R. Dunwoody)*
2. Cavvies Clown 8-12-0 *(S. Sherwood)*
3. Beau Ranger 10-12-0 *(P. Scudamore)*

SP: 10/1; 6/1; 33/1 15 ran
D. Nicholson 6:10

1989 £66,635

1. **Desert Orchid** 10-12-0 *(S. Sherwood)*
2. Yahoo 8-12-0 *(T. Morgan)*
3. Charter Party 11-12-0 *(R. Dunwoody)*

SP: 5/2; 25/1; 14/1 13 ran
D. Elsworth 1½:8

1990 £67,003

1. **Norton's Coin** 6-12-0 *(G. McCourt)*
2. Toby Tobias 8-12-0 *(M. Pitman)*
3. Desert Orchid 11-12-0 *(R. Dunwoody)*

SP: 100/1; 8/1; 10/11 12 ran
S. Griffiths ¾:4

CHAMPION HURDLE (Cheltenham, 2m)

1946 £980

1. **Distel** 5-11-10 *(R. J. O'Ryan)*
2. Carnival Boy 5-11-10 *(F. Rimell)*
3. Robin O'Chantry 6-12-0 *(J. Goodgame)*

SP: 4/5; 7/2; 100/6 8 ran
C. Rogers, in Ireland 4:½

1947 £1,035

1. **National Spirit** 6-12-0 *(D. Morgan)*
2. Le Paillon 5-11-10 *(A. Head)*
3. Freddy Fox 8-12-0 *(R. Smyth)*

SP: 7/1; 2/1; 8/1 13 ran
V. Smyth 1:2

1948 £2,068

1. **National Spirit** 7-12-0 *(R. Smyth)*
2. D.U.K.W. 5-11-10 *(J. Maguire)*
3. Encoroli 5-11-10 *(M. Connors)*

SP: 6/4; 5/1; 20/1 12 ran
V. Smyth 2:¾

1949 £2,299

1. **Hatton's Grace** 9-12-0 *(A. Brabazon)*
2. Vatelys 9-12-0 *(R. Bates)*
3. Captain Fox 4-11-0 *(K. Mullins)*

SP: 1007; 10/1; 100/9 14 ran
M. V. O'Brien, in Ireland 6:1

1950 £2,427

1. **Hatton's Grace** 10-12-0 *(A. Brabazon)*
2. Harlech 5-11-12 *(M. Molony)*
3. Speciality 5-11-12 *(K. Mullins)*

SP: 5/2; 9/2; 100/6 12 ran
M. V. O'Brien, in Ireland 1½:2

1951 £3,615

1. **Hatton's Grace** 11-12-0 *(T. Molony)*
2. Pyrrhus III 8-12-0 *(A. Gill)*
3. Prince Hindou 5-11-12 *(M. Larraun)*

SP: 4/1; 11/2; 9/2 8 ran
M. V. O'Brien, in Ireland 5:½

1952 £3,632

1. **Sir Ken** 5-11-12 *(T. Molony)*
2. Noholme 5-11-12 *(B. Marshall)*
3. Approval 6-12-0 *(D. Dillon)*

SP: 3/1; 100/7; 9/1 16 ran
W. Stephenson 2:4

1953 £3,479

1. **Sir Ken** 6-12-0 *(T. Molony)*
2. Galatian 6-12-0 *(B. Marshall)*
3. Teapot II 8-12-0 *(P. Taaffe)*

SP: 2/5; 4/1; 100/9 7 ran
W. Stephenson 2:1½

1954 £3,657

1. **Sir Ken** 7-12-0 *(T. Molony)*
2. Impney 5-11-12 *(M. Pumfrey)*
3. Galatian 7-12-0 *(P. Taaffe)*

SP: 4/9; 9/1; 10/1 13 ran
W. Stephenson 1:3

1955 £3,717

1. **Clair Soleil** 6-12-0 *(F. Winter)*
2. Stroller 7-12-0 *(T. P. Burns)*
3. Cruachan 7-12-0 *(G. Slack)*

SP: 5/2; 7/2; 50/1 21 ran
R. Price hd:4

1956 £3,300

1. **Doorknocker** 8-12-0 *(H. Sprague)*
2. Quita Que 7-12-0 *(Mr J. Cox)*
3. Baby Don 6-12-0 *(T. Molony)*

SP: 100/9; 33/1; 100/8 14 ran
W. Hall ¾:4

1957 £3,729

1. **Merry Deal** 7-12-0 *(G. Underwood)*
2. Quita Que 8-12-0 *(Mr J. Cox)*
3. Tout ou Rien 5-11-12 *(R. Emery)*

SP: 28/1; 15/2; 100/8 16 ran
A. Jones 5:5

1958 £4,812

1. **Bandalore** 7-12-0 *(G. Slack)*
2. Tokoroa 7-12-0 *(D. Dick)*
3. Retour de Flamme 5-11-12 *(J. Lindley)*

SP: 20/1; 5/1; 11/2 18 ran
J. Wright 2:3

1959 £4,587

1. **Fare Time** 6-12-0 *(F. Winter)*
2. Ivy Green 9-12-0 *(P. Taaffe)*
3. Prudent King 7-12-0 *(T. P. Burns)*

SP: 13/2; 40/1; 13/2 14 ran
R. Price 4:1

1960 £4,290

1. **Another Flash** 6-12-0 *(H. Beasley)*
2. Albergo 6-12-0 *(D. Page)*
3. Saffron Tartan 9-12-0 *(T. P. Burns)*

SP: 11/4; 11/2; 3/1 12 ran
P. Sleator, in Ireland 2:3

1961 £5,211

1. **Eborneezer** 6-12-0 *(F. Winter)*
2. Moss Bank 5-11-12 *(J. J. Rafferty)*
3. Farmer's Boy 8-12-0 *(D. Nicholson)*

SP: 4/1; 7/4; 8/1 17 ran
R. Price 3:1½

1962 £5,143

1. **Anzio** 5-11-12 *(G. W. Robinson)*
2. Quelle Chance 7-12-0 *(D. Dick)*
3. Another Flash 8-12-0 *(H. Beasley)*

SP: 11/2; 11/2; 11/10 14 ran
F. Walwyn 3:1½

1963 £5,585

1. **Winning Fair** 8-12-0 *(Mr A. Lillingston)*
2. Farrney Fox 8-12-0 *(P. Powell)*
3. Quelle Chance 8-12-0 (B. Wilkinson)

SP: 100/9; 10/1; 100/7 21 ran
G. Spencer, in Ireland 3:nk

1964 £8,161

1. **Magic Court** 6-12-0 *(P. McCarron)*
2. Another Flash 10-12-0 *(H. Beasley)*
3. Kirriemuir 4-11-4 *(G. W. Robinson)*

SP: 100/6; 6/1; 100/6 24 ran
T. Robson 4:¾

1965 £8,042

1. **Kirriemuir** 5-11-12 *(G. W. Robinson)*
2. Spartan General 6-12-0 *(T. Biddlecombe)*
3. Worcran 7-12-0 *(D. Nicholson)*

SP: 50/1; 8/1; 8/1 19 ran
F. Walwyn 1:1½

1966 £7,921

1. **Salmon Spray** 8-12-0 *(J. Haine)*
2. Sempervivum 8-12-0 *(J. King)*
3. Flyingbolt 7-12-0 *(P. Taaffe)*

SP: 4/1; 20/1; 15/8 17 ran
R. Turnell 3:¾

1967 £8,857

1. **Saucy Kit** 6-12-0 *(R. Edwards)*
2. Makaldar 7-12-0 *(D. Mould)*
3. Talgo Abbess 8-12-0 *(F. Carroll)*

SP: 100/6; 11/4; 100/8 23 ran
M. H. Easterby 4:1

1968 £7,798

1. **Persian War** 5-11-12 *(J. Uttley)*
2. Chorus 7-12-0 *(A. Turnell)*
3. Black Justice 6-12-0 *(B. Scott)*

SP: 4/1; 7/2; 100/6 16 ran
C. Davies 4:5

1969 £7,876

1. **Persian War** 6-12-0 *(J. Uttley)*
2. Drumikill 8-12-0 *(B. Brogan)*
3. Privy Seal 5-11-12 *(J. Cook)*

SP: 6/4; 100/7; 33/1 17 ran
C. Davies 4:2½

1970 £7,739

1. **Persian War** 7-12-0 *(J. Uttley)*
2. Major Rose 8-12-0 *(J. Gifford)*
3. Escalus 5-11-12 *(D. Mould)*

SP: 5/4; 8/1; 25/1 14 ran
C. Davies 1½:1½

1971 £7,466

1. **Bula** 6-12-0 *(P. Kelleway)*
2. Persian War 8-12-0 *(J. Uttley)*
3. Major Rose 9-12-0 *(T. Biddlecombe)*

SP: 15/8; 9/2; 4/1 9 ran
F. Winter 4:1

1972 £15,648

1. **Bula** 7-12-0 *(P. Kelleway)*
2. Boxer 5-11-12 *(J. Uttley)*
3. Lyford Cay 8-12-0 *(D. Cartwright)*

SP: 8/11; 25/1; 66/1 12 ran
F. Winter 8:3

1973 £14,563

1. **Comedy of Errors** 6-12-0 *(W. Smith)*
2. Easby Abbey 6-12-0 *(R. Barry)*
3. Captain Christy 6-12-0 *(H. Beasley)*

SP: 8/1; 20/1; 85/40 8 ran
F. Rimell 1½:2

1974 £14,023

1. **Lanzarote** 6-12-0 *(R. Pitman)*
2. Comedy of Errors 7-12-0 *(W. Smith)*
3. Yenisei 7-12-0 *(H. Beasley)*

SP: 7/4; 4/6; 100/1 7 ran
F. Winter 3:8

1975 £14,459

1. **Comedy of Errors** 8-12-0 *(K. White)*
2. Flash Imp 6-12-0 *(T. Stack)*
3. Tree Tangle 6-12-0 *(A. Turnell)*

SP: 11/8; 12/1; 10/1 13ran
F. Rimell 8:hd

1976 £14,530

1. **Night Nurse** 5-12-0 *(P. Broderick)*
2. Bird's Nest 6-12-0 *(A. Turnell)*
3. Flash Imp 7-12-0 *(R. Mann)*

SP: 2/1; 100/30; 40/1 8 ran
M. H. Easterby 2½:8

1977 £18,147

1. **Night Nurse** 6-12-0 *(P. Broderick)*
2. Monksfield 5-12-0 *(T. Kinane)*
3. Dramatist 6-12-0 *(W. Smith)*

SP: 15/2; 15/1; 6/1 10 ran
M. H. Easterby 2:2

1978 £21,327

1. **Monksfield** 6-12-0 *(T. Kinane)*
2. Sea Pigeon 8-12-0 *(F. Berry)*
3. Night Nurse 7-12-0 *(C. Tinkler)*

SP: 11/2; 5/1; 3/1 13 ran
D. McDonogh, in Ireland 2:6

1979 £22,730

1. **Monksfield** 7-12-0 *(D. T. Hughes)*
2. Sea Pigeon 9-12-0 *(J. J. O'Neill)*
3. Beacon Light 8-12-0 *(J. Francome)*

SP: 9/4; 6/1; 22/1 10 ran
D. McDonogh, in Ireland ¾:15

1980 £24,972

1. **Sea Pigeon** 10-12-0 *(J. J. O'Neill)*
2. Monksfield 8-12-0 *(D. T. Hughes)*
3. Bird's Nest 10-12-0 *(A. Turnell)*

SP: 13/2; 6/5; 11/1 9 ran
M. H. Easterby 7:1½

1981 £32,260

1. **Sea Pigeon** 11-12-0 *(J. Francome)*
2. Pollardstown 6-12-0 *(P. Blacker)*
3. Daring Run 6-12-0 *(Mr T. Walsh)*

SP: 7/4; 9/1; 8/1 14 ran
M. H. Easterby 1½:nk

1982 £37,043

1. **For Auction** 6-12-0 *(Mr C. Magnier)*
2. Broadsword 5-12-0 *(P. Scudamore)*
3. Ekbalco 6-12-0 *(D. Goulding)*

SP: 40/1; 100/30; 7/2 14 ran
M. Cunningham, in Ireland 7:1½

1983 £34,865

1. **Gaye Brief** 6-12-0 *(R. Linley)*
2. Boreen Prince 6-12-0 *(N. Madden)*
3. For Auction 7-12-0 *(Mr C. Magnier)*

SP: 7/1; 50/1; 3/1 17 ran
Mrs M. Rimell 3:7

1984 £36,680

1. **Dawn Run** 6-11-9 *(J. J. O'Neill)*
2. Cima 6-12-0 *(P. Scudamore)*
3. Very Promising 6-12-0 *(S. Morshead)*

SP: 4/5; 66/1; 16/1 14 ran
P. Mullins, in Ireland ¾:4

1985 £38,030

1. **See You Then** 5-12-0 *(S. Smith Eccles)*
2. Robin Wonder 7-12-0 *(J. J. O'Neill)*
3. Stans Pride 8-11-9 *(S. Morshead)*

SP: 16/1; 66/1; 100/1 14 ran
N. Henderson 7:3

1986 £41,435

1. **See You Then** 6-12-0 *(S. Smith Eccles)*
2. Gaye Brief 9-12-0 *(P. Scudamore)*
3. Nohalmdun 5-12-0 *(J. J. O'Neill)*

SP: 5/6; 14/1; 20/1 23 ran
N. Henderson 7:1½

1987 £43,205

1. **See You Then** 7-12-0 *(S. Smith Eccles)*
2. Flatterer 8-12-0 *(J. Fishback)*
3. Barnbrook Again 6-12-0 *(S. Sherwood)*

SP: 11/10; 10/1; 14/1 18 ran
N. Henderson 1½:1

1988 £52,225

1. **Celtic Shot** 6-12-0 *(P. Scudamore)*
2. Classical Charm 5-12-0 *(K. Morgan)*
3. Celtic Chief 5-12-0 *(R. Dunwoody)*

SP: 7/1; 33/1; 5/2 21 ran
F. Winter 4:3

1989 £50,207

1. **Beech Road** 7-12-0 *(R. Guest)*
2. Celtic Chief 8-12-0 *(G. McCourt)*
3. Celtic Shot 7-12-0 *(P. Scudamore)*

SP: 50/1; 6/1; 8/1 15 ran
G. Balding 2:1

1990 £50,047

1. **Kribensis** 6-12-0 *(R. Dunwoody)*
2. Nomadic Way 5-12-0 *(P. Scudamore)*
3. Past Glories 7-12-0 *(J. Quinn)*

SP: 95/40; 8/1; 150/1 19 ran
M. Stoute 3:¾

TIMEFORM HURDLE (4-y-o) (Chepstow 2m)

1969	Country Retreat 11-3: 7/1	F. Walwyn	*M. Gifford*	9
1970	Harlech Lad 10-13: 5/1	J. Cann	*W. Smith*	16
1971	Boy Tudor 10-4: 25/1	R. Hezlet	*P. Kelleway*	14
1972	Freethinker 10-5: 7/1	F. Winter	*J. Francome*	9
1973	Bumble Boy 11-2: 6/1	W. Marshall	*W. Smith*	13
1974	Southern Darling 10-5: 8/1	J. Gifford	*R. Champion*	15
1975	Night Nurse 11-5: 11/10	M. H. Easterby	*P. Broderick*	16
1976	Romping To Work 10-7: 12/1	J. Edwards	*P. Blacker*	11
1977	Levaramoss 12-0: 15/2	A. Ingham	*B. R. Davies*	12
1978	Sean 11-0: 11/2	F. Rimell	*J. Burke*	8
1979	McAdam 10-5: 4/6	F. Rimell	*C. Tinkler*	4
1980	Gay George 11-10: 1/2	F. Walwyn	*W. Smith*	5
1981	York Cottage 10-3: 3/1	N. Gaselee	*R. Linley*	11
1982	Monza 10-5: 16/1	P. Cundell	*R. Rowe*	9
1983	Ra Nova 10-13: 4/1	Mrs N. Kennedy	*P. Farrell*	7
1984	Statesmanship 10-9: 14/1	R. Hannon	*P. Scudamore*	10
1985	Nebris 11-1: 15/8	R. Akehurst	*H. Davies*	10
1986	Tingle Bell 10-1: 10/1	G. Moore	*M. Hammond*	10
1987	Framlington Court 11-6: 7/2	P. Walwyn	*D. Browne*	7
1988	Rivers Secret 9-10: 8/1	Denys Smith	*A. Smith*	16
1989	Peer Prince 11-8: 11/4	G. Pritchard-Gordon	*S. Smith Eccles*	8

BOBBY RENTON MEMORIAL NOVICES CHASE
(Wetherby 2m 50yds)

1976	Victor's Slave 5-11-0: 2/1	A. Dickinson	*M. Dickinson*	8
1977	Pavement Artist 5-11-0: 6/4	H. T. Jones	*S. Smith Eccles*	8
1978	Night Nurse 7-11-1: 9/4	M. H. Easterby	*I. Watkinson*	7
1979	Hard Tarquin 7-11-10: 11/10	E. O'Grady (Ir)	*T. Ryan*	9
1980	Alick 5-11-0: 10/1	M. H. Easterby	*J. J. O'Neill*	12
1981	Pay Related 7-11-1: 5/4	M. H. Easterby	*A. Brown*	11
1982	Basils Choice 7-11-3: 8/13	M. Dickinson	*R. Earnshaw*	6
1983	Homeson 6-11-3: 3/1	J. Gifford	*R. Rowe*	9
1984	Rentaghost 6-11-1: 11/8	T. Barron	*R. Lamb*	6
1985	Music Be Magic 6-11-1: 6/4	G. Richards	*N. Doughty*	10
1986	Slieve Felim 6-11-5: 2/9	W. A. Stephenson	*R. Lamb*	3
1987	Yeoman Broker 6-11-1: 13/2	J. Gifford	*R. Rowe*	12
1988	Rapier Thrust 6-11-1: 8/13	J. FitzGerald	*M. Dwyer*	5
1989	Mister Point 7-11-12: 1/1	M. H. Easterby	*R. Marley*	7

FLAVEL-LEISURE HURDLE (4-y-o) (Newbury 2m 100yds)

1980	Gay George 11-3: 8/13	F. Walwyn	*W. Smith*	8
1981	Ra Tapu 11-3: 6/1	P. Mitchell	*R. Hughes*	12
1982	Royal Vulcan 11-3: 9/4	N. Callaghan	*J. J. O'Neill*	9
1983	Connaught River 11-3: 12/1	D. Nicholson	*P. Scudamore*	12
1984	Statesmanship 11-3: 4/1	R. Hannon	*P. Scudamore*	9
1985	Ace of Spies 11-0: 100/30	L. Kennard	*B. Powell*	4
1986	Saffron Lord 11-3: 3/1	L. Kennard	*B. Powell*	8
1987	Celtic Chief 11-0: 7/2	Mrs M. Rimell	*P. Scudamore*	7
1988	Kribensis 11-7: 4/5	M. Stoute	*R. Dunwoody*	7
1989	Jopanini 11-0: 4/1	D. Thom	*D. Murphy*	9

GLYNWED INTERNATIONAL HANDICAP CHASE (Newbury 2½m)

1961	Frenchman's Cove 6-11-0: 100/30	H. T. Jones	*S. Mellor*	10
1962	Fortria 10-10-7: 4/11	T. Dreaper (Ir)	*P. Taaffe*	4
1963	King's Nephew 9-11-0: 5/2	F. Cundell	*D. Mould*	12
1964	No race			
1965	Abandoned because of fog			
1966	Kapeno 9-11-0: 100/7	P. Cazalet	*Mr N. Gaselee*	10
1967	Rondetto 11-10-7: 7/4	R. Turnell	*J. Haine*	5
1968	Chaou II 5-10-11: 3/1	P. Cazalet	*D. Mould*	5
1969	Moonduster 10-11-11: 5/2	F. Rimell	*T. Biddlecombe*	8
1970	Moonduster 11-10-12: —	F. Rimell	*C. G. Davies*	w.o.
1971	Into View 8-11-10: 8/13	F. Winter	*P. Kelleway*	3
1972	Spanish Steps 9-11-1: 11/10	E. Courage	*P. Blacker*	4
1973	Crisp 10-11-6: 4/5	F. Winter	*R. Pitman*	6
1974	Pendil 9-12-0: 1/3	F. Winter	*R. Pitman*	4

1975	Game Spirit 9-11-6: 2/7	F. Walwyn	*W. Smith*	2
1976	Game Spirit 10-11-6: 3/1	F. Walwyn	*W. Smith*	4
1977	Fort Devon 11-11-1: 10/11	F. Walwyn	*W. Smith*	4
1978	Party Line 9-11-10: 5/6	H. Poole	*R. R. Evans*	3
1979	Jack of Trumps 6-12-0: 1/1	E. O'Grady (Ir)	*Mr N. Madden*	3
1980	Stopped 8-11-1: 2/1	F. Winter	*B. de Haan*	9
1981	Fairy King 8-10-9: 1/1	J. FitzGerald	*S. Smith Eccles*	9
1982	Observe 6-10-7: 16/1	F. Winter	*B. de Haan*	9
1983	The Mighty Mac 8-10-13: 8/11	M. Dickinson	*Mr D. Browne*	6
1984	Observe 8-11-3: 4/1	F. Winter	*J. Francome*	7
1985	Tom's Little Al 9-11-7	W. Williams	*P. Scudamore*	2
1986	Voice of Progress 8-11-5: 3/1	D. Nicholson	*R. Dunwoody*	7
1987	Brave Hussar 9-10-0: 8/1	R. Curtis	*C. Llewellyn*	5
1988	Pegwell Bay 7-11-2: 2/1	T. Forster	*C. Llewellyn*	6
1989	Joint Sovereignty 9-10-11: 11/10	P. Hobbs	*P. Hobbs*	3

UNITED HOUSE CONSTRUCTION HANDICAP CHASE (Ascot 2m)

1982	Artifice 11-10-7: 5/1	J. Thorne	*S. Smith Eccles*	7
1983	Western Rose 11-10-0: 11/10	Mrs M. Rimell	*S. Morshead*	2
1984	Little Bay 9-12-3: 2/1	G. Richards	*J. Francome*	7
1985	Admiral's Cup 7-10-7: 2/1	F. Winter	*B. de Haan*	4
1986	Far Bridge 10-10-7: 13/2	G. Balding	*S. Smith Eccles*	7
1987	Long Engagement 6-10-7: 12/1	D. Nicholson	*R. Dunwoody*	7
1988	Vodkatini 9-11-10: 6/1	J. Gifford	*P. Hobbs*	6
1989	Prize Asset 9-11-3: 100/30	P. Hobbs	*S. Earle*	9

CHARLIE HALL MEMORIAL WETHERBY PATTERN CHASE
(Wetherby 3m 100yds)

1969	Arcturus 8-11-10: 11/4	N. Crump	*P. Buckley*	3
1970	Kildrummy 5-11-7: 100/30	W. Crawford	*R. Barry*	8
1971	Abandoned because of snow and frost			
1972	Coxswain 7-11-10: 4/5	W. A. Stephenson	*Mr G. Macmillan*	8
1973	Dunrobin 6-11-5: 4/5	W. Crawford	*S. P. Taylor*	6
1974	Tamalin 7-11-9: 9/4	G. Richards	*J. J. O'Neill*	7
1975	Davy Lad 5-11-7: 2/5	M. O'Toole (Ir)	*D. T. Hughes*	5
1976	Set Point 8-11-9: 20/1 } dh	Lady Herries	*T. Stack*	6
	Current Gold 5-11-7: 4/1 } dh	G. Richards	*D. Goulding*	
1977	Goolagong 7-11-9: 8/1	N. Crump	*Mr H. Orde-Powlett*	8
1978	Fighting Fit 6-11-9: 6/5	K. Oliver	*R. Lamb*	5
1979	Sparkie's Choice 6-11-9: 9/2	N. Crump	*C. Hawkins*	8
1980	Manton Castle 6-11-9: 16/1	M. Camacho	*G. Holmes*	9
1981	Gay Return 6-11-10: 12/1	E. O'Grady (Ir)	*T. Ryan*	11
1982	Righthand Man 5-11-7: 11/10	M. Dickinson	*G. Bradley*	10
1983	Wayward Lad 8-11-10: 1/3	M. Dickinson	*R. Earnshaw*	3
1984	Burrough Hill Lad 8-11-9: 10/11	Mrs J. Pitman	*P. Tuck*	4
1985	Wayward Lad 10-11-6: 1/1	Mrs M. Dickinson	*G. Bradley*	4
1986	Forgive'N Forget 9-11-10: 5/2	J. FitzGerald	*M. Dwyer*	6
1987	Cybrandian 9-11-2: 7/4	M. H. Easterby	*C. Grant*	4
1988	High Edge Grey 7-11-2: 13/2	K. Oliver	*T. Reed*	10
1989	Durham Edition 11-11-2: 33/1	W. A. Stephenson	*A. Merrigan*	7

WHITBREAD WHITE LABEL HANDICAP HURDLE
(Cheltenham 2m)

1984	Robin Wonder 6-11-4: 7/4	D. Elsworth	*R. Arnott*	9
1985	Jim Thorpe 4-10-0: 8/1	G. Richards	*D. Coakley*	12
1986	Robin Wonder 8-11-10: 9/1	D. Elsworth	*G. Bradley*	9
1987	Celtic Shot 5-10-6: 9/4	F. Winter	*P. Scudamore*	9
1988	South Parade 4-11-0: 9/2	G. Balding	*G. Bradley*	10
1989	Highland Bounty 5-10-4: 14/1	S. Dow	*S. Turner*	10

MACKESON GOLD CUP HANDICAP CHASE (Cheltenham 2½m)

1960	Fortria 8-12-0: 8/1	T. Dreaper (Ir)	*P. Taaffe*	19
1961	Scottish Memories 7-10-12: 9/2	A. Thomas	*C. Finnegan*	17
1962	Fortria 10-12-0: 5/1	T. Dreaper (Ir)	*P. Taaffe*	25
1963	Richard of Bordeaux 8-10-5: 20/1	F. Walwyn	*H. Beasley*	20
1964	Super Flash 9-10-5	F. Cundell	*S. Mellor*	9
1965	Dunkirk 8-12-7: 11/10	P. Cazalet	*W. Rees*	8

1966	Pawnbroker 8-11-9: 7/2	W. A. Stephenson	*P. Broderick*	5
1967	Charlie Worcester 10-10-11: 7/1	R. Price	*J. Gifford*	13
1968	Jupiter Boy 7-10-3: 9/1	F. Rimell	*E. P. Harty*	13
1969	Gay Trip 7-11-5: 8/1	F. Rimell	*T. Biddlecombe*	14
1970	Chatham 6-10-3: 33/1	F. Rimell	*K. White*	17
1971	Gay Trip 9-11-3: 8/1	F. Rimell	*T. Biddlecombe*	10
1972	Red Candle 8-10-0: 20/1	G. Vallance	*J. Fox*	11
1973	Skymas 8-10-5: 7/1	B. Lusk (Ir)	*T. S. Murphy*	15
1974	Bruslee 8-10-7: 2/1	M. Scudamore	*A. Turnell*	11
1975	Clear Cut 11-10-9: 13/2	M. Camacho	*D. Greaves*	13
1976	Cancello 7-11-1: 4/1	N. Crump	*D. Atkins*	13
1977	Bachelor's Hall 7-10-6: 11/2	P. Cundell	*M. O'Halloran*	16
1978	Bawnogues 7-10-7: 5/1	M. Tate	*C. Smith*	11
1979	Man Alive 8-10-9: 6/1	G. Richards	*R. Barry*	11
1980	Bright Highway 6-11-1: 5/1	M. J. O'Brien (Ir)	*G. Newman*	15
1981	Henry Kissinger 7-10-13: 5/1	D. Gandolfo	*P. Barton*	11
1982	Fifty Dollars More 7-11-0: 11/1	F. Winter	*R. Linley*	11
1983	Pounentes 6-10-6: 7/1	W. McGhie	*N. Doughty*	9
1984	Half Free 8-11-10: 5/2	F. Winter	*R. Linley*	10
1985	Half Free 9-11-10: 9/2	F. Winter	*R. Linley*	10
1986	Very Promising 8-11-13: 7/1	D. Nicholson	*R. Dunwoody*	11
1987	Beau Ranger 9-10-2: 13/2	M. Pipe	*M. Perrett*	14
1988	Pegwell Bay 7-11-2: 6/1	T. Forster	*P. Scudamore*	13
1989	Joint Sovereignty 9-10-4: 10/1	P. Hobbs	*G. McCourt*	15

FOODBROKERS & PRIMULA FIGHTING FIFTH HURDLE
(Newcastle 2m)

1969	Mugatpura 6-11-7: 1/1	F. Walwyn	*G. W. Robinson*	7
1970	Inishmaan 4-11-2: 5/1	F. Rimell	*T. Biddlecombe*	11
1971	Dondieu 6-11-7: 4/5	Denys Smith	*B. Fletcher*	11
1972	Comedy of Errors 5-11-7: 11/8	F. Rimell	*W. Smith*	8
1973	Comedy of Errors 6-12-0: 8/11	F. Rimell	*W. Smith*	7
1974	Comedy of Errors 7-11-10: 8/13	F. Rimell	*K. White*	5
1975	Night Nurse 4-11-5: 6/4	M. H. Easterby	*P. Broderick*	4
1976	Bird's Nest 6-11-10: 4/1	R. Turnell	*S. C. Knight*	6
1977	Bird's Nest 7-11-10: 5/2	R. Turnell	*A. Turnell*	5
1978	Sea Pigeon 8-11-10: 4/6	M. H. Easterby	*I. Watkinson*	4
1979	Bird's Nest 9-11-9: 5/4	R. Turnell	*A. Turnell*	5
1980	Sea Pigeon 10-12-0: 7/4	M. H. Easterby	*A. Brown*	7
1981	Ekbalco 5-11-5: 7/2	R. Fisher	*D. Goulding*	7
1982	Donegal Prince 6-11-5: 10/1	P. Kelleway	*P. Tuck*	6
1983	Gaye Brief 6-12-0: 4/9	Mrs M. Rimell	*S. Morshead*	5
1984	Browne's Gazette 6-11-9: 1/2	Mrs M. Dickinson	*D. Browne*	8
1985	Out of The Gloom 4-11-6: 9/1	R. Hollinshead	*J. J. O'Neill*	9
1986	Tom Sharp 6-11-0: 7/2	W. Wharton	*S. J. O'Neill*	10
1987	Floyd 7-11-6: 5/6	D. Elsworth	*C. Brown*	7
1988	Floyd 8-11-6: 9/4	D. Elsworth	*S. Sherwood*	6
1989	Kribensis 5-11-9: 4/7	M. Stoute	*M. Dwyer*	5

RACECALL ASCOT HURDLE (Ascot 2½m)

1972	Bula 7-11-8: 4/5	F. Winter	*P. Kelleway*	6
1973	Moyne Royal 8-11-8: 13/8	A. Pitt	*D. Mould*	6
1974	Lanzarote 6-11-8: 8/15	F. Winter	*R. Pitman*	4
1975	Lanzarote 7-11-8: 6/4	F. Winter	*J. Francome*	4
1976	Dramatist 5-11-8: 6/4	F. Walwyn	*W. Smith*	6
1977	Dramatist 6-11-4: 1/3	F. Walwyn	*W. Smith*	5
1978	Kybo 5-11-8: 2/9	J. Gifford	*G. Enright*	4
1979	Connaught Ranger 5-11-8: 8/11	F. Rimell	*C. Tinkler*	10
1980	Connaught Ranger 6-11-8: 11/4	F. Rimell	*J. Burke*	8
1981	Lumen 6-10-13: 14/1	J. Gifford	*R. Rowe*	7
1982	Al Kuwait 6-10-13: 1/1	F. Winter	*J. Francome*	4
1983	Dawn Run 5-10-13: 1/3	P. Mullins (Ir)	*J. J. O'Neill*	7
1984	Gaye Brief 7-10-11: 4/6	Mrs M. Rimell	*R. Linley*	5
1985	Gaye Brief 8-10-11: 13/8	Mrs M. Rimell	*R. Linley*	9
1986	Ibn Majed 4-10-11: 9/2	C. Spares	*J. McLaughlin*	5
1987	Sabin du Loir 8-10-11: 5/2	M. Pipe	*P. Scudamore*	7
1988	Sabin du Loir 9-10-11: 1/2	M. Pipe	*P. Scudamore*	6
1989	Nodform 5-10-11: 12/1	J. Gifford	*R. Rowe*	5

HURST PARK NOVICES' CHASE (Ascot 2m)

1965	Stalbridge Colonist 6-11-4: 6/1	K. Cundell	*W. Rees*	9
1966	Sir Thopas 5-11-6: 1/1	R. Turnell	*J. King*	7
1967	Get Stepping 6-11-4: 4/1	R. Turnell	*J. King*	9
1968	Rehearsed 6-11-4: 15/2	R. Turnell	*W. Rees*	10
1969	Louis Napoleon 6-11-4: 11/4	F. Cundell	*S. Mellor*	8
1970	Table Mountain 5-11-1: 7/2	F. Rimell	*K. White*	9
1971	Shell Streak 4-10-6: 9/2	S. Pattemore	*R. Champion*	7
1972	Killiney 6-11-4: 11/8	F. Winter	*R. Pitman*	3
1973	Cool Million 5-11-1: 11/2	F. Walwyn	*A. Branford*	8
1974	Isle of Man 7-11-9: 4/9	F. Walwyn	*W. Smith*	4
1975	Hardier 7-11-9: 1/6	H. T. Jones	*I. Watkinson*	2
1976	Supreme Halo 6-11-4: 4/6	R. Smyth	*C. Read*	7
1977	Pavement Artist 5-11-8: 9/4	H. T. Jones	*S. Smith Eccles*	4
1978	Ramblix 6-11-4: 11/10	F. Winter	*J. Francome*	3
1979	Kybo 6-11-4: 5/4	J. Gifford	*R. Rowe*	3
1980	Little Bay 5-11-4: 4/6	G. Richards	*R. Barry*	4
1981	Run With Pride 6-11-7: 100/30	M. O'Toole (Ir)	*N. Madden*	7
1982	Jubilee Medal 5-11-1: 7/1	N. Henderson	*J. Francome*	6
1983	Monza 5-10-10: 6/4	P. Cundell	*R. Rowe*	3
1984	Townley Stone 5-11-8: 9/4	J. Webber	*G. McCourt*	7
1985	Desert Orchid 6-11-4: 4/9	D. Elsworth	*C. Brown*	4
1986	Ten of Spades 6-11-4: 8/1	S. Mellor	*G. Charles Jones*	8
1987	Barnbrook Again 6-11-8: 5/6	D. Elsworth	*S. Sherwood*	5
1988	Fred The Tread 6-11-4: 8/1	T. Casey	*R. Dunwoody*	5
1989	Young Snugfit 5-11-8: 11/8	O. Sherwood	*J. Osborne*	5

H & T WALKER GOLD CUP HANDICAP CHASE (Ascot 2½m)

1981	Wayward Lad 6-11-10: 9/4	M. Dickinson	*R. Earnshaw*	8
1982	Pay Related 8-11-2: 7/1	M. H. Easterby	*J. J. O'Neill*	6
1983	The Tsarevich 7-11-6: 9/2	N. Henderson	*Mr J. White*	6
1984	Cybrandian 6-10-9: 6/4	M. H. Easterby	*A. Brown*	6
1985	Very Promising 7-11-7: 6/1	D. Nicholson	*P. Scudamore*	7
1986	Church Warden 7-10-7: 12/1	D. Murray-Smith	*R. Dunwoody*	6
1987	Weather The Storm 7-11-10: 6/1	A. Moore (Ir)	*T. Taaffe*	11
1988	Saffron Lord 6-11-3: 8/11	J. Gifford	*R. Rowe*	5
1989	Man O'Magic 8-11-5: 9/1	K. Bailey	*M. Perrett*	11

AURELIUS HURDLE (3-y-o) (Ascot 2m)

1968	Soloning 11-0: 9/4	F. Winter	*H. Beasley*	9
1969	Varma 11-0: 11/2	M. Masson	*D. Mould*	16
1970	Fount of Youth 11-0: 10/1	S. Ingham	*J. Uttley*	12
1971	Westward Lad 11-0: 7/1	F. Walwyn	*B. Brogan*	11
1972	Golden Jet 10-7: 33/1	P. Bailey	*Jeff Williams*	22
1973	Supreme Halo 10-11: 2/7	R. Smyth	*P. Skelton*	3
1974	Abandoned because of waterlogged state of course			
1975	Cabar Feidh 11-0: 7/1	P. Calver	*R. Linley*	11
1976	Rushmere 11-0: 9/2	J. Gifford	*R. Champion*	9
1977	Rodman 11-0: 11/10	F. Winter	*J. Francome*	17
1978	Larryr 11-0: 10/1	N. Callaghan	*J. King*	8
1979	Gleason 11-0: 8/13	M. H. Easterby	*A. Brown*	5
1980	Lir 11-0: 9/2	A. Moore	*G. Moore*	10
1981	Goldspun 11-0: 1/1	D. Nicholson	*P. Scudamore*	11
1982	Connaught River 11-0: 4/5	D. Nicholson	*P. Scudamore*	5
1983	Statesmanship 11-1: 100/30	P. Bailey	*R. Linley*	10
1984	Jamesmead 11-1: 7/2	D. Elsworth	*C. Brown*	14
1985	Thawhorn 11-4: 7/4	T. Carberry (Ir)	*F. Berry*	8
1986	Sprowston Boy 11-1: 7/2	P. Kelleway	*R. Rowe*	10
1987	Calapaez 11-8: 5/4	Miss B. Sanders	*C. Brown*	8
1988	Nomadic Way 11-8: 6/5	B. Hills	*K. Mooney*	10
1989	Major Inquiry 11-8: 6/4	D. Elsworth	*G. Bradley*	11

HENNESSY COGNAC GOLD CUP HANDICAP CHASE
(Newbury 3m 2f 82yds)

1957	Mandarin 6-11-0: 8/1	F. Walwyn	*P. Madden*	19
1958	Taxidermist 6-11-1: 10/1	F. Walwyn	*Mr J. Lawrence*	13
1959	Kerstin 9-11-10: 4/1	C. Bewicke	*S. Hayhurst*	26
1960	Knucklecracker 7-11-1: 100/7	D. Ancil	*D. Ancil*	20

1961	Mandarin 10-11-5: 7/1	F. Walwyn	*G. W. Robinson*	22
1962	Springbok 8-10-8: 15/2	N. Crump	*G. Scott*	27
1963	Mill House 6-12-0: 15/8	F. Walwyn	*G. W. Robinson*	10
1964	Arkle 7-12-7: 5/4	T. Dreaper (Ir)	*P. Taaffe*	9
1965	Arkle 8-12-7: 1/6	T. Dreaper (Ir)	*P. Taaffe*	8
1966	Stalbridge Colonist 7-10-0: 25/1	K. Cundell	*S. Mellor*	6
1967	Rondetto 11-10-1: 100/8	R. Turnell	*J. King*	13
1968	Man of The West 7-10-0: 20/1	F. Walwyn	*G. W. Robinson*	11
1969	Spanish Steps 6-11-8: 7/1	E. Courage	*J. Cook*	15
1970	Border Mask 8-11-1: 7/1	P. Cazalet	*D. Mould*	12
1971	Bighorn 7-10-11: 7/1	C. V. Miller	*D. Cartwright*	13
1972	Charlie Potheen 7-11-4: 10/1	F. Walwyn	*R. Pitman*	13
1973	Red Candle 9-10-4: 12/1	G. Vallance	*J. Fox*	11
1974	Royal Marshal II 7-10-0: 11/2	T. Forster	*G. Thorner*	13
1975	April Seventh 9-11-2: 11/1	R. Turnell	*A. Turnell*	13
1976	Zeta's Son 7-10-9: 12/1	P. Bailey	*I. Watkinson*	21
1977	Bachelor's Hall 7-10-10: 11/2	P. Cundell	*M. O'Halloran*	14
1978	Approaching 7-10-6: 3/1	J. Gifford	*R. Champion*	8
1979	Fighting Fit 7-11-7: 15/2	K. Oliver	*R. Linley*	15
1980	Bright Highway 6-11-6: 2/1	M. J. O'Brien (Ir)	*G. Newman*	14
1981	Diamond Edge 10-11-10: 9/2	F. Walwyn	*W. Smith*	14
1982	Bregawn 8-11-10: 9/4	M. Dickinson	*G. Bradley*	11
1983	Brown Chamberlin 8-11-8: 7/2	F. Winter	*J. Francome*	12
1984	Burrough Hill Lad 8-12-0: 100/30	Mrs J. Pitman	*J. Francome*	13
1985	Galway Blaze 9-10-0: 11/2	J. FitzGerald	*M. Dwyer*	15
1986	Broadheath 9-10-5: 6/1	D. Barons	*P. Nicholls*	15
1987	Playschool 9-10-8: 6/1	D. Barons	*P. Nicholls*	12
1988	Strands of Gold 9-10-0: 10/1	M. Pipe	*P. Scudamore*	12
1989	Ghofar 6-10-2: 5/1	D. Elsworth	*H. Davies*	8

GERRY FEILDEN HURDLE (Newbury 2m 100yds)

1951	Campari 4-11-0: 100/7	R. Price	*F. Winter*	11
1952	Pont Cordonnier 5-10-2: 13/8	V. Smyth	*F. Crouch*	9
1953	Straight Cut 4-10-1: 7/1	T. R. Rimell	*K. Mullins*	9
1954	Syrte 4-12-2: 7/2	R. Price	*F. Winter*	11
1955	Punjab 4-10-1: 9/4	T. Farmer	*H. Sprague*	6
1956	Hilarion 8-11-4: 9/1	W. Wightman	*M. Scudamore*	10
1957	Fare Time 4-10-12: 4/1	R. Price	*J. Gilbert*	13
1958	Retour de Flamme 5-12-4: 9/2	S. Warren	*D. Dick*	12
1959	Langton Heath 5-11-4: 100/8	T. Griffiths	*R. Martin*	16
1960	Rough Tweed 6-10-4: 7/1	N. Crump	*H. East*	15
1961	Anzio 4-11-1: 11/4	F. Walwyn	*H. Beasley*	14
1962	White Park Bay 7-11-4: 2/1	P. P-Gallwey	*J. Gifford*	14
1963	Salmon Spray 5-10-8: 5/4	R. Turnell	*J. Haine*	11
1964	Golden Sailor 5-10-4: 100/8	G. Vergette	*D. Nicholson*	22
1965	Lanconello 6-10-5: 5/2	K. Piggott	*J. Haine*	11
1966	Hanassi 6-10-6: 9/1	J. Goldsmith	*A. Turnell*	19
1967	Secret Agent II 5-10-10: 11/2	J. Benstead	*J. Gifford*	16
1968	Bric-Brac 9-11-6: 5/1	H. Hannon	*J. Guest*	9
1969	Viroy 5-11-6: 8/1	R. Price	*J. Gifford*	14
1970	Coral Diver 5-12-0: 1/1	F. Rimell	*K. White*	12
1971	Eric 4-10-8: 25/1	V. Cross	*J. Nolan*	11
1972	Comedy of Errors 5-12-0: 8/11	F. Rimell	*W. Smith*	10
1973	Lanzarote 5-11-10: 1/3	F. Winter	*R. Pitman*	7
1974	Flash Imp 5-11-6: 11/2	R. Smyth	*J. King*	5
1975	Dramatist 4-11-1: 10/1	F. Walwyn	*W. Smith*	9
1976	Beacon Light 5-12-0: 6/1	R. Turnell	*A. Turnell*	9
1977	Decent Fellow 4-11-9: 1/1	G. Balding	*R. Linley*	5
1978	Connaught Ranger 4-11-9: 6/1	F. Rimell	*J. Burke*	7
1979	Celtic Ryde 4-11-5: 5/4	P. Cundell	*M. O'Halloran*	7
1980	Pollardstown 5-11-8	S. Mellor	*P. Blacker*	8
1981	Heighlin 5-11-8: 4/1	D. Elsworth	*S. Jobar*	6
1982	Royal Vulcan 4-11-0: 4/6	N. Callaghan	*J. J. O'Neill*	8
1983	Buck House 5-11-8: 4/1	M. Morris (Ir)	*T. Carmody*	7
1984	Ra Nova 5-11-3: 11/8	Mrs N. Kennedy	*M. Perrett*	7
1985	Gala's Image 5-11-0: 9/2	Mrs M. Rimell	*R. Linley*	8
1986	Barnbrook Again 5-11-0: 7/2	D. Elsworth	*R. Arnott*	7

1987	Celtic Chief 4-11-0: 8/11	Mrs M. Rimell	*P. Scudamore*	9
1988	Kribensis 4-11-6: 8/11	M. Stoute	*R. Dunwoody*	5
1989	Cruising Altitude 6-11-3: 6/5	O. Sherwood	*J. Osborne*	8

DIPPER NOVICES' CHASE (Newcastle 2½m)

1980	Little Owl 6-11-5: 9/4	M. H. Easterby	*J. J. O'Neill*	13
1981	Abandoned because of frost			
1982	Rosewell Riever 9-11-6: 16/1	P. Monteith	*D. Nolan*	9
1983	Lettoch 6-11-10: 4/5	M. Dickinson	*G. Bradley*	6
1984	Jimbrook 7-11-6: 11/4	M. H. Easterby	*A. Brown*	6
1985	Abandoned because of snow			
1986	Joint Sovereignty 6-11-10: 4/5	J. FitzGerald	*M. Dwyer*	4
1987	Jim Thorpe 6-11-13: 15/8	G. Richards	*P. Tuck*	6
1988	Cool Strike 7-11-6: 9/2	G. Moore	*B. Storey*	6
1989	Blazing Walker 5-11-9: 8/11	W. A. Stephenson	*C. Grant*	6

EDWARD HANMER MEMORIAL CHASE (Haydock 3m)

1959	John Jacques 10-12-0: 5/1	N. Crump	*G. Scott*	11
1960	Badanloch 9-11-11: 11/8	G. Owen	*S. Mellor*	4
1961	Loch Sloy 7-11-7: 5/4	T. Robson	*M. Batchelor*	5
1962	Dancing Rain 7-10-4: 20/1	P. Upton	*E. Kelly*	11
1963	Prudent Barney 9-10-12: 5/1	R. Renton	*J. Gifford*	7
1964	Bodger 9-10-0: 100/30	G. Owen	*R. Langley*	3
1965	Forest Prince 7-11-7: 11/10	N. Crump	*G. Scott*	7
1966	Falls of Cruachan 10-12-0: 6/4	N. Crump	*P. Buckley*	5
1967	Abandoned because of foot and mouth epidemic			
1968	Two Springs 6-10-8: 4/5	G. Owen	*R. Edwards*	3
1969	Fearless Fred 7-11-10: 5/2	F. Rimell	*T. Biddlecombe*	5
1970	Supermaster 7-11-4: 5/1	W. A. Stephenson	*J. Enright*	9
1971	Red Sweeney 7-10-8: 5/1	G. Richards	*E. Fenwick*	10
1972	L'Escargot 9-11-7: 10/11	D. L. Moore (Ir)	*T. Carberry*	4
1973	Abandoned because of frost			
1974	Pendil 9-11-12: 1/3	F. Winter	*R. Pitman*	3
1975	Bula 10-12-0: 10/11	F. Winter	*J. Francome*	4
1976	Bula 11-12-0: 8/13	F. Winter	*J. Francome*	3
1977	Abandoned because of frost			
1978	Bawnogues 7-10-7: 9/4	M. Tate	*C. Smith*	8
1979	Silver Buck 7-11-6: 20/21	A. Dickinson	*T. Carmody*	3
1980	Silver Buck 8-12-0: 8/15	M. Dickinson	*T. Carmody*	4
1981	Silver Buck 9-11-12: 5/2	M. Dickinson	*J. Francome*	5
1982	Silver Buck 10-12-0: 8/11	M. Dickinson	*R. Earnshaw*	5
1983	Abandoned because of frost			
1984	Wayward Lad 9-12-0: 8/15	Mrs M. Dickinson	*R. Earnshaw*	5
1985	Forgive'N Forget 8-12-0: 2/1	J. FitzGerald	*M. Dwyer*	3
1986	Forgive'N Forget 9-12-0; 10/11	J. FitzGerald	*M. Dwyer*	3
1987	Beau Ranger 9-10-12: 6/4	M. Pipe	*P. Scudamore*	3
1988	Beau Ranger 10-11-13: 13/8	M. Pipe	*P. Scudamore*	8
1989	Golden Friend 11-10-10: 9/2	J. McConnochie	*G. McCourt*	5

TINGLE CREEK HANDICAP CHASE (Sandown 2m 18yds)

1969	Spanish Steps 6-11-13: 5/2	E. Courage	*J. Cook*	11
1970	Even Keel 8-12-3: 7/1	K. Oliver	*B. Brogan*	10
1971	Happy Medium 9-10-2: 33/1	R. Armytage	*Lord Oaksey*	8
1972	Pendil 7-12-3: 5/4	F. Winter	*R. Pitman*	8
1973	Tingle Creek 7-12-5: 5/2	H. T. Jones	*D. Mould*	6
1974	Dorlesa 6-10-4: 8/1	A. Dickinson	*M. Dickinson*	10
1975	Easby Abbey 8-10-10: 6/4	M. H. Easterby	*R. Barry*	6
1976	No Race			
1977	Tree Tangle 8-11-5: 2/1	R. Turnell	*A. Turnell*	4
1978	Abandoned because of frost			
1979	Artifice 8-11-11: 7/4	J. Thorne	*R. Hoare*	5
1980	Stopped 8-11-10: 7/4	F. Winter	*B. de Haan*	5
1981	News King 7-10-13: 11/8 (at Kempton)	F. Winter	*J. Francome*	6
1982	News King 8-11-11: 9/4	F. Winter	*J. Francome*	3
1983	Abandoned because of frost			
1984	Far Bridge 8-10-0: 11/2	G. Balding	*B. Reilly*	4
1985	Lefrak City 8-10-1: 2/1	T. Forster	*R. Dunwoody*	5

1986	Berlin 7-11-2: 11/8	N. Gaselee	*D. Browne*	7
1987	Long Engagement 6-10-2: 3/1	D. Nicholson	*R. Dunwoody*	5
1988	Desert Orchid 9-12-0: 5/2	D. Elsworth	*S. Sherwood*	5
1989	Long Engagement 8-10-0: 9/2	D. Nicholson	*B. Powell*	4

WILLIAM HILL HANDICAP HURDLE (Sandown 2m)

1970	Bula 5-12-1: 3/1	F. Winter	*P. Kelleway*	18
1971	Churchwood 7-11-9: 13/2	M. Goswell	*D. Barrott*	13
1972	True Luck 5-10-13: 11/1	F. Rimell	*T. Biddlecombe*	15
1973	St Columbus 6-11-9: 13/2	W. Marshall	*A. Turnell*	16
1974	Supreme Halo 4-10-10: 6/1	R. Smyth	*J. King*	21
1975	Fighting Taffy 8-11-6: 25/1	P. Upton	*M. Gifford*	16
1976	No Race			
1977	Narribinni 5-9-9: 14/1	D. Kent	*A. Webb*	13
1978	Abandoned because of frost			
1979	Golden Vow 5-10-0: 7/1	R. Hartop	*A. Webber*	12
1980	Ekbalco 4-10-0: 4/1	R. Fisher	*D. Goulding*	17
1981	Celtic Ryde 6-11-13: 9/2 (at Kempton)	P. Cundell	*J. Francome*	15
1982	Allten Glazed 5-10-2: 5/1	M. Naughton	*Mr D. Browne*	16
1983	Abandoned because of frost			
1984	Prideaux Boy 6-10-3: 6/1	G. Roach	*R. Dunwoody*	14
1985	Chrysaor 7-10-8: 16/1	S. Christian	*R. Beggan*	12
1986	Aonoch 7-11-7: 16/1	Mrs S. Oliver	*Jacqui Oliver*	17
1987	Celtic Shot 5-10-6: 6/4	F. Winter	*P. Scudamore*	12
1988	Corporal Clinger 9-10-7: 9/2	M. Pipe	*M. Perrett*	13
1989	Liadett 4-10-0: 12/1	M. Pipe	*J. Lower*	6

A. F. BUDGE GOLD CUP HANDICAP CHASE (Cheltenham 2½m)

1963	Limeking 6-10-12: 100/9	D. Morgan (Ir)	*T. Taaffe*	14
1964	Flying Wild 8-10-6: 100/8	D. L. Moore (Ir)	*T. Carberry*	7
1965	Flyingbolt 6-12-6: 5/2	T. Dreaper (Ir)	*P. Taaffe*	11
1966	The Laird 5-10-9: 13/2	R. Turnell	*J. King*	8
1967	Abandoned because of foot and mouth epidemic			
1968	Tassilo 10-10-1: 8/1	F. Walwyn	*A. Branford*	14
1969	Titus Oates 7-11-13: 9/4	G. Richards	*R. Barry*	11
1970	Simian 8-11-8: 4/1	Miss A. Sinclair	*D. Moore*	7
1971	Leap Frog 7-12-1: 3/1	T. Dreaper (Ir)	*V. O'Brien*	12
1972	Arctic Bow 7-10-12: 9/2	R. Turnell	*A. Turnell*	11
1973	Pendil 8-12-7: 8/11	F. Winter	*R. Pitman*	8
1974	Garnishee 10-10-6: 12/1	H. T. Jones	*D. Mould*	9
1975	Easby Abbey 8-11-10: 5/1	M. H. Easterby	*R. Barry*	9
1976	Abandoned because of frost			
1977	Even Melody 8-11-2: 8/1	N. Crump	*C. Hawkins*	11
1978	The Snipe 8-10-0: 20/1	J. Webber	*A. Webber*	14
1979	Father Delaney 7-10-10: 12/1	M. H. Easterby	*A. Brown*	12
1980	Bueche Giorod 9-10-0: 14/1	Mrs J. Pitman	*B. Smart*	15
1981	Abandoned because of snow			
1982	Observe 6-10-11: 11/2	F. Winter	*J. Francome*	15
1983	Fifty Dollars More 8-11-10	F. Winter	*R. Linley*	13
1984	Beau Ranger 6-9-10: 8/1	J. Thorne	*J. Hurst*	10
1985	Combs Ditch 9-11-9: 13/2	D. Elsworth	*C. Brown*	7
1986	Oregon Trail 6-10-7: 3/1	S. Christian	*R. Beggan*	6
1987	Bishops Yarn 8-10-7: 100/30	G. Balding	*R. Guest*	5
1988	Pegwell Bay 7-10-13: 7/2	T. Forster	*B. Powell*	10
1989	Clever Folly 9-10-4: 4/1	G. Richards	*N. Doughty*	6

CHARLES HEIDSIECK CHAMPAGNE BULA HURDLE
(Cheltenham 2m)

1963	Scottish Memories 9-11-11: 6/4	A. Thomas	*C. Finnegan*	7
1964	Magic Court 6-12-1: 4/7	T. Robson	*P. McCarron*	6
1965	Salmon Spray 7-12-1: 3/1	R. Turnell	*J. Haine*	5
1966	Sempervivum 8-11-11: 8/11	F. Walwyn	*G. W. Robinson*	4
1967	Abandoned because of foot and mouth epidemic			
1968	Solway Sands 4-11-6: 33/1	J. McMurchie	*B. Fletcher*	7
1969	Celtic Gold 7-12-1: 9/2	W. A. Stephenson	*T. S. Murphy*	7
1970	Pendil 5-11-8: 7/2	F. Winter	*P. Kelleway*	6
1971	Canasta Lad 5-11-8: 5/1	P. Bailey	*J. King*	8

1972	Bula 7-11-12: 8/13	F. Winter	*P. Kelleway*	8
1973	Comedy of Errors 6-11-12: 2/5	F. Rimell	*W. Smith*	5
1974	Comedy of Errors 7-11-10: 6/4	F. Rimell	*K. White*	4
1975	Sea Pigeon 5-11-2: 5/1	G. Richards	*J. J. O'Neill*	7
1976	Abandoned because of frost			
1977	Bird's Nest 7-11-6: 11/4	R. Turnell	*A. Turnell*	10
1978	Bird's Nest 8-11-6: 1/1	R. Turnell	*A. Turnell*	5
1979	Celtic Ryde 4-11-3: 11/4	P. Cundell	*M. O'Halloran*	5
1980	Bird's Nest 10-11-6: 5/2	R. Turnell	*A. Turnell*	7
1981	Abandoned because of snow			
1982	Ekbalco 6-11-10: 2/1	R. Fisher	*J. J. O'Neill*	5
1983	Amarach 5-11-6: 7/2	R. Fisher	*J. Duggan*	9
1984	Browne's Gazette 6-11-4: 7/2	Mrs M. Dickinson	*Mr R. Beggan*	5
1985	Corporal Clinger 6-11-2: 20/1	M. Pipe	*P. Leach*	9
1986	Floyd 6-11-2: 7/2	D. Elsworth	*C. Brown*	8
1987	Pat's Jester 4-11-2: 11/2	R. Allan	*P. Niven*	8
1988	Condor Pan 5-11-2: 12/1	J. Bolger (Ir)	*C. Swan*	8
1989	Cruising Altitude 6-11-4: 8/11	O. Sherwood	*J. Osborne*	8

FREEBOOTER NOVICES' CHASE (Doncaster 2m 150yds)

1980	Alick 5-11-3: 5/2	M. H. Easterby	*A. Brown*	8
1981	Abandoned because of snow			
1982	Abandoned because of frost			
1983	Noddy's Ryde 6-11-8: 4/5	G. Richards	*N. Doughty*	8
1984	Abandoned because of fog			
1985	Music Be Magic 6-11-11: 4/6	G. Richards	*N. Doughty*	3
1986	Dan The Millar 7-11-11: 4/5	Mrs M. Dickinson	*G. Bradley*	4
1987	Prideaux Boy 9-11-4: 1/1	G. Roach	*A. Webb*	6
1988	Nohalmdun 7-11-11: 4/6	M. H. Easterby	*R. Marley*	4
1989	Antinous 5-11-8: 11/10	M. H. Easterby	*L. Wyer*	4

S.G.B. HANDICAP CHASE (Ascot 3m)

1965	Vultrix 7-12-1: 6/4	F. Cundell	*S. Mellor*	7
1966	Arkle 9-12-7: 1/3	T. Dreaper (Ir)	*P. Taaffe*	5
1967	Abandoned because of foot and mouth epidemic			
1968	Abandoned because of waterlogged state of course			
1969	Straight Fort 6-12-0: 7/2	T. Dreaper (Ir)	*P. Taaffe*	7
1970	Glencaraig Lady 6-11-13: 4/1	F. Flood (Ir)	*R. Coonan*	10
1971	Spanish Steps 8-12-1: 4/1	E. Courage	*W. Smith*	12
1972	Soloning 7-10-12: 6/1	F. Winter	*R. Pitman*	16
1973	Mocharabuice 10-10-6: 7/1	T. Forster	*G. Thorner*	9
1974	Rough House 8-10-7: 11/1	F. Rimell	*J. Burke*	14
1975	What A Buck 8-10-4: 9/2	D. Nicholson	*J. King*	9
1976	Abandoned because of frost			
1977	Midnight Court 6-12-0: 6/5	F. Winter	*J. Francome*	8
1978	Grand Canyon 8-11-1: 15/8	D. Kent	*R. Barry*	10
1979	Raffi Nelson 6-10-1: 5/2	N. Henderson	*S. Smith Eccles*	6
1980	Henry Bishop 7-11-0: 7/1	J. Gifford	*R. Champion*	4
1981	Abandoned because of snow			
1982	Captain John 8-11-13: 11/8	M. Dickinson	*R. Earnshaw*	8
1983	The Mighty Mac 8-11-10: 13/8	M. Dickinson	*Mr D. Browne*	7
1984	Canny Danny 8-11-8: 6/4	J. FitzGerald	*M. Dwyer*	7
1985	Door Latch 7-10-2: 11/4	J. Gifford	*R. Rowe*	8
1986	Door Latch 8-11-1: 6/1	J. Gifford	*R. Rowe*	12
1987	Cavvies Clown 7-10-11: 10/1	D. Elsworth	*R. Arnott*	12
1988	Ballyhane 7-10-4: 13/8	J. Gifford	*P. Hobbs*	5
1989	Solidasarock 7-10-0: 33/1	R. Akehurst	*L. Harvey*	12

H.S.S. HIRE SHOPS HURDLE (Ascot 2m)

1965	Compton Martin 6-11-4: 5/2	G. Todd	*S. Mellor*	5
1966	Abandoned because of waterlogged state of course			
1967	Abandoned because of foot and mouth epidemic			
1968	Abandoned because of waterlogged state of course			
1969	Moyne Royal 4-10-5: 10/1	R. Akehurst	*B. Leyman*	12
1970	Bowie's Brig 4-10-8: 5/2	A. Pitt	*B. Brogan*	7
1971	Flower Picker 5-11-6: 100/30	F. Walwyn	*A. Branford*	7
1972	Ruisselet 5-11-6: 4/1	R. Price	*P. Kelleway*	22
1973	Lanzarote 5-11-13: 4/11	F. Winter	*R. Pitman*	7

1974	Tree Tangle 5-11-13: 11/10	R. Turnell	*A. Turnell*	9
1975	Grand Canyon 5-11-9: 8/1	D. Kent	*P. Haynes*	10
1976	Abandoned because of frost			
1977	Kybo 4-11-8: 13/2	J. Gifford	*G. Enright*	12
1978	Kybo 5-11-13: 11/4	J. Gifford	*R. Champion*	10
1979	Walnut Wonder 4-10-8: 33/1	L. Kennard	*L. Vincent*	8
1980	Heighlin 4-11-8: 6/4	D. Elsworth	*S. Jobar*	11
1981	Abandoned because of snow			
1982	Carved Opal 4-10-11: 7/1	F. Winter	*C. Brown*	6
1983	Admiral's Cup 5-11-6: 9/4	F. Winter	*J. Francome*	11
1984	See You Then 4-11-8: 11/10	N. Henderson	*J. Francome*	5
1985	First Bout 4-11-8: 5/1	N. Henderson	*S. Smith Eccles*	7
1986	Nohalmdun 5-11-4: 13/8	M. H. Easterby	*P. Scudamore*	5
1987	Osric 4-10-8: 11/4	M. Ryan	*G. McCourt*	7
1988	Celtic Chief 5-11-8: 2/5	Mrs M. Rimell	*R. Dunwoody*	7
1989	Forest Sun 4-10-8: 7/2	G. Balding	*J. Frost*	7

YOUNGMANS LONG WALK HURDLE (Ascot 3¼m)

1965	Minute Gun 8-10-11: 100/8	W. Shand-Kydd	*R. Pitman*	26
1966	Sir Edward 6-10-9: 7/2	R. Price	*J. Gifford*	18
1967	Abandoned because of foot and mouth epidemic			
1968	Abandoned because of waterlogged state of course			
1969	Candid Camera 6-10-6: 100/8	E. Goddard	*J. Guest*	22
1970	Rouge Autumn 6-10-5: 9/2	F. Rimell	*K. White*	20
1971	St Patrick's Blue 6-11-12: 7/2	D. Tatlow	*W. Smith*	12
1972	Highland Abbe 6-11-12: 11/1	L. Kennard	*Mr R. Smith*	8
1973	Soloning 8-11-8: 9/2	F. Winter	*R. Pitman*	10
1974	Go Bingo 5-11-12: 9/4	S. Hall	*D. Munro*	6
1975	Lanzarote 7-12-5: 4/9	F. Winter	*J. Francome*	7
1976	Abandoned because of frost			
1977	John Cherry 6-10-11: 11/8	H. T. Jones	*S. Smith Eccles*	10
1978	Kelso Chant 6-11-7: 10/1	B. Wilkinson	*S. Charlton*	14
1979	John Cherry 8-10-11: 6/1	H. T. Jones	*S. Smith Eccles*	12
1980	Derring Rose 5-11-11: 7/1	F. Winter	*J. Francome*	9
1981	Abandoned because of snow			
1982	Mayotte 7-10-11: 15/8	R. Holder	*P. Richards*	11
1983	Crimson Embers 8-10-11: 14/1	F. Walwyn	*S. Shilston*	11
1984	Kristenson 7-10-8: 7/2	R. Fisher	*M. Williams*	11
1985	Misty Dale 7-10-8: 9/4	Mrs J. Pitman	*P. Tuck*	8
1986	Out of The Gloom 5-10-8: 4/1	R. Hollinshead	*P. Scudamore*	5
1987	Bluff Cove 5-10-8: 14/1	R. Hollinshead	*R. Dunwoody*	10
1988	French Goblin 5-11-1: 3/1	J. Gifford	*P. Hobbs*	10
1989	Royal Athlete 6-10-8: 33/1	Mrs J. Pitman	*D. Gallagher*	11

CORAL WELSH NATIONAL HANDICAP CHASE (Chepstow 3¾m)

1948	Bora's Cottage 10-10-2: 100/8	R. Price	*E. Reavey*	16
1949	Fighting Line 10-10-9: 7/1	K. Cundell	*R. Francis*	15
1950	Gallery 12-10-8: 7/2	W. Bissill	*A. Mullins*	12
1951	Skyreholme 8-10-13: 7/2	N. Crump	*A. Thompson*	16
1952	Dinton Lass 10-10-0: 10/1	J. Roberts	*A. Mullins*	16
1953	Stalbridge Rock 10-11-3: 6/1	H. Dufosee	*R. McCreery*	15
1954	Blow Horn 10-10-6: 100/8	T. Jarvis	*J. Hunter*	17
1955	Monaleen 10-9-7: 20/1	H. T. Smith	*P. Fitzgerald*	17
1956	Crudwell 10-11-6: 100/9	F. Cundell	*R. Francis*	16
1957	Creeola II 9-10-5: 3/1	F. Rimell	*M. Scudamore*	11
1958	Oscar Wilde 8-9-13: 20/1	W. Wightman	*B. Lawrence*	14
1959	Limonali 8-10-2: 100/8	E. C. Morel	*D. Nicholson*	10
1960	Clover Bud 10-10-10: 7/1	G. Llewellin	*D. Nicholson*	14
1961	Limonali 10-11-12: 7/4	I. Lewis	*D. Nicholson*	9
1962	Forty Secrets 8-10-11: 6/1	E. Jones	*J. Gifford*	15
1963	Motel 9-10-6: 7/1	W. Lowe	*P. Cowley*	10
1964	Rainbow Battle 8-10-0: 3/1	W. A. Stephenson	*P. Broderick*	11
1965	Norther 8-11-0: 9/2	D. Jenkins	*T. Biddlecombe*	11
1966	Kilburn 8-11-2: 11/4	C. Nesfield	*T. Norman*	11
1967	Happy Spring 11-10-4: 6/1	J. S. Wright	*K. White*	6
1968	Glenn 7-10-4: 11/2	F. Rimell	*E. P. Harty*	8
1969	Abandoned because of snow			
1970	French Excuse 8-10-9: 3/1	F. Rimell	*T. Biddlecombe*	11

1971	Royal Toss 9-10-12: 15/8	H. Handel	*P. Cowley*	13
1972	Charlie H 10-11-3: 11/2	R. Turnell	*J. Haine*	9
1973	Deblin's Green 10-9-12: 20/1	G. Yardley	*N. Wakley*	16
1974	Pattered 8-10-2: 25/1	E. Jones	*K. White*	24
1975	Abandoned because of waterlogged state of course			
1976	Rag Trade 10-11-2: 17/2	F. Rimell	*J. Burke*	17
1977	Abandoned because of waterlogged state of course			
1978	Abandoned because of frost			
1979	Abandoned because of snow			
1979	(Dec 22) Peter Scot 8-10-2: 8/1	D. Gandolfo	*P. Barton*	15
1980	Narvik 7-10-11: 15/1	N. Crump	*J. Francome*	18
1981	Peaty Sandy 7-10-3: 3/1	Miss H. Hamilton	*Mr G. Dun*	23
1982	Corbiere 7-10-10: 12/1	Mrs J. Pitman	*B. de Haan*	10
1983	Burrough Hill Lad 7-10-9: 100/30	Mrs J. Pitman	*J. Francome*	18
1984	Righthand Man 7-11-5: 6/1	Mrs M. Dickinson	*G. Bradley*	18
1985	Run And Skip 7-10-8: 13/1	J. Spearing	*P. Scudamore*	18
1986	Stearsby 7-11-5: 8/1	Mrs J. Pitman	*G. Bradley*	17
1987	Playschool 9-10-11: 5/1	D. Barons	*P. Nicholls*	13
1988	Bonanza Boy 7-10-1: 9/4	M. Pipe	*P. Scudamore*	12
1989	Bonanza Boy 8-11-11: 15/8	M. Pipe	*P. Scudamore*	12

CURRAN GROUP FINALE HURDLE (3-y-o) (Chepstow 2m)

1971	Ballytruckle 11-0: 15/2	D. Gandolfo	*G. Thorner*	8
1972	Lightning Trial 11-0: 7/1	F. Rimell	*W. Smith*	16
1973	Fighting Kate 10-7: 12/1	H. Nicholson	*R. Dickin*	19
1974	Philominsky 11-0: 6/1	W. Marshall	*M. Wagner*	21
1975	Tiepolino 11-3: 4/1	J. Gifford	*R. Champion*	23
1976	Decent Fellow 11-0: 20/1	G. Balding	*R. Linley*	18
1977	Rodman 11-3: 2/11	F. Winter	*J. Francome*	12
1978	Abandoned because of snow			
1979	Good Ruler 11-0: 10/1	G. Beeson	*R. Goldstein*	14
1980	Broadsword 11-3: 15/8	D Nicholson	*P. Scudamore*	16
1981	Brave Hussar 11-0: 6/5	R. Turnell	*A. Turnell*	15
1982	Primrolla 11-0: 3/1	D. Nicholson	*H. Davies*	14
1983	Dodgy Future 11-0: 2/1	S. Mellor	*M. Perrett*	14
1984	Out of The Gloom 11-0: 7/1	R. Hollinshead	*J. J. O'Neill*	13
1985	The Footman 11-0: 11/1	D. Elsworth	*G. Bradley*	12
1986	High Knowl 11-0: 4/5	M. Pipe	*P. Scudamore*	9
1987	South Parade 11-3: 15/8	G. Balding	*G. Bradley*	7
1988	Enemy Action 11-3: 8/15	M. Pipe	*P. Scudamore*	9
1989	Crystal Heights 11-0: 33/1	J. G. Retter	*B. Powell*	10

KING GEORGE VI RANK CHASE (Kempton 3m)

1947	Rowland Roy 8-11-13: 5/1	F. Walwyn	*B. Marshall*	10
1948	Cottage Rake 9-12-6: 13/8	M. V. O'Brien (Ir)	*A. Brabazon*	9
1949	Finnure 8-11-10: 9/2	G. Beeby	*R. Francis*	4
1950	Manicou 5-11-8: 5/1	P. Cazalet	*B. Marshall*	7
1951	Statecraft 6-11-11: 100/6	P. Cazalet	*A. Grantham*	6
1952	Halloween 7-11-13: 7/4	W. Wightman	*F. Winter*	6
1953	Galloway Braes 8-12-6: 9/4	A. Kilpatrick	*R. Morrow*	7
1954	Halloween 9-11-10: 9/2	W. Wightman	*F. Winter*	8
1955	Limber Hill 8-11-13: 3/1	W. Dutton	*J. Power*	8
1956	Rose Park 10-11-7: 100/6	P. Cazalet	*M. Scudamore*	6
1957	Mandarin 6-12-0: 7/1	F. Walwyn	*P. Madden*	9
1958	Lochroe 10-11-7: 7/2	P. Cazalet	*A. Freeman*	7
1959	Mandarin 8-11-5: 5/2	F. Walwyn	*P. Madden*	9
1960	Saffron Tartan 9-11-7: 5/2	D. Butchers	*F. Winter*	10
1961	Abandoned because of frost			
1962	Abandoned because of frost			
1963	Mill House 6-12-0: 2/7	F. Walwyn	*G. W. Robinson*	3
1964	Frenchman's Cove 9-11-7: 4/11	H. T. Jones	*S. Mellor*	2
1965	Arkle 8-12-0: 1/7	T. Dreaper (Ir)	*P. Taaffe*	4
1966	Dormant 9-11-0: 10/1	J. Wells-Kendrew	*J. King*	7
1967	Abandoned because of foot and mouth epidemic			
1968	Abandoned because of waterlogged state of course			
1969	Titus Oates 7-11-10: 100/30	G. Richards	*S. Mellor*	5
1970	Abandoned because of snow			

1971 The Dikler 8-11-7: 11/2	F. Walwyn	*B. Brogan*	10
1972 Pendil 7-12-0: 4/5	F. Winter	*R. Pitman*	6
1973 Pendil 8-12-0: 30/100	F. Winter	*R. Pitman*	4
1974 Captain Christy 7-12-0: 5/1	P. Taaffe (Ir)	*R. Coonan*	6
1975 Captain Christy 8-12-0: 11/10	P. Taaffe (Ir)	*G. Newman*	7
1976 Royal Marshal II 9-11-7: 16/1	T. Forster	*G. Thorner*	10
1977 Bachelor's Hall 7-11-7: 9/2	P. Cundell	*M. O'Halloran*	9
1978 Gay Spartan 7-11-10: 3/1	A Dickinson	*T. Carmody*	16
1979 Silver Buck 7-11-10: 3/1	A. Dickinson	*T. Carmody*	11
1980 Silver Buck 8-11-10: 9/4	M. Dickinson	*T. Carmody*	8
1981 Abandoned because of frost			
1982 Wayward Lad 7-11-10: 7/2	M. Dickinson	*J. Francome*	6
1983 Wayward Lad 8-11-10: 11/8	M. Dickinson	*R. Earnshaw*	5
1984 Burrough Hill Lad 8-11-10: 1/2	Mrs J. Pitman	*J. Francome*	3
1985 Wayward Lad 10-11-10: 12/1	Mrs M. Dickinson	*G. Bradley*	5
1986 Desert Orchid 7-11-10: 16/1	D. Elsworth	*S. Sherwood*	9
1987 Nupsala 8-11-10: 25/1	F. Doumen (Fr)	*A. Pommier*	9
1988 Desert Orchid 9-11-10: 1/2	D. Elsworth	*S. Sherwood*	5
1989 Desert Orchid 10-11-10: 4/6	D. Elsworth	*R. Dunwoody*	6

TOP RANK CHRISTMAS HURDLE (Kempton 2m)

1969 Coral Diver 4-12-0: 9/4	F. Rimell	*T. Biddlecombe*	6
1970 Abandoned because of snow			
1971 Coral Diver 6-12-5: 7/4	F. Rimell	*T. Biddlecombe*	4
1972 Canasta Lad 6-12-1: 4/7	P. Bailey	*J. King*	6
1973 Lanzarote 5-12-1: 1/6	F. Winter	*R. Pitman*	4
1974 Tree Tangle 5-12-1: 30/100	R. Turnell	*A. Turnell*	5
1975 Lanzarote 7-11-13: 1/1	F. Winter	*J. Francome*	5
1976 Dramatist 5-11-10: 9/1	F. Walwyn	*W. Smith*	6
1977 Beacon Light 6-11-10: 5/2	R. Turnell	*A. Turnell*	3
1978 Kybo 5-11-7: 5/4	J. Gifford	*R. Champion*	6
1979 Bird's Nest 9-11-10: 6/4	R. Turnell	*A. Turnell*	5
1980 Celtic Ryde 5-11-6: 2/1	P. Cundell	*J. Francome*	7
1981 Abandoned because of frost			
1982 Ekbalco 6-11-13: 1/2	R. Fisher	*J. J. O'Neill*	4
1983 Dawn Run 5-10-12: 9/4	P. Mullins (Ir)	*J. J. O'Neill*	4
1984 Browne's Gazette 6-11-3: 11/8	Mrs M. Dickinson	*D. Browne*	7
1985 Aonoch 6-11-3: 14/1	Mrs S. Oliver	*J. Duggan*	9
1986 Nohalmdun 5-11-3: 15/8	M. H. Easterby	*P. Scudamore*	7
1987 Osric 4-11-3: 12/1	M. Ryan	*G. McCourt*	8
1988 Kribensis 4-11-3: 4/9	M. Stoute	*R. Dunwoody*	7
1989 Kribensis 5-11-3: 4/6	M. Stoute	*R. Dunwoody*	8

ROWLAND MEYRICK HANDICAP CHASE (Wetherby 3m 100yds)

1957 Symaethis Nephew 7-10-0: 100/8	R. Renton	*B. Wilkinson*	6
1958 Dondrosa 6-10-9: 10/1	F. Taylor	*T. Kellett*	6
1959 Pendle Lady 9-10-6: 10/1	A. Watson	*M. Towers*	10
1960 Merryman II 9-12-6: 3/1	N. Crump	*G. Scott*	5
1961, 1962, 1963, 1964 and 1965 Abandoned because of frost			
1966 Tudor Fort 6-10-4: 7/1	N. Crump	*P. Buckley*	9
1967 Abandoned because of foot and mouth epidemic			
1968 Chancer 6-9-13: 10/1	W. Hall	*P. Vaughan*	6
1969 Chesapeake Bay 6-10-13: 4/1	N. Crump	*P. Buckley*	6
1970 Excess 8-10-9: 6/5	H. T. Jones	*S. Mellor*	6
1971 Great Noise 7-9-7: 7/2	W. Hall	*D. Taylor*	7
1972 Jomon 6-11-6: 9/2	H. T. Jones	*T. Stack*	8
1973 Tartan Ace 6-10-5: 6/4	W. A. Stephenson	*T. Stack*	7
1974 Glen Owen 7-10-2: 10/1	N. Crump	*P. Buckley*	6
1975 The Gent 7-10-9: 6/1	W. A. Stephenson	*T. Stack*	6
1976 Irish Tony 8-10-9: 9/2	N. Crump	*D. Atkins*	8
1977 Set Point 9-11-5: 5/2	Lady Herries	*D. Munro*	5
1978 Rambling Artist 8-10-11: 6/1	A. Gillam	*D. Goulding*	7
1979 Ballet Lord 8-11-10: 7/1	N. Crump	*C. Hawkins*	7
1980 Sunset Cristo 6-10-11: 9/4	R. Hawkey	*C. Grant*	6
1981 Abandoned because of snow and frost			
1982 Richdee 6-10-6: 5/1	N. Crump	*C. Hawkins*	8
1983 Phil The Fluter 8-10-0: 12/1	H. Wharton	*S. Keightley*	7

1984 Forgive' N Forget 7-11-7: 4/6	J. FitzGerald	*M. Dwyer*	4
1985 Fortina's Express 11-10-6: 14/1	W. A. Stephenson	*C. Hawkins*	5
1986 The Thinker 8-11-6: 12/1	W. A. Stephenson	*R. Dunwoody*	8
1987 Yahoo 6-10-4: 11/8	J. Edwards	*T. Morgan*	5
1988 Whats What 9-10-1: 3/1	B. Bousfield	*P. Niven*	5
1989 Durham Edition 11-10-6: 5/1	W. A. Stephenson	*A. Merrigan*	7

CASTLEFORD HANDICAP CHASE (Wetherby 2m 50yds)

1975 Tingle Creek 9-12-0: 4/9	H. T. Jones	*I. Watkinson*	3
1976 Skryne 6-11-7: 2/1	P. Bailey	*R. Barry*	6
1977 Crofton Hall 8-11-0: 6/5	J. Dixon	*J. J. O'Neill*	6
1978 Lord Greystoke 7-10-11: 9/2	G. Richards	*R. Barry*	4
1979 Rathgorman 7-11-2: 6/4	A. Dickinson	*K. Whyte*	7
1980 Rathgorman 8-11-10: 13/8	M. Dickinson	*K. Whyte*	5
1981 Abandoned because of snow and frost			
1982 Little Bay 7-10-8: 9/2	G. Richards	*R. Barry*	6
1983 Badsworth Boy 8-12-0: 10/11	M. Dickinson	*G. Bradley*	5
1984 Ryeman 7-11-10: 5/2	Mrs M. Dickinson	*G. Bradley*	5
1985 Our Fun 8-10-11: 9/4	J. Gifford	*R. Rowe*	4
1986 Little Bay 11-11-7: 9/1	G. Richards	*P. Tuck*	8
1987 Pearlyman 8-12-7: 1/1	J. Edwards	*T. Morgan*	5
1988 Midnight Count 8-12-2: 15/8	J. Gifford	*P. Hobbs*	4
1989 Ida's Delight 10-10-7: 17/2	J. Charlton	*B. Storey*	5

BLACK AND WHITE WHISKY CHAMPION CHASE
(Leopardstown 2½m)

1986 Very Promising 8-12-0: 5/4	D. Nicholson	*R. Dunwoody*	7
1987 Weather The Storm 7-12-0: 4/1	A. Moore (Ir)	*T. Taaffe*	6
1988 Maid of Money 6-11-9: 12/1	J. Fowler (Ir)	*A. Powell*	6
1989 Maid of Money 7-11-9: 11/10	J. Fowler (Ir)	*A. Powell*	4

BOOKMAKERS HURDLE (Leopardstown 2m)

1986 Derrymore Boy 4-11-3: 8/1	P. Mullins (Ir)	*A. Mullins*	10
1987 Cloughtaney 6-12-0: 3/1	P. Mullins (Ir)	*A. Mullins*	7
1988 Grabel 5-11-9: 7/1	P. Mullins (Ir)	*Mr W. Mullins*	5
1989 Grabel 6-11-9: 8/11	P. Mullins (Ir)	*A. Mullins*	5

THE LADBROKE (Leopardstown 2m)

1969 Normandy 4-11-2: 15/2	F. Rimell	*T. Biddlecombe*	15
1970 Persian War 7-12-0: 5/4	A. Pitt	*J. Uttley*	11
1971 Kelanne 7-11-6: 20/1	W. Marshall	*W. Smith*	16
1972 Captain Christy 5-11-6: 15/2	P. Taaffe (Ir)	*H. Beasley*	13
1973 Comedy of Errors 6-12-0: 4/5	F. Rimell	*W. Smith*	9
1974 Comedy of Errors 7-12-0: 11/10	F. Rimell	*K. White*	8
1975 Night Nurse 4-11-5: 6/4	M. H. Easterby	*P. Broderick*	9
1976 Master Monday 6-10-2: 25/1	L. Quirke (Ir)	*J. P. Harty*	19
1977 Decent Fellow 4-11-4: 4/1	G. Balding	*R. Linley*	18
1978 Chinrullah 6-10-6: 8/1	M. O'Toole (Ir)	*G. Newman*	12
1979 Irian 5-10-0: 25/1	A. Moore (Ir)	*Mrs A. Ferris*	20
1980 Carrig Willy 5-10-0: 33/1	M. O'Toole (Ir)	*T. Quinn*	26
1981 No Race			
1982 For Auction 6-10-10: 9/1	M. Cunningham (Ir)	*Mr C. Magnier*	20
1983 Fredcoteri 7-10-0: 10/1	A. Moore (Ir)	*T. Taaffe*	15
1984 Fredcoteri 8-10-4: 8/1	A. Moore (Ir)	*T. Taaffe*	18
1985 Hansel Rag 5-10-0: 14/1	A. Redmond (Ir)	*A. Powell*	20
1986 Bonalma 6-10-13: 5/1	A. Moore (Ir)	*T. Taaffe*	23
1987 Barnbrook Again 6-11-8: 5/2	D. Elsworth	*C. Brown*	22
1988 Roark 6-11-1: 5/1	A. Moore (Ir)	*T. Taaffe*	15
1989 Redundant Pal 6-10-0: 16/1	P. Mullins (Ir)	*P. Kavanagh*	17
1990 Redundant Pal 7-11-5: 20/1	P. Mullins (Ir)	*C. O'Dwyer*	27

SAVE & PROSPER MANDARIN HANDICAP CHASE (Newbury 3m 2f 82yds)

1963 Mill House 6-12-5: 5/6	F. Walwyn	*G. W. Robinson*	6
1964 Out And About 9-10-5: 7/1	K. Cundell	*B. Gregory*	6
1965 Mill House 8-12-7: 6/4	F. Walwyn	*G. W. Robinson*	7
1966 Abandoned because of snow and frost			
1967 What A Myth 10-11-9: 5/2	R. Price	*P. Kelleway*	11

1968	Abandoned because of snow and frost			
1969	The Otter 8-10-11: 100/8	R. Denning	*B. Scott*	12
1970	Lord Jim 9-10-0: 4/1	F. Walwyn	*G. W. Robinson*	12
1971	The Pantheon 8-11-6: 6/1	F. Rimell	*T. Biddlecombe*	6
1972	Royal Toss 10-11-1: 3/1	H. Handel	*N. Wakley*	9
1973	Abandoned because of fog			
1974	Midnight Fury 7-10-3: 4/1	F. Winter	*V. Soane*	7
1975	Moonlight Escapade 8-10-5: 9/2	C. V. Miller	*D. Cartwright*	6
1976	Roman Holiday 12-10-6: 11/1	C. Bewicke	*V. Soane*	7
1977	Abandoned because of frost			
1977	(Dec 31) Master Spy 8-11-7: 2/1	T. Forster	*G. Thorner*	6
1978	Tommy Joe 8-11-4: 2/1	A. Dickinson	*T. Carmody*	8
1979	Zongalero 9-10-6: 5/2	N. Henderson	*B. R. Davies*	6
1981	Master Smudge 9-11-7: 9/1	A. Barrow	*R. Linley*	7
1982	Night Nurse 11-11-12: 11/2	M. H. Easterby	*J. J. O'Neill*	8
1983	Earthstopper 9-11-1: 9/2	J. Gifford	*Mr G. Sloan*	7
1983	(Dec 31) Observe 7-11-7: 8/13	F. Winter	*J. Francome*	6
1984	Maori Venture 8-11-5: 4/1	A. Turnell	*S. C. Knight*	5
1985	Abandoned because of frost			
1987	Maori Venture 11-11-3: 4/1	A. Turnell	*S. C. Knight*	6
1988	Contradeal 11-11-10: 9/4	F. Walwyn	*K. Mooney*	6
1988	(Dec 31) Ten Plus 8-11-10: 11/10	F. Walwyn	*K. Mooney*	4
1989	Polyfemus 7-10-5: 3/1	M. Robinson	*J. White*	7

L'OREAL HANDICAP HURDLE (Newbury 2m 100yds)

1971	Broken Melody 7-10-3: 8/1	D. Gandolfo	*J. Haine*	16
1972	Dan'l Widden 6-10-2: 20/1	S. Morant	*A. Branford*	19
1973	Abandoned because of fog			
1974	Sycamore 4-10-9: 11/2	J. Gifford	*R. Pitman*	8
1975	Fighting Taffy 7-11-1: 11/2	P. Upton	*P. Blacker*	11
1976	Fighting Kate 6-10-12: 5/2	H. Nicholson	*R. Dickin*	17
1977	No Race			
1977	(Dec 31) Pinchow 6-10-3: 11/2	D. Kent	*P. Haynes*	13
1978	Western Rose 6-11-4: 100/30	F. Rimell	*J. Burke*	12
1979	Jack O'Lantern 4-10-4: 3/1	P. Cundell	*M. O'Halloran*	12
1981	News King 7-11-9: 7/1	F. Winter	*Mr O. Sherwood*	16
1982	Mr Moonraker 5-10-0: 9/2	Miss S. Morris	*M. O'Halloran*	15
1982	Great Light 5-10-12: 6/1	J. Jenkins	*J. J. O'Neill*	12
1983	Cool Decision 6-11-7: 11/2	Miss S. Hall	*R. Earnshaw*	16
1984	Flarey Sark 7-10-8: 7/1	R. Fisher	*J. Doyle*	11
1985	Abandoned because of frost			
1987	Juven Light 6-10-9: 2/1	R. Akehurst	*S. Smith Eccles*	10
1988	Tivian 8-11-0: 10/1	I. Matthews	*G. McCourt*	7
1988	(Dec 31) Afaristoun 4-10-10: 2/1	J. Edwards	*T. Morgan*	5
1989	Fragrant Dawn 5-11-0: 5/2	J. FitzGerald	*M. Dwyer*	16

NEW YEAR'S DAY HURDLE (Windsor 2m 30yds)

1975	Flash Imp 6-12-3: 6/4	R. Smyth	*P. Beasant*	5
1976	Comedy of Errors 9-12-1: 10/11	F. Rimell	*K. White*	8
1977	Strombolus 6-11-9: 12/1	P. Bailey	*R. Barry*	6
1978	Beacon Light 7-12-1: 4/5	R. Turnell	*A. Turnell*	6
1979	Abandoned because of snow			
1980	Abandoned because of frost			
1981	Celtic Ryde 6-11-8: 4/9	P. Cundell	*H. Davies*	9
1982	Celtic Ryde 7-11-8: 1/5	P. Cundell	*H. Davies*	5
1983	Sula Bula 5-11-0: 10/11	M. H. Easterby	*Mr T. Easterby*	6
1984	Secret Ballot 9-11-4: 14/1	A. Turnell	*E. Waite*	6
1985	Ra Nova 6-11-10: 11/8	Mrs N. Kennedy	*R. Dunwoody*	8
1986	Southernair 6-11-4: 9/2	P. Haynes	*A. Webb*	5
1987	Ra Nova 8-11-4: 9/2	I. Matthews	*M. Perrett*	7
1988	Celtic Shot 6-11-4: 5/2	F. Winter	*P. Scudamore*	10
1989	Wishlon 6-11-4: 9/2	R. Smyth	*I. Shoemark*	5
1990	Aldino 7-11-7: 3/1	O. Sherwood	*J. Osborne*	5

ANTHONY MILDMAY, PETER CAZALET MEMORIAL TROPHY HANDICAP CHASE (Sandown 3m 5f 18yds)

1952	Cromwell 11-11-10: 9/2	P. Cazalet	*B. Marshall*	12
1953	Whispering Steel 8-11-3: 7/1	A. Kilpatrick	*R. Emery*	16

1954	Domata 8-10-12: 6/1	F. Cundell	*A. Corbett*	10
1955	Abandoned because of snow and frost			
1956	Linwell 8-9-9: 4/1	C. Mallon	*R. Hamey*	10
1957	Much Obliged 9-10-12: 100/8	N. Crump	*H. East*	20
1958	Polar Flight 8-10-7: 11/2	G. Spann	*G. Slack*	14
1959	Abandoned because of snow and frost			
1960	Team Spirit 8-9-10: 10/1	D. L. Moore (Ir)	*G. W. Robinson*	12
1961	Mac Joy 9-10-7: 25/1	K. Bailey	*M. Scudamore*	13
1962	Duke of York 7-10-12: 6/1	J. Tilling	*Mr D. Scott*	18
1963	Abandoned because of snow and frost			
1964	Dormant 7-10-12: 11/4	N. Crump	*P. Buckley*	9
1965	Freddie 8-10-5: 2/1	R. Tweedie	*P. McCarron*	12
1966	What A Myth 9-12-0: 4/1	R. Price	*P. Kelleway*	5
1967	Abandoned because of frost			
1968	Stalbridge Colonist 9-12-0: 7/1	K. Cundell	*S. Mellor*	18
1969	Abandoned because of fog			
1970	Larbawn 11-11-13: 9/1	M. L. Marsh	*J. Gifford*	8
1971	Abandoned because of frost			
1972	Royal Toss 10-11-4: 5/2	H. Handel	*N. Wakley*	9
1973	Midnight Fury 7-10-0: 12/1	F. Winter	*V. Soane*	9
1974	High Ken 8-10-4: 16/1	J. Edwards	*B. R. Davies*	10
1975	Money Market 8-10-11: 6/1	C. Bewicke	*J. King*	11
1976	Money Market 9-11-0: 3/1	C. Bewicke	*R. Barry*	9
1977	Zeta's Son 8-11-7: 11/2	P. Bailey	*R. Barry*	12
1978	Shifting Gold 9-11-4: 11/8	K. Bailey	*J. Francome*	5
1979	Abandoned because of snow and frost			
1980	Modesty Forbids 8-10-2: 9/1	J. Gifford	*R. Rowe*	13
1981	Peter Scot 10-10-9: 6/1	D. Gandolfo	*P. Barton*	9
1982	Abandoned because of frost and snow			
1983	Fifty Dollars More 8-11-5: 4/6	F. Winter	*R. Linley*	5
1984	Burrough Hill Lad 8-10-9: 11/8	Mrs J. Pitman	*J. Francome*	9
1985	West Tip 8-10-1: 11/4	M. Oliver	*R. Dunwoody*	5
1986	Run And Skip 8-11-1: 7/2	J. Spearing	*P. Scudamore*	8
1987	Stearsby 8-11-5: 11/8	Mrs J. Pitman	*G. McCourt*	7
1988	Rhyme 'N' Reason 9-10-7: 11/8	D. Elsworth	*C. Brown*	6
1989	Mr Frisk 10-10-13: 3/1	K. Bailey	*R. Dunwoody*	7
1990	Cool Ground 8-10-5: 6/1	N. Mitchell	*A. Tory*	12

BIC RAZOR LANZAROTE HANDICAP HURDLE (Kempton 2m)

1978	Nougat 8-11-11: 8/1	J. Gifford	*G. Enright*	13
1979	Love From Verona 5-10-1: 12/1	R. Sheather	*R. Cochrane*	14
1980	Danish King 6-10-3: 4/1	R. Turnell	*A. Turnell*	10
1981	Walnut Wonder 6-10-6: 7/1	L. Kennard	*A. Webber*	12
1982	Knighthood 7-10-0: 10/1	R. Turnell	*S. C. Knight*	14
1983	Brave Hussar 5-10-7: 16/1	J. Gifford	*R. Rowe*	16
1984	Janus 6-11-1: 5/1	Mrs N. Smith	*C. Brown*	10
1985	Abandoned because of snow and frost			
1986	Prideaux Boy 8-11-10: 11/1	G. Roach	*M. Bowlby*	14
1987	Stray Shot 9-9-10: 16/1	G. Hubbard	*Miss G. Armytage*	9
1988	Fredcoteri 12-11-4: 15/2	G. Moore	*M. Hammond*	11
1989	Grey Salute 6-10-7: 9/4	J. Jenkins	*R. Dunwoody*	8
1990	Atlaal 5-10-3: 10/1	J. Jenkins	*R. Dunwoody*	13

MANDOR FLEXIBLE DOORS PREMIER LONG DISTANCE HURDLE (Haydock 3m)

1970	Clever Scot 5-10-9: 4/1	C. Davies	*B. R. Davies*	8
1971	Colonel Imp 9-11-9: 3/1	D. Smith	*B. Fletcher*	7
1972	Notification 7-11-9: 8/1	F. Rimell	*K. White*	8
1973	Be My Guest 5-11-10: 5/2	B. Wilkinson	*B. Fletcher*	7
1974	Abandoned because of waterlogged state of course			
1975	Moyne Royal 10-11-9: 4/6	A. Pitt	*J. King*	7
1976	Abandoned because of waterlogged state of course			
1977	Abandoned because of waterlogged state of course			
1978	Abandoned because of frost			
1979	Abandoned because of frost			
1980	Abandoned because of waterlogged state of course			
1981	Richdee 5-11-5: 11/2	N. Crump	*C. Hawkins*	10
1982	Shell Burst 7-11-5: 4/1	L. Kennard	*H. Davies*	12

1983 Here's Why 6-11-13: 5/1	J. Gifford	*J. J. O'Neill*	9
1984 Abandoned because of frost			
1985 Abandoned because of frost			
1986 Sheer Gold 6-11-6: 7/2	G. Balding	*G. Bradley*	10
1987 Aonoch 8-12-0: 2/1	Mrs S. Oliver	*J. Duggan*	5
1988 Abandoned because of snow			
1989 Out of The Gloom 8-11-7: 3/1	M. Pipe	*P. Scudamore*	10
1990 Mrs Muck 9-11-2: 13/8	N. Twiston-Davies	*G. Bradley*	7

DAILY MAIL RACECALL CHAMPION HURDLE TRIAL (Haydock 2m)

1981 Starfen 5-11-12: 5/2	M. H. Easterby	*Mr T. Easterby*	6
1982 Gaye Chance 7-12-0: 7/2	Mrs M. Rimell	*S. Morshead*	7
1983 Ekbalco 7-12-0: 8/13	R. Fisher	*J. J. O'Neill*	3
1984 Abandoned because of frost			
1985 Abandoned because of frost			
1986 Humberside Lady 5-11-6: 4/1	G. Huffer	*M. Dwyer*	7
1987 Nohalmdun 6-12-0: 2/5	M. H. Easterby	*L. Wyer*	5
1988 Abandoned because of snow			
1989 Vicario di Bray 6-11-8: 11/1	J. J. O'Neill	*M. Dwyer*	6
1990 Bank View 5-11-8: 33/1	N. Tinkler	*G. Bradley*	7

PETER MARSH HANDICAP CHASE (Haydock 3m)

1981 Little Owl 7-11-3: 4/6	M. H. Easterby	*Mr A. J. Wilson*	6
1982 Bregawn 8-10-7: 11/2	M. Dickinson	*R. Earnshaw*	8
1983 Ashley House 9-10-7: 11/8	M. Dickinson	*R. Earnshaw*	7
1984 Abandoned because of frost			
1985 Abandoned because of frost			
1986 Combs Ditch 10-11-8: 3/1	D. Elsworth	*C. Brown*	7
1987 The Thinker 9-11-10: 9/2	W. A. Stephenson	*R. Lamb*	6
1988 Abandoned because of snow			
1989 Bishops Yarn 10-10-12: 13/2	G. Balding	*R. Guest*	4
1990 Nick The Brief 8-10-9: 15/8	J. Upson	*M. Lynch*	6

FOOD BROKERS FINESSE HURDLE (4-y-o) (Cheltenham 2m)

1985 Out of The Gloom 11-7: 11/4	R. Hollinshead	*J. J. O'Neill*	10
1986 Tangognat 11-7: 7/4	R. Simpson	*P. Scudamore*	11
1987 Abandoned because of frost			
1988 Jason's Quest 11-0: 16/1	J. Baker	*M. Williams*	9
1989 Highland Bud 11-3: 4/1	D. Nicholson	*R. Dunwoody*	6
1990 Sayyure 11-8: 3/1	N. Tinkler	*G. McCourt*	4

CHARTERHOUSE MERCANTILE CHASE (Cheltenham 3m 1f)

1980 Raffi Nelson 7-11-6: 5/2	N. Henderson	*S. Smith Eccles*	7
1981 Little Owl 7-11-12: 8/11	M. H. Easterby	*Mr A. J. Wilson*	6
1982 Lesley Ann 8-11-12: 5/2	D. Elsworth	*C. Brown*	3
1983 Combs Ditch 7-11-9: 6/1	D. Elsworth	*C. Brown*	6
1984 Everett 9-11-8: 15/8	F. Walwyn	*S. Shilston*	6
1985 West Tip 8-11-6: 5/2	M. Oliver	*R. Dunwoody*	4
1986 Misty Spirit 7-11-6: 9/1	D. Lee	*S. Smith Eccles*	6
1987 Abandoned because of frost			
1988 Twin Oaks 8-11-6: 6/1	D. Murray-Smith	*P. Croucher*	3
1989 Deep Moment 7-11-3: 12/1	Mrs M. Rimell	*D. Browne*	4
1990 Toby Tobias 8-11-6: 5/4	Mrs J. Pitman	*M. Pitman*	4

ROSSINGTON MAIN NOVICE HURDLE (Doncaster 2m 150yds)

1971 Pry 5-11-2: 7/1	G. Balding	*E. Harty*	6
1972 The Bugler 4-10-5: 10/1	J. Astor	*R. Griffin*	10
1973 Dark Sultan 5-11-7: 5/1	P. Chisman	*R. Barry*	18
1974 Charlie Mouse 5-11-2: 14/1	T. Forster	*G. Thorner*	22
1975 Sea Pigeon 5-11-12: 13/8	G. Richards	*R. Barry*	13
1976 Grand Canyon 6-12-0: 1/2	D. Kent	*P. Haynes*	6
1977 French Hollow 5-11-12	A. Dickinson	*M. Dickinson*	12
1978 Newgate 5-11-12: 5/1	A. Scott	*R. Lamb*	11
1979 No Bombs 4-10-8: 3/1	M. H. Easterby	*N. Tinkler*	11
1980 Pulse Rate 4-10-8: 21/20	M. H. Easterby	*A. Brown*	8
1981 Hard About 5-11-7: 3/1	E. O'Grady (Ir)	*T. Ryan*	8
1982 Gaye Brief 5-11-7: 3/1	Mrs M. Rimell	*S. Morshead*	16
1983 Cardinal Flower 6-11-4: 7/4	A. Scott	*J. J. O'Neill*	8

1984	Abandoned because of snow			
1985	Abandoned because of snow and frost			
1986	Shean Lad 6-11-7: 50/1	Miss L. Siddall	*P. Tuck*	15
1987	Abandoned because of frost			
1988	Drumlin Hill 5-11-0: 15/2	F. Winter	*P. Scudamore*	9
1989	Cruising Altitude 6-11-7: 5/4	O. Sherwood	*S. Sherwood*	5
1990	Peanuts Pet 5-11-0: 4/5	B. McMahon	*T. Wall*	6

WILLIAM HILL GOLDEN SPURS HANDICAP CHASE
(Doncaster 3m 122yds)

1948	Cool Customer 9-12-7: 4/1	J. Fawcus	*P. Murphy*	17
1949	Old Morality 7-10-1: 33/1	F. Rimell	*R. Turnell*	11
1950	Freebooter 9-11-11: 5/2	R. Renton	*J. Power*	14
1951	Arctic Gold 6-11-0: 5/1	G. Balding	*T. Molony*	10
1952	No Race			
1953	Knock Hard 9-11-7: 5/1	M. V. O'Brien (Ir)	*T. Molony*	9
1954	Abandoned because of frost			
1955	Bramble Tudor 7-11-3: 6/1	J. Wight	*R. Curran*	14
1956	Abandoned because of snow and frost			
1957	E.S.B. 11-11-10: 10/1	F. Rimell	*T. Molony*	13
1958	Hall Weir 8-10-10: 11/4	F. Cundell	*W. Rees*	17
1959	Abandoned because of frost			
1960	Knightsbrook 8-11-1: 11/4	W. Hall	*G. Slack*	10
1961	Chavara 8-10-7: 10/1	G. Owen	*S. Mellor*	13
1962	Nicolaus Silver 10-11-9: 100/8	F. Rimell	*H. Beasley*	15
1963	Abandoned because of frost			
1964	King's Nephew 10-11-10: 7/4	F. Cundell	*S. Mellor*	9
1965	King of Diamonds 7-10-4: 20/1	G. Vergette	*J. Kenneally*	12
1966	Freddie 9-11-7: 2/1	R. Tweedie	*P. McCarron*	12
1967	Spear Fir 8-10-6: 100/6	R. Fairbairn	*J. Leech*	12
1968	Sixty Nine 8-12-0: 7/1	Denys Smith	*B. Fletcher*	16
1969	Playlord 8-11-6: 100/8	G. Richards	*R. Barry*	15
1970	Freddie Boy 9-11-3: 100/9	F. Winter	*R. Pitman*	11
1971	Two Springs 9-10-10: 11/1	G. Owen	*R. Edwards*	14
1972	Slaves Dream 8-10-6: 8/1	R. Hall	*M. Dickinson*	9
1973	Charlie Potheen 8-11-10: 9/2	F. Walwyn	*T. Biddlecombe*	10
1974	Cuckolder 9-10-1: 15/2	R. Turnell	*A. Turnell*	11
1975	Rough House 9-10-5: 9/2	F. Rimell	*J. Burke*	9
1976	Abandoned because of frost			
1977	Abandoned because of frost			
1978	Autumn Rain 7-10-2: 12/1	A. Dickinson	*C. Tinkler*	7
1979	Abandoned because of snow			
1980	Jer 9-10-0: 9/2	P. Bevan	*P. Tuck*	8
1981	Tragus 9-10-13: 6/1	D. Morley	*B. R. Davies*	10
1982	Bregawn 8-11-6: 11/8	M. Dickinson	*J. Francome*	9
1983	Get Out of Me Way 8-10-0: 7/2	G. Thorner	*P. Barton*	9
1984	Abandoned because of snow			
1985	Abandoned because of snow and frost			
1986	Abandoned because of frost			
1987	Abandoned because of frost			
1988	Bob Tisdall 9-12-5: 16/1	J. Edwards	*T. Morgan*	21
1989	Proverity 8-11-8: 100/30	J. Edwards	*T. Morgan*	11
1990	Man O'Magic 9-11-0: 7/2	K. Bailey	*M. Perrett*	11

WEST OF SCOTLAND PATTERN NOVICE CHASE (Ayr 2½m)

1976	Stay-Bell 7-11-4: 2/1	Mrs S. Chesmore	*R. Barry*	5
1977	Zarib 9-11-5: 13/8	F. Rimell	*R. Evans*	11
1978	Ballet Lord 7-11-0: 5/2	N. Crump	*C. Hawkins*	7
1979	Abandoned because of frost and snow			
1980	Little Owl 6-11-10: 8/11	M. H. Easterby	*J. J. O'Neill*	7
1981	Wayward Lad 6-11-0: 9/4	M. Dickinson	*T. Carmody*	8
1982	Seamus O'Flynn 7-11-0: 2/1	M. Dickinson	*G. Bradley*	6
1983	Branding Iron 6-11-0: 15/8	M. Dickinson	*R. Earnshaw*	8
1984	Abandoned because of snow and frost			
1985	Abandoned because of frost			
1986	Abandoned because of frost			
1987	Abandoned because of frost			
1988	Randolph Place 7-11-7: 13/8	G. Richards	*P. Tuck*	7

1989	Southern Minstrel 6-11-7: 7/2	W. A. Stephenson	*A. Merrigan*	3
1990	Carrick Hill Lad 7-11-11: 11/10	G. Richards	*N. Doughty*	4

RACEPHONE NATIONAL HANDICAP CHASE
(Warwick 3½m 180yds)

1974	Clarification 7-10-0: 3/1	R. Armytage	*J. Glover*	14
1975	Abandoned because of waterlogged state of course			
1976	Jolly's Clump 10-10-6: 3/1	H. T. Jones	*I. Watkinson*	10
1977	Cornish Princess 9-10-2: 50/1	W. Turner	*Mr R. Hoare*	22
1978	Abandoned because of frost			
1979	Abandoned because of snow and frost			
1980	Abandoned because of frost			
1981	Colonel Christy 6-9-10: 9/1	H. O'Neill	*G. Gracey*	12
1982	Loving Words 9-10-10: 9/1	J. Thorne	*R. Hoare*	12
1983	Bonum Omen 9-10-13: 9/4	F. Walwyn	*K. Mooney*	12
1984	Abandoned because of frost			
1985	Abandoned because of snow and frost			
1986	Knock Hill 10-10-5: 8/1	J. Webber	*A. Webber*	15
1987	Abandoned because of snow and frost			
1988	Abandoned because of snow			
1989	Memberson 11-10-7: 15/2	P. Dufosee	*Mr G. Upton*	11
1990	Midnight Madness 12-11-1: 16/1	D. Bloomfield	*R. Greene*	18

RACECALL GAINSBOROUGH HANDICAP CHASE
(Sandown 3m 118yds)

1954	Shaef 10-11-7: 5/4	J. Gosden	*B. Marshall*	3
1955	Abandoned because of snow			
1956	Abandoned because of frost			
1957	Rose Park 11-12-5: 8/13	P. Cazalet	*G. Nicholls*	7
1958	Pelopidas 8-11-11: 7/2	H. Nicholson	*D. Dick*	5
1959	Saffron Tartan 8-11-11: 2/5	M. V. O'Brien (Ir)	*T. Taaffe*	3
1960	Double Star 8-11-11: 4/9	P. Cazalet	*A. Freeman*	3
1961	Carraroe 9-11-7: 5/1	C. Mitchell	*R. Jenkins*	4
1962	Blue Dolphin 9-11-5: 10/11	P. Cazalet	*W. Rees*	5
1963	Abandoned because of snow and frost			
1964	Mill House 7-12-5: 1/7	F. Walwyn	*G. W. Robinson*	5
1965	Mill House 8-12-5: 8/13	F. Walwyn	*G. W. Robinson*	4
1966	What A Myth 9-11-9: 10/11	R. Price	*P. Kelleway*	6
1967	Mill House 10-11-9: 6/5	F. Walwyn	*G. W. Robinson*	4
1968	The Laird 7-11-9: 5/1	R. Turnell	*J. King*	3
1969	Stalbridge Colonist 10-11-9: 2/1	K. Cundell	*S. Mellor*	3
1970	Spanish Steps 7-12-0: 10/11	E. Courage	*J. Cook*	3
1971	Titus Oates 9-12-0: 10/1	G. Richards	*R. Barry*	3
1972	Crisp 9-12-0: 11/10	F. Winter	*R. Pitman*	3
1973	Royal Toss 11-11-9: 2/1	H. Handel	*N. Wakley*	3
1974	Kilvulgan 7-10-9: 5/2	R. Turnell	*A. Turnell*	6
1975	Abandoned because of waterlogged state of course			
1976	Bula 11-12-0: 1/3	F. Winter	*J. Francome*	3
1977	Master H 8-10-8: 11/1	M. Oliver	*Mr J. Weston*	7
1978	Master H 9-11-3: 4/1	M. Oliver	*J. Francome*	6
1979	Diamond Edge 8-11-3: 11/4	F. Walwyn	*W. Smith*	11
1980	Diamond Edge 9-12-0: 11/4	F. Walwyn	*W. Smith*	7
1981	Tragus 9-10-7: 9/2	D. Morley	*B. R. Davies*	8
1982	Bregawn 8-10-7: 3/1 (at Kempton)	M. Dickinson	*R. Earnshaw*	9
1983	Observe 7-11-3: 11/8	F. Winter	*J. Francome*	5
1984	Burrough Hill Lad 8-11-10: 11/8	Mrs J. Pitman	*J. Francome*	5
1985	Burrough Hill Lad 9-12-0: —	Mrs J. Pitman	*J. Francome*	w.o.
1986	Burrough Hill Lad 10-12-0: 100/30	Mrs J. Pitman	*P. Scudamore*	6
1987	Desert Orchid 8-11-10: 11/4	D. Elsworth	*C. Brown*	6
1988	Charter Party 10-10-11: 100/30	D. Nicholson	*R. Dunwoody*	11
1989	Desert Orchid 10-12-0: 6/5	D. Elsworth	*S. Sherwood*	4
1990	Abandoned because of waterlogged state of course			

SCILLY ISLES NOVICES' CHASE (Sandown 2½m 68yds)

1964	Buona notte 7-12-1: 2/5	R. Turnell	*J. Haine*	6
1965	The Braggart 7-10-12: 100/7	H. T. Jones	*T. Biddlecombe*	13

1966	Abandoned because of waterlogged state of course			
1967	Bowgeeno 7-11-11: 2/1	R. Turnell	*J. King*	9
1968	Aurelius 10-11-8: 4/6	K. Cundell	*S. Mellor*	6
1969	Abandoned because of snow			
1970	Royal Relief 6-12-0: 13/8	E. Courage	*J. Cook*	6
1971	Black Magic 7-12-0: 6/4	P. Cazalet	*R. Dennard*	8
1972	Potentate 7-11-8: 7/4	J. Gifford	*D. Barrott*	6
1973	Killiney 7-12-0: 1/10	F. Winter	*R. Pitman*	3
1974	Even Up 7-11-8: 100/30	Mrs D. Oughton	*G. Thorner*	8
1975	Abandoned because of waterlogged state of course			
1976	Skryne 6-11-9: 2/1	P. Bailey	*R. Barry*	5
1977	Flitgrove 6-11-4: 10/1	D. Nicholson	*J. King*	5
1978	Space Project 8-11-9: 7/1	R. Brown	*R. Hyett*	6
1979	Abandoned because of frost			
1980	Beacon Light 9-11-12: 1/2	R. Turnell	*A. Turnell*	6
1981	Clayside 7-11-9: 13/8	M. H. Easterby	*A. Brown*	7
1982	Sea Image 7-11-8: 11/4 (at Kempton)	F. Winter	*J. Francome*	8
1983	Kilbrittain Castle 7-11-0: 6/4	F. Walwyn	*W. Smith*	5
1984	Norton Cross 6-11-10: 2/1	M. H. Easterby	*A. Brown*	6
1985	Karenomore 7-11-5: 9/4	M. H. Easterby	*J. J. O'Neill*	5
1986	Berlin 7-11-10: 5/2	N. Gaselee	*D. Browne*	6
1987	First Bout 6-11-5: 11/10	N. Henderson	*S. Smith Eccles*	6
1988	Yeoman Broker 7-11-0: 7/4	J. Gifford	*R. Rowe*	5
1989	The Bakewell Boy 7-11-6: 6/1	R. Frost	*J. Frost*	4
1990	Abandoned because of waterlogged state of course			

OTELEY HURDLE (Sandown 2m)

1949	National Spirit 8-12-5: 1/3	V. Smyth	*B. Marshall*	5
1950	National Spirit 9-12-7: 1/4	V. Smyth	*D. Dillon*	5
1951	Abandoned because of waterlogged state of course			
1952	Telegram II 5-11-5: 3/1	F. Walwyn	*D. Dick*	8
1953	Abandoned because of snow			
1954	Fastnet Rock 7-11-9: 7/4	C. Jellis	*A. Freeman*	6
1955	Abandoned because of snow			
1956	Abandoned because of frost			
1957	Vermillion 9-12-5: 10/11	R. Price	*F. Winter*	6
1958	Retour de Flamme 5-11-13: 4/1	S. Warren	*J. Lindley*	8
1959	Fare Time 6-12-3: 1/3	R. Price	*F. Winter*	6
1960	Fare Time 7-12-3: 1/1	R. Price	*F. Winter*	7
1961	Eborneezer 6-12-3: 6/1	R. Price	*F. Winter*	5
1962	Snuff Box 5-10-10: 9/2	J. Benstead	*J. Gilbert*	9
1963	Abandoned because of snow and frost			
1964	Kirriemuir 4-10-12: 8/15	F. Walwyn	*D. Mould*	7
1965	Magic Court 7-12-5: 6/4	T. Robson	*P. McCarron*	12
1966	Abandoned because of waterlogged state of course			
1967	Chenonceaux 6-10-7: 100/6	K. Cundell	*D. Briscoe*	11
1968	Into View 5-10-8: 50/1	F. Winter	*E. P. Harty*	15
1969	Abandoned because of snow			
1970	Major Rose 8-10-10: 1/1	R. Price	*J. Gifford*	7
1971	Major Rose 9-11-4: 15/8	R. Price	*P. Kelleway*	5
1972	Phaestus 6-11-4: 5/2	F. Rimell	*K. White*	9
1973	Lanzarote 5-11-2: 15/8	F. Winter	*R. Pitman*	4
1974	Lanzarote 6-11-12: 1/6	F. Winter	*R. Pitman*	3
1975	Abandoned because of waterlogged state of course			
1976	Sea Pigeon 6-11-12: 2/1	G. Richards	*J. J. O'Neill*	8
1977	Bird's Nest 7-12-2: 30/100	R. Turnell	*A. Turnell*	4
1978	Sea Pigeon 8-11-12: 2/1	M. H. Easterby	*J. J. O'Neill*	5
1979	Abandoned because of frost			
1980	Pollardstown 5-12-2: 9/4	S. Mellor	*P. Blacker*	4
1981	Celtic Ryde 6-11-12: 1/6	P. Cundell	*J. Francome*	4
1982	Heighlin 6-11-4: 8/11 (at Kempton)	D. Elsworth	*S. Jobar*	8
1983	Cima 5-11-4: 8/1	J. Old	*S. Morshead*	5
1984	Sula Bula 6-11-5: 5/1	M. H. Easterby	*Mr T. Easterby*	8
1985	Desert Orchid 6-11-5: 2/1	D. Elsworth	*C. Brown*	8
1986	See You Then 6-11-12: 3/1	N. Henderson	*S. Smith Eccles*	9
1987	Prideaux Boy 9-11-0: 9/4	G. Roach	*M. Bowlby*	7

Year	Winner	Trainer	Jockey	Runners
1988	Celtic Chief 5-11-2: 4/1	Mrs M. Rimell	*R. Dunwoody*	7
1989	Aldino 6-10-7: 4/1	O. Sherwood	*S. Sherwood*	6
1990	Abandoned because of waterlogged state of course			

GAME SPIRIT HANDICAP CHASE (Newbury 2m 160yds)

Year	Winner	Trainer	Jockey	Runners
1953	Marcianus 7-11-7: 13/2	G. Beeby	*R. Francis*	8
1954	Big Bill 8-11-12: 6/4	P. P-Gallwey	*E. Fisher*	6
1955	Belliquex 6-9-12: 20/1	C. Cooper	*E. Kelly*	9
1956	Abandoned because of frost			
1957	Buttercleugh 6-11-6: 11/10	C Bewicke	*G. Milburn*	3
1958	Highland Bard 7-10-10: 9/2	C. Bewicke	*G. Milburn*	13
1959	Chatelet 7-10-0: 100/7	R. Renton	*B. Wilkinson*	13
1960	Threepwood 7-10-9: 8/1	C. Bewicke	*G. Milburn*	8
1961	Richard of Bordeaux 6-10-7: 1/1	F. Walwyn	*F. Winter*	5
1962	Sea Horse 8-11-5: 4/1	W. Marshall	*P. Jones*	10
1963	Abandoned because of snow and frost			
1964	Irish Imp 7-12-7: 4/9	F. Walwyn	*G. W. Robinson*	7
1965	Dunkirk 8-11-10: 9/2	P. Cazalet	*D. Dick*	9
1966	Flash Bulb 9-11-9: 9/2	R. Turnell	*J. Haine*	14
1967	Vulmidas 10-10-9: 6/1	J. Barclay	*Mr T. Pinner*	7
1968	Stonehaven 8-12-3: 4/1	R. Armytage	*S. Mellor*	6
1969	Abandoned because of frost			
1970	Abandoned because of snow and frost			
1971	Royal Relief 7-12-1: 11/4	E. Courage	*J. Cook*	6
1972	Straight Fort 9-11-3: 4/6	J. Dreaper (Ir)	*E. Wright*	3
1973	Pendil 8-12-0: 4/7	F. Winter	*R. Pitman*	8
1974	Abandoned because of waterlogged state of course			
1975	Shock Result 9-10-1: 25/1	R. Turnell	*A. Turnell*	5
1976	Uncle Bing 7-10-0: 16/1	G. Doidge	*J. Burke*	8
1977	Isle of Man 10-11-7: 5/2	F. Walwyn	*W. Smith*	6
1978	Abandoned because of frost			
1979	Casbah 12-10-5: 20/1	T. Forster	*G. Thorner*	5
1980	Gambling Prince 7-10-1: 100/30	Mrs G. Jones	*J. Suthern*	7
1981	Abandoned because of frost			
1982	News King 8-11-7: 7/4	F. Winter	*J. Francome*	5
1983	Abandoned because of snow and frost			
1984	Ragafan 7-10-7: 6/1	R. Smyth	*R. Hughes*	5
1985	Abandoned because of snow			
1986	Abandoned because of snow			
1987	Pearlyman 8-11-7: 3/1	J. Edwards	*P. Scudamore*	6
1988	Very Promising 10-11-6: 5/4	D. Nicholson	*R. Dunwoody*	5
1989	Mr Key 8-10-7: 14/1	D. Murray-Smith	*S. Sherwood*	6
1990	Feroda 9-11-2: 10/11	A. Moore (Ir)	*T. Taaffe*	4

TOTE GOLD TROPHY HANDICAP HURDLE (Newbury 2m 100yds)

Year	Winner	Trainer	Jockey	Runners
1963	Rosyth 5-10-0: 20/1	R. Price	*J. Gifford*	41
1964	Rosyth 6-10-2: 10/1	R. Price	*J. Gifford*	24
1965	Elan 6-10-7: 9/2	J. Sutcliffe, jnr	*D. Nicholson*	21
1966	Le Vermontois 5-11-3: 15/2	R. Price	*J. Gifford*	28
1967	Hill House 7-10-10: 9/1	R. Price	*J. Gifford*	28
1968	Persian War 5-11-13: 9/2	C. Davies	*J. Uttley*	33
1969	Abandoned because of frost			
1970	Abandoned because of snow and frost			
1971	Cala Mesquida 7-10-9: 33/1	J. E. Sutcliffe	*J. Cook*	23
1972	Good Review 6-10-9: 8/1	J. Dreaper (Ir)	*V. O'Brien*	26
1973	Indianapolis 6-10-6: 15/2	J. E. Sutcliffe	*J. King*	26
1974	Abandoned because of waterlogged state of course			
1975	Tammuz 7-10-13: 18/1	F. Walwyn	*W. Smith*	28
1976	Irish Fashion 5-10-4: 16/1	M. Cunningham (Ir)	*R. Barry*	29
1977	True Lad 7-10-4: 14/1	W. Swainson	*T. Stack*	27
1978	Abandoned because of frost			
1979	Within The Law 5-11-4: 25/1	M. H. Easterby	*A. Brown*	28
1980	Bootlaces 6-10-9: 20/1	D. Barons	*P. Leach*	21
1981	Abandoned because of frost			
1982	Donegal Prince 6-10-8: 13/1	P. Kelleway	*J. Francome*	27
1983	Abandoned because of snow and frost			
1984	Ra Nova 5-10-6: 16/1	Mrs N. Kennedy	*P. Farrell*	26
1985	Abandoned because of snow			

1986	Abandoned because of snow			
1987	Neblin 8-10-0: 10/1	G. Balding	*S. Moore*	21
1988	Jamesmead 7-10-0: 11/1	D. Elsworth	*B. Powell*	19
1989	Grey Salute 6-11-5: 8/1	J. Jenkins	*R. Dunwoody*	10
1990	Deep Sensation 5-11-3: 7/1	J. Gifford	*R. Rowe*	17

BYRNE BROTHERS COMPTON CHASE (Newbury 3m)

1966	Woodland Venture 6-12-12: 11/8	F. Rimell	*T. Biddlecombe*	4
1967	Sir Giles 6-12-2: 8/13	F. Walwyn	*D. Nicholson*	5
1968	Domacorn 6-11-13: 4/5	F. Rimell	*T. Biddlecombe*	7
1969	Abandoned because of frost			
1970	Abandoned because of frost and snow			
1971	Lucky Edgar 6-11-2: 11/2	R. Smyth	*J. Woodman*	7
1972	Game Spirit 6-11-13: 7/2	P. Cazalet	*D. Mould*	5
1973	Echo Sounder 6-11-9: 3/1	H. Payne	*N. Flanagan*	5
1974	Abandoned because of waterlogged state of course			
1975	Charlie Mouse 6-11-13: 5/4	T. Forster	*G. Thorner*	10
1976	Zeta's Son 7-11-9: 3/1	P. Bailey	*R. Barry*	7
1977	Double Negative 7-12-2: 11/2	F. Rimell	*S. Morshead*	8
1978	Abandoned because of frost			
1979	Gaffer 7-10-12: 3/1	F. Walwyn	*W. Smith*	8
1980	Silver Buck 8-11-5: 8/13	A. Dickinson	*T. Carmody*	6
1981	Abandoned because of frost			
1982	Royal Judgement 9-11-5: 9/2	J. Gifford	*R. Rowe*	3
1983	Abandoned because of snow and frost			
1984	Brown Chamberlin 9-11-5: 4/6	F. Winter	*J. Francome*	2
1985	Abandoned because of snow			
1986	Abandoned because of snow			
1987	Golden Friend 9-11-4: 4/1	Mrs M. Rimell	*D. Browne*	6
1988	Golden Friend 10-11-4: 11/10	Mrs M. Rimell	*D. Browne*	5
1989	Ten Plus 9-11-4: 8/13	F. Walwyn	*K. Mooney*	3
1990	Barnbrook Again 9-11-2: 11/4	D. Elsworth	*H. Davies*	4

SIDNEY BANKS MEMORIAL NOVICES HURDLE (Huntingdon 2½m)

1976	Grand Canyon 6-12-0: 1/1	D. Kent	*P. Haynes*	6
1977	Abandoned because of waterlogged state of course			
1978	Abandoned because of frost			
1979	Abandoned because of waterlogged state of course			
1980	Abandoned because of flooding			
1981	Glamour Show 5-11-2: 6/1	J. Gifford	*R. Champion*	8
1982	Angelo Salvini 6-11-4: 7/1	M. H. Easterby	*A. Brown*	18
1983	Abandoned because of snow			
1984	The Pawn 5-11-2: 9/2	M. Ryan	*H. Davies*	15
1985	Sheer Gold 5-10-11: 7/4	G. Balding	*B. Reilly*	11
1986	Abandoned because of snow and frost			
1987	Robin Goodfellow 6-11-4: 7/1	G. Balding	*G. Bradley*	8
1988	Nick The Brief 6-11-4: 9/2	T. Casey	*E. Buckley*	16
1989	Celtic Barle 5-11-2: 12/1	T. Casey	*M. Lynch*	7
1990	Abandoned because of waterlogged state of course			

DAILY TELEGRAPH HURDLE (Ascot 3m)

1971	Bannon's Star 9-10-12: 12/1	J. Gifford	*D. Barrott*	8
1972	Highland Seal 9-10-12: 11/2	R. Dening	*T. Jones*	9
1973	True Luck 6-12-2: 11/10	F. Rimell	*K. White*	6
1974	Abandoned because of waterlogged state of course			
1975	Adulation 9-10-10: 7/1	D. Kent	*P. Haynes*	13
1976	Sunyboy 6-12-5: 9/4	F. Walwyn	*W. Smith*	5
1977	Garliestown 10-11-5: 14/1	M. Tate	*C. Smith*	6
1978	Abandoned because of frost			
1979	Abandoned because of frost			
1980	Ross du Vin 9-11-5: 15/2	J. Gifford	*C. Kinane*	9
1981	Richdee 5-11-12: 9/1	N. Crump	*C. Hawkins*	10
1982	Crimson Embers 7-11-5: 7/4	F. Walwyn	*S. Shilston*	8
1983	Abandoned because of frost			
1984	Mayotte 9-11-13: 11/2	R. Holder	*P. Richards*	8
1985	Rose Ravine 6-11-9: 100/30	F. Walwyn	*R. Pusey*	10
1986	King's College Boy 8-11-9: 6/1	N. Vigors	*D. Browne*	4
1987	Model Pupil 7-11-9: 9/2	O. O'Neill	*G. Bradley*	8

1988	Miss Nero 7-11-3: 7/1	R. Lee	*B. Dowling*	11
1989	Calapaez 5-11-13: 6/5	Miss B. Sanders	*S. Sherwood*	6
1990	Ryde Again 7-11-0: 11/4	P. Cundell	*G. McCourt*	11

OLD ROAD SECURITIES REYNOLDSTOWN NOVICES CHASE
(Ascot 3m)

1971	Orient War 8-12-0: 6/5	F. Walwyn	*S. Mellor*	4
1972	Colebridge 8-11-11: 10/11	J. Dreaper (Ir)	*E. Wright*	5
1973	Killiney 7-12-0: 1/4	F. Winter	*R. Pitman*	3
1974	Abandoned because of waterlogged state of course			
1975	Brown Lad 9-11-9: 10/11	J. Dreaper (Ir)	*T. Carberry*	5
1976	Ghost Writer 9-12-0: 7/4	F. Walwyn	*W. Smith*	7
1977	Lanzarote 9-12-0: 4/9	F. Winter	*J. Francome*	6
1978	Abandoned because of frost			
1979	Abandoned because of snow			
1980	Little Owl 6-12-0: 11/10	M. H. Easterby	*J. J. O'Neill*	9
1981	Easter Eel 10-12-0: 8/11	F. Winter	*J. Francome*	7
1982	Richdee 6-11-10: 3/1	N. Crump	*C. Hawkins*	12
1983	Abandoned because of frost			
1984	Duke of Milan 7-11-12: 11/4	N. Gaselee	*S. Smith Eccles*	5
1985	Drumadowney 7-11-8: 3/1	T. Forster	*H. Davies*	8
1986	Bolands Cross 7-11-8: 2/1	N. Gaselee	*P. Scudamore*	7
1987	Tawridge 7-11-12: 2/1	A. Turnell	*S. C. Knight*	5
1988	Kissane 7-11-8: 4/1	J. Edwards	*T. Morgan*	6
1989	Vulgan Warrior 8-11-8: 8/1	S. Christian	*J. Osborne*	6
1990	Royal Athlete 7-11-8: 11/4	Mrs J. Pitman	*M. Pitman*	7

CHARTERHOUSE MERCANTILE HANDICAP CHASE
(Ascot 3m)

1966	Highland Wedding 9-10-12: 4/1	G. Balding	*O. McNally*	12
1967	No Race			
1968	Regal John 10-10-11: 6/1	R. Price	*J. Gifford*	7
1969	Abandoned because of frost			
1970	French Tan 8-11-9: 4/1	A. Watson (Ir)	*P. Taaffe*	8
1971	The Laird 10-11-10: 6/1	R. Turnell	*J. King*	8
1972	Prairie Dog 8-10-1: 5/1	F. Walwyn	*B. Brogan*	6
1973	Balinese 8-11-1: 5/2	R. Turnell	*A. Turnell*	6
1974	Abandoned because of waterlogged state of course			
1975	Ten Up 8-11-6: 7/4	J. Dreaper (Ir)	*T. Carberry*	8
1976	April Seventh 10-11-7: 15/8	R. Turnell	*A. Turnell*	6
1977	Ghost Writer 10-11-5: 3/1	F. Walwyn	*W. Smith*	8
1978	Abandoned because of frost			
1979	Abandoned because of snow			
1980	Master Spy 11-10-11: 9/1	T. Forster	*Mr T. Thomson Jones*	7
1981	Aldaniti 11-11-7: 14/1	J. Gifford	*R. Champion*	8
1982	Cavity Hunter 9-10-3: 5/1	M. Dickinson	*R. Earnshaw*	9
1983	Abandoned because of frost			
1984	Tracys Special 7-10-5: 100/30	A. Turnell	*S. C. Knight*	5
1985	Greenwood Lad 8-10-6: 10/1	J. Gifford	*R. Rowe*	7
1986	Brunton Park 8-10-4: 14/1	Mrs M. Dickinson	*G. Bradley*	8
1987	Castle Warden 10-9-12: 10/1	J. Edwards	*Mr M. Richards*	10
1988	Aquilifer 8-10-1: 5/2	D. Murray-Smith	*P. Croucher*	8
1989	Proud Pilgrim 10-10-9: 6/1	J. FitzGerald	*M. Dwyer*	10
1990	Ten of Spades 10-10-0: 11/2	F. Walwyn	*K. Mooney*	7

TOTE EIDER HANDICAP CHASE (Newcastle 4m 1f)

1952	Witty 7-9-8: 100/8	W. Hall	*G. Slack*	11
1953	Gigolo 8-11-7: 10/11	J. Wight	*Mr A Moralee*	7
1954	Gentle Moya 8-9-10: 7/2	C. Bewicke	*Mr J. Straker*	13
1955	Abandoned because of snow			
1956	Abandoned because of snow and frost			
1957	Wyndburgh 7-10-4: 100/8	P. Wilkinson	*M. Batchelor*	15
1958	Wyndburgh 8-11-1: 9/4	P. Wilkinson	*M. Batchelor*	10
1959	Turmoil 9-10-0: 7/1	T. Hudson	*J. Hudson*	14
1960	Abandoned because of snow and frost			
1961	Carmen IV 9-11-3: 5/1	R. Brewis	*Mr R. Brewis*	13
1962	Ballydar 9-10-10: 13/2	N. Crump	*P. Buckley*	11
1963	Abandoned because of snow and frost			

1964	Vice Regent 7-9-12: 6/1	T. Scott	*S. Hayhurst*	5
1965	Pontin-Go 13-9-9: 10/1	W. Marshall	*J. Lehane*	16
1966	Highland Wedding 9-10-11: 6/1	G. Balding	*O. McNally*	10
1967	Highland Wedding 10-12-0: 1/1	G. Balding	*O. McNally*	7
1968	Abandoned because of snow and frost			
1969	Highland Wedding 12-11-11: 7/4	G. Balding	*R. Champion*	10
1970	China Cloed 7-9-10: 7/2	K. Oliver	*P. Ennis*	8
1971	Abandoned because of waterlogged state of course			
1972	Fair Vulgan 8-9-7: 6/1	H. Bell	*M. Barnes*	8
1973	Abandoned because of snow and frost			
1974	Scarlet Letch 9-10-4: 4/1	R. Brewis	*P. Mangan*	11
1975	Abandoned because of waterlogged state of course			
1976	Forest King 7-10-0: 11/10	K. Hogg	*D. Munro*	12
1977	Set Point 9-11-11: 6/4	Lady Herries	*D. Munro*	6
1978	Abandoned because of snow			
1979	Abandoned because of frost and snow			
1980	Abandoned because of waterlogged state of course			
1981	Waggoners Walk 12-10-2: 6/1	Miss C. Mason	*R. Earnshaw*	12
1982	Lasobany 9-10-0: 5/1	H. Bell	*P. Tuck*	14
1983	Abandoned because of frost			
1984	Lucky Vane 9-10-11: 11/4	G. Balding	*J. Burke*	14
1985	Abandoned because of snow and frost			
1986	Abandoned because of snow and frost			
1987	Peaty Sandy 13-11-11: 11/4	Mrs H. Hamilton	*Mr A. Dudgeon*	9
1988	Star of Screen 8-10-7: 5/2	J. Edwards	*T. Morgan*	8
1989	Polar Nomad 8-9-11: 11/2	W. A. Stephenson	*J. O'Gorman*	10
1990	Jelupe 8-10-0: 13/2	R. Sandys-Clarke	*R. Sandys-Clarke*	13

FOOD BROKERS PERSIAN WAR NOVICE HURDLE
(Chepstow 2½m)

1977	The Dealer 7-12-0: 15/8	F. Winter	*J. Francome*	14
1978	Ballyfin Lake 7-11-10: 15/2	F. Winter	*J. Francome*	12
1979	Abandoned because of snow and frost			
1980	Broadleas 6-11-10: 11/4	J. Gifford	*R. Rowe*	14
1981	Abandoned because of waterlogged state of course			
1982	Arabian Music 7-11-10: 10/1	J. Gifford	*R. Rowe*	10
1983	Abandoned because of frost			
1984	Brown Trix 6-11-7: 7/1	F. Winter	*J. Francome*	10
1985	Abandoned because of snow and frost			
1986	Abandoned because of frost			
1987	Bonanza Boy 6-11-3: 11/4	P. Hobbs	*P. Hobbs*	13
1988	Sir Blake 7-11-10: 10/1	D. Elsworth	*C. Brown*	8
1989	Abandoned because of waterlogged state of course			
1990	Abandoned because of waterlogged state of course			

NOTTINGHAMSHIRE NOVICES CHASE (Nottingham 2m)

1974	The Sundance Kid 7-11-9: 4/1	H. T. Jones	*Mr C. T. Jones*	10
1975	Traite de Paix 7-11-13: 6/1	A. Jarvis	*S. Taylor*	7
1976	Sycamore 7-11-1: 6/1	J. Gifford	*P. Blacker*	6
1977	Abandoned because of waterlogged state of course			
1978	Abandoned because of frost			
1979	Abandoned because of snow			
1980	Beacon Light 9-11-11: 4/9	R. Turnell	*A. Turnell*	5
1981	Palace Dan 5-10-7: 2/1	F. Rimell	*S. Morshead*	7
1982	Sailor's Return 6-11-11: 4/1	D. Nicholson	*P. Scudamore*	10
1983	Bold Yeoman 7-11-1: 25/1	J. Gifford	*H. Davies*	7
1984	Noddy's Ryde 7-11-10: 8/11	G. Richards	*N. Doughty*	5
1985	Abandoned because of snow			
1986	Abandoned because of snow and frost			
1987	Kouros 8-11-5: 20/1	O. Brennan	*M. Brennan*	6
1988	Danish Flight 9-11-5: 5/1	J. FitzGerald	*M. Dwyer*	4
1989	Phoenix Gold 9-11-5: 15/8	J. FitzGerald	*P. Scudamore*	6
1990	Cashew King 7-11-10: 7/4	B. McMahon	*T. Wall*	6

ARKLE PERPETUAL CUP CHASE (Leopardstown 2¼m)

1969	King's Sprite 7-11-9: 100/7	G. Wells	*P. Black*	8
1970	Not run			
1971	Dim Wit 6-11-9: 3/1	P. Mullins	*M. Curran*	7

1972	Ormond King 7-11-9: 11/5	C. Powell	*B. Hannon*	12
1973	Good Review 7-12-0: 4/9	J. Dreaper	*V. O'Brien*	4
1974	Ten Up 7-12-0: 4/7	J. Dreaper	*T. Carberry*	6
1975	Spanish Tan 7-11-6: 12/1	F. Flood	*F. Berry*	13
1976	Troubled Times 7-11-2: 6/1	P. McCreery	*D. Hughes*	6
1977	Siberian Sun 6-11-9: 9/2	F. Flood	*F. Berry*	8
1978	Kilmakillogue 9-11-2: 4/6	E. O'Grady	*Mr W. Madden*	7
1979	Chinrullah 7-11-2: 5/4	M. O'Toole	*D. Hughes*	13
1980	Anaglogs Daughter 7-10-12: 7/1	W. Durkan	*M. Mulligan*	11
1981	Light The Wad 8-11-7: 5/4	D. Hughes	*F. Leavy*	6
1982	Sean Ogue 6-11-5: 1/2	M. O'Brien	*P. Walsh*	4
1983	Pearlstone 7-10-11: 4/1	P. Mullins	*A. Mullins*	14
1984	Bobsline 8-11-9: 4/5	F. Flood	*F. Berry*	10
1985	Buck House 7-11-9: 7/4	M. Morris	*T. Carmody*	6
1986	Passage Creeper 9-10-13: 3/1	J. Dreaper	*K. Morgan*	7
1987	Barrow Line 10-12-0: 4/5	P. Hughes	*F. Berry*	10
1988	Wolf of Badenoch 7-11-6: 11/10	J. Mulhern	*T. Carmody*	5
1989	Abbenoir 7-11-6: 10/1	F. Flood	*R. Byrne*	5
1990	On The Other Hand 7-11-6: 5/2	J. Mulhern	*T. Carmody*	8

WESSEL CABLE CHAMPION HURDLE (Leopardstown 2m)

1977	Master Monday 7-12-0: 20/1	L. Quirke (Ir)	*J. P. Harty*	16
1978	Prominent King 6-11-4: 6/1	K. Prendergast (Ir)	*R. Coonan*	16
1979	Connaught Ranger 5-11-5: 5/1	F. Rimell	*C. Tinkler*	12
1980	Twinburn 5-11-5: 7/4	A. Redmond (Ir)	*T. Quinn*	13
1981	Daring Run 6-11-8: 13/8	P. McCreery (Ir)	*Mr T. M. Walsh*	13
1982	Daring Run 7-12-0: 9/4	P. McCreery (Ir)	*Mr T. M. Walsh*	13
1983	Royal Vulcan 5-11-5: 2/1	N. Callaghan	*J. J. O'Neill*	7
1984	Dawn Run 6-11-9: 4/5	P. Mullins (Ir)	*J. J. O'Neill*	8
1985	Fredcoteri 9-11-4: 5/1	A. Moore (Ir)	*T. Taaffe*	8
1986	Herbert United 7-11-4: 8/1	D. McDonogh (Ir)	*H. Rogers*	11
1987	Deep Idol 7-11-9: 12/1	P. Osborne (Ir)	*B. Sheridan*	7
1988	Classical Charm 5-11-3: 9/1	J. O'Connell (Ir)	*K. Morgan*	8
1989	Kingsmill 6-11-7: 8/1	T. Stack (Ir)	*D. Murphy*	12
1990	Nomadic Way 5-11-4: 3/1	B. Hills	*B. Powell*	8

FAIRLAWNE CHASE (Windsor 3m)

1962	Hedgelands 9-11-7: 4/1	C. Mitchell	*J. Gifford*	9
1963	Certain Justice 10-11-1: 4/1	A. Neaves	*T. Baldwin*	4
1964	Sir Daniel 8-11-4: 11/10	P. Cazalet	*W. Rees*	6
1965	Anglo 7-11-2: 8/11	F. Winter	*T. Norman*	6
1966	No Race			
1967	Abandoned because of frost			
1968	Bassnet 9-11-4: 6/1	A. Kilpatrick	*D. Nicholson*	6
1969	The Laird 8-11-7: 4/5	R. Turnell	*J. King*	4
1970	Specify 8-11-4: 100/8	D. Weeden	*T. Biddlecombe*	5
1971	Into View 8-12-0: 4/9	F. Winter	*P. Kelleway*	2
1972	Cardinal Error 8-11-0: 8/1	F. Winter	*J. Francome*	5
1973	Spanish Steps 10-12-0: 7/4	E. Courage	*B. R. Davies*	3
1974	Game Spirit 8-11-4: 1/3	F. Walwyn	*T. Biddlecombe*	5
1975	Bula 10-12-0: 8/13	F. Winter	*J. Francome*	5
1976	Bula 11-12-0: —	F. Winter	*J. Francome*	2
1977	Abandoned because of waterlogged state of course			
1978	Abandoned because of frost			
1979	Joint Venture 10-11-8: 33/1	J. Old	*J. Francome*	4
1980	Border Incident 10-12-0: 4/11	R. Head	*J. Francome*	3
1981	Abandoned because of frost			
1982	Venture To Cognac 9-11-12: 11/10	F. Winter	*Mr O. Sherwood*	4
1983	Abandoned because of snow			
1984	Everett 9-11-12: 4/5	F. Walwyn	*S. Shilston*	4
1985	Abandoned because of snow and frost			
1986	Abandoned because of snow and frost			
1987	Western Sunset 11-11-12: 5/4	T. Forster	*H. Davies*	5
1988	Rhyme 'N' Reason 9-11-4: 15/8	D. Elsworth	*B. Powell*	5
1989	Bartres 10-11-8: 1/1	D. Murray-Smith	*G. Bradley*	5
1990	Abandoned because of flooding			

KINGWELL HURDLE (Wincanton 2m)

1971	Bula 6-11-13: 2/5	F. Winter	*R. Pitman*	7
1972	Bula 7-12-3: 11/10	F. Winter	*P. Kelleway*	9
1973	Bula 8-12-3: 2/7	F. Winter	*P. Kelleway*	3
1974	Lanzarote 6-12-3: 1/3	F. Winter	*R. Pitman*	7
1975	Lanzarote 7-12-3: 1/4	F. Winter	*R. Pitman*	12
1976	Lanzarote 8-12-0: 1/3	F. Winter	*J. Francome*	7
1977	Dramatist 6-11-7: 4/9	F. Walwyn	*W. Smith*	7
1978	Abandoned because of snow			
1979	Western Rose 7-12-0: 11/8	F. Rimell	*C. Tinkler*	9
1980	Random Leg 5-11-5: 4/1	J. Gifford	*R. Rowe*	7
1981	Jugador 6-11-7: 15/2	D. Kent	*P. Haynes*	11
1982	Walnut Wonder 7-11-7: 4/1	D. Elsworth	*C. Brown*	6
1983	Migrator 7-11-7: 8/1	L. Kennard	*R. Linley*	14
1984	Desert Orchid 5-11-2: 2/1	D. Elsworth	*C. Brown*	9
1985	Abandoned because of snow and frost			
1986	Abandoned because of frost			
1987	Hypnosis 8-11-2: 25/1	D. Elsworth	*P. Scudamore*	6
1988	Floyd 8-11-8: 9/2	D. Elsworth	*C. Brown*	8
1989	Floyd 9-11-8: 10/11	D. Elsworth	*R. Dunwoody*	5
1990	Kribensis 6-11-12: 4/6	M. Stoute	*R. Dunwoody*	8

RACING POST HANDICAP CHASE (Kempton 3m)

1949	Royal Mount 10-11-5: 15/8	J. Powell	*P. Doyle*	5
1950	Printers Pie 6-11-2: 4/1	G. Wilson	*I. Stephens*	7
1951	Cadamstown 11-10-9: 6/1	V. Brunt	*J. Dowdeswell*	7
1952	Mont Tremblant 6-11-5: 6/4	F. Walwyn	*D. Dick*	7
1953	Wigby 7-11-0: 5/2	F. Cundell	*R. Francis*	4
1954	Claude Duval 9-10-13: 7/2	P. Thrale	*J. Beasty*	5
1955	Halloween 10-12-6: 11/10	W. Wightman	*F. Winter*	5
1956	Abandoned because of snow and frost			
1957	Pointsman 9-12-1: 3/1	A. Kilpatrick	*R. Morrow*	7
1958	Lochroe 10-11-13: 9/4	P. Cazalet	*Mr E. Cazalet*	5
1959	Stanton Johnie 9-9-12: 20/1	D. Ancil	*R. Hirons*	3
1960	Dandy Scot 10-11-4: 4/11	R. Price	*F. Winter*	4
1961	Pouding 8-10-8: 7/4	F. Walwyn	*F. Winter*	6
1962	Frenchman's Cove 7-11-13: 4/5	H. T. Jones	*S. Mellor*	4
1963	Dark Venetian 8-10-10: 6/1	R. Bassett	*D. Bassett*	7
1964	Abandoned because of frost			
1965	The Rip 10-12-0: 7/4	P. Cazalet	*D. Dick*	6
1966	Kapeno 9-11-1: 100/30	P. Cazalet	*D. Mould*	9
1967	Maigret 10-10-4: 9/1	I. Herbert	*J. Haine*	5
1968	Different Class 8-11-9: 30/100	P. Cazalet	*D. Mould*	2
1969	Bassnet 10-11-9: 3/1	R. Price	*J. Gifford*	8
1970	Titus Oates 8-11-12: 3/1	G. Richards	*S. Mellor*	9
1971	The Laird 10-11-0: 11/8	R. Turnell	*J. King*	3
1972	Crisp 9-12-0: 9/4	F. Winter	*R. Pitman*	5
1973	Pendil 8-12-0: 1/7	F. Winter	*R. Pitman*	3
1974	Pendil 9-12-0: 1/6	F. Winter	*R. Pitman*	3
1975	Cuckolder 10-10-0: 6/1	R. Turnell	*A. Turnell*	5
1976	Canadius 7-10-9: 4/1	G. Richards	*J. J. O'Neill*	4
1977	Don't Hesitate 7-9-9: 20/1	P. Cundell	*M. O'Halloran*	7
1978	Fort Devon 12-12-0: 10/11	F. Walwyn	*W. Smith*	5
1979	Strombolus 8-10-10: 16/1	P. Bailey	*R. Champion*	14
1980	Father Delaney 8-10-11: 9/1	M. H. Easterby	*A. Brown*	10
1981	Sugarally 8-10-0: 9/2	G. Fairbairn	*P. Scudamore*	8
1982	Two Swallows 9-10-9: 6/1	R. Armytage	*A. Webber*	7
1983	Manton Castle 9-11-7: 15/2	J. Gifford	*H. Davies*	10
1984	Tom's Little Al 8-10-3: 6/1	W. R. Williams	*C. Brown*	10
1985	Abandoned because of frost			
1986	Abandoned because of frost			
1987	Combs Ditch 11-11-7: 11/10	D. Elsworth	*C. Brown*	4
1988	Rhyme 'N' Reason 9-10-11: 7/2	D. Elsworth	*B. Powell*	12
1989	Bonanza Boy 8-11-1: 5/1	M. Pipe	*P. Scudamore*	11
1990	Desert Orchid 11-12-3: 8/11	D. Elsworth	*R. Dunwoody*	8

TOTE PLACEPOT HURDLE (4-y-o) (Kempton 2m)

1965	Bronzino 10-10: 11/2	G. Todd	*R. Broadway*	10

1966 Harwell 11-10: 11/10	A. Thomas	*H. Beasley*	12
1967 Acrania 11-1: 20/1	G. Harwood	*H. Beasley*	16
1968 St Cuthbert 11-3: 9/4	F. Rimell	*T. Biddlecombe*	12
1969 Rabble Rouser 10-10: 25/1	R. Akehurst	*R. Atkins*	25
1970 Frozen Alive 11-5: 7/2	H. T. Jones	*S. Mellor*	15
1971 Melody Rock 11-3: 11/8	R. Price	*T. Biddlecombe*	7
1972 Official 11-8: 4/1	G. Balding	*R. Bailey*	12
1973 Padlocked 11-8: 6/4	R. Price	*P. Kelleway*	10
1974 Supreme Halo 11-8: 6/1	R. Smyth	*J. King*	26
1975 Wovoka 11-1: 14/1	I. Dudgeon	*R. Floyd*	14
1976 Soldier Rose 10-13: 2/1	R. Price	*P. Kelleway*	14
1977 Rathconrath 10-10: 3/1	F. Winter	*J. Francome*	13
1978 Bootlaces 10-10: 10/1	D. Barons	*P. Leach*	16
1979 Pollardstown 11-3: 13/8	S. Mellor	*P. Blacker*	11
1980 Hill of Slane 11-3: 2/1	A. Jarvis	*A. Turnell*	7
1981 Ra Tapu 10-10: 12/1	P. Mitchell	*R. Hughes*	12
1982 Morice 10-10: 4/1	R. Hannon	*A. Turnell*	8
1983 Jorge Miguel 10-0: 10/1	G. Pritchard-Gordon	*R. Earnshaw*	15
1984 Clarinbridge 10-10: 11/4	J. Bolger (Ir)	*B. Nolan*	11
1985 Abandoned because of frost			
1986 Abandoned because of frost			
1987 Framlington Court 10-10: 6/1	P. Walwyn	*D. Browne*	10
1988 Russian Affair 11-0: 7/1	R. Akehurst	*D. McKeown*	12
1989 Royal Derbi 11-3: 10/1	N. Callaghan	*H. Davies*	6
1990 Philosophos 11-0: 33/1	J. Baker	*W. McFarland*	11

R.O.A. RENDLESHAM HURDLE (Kempton 3m)

1980 Derring Rose 5-10-11: 50/1	A. Jarvis	*A. Turnell*	6
1981 Derring Rose 6-11-6: 11/10	F. Winter	*J. Francome*	7
1982 Hill of Slane 6-11-3: 7/2	A. Jarvis	*A. Turnell*	10
1983 Mellie 8-11-7: 33/1	R. Blakeney	*S. Morshead*	15
1984 Gaye Chance 9-11-5: 4/6	Mrs M. Rimell	*S. Morshead*	6
1985 Abandoned because of frost			
1986 Abandoned because of frost			
1987 Aonoch 8-12-0: 6/4	Mrs S. Oliver	*J. Duggan*	9
1988 King's College Boy 10-11-5: 15/8	Mrs M. Dickinson	*G. Bradley*	8
1989 Cliffalda 6-11-9: 11/4	J. Edwards	*T. Morgan*	5
1990 Old Dundalk 6-11-3: 33/1	D. Murray-Smith	*M. Bowlby*	7

NATIONAL SPIRIT CHALLENGE TROPHY HURDLE
(Fontwell 2¼m)

1971 Varma 5-11-10: 5/2	M. Masson	*D. Mould*	9
1972 St Patrick's Blue 7-11-12: 7/2	D. Tatlow	*D. Mould*	8
1973 Brantridge Farmer 5-11-3: 6/1	Miss A. Sinclair	*R. Rowell*	7
1974 Brantridge Farmer 6-11-12: 4/5	F. Walwyn	*T. Biddlecombe*	7
1975 Bladon 5-11-10: 14/1	F. Winter	*R. Kington*	8
1976 Comedy of Errors 9-12-0: 4/6	F. Rimell	*J. Burke*	6
1977 Comedy of Errors 10-12-0: 1/2	F. Rimell	*J. Burke*	6
1978 Kybo 5-11-12: 7/2	J. Gifford	*R. Champion*	11
1979 Bird's Nest 9-12-0: 4/1	R. Turnell	*A. Turnell*	8
1980 Snowtown Boy 5-11-8: 1/7	F. Winter	*J. Francome*	6
1981 Random Leg 6-11-11: 33/1	J. Gifford	*R. Champion*	6
1982 Mr Moonraker 5-11-10: 13/2	Miss S. Morris	*P. Carvill*	6
1983 Abandoned because of frost			
1984 Cut A Dash 5-11-7: 8/11	Mrs N. Smith	*J. Francome*	8
1985 Abandoned because of frost			
1986 Abandoned because of frost			
1987 Corporal Clinger 8-11-9: 8/11	M. Pipe	*P. Scudamore*	7
1988 Vagador 5-10-12: 9/4	G. Harwood	*M. Perrett*	5
1989 Beech Road 7-10-12: 4/1	G. Balding	*R. Guest*	3
1990 Vagador 7-10-9: 11/4	G. Harwood	*M. Perrett*	5

VICTOR LUDORUM HURDLE (4-y-o)
(Haydock 2m)

1962 Pillock's Green 10-13: 5/1	F. Rimell	*H. Beasley*	9
1963 Abandoned because of frost			
1964 Makaldar 11-3: 8/11	P. Cazalet	*D. Mould*	11
1965 Anselmo 11-3: 13/8	K. Piggott	*T. Carberry*	15

1966	Harwell 11-3: 4/9	A. Thomas	*H. Beasley*	9
1967	Persian War 11-3: 5/4	B. Swift	*J. Uttley*	9
1968	Wing Master 11-3: 8/1	J. Bower	*R. Reid*	6
1969	Coral Diver 11-0: 7/2	F. Rimell	*T. Biddlecombe*	11
1970	Abandoned because of snow and frost			
1971	Nerak 11-0: 3/1	S. Norton	*S. A. Taylor*	13
1972	North Pole 11-0: 100/30	F. Rimell	*K. White*	7
1973	Mythical King 11-4: 5/1	J. Gifford	*D. Barrott*	13
1974	Relevant 11-4: 10/1	R. Edwards	*G. Griffin*	15
1975	Zip Fastener 11-4: 5/1	F. Rimell	*J. King*	11
1976	Sweet Joe 11-9: 5/1	H. T. Jones	*I. Watkinson*	11
1977	Rathconrath 11-9: 7/2	F. Winter	*J. Francome*	12
1978	Mixed Melody 11-4: 12/1	G. Richards	*D. Goulding*	13
1979	Exalted 11-4: 5/2	J. Bolger (Ir)	*J. P. Harty*	13
1980	Jubilee Saint 11-4: 6/1	Miss S. Hall	*D. Goulding*	8
1981	Abandoned because of waterlogged state of course			
1982	Azaam 11-4: 14/1	R. Fisher	*D. Goulding*	11
1983	Wollow Will 11-9: 8/13	F. Winter	*J. Francome*	8
1984	Childown 11-9: 9/4	N. Henderson	*S. Smith Eccles*	11
1985	Wing And A Prayer 11-10: 4/7	J. Jenkins	*J. Francome*	8
1986	Abandoned because of frost			
1987	Cashew King 11-4: 10/1	B. McMahon	*T. Wall*	6
1988	Royal Illusion 11-10: 20/1	G. Moore	*M. Hammond*	13
1989	Liadett 11-10: 7/4	M. Pipe	*J. Lower*	7
1990	Ninja 11-4: 5/1	D. Nicholson	*R. Dunwoody*	5

TIMEFORM CHASE (Haydock 2½m)

1981	Little Owl 7-11-10: 4/5	M. H. Easterby	*Mr A. J. Wilson*	4
1982	Wayward Lad 7-11-12: 2/5	M. Dickinson	*R. Earnshaw*	4
1983	Fifty Dollars More 8-11-8: 13/8	F. Winter	*R. Linley*	4
1984	Forgive'N Forget 7-11-0: 5/2	J. FitzGerald	*M. Dwyer*	6
1985	Forgive'N Forget 8-11-8: 4/7	J. FitzGerald	*M. Dwyer*	7
1986	Abandoned because of frost			
1987	Abandoned because of snow			
1988	Raise An Argument 9-11-4: 7/2	Mrs M. Dickinson	*J. Osborne*	7
1989	Southern Minstrel 6-11-0: 1/1	W. A. Stephenson	*A. Merrigan*	3
1990	Tartan Takeover 8-11-0: 2/1	G. Richards	*M. Dwyer*	5

GREENALL WHITLEY HANDICAP CHASE (Haydock 3m)

1968	Half Awake 8-10-13: 7/2	D. Thomson	*T. Stack*	9
1969	Two Springs 7-10-4: 5/1	G. Owen	*R. Edwards*	6
1970	Abandoned because of snow and frost			
1971	Rainbow Valley 8-10-13: 7/2	A. Dickinson	*M. Dickinson*	6
1972	Young Ash Leaf 8-11-8: 6/1	K. Oliver	*T. Stack*	9
1973	Tregarron 6-10-6: 7/1	K. Oliver	*C. Tinkler*	11
1974	Glanford Brigg 8-10-7: 4/1	J. Hardy	*S. Holland*	12
1975	The Benign Bishop 8-11-8: 4/1	K. Oliver	*R. Barry*	6
1976	Royal Frolic 7-10-12: 3/1	F. Rimell	*Mr S. Morshead*	7
1977	General Moselle 8-10-3: 15/2	H. Wharton	*I. Watkinson*	10
1978	Rambling Artist 8-10-6: 3/1	T. Gillam	*J. J. O'Neill*	8
1979	Alverton 9-11-5: 2/1	M. H. Easterby	*J. J. O'Neill*	13
1980	Cavity Hunter 7-11-1: 4/1	A. Dickinson	*R. Lamb*	9
1981	Sunset Cristo 7-11-7: 5/1	R. Hawkey	*C. Grant*	8
1982	Scot Lane 9-10-0: 14/1	M. Tate	*C. Smith*	12
1983	Righthand Man 6-10-9: 9/4	M. Dickinson	*R. Earnshaw*	10
1984	Midnight Love 9-10-3: 14/1	D. Smith	*C. Grant*	10
1985	Earls Brig 10-10-6: 3/1	W. Hamilton	*P. Tuck*	9
1986	Abandoned because of frost			
1987	Abandoned because of snow			
1988	Yahoo 7-10-10: 11/4	J. Edwards	*T. Morgan*	8
1989	Eton Rouge 10-10-1: 11/2	Mrs M. Rimell	*J. Bryan*	4
1990	Rinus 9-10-4: 11/2	G. Richards	*R. Dunwoody*	11

GEOFFREY GILBEY MEMORIAL HANDICAP CHASE
(Newbury 2½m)

1970	Simian 8-10-10: 11/8	Miss A. Sinclair	*D. Moore*	6
1971	Into View 8-11-9: 6/5	F. Winter	*P. Kelleway*	9
1972	The Laird 11-11-10: 13/2	R. Turnell	*J. King*	7

1973	Crisp 10-12-1: 15/8	F. Winter	*R. Pitman*	9
1974	Bula 9-11-4: 1/1	F. Winter	*J. Francome*	11
1975	Game Spirit 9-11-8: 9/2	F. Walwyn	*W. Smith*	8
1976	Black Andrew 8-10-5: 1/1	F. Walwyn	*M. Floyd*	5
1977	Even Dawn 10-11-1: 3/1	B. Lunness	*G. Holmes*	8
1978	Midnight Court 7-12-0: 4/5	F. Winter	*J. Francome*	8
1979	Harry Hotspur 9-10-1: 4/1	Mrs D. Oughton	*S. Smith Eccles*	7
1980	Bachelor's Hall 10-10-13: 11/4	P. Cundell	*A. Brown*	7
1981	Dramatist 10-11-0: 7/2	F. Walwyn	*W. Smith*	7
1982	Straight Jocelyn 10-11-7: 11/4	R. Armytage	*B. R. Davies*	6
1983	Kathies Lad 6-10-6: 5/4	A. Jarvis	*P. Scudamore*	6
1984	Classified 8-10-11: 6/1	N. Henderson	*C. Mann*	11
1985	Western Sunset 9-10-12: 5/2	T. Forster	*H. Davies*	10
1986	Abandoned because of frost			
1987	Abandoned because of snow			
1988	Pegwell Bay 7-11-10: 21/20	T. Forster	*C. Llewellyn*	4
1989	Eastshaw 7-10-3: 9/4	T. Forster	*C. Llewellyn*	6
1990	Gembridge Jupiter 12-10-9: 9/1	C. C. Trietline	*P. Dever*	8

PHILIP CORNES SADDLE OF GOLD HURDLE FINAL

(Newbury 3m 120yds)

1977	Kas 5-10-12: 9/4	P. Ashworth	*K. Gray*	14
1978	Lighter 5-10-12: 1/1	J. Edwards	*P. Blacker*	8
1979	Quarry Stone 6-11-0: 4/1	J. Cox (Ir)	*T. McGivern*	12
1980	Woodford Prince 7-11-0: 11/2	P. Cundell	*J. Francome*	10
1981	Gaye Chance 6-11-5: 11/1	F. Rimell	*S. Morshead*	15
1982	Angelo Salvini 6-11-5: 4/1	M. H. Easterby	*S. C. Knight*	10
1983	Inish Glora 7-11-5: 5/2	G. Thorner	*R. Kington*	14
1984	Bucko 7-11-0: 7/1	J. FitzGerald	*R. O'Leary*	13
1985	Lonach 7-11-5: 7/2	G. Balding	*R. Linley*	8
1986	Pike's Peak 5-11-5: 11/8	N. Henderson	*S. Smith Eccles*	16
1987	Abandoned because of snow			
1988	Crumpet Delite 8-11-5: 4/1	Mrs J. Pitman	*M. Pitman*	13
1989	Pertemps Network 5-11-5: 4/5	M. Pipe	*P. Scudamore*	5
1990	Miinnehoma 7-11-5: 1/1	M. Pipe	*P. Scudamore*	6

PHILIP CORNES NICKLE ALLOYS NOVICE CHASE

(Newbury 2½m)

1957	Merchant Prince 7-11-7: 9/2	G. Beeby	*D. Dick*	9
1958	Devon Dumpling 6-11-4: 7/1	R. Renton	*B. Wilkinson*	11
1959	Wayward Bird 10-11-10: 7/4	D. Ancil	*D. Ancil*	15
1960	Mariner's Dance 7-12-0: 4/9	P. Cazalet	*A. Freeman*	12
1961	King's Nephew 7-12-0: 6/5	F. Cundell	*M. Scudamore*	7
1962	Forgotten Dreams 8-11-7: 6/4	A. Thomas	*J. Gifford*	9
1963	Rue de Paris 6-11-4: 5/1	H. T. Jones	*S. Mellor*	12
1964	Vultrix 6-11-10: 11/4	F. Cundell	*F. Winter*	10
1965	Abandoned because of snow			
1966	Sunny Bright 9-11-10: 8/1	M. Goswell	*D. Moore*	16
1967	Woodbow 7-11-4: 7/2	F. Winter	*R. Pitman*	9
1968	Cottager 8-11-7: 5/2	F. Winter	*Mr N. Gaselee*	6
1969	Fishers Lodge 5-10-10: 20/1	A. Kilpatrick	*B. Scott*	11
1970	Soldo 9-11-4: 13/2	P. Cazalet	*D. Mould*	11
1971	Stradivarius 7-11-12: 3/1	L. Kennard	*W. Smith*	7
1972	Cuckolder 7-11-8: 5/2	R. Turnell	*A. Turnell*	6
1973	Carroll Street 6-11-4: 6/1	G. Balding	*C. Mellerick*	6
1974	Even Up 7-11-12: 8/11	Mrs D. Oughton	*R. Smith*	10
1975	Lord Browndodd 7-11-8: 5/2	P. Cundell	*J. Francome*	12
1976	Summer Dance 9-11-4: 5/1	R. Turnell	*A. Turnell*	5
1977	Young Arthur 8-11-4: 5/4	D. Kent	*P. Haynes*	11
1978	Alverton 8-11-8: 100/30	M. H. Easterby	*I. Watkinson*	8
1979	Prominent King 7-11-8: 5/2	M. H. Easterby	*A. Brown*	10
1980	Flying Gamble 7-11-4: 10/1	I. Wardle	*A. Brown*	15
1981	Captain John 7-11-8: 11/2	A. Goodwill	*J. Pearce*	12
1982	Leckie 7-11-12: 2/1 } dh	R. Armytage	*B. R. Davies*	8
	Ivory Thrust 8-11-4: 10/1 } dh	K. Bailey	*K. Mooney*	
1983	Leander Blue 6-11-8: 8/1	D. Nicholson	*P. Scudamore*	10
1984	Simon Legree 7-11-12: 6/1	J. Gifford	*R. Rowe*	9
1985	Sign Again 7-11-4: 5/2	J. Fox	*S. Moore*	11

1986	Abandoned because of frost			
1987	Abandoned because of snow			
1988	Loddon Lad 6-11-4: 14/1	D. Nicholson	*R. Dunwoody*	7
1989	Admirals All 6-11-4: 1/1	C. Brooks	*P. Scudamore*	6
1990	Comandante 8-11-8: 5/4	J. Gifford	*P. Hobbs*	6

VINCENT O'BRIEN IRISH GOLD CUP CHASE (Leopardstown 3m)

1987	Forgive'N Forget 10-12-0: 5/4	J. FitzGerald	*M. Dwyer*	9
1988	Playschool 10-12-0: 2/1	D. Barons	*P. Nicholls*	5
1989	Carvill's Hill 7-12-0: 9/4	J. Dreaper (Ir)	*K. Morgan*	9
1990	Nick The Brief 8-12-0: 5/1	J. Upson	*M. Lynch*	6

WILLIAM HILL IMPERIAL CUP HANDICAP HURDLE
(Sandown 2m)

1947	Tant Pis 5-9-10: 20/1	J. Goldsmith	*H. Nicholson*	33
1948	Anglesey 6-11-8: 4/1	S. Ingham	*J. Gilbert*	12
1949	Secret Service 6-11-11: 20/1	F. Walwyn	*J. Gilbert*	17
1950	Secret Service 7-11-10: 100/8	F. Walwyn	*T. Cusack*	13
1951	Master Bidar 6-10-11: 100/7	R. Smyth	*R. Emery*	21
1952	High Point 6-10-4: 10/1	J. Dennistoun	*H. Sprague*	19
1953	High Point 7-10-7: 10/1	J. Dennistoun	*H. Sprague*	19
1954	The Pills 6-10-5: 20/1	P. Rice-Stringer	*J. Dowdeswell*	26
1955	Bon Mot II 6-10-11: 11/2	S. Wootton	*M. Haynes*	32
1956	Peggy Jones 6-10-10: 100/9	S. Palmer	*A. Oughton*	22
1957	Camugliano 7-10-10: 20/1	H. T. Smith	*R. Emery*	29
1958	Flaming East 9-10-5: 100/9	G. Vallance	*Mr J. Lawrence*	23
1959	Langton Heath 5-10-9: 100/6	T. Griffiths	*R. Martin*	21
1960	Farmer's Boy 7-11-7: 25/1	W. Stephenson	*D. Nicholson*	20
1961	Fidus Achates 6-10-4: 25/1	M. James	*C. Chapman*	23
1962	Irish Imp 5-10-12: 10/1	R. Smyth	*G. Ramshaw*	26
1963	Antiar 5-11-2: 7/1	P. Cazalet	*D. Mould*	21
1964	Invader 6-11-4: 6/1	L. Dale	*T. M. Jones*	15
1965	Kildavin 7-10-7: 100/7	J. Sutcliffe, jnr	*J. King*	19
1966	Royal Sanction 7-10-1: 10/1	F. Winter	*R. Pitman*	18
1967	Sir Thopas 6-11-8: 100/9	R. Turnell	*J. Haine*	20
1968	Persian Empire 5-11-4: 4/1	C. Davies	*B. Scott*	18
1969	Abandoned because of waterlogged state of course			
1970	Solomon II 6-11-1: 11/2	D. Barons	*B. R. Davies*	17
1971	Churchwood 7-11-3: 10/1	M. Goswell	*D. Barrott*	12
1972	Spy Net 5-10-0: 15/1	L. Dale	*G. Lawson*	18
1973	Lanzarote 5-12-4: 5/2	F. Winter	*R. Pitman*	14
1974	Flash Imp 5-10-9: 5/1	R. Smyth	*J. King*	17
1975	Abandoned because of waterlogged state of course			
1976	Nougat 6-10-6: 7/1	J. Gifford	*G. Enright*	11
1977	Acquaint 6-11-2: 16/1	F. Winter	*Mr N. Henderson*	20
1978	Winter Melody 7-11-3: 12/1	J. Hanson	*W. Smith*	15
1979	Flying Diplomat 8-10-6: 5/1	A. Smith	*Mr T. Thomson Jones*	9
1980	Prayukta 5-11-0: 14/1	F. Winter	*J. Francome*	16
1981	Ekbalco 5-11-3: 8/1	R. Fisher	*D. Goulding*	14
1982	Holemoor Star 5-11-7: 2/1 (at Kempton)	Miss S. Morris	*M. O'Halloran*	7
1983	Desert Hero 9-9-8: 20/1	F. Walwyn	*R. Chapman*	16
1984	Dalbury 6-9-12: 9/2	P. Haynes	*P. Corrigan*	13
1985	Floyd 5-10-3: 13/8	D. Elsworth	*C. Brown*	16
1986	Insular 6-9-10: 14/1	I. Balding	*E. Murphy*	19
1987	Inlander 6-10-3: 10/1	R. Akehurst	*S. Smith Eccles*	23
1988	Sprowston Boy 5-10-11: 10/1	P. Kelleway	*S. McCrystal*	15
1989	Travel Mystery 6-10-0: 3/1	M. Pipe	*P. Scudamore*	8
1990	Moody Man 5-10-13: 20/1	P. Hobbs	*P. Hobbs*	15

CROWN BERGER HURDLE (5-y-o) (Chepstow 2m)

1971	Killiney 11-0: 5/2	F. Winter	*E. P. Harty*	8
1972	Celtic Cone 11-0: 4/6	F. Cundell	*A. Turnell*	13
1973	Dark Sultan 11-0: 5/4	P. Chisman	*R. Barry*	8
1974	True Song 11-0: 7/1	D. Underwood	*G. Old*	13
1975	Border Incident 11-0: 7/4	R. Head	*J. Francome*	10
1976	Winter Melody 11-0: 15/2	J. Hanson	*A. Bowker*	15
1977	French Hollow 11-0: 6/4	A. Dickinson	*M. Dickinson*	17

1978	Gruffandgrim 11-0: 5/1	F. Winter	*J. Guest*	9
1979	Applalto 11-0: 10/1	R. Armytage	*H. J. Davies*	8
1980	Run Hard 11-0: 7/2	R. Turnell	*S. C. Knight*	9
1981	Passing Parade 11-0: 5/2	M. O'Toole (Ir)	*P. Scudamore*	11
1982	Gaye Brief 11-0: 1/1	Mrs M. Rimell	*P. Scudamore*	8
1983	Very Promising 11-0: 100/30	Mrs M. Rimell	*S. Morshead*	12
1984	Aonoch 11-0: 4/5	R. Fisher	*J. Duggan*	10
1985	Maganyos 11-0: 17/2	N. Henderson	*S. Smith Eccles*	8
1986	Canute Express 11-5: 5/4	H. Scott (Ir)	*Mr L. Wyer*	12
1987	Positive 11-5: 8/1	K. Bailey	*P. Croucher*	7
1988	Rymster 11-5: 9/4	N. Henderson	*G. McCourt*	12
1989	Dis Train 11-5: 4/1	Mrs J. Pitman	*M. Pitman*	6
1990	Sacre d'Or 11-5: 14/1	J. Mackie	*S. O'Neill*	12

WATERFORD CRYSTAL SUPREME NOVICES' HURDLE

(Cheltenham 2m)

1948	(D.1) Vulgan 5-10-10: 9/2	J. de Moraville	*R. Black*	13
	(D.2) Jean's Last 6-11-0: 7/4	F. Walwyn	*B. Marshall*	21
1949	(D.1) French Wedding 4-10-7: 11/2	G. Wilson	*J. Brogan*	14
	(D.2) Tough Guy 4-10-0: 4/1	I. Anthony	*D. Dillon*	18
1950	(D.1) Tsaoko 5-11-8 4/9	F. Armstrong	*M. Molony*	9
	(D.2) Sir Charles 4-10-4: 25/1	J. Scudamore	*Mr M. Scudamore*	15
1951	(D.1) Red Stanger 4-10-12: 100/8	R. Smyth	*D. Dillon*	20
	(D.2) Oukilele II 4-10-12: 6/1	G. Archibald	*F. Winter*	13
1952	(D.1) Cockatoo 6-11-3: 4/1	M. V. O'Brien (Ir)	*Mr A. O'Brien*	13
	(D.2) Evian 4-10-7: 10/1	G. Archibald	*F. Winter*	14
1953	(D.1) Assynt 5-11-1: 9/4	D. Morgan (Ir)	*E. Newman*	18
	(D.2) Dessin 7-11-8: 100/9	F. Hudson	*J. Gilbert*	17
1954	(D.1) Stroller 6-11-8: 13/8	M. V. O'Brien (Ir)	*P. Taaffe*	18
	(D.2) Tasmin 4-10-7: 5/1	M. Count (Fr)	*R. Emery*	18
1955	(D.1) Vindore 6-11-12: 1/1	M. V. O'Brien (Ir)	*Mr A. O'Brien*	19
	(D.2) Illyric 6-11-8: 3/1	M. V. O'Brien (Ir)	*T. P. Burns*	23
1956	(D.1) Boy's Hurrah 8-11-8: 9/4	M. V. O'Brien (Ir)	*T. P. Burns*	17
	(D.2) Pelargos 5-11-6: 6/4	M. V. O'Brien (Ir)	*T. P. Burns*	22
1957	(D.1) Tokoroa 6-12-1: 5/4	F. Rimell	*D. Dick*	10
	(D.2) Saffron Tartan 6-11-12: 10/11	M. V. O'Brien (Ir)	*T. P. Burns*	12
1958	(D.1) Admiral Stuart 7-11-12: 6/5	M. V. O'Brien (Ir)	*T. P. Burns*	19
	(D.2) Prudent King 6-11-8: 3/1	M. V. O'Brien (Ir)	*T. P. Burns*	19
1959	(D.1) York Fair 5-11-10: 4/5	M. V. O'Brien (Ir)	*T. P. Burns*	16
	(D.2) Albergo 5-11-6: 9/1	C. Magnier (Ir)	*D. Page*	19
1960	(D.1) Blue Mountain 6-11-8: 5/1	G. Todd	*R. Broadway*	20
	(D.2) Bastille 5-11-6: 33/1	T. Masson	*W. Woods*	18
1961	(D.1) Beau Normand 5-11-6: 5/1	R. Turnell	*W. Rees*	18
	(D.2) Greektown 5-12-2: 100/8	W. Stephenson	*M. Scudamore*	15
1962	(D.1) Tripacer 4-10-12 : 20/1	D. L. Moore (Ir)	*T. Carberry*	18
	(D.2) Clerical Grey 4-11-12: 100/8	P. Murphy (Ir)	*G. W. Robinson*	18
1963	(D.1) Honour Bound 5-11-10: 3/1	F. Rimell	*T. Biddlecombe*	18
	(D.2) Buona notte 6-11-8: 7/2	R. Turnell	*J. Haine*	15
	(D.3) Deetease 5-12-2: 9/1	B. Foster	*C. Chapman*	18
1964	(D.1) Flyingbolt 5-12-2: 4/9	T. Dreaper (Ir)	*P. Taaffe*	11
	(D.2) Elan 5-12-2: 9/2	J. Sutcliffe, jnr	*D. Dick*	18
1965	(D.1) Red Tears 5-11-6: 7/1	H. T. Jones	*S. Mellor*	19
	(D.2) Havago 6-12-4: 11/8	P. Sleator (Ir)	*H. Beasley*	15
1966	(D.1) Beau Caprice 12-12-2: 6/1	F. Walwyn	*T. Jennings*	14
	(D.2) Fosco 5-11-6: 7/2	M. Goswell	*D. Moore*	19
1967	(D.1) Chorus 6-11-12: 15/2	H. T. Jones	*J. Haine*	20
	(D.2) Early to Rise 7-11-12: 11/2	R. Turnell	*J. King*	14
1968	(D.1) King Cutler 5-12-0: 85/40	Denys Smith	*B. Fletcher*	12
	(D.2) L'Escargot 5-12-4: 13/2	D. L. Moore (Ir)	*T. Carberry*	11
1969	(D.1) Normandy 4-11-2: 10/1	F. Rimell	*T. Biddlecombe*	28
	(D.2) Private Room 5-11-10: 10/1	F. Walwyn	*G. W. Robinson*	20
1970	(D.1) Ballywilliam Boy 5-12-0: 4/1	P. Sleator (Ir)	*R. Coonan*	20
	(D.2) Bula 5-12-0: 3/1	F. Winter	*P. Kelleway*	21

1971	(D.1) Persian Majesty 4-10-13: 13/2	R. Price	*T. Biddlecombe*	10
	(D.2) Barnard 7-12-0: 4/1	F. Walwyn	*J. Haine*	13
1972	Noble Life 5-11-6: 16/1	C. Grassick (Ir)	*T. Murphy*	18
1973	King Pele 4-10-10: 13/2	G. P-Gordon	*D. Nicholson*	20
1974	Avec Moi 5-11-6: 5/4	Miss A. Sinclair	*R. Rowell*	16
1975	Bannow Rambler 6-11-8: 9/2	P. Berry (Ir)	*F. Berry*	18
1976	Beacon Light 5-11-8: 14/1	R. Turnell	*A. Turnell*	11
1977	Mac's Chariot 6-11-8: 7/1	M. O'Toole (Ir)	*D. T. Hughes*	16
1978	Golden Cygnet 6-11-8: 4/5	E. O'Grady (Ir)	*Mr N. Madden*	18
1979	Stranfield 6-11-8: 16/1	D. McDonogh (Ir)	*T. Kinane*	16
1980	Slaney Idol 5-11-8: 9/1	L. Browne (Ir)	*T. Carmody*	27
1981	Hartstown 6-11-8: 2/1	M. O'Toole (Ir)	*N. Madden*	16
1982	Miller Hill 6-11-8: 20/1	D. Hughes (Ir)	*T. Morgan*	19
1983	Buck House 5-11-8: 8/1	M. Morris (Ir)	*T. Carmody*	22
1984	Browne's Gazette 6-11-8: 11/2	M. Dickinson	*Mr D. Browne*	18
1985	Harry Hastings 6-11-8: 14/1	J. S. Wilson	*C. Grant*	30
1986	River Ceiriog 5-11-8: 40/1	N. Henderson	*S. Smith Eccles*	29
1987	Tartan Tailor 6-11-8: 14/1	G. Richards	*P. Tuck*	20
1988	Vagador 5-11-8: 4/1	G. Harwood	*M. Perrett*	26
1989	Sondrio 8-11-8: 25/1	M. Pipe	*J. Lower*	21
1990	Forest Sun 5-11-8: 7/4	G. Balding	*J. Frost*	18

ARKLE CHALLENGE TROPHY CHASE (Cheltenham 2m)

1969	Chatham 5-11-0: 10/1	F. Rimell	*T. Biddlecombe*	10
1970	Soloning 5-11-0: 4/1	F. Winter	*P. Kelleway*	13
1971	Alpheus 6-11-8: 15/1	T. Dreaper (Ir)	*E. Wright*	11
1972	Pendil 7-12-1: 10/11	F. Winter	*R. Pitman*	10
1973	Denys Adventure 8-12-1: 8/1	T. Forster	*G. Thorner*	10
1974	Canasta Lad 8-11-11: 2/1	P. Bailey	*J. King*	10
1975	Broncho 6-11-11: 8/1	A. Dickinson	*C. Tinkler*	12
1976	Roaring Wind 8-11-8: 11/1	R. Cambidge	*R. Crank*	16
1977	Tip the Wink 7-11-8: 15/2	P. Taylor	*D. T. Hughes*	10
1978	Alverton 8-11-8: 5/2	M. H. Easterby	*G. Thorner*	12
1979	Chinrullah 7-11-8: 10/11	M. O'Toole (Ir)	*D. T. Hughes*	8
1980	Anaglogs Daughter 7-11-8: 9/4	W. Durkan (Ir)	*T. Carberry*	9
1981	Clayside 7-11-8: 5/2	M. H. Easterby	*A. Brown*	13
1982	The Brockshee 7-11-8: 12/1	A. Moore (Ir)	*T. Carberry*	19
1983	Ryeman 6-11-8: 16/1	M. H. Easterby	*A. Brown*	16
1984	Bobsline 8-11-8: 5/4	F. Flood (Ir)	*F. Berry*	8
1985	Boreen Prince 8-11-8: 15/2	A. McNamara (Ir)	*N. Madden*	16
1986	Oregon Trail 6-11-8: 14/1	S. Christian	*R. Beggan*	14
1987	Gala's Image 7-11-8: 25/1	Mrs M. Rimell	*R. Linley*	19
1988	Danish Flight 9-11-8: 11/2	J. FitzGerald	*M. Dwyer*	12
1989	Waterloo Boy 6-11-8: 20/1	D. Nicholson	*R. Dunwoody*	14
1990	Comandante 8-11-8: 9/2	J. Gifford	*P. Hobbs*	14

WATERFORD CRYSTAL STAYERS' HURDLE (Cheltenham 3m 1f)

1972	Parlour Moor 8-11-12: 13/2	H. T. Jones	*M. Gifford*	11
1973	Moyne Royal 8-11-12: 10/1	A. Pitt	*D. Mould*	8
1974	Highland Abbe 8-11-12: 15/2	L. Kennard	*R. Smith*	15
1975	Brown Lad 9-11-12: 7/2	J. Dreaper (Ir)	*T. Carberry*	12
1976	Bit of a Jig 8-11-12: 2/1	M. O'Toole (Ir)	*D. T. Hughes*	12
1977	Town Ship 6-11-12: 5/2	M. H. Easterby	*T. Carberry*	11
1978	Flame Gun 6-11-12: 14/1	E. O'Grady (Ir)	*Mr N. Madden*	13
1979	Lighter 6-11-12: 14/1	J. Edwards	*P. Blacker*	14
1980	Mountrivers 6-11-12: 7/1	E. O'Grady (Ir)	*T. Ryan*	19
1981	Derring Rose 6-11-12: 3/1	F. Winter	*J. Francome*	14
1982	Crimson Embers 7-11-12: 2/1	F. Walwyn	*S. Shilston*	11
1983	A Kinsman 7-11-12: 50/1	J. Brockbank	*T. G. Dun*	21
1984	Gaye Chance 9-11-10: 5/1	Mrs M. Rimell	*S. Morshead*	14
1985	Rose Ravine 6-11-5: 5/1	F. Walwyn	*R. Pusey*	22
1986	Crimson Embers 11-11-10: 12/1	F. Walwyn	*S. Shilston*	19
1987	Galmoy 8-11-10: 9/2	J. Mulhern (Ir)	*T. Carmody*	14
1988	Galmoy 9-11-10: 2/1	J. Mulhern (Ir)	*T. Carmody*	16
1989	Rustle 7-11-10: 4/1	N. Henderson	*M. Bowlby*	21
1990	Trapper John 6-11-10: 15/2	M. Morris (Ir)	*C. Swan*	22

KIM MUIR MEMORIAL CHALLENGE CUP HANDICAP CHASE (Amateur Riders) (Cheltenham 3m)

1946	Astrometer 8-10-13: 5/4	C. Rogers (Ir)	*D. Baggallay*	14
1947	Abandoned because of snow and frost			
1948	Double Bridge 7-10-10: 20/1	J. Powell	*J. Gale*	16
1949	Jack Tatters 11-12-2: 4/1	F. Walwyn	*Lord Mildmay*	11
1950	Morning Cover 9-10-10: 6/1	G. Wilson	*A. Parker*	6
1951	Mighty Fine 9-11-11: 2/1	F. Rimell	*P. Chisman*	9
1952	Menzies 10-10-11: 4/1	S. Mercer	*P. Chisman*	9
1953	Crudwell 7-11-11: 5/4	F. Cundell	*A. Corbett*	10
1954	Arctic Gold 9-12-3: 6/1	G. Balding	*F. Greenway*	11
1955	Gay Monarch II 9-11-3: 100/8	F. Rimell	*R. Watson*	15
1956	Filon d'Or 9-10-10: 20/1	H. Cousins	*A. Moralee*	11
1957	Mighty Apollo 8-10-13: 25/1	D. Machin	*R. Brewis*	16
1958	Lochroe 10-12-2: 10/11	P. Cazalet	*E. Cazalet*	11
1959	Irish Coffee 9-10-13: 100/30	C. McCartan (Ir)	*G. Kindersley*	12
1960	Solray 6-11-3: 7/1	F. Cliffe	*N. Upton*	9
1961	Nicolaus Silver 9-10-5: 10/1	F. Rimell	*W. Tellwright*	11
1962	Carrickbeg 6-9-12: 7/1	D. Butchers	*G. Pitman*	10
1963	Centre Circle 8-10-12: 6/1	D. Ancil	*B. Ancil*	18
1964	Jim's Tavern 7-10-4: 10/1	J. Hicks	*G. Pitman*	11
1965	Burton Tan 10-11-3: 10/1	R. Collie	*E. Collie*	15
1966	Jimmy Scot 10-10-9: 6/1	F. Walwyn	*J. Lawrence*	14
1967	Chu-Teh 8-10-8: 9/2	K. Cundell	*N. Gaselee*	11
1968	Chu-Teh 9-10-6: 3/1	K. Cundell	*D. Crossley-Cooke*	8
1969	Pride of Kentucky 7-10-4: 100/8	E. Courage	*R. Charlton*	13
1970	Rainbow Valley 7-10-12 : 10/1	A. Dickinson	*M. Dickinson*	20
1971	Black Baize 6-10-6: 13/8	W. Shand Kydd	*J. Lawrence*	9
1972	The Ghost 7-11-11: 5/2	V. Cross	*J. Mead*	15
1973	Hinterland 7-10-7: 5/2	T. Forster	*W. Foulkes*	22
1974	Castleruddery 8-10-5: 14/1	P. McCreery (Ir)	*T. Walsh*	19
1975	Quick Reply 10-11-1: 15/2	H. Bell	*R. Lamb*	17
1876	Prolan 7-11-7: 3/1	E. O'Grady (Ir)	*T. Walsh*	14
1977	Double Negative 7-10-9: 11/2	F. Rimell	*P. Brookshaw*	16
1978	Abandoned because of snow			
1979	Redundant Punter 9-9-12: 14/1	T. Forster	*D. Jackson*	20
1980	Good Prospect 11-10-12: 9/2	J. Edwards	*A. J. Wilson*	12
1981	Waggoners Walk 12-10-3: 7/1	Miss C. Mason	*C. Cundall*	20
1982	Political Pop 8-12-0: 15/2	M. Dickinson	*D. Browne*	18
1983	Greasepaint 8-11-5: 8/1	M. Cunningham (Ir)	*C. Magnier*	16
1984	Broomy Bank 9-11-4: 16/1	J. Edwards	*A. J. Wilson*	18
1985	Glyde Court 8-10-5: 11/1	F. Winter	*S. Sherwood*	18
1986	Glyde Court 9-11-0: 13/2	F. Winter	*J. Queally*	20
1987	The Ellier 11-10-5: 16/1	N. Tinkler	*Miss G. Armytage*	16
1988	Golden Minstrel 9-11-1: 7/1	J. Gifford	*T. Grantham*	13
1989	Cool Ground 7-10-0: 7/2	N. Mitchell	*A. Tory*	16
1990	Master Bob 10-10-1: 20/1	N. Henderson	*J. Berry*	17

CHELTENHAM GRAND ANNUAL CHALLENGE CUP HANDICAP CHASE (Cheltenham 2m)

1946	Loyal King 6-11-12: 7/2	C. Rogers (Ir)	*D. L. Moore*	11
1947	Rope Trick 6-10-8: 100/7	C. Bewicke	*D. Doyle*	12
1948	Clare Man 7-10-3: 20/1	W. Nightingall	*C. Hook*	20
1949	Abandoned because of frost			
1950	Norborne 6-11-4: 8/1	E. Champneys	*E. Reavey*	11
1951	Merry Court 6-10-11: 10/1	T. Yates	*T. Molony*	11
1952	Marcianus 6-11-2: 7/1	G. Beeby	*T. Molony*	12
1953	Rose & Crown 6-10-0: 33/1	F. Walwyn	*J. Bullock*	13
1954	Hipparchus 5-10-1: 100/1	P. Rice-Stringer	*J. Dowdeswell*	11
1955	Abandoned because of snow			
1956	Rosenkavalier 7-10-6: 8/1	R. Turnell	*H. Sprague*	11
1957	Sir Edmund 7-10-12: 6/1	A. Kilpatrick	*R. Morrow*	11
1958	Top Twenty 9-10-7: 10/1	C. Magnier (Ir)	*F. Shortt*	18
1959	Top Twenty 10-12-6: 9/2	C. Magnier (Ir)	*F. Winter*	12
1960	Monsieur Trois Etoiles 8-11-6: 3/1	J. Brogan (Ir)	*F. Carroll*	9
1961	Barberyn 6-11-0: 3/1	W. Stephenson	*M. Scudamore*	10
1962	Moretons 9-10-12: 100/8	P. Cazalet	*W. Rees*	14

1963	Anner Loch 8-10-6: 7/1	J. Hicks	*D. Nicholson*	13
1964	Richard of Bordeaux 9-11-3: 9/1	F. Walwyn	*G. W. Robinson*	14
1965	Fort Rouge 7-11-0: 13/2	K. Oliver	*G. Milburn*	10
1966	Well Packed 8-10-11: 100/7	R. Renton	*Mr T. Stack*	12
1967	San Angelo 7-11-1: 10/1	E. Courage	*J. Buckingham*	13
1968	Hal's Farewell 7-10-10: 5/1	P. Bailey	*J. King*	10
1969	All Glory 8-10-0: 10/1	J. Edwards	*Mr A. Robinson*	10
1970	Fortina's Palace 7-11-11: 10/1	M. Scudamore	*P. Jones*	18
1971	Khan 7-10-8: 2/1	M. Burke (Ir)	*F. Carroll*	8
1972	Tudor Dance 6-10-2: 4/1	R. Turnell	*J. King*	15
1973	Coolera Prince 8-10-10: 8/1	H. Handel	*N. Wakley*	15
1974	Dulwich 7-10-13: 100/30	C. Davies	*M. Salaman*	9
1975	Abandoned because of waterlogged state of course			
1976	Dulwich 9-11-7: 9/4	C. Davies	*B. R. Davies*	10
1977	Tom Morgan 8-11-6: 9/4	K. Oliver	*T. Stack*	9
1978	Young Arthur 9-11-4: 3/1	D. Kent	*A. Webb*	8
1979	Casbah 12-11-13: 5/1	T. Forster	*G. Thorner*	10
1980	Stopped 8-11-12: 7/2	F. Winter	*B. de Haan*	13
1981	Friendly Alliance 8-10-7: 11/2	F. Winter	*J. Francome*	11
1982	Reldis 8-10-0: 9/1	D. Gandolfo	*P. Barton*	16
1983	Churchfield Boy 7-10-0: 8/1	M. Cunningham (Ir)	*J. P. Byrne*	18
1984	Mossy Moore 8-10-0: 11/2	B. Chinn	*J. J. O'Neill*	13
1985	Kathies Lad 8-11-10: 7/1	A. Jarvis	*S. Smith Eccles*	19
1986	Pearlyman 7-11-5: 14/1	J. Edwards	*G. Bradley*	19
1987	French Union 9-11-3: 13/2	D. Nicholson	*R. Dunwoody*	16
1988	Vodkatini 9-10-13: 4/1	J. Gifford	*R. Rowe*	14
1989	Pukka Major 8-10-2: 4/1	T. T. Jones	*P. Scudamore*	17
1990	Katabatic 7-10-8: 11/4	A. Turnell	*H. Davies*	13

SUN ALLIANCE NOVICES' HURDLE (Cheltenham 2½m)

1971	Midsprite 5-11-12: 7/1	H. T. Jones	*M. Gifford*	20
1972	Even Dawn 5-11-6: 40/1	Mrs E. Gaze	*R. Hyett*	17
1973	Willie Wumpkins 5-11-6: 11/1	A. Maxwell (Ir)	*P. Colville*	15
1974	Brown Lad 8-11-8: 2/1	P. Osborne (Ir)	*R. Barry*	25
1975	Davy Lad 5-11-7: 5/2	M. O'Toole (Ir)	*D. T. Hughes*	20
1976	Parkhill 5-11-7: 4/1	M. O'Toole (Ir)	*D. T. Hughes*	21
1977	Counsel Cottage 6-11-8: 6/1	P. Mullins (Ir)	*S. Treacy*	26
1978	Mr Kildare 5-11-7: 8/11	L. Browne (Ir)	*T. Carmody*	20
1979	Venture To Cognac 6-11-8: 4/1	F. Winter	*Mr O. Sherwood*	29
1980	Drumlargan 6-11-8: 5/2	E. O'Grady (Ir)	*T. Ryan*	27
1981	Gaye Chance 6-11-8: 7/1	F. Rimell	*S. Morshead*	21
1982	Mister Donovan 6-11-8: 9/2	E. O'Grady (Ir)	*T. Ryan*	21
1983	Sabin du Loir 4-10-8: 16/1	M. Dickinson	*G. Bradley*	27
1984	Fealty 4-10-12: 33/1	P. Brookshaw	*S. O'Neill*	29
1985	Asir 5-11-7: 9/1	P. Kelleway	*Mr R. Beggan*	27
1986	Ten Plus 6-11-7: 5/2	F. Walwyn	*K. Mooney*	28
1987	The West Awake 6-11-7: 16/1	O. Sherwood	*S. Sherwood*	28
1988	Rebel Song 6-11-7: 14/1	O. Sherwood	*S. Sherwood*	25
1989	Sayfar's Lad 5-11-7: 12/1	M. Pipe	*M. Perrett*	22
1990	Regal Ambition 6-11-7: 3/1	M. Pipe	*P. Scudamore*	22

THE QUEEN MOTHER CHAMPION CHASE (Cheltenham 2m)

1959	Quita Que 10-12-0: 4/9	D. L. Moore (Ir)	*J. Cox*	9
1960	Fortria 8-12-0: 15/8	T. Dreaper (Ir)	*P. Taaffe*	7
1961	Fortria 9-12-0: 2/5	T. Dreaper (Ir)	*P. Taaffe*	5
1962	Piperton 8-12-0: 100/6	A. Thomlinson	*D. Dick*	7
1963	Sandy Abbot 8-12-0: 5/1	G. Owen	*S. Mellor*	5
1964	Ben Stack 7-12-0: 2/1	T. Dreaper (Ir)	*P. Taaffe*	5
1965	Dunkirk 8-12-0: 8/1	P. Cazalet	*D. Dick*	6
1966	Flyingbolt 7-12-0: 1/5	T. Dreaper (Ir)	*P. Taaffe*	6
1967	Drinny's Double 9-12-0: 7/2	R. Turnell	*F. Nash*	8
1968	Drinny's Double 10-12-0: 6/1	R. Turnell	*F. Nash*	5
1969	Muir 10-12-0: 15/2	T. Dreaper (Ir)	*B. Hannon*	11
1970	Straight Fort 7-12-0: 7/4	T. Dreaper (Ir)	*P. Taaffe*	6
1971	Crisp 8-12-0: 3/1	F. Winter	*P. Kelleway*	8
1972	Royal Relief 8-12-0: 15/8	E. Courage	*W. Smith*	5
1973	Inkslinger 6-12-0: 6/1	D. L. Moore (Ir)	*T. Carberry*	6
1974	Royal Relief 10-12-0: 6/1	E. Courage	*W. Smith*	6

1975 Lough Inagh 8-12-0: 100/30	J. Dreaper (Ir)	*S. Barker*	8
1976 Skymas 11-12-0: 8/1	B. Lusk (Ir)	*M. Morris*	7
1977 Skymas 12-12-0: 7/2	B. Lusk (Ir)	*M. Morris*	8
1978 Hilly Way 8-12-0: 7/1	P. McCreery (Ir)	*T. Carmody*	10
1979 Hilly Way 9-12-0: 7/1	P. McCreery (Ir)	*Mr T. Walsh*	9
1980 Another Dolly 10-12-0: 33/1	F. Rimell	*S. Morshead*	7
1981 Drumgora 9-12-0: 25/1	A. Moore (Ir)	*F. Berry*	9
1982 Rathgorman 10-12-0: 100/30	M. Dickinson	*K. Whyte*	9
1983 Badsworth Boy 8-12-0: 2/1	M. Dickinson	*R. Earnshaw*	6
1984 Badsworth Boy 9-12-0: 8/13	M. Dickinson	*R. Earnshaw*	10
1985 Badsworth Boy 10-12-0: 11/8	Mrs M. Dickinson	*R. Earnshaw*	5
1986 Buck House 8-12-0: 5/2	M. Morris (Ir)	*T. Carmody*	11
1987 Pearlyman 8-12-0: 13/8	J. Edwards	*P. Scudamore*	8
1988 Pearlyman 9-12-0: 15/8	J. Edwards	*T. Morgan*	8
1989 Barnbrook Again 8-12-0: 7/4	D. Elsworth	*S. Sherwood*	8
1990 Barnbrook Again 9-12-0: 11/10	D. Elsworth	*H. Davies*	9

CORAL GOLDEN HANDICAP HURDLE FINAL
(Cheltenham 3m 1f)

1974 Kastrup 7-10-3: 10/1	D. Barons	*G. Thorner*	22
1975 Saffron Cake 6-10-7: 13/1	L. Kennard	*E. Wright*	24
1976 Good Prospect 7-11-10: 10/1	J. Edwards	*R. R. Evans*	17
1977 Outpoint 7-11-3: 10/1	F. Winter	*P. O'Brien*	27
1978 Water Colour 9-10-1: 11/1	M. Tate	*K. Whyte*	23
1979 Willie Wumpkins 11-10-4: 25/1	Mrs T. Pilkington	*Mr A. J. Wilson*	22
1980 Willie Wumpkins 12-10-7: 10/1	Mrs T. Pilkington	*Mr A. J. Wilson*	19
1981 Willie Wumpkins 13-10-8: 13/1	Mrs T. Pilkington	*Mr A. J. Wilson*	20
1982 Tall Order 8-10-2: 15/1	L. Foster	*A. Stringer*	31
1983 Forgive'N Forget 6-11-6: 5/2	J. FitzGerald	*M. Dwyer*	23
1984 Canio 7-10-9: 20/1	R. Hodges	*J. Francome*	31
1985 Von Trappe 8-10-6: 12/1	M. Oliver	*R. Dunwoody*	30
1986 Motivator 6-10-7: 15/2	M. Ryan	*G. McCourt*	31
1987 Taberna Lord 6-11-5: 10/1	A. J. Wilson	*L. Harvey*	31
1988 Pragada 5-11-0: 16/1	J. Gifford	*R. Rowe*	29
1989 Rogers Princess 7-10-0: 8/1	M. Tate	*S. Keightley*	27
1990 Henry Mann 7-11-9: 20/1	S. Christian	*A. Mulholland*	27

SUN ALLIANCE CHASE (Cheltenham 3m)

1964 Buona notte 7-12-4: 11/8	R. Turnell	*J. Haine*	16
1965 Arkloin 6-11-7: 100/7	T. Dreaper (Ir)	*L. McLoughlin*	17
1966 Different Class 6-11-12: 10/1	P. Cazalet	*D. Mould*	17
1967 Border Jet 7-11-0: 4/1	R. Price	*J. Gifford*	19
1968 Herring Gull 6-11-12: 9/1	P. Mullins (Ir)	*J. Crowley*	16
1969 Spanish Steps 6-11-12: 100/8	E. Courage	*J. Cook*	22
1970 Proud Tarquin 7-11-12: 100/7	T. Dreaper (Ir)	*P. Taaffe*	17
1971 Tantalum 7-11-7: 14/1	M. Pope	*D. Nicholson*	16
1972 Clever Scot 7-11-7: 11/1	H. T. Jones	*D. Mould*	18
1973 Killiney 7-11-3: 8/15	F. Winter	*R. Pitman*	9
1974 Ten Up 7-11-0: 7/2	J. Dreaper (Ir)	*T. Carberry*	12
1975 Pengrail 7-11-0: 12/1	F. Winter	*J. Francome*	11
1976 Tied Cottage 8-11-0: 12/1	D. L. Moore (Ir)	*T. Carberry*	15
1977 Gay Spartan 6-11-4: 13/2	A. Dickinson	*M. Dickinson*	15
1978 Sweet Joe 6-11-4: 12/1	H. T. Jones	*S. Smith Eccles*	17
1979 Master Smudge 7-11-4: 16/1	A. Barrow	*R. Hoare*	17
1980 Lacson 8-11-4: 16/1	R. Hawker	*S. C. Knight*	17
1981 Lesley Ann 7-11-4: 25/1	D. Elsworth	*C. Brown*	17
1982 Brown Chamberlin 7-11-4: 7/1	F. Winter	*J. Francome*	15
1983 Canny Danny 7-11-4: 33/1	J. FitzGerald	*N. Madden*	14
1984 A. Kinsman 8-11-4: 10/1	J. Brockbank	*T. G. Dun*	18
1985 Antarctic Bay 8-11-4: 6/4	P. Hughes (Ir)	*F. Berry*	11
1986 Cross Master 9-11-4: 16/1	T. Bill	*R. Crank*	30
1987 Kildimo 7-11-4: 13/2	G. Balding	*G. Bradley*	18
1988 The West Awake 7-11-4: 11/4	O. Sherwood	*S. Sherwood*	14
1989 Envopak Token 8-11-4: 16/1	J. Gifford	*P. Hobbs*	15
1990 Garrison Savannah 7-11-4: 12/1	Mrs J. Pitman	*B. de Haan*	9

NATIONAL HUNT CHASE (Amateur Riders) (Cheltenham 4m)

1946 Prattler 11-12-3: 33/1	T. Yates	*Major D. Daly*	20

1947	Maltese Wanderer 8-12-3: 6/1	T. Yates	*Major D. Daly*	20
1948	Bruno II 8-12-3: 20/1	W. A-Gray	*Major G. Cunard*	37
1949	Castledermot 7-12-7: 6/4	M. V. O'Brien (Ir)	*Lord Mildmay*	17
1950	Ellesmere 7-12-7: 100/30	K. Cundell	*A. Corbett*	26
1951	Cushendun 6-12-4: 10/1	R. Renton	*P. Chisman*	18
1952	Frosty Knight 6-12-0: 15/2	I. Straker	*C. Straker*	19
1953	Pontage 7-12-4: 9/4	D. L. Moore (Ir)	*J. Cox*	22
1954	Quare Times 8-12-4: 5/2	M. V. O'Brien (Ir)	*J. Cox*	26
1955	Reverend Prince 9-12-0: 33/1	P. Dufosee	*C. Pocock*	26
1956	Rosana III 7-12-0: 9/1	J. Everitt	*J. Everitt*	22
1957	Kari Sou 8-12-0: 100/6	A. Thomlinson	*A. Lillingston*	24
1958	Spud Tamson 7-12-4: 13/2	T. Dun	*G. Dun*	28
1959	Sabaria 8-12-0: 5/2	R. Turnell	*J. Lawrence*	17
1960	Proud Socks 8-12-0: 100/6	V. Bishop	*H. Thompson*	22
1961	Superfine 8-12-4: 10/1	F. Cundell	*Sir W. P-Brown*	33
1962	Go Slow 7-12-7: 10/1	A. Piper	*G. Small*	26
1963	Time 8-12-0: 8/1	W. Stephenson	*I. Balding*	35
1964	Dorimont 10-12-1: 4/1	T. Taaffe (Ir)	*C. Vaughan*	30
1965	Red Vale II 11-12-0: 100/8	A. Piper	*G. Small*	26
1966	Polaris Missle 7-11-9: 100/6	H. Thorne	*M. Thorne*	29
1967	Master Tammy 9-11-7: 100/7	G. Guilding	*B. Fanshawe*	24
1968	Fascinating Forties 9-11-7: 9/1	G. Owen	*M. Dickinson*	22
1969	Lizzy The Lizard 10-12-0: 10/1	A. Hartnoll	*G. Cann*	35
1970	Domason 7-12-1: 10/1	H. Dufosee	*R. Alner*	18
1971	Deblin's Green 8-11-7: 9/2	G. Yardley	*J. Edmunds*	20
1972	Charley Winking 7-12-0: 20/1	I. Scott	*D. Scott*	23
1973	Foreman 7-12-1: 11/2	H. T. Jones	*W. Shand-Kydd*	25
1974	Mr Midland 7-12-4: 7/2	E. O'Grady (Ir)	*M. Morris*	17
1975	Abandoned because of waterlogged state of course			
1976	Sage Merlin 8-12-7: 5/2	J. Hardy	*P. Greenall*	22
1977	Alpenstock 10-12-4: 14/1	S. Mellor	*C. Saunders*	21
1978	Gay Tie 5-11-9: 10/1	M. O'Toole (Ir)	*J. Fowler*	17
1979	Artic Ale 8-12-0: 20/1	D. Moore (Ir)	*J. Fowler*	25
1980	Waggoners Walk 11-12-4: 10/1	Miss C. Mason	*A. Fowler*	23
1981	Lucky Vane 6-12-7: 13/1	G. Balding	*S. Bush*	21
1982	Hazy Dawn 7-12-7: 8/1	P. Mullins (Ir)	*W. Mullins*	26
1983	Bit Of A Skite 7-12-0: 5/1	E. O'Grady (Ir)	*F. Codd*	29
1984	Macks Friendly 7-12-7: 11/4	P. Mullins (Ir)	*W. Mullins*	18
1985	Northern Bay 9-12-4: 12/1	T. Bill	*A. Fowler*	20
1986	Omerta 6-12-7: 9/4	H. Scott (Ir)	*L. Wyer*	22
1987	Mighty Mark 8-12-7: 8/1	F. Walton	*J. Walton*	30
1988	Over The Road 7-12-4: 10/1	T. Casey	*T. Costello*	28
1989	Boraceva 6-12-7: 4/1	G. Balding	*S. Mullins*	21
1990	Topsham Bay 7-12-0: 40/1	D. Barons	*P. Hacking*	25

MILDMAY OF FLETE CHALLENGE CUP HANDICAP CHASE

(Cheltenham 2½m)

1951	Slender 9-10-11: 7/1 } dh	R. Price	*F. Winter*	9
	Canford 9-12-2: 100/8 } dh	I. Anthony	*G. Kelly*	
1952	Portarlington 7-10-8	W. Stephenson	*K. Mullins*	10
1953	Sy Oui 8-10-3: 100/8	R. Price	*F. Winter*	17
1954	Tudor Line 9-10-12: 11/4	R. Renton	*G. Slack*	11
1955	Mont Tremblant 9-12-7: 11/2	F. Walwyn	*D. Dick*	19
1956	Pondapatarri 7-11-0: 100/6	G. Beeby	*R. Emery*	21
1957	Madras 7-10-2: 100/7	M. L. Marsh	*J. Bullock*	12
1958	Caesar's Helm 7-11-6: 9/2	R. Renton	*F. Winter*	14
1959	Siracusa 6-10-12: 9/4	R. Renton	*B. Wilkinson*	12
1960	Devon Customer 8-10-4: 100/7	S. Bowler	*J. Guest*	12
1961	Malting Barley 6-10-4: 5/1	G. Balding	*O. McNally*	8
1962	Spring Greeting 7-10-6: 100/8	C. Bewicke	*J. Lehane*	19
1963	Milo 8-10-4: 11/2	H. Blagrave	*J. Gifford*	19
1964	Take Plenty 8-10-1: 100/9	T. Forster	*R. Vibert*	12
1965	Snaigow 6-10-3: 100/6	C. Bewicke	*J. Lehane*	15
1966	Tibidabo 6-10-4: 7/1	A. Freeman	*J. King*	12
1967	French March 7-9-9: 25/1	T. Hanbury	*Mr B. Hanbury*	14
1968	Merrycourt 7-10-3: 20/1	R. Renton	*J. Gifford*	14
1969	Specify 7-11-2: 5/1	D. Rayson	*B. R. Davies*	8

1970 Verona Forest 7-11-0: 25/1	N. Crump	*G. Scott*	19
1971 Hound Tor 7-10-2: 14/1	G. Harwood	*M. Gifford*	10
1972 Mocharabuice 9-10-7: 11/2	T. Forster	*G. Thorner*	17
1973 Vulgan Town 7-10-0: 9/2	G. Balding	*J. Haine*	15
1974 Garnishee 10-10-10: 9/2	H. T. Jones	*D. Mould*	7
1975 Summerville 9-10-13: 4/1	R. Turnell	*A. Turnell*	13
1976 Broncho II 7-11-1: 7/2	A. Dickinson	*M. Dickinson*	14
1977 Uncle Bing 8-12-5: 9/2	R. Head	*J. Francome*	7
1978 King Or Country 7-10-9: 7/1	D. Barons	*P. Leach*	16
1979 Brawny Scot 9-10-0: 10/1	G. Fairbairn	*R. Lamb*	15
1980 Snowshill Sailor 8-10-4: 8/1	R. Turnell	*A. Turnell*	14
1981 Political Pop 7-10-0: 15/8	M. Dickinson	*R. Earnshaw*	12
1982 Doubleuagain 8-10-0: 11/1	A. Geraghty (Ir)	*F. Berry*	13
1983 Mr Peapock 7-9-7: 20/1	T. Hallett	*L. Bloomfield*	15
1984 Half Free 8-11-6: 16/1	F. Winter	*R. Linley*	16
1985 The Tsarevich 9-11-7: 5/1	N. Henderson	*J. White*	16
1986 The Tsarevich 10-11-5: 8/1	H. Henderson	*J. White*	16
1987 Gee-A 8-9-10: 33/1	G. Hubbard	*Miss G. Armytage*	18
1988 Smart Tar 7-10-2: 11/1	M. Wilkinson	*C. Llewellyn*	15
1989 Paddyboro 11-10-7: 9/2	J. Gifford	*R. Rowe*	10
1990 New Halen 9-9-7: 66/1	P. James	*E. Tierney*	14

DAILY EXPRESS TRIUMPH HURDLE (4-y-o) (Cheltenham 2m)

1950 Abrupto 11-6: 9/2	E. Diggle (Fr)	*R. Mantelin*	19
1951 Blue Song II 10-7: 6/1	G. Pelat (Fr)	*F. Thirion*	12
1952 Hoggar 10-10: 13/2	J. Cunnington (Fr)	*R. Triboit*	15
1953 Clair Soleil 11/4: 8/1	F. Mathet (Fr)	*F. Winter*	13
1954 Prince Charlemagne 10-10: 11/4	T. Carey	*L. Piggott*	12
1955 Kwannin 10-10: 2/1	A. Head (Fr)	*P. Delfarguiel*	12
1956 Square Dance 10-12: 13/2	F. Walwyn	*M. Scudamore*	11
1057 Meritorious 10-12: 20/1	P. Thrale	*D. Dillon*	14
1958 Pundit 11-4: 5/2	S. Ingham	*H. Sprague*	14
1959 Amazons Choice 10-10: 7/1	P. Thrale	*J. Gilbert*	13
1960 Turpial 10-10: 7/1	P. Cazalet	*A. Freeman*	13
1961 Cantab 10-10: 4/1	R. Price	*F. Winter*	15
1962 Beaver II 10-10: 100/6	R. Price	*J. Gifford*	11
1963 No Race			
1964 No Race			
1965 Blarney Beacon 11-4: 8/1	R. Smyth	*G. Ramshaw*	7
1966 Black Ice 11-4: 9/2	A. Thomas	*H. Beasley*	11
1967 Persian War 11-8: 4/1	B. Swift	*J. Uttley*	13
1968 England's Glory 10-10: 9/2	S. Ingham	*J. Uttley*	16
1969 Coral Diver 11-4: 3/1	F. Rimell	*T. Biddlecombe*	26
1970 Varma 11-4: 100/7	M. Masson	*B. Barker*	31
1971 Boxer 11-3: 100/30	R. Smyth	*J. Uttley*	18
1972 Zarib 11-0: 16/1	F. Rimell	*W. Smith*	16
1973 Moonlight Bay 11-0: 85/40	R. Price	*J. Haine*	18
1974 Attivo 11-0: 4/5	C. Mitchell	*R. G. Hughes*	21
1975 Royal Epic 11-0: 20/1	V. Cross	*F. McKenna*	28
1976 Peterhof 11-0: 10/1	M. W. Easterby	*J. J. O'Neill*	23
1977 Meladon 11-0: 6/1	A. Maxwell (Ir)	*T. Carberry*	30
1978 Connaught Ranger 11-0: 25/1	F. Rimell	*J. Burke*	14
1979 Pollardstown: 12/1	S. Mellor	*P. Blacker*	28
1980 Heighlin 11-0: 40/1	D. Elsworth	*S. Jobar*	26
1981 Baron Blakeney 11-0: 66/1	M. Pipe	*P. Leach*	29
1982 Shiny Copper 11-0: 66/1	Mrs N. Smith	*A. Webb*	29
1983 Saxon Farm 11-0: 12/1	S. Mellor	*M. Perrett*	30
1984 Northern Game 11-0: 20/1	E. O'Grady (Ir)	*T. Ryan*	30
1985 First Bout 11-0: 5/1	N. Henderson	*S. Smith Eccles*	27
1986 Solar Cloud 11-0: 40/1	D. Nicholson	*P. Scudamore*	28
1987 Alone Success 11-0: 11/1	N. Henderson	*S. Smith Eccles*	29
1988 Kribensis 11-0: 6/1	M. Stoute	*R. Dunwoody*	26
1989 Ikdam 11-0: 66/1	R. Holder	*N. Coleman*	27
1990 Rare Holiday 11-0: 25/1	D. K. Weld (Ir)	*B. Sheridan*	30

CHRISTIES FOXHUNTER CHALLENGE CUP (Hunter Chase)
(Cheltenham 3¼m)

1946 Koilo 9-12-0: 6/1	H. Jackson	*H. Jackson*	16

1947	Lucky Purchase 9-12-0: 7/1	S. Banks	*J. Nichols*	26
1948	State Control 8-12-0: 7/2	H. Llewellyn	*H. Llewellyn*	38
1949	Abandoned because of frost			
1950	Greenwood 13-12-0: 100/7	J. Evans	*J. Stuart-Evans*	25
1951	Halloween 6-12-0: 11/8	W. Wightman	*R. Smalley*	26
1952	Parasol II 7-12-0: 8/1	A. Walton	*I. Kerwood*	19
1953	Dunboy II 9-12-0: 3/1 } dh	P. Bruce	*C. Scott*	22
	Merry 13-12-0: 100/7 } dh	A. Kerr	*G. Kindersley*	
1954	Happymint 9-12-0: 7/1	J. Wight	*A. Moralee*	21
1955	Abandoned because of snow			
1956	The Callant 8-12-0: 11/8	J. Wight	*J. Scott-Aiton*	17
1957	The Callant 9-12-0: 10/11	J. Wight	*J. Scott-Aiton*	9
1958	Whinstone Hill 9-12-0: 7/1	R. Brewis	*R. Brewis*	16
1959	Some Baby 10-12-0: 100/8	T. Rootes	*J. Thorne*	15
1960	Whinstone Hill 11-12-0: 11/8	R. Brewis	*R. Brewis*	15
1961	Colledge Master 11-12-0: 7/2	L. Morgan	*L. Morgan*	17
1962	Colledge Master 12-12-0: 9/2	L. Morgan	*L. Morgan*	17
1963	Grand Morn II 9-12-0: 15/2	G. Shepheard	*R. Bloomfield*	20
1964	Freddie 7-11-7: 1/3	R. Tweedie	*A. Mactaggart*	10
1965	Woodside Terrace 12-11-7: 33/1	R. Woodhouse	*R. Woodhouse*	19
1966	Straight Lady 10-11-7: 100/8	W. Shepherd	*R. Shepherd*	21
1967	Mulbarton 11-12-0: 1/1	I. Pattullo	*N. Gaselee*	13
1968	Bright Beach 8-11-11: 5/1	G. Dun	*C. MacMillan*	12
1969	Queens Guide 8-11-7: 10/1	W. Wade	*G. Wade*	10
1970	Highworth 9-11-7: 15/2	R. Woodhouse	*R. Woodhouse*	13
1971	Hope Again 9-11-7: 16/1	D. Windell	*R. Smith*	18
1972	Credit Call 8-12-0: 7/4	W. A. Stephenson	*C. Collins*	9
1973	Bullock's Horn 10-12-0: 5/1	R. Turnell	*Lord Oaksey*	20
1974	Corrie Burn 8-12-0: 20/1	G. Fairbairn	*I. Williams*	16
1975	Real Rascal 12-11-10: 8/1	Mrs B. Surman	*G. Hyatt*	16
1976	False Note 10-11-9: 11/4	J. Horton	*B. Smart*	16
1977	Long Lane 9-11-11: 9/4	R. Shepherd	*R. Shepherd*	16
1978	Mountolive 8-12-0: 13/2	R. Shepherd	*R. Shepherd*	17
1979	Spartan Missile 7-12-0: 9/4	J. Thorne	*J. Thorne*	10
1980	Rolls Rambler 9-12-0: 9/4	F. Winter	*O. Sherwood*	7
1981	Grittar 8-12-0: 12/1	F. Gilman	*R. Saunders*	17
1982	The Drunken Duck 9-12-0: 12/1	B. Munro-Wilson	*B. Munro-Wilson*	19
1983	Eliogarty 8-12-0: 3/1	B. Kelly (Ir)	*Miss C. Beasley*	16
1984	Venture To Cognac 11-12-0: 7/1	F. Winter	*O. Sherwood*	21
1985	Elmboy 7-12-0: 10/1	W. Mawle	*A. Hill*	17
1986	Attitude Adjuster 6-12-0: 10/1	M. Morris (Ir)	*T. Walsh*	14
1987	Observe 11-12-0: 14/1	F. Winter	*C. Brooks*	14
1988	Certain Light 10-12-0: 10/1	Mrs A. Campbell	*P. Hacking*	9
1989	Three Counties 12-12-0: 6/1	Mrs M. Rimell	*Miss K. Rimell*	16
1990	Call Collect 9-12-0: 7/4	J. Parkes	*R. Martin*	15

RITZ CLUB NATIONAL HUNT HANDICAP CHASE

(Cheltenham 3m 1f)

1948	Cavaliero 7-11-10: 7/1	F. Rimell	*E. Vinall*	21
1949	Frere Jacques II 7-10-6: 20/1	F. Rimell	*E. Vinall*	13
1950	Silver Fame 11-12-7: 5/4	G. Beeby	*M. Molony*	11
1951	Land Fort 7-11-8: 8/1	F. Rimell	*J. Bullock*	14
1952	Royal Tan 8-11-8: 7/2	M. V. O'Brien (Ir)	*Mr A. O'Brien*	11
1953	Four Ten 7-10-7: 4/1	J. Roberts	*T. Cusack*	12
1954	Holly Bank 7-10-13: 7/2	F. Rimell	*Mr P. Brookshaw*	12
1955	Limber Hill 8-11-2: 7/1	W. Dutton	*T. Molony*	19
1956	Kerstin 6-10-5: 100/9	C. Bewicke	*G. Milburn*	14
1957	Sentina 7-10-4: 3/1	T. Dreaper (Ir)	*P. Taaffe*	12
1958	Sentina 8-11-7: 7/1	T. Dreaper (Ir)	*T. Taaffe*	14
1959	Winning Coin 7-11-4: 100/9	G. Beeby	*D. Dick*	14
1960	Isle of Syke 9-10-5: 100/8	A. Kilpatrick	*A. Keen*	12
1961	Ravencroft 8-10-3: 9/2	F. Walwyn	*F. Winter*	10
1962	Longtail 7-11-0: 100/7	R. Curran	*S. Mellor*	18
1963	Team Spirit 11-11-4: 100/8	F. Walwyn	*G. W. Robinson*	24
1964	Prudent Barney 10-10-11: 10/1	R. Renton	*T. Biddlecombe*	10
1965	Rondetto 9-11-10: 11/2	R. Turnell	*J. Haine*	20
1966	Arkloin 7-12-5: 5/2	T. Dreaper (Ir)	*P. Taaffe*	12
1967	Different Class 7-11-13: 13/2	P. Cazalet	*D. Mould*	16

1968	Battledore 7-10-10: 3/1	W. A. Stephenson	*C. Stobbs*	8
1969	Chancer 7-11-0: 6/1	W. Hall	*P. McCarron*	13
1970	Charter Flight 8-11-9: 100/8	R. Turnell	*A. Turnell*	16
1971	Lord Jim 10-10-8: 8/1	F. Walwyn	*J. Haine*	14
1972	Jomon 6-10-12: 8/1	H. T. Jones	*D. Mould*	15
1973	The Chisler 7-10-10: 6/1	A. Dickinson	*M. Dickinson*	13
1974	Cuckolder 9-10-13: 6/1	R. Turnell	*A. Turnell*	11
1975	King Flame 9-10-6: 12/1	R. Head	*J. Francome*	14
1976	Barmer 8-10-3: 20/1	R. Blakeney	*J. McNaught*	14
1977	Gay Vulgan 9-11-4: 4/1	F. Walwyn	*W. Smith*	12
1978	Abandoned because of snow			
1979	Fair View 9-10-4: 12/1	G. Fairbairn	*R. Lamb*	13
1980	Again The Same 7-11-1: 10/1	J. Edwards	*Mr A. J. Wilson*	16
1981	Current Gold 10-10-7: 10/1	G. Richards	*N. Doughty*	16
1982	Scot Lane 9-10-12: 15/2	M. Tate	*C. Smith*	18
1983	Scot Lane 10-11-7: 20/1	M. Tate	*C. Smith*	19
1984	Tracys Special 7-11-1: 5/1	A. Turnell	*S. C. Knight*	12
1985	West Tip 8-10-13: 6/1	M. Oliver	*R. Dunwoody*	20
1986	Charter Party 8-10-10: 12/1	D. Nicholson	*P. Scudamore*	16
1987	Gainsay 8-10-5: 10/1	Mrs J. Pitman	*B. de Haan*	12
1988	Aquilifer 8-10-12: 9/2	D. Murray-Smith	*P. Croucher*	16
1989	Dixton House 10-11-0: 13/2	J. Edwards	*T. Morgan*	16
1990	Bigsun 9-10-11: 15/2	D. Nicholson	*R. Dunwoody*	14

CATHCART CHALLENGE CUP CHASE (Cheltenham 2½m)

1946	Leap Man 9-12-0: 100/7	F. Walwyn	*B. Marshall*	14
1947	Abandoned because of snow and frost			
1948	Jack Tatters 10-12-3: 9/2	F. Walwyn	*B. Marshall*	13
1949	Abandoned because of frost			
1950	River Trout 7-12-1: 8/13	J. Dennistoun	*M. Molony*	10
1951	Semeur 5-11-5: 11/8	F. Walwyn	*B. Marshall*	10
1952	Coolrock 7-11-13: 11/8	F. Walwyn	*B. Marshall*	5
1953	Arctic Gold 8-11-8: 4/1	G. Balding	*G. Kelly*	10
1954	Royal Approach 6-11-13: 10/11	T. Dreaper (Ir)	*P. Taaffe*	6
1955	Abandoned because of snow			
1956	Amber Wave 8-11-8: 6/1	E. Champneys	*M. Scudamore*	10
1957	Rose's Quarter 10-12-4: 3/1	G. Beeby	*D. Dick*	7
1958	Quita Que 9-11-8: 10/11	D. Moore (Ir)	*J. Cox*	7
1959	Gallery Goddess 8-11-3: 11/2	C. Mallon	*F. Winter*	7
1960	Dove Cote 10-11-8: 2/1	J. Wight	*M. Batchelor*	8
1961	Quita Que 12-11-3: 8/11	D. Moore (Ir)	*G. Robinson*	7
1962	Hoodwinked 7-12-1: 8/1	N. Crump	*D. Nicholson*	8
1963	Some Alibi 8-12-1: 9/4	F. Walwyn	*G. Robinson*	13
1964	Panisse 9-11-12: 7/2	W. Stephenson	*M. Scudamore*	10
1965	Scottish Memories 11-11-8: 4/9	P. Sleator (Ir)	*H. Beasley*	5
1966	Flying Wild 10-11-3: 5/4	D. Moore (Ir)	*T. Carberry*	6
1967	Prince Blarney 7-11-8: 100/8	J. Barclay	*R. Barry*	5
1968	Muir 9-11-12: 10/11	T. Dreaper (Ir)	*P. Taaffe*	8
1969	Kinloch Brae 6-12-4: 3/1	W. O'Grady (Ir)	*T. Hyde*	8
1970	Garrynagree 7-11-3: 2/1	T. Dreaper (Ir)	*P. Taaffe*	6
1971	The Laird 10-12-4: 2/1	R. Turnell	*J. King*	5
1972	Soloning 7-12-1: 6/5	F. Winter	*R. Pitman*	8
1973	Inkslinger 6-12-4: 21/20	D. Moore (Ir)	*T. Carberry*	4
1974	Soothsayer 7-11-3: 11/8	F. Winter	*R. Pitman*	7
1975	Abandoned because of waterlogged state of course			
1976	No Race			
1977	No Race			
1978	Abandoned because of snow			
1979	Roller-Coaster 6-11-9: 6/4	F. Winter	*J. Francome*	5
1980	King Weasel 8-11-9: 5/2	M. H. Easterby	*J. J. O'Neill*	6
1981	Lord Greystoke 10-11-6: 7/2	G. Richards	*N. Doughty*	8
1982	Dramatist 11-11-8: 15/8	F. Walwyn	*W. Smith*	6
1983	Observe 7-11-8: 1/2	F. Winter	*J. Francome*	7
1984	The Mighty Mac 9-11-8: 4/7	M. Dickinson	*Mr D. Browne*	7
1985	Straight Accord 10-11-8: 15/2	F. Walwyn	*S. Shilston*	8
1986	Half Free 10-11-8: 11/8	F. Winter	*S. Sherwood*	6
1987	Half Free 11-11-12: 5/4	F. Winter	*P. Scudamore*	4
1988	Private Views 7-11-0: 7/1	N. Gaselee	*B. Powell*	8

1989	Observer Corps 8-11-0: 66/1	J. Edwards	*T. Morgan*	9
1990	Brown Windsor 8-11-3: 13/8	N. Henderson	*J. White*	8

RACEGOERS CLUB COUNTY HANDICAP HURDLE
(Cheltenham 2m)

1946	Vidi 5-11-10: 6/1	R. Hobbs	*D. Butchers*	27
1947	Abandoned because of snow and frost			
1948	Cape Light 5-11-1: 2/1	I. Anthony	*J. Maguire*	21
1949	Abandoned because of frost			
1950	Blue Raleigh 7-10-0: 25/1	R. Renton	*J. Power*	19
1951	Southwick 7-10-3: 100/7	J. Whiting	*G. Spann*	21
1952	Ballymacan 5-10-12: 100/7	N. Crump	*B. Marshall*	21
1953	Teapot II 8-12-7: 4/1	C. Magnier (Ir)	*P. Taaffe*	16
1954	Bold Baby 8-12-0: 13/8	M. Dawson (Ir)	*P. Powell, jnr*	14
1955	Abandoned because of snow			
1956	Pommell 9-10-11: 100/7	J. C. Waugh	*S. Boddy*	18
1957	Flaming East 8-10-5: 100/6	G. Vallance	*P. Pickford*	19
1958	Friendly Boy 6-10-5: 3/1	J. Osborne (Ir)	*W. Brennan*	18
1959	Approval 13-11-2: 10/1	S. Mercer	*D. Leslie*	20
1960	Albergo 6-12-5: 7/4	C. Magnier (Ir)	*D. Page*	26
1961	Most Unusual 6-10-7: 100/7	W. Ransom	*J. Gifford*	23
1962	Sky Pink 5-10-11: 100/8	R. Price	*F. Winter*	20
1963	Bahrain 6-10-6: 11/2	D. L. Moore (Ir)	*T. Carberry*	19
1964	Icy Wonder 5-10-2: 11/2	V. Cross	*J. King*	17
1965	Mayfair Bill 6-10-4: 100/7	R. Turnell	*A. Turnell*	25
1966	Roaring Twenties 6-11-2: 10/1	K. Oliver	*G. Milburn*	16
1967	Cool Alibi 5-10-9: 20/1	J. Bower	*R. Reid*	28
1968	Jolly Signal 6-10-11: 6/1	E. Jones	*J. Uttley*	16
1969	Gay Knight 5-10-3: 100/7	L. Kennard	*A. Branford*	27
1970	Khan 6-9-11: 100/8	Miss D. Harty (Ir)	*Lord Petersham*	32
1971	Carry Off 7-10-1: 25/1	N. Angus	*D. Goulding*	24
1972	Cold Day 6-10-8: 15/1	Mrs E. Gaze	*R. Hyett*	25
1973	Current Romance 7-10-7: 20/1	H. Nicholson	*D. Nicholson*	31
1974	True Song 5-11-2: 14/1	D. Underwood	*G. Old*	20
1975	Abandoned because of waterlogged state of course			
1976	Java Fox 6-10-1: 16/1	R. Cambidge	*Mr G. Jones*	13
1977	Kilcoleman 5-10-7: 14/1	J. Boyers (Ir)	*T. Kinane*	26
1978	Abandoned because of snow			
1979	Monte Ceco 6-10-12: 6/1	F. Rimell	*C. Tinkler*	20
1980	Prince of Bermuda 5-10-0: 9/1	R. Turnell	*S. C. Knight*	18
1981	Staplestown 6-10-7: 11/2	E. O'Grady (Ir)	*T. Ryan*	25
1982	Path of Peace 6-10-6: 4/1	C. Thornton	*J. J. O'Neill*	23
1983	Robin Wonder 5-10-3: 10/1	D. Elsworth	*J. Davies*	29
1984	Hill's Guard 5-10-11: 6/1	A. Scott	*A. Stringer*	19
1985	Floyd 5-10-5: 5/2	D. Elsworth	*C. Brown*	27
1986	Jobroke 6-10-3: 6/1	M. H. Easterby	*J. J. O'Neill*	29
1987	Neblin 8-11-0: 14/1	G. Balding	*R. Guest*	24
1988	Cashew King 5-10-4: 9/1	B. McMahon	*T. Wall*	24
1989	Willsford 6-10-8: 11/1	Mrs J. Pitman	*M. Bowlby*	21
1990	Moody Man 5-11-2: 9/1	P. Hobbs	*P. Hobbs*	20

BUILDER GROUP GOLD CUP HANDICAP HURDLE
(Lingfield 2½m)

1984	Jorge Miguel 5-10-6: 15/2	G. Pritchard-Gordon	*S. Smith Eccles*	12
1985	Going Broke 5-10-0: 13/2	D. Murray-Smith	*C. Brown*	14
1986	Inlander 5-9-7: 9/2	J. Davies	*Mr S. Woods*	16
1987	Tigerwood 6-10-10: 13/2	R. Akehurst	*R. Guest*	15
1988	Carnival Air 9-10-0: 8/1	K. Bailey	*P. Croucher*	18
1989	Predominate 8-10-4: 10/1	O. Sherwood	*S. Sherwood*	14
1990	Nahar 5-10-7: 9/2	S. Dow	*H. Davies*	9

ODDBINS HANDICAP HURDLE (Liverpool 3m 1f)

1985	Gembridge Jupiter 7-10-3: 12/1	C. Trietline	*J. Suthern*	21
1986	Ishkomann 7-10-9: 11/1	J. Spearing	*G. McCourt*	14
1987	Mandavi 6-10-4: 12/1	N. Henderson	*M. Bowlby*	20
1988	Rapier Thrust 6-11-3: 8/1	J. FitzGerald	*M. Dwyer*	16
1989	Slalom 8-12-0: 9/1	M. Robinson	*J. White*	17
1990	Sip of Orange 8-10-3: 5/1	J. FitzGerald	*M. Dwyer*	21

SEAGRAM 100 PIPERS TOP NOVICES' HURDLE (Liverpool 2m)

1976	Beacon Light 5-11-6: 4/1	R. Turnell	*A. Turnell*	13
1977	Irish Rambler 6-11-0: 3/1	J. Crowley (Ir)	*J. Crowley*	21
1978	Prousto 5-11-5: 4/1	A. Jarvis	*J. J. O'Neill*	13
1979	Rimondo 4-10-10: 8/1	E. Carter	*J. J. O'Neill*	20
1980	Jugador 5-11-5: 17/2	D. Kent	*B. R. Davies*	22
1981	Burns 5-11-5: 14/1	F. Walwyn	*W. Smith*	18
1982	Bright Oassis 6-11-5: 14/1	K. Bailey	*A. Webb*	17
1983	Very Promising 5-12-3: 7/4	Mrs M. Rimell	*S. Morshead*	13
1984	Browne's Gazette 6-11-11: 10/11	M. Dickinson	*Mr D. Browne*	14
1985	Sailor's Dance 5-11-0: 12/1	F. Winter	*J. Duggan*	18
1986	I Bin Zaidoon 5-11-0: 14/1	Mrs J. Pitman	*G. McCourt*	17
1987	Convinced 5-11-0: 100/30	M. Pipe	*P. Scudamore*	14
1988	Faraway Lad 5-11-0: 10/1	O. Sherwood	*S. Sherwood*	14
1989	Young Benz 5-11-0: 3/1	M. H. Easterby	*L. Wyer*	11
1990	Fidway 5-11-0: 16/1	T. Thomson Jones	*S. Smith Eccles*	15

MARTELL CUP CHASE (Liverpool 3m 1f)

1984	Royal Bond 11-11-5: 11/2	A. Moore (Ir)	*T. Taaffe*	4
1985	Wayward Lad 10-11-5: 6/1	Mrs M. Dickinson	*J. Francome*	6
1986	Beau Ranger 8-11-5: 40/1	J. Thorne	*H. Davies*	4
1987	Wayward Lad 12-11-5: 7/1	Mrs M. Dickinson	*G. McCourt*	6
1988	Desert Orchid 9-11-5: 3/1	D. Elsworth	*S. Sherwood*	4
1989	Yahoo 8-11-5: 5/1	J. Edwards	*T. Morgan*	8
1990	Toby Tobias 8-11-9: 1/1	Mrs J. Pitman	*M. Pitman*	5

JOHN HUGHES MEMORIAL TROPHY HANDICAP CHASE
(Liverpool 2¾m)

1949	Cadamstown 9-11-4: 20/1	J. Powell	*J. Brogan*	24
1950	Culworth 9-10-12: 7/1	W. Hall	*R. Curran*	16
1951	Culworth 10-11-6: 5/1	W. Hall	*R. Curran*	18
1952	Ballymagillan 6-10-9: 7/2	T. Dreaper (Ir)	*P. Taaffe*	15
1953	Irish Lizard 10-10-4: 100/8	H. Nicholson	*R. Francis*	17
1954	Little Yid 12-10-11: 3/1	R. Renton	*G. Slack*	17
1955	Stormhead 11-11-12: 10/1	W. Hall	*P. Farrell*	14
1956	John Jacques 7-11-4: 13/2	W. Wharton	*J. Power*	10
1957	Roughan 9-10-8: 100/7	N. Crump	*H. East*	14
1958	Roughan 10-11-0: 11/2	N. Crump	*F. Winter*	16
1959	Clanyon 11-11-2: 6/1	W. J-Powell	*G. Underwood*	19
1960	Fresh Winds 9-11-1: 100/7	R. Whiston	*S. Mellor*	21
1961	Cupid's Charge 6-11-3: 9/1	P. Cazalet	*W. Rees*	13
1962	Dagmar Gittell 7-10-11: 100/8	R. Renton	*J. Gifford*	22
1963	Barberyn 8-11-9: 7/1	W. Stephenson	*M. Scudamore*	20
1964	Red Tide 7-10-6: 10/1	R. Turnell	*J. King*	14
1965	Hopkiss 7-10-12: 11/2	A. Kilpatrick	*E. P. Harty*	13
1966	Walpole 10-11-5: 10/1	R. Price	*J. Gifford*	24
1967	Georgetown 7-10-7: 100/8	N. Kusbish	*P. Mahoney*	23
1968	Surcharge 10-10-8: 100/8	J. Barclay	*S. Davenport*	16
1969	Dozo 8-10-5: 10/1	G. Balding	*E. P. Harty*	20
1970	Charter Flight 8-11-12: 9/2	R. Turnell	*J. Haine*	23
1971	Rigton Prince 10-11-1: 8/1	W. A. Stephenson	*J. Enright*	15
1972	Sunny Lad 8-10-8: 8/1	F. Rimell	*K. White*	17
1973	Inch Arran 9-11-2: 8/1	P. Cazalet	*D. Mould*	14
1974	Clear Cut 10-11-8: 8/1	W. Hall	*J. J. O'Neill*	18
1975	Our Greenwood 7-12-0: 11/2	J. Dreaper (Ir)	*T. Carberry*	18
1976	Lictor 9-10-0: 20/1	E. Courage	*D. Sunderland*	12
1977	Churchtown Boy 10-10-0: 9/1	M. Salaman	*C. Read*	26
1978	Canit 8-10-0: 8/1	F. Rimell	*C. Tinkler*	15
1979	Artic Ale 8-10-8: 12/1	D. Moore (Ir)	*Mr J. Fowler*	23
1980	Uncle Bing 11-11-11: 17/2	R. Head	*J. Francome*	24
1981	Mr Marlsbridge 8-10-10: 10/1	D. Gandolfo	*P. Barton*	18
1982	Beacon Time 8-10-9: 13/2	F. Walwyn	*K. Mooney*	26
1983	Tiepolino 11-10-4: 16/1	K. Bishop	*H. Davies*	19
1984	Fabulous 11-10-0: 33/1	J. S. Wilson	*A. Stringer*	23
1985	Smith's Man 7-10-0: 10/1	Mrs J. Pitman	*M. Perrett*	21
1986	Glenrue 9-10-2: 20/1	T. Casey	*R. Dunwoody*	22
1987	Strath Leader 9-11-10: 12/1	J. Edwards	*T. Morgan*	15
1988	Wiggburn 9-10-2: 12/1	Mrs A. Hewitt	*M. Williams*	19

1989	Villierstown 10-11-10: 5/2	W. A. Stephenson	*S. Sherwood*	7
1990	Wont Be Gone Long 8-10-2: 25/1	N. Henderson	*R. Dunwoody*	30

MUMM CLUB NOVICES' CHASE (Liverpool 3m 1f)

1981	Bregawn 7-11-8: 7/4	M. Dickinson	*R. Earnshaw*	8
1982	Burrough Hill Lad 6-11-5: 9/1	Mrs J. Pitman	*P. Tuck*	10
1983	Everett 8-11-9: 7/2	F. Walwyn	*S. Shilston*	5
1984	Baron Blakeney 7-11-6: 14/1	M. Pipe	*Mr O. Sherwood*	8
1985	Rhyme 'N' Reason 6-11-3: 11/8	D. Murray-Smith	*G. Bradley*	12
1986	Stearsby 7-11-6: 11/4	Mrs J. Pitman	*G. Bradley*	11
1987	Against The Grain 6-11-3: 8/1	D. Nicholson	*R. Dunwoody*	13
1988	Delius 10-11-3: 9/1	R. Lee	*B. Dowling*	13
1989	Swardean 7-11-3: 16/1	R. Lee	*B. Dowling*	13
1990	Royal Athlete 7-11-9: 5/2	Mrs J. Pitman	*M. Pitman*	11

SEAGRAM FOX HUNTERS' CHASE (Liverpool 2¾m)

1947	Lucky Purchase 9-12-0: 100/30	S. Banks	*J. Nichols*	6
1948	San Michele 8-12-0: 7/1	G. Cunard	*G. Cunard*	12
1949	Ballyhartfield 10-12-0: 7/2	J. Makin	*J. Straker*	5
1950	Hilmere 17-12-0: 100/7	L. Dalton	*P. Brookshaw*	14
1951	Candy II 9-11-7: 10/1	R. Brewis	*R. Brewis*	17
1952	Pampeenne II 9-12-0: 7/2	H. Alexander	*H. Alexander*	11
1953	Solo Call 9-12-0: 6/1	M. Brewis	*M. Brewis*	7
1954	Dark Stranger 9-12-0: 10/1	L. Colville	*J. Bosley*	14
1955	Happymint 10-12-0: 9/2	J. Wight	*A. Moralee*	13
1956	Mr Shanks 9-12-0: 5/2	J. Keith	*J. Everitt*	8
1957	Colledge Master 7-12-0: 11/10	L. Morgan	*L. Morgan*	6
1958	Surprise Packet 9-12-0: 2/1	Mrs S. Richards	*T. Johnson*	13
1959	Merryman II 8-12-0: 5/2	N. Crump	*C. Scott*	10
1960	April Queen 9-12-0: 100/7	M. Fear	*J. Daniell*	8
1961	Colledge Master 11-12-0: 4/6	L. Morgan	*L. Morgan*	8
1962	Dominion 10-12-0: 8/1	K. Beeston	*C. Foulkes*	12
1963	Sea Knight 8-12-0: 13/2	W. A. Stephenson	*P. Nicholson*	15
1964	Aerial III 8-12-0: 5/2	R. Armytage	*J. Daniell*	8
1965	Sea Knight 10-11-9: 8/1	W. A. Stephenson	*P. Nicholson*	14
1966	Sulbaltern 12-12-0: 100/7	C Alexander	*J. Lawrence*	13
1967	Minto Burn 11-11-7: 5/1	Miss B. Johnson	*B. Surtees*	10
1968	Juan 12-11-7: 11/4	P. Wills	*P. Wills*	8
1969	Bitter Lemon 8-11-11: 7/1	V. Rowe	*V. Rowe*	15
1970	Lismateige 7-11-7: 6/1	P. Wates	*A. Wates*	5
1971	Bright Willow 10-11-11: 5/1	G. Cure	*R. Chugg*	15
1972	Credit Call 8-12-0: 8/13	W. A. Stephenson	*C. Collins*	8
1973	Bullock's Horn 10-12-0: 7/2	R. Turnell	*Lord Oaksey*	14
1974	Lord Fortune 11-11-9: 7/2	Mrs J. Brutton	*D. Edmunds*	10
1975	Credit Call 11-11-7: 6/1	W. A. Stephenson	*J. Newton*	10
1976	Credit Call 12-11-9: 5/4	Mrs R. Newton	*J. Newton*	9
1977	Happy Warrior 10-12-0: 6/1	F. Winter	*N. Henderson*	20
1978	Spartan Missile 6-12-0: 15/8	J. Thorne	*J. Thorne*	19
1979	Spartan Missile 7-12-7: 8/15	J. Thorne	*J. Thorne*	15
1980	Rolls Rambler 9-12-5: 100/30	F. Winter	*O. Sherwood*	24
1981	Grittar 8-12-5: 7/4	F. Gilman	*R. Saunders*	25
1982	Lone Soldier 10-12-0: 25/1	J. Docker	*P. Greenall*	12
1983	Atha Cliath 8-12-0: 5/1	P. Mullins (Ir)	*W. Mullins*	8
1984	Gayle Warning 10-12-0: 85/40	J. Dudgeon	*A. Dudgeon*	17
1985	City Boy 10-12-0: 4/1	Mrs J. Mann	*T. Thomson Jones*	18
1986	Eliogarty 11-12-0: 11/1	D. Murray Smith	*Miss C. Beasley*	20
1987	Border Burg 10-12-0: 7/2	J. Delahooke	*A. Hill*	25
1988	Newnham 11-12-0: 50/1	M. Johnson	*S. Andrews*	23
1989	Call Collect 8-12-0: 5/1	J. Parkes	*R. Martin*	16
1990	Lean Ar Aghaidh 13-12-0: 5/1	S. Mellor	*D. Gray*	25

SANDEMAN HANDICAP CHASE (Liverpool 2½m)

1977	Batchelor's Hall 7-9-9: 18/1	P. Cundell	*M. O'Halloran*	18
1978	King Or Country 7-11-2: 11/2	D. Barons	*P. Leach*	15
1979	King Or Country 8-12-1: 7/2	D. Barons	*P. Leach*	11
1980	Carrow Boy 8-10-5: 12/1	W. Durkan (Ir)	*M. Mulligan*	10
1981	Swift Albany 7-10-3: 7/1	R. Robinson	*C. Pimlott*	16

1982	Polars Laddie 9-10-0: 33/1	R. Goldie	*A. Dickman*	10
1983	King Or Country 12-10-4: 9/1	D. Barons	*H. Davies*	12
1984	Gambling Prince 11-10-0: 20/1	Mrs G. Jones	*J. Burke*	12
1985	Beau Ranger 7-11-3: 5/2	J. Thorne	*J. Hurst*	8
1986	Fifty Dollars More 11-11-8: 7/1	F. Winter	*S. Sherwood*	9
1987	Gee-A 8-10-9: 13/2	G. Hubbard	*Miss G. Armytage*	13
1988	Worthy Knight 7-10-0: 14/1	B. McLean	*B. Storey*	8
1989	Golden Freeze 7-11-10: 4/1	Mrs J. Pitman	*M. Bowlby*	8
1990	Sure Metal 7-10-0: 100/1	D. McCain	*B. Storey*	13

PERRIER JOUET NOVICES CHASE (Liverpool 2m)

1954	Evian 6-11-4: 100/6	M. V. O'Brien (Ir)	*E. McKenzie*	11
1955	Wise Child 7-12-0: 11/4	C. Bewicke	*G. Milburn*	17
1956	Sir Ken 9-12-0: 1/1	W. Stephenson	*T. Molony*	7
1957	Northern King 6-11-4: 11/2	E. Cousins	*M. Pumfrey*	9
1958	Just Awake 6-12-0: 110/7	P. Cazalet	*A. Freeman*	14
1959	Liquidator 7-11-4: 100/7	W. Hall	*P. Farrell*	13
1960	Cupid's Charge 5-11-0: 100/6	P. Cazalet	*A. Freeman*	13
1961	Peacetown 7-11-11: 7/1	G. Owen	*S. Mellor*	8
1962	Rye Light 10-11-8: 5/1	W. Hall	*P. Farrell*	14
1963	Border Sparkle 7-11-8: 13/2	N. Robinson	*T. McGinley*	9
1964	Brand Z 9-11-8: 11/2	F. Cundell	*R. Edwards*	6
1965	Oedipe 7-11-11: 5/2	P. Cazalet	*S. Mellor*	11
1966	Roe Gemmel 7-11-8: 100/7	R. Fairbairn	*Mr G. Macmillan*	20
1967	Glenn 6-11-11: 7/2	F. Rimell	*T. Biddlecombe*	11
1968	Brian's Best 8-11-11: 10/1	G. Owen	*R. Edwards*	13
1969	Rainbow Cottage 6-11-8: 100/8	W. A. Stephenson	*T. S. Murphy*	14
1970	Tenterclef 8-11-4: 5/1	P. Ransom	*B. Brogan*	6
1971	Vegeo 8-11-4: 16/1	W. Stephenson	*D. Nicholson*	12
1972	Explicit 8-12-0: 9/2	L. Shedden	*T. Stack*	11
1973	Line Regiment 9-11-4: 14/1	W. D. Francis	*J. Bourke*	6
1974	Winter Rain 6-12-0: 9/4	A. Dickinson	*M. Dickinson*	15
1975	Tom Morgan 6-12-0: 3/1	K. Oliver	*C. Tinkler*	9
1976	Vaguely Attractive 7-11-3: 15/1	S. Murphy (Ir)	*Mr J. Fowler*	11
1977	Siberian Sun 6-11-9: 11/2	F. Flood (Ir)	*F. Berry*	10
1978	Another Dolly 8-11-9: 11/4	F. Rimell	*J. Burke*	4
1979	Night Nurse 8-11-3: 1/1	M. H. Easterby	*J. J. O'Neill*	4
1980	Western Rose 8-11-3: 15/2	F. Rimell	*S. Morshead*	7
1981	Irian 7-11-3: 10/1	A. Moore (Ir)	*F. Berry*	10
1982	Brave Fellow 8-11-3: 9/2	J. FitzGerald	*P. Charlton*	11
1983	Ryeman 6-11-11: 10/11	M. H. Easterby	*A. Brown*	8
1984	Noddy's Ryde 7-11-10: 1/2	G. Richards	*N. Doughty*	12
1985	Pan Arctic 6-11-3: 100/1	T. Bill	*P. Hobbs*	10
1986	Pearlyman 7-11-13: 4/1	J. Edwards	*P. Barton*	10
1987	Dan The Millar 8-11-13: 5/2	Mrs M. Dickinson	*G. Bradley*	9
1988	Jim Thorpe 7-11-8: 11/4	G. Richards	*C. Grant*	7
1989	Feroda 8-11-8: 13/8	A. Moore (Ir)	*T. Taaffe*	6
1990	Boutzdaroff 8-11-1: 8/1	J. FitzGerald	*D. Byrne*	14

WHITE SATIN NOVICES' HURDLE (Liverpool 3m 1f)

1988	Rustle 6-11-7: 13/8	N. Henderson	*M. Bowlby*	12
1989	Boreen Belle 7-11-2: 10/1	W. Harney (Ir)	*C. Swan*	14
1990	Dwadme 5-11-4: 5/1	O. Sherwood	*J. Osborne*	10

HEIDSIECK DRY MONOPOLE HANDICAP CHASE
(Liverpool 3m 1f)

1977	Our Edition 10-11-13: 7/2	S. Mellor	*S. Jobar*	12
1978	Mr Snowman 9-10-10: 5/1	T. Forster	*G. Thorner*	8
1979	Silent Valley 6-9-10: 16/1	I. Jordon	*J. Allen*	12
1980	New Colonist 8-10-3: 9/4	A. Dickinson	*T. Carmody*	10
1981	Megan's Boy 8-11-5: 11/2	E. Carter	*P. Charlton*	12
1982	Silent Valley 9-10-13: 16/1	I. Jordon	*P. Scudamore*	11
1983	Fauloon 8-10-7: 8/1	F. Walwyn	*W. Smith*	13
1984	Straight Accord 9-11-8: 9/2	F. Walwyn	*S. Shilston*	9
1985	Green Bramble 8-10-3: 5/2	N. Henderson	*S. Smith Eccles*	11
1986	Arctic Beau 8-10-1: 10/1	J. Thorne	*R. Dunwoody*	7
1987	Gainsay 8-10-11: 7/2	Mrs J. Pitman	*M. Pitman*	10
1988	Rinus 7-10-2: 7/2	G. Richards	*R. Dunwoody*	8

1989	Travel Over 8-10-1: 3/1	Mrs M. Dickinson	*M. Hammond*	6
1990	One More Knight 7-10-12: 10/1	Mrs I. McKie	*L. Harvey*	12

MARTELL HANDICAP HURDLE (Liverpool 2½m)

1989	Hill Street 7-10-5: 10/1	J. FitzGerald	*M. Dwyer*	15
1990	Sayparee 5-11-3: 10/1	M. Pipe	*P. Scudamore*	14

GLENLIVET ANNIVERSARY HURDLE (4-y-o) (Liverpool 2m)

1976	Cooch Behar 11-0: 4/1	C. Kinane (Ir)	*L. O'Donnell*	8
1977	Decent Fellow 11-3: 7/2	G. Balding	*R. Linley*	11
1978	Beparoejojo 11-0: 10/1	J. Bolger (Ir)	*D. T. Hughes*	11
1979	Pollardstown 11-7: 10/11	S. Mellor	*P. Blacker*	9
1980	Starfen 11-0: 3/1	M. H. Easterby	*J. J. O'Neill*	20
1981	Broadsword 11-3: 6/5	D. Nicholson	*P. Scudamore*	10
1982	Prince Bless 11-0: 12/1	Mrs N. Smith	*M. O'Halloran*	12
1983	Benfen 11-0: 16/1	M. H. Easterby	*A. Brown*	9
1984	Afzal 11-0: 9/1	R. Hollinshead	*G. McCourt*	17
1985	Humberside Lady 10-9: 15/2	G. Huffer	*M. Dwyer*	15
1986	Dark Raven 11-0: 7/2	D. Weld (Ir)	*T. Carmody*	16
1987	Aldino 11-0: 11/1	O. Sherwood	*S. Sherwood*	13
1988	Royal Illusion 11-0: 9/1	G. Moore	*M. Hammond*	14
1989	Vayrua 11-0: 12/1	G. Harwood	*M. Perrett*	9
1990	Sybillin 11-0: 25/1	J. FitzGerald	*D. Byrne*	18

CAPTAIN MORGAN AINTREE CHASE (LIMITED HANDICAP)
(Liverpool 2m)

1976	Menehall 9-10-0: 25/1	F. Walwyn	*M. Floyd*	10
1977	Skymas 12-12-0: 5/1	B. Lusk (Ir)	*M. Morris*	9
1978	Even Melody 9-11-6: 11/1	N. Crump	*C. Hawkins*	14
1979	Funny Baby 8-10-7: 9/1	G. Fairbairn	*R. Lamb*	8
1980	Drumgora 8-10-7: 8/1	A. Moore (Ir)	*T. McGivern*	10
1981	Western Rose 9-10-7: 8/1	F. Rimell	*S. Morshead*	11
1982	Little Bay 7-10-7: 14/1	G. Richards	*J. J. O'Neill*	12
1983	Artifice 12-11-0: 9/1	J. Thorne	*P. Scudamore*	9
1984	Little Bay 9-11-7: 11/4	G. Richards	*J. Francome*	7
1985	Kathies Lad 8-11-7: 6/5	A. Jarvis	*S. Smith Eccles*	8
1986	Kathies Lad 9-10-13: 11/8	A. Jarvis	*S. Smith Eccles*	6
1987	Sea Merchant 10-10-7: 9/1	W. A. Stephenson	*R. Lamb*	9
1988	Prideaux Boy 10-10-7: 25/1	G. Roach	*A. Webb*	13
1989	Feroda 8-10-7: 9/1	A. Moore (Ir)	*T. Taaffe*	9
1990	Nohalmdun 9-10-7: 11/1	M. H. Easterby	*L. Wyer*	12

SANDEMAN AINTREE HURDLE (Liverpool 2½m)

1976	Comedy of Errors 9-11-9: 2/1	F. Rimell	*K. White*	10
1977	Night Nurse 6-11-11: 4/5 } dh	M. H. Easterby	*P. Broderick*	10
	Monksfield 5-11-5: 7/2 } dh	D. McDonogh (Ir)	*D. T. Hughes*	
1978	Monksfield 6-11-11: 9/4	D. McDonogh (Ir)	*D. T. Hughes*	7
1979	Monksfield 7-11-11: 5/4	D. McDonogh (Ir)	*D. T. Hughes*	4
1980	Pollardstown 5-11-5: 2/1	S. Mellor	*P. Blacker*	3
1981	Daring Run 6-11-9: 9/4	P. McCreery (Ir)	*Mr T. Walsh*	7
1982	Daring Run 7-11-9: 2/1	P. McCreery (Ir)	*Mr T. Walsh*	5
1983	Gaye Brief 6-11-11: 11/8	Mrs M. Rimell	*R. Linley*	6
1984	Dawn Run 6-11-6: 4/6	P. Mullins (Ir)	*A. Mullins*	8
1985	Bajan Sunshine 6-11-6: 11/1	M. Tate	*P. Scudamore*	7
1986	Aonoch 7-11-9: 16/1	Mrs S. Oliver	*J. Duggan*	9
1987	Aonoch 8-11-9: 5/2	Mrs S. Oliver	*Jacqui Oliver*	7
1988	Celtic Chief 5-11-6: 4/5	Mrs M. Rimell	*R. Dunwoody*	9
1989	Beech Road 7-11-9: 10/1	G. Balding	*R. Guest*	12
1990	Morley Street 6-11-6: 4/5	G. Balding	*J. Frost*	6

MUMM PRIZE NOVICES' HURDLE (Liverpool 2½m)

1985	Out of The Gloom 4-11-0: 11/4	R. Hollinshead	*J. J. O'Neill*	14
1986	Canute Express 5-11-9: 3/1	H. Scott (Ir)	*Mr L. Wyer*	15
1987	The West Awake 6-11-9: 11/8	O. Sherwood	*S. Sherwood*	11
1988	Sir Blake 7-11-5: 2/1	D. Elsworth	*B. Powell*	13
1989	Morley Street 5-11-5: 7/2	G. Balding	*J. Frost*	10
1990	Vazon Bay 6-11-0: 33/1	Mrs J. Pitman	*M. Pitman*	10

RAPID RACELINE SCOTTISH CHAMPION HURDLE (Ayr 2m)

1966	Blue Venom 7-11-1: 7/1	P. Adams	*Mr P. Adams*	5
1967	Originator 6-11-1: 13/2	J. Barclay	*E. Wilson*	13
1968	Al-'Alawi 5-10-8: 9/1	T. Robson	*P. McCarron*	19
1969	Mugatpura 6-11-3: 9/2	F. Walwyn	*T. Jennings*	13
1970	Easter Pirate 6-10-0: 100/6	R. Fairbairn	*S. Hayhurst*	17
1971	Dondieu 6-11-11: 3/1	Denys Smith	*B. Fletcher*	9
1972	Coral Diver 7-11-11: 3/1	F. Rimell	*K. White*	7
1973	Captain Christy 6-12-0: 2/1	P. Taaffe (Ir)	*H. Beasley*	5
1974	Santon Brig 5-11-3: 6/4	A. Dickinson	*M. Dickinson*	3
1975	Comedy of Errors 8-12-0: 1/5	F. Rimell	*K. White*	5
1976	Night Nurse 5-12-0: 1/4	M. H. Easterby	*P. Broderick*	2
1977	Sea Pigeon 7-11-4: 4/9	M. H. Easterby	*J. J. O'Neill*	3
1978	Sea Pigeon 8-12-0: 7/4	M. H. Easterby	*J. J. O'Neill*	7
1979	Bird's Nest 9-11-8: 100/30	R. Turnell	*A. Turnell*	5
1980	Secret Ballot 6-10-7: 11/2	R. Turnell	*A. Turnell*	7
1981	Bird's Nest 11-11-6: 6/1	R. Turnell	*A. Turnell*	5
1982	Gay George 6-11-7: 4/6	F. Walwyn	*W. Smith*	5
1983	Royal Vulcan 5-11-13: 7/2	N. Callaghan	*P. Scudamore*	6
1984	Rushmoor 6-10-13: 3/1	R. Peacock	*P. Scudamore*	8
1985	Sailor's Dance 5-11-1: 5/2	F. Winter	*J. Duggan*	4
1986	River Ceiriog 5-10-9: 4/1	N. Henderson	*S. Smith Eccles*	7
1987	Positive 5-10-8: 11/2	K. Bailey	*P. Croucher*	6
1988	Pat's Jester 5-11-1: 5/1	R. Allan	*B. Storey*	8
1989	Aldino 6-12-0: 13/2	O. Sherwood	*S. Sherwood*	6
1990	Sayparee 5-10-7: 11/2	M. Pipe	*J. Lower*	13

EDINBURGH WOOLLEN MILL FUTURE CHAMPIONS NOVICES CHASE (Ayr 2m)

1971	Chorus 10-11-7: 11/2	H. T. Jones	*S. Mellor*	11
1972	Avondhu 9-11-7: 8/1	P. Chesmore	*P. Brogan*	11
1973	The Benign Bishop 6-12-1: 11/4	K. Oliver	*R. Barry*	13
1974	Winter Rain 6-12-1: 4/7	A. Dickinson	*M. Dickinson*	6
1975	Easby Abbey 8-11-7: 5/4	M. H. Easterby	*R. Barry*	6
1976	Cromwell Road 6-12-1: 5/2	G. Richards	*D. Goulding*	11
1977	Crofton Hall 8-11-8: 5/1	J. Dixon	*J. J. O'Neill*	5
1978	King Weasel 6-11-1: 1/2	M. H. Easterby	*J. J. O'Neill*	4
1979	Night Nurse 8-12-0: 5/6	M. H. Easterby	*J. J. O'Neill*	6
1980	Don't Forget 6-11-3: 8/1	W. A. Stephenson	*R. Lamb*	6
1981	Little Bay 6-11-11: 5/2	G. Richards	*R. Barry*	9
1982	Full Sutton 9-11-3: 5/1	D. Kent	*B. R. Davies*	6
1983	Mountain Hays 8-11-8: 11/10	M. H. Easterby	*A. Brown*	5
1984	Noddy's Ryde 7-11-11: 4/11	G. Richards	*N. Doughty*	8
1985	Buck House 7-11-10: 4/6	M. Morris (Ir)	*T. Carmody*	10
1986	Amber Rambler 7-11-3: 5/1	H. Wharton	*S. Youlden*	5
1987	General Chandos 6-11-3: 8/1	J. Bradburne	*Mr J. Bradburne*	6
1988	Jim Thorpe 7-11-10: 9/4	G. Richards	*M. Dwyer*	6
1989	Southern Minstrel 6-11-13: 5/4	W. A. Stephenson	*C. Grant*	7
1990	Celtic Shot 8-11-13: 5/2	C. Brooks	*G. McCourt*	12

WILLIAM HILL SCOTTISH GRAND NATIONAL CHASE
(Ayr 4m 120yds)

1947	Rowland Roy 8-11-2: 6/1	F. Walwyn	*Mr R. Black*	15
1948	Magnetic Fin 9-10-5: 100/8	W. Hall	*L. Vick*	12
1949	Wot No Sun 7-11-5: 2/1	N. Crump	*A. Thompson*	10
1950	Sanvina 10-12-2: 25/1	J. Wight	*Mr K. Oliver*	19
1951	Court Painter 11-9-7: 20/1	C. Bewicke	*F. Carroll*	13
1952	Flagrant Mac 8-11-12: 100/8	R. Renton	*J. Power*	17
1953	Queen's Taste 7-10-2: 100/6	H. Clarkson	*Mr T. Robson*	21
1954	Queen's Taste 8-10-9: 10/1	H. Clarkson	*G. Slack*	15
1955	Bar Point 8-10-2: 20/1	R. Renton	*D. Ancil*	18
1956	Queen's Taste 10-11-0: 8/1	H. Clarkson	*R. Curran*	14
1957	Bremontier 10-10-12: 10/1	P. Taylor	*A. Rossio*	13
1958	Game Field 8-11-10: 9/1	J. Fawcus	*J. Boddy*	14
1959	Merryman II 8-10-12: 100/8	N. Crump	*G. Scott*	18
1960	Fincham 8-10-0: 9/4	J. White	*M. Batchelor*	8
1961	Kinmont Wullie 7-10-7: 8/1	W. A. Stephenson	*C. Stobbs*	18
1962	Sham Fight 10-10-10: 100/6	T. Robson	*T. Robson*	18

1963	Pappageno's Cottage 8-10-9: 100/8	K. Oliver	*T. Brookshaw*	18
1964	Popham Down 7-10-0: 8/1	F. Walwyn	*J. Haine*	14
1965	Brasher 9-10-5: 4/1	T. Robson	*J. FitzGerald*	9
1966	African Patrol 7-10-7: 10/1	R. Fairbairn	*J. Leech*	17
1967	The Fossa 10-9-12: 8/1	F. Rimell	*A. Turnell*	18
1968	Arcturus 7-10-4: 4/1	N. Crump	*P. Buckley*	10
1969	Playlord 8-12-0: 9/1	G. Richards	*R. Barry*	17
1970	The Spaniard 8-10-0: 8/1	K. Oliver	*B. Brogan*	10
1971	Young Ash Leaf 7-10-2: 12/1	K. Oliver	*P. Ennis*	21
1972	Quick Reply 7-9-9: 11/1	H. Bell	*M. Barnes*	17
1973	Esban 9-9-11: 16/1	R. Clay	*J. Bourke*	21
1974	Red Rum 9-11-13: 11/8	D. McCain	*B. Fletcher*	17
1975	Barona 9-10-0: 33/1	R. Armytage	*P. Kelleway*	17
1976	Barona 10-10-2: 12/1	R. Armytage	*P. Kelleway*	23
1977	Sebastian V 9-10-2: 9/2	H. Bell	*R. Lamb*	18
1978	King Con 9-9-13: 33/1	G. Renilson	*Mr P. Craggs*	21
1979	Fighting Fit 7-10-10: 9/1	K. Oliver	*C. Hawkins*	19
1980	Salkeld 8-10-0: 14/1	N. Crump	*D. Atkins*	23
1981	Astral Charmer 8-9-10: 66/1	H. Bell	*J. Goulding*	21
1982	Cockle Strand 9-9-11: 9/1	K. Oliver	*D. Dutton*	15
1983	Canton 9-10-2: 16/1	N. Crump	*K. Whyte*	22
1984	Androma 7-10-0: 7/1	J. FitzGerald	*M. Dwyer*	19
1985	Androma 8-10-0: 11/1	J. FitzGerald	*M. Dwyer*	18
1986	Hardy Lad 9-10-0: 28/1	B. Wilkinson	*M. Hammond*	24
1987	Little Polveir 10-10-0: 12/1	J. Edwards	*P. Scudamore*	11
1988	Mighty Mark 9-10-5: 9/1	F. Walton	*B. Storey*	17
1989	Roll-A-Joint 11-10-0: 4/1	C. Popham	*B. Powell*	11
1990	Four Trix 9-10-0: 25/1	G. Richards	*D. Byrne*	28

GOLDEN EAGLE NOVICES CHASE (Ascot 2½m)

1974	Colondine 7-11-3: 7/1	I. Dudgeon	*D. O'Donovan*	13
1975	Galloway Edition 6-11-3: 100/30	G. Balding	*J. Fox*	8
1976	The Snipe 6-11-3: 85/40	J. Webber	*A. Webber*	5
1977	Autumn Rain 6-11-3: 7/4	A. Dickinson	*M. Dickinson*	6
1978	Valiant Charger 7-11-3: 100/30	F. Winter	*J. Francome*	12
1979	Sweet September 7-11-3: 8/13	R. Turnell	*A. Turnell*	12
1980	O'er The Border 6-11-3: 7/1	P. Calver	*P. Haynes*	16
1981	Spring Chancellor 6-11-3: 33/1	W. A. Stephenson	*P. Scudamore*	14
1982	New Lyric 7-11-3: 13/2	D. Nicholson	*P. Scudamore*	9
1983	Gallaher 7-11-3: 100/30	F. Walwyn	*W. Smith*	7
1984	Just For The Crack 6-11-3: 20/1	K Bailey	*A. Webber*	3
1985	Townley Stone 6-11-7: 8/1	J. Webber	*G. McCourt*	7
1986	Oregon Trail 6-11-10: 2/1	S. Christian	*K. Mooney*	5
1987	Foyle Fisherman 8-11-3: 9/1	J. Gifford	*R. Rowe*	8
1988	Saffron Lord 6-11-8: 2/1	J. Gifford	*R. Rowe*	3
1989	Abandoned because of snow			
1990	Okeetee 7-11-4: 40/85	C. Brooks	*B. de Haan*	3

KEITH PROWSE LONG-DISTANCE HURDLE
(Ascot 3m)

1974	Moyne Royal 9-12-3: 11/2	A. Pitt	*J. King*	20
1975	Lanzarote 7-11-12: 5/2	F. Winter	*R. Pitman*	10
1976	Good Prospect 7-11-3: 5/2	J. Edwards	*A. Turnell*	7
1977	Mark Henry 6-11-3: 7/1	W. Elsey	*T. Stack*	12
1978	Flame Gun 6-11-12: 11/2	E. O'Grady (Ir)	*Mr N. Madden*	11
1979	Prominent King 7-11-12: 13/8	M. H. Easterby	*J. J. O'Neill*	9
1980	Derring Rose 5-11-12: 4/1	A. Jarvis	*A. Turnell*	9
1981	Shell Burst 6-11-0: 20/1	L. Kennard	*H. Davies*	13
1982	Gaye Chance 7-11-12: 7/4	Mrs M. Rimell	*P. Scudamore*	7
1983	Sandalay 5-11-3: 8/1	P. Cundell	*P. Charlton*	11
1984	Alastor O Mavros 5-11-3: 9/1	J. Gifford	*H. Davies*	6
1985	Bajan Sunshine 6-12-2: 4/1	M. Tate	*P. Scudamore*	9
1986	Gaye Brief 9-12-2: 4/1	Mrs M. Rimell	*P. Scudamore*	11
1987	Mrs Muck 6-11-2: 9/4	N. Twiston Davies	*P. Scudamore*	10
1988	Gaye Brief 11-12-2: 14/1	Mrs M. Rimell	*D. Browne*	6
1989	Abandoned because of snow			
1990	Battalion (USA) 6-11-7: 100/30	C. Brooks	*B. de Haan*	8

PEREGRINE HANDICAP CHASE (Ascot 2½m)

1976 Game Spirit 10-11-12: 7/4	F. Walwyn	*W. Smith*	5
1977 Cloud Park 8-10-0: 8/1	M. Tate	*J. J. O'Neill*	8
1978 Royal Epic 7-11-3: 8/1	V. Cross	*J. King*	6
1979 Breemount Don 6-11-8: 3/1	F. Winter	*J. Francome*	10
1980 Tiepolino 8-12-4: 9/2	P. Cundell	*H. Davies*	6
1981 Fairy King 8-10-2: 3/1	J. FitzGerald	*A. Brown*	16
1982 Shady Deal 9-10-3: 3/1	J. Gifford	*R. Rowe*	5
1983 Richdee 7-11-7: 3/1	N. Crump	*C. Hawkins*	6
1984 Tom's Little Al 8-10-9: 4/1	W. Williams	*P. Scudamore*	6
1985 Restless Shot 10-10-2: 12/1	J. Webber	*J. Burke*	9
1986 Ryeman 9-11-3: 7/1	M. H. Easterby	*J. J. O'Neill*	9
1987 Desert Orchid 8-12-4: 7/4	D. Elsworth	*C. Brown*	7
1988 Dunkirk 12-10-2: 8/1	M. Francis	*M. Richards*	6
1989 Abandoned because of snow			
1990 Ida's Delight 11-11-2: 11/4	J. Charlton	*B. Storey*	6

WELSH CHAMPION HURDLE (Chepstow 2m)

1969 Persian War 6-12-0: 4/6	C. Davies	*J. Uttley*	9
1970 Frozen Alive 4-10-12: 5/1	H. T. Jones	*S. Mellor*	6
1971 Bula 6-12-0: 1/2	F. Winter	*P. Kelleway*	6
1972 Canasta Lad 6-11-8: 7/1	P. Bailey	*J. King*	5
1973 Comedy of Errors 6-12-0: 11/4	F. Rimell	*W. Smith*	6
1974 Canasta Lad 8-11-4: 11/4	P. Bailey	*J. King*	5
1975 Lanzarote 7-11-4: 13/8	F. Winter	*R. Pitman*	6
1976 Night Nurse 5-11-11: 1/5	M. H. Easterby	*P. Broderick*	3
1977 Night Nurse 6-11-12: 1/1	M. H. Easterby	*P. Broderick*	3
1978 Abandoned because course waterlogged			
1979 Monksfield 7-12-0: 2/7	D. McDonogh (Ir)	*D. T. Hughes*	3
1980 Sea Pigeon 10-12-0: 4/6	M. H. Easterby	*J. J. O'Neill*	5
1981 Pollardstown 6-11-9: 8/11	S. Mellor	*P. Blacker*	4
1982 Ekbalco 6-11-9: 2/1	R. Fisher	*J. J. O'Neill*	7
1983 Royal Vulcan 5-11-13: 9/4	N. Callaghan	*D. Goulding*	3
1984 Ra Nova 5-11-8: 11/10	Mrs N. Kennedy	*M. Perrett*	4
1985 Browne's Gazette 7-11-13: 8/13	Mrs M. Dickinson	*D. Browne*	7
1986 Abandoned because course waterlogged			
1987 High Knowl 4-11-0: 6/1	M. Pipe	*J. Lower*	9
1988 Past Glories 5-11-6: 8/1	W. Elsey	*P. Farrell*	5
1989 Celtic Shot 7-11-6: 1/7	C. Brooks	*P. Scudamore*	2
1990 Beech Road 8-12-1: 1/3	G. Balding	*R. Guest*	4

JAMESON IRISH GRAND NATIONAL HANDICAP CHASE
(Fairyhouse 3½m)

1946 Golden View II 11-12-7: 7/1	R. O'Connell	*M. Molony*	11
1947 Revelry 7-11-5: 6/1	J. Doyle	*D. L. Moore*	17
1948 Hamstar 8-9-7: 6/1	W O'Grady	*E. Kennedy*	17
1949 Shagreen 8-10-0: 5/1	T. Dreaper	*E. Newman*	20
1950 Dominick's Bar 6-10-6: 8/1	T. Hyde	*M. Molony*	12
1951 Icy Calm 8-10-3: 100/6	W. O'Grady	*P. Doyle*	19
1952 Alberoni 9-10-1: 6/1	M. V. O'Brien	*L. Stephens*	11
1953 Overshadow 13-10-4: 20/1	C. Magnier	*A. Power*	15
1954 Royal Approach 6-12-0: 1/1	T. Dreaper	*P. Taaffe*	11
1955 Umm 8-10-5: 100/7	G. Wells	*P. Taaffe*	16
1956 Air Prince 12-10-0: 20/1	J. McClintock	*T. O'Brien*	19
1957 Kilballyown 10-9-10: 10/1	P. Norris	*G. W. Robinson*	26
1958 Gold Legend 8-9-7: 100/8	J. Brogan	*J. Lehane*	21
1959 Zonda 8-10-6: 5/1	M. Geraghty	*P. Taaffe*	15
1960 Olympia 6-9-11: 6/1	T. Dreaper	*T. Taaffe*	16
1961 Fortria 9-12-0: 17/2	T. Dreaper	*P. Taaffe*	14
1962 Kerforo 8-10-3: 9/1	T. Dreaper	*L. McLoughlin*	11
1963 Last Link 7-9-7: 7/1	T. Dreaper	*P. Woods*	10
1964 Arkle 7-12-0: 1/2	T. Dreaper	*P. Taaffe*	4
1965 Splash 7-10-13: 6/4	T. Dreaper	*P. Woods*	4
1966 Flyingbolt 7-12-7: 8/11	T. Dreaper	*P. Taaffe*	6
1967 Vulpine 6-11-6: 7/1	P. Mullins	*M. Curran*	12
1968 Herring Gull 6-11-13: 5/2	P. Mullins	*J. Crowley*	12
1969 Sweet Dreams 8-9-10: 10/1	K. Bell	*R. Coonan*	18
1970 Garoupe 6-9-9: 10/1	F. Flood	*C. Finnegan*	13

1971	King's Sprite 9-9-13: 7/1	G. Wells	*A. Moore*	19
1972	Dim Wit 7-10-13: 15/2	P. Mullins	*M. Curran*	14
1973	Tartan Ace 6-9-7: 10/1	T. Costello	*J. Cullen*	14
1974	Colebridge 10-11-2: 11/5	J. Dreaper	*F. Wright*	10
1975	Brown Lad 9-10-5: 6/4	J. Dreaper	*T. Carberry*	8
1976	Brown Lad 10-12-0: 7/2	J. Dreaper	*T. Carberry*	15
1977	Billycan 7-10-0: 8/1	A. Maxwell	*M. Morris*	20
1978	Brown Lad 12-12-2: 5/1	J. Dreaper	*G. Dowd*	19
1979	Tied Cottage 11-10-2: 13/2	D. Moore	*Mr A. Robinson*	20
1980	Daletta 7-11-4: 11/1	G. St J. Williams	*J. P. Harty*	25
1981	Luska 7-9-9: 11/1	P. Mullins	*T. Finn*	20
1982	King Spruce 8-10-2: 20/1	M. O'Brien	*G. Newman*	25
1983	Bit Of A Skite 7-9-7: 7/1	E. O'Grady	*T. Ryan*	27
1984	Bentom Boy 9-9-9: 33/1	W. Rooney	*Mrs A. Ferris*	29
1985	Rhyme 'N' Reason 6-10-6: 6/1	D. Murray-Smith (Eng)	*G. Bradley*	23
1986	Insure 8-9-7: 16/1	P. Hughes	*M. Flynn*	15
1987	Brittany Boy 8-10-0: 14/1	K. Hitchmough	*T. Taaffe*	26
1988	Perris Valley 7-10-0: 12/1	D. Weld	*B. Sheridan*	18
1989	Maid of Money 7-11-6: 10/1	J. Fowler	*A. Powell*	22
1990	Desert Orchid 11-12-0: 1/1	D. Elsworth	*R. Dunwoody*	14

PIPER CHAMPAGNE GOLDEN MILLER CHASE (LIMITED HANDICAP) (Cheltenham 3¼m)

1980	Lacson 8-10-11: 13/2	R. Hawker	*S. C. Knight*	10
1981	Master Smudge 9-10-13: 5/2	A. Barrow	*R. Linley*	6
1982	Scot Lane 9-11-7: 10/1	M. Tate	*C. Smith*	13
1983	Abandoned because course waterlogged			
1984	Plundering 7-10-0: 5/1	F. Winter	*B. de Haan*	10
1985	Aces Wild 7-10-5: 4/1	F. Winter	*J. Duggan*	10
1986	Charter Party 8-11-9: 11/4	D. Nicholson	*P. Scudamore*	9
1987	Golden Friend 9-11-4: 15/8	Mrs M. Rimell	*D. Browne*	5
1988	Ten of Spades 8-11-3: 11/8	Mrs M. Rimell	*P. Scudamore*	5
1989	Smart Tar 8-10-5: 9/2	M. Wilkinson	*C. Llewellyn*	9
1990	Royal Cedar 9-10-13: 3/1	J. McConnochie	*R. Dunwoody*	7

SOUTH WALES SHOWERS MIRA SILVER TROPHY CHASE (Cheltenham 2½m)

1986	Mr Moonraker 9-11-2: 7/2	L. Kennard	*B. Powell*	7
1987	Duke of Milan 10-10-2: 11/2	N. Gaselee	*S. Sherwood*	5
1988	Beau Ranger 10-11-0: 11/10	M. Pipe	*P. Scudamore*	5
1989	Norton's Coin 8-11-0: 20/1	S. Griffiths	*R. Dunwoody*	8
1990	Barnbrook Again 9-11-10: 6/4	D. Elsworth	*H. Davies*	5

EBF NOVICES' HANDICAP HURDLE FINAL (Cheltenham 2m)

1981	Mr Foodbroker 6-9-7: 4/1	D. Kent	*J. Lovejoy*	14
1982	Allten Glazed 5-10-10: 14/1	M. Naughton	*G. Bradley*	16
1983	Talkabout 6-10-10: 12/1	G. Fletcher	*J. J. O'Neill*	17
1984	Golden Fancy 7-10-6: 25/1	I. Vickers	*R. Lamb*	9
1985	Cats Eyes 5-11-10: 10/1	M. Pipe	*P. Leach*	17
1986	Atrabates 6-11-7: 7/1	O. Sherwood	*S. Sherwood*	19
1987	Teletrader 6-11-9: 6/1	R. Hodges	*H. Davies*	14
1988	Western Dandy 5-9-7: 33/1	N. Gaselee	*A. Adams*	24
1989	For The Grain 5-11-10: 14/1	J. Wilson	*L. Wyer*	18
1990	Vazon Bay 6-12-0: 7/1	Mrs J. Pitman	*M. Pitman*	12

STEEL PLATE AND SECTIONS YOUNG CHASERS CHAMPIONSHIP FINAL (Cheltenham 2½m)

1980	Drusus 6-11-11: 10/11	F. Rimell	*J. King*	8
1981	Sea Captain 7-12-0: 9/4	R. Head	*H. Davies*	6
1982	Masterson 7-11-7: 6/1	Mrs M. Rimell	*P. Scudamore*	7
1983	Abandoned because course waterlogged			
1984	Gambir 6-11-8: 1/1	D. Nicholson	*P. Scudamore*	5
1985	Clutterbuck 7-11-8: 6/4 } dh	F. Winter	*R. Linley*	6
	Connaught River 6-11-4: 6/1 } dh	D. Nicholson	*P. Scudamore*	
1986	Arctic Stream 7-11-11: 6/4	F. Walwyn	*K. Mooney*	5
1987	Summons 8-12-0: 4/1	J. Gifford	*R. Rowe*	8
1988	Private Views 7-11-11: 8/13	N. Gaselee	*K. Mooney*	6

1989	Pin's Pride 7-11-4: 14/1	J. Gifford	*E. McKinley*	6
1990	Elfast 7-11-4: 11/10	J. Webber	*M. Lynch*	3

BOLLINGER CHAMPAGNE NOVICES HANDICAP CHASE
(Ascot 2½m)

1967	Three No Trumps 8-10-7: 2/1	P. Cazalet	*D. Mould*	10
1968	Gay Trip 6-11-7: 100/30	F. Rimell	*T. Biddlecombe*	7
1969	Beau Champ 7-12-0: 6/1	F. Winter	*H. Beasley*	9
1970	Into View 7-12-0: 11/8	F. Winter	*P. Kelleway*	6
1971	Bobby Corbett 6-10-10: 14/1	K. Oliver	*P. McCarron*	10
1972	Balinese 7-11-7: 10/1	R. Turnell	*D. R. Hughes*	8
1973	Proper Charlie 8-11-7: 20/1	C. V. Miller	*D. Cartwright*	4
1974	Winter Rain 6-10-4: 15/8	A. Dickinson	*M. Dickinson*	12
1975	Floating Proud 6-10-6: 9/2	F. Winter	*R. Pitman*	11
1976	Grangewood Girl 7-10-10: 11/2 11/2	Mrs A. Finch	*J. Fox*	14
1977	Commandant 5-10-5: 14/1	G. Balding	*S. McNally*	12
1978	Race abandoned			
1979	Bennachie 6-10-8: 9/1	A. Scott	*R. Lamb*	7
1980	Mister Bosun 7-10-6: 9/1	J. Thorne	*R. Hoare*	15
1981	Prayukta 6-11-10: 8/1	F. Winter	*J. Francome*	12
1982	Masterson 7-10-12: 4/1	Mrs M. Rimell	*R. Linley*	12
1983	Another Breeze 8-11-3: 7/2	N. Gaselee	*Mr A. J. Wilson*	7
1984	The Thatcher 6-10-4: 4/1	J. Gifford	*P. Hobbs*	9
1985	Townley Stone 6-12-2: 4/1	J. Webber	*G. McCourt*	8
1986	Repington 8-10-3: 9/1	N. Crump	*C. Hawkins*	13
1987	Barryphilips Disco 10-10-0: 7/1	R. Whitaker	*R. Beggan*	10
1988	Ballyhane 7-11-10: 11/2	J. Gifford	*R. Rowe*	6
1989	Man O'Magic 8-10-0: 14/1	K. Bailey	*M. Perrett*	17
1990	Sword Beach 6-10-1: 6/4	M. H. Easterby	*L. Wyer*	6

WHITBREAD GOLD CUP HANDICAP CHASE
(Sandown 3m 5f 18yds)

1957	Much Obliged 9-10-12: 10/1	N. Crump	*H. East*	24
1958	Taxidermist 6-10-8: 100/6	F. Walwyn	*Mr J. Lawrence*	31
1959	Done Up 9-10-13: 100/6	R. Price	*H. Sprague*	23
1960	Plummers Plain 7-10-0: 20/1	L. Dale	*R. Harrison*	21
1961	Pas Seul 8-12-0: 8/1	R. Turnell	*D. Dick*	23
1962	Frenchman's Cove 7-11-3: 7/2	H. T. Jones	*S. Mellor*	22
1963	Hoodwinked 8-10-9: 100/7	N. Crump	*P. Buckley*	32
1964	Dormant 7-9-7: 11/4	N. Crump	*P. Buckley*	11
1965	Arkle 8-12-7: 4/9	T. Dreaper (Ir)	*P. Taaffe*	7
1966	What a Myth 9-9-8: 5/4	R. Price	*P. Kelleway*	8
1967	Mill House 10-11-11: 9/2	F. Walwyn	*D. Nicholson*	13
1968	Larbawn 9-10-9: 8/1	M. L. Marsh	*M. Gifford*	16
1969	Larbawn 10-11-4: 9/2	M. L. Marsh	*J. Gifford*	18
1970	Royal Toss 8-10-0: 20/1	H. Handel	*R. Pitman*	17
1971	Titus Oates 9-11-13: 11/1	G. Richards	*R. Barry*	18
1972	Grey Sombrero 8-9-10: 16/1	D. Gandolfo	*W. Shoemark*	28
1973	Charlie Potheen 8-12-0: 11/4	F. Walwyn	*R. Barry*	21
1974	The Dikler 11-11-13: 5/1	F. Walwyn	*R. Barry*	16
1975	April Seventh 9-9-13: 16/1	R. Turnell	*S. C. Knight*	12
1976	Otter Way 8-10-10: 15/2	O. Carter	*J. King*	14
1977	Andy Pandy 8-10-12: 4/1	F. Rimell	*J. Burke*	15
1978	Strombolus 7-10-0: 7/1	P. Bailey	*T. Stack*	15
1979	Diamond Edge 8-11-11: 7/1	F. Walwyn	*W. Smith*	14
1980	Royal Mail 10-11-5: 8/1	S. Mellor	*P. Blacker*	12
1981	Diamond Edge 10-11-7: 5/1	F. Walwyn	*W. Smith*	18
1982	Shady Deal 9-10-0: 4/1	J. Gifford	*R. Rowe*	9
1983	Drumlargan 9-10-10: 11/1	E. O'Grady (Ir)	*Mr F. Codd*	15
1984	Special Cargo 11-11-2: 8/1	F. Walwyn	*K. Mooney*	13
1985	By The Way 7-10-0: 11/2	Mrs M. Dickinson	*R. Earnshaw*	20
1986	Plundering 9-10-6: 14/1	F. Winter	*S. Sherwood*	16
1987	Lean Ar Aghaidh 10-9-4: 6/1	S. Mellor	*G. Landau*	9
1988	Desert Orchid 9-11-11: 6/1	D. Elsworth	*S. Sherwood*	12
1989	Brown Windsor 7-10-0: 12/1	N. Henderson	*M. Bowlby*	18
1990	Mr Frisk 11-10-5: 9/2	K. Bailey	*Mr M. Armytage*	13

SWINTON INSURANCE BROKERS TROPHY HANDICAP HURDLE (Haydock 2m)

1978	Royal Gaye 5-10-0: 20/1	F. Rimell	*C. Tinkler*	20
1979	Beacon Light 8-11-1: 12/1	R. Turnell	*A. Turnell*	17
1980	No Bombs 5-10-9: 7/1	M. H. Easterby	*J. J. O'Neill*	14
1981	Gaye Chance 6-10-10: 13/2	F. Rimell	*S. Morshead*	18
1982	Secret Ballot 8-10-3: 10/1	R. Turnell	*A. Turnell*	17
1983	Abandoned because course waterlogged			
1984	Bajan Sunshine 5-10-13: 6/1	M. Tate	*P. Scudamore*	15
1985	Corporal Clinger 6-10-3: 11/2	M. Pipe	*P. Leach*	21
1986	Prideaux Boy 8-11-2: 15/2	G. Roach	*M. Bowlby*	20
1987	Inlander 6-10-8: 4/1	R. Akehurst	*S. Smith Eccles*	8
1988	Past Glories 5-11-9: 16/1	W. Elsey	*P. Farrell*	23
1989	State Jester 6-10-0: 14/1	W. Elsey	*J. Quinn*	18
1990	Sybillin 4-10-1: 8/1	J. FitzGerald	*D. Byrne*	14

HORSE AND HOUND CUP FINAL CHAMPION HUNTERS CHASE (Stratford 3¼m)

1959	Speylove 10-11-12: 25/1	V. Bishop	*J. Jackson*	15
1960	Bantry Bay 9-12-3: 6/1	H. Dufosee	*M. Tory*	17
1961	Bantry Bay 10-12-0: 8/1	H. Dufosee	*M. Tory*	8
1962	Baulking Green 9-12-0: 11/2	J. Reade	*R. Willis*	16
1963	Baulking Green 10-12-0: 7/4	T. Forster	*A. Frank*	17
1964	Royal Phoebe 8-11-7: 100/7	R. Whiston	*M. Gifford*	13
1965	Baulking Green 12-12-0: 4/7	T. Forster	*G. Small*	8
1966	Santa Grand 7-11-11: 7/1	W. A. Stephenson	*C. Collins*	10
1967	Cham 10-12-0: 3/1	F. Cundell	*J. Lawrence*	16
1968	Green Plover 8-11-9: 33/1	J. Ford	*A. Maxwell*	8
1969	Touch of Tammy 9-11-12: 11/4	G. Guilding	*R. Guilding*	14
1970	Some Man 8-12-0: 8/1	H. Poole	*R. Knipe*	15
1971	Credit Call 7-12-0: 4/1	W. A. Stephenson	*G. Macmillan*	10
1972	Credit Call 8-12-0: 1/1	W. A. Stephenson	*C. Collins*	11
1973	Credit Call 9-12-0: 4/7	W. A. Stephenson	*C. Collins*	5
1974	Stanhope Street 8-11-7: 2/1	H. Counsell	*B. Venn*	12
1975	Credit Call 11-12-0: 11/2	W. A. Stephenson	*J. Newton*	12
1976	Otter Way 8-12-0: 7/4	O. Carter	*G. Cann*	10
1977	Devil's Walk 9-12-0: 50/1	M. Bishop	*T. Rooney*	16
1978	Rolls Rambler 7-12-0: 8/11	F. Winter	*N. Henderson*	9
1979	Spartan Missile 7-12-0: 4/7	J. Thorne	*J. Thorne*	8
1980	Rolls Rambler 9-12-0: 13/8	F. Winter	*O. Sherwood*	16
1981	Ottery News 8-12-0: 7/4	O. Carter	*A. J. Wilson*	12
1982	Loyal Partner 8-12-0: 7/1	T. Clay	*T. Clay*	10
1983	Otter Way 15-12-0: 20/1	O. Carter	*A. J. Wilson*	17
1984	Prominent King 12-12-0: 7/1	M. H. Easterby	*T. Easterby*	20
1985	Flying Ace 9-12-0: 5/1	A. Calder	*Miss D. Calder*	10
1986	The Pain Barrier 7-12-0: 12/1	O. Sherwood	*Miss A. Langton*	10
1987	Three Counties 10-12-0: 9/4	Mrs M. Rimell	*Miss K. Rimell*	11
1988	Three Counties 11-12-0: 5/2	Mrs M. Rimell	*Miss K. Rimell*	14
1989	Mystic Music 10-11-9: 2/1	Miss H. Wilson	*K. Anderson*	16
1990	Mystic Music 11-11-9: 8/11	Miss H. Wilson	*K. Anderson*	9

CHEPSTOW

First October Meeting, 1990

Saturday, October 6th

THE TIMEFORM HURDLE

A Free Handicap for four years old only
£10,000 added to stakes
Distributed in accordance with Rule 194 (iv)(a)
(Includes a fourth prize)

for four years old only
about TWO MILES

£100 to accept

Lowest weight .... 10st; Highest weight not less than 12st
Penalties, after June 9th, a winner of a hurdle race 4lb
Half penalties for horses originally handicapped at or above 11st 7lb

TIMEFORM have generously contributed towards the prize money for this race, including a trophy value £500, at the option of the winner
The Stewards of the Jockey Club have modified Rule 95 (iii) so that it shall not apply to this race

Weights published June 14th

	st	lb		st	lb
Rare Holiday	12	0	Royal Square (CAN)	11	0
Sybillin	11	13	Sartorius	11	0
Ninja	11	12	Calicon	10	12
Vestris Abu	11	10	Dark Desire	10	12
Philosophos	11	9	Il Trovatore (USA)	10	12
Orbis (USA)	11	8	Major Inquiry (USA)	10	12
Lucky Verdict	11	7	Ambuscade (USA)	10	11
Sayyure (USA)	11	7	Green's Fine Art	10	11
Magic Million	11	6	Official Reception (USA)	10	11
Bally Rue (USA)	11	2	Silver King (FR)	10	11
Midfielder	11	2	Stigon	10	11
On Deposit	11	1	Bescaby Boy	10	10

	st	lb
Spring Hay	10	10
Rouyan	10	9
Stone Flake (USA)	10	9
Carbisdale	10	8
Question of Degree	10	7
Cornet	10	6
Cyphrate (USA)	10	6
Ivors Guest	10	6
Good Spark	10	4
In-Keeping	10	4
Rambo Castle	10	4
Crystal Heights	10	3
Tiger Claw (USA)	10	3
Dancing River	10	2
Houghton	10	2
Obeliski	10	2
General Pershing	10	1
Olnistar (FR)	10	1
Shadeux	10	1
Tri Folene (FR)	10	1
Champagne Lad	10	0
Sea Buck	10	0
Gay Ruffian	9	13
Shamirani	9	13
Valiant Boy	9	12
Badrakhani (FR)	9	12
Go Nobley	9	11
Cockstown Lad	9	10
Coe	9	10
Deltic (USA)	9	10
Joe Bumpas	9	10
Lissahane Lass	9	10
Stage Player	9	10
The Lighter Side	9	10
Able Leader	9	9
Groom Star (USA)	9	9
Leigh Boy (USA)	9	9
Man For All Season (USA)	9	9
Sagaman (GER)	9	9
Stay Awake	9	9
Crossroad Lad	9	8
Precious Boy	9	7
Southend Scallywag	9	7
Valiant Dash	9	6
As Good As Gold	9	5
Ballywillwill	9	5
Corn Lily	9	5
Dale Park	9	5
Mr Dormouse	9	5
New Arrangement	9	5
Royal Wonder	9	5
Bay Tern (USA)	9	4
Blake's Progress	9	4
Kami King	9	4
Logamimo	9	4
Rochallor	9	4
Beekman Street	9	3
Grey Fellow	9	3
Sharpgun (FR)	9	3
Sleepline Royale	9	3
Peristyle	9	2
Fisherman's Croft	9	1
Bold Choice	9	0
Carmagnole (USA)	9	0
Iveagh House	9	0
March On	9	0
None So Wise (USA)	9	0
Straw Blade	9	0
Island Jetsetter	8	13
Miss Pokey	8	13
Letterewe	8	12
Non Permanent	8	12
Old Virginia	8	12
Fistful of Bucks	8	11
Premier Princess	8	11
Softly	8	11
Hiram B Birdbath	8	10
Kenilworth Castle	8	10
Mister Lawson	8	10
Zucchini	8	10
Ardour	8	9
Deb's Ball	8	9
Easy Over (USA)	8	9
Elder Prince	8	9
Go Go Gorgeous	8	9
Nineofus	8	9
Oti (USA)	8	9
Return To Romance	8	9
The Widget Man	8	9
Blakesware Gold	8	8
Persian Luck	8	8
Basic Fun	8	7
Catch The Cross	8	7
Muirfield Village	8	7
Punchbag (USA)	8	7
Apollo King	8	6
Millie Belle	8	6
Ockley	8	6
Out Run	8	6
Star of The Glen	8	6
Billsha	8	5
Monaru	8	5

	st	lb		st	lb
Rocquaine	8	5	Bollin Gorgeous	8	2
Seattle Pride (CAN)	8	5	Bradmore's Vision	8	2
Spring Rag	8	5	City Index (USA)	8	2
Barley Mow	8	4	Lasting Memory	8	2
Beau Rolando	8	4	Polder	8	2
Hellenic Prince	8	4	Rustino	8	2
Highfield Prince	8	4	White River	8	2
Irish Ditty	8	4	Will James	8	2
Kosciosko (USA)	8	4	Far Out	8	1
Lava Falls (USA)	8	4	Galwex Lady	8	1
Pocketed (USA)	8	4	High Stoy	8	1
Blackguard (USA)	8	3	La Castana	8	1
Kowza	8	3	Birmingham's Pride	8	0
Mo Ichi Do	8	3	Dutch Majesty	8	0
Ruby Davies	8	3	Fit For Counsel	8	0
Snugfit's Image	8	3	Gargoor	8	0
Ultra Violet (FR)	8	3	Major Fredie	8	0
Welshman	8	3	Nearctic Bay (USA)	8	0
Zamore	8	3	Oasis	8	0
Able Vale	8	2	Outstanding Bill	8	0
Bharkat	8	2	Sonalto	8	0

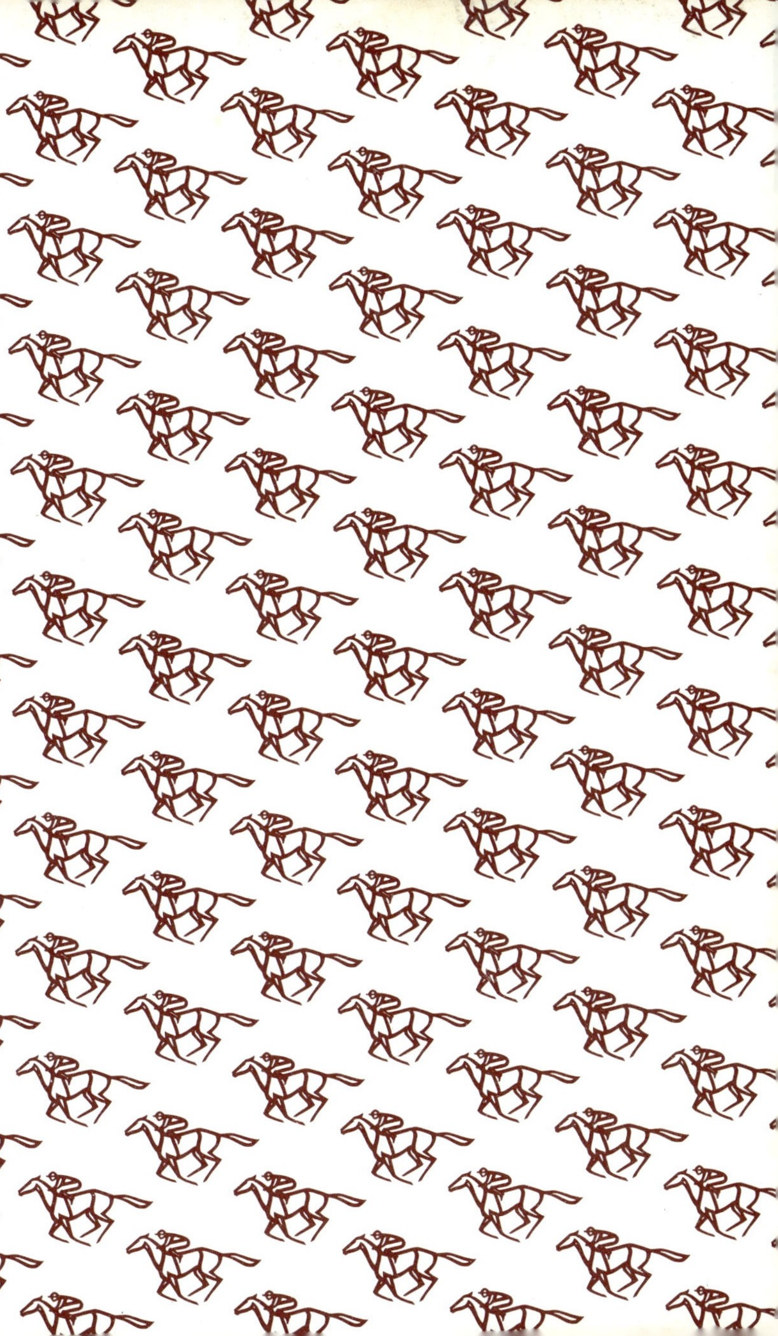